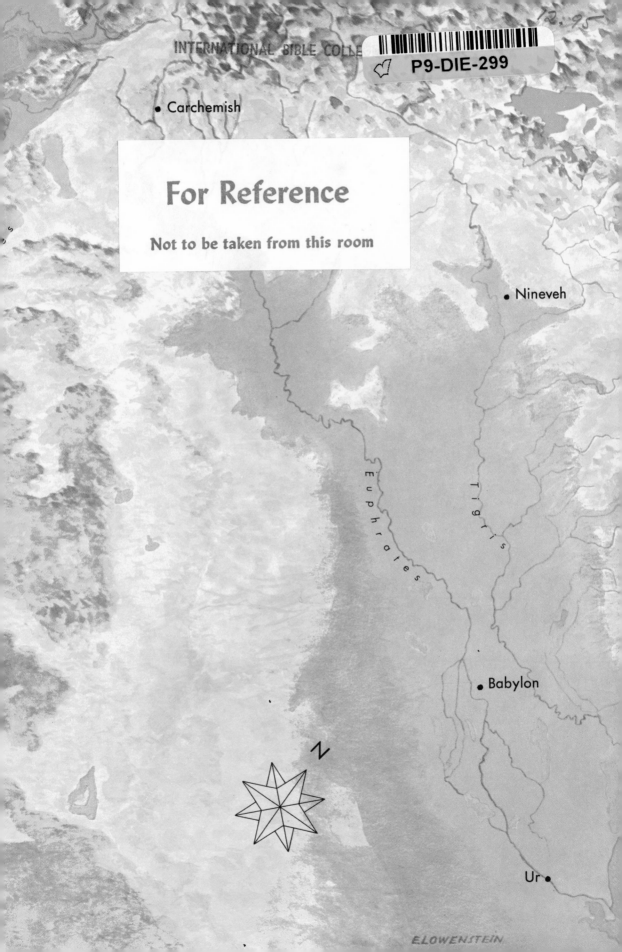

Carchemish

Nineveh

Euphrates

Tigris

Babylon

N

Ur

ELOWENSTEIN

THE INTERPRETER'S BIBLE

THE INTERPRETER'S BIBLE

IN TWELVE VOLUMES

VOLUME I

General Articles on the
BIBLE

General Articles on the
OLD TESTAMENT

The Book of
GENESIS

The Book of
EXODUS

THE
INTERPRETER'S BIBLE

—

The Holy Scriptures

IN THE KING JAMES AND REVISED STANDARD VERSIONS
WITH GENERAL ARTICLES AND
INTRODUCTION, EXEGESIS, EXPOSITION
FOR EACH BOOK OF THE BIBLE

IN TWELVE VOLUMES

VOLUME
I

דבר־אלהינו יקום לעולם

NEW YORK *Abingdon Press* NASHVILLE

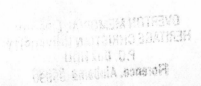

ISBN 0-687-19207-2
Library of Congress Catalog Card Number: 51-12276

The text of the Revised Standard Version of the Bible
(RSV) and quotations therefrom are copyright 1946, 1952
by Division of Christian Education of the National Council of the Churches of Christ in the United States of
America. Scripture quotations designated "ASV" are
from the American Standard Version of the Revised
Bible, copyright renewed 1929 by the International Coun-
cil of Religious Education. Those designated "Moffatt"
are from *The Bible, A New Translation,* by James Mof-
fatt, copyright in the United States, 1935, by Harper &
Brothers, New York; copyright in countries of the
International Copyright Union by Hodder & Stoughton,
Ltd., London. Those designated "Amer. Trans." or
"Goodspeed" are from *The Complete Bible, An Ameri-
can Translation,* by J. M. Powis Smith and Edgar J.
Goodspeed, copyright 1939 by the University of Chicago.

W
SET UP, PRINTED, AND BOUND BY THE
PARTHENON PRESS, AT NASHVILLE,
TENNESSEE, UNITED STATES OF AMERICA

CONSULTING EDITORS

ALEXANDER C. PURDY
Professor of New Testament, Hartford
Theological Seminary

GEORGE W. RICHARDS
President Emeritus and Professor Emeritus of Church History, Theological Seminary of the Evangelical and Reformed Church

R. B. Y. SCOTT
Professor of Old Testament Language and Literature, Faculty of Divinity, McGill University

W. AIKEN SMART
Professor of Biblical Theology, Emory University

HORACE G. SMITH
President and Professor of Preaching, Garrett Biblical Institute

WILLARD L. SPERRY
Dean of the Divinity School, Chairman of the Board of Preachers, Harvard University

JOHN S. STAMM
Bishop of the Evangelical United Brethren Church

W. TALIAFERRO THOMPSON
Professor of Christian Education, Union Theological Seminary, Richmond

HOWARD THURMAN
Minister, The Church for the Fellowship of All Peoples, San Francisco

LESLIE D. WEATHERHEAD
Hon. Chaplain to His Majesty's Forces, Minister, The City Temple, London

AMOS N. WILDER
Professor of New Testament Interpretation, Chicago Theological Seminary and Federated Theological Faculty of the University of Chicago

CONTRIBUTORS

WILLIAM F. ALBRIGHT
Professor of Semitic Languages, Johns
Hopkins University
General Article
The Old Testament World

E. L. ALLEN
Lecturer in Divinity, University of
Durham
Exposition ....Ezekiel

BERNHARD W. ANDERSON
Professor of Old Testament Interpreta-
tion, Colgate-Rochester Divinity School
Introduction and Exegesis ......Esther

GAIUS GLENN ATKINS
Professor Emeritus of Homiletics, Auburn
Theological Seminary
Exposition ....Ecclesiastes

JOHN W. BAILEY
Professor Emeritus of New Testament
Interpretation, Berkeley Baptist Divinity
School
Introduction and Exegesis
I and II Thessalonians

FRANK H. BALLARD
Minister, Hampstead Garden Suburb Free
Church, London
Exposition ....Psalms 90–150

ALBERT E. BARNETT
Professor of New Testament Interpreta-
tion, Candler School of Theology,
Emory University
Introduction and Exegesis .....II Peter
Introduction and Exegesis ....Jude

GEORGES AUGUSTIN BARROIS
Associate Professor of Biblical Literature
and Theology, Princeton Theological
Seminary
General Article
Chronology, Metrology, etc.

FRANCIS W. BEARE
Professor of New Testament Studies,
Trinity College, Toronto
Introduction and Exegesis ...Ephesians
Introduction and Exegesis ...Colossians

OSCAR F. BLACKWELDER
Minister, Lutheran Church of the Refor-
mation, Washington, D.C.
Exposition ....Galatians

HAROLD A. BOSLEY
Minister, First Methodist Church,
Evanston, Illinois
Exposition ....Micah

WALTER RUSSELL BOWIE
Professor of Homiletics, The Protestant
Episcopal Theological Seminary in
Virginia
General Article
The Teaching of Jesus: III. The Parables
Exposition ....Genesis
Exposition ....Luke 1–6

RAYMOND A. BOWMAN
Associate Professor, Department of Ori-
ental Languages and Literature, Univer-
sity of Chicago
Introduction and Exegesis ....Ezra
Introduction and Exegesis ...Nehemiah

JOHN BRIGHT
Professor of Hebrew and the Interpretation of the Old Testament, Union Theological Seminary, Richmond
Introduction and Exegesis ......Joshua

GEORGE ARTHUR BUTTRICK
Minister, Madison Avenue Presbyterian
Church, New York
General Article
The Study of the Bible
Exposition ....Matthew
Exposition ....Luke 13–18
Exposition ....Philemon

ALBERT GEORGE BUTZER
Minister, Westminster Presbyterian
Church, Buffalo
Exposition ....Numbers

HENRY J. CADBURY
Professor of Divinity, The Divinity
School, Harvard University
General Article ... The New Testament
and Early Christian Literature

GEORGE B. CAIRD
Professor of New Testament Literature
and Interpretation, McGill University
Introduction and Exegesis
I and II Samuel

RAYMOND CALKINS
Minister Emeritus, First Church in Cambridge, Congregational, Cambridge, Massachusetts
Exposition .... II Kings

JAMES W. CLARKE
Minister, Second Presbyterian Church, St.
Louis
Exposition ...... I and II Thessalonians

JAMES T. CLELAND
Professor of Preaching and Preacher to
the University, The Divinity School, Duke
University
Exposition .... Ruth
Exposition .... Nahum
Exposition .... Zechariah 9-14

HENRY SLOANE COFFIN
President Emeritus, Union Theological
Seminary, New York
Exposition .... Isaiah 40-66

ERNEST C. COLWELL
President, University of Chicago
General Article .... The Text and
Ancient Versions of the
New Testament

J. HARRY COTTON
Professor of Philosophy, Wabash College
Exposition .... Hebrews

GERALD R. CRAGG
Minister, Erskine and American United
Church, Montreal
Exposition .... Romans

CLARENCE T. CRAIG
Dean, Drew Theological Seminary
General Article .... The Teaching
of Jesus: I. The Proclamation
of the Kingdom
Introduction and Exegesis
I Corinthians

ROBERT C. DENTAN
Professor of the Literature and Interpreta-
tion of the Old Testament, Berkeley
Divinity School, New Haven
Introduction and Exegesis
Zechariah 9-14
Introduction and Exegesis ..... Malachi

BURTON S. EASTON
Professor Emeritus of Literature and Interpretation of the New Testament, General Theological Seminary
Introduction and Exegesis .... James

PHILLIPS P. ELLIOTT
Minister, First Presbyterian Church,
Brooklyn
Exposition .... Judges

W. A. L. ELMSLIE
Principal and Professor of Hebrew and
Old Testament Theology and Literature,
Westminster College, Cambridge
Introduction and Exegesis
I and II Chronicles
Exposition .... I and II Chronicles

MORTON SCOTT ENSLIN
Professor of New Testament Literature
and Exegesis, Crozer Theological Semi-
nary
General Article
New Testament Times: II. Palestine

HERBERT H. FARMER
Professor of Divinity, University of
Cambridge
General Article .... The Bible:
Its Significance and Authority

THEODORE P. FERRIS
Rector, Trinity Church, Boston
Exposition .... Acts

FLOYD V. FILSON
Professor of New Testament Literature
and History, McCormick Theological
Seminary
Introduction and Exegesis
II Corinthians

HUGHELL E. W. FOSBROKE
Dean Emeritus, General Theological
Seminary
General Article
The Prophetic Literature
Introduction and Exegesis .... Amos

CONTRIBUTORS

CHARLES T. FRITSCH
Associate Professor of Old Testament, Princeton Theological Seminary
Introduction and Exegesis ....Proverbs

FRED D. GEALY
Professor of New Testament Greek, Perkins School of Theology, Southern Methodist University
Introduction and Exegesis
I and II Timothy and Titus

CHARLES W. GILKEY
Dean Emeritus of the University Chapel, Professor of Preaching, University of Chicago
Exposition ....Ezra
Exposition ....Nehemiah

S. MacLEAN GILMOUR
Professor of New Testament Literature and Criticism, Queen's Theological College
Introduction and Exegesis ....Luke

EDGAR J. GOODSPEED
Professor Emeritus of Biblical and Patristic Greek, University of Chicago
General Article
The Canon of the New Testament

ARTHUR JOHN GOSSIP
Emeritus Professor of Christian Ethics and Practical Training, University of Glasgow
Exposition ....John

FREDERICK C. GRANT
Professor of Biblical Theology, Union Theological Seminary, New York
Introduction and Exegesis ....Mark

ROBERT M. GRANT
Professor of New Testament Language and Interpretation, School of Theology, University of the South
General Article....The History of the Interpretation of the Bible:
I. Ancient Period

WILLIAM H. P. HATCH
Professor Emeritus of the Literature and Interpretation of the New Testament, Episcopal Theological School
General Article ...The History of the Early Church: II. The Life of Paul

ELMER G. HOMRIGHAUSEN
Professor of Christian Education, Princeton Theological Seminary
Exposition ....I and II Peter
Exposition ....Jude

PAUL WAITMAN HOON
Minister, First Methodist Church, Germantown, Philadelphia
Exposition .... I, II, and III John

STANLEY ROMAINE HOPPER
Professor of Christian Ethics, Drew Theological Seminary
Exposition ....Jeremiah

LYNN HAROLD HOUGH
Sometime Dean, Drew Theological Seminary
Exposition ....Revelation

WILBERT F. HOWARD
Principal, Handsworth College, Birmingham
Introduction and Exegesis ....John

ARCHIBALD M. HUNTER
Professor of Divinity and Biblical Criticism, King's College, Aberdeen University
Introduction and Exegesis ......I Peter

JAMES PHILIP HYATT
Professor of Old Testament, School of Religion, Vanderbilt University
Introduction and Exegesis ....Jeremiah

WILLIAM A. IRWIN
Professor of Old Testament Language and Literature, Perkins School of Theology, Southern Methodist University
General Article
The Literature of the Old Testament
General Article
The Wisdom Literature

ARTHUR JEFFERY
Professor of Semitic Languages, Columbia University
General Article
The Canon of the Old Testament
General Article ....The Text and Ancient Versions of the Old Testament
Introduction and Exegesis ......Daniel

SHERMAN E. JOHNSON
Professor of Literature and Interpretation of the New Testament, Episcopal Theological School
Introduction and Exegesis .... Matthew

GERALD KENNEDY
Bishop, The Methodist Church, Portland Area
Exposition .... Daniel

HUGH THOMSON KERR
Pastor Emeritus, The Shadyside Presbyterian Church, Pittsburgh
Exposition .... Song of Songs

G. G. D. KILPATRICK
Principal, The United Theological College, Montreal
Exposition .... Isaiah 1–39

JOHN KNOX
Professor of New Testament, Union Theological Seminary, New York
Exposition .... Luke 7–12
Introduction and Exegesis .... Romans
Introduction and Exegesis ... Philemon

NORMAN F. LANGFORD
The Board of Christian Education, Presbyterian Church in the U.S.A.
Exposition .... Joel
Exposition .... Obadiah

ARTHUR C. LICHTENBERGER
Bishop Coadjutor of Missouri
Exposition .... Esther

GANSE LITTLE
Minister, Broad Street Presbyterian Church, Columbus, Ohio
Exposition .... II Samuel

SIDNEY LOVETT
Chaplain of Yale University
Exposition .... Amos

HALFORD E. LUCCOCK
Professor of Homiletics, The Divinity School, Yale University
Exposition .... Mark

G. H. C. MACGREGOR
Professor of Divinity and Biblical Criticism, University of Glasgow
Introduction and Exegesis .... Acts

G. PRESTON MACLEOD
Minister, Knox United Church, Calgary, Alberta
Exposition .... Colossians

JOHN MARSH
Professor of Christian Theology, The University, Nottingham
Introduction and Exegesis .... Numbers

JOHN MAUCHLINE
Professor of Old Testament Language and Literature, University of Glasgow
Introduction and Exegesis ...... Hosea

HERBERT G. MAY
Professor of Old Testament Language and Literature, Graduate School of Theology, Oberlin College
Introduction and Exegesis ...... Ezekiel

S. VERNON MCCASLAND
Professor of Religion, University of Virginia
General Article .... New Testament Times: I. The Greco-Roman World

JOHN T. MCNEILL
Professor of Church History, Union Theological Seminary, New York
General Article .... The History of the Interpretation of the Bible: II. Medieval and Reformation Period

THEOPHILE J. MEEK
Professor of Oriental Languages, University College, University of Toronto
Introduction and Exegesis
Song of Songs
Introduction and Exegesis
Lamentations

WILLIAM PIERSON MERRILL
Pastor Emeritus, Brick Presbyterian Church, New York
Exposition .... Lamentations

BRUCE M. METZGER
Associate Professor of New Testament, Princeton Theological Seminary
General Article
The Language of the New Testament

NATHANIEL MICKLEM
Principal and Professor of Dogmatic Theology, Mansfield College, Oxford
Introduction and Exegesis .... Leviticus
Exposition .... Leviticus

CONTRIBUTORS

PAUL S. MINEAR
Professor of New Testament, Andover
Newton Theological School
General Article .... The History of the
Early Church: III. Paul the Apostle

JAMES MUILENBURG
Professor of Hebrew and Cognate Languages, Union Theological Seminary,
New York
General Article
The History of the Religion of Israel
Introduction and Exegesis
Isaiah 40–66

JACOB M. MYERS
Professor of Old Testament, Lutheran
Theological Seminary, Gettysburg
Introduction and Exegesis ...... Judges

MORGAN P. NOYES
Minister, Central Presbyterian Church,
Montclair, New Jersey
Exposition .... I and II Timothy
Exposition .... Titus

J. EDGAR PARK
President Emeritus, Wheaton College,
Norton, Massachusetts
Exposition .... Exodus

PIERSON PARKER
Professor of New Testament, General
Theological Seminary
Exposition .... Deuteronomy

ALFRED M. PERRY
Professor of New Testament Language
and Literature, Bangor Theological Seminary
General Article
The Growth of the Gospels

ROBERT H. PFEIFFER
Lecturer on Semitic Languages and Curator of Semitic Museum, Harvard University; Professor, Boston University
School of Theology
General Article .... The Literature
and Religion of the Apocrypha
General Article .... The Literature
and Religion of the Pseudepigrapha

HAROLD COOKE PHILLIPS
Minister, First Baptist Church, Cleveland
Exposition .... Hosea

EDWIN MCNEILL POTEAT
Minister, Pullen Memorial Baptist Church,
Raleigh, North Carolina
Exposition .... Psalms 42–89

GORDON POTEAT
Minister, Tourist Church, Daytona Beach,
Florida
Exposition .... James

ALEXANDER C. PURDY
Professor of New Testament, Hartford
Theological Seminary
Introduction and Exegesis .... Hebrews

O. S. RANKIN
Professor of Old Testament Language,
Literature and Theology, New College,
University of Edinburgh
Introduction and Exegesis .. Ecclesiastes

JAMES REID
Minister, Formerly of St. Andrew's Presbyterian Church, Eastbourne, Sussex
Exposition .... II Corinthians

MARTIN RIST
Professor of New Testament Literature
and Interpretation, Iliff School of Theology
Introduction and Exegesis ... Revelation

THEODORE H. ROBINSON
Professor Emeritus of Semitic Languages,
University College, Cardiff
General Article .. The History of Israel

J. COERT RYLAARSDAM
Associate Professor of Old Testament
Theology, The Federated Theological
Faculty of the University of Chicago
Introduction and Exegesis ..... Exodus

WILLIAM SCARLETT
Bishop of Missouri
Exposition .... Jonah

PAUL SCHERER
Professor of Homiletics, Union Theological Seminary, New York
Exposition .... Job
Exposition .... Luke 19–24

ROLLAND W. SCHLOERB
Minister, Hyde Park Baptist Church,
Chicago
Exposition .... Proverbs

xiii

JOHN C. SCHROEDER
    Master, Calhoun College, Yale University
       Exposition .... I Samuel

J. R. P. SCLATER
    Minister, Old St. Andrew's Church,
    Toronto
       Exposition .... Psalms 1–41

ERNEST F. SCOTT
    Professor Emeritus of Biblical Theology,
    Union Theological Seminary, New York
       General Article .... The History of the
           Early Church: I. The Beginnings
       Introduction and Exegesis .. Philippians

R. B. Y. SCOTT
    Professor of Old Testament Language and
    Literature, Faculty of Divinity, McGill
    University
       Introduction and Exegesis .. Isaiah 1–39

MASSEY H. SHEPHERD, JR.
    Professor of Church History, Episcopal
    Theological School
       General Article .... The History
           of the Early Church: IV. The
           Post-Apostolic Age

HENRY HERBERT SHIRES
    Bishop Suffragan of California
       Exposition .... Deuteronomy

JOHN SHORT
    Minister, Richmond Hill Congregational
    Church, Bournemouth
       Exposition .... I Corinthians

CUTHBERT A. SIMPSON
    Sub-dean and Professor of Old Testament
    Literature and Interpretation, General
    Theological Seminary
       General Article
           The Growth of the Hexateuch
       Introduction and Exegesis ..... Genesis

JOSEPH R. SIZOO
    President, New Brunswick Theological
    Seminary
       Exposition .... Joshua

JAMES D. SMART
    Minister, Rosedale Presbyterian Church,
    Toronto
       Introduction and Exegesis ...... Jonah

LOUISE PETTIBONE SMITH
    Professor of Biblical History, Wellesley
    College
       Introduction and Exegesis .... Ruth

NORMAN H. SNAITH
    Tutor in Old Testament Languages and
    Literature, Wesley College, Leeds
       General Article
           The Language of the Old Testament
       Introduction and Exegesis
                 I and II Kings

RALPH W. SOCKMAN
    Minister, Christ Church, New York
       Exposition .... I Kings

THEODORE CUYLER SPEERS
    Minister, Central Presbyterian Church,
    New York
       Exposition .... Zechariah 1–8

WILLARD L. SPERRY
    Dean of the Divinity School, Chairman
    of the Board of Preachers, Harvard Uni-
    versity
       Exposition .... Haggai
       Exposition .... Malachi

RAYMOND T. STAMM
    Professor of New Testament Language,
    Literature and Theology, Lutheran The-
    ological Seminary, Gettysburg
       Introduction and Exegesis .... Galatians

ROBERT HARVEY STRACHAN
    Professor Emeritus of New Testament
    Language and Literature, Westminster
    College, Cambridge
       General Article
           The Gospel in the New Testament

CHARLES L. TAYLOR, JR.
    Dean and Professor of Literature and In-
    terpretation of the Old Testament, Epis-
    copal Theological School
       Introduction and Exegesis ..... Nahum
       Introduction and Exegesis .. Habakkuk
       Introduction and Exegesis .. Zephaniah

VINCENT TAYLOR
    Principal and Tutor in New Testament
    Language and Literature, Wesley College,
    Leeds
       General Article
           The Life and Ministry of Jesus

CONTRIBUTORS

WILLIAM R. TAYLOR
Principal and Professor, Department of Semitics, University College, University of Toronto
Introduction and Exegesis ......Psalms

SAMUEL TERRIEN
Associate Professor of Old Testament, Union Theological Seminary, New York
General Article....The History of the Interpretation of the Bible: III. Modern Period
Introduction and Exegesis ....Job

D. WINTON THOMAS
Regius Professor of Hebrew, University of Cambridge
Introduction and Exegesis .....Haggai
Introduction and Exegesis
Zechariah 1–8

JOHN A. THOMPSON
Professor of Old Testament Language and Exegesis, Evangelical Theological Seminary, Cairo, Egypt
Introduction and Exegesis ....Joel
Introduction and Exegesis ....Obadiah

HOWARD THURMAN
Minister, The Church for the Fellowship of All Peoples, San Francisco
Exposition ....Habakkuk
Exposition ....Zephaniah

THEODORE O. WEDEL
Canon of Washington Cathedral and Warden of the College of Preachers, Washington, D.C.
Exposition ....Ephesians

ROBERT R. WICKS
Dean Emeritus of the University Chapel, Princeton University
Exposition ....Philippians

ALLEN WIKGREN
Associate Professor of New Testament Language and Literature, The Divinity School and Federated Theological Faculty of the University of Chicago
General Article .....The English Bible

AMOS N. WILDER
Professor of New Testament Interpretation, Chicago Theological Seminary and Federated Theological Faculty of the University of Chicago
General Article ......The Teaching of Jesus: II. The Sermon on the Mount
Introduction and Exegesis
I, II, and III John

ROLLAND E. WOLFE
Professor of Biblical Literature, Western Reserve University
Introduction and Exegesis ....Micah

G. ERNEST WRIGHT
Professor of Old Testament History and Theology, McCormick Theological Seminary
General Article ....The Faith of Israel
Introduction and Exegesis
Deuteronomy

HOW TO USE THE INTERPRETER'S BIBLE

The Interpreter's Bible is a guidebook to the city of the Bible. To some readers the Bible is a foreign city: they can find in this commentary, if it is properly used, a veritable "open-sesame." To other readers the Bible is a familiar place: even they may find by means of these volumes treasures which they never dreamed were just around the corner. The Bible has towers and streets and rivers, plazas and libraries and shrines, incalculably more historic and lifegiving than any London or New York. It amply justifies a multivolume work, involving twelve years of labor by over one hundred exegetes and expositors, with a commensurate outlay of money. Justifies? Nay, requires it in every century; for the Bible offers that enrichment and fellowship which other cities promise but fail to provide. It is more than a "city of refuge": it is the home of the "beloved community" of God in Christ.

Here then is a commentary guidebook to the city of the Bible. How is the guidebook planned? How should it be used? The editors "have a concern," as the Quakers might say, that *The Interpreter's Bible* shall be rightfully employed, and that none of its values shall be missed. The general reader, the teacher, and the preacher of the Bible, if they understand the scheme and purpose of these volumes, can all here find unusual resource.

The Prefaces

Is it too much to ask that the Prefaces be read? In many a book the preface is more than the front door: it is both the clue to the book's intention and the story of the author's pilgrimage. The Prefaces to these volumes, though they bear two individual names, are in large degree the statement of editors and publishers. There the reader is told that this work travels by a dual directional beam, honest scholarship within the Protestant evangelical faith. Every book is written in some faith. The cult of "objectivity" would be empty even if it were possible, for only faith gives content to any study; so our editors and contributors eagerly confess, as men under a saving conviction, that God in Christ "for us men, and for our salvation, came down . . . and was made man." That faith itself demands honesty of scholarship, for the Spirit of Christ guides men's minds without coercing them, and requires that we "speak every man truth with his neighbor." The Bible is not a series of phonograph records traced on helpless human wax by a compulsive needle, but genuinely an inspiration from which new light breaks age on age under the leading of that selfsame Spirit. The Prefaces tell further how the whole work was planned, how writers were chosen, why liberty of interpretation was given them under what gentle constraints, and the rules that were followed in the arduous task of editing. So we plead, for the reader's own understanding, that the Prefaces be read.

The Working Page

A sequential reading of the whole work is probably too exacting a request. Many a reader will be a hard-pressed teacher or preacher who will turn in the Commentary to the page that bears on his immediate task. So we now write to him. The working page is in three parts. The second is pendant on the first, and the third on the other two; and the proper method of study is therefore by a downward movement of the eye.

At the top of the page, in clear type, the King James Version and the Revised Standard Version of the passage under consideration are set side by side. Comparison and contrast can thus be made almost at a glance. The King James Version is not only a devotional classic in its own enduring right, which in majestic cadence worships God in the beauty of holiness, but is so inevitably true in many of its translations as almost to have added new power to the original word. For this reason, and because it is hallowed in memory, it is placed first on each working page. The Revised Standard Version stands alongside it because, by the general consent of scholars, it is the most accurate revision of the King James Version; and one which, moreover, has been intent on preserving the priceless values of the Tyndale–King James tradition. As compared with prior translations, the Revised Standard Version has the advantage of recently discovered manuscripts such as the papyri obtained by Chester Beatty, and the further advantage of newer knowledge of the original languages such as has followed from Adolf Deissmann's brilliant deduction that the New Testament was written in koine (vernacular) Greek. Contributors have been left free to use or quote from either version. Many have turned to the Revised Standard Version because that provides the more accurate rendering. Sometimes a contributor has stressed a difference between the two versions; sometimes he has proposed a third translation. At such junctures, to conserve time and space, we have not asked him to enter into lengthy explanations. The two versions themselves, set side by side, provide the key.

Midway in the working page, immediately below the scripture passage under study, is the Exegesis. Many readers, even teachers and preachers, are prone to overlook the setting of a phrase and the exact meaning of a word. A reader who casts his eye on a line of scripture and accepts what it "seems to mean" is dealing in astrology or pre-Copernican astronomy rather than in the present wonder of heavenly truth. Truth depends, not alone on accuracy of meaning, but on its total setting—on what a word or phrase meant for its original speaker in the original time and occasion. Such neglect of meaning has become a minor scandal, for thus the Bible has been twisted to support arbitrary notions and contemporary trends:

> What damned error, but some sober brow
> Will bless it, and approve it with a text?

The reader will notice that the expositors in these volumes, though the editors have given them a large liberty, have based their interpretations on the Exegesis. In no other way can any interpreter "rightly" divide "the word of truth." So the editors plead for a careful and grateful use of the Exegesis. Preachers who thus "search the Scriptures" will gain more, and better, sermons than they lose.

Below the Exegesis is the Exposition. The nature and strategy of these interpretations should be understood, for otherwise their resource cannot be tapped. They are not ready-made outlines for sermons or addresses, or even homilies for general reading. Such aids, like the schoolboy's "prop," could be the defeat of knowledge rather than its enhancement; and they could make Bible teaching a poor desultory effort or a secondhand purchase. The expositions are rather "openings": they point a path rather than impose a pattern. They are not a crutch, but a spur. They hint the relevance of the Scriptures for our time and for all time, and they invite the student to "take the hint." They are not bereft of illustration, for one of the values of these volumes is that they provide both an index and a corpus of illustrative material; but even the illustrations are given not as a lift for lazy legs, but as a challenge to the reader's quest. The exegetes have been chosen for their knowledge, honesty, and reverence; the expositors have been chosen for their readiness to be true to the Exegesis and for their gift of kindling suggestion. So for the teacher the Expositions are not an ambulance but a guide. Yet the average reader will find in them, when they are coupled with the scripture text, leading in his meditations.

The Introductions

But though the average owner of these volumes may turn first, because of the necessities of his daily task, to the working page, it would be unfortunate both for him and for those whom he would teach, if he were content to stay within such limits. The Introductions to the various Bible books are an invaluable library, especially for a teacher of the Scriptures. If gathered into one volume they would give as comprehensive knowledge in that field as has ever been published in one book. They answer questions which, while unanswered, leave the working page in bondage. Here are such questions: Who wrote this book? When was it written? Where was it written? Under what conditions and in the midst of what events? The Holy Spirit does not denature a writer's personal traits or make him utterly independent of his time. He lives indeed under the aspect of eternity, for God is pleased to use him, but he is used as the servant of God in his own place and age. A writer in our time, however obedient to the divine summons, could hardly forbear any mention of communism. So Bible writers addressed themselves to the case in point, and found in contemporary events God's stern or gentle providence. The Introductions answer these inescapable questions. So a wise reader will regard the words "See Intro." as a command to be eagerly obeyed.

The Bible teacher in particular will find the Introductions an indispensable aid. What happenings, God's handwriting in history, brought Amos from his flocks and sycamore trees to the king's palace and the haunts of the "prophets"? What appearance did his land wear, and what culture prevailed? Amos is a partly closed book until such questions are answered. What did men believe about human suffering when Job was written, and what travail of soul gave us that sublime drama? What history, with its successive hammerings of conquest until Israel became a blood-stained anvil, provides the background for the apocalypse of Daniel? What transpirings dictated the mood under which Paul wrote the Epistle to the Romans? Who was the author of Matthew, and when was that book composed: in Jerusalem about seventy years after Jesus as scholars long supposed, or in Syria toward the turn of the first century as now appears? When such questions are answered, the prayer

> O may these heavenly pages be
> My ever dear delight;
> And still new beauties may I see,
> And still increasing light

is fulfilled; and the preacher or teacher becomes "a workman that needeth not to be ashamed."

There is danger that any reader of the Bible will read it by verses. The Introductions, showing the relation of the parts to the whole, rescue him from that danger. There were no verses in the original manuscripts. Indeed in the Greek text there were no spaces between the words. The Synoptic Gospels were intended for the instruction of young beginners in the Christian faith, and were written in stories and paragraphs rather than in verses. To cite another instance: Deutero-Isaiah consists in part of "oracles"—stanza-jets of white-hot prophecy. Perhaps preachers should preach on the proper units of Scripture rather than on phrases or verses torn, sometimes with violence or disfigurement, from their context. Certainly Bible classes and congregations would be edified if the interpreter oftener expounded a whole book. Then Jonah would be seen for what it is, a stirring challenge to a missionary faith that shall make the whole world one family around the feet of God. Then Luke-Acts would be seen in its original wholeness—the deeds of the Spirit of Christ recorded in proper sequel to his deeds in the flesh.

There are two other features of the Introduction that give outstanding help. First, there is an outline immediately following the title, in which the general reader or teacher will find guidance as he studies what follows, and which provides a pondered scheme for any instruction he may wish to give. Second, there is a good bibliography at the end of each Introduction, whereby the reader may pursue further study. *The Interpreter's Bible* is vast in scope, comprising in all about eight million words; but it is still hardly more than a primer when compared with all that has been written on the Scriptures through the centuries. Therefore the bibliographies. The Introduction to Matthew, for instance, divides the bibliography into three parts—commentaries, other works, and books that discuss the most important ancient sources. So the editors earnestly recommend the reading of the Introductions. The man who lives only within the working page of *The Interpreter's Bible* is hardly better than one who knows his own house and street but is ignorant of his city.

The General Articles

Just as the Introductions provide a necessary background for the working page, so the General Articles explain and illumine the Introductions. The simile in the preceding paragraph could be extended: the man who knows his own city without knowing his nation and world would still be ignorant. Who can understand Chicago without any knowledge of the streams of immigration by which its life has been fed, or of the prairies and lakes that sustain it, or of its problems of government? But many a reader of the Bible is correspondingly ignorant of its wider setting. This hinterland of Scripture sustains it, almost as streams of immigration and the fertility of prairies maintain an American city. Take the instances. In what sense is Scripture inspired? Two articles answer that question: "The Bible: Its Significance and Authority"; and another, which is actually three articles in one, "The History of the Interpretation of the Bible." From what wider history has the Old Testament come to us? Two articles satisfy that query: "The Old Testament World" and "The Faith of Israel." The former shows the origins of the Hebrew people in the Fertile Crescent, and how their history was affected by the political and military adventures of encompassing empires; the latter provides criteria without which no reader can properly judge "the Law, the Prophets, and the Writings."

Instances regarding the New Testament could be cited with as sharp or sharper point. Perhaps Volume VII should have been entitled Mark-Matthew, and Volume VIII Luke-Acts. The editors held to the traditional order lest they be accused of iconoclasm or hankering after novelty, but the new titles might still have been justified; for sudden illumination falls on the New Testament when the reader comes to terms with the chronological order of its books— many of the epistles first, then Mark a full generation after Jesus, then Luke-Acts and Matthew after almost another generation, then John and the other books. Another wave of light breaks when the reader realizes that not the epistles only, but the Gospels also, stem from the life of the early church. So the article on "The Growth of the Gospels" and those on "The History of the Early Church" are literally and urgently a "priority"; that is to say, an indispensable asset for which other assets must, if necessity dictates, for a time be sacrificed. Any reader,

student, or would-be interpreter, will find added value in the General Articles in that they also begin with a synopsis and end with a bibliography.

The articles instanced are not more valuable than the others: they are used only as example, and they would themselves be incomplete without their companion articles. This feature alone of the Commentary comprises about half a million words, a small library in itself. The order of the articles and their location, whether in Volume I or Volume VII, have been carefully pondered; and each author has been chosen for his knowledge of a particular field. Here as in a panorama pass in review the history, the tides of immigration, the world-terrain of the city of the Scriptures. If a reader is ignorant of this vast and teeming hinterland, the Scriptures may baffle rather than inspire. In New York City the name Stuyvesant Square is only a name until a man knows the early history of New York, the teeming East Side with its belts of population, the bond between the U.S.A. and Europe, barges on the Hudson carrying coal from Pennsylvania, and grain elevators fed from the harvests of North Dakota. This illustration is not invincible, for the Bible has a power of its own to pierce man's ignorance; but that power finds swifter and surer release when the Bible reader knows the background of the Book.

Maps and Indexes

The maps in *The Interpreter's Bible* deserve more than casual mention. They picture the word-truth of working page, Introduction, and General Article. For when the pilot of the plane says through the loudspeaker, "Such-and-such a mountain is now on our right," the passenger can say to himself, if he has a map before him, "I see where we are!" *The Interpreter's Bible* provides a map for almost every book of the Bible. These are in black-and white outline for clarity, and placed in proper context. Certain additional maps of the same kind have been given, such as that of Jerusalem in New Testament times, this particular map having been set just before the General Articles in Volume VII. There are also four large maps in color. On the front end-pages of the Old Testament volumes is a color map of the early Old Testament world, featuring the Fertile Crescent; and on the back end-pages of the same volumes, a map of Palestine in the middle period of Old Testament history. As for the New Testament volumes, the color map on the front end-pages shows the Eastern Mediterranean world in New Testament times, and that on the back end-pages shows Palestine in New Testament times. These color maps have been specially drawn for *The Interpreter's Bible* in such a way as to emphasize the land contours. The maps of Palestine are portrayed as if seen from the east, from "the wilderness beyond Jordan," because the mountains and valleys are more clearly marked when viewed from such an angle. By the help of these maps the Bible reader can say of the journey of Abraham from Ur of the Chaldees, "I see where he trekked"; and of the fateful travel of the man who "fell among thieves," he can exclaim, "I understand now how he went *down* from Jerusalem to Jericho!"

The Indexes to the twelve volumes, found in Volume XII, are designed for their practicality. They provide far more than an aid to reading memory or a ready-finder. They are a guide to topical study, whether the topic be theological, historical, or homiletic. There will be three indexes for which over three hundred and fifty pages are allotted. The first index (first in importance, though last in order) is general—so named and so planned, with every subject and name appearing in its alphabetical place, to eliminate needless shuttling from index to index; yet so implemented with subentries, repeated entries, and cross references that one can find all facets of such topics as "redemption," which instantly commend themselves for study, carefully displayed under one heading. The second index will list scripture passages referred to out of context, so that a reader studying a passage in Romans may know, for example, if that same verse has been discussed in the volume on Galatians. No attempt has been made to avoid duplication, as, for instance, in the Exegesis and Exposition of parallel passages in the Synoptic Gospels; for the editors have felt that such duplication adds value to the Commentary by giving two interpretations (to cite a case in point) rather than one of the parable of the lost sheep. The third

index consists of illustrations. There is a wealth of such material in these volumes, of far better quality and far vaster scope than any "book of illustrations" has provided; and this particular index offers this wealth at quick avail.

A house in Bruges has a motto inscribed on a rafter near the front door: "There Is More Within." This brief guide to *The Interpreter's Bible* only echoes that motto or, at best, only summarizes some main values. The very paper on which the Commentary is printed has been chosen with costly care for its lasting whiteness, lightness, and strength; and the bindings likewise have durability corresponding to their worthy and attractive appearance. Yet these externals only hint the inner treasure, for there is hardly a page that does not lead out and on, like a Columbus voyage, into a new world.

There is only one Book. That Book is the noun; other books are but poor adjectives. God renews in this Book, age on age, his covenant with his people. For fifty or sixty years there has been, at least in the English language, no comprehensive commentary on the Holy Scriptures. Now comes this Commentary, with better manuscripts as initial resource and with better knowledge than other commentaries could have claimed. It appears at a crucial juncture in history, when (if our human eyes can judge) one age is dying, and another is being born from a "holy void." No age can safely neglect the Book, least of all an age in transition; for an age that has struck its tents and is on the move needs even more than other ages a pillar of cloud by day and a pillar of fire by night. The Bible tells of Israel, the chosen people through whom God's purpose has been made known to our world; it tells of Christ, than whom there is "no other name . . . by which we must be saved." There are signs that our era is turning from ruinous doctrines of self-help to a new obedience to God's will and power, from man's exploitive skill to a trust in God's mercy in Jesus Christ. We pray that *The Interpreter's Bible* may hasten that turning, and prepare the way along which Christ shall come to reign in love, "King of kings, and Lord of lords."

GEORGE ARTHUR BUTTRICK

BOOK EDITOR'S PREFACE

The Interpreter's Bible is presented as the embodiment of a comprehensive Christian biblical scholarship. Eminent scholars and interpreters living in different parts of the world, but at one in their zeal for truth, have been drawn upon to contribute to this Commentary. The list of those who have had a part in its making is a roster of persons renowned for distinguished leadership in the field of biblical interpretation. To each of these contributors every encouragement has been extended by the Editorial Board, so that out of the richness of their ripened scholarship, and out of the warmth of their expositional interpretation, *The Interpreter's Bible* may go forth to accomplish the mission for which it was created—to interpret anew the timeless truth of God's holy Word.

It will be expected, of course, that among 125 different writers there will be a certain diversity of interpretation, not only about passages of Scripture whose meanings have always been debated, but even about "accepted" passages. It is the glory of Protestantism that each believer has the right to be guided by his own mind and conscience under God's Spirit in matters of faith and its interpretation. The Protestant principle of "the priesthood of all believers" so affirms, and thus grants to every Christian the right to hold and to declare his own sense of Christian truth, provided he keeps within the bond of corporate love and prayer. There is real merit in honestly differing points of view, granted this fundamental concern for the fellowship of believers.

This advantage has been sought in *The Interpreter's Bible*. Although uniformity of presentation has of course been called for, according to the general plan of the Commentary, in the interpretation itself the exegetical and expository skill of the separate contributors has been depended upon to have full play in all those ways which would make for a deeper appreciation of the sacred Word. At the same time every effort has been made to see that all interpretation be constructive and edifying, and that nothing captious or capricious appear. The writers have been encouraged to speak the truth in love by such light as God has given to their reverent and disciplined minds. Truth always has a self-evidencing power, nowhere more so than in the pages of sacred Scripture, and the overwhelming fact is not that Christian scholars and exegetes differ from each other in interpreting biblical truth, but that they so heartily agree in all its essentials.

The Bible is a book of infinite variety, and both those who would read and those who would interpret the riches of its truth must be prepared, like the scribes of old, to discover within it treasures both new and old. The thoughts of God are always wider than the measure of man's mind; but that mind, with understanding reverence, has the power given it by the Creator to read God's thoughts after him in his holy Word.

Long ago a scholarly father of the church said that the Bible ought to be read by the light of that same Spirit through whom it was written. This is true, and of all men's interpretations we must say,

> They are but broken lights of thee,
> And thou, O Lord, art more than they.

God abides; his Word abides; and his Holy Spirit, coming imperceptibly like the morning light or in sudden lightning flash, is the best interpreter of his Word. So from many minds and much labor and consecration this great work goes forth, in the prayer that it may redound to the glory of God and advance the cause of Christian life and truth in the world.

NOLAN B. HARMON

EDITOR'S PREFACE

For fifty years no full-scale commentary has been produced in the English language on the whole Bible. Exegetical studies on the one hand and expository aids on the other have appeared, not with a "great gulf fixed" between them, but with too little mutual concern. Both scholarship and preaching have suffered from the separation: perhaps scholarship has tended to barren erudition, and preaching to "vain imaginings"—vain because of somewhat tenuous contact with the meaning of Scripture. Preachers, teachers, and other students of the Bible need a threefold resource: namely, introduction to Scripture and the individual books, exegesis of the text, and relevant exposition. We hope not only that *The Interpreter's Bible* will meet this need, but that it may disclose unsuspected treasures for those who would bring forth "things new and old" from the "unsearchable riches" of the Book.

Recent decades have seen a notable increase in biblical knowledge. New manuscripts of portions of both the Old and the New Testaments have been found, of considerably earlier date than those on which the standard text had previously been based, with consequent gain both in textual study and historical criticism. Archaeology, the scrutiny of ancient papyri, and research in comparative philology and literature and religion have all thrown light on the meaning of the Scriptures. Careful and reverent investigation has dated the various books of the Bible with far greater accuracy than was formerly possible; and this new chronology has been a lamp to our feet—as witness our fresh understanding of Isaiah, or of Matthew and Luke when these Gospels are compared with their Marcan source. Study of the text, especially in the light of Deissmann's brilliant realization that the New Testament manuscripts are written in vernacular rather than in literary Greek or in some special biblical vehicle, has brought the meaning of word and phrase into sharper focus. Form criticism has helped us to see how the traditions of the Hebrew fathers, the laws of the priests, the poems of the prophets and psalmists on the one hand, and the records of the teaching of Jesus on the other, have taken form and color, perhaps inevitably, from the life-situation respectively of the Hebrew community and the first-century church—an insight that is our gain rather than our loss. Above all, present theological trends have confirmed and renewed the faith of the church in the Bible as the very Word of God. So revolutionary is this whole body of knowledge that many of the older commentaries, despite their integrity in labor, are in some regards out-of-date.

But more than scholarship is needed in a true commentary. The gospel is eternal: from age to age we may catch new accents in God's Word to men, but the Word itself is from the foundation of the world. Similarly we may trace new marvels in the realm of light, as astrology gives place to the ever-growing wonder of astronomy, but the light abides unchanging, blessing all men's eyes, shining in every lowly place, even though we may understand only that light is light. Growing knowledge about the Bible is not enough to save us, any more than bricks are enough to make a home. The Spirit of the crucified and risen Lord must dwell in the knowledge, or the knowledge itself becomes a prison. Therefore a double demand confronts every commentary on the Scriptures: first, to be true to the clearer understanding that waits on reverent study, since God always has "new light to break from his Word"; and second, to avow its unwavering fealty to God's Incarnate Word by whose forgiving grace all men live. *The Interpreter's Bible* earnestly desires to meet this double demand: it would be honest in the truth that makes men free, and it would cleave to the evangel of Christ born, crucified, and risen "for us men and for our salvation."

The name *The Interpreter's Bible* was chosen not only because it shows well the purpose of these volumes, but because it carries pleasing echoes of "The Interpreter's House" where Christian, in Bunyan's inspired record, learned the deeper meanings of the gospel. The editors whose names appear facing the title page of the Commentary have come from different denominational backgrounds, and the writers represent almost every branch of the Christian church. For several years they have labored on this project, with a sense of mission and in prayer. Not only has there been no difference in spirit; there has been mutual trust deepening into friendship in the grace of Christ. Thus divergences in opinion have only added zest, comradeship, and wisdom in the task.

Slowly the Commentary has grown. Thirty-six consultants, drawn from all the larger Protestant groups in the English-speaking world, helped to guide the initial steps. The titles of general articles and the subjects of maps were determined. A style book was prepared to help contributors and to give consistency in form. The total number of words in the Commentary was estimated at approximately eight million. These were allotted in carefully planned proportions to general articles, and to the introduction, exegesis, and exposition of the separate books of the Bible. The contributors were then chosen; they represent the best exegetical and expository skill of our time. Manuscripts were carefully read, in each instance by both an exegetical and an expository editor, and changes made in co-operation with the respective authors. Questions of policy, foreseen and unforeseen, were honestly faced and carefully answered. Type forms were selected for the three-part arrangement of text, exegesis, and exposition which itself resulted from the study of twenty samples. Finally the copy for the first-published volume, Matthew–Mark, was sent to the printer—the "first fruits" of long labor and unrelinquished hope.

Some further remarks on the page format may be in order, for here also the Commentary breaks new ground, in line with the editorial resolve that *The Interpreter's Bible* shall provide comprehensive yet quickly available help to the student and teacher. At the top of the page in parallel columns are the King James Version and the Revised Standard Version of the scripture passages under discussion, so that the differences in the two versions may instantly be seen. Below these are the exegetical comments, printed across the page, with the key phrases struck off in bolder type, like the "notes" appended to a Shakespearean text. Below these is the exposition, printed in two columns, and so written that it may give prompting and "opening" to the interpreter. Each book of the Bible is prefaced by a succinct but well-informed introduction. General articles offer similar introduction to the whole book. A wide roster of maps gives visual aid. The Hebrew, Aramaic, and Greek terms are quoted where these are needed for clarity, but their use has been held to a minimum in favor of the easier-to-understand "transliteration." We believe that the reader who does not know the original languages will find no undue obstacle. The Hebrew and Greek letter fonts have been chosen to accord with the clear and attractive Baskerville type of the English text.

The editor would be recreant in debt of gratitude should he fail to acknowledge the invaluable help of his colleagues. The associate editors have worked unflaggingly, and with such stanch friendliness that it would be hard to imagine a more kindling *esprit de corps*. The consulting editors not only served as judicious advisers and critics in the planning of fundamental policies but have continued to provide wise counsel and encouragement. Contributors have exercised in Christian restraint the freedom they have been gladly accorded. They have expressed individual conviction, as the editors have urged, but have honored differing convictions; and they have not only accepted, but have sought and welcomed, editorial suggestion. Thomas Nelson and Sons and the International Council of Religious Education have given outright use not only of the Revised Standard Version of the New Testament already published, but also of the earlier drafts and the final version of the Old Testament while still in preparation—an extraordinary act of co-operation which has greatly enhanced the value of the

Commentary. Thomas Nelson and Sons have also generously granted use of their black and white maps in sufficient number to illuminate each book of the Bible. Mr. Emil Lowenstein has prepared the excellent colored "dimensional maps" for the end pages of the volumes.

Special appreciation has been earned by the publishers. They have shown as true a sense of mission as any editor or writer. They have steadfastly refused to spare expense, even though they are well aware that their great financial investment may never be returned and certainly cannot be recovered in this generation. The members of their official Board of Publication caught the vision of service to all Christendom, and authorized the project without limitation upon its cost. Dr. B. A. Whitmore and Dr. Fred D. Stone, Publishing Agents at the time of its inception, and Mr. Lovick Pierce and Dr. Roy L. Smith, their successors, have given wise counsel and direction to the whole endeavor. Dr. Nolan B. Harmon has served both as a member of the Editorial Board and in his official capacity as Editor of Abingdon-Cokesbury Press. Others should be mentioned by name: Mr. Pat Beaird, manager of the Press, who has given able over-all guidance and enthusiasm; Mr. Gordon Duncan, who wrote the style book and has provided constant help in that field; the Rev. Charles L. Wallis, who is responsible for the extensive indexes appearing in the final volume; Mr. E. Sinclair Hertell, who has corrected the copy; Miss Bernice Coller, who has prepared all manuscripts for the printer and compassed the exceedingly hard task of page-setting; and Miss Elizabeth Stouffer, who has been not only secretary to the whole Board but also a competent editorial assistant. A special word of gratitude is due the printers, binders, Linotype operators, proofreaders, and others who have contributed their skill and by their eager interest become partners in the enterprise. It is difficult to believe that any endeavor could have found a more harmonious and indefatigable "task force" than *The Interpreter's Bible*. For the editor the experience will always be a spring of gratitude.

Surely no commentary on the Bible has appeared at a more crucial juncture in history. We live at the end of an age. Accustomed patterns in statecraft and commerce, as in the church itself, are dissolving: "The old order changeth, yielding place to new." Only dimly can any man foresee the "shape of things to come." But one truth is paramount: God has spoken once and for all in Jesus Christ. In him alone can the world cohere. Each new age will not be new, but only "chaos and old night," if it does not worship Christ as Savior and sovereign Lord. The Holy Scriptures are sun by day and stars by night in every era of man's pilgrimage. Therefore a new commentary on the Bible is both timely and indispensable, for, in every unknown tomorrow, "thy word is a lamp unto my feet." It is our ardent prayer that *The Interpreter's Bible* may be used of God in the travail of our times for the coming of the kingdom of his Son.

GEORGE ARTHUR BUTTRICK

ABBREVIATIONS AND EXPLANATIONS

ABBREVIATIONS

Canonical books and bibliographical terms are abbreviated according to common usage

Amer. Trans. — *The Bible, An American Translation*, Old Testament, ed. J. M. P. Smith
Apoc.—Apocrypha
Aq.—Aquila
ASV—American Standard Version (1901)
Barn.—Epistle of Barnabas
Clem.—Clement
C.T.—Consonantal Text
Did.—Didache
Ecclus.—Ecclesiasticus
ERV—English Revised Version (1881-85)

Exeg.—Exegesis
Expos.—Exposition
Goodspeed—*The Bible, An American Translation*, New Testament and Apocrypha, tr. Edgar J. Goodspeed
Herm. Vis., etc.—The Shepherd of Hermas: Visions, Mandates, Similitudes
Ign. Eph., etc.—Epistles of Ignatius to the Ephesians, Magnesians, Trallians, Romans, Philadelphians, Smyrnaeans, and Polycarp

KJV—King James Version (1611)
LXX—Septuagint
Macc.—Maccabees
Moffatt—*The Bible, A New Translation*, by James Moffatt
M.T.—Masoretic Text
N.T.—New Testament
O.T.—Old Testament
Polyc. Phil.—Epistle of Polycarp to the Philippians
Pseudep. — Pseudepigrapha
Pss. Sol.—Psalms of Solomon

RSV—Revised Standard Version (1946-52)
Samar.—Samaritan recension
Symm.—Symmachus
Targ.—Targum
Test. Reuben, etc.—Testament of Reuben, and others of the Twelve Patriarchs
Theod.—Theodotion
Tob.—Tobit
Vulg.—Vulgate
Weymouth—*The New Testament in Modern Speech*, by Richard Francis Weymouth
Wisd. Sol.—Wisdom of Solomon

QUOTATIONS AND REFERENCES

Boldface type in Exegesis and Exposition indicates a quotation from either the King James or the Revised Standard Version of the passage under discussion. The two versions are distinguished only when attention is called to a difference between them. Readings of other versions are not in boldface type and are regularly identified.

In scripture references a letter (*a*, *b*, etc.) appended to a verse number indicates a clause within the verse; an additional Greek letter indicates a subdivision within the clause. When no book is named, the book under discussion is understood.

Arabic numbers connected by colons, as in scripture references, indicate chapters and verses in deuterocanonical and noncanonical works. For other ancient writings roman numbers indicate major divisions, arabic numbers subdivisions, these being connected by periods. For modern works a roman number and an arabic number connected by a comma indicate volume and page. Bibliographical data on a contemporary work cited by a writer may be found by consulting the first reference to the work by that writer (or the bibliography, if the writer has included one).

GREEK TRANSLITERATIONS

α = a	ε = e	ι = i	ν = n	ρ = r	φ = ph
β = b	ζ = z	κ = k	ξ = x	σ(ς) = s	χ = ch
γ = g	η = ē	λ = l	o = o	τ = t	ψ = ps
δ = d	θ = th	μ = m	π = p	υ = u, y	ω = ō

HEBREW AND ARAMAIC TRANSLITERATIONS

I. HEBREW ALPHABET

א = '	ה = h	ט = ṭ	מ(ם) = m	פ(ף) = p, ph	שׁ = s, sh
ב = b, bh	ו = w	י = y	נ(ן) = n	צ(ץ) = ç	ת = t, th
ג = g, gh	ז = z	כ(ך) = k, kh	ס = ş	ק = q	
ד = d, dh	ח = ḥ	ל = l	ע = '	ר = r	

II. MASORETIC POINTING

Pure-long	Tone-long	Short	Composite *sh°wa*	
ָ = â	ַ = ā	ַ = a	ֱ = ᵉ	NOTE: (*a*) The *páthaḥ* furtive is transliterated as a *ḥateph-páthaḥ*. (*b*) The simple *sh°wa*, when vocal, is transliterated ᵉ. (*c*) The tonic accent, which is indicated only when it occurs on a syllable other than the last, is transliterated by an acute accent over the vowel.
ֵ = ê	ֵ = ē	ֶ = e	ֳ = ᵒ	
or ִ = î		ִ = i	ֲ = ᵃ	
וֹ or ֹ = ô	ֹ = ō	ָ = o		
וּ = û		ֻ = u		

TABLE OF CONTENTS

VOLUME I

GENERAL ARTICLES ON THE BIBLE

GENERAL ARTICLES ON THE OLD TESTAMENT

THE INTERPRETER'S BIBLE

THE BOOK OF GENESIS

THE BOOK OF EXODUS

MAPS

GENERAL ARTICLES

on

THE BIBLE

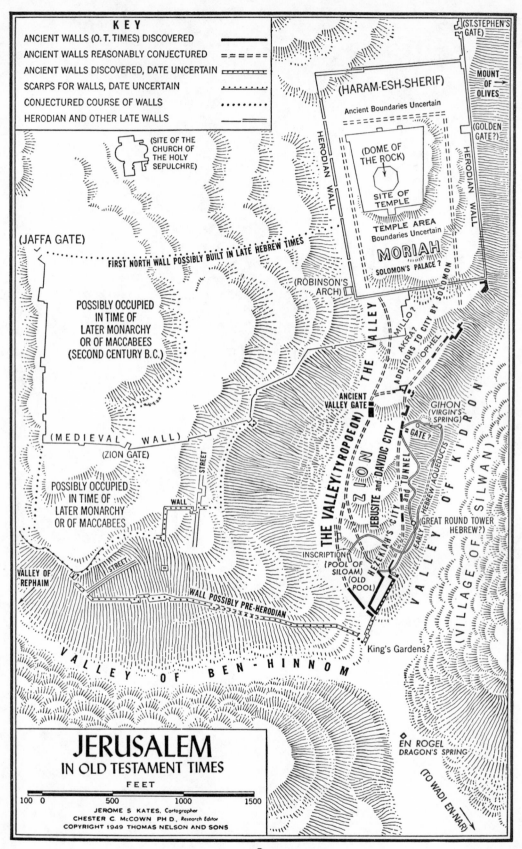

KEY

ANCIENT WALLS (O.T. TIMES) DISCOVERED	
ANCIENT WALLS REASONABLY CONJECTURED	
ANCIENT WALLS DISCOVERED, DATE UNCERTAIN	
SCARPS FOR WALLS, DATE UNCERTAIN	
CONJECTURED COURSE OF WALLS	
HERODIAN AND OTHER LATE WALLS	

(SITE OF THE CHURCH OF THE HOLY SEPULCHRE)

(ST. STEPHEN'S GATE)

(HARAM-ESH-SHERIF)

Ancient Boundaries Uncertain

(DOME OF THE ROCK)

SITE OF TEMPLE

TEMPLE AREA
Boundaries Uncertain

MORIAH

SOLOMON'S PALACE?

MOUNT OF OLIVES →

(GOLDEN GATE?)

(JAFFA GATE)

FIRST NORTH WALL POSSIBLY BUILT IN LATE HEBREW TIMES

(ROBINSON'S ARCH)

POSSIBLY OCCUPIED IN TIME OF LATER MONARCHY OR OF MACCABEES (SECOND CENTURY B.C.)

MILLO?

AKRA?

ADDITIONS TO CITY BY SOLOMON

OPHEL

ANCIENT VALLEY GATE

THE VALLEY (TYROPOEON)

ZION

JEBUSITE and DAVIDIC CITY

GATE?

HEZEKIAH'S 2nd TUNNEL

EARLY HEBREW AQUEDUCTS

GIHON (VIRGIN'S SPRING)

(GREAT ROUND TOWER HEBREW?)

(MEDIEVAL WALL)

(ZION GATE)

POSSIBLY OCCUPIED IN TIME OF LATER MONARCHY OR OF MACCABEES

STREET

WALL

STREET

VALLEY OF REPHAIM

STREET

WALL POSSIBLY PRE-HEBREW TIMES

INSCRIPTION (POOL OF SILOAM) (OLD POOL)

(VALLEY OF SILWAN)

(VILLAGE OF SILWAN)

VALLEY OF KIDRON

King's Gardens?

VALLEY OF BEN-HINNOM

EN ROGEL DRAGON'S SPRING

(TO WADI EN-NAR)

JERUSALEM
IN OLD TESTAMENT TIMES

FEET

100 0   500   1000   1500

JEROME S. KATES, Cartographer
CHESTER C. McCOWN PH.D., Research Editor
COPYRIGHT 1949 THOMAS NELSON AND SONS

THE BIBLE: ITS SIGNIFICANCE AND AUTHORITY

by HERBERT H. FARMER

From the earliest period of its history the Christian church has regarded the Scriptures as being in some sense the special revelation of God, and therefore as being in some sense the final standard or norm of Christian truth. The Old Testament seems to have been accepted from the beginning as an authoritative revelation of God, and it was not very long before the writings which came ultimately to form the New Testament were also in circulation, carrying a similar, though not precisely assessed, authority. No consistent or unanimous answer has, however, been given by the church to the question in what sense exactly the Scriptures are the revelation of God and the standard of truth. This article is intended to be a contribution to the answering of this question as it confronts the Christian believer today. It is written from the angle of Christian faith and experience as these are shared and known within the fellowship of the Christian church: that is to say, it accepts as a datum the uniquely normative status which the church has always assigned to the Bible, and it endeavors to explore its meaning and bearings in relation to the Christian faith taken as a whole. In other words, the question of the Bible is here considered as a theological question; the answering of it involves raising the question as to what the Christian faith essentially is, for only on that basis

can we determine the essential significance and authority of the Bible.

It is, of course, possible to approach the Bible from other angles, in relation to other interests and beliefs. The books of the Bible are so various, and cover alike in their origin and content so vast a period of time, that they provide invaluable material for the historian, the archaeologist, the anthropologist, and many others. Each of these, in using the biblical material, in effect asks and answers the question of the significance and authority of the Bible for his particular study. Such different approaches may provide important material for the Christian theologian inquiring into the significance and authority of the Bible for the Christian faith; indeed, there is no reason why the Christian theologian himself should not on occasion study the Bible, not as a theologian, but as a historian, an archaeologist, or an anthropologist. The question whether in pursuing such studies he should seek to divest himself of his Christian convictions and presuppositions we need not explore. The point is that however much the various ways of studying the Bible may interact, the special interest of the Christian theologian as such, and the one which governs this article, remains quite distinct: we raise the question of the significance and authority of the Bible as part of the wider theological

3

question of the essence of the Christian faith which the church is commissioned to proclaim to the world.

This being the line of approach, we are immediately confronted with a difficulty. As has been said, we can determine in what sense exactly the Bible has the pre-eminent normative status in the church's life, which has always been given to it, only on the basis of our general understanding of the Christian faith. But, it may be said, if the Bible has such a status, how can we reach a general understanding of the essence of the Christian faith prior to and independently of our understanding of that status? We appear to be involved in a circle. If the Bible is the final standard, then we can know nothing for certain concerning the essentials of the Christian faith apart from it; yet if we know nothing for certain about the essentials apart from the Bible, how can we know for certain this particular "essential," namely, that the Bible is such a standard, and how can we know the right way to use it as such a standard? It is obviously no way out of the difficulty to quote the Bible itself as an authoritative witness to its own supreme normative status, for apart from the fact that it makes no claim to such a status, it is clear that even if it did, to concede the claim on the ground of its own *ipse dixit* would be to beg the whole question. (The statement made in II Tim. 3:16 cannot be taken as such a claim, for it gives no indication as to what exactly is meant by the words "inspired by God," or what writings are to be regarded as so inspired. Furthermore, the verse does not do more than declare that inspired scripture is "profitable for teaching, for reproof, for correction, and for training in righteousness"—a statement which nobody would wish to question, whatever his views on the Bible might be. To declare that certain writings are profitable, and to declare them to be in some sense a final standard or norm, are two very different things.)

The difficulty, however, is more apparent than real, and arises out of a failure to distinguish between two types of standard or norm. There are what may be called extrinsic or static norms, and there are what may be called intrinsic or organic norms. An example of the former is the measuring rod or yardstick, which exists independently of the objects it measures: it is brought to the objects, or they are brought to it, and the transaction being concluded, the two continue to exist independently. An example of the latter is the indwelling normative principle which informs a living organism, so that it grows to and is preserved in its distinctive maturity amidst the changes and challenges of its environment. An organism has within it something which can only be thought of as a kind of "spirit of the whole," which keeps all the various biochemical processes in a specific unity or balance with one another. Such a normative principle obviously has no existence apart from the organism, and the organism has no existence apart from it: the organic processes, and the normative principle which informs them and binds them into a unity, though distinguishable in thought, constitute a single, indivisible reality. A better example, for our purpose, of an intrinsic norm (better because it takes us into the realm of the personal) is that impalpable and indefinable, but very real, something which we think of as the spirit of a nation or an institution. Such a statement as "It is un-American, or un-English, to do so-and-so" (despite the deplorable misuse to which it is sometimes put) rests on the recognition of a normative factor within the national life which is really "there," impossible though it be to give it either precise definition or exact location. It is an immanent or intrinsic norm, dwelling within and informing a people in a characteristic way, and having no existence whatever apart from them. This is not to say that there are no explicit formulations of the norm to which appeal can be made when occasion demands. The laws of a people, the constitutional practice (written or unwritten) which directs the form and process of its government, its recorded history, its highest and most distinctive cultural products, especially its literature—all these are in large degree permanently and publicly accessible, just as the yardstick is. Nevertheless the norm, even in its written expression, never becomes—like the yardstick—extrinsic to the things it informs and measures, for nobody can understand it, still less rightly interpret and use it, who does not share in the spirit of the people, the *esprit de corps*, which it not only expresses but also creates and fosters.

The normative relation of the Bible to the faith and life of the church is clearly of the intrinsic kind. It is, we must insist, not the less a true norm for being intrinsic; indeed, it is not the less a final norm, in the sense that no question of faith or conduct can be deemed to be rightly determined which is not thought out with the Bible, as it were, being present throughout the discussion and taking a dominant and authoritative part in it. Nevertheless, what the Bible says can be rightly interpreted only by those who livingly share in the distinctively Christian life within the fellowship of the church; for this life, though it could not arise or be preserved without the Bible, always includes far more than is or ever could be contained in or expressed through a written record. These are matters which will be more fully explored in the course of this article; it is enough at the moment to insist that if we think of the Bible as exercising an intrinsically normative function within the life of the church, the difficulty about circular reasoning disappears. If it is true that we cannot rightly apprehend the essentials of the Christian faith and life without using the Bible as an authoritative source and norm, it is equally true that we cannot apprehend the Bible as such a source and norm, still less rightly use it, apart from a living participation in the church's faith and life. This is not to argue in a circle, because the Bible, in its function as norm, and the church's faith and life are organically one, and form a single, indivisible whole.

This suggests the plan we may follow in seeking to grasp and expound the significance and authority of the Bible. We shall start from the thought just indicated, that the Christian faith and life as manifested within and sustained by the fellowship of the church constitute an organic whole which, in spite of its many variant developments in the course of the centuries and its many aberrations from its own ideal, has persisted in a recognizably distinct form throughout—a whole in which we ourselves now share, and within which the Bible has an immanently normative place and function. The task of the Christian will then be so to expound faith that (a) it is seen to be in harmony with the actual content of the Bible itself, for clearly if what is set forth as "normal" Christianity (in the sense of being "regular or usual or not deviating from the common type") is not in harmony with what is acknowledged to be "normative" (in the sense of setting up a standard), then the unity of the organism of Christian faith and life is seriously broken; (b) the normative function of the Bible within the whole is fully preserved and explained; and (c) the way in which that normative function is to be exercised is made clear.

The plan will be to speak first of the essence of the Christian faith, and then to develop this in relation to points (a), (b), and (c) in turn.

I. Normal or Essential Christianity

The necessity of starting from the thought of the Christian faith and life within the church as an organic whole might suggest that nothing less than an exposition of the whole content of the faith is required if we are to understand the significance and authority of the Bible within it. Fortunately that is not so. Just because we are dealing with an organic whole, and are particularly interested in the normative factors within it, all that is required is a grasp of that central and controlling truth which imparts and preserves to the whole its specifically Christian character, distinguishing it once and for all from other religious "wholes," no matter what partial identities or similarities there may otherwise be.

There can hardly be division of opinion as to what this central and controlling "essence" of Christian faith and life is. It is belief in the Incarnation—the conviction that God himself came, and comes, into human history in the person of Jesus Christ. Jesus Christ is God himself in action within history "for us men and for our salvation," in a way that is unique, final, adequate, and indispensable. "There is none other name under heaven given among men, whereby we must be saved" (Acts 4:12); "God so loved the world, that he gave his only begotten Son" (John 3:16); "God was in Christ, reconciling the world unto himself" (II Cor. 5:19). There have, of course, been great differences among Christians as to the precise significance and implications of this central affirmation of the Incarnation, the grounds for making it, the way in which the divine action it describes is wrought out in men's lives; and some have interpreted it in ways that have seemed to others to be destructive of its distinctively Christian meaning. But it hardly can be questioned that unless a man is prepared to make the affirmation in some sense or other, then, no matter how much he may in fact owe to Christian teaching, or may accept and exemplify Christian moral values, any claim he may make to be a specifically Christian believer, with a specifically Christian gospel to preach, is, to say the least, extremely dubious. This is not a merely personal view; on the contrary, it is hardly more than a report of evident historical truth. However much and rightly we may dislike heresy hunting, and whatever difficulty may arise in border line cases, the fact remains that the belief in the Incarnation has been the central, distinctive, all-controlling belief of the Christian movement all down the ages; it is the heart and center of what may be called "historic" Christianity, meaning by that simply Christianity as a movement having a distinctive character and being identifiable as such, in spite of all its variant and even conflicting forms, throughout the centuries.

The statement of the dogma of the Incarnation just made—that God himself came, and comes, into human history in the person of Jesus Christ—does not, however, suffice without further explication to bring out the distinctive essence of the Christian faith as this is determinative of the significance and authority of the Bible within it. To do this we must concentrate on two things in the statement—the word "into" and the phrase "came, and comes." We shall take each in turn.

A. God's Action "into" History.—There are two ways in which the word "into" might be interpreted. These may be made plain by a somewhat fantastic illustration. Suppose that I am dropped from an airplane into the midst of a savage people, with the commission to transform their life into something very much higher, and suppose that I am given power to effect whatsoever I will. I am, as it were, a savior come down "for these men and for their salvation." How shall I go to work? I can do either of two things.

In the first place, I can, if I choose, put into operation at once the higher civilized life which I represent. Using the unlimited resources at my disposal, I can break up the tribal organization of these people, pour scorn on their traditions, prohibit their low moral codes, annihilate their primitive culture—in one gigantic upheaval and revolution pound everything to pieces and then force the pieces into the mold of my own plans and ideals. Suppose that, impossible though it is, I succeed in doing this. Is it not clear that while in one sense I have acted *into* their history, in another sense I have not acted into *their* history at all? For what I have done is to negate and annihilate *their* history and put something radically discontinuous and new in its place. To make what may seem a fine distinction—though it is really an important one and exactly expresses the point— my coming as their savior has been *into* their history, but not *in and through* it: it has been, as it were, down the vertical, but not along the horizontal. In a similar way, a bomb which drops from the sky and destroys my house, while in one sense it is an event in the history of the house, in another sense it is not, for it is in fact the end of the history of the house. There is "before" but no "after"; indeed, strictly speaking, there is no "before," for nothing in its previous history had anything to do with the coming of the bomb. That dropped from the skies, a bolt from the blue.

The alternative line of action has already been indicated by contrast. Instead of annihilating the tribe's whole manner of life, I may take the trouble to "get inside" it, to make myself one with it, to work from within it, to re-create it on the basis of whatsoever there is of good in it, whatsoever is usable in relation to the higher mode of life to which I am commissioned to lift it. The effect of this will be that the new mode of life, though new, will still have the impress of the tribe's own distinctive history and character upon it. It will be saving action not merely *into* their history, but also *in and through* it. There will be continuity between the new life and the old—the pattern will, so to speak, run on, the fabric will come off the loom in one piece; it will still be *their* history. And yet at the same time there will be radical discontinuity, for my dropping from the airplane, and all that I bring with me, will not have been anything that their previous history could have produced by itself. If I had not dropped from above, their history would have continued indefinitely on its former degraded level. There is continuity, yet also discontinuity.

To return now to the fundamental Christian affirmation of the Incarnation. The Christian faith, when it has been true to itself, has always maintained that God's saving action in Christ was along the line of the second alternative in our fantastic parallel. It was action *into* history in that Christ's coming was something radically new, an irruption "vertically" from above, something which, without God's deliberate intention thus personally to come among men, could not have happened, something utterly beyond the resources of human history to bring forth. On the other hand, it was also action *in and through* history—along the "horizontal": there was real continuity with what had gone before in the ordinary web and texture of human affairs, and with what came afterward. The Incarnation was real history, yet not merely history: there was real continuity, yet also radical discontinuity.

The phrase "when it has been true to itself," which was used at the beginning of the last paragraph, may sound somewhat question begging. But if we allow Christianity to define itself by its own dominant historical manifestations, there can be no question that the insistence on both the "into" and the "in and through" aspects of the Incarnation—the repudiation on the one hand of any tendency to assert discontinuity at the expense of continuity, and on the other hand of any tendency to assert continuity at the expense of discontinuity—has characterized the main tradition of the faith. And this is the more clear when we realize that this main tradition has had continually to assert itself against the two opposed tendencies just referred to, both in their obvious and more subtle forms—just as in the compass the holding power of the magnetic north is most clearly evidenced by the oscillations of the needle on either side of it. Thus the distinction usually drawn between the Antiochian and the Alexandrian schools of christological thought in the early centuries obviously represents in a broad way the two sides of the antithesis. The Antiochian school tended to lay the major emphasis on the humanity of Jesus—that is, on his continuity with history. The extreme wing of this school was adoptionism, with its teaching that Jesus was merely an unusually good man in whom the divine Spirit was able to dwell in greater degree than in other men, though not in a way that was essentially different—which comes as near to denying discontinuity as is compatible with making any plausible claim to a distinctively Christian gospel of the Incarnation. The Alexandrian school tended to lay the major emphasis on the divinity of Jesus, that is, on his discontinuity with history. On the extreme wing of this school was Docetism, with its assertion that the human side of Jesus was mere "seeming," a phantasm of humanity—which comes as near denying continuity as is compatible with making any plausible claim to a distinctively Christian gospel of the Incarnation. In the end the problem defined itself (as the Formula of Chalcedon indicates) as the problem of asserting both the continuity and the discontinuity—the genuine humanity rooted in history and the genuinely divine irruption "into" history—without impairing the unity of the Savior's person. In our own day it is possible to discern the same tension between continuity and discontinuity. Labels can be very unjust to individual thinkers, but broadly speaking, the reaction of the movement associated with the name of Karl Barth, against what is vaguely called liberal Protestantism, as represented, say, by Ernst Troeltsch or Adolf von Harnack, is, especially in the realm of Christology, the vigorous reassertion of discontinuity against a too exclusive emphasis on continuity; of the "into" or "vertical" against a falsifying preoccupation with the "in and through" or "horizontal" (see below, p. 11).

B. God's Continuing Action in Christ.—It was said above that God came, and comes, into human history in the person of Jesus Christ. The phrase "and comes" is important.

The Christian faith affirms that God's saving action "into" and "in and through" history in Jesus Christ did not come to an end with the death of Jesus on Calvary. The action still continues. It is still going on through the church, of which Christ is the living head, and in which he is present through the Holy Spirit as the creative and constitutive principle of its being and life. There are deep theological problems involved in this affirmation, into which it is not our business to enter here; but there can be no question that this conviction of the continuing, redeeming presence of Christ in the world is axiomatic in the Christian faith and life. It is only in relation to this belief that the meaning and the centrality of the Resurrection in the Christian gospel can be understood. The essence of the Christian faith concerning the Resurrection, as it is set forth in the New Testament, is not that Christ survived death according to some general capacity for survival inherent in the human soul as such, but rather that God raised him up; that is to say, the Resurrection was part of God's mighty act of redemption to save mankind and establish his kingdom. Furthermore, it is part of the same act of redemption that Christ thus raised up has not passed into the "beyond," out of touch with men except as an inspiring memory. On the contrary, he has been raised to "God's right hand," and this means that he is now accessible, as a living, active presence mediated through the Holy Spirit, to all who give themselves to him in discipleship and faith.

We may put it like this: the Resurrection and the Ascension constitute the link between two periods in the continuous "biography" of the Redeemer—the period in which he dwelt among men in the flesh, subject to the limitations of time and space, and of which the culmination was his crucifixion and burial, and the period in which in some mysterious way he transcends those limits and becomes the unseen and living Lord and Savior of all who hear his call and seek to obey it in penitence and trust and in mutual love. It would be misleading, if natural, to say that the first period was the earthly period while the second is the heavenly, for in both the sphere of his saving work, of God's saving action in him, is human life and human history. From this point of view it is legitimate to say that the Christian church as the fellowship created and sustained in history by Christ through the Holy Spirit is the extension of the Incarnation. In this sense the church is part of the historical biography of Christ.

In the light of this understanding of the essential Christian faith we can now take up the question of the significance and authority of the Bible within the total organism of the church's life. Each of the three points (a), (b), and (c), set forth above, will be considered in turn:

II. The Essence of the Faith Harmonious with the Content and Structure of the Bible

It was said that our task must be so to understand the Christian faith that we can see it to be deeply grounded in and harmonious with the content of the Bible, for otherwise typical Christianity would not be in accord with its own acknowledged norm, and the unity of the organism of Christian faith and life would be seriously disrupted.

If then we concentrate on the central truth of the Incarnation, and in particular on its dual aspect of continuity-discontinuity, we find that this is in fact very deeply grounded in the whole structure and content of the Bible. Indeed, the Bible might be said to be built up throughout, in a way that is quite without parallel, on the continuity-discontinuity theme, the theme beginning with ancient Israel and reaching its consummation (at the same time disclosing its

7

deep, underlying meaning) in the divine saving action in Christ. This may be expounded under three heads.

A. Continuity-Discontinuity in the Old Testament.—The picture of the people of Israel with which the Old Testament presents us through the wide variety of its contents—historical narratives, legal and liturgical codes, poetry, hymns, proverbs and maxims, utterances of great prophetic souls speaking in the name of God—is obviously the picture of a people whose life is continuous with the life of mankind generally. This is true in the first place in respect of the ordinary human nature of the persons concerned. To enter into the world of ancient Israel as it is disclosed to us in the pages of the Old Testament is to enter the same world of human actions and motives, loves and hates, passions and sins, hopes and fears, as we ourselves know: the people and the situations which confront them are recognizably "everyman" and the situation of "everyman." This is one reason why the Old Testament can still come alive for —and speak to—the perceptive and receptive mind today; and one reason also why it can always be read, if anyone chooses, simply as great literature. In the second place, it is true in respect of the forces which play upon Israel as a nation and determine the course of its history. To understand the history of Israel it is as necessary to take note of the economic, social, political, international forces which were operating in the ancient world as it would be to understand the history of any other people of that time: we must know something of Egypt, Assyria, Babylon, Rome, of Sennacherib, Cyrus, Darius, and Alexander. The history of Israel thus takes its place in and is continuous with what may be called the wider secular history of mankind, and can be studied by the methods of ordinary historical inquiry.

On the other hand, the picture is equally, and indeed much more, the picture of a people whose life is profoundly discontinuous with the life of the rest of mankind. This profound discontinuity comes to expression in the quite distinctive religious idea and experience of "the covenant." Covenant signifies a relationship of a personal and ethical kind which God, who has all peoples and all history in his grasp, has entered into with Israel, and with Israel alone, in order to fulfill his purpose in the world. God himself has taken the initiative in setting up this relationship, which, because it is set up with Israel only, puts that people, in respect of the forces which determine its history, in a position of radical discontinuity with the rest of the world. It is a people apart, the chosen people, marked out by God for signal honor and responsibility. By great acts of deliverance and disciplinary judgment, and through the mouths of prophets and teachers whom he inspires to interpret those acts, God calls and continually recalls the people of Israel into obedience to and trust in himself, promising them, as they respond to the call, his blessing and guidance so that they may in turn be a blessing and a guide to men. This strange, deep notion of the covenant relationship thus focuses in itself four elements which taken together form the heart and kernel of Old Testament religion: the apprehension of the one God as (a) personal, (b) actively working out a purpose in history, (c) taking the initiative in making himself known to men, so that they can in some measure co-operate with and understand his activity in history, and (d) calling a particular community into a unique relationship with himself so that it may be his agent in the world.

B. Continuity-Discontinuity Between the Old and New Testaments.—There is a second and even more deep-going continuity-discontinuity which the Bible exhibits to us: it comes into being, as it were, within the first. The covenant community of Israel, which God called out from and so made discontinuous with the rest of mankind, is set before us as failing to respond fully to that call. In varying ways and degrees, with recurrent backslidings after partial and temporary recoveries, it goes counter to the divine purpose, so that if it serves the divine purpose at all it does so very imperfectly, and then not so much as a willing agent as an unwilling, and even unwitting, instrument. Nevertheless, the divine purpose of saving the world through the elect people of Israel, being divine, cannot really be frustrated. By a new initiative in the coming of Christ, God brings into being in the midst and out of the midst of the old covenant people a *new* covenant people, a new Israel, to be what the old Israel had been called, but had failed, to be (except in the prayers and hopes of a remnant of elect souls) : namely, the servant and medium of his redeeming purpose toward mankind—to be "a chosen race, a royal priesthood, a holy nation, God's own people," that they might "declare the wonderful deeds of him who called [them] out of darkness into his marvelous light" (I Pet. 2:9; cf. also Exod. 19:5-6) . This new divine initiative and its decisive significance are emphasized in the sharpest possible way by the break in the Bible between the Old and New Testaments. "Testament" means "covenant," so that the Old Testament should in strictness be called the scriptures of (that is, the writings and records concerning) the old covenant, and the New Testament should be called the scriptures of (that is, the writings and records concerning) the new covenant.

Here, it may be repeated, is a new and even more deep-going continuity-discontinuity. Let us develop each side of the antithesis in turn.

First, the continuity: That the word "testament" or "covenant" is used of both main sections of the Bible indicates the continuity of the one with the other. It indicates that the story runs on, that the Bible throughout is concerned with essentially the same community —the covenant community, constituted as such by the redeeming purpose of God, conscious of itself as set apart in the midst of mankind, though otherwise continuous with it. This gives the Bible, despite the multiplicity and variety of its contents, and above all, despite the break between the Old and New Testaments, a singular and indiscerptible unity. The New Testament writings do indeed set forth the church as the distinctively *new* Israel of God, the people of the *new* covenant, but if the main emphasis is on the word "new," that is because the unbroken continuity with what has gone before, which is implicit in the words "Israel" and "covenant," is not felt to need any emphasis. Unostentatiously and without discussion, the writers assume themselves heir to the "commonwealth of Israel" and "the covenants of promise" (Eph. 2:12).[1] The church, the new Israel, is not a substitute for the old covenant community, brought in, as it were, from elsewhere; rather it springs from the loins of the old community. It is its true heir; it carries, so to speak, its heredity; it is the evidence not of its having ceased to be, but of its unbroken and unbreakable persistence. It is all this because the divine purpose and call which laid hold of Israel in the beginning, and constituted it the covenant people for the salvation of mankind, still grasps it, only now under the form of the church.[2] In what then does this "newness" consist?

This brings us to the second point, the discontinuity: the "newness" of the new covenant community, according to the New Testament, is radical and manifests itself in the following main ways:

(a) It manifests itself in *the way in which the covenant community is established and maintained in its relationship to God.* As the New Testament writers look back on the previous history of the covenant people, they see a dense shadow lying across it—the shadow of men's sinful disobedience to God and consequent alienation from him. They see, of course, other things as well: as we have said, they as-

sume themselves heirs to the hopes and promises of what they recognize to be a unique and glorious past, a past which has prepared the way for the coming of the Savior. But the unsolved problem of sin stands out in somber relief, for it is because of sin that the covenant people has failed to be the effective servant of the divine purpose in the world. In the new covenant relationship this problem is solved, the shadow removed, not indeed by the members of the new community being made sinless, but by their being put *as sinners* into an entirely new relationship to God in respect of their sin. This is brought about by God's new action in Christ. God reconciles sinful men to himself, makes them "at one" with himself through Christ, and supremely through his death at Calvary; and the new covenant community consists of men and women who are thus reconciled to him. But this is not all. The New Testament faith, as has already been said, is that Christ is the risen, living, and ever-present Lord of the new covenant community; as such he is, through the Holy Spirit, ever operative in the hearts and lives of its members. The new community lives and moves and has its being in Christ, its divine Savior and Lord, in a way that the old covenant community never lived and moved and had its being in the prophets through whom the divine word came to it. The word of God, formerly uttered by a person, has now become the living, saving person himself. (See p. 29 on the use of the phrase "the word of God" and on its application to Christ.) This is indeed a new sort of covenant, constituting a new covenant people. There is still a further point: while the new relationship to God is a community relationship, it is also a relationship of an intensely individual and personal kind between each member and God through the Savior. Repentance, forgiveness, faith, growth in Christian character, all these spring out of the living encounter with God in Christ within the innermost places of each man's heart; nevertheless—it must be reiterated at once—even as individual transactions with God they become possible only because the word of the gospel meets the believer through the new covenant community and calls him to and establishes him in its fellowship. The New Testament is at one and the same time the most individualistic and the most community-conscious book in the world, which is some evidence perhaps of the richness and adequacy of the truth it contains. (Most of this theme is contained in two key passages of scripture: Jer. 31:31-34, where the new covenant relationship is promised and its nature defined; I Cor. 11:25—see also Matt. 26:28; Mark 14:24; Luke 22:20—where the establishment of the

[1] It is important to note that among the promises was the promise of a *new* covenant with Israel, so that the very newness of the church constituted a significant element in its unity and continuity with what had gone before. See Jer. 31:31-32.

[2] See C. H. Dodd, *The Bible Today* (Cambridge: University Press, 1946), ch. i.

new covenant is associated through the Last Supper with the death of Christ and the forgiveness of sins.)

(b) The newness manifests itself in *the scope of the covenant community*. It is no longer a community whose membership is defined in any sense whatever in terms of race or nation; it is now defined in terms only of a man's—that is, any man's—relationship to God through Christ. It is, therefore, in principle a universal society in which every social and national boundary or cleavage is broken through. It is perhaps difficult for those reared in the Christian tradition to realize how radically new this universalism was. There are, to be sure, a number of striking utterances in the Old Testament concerning the universal mission of Israel: she is called to be the agent of the divine purpose in history toward all mankind, and through her the nations of the earth will be brought to the true knowledge and worship of the Most High.[3] But the Old Testament never succeeded in universalizing the notion of the covenant community itself. That remained essentially bound up with Jewish national feeling, with the inevitable result—since national feeling, especially under the stress of national misfortune, is one of the most powerful to which men are subject—that the universalistic elements in the prophetic teaching were almost completely overridden.[4] That the church of the New Testament broke away from this narrow nationalism, while at the same time defining itself in covenant terms and exulting in its continuity with the people of the old covenant, is a most remarkable thing, and is explicable only as the result of the impact of the transcendent personality of Jesus Christ.

(c) The newness manifests itself in *the finality of the covenant community*. Throughout the New Testament the conviction rules that the church is something final, conclusive, in the working out of God's purpose in the world through the covenant community. The old covenant was succeeded by the new covenant in Christ, but the latter cannot be succeeded by one still newer, and so itself in course of time become old—it is "once for all." A full explication of the finality of Christianity, such as would exclude the many possible misinterpretations of

[3] The relevant passages may be found conveniently brought together in H. H. Rowley, *The Missionary Message of the Old Testament* (London: The Carey Press, 1945).

[4] See C. R. North, *The Old Testament Interpretation of History* (London: The Epworth Press, 1946), p. 178: "The Jews were unable to shake themselves entirely free from the principle of nationalism in religion. Even Jeremiah, for all his New Covenant oracle, did not succeed in doing that. He conceived of the future kingdom of God as somehow bound up with the restoration of His own people."

it, is beyond the scope of this article; it is sufficient to point out three things:

First, finality is necessarily involved in the New Testament view of the person and work of Christ. The categories applied to him cannot be used of one concerning whom the possibility can be even theoretically entertained that he might be superseded.

Second, the finality is not a completed finality. This has the sound of self-contradiction, but it does no more than express the conviction which runs throughout the New Testament, that God's action in history through Christ is not yet a completed action. It has assuredly begun in what is a radically new initiative, but the consummation of it in the fully realized kingdom of God is yet to be, "according to his purpose which he set forth in Christ as a plan for the fullness of time, to unite all things in him, things in heaven and things on earth" (Eph. 1:9-10).

Third, the finality lies in the fact that the new covenant fulfills the old covenant. It is important in this context to give the notion of fulfillment its proper meaning. It might be taken to mean simply that under the old covenant the Jews developed certain religious longings and aspirations which were never fully satisfied, but which under the new covenant were fully satisfied. Or it might be taken to mean that in course of time certain religious and theological problems or tensions emerged in the old covenant period which were not then resolved, but which were later resolved by the coming of Christ. Both these thoughts are valid and important aspects of the full notion of fulfillment as applied to the work of Christ (see p. 27). But they do not express the distinctive New Testament idea of Christ as fulfillment which is here in mind. It might be said that taken by themselves they are too anthropocentric. The primary emphasis of the New Testament is much more theocentric: that is to say, the emphasis is not so much on Christ as meeting the unsatisfied aspirations, or resolving the outstanding problems, of religious men, as on Christ fulfilling God's purpose. He is God's fulfillment before he is man's. God had planned and intended from the beginning to come in Christ; his dealings with the old covenant people from the call of Abraham onward were in pursuit of that plan and intention; the plan and intention were fulfilled when "in the fullness of time" he did in fact come in Christ. In all his dealings with the covenant people God, so to say, had Christ in mind. Christ came and died and rose again "according to the definite plan and foreknowledge of God" (Acts 2:23). "He was destined before the foundation of the world but was made manifest at the end of the times"

(I Pet. 1:20). In other words, there comes to expression in the New Testament idea of Christ as fulfillment the characteristic biblical thought of God as purposively active in history, and above all in the history of the covenant people. It is this that lies behind the frequent application by the New Testament writers to Christ's advent and life and death of such phrases as "according to the scriptures" or "spoken of by the prophets" or "according to the promises." There is no hint in such phrases, it is superfluous to say, of a fatalistic or mechanical necessity. Nor is there any suggestion that the Old Testament writings thus referred to resulted from some occult gift of clairvoyance in those who wrote them. The controlling thought in such phrases is, once again, the thought of God actively at work in history, and more particularly of his making his mind and purpose known, in some way and in some degree, to prophetic souls. This making known is indeed part of the working out of his purpose, for the work and witness of the prophets are part and parcel of the historic process itself. The interpretation of events that they proclaim in the name of God is itself a creative event. The phrase "in some way and in some degree" has been used because the New Testament writers offer no information as to how or to what extent the divine purpose was made known; this is because their emphasis is primarily on the fact of the divine activity in the history of the covenant people and in the witness of the prophets, preparing the way for Christ, and only secondarily on the human agents whom he chose to speak to and to use "at sundry times and in divers manners" (Heb. 1:1).

C. Continuity-Discontinuity in the Person of Christ.—What, then, is the source and ground of this radical newness in the covenant relationship which constitutes the church the new Israel of God? The answer which the New Testament gives to this question is implicit in what has just been said: the newness derives from the radical, the incommensurable, newness of Jesus Christ. The New Testament unequivocally teaches that—to repeat the words used at the beginning of this article—God himself came, and comes, in Jesus Christ in a saving self-giving and self-disclosure which are unique, final, adequate, and indispensable. The point, however, which should be emphasized here is that there is in the New Testament the clearest testimony to both the continuity and the discontinuity, both the "in and through" aspect and the "into" aspect, of the person of Christ. It is here that the continuity-discontinuity theme of the Bible reaches its profoundest depth, and at the same time its central point

—that which holds together and gives a unitary meaning to the whole biblical history.

On the one hand, Jesus Christ is emphatically and unreservedly set forth as a fully human and historic individual. He is a Jew, his whole being and life rooted in, fashioned in, and conditioned by the history and tradition, the distinctive religious, moral, cultural character of the Jewish people, including in this, above all, its consciousness of being called of God to a special place in his purpose. And even as the life of the Jewish community was conditioned by the wider secular events and circumstances of the time, particularly those connected with the imperial activities of Rome, so also was his life. Much of his teaching can only be fully comprehended when it is taken in the context of the Roman occupying power and of the relation of the Jews to it; his death is brought about by the co-operation of the Jewish and Roman authorities. There is a wealth of meaning in the fact that Luke dates the beginning of the active ministry of Jesus with the words "in the fifteenth year of the reign of Tiberius Caesar, Pontius Pilate being governor of Judea, and Herod being tetrarch of Galilee, and his brother Philip tetrarch of Iturea and of the region of Trachonitis, and Lysanias the tetrarch of Abilene, Annas and Caiaphas being the high priests" (Luke 3:1-2).

On the other hand, with equal emphasis Jesus Christ is set forth as being not merely historic and human: his person and work cannot be comprehended in their essential nature simply in terms of the history of the old covenant people and of the interplay of this with the wider history of mankind. He is not even set forth as the last and greatest of the great prophets with whom had been so closely bound up, in the past, God's dealings with Israel. On the contrary, he is presented throughout as one who, by virtue of his unique and mysterious office as the Messiah, is the redeeming God himself in action to set up his kingdom, in a way for which there is, and in the nature of the case can be, no parallel. In accordance with this he is made the object of religious devotion, of utter faith and obedience, such as the writers would normally direct only to God himself.

It is hardly necessary to say that the New Testament makes no attempt to work out this paradoxical faith concerning the Jewish and human "continuity" and the divine "discontinuity" of Christ into a theoretical doctrine of his person; the deep, underlying theological problems are not raised, for example, how this religious devotion to Christ and a strict monotheism are to be reconciled. There is little in the New Testament to suggest the christological doctrines which were later wrought out in the discussions of the Greek fathers and are enshrined in the Nicene and Chalcedonian formulas. Indeed, it is perhaps a trifle misleading to describe the New Testament belief concerning Christ as a doctrine of the Incarnation, unless the word "Incarnation" is carefully interpreted to mean that Christ in his divine-earthly life was veritably a man in the wholeness of a man's being as an embodied and historic person—which was the sense in which the word was used at the beginning of this article and the sense which the phrase "became flesh" bears in the first chapter of the Fourth Gospel (John 1:13). Apart from such careful use, the word "Incarnation" is perhaps a little apt, for etymological reasons, to suggest the underlying dualism of Greek thought, with its readiness to think of the Incarnation as the ingress of a divine principle into a mortal envelope of flesh essentially alien to it. Nothing could be farther from the thought of the New Testament than that. We could keep much nearer to the New Testament thought if we had an abstract noun in English corresponding to the Greek word ἐνανθρώπησις, or if we could coin a word and speak of the divine "inhumanization" or even "inhistorization," rather than of the Incarnation.

The purpose of the first main section of this article should be now evident: to show that the central Christian affirmation of the Incarnation, with its insistence that the divine action in Christ is both "in and through" and "into" history, both continuous and discontinuous with history, is intimately and indissolubly bound up with the whole distinctive content and structure of the Bible. Normal or typical Christianity is thus seen to be profoundly and organically one with what it has always asserted to be in some sense its standard and norm. By the same argument, the assertion made at the beginning, that the normative relation of the Bible to the faith and life of the church is of the intrinsic or organic kind, is illustrated and reaffirmed. The faith and life of the church as centered in God's unique action in Christ can in fact no more be torn apart from the Bible and remain their distinctive selves than a plant can be torn from the soil and remain a living plant.

The close connection between the central and distinctive Christian affirmation concerning Christ and the view taken of the Scriptures can be illustrated from the early history of the church. Thus it is significant that Marcion, who had strongly Docetist leanings (i.e., emphasized the "into" aspect of the divine action in Christ at the expense of the "in and through" aspect, the divine at the expense of the human), also rejected the Old Testament. On the other hand, the adoptionists (those who emphasized the "in and through" aspect at the expense of the "into," the human at the expense of the divine) find their first representatives among the Ebionites, who had no awareness of the essential newness of the Christian revelation which ultimately found expression in the idea and the compilation of a New Testament. The mission of Jesus was held to be merely to purify and revive the old revelation. Thus Paul of Samosata was acutely characterized by some of the fathers as "neo-Jewish" and "Ebionitic."

Before proceeding, it may be worth while, in order to avoid misunderstanding, to emphasize that in setting forth the biblical conception of the church as the new Israel, the new covenant people, we have inevitably thought of the church in terms of its ideal as this is defined by God's intention and purpose toward it and toward mankind through Christ. That is to say, we have inevitably thought in terms of the true church, which does not necessarily coincide exactly with this or that institution in history which has in fact called itself a church or the church. There are difficult problems here with which every Christian thinker is familiar, but the line of thought which has been pursued is not really affected by them. We must believe that somewhere within the empirical and institutional churches the true church of God is always in being; and the thesis of this article is that its essential and distinctive nature, purpose, and message, and particularly the relation of these to its own acknowledged norm in the Bible, can be rightly comprehended only on the basis of what has already been said above, and along the lines of thought which we now go on to pursue.

III. The Normative Function of the Bible Within the Church

This central section of the inquiry can be begun with the statement made in connection with the phrase "and comes," namely, that the creative and constitutive principle of the church is the living Christ himself, who in all things rules and directs its faith and life through the Holy Spirit (see p. 7).

This statement clearly involves that Christ is the final and absolute authority for the faith and life of the church, and therefore for the faith and life of every individual member. To say this does not in any way depart from the truth that God is the sole absolute authority for men, but rather expresses it in its specifically Christian form; for, as we have seen, it is precisely the distinctive Christian affirmation that Christ is the personal self-manifestation of God to men. But we have also accepted as the datum of this inquiry that the Bible is in some sense the supreme standard and norm. Obviously our task is to relate these two statements, which, in their apparent assertion of two finalities, seem at first sight to be contrary. As a matter of fact, as will be seen, it is only by relating them to one another that we can rightly understand in what sense the Bible is the supreme standard and norm, and on what its authority rests. But before going on to this, it is necessary to insist on the importance of being once and for all clear that whatever place may be assigned to the Bible as standard and norm, the truth that Christ, the living Christ speaking through the Holy Spirit, is the supreme authority must not be qualified in any way whatsoever. Only by holding firmly to this truth can the essential and unique quality of the Christian faith and life be preserved. It is a faith and life centered in the person of Christ, apprehended as God himself personally and livingly encountering us and dealing with us. It is not centered in a book, as in Islam; or in a code of behavior, as in Confucianism; or in a system of philosophical or theological truth, as in Vedantic Hinduism; or in a rigidly authoritarian institution such as the Christian church in its Roman form has in large measure become. It is, of course, unhappily true that Christianity has often been set forth in a way that moves far too much in the direction of one or other of these possibilities. Thus it has been presented in a way to give the impression that it is essentially a religion of a book (as when unquestioning acceptance of the inerrancy of the Bible has been made *de fide*) ;[5] or that it is merely a matter of living according to the ethical teaching of the New Testament, particularly of the Sermon on the Mount, other distinctive New Testament beliefs being relatively unimportant (as in some of the shallower forms of what is called liberal modernism) ; or that it is a matter of accepting an elaborate scheme of doctrines (as in certain forms of "scholastic" Protestantism) ; or, in the way already indicated, of submitting to an authoritarian institution (as in Roman Catholicism). One may venture to think, however, that the distinctive Christian relationship of personal trust in and obedience to the living Christ has usually lain within these faulty presentations and aberrations, and given them, in spite of themselves, a characteristically Christian vitality and power.

Let us turn now to the problem of the relation of the authority of the Bible to the authority of Christ. The position to be put forth is that we can only understand and justify the supremely normative status of the Bible within the church's life, while at the same time not qualifying in any way Christ's supreme authority, by doing two things. First, we must show that the biblical writings are indispensable to the present, living relationship of Christ to the church—the new covenant community—and its members: in other words, we must show that the normative relation of the Bible to the church is an essential part of the normative relation of the living Christ to it. The special problem here is to see how printed documents from the past can enter into a present, living, personal relationship, particularly in view of the fact that Christ himself left no written records. Second, we must show why nothing else but the Bible thus indispensably participates in the authority of the living Christ. The special problem here is to see why later writings, some of them on the highest level of inspiration, which have been produced as part of the ongoing life of the church throughout the ages, should not enter as indispensably into the living authority of Christ as those which are in the New Testament. The Roman Church maintains that they do, at least in so far as they help to form that ecclesiastical tradition which it expressly puts on a level with scripture as constituting, with the latter, the normative factors governing the authoritative and final pronouncements of the Papacy.[6] If we reject this view, as the Protestant church has always rightly done, we must be clear why we do so, why we give only the biblical writings so unique a place. The two points will be discussed in turn.

A. The Bible as Essential to the Normative Relationship of the Living Christ to the Church. —We can understand the way in which the Bible, as a collection of documents and records from the past, enters indispensably into the present lordship of the living Christ only in the light of our general understanding of why a historic incarnation was necessary at all to God's saving work for men. In other words, the question is fundamentally a theological one, involving our whole doctrine of salvation, which in turn involves the doctrine of God, of man, of sin—in short, of the whole organism of Christian truth. The close connection between our view of the Bible and our view of salvation can be seen by reflecting that to assert the necessity for a historic incarnation is not the same thing as to assert the necessity for trustworthy records

[5] Cf. William Chillingworth's famous dictum, "The Bible alone is the religion of Protestants."

[6] See the decree concerning the canonical Scriptures in "The Canons and Decrees of the Council of Trent" in Philip Schaff, *Creeds of Christendom* (New York: Harper & Bros., 1877), II, 79. In practice, as has often been remarked, the Roman Church sets tradition above scripture as the authoritative source of truth, for scripture is acknowledged to require interpretation and exposition, whereas the teaching of the church concerning their interpretation and exposition is infallible and irreformable (that is, never to be examined in the light of Scripture itself). See "Dogmatic Decrees of the Vatican Council," 1870, *ibid.*, II, 271.

concerning it. One might hold a doctrine of salvation which established or presupposed the necessity for a historic incarnation, but which made superfluous a trustworthy record of the events associated with it: all that would be required on such a view would be credible witness of the bare fact that such incarnation had taken place. There have been doctrines of Christ's saving work of this type. Thus the view which finds expression in the writings of some of the Greek fathers, that the essence of Christ's saving work was that he introduced the divine, incorruptible life into the corrupt and perishing body of humanity, and that our benefiting from that work takes place through participation in the sacraments, while obviously asserting the necessity of the Incarnation, leaves no indispensable place for a collection of records like the Bible. Similarly, certain types of substitutionary views of Christ's saving work (particularly when the view is elaborated into a scheme of soteriological doctrine which every man must believe in order to be saved) do not seem indispensably to involve the sort of records we have in the Bible. The clearest example is once again afforded by the Roman Church, which makes the saving process rest essentially on a man's committing himself to the whole hierarchical and dogmatic system of the church in an act of *fides implicita*, or, as Luther dubbed it, "blind faith." In accordance with this, the Roman Church has not only never given the biblical records an indispensable place in its understanding of the work of Christ, but has also on the whole discouraged its lay members from acquiring knowledge of them.

If, however, we so understand God's saving work through Christ that *it requires as an indispensable element in it the encounter, continually re-enacted, with the concrete individuality of the historic Savior,* then we can see at once why the biblical documents become an indispensable factor in Christ's living relationship to the church. For without the Bible such encounter could not take place. It is obviously not possible fully to elaborate in this article such an account of the saving work of Christ; all that is possible, and indeed all that is necessary for our purpose, is to summarize what has been set forth elsewhere.[7]

The main point is what may be called the "radical personalism" of the Christian message, a personalism which is itself in profoundest harmony with the biblical revelation. According to this radical personalism, the essential nature of man consists in the fact that God has made him a finite person in order that he may enjoy personal fellowship with God and with other

[7] Herbert H. Farmer, *God and Men* (New York and Nashville: Abingdon-Cokesbury Press, 1947), chs. iii-iv.

finite persons. It is this purpose of God which has brought the process of what we call "history" into being, for history is but another name for the sphere in which finite persons can live freely as persons, the sphere, that is to say, in which their decisions and deeds can have real significance either as co-operative with or as opposed to God's purpose for them and through them. Sin, on account of which God's saving action in Christ is made necessary, has to do with this profound relationship to God which lies at the root of man's whole distinctive nature as a personal being. By the word "sin" we indicate the fact that men have rejected and do reject God's claim upon them for their obedience and trust, and the claim of their fellows upon them for their love, this latter claim being itself part of God's claim. Men are able to make this rejection because in such a personal world there is real freedom; without such freedom to reject claims it would not be a personal world. Because sin has thus to do with the ultimate core and basis of man's distinctively personal life, its effects upon the personality are disastrous and inevitable. The worst and most disabling effect is blindness. Men become increasingly unable to see the truth concerning themselves, to discern the true meaning and direction of their life, and of history generally; they become increasingly unable to know what God's will for them and claim upon them are, and indeed to know that there is a personal God at all, still less one who may be joyfully obeyed and trusted. This is the worst and most disabling effect of sin because it is precisely the prerogative of a *personal* being to walk in freedom according to the light of truth within his own soul. It follows from this that only as the blindness is being continuously healed, only as a man is brought again and again to the light and kept in the light, can the evil of his sin-corrupted existence even begin to be set right. And by the same argument a man cannot cure his own blindness, for to cure it he would first require the capacity to see the truth about God and about himself which his blindness now denies him. If God does not act in a way that is effectively revealing, effectively healing of his blindness, there is no hope.

All this indicates the conditions which the divine saving action in relation to sin, if it was to be effective, had to fulfill. It had to be action which lays bare to men the real nature of the personal—that is, the historical—world, in such a way that their blindness is overcome. Yet this must not be in a way that coerces and overrides their minds, for if it did that it would be false to the real nature of the personal world, and so far from unveiling it, would obscure it. It must be effective, yet not overriding—not overviding, precisely in order to be a truly effective way of dealing with men as persons.

It is difficult, to say the least, to see how a saving disclosure of the truth of the kind just indicated could take any form other than that which Christianity affirms it did in fact take in Christ, the form, that is, of a full and concrete embodiment in a human personal life, lived in the midst of, and confronting men in the midst of, those very events and relationships which constitute their historical existence as persons. Only thus could it deal with the corruption and darkness which sin causes, and only thus could it remain true to the personal world by continuously evoking in men a new inward perception and response. In particular, it was most necessary that it should thus confront us in the midst of and in closest relationship with human existence as corrupted and darkened and embittered by sin, for it is in the midst of human existence as thus corrupted and darkened and embittered that the saved man has to live the new life into which he is called, and for which he is empowered by God. Certainly the mere announcement of general truths or doctrines concerning the nature of God and his purpose for men, or concerning sin, could not effect these things, even if uttered with power and eloquence by some prophetic personality.

To suppose that it could—to suppose that it could be anything more than a merely ameliorative factor—would be to show a very inadequate grasp both of the nature of personality and of the effects of sin upon it. General truths cannot get right inside men, so to speak, and continue to get right inside them, in their sinful state and situation—challenging the will, stirring the deep springs of feeling, breaking up the obstinate resistances of pride and self-justification; general truths cannot pierce the hard crusts of egotism, with its fears and hates and insincerities, and when the crust re-forms, pierce it again, letting in the light and again letting in the light, bringing men again and again to a true and deep penitence, making credible a divine pardon which will neither indulge nor yet be turned aside by their sinfulness. Only truth in unclouded personal embodiment and action, encountering and challenging men in the actual historical situations which are the real stuff of their personal existence, can work real redemption.

It is hardly necessary to point out that what has just been said is not offered as a full statement of the doctrine of our redemption by Christ. It is meant only to set forth a basic general principle which must underlie all our understanding of Christ's saving and sanctifying work, and which is especially relevant to the problem under discussion. The point is that

if this general principle is valid, it makes clear why an encounter, continually renewed, with the concrete individuality of the historic Christ is an indispensable factor in his present relationship to the church and to its individual members. Furthermore, it makes clear why a historical record is indispensable also, for without a historical record such an encounter could not take place.

We may reach the same truth from a different angle. We have spoken of the risen and living Christ directing the faith and life of the church and of its members through the Holy Spirit. The significance of this statement, however, both theologically and for the Christian life, depends on the content we give to the term Christ: it depends on whether we can give it a content which differentiates it significantly from the meaning which we attach to the term Holy Spirit. If we mean by the living Christ merely the Spirit of God conceived as working for the realization of certain values vaguely called Christian, or even more vaguely called spiritual, then the proposition that Christ rules through the Holy Spirit becomes the meaningless tautology that the Spirit rules through the Spirit. Futhermore, it becomes all too easy, as experience shows, for the religious life to run out into a sentimental nebulosity, lacking all positive direction and drive, or else, if it achieves positive direction, to do so by becoming an unchecked individualism for whose merely private "hunches" the authority of the Spirit's leading is claimed. But if we mean by Christ as risen and living the same Christ as he who meets us in the pages of the Gospels, with all the sharp personal characterization and definition of concrete historic existence, then to say that Christ rules through the Holy Spirit is to say something highly significant. For on the one hand, the Spirit takes on the character of Christ, and so ceases to be merely a vague divine principle dimly conceived as indwelling human nature and lending sanction to any strong impulse from the subconscious regions of the personality; and on the other hand, the rule of Christ becomes a truly personal rule operating through the quickened insight of the believer in relation to his personal situation, and not through a merely slavish imitation of or legalistic obedience to the deeds and words of Christ as recorded in the Gospels. The Spirit takes of the things of Christ and shows them to us, and the fruits of the Spirit are the virtues of Christ. But this means that there has to be a Christ—a historic Christ—for the Spirit to show us; and that in turn means that there has to be a historical record.

The argument so far might seem only to demonstrate the indispensability of the Gospels to Christ's saving and ruling presence in the church. But in view of all that has been maintained throughout this article concerning the divine action in Christ, it is clear that the gospel records of the life of the Redeemer could not possibly suffice by themselves to present us with the whole content and full import of that action. To suppose that they could would be to fail to give **proper** weight to that "in and through" or "continuity" aspect of the divine action which is essential to a truly historic incarnation and revelation. It would also be to display ignorance of the gospel records themselves, for it does not require much study of the Gospels to see that they cannot be understood apart from what went before in the history of the old covenant people, as set before us in the Old Testament, and apart from what came after in the coming into existence of the new covenant community, as set before us in the documents of the New Testament other than the Gospels. Once we grant the necessity of the gospel records to God's dealings with us through Christ, we grant in principle the necessity of more than just those records; we grant the necessity of a whole Bible. At the moment I say no more than "a" whole Bible, for the question of the limits of the canon of scripture is yet to be discussed. But, with that reservation, Luther's dictum stands, "the Bible is the manger in which Christ is laid."

There is, however, a latent assumption in the position which has been laid down which raises serious difficulties, and which therefore we must examine with some care. The assumption is that the Gospels are in fact such records that when we read them we can be sure that we are encountering the actual historic person of whom they claim to give an account. There was a time when this was not felt to be an assumption, for most Christians accepted without any question the doctrine of the inerrancy of the scripture writings. It was believed that God had so operated on the minds of the sacred writers that they did not write down anything which was not strictly accurate in every particular. Whatever was set down in the Gospels actually happened as therein set down. This is no longer a tenable view. It is untenable for two reasons.

The first has to do, once again, with the central Christian assertion of the Incarnation. A completely inerrant record could have been produced only if God had suspended the normal processes of memory and composition in the minds of the writers, and used the latter not as co-operating human persons, but as passive instruments like a pen. But to suppose that such a diminution of the full humanity of the evangelists was necessary to the working out of

God's saving purpose in Christ is to deny the full historic humanity of the Savior himself: it is to deny the "in and through" aspect of God's action, and so is a partial denial of the Incarnation. For to assert the full humanity of Christ is to assert the full humanity of all the conditions affecting human life under which and in the midst of which he lived and died, under which he effected, and effects, his saving work. Among such conditions must be included the normal mental processes, both of those who kept company with him and whose memory made the writing of the Gospels possible, and of those who actually wrote the Gospels. This is not to deny that God gave these men guidance and inspiration in their work; it is merely to assert that the guidance and inspiration were given without impairing their full humanity as persons, and without setting up supernatural infallibilities in the midst of mankind—a truth far more honoring to the wisdom and patience of God than a statement like that of the Lutheran theologian Quenstedt to the effect that

there is in Canonical Scripture no untruth, no falsity, no error, not even in the smallest particular, either in deed or word; but all and everything contained in it is of the highest possible truth, whether it be a matter of Dogma, Morals, History, Chronology, Topography, or Nomenclature. And no ignorance, no lack of thought, no forgetfulness, nor lapse of memory, either can or ought to be attributed to the amanuenses of the Holy Spirit in their recording of the sacred text.[8]

The second reason has to do with the evidence afforded by the Gospels themselves, and calls for fuller treatment. Scholarly research into the Gospels has convincingly shown that they cannot be accepted in detail as they stand. The evidence is clear that they contain inaccuracies, inconsistencies, interpolations, omissions, overstatements, and so forth—in short, precisely the sort of thing that normal mental processes produce. Moreover, it has become clear that the Gospels were written from the angle of an overmastering religious faith in Christ as the Savior sent from God; indeed, they were intended to convey that faith, and they were not composed as biographies in the modern sense. This immediately raises the question whether we must not allow for the possibility that this faith has colored and distorted the historical facts which the Gospels purport to describe. Where facts and interpretations of facts by religious faith are so inextricably bound up together,

[8] Quoted by H. F. D. Sparks, *The Old Testament in the Christian Church* (London: Student Christian Movement Press, 1944), p. 18.

how can we have any assurance concerning the facts?

Before taking up these two sources of doubt, it will be worth while to digress for a moment to insist that the work of critical scholarship on the Gospels to which reference has just been made has no necessary connection with a certain view which has been characteristic of some schools of liberal thought. This is the view which rejects forthwith some elements in the Gospels (particularly the miraculous elements) on the basis of the alleged inescapable requirements of sound philosophy and sound science. It is not necessary to discuss these alleged inescapable requirements here; it is enough to state that not many competent authorities in this sphere of philosophical and theological thought would now find them anything like so inescapable as they have been asserted by some to be. Rather, it has come to be recognized that the rejection of the miraculous elements in the Gospels on this particular basis was a much too hasty surrender of the biblical and Christian outlook to what has proved to be in large measure merely a prevailing fashion of thought.[9] Nevertheless, to admit, as we must, the *general* possibility and the historical actuality of the "mighty works" of Jesus does not commit us to the acceptance of every *particular* in the gospel account of them. There may be other reasons—as in some cases there certainly are—for rejection, or at least hesitation; reasons which arise out of that close and reverent study of the documents themselves which is demanded from us by the Christian faith in God's saving action "in and through" history. For as T. W. Manson has well said, this faith means "that history takes on a new significance, that the outstanding events in which the voice of God has been heard, or his hand discerned, must be studied with the same passion for accuracy that the scientist gives to a chemical analysis"[10]— though, it may be well to add, not by the same methods or on the same presuppositions. In biblical study we are now in a "postliberal" period, but we can never pass into a "postcritical" one, for the obligation to use every resource of scholarship upon our documents in order to know, so far as we are able, what really did happen, springs, it must be repeated, from the nature of the gospel itself as a gospel of God's action in history.[11]

Let us return now to the two causes of doubt

above mentioned concerning the capacity of the Gospels to confront us with the historic person of Jesus.

1. The Trustworthiness of the Gospel Records.—With regard to the first cause of doubt it can be said that the fact that critical scholarship lays bare in the Gospels as they stand a number of inconsistencies, inaccuracies, and so forth, is not able by itself to support the conclusion suggested, namely, that we cannot arrive at assured knowledge of the historical facts. It does not do more than define the task with which reverent critical scholarship is confronted, a hard enough task, to be sure, and one which requires the full and responsible use of all the resources available, but not a task which is foredoomed to failure. On the contrary, if we share the Christian faith about Christ, we are entitled to believe that since it is a task which God has laid upon us through the inevitable developments of scholarship, it is destined to succeed. There is no reason to think that the Holy Spirit does not take the things of Christ and show them to scholars as much as to other believers.[12] In any case, the question of success or failure must not be prejudged: it must be decided by the outcome of the enterprise itself. At this point, however, we are met by the allegation made by some that the outcome is already clear enough, that so soon as we surrender belief in the absolute trustworthiness of the gospel records, and begin to try, by methods of critical research, to establish what "really happened," we find ourselves lost in a quagmire of conflicting suggestions and theories. Every critical scholar, it is said, creates his own picture of Jesus and of the events of his life, selecting his material according to his own fancy, accepting this, rejecting that, explaining away something else, as his own sense of "what must have happened" may dictate. The real Jesus vanishes behind a cloud of conflicting theories and suppositions. The answer to this allegation is simply that it is not true, or in so far as it is true, it is true with the crucial qualification that it is so in the main only of those pictures of Jesus set forth by unbelieving and frequently not very well-equipped critics. Those who for one reason or another desire to retain the old view of the literal inerrancy and absolute trustworthiness of the records are always inclined to exaggerate the extent to which the modern critical study of the Gospels undertaken by Christian scholars has issued only in the multiplication of perplexities. In some ways the exact reverse is true. A fuller, more concrete, more consistent, and historically more credible

[9] See below, p. 26. For a general discussion of miracles in relation to science, see Herbert H. Farmer, *The World and God* (New York: Harper & Bros., 1935).

[10] "The Failure of Liberalism to Interpret the Bible as the Word of God," in *The Interpretation of the Bible*, ed. C. W. Dugmore (London: Society for Promoting Christian Knowledge, 1944), p. 104.

[11] See Dodd, *The Bible Today*, p. 26.

[12] See below, p. 18, about the value for the Christian life of the questions raised by modern research into the Gospels.

portrait of Jesus than has been possible hitherto is now available to us, mainly as the result of the researches of modern scholars. To be sure, there is always a certain fluidity in the picture: it changes as this or that line of inquiry is pursued, this or that hypothesis is put forward, discussed, tested, modified, partially rejected, partially accepted and incorporated in the picture which is being formed; nevertheless, it remains substantially and recognizably the picture of the same transcendent Person. The process might be compared to the changes which pass over a landscape as the clouds float across the sky; the light falls first here, then there, partially obscuring, partially revealing, yet always disclosing the same landscape and its loveliness. In the oft-quoted words of Browning:

That one Face, far from vanish, rather grows,
Or decomposes but to recompose,
Become my universe that feels and knows.[13]

It may indeed be maintained, as it was years ago by Wilhelm Herrmann, that in so far as historical research raises questions as to what exactly happened in the earthly life of Jesus Christ, it does a real service to the Christian faith. It serves to shake the Christian again and again out of what Herrmann calls "the lazy acquiescence of the natural man," and to guard him against being arrested in some supposedly final resting place in his knowledge of God through Christ. Herrmann writes:

Historical work on the New Testament . . . destroys certain false props of faith, and that is a great gain. The Christian who imagines that the reliability of the records as historical documents gives certainty to his faith, is duly startled from his false repose by the work of the historian, which ought to make it clear to such a man that the possession of Christianity cannot be obtained so cheaply as he thinks.[14]

Furthermore, the fact that historical research is always raising questions about Jesus Christ con-

[13] "Epilogue: Dramatis Personae"; cf. C. H. Dodd, *History and the Gospel* (New York: Charles Scribner's Sons, 1938), ch. iii. Having discussed the various groups of material, as reconstructed by form criticism, which have gone to the making of the Gospels, Dodd concludes: "They do set Jesus before us as a clear-cut Figure in word and action. And although the points of view differ, we cannot avoid the impression that it is the same picture that we are seeing from them all" (p. 92). Again: "In the fourth decade of the first century the Christian Church grew up around a central tradition, which, however it is expressed—in preaching, in story, in teaching and in liturgical practice—yields a coherent picture of Jesus Christ, what He was, what He stood for, what He said, did and suffered" (p. 110).

[14] *The Communion of the Christian with God*, tr. J. Sandys Stanton (2nd ed.; London: Williams & Norgate, 1906), pp. 76-77.

tinually compels the church and the individual believer to explore afresh the significance of Jesus Christ, continually compels us to ask ourselves whether we are really grasping "what He was, what He stood for, what He said, did and suffered," whether we are really entering into the riches which are offered us in him. A good example of this kind of service is the way in which many at the beginning of the twentieth century, who were inclined to settle down too easily in the liberal view of Jesus as a supreme teacher and exemplar of the fatherhood of God and the brotherhood of man and as such taking his place in the continuous upward "progress" of mankind to better things, were shaken out of that position by the work of scholars such as Johannes Weiss, Albert Schweitzer, and Alfred Loisy, who compelled attention to the dominant place of eschatological belief in the Gospels and in the New Testament generally. In view of all this, it is wrong to regard the tension between Christian faith and historical research as a burden of which, if it were possible, we would rather be relieved. On the contrary, one may think rather that it is of the good providence of God that the Gospels have come down to us in their present form, requiring ever-renewed study and exploration.

2. The Gospels as Faith Documents.—The second source of difficulty proves on examination to be of no greater weight, though it looks at first sight very formidable. The suggestion is that it is impossible for us to encounter the historic Jesus when we read the Gospels, because we have in them an account written from the angle of faith in him: that is to say, we are presented (so it is alleged) not with the facts as such, but with a religious interpretation of them, an interpretation which may well lead in places to distortion and misrepresentation.

In reply to this allegation it is necessary to consider whether there does not lurk behind it an untenable theory of knowledge. The error is to suppose that if we are really to get to know a reality of any sort, then we must somehow get to know it "in and for itself" as bare fact, that is, out of relation to the impression it makes upon us or upon anybody else. Thus—to take an example from another sphere—it is supposed, on this view, that when I look at a rose, the color, fragrance, and beauty of it are merely impressions in my mind which the rose causes, but which are not aspects of its essential being. The impressions are a sort of curtain behind which the real rose—the "rose in itself" —remains hidden. In so far as the real rose is pictured at all, it is pictured as merely a source of energy which, radiating from it, causes vibratory impulses to run up the nerves to the brain cells, where they are transformed into sensory and aesthetic impressions. The latter, however, are "no more like the real rose than the knock on the door is like the postman." It is out of place here to discuss this phenomenalist theory of knowledge: its deficiencies have often enough been discussed by the philosophers. It is sufficient to make the obvious point which this theory involves, that we cannot really know any object at all, for obviously we cannot know an object unless it makes some impact upon us; yet on this view, directly it makes such an impact, it goes into hiding, so to speak, behind it. It is much more satisfactory to suppose (as we do normally suppose) that it *is* the real rose which is given to us in its color, shape, scent, and beauty. It is part of the reality of the object we call a rose that it is in a world along with conscious minds which are in rapport with their world through a nervous system, and that when it encounters such minds it offers itself, as it were, to them as color, shape, scent, and beauty. It does not hide behind these, but rather completes itself in them, discloses its reality and significance through them.

Now a similar and equally unsatisfactory theory of knowledge may lie behind the notion we are considering, namely, that since we have in the Gospels a report and interpretation of Jesus and of the events of his life, written down by those who had a profound religious faith concerning him, therefore the real, historic facts are inaccessible to us. We are asked, in effect, to suppose that there was a Jesus "in and for himself" independently of the relations he entered into with other people and the impact he made upon them, and that this, and this alone, was the "real" Jesus. But the truth is that there are no persons "in and for themselves." To be a person in history is to be in relation with other persons, to act and react with them in a continuous interplay of reciprocal meanings, valuations, and interpretations. And the "reality" of a person can in greater or less degree be truly known through these relationships: he discloses himself, gives himself to others, through thus meeting with them. If he cannot be so known, then he cannot be known as a person at all. By the same argument, there are in history no such things as bare facts or events, for history is the sphere of persons in relationship with one another, and events, in so far as they are factors in history, and not merely in impersonal nature, are all events having meaning to, and interpreted by, persons. There is therefore no reason to think that because in the Gospels we are presented with an account of Jesus as he entered into the religious faith of men and women with whom he had the closest personal relationships, that we cannot encounter his historical reality through that account. If we do so

suppose, it can only be on grounds which make it impossible to know the world of history at all, either in the past or in the present; and the labors of historians, in so far as they go beyond the merely external cataloguing of dates, become a perpetual chasing of what can never be attained.

It may be said, however, that even if all this is granted, the interpretation of Jesus that lies behind and within the Gospels and the New Testament generally may, for all we know, be false and distortingly imposed upon the facts, so that while it cannot be denied that we *may* know the real Jesus through them, nevertheless we can never be sure that we *do*. The answer to this is to point out that it has never been maintained by the Christian faith that it is possible to know with growingly unassailable conviction the reality of Jesus as he is apprehended by that faith merely by reading and studying the Gospels and the New Testament in a completely detached way, if indeed that is ever possible. It is part of the faith that a transcendent factor is involved, namely, the risen Christ working through the Holy Spirit in the Christian community. All we have been concerned to show is that if it is true, as we have maintained it to be, that it is an essential part of Christ's work for us that we should encounter and continually re-encounter him in his historic self-manifestation, then the difficulty which some feel that we cannot so encounter him because of the nature of the records is not a reasonable one, for it rests on very questionable epistemological presuppositions. It is clear, indeed, that if the Christian faith is valid and Christ does in fact have the transcendent significance claimed for him, then only an account written from the angle of that faith could convey a historically trustworthy impression of him. Furthermore, this impression will not be nullified by the fact that doubtfully accurate statements enter here and there into the account—the total impact of the man Jesus Christ, as he evokes and sustains faith in himself, will still remain unimpaired. On the other hand, even if the Christian faith were false, it would still not follow that because the Gospels are written from the angle of such a mistaken belief, they therefore cannot convey to us a good deal of the real historic quality of Christ's personality and life. For this at least we know for certain, that Jesus Christ was the historic person who evoked that faith. Nothing can alter that remarkable fact and all that has flowed from it; and no study of Jesus Christ which claims to be historically grounded, but which does not earnestly seek to do justice to that fact, is worth consideration. In that fact more than in any other the real Jesus is disclosed. It is at this point that many studies of Jesus Christ made by skeptical minds fail, and must be judged unscientific. They seek to appraise the story of Jesus without giving due weight to the faith he evoked and to the Christian movement which sprang from him. It may be stated as a definite principle for the study of the Gospels that those reconstructions of the life of Jesus Christ, which, if true, would leave the Christian movement and its faith, as it were, in mid-air, must be false.

This leads to a word on the question of how written records from the past, or rather the reading and exposition of them, can be taken up into, and share in, Christ's present living and ruling relationship to the church.

3. *How Written Records Enter into Christ's Living Relationship to the Church.*—It might be considered sufficient answer to the question to say, as has already been implied, that it is the work of the Holy Spirit to bring this about; but to say that and nothing more carries perhaps too much the suggestion of a merely incomprehensible and miraculous tour de force. We get a little light on the matter by looking at it from the angle of the whole Christian faith concerning Christ, even though in the last analysis the way of the Spirit's working must remain a mystery. To look at it from this angle has the further advantage of enabling us to see once again how the significance and authority of the Bible are inseparably bound up with the whole organism of Christian faith and experience, and cannot rightly be understood apart from it.

If the Christian faith concerning Christ is true, then he stands in his historical and human self-manifestation, despite the ever-lengthening interval between that manifestation and those who come after him, in a peculiarly deep relationship of contemporaneousness to all men. This is true in three ways:

In the first place, if the Christian faith concerning him is valid, then the Christ who encounters us in the pages of the New Testament, while he has the concrete individuality of historic personality, is the true universal of human nature. We implicitly recognize this in the way in which we believe it to be possible and desirable for any man to be Christlike without losing his distinctive individuality. This means that Christ is profoundly and uniquely related to the inner being of every man in every age. He is the realization in concrete, historical reality of that norm which God made constitutive of human nature when he created man, and which, though it is frustrated and perverted by sin, can never be entirely destroyed.

In the second place, if the Christian faith concerning him is valid, the Christ who meets us in the pages of the New Testament, being the Incarnation of the very nature and purpose of the personal God, is profoundly and uniquely related to the outward environment of all men, particularly the environment of personal relationships which constitutes what we call history. The ultimate reality with which men have to deal in their present situations and tasks is a personal order, deriving its essential nature and meaning from a personal divine will whose character and direction are manifested fully in the person of Christ. Christ is, as it were, a clear and focused, a "concreted," revelation of that of which the historical existence of men—life as they have every day to live it and meet it—is a clouded and distorted one.

These first two points might be expressed together by saying that Christ is every man's contemporary because the whole of reality, particularly in its relation to the world of persons —both in its inward and its outward manifestations—is Christ-grained, Christ-patterned (John 1:1-18; Col. 1:15-19).

In the third place, if the Christian faith concerning him is valid, Christ is men's contemporary, not merely because he is the expression in concrete individuality of the "essence" of man and of the personal order, but also because he is a living, personal purpose and presence who, through the Holy Spirit, is seeking actively and personally now to encounter men and claim them.

All these aspects of what has been called the contemporaneousness of Christ, which are implicit in the Christian faith concerning him, shed at least a little light on the way in which the Gospels and the New Testament cease to be "dead" and "dated" documents from the past, and become part of the present saving ministry of the Redeemer. It is not a question of leaping over a gap of almost two thousand years out of Britain or the United States of today into first-century Palestine, and sitting at the feet of one who, however impressive, is alien to us. That would be the situation if Jesus were an ordinary man with no unique significance. But it is the Christian faith and experience that he is not an ordinary man: rather, there is incarnate in him the divine will and purpose which lie behind and are at work in every human life and all history.

We may give other expression to the same truth—the truth that Christ's relationship to the Christian man is at one and the same time that of a historical figure in the past depicted in the Gospels and that of a contemporaneous reality deeply related to his inward being and his outward environment—by insisting, as Christianity has always insisted, that Christ's saving work and presence are mediated through the

Christian fellowship, through the new covenant community. The Christian fellowship is a community which is as fully contemporaneous with the believer as are the living men and women who constitute its membership and meet him in day-to-day "I-thou" relationships; but at the same time it is deeply and consciously rooted in and continuous with a past which runs back through the centuries to the historical Christ himself. And both these aspects are inseparably involved in its function as mediating Christ. When I participate in the life of the church, I encounter Christ actively disclosing himself to me now in and through an order of living personal relationships which, despite its faults and failings—nay, in some measure because of its faults and failings, or rather, because of the opportunity for distinctively Christian forbearance and forgiveness which these afford—manifestly bears the mark of his mind and spirit. Christ looks at me, as it were, through the eyes of contemporary men and women in whom he dwells. But I also encounter the historic Christ of long ago; for the church's long past, which goes right back to the first disciples whom he gathered around him in Palestine, and without the explicit consciousness of which it would not be what it is, now becomes my past, my memory, my history.[15] This is why the study and exposition of the Scriptures, particularly the New Testament, within the worshiping fellowship of the church, is something so very different from the study of them by one whose interest is merely in historical or antiquarian research. Such study and exposition are integrally one with the life of the fellowship itself: they illumine and are reciprocally illumined by the whole organism of redeemed personal relationships which the New Testament calls the body of Christ. Perhaps the supreme illustration of these truths is the sacrament of the Last Supper. In the symbolism of this solemn and central rite the church deliberately goes back through the centuries to the Redeemer's earthly life; it obeys his direct injunction spoken by his human lips so many hundreds of years ago; it re-enacts his words and deeds as recorded in the Scriptures, which are read at the rite itself. Nevertheless, it is the faith and experience of the church that the rite is never a mere recalling of the past; it is not mere commemoration. In and through it there is a present communion with the risen and living Lord.

B. Limits of the Canon.—We now turn to the second of the two questions which arise in connection with the understanding of the norma-tive place of the Bible within the church, namely, why the writings which are essential to the present efficacy of Christ's saving and ruling office in the church should be limited to the present contents of the Bible. This is to raise —from the theological angle—the question of the limits of the canon.[16]

So far as the Old Testament is concerned, the question is not a difficult one in principle, nor an important one in practice. In principle, it would be impossible to deny a place in the Old Testament to any writing which was manifestly important as participating in and witnessing to, and so enabling us more fully to grasp, the divine activity in the history of the old covenant people preparing and leading up to the coming of Christ. In practice, the question has no importance because the advent of Christ itself put a final limit to the old covenant history considered as preparatory to that advent. There cannot, therefore, be any more candidates for canonicity, except in the extremely remote contingency of a new manuscript belonging to the Old Testament period being discovered. Though this is an eventuality so improbable as to be hardly worth considering, nevertheless it is clear that if it did happen, the church would have to consider the claim of the writing in question to be included in the canon. The only question which might be considered to remain open is that of the Apocrypha, or rather, of those books in the Apocrypha which help to bridge the gap between the two Testaments, and therefore to give knowledge of the history of the old covenant people immediately prior to the Incarnation itself (e.g., I and II Maccabees). In principle, there is no reason why the churches which now exclude the Apocrypha from the Bible should not at any time reconsider the matter from this angle; but there does not appear to be any reason why they should do so, for the books are in any case available to Christian scholars and thinkers, and none of them is so strong a candidate (though some might well be thought stronger candidates than, say, the Song of Songs or Esther) as to make it worth while to open up what would probably prove a thorny and divisive question.

The question of the limits of the canon is not so easily disposed of in relation to the New Testament. The church as the new covenant community is still going on, so that there is not, as there is in the case of the Old Testament, an inevitable chronological limit to the writings which might be considered to be candidates for canonicity. Why, then, should not later writings

---

[15] Cf. Nicolas Berdyaev, *The Meaning of History*, tr. George Reavey (New York: Charles Scribner's Sons, 1936), p. 16.

[16] See also articles "The Canon of the Old Testament" (pp. 32-45); "The Canon of the New Testament" (pp. 63-71).

than those at present comprising the New Testament, some of them on a very high level of inspiration, which have been produced as part of the ongoing life of the church throughout the ages, enter as indispensably into the present living relationship of Christ to his people?

To answer this question we must go back once again to the central Christian affirmation of the Incarnation. We must again insist that the divine saving action in Christ was "in and through" as well as "into" history. This "in-and-through-ness" implies that we must include in the scope of that action more than the human person of Christ. We must include in some measure the other human persons and events in immediate relation to which his life, death, and resurrection were wrought out and the new revelation made. If we do not thus widen the scope of the divine action, we must suppose either that it was a matter of chance whether the revelation in Christ would prove effective as a revelation, or that its effectiveness was independent of genuine historical conditions—in other words, that there was no real historic Incarnation at all.

The question is: In what measure must we include the human persons and events in relation to which the life of the Redeemer was wrought out? This raises some formidable problems, as, for example, in what sense must we include the betrayal by Judas and the rejection by the Jerusalem authorities in the divine plan to enter history and save mankind through Christ. Such questions run out into some of the oldest and most intractable problems of philosophical theology, but fortunately there is no need to consider them here. Our interest is simply in God's bringing into existence the new covenant community of saved men and women which should be both the first fruits and the agent of God's saving purpose toward mankind in Christ. Clearly, if this was to be accomplished, it was necessary that the divine action should include the provision of men who would not only keep company with Christ in the actual unfolding of his historic life, death, and resurrection, but also discern the transcendent meaning of these events, and be sent forth to bear witness to it. The calling of such men, and the continual quickening of their minds and hearts to fulfill the calling, we can think of only as the mysterious work of the Holy Spirit. As Christ himself said, when Peter confessed that he was the Christ, "Flesh and blood hath not revealed it unto thee, but my Father which is in heaven" (Matt. 16:17). But whatever the mystery of the divine working, the indispensability of these men is obvious. Only in their response does the divine intention and act of revelation complete itself. Had there been no such men,

the story of Jesus would not have become a revelation to humanity; it would not have become the Word of God. It would have echoed and re-echoed, like a sound which passes unheard in a primeval forest. It would have been like a bridge which had been begun from one side of a river, but which never reached the other side.[17]

So the first apostles come into view as essentially and indispensably involved in the process of a historic incarnation and revelation.

The word "apostle" in New Testament usage is nowhere exactly defined, but it seems clear that in essence it signifies precisely those who were called to play this crucial part in the totality of the divine action in Christ. Perhaps the best description of their function is given in the words: "That which . . . we have heard, which we have seen with our eyes, which we have looked upon, and our hands have handled, of the Word of life. . . . That which we have seen and heard declare we unto you" (I John 1:1, 3; cf. I Cor. 9:1, "Am I not an apostle? . . . have I not seen Jesus Christ our Lord?") There is, however, an important element to be added to this description, the element indicated by the word apostle itself. It is an essential part of the content of the divine revelation, and of its apprehension by those whose eyes saw and whose hands handled the Word of life, that these last should be sent, and be conscious of themselves as sent, to declare it to the world. In the sending of the apostles, and through the sending of the apostles, the purpose of God as manifested in Christ is set forth as a redemptive purpose which is impelled by its essential nature to go out to all mankind. "As my Father hath sent me, even so send I you" (John 20:21). Obvious as this may appear to be, it is of the greatest importance for a right doctrine of redemption and of the church. Christian thought has been too much dominated by what someone has called "the ark" view of salvation, the view, that is, that being saved consists in being rescued from something, whereas it consists just as much in being sent to do something; the "being-sent-to-do" is essentially part of the "being-rescued-from." "Apostolicity" or "being-sent-ness" lies therefore at the very heart of the Christian revelation, springing as it does from what one may perhaps venture to call the "apostolic" activity of God—God in his saving purpose *sends* the Son, and the Son *sends* those who respond to his revelation and call.

The first apostles, then, stand in a distinctive

[17] Emil Brunner, *Revelation and Reason*, tr. O. Wyon (Philadelphia: Westminster Press, 1946), p. 122. My thought at this point is indebted to Brunner.

position within the divine saving revelation in Christ, and in the bringing into existence of the new covenant community. They participate in the historic actuality of the Incarnation, and it is an essential element in the participation that they are sent into the world to bear witness to it. The bearing witness had to be in the first instance oral—the preaching of the gospel—but it is evident that if any of the apostolic circle gave any sort of expression to the message in writing, or was the immediate source or inspiration of such writing, the writing in question would have a special significance and status. It would itself be part of, an immediate deposit of, the great originative historic event itself, and no writing subsequently produced by others could possibly have the same significance and status.

That it was not long before written documents (especially compilations of the incidents and sayings of the Master's life) appeared and were being circulated within the new community is easily understandable; there is no need to try to analyze the process here. And it is as easily understandable that in due course, when the young community moved out into the Greek world, when the many currents of thought in that world began to play upon it, and when at the same time Christian writings—some of them of secondary and doubtful value—began to multiply and gain currency, the need was felt to establish a select body or canon of writings which should express and preserve once and for all, in as pure a form as possible, the story of the originative events of the Savior's life and death and resurrection, and the apostolic testimony concerning them. Such a collection of writings would inevitably be thought of as the completion of the Old Testament canon which was already in use, and would act both as a continuous source and a corrective standard of the church's teaching and life. But the process in its broad outline—much of its detail is obscure—is not only easy to understand; it must be judged to be wholly right and justified. The necessity for authoritative writings of some sort is implicit in the idea of a historic revelation and redemption; without such writings the historic events, along with their crucial significance for men, would have been lost in alien systems of thought, or in embroidered legends, or in theosophical and mystical speculations, if indeed the knowledge of them had not faded away altogether into oblivion, their memory and influence gradually dissipated and dissolved into the unregenerate life of mankind.

Furthermore, it was right instinct which led the church in course of time to formulate the principle that from among the writings which the general mind of the community had already,

by the unconscious selection of use, declared to be valuable and worth preserving, only those should be finally admitted to the canon which were apostolic in origin, for as we have seen, the apostles do stand apart: they are within the circle of the divine revelation in Christ, within the process of the Incarnation itself, and any testimony of theirs shares in the same distinctive status. The criterion of apostolicity, however, having been thus justifiably laid down, the task of applying it correctly was no easy one, and the question still remains whether in point of fact it was so applied. This is a large question, involving matters of New Testament scholarship and research into which it is not necessary to enter. But the judgment seems warranted that if we do not identify apostolic origin with direct apostolic authorship, and if we frankly allow for legitimate doubt in respect of some of the writings included in our New Testament (e.g., II Peter, James, Jude, Revelation), the church on the whole decided well. Broadly speaking, the New Testament *is* an apostolic book and therefore shares in the unique status of the apostolic circle in relation to the Incarnation. And in the New Testament we do find ourselves confronting the historic person of the Redeemer in his unique creative and re-creative impact upon men, bringing into existence the new covenant community and sending and empowering it to bear witness to him throughout the world, in a way in which we do not confront him in other early writings of the church, even the most beautiful and helpful. While it is obviously impossible to maintain that the New Testament would not have played a part in the life of the Christian community and in the lives of its individual members if it had included some writings which it does not now include, or had excluded some it now contains, it is beyond question that the New Testament, taken as a whole, has been and is indispensable to God's giving to every new generation the riches which are in Christ. On the principles here laid down, the exact boundaries of the New Testament canon may be held to be debatable, yet the distinctiveness and indispensability of what lies centrally and solidly within those boundaries remain quite clear and undeniable. In a similar way, although the precise limits of the sun when it rides the heavens at noon cannot be discerned with our eyes, there is no doubt in what part of the heaven it is, or that it gives light and warmth and healing to mankind.

The absence of boundaries which we can exactly define and justify might perhaps be looked upon as bearing witness once more to the thoroughgoing historical reality of the revelation which lies at the center of the Christian faith. It bears witness once more to the "in and through" aspect of it. The same witness is borne by the nature of the writings comprised within the New Testament. None of them, of course, was written for the purpose of finding a place in an authoritative canon defined in accordance with a prior idea as to what such a canon should be and should provide. They were written simply to meet the actual situations which confronted the new faith as it went out into the world in the persons of those who committed themselves to it. As such they are rooted in the historic process itself, even as is the Incarnation with which they are integrally bound up.

IV. The Nature of the Authority of the Bible

This article has maintained that there is only one final and absolute authority for the faith and life of the church, and therefore for the faith and life of the individual members within it: namely, the living Christ speaking through the Holy Spirit. It has sought to show that the reason why the New Testament participates indispensably in the authority of the living Christ is that the faith and witness of the apostolic circle are part of the original act of divine revelation "into" and "in and through" history. If we desire to hear God's word to us in Christ and to be kept from straying again into the darkness from which he came to deliver us, we must always begin with the New Testament and to it we must ever return, for that is but to begin with Christ and to return to him. This commits us to the study of the Old Testament as well, for the coming of Christ, and the bringing into existence of the new covenant community through him, are continuous with the life and history of the old covenant community and cannot be fully comprehended apart from them.

The question to which we now address ourselves is how, in view of all that has been said, the Scriptures are to be used so that their normative function may be rightly exercised.

A. The Authority of the Bible Not Different from That of Christ.

—The first thing that has to be said is that the authority of the Bible, being bound up with the authority of the living Christ himself, cannot be a different sort of authority from his. If, then, we ask what sort of authority Christ seeks to exercise over men, the primary appeal must be to the New Testament. This is in accordance with the principles already laid down. In any case, to ascribe to the biblical writings, and particularly to the New Testament, a kind of authority which it is not even hinted that Christ ever claimed for himself, or wanted to claim, would be to put a contrariety at the very sources of our faith.

When we examine the Gospels, we find that at no point did Christ attempt to exercise an external, overriding authority, to whose pronouncements men are required to submit without investigation or criticism, and altogether apart from any inward endorsement and response within their own minds. On the contrary, we meet the exact reverse—a steadfast refusal to do so, and even a deliberate avoidance of any relationship which might perhaps wear that coercive appearance. This characteristic of Christ's life and teaching is so manifest throughout the Gospels that illustration is hardly necessary. It is indeed so characteristic of him, and at the same time so contrary to the natural instincts of men, that it constitutes one of the evidences of the truth of the record. One may refer only to his refusal to provide a sign from heaven, when asked so to do; to his refusal to answer the question on what authority he did "these things," on the ground that his questioners were not sincere; to such sayings as "He that hath ears to hear, let him hear," and "Why do you not judge for yourselves what is right?" In John Oman's words:

> The great demonstration of the Christ is just that He never sets Himself, as the absolute external authority of the perfect truth, in opposition to the imperfect authority of the finite and sinful spirit within, but that He has only one appeal, which is to the likeness of God and the teaching of God within. Jesus speaks indeed with authority. He is not as the Scribes. They had authorities, but no authority. They had nothing to speak from direct, and nothing to appeal to direct. Jesus, on the other hand, speaks from man to man the truth He has seen and to which his hearers cannot be blind, unless they close their eyes. . . . His "I say unto you" did not end inquiry, but begin it. Hear something, it said, which the humble heart will recognise as true, and which the experience of obedience will confirm. And surely herein is the weightiest proof of the perfect truth. It does not dominate and silence the inward voices, but awakes them and makes them its chief witness.[18]

The rest of the New Testament is in harmony with this. In the Acts the apostles are plainly set before us as men of authority in the infant church, yet their authority is not of the magisterial kind working by dictation and coercion, but rather of a kind which works by persuasion through love, as can be seen in the proceedings of the so-called Council of Jerusalem recorded in Acts 15. The same note appears in the epistles of Paul, wherein the writer, though ready to speak with great force and conviction, nevertheless seeks to persuade his readers by argument and exposition, appealing to them to "judge

[18] *Vision and Authority* (new and rev. ed.; London: Hodder & Stoughton, 1928; New York: Harper & Bros., 1929), pp. 107, 112. Used by permission.

for yourselves what I say" (I Cor. 10:15), and commending the truth "to every man's conscience in the sight of God" (II Cor. 4:2).

It follows that it is a most grave disloyalty to Christ, and to the Scripture which he uses to speak to men, to turn the latter into an overriding authority of the extrinsic, "yardstick" sort, whether by ascribing to it a miraculous infallibility whose statements none may question or investigate, or by forcing it—usually by strained exegesis—to stand sponsor for a system of doctrine the acceptance of which is demanded as essential to salvation (as in some types of Protestant orthodoxy), or by using it as a kind of *sortes Vergilianae* or means of divination (as in certain kinds of foolish, intense piety we all know).

By the same argument, we are brought to see what is the right use of the Scripture, and what is true loyalty to it. We betake ourselves to the Scripture as part of our betaking ourselves to the feet of Christ, in the humble faith that in him, and therefore in the Scripture through which he chooses to encounter us, is the final truth for our lives; yet well knowing that only as this truth becomes veritably our truth, the truth which compels our allegiance through our own sincerest thought in relation to our own contemporary world, is Christ's purpose—and therefore the Scripture's purpose—fulfilled in us.

There are, however, two possible objections to this position which must be faced.

First, it is sometimes urged that thus to understand the authority of Scripture is in effect to destroy it altogether; for, it is said, if we accept in the Scripture only what compels our own assent, we are exposed to the danger of an unchecked individualism by which each takes or leaves what his own judgment may dictate. The answer to this is to insist once again on the double truth that Scripture is a norm which is intrinsic to the life of the whole Christian community, and that its normative function is inseparable from the ever-present ministry of the living Christ through the Holy Spirit. It is to the insight of the individual that Christ speaks, but to picture the individual Christian to whom Christ thus speaks as an isolated and self-contained unit shut up within the circle of his own mental processes is to deny in effect the two truths just stated. The Christian man who is being brought by Christ into the new life of reconciliation with God is by that fact incorporated in the new covenant community, and it is only as such that he can properly understand and use the Scriptures. This is itself a continuous and effective check upon eccentric individualism. But in addition, the Christian man, along with the community of which he is part, is under the promised guidance of the Holy Spirit. To fear an uncontrolled and destructive individualism is therefore to express an ultimate unbelief in the effectiveness of God's revelation in Christ and in his power to authenticate that revelation to any who seek to open their minds to it. (The truths contained in this paragraph are implicit in Eph. 4:11-16.)

In this connection it is perhaps not without significance that it was during the era when Protestantism generally assumed the literal inerrancy of Scripture, and used it in an externally authoritarian way, that it broke up into a multitude of sects; whereas it has been in more recent times, since biblical scholarship released us from this bondage and gave us the true freedom of the Scripture, that the process has shown a marked tendency to be reversed. The various churches have begun to draw together, and have increasingly discovered a fundamental unity of belief. *Post hoc, ergo propter hoc* is no doubt a precarious argument, but these facts certainly suggest that the view that an authoritarian use of Scripture is necessary to preserve us from a divisive individualism is not borne out by experience.

Second, it may be said that thus to throw the Christian believer back upon his own inward sense of truth is to fail to take account of his actual situation as a weak and sinful man, who, because of his weakness and sinfulness, needs an authoritative guidance and direction transcending his own powers. To adapt some words written elsewhere, the cry for firm and trustworthy direction as to what a man should do and believe springs from the reality of the human situation. Sin is always with us, and sin obscures God. Terrible things happen, and the soul begins to doubt the truth of its highest vision. Testing situations arise when a man is called to stake even his life, and then he begins to waver and to ask for some other assurance than his own inward conviction that the sacrifice he is called upon to make is really worth while. It is these facts of man's spiritual immaturity and spasmodic and erratic growth into the truth, his muddled insights, his shadowed and chaotic life, his sinful failures and disloyalties—everything in his nature which clouds and obscures vision—which evoke the cry for an authority which shall tell him once and for all what he must believe, what he must do, and what he may hope for.[19] If the Scriptures do not answer this cry and meet this need, of what essential value are they to him? But how can they do so if he is thrown back in the end on his own feeble understanding of them?

[19] See Herbert H. Farmer, *The Servant of the Word* (New York: Charles Scribner's Sons, 1942), pp. 83-84.

The answer to this can only be to reaffirm what has already been said, namely, that in Christ God has in fact given the truth in such a form that it is able to reach men even in the darkness and weakness of their sinfulness, without, however, overriding their minds in an impersonally authoritarian way. In this work of Christ, as we have seen, the Scriptures play an instrumental and indispensable part in co-operation with the Holy Spirit. This is fundamentally a matter of faith; but it is also in sufficient measure a matter of proved experience. And this further should be added: The clamor for an authoritarian direction which shall dispel all our doubts and perplexities, exempt us from ever making mistakes, and therefore from learning from them humility and patience and charity for others, relieve us of any necessity to make up our own minds, or to venture on decisions of faith which take us out, like Abraham, into the unknown—such clamor may itself be a manifestation of our unregenerate state, of that anxiety and unbelief which lie somewhere at the heart of sin. Indeed, we may assert that it is such a manifestation, for certainly there is no evidence, either in Scripture or in experience, that that sort of direction is in fact provided for us. Nevertheless, there is always a true succor for our need, even if it is at times not so much the succor of clear vision as of faith renewed, faith in the overshadowing and pardoning love of God from which nothing can separate us, not even our sin, still less our perplexities, immaturities, and mistakes.

B. Some Principles of Discrimination and Interpretation.—When once we have set to one side the infallibility of the Scriptures, and have fully admitted that the Christian believer or theologian in his use of them must be guided in the last resort by his own conviction of truth, we admit in principle the right to set to one side some of the biblical content. But on the other hand, if the Bible is the record of the divine revelation in history, and as such part of the revelation, there must be within it that from which the Christian is not at liberty to depart without gravely imperiling, if not destroying, the notion of an objective historical revelation available in an accessible and relevant form. It is the task of theology, and that which gives its work vitality and value in every new generation, to keep these two things—the critical discrimination of the content of the Bible, and the faith that there is within that content that which is objectively and finally given—in continuous tension with one another.[20] Though this is a tension which can never be completely overcome, some broad

[20] Cf. p. 18 regarding the value of the questions raised by the historical criticism of the Bible.

principles may be laid down in relation to it on the basis of the general position set forth in this article.

(a) It is perhaps hardly necessary to say at this time of day that the Christian is free to reject beliefs concerning the facts of the natural order which find expression in the Bible, but which are contrary to the established and tested findings of competent scientific research. To suppose that we must accept every biblical belief about the facts of nature would be to ignore both the historic character of the Christian revelation and the distinctive content of it: the historic character of it requires, as has been said so often already, that it should be "in and through" human life, that is, at the level of general knowledge and culture obtaining at the time it is made; the content of the revelation, on the other hand, being Christ the redeemer and reconciler, is plainly unaffected by the question whether a man is, say, a medieval Christian believing, with the biblical writers, that the earth is flat, or a modern Christian believing, contrary to the biblical writers, that it is round. No doubt we have always to be on our guard against accepting too easily and uncritically the views of scientists on this or that matter. It is especially necessary to discriminate between experimentally established facts and those theoretical interpretations of facts which at best are never more than probable hypotheses, and which in many cases fall outside the scope of strict science and become essentially philosophical in character. But the obligation to be thus cautious in the interest of truth is a general one and rests upon all men, not merely on the Christian believer, though no doubt the Christian believer has an added incentive to watchfulness because of his concern that the essential truth of the biblical revelation shall not be set to one side by speculations falsely claiming the authority of science. However difficult it may be in some cases to determine the boundary between fully accredited fact, probable hypothesis, and philosophical speculation, particularly when, as is sometimes the case, they are intertwined with one another, the general principle that has been laid down is clear and indubitable, namely, that scriptural views on such matters as natural science is competent to investigate and determine cannot be regarded, on a right view of the Scriptures, as binding.

(b) The distinction must be made, whenever appropriate, between the content of the biblical revelation and the symbols through which it is expressed. The latter may belong, like views on the facts of nature, to the culture and thought forms of the time, and we are free, if we will, to set them to one side and find other symbols and forms of expression. It is another of the great services of the historical approach to the Bible that it often enables us to recover, in a way that was not possible before, the meaning which a particular form of expression had to those who used it and to those to whom it was addressed. This gives us a firmer grasp of the meaning intended (guarding us against reading into it our own meanings), and at the same time it releases us from bondage to the symbol itself. A notable example of this is the understanding we now have of the symbolism of the book of Jonah, an understanding through which the full force of its teaching has been recovered, releasing us once and for all from the preposterous notion that acceptance of the fish episode as historic fact is somehow part of a sound Christian faith. Another illustration is the understanding we now have of the metaphorical element in such key words of Paul's thought as "justification" (a symbol from the law courts), "adoption" (a symbol from contemporary social custom), and "redemption" (a symbol from the institution of slavery).[21]

(c) That the revelation set forth in the Bible is a developing revelation is implicit in the idea of the New Testament as the fulfillment of the Old and is plainly evident from the content of Scripture itself. This means that we have not merely the right but the duty to discriminate within the scripture records between different levels in the apprehension of God's nature and purpose and to reject the lower levels once and for all in favor of the higher. For only by so doing can we once again be loyal to the notion of a revelation which God has given through the medium of historical events, and to the faith that Christ himself is the final source and norm of all truth in this sphere.[22]

At the same time it must be recognized that it is not always easy to make such a discrimination between lower and higher levels. Difficulty arises for two reasons.

The first is that though we may rightly speak of development in the apprehension of God set forth in the biblical history, nevertheless the development is not a straight linear advance, such as it has sometimes been represented to be by thinkers too much dominated by the uncritical nineteenth-century notion of an inevitable and always mounting progress in human affairs. In the biblical history we do not see depicted the "evolution of religion," but the

wrestling of the living God with real human persons, who have wills of their own and are liable to all the perversities of mind and heart which characterize human persons. The earlier is therefore not necessarily on a lower level than the later: there is retrogression as well as progression; and the task of discrimination can never be simply a matter of establishing, if we can, a chronological sequence. Something of direct religious insight and evaluation has also to come into play, enabling us to differentiate between what is essentially sound and of permanent value, even though relatively undeveloped, and what is essentially unsound, even though otherwise on a much higher cultural level. The Bible itself justifies us in making such a differentiation and helps us to make it, for it is an essential part of the witness of the prophetic minds, whose message it preserves, to recall their contemporaries from their perpetual wanderings into error and darkness to, as it were, the highway of God's unfolding disclosure of himself to them through the working out of his purpose in their history. It is indeed part of the value of the Bible to us that it thus mediates the purpose of God to us through a record of men's continual disloyalties to and departures from it, for the same tendencies to stray into error are always present within the human soul. And it is also part of its value that though what we have called the highway of God's revelation of truth is indicated, there is always need for our own insight and discrimination to be brought into play if we are to discern it and find in it a directive for our own life.

The second reason has to do with the ambiguity in the meaning of the term "fulfillment," to which reference was made earlier (see p. 10). When we say that the New Testament fulfills the Old we may mean that it provides answers to certain fundamental religious questions which the Old Testament leaves unanswered or answers unsatisfactorily. Clearly such fulfillment supersedes the Old Testament so far as the *answers* to these questions are concerned, though the Old Testament record in relation to such questions may still have great value in making clear what they are and how they arise, and in warning against those partial or false solutions which the New Testament once and for all sets to one side. C. H. Dodd, in a chapter headed "The New Testament as the Fulfillment of the Old," lists five such fundamental questions.[23]

On the other hand, we may think of the New Testament as fulfilling the Old in such a way that what is fulfilled is not completely set to one side, but, on the contrary, is validated and

---

[21] Cf. Adolf Deissmann, *Paul*, tr. William E. Wilson (2nd ed.; New York: George H. Doran, 1926), pp. 167 ff.

[22] Christ's "Ye have heard that it was said by them of old time, . . . but I say unto you" is a clear recognition of different levels in the divine revelation to and through the covenant people. That history must be a development process in order to be a true meeting place between God and men as persons, I have sought to show in my book *The World and God*, p. 300.

[23] *The Authority of the Bible* (New York: Harper & Bros., 1929), pp. 205-23.

its true significance and value preserved and made plain. Moreover, that which is thus fulfilled may in a measure reciprocally illumine and illustrate that which fulfills it. An example will help to make this clear. In Hosea's loyal and tender relationship with his erring wife, and in the new discernment of God's nature and purpose which came to him through that tragic experience, we can see, as we look back on it from the standpoint of the New Testament revelation, both a true likeness to Christ and at least a partial discernment of the truth which was fully disclosed in him. And because of this continuity of truth between the two, because the incomplete and the partial, so far from being abrogated, is taken up and reaffirmed in that which fulfills it, we can even use the story of Hosea (as many a preacher must have done) to illustrate, and by illustrating to illumine, the truth which is in Christ. In a similar way, the faith of Abraham, the sympathetic and pitiful imagination of David, the deep concern of the Mosaic law for the weak and needy, the penitence of the psalmist, the "servant passages" of Isaiah, and much else in the Old Testament, can be understood in a new way in the light of Christ; and they may even help us to apprehend and appropriate that light more fully.

It is along these lines that we can find room in our use of the Old Testament for something that might be called a "typology," but it is obviously a very different typology from that which can be amply illustrated from the history of scriptural interpretation—namely, that which fancifully and ingeniously reads into almost anything in the Old Testament oblique Christian references and meanings, without any regard to what a sound exegesis would show to be the real meaning and intention of the text. The hold which typological and allegorical methods of interpretation (seldom clearly distinguished from one another) have had on the minds of students of Scripture all down the history of the church can be sympathetically regarded as an endeavor to assert the continuity of the Old and New Testaments and the divine unity of Scripture. But it too often rested on what we now see to be (i) an inevitably inadequate exegetical equipment; (ii) a defective sense of the meaning of a historical revelation, which made it seem necessary to find an equal place in the divine revelation for everything in the Old Testament (even for the voluptuous love lyric called the Song of Songs—usually interpreted as an allegory of the relation of Christ to the church); and (iii) a failure to realize that if there is continuity between the Old and New Testaments, there is also a radical discontinuity between them.

(d) It is important in discriminating the biblical material to be sure that we are not doing so on the basis of theological or philosophical presuppositions and principles which have been adopted on grounds extraneous to the biblical revelation, which have never been thoroughly scrutinized in the light of that revelation, and which may in fact be contrary to it. Thus—to give some examples—whatever we may make of the difficult question of the miracle stories in the Bible, we must seek to be sure that the position we adopt in regard to it is not based on a general philosophical position which not only starts elsewhere than in the fundamental biblical view of God as personally active in the world he has made, but must also, if logically wrought out, gravely impugn that view. Or again, whatever we may make of the eschatological elements in the New Testament, we must seek to be sure that we are not bringing to the interpretation of them a view of history which owes much more to current notions of evolution and progress than to serious wrestling with the distinctively biblical view of the relation of time and eternity. Or again, we must take care that the very somber view which is taken throughout the Bible of man's status as a sinner before God is not unconsciously toned down and reinterpreted, if not almost completely explained away, on the basis of an optimistic, semipantheistic humanism which, if it is true, really takes the heart out of the distinctive biblical message of man's redemption.

The problem of rightly relating to one another the special interests and problems of philosophy and a theology which is seeking to be true to the Bible is a difficult one, and affords another of those tensions which keep theological work alive. It is not possible to avoid the use of philosophical categories (such as time, eternity, cause, purpose, personality) in building up a systematic theology; moreover, the general cosmological framework into which the Christian theologian, and even preacher, inevitably seeks to fit his Christian convictions is bound to contain elements of which the Bible knows nothing, on which it sheds little direct light, and to which in some measure a philosophical evaluation must be applied if they are to be rightly assessed (as the facts of biological evolution). Nevertheless, the general principle, however difficult to apply, remains clear, namely, that we must be continually interrogating ourselves to see whether we are allowing the Bible in its basic affirmations to be determinative of our thinking, or whether we are making some other view the criterion to which (perhaps unconsciously) we compel all else, including the Bible itself, to submit. The point may be put another way by saying that the principles by which we discriminate the biblical material must be supplied by the Bible itself, or at least be in fundamental harmony with it, and not be taken over uncritically from elsewhere.[24]

(e) A special word may perhaps be said concerning the application to the Gospels and to the New Testament epistles of the principles which we have discussed. The view herein set forth certainly implies that we are not under obligation to accept without question every belief and teaching which is ascribed to Christ, or finds place in the epistles, as though a quotation from these were sufficient to settle every problem, or at least to supply the quite indisputable premise of every argument. Many, however, will feel a particular shrinking from claiming the right to exercise such a discriminatory judgment on the New Testament; it seems like tampering with the very springs of Christian truth. This feeling must certainly be honored to the extent of insisting most strongly that the work of discrimination within the New Testament requires always the greatest care and humility of spirit, and a constant readiness to review one's judgment, lest aught of the new and challenging truth be lost. But if the feeling is allowed to issue in a total prohibition against setting to one side anything in the New Testament, we are in effect back in that wrong view of the authority of Scripture which in fact involves a far greater disloyalty to it than the possible errors against which such a view is alleged to give protection.

The duty and the right to discriminate (always, it may perhaps be well to say again, from within the fellowship of the church and under the promised guidance of the Holy Spirit) are perhaps not so difficult to affirm in relation to the epistles as in relation to the Gospels, for the writers of the epistles, great as they were and commandingly unique as is their function in the economy of God's revelation in Christ, were in their degree sinful and fallible men. They were seeking to appropriate and express, in relation to their own historical situations and under a divine guidance which certainly did not confer either infallibility or sinless perfection, the riches given in Christ; and it is obvious that what they say does not provide us with a perfectly harmonious system of thought and belief, though there is, of course, a deep underlying unity. In the Gospels, however, we believe ourselves to encounter the perfect One, the incarnate Son of God. Therefore, if we feel led to question beliefs and teachings ascribed to him, it can never be in such a way as even distantly to hint or imply that we know better than he concerning the deep things of God. It can only

[24] See Herbert H. Farmer, "Some Reflections on Professor Wieman's New Book," *Journal of Religion*, XXVII (1947), 114.

be for one or both of two reasons: (i) because we see that the belief in question is not integrally part of the saving truth Christ came to disclose, but is rather part of the mental furniture of any first-century Jew, and so enters indispensably into his historic humanity, or (ii) because we have good reason to think that Christ's teaching has been inadequately or inaccurately reported. An example of (i) might be found in the belief held in demons and demon possession, which Christ apparently shared. Some Christians today reject this belief, and whether we agree with them in this or not, it must be conceded that they are within their rights so to do, provided only that they are prepared to maintain the position that belief in demon possession is not integral to "saving truth," and that the holding of this belief was part of Christ's historic humanity as a first-century Jew. An example of (ii) might be found in some aspects of Christ's reported eschatological teaching. There is evidence to suggest that contemporary apocalyptic ideas and schemes of thought have entered more or less distortingly into the reports given us in the Gospels. The so-called Little Apocalypse of Mark 13, for example, has a symmetry which makes it more than a little dubious whether it can be accepted as it stands and in its entirety as an authentic utterance of Christ.

C. *The Bible as the Word of God.*—It may well be asked, in view of all that has been said, in what sense, if any, we can properly speak of the Bible as the Word of God. When the Scriptures were regarded as literally inerrant, the writers being passive instruments in God's hands, there was a clear and definite sense in which the Scriptures could be called the Word of God. God wrote the Scriptures, and they were therefore his written Word. But when this view is rejected, and we regard it as both a right and a duty to exercise a discriminatory judgment on the Scriptures, the time-honored phrase, the Word of God, if we continue to use it, obviously calls for fresh exposition and definition. The need becomes the more evident when inquiry reveals that both in the Bible itself and in theological usage the phrase, the Word of God, has had a number of variant though not unrelated meanings.

In the New Testament the concept of the "word" (used *simpliciter*, or in variant phrases such as "Word of God" or "word of the Cross" or "word of the Gospel," etc.) seems to bear the following main meanings: (a) the content of the gospel message, as disclosed to mankind by God through Christ, and as witnessed to in the preaching of the apostles—see Mark 4:14-20; Acts 16:6; Rev. 1:2; Acts 15:7; I Cor. 1:18; Phil. 2:16; (b) the total truth for life, conduct, and belief, which is implicit in the gospel proclamation, and which must be accepted if the full riches of the gospel are to be enjoyed—see Col. 1:5; Tit. 1:9; I Pet. 2:8; 3:1; Jas. 1:22; II Cor. 4:2; (c) God's active power as manifested in the creation and preservation of the world—see II Pet. 3:5; Heb. 1:3; (d) God's activity in salvation, both within the hearts and minds of believers and in the church—see Heb. 4:12; 6:5; Jas. 1:18; Eph. 5:26; Col. 3:16; and finally (e)—the distinctively Johannine thought—the expression of God's eternal being in an eternally outgoing activity of creative reason, which creates the world, gives life and understanding to men, and finally becomes incarnate in Jesus Christ—see John 1:1-4, 14; I John 1:1; Rev. 19:13.

It is not difficult to see what is the dominant and unifying thought of all these usages: the Word of God signifies the revealing activity of the living and personal God in creation and toward men, particularly as this is manifest and operative in the gospel—"gospel" being here used as an all-inclusive term to signify (a) the content of the gospel, namely, that God himself came in a supreme, saving act of self-giving and self-disclosure in Christ, (b) the declaration of the gospel through the preaching and teaching of its primary witnesses, and (c) the making of the gospel effective in the hearts and lives of those who believe. To this wealth of meaning—all of it centering in the thought of the revealing activity of God toward men—the symbol of the Word is singularly appropriate; it would be difficult to think of one more compendiously adequate. For the spoken word springs from, is sustained by, and directly expresses the personality of the speaker in his purposeful activity, as nothing else does—his reasoned thought, his desire to unveil his mind, his intention to challenge and draw a response from the mind and will of another person. And speech can be most deeply penetrative in its effects on those who hear it. No doubt the symbol of the Word becomes somewhat strained when it is applied, as in the Johannine literature, to the divine Redeemer himself, for "word" normally signifies the expression and act of personality, not the personality itself. The strain is evidenced by the fact that this usage stands rather apart in the New Testament, and by the fact that many people find the conception of Christ as "the Word of God" (particularly as expounded in John 1) somewhat mystifying. But when once the meaning is grasped, the sense of strain in calling Christ himself the Word is lost in the appropriateness of the symbol along the lines just indicated. Moreover, to call Christ himself the Word of God has this advantage: that it emphasizes the point already insisted on so much, that the supreme source and norm of Christian truth are not words written down and preserved between the covers of a book (important as these are, for the reasons which have been given), but Christ who is the living Word.

It was much later in the history of Christian thought that the tendency arose to equate the Scriptures with the Word of God. The tendency was especially manifest in Protestant circles after the Reformation, though it should be noted that in these circles the phrase the "Word of God" was also used in the New Testament sense indicated above, as a study of the various confessions shows. It is noteworthy that Calvin never identified Scripture with the Word of God. It is broadly true to say that in the Protestant tradition the New Testament usage of the phrase is preserved alongside the increasingly dominant usage of it to indicate the Scriptures as such, the two usages not being very clearly related to one another.

It follows from this brief inquiry that it would not be in the least contrary to Scripture itself but rather in harmony with it, nor would it be contrary to anything essential in the Christian faith, if we ceased altogether to speak of the Scriptures as the Word of God, and if we reserved the phrase, as the New Testament does, for God's great saving act of revelation in Christ and for the gospel message proclaiming it to mankind.

However, the course of thought which has been pursued in this article may perhaps be taken to afford sufficient ground for adhering to what has become the Protestant tradition of speaking of the Bible as the Word of God, though it at the same time defines the sense in which we may do so. For we have maintained that the Scriptures do enter indispensably into that revealing and saving activity of God in the incarnate Redeemer and in the gospel message concerning him, which is what the symbol of the Word of God properly denotes. God, as it were, continually takes the written word of the Bible up into his own living Word, so that it becomes vitally one, though not identical, with it. To speak of the Scriptures as the Word of God, for all the misrepresentation and misuse to which such a usage is admittedly exposed, does at least forbid us to minimize or overlook this vital union and its necessity. Nor, it must be emphasized again, is this indispensable union of the Scriptures with the saving Word of God in Christ and in the gospel message impaired in the least by the fact that we must use our own best knowledge and judgment to interpret them. On the contrary, our freedom to do this is used by God, in his patience and wisdom, to turn the *littera scripta* into a living encounter with us as persons, whom he must save as persons, if we are to be saved at all.

D. The Bible as the Authoritative Basis of Preaching.—The proclamation of the gospel through preaching has from the beginning been recognized to be an indispensable factor in God's saving activity toward men in Christ. This necessity of preaching arises primarily out of the nature of the gospel itself as a message concerning God's coming into the world in a historic event, a historic Incarnation. An event can become known only by being borne witness to, by being proclaimed, by the story being told. Nobody can come to the knowledge of an event by his own reflection, by excogitation. And if the significance of the event is that in it God comes to encounter men as persons in the challenge and the succor of redeeming love, then another reason for preaching can be seen: namely, that preaching is in a superlative degree the deliberate challenge of one person to another, the encounter of one person with another. God takes the human personal encounter involved in bearing witness to the Event up into his own personal encounter with men through the Event. Here also he makes the human word vitally one, though not identical, with the divine Word. Once again the appropriateness of the symbol "Word" to indicate the total divine activity in Christ toward men becomes apparent.[25]

It follows from this that preaching in its essential idea is not necessarily required to be based upon scriptural texts or passages. All that is required is that it should be, in whatever form is appropriate to the occasion, a bearing witness to, a setting forth of, the Word of the gospel, the Word which is Christ. However, this requirement, when taken along with all that has been said concerning the part played by Scripture in mediating the Word of God, does make the deliberate yoking of the preacher's message to the content of the Scripture indispensable to the effective prosecution of his task, whether or not in fact he starts from, or indeed makes any explicit reference to, a scripture text or passage. The long tradition of the church that preaching shall as a rule be "from the Scriptures" is therefore justified. But, of course, by the same argument it must be genuinely "from the Scriptures." The danger earlier referred to is always present, that even when the preacher does "take a text," he fails really to submit his mind to it, but rather reads into it contemporary con-

ceptions and beliefs, using the scripture words merely as a perch on which his own ideas, like a lot of twittering birds, may alight and preen themselves.

The basing of preaching on Scripture imparts to it a weight and authority which the preacher in himself could not hope to command. This authority, it must be insisted once more, is not of the external, overriding kind; always it makes itself felt through the *testimonium spiritus sancti internum* working through the quickened insight of the hearer. But it is nevertheless a real authority. It derives from the inherent and proved power of the Scriptures to disturb the heart of a man with a renewed sense of sinfulness and need, to challenge him with a sense of the seriousness of the issues which are at stake in human existence, to solemnize him with a sense of the living God coming to him in the majestic person of the Redeemer. It derives too from the fact that Scripture comes to the hearer as an inseparable part of the total life and witness of the Christian church, and so carries with it the authority of the church's agelong experience and testimony. By taking his stand upon the Bible and preaching thence, the preacher utters the prayer, and expresses the faith, that the thin, shallow trickle of his own words will be taken up into the living Word of him, concerning whom it was said that his voice was "as the sound of many waters."

V. Selected Bibliography

BRUNNER, EMIL. *Revelation and Reason,* tr. Olive Wyon. Philadelphia: Westminster Press, 1946.

CUNLIFFE-JONES, HUBERT. *The Authority of the Biblical Revelation.* London: James Clarke & Co., 1945.

DODD, C. H. *The Authority of the Bible.* New York: Harper & Bros., 1929.

————. *The Bible Today.* New York: The Macmillan Co., 1947.

DUGMORE, C. W., ed. *The Interpretation of the Bible.* London: Society for Promoting Christian Knowledge, 1944.

LILLEY, A. L. *Religion and Revelation.* New York: The Macmillan Co., 1932.

PHYTHIAN-ADAMS, W. J. *The People and the Presence.* London: Oxford University Press, 1942.

RICHARDSON, ALAN. *Christian Apologetics.* New York: Harper & Bros., 1947.

ROBINSON, H. WHEELER. *Redemption and Revelation in the Actuality of History.* New York: Harper and Bros., 1942.

————. *Inspiration and Revelation in the Old Testament.* Oxford: Clarendon Press, 1946.

ROWLEY, H. H. *The Relevance of the Bible.* New York: The Macmillan Co., 1944.

[25] For a further exposition of this see Farmer, *The Servant of the Word.*

THE CANON
OF THE OLD TESTAMENT

by ARTHUR JEFFERY

Readers of the Bible are usually inclined to take for granted the contents of the Book as it comes to them in its printed form, without thinking to ask why it contains just so many books, arranged in what seems to be an invariable order. Some readers are aware that in certain churches lessons are at times read from the Apocrypha, which, however, are not contained in most of the printed editions they see, but why this should be they do not know. The answer is that the various churches recognize a canon of Scripture which decides for them what books are to be included or excluded and in what order they are to be arranged.

I. The Christian Inheritance of the Hebrew Scripture

Part of the inheritance of Christianity from Judaism was a scripture. Jesus in his preaching constantly referred to this scripture, and the disciples followed him in this practice. They accepted as a religious fact which directly concerned them the existence among the Jews of a body of writings received as sacred and authoritative.

This body of writings did not profess to include all the religious books that had appeared during the history of the Jewish people. It did not include all the religious documents which were in circulation among the Jews at that period. It was a body of writings which had been brought together by a process of selection, given an authority not possessed by their other religious literature, and invested with a sanctity which set it apart as in some particular way connected with the official religious life of the people.

In this there was nothing unique. We find the same factors at work among other peoples producing the sacred books of other religions. Save in such cases as the Manichaean scriptures or the *Qur'ān*, which were produced in conscious imitation of an earlier canonical scripture, we find that the "scripture" of a religion consists of a body of writings of different age and authorship, formed by a gradual process of selection, and little by little acquiring sanctity and authority. The writings assembled in such sacred books are of various kinds, some historical, some didactic, some hortatory, some perhaps magical, but they gain their authority because the community feels that in them is enshrined something that is of vital significance for the practice of the religion whose sacred books they are.

When New Testament writers use such phrases as ἐν ταῖς γραφαῖς, or γραφαὶ ἅγιαι, or (τὰ) ἱερὰ γράμματα, and Jewish writers such as Josephus, Philo, and the author of I Maccabees, speak of αἱ ἱεραὶ βίβλοι, or τὰ βιβλία τὰ ἅγια, or τὰ ἱερὰ γράμματα, they are testifying to the existence of such a collection among the Jews. The same idea of a well-recognized collection is implicit in the Talmudic expression *miqrā'*, "reading," used of writings publicly read in the synagogue services. The Christians took over from the Jews this collection of "sacred writings," and later formed an additional collection of their own, which in turn came to acquire sanctity and authority. With the development of the church, and the use of these documents as standards of doctrine and discipline, Christian writers began to make use of the Greek word κανών in a technical sense, and to speak of a canon of scripture.

Though the use of the word "canon" in connection with an authoritative body of scripture is of Christian origin, the conception which it crystallized in a convenient technical term was in operation long before any precise term was used. We have the conception wherever in a religious community there comes into existence a collection of writings marked off as especially sacred and authoritative, and so in modern books we speak of the Zoroastrian canon, or the Taoist canon, and distinguish in Buddhism between the Sanskrit, Pali, Tibetan, and Chinese canons. In none of these religions is the term used in the native sources, but the conception is there. When in any religion the stage is reached where the community is conscious that the authentic voice of religious authority is no longer heard, the writings which had been produced in that past in which such an authentic voice had been heard and recognized tend to be marked out by that fact and so to be set aside as the writings sacred to the community. This would not preclude the possibility of adding to them at some future time other writings in which once again the sure voice of religious authority was heard, nor indeed of the adding to them of historical records, or memorials of the past of the community, without which much of the meaning of "the word of prophecy" might be lost. Furthermore, the conception is not incompatible with some diversity of opinion as to the extent of such a corpus of sacred writings, as to what should be included and what omitted.

While Christian theologians may recognize in the process of scriptural canonization the official act of the church and the providential work of the Holy Spirit (see article, "The Bible: Its Significance and Authority," pp. 3-31), historians can merely state that a canon of scripture is not something given, but something humanly devised. From the historical point of view the canon is the result of human decision as to which among the religious writings existing in a community are those in which it recognizes the authentic voice of religious authority speaking to man. It is likewise clear that canonization is something entirely apart from the process of collection, and that it is not necessarily connected with the public use of a body of writings. We have ample evidence of the collection and use in a community of religious writings which have never become part of any canonical collection of scripture. In general it is the effort to preserve the community from some threat to its religious life, whether from heresy or false teaching or some such calamity, that leads it to place the seal of its approval on certain writings to the exclusion of others, already collected and in use, as being those alone in which it recognizes the authentic voice of authority. It is possible to think of a wider and a narrower sense of the word "canonization." It may be argued that a collection of writings may come into use in a religious community and by custom and general recognition come to be regarded as of religious authority, without there ever having been any formal pronouncement as to its canonization. In this wider sense we could speak of a growing canon, as at different periods we find different groups of writings attaining an authoritative position. In the stricter sense, however, canonization means a definite formulation whereby a body of writings is set aside because those writings are recognized as authoritative.

II. Growth of the Hebrew Writings

The story of the growth of Hebrew literature is in no fundamental way different from that of the growth of literature among other peoples. Everywhere the beginnings of national literature are oral. As the people attain to literacy there is the tendency to put this national literature—the tales of origins, the annals of the kings, the deeds of the heroic age, the oracles of the shrines, the priestly liturgies, the popular religious songs, the wisdom of the sages, and so forth—into written form. These types are common to many peoples in the ancient world. Among the Israelites we can recognize several such types of literary endeavor slowly developing to form a body of writings preserved in a fixed form: (a) fragments of early song; (b) archives and chronicles; (c) laws; (d) prophecies; (e) history; (f) cult books; (g) wisdom books. Parallels to all of these types can be found in the literature of the surrounding peoples. Not all the literature that was produced in ancient Israel is contained in the Old Testament as we know it, nor even in the wider range of the apocryphal and pseudepigraphal books. Some of it was produced as early as the tenth century B.C., and some of it as late as the last century before the Christian Era. Some of it has survived only in very fragmentary form. Most of it is anonymous, some of it pseudonymous, and even that which appears under a definite name is commonly found to be interpolated with material from other sources. Some of it is definitely religious, and some of it would not strike us at first as being religious literature at all. Two main questions should therefore be asked: How and why did the various books of the present Old Testament come to be considered as having such religious authority as to be included in a canon of scripture, and how and why did other books come to be excluded from that canon?

III. The Word Canon

The Greek word κανών comes from a Semitic word meaning "reed." The reed was one of man's earliest measuring instruments, so that κανών, whose earliest meaning in Greek was "straight rod," came to designate specifically "measuring rod" such as was used by carpenters, and then metaphorically, like the Latin *norma* or *regula*, came to stand for that which regulates, rules, or serves as a norm or pattern for other things. Later in literary criticism the Alexandrian grammarians referred to their collection of ancient writings as a κανών, because this collection was the standard for pure language and the model for composition. From this, by an easy step, came its use in ethics for the standard of good living. It is in this ethical sense that the word is used in the New Testament (Gal. 6:16; II Cor. 10:13-16) as the rule for conduct or doctrine, and in the early church for the "rule of faith and conduct." As the rule of faith was based on the scriptures we find the word associated with scripture as early as Origen. According to the usage of the early ecclesiastical writers, however, there is some confusion among three meanings of the words "canonical scripture." Sometimes it seems to mean that the books were constituted into a standard, that is, they were the κανών by which other things were to be judged. Sometimes the idea seems to be that they were books which corresponded to a standard, namely, the standard of faith. And sometimes it would appear to mean that these are the books which have been taken up into an authoritative catalogue. In all three cases, however, there is the recognition of a definite body of literature considered to be canonical.

IV. The Various Witnesses of the Canon

While the Christians took over a scripture from the Jews, they did not take over any well-defined collection. In fact, in the latter part of the second century we find a Christian bishop, Melito of Sardis, puzzled as to the exact number and order of the Old Testament books, and undertaking a journey to the East "accurately to ascertain" what the truth of the matter might be. In the early Christian centuries, indeed, there was some dispute among the Jews themselves as to the extent of the canon, though Jewish consensus was in favor of the collection we have in our Protestant Bible. The earliest Christian communities had largely followed Alexandrian usage, but after Origen's labors on the text, the Greek-speaking churches tended to follow the Jewish consensus, and this attitude was supported by Jerome. In the Latin-speaking churches, however, the authority of Augustine drew the communities away from Jerome to the wider canon that had been current in Alexandria, and the Greek churches soon followed. With the Reformation, the Protestant groups swung back again to the Jewish consensus, and, in opposition, the Council of Trent formally declared in favor of the Alexandrian usage as sanctioned by Augustine.

The question of the extent of the canon can thus be approached historically only by considering what evidence is available concerning the assembling of these writings which were considered to have religious authority.

A. Hebrew Scriptures.—The Hebrew text of the Old Testament presents a corpus of writings already selected and arranged. There are in it some indications of the way in which these writings came to be set aside as sacred and authoritative:

(a) The law codes in Israel, as those of Hammurabi in Babylon and of Manu in India, were placed under religious sanction (Exod. 20:1; cf. 24:3-8), and we have references to the tablets on which the law was written being placed in association with the ark and especially venerated. Since it was customary among the surrounding peoples to deposit at shrines documents of an official nature, there is nothing improbable in the accounts of Moses (Deut. 31:9 ff.), Joshua (24:25-26), and Samuel (I Sam. 10:25) writing covenants and laying them up at the sanctuary.

(b) In II Kings 22:3 ff. we read how in the reign of Josiah, Hilkiah the high priest came upon such a book of law in the sanctuary, the reading of which caused great consternation, resulting in wide reforms and a solemn covenant of king and people to abide by the words written in this book, which they were conscious of not having followed. We have here a clear account of a document being regarded as a *regula*.

(c) The writings of the later prophets and the psalmists show acquaintance with the books of their predecessors, and give us good evidence that during and after the Exile there were in circulation some literary pieces regarded as those in which the authentic voice of religious authority was heard.

(d) In the account of the return from the Exile we read of how Ezra came with the law of his God in his hand (Ezra 7:14, 25), a law which he was to administer among the people; while in Neh. 8–10 we have an account of how the law was read aloud by Ezra in popular assembly, and solemnly sealed and accepted as the authoritative *regula* for community life.

In all of this there is no hint of a canon of scripture, but there are some of the elements out of which such a canon could arise. We find writings considered as sacred and tending to be collected, though there was no fixed body of them, since the Chronicler made use of some which were not preserved in the final collection. We find the sense of writings being authoritative as a *regula*. We find official pronouncement of certain writings as authoritative, though what Ezra is said to have "canonized" was a body of laws, and so not the Pentateuch as we have it, which contains much besides law and indeed includes material from a time later than that of Ezra. The canon of scripture had not yet come into existence.

B. The Hellenistic Bible.—As early as the third century B.C. the Jews of the Diaspora needed a Greek version of their religious writings, and finally came to have a Hellenistic Bible known to us as the Septuagint. Different parts of it were translated at different times and under different circumstances, but we have actual fragments of it from as early as the middle of the second century B.C., and considerable manuscripts from the fourth century A.D., whereas we have no considerable manuscripts of the Hebrew Bible earlier than the ninth century A.D. The Hellenistic Bible contains all the writings that are in our Hebrew Bible, though it arranges the material somewhat differently and adds some material not found in any Hebrew manuscripts of the Bible.

The additional material in the Septuagint consists of (a) translations of other Hebrew writings, e.g., Ecclesiasticus (Ben Sirach), Judith, I Maccabees; (b) works composed in Greek, e.g., I Esdras, Tobit, Wisdom of Solomon, Baruch, II Maccabees; (c) supplements in Greek to certain of the Hebrew writings, e.g., the additions to Esther, Susanna, the Song of the Three Children, and Bel and the Dragon, which are supplements to Daniel; (d) a fringe of writings which appear in some manuscripts but not in others, e.g., Prayer of Manasses, III and IV Maccabees. It is possible that such books as Enoch, II Esdras (IV Ezra), the Testaments of the Twelve Patriarchs, and the Psalms of Solomon, also once belonged to this fringe.

The witness of the Septuagint is important on account of its age and because it shows quite clearly that there was as yet no fixed canon. It treats its extra writings as on a level with those in the Hebrew Bible, and in its manner of translating suggests clearly that its translators were not working on a text which they considered as fixed *ne varietur*. Its fringe also reveals the fact that there was as yet no certainty as to the exact range of books that should be included in the collection.

C. The Samaritan Pentateuch.—The Samaritans have a Pentateuch, in their own script, which for the most part agrees closely with the Pentateuch in the Hebrew Bible, though it has certain peculiarities of its own, and certain curious resemblances to the text of the Septuagint. We have no actual evidence as to when and where this text was formed, but it is a reasonable inference that the Samaritans provided themselves with such a text after their breach with the Jews. It is furthermore reasonable to infer that at the time they made their copy the Pentateuch was a writing not only recognized officially as authoritative but already approaching a fixed form. The question is the date at which the Samaritan copy was made.

The usual assumption is that it was made somewhere around 432 B.C., when Manasseh, the son-in-law of Sanballat, went off to found a community in Samaria, as related in Neh. 13:28 and Josephus *Antiquities* XI. 7. 2; 8. 2. Josephus himself, however, dates this event in the days of Alexander the Great, and though there is a notorious confusion in Josephus at this point, he may be right about the Gerizim temple dating from 332, and that may have been the date of the copying of their Pentateuch. Recent scholarship, however, is inclined to think that the real schism between the peoples did not take place till Hasmonean times, when the Gerizim temple was destroyed in 128 B.C. The script of the Samaritan Pentateuch, its close connections at many points with the Septuagint, and its even closer agreement with our present Hebrew text, all suggest a date about 122 B.C.

In any case, the Samaritan Pentateuch, while it constitutes evidence that the Pentateuch, in a form not very different from its present one, was at that time a document having official sanction which could be taken over as something recognized as authoritative is, however, no evidence that there were not other collections of writings also in existence which were equally regarded as authoritative, but which the Samaritans felt no need to take over.

D. Ben Sirach (ca. 180 B.C.).—The Wisdom of Jesus ben Sirach, or Ecclesiasticus, seems to have been written in Hebrew about 180 B.C., and fragments of the text in the original language have been recovered. In its complete form, however, it exists only in the Greek translation made in Alexandria about 130 B.C. by the author's grandson. Ben Sirach seems to regard himself as writing a genuine continuation of the Prophets and of the books of Wisdom (Ecclus. 24:32-34), and to have no consciousness of the existence of a scripture collection that is closed and to which no additions can be made. He knows of the Law as something quite apart and to be regarded in a very special way, but whether the Law as he knows it is to be identified with our Pentateuch is something which cannot be determined. In chs. 44 and 49 he makes a survey of the national heroes, and it is significant that he mentions them in a particular order. In chs. 44–45 he follows the Pentateuch; in 46:1-12, Joshua and Judges; in vss. 13-20, Samuel. Ch. 47 begins with a list drawn from the books of Kings and Chronicles, and this combination continues to 49:6. In 49:7 we meet with Jeremiah, in vss. 8-10, Ezekiel and the Twelve, while vss. 11-13 depend on Ezra-Nehemiah, and vss. 14-16 may indicate a knowledge of some of the books on the fringe of the Septuagint. There is no mention of Daniel, Esther, or Ezra, but Ben Sirach knows of certain praises of David (47:8), songs, proverbs, and parables of Solomon (47:17), and prophecies of Isaiah (48:22 ff.). He may be merely reproducing a list from oral tradition, but his order suggests that he is using source material from a collection very similar in arrangement to that in the Hellenistic Bible, a collection which is not yet on the same level of authority as the Law, but is in a sense parallel to it.

The witness of the grandson who translated the book is more definite. He composed a prologue to his translation in which he thrice refers to the sacred books of his people:

(a) Since many great things have been communicated to us by the Law and the Prophets and the others who followed in their steps. . . .

(b) My grandfather, Jesus, having long devoted himself to the reading of the Law and the Prophets, and the other books of our fathers, and having gained great familiarity with them, was led himself to write somewhat. . . .

(c) And not only these things, but the Law itself, and the prophecies, and the rest of the books, have no small difference when spoken in their originals.

Here we have quite definite testimony to the existence of collections of writings which are regarded with particular reverence as having been handed down from the fathers. Moreover, there are three groups of these, the Law, the Prophets, and the other Writings, which is sig-

nificant inasmuch as in our Hebrew Bible the various books are arranged in three groups labeled the Law, the Prophets, and the Holy Writings (Hagiographa). Yet this writer does not feel that there is anything to hinder his grandfather's work from being added to the religious literature of his people. As a matter of fact, it is claimed that there is Maccabean material in our Hebrew Bible which was written later than the time of Sirach.

E. Simeon ben Shetach (ca. 75 B.C.).—If the evidence of the Talmud can be trusted, this celebrated Pharisee, who lived in the first half of the first century B.C., quoted Eccl. 7:12 with the introductory formula, "it is written," a phrase used only in quoting scripture; quoted Prov. 23:25 with the words "scripture saith," and perhaps quoted Sirach the same way. If this is not just a case of later usage being attributed to Simeon, it means that certain books in the Hagiographa were being quoted as scripture at the beginning of the first century B.C., and that perhaps Sirach was included among them.

F. The Books of Maccabees (ca. 90-50 B.C.).—Our interest in I Maccabees, which seems to have been written in Hebrew somewhere between 90 and 70 B.C., is that it depicts the whole Maccabean struggle as due to zeal for the Law. For this author and his contemporaries the Law was not only a *regula* but something for which men would fight and die. He knew the Law as something in written form and in the hands of the people, for in 1:56 he tells us that whenever the officials of Antiochus found copies of the book of the Law they tore them up and burned them, and in 3:48 he says that when the people gathered together at Mizpeh "they unrolled the roll of the Law." Whether this Law coincided with our Pentateuch we have no means of knowing. Beyond the Law he shows acquaintance with stories from Exodus, Joshua, Judges, Samuel, Kings, and he is familiar with the story of Daniel. These he may have known, however, from oral tradition, though the words in 12:9, "We find encouragement in the sacred books that are in our keeping," suggest that other sacred writings in addition to the Law were in circulation among the people. He seems to quote from Ps. 79:3 in 7:17, and has reminiscences of other psalms and of Jeremiah. There is no evidence, however, that he knew the Psalter and the Prophets as we have them.

II Maccabees is a Greek writing apparently of Alexandrian origin, dating from the middle of the first century B.C., or maybe earlier, and while it is so rhetorical as to be of very little use for historical purposes, its author's ideas of scripture probably reflect those of his milieu. As to the extent of scripture known to him, we note that: (*a*) the law of Moses is to him fundamental to the whole social and religious life of his people; (*b*) he is acquainted with the narratives of Kings; (*c*) he is familiar with the custom of singing psalms, though we have no evidence that he used our Psalter; (*d*) Jeremiah is to him a writing prophet; (*e*) he is familiar with the stories of Nehemiah and of Esther. As to his evidence in regard to collected scripture we may note that: (*a*) in 8:23, when Judas was assembling and encouraging his followers to resist Nicanor, after dividing them he "read out of the holy book," which obviously must be some scripture; (*b*) in 15:9, Judas encouraged his men "from the Law and the Prophets," which are clearly regarded as valuable documents of national importance, and of course may be the "book" of 8:23; (*c*) in 2:13-15, we have the following passage: "The same things were reported also in the writings and memoirs about Nehemiah, how, in forming a library, he gathered together the books about the kings and prophets, and those of David, and epistles of kings about gifts. In like manner also Judas gathered together for us all those [books] that had been scattered because of the war that had come to pass, and they are with us."

A great deal more has at times been drawn from this passage than it will warrant, but one cannot resist the conclusion that we have here a more advanced conception of a canonical collection than we have met hitherto. The "holy book" of 8:23 is clearly a writing held sacred, which is one prime requisite of canonicity. The author uses the phrase "the Law and the Prophets" precisely as does the New Testament, and he probably knew these as two collections, though it does not follow that they included what we now have in these sections in our Hebrew Bible. The reference to the work of Nehemiah and Judas also suggests that there existed at that time a collection of "writings" of the type that we know in the Hebrew Bible, though there is no reference to canonization, nor can we assume that what he meant by "David" or "kings and prophets" coincided with what we mean by them.

G. Philo Judaeus (ca. A.D. 40).—Being an Alexandrian, Philo normally used the Septuagint, though he seems to have known the Hebrew text. His evidence is to be dated about A.D. 40, and the free and easy way in which he deals with scripture is clear evidence that to him the text is not sacrosanct, though it may be sacred. He quotes from or refers to every book of the Hebrew Bible save Ezekiel, Daniel, Ruth, Esther, Lamentations, Ecclesiastes, and Song of Songs. For him the Law is definitely our Pentateuch, and he actually refers to four of its five parts by their names. All scripture, however, not only the Law, is inspired, and he speaks of "most holy scriptures," "sacred oracles," "sacred word," and so forth, in a way that leaves no doubt that these were writings in collected form having a definite place of religious authority in the community. It is significant that he never quotes from the extra books of the Hellenistic Bible, or from those which were disputed in the rabbinical schools.

The commonly adduced passage from *The Contemplative Life* III, which makes Philo bear witness to the threefold division of Law, Prophets, and other writings, is no work of Philo, but a tractate of the third or fourth century A.D.

H. The New Testament (ca. A.D. 50-150).—There are abundant references to scripture in the New Testament. That these scripture books were regarded as *sacred* is evidenced not only by the fact that they are called "holy writings" (Rom. 1:2; II Tim. 3:15), and referred to as God-given (II Tim. 3:16; Matt. 22:43; Acts 4:25), but also by the fact that their character is such that it is sufficient to say "it is written" (Matt. 4:6; Gal. 3:13; etc.). That they were regarded as *authoritative* is equally clear from the way in which appeal is made to them (Matt. 21:42; Rom. 11:2). This authority applies to all parts of the Old Testament. In Heb. 3:7 it refers to Exodus and Numbers, but in Heb. 10:15 the reference is to Jeremiah, in Acts 2:16 to Joel, in Rom. 9:25 to Hosea, while in Acts 4:25; 13:34; Heb. 13:5 it is to the Psalms. Yet here again, scripture though sacred is not sacrosanct. Quotations are given inaccurately, passages from different books are run together in one quotation, and passages are given as quotations from scripture which cannot be found in our Old Testament, not even the extra books, and are best regarded as Old Testament reminiscences (e.g., Luke 11:49; John 7:38; Eph. 5:14; Jas. 4:5). As to the extent of scripture, we find that the Law is scripture in a special sense, so that it may stand for the whole Old Testament, and the Psalms and Isaiah may be quoted as the Law. The Law and the Prophets are frequently mentioned together and are apparently of equal authority, both seeming to be read regularly in the synagogues (Acts 13:15). In Luke 24:44 we find the Psalms on a level with the Prophets and the Law. Quotations or reminiscences of all the books in the Old Testament have been recognized, except from Obadiah, Nahum, Zephaniah, Esther, Ecclesiastes, Song of Songs, Ruth, Lamentations, Ezra, Nehemiah, and Chronicles. There are also references to or reminiscences of I Maccabees, Enoch, Wisdom of Solomon, Sirach, the Martyrdom of Isaiah, the Assumption of Moses, and the Apocalypse of Elias. These writings, both of the regular Hellenistic Bible and of those on the fringe, seem for the most part to be known as written sources, and to be treated in no fundamental way differently from the books of the Hebrew Bible. The writers of the New Testament could thus not have been conscious of the existence of any fixed canon of such writings. The special treatment accorded to the Law would suggest that it was recognized as having some special sanctity and authority, but not that its authority was different in nature from that of the other books. The evidence frequently adduced to prove that the New Testament knows the tripartite division of our Hebrew Bible is insufficient to prove this.

The evidence of the New Testament thus points to the existence of a recognized collection, but one wider than that of the Hebrew Bible. Its quotations are most commonly, but not exclusively, from the Hellenistic Bible. It regards scripture as sacred but not yet sacrosanct, though it treats it as something that has long been held as sacred, and is apparently all of equal inspiration, not, as sometimes held, of three degrees of inspiration.

J. Josephus (ca. A.D. 100).—The witness of Josephus is contemporary with that of parts of the New Testament, and like its writers, he prefers the Hellenistic Bible, utilizing Esdras, I Maccabees, and the additions to Esther as readily as he does the books of the Hebrew Bible. It is in his *Against Apion* I. 8 that he makes his important contribution to the question of the canon:

There are not with us myriads of books disagreeing and contradicting one another, but only two-and-twenty books containing the record of all time, and which rightly are believed in. Of these, five are those of Moses, which contain the laws and the tradition as to the origin of mankind till his death. This period falls little short of three thousand years. From the death of Moses till Artaxerxes, who was king of the Persians after Xerxes, the prophets who came after Moses wrote of the things that came to pass in their times, in thirteen books. The remaining four [books] contain hymns to God and maxims of life for men. From Artaxerxes to our own time all things have been recorded, but not esteemed worthy of like credit with those which preceded them, because of there not being an exact succession of prophets. There is practical proof of how we treat these same writings, for though so long a time has now elapsed, no one has dared either to add to them or to make any change. But it is natural to all Jews straightway from the day of birth to consider these as the teachings of God, and to stand by them, and if needful gladly to die on their behalf.

It is immediately clear that Josephus speaks with two voices. As a historian presenting his case to a Hellenistic public, he uses the whole range of writings in the Hellenistic Bible, claiming that the whole history of his people is contained in τὰ ἱερὰ γράμματα (*Preface to Antiquities* III), and that he has written his history ὡς αἱ ἱεραὶ βίβλοι περὶ πάντων ἔχουσιν τὴν ἀναγραφήν (*Antiquities* XX. 11. 2), but he knows that there is a narrower acceptation of the range of scripture, and when speaking as a pious Jew, he confines scripture to the range of the twenty-two books in the Hebrew Bible. With regard to this narrower range we notice that:

(a) He considers the process of selection among the writings as having already come to an end, the community possessing a collection of sacred writings limited in number, to which no further additions can be made. Moreover, the textual form of this collection is fixed, so that no one would dare to make any change therein.

(b) The writings in this collection have more than human authority, must be believed in and stood by, and if necessary one must be prepared to die for them.

(c) A principle had governed the selection of these writings, for only such were included as were considered to have been written in past days when the genuine voice of prophecy could still be heard. Josephus defines the period as from Moses to Artaxerxes, and apparently regards the historical works as written by the prophets.

(d) While his division of the parts is the Hellenistic division, he nevertheless clearly recognizes a tripartite division of scripture—law, prophets, hymns and maxims.

K. II Esdras (IV Ezra, ca. A.D. 90-120).—The main portion of this writing seems to date from about A.D. 90, and in it the Law is the essential part of scripture, though it knows of Daniel, Enoch, Job, Isaiah, and Jeremiah, and enumerates the Twelve in the Septuagint order. Ch. 14, however, is a later insertion, perhaps to be dated at A.D. 120, and in vss. 19-48 we have a strange story of Esdras complaining that the law of Moses has been burned so that no man knows what things were done of God, and he prays that the Holy Spirit may come upon him so that he may write out again the things that were in the law. He is instructed to go into seclusion for forty days, taking many tablets and five good scribes. Then after drinking from a mystic cup, he spends the days dictating to the scribes some ninety-four books, the first twenty-four of which he is to publish, and the other seventy to reserve as occult books which will be shown only to the wise. This story had immense popularity in the Christian church, but its interest to us is that it testifies to the fact that there was a collection of twenty-four writings recognized as having authority and as such in public religious use, in contradistinction to other writings which, while equally religious, were not considered proper for such public use. The number twenty-four is interesting, as it is the number of the books in the Hebrew Bible as against the twenty-two of Josephus.

L. The Rabbinical Tradition.—The Mishnah of the two Talmuds might be expected to contain the rabbinical tradition concerning their canon of scripture, but though the Mishnah was assembled by R. Yehuda Hannasi at the end of the second century A.D. (between 180 and 200), we can never be sure that in any given passage there has not been later interpolation, so that its witness to the canon can be consulted only under reserves. In the Mishnah there are quotations from every book of the Hebrew Bible save Nehemiah, Daniel, Obadiah, Nahum, Habakkuk, and Zephaniah. The tripartite division of the writings is clearly recognized, though all parts are equally scripture. The extent of the collection, however, was not decided, for there was still discussion as to whether certain writings should be included or rejected, though the Mishnah itself, while it records the discussion, is satisfied that the disputed books are true scripture. From the Gemara we gather that in some quarters the discussion regarding certain books was still dragging on in the fourth century.

In the classical passage Yadayim 3:5 there is evidence of a dispute over the inclusion of Ecclesiastes and Song of Songs in the list of accepted books, and from the Gemara we learn that some did not admit Proverbs, Esther, Ezekiel, and Ruth, though the Mishnah includes them all. Whether the rabbis also included any of the books in the wider list of the Hellenistic Bible is both affirmed and denied. Ben Sirach certainly seems to be quoted as scripture in Erubin 65a and Baba Kamma 92b, and the very violence of Akiba's language against Ben Sirach in Yer. Sanh. X. 28a shows that many in his day must have been using it as if it were accepted scripture. In Origen's time the book of Baruch was also apparently recognized, at least in some rabbinical circles, for he includes it in his list of the twenty-two books recognized as making up the Hebrew Bible. In Baba Bathra 14b we have a Baraita which may date from as early as A.D. 180, and which, besides taking for granted in all its discussion the tripartite division into Law, Prophets, and Hagiographa, contains statements concerning the order of the books in these latter groups:

Our masters teach—the order of the Prophets is this: Joshua, Judges, Samuel, Kings, Jeremiah, Ezekiel, Isaiah, the Twelve, . . . and the order of the Hagiographa is this: Ruth, the book of Psalms, Job and Proverbs, Ecclesiastes, Song of Songs, Lamentations, Daniel and the roll of Esther, Ezra and Chronicles.

Here we have the order of our Hebrew Bible, and as the early form of these writings would have been on individual rolls where the order is of no importance, this Baraita suggests the beginning of arrangements in codex form, or at least of large rolls, where writings necessarily have to be placed in a certain order.

In the rabbinical discussions over the disputed books there is constant recurrence of the phrase "defiling the hands." The handling of books recognized as authoritative scripture causes such defilement, whereas that of other religious writings does not cause it. There has been much discussion concerning the meaning of this phrase, but the essential point is that it implies a recognition of special sanctity for some writings but not for others, and such special sanctity is a mark of canonicity. Yadayim 3:5 indicates the date at which the decision was made regarding what writings possessed this mark and what writings did not:

R. Simeon b. Azzai [ca. A.D. 100] said, I have heard a tradition from the seventy-two elders, on the day when they made R. Eleazar b. Azariah head of the college, that the Song of Songs and Ecclesiastes both defile the hands.

The reference is to the temporary deposition of Gamaliel II from the headship of the "college," when Eleazar b. Azariah was elected for a time to his place—an event that is often referred to as "that day." The "college" was sitting at the time at Jabneh (Jamnia), and it seems to have been under the brief presidency of Eleazar when the influence of Akiba and Joshua was so strong that many hitherto undecided points were settled. The reference above suggests that this question of the disputed books came up at that time and a decision was reached concerning the extent of the canon. This decision finally prevailed in spite of some rumblings of dissent which were still heard occasionally in later years. This decision is usually dated as about A.D. 90, but may have been nearer A.D. 100, and we must remember that it was only the decision of an "academy" and not an official ratification such as that of a "council," even though the weight of authority of the "academy" gained general acceptance for it.

M. The Apostolic Fathers.—We have no scripture lists recorded in any of the works of the Apostolic Fathers, but from their writings we can perhaps estimate the extent of their canon. They quote from or refer to as scripture: Genesis, Exodus, Leviticus, Numbers, Deuteronomy, Joshua, Judges, I, II, III, IV

Kings, I, II Paralipomena, Esther, Job, Psalms, Proverbs, Ecclesiastes, Song of Songs, Isaiah, Jeremiah, Ezekiel, Daniel, Hosea, Joel, Amos, Jonah, Habakkuk, Zephaniah, Zechariah, Malachi, II Maccabees, Judith, Tobit, Sirach, Wisdom of Solomon, II Esdras (IV Ezra), and Enoch. There are no quotations from Ruth, Ezra-Nehemiah, Lamentations, Obadiah, Micah, or Haggai, nor are there any from Baruch or I Maccabees. It is at least notable that out of eight Old Testament books from which there is no quotation, six are also books not quoted in the New Testament. The extra books of the Hellenistic Bible, even Enoch, are used with apparently no feeling that they are not genuine scripture, and in this also the Apostolic Fathers are in harmony with the New Testament.

N. *Melito of Sardis (ca. 170).*—It is somewhat curious that the Christian bishop of an important city like Sardis, in the second half of the second century, did not know the extent of the Jewish canon and undertook a journey to the East to discover the truth of the matter. Possibly the explanation is that he used the Hellenistic Bible but was conscious of Jewish criticism directed against it and wished to learn what range of scripture the rabbis accepted. The result of his inquiry is recorded by Eusebius (*Church History* IV. 26. 14) in a list commonly known as the Canon of Melito:

When, therefore, I went to the East, and came as far as the place where these things were proclaimed and done, I accurately ascertained the books of the Old Testament, and send them to thee here below. The names are as follows: Of Moses, five books—Genesis, Exodus, Numbers, Leviticus, Deuteronomy. Jesus Nave, Judges, Ruth. Four of Kings. Two of Paralipomena. Psalms of David. Proverbs of Solomon and the Wisdom, Ecclesiastes, Song of Songs, Job. Of Prophets, Isaiah, Jeremiah. Of the Twelve Prophets one book. Daniel, Ezekiel, Esdras. From these I have, therefore, made the selections which I have divided into six books.

This order is strange in that it agrees neither with the Hebrew nor with the Septuagint though it is closer to the Hellenistic usage. That Melito should put the disputed Ezekiel along with Daniel, and omit Esther altogether, suggests that he obtained his list from circles aware of the disputed position of these books, though he does not say that he received it from Jews, and he may have been quoting only from an Antiochene source.

O. *Origen (185-254).*—Origen's witness is of peculiar significance because he was instructed by Jewish teachers. That scripture was recognized as a body of authoritative religious writing to be used as a *regula* is apparent throughout his writings, and the extent of this body of

authoritative scripture recognized by him is quoted by Eusebius *Church History* VI. 25. 2 from his exposition of Ps. 1, where, after remarking that the writings of the Hebrew canon are twenty-two according to the number of letters in their alphabet, Origen says:

These twenty-two books, according to the Hebrews, are as follows: that which is called Genesis, but by the Hebrews, from the beginning of the book, Bresith, which means "in the beginning." Exodus, Welesmoth, which means, "these are the names." Leviticus, Waikra, "and he called." Numbers, Anmesphekodeim. Deuteronomy, Elle addebarim, that is, "these are the words." Jesus the son of Nave, in Hebrew, Joshua ben Nun. Judges and Ruth in one book, with the Hebrews, which they call Sophetim. Of Kings: the First and Second, one book, with them called Samuel, "the called of God." The Third and Fourth of Kings, also in one book with them, and called, Wahammelech Dabid, which means "and King David." The First and Second Book of the Paralipomena, contained in one volume with them, and called Dibre Hamaim, which means the words, i.e. "the records of days." The First and Second of Esdras, in one, called Ezra, that is, "an assistant." The Book of Psalms, Sepher Tehillim. The Proverbs of Solomon, Misloth. Ecclesiastes, Coheleth. The Song of Songs, Sir Hasirim. Isaiah, Iesaia. Jeremiah, with the Lamentations and his Epistle, in one, Jeremiah. Daniel, Daniel. Ezekiel, Jeezkel. Job, Job. Esther, also with the Hebrews, Esther. Besides these there are also the Maccabees, which are inscribed "Sarbeth sarbane el."

His order is that of the Hellenistic Bible, but obviously he had before him the Hebrew text. He says the number is twenty-two, but he enumerates only twenty-one, so that the omission of the Twelve is probably a scribal error. Baruch seems to have been included with Jeremiah, and it is perhaps significant that Esther is mentioned last of all. Maccabees is separated from the list but why it should be mentioned at all is strange.

P. *Athanasius (365).*—In the *Festal Epistles* for the year 365 Athanasius gives an enumeration of the canonical books of the Old Testament:

According to their order these are the names. First Genesis, then Exodus, Leviticus, Numbers, Deuteronomy. These are followed by Joshua son of Nave, Judges and then Ruth. Afterwards four books of the Kingdoms, of which they make the first two one book, and the third and fourth one book. After them Paralipomenon, two books as one. Then Esdras, first and second as one, likewise. After this the Psalms, then Proverbs, Ecclesiastes, Song of Songs. Then Job and afterwards Prophets, of whom Twelve make up one book, and besides Isaiah, Jeremiah, with which are Baruch, Lamentations and an Epistle. Then Ezekiel and Daniel. So far the books of the Old Testament.

THE CANON OF THE OLD TESTAMENT

This list is clearly dependent on the Hellenistic Bible, though it enumerates only the writings of the Hebrew Bible, save that, like Origen, it knows Baruch as going with Jeremiah. Again we find Esther missing, and this time it can be no oversight, for a little later on Athanasius gives another list of books which it is edifying to read, but which are not authoritative, that is, not canonical, and among these are Wisdom of Solomon, Sirach, Esther, Judith, and Tobit.

Q. Jerome (329-420).—The place of honor as an authority on scripture was held in the Latin-speaking church by Jerome who, like Origen, had Jewish teachers. In his commentary on Ecclesiastes he shows his awareness of the fact that the position of this book was disputed, though he records no objections to Esther. In his preface to Daniel he writes:

I call attention to this, that, among the Hebrews, Daniel is not reckoned with the Prophets, but with those who wrote the Hagiographa. For all Scripture is by them divided into three portions, the Law, the Prophets, and the Hagiographa, that is, into five, and eight, and eleven books.

This is precisely the division of the Hebrew Bible as we have it. Then in his *Prologus Galeatus* prefaced to the books of Samuel-Kings he gives his famous catalogue:

First among them is a book called *Bresith* which we call Genesis. Second, *Hellesmoth,* which is called Exodus. Third, *Vaiecra,* that is, Leviticus. Fourth *Vaiedabber,* which we name Numbers. Fifth, *Addabarim,* which signifies Deuteronomy. These are the five books of Moses which are properly called the *Torah.* They make a second order of the Prophets, and begin with *Hiesu,* son of Nave, who among them is called *Josue ben Nun.* Then they add *Sophtim,* that is, book of Judges, and with that they include *Ruth,* because it narrates a history that took place in the days of the Judges. Third follows *Samuel,* which we say to be the first and second books of Kings. Fourth *Malachim,* that is, Kings, which continue the third and fourth books of Kings. . . . Fifth, *Esaias.* Sixth, *Hieremias.* Seventh, *Hiezecihel.* Eighth, the book of the Twelve Prophets, which among them is called *Thare-asar.* The third order has the Hagiographa. And first it begins with the book of Job. Second, David, comprising five groups of Psalms in one volume. Third is Solomon, having three books, Proverbs, which they call *Masaloth,* and Ecclesiastes, that is, *Accoeleth,* and Song of Songs, which is named *Sir-assirim.* The sixth is Daniel; the seventh, *Dabre-iamim,* that is, words of the days, but which we can more significantly call the chronicles of all divine history, and which among us is known as the first and second of *Paralipomenon.* The eighth is *Ezras,* which, as among the Greeks and Latins is divided into two books. Ninth, Esther. Thus the books of the Old Testament make up twenty-two books—five of Moses, eight of Prophets, and nine of Hagiographa.

Nevertheless not a few reckon Ruth and Lamentations among the Hagiographa, and consider these two as being outside the number, making up the number of books to twenty-four.

Here again we have the tripartite division recognized as fundamental, but the arrangement of the books is influenced by that of the Hellenistic Bible, and again Esther comes last. Later on Jerome mentions Wisdom of Solomon, Sirach, Judith, Tobit, and I and II Maccabees, but acknowledges that they are not in the canon. He freely uses the word canon, so that we are quite sure that his lists represent his understanding of what was in his day regarded as canonical in the strict sense.

R. The Eastern Churches.—The churches of Eastern Christendom were as a rule much closer to Jewish communities than the Greek-speaking or the Latin-speaking churches, but in this matter of the canon they have preserved considerable independence as to the extent of canonical scripture, though they differ not at all from either the Jews or the churches of Western Christendom regarding the authority of canonical scripture as a *regula.*

1. The Syriac-Speaking Church.—Some Syriac-speaking groups which remained in communion with Constantinople accepted the Septuagint as used in the Byzantine church, but those which stood independent, whether Monophysite or Nestorian, accepted the Peshitta as their official scripture version. The Peshitta represents a revision of earlier versions into Syriac, and may be dated in the fourth century. Originally it would seem to have had only the books of the Hebrew Bible, for Isho'dad of Merv in his commentaries knows that the number of books in the Old Testament must be twenty-two, and two authors of the latter part of the fourth century, Aphraates and Ephraem Syrus, though they know the extra books, do not quote from them or comment on them as they do in the case of the others. Early in the fifth century Theodore of Mopsuestia—who, though himself Greek-speaking, was regarded especially by the Nestorians as *the* great expositor of scripture—divided scripture into three classes, books *perfectae auctoritatis,* books *mediae auctoritatis,* books *nullius auctoritatis.* The latter included numerous works of piety which circulated in the Eastern churches, but in the second we find Job, Tobit, I Esdras, Judith, Esther, Wisdom of Solomon, II Maccabees, Song of Songs, Chronicles, and Ezra-Nehemiah. Chronicles, indeed, seems to have been omitted from the original Peshitta, and in the Syrian Masorah there are no Masoretic notes for Chronicles or Ezra-Nehemiah, nor in the Nestorian Bibles for Esther. There is considerable variety in the

41

Syriac manuscripts, both Jacobite and Nestorian, as to the extra books that are included. As late as the end of the thirteenth century, in the *Nomocanon* of Bar-Hebraeus, we have a quotation from Canon 81 of the Canons of the Apostles regarding the scripture which all clergy and laymen ought to have, and the list runs for the Old Testament as follows:

Five books of Moses, Joshua, Judges, Ruth, Judith, four books of Kings, two of Chronicles, two of Ezra, Esther, Job, David, five of Solomon, and sixteen Prophets. Of books without there is to be Bar Sira for the teaching of the young.

2. The Armenian Church.—There is quite a variety of lists of scripture to be found in Armenian ecclesiastical literature, and the oldest manuscripts differ considerably as to the books which they contain. We have, however, a synodal statement on the extent of the canon recognized in the Armenian church, which perhaps ought to be taken as the norm rather than the richer variety to be found in the manuscripts or in later lists. At the Synod of Partav in 768 we find in Canon 22:

As holy books of the Old Testament shall be reckoned—Genesis, Exodus, Leviticus, Numbers, Deuteronomy, Joshua, Judges, Ruth, four books of Kings, two books of Paralipomenon, two books of Esdras, Tobit, Judith, Esther, Maccabees, four books of Solomon (that is, Proverbs, Ecclesiastes, Wisdom and Canticles), Job, Psalms of David, the Twelve Prophets, Isaiah, Jeremiah with Baruch, Ezekiel, Daniel, and the Wisdom of Sirach.

3. The Abyssinian Church.—An even greater variety of books is to be found in the early biblical manuscripts in Ethiopic, and the Abyssinian church has a wider range of scripture than any other Eastern church. Fundamentally its version depends on the Septuagint, but other influences have come in with later revisions. There seems to have been no authoritative decision in this church as to the extent of its canon, but the selections of the scribes of the biblical manuscripts seem to have been always from the following list:

Eight books of the Octateuch; Kufale or little Genesis, one book; five books of Kings and Chronicles; Job; five books of Solomon; four books of greater Prophets; twelve books of minor Prophets; two books of Ezra; one book of Maccabees; Tobit; Judith; Asenath; Esther; Ecclesiasticus; the Psalter; Uzziah; Enoch; Baruch; third (or fourth) Ezra.

4. The Coptic Church.—We have no early lists of the books received as canonical in the Coptic church, but from the *Nomocanon* of the thirteenth-century writer Ibn al-'Assal it is clear that the Copts accepted the authority of the above-mentioned Canons of the Apostles. The text of the relevant canon therefrom differs somewhat in the various Coptic and Arabic sources available to us, but a comparison of them gives us the following list as that generally accepted in the Coptic church:

Pentateuch, five books; Joshua; Judges with Ruth; four books of Kings; two books of Paralipomena; Ezra and Nehemiah; Job; the Psalms; Proverbs; Ecclesiastes; Song of Songs; the twelve minor Prophets; the four greater Prophets (i.e., Isaiah, Jeremiah, Ezekiel, Daniel); Wisdom; Judith; Tobit; Esther; three books of Maccabees; Ecclesiasticus.

This list is derived from the Hellenistic Bible, whose wider range of writings, as might have been expected, has in general prevailed in the various areas that were formerly under the control of the Byzantine church. There has been at times discussion, e.g., in the Russian church, regarding the authority and canonicity of the so-called Deuterocanonical writings, and the various lists of books of scripture in the early Byzantine writers differ considerably, but the prevailing usage in the Greek and Russian churches has been to accept the Hellenistic Bible, and it was one form of the Hellenistic Bible that was formally pronounced as canonical in the Roman Catholic Church.

V. Conclusion

The result of examining these various witnesses may be summarily stated.

A. Preparation for Canonization.—There was a preparation for canonization by a progressive assembling of religious writings in which the community felt that the voice of religious authority could be heard, and this assembling among the Jews crystallized in three stages:

(a) The Law, which at first meant merely the codes embodying the social and religious rules to be obeyed by the community, came to include the narratives of the early history and antiquities of the people, which were felt to be necessary to make the codes meaningful, and the whole was called Torah, or instruction. This later came to be divided into five sections, giving us the Pentateuch. That the Law was recognized as an entity, though not necessarily as a canonized entity, earlier than the other writings, is suggested by the facts (i) that the Samaritans took over only the Law; (ii) that the word Torah could later be used to cover all scripture; (iii) that among the Jews it has a place of unique regard; (iv) that it seems always to have been given first attention in the various translations. Some of the material now in our Pentateuch may have come to be regarded as sacred and authoritative at a fairly early date, but the Septuagint shows that some little additions were made to the Hebrew text later than the date of its translation into Greek, about 250 B.C., so that its text could not have been sacrosanct then. The Mishnah, however, about A.D. 200 assumes the present Hebrew text as something given. Much of the halakah therein is based on a text substantially that of our Pentateuch, so that we are driven back to about 200 B.C. as the date when the text must have been for all practical purposes fixed. This date is confirmed by the fact that the New Testament regards the Law as something known as a definite *regula* long held to be authoritative, no jot or tittle of which could be lightly changed. The end of the third century B.C., therefore, may be considered to be the date of the fixing of the text of the Pentateuch.

(*b*) The Prophets is the group of documents including the writings of the prophets themselves and the history within whose framework the prophets lived and labored. We have no means of telling when the writings of this second group began to form into a collection. The citation of earlier prophets by later ones is evidence that there were little collections in circulation earlier than the final collection. Ben Sirach certainly knew of scripture writings other than the Law in circulation about 200 B.C., and his grandson knew of a collection named "Prophets." The books of Maccabees know of a collection of "Prophets" besides the Law, and in the New Testament we have evidence of the custom of public reading of sections from the Prophets at synagogue services. This, however, does not necessarily presuppose the existence of a fixed body of writings from which nothing could be subtracted nor anything added. By the time of Josephus, however, the limits of such a collection had been set and a theory elaborated as to when true prophecy had come to an end. If we have to date Zech. 12–14 in 135 B.C., the collection could not have reached its final form before that date, and yet the semiofficial character of the undertaking evident in the Septuagint version of the Prophets would point to the existence of some generally recognized body of prophetic writings when that translation was made.

(*c*) The Hagiographa is a collection of miscellaneous writings, some of which may have begun to win recognition as early as parts of the prophetic collection. The New Testament quotes the Psalms as scripture, Ben Sirach knows of a collection besides the Law and the Prophets, and his grandson actually mentions such a group. So also the books of Maccabees refer to religious books in circulation which are neither Law nor Prophets. Josephus knows a fixed list of them. That this collection grew from small beginnings is clear. The Psalter is made up of smaller collections, and several documents have gone into the making of Proverbs. Some of this material may be dated as early as the sixth century B.C., but much of it is later, coming from a time when there was a general feeling that the creative period was past, so that these books are for the most part (i) paraphrase or elucidation or continuation of older texts, (ii) works put forth in the name of some great figure of the past, (iii) midrashim on some particular events in the past history of the people.

B. Official Canonization.—Older writers on the canon frequently speak of three separate canonizations, corresponding to the three stages in the collection of the writings, but we have no actual evidence that any one of these three parts was ever regarded as alone canonical. As collections, they were formed and limited at different times, and one part may have come to have a reputation as authoritative earlier than others, but the official pronouncing of them as canonical was a pronouncement that covered all three parts. Josephus knows that the officially received canon was a collection of twenty-two books, a figure which occurs again in Origen and is known to Jerome. II Esdras (IV Ezra) says it was of twenty-four books, which is the rabbinical number and the number given by Jerome in his preface to Daniel; the difference, Jerome says, depending on counting or not counting Ruth and Lamentations as separate. This official pronouncement was made at the Assembly at Jamnia, although it was not universally accepted.

C. Resistance to Official Canonization.—The Hellenistic Bible continued to perpetuate a larger collection, and the various translations from the Septuagint—the Coptic, the Armenian, the Ethiopic—carried yet further this larger collection. On the other hand, we find that some books admitted in the Jewish tradition (twenty-two or twenty-four) were not included elsewhere, for example, Esther and Chronicles in the earlier Syriac tradition. Even among the Jews, quite apart from the echoes in the Talmud of discussions over the standing of certain books, we know from Yadayim 4:6 that the Sadducees did not accept without demur this limitation of the books, and we are told that the Essenes had books of their own which the postulant for admission to their sect had to swear to preserve.

When we inquire more carefully into the canonization of the twenty-two or twenty-four books among the Jews, we discover the following facts:

(*a*) It bears traces of the handiwork of the scribes, the Sopherim. The whole discussion regarding the "defiling of hands" in connection with the scrolls of the scriptures, whether they defiled when written in Aramaic or only when in Hebrew, whether the spaces above and below the letters defile, or the erasures, or the blanks at the end, all these things show the preoccupation of the Sopherim, and it was apparently their work that led to official action regarding sacred scripture.

(b) It was a Pharisaic ordinance and regulation which the Sadducees did not accept without protest, and which they actually accused the Pharisees of inventing.

(c) It originated in Palestine. The oft-suggested antithesis between the Alexandrine and the Palestinian canon is fictitious. There never were two canons. In New Testament times we find such a book as Enoch in use both in Alexandria and in Palestine. In Palestine there came about a definite narrowing of the range of the books to be included in the finally fixed collection, and this was the only official canonization of the books of the Old Testament.

The discussions regarding the inclusion or noninclusion of certain books show that the idea of a canonization of a limited number of books must have been in the minds of the rabbis for some time. That it was not a settled question in 130 B.C. is clear from the prologue of the grandson of Ben Sirach, nor could it have been settled in 114 B.C. when Lysimachus of Jerusalem translated Esther into Greek, for had there been a recognized collection he would hardly have felt at liberty to add to that book the legendary embellishments we find there. As the question of the disputed books divided the schools of Hillel and Shammai, it must have been a live question in the first century A.D., and probably was so fairly early in that century.

When we ask why the question should have arisen in an acute form just at that time, we find two answers given:

(a) When men felt that the genuine voice of religious authority was no longer to be heard, it was a matter of some importance to assemble those writings in which the community agreed it had been heard. This feeling, however, had long been present in Israel, and there must have been something that made it suddenly a matter of urgency to settle for the community the question of canonicity. One theory is that it was the rise of apocalyptic. The apocalyptic books with their grandiose visions of the future tended to wean men's minds from the past in which the religious life of the community was rooted, and in a subtle way to supersede the older literature. The law had been given through Moses, but these books went behind Moses to supposed writings of Enoch and Seth and Noah, to testaments of Adam and Abraham, which as such laid claim to be superior books. II Esdras (IV Ezra) boldly asked that the seventy extra books that Ezra produced be kept apart and delivered only to those who were wise among the community, "for in [such books] is the spring of understanding, the fountain of wisdom, and the stream of knowledge" (II Esdras 14:47). To check this apocalyptic the Sopherim elaborated a theory of inspiration; they said that inspiration belonged to the prophetic office, which began with Moses, and ended, as we learn from Josephus, in the time of Artaxerxes Longimanus, or according to the rabbinical writings, in the time of Alexander the Great. Therefore all books supposed to have been written before Moses, or those written later than the period of the prophets, were to be excluded. Thereafter the writings which were accepted into the canon gained their place only because they were supposed to have been written during the period of prophetic activity. This theory excluded Ben Sirach and the books of Maccabees, but Maccabean pieces included in the Psalter got in because they were covered by the name of David. Daniel and Job were considered to be of prophetic origin, and all that was ascribed to Isaiah and Zechariah found a place in the collection, however much later some of this material may be. Song of Songs, Proverbs, and Ecclesiastes were covered by the name of Solomon, and the exclusion of Wisdom and the Psalms of Solomon, which also bore the name of Solomon, can be explained only on the ground of language, since Greek was known to have been a language that was not used in the prophetic period. Esther, however, being in Hebrew, was considered to have come from that period. Lamentations found a place because of its association with Jeremiah, and Baruch must have been excluded for the same reason that excluded Wisdom of Solomon.

(b) The other theory is that the question assumed so acute a form as to demand immediate resolving at that particular time, because of the rise and circulation of a body of Christian writings. Just as the necessity of excluding Gnostic writings led to the formulation of a canon of the New Testament books, so the rise of what in Jewish eyes was the Christian heresy brought about a Jewish formulation of a canon of scripture in a definite attempt to exclude those Christian writings which were exercising a dangerous fascination for many Jews. With the attempt to exclude these books came the necessity of settling on a standard for canonicity, and by the selection of the criterion of prophetic inspiration, which ceased in the time of Artaxerxes, there followed automatically the exclusion of such books as Sirach, Maccabees, and so forth, and of course the new Christian books which were making their claim to be inspired books and to speak with the same note of religious authority. This second theory would seem to be supported by the fact that the earliest pronouncement on what does and what does not defile the hands specifically mentions the Gospels. This passage is the Tosephta Yadayim 2:13:

The Gospels and the books of the Minin do not defile the hands. The books of Ben Sira and all the books that have been written since his time do not defile the hands.

With this may be associated the discussion in Tosephta Shabbath 12(14):5, on what things may legally be rescued from a burning building on the sabbath day, where we read that scriptures may be rescued but not Gospels or the books of the Minin (i.e., heretics), even though they contain names of God. It has been pointed out that while the earliest mention of an ordinance against Christian and heretical books dates from between A.D. 70 and 90, it is in the years 100 to 130 that we find all the Jewish leaders inveighing violently against the heretics and their books. Suddenly, in the second half of the second century, polemic against the Christians abruptly ceased, so that when the Mishnah was redacted at the end of the century, it included none of the defensive ordinances against Christianity such as are in the Tosephtas and Baraitas. The distinction had been made so clear between Jewish scripture and Christian scripture that the latter had become of little danger to the Jewish community, and thus from now on we hear nothing within Judaism concerning the canon of scripture save some echoes of controversy as to whether some of the books included when the canon was defined had not better have been left out. Christians continued to use the larger collection, but when Jewish revisions of the Greek were made, they limited themselves to those books in the now definitely fixed Hebrew canon.

VI. Selected Bibliography

BENTZEN, AAGE. *Introduction to the Old Testament.* Copenhagen: G. E. C. Gad, 1948. Vol. I, pp. 20-41.

BUDDE, KARL. Article, "Canon, Old Testament," in T. K. Cheyne, ed., *Encyclopaedia Biblica.* New York: The Macmillan Co., 1899. Vol. I, pp. 649-74.

BUHL, FRANTS. *Canon and Text of the Old Testament,* tr. John Macpherson. Edinburgh: T. & T. Clark, 1892.

EISSFELDT, OTTO. *Einleitung in das Alte Testament.* Tübingen: J. C. B. Mohr, 1934. Pp. 614-30.

MARGOLIS, M. L. *The Hebrew Scriptures in the Making.* Philadelphia: Jewish Publication Society of America, 1922.

OSTBORN, GUNNAR. *Cult and Canon: A Study in the Canonization of the Old Testament.* Uppsala: A.-B. Lundequistska, 1951.

PFEIFFER, R. H. *Introduction to the Old Testament.* New York: Harper & Bros., 1941. Pp. 50-70.

RYLE, H. E. *The Canon of the Old Testament.* 2nd ed. London: Macmillan & Co., 1925.

SMITH, W. ROBERTSON. *The Old Testament in the Jewish Church.* 2nd ed. rev. New York: D. Appleton & Co., 1892.

STRACK, H. L. Article, "Canon of Scripture," in S. M. Jackson, ed., *The New Schaff-Herzog Encyclopedia.* New York: Funk & Wagnalls, 1908. Vol. II, pp. 388-93.

WILDEBOER, G. *The Origin of the Canon of the Old Testament,* tr. B. W. Bacon. London: Luzac & Co., 1895.

WOODS, F. H. Article, "Old Testament Canon," in James Hastings, ed., *A Dictionary of the Bible.* New York: Charles Scribner's Sons, 1900. Vol. III, pp. 604-16.

ZEITLIN, S. *An Historical Study of the Canonization of the Hebrew Scriptures.* Philadelphia: Jewish Publication Society of America, 1933.

TEXT AND ANCIENT VERSIONS
OF THE OLD TESTAMENT

by ARTHUR JEFFERY

Modern English versions of the Old Testament are based in the first instance on the Masoretic text of the canonical Hebrew Scripture (see articles, "The Canon of the Old Testament," pp. 32-45, and "The English Bible," pp. 84-105). The Masoretic text was established from the fifth to the tenth centuries of the Christian Era by several generations of Jewish scholars, most of whom were called "Masoretes" (from the word Masorah, "tradition").

Of none of the documents received into the canonical collection of Hebrew Scripture do we possess the original autograph; nor do we possess the original text of the collection as it was written out at the time of its acceptance as canonical. Thus a history of the text of the Old Testament, however we may divide it for convenience of study, falls chronologically into three periods: (*a*) the history of the text of the original documents before the time of their definite acceptance into a canonical collection; (*b*) the history of the text of this canonical collection till the time of its receiving a fixed form at the hands of the Masoretes; (*c*) the history of the Masoretic text from the date of its fixing till the appearance of the printed editions we now use. It will never be possible to write the complete history of the text, with all the changes it underwent throughout this long period of transmission, for history must be based on evidence, and at all too many places in our survey the evidence available to us is too fragmentary and uncertain to permit more than conjectures.

I. Primitive Documents

Some of the material that is now contained in the canonical books of the Old Testament was doubtless handed down orally from generation to generation for a considerable time before any attempt was made to set it down in writing. In the case of other religions also we know of sacred poetry and legend, sacred laws, liturgies, and rituals being handed down and preserved throughout many generations in unwritten form. In all such cases there can be no doubt that during the period of oral transmission the text underwent many modifications. Sometimes a given text has been transmitted in two or more parallel forms, and this fact enables us to see how various types of error and change may occur. The claim has been made that a special providence preserved the documents of the Old and the New Testaments from all contamination by the various types of corruption which normally affect documents during the long process of their transmission. Precisely the same claim is made by other religions for their scriptures, but the evidence in our hands makes it quite clear that in all cases such claims are baseless. The text of the Old Testament in its *written* form has demonstrably been subject to alteration and modification in the process of transmission, and there is no reason to think that it did not suffer similarly during the period of oral transmission before it was recorded in written form. This does not necessarily mean that the text has been altered with evil intent. The correctors may have meant well. Obsolete words tend to be replaced by words in more common use; expressions which the taste of a later day finds objectionable tend to be toned down or replaced; explanatory glosses come to be added as an aid to understanding a text. Although such modifications are made with good intent, they constitute a tampering with the text and must be technically considered as cases of textual corruption.

How early any of the Old Testament material was written down, or in what form, we cannot say with certainty. Written material of a religious nature was found in the Near East at an early period, perhaps as early as the fourth millennium B.C. The Pyramid texts of the early dynasties in Egypt present material which strongly suggests that it is derived from written material of the predynastic period. Temple records in Mesopotamia may be even earlier than this. A publication by Maurice Dunand[1] suggests that in Canaan pictographic script may have been in use, at least at Byblos, not very much later, while a pseudo-hieroglyphic script was certainly in use there before the end of the third millennium B.C. There is thus nothing inherently impossible in the suggestion that written religious documents may have been in circulation in Palestine during the patriarchal period. The alphabetic use of cuneiform signs in the Ras Shamra texts, the alphabetic adaptation of Egyptian signs in the Sinai inscriptions from Serabīt el-Khādem, the possibility that the acrophonetic system of reading hieroglyphs in Egypt may have given rise to an alphabetic system of signs there earlier than the Eighteenth Dynasty, and the evidence adduced by Dunand in the above-mentioned book, suggesting that the Phoenician alphabet may go back as far as the fifteenth century B.C., make it not only possible but even probable that in Mosaic times an alphabetic script would have been used in Palestine for recording religious documents. It is thus beside the point to discuss whether our Old Testament may in places present features of documents transcribed from originals which Moses wrote in cuneiform on clay tablets, or from documents on papyrus, in some form of hieratic script, in which he brought from Egypt the story of the bondage and recorded the tale of the desert wanderings and the laws given at Sinai. Literary criticism suggests that the earliest material we actually have in our Old Testament documents dates from the tenth century B.C., and as we have several examples of writing in

[1] *Byblia Grammata* (Beyrouth: 1945).

an alphabetic script from Palestine of the early Iron Age (*ca.* 1200-900 B.C.), examples which suggest that writing was then used for everyday purposes, it is reasonable to assume that if our documents took written form in this period, they would have been written in the same way.

References to writing in the Old Testament are not numerous. In Genesis there is no allusion to writing, but in Exodus the JE document represents Moses as practicing the art (Exod. 17:14; 34:28). The more frequent references in the Prophets indicate that writing was common in their time. The oft-quoted "pen of the writer" in Judg. 5:14 is no evidence, for ספר שבט means rather the scribe's staff of office. The יכתב of Judg. 8:14, however, may be proof that youths in Gideon's time were taught to write, while David is described not only as having secretaries on his staff (II Sam. 8:17; 20:25; cf. II Kings 12:11 [Heb. 10]), but also as himself writing and sending a message (II Sam. 11:14-15). The Gezer calendar of the ninth (or perhaps the tenth) century B.C., the Mesha' inscription in Moabitish of the ninth century, and the business documents on ostraca from Samaria of the eighth century, all of which are in dialects closely related to biblical Hebrew, show us what the script in use in this age was like. The earliest documents in Hebrew at present known are the Siloam inscriptions of the eighth century, the Ophel ostracon of the seventh century, numerous stamps on jar handles, seals from various sites and dates between 650 and 500 B.C., and the Lachish letters on ostraca from the sixth century. All these use that same type of script.

The Siloam inscriptions are incised on stone, as are the Gezer calendar and the Moabite inscription. Religious inscriptions carved on stone are known from very early periods in the Near East. In the Old Testament itself we read of Moses having his laws on tables of stone (Exod. 31:18; 34:1, 28), while laws written on stones were set up beyond Jordan (Deut. 27:2-3; Josh. 8:30-32). Inscriptions carved on wood and metal are also known from early times. The לוח of Isa. 30:8 and Hab. 2:2 was doubtless of wood, and perhaps the גליון of Isa. 8:1 was of metal. The cuneiform religious texts are commonly on clay, and that such a material was used for writing in Israel is evidenced not only by the stamped jar handles and seals, but also by the notice that Ezekiel was directed to draw his plan of Jerusalem on a tile (לבנה, Ezek. 4:1). Writing that is painted, not incised, is known from quite early times in Egypt, and on a variety of materials. This method of writing served to introduce new materials such as linen, leather, ostraca, and papyri, and with these developed the use of ink. Ostraca were used mostly for nonliterary documents. We have representations on both Mesopotamian and Egyptian monuments of scribes using leather or parchment scrolls. The Letter to Aristeas (ca. 110 B.C.) assumes that it was customary for scripture books to be copied on parchment. The story of the cutting and burning of the roll of which we read in Jer. 36:23 suggests papyrus rather than leather, and indeed the Greek translation assumes that it was a papyrus roll. Papyrus was used in Egypt at an early date. The story of Wen Amon (ca. 1110 B.C.) shows that large quantities of this writing material were being imported into Byblos, a fact which suggests its common use in other centers also. As a matter of fact, a number of seals in the collection of the Palestine Museum bear evidence of having been impressed on papyrus documents. It is probable that the early documents of the Old Testament would have been written on papyrus. The sense that we have in some parts of the Old Testament of dealing with dismembered fragments whose arrangement and piecing together had presented difficulties to the collectors has its parallel in the difficulties scholars have in dealing with the Greek papyri, and perhaps can best be explained by the assumption that much of the original material came to the collectors written on this type of perishable material.

The kind of writing instrument employed would depend on the material being used. Metal implements were used for incising inscriptions on stone and metal. Job 19:24 speaks of an "iron pen" (עט ברזל) with which he would engrave his words, and the same expression is used in Jer. 17:1 for the pen which is to engrave the sin of Judah. The חרט, or "graving tool," which in Exod. 32:4 is the instrument whereby the golden calf was fashioned, in Isa. 8:1 is used for the "pen" with which the prophet was to write his message. The stylus (στύλος) was a pointed instrument for writing on clay or wax. A brush could be used for writing on various types of material with either paint or ink. The popular instrument for writing, however, was the reed pen, such as is pictured in the hands of scribes in early Egyptian tombs. This is the κάλαμος (III Macc. 4:20) for which the Hebrew equivalent is עט (Ps. 45:2 [Heb. 1]; Jer. 8:8). The point wore down and had to be recut, whence comes the importance of the "scribe's knife" (Jer. 36:23), which he also used for making erasures. The Samaritan ostraca and the Lachish letters are written with ink, and Baruch tells how he wrote the words of the prophet in ink (Jer. 36:18). Along with his knife, the scribe carried in his girdle the inkhorn (Ezek. 9:2).

Though individual oracles or poems, records or literary pieces, would be written on convenient papyrus sheets, the normal *book* form at the time of these early Old Testament documents was the scroll or roll, whether of papyrus, leather, or parchment. Such are represented on Egyptian and Mesopotamian monuments, and in the well-known scene on the Arch of Titus a man is pictured carrying one of these rolls. That the Hebrew ספר, "book," was a scroll is clear from Isa. 34:4, where we read that the heavens are to be rolled up like a ספר. So the מגלה of Jer. 36:14 is in Ezek. 2:9 called "the roll of a book." In ancient times such scrolls or rolls were usually small in size, and it may be that the dividing of certain parts of the Old Testament is due to the fact that only so much writing could be contained conveniently in a normal-sized roll. The cursive character of the writing on the ostraca, which is also reflected in the style of the writing in the Siloam inscription, suggests extensive practice of writing, so that we may think of the early documents we are considering as having been written in cursive fashion by professional or semiprofessional scribes. In Jer. 36:18 the prophet pronounces the words with his mouth and Baruch writes them in the scroll, but it is by no means unlikely that some of the early documents whose content was later incorporated in the Old Testament may have been written by their authors and not dictated. The three words for "scribe" used in the Old Testament, ספר, שטר, and מפסר, all seem to be words borrowed from Mesopotamia, and to be used as the titles of officials, but this does not prove that private writers may not have been common.

The oldest specimens of Hebrew writing that we possess are all in what we may call the Canaanite characters, such as were used in the old Phoenician inscriptions and on the Moabite stone. These are also used in the writing on the Samaritan ostraca and in the Lachish letters, and would doubtless have been used for writing the originals of the Old Testament documents of the earliest period. These characters continued to be used on coins as late as the Jewish revolt of A.D. 132-35, and in a modified form are still used by the Samaritans for their religious books. When the Aramaeans came into Asia Anterior and began to write their Aramaic language, they also made use of these Canaanitish characters, but in their hands the characters underwent certain modifications. We can see the earlier forms in the inscriptions from Zendjirli of the eighth century B.C., but by the time we reach the Elephantine papyri of the fifth century, these Aramaic characters have a definite style of their own. A little before the time of Christ we find some inscriptions in Hebrew, such as that at 'Araq al-Amīr, which are written in this Aramaic form of the script, and in the early centuries after Christ the writing on the Jewish ossuaries and the inscriptions, such as that of the mosaic at 'Ain Dūk, are also in this script. The Elephantine papyri were written for, if not actually by, Jews, and there is reason to believe that with the increasing use of the Aramaic language in Palestine this Aramaic form of script gradually superseded the older Canaanitish form in documents for official usage, though the survival of it in Samaritan and the fragments of Leviticus from the 'Ain Feshka cave suggest that the old script for long continued in popular use alongside it. Every manuscript of the Old Testament that has survived, including the Nash papyrus and the Dead Sea scrolls, which are our oldest specimens of biblical manuscripts in Hebrew, and may be pre-Christian, are written in a variety of this Aramaic type of script known as the "square script." There are in the Bible certain passages that are in the Aramaic language, and it is not improbable that they, along with some of the postexilic material in Hebrew, may have been originally written in the Aramaic script. It seems certain that by the time our documents were gathered together in a form ready for canonization, they would all have been written in this script. Some readings in our present text are due to the confusion of letters which are similar in the square script but not in the older script and are not represented in the Septuagint which fact points to the same conclusion.

At the time the Pentateuch was first translated into Greek it was still in the older style of script. This is clear from the fact that certain of the mistakes of translation in that version are best explained as due to the confusion of letters which are much alike in the old script but which would not have been likely to be confused in the Aramaic script. Outside the Pentateuch, however, there are mistakes of translation in the Septuagint which seem to be due to confusion of those letters which are similar in form in the Aramaic script. Josephus at one place [2] speaks of copies of the Law in the old script, though elsewhere [3] he seems to know of books in the Aramaic character. That the Samaritans made their copy of the Pentateuch in the old characters suggests that about 122 B.C. manuscripts of the Pentateuch were still circulating in that style of script. In the Gospels, however, we find the *yōdh* referred to as the smallest letter (Matt. 5:18), which it was in the Aramaic square script but not in the old script. As this is the period when we begin to find Jewish inscriptions appearing in the Aramaic characters, we may perhaps date the complete

change-over into this type of script as having taken place in the first century B.C. Later Jewish writers found it necessary to explain this change in script to the square, or what they called the "Assyrian" script, and so we have the curious passages in the Talmud, B. Sanhedrin 21*b*, Yer. Meg. I. 71*b*-*c*, and Tosephta Sanhedrin 4:7-8.

The text at this early period would have been a bare consonantal text, though with a beginning of the use of the *matres lectionis*. Some of the inscriptions, such as the Mesha' stone and the great Siloam inscription, have a dot as word divider, and this is found in the Samaritan ostraca. No such device, however, is used in the Lachish letters, and the fact that numerous translations in the Septuagint depend on a different word division from that in our present Hebrew text makes it fairly certain that the earliest manuscripts would have had neither marks for word division nor signs of verse division, though they may have had some simple form of paragraphing such as may be seen in the Dead Sea scrolls. The inscriptions reveal the practice of abbreviation, and there are certain phenomena in our present text which suggest that various types of abbreviation were used in earlier copies, which later generations of scribes did not fully understand.

II. The Early Collection

In the wider sense the history of the text commenced when the first material came to be composed. Some of this, as we have seen, may have circulated in oral form long before it was written down, and even when reduced to written form may have had considerable circulation before it came to be regarded as scripture material, and as such copied for community use. In the narrower sense, therefore, the history of the text, as a text of canonical scripture, begins only when a group of documents comes to be copied as a collection of writings of religious authority. Even then there will normally be a long period of transmission before any attempt is made to fix the text in a definite form. Some documents in the collection may circulate in a contracted, or maybe in an expanded, form. Owners will correct, interpolate, or annotate their copies. Some will order to be copied for them only those portions which have interest to them, or may have portions from different sources copied into one and the same manuscript. The characteristic of this period is the free and uncontrolled transmission of the text by copyists who took liberties with their text in a way that was not possible after canonization. Also with continuous copying over a long period it was inevitable that there would

[2] *Antiquities* XII. 2. 4.
[3] *Ibid.*, XII. 2. 1.

creep into the text the usual types of textual corruption.

A study of the parallel passages in the Old Testament reveals the freedom with which the text was then treated. A comparison of II Sam. 22 with Ps. 18, of Ps. 14 with Ps. 53, of Ps. 31: 2-4a [Heb. 1-3a] with Ps. 71:1-3, of Ezra 2 with Neh. 7:6 ff., or the parallel accounts in Samuel-Kings and those in Chronicles, shows us not only the wording of statements, but even names and numbers, differing in a way that can be explained only as alterations made during transmission. Curious repetitions within certain books suggest that the text we have is a copy based on two or more manuscripts which the copyist had at his disposal, while other mistakes suggest repeated copying at different times. Some corruptions would seem to have arisen from the process of transcribing texts from the old style of writing to the new square script. Others arise from the usual sources of copyists' errors—confusion of letters or groups of letters, wrong repetition or omission, transposition, false writings under the influence of neighboring words or sentences, incorporation of glosses, and so forth. Some are due to a copyist's exercising his own judgment instead of merely copying, as when he introduces wrong word division or word connection or a false vocalization, or when he corrects passages, either by attempting to fill out abbreviations, or replacing words by synonyms, or making alterations on the ground of etymology. Sometimes explanatory glosses are added, sometimes the text is expanded by the citation of parallel passages, and occasionally there are tendential alterations, such as the interchange of the names Gerizim and Ebal during the Samaritan controversy. In the poetical and prophetic books we are frequently conscious of dislocation in the text. One cause of this may well be that in such books, where there was no such guide as is present in narrative material, copyists working at the task of copying deteriorated scrolls often had difficulty in recognizing the order of the leaves and fragments lying before them, and so tended to join pieces together on the ground of catchwords, with the result that in places quite unrelated materials are joined and related materials separated.

As the collection grew in importance to the community because of its religious significance, there inevitably came into being a body of men who in a special way interested themselves in the care of the material in the collection. We find this happening in the case of other religions, for example, in the growth of the group of the *Qurrā'* in early Islam, who devoted themselves to caring for the text of the *Qur'ān*. Among the Jews this group of men came to be known as Sopherim, that is, bookmen or scribes. Tradition associates the name of Ezra with the formal organization of the Sopherim, but it is fairly certain that for long they would have had no formal organization, being simply individuals interested in scripture, who were thus drawn together, until presently they found themselves regarded by the community as in some special sense the guardians and custodians of scripture. They were by no means mere copyists, as the name scribe might seem to imply, but were "bookmen," interested in everything that concerned the preservation and interpretation of the national and religious literature of their community. It is possible that they came to be recognized as a more or less organized body during the experience of the Exile, but it was later, when the community had come to recognize that its religion, both in belief and practice, was founded on the authority of scripture, that they really came into prominence and had that special position which is reflected in the New Testament references.

From the material in our hands it is possible to indicate some aspects of their various labors in connection with the text. It was under them that the change-over from the old style writing to the new was completed, and in their hands the manuscript form of the "square" script developed. With them the collection began to take shape as a body of religious literature. The text as we have it bears manifold signs of the hand of "the redactor," so it is evident that pious men were exercising great care in selecting, arranging, and editing material to form a body of scripture that would one day be officially canonized. No thought of such canonization was in their minds, but they were doing the necessary work preliminary to such canonization. The earliest versions of the Old Testament were also doubtless due to members of this class. Though the Greek and Syriac translations were later revised by Christians, the underlying work on them was done by Jews, and like the Aramaic Targums, they seem at first to have been quite unofficial undertakings which arose from the needs of communities to whom the Hebrew original was not easily intelligible. Different sections of these versions were translated at different times and in different places, and they vary considerably in both accuracy and style, but their translators would certainly have come from among those individuals whose special interest was the text. If we admit the possibility that some of the documents in our Hebrew Bible are translations from Aramaic originals, the task of rendering them into the sacred tongue would also have been the work of members of this group.

The rise of the synagogue presented a special

problem, for numbers of copies of the Torah, and to a lesser extent of the Prophets, would be needed for the synagogues. Great care had to be taken to ensure the correctness of the text thus copied and the Sopherim came to be more and more occupied with textual details. First there was the question of orthography, of improvements such as the introduction of final forms for certain letters, of the increased use of the *matres lectionis* to ensure correct readings, of perfecting the manuscript hand with its "tittles" and other small peculiarities. Then there was the choice of a standard text to be read in all centers of the community. Along with this came the task of marking clearly the larger and smaller sense divisions in the text, since a correct interpretation would often depend on such marking.

Increased reverence for the scriptural books led to a certain amount of correction made in the interests of piety. To safeguard the divine name little alterations were made, names of heathen deities were disfigured, small changes were introduced in order to avoid anthropomorphisms, and euphemisms were substituted for words and expressions which the Sopherim considered offensive or inelegant. One special class of these euphemisms is that known as the *Tiqqûnê Ṣôpherim,* to eighteen of which attention is called by marginal notes in some of our oldest manuscripts (Gen. 18:22; Num. 11:15; 12:12; I Sam. 3:13; II Sam. 16:12; 20:1; I Kings 12:16; II Chr. 10:16; Jer. 2:11; Ezek. 8:17; Hos. 4:7; Hab. 1:12; Zech. 2:12 [Heb. 8]; Mal. 1:12; Ps. 106:20; Job 7:20; 32:3; Lam. 3:20). It is probable also that the curious uniformity of language in the Old Testament, which is quite extraordinary in a collection of documents of such varied dates, is due to an attempt by the Sopherim to secure linguistic uniformity in their text, just as in the case of the *Qur'ān* we read how Uthman's committee was appointed expressly to secure such uniformity in the final redaction. It has been suggested that the Sopherim of this period, conscious of numerous variant readings from manuscripts other than that which they chose as their standard text, and desiring to record these variants, simply inserted them into the text, thus producing the very curious redundancies often evident in the present Bible, and which in modern days should be indicated by brackets.

III. The Completed Collection

With the closing of the canon (*ca.* A.D. 100), we enter the period of the later Sopherim, the chief feature of whose work is the "stereotyping" of the text. The closing of the canon defined what books the Jews accepted as having authority, and it must have become evident soon thereafter that a closer definition of the text was also necessary. The New Testament quotes scripture often from the Septuagint, sometimes from what is virtually the present Hebrew text, and sometimes in a form that agrees with neither. Likewise, the early Christian writers handled the text very freely, so that the controversy with the growing Christian church was doubtless one factor contributing to the sense of need for a text fixed *ne varietur.* It would seem that much of the work directed to this end was accomplished under the direction of R. Akiba and his colleagues. By the middle of the second century A.D. the text of the Hebrew Bible, as regards the consonants and the first stage of voweling represented by the introduction of consonantal letters indicating vowel sounds, was probably very little different from that which we have today. While the old Greek version of the Septuagint shows in a great many passages that it was translated from a text which differed considerably from ours, the new Greek versions of Aquila, Theodotion, and Symmachus, that were made between A.D. 120 and 200 rarely show readings based on a consonantal text different from that of our Hebrew Bible. Moreover, the quotations in the rabbinical writings, though they do occasionally have variant readings, show that the text used by the rabbis was in all essentials the text we have today. Thus with the closing of the canon there was also a fixing of the text. A uniform text necessarily depends on the choosing of a standard exemplar to which all copies must conform, and this choice was probably the work of the Sopherim. We have no tradition, however, as to how or where this standard copy was selected. It was a text that had a number of peculiarities, some of which must be relatively old since they are referred to in the Talmud, and all these were now faithfully transmitted as part of the uniform text, precisely as all the peculiarities of Uthman's standard exemplar of the *Qur'ān* are still preserved in modern editions.

Any such exemplar chosen as the standard would represent only one form of text tradition. We may assume that in the eyes of the Sopherim the text chosen represented the best tradition available to them, but it was not the only tradition. The Samaritan Pentateuch in many passages seems to be following a different tradition, particularly where its numerous differences in orthography, in the minutiae of grammar, in names and numbers, and in the way its redactor takes over the results of exegesis into the text, have external attestation. The earlier parts of the Septuagint version were certainly translated from a text that differed in many particulars from that chosen as standard by the Sopherim, but even in the parts that were translated much later there is similar evidence. The text of some books, for example, Ezekiel and Job, is shorter in the Septuagint than in the present Hebrew text, while in other books it contains passages which have dropped out of the Hebrew original. Its tradition on numbers frequently differs from the Hebrew, and in places it has preserved a better form of proper names. Its arrangement of material also in some places is considerably different. On the other hand, many little details, such as tendentious changes in name (e.g., מריבעל to מפיבשת; LXX: Μεφιβόσθε) , show that the text underlying the Greek had undergone somewhat the same process of revision as had the Hebrew. In the rabbinical writings also we occasionally hear of other codices whose reading did not always agree with those of the standard text. Thus we have a number of striking variants quoted from a codex said to have belonged to R. Meir, and a list of variants from a codex of the Pentateuch said to have been brought from Jerusalem to Rome and there housed in the synagogue of Severus. In both the Mishnah and Gemara we find quotations from the Old Testament whose wording differs from that in our present text, and the further we move back historically in the rabbinical writings the greater becomes the divergence from the present text. It is therefore possible that the research initiated by Blau and Aptowitzer in this field may reveal further traces of an earlier type of text. The text of the Nash papyrus, already mentioned, is closer to that followed by the Septuagint than to that of the Masoretes. In Yer. Ta'anith 4:2 we have reference to three codices known as Me'ônî, Za'aṭûṭî and Hî', but it is doubtful if these can be considered traces of variant text tradition.

Even though the Sopherim of this period were working on a text that was accepted as standard, the technique of perfect transmission was not attained immediately. They seem to have recognized that it was not a perfect text, and modern scholarship suggests that we can detect certain euphemistic and dogmatic revisions, conflations, eliminations of unpropitious names, corrections of unfulfilled prophecies, due to their hands, as well as scribal alterations resulting from a failure to distinguish clearly the guttural letters, exchange of consonants, and perhaps some changes due to the universal scribal fondness for wordplay. As their technique improved, however, they learned to leave the text as it was and simply mark it to suggest corrections or emendations.

A. Textual Markings.—Various classes of textual markings have been preserved.

(a) The *Puncta extraordinaria*. Fifteen words in the printed Bible, following the manuscripts, are marked by being dotted, viz., וביניך in Gen. 16:5; אליו in Gen. 18:9; ובקומה in Gen. 19:33; וישקהו in Gen. 33:4; את־צאן in Gen. 37:12; ואהרן in Num. 3:39; רחקה in Num. 9:10; אשר in Num. 21:30; ועשרון in Num. 29:15; לנו ולבנינו in Deut. 29:28; יצא in II Sam. 19:20; המה in Isa. 44:9; והיכל in Ezek. 41:20; מחקצעות in Ezek. 46:22; and לולא in Ps. 27:13. This dotting of letters is a well-known scribal method of indicating erasures, and the rabbinical notes on these words in Sifre (Num. 9:10) and Midrash Rabba (Num. 3:39) make it clear that later authorities thought these words were spurious additions to the text. It is probable that many other words were so marked in old manuscripts.

(b) The *Miqra' Ṣôpherîm*, and *'Iṭṭûr Ṣôpherîm*, referred to in Nedarim 37b, which were directions to the reader as to the correct pronunciation of words or groups of words in the text.

(c) The *Piṣqâ'*, or blank space left in the text, apparently to mark omissions. Some twenty-eight of these have been noted in the manuscripts, e.g., at Gen. 35:22; I Sam. 14:19; Ezek. 3:16.

(d) The *Qerê wā-Kethîbh* where a mark in the text refers the reader to the margin which gives the correct reading to be used in place of what is written in the text.

There are three groups of material in this class:

(i) *Qaryān wā-lô' Kethîbhān*—words which are to be read though they are not in the text; that is, they mark scribal omissions, e.g., Judg. 20:13; Ruth 3:5, 17; II Sam. 8:3; 16:23.

(ii) *Kethîbhān wā-lô' Qaryān*—words which though written in the text must be omitted in the reading; that is, they mark mistaken scribal additions to the text, e.g., Ruth 3:12; Jer. 38:16; 51:3.

(iii) *Qerê*—where nothing is omitted and nothing is added, but the reading in the margin is suggested as an improvement on what is written in the text. Sometimes the *Qerê* is suggested from motives of piety, sometimes it is a grammatical correction or a supplementing of the older orthography, sometimes it is a critical emendation of what was considered a mistake in the text, and sometimes it seems to be a variant reading, either a reading from a parallel passage or a variant that has come down in another tradition. Some of these *Qerê* are quite ancient but others would seem to be very late and belong to the period of the Masoretes.

B. Verse and Sense Divisions.—Another feature of the work of the Sopherim of this period was the completion of the task of marking verse and sense divisions in the text. Some simple form of paragraphing had appeared earlier, but to this period belongs the consistent carrying through of word division, and with it the consistent use of the final forms of letters ך, ם, ן, ף, ץ. The fact that not only the Syriac version but also the Targums sometimes agree with the Septuagint word division and not with that of our printed Hebrew text indicates that this fixing of the word division was a gradual process. Verse divisions are assumed in the rabbinical prescription (Megillah 4:5) that in public reading the translator is to translate only one verse at a time from the Pentateuch, but may translate three verses at a time from the Prophets. Some system of marking verse endings was probably devised, and although the ṣōph-pāṣûq sign of the printed text is mentioned only in late writings, it may have been used at an early period.

It is clear that there was considerable difference between the verse divisions used in Babylonia and those current in Palestine, and there may have been differences among the various schools within those countries, just as we find later in the schools of Baṣra, Kūfa, and Damascus over the verse division of the Qur'ān. The Hebrew text used by Jerome had certain larger sense divisions marked by some form of paragraphing, probably like that of the pārāshiyyôth mentioned in the Mishnah as subdivisions of the Law and the Prophets. The practice of reading regular "lessons" in the synagogue gave rise to liturgical divisions of the text—divisions which might or might not coincide with some of the natural paragraphing divisions. The passage in Luke 4:16-21 does not prove that there were fixed pericopes from the Prophets read as lessons in the synagogue beside the lessons from the Law, though it suggests that there was a recognized portion for the day, and this suggestion is strengthened by the fact that the earliest Midrashim seem based on a system of fixed lessons from both the Law and the Prophets. Since the Mishnah does not regulate this matter, it may be that there was considerable latitude in the selection and arrangement of these pericopes. They would, however, tend to be marked in the text.

C. Peculiarities of Orthography.—Certain peculiarities of orthography the Sopherim apparently inherited with their standard copy and transmitted as an essential part of the text they had received. Some of these eccentricities seem to have existed at an early age. They include:

(a) Anomalous forms, for example, הוא instead of היא in nearly two hundred places, mostly in the Pentateuch; some defective writings, and some cases of the wrong insertion or omission of matres lectionis, as in Ps. 140:13; I Kings 8:48; Deut. 22:23, 28; 32:13; Hos. 4:6; 8:12; 9:16; Mic. 3:2.

(b) Literae majusculae et minusculae, for example, the extra large צ in Deut. 32:4, or the extra small ה in Gen. 2:4. There are said to be thirty cases of such majusculae and thirty-two cases of minusculae. Sometimes the use of the large letters resembles our use of capitals, but frequently they seem to be nothing more than scribal peculiarities.

(c) Literae suspensae, where certain letters are written above the line, that is, are as it were suspended, as in Judg. 18:30; Ps. 80:14; Job 38:13, 15.

(d) Inverted nun, where the letter נ is inverted and reversed, in Num. 10:35, 36; and seven times in Ps. 107.

(e) Oddities, such as a final ם in the middle of a word in Isa. 9:6; a ו cut off in the middle in Num. 25:12; an initial מ instead of a final in Neh. 2:13; an adhering ק in Exod. 32:25; Num. 7:2; an initial נ instead of a final in Job 38:1.

Similar orthographical peculiarities may be noticed in the standard text of the Qur'ān, and the simplest explanation of them is to take them as scribal peculiarities in the ancient standard exemplar which later scribes regarded as sacrosanct, and therefore to be transmitted faithfully even in its peculiarities.

IV. The Masoretes

According to Aboth 3:13, R. Akiba used to speak of מסרת as a fence to the Torah, and this word has given a name to those scholars who succeeded to the Sopherim, and who from about A.D. 500 onward concerned themselves with the safeguarding and transmission of the traditional text. They are the בעלי המסרת, the Masoretes. The name Masoretes is sometimes used to include all the work of the Sopherim, but is more commonly used in a narrower sense as a name for those who took up where the Sopherim left off, codifying and arranging what had already been done on text, and compiling the great apparatus of critical, comparative, interpretative, and statistical annotations that go under the name of the Masorah. Their labors led to several achievements.

A. Statistical Masorah.—There was a rabbinical conceit (Kiddushin 30a) that the Sopherim were so called because they counted the letters of the Torah. Though this derivation is unsound, it shows that the rabbis were aware that these scribes were using statistical devices as a help in checking the accuracy of transcription. The Indian scribes who copied the Vedas and the Moslem scribes who copied the Qur'ān used the same device. They counted the number of words, the number of letters, marked middle words and middle letters of passages or books, noted places where anomalous forms or noteworthy phenomena occurred. This practice may have begun early, but it was the Masoretes who gave it its definite form. They marked the middle verses of books, as at Josh. 13:26; Judg. 10:8; Isa. 33:21; etc.; they indicated that the middle verse of the Old Testament is Jer. 6:7; they stated the number of letters in the various books; they marked with a ל the *hapax legomena;* they noted the number of times the divine name occurs; they made lists of places where a word is written fully or defectively; they recorded the number of occurrences of certain grammatical peculiarities, and so forth. These annotations were later gathered together under special rubrics and recorded in the manuscripts. They are of textual importance not only because they served as checks to the scribes who were writing copies, but also because they preserve evidence of these curious features of the text that was accepted as standard.

B. Exegetical Masorah.—Since the Scriptures were read not as dead documents, but as part of the living religion of the people, an important task of those who cared for the transmission of the text was to ensure correct interpretation of the text as it was read. Various devices were used to secure this aim:

(*a*) Text division. The paragraphing that had been introduced earlier was now systematized. The *pārāshiyyôth* are carefully marked, the "open" by a פ (פתוחות), and the "closed" by a ס (סתומות); the "open" having a large blank space left before it commences, and the "closed" a small blank space. The manuscripts are uniform in the marking of these in the Law, though there is less regularity in the case of the Prophets and the Hagiographa. The Masoretes made lists of these sections with catchwords to indicate the beginning and closing of each. With the systematization of the form of worship in the synagogue came the custom of reading regular "lessons" from the Law and the Prophets. Those from the Law were called *Şedhārîm;* in Babylonia they were so arranged that the whole Pentateuch would be read through in a year, in Palestine for a three-year cycle. The schools differed somewhat as to where these divisions should fall, but marks were made in the manuscripts to indicate them. It was to be expected that they would correspond with some of the paragraphing divisions, and where they coincided with an "open" section they were marked by פפפ, and when with a "closed" section, by ססס. These signs stand in the printed text.

The verse divisions, which had been fluid at the time that the Greek and Syriac versions were made, the Masoretes attempted to fix, and they marked them with the *Şillūq* and *Şôph pāsūq.* The schools, however, differed on this matter,

for we read in Kiddushin 30*a* that the Palestinians had shorter verses than the Babylonians. As early as the Septuagint translation there were rubrics at the beginnings of some books and parts of books, and these the Masoretes systematized. They also noted on the margins of the manuscripts the *haphṭārôth,* or lessons from the Prophets, which were to be read in connection with each *pārāshāh* of the Law.

(*b*) Vocalization. The first step toward vocalization of the text had appeared in the use of the *matres lectionis,* or vowel letters, and this, when consistently carried through, was sufficient for an intelligent reading of the text. The modern Hebrew newspapers and printed books, just as the vast majority of Arabic and Syriac books, have no vocalization other than the vowel letters, and are familiarly read by anyone acquainted with the language. The scriptures, however, were sacred, and piety felt itself under obligation to avoid any possibility of misinterpretation by inserting signs to mark the complete vocalization of each word. Jerome had felt the need for such signs, and apparently it was felt also in the schools of Babylonia. As early as the fifth century A.D. the Nestorians had worked out a system of pointing for their Syriac Bible, and their system was later adapted for use with the Arabic script. It was apparently in Babylonia in the sixth and seventh centuries A.D. that the Jewish schools, under the same influence, began to work out their system of vocalization, with the intention of preserving the traditional pronunciation current among them. The Qaraites, who arose in the eighth century, presuppose in their controversy with the rabbinical schools a system of pointing known and observed, but we have no rabbinical tradition as to how it arose, save the later attempts to prove that the vowel points were given to Moses on Sinai.

Three systems of vocalization are known to us: (i) a Palestinian, whose signs closely resemble the Nestorian signs. It is known from manuscripts ranging from the sixth to the tenth centuries, and is a supralinear system, used at first only to point ambiguous words; (ii) a Babylonian, which is also a supralinear system, with signs that have certain points of contact with the Jacobite system used for Syriac, and may be a development from the Palestinian; (iii) a Tiberian, an infralinear system, probably of Mesopotamian origin, which is the system now in common use. Once the system of vocalization had been fixed, there grew up for it a statistical Masorah similar to that in use for the consonantal text.

(*c*) Accentuation. A further system of signs was devised in order to show the reader correct pronunciation, and later, correct cantillation of the text. These signs mark the stress or accent where that is necessary, and serve, like our marks of punctuation, to guide the reader to the logical or syntactical relations of one part of a sentence to another. There are two traditions with regard to this accentuation, a Babylonian and a Palestinian, the latter having two systems, one for the poetical and another for the prose books. They seem to be of the same age as the signs for vocalization, and their forms suggest that they were derived from similar signs used in Greek biblical manuscripts to regulate the public reading of the text. Later there grew up a statistical Masorah for the accents.

(d) Admonition. At places admonitory signs were placed in the text for the guidance of the reader. Thus where the words אלה; אל; אדני; אלהים occur in senses other than that of the divine name, e.g., Gen. 19:2; 31:53; Deut. 32:17, 21; etc., a sign חול is set to call the attention of the reader to the fact that here the words are secular and do not demand the reverent treatment accorded to the divine name. At the conclusion of Isaiah, Malachi, Lamentations, and Ecclesiastes the sign יתקק occurs, preceded by the beginning of the last verse but one, to warn the reader to go back and read that verse again so as to avoid finishing a pericope with something of bad omen.

C. Text-Critical Masorah.—Other classes of notes in the Masorah are in the nature of critical remarks on the text, indicating that though the Masoretes felt that they were committed to the transmission of a certain text tradition, they were aware that their text was not perfect, and knew that there were other text traditions whose readings sometimes differed from theirs. These notes are of several kinds:

(a) The Qeryān. We have already noticed that some of the Qerê notes are ancient, but a goodly proportion of those in our manuscripts seem to come from this later period of the Masoretes. In any case, their present arrangement and detail are due to the labors of the Masoretes.

(b) The Ṣebhîrîm. C. D. Ginsburg collected some 350 of these from the manuscripts, and many are marked in our printed texts, e.g., Gen. 19:8, 33; 49:13; Exod. 22:24; Num. 8:4; 9:6; II Kings 9:19. It is clear that they refer to variant readings, but whether they are intended to mark emendations to be adopted by the reader, or suggested emendations the reader is warned to avoid, or variants from other codices, is still a matter of dispute.

(c) Variants. When the standard exemplar was chosen it was only one among many copies then existing, and variant readings from other early manuscripts would continue to be remem-

bered, just as in the parallel case of the Qur'ān. Moreover, even the greatest care taken with regard to transmission did not prevent variants from appearing in copies which were supposed to follow the standard exemplar, nor suppress the memory that there had been various traditions on how the text should be voweled. The variants from the manuscript of R. Meir and from that in the Severian synagogue have already been mentioned. The Masoretes collected and tabulated these variants, and listed other variants from famous old copies such as the Mahzôrā' Rabbā', the Múgāh, the Hilleli, the Zanbúkî, the Jericho Pentateuch, the Sharqî (or Babhlî), and so forth. There were differences in tradition between the Babylonian and the Palestinian schools, and certain of their readings are recorded as Madinḥay (Eastern) and Ma'arbay (Western). Curiously enough, some of these variants have crept into the text where they can be recognized by the anomalous spellings.

(d) The Pâṣēq (divider). This sign occurs almost five hundred times in the printed text, and seems to belong to this class of Masoretic signs, though its origin and significance are still disputed.

(e) Curiosa. Marks were also used by the Masoretes to call attention to various things they thought of interest in the text, such as the occurrence of redundant letters, the number of years covered by the events mentioned in a section, the fact that in Ruth all the verses save eight begin with the letter ו.

These Masoretic notes were written in the manuscripts, sometimes in the space between the columns, sometimes on the margins, and only later were they systematized. One form of systematization was to group the notes in the text. This took three forms: (i) Initial Masorah, that is, tabulations placed before the text proper begins, sometimes written in fantastic forms around the large initial letter of a book. (ii) Marginal Masorah, comprising the masora parva, a system of symbols written on the side margins, or between columns, or more rarely between the lines, and unintelligible without the key; and the masora magna, written on the upper and lower margins. (iii) Final Masorah, made up of tabulations, often arranged alphabetically, placed at the end of the text. A second form of systematization was to digest these Masoretic notes into manuals such as the Oklāh wa Oklāh, or the Diqdûqê ha-Ṭe'amîm, or the Minhath Shay.

Since no two manuscripts ever have precisely the same collection of Masoretic notes, it is evident that the Masorah never reached the stage of fixation. Various strata within it can be recognized. There is an old period where the language is Hebrew, a middle period where the language is Aramaic, and a later period where the notes are again in Hebrew. Most of our Masoretic material is from the Palestine schools, but the work of Paul Kahle and his students has in recent years brought considerable accessions to our knowledge of the Masorah of the Babylonian schools. It was the school of Tiberias which finally came to dominate these textual studies. In the first half of the tenth century the tradition of the Tiberian school was embodied in two rival codices, one of Moses ben David ben Naphtali, the other of Aaron ben Moses ben Asher. The latter of these finally won acceptance, in spite of opposition from Babylonia, and provided the textus receptus with which for all practical purposes the period of the Masoretes comes to a close. Later small improvements and additions by the Naqdanim made in the thirteenth and fourteenth centuries are of minor importance. Here we reach the printed text. Jacob ben Ḥayyim ben Adonijah, who edited the second edition of the Bomberg Bible (Venice, 1524-25), collated a great number of manuscripts and systematized their Masoretic notes in an attempt to provide a definitive edition of this textus receptus. His critical method, however, was not faultless, and the Ben Asher text he produced is contaminated in places by that of Ben Naphtali.

V. The Printed Text

Jacob ben Ḥayyim based his text on relatively late manuscripts. We have an abundance of manuscripts of the Hebrew Old Testament, some of them synagogue rolls, but the majority in codex form. The Dead Sea scroll of Isaiah may prove to be from the first century B.C.; otherwise the earliest manuscripts bear dates of the ninth and tenth centuries A.D., but there is doubt whether some of these are as old as they claim to be. Considerable collections of variants from these manuscripts have been gathered by Benjamin Kennicott, G. B. de Rossi and C. D. Ginsburg. In spite of their late date they are the basis for the printed text. The earliest printed part of the Bible was the Bologna Psalter of 1477. The early prints, however, have only a typographical interest. Then we come to the Bomberg Bible printed at Venice in 1524-25. Jacob ben Ḥayyim's work on that edition has been the foundation on which most later printed editions have been based. Ginsburg's texts, both that of 1894 and that of 1926, and the first and second editions of Rudolf Kittel's *Biblia Hebraica*, started from the Ben Ḥayyim text. The first Christian edition of the Hebrew text was that in Cardinal Ximenes' *Complutensian Polyglot* of 1520. The

Amsterdam editions of Athias (1661) and Leumsden (1667) were based on a comparison of the Complutensian text with the Ben Ḥayyim text. A new edition of the Amsterdam text by Van der Hooght in 1795, and revised by Letteris in 1852, is the commonly used text that has for the last century been circulated by the British and Foreign Bible Society. For the third edition of Kittel's *Biblia Hebraica,* Paul Kahle used the Leningrad manuscript, which is a very accurate copy of the ben Asher type of text, and presents the best Hebrew Bible so far available. N. H. Snaith is at present engaged in preparing for the British and Foreign Bible Society a new text to replace the Letteris edition, and which will seek both to get behind the Ben Ḥayyim model to a more correct Masoretic text, and at the same time avoid the too great reliance on one manuscript, which some scholars feel is a defect in the work of both Baer and Kahle. A large edition of the Hebrew Bible is also being planned by a group of scholars at the Hebrew University of Jerusalem.

VI. The Ancient Versions

The early versions are important for the history of the text in so far as they provide evidence of the type of text from which they were translated. In the case of the Old Testament we are in the position of having manuscripts of certain of the versions considerably older than the majority of our manuscripts of the Hebrew text. The versions, however, present their own problem. Each of them has its individual textual history. In the process of transmission they were subject to the same sources of textual corruption as was the Hebrew text, were redacted, emended, interpolated, so that the recovery of their original forms, which alone would be evidence of the type of text from which they were translated, is a critical problem of great delicacy. These versions, moreover, are more often than not the work of several hands, and translators vary enormously in their method of translation, a fact which in its turn affects the possibility of restoring the original underlying the translation. We still lack satisfactory critical editions of most parts of all these early versions.

A. The Samaritan Pentateuch.—The Samaritan Pentateuch is not really a version, being the Hebrew text written out in Samaritan characters, and so only a Samaritan recension. It differs from the text of our printed Hebrew Bibles in some six thousand places, in about a third of which it agrees with the Septuagint, and in some cases with the Syriac and Latin versions. Many of the variants are nothing but scribal errors, and of these a goodly number are due to confusions among those letters which the Samaritans no longer distinguished in pronunciation. Some are brought about by a fuller use of the *matres lectionis,* and so are also merely orthographic variants. Others arise from the desire of the copyist to avoid anthropomorphisms, to remove anomalous forms, to harmonize passages, to make grammatical corrections or to correct mistakes in the Hebrew text, or to express the meaning more clearly or forcefully. Some variants represent a deliberate tampering with the text in favor of Samaritan views, for example. the substitution of Gerizim for Ebal in Deut. 27:4, and other such changes and interpolations intended to emphasize the importance of their shrine in Samaria as against that in Jerusalem. Other interpolations are due to material being supplied from parallel passages. When allowance has been made for all such variants, there still remains a body of readings where the Samaritan text presents a different textual tradition. In some cases we may be dealing with glosses that represent a traditional exegesis within the community, and it is possible that some cases represent dialectal peculiarities. There remain, however, a good many passages where the textual critic must take into consideration the possibility that the Samaritan presents a better and more likely original reading than the Masoretic text, particularly where such readings agree with one of the other versions. No one of the manuscripts of the Samaritan Pentateuch appears to be older than the thirteenth century, but they would seem to represent a text current in the second century. The best edition is the five-volume work of August von Gall (1914-18).

The *Samareitikon,* quoted some fifty times in the *scholia* to Origen's Hexapla, would seem to refer to a Greek rendering made in Egypt of material from the Samaritan Pentateuch. The Samaritan Targum is a version of the Pentateuch in Samaritan Aramaic. It cannot be earlier than the fourth century A.D. It has striking agreements with the Targum of Onkelos, but also striking differences, and so is probably a local rendering of a common oral Palestinian tradition. It has no great value for textual studies. The Samaritan book of Joshua is not the Hebrew Joshua but an apocryphal work.

B. The Aramaic Targums.—In the true sense, the earliest versions of any portion of the Old Testament were Aramaic translations. They were produced to meet the needs of Jewish communities whose knowledge of Hebrew was insufficient to make fully intelligible to them the scripture as read in public or in private. Aramaic is a language closely akin to Hebrew but sufficiently different from it to make documents in the one language unintelligible to people who spoke colloquially only the other. From the eighth century B.C. Aramaic had begun to spread widely in the Near East and gradually to supersede the other Semitic languages both in popular and in official use. We find it appearing even in the text of the Hebrew Bible in certain chapters of Ezra and Daniel. The documents surviving to us from the Jewish community that dwelt at Elephantine in the Persian period are in Aramaic; a number of Aramaic expressions are used in the New Testament, and it is the language of the Gemara of the Talmud. Where Jewish communities were predominantly Aramaic speaking there would arise the need of translation from Hebrew into the locally spoken Aramaic. Perhaps we may see a beginning of this practice in Neh. 8:8, where it says, "They read the book of the law of God distinctly, and they gave the sense so that they understood the reading."

The word Targum means "translation." In early cuneiform inscriptions we read of the *targamānû* who interpreted for foreigners at the court, and who was the forerunner of the modern consular dragoman. His translations were for the most part oral, and it would seem that in Jewish circles the *Turgᵉmān* or *Mᵉthurgᵉmān* at first stood by the reader, and as the scripture was read, gave the sense in the local Aramaic dialect. Before long the office became so important as to need regulation. The regulation is recorded in Megilla 4:4, which says the translation is to be verse by verse for the Law, and section by section for the Prophets. This practice died out only when Aramaic itself ceased to be the vernacular of the congregations. The Targums which have survived are all of Palestinian origin. Undoubtedly the rendering was at first quite free, each *Mᵉthurgᵉmān* making his translation as he went along. In time, however, conventional ways of translating various passages would come to be recognized as the accepted Targum. For long there was a strong prejudice against writing these Targums, and when they did come to be written down, they represented the labors of many minds, even though the actual fixing of the form may have been the work of one man. Neither Origen nor Jerome seems to have known of any written Targum, though we have reference to a written Targum on Job in the days of Gamaliel I. The most important Targum was that on the Pentateuch. There seems to have been an old paraphrastic Targum to the Pentateuch of the second century A.D., which has come down to us in two forms. In Babylonia it was worked over both in language and in form, and under the name of Targum of Onkelos became the official Babylonian Targum. It is on the whole a literal translation, turning to paraphrase only in the poetical portions, but it was brought into conformity with the text fixed by Akiba's school, and edited to remove all anthropomorphisms and expressions thought to be unseemly. A Masorah grew up in connection with this Targum. In Palestine itself the older Targum had a final redaction in the seventh century to form the Targum of pseudo-Jonathan. Both in diction and content this more closely resembles the older Targum than does that of Onkelos. It was the Jerusalem Targum. Fragments of another Jerusalem Targum have survived, though it is difficult to say whether it represents a separate Targum or another recension of some of the pseudo-Jonathan material. The chief Targum to the Prophets also received its final form in Babylonia, though it originated in Palestine. It is probably of the second century, and goes under the name of Jonathan ben Uzziel, though in its present form it cannot be earlier than the fifth century. Portions of a Jerusalem Targum to the Prophets are also extant. The Targums to the Hagiographa seem to be of Palestinian origin. Those to Psalms and Job are early and contain a number of variants from the Masoretic text, some of which agree with the Septuagint or the Peshitta. That on Proverbs is but a working over of the Peshitta version. To Esther there are two Targums which, like those to the Megilloth in general, are in the nature of haggadic paraphrase. There is a haggadic Targum to Chronicles, but apparently none to Ezra-Nehemiah or to Daniel.

C. The Greek Versions.—Although the history of the Greek versions is for the most part a history of their use in the Christian church, they were produced in the first instance to serve Jewish groups, particularly those in the Diaspora, whose language of daily intercourse and of literary expression was Greek. That such groups normally used Greek in connection with their religious life is made evident by the number of tombstone and synagogue inscriptions that are in Greek. Paul on his missionary journeys addressed congregations of Jewish people in Greek. The writer of the Epistle to the Hebrews, like the writer of the encyclical letter of I Peter, in addressing Jews of the Diaspora uses Greek. Doubtless in all these communities there would have been some who understood Hebrew, but there would also have been many who would need a translation of the Hebrew scriptures into the locally used Greek. As in the case of the Aramaic Targum this need would in all probability have been met at first by someone standing up by the reader and making a running translation verse by verse, or section by section, as the scripture was read. The Greek version would thus have begun as a Greek Targum. Since Alexander's time, however, Greek had come to be more and more a world

language, and we cannot set aside the possibility that some Jewish groups, quite apart from practical considerations within the community, might have wished to have their scripture made available to non-Jews in the Greek, which was the cultural language of their day.

It would seem that the need for a Greek version of the Hebrew scriptures first became apparent in Egypt, for ·it is there that from about the middle of the third century B.C. we begin to come upon traces of such versions. They were not official versions, and at times they seem to be somewhat paraphrastic renderings of the Hebrew. Apparently the Law was the first section to receive attention and to be translated with considerable care. Different translations of the Law circulated in written form, and about the middle of the second century B.C. an attempt was made to supersede them by an official version of the Law in Greek. The Letter of Aristeas (*ca.* 110 B.C.), which purports to be an account of the way in which a translation into Greek was made by seventy-two learned elders from Palestine for the royal library of Ptolemy Philadelphus (285-247 B.C.), is really an account of this later venture. It makes quite clear (*a*) that there were in use among the Jews of Egypt certain Greek versions of the Law which for one reason or another were considered to be unsatisfactory; (*b*) that at Alexandria a "revision committee" had made a concerted effort to produce a more satisfactory version; and (*c*) that a serious attempt was made to have this revised version generally accepted.

From the story of the seventy-two translators this version later came to bear the name Septuagint (LXX). Both Philo and Josephus speak of it in words of high praise; Philo, indeed, goes so far as to say that its authors were not mere translators but could justly be called prophets. Not so long after this, however, we find the rabbis asserting that the day on which the elders wrote out the Law for Ptolemy in Greek was disastrous for Israel. There are two reasons for this change of opinion. The first is that meanwhile, under the influence of Akiba's school, a new recension of the Hebrew text had been made, so that the Greek whose fidelity to the older form of Hebrew text had filled Philo with amazement was now outdated. Second, the Christian church had taken over the Greek translation as its own text of the Old Testament, and had applied the name "Septuagint" (previously used only for the Law) to all parts of the Greek Bible, including the books which had received no place in the Hebrew canon fixed at Jamnia. Moreover, the church in its preaching was insistent that this Greek text was the authentic word of God. As a result of these developments, the Jews made new Greek translations which followed the newly established Hebrew text, and since they took no further interest in the Septuagint, the history of this Greek version from then on became that of a text transmitted in the Christian community by the hands of Christian scribes.

Though the Law was the first part to be translated into Greek, and may have been circulating as early as 250 B.C., we have evidence of a Greek version of other parts of the Old Testament early in the second century B.C., and the grandson of Jesus ben Sirach, writing about 130 B.C., mentioned "the Law, and the Prophets, and the rest of the books" as current in a Greek version. To judge by the Septuagint that has come down to us, the historical books were translated with much more freedom than had been the case with the Law, and the translators of the Prophets frequently gave a mere paraphrase of the text. The Psalter has been well translated, though an extra psalm was added to the collection. The rest of the Hagiographa give the impression of having been translated as individual books at different times and by different hands. A number of details suggest that though the Law and most of the Hagiographa were translated in Egypt, the Prophets may have been translated in Asia.

As the Septuagint continued to be copied by Christian scribes, it did not escape the usual types of scribal corruption. In places, indeed, there was a little tampering with the text in the interests of Christian teaching. For example, in Ps. 96:10 (LXX 95:10) some scribes added ἀπὸ ξύλου to the words ὁ κύριος ἐβασίλευσεν to make it clear that the reference is to the Messiah ruling from the cross. What is more important, however, is that no uniform text of the Septuagint circulated in the early church. Origen was well aware of this, as well as of the fact that the texts used in the church by no means represented the Hebrew text in the hands of the Jews, whereas there were other Greek translations which did follow that text. Origen, therefore, set himself to gather materials as a basis for providing a uniform text of the Greek Old Testament for use in the church. This was his great Hexapla, in whose six columns he assembled the Hebrew text used by his Jewish teachers, a Greek transliteration of the same, the versions of Aquila, Symmachus, and Theodotion, and a text of the Christian Septuagint with his own critical emendations. For some of the books, where he had the material, he added a fifth, sixth, and even seventh Greek version. His own work was in the fifth column, and he carefully marked his emenda-

tions and his critical work on the text. This was not his critical edition of the Septuagint, but only his preparation for such an edition. Later scribes, however, most unfortunately treated this fifth column as though it were a true Septuagint text, and copied it without including the critical signs. Thus, we do not know what manuscripts Origen used for the text of his fifth column. Moreover, except for those passages where we have help from the Syro-Hexapla or some other source, we are unable to distinguish with certainty between his text and his emendations.

Origen was not the only scholar who attempted a revision of the Septuagint. When Jerome took up his work in the fourth century, there were four types of text of the Greek Old Testament in circulation: (a) the unrevised text as it had been circulating in various forms before Origen's day; (b) the hexaplarian text that had been derived from Origen's fifth column; (c) a recension made by Lucian of Antioch, about 300, which appears to have been much used in the area between Antioch and Constantinople; and (d) a Hesychian revision, of approximately the same date as that of Lucian, which was in use in Egypt. Manuscripts of the Septuagint are numerous, but it is only in modern times that research has reached a point where it is possible to classify them according to their type and lay the foundation for a critical edition.

Of the three versions made from the revised Hebrew text of the first century A.D., and utilized by Origen in his Hexapla, only fragments survive. That made by Aquila of Pontus, about 130 A.D., apparently under the influence of the school of Akiba, was an extremely literal translation, so literal that it is not Greek but jargon, rendering the Hebrew into Greek word by word with no regard for Greek idiom. That of Symmachus the Ebionite, made about 170, is in good Greek, and was highly regarded by Jerome. Both Symmachus and Aquila translated directly from the Hebrew text, but the new version of Theodotion, about 185, was rather a revision of an earlier Greek translation in the light of the current Hebrew text. What survives of these was printed by Frederick Field in his edition of Origen's Hexapla, and only small fragments have come to light since that time.

D. The Syriac Versions.—Just as Greek-speaking Jews and Christians needed an Old Testament in Greek, so Syriac-speaking Jews and Christians came to need a version in their vernacular. All the early Syriac manuscripts represent a version which has been known since the ninth century as the Peshitta ("common" or "simple"). These manuscripts come from the fifth and sixth centuries, but the quotations in Aphraates and Ephraem Syrus represent the same version, which was clearly the text commonly used in the Syriac-speaking churches from the fourth century onward, and may have originated as early as the second century. Of its origin we know nothing. Even so great a scholar as Theodore of Mopsuestia (d. 428) did not know when or by whom it was made. Nor do we know whether its name means "common" in the sense of a vulgate edition, or "simple," in contrast with the Syro-Hexapla. Its manuscript tradition is not uniform, but the version gradually took on a stereotyped form in the language of Edessa, which was used for a great proportion of Syriac ecclesiastical literature. A number of details suggest that it was originally a Jewish version, perhaps at first a Syriac Targum, but it was taken over by the Syriac-speaking Christians, and in its transmission has been influenced by the Septuagint. The translation is by different hands and varies considerably in the different books. The translation of the Pentateuch is fairly literal, whereas that of Ruth is a mere paraphrase. There is a Masorah to the Peshitta which, however, differs somewhat in Jacobite manuscripts from what is given in Nestorian manuscripts. There is no Masorah to Chronicles, Ezra-Nehemiah, or Esther, a fact which suggests that they were later additions to the Syriac Bible. The text of Chronicles, indeed, resembles a Targum. The text of the Peshitta has been more than once revised but never in a systematic fashion.

The manuscripts present considerable variety in the number of books and in the order in which they are placed. Some manuscripts have, after the Pentateuch, a *Liber Sessionum,* comprising the books of Joshua, Judges, Job, Samuel and Kings, Proverbs, Ecclesiasticus, Ecclesiastes, Ruth, and Song of Songs. In other manuscripts Ruth, Esther, Judith, and Susannah are grouped together as the Book of Women. The Psalter is commonly found divided into twenty sections. Many manuscripts contain as well a variety of pseudepigraphic works.

The Peshitta was translated from the Hebrew, but all the other Syriac versions were made from the Septuagint. Paul of Tella in 616-17 translated into Syriac Origen's Hexapla, which is the above-mentioned Syro-Hexapla. Of these other versions, whether Nestorian or Jacobite, and of the Melkite version known as the Christian-Palestinian, we have only fragments.

E. The Latin Versions.—Very little is known about the origin of the Latin versions save that they were translated from the Septuagint. Latin was the vernacular of the church in North Africa westward from Cyrenaica, and apparently a number of Latin translations of various parts of the Old Testament were produced in the second century for the use of Christian communities in this area. Only fragments of these remain. The text underlying them has some striking resemblances to the type of text we find in Lucian's recension of the Greek. Jerome made a revision of this Old Latin translation. At first he labored at revising it from the Septuagint, but later he worked from the Hebrew text. His Vulgate, however, is not a direct translation from the Hebrew, for he felt obliged to consider the feelings of a church used to the Old Latin translations, and consequently he used the Old Latin and the Greek versions as well as the Hebrew, and thus produced a curiously mixed text. It met with considerable opposition when it appeared, but by the seventh century it had become the Bible of the Roman Church. It has undergone several recensions, and a truly critical edition of it is now in progress.

F. The Coptic Versions.—The Christians of Egypt, like the Egyptian Jews, used the Greek Bible. With the spread of Christianity among communities less familiar with Greek there came the need of a translation into the vernacular of the people. In the third and fourth centuries a number of translations of portions of the Bible were made into different dialects of Coptic. The first to attain a fixed form was that in the Sahidic dialect of Upper Egypt. It was made from the Septuagint, perhaps from the Hesychian recension, though there has been revision from the Hebrew, or from some source that knew the Hebrew. As various books were translated at different times by different hands, we should perhaps speak of the Sahidic versions. Later came a translation into the Bohairic dialect of Lower Egypt. This is the version which is used today in the Coptic churches. There are fragments of translations into other dialects, such as the Fayyumic of Middle Egypt, and the Akhmimic, formerly spoken around Akhmim in Upper Egypt.

G. The Armenian Version.—This is a uniform version made from the Septuagint in the fifth century for the use of the national Armenian church. Legend tells of early saints laboring at a translation from the Syriac, but the current version is clearly a translation from Greek manuscripts of the hexaplarian type, though this has been revised from the Peshitta so as to supplement and correct the Septuagint. In places it supports the Septuagint against the Peshitta, and in places it follows the Masoretic text against both, so that some have thought that its revisers must have used the Hebrew also.

The manuscripts differ widely in extent and arrangement. Various groups of apocryphal and pseudepigraphic material are included in most manuscripts, and commonly the manuscripts have prefaces to the various books.

H. The Arabic Versions.—It is not certain that any portion of the Bible was translated into Arabic before the Moslem conquest in the seventh century. After the Moslem conquest Arabic translations were needed by both Jewish and Christian communities, and we have a bewildering variety of translations of various portions of the Bible, some made directly from the Hebrew, others from the Greek, Syriac, Coptic, Samaritan, and even from the Latin. We read of John I, Jacobite patriarch of Antioch (d. 648), laboring at such a translation; and another John, bishop of Seville in Spain (*ca.* 724), is said to have made one for Arabicized Christians and Moors in the West. Moslem writers refer to a number of Arabic versions made in the ninth and tenth centuries. For the Jews, Saadia Gaon (d. 942) made a translation of most of the books of the Old Testament. It is a free translation, frequently following the Targums, and is curious in that it has a tendency to use Arabic technical terms, and to replace biblical place names by others more familiar to his contemporaries. Saadia's version was used by the Samaritans in making their Arabic version from the Samaritan Pentateuch; the Qaraites, however, rejected it, and made numerous translations of their own. The translations from Greek, Syriac, and Coptic are all Christian, some Nestorian, some Jacobite, and some Melkite. The most famous of them is that which bears the name of Ibn al-Assal. Critical work on the Arabic versions has only begun.

J. The Ethiopic Version.—This is a Christian version made originally from the Septuagint for the use of the native church of Abyssinia. Some translation work would seem to have been done as early as the fifth century, but the texts we have represent later translations by several hands, some of whom used the Syriac, and perhaps also the Hebrew, as an aid in their endeavor to give a faithful rendering of the text. The work was probably completed before the eighth century, but was afterwards revised on the basis of Arabic versions, so that all the extant manuscripts present a mixed text. This version has, even from early times, included a number of writings, such as Jubilees and Enoch, not usually included in the canon of the Old Testament.

K. The Georgian Version.—In its early days the Georgian church depended very largely on the Armenian church. For this reason its Bible is a translation from the Armenian, though it has been influenced by the Syriac in revision even more than the Armenian itself. The translation dates from the fifth century and is by many hands. There have been various later recensions, at least of some of the books, but too little critical work has been done on this version to permit any certain conclusions as to its history.

Other versions in these various languages, as in other languages of the East and the West, are too late to be of any interest for the recovery of the text.

L. Conclusion.—In spite of these defects the older versions are useful tools to the student of the Old Testament, providing him with valuable evidence on such important matters as text, exegesis, and canon.

(*a*) A translation presupposes a text from which it has been translated, and it is often possible to reconstruct with a fair degree of accuracy the original text from which a passage has been translated. Manuscripts, even of books of Scripture, are subject in transmission to accident, to interpolation, to alteration, and to various types of textual corruption. In the case of the Old Testament, many manuscripts of the versions, which are much older than most of the manuscripts of the Hebrew text, at times reveal places where lacunae, conflations or transpositions, and other kinds of scribal confusions and alterations have affected the present Hebrew text.

For example, in Josh. 15:59; Judg. 16:13 ff.; I Sam. 12:8; 14:42, lacunae in the Hebrew text, due apparently to homoeoteleuton, can be supplied from the Greek. In Gen. 4:8, the words of Cain are not given, though the ויאמר leads us to expect them. The Samaritan text supplies, "Let us go into the field," and this is the reading in the Septuagint, the Targum, the Peshitta, and the Latin of both the Vulgate and Jerome. In II Sam. 24:6, "unto the land of Tahtim-hodshi" is meaningless, but the Greek, "unto the land of the Hittites, even to Kadesh," enables us to correct תחתים חדשי to החתים קדשה. In Job 7:20, we have a scribal alteration of the text from motives of piety, which makes our text represent Job as saying, "I am a burden to myself." The Greek ἐπὶ σοί, however, shows that the present awkward עלי was originally עליך, "unto thee." In Ps. 16:2 our text reads אמרת, "thou hast said," and so the King James Version has to supply "O my soul" to explain the feminine singular. The Septuagint (15:2) has εἶπα, "I said," that is, אמרתי, which gives us the original reading. In Prov. 10:10*b*, "but a prating fool shall fall" has been copied by the scribe from vs. 8*b* in mistake for the original ending of this verse. The original ending, however, is preserved in the Septuagint, ὁ δὲ ἐλέγχων μετὰ παρρησίας εἰρηνοποιεῖ.

Both the Septuagint and the Peshitta show in many passages that the text before their translators was in *scriptio continua* without word separation, for the translator has divided in a way which makes sense (sometimes better sense) but which is different from the way in which the words are separated in the standard Hebrew text. For example, in Jer. 46:15 our text reads מדוע נסחף, but the Septuagint ἔφυγεν ὁ ἆπις shows that they divided it מדוע נס חף, "why hath Apis fled?" In Ps. 44:4 our text reads אלהים צוה, but the Septuagint ὁ θεός μου, ὁ ἐντελλόμενος shows that they divided it אלהי מצוה, as did the Peshitta.

There are also many places where the versions show that in the text before the translator the *matres lectionis* were used differently from the way in which we find them in our present Hebrew text. For example, in Job 19:18 our text has עוילים, "young children," but the Septuagint εἰς τὸν αἰῶνα assumes a text עולם. In the superscription to Ps. 5 we have אל-הנחילות, "on wind instruments," but the Septuagint ὑπὲρ τῆς κληρονομούσης, "for an inheritance," assumes a text אל-הנחלות.

(*b*) A translator is endeavoring to give the meaning of the text before him, so that his translation shows how he himself understood the text and possibly how it was generally understood in his day or in his area. As he stands many generations nearer the original than we do, his understanding of the text before him can often aid us in matters of exegesis. For example, in Dan. 10:1 the King James Version follows the later Jewish commentators in translating וצבא גדול as "but the time appointed was long." The Greek versions, the Peshitta, and the Vulgate, however, show that צבא was taken in their day to have its usual meaning of "force," and the Revised Standard Version has gone back to this by translating "great conflict."

(*c*) Finally, a version is useful in throwing light on such questions as the arrangement and order of books within the collection, the presence or absence of certain books in one locality or another, and at times can give us evidence as to the type of text in use in different areas at different periods.

VII. Selected Bibliography

BUHL, FRANTS. Article, "Bible Text," in S. M. Jackson, ed. *The New Schaff-Herzog Encyclopedia*. New York: Funk & Wagnalls, 1908. Vol. II, pp. 94-99.

————. *Canon and Text of the Old Testament*, tr. John Macpherson. Edinburgh: T. & T. Clark, 1892.

DRIVER, S. R. *Notes on the Hebrew Text of the Books of Samuel*. Oxford: Clarendon Press, 1890.

GEDEN, A. S. *Outlines of Introduction to the Hebrew Bible*. Edinburgh: T. & T. Clark, 1909.

GINSBURG, C. H. *Introduction to the Masoretico-Critical Edition of the Hebrew Bible*. London: Trinitarian Bible Society, 1897.

GORDIS, ROBERT. *The Biblical Text in the Making*. Philadelphia: Dropsie College for Hebrew & Cognate Learning, 1937.

GOTTHEIL, RICHARD. Articles, "Bible Editions" and "Bible Translations," in *The Jewish Encyclopedia*. New York: Funk & Wagnalls, 1906. Vol. III, pp. 154-62, 185-97.

KAHLE, PAUL. *The Cairo Geniza*. London: British Academy, 1947.

KENNEDY, JAMES. *An Aid to the Textual Amendment of the Old Testament*. Edinburgh: T. & T. Clark, 1928.

KENYON, FREDERIC GEORGE. *Recent Developments in the Textual Criticism of the Greek Bible*. London: British Academy, 1933.

————. *The Text of the Greek Bible*. London: Duckworth, 1937.

NAVILLE, E. H. *The Text of the Old Testament*. London: British Academy, 1916.

NESTLE, E. Article, "Bible Versions," in S. M. Jackson, ed., *The New Schaff-Herzog Encyclopedia*. New York: Funk & Wagnalls, 1908. Vol. II, pp. 115-29.

OTTLEY, R. R. *A Handbook to the Septuagint*. London: Methuen & Co., 1920.

REIDER, JOSEPH. *Prolegomena to a Greek-Hebrew and Hebrew-Greek Index to Aquila*. Philadelphia: Dropsie College for Hebrew & Cognate Learning, 1913.

ROBERTS, B. J. *The Old Testament Text and Versions*. Cardiff: University of Wales Press, 1951.

STRACK, H. L. Article, "Text of the Old Testament," in James Hastings, ed. *Dictionary of the Bible*. New York: Charles Scribner's Sons, 1904. Vol. IV, pp. 726-32.

SWETE, H. B. *An Introduction to the Old Testament in Greek*. Cambridge: University Press, 1914.

WEIR, T. H. *A Short History of the Hebrew Text of the Old Testament*. London: Williams & Norgate, 1899.

THE CANON
OF THE NEW TESTAMENT

by EDGAR J. GOODSPEED

Christianity originated and developed in the presence of the Jewish scriptures, or what we know as the Old Testament, first in their original Hebrew but very soon in the Greek version of them which we call the Septuagint. It was this Greek form of the Jewish scriptures, including as it did the books known as the Apocrypha, that became the basis of the Bible of the early church, and was gradually supplemented by a collection of Christian writings which we know as the New Testament. How did this Christian collection arise? What steps can we trace in its origin and growth? These books were written in Greek at various stages of the progress of the Greek mission, and they came to be accepted as a standard list or canon of Christian authorities. But what led to their collection into a definite body, and their association with the older Jewish scriptures in what we know as the Bible? The story of their collection and authorization is called the history of the canon.

I. Early Collections

That the early church should have made itself an authoritative scripture and placed it side by side with the Old Testament is from some points of view strange. It already had an extensive literature in the Jewish scriptures, which did not yet form a single book, as with us, but took the form of twenty-five or thirty separate scrolls. The basic conviction of primitive Christianity, moreover, was that it possessed an inner guide, the Spirit of God, the mind of Christ, far superior to written rules and records. Yet despite these facts, it gradually came to acknowl-

edge a Christian collection of books, which it revered just as much as it did the old Hebrew scriptures, and even more, for as Adolf von Harnack observed, the Old Testament was always interpreted to agree with the New, not the New to agree with the Old.

The books of the New Testament were not recognized as scripture from the moment of their origin, but came only gradually to such recognition. The letters of Paul were written to meet definite acute situations in the life of the Pauline churches, and when those situations had passed the letters lost interest for the next generation. It is a striking fact that the Gospels of Matthew, Mark, and Luke and even the Acts of the Apostles show no acquaintance with the letters of Paul. But the Revelation of John reflects them in a startling manner, for though it is an apocalypse it opens with a collection of Christian letters to churches, seven in number, preceded by a general letter to all seven. These letters were not really sent individually to the churches addressed in them, and then later reassembled by the writer through an afterthought; they were frankly and obviously written as a collection, and published as the portal of the Revelation. The writer has evidently seen the Pauline collection of seven letters to Christian churches and has been so impressed that he makes that literary device the façade of his apocalypse. The fact that he begins with a general letter to all seven strongly suggests that the Pauline collection as he knew it, toward A.D. 95, began with a general letter to all seven of the churches Paul wrote to; and indeed Ephe-

63

sians is most naturally understood as just such a general letter. (See Vol. IX, pp. 356-58 and on Ephesians, Vol. X.)

The letter of Clement of Rome to the Corinthians, written about A.D. 95, also gives clear evidence of acquaintance with a collection of Paul's letters, which probably included Ephesians, Romans, I and II Corinthians, Galatians, Philippians, Colossians, I and II Thessalonians, and Philemon, the last being included as a church letter to the Laodiceans. This made a collection of ten letters to seven churches, Ephesians being the introductory letter to Christians generally. This letter collection was not thought of as scripture. It was read for its religious value, with no thought as yet that it was authoritative or inspired.

The rise of the Synoptic Gospels—Mark and the Gospels of Matthew and of Luke so largely based upon it—between A.D. 70 and 90 was followed soon after A.D. 100 by the Gospel of John, in which the gospel narrative was strongly colored by ideas gathered from the collected letters of Paul. The new Gospel was designed to meet the religious needs of the Greek public which had become the field of the Christian mission, and soon after its appearance, certainly by A.D. 120, it was combined with the three earlier Gospels into the great quartet we know so well. The primary object of making and publishing this collection was to bring the immense religious values of all the Gospels freshly to the attention of Greek Christianity, but in the course of a generation they won a place in Christian worship side by side with the Jewish Bible, and by A.D. 150 these "memoirs of the apostles," as they were called, were read at services of public worship in Rome along with the writings of the prophets.

A few years earlier Marcion, an original and energetic layman of Sinope in Pontus, anxious to unite the scattered churches and shake off Judaism, had undertaken to replace the Jewish scriptures in Christian worship by a Christian scripture made up of the Gospel of Luke and the ten letters of Paul. Partly as a result of this Marcionite usage the letters of Paul came to hold a place side by side with the four Gospels in public worship. This stage is reflected in Athenagoras, the Athenian apologist (ca. A.D. 177), who makes use of the fourfold Gospel and the ten letters of Paul as Christian authorities, though for him they fall a little short of being inspired scripture like the prophets. Theophilus of Antioch (A.D. 180-90) goes a little further in his esteem for the Gospels, though even he does not quite admit them to what he calls the Holy Scriptures. He highly valued the letters of Paul, but not quite so highly as he did the Gospels. So in his day in Antioch the Jewish scriptures were still pre-eminent, though the Gospels too were considered inspired, and to a less degree the letters of Paul. With Theophilus we are in fact on the threshold of the New Testament.

The martyrs at Scili in North Africa, in A.D. 180, say that they kept the letters of Paul in their church chest, with their church "books" (βιβλία, or "Bible"), by which they must have meant the Jewish scriptures and the four Gospels. We gather thus that the Gospels were in their Bible and that Paul's letters were not; but these letters were in the chest, and therefore were evidently read in church from time to time. In the Scilitan chest, in fact, we can see Paul's letters actually entering the Bible. They were not yet in the "books," but they were in the chest which contained the books.

In A.D. 170-80 Melito of Sardis speaks of the Jewish scriptures as the books of the Old Covenant, or Testament, being evidently on the verge of using the phrase "Old Testament" in a literary sense just as we do. From that use it would seem a short step to using the phrase "New Testament" in the same sense. How did that step come to be taken?

II. The First New Testament

The series of sectarian movements that successively obscured the sky of second-century Christianity—Docetism, Marcionism, Gnosticism, Montanism—led at length to a powerful effort on the part of general, nonschismatic Christianity to exert and express itself. Marcion had attempted to organize the churches, but in too drastic and partisan a spirit. A generation after his day the pretensions of Montanism, with its exaggerated claims of prophetic gifts, precipitated a general movement toward standardization and co-operation among the churches. Types of polity, doctrine, and scripture which had established themselves in historic churches were now recognized as standard and were adopted by all. The Gospels and the letters of Paul were already being read in public worship; now they are definitely recognized as forming the core of a New Testament scripture to stand side by side with the Old. The two collections are supplemented and bound together by the book of Acts and two or three or four letters which bore the names of apostles, Peter, John, Jude. The new scripture was concluded by one or two apocalypses—John, Peter, Hermas.

The sources of our information at this stage of the development of the canon are Irenaeus, Tertullian, and a document containing a list of New Testament books which is known as the Muratorian Fragment. Irenaeus of Lyons wrote his *Refutation of Gnosticism* probably between

180 and 189. He accepted I Peter and I John (the latter including II John and probably III John as well, which are after all little more than covering letters for I John). He accepted the Revelation of John and the Shepherd of Hermas. Tertullian of Carthage wrote his voluminous works between A.D. 197 and 223. He used I Peter, I John, and Jude as scripture, and accepted the Revelation of John, and at first the Shepherd of Hermas, though later in life he rejected it with the utmost scorn. The Muratorian Fragment on the canon, so called after the Italian scholar who first published it from a Milan manuscript in 1740, is of unknown authorship, though it may be from the hand of Victor, bishop of Rome about A.D. 200. At any rate it seems clearly to be a Roman canon of about that period and has an authoritative ring. It includes two letters of John and one of Jude, and the Revelations of John and of Peter, but admits that some will not have the Revelation of Peter read in church.

It is clear that Lyons, Carthage, and Rome were not wholly agreed toward the end of the second century upon the precise contents of their New Testaments, though the major bodies of scripture making it up were well recognized, and all contained I John and the Revelation of John. It is most striking that with all of them the letters of Paul included the letters to Timothy and to Titus (but not the Epistle to the Hebrews). It seems clear, however, that Timothy and Titus were written in the second century to disclaim Marcion and contemporary schisms, just as the baptismal confession now adopted (the "Apostles' Creed") disavowed the main items in Marcion's heretical views.

III. Early Alexandrian Canons

The end of the second and beginning of the third centuries witnessed the activity of Clement of Alexandria, the head of the famous Christian school there. Egypt was the home of the early apocryphal gospels of the Hebrews and of the Egyptians, which were evidently in use in Egypt by A.D. 150, before the four Gospels were introduced there and gradually superseded them. The loss of his famous work called the *Outlines*, which contained accounts of the books of scripture, impairs our view of Clement's position on scripture, but from his other works we can see that he accepted a larger list of New Testament books than was accepted at Rome. He knew the four Gospels and regarded them as scripture; but he was also acquainted with the gospels of the Hebrews and of the Egyptians and the Traditions of Matthias, though he did not think of them as scripture. His list of Paul's letters included not only the ten of the original list and the three Pastorals, I and II Timothy,

and Titus, but also the Epistle to the Hebrews. This raised the number of Pauline letters to fourteen.

Besides the four Gospels and these fourteen letters of Paul, Clement also accepted an enlarged body of general letters, for he accepted not only I Peter, I and II John, and Jude, but also I Clement and Barnabas, as works of apostolic authority. We remember that I and II Clement stand at the end of the New Testament in the Alexandrian manuscript of the fifth century, and that Barnabas follows the Revelation of John in the Sinaitic manuscript of the fourth. These are our oldest complete manuscripts of the Greek New Testament. They evidently reflect Egyptian canons of the fourth and fifth centuries.

Clement has a striking list of apocalypses in his scripture, for he accepted not only the Revelation of John, but also that of Peter and the Shepherd of Hermas. The Shepherd had been written in Rome and was at first highly prized there; but the prophetic pretensions of Montanism soon led to its eclipse. What Clement thought of the Acts is not entirely clear. He used it freely and spoke of it as the work of Luke. In fact, he used it very much as he did the general letters, taking its acceptance for granted.

But Clement also made free use of the so-called Preaching of Peter, perhaps the earliest of Christian apologies. "Peter says in his Preaching" is the way Clement quotes it. He once quotes a line from the Teaching of the Apostles as scripture, and cites as scripture other ancient sayings which are otherwise unknown. So we are unable to define his canon sharply. He had no such rigid list of New Testament books as the churches of Rome and Africa had in his day. He shows the New Testament scripture not yet fully formed in Egypt, but in process of formation.

IV. The Times of Origen

Severus' persecution in A.D. 202 forced so many Christian leaders out of Alexandria that a youth of eighteen named Origen became head of the Christian school there, and for more than fifty years he wrote and taught, first in Alexandria and later in Caesarea. A rich friend named Ambrosius in later years provided him with such a number of stenographers and copyists that everything he wrote was immediately published, and so Origen became the most voluminous of Christian writers. He realized the confusion in the churches about the precise contents of the New Testament, and while he did not seek to settle the problem, he analyzed it by classifying the canonical books as "accepted" or "disputed." The accepted or acknowledged books—that is, accepted by all churches—were twenty-two in number: the four Gospels, fourteen letters of Paul, the Acts of the Apostles, two general letters (I Peter and I John), and one apocalypse (the Revelation of John). We know that Hebrews was not yet accepted in the West, but Origen included it in his list of acknowledged books nevertheless.

Origen's own New Testament, however, was larger than this; it included also the "disputed" books, that is, some books which he knew some churches did not accept. These were James, II and III John, Jude, II Peter, and Barnabas. James and II Peter appear first in the New Testament in this "disputed" list. And to the Revelation of John, Origen added the Shepherd of Hermas, so that the contents of his own New Testament, comprising both the acknowledged and the disputed books, were therefore exactly those of the Sinaitic manuscript, the oldest complete Greek Testament known, written about a century after Origen's death, which ends with Barnabas and the Shepherd of Hermas.

Origen's Roman contemporary Hippolytus (ca. 235), however, was more conservative. Like his teacher Irenaeus, Hippolytus accepted as his New Testament only twenty-two books. He did not accept Hebrews as one of the letters of Paul, and included only three general letters (I Peter, I and II John) and one apocalypse, that of John, in his New Testament. Yet Hippolytus knew and used a number of other Christian books which were sometimes included by others —Hebrews, the Shepherd, the Revelation of Peter, II Peter, the Acts of Paul, James, and Jude.

The Roman church had always been a Greek church, and it was so still in the days of Hippolytus. But he was the last Roman father to write in Greek. About the middle of the third century we find Novatian of Rome and Cyprian of Carthage writing to each other in Latin, and Latin remained thenceforth the language of the church at Rome. Their letters and treatises show that they, like Hippolytus, still held the primitive Roman canon of twenty-two books, unshaken by the example of the Alexandrian fathers, Clement and Origen.

Origen was driven from Alexandria by his own bishop in A.D. 230, and withdrew to Caesarea; a year later Dionysius became head of the famous school at Alexandria, continuing in that position until A.D. 247, when he became bishop of Alexandria. His episcopate lasted for seventeen years, A.D. 247-264, and he met the troubled situation of his times with such skill and vigor that he came to be considered Dionysius the Great. He wrote about the Revelation of John with such penetration and force

that he considerably modified Eastern opinion of it; for while he had the highest esteem for the book, he could not agree that it was written by the author of the Gospel of John. This keen perception of his led to the rejection of the Revelation by a large part of the Eastern church; of the manuscripts of the Greek Testament extant today about two thirds omit it.

V. Eusebius of Caesarea

A few years later the Christian library established at Caesarea by Pamphilus was visited and studied by Eusebius, who afterward became bishop of Caesarea, attended the Council of Nicaea in 325, and wrote a life of Constantine. In his great *Church History*, completed in A.D. 326, he fortunately included an account of the principal writers and writings of the three preceding centuries, particularly where they spoke on the books of the New Testament. He was well aware of the wide disagreement among churches and Christian leaders as to just what books should be included in the canon, and he followed Origen in seeking to organize the whole body of such literature in such a way as to do justice to all sides. But while he followed Origen's division of the books into "acknowledged" and "disputed," he divided the latter class into those that he accepted and those that he rejected. In order to find his own New Testament list, therefore, we must take his "acknowledged" list and add to it the books in his "disputed" list which he did not call "rejected."

Eusebius accepted the four Gospels and the Acts, fourteen letters of Paul (including Hebrews), I John, I Peter. Of the disputed books, Eusebius accepted James, Jude, II Peter, II and III John, and as he put it, "if it really seem proper," the Revelation of John. This lingering doubt about the Revelation echoes the suspicion Dionysius had raised two generations before. It means much, however, that Eusebius admitted the Revelation to his "acknowledged" list. These built up his own New Testament to just the proportions of ours today.

The disputed books which Eusebius listed as "rejected" were the Acts of Paul, the Shepherd, the Revelation of Peter, the Letter of Barnabas, the Teaching of the Apostles. In referring to the Revelation of John, after acknowledging it "if it seem proper," he adds, "which some reject, but which some class with the accepted books."

He has another list of books definitely heretical, such as the Gospel of Peter, the Gospel of Thomas, the Traditions of Matthias, the Acts of Andrew, and the Acts of John. His objection to these books was that they were not of apostolic origin, such origin being decided on the basis of use by earlier church writers and freedom from schismatic bias.

VI. Egypt in the Fourth Century

A. The Clermont Manuscript List.—In the Codex Claromontanus, a sixth-century Greek-Latin manuscript of Paul's letters, some scribe inserted, just before Hebrews, a Latin list of the books of the Old and New Testaments. One gathers from its contents that it must have been translated from a Greek list of the books recognized as scripture in Egypt about A.D. 300. It includes the four Gospels and ten letters of Paul (evidently skipping Philippians, I and II Thessalonians, and probably Hebrews by mistake). It goes on with eight general letters (I and II Peter, James, I, II, and III John, Jude, and Barnabas). The list ends with three apocalypses and two books of acts—the Revelation of John, the Acts of the Apostles, the Shepherd of Hermas, the Acts of Paul, the Revelation of Peter. But a later hand has put a dash before I Peter (probably to indicate that the general letters began with it), and before Barnabas, the Shepherd, the Acts of Paul, and the Revelation of Peter (probably on the ground that these four were of questionable canonicity). Here we have plainly reflected a time when there was a group of books on the very edge of the New Testament, about which agreement had not been reached.

B. Athanasius.—This great bishop of Alexandria, in his annual Easter letter to the churches of his diocese in A.D. 367, gave a list of the books of scripture. His New Testament consisted of the four Gospels, the Acts, seven general letters, James, I and II Peter, I, II, and III John, and Jude; fourteen letters of Paul (including Hebrews), and the Revelation of John. This is just our canon today. But Athanasius adds a supplementary list of books "to be read by those just coming forward to receive oral instruction in religion." Of these, five are from the Apocrypha, the others being the Teaching of the Apostles and the Shepherd of Hermas. Athanasius had made use of the Shepherd in his early writings, but by 367, when he was more than seventy years old, he had given up the idea that it could be regarded as scripture. Athanasius' visits to the West had restored his confidence in the Revelation of John, though even there the Gothic New Testament of Ulfilas, a younger contemporary of Athanasius, did not include it.

C. Coptic New Testaments.—Of the Coptic versions, the oldest, the Sahidic, which began to take shape between A.D. 250 and 350, contained all the books of Athanasius' canon. But the Shepherd and I Clement also passed very early into Sahidic, and may have been regarded as scripture in Sahidic circles. The Acts of Paul was also translated into an Akhmimic-Sahidic version, which was until recently the chief source of its text.

D. Greek Uncial Codices.—Our three oldest and most complete manuscripts of the Greek New Testament also throw some light on the New Testament in Egypt in the fourth and fifth centuries. The oldest of them, the Vatican Codex, unfortunately breaks off at Heb. 9:14, so we cannot tell what books it may have had at the end. The Sinaitic Codex, written around A.D. 350 or soon after, ends with Barnabas and the Shepherd of Hermas, breaking off about one fourth of the way through the Shepherd. The Alexandrian Codex of the fifth century contains I and II Clement after the Revelation of John, but breaks off a little past the middle of II Clement. There was evidently uncertainty in Egypt about the precise contents of the New Testament even after the statement of Athanasius in A.D. 367. But later manuscripts settled down on the Athanasian list, except for the Revelation, which only about one third of the Greek manuscripts of the whole New Testament included.

VII. The Syriac New Testament

A. Tatian.—No less ancient in its origins than the Latin New Testament was the Syriac version, which had grown up and come to be accepted in the native church of Syria. There Tatian, soon after A.D. 170, had put forth a Syriac harmony of the Gospels called the Diatessaron. The Greek church of Antioch took measures a generation later to introduce the four separate Gospels into Syriac Christianity, but the Diatessaron maintained its ascendancy for almost two centuries longer. We know this because it is the form of the Gospels in the New Testament set forth in the fourth century Teaching of Addai. This work regards as also canonical only the letters of Paul and the Acts of the Apostles. Syriac Christianity was evidently behind the Greek and Latin churches in the forming of its New Testament.

B. Afrahat and Efrem.—About the middle of the fourth century Afrahat accepted the Diatessaron, the fourteen letters of Paul, with perhaps also the apocryphal III Corinthians, and the Acts of the Apostles. In the third quarter of the fourth century Efrem, a great figure in Syriac Christianity, had the same New Testament canon, and wrote a commentary on the Diatessaron and the fifteen letters of Paul, including III Corinthians. In fact this last book was carried over from Syriac into the ancient Armenian canon. Efrem knew other books accepted elsewhere as canonical, as well as the four separate Gospels, but the seventeen books listed above formed his New Testament. That the four separate Gospels, however, were gradually coming into favor in the Syrian churches is confirmed by a Syriac canon list of about A.D. 400, which consists of the four separate Gospels, the Acts, and fourteen letters of Paul, and ends with the words, "This is all." Evidently the Diatessaron and III Corinthians are on the way out.

C. Rabbula and the Peshitta New Testament. —A marked revision of the text and contents of the Syriac New Testament took place after A.D. 411, when Rabbula became bishop of Edessa (411-35). The result was the Peshitta New Testament, which from that time on was the authorized form in Syriac circles. It exists in many manuscripts, some from the fifth and sixth centuries, and includes the four Gospels, the Acts, three general letters (James, I Peter, I John) and fourteen letters of Paul. The substitution of the new scripture for the old was systematically carried out. When Theodoret became bishop of Cyrrhus on the Euphrates in 423, he made it his business to collect two hundred copies of the Diatessaron from his churches and put the four separate Gospels in their place. This work of substitution was so complete that no copy of the Syriac Diatessaron has yet been found. As a result, the Peshitta became almost at once the prevalent New Testament in Syria, for in the Syrian schisms of 431 and 489 it was accepted by both sides, and in all the subsequent centuries the Syrians have carried it with them in their migration over the world.

D. Later Syriac Versions.—To be sure the Peshitta underwent a series of revisions, the first of them (the Philoxenian) made in A.D. 508 by a certain Polycarp for a west Syrian bishop named Philoxenus, for whom the version was named. Being based on Greek manuscripts, it conformed to the Greek New Testament canon, and included all seven general letters and even the Revelation of John. Again in A.D. 616, this version was itself revised at Alexandria by Thomas of Harkel, on the basis of the Greek text. He naturally retained the Greek canon of scripture which he found in Philoxenus' version. In the sixth century another Syriac version was made, probably through agencies sponsored by Antioch, the Greek center of Syrian Christianity. The new version appeared in the Palestinian dialect of Syriac which prevailed about Antioch, and while we know it chiefly from the readings given in church lesson books, it is clear that it contained not only the four Gospels, the Acts, and fourteen letters of Paul, but also I and II Peter and I John, and hence probably all seven of the general letters. It did not contain the Revelation, however. The version was revived in the eleventh century, and from this period most of the surviving manuscripts of it come. In the twelfth century Dionysius bar

Salibi wrote a commentary on the Revelation, but in spite of this tacit acceptance of that book, and despite the three versions just mentioned, the Peshitta continued to prevail among the Syrians as they scattered over the world, and it has never admitted the other four general letters nor the Revelation to its canon.

VIII. The Work of the Councils

The church councils did not so much form the New Testament canon as recognize views about it that had taken shape in church usage. In A.D. 363 the Synod of Laodicea in Asia Minor forbade in Canon 59 the reading of uncanonical books. Canon 60, giving a list of canonical books, is probably a later addition, though from the fourth century. It contains all the books of our present New Testament except the Revelation. The Council of Hippo in Africa in A.D. 393 gives exactly our present list of twenty-seven books as scripture. The Synod of Carthage in A.D. 397 gives our present list of New Testament books, but adds that on martyrs' days their martyrdoms may be read. The next Council of Carthage, A.D. 419, repeats the list previously given, simply shifting Hebrews into the Pauline list.

The fathers of the fourth and fifth centuries differed among themselves about the unsettled status of Hebrews, the general letters, and the Revelation. Chrysostom (fl. 407), the greatest of the Greek preachers, the presbyter of Antioch who became patriarch of Constantinople, reflects his Syrian origin in his canon, which includes only the twenty-two books of the Peshitta canon. Theodoret of Cyrrhus (A.D. 386-458) had the same Antiochian canon as Chrysostom. But another man of Antioch, Theodore of Mopsuestia (fl. 428), had no general letters (as well as no Revelation) in his New Testament, standing with the Syriac canon of about A.D. 400 already mentioned. Gregory of Nazianzus (A.D. 329-89) accepted the seven general letters, but not the Revelation, agreeing with the (supposed) Canon 60 of the Synod of Laodicea, and the later list of sixty canonical books. Amphilochius of Iconium (fl. 394) accepted four Gospels, the Acts, fourteen letters of Paul; his statement continues: "Of general letters, some say seven, others only three, one of James, one of Peter, and one of John. . . . The Revelation of John some accept but the majority call it uncanonical." It was in his day that the first Latin father we know of accepted Hebrews—Hilary of Poitiers (fl. 367). But Amphilochius concurs with Chrysostom, Theodore, and Gregory in refusing to accept the Revelation. As we have seen, this is the position of the great majority of Greek manuscripts of the New Testament.

In fact, the Revelation divided the church in the East late in the fourth century, when Basil (*fl.* 379), Gregory of Nyssa (*fl. ca.* 394), and Epiphanius of Constantia in Cyprus (*fl.* 403) followed Athanasius in accepting the Revelation. Of the four "doctors" of the Eastern church (Gregory of Nazianzus, Athanasius, Chrysostom, and Basil), two accepted the Revelation and two rejected it. Even today the Greek church uses no readings from the Revelation in its church lessons.

The West meanwhile questioned not the Revelation but Hebrews. In the middle of the third century, as we have seen, Western Christianity was still refusing Hebrews and all but three general letters—I Peter, I and II John. The Eastern churches were going on, especially in Alexandria, to a larger New Testament; and this fuller canon gradually penetrated the West as well. A North African list of about A.D. 359, a hundred years after Cyprian, contained all of our New Testament except Hebrews, James, and Jude. Hilary of Poitiers (*fl.* 367), Ambrosiaster (the times of Damasus, 366-84), Lucifer of Cagliari (*fl.* 371), and Priscillian of Saragossa (*fl.* 385) accepted Hebrews as part of the New Testament. Pelagius of Britain (*ca.* 410) did not include it among Paul's letters, but the authority of Ambrose, Rufinus, Jerome, and Augustine assured its acceptance in the West. For Jerome put it into his Vulgate Latin version, begun in A.D. 382, though he admitted that "the custom of the Latins" did not accept it. Augustine was doubtful about its being the work of Paul, but admitted that he was following the Eastern churches in accepting it. It was his influence that led the councils of Hippo (393) and Carthage (397, 419) to put it into their New Testaments.

IX. *Further Developments*

The full list of seven general letters was even more reluctantly accepted in the West. Hilary, Lucifer, and Ambrose accepted three or four of these letters, while Rufinus, Augustine, and Jerome acknowledged all seven. The work of Jerome in producing the authoritative Vulgate version at the instance of Pope Damasus I had of course the effect of fixing the New Testament canon of twenty-seven books for Latin Christianity.

The papal decretals of Damasus, Gelasius, and Hormisdas, all now known to be from the sixth century, reflect this Vulgate canon, though in A.D. 560, Cassiodorus found and copied from some old book a New Testament list of twenty-two books just like that of the Peshitta—a fact to be accounted for perhaps by the origin of his family in Syria.

Improvements in book forms in the Latin world helped to establish this canon, for while the Greeks very seldom produced a one-volume New Testament, Latin scribes had no difficulty in doing so, and such manuscript copies of the New Testament in Latin became very numerous. In Greek, however, the Gospels were likely to form one volume, the letters of Paul another, the Acts and general letters a third, and the Revelation a fourth. Indeed, Leontius of Byzantium, lecturing in Jerusalem in A.D. 530, says the New Testament consists of six volumes—Matthew-Mark, Luke-John, Acts, the seven general letters, the letters of Paul, and the Revelation. In both Greek and Latin churches the Athanasian canon of twenty-seven books had prevailed.

While the Syrian church steadfastly maintained its short canon of twenty-two books, the influence of Alexandria had made itself felt in the Ethiopic canon of thirty-five books, our twenty-seven being supplemented by the so-called "Clement" and the Synodus—"Clement" including among other things an expanded form of the Revelation of Peter, which, as we have seen, had found a place in the Muratorian canon, in that of Clement, in the Clermont list and in other ancient canons. A somewhat similar appendix to the New Testament is mentioned in a Greek list (*ca.* A.D. 400) of New Testament books which contained eight books of the Apostolical Constitutions—condensations of church law which it was convenient to have copied with the New Testament scriptures. But after the sixth century nothing more is heard of this appendix in Greek circles.

The Middle Ages made no changes in these three standard canons, Greek-Latin, Syriac, and Ethiopic, though some incidents are of interest. In the sixth century Andreas of Caesarea in Cappadocia wrote a commentary on the Revelation of John, which he evidently considered a New Testament book. This was the first commentary on Revelation written in the East. In the same century Cosmas, called Indicopleustes because of his voyages to the shores of India, reported that in Syria only three general letters were accepted, and he himself regarded all seven with suspicion. A ninth-century list bearing the name of Nicephorus (*fl.* 828), which gives the number of lines (*stichoi*) in each book, has the Revelation in its "disputed" list. On the other hand, Photius, patriarch of Constantinople in the ninth century, in the collection of 280 book reviews known as his *Bibliotheca*, accepts the Revelation as part of the New Testament.

Another ninth-century figure, Arethas of Caesarea, who played his part like Photius in the Greek revival of the period, expanded Andreas' commentary on the Revelation. His commentary accompanies the Revelation in many manuscripts, for example in the Elizabeth Day McCormick manuscript.

In the West Jerome's Vulgate version, supported as it was by Augustine, came slowly into use, not establishing its supremacy over Old Latin texts until the ninth century. The oddest variation the Western canons exhibit is the inclusion in about a hundred manuscripts of the spurious letter to the Laodiceans, a meaningless string of Pauline phrases, probably composed in Greek, but extant only in translation. It is found in Old Latin texts as well as Vulgate copies from the sixth century down. Jerome said that all rejected it; but the Spanish Priscillian (fl. 385), his contemporary Philaster of Brescia, and Pope Gregory the Great (ca. 900) thought it a genuine work of Paul, though not scripture. The British Alfric, abbot of Cerne (989), regarded it as a fifteenth letter of Paul. John of Salisbury (1165) too held it to be Paul's. It was translated into Old English and German, and followed Galatians in all the High German Bibles from 1466 until Luther, while even later the French scholar Faber Stapulensis (fl. 1536) listed it among the letters of Paul.

Other eddies in the stream of scripture transmission may be mentioned. The Visigoths brought Ulfilas' version of the New Testament to Spain, where its omission of the Revelation was denounced in the fourth Council of Toledo in A.D. 633. Some Latin New Testaments on the other hand included the Shepherd of Hermas in Latin. But in 1441 Pope Eugene IV reaffirmed the canon of Augustine and Jerome, including the Revelation and omitting the Shepherd.

In the Middle Ages the Latin Bible passed still more definitely into the hands of the clergy. Translations into the vulgar tongues were generally forbidden in the thirteenth, fourteenth, and fifteenth centuries, the church presuming to be the sole interpreter of scripture. Nevertheless, a German Bible translated from the Latin in the fourteenth century began to appear in print in 1466, and Wycliffe's English version was completed in 1382. Problems of authenticity and canonicity were neglected until at length in 1546 the Council of Trent definitely shut the door on any further inquiry. It was Erasmus who in the preface to his Greek Testament in 1516 broke sharply with the church position and called for translations of the Bible into all the vernaculars, thus inviting the work of Luther (1522) and Tyndale (1525).

X. New Testament Apocrypha

The term Apocrypha—"secret" or "hidden" —strictly applies only to the books of the Greek Old Testament which Jerome did not find in the Hebrew Old Testament, and which Luther actually separated and printed in a group by themselves in his translation of 1534, being followed in this by all the Protestant English Bibles from Coverdale to the King James Version. There is no such appendix to the New Testament, but the term may be applied to a number of books, one or more of which have been included at one time or another in New Testament manuscripts or in lists of New Testament books.

The Shepherd of Hermas and the Revelation of Peter found place in some lists or manuscripts. The Shepherd of Hermas in a Latin version influenced even Dante around 1300. From the time of its completion at Rome about A.D. 100, the Shepherd was very popular. It was accepted then as scripture. In Alexandria too Clement and Origen held it to be scripture, as did the maker of the original of the Clermont list in Egypt about A.D. 300. Eusebius classed it among the disputed books which were rejected. Athanasius recommended it for use by new converts, but did not admit it to the New Testament. Yet it found a place at the end of the New Testament in the Sinaitic manuscript about A.D. 350. In the West Irenaeus held it to be scripture, as did Tertullian at first, though he later repudiated it. The Muratorian writer definitely excluded it, as recently written and not apostolic. But it was translated early into Latin, and in the Middle Ages was often copied as part of the Latin Bible.

The Revelation of Peter was accepted as scripture by the Muratorian writer and by Clement of Alexandria, but not by Hippolytus at Rome. Eusebius placed it among the disputed and rejected books. Sozomen (ca. 450) says it was read annually on Good Friday in the churches of Palestine in his day. It stood in the Clermont list, but with a dash, perhaps to cancel it. Another work bearing the name of Peter, the Preaching of Peter, was accepted by Clement of Alexandria and Heracleon, but not by Origen or Eusebius.

The Teaching of the Apostles was also treated as scripture by Clement, but not by Origen or Eusebius. Athanasius said it might be read, like the Shepherd, by new converts. The Letter of Barnabas was accepted by Clement and Origen as scripture and stands after the Revelation of John in the Sinaitic manuscript. The Clermont list has it as the end of the general letters. The "Stichometry of Nicephorus" (850) put it among the disputed books. Jerome thought it was written by Barnabas but was not scripture.

The letter of Clement of Rome to the Corinthians was accepted as scripture by Clement of Alexandria, and with the so-called II Clement found a place at the end of the Alexandrian manuscript of the New Testament and in a twelfth-century Syriac manuscript of the New Testament. The Acts of Paul found a place in the Clermont list, though marked off with a dash. Laodiceans appeared in some Latin New Testaments, and III Corinthians was in Efrem's Syriac New Testament in the fourth century. But no ancient list included all these different documents.

XI. Selected Bibliography

GOODSPEED, EDGAR J. *The Formation of the New Testament*. Chicago: University of Chicago Press, 1927.

GREGORY, C. R. *The Canon and Text of the New Testament*. Edinburgh: T. & T. Clark, 1907.

HARNACK, ADOLF VON. *The Origin of the New Testament*, tr. J. R. Wilkinson. New York: The Macmillan Co., 1925.

JACQUIER, EUGÈNE. *Le Nouveau Testament dans l'Église chrétienne*. Paris: Victor Lecoffre, 1911. Vol. I, "Préparation, formation, et definition du canon du Nouveau Testament."

LEIPOLDT, JOHANNES. *Geschichte des neutestamentlichen Kanons*. Leipzig: J. C. Hinrichs, 1907-8.

MOORE, E. C. *The New Testament in the Christian Church*. New York: The Macmillan Co., 1904.

SOUTER, ALEXANDER. *The Text and Canon of the New Testament*. New York: Charles Scribner's Sons, 1913.

WESTCOTT, B. F. *A General Survey of the History of the Canon of the New Testament*. London: Macmillan & Co., 1866.

ZAHN, THEODOR. *Forschungen zur Geschichte des neutestamentlichen Kanons*. Erlangen: A. Deichert, 1881-1900.

TEXT AND ANCIENT VERSIONS
OF THE NEW TESTAMENT

by ERNEST C. COLWELL

When the modern minister wishes to use a New Testament, he turns to a printed book. This is true whether he reads the New Testament in English, French, Russian, or Greek. He knows—if he stops to think about it at all—that the early Christians had no printed books but used handwritten copies of the New Testament. He may not know that the early Christian use of handwritten books is reflected even today in variations in the content of the various printings of the New Testament.

I. The Nature and Origin of Variant Readings

The easiest way to get rid of variations and to attain accuracy would be to print from the original copy of each book of the New Testament, and to get universal agreement to use that printing. But the original documents are all gone—sunk without a trace in the vast and misty sea of the past. From time to time the claim is made that an "original" has been found. St. Mark's Church in Venice claimed to possess the original of the Gospel of Mark. Investigation revealed that what it had was a copy of Jerome's fourth-century revision of a Latin translation of the Gospel of Mark.

The falsity of these claims to possess an "original" can easily be demonstrated by competent scholars. Edgar J. Goodspeed of the University of Chicago was once offered the "original" of Pilate's report on the Crucifixion to the Emperor Tiberius. It had been "discovered" in an Italian city, and came into the hands of an Italian living in Schenectady, New York. Inspection showed that the parchment on which it was written had served as the cover of a modern book, that the scribe used all the modern marks of punctuation, that the ink was still on the surface of the parchment, that the alphabet employed was taken from modern Greek printing and was one which had never been employed in Greek handwriting, least of all in the first century A.D.

The originals of each book of the New Testament have vanished. There is nothing surprising in this. Many of these books were in all probability written on papyrus, which is no more durable than modern paper. Moreover, they were written to be read at group meetings, not to be deposited in archives. They were read and reread until they were worn out. Then they were discarded. The originals had been discarded before they became canonical.

But before the originals were discarded, they were copied. Before the originals were worn out, their copies had been copied, some of them many times. Not all Christians could read, but the size of the reading public of the Gospels, for example, was not limited to the number of literate Christians. In that ancient world reading meant reading aloud, and scores of illiterate Christians could hear the gospel read. The "lessons" from the Old and New Testament in our church service today go back to this ancient custom. By the second half of the second century this custom was well established.

Almost all the early Christians were traveling salesmen for their religion, and this increased the demand for copies of the New Testament books. Imagine a citizen of Carthage converted to Christianity while on a trip to the city of Rome. As he starts back to Carthage, the members of the church—his new-found brothers—equip him with helps for the maintenance and spread of his faith. These helps may have included some books of the "Bible" (which for them was the Old Testament in Greek) and a copy of the Christian Gospel written in Rome by one of their own number, John, who was also called Mark. This last would be copied by amateur scribes whose zeal surpassed their ability. To them, as to modern ministers, it was the gospel that mattered, not the exact wording. Thus the man from Carthage went back home with a copy of Mark which differed somewhat from its source.

The Christian convert from Carthage is a product of imagination, but the disagreement of one handwritten copy of the New Testament from another handwritten copy is not imaginary. No two of these manuscripts agree completely. In some cases the disagreement is extensive. These variations, or "variant readings," create difficulties for the modern publisher who would like to print an edition of the New Testament. Before he begins printing, he must decide which of the handwritten copies he will follow as regards those points where they disagree with each other. The editor might escape this arduous task if these disagreements were insignificant in number or in nature. It does not take long to show that they are not.

A. *Amount of Disagreement in Variant Readings.*—To start at the bottom of the list with the least significant variants we note those which are unique. Each manuscript has some readings of its own ("singular readings"). If we were to compare one human being with all the rest of the human race, we would find some details in which he differed from all other human beings. The best known of these singular items is his fingerprints. Thus one manuscript, when compared with all other manuscripts in existence, has some singular readings, as distinctive as fingerprints. One of the manuscripts at the University of Chicago contains only the Gospel of Mark. But in this Gospel it has 181 variant readings which do not occur in any other manuscript.[1]

Or take another approach to the question of the amount of difference between these New Testaments. Any person compared with any other person will differ from that person in various ways. Mr. A will be tall, skinny, dark, and handsome. Mr. B will be short, fat, blond, and ugly. The range of difference when two people are compared will be greater than that found when one person is compared with the human race. Generally speaking, two members of the same family differ less than two members of the same tribe, and these differ less than inhabitants of different continents. As with people, so with manuscripts. Every manuscript in existence differs from any other specific manuscript in a large number of passages. The range of this variation is quite wide.

Two specific manuscripts that are members of a closely related family differ from each other in matters other than spelling 25 times in Mark, the shortest of the Gospels.[2] Two other manuscripts that belong to the same type of text but not to a family are the manuscripts 2427 and Vaticanus (B), members of the Beta text type. In the Gospel of Mark these two have no closer kin, yet they differ in that one Gospel 873 times. Again, two manuscripts that belong to different text types may differ from each other as much as 14,040 times in the four Gospels.[3] Although reduction in these totals might be required to compensate for errors in computation, the totals are still impressive. The amount of variation is large enough to fatigue the memory of the student, and to appall the prospective editor.

There is a third method of estimating the amount of differences between copies of the New Testament. Suppose one wanted a record of all human variations from some one standard without regard to the number of people exhibiting each variation. In manuscript study this means taking some one form of the New Testament as the base or "text" and recording all known variations from it in what is called a "critical apparatus." This is not done very often. Konstantin von Tischendorf did it in 1869. Again, in 1913 Hermann von Soden printed the variations from his Greek New Testament. The listing required 893 pages. Since the number of variations listed per page ranges from 39 to 61, and averages more than 50, one estimates that von Soden knew about 45,000 different readings in the New Testament which he regarded as worth printing.

The extant manuscripts, most of them as yet unstudied in detail, must contain several times that number. The vast majority of these will be

[1] University of Chicago MS 972, Gregory's 2427.

[2] 1219 and Π, members of "Family Pi."

[3] Bezae (D) and 2427 differ in Mark 11 a total of 117 times. The figure given in the text is an estimate based on the assumption that the same rate of variation would hold throughout the Gospels.

rejected by any editor. This may console the pious, but it does not help the editor who has to winnow the chaff from such a vast heap before he begins printing his New Testament.

B. Variations Created by Scribes.—Before the publisher can make an intelligent decision between these numerous variants, he has to study them carefully and extensively. To help him appraise these variants scholars group them in various ways. Some of these classifications are technical, complicated, and obscure to the beginner. To make as clear as possible the nature of these variants, we may classify them here on the basis of the cause of the particular variation.

1. Harmonization.—The desire for consistency created many of these variant readings. The Christian scribe expected one Gospel to agree with another; he anticipated that a New Testament book would agree with an Old Testament book. Where he found disagreement or inconsistency in the manuscript he was copying, he automatically assumed that it was in error and "corrected" the error by bringing the divergent passages into harmony. This harmonization is found in varying degree in almost all manuscripts, and in almost all the books of the New Testament. It is commonest in the first three Gospels because they have the largest amount of parallel material.

The objective situation in this area can be described as follows: 92 per cent of the Gospel of Mark appears in the Gospel of Matthew, and much more than half of it appears also in the Gospel of Luke. In some copies of the Gospels there are striking variations from Gospel to Gospel in these parallel passages. In other copies of the Gospels all three of the Gospels agree. Since we know from a study of the church fathers that Matthew was much more popular than Mark, we would expect to find Matthew's form of a story affecting Mark's form of the same story. Actually examples of this are numerous.

In the account of the healing of the man with the withered hand, Matthew's Gospel (12:13) reads, "Then he said to the man, 'Stretch out your hand.' And the man stretched it out, and it was restored, whole like the other." None of the copies of Matthew conclude otherwise than "restored, whole like the other." In Mark's Gospel (3:5), most copies, including all the earliest ones, read, "And said to the man, 'Stretch out your hand.' He stretched it out, and his hand was restored." Other copies of Mark, including eleven dating from the seventh to the ninth centuries, add "whole like the other." Thus they agree with Matthew. In Luke's Gospel (6:10) some copies read, "And he did so and his hand was restored." Many copies add the word "whole"; still more copies

add the words "like the other." Since there is no variation in Matthew, we assume that we have Matthew's original wording, "restored, whole like the other." In Mark and Luke we assume that the text originally lacked these words and that they were added to harmonize these Gospels with Matthew. If the long form of Mark and Luke is assumed to be original, no good reason for the widespread omission can be found. If it is said that omission by error needs no explanation, the answer is that the error did not occur in *any* of the copies of Matthew, and that this same difference between copies of Matthew and the copies of Mark and Luke occurs in scores of other passages.

In the prediction of the last days, Mark's Gospel (13:14) reads, "But when you see the desolating sacrilege set up where it ought not to be (let the reader understand), then let those who are in Judea flee to the mountains." The verse appears in this form in the two fourth-century copies (B and ℵ) that Westcott and Hort favored, in the fifth-century Washington manuscript of the Gospels (W), in the contemporary but frequently divergent Codex Bezae (D), in the oldest copy in Syriac, in some Old Latin copies, in most copies of Jerome's Latin Vulgate, in the two major Egyptian versions, in the Armenian and the Old Georgian, in an explicit statement by Augustine, and in a few other copies. But the overwhelming majority of the copies of Mark add the words "spoken of by the prophet Daniel" after "sacrilege." In Matt. 24:15-16 all copies agree in reading "sacrilege spoken of by the prophet Daniel." In passages where Matthew has no parallel in Mark, he makes frequent reference to Old Testament prophecy. This supports the judgment of manuscript students that the appearance of Daniel in some copies of Mark 13:14 is due to harmonization with the parallel in Matthew. The student of the English Bible can observe the difference by comparing the King James Version in these passages with the Revised Standard Version or Goodspeed's American translation.

In these examples of harmonization we see the intentional creation of variants. This is not to say that the scribe intended to create a new reading; what he intended was the correction of what he mistakenly identified as an erroneous reading. Reverence for scripture was a help rather than a hindrance to such action. The "errors" which harmonization removed were inconsistencies or disagreements between the parts of scripture. More serious alleged errors were weeded out just as ruthlessly by many scribes.

2. Removal of Heresy.—A Christian scribe copying the Gospel of Matthew was surprised to find Jesus quoted as saying that the exact date of the end of the world was a secret from him, "But of that day and hour no one knows, not even the angels of heaven, nor the Son, but the Father only" (Matt. 24:36). The scribe knew that "the Son" referred to Jesus; he knew that Jesus was omniscient; therefore he knew that someone had made a mistake in writing this sentence. So he corrected it by omitting the words "nor the Son." In making this change he felt sure that he was restoring the original reading. Scholars today would disagree with him. They regard the absence of the words "nor the Son" as a variation—albeit an early one—from the original text of Matthew.

In Luke's account of the arrest a statement is made which wounded the sensibilities of some devout Christians. "Also other criminals, two, were led away to be put to death with him" (Luke 23:32). This statement is made in a very different and completely innocuous form in the Gospels of Matthew and Mark. The Lukan wording with its implication that Jesus was a criminal was regarded as erroneous by some scribes. They avoided this implication by changing the word order of the Greek so that it read, "Two others also, who were criminals, were led away to be put to death with him." Still other Christian copyists made the "correction" sure by omitting the word "criminals" altogether, so that the verse reads, "Also two others were led away to be put to death with him."

3. Clarification.—Reverence for the Gospels supported the creation of another class of variations: the explanatory notes. These may have started in the margins of the book, or in parenthetical expressions written between the lines. From either of these positions they could easily move into the text itself. One scribe who mistook the explanatory note for a "correction" of the text would be enough to introduce the new reading. In fact, explanation and correction often appear in the same position on the page; thus the scribe's mistake was an easy one to make.

In Mark 4:11-12 the American Standard Version reads: "Unto you is given the mystery of the kingdom of God: but unto them that are without, all things are done in parables: that seeing they may see, and not perceive; and hearing they may hear, and not understand; lest haply they should turn again, and it should be forgiven them." The vague reference of the impersonal pronoun "it" in "it should be forgiven them" is no less vague in the Greek, which has the verb without a subject. A fair number of Greek copies of Mark have the passage in this obscure form, but some scribes added the words "their sins" to clear up the passage. This

clearer form occurs in the majority of the copies, and may be seen in the King James Version: "and their sins should be forgiven them."

In John 5 the story is told of a healing at the pool called Bethesda. In the form of the story which appears in a score of early witnesses (including the earliest versions and some very early patristic evidence) the sick man's answer to Jesus refers to things which were undoubtedly clear to both him and Jesus but could not possibly be clear to later generations of readers: "The sick man answered him, 'Sir, I have no man to put me into the pool when the water is troubled, and while I am going another steps down before me'" (John 5:7). Up to this point nothing has been said as to the nature of the troubling of the water or the importance of being first. The obscurity is cleared up in the vast mass of later copies by the addition of the following explanatory note early in the story (KJV; RSV mg.): ". . . waiting for the moving of the water; for an angel of the Lord went down at certain seasons into the pool, and troubled the water: whoever stepped in first after the troubling of the water was healed of whatever disease he had."

4. Unintentional Variation.—The three causes of variation discussed so far (harmonization, removal of heresy, and clarification) are all the result of conscious changes; these are what are called intentional variations. But scribes who copied the New Testament were as liable to human weakness as scribes who copied Homer. Like Homer himself, they occasionally nodded. One very common error of the eye led to the omission of a passage by mistake. If two successive lines began with the same word, the scribe's eye might slip from one to the other with the consequent omission of a line of text. This occurred in very early manuscripts, and in late medieval copies. In most copies, Mark 10:46 reads, "And they came to Jericho; and . . . ." In a fourth-century New Testament, the famous Codex Vaticanus (B), "And they came to Jericho" would fill one line. The scribe's eye jumped to the "and" which began the next line; so "and they came to Jericho" is omitted by this manuscript. This copy also contains examples of the omission of a line due to the identity of its ending with that of an adjacent line (homoeoteleuton).

Sometimes the scribe skipped over a word but caught his error before he reached the end of the sentence. In Greek, word order is very free. Thus the scribe could insert the omitted word as soon as he discovered it was missing. In this way he created a variation in word order. These variations are often without significance for meaning, but occasionally affect the sense vitally. Even when they do not drastically affect the sense, they cause difficulties for the printer who wants to publish an exact copy of the New Testament.

The fallibility of the scribe's eyesight led him to duplicate passages as well as to omit them. These variations are usually easily identifiable as errors. The scribe who wrote the Four Gospels of Karahissar, a thirteenth century copy of the Gospels in Greek, duplicated one line of the genealogy in Matt. 1:15-16. In his copy we read, "And Matthan begat Jacob; and Jacob begat Jacob; and Jacob begat Joseph. . . ." The frequent repetition of the verb "begat" misled him into the repetition of "begat Jacob; and Jacob."

In a few passages the variation is of such a nature that it can be explained either as omission by error, or as addition by error. In Matt. 27:17, the Revised Standard Version reads: "Pilate said to them, 'Whom do you want me to release for you, Barabbas or Jesus who is called Christ?'" In a few copies of this passage we find, "Whom do you want me to release for you? Jesus Barabbas? or Jesus who is called Christ?" Let us assume that the original did not read the word "Jesus" before "Barabbas." It could have been created there by the erroneous duplication of the last syllable of the Greek word "you." This word in this passage would be YMIN, and IN is an abbreviation frequently employed for "Jesus." If a scribe by error wrote YMININ, the result would be ". . . for you? Jesus Barabbas?" But let us take the other position and assume that the original read the word "Jesus" before "Barabbas." Then the scribe could easily by error have omitted the second IN and thus created the reading ". . . for you? Barabbas? . . ." In such circumstances either additional data or other criteria for judgment are needed before the printer can decide which form to follow.

Variations between copies of the New Testament were created also by scribes who were poor spellers. In this regard ancient stenographers resemble their modern counterparts at their worst. Quite a few vowels and diphthongs were pronounced alike in Greek, and not until the printing press was invented did uniform spelling become possible. In the Four Gospels of Karahissar there are 271 of these misspellings.

The presence of these "ear-spellings" in a copy has often been claimed as evidence that it was written from dictation. But one's confidence in this claim may well be shaken by the discovery that when composing on the typewriter, one can easily think "their" and write "there," etc., or by the observation of similar errors made by typists who are following clear copy. Slight variations of this and similar types account for almost fifty per cent of the variant readings found in the ordinary handwritten copy of the Greek New Testament.

5. Change of the Rare to the Familiar.— Modern psychologists have taught us that we often see what we expect to see, the familiar object, even when it is not there. The scribes who copied the New Testament were subject to this failing also, and because of it, created variations in some copies of the New Testament. This is strikingly illustrated in Mark 6:20, in the story of John the Baptist's imprisonment. One of the commonest words in Greek, as in English, is the verb "do." Relatively rare in Greek, as in English, is the verb "to be perplexed." It occurs only six times in the New Testament. In the Greek these two verbs look much alike in the third person singular of the imperfect tense of the indicative mood. "He did" is ἐποίει; "he was perplexed" is ἠπόρει. On the one hand, the famous manuscripts Vaticanus, Sinaiticus, Koridethi, and a few others with the Egyptian version read, "When he [Herod] heard him [John], he was much perplexed; and yet he heard him gladly." This is to be seen in the Revised Standard Version, also in Goodspeed's translation. On the other hand, the overwhelming majority of copies read with the King James Version, "And when he [Herod] heard him [John], he did many things, and heard him gladly."

There can be little doubt that the scribes misread the rare word "perplexed" as the familiar word "did." This can be seen actually happening in a copy of the Gospel of Mark at the University of Chicago. This manuscript, called "The Archaic Mark," originally read "perplexed," but has been "corrected" to read "did."

C. Variations Created by Editors.—Up to this point we have been considering variations caused by scribes. Two other classes of people worked their will upon the New Testament: editors and translators. At times the results of their work included the creation of new variants. Scribes were discussed first because they are more numerous, but not because the time sequence is scribes, editors, translators. Only the first few scribes preceded all editors and translators; after that they all overlap in time. Thus, for example, in the fifty years from A.D. 150 to 200, the New Testament was being translated, edited, and copied.

Much of what has been said about scribes is true also of editors. An editor is just a superscribe who hires other scribes to multiply copies of the New Testament under his direction. An editor would differ from a scribe in the rigor with which he applied his principles throughout the text of the New Testament. If he preferred participle and verb to verb and verb, the editor would choose the former rather consistently. If he felt that a short form was primitive, he would take it whenever he could. An editor who favored smoothness would add expletives throughout the work. As will be seen later, we have in existence groups of manuscripts which exhibit some of these characteristics so consistently that we are constrained to attribute them to the work of editors.

An editor would differ also from a scribe in the degree of conscious purpose with which he changed particular copies or particular passages. In that purpose most editors would certainly include a desire for unity. This desire might express itself as a concern for the widest possible circulation of the new edition, or for the destruction of rival editions. Yet this very desire might lead to the use of several previously distinct strains in the production of the new edition. A New Testament of one type might be corrected by one of a very different sort. This led to the creation of new readings when the editor blended the readings of the two manuscripts.

Westcott and Hort called such a hybrid a "conflate reading," and identified eight of them as the work of the editors who produced a fourth-century edition which they called "Syrian." In Mark 9:49 these editors created the reading, "For every one shall be salted with fire, and every sacrifice shall be salted with salt." Earlier editions of the passage are known. One reads, "For every one will be salted with fire"; another, "For every sacrifice shall be salted with salt." We have seen that editors resembled scribes, and we find individual scribes occasionally blending readings in this same fashion. In Acts 6:8 many copies read "full of grace"; many others "full of faith." But one copy reads, "full of grace and faith."

D. Variations Created by Translators.—By the time the apostle Paul came to his martyrdom, the overwhelming majority of the Christians spoke Greek, either as a native tongue or as a second language. But as Christian missionaries pushed beyond the cities into small provincial villages, the demand for a New Testament in the native tongue of these new converts increased. By A.D. 200, the New Testament was available in Latin, in Egyptian, and in Syriac. The gradual decline in knowledge of Greek among Christians contributed to the development of particular forms of the New Testament in several languages.

Translating the New Testament, even when it is done with care, creates new variations in its content. Many of the early translations were not made with much care. Augustine says of the making of the early Latin translations:

For the translations of the Scriptures from Hebrew into Greek can be counted, but the Latin translators are out of all number. For in the early days of the faith every man who happened to get his hands upon a Greek manuscript, and who thought he had any knowledge, were it ever so little, of the two languages, ventured upon the work of translation.[4]

It is interesting to note that one of these Latin versions is probably the longest form of the Gospels in existence while an equally ancient Syriac translation is the shortest form in existence.

Sometimes the translator creates a reading unwittingly. In the account of the Lord's Supper in the King James and the American Standard Version (Matt. 26:27) the Lord says to his disciples as he hands them the cup, "Drink ye all of it." Sermons on this text have sometimes expounded it as an exhortation to *complete* devotion, devotion unto death, as though the meaning were, "drink the cup to the dregs." To avoid such a misunderstanding, Weymouth reads "Drink, all of you"; the Twentieth Century New Testament translates "Drink from it, all of you"; Goodspeed reads "You must all drink from it"; and the Revised Standard Version has "Drink of it, all of you."

When Tyndale translated a Greek verb meaning "wrapped up" in Luke 2:7 as "wrapped hym in swadlynge cloothes," he created a new reading for the New Testament. For it survived through the King James Version to the English Revised Version and the American Standard Version. "Clothes" is a survival of the old spelling of "cloths"; thus the "swaddling-cloths" were not garments, and the passage is much more accurately translated in the modern speech versions as "wrapped him up." The Revised Standard Version reads "swaddling cloths."

Other variants created by translators are less innocent. The Revised Standard Version often smooths out the language of the original beyond recognition; especially is this true in the Gospels of Mark and Luke. The "and . . . and . . . and" of Mark's Gospel is polished up to suit sensitive English ears and leaves no trace of the style of the original for the student of Mark. Likewise, the "and it came to pass" of the older version—which actually exists in the New Testament itself—was dropped.

E. Standardization of the Text.—Editors and translators create "standard" editions which spread a particular pattern of variations widely but check the development of new variations.

⁴ *On Christian Doctrine* II. 11.

A few editors tried to standardize the New Testament as early as the second century. A Greek-Latin manuscript from the fifth century, which is supported by some copies of second-century Latin translations, contains one of the earliest standard texts. This particular type is harmonized and inclusive—long, rather than short. It is a part of what used to be called the Western Text. But standardization began to succeed about the end of the fourth century, progressed unevenly through the Middle Ages and found its period of greatest success from the invention of printing in the fifteenth century to the middle of the nineteenth century. The earliest datable standard version was the revision of the earlier Latin versions made by Jerome at the request of Pope Damasus I about A.D. 380. Jerome claimed that when he began his work there were as many different forms of the Latin New Testament as there were individual copies. To reform the Latin New Testament by making a new revision was one thing; to get it universally used, another. The triumph of this Latin Vulgate New Testament was gradual and partial; it reached its climax in the days of the Counter Reformation. In A.D. 1546, by a vote of the majority of the clerics assembled at Trent, it was decided that Jerome's Latin revision was *the* New Testament.

Early in the fifth century A.D. an energetic leader of the Syriac-speaking church, Rabbula, prepared a new form of the Syriac New Testament. With the aid of the hierarchy in Syria, earlier forms of the New Testament were collected and destroyed. One bishop reported that he found and destroyed over two hundred copies of Tatian's harmonized gospel (the Diatessaron). In this liquidation of competing forms of the Bible, and in the care with which the new standard version was copied, the Syrian Christians are very similar to the Jewish scribes who worked on the standard form of the Hebrew Old Testament. This fifth-century Syriac New Testament, called Peshitta or vulgate, won its victory rapidly and maintained its dominance effectively. The manuscripts in which it appears differ from one another very little.

In Egypt the form of the New Testament which won a dominant position owed much to the scholarly achievements of Christians at Alexandria. Here under Clement and Origen, the young Christian movement learned much of the lore of the Greeks. At Alexandria the study of the manuscripts of the pagan classics reached its peak. It is not surprising, therefore, that Alexandrian Christians are given credit for developing the version which is today the preference of most scholars. "Develop" is the exact word, for its witnesses are seldom unanimous. By the fifth century this New Testament, called variously the Alexandrian or the Beta or the Neutral, held a dominant position in Egypt. Its career was cut short by the Mohammedan conquest of Egypt in the seventh century.

Long before the seventh century, the leadership of the Greek world had passed to Constantinople. Here there emerged a form of the New Testament distinct both from that of Alexandria and from that known in the West before Jerome. Today we know but little of its origin, and very little more of the steps by which it developed into the form in which we find it in the tenth century ruling all Greek Christendom. Like the Latin and Syriac vulgates, like the Alexandrian New Testament, there is little in this Byzantine New Testament that is distinctive; and there is relatively little that was created by the makers and revisers of this revision. Most of its readings existed in the second century. The pattern in which earlier forms were mixed at Constantinople is, however, a distinct pattern. From the tenth to the fourteenth centuries, at least four distinguishable revisions of this Greek vulgate were produced. One of its forms appears in the first printings of the New Testament (notably in those of Erasmus, Elzevir, and Stephanus), and through them determines the content of the sixteenth-century translations into English, which in their turn determined the content of the King James Version and the English New Testament down to A.D. 1880.

II. Choosing Between Variant Readings

The individual Christian, or the translator or editor or printer who is his deputy, must choose a New Testament from a bewildering variety of New Testaments. How shall he choose?

A. Methods Not Now Generally Approved. 1. By Custom.—For three centuries after the printing of the first Greek New Testament in A.D. 1525, the choice of a New Testament was decided by custom. The content of the earliest printings was based largely on what lay at hand. These editions became the source of the popular versions, including all the great English translations of the sixteenth century. The long-continued vogue of the King James Version sanctified the Greek text from which it was made. When, therefore, in the eighteenth and nineteenth centuries, scholars found ancient manuscripts that differed widely from the received text and challenged its supremacy, the answer was that the text which the church was using was the correct New Testament. Its champions voted for the customary, but they found other arguments to support their position.

The Protestant champions argued (*a*) that the Holy Spirit would not permit the church to accept an inferior or corrupt New Testament;

(b) that other New Testaments smelled of heresy; (c) that no record exists of the making of this text or of its adoption by the church—an indication that it is primitive in origin and in its use by the church; and (d) that more manuscripts in Greek and in other languages, and more church fathers support this New Testament than support any other.

2. By Majority Vote.—The one objectively supported argument was the claim that this New Testament had the largest number of adherents among the manuscripts. This is the argument from recent usage in another form. Why is it that the type of New Testament published by Erasmus and his successors in the sixteenth century is generally supported by hundreds and hundreds of copies of the New Testament? Because Erasmus chose the current form of the New Testament to print. That form had won a dominant position by the tenth century; most of the manuscripts in existence today were written after the tenth century. Thus if the selection of a New Testament is determined by majority vote of the copies in existence, the decision would inevitably be in favor of a late medieval form of the Greek New Testament. This New Testament indeed deserves to be called the Greek Vulgate. (It has other names as well: "the Syrian Text," "the Ecclesiastical Text," "the Koine," "the Textus Receptus," "the Byzantine Text," "the Traditional Text," and "the Received Text.") Is not the sheer weight of the witnesses to this commonly used New Testament decisive in its favor?

This was the one question which the champions of other forms of the New Testament had to answer. Their answer was a resounding negative.

The opponents of the Greek Vulgate forced its rejection by turning a spotlight on the significance of the family tree, of genealogy, in the world of manuscripts. Suppose that there are only ten copies of a book and that nine are all copies from one; then the majority can be safely rejected. Or suppose that nine of the ten are copied from a lost manuscript, and that this lost manuscript and the other one were both copied from the original; then the vote of the majority would not outweigh that of the minority. These arguments show clearly that a majority of manuscripts is not *necessarily* to be preferred as correct.

It is the quality of a New Testament that counts, not the quantity of its adherents. Witnesses should not be counted but weighed. Scribes could recopy a poor New Testament a hundred times without making it a good New Testament. In the scales of judgment this majority text (from which the King James Version was translated) has been shown to be a relatively corrupt New Testament, outweighed by others with fewer adherents. It is a harmonized text, a polished text, an annotated text.

3. By Date.—Another simple solution to the difficulty is to choose the oldest manuscript and follow it faithfully. If the history of the New Testament were a record of steady deterioration, this could be done. But the opening period in the transmission of the New Testament is marked by a splurge of deterioration, and that period (to A.D. 150) is older than the oldest manuscript in existence. If we had a New Testament from the second century, we could have no assurance that other second-century manuscripts were like it or any confidence that it was like the original New Testament.

4. By Quality.—If the oldest is not certainly the best, since age and virtue are not co-ordinates, why not select the best manuscript or text type—whatever its age may be—and follow it? This cannot be done because no manuscript or text type is of the same quality throughout. All the manuscripts and text types are the result of crossbreeding and a consequent mixture in ancestry. No text or document is homogeneous enough to justify judgment on the basis of a part of its readings for the rest of its readings. Some manuscripts and text types can be justified in part of their readings even when they have to be generally repudiated.

The mixture in quality in manuscripts is due partly to the absence of single-volume New Testaments in the first two centuries. At the beginning each book was copied as a single book and circulated alone. By A.D. 200, or soon after, the four Gospels probably were copied together, as were the letters of Paul. But it is doubtful that any single book contained Gospels, Acts, and Paul much earlier than A.D. 300. When these books were put together into one book, they had various separate ancestries. Thus the fourth-century New Testaments resemble a freight train in which one car is New York Central, one is Pennsylvania, one is Chesapeake and Ohio, one is Atlantic Coast Line, etc. This is mixture by distinct blocks of text, the quality of one section being quite different from that of another.

This type of mixture occurred even in the four Gospels. The celebrated Washington manuscript, "the Freer Gospels," from the late fourth or early fifth century in Egypt has this type of content. Matthew has the Byzantine text type; the Gospel of John has the "Neutral" text type; Mark 1:1–5:30 has an "African" text type; Mark 5:31 to the end has the so-called Caesarean text type; Luke 1:1–8:12 has the "Neutral" text type; and Luke 8:13 to the end has the Byzantine text type. This is mixture in large blocks.

But it is simple and unified compared to another and more common type of mixture which could be called repair shop mixture. Suppose some wooden Chesapeake and Ohio freight cars were growing old; some of the slats that make up the sides of the cars were broken, some rotted, etc. The cars go to the shops. In the shops are a number of old freight cars bought from the Pennsylvania Railroad. These are dismantled and used to patch the Chesapeake and Ohio cars, which are returned to service. Again they wear out; again they go to the shops. This time the supply of repair parts comes from some old New York Central boxcars. The Chesapeake and Ohio cars are repaired and go back into service. After this has happened four or five times, no railroad detective could trace the ancestry of the train.

5. By Genealogy.—This mixture in ancestry and quality blocks the path to another solution —the retracing of the genealogy from children to parents to grandparents and so on all the way back to the original. Multiple or mixed ancestry is the rule in these large groups. Most of the manuscripts are no closer than forty-second cousins or great-great uncles. This combination of promiscuity and gaps in the generations baffles the constructor of family trees. In short, we are dealing not with a family, close-knit in intimate relationships, but with a nation, a nation to which immigrants have come from many countries. Genealogy will help us reach some of the way stations, but it will never take us back through the jungle of mixture to the original New Testament.

6. By Agreement with Church Fathers.—Nor can one appeal from confusion in the New Testaments themselves to the testimony of the earliest church fathers. What has been said above about the "oldest manuscript" can be said also about the oldest fathers. They disagree with one another, and even with themselves. Many of them can be quoted on both sides of the question in passage after passage. Even as late as the end of the second century, scholarly Christians are treating the scriptures with considerable freedom. In the *Miscellanies* I. 19 Clement quotes I Cor. 13:12 simply as, "For now we see as in a mirror," rather than as, "For now we see as in a mirror darkly." Consistently throughout both the *Instructor* and the *Miscellanies* he omits "darkly" when quoting this passage. There is evidence, however, that he knew the verse in its longer form. The word translated "darkly" means "a dark saying" or "a riddle." The omission probably grows out of Clement's reluctance to assert that the Christian, the true gnostic, now sees only in riddles or enigmas. In general, this freedom in quotation makes it difficult to determine just what form of the New Testament the early fathers were using. It is as necessary to check the fathers by the manuscripts as it is to check the manuscripts by the fathers.

7. By Geographical Distribution.—One of the great students of manuscripts cast a wistful eye at the possibility of geographical evidence as a clue to the original. F. C. Burkitt used to say that where the Old Syriac from the eastern end of the Christian world agreed with the Old Latin from the western end of the world, the original New Testament brought them together. This argument rests on the assumption that Syria and Africa were isolated from each other in so far as the copying of the New Testament was concerned. But we cannot be sure of this isolation; the Greek forerunner of the Old Syriac—itself not the original New Testament —could have been carried to the West to influence the making of the Old Latin Version.

No single or simple answer is possible. We cannot choose our New Testament by counting noses, or by venerating age, or by the selection of a paragon, or by constructing a family tree, or by preferring an early Christian who commented on the New Testament to one who copied it, or by assuming the independence of voters who live in distant towns.

B. The Best Method a Triple One.—The answer is complex. We choose our New Testament by taking three steps. First of all we study the relationship of one New Testament to other New Testaments. This is sometimes called the external study of manuscripts. Then we study the relationship of one particular form of a passage to the alternative forms of the passage. This is the internal evidence. Finally, if neither of these helps us and the passage still does not make sense, we make the shrewdest guess we can as to the original form of the passage. This is conjectural emendation.

1. External Study.—It may seem silly to say that family trees cannot solve our problem and then say that we begin the solution with family trees. For the student of textual criticism the making of family trees is not wisdom, but it is the beginning of wisdom. He starts his investigation with a particular manuscript of the New Testament. Either members of its family still survive or they do not. If they do, he charts the family tree. Then he can forget the individual members of the family and quote only the family from there on. This clears out a lot of underbrush. But if the other members of the immediate family have not survived, the student profits from comparing his manuscript with others—even though he cannot reconstruct the family tree. Although exact location cannot be recovered, more general locations within larger groups of manuscripts are a real possibility. The study of these larger and looser kinships illuminates the history of the transmission of the New Testament. In the second place, the study of the relationship of the first manuscript to others educates the student in the habits of scribes and in the characteristics of individual manuscripts.

2. Internal Evidence.—Variant readings have been appraised by the experts through the generations of scholarly study according to longer or shorter lists of rules, or "canons of internal criticism." These rules were supposed to guide the student in choosing between alternative forms of the same passage. But they furnish no sure guide. One scholar tells us to prefer the shorter and less elegant reading. But if the shorter reading should be more elegant than the longer reading, what can the poor student do? No rule will save him.

These lists of rules have shrunk steadily in the last one hundred and fifty years. Tischendorf was content with five. Hort has been followed by many moderns in emphasizing only two. These two are: (*a*) that reading is to be preferred which best suits the context, and (*b*) that reading is to be preferred which best explains the origin of all others. Fenton John Anthony Hort was never satisfied with short words if he could find a long one; so he called these rules: (*a*) "Intrinsic Probability," and (*b*) "Transcriptional Probability."

These two rules are nothing less than concentrated formulas of all that the textual critic must know and bring to bear upon the solution of his problem. The first rule about choosing what suits the context exhorts the student to know the document he is working on so thoroughly that its idioms are his idioms, its ideas as well known as a familiar room. The second rule about choosing what could have caused the other readings requires that the student know everything in Christian history which could lead to the creation of a variant reading. This involves knowledge of institutions, doctrines, and events. This is knowledge of complicated and often conflicting forces and movements. Christianity from the beginning was a vital and creative movement. It outran the formation of patterns and fences. It experienced the love of God first and formulated it afterward. No single line can chart its course; no one orthodoxy encompasses it.

In this complexity the student is guided not by rules, but by knowledge and judgment. He is guided by his knowledge of scribes and manuscripts, of Christian history and institutions and theology, and of the books whose textual form he is striving to perfect. He is guided also by his own judgment, a quality through which the application of reason to knowledge becomes an art.

3. Conjectural Emendation.—The quality of judgment is needed in the decision as to the use of conjectural emendation in the study of the New Testament. If after external and internal evidence has been studied, the passage in question still yields no sense in any of the forms preserved in the manuscripts, a shrewd guess as to the nature of a possible primitive error is legitimate.

The careless use of conjecture is as indefensible as the refusal to use it at all. There can be no doubt that some readings preserved in our manuscripts were created by the conjectures of ancient editors. To use their conjectures in various passages because they are recorded in manuscripts and are therefore objective, and to refuse to make our own best guess when the situation requires it, is not a case of good judgment. Those scholars whose stubborn devotion to objectivity and the evidence of the manuscripts leads them to reject all conjecture deserve A. E. Housman's indictment: they "use MSS as drunkards use lamp-posts,—not to light them on their way but to dissimulate their instability." [5] In general, the students of the manuscripts and the translators have used conjecture parsimoniously; it is seldom that a modern edition of the New Testament will contain more than two or three conjectures. For in view of the wealth of manuscript evidence, it is probable that the original reading has survived.

4. Two Illustrations.—No statement of theory is complete unless it contains examples of its application. The larger variations are the easier to describe, and a review of these suggests the choice of the story of the adulterous woman found in some New Testaments in John 7:53–8:11. Was this or was it not a part of the original Gospel of John?

The Freer Gallery of Art in Washington contains a justly famous Greek manuscript of the four Gospels from the fourth or fifth century A.D. It is the habit of the gallery to provide souvenir postcards for interested visitors. For some time they distributed a postcard of this manuscript of the four Gospels. The photographed page begins at John 7:46 in the middle of the word "servants" and ends in 8:16 with the word "sent." On the back of the card appears a translation of John 8:3-11. This translation is sensational because *not a word of it appears on the other side of the card*. The Washington Gospels do not contain the story of the adulterous woman anywhere. The treacherous character of ignorance is shown by the

[5] *M. Manilii Astronomicon; Liber Primus* (2nd ed.; Cambridge: Cambridge University Press, 1937), p. liii.

fact that the maker of the card chose this page to photograph because the story of the adulterous woman was one of his favorite scripture passages. He chose the page of the manuscript that began before it and ended after it, assumed that it contained it, and copied the story from a printed King James Version.

The external evidence on this passage is as follows:

(*a*) It is absent from all Greek manuscripts earlier than the ninth century, with the exception of a fifth-century Greek-Latin manuscript.

(*b*) No Greek commentator before the twelfth century comments on this passage, although many comment on its context.

(*c*) It appears in the majority of Greek manuscripts after the tenth century.

(*d*) It appears in various locations: (i) after John 7:53 most frequently; (ii) after Luke 21 in Family 13; (iii) after John 7:36 in MS 225; (iv) at the end of John in a dozen Greek and many Armenian manuscripts; (v) in the margins of many manuscripts at John 7:53.

(*e*) It is marked as an insertion in scores of Greek manuscripts.

(*f*) It appears in widely varying forms. The student who is comparing the Gospel of John with a printed text is usually amazed at the amount of variation that begins as soon as he enters this story. Nine distinct forms of it are well attested in Greek.

(*g*) It is known in the Latin West earlier than the fourth century; known to Ambrose, Augustine, and Jerome, who said that many Greek and Latin manuscripts contained it; it appears in half a dozen pre-Vulgate Latin manuscripts and in the Latin Vulgate.

(*h*) It is known in some form in Syria by the middle of the third century. It is quoted in the Syriac Teaching of the Apostles and in the Apostolic Constitutions which are based on that.

This external evidence is best explained by the assumption that this story was no part of the original Gospel of John but entered the Greek New Testament through the Latin versions. This assumption is supported by the internal evidence.

If we apply the test of suitability to context, the vote is still negative. This woman is the only sinner in the Fourth Gospel. Sin defined as immorality does not exist in this Gospel. Nowhere else does the Fourth Evangelist suggest the quality of pity, mercy, or compassion. There are no "publicans and sinners" in John's gospel. John had no repentance or forgiveness of sins. No person of notorious character is introduced. Nowhere is any group of sinners mentioned as companions of Jesus.

Detailed studies of vocabulary and style show that this story is as alien to John in form as it is in idea.

Furthermore, the story does not fit the context because it interrupts the narrative. If this story is absent, then the great day of the feast of Tabernacles is signalized by Jesus' twin declarations that he is the Water of Life and that he is the Light of the World. These sayings correspond to two symbolic acts performed on that day: the pouring of the water, and the lighting of the golden lamps. If the story of the adulterous woman is interposed, the first passage alone falls within the time of the feast, and the second is deferred till the day after its conclusion. Moreover, the two sayings are then separated by an unrelated incident.

The second test has little force here. Does its presence or its absence in the original best explain the other? It is hard to imagine a good reason for its wholesale omission. But Augustine's imagination was strong enough to think up a reason:

Some of little faith, or rather enemies of the true faith, I suppose from a fear lest their wives should gain impunity in sin, removed from their manuscripts the Lord's act of indulgence to the adulteress.[6]

The generality of the "omission" in early Greek sources can hardly be explained this way. Nor is Augustine's argument supported by the evidence from Luke's Gospel, where even greater acts of compassion are left untouched by the scribes who lack this story in John. The external evidence and the evidence from intrinsic probability show that this story was no part of the original Gospel of John.

As an example of conjectural emendation, we may consider a suggested correction of John 19:29. In this account of the Crucifixion the King James Version and the Revised Standard Version agree in the use of the word "hyssop." "A bowl full of vinegar stood there; so they put a sponge full of the wine on hyssop and held it to his mouth." Goodspeed translates this "on a pike," and gives the following commentary:

Matthew and Mark speak of a reed or stick . . . being used for the purpose. But hyssop was a low grassy plant, seldom over two feet high, and how it could be used for such a purpose is hard to see. It is mentioned in I Kings 4:33 as the most insignificant of plants. . . . Modern scholars are inclined to dismiss the word "hyssop" as a graphic error (Souter) for the Greek word ὑσσῷ [*hysso*], a pike, which would be the most practical and natural thing to use in such a situation. If this . . . was the original reading, it must have been changed very early to hyssop, under the influence of the use of hyssop before the Passover to sprinkle the blood of

[6] *Ad Pollentium de Adulterinis Conjugiis* II. vii. 6.

the Passover lamb upon the doorposts (Exod. 12:22).[7]

In such a case the reader must judge whether John, who had read Mark, would care more for accuracy in historical detail or more for symbolic allusion. In other words, is the nature of the Fourth Gospel in general such as to support or reject this conjecture?

With these brief examples we leave the discussion of method. The method begins by the comparison of manuscript with manuscript—a study of external relationships. But since the student cannot accurately reconstruct the archetype or source of each large group, he turns to the appraisal of variants in specific passages. Here he tries to select that reading which best suits its context and best explains the origin of the other readings in the same passage. Beyond this, the student must make the best-informed and most judicious guesses possible to him.

III. Summary

The problem that confronts the printer or translator of the New Testament is one of selection from variant readings of the same passage. A lengthy study of the causes of these variants illuminates the history of the New Testament in the period when it was written by hand and also illustrates the method by which the problem is solved in particular passages. The method is basically one of reversing the flow of history. In history, as manuscript begets manuscript the number of variant readings is increased. In manuscript study (textual criticism to the scholar) variant readings are decreased until a reading is selected which may be regarded as the original with a high degree of probability.

The raw materials for this work are the handwritten copies of the New Testament, whether in Greek or in other languages, plus the copies of the fathers who quote the New Testament. Most essays of this sort devote considerable time to summary catalogues of these documents. In this article no effort has been

made to present such a catalogue. The handbooks noted in the bibliography, especially those by Kenyon and Vaganay, provide extensive though not comprehensive information on these "materials of New Testament criticism." Since the discovery of hitherto unknown materials proceeds apace, all such lists are out of date within five years of publication. Only the specialist can be expected to keep abreast of this flood.

The minister and the educated layman cannot learn anything comprehensive and accurate about the manuscripts themselves from brief statements. Here of all places a little knowledge is exceedingly dangerous. The nonspecialist should know that we have several thousand manuscripts of the New Testament in Greek and other thousands in more than half a dozen important translations into other languages, with at least a score of church fathers to be studied either in printed "critical" editions or in handwritten copies. Beyond this the nonspecialist must clearly understand the nature of the problem and the methods by which we are steadily though slowly arriving at more accurate solutions.

[Other helpful discussions of the text of the New Testament can be found in the Introduction to the several New Testament books. See especially Vol. VII, pp. 244-46; Vol. VIII, pp. 19-22.]

IV. Selected Bibliography

COLWELL, ERNEST C. *The Study of the Bible.* Chicago: University of Chicago Press, 1937. Chs. ii-iii.

GOODSPEED, EDGAR J. *The Making of the English New Testament.* Chicago: University of Chicago Press, 1925.

KENYON, FREDERIC GEORGE. *The Text of the Greek Bible.* London: Duckworth, 1937.

LAKE, KIRSOPP. *The Text of the New Testament,* ed. Silva New. London: Christophers, 1928.

PRICE, IRA MAURICE. *The Ancestry of Our English Bible: An Account of Manuscripts, Texts, and Versions of the Bible,* ed. W. A. Irwin and Allen Wikgren. New York: Harper & Bros., 1949.

VAGANAY, LEO. *An Introduction to the Textual Criticism of the New Testament,* tr. B. V. Miller. St. Louis: B. Herder Book Co., 1937.

[7] *Problems of New Testament Translation* (Chicago: University of Chicago Press, 1945), pp. 115-16. Used by permission.

THE ENGLISH BIBLE

by ALLEN WIKGREN

The Bible is by far the most translated book in the world. The Jews translated their scriptures into Greek and other languages, and the early Christians naturally felt the need of bringing the biblical message to every people in its own tongue.[1] The modern missionary movements continued and expanded these efforts until now the Bible has been rendered into well over a thousand languages and effectively circulated in printed form throughout the entire world.

I. Beginnings

The story of the English Bible begins with the introduction of Christianity into Britain. When and how that happened are obscure, but in the early third century Tertullian and Origen witness to the existence of British Christianity, the former stating that there were places in Britain subject to Christ which Roman arms could not penetrate. Initial gains by the church were wiped out by the Teutonic invasions of the fifth century, but significant advance began again with the coming in A.D. 597 of missionaries sent out by Pope Gregory, and Christianity became firmly established.

In Britain, as elsewhere, missionary work proceeded at first almost entirely by means of the spoken word. Any translation of the Bible consisted of a free and extemporaneous treatment of the Latin text in vernacular speech. In sermon and minstrel song the Scriptures thus first became known in the earliest English form, that is, Anglo-Saxon; and soon partial translations and paraphrases were put into writing in homilies, commentaries, and glosses in Latin manuscripts. A complete translation, however, is unknown in this Anglo-Saxon period. No real popular demand for such a production existed since few people could read, and manuscripts were too expensive for the average person to buy. A Bible for laymen was also unthinkable in the medieval church, which saw in the wide use of the Bible a threat to unity and to ecclesiastical control over the interpretation of the text, as well as a profanation of the Scriptures through such rough dialects as the Anglo-Saxon. Yet much of the biblical contents was made known through ritual, art, religious drama, and Bible picture books, the so-called *Biblia pauperum* or "Bibles of the poor."

In the earlier period, therefore, we have hardly more than a number of interesting traditions. A certain Caedmon, a seventh-century cowherd of northern England, overnight became divinely inspired and commissioned to sing versifications of the biblical stories as they were translated for him into Anglo-Saxon. Remains (although later) of such metrical paraphrases are to be found. In southern England at the same time, that is, about A.D. 700, Abbot Aldhelm is reported by King Alfred the Great to have used the minstrel technique effectively to procure an audience, and Cynewulf, greatest of Anglo-Saxon poets, also contributed numerous biblical allusions. The Venerable Bede is supposed to have translated the Lord's Prayer and the Apostles' Creed for the benefit of priests who were a bit weak in their Latin, and to have urged a contemporary churchman, Egbert, to similar activity. To Egbert is ascribed a translation of the Gospels, and a disciple, Cuthbert, credits Bede with a version of the Gospel of

[1] See pp. 32-83 in this volume.

John, the work being dramatically completed in Bede's dying moments. By the middle of the eighth century, then, probably all the Gospels existed in Anglo-Saxon. In the late ninth century King Alfred apparently promoted biblical study and translation, and to him is attributed among other things an Anglo-Saxon version of the Decalogue, which headed his "Book of Laws," and an unfinished version of the Psalter.

Of extant Anglo-Saxon versions the earliest is probably the British Museum's Vespasian Psalter, a ninth-century Latin text with a crude, interlinear gloss representing middle England speech. A similar manuscript in the Bibliothèque Nationale, the Paris Psalter, contains a southern gloss. It has been ascribed to Alfred the Great, but in its present form appears to be a century or two later. About a dozen such Psalters are known from the ninth and tenth centuries. Other early remains consist of a tenth-century partial gloss of Proverbs and eight copies of the Gospels in various dialects. One of these, the famous Lindisfarne Gospels, is a British Museum manuscript copied by Eadfrid, bishop of Lindisfarne, about A.D. 687 and glossed in northern speech. It is also beautifully illuminated. A similar tenth-century text, named the Rushworth Gospels after its donor, is in the Bodleian Library at Oxford. The other extant manuscripts are all probably copies or descendants of a West-Saxon document of about A.D. 1000, ascribed by a note or colophon to Aelfric, later Archbishop of Canterbury, who is known at about this time for his activity in making the Scriptures available in English. These Gospels contain only the Anglo-Saxon text and deserve rather to be called translations. Aelfric did make a condensed version of the Pentateuch and translations of several Old Testament books in a free and idiomatic style. His sermons and commentaries also contain translation of scriptural text, and he claims to have made use of earlier Anglo-Saxon versions. Similar sermonic efforts of this and later periods also exist in such works as the *Blickling Homilies*.

Further translation was discouraged by the Norman Conquest in 1066. But some metrical paraphrases based on Genesis and Exodus circulated in the twelfth and thirteenth centuries, and a similar version of the Gospels and Acts is preserved in an Oxford manuscript of some twenty thousand lines known as the "Ormulum," after the author, Orm, an Augustinian monk who gave as the motive for his efforts, "that all young Christian folks may depend upon the gospel only, and may follow with all their might its holy teaching, in thought and word and deed."

In the face of the French usage of the time the Anglo-Saxon persisted, and re-emerged, though greatly changed, in the fourteenth century, when political events had produced a new national unity and consciousness, and literary activity blossomed forth in Chaucer and others. The language was now less confused by dialectical variations.

In this new era we have a Psalter in Latin and English dated about 1320 and doubtfully attributed to the poet William of Shoreham; and from perhaps a few years later comes a gloss found in another Latin Psalter and accredited to Richard Rolle, the "Hermit of Hampole." The latter was copied several times for a century or so. Other ventures of some popularity were the translation (*ca.* 1360) of a French text and commentary on Revelation, and a little later a French-Latin collection of gospel narratives which were formed into a kind of harmony of the life of Jesus and used as late as the fifteenth century.

The language of these early versions, especially of the pre-Norman period, is of course quite strange to us, being as close or closer to modern Germanic languages' than to modern English. If these versions exerted any influence upon the later English Bible, it was mostly in simplicity and directness of tone and expression.

II. The Wycliffite Bible

So far as we know, the first complete English Bible was due to the influence and activity of John Wycliffe (1324?-1384), the able and eloquent Oxford scholar called the "morning star of the Reformation" because of the religious convictions which he developed and propagated. In common with later Protestantism he emphasized the necessity of providing the layman with the opportunity of reading the Bible. Since he was also active in efforts for social justice, his appeal was widespread among the common people. After his forced retirement to Lutterworth in 1382 and his death in 1384, his followers, the "poor priests" or "Lollards," carried on his work in an influential traveling ministry of teaching, preaching, and distribution of the Scriptures. Wycliffe managed to survive the attack of his enemies and to die a natural death. But his writings were banned, and the Council of Constance in 1415 officially ordered his body as well as his books burned. The cause of religion was thus "advanced" by the digging up and burning of his bones in 1428, the ashes being thrown into the river Swift.

The dispersal of Wycliffe's remains was symbolic, however, of real religious progress through the spread of the Scriptures which he brought about. The Wycliffite Bible has justly been described as an event rather than merely a book, both on this account and because of its effect upon English prose style. While Wycliffe's exact part in the project is obscure, he nevertheless appears to have been the moving spirit behind it. A pupil and colleague, Nicholas of Hereford, may have done most of the work, assisted perhaps by another friend, John Purvey. The latter also is credited, though uncertainly, with the revision which appeared about the year 1388 or later and became the popular and standard form. The original seems to have been completed in 1382, or a little later, and was more literal than the revision. The translation was made from the current Latin text, and so included the Old Testament apocryphal books.

A definitive attempt to distinguish the original Wycliffite Bible from the "Purvey revision" was not made until 1850, when J. Forshall and F. Madden published the complete text of both in four volumes, representing the result of twenty-two years of work and the examination of 170 manuscripts.[2] Strangely enough, this also was the first printing of the complete version, only the New Testament having been previously so published, the Purvey form in 1731 and the earlier form in 1848. Printing had been introduced into England in 1477 by William Caxton, and much scripture circulated in other publications, for example, in his own translation of the *Golden Legende,* which contained the first printing in 1483 of portions of the English Bible. But an edict of 1408 forbidding unauthorized translation and publication in English or other languages appears effectively to have discouraged printing of the Bible as such in the fifteenth century.

The fact of the survival of so many manuscripts of the Wycliffite Bible in spite of opposition and destruction indicates its widespread influence. Some of its diction and phraseology and much of its spirit lived on in the mainstream of subsequent translation and revision.[3] Replacing a number of similar and fragmentary attempts at translation made in the same period, it remained the only English Bible until the sixteenth century.

III. Early Translation into Other Languages

In the manuscript era a development of vernacular versions similar to that in England occurred also in the other countries of western Europe. Early French activity seems to have culminated in a Norman-French Bible made at the University of Paris and used in northern France around 1250. In Germany early fragmentary translation is exemplified by the

Monsee fragment of Matthew, by a gospel harmony, and by an old Saxon poem *Heiland* ("Savior"), of the ninth century. Translations multiplied so rapidly that before the time of Luther about fifty complete German editions had been produced! In most of the Western countries, owing doubtless to the earlier impact of the Reformation, printed editions of the Scriptures appeared sooner than in England. Beginning with the Strasbourg German Bible of Mentel in 1466, there were eighteen printings in German before the important Luther New Testament of 1522 and Bible of 1534. In French the first printing, a New Testament, occurred about 1478 at Lyons, and the complete Bible appeared in 1487. Even before this, the Italians (1471) and Dutch (1477) had their Bible in the printed vernacular. Swedish, Bohemian, Slavonic, Russian, and Danish printing in whole or in part preceded English. Other subsequent editions of non-English scripture will be mentioned in connection with the English versions upon which they exerted an influence.

IV. William Tyndale and the First Printed New Testament

With the sixteenth century we enter into the most creative period in the history of the English Bible. It was a time of bitter Protestant-Catholic conflict, of widespread ignorance of the Scriptures, even among the clergy, and of initial opposition to vernacular translations in England by both Catholic and Anglican alike. But forces were at work in the Renaissance and Reformation which in a very few years led to the legal dissemination of the Bible in English. The momentous discovery of printing took place. The Scriptures were made known in their original languages, the first printed Hebrew Bible appearing in 1488 and the first Greek New Testament, the edition of Erasmus, in 1516. Scholars like Erasmus and reformers like Luther spoke and worked for the right of all to read the sacred text. The vernacular languages, including English, had developed to the point where they could be used as literary mediums. They, as well as Hebrew and Greek, were studied in the newly founded universities. These and other factors combined to set the stage for the production of the first printed English Bible.

At this time William Tyndale, born about 1492 or earlier, and educated at Oxford and Cambridge, came upon the scene. His experience as chaplain and tutor led him to the conviction that "it was impossible to stablysh the laye people in any truth, except the scripture were playnly layde before their eyes in their

---

[2] *The Holy Bible, Containing the Old and New Testaments, with the Apocryphal Books, in the Earliest English Versions Made from the Latin Vulgate by John Wycliffe and His Followers* (Oxford: University Press, 1850).

[3] E.g., "compass sea and land," "son of perdition," "God forbede," "peradventure."

mother tonge." [4] And to a prominent churchman of his time he addressed his well-known words: "If God spare my lyfe, ere many yeares I wyl cause a boye that dryveth the plough shall know more of the scripture than thou doest!" [5] For the task which he set himself Tyndale was well qualified both by an excellent knowledge of Greek and Hebrew and by an ability to write English of such felicity of phraseology and simple, graceful style that it has become immortalized in the English Bible.

Another necessary quality which Tyndale possessed was perseverance in the face of opposition, calumny, and persecution. For the clergy, with government support, were still opposed to translation in general, and in particular disliked Tyndale's developing Protestant views. His vigorous denunciation of the clergy did not help his cause. His own account tells of inability to find support for his project in England from Bishop Tunstall of London, and of the necessity of going to the Continent to pursue the work. He was befriended by a London merchant, Humphrey Monmouth, in whose home he apparently began his translation. There also he may first have become informed about the tenets of Lutheranism, and been led to realize "not only that there was no rowme in my lorde of londons palace to translate the new testament, but also that there was no place to do it in all englonde." [6]

In 1524, therefore, Tyndale left for Hamburg, and by the middle of 1525 his New Testament was complete and printing was begun at Cologne. A quarto edition was interrupted by the authorities at the instigation of a bitter enemy of the reformers, Cochlaeus (Johan Dobneck). From it only a thirty-one leaf fragment of Matthew in the British Museum is extant, although it is believed that three thousand copies were published after the work was resumed at Worms. Here also an anonymous octavo edition of the same size was first published. So vigorous was the opposition of the English authorities, however, and so zealously did king and bishops collaborate to destroy the Tyndale publications as they were smuggled into England, that only two copies of this octavo issue survived, and one of these is very fragmentary. One, lacking only the title page, is in the Baptist College at Bristol, England. The other is preserved in the library of St. Paul's Cathedral, London. Tyndale, however, was enabled to continue for some time by the support of certain London merchants, in particular of one Augustine Packynton, who contrived to raise money by selling New Testaments to the Bishop of London for burning, thus keeping both Tyndale and the bishop's bonfire going.

Tyndale's association with Luther at Wittenberg and his manifest indebtedness to Luther's German New Testament were special reasons for official condemnation. The single-column, Gothic black-letter type, the prologue, prefaces, and marginal notes showed the influence of the reformer's edition. The authorities were also provoked by the substitution of new terms for certain ecclesiastically sacred ones, such as "elder" for "priest," "repentance" for "penance," "congregation" for "church," etc.

A revision by Tyndale was issued in 1534; and another corrected edition published in 1535 became the basis for all later revision. The Greek text underlying the work remained close to the Erasmus editions of 1519 and 1522, unfortunately for the accuracy of the English New Testament for years to come.

Tyndale also undertook to translate the Old Testament and made a significant contribution to that end, although unable to complete the work before his death. He published the Pentateuch in 1530 and Jonah in 1531. But the authorities finally apprehended him through the treachery of a friend, and after an imprisonment of a year and a half near Brussels (during which he probably completed the text through Chronicles), he was strangled and burned at the stake on October 6, 1536. His famous dying prayer, according to Foxe, was "Lord, open the King of England's eyes." [7] Meanwhile, the situation in England had already changed for the better under Cromwell, who had even sought Tyndale's release, and a complete English Bible was now in relatively unimpeded circulation.

The creative nature of Tyndale's work cannot be overestimated. Though he freely consulted the Vulgate, Luther, and Erasmus' new Latin version, and was doubtless influenced here and there by the current Wycliffite English, his production is characterized by great originality and vigor. It became, in fact, a foundation for all subsequent efforts of revision, so much so that 80 per cent or more of the English down through the Revised Version has been estimated to be basically his in those portions of the Bible in which he wrought with such skill and devotion. [8]

[4] Alfred W. Pollard, Records of the English Bible (Oxford: Henry Frowde, 1911), p. 95.
[5] John Foxe, The Acts and Monuments of the Church (ed. M. Hobart Seymour; New York: Robert Carter & Bros., 1855), p. 542.
[6] Pollard, op. cit., pp. 97-98.

[7] Op. cit., p. 544.
[8] Recent special studies include Henry Guppy, William Tindale and the Earlier Translators of the Bible into English (London: Longmans, Green & Co., 1925); J. F. Mozley, William Tyndale (New York: The Macmillan Co., 1937); S. L. Greenslade, ed., The Work of William Tindale (London: Blackie & Son, 1938).

V. George Joye

A former friend and collaborator of Tyndale's, George Joye, deserves mention at this point as a contributor to the growing number of biblical books printed in English. Joye had incurred Tyndale's disfavor by bringing out unauthorized revisions of the latter's New Testament in 1534 and 1535, and a sharp controversy ensued between the two. He should apparently be credited, however, with the translation and publication of a portion of the Old Testament extending from Psalms through Lamentations. This includes a rendering of Isaiah from the Latin (1531) which exerted some influence upon Coverdale's version of 1535, a translation of Jeremiah and Lamentations (1534) which included the "Song of Moses" to "magnify ye our Lorde for the fall of our Pharao the bishop of Rome," probably an edition of Proverbs and Ecclesiastes (1535), and a Psalter (1534), some readings of which have continued down through the King James Version. He has recently been credited with the possible authorship of the first Psalter printed in English, a translation from Latin pseudonymously published in 1530.[9] Joye's style is rather free, a reflection of his attitude appearing in a declaration that "as for me I had as lief put the trwthe in the text as in the margent," and "I wolde the scripture were so purely and playnly translated that it neded nether note, glose nor scholia, so that the reder might once swimme without a corke."[10]

VI. Miles Coverdale and the First English Bible

The completion and publication of the first complete printed English Bible was, however, the work of Miles Coverdale (1488-1568). Coverdale had studied at Cambridge, had become a priest and friar, and had apparently also found it discreet to spend some years outside of England because of Protestant convictions. He became acquainted with Tyndale and his work, and may have been encouraged to attempt a complete edition, of the English Scriptures, while still abroad, by statements of King Henry VIII favorable to an English Bible "by great lerned and Catholyke persones," and by activities of similar import by Archbishop Latimer and Thomas Cromwell. The edition which he published in 1535, printed perhaps at Cologne or Marburg, was not authorized in any way, but

Coverdale dedicated it to the king and queen in polite and flattering phraseology, and it met with no serious opposition. (The elaborate woodcut title page by Holbein shows the king handing out the Bible to the clergy.) This toleration is particularly noteworthy because Tyndale's translation was the basis of the work in the New Testament and Pentateuch.

Hostility toward the version was doubtless lessened by Coverdale's mild disposition and tractable attitude. In his dedication he declares, "I have nether wrested nor altered so moch as one worde for the mayntenaunce of any maner of secte." In notes and prologues he eliminated controversial data, and in the text he restored most of the ecclesiastically favored terms which Tyndale had altered. It is quite possible also that the first edition was anonymous, and that the dedicatory "Epistle unto the Kynges hyghnesse," signed by Coverdale, first appeared in a 1537 reprinting by James Nicolson. The original title page read: "Biblia: The Bible / that is, the holy Scripture of the Olde and New Testament, faithfully and truly translated out of Douche and Latyn in to English. M.D.XXXV." Other editions of the same year printed in England omitted the reference to Dutch (i.e., German) and Latin, which implied Lutheran and Catholic connections, and modified a prefatory reference to dependence upon Luther.

Actually, Coverdale did translate from the Latin and German in those sections of the Old Testament in which he did not use Tyndale. It is generally doubted that he knew much if any Hebrew, but his acquaintance with German was good. He states in his dedication that he translated out of "fyve sundry interpreters"; and besides Tyndale, these have been identified as the Vulgate, Luther, Pagninus' rather literal Latin translation of 1528, and the Zurich Swiss-German Bible of 1527-29 by Leo Juda, Zwingli, and others. The Vulgate rather than the Hebrew order of books was used in the Old Testament, and the Apocrypha are included, although their authority is questioned. The format and type resembled Tyndale's, but the text was set in double columns and decorated with sixty-eight woodcuts, and chapter summaries were introduced.

In general, the Tyndale portions of the edition are superior in quality, but Coverdale often improved the phrasing by reason of a special aptitude for euphonious English and for a fluent, although frequently diffuse, form of expression. While the work is uneven in this respect, some permanent contribution was thus made to the language of the English Bible, here as well as in later improvements of his which appeared in three editions of the Latin-English New Testament (1538) and in the Great Bible

---

[9] Charles C. Butterworth, *The Literary Lineage of the King James Bible* (Philadelphia: University of Pennsylvania Press, 1941), pp. 64-70, 87-91. The version was fairly popular, especially in connection with various devotional books known as "primers," and together with an independent version of the Psalter, found in the latter, it represents frequent literary linkage between the Wycliffite and later forms.

[10] Pollard, *op. cit.*, pp. 194-95.

of 1539. In particular, his version of the Psalter, as it appears in the latter, has remained a part of the Anglican Prayer Book to this day. Phraseology appearing here first with Coverdale included "Thou anoyntest my heade with oyle"; "the valley of the shadowe of deeth"; "but the way of the vngodly shal perishe" (see also table on pp. 101-4).

VII. The First Licensed Bible, 1537

Developing opinion in favor of an English Bible available to all without fear or favor now appeared in the renewal of a request to the king by the bishops. With a new translation by the bishops in mind, an injunction was actually drawn up in 1536, but not published until 1538, instructing the clergy to provide both a Latin and English Bible for every parish church. Meanwhile, two Bibles were published in 1537 which claimed to be licensed by the king. One, the printing of Coverdale by James Nicolson, probably merely assumed this status; the other, of obscure origin, but published under the name of Thomas Matthew, perhaps at Antwerp, obtained official support.[11]

Although this version largely followed Tyndale, incorporating also here for the first time his Old Testament translations of Joshua through Chronicles, and even reintroducing his prologues and notes, Cranmer, in his intercession with Cromwell to obtain royal approval, intimated that this was a "new Bible, both of a new translacion and of a new prynte," and claimed that "so farre as I have redde thereof I like it better than any other translacion heretofore made." Rather than cast aspersions upon Cranmer's Bible reading, we may suppose that he was motivated by the desire to have something to serve until the production of the projected bishops' version, which in his appeal to Cromwell he pessimistically dated at "a day after domesday." Whether king or counselors were acquainted with the facts about the revision is uncertain, but the mysterious circumstances of its origin may reflect an attempt to cover up the rather embarrassing approval of a Bible so largely the work of a man whose translations were officially condemned and who himself had just been burned at the stake as a heretic.

Although a Thomas Matthew of Colchester is known in connection with earlier biblical study, the work on the Bible of 1537 is generally attributed to John Rogers, a Cambridge graduate and friend of Tyndale, who in 1555 became the protomartyr in the persecution of Protestants under Bloody Mary. There is little departure from the Tyndale text, but the influence of Olivétan's French Bible of 1535 and Lefèvre's French Bible of 1534 is evident in the marginalia, in a new preface to the Apocrypha, and in the added "Prayer of Manasses." Whatever the true circumstances of its origin and publication, the Matthew Bible is notable for its official status, for its use of the heretofore unpublished Tyndale portions of the Old Testament, and for the fact that it became the chief basis for future revisions.

VIII. The Taverner Bible of 1539

In 1539 a revision of the Matthew Bible, minus most of the notes and polemic data, was issued by Richard Taverner at the instigation of Cromwell or of the king's printer, Thomas Barthlet. The title was as follows: "The Most Sacred Bible: Whiche is the holy scripture, conteyning the old and new testament, translated in to English, and newly recognised with great diligence after most faythful exemplars, by Rychard Taverner. ... Prynted at London in Fletestrete. ... by Iohn Byddell, for Thomas Barthlet. ... M.D.XXXIX." Taverner was a Cambridge and Oxford student who had been interested for some time in the English Bible. He knew Greek well, and especially therefore in the New Testament he introduced some independent renderings of real merit, several of which entered into subsequent English revisions. But this version was soon superseded by another revision and therefore exercised relatively little influence within the mainstream of the English Bible. It does have the honor of being the first to be printed completely in England.

IX. The First Authorized Bible: The Great Bible of 1539

A more significant revision appeared in the same year with the "Great Bible," so called from its size, or "Cranmer's Bible," from a preface to the second edition (1540) written by the archbishop. It may owe its origin mainly to a reaction of the clergy against the Matthew Bible, whose true content they had discovered. Yet it was undertaken by Coverdale at Cromwell's request. There was some episcopal supervision in the fourth and sixth of the seven editions which were published, and the title page refers the work to "dyverse excellent learned men." Who these were is unknown, unless the reference is to those responsible for the various earlier translations and other sources used in the revision. For, in particular, use was made of Munster's Latin Old Testament (1534-35), the Vulgate, and especially in the 1540 edition, of Erasmus' Latin New Testament and the Complutensian

[11] The title page read: "The Byble, which is all the holy Scripture: In whych are conteyned the Olde and Newe Testament, truly and purely translated into Englysh by Thomas Matthew . . .M.D.XXXVII. Set forth with the Kinges most gracyous lycence."

Polyglot.[12] As the first and, in fact, the only formally "authorized" English Bible, it is of special significance in our story. The 1540 and subsequent editions carried on the title page the explicit words: "This is the Byble apoynted to the use of the churches." [13]

Except for its larger size, the Great Bible does not differ much in format from previous revisions. However, the reactions against controversial prologues and marginalia now resulted in the removal of all such adjuncts to the text. Coverdale himself had projected explanatory notes for the first edition and was very much disappointed, as he wrote to Cromwell, that "the darck places of the text (vpon the which I haue allwaye set a hande) shulde so passe vndeclared." [14] The pointing hands actually appeared in the margins of the first three editions, but the notes were never made. There was no dedication, but a special feature serving the same purpose was an elaborate title page woodcut, often wrongly attributed to Holbein,[15] which shows King Henry VIII receiving and distributing the "Word of God" through his ministers Cranmer and Cromwell to the people amid their shouts of *Vivat Rex* and "God save the King." Private interpretation of the Bible was still feared, however, as indicated by statements in the preface and in royal proclamations of 1541 and later. The reference of difficulties to men of higher judgment in the Scriptures was recommended, and disputations were forbidden, especially in taverns and alehouses. The people now had a certain access to the Bible in the church and they were making the most of it; the authorities thought they were making too much of it.

Beginning about this time, however, and extending to the end of the reign of Henry VIII, a Catholic reaction set in which effectively halted the publication of the Bible in England for some years. The year 1540 saw the execution of Cromwell and the burning of both Protestants and papists for heresy. In 1543 restrictions were placed upon the reading of the Bible, and in

1546 a general burning of Bibles commenced. The authorized Great Bible alone was allowed, and its reading was limited to the upper classes. Although the brief reign of Edward VI afforded the Protestant forces some opportunity for recovery and advance, and the restrictions on the Bible were removed, the intemperate form of some of the Protestant iconoclasm of the period, when added to the previous Cromwellian "terror," made inevitable the continuation of reaction upon the accession of Mary Tudor in 1553. The situation was again reversed. A severe Catholic persecution ensued, which resulted in some three hundred martyrs, including men like Cranmer, Ridley, and Latimer. Many, among them Coverdale, took refuge on the Continent, and not a few gathered in Geneva, where they found a sympathetic welcome. Among these refugees the next great contribution to the promulgation of the Scriptures in English was made in the preparation and publication of the so-called "Geneva Bible."

X. The Geneva Bible

The purpose and character of the new Geneva revision reflect this geographically concentrated Protestantism. Calvin, Knox, Beza, and for a time Coverdale were in touch with the work. Important contacts were probably made with a group of scholars revising the French Bible of Olivétan.[16]

Although no names appear on the New Testament, which was published in 1557, the work is mainly credited to William Whittingham, a brother-in-law of Calvin, who was an able scholar and the successor of John Knox as minister to the English congregation at Geneva. The Old Testament was done by a group including Anthony Gilby, Thomas Sampson, and others of uncertain identity.

Notwithstanding the valuable contribution of those who participated, the result was definitely a revision of previous work. In the New Testament, Tyndale's 1534 edition was the chief basis, with important suggestions from Beza's Latin text and commentary of 1556.[17] The Old Testament consisted of a revision of the Great Bible by a careful reference to the Hebrew and with the guidance of the Latin editions of Pagninus, Münster, and Leo Juda. The Old Testament was published together with a careful revision of the New Testament in 1560, the

[12] A Hebrew-Greek-Latin edition of the Bible (Latin-Greek in the New Testament) published in four volumes at Complutum (Alcalá de Henares), Spain by Cardinal Ximenes in 1522-26.

[13] The original (1539) title page read: "The Byble in Englyshe, that is to saye the content of all the holy scrypture, bothe of ye olde and newe testament, truly translated after the veryte of the Hebrue and Greke textes, by ye dylygent studye of dyverse excellent learned men, expert in the forsayde tonges. Prynted by Rychard Grafton and Edward Whitchurch. Cum privilegio ad imprimendum solum. 1539."

[14] Pollard, *op. cit.*, p. 245.

[15] This is the conclusion of H. R. Willoughby's careful investigation as recorded in a quatrocentennial publication, *The First Authorized English Bible and the Cranmer Preface* (Chicago: University of Chicago Press, 1942).

[16] So David Daiches, *The King James Version of the English Bible* (Chicago: University of Chicago Press, 1941). He shows that it was the model for a table on Hebrew names and on "the chief and principal matters of the whole Bible."

[17] B. F. Westcott, *A General View of the History of the English Bible* (3d ed., rev. W. A. Wright; London: Macmillan & Co., 1905), has shown that in I John at least two thirds of the new renderings are from Beza.

first edition of the complete Geneva Bible, or, as it is sometimes called from the translation in Gen. 3:7, the "Breeches Bible." [18] The title page of the 1560 Bible read: "The Bible and Holy Scriptures conteyned in the Olde and Newe Testament. Translated according to the Ebrue and Greke, and conferred with the best translations in divers languages. With most profitable annotations vpon all the hard places, and other things of great importance as may appear in the Epistle to the Reader. At Geneva. Printed by Rouland Hall. M.D.LX." To Queen Elizabeth, who had succeeded to the throne in 1558 and had re-established the Church of England, the Geneva Bible was optimistically dedicated, along with some pious exhortation on building the church and putting all papists to the sword.

The new revision was the most scholarly and accurate English Bible so far produced, and represented the most creative development since Tyndale. The revisers themselves in their preface modestly explain how "in respect of this ripe age and cleare light which God had now reveiled, the translations required greatly to be perused and reformed," and give a strong Protestant statement of the importance of an English Bible for the common man. The understanding of the text was furthered by a profuse marginal commentary, again of strongly Protestant, even sometimes Calvinistic, tenor. "I have endevered so to profitt all therby," ran the preface of the 1557 New Testament, "that both the learned and others might be holpen. . . ."

The marginal notes contributed greatly to the popularity of the version among Protestants in general. Royalty and clergy, however, and especially Roman Catholic circles, were disturbed by certain of the interpretations. A note on Exod. 1:19 approving of the midwives' lying to Pharaoh was considered a reflection on royal prerogatives. The Pope naturally objected to being identified with "the angel of the bottomless pit" (Rev. 9:11), as "Antichrist the Pope, king of hypocrites and Satan's ambassadour." But not all notes were polemic, and their apparent bias can rarely be said to extend into the text itself. Alternative translations, exposition, and explanations of various kinds all made up the "most profitable annotations vpon all the hard places."

Several other novel features contributed to the usefulness and popularity of this Bible. Roman type was used for the first time. Division of the chapters into verses first appeared in English and became the basis of all versification in later English Bibles. The Hebrew Old Testament had long been divided (by Jewish scholars, the Masoretes) into sections or paragraphs

but these were supplanted in the Complutensian Polyglot of 1522-26 by the Vulgate chapter division, probably devised by Stephen Langton in the thirteenth century for Old and New Testaments. This appeared in all English Bibles. The versification of Old Testament and Apocrypha, originating with the Masoretes, appeared in Pagninus' Latin of 1528, and was taken over by the Geneva version in substantially the same form in which it is given in a later (1556-57) edition. The New Testament versification was made by Robert Estienne for his Greek edition of 1551, from which it was probably incorporated into the Geneva via Beza's Latin of 1556. The practice of italicizing English words not represented in the original text was introduced from Pagninus and Beza, a practice which was to continue down through the Revised Version. The convenient quarto size and consequently cheaper price also contributed to its popularity; and besides the marginal commentary, a variety of "helps," including maps, tables, woodcuts, chapter summaries, running titles, and, after 1579, a Calvinistic catechism, added to its usefulness.

As a result of these various features and the superior and attractive character of the version itself, the Geneva Bible enjoyed an immediate and widespread reception and usage. It soon became the household Bible of English-speaking Protestantism and so remained for nearly a century. It was the Bible of Shakespeare, of John Bunyan, of Cromwell's army, of the Puritan pilgrims, and of King James himself. It even colors a scripture quotation in the preface of the King James Version! About 180 editions of various sorts, 96 complete, were published, 8 of them appearing after the publication of the King James Version in 1611. Although never officially endorsed, it exerted a fundamental influence upon its "authorized" successors.

XI. The Second Authorized Bible: The Bishops' Bible of 1568

The popularity and superiority of the Geneva Bible were irksome to the church and state. Elizabeth's policy of toleration also had made it possible for all previous versions to circulate, and the Great Bible was unable to maintain a position commensurate with its official prerogative. An attempt was made, therefore, to produce a revision which might supplant the Geneva and other competing editions. Archbishop Parker, who became the leader of the undertaking, really a revival of Cranmer's project, formed a committee of revisers in 1564; [19] and

---

[18] The term "breeches" had occurred here, however, in Wycliffe and in Caxton's *Golden Legende*.

[19] A fairly accurate, although not quite certain or complete, list has been compiled from an account by Parker and from the revisers' initials affixed to the various parts of the work. A reconstruction is given by Pollard, *op. cit.*, pp. 30-31, and in some handbooks.

since the majority were bishops, the new version was naturally called "The Bishops' Bible."

After about four years of effort by the members of the committee to whom the work had been parceled out, the first edition was published in 1568 in a very large and impressive folio. The title was simply "The holie Bible conteyning the olde Testament and the newe." Although there was no dedication, a woodcut portrait of Queen Elizabeth appeared on the title page. The Cranmer preface to the Great Bible was reproduced and another long one added by Parker. Extensive external equipment included tables of content, a chronology, genealogies, maps, pictures, an almanac, numerous decorative woodcuts, two engravings, and marginal annotations. The customary black-letter type was employed, but Roman type served the function of the italics which had been used in the Geneva Bible.

Officially the revision was to be based on the Great Bible and there was to be only such necessary variation from it as was demanded by the Hebrew or Greek. This purpose is stated in a set of "Observacions respected of the Translators," which also enjoined the use of the Latin of Pagninus and Münster as guides. It was suggested too that unedifying text like genealogies should be marked for possible omission in public reading, that "all such wordes as soundeth in the Olde Translacion to any offence of Lightnes or obscenitie be expressed with more convenient termes and phrases," and that no "determinacion in places of controversie" or "bitter notis vppon any text" be included.[20] The real result was a revision of very uneven character, due to the exercise of individual freedom by the translators without adequate editorial supervision of the whole work. While some sections are therefore close to the Great Bible, especially in the Old Testament and Apocrypha, others depart freely from it. In some of these the influence of the Geneva Bible is apparent; even many of its marginalia were taken over. John Eadie[21] found that out of fifty notes in I Corinthians all but seven were from the Geneva. In Galatians twenty-two notes, all but two alternative translations, are used. The notes in general are explanatory or historical with some alternative renderings and some exhortation. The most famous is doubtless that on the gold of Ophir in Ps. 45:9: "Ophir is thought to be the Islande in the west coast, of late founde by Christopher Columbo: from whence at this day is brought most fine golde." The preface attributes the verse division to the Pagninus Bible. But the version was in general unpro-

gressive, and ignored many improvements in the Geneva text. Nor was the phraseology as simple and direct as in the latter, although Parker had been asked to avoid "ink horn terms."

In spite of its defects, the Bishops' Bible became the second "authorized" English version, for, although never so officially designated by the queen, it was endorsed by a convocation which in 1571 ordered its possession and use by every bishop and archbishop. While this injunction does not seem generally to have been obeyed, the version eventually displaced the Great Bible as the one "appoynted to be read in the Churches," and from 1577 on "as set forth by authoritie." As has been already intimated, however, it failed to oust the Psalter of the Great Bible. The second edition of 1572 gave both in parallel columns, the preface rather timidly inviting the reader to compare the two. But in all subsequent printings except one, the Psalter of the Great Bible alone was retained!

Although the Bishops' Bible was thus ecclesiastically acceptable, and about twenty editions of it were printed over the period from 1568 to 1606, it failed to replace the Geneva version in popular esteem and usage. The second edition served, however, as the official basis of the revision which was destined to do so, and in this way a number of readings which originated with the Bishops' Bible were perpetuated.

XII. The First Roman Catholic Bible in English

Meanwhile, another influential achievement occurred in the form of a Roman Catholic Bible in English. Back of this startling venture were Catholic refugees from England led by William Cardinal Allen, president and founder of the English college at Douai, France, then temporarily removed to Reims. The reasons for such a translation were given by Allen as Protestant distortion of the meaning of the text and the fact that Catholic preachers were at a disadvantage in quoting the Bible in English without a version of their own. Approval of lay use of the Bible was definitely not intended. In fact, the undertaking was not at first officially sanctioned by the church at all, but was doubtless a part of the Jesuit program of recapturing England for Catholicism.

The translation was made chiefly by Gregory Martin, and revised by Allen, both Oxford men. Although completed by 1582, only the New Testament was then published at Reims, the Old Testament being delayed until 1609-10 by lack of funds. By this time the college had moved back to Douai, and the version is therefore known as the Douay or Reims-Douay Bible. A complete Bible was not issued until 1633-35 at Rouen. Roman type and marginal versifica-

---

[20] Pollard, op. cit., pp. 297-98.
[21] The English Bible (London: Macmillan & Co., 1876).

tion are used, and the text is paragraphed, but not by verses as in the Bishops' and Geneva Bibles. Annotations by Allen in the form of marginalia and notes at the ends of chapters rival the Geneva in profuseness and exceed it in polemic nature. The Protestant "hereticks" and the Genevan commentators in particular are constantly, though not lovingly, in mind. The note on Matt. 6:24, for example, gives as the first interpretation of "two masters": "Two religions, God and Baal, Christ and Calvin, Masse and Communion, the Catholike Church and Heretical Conventicles."

The title page of the version proclaims it to be translated out of the "authentical Latin," referring, of course, to the Vulgate. The preface was to a certain extent right in claiming that this preserved a less corrupt text than the late Greek which lay behind the English translations to this time. The reading in Luke 2:14 ("and in earth peace to men of good will") and the omission of the doxology in Matt. 6:13 are conspicuous examples (see tables on pp. 102-3). Here and elsewhere there is coincidence with the Wycliffite version, since it too was made from the Vulgate. As the title page suggests, the Greek, Hebrew, and "other editions in divers languages" were also consulted. This is especially true in the New Testament, where even the influence of Geneva readings is apparent. But the version was often a slavishly literalistic rendering, at times merely a transliteration, of the Latin. To be understood it needed itself to be translated in such passages as "Give us today our supersubstantial bread" (Matt. 6:11), or, "But he exinanited himself" (Phil. 2:7).

The version was not without improvements, especially in its treatment of the Greek article, and it exerted a considerable influence upon the King James revision, in which many of its Latinisms were adopted. Its chief significance lay of course in Roman Catholic circles, where it was not only the first translation into English, but was eventually accorded official recognition and became the basis of all subsequent revision.

XIII. The King James Version of 1611

The climax and culmination of these early efforts in translation and revision was reached in the King James Version of 1611.

A number of factors combined to set the stage for the undertaking. The long reign of Elizabeth (1558-1603), with its partial settlement of the Protestant-Catholic controversy and defeat of the Spanish Armada (1588), ushered in a period of comparative peace and quiet that became notable for intellectual and literary effort. When James I came to the throne in 1603, he brought with him pronounced Protes-

tant views and a personal interest in biblical study and translation. The Bishops' Bible had failed to displace the Geneva, and the Puritans were objecting, among other things, to the "authorized" versions. It was to hear their complaints that James called the Hampton Court Conference of 1604, which became the immediate occasion for the new revision. For when the Puritans gained little in other matters, the criticism of the English Bibles was broached, and John Reynolds, Puritan president of Corpus Christi College, Oxford, moved that there might be a new translation of the Bible. Although there was no immediate action on this petition, the idea appealed to the king, and as the preface to the version itself puts it, "yet even hereupon did his Maiestie beginne to bethinke himself of the good that might ensue by a new translation, and presently after gave order for this translation which is now presented unto thee." Whatever his motives, King James supported the project so vigorously that by July, 1604, a translation committee of fifty "learned men" and a list of rules of procedure had been provided.[22]

Although our knowledge of the earliest period of the work is vague, the purposes of the revision may be learned from the rules of procedure and from the preface. The latter, a long and learned document by one of the revisers, Miles Smith, is unfortunately omitted from the version as usually printed.[23] Its presence would clear up many misunderstandings about the character and intent of the revision. The reader would learn that an English Bible still needed justification and that strong opposition was expected to any revision of the current version:

Many mens mouths haue bene open a good while (and yet are not stopped) with speeches about the Translation so long in hand . . . : and aske what may be the reason, what the necessitie of the employment.

They would learn that the new version was a scholarly revision of previous work with a modest hope of improvement and no thought of finality:

Truly (good Christian Reader) wee neuer thought from the beginning, that we should neede to make a new Translation, nor yet to make of a bad one a good one, . . . but to make a good one better, or out of many good ones, one principall good one, not

---

[22] About fifty of the group are known. But our fullest list has forty-seven names. It may be found in Pollard, *op. cit.*, pp. 49-53; Butterworth, *op. cit.*, pp. 208-9. A full statement of the rules of procedure may be found in Pollard, pp. 53-55, and in various handbooks.

[23] It is reproduced in Pollard, *op. cit.*, pp. 340-77. E. J. Goodspeed has published it with a facsimile and introduction: *The Translators to the Reader* (Chicago: University of Chicago Press, 1935).

justly to be excepted against; that hath bene our indeauour, that our marke. . . . So, if we building vpon their foundation that went before vs, and being holpen by their labours, doe endeuour to make that better which they left so good; no man, we are sure, hath cause to mislike vs; they, we perswade our selues, if they were aliue, would thanke vs.

The rules of procedure more specifically indicated that the Bishops' Bible was to be followed and "as little altered as the Truth of the original will permit"; that certain other translations should be used where they agreed better with the text, viz., "Tindoll's, Matthew's, Coverdale's, Whitchurch's [the Great Bible, so named from a printer], Geneva"; that "the old Ecclesiastical words [were] to be kept," and that no marginal notes were to be used except for necessary explanation of the Hebrew or Greek. Most of the remaining fifteen rules dealt with method of procedure, providing that the committee be divided into six companies operating two each at Oxford, Cambridge, and Westminster on allotted sections of the text, that they should confer on the results, and that a special committee should make a final review of the work. It is questionable whether the last two of these provisions were adequately carried out. Although its beginning was unaccountably delayed for about four years, the revision was completed within three years and ready for publication by 1611.

The historic edition which issued from the press of Robert Barker was a large folio volume very similar to the Bishops' Bible in appearance. The type and the chapter and verse division were essentially the same. Running titles and prefatory chapter summaries were included, many reflecting the influence of the Geneva Bible. There were several tables and charts. The Apocrypha were given without any distinguishing comments. A flattering dedication to King James was naturally a feature, and an elaborate engraved title page described the version as "The Holy Bible, Conteyning the Old Testament and the New: Newly Translated out of the Originall tongues; & with the former Translations diligently compared and revised, by his Maiesties speciall Commandement. Appointed to be read in Churches."

A second edition partly printed in the same year and published in 1613 has caused some confusion as to priority because of the use of leaves of the earlier edition in copies of the later. The editions differed in over four hundred readings and in other features. (They are sometimes called the "He Bible" and "She Bible" from their respective renderings of the reference in Ruth 3:15.) Although the King James Version has come to be known as *the*

authorized version, no official action of authorization is known to exist. Either the record of such an act was destroyed by fire or, as with the Bishops' Bible, the official sponsorship was considered sufficient recognition. The King James Bible therefore became the third "authorized" English Bible.

Although officially a revision of the Bishops' Bible, especially of the second edition of 1572, the King James Version derived comparatively little from that except as it contained the cumulative result of previous work. The other translations mentioned in the rules, especially the Tyndale and Geneva versions, contributed much more, and among unnamed sources the contributions of the Reims New Testament, Luther's German Bible, and various Latin translations such as Pagninus, Münster, Tremellius-Junius, and Beza are very apparent. In general, however, the total result is still basically the inherited Tyndale-Coverdale text. The Geneva was of next greatest influence. In the Lord's Prayer the two are identical except for two minor words.[24] The revisers, of course, added their own improvements, centering particularly in the choice of words, enrichment of vocabulary, and the enhancement of the rhythmic quality of the text. While this contribution varied greatly from place to place, the result was a version generally superior to its predecessors in accuracy of translation and refinement of literary style.

But the revision had also its weaknesses, several of them a part of its inheritance. The underlying text was still far from satisfactory. There was no standard edition of the Hebrew Masoretic text of the Old Testament. In the New Testament the late and corrupt text of Erasmus as popularized and slightly modified by Stephanus and Beza was necessarily used, since nothing better was available. The variety introduced into the rendering of the same words was often unnecessary and misleading, especially when extended to proper names and to identical passages in the Synoptic Gospels and elsewhere, where literary relationships were thus obscured.[25] Conversely, certain real distinctions were not observed, a famous example being the inherited translation in John 10:16 of two different Greek words as "fold," where the second should have been "flock," apparently, as in

[24] A good treatment of the varied literary relationship will be found in Butterworth, *op. cit.* In the latter part of the Old Testament he found that "often as much as half the text is taken word for word from the Geneva Bible" (p. 165).

[25] Cf., e.g., Isa. 35:10 and 51:11; Matt. 26:41 and Mark 14:38; etc. The bewildering variety in proper names still remains, e.g., Elijah and Elias; Jeremiah, Jeremias, and Jeremy; Judas, Judah, and Jude; Luke and Lucas; etc.

the Vulgate, in the interests of *one* church. No systematic representation of measurements is used, several of differing quantity being rendered simply as "measure." Coinage is generally resolved into British equivalents, but again, indefinite terms such as "pieces of silver" (Luke 15:8) or "piece of money" (Matt. 17:27) are often used where the original is definite. "Lamp" and "lampstand"—to cite another example of modernization—had long been translated as "candle" and "candlestick." Failure to give proper recognition to certain Greek usages is attributable to the still unsatisfactory knowledge of the original languages. Other defects included obscurities, archaisms, solecisms in the English, failure to recognize and represent all Hebrew poetical forms, and, especially in the earlier editions, many printing errors. A famous misprint still remaining in the version is "at" for "out" in "strain at a gnat" (Matt. 23:24). Obscure or archaic expressions abound, e.g., "prevent" for "go before"; "to wit" for "to know"; "damnation" for "judgment"; "cleanness of teeth" for "famine" (a Hebraism); "carriage" for "baggage"; etc. Lists of dubious readings of all sorts may be found in Philip Schaff, *A Companion to the Greek Testament and the English Version* (New York: Harper & Bros., 1883), and elsewhere.

But no one reads the King James Version in its original form. Many archaisms, misspellings and other errors were corrected in subsequent editions.[26] Criticism of the version, as anticipated, was severe, and led to several revisions. That of 1629 first omitted the Apocrypha. (The fortunes of the Apocrypha would require too much space to relate here. An ordinance of 1615 threatened a year's imprisonment to printers who omitted them. But after sporadic omission for two centuries, they were generally dropped as of supposedly inferior value and no part of the original—i.e., Hebrew—canon.) The most extensive revisions were made by Thomas Paris at Cambridge in 1762 and by Benjamin Blayney at Oxford in 1769. The latter became the standard form, and after this few changes were made. The original edition, in spite of the stricture on marginalia, had included about 9,000 cross references and some 8,000 other notations, mostly the literal Hebrew and Greek, but some explanatory, as the preface indicated and sought to justify. The revisions added to this number constantly, so that by the

time of the Blayney edition the notes, increased especially by an indiscriminate multiplication of cross references, totaled about 65,000. Archbishop Ussher's chronology was added in Lloyd's 1701 edition. The various editions, of which about 50 were published by 1640, differed in size and format, and as early as 1612 both a folio and quarto were issued in Roman type.

With the gradual improvement of the version the clamor against it died down to a great extent. Officially it replaced the Bishops' Bible, and after fifty years or so the Geneva Bible, in popular use. Political strife served also to distract attention from biblical revision for some time. The result was that the King James Bible remained for two and a half centuries the Bible of English-speaking Protestantism and exerted a wide and lasting influence not only in religion but also in literature and every other area of contemporary culture.[27]

The version also became widely recognized for its own intrinsic literary value, and many came to regard it as the greatest monument of English prose. A good part of its appeal is attributable to the literary genius exemplified in the original writings, and to the reproduction of much of the flavor of the vivid and concrete word-picture character of Semitic expression, with its striking imagery, metaphors, personifications, proverbs, parables, etc. These have often become a part of our speech, as in terminology like "lick the dust," "skin of his teeth," "salt of the earth." And long familiarity fails to dull the beauty of such natural imagery as is found in Ps. 23, or the human appeal of a parable like that of the prodigal son.[28]

XIV. The Revised Version

But great progress was made after 1611, especially in the nineteenth century, both in the discovery and publication of better Hebrew and Greek texts and in fields such as archaeology, linguistics, comparative religion, etc., with the result that new light was thrown upon the understanding of the biblical text and its proper translation. Discovery or first real use of such early manuscripts as Vaticanus, Alexandrinus, Beza, and Sinaiticus had marked influence. The

---

[26] Later editions often added their own errors, however, and several have been nicknamed after some particular slip. A list of such "Queer and Interesting Bibles" may be seen in Laura H. Wild, *The Romance of the English Bible* (New York: Doubleday, Doran & Co., 1929), Appendix II. All of the changes from the 1611 edition are noted in *The Cambridge Paragraph Bible* (Cambridge: Cambridge University Press, 1873).

[27] For its pervasive influence in literature see the discussion and bibliographies in Margaret B. Crook, ed., *The Bible and Its Literary Associations* (New York: Abingdon Press, 1937); A. S. Cook, *Biblical Quotations in Old English Prose Writers* (New York: The Macmillan Co., 1898); *The Bible and English Prose Style* (Boston: D. C. Heath & Co., 1892).

[28] Many good treatments of this aspect of the subject exist; e.g., Josiah H. Penniman, *A Book About the English Bible* (New York: The Macmillan Co., 1919); C. A. Dinsmore, *The English Bible as Literature* (Boston: Houghton Mifflin Co., 1931); W. O. Sypherd, *The Literature of the English Bible* (New York: Oxford University Press, 1938).

steady accumulation of thousands of variant readings in the New Testament, many of which were obviously older and better, led eventually to the first total disregard of the "received" text by Karl Lachmann in 1831. Great advance was made by the work of Konstantin von Tischendorf, Samuel Tregelles, and others, and after nearly thirty years of labor, Westcott and Hort in 1881 published a text of the fourth century or earlier. The Old Testament text had been vocalized and standardized by the seventh or eighth century A.D. in what was not a truly critical form. A tenth-century copy of it by Ben Asher became the prevalent text and mainly underlies the English and other translation to this time as well as to the present. But variation in text was publicized in the earlier period through the polyglots, which gave the Latin, Greek, Syriac, Aramaic, and other versions, and through such editions as those of Benjamin Kennicott (Oxford, 1776-1780) and J. B. de Rossi (Parma, 1784-88).[29] Advance in the other areas mentioned frequently threw doubt upon the accuracy of the translation. The lapse of time had rendered many more words and expressions obsolete or generally unintelligible. Bishop Robert Lowth's lectures on Hebrew poetry in the middle eighteenth century first revealed the true literary character of much of the biblical text. The decipherment of hieroglyphic and cuneiform writing in the first half of the nineteenth century had made possible for the first time the reading of the ancient records of Medes, Persians, Babylonians, Assyrians, and Egyptians, with consequent illumination of Hebrew history and literature.

The effect of these influences appeared in renewed agitation for a revision of the King James Version and in numerous attempts on the part of private individuals and groups to anticipate such an undertaking by issuing new translations and revisions of their own. From about the middle of the eighteenth century these became increasingly numerous, and every sort of experiment was tried with style and format. One scholar estimates that nearly 100 such editions, mostly of the New Testament, were produced in the 259 years between 1611 and the beginning of work on the Revised Version, over half of them in the nineteenth century.[30] These ventures served to call attention to such defects in the current Bible as have been already briefly indicated, and some of them were of real merit as illustrative of the possibilities involved in a new revision. Among the most interesting and valuable are the following (New Testament and British, unless otherwise indicated) : W. Mace (1729), William Whiston (1745), John Wesley (1755), Philip Doddridge (1765), Edward Harwood (1768), William Newcome (1796), Anthony Purver (1764), Gilbert Wakefield (1789-91), Nathaniel Scarlett (1798), Charles Thomson (a translation of the Greek Bible, Philadelphia, 1808), Noah Webster (New Haven, 1833), Granville Penn (1836-37), Asahel Kendrick (1842), Alford, Moberly, Humphrey, Ellicott and Barrow (Gospel of John and Pauline Epistles, 1857-61), Thomas J. Conant (New Testament and parts of the Old Testament, editions of the American Bible Union, 1860-71), G. R. Noyes (Boston, 1869), Henry Alford (1870), Julia Smith (Bible, Hartford, 1876). The Bible of Thomson, who was secretary of the Continental Congress, was the first complete English translation by an American.

Scholars also published lists of the deficiencies in the Authorized Version and sought to estimate the probable nature and amount of revision that would be necessary. While defenders of the current version were not lacking, and efforts to find official support for revision failed in 1856, the tide of opinion could not be stayed much longer.

The first official step was taken on February 10, 1870, when at a meeting of the convocation of Canterbury, Bishop Samuel Wilberforce of Winchester proposed the appointment of a committee to report on the desirability of a revision of the New Testament. This, as amended to include the Old Testament, was approved, and the committee named soon brought in a favorable report in the form of five resolutions which suggested the general purpose and procedure of the work. It is clear that the revision was considered to be mainly textual (including the margin), that only necessary changes were to be adopted, and that the style of the King James Version was to be retained. Another committee was then authorized to proceed with more detailed plans for the project and its personnel. Nucleus sections for Old and New Testament were quickly formed, a list of rules of procedure for guidance was drawn up, and by June 22, 1870, the work on the New Testament had got under way with an initial meeting at Westminster Abbey.

The men who undertook the task of revision constituted an able and distinguished group,[31]

---

[29] See p. 56.

[30] E. J. Goodspeed, The Making of the English New Testament (Chicago: University of Chicago Press, 1925), p. 78.

[31] For a list of the members see H. Wheeler Robinson, The Bible in Its Ancient and English Versions (Oxford: Clarendon Press, 1940), pp. 243-45. The twenty-four to twenty-eight members who were active in the ensuing ten years included for the Old Testament group T. K. Cheyne, A. B. Davidson, S. R. Driver, F. Field, C. D. Ginsburg, J. McGill, A. H. Sayce, R. Payne Smith, W. Wright; and for the New Testament, H. Alford, J.

and included representatives of various denominations other than the Anglican. Co-operation with American "divines" was also invited from the beginning, and an American group of about nineteen active members was formed under the leadership of Philip Schaff, arrangements being made for collaboration with the British.[32] The rules of procedure adopted added certain specifications to the original resolutions. The text was to be gone over twice, decisions in doubtful places depending upon a majority in the preliminary revision and by a two-thirds vote in the second. Rejected readings of the King James Version were to be placed in the margin; the headings of chapters and pages, paragraphing, italics, and punctuation were to be revised; and reference was to be made when desirable "to Divines, Scholars and Literary Men, whether at home or abroad, for their opinions."

The work continued for ten and a half years on the New Testament and about fourteen on the Old. A much needed revision of the Apocrypha was also made. The expenses were borne by the university presses of Cambridge and Oxford, the publishers and copyright owners; but the revisers themselves received no remuneration.

The New Testament was published on May 17, 1881, and met with an enthusiastic initial reception. People stood in line for copies. A million copies had been ordered in advance, and some three million were sold in England and the United States within the first year. The book was first put on sale in the United States on May 20, and two days later two Chicago newspapers printed the complete text for their readers. The Old Testament appeared, with less demonstration, as a part of the whole Bible on May 19, 1885. The Apocrypha were published in 1895.

Purchasers found themselves in possession of a text in which the number of changes far exceeded all previous estimates. Of some 180,000 words in the New Testament, for example, alterations amounted to an estimated 30,000, or an average of four and a half per verse. While the revisers did attempt to retain the style and flavor of the King James Version, they did not hesitate to remove obscurities, archaisms, and inconsistencies in the text. Wide variation was due to the increased accuracy of

Angus, J. Eadie, C. J. Ellicott (chairman), F. J. A. Hort, B. H. Kennedy, J. B. Lightfoot, W. Milligan, W. F. Moulton, R. Scott, R. C. Trench, B. F. Westcott.

[32] The American committee included T. J. Conant, W. H. Green, C. M. Mead, Josiah Strong, Ezra Abbott, Timothy Dwight, J. Hadley, A. C. Kendrick, M. B. Riddle, J. H. Thayer, and T. D. Woolsey. M. B. Riddle published *The Story of the Revised American Standard Version* (Philadelphia: Sunday School Times Co., 1908).

the underlying text which they used, especially in the New Testament. Hort persuasively urged upon the committee the text upon which he and Westcott had labored so many years, and it exerted a great influence, though far from being consistently followed. Many of its rejected readings, however, were placed in the margin.

The English was given in two columns, improved by division into sense paragraphs and with verse numbers in the margin. Poetry was better represented; italics were reduced in number and systematized. Chapter summaries and headings were omitted entirely. At first the marginal cross references were also dropped, but popular demand led to their restoration in 1898 and in subsequent editions. The usual marginal notes appeared, the textual variants and alternative renderings occupying a much larger space. The enormous amount of new evidence which could be brought to bear upon the problems of translation made the marginalia of value to the student interested in accuracy and comprehension. The better text was often represented in the margin. A list of about three hundred readings preferred by the American Committee, but not adopted by the English revisers, was given in an appendix.

It was not long, however, before the number and character of the changes in the revision provoked a strong reaction. The work had already been under attack before publication, but now criticism became more specific as well as voluble. Members of the revision committee itself joined in denouncing the results, as the merits and demerits of the version were argued. Charges of unnecessary departure from the familiar phraseology, undue literalism, elaborate overcorrection, destruction of beauty and rhythm, impoverishment of the English language, and the like, flew thick and fast. Prime Minister Gladstone spoke against its authorization, and it was coolly received by its sponsor, the convocation of Canterbury. Champions of the enterprise were numerous, however, and not a few felt that the revision did not depart sufficiently from the traditional text either in the choice of readings or in the modernization of the English.

It is quite true that the revisers went beyond their expressed purposes. Charges of overliteralism and overconsistency could often be substantiated. The total effect was frequently to spoil a certain natural vigor and beauty without rewriting the translation in a really creative fashion. This resulted in an artificial product for the day in which it was made. Yet the vast number of improvements in accuracy, clarity, and consistency are undeniable, and much opposition to the revision must be attributed to traditional associations. Certain alterations in the text, such as the omission of the doxology at the end of the Lord's Prayer (Matt. 6:13), were very disconcerting to those unacquainted with the facts about textual study. Examples of greater accuracy and clarity are legion. Cf., e.g.,

II Cor. 8:1 KJV "We do you to wit."

RV "We make known to you."

Luke 3:23 KJV "And Jesus himself began to be about thirty years of age."

RV "And Jesus himself, when he began to teach, was about thirty years old."

Isa. 9:1 KJV ". . . and afterward did more grievously afflict her."

RV ". . . in the latter time hath he made it glorious."

In spite of opposition the Revised Version eventually became widely used, especially in church schools and for purposes of study, and particularly in the United States. It officially displaced the King James Version at Canterbury and Westminster. After a stipulated wait of fourteen years, an American edition was published on August 26, 1901, incorporating the readings of the American appendix in the text and making an equal number of other changes. In general, these show more progress away from traditional and archaic forms of expression, and they substitute American for British idiom where the two differ. The American committee also restored (revised) running headlines, included a new set of sensible marginal references, and further improved the use of italics and punctuation.[33]

The Revised Version, however, failed to displace the King James Version to a degree comparable to that in which the latter had overcome rival versions. This was due to the defects which have been mentioned, to the disadvantage of copyright restrictions which made the revision more expensive to buy, and to the fact that it faced the formidable opposition of a version which had been hallowed by religious usage and literary associations for well over two centuries. To overcome the last circumstance alone only a phenomenal production could have sufficed. The Revised Version was not such: it went too far to be acceptable as a mere revision of the King James Version; it did not go far enough to be accepted on its own merits as a new and modern translation.

XV. The Modern Speech Versions

The recognition of the defects in the Revised Version and the continuing increase of knowl-

edge in the areas pertaining to translation led to renewed efforts to provide more satisfactory, and in particular, more modern, results. Several new manuscript discoveries, such as the Sinaitic Syriac, together with progress in textual study served further to discredit the traditional Greek text. In Egypt especially, at the turn of the century and in subsequent years, great numbers of papyrus documents were unearthed, which reflected every aspect of the life of the people of the ancient world in which much of the Bible and particularly the New Testament was written. These discoveries were a special stimulus to translation activity, since the documents revealed that the New Testament was written in general in the ordinary, everyday Greek of the time and indicated the true or exact meaning of many of its words and idioms for the first time. The new knowledge was soon incorporated in grammatical and lexical works, and modern speech translations began to appear, which not only sought to exploit the new information on specific points, but tried also to exemplify in their English the fact that the New Testament books were originally written to be understood by ordinary folk and ought to be kept in the language of the people. This conviction was fortunately extended to cover the Old Testament too, where archaeological discoveries and study had also opened up new vistas for the understanding of the Hebrew text.

Only a few of the outstanding versions produced in this modern period can be mentioned. Ferrar Fenton published a Bible (1883-1900) in the modern English of Great Britain which enjoyed considerable popularity. A pioneering effort was the *Four Gospels* of F. A. Spencer, published in 1898. The rest of the New Testament was translated in 1937. F. S. Ballentine first sought to employ American idiom in an 1898 Bible, which in the preface he described as "a plainer Bible for plain people in plain American." From the same viewpoint, and consistently good, was the *Twentieth Century New Testament* published anonymously by a group of scholars in a tentative form in 1898-1901 and in a definitive edition in 1904. British idiom is represented in a New Testament translation made by R. F. Weymouth, a competent Greek scholar, from his own *Resultant Greek Testament,* and issued posthumously in 1903. Couched in modern, dignified but often diffuse English, and furnished with an extensive apparatus of notes, it became especially popular in England, and a fourth edition revised by three English scholars was published in 1924. One of the most popular of the new versions has been that of James Moffatt, who translated the entire Bible into modern speech of free style. The New Testament (1913), based on von Soden's

---

[33] The title page read identically with the English except for the date, "Revised A.D. 1881-1885," and the following lines: "Newly Edited by the American Revision Committee, A.D. 1901, Standard Edition. New York: Thomas Nelson & Sons." The text was copyrighted by the publishers.

text, was of greater value and vogue than the Old. The latter was issued in 1924, and a complete Bible in 1926. William G. Ballantine issued a translation in 1923 (rev. ed., 1934) based on the Nestle text and known as the *Riverside New Testament*. It is closer to the traditional English than most modern versions but has a number of independent readings of merit. A two-volume edition of the New Testament ably and rather conservatively translated by Helen Barrett Montgomery was issued to commemorate the one-hundredth anniversary of the American Baptist Publication Society in 1923-24, and is known as the *Centenary New Testament*. Rivaling the Moffatt New Testament in value and popularity is the edition of Edgar J. Goodspeed. His is again a fairly free rendering and represents, as its subtitle indicates, *An American Translation*. The New Testament was published in 1923, a translation of the text of Westcott and Hort; and a revision of it by Goodspeed is in process. The Old Testament was likewise, but more conservatively, rendered into American idiom by a group of scholars under the leadership and editorship of J. M. P. Smith and published in 1927.[34] The complete Bible appeared in 1931, and a new translation of the Apocrypha prepared by Goodspeed was incorporated into an edition issued in 1939. Independent readings of merit often occur in other modern speech versions, such as Verkyl's New Testament (1945) and the Jehovah's Witnesses' edition of the New Testament (1950).

Besides using modern diction, these various editions generally sought to incorporate improvements in format and mechanics. The text is often logically paragraphed, chapter and verse numbers are returned to the margin, poetry is distinguished from prose, Old Testament quotations in the New Testament are differentiated, cross references are much reduced in quantity and relegated to the bottom of the page, direct speech is sometimes paragraphed. Marginal notes are usually few, if any. A free, idiomatic rendering is not concerned about literal meanings. Most modern speech versions could be improved, however, by a few marginal annotations on important textual variants and problem passages.

Translation and revision have continued for a variety of reasons. Some of it reflects the prolongation of efforts to improve the King James Version. Thus the American Bible Union work was carried forward until the whole Bible had been completed, a third revision of the 1864 New Testament being published in 1891 by Hovey, Broadus, and Weston, and a revised Bible being issued in 1912. Charles F. Kent

produced a meritorious translation of parts of the New Testament for his *Shorter New Testament,* published in 1919; and in the same year the "Concordant Version" of all except the Gospels was issued, based upon a text reconstructed from the three manuscripts, Vaticanus, Sinaiticus, and Alexandrinus. The Gospels appeared in 1924. Several translations of individual manuscripts have also been published. We cannot deal with these or with the many extant translations of parts of the Bible. In 1933, George Lamsa and C. C. Torrey each issued versions of the four Gospels, supposedly reflecting new insights into the meaning of the text arising out of a fuller knowledge of its Semitic backgrounds and of Semitic documents hypothetically lying behind the Greek, especially of the Gospels, the first half of Acts and Revelation. Lamsa's translation was really nothing but a rendering of the late (Peshitta) Syriac, itself a translation from Greek; Torrey's was a more or less ingenious attempt to reconstruct and translate an underlying Semitic text. In 1941 a group of British scholars produced the *New Testament in Basic English.* In spite of obvious defects due to the limited vocabulary of less than a thousand words, the work was well done. But one is disturbed—thinking of the children whom the volume was in part supposed to serve—by passages such as "Happy are the sad." A similar translation of the Old Testament was produced subsequently and the two were published together in 1949 as *The Basic Bible.*

XVI. Jewish and Roman Catholic Versions

Work has also continued in non-Protestant areas. Jewish efforts in Old Testament translation began in England with versions of the Pentateuch by Isaac Delgado and David Levi in 1785 and 1787 and complete editions more or less in the King James style by Benisch (1851-56) and Friedlander (1884). They continued in the United States with the 1853 editions of Isaac Leeser, widely used in both countries, and culminated in the version published by the Jewish Publication Society in 1917. The last was the work of a committee of scholars which began operations in 1892 and which took full account of the various English versions previously mentioned.[35]

Among Roman Catholics the Reims-Douay version was soon subject to several revisions, the most important of which was that of the Douai scholar, Richard Challoner. His revision, which practically amounted to a new translation, was published in 1749-50 and showed extensive influence of the King James Version. It

---

[34] The other collaborators were Leroy Waterman, Theophile J. Meek, and Alexander R. Gordon.

[35] A fuller account of Jewish efforts is given in Max L. Margolis, *The Story of Bible Translations* (Philadelphia: Jewish Publication Society, 1917).

became the standard text, especially in the Old Testament. A revision of Challoner by McMahon (New Testament, 1781; Bible, 1791) was approved by Archbishop Troy of Dublin. Archbishop F. P. Kenrick of Philadelphia also edited a revised text (New Testament, 1851; Bible, 1862), and a committee of about twenty-seven scholars, under the patronage of the "Episcopal Committee of the Confraternity of Christian Doctrine," completed, after five years of work, a revision of the New Testament which was published in 1941. This, although retaining much of the traditional language and style, makes some concession to modern speech. A similar but more independent and effective result was attained in the 1944 New Testament of Ronald A. Knox, a British scholar. In his free style he also published in 1948 Vol. I (Genesis to Esther) of the Old Testament. Vol. II (Job to Maccabees) appeared in 1950. While these revisions take account of the Hebrew and Greek texts, their official basis remains the Latin Vulgate. Independent translations, however, have been made directly from the original languages, the most important of which is the Westminster Version edited by C. Lattey and J. Keating. This was published serially between 1913 and 1935, and a one-volume edition, reduced in format and slightly revised, was issued in 1948. The Confraternity Committee has also undertaken a complete retranslation from the original languages, following the pattern of its New Testament but giving up "deliberate compromise with earlier usage." Genesis (1948) and the Psalms and Canticles (1950) have already appeared.

XVII. The Revised Standard Version

The effect of the new data bearing upon translation eventually found expression also in the institution of "official" projects both in the United States and England for a revision of the Revised Version. The defects of the latter had been highlighted by the modern speech publications, and with the lapse of time new progress was made in all disciplines bearing upon accuracy of translation. New manuscripts such as the Washington and Koridethi Gospels and the Chester Beatty papyri were discovered and published. Scholars began to show some diminution of confidence in Hort's textual theories and results, at least so far as they pretended to restore the most primitive text of the New Testament. Great progress was made in the study of the Septuagint text of the Old Testament. Significant linguistic study and archaeological discovery continued. In the United States, when the American Standard Version copyright expired, it was transferred by the publishers to the International Council of Religious Educa-

tion, and through this representative Protestant organization, two committees of scholars, with Luther A. Weigle as chairman of both, were appointed to undertake revisions of the New and Old Testaments respectively.[36]

The work was begun in 1930 and, except for a few lean years (1932-37), had continued to the time of publication. The New Testament was published in February, 1946, and the Old Testament will have only just appeared when this article is published (1952). Recognizing the deficiencies of the Revised Version, the new version aims not only to be a clear, idiomatic, and "readable" translation based on the best available text, but also to preserve the great values of the Tyndale-King James tradition for use in public and private worship. If the whole can be judged by the New Testament part (which alone is available at the moment of writing), the revisers have gone far toward the achievement of these purposes. The modern format and the dropping of the antique forms of the personal pronouns and verbal endings except in address to the deity and a few other places give the impression of a modern speech version, and this is borne out frequently by the phraseology; but in general, and especially in the familiar passages, the Revised Version is closely followed and modernized. An occasional reading is adopted from the King James Version. Opinion of critical readers has differed on a number of specific passages, both as regards text and translation, but not on the general acceptability of the work. Some feel that the revision did not go far enough in its adoption of modern idiom; others, replying, contend that great progress has been made in that direction without the sacrifice of so much of the traditional English as to alienate the majority of readers and to render the volume unacceptable for ecclesiastical usage. The fact that the committee of scholars which prepared the Revised Standard Version will continue, with necessary changes in membership, as a permanent committee of the National Council of the Churches of Christ in the U. S. A., into which the International Council of Religious Education has merged, makes provision for progressive revision to eliminate such deficiencies as may still remain in it.

In England, also, a movement for a revision designed for modern readers has been initiated. The matter was discussed in the General As-

---

[36] A statement of the purpose and circumstances of the work, of the committee members and denominational representatives, etc., will be found in a pamphlet written by the revisers: *An Introduction to the Revised Standard Version of the New Testament* (Chicago: International Council of Religious Education, 1946). A good summary of the progress in areas related to translation is here given.

sembly of the Church of Scotland; and the upper house of the convocation of Canterbury on May 20, 1947, authorized the appointment of an interdenominational committee to work with the Cambridge and Oxford presses upon such a project. The books of the Bible (including the Apocrypha) have been allotted to translators. The present secretary of the committee is J. K. S. Reid, and the work is under the general direction of C. H. Dodd. It is unfortunate that the British and American revisions are, apparently, entirely independent of each other.

XVIII. Story Without End

This brings us to the end of a story which has no end, for the task of revision will never be completed. We have mapped out some of the main tributaries and sources which have poured into the mainstream of our English Bible. We have had a glimpse of the devoted efforts which have given it to us both in the traditional text in which especially it has permeated our English-speaking culture, and in the subsequent forms which have sought to bring it to us in the most accurate and intelligible representations of its original thought. As certainly as the Bible remains the great classic of the Judeo-Christian faith and, indeed, the pre-eminent religious classic of all faiths, so surely will go on the work of making it known to all men, "each in his own tongue."

XIX. Tables of Illustrative Readings

KEY TO ABBREVIATIONS

Lin	Lindisfarne Gospels
Sh	Shoreham Psalter
Lu	Luther's New Testament (1522)
W¹	First Wycliffite Bible (*ca.* 1382)
W²	Second Wycliffite Bible (*ca.* 1400; Purvey revision?)
T	Tyndale's New Testament (1525-26)

C	Coverdale Bible (1535)
Ma	Matthew Bible (1537)
Ta	Taverner Bible (1539)
Gr	Great Bible (1539)
Ge	Geneva Bible (1560)
Ge²	Geneva Bible (1579)
B¹	Bishops' Bible (1568)
B²	Bishops' Bible (1572)
R-D	Reims-Douay Bible (1609-10)
KJV	King James Version (1611)
ERV	English Revised Version (1881-85)
ASV	American Standard Version (1901)
RV	Revised Version (English and American)
RSV	Revised Standard Version (1946-52)
We	Weymouth New Testament (1903)
M	Moffatt New Testament (1913), Old Testament (1924)
G	Goodspeed New Testament (1923)
Am	American Translation, Old Testament (1931)

SOURCES OF THE READINGS

The readings in the following tables have been taken directly from actual copies of the Bibles listed, with the following exceptions: The Wycliffe and Shoreham Psalter passages are from the edition of Forshall and Madden; the Tyndale Lord's Prayer is from the photographic facsimile of the quarto fragment published by the Clarendon Press in 1926; the other Tyndale passages are from the "verbatim" edition of Samuel Bagster (London, 1836); the Lindisfarne selection is reproduced from J. I. Mombert, *A Handbook of the English Versions of the Bible* (2nd. ed.; New York: D. Appleton & Co., 1890), p. 7. The original form is reproduced, except that commas are substituted for virgules, and italicized words are not so indicated.

Thanks are accorded to the libraries of the University of Chicago and to the Newberry Library, Chicago, for the generous opportunity afforded of consulting the rare Bibles in their respective collections.

PSALM 23:1-3a

Sh	Our Lord gouerneth me, and nothynge shal defailen to me; in the stede of pasture, he sett me ther.
W¹	The Lord gouereneth me, and no thing to me shal lacke; in the place of leswe where he mc ful sette.
W²	The Lord gouerneth me, and no thing schal faile to me; in the place of pasture there he hath set me.
C	The Lorde is my shepherde, I can wante nothinge. He fedeth me in a grene pasture,
Ma	The Lord is my shepherde, I can want nothynge. He fedeth me in a grene pasture,
Ta	The Lord is my shepherde, I can wante nothynge. He fedeth me in a grene pasture,
Gr	The Lorde is my shepherde, therfore can I lack nothyng. He shall fede me in a grene pasture,
Ge	The Lord is my shepherd, I shal not want. He maketh me to rest in grene pasture,
B	God is my sheephearde, therfore I can lacke nothyng: He wyll cause me to repose my selfe in pasture full of grasse,

R-D Our Lord ruleth me, and nothing shal be wanting to me: in place of pasture there he hath placed me.

KJV The Lord is my shepheard; I shall not want. He maketh me to lie downe in greene pastures:

ERV The Lord is my shepherd, I shall not want. He maketh me to lie down in green pastures:

ASV Jehovah is my shepherd; I shall not want. He maketh me to lie down in green pastures;

RSV The Lord is my shepherd, I shall not want; He makes me lie down in green pastures.

Am The Lord is my shepherd; I shall not want; In green pastures he makes me lie down;

PSALM 23:1-3a

Sh He norissed me vp water of fyllynge; he turned my soule fram the fende

W[1] Ouer watir of fulfilling he nurshide me; my soule he conuertide.

W[2] He nurschide me on the watir of refreischyng; he conuertide my soule.

C and ledeth me to a fresh water. He quickeneth my soule,

Ma and ledeth me to a fresh water. He quickeneth my soule,

Ta and leadeth me to a fresh water. He quickeneth my soule,

Gr and leade me forth besyde the waters of comforte. He shall conuerte my soule.

Ge and leadeth me by the stil waters. He restoreth my soule.

B and he wyll leade me vnto calme waters. He wyll conuert my soule.

R-D Vpon the water of refection he hath brought me vp, he hath conuerted my soule.

KJV He leadeth mee beside the still waters. He restoreth my soule:

ERV He leadeth me beside the still waters. He restoreth my soul.

ASV He leadeth me beside still waters. He restoreth my soul.

RSV He leads me beside still waters; he restores my soul.

Am Beside refreshing waters he leads me. He gives me new life;

PROVERBS 15:17

W[1] Betere is to be clepid to wrtis with charitie, than to a fat calf with hate.

W[2] It is betere to be clepid to wortis with charitie, than with hatrede to a calf maad fat.

C Better is a meace of potage with loue, then a fat oxe with euell will.

Ma Better is a messe of potage with loue, then a fat oxe with euell wyll.

Ta Better is a messe of potage with loue, then a fat oxe with euyl wyll.

Gr Better is a measse of potage with loue, than a fat oxe with euell will.

Ge Better is a dinner of grene herbes where loue is, than a stalled oxe and hatred therewith.

B Better is a dynner of hearbes with loue, then a fat oxe with euyll wyll.

R-D It is better to be called to herbes with charitie, then to a fatted calfe with hatred.

KJV Better is a dinner of herbes where loue is, then a stalled oxe and hatred therewith.

RV Better is a dinner of herbs where love is, than a stalled ox and hatred therewith.

RSV Better is a dinner of herbs where love is than a fatted ox and hatred with it.

Am Better a dish of herbs, where love is, Than a fatted ox, and hatred with it.

M Better a dish of vegetables, with love, than the best beef served with hatred.

THE LORD'S PRAYER: MATTHEW 6:9-13

Lin Fader uren thu in Heofnas, Sie gehalgud Nama thin; To Cymeth ric thin; Sie fillo thin

Lu Unser vater ynn dem hymel. Deyn name sey heylig. Deyn reych kome. Deyn wille geschehe

W[1] Oure fadir that art in heuenes, halwid be thi name; thi kyngdom cumme to, be thi wille don

T O oure father, which art in heven halewed be thy name. Let thy kyngdom come. Thy wyll be fulfilled,

KJV Our father which art in heauen, hallowed be thy name. Thy kingdome come, Thy will be done.

Lin Suae is in Heofne and in Eortha. Hlaf userne oferwirtlic sel us to daeg; and forgev us scyltha urna,

Lu auff erden wie ynn dem hymel. Unser teglich brott gib vnns heutt, und vergib vns vnsere schulde,

W[1] as in heuen so in erthe. ȝiv to vs this day oure breed ouer other substaunce; and forȝeue to vs oure dettis,

T   as well in erth, as hit ys in heven. **Geve vs this daye oure dayly breade. And forgeve vs oure** treaspases,

KJV   in earth, as it is in heauen. **Giue vs this day our daily bread. And forgiue vs our debts,**

Lin   suae we forgefon scylgum urum. And ne inlead writh in **Cosnunge.** Al gefrigurich from evil.

Lu   wie wyr vnsern ſchuldigen vergeben, vnnd fure vnns nitt ynn versuchung, sondern erlose vns von dem vbel,

W1   as we forȝeue to oure dettours; and leede vs nat in to temptacioun, but delyuere vs fro yuel.

T   even as we forgeve them whych treaspas vs. Lede vs nott in to temptacion, but delyvre vs from yvell,

KJV   as we forgiue our debters. And lead vs not into temptation, but deliuer vs from euil:

LUKE 2:14

W   Glorie be in the hiȝeste thingis to God: and in erthe pees be to men of good wille.

T   Glory to God an hye, and peace on the erth: and vnto men reioysynge.

C   Glory be vnto God an hye, and peace vpon earth, and vnto men a good wyll.

Ma   Glory to God on hye, and peace on the erth, and vnto men reioysing.

Ta   Glorye to God on hye, and peace in the erth, in men reioysynge.

Gr   Glory to God on hye, and peace on the erth. and vnto men a good wyll.

Ge   Glorie be to God in the high heauens, and peace in earth, and towards men good wil.

B1   Glorie to God on hye, and peace on the earth, and vnto men a good wyll.

B2   Glorie to God in the hyghest, and peace on the earth, and among menne a good wyl.

R-D   Glorie in the highest to God: and in earth peace to men of good vvill.

KJV   Glory to God in the highest, and on earth peace, good wil towards men.

RV   Glory to God in the highest, and on earth peace among men in whom he is well pleased.

RSV   Glory to God in the highest, and on earth peace among men with whom he is pleased!

We   Glory be to God in the highest heavens, And on earth peace among men who please him!

M   Glory to God in high heaven, and peace on earth for men whom he favours!

G   Glory to God in heaven and on earth! Peace to the men he favors!

ROMANS 3:25a

W1   Whom God purposide an helpere by feith in his blood,

W2   whom God ordeynede forȝyver bi feith in his blood,

T   whom God hath made a seate of mercy thorow faith in his bloud,

C   whom God hath set forth for a Mercy seate thorow faith in his bloude,

Ma   whom God hathe made a seate of mercy thorow fayth in hys bloud,

Ta   to whome God hathe made a seate of mercye, thorowe fayth in his bloude,

Gr   whom God hath set forth to be the obtayner of mercy thorow fayth, by the meanes of hys bloude,

Ge   whom God hathe set forthe to be a reconciliation through faith in his blood,

B   whom God hath set foorth to be a propitiation, through fayth in his blood,

R-D   Whom God hath proposed a propitiation, by faith in his bloud,

KJV   Whom God hath set forth to bee a propitiation, through faith in his blood,

ERV   whom God set forth to be a propitiation, through faith, by his blood,

ASV   whom God set forth to be a propitiation, through faith, in his blood,

RSV   whom God put forward as an expiation by his blood, to be received by faith.

We   whom God put forward as a Mercy-Seat, rendered efficacious through faith in His blood,

M   whom God put forward as the means of propitiation by his blood, to be received by faith.

G   For God showed him publicly dying as a sacrifice of reconciliation to be taken advantage of through faith.

I CORINTHIANS 13:4-5a

W1   Charite is pacient, it is benynge or of good will, . . . , it doth not gyle, it is not **inblownyn** with pride,

W2   Charite is pacient, it is benynge; . . . , it doeth not wickidli, it is not blowun,

T   Love suffreth longe, and is corteous. . . . Love doth nott frawardly, swelleth not,

C	Loue is pacient and curteous, . . . , loue doth not frowardly, is not puft vp,
Ma	Loue suffreth longe, and is corteous. . . . , Loue doth not frowardly, swelleth not,
Ta	Loue suffreth longe, is curteous. . . . , Loue doth not frowardely, swelleth not,
Gr	Loue suffreth longe, and is curteous. . . . , Loue doth not frowardly, swelleth not,
Ge	Loue suffreth long, it is bountiful: . . . : loue doeth not boast itself; it is not puffed vp;
B¹	Loue suffreth long, and is curteous. . . . , loue doth not frowardely, swelleth not,
B²	Charitie suffereth long, and is curteous: . . . , charitie doth not frowardly, swelleth not,
R-D	Charitie is patient, is benigne: . . . , dealeth not peruersly: is not puffed vp,
KJV	Charitie suffereth long, and is kinde: . . . : charitie vaunteth not itselfe, is not puffed vp,
RV	Love suffereth long, and is kind; . . . ; love vaunteth not itself, is not puffed up,
RSV	Love is patient and kind; love is not . . . boastful; it is not arrogant or rude.
We	Love is patient and kind; . . . Love is not forward and self-assertive, nor boastful and conceited.
M	Love is very patient, very kind. . . . Love makes no parade, gives itself no airs,
G	Love is patient and kind. Love is not . . . boastful. It does not put on airs.

Hebrews 11:1a

W¹	Forsothe faith is the substaunce of thingis that ben to be hopid,
W²	But faith is the substaunce of thingis that ben to be hopid,
T	Faith is a sure confidence off thynges which are hoped for,
C	Faith is a sure confidence of thinges which are hoped for,
Ma	Fayth is a sure confydence of things which are hoped for,
Ta	Faith is a sure confydence of thynges whiche are hoped for,
Gr	Fayth is a sure confydence of thynges, whych are hoped for,
Ge	Fayth is that, which causeth those things to appeare in deed which are hoped for,
Ge²	Now faith is the grounde of things, which are hoped for,
B	Fayth is the grounde of thynges hoped for,
R-D	And faith is, the substance of things to be hoped for,
KJV	Now faith is the substance of things hoped for,
ERV	Now faith is the assurance of things hoped for,
ASV	Now faith is assurance of things hoped for,
RSV	Now faith is the assurance of things hoped for,
We	Now faith is a well-grounded assurance of that for which we hope,
M	Now faith means we are confident of what we hope for,
G	Faith means the assurance of what we hope for,

Hebrews 11:1b

W¹	and an argument or certaynte of thingis not apperinge.
W²	and an argument of thingis not apperynge.
T	and a certayntie of thynges which are not sene.
C	and a certaynte of thinges which are not sene.
Ma	and a certayntie of thynges whych are not sene.
Ta	and a certaynte of thinges whiche are not sene.
Gr	and a certayntie of thynges whych are not sene.
Ge	and sheweth euidently the thinges which are not sene.
Ge²	and the euidence of things which are not sene.
B	the euidence of thynges not seene.
R-D	the argument of things not appearing.
KJV	the euidence of things not seen.
ERV	the proving of things not seen.
ASV	a conviction of things not seen.
RSV	the conviction of things not seen.
We	and a conviction of the reality of things which we do not see.
M	convinced of what we do not see.
G	it is our conviction about things that we **cannot see.**

XX. Selected Bibliography

BUTTERWORTH, CHARLES C. *The Literary Lineage of the King James Bible*. Philadelphia: University of Philadelphia Press, 1941.

DAICHES, DAVID. *The King James Version of the English Bible*. Chicago: University of Chicago Press, 1941.

DARLOW, T. H., and MOULE, H. F. *Historical Catalogue of the Printed Editions of Holy Scripture in the Library of the British and Foreign Bible Society*. London: The Bible House, 1903-11.

EADIE, JOHN. *The English Bible*. London: Macmillan & Co., 1876.

GOODSPEED, E. J. *The Making of the English New Testament*. Chicago: University of Chicago Press, 1925.

GUPPY, HENRY. *A Brief Sketch of the History of the Transmission of the Bible*. Manchester: Manchester University Press, 1936.

KENYON, FREDERIC GEORGE. *Our Bible and the Ancient Manuscripts*. New York: Harper & Bros., 1940.

PENNIMAN, JOSIAH H. *A Book About the English Bible*. New York: The Macmillan Co., 1919.

POLLARD, ALFRED W. *Records of the English Bible*. Oxford: Henry Frowde, 1911.

PRICE, IRA MAURICE. *The Ancestry of Our English Bible*. Ed. W. A. Irwin and Allen Wikgren. New York: Harper & Bros., 1949.

ROBINSON, H. WHEELER, ed. *The Bible in Its Ancient and English Versions*. Oxford: Clarendon Press, 1940.

SCHAFF, PHILIP. *A Companion to the Greek Testament and the English Version*. New York: Harper & Bros., 1883.

SIMMS, P. MARION. *The Bible in America*. New York: Wilson-Erickson, 1936.

WEIGLE, LUTHER A. *The English New Testament from Tyndale to the Revised Standard Version*. New York and Nashville: Abingdon-Cokesbury Press, 1949.

WESTCOTT, B. F. *A General View of the History of the English Bible*. 3rd ed., rev. W. A. Wright. London: Macmillan & Co., 1905.

WILD, LAURA H. *The Romance of the English Bible*. Garden City: Doubleday, Doran & Co., 1929.

An Introduction to the Revised Standard Version of the New Testament. Chicago: International Council of Religious Education, 1946.

HISTORY OF THE INTERPRETATION
OF THE BIBLE

I. ANCIENT PERIOD

by ROBERT M. GRANT

During the early centuries of the life of the Christian church, its Bible was the Greek version of the Old Testament known as the Septuagint. According to legend, it had been translated entire by seventy-two Hebrew scholars whose results were completely in agreement. The translation, like the original Hebrew text, was regarded as verbally inspired by God. Only in the course of the second century did the Greek New Testament come to possess a status equivalent to that of the Septuagint. The Greek Old Testament remained basic. But the religious ideas of the Old Testament, even in Greek dress, were not entirely in harmony with those of the New Testament or of early Christian theology. The experience of the children of Israel in the distant past, in nomadic or agricultural cultures, was different from the experience of Christians in the crowded half-Hellenized cities of the Roman Empire. The Christian, striving to express the meaning of his faith, might have abandoned the Old Testament, admitting that "time makes ancient good uncouth"[1] had he not possessed a boundless veneration for the mysterious wisdom of the past, as well as methods of reinterpreting that wisdom and of making it comprehensible for his own times.

I. Sources

Some of these methods of interpretation were traditional in the Judaism out of which Chris-

tianity arose; others were gifts of the Hellenistic schools; and others were standards of interpretation ultimately developed within the church itself. Let us first consider Jewish methods of exegesis. Within the Old Testament we can trace the reinterpretation of the cardinal events of religious history. Along with a progressive revelation went a progressive interpretation,[2] especially in the writings of the prophets. Still later the prophets themselves were reinterpreted in the works of the apocalyptic writers of Judaism. Not the Old Testament as we view it in the light of historical research, but the Old Testament explained by apocalyptic interpretation, was the Bible of the earliest church.[3] The earliest Christians did not understand the Bible from its text alone, but from the mass of legends and legal decisions which had gathered about it in the previous two or three centuries. The stories are usually called "haggada"; under this heading may be classified all the nonlegal interpretations of scripture.[4] Beside them stood the "halakah," interpretations by which the Scriptures could be made to govern every detail of Jewish civil and religious life.[5] Both types of exegesis are found in early Christianity. Both are based on the literal meaning of a text, usually taken out of context, but never con-

[1] See Robert M. Grant, "The Place of the Old Testament in Early Christianity," *Interpretation*, V (1951), 186-202.

[2] J. A. Bewer, "Progressive Interpretation," *Anglican Theological Review*, XXIV (1942), 89-100.
[3] Ethelbert Stauffer, *Die Theologie des Neuen Testaments* (Stuttgart: W. Kohlhammer, 1947), pp. 1 ff.
[4] See Louis Ginzberg, *The Legends of the Jews* (Philadelphia: Jewish Publication Society, 1908-38).
[5] See Herbert Danby, *The Mishnah* (Oxford: Clarendon Press, 1933); also Vol. VII, pp. 109-12.

tradicted. For in Jewish eyes the whole Bible was verbally inspired by God. There could be no question of contradiction or error.

Not all Jews, however, were completely true to their inherited tenets. Those who lived outside Palestine had a tendency to make the Bible say what their more enlightened neighbors said. They admired the "assured results" of Greek philosophy and wanted to enjoy a synthesis between philosophy and religion. The most prominent "modernist" of ancient Judaism was Philo of Alexandria. While he once called Jerusalem his native city,[6] his intellectual life was largely centered in Hellenistic Alexandria. It was there that forerunners whom he occasionally mentions had learned to interpret the Old Testament allegorically.

The allegorical method is as old as the rise of Greek philosophy, and probably owes its existence to it. With the development of the Ionian philosophy of nature, it became impossible for an intelligent man to continue to take myths literally. It was especially difficult to accept Homer and Hesiod, in whose writings the immoralities of the gods were described.[7] And from the sixth century B.C. until the end of antiquity—and in the Renaissance—there were many writers who attempted to get rid of the difficulties by claiming that the poets were really writing about something else. This "something else" was usually thought to be the nature of the physical universe (Iliad, Theogony) or of ethics (Odyssey, Works and Days). Plato or Epicurean literalists might criticize mythology; it could be claimed that this criticism was due to misunderstanding. Among Stoic writers, who combined a fairly complete rationalism with a cautious enthusiasm for the status quo, the allegorical method was especially popular. In the first century of our era one of them set forth his underlying principles as follows:

You, O son, can refer the mythical traditions concerning the gods to the elements which are typified, in the belief that the ancients were not ordinary men, but that they too were able to understand the nature of the world and were disposed to philosophize about it through symbols and dark sayings.[8]

So also a Jew, reading his Greek Old Testament and finding it full of anthropomorphic expressions, might come to believe that God had spoken to men through symbols and dark sayings. And he would observe the fact that the heroes of the Old Testament, like those of Homer, lived on a different plane from men of his own time. Their lives seemed simpler. They must have been types or examples. And an etymological analysis of their names might prove to the analyst (if to no one else) that they were really personified virtues. Philo makes such a study, and it is so unconvincing that recent critics have doubted his knowledge of the Hebrew language.[9]

The allegorical method has very little rational justification, but it was highly popular in antiquity. It made possible the retention of Homer as a schoolbook in spite of the criticism of the intelligentsia. Within Christianity and Judaism it was the first line of defense for the Old Testament. Even as early as the first century the method is used at least twice. The first and more famous instance is found in Gal. 4:21-24: "Tell me, you who desire to be under law, do you not hear the law? For it is written that Abraham had two sons, one by a slave and one by a free woman. But the son of the slave was born according to the flesh, the son of the free woman through promise. Now this is an allegory: these women are two covenants." Here Paul, interpreting the history of the Old Testament as full of types or examples for us—"whatever was written in former days was written for our instruction" (Rom. 15:4)—goes so far as to use the Greek word for "allegory." These things, he says, were meant allegorically by the writers of scripture. Modern readers may doubt the accuracy of Paul's exegesis; but in its day it made the Old Testament meaningful for many Greek-speaking Jews and Christians.

The other example is in the Revelation of John. As a whole, this apocalypse is written in a style and form intentionally enigmatic. In a description of the fall of the great city Jerusalem, the author explains that allegorically it is called Sodom and Egypt, for the Lord was crucified there (Rev. 11:8). He knows that in his Old Testament Jerusalem is sometimes called Sodom because of its wickedness (e.g., Isa. 1:9); he himself contributes the identification with Egypt.

II. Beginnings

In the New Testament allegorical exegesis is not ordinarily used. Most of the New Testament writers stand close to Judaism and interpret the Old Testament literally. Nevertheless there is a certain air of freedom about their exegesis which is not found among the rabbis. Where does this freedom come from? It comes from Jesus himself. Jesus was the creator of Christian biblical interpretation. His exegesis has within it a double attitude to his Bible,

[6] Legation to Gaius 278.

[7] Fritz Wehrli, Zur Geschichte der allegorischen Deutung Homers im Altertum (Basel: 1928), p. 88.

[8] Cornutus, Theologiae graecae compendium 31.

[9] Edmund Stein, Die allegorische Exegese des Philo aus Alexandreia (Giessen: Alfred Töpelmann, 1929), pp. 20 ff.

though later interpreters develop only single aspects of his thought.

This double relationship to the Old Testament has troubled commentators on the Gospels since ancient times. On the one hand, Jesus takes the Old Testament as it stands and insists on its permanent authority. On the other, he ventures to criticize it, to reinterpret it, to attack not only traditional interpretations but even scripture itself. Is not such an attitude paradoxical? By critical methods can we get rid of one or the other aspect of Jesus' interpretation? Unfortunately, only an arbitrary criticism can water down the difficulty which we face.

Well-attested sayings of the Lord prove that his relationship to the Jewish scriptures was bipolar. Brought up in a conservative Jewish family, he respected the authority of the law. To a man who wanted to "inherit eternal life" Jesus quoted the second table of the Decalogue (Mark 10:19).[10] He could attack the tradition of the Pharisees by claiming that they abandoned the "commandment of God" (Mark 7:8-9). While there were those who argued that he was destroying the law, he could be remembered as saying that he intended only to reinterpret it. His aim was revitalization, not destruction. David was not the only writer of scripture to speak "in the Holy Spirit" (Mark 12:36); Moses and the other prophets must have spoken or written in the Spirit as well. The testimony of the Spirit could not be rejected.

At the same time, Jesus freely criticized the Old Testament. His reinterpretation of the sabbath (Mark 2:27; 3:4) is at least implicitly contradictory to the fourth commandment (Exod. 20:8-11). And in his rejection of the possibility of divorce he stands opposed to Deut. 24:1 (Moses' bill of divorcement), claiming that it is based on the "hardheartedness" of the people. He relegates the verse to a secondary place compared with Gen. 2:24 ("they shall be one flesh"). He contrasts the word of Moses with the word of God. For the normal Jewish interpreter such a contrast was inconceivable. Again, in the Sermon on the Mount we find a whole series of such contrasts: "You have heard that it was said to the ancients . . . but I say. . . ." Jesus speaks with the authority of a prophet, and of one greater than a prophet.

Above all, in the Last Supper Jesus interprets the Old Testament idea of a covenant, and of a new spiritual covenant, in relation to himself and his disciples. It is this interpretation which provides a seed for the growth of the later Christocentric exegesis of the Old Testament. Paul, for example, not only repeats the words of the Lord at the Last Supper (I Cor. 11:24-25), but goes on to take the whole experience of Israel at the Exodus as typical of the later experience of Jesus and his church (I Cor. 10:1 ff.). At a later date the evangelist John interprets the Eucharist in terms of the "bread of heaven," the manna which the Israelites ate in the desert.

One book of the New Testament is almost entirely devoted to interpretation of the meaning of Jesus in terms of the Old Testament. This book is the Epistle to the Hebrews. It finds its starting point in the resemblances between Jesus and the mysterious Melchizedek of Gen. 14:18-20. Unlike the other actors on the stage of the patriarchal histories, Melchizedek suddenly appears and as suddenly disappears. He comes only to bless Abraham. And in his career, "without beginning of life or end of days," the author of Hebrews could find pretypified the work of Jesus. Again, he can compare this work with the sacrificial cultus of the Levitical priesthood, and see how closely related both sacrifices are—and how much more efficacious that of Jesus is.[11]

In the New Testament as a whole, the Old Testament is treated as a book of hope. Christians, following the example of Jesus and building upon it, gradually came to reject the Jewish law as law. But since it was the inspired word of God, it must (they believed) contain a deeper meaning. This meaning they found in types of Christ and of his church. "As Moses lifted up the serpent in the wilderness, so must the Son of Man be lifted up" (John 3:14). And the author of I Peter expresses the normal Christian belief that the prophets could not be understood without the spirit of Christ (I Pet. 1:10-11; cf. II Cor. 3:12-18).

III. The Second Century and the Problem of Authority

As the Christian church expanded into the world of Hellenistic culture, there were many within it who hoped that its Jewish chrysalis could be discarded. Most of the heretical minority groups of the second century were militantly anti-Jewish. Marcion, for example, was convinced that he could distinguish between the essence of Christianity and the additions which the Jewish disciples of Jesus had made. He accepted only one gospel, that of Luke, and with the scissors of criticism removed what he considered the interpolations of Judaizers. Such a man naturally attacked the Old Testament with vigor. It was irrational and immoral. When defenders of the book tried to interpret it allegorically, their attempts were greeted with de-

---

[10] See Robert M. Grant, "The Decalogue in Early Christianity," *Harvard Theological Review*, XL (1947), 1-17.

[11] R. K. Yerkes, "Atonement," *Anglican Theological Review*, XXIX (1947), 28-33.

rision. But in the second century allegorization was inevitable if Christianity was to be preserved and not transformed. And in upholding allegorization it became necessary to insist on the right of the church to interpret the true meaning of scripture. Only those who had received the apostolic teaching through the apostolic succession could be trusted as interpreters. There is a considerable measure of truth in this contention. Without sympathy, there could be no possibility of understanding. Those who did not share the life of the main stream of Christianity could not understand the books which came from an earlier level of the same river.

Late in the second century Irenaeus, bishop of Lyons, set forth this principle in his work against heresies. It was a principle not so much invented as developed and defended in the heat of controversy.

When they are refuted from the scriptures, they shift their ground and censure the scriptures, declaring that they are wrong or are not authoritative, or that there are various readings, and that the truth cannot be discovered from these by those who do not know the tradition.[12]

By "tradition" the Gnostics meant their own secret oral tradition, unknown to the church as a whole. Irenaeus replies that the church is the guardian of scripture, that the orthodox tradition is known to all, and that it alone is true. The same point of view was espoused at Carthage by Tertullian and expressed in the language of Roman law. When questions of interpretation arise, the church can enter a "prescription," a petition based on the fact that the Scriptures are the legal property of the church. The prescription is intended to make the position of heretics so precarious that their case will never come to court. Why argue with them when it is not always certain that we are to be victorious?

They put forward the scriptures and by their audacity make an immediate impression on some people. . . . If their strength consists in the fact that they are able to possess them, we must see to whom the scriptures belong, so that no one is admitted to them who is not legally competent.[13]

By this argument Tertullian seeks to transfer the battle to a ground where the church can feel more confident of success.

A Christian might well admit that heretics did not have the right to interpret the Bible. But how were those within the church to interpret it? What standard were they to use? Irenaeus and Tertullian agree in answering that the only correct exegesis is to be made according

[12] *Against Heresies* III. 2. 1.
[13] *Prescription Against Heretics* 15.

to the "rule of faith"—essentially the common Christian creed. And in the subsequent history of interpretation the rule of faith plays a prominent part. Indeed, theology and exegesis were never divorced in antiquity. The best example of their union is found in the *Commonitorium* of Vincent of Lérins (fifth century), where the rule is laid down that interpretation must be made according to the Catholic faith. What is the Catholic faith? It is what has been held "everywhere, always, and by everyone." [14] Obviously this definition represents an ideal rather than an actuality; and in practice it eventually proved unworkable. But it represents an ancient attempt to base interpretation by authority on the rational ground of universal consent.

Such an appeal to external authority, even though Bible and church were not regarded as independent entities, was not altogether satisfactory. It did not give any guidance in internal disputes. In the quarrels between the exegetical schools of Alexandria and Antioch it could not be employed. Many passages in scripture received little illumination from the rule of faith, and therefore some other standard was necessary. The lack of such a standard, among other things, accounts for the inconclusiveness of the disputes between Alexandria and Antioch.

IV. Alexandria and Antioch

The conflict between Alexandria and Antioch was not entirely a matter of exegetical theory. The two cities were respectively second and third in the Roman Empire; [15] and one may suspect the existence of a rivalry like that between New York and Chicago. Again, the theological viewpoints of the two churches were quite different. Their emphases were divergent especially in matters of Christology.[16] Alexandria may be called Platonist, while Antioch was Aristotelian. To say this is to oversimplify the situation, but the statement is essentially true.

In the biblical interpretation the two schools were divided over the problem of the allegorization of scripture. To the Alexandrians it seemed that God had intentionally placed stumbling blocks in the Bible in order to awaken men's minds. There were hidden truths behind the literal meanings. Following the Jewish exegete Philo, Clement of Alexandria finds hidden meanings throughout the Old Testament.

The gnostic [or, as Clement uses the term, true Christian] does not merely lend his ear to the words of scripture; he opens his very soul to what is hid-

[14] *Commonitorium* II. 3.
[15] K. O. Müller, *Antiquitates Antiochenae* (Göttingen: 1839), p. 2.
[16] See R. V. Sellers, *Two Ancient Christologies* (London: Society for Promoting Christian Knowledge, 1940).

den under the words: realities to know and actions to do.[17]

But Clement was no systematizer. Indeed, his longest extant work is called *Scrapbooks* or *Miscellanies.* Any genuine theoretical analysis of allegorization had to be supplied by his successors at Alexandria. And it is in the *On First Principles* of Origen that we find this analysis set forth:

Wherever in the narrative [of scripture] the accomplishment of some particular deeds did not correspond with the sequence of the intellectual truths, the scripture wove into the story something which did not happen, occasionally something which could not happen, and occasionally something which might have happened but in fact did not.[18]

Therefore the difficulties of scripture themselves suggest the existence of a deeper meaning. Origen gives examples of such difficulties from the Old Testament. There are days described in Genesis before the creation of sun and moon; obviously this is impossible; equally obviously there must be a hidden meaning. Surprisingly, he finds these difficulties also in the New Testament: "Even the gospels are full of passages of this kind, as when the devil takes Jesus up into a high mountain. . . ."[19] The devil shows Jesus all the kingdoms of the earth (Matt. 4:8); obviously again, there is no mountain from which all the kingdoms can be seen; therefore the story does not mean what it says. Furthermore, the Gospels disagree among themselves in regard to the order of events in Jesus' life. In theory, scripture is entirely self-consistent and accurate. The history it seems to portray is not consistent or accurate. Therefore there must be an allegorical meaning. In fact, because in the Septuagint Prov. 22:20-21 reads, "Do thou thrice record them . . . that thou mayest answer with words of truth," there is a threefold meaning in scripture. This meaning is literal, moral, and spiritual (allegorical).

Some of the difficulties which Origen finds in the Gospels are rather naïve. He claims that several of the Lord's commandments are impossible to obey, and gives as examples the admonitions to salute no one on the road (Luke 10:4), to turn the other cheek (Matt. 5:39), and to pluck out the right eye (Matt. 5:29). How can you tell which eye offended?[20] At the same time, he is not always true to his own principles. He insists on the historicity of the story of the witch of Endor (I Sam. 28), and

relies on the Septuagint, which called her a ventriloquist. The story in scripture cannot be false. Samuel really appeared.[21] The reason for his opponent's caution is that unless he can attack the veracity of the witch on historical grounds, it will seem that she, a demon, has authority over the soul even of a prophet. But if Origen is not willing to allegorize this difficult story, on what grounds can he allegorize other stories which are no more difficult? Eustathius of Antioch was not slow to point out this inconsistency.[22]

The real purpose of Alexandrian allegorization was avoidance of the anthropomorphisms of the Old Testament, which simple-minded Christians took literally. Here the aim of the school was twofold. The Alexandrians were eager to defend Christianity from the criticisms of its cultured despisers. For centuries, philosophers of every school had been pointing out the nonanthropomorphic character of God. Surely Christianity, the true philosophy, was in harmony with their teaching. But by presenting Christian theology in apologetic form, the Alexandrians actually altered its teaching. Biblical allegorization was one of the principal methods of this theological movement.

The theological bias of Alexandrian theology was clear to ordinary Egyptian Christians, one of whom wrote a work called *Refutation of the Allegorists.*[23] At the same time, Tertullian and others like him fought for the corporeality of God in an effort to avoid the excessive spiritualization characteristic of Alexandria. But the most important adversaries of Origen and his school were the exegetes of Antioch.

The school of Antioch was noted for its literal and grammatical interpretation of the Bible. The earliest representative of it whom we know is Theophilus, bishop of Antioch about 180, whose second and third books dedicated to a certain Autolycus are full of literal exegesis of the Old Testament. Later Antiochians were expert in the study of Hebrew or of the Greek text of the Old Testament. Their exegesis, under the influence of the prominent Jewish community of the city, was ordinarily soberly literal. The great period of the school came late in the fourth century, when Diodorus of Tarsus taught his pupils, Theodore of Mopsuestia and John Chrysostom of Antioch, later metropolitan of Constantinople.

Theodore was less orthodox and more original than his master or his fellow disciple. And it must be admitted that where he is original

[17] *Miscellanies* VII. 11. 60. 3-4; Claude Mondésert, *Clément d'Alexandrie* (Paris: Aubier, 1944), p. 110.
[18] IV. 2. 9.
[19] *Ibid.,* IV. 3. 1.
[20] *Ibid.,* IV. 3. 3.

[21] Albert Jahn, *Des h. Eustathius . . . Beurtheilung des Origenes betreffend die Auffassung der Wahrsagerin* (Leipzig: J. C. Hinrichs, 1886), p. 5.
[22] *Ibid.,* pp. 21 ff.
[23] Nepos, in Eusebius *Church History* VII. 24. 2.

he is usually wrong; where he is right he simply reproduces the general outlook of the Antiochian school. As a whole, the school rejected allegorization. In commenting on Gal. 4:24, Theodore takes the opportunity to attack Origen for his misuse of scripture. He contrasts Origen's denial of the reality of the events described in Genesis with the apostle's use of events as examples. On Origen's view, he claims, the reality of the fall of man is denied, and so is the reality of redemption. Paul, on the other hand, interpreted all these events as historical. Theodore also wrote five books "On Allegory and History Against Origen." These are lost, as is the work of Diodorus called "What Is the Difference Between Theory and Allegory?" (By "theory" the school of Antioch meant the genuine meaning of the text.)

To the Alexandrians the literal meaning of a text did not include its metaphorical meaning. The literal meaning of "the arm of God" is that God really has an arm. Such an interpretation is an example of what Whitehead has called "misplaced concretion." The Alexandrians used this concretion as a means for introducing their own theological views. At Antioch, on the other hand, the meaning of a passage, its "theory," included both metaphor and simple statement. Obviously their analysis is the more natural of the two. The literal meaning of scripture cannot exclude metaphor. It is to Theodore's credit that he insisted on this position. In his view

every passage of the Bible is provided with a literal meaning, whether proper or metaphorical. To deny this would be to suppose that the Holy Spirit would sometimes have spoken in order to say nothing. . . . Consequently, according to Theodore, all the biblical narratives, all the laws, even the ceremonial laws, must be interpreted in their simple literal meaning.[24]

With a similar emphasis on literalism, Theodore declared that most of the prophecies of the Old Testament had a reference to future events within Jewish history, and not to Christ. Only Pss. 2; 8; 45; 110 are psalms which predicted Christ.

Theodore's actual results in exegesis are not so different from those of the Origenists as one might expect. One reason for this similarity is to be found in the fact that typology, which he frequently employs, is not entirely unlike allegorization. Again, he constantly stresses the metaphorical meaning of passages of scripture, while continuing to regard this meaning as literal. At the same time, his use of genuine allegorization is extremely limited.

Chrysostom, on the other hand, as a popular preacher, feels more free to interpret the Bible allegorically. He too avoids the excesses of Alexandria.

We are not irresponsible exponents of the laws on this matter, but may only apply the system of allegorical interpretation when we are following the mind of Scripture. . . . And this is the universal law of Scripture when it speaks in allegories, viz., to supply the interpretation of the allegory.[25]

But Chrysostom does not propose to employ a simple literalism:

We must not examine the words as bare words, else many absurdities will follow, but we must mark the mind of the writer.[26]

Thus he endeavors to steer a middle course between the fancies of allegorists and the absurdities of simple literalists. He lays emphasis on the metaphorical language of scripture.

In this connection it may be appropriate to refute a dictum of Cardinal Newman. In discussing his theory of development in Christian thought, Newman said, "It may be almost laid down as an historical fact that the mystical interpretation and orthodoxy will stand or fall together." But the Alexandrians were led astray by their exegetical method quite as often as the Antiochians. The second-century Gnostics were ardent allegorizers. The fathers of Antioch, on the other hand, had a sounder understanding of the Bible than most of their rivals.

V. Jerome and Augustine

The greatest exegete of the ancient church, Jerome, derived much of his method from Antiochian sources.[27] Jerome's most important accomplishment, the translation of the Old Testament from Hebrew into Latin, testifies to the interest in the original text which he shared with the school of Antioch. Like the Antiochians, he was vigorously attacked. Augustine, for example, regarded the Septuagint as inspired and authoritative, and viewed Jerome's work as mistaken. Eventually the new version won its way, however, and for centuries it was the only translation authorized by the Roman church. Most new versions are opposed by backward-looking Christians, but few are greeted with the abuse which the Vulgate at first encountered. Jerome was called a forger and a betrayer of his religion.

Jerome's development as an interpreter of scripture is of considerable interest, for origi-

[24] Louis Pirot, *L'oeuvre exégétique de Théodore de Mopsueste* (Rome: Pontificii Instituti Biblici, 1913), p. 180.

[25] F. H. Chase, *Chrysostom* (Cambridge: Deighton, Bell, & Co., 1887), p. 61.

[26] *Ibid.*, p. 157.

[27] A. Vaccari, "I Fattori Della Esegesi Geronimiana," *Biblica*, I (1920), 457-80.

nally he was a convinced Origenist. His first exegetical work, a commentary on Obadiah, was thoroughly allegorical. Later, however, when he studied Hebrew and lived in Palestine, he came under the influence of Jewish teachers and of the school of Antioch, and he turned to a more sober and literal exegetical method. This change was also due in large measure to the concentration on the text of scripture which his work of translation required. In his later writings he constantly insisted on the "Hebrew truth" of the Old Testament, although with the Antiochians he held that there were spiritual and typological meanings which his Jewish opponents failed to understand. He believed that a bare literalism was barren. At the same time, he refused to interpret the Bible against the letter. "There are many things in scripture which sound incredible and yet are true." [28]

When historical questions came to his attention, he was not remarkably at ease in handling them. The most striking instance of this difficulty is to be found in his correspondence with Augustine over the dispute between Peter and Paul at Antioch.[29] Following Origen, Jerome held that Peter and Paul had simply staged a dispute in order to give dramatic proof to Gentile Christians that the law had been abolished. If Paul ever observed the law, it was merely for convention's sake. A lengthy controversy arose when Augustine declared that such a staged dispute would have been dishonest. Historical criticism was rare in the ancient church,[30] and neither of the fathers should be blamed too severely for lack of interest in something they considered irrelevant.

There is a considerable difference between Jerome and his contemporary, Augustine, as far as attitude to the interpretation of scripture is concerned. Jerome is a scholar, and while his outlook lacks the range of Augustine, he is ordinarily more accurate in matters of detail. Augustine, on the other hand, is a theologian, and in his comments on the meaning of the Bible there is greater depth and religious insight than in those of Jerome. On questions such as the correctness of the new translation of the Old Testament, Jerome's judgment is superior. In general, Augustine goes to the heart of scripture. He takes account of critical problems but does not consider them all-important.[31]

[28] *Letters* LXXII.
[29] J. Schmid, *SS. Eusebii Hieronymi et Aurelii Augustini Epistulae Mutuae* (Bonn: P. Haustein, 1930), pp. 14 ff.
[30] See Robert M. Grant, "Historical Criticism in the Ancient Church," *Journal of Religion*, XXV (1945), 183-96.
[31] A. A. Gilmore, "Augustine and the Critical Method," *Harvard Theological Review*, XXXIX (1946), 141-64.

Augustine's entire early career may be regarded as a search for a tenable exegetical method. Only when he discovered and accepted allegorization, under the guidance of Ambrose, was he able to enter into traditional Christianity. Before that time he was a halfhearted Manichaean. Like Marcion, his Manichaean teachers insisted on a literal interpretation of the Old Testament in order to prove its absurdity. They emphasized anthropomorphic expressions in order to ask ironically whether God has hair and nails. They criticized the morality of the patriarchs. As for the New Testament, they again followed Marcion in their claim that the text had been interpolated by Judaizers.[32] Augustine began to suspect their veracity when they proved unable to provide a copy of the original, genuine text. But Old Testament problems continued to disturb him. Only the sermons of Ambrose of Milan were able to bring him to a fresh view of the Old Testament. Ambrose constantly quoted II Cor. 3:6; "The letter kills, but the spirit gives life." This justification of the allegorical method was not intended by Paul, who was discussing the law of Moses as contrasted with the free Spirit of God. But the exegesis of Ambrose made Christian faith possible for Augustine.

Once within the church, Augustine believed that he ought to set down the principles of an exegesis which would be at the same time scholarly and also centered in theology. In the year 397 he composed most of his *Christian Doctrine*. This work is an attempt not only to insist on the importance of sound learning for the interpreter, but also to stress the primacy of a single theological principle running throughout scripture:

Whoever seems to himself to have understood the divine Scriptures in such a way that he does not build up that double love of God and neighbor, has not yet understood.[33]

This is the fundamental principle. If there remain unsolved questions of exegesis, the interpreter is to consult the rule of faith, the orthodox teaching of the church, as well as the context of scripture. He must also beware of taking figurative language literally, or literal language figuratively. The authors of scripture made use of all the rhetorical forms known to grammarians.

In his *The Harmony of the Gospels* Augustine makes a suggestion to explain the differences in the order of events in the Gospels. This suggestion, if consistently applied, would have undermined the ancient theory of verbal inerrancy. The reason for the differences, he

[32] Augustine *Confessions* III. 7; V. 11.
[33] I. 36.

says, is to be found in the nature of memory. What comes into our mind is not what we will, but as it is given. Therefore each evangelist gives the events in the order which God desired for him; these orders need not be the same.[34] Obviously, then, we cannot tell—and we should not try to tell—which order is the historical order of events. Augustine's entire book shows how little he, or the ancient church generally, was interested in historical questions.

With Jerome and Augustine the history of interpretation in the ancient church really comes to an end. Jerome makes use of the insights of the school of Antioch, combines them with his own phenomenal learning, and produces the Vulgate. In this translation are summed up the achievements of the Antiochian fathers. Augustine, on the other hand, modifies the allegorical method of Alexandria while retaining its fundamental point of view and its emphasis on systematic theology. Both Jerome and Augustine, writing in Latin, point the way forward to the Middle Ages. But ancient exegesis had not come to a full stop. There remained the task of assimilation.

VI. Handbooks

In the third book of his *Christian Doctrine*, Augustine makes use of a book of seven rules composed by a certain Tyconius. The rules are intended to cover every situation in which an allegorical interpretation might seem to be demanded. Like their contemporary Jewish equivalents (e.g., the thirty-two rules of Rabbi Eliezer, son of Rabbi Jose), they are rather far-fetched. Their chief purpose is to give some rational ground for allegorization. Thus the first rule, "Of the Lord and his body," shows that often in scripture what is said of Christ applies also to his body, the church. Another rule, "Of times," is really an attempt to solve difficulties without recourse to criticism. If one Gospel says the Transfiguration was eight days after the scene at Caesarea Philippi, while another says it was six, the difference can easily be explained. The first gives the whole period of time, while the second gives only a part. The same rule takes care of the difference between "on the third day" and "after three days" in the resurrection narratives. Another rule, "On recapitulation," provides the traditional explanation of the double account of creation in the book of Genesis.

Perhaps the most interesting feature about these rules lies not in the rules themselves, but in the fact that Augustine thought it worth while to use them. As the great period of ancient exegesis draws to its close, biblical interpretation, like other manifestations of intellectual

[34] II. 21.

life, is becoming more and more stereotyped. It is becoming fixed in rules. To be sure, the works of the great commentators like Origen are preserved, but most interpreters read them in "catenas," chains of exegetical materials in capsule form.[35] The freshness of early exegesis has gone. Theodore of Mopsuestia is condemned not so much for being wrong as for being original. It is noteworthy that his commentaries survived only in the Syriac language and in Latin under the name of Ambrose.

Through manuals of interpretation, perhaps more than in any other way, the exegetical outlook of antiquity was able to influence the thought of the medieval church. When Cassiodorus in the sixth century compiled an introduction to sacred studies, he recommended five earlier writers. They were Tyconius, Augustine (*Christian Doctrine*), Adrian, Eucherius, and Junilius.[36] Augustine and Tyconius have already been mentioned. Let us now consider the last three names.

Eucherius of Lyons, who died about 450, wrote a handbook on the interpretation of scripture which summed up for the Western church the methods of Origen without his theological acumen. This book was called *Rules for Allegorical Interpretation*. Eucherius begins with an introduction in which he sets forth his theory of exegesis. First he proves the existence of symbolic language in scripture. Next he justifies its existence by the necessity of keeping pearls from swine; for this reason anthropomorphisms are found in the Bible. He finds a threefold meaning in scripture: historical, tropological, and anagogical. This division, found in various forms as early as Origen, is sometimes made fourfold, as Eucherius says, by the addition of allegory.[37] "Tropology" involves a moral meaning, while the "anagogical" refers to a secret and heavenly meaning. As an example, he offers "And the waters which are above the heavens shall praise the name of the Lord" (Ps. 148:4). "Heaven" historically or literally means the sky, tropologically, heavenly life; "waters" allegorically mean baptism, anagogically, the angels. Most of Eucherius' work is devoted to explaining away anthropomorphic expressions and to giving the allegorical meaning of animals and forces of nature in the Bible. He is perhaps farthest from reality in his last chapter, on numbers. But the text of his work as printed in Migne has been interpolated by

[35] See G. Heinrici, "Catenae," *New Schaff-Herzog Encyclopedia of Religious Knowledge* (New York: Funk & Wagnalls, 1908), II, 451-53.

[36] *Institutiones* I. 10.

[37] *Corpus Scriptorum Ecclesiasticorum Latinorum*, XXXI, 5. See Ernst von Dobschütz, "Vom vierfachen Schriftsinn," in *Harnack-Ehrung* (Leipzig: J. C. Hinrichs, 1921), pp. 1-13.

ingenious number-allegorists of later times. His own work, recovered by Wotke, does not do much more than give biblical examples of the use of some numbers between one and one hundred.

The two other handbooks reflect not the school of Alexandria, but that of Antioch. The *Introduction to the Sacred Scriptures* of Adrian seems to have been written shortly before Eucherius' work.[38] It is divided into three parts because there are three characteristics of Hebrew expressions, based on meaning, phraseology, and composition. "Meaning" involves the problem of anthropomorphisms; "phraseology" is concerned with metaphorical expressions and explains them in terms of biblical usage; "composition" considers rhetorical forms in relation to the interpretation of scripture. Adrian concludes his work with a brief general discussion of holy scripture and interpretation. In this the influence of the school of Antioch is clear. He states that there are two forms in the divine scripture: prophetical and historical. Each of these deals with past, present, and future. While literal exegesis is primary, we must go farther, beyond the mere unsymbolical analysis of the letters. Like other Antiochians, Adrian is not content with simple literalism. He stands close to Chrysostom.

Finally we have the *Rules for the Divine Law* of Junilius Africanus, written about 550, in which the peculiar ideas of Theodore of Mopsuestia concerning the canon of the Bible are combined with a systematic treatment of exegesis. This analysis is made on the basis of the Aristotelian rhetoric which flourished in sixth-century Syria. Junilius nods in passing to the Augustinian principle of love of God and neighbor, but he makes little use of it. His rules were widely influential in the early Middle Ages.[39] At the end of his work he sets forth an Aristotelian principle which doubtless made his theories palatable to scholastic-minded Christians. After proving the divine inspiration of scripture from the truth and consistency of the Bible, he finds that he has left little place for faith. The reason for this is that our religion is superrational, but not irrational: "What reason teaches, faith understands, and where reason fails, faith leads the way." Faith and reason are never opposed to each other. The separation of exegesis from theology has begun.

The study of the interpretation of the Bible in the ancient church is a vast field. We have skimmed the surface, but enough has been said to make plain the fact that the problems of ancient interpreters were much like our own. The debate between Alexandria and Antioch is a perennial one, now to some extent by-passed by the idea of development within biblical thought, but never entirely settled. Yet at the end of antiquity little fresh investigation of the meaning of scripture was being made. Interpreters were content to regard themselves as dwarfs on the shoulders of giants, and to seek all their inspiration in the past. The vigor and originality of Origen or Theodore of Mopsuestia had been lost; the authoritarianism of Vincent of Lérins had taken its place. Even Augustine felt that toward the end of his life he ought to publish *New Treatments* of any points, exegetical or theological, in which he might have slipped into heterodoxy. Satisfactory exegesis could not be carried on in such an atmosphere.

At the same time, enough of the exegetical work of the earlier fathers was preserved so that their disagreements could be seen. There was almost no exegetical point on which they unanimously agreed. And this measure of difference helped, when learning once more flourished, to keep the interpretation of the Bible alive. In the writings of the fathers we find no enduring exegetical method. We find attempts to solve difficulties by means of the best tools available. But the fathers rarely if ever considered the possibility that a passage of scripture meant something different to its writer from what it meant in their own day. For this reason the tools employed by the fathers are not those which later interpreters were to find most useful.[40]

[38] Friedrich Goessling, *Adrians* ΕΙΣΑΓΩΓΗ ΕΙΣ ΤΑΣ ΘΕΙΑΣ ΓΡΑΦΑΣ (Berlin: H. Reuther, 1887), p. 13.

[39] Heinrich Kihn, *Theodor von Mopsuestia und Junilius Africanus als Exegeten* (Freiburg im Breisgau: Herder, 1880), pp. 302 ff.

[40] A selected bibliography on the history of biblical interpretation will be found on p. 141. Editors.

HISTORY OF THE INTERPRETATION
OF THE BIBLE

II. MEDIEVAL AND REFORMATION PERIOD

by JOHN T. MCNEILL

The purpose of this article is to mark a few guideposts on the course of Bible interpretation through the centuries from Vincent of Lérins to Luther and Calvin and their contemporaries. The conception of the Bible as holy writ, resting upon divine authority, and entirely distinct from other human writings, had been increasingly affirmed from the second century to the fifth. The canon of Scripture was defined in controversy with Gnostics who were inventing their own scriptures. The process involved for the Catholic church the assertion of the principle of tradition as the basis of selection of authoritative books. As the test of canonicity, tradition tended to assume an authority superior to that of Scripture itself. But once the canon was established, the accepted books were held in peculiar reverence, and the balance of authority between the Scripture and tradition seems to have been in some degree altered in favor of the former. During the decade that followed the death of Augustine (430), Vincent of Lérins in his *Commonitorium* (434) asserted the primacy of Scripture, but stressed the necessity of interpreting it in accordance with tradition. Vincent would defend the church against heretics and fortify Christian faith, "first, by the authority of the divine law [Scripture], and secondly by the tradition of the Catholic church." The canonical Scriptures are admittedly "sufficient for everything," but they are variously misinterpreted. He therefore holds it

urgently necessary "that the rule of interpretation of the Prophets and Apostles be laid down in accordance with the norm of ecclesiastical and Catholic understanding [*sensus*]." This is the position that was to have general adherence in the medieval church.

Already, then, the Bible, as delimited in the canon, was fully recognized as the Book of God. In the language of the church fathers it was "the sacred writings," "the divine law," "the sacred page," "the word of God." In accordance with this conception it afforded the chief public reading in church and monastic services, and the series of lections for public worship was already substantially determined. Furthermore, the Scriptures furnished the principal inspiration of those Christians who seriously engaged in the cultivation of their own personal piety. Searching the Scriptures for edification became a feature of life in the early monastic communities. The *lectio divina* (divine reading) was a common exercise of monks before and after Benedict. It involved an intensive devotion to the study of Scripture. The Rule of Benedict itself, almost from beginning to end, offers remarkable evidence of the functioning of scriptural knowledge and suggestion in the monastic mind. In his last chapter Benedict speaks depreciatively of what he has written by comparison with the Scriptures and the fathers and monastic writers; and here he asks rhetorically: "For what page or what word of divine authority of the Old and the New Testament is not a perfect norm [*rectissima norma*] of human life?"

Benedict's use of scripture passages is direct and practical. It is noteworthy that he does not follow his master and Vincent's contemporary, John Cassian, in utilizing allegorical or other nonliteral senses. Cassian, explaining the true meaning of scripture, had compared the spiritual sense with the literal by reference to the son of the free woman and of the bondwoman in the Abraham story, and to the "double garments" referred to in the Vulgate rendering of Prov. 31:21. Cassian also subdivided the spiritual interpretation much in the fashion of medieval writers. From I Cor. 14:6, "What shall it profit except I speak either by revelation or by knowledge or by prophecy or by doctrine," he deduces the four senses, allegorical, tropological, anagogical, and historical.[1] There are, of course many passages in Cassian which employ simply the historical or literal sense in the manner of Benedict. In a well-known epigram Gregory the Great commends Benedict's lack of schooling. In using the Bible for simple direction the good abbot may have been unaware that his writing favored the Aristotelian Antiochian literal interpreters against the Platonic-Philonic Alexandrian allegorists.

I. The Middle Ages

A. The Period of Gregory and Bede.—The allegorists, to be sure, had not carried all before them in the ancient church, and though allegory flourished in most of the medieval Latin commentaries, it was, as we shall see, frequently criticized and sometimes completely abandoned. Moreover, a change was coming over the spirit of interpretation as the institutions and doctrines of the church became more rigid. Allegory would no longer be used with the originality and ecclesiastically dangerous freedom that marked some passages of Origen and even of Ambrose, but rather, in the spirit of Vincent's canon, under the governing idea of the ecclesiastical tradition. This tradition was now enshrined mainly in the writings of the fathers. Through the period of Gregory the Great and the Venerable Bede some measure of originality and independence remains. Thereafter, for six or seven centuries, the dominant type of biblical interpretation rested upon direct or indirect quotation of the patristic literature and was equally dependent and repetitious. In some quarters, however, freedom and originality were not wanting.

Gregory the Great lent his influence to the side of the spiritual as opposed to the literal exegesis. Five centuries after him Guibert de Nogent found in Gregory's writings "the keys to this art," that is, the art of expounding spiritual senses. "Allegory," says Gregory, expounding the Song of Songs, "makes a kind of machine for the soul far off from God by which it may be raised up to him."[2] His use of the method may be illustrated from the *Moralia*, his lectures on the book of Job. In the dedicatory epistle to Leander which precedes this work, he states that he is responding to the request

that I would not only expound the words of the history in allegorical senses, but that I would direct the sense of the allegories into an exercise in morality, adding to this something more difficult, that I would surround the several meanings with testimonies and that the testimonies presented, if perchance they should seem involved, should be untangled by the insertion of additional expositions.[3]

In the preface to this work Gregory gives us his high conception of the authorship of scripture. He refuses to become involved in an investigation of the human authorship of the book of Job, since it is the work not of a man, but of the Holy Spirit:

But who was the writer, it is utterly useless to ask; since at any rate the Holy Spirit is trustworthily believed to have been the Author of the book. He, therefore, who dictated the things to be written, himself wrote them. He himself wrote them who was both the Inspirer in that writer's work, and by the utterance of the writer has passed on to us his acts for our imitation. If we were reading the words of some great man whose letters we had received, yet were to ask by what pen they had been written, it would truly be ridiculous, to know the author of the epistles and understand his meaning, and yet to make search to know with what sort of pen the words were set down. Thus when we understand the matter, and hold that the Holy Spirit was its Author, in seeking out the writer, what else are we doing than in reading a letter to inquire about the pen?[4]

We are soon plunged into a maze of Gregory's spiritual expositions. We learn that the three friends of Job are the heretics, and that when they come to Job, they are returning to holy church; Job himself maintains a semblance to the Redeemer to come. His name means "grieving," a forecast of the Mediator's passion and of the travails and afflictions of holy church in this life. Job's seven thousand sheep are innocent thoughts; the three thousand camels are

---

[1] *Conferences* XIV. 8. *Corpus Scriptorum Ecclesiasticorum Latinorum*, XIII, ii, pp. 404 ff. See above, p. 113 and below, p. 121.

[2] *Exposition of the Song of Songs.* Prologue, 2. Jacques P. Migne, *Patrologia Latina*, LXXIX, 473.

[3] Migne, *op. cit.*, LXXV, 512.

[4] *Ibid.*, 517.

high and vain notions; the five hundred oxen are virtues, and the five hundred she-asses are wanton inclinations. In the words of Job, "My sighing cometh before I eat," we see the groaning of sorrow before the gladness of contemplation. Arcturus, Orion, the Pleiades, and the chambers of the south in Job 9:9 represent respectively the church, the martyrs, the doctors, and the Holy Spirit. One might go on enumerating countless instances of what seems a needless insistence upon the items of ecclesiastical life, and in some cases sheer wresting of scripture meanings; but there is no doubt of the deep sincerity of the author's mind in these matters. He was not merely indulging a wayward imagination. Like other serious allegorists, he is deeply concerned for the reader's ethical and spiritual enrichment and the support of the orthodox faith. He is never far from the demands of practical piety. "What," he asks, "are the sayings of truth if we do not take them as food for the nourishment of the soul?"

The dogmatic control of the spiritual senses of scripture was to be more fully developed in later times. It would result in a long series of scripture commentaries which contain extended catenae of quotations from accepted church fathers. The Venerable Bede is one of the first to profess in his interpretations a substantial dependence upon the fathers. He speaks of scripture study as medicine for the soul. In his exegesis the purpose of edification is completely dominant. He rests his *Commentary on Luke* upon the works of Ambrose, Augustine, Jerome, and Gregory. But while Bede patiently seeks out tradition as conveyed by these fathers, he exhibits also a considerable body of independent interpretation, and at least regards it as legitimate that he should express his own judgments. In the letter to Acca, bishop of Hexham, that accompanies his *Commentary on Luke,* he adds to his expression of reverence for the fathers the modest statement:

A few items, too, which (as I may say in the words of your Holiness) the Author of Light disclosed to me, I have added, as seemed appropriate, by my own labor. Even though I am not able to spend (as you yourself phrased it) days and sleepless nights in meditation on the Divine Law, yet I have no doubt that I have devoted myself to the Scriptures with no slight zeal, and that I have been able to see, that is, to perceive and discern, not in this book alone, but in every passage, only those things which the Author of Light deigned to show me.[5]

This sense of something of the nature of a direct illumination in Bede may remind us of the teaching of John Calvin regarding the

testimony of the Holy Spirit enlightening the devout reader. It was from Ambrose and Augustine that Bede derived his interpretation of the parable of the prodigal son in Luke 15. The prodigal is worldly philosophy which, unsatisfied, having deserted its true master, Christ, yet hungers after truth, while the faithful Christians receive the bread of the word in the father's house, which is identified with the church. Glunz points out that the Vulgate text was affected by this type of interpretation. Some interpreters, applying Alcuin's realistic principle *substantia commune est nomen omnium rerum quae sunt,*[6] felt that the text itself ought to contain a reference which could be directly used to signify "church," and so interpolated the phrase *in domo* in the text of Luke 15:17. The father's "house" is the church from which the prodigal son has departed. Thus hermeneutic presuppositions were forcing alterations in the text itself. Glunz connects this interpolation with the attention given to the interpretations of Ambrose and Bede in the school of Alcuin, whose study of the Bible marks the beginning of the more typical medieval exegesis.

B. Development of Allegory.—Alcuin represents a type of interpretation which not only relies upon the fathers but sincerely attempts to restrict itself to patristic authority. He explains that as physicians do not create their medicines but procure them from a variety of sources, so he proposes to use Augustine, Ambrose, Gregory, Bede, and other holy fathers. Originality is confined to selection. He "wanders through the blossoming fields" of the patristic literature with a humble heart and a bowed head, and culls passages in reliance upon his own judgment, being cautious to set down nothing contrary to the interpretations of the fathers.[7]

Many followed Alcuin's method of interpretation. Rabanus Maurus, his most distinguished pupil, searched the fathers with even more diligence than Alcuin, and favored spiritual interpretations calculated to support the structure and dogma of church tradition. Thus the four wheels of Ezekiel's chariot are the Law, the Prophets, the Gospels and the Apostles.[8] He

---

[5] *Ibid.*, XCII, 305. H. H. Glunz has called attention to this passage, and gives a condensed translation of it in *History of the Vulgate in England from Alcuin to Roger*

Bacon (Cambridge: Cambridge University Press, 1933), p. 80.

[6] "Substance is the common name of all the things that are." Migne, *op. cit.,* VI, 418; cf. Glunz, *op. cit.,* pp. 87 ff.

[7] *Commentary on the Gospel of St. John,* Migne, *op. cit.,* C, 743, and Glunz, *op. cit.,* pp. 81 ff. Alcuin was deeply concerned to combat the prevailing neglect of the Scriptures in the schools. In 797 he wrote to the church of Canterbury urging the appointment of competent teachers, "lest the Word of God be lacking among you." "Ignorance of Scripture," says Alcuin, "is ignorance of God." Migne, *op. cit.,* C, 250.

[8] Migne, *op. cit.,* CX, 525 ff.

tells us that the book of Esther contains in manifold ways the sacraments of Christ and the church. Esther, as typifying the church, frees her people from peril; Haman stands for *iniquitas,* and Ahasuerus is a type of Christ.[9] In such interpretations the typology of Rabanus is only remotely similar to that employed by the Protestant reformers: it relies largely upon etymologies, many of which are erroneous. Rabanus is, however, an exponent of the four senses of scripture. These are, he explains in the preface to his book *Allegories on Holy Scripture,* four daughters of one mother, Wisdom. He here refers to the historical interpretation as milk, the allegorical as bread, the anagogical as savory nourishment, and the tropological as exhilarating wine. Elaborating numerous comparisons, he observes: "In the house of our soul history lays the foundation, allegory erects the walls, analogy sets on the roof, and tropology provides the ornaments."[10] With his dependence upon the church fathers, he is harsh toward the exponents of fresh opinions.

Walafrid Strabo (d. 849), who became abbot of Reichenau, carried on the Alcuin tradition after Rabanus. The *Glossa Ordinaria,* a universal commentary on scripture, was assumed in the later Middle Ages to be the work of Walafrid. In fact it was substantially of later origin, but it well illustrates the tendency of the Alcuin school. It is a compilation of extracts from the fathers, usually with the name of the original author indicated. Many Bible passages are left unnoticed, but a large body of material is presented.[11] The *Glossa Ordinaria* was one of those useful works which, while possessing no claim to originality, have exercised great influence. It is a mark of weakness in the later scholastics that they recognized this anthology as an authoritative work of interpretation. Thomas Aquinas honors it with countless citations.

Not only the monastic scholars but, as we should expect, the zealous reformers of monasticism in the early Middle Ages, have much to say about the Scriptures and urgently seek to give reality to the *lectio divina.* Benedict of Aniane (d. 821) seizes upon the passage in the final chapter of the Rule of Benedict of Nursia which has been quoted above (p. 115), and sets it in the first paragraph of his *Concordia Regularum.*[12] The brilliant leadership of Odo of Cluny (d. 942) gave a new impulse to monasticism in the early tenth century. Odo undertook in early life, even before he had become a

monk, to labor upon interpretations of the Bible. But he felt serious scruples, and under the criticism of his clerical associates at Tours, shrank from independent opinions. His chief contribution was his *Epitome Moralium,* a condensation of Gregory's work on Job. In another work, the *Collationes,* he gives further evidence of his interest in the Bible. In the opening section of this work Odo says, "If there is anything which can keep a wise man steadfast amid worldly turmoil, it is most of all, I believe, meditation on the Scriptures. . . . Indeed, the intention of all scripture is to restrain us from the depravity of this life."[13] This is the true spirit of monastic injunctions regarding the Scriptures. It does not directly conduce to technical study of the text or to independent intellectualizing of its meaning. The monk is a seeker after spiritual security. Similar is the attitude of Gerard de Brogne (d. 959), a reformer of monasticism in the region of Ghent in the Netherlands. Gerard became a preacher, thereby attracting recruits to his movement. His early biographer tells us that he sought "by opening the fountain of the Scriptures to water their dry minds," and to induce the spiritually weak brethren to "take the life-giving herb of the divine word" for the healing of their vices.[14]

The Norman monk and prelate, Lanfranc (d. 1089), who played an important part in the church of England, like Alcuin and his followers relied upon the patristic writings and resented any attempt to evade that authority. Thus he was a determined opponent of Berengar (d. 1088), who in a dialectical manner introduced new interpretations of the passages of scripture concerning the Lord's Supper. This to Lanfranc was "pertinacious arrogance." Lanfranc, however, exhibits a great interest in improving the Vulgate texts, and the copying of the Scriptures flourished in the monasteries that fell under his influence.

C. Toward a More Historical Exegesis.—There were other authors, however, who were nonconformists with respect to the senses of scripture and to the fashion of dependence upon the fathers. This is true of the illustrious Irishman, Johannes Scotus Erigena (d. in or after 877). The philosophical mind of Erigena is not satisfied with the sharp distinction between the word and its spiritual meaning assumed by the Alcuin school. What is needed is sound intellectual understanding of the text. The language itself has everything in it if only the mind is taught to draw it forth. This position encourages the labor of interpretation and at the same time the effort to obtain the best

---

[9] *Ibid.,* CIX, 635 ff.

[10] *Ibid.,* CXII, 849.

[11] The work occupies about two thousand columns in Migne, *op. cit.,* CXIII, CXIV.

[12] Migne, *op. cit.,* CIII, 718.

[13] *Ibid.,* CXXXIII, 520.

[14] Glunz, *op. cit.,* p. 38; text in *Monumenta Germaniae Historica, Scriptores* (Hannover: Hahn, 1888), XV, 671.

possible text. Erigena himself examined textual variants, seeking a fuller understanding of scripture.[15]

The gifted monk of St. Gaul, Notker Balbulus (d. 912), also favored a more critical interpretation and was somewhat disinclined to allegory. In a sort of bibliographical guide to commentaries on the Scriptures, Notker dryly remarks that the Venerable Bede, in his comments on Tobias and Esdras, wrote what was pleasant rather than what was required and tried to turn a simple story into allegory.[16]

Christian of Stavelot (d. 850), commonly called Druthmar, at the beginning of his commentary on Matthew, wrote:

I have studied to follow the historical more than the spiritual sense because it seemed to me irrational to seek for spiritual knowledge in any book and to be utterly ignorant of the historical, since history is the foundation of all knowledge [quum historia fundamentum omnis intelligentiae sit].[17]

Druthmar does not revel in allegory, but he likes to offer brief historical notes on place names, and simple expositions of unusual words. On the other hand, he takes a great interest in edifying etymologies and typological identifications. In Matthew's genealogy, for example, Abraham "signifies" the Father, Isaac the Lord Jesus Christ.[18]

In the twelfth century we have a number of commentators who show a marked departure from the current methods of exegesis. Among these is Rupert of Deutz (d. 1135). This learned abbot commented on many Old and New Testament books, and wrote a quite remarkable treatise, On the Victory of God's Word (1127). Christ, for Rupert as for Luther, is the center of all scripture. On Rev. 12:21 and Eph. 2:20 he remarks that the prophets are foundations, the apostles foundations of foundations, and Christ the foundation of all foundations.[19] In his Victory of God's Word he argues that "the Word of God is the Son of God," and that the Scriptures are necessary to salvation and sufficient for faith. In our natural ignorance of God they are our one light, and the guide to theology. The Scripture is not a book of dark mysteries, but essentially simple, and suitable for the unlearned. The teacher of the Word should be one taught of God, and trained for

the combat like Job's war horse. We receive the Word as from the mouth of God.[20] In the preface to his Commentary on John's Gospel Rupert rejects the view that Augustine is a sufficient authority, and affirms the right of other Christians to expound the books. Nor is it necessary to rest on the authority of Gregory for Job.[21] He is more typically medieval when he makes the seven days of creation a forecast of the seven gifts of the Holy Spirit. He laid a novel emphasis in his soteriology upon the work of the Holy Spirit, and his doctrine of the Eucharist was under suspicion as a reflection of the heresy of Berengar.[22]

The work of the Victorines was also startling. Both Hugh (d. 1141) and Andrew (d. 1175) of St. Victor profited by the Old Testament scholarship of the new school of French rabbis who followed Solomon Rashi (d. 1105) of Troyes. Half a century ago Nicholas of Lyra was regarded as the first Christian greatly indebted to Rashi. Recent scholarship has shown a powerful leaven of Rashi's literal, rational exegesis upon the Christian scholars of the twelfth century. Beryl Smalley's revealing book, The Study of the Bible in the Middle Ages,[23] strongly supports this view, and also reinforces the evidence that, from Rabanus Maurus down, Jewish scholars were frequently consulted by Christians. In view of what is now known of Rashi's Jewish and Christian influence in many lands, it would be difficult to name a more important writer in the whole history of interpretation. Herman Hailperin[24] has clarified this matter further. He points out that amid the anti-Jewish enactments and riots of the early thirteenth century, when the Talmud and Rashi's commentaries were burned at Paris, Christians were busy translating parts of both. A century earlier Bernard of Clairvaux was anxious about this intellectual traffic with Jews. He rebuked a young scholar for "gnawing crusts with the lettered Jews": "crust" is here the letter of the bread of scripture.

Of the three great Victorines, Hugh was a Saxon, Richard a Scot, and Andrew an Englishman. Hugh went for help to the rabbis and worked mainly on the Old Testament. He rebuked those who despised the letter. "Subtract the letter, and what is left?" he cogently asks. He advises, "Do not despise what is lowly in

[15] Glunz, op. cit., pp. 108 ff.

[16] De Interpretibus Divinarum Scripturarum. Migne, op. cit., CXXXI, 997.

[17] Migne, op. cit., CVI, 1262; the commentary has been examined by M. L. W. Laistner, "A Ninth-Century Commentator on the Gospel According to Matthew," Harvard Theological Review, XX (1927), 129-49, with attention chiefly to text.

[18] Migne, op. cit., CVI, 1268.

[19] Ibid., CLXIX, 1198.

[20] De Victoria Verbi Dei, chs. i-iv. Migne, op. cit., CLXIX, 1217-29.

[21] Migne, op. cit., CLXIX, 201-2.

[22] A. J. Macdonald, Berengar and the Reform of Sacramental Doctrine (London: Longmans, Green & Co., 1930), pp. 399-400. For Rupert's theology see the article on him in Dictionnaire de Théologie Catholique (Paris: Letouzey et Ané, 1903), XIV, 169-205.

[23] Oxford: Clarendon Press, 1941.

[24] "The Hebrew Heritage of Mediaeval Christian Biblical Scholarship," Historia Judaica, V (1943), 133-54.

God's Word." He criticizes the interpretation of Isa. 4:1, "seven women shall take hold of one man," as referring to the seven gifts of the Spirit, without acknowledging that the prophet means something literal as well. Hugh would select among patristic commentaries "that which has been certainly intended by the author," or if that is unclear, what is admissible and in accord with the faith. On Ecclesiastes he blames those who "strive superstitiously to find a mystical sense and a deep allegory where none is." Possessed of a fine imagination, he was able to illuminate the literal meaning without "toiling after tropologies." Beryl Smalley writes, "His great service to exegesis was to lay more stress on the literal interpretation *relatively* to the spiritual." [25] In *De Arca Noe Morali* [26] he explains his classroom drawings designed to show the ark just as Noah built it. But Hugh is no mere literalist. He employs with the Alexandrians the allegorical and tropological as well as the literal sense. "The Ark signifies the church," he here observes, "and the church is Christ's body; so I have drawn the whole person of Christ, head and members. . . ." [27]

Richard (d. 1173) and Andrew had more knowledge of Hebrew than Hugh. Richard, like Bernard of Clairvaux, wrote against the Jewish literal, and to him therefore false, interpretation. Richard asks his readers not to be surprised if something has escaped the fathers. What has escaped them is the value of the literal meaning. He implies that Gregory was mistaken in saying that the second vision of Ezekiel had no meaning according to the letter. Yet this independence is asserted with great deference to the patristic authors. The earlier reapers who have filled their volumes with corn have left gleanings for the poor! We honor the fathers by seeking the truth beyond their reach. "Do not ask whether what I say is new, but whether it is true." Richard will not be misled, however, by Jewish tradition to question the authority of the Scriptures. In a slap at Andrew, he warns that Josephus is not to be taken as authoritative simply on the ground that he is a Jew.[28]

Andrew was the most radical of the champions of rational literalism. He was the Abélard of Bible scholars. Beryl Smalley even calls him a humanist. He writes with no interest in a theological pattern but in joy of the perusal of these revered documents of antiquity. "A pleasant toil, a toilsome pleasure," he esteems the task, and he is sustained by a hearty assurance that there is truth yet to spring forth from the

Word. With perfect freedom he may set down phrases like these: "We follow the Jews and Josephus rather than Bede," or "Men of great authority give this opinion; . . . they are misled." The historical method may involve historical speculation and conjecture. How could Moses know what happened at Creation? Conceivably by revelation of the Holy Spirit. Possibly, however, the history was handed down from Adam, and Moses obtained it by painstaking research (*diligenter investigare curavit*). Andrew makes the most of the fragmentary biographical details furnished by Old Testament books about their authors. Isaiah is distinguished for seven things: his noble race, polished eloquence, dignified office, royal connection, worth of character, constancy, and holiness. This approach is far removed from Gregory's estimate of the human author of Job as of the same importance as the pen that wrote the book. It is probable that if Andrew could have stepped into the study of Lorenzo Valla, he would have been intellectually at home; while in the company of his elder contemporary, Bernard of Clairvaux (d. 1153), he would certainly have been embarrassed.[29]

D. Tension Between History and Allegory.—Bernard's sermons on the Song of Songs exhibit the exegesis of edification unalloyed by history. With the eloquence of free discourse, they gather into a loose relation to the text of the book a body of mystical reflections upon God, angels, and human life. Allegory prevails, but ascetic morality is often, if sometimes tardily, introduced. "I thought," says Bernard, wearied with his own lucubrations, "that we should quickly traverse this forest shady with allegories and reach the level ground of moral meanings." Bernard's allegorical exuberance carries him far indeed from the embarrassing literal sense of the book. The words, "the virgins love thee," send him off to elaborate the diverse reasons why God is loved by angels, archangels, virtues, powers, principalities, dominations, cherubim, and seraphim. The phrase, "go forth and pasture thy kids," causes him to shed "a torrent of tears": the bride is being rebuked and sent away in anger under a command to indulge the fleshly desires. "But whither are we being borne?" he not inappropriately interjects.[30]

Bernard in his exhortation to Pope Eugenius III presents a doctrine of the two swords of Luke 22:38. Alcuin had used this passage, giving both swords to Charlemagne, not yet emperor, for defense of Christendom from without and from within. In Bernard the swords are "spir-

[25] Smalley, *op. cit.*, p. 77.
[26] Migne, *op. cit.*, CLXXVI, 617 ff.
[27] *Ibid.*, CLXXVI, 622.
[28] Smalley, *op. cit.*, p. 84.

[29] On Andrew see Smalley, *op. cit.*, ch. iv. Miss Smalley has used MS sources.
[30] *Sermons on the Canticles*, XVI. 1; XXXIV. 3, 5; XXXV. 2. Migne, *op. cit.*, CLXXXIII, 849, 959 ff.

itual" and "material," and they are wielded respectively by the church and by the soldier at the bidding (*nutum*) of the clergy and at the command (*iussum*) of the emperor.[81] This passage was to be habitually invoked in support of papal claims by Innocent III and his successors. Here it may be said that a study of the use of scripture passages in asserting papal authority through the period from Pope Gregory VII to the Reformation would certainly reveal an important current in the history of interpretation. The texts principally relied upon were the "dominical charge" in Matt. 16:17-19; the commission of Jeremiah, "I have this day set thee over the nations and over the kingdoms" (Jer. 1:10); the two lights set in the firmament at creation (Gen. 1:16-18), of which the sun is the papacy and the moon is the secular ruler; and the "two swords" passage. The last two represent pure allegory. Many other passages were employed to give scriptural basis to the papal claims. But these interpretations were disputed by opponents of the papacy, notably by Dante in *De Monarchia* (ca. 1309).

Reference has been made above to the different senses of scripture recognized by our authors. Guibert de Nogent (d. 1124), in a book on the construction of sermons, speaks of the four senses as the rules by which every page of scripture turns as on so many wheels:

That is to say: *history*, which speaks of things done; *allegory*, in which one thing is understood by another [*ex alio aliud*]; *tropology*, that is, the moral way of speaking, in which the ordering of morals is treated; *anagoge*, or the spiritual understanding by which, discussing what is lofty and heavenly, we are led to things above.[82]

Hugh of St. Cher wrote: "History tells what happened; allegory teaches what is to be understood; anagogy, what is to be sought after; tropology, what is to be done." [83]

The main tension seems to have been between allegory and history, and most writers were partisans of one or the other of these. Joachim of Floris (d. 1202) carried allegory to an extreme, presenting a revolutionary doctrine of the church. But the moral sense emerged into new prominence in the twelfth and thirteenth centuries. Even before the Vic-

torines, Guibert remarked that the need of the age was no longer for allegory but rather for tropology, the moral sense. The great commentators, Peter Comestor (d. 1179?), chief author of the *Historia Scholastica*, Peter Cantor (d. 1197), and Stephen Langton (d. 1228), constitute what Grabmann and Beryl Smalley have called the "biblical moral school." The lectures of these professors were taken down in shorthand and afterward polished, as Beryl Smalley shows in her discriminating chapter on the three. The *Historia Scholastica* [34] is a Bible with extensive comments; it was very widely circulated, and was printed in 1473 at Augsburg. At the outset Peter Comestor says: "Holy Scripture is God's dining room, where the guests are made soberly drunk." [35] The foundation is history, which divides into annals, calendars, and ephemera (the records of years, months, and days); the walls are allegory, which makes one event the figure of another; the roof is tropology, which from what has been done suggests what we ought to do. This passage may be compared with the language of Rabanus Maurus quoted above. With a similar view Langton makes the words, "Thy silver is become dross" (Isa. 1:22) apply to the work of scholars who turn from tropological and moral to "curious" questions.[36]

E. The Scholastic Age.—We are now in the age of the universities, the friars, and the great Scholastics. Robert Grosseteste (d. 1253) taught the young Franciscans of Oxford to love and labor over the Scriptures. Dominic was himself an intense Bible student; and Ray C. Petry has shown that Francis of Assisi searched the Scriptures for testimony of Jesus, while he found there also the justification of the Friars Minor. Francis uses very effectively the literal sense. But Petry in his chapter on "The Last Times and the Kingdom of God" exhibits what is really the Franciscan appropriation of anagogy.[37] Certain of the Spiritual Franciscans were to carry this eschatological strain, with the aid of Joachim, to a fanatical pitch, while others in a more literal apocalypticism identified in the contemporary scene the enemies of God. At Oxford and Paris a sober and rational interpretation was carried on by Franciscan and Dominican professors. We are not here concerned with the work of the Paris correctors, such as William de la Mare and Gerard of

---

[81] *De Consideratione* IV. 3. 7; Migne, *op. cit.*, CLXXXII, 776.

[82] *Quo Ordine Sermo Fieri Debet.* Migne, *op. cit.*, CLVI, 25-26.

[83] *Opera* (Venice: Nicolaus Pezzana, 1703), I, 2. The mnemonic verses quoted by Nicholas of Lyra, and very frequently by later writers, that call to mind this "four-horse chariot" (*quadriga*), as Luther called it, ran thus:

Litera gesta docet
quid credas allegoria
moralis quid agas
quo tendas anagogia.

[34] Migne, *op. cit.*, CXCVIII, 1053-1722. Hans Vollmer has edited Latin and German versions: *Materialien zur Bibelgeschichte . . . des Mittelalters* (Berlin: Weidmann, 1912-16), II, i, ii.

[35] Migne, *op. cit.*, CXCVIII, 1053.

[36] Smalley, *op. cit.*, p. 199.

[37] *Francis of Assisi, Apostle of Poverty* (Durham: Duke University Press, 1941), chs. iv, v; cf. Ernst Benz, *Ecclesia Spiritualis* (Stuttgart: W. Kohlhammer, 1934), Part III.

Huy: but their rather unsuccessful attempts to purge the text are evidence of the importance of the problem of Bible text in the Scholastic age. The chapter general of the Dominicans in 1256 complained of their lack of success. Roger Bacon thought they did more harm than good, and at the same time criticized the weakness of academic study of Scripture. But the fact is that the Scholastics had something of a new scholarly power of biblical interpretation; and it is contrary to fact to say that Aristotle crowded the Scriptures out of their thoughts.

It is doubtful whether any theologian has ever surpassed Thomas Aquinas in familiarity with the language of the Latin Bible. There is a legend that he memorized it throughout while detained by his brothers from entering the Dominican order. In the *Summa Theologica*, before taking up the doctrine of God, he presents a doctrine of sacred Scripture. Here he examines the question "Whether Scripture has more senses than the literal," and after references to Augustine and Gregory, responds (condensed):

God is the Author of Holy Scripture. He has given a meaning not only to the words but to the things they signify, so that the things signified in turn signify something else. Primarily, words signify things, which is the historical sense; secondarily, the things signify other things, and we get the spiritual sense. The latter is of three sorts. The Old Law is allegorically interpreted in the New Law, but the interpretation of matters affecting Christ and our obligation is tropological, and that which deals with the eternal glory is the anagogical or celestial sense. The literal sense is that which the author intends, but God being the Author, we may expect to find in Scripture a wealth of meaning.[38]

Thomas here quotes with approval Augustine's statement, "On the literal sense alone can we base arguments," and this principle is habitually observed in the *Summa*. But his *Catena aurea*, or *Commentary on the Four Gospels Collected Out of the Works of the Fathers*,[39] an assemblage of quotations from numerous authors ranging from Origen to the twelfth-century *Interlinear Gloss*, shows how highly he prized the nonliteral senses. The locusts and wild honey that nourished John the Baptist (Matt. 3:4) point to the fact that his speeches were sweet as honey but of short flight, like that of locusts, and his camel's hair garment represents the church of the Gentiles. In Matt. 8:20 the foxes and the birds are respectively deceitful and proud demons, or (by another authority) they signify heretics and Jews. The four thousand of Mark 8:9, 20 are men perfect in the four virtues; the five thousand of Mark 8:19 are men enslaved to the five senses. Similar interpretations abound in the *Meditations* of Thomas, where many Old Testament passages are employed to sustain medieval doctrines.[40] For Thomas the teaching of the church is to be adhered to "as an infallible and divine rule." [41] As a commentator the Angelic Doctor too often plays a role of conservative dependence on less competent minds than his own.

F. Rashi and Nicholas of Lyra.—Resistance to allegorical excess seems to have owed much to Rashi and his Christian disciples. The age of Aquinas produced an anonymous Christian commentary on the Song of Songs which follows Rashi closely, and except at the very end makes no reference to Christ.[42] Rashi was given Christian reincarnation in Nicholas of Lyra (d. 1340), a Norman Franciscan and Sorbonne doctor. His great commentary, *Postillae Perpetuae in Vetus et Novum Testamentum*, reflects on almost every page of its fifty books the opinions of Rashi ("Rabbi Solomon"). Lyra makes no profession of novel purpose. He recites respectfully the now traditional description of the four senses, and quotes the passage of Aquinas on this topic, to which reference has been made. But he labors to bring out the historic meaning of the Hebrew and Greek. Herman Hailperin, in a study of Rashi's influence on Lyra,[43] rates highly his appreciation of the nuances of Hebrew and interest in Bible customs, in which he followed Rashi. Sometimes he rejects Rashi's view and goes over his head to the Targums. More often he prefers Rashi to Jerome or some other Christian authority. Yet in doctrinal matters Lyra, much more than Andrew of St. Victor, stands on guard for the Christian tradition.

It is of interest that the Waldenses, who long before Nicholas had taken their stand on the Scriptures literally understood as sufficient for salvation, and had condemned as "Pharisees" the conventionally allegorical commentators who supported "idolatry" by their interpretations, made considerable use of the *Postillae*.[44] In this they were followed by the Reformers. Lyra calls Rashi the commentator "whose teach-

---

[38] Part I, question 1, Art. 10.
[39] Oxford: James Parker & Co., 1874.
[40] The *Meditations* has been edited in Latin and English by P. D. Mezard and E. C. McEniry (Columbus, Ohio: 1940). See pp. 37, 63 ff., 154, 438, 482.
[41] Cf. Hugh Pope, "His Principles of Biblical Interpretation" in Aelred Whitacre *et al*, *St. Thomas Aquinas* (Oxford: Basil Blackwell, 1924), pp. 125-39.
[42] Smalley, *op. cit.*, p. 262.
[43] "Nicolas de Lyra and Rashi: The Minor Prophets," *Rashi Anniversary Volume* (New York: American Academy for Jewish Research, 1941), pp. 115-47.
[44] Louis I. Newman, *Jewish Influence on Christian Reform Movements* (New York: Columbia University Press, 1925), pp. 74-78, 213-39.

ing is reported most authentic among modern Jews." Luther refers to Lyra as "an excellent man, a good Hebraist, and a steadfast Christian." [45] The unknown author of the immortal jingle

> Si Lyra non lyrasset
> Lutherus non saltasset

oversimplifies the relationship. As Lyra was indebted to others than Rashi, so Luther was indebted to many interpreters besides Lyra. But in both cases the debt to the predecessor named was primary. Many sixteenth-century commentators besides Luther, humanist, Roman Catholic, and Protestant, used the *Postillae* with appreciation.

The way to the Reformation interpretation of scripture was led not only by Lyra but by the work of Lorenzo Valla (d. 1457), Gianozzo Manetti (d. 1459), John Wessel Gansfort (d. 1489), John Colet (d. 1519), Jacques Lefèvre (d. 1536), Erasmus (d. 1536), and other humanists who by their Greek and Hebrew studies laid the foundation for a philological understanding of the Scriptures. The effect of their work—not always its purpose—was to give a new prominence to the literal and historical sense. By the time of Luther's early commentaries the shackles of tradition were already weakened.

II. The Reformation

A. Martin Luther.—In his *Address to the German Nobility* (1520) Luther vehémently denounced the view that the interpretation of scripture belongs to the pope alone. It belongs, he says in effect, to pious and competent Christians. It is, moreover, a task that is never completed. In the *Commentaries on the Psalms* (1519-21) he states the matter thus:

I came to this opinion, that no man's interpretation, (assuming it to be pious) ought to be rejected unless by the law of retaliation one chooses to be rejected in turn. He is lacking in some things, you in more; I see many things missed by Augustine, and I know men will see many things that I myself do not see. . . . Our life is a beginning and a going forward, not a consummation.[46]

Interpretation is thus in a degree fluid, and it cannot be held static by ecclesiastical authority. "The Church," says Luther, "is a daughter born of the Word, not the mother of the Word." [47] He many times insists that he is doing nothing final either in translation or in interpretation.

Yet he is assured and unyielding on the main principles by which he is guided, and which form the bases of his theology. Thus in his *Preface to Romans,* having stressed the priority of faith to works and the Pauline meaning of "flesh" as sin and unbelief, he adds:

Without such an understanding of these words you will never understand this letter of St. Paul, or any other book of Holy Scripture. Therefore, beware of all teachers who use these words in a different sense, . . . even Jerome, Augustine, Ambrose, Origen and men like them or above them.[48]

Luther has praise and blame for many commentators. He recognizes the indispensable service of humanism to interpretation:

As for me, I am persuaded that without skill in literature genuine theology cannot stand, just as hitherto in the ruin and prostration of letters it too has miserably fallen and been laid low. Indeed I see that the remarkable disclosure of the Word of God would never have taken place had He not first prepared the way by the rediscovery of languages and sciences, as by Baptist forerunners.[49]

But his reported saying, "The inseparable companion of Holy Scripture is the Holy Spirit," [50] reveals what is really the governing, if somewhat intangible, principle of authority. Again, Luther strongly affirms and constantly exemplifies the view that Christ is the center around which all Scripture revolves—the *punctus mathematicus sacrae scripturae,*[51] and that the entire Bible has meaning by virtue of, and in proportion to, its emphasis upon the gospel of Christ. His prefaces to the Old Testament, and to its several books, bring out this point clearly, and in his commentaries on Genesis, Isaiah, and the Psalms we are never long unreminded of it. Thus in Ps. 2 "the kings of the earth" are Herod and Pilate; Christ speaks of the church in "my holy hill of Zion"; the "rod of Iron" is the gospel, an opinion which he labors to illustrate with allegorical detail.[52]

Luther frequently expresses a preference for the grammatico-historical interpretation, or literal sense, but it would be a basic error to suppose that he was always content to follow it. Indeed we find him often quite hospitable to the stock allegories of the fathers, and fertile

[45] *Sämmentliche Werke* (Erlangen: Carl Hender, 1845), XXXVII, 4.
[46] *Werke* (Weimar: Hermann Böhlan, 1892), V, 23.
[47] *Lectures on Genesis,* 7:16-24. *Werke,* Weimar edition, XLII, 324.

[48] *Works of Martin Luther,* tr. C. M. Jacobs (Philadelphia: Muhlenberg Press, 1932), VI, 453. Original in Luther's *Werke,* Weimar edition, *Deutsche Bible,* VII (1931), 12.
[49] Letter to Eoban Hess, March 29, 1523. *Werke,* Weimar edition, *Luthers Briefwechsel,* III, 50.
[50] *Werke,* Weimar edition, *Tischreden,* V, 397 (No. 5904).
[51] *Ibid.,* II, 439 (No. 2383).
[52] *Werke,* Weimar edition, V, 47 ff.

in inventing his own. There are sections of his commentaries that are surprisingly medieval in this respect. In his *Lectures on Genesis* (1535-45) he inserts (at ch. 9) a disquisition on allegories and his use of them. He had been led, he tells us, into allegorical interpretations by Origen, Jerome, and Augustine, but finding that he was following a vain shadow, began to detest allegories. Müntzer and the Anabaptists have been wrong in turning everything into allegory. Allegories are to be permitted only if they observe the analogy of faith. Some of the fathers leave out faith; and it is rash impudence and ambition to assert papal supremacy on the allegory of the sun and moon. When Luther here adopts from the ancients the view that the ark of Noah typifies Christ, with whom we are saved from the flood, and points with approval to their observation that the ark like the human body is six times as long as it is wide, we fear that he is still pursuing the "shadow." But he sums up his thought on the subject in a lucid and revealing statement:

I have often said what theology was when I entered upon this kind of study. They used to say, "The letter killeth" (II Cor. 3:6). Therefore I disliked Lyra most of all interpreters because he followed so diligently the literal meaning. But now, in commendation of this very thing, I prefer him to almost all interpreters of Scripture. And I admonish you with the utmost earnestness, seek to be diligent in appraising historical matters. But if ever you wish to use allegory, do so observing the analogy of faith; that is, accommodate it to Christ, the church, faith, and the ministry of the Word.[53]

Despite inconsistencies and traditional and unfruitful interpretations, Luther's powerful mind produced a new and vitalizing presentation of scripture in which the Old Testament is made to support the teaching of the New. In his doctrine of salvation the law, nevertheless, stands in dramatic antithesis to the gospel: it convinces us of sin, for which the gospel offers forgiveness. Thus the whole Bible becomes significant as a testimony to those central convictions that he regards as the essentials of Christianity. Luther's theology dominates his evaluation of the scripture books. He feels free to hold certain of them in far higher esteem than others. In the

New Testament itself he has little use for James and Revelation, since they fail to supply corroboration of the gospel as he understands it. According to a passage in the *Table Talk*, it was his habit to read the Bible through twice a year.[54] At any rate, he was completely familiar with all of it. With great readiness he can match passage with passage. His sermons flash with insights that are the fruits of eager study and reveal the resources of scripture for the Christian life.

B. John Calvin.—Calvin's masterly knowledge of the language and thought of the Bible is the key to his power as a theologian. His commentaries form the major portion of his writings; and virtually all his treatises proceed by a series of references to scripture passages. He omitted from formal exposition only one book of the New Testament and eight of the Old. He makes some use of every scripture book, though he almost completely neglects the Song of Songs and Revelation. Of the latter he is reported to have said that he was totally unable to find its meaning.[55] In the *Institutes* he quotes the New Testament 3,098 times, the Old 1,755 times.[56] Henri Clavier, in a careful examination of Calvin's biblicism, finds a distinction between the Word and the Scripture. The Word is God's communication of himself: in the Scripture it becomes precise.[57] For Calvin, as for Aquinas, "the Author of Scripture is God": he affirms its "complete credit and authority." He would like to assert the inerrancy of the Scriptures, but in fact admits minor errors. In Eph. 4:8 Paul misquotes Ps. 68:18, even seeming to reverse the psalmist's meaning. Calvin argues that the apostle is not repeating the words but pursuing the matter itself, and he uses other verses of the psalm to enforce his point.[58] From Ps. 8:6 and Heb. 2:7 "we see with what freedom the apostles permitted themselves to quote scripture passages.[59] The apostles were not so scrupulous (in quotations) as to decline to accommodate their language to the uninformed.[60] Praiseworthy as is the teaching of II Peter, its inferior style may be explained on the ground that the apostle in his old age dictated it to some disciple.[61] Classical authors are employed to give perspective on the lan-

[53] *Werke,* Weimar edition, XLII, 377. Luther has here indicated broadly what he means by the "analogy of faith," a term employed by Augustine. In Rom. 12:6, κατὰ τὴν ἀναλογίαν τῆς πίστεως, certainly a different sense is intended than that understood in hermeneutics. In the latter the term was used as a cable by which interpretation could be moored to orthodox belief. On the progress of Luther's thought concerning the senses of scripture there are some valuable pages in J. M. Reu, *Luther's German Bible* (Columbus, Ohio: Lutheran Book Concern, 1934), pp. 124 ff.

[54] *Tischreden,* II, 244 (No. 1877).
[55] Jean Bodin, *Method for the Easy Comprehension of History,* tr. Beatrice Reynolds (New York: Columbia University Press, 1945), p. 291.
[56] Henri Clavier, *Études sur le calvinisme* (Paris: Fischbacher, 1936), p. 87.
[57] *Ibid.,* p. 108.
[58] *Opera, Corpus Reformatorum* (Brunsvig: C. A. Schwitschke, 1863), LI, 194.
[59] *Ibid.,* XXXI, 92.
[60] *Ibid.,* LV, 159. On Heb. 11:21.
[61] *Ibid.,* LV, 441.

guage of scripture. For example, on καλοῦ ἔργου in I Tim. 3:1 he remarks:

I doubt not that he alludes to the ancient Greek proverb, often quoted by Plato, δύσκολα τὰ καλά, which means in Greek, "Those things that are beautiful (*pulchra*) are also arduous and difficult." [62]

Thus, he is sometimes led, though not willingly, to the view that it is not the letter of scripture, but the substance of doctrine in it, that is *verbum Dei*. His oft-quoted designation of the apostles as "authentic amanuenses of the Holy Spirit," [63] and his statement that the Scriptures are "given to us by the very mouth of God" [64] must be read in the light of his commentaries, which exhibit no such assumption of verbal infallibility as these words seem to imply. The Bible authors are inspired indeed; they are inspired personalities writing out of their conscious experiences and in historic settings that are significant to the interpreter.

In his handling of scripture Calvin habitually draws together both Testaments. So much is this the case that many expounders of his thought have overlooked his repeated affirmations of a progressive revelation in the Bible. God, Calvin argues, has employed an order and economy in dispensing his covenant of mercy, making additional revelations "from day to day." The promise to Adam was as a feeble spark; the light enlarged in course of time until the coming of Christ, the Sun of Righteousness, who illumined the whole world. [65] Calvin sometimes represents Bible writers as accommodating their messages to the mental capacities of their original readers. Thus Moses in Gen. 1:16 implies that the moon is next in size to the sun among the heavenly bodies. Astronomy, in denying this, is not to be reprobated, nor did Moses mean to condemn that admirable science. But he was a teacher of uneducated people, and descended to the level of their understanding. Meanwhile the splendor of moonlight should teach us the beneficence of God. [66] Calvin presents at length the evidence of "the superior excellence of the New Testament over the

Old." [67] But he links the two intimately, and sometimes overstates the Christian element in the Old Testament, while on the other hand he sometimes employs the harsher passages of the early books to the detriment of the doctrine of grace. [68] Furthermore, he uses typology to mark the relationship between the Old Covenant and the New; for instance, in making the land of Canaan a figure of the eternal inheritance. [69] Apart from this discovery of "types" of the gospel in the rites and narratives of the Old Testament, he is firm in his avoidance of nonliteral meanings. Where it is necessary to explain a manifest allegory in the text, he handles the matter with circumspect precision, and minimizes the allegorical element. In his commentary on Galatians he points out that ever since the early fathers, men have by allegory "changed into curious shapes the sacred Word." Here he states that "the true meaning of scripture is the natural and obvious meaning"; to it we ought to adhere firmly. Paul, when in Gal. 4:22-25 he allegorizes Gen. 16, does not imply that Moses wrote with the purpose that his history should be turned into allegory. [70] Calvin objects to the traditional "frigid" interpretation that would identify the four chariots of Zech. 6:1-3 with the four Gospels. [71] On the use of Isaiah's Trisagion (6:3) as an argument to quell the Arians, he remarks stiffly: "I should prefer to employ firmer evidence." [72]

In the preface to his first commentary (Romans, 1539), Calvin reminds his friend Grynaeus of a conversation in which the two had discussed the qualities needed in an exegete. They had agreed that these were clearness and brevity, and that it was "his particular duty to exhibit the spirit of the writer." Calvin was not forgetful of these principles. "Brevity" is a relative term, but though his commentaries are extensive, they are written with economy of language. What is attempted is a searching out of the meaning of the text, as the scripture writer understood it. The resources of humanistic learning are employed, historical data are freely used, and at points of difficulty the opinions of earlier commentators are sifted. Doctrinal interest is keen, and we are made aware of what has been referred to above as the "analogy of faith." For Calvin this calls

[62] *Ibid.*, LII, 279.

[63] *Institutes*, IV. 8. 9.

[64] *Ibid.*, I. 7. 5. But compare his *Homilies on I Samuel*, Homily 42, where prophets and pastors in the church are referred to as "the very mouth of God." *Opera*, XXIX, 705.

[65] *Institutes*, II. 10. 20; 11. 2-5; cf. P. T. Fuhrmann, *God-Centered Religion* (Grand Rapids: Zondervan Publishing House, 1942), p. 84.

[66] *Opera*, XXIII, 22. There is a very similar passage in Aquinas (*Summa Theologica*, Part I, question 68, Art. 3): "But it is to be borne in mind that Moses was speaking to a rude people [*rudi populo loquebatur*] and, to condescend to their weak capacity, he set forth to them only what was clearly apparent to their senses [*sensui manifeste apparuit*]."

[67] *Institutes* II. 11. 12. The treatment of this point by Rupert E. Davies, *The Problem of Authority in the Continental Reformers* (London: Epworth Press, 1946), pp. 111 ff., tends to minimize the differences noted by Calvin.

[68] See e.g., his *Commentary on Joshua*, 10:18; *Opera*, XXV, 502.

[69] *Institutes* II. 11. 1-4.

[70] *Opera*, L, 237.

[71] *Ibid.*, XLIV, 202.

[72] *Ibid.*, XXXVI, 129.

forth a great emphasis upon the scripture testimony to the sovereignty of God, and an exaggeration of the arguments for predestination. But this does not eclipse the objective of a clear understanding of the writer's meaning. In order to appreciate Calvin's commentaries one does not have to subscribe to his entire theology. Indeed, F. A. G. Tholuck remarks that he "is by no means solicitous to insist, in all cases, and with zeal, upon that meaning which tends most to the confirmation of Christian truths." [73] We may say that he follows the clues like a detective, until he is assured that he possesses the writer's secret. Philological and other aids are subordinated to the one purpose, the discovery and elucidation of the message. This is of course presented as in essence a divine message, with a bearing upon all history, and upon the reader's life. The task that he sets himself is by no means merely a verbal exercise. He keeps in view the book as a whole, the Scriptures as a whole, and to some degree the body of human thought. He can sum up the teaching of Romans in a sentence: "There is only one righteousness for men, the mercy of God in Christ; and this offered through the gospel is received by faith." [74] But if necessary, he will wrestle with a word through three paragraphs. He believes that at the best a "partial ignorance" will remain. Besides, no accumulation of rational argument without "the inward testimony of the Holy Spirit" can accredit the Scriptures to the reader.[75] It is "the spirit of the writer" that is to be discovered, and the Holy Spirit that inspired him to write must guide the inquirer. In one place Calvin remarks that the Holy Spirit is not mistakenly called "a spirit of discernment [discretionis]." [76] If we bear in mind the sweep of his conception, we may apply to Calvin's interpretation of scripture the canon of J. A. Ernesti: "Interpretation is the art of teaching the real sentiment contained in any form of words, or of effecting that another may derive from them the same idea that the writer intended to convey." [77]

C. Other Reformation Interpreters.—On the Continent, scripture commentaries were numerous in the sixteenth century. Those of Melanchthon, Bucer, Zwingli, Oecolampadius, and Bullinger won the measured approval of Calvin. He thought Melanchthon too selective, Bucer too elaborate, Zwingli too discursive,

Oecolampadius and Bullinger nearer to his own ideal.[78] The prodigiously productive pen of Matthias Flacius, in his *Key to Scripture* (1567), carried forward Lutheran biblical scholarship and urged fresh labor on the historical meaning of the text.[79] In England and Scotland the vernacular Bible flourished but few commentaries were written in the sixteenth century. Luther's views were reflected in Tyndale's prefaces. In a treatise of 1528 Tyndale states that "Scripture hath but one sense, which is the literal sense," and that the explanation of its "proverbs, similitudes, riddles, and allegories" falls within literal interpretation.[80] Anglicans of the period generally adopt this conception. Jewel's (posthumous) *Commentary on I and II Thessalonians* offers a good example of this method. In his *Treatise on Holy Scripture* (1570) Jewel stresses the simplicity of most of the Bible and its unique instructional value even for untrained minds.[81] William Whitaker, in a learned treatise, reiterates Tyndale's position just noted, and enforces the reformers' contention for the unique authority and sufficiency of the Scriptures.[82] Negatively applying a rigorous doctrine of scripture authority, Thomas Cartwright and the Elizabethan Puritans rejected all nonscriptural elements in Anglican worship and polity. Hooker assailed this position, and advanced the claims of reason. He holds that the perfection of scripture is limited by the purpose for which it is given. Not every act which it does not enjoin is sin. Hooker is dissatisfied with Calvin's teaching that scripture is authenticated only by the inward witness of the Spirit: too much is thereby left to private waywardness. We should test by reason what we are taught by the Spirit.[83] In his view that church polity is not prescribed in the Scriptures, and therefore mutable, Hooker is on the same ground as Luther: his subjection of interpretation to "reason" would have alarmed Luther and links him with later critical interpreters.[84]

---

[73] "Calvin as an Interpreter of Holy Scripture" (1831), in Calvin, *Commentary on Joshua*, tr. Henry Beveridge (Edinburgh: Calvin Translation Society, 1854), p. 350.

[74] *Opera*, XLIX, 1.

[75] *Institutes* I. 7. 4.

[76] *Opera*, XLVIII, 401. On Acts 17:11.

[77] *Principles of Biblical Interpretation*, tr. C. H. Terrot (Edinburgh: Thomas Clark, 1832), I, 6.

[78] Preface to *Romans* cited above, and letter to Viret, May 19, 1540.

[79] *Clavis Scripturae Sacrae*, Antwerp, 1567; cf. Wilhelm Preger's chapter on this work, *Matthias Flacius Illyricus und seine Zeit* (Erlangen: Theodor Bläsing, 1859), pp. 478-91.

[80] *Doctrinal Treatises of William Tyndale*. Parker Society Publications (Cambridge: University Press, 1848), XLII, 304.

[81] Works of John Jewel, Vol. IV. Parker Society Publications (Cambridge: University Press, 1850), XXVI, 1162-88.

[82] *A Disputation on the Holy Scripture*, 1588. Tr. William Fitzgerald, Parker Society Publications (Cambridge: University Press, 1849), XLV. See especially p. 405.

[83] *Laws of Ecclesiastical Polity* II. 4; III. 7.

[84] A selected bibliography on the history of biblical interpretation will be found on p. 141. Editors.

HISTORY OF THE INTERPRETATION OF THE BIBLE

III. MODERN PERIOD

by SAMUEL TERRIEN

While Luther and Calvin in their respective ways approached the biblical text with a freedom and a critical acumen that were exceptional for their time, they did not concern themselves primarily with the literary and historical problems which are related to the scriptural documents themselves. Although the Protestant Reformation spurred in every land an unprecedented interest in the Bible, the dogmatic intolerance of the post-Reformation period was not favorable to the development of biblical studies. Energies of the Protestant divines were diverted into struggles for survival, as in France, or were spent in the most bitter controversies over doctrinal, ecclesiastical, and political matters, as in Switzerland, the Netherlands, the German states, England, and Scotland. In countries dominated by Roman Catholic power the canons of the Council of Trent (1546) made it clear that any interpretation of scripture had to be tightly fitted into the Procrustean bed of the official dogma.

Ever since the early days of the Renaissance, however, revolutionary ideas were in the air, and their force was bound to meet and ultimately to strike at the authority of the Bible itself. In the long run their impact had not only a destructive but also an unexpectedly constructive effect. It handed back the Bible to man and taught him how to recognize its uniqueness and its relevance.

I. The Rise of Biblical Criticism (ca. 1650-1800)

Three cultural developments have ushered in the modern period of biblical interpretation.

In the first place, the Ptolemaic conception of the universe, which had been quite satisfactorily harmonized with the biblical cosmogony, was undermined by the geographical discoveries of the Portuguese and others, and also by the astronomical observations of Copernicus (1473-1543), whose theory of the heliocentricity of the planetary movements was condemned by the pope as contrary to scripture. The various contributions of Giordano Bruno (1550-1600), Kepler (1571-1630) and Galileo (1564-1642) led in due course to the theory of universal gravitation as formulated by Newton (1642-1727). Thus, the natural scientists turned away from biblical teaching, and biblical interpreters could no longer claim with intellectual integrity that the Bible provided a scientifically accurate picture of the cosmos.

In the second place, the humanists' boldness in investigating the text, composition, and authorship of the ancient documents, as initiated by Lorenzo Valla's devastating work on the so-called "Donation of Constantine" (1440), received a new impulse from the epistemological reflections of philosophers like Bacon (1561-1626) and Descartes (1596-1650). The use of the experimental method, together with the dawn of rationalism, soon influenced the minds of the biblical interpreters themselves.

In the third place, the very intransigency of Lutheran and Calvinistic scholasticism produced exegetical reactions like those of Arminius (1560-1609), Grotius (1583-1645), Calixtus (1586-1656), and others, who in various ways doubted that the dogmatic orthodoxy of their time was based upon a correct appreciation of the scriptural meaning. Likewise, the mysticism of Böhme (1575-1624), the pietism of Spener (1635-1705), together with the stress laid by Cocceius (1603-69) on the progressive character of revelation, these and other factors played their respective parts in unshackling the minds of Protestant theologians from the strait jacket of bibliolatry. For more than three centuries thereafter, scholars have wrestled with the numerous problems of text, composition, sources, date, and occasion of the biblical books. Such investigations may have appeared at times to be irrelevant; yet they were indispensable to the task of interpretation.

A. Textual and Philological Research.—The emergence of the new era was marked by first attempts at discovering the exact wording and meaning of the scriptural text. In 1538, Elijah ben Asher (Elias Levita) had shocked the scholarly world by proving conclusively that the vowel points and accents of the Hebrew Bible were of considerably later date than the fixation of the consonantal text, none of them earlier than the sixth century A.D.[1] Several Protestant Hebraists, such as William Fulke (1538-89), John Lightfoot (1602-75), and John Owen (1616-83), accepted the thesis of ben Asher as valid and yet, like him, they continued to believe in the verbal inspiration of both Masoretic text and pointing. Others, such as Johannes Piscator (1546-1625) and Johannes Buxtorf the Elder (1564-1629), vainly tried to defend the high antiquity of the pointing. With courage and integrity, however, Louis Cappel (1585-1658), against the strong opposition of his coreligionists, succeeded in proving not only that the chronological conclusions of ben Asher were correct, but also that the consonantal text itself

was far from reliable.[2] On the ground of his study of the *Qerê* and *Kethîbh,* of the Oriental and Occidental texts, of the Samaritan Pentateuch, of the Septuagint version, of the Old Testament quotations in the New Testament, and so forth, Cappel deserves to be called the first textual critic of the Old Testament; in addition, his work considerably influenced the literary critics of subsequent generations.

A similar type of investigation was taking place at the same time in the field of New Testament scholarship. The first editions of the Greek text by Erasmus (1516), Ximenes ("Complutensian," 1522), and Simon de Colines (1534) revealed the fact that the various manuscripts differed widely among themselves. Robert Estienne, in his third edition of the Greek text (1551), collated for the first time not only variants from the fourth (1527) and fifth (1535) editions of Erasmus' Greek New Testament, together with the marginal readings of the Complutensian, but also the witness of fifteen manuscripts. In addition, Theodore of Beza utilized in his numerous editions of the Greek text (1565, etc.) the witness of several ancient versions, and Lucas Brugensis (1580) noted the importance of the citations of the New Testament found in the patristic literature. The wide acceptance of the Textus Receptus (an expression which in England referred to the 1550 edition of Estienne and in continental Europe to the 1663 edition of the Elzevir brothers) somewhat retarded the development of New Testament textual criticism, but the appearance in England of the Codex Alexandrinus (1628) provided a new impulse, and the contributions of Brian Walton (1657), Etienne Courcelles (1658), John Fell (1675), and especially John Mill (1707), prepared the ground for scientific attempts to recapture as accurately as possible the wording of the original text.

The development of textual criticism, which raised in the fields of both Old and New Testaments problems of a specific and quite unrelated nature, profoundly impressed the minds of biblical interpreters, and not only destroyed belief in verbal inspiration but also opened the way to an empirical investigation into the authorship, date, composition, and meaning of each of the biblical books.

B. The Rationalistic Principle of Interpretation.—It is significant that an independent approach to the interpretation of the Bible was initiated not by biblical interpreters them-

---

[1] *Massôreth hammassôreth* (Venice, 1538).

[2] See especially *Arcanum Punctationis Revelatum* (Leiden, 1623); *Diatriba de Veris et Antiquis Hebraeorum Literis* (Amsterdam, 1645); *Critica Sacra* (Paris, 1650); *Epistola Apologetica* (Saumur, 1651).

selves, but by political philosophers like Hobbes and Spinoza.

In his *Leviathan* (1651), Thomas Hobbes implied that the Bible was not the Word of God but merely contained the record of some men who had been inspired by God. He wrote:

When God speaketh to man, it must be either immediately; or by mediation of another man, to whom he had formerly spoken by himself immediately. How God speaketh to a man immediately, may be understood by those well enough, to whom he hath so spoken; but how the same should be understood by another, is hard, if not impossible to know. For if a man pretend to me, that God hath spoken to him supernaturally, and immediately, and I make doubt of it, I cannot easily perceive what argument he can produce, to oblige me to beleeve it. . . . For to say that God hath spoken to him in the Holy Scripture, is not to say God hath spoken to him immediately, but by mediation of the Prophets, or of the Apostles, or of the Church, in such manner as he speaks to all other Christian men. . . . How then can he, to whom God hath never revealed his Wil immediately (saving by the way of natural reason) know when he is to obey, or not to obey his Word, delivered by him, that sayes he is a Prophet? [3]

In using such language, Hobbes was in fact denying the theological authority of Scripture as it was then understood, and he was also formulating a rationalistic and subjective principle of interpretation. He still maintained that the canon referred to "the Rules of Christian life" (ch. xxxiii), but he was interested more in the relationship which should exist between the Bible and "a Christian Commonwealth" than in the biblical basis of Christian faith. However, the exegesis of Hobbes was often penetrating, as revealed, for instance, by his analysis of faith and obedience in their relation to salvation (ch. xliii) or by his statement that the immortality of the soul is a category of grace and not of nature (ch. xliv). On literary and historical matters he displayed a certain degree of independence when he expressed skepticism over the Mosaic authorship of the Pentateuch in its present form (ch. xxxiii); but on the whole he was traditionally conservative. "I see not . . . any reason to doubt, but that the Old, and New Testament, as we have them now, are the true Registers of those things, which were done and said by the Prophets, and Apostles." [4]

Baruch Spinoza, in his famous *Tractatus Theologico-Politicus* (1670), attempted to liberate the field of philosophical endeavor from the claims of theologians and to examine critically the way in which Christian dogmatists used the Bible in order to bolster their doctrinal speculations.

I grant that they are never tired of professing their wonder at the profound mysteries of Holy Writ; still I cannot discover that they teach anything but speculations of Platonists and Aristotelians, to which (in order to save their credit for Christianity) they have made Holy Writ conform; . . . showing conclusively, that never even in sleep have they caught a glimpse of Scripture's Divine nature. . . . Their belief in the Bible is a formal assent rather than a living faith. [5]

Thereupon, Spinoza pleaded for a right understanding of Scripture, which cannot be obtained without a careful examination and close criticism of the text, and is identical with our natural understanding. He concluded, "I found nothing taught expressly by Scripture, which does not agree with our understanding. . . . I became thoroughly convinced that the Bible leaves reason absolutely free." [6] In order to grasp the thought of the Bible, the interpreter must look at any biblical book exactly as a naturalist observes the phenomena of nature, and when he has obtained every possible bit of information concerning its date, authorship, composition, occasion, and purpose of writing, he must then proceed to seek the sense of the words themselves without asking whether or not they express an acceptable truth. Man must listen to Scripture rather than appeal to it.

Although Spinoza's strictly rationalistic presuppositions constitute obvious limitations to his exegetical method and achievements, one must admit that a great many of his reflections are still valid in our time. Indeed, some of his remarks, such as those on the characteristics of Hebrew expression, and on the importance of understanding Hebrew manners of speech in order to interpret correctly not only the Old Testament but also the New Testament, are not yet fully appreciated.

Like Hobbes, Spinoza discussed freely the Mosaic authorship of the Pentateuch; he also examined objectively the literary incoherencies, historical contradictions, and especially the chronological difficulties of Genesis. But he was not merely a rationalistic exegete.

Those who look upon the Bible as a message sent down by God from Heaven to men, will doubtless cry out that I have committed the sin against the Holy Ghost because I have asserted that the Word of God is faulty, mutilated, tampered with, and inconsistent; that we possess it only in fragments, and that the original of the covenant which

[3] Reprinted from ed. of 1651 (Oxford: Clarendon Press, 1909), pp. 287-88.

[4] *Ibid.*, p. 298.

[5] *The Chief Works of Benedict de Spinoza*, tr. R. H. M. Elwes (London: George Bell & Sons, 1883), I, 7-8.

[6] *Ibid.*, I, 9.

God made with the Jews has been lost. However, I have no doubt that a little reflection will cause them to desist from their uproar: for not only reason but the expressed opinions of prophets and apostles openly proclaim that God's eternal Word and covenant, no less than true religion, is Divinely inscribed in human hearts, that is, in the human mind, and that this is the true original of God's covenant, stamped with His own seal, namely, the idea of Himself, as it were, with the image of His Godhood.[7]

One may detect a certain element of philosophical naïveté and of theological shallowness in such a statement, but one must recognize at the same time that there is in it no trace of prejudice or hostility.

C. The Beginnings of Literary Analysis.—Four years after the publication of *Leviathan* there appeared anonymously a pamphlet called *Praeadamitae* (1655), in which the bold thesis was presented that mankind had been created long before Adam, and that the Pentateuch was the work of more than one author. Isaac de la Peyrère, who later acknowledged authorship, was arrested by the Inquisition, and his book was publicly burned. But his ideas were not forgotten. In the subsequent generation the French Oratorian, Richard Simon, became the true father of biblical criticism. Theologically conservative, Simon did not attack the traditional views of revelation, but in a series of scholarly treatises [8] he applied to the whole of Scripture the hermeneutic principles of Spinoza, and he claimed the right to investigate the Bible as one looks at any other literary piece of the ancient world.

None can doubt but that the truths contained in the Holy Scripture are infallible and of Divine authority; since they proceed immediately from God, who in this has onely made use of the ministry of Men to be his Interpreters. So there is no person either Jew or Christian, who does not acknowledge that the Scripture being the pure word of God, is at the same time the first principle and foundation of Religion. But as Men have been the Depositories of these sacred Books, as well as all others, and their first Originals have been lost, it was in some sort impossible, but that there must needs happen some changes, as well by reason of the length of time, as the carelessness of Transcribers.[9]

Thus, the study of the additions or corrections which may have been made in the original

---

[7] *Ibid.*, I, 165.

[8] *Histoire critique du Vieux Testament* (Paris, 1678); *Histoire critique du texte du Nouveau Testament* (Rotterdam, 1689); *Histoire critique des principaux commentateurs du Nouveau Testament* (Rotterdam, 1689); and *Nouvelles observations sur le texte et les versions du Nouveau Testament* (Paris, 1695).

[9] *A Critical History of the Old Testament* (London: Jacob Tonson, 1682), pp. 1-2.

writings is legitimate, although Simon insisted that these "alterations . . . are of as great Authority as the rest of the Text," and that "Spinoza has shown his ignorance, or rather malice in crying down the Authority of the *Pentateuch,* by reason of some alterations . . . therein, without considering the quality of the Authors of these alterations." [10]

Simon's purpose was mainly to study the Bible with objectivity. "As for the Writers of our times, whether Catholic or Protestant, I have found none that are wholly free from prejudice." Although he was not strictly speaking a biblical interpreter, he considerably influenced subsequent exegetes, and many of his views have been vindicated. For instance, he concluded rightly that the Old Testament did not receive its present form until after the Exile, and he defended the Hellenistic idiom of the New Testament against the attacks of the Greek purists.

The name of Richard Bentley deserves mention, for his *Dissertations upon the Epistles of Phalaris* (1699) taught biblical scholars how to apply with the strictest method the principle of internal evidence—the principle according to which characteristics of a document are induced from the observation of its contradictions, chronological allusions, literary inconsistencies, and the like. That principle had already been employed, perhaps unwittingly, by Vitringa in his *Observationes sacrae* (1683), and received notoriety when Henning Witter separated the two stories of creation in Gen. 1–2 by recognizing the presence of repetitions and contradictions within the two chapters, and the use of different names for designating the deity (see article "The Growth of the Hexateuch," pp. 188-90).

The same observation on the alternation of the names YHWH and Elohim was one of the clues which led the physician Jean Astruc to distinguish in Genesis two main sources, two secondary sources, and the traces of about twelve other documents.[11] Although many of Astruc's hypotheses were later abandoned, he must receive credit for initiating the documentary theory of Pentateuchal composition.

In spite of his claims to originality, Johann Eichhorn [12] was dependent upon Astruc's discoveries,[13] and probably also upon the lectures of

---

[10] *Ibid.*, preface.

[11] *Conjectures sur les mémoires originaux dont il paroît que Moyse s'est servi pour composer le livre de la Genèse* (Bruxelles: Fricx, 1753). The book appeared anonymously.

[12] "Ueber Mosis Nachrichten von der Noachischen Fluth," *Repertorium für Biblische und Morgenländische Litteratur*, V (1779), 188.

[13] See discussion of Adolphe Lods, "Astruc et la critique biblique de son temps," *Revue d'Histoire et de Philosophie Religieuses*, IV (1924), 222 ff.

Johann Michaelis, his own teacher at Göttingen. Nevertheless, Eichhorn's work was epoch-making in the field of literary criticism.[14] At the same time, Johann Semler, who was not only a literary critic but also a perceptive and extremely versatile historian, recognized the historical nature of the development of the canon,[15] and anticipated the historical method of the nineteenth century by insisting on the importance of circumstantial environment for the correct exegesis of the biblical books.

D. The Deists' Explanations of Jesus.—Meanwhile, some of the English deists had attempted to explain the life and teaching of Jesus according to their views of "natural religion." Thomas Woolston (1670-1733) dismissed many of the miracle narratives as "most romantick tales." His purpose was clearly stated: "I will shew, that the Miracles of healing all manner of bodily Diseases, which Jesus was justly famed for, are none of the proper Miracles of the Messiah, nor are they so much as a good Proof of Jesus's divine Authority to found and introduce a Religion into the World."[16] His comments on the resurrection narratives anticipated the rationalistic interpretations of Hermann Samuel Reimarus, whose work was first published by Lessing as *Fragmente des wolfenbüttelschen Ungenannten* in 1774-78. Lessing himself in *Nathan der Weise* (1779) sought to be objective and made pertinent remarks on the oral tradition which preceded the written Gospels, but he did not penetrate very far in his attempts to understand "the religion of Christ" as opposed to "the Christian religion." Many of the exegetical treatises of this period reflect the age of the Enlightenment, when faith was deemed to be irreconcilable with reason. It would be wrong to assume however that all the interpreters of the eighteenth century were representatives of the deistic and rationalistic trends.

E. The Historical Approach to the New Testament.—Already in 1730 Johann Wettstein, who had been under the influence of Richard Bentley in Cambridge, published anonymously his *Prolegomena ad Novi Testamenti graeci editionem accuratissimam* (Amsterdam, 1730), and finally the Greek text of the New Testament (Amsterdam, 1751-52). In addition to his significant contribution to textual criticism, he expressed in his *Libelli ad Crisin atque Interpretationem Novi Testamenti* brilliant views on the importance of the historical environment for the correct understanding of Jesus and of the apostles. He held that scriptural interpretation should always respect the thinking

habits and the linguistic peculiarities of writers contemporary with the authors of the books under investigation, and that the exegesis of the Gospels is greatly helped by the study of the rabbinical literature.

Like Wettstein, J. A. Bengel was a historical interpreter. The influence of Pietism had made him reject the wooden exegesis of dogmatic orthodoxy, but he was not a rationalist. He attempted to penetrate to the human warmth and the inner life of the biblical writers themselves. His *Gnomon Novi Testamenti in quo ex nativa verborum vi simplicitas, profunditas, concinnitas, salubritas sensuum coelestium indicatur* (1742), which influenced John Wesley's *Notes on the New Testament* (1755), is a work of merit based on strict textual and philological research and animated by a profound devotion to Christian faith.

F. A New Appreciation of Hebrew Poetry.—While the seventeenth-century scholastics looked at the Bible only from a dogmatic point of view and most of the eighteenth-century exegetes were concerned chiefly with matters of text, literary composition, and rationalistic explanations of scripture, a few men began to realize that a great deal of the Old Testament was written in a poetic style, and that an exegetical method which might be adequate for the prose sections of the Bible should be considered inadequate for the interpretation of the poetic books.

As early as 1753, Robert Lowth, bishop of London, opened a new path in this hitherto neglected field with his *De Sacra Poesi Hebraeorum*.[17] Although Lowth may conceivably have been prejudiced in his approach by a profound knowledge of Greek and Latin poetry, he grasped amazingly well not only the technical aspects of Hebrew prosody, especially the use of parallelism, but also the spirit of the Hebrew poetic idiom. He appreciated "the sublime of [its] passion"; he recognized "the peculiar characters of the different prophets";[18] in brief, he led the way to the historical concreteness which characterized biblical exegesis subsequently.

It was Johann Gottfried von Herder, nevertheless, who made in this domain the most outstanding contribution,[19] for he showed that the Hebrew tongue was essentially a poetic medium of expression and that even the so-called prose books of the Bible had to be read as poetically written. His analysis of the traditions of Genesis or of the story of Jonah, in this respect, steers subtly away from traditional literalism without

[14] *Einleitung ins Alte Testament* (Leipzig, 1770-73).

[15] *Abhandlung von freier Untersuchung des Canon* (Halle, 1771-76).

[16] *A Discourse on the Miracles of Our Saviour* (6th ed.; London: Printed for the Author, 1729), p. 7.

[17] English tr., *Lectures on the Sacred Poetry of the Hebrews* (London, 1787).

[18] See his *Isaiah, A New Translation* (London, 1778).

[19] *Vom Geist der Ebräischen Poesie* (1782-83); tr. James Marsh, *The Spirit of Hebrew Poetry* (Burlington: E. Smith, 1833).

moving recklessly toward the rocks of rationalistic subjectivism. In spite of some exegetical limitations due to his illusions on human nature, Herder may still teach a great deal to biblical interpreters who have not begun to understand the deep interweaving which unites theological formulation and poetic diction. In addition, Herder's relationship to the romantic movement enabled him to appreciate the culture of the ancient Near East as it was known in his time and this made him a forerunner of the twentieth-century "school of comparative religion."

II. Literary and Historical Achievements (1800-1925)

Theological thinking generally, and biblical interpretation particularly, at least as far as the New Testament is concerned, were dominated for many decades of the nineteenth century by the influence of Friedrich Schleiermacher, who combined in a subjective synthesis rationalistic principles of exegesis with a Christocentric faith. As the deists had done, Schleiermacher rejected the uniqueness of the Bible, both as a monument of literature and as the authority for theological formulation. He noted that after the first bloom of Christianity had withered,

the sacred scriptures . . . were regarded as a finished codex of religion. . . . All who still feel the life of religion in themselves or perceive it in others, have ever protested against this unchristian proceeding. The sacred scriptures have, by their native power, become a bible, and forbid no other book to be or to become a bible. Anything written with like power they would willingly allow to be associated with themselves.[20]

Biblical authority is thus superseded by "that which flows immediately from the person of Jesus Christ." Unfortunately, Schleiermacher's view of Jesus, as shown by his posthumously published *Leben Jesu* (1864), was chiefly a rationalistic truncation of the gospel record, in the line of the interpretation of Reimarus, and in some respects quite similar to that of Paulus (1828). Schleiermacher's theology was largely responsible for initiating "the quest for the historical Jesus." At the same time, his neglect and almost total ignorance of Old Testament religion and revelation [21] may be one of the causes for which nineteenth-century interpreters

allowed the Old Testament to stand at the periphery of their preoccupations and left it to the literary critics.

A. The Search for the "Jesus of History."—Although an erudite exegete like Wilhelm de Wette had warned that any attempt to seek a chronological and psychological structure in the life of Jesus was bound to end in failure on account of the very nature of the available sources, the biographical approach flourished almost until the middle of the twentieth century. Perhaps the amazing success of David Strauss's *Leben Jesu* (1835) is chiefly responsible for the emergence of this trend. Strauss's representation of Jesus as a wise man is the result of rationalistic oversimplification, but many of his views are remarkably sound and have become widely accepted. He understood the motives which played a part in the growth of the gospel tradition and the principle of selection by which some details rather than others were kept alive and amplified in the memory of the early Christians. He clearly saw the differences which separate the Synoptics from the Fourth Gospel, and he rightly observed the eschatological aspect of the teaching of Jesus. In many ways Strauss anticipated the work of twentieth-century critics.[22] Moreover, the scandal produced by his *Life of Jesus* had one beneficial and lasting effect: it compelled scholars to evaluate anew the historical significance of the Gospels and their literary interrelationship. This type of study led to the formulation first of the Marcan hypothesis,[23] and later of the two-document hypothesis.[24] It also incited research on the origins of the whole New Testament literature.

Profoundly influenced by Hegel's philosophy of history, Ferdinand Christian Baur reinterpreted the birth of Christianity as the result of a conflict between a thesis (Jewish Christianity) and an antithesis (pagan Christianity) which resolved itself in a second-generation synthesis (Catholic Christianity).[25] This view of the de-

---

[20] *Reden über die Religion* (Berlin, 1799); tr. John Oman, *On Religion* (London: Kegan Paul, Trench, Trubner & Co., 1893), p. 249.

[21] See, e.g., the paucity of his remarks on the "biblical account of creation" (*Der Christliche Glaube* [1821-22], §40), or the prejudiced character of his views on the "Mosaic Law" as part of the "divine economy of salvation" (*ibid.*, §13).

[22] F. C. Conybeare, *History of New Testament Criticism* (New York: G. P. Putnam's Sons, 1910), pp. 141-42. See also the comments of Joachim Wach, *Das Verstehen. Grundzüge einer Geschichte der hermeneutischen Theorie im 19. Jahrhundert* (Tübingen: J. C. B. Mohr, 1929), II, 271-76.

[23] Initiated by Christian Hermann Weisse in *Die evangelische Geschichte* (Leipzig: Breitkopf & Härtel, 1838).

[24] Formulated chiefly by Heinrich Holtzmann in *Die synoptischen Evangelien, ihr Ursprung und geschichtlicher Character* (Leipzig: Wilhelm Engelmann, 1863), and Bernhard Weiss in *Das Leben Jesu* (Berlin: W. Hertz, 1882). See article "The Growth of the Gospels," Vol. VII, pp. 60-74.

[25] *Paulus der Apostel Jesu Christi* (Stuttgart: Becher & Müller, 1845); *Kritische Untersuchungen über die kanonischen Evangelien* (Tübingen: L. F. Fues, 1847).

velopment of the early church was not altogether wrong; unfortunately Baur used it as a criterion for determining the date and authenticity of the various New Testament writings, and this course led him to adopt a rather negative attitude toward the authenticity of the Pauline epistles, of which only Romans, I and II Corinthians, and Galatians he ascribed to the Apostle to the Gentiles. Consequently, Baur's reconstruction of Pauline theology was quite fragmentary.

In the meantime, the skeptical, imaginative, or merely "liberal" lives of Jesus appeared in an astoundingly large number throughout the second half of the nineteenth century.[26] The most popular among them was probably *La Vie de Jésus* (1863) by Ernest Renan—chiefly a sentimental romance. "There is a kind of insincerity in the book from beginning to end."[27] But some of Renan's later contributions[28] often reveal an interpretative perspicacity based on a profound knowledge of Jewish thought in the first century A.D.

The question of the Jesus of history seemed to float on stagnant waters until 1892, when Johannes Weiss analyzed *Die Predigt Jesu vom Reiche Gottes* and pointed out the eschatological, otherworldly, transcendental character of the kingdom of God as preached in the Gospels. The exclusively eschatological interpretation, however, was seriously qualified by Wilhelm Bousset,[29] who called attention to the diversity of forms in which Jewish apocalypticism presented itself to the popular mind in the New Testament times. Bousset maintained that hope in the proximate advent of a transcendental kingdom affects one's attitude to the present reality in such a thorough fashion that it becomes permissible to speak of a spiritualization of eschatology. Faith in God as a living and trustworthy father was combined in the teaching of Jesus with a genuine enjoyment of life upon this earth. This emphasis represents his main preoccupation more accurately than the admittedly eschatological bent of some of his sayings. In contrast with the Jewish apocalyptists and John the Baptist, Jesus fully lived in the present age, and he hailed the kingdom in his experience of filial communion with God and of brotherly fellowship with men.

Such an interpretation exercised a peculiar appeal to the average nineteenth-century Protestant. It found brilliant exponents and popularizers, none more so perhaps than Adolf von Harnack, who in his famous lectures entitled *Das Wesen des Christentums* (1899-1900) reduced Christianity to the religion of Jesus and that, in turn, to an individualistic harmony between God and man.

The kingdom of God comes by coming to the individual, by entering into his soul and laying hold of it. True, the kingdom of God is the rule of God; but it is the rule of the Holy God in the hearts of individuals; *it is God Himself in His power*. From this point of view everything that is dramatic in the external and historical sense has vanished; and gone, too, are all the external hopes for the future. . . . It is not a question of angels and devils, thrones and principalities, but of **God and the soul, the soul and its God**.[30]

In brief, Harnack was attempting to transform the gospel into a mere belief in "the fatherhood of God" and in "the infinite value of the human soul."

Reviewing critically the whole nineteenth-century attempt to recapture the "historical Jesus," Schweitzer sharpened the issue to an extreme degree. He maintained that the "liberal" search led to the "thoroughgoing skepticism" of Wilhelm Wrede.[31] Wrede denied that Jesus ever thought of himself as the Messiah. After his death, however, the disciples, who had become convinced of his messiahship, created the fiction of the "messianic secret" in order to explain how it had happened that he never declared himself publicly as "the one who was to come." Against this view Schweitzer reacted violently by pushing Weiss's emphasis to a "thoroughgoing eschatology."[32] He found it impossible "to suppose that Jesus could come to mean more to our time by entering into it as a man like ourselves . . . because such a Jesus never existed." He conceded that "historical knowledge can no doubt introduce greater clearness into an existing spiritual life," but he added that "it cannot call spiritual life into existence."[33] Schweitzer, nonetheless, paid high tribute to German research on the life of Jesus, and held it to be "one of the most significant events in the whole mental and spiritual life of humanity."[34] His implicit conclusion called for

---

[26] See Albert Schweitzer, *The Quest of the Historical Jesus*, tr. W. Montgomery (New York: The Macmillan Co., 1950).

[27] *Ibid.*, p. 191.

[28] See particularly *Les Apôtres* (1866), *Saint-Paul* (1869), *L'Antéchrist* (1873), and *Les Evangiles et la seconde génération chrétienne* (1877).

[29] *Jesu Predigt in ihrem Gegensatz zum Judentum* (Göttingen: Vandenhoeck & Ruprecht, 1892).

[30] *What Is Christianity?* tr. Thomas Bailey Saunders (2nd ed.; New York: G. P. Putnam's Sons, 1901), pp. 60-61.

[31] *Das Messiasgeheimnis in den Evangelien* (Göttingen: Vandenhoeck & Ruprecht, 1901).

[32] Schweitzer, *Das Messianitäts-und Leidensgeheimnis* (Tübingen: J. C. B. Mohr, 1901).

[33] *Quest of the Historical Jesus*, p. 399.

[34] *Ibid.*

a return to New Testament Christianity as a whole.

We are experiencing what Paul experienced. In the very moment when we were coming nearer to the historical Jesus than men had ever come before, and were already stretching out our hands to draw Him into our own time, we have been obliged to give up the attempt and acknowledge our failure in that paradoxical saying: "If we have known Christ after the flesh yet henceforth know we Him no more." And further we must be prepared to find that the historical knowledge of the personality and life of Jesus will not be a help, but perhaps even an offence to religion.[35]

The religion of Jesus must make room once more for the *religio de Christo*.

B. The Graf-Wellhausen School of Old Testament Criticism.—The first documentary theory of the Hexateuch's composition as it was popularized by Eichhorn's *Einleitung* (1780-83) did not hold the field of scholarship without widespread challenge and much opposition. Rival hypotheses of various kinds were proposed, such as the conjecture of the fragments,[36] for example, and especially that of the complements and interpolations which was defended by Wilhelm de Wette.[37] The documentary theory, however, slowly regained ground under the various modifications introduced by Hermann Hupfeld,[38] who mistakenly continued to maintain that the First Elohist (later known as the Priestly Code) was the earliest of the documents. The postexilic dating of the Priestly Code was first recognized by Édouard Reuss in 1833, but was finally established by Karl Graf,[39] and endorsed by Abraham Kuenen and August Kayser.[40] The preparatory work was thus accomplished when Julius Wellhausen came on the scene and gave the classical exposition of the Hexateuch's literary origin and development.[41]

As a result of Wellhausen's lucid and in many ways brilliant demonstration[42] which, like

Baur's work on the early church, reveals the influence of Hegelian philosophy, a radically new conception of Israel's history dawned on the mind of the exegetes. While the Yahwist and Elohist documents were ascribed to a relatively early date, the Law as a whole came to be considered no longer as "the starting point for the history of ancient Israel," but rather as a priestly program conceived for the restoration of postexilic Judaism. It was felt that nothing could be known with certainty about the history and religion of Israel before the time of David. Ignoring the theological structure which undergirds the Yahwist's conception of history, critics assumed that Israel's faith in Yahweh began and developed according to normal evolutionary processes, such as those which are observable among all primitive societies. Consequently, traces of animism, totemism, polydaemonism, and polytheism were culled from the descriptions of rites and beliefs associated by the biblical writers with the Hebrew fathers, and this composite picture of "popular religion" was presented as corresponding adequately to the normative Yahwism of the early period. The "genius" of the eighth- and seventh-century prophets raised the practical monolatry of Yahweh to the level of a consciously formulated henotheism, which then was purified and made triumphant in the form of ethical monotheism under the impact of the Babylonian exile. The Psalter and the wisdom literature were ascribed en bloc to postexilic Judaism, at a time when religious individualism had at last conquered the consciousness of the Second Temple worshipers and teachers. Indeed, many of the psalms were thought to have been inspired by the Maccabean rebellion.

Such a reconstruction of the development of Old Testament religion, partial and unsatisfactory as it may have been at many points, produced a remarkable result: it created an unprecedented interest in the personalities of the prophets. For the first time the figures of Amos, Hosea, Isaiah, and their successors emerged concretely and powerfully against the vivid background of economic, political, psychological, and sociological forces. While the thunders and the flames of Sinai were lost in the dimness of the past, the prophets came into their own as living men of history.[43]

To ignore or to underestimate the significance of the literary and historical achievements

---

[35] *Ibid.*, p. 401.

[36] See article "The Growth of the Hexateuch," pp. 188-89; also, Joseph Coppens, *The Old Testament and the Critics*, tr. Edward A. Ryan and Edward W. Tribbe (Paterson, N. J.: St. Anthony Guild Press, 1942), pp. 11 ff.

[37] De Wette remained famous for having applied the formula of "pious fraud" to the seventh-century composition and discovery of the Deuteronomic Code.

[38] *Die Quellen der Genesis und die Art ihrer Zusammensetzung* (Berlin: Wiegandt & Grieben, 1853).

[39] *Die geschichtlichen Bücher des Alten Testaments* (Leipzig: T. O. Weigel, 1866).

[40] *Das vorexilische Buch der Urgeschichte Israels und seine Erweiterungen* (Strassburg: C. F. Schmidt, 1874).

[41] *Die Composition des Hexateuchs* (Berlin: G. Reimer, 1885; first published in the form of articles in 1876-77).

[42] See especially *Israelitische und Jüdische Geschichte* (3rd ed.; Gütersloh: G. Reimer, 1897), Eng. tr., *Sketch of the History of Israel and Judah* (London: Black,

1891); and *Prolegomena zur Geschichte Israels* (3rd ed.; Berlin: Georg Reimer, 1886), tr. J. Sutherland Black and Alan Menzies, *Prolegomena to the History of Israel* (Edinburgh: A. & C. Black, 1885). See also article "The Growth of the Hexateuch," pp. 189-90.

[43] See the works of C. H. Cornill, W. Robertson Smith, George Adam Smith, Bernhard Duhm, *et al.*

of the Graf-Wellhausen school would constitute a grievous error. In spite of many modifications of detail, the documentary hypothesis still stands in its general lines after years of minute analysis and inquiry. However, the conception of the origin and development of Israel's religion, and especially of the nature of the Yahwistic faith, which was proposed by Wellhausen and his disciples, soon suffered profound revisions.

C. New Sources of Knowledge.—Both in the field of the Old Testament and in that of the New Testament the acquisition of a vast amount of archaeological data produced a considerable enlargement of the picture of the ancient world, against which stood out in a new light the life of Israel and of the early church. Modern archaeology of the ancient Near East began when Napoleon Bonaparte brought a hundred artists and scholars to the sleeping ruins of the Nile Valley in 1798. The deciphering of hieroglyphics by Champollion in 1822, and of the cuneiform script by Rawlinson in 1846, inaugurated the manifold and complex work of interpreting thousands of texts which were soon being unearthed from the sands of Egypt and Mesopotamia. This development led to a new conception of the classical Orient. The Bible could no longer be considered as the earliest book of mankind's culture. Its religion could not any more be viewed in its "splendid isolation."

Meanwhile, in 1838 and 1852, Edward Robinson surveyed systematically the western lands of Asia Anterior and laid the foundations of biblical geography.[44] Scientific research in biblical Hebrew, which had been inaugurated by Wilhelm Gesenius,[45] was advancing steadily through the study of comparative Semitic philology which the archaeological discoveries of Mesopotamian and other documents made possible on a scale hitherto unknown.[46] Likewise, New Testament exegetes became aware of the Aramaic background of the language used in the Gospels and Acts, especially through the investigations of Emil Kautzsch and Gustaf Dalman.[47] From Adolf Deissmann[48] and others

they also learned to analyze the Greek of the New Testament in the light of a better appreciation of the dialects and especially of the Hellenistic tongue as it came to light through the discovery of papyri and ostraca.[49] Perhaps Deissmann's insistence on the popular character of the koine, necessary as this was, suffered from a certain degree of exaggeration and did not do full justice to the scholarly modes of expression common in the Jewish literature with which at least some of the New Testament writers were apparently acquainted.

The importance of the rabbinical teaching and preaching for the exegesis of the Gospels, which had been long ago sensed by John Lightfoot,[50] received in due course a wide and scrutinizing attention that led to the outstanding work of Hermann L. Strack and Paul Billerbeck.[51]

Finally, efforts to restore the primitive text of the Bible proceeded on a broad scope and at an accelerated pace. Tischendorf's discovery in 1844 of the Codex Sinaiticus and the labors of many other textual critics[52] led to the establishment of scientifically edited texts of the Hebrew Bible, the Septuagint, and the Greek New Testament.

Thus, archaeological excavations, with their cultural and particularly their epigraphic yields, as well as research in comparative philology and textual criticism, brought interpreters more closely than ever to the literal meaning of the biblical writings. The addition of these new sources of knowledge was largely responsible for the inception of new methods of interpretative investigation.

D. Modern Methods of Interpretation.—In contrast to mere literary critics who were interested almost exclusively in the composition of the scriptural documents and the analysis of their respective sources and too little concerned with the meaning of their contents, several scholars felt the need of adapting or refining the old, and of devising new methods of approach to the Scriptures. They turned to the history of the oral tradition, the comparative study of religion or history of religion, and the analysis of form or form criticism. The cautious application of these methods produced a harvest of fruitful results which, in the mid-century, were still being formulated and evaluated.

In the field of Old Testament study Hermann

[44] *Biblical Researches in Palestine, Mount Sinai and Arabia Petraea* (New York: J. Leavitt, 1841, etc.).

[45] *Hebräisches . . . Handwörterbuch* (1812, etc.); *Hebräische Grammatik* (1813, etc.); *Thesaurus Philologicus Criticus Linguae Hebraeae et Chaldaeae Veteris Testamenti* (1829-53).

[46] See article "The Language of the Old Testament," pp. 220-32.

[47] *Grammatik des jüdisch-palästinischen Aramäisch* (Leipzig: J. C. Hinrichs, 1894); *Die Worte Jesu* (Leipzig: J. C. Hinrichs, 1898).

[48] *Bibelstudien* (Marburg: N. G. Elwert, 1893); and especially *Licht vom Osten* (Tübingen: J. C. B. Mohr, 1908), tr. Lionel R. M. Strachan, *Light from the Ancient East* (London: Hodder & Stoughton, 1910).

[49] See article "The Language of the New Testament," Vol. VII, pp. 43-59.

[50] *Horae Hebraicae et Talmudicae* (Cambridge and London, 1658-78).

[51] *Kommentar zum Neuen Testament aus Talmud und Midrasch* (Munich: C. H. Beck, 1922-28).

[52] See articles "The Text and Ancient Versions of the Old Testament," pp. 46-62; "The Text and Ancient Versions of the New Testament," pp. 72-83.

Gunkel,[53] followed by Hugo Gressmann,[54] Alfred Jeremias [55] and others, while paying high tribute to the accomplishments of literary criticism, realized that Wellhausen and his school were too passively subservient to the literary documents alone in their reconstruction of religious history. Gunkel rightly maintained that rites, customs, and even beliefs which are recorded in relatively late sources may actually belong to an extremely early age. He therefore endeavored to reach the contents and—whenever possible—the history of the oral tradition which lay behind the written documents themselves. In addition, just as Wellhausen had studied the religion of the pre-Islamic Arabs,[56] Gunkel and his disciples analyzed the Egyptian, Babylonian, and Persian religions in an attempt to discover the foreign influences which may have played upon the development of Old Testament religion. By so doing they brought sharply into focus the way in which Israel, as part of the ancient world, was constantly in danger of being corrupted by surrounding paganism and yet asserted against it the distinctive power of her own faith.

Finally, Gunkel paid particular attention to the literary forms of the Old Testament writings, and by initiating the method of form criticism made his most brilliant contribution. He showed conclusively that Hebrew literature followed precise aesthetic patterns or structures characterizing specific literary categories or genres (*Gattungen*), which did not emerge *in vacuo* but were born over the centuries from the requirements of a "life situation" (*Sitz im Leben*). Naturally, the method of form criticism or form analysis is not separate in its application from the method of "history of religion." Gunkel's study of the Psalter, for instance, revealed that an objective classification of the psalms into hymns, laments, royal songs, and so forth, may be obtained from the investigation of the poetic structure and also from a comparison with the cultic poems of Egypt and Mesopotamia. The combined application of the two methods revitalized the exegesis of the psalms by showing that they answered precise needs in concrete environments.

Gunkel himself made it clear that his interest in the history of the ancient religions and in the form criticism of the Old Testament books was dependent upon his belief in the Christian significance of the Bible as a whole.

Before our eyes, uplifting us and bearing us onward, stood a wondrous picture—the Religion of the Bible in all its glory and dignity. We had come to see that such a phenomenon can be understood only when it is understood in its history, in its growth and becoming. It seemed to us to be a sublime task to understand this religion in its depth and breadth, to trace it through its winding course, to be present at the birth of its deepest thoughts.[57]

The expression "to be present at" reveals a certain historical warmth, but also detachment, for it has nothing to do with "being personally involved in." Although Gunkel acknowledged that if "the Bible [ceased] to be the foundation of the Christian Church, Bible scholarship would also receive a fatal blow," [58] he was not concerned directly with the theological relevance of the Hebrew Scripture for Christians.

Methods of comparative religion and of form criticism were soon applied also to the New Testament writings. The pioneering works of Franz Cumont [59] and James Frazer [60] on the transformations wrought in Greco-Roman culture by the seemingly irresistible attraction of the Oriental religions, together with the results of Richard Reitzenstein's research on the Hermetic literature,[61] led to a re-evaluation of the way in which the Christian gospel, especially in its Pauline form, was preached to the Mediterranean world. Pursuing the superficial appearances of the parallels, such as in Paul's use of technical terms common in the mystery cults or in his emphasis on the rites of baptism and of a sacramental meal, some critics viewed the phenomenon of early Christianity as nothing more than another mystery religion. Wrote Alfred Loisy:

The scheme of Messianic salvation, of which the Galilean prophet thought himself the destined head, became a myth of universal salvation. . . . [Jesus] was a saviour-god . . . : like Adonis, Osiris, and Attis he had died a violent death, and like them

[53] See especially *Schöpfung und Chaos in Urzeit und Endzeit* (Göttingen: Vandenhoeck & Ruprecht, 1895, etc.); *Genesis übersetzt und erklärt* (Göttingen: Vandenhoeck & Ruprecht, 1901, etc.); *Einleitung in die Psalmen*, ed. J. Begrich (Göttingen: Vandenhoeck & Ruprecht, 1933).

[54] *Altorientalische Texte und Bilder zum Alten Testamente* (Tübingen: J. C. B. Mohr, 1909, etc.); *Der Ursprung der israelitisch-jüdischen Eschatologie* (Göttingen: Vandenhoeck & Ruprecht, 1905); *Der Messias* (Göttingen: Vandenhoeck & Ruprecht, 1929).

[55] *Das Alte Testament im Lichte des alten Orients* (Leipzig: J. C. Hinrichs, 1904, etc.), tr. C. L. Beaumont, *The Old Testament in the Light of the Ancient East* (London: Williams & Norgate, 1911).

[56] See especially *Reste Arabischen Heidentums* (Berlin: Georg Reimer, 1887, etc.).

[57] "The 'Historical Movement' in the Study of Religion," *The Expository Times*, XXXVIII (1926-27), 533.

[58] *Ibid.*, p. 534.

[59] *Les religions orientales dans le paganisme romain* (Paris: Ernest Leroux, 1907).

[60] *The Golden Bough*, Part III, *The Dying God*, Part IV, *Adonis Attis Osiris* (London: Macmillan & Co., 1911, 1914).

[61] *Die hellenistischen Mysterienreligionen* (Leipzig: B. G. Teubner, 1910).

he had returned to life; like them, he had prefigured in his lot that of the human beings who should take part in his worship, and commemorate his mystic enterprise; like them, he had predetermined, prepared, and assured the salvation of those who became partners in his passion.[62]

Yet, many adherents of the *religionsgeschichtliche Schule* came to adopt a more balanced conception of the part played by Hellenistic syncretism in the New Testament interpretation of the death and resurrection of Christ, especially after Deissmann[63] re-emphasized cautiously the influence exercised over Pauline thought by the specifically Jewish element.

The need to study the forms of the oral tradition that lay behind the written Gospels had already been sensed by Eichhorn (1794), Krummacher (1805), and especially Gieseler (1818). It was, however, primarily on account of Gunkel's brilliant application of the form critical method to the study of the Genesis sagas (1901) that New Testament scholars turned their attention to the history of the gospel tradition.[64] Martin Dibelius, who had prepared the way in 1911 by his studies on John the Baptist,[65] applied the new method on an inclusive scale,[66] simultaneously with Karl Ludwig Schmidt,[67] and the work of these two scholars was soon followed by the contribution of Rudolf Bultmann.[68] Accepting the artificial character of the Marcan framework,[69] as well as the fragmentary, independent, and self-contained nature of the stories about Jesus which circulated among the early Christians, form critics attempted to classify these stories according to their respective "forms" as sayings, paradigms, wonder tales, legends, and myths. They showed how these forms arose and were preserved to satisfy the homiletical and practical needs of the early communities (cf. Gunkel's *Sitz im Leben*). Furthermore, they claimed that the original tradition could be recovered through the study of the laws by which the forms were transmitted. Unfortunately the classifications proposed by the various leaders of the school are far from identical, and they are based not exclusively on considerations of form, but on the analysis of the contents as well. The claims to objectivity made by the exponents of form criticism are therefore somewhat exaggerated. In addition, form critics have made a number of gratuitous assumptions concerning the needs and social requirements of the various Christian groups. Finally, they have shown a tendency to neglect almost completely the results of literary criticism itself. In spite of these and other limitations,[70] the form critics have rendered a great service to exegesis by insisting rightly on the theological and especially kerygmatic, rather than the primarily historical, purpose of the gospel writers.

It was precisely at this same time that the theology of Karl Barth began to sweep Europe.[71] While exegetes were slowly realizing that both the Old Testament and the New Testament were the products of faith, systematic theologians were suddenly returning to the Bible in an attempt to recover its authority by listening through its pages to the perennial "word of God." The confluence of these two originally independent trends characterizes the contemporary period of interpretation.

III. Biblical Exegesis at the Mid-Century (1925-1950)

Technical research in archaeology, in philology, in textual, literary, and form criticism produced in these years such an enormous amount of material[72] that most biblical interpreters became extraordinarily specialized. Many of the most significant contributions dealt with fragmentary problems of translation and interpretation of isolated passages. It is thus difficult and somewhat reckless to characterize the prevailing trends. Still, it is possible to observe a threefold tendency: (a) for some books of the Bible, at least, a return to relatively conservative conclusions on matters of composition and date; (b) an increased readiness to accept the historical reliability of the documents; and (c) a re-

[62] "The Christian Mystery," *The Hibbert Journal*, X (1911), 51. See also Wilhelm Bousset, *Kyrios Christos* (Göttingen: Vandenhoeck & Ruprecht, 1913, etc.).

[63] *Paulus* (Tübingen: J. C. B. Mohr, 1911, etc.), tr. Lionel R. M. Strachan, *Paul* (London: Hodder & Stoughton, 1912).

[64] See Maurice Goguel, "Une nouvelle école de critique évangélique," *Revue de l'Histoire des Religions*, XCIV (1926), 114-60.

[65] *Die urchristliche Überlieferung über Johannes dem Taüfer* (Göttingen: Vandenhoeck & Ruprecht, 1911).

[66] *Die Formgeschichte des Evangeliums* (Tübingen: J. C. B. Mohr, 1919, etc.), tr. Bertram Lee Woolf, *From Tradition to Gospel* (New York: Charles Scribner's Sons, 1935).

[67] *Die Rahmen der Geschichte Jesu* (Berlin: Trowitzsch & Sohn, 1919).

[68] *Die Erforschung der synoptischen Evangelien* (Göttingen: A. Töpelmann, 1925).

[69] A fact which had long been recognized by such scholars as Johannes Weiss (*Das älteste Evangelium* [Göttingen: Vandenhoeck & Ruprecht, 1901]) and Maurice Goguel (*L'Évangile de Marc* [Paris: Ernest Leroux, 1909]).

[70] See Vincent Taylor's critique of the form critical method in *The Formation of the Gospel Tradition* (London: Macmillan & Co., 1933).

[71] Barth's *Der Römerbrief* (München: C. Kaiser, 1923), with its brilliant insights, is more an illustration of theological eisegesis than a monument of exegesis.

[72] See among others Harold R. Willoughby, ed., *The Study of the Bible Today and Tomorrow* (Chicago: University of Chicago Press, 1947).

born awareness of the primarily theological intentions of the biblical writers.

A. Trends in Old Testament Study.—The documentary hypothesis of Hexateuchal composition triumphantly survived the attacks of the previous four decades.[73] With minor differences as regards the contents, characteristics, and dates of the various strata,[74] the majority of scholars accepted on the whole the literary results of the Graf-Wellhausen analysis.[75] Most of the exegetes were pursuing the study of the oral traditions along the lines indicated by Gunkel, but they were also aware of the theological purpose which animated the editors and redactors of these traditions. Gerhard von Rad,[76] and to a limited extent Martin Noth,[77] have shown that the Yahwist, although he was the earliest writer of the Hexateuch (the date of J, incidentally, for various reasons was being pushed back from 850-750 to *ca.* 950 B.C. or even earlier), conceived his work as the history of the "grand design of salvation," and he tried to substantiate the old covenantal creeds—represented, for instance, by the archaic liturgy of Deut. 26:5-9—by collecting a multitude of originally independent traditions and by organizing them into a structure of *Heilsgeschichte*. He preached on the one hand the power of Yahweh, his saving grace and ethical requirements, and on the other hand, the sinful nature of man and the mission of Israel. The Yahwist's categories of thinking were therefore strictly theological, for he dealt first and last with God's purpose in mankind's history. In this respect exegesis in the mid-century divorced itself from the Wellhausenian reconstruction of Israel's religion, and while it recognized of course the existence of a development throughout the centuries of biblical life, it refused a priori to associate early expressions of belief with a so-called "primitive" theology which had to be superseded by the so-called "insights" of the great prophets.[78] The tendency was to emphasize, not from dogmatic presuppositions, but from the understanding of the texts themselves in the light of the archaeological evidence,[79] the uniqueness of Yahwism as compared to the other religions of the ancient Near East, and the unity of the Old Testament revelation of God in spite of its diversity.

Likewise, if the antiquity of the oral traditions concerning the pre-Mosaic age, for instance, became apparent from an analysis of the forms in which they have been preserved, the question of their historical validity was reopened on a new basis. The exact chronology of the patriarchal age was still a matter of debate, but extensive research [80] tended to show that the patriarchal traditions are not the product of late imagination, for they correspond remarkably well to the *Sitz im Leben* which is revealed by extrabiblical documentation. Such views were by no means acceptable to all, but the very fact that they were presented seriously by responsible critics who were not prone to use archaeology for the sake of defending fundamentalism or any kind of dogmatic orthodoxy constituted a strong reinforcement of the trend toward historical conservatism. Moreover, it became increasingly clear that the covenantal requirements of early Yahwism were primarily of a theological and ethical nature in contradistinction to the ritual characteristics of the agrarian syncretism which corrupted the popular religion of Israel after the conquest.

The work of the prophets was thus brought into a new light. They inherited their "ethical monotheism" from their predecessors, but they deepened its implications under the stress of historical crisis. It seems that Amos and his successors built upon the theology of Yahweh's presence as it was made concrete within the people, and of Yahweh's lordship over nature and history.[81] The basic agreement between

[73] Especially those of Klostermann (1908-12), Eerdmans (1908-12), Wiener (1910-12), Naville (1921), Sanda (1924), D. B. Macdonald (1933), Cassuto (1934), and Olmstead (1943). The existence of the Elohist, which Volz (1933) and Rudolph (1938) had tried to discard, appears to be vindicated.

[74] Proposed respectively by Eissfeldt (1922), Morgenstern (1927), and Pfeiffer (1930-41).

[75] See Aage Bentzen, *Introduction to the Old Testament* (Copenhagen, G. E. C. Gad, 1948); Artur Weiser, *Einleitung in das Alte Testament* (Göttingen: W. Kohlhammer, 1949); Adolphe Lods, *Histoire de la littérature hébraïque et juive* (Paris: Payot, 1950); also Cuthbert A. Simpson, *The Early Traditions of Israel* (New York: The Macmillan Co., 1948).

[76] *Das formgeschichtliche Problem des Hexateuch* (Stuttgart: W. Kohlhammer, 1938); *Deuteronomium-Studien* (Göttingen: Vandenhoeck & Ruprecht, 1947); *Das erste Buch Mose* (Göttingen: Vandenhoeck & Ruprecht, 1949).

[77] *Überlieferungsgeschichte des Pentateuch* (Stuttgart: W. Kohlhammer, 1948).

[78] "Only the most extreme criticism can see any appreciable difference between the God of Moses in JE and the God of Jeremiah" (W. F. Albright, "The Ancient Near East and the Religion of Israel," *Journal of Biblical Literature*, LIX [1940], 111).

[79] See G. Ernest Wright, "The Present State of Biblical Archeology," in Harold R. Willoughby, ed., *Study of Bible Today and Tomorrow*, pp. 92 ff.

[80] See W. F. Albright, *From the Stone Age to Christianity* (2nd ed.; Baltimore: Johns Hopkins Press, 1946); *The Archaeology of Palestine* (Harmondsworth: Pelican Books, 1949); R. de Vaux, "Les patriarches hébreux et les découvertes modernes," *Revue Biblique*, LIII (1946), 321-48, LV (1948), 321-47, LVI (1949), 5-36; H. H. Rowley, *From Joseph to Joshua* (London: Oxford University Press, 1950).

[81] See G. Henton Davies, "The Yahwistic Tradition in the Eighth-Century Prophets," and N. W. Porteous, "The Basis of the Ethical Teaching of the Prophets," in H. H. Rowley, ed., *Studies in Old Testament Prophecy* (Edinburgh: T. & T. Clark, 1950), pp. 37 ff., 143 ff.

Yahwism and prophetism was stressed on various levels, one of which is the *Glaubensideologie*, which is found some fifty-two times before Amos; another, the covenantal emphasis on obedience; and a third, the *da'ath 'elōhîm*, or knowledge of God, which became the keystone of Hosea's religion. The prophets were able to perceive their special "word" because they were steeped in the Yahwistic tradition.

Intensive research on the prophetic books, especially that pursued by Scandinavian scholars, was less intent than in the previous generation upon trying to isolate the *ipsissima verba* of the prophetic figures and more eager to interpret correctly the meaning of the books in their totality. All these studies revealed in various degrees the three characteristics of the period: they showed a new respect for the validity of the Masoretic text; [82] they assumed a somewhat reactionary stand on the integrity of composition; [83] and they laid the exegetical emphasis on the theological meaning of the prophetic message. The work of Christopher R. North on the suffering servant [84] deserves special notice, for a strong case was made therein for a messianic-soteriological interpretation of the servant—although not in the Davidic sense of Isa. 9 and 11—along lines which lead directly to the New Testament application. North went so far as to state that Deutero-Isaiah was a "myth" prophet in the predictive sense, who pictured the servant not at all as Israel (which had failed), but as an individual figure who would come on this earth and whose chastisement would bring peace to the Gentiles. The theological interest of these exegetes is equally visible in monographs on the Hagiographa, particularly Job and the Psalms.

B. New Testament Criticism in Transition.— Spurred by the discovery of new fragments of manuscripts, particularly those of the Chester Beatty papyri, a considerable amount of work was accomplished in the textual criticism of the New Testament. The extremely complex relationship of the manuscript families was studied on an objective basis, and a scientific text superseding the editions of Tischendorf, of Westcott and Hort, and of Nestle, was in process of establishment. Linguistic studies were intensely carried forward, particular emphasis being laid on the theological keywords, as in Gerhard Kittel's *Theologisches Wörterbuch zum Neuen*

Testament, a monument of invaluable information under the editorship of Gerhard Friedrich.

Synoptical exegesis appeared at the same time to avoid the excesses of literary criticism as well as the extremes of form criticism, while taking full advantage of the contributions which both methods may offer.[85] Such a fact as that the testimony of eyewitnesses lies at the origin of the oral tradition was increasingly recognized. The ecclesiastical nature and the theological purpose of the gospel literature were taken into serious consideration at every point of the exegetical analysis. Considerable attention was given to the Fourth Gospel,[86] the composition of which was now often ascribed to a first-century date. While the problem of the validity of the sources used by the Johannine evangelist remains extremely complex, the trend here also was in the direction of a qualified conservatism [87] and gave more confidence in the historical accuracy of the narrative.

Intensive studies were also pursued on the book of Acts and the early church,[88] and particular attention was given to the early sermons and to the historical value of the narratives concerning Paul. Although lives of Jesus were written between the two world wars,[89] scholars were slowly coming to recognize the impossibility of the merely biographical inquiry. The familiar and worn-out antitheses of the nineteenth and early twentieth centuries, like those of Jesus or Paul, Synoptics or Fourth Gospel, eschatology or earthly kingdom, and so forth, were overshadowed by more balanced views which were not reached from an artificially synthetic approach but were derived from conscientious sifting and evaluation of previous exegetical contributions.[90]

---

[85] See, e.g., F. C. Grant, *The Earliest Gospel* (New York and Nashville: Abingdon-Cokesbury Press, 1943).

[86] See among others R. H. Strachan, *The Fourth Gospel* (London: Student Christian Movement Press, 1917); W. Bauer, *Das Johannesevangelium* (Tübingen: J. C. B. Mohr, 1925); W. F. Howard, *The Fourth Gospel in Recent Criticism and Interpretation* (London: Epworth Press, 1931); Philip Menoud, *L'Évangile de Jean d'après les recherches récentes* (Paris: Neuchatel, 1943); E. C. Hoskyns and F. N. Davey, *The Fourth Gospel* (London: Faber & Faber, 1948); Rudolf Bultmann, *Das Evangelium des Johannes* (11th ed.; Göttingen: Vandenhoeck & Ruprecht, 1950).

[87] A fact which had already been recognized by Maurice Goguel in his *Vie de Jésus*; see *The Life of Jesus*, tr. Olive Wyon (New York: The Macmillan Co., 1933), pp. 156-57 and, in the revised French edition, *Jésus* (Paris: Payot, 1950), pp. 107-10.

[88] *The Beginnings of Christianity*, ed. F. J. Foakes Jackson and Kirsopp Lake (London: Macmillan & Co., 1920-33). See also C. H. Dodd, *The Apostolic Preaching and Its Developments* (London: Hodder & Stoughton, 1936).

[89] See Chester C. McCown, *The Search for the Real Jesus* (New York: Charles Scribner's Sons, 1940).

[90] See, e.g., W. G. Kümmel, *Verheissung und Erfüllung, Untersuchungen zur eschatologischer Verkündigung Jesu*

---

[82] The legitimacy of this attitude has received unexpected support from the discovery of the 'Ain Feshka MS of Isaiah.

[83] E.g., Artur Weiser accepted the authenticity of Mic. 5-6; 7:1-7 in addition to 1-3. See *Das Buch der zwölf Kleinen Propheten* (Göttingen: Vandenhoeck & Ruprecht, 1949), I, *ad loc.*

[84] *The Suffering Servant in Deutero-Isaiah* (London: Oxford University Press, 1948).

Several dangers arose, however, when radical form critics, such as Bultmann,[91] were at times inclined to disregard the importance of historical research altogether, simply because the historical event of God's revelation in Jesus Christ is known and transmitted only through the kerygmatic word. On much safer grounds appeared to be such an interpreter as Oscar Cullmann,[92] who squarely placed the Christian event in the whole biblical *Heilsgeschichte*, insisted upon the "temporally unique character of the central event," and at the same time pointed out the peril of the ever-recurrent heresy of Docetism. It is on account of this awareness that, in the words of C. H. Dodd,

we turn back to the unfinished "quest of the historical Jesus"; for we cannot escape it, in spite of the flourishes against *"Historismus"* with which our period opened. As the great tradition reveals itself afresh in its wholeness and essential unity, the yawning gap which earlier criticism left between the Jesus of History and the emergent Church disappears, and we begin to see that to make a separation between the historical and the theological understanding of the Gospel is to put asunder what God hath joined.[93]

C. Toward the Formulation of a Biblical Theology.

—Exegetes at the mid-century were thus aware of their theological responsibility. Old Testament scholars no longer apologized for the fact that the Hebrew Scripture is part of the Christian canon; they were not on the whole tempted to divorce a structural exposition of the various Hebrew formulations of faith from the historical account of the Hebrew religion in its development and diversity. Until 1950, no treatise had superseded Walther Eichrodt's inclusive explication of the way in which the Hebrew revelation of God, man, sin, and salvation is focused on the covenant;[94] however, several monographs on limited subjects[95] show that interpreters were cautiously beginning to draw lines across the centuries in an effort to grasp the homogeneity of Israel's religious growth. The task could not be accomplished without further discussion on methodology.[96]

Similarly, books were appearing with the title of "Theology of the New Testament,"[97] though many of them still treated the early Christian thought in fragmentary fashion—Paulinism, Johanninism, and so forth. There was, however, a real need for a presentation of the great themes—God, man, sin, salvation, kingdom, and church—in their "growth and variety" from Paul to Hebrews and II Peter, along the lines drawn by F. C. Grant, who insisted rightly that in spite of the diversity of expression, "the faith is one" and "the fundamental outlook of the primitive church was certainly consistent and increasingly homogeneous."[98]

The next step was to be taken when a truly "biblical" theology, a theology of the Bible as a whole, should reveal how the unresolved tensions of Hebrew faith—particularism and universalism, grace and law, individual and community, church and world, history and eschatology—are displaced, overcome, and transfigured by what proved to be at once the scandal and the creativity of the Christ-event. The fulfillment of this task demanded a restatement of exegetical purpose and methodology.

D. Discussions on Hermeneutics.

—One cannot review the history of biblical interpretation without observing that exegetes have been too often influenced in their work by epistemological presuppositions of which they themselves were more or less unaware. "Historical" exegesis, for example, which vehemently claimed to have reached the highest possible degree of objectivity was chiefly dominated by philosophical premises of a naturalistic type. Not only have the allegorical or "spiritual," and, to a lesser extent, typological interpreters practiced eisegesis rather than exegesis, but also many self-styled "exegetes" have done so: for instance, the "liberal" students who spiritualized the eschatological element in the teaching of Jesus or the "neo-orthodox" theologians who dismissed the "mythological frame" as alien to the New Testament.

(Basel: H. Majer, 1945; "Abhandlungen zur Theologie des Alten und Neuen Testaments").

[91] At least in his extremely controversial remarks on the Christian myth in "Neues Testament und Mythologie," in *Kerygma und Mythos; ein theologisches Gespräch*, ed. Hans W. Bartsch (Hamburg: Reich & Hedrich, 1948), pp. 15-53. See the critique of Amos N. Wilder, "Mythology and the New Testament," *Journal of Biblical Literature*, LXIX (1950), 113-27.

[92] *Christus und die Zeit* (Zurich: Zollikon, 1946), tr. F. V. Filson, *Christ and Time* (Philadelphia: Westminster Press, 1950).

[93] "Thirty Years of New Testament Study," *Union Seminary Quarterly Review*, V (1950), 12.

[94] *Theologie des Alten Testaments* (Leipzig: J. C. Hinrichs, 1933-39).

[95] Such as J. J. Stamm, *Erlösen und Vergeben im Alten Testament* (Bern: A. Francke, 1940); Christopher North, *The Old Testament Interpretation of History* (London: Epworth Press, 1946); H. H. Rowley, *The Biblical Doctrine of Election* (London: Lutterworth Press, 1950).

[96] See James D. Smart, "The Death and Rebirth of Old Testament Theology," *Journal of Religion*, XXIII (1943), 1-11, 125-36; N. W. Porteous, "Towards a Theology of the Old Testament," *Scottish Journal of Theology*, I (1948), 136-49; Robert C. Dentan, *Preface to Old Testament Theology* (New Haven: Yale University Press, 1950).

[97] See Ethelbert Stauffer, *Die Theologie des Neuen Testaments* (Stuttgart: W. Kohlhammer, 1947); Rudolf Bultmann, *Theologie des Neuen Testaments* (Tübingen: J. C. B. Mohr, 1948-51).

[98] *An Introduction to New Testament Thought* (New York and Nashville: Abingdon-Cokesbury Press, 1950), p. 42.

It is unfortunate that much of the mid-century discussion on hermeneutic principles originated with men who disparaged the work of the historico-critical schools in a one-sided way and proposed in its stead a "suprahistorical," "dogmatic," "pneumatic," "ecclesiastic," or strictly "theological" exegesis.[99] In general, however, the sounder view was being maintained that the exegete must be concerned at all times with the philological, grammatical, literal meaning of the text as it is related to the historical framework of composition.[100] But his task does not end there. The exegete cannot and should not deny that the meaning of a text has grown in the whole scriptural context and needs therefore to be viewed in the light of that context. For instance, if the exegete analyzes the expression *imago dei,* he must realize that the priestly school which was originally responsible for it wrote at a time of grave national distress; he must remember that the final editors of the Pentateuch preserved this expression in a story which is now placed side by side with the J accounts of the Creation and the Fall, thereby suggesting a subtle equilibrium between contrasting emphases; he must also take into central consideration the fact that the New Testament places upon the famous text of Genesis its culminating, teleological interpretation. In other words, the exegesis of a passage includes not only "The determination of the text; . . . The literary form of the passage; . . . The historical situation, the Sitz im Leben; . . . The meaning which the words had for the original author and hearer or reader"; but also, ". . . The understanding of the passage in the light of its total context and the background out of which it emerged." [101] This "total context" should mean "the total Scripture." The theologically-minded exegete will therefore en-

ter into the biblical world through his participation in the κοινωνία of the people of God. Considering the object of his science, he will know that a neutral, detached, "objective" attitude would become in effect "unscientific." In this sense "theological" exegesis is not only legitimate but also indispensable; however, it cannot be divorced from the literal interpretation, which at all times must restrain the vagaries of subjective imagination too often "deified" as "the inner testimony of the Holy Spirit," and must resist even the pressure of a particular ecclesiastic tradition.[102] In any event, the interpreter should study in considerable detail the history of interpretation, thereby obtaining a clear sense of his responsibility, and perhaps also some humility.

IV. Selected Bibliography

BURGHARDT, W. J. "On Early Christian Exegesis," *Theological Studies,* XI (1950), 78-116.

CARPENTER, J. ESTLIN. *The Bible in the Nineteenth Century.* New York: Longmans, Green & Co., 1903.

COPPENS, JOSEPH. *The Old Testament and the Critics,* tr. Edward A. Ryan and Edward W. Tribbe. Paterson, N. J.: St. Anthony Guild Press, 1942.

DUGMORE, CLIFFORD WILLIAM, ed. *The Interpretation of the Bible.* London: Society for Promoting Christian Knowledge, 1944.

FARRAR, FREDERIC WILLIAM. *History of Interpretation.* New York: E. P. Dutton & Co., 1886.

GILBERT, GEORGE HOLLEY. *Interpretation of the Bible.* New York: The Macmillan Co., 1908.

GLUNZ, H. H. *History of the Vulgate in England from Alcuin to Roger Bacon.* Cambridge: Cambridge University Press, 1933.

GRANT, ROBERT M. *The Bible in the Church.* New York: The Macmillan Co., 1948.

ROWLEY, H. H., ed. *The Old Testament and Modern Study.* Oxford: Clarendon Press, 1951.

SCHWEITZER, ALBERT. *The Quest of the Historical Jesus,* tr. W. Montgomery. New York: The Macmillan Co., 1950.

SMALLEY, BERYL. *The Study of the Bible in the Middle Ages.* Oxford: Clarendon Press, 1941.

SPICQ, C. *Esquisse d'une histoire de l'exégèse latine au moyen âge.* Paris: J. Vrin, 1944.

WACH, JOACHIM. *Das Verstehen, Grundzüge einer Geschichte der hermeneutischen Theorie im 19. Jahrhundert.* Tübingen: J. C. B. Mohr, 1926-33.

WASZINK, J. H. "Allegorese," *Reallexikon für Antike und Christentum I.* Stuttgart: Hiersemann, 1950. Pp. 283-93.

WILLOUGHBY, HAROLD R., ed. *The Study of the Bible Today and Tomorrow.* Chicago: University of Chicago Press, 1947.

[99] See, e.g., Albrecht Oepke, *Geschichtliche und übergeschichtliche Schriftauslegung* (Gütersloh: C. Bertelsmann, 1931); see also Karl Barth's well-known stand, as reaffirmed in his *Kirchliche Dogmatik* (München: C. Kaiser, 1948), Vol. III, Bd. 2, pp. vii-ix.

[100] See, among many others, H. Cunliffe-Jones, *The Authority of the Biblical Revelation* (London: James Clarke & Co., 1945); Floyd V. Filson, "Theological Exegesis," *The Journal of Bible and Religion,* XVI (1948), 212-15; Oscar Cullmann, "La nécessité et la fonction de l'exégèse philologique et historique de la Bible," *Verbum Caro,* III (1949), 2-13.

[101] From "Guiding Principles for the Interpretation of the Bible, As accepted by the ecumenical Study Conference, held in Oxford from June 29th to July 5th 1949." Studies on "The Bible and the Church Message to the World," as quoted by G. Ernest Wright, "The Problem of Archaizing Ourselves," *Interpretation,* III (1949), 458.

[102] See article "The Bible: Its Significance and Authority," pp. 3-31.

CHRONOLOGY, METROLOGY, ETC.

by GEORGES AUGUSTIN BARROIS

I. Chronology

A. From Creation to Abraham.—The genealogy of the early patriarchs (Gen. 5; 11:10-32) is cast into a chronological scheme whose figures according to the standard Hebrew text (followed by the King James Version) conflict with those in the Greek and Samaritan versions. In each division of Table I, column A shows the age of the patriarchs at the birth of their heir; column B, the number of their years thereafter; column C, their total lifetime.

The scheme of Gen. 5 and 11:10-32 is strictly genealogical. This means that the summation of the figures shown in column A should give the number of years elapsed since the Creation. Hence the dates, *anno mundi*, 1656 for the Flood (Noah's six hundredth year) and 1946 for Abraham's birth.

Such figures cannot be reconciled with the conclusions or hypotheses of modern science concerning the age of the world or the average life span of primitive man, unless it is assumed that the reckoning of times by the biblical authors or translators follows symbolical preconceptions whose nature or ratio cannot be ascertained. The analogy of early Mesopotamian dynastic lists may to a certain extent substantiate this assumption.

According to the Greek chronology, Methuselah survived the Flood by fourteen years, in contradiction to Gen. 7:23. The Hebrew dates his death in the year of the Flood. The fresh start to be made by Noah and his sons is further emphasized in the Samaritan, where Jared, Methuselah, and Lamech are made to die the year of the Flood, being presumably wiped out by the cataclysm.

The low figures in column A of the Hebrew chronology, from Arpachshad to Nahor, account for the abnormal fact that all the patriarchs from Noah to Terah were still alive when Abraham was born. According to the Greek and the Samaritan, all of Abraham's forebears had died when he started on his journey to Canaan, as if to stress the beginning of a new era in biblical history.

Events recorded in the biblical narratives covering this period cannot be synchronized with events of world history. However, the story of the Flood is paralleled in early Mesopotamian literature by traditions which became embodied in the epic of Gilgamesh around the eighteenth century B.C. The story of the Tower of Babel possibly refers to the construction or the restoration of the temple tower Etemenenki at Babylon, the age of which is not ascertainable, although it antedates the second millennium B.C.

142

B. *From Abraham to the Exodus.*—The biblical data consist of a few genealogical indications shown in Table II.

That the genealogies were regarded as complete is confirmed by the prophecy of Gen. 15:16, according to which the fourth generation after Jacob was to return to Canaan. However, the numerical indications recorded in column A of Table II are defective, and this makes it impossible directly to calculate the total length of the period, which has to be inferred from the following data:

Gen. 12:4—Abraham's entry into Canaan, at 75 years
Gen. 47:9—Jacob's migration to Egypt, at 130 years
Exod. 12:40 (Heb.) —Sojourn in Egypt, 430 years
Exod. 12:40 (LXX, Samar.) —Sojourn in Canaan and Egypt, 430 years

Thus the years from the birth of Abraham to the Exodus can be tabulated as shown in Table III.

The abnormal longevity of the patriarchs and the excessive number of years assigned to the generations from Abraham to Moses point to-

TABLE I. GENEALOGY OF THE EARLY PATRIARCHS

PATRIARCH	HEBREW			SAMARITAN			LXX (Ed. Rahlfs)		
	A	B	C	A	B	C	A	B	C
Adam	130	800	930	130	800	930	230	700	930
Seth	105	807	912	105	807	912	205	707	912
Enosh	90	815	905	90	815	905	190	715	905
Kenan	70	840	910	70	840	910	170	740	910
Mahalalel	65	830	895	65	830	895	165	730	895
Jared	162	800	962	62	785	847	162	800	962
Enoch	65	300	365	65	300	365	165	200	365
Methuselah	187	782	969	67	653	720	167	802	969
Lamech	182	595	777	53	600	653	188	565	753
Noah	500	450	950	500	450	950	500	450	950
Shem	100	500		100	500	600	100	500	
Flood	1656			1307			2242		
Arpachshad	35	403		135	303	438	135	430	
[Kainan]							130	330	
Shelah	30	403		130	303	433	130	330	
Eber	34	430		134	270	404	134	370	
Peleg	30	209		130	109	239	130	209	
Reu	32	207		132	107	239	132	207	
Serug	30	200		130	100	230	130	200	
Nahor	29	119		79	69	148	79	129	
Terah	70		205	70		145	70		205
Abraham's birth	1946			2247			3312		

TABLE II. GENEALOGY FROM ABRAHAM TO THE EXODUS

REFERENCE	PERSON	A AGE AT BIRTH OF HEIR	B TOTAL LIFETIME		
			HEBR.	SAMAR.	LXX
Gen. 21:5; 25:7	Abraham	100	175		
Gen. 25:26; 35:28	Isaac	60	180		
Gen. 47:28	Jacob		147		
Exod. 6:16	Levi		137		
Exod. 6:18	Kohath		133		130
Exod. 6:20	Amram		137	136	132
Deut. 34:7	Moses		120		

TABLE III. YEARS FROM THE BIRTH OF ABRAHAM TO THE EXODUS

PERIOD	HEBR. (KJV)	LXX SAMAR.
From Abraham's birth to his entry into Canaan	75	75
From Abraham's entry into Canaan to Jacob's migration	215	215
From Jacob's migration to the Exodus	430	215
Total duration	720	505

ward the artificial character of the biblical chronology, which aims at making the sojourn in Egypt exactly the double of (Hebrew), or equal to (LXX, Samaritan), the sojourn in Canaan.

The symbolic nature of the chronology of the patriarchs from Abraham to Moses makes it inadvisable to use the figures of the Bible for the computation of historical synchronisms, lest re-sults thus obtained should at best prove coincidental, and possibly misleading.

Most exegetes have abandoned the identification of Amraphel (Gen. 14:1) with Hammurabi. The once favored synchronism Abraham-Hammurabi is therefore uncertain, even though it might obtain some support from linguistic and onomastic parallels between the patriarchal stories of Genesis and the cuneiform texts of

TABLE IV. SYNCHRONISMS OF HEBREW AND ORIENTAL HISTORY

HEBREW HISTORY	ORIENTAL HISTORY
	Cuneiform documents of Mari, 18th century
	Hammurabi, 1728-1686 (dates revised after data from the Mari texts)
Hebrew Patriarchs in Canaan	
	Cuneiform documents of Nuzi, 15th century

TABLE V. SYNCHRONISMS OF HEBREW AND EGYPTIAN HISTORY

HEBREW HISTORY	EGYPTIAN HISTORY
	THE HYKSOS (XV DYNASTY) *
Hebron built 7 years before Zoan (Num. 13:22)	
Migration of the Hebrews into Egypt [?]	Capital Avaris (Zoan), founded 1675
	Conquer Xois, 1594
	Expelled by Ahmose, 1567
	XVIII DYNASTY, 1546-1319
	Thutmose III, 1490-1436; campaigns in Syria
14th century; Jericho besieged twice and destroyed (Garstang)	Amenophis III, 1413-1377
Hypothesis of a partial Exodus and settlement of tribes in central Palestine	Amenophis IV (Akhenaton), 1377-1360 (Cuneiform documents of Tell el-Amarna, 14th century)
	XIX DYNASTY, 1319-1200
The king "which knew not Joseph" (Exod. 1:8), possibly Seti I	Seti I, 1319-1301
The Exodus, after 1300	Ramses II, 1301-1234
Final destruction of Jericho (Vincent) and Joshua's conquest of Palestine, shortly after 1250	Merneptah, 1234-1227, defeats Israel in Palestine, the 5th year of his reign
	XX DYNASTY, 1200-1085
	Invasion of Egypt by the Sea Peoples, defeated by Ramses III, 1195-1164, and settlement of the Philistines in the Palestinian lowlands
The Philistines, hostile neighbors of Israel in the story of Samson (previous mentions of the Philistines in the Bible are anachronisms)	
David, king in Hebron, 1002-995	
David, king in Jerusalem, 995-962	
Reign of Solomon, 962-922	
Construction of the temple, from the 4th to the 11th year of Solomon (I Kings 6:1, 38), 959-952	

* Dynasties XVI-XVII are local (Theban) dynasties.
Chronology of the Hyksos according to H. E. Winlock, *The Rise and Fall of the Middle Kingdom in Thebes* (New York: The Macmillan Co., 1947). New Empire dates after Borchardt-Edgerton.

Mari (eighteenth century). On the other hand, the customs of the early Hebrews, as described chiefly in the Jacob narratives, conform best to the social and legal conditions revealed by the cuneiform documents of Nuzi (fifteenth century).

Synchronisms with Egyptian history are equally hypothetical. It is generally assumed that the migration of the Hebrews into Egypt may have occurred while the Hyksos kings of the Fifteenth Dynasty had their capital in the Delta, according to the tradition of Manetho, an Egyptian priest of the third century B.C. The Exodus most likely took place during the reign of Ramses II. The interval, which exceeds two and one half centuries, seems, however, not to be in harmony with the genealogical scheme of the Bible, which counts only four generations from Jacob to Moses.

Although archaeologists still disagree upon the circumstances and date of the destruction of Jericho, miscellaneous data support the dating of Joshua's conquest of Palestine shortly after 1250 B.C.

The hypothetical and provisional character of the dates shown in Tables IV and V should be kept in mind.

C. From the Exodus to Solomon.—Chronological indications from the historical books according to the Hebrew (followed by the King James Version), together with the Greek variants (Rahlfs' text of Septuagint), may be tabulated in years as shown in Table VI.

The chronology of the entire period tends to reckon with units, multiples, or fractions of 40 years. In I Kings 6:1 the period extending from the Exodus to the construction of the temple in the fourth year of Solomon lasts 480 years (Hebrew and King James Version), or 440 years (Greek), that is, respectively, 12 or 11 units of 40 years. However, this conflicts with the detailed chronology of the historical books recorded in the above table. The summation of the figures in the Hebrew column gives a total of 590 years from the Exodus to the death of Solomon, that is, 554 years to the construction of the temple, over against the 480 years of I Kings 6:1 in the Hebrew tradition. The last number may be explained as follows: The years of oppression, including the three years of Abimelech, who was never regarded as a legitimate ruler, amount to 114. There are therefore 554—114=440 years of Hebrew rule from the Exodus to the construction of the temple, which is precisely the number read by the Septuagint in I Kings 6:1. The Hebrew adds 40 years to cover the unrecorded duration of the leadership of Joshua, and the reign of Saul, thus making up the sum total of 480 years.

The summation of the figures of the Greek

TABLE VI. BIBLICAL CHRONOLOGY FROM THE EXODUS TO SOLOMON

	HEBR.	LXX
A. The years of the Wandering (Num. 32:13)	40	
Leadership of Joshua	?	
B. Oppression. Cushan-rishathaim (Judg. 3:8)	8	
Othniel (Judg. 3:11)	40	50
Oppression. Eglon, king of Moab (Judg. 3:14)	18	
Ehud (Judg. 3:30)	80	
Oppression. Jabin, king of Hazor (Judg. 4:3)	20	
Deborah-Barak (Judg. 5:31)	40	
Oppression. The Midianites (Judg. 6:1)	7	
Gideon (Judg. 8:28)	40	
Rule of Abimelech (Judg. 9:22)	3	
Tola (Judg. 10:2)	23	
Jair (Judg. 10:3)	22	
Oppression. The Ammonites (Judg. 10:8)	18	
Jephthah (Judg. 12:7)	6	
Ibzan (Judg. 12:9)	7	
Elon (Judg. 12:11)	10	
Abdon (Judg. 12:14)	8	
Oppression. The Philistines (Judg. 13:1)	40	
Samson (Judg. 15:20; 16:31)	20	
C. Eli, priest in Shiloh (I Sam. 4:18)	40	20
Samuel. Ark in Kirjath-jearim (I Sam. 7:2)	20	
Saul, king	?	
David, king in Hebron (I Kings 2:11)	7 ⎫ 40	
David, king in Jerusalem (I Kings 2:11)	33 ⎭	
Solomon, king (I Kings 11:42)	40	

TABLE VII. COMPARATIVE CHRONOLOGY OF THE KINGS OF JUDAH AND ISRAEL FROM SOLOMON TO THE EXILE

Kings of Judah	Regnal Years	B.C.	Dated Events	Kings of Israel	Regnal Years	B.C.
Rehoboam	8 (17)	922-915	Sheshonk of Egypt, XXII Dynasty (Lybian), raids Palestine, the 5th year of Rehoboam, ca. 918 B.C. (I Kings 14:25; II Chr. 12:2)	Jeroboam	22	922-901
Abijam	3	915-913				
Asa	41	913-873		Nadab	2	901-900
				Baasha	24	900-877
				Elah	2	877-876
				Zimri	7 days	876
Jehoshaphat	25	873-849	Omri builds Samaria after 6 years of reign in Tirzah, ca. 870 B.C. (I Kings 16:23-24)	Omri	8 (12)	876-869
			Shalmaneser III of Assyria, 859-824 B.C., fights Ahab and the Syrian confederates at Qarqar, ca. 853 B.C., *Monolith of Shalmaneser*	Ahab	20 (22)	869-850
				Ahaziah	2	850-849
Jehoram	8	849-842	According to II Kings 3:7-27, the death of Jehoshaphat occurred some time after the accession of Joram of Israel, since both kings personally joined in the war against Moab	Joram	8 (12)	849-842
Ahaziah	1	842	Ahaziah of Judah and Joram of Israel slain the same day by Jehu, 842 B.C. (II Kings 9:21-28)			
Athaliah, queen	6 (7)	842-837	*Ca.* 841 B.C. Jehu pays tribute to Shalmaneser III of Assyria, 859-824 B.C. (*Black Obelisk*, and *Annals*)	Jehu	28	842-815
Jehoash	38 (40)	837-800		Joahaz	15 (17)	815-801
Amaziah	18 (29)	800-783		Joash	16	801-786
Azariah (Uzziah)	42 (52)	783-742		Jeroboam	41	786-746
Jotham, regent	8?	750-742		Zechariah	6 mos.	746-745
				Shallum	1 mo.	745
Jotham, king	8 (16)	742-735	*Ca.* 738 B.C. Menahem pays tribute to Pulu (Tiglath-pileser III) of Assyria, 745-727 B.C. (II Kings 15:19, and Assyrian documents)	Menahem	8+ (10)	745-738
				Pekahia	2	738-737
Ahaz	21±(16)	735-715	Pekah and Rezon of Syria besiege Jerusalem, ca. 734 B.C. (II Kings 16:5)	Pekah	6- (20)	737-732
			Ca. 733-732 B.C., campaign of Tiglath-pileser III in Palestine (*Annals*)			
			Hoshea, enthroned by Tiglath-pileser III, *ca.* 732 B.C.; pays tribute to Shalmaneser V of Assyria, 727-722 B.C. (II Kings 17:3); taken into captivity, *ca.* 724 B.C. (II Kings 17:4)	Hoshea	9	732-724
			3 years' siege of Samaria (II Kings 17:5) ends between December 722, accession of Sargon II of Assyria, 722-705 B.C., and the spring of 721 B.C. (Assyrian documents)			

TABLE VII. Concluded

Kings of Judah	Regnal Years	B.C.	Dated Events	Kings of Israel	Regnal Years	B.C.
Hezekiah	29	715-687	Sennacherib of Assyria, 705-681 B.C., invades Judah, the 14th year of Hezekiah, *ca.* 701 B.C. (II Kings 18:13, and Assyrian documents)			
Manasseh	45 (55)	687-642	Taken prisoner by king of Assyria, possibly Esarhaddon, 681-669 B.C., or rather, Ashurbanipal, 669-626 B.C. (II Chr. 33:11)			
Amon	2	642-640				
Josiah	31	640-609	Deuteronomic reform, the 18th year of Josiah, *ca.* 622 B.C. (II Kings 22:3; 23:23; II Chr. 34:8; 35:19)			
			612 B.C., fall of Nineveh, beginning of Neo-Babylonian Empire; Assyrian kings fight till 609 B.C.			
			Josiah killed in battle at Megiddo, against Necho of Egypt, XXVI (Saite) Dynasty (II Kings 23:29; II Chr. 35:22-24)			
Jehoahaz	3 mos.	609	Taken into captivity by Necho (II Kings 23:33-34; II Chr. 36:3)			
Jehoiakim	11	609-598	Enthroned by Necho (II Kings 23:34; II Chr. 36:4)			
			1st year of Nebuchadrezzar of Babylon, 605-562 B.C., 4th of Jehoiakim,, *ca.* 605 B.C., prophecy on the ruin of Judah (Jer. 25:1)			
			7th year of Nebuchadrezzar, *ca.* 599 B.C., deportation of 3,023 Jews (Jer. 52:28)			
Jehoiachin	3 mos.	598	Taken into captivity the 8th year of Nebuchadrezzar, *ca.* 598 B.C. (II Kings 24:12; II Chr. 36:10)			
Zedekiah	11	598-587	Enthroned by Nebuchadrezzar (II Kings 24:27)			
			18th year of Nebuchadrezzar, 10th of Zedekiah, *ca.* 588 B.C., Jerusalem besieged (Jer. 32:1-2); deportation of 832 persons from Jerusalem (Jer. 52:29)			
			19th year of Nebuchadrezzar, 587 B.C., Jerusalem destroyed (II Kings 25:8; Jer. 52:12-13)			
			23rd year of Nebuchadrezzar, *ca.* 583 B.C., deportation of 745 Jews (Jer. 52:30)			
			Jehoiachin received by Evil-merodach (Awel-Marduk) of Babylon, 562-560 B.C., in the year of his accession (Jer. 52:31)			

gives a total of 580 years for the entire period, that is, 544 years from the Exodus to the construction of the temple, and consequently 544—114=430 years of Hebrew rule. The period from the Exodus to the construction of Solomon's temple is thus regarded as strictly equal to the sojourn of the Hebrews in Canaan and in Egypt according to Exod. 12:40 (LXX).

The above remarks demonstrate the conventional character of the biblical chronology of this period, and the inadvisability of using its figures for the computation of historical synchronisms. Attempts at relating the chronology of Joshua-Judges to the vicissitudes of the fast dwindling power of Egypt lead to highly questionable results.

The dates of David and Solomon, if one is to assume the historicity of the numbers of their regnal years, may be deduced from the chronology of their successors, the kings of Judah and of Israel.

Thus the period from the Exodus to the death of Solomon can be outlined as shown at the end of Table V.

The generally accepted date for the death of Solomon, and consequently Rehoboam's accession and the schism, is 933-932 B.C. Modern historians tend to depart from this date for the following reasons: II Chr. 16:1 states that Baasha was still reigning in the thirty-sixth year of Asa. If one were to follow the chronology of the author of Kings, the thirty-sixth year of Asa would fall after Baasha's death. If the indication of the Chronicler is to be taken into account, and if the number of the regnal years of the Israelite kings is not to be increased drastically, the reign of Rehoboam ought to be shortened by a decade or so. Thus the death of Solomon would have taken place *ca.* 922 B.C.[1]

[1] Cf. William F. Albright's discussion in "The Chronology of the Divided Monarchy of Israel," *Bulletin of the American Schools of Oriental Research,* No. 100 (1945), p. 20, n. 14.

D. From Solomon to the Exile.—The biblical data consist of a double set of chronological indications recorded in I and II Kings and parallels. (*a*) Regnal years of each king, sometimes with their age when enthroned. (*b*) Synchronisms between the kings of Judah and the kings of Israel, sometimes with synchronisms with the history of Egypt and Mesopotamia.

These data are drawn from official annals of the kingdoms and, on account of their historical character, can be used as the framework of the chronological succession of the kings of Judah and Israel, with reference to events known and dated from other sources such as the fall of Samaria, which occurred shortly after the accession of Sargon II of Assyria.

However, the interpretation of the data is made difficult for the following reasons: (*a*) There are occasional divergent readings in the Hebrew and the Greek. (*b*) There is also frequent disagreement between the synchronisms recorded in the Bible and the absolute numbers of regnal years.

Whereas Wellhausenian critics inclined to give up the synchronisms as purely conventional and therefore unreliable, Joachim Begrich has proved conclusively that most of the variants

TABLE VIII. COMPARATIVE CHRONOLOGY OF HEBREW AND PERSIAN HISTORY AFTER THE EXILE

PERSIAN KINGS	DATED EVENTS
Cyrus, 539-530 B.C. (counting from the conquest of Babylon)	Edict for the return of the Jews, the 1st (formal) year of Cyrus, *ca.* 538 B.C. (Ezra 1:1)
	Zerubbabel undertakes to restore the temple, the 2nd year after the return, *ca.* 537 B.C. (Ezra 3:8) ; work interrupted (Ezra 4:5, 24)
Cambyses, 530-522 B.C.	Jewish community established at Elephantine, before 525 B.C. (conquest of Egypt) ; papyri range from 500 to 400 B.C.
Darius I, 522-486 B.C.	Work at the temple resumed the 2nd year of Darius, *ca.* 520 B.C. (Ezra 4:24; Hag. 1:15) ; completed the 6th year of Darius, *ca.* 516 B.C. (Ezra 6:15)
Xerxes I (Ahasuerus) 486-465 B.C.	Opposition to the Jews (Ezra 4:6)
Artaxerxes I, Longimanus, 465-424 B.C.	Opposition to the Jews (Ezra 4:7-23)
	Return of Ezra, the 7th year of Artaxerxes, *ca.* 458 B.C. (Ezra 7:7, according to the actual order of the book)
	Nehemiah, governor of Judah, from the 20th to the 32nd year of Artaxerxes, *ca.* 445-433 B.C. (Neh. 2:1; 5:14)
	Nehemiah back to Persia the 32nd year of Artaxerxes, *ca.* 433 B.C., and 2nd mission to Palestine (Neh. 13:6)
Xerxes II, 424-423 B.C. Darius II, 423-404 B.C.	
Artaxerxes II, Mnemon, 404-358 B.C.	Return of Ezra, the 7th year of Artaxerxes, *ca.* 397 B.C. (Ezra 7:7, as suggested by several exegetes for reasons of internal evidence)
Artaxerxes III, 358-338 B.C. Arses, 338-336 B.C. Darius III, Codomannus, 336-331 B.C.	

and of the so-called erroneous synchronisms resulted from several attempts at systematizing historical data, and had an objective value.[2] At the same time, he was successful in explaining

[2] *Die Chronologie der Könige von Israel und Juda* (Tübingen: J. C. B. Mohr, 1929).

rationally the origin of many discrepancies. Yet his effort to fit all data goes too far, and the proportion of trivial errors in the transmission of the text is probably greater than he would admit.

Some of the difficulties are of a historical

TABLE IX. COMPARATIVE CHRONOLOGY OF HEBREW AND HELLENISTIC HISTORY TO THE ROMAN CONQUEST

HELLENISTIC KINGS		DATED EVENTS
PTOLEMIES (Egypt)	SELEUCIDS (Asia Minor and Syria)	(Fall of Tyre, *ca.* 332 B.C.)
(Alexander the Great, 336-323 B.C.)		
Ptolemy I, Soter, 323-283 B.C.	Seleucus I, Nicator, 312-280 B.C.	Seleucid Era begins, October, 312 B.C.
Ptolemy II, Philadelphus, [285]283-246 B.C.	Antiochus I, 280-261 B.C. Antiochus II, 261-247 B.C.	In Alexandria, version of the LXX Papyri of Zeno, agent of Ptolemy II
Ptolemy III, 246-221 B.C.	Seleucus II, 247-226 B.C. Seleucus III, 226-223 B.C.	
Ptolemy IV, 221-203 B.C.	Antiochus III, the Great, 223-187 B.C.	Following the battle of Panion, Palestine, lost to the Ptolemies, passes under the control of the Seleucids, 198 B.C.
Ptolemy V, 203-181 B.C.	Seleucus IV, 187-175 B.C.	
Ptolemies continue under Roman protectorate until 30 B.C., when Egypt becomes a Roman province	Antiochus IV, Epiphanes, 175-163 B.C.	Persecution of the Jews, pollution of the temple, 167 B.C. (I Macc. 1:57)
		THE MACCABEES
	Antiochus V, 163-162 B.C.	Judas, 166-160 B.C.; temple purified, 164 B.C. (I Macc. 4:52)
	Demetrius I, 162-150 B.C.	Jonathan, 160-142 B.C., high priest, 152 B.C. (I Macc. 10:21)
	Alexander Balas, usurper, 150-145 B.C. Antiochus VI, 145-142/1 B.C.	
	Demetrius II, 145-139/8 B.C.	Simon, 142-134 B.C.; recognized by Demetrius, 142 B.C. (I Macc. 13:41)
	Antiochus VII, Sidetes, 139/8-129 B.C.	John Hyrcanus I, 134-104 B.C.
		Judas Aristobulus I, 104-103 B.C.
		Alexander Jannaeus, 103-76 B.C.
	Seleucids continue amidst rivalries until Syria becomes a Roman province, 65 B.C.	Alexandra, queen, 76-67 B.C.
		Aristobulus II, 67-63 B.C.
		Pompey takes Jerusalem, 63 B.C.
		Maccabean dynasty continues nominally: Hyrcanus II, 63-40 B.C. Antigonus Mattathias, 40-37 B.C.
		Antipater and his son Herod rise to effective power

TABLE X. NEW TESTAMENT EVENTS SYNCHRONIZED WITH ROMAN AND
PALESTINIAN HISTORY AFTER THE ROMAN CONQUEST

ROME	PALESTINE			NEW TESTAMENT
	ITURAEA, TRACHONITIS, ETC.	GALILEE	JUDEA	
First Triumvirate, 60 B.C.: Pompey, Caesar, Crassus	Conquest of Jerusalem by Pompey, 63 B.C. Hyrcanus II, 63-40 B.C.			
Second Triumvirate, 43 B.C.: Antony, Octavius, Lepidus	Antigonus Mattathias, 40-37 B.C.			
Augustus (Octavius), 31 B.C.–A.D. 14	Herod the Great, nominated, 40 B.C.; began to reign 37 B.C.; died, spring of 4 B.C.			Jesus born before the spring of 4 B.C.
Tiberius, A.D. 14-37	Philip, 4 B.C.–A.D. 34	Herod Antipas, 4 B.C.–A.D. 40	Archelaus, 4 B.C.–A.D. 6	
			Procurators, A.D. 6-41 (Pontius Pilate in office, A.D. 26-36)	Baptism of Jesus, the 15th year of Tiberius, A.D. 28/29 Crucifixion (year uncertain) Damascus controlled by Aretas, ca. A.D. 37-40; conversion of Paul (II Cor. 11:32)
Caligula, A.D. 37-41	Agrippa I, A.D. 34-44	Agrippa I, A.D. 40-44		
Claudius, A.D. 41-54			Agrippa I, A.D. 41-44	The apostles persecuted (Acts 12)
			Procurators, A.D. 44-66	Gallio proconsul in Achaia, A.D. 51-52; Paul in Corinth (Acts 18:12)
Nero, A.D. 54-68	Agrippa II, A.D. 53-93	Agrippa II, A.D. 54/5-93	(Felix in office, A.D. 52-60; Festus, in office, A.D. 61-62)	Paul arrested under Felix, in prison for 2 years, appears before Festus (Acts 24:27–25:27)
Galba, Otho, Vitellius, A.D. 68		First revolt of the Jews, begins A.D. 66		
Vespasian, A.D. 69-79		Fall of Jerusalem, A.D. 70 Fall of Masada, A.D. 73		
Titus, A.D. 79-81 Domitian, A.D. 81-96 Nerva, A.D. 96-98 Trajan, A.D. 98-117 Hadrian, A.D. 117-138		Second revolt of the Jews, A.D. 132-135 Foundation of Colonia Aelia Capitolina over the ruins of Jerusalem, A.D. 136		

nature, such as the confusion of the period extending from the death of Baasha to the accession of Omri, or the obscurity of the circumstances which marked the accession of the kings of Judah from Jehoash to Jotham.

Technical difficulties are equally perplexing. Such is the relation of regnal years to calendar years. It is generally admitted that the Hebrew annalists practiced antedating—that is, counting as first year of the king the remaining portion of the calendar year in which his accession took place. Postdating, however, may have prevailed in Judah from Manasseh to Zedekiah, the first official year being then the full calendar year following the accession.

Another difficulty arises from the reckoning of New Year's Day. The year normally began with the autumnal equinox. One may question Begrich's affirmation that the practice of beginning the year in the spring was introduced in Judah before 620 B.C.

In Table VII the initial and final dates of reigns are borrowed from William F. Albright, who revised the chronology of Begrich in the light of intervening publications.[3] In the columns of regnal years figures in parentheses are those of the Hebrew Bible (and King James Version), before adjustment. Horizontal lines mark interruptions in the normal succession of the kings. All dates are approximate.

E. From the Exile to the Roman Conquest.— Whereas the books of Kings and parallels constitute a suitable framework for the chronology of the Hebrew kingdoms, the documentation of the period extending from the Exile to the Roman conquest is scanty and discontinuous. The books of Ezra and Nehemiah, which may be described as a collection of miscellaneous documents without a strict chronological order, contain a few synchronisms with Persian history.

After a gap of more than two centuries, a few dates of interest for the history of the Hebrews under the rule or in the sphere of influence of the Hellenistic kingdoms of Egypt and Syria are available in the books of the Maccabees and in the writings of Josephus.

In Tables VIII and IX the chronology of the Persian and Hellenistic kingdoms is used as the

[3] *Op. cit.*, pp. 16-21.

framework for dated events from Hebrew history.

F. From the Roman Conquest to the Destruction of Jerusalem.—The succession of events which brought about the overthrow of the republican institutions of the Romans and the list of the emperors, as well as of the local rulers appointed or recognized by Rome for the control of Palestine, constitute the framework of a chronology of the Gospels and early apostolic history.

Unfortunately, the chronological indications given by the Gospels and the Acts of the Apostles are few and of difficult interpretation. The date of the birth of Jesus is not known with certainty. Our Christian Era, derived from the chronology of Dionysius Exiguus, is several years late. According to Matt. 2:1, 19 Jesus was born *some time before* the death of Herod, which occurred in the spring of 4 B.C. Luke 2:2 dates the birth of Jesus with reference to a census taken by Cyrenius (Quirinius), governor of Syria. No precision can be obtained from this statement on account of unsettled difficulties of interpretation and even of translation.

The extensive synchronism recorded by Luke 3:1 dates the baptism of Jesus and the beginning of his ministry from the fifteenth year of Tiberius, that is, A.D. 28/29, depending on the reckoning of the first regnal year as A.D. 14 or, postdating, 15. A few exegetes, interpreting strictly the statement that Jesus was "about thirty years of age" (Luke 3:23), have suggested that the years of Tiberius be counted from the time when he was associated with the government of Augustus, ca. A.D. 11-12, and that the date of the baptism should be antedated accordingly. This manner of reckoning, however, finds little support in the literature of the age.

On the other hand, John 2:20 states that in the time of the (first) passover recorded (John 2:13, 23) forty-six years had elapsed since the beginning of the construction of the temple, in the eighteenth year of Herod (20/19 B.C.). If one starts from 19 B.C., the forty-sixth year is A.D. 27.

John's various references to Jewish festivals have been used to fix the duration of the ministry of Jesus, and consequently the date of his

TABLE XI. JEWISH FESTIVALS MENTIONED IN THE FOURTH GOSPEL

KJV	HYPOTHESIS 1	HYPOTHESIS 2	HYPOTHESIS 3
John 2:13 passover	passover 28	passover 28	passover 28
John 5:1 a feast			=passover 29
John 6:4 passover	text emended	passover 29	passover 30
John 7:2 tabernacles			
John 10:22 dedication			
John 11:55 passover	passover 29	passover 30	passover 31
Total duration of the public life	over one year	over two years	over three years

death. According to divergent interpretations, the interval between the Baptism and the Crucifixion is over one year, or over two years, or over three years.

On account of these variations, Table X records only those events from the Gospels or the Acts which can be synchronized *objectively* with the course of general history.

Table XI shows alternate arrangements of the recording of Jewish festivals during the public life of Jesus, the last Passover referred to by John 11:55 coinciding with the time of the Passion. The dates, entirely hypothetical, assume that the Baptism took place in the early months of A.D. 28.

II. Calendars

A. Hebrew Calendar.—The Hebrew calendar was based on the empirical observation of the phases of the moon. The year consisted of twelve lunar months, which were counted each from the first appearance of the crescent of the new moon (neomenia). The lunar year being approximately eleven days shorter than the solar year, it was necessary to repeat the last month every two or three years in order to keep calendar dates in accordance with the seasons. The scientific determination of the neomenias and of the leap year of thirteen months was probably not introduced until after the Talmudic period.

The Israelites first called their months by Canaanite names, four of which are recorded in the Bible. Postexilic and late Judaism adopted Babylonian names, which were transliterated in Hebrew, and are still in use in the modern Jewish calendar. Table XII gives both series. The correspondence with the months of the Julian calendar is only approximate.

The first day of *niṣān* marks the beginning of the year with regard to the computation of passover. For other purposes the year began in autumn, on the first of *tishrî*, which was solemnized as New Year's Day (*rôsh hashshānāh*).

The ancient Hebrews had no era for the recording of dates, which were computed by reference to some memorable event such as, under the monarchy, the accession year of the reigning king.

The sabbath or seventh day of the week now begins on Friday at dusk, since the days arè counted from sunset to sunset. The periodic week replaced sometime before the Exile the ancient division of each month according to the phases of the moon.

B. Hellenistic Calendar.—A calendar of Macedonian origin was introduced by the Hellenistic rulers of Palestine, but was not generally accepted by the Jews. The lunar months of the original Macedonian calendar had been transformed in Egypt into months of thirty days, to which five days were added after the twelfth month to approximate the solar year. In the regions ruled by the Seleucids the Macedonian calendar was harmonized with the Neo-Babylonian calendar of twelve lunar months, and an additional month on leap years. Thus the correspondence of Seleucid and Neo-Babylonian dates can be established with some accuracy.

In Antioch, following the adoption of the Seleucidan Era (312 B.C.), New Year's Day was the first of Ὑπερβερεταῖος (=*tishrî*). During the Roman period, the Syro-Macedonian months were often equated to the Julian months, in this manner:

Ὑπερβερεταῖος	October
Δῖος	November
Ἀπελλαῖος	December
Αὐδυναῖος	January
Περίτιος	February
Δύστρος	March
Ξανθικός	April
Ἀρτεμίσιος	May
Δαίσιος	June
Πάνημος	July
Λῷος	August
Γορπιαῖος	September

TABLE XII. HEBREW CALENDAR

CANAANITE	BABYLONIAN	JULIAN
'ābhibh	niṣān	March-April
ziw	'iyyār	April-May
	ṣîwān	May-June
	tammûz	June-July
	'ābh	July-August
	'elûl	August-September
'êthānîm	tishrî	September-October
bûl	marheshwān	October-November
	kislēw	November-December
	ṭēbhēth	December-January
	shebhāṭ	January-February
	'adhār (repeated on leap years)	February-March

In Babylon, however, the beginning of the year continued to be celebrated in the spring. In free cities having particular eras, the first of Δῖος, which in Macedonia was regarded as New Year's Day, was often caused to coincide with the anniversary of the era.

C. Festivals.—In addition to the sabbath and the neomenia, the Jews kept the following festivals:

Pésaḥ, Passover, 14th-15th of *nîsān,* and the following seven days
Shâbhû'ôth, Pentecost, the 50th day after *pésaḥ*
Rôsh hashshānāh, New Year's Day, 1st of *tishrî*
Yôm kippûr, Day of Atonement, 10th of *tishrî*
Sukkôth, Tabernacles, 15th-23rd of *tishrî*
*Ḥ*anukkāh,* dedication of the temple by Judas Maccabee (165 B.C.), 25th of *kislēw* and the following seven days
Pûrîm, commemoration of the events recorded in the book of Esther, 14th-15th of *'adhār* (second *'adhār* on leap years)

Table XIII gives by way of illustration the dates of the main festivals according to the standard computation of the modern Jewish calendar. Years are counted according to the so-called "World Era," introduced by the Talmudists. Leap years are marked with an asterisk.

III. Metrology

A. Measures of Length.—In the Old Testament standard units of length are named by reference to parts of the human body. (See Table XIV.)

Surveyors and architects used a measuring "reed," the length of which was expressed in cubits. In Judg. 3:16 the Hebrew גמד (*gômedh*), otherwise unknown, is interpreted "cubit" in the King James Version.

The current ratio between the units of length is shown in the following chart:

1 cubit	= 2 spans
	= 6 handbreadths
	= 24 fingers
1 span	= 3 handbreadths
	= 12 fingers
1 handbreadth	= 4 fingers

TABLE XIII. JEWISH FESTIVALS

Anno Mundi	5713	5714*	5715	5716	5717*	5718	5719*	5720
Rôsh hashshānāh 1 tishrî	Sep. 20 1952	Sep. 10 1953	Sep. 28 1954	Sep. 17 1955	Sep. 6 1956	Sep. 26 1957	Sep. 15 1958	Oct. 3 1959
Yôm Kippûr 10 tishrî	Sep. 29	Sep. 19	Oct. 7	Sep. 26	Sep. 15	Oct. 5	Sep. 24	Oct. 12
Sukkôth (first day) 15 tishrî	Oct. 4	Sep. 24	Oct. 12	Oct. 1	Sep. 20	Oct. 10	Sep. 29	Oct. 17
Ḥanukkāh (first day) 25 kislēw	Dec. 13	Dec. 2	Dec. 20	Dec. 10	Nov. 29	Dec. 18	Dec. 7	Dec. 26
Pûrîm (first day) 14 'adhār	Mar. 1 1953		Mar. 8 1955	Feb. 26 1956		Mar. 6 1958		Mar. 13 1960
14 'adhār II (on leap years)		Mar. 19 1954			Mar. 17 1957		Mar. 24 1959	
Pésaḥ (first night) 14 nîsān	Mar. 30	Apr. 17	Apr. 6	Mar. 26	Apr. 15	Apr. 4	Apr. 22	Apr. 11
Shâbhû'ôth 6 sîwān	May 20	Jun. 7	May 27	May 16	Jun. 5	May 25	Jun. 12	Jun. 1

TABLE XIV. OLD TESTAMENT STANDARD UNITS OF LENGTH

HEBREW	KJV	RSV
אמה *'ammāh*	cubit	cubit
זרת *zéreth*	span	span
טפח *tôphaḥ, tĕphaḥ*	handbreadth	handbreadth
אצבע *'eçba'*	finger	finger

The cubit which was to be used in Ezekiel's new Jerusalem is described as equal to a "cubit and a handbreadth" of the current system (Ezek. 40:5; 43:13). This is not to be interpreted as an innovation, but rather as a return to a system of measures used for the buildings of Solomon (II Chr. 3:3) which may be restored as follows:

1 cubit	=	2	spans
	=	7	handbreadths
	=	28	fingers
1 span	=	3½	handbreadths
	=	14	fingers
1 handbreadth	=	4	fingers

The value of the cubit cannot be determined directly, but only by deduction. The inscription of Siloam attributes to the aqueduct of Hezekiah a length of 1,200 cubits. The actual measurement of the aqueduct, from the spring to the pool, being 533.1 meters, or 1,749 feet, the value of the cubit is therefore 444.25 millimeters, or 17.49 inches. Hence the Hebrew system of linear measures may tentatively be expressed as shown in Table XV.

In the New Testament the following terms are used for measures of length:

πῆχυς, "cubit." Considered as equivalent to 1½ feet of the Hellenistic system of measures.

ʼοργυιά, "fathom." Approximately 1.84 meters, or 72.44 inches.

B. Measures of Distance.—In the Old Testament distances are not measured directly, but are suggested by such expressions as "three days' journey" (Gen. 30:36), "seven days' journey" (Gen. 31:23).

Distance is measured in the New Testament according to the following:

στάδιον, "furlong" (KJV), "stadion," or an evaluation of distance in "miles" (RSV). The Alexandrine stadion equals 184.83 meters, or 606 feet 2 inches.

μίλιον, "mile." The Roman mile was usually considered as equal to 8 stadia, thus approximately 1,478 meters, or 4,879 feet. The Jews, however, regarded it as the equivalent of ¼ of a parasang (a Persian measure of distance), or 7½ stadia, thus approximately 1,386 meters, or 4,546 feet.

ὁδὸς σαββάτου, "a sabbath day's journey" (Acts 1:12). According to Josephus, this is a distance of 6 stadia, thus about 1,109 meters, or 3,637 feet.

C. Measures of Area.—Only one specific measure of area is found:

צמד, çémedh, "acre" (I Sam. 14:14; Isa. 5:10). As much land as a team of oxen (çémedh) can plow in one day.

The area of a piece of ground can also be determined by the quantity of seed required for sowing (I Kings 18:32).

D. Measures of Capacity.—Table XVI shows Old Testament measures of capacity.

Hômer and kōr have the same capacity; also ʼêphāh and bath; ʼômer and ʼissārôn are synonyms. In Ezekiel, and later, the kōr is reserved for liquids. In Isa. 40:12 שלש, shālish, "one third" (of an ʼêphāh), is rendered by "measure" in the King James and Revised Standard Versions.

TABLE XV. HEBREW SYSTEM OF LINEAR MEASURES

MEASURE	COMMON SCALE		EZEKIEL'S SCALE	
	millimeters	inches	millimeters	inches
cubit	444.25	17.49	518.29	20.405
span	222.12	8.745	259.14	10.202
handbreadth	74.04	2.915	74.04	2.915
finger	18.51	0.728	18.51	0.728

TABLE XVI. OLD TESTAMENT MEASURES OF CAPACITY

HEBREW		KJV	RSV	MEASURE
חמר	hômer	homer	homer	dry
כר	kōr	measure, cor	measure, cor	dry and liquid
לתך	léthekh	half homer	lethech	dry
איפה	ʼêphāh	ephah, measure	ephah, measure	dry
בת	bath	bath	bath	liquid
סאה	sᵉʼāh	measure	measure	dry
הין	hin	hin	hin	liquid
עמר	ʼômer	omer	omer	dry
עשרון	ʼissārôn	tenth deal	tenth part (of ephah)	dry
קב	qabh	cab	kab	dry and liquid
לג	lōgh	log	log	liquid

The ratio between the units of capacity is known from biblical and extrabiblical sources, mostly Hellenistic. It is shown in the following lists:

DRY MEASURES

1 ḥômer (kōr)	=	2	léthekh
	=	10	'êphāh
	=	30	s⁰'āh
	=	100	'ômer ('issārôn)
	=	180	qabh
	=	720	lōgh
1 léthekh	=	5	'êphāh
	=	15	s⁰'āh
	=	50	'ômer
	=	90	qabh
	=	360	lōgh
1 'êphāh	=	3	s⁰'āh
	=	10	'ômer
	=	18	qabh
	=	72	lōgh
1 s⁰'āh	=	3 1/3	'ômer
	=	6	qabh
	=	24	lōgh
1 'ômer ('issārôn)	=	1 4/5	qabh
	=	7 1/5	lōgh
1 qabh	=	4	lōgh

LIQUID MEASURES

1 kōr	=	10	bath
	=	60	hîn
	=	180	qabh
	=	720	lōgh
1 bath	=	6	hîn
	=	18	qabh
	=	72	lōgh
1 hîn	=	3	qabh
	=	12	lōgh
1 qabh	=	4	lōgh

The evaluation of the Hebrew measures of capacity in units of modern systems remains thus far uncertain. Two restored jars from Lachish, marked respectively with a royal seal and a private seal, have been assumed to contain one bath each, on account of their similarity with a jar stamped bath lammélekh, "royal bath," of which only fragments were recovered.[4] The latter, however, was certainly

[4] Charles H. Inge, "Post Scriptum on Ancient Hebrew Inscriptions," Palestine Exploration Quarterly for 1941, pp. 106-9.

smaller than the former two. William F. Albright has shown that the big Lachish jars were possibly twice as capacious as the jars labeled "royal bath."[5]

The average volume of the two restored jars from Lachish is 2,806.096 cubic inches, equivalent to 45.982 liters, or 12.147 U.S. gallons. If, according to Albright's hypothesis, they represent a double bath standard, the system of Hebrew measures of capacity may tentatively be expressed as shown in Table XVII.

The hypothetical character of Table XVII must be kept in mind. It does not agree with evaluations of Hebrew measures in terms of Hellenistic or Roman standards, e.g., bath= μετρητής (approximately 39 liters, or 10.3 U.S. gallons), and lōgh=sextarius (approximately 0.53 liters, or 1.12 U.S. pints). Such evaluations, formulated by ancient authors, do not express a strict equivalence, but rather a comparison, as we assimilate the yard to the meter, or the quart to the liter.

Measures of capacity in the New Testament fall into two classes:

a) Names of measures transcribed from the Hebrew:

βάτος, "measure" = Hebrew bath
κόρος, "measure" = Hebrew kōr
σάτον, "measure" = Hebrew s⁰'āh

b) Hellenistic and Roman measures:

μετρητής, "firkin" (KJV); "measure" (RSV). Liquid measure. About 39 liters, or 10.3 U.S. gallons.
χοῖνιξ, "measure" (KJV), "quart" (RSV). Dry measure. About 1.08 liters, or 0.98 U.S. dry quart.
μόδιος (Latin modius), "bushel" (Matt. 5:15). Dry measure. About 8.49 liters, or 7.68 U.S. dry quarts.
ξέστης (Latin sextarius), "pot" (Mark 7:4). Dry and liquid measure. About 0.53 liter, or 0.96 U.S. dry pint, or 1.12 U.S. liquid pints.

In the last two instances, however, the stress is not on the metrological value of the units mentioned.

[5] "The Excavation of Tell Beit Mirsim," Annual of the American Schools of Oriental Research, XXI-XXII (1941-43), 58, n. 7.

TABLE XVII. HEBREW MEASURES OF CAPACITY

HEBREW	CUBIC INCHES	LITERS	U.S. LIQUID MEASURES	U.S. DRY MEASURES
ḥômer = kōr	14,030.480	229.913	60.738 gal.	6.524 bu.
léthekh	7,015.240	114.956	30.369 gal.	3.262 bu.
'êphāh = bath	1,403.048	22.991	6.073 gal.	20.878 qt.
s⁰'āh	467.682	7.663		6.959 qt.
hîn	233.841	3.831	1.012 gal.	
'ômer = 'issārôn	140.304	2.299		2.087 qt.
qabh	77.947	1.277	1.349 qt.	1.159 qt.
lōgh	19.486	0.319	0.674 pt.	

E. Measures of Weight.—Old Testament measures of weight and their equivalents may be seen in Table XVIII.

The current ratio between the units of weight, as established from biblical and extrabiblical evidence, is shown as follows:

$$1 \ kikk\bar{a}r = \quad 60 \ m\bar{a}neh$$
$$= \ 3{,}000 \ sh\acute{e}qel$$
$$= \ 6{,}000 \ b\acute{e}qa`$$
$$= 60{,}000 \ g\bar{e}r\bar{a}h$$
$$1 \ m\bar{a}neh = \quad 50 \ sh\acute{e}qel$$
$$= \quad 100 \ b\acute{e}qa`$$
$$= \ 1{,}000 \ g\bar{e}r\bar{a}h$$
$$1 \ sh\acute{e}qel = \quad 2 \ b\acute{e}qa`$$
$$= \quad 20 \ g\bar{e}r\bar{a}h$$
$$1 \ b\acute{e}qa` = \quad 10 \ g\bar{e}r\bar{a}h$$

This system may have superseded another scale of weights, which Ezekiel would have restored in his ideal theocracy (Ezek. 45:12), and which may be expressed as follows:

$$1 \ kikk\bar{a}r = \quad 60 \ m\bar{a}neh$$
$$= \ 3{,}600 \ sh\acute{e}qel$$
$$= \ 7{,}200 \ b\bar{e}qa`$$
$$= 72{,}000 \ g\bar{e}r\bar{a}h$$
$$1 \ m\bar{a}neh = \quad 60 \ sh\acute{e}qel$$
$$= \quad 120 \ b\acute{e}qa`$$
$$= \ 1{,}200 \ g\bar{e}r\bar{a}h$$
$$1 \ sh\acute{e}qel = \quad 2 \ b\acute{e}qa`$$
$$= \quad 20 \ g\bar{e}r\bar{a}h$$
$$1 \ b\acute{e}qa` = \quad 10 \ g\bar{e}r\bar{a}h$$

The value of the *shéqel*, which is the basic unit of both systems, can be determined inductively from stone weights discovered in the course of archaeological excavations. The following averages were obtained from lists of weights compiled in 1932, and from material recently discovered at Beth Zur, Ain Shems,

Megiddo, Lachish, Tell Beit Mirsim, and Tell en-Nasbeh.[6] Dubious or defective samples have been excluded.

A first series of weights bears the conventional sign for *shéqel*, followed eventually with an indication of the number of standard units. Frequent multiples are 2, 4, 8, and 16 shekels. Average weight: 11.424 grams, or 176.29 grains. Uninscribed weights are often slightly lighter.

Some weights marked פים, *páyim*, average 7.624 grams, or 117.65 grains. If *páyim* is correctly interpreted "two thirds," the corresponding unit would be 11.436 grams, or 176.47 grains. These weights, together with a few uninscribed samples, might therefore be regarded as current fractions of the *shéqel* standard.

A few weights marked בקע, *béqa`*, average 6.112 grams, or 94.32 grains. Some uninscribed weights come close to these figures. If the *béqa`* weights are considered as half shekels (see above), the corresponding unit would be a weight of 12.224 grams, or 188.64 grains, noticeably heavier than the units of the previous series. They seem to represent a different standard.

A few weights marked נצף, *néçeph*, average 9.875 grams, or 152.39 grains, and compare with some uninscribed material. They are considerably lighter than the *shéqel* weights, and probably belong to a different standard.

Table XIX gives the equivalents of the entire series of Hebrew weights in metric notation and in weights avoirdupois.

[6] Georges A. Barrois, "Métrologie dans la Bible," *Revue Biblique*, XLI (1932), 50-76. O. R. Sellers, *The Citadel of Beth Zur* (Philadelphia: Westminster Press, 1933), p. 60. Elihu Grant and G. E. Wright, *Ain Shems Excavations V* (Haverford: 1939), p. 159, Pls. LII-LIII. R. S. Lamon and G. M. Shipton, *Megiddo, Seasons of 1925-34, Strata I-V* (Chicago: University of Chicago Press, 1939), Pl.

TABLE XVIII. OLD TESTAMENT MEASURES OF WEIGHT

HEBREW	KJV	RSV
כככר *kikkār*	talent	talent
מנה *māneh*	pound, maneh	mina
שקל *shéqel*	shekel	shekel
בקע *béqa`*	bekah, half a shekel	beka, half a shekel
גרה *gērāh*	gerah	gerah

TABLE XIX. EQUIVALENTS OF HEBREW WEIGHTS

HEBREW	COMMON SCALE (1 māneh = 50 shekels)		EZEKIEL'S SCALE (1 māneh = 60 shekels)	
	Metric	Avoirdupois	Metric	Avoirdupois
kikkār	34.272 kg.	75.558 lb.	41.126 kg.	88.485 lb.
māneh	571.2 g.	20.148 oz.	685.44 g.	24.178 oz.
shéqel	11.424 g.	176.29 gr.	11.424 g.	176.29 gr.
béqa`	5.712 g.	88.14 gr.	5.712 g.	88.14 gr.
gērāh	0.571 g.	8.81 gr.	0.571 g.	8.81 gr.

Few allusions are made to weights in the New Testament. The words τάλαντον, "talent," and μνᾶ (Hebrew *māneh*), "pound," refer, not to weights, but to sums of money (see below).

In John 12:3; 19:39, λίτρα is a Greek interpretation of the Roman *libra*, "pound," about 326 grams, or 0.719 pound avoirdupois.

IV. Numismatics

A. Early Means of Exchange.—Among the Canaanites and the Hebrews, largely devoted to pastoral life, the sheep, or its equivalent in precious metal, constituted the earliest standard for commercial transactions. Thus the Septuagint translates the Hebrew קשׂיטה, *qesîṭāh*, by ἀμνός, ἀμνάς, "lamb" or "ewe." The ingots of metal had to be weighed out in each transaction, since their value and purity were not officially guaranteed. Hence sums of money were counted according to standards of weight, as in Gen. 23:16. In the King James Version the rendering of קשׂיטה, *qesîṭāh*, and כסף, *késeph*, "silver," by "pieces of money," or "pieces of silver," constitutes an anachronism, inasmuch as it assumes the early use of coined currency, which was not extant among the Hebrews until after the Exile.

B. Persian Period.—Coins are mentioned for the first time in the books of Ezra and Nehemiah, and in I Chr. 29:7, where their use is attributed to David by anachronism.

The Hebrew words אדרכנים, *'adharkōnîm*, and דרכמונים, *darkemōnîm*, "drams," probably refer to the Persian daric, a gold coin issued by Darius, weighing 8.41 grams, or 130 grains.

Silver coins weighing 5.60 grams, or 86.4 grains, corresponding to one twentieth of the weight of silver equivalent to the gold standard, were known as silver darics, or Median shekels. It is not clear whether Neh. 5:15 and 10:32 refer to these Median shekels or to weighed silver. The interpretation of מנה, *māneh*, "pound of silver" (Ezra 2:69; Neh. 7:70-72), as a sum of 100 Median shekels is also uncertain.

A few silver coins of uncertain denomination found in southern Palestine bear the Hebrew letters יהד, interpreted *Yehûdh*, the Persian province of Judea.

C. Hellenistic Period.—Greek currency prevailed in Palestine after the conquest of Alexander the Great. The standard was the silver drachma, the weight of which was reduced from 4.32 grams, or 66.6 grains, to 3.41 grams, or 52.6 grains, in Egypt, Palestine, and the provinces

CIV. David Diringer, "The Early Hebrew Weights Found at Lachish," *Palestine Exploration Quarterly for 1942*, pp. 82-103. W. F. Albright, "The Excavation of Tell Beit Mirsim," *Annual of the American Schools of Oriental Research*, XXI-XXII (1941-43), 76-77. Chester C. McCown in *Tell en-Nasbeh* (Berkeley, Calif.: The Palestine Institute of Pacific School of Religion and the American Schools of Oriental Research, 1947), I, 259.

ruled by the Ptolemies. The usual denominations were:

tetradrachma = 4 drachmas
didrachma = 2 drachmas
drachma
hemidrachma = ½ drachma

The gold stater, weighing approximately 8.60 grams, or 132.7 grains, equivalent in theory to 20 drachmas, was rated according to variable banking conditions.

Bronze currency in various denominations was issued to meet the needs of local trade. Its relative value with regard to silver was subject to frequent fluctuations.

When Palestine passed under the Syrian rule (198 B.C.), the coins of the Seleucids replaced Ptolemaic currency. However the mints of Askelon and Gaza continued to strike their own silver and bronze.

D. Maccabean Period.—In 142 B.C. the Palestinian Jews gained recognition as an autonomous community in the frame of the Seleucid state and were granted the right of coinage, apparently limited to bronze currency. Coins were struck in the name of the Hasmonaean high priests (the Maccabees) and of the community of the Jews, with legends in archaic Hebrew letters. Alexander Jannaeus and his widow Alexandra issued a currency with bilingual legends (Hebrew and Greek), in which they assumed the titles of king and queen.

E. Roman Period. 1. Coinage of the Roman Administration (63 B.C.–A.D. 66).—The introduction of Roman money followed the conquest of Palestine by Pompey (63 B.C.). The basic bronze currency was the object of frequent adjustments, and the silver coinage, introduced in the third century B.C., had continually deteriorated. The denarius, originally worth 4.53 grams, or 70 grains of silver, weighed 3.88 grams, or 60 grains, at the end of the third century B.C., to be reduced further to 3.43 grams, or 53 grains, under Nero. Gold was rare at all times, the official rate of exchange being 25 silver denarii for 1 aureus, or gold denarius.

The following charts show the relative value of usual silver and bronze coins in the time of Augustus:

SILVER COINS

denarius	= 16 asses
quinarius	= 8 asses
sestertius	= 4 asses

BRONZE COINS

sestertius	= 4 asses
dupondius	= 2 asses
as	
semis	= ½ as
quadrans	= ¼ as

TABLE XX. HELLENISTIC CURRENCY MENTIONED IN THE NEW TESTAMENT

HELLENISTIC CURRENCY		KJV	RSV	APPROXIMATE VALUE
τάλαντον	6,000 drachmas	talent	talent	$960.00
μνᾶ	100 drachmas	pound	pound	16.00
στατήρ	tetradrachma	piece of money	shekel	
δίδραχμον	didrachma (paid to the temple)	tribute money	half shekel	
δραχμή	drachma	piece of money	silver coin	0.16

TABLE XXI. ROMAN CURRENCY MENTIONED IN THE NEW TESTAMENT

ROMAN CURRENCY		KJV	RSV	APPROXIMATE VALUE
δηνάριον	denarius	penny	denarius, coin	$ 0.20
ἀσσάριον	as	farthing	penny	
κοδράντης	quadrans	farthing	penny	

Whereas Rome reserved to itself the privilege of silver coinage, Palestinian mints were allowed to strike bronze coins of the usual denominations. This currency may be divided into three categories: (a) coins of the cities holding a charter of franchise; (b) coins of Herod and the Herodians, viz., the tetrarchs, Agrippa I and Agrippa II; (c) coins of the governors of Judea (the procurators).

2. Coinage of the First Jewish Revolt (A.D. 66-70).—Silver shekels of the average weight of 14.27 grams, or 220.2 grains, were struck together with half shekels and quarter shekels of the same type and standard. Owing to the increasing scarcity of silver, bronze tokens of half and quarter shekels were issued the fourth year of the revolt. These coins have been attributed erroneously to Simon Maccabee.

Coins commemorating the victory of Rome over the Jewish nationalists were struck in the name of Vespasian, with the legend *Iudaea capta,* "Judea conquered."

3. Coinage of the Second Jewish Revolt (A.D. 132-35).—The coins of the second revolt fall into three categories: (a) tetradrachmas, often restruck on imperial silver; (b) restruck silver denarii; (c) bronze coins, most of them restruck on imperial brass. This currency was issued in the name of the Jewish leader, Simon Bar Cocheba, who assumed the title of *nāsî',* or "prince" of Israel. One denarius and several bronze coins bear the name and title of "Eleazar the Priest," of uncertain identity.

Local currency issued after the victory of Hadrian over the Jews (A.D. 136) bears the new name of Jerusalem, which had become officially *Colonia Aelia Capitolina.*

F. Appendixes. 1. Money in the New Testament.—References are made to Hellenistic and Roman currency, the denominations proper to Roman money being translated into Greek. Tables XX and XXI show the English translations and the approximate value of the currency mentioned in the New Testament.

According to the equivalence formulated in Mark 12:42, two lepta, "mites" (KJV), or "copper coins" (RSV), make up a quadrans. It is doubtful, however, whether or not the lepton belongs to the Roman series of bronze coins.

The values in American currency in the above tables are those given in the footnotes of the Revised Standard Version. They are not altogether consistent, and may be regarded at best as rough approximations. They seem to be based on the weight of the coins, but the variability and deterioration of ancient standards do not make a rigorous evaluation possible. Furthermore, the purchasing power of Hellenistic and Roman currencies cannot be determined to any reasonable degree of accuracy.

2. *Illustrations of Selected Coins Current in Ancient Palestine*

a) Persian

1. Persian daric, gold
Obv. Kneeling figure of king holding spear and bow.
Rev. Incuse square.

2. Local mint, bronze
Obv. Bearded head wearing crested helmet.
Rev. Male figure seated on winged wheel. יהד
(Judea).

b) Hellenistic

3. Alexander: tetradrachma, silver
Obv. Head of Hercules.
Rev. Zeus Aetophoros. Βασιλεως Αλεξανδρου.

4. Ptolemy I: tetradrachma, silver
Obv. Diademed head of Ptolemy.
Rev. Eagle on thunderbolt. Πτολεμαιου Βασι-
λεως.

5. Antiochus III: tetradrachma, silver
Obv. Diademed head of Antiochus.
Rev. Apollo seated on omphalos. Βασιλεως
Αντιοχου.

c) Maccabean

6. John Hyrcanus I: bronze
Obv. Wreath. יהוחנן הכהן הגדל וחבר היה(ו)דים
(Johanan the high priest and the community
of the Jews).
Rev. Pomegranate and cornucopias.

7. Alexander Jannaeus: bronze
Obv. Anchor. Βασιλεω[ς Αλεξανδρ]ου.
Rev. Lily. יהונתן המלך (Jonathan the King).

8. Alexander Jannaeus: bronze
Obv. Palm. יהונתן המלך (Jonathan the King).
Rev. Lily.

9. Alexander Jannaeus: bronze

Obv. Wreath. (יהד(ים) יהד(ים) יתן הכהן הגדל וחבר היהד (Jona-
than the high priest and the community of the
Jews).
Rev. Pomegranate and cornucopias.

10. Alexander Jannaeus: bronze

Obv. Anchor. Βασ[ιλεω]ς Αλεξανδρου.
Rev. Wheel. יהונתן המלך (Jonathan the King).

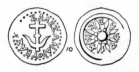

11. Antigonus Mattathias: bronze

Obv. Cornucopias. (דל) וחבר מתתיה הכהן ג
[?]היהודה (Mattathias the high priest and the
community of the Jews).
Rev. Ivy wreath. Βασ[ιλ]εως Αντιγονου.

12. Antigonus Mattathias: bronze

Obv. Unidentified object.
Rev. Seven-branched candlestick. [Βασιλ]εως
Αν[τιγονου].

d) Roman

HEROD AND THE HERODIANS

13. Herod the Great: bronze

Obv. Tripod. Βασιλεως Ηρωδου.
Rev. Tiara surmounted by star and palms.

14. Herod the Great: bronze

Obv. Caduceus. Βασιλεως Ηρωδου.
Rev. Pomegranate with leaves.

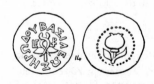

15. Herod the Great: bronze

Obv. Wreath. Βασιλεως Ηρωδου.
Rev. Tripod and palms.

16. Herod the Great: bronze

Obv. Cornucopia. Βασιλ. Ηρωδ.
Rev. Eagle.

17. Herod Agrippa I: bronze

Obv. Umbrella. Βασιλεως Αγριπα.
Rev. Three ears of barley.

18. Herod Agrippa I: bronze

Obv. Head of Agrippa. Βασιλευς μεγας Αγριπ-
πας Φιλοκαισαρ.
Rev. City goddess holding cornucopia, leaning
on boat rudder. Καισαρια η προς [Σεβαστ]ω
λιμενι (Caesarea on the Sea).

19. Herod Agrippa II: bronze

Obv. Head of Vespasian. Αυτοκρ. Ουεσ. Καισαρι
Σβαστω (*sic*).
Rev. Tyché holding cornucopia and ears of
barley. Ετ ΔΙ (Year 14, era of Tiberias=A.D.
74). Βα. Αγριππα.

FREE CITIES. EMPERORS. PROCURATORS

20. Ascalon: hemidrachma, silver

Obv. Bust of city goddess.
Rev. War galley. Ασ. ιερας (Ascalon Holy) LBΣ
(Year 202, Seleucid era=111-110 B.C.).

21. Ascalon: tetradrachma, silver

Obv. Cleopatra VII.
Rev. Eagle on thunderbolt, dove. Ασκαλ[ωνος
ιε]ρας ασυλου (Ascalon Holy, Sacred) LNE
(Year 55, era of 84 B.C.=29 B.C.).

22. Ascalon: bronze

Obv. Bust of city goddess.
Rev. War galley. ΣOP (Year 176, era of 104 B.C.
=A.D. 72) Aσ (Ascalon).

23. Tiberius: denarius, silver

Obv. Head of Tiberius. TI.CAESAR DIVI AVG.F. AVGVSTVS.

Rev. Livia (?), holding scepter. PONTIF. MAXIM.

24. Pontius Pilate, Procurator: bronze

Obv. Ladle. Τιβεριου Καισαρος LIΣ (Year 16 of Tiberius=A.D. 29-30).

Rev. Three ears of barley. Ιουλια Καισαρος.

25. Pontius Pilate, Procurator: bronze

Obv. Augur wand. Τιβεριου Καισαρος.

Rev. Wreath. LIZ (Year 17 of Tiberius=A.D. 30-31).

26. Antonius Felix, Procurator: bronze

Obv. Palm. LE (Year 5 of Nero=A.D. 58-59) Καισαρος.

Rev. Wreath. Νερωνος.

First Revolt

27. Shekel, silver

Obv. שקל ישראל (Shekel of Israel) א (Year 1= A.D. 66-67).

Rev. Three pomegranates. ירושלם קדשה (Jerusalem Holy).

28. Half shekel, silver

Obv. חצי השקל (½ shekel) שב (Year 2=A.D. 67-68).

Rev. ירושלים הקדושה (Jerusalem the Holy).

29. Token, half shekel, bronze

Obv. Citron between two bundles of twigs. שנת ארבע (Year 4=A.D. 69-70) חצי (one half).

Rev. Palm tree, two baskets. לגאלת ציון (For the redemption of Zion).

30. Bronze
Obv. Amphora. שנת שתים (Year 2=A.D. 67-68).
Rev. Vine branch. חרת ציון (Liberty of Zion).

31. Bronze
Obv. Bundle of twigs between two citrons. ארבע
שנת (Year 4 =A.D. 69-70).
Rev. Cup. לגאלת ציון (For the redemption of
Zion).

32. Imperial: sestertius, bronze
Obv. Head of Vespasian. IMP.CAES.VESPA-
SIAN.AUG. P.M. TR.P. P.P. COS.III.
Rev. Judea guarded by soldier under palm tree.
IVDAEA CAPTA S.C. Struck at Rome, A.D.
71.

33. Imperial: bronze
Obv. Head of Titus. Αυτοκρ. Τιτος Καισαρ.
Rev. Palm tree, Nike. Ιουδαιας εαλωκυιας (Judea
conquered). Struck in Palestine.

SECOND REVOLT

34. Tetradrachma, silver
Obv. Star above temple (or Torah shrine ?)
שמעון (Simon).
Rev. Citron and bundle of twigs. לחרות ירושלם
(For the liberty of Jerusalem).

35. Denarius, silver
Obv. Wreath. שמע (Simon).
Rev. Jug and palm. שב לחר ישא (*sic*) (Year 2
of the liberty of Israel=*ca*. A.D. 133).

36. Silver
Obv. Wreath. שמעון (Simon).
Rev. Three-stringed lyre. לחרות ירושלם (For the
liberty of Jerusalem).

163

37. Silver

Obv. Bunch of grapes. שמ[ע]ון (Simon).

Rev. Two trumpets. לחרות ירושלם (For the liberty of Jerusalem).

38. Bronze

Obv. Bunch of grapes. שנת א[ח]ת לגאלת ישר (First year of the redemption of Israel=*ca.* A.D. 132).

Rev. Palm tree. אלעזר הכהן (Eleazar the Priest).

39. Bronze

Obv. Vine leaf. שנת אחת [לג]אלת ישראל (First year of the redemption of Israel).

Rev. Palm tree. שמעו[ן] נשיא ישראש (*sic*) (Simon Prince of Israel).

40. Bronze

Obv. Head of Hadrian. IMP. CAES. TRAI. HADRIAN. AVG.

Rev. Jupiter and two female deities in a distyle temple. COL(onia) AEL(ia) CAP(itolina).

THE STUDY OF THE BIBLE

by GEORGE ARTHUR BUTTRICK

Perhaps this article is carrying coals to Newcastle, for presumably the man who buys and reads *The Interpreter's Bible* already knows how to study the Bible. But the presumption may not be justified. Preachers and teachers of the Book may come to the Scriptures by the wrong door: not always do they read it that it may read them. In any event, people who use *The Interpreter's Bible* are the very people who must guide others in the study of the Bible. So these lines, if rightly written, may have at least an indirect value.

I. Barriers to Bible Study

Sometimes the church has seemed intent to discourage the study of the Bible. It binds the Book in funereal black. It prints the text in type almost too small to read. It clutters the sacred page with side references and footnotes. It cuts its natural paragraphs, as if with ruthless shears, into verses—a violence from which apostle and evangelist would have recoiled. It makes its poetry look like prose. The years have gone far to defeat the Reformation hope that the Bible might become an open book for the "man behind the plow."

Even more serious failures must be laid on the church's conscience. The Bible is a library, and the library is itself an anthology. The library comprises religious interpretations of history, hymns, idyls, sermons, letters; and it covers a period of several centuries. Then why are its books arranged so as to hide true chronology? If the Old Testament were so printed that Amos and Hosea came first, with the Pentateuch in its place of comparatively late authorship, the reader could no longer assume that the books of the Law (whatever their elements of antiquity) came from the childhood of the race. If the New Testament set most of the epistles first, followed by Mark, and if Luke and Matthew were shown as the work of the church toward the end of the first century, the reader would not be misled into believing that

the Synoptic Gospels are simple biographies of Jesus. Rather he would be prepared to study them for what they are, namely, primers for catechumens in the Christian faith.

Preachers have urged people to "read the Bible." People have tried, and have often been baffled. For though some passages are so clear that "he that runs may read," there are others (as in the Epistle to the Romans) so hard that to tell a beginner, "Read the Bible" is as unfair as if an elementary-school teacher were to say to his class, "Study Euclid." The Bible is not an easy book to read. Its gold is given sometimes in nuggets, as in the twenty-third psalm or the Sermon on the Mount; but more often it comes in ore to be dug, smelted, and refined. Books which give a brief introduction to each biblical book and place it in its approximate chronological order perform a necessary service and meet a claim long overdue, for they enable the reader to answer such questions as, "Who wrote this book, and why, and when, and where?" Surely the time has come to strike from the Bible the fetters which the church itself has wittingly or unwittingly forged.

II. Nature and Purpose of the Book

Then how should a man study the Bible? He must begin with the right presuppositions. To pretend that he can completely suspend judgment until the whole Bible has been read and pondered is just that—a pretense. Judgments, based on deepest experience, have long ago been formed, and are now part of widespread conviction. In any event, there is no adventure without an initial faith. Every reader must make some assumption about the Bible, if only that it is a book. Even in that assumption he would be wrong, for the Bible is both a library of books and *the* Book, as ages of experience have testified. The man who said of the dictionary that it "has great variety but little plot" is an instance of what happens when a book is read with wrong assumptions. A student who expected to find a historical romance in a book of mathematics, or sober history in a volume of Shakespeare's plays, would be both puzzled and affronted in the reading. So with any man who expects to find in the Bible what it was never intended to give.

The Bible is not merely "great literature." It has glowing passages that are supreme in the realm of letters, as many a pre-eminent literary artist has been quick to see. Nevertheless Bible authors would have been dismayed by the suggestion that they had a literary purpose. The danger of all books that treat the Bible as "literature" is precisely that they may distract the reader from the Bible's deeper intent. Indeed it could be argued that the Bible is on guard *against* literature, and against all other "words of man's wisdom" that might offer to the reader a refuge from the tremendous onsets of God.

The Bible is not a book of science. If this fact had been acknowledged and remembered, many a conflict that has brought discredit on both science and religion could have been avoided. The 139th psalm is true whether the earth is flat or round. The parable of the prodigal son is the history of men and man, though the Bible may seem to be falsified by "evolution," and though "evolution" may yield place to a doctrine of "contingency" not essentially different from Genesis! Science, however necessary, is sensate, and cannot sound the depths. It is of the analytic mind, and therefore cannot serve the wholeness of man's nature. It can give some answer to "How?" but none to "Why?" Only faith can say why, and every man must live by some faith. So the story of the Tower of Babel, though it is not a scientific account of the origin of languages, is tragic truth concerning that pride in man which destroys the work of man's own hands, whether in Babel or Berlin; and which always brings such confusion of tongues that Russia cannot understand the United States or Hitler's Germany comprehend the motives of Norway. The Bible is not a book of science. It has mightier business on hand. It will be read when our meticulous science has been forgotten.

The Bible is not a book of history, even though that fact may not be as readily acceptable as the two above cited. Such books as Samuel and Kings are frequently described as "historical books" and the Gospels are called "lives" of Jesus; but both titles, despite their measure of truth, are misnomers. For when the Bible authors write history they are not intent to provide an "objective story." It is doubtful if such objectivity would be desirable, even if it were possible; but in any event, the Bible does not covet it. Its "history" is written in such a way as to show how a certain nation and its individ-

uals were apprehended by God. This fact holds not less, but almost more, of the Gospels; for manifestly these four priceless books are too scant and disjointed ever to pose as complete "biographies of Jesus." Rather are they central in the prime intent of all scripture revelation: with one voice they say, "Here God came and laid his hand on men!"

The Bible, despite frequent avowals, is not in original instance a book of "man's quest for God." Initially, in prime purpose it is intent to show that no quest on man's part is possible except under God's prompting. Our search for him is quickened by his prior finding of us. The Bible is not a book of "comparative religion," for it tells of a revelation that is precisely *beyond* compare: "The LORD our God is one LORD: And thou shalt love the LORD thy God with all thine heart, and with all thy soul, and with all thy might"; and (in that love) "thy neighbor as thyself" (Deut. 6:4-5; Lev. 19:18). The one word of the Bible is: "Halts by me that footfall."[1] Its whole story is of the siege of Mansoul by "this tremendous Lover."[2] It is not an earthbound book either of literature or science, history or human quest: its sole and all-comprehending purpose is to tell of the invasion of earth by heaven's succor and demand. The reader is not required in any dark coercion to believe this claim "sight unseen," but he should understand the claim. Moreover, it is fair to ask that he expose himself to it. So the study of the Bible requires him to say, whether neophyte or theologian, "Generations of people have said that God has found them through this Book. I will be neither servile nor embattled, but will give the Book its chance with me." A man must approach the study of the Bible with the right presuppositions.

III. The Meaning of Inspiration

This faith that the Bible is a book of God's self-revealing, and thereafter of man's search for God, does not demand the acceptance of any arbitrary doctrine of inspiration. But it does print the words "veritably inspired" over all Scripture. For the men who wrote the Bible contend that God found them: that is why they wrote. Likewise, hosts who have read the Bible testify that through it God has found them also: that is why they have continued to read. But none of this need be equated with the theory of verbal inerrancy. Of that latter doctrine, which has repelled thousands of youth who might otherwise have been won to eager study of the Scriptures, we had better say just what Jesus said of similar doctrines, "Ye [make] the

[1] Francis Thompson, "The Hound of Heaven."
[2] *Ibid.*

word of God of none effect through your tradition" (Mark 7:12-13).

Anyone who will trouble to read in this Commentary the three articles on "The History of the Interpretation of the Bible" will understand that the doctrine of literal inspiration is an interloper in the "Interpreter's House," and far too weak to dispossess the proper tenant. What aberrations are invited by this rigid theory —belief in a flat earth, belief in a host of demons inhabiting the middle air! What crimes are condoned—all the way from killing witches to approving the institution of slavery! An unprejudiced reader would see, if left alone, that the doctrine of literal infallibility has been imposed on the Book. The writers do not write as men who are the blind and helpless instruments of God. Luke in his prologue tells of choosing his method and plan, and nobody could pretend that the respective personal traits of Matthew or Paul have been canceled by inspiration. Yet surely nobody could sincerely expose himself to these writings and deny inspiration—by whatever name. We must say of every Bible author what Browning said of Bunyan and *The Pilgrim's Progress,* and say it with profounder conviction: " 'Tis my belief, God spoke: no tinker has such powers." [3]

Is the theory of literalism a fear? Perhaps it is a worthy fear. The creaturely mind seeks refuge in a simplicity. Marxism is a prime instance: man is the spawn of the economic system, so all that is needed is a changed system, and, presto, heaven on earth! So in religion also men have coveted an impossible simplicity. What could be simpler than the doctrine that here is the literal and explicit Word of God? Actually we show not reverence, but a mild blasphemy, when we assume that God turns a man into a typewriter; and certainly the theory is a disparagement also of human nature. But it seems simple and safe. It lifts from the mind a burden of painful study under the guidance of the Holy Spirit. Yet the theory has elements of worth, for how could it have come if men had not found God in scripture? And is not God the sovereign Lord? When a man sees God in the temple "high and lifted up," he may be forgiven for insisting that every stone now has inviolable sacredness—though the stones still crumble.

The emphasis in the phrase "literal inspiration" is not on the adjective, but on the noun; and there all Christian conviction finds common ground. The Old Testament tells of God choosing a nation to make covenant with them, not that they might bask in his favor, but that they might make his name and nature known among men. The history and songs of that nation are

[3] "Ned Bratts."

witness to the covenant, for through them God has found our race. The prophets tell of the national failure to keep the covenant, and of the holy grace that renewed it. The New Testament tells how the covenant, even God himself, came to earth in a Man—the mercy of the covenant being sealed in his death ("This . . . is the new covenant in my blood"), the power of the covenant being proved in his resurrection. The Book is a record of the self-revelation of God. Thus the record *becomes one* with the revelation, in even closer bond than the announcement of good news becomes one with the glad tidings it proclaims. In that fact, at long last, is the inspiration of the Scriptures. The surge of God's ocean moves through its pages: "That Voice is round me like a bursting sea." [4] We need not try to define inspiration in terms more exact, whether "literal" or "plenary"; for if God could be defined by man, God would no longer be God. God is his own evidence. God is his own interpreter. So the Bible is *the Book,* the central sun from which all other books receive their light.

Now we can understand the reason why lowly folk find revelation in the Bible (or are found by revelation), despite all fetters of printing and verse-snippets and scrambled chronology which the church has fastened on it, and despite all ignorance in the reader. For God speaks through the Book: it is the voice of his self-revealing grace. It is his inbreathing (inspiration), more intimately than a man's voice is the breath and presence of the man. Yet the Bible is never to be confused with man's voice. So when a reader comes to the Book in humility saying, "For thee only do I wait," God finds him despite every barrier. The old-time boxes of Bible texts were not all folly. Many of us can remember them, a text on each tiny roll of paper, and how the godly in time of crisis would "draw a text," and thus consult the oracles of God. Of course the texts were chosen beforehand, from such shining chapters as Ps. 91; Isa. 40; John 14; and Rom. 8. Imagine the consternation and tumult had the texts been culled from the "begats," or from the Levitical laws, or from "Beware of dogs"! But even allowing for the carefulness of prior choice, the striking fitness of the counsel or comfort in the "drawn text" cannot be explained merely as "coincidence." That word is a description, not an explanation. The explanation goes back to the fact of inspiration. God had already found men in those passages from his Book. Therefore they were chosen for the box; therefore they "found" men again in the day of crisis.

So the way to study the Bible is to come to it with the right presuppositions. This does not

[4] Thompson, *op. cit.*

mean "begging the question," but it does mean awareness of the fact that the Book is not primarily literature or science or history, or the record of man's search: men tell in the Book how God took them unawares. Men have claimed to find in it, with shining and martyred grace to support the claim, the very oracle of God. The reader, however skeptical, must at least make acknowledgment of that radiant claim.

IV. Rewards of Bible Study

But though neither the barriers that have been built around the Book nor ignorance in the reader can stay the holy and redeeming onsets of God in scripture, the barriers and ignorance cannot be made a virtue. The stars can speak of God to people unversed in astronomy; but other factors being equal, the astronomer with his Mount Wilson observatory is likelier to bow before God's wonders in the sky. It must be granted that other factors are not always equal, and that the astronomer can miss the celestial woods in his absorbed study of the celestial trees. Is it not a word of T. E. Lawrence that though the Arabs know little of astronomical science, they can still find God between the stars? Knowledge is always under threat from pride of the mind, not least Bible knowledge. Thus even the study of the Scriptures can be the occasion, though not the cause, of a man's damnation. But knowledge and reverence are *not* antithetic terms: knowledge can lead to deeper reverence. Festus was mistaken when he said to Paul, "Much learning doth make thee mad" (Acts 26:24). There is no premium on ignorance. Granted that a Bible student continues to say, "For thee only do I wait," more knowledge will bring more godliness.

The Bible shines with brighter light if the reader knows the correct text of the Bible and its original meaning. For such knowledge we are dependent upon the lower or textual critic and the lexicographer. Their study is not criticism in the sense of carping. It is not scrutiny for the purpose of detecting error, but rather a study of manuscripts and a grateful exploring of the treasure of meaning in Bible word and phrase. The student should be quick to welcome the light that has thus broken from God's Book. Instances are legion. Ps. 139 is probably composite; and the main poem, when set free, gains in clarity and searching power, while the associated scripture reveals its own treasure. Isa. 53 has extra poignancy and power when it is understood in its context and its alternate phrases are read as a colloquy between Yahweh and the kings of the earth. The verb used in the phrase "They have their reward" in Matt. 6:5, concerning ostentation in prayer, was used in writing receipts, so that the phrase is equivalent to our "They have a receipt for it"; but the reward in Matt. 6:6, promised to sincere and lowly prayer, is represented by a different and more generous word (ἀποδώσει): "Thy Father shall render back [or grant] unto thee." When the student further finds that "openly" is a gloss (surely prompted by man's false pride?), the whole passage stabs the soul awake. The new commandment of Jesus is new in very truth when his word love (ἀγάπη) is properly construed, namely, not as any earth-bound sexual love (ἔρως) or friendship love (φιλία) which can decay or break under strain, but as God's own love come to earth in Jesus Christ. The word "keep" (the Greek φρουρήσει) becomes almost apocalypse when we understand its implications: something precious that must be kept in some sure and secret place, with a sentinel set to guard it; "The peace of God . . . shall keep [sentinel] your [precious] hearts and minds in [the sure and secret place which is] Christ Jesus" (Phil. 4:7). As for the importance of understanding the unity of a passage, let the reader reread I Cor. 13 from its proper beginning in I Cor. 12:27, and see if the meaning of that great hymn to Christian love does not glow with purer fire.

Similarly, the voice of God speaks more clearly in the Bible when the reader understands higher criticism. Again the term may be a misfortune, for we misconstrue "criticism" to mean censoriousness, whereas actually it means appreciation. Higher criticism enables the Bible reader to appreciate the background of a given Bible book. Do we not rightly ask of any other book: "Who wrote it? For whom—Chinese or Britishers? Is it old or new? What purpose prompted the book?" These questions are valid also for the inspired Book; for when God speaks through a man, God does not destroy the man, but employs the man's individual traits in divine humility, and awaits the man's consent. "Whom shall I send, and who will go for us?" (Isa. 6:8.) Job is dramatic poetry, surely mightier even than the *Antigone,* and should so be read. Ruth is an idyl, with just as much truth as if it had been history: did not Jesus tell stories, and so convict the world of truth? Daniel in its later chapters is apocalypse, a philosophy of past history cast into the form of visions, as springboard for the prediction and sure hope of the coming Deliverer; and honest study of the book should long ago have rescued it from calamitymongers who try to find in it cabalistic symbols of current events. Isaiah is not one book, as a cursory reading of the Bible would assume, for there is a gap of centuries between the end of ch. 39 and the beginning of ch. 40; and when chs. 1–39 and chs. 40–66 are treated as two separate units, and each is understood under its rightful authorship and era, new worlds open to the student of the Bible. The Gospel of Matthew must be dated perhaps as late as A.D. 95, and may have been written in the Syrian church. It reflects the turmoil of its time—the uncertain tenure of the new faith in the Roman Empire, for instance, and the strife between synagogue and church; and when the Gospel is thus read, it gathers fresh meanings and a fervent power. Each Bible book, such as an epistle of Paul, was first written for its own time, even though it holds truth for all time; and the study of the Bible requires a knowledge of the background of each book. This knowledge is an "opening" for God's Word.

Study of the meaning of word and study of the background of the book: these two realms, even though thoroughly mastered, are still only provinces of the total kingdom of Bible study. There are wider reaches of knowledge. Further study is indispensable as the knowledge of our world is indispensable to a student seeking to understand the United States. Let us take certain phrases to see how they carry questions into this wider realm. "In the year that king Uzziah died I saw also the Lord" (Isa. 6:1). Who was King Uzziah, and why should his death have been a mark deep-scored in Isaiah's memory? That Bible passage, along with how much else in the Old Testament, cannot be understood without a study of the history of Israel. "And they went forth with them from Ur of the Chaldees, to go into the land of Canaan" (Gen. 11:31). There we realize that the whole history of Israel, though held within the special covenant of God, was yet an emergent from the far vaster history of the ancient world. Abraham's trek, his going out, "not knowing whither he went" (Heb. 11:8), in obedience to an imperious Voice, becomes for us an affair of more poignant courage when we trace his journeyings within and around the Fertile Crescent. "The abomination that maketh desolate" (Dan. 11:31; 12:11): that phrase leads directly to the desecration of the Jewish temple by Antiochus, and gives reminder that the history of Israel throughout its course was interlocked with that of surrounding lands. So with the New Testament. Who were the Pharisees, the Sadducees, the Zealots? Who was King Agrippa before whom Paul appeared, and how was Agrippa's land linked with Judea? Why were the merchants of Ephesus so intent to defend the worship of Diana of the Ephesians against the inroads of the new Christian faith? What kind of praise and polity in the early church is implied in such a sentence as "They continued steadfastly in the apostles' doctrine and fellowship, and in breaking of bread, and in prayers" (Acts 2:42)? This Commentary offers concentric circles of knowledge to the student—understanding of the meaning of word and phrase, understanding of the book in which word and phrase occur, and understanding of the national and world history from which the book sprang to speak aloud the Word of God.

The Bible is far from easy reading. It can be understood, but "not without dust and heat." Why should any man shrink from the task? So rich is the treasure, "a pearl of great price," even the kingdom of God, that a man to gain it should count the pain all joy and the world well lost. A neighbor spends years to master the mechanics of the radio, and we do not laugh at him. Another devotes half a lifetime to Shakespeare or Beethoven, and we count him no fool. Then why is not all life well spent on the study of the Bible? This is the Book through which God moves in ocean might—now in the calm of a sunset sea, now in judgment storm, now in the tidal mercy that floats all our beached vessels. This is the only Book of Jesus Christ, whose life is the "master light of all our seeing," whose tragic cross is the taking away of the sins of the world, whose resurrection is the hope of men aghast at death's blight. Why is not all life well spent in the study of such a Book? If choice had to be made between this Book and all others, there would be no choice: who would not choose the sun against ten million candles?

V. Bible Study and Prayer

But this should be said, even at risk of seeming to disavow the foregoing plan for lifelong study of the Book: knowledge is not the prime essential in Bible study. Neither is ignorance: the church has been shamed, and men beyond the church alienated from the Book, by "proof texts" quoted to support a hundred aberrations —white supremacy, the prevalence of poverty, dire prophecies a thousand times falsified and a thousand times renewed. No man should offer suffrages to a darkened mind. Yet the reader should confront the fact that a professor erudite in the Scriptures may miss salvation, while the lowly saint on his knees before the Book may know the Presence and almost feel the Hand.

The dilemma of scholarship has become acute in our time, namely this: that knowledge must be pursued, but is always open to mistake and is never complete. Wisdom can tarry while facts multiply. Already in almost any field, including the field of Bible study, the glut of facts is such that no man can digest them. As for the meaning of Bible words and phrases, that study leads out into a study of languages—not only of Hebrew and Greek, but of cognate tongues. As for the study of the background of the Bible, that soon involves the student in archaeology, and that in its turn leads to anthropology and a dozen allied inquiries of like scope. This knowledge must be pursued; but it is constantly outmoded and never complete. Thus the study of the Gospels has moved somewhat as follows: simple records (as was supposed) became the Synoptic problem and the Johannine problem; and these led to a painful probing into questions of date, authorship, and sources; and that, in turn, to a realization that the church, instead of being simply and solely produced by the Gospels, also produced them under the very Spirit of Christ; and that recognition has led in our time to form criticism and an attempt to disentangle from all additions and redactions "the core of tradition." Only a naïve optimist could pretend that the process will end in some impregnable rock of knowledge. Yet only an equally naïve pessimist could pretend that the quest has been in vain, or that any man has honorable discharge from the study of the Bible. The inevitable incompleteness of Bible knowledge does not permit us to sell out to some obscurantism. It means rather that we should pursue the quest

> beyond the sunset, and the baths
> Of all the western stars, until [we] die,[5]

accepting the burden of our finitude.

> A man's reach should exceed his grasp,
> Or what's a heaven for?[6]

But this impossibility of ever mastering all the facts, not to mention the distortion that besets all knowledge, still poses a dilemma for scholarship, including Bible scholarship. Must a man forever be cheated of Bible light? No, for there is another way of knowing, and this is the prime essential in Bible study: "I know whom I have believed" (II Tim. 1:12). Middleton Murry, in a glowing sentence, has quoted of Christ, "Look upon him, till he look back upon us again."[7] It is reminiscent of an account given by a medieval saint of his prayers: "I look at Jesus, and he looks back at me." Every man looks on Christ. That is why every man knows of any painted picture of Christ that it falls far short of truth. "Look upon him": only in that rapt prayer can the Bible be studied. Thus lowly saints unversed in knowledge about the Scriptures are still found of God as they read, while "Bible scholars" may grope through a deserted shrine.

[5] Tennyson, "Ulysses."
[6] Browning, "Andrea Del Sarto."
[7] *Jesus, Man of Genius* (New York: Harper & Bros., 1926), p. 372.

VI. Yet More Light

The study of the Bible is therefore, at long last, a meditation on the word and the paragraph, an exposing of the soul to the Book's healing light. The reader prays, "Open thou mine eyes, that I may behold wondrous things out of thy law" (Ps. 119:18). He looks on Jesus meanwhile and asks, "What does this word mean for me?" He asks again and again, not shrinking from any cauterizing needle, not rejecting any proffered grace, not disobeying any commission. For if a man is unwilling to follow God's sign, why should God give it? Then the reader asks the wider question, "What does this mean for my land and era?" and thus sees his world, with all its raucousness, forgotten reverence, and yearning, under the judgment and mercy of God. Not without cause, and not without effect, have men found in every age that prayer and Bible study are necessarily joined. Necessarily—both by man's need and God's ordination. Age on age the church has wisely made demand of its catechumens that they be "faithful in prayer and in the study of the Scriptures."

So to this conclusion we have been led: the study of the Scriptures is under the light and leading of the Holy Spirit. That doctrine has of late been neglected in the church: therefore our gardens have become sand. Veritably at Pentecost the Spirit of Christ was given to his followers; veritably the gift is renewed to all who seek him. There are many words that Jesus had too scant time to speak during the days of his flesh; many words he could not speak because men were deaf; many words he had to keep until the occasion (our occasion) summoned them. All these words are hidden in God's Holy Word, but only his Spirit can call them into life: "When he, the Spirit of truth, is come, he will guide you into all truth; for . . . he shall take of mine, and shall show it unto you" (John 16:13, 15). Therefore we "look upon him"; therefore we pray, "Come, Holy Spirit"; for only through God's gift granted in worship and prayer can any man truly study the Bible or be found of its eternal verity.

Is there not a picture of Luther busy at his New Testament at the very moment when its light broke on him like morning after a weary night? Word by word he is tracing the Word—not without the discipline of a student, for he brought to the endeavor a close knowledge of Latin, Greek, and Hebrew; yet not without fervent prayer for the Spirit's guidance. The chain by which the Bible had once been bound to a lectern lies broken. Luther comes now to the moment of revelation. The sun's rays slant through the lattice, token of a deeper light that soon will pierce him. Then the word: "Therefore being justified by faith, we have peace with God through our Lord Jesus Christ" (Rom. 5:1). Luther brought agony of soul to that quest, and he brought scholarship. But he brought more—the essential things; for he was in a cloister, and for every man the cloister is the place of prayer:

> Come, Holy Ghost, our hearts inspire
> And lighten with celestial fire.[8]

Thus the page glows. Thus God finds the longing soul through the Book which he alone could give. Thus is the joy once more fulfilled: "Thy word is a lamp unto my feet" (Ps. 119:105).

[8] "Veni Creator Spiritus."

VII. Selected Bibliography

CLARKE, WILLIAM NEWTON. *Sixty Years with the Bible.* New York: Charles Scribner's Sons, 1909.

COLWELL, ERNEST C. *The Study of the Bible.* Chicago: University of Chicago Press, 1937.

DODD, C. H. *The Authority of the Bible.* New York: Harper & Bros., 1929.

————. *The Bible Today.* New York: The Macmillan Co., 1947.

GOODSPEED, E. J. *The Story of the Bible.* Chicago: University of Chicago Press, 1936.

PEAKE, A. S. *The Bible: Its Origin, Its Significance, and Its Abiding Worth.* 5th ed. New York: Hodder & Stoughton, 1914.

RICHARDSON, ALAN. *Preface to Bible Study.* Philadelphia: Westminster Press, 1944.

GENERAL ARTICLES

on the

OLD TESTAMENT

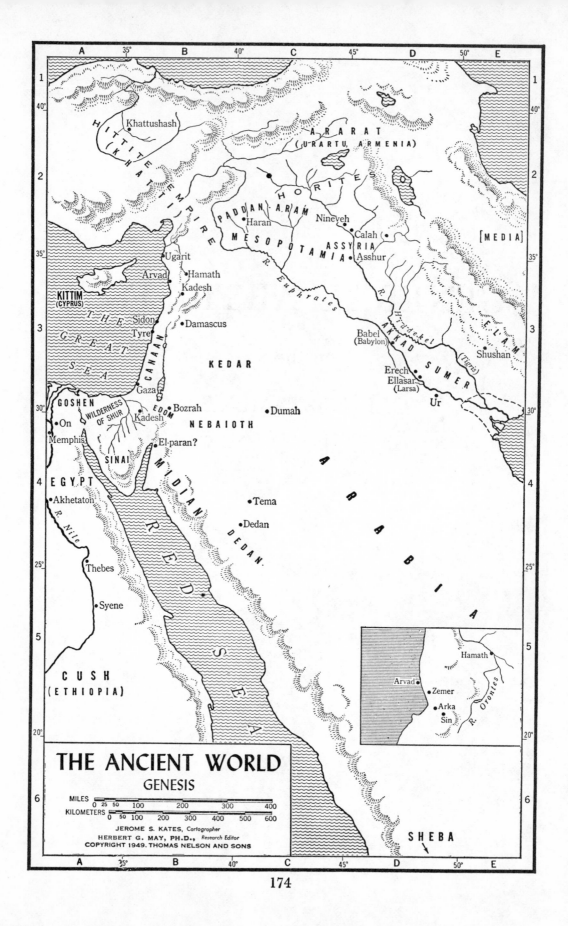

THE ANCIENT WORLD
GENESIS

MILES 0 25 50 100 200 300 400
KILOMETERS 0 50 100 200 300 400 500 600

JEROME S. KATES, *Cartographer*
HERBERT G. MAY, PH.D., *Research Editor*
COPYRIGHT 1949, THOMAS NELSON AND SONS

THE LITERATURE
OF THE OLD TESTAMENT

by WILLIAM A. IRWIN

When the Hebrew tribes broke into Palestine in the long series of incursions and infiltrations that reached flood tide sometime during the fourteenth or thirteenth century B.C., they projected themselves into a course of culture that was already very old. Of their own level of civilization little is known. At times they have been regarded as unspoiled nomads directly out of the Arabian Desert, and consequently possessed of a culture not far above the barbaric; again, they have been associated with the widely diffused Habiru peoples who then lived or had lived in varying status in several of the civilized lands of the ancient Near East. Probably the safest guess is a theory that provides room for a combination of these views. Nonetheless, the conquest of Palestine was epochal for their culture, as it was to prove also, in the long perspective of the centuries, for civilization as a whole. The little land to which they made claim lay right athwart the great highroads of the ancient world. Up and down its valleys and along its strip of coastal plain went the commerce as well as the pomp and circumstance of the empires of the time, rich argosies of products from the looms and shops of Egypt and Babylonia that bore also undeclared imports of spiritual treasures from the civilizations of "the gorgeous East."

I. Ancient Near-Eastern Culture

The great story of the achievements of the older Orient is not our present theme. We must restrain comment on the incredibly superb metalworking of Sumer, and the temples of Egypt and of Babylonia, different as they were in their architectural genius, yet alike in their housing of a ritual and liturgy that grew ornate and magnificent with the lengthening centuries. The palaces, the pyramids, the splendor of well-planned royal cities, the wealth and ease and the refinement that leisure can encourage—and much more may be recalled only as colorful and pregnant background possessed of immense relevance for the quasi-barbarian invaders of Palestine's narrow strip of fertility between the desert and the sea. It is more acute loss, however, that we may only allude to the slow dawning of a science that in some departments presently became empirical, and to the speculative thought of these lands that age after age wrestled with the persistent problem, in course of time to become Israel's obsession also—What is man? What is his place in a world of wonder and unfathomed mystery?

It was a very old and ripe culture into which the Hebrews came. More significantly still, it was a literate civilization. All literatures have their beginnings in oral traditions of one sort or another; and this unwritten heritage was of peculiar significance to the Orient. Note must soon be taken of its function in Israel. But by the time of the Hebrew conquest, the great lands of the Near East had long since passed beyond that stage of development. Business, government, law, ritual, and the outreach of thought had all invoked the art of the scribe for so many centuries that it had become normal and undeserving of remark. As the modern world has its classics, so then likewise, famous old poems and myths circulated afar, and won a renown which justly has revived in our own day. In the history of human culture they were documents of a very high relevance.

II. The Pre-Israelite Culture of Palestine

The immediate context of the emerging Hebrew nationality was also notable. The Canaanites have received less than their due. Religious

175

practices which rightly shocked Israel's austere morality have through the medium of Old Testament condemnation provoked contempt and disregard for the pre-Israelite culture of Palestine, but accumulating facts compel more generous appraisal. The Canaanites were a people of unusual ability. Through more than a thousand years they had built up in Palestine a great civilization. The wealth and refinement of their cities astonished Egyptian conquerors. Their inventive genius originated three novel systems of writing; two of these were alphabetic, and of these one was destined to supplant the venerable systems of Egypt and Babylonia, and to become in its lineal descendants the medium of written record and communication for the entire Western culture even to this day. These alphabetic characters were ready, waiting when the Israelites arrived, tempting alert spirits to invoke them for expression and for annals. But stimulus and example were also at hand. It has long been recognized that a considerable portion of the Old Testament legal system, notably the social legislation in Exod. 21–23, was originally Canaanite but received Israel's characteristic stamp. The Canaanites shared also, it would appear, in the intellectual activity of the Orient known as "wisdom." Yet most astonishing is the group of documents uncovered at Ras Shamra on the northern coast of Syria in 1929 and subsequent years (see article, "The Old Testament World," pp. 259-61). They turned out on decipherment to consist largely of ancient religious poems, epics, and myths intimately related to the cultus—nothing less in fact than a portion of the long-lost literature of the ancient Canaanites! That the documents date from the period when the Hebrews were in the early stages of their thrust into Palestine is but incidental; the significant fact is that they give us an all too tantalizing glimpse of the intellectual and religious culture and practice that were to be Israel's pervasive atmosphere for centuries. Their actual influence is attested in the notable series of parallels, allusions, and even near-quotations steadily being recognized in the Old Testament down to its later portions.

The Hebrews, then, had august guides, and the stimulus of a great and ancient culture so all-comprehending as to constitute their native air, when presently they set out themselves to create a literature that was to prove itself one of the greatest achievements of the human spirit. Yet it would be an error to limit our perspective to non-Hebraic facts and forces. Basic to all was the inherent genius of the Hebrews themselves, although it is highly dubious that as yet any of them or of their contemporaries could have suspected the possibilities that lay in germ in these uncouth shepherds and desert wanderers whose immediate purpose was to dispossess the Canaanites, the legal owners of the land. The reality of national traits cannot be denied, even though their origin lies hidden in the mystery of human biology; and Israel's incomparable contribution to human culture will not be comprehended if it is not freely recognized that they were a people of remarkable endowments.

III. Earliest Fragments of Hebrew Literature

It is more directly to the point, however, to speak of fragments of the Hebrew literary heritage so old as apparently to antedate the settlement in Palestine. Poetic scraps such as the Song of the Well, the taunt against Heshbon, and the vivid bit of description of the boundaries of Moab, preserved in Num. 21, are placed by the narrator in the time of the Wandering, a date there is no good reason for disputing. How long before the Conquest the Song of Lamech (Gen. 4:23-24) and the curse of Canaan (Gen. 9:24-27) may have originated no one can say. But it is freely admitted that some nucleus of the Song of Moses (or Miriam?) in Exod. 15 was actually composed for the triumphant celebration it memorializes. Balaam's oracles (Num. 23–24) are other extended poetic traditions which can with reasonable confidence be assigned in greater or lesser bulk to the period with which the record associates them.

The earliest Hebrews also accumulated a body of traditions about the great figures and events of their history. To these we are indebted in some undetermined measure for our stories about the patriarchs. The superb character of these narratives is, consciously or otherwise, recognized by all; but the critical study of them is yet far from finality, indeed much farther than was once supposed. Even among prominent scholars opinions differ widely, all the way from a relative conservatism [1] to a belief that the stories have grown up in a way typical of most early traditions: a small nucleus of historic events—which cannot now be precisely determined—overlaid with legendary embellishments.[2] However this may be, the account of Abraham's successful pursuit of the four marauding kings who had carried off his nephew Lot (Gen. 14) has archaic features that indicate dependence on an actual historic source. The whole body of these narratives has indeed received in recent years small, quite indefinite, but significantly corroborative, support from various aspects of our growing knowledge of the ancient East. We can no longer doubt their factual basis, but he would be a bold spirit

[1] See H. H. Rowley, *From Joseph to Joshua* (London: Oxford University Press, 1950).

[2] See Aage Bentzen, *Introduction to the Old Testament* (Copenhagen: G. E. C. Gad, 1948).

who would undertake to delineate that basis. Much the same is to be said of the stories of Jacob; they fit at numerous points what we know from other sources. Yet we wrong this whole body of literature when we appraise it primarily as history, for it was composed for a variety of purposes, most of them quite apart from systematic record of the past. Nonetheless it is apparent that the origins of these stories carry us far back in Israel's career, so that the traditions provided a significant portion of the nation's cultural heritage when at length the Hebrew tribes emerged into actual history. It is highly improbable that any of these various elements had been committed to writing before the Conquest; they existed rather as an oral literature, more accurately, as folk traditions. The art of writing was already very ancient and was widely diffused; it had long been practiced in Palestine. But such meager knowledge as we possess relevant to the point does not encourage the assumption that literacy was general at this time in Israel.

IV. Epics of the Conquest

The heroic age of the Conquest and settlement added greatly to the people's store of subjects worthy of celebration in song and story. It was an age of precisely the conditions that have universally created ballads and hero tales, a protracted time of turmoil where battle lines were not drawn, but the enemy might be confronted at any chance turning: a time of notable victories against great odds, of common rustics who in emergency proved of such epic stuff that an otherwise unknown Shamgar ben Anath could slay of the well-armed Philistines six hundred men with an ox goad and so work deliverance for Israel; a time, too, of notable champions who, like Samson, grew legendary with the passing years. From some such source the account of Joshua's triumph was later composed. The old sources are still clearly visible in the book of Judges, although overlaid with the historical interpretation of later ages.

The most notable poetic monument of this time is the Song of Deborah (Judg. 5). It has suffered from subsequent editing; but its archaisms, its vivid realism and passion, and its obvious verisimilitude, carry conviction of the contemporaneity of its original. It is a stirring composition in which even yet one feels the anxious concern of the ill-armed tribesmen gathering for battle against Sisera's chariotry, and the excitement and thrill of the victory:

The kings came; they fought.
Then fought the kings of Canaan,
At Taanach, by the waters of Megiddo.
They took no spoil of silver.

From heaven fought the stars,
from their courses they fought against Sisera.
The river Kishon swept them away,
the river of the valiant, the river Kishon.

Fragments of folk poetry have survived in the tales of Samson: his riddle and his answer to the Philistine youths, and his boast of victory at Lehi (Judg. 14:14, 19; 15:18). They are the sort of popular jingle that comes naturally out of a rustic community; they could have arisen at any time, but it is best to relate them to this stage of Israel's development. Through this period, too, the heroic episodes of the nation's past were being recorded in poems that may very well have been chanted in popular gatherings, much like the medieval minstrelsy. It is not known how extensive these were, or whether they approximated the character of a national epic. Mere scraps of the total have been preserved as citations in some of the narrative books, where they are ascribed to the book of Jashar and the book of the Wars of the Lord. They were still receiving accretions as late as the time of Solomon, it would appear, but beyond that nothing is known.

Not less significant is Jotham's fable (Judg. 9:8-15) about the trees seeking a king but finding only the worthless bramble willing to waste time in politics! It is a characteristic piece of the plant and animal fables of the ancient East, of which we have little else from Israel, and along with a few other traces reveals that in this relatively early time Canaanite "wisdom" activity, however slight or extensive it may have been, was contributing to the literary development of the Hebrew people.

V. Canaanite Influence

Since the days of the biblical writers themselves it has been recognized that Canaanite religion made a powerful appeal to the Hebrews, so that the rival claims of pagan deities over against the worship of Israel's own God constituted a disturbing and to some extent a creative stress in religious thought for many centuries—indeed, until the triumph of normative Judaism subsequent to Ezra's reform. The Canaanite religion was old and rich in ritual and liturgy. In spite of features which Israel's better thought repudiated, it had much to teach the newcomers. And so it is that certain of the psalms, for example, which we use to this day, are really Canaanite religious poems taken over and adapted by Israel. It has been claimed likewise that the amazing group of love lyrics which make up the Song of Songs trace back through some undetermined process of adaptation to songs of the Canaanite cultus. Obviously no one can mark the point in the long centuries of Israel's exposure to Canaanite culture when any given poem was so appropriated by the Hebrews, but it is important to realize that here lay one of the potent stimuli to the nascent Hebrew literary genius, which in some way must have been felt as early as the days of the judges.

Yet it was not in hymns and songs alone that this pervasive influence was effective. There were numerous sacred places up and down the length of the land; several of these are mentioned in the Old Testament, and certain others have come to light through archaeological investigation. Each was a center of ritualistic procedure. Details of their interrelationship escape us. Certainly there was some general pattern of practice; but also it is more than probable that the atomistic politics of Canaan entailed a corresponding independence on the part of the priests in the several petty states. Then presently the Yahweh cult likewise came to recognize several places of worship. The old shrine at Shiloh was a center for the tribesmen so early that its origin is unknown: and apparently Shechem was still earlier in religious significance. In course of time another was established at Dan in the far north, and still others at Gilgal, Gibeon, Bethel, and Beer-sheba. The peasant Micah had a private sanctuary for Yahweh in his own home (Judg. 17–18), and there is no reason to suppose that his was unique. Indeed, after the destruction of Shiloh, we hear of just such local and personal places of worship. David provided quasi-national establishment for the cultus in Jerusalem. Yet numbers of Canaanite sacred places were still in some way revered by devout Israelites. Doubtless the situation was comparable with what still exists in Palestine, where very old, originally pagan, sacred places have been taken over as Moslem or Christian sites. Just so the Hebrews worshiped at numerous ancient holy places. In this diversity and wealth of ritual practice we are to see the origins of much of what now stands in the late Priestly Code. The characteristic conservatism and traditionalism of the priesthood evidently preserved in memory—perhaps also in small measure in written documents—generation after generation the ancient modes of worshiping its God, until at length the tragedy of national collapse aroused exiled priests to organize this diverse material in final form.

Something similar may be said of the legal corpus. Whatever rules and regulations the Hebrews possessed at the time of their entrance into Palestine, it is clear these would not fit the new circumstances. But the Canaanites had been for a millennium evolving codes for Palestinian life. What more inevitable than that this ancient legislation should continue, more particularly since the view must be revised that Israel practically exterminated the former inhabitants of the land? In the social upheaval of the troublous times of the settlement, when the two peoples were finding a somewhat tumultuous *modus vivendi*, it is more than probable that much of the Canaanite body of laws would be sloughed off and finally lost. Nonetheless, in the case law now found in Exod. 21–23 we are by common consent to recognize fragments of the Canaanite code, doubtless revised and adapted to Hebrew needs, but still patently Canaanite. Obviously we have no knowledge of the time and circumstance of the origin of this legislation; also the date of its full acceptance by Israel is so uncertain that scholars differ markedly. It suffices that here lay one more source of our Old Testament literature.

VI. Cultural Significance of the Monarchy

The establishment of the monarchy was epochal for Israel's culture to a degree not commonly realized; indeed, it may be said to mark the beginning of that culture, if defined in a narrower sense. Saul deserves more respect than he generally receives; it was he who first gave the Hebrew tribesmen a few years' experience of the security, even against the powerful Philistine menace, that was possible through political unity. Yet to the end he remained a rustic, ruling his domain in simple state, more like a landed squire than a king. It was the destiny of David to raise his people from abject conquest by the Philistines to near-imperial status as the first power on the eastern seaboard of the Mediterranean. More to our present interest, he established his capital in the ancient fortress city of Jerusalem, came into relations—not always wholesome—with the long-civilized people of the city, and doubtless unconsciously laid the foundations for all the subsequent refinement of Israel's life.

The urbanization went on apace through Solomon's reign. That this was a period of grandeur and wealth is freely recognized; the Hebrew historian himself was dazzled by it (I Kings 4:20-34). But there was much that does not immediately meet the eye. The visit of the queen of Sheba was a showy affair that roused the narrator to grandiloquence. He says little, however, about a quiet and perhaps embittered man, banished to his country estate on pain of death if ever he set foot in the capital. Yet this man, if the identification is proper—in any case, some man of the time while Solomon disported himself in gaudy show—was busy writing. Away from the pomp of the court, at work in some Palestinian home devoid of our simplest conveniences, doubtless equipped with a common reed pen and a roll of papyrus, he was writing the first real history ever composed by man. He may have entertained notions of the superiority of his methods over the annals and royal chronicles of former times; certainly he could not have dreamed of the consequences of his work. For he, and not Herodotus five hundred years later, was the real "Father of History." His theme was that of the kingship in Israel, perhaps the reign of Saul, but certainly that of David, which we have now in II Sam. 9–20. He told of events that he knew well from his own participation; and he related them with such superb skill as even yet might well set an example for historians. His selection of facts was much too narrow; there are hosts of questions that concern the modern historian of which he said nothing. But within the scope of his plan he wrote his narrative in lucid simplicity, with a compelling realism of the interplay of human personalities. Here was something new in Israel's literary career: so far as we know, the first continuous prose. It was Israel's first book.

Yet this is but part of the real brilliance of Solomon's time. For it was the age of Israel's first thrilled experience of the delights of the mind. Solomon's far-famed "wisdom" is to be understood as in some way a part of a notable intellectual awakening, doubtless fostered and participated in by the king himself. His 3,000 proverbs and 1,005 songs (I Kings 4:32), however far a carping skepticism may discount them, were yet, on the background of the erstwhile rural culture of his people, indicative of a profound revolution. There was a new ferment stirring in the Hebrew consciousness such as to make this, in spite of the monarch's maladroit politics, a golden age of promise.

That promise did not long delay. The true mission of Israel had come to such self-consciousness that the political debacle of the following centuries could not dim or abate its vigor. The first great historian's work set a vogue. It must have been very soon after this that the hero tales of the "judges" were committed to writing and arranged in some sort of pristine ancestor of the present book of Judges. But still the historic instinct was not satisfied. The old tales and traditions of the nation's early days, its patriarchs, the oppression in Egypt from which the Lord had brought them out by a strong hand and an outstretched arm—all these called to an aroused sense of the meaning of the past. The still older stories of a remote past before Israel had its beginning likewise beckoned to historic research, tales of the great flood, of the antediluvian celebrities, of the beginnings of civilization, of the fabled tower in Shinar from which the human race was dispersed over the face of the earth. The information was gleaned in various ways from the great ancient cultures of Israel's world and passed current in a land through which flowed the tides of the best thought of the time. And all called to an aroused realization of the significance of the past, and quickened the insight that was to be one of Israel's great contributions, the sense of history.

The immediate result was the work now interwoven in much of our Pentateuch and commonly referred to as the J and E documents (see article, "The Growth of the Hexateuch," pp. 192-97). They were conceived on the grand scale, nothing less in fact than world history. And in this once more we come in touch with the revolutionary character of Israel's historians; for one goes far in the stream of historiography before uncovering other writers whose intellects attempted such scope. It may perhaps be objected that J and E were only histories of Israel in a world setting. Yet the long introduction beginning with the creation of the world and the dispersion of the races of man, as well as the steady consciousness of wider contacts that confronts one constantly in these histories, justifies the more challenging description. And like the nameless historian of David's reign, they tell their story with the high literary art which now we may recognize as one of the excellences of Hebrew writing.

Yet these qualities do not exhaust the astonishing character of these ancient Hebrew works produced in the midst of physical conditions that to sophisticated tastes seem little better than barbaric. They have lived to this remote day by their intrinsic worth alone, high among the treasures of man's heritage. For along with other merits they were theological philosophies of history, the first such undertaking that had ever dawned upon human thought. They set a model for subsequent Hebrew historians, so that it is scarcely an exaggeration to claim that the theme of the Old Testament throughout is a survey of human life *sub specie aeternitatis*. These Hebrew thinkers remained for many ages alone in their field, and when eventually speculation about meaning in history did seize the imagination of a wider circle of scholars, these paid unconscious tribute to the unknown philosophers of Israel who had begun the study. It is mildly amusing for the student of the Old Testament to observe current discussions tracing the course of this speculation only from Augustine onward, apparently oblivious of his dependence on the Bible, that is, ultimately on Israel's historians. There is a tendency to dismiss all this phase of thought as transcendentally based, whereas the scope of the Hebrew historians' narrative should have indicated the factual ground of their conclusions. Actually they surveyed an expanse which only through the archaeological and anthropological discoveries of the past hundred years the modern world has been able to rival—and the significance of these newer facts has as yet very imperfectly made its impact upon the thought of this century. While it is true that the psychological sciences began with the Greeks, yet in a large way the Hebrews in their theological interpretation of history were first in the application of empirical methods to the processes of thought.

Israel had become pen conscious. Besides these two great documents, the years of the kingdoms witnessed the production of a diversity of books, temple records, national annals, architectural specifications, stories of the prophets such as those that have enriched us with copious tales of Elijah and Elisha, and a variety of works of transient relevance. Out of such sources the material of the present books of Kings was slowly growing, although it is doubtful that they were assembled until much time had passed, and certainly they did not reach final form until the Exile. Someone has counted twenty-four books mentioned by name in the Old Testament, all of which have disappeared except for such citation; most familiar are the books of the Chronicles of the Kings of Judah or of Israel, mentioned in the books of Kings as supplementary sources. What a prize if only archaeology might turn up a copy of some one of these! But it is a vain hope; we must content ourselves with names that witness a vigorous literary activity in the days when monarchs sat enthroned in Jerusalem and in Samaria.

Nor may we overlook the temple in Jerusalem and other shrines of greater or less repute through the land. Allusion has already been made to them as centers of Canaanite literary stimulus; but their influence by no means waned with their growing orthodoxy. The ritual performed day in and day out, century after century, was one of the potent though generally unobtrusive aspects of ancient life. Hymns and liturgies were tested for their effectiveness, and gradually grew into a sifted body of religious lyrics, many of them in course of time to be preserved for us in that classic of the inner life, the book of Psalms. The "wise men" likewise had a continuing activity; we hear of them occasionally, and not always in flattering terms. The heading of Prov. 25 testifies that an organic group of them was engaged in the days of Hezekiah in something resembling the work of a present-day committee. The distilled wisdom of their sage observations on human life has also gone into the total of our heritage from ancient Israel.

A side light, pitifully small but priceless in its uniqueness, is provided by the documents written in ink on potsherds which archaeology has already turned up in Judah and on the site of Samaria. A single ostracon from the hill of Ophel, at Jerusalem, half obliterated by the action of the centuries, appears to contain a list of commodities, perhaps for use in the cultus. The group from Samaria, dating from the eighth century B.C., likewise lists materials, constituting, it would seem, a sort of acknowledgment of payment of taxes in kind. But most remarkable are the ostraca from the site of ancient Lachish. They are a series of letters written by at least two officers of the garrison at the time of Nebuchadrezzar's advance to the attack on Jerusalem. They possess a genuine thrill for the student of the Old Testament, in part for the names they mention, some of which have been long familiar, but even more for turns of expression and idiomatic structure which seem to come right out of the Hebrew Bible, though in reality their significance is the reverse: the Bible was written in the living language of the time. But of all the ostraca alike, the importance for our present interest is their testimony to Israel's literate culture. The art of writing was a common acquisition.

VII. The Literary Prophets

With the line of prophets beginning about the middle of the eighth century, Israel's literature reached its maturity. The prophets brought Hebrew writing to such excellence that the period of approximately two hundred years, from Amos and Isaiah to Second Isaiah, is well considered Israel's classic age. They imparted an impulse that through several minor figures down to Second Zechariah (Zech. 9–14) was felt for many ages, and in the considerably modified form called now "apocalypse" passed over into Christian usage. Indeed, both this and true prophecy have continued potent forces to the present.

The study of the prophets is not easy, for practically all the books bearing their names are composite. Those of the great prophets, in particular, and several of the so-called minor prophets also in striking degree, are expanded with relatively large bulks of matter of diverse authorship, and generally of most indefinite origins. In the form in which they have come to us they are a deposit of Jewish piety through many centuries. Actually there are reasons to believe that the process of accretion was not complete until near Christian times. Within this diverse mass, then, precise identification of the words of the original prophet remains even yet a contentious issue. Nonetheless, on one basic matter there is full agreement. The prophets were poets. This does not preclude the possibility that as well they uttered prose oracles; but how much, if any, of the prose material now found in their books is genuine continues uncertain. Their poems are short—by comparison with some of the famous literature of later times, very short. There is an effort growing out of the study of literary types in the Old Testament to show that the critical process of fragmentation went too far, and instead certain shorter books, as Joel and Habakkuk, constitute complete, unified literary compositions of an established form. But granting whatever cogency one may to such contentions, it is uncertain how far this form is the work of later editors using composite materials, and how far it stems from the original prophet. In any case, it is incontestable that some at least of the prophetic oracles are and always have been no more than two, three, or four lines. From this minimum they range in bulk upward, admittedly in many cases to whole chapters or somewhat more.

It is the habit to distinguish this line of prophets from their predecessors as "the writing prophets." Yet we shall fail to understand them if we overlook the fact that they were, prior to the Exile at least, just as truly concerned with oral utterance as were Samuel, Nathan, Elijah, and the rest. How their spoken words came into written form is an interesting but largely futile speculation. Certain Scandinavian scholars emphasize oral tradition, claiming that the oracles were so preserved for ages. It is a fruitful insight, but in grave danger of excess; for we know that Jeremiah had his words committed to writing while as yet he was but in midcareer (Jer. 36), and this book was certainly the lineal predecessor of the present book of Jeremiah. It has been pointed out also that Isa. 8:16 is susceptible of the meaning that in a similar time of menace Isaiah took the same course. But certainly, of the rest nothing more is known than can be deduced from the form and condition of the books themselves, which commonly evidence a long period of collecting and editing, but reveal nothing about the original writing. However, the question is for our present concern largely irrelevant. The prophets were great literary creators, whoever did the actual inditing of their words.

It will be apparent that the common description of the prophets as preachers is susceptible of grave perversion. Yet in one regard it provides real insight; the consciousness of an immediate audience lay ever upon the prophet; in prophecy's earlier stages at least, it was his impelling drive. And his oracles, however polished and finished, were poured out in an intense effort to sweep along and bring moving conviction to living contemporaries who sat or stood, listening and watching with various reactions. The prophetic poems have thus a common type; they are characterized by an impetuosity and

intensity of utterance, a sense of terrible urgency: the issues of life and death hung in the balance, a mortal threat was already on the way —if only something might be done while yet there was time! The prophetic method then was not so much that of reasoned development of a theme to carry an audience by logical steps to a rational conclusion; it was rather to overwhelm and overawe, to impress by telling words, by skillfully turned expressions, by lines that would re-echo in memory till action was provoked. For the prophet's mission could brook no interruption. The awful majesty and holiness of God, over against the injustices, the paganisms, the political stupidities of contemporary society— these were the two poles between which his soul was racked in an agony of spiritual torment. As time passed, prophecy took on a more calm demeanor, yet its inner fervor was never abated, not even when it expressed itself in the apocalyptic visions of the book of Daniel.

It is tempting to pause over the majesty and finished art of Isaiah, the wistful, haunting beauty of Jeremiah's poetry, the rare occasions when Ezekiel's muse takes flight above common levels, and, as in his description of the imminent fall of Jerusalem (Ezek. 7), reveals that under stress even he can feel the touch of celestial fire. With the second Isaiah the prophetic poetry reached the highest level of exaltation, reasoned force and pure beauty (see article, "The Prophetic Literature," pp. 201-11).

VIII. Deuteronomy and the Historians

The book of Deuteronomy—everyone is familiar with the common view that the book found in the temple in 621 B.C. (II Kings 22) constitutes its major bulk—demonstrates afresh the growing literary self-consciousness of the nation. For while basically a book of laws, a sort of Revised Statutes of ancient Judah, it is set in a homiletic framework where the writer argues the claims of God upon Israel and the importance of national faithfulness. Its temper is a strange blend of prophetic and legal; yet unlike the works of the prophets it was clearly composed for private study. The author's subject parallels the theme of the prophets, but he differs from them in that he expounds and reasons. Here, and not in their oracles, is found Israel's first homiletic literature, for Deuteronomy is a great sermon, or series of sermons.

Writing of this sort implies, and to be effective entails, literary mastery beyond that of the narrator or oracular poet. It is the art of the essayist. Deuteronomy is Israel's first attempt at belles-lettres; and in the hands of this writer the attainment is high. The book has a notable style, which in fact set a vogue for a "school" of writers and editors. If one were obliged to characterize it in a single term, that word would be "flow"; it has a rounded fluency, a rhythmic dignity, that impart majesty and elevation. The author delights in words, in their cadences and overtones. He piles them up in synonyms, he entwines them in ornate patterns, he balances them in polished phrases, until at times, half entranced with their music, he almost loses his line of thought in their enchanting beauty. Yet ponderous as his style threatens to become, his greatness is apparent in the sustained interest and sheer beauty he attains. He may be charged with breaking the rules of good writing—and then he writes better than the masters. Through his balance and rhythm, his sense of form and proportion, and in his love of the allusive, pictorial quality of words, his prose becomes lyric.

IX. The Exile and Its Sequel

The Exile was the Great Divide in Hebrew history. It was at once the most terrible and the most transforming experience that befell ancient Israel. From this point onward all streams run in different and generally in deeper channels. The course of literature likewise was diverted, although not always for the better; what was gained in moral earnestness and religious fervor was not uncommonly lost in literary art. One of the notable features of this later time was the great editorial activity mentioned briefly above, the marks of which are apparent on most books of the Old Testament. It signifies the attainment of a complete literary self-consciousness; the Jews had now become "the people of the book." It was a labor which along its exegetical and homiletic lines produced later the Mishnah, the Midrashim, and a great bulk of other writing, indeed down to our own day. Acceptance of an ancillary relationship implies admission of inferiority; and notwithstanding flashes of creative writing by completely unknown authors, as for example the magnificent poetry of Isa. 60–62, we find ourselves here in the lesser light of the epigoni.

The best narrative of the postexilic period is in the books of Jonah and Ruth, granted that the latter is actually to be dated here; it in particular is a charming idyl of simple life in Judah in the days of long ago. The only work worthy of mention alongside these, until perhaps the time of I Maccabees, is the memoirs of Nehemiah, now incorporated in the book of his name. It is rich in unconscious character delineation, the account of the difficulties and endeavors of an intensely loyal, unselfish, and altogether high-minded Jew, who at the same time could be amusingly smug. The books of Chronicles are the most obvious historical narrative of the period, but of them as literary art the less said the better. The writer has forgotten how the times of the kingdoms produced authors even more intense than he in their moral convictions, yet by very reason of that intensity great as literary men.

A prime treasure of this time is the book of Psalms. Enough has been said of its remote origins; psalmody was very old in the Orient and expressed itself early in Israel. Of prior collections of such sacred lyrics we know nothing save as their presence in whole or in part is declared in the present Psalter; for the book of Psalms is an anthology of Israel's hymns and liturgies, which received its final editing into 150 poems somewhere in this long, indefinite period of which we are speaking. Activity was not confined, however, to externals: psalm writing continued, probably until the Maccabean period.

The wisdom books likewise were edited in postexilic times. And of their greatness, particularly that of Job, there can be no two opinions, yet we can afford to dismiss them with this brief mention, since they are dealt with elsewhere (see article, "The Wisdom Literature," pp. 212-19).

Much attention has been given in recent years to the forms of Hebrew literature. Beginning with a structural analysis of the Psalms, it has broadened out to the prophetic books and to the narratives. As a result we have discovered that there existed clearly recognized literary forms of a wide diversity: hymns, thanksgivings, lamentations, liturgies, wedding poetry, war poetry, peasant songs, imprecations, prophetic and priestly oracles, and a variety of tales. The form was of as precise a structure as that of the modern sonnet. The investigation contributes to an enhanced realization of the self-conscious art of Israel's writers. It promises to transform considerably the method of literary criticism.

X. Style of Old Testament Literature

A literature so diverse as that of the Old Testament may well baffle rational appraisal and in addition to its diversity of type and theme, it possessed also a wide range of merit. Nonetheless, the important matter is to realize its prevailing excellence. For those who possess historic perspective it stands out easily as the greatest literature of the ancient East. The writers of Egypt and of Mesopotamia, notwithstanding their indisputable importance in the history of culture, yet at their best only imperfectly approached the level where Israel's literary men moved easily as masters. Nor is this all. The Old Testament has continued to this day a high treasure of our cultural heritage by reason of its historical significance, it is true, but primarily through its literary beauty and power.

After all that has transpired in more than two thousand years, we must yet appoint a place with the mighty for these unknown men of the rugged hills of Judah and the narrow vales of Israel. They lived in conditions of stark simplicity; but herein they are themselves a symbol of their own deepest meaning: man's life consists not in things, but "out of the abundance of the heart the mouth speaks."

The Hebrew storytellers manifest an uncanny sense of the appropriate. They fall occasionally, it is true, into tedious repetition, which indeed may have been effective for ancient audiences; but apart from this, they are masters of the art of commanding and holding interest. Their compactness and speed of movement are remarkable. The tragedy of Queen Jezebel, with its shallow taunts, its cold brutality, its callous indifference, and the ghastly sequel, is all told in the brief compass of six biblical verses (II Kings 9:30-35). They know also the power of suspense and surprise. They can paint a picture with a few bold strokes so that it stands out clear as a vignette. And permeating all is the utter simplicity of their themes, and the realism and deep psychological insights of their flowing tale. An excellent illustration for study of Hebrew narrative is Gen. 24, a simple story of Abraham's servant going to Mesopotamia to find a wife for Isaac. What a picture is sketched when, having arrived at his destination, the servant "made the camels kneel down outside the city by a well of water at the time of evening, the time when women go forth to draw water"! Even more effective, for those who can apply a touch of disciplined imagination, is the conclusion where, leaving the servant slowly wending his way back to southern Palestine with Rebecca in his entourage, the scene shifts, and Isaac is depicted going out "to muse in the field at eventide; and he lifted up his eyes, and behold, the camels were coming"! What surprise too when the servant stood praying beside the well, and he had scarcely ended his prayer when down came Rebecca with her pitcher—and fulfilled his prayer to the letter! Rebecca's family brought the stranger home, made him comfortable with all the attention of Oriental hospitality, and set food before him. But he put it away with the remark, "I will not eat until I have told my errand." An errand to them? This stranger with every mark of wealth and distinction? And his first words are, "I am Abraham's servant"—Abraham, their kinsman who had gone out years ago; the West had swallowed him up with never a word come back to tell whether he was living or long since dead; and now—"the Lord has blessed my master greatly, and he has flocks and herds, and men-servants and maid-servants, and silver and gold."

But greatest is the Joseph story, which might well delay us long. To these other excellences it adds superb character delineation. The greatness of the story lies in the majesty and magnanimity of Joseph. Also the author manifests a skillful mastery of his plot. Joseph fell lower and lower in his troubles until with a change of fortune such as could be credible only of the Orient he found himself master of the greatest land of the time. Then presently he had opportunity for vengeance on the callous brothers who had sold him a slave into years of misery. But vengeance? It seems so; until we discover that Joseph has cleverly maneuvered them into a position where once again they can serve their selfishness at the expense of a little brother. What will they do? The answer is in Judah's plea, one of the most moving passages in the Old Testament. "And so Joseph could not restrain himself before those who stood by, and he commanded, 'Let every man go out from me'; and there stood no man with him while Joseph made himself known to his brothers. And he wept aloud . . . and he said, 'I am Joseph; is my father still alive?'" Ah! "that old man," his father, of whom he had inquired from the brothers as often as he had opportunity, would he yet see him after these long years of separation? Old peasant as he was, in the far land of Palestine: of him, in his magnificence, Joseph was not ashamed but introduced him proudly to Pharaoh himself. In Joseph's wistful longing for his father, in the deep satisfaction with which he gave directions, "Go up and tell my father, The Lord has made me master of all the land of Egypt," we see the golden thread of the narrative binding all together in the depth and nobility of Joseph's character.

Of other types of prose we may remark only their near-poetic quality. The authors' feeling for the resonance of words and their sense of form and rhythm are such that commonly they fall, unconsciously it would seem, into lyric. The rhythmic sentences of Deuteronomy have the cadence of music as the author warns of prosperous years in the land of promise (Deut. 6:6-12) ; his feeling for nature, his love of the marvelous little land that God had given to his fathers, and his literary instincts all combine in a gem of description, prose in form, but of purest poetry (Deut. 8:7-9). Yet perhaps this deep poetic feeling of the Hebrew writers is most strikingly illustrated by Koheleth, that "gentle cynic" (Ecclesiastes), who looked on life with a mildly blasé, certainly completely disillusioned, but withal amused, tolerance.

Little wonder then that the recognized poets of the Old Testament give us sheer lyric beauty. They reveled in the scenery of their little land, but they always made nature subservient to a higher theme—that of God's glory and will.

The device of parallelism proved in their hands an effective expression of that rounded measure lacking which an alleged poet writes at the best only exalted prose, and on lower levels, pure banality. They also used assonance and alliteration; occasionally they ventured a sort of rhyme; they played with words in a way that we might call "punning" were they not so solemnly serious; they employed refrains and measured reiteration; they grouped their lines also in simple strophic structures of twos, threes, fours, or in even larger units—a fact which adds to the sense of form and at times provides subtle overtones to the thought.

The curse of not a few contemporary writers is that with notable mastery of their art they yet have nothing to say! To their qualities of great expression the Hebrews added robust and profound thought. Their theme was one, whatever their immediate topic; and it is the greatest theme that can engage human thought. In some way the mystery of human life had been impressed upon them. What is man? Man in his deepest being, man over against and in relation to that supreme mystery of Being from which all things and all beings proceed? Here lay their interest, their obsession. Age after age, in varying mood, form and emphasis, the Hebrew writers discussed directly or through implication this and this only. Some lost the greatness in a petty selfishness; some were content to mouth ancient sentiments, and at best to stand on the gains of former ages. But on the whole they were creative thinkers of the highest order.

On the same theme much has been written in subsequent centuries by way of commentary or expansion, much too in quite other traditions. Yet it is no ex parte bias that would claim Israel's insights to be unrivaled in primacy and importance to this day. They were taken up, obviously, into rabbinical Judaism; they became the essential core of Christianity; along these two lines, and supported by Islamic thought likewise in its central impulse Hebraic, they have shaped the culture of all the West, and are at this day the vital impulse in our groaning and travailing toward a better world.

XI. Selected Bibliography

BENTZEN, AAGE. Introduction to the Old Testament. Copenhagen: G. E. C. Gad, 1948.

BEWER, JULIUS A. The Literature of the Old Testament in Its Historical Development. Rev. ed. New York: Columbia University Press, 1933.

FRANKFORT, HENRI, et al. The Intellectual Adventure of Ancient Man. Chicago: University of Chicago Press, 1946.

GRAY, GEORGE BUCHANAN. The Forms of Hebrew Poetry. London: Hodder & Stoughton, 1915.

HEMPEL, JOHANNES. Die Althebräische Literatur und ihr hellinistischjüdisches Nachleben. Potsdam: Akademische Verlagsgesellschaft, 1930.

MACDONALD, D. B. The Hebrew Literary Genius. Princeton: Princeton University Press, 1933.

PRITCHARD, J. B. Ancient Near Eastern Texts Relating to the Old Testament. Princeton: Princeton University Press, 1950.

PFEIFFER, ROBERT H. Introduction to the Old Testament. New York: Harper & Bros., 1941.

ROBINSON, THEODORE H. The Poetry of the Old Testament. London: Duckworth, 1947.

WILD, LAURA H. A Literary Guide to the Bible. New York: George H. Doran Co., 1922.

THE GROWTH OF THE HEXATEUCH

by CUTHBERT A. SIMPSON

The term Hexateuch is of modern origin and designates the first six books of the Old Testament. It conveniently registers the fact, established by critical investigation, that the documents of which these six books are composed did not end with the death of Moses (Deut. 34) but continued with an account of the Israelite settlement in Palestine. The word Pentateuch, used in Origen's commentary on John 4:25, refers to the first five books only. In the Jewish tradition these books are called "Torah" or "Law" and they stand by themselves, while the book of Joshua is included among the "Former Prophets." That Joshua should have come to be regarded as the author of the book bearing his name as its title—a tradition first recorded in the pages of the Talmud (Baba Bathra 14b) —is easily understandable.

I. The Traditional Authorship of the Pentateuch

The ascription of the Pentateuch to Moses, explicit in the various English versions of the Bible, rests upon a tradition of obscure origin. The books themselves do not claim him as their author. Indeed, it may be argued that the attribution of certain specific passages to him—e.g., Exod. 24:4; 34:27; Num. 33:2; Deut. 31:9—rather suggests that these passages are unique in this respect, and that the Pentateuch as a whole does not come from his hand. It is not until we come to Chronicles, with its continuation in Ezra and Nehemiah, that we find reference to "the law of Moses," meaning the Pentateuch (II Chr. 23:18; 30:16; Ezra 3:2; 7:6; Neh. 8:1; cf. "the book of Moses," II Chr. 35:12; Ezra 6:18; Neh. 13:1). The tradition of Mosaic authorship thus appears to have been current about 250 B.C. In view of the absence of earlier testimony one can scarcely maintain that it took form much before that date, nearly a thousand years after Moses' death.

II. The Beginnings of Pentateuchal Criticism

Apart from Jerome's identification of Deuteronomy with the law book of Josiah, there appears to have been no challenging of the tradition on critical grounds [1] until the eleventh century, when two rabbis, Isaac and Ibn Ezra, ventured to question the Mosaic authorship of certain passages,[2] with, however, no immediate result. It was not until 1520 that the matter was raised again by Carlstadt, who, in his *De Canonicis Scripturis,* called attention to the fact that the style of the Old Testament narrative remained unchanged after the account of the death of Moses, and suggested that this might have some bearing upon the question of the authorship of the Pentateuch. In the two centuries which followed, a number of scholars raised further questions on other grounds, noting (a) the occurrences of two or more versions of what appeared to be the same incident, (b) the inconsistencies in the narrative, and (c) its recurring chronological difficulties.

III. The Composite Character of the Hexateuch

It will be convenient at this point to list some of the more outstanding instances of these

[1] The doctrinal and ethical implications of certain of the tales in Genesis did cause some searching of heart for the author of the Clementine Homilies, and led him to attempt a modification of the tradition; but this was not criticism as the word is now understood.

[2] For particulars see Cuthbert A. Simpson, *The Early Traditions of Israel* (Oxford: Blackwell, 1948), p. 19.

phenomena,[3] not all of which, however, were noted by the critics of the sixteenth and seventeenth centuries:

A. Parallel Narratives and Laws.— (a) Abraham twice met what appeared to be a dangerous situation by representing his wife to be his sister (Gen. 12:10-20; 20:1-18), and Isaac once resorted to the same expedient (Gen. 26:6-11). (b) Abraham three times received the promise of a son (Gen. 15:4; 17:16; 18:10), and (c) four explanations of that son's name, Isaac, meaning, "he laughs," are given (Gen. 17:17-19; 18:12-13; 21:6a, 6b). (d) Hagar is twice expelled from Abraham's household on account of Sarah's jealousy, to find herself at a well in the desert where she is succored by an angel who tells her that she is to be the mother of a great people (Gen. 16:4-14; 21:9-21). (e) Jacob twice gives the name Bethel to a place formerly called Luz (Gen. 28:19; 35:6, 15). (f) Jacob's name is twice changed to Israel (Gen. 32:28; 35:10). It might, of course, be argued that these phenomena can be accounted for by assuming that Moses had composed the book of Genesis from existing documents or divergent oral traditions. The fact that similar duplications occur in the record of events in which he was himself involved is less easily explained: (g) The name Yahweh is twice revealed to Moses (Exod. 3:14-15; 6:2-3). (h) On each occasion this revelation is accompanied by a promise that God would deliver Israel from Egypt (Exod. 3:7-8; 6:5-6) and (j) Moses is commissioned to this end (Exod. 3:10-18; 6:11). (k) Moses twice hesitates to accept this appointment (Exod. 4:10-13; 6:12), and (l) twice receives Aaron as his spokesman (Exod. 4:14-16; 7:1-2). While it is, of course, possible that Moses was reluctant to undertake the task assigned to him and that it was necessary for God to speak to him twice, it is, to say the least, curious that no reference whatever is made on the "second" occasion to the "former" experience. (m) Twice the quails are given (Exod. 16:13; Num. 11:4-6, 31-32), and (n) twice water is brought from the rock (Exod. 17:1-7; Num. 20:1-13).

The questions raised by the numerous repetitions in the legislation are less disturbing, for such repetitions could be accounted for on the theory that certain laws had, for whatever reason, been promulgated more than once. Nevertheless, it is curious that during the stay of the people at Sinai—a period of less than a year according to the present narrative (Exod. 19:1; Num. 10:11)—Moses should have found it necessary to command (o) three times the observ-

[3] With the permission of the publisher, considerable use, in this and the next three sections, has been made of Simpson, *Early Traditions of Israel*, pp. 26-31, 38-40.

ance of the feasts of unleavened bread (Exod. 23:15; 34:18; Lev. 23:6), of weeks or harvest (Exod. 23:16a; 34:22a; Lev. 23:15), and of ingathering or tabernacles (Exod. 23:16b; 34:22b; Lev. 23:33-36; cf. Lev. 23:39-43), and (p) six times the keeping of the sabbath (Exod. 20:8-10; 23:12; 31:13-17; 34:21; 35:1-3; Lev. 23:3).

B. Inconsistencies Within Narratives and Laws.— (a) According to Gen. 1:26-27 man and woman were created together after the rest of creation, herbs, trees, fish, birds, and animals, had been completed; according to Gen. 2:7 man was created first, then the trees (vs. 9), then the animals (vs. 19), and finally woman, formed from a rib of the man (vss. 21-22). (b) According to Gen. 6:19-20 Noah was commanded to take into the ark with him one pair of each kind of animal, birds, cattle, etc.; contrast 7:2-3, where he is commanded to preserve alive seven pairs of clean beasts to one pair of unclean. (c) Gen. 7:12 records that the rain of the Flood was on the earth for 40 days; in 7:24 it is stated that the waters prevailed upon the earth 150 days. (d) According to Gen. 41:34 Joseph advises Pharaoh to prepare for the coming famine by storing up one fifth of the grain yield during the intervening plenteous years; according to vs. 35 he advised him to gather all the food. (e) Moses' father-in-law is named Reuel in Exod. 2:18, 21 and Num. 10:29—unless the name here is Hobab—and Jethro in Exod. 3:1; 4:18; 18:1-12. (f) According to Exod. 25:10-22 Moses, while on the holy mount, received directions for the making of the ark. These directions were carried out by Bezaleel (37:1-9) after Moses had brought down from the mount the second set of the tables of the law (34:29), which were placed in the ark (40:20) upon the completion of the tabernacle. According to Deut. 10:1-5 Moses himself made the ark after the incident of the golden calf, before going up the mount to have the ten words inscribed on a new set of tables, and these were placed in the ark immediately upon his return. (g) According to Num. 2 the sacred tent was in the midst of the camp, while Exod. 33:7 (cf. Num. 11:24-30; 12:4) states that it was pitched outside the camp. (h) According to Num. 13:27 the spies report to Moses that the land of Palestine is extremely fertile; yet in vs. 32 they say that it "eateth up the inhabitants thereof"—that is, that the people are weak and undernourished; yet, a further contradiction, the same verse describes them as "men of great stature." (j) According to Num. 22:20 God gave Balaam permission to accompany the princes of Balak, yet in vs. 22 it is stated that "God's anger was kindled because he went." (k) According to Josh. 2:15 Rahab's house was on the wall of Jericho, which (6:20) collapsed when the people shouted; yet (6:22) Joshua commanded the spies whom Rahab had befriended to go to her house and bring her out, which they did (6:23).

There are also numerous inconsistencies in the laws. These are, however, of another nature than the contradictions in the narrative, and are in themselves of little weight against the tradition of single, Mosaic authorship. For it could be held that the promulgation of a new law by implication repealed any earlier command to which it stood in contradiction, especially since the Pentateuch assumes that Moses' career as lawgiver extended over a period of forty years. Nevertheless, it must be said that adequate grounds for postulating such a legal development within this relatively brief period would seem to be lacking. And when it is found that certain of the laws have a marked affinity with certain parts of the narrative which, as regards both style and content, are clearly distinct from other parts of the narrative with which other laws are in agreement, it is reasonable to infer that the inconsistencies in the laws and the inconsistencies in the narrative point in the same direction.

As a concrete instance [4] Exod. 20:24 may be noted. Here the erection of an altar—and so the establishment of a sanctuary—is permitted in every place where Yahweh records his name. This is congruent with such passages as Gen. 12:7; 22:9; 26:25; 35:7. It is inconsistent with Deut. 12 where only one sanctuary is recognized as legitimate. If it be argued that the law in Exod. 20:24 was implicitly repealed by Deut. 12, reference need only be made to such passages as Judg. 6:24, 26; I Sam. 14:35 where the fact that the erection of altars is recorded without reprobation indicates that Exod. 20:24 was regarded as still valid—and therefore that Deut. 12 was unknown. Nor can it be held that Deut. 12 did not come into effect until the Jerusalem temple was built, for in the present form of the narrative a central sanctuary was provided by the making of the tabernacle (Exod. 40) which, it is recorded in Josh. 18:1, after the conquest of Canaan was set up permanently at Shiloh.

C. Chronological Difficulties.— (a) In Gen. 12:11 Sarah is represented as a woman of such physical attractiveness as to be an object of desire to the Pharaoh. Gen. 17:17 states that she was ten years younger than Abraham; she would therefore have been at least sixty-five

[4] In this connection see p. 190, where the legislation in Exodus—except that in chs. 20-23 and 34—Leviticus and Numbers is shown to be related to certain parts of the narrative in Genesis, and to be inconsistent with other parts of it.

at this time since it is stated in 12:4 that Abraham was seventy-five years old when he came to Palestine. (b) According to Gen. 25:26 Isaac was sixty years old when Jacob and Esau were born; by 26:34 he was a hundred when he blessed Jacob on his deathbed (cf. 27:2, 4), but according to 35:28 he did not die until he was a hundred and eighty. He was, accordingly, eighty years dying. (c) Jacob had returned to Palestine before his father died (33:18), and was present at his funeral (35:29); his stay with Laban had been for only twenty years (31:41); chs. 34-35, according to the present record, thus cover a period of some sixty years. Against this is the notice in 37:2 that Joseph was seventeen years old when he first began to annoy his brothers; he had been born nine years after his father, having served Laban seven years (29:20-30), had married Leah and Rachel (cf. 29:31-35; 30:9-21), that is, four years before the return to Palestine. In the light of this chronology the events in chs. 34-35 had not covered more than thirteen years. (d) If it is argued that the notice of Isaac's death has been misplaced, other difficulties result. For Joseph, sold into Egypt at the age of seventeen, was thirty years old when he came to power (41:46), spent seven years preparing for the famine (41:29-30), and brought his father to Egypt two years later (45:11), that is, twenty-two years after he had been sold to the Ishmaelites. Isaac would then be a hundred and fifty-five years old, with still twenty-five years to live. His name is not included in the list of those going into Egypt (46:8-27). If we admit that the notice of Isaac's death has simply been misplaced, then we must suppose that, according to the narrator, Jacob had returned from Egypt to be present at his funeral. But Jacob was a hundred and thirty years old when he went to Egypt (47:9), and died seventeen years later (47:28), and so eight years before his father.

(e) Chronological difficulties of a somewhat different nature are involved in Exod. 1-12. According to 12:40 the Israelites had been in Egypt for 430 years. Since according to the present narrative (as it has been seen) Joseph was thirty-nine when they arrived, only seventy-one years of this period had elapsed when he died at the age of a hundred and ten (Gen. 50:26). According to Exod. 7:7 Moses, whose birth is recorded in 2:2, was eighty years old at the time of the Exodus. Hence, allowing a good margin for the events recorded in 1:9-22, some two hundred and fifty years are "covered" in 1:6-8.

(f) According to Num. 10:11 the Israelites left Sinai in the second month of the second year, reckoning from the Exodus (cf. Exod. 19:1, where this reckoning is explicit). They arrived at Kadesh (Num. 20:1) in the first month, presumably of the third year, since no dates are mentioned between chs. 10 and 20. Aaron's death is recorded in 20:23-28, and 33:38 places this in the fifth month of the fortieth year after the Exodus. Thus a period of something more than thirty-seven years is "covered" by 20:1-22 (with this cf. Deut. 2:14; Num. 21:12-13).

It is the presence in the text of difficulties and inconsistencies such as these which makes it impossible to accept the traditional theory that the Pentateuch is the work of one man. The critics of the sixteenth and seventeenth centuries were thus led to attempt the formulation of a theory of sources. They did not, however, discover the clue which ultimately was to make possible the isolation of those sources, and so the determination of their origin and character.

IV. The Rise of Scientific Criticism

In 1753, Jean Astruc,[5] a physician of Montpellier, published a monograph on the sources of Genesis.[6] He noted the alternating use of God and Yahweh to designate the deity as an indication of diversity of authorship, and using this as his criterion, resolved Genesis into two main documents, postulating at the same time a number of minor sources.

Some twenty-five years later Johann Gottfried Eichhorn, who had independently reached the same general conclusions as Astruc, published his introduction to the Old Testament. He advanced a step beyond Astruc, however, in that he attempted to establish the existence of additional characteristics, both of style and content, marking each source. Nevertheless, he failed to recognize that the sources of which Genesis was composed were to be found underlying the remaining books of the Hexateuch.

In the century that ensued, investigation of the Hexateuch followed three main lines. One of them attempted to reconstruct the documents from which the books had been composed; the second rejected the theory of continuous source documents and instead developed, in one form or another, a "fragment-hypothesis," which maintained that the present narrative was a compilation of numerous brief, independent, and often contradictory units of tradition. The third theory, lying midway between the document-hypothesis and the fragment-hypothesis,

was that of supplementation. According to this theory, underlying the present narrative there was but one continuous source document, which had, however, been supplemented from time to time by the insertion of fragments of diverse origin.

The work of the century found a summing up in the "new document-hypothesis" of Hermann Hupfeld, who, in 1853, exactly one hundred years after the appearance of Astruc's *Conjectures,* published the results of his investigations into the sources of Genesis,[7] following this a few years later with a similar analysis of the remaining books of the Pentateuch. In its developed form this new document-hypothesis maintained that the groundwork of the Pentateuch was a document which in Genesis referred to God as Elohim. This Hupfeld designated E^1 (today it would be symbolized by P). He believed (erroneously, as it will be seen) that this was the earliest of the component documents. Next in origin was the second E document, designated E^2—roughly equivalent to the modern E. Still later a third document was written which used the name Yahweh, and which Hupfeld[8] designated J. These three documents were combined by a redactor to form a composite work which would today be symbolized by PEJ (for Hupfeld, E^1E^2J). The latest document of the four was Deuteronomy, which was added to this composite work in order to form the present Pentateuch.

It may be noted here that the solution of the problem of the growth of the Hexateuch involves two things: the books must be analyzed into their component sources, and the chronological relationship of the sources must be determined. In the century ending with Hupfeld the first of these tasks had been substantially accomplished—though subsequent investigation was to modify the results in certain details, and was to reveal a process of literary development within the sources themselves; little of value had been achieved as regards the second task. This was due to the fact that Hupfeld, like his predecessors, had approached the problem through Genesis. This book, being practically pure narrative, furnished of itself little or no indication as to the chronological order of the documents of which it was composed. It was therefore easy enough to assume that the document which furnished the opening chapter of the book, and also served as the framework into which the material from the other documents

[5] Astruc's conclusions had been anticipated by Vitringa (1683) and by H. B. Witter (1711), but their work seems to have remained practically unknown until attention was called to it by Adolphe Lods; see his *Israel from Its Beginnings to the Middle of the Eighth Century,* tr. S. H. Hooke (London: Kegan Paul, Trench, Trubner & Co., 1932), p. 10, and his *Jean Astruc et la critique biblique au XVIII⁰ siècle* (Strasbourg: Istra, 1924).

[6] *Conjectures sur les mémoires originaux dont il paroît que Moyse s'est servi pour composer le livre de la Genèse* (Bruxelles: Fricx, 1753).

[7] *Die Quellen der Genesis und die Art ihrer Zusammensetzung* (Berlin: Wiegandt & Grieben, 1853).

[8] German scholars used J to represent the Hebrew letter *yodh,* the first letter of the divine name (יהוה) here transliterated Yahweh; hence the document using this name in Genesis is called J, not Y.

had been fitted, was chronologically the first of the series.

V. The Graf-Wellhausen Hypothesis

In 1865-66 Karl H. Graf published the results of his critical work on the historical books of the Old Testament.[9] He approached the problem of the Hexateuch not by way of Genesis, but through a comparative study of the laws. He maintained that the Book of the Law "found" in the temple in the reign of Josiah (II Kings 22:8) was the Deuteronomic Code, D; that the laws in Exod. 13–23 and 34 were earlier than D, as was the "prophetic" narrative, JE, in which they were embedded; that the laws of the P Code—Hupfeld's E[1]—were of post-exilic origin, but that the narrative of P was the oldest part of the Hexateuch. With it the Deuteronomist had combined JE and his own work. To this Ezra had added the P legal code, together with some supplementary narrative material.

The great Dutch scholar Abraham Kuenen immediately discerned both the strength and the weakness of Graf's hypothesis, and pointed out to him in a private letter that the narrative and the laws of P were so obviously interdependent that it was impossible to suppose that they had originated some centuries apart. Graf accepted this criticism and modified his theory accordingly, which at once received the public support of Kuenen,[10] and, a few years later, of Julius Wellhausen.[11] The theory, which has come to be known as the Graf-Wellhausen hypothesis, may in its broad outlines be stated as follows:

The Hexateuch is composed of four originally separate documents, of which the earliest is that known as J, so called because of its use of the name Yahweh in the narratives of Genesis. The second is E, so called because of its use of Elohim prior to the specific revelation of the name Yahweh to Moses, recorded in Exod. 3:14-15. These two documents were combined, with the necessary harmonization, to form a single narrative, JE, by a redactor, R[JE]. The third document in point of time is Deuteronomy, D, which is identical in whole or in part with the lawbook found in the temple in the reign of Josiah. The combination of JE with D to form JED was effected by a redactor, R[D], who in the process added a considerable amount of material to the older narratives. While his additions to the account of the patriarchal and Mosaic periods are severely limited in scope, and are for the most part of a theological character, those to the narrative of the Conquest are of such a nature as to alter radically the representations of JE. For this and other reasons it is probable that the Deuteronomic redaction was carried through by different hands, possibly at different times. The fourth document is P, so symbolized because of the great amount of priestly legislation it contains. It is postexilic in origin, and was conflated with JED by a redactor, R[P], to form JEDP. This, allowing for the insertion of some supplementary legislative material, an occasional narrative, and possibly for some minor Deuteronomic additions, was substantially the present Hexateuch.

The evidence upon which this hypothesis rests can be only briefly summarized here. Some of the textual phenomena which led to its formulation have already been indicated, but it is in Exod. 6:2-3 that the key to the composition of the Hexateuch is found. There it is stated that God had appeared to Abraham, Isaac, and Jacob as El Shaddai, but had not been known to them by his name Yahweh. Gen. 17:1 and 35:11, recording God's revelation of himself as El Shaddai to Abraham and Jacob respectively—the analogous revelation to Isaac is missing, presumably dropped in the process of conflating the documents because of redactional exigencies—obviously belong to the same source as Exod. 6:2-3; and those stories in Genesis in which the name Yahweh is known to the actors must come from another source.

Gen. 17:1; 35:11; and Exod. 6:2-3 thus provide a point of departure. Gen. 17:1, with which the rest of that chapter is continuous, states explicitly that Abraham was at the time ninety-nine years old. Now we have already seen how the recorded ages of the patriarchs give rise to serious chronological difficulties in the narrative of Genesis, a fact which suggests that the passages in which their ages are given come from another hand than the stories thus rendered incredible. This points to the conclusion that the age verses, and the material inseparable from them, are from the same source as Gen. 17.[12] This material is sufficiently extensive to make it possible to discern something of the style of its author, to note many of his characteristic expressions, and to detect certain of his preconceptions, theological and other. Working with these criteria we are able to isolate from Genesis a body of material informed by a peculiar theory of revelation. In this material it is

---

[9] *Die geschichtlichen Bücher des Alten Testaments* (Leipzig: T. O. Weigel, 1866).

[10] In *The Religion of Israel*, tr. Alfred H. May (London: Williams & Norgate, 1874-75). The original, entitled *Godsdienst van Israels*, appeared in 1869-70.

[11] In a series of articles in *Jahrbücher für deutsche Theologie*, XXI and XXII (1876-77), published in book form as *Die Composition des Hexateuchs* (Berlin: G. Reimer, 1885).

[12] Gen. 12:4b-5; 16:15-16; 23; 25:7-10, 17, 19-20, 26b; 26:34-35; 35:28-29; 37:2a; 41:46a; 47:7-11, 28; 49:29-32; 50:12-13, 22b; Exod. 7:7; etc.

not once recorded that the patriarchs offered sacrifice. In view of the frequent and indeed casual reference to the practice in other parts of the book (e.g., Gen. 12:7; 22:9; 26:25; 35:7, cited above), it is not likely that this silence is accidental. Its significance becomes apparent when it is found that the books of Exodus, Leviticus, and Numbers contain a mass of detailed regulations concerning the modes and dates of sacrifices (Exod. 29:38-42; Lev. 1:2–5:19; Num. 15:1-41; 29:1-39). These regulations are promulgated *de novo;* that is, the assumption underlying them is that hitherto the institution of sacrifice had been unknown. It may reasonably be inferred that they are related to the material in Genesis in which sacrifice is not mentioned. Again, the concern for the proper performance of the cult which finds expression in the regulations regarding sacrifice is also characteristic of the great mass of legislation in Exodus—except that in chs. 20–23 and 34—Leviticus and Numbers. Furthermore, this legislation is cast in the same pedantic style as the material dealing with sacrifice. It is difficult to avoid the conclusion that it comes from the same source.

It is this material which constitutes the P document. A comparison of its laws with those found elsewhere in the Pentateuch leaves no room for doubt that they form the latest stratum of the legal material. The document is thus the latest of the four of which the Hexateuch is composed.

When the P material has been removed from Genesis, the presence of duplications and inconsistencies, and the alternating use of the Lord (Yahweh) and God (Elohim), in the narrative remaining indicate that it comes in the main from two different sources. Using the names employed in referring to or addressing the Deity as our criterion—though allowance must be made for occasional redactional alteration, e.g., in Gen. 40–50 (see the Exeg. thereon) — and correlating passages which reveal similarities of style and identity of interest in certain localities, we are able to reconstruct, with, of course, numerous lacunae, two narratives, the documents J and E. An examination of the non-P material in Exodus-Joshua reveals the fact that these documents are component parts of the Hexateuch—with which Judg. 1:1–2:5 really belongs—as a whole. The dependence of E upon J, noted below, indicates the priority of the latter.

The evidence for the literary independence of Deuteronomy, D, is of a character similar to that for the once separate existence of J, E, and P: (a) The style of the book has marked peculiarities which set it off both from the natural simplicity of J and E and from the formal phraseology of P; and (b) the religious tone of the D legislation stands in marked contrast to the simple cult requirements and matter-of-fact secular enactments of the JE codes (Exod. 20:23–23:19; 34:10-27) on the one hand, and to the advanced ceremonialism of P on the other.

The peculiar style and the religious ideas which characterize D are found also in certain passages in the other books of the Hexateuch. These passages are not only unnecessary to the continuity of the reconstructed source documents, but frequently inject an element of inconsistency into their context. They are accordingly assumed to have come from the hand of a redactor, or redactors, belonging to the same circle as the authors of Deuteronomy—R^D.

That D is later than JE—the narrative built up by R^{JE} through a conflation of the two documents, J and E—is indicated by the fact that the historical recapitulation in the opening chapters of Deuteronomy is dependent upon JE. Furthermore, D incorporates and frequently expands much of the legislative material now forming part of JE.

The priority of D to P is indicated not only by the fact that the laws of the latter are in many cases a development of those of the former, but especially by a comparison of their respective theories as to the priesthood. In D, Levite and priest are practically synonymous terms, and all priests are of equal rank. In P, the Levites are not priests, but ministers of subordinate rank; and at the head of the priesthood stands the high priest, unknown to D. Any suggestion that D is a simplification of P is contradicted by the known fact that the hierarchical system of P remained in force until the destruction of the temple in A.D. 70.

VI. The Structure of the Documents

The Graf-Wellhausen hypothesis has commanded the assent of the great majority [13] of Old Testament critics for more than sixty years, and has served as the point of departure for investigation of the internal structure of the several sources. This investigation, indeed, began as soon as the hypothesis had been formulated. Wellhausen [14] himself pointed out that the account of the rise of nomadism, of the discovery of music, and of the beginning of metalworking in Gen. 4:16-24, derived from the J document, was an account of the origin of certain skills which the author implies had continued in un-

---

[13] For the theories held by the dissenting minority see Simpson, *Early Traditions of Israel,* pp. 44-46; also Robert H. Pfeiffer, *Introduction to the Old Testament* (New York: Harper & Bros., 1941), pp. 140-41.

[14] In *Die Composition des Hexateuchs* mentioned above.

broken existence until his own day. This little narrative was accordingly irreconcilable with the story of the Flood (Gen. 6:5–9:19), one strand of which was also derived from J.

This is but one of the numerous internal inconsistencies which Wellhausen observed, not only in J but also in E and P. They were evidence that the original documents had, each of them, undergone elaboration before being combined into a single narrative. These successive strata of material Wellhausen represented by the symbols J^1, J^2, E^1, E^2, P^1, etc. He was, however, careful to insist upon the provisional character of his conclusions, and left most points of detail to be determined by future investigation.

Wellhausen was followed by Karl Budde,[15] who argued that the J narrative in Gen. 1–11 was composed of two originally independent documents which had been woven together by a redactor. Kuenen[16] likewise recognized divergent accounts of the earliest generations of men in the J material in these chapters, though he was inclined to dissent from Budde's theory of two originally independent documents. He was of the opinion that the inconsistencies, not only in these chapters but in the rest of the J document, were due to the systematic elaboration of one basic narrative. The E material in the Hexateuch, he maintained, had been similarly elaborated—a theory which was further developed by Otto Procksch[17] some years later.

In the quarter of a century following the appearance of Kuenen's treatise on the Hexateuch the study of the separate documents did little more than confirm the fact to which Wellhausen had called attention—that before they had been combined into a single narrative the original documents had in each case been expanded by the introduction of secondary material. The historical circumstances which had given rise to these revisions, the purpose for which they had been undertaken, and the nature of the process by which they had been carried through remained, however, undetermined. A growing disagreement inevitably resulted, not only as to the extent of the supplementary material and, in some cases, as to its affinity, but also as regards the primary form of the documents themselves, the outlines of which, particularly of J and E, became less and less distinct.

Indeed, Hermann Gunkel, in his great and epoch-making commentary on Genesis,[18] explicitly maintained that it was impossible to answer such questions in detail. Following Budde, he distinguished two independent strands in the J narrative of chs. 1–11; similarly, he found two independent strands in the J material dealing with the patriarchs, though he was unable to decide whether or not these were continuous with the strands in the earlier chapters. He was inclined to regard the question as of little importance, for his interest was in the individual units—myths, legends, poems, genealogical tables, and notices—of which the documents were composed. It was to these that he directed his attention.

Through his brilliant and penetrating analysis Gunkel achieved certain results of fundamental importance: (a) he established once and for all the diverse and independent origins of the literary units which make up the source documents of Genesis; (b) he demonstrated that their present form was in most cases the result of gradual growth and adaptation; (c) he revealed the frequently intricate process by which legends of non-Israelite provenance had become an integral part of the Israelite tradition; and (d) he made clear the fact that the tradition in its final form was complex in the extreme—the product of centuries of assimilation and development of material drawn from many sources.

A few years later Hugo Gressmann,[19] applying Gunkel's techniques to the account of the Exodus and the events which followed, threw fresh light upon the narrative of the remaining books of the Pentateuch.

Nevertheless, the work of these two scholars was not pure gain, for in reviving (albeit in modified form) the fragment-hypothesis and the supplementation-hypothesis of the late eighteenth and early nineteenth centuries, they inevitably tended to overlook the fact that the growth and development of the national tradition had been conditioned by political events—such as, for example, the formation and extension of intertribal confederacies—and to underestimate, therefore, the extent to which the articulation of the tradition had been a process consciously and deliberately undertaken.[20]

Now, it must be realized that if the J and E documents should turn out to be not carefully articulated historical narratives—however legendary much of their content may be—but merely collections of legends and other material, so loosely put together that it is frequently doubt-

---

[15] *Die biblische Urgeschichte* (Giessen: J. Ricker, 1883).

[16] *An Historico-critical Inquiry into the Origin and Composition of the Hexateuch*, tr. P. H. Wicksteed (London: Macmillan & Co., 1886).

[17] *Das nordhebräische Sagenbuch: die Elohimquelle* (Leipzig: J. C. Hinrichs, 1906).

[18] *Genesis übersetzt und erklärt* (Göttingen: Vandenhoeck & Ruprecht, 1901; "Göttinger Handkommentar zum Alten Testament").

[19] *Mose und seine Zeit* (Göttingen: Vandenhoeck & Ruprecht, 1913).

[20] For instances of Gunkel's failure in this respect see Simpson, *Early Traditions of Israel*, pp. 46-47.

ful to which collection a certain legend may belong, there would be little reason to hope that they would be of much value as source material for reconstructing the history of Israel, or for tracing the course of their religious development. In such a case the study of the narrative of the Hexateuch—the study of the laws is another matter—would be not much more than an academic exercise; it certainly could contribute little to the business of living. And this was precisely what seemed to be emerging from the critical efforts of twenty-five years. Scholars had lost their way in a kind of literary morass, their work was in danger of degenerating into pure irrelevancy, and seemed to the ordinary man to have brought little more than intolerable confusion.

It was in explicit revolt against this confusion that Rudolf Smend in 1912 published his work on the Hexateuch.[21] In this he advanced the theory that the narrative, apart from the Deuteronomic material contained in it, was the result of the conflation not of three, but of four documents, J^1, J^2, E, and P. Of these, J^1 and J^2 had first been combined by a redactor, R^J, whose narrative was then fused with E by R^E. To this, R^D had later added Deuteronomy. Finally, R^P had combined R^D's work with P.

Working with this apparatus, Smend was able to assign practically all the material to one or other of his primary sources; secondary material, whether elaboration of one of the component narratives or redactional harmonization and linking, he reduced to a bare minimum.

Smend's methods and conclusions, with certain minor modifications, were accepted by Otto Eissfeldt in his analysis of the narrative of the Hexateuch[22] which he published ten years later. To avoid, however, any suggestion that the second source, J^2, was merely an elaboration of the first, he substituted the symbols L and J for Smend's J^1 and J^2, L signifying lay source (*Laienquelle*). In employing this symbol he was able to call attention to the fact that it was the least theological of the narratives, and also to place it in sharp contrast to the final one of the series, the Priestly Code.

The analytical work of these two scholars was characterized by an extraordinary penetration. Nevertheless, the order which Smend brought out of the confusion was artificial in the extreme. The narratives as he reconstructed them suffered in places from an internal inconsistency, so marked as to be impossible.[23] At the same time they were so similar in the ground

they covered that they could only have been written by men depending upon a common tradition, the content and scope of which remained fixed for some four centuries. And there is a further point to be noted. In Smend's analysis the authors of the four documents, J^1, J^2, E, and P (in Eissfeldt's terminology, L, J, E, P), had effected an almost identical articulation of their material, so that it was possible for a redactor to conflate the first two with practically no adaptation or connecting links, and then for a second redactor, with the same ease, to combine this narrative with the third. The question inevitably arises, "Why, if they were indeed so similar, were the pre-exilic narratives ever combined?"

These facts suggest that Smend, troubled by the literary confusion which confronted him, allowed himself to be swayed by his desire to find a solution to the problem of the Hexateuch along the neat and orderly lines of a document-hypothesis uncontaminated by the heresy of supplementation, and so failed to allow sufficiently for the presence of material which does not belong to any of the narratives in their original form. He took little account of the steady and dynamic expansion to which the tradition had been subjected, even after it had first been committed to writing. As a result he failed, as Gunkel had failed, to discern the extent to which this process reflected, and had been conditioned by, political and religious developments. His analysis was, in short, a purely literary performance.

VII. The Two Editions of the J Document

All this seems to suggest that, for a solution of the problem of the Hexateuch, full account must be taken of the political and religious developments which Gunkel and Smend too easily ignored. To this conclusion Wellhausen was again the first to point the way when, arguing from certain duplications in the narrative of the Exodus and from the general impression of the crucial importance of Kadesh which the narrative nevertheless conveyed even in its present form, he maintained that the tradition of Israel had originally known nothing of a journey to, or of the lawgiving at, Sinai, but had told of the people going directly to Kadesh from the Red Sea.[24]

The phenomena to which Wellhausen called attention did not of themselves necessarily point to this conclusion. But Eduard Meyer,[25] taking up where Wellhausen had left off, delivered him

[21] *Die Erzählung des Hexateuch* (Berlin: Georg Reimer, 1912).

[22] *Hexateuch-Synopse* (Leipzig: J. C. Hinrichs, 1922).

[23] Instances are given in Simpson, *Early Traditions of Israel*, pp. 47-48.

[24] *Prolegomena to the History of Israel*, tr. J. Sutherland Black and Allan Menzies (Edinburgh: A. & C. Black, 1885), pp. 342-43.

[25] *Die Israeliten und ihre Nachbarstämme* (Halle: Max Niemeyer, 1906), pp. 1-103.

from a possible charge of undue impressionism. He established the existence in the Hexateuch of a document, J^1, which told of the Israelites journeying directly to Kadesh from the Red Sea, and showed that this document had been elaborated by a later writer, J^2, who added the material telling of the journey of Israel to Sinai and of the lawgiving there.

Having established this point, Meyer proceeded to argue that the southern tribes had entered Palestine not from the east by crossing the Jordan, but from the south.[26] His argument was based not upon a reconstruction of an early narrative of the Conquest—which indeed he believed to be irrecoverable—but upon the geographical position of the tribes of Judah and Simeon, cut off as they were from the north until the rise of the monarchy; upon the political situation in the time of Saul and earlier; and upon the narrative reflecting a movement northward from Kadesh in Num. 21:1-3, and its variants in Num. 14:39-45 and Exod. 17:8-16.

In analyzing the narrative of the Conquest,[27] beginning with Num. 13 and ending with Judg. 2:5, one may isolate what is probably the earliest account of an invasion of Palestine from the south (as postulated by Meyer). This appears to belong to the same stratum of the J material as the Kadesh narrative of the Exodus. We thus have an account of the Exodus and the Conquest which embodies the tradition of the southern tribes only.

Just as the Kadesh narrative of the Exodus was elaborated by the addition of material telling of the Israelites going to Sinai following the deliverance at the Red Sea, so the account of an invasion of Palestine from the south has been enlarged by the addition of material telling of all the tribes proceeding from Kadesh to the land of Moab, of their miraculous crossing of the Jordan at Jericho, and of their conquest, under the leadership of Joshua, of the land occupied in historical times by Ephraim and Benjamin. Following this the narrative reverts to the earlier account—now preserved in Judg. 1—of the conquest of the south, though with the order of events changed to make it fit the new representation that it was a movement not northwards from Kadesh, but southwards from Joshua's (supposed) headquarters in the vicinity of Jericho.

This secondary conquest material seems to belong to the same stratum of J as does the Sinai material, that is, J^2. Since it is concerned with Benjamin and Ephraim, one may tentatively infer that the specific tradition upon which J^2 had drawn in his elaboration of the

southern J^1 narrative was the tradition of those two tribes.

Further support for this inference is furnished by an analysis of Genesis which takes full account of the duplications and inconsistencies in the J material noted by Wellhausen, Budde, and Kuenen, for which Smend and Eissfeldt sought to account by postulating two originally independent documents, both characterized by expressions and modes of thought which earlier critics had noted as indications of J.

By this analysis a narrative is isolated which contains traditions most of which bear the marks of having been current either in the vicinity of Hebron, the capital of the southern tribes, or in the land east of the Jordan. Significantly, the author of this narrative nowhere reveals any firsthand knowledge of the traditions of the Joseph-Rachel tribes, Ephraim, Manasseh, and Benjamin. It is thus a southern document, with certain east-Jordan affinities, and it appears to belong to the same stratum of the J tradition as the Exodus Kadesh narrative and the related account of the conquest of the south.

This J^1 material in Genesis has been subjected to the same kind of elaboration as the J^1 narrative of the Exodus and the Conquest. There has been added to it a great deal of material which reveals for the most part an interest in legends which are rooted in the north. This material is from the same stratum as that dealing with Sinai and the conquest of the north.

The conclusion demanded by the observation of these phenomena would seem to be that the inconsistencies and repetitions within the J material of the Hexateuch, to which Wellhausen first called attention in 1876, are due to the fact that the document is based on a very simple narrative, J^1, embodying the tradition of the southern tribes; and that this was later elaborated by another writer, J^2, who added to it the tradition of the Joseph tribes, reconciling the two traditions as best he could.

The "second edition" of the J document itself received some further additions, but this elaboration did not have the systematic character which marks the work of J^2. It was the completed J document—J^2 plus supplements—which was ultimately conflated with the E document to form the narrative JE.

This conclusion, it may be noted, is within the framework of the Graf-Wellhausen hypothesis, and indeed is in substantial agreement with the suggestions advanced, however tentatively, by Wellhausen himself. It rejects the theory—also congruent with the Graf-Wellhausen hypothesis—espoused in different forms by Budde, Smend, and others, that the J narrative is the

---

[26] Ibid., pp. 72-77.

[27] Simpson, *Early Traditions of Israel*, pp. 230-329.

product of an interweaving of two originally separate and independent documents.

Pfeiffer's variant to this latter theory should also be noted.[28] He feels that the non-P material in Gen. 1:1–11:9 is so unlike the J stories of the patriarchs that it cannot originate from the same hand. He therefore derives it, together with certain other stories in Genesis, such as chs. 14; 19; 34; and 38, from a document of Edomite origin which he designates S (=South or Seir), and which he believes to have been added to JEDP *ca.* 400 B.C. When, however, it is clearly recognized (see Exeg. of Genesis) that the non-Israelite traditions taken over by the Hebrew writers were of widely diverse origin, the difference in tone and character in the material generally attributed to J is sufficiently accounted for; and, at the same time, the difficulty inherent in Pfeiffer's theory—that at so late a date as 400, stories of non-Israelite origin, and of such dubious morality as those in Gen. 34 and 38, should have been intruded into the national tradition—is avoided.

VIII. The Purpose of J¹

An examination of the narrative in the books of Judges and Samuel reveals the same structural pattern as that which appears in the pre-exilic narrative of the Hexateuch—J¹ elaborated by J² and E. It is significant, however, that evidence for two strata of material in J comes to an end with II Sam. 8:15, that is, shortly after David had moved his capital from Hebron to Jerusalem.[29]

It may reasonably be inferred that the J¹ document was written about this time, that is, about the year 1000. Furthermore, in view of the interest of J¹ in Hebron,[30] David's first capital, it seems not unlikely that one of the author's purposes in writing history was a desire to record the events which brought greatness to that city and its sanctuary—a greatness now threatened by David's move to Jerusalem. His secondary aim was to bring into an ordered relationship the various local legends current at various holy places in Palestine,[31] and to unify them with the tradition which Israel had brought from the desert. He had then gone on to record the feats of certain heroes (judges), leading up to the rise of the monarchy and David's accession to the throne.

[28] *Introduction to O.T.*, pp. 159-67.

[29] It seems probable that the story in II Sam. 21:1-11 belongs to the earlier stratum. It is obvious, however, that this story, which tells of an incident that must have occurred early in David's reign, has been moved from its original position in the narrative, for whatever reason.

[30] See Exeg. of Genesis; note also the J material in the story of the spies (Num. 13:17-33) and the sequel to this in Judg. 1:10-20.

[31] See Intro. and Exeg. of Genesis.

Underlying his whole narrative is one consistent theme, that of the relation in which Israel stood to the Lord, the God of Sinai. Yahweh had in his call of Abraham chosen Israel to be his people; he had delivered them from the oppression of the Egyptians; he had reaffirmed his choice of them through Moses, revealing his essential righteousness and demanding justice in all the relationships of life; he had settled them in the good land of Palestine, and had protected them against their enemies; and now he had made them into a nation, giving them David as their king to execute "justice and righteousness unto all his people" (II Sam. 8:15 ASV). It was the relationship in which they stood to the Lord that gave significance to Israel—that and nothing else.

IX. The Purpose and Methods of J²

The J¹ document was written when the future seemed filled with hope. Some seventy-five years later, *ca.* 930, the political unity of north and south which David had achieved was shattered, the people whom the Lord had chosen and brought into a peculiar relationship with himself were organized into two kingdoms, and the spiritual unity of Israel was threatened.

It may reasonably be assumed that the J material following II Sam. 8:15 comes in the main from the hand of J². Its concluding section is the account of the disruption of the kingdom,[32] which ends with the words, "So Israel rebelled against the house of David unto this day" (I Kings 12:19).

This suggests that the literary activity of J² was, to some extent at any rate, motivated by this event. Furthermore, the content of his narrative shows that he was also eager to preserve the spiritual unity of Israel. He saw that the real unity of the people inhered not in the state, but in the will of the Lord who had brought them into a unique relationship with himself.

This had indeed been the theme of the J¹ narrative, but something more than this was needed to meet the situation which the disruption of the kingdom had brought about. For the J¹ document embodied only the tradition of the southern tribes, and stressed the fact of God's activity in the history of Israel with reference only to events in which those tribes had been involved—the Exodus, the deliverance at the Red Sea, the ministry of Moses at Kadesh, and the conquest of the south. The northern tribes had had no part in these events.

[32] Gustav Hölscher, "Das Buch der Könige, seine Quellen und seine Redaktion," ΕΥΧΑΡΙΣΤΗΡΙΟΝ, *Studien zur Religion und Literatur des Alten und Neuen Testaments*, ed. Hans Schmidt (Göttingen: Vandenhoeck & Ruprecht, 1923), I, 181-82.

They had entered Palestine by an independent movement [33] from the east across the Jordan, not from the south. Their knowledge of Moses and his work was limited to what they had learned from the southern tribes in Palestine, for their ancestors had not come under his influence. Consequently, Kadesh had no place in their complex of associations; Sinai was for them the center of the Lord's activity (cf. Judg. 5:5), and the Lord was to them still primarily the God of the storm, the God of war. Their awareness of him as the God of justice and righteousness was less insistent than was the awareness of the southern tribes to whose ancestors this truth had been revealed through Moses.

J[2] accordingly undertook the task of revising the J[1] narrative so that it would appeal more directly to the people of the north, and bring home to them the fact of the spiritual unity of the nation as a whole—a unity which inhered in the will of God.

J[1] had begun the process of uniting legends long current in Palestine to the desert tradition of Israel. J[2] continued this process. He first dealt with certain tales which had originated centuries earlier in Babylonia—the Marduk creation myth,[34] the saga of Eden, the garden of God, and the story of the Flood. These had found their way to Palestine, and had long since become a part of the cultural heritage into which the Joseph tribes had entered— though the fact that J[1] made no use of them would seem to indicate that they were unknown in the south. J[2] could not ignore them without endangering the strong tendency toward monotheism, which even at this time characterized Yahwism. He therefore took them over, and, with the necessary theological and moral adaptation,[35] incorporated them into the J[1] narrative, with which he was working.

He then proceeded to expand and elaborate J[1]'s relatively simple narrative of the patriarchs. His additions were made for various reasons: (a) to explain the relationship in which Israel stood to neighboring peoples—for example, the notices which form the nucleus of the much-expanded genealogical tables in Gen. 10, and the stories now preserved, along with parallel material from other documents, in chs. 16; 24; and 27; (b) to account for the existence of certain northern tribes which had apparently been unknown to J[1]—the J material in Gen. 30:1-24, and 35:16-20; (c) to bring out the fact —of which J[1] appears to have been ignorant— of the connection of Joseph with Shechem, and to witness to the power and prestige of the tribes claiming descent from him—the material from J[2]'s hand in Gen. 37–50. Other minor additions were designed, (d) to make more explicit the fact of the Lord's care for the patriarchs; (e) to mitigate the somewhat dubious behavior which had been attributed to them in some of the older stories—for example, Jacob's tricky outwitting of Laban (Gen. 30:31– 31:35) and Judah's relations with Tamar (ch. 38); and (f) simply to improve the literary quality of the narrative.

This revision of the earlier account of the primeval world and of the patriarchs was a relatively simple matter, and involved little change in the order of events as they had been there set down. J[2]'s elaboration of the story of the oppression in Egypt, the birth and commissioning of Moses, and the events preceding the Exodus was limited for the most part to making more explicit its religious significance. When, however, he came to deal with the life of Israel in the desert and the Conquest, he was compelled to subject his predecessor's narrative to more drastic treatment.

As has already been noted, the tradition of the Joseph tribes knew nothing of Kadesh; for them Sinai was the only desert center of the Lord's activity. If the southern tradition of Moses as the great exponent of Yahwism was to find something more than formal acceptance among the northern tribes—if, that is, it was to become a real and essential part of their religion—it was necessary that Moses should be connected with Sinai. J[2] accordingly revised the J[1] narrative by representing the Israelites as proceeding from the Red Sea, not at once to Kadesh, but first to Sinai, where, through the mediation of Moses, the Lord entered into a covenant with them. There can be little doubt that, as Eduard Meyer [36] has argued, the covenant idea in Israel was at least partly derived from the cult of Baal-berith—the Lord of the Covenant—the tutelary deity of Shechem. Hence, J[2] not only transferred the scene of Moses' essential activity from Kadesh to Sinai to make it definitive for the northern tribes; he also stated it in terms which related it dynamically to their own experience.

[33] Cf. A. T. Olmstead, *History of Palestine and Syria to the Macedonian Conquest* (New York: Charles Scribner's Sons, 1931), chs. xv and xvii.

[34] No trace of this is found in the extant J material in Genesis. There can be little doubt, however, that, as Karl Marti has argued (*Das Buch Jesaja* [Tübingen: J. C. B. Mohr, 1900], pp. 338-39), the J[2] narrative opened with a version of this myth, which was later dropped by R[p] in favor of the revision of it made by P, now contained in Gen. 1:1–2:4a; see Simpson, *Early Traditions of Israel*, p. 491.

[35] For the details of this adaptation see Exeg. of Gen. 1-3; 6:5–8:22. It may be noted that the inconsistency in J between the flood story and Gen. 4:19-22 is in this way accounted for.

[36] *Israeliten und ihre Nachbarstämme*, pp. 542-61.

J² then told of the Israelites moving to Kadesh, thus reverting to the J¹ narrative which he followed, with some minor elaboration, up to the departure of the tribes from Kadesh for the conquest of Palestine. At this point, since he was making basic to his history a tradition familiar among the Joseph-tribes, of an entry into the land near Jericho, he was compelled to abandon the J¹ account of a movement northward from Kadesh. Instead, he told of the people proceeding to the east of the Jordan. There, after the king of Moab had tried in vain to persuade the seer Balaam to curse Israel—J² is here incorporating into the national tradition a legend, probably of pre-Israelite origin, which had been taken over by the east-Jordan tribes—Moses died and Joshua succeeded him. Under his leadership the Jordan was crossed and the country conquered.

In writing this account of the conquest J² made use of various local traditions which may well have been preserved, as Martin Noth [37] suggests, in the sanctuary at Gilgal. He then reverted once more to the J¹ narrative, and told of the conquest of the south, continuing with the account (considerably elaborated) of the judges, of the rise of the monarchy, of the Davidic kingdom and its disruption, ending his history with I Kings 12:19.

This is the narrative from which, with some minor additions, the J material in the Hexateuch is derived. Written for a definite purpose —to preserve the spiritual unity of Israel from the dangers which threatened it consequent upon the disruption of the kingdom—it resulted from and reflects the political events of the eleventh and tenth centuries. It may accordingly be dated [38] about the year 900, one hundred years later than the J¹ document upon which it is largely based.

X. The Tradition of the E Document

The E document begins with the story of Abraham. In the sequence of the events which it records through the patriarchal period, the Exodus, and the Conquest, it is much the same as J², a fact which indicates that it is in some way dependent upon that document. There are, however, certain significant differences of representation. (a) The name Yahweh (the Lord) does not occur in the stories of the patriarchs. Instead E uses Elohim (God). According to him the name Yahweh was unknown until it was revealed to Moses (Exod. 3:14-15). (b) Hebron is never mentioned and Abraham is

represented as having his home in Beer-sheba. It may be noted that J² had connected Abraham with this place, though at the same time preserving in a modified form the J¹ tradition which had associated him exclusively with Hebron. (c) The scene of the covenant between the Lord and Israel is not Mount Sinai, which is never mentioned, but Mount Horeb. Nor is it possible to hold that Horeb is merely another name for Sinai, for the implication of the E narrative is that it was situated much nearer to Egypt. [39] (d) Kadesh is never mentioned, and the work of Moses is associated exclusively with Horeb. (e) The crossing of the Jordan was made not at Jericho, as J² had represented, but at Adamah, [40] at the junction of the Jabbok and the Jordan. (f) Following the crossing of the Jordan the Israelites went straight to Shechem, where, in accordance with a command given by Moses before his death (Deut. 11:29-30; 27:2-8; note "on the day when ye shall pass over the Jordan," in 27:2), the covenant with the Lord was renewed (Josh. 8:30-35). It should be noted that neither of the passages here cited is in its original form. [41] Both were tampered with because the Samaritans were appealing to them in support of their claim that Shechem, not Jerusalem, was the central sanctuary referred to in the Deuteronomic Code (e.g., Deut. 12:5). (g) The conquest of Palestine thus began not at Jericho, but at Shechem— though E says nothing of any fighting at Shechem—and so was a movement from north to south. (h) There are even greater differences in the material now preserved in Judges, and especially in Samuel, particularly in the account of the rise of the monarchy. The document seems to continue through the books of Kings. [42] If, however, it first appeared about 700, as is suggested below, the material following II Kings 17 must be from a second hand.

There can be little doubt that the group whose tradition forms the basis of the E document was of another origin than the group upon whose tradition J² had drawn in his elaboration of J¹. For the one, the holy mount was Horeb, for the other, Sinai. Up to a point, therefore, their history had been different. But in Palestine the Horeb group had come to know the southern tradition of the patriarchs, of Moses, and of the Exodus. This they had gradu-

---

[37] *Das Buch Josua* (Tübingen: J. C. B. Mohr, 1938; "Handbuch zum Alten Testament"), p. xi.

[38] The date usually assigned is 850 B.C. See, however, W. F. Albright, *From the Stone Age to Christianity* (2nd ed.; Baltimore: Johns Hopkins Press, 1946), p. 190.

[39] August von Gall, *Altisraelitische Kultstätten* (Giessen: J. Ricker, 1898), pp. 1-22. See also Simpson, *Early Traditions of Israel*, p. 613.

[40] See Adam C. Welch, *Deuteronomy, the Framework to the Code* (London: Oxford University Press, 1932), pp. 175-82. Also Simpson, *op. cit.*, pp. 285, 293, 316, 644.

[41] See Meyer, *Israeliten und ihre Nachbarstämme*, p. 546; cf. Smend, *Die Erzählung des Hexateuch*, pp. 264-67.

[42] See Hölscher, "Das Buch der Könige."

ally made their own as they had come to have their part in the peculiar relationship with the Lord into which Israel had been taken. The result of this fusion of the southern tradition with their own remembered history would be a tradition, preserved at some point in the north —probably Shechem, in view of the unique position accorded to that sanctuary in E—which differed markedly both in form and content from the tradition created by J², and which, it may be assumed, had become (so to speak) the official history of Judah, Benjamin, and Ephraim.

XI. The Purpose of E

It seems unlikely that this new and composite tradition would, before it was committed to writing, have followed the J² order of events as closely as the E document does. That document would thus seem to have been written by one who had only recently come into contact with the earlier narrative, and had believed it to be inaccurate. Certainly it did not present the national tradition as he was familiar with it. He therefore undertook the task of recasting it to bring it into closer agreement with the tradition of Shechem. At the same time, he utilized the opportunity thus offered to soften some of the anthropomorphisms of J, and to remove certain tales which the conscience of the people, as it had developed over a period of some two centuries, now found to be morally objectionable (cf. J²'s treatment of J¹ in this respect).

It can scarcely be supposed that the author was motived purely by an abstract concern for historical accuracy. Such an interest would have been impossible in his age and environment. He was, rather, dealing with a crisis in the life of the nation, and it seems probable that this was the fall of the northern kingdom.

The fact is sometimes overlooked that the destruction of the state, disastrous as it was, released the religious leaders of the north from certain responsibilities which had been growing more and more intolerable, and left them free to reconstitute the community on a religious basis—free to begin the transformation of North Israel into a church. Conscious of their common heritage, they will have at least attempted a *rapprochement* with the leaders in the south. How far they succeeded must remain doubtful. The priesthood of Jerusalem—the officials of an "established church"—may not, at the moment, have been particularly interested. It may indeed have been their intransigent refusal to meet the northerners halfway that led to the writing of the E document with its disregard of Kadesh and Hebron, and its attribution

to Jacob of an importance, both political and religious,[43] equal to that of Abraham.

The E document thus appears to have been written about the year 700,[44] and to be the result of, and to reflect, the political events of the eighth century.

XII. The Conflation of J and E

When Jerusalem fell in 586, the religious leaders of the south found themselves in much the same position, and were confronted with much the same problems, as the northerners had been in 722. Once more a *rapprochement* was attempted; this time, it would seem, with greater success. The existence of two mutually contradictory histories of the nation was an obstacle to the desired unity between the north and the south, so the two documents, J and E, were conflated in such a way as to preserve the salient features of each. On the whole, however, the point of view of J predominated. This new document, JE, became the "official" history of Israel.

XIII. The Origin and Purpose of Deuteronomy

The opinion that Deuteronomy in whole or in part is identical with the Book of the Law found in the temple in the reign of Josiah (II Kings 22:8) was first advanced by Jerome, and again by Thomas Hobbes in the *Leviathan* some twelve hundred years later.[45] In the course of the nineteenth century, however, this identification became almost an axiom of Hexateuchal criticism. It has, nevertheless, been called into question in the past twenty-five years by Adam C. Welch,[46] Theodor Oestreicher,[47] Gustav Hölscher,[48] and others.

There can be no doubt that the redactor who put the account of Josiah's reformation (II Kings 22:3–23:25) into its final form intended to, and did, convey the impression that it was a carrying out of the provisions of Deuteronomy. Hölscher[49] has shown, however, that this account is not a unity, but is an elaboration of a

---

[43] See Exeg. of Gen. 48:22.

[44] The date usually assigned to E is 750. But the historical situation at that time seems to have held nothing which would account for the writing of a document departing so markedly and deliberately from the J tradition. Hölscher ("Das Buch der Könige," pp. 205-6), it may be noted, believes that it was written during the Exile.

[45] See J. Estlin Carpenter and George Harford, *The Composition of the Hexateuch* (London: Longmans, Green & Co., 1902), pp. 35, 38.

[46] *The Code of Deuteronomy* (London: James Clarke & Co., 1924).

[47] *Das deuteronomische Grundgesetz* (Gütersloh: C. Bertelsmann, 1923).

[48] "Komposition und Ursprung des Deuteronomiums," *Zeitschrift für die alttestamentliche Wissenschaft*, XL (1922), 161-255.

[49] "Das Buch der Könige," pp. 206-13.

more simple narrative telling of Josiah's purging of the temple of the symbols of Assyrian influence which had been introduced by Manasseh (II Kings 21:4-5). In 621 the Assyrian Empire was breaking up, and Josiah recognized that the opportunity had come for a reaffirmation of the nation's ancient faith in the Lord, and acted accordingly.[50]

If this is a valid reconstruction of the event, then Josiah's reform was not the implementation of the provisions of the Deuteronomic Code, and the code itself must have had another origin than that usually assigned to it. Some light is thrown on this question by Welch, who both argues for the northern provenance of the code,[51] and maintains that many of its provisions come from an earlier period than the time of Josiah.[52]

A likely occasion for its compilation would seem to be the fall of Samaria in 722, and, like E, it may well have been a product of the movement for the reconstruction of the northern community already referred to. If this is the case, then it is reasonable to assume that the code was the fundamental law of the north at the time of the fall of Judah.

The extent to which this movement, with its insistence that the Lord was the only God for Israel (cf. Deut. 13; 17:2-7), had affected the south prior to 586 cannot be determined. But the present form of the account of Josiah's reformation, linking it as it does with Deuteronomy, may well echo a historical fact—that Josiah had been influenced by what the Deuteronomists had achieved in purifying the religious life of the north.

It has already been suggested that, following the fall of the state, the religious leaders of the south effected a *rapprochement* with the north. This involved ultimately their acceptance of the code of Deuteronomy, which was incorporated into the JE narrative, possibly displacing the code known as the Book of the Covenant (Exod. 20:22–23:19). This code, a compilation of enactments of diverse origin, seems to have been first incorporated into the national history just before the account of Moses' death; and later to have been moved to its present position to make room for the code of Deuteronomy. However that may be, the fact that the latter code was eventually integrated with the JE narrative is evidenced by the presence of E material in Deut. 11:29-30—adapted to make it part of the introduction to the code—and in Deut. 27:2, 5-8; of J material in Deut. 31:14-15, 23; and of both J and E in Deut. 34.

[50] See Oestreicher, *Das deuteronomische Grundgesetz,* pp. 9, 33, 37, 39-43.
[51] *The Code of Deuteronomy,* pp. 185, 190-92.
[52] *Ibid.,* pp. 45, 51, 99, 113, 130-31.

This new document, JED, was then elaborated by a succession of editors, who added such parts of Deut. 1:1–11:25; 27:11–31:13; 31:24–32:47; 33, as had not already found a place in D prior to its conflation with JE. They may in this process of elaboration have dropped some earlier material. They also made other additions and changes of varying degrees of importance, both in the narrative and in the code.

JED is thus the product of the Exile, and became the official history, so to speak, of the Palestinian-Jewish community. In its final form —and perhaps considerably earlier—it contained the law of the central sanctuary. It may well be, in view of the implications of Deut. 11:26-31; 27:2-8; Josh. 8:30-35; 24:1-27,[53] that this originally referred not to Jerusalem but to Shechem. That is, during the Exile, following the integration of the north and south, Jerusalem fell into the background, and men looked to Shechem for leadership. For it was the priests and prophets of Shechem who had responded selflessly to the situation resulting from the fall of the state in 722, and, thus responding, had been able by the grace of God to rebuild a broken community. It was the priests and prophets of Shechem who played the role of the good Samaritan, and brought help and healing to the bewildered people of the south a century and a quarter later. Jerusalem had fallen despite its supposed inviolability, and its priesthood had been carried into exile. It is little wonder that the prestige of Jerusalem passed to the north—at least for a time.

XIV. The Origin and Purpose of P

In Babylonia the priests of Jerusalem were not idle. They assumed the leadership of the exiled Jews, and giving a new significance to certain ancient institutions—the observance of the sabbath, the practice of abstaining from certain foods, and the custom of circumcision— welded their community into a self-conscious unity. At the same time they brought together into a new code a number of pre-exilic laws, giving it a hortatory tone throughout, and insisting that "holiness" was the dominant element in the relationship between the Lord and his people. Holiness was demanded from Israel by the holiness of the God who had chosen them. Hence, this code, preserved with some secondary material in Lev. 17–26, has been called the Holiness Code.

The interest of this group was naturally focused upon Jerusalem, and it was due to their influence that, in the favorable circumstances which followed the rise of the Persian Empire, the temple in Jerusalem was rebuilt in 516, and the ancient cult restored.

[53] See Simpson, *Early Traditions of Israel, ad loc.*

It is difficult to recover the actual course of events during the next seventy-five years, so completely has the Chronicler confused the record now contained in the books of Ezra and Nehemiah. Nevertheless, a critical examination of the memoirs of Nehemiah [54] leaves one with the inescapable impression that when Nehemiah arrived in Jerusalem he found the city in a sorry state, divided in its leadership, largely controlled by a priesthood which was content to keep the temple going, but had lost its vision of the city as the dynamic center of a religion of world-wide significance.

Nehemiah's appointment as governor of Judah by the Persian king meant that Judah was made politically independent of Samaria. The governor of that province opposed Nehemiah's efforts to restore Jerusalem's self-respect. Nevertheless, the walls were rebuilt and measures taken for the security of the city (Neh. 2:17–6:15).

We have no way of knowing whether the political opposition to Nehemiah and his policy on the part of the governor of Samaria was reinforced by ecclesiastical opposition from the religious community finding its center in Shechem—the Deuteronomist community. This may have been the case. On the other hand, the hostility may have begun with the Jerusalemites, who saw in the continued prestige of Shechem a threat to their aim of making Jerusalem the center of the religion of Israel. However that may be, such hostility did eventually develop. The Priestly Code in its original form [55] was adopted as the manifesto of the Jerusalem group, backed by the influence of the Babylonian Diaspora. It contained the P narrative of Genesis, the account of the oppression in Egypt, the call of Moses, the plagues, the Passover and the Exodus, the passage through the Red Sea, the arrival at Sinai, the making of the tabernacle, the setting apart of the priesthood, the numbering of the people, the departure from Sinai, the sending of the manna and the quails, and the P narrative from Num. 13 through the account of the division of the land in Joshua. It thus provided divine sanction for the sabbath, the prohibition of eating blood, and circumcision. In its description of the tabernacle it is dependent upon the plan of the Jerusalem temple for the uniqueness of which it thus by implication claims divine authority. And it makes a similar claim for its priesthood.

The adoption of the Priestly Code made clear and definite the points at issue between the south and the north. There can be no doubt that many were persuaded to transfer their allegiance from Shechem to Jerusalem. Evidence for this is provided not only by the general Deuteronomic editing of the history of the monarchy (cf. I Kings 15:14; 22:43; II Kings 15:35; etc.), which assumes that Jerusalem, not Shechem, was the place the Lord had chosen "to cause his name to dwell there" (Deut. 12: 11), but particularly by the implied claim of the account of Josiah's reformation, in its final form, that Deuteronomy was a southern document, and that it was implemented by the suppression of all sanctuaries outside of Jerusalem (II Kings 23:8).

Nevertheless, this acceptance by the Deuteronomists (or a group of them) of the claims of the Jerusalem priesthood was by no means a simple act of submission. The Jerusalemites on their part seemed to have been forced to make a considerable concession when they accepted as authentic the sacred document of the north, JED. This was eventually conflated with the P Code, and the structural form of the present Pentateuch at last emerged. To this new document other laws, including the Holiness Code, were added from time to time as circumstances demanded. Indeed, it seems likely that additions had already been made to P in the interval between its promulgation and its fusion with JED. Other narratives were also inserted here and there, for instance, the story in Gen. 14.

The agreement between the north and the south which produced the Pentateuch did not, however, settle finally the fundamental point at issue. Shechem's claim to be the one legitimate sanctuary of the God of Israel continued to be voiced. Whether or not it issued in action—the offering of sacrifice at Shechem—formal schism was avoided for some time. But eventually the break occurred. In the reign of Darius III (338-32) [56] a temple was erected on Mount Gerizim at Shechem, where—according to E—Israel, as commanded by Moses (Deut. 11:29-30; 27:2-7), had offered the first sacrifice following its entry into Palestine (Josh. 24:1-25; 8:30-35; see above), and the tie with Jerusalem was broken.

Nevertheless, the Samaritans retained the Pentateuch as their scriptures. Joshua, however, was not accepted, perhaps because of the redactional transposition of Josh. 8:30-35. This passage in its present form substitutes Ebal for Gerizim as the place of sacrifice (vs. 30); and

[54] See Gustav Hölscher, "Die Bücher Esra und Nehemia," Die Heilige Schrift des Alten Testaments, ed. E. Kautzsch and A. Bertholet (4th ed.; Tübingen: J. C. B. Mohr, 1923), II, 491-562.

[55] See Gustav Hölscher, Geschichte der israelitischen und jüdischen Religion (Giessen: Alfred Töpelmann, 1922), pp. 141-43.

[56] Josephus (Antiquities XI. 8. 2) ascribes the erection of the temple to Sanballat, Nehemiah's contemporary, who lived a century earlier. It seems likely that his error lies here, not in his placing of the event in the reign of Darius III.

in its present position places both mountains near Gilgal. It thus carries further the polemic against Shechem, begun by some Jerusalemite redactor who added to the command of Moses in Deut. 11:30 the words "in the land of the Canaanites that dwell in the Arabah, over against Gilgal" (ASV).

XV. Summary

The conclusions advanced in this article stand within the framework of the Graf-Wellhausen hypothesis. This as it was first formulated was primarily a literary analysis, but Wellhausen himself initiated the investigation which was to show how the documents, both in their origin and in their development, were related to the history of Israel as it is known to us. The results of this investigation may be summarized as follows:

(a) The primary material in the Hexateuch is the narrative of J[1], embodying the tradition of the southern tribes, and written about the year 1000 when the prestige of Hebron, their center, was fading before Jerusalem.

(b) About a century later this material was expanded and elaborated by J[2], who added to it certain traditions of the north. His purpose was to preserve the spiritual unity of Israel which had been endangered by the disruption of the kingdom.

(c) Around the year 700, following the fall of Samaria, this J[2] tradition was recast by E to bring it into closer agreement with the originally independent tradition of a group centering at Shechem.

(d) The *rapprochement* between the north and the south following the fall of Jerusalem made it desirable that these two forms of the national tradition should be unified. To this end the two documents J and E were conflated into JE sometime in the course of the sixth century, or perhaps early in the fifth.

(e) The code of Deuteronomy was the creation of the same movement as that which produced the E document. It was designed to provide authoritative guidance for the people of the north, left bewildered and broken by the catastrophe of 722. It was accepted by the south after 586, and was later combined with JE. This new document, JED, embodying the national historical and legal tradition, and centering upon Shechem, was eventually accepted as authoritative by the Palestinian community of Israel.

(f) The Priestly Code was the manifesto of those who, influenced by the ideas of the Babylonian Diaspora, were concerned to make Jerusalem the religious center of Israel. It was officially adopted in Jerusalem about the beginning of the fourth century, and was thus a part of the program developed to continue the work that Nehemiah had begun.

(g) To secure its acceptance by the group which looked to Shechem, P was eventually conflated with JED, and, allowing for certain relatively minor additions, the present Hexateuch, JEDP, was completed.

XVI. Selected Bibliography

CARPENTER, J. ESTLIN, and HARFORD, GEORGE, eds. *The Composition of the Hexateuch*. London: Longmans, Green & Co., 1902.

CHAPMAN, ARTHUR THOMAS. *An Introduction to the Pentateuch* ("The Cambridge Bible"). Cambridge: Cambridge University Press, 1911.

GALLING, KURT. *Die Erwählungstraditionen Israels*. Giessen: Alfred Töpelmann, 1928.

HARFORD, JOHN BATTERSBY. *Since Wellhausen*. Privately published, 1926. Reprint of articles appearing in *The Expositor*, Ser. 9, Vol. IV (1925).

NOTH, MARTIN. *Überlieferungsgeschichte des Pentateuch*. Stuttgart: W. Kohlhammer, 1948.

PFEIFFER, R. H. *Introduction to the Old Testament*. New York: Harper & Bros., 1941. "The Pentateuch," pp. 129-289.

RAD, GERHARD VON. *Das formgeschichtliche Problem des Hexateuchs*. Stuttgart: W. Kohlhammer, 1938.

SIMPSON, CUTHBERT A. *The Early Traditions of Israel*. Oxford: Blackwell, 1948.

SIMPSON, DAVID CAPELL. *Pentateuchal Criticism*. London: Hodder & Stoughton, 1944.

WELLHAUSEN, JULIUS. *Die Composition des Hexateuchs und der historischen Bücher des Alten Testaments*. 2nd. ed. Berlin: G. Reimer, 1889.

THE PROPHETIC LITERATURE

by HUGHELL E. W. FOSBROKE

In the tradition of Judaism the Hebrew scriptures consist of three parts: Law, Prophets, and Writings. The second part is subdivided into Former Prophets, four books which in the English Bible appear as Joshua, Judges, I and II Samuel, and I and II Kings; and Latter Prophets, also four books, Isaiah, Jeremiah, Ezekiel, and The Twelve (The Minor Prophets constituting a single volume). It is of this subdivision, Latter Prophets, that the term "prophetic literature" is used, a subdivision to which there corresponds in the English Bible the sequence of books from Isaiah to Malachi (except for Lamentations and Daniel, which Hebrew tradition places among the Writings).

I. The Ministry of the Spoken Word

It should be noted first of all that the very use of the words "literature" or "book" in this connection may easily give rise to a serious misunderstanding, for these terms would seem to suggest that the prophets were in the first instance literary figures. So, too, the phrase "writing prophets," which is widely current, lends color to the idea that a prophet's chief activity was the composition of a book. True enough, an Isaiah could and did commit to writing his memoirs of the two great crises of his ministry (Isa. 6–8; 28–31), but this he did evidently as an afterthought in the face of apparent failure. Jeremiah dictated his poems to Baruch (Jer. 36), but this only after some years of his ministry had elapsed. Even the shepherd Amos himself may have written down or dictated to another the visions now recorded in chs. 7–8 of the book that bears his name. But in all these cases writing is a secondary activity. The ministry of the prophets was in the first instance a ministry of the spoken word.

The phrase "spoken word" points, then, to what is of primary importance in any consideration of the work of the prophets. There is a vast difference between the language of sound and the language of sight. Writing is comparatively modern—its history hardly more than five or six thousand years—while speech is as old as human nature. The whole man expresses himself in speech as he cannot do in the written word. Over and above the meaning of what a man says there is conveyed by the voice a sense of the vague intimacies of existence, something of the very self. Again, the spoken word embodies, as the written word cannot, a "dominating reference to an immediate situation";[1] it is contemporary with the particular situation or experience of which it speaks. There is, for example, a tremendous difference in the effect of the phrase "a warm day" as it falls from the lips of a damp and drooping human being and as it appears in the impersonal abstraction of the weather report.

Now it is this spoken word that biblical scholarship seeks first of all to recover as it sets about tracing the growth and development of the prophetic literature. In this it is concerned with much more than any merely literary distinctions. It endeavors to enter into the specific immediacy of the situation in which the words were uttered, and to catch the overtones of feeling in which the something more than the surface meaning of the words declared itself.

II. The Beginnings of Prophecy

This effort to recapture the accents of the living voice of the prophet would be an almost impossible task if it were not for our knowledge

[1] A. N. Whitehead, *Modes of Thought* (New York: The Macmillan Co., 1938), p. 53.

of the beginnings of prophecy and the way in which these beginnings have given characteristic form to prophetic utterance. It is in the account of Samuel's choice of Saul to be king over Israel that the prophets as a group make their earliest appearance in the Old Testament. They are there pictured as a company of men coming down from a sanctuary to the accompaniment of lute, timbrel, flute, and harp, and responding to this abundant musical stimulus with ecstatic cries (I Sam. 10:5-6). The ecstasy of these prophets had so contagious an effect that Saul was caught by it and associated himself with them in their prophesying (I Sam. 10:10).

That the word "prophesy" in this connection denotes the behavior of those who were beside themselves is clearly shown in the description of Saul's conduct later on. "The evil spirit from God came upon Saul, and he prophesied in the midst of the house"; and then, as the story unfolds, the king proceeded to cast his spear at David in an effort to pin the young musician to the wall (I Sam. 18:10-11). Again, a late legend describes a striking effect of contact with the prophets. Saul "stripped off his clothes also, and prophesied before Samuel in like manner, and lay down naked all that day and all that night" (I Sam. 19:24).

III. Ecstatic Prophetism in Extrabiblical Sources

The orgiastic character of early prophetism has of course long been recognized, though even now some scholars would minimize its significance. In modern times, however, the affinity of ecstatic prophetism with similar phenomena in other religions has been more closely studied. An Egyptian papyrus of the eleventh century B.C. speaks of the existence of such prophetism at Byblos, a Phoenician city on the coast of Canaan, an interesting fact in view of the appearance of the prophets of the Phoenician Baal in the Elijah stories. These "leaped upon the altar" and "cut themselves after their manner with knives and lancets, till the blood gushed out upon them" (I Kings 18:25-29).

There are references to the same phenomenon in classical and postclassical literature, e.g., Herodotus History II. 61, Lucian Asinus 37, Apuleius Metamorphoses VIII. 24-29. Significantly enough, these point to Syria and Asia Minor as the peculiar habitat of this form of religious frenzy. On the other hand, it has become increasingly clear that ecstatic prophetism did not originate in the ancient Semitic world. No traces of it are found among the pre-Mohammedan Arabs. Greek writers, so quick to observe the bizarre customs of bar-

barians, do not appear to have found it in Babylonia. Herodotus speaks of its occurrence in Egypt; he insists, however, that it is associated not with native Egyptians but with the Carians from Asia Minor. Islam adopted this strange form of mystic rapture only after Mohammedanism had made itself at home in the regions to the north and east of Arabia. All the evidence of geographical distribution therefore suggests that ecstatic prophetism was no part of Israel's desert life, but had established itself in Canaan before Israel's entrance into the land and was part of the heritage, religious and cultural, which the nomad tribes appropriated.

IV. The Transformation of Ecstatic Prophetism

In the biblical narratives, to be sure, ecstatic prophetism is pictured only as it is in process of being transformed by the spirit of Israel's religion. To feel the full force of the contrast between this spirit and the genius of the group ecstasy of which it made use, it is necessary to turn to descriptions of this phenomenon that are found in extrabiblical sources.

In the second-century romance popularly known as The Golden Ass, Apuleius gives an account of a strange group of men in attendance upon a Syrian goddess. He speaks of them as "shouting and dancing like mad persons to the sound of the pipe," as spinning "round so that their hair flew out in a circle," as biting their own flesh and wounding themselves while "one more mad than the rest . . . feigned a swoon and frenzy." [2] The writer is a satirist and he rightly insists on the exhibitionist and mercenary character of the performance, but perhaps makes too much of the note of pretense. In such matters the line between the simulated and the genuine cannot be sharply drawn even by the participants themselves, as Browning has clearly shown in "Mr. Sludge, 'The Medium.'" Characteristic, at any rate, of the group ecstasy are the frantic dancing to the sound of the pipe, the howling, the shouting, and the self-wounding; and especially significant is the conduct of the man who "feigned a swoon," not only because of the parallel with Saul lying naked all that day and all that night, but because the swooning was evidently one of the ways in which the mystic rapture could find its complete fulfillment.

Still further knowledge of this strange phenomenon of group ecstasy is gained by consideration of the worship of Dionysus, the god of vegetation and of the vine in particular. Belief in this deity came to Greece from Phrygia by way of Thrace, and the connection

[2] VIII. 27.

with Asia Minor may suggest that this region was the original home of ecstatic prophecy. In *The Bacchae*, Euripides gives the most vivid portrayal of the behavior of the Dionysus worshipers, and there are also references to their wild revels in other classical writings. Edwin Rohde's penetrating analysis of the mood of these devotees is especially illuminating:

The worshippers, too, in furious exaltation and divine inspiration, strive after the god; they seek communion with him. They burst the physical barriers of their soul. A magic power takes hold of them; they feel themselves raised high above the level of their everyday existence; they seem to *become* those spiritual beings who wildly dance in the train of the god. Nay, more, they have a share in the life of the god himself; nothing less can be the meaning of the fact that the enraptured servants of the god call themselves by the name of the god.[3]

Now, it is true that in its desert days Israel had had its own experience of possession. The wild exultation of the battle frenzy speaks clearly through such a poem as the Song of Deborah. The power of the dread storm-god seized upon the warriors, lifted them to new levels of achievement as, careless of what might befall them, they hurled themselves upon the foe. A passage in the book of Amos puts in significant parallelism the prophets and the Nazirites, who were perhaps originally dedicated long-haired warriors (Amos 2:11).

But this fighting rapture differed from ecstatic prophetism in three important respects.

In the first place there was always about the coming in power of Yahweh, the God of Israel, an element of the incalculable. It was as unpredictable as the advent of storm or earthquake. But ecstatic prophetism could be induced by a definite technique of music, dance, and other forms of ryhthmic movement. The presence of deity could be compelled from the human side, whereas in Yahwism the initiative lay with God and not with man. The spirit of Yahweh leaped suddenly and unexpectedly upon Samson and he rent the lion as he would have rent a kid (Judg. 14:6).

In the second place, in Yahwism the energy that seized upon men used them for ends beyond themselves. They became the instruments of the power that laid hold of them. Their activity was directed outward and issued in such definitely practical achievement as that represented by fighting in battle. Nor was fighting the only outlet for the heightened sense of power. Late, but thoroughly in keeping with the genius of primitive Yahwism, is the account of Bezaleel, one of the artificers of the tabernacle, "See, the LORD hath called by name Bezaleel the son of Uri, the son of Hur, of the tribe of Judah; and he hath filled him with the spirit of God, in wisdom, in understanding, and in knowledge, and in all manner of workmanship" (Exod. 35:30-31). In the non-Israelite ecstasy, however, the energy was directed inward. The recipients became, as it were, the containers rather than the instruments of the divine energy. The enlargement and extension of one's own being was an end in itself. The experience of possession by deity was sought for its own sake. Psychologically, as well as in other respects, there is a world of difference between activity which issues in the rending of a lion and that which finds an outlet in wounding one's self. It is not fanciful to see in the prostrate swooning figure of a man sunk in cataleptic trance, or in the howling dervish achieving complete revolution round his own axis, fitting symbols of the way in which religious introversion can reach its climax.

Sometimes, to be sure, the abnormal visionary or auditory experiences which were thus induced could be regarded as forecasting the future; the ravings could become in part intelligible, or could be interpreted as if they were, and considered to have predictive value. But what thus found expression was simply a dominant wish of the group, "Go up to Ramoth-gilead, and prosper" said the four hundred prophets to Ahab (I Kings 22:12). "They speak a vision of their own heart" says the book of Jeremiah (23:16). Ecstasy meant not an escape from self, but imprisonment within the circle of one's own desires.

In the third place, what was sought in ecstasy was actual identification with the life of the god. The worshipers in their frenzied exaltation seemed to become one with deity. They are *entheoi*, god-indwelt. This is abundantly clear in the case of the Dionysus cult in Greece and its antecedents in Thrace. So, as Rohde points out, "The enraptured servants of the god call themselves by the name of the god."[4] The worshipers of Bacchus are Bacchae. So participants in the Bacchus festival set horns upon their heads. The enthusiasts express their sense of identification with the god by assuming as far as possible his appearance. Now, this belief in the fusion of the human and the divine rests upon a conception of the relationship between god and man entirely foreign to Yahwism. In this the distinction between the two was from the beginning so absolute as to

---

[3] *Psyche*, tr. W. B. Hillis (New York: Harcourt, Brace & Co., 1925), p. 258.

[4] *Ibid.*

forbid the suggestion that even for a moment a human being could live the life of divinity. It is the spirit of Yahweh, not Yahweh himself, that comes upon Saul and joins him to the prophets. In him is God-given power, but not the being of God himself.

On these grounds, then, as on the grounds of geographical distribution, it becomes increasingly clear that ecstatic prophetism, with its self-initiated effort to take possession of deity for its own enjoyment, was not a native product of Israel's religion, but like much else in Canaan was taken over by Yahwism and radically transformed. It is indeed a far cry from the bands of ecstatics to the great solitary figures of a Hosea, a Micah, or a Jeremiah; from the hardly intelligible ravings of enthusiasts to the terrible clarity of an Amos or an Isaiah; from the devotees who found a refuge from the actual in the vaporings of their own excited fantasy to the men who accepted fearlessly the dread impact of austere reality. One of the things which is not accounted for by those who would make the distinctive character of Israel's religion begin with the eighth-century prophets is the extraordinary dynamic needed to effect this transformation of ecstatic prophetism into the later prophecy.

V. The Note of Ecstasy in the Ministry of the Prophets

Yet along with this remarkable change certain characteristics of the older prophetism persisted in the ministry of the later prophets, and the recognition of these characteristics as giving form to their utterance has a very definite bearing upon the interpretation of the books that bear their names.

The visions of an Isaiah or an Amos are evidently born of ecstatic experience. Amos, for example, sees "a basket of summer fruit" (Amos 8:1-2). He finds himself staring at it, everything for the moment invested with enhanced significance. In his inner consciousness there sounds a voice, "Amos, what seest thou?" There is here something more than meets the eye. In Hebrew the word for "summer fruit" closely resembles that for "end," and to a heart charged with the sense of impending doom such a word has an ominous ring. There breaks upon his inner hearing the solemn pronouncement, "The end is come upon my people of Israel." This suggestibility resulting in the trancelike condition is that of the ecstatic. Again abnormal powers of sight and hearing, an intense emotional impressionability, the sense of compulsion from without—"The LORD spake thus to me with a strong hand" (Isa. 8:11)—alike re-

veal the kinship of the great prophets with the members of the earlier dervishlike companies. Jeremiah, announcing the coming of the invader, cries, "How long shall I see the standard, and hear the sound of the trumpet?" (Jer. 4:21.) His imagination is aflame with vivid anticipation of the terrors that are to come. There is a direct response to stimulus and the expression of that response is instantaneous and unreflecting. The prophet speaks of things immediately seen, heard, and felt. Very different in tone are passages which are the result of literary effort. Take the following from the book of Amos (1:2):

The LORD will roar from Zion,
And utter his voice from Jerusalem;
And the habitations of the shepherds shall mourn,
And the top of Carmel shall wither.

The passage is in part found also in the book of Joel (3:16); the reference to Zion and Jerusalem suggests that if God declares himself, there will be some association with the Holy City; the shepherd of Tekoa must speak, as it were, in the name of the church. For these reasons it is unlikely that the passage can be taken as coming from Amos himself. But it is almost as important to note that the imagery is confused. The first half of the verse uses the roaring of the lion and the thunder as symbols of God's majesty and power; but neither of these would produce the drought of which the second half of the verse speaks. The writer has not immediately heard or felt these things. His language is conventional. This is not to deny the great value of the expression of his conviction that the God who manifests himself with destroying power is none other than the God who is known in the ordered ways of the sanctuary.

A second notable sign of the ecstatic background of prophecy is the use of the pronoun of the first person singular for the divine utterance upon the prophet's lips:

I found Israel
Like grapes in the wilderness (Hos. 9:10).

And when ye spread forth your hands,
I will hide mine eyes from you;
Yea, when ye make many prayers,
I will not hear (Isa. 1:15).

I will bring evil from the north,
And a great destruction (Jer. 4:6).

God himself speaks through the prophet. The human "I" has for the moment been surrendered to the divine speaker. This experience is both like and unlike that of the earlier ecstatic. It is not a fusion of the human and the divine in which the subject loses all consciousness of anything but the sense of its own heightened existence. The prophet is a mediator between God and the world, the vehicle through which the dynamic word passes on to human life. As the initiative is not with a man's self but with Yahweh, so the end is beyond self. But this capacity for surrender to another has its very evident kinship with the intense emotional susceptibility of the ecstatic. The full significance of this astounding phenomenon of the immediacy of the divine utterance is hardly realized by the ordinary reader. It is assumed that the prophet is simply reporting verbatim a message previously conveyed to him. Color is lent to this interpretation by the prefatory formula, "Thus saith the LORD," which might often be better rendered, "Thus did the LORD say." But this clause is generally the contribution of those who have transmitted to us in writing the oracles of the prophets. For the original hearers there was no need of such an introductory statement. There was that about the look and bearing of the prophet and the content of his message which made it abundantly clear that Another than himself was speaking. What men felt as they listened was the actual presence and power of the living God. It is of course evident that at times the prophet speaks in his own person, though nonetheless as the messenger of God. Only it is in the moments of entire possession by the divine voice that the relation to the older ecstatic prophetism can be most clearly noted, while the quality of these utterances in which God himself speaks in the first person bears striking testimony to the transforming power of Israel's religion.

Again, the persistence of the ecstatic element had much to do with determining the form of prophetic utterance. It has long been recognized that the prophet was a poet, but this has often been taken to mean that the poetry was the result of his literary elaboration of his message. This, however, is to forget the spontaneous immediacy of the prophet's delivery. His word was the child of the moment of inspiration. He spoke under the compelling power of the Other than self. In strangely heightened emotional response to the invasion of his being, his improvisation took rhythmic form, was indeed poetry in the fullest sense of the word. But obviously the mood could not be prolonged to the production of poems of considerable length and involved structure. The typical prophetic utterance was therefore a brief oracle in which a single truth was expressed with direct simplicity and ravished intensity.

A good illustration of the contrast between the original brevity and directness of the prophet's speech and the language of the more deliberate and conscious development of his thought may be found in Jer. 2. Imbedded in the opening verses is a poem of characteristic tenderness:

I remember thee, the kindness of thy youth,
The love of thine espousals,
When thou wentest after me in the wilderness,
In a land that was not sown.
Israel was holiness unto the LORD,
And the firstfruits of his increase:
All that devour him shall offend;
Evil shall come upon them (Jer. 2:2-3).

Even in the translation the rhythm is unmistakable, three thought units followed by two. The rhythm can be discerned again in vss. 14 ff., as the prophet pictures the distressful fate that is to overtake the nation, "Israel a servant," "his land waste," "his cities . . . burned." The theme is a simple one, the pitiful contrast of then and now, of the days when Israel walked in loving loyalty with Yahweh, sheltered from harm amid the perils of the wilderness, and the desolation that is to befall a people that have forgotten their God. But between the parts of this poem there is a long passage which halts between prose and poetry, for while it has a certain rhythmic swing, no regularity of the rhythm can be discerned: "What iniquity have your fathers found in me, that they are gone far from me, and have walked after vanity, and are become vain? Neither said they, Where is the LORD that brought us up out of the land of Egypt, that led us through the wilderness, through a land of deserts and of pits, through a land of drought, and of the shadow of death, through a land that no man passed through, and where no man dwelt? . . . Be astonished, O ye heavens, at this, and be horribly afraid, be ye very desolate, saith the LORD. For my people have committed two evils; they have forsaken me the fountain of living waters, and hewed them out cisterns, broken cisterns, that can hold no water" (Jer. 2:5-6, 12-13). The changes are rung effectively on the baseness and the folly of a people forsaking their God who has done so much for them. The author enforces his point with moving eloquence, but his style is that of the preacher rather than the poet. The treatment of the desert by the two writers is significant. The poet is content with the single revealing epithet, "a land that was not sown"; but that epithet seizes at once the essential feature of the desert, its oblivion of human effort, a land where none would ever speak of mother earth and where man remains a stranger and a wanderer. It is interesting to see the phrase recurring more than once in T. E. Lawrence, *Seven Pillars of Wisdom*.[5] "The wilderness," says the biblical writer, "a land of deserts and pits, . . . a land of drought and deep darkness, . . . a land that none passes through, where no man dwells" (Jer. 2:6), and the method of enumeration has its own rhetorical adequacy, but it does not give the feel of the desert as the poet's single phrase does. The difference in tone and style of the prose passage would seem to justify the contention of some scholars that it is not from Jeremiah himself, but from a later writer on whom the prophet's message had made so profound an impression that he was inspired to translate it into the idiom of his own day.

VI. The Form of Prophetic Utterance

The prophets themselves did not compose speeches or even poems in which they developed a theme with some degree of logical consistency. Their utterances were brief, pregnant oracles charged with an emotional intensity which found expression in a rhythmic form probably maintained unchanged through any particular deliverance. That is to say, change in rhythm, in mood, in imagery, is a likely indication that a new oracle is to be reckoned with. Often, too, these changes will be found to coincide with the occurrence of the introductory formula "Thus did the Lord say," or the concluding phrase "saith the Lord," and it would seem likely that editors have thus preserved the tradition of the separate origin of the oracles. Some of these may have been afterward committed to writing by the prophet himself. This is certainly true in the case of Isaiah (30:8). Jeremiah, as has been noted, dictated his poems to Baruch (Jer. 36). But for the most part they would have lived in the memories of hearers who in the course of time recorded them on ostraca, parchments, or whatever materials were available. Such fragmentary records, generally associated with a significant name, would be cherished and no doubt copied and recopied. A man into whose possession a small collection of these oracles came would take delight in adding to it other utterances reputed to be by the same author, and he would not question too curiously their source. Enough that the words rang true. Superimposed upon this first stage, the process of informal growth is the work of those who, feeling that the oracles were of timeless value,

sought to relate them to the conditions of their own day and age, adding, therefore, interpretation, explanation, and commentary.

VII. The Spoken Word Committed to Writing

No small part of the contribution thus made was concerned with the necessity of taking account of that difference between the spoken and the written word to which reference has already been made. For those who heard the prophet speak, the particular situation known to all would make abundantly clear the meaning of what he said. The later reader, unfamiliar with the circumstances, might easily be bewildered, and it is often with his need of enlightenment that the editors are concerned. For example, at a critical moment in the history of the little kingdom of Judah, Jeremiah delivered this oracle:

> Weep ye not for the dead,
> Neither bemoan him;
> But weep sore for him that goeth away:
> For he shall return no more (Jer. 22:10).

The good king Josiah had been slain in battle by Pharaoh-Necho, king of Egypt. By this same victor, Jehoahaz, Josiah's son, whom the people had placed upon the throne in his father's place, had been summoned to Riblah and there put in bonds. No one who heard Jeremiah speak could fail to understand the reference to this situation and the unequivocal announcement of the fate that was in store for the young king. But at a later time this oracle in the hands of a reader would be obscure. So there has been added in plain prose the explanatory statement: "For thus saith the Lord touching Shallum [another name for Jehoahaz] the son of Josiah king of Judah, which reigned instead of Josiah his father, which went forth out of this place; He shall not return thither any more: but he shall die in the place whither they have led him captive, and shall see this land no more" (Jer. 22:11-12).

Or to take another illustration, there came a moment when the prophet Isaiah, finding himself in the presence of the wealthy landowners and nobles of his day, hurled in their teeth this bitter challenge:

> Ye have eaten up the vineyard;
> The spoil of the poor is in your houses.
> What mean ye that ye beat my people to pieces,
> And grind the faces of the poor? (Isa. 3:14*b*-15.)

Those who heard the prophet were in no doubt that the burning indignation was that of the great God himself. It was he who had spoken upon Isaiah's lips. But there is now

[5] Garden City: Garden City Publishing Co., 1938.

prefixed to this oracle a four line verse in which Yahweh himself does not speak but is spoken of in the third person:

The Lord standeth up to plead,
And standeth to judge [his] people [6]
The Lord will enter into judgment
With the ancients of his people, and the princes thereof (Isa. 3:13-14a).

The tone is rather different from that of the oracle. There is not the same effect of charged intensity. This and the change in person would seem to make it not unlikely that the verse was composed with a view to providing for the reader a setting for the oracle which would help him better to grasp its meaning. In so doing, the writer has enunciated an important and sublime truth, as he makes Isaiah's utterance a particular instance of that constant subjection of the national life to the divine judgment which men all too easily forget. It is not without significance that the Hebrew text in vs. 13 reads "peoples" instead of "his people." Someone felt that it is nothing less than the world with which God is thus concerned, and he has therefore given the passage this wider reference. So a nameless scribe has helped to give to Isaiah's fearless challenge of the leaders of his day its meaning for the whole of human life.

VIII. The Development of the Implications of Prophetic Prediction

In the case of the great prophets of the pre-exilic period, the recognition of the distinction between their oracles and the additions that have been made serves to bring out more clearly the arresting fact that Amos, Hosea, Micah, Isaiah, Jeremiah, and Ezekiel are all alike in this—they announce the final doom that is to overtake the nation. "The God of Israel is about to destroy his people for their sins" might well be taken as the summary of the message of every one of them. To these prophets it was thus given to discern in the actual course of events the supreme truth of the absolute righteousness of God. They did not set this forth in abstract propositions, as theory which might later win general acceptance, for it was truth pressing in upon life, declaring itself with appalling power in the immediate situation. This realism of their message in the exactness of its relationship to the circumstances of their own day invested what they said with a dread intelligibility for those who heard them speak. But for the reader of a later and a different time there was need of comment

[6] Greek, "his people"; Hebrew, "peoples."

and explanation of the kind to which reference has been made. There was also need of a further unfolding of the implications of the truth to which the prophets had borne their startling witness. Questions would be asked. Could the will of the righteous God be bent only on destruction? Were not the prophets sustained in their harsh and forbidding ministry by the hope that the nation might repent and so the final catastrophe be averted? And indeed in the books of the prophets there are to be found moving exhortations to the people to turn from their evil ways. There is, however, grave difficulty in taking the exhortations as coming from the prophets themselves. The unhesitating certainty with which they declare that the fate of the nation is sealed would make somewhat unreal any suggestion that the disaster could be averted by repentance. The prophets speak because they know that doom is inevitable. When, however, due account is taken of the distinctive character of these oracles of doom with their note of ecstatic utterance and their trenchant brevity, and it is further noted that introductory formulas often mark the exhortations as separate deliverances, it seems at least very probable that these have been added to the original oracles of doom by those who sought to relate the prophet's revelation of God more definitely to human needs; teachers for whom, too, the distinctions within the nation, which have their roots in Isaiah's reference to the remnant, had become a basic postulate. An interesting illustration is found in Amos 5. In the midst of invective and predictions of woe there is a powerful appeal to the moral consciousness. Part of it runs as follows:

Seek good, and not evil, that ye may live;
And so the Lord, the God of hosts, shall be with you, as ye have spoken.
Hate the evil, and love the good, and establish judgment in the gate:
It may be that the Lord God of hosts will be gracious unto the remnant of Joseph (Amos 5:14-15).

The reference to the remnant of Joseph points at once to a later date than that of Amos. The "may be" is quite out of keeping with the categorical note which characterizes the prophet's utterances generally. Some commentators therefore regard this call to repentance as coming from a later hand. But let it be said at once that to hold this view does not mean that the passage in question is robbed of its significance. It is simply to distinguish between the task committed to the prophet of setting forth unfalteringly the inexorable nature of the divine righteousness and that of another who, taking home to his heart the truth enunciated by

Amos, draws out more richly its bearing upon human living.

In ways like these many writers of varied outlook played their part in the growth of the books of the prophets. To them we owe the transmission to our own day of the original oracles of the great outstanding figures in the history of religion who in an especial way are rightly known as *the* prophets—Amos, Hosea, Isaiah, Micah, Jeremiah, Ezekiel, and the rest. But more than that, they discerned the timeless value of these oracles; they attempted by explanation and interpretation to relate them to the needs and questions of later times; in a word, they developed the truth embodied in the earlier writings and thus helped to invest them with that wealth of meaning which has been theirs through all the centuries down to our own time.

IX. Prophecies of the New Order

There is, however, another important element to be reckoned with in the development of the prophetic literature. In each book there are found substantial additions of quite different character from the passages thus far considered. Instead of dire prediction of the destruction of the nation, with its teaching about the divine transcendence and the righteousness of God and the inviolable holiness of his love, or the development of these truths by way of exhortation to repentance, there is found in these further additions the unfaltering conviction of the greatness of Israel's future, of its primacy among the peoples, of the world-wide significance of its history.

To be sure, a link between what may be called the negative note of the oracles and the positive tone of these hopeful predictions was provided by making these latter speak of the restoration which will follow upon the time of disaster and the repentance which this brings about. In fact, many of them were first uttered at a time subsequent to the fall of Jerusalem in 586 B.C. and the end of Israel's career as a nation, notably those found in Isa. 40–66. But some of them date from earlier times, and it is not unlikely that nearly all of them once had their own independent currency. They too spring from the background of primitive ecstatic prophetism, though along a line of development quite different from that represented by the great solitary figures with whose names we are familiar. A piece of historical narrative in I Kings 22 throws light on this twofold development. At the suggestion of Jehoshaphat, Ahab consulted the prophets of Yahweh, four hundred in number, about an expedition he was planning for the recapture of Ramoth-gilead from the Syrians. With one voice the four hundred predicted the success of his siege of that city. But at the prompting of Jehoshaphat, Ahab made further inquiry of one Micaiah ben Imlah, also a prophet, though one who held himself aloof from the group and was known for his contempt for the king. While Micaiah was being summoned, the four hundred prophets in their state of ecstasy continued to forecast Ahab's success. Their strange inspiration characteristically came to a focus in the behavior of one Zedekiah ben Chenaanah. He fashioned horns of iron and dramatically represented the irresistible bull-like rush with which the king was to overwhelm his foes. Over against the group stood the solitary figure of Micaiah, like them the subject of ecstatic vision, but in total opposition as he announced the disaster that was to overtake the royal expedition. Like Elijah of his own day, he was the forerunner of the great prophets of the eighth century and their successors. In him can be noted the same surrender of the heightened consciousness of the individual to the will of the righteous God that led them to announce exultantly the overthrow of self-seeking human power, though it involved tragic results for their own people.

On the other hand, the kind of identification with a people's natural hope of victory, represented by the group ecstasy of the four hundred, and finding expression in the symbolic activity of Zedekiah, was to undergo radical transformation as the implications of Yahweh's relation to the course of history were more clearly understood. The God of Israel was indeed the transcendent God of righteousness who would make no compromise with evil. That righteousness must flame forth hotly against all iniquity, even to the destruction of his people. But nonetheless this was the God who had brought Israel into strangely intimate relationship to himself. In the Exodus his power had been declared in their deliverance from the Egyptian oppressors. He had entered into their history and invested it with positive worth and significance. In Canaan, Israel had gradually learned that the life of nature as it ministered to human need was the beneficent manifestation of the power of this same God. It was he who gave them "corn, and wine, and oil" (Hos. 2:8). If this primary truth of man's dependence upon the goodness of God could be unfalteringly maintained, and right human effort could be seen as a faithful and humble acceptance of God's gifts and response to his activity, the hopes and aspirations of a people could take on new meaning. To these hopes and aspirations thus transfigured, group prophecy, speaking on the lips of individuals, was to give inspired expression. Instead of the simple, "Go up . . . and prosper," representing naïve belief in the successful employment of human resources of wealth and wisdom, no matter what might be the character and motives of those who made use of them, there was to be the assertion of the ultimate triumph of the God of righteousness in a victory in which his people were to have their humble but significant part. Always there was the danger that this victory would be thought of as primarily redounding to the material advantage of the nation and to its exaltation. False prophets would subordinate God to man's selfish aims and desires. An Amos must therefore denounce those who lightheartedly hailed the day of Yahweh's final manifestation of power as the day of the fulfillment of their own fond hopes (Amos 5:18). But this perversion upon the part of many of what was involved in God's participation in the human adventure did but throw into sharper relief the prophecies of those to whom God's righteous goodness was the supreme and determining factor in the movement of history. These men of deep spiritual understanding were the authors of many of the great passages in the books of the prophets that again and again have sustained the faith and hope of those who in the face of human failure have held fast to a belief in God's ultimate victory.

An excellent example of this transformed product of group prophecy is found in the book of Isaiah. The passage runs as follows: "And it shall come to pass in the last days, that the mountain of the Lord's house shall be established in the top of the mountains, and shall be exalted above the hills; and all nations shall flow unto it. And many people shall go and say, Come ye, and let us go up to the mountain of the Lord, to the house of the God of Jacob; and he will teach us of his ways, and we will walk in his paths: for out of Zion shall go forth the law, and the word of the Lord from Jerusalem. And he shall judge among the nations, and shall rebuke many people: and they shall beat their swords into plowshares, and their spears into pruning hooks: nation shall not lift up sword against nation, neither shall they learn war any more" (Isa. 2:2-4).

The same prophecy is found almost word for word in the book of the prophet Micah (4:1-3). Biblical scholarship in the past has long debated whether Isaiah or Micah was the original author; but it is now generally agreed that the passage is of quite independent authorship. In fact, in tone and idiom, as well as in content, it differs very markedly from the authentic oracles of both these prophets. Both of them foretell unequivocally the destruction that is to befall Jerusalem. Isaiah sees the nation as priding itself upon the abundance of its material resources, and its leaders by their brutal disregard of the elementary principles of justice as flaunting their arrogance in the face of the majesty of God. Upon such a people irrevocable doom must fall, doom which will inevitably involve the fall and destruction of the capital. Micah denounces Zion as a city built with blood, where the greed of princes, priests, and prophets complacently claims the divine protection; and the prophet sees this Jerusalem in ruins, its site a desolate jungle.

But Jerusalem is nonetheless the place of the special manifestation of Yahweh's power, though that power must destroy. It remains possessed of an awful distinction. It was fitting, then, that a prophecy which superbly sets forth the true destiny of the city should be placed alongside oracles that foretold its destruction. In the face of his people's failure to respond rightly to its divine vocation, someone has introduced this utterance of an unknown author, as if to say that God's purpose cannot in the end be defeated. So there has been preserved a prophecy in which crude nationalism has been transmuted into a vision of the true meaning of Israel's unique calling, to mediate to the world the knowledge of the one God, with the result that in the light of that knowledge all peoples are to dwell at peace one with another.

It is not always that the authors of passages such as this so completely transcend the natural self-centered longing of a people for its own security and prosperity. At times the delight in the material benefits which may be expected to accrue as the accompaniment of a right relationship to God seems to be given undue prominence as in such a verse as Isa. 60:5,

The abundance of the sea shall be converted unto thee,
The forces of the Gentiles shall come unto thee.

But again and again it is in world vision far transcending national self-interest that the hope of the future comes to its climax. So in the description of the ideal ruler in Isa. 11:1-9, a beginning is made with the memory of the glorious reign of David, but an end is found in the assurance that the earth shall be "full of the knowledge of the Lord, as the waters cover the sea." Whether the thought is of what is done for Israel or of what is done for the world through Israel, invariably it is the sense of the divine activity that dominates the outlook, and life is seen in the light of God's purpose of righteousness and love rather than in the light of what man's unaided effort can make of it.

It is this sense of God ceaselessly at work in his world that affords the vital connection between these prophecies of well-being and the oracles of doom. Indeed, it was the unfailing fidelity of the great prophets to their discernment of God, declaring his righteous power in the ending of Israel's career as a nation through the rise of the empires of Assyria and Babylonia, that provided the firm ground for the hope of the future. So an unknown author in the splendid prophecies of restoration in the second part of the book of Isaiah makes startling appeal to the truth that his predecessors had made so abundantly clear. In a brief poem embedded in Isa. 42:24-25 he asks,

> Who gave Jacob for a spoil,
> And Israel to the robbers . . . ,
> Poured upon him the fury of his anger,
> And the strength of battle?

This apparently harsh reminder that it was their own God who had smitten them is an integral part of the message of consolation. It was no unknown deity who had overwhelmed them, no inexplicable fate against which they must blindly and helplessly struggle. A stricken, broken fragment of a people, they were still in the hands of the one God who in the dire misfortune that had befallen them had manifested that awful righteousness of which their own prophets had spoken.

X. In Many and Various Ways

Both types of prophecy, then, have their distinctive contribution to make to the understanding of God's ways with man. The one enters into the heart of human life, and discerning even in the egoism and the selfishness of human striving simply the perversion of God-given instincts, keeps its thought steadfastly fixed upon what God can do through man, and thus sees human aspiration purified and ennobled and human effort invested with new and lasting value. But the power of this prophecy of the good that will come to keep its vision of God undimmed rests in no small degree upon the faithfulness of the few and lonely souls to whom the absolute holiness of God was all in all, so that for its sake they could face and proclaim the dissolution of all the ties of home and family and country that for most men are what make life worth living. They lived noble lives with the pervading sense of that presence and might which claimed their whole being. They had been drawn out of themselves into union with overwhelming power; they had made complete surrender to the righteousness and truth that they had found at the heart of that power. They had looked into the face of tragedy, seen life at its darkest, and yet could rest in their intense awareness of God and of the world as subject to his sovereign sway.

To speak then of the prophetic literature is to call to mind first of all the great prophets after whom the several books that compose that literature are named. In these books are preserved their authentic oracles, and in each case these oracles constitute the nucleus about which additions by way of explanation, interpretation, and supplement have gathered. It was their ministry that enabled Israel's life as a people to survive the catastrophic end of its career as a nation and thus to be the vehicle of God's continued revelation of himself. But that continued revelation was in no small degree given through the work of the nameless authors who were responsible for the further growth and development of the books. Some of these were prophets and poets in their own right, and their glowing pictures of what the future may hold in store still direct and enrich the faith and hope of the Christian church. Others made their contribution by way of inspired interpretation of the great utterances of those who had gone before. Still others played the humbler role of bringing all this varied material together. The title "editor" that is sometimes given them hardly does justice to the loving insight and care that informed their labors and bear their own testimony to the working of the "one and the selfsame Spirit, dividing to every man severally as he will" (I Cor. 12:11).

If, then, on the one hand biblical scholarship has helped to make more clear the unparalleled greatness of the prophets whose names have come down to us, it has on the other hand made it plain that many unknown writers had their place in shaping the prophetic literature. To no one man, not even to the greatest of the prophets, is it given to know the whole of God's revelation of himself. There is a splendid onesidedness about the prophet that is bound up with his unhesitating loyalty to the truth of his own immediate vision. That one-sidedness is in no small measure made part of a larger understanding of God's way with man by those through whose labors the prophets' utterances have been transmitted. Theirs was not the piercing original insight of high spiritual genius; they were no doubt often simply representative of the better thought and temper of their own day; but their hearts nonetheless sought God, and his Spirit used them for the enrichment of his revelation of himself through the discipline of his people. "The Bible itself is a monument of the principle that the validity of individual intuitions must be checked by the conscience and insight of the religious community."[7] That principle finds pre-eminent expression in the growth and development of the books of the prophets through whom God spoke of old, "in many and various ways" (Heb. 11:1).

[7] B. H. Streeter, *The God Who Speaks* (New York: The Macmillan Co., 1936), p. 169.

XI. Selected Bibliography

GUILLAUME, ALFRED. *Prophecy and Divination Among the Hebrews and Other Semites.* New York: Harper & Bros., 1938.

LODS, ADOLPHE. *The Prophets and the Rise of Judaism,* tr. S. H. Hooke. New York: E. P. Dutton & Co., 1937.

MOWINCKEL, SIGMUND. *Prophecy and Tradition.* Oslo: J. Dybwad, 1946.

ROBINSON, THEODORE H. *Prophecy and the Prophets in Ancient Israel.* New York: Charles Scribner's Sons, 1923.

SCOTT, R. B. Y. *The Relevance of the Prophets.* New York: The Macmillan Co., 1944.

SKINNER, JOHN. *Prophecy and Religion.* Cambridge: The University Press, 1922.

SMITH, J. M. P. *The Prophets and Their Times.* 2nd ed. rev. William A. Irwin. Chicago: University of Chicago Press, 1941.

THE WISDOM LITERATURE

by WILLIAM A. IRWIN

Wisdom is very old in the Orient. At this day we have the collected sayings of Ptahhotep, an Egyptian sage of about the twenty-third century B.C., and we know of the famous Imhotep who preceded him by several hundred years. From such early expression, wisdom continued through the course of Egypt's ancient history. It had a comparable development and popularity in Babylonia. A considerable wisdom literature from both lands has been preserved to the present.

I. Wisdom in the Ancient Near East

Oriental wisdom suffers under deep and widespread misunderstanding. It is supposed to consist of maxims of the sort that constitute a considerable bulk of the biblical book of Proverbs. While this type of sayings was a normal expression of the wise men, it constituted only a part of their activity. The introduction to the book of Proverbs, giving as it does a sort of curriculum of the wisdom schools, provides some concept of the diversity of expression of the ancient sages. The mention of riddles is particularly worth notice. For us they are merely a form of bucolic humor, or serve for the amusement of schoolboys. But in the ancient world the riddle was a serious mode of scholarly investigation and teaching. We grasp its significance by recalling the phrase "The riddle of the universe."

There was also in Babylonia a considerable use of plant and animal fables that expressed the ancient thinkers' engrossment in the problem of man's obvious similarity to and dissimilarity from the lower creatures. Moreover, it is not generally recognized that the maxims, which unfortunately focus the attention of every casual observer of ancient wisdom, are in actuality an expression of the problem of ethics, a very early and simple expression, but nonetheless concerned with the study of human conduct. The ancient sage ignored the prolegomena which we consider essential. He had scarcely realized as yet that there could be a problem of ends and sanctions; consequently, he merely assumed the nature of the good life and the reasons for pursuing it. But given these objectives, which to him seemed obvious, the wise man studied types of conduct and their significance as conducive to or destructive of life's good.

Furthermore, wisdom undertook in relatively ancient times an examination of the ultimate worth of human life, with dawning apprehensions of the metaphysical problems entailed. On a little study it becomes apparent that wisdom was the organized thinking of the East. One might describe it as the scholarship of the time, for the wise man was necessarily conversant with the outreach of contemporary knowledge. But also he did serious thinking about it, asking meanings and relations. He was the ancient philosopher, though we must understand that wisdom had its practical side and application, so that it covered more in this direction than philosophy has come to comprise for us. On the other hand, it was less than modern philosophy, for thought has expanded with the advance of the ages to include problems and areas of truth that had never dawned on the imagination of the ancient scholar. The close and direct relationship between Oriental wisdom and subsequent thought is declared in the word that has become technical with us, for philosophy is *philosophia*—by which the Greeks confessed their debt to the older speculative thought that had its most notable expression in the wisdom of the Orient.

Wisdom, then, was not limited to the great cultures in the older world. Man instinctively asks the meaning of all that comes within the scope of his experience; not least he asks about himself. It is not relevant, thus, to inquire what lands of the ancient world had wise men —in addition to Babylonia and Egypt we hear a little about them in Assyria and in Edom— but only to know what expression their wisdom found, and how far they pushed their investigations. Indeed, it is now realized that even savage man had his philosophy.

II. Wisdom in Early Israel

Little is known of the wisdom of the Canaanites. The fragments of their literature found at Ras Shamra, in north Syria, contain none. But the high attainments of their civilization, along with certain allusions and records in the Old Testament, make it quite clear that a vigorous, self-conscious wisdom movement had long functioned in Palestine before the Hebrews entered. And this fact is basic to an understanding of Israel's wisdom.

In the Song of Deborah the archaic poet gloats over the death of Sisera; in imagination he pictures the king's mother in the royal palace at Harosheth-haggoyim, peering out the window and anxiously inquiring,

> Why is his chariot so long coming,
> why tarry the wheels of his chariots?

To this her wise women made answer, assuring her that the delay was but evidence of complete victory (Judg. 5:28-30). What the normal function of these "wise women" may have been we can only guess. Their presence at this time and place, however, provides a brilliant flash of illumination upon an established institution. It is to be noted that they were wise *women;* hitherto our study has encountered only men in this profession. But that this is no casual accident in Palestinian practice is shown by two other stories.

When Joab would win David's consent to the return of Absalom from exile, he sent to Tekoa for "a wise woman." And she, when she came, behaved with the astuteness and skill of a professional, quoting ancient lore that bears every mark of the traditional maxims of the wisdom movement (II Sam. 14:14). When the revolt that grew out of the Absalom incident was near collapse, again a wise woman took decisive action. Evidently on her own initiative and by virtue of her professional renown, she negotiated with Joab and agreed to the execution of the leader of the insurrection. Then she "went to all the people in her wisdom" and had them perform what she had promised. "In her wisdom" clearly means in her recognized position and acquired fame as one of the "wise." Nor is this all; in her conversation with Joab she told how in early times it used to be said, "They always ask counsel at Abel" (II Sam. 20:16-22). This insignificant little town, up on the borders of Israelite holdings and evidently little changed from its Canaanite days, had in the tenth century B.C. a tradition of ancient repute for its wisdom.

These passages, though all too brief to satisfy us, yet make clear that a Canaanite wisdom movement carried over into Israel. And this circumstance in turn explains the prestige of "wise" persons there when as yet the nation had scarcely emerged beyond a rural culture. Further light in this direction is obtained by consideration of Samson's riddle (Judg. 14:12-19). In and of itself it is commonplace: merely a bit of rustic play of wits. But as a riddle it implies the entire long course of Oriental wisdom. Indeed more; its debasement here to countrymen's buffoonery carries an implication of many years of use through which this could come about. One may not, however, draw the tempting conclusion that here we have evidence of a wisdom movement already very old in Israel; it is more probable that the development took place in pre-Hebrew times. It is relevant to mention also Jotham's fable (Judg. 9:8-15), which tells of the acceptance of kingship by the worthless bramble, after the vine, the olive, and the fig tree had refused it. Respectable people are too busy for politics, and so the way is left open for reprobates! Here is an excellent example of the Oriental plant fable—in fact, the one pure fable of this sort in the Old Testament—providing further evidence of the complete acclimatization of the wisdom movement in Palestine when Israel was yet a newcomer in the land.

Too little is told for us to understand the full nature of this earliest Israelite movement. Social circumstances and the implication of our few passages both alike point toward its having stressed practical discretion rather than metaphysical and ethical speculation. And certainly this is borne out by the function of men such as Ahithophel and Hushai. Of the former it is recorded that "the counsel which he counseled in those days, was as if one inquired of the word of God" (II Sam. 16:23). The conviction cannot be avoided that his relation to David was in a class with the sporadic advice given by the woman of Tekoa; he was a "wise man."

III. The Wisdom of Solomon

On this entire background we are enabled to understand the far-famed wisdom of Solomon. The story of the disputed baby (I Kings 3:16-27), which the historian narrates as an example, implies for us little more than native astuteness and a practical knowledge of psychology. Yet it will be recognized that these qualities fall within the scope of ancient wisdom. More to our purpose is it to consider Solomon's historic place in Israel's evolving culture. His people were but a generation away from rural life. David had won for them a famous old city, and had made it a center for the nation; yet notwithstanding such graces and vices of city life as he may have fostered, he remained to the end essentially a country man. But Solomon was city-bred, with connections through his mother, apparently, far back in the old pre-Hebrew culture of the city. What influences may have molded his youth we do not know, but his tastes soon led his kingdom to such magnificence, such unheard-of graces and external splendor, as to dazzle even the staid historian of his reign (I Kings 4:20-28). His "wisdom," too, becomes lucid in the light of its long history in the Orient: simply, he was a scholar. It is immensely to his credit that in an age and environment such as his he realized the delights and supremacy of the things of the mind. It was of epochal significance for his kingdom; here was the dawning of Israel's cultural life in the narrower sense, with results and implications that go far beyond our present task.

True to the supranational character of scholarship, Solomon was reputed in all lands, his enthusiastic biographer relates, and his wisdom surpassed that of the sons of the East and of Egypt (I Kings 4:30-31). How proficient he may have been, engrossed as he was in affairs of state, it is impossible to say. Men came from distant lands, we are told, to hear his wisdom: doubtless foreign scholars induced by Solomon's generosity to live and work in Jerusalem. Probably we shall not be far from the facts if we regard him as patron of the arts and sciences, who made Jerusalem a center of learning, however modest, and doubtless in his spare time indulged his interests with excursions into scholarly matters. He can be thought of along with Akhenaton, Harun ar-Rashid, Charlemagne, and many other monarchs whose tastes lay in the things of the mind, and who made their courts brilliant with intellectual life, centers of the best things of their times.

The biblical historian summarizes all in the claim that Solomon was author of 3,000 proverbs and 1,005 songs, and that he spoke of plants and animals—evidently plant and animal fables, such as already mentioned; but unfortunately none are preserved, for the few reminiscences of such wisdom in the book of Proverbs (30:18-19, 24-31) are not ascribed to him. Similarly, his songs are not in the present Song of Songs. Both we must consider lost through the accidents of the centuries; but the proverbs are another matter.

IV. The Earliest Core of Proverbs

Prov. 10–21 contain a collection of maxims that bears his name, and ch. 25 claims to begin another that was copied by Hezekiah's men: that is, a full hundred years before the destruction of the Judean kingdom these were already ascribed to Solomon. The collections are such as to be impossible of dating by internal evidence; besides, being devoid of continuous thought, they lent themselves readily to free editorial treatment. And so no one can say of any one proverb that it did or did not belong to the original collection; and of the total we have only such tenuous evidence as here surveyed for its Solomonic origin. Nonetheless, the situation is comparable with that in the Psalter, where we have reacted strongly against the marked skepticism of a former age. There is no adequate reason for denying that chs. 10–21 contain an undetermined nucleus that is Solomonic, an adjective which again we must interpret generously as meaning "produced under Solomon's inspiration."

The form of the maxims is normally a single line, of two parallel members, that makes a pungent observation on some aspect of human conduct, petty or important. It has been claimed that they are not poetic in form, but since parallelism is the usual formal mark of Hebrew poetry, it is difficult to see the grounds of the objection. Certainly when they attain the bulk of two or more lines, one must admit their form is poetic. Probably they should be thought of as comparable with the popular proverbs of the Western world, which commonly strain after a pseudopoetic form but seldom attain anything higher than popular jingle.

The proverbs are not easy reading. Their atomistic structure, lacking context and sequence, baffles the mind with a multitude of unrelated details. However, they were intended not for continuous reading but for prolonged study. They are a concentrate of ancient learning, a crystallization of the sages' long study of courses of conduct and their outcome, and for proper understanding they demand to be redissolved in copious quantities of personal episode. When each is enlarged, through a process of chastened imagination, to the bulk of a whole chapter, then they take on life and impact. Indeed, it is possible that some such method characterized their actual use in antiquity; for they give the impression of being notes of the wise men's teaching. In their corporate character the sages had watched through the centuries the course of history, the rise and fall of kingdoms, and the outcome of individual courses of life. Society was for them a sort of test tube in which they observed experiments in ethics. And in their maxims they set forth the distilled essence of their results. This extra-temporal character of the wisdom movement constituted one of its great contributions: its sense of the continuity and unity of scholarship across the millenniums, indifferent to national bounds, and of the ongoing process of human life that was working itself out to inherently determined results. Symbolic of this is a late Egyptian document that cites the work of famous wise men a thousand years and more in the past.

V. Pre-Exilic Wisdom

The temper of the pre-exilic Hebrew wisdom, in so far as we may cautiously identify it in the book of Proverbs and whatever other source that can be adduced, was not comparable to the religious compulsion which animated the prophets. It lacked their flaming passion; in a word, their inspiration. The wise men took life as it was, and regarded it in a somewhat detached way. At times they were half amused, at times just a little cynical. Life, they were convinced, works itself out according to its own laws, and the man who cannot govern his way to take proper account of them is a fool. Religious realities are to be respected, still only as part of the total of circumstance which the wise man will appraise in planning his conduct.

The course of the wisdom movement subsequent to Solomon is vaguely discernible from a few allusions. Yet in seeking to trace its character and achievements, it is highly important to avoid a fragmentation of Hebrew intellectual life. While one may study separately the three famous forms of leadership of thought in the Old Testament, those of the priest, the prophet, and the wise man, it must be recognized that Israel's life was diverse only within a comprehensive unity. We shall understand it by comparison with the present, where all differing points of view and emphasis blend into a composite that is the spirit of our times. And so while the prophet bitterly criticized priest and politician, the wise man followed his own course, and the priest felt himself superior to both, yet all alike were members of the Hebrew community, sharing its outlook and contributing, each in his own way, for better or worse, to its intellectual and spiritual being and end. In particular, the wise man, as custodian of the nation's intellectual heritage, and concerned with the total of truth in its significance for ongoing life and faith, was intimately a part of all, contributing to all in a comprehensiveness which too often today we are prone to overlook. However, just as a history of philosophy is legitimate, although the philosopher's conclusions have frequently had profound effect on religious belief, on political faith and practice, and on the deep unvoiced convictions of the people as a whole, so likewise we may concern ourselves with assembling the too meager evidences of the continuing work of the ancient sages.

Mention of King Hezekiah's men, already referred to, is highly illuminating. Scholarship then continued under royal patronage. There is an odd little wisdom passage in Isa. 28:23-29, which few scholars would attribute to the prophet. The book of Job, though certainly of a later period, contains allusions to an ancient wisdom that may very well be relevant to the time now under discussion (Job 8:8-12; 15:10; 22:15). It is commonly recognized also that certain of the psalms belong more with the wisdom movement than with the cultus; but the period of their composition is highly uncertain. Thus Ps. 15 is intimately of a piece with the ethical maxims of the Orient, a feature which Ps. 24 shares in part. Ps. 1 is a didactic treatment of the "two ways"—the theme of the much later Didache. Pss. 16; 49; 73 are of the speculative character that is the essence of wisdom. Ps. 19 apparently contains a remnant of the best riddle—in the technical sense of the term—to be found in the Old Testament. Vs. 2 reads, "Day unto day utters speech, and night unto night proclaims knowledge"; but vs. 3 contradicts this flatly, "There is no speech and no language; their voice is not heard." It has been suggested that originally the psalm posed a question to the effect, "What is it that speaks, day by day and night after night, yet has no speech or voice or language?" Answer: "The heavens, which declare the glory of God, and the firmament which shows his workmanship."

VI. Postexilic Wisdom

A. Proverbs.—The Exile was of profound relevance for Hebrew life and thought. All aspects of the people's experience were deepened, a transformation in which the wisdom movement shared to the full. Later wisdom, in so far as we can identify it, is markedly religious —with the exception of Ecclesiastes. The reiterated comment, which is found first in Prov. 1, is a symbol of postexilic wisdom: "The fear of the LORD is the beginning of wisdom." Wisdom was a quest of value in life; and so here the sages set forth their reasoned conclusion that supreme and enduring satisfaction can be found only along religious lines. Yet the religious outlook is in general noncultic. A unique passage enjoins payment of religious dues (Prov. 3:9-10); and Ecclesiastes somewhat cynically advised meticulous payment of vows, though qualifying this with the comment that it is better not to vow at all (Eccl. 5:4-5). It is related also that Job sacrificed regularly on behalf of his sons (Job. 1:5). But these are the exception. In general, the emphasis of these later wise men might be supposed to have originated with the prophets who state baldly that the Lord never desired sacrifices; it accords fully with the famous summary of religious duty in Mic. 6:6-8.

Whatever uncertainty attaches to the rest of the book, Prov. 1–9 are generally regarded as postexilic. Apart from placing them somewhere midway in this period, scholars generally refuse to date them more precisely. They begin with a notable catalogue of the proficiency of the trained wise man. They have much to say about the menace of the "strange woman." They contain some maxims of the traditional sort, and frequently follow the usage of twenty previous centuries in bearing the address "My son." They fall into somewhat clearly recognizable sections that may, again with some play of imagination, be described as separate lectures of the ancient teacher. But altogether, their most notable feature is in the exquisite lyric in 3:13-20 and the more lengthy treatment of the same subject in chs. 8–9. Wisdom is described as superior to wealth and precious treasures, which had been precisely the desiderata of the earlier sages. Careful reflection makes it apparent that the term here means the finer, intangible riches of life, the things of the heart and mind. The refined Hebrew wisdom of this late time has penetrated to the insight that life's nonmaterial values transcend all: only in things of the spirit does life attain meaning. Ch. 8 gives this a cosmic setting. God "possessed" wisdom before creation—it was an attribute of his; life's goodness and beauty and all its unseen realities are of the character and being of God. He created the world as an expression of this "wisdom"; and now it stands in the busiest places, wherever men are, calling to them, inviting them to turn aside from lesser things and to seek the serene worth that is found in the ways of God. Here, it may be remarked in passing, is the sages' doctrine of divine revelation, and it is one that has not yet been surpassed or superseded.

B. Job.—By common consent the book of Job is the greatest of Israel's wisdom books, and a supreme treasure of our literary heritage. The greatness of the theme at once attracts attention, for the writer here sets out to pursue

Things unattempted yet in prose or rhyme—

nothing less, in fact, than to

assert eternal Providence,
And justify the ways of God to men.[1]

[1] Milton, *Paradise Lost*, Bk. I.

The tragic figure of Job stirs universal sympathy —that lordly and blameless sheik who lived in ease and happiness, yet was stricken in a moment with loss of all. His sons and daughters were taken from him, his property destroyed, and then he himself was afflicted with a loathsome disease. So he sits, in the city refuse ground, tormented with pain, and tried to the breaking point by his three friends who lecture him on the wickedness that must have brought him to such sorry plight, while he, in a horror of loneliness and despair, gropes for some ground of faith in the God whose goodness had been the light of former days.

One may summarize the theme of the book in the question, "Why do the righteous suffer?" More pertinent is it to realize that it is a theodicy; it probes into the mystery of God's government of the world and its meaning as a revelation of his own nature. Yet the greatness of the book is that with a subject so exalted it yet moves among simple things: a very sick man, and his obsessions and querulous musings, and his friends who in their smug orthodoxy believe that they have the answers to all life's deepest issues and to the ultimate meaning of the universe. To follow through their lengthy speeches and the still longer ones of Job, adorned as they are with Oriental flights of fancy, and to study the subtle contribution of each to the advance of the discussion toward a conclusion which, we may presume, the author envisaged from the beginning—to do this is a new experience in Old Testament study, where apart from narratives the matter falls generally into relatively brief and somewhat independent passages.

It is well known that the bulk of the book is in poetry. Its art is a delight. The author embellishes his pages with vignettes of ancient life; he draws upon his deep knowledge of psychology; he carries one along with allusion and citation from his wide reading in the great literature of the Orient; and still more, his lines are superb in their finished form, their resonant assonances, their majestic structures, and their confident use of all the devices and figures that enhance great poetry. Certain of his lines have passed into general use as gems of literary art. Think of these:

When the morning stars sang together
and all the sons of God rejoiced (38:7).

What pure poetry in the phrase, "the eyelids of the dawn" (3:9)! What majesty in the description of the war horse, pawing the valley in his impatience, while he hears the trumpet and the clash of swords, and "smells the battle far off" (39:19-25)!

The book is in semidramatic form. Indeed, its stated dramatis personae and their conversation have led some readers to regard it as modeled on Greek drama. It is impossible to say what the writer intended to achieve, but certainly the action normally expected in drama is lacking. It is sufficient for us that the movement of thought is dramatic. And what a flight of fancy when at length the Lord himself is introduced, appearing in the whirlwind to challenge Job, "Gird up now your loins like a man!" And then there follows a magnificent account of the great works of God since the time when he

> shut up the sea with doors when it broke forth as if it had issued from the womb (38:8).

The origin of the book has given rise to considerable speculation. Its locale out on the fringe of the desert, its indifference to Old Testament law and ritual, and its strange linguistic features have suggested the hypothesis of a foreign origin. One claim is that it is a translation of an Arabic poem, another that it is a product of Edomite wisdom. But to attribute this supreme achievement of the literary and intellectual life of the ancient world to such sources is just out of the question. Unless better evidence is forthcoming, we may safely hold that the one people in the ancient world qualified to produce such a work was Israel. Job is Hebraic through and through. Its linguistic peculiarities may safely be set down to dialectal divergence from the familiar Hebrew of Jerusalem. Presumably, then, some concession is to be made to the theories just now mentioned; the author was a Jew not of Jerusalem, but of some other part of the world.

The traditional and still commonly accepted interpretation of the book is the obvious one: that it reaches the answer to its problem in the speeches of the Lord. And that answer, so it is held, is that man may trust a God whom he cannot understand. But this line of exposition runs foul of two acute difficulties. Excellent as such a sentiment may be, it can be extracted from these chapters only by violence—or by pietistic eisegesis, which is the same thing. Their patent import and emphasis is that God is mighty, and man has no right to ask questions about his conduct. God is the "completely other," so far above man and so distinct from him that his righteousness also is of a different kind; it is folly to suppose, much less demand, that he be righteous by human standards. For man there is only submission and acceptance, a view which, it may be remarked, is precisely that of the friends in the dialogue, hence the view

which Job (and so, presumably, the poet) passionately repudiates. The other objection to this interpretation is that it has uniformly led scholars to overlook an aspect of the dialogue that becomes obvious as soon as it is approached in its own right, freed from presuppositions as to its place in the book. In the dialogue Job's experience is a pilgrimage of faith and hope. But to our astonishment the standard commentators uniformly treat the Job of the dialogue as a static figure. Some, it is true, speak of his progress of thought, but their demonstration leaves it microscopic; for they single out passages from his speeches indiscriminately at any point in the book, and piece them together as Job's "position." In reality Job has no position, but a progress. From an initial theology not unlike that of the friends, he moves on under the spur of their taunts, first into deep pessimism and rebellion, then gradually to a dawning hope which through notable apprehensions of faith comes to clarity in his great affirmation,

> He knows the way I take;
> when he has tried me, I shall come forth as gold (23:10).

The book takes on vital meaning when we regard it in some such light as this. An old folk tale about the righteous sufferer circulated in Israel; following a method familiar to us from the work of great creative writers of far-subsequent ages, a poet-thinker took this as stimulus and point of departure for the discussion that now constitutes the dialogue. Originally this was of greater extent than at present, and carried the thought onward to Job's restoration. Through some unrecorded misadventure the conclusion of the poem was lost and other parts preserved only in fragments: later editors put together these tattered remnants in what are now called chs. 25–27. But the discussion was of such importance and power as to inspire a series of lesser men to add their views on the subject. Relatively early a series of mutually independent poems were appended; they now go under the name of Elihu. This was before the injury to the manuscript of the dialogue, for the first speech of Elihu (chs. 32–33) traces lightly the course of the discussion right through to the original conclusion. It was some time later that the speeches of the Lord were added by a poet of imagination and skill who saw dramatic possibilities in letting Job have his wish to meet the Lord in open debate. His description of the encounter is a high example of the art of the Hebrew poets. The epilogue was added by lesser men, and apparently someone prefixed the prologue in order to round out the entire episode.

C. Ecclesiastes.—Contrary to a former view, the book of Ecclesiastes is to be regarded as in the main the unified work of a single author. Eccl. 12:12-14 has been added, a sort of pious colophon; the proverbial sayings occurring throughout the book also give an impression of having been expanded, if indeed they are not in some cases intruded in entirety. But for the rest, the book consists of reasoned and orderly views of life's ultimate meaning set forth by some thoughtful and eminently honest man of an indeterminate late period of Old Testament times. His views in part resemble the hedonistic conclusions of Egyptian pessimists of more than seventeen centuries before. It is claimed, too, that he was influenced by Greek thinking; if so, this is clearest in his cyclical theory of history (3:1-17). In any case, he was a thoughtful, educated man who was familiar with the literature and thought of the ancient world.

The author's problem is to find some redeeming value in human life. He gives his conclusion at the outset, though not in a priori thinking, but merely as his way of presenting his views: "Vanity of vanities; all is vanity." The word here translated "vanity" means both worthlessness and transience. It has the latter force in 11:10, but elsewhere the other is closer to the author's thought. His conviction, then, is that life has no worth. This he expounds with several considerations. He points out the cyclical character of nature and life (1:1-11); he tells of his experiment with himself, how he tried various experiences in hope of finding life's secret (1:12–2:23); he speaks of the uncertainty of family and personal fortune (4:4-7; 6:3-8), since a wise man may be succeeded by a fool. In a passage that reveals his generous instincts he tells of rampant injustice (4:1-3, 8) but—unlike the prophets whom it aroused to fiery action—he was merely thrown into deeper dejection. For he is convinced, doubtless on account of his cyclical view of life, that the total of human misery is a constant quality, so that it is hopeless to seek to do anything about it. He concedes that wisdom surpasses folly as light surpasses darkness (2:13), yet for him what is the use? Here we find a clue to his pessimism; he lacks the cosmic view of wisdom so remarkably set forth in Prov. 8; for him wisdom is about equivalent to individual education. As a consequence, it has no permanence. Life is atomistic and futile, never achieving anything of lasting worth. Always it deceives with glimpses of reality and understanding that are never attained, but it ever starts afresh with each new individual from the same unchanging beginning. What then remains? Only to enjoy the passing moment, and avoid serious thought.

The author is from some points of view a figure to stir something akin to pity. An eminently attractive personality, genial, kindly, supremely honest, with deep social feelings and keen intellectual tastes, he could yet find no worth in life. It was all vanity and vexation of spirit, a mere chasing after wind. How one wishes he might have realized, as did the wise man in Prov. 8, that across the ages human life is building up values that endure, and that these compel a metaphysical answer to all our questing. But then there have always been men of his outlook; they are still with us, and some of them are called philosophers. They insist that they are the ones who take account of all available truth; it is the religious man who is deceiving himself with wishful thinking and a biased selection of facts. But whatever is to be our judgment of his thinking, there can be no doubt that Ecclesiastes was a writer possessed of genuine skill and poetic feeling. His lucidity remains a challenge and a warning to those who too easily reconcile their faith with the perplexities and boredom of human existence.

VII. Conclusion

The vitality of the Jewish sages at a later age is revealed by two books which were not included in the Hebrew canon: Ecclesiasticus and the Wisdom of Solomon (see article "The Literature and Religion of the Apocrypha," pp. 408-11, 406-8). Along with comments of the maxim type, both books took over the concept of cosmic wisdom that had been so strikingly set forth in Prov. 8–9. Ecclesiasticus identified this primordial wisdom with the Torah, a view which is not to be regarded as a mark of the triumph of legalism so much as a logical conclusion drawn from Jewish theological concepts. The author of the Wisdom of Solomon was equally dependent on the ancient sages; his thought was similar to that of Proverbs, but he dressed it up in Stoic phraseology.

The nature of the wisdom concept was such that it was easily carried over into the New Testament. When the early Christians began to wrestle with the problem of understanding the nature and place of their divine Lord, they found an interpretation ready at hand in the age-old speculations of the wise men. Contrary to widely held opinion, the prologue to the Fourth Gospel is more Hebraic than Hellenic. Apart from its featuring the word *logos*, it is almost completely derived from Prov. 8; it is a reshaping, in terms still bearing the stamp of their origin, of the concept of the pre-existent divine wisdom that had made the world and took delight in the sons of men. Some years earlier Paul had taken the same course of interpreting his Savior as "Christ the power of God and the wisdom of God" (I Cor. 1:24). The christological speculation of the church is rooted in the Old Testament in a far more profound way than mere grasping after "messianic prophecy" has permitted Christian thought to apprehend.

VIII. Selected Bibliography

BAUMGARTNER, WALTER. *Israelitische und altorientalische Weisheit.* Tübingen: J. C. B. Mohr, 1933.

DRIVER, S. R., and GRAY, G. B. *A Critical and Exegetical Commentary on the Book of Job* ("International Critical Commentary"). New York: Charles Scribner's Sons, 1921.

GRESSMANN, HUGO. *Israels Spruchweisheit im Zusammenhang der Weltliteratur.* Berlin: Karl Curtius, 1926.

GUNN, B. G. *The Instruction of Ptah-hotep and the Instruction of Ke'gemni.* New York: E. P. Dutton & Co., 1909.

HUMBERT, PAUL. *Recherches sur les sources égyptiennes de la littérature sapientale d'Israël.* Neuchâtel: Secrétariat de l'Université, 1929.

MACDONALD, D. B. *The Hebrew Philosophical Genius.* Princeton: Princeton University Press, 1936.

OESTERLEY, W. O. E. *The Wisdom of Egypt and the Old Testament.* New York: The Macmillan Co., 1927.

RANKIN, O. S. *Israel's Wisdom Literature.* Edinburgh: T. & T. Clark, 1936.

RANSTON, HARRY. *The Old Testament Wisdom Books and Their Teaching.* London: Epworth Press, 1930.

RYLAARSDAM, J. COERT. *Revelation in Jewish Wisdom Literature.* Chicago: University of Chicago Press, 1946.

THE LANGUAGE
OF THE OLD TESTAMENT

by NORMAN H. SNAITH

Most of the Old Testament was originally written in Hebrew. The small residue was written in a dialect of Aramaic known as biblical Aramaic, and comprises three main pieces (Dan. 2:4b–7:28; Ezra 4:8–6:18; 7:12-26), an odd verse in the middle of Jeremiah (10:11, presumably an early gloss), and two words in Genesis (31:47; "Heap of Witness," the name given by Laban to the Mizpah stone which Jacob's clansmen set up in Gilead). The fact that the central portion of the book of Daniel is written in this dialect led ancient scholars to call it Chaldee, under the impression that this was the tongue spoken by the Jewish exiles in Chaldea (Babylonia).

I. The Semitic Languages

Both Hebrew and Aramaic belong to the Semitic family of languages. These are called "Semitic" because, according to the ancient Hebrew ethnological tables of Gen. 10–11, most of the peoples who have spoken them were descended from Shem, son of Noah. The Semitic languages may be roughly grouped according to four geographical areas: (*a*) *Eastern* —Akkadian (the modern name for Assyrian and Babylonian); (*b*) *Western*—Hebrew and the languages of ancient Palestine and Trans-Jordan; (*c*) *Northern*—the various Aramaic dialects, including the later Syriac; (*d*) *Southern*—Arabic and Ethiopic.

As a written language, Akkadian is the earliest member of the Semitic family. Then comes the recently discovered Ugaritic, so called from the site of Ugarit discovered in 1929 at Ras Shamra on the Syrian seacoast. These two languages both used cuneiform (wedge-shaped) scripts, and were written from left to right. Akkadian cuneiform is syllabic and ideographic, while Ugaritic cuneiform is consonantal-alphabetical.

Next in chronological order as a written language comes Hebrew, with Aramaic not far behind, though as a spoken language Aramaic is certainly earlier than the Hebrew of the Old Testament. During and after the Exile, Aramaic was used by the Jews both in Babylonia and in Palestine, while the closely allied Syriac became the language of the Christians of the East.

Arabic came into prominence with the rise of Islam from the seventh century A.D., and in the Middle Ages was the medium through which the learning of the Greeks became known in the West. Today Arabic is the major spoken Semitic language, having in addition a marked influence on Urdu (Hindustani), and to a lesser degree on some of the languages of West Africa. Modern Abyssinian is a development from Ethiopic. Small ethnoreligious groups still speak Aramaic and Syriac, while the rise of modern Hebrew is a recent phenomenon.

II. The Consonantal Script and the Vowels

Apart from Akkadian, Semitic languages have used consonantal scripts only, and other means have had to be devised to express the vowel sounds. Even Akkadian did not need vowel signs, for its script, being syllabic, included vocalic sounds in the notation of consonants.

Other Semitic languages, especially Hebrew, pressed certain consonants into service to represent unchangeably long vowels (see article, "Text and Ancient Versions of the Old Testament," pp. 46-62). When this device was found to be inadequate, special signs were created and placed above, within, or below the consonants in order to represent all vocalic sounds. Hebrew was written for centuries without vowels, and this custom is still followed in the scrolls which are used in the synagogues.

The lack of vowel signs has in general occasioned no great difficulty, though there are instances where it has given rise to misunderstandings. For example, in Gen. 47:31, the Hebrew says that the aged Israel bowed down on the top of the bed (*miṭṭāh*), but the Septuagint reads that he bowed down on the top of his staff (*maṭṭeh*), and this rendering was quoted in Heb. 11:21. Likewise, in I Kings 19:2-3 the Hebrew tells how Jezebel threatened Elijah with reprisals for his slaughter of her prophets; the Consonantal Text has וירא which the Masoretes read as *wayyar'* ("And he saw") and the Septuagint as *wayyîrā'* ("And he was afraid").

III. Main Characteristics of Hebrew Morphology

Like all Semitic languages, Hebrew is built up on a three-consonant (or triliteral) verbal root system. There are indications that there was also a two-consonant system, but any attempt to recover it is largely conjectural. The three consonants carry the meaning, while the vowels, together with consonants either prefixed or suffixed, are used to conjugate the verb in various forms, voices, moods, tenses, and to derive nouns and adjectives (though Hebrew is notoriously weak in the latter).

The verb has seven main forms with a number of others in occasional use. The main forms are the ordinary active with its passive, an intensive or causative form with its passive, a causative, declarative, or progressive-stative form with its passive, and an intensive-reflexive, reciprocal, or "pretensive" form.

The way in which these forms may be obtained by variations in vowels and by additions of consonants will be seen in the following words.

The triliteral root גנב (*gānabh*) means "he stole"; *yignōbh* means "he will [may] steal"; *gônēbh* (active participle) is "one who steals," while the noun *gannābh* is a professional or persistent "thief" and *genēbhāh* is a "thing stolen"; *ginnēbh* means transitively "he stole away" (e.g., "the hearts"), but *hithgannēbh* signifies, intransitively, "he stole away" (i.e., "he went away by stealth"); finally, Joseph told Pharaoh *gunnōbh gunnabhtî*, "I was truly stolen away" (Moffatt, "really kidnapped"; Gen. 40:15).

Likewise the three-consonant verb שמר

(*shāmar*) means "he kept," "tended" (e.g., "flock"), "watched," "observed"; *nishmar* signifies "he was on his guard," or "he was kept"; while *hishtammēr* means "he kept himself [from]." Apart from these verbal forms, several nouns may be derived, like *mishmār*, "jail," "prison," and later, "guard post"; *shomrāh* and *mishméreth* are "guard," "watch," while *'ashmŏreth* means "watch" (division of time).

For the most part the same three consonants carry always the same meaning, though, as in every language, there are changes with the passing centuries. Sometimes the same three consonants have meanings which seem to be mutually incompatible. One cause of this phenomenon is that each of the two Hebrew letters ח and ע represents what were originally two distinct gutturals, though the distinction came to be lost in Hebrew. These are still expressed by different signs in Arabic and in Ethiopic. For instance, the Hebrew consonants h-r-b mean either "be waste," "desolate" or "attack," "smite down." The explanation is to be seen in the Arabic equivalents, where *hariba* (with the heavy *hēth*) means "be waste," while *haraba* (with the light *hēth*) means "plunder." Thus the Hebrew noun *hôrebh* (heavy *hēth*) means "desolation," while *hérebh* (light *hēth*) means "sword."

A second reason is that Hebrew is not a pure language: to some extent it occupied a central place in the Semitic world, where East and West overlapped. For instance, the root *q-ç-r* can mean both "be short" and "reap" or "harvest." The former is the meaning in Arabic, while the latter is the meaning in Akkadian.

A third reason is the way in which consonants interchange from language to language. In the Indo-Teutonic group of languages we have the regular interchanges of consonants according to the correspondences known as Grimm's law; e.g., the English *thrash* and the German *dreschen*, or again, *father* and *Vater*. Among the similar Semitic rules there are those affecting the Hebrew consonant צ, which is represented in Arabic by no less than three consonants, *çād* (an emphatic *s*), *ḍād* (an emphatic *d*), and *ẓā* (an emphatic *z*). There are thus three Hebrew roots *ç-r-r*. In Arabic the first is *çarra* ("bind"), so that the Hebrew *çerôr* means "bundle," "parcel," and *çar* means "straits," "distress." The second is *ḍarra* ("harm," "damage") so that the Hebrew *çar* means "foe," "adversary," and *çārāh* means "vexer," i.e., "rival wife." The third is *ẓarra* ("be sharp"), whence the Arabic *ẓurar* is "a sharp-edged stone." In Hebrew, as a relic of the Stone Age, *çerôr* means "pebble," and *çôr* is "knife," presumably dating back to a time when the first Hebrew cutting instruments were flint knives.

IV. Hybrid Character of the Hebrew Language

The fact that Hebrew is a mixed language and has features common to other Semitic languages is to be seen also in the duplicate forms of the first person singular pronoun "I." There are two forms in common use, with no distinction between them as regards meaning, but only as regards style or preference. Each form belongs to its own group, but the two groups overlap in Hebrew. The first form is *'ānôkhî,* found in Akkadian and also in Phoenician and Ugaritic. Probably it belonged originally to the east, but came west with that Babylonian influence which was especially strong in Palestine during the middle part of the second millennium, and was formative in the development of the speech of Syria (Amurru, according to the Assyrian geographers) out of which the Palestinian tongues sprang. The second is *'anî,* and is found in Aramaic, also in Arabic and Ethiopic. It apparently belonged to the north and the south, and was probably brought into Canaan by the Hebrews or by some other group of invaders with Aramaean associations. When the Hebrews entered Palestine, they seem to have spoken some Aramaean-Arabic language, which in time was fused with the Canaanite already there. Perhaps the book of Job with its strong Aramaic-Arabic flavor is a development of the original speech of the Hebrews of the desert. In Isa. 19:18 Hebrew is rightly called "the language of Canaan," for the Ras Shamra (Ugarit) tablets, the glosses on the Tell el-Amarna tablets, and the ninth-century Moabite stele of King Mesha, all show that the Canaanite element is dominant in biblical Hebrew. The conqueror conquered the inhabitants, but the land itself to a large extent conquered him. Both ethnologically and linguistically it is plain that the land of Canaan conquered, with its already mixed blood, language and traditions. It is plain also from the Old Testament that Canaan would have conquered religiously also had it not been for the prophets whom God "rose early to send." The physical characteristics which we tend to associate with the Jew are actually Hittite, as the Hittite bas-reliefs show. The true Semitic type is to be seen sometimes in the leaner, hawk-eyed Spanish Jew, possibly because an admixture of Moorish blood has brought him back closer to the purer Semitic strain. Ezekiel was in the main right when he said, "Thy birth and thy nativity is of the land of the Canaanite; the Amorite [i.e., the original Syrian stock, cf. Assyrian "Amurru"] was thy father, and thy mother was an Hittite" (Ezek. 16:3 ERV).

The hybrid origin of the Hebrew language is nowhere more clear than in the verbal system.

It used to be said that Hebrew had only two tenses, in this respect being similar to classical Arabic: a "perfect" tense, used of an action thought of as having been completed, and an "imperfect" tense, used of an action thought of as being incomplete. It was also held that the inadequacy of this tense system is compensated for to a considerable extent by the construction known as "imperfect with strong *waw*" (or "*waw* conversive" or "*waw* consecutive"), whereby the imperfect occurring with the copula at the beginning of a clause is translated as if it were the perfect; and similarly, though contrariwise, with the "perfect with strong *waw.*" We know now [1] that this strong *waw* construction is Akkadian so far as some of its unique features are concerned. It was always hard to explain why the tone should sometimes move forward in the imperfect with strong *waw.* A modern explanation is that the tense is not really the imperfect *yiqtōl* at all, with the accent on the last syllable, but a preterite *yiqtōl,* with the accent on the first syllable, preserved in the Akkadian preterite *iqtul.* Similarly what was thought to be the perfect with strong *waw* is not the perfect of Aramaic, Arabic, and Ethiopic, but is the Akkadian "permansive," definitely a present-future tense.

Perhaps we have here an explanation of the so-called "prophetic perfect" of Hebrew. This is an apparent perfect tense used of an action which is in the future, either immediate or not so immediate, but certainly to be fulfilled in the mind of the prophet. It is used chiefly of the word of God as spoken by the prophet concerning future weal or woe. The prophet Isaiah says in 5:13, "Therefore my people are gone into exile" (Amer. Trans.), by which he means that it is absolutely certain that they will go. Or again, a strict translation of Num. 24:17 is "There hath risen a star out of Jacob, and a scepter shall arise out of Israel." Here we have a perfect with a strong *waw* following an apparent perfect, but the English versions have rightly realized that it is not a true perfect, and they have rendered, "shall arise." Actually the tense is a permansive, referring to the future whether immediate or remote.

In the hands of the prophets this so-called "prophetic perfect" developed into a most powerful mode of expression, and it seems to have gathered to itself something of the significance of all the time categories, present, past, and future. For instance, the prophet known as Deutero-Isaiah regularly uses the "prophetic perfect" to say that God "hath redeemed" Jacob-Israel (Isa. 43:1; 44:22, 23; 48:20; 52:9). But this redemption has not yet

[1] G. R. Driver, *Problems of the Hebrew Verbal System* (Edinburgh: T. & T. Clark, 1936), pp. 85-97.

taken place. The prophet regards it as belonging to the immediate future, and at the same time as being absolutely and finally determined. It is out of this combined idea of an action fully determined by God in the past, but due for realization in the immediate future, that the peculiar features of the prophetic eschatology developed. The prophets spoke of the last things (eschatology), of the consummation of the will of God, with a sense of immediacy. These last things were to come to pass almost "now." The prophets could say that God "hath redeemed Israel," because it was always being realized as true. The whole history of Israel in times past echoed no other refrain than, "God hath redeemed Israel." Any man who had eyes to see could look and see that it was true now; and the prophet could see equally that it was true tomorrow. God is always redeemer. In this sense the development from prophecy to apocalypse is a widening of the prospect from the historical to the eternal. God is immanent to redeem and save not only in the long process of history, but always now, immediately now. The prophetic doctrine of the last things with its salvation in the indefinite future becomes the apocalyptic doctrine of salvation in the immediate future, i.e., the present-future of the permansive tense, so to speak, the eternal tense of the ever present-imminent "now."

We thus see that the hybrid nature of the language and of the people is witness both to their very ordinary beginnings and to their extraordinary development. The study of the language emphasizes the statement made in various forms that Israel in herself was no different from any others of the peoples which surrounded her. Everything, therefore, that Israel ever came to be was due not to herself but to the grace of God. Israel was certainly chosen by God to be "a peculiar people to himself" (Deut. 7:6; "a people of *ṣegullāh*," i.e., acquired property, and so made especially his own while not being his own originally), but, as the passage continues to say, it was not because of any merit in them, e.g., it was not because they were greater in number than any people, for they were few.

It used to be claimed that just as the Greeks had a genius for beauty and so taught the world what true beauty is, so the Romans had a genius for law and gave to the world the idea of law. And similarly, the Hebrews had a genius for religion and so taught the world the true religion. This is contrary to the attitude of the Old Testament. The Hebrews, according to the Old Testament, had no natural genius for religion. On the contrary, they were essentially wayward, and it was only the continued mercy of God to a special degree that enabled even a

remnant of them to be faithful to the true God. The language shows that they were a mixed race, and by no means a people especially marked by a preserved purity of blood or ethos. Whatever they came to be was of God, and all was of grace. It was God himself who raised up the prophets. These men, like Amos, were not prophets because their fathers had been prophets, nor because of their occupations or of anything that was peculiarly theirs. They were prophets because God had called them, invaded their lives, and raised them up to be the men they became, to call the people back to him in repentance.

V. Hebrew Versus Aramaic

In some respects the whole story of Hebrew during biblical times is a fight against Aramaic. We know that more and more during the time of the Persian domination (538-331 B.C.), Aramaic supplanted Hebrew, chiefly because it was the language in which official Persia spoke to her western satrapies. But the fight between Hebrew and Aramaic did not begin then. It originated when the Israelites first entered Palestine. They spoke then a dialect which had much closer affinities with Aramaic than with Hebrew.[2] This accounts for the so-called Aramaisms which appear in the Old Testament, mostly in north Israelite literature, even as early as Judg. 5:11 (*yetannû* for the true Hebrew *yeshannû*, "they shall repeat," "rehearse"). Aramaisms are to be found also in Hosea and in the Song of Songs, parts of which are probably northern in origin. Similarly, there is the famous shibboleth test of Judg. 12:6, where the Ephraimites apparently used the Arabic "*s*" as against the "*sh*" of the Hebrew.

There was thus always a strong tendency in the north toward Aramaic, strengthened by the Gileadite emphasis on the old desert ways. With the Assyrian settlements of deportees from 721 B.C. onward, the Aramaic influence increased enormously, and doubtless from these days the language penetrated more and more into the south, where the original inhabitants seem to have been less disturbed by the invasion under Joshua. When the Babylonian exiles returned, they came back with their Hebrew into a largely Aramaic-speaking country. Nehemiah complained of the mixed speech, and of children who "spake half in the speech of Ashdod, and could not speak in the Jews' language" (Neh. 13:24). After the Exile, Hebrew survived among the intelligentsia, both as a religious language and as a literary language; this has been the case not only in the early

[2] D. W. Thomas, "The Language of the Old Testament," in *Record and Revelation*, ed. H. Wheeler Robinson (Oxford: Clarendon Press, 1938), p. 377.

postexilic times, but also right down to the present day. Nevertheless, Aramaic was the common language of ordinary folk, and it grew more and more necessary for the Scriptures themselves to be rendered into Aramaic in order that the hearer should understand what he heard.

VI. Semantic Changes of Religious Terms

The Old Testament is the product of many generations, and scarcely a page of it is to be found in the state in which it left the hand of the first writer. The fact is that no book in the world has been more deliberately kept up to date throughout many centuries. This was helped by the fact that all Hebrew writings of olden time are anonymous, the various titles which we now read having been supplied by editors. Men of God kept on re-editing the ancient texts in order to make sure that the Word of God should speak as clearly as possible to every generation in spite of all the changing circumstances of the years. Especially, the editors knew that Yahweh was a God of salvation, so that again and again when they did not find his saving power sufficiently emphasized in the writings that came down to them, they inserted passages to that effect. These additions are often found at the end of books, such as the last verses of Amos.

It is important on other grounds to recognize that the Hebrew of the Old Testament has come from widely separated centuries. Words change their meanings as the generations pass away. For instance, in pre-exilic writings the word *qeṭôreth* means "sacrifice" (e.g., Isa. 1:13), whereas in postexilic writings it means "incense" (e.g., Exod. 25:6; I Chr. 28:18). This particular instance is important for two reasons. It makes it quite clear that Isaiah of Jerusalem denounced sacrifice in no uncertain terms: he said that it was an abomination to God. And again, it agrees with what we know otherwise, namely, that there was no incense in Solomon's temple, but that this was an innovation of postexilic times, due presumably to Babylonian influence on the returning exiles.

Or again, and once more in connection with sacrifice, there is a word *minḥāh,* used both early and late. In Arabic the verb *manaḥa* means "lend," "give a gift," and the noun *minḥat* is used of a loan or gift, especially of a she-camel, a sheep, or a goat for milking. The verb itself is not found in Hebrew, but the noun *minḥāh* means "gift," "present," and it is used especially of tribute paid to an overlord or king (Judg. 3:15; Ps. 72:10). This noun is used in Gen. 4:3 of both the animal offering brought by Abel and of the cereal or fruit offering brought by Cain. Here the word un-doubtedly means "tribute offering," a gift to God wholly given to him, and not largely consumed by the offerer at a sacred meal, as some other "sacrifices" were. This is the pre-exilic use of the word, but in postexilic writings the word denotes the cereal offering (ERV "meal-offering") which accompanied every flesh sacrifice on the altar of the second temple. In the King James Version the translation is "meat offering," misleading to us today, but in the sixteenth century this phrase actually meant "food offering," involving a wider use of the word "meat" than in modern times. This older use still appears often in common English speech and also, e.g., in John 6:27.

Or yet again, in connection with sacrificial terms, there is a word *'āshām,* which is used in postexilic times, especially in the Priestly Code, to denote a particular type of offering brought in connection with the expiation of certain offenses (Lev. 5; etc.). The King James Version translates, "trespass offering," and the English Revised Version, "guilt offering." The *'āshām* had its place in connection with such offenses against God or man as could be estimated in damages and so covered by compensation. It is this idea of "compensation," "substituted payment," which is at the heart of the word. This particular type of offering was unknown before the second temple, so that when we find the word, for instance, in Isa. 53:10, we must remember that there is no reference here to the guilt offering of later postexilic times. The meaning is, "When you realize that he [or "his life"] is a substitute for yours," i.e., when you realize that he suffers instead of you.

VII. The Main Motif of Words

Proper understanding of the Old Testament may be enhanced by a careful study of Hebrew words. While it must be recognized that words can change their meaning in strange and unexpected ways through the centuries, yet in all languages there is a fundamental motif in a word which tends to endure, whatever other changes the years may bring. This fundamental "theme" of a word is often curiously determinative of later meanings.

The Hebrew word *hēpheç* is a case in point. The original meaning of this word is "attention." In Arabic it came to mean "excited attention" and so "excitement," but in Hebrew the development was "delighted attention" and so "delight." As the years passed by, the word came to be used to mean "good pleasure," "purpose," e.g., "the purpose of the LORD will prosper in his hands" (Isa. 53:10), with the suggestion of wholehearted and complete attention. The idea of full attention is to be understood in Prov. 31:13, "And she worketh at the *business* of her hands." In course of time the word came to mean "affair," "matter," e.g., "There is a time for every affair" (Eccl. 3:1; etc.), and in the Mishnah it referred merely to a "thing," having lost all definitive meaning. The word thus ultimately decayed, but it did not lose its motif of "complete attention" until its deterioration from the third century B.C. onward. The name Hephzi-bah, for instance, does not mean merely "my delight is in her," but "my whole delight is in her."

Another example is the first word of Ps. 1. This can be used to illustrate the way in which the ancient Hebrews thought. In the English versions this word is rendered "blessed." The Hebrew is *'ashrê,* literally, "happinesses of." The noun *'āshûr* means "footstep," and this meaning is confirmed in Arabic and Ethiopic. Further, *'asher* is the Hebrew relative particle. The explanation of these wide divergences is that the three-consonant root from which all these words are derived *('-sh-r)* means "go straight ahead," "advance." It is thus easy to see how the noun comes to mean "footstep." Many scholars are of the opinion that the Hebrew relative particle was once used as a relative of place only, like its Akkadian counterpart *ashru,* but that the Hebrew relative particle developed so as to become a general relative for all purposes. All this shows how apt is the use of the first word. The psalm tells of the true way as distinct from the false. The happy man is the man who goes straight ahead, because, as the last verse says, "the LORD knoweth the way of the righteous," while "the way of the wicked shall perish." The meaning of the last word (אבד, "perish") is to be seen in Job 6:18, where it is used of a desert caravan turning aside in a last desperate effort to find water, and wandering till it is lost and dies in the desert; or again in the firstfruits declaration of Deut. 26:5, "An Aramaean ready to perish was my father," where the word *'ôbhēdh* (participle) is practically untranslatable. It means "wandering," and also doomed as a desert wanderer who one day will be lost to perish in the desert. And still further, to complete the picture of the last verse of the psalm, there is plenty of evidence to show that the Hebrew *yādha'* ("know") tends to be used of personal intimacy rather than of intellectual knowledge. God is personally acquainted with this road of the righteous, knows every step of it, and has a real concern for every wayfarer.

This personal aspect of Old Testament religion comes to the forefront again in a word which is often wrongly rendered in the English versions. The word is *pésha'.* This is very frequently translated "transgression," but its true meaning is "rebellion." When, therefore, the prophets use this term, a favorite word with them, they are thinking not so much of transgressing a code, however excellent, as of deliberate rebellion against a person, and that person the savior God himself. This emphasis makes a very great deal of difference in the Old Testament conception of sin. It makes the main emphasis religious rather than ethical. In this respect Old Testament ethics differ from the traditional Greek ethics which have been the norm for our Western world. In all sound ethical systems the emphasis comes to be placed on the attitude of mind of the wrongdoer rather than on the action itself. This is true of the Greek system equally with the Hebrew. In general humanitarian or secular ethics there is also the emphasis that the wrongdoer has transgressed a particular code or some element in the system. In the Old Testament this second point of emphasis, certainly so far as the prophets are concerned, lies in the fact that the wrongdoer has turned his back on the savior God, and is going his own way instead. "We have turned every one to his own way" (Isa. 53:6). Sin, therefore, is regarded as all the more serious because the wrongdoer, as Elihu said, though wrongly, of Job "addeth rebellion [*pésha'*] to his sin [*haṭṭâ'th,* "error," "mistake"]" (Job 34:37).

Corresponding to "rebellion," "turning every one to his own way," the regular word in common use by the prophets for "repent" is *shûbh* ("return," "turn back"). When Isaiah calls his son *She'âr-yāshûbh,* his meaning is not, as is often popularly thought, "a remnant shall return from exile," but "a remnant shall turn back to God," i.e., a remnant shall repent.

Another word used in this connection, though less frequently, is *niham,* generally translated "repent" (in the passive form) and "comfort" (in the intensive form). Actually the word means "to take a breath of relief," the implication being "to breathe hard [as of a horse]," as is shown in Arabic.[3] The word therefore has to do with "change of attitude," "change of mind," any other association being accidental. If therefore the word must be translated "comfort," then it refers to "comfort out of sorrow," and so cessation from lamentation and weeping because the troubles are over (Isa. 40:1). When the word is translated "repent," as frequently of God, it means "change of mind or intention," and has no necessary connection with sorrow or regret. We see thus what an apt rendering the Greek μετανοεῖν is, with its corresponding noun μετάνοια. This verb is used

[3] D. W. Thomas, "A Note on the Hebrew Root *Nācham," Expository Times,* XLIV (1933), 191. Also N. H. Snaith, "The Meaning of 'The Paraclete,' " *ibid.,* LVII (1945), 47-50.

occasionally in the Septuagint as the equivalent of the Hebrew verb *niham,* eight times in the sense of "change one's mind," and about thirteen times where the idea of "repent," "be sorry," is also involved. Both verb and noun occur frequently in the New Testament, and both of them definitely involve a change of mind and intention, as the etymology suggests. The idea of sorrow for past sin, though necessary enough from the religious point of view, is not conveyed in the word itself. The emphasis is that, with whatever accompaniment, the man should change his attitude, turn right around, and go back along the road into which he ought never to have gone away from God.

There is another matter which arises in connection with Hebrew ideas of sin, and here again a study of the key words shows that Hebrew thought differs from our Western ways of thinking. We make a clear distinction between sin as the wrong act itself, the guilt which thereafter rests upon the sinner, and the consequences of the sin which fall sometimes on the sinner and usually on the innocent. The Hebrews tended to include all three aspects under the same word. The outstanding example is to be found in Gen. 4:13, where Cain says, "My *ʿāwôn* is greater than I can bear." This word *ʿāwôn* is most often translated "iniquity," but in Gen. 4:13 the English translators have rightly seen that the reference is to the consequences of Cain's wrongdoing, and they have translated it by "punishment." It is very often quite difficult to decide the precise meaning of the word in any particular case as between the three elements. In this particular passage the Vulgate has *iniquitas,* while the Septuagint has αἰτία ("blame," "guilt"). The difficulties of classification are plain from the variations of the references given under the three heads by such authorities as Buhl, Siegfried-Stade, and Brown-Driver-Briggs.

Further complications are introduced with the word *ḥaṭṭāʾth* ("error," "sin," "mistake"). This word is used mainly for the wrong action itself and occasionally for the guilt of it (Zech. 14:19). It is also used for the postexilic "sin offering," of which, in the ritual of the second temple, there was more than one grade. This further meaning of the Hebrew *ḥaṭṭāʾth* needs to be remembered when we come to interpret such a passage as II Cor. 5:21, "For our sake he made him to be sin who knew no sin." Inasmuch as Paul is thinking of the Greek ἁμαρτία in terms of the Hebrew *ḥaṭṭāʾth,* he does not confine himself to thinking of the guilt and of the consequences. He may be thinking of Christ as a sin offering in the sense that what Christ did on the Cross takes away the sin which stands between us and God, and thus re-establishes the proper relationship between God and us. The translation might be, "Made him to be a sin offering, who knew no sin"; that is, although he himself was wholly guiltless, yet he did more than bear the consequences of our sin; his suffering was a *ḥaṭṭāʾth,* a sin offering, putting us in a right relationship with God.

A proper appreciation of the root meaning of words is useful generally in the understanding of the Old Testament, as much in secular passages as in directly religious contexts. For instance, in Song of S. 4:1 and again in 6:5, the hair of the maid is likened to "a flock of goats that come in sight from mount Gilead." The Hebrew word for "flock" is *ʿēdher,* which is derived from the root *ʿ-d-r* ("to lag behind"). We have, then, the splendid picture of a flock of goats streaming out as it comes into sight on the mountainside, as happy a simile as could be found anywhere for describing the maid's flowing hair.

VIII. Hebrew Poetry and Theological Expression

A substantial portion of the Old Testament is written in poetry. According to official Jewish tradition there are three poetical books, Job, Proverbs, and Psalms. In addition, there is a small number of pieces which traditionally are spaced out as poetry, the chief of which are the two ancient sabbath canticles (Exod. 15:1-18; Deut. 32:1-43), together with the song of Deborah (Judg. 5). Much of the writings of the prophets is in verse also; indeed some scholars maintain that the prophets never wrote or spoke except in verse, and that this criterion should be applied as a test for genuineness. For instance, Gustav Hölscher boldly calls his commentary on Ezekiel *Hezekiel, der Dichter und das Buch* (Giessen: Alfred Töpelmann, 1924), and a similar attitude is taken by W. A. Irwin, *The Problem of Ezekiel* (Chicago: University of Chicago Press, 1943).

Hebrew poetry has no rhymes. Its two characteristics are rhythm and parallelism and thus it follows the same pattern as Babylonian psalmody,[4] or Ugaritic prosody.[5]

A. Rhythm.—The rhythm is provided by stressed syllables, the unstressed syllables being neglected for this purpose. The lines are divided into two sections, and sometimes into three. The commonest rhythms contain two or three stressed syllables in the section. The three-three rhythm is very common, especially with occasional two-stress sections interspersed as

[4] G. R. Driver, "The Psalms in the Light of Babylonian Research," in *The Psalmists,* ed. D. C. Simpson (London: Oxford University Press, 1926), pp. 109-75.

[5] See, e.g., the translations given by Cyrus H. Gordon, *Ugaritic Literature* (Rome: Pontificium Institutum Biblicum, 1949).

though for the sake of variation. One of the best examples of three-three rhythm is Ps. 105. Perhaps the most striking Hebrew rhythm is the three-two rhythm, where the line is divided into two sections of unequal length, producing a peculiar halting rhythm much used in laments. For this reason Budde called it the *qînāh* ("lament") rhythm. Ps. 17:8-11 is composed in this rhythm, and this particular portion of the psalm can thus be seen to be wholly distinct from the verses which precede it. The whole of the book of Lamentations is in this rhythm, each chapter comprising a *qînāh* poem, the first four being acrostics of various types.[6]

The change of rhythm is often indicative of a new paragraph entirely unconnected with what has gone before. For instance, the rhythm changes at Isa. 42:18. Previously the rhythm has been three-two with an occasional three-three, but after vs. 10 there is no two-stress section until vs. 24, which may contain one. There is a new section beginning at vs. 18. The "blind" of vs. 18 are not the "blind" of vs. 16. In vs. 16 they are all the exiles, but in vs. 18 they are those who do not understand the true significance of the Exile.

Another case where there is a change of rhythm is Isa. 46:3. The first two verses of this chapter are quite separate from what follows. They refer to an attempt to carry the idol gods of Babylon away to safety before the fall of the city. The next verses tell the story of God's continued care for Israel, how he carried Israel as a woman carries her unborn child, and how in time to come he will bring her to new birth. The exile, elsewhere spoken of under the figure of death and resurrection (Isa. 53:9-10; Ezek. 37:1-10) or as being swallowed up and disgorged by a sea-monster (Jer. 51:34; Jonah 1:17; 2:10), is here represented under the figure of a new birth.

B. Parallelism.—There are three types of parallelism in Hebrew poetry. The first is "synonymous," where the statement of the first line is repeated in the second, but with other words:

Thou shalt break them with a rod of iron:
Thou shalt dash them in pieces like a potter's vessel
(Ps. 2:9).

The second is "antithetic," where two opposite thoughts are expressed in the two lines, often with exact contrariness:

Weeping may tarry for the night,
But joy cometh in the morning (Ps. 30:5).

[6] For a detailed study of the structure of Hebrew poetry see G. B. Gray, *The Forms of Hebrew Poetry* (London: Hodder & Stoughton, 1915). A less detailed study is the more recent T. H. Robinson, *The Poetry of the Old Testament* (London: Duckworth, 1947), pp. 20-46.

The third is "climbing," where part of the first line is repeated in the second, and something further is added:

The floods have lifted up, O LORD!
The floods have lifted up their voice (Ps. 93:3).

An example of this climbing parallelism which extends over three lines is:

The voice of the LORD is upon the waters:
The God of glory thundereth:
Even the LORD upon many waters (Ps. 29:2 ERV).

Some scholars identify as a fourth type an extension of climbing parallelism which dispenses with the repetition (e.g., Ps. 121:2); others do not recognize in it any parallelism.

There are instances where it is theologically important to analyze the use of parallelism in Hebrew poetry. In Isa. 40:31, we have two three-three lines, in each of which there is an almost exact parallelism. The first line is, "But they that wait upon the LORD shall exchange strength . . . ," and the second line is, "They shall run, and not be weary; they shall go [travel] and not faint." In the first half of the first line the word translated "renew" in the English versions actually means "exchange." It is the same root as that which is used in the word "Caliph," he who is the successor to Mohammed, the new leader who takes the place of the old. Further, the word "their" is an unwarranted interpolation. The translators, in their zeal to make the passage more intelligible, have changed its meaning. The whole point of the passage is that human strength, even of the lustiest and the most vigorous, is of no avail, but God will give them new strength, different strength, his own strength. They will then grow pinions like the eagles, those high-soaring, distance-devouring watchers of the desert. It is often admitted, though with some regrets as for a good poet who has nodded, that there is an anticlimax in this verse, from flying to running and finally to walking. This, as we have seen, is a mistaken exegesis since it ignores the parallelism of the verse. Further, the root *h-l-k* does not mean only "walk"; it also means "go on a journey," "travel," and it is better to understand it here in this wider sense.

IX. Modern Recovery of Hebrew Words

Reference has been made above, in illustration of the hybrid nature of Hebrew, to the fact that the same three consonants sometimes represent more than one root, and so carry widely different and wholly unrelated meanings. Sometimes the more infrequent root has been forgotten because of the frequent occurrence of the other. Considerable progress has been made of recent years in the recovery of roots thus forgotten.

There are instances where the Septuagint translators evidently knew of the existence in Hebrew of these other roots. For instance, the Septuagint reads γέρας in Prov. 30:17, supported by the Syriac, the Targum, and Rashi. Evidently they recognized here in the word ליקהת (usually translated "obedience"), a root להק meaning "old age." This root is found in this sense in Ethiopic, while the corresponding Arabic root is used of hair being white.[7] Or again, in Isa. 48:10, the word çeraphtîkhâ is translated "I have refined thee," but the Septuagint has πέπρακα, which may be explained from another similar Semitic root, presumably preserved by the Egyptian Jews after it had been lost by other Hebrew-speaking groups. This other root is represented by the Akkadian sarâpu, with which one may compare the Arabic çarafa, meaning "buy." There is therefore no need to seek to emend the verse either in this section or the next. Another instance[8] is to be found in Dan. 7:22, where the Aramaic meṭâth is rendered ἐδόθη ("was given"). The context suggests that some such translation is desirable, and Nöldeke referred[9] to the fourth form of the Arabic root 'aṭay. This suggestion has its difficulties, but there is an Ethiopic root matawa, meaning "gave," and it seems likely that the Egyptian Jews still knew this word.[10] Yet again, in Isa. 44:28, there is no reason to doubt the correctness of the Hebrew text in the word rô'î ("my shepherd"), but the Septuagint has φρονεῖν, evidently recognizing a Syriac root, from which we get the noun ra'yón ("thought").[11] This instance, however, may not actually involve a newly discovered root since it is probably connected with an Aramaic root which was used by late Hebrew writers, e.g., Ps. 139:2, 17, in the sense of "purpose," "aim," or again, ten times in Ecclesiastes with the meaning "longing," "striving." In this case the history of the word would be similar to that of the noun hêpheç mentioned above.

A similar case is Ps. 25:14. Here the Septuagint has κραταίωμα for the Hebrew סוד. The English versions have "secret," i.e., "secret counsel," but the Greek translators evidently knew the meaning, "chieftaincy," comparable to the Arabic sudu. This is probably not an indication of another root, but rather evidence of a wider range of meaning, for all words have both width and depth. They represent wedges rather than pin points, and can develop along one line into what appear to be strange fields. As Driver has pointed out,[12] the original meaning of the root סוד is "blackness," as is evidenced both in the Hebrew of Ecclus. 40:29 and in the Arabic sawida ("was black"). From this idea of "blackness" the root branched out in two directions; on the one hand, the idea of secrecy, either in a good sense (Amos 3:7; etc.) or in a bad sense (Ecclus. 41:23). But the Arabic sayyid means "lord," "chief," and sudu is "authority." Driver thinks that this meaning has developed through the idea of the leader who is in the secret counsels of the group, but Fritz Hommel more likely suggests[13] that Arabic sayyid means "speaker," as one who gives the decision of the converse which those in secret have held. The Syriac sowud means "friendly, confidential speech," and 'estawad is the regular Syriac equivalent of the Greek ὁμιλία ("conversation"), whence the English "homily." But whatever the steps of the development may have been, it seems clear that the Egyptian Jews knew of a development of the word in Hebrew comparable to that in Arabic.

In Hos. 7:16 Arabic again helps in the elucidation of an almost unintelligible passage.[14] The Hebrew root זעם means "be angry," but the Arabic za'um ("stammerer") suggests that it had also a wider meaning. If this is so, then the proper translation is, "Their princes fall by the sword because of the stuttering of their tongues," the unusual meaning having been explained in a gloss, as Budde pointed out, "that is, their stammering in the land of Egypt."

Or again, an interesting question is raised by G. R. Driver[15] concerning the Hebrew word higgāyôn. The word is usually connected directly with the root הגה ("moan," "growl," "mutter," "muse," "speak"), and is understood to describe a particular type of song, a "medita-

---

[7] D. W. Thomas, "A Note on Liqqᵉhath in Proverbs xxx.17," Journal of Theological Studies, XLII (1941), 154-55. The root was at first suggested by G. R. Driver in connection with I Sam. 19:20.

[8] G. R. Driver, reviewing Joseph Ziegler's Untersuchungen zur Septuaginta des Buches Isaias, Journal of Theological Studies, XXXVI (1935), 83. This and other instances of the recovery of long-lost Hebrew roots are given by D. W. Thomas, "The Language of the Old Testament," in Record and Revelation, ed. H. Wheeler Robinson, pp. 391-99.

[9] See Francis Brown, S. R. Driver, and C. A. Briggs, A Hebrew and English Lexicon of the Old Testament (Boston: Houghton & Mifflin, 1906), ad loc.

[10] G. R. Driver, "Supposed Arabisms in the Old Testament," Journal of Biblical Literature, LV (1936), 102-3.

[11] G. R. Driver, Journal of Theological Studies, XXXVI (1935), 82.

[12] "Notes on the Psalms. I. 1-72," Journal of Theological Studies, XLIII (1942), 150; see also his "Supposed Arabisms in the Old Testament," Journal of Biblical Literature, LV (1936), 102, 113-14.

[13] "Das Samech in den mināo-sabäischen Inschriften," Zeitschrift der deutschen Morgenländischen Gesellschaft, XLVI (1892), 529.

[14] See G. R. Driver, "Linguistic and Textual Problems: Minor Prophets I," Journal of Theological Studies, XXXIX (1938), p. 157.

[15] "Notes on the Psalms. I. 1-72," Journal of Theological Studies, XLIII (1942), 151.

tion." What is its exact significance in Ps. 9:16 (Hebrew 9:17) where it occurs as a musical note in connection with the hitherto unexplained *selāh?* Driver points out that the Arabic *higā'ū* means "alphabet," and that this meaning has support in the Syriac *hegyana.* Does the Hebrew word, then, also have a special technical meaning, "an acrostic poem," as indeed Pss. 9 and 10 at one time evidently were?

One of the most helpful examples of this type of suggestion is that by D. W. Thomas [16] of a second root ידע. This root is very common indeed with the meaning "know," but there is another similar root *wadu'a* in Arabic, which means, "be still," "quiet," "humiliated." In Hos. 9:7, therefore, the Septuagint is right in translating κακωθήσεται. The meaning of the Hebrew actually is, "Israel shall be humiliated." A similar translation is possible in Isa. 9:7 but the most interesting of Thomas' suggestions is in connection with the obscure phrase in Isa. 53:11, a suggestion all the more welcome because of the general interest in the passage. The phrase "by his knowledge" is difficult. One can retain it, though barely, by assuming God to be the subject, but if "by his humiliation" is read, then we have an admirable rendering, and this is exactly the sense which is required.

X. The Old Testament of the Early Church

The original Christian Old Testament was not in Hebrew, but in Greek—the Septuagint (see article, "Text and Ancient Versions of the Old Testament, pp. 46-62).

Here we have a matter of an importance which can scarcely be exaggerated: Has the Greek Bible had any effect on Christian theology because it was written in Greek? When Protestantism went back to the Hebrew Bible, did this have any effect on Protestant theology? Does it make any difference to the Old Testament and our understanding of it if we read it as a Hebrew book with a Hebrew setting? And has this any effect on the interpretation of the New Testament?

The answer is that it makes a very great deal of difference in our interpretation of both Testaments if we neglect the fact that the Old Testament was written originally in Hebrew.

It is often said that the New Testament was written in koine Greek, that is, in the ordinary "common" Greek of the period, the lingua franca which was common to large parts of the Roman Empire (see "The Language of the New

[16] "The Root *Yādha'* in Hebrew," *Journal of Theological Studies,* XXXV (1934), 302, and in several subsequent issues, especially, "More Notes on the Root *Yādha'* in Hebrew," XXXVIII (1937), 404-5; and "A Note on the Meaning of *Yādha'* in Hosea ix.7 and Isaiah ix.8," XLI (1940), 43-44.

Testament," Vol. VII, pp. 43-59). This is substantially true so far as the syntax is concerned, although every national will tend to write in the idiom of his mother tongue. This happens today. If, for instance, one's knowledge of German is limited, it is much easier to understand German as spoken, say by a Czech, simply because he tends to follow the order of his own language, and does not heap up his verbs at the end of the sentence after the German fashion. It is true also so far as ordinary "secular" words are concerned. In respect of these words the recovery of papyri from ancient settlements of Egypt during the present century has been invaluable. But when we come to "religious" words, then we need to remember that many of the first Christians were thoroughly acquainted with the Septuagint, and may well have used certain Greek words in special ways, different from the ways in which they were commonly used in ordinary Greek. Especially do we need to remember that Paul, the most prolific of the New Testament writers, knew both his Greek Bible and his Hebrew Bible. He was a thorough Jew, sedulously trained in the rabbinical schools, and at the same time a man deeply influenced by the ideas of the Hellenistic (Greek-speaking) Jews of the Dispersion. For instance, in I Cor. 2:16 he quotes the Septuagint of Isa. 40:13 with its "mind" (νοῦς) instead of the "spirit" (*rûah*) of the Hebrew. In the earlier part of the chapter the apostle speaks continually of "spirit," but it is necessary for the sake of his argument that he should change over his terminology from "spirit" to "mind." His knowledge of both the Hebrew Bible and the Greek Bible aided him here in this point, because Isa. 40:13 is precisely the one case in the Old Testament where the Hebrew *rûah* is rendered in the Septuagint by the Greek νοῦς.

It is probable, therefore, that there are many New Testament words which may well have to be interpreted as Hebrew—Septuagint words—rather than according to the meaning which is usual in the ordinary nonbiblical Greek of the period. Further, if there are such words, then they are likely to be the most important words so far as interpretation and doctrine are concerned. In these cases the proper approach will be first to ascertain the meaning of the original Hebrew word, then to study its equivalent in the Septuagint, and finally to determine its sense in the New Testament. The problem of New Testament exegesis is coming to be more and more the extent to which this method is sound and necessary, and there is at present considerable difference of opinion in this matter.

In respect of some words the position is quite clear, and there can be no doubt that the Old

Testament, first in the Hebrew and then in the Greek, is essential to the understanding of the New Testament. What, for instance, is the meaning in the New Testament of the verb ἱλάσκεσθαι and its compounds and derivatives? Does it carry the meaning of classical Greek, or that of Septuagint Greek? In classical Greek the verb means primarily to placate a person, and secondarily to expiate a sin, the object being personal in the first case and impersonal in the second. In the Septuagint the meaning [17] is not at all that of placating an angry God. The temple ritual is not looked upon in the Septuagint as being a means to this end, but rather as a means of delivering man from sin. Here the Septuagint is true to the Hebrew *kôpher*, which does not mean "propitiation." It involves an act whereby guilt or defilement is removed. The idea of placating an angry God is foreign to the word and is definitely wrong. We should have been saved from a great deal of unchristian theology if this had been realized from the beginning. Here, as perhaps elsewhere, New Testament words have been translated as if they were pagan Greek words, and the doctrine of the Atonement has been given a pagan setting.

Another clear case is the Greek ψυχή. This word etymologically has to do with breathing, as the verb ψυχεῖν shows. It stands, therefore, primarily in the first place for the "breath-soul," that which is the clearest outward evidence of life, and leaves the body at death with the blood.[18] The word thus comes to be used for "life," e.g., "to fight for one's life" is μάχεσθαι περὶ ψυχῆς.[19] But even in Homer the word is used for that part of a man which is said to survive death, and so for the departed soul. Thus the word comes readily to stand for "the immortal soul" of man. It is used also, though not commonly, of sensual desire, appetite, and sometimes, though rarely, of animals (Isocrates *Orations* II. 12). Finally it is used, especially by Plato, of the organ of thought and judgment (i.e., as the organ of νοῦς).

In the Septuagint the word ψυχή is used regularly for the Hebrew *néphesh*. This word originally also had to do with breathing (cf. Akkadian *napâshu*, "to get breath," and the fifth form of the Arabic *nafusa*, "breathe," "sigh"). It is therefore used of "that which breathes and lives" in man. It is also used regularly of the appetites, and sometimes of animals. In Gen. 1:20 the phrase *néphesh ḥayyāh* means "a living being." The word

néphesh is used in "risking one's *life*" (Judg. 5:18) and more than once in "taking one's *life* in one's hand" (Judg. 12:3; etc.). While the word is used regularly of the seat of the emotions and passions, there is no definite evidence that it is used in connection with mental activities. There are six cases which some allege to be examples of this (e.g., Esth. 4:13), but these are all doubtful and can be more readily explained otherwise.

The great difference between Greek ideas and Hebrew ideas is that the Greeks came to think of the ψυχή as being something in itself, and as continuing after death, whereas the Hebrews did not think of *néphesh* in this way. At death the *néphesh* ceased to exist, and while the Hebrews did speak of Sheol as the abode of the dead, yet there was no real life there, no *néphesh*, not anything, and the whole idea was negative. It follows, therefore, that since the word "soul" in the English translations stands for the Hebrew *néphesh*, there is not one single instance in the Old Testament where the word "soul" should be thought of as that which survives death. When the Bible writer says, according to the English versions, that God "breathed into his [i.e., the man's] nostrils the breath of life; and man became a living soul" (Gen. 2:7), he does not mean that God thereby gave to man an immortal soul. He means that God, having formed man from the dust of the earth, shaping him as the potter shapes the clay, breathed into him his own life-giving breath, so that this shape of dust became alive.

The New Testament follows the Septuagint and uses the word ψυχή as referring to something which is connected with this life only, and not with any life after death. The "natural man" of I Cor. 2:14 is ψυχικός in the Greek, i.e., the man of ψυχή, and he is contrasted with the "spiritual" (πνευματικός) man. In the New Testament ψυχή does not survive death, but πνεῦμα ("spirit") does. For instance, Heb. 4:12 speaks of the word of God as the sharp two-edged sword, "piercing even to the dividing asunder of soul and spirit," i.e., of ψυχή and πνεῦμα, separating that which ceases at death (ψυχή) from that which survives death (πνεῦμα). It is true that in the Old Testament man is sometimes spoken of as having a "spirit" (Hebrew *rûaḥ*; Greek πνεῦμα), though this is a late usage. In any case, this "spirit" is withdrawn at death by God, and no longer belongs to man. If, therefore, the belief in the immortality of the human soul is held to be a Christian doctrine, then it should be realized that it is not a biblical doctrine. The biblical doctrine is of a resurrection life for those who "have the Spirit" and are "in Christ," with variations as to the

---

[17] C. H. Dodd, *The Bible and the Greeks* (London: Hodder & Stoughton, 1935), pp. 82-95; especially the short summary on p. 93.

[18] Homer *Iliad* XIV. 518.

[19] Homer *Odyssey* XXII. 245.

fate of the wicked and unrepentant between "the outer darkness" and a resurrection to judgment and the fires of destruction.

Another important New Testament word is the verb δικαιοῦν and its derivatives. The phrase δικαιοῦν τὸν ἀσεβῆ in classical Greek means "to condemn the impious," [20] but in the Septuagint of Isa. 5:23 it means "to put the impious in the right," being used of unjust judges who give the verdict to those who are oppressing the poor. Paul uses the phrase in Rom. 4:5 in the Septuagint sense and not in the classical Greek sense. One can go further and maintain that the noun δικαιοσύνη, usually translated "righteousness," should be regarded in many places in the New Testament as belonging to the vocabulary of salvation rather than to that of ethics.[21] The argument is that the Septuagint word δικαιοσύνη has a wider use than merely ethical, since it represents the Hebrew çedhāqāh, a word which "always tends away from the more abstract and intellectual Greek conception of justice, in the direction of something warmer and more humane," [22] and indeed in many cases is equivalent to "salvation" [23] (e.g., Isa. 45:8, 23; 46:13; 51:5, 6; etc.). In fact, in the Tosephta Sanhedrin 1:3 çedhāqāh is actually contrasted with dîn ("strict justice").

In Rom. 6:16 we read "either of sin, which leads to death, or of obedience, which leads to δικαιοσύνη." Here we have the regular Old Testament prophetic contrast between sin and obedience, and also a contrast between death and δικαιοσύνη. In view of the Septuagint usage of the word we are encouraged here to see a contrast between death and life, in the sense of that salvation-life of which Paul continually speaks. Paul indeed uses the word in three senses. When he speaks of "the righteousness which is by the law," he means that ethical rightness which comes from obeying the code; when he speaks of "the righteousness which is by faith," he means that "righteousness [çedhāqāh] of God" which is shown chiefly in God's mighty works of salvation; and when he speaks of the righteousness of the man who is in Christ, he means all those good works which are the fruits of the spirit.

To say that these words should be interpreted by their Septuagint usage, as carrying something of the original Hebrew meaning, effects in more than one case a complete transformation in interpretation. Especially is this true in respect of the δικαιοῦν group, and also in respect of πνεῦμα and its companion words, since in this latter case we must think primarily in terms of the transforming, rather than of the sublimating, power of the Spirit of God.

Yet another New Testament word of great importance is the verb πιστεύειν and its derivatives. In classical Greek the general meaning is "to believe in," "trust in" a person or a thing, and "to believe" a statement. Similarly for the noun, but mostly in a subjective sense of "faithfulness," "trustworthiness," or as signifying "that which gives confidence." In the New Testament the noun is used some four times in a passive sense of "fidelity" or "a pledge of fidelity," and similarly for the verb. Then there is the case of Jas. 2:18-20, where the noun is used of "belief in God" in much the same sense as it is used in Euripides *Medea* 414, where the chorus bemoans the deceitful counsels of men, deceitful because "faith in the gods is no longer firm" (οὐκέτι πίστις ἄραρε). The meaning here is thus a more or less intellectual acceptance of the proposition that the gods exist, together with the assumption that such a belief ought to issue in honorable dealing between man and man.

But the main New Testament use of both verb and noun is, however, determined by the Septuagint. Here the noun stands almost without exception for the Hebrew noun 'emûnāh, but always for one of the four nouns from the root '-m-n. The fundamental meaning of this root is "reliability," "steadfastness," and the causative form of the verb means "to have full reliance upon." This is determinative for the Pauline use of both verb and noun. Paul means an utter and complete reliance upon God. There is, of course, a transformation, as always, between the Old Testament and the New Testament because of the revelation of God manifested in Jesus Christ, but it is a transformation on the Old Testament basis of "reliance," "firm trust."

There is another Hebrew noun derived from the root '-m-n, namely, the noun 'emeth. This noun is represented in the Septuagint generally by ἀλήθεια ("truth"), but occasionally by πίστις ("trust"). This latter rendering is found only in Proverbs, with its speculative atmosphere, more prominent in the Greek Proverbs than in the Hebrew Proverbs, and in the latter part of Jeremiah, that is, that part of Jeremiah for which the second translator was responsible.[24] What is important here is that to the Hebrews "truth" is not anything abstract and theoretical, but something concrete that can be relied on, that can be trusted. Thus "truth" is the objective side of "faith"; that is, 'emeth-ἀλήθεια is the ground and basis of 'emûnāh-πίστις. In

[20] Dodd, *op. cit.*, p. 52.
[21] N. H. Snaith, *The Distinctive Ideas of the Old Testament* (Philadelphia: Westminster Press, 1946), pp. 207-22.
[22] Dodd, *op. cit.*, p. 45.
[23] Snaith, *op. cit.*, p. 115.

[24] H. St. John Thackeray, *The Septuagint and Jewish Worship* (London: British Academy, 1921), pp. 116-17.

the Fourth Gospel, therefore, "truth" is not a true idea so much as a person to be relied on. When Jesus says that he is the way, the truth, and the life, he means that he is the way in which we must walk, he is the one on whom we must rely, and he is the means by which we live—all of it wholly practical and this-worldly; not "this-worldly" in the sense of being divorced and separate from what is "otherworldly," but "this-worldly" because God has broken into this world, in order that the kingdoms of this world might become the kingdom of our God and of his Christ. After all, that is indeed what the Bible is about.

XI. Selected Bibliography

DODD, C. H. *The Bible and the Greeks.* London: Hodder & Stoughton, 1935.

DRIVER, G. R. *Problems of the Hebrew Verbal System.* Edinburgh: T. & T. Clark, 1936.

—— "The Modern Study of the Hebrew Language," in *The People and the Book,* ed. A. S. Peake. Oxford: Clarendon Press, 1925. Pp. 73-120.

ROWLEY, H. H. *The Aramaic of the Old Testament.* London: Oxford University Press, 1929.

SNAITH, N. H. *The Distinctive Ideas of the Old Testament.* Philadelphia: Westminster Press, 1946.

THOMAS, D. W. "The Language of the Old Testament," in *Record and Revelation,* ed. H. Wheeler Robinson. Oxford: Clarendon Press, 1938. Pp. 374-402.

THE OLD TESTAMENT WORLD

by WILLIAM F. ALBRIGHT

If we examine Bible handbooks and histories written over a century ago, we shall find that their chief source of information with regard to the historical and cultural background of the Old Testament was the latter itself. A few scattered details about the kings of Egypt, Assyria, Babylonia, and Tyre, some miscellaneous information about the religions and customs of these countries, some parallels from Greek life and culture, a number of allusions to old-fashioned practices in modern Arab lands—and that was practically all. Yet a new day was beginning to dawn. When Gardner Wilkinson published his popular three-volume work, *The Manners and Customs of the Ancient Egyptians* (1836), utilizing the publications of Jean

Champollion and Ippolito Rosellini (which had just begun to appear in stately folios), a sensation was created, and scholars were occupied for the next generation trying to employ the new material in biblical research. Only seven years later the discoveries of Paul Botta and Austen Layard in the mounds of Assyria began to dim the luster of the Egyptian monuments, but they proved harder than the earlier Egyptian finds for scholars to digest. It was not until the 1870's that we find reasonably accurate information from both Egyptian and Mesopotamian antiquity appearing in the better informed biblical handbooks.

This is not the place to give a detailed survey of the progress achieved by archaeological research in Bible lands during the past three quarters of a century. It is enough to contrast the paucity of reliable publications of monuments and objects then available with the wealth of material now at the disposal of the biblical scholar who possesses the necessary command of modern languages. Egyptian and Akkadian (Semitic Babylonian) documents can now be read almost as accurately as Greek and Latin texts (where the uncertainty of the transmitted text compensates for occasional doubt as to the meaning of a word or passage in either of the former). The new languages which have been deciphered during the past generation, such as Hittite, can be read fairly well if there is enough inscriptional material available for scholars to study. Even the Ugaritic dialect of Canaanite, written in a previously unknown script, yielded its secrets rapidly after its initial discovery in 1929, and the still more obscure syllabic script of earlier Byblos seems to be on the verge of decipherment. The art of excavation has made such strides that it has become a true science of stratigraphy, yielding historical insights quite as valuable in their way as the material provided by ancient documents.

I. The Sources of Our Knowledge

A. Archaeology.—Scientific archaeology does not go back very far. No early excavator recognized the existence of true mounds, in which successive occupation and destruction had left superimposed layers of debris, which specialists call "strata," until Heinrich Schliemann began the excavation of Troy in 1870. Few even then took the gifted German amateur seriously, and it was not until 1890 that Flinders Petrie made the first soundings in the Palestinian mound of Tell el-Hesi, where he recognized clear stratification and determined the significance of pottery, whole or broken, for dating. Since that time archaeological stratigraphy has developed to a high level of excellence, closely paced by pottery chronology and historical architecture. Museum techniques have also progressed enormously, aided by the resources of modern science. We can accordingly speak of archaeology as a science in the same way that we can use the term "science" of structural geology or geomorphology. Used in this way the word "archaeology" does not ordinarily include the study of the written documents unearthed by the excavator. For the investigation of written remains we must turn to the philological disciplines.

B. Philology.—To decipher inscriptions requires knowledge and ingenuity, but to interpret their meaning in detail and to classify the results of interpretation in historically usable form require all the resources of modern linguistics and philology. Decipherment often demands guessing at meaning, but the time soon arrives when guessing becomes unscientific and when the investigator must employ the same rigorous procedure that any scientist must follow if his results are to be logically consistent. The grammar of any new language must be worked out by scrupulous analysis and classification of the observed phenomena of the language. In other words, the scholar must start with passages which make sense and must study spelling, forms, and inflections of words, and syntactical constructions. His results must then be tested in other clear passages by application of the experimental technique. After sufficient inductive collection of data, formulation of rules which satisfy the data, and experimental verification of these rules, the scholar may begin to apply his rules to the interpretation of more difficult passages. Eventually a complete system of grammar emerges, in which virtually all linguistic facts fit neatly into their places. Naturally documents from different periods and places may diverge linguistically from one another, so that the trained investigator must learn to distinguish between historical periods and dialects within a language. Since comparatively few archaeologists or biblical scholars possess the necessary linguistic and philological training, many of them hold impossible philological views. It must be remembered that in order to determine the meaning of a difficult or obscure word, all passages where this word occurs must be carefully examined, all possible ways of explaining it through comparison with similar words in other languages must be explored; nor may one assume strange phonetic or other changes unless one can show that such changes are normal in the period and language or dialect in question. Linguistic law is not adjusted to mathematical requirements like the laws of physics, nor is it promulgated by decree, like civil legislation; but it is quite as rigorous, unless its operation is suspended or canceled by the operation of another principle which cuts across it. The chief requirements of the interpreter of ancient inscriptions may be summed up as (a) accuracy in copying and transcribing; (b) methodical rigor in making or in using grammars and dictionaries, as well as in studying the pertinent work of all competent scholars; (c) willingness to go to any amount of trouble to obtain information bearing on any given problem. The results must make sense to specialists in the life of the ancient world before they can safely be adopted by scholars in other fields.

II. The Geographical and Economic Background

A. The Ancient Near East.—All the countries which play an important role in the Old Testament lie in several heterogeneous geographical areas clustered around the points where Asia, Africa, and Europe meet. The region in question is roughly comprised between 20° and 40° north latitude and between 25° and 50° east longitude; it includes all of Palestine, Syria, Mesopotamia, and Egypt, all but the extreme north of Asia Minor, most of Armenia, western Media, Elam, all Arabia except the extreme south and southeast, northern Nubia, eastern Libya, Cyprus, Crete, and the eastern islands of the Aegean. Around is a peripheral area including many lands, such as southern Ethiopia, South Arabia, and the land of the Scythians (southern Russia), which play some part in the Old Testament, but which are seldom in the center of the stage. In order to make the extent of this central region clear, we may compare it with one of exactly the same extent in eastern North America, between 20° and 40° north latitude, and between 75° and 100° west longitude; this region includes all the southeastern states south of the Mason and Dixon line, the southern halves of Ohio, Indiana, Illinois, nearly all Missouri, nearly all Kansas, Oklahoma, eastern Texas, northeastern Mexico (with Mexico City), the Gulf of Mexico, Yucatan, Cuba, and most of the Bahamas. It is, in other words, far from being a restricted territory, even though Palestine itself, lying in the center, is no larger than Vermont.

B. Palestine and Syria.—Palestine and Syria form a continuous narrow strip over five hundred miles long between the Mediterranean and the desert. The dominant feature of their terrain is the great north-south cleft, dating from the Pliocene Age, which divides both countries into eastern and western halves. In southern Syria this cleft forms the deep and wide Baq'ah, which separates Mount Lebanon from the Anti-Lebanon range. In Palestine the same cleft is continued as the valley of the Jordan and the Dead Sea, the Hebrew Arabah and the Arab Ghor. Palestine and Syria provide typical examples of Mediterranean climate, lying as they do east of a wide stretch of sea between latitudes 30° and 35°. As in southern and central California, each year is divided into a dry season and a rainy season. In the winter the tilt of the earth draws Palestine into the zone characterized by rain-bearing westerly winds; in the summer the southward swing of the earth carries it out of this zone into one of dry west winds. In northern Phoenicia there are relatively heavy winter rains in normal years, but the amount of rainfall decreases steadily as one moves south, until it becomes insufficient in the area of Beer-sheba to permit more than one good crop of winter grain every three years. On the western slopes of the mountains there is ample rain, but on the eastern side, in the rain shadow, rainfall rapidly diminishes until it becomes negligible. The same cycle is resumed east of the great Pliocene cleft, and the clouds decrease their yield of rain progressively as we go eastward into the Syrian Desert. The failure of winter rain, especially in March or April, brings with it great distress, and low rainfall prolonged over several seasons entails inevitable famine. The people of Palestine and Syria are in fact so dependent on the seemingly capricious rainfall for existence that it is scarcely surprising that the great storm-god Baal (Hadad) was the head of the Canaanite pantheon.

Palestine and Syria are countries rich by nature, but this wealth was of such character that it was unevenly exploited and it often vanished entirely. Oil, wine, and honey were by far the stablest crops, since olive trees and vines grew almost everywhere and could strike root deep into the porous limestone soil of the hill country, while the luxuriant growth of wild flowers provided food for innumerable swarms of bees. Next in order of importance came herds of cattle, especially of sheep and goats, which remained close to perennial streams and springs during the summer months, but might be driven out to graze deep in the Southland (Negeb) and far out into the Syrian Desert in winter and spring. The third chief source of livelihood was winter grain, sown in the autumn and harvested in late spring or early summer. In ancient days barley was more important than wheat, while *durah (emmer)*, now an important summer crop, was little grown. Today wheat is grown much more widely than barley. The fourth chief class of food products was composed of various fruits and vegetables, both of which were much more restricted in variety than today. Citrus fruits and bananas were unknown; peaches and apricots seem also to have been unknown. Figs, grapes, and almonds were staples, and the lack of many succulent modern fruits was partly compensated by extensive growing of very inferior apples and of sycamore figs (*djummeiz*), which had to be punctured while green (giving Amos a secondary occupation) in order to become really edible. Vegetables were also much less common than today; such staples as tomatoes and potatoes were wholly unknown. Onions and garlic, lentils and horse beans (*ful*), chick-peas, watermelons, vegetable marrows, and cucumbers were leading crops.

Only two important types of raw material were exported from Palestine and Syria in high antiquity: cedar, fir, and other coniferous wood from Lebanon, Casius, and Amanus; copper and some iron from Trans-Jordan and Syria. On the other hand, commerce flourished in most periods. To judge from our evidence regarding the diffusion of culture in the ancient Near East, Syria and Palestine began to have a fairly extensive carrying trade toward the end of the fourth millennium, when Egyptian art and craftsmanship show profound influence from the Euphrates Valley. The cedar trade between Lebanon and Egypt may be traced back by discoveries at Byblos to the beginning of the third millennium. Trade continued to grow apace through the third millennium, as demonstrated by finds scattered through all the lands of the Near East. In the early second millennium there was a great expansion of trade northward into the heart of Asia Minor, while the caravan trade through Palestine and Syria gained steadily in importance. In the early first millennium the Phoenicians developed a previously undreamed-of expansion of commerce throughout the Mediterranean and even beyond it. The entire Israelite and Aramaean hinterland was enriched by the by-products of this commercial activity. Eastward the Aramaeans became the heirs of the old caravan trade, which they developed to new levels of business enterprise.

C. Mesopotamia.—Mesopotamia is much greater in area than Palestine and Syria, but only a very small fraction of that area receives sufficient water from rainfall and irrigation to support human life. In northern Assyria there is enough rain to take care of winter crops in good seasons; elsewhere in Mesopotamia irrigation is absolutely necessary. The two great rivers, Euphrates and Tigris, together with their eastern tributaries, the Balikh and Khabur (Habur), the Upper and Lower Zab, 'Adheim and Diyala, were the only important sources of life in most of Mesopotamia. Hence distances between settlements were great, and narrow strips of irrigated terrain were separated by wide stretches of desert. Only in Babylonia, where the rivers ran nearly parallel (and for most of the distance much nearer together than today), from Eshnunna to Eridu, a distance of over two hundred miles in a straight line, was there an area of more than ten thousand square miles which could be irrigated almost throughout in successive years (not all, of course, simultaneously). Hence Babylonia probably supported more than half the entire population of Mesopotamia in the second millennium B.C. Some idea of the distance between points in greater Mesopotamia may be gained from the following figures: from Babylon to Nineveh was about 280 miles in a straight line and at least 350 by road; from Ur at the lower end of the Euphrates to Carchemish at the upper end there was a distance of some 625 miles in a straight line, but by road up the Euphrates the distance was nearer a thousand miles—which is, incidentally, practically the same distance as from Carchemish to Memphis, capital of Lower Egypt.

In Mesopotamia irrigation made it possible to grow enormous crops of grain and vegetables, while adjacent plains and hills supported great flocks of sheep and goats, as well as extensive herds of cattle. Wood, stone, and metals for construction and manufacture were almost wholly wanting, so the natives of the two river valleys were compelled to trade with their neighbors or to raid them periodically in order to obtain these necessary products. Since the nature of irrigation culture, especially in Babylonia, made the growth of organized states inevitable, empires arose. Wealth brought concentration of craftsmanship; the latter created suitable articles for foreign trade, which in its turn brought continuous pressure from the merchants for military control of trade routes and foreign customers. The cuneiform epic entitled "The King of Battle," composed not long after the fall of the Dynasty of Akkad (*ca.* twenty-third century B.C.), gives a vivid impression of the interaction between merchants and warriors in pressing for imperial expansion.

D. Egypt.—Egypt is a unique geographical phenomenon. The Nile flows north from the mountains of Abyssinia, where the equatorial rainfall and the melting of the winter snow might be expected to produce disastrous spring floods like those which are characteristic of Mesopotamia. However, the Nile flows through hundreds of miles of swamps in the southern Sudan, and the latter act as run-offs and catchment basins in a natural "Nile Valley Authority," which regularizes the Nile flood to an extent nowhere else paralleled. The damage caused by exceptionally high flood levels was so small compared to the increased irrigation which high Niles made possible that they were considered a great blessing. Low Niles were followed by widespread suffering and a succession of them meant a terrible famine, such as has occurred several times in Egypt's long history. The Nile not only brought fructifying water and fertilizing silt; it also provided an unequalled natural highway, since there were no rapids north of the first cataract near Elephantine. The even current of the Nile bears boats and rafts northward, while the regular etesian winds from the north make it possible to sail south with a minimum of rowing, even if at a slow rate of speed. On both sides of the narrow valley are broad stretches of desert, extending to the Red Sea on the east and as far as the Atlantic on the west. During the last three millenniums B.C. these deserts were just as inhospitable to man as they are today. With the highway of the Nile connecting all parts of Egypt from Elephantine to Tanis, some five hundred miles by air and a good eight hundred by boat, it is not surprising that Egypt became an exceedingly homogeneous land. From one end of Egypt to the other there was little perceptible difference in race, language, or customs. The delta was of course more accessible to foreign influences, both because of the rich commerce to which its wealth gave rise, and because of land and sea roads which gave easy access to Palestine, Libya, and the islands of the Mediterranean.

Egypt's natural wealth was proverbial in the ancient world; the Mitannian King Tusratta wrote to the king of Egypt about 1380 B.C., remarking in connection with his repeated pleas for more gold, "In my brother's land gold is as abundant as dirt." When we realize that its irrigable extent has changed in the past century and a half from less than six thousand square miles to about fourteen thousand in 1950, it becomes easier to understand how productive the soil is. However, this productivity depended largely on the upkeep of dams and canals, the draining of marshes and the irrigation of the Fayyum; it must have varied surprisingly in different periods. In the last century and a half the population of Egypt has grown from not over two million to about eighteen million. H. E. Winlock in 1947 estimated the total population about 2000 B.C. as not over a million, and I should be inclined to estimate its size in the reign of Ramses III (early twelfth century B.C.) as about three million. These figures may seem small, but they average ten times the probable population of Palestine in the same periods. This ratio corresponds to the actual average relation between the populations of Egypt and Palestine in the past century and a half.

E. Anatolia, Armenia, and Iran.—Northwest, north, and east of the "Fertile Crescent," to use Breasted's famous expression describing Mesopotamia, Syria, and Palestine, lies a wide zone of mountain ranges separated from one another by valleys and plateaus. In this zone lies the peninsula of Anatolia, commonly called Asia Minor, northwest and north of Syria. East of it is Armenia, north of Mesopotamia. Southeast of Armenia and east of Mesopotamia lies Iran, or Persia. All three countries are mountainous and suffer more or less from inadequate rainfall, which makes irrigation necessary if they are to sustain strong organized states. In antiquity these lands were thinly peopled in most periods, but the hardy mountaineers who inhabited them were excellent fighters. Asia Minor was the seat of the Hittites, and it was always important because of its situation as a land bridge between Europe and southwestern Asia. The rich silver, lead, and tin mines of Anatolia attracted merchants and conquerors from Mesopotamia as early as the Dynasty of Akkad (*ca.* twenty-third century) if not before.

Armenia took little part in international affairs during the third and second millenniums, owing doubtless to the inhospitable forests with which most of it was then covered, as well as to the wildness of its few inhabitants. How primitive its customs were in the middle of the second millennium we learn from Hittite sources, which mention polyandry and even cannibalism among them. In the early first millennium B.C. Armenia gained a dominant position, thanks to the energy of the people of Urartu (Ararat), whose kings nearly brought Assyria to its knees in the eighth century.

Iran was a large and rich country, with a sedentary culture quite as old as that of Asia Minor, though no great state is known to have arisen there before the emergence of the Median Empire in the seventh century B.C. At Iran's southwestern corner lay Elam, with its ancient capital at Susa (Shushan), but Elam was geographically so much more closely associated with Babylonia that it is somewhat misleading to speak of it as Iranian. At the same time, close ethnic and geographical ties bound the Elamites to their neighbors on the north, east, and south, so Elam was able to exercise a disproportionate cultural influence on the Iranians, even down into the Achaemenian Age (sixth to fourth centuries). Though little is known about early Iranian commerce, there can be no doubt that it went back to very ancient times, as attested by the wide diffusion of pottery and other artifacts. In the second half of the third millennium a rich irrigation culture sprang up to the east of Iran in the Indus Valley; it is shown by archaeological finds to have been roughly contemporaneous with the empire of Akkad (twenty-fourth to twenty-second centuries). Early in the second millennium this civilization was destroyed by an irruption of the Indo-Aryans (see below, p. 240), part of whom swept westward through Iran into Mesopotamia. From this time on Iran became partly Aryanized, and after the Iranian irruption at the end of the second millennium (see pp. 268-69), Iran became almost wholly Aryanized in language and culture.

F. Arabia.—South of the Fertile Crescent lies the peninsula of Arabia, which has from time immemorial been associated with the purest Semitic stock known to exist anywhere. From Palmyra in the northern part of the Syrian Desert to the coast of Hadhramaut (Hazarmaveth) is an air flight of over fifteen hundred miles, and it must have meant a good two thousand miles for a camel caravan. Most of Arabia is more or less complete desert, with broad stretches of sandy waste (Nefud); but the mountain valleys of Yemen (Sheba) and the Western Aden Protectorate are fertile, with relatively heavy rainfall. The valley of Hadhramaut is richly supplied with underground water, and there are numerous oases scattered through the Hedjaz in west-central Arabia and the Nedjd in east-central Arabia. In the north there are some large oases, such as Palmyra (Tadmor), Djof (Dumah), and Teima (Tema). Gold and copper were the most important mineral products of ancient Arabia, and in the first millennium B.C. the spices of South Arabia became a source of exceedingly lucrative caravan trade with the Fertile Crescent and the lands of the Mediterranean.

The critical point in the history of Arabia fell in the latter part of the second millennium B.C., when the camel, previously common in its wild state, became effectively domesticated for use in caravans. On account of this development it became possible for caravans to plunge out into the desert, relying on a new water supply every third or fourth day. The ass caravans which were the only means of desert transport in the early second millennium were dependent on obtaining water daily, or at most every other day. Camels, moreover, flourish on desert thorns and tamarisk twigs, while asses require grass or fodder. From about 1100 B.C. the use of camels increased steadily and rapidly, and by the eighth century spice caravans from South Arabia had become a characteristic feature of desert life.

III. The Ethnic Background

A. Prehistoric Men.—Great progress is now being made in the domain of prehistory, and the complex picture of prehistoric man is beginning to take definite form. The rapid succession of unexpected discoveries of fossil man in Palestine, in China, in Java, and in South Africa since 1925 led some of the more reckless spirits to construct a separate species for each new fossil type, until current handbooks swarmed with the names of distinct human species. However, more cautious counsels are now beginning to prevail, thanks to the entry into the debate of such first-class geneticists as Theodosius Dobzhansky and genetically competent paleontologists as G. G. Simpson, who insist on the absurdity of multiplying species of hominids. Since the early 1940's this crusade for moderation has been gaining ground rapidly among physical anthropologists. It is now quite generally recognized that many archaic (paleoanthropic) features of anatomy from extinct types of man survive in modern (neoanthropic) types. Skeletons of fossil man from the Middle Paleolithic discovered by Dorothy Garrod and Theodore McCown in Palestine show all sorts of anatomical variation from almost pure Neanderthaloid to a type with well-developed characteristics of Homo sapiens. Yet all these skeletons belong to a single restricted population. It thus appears more and more likely that all surviving types of man are races of Homo sapiens which developed their present peculiarities partly through intermixture with previously existing races or subspecies (*Homo neanderthalensis, Homo soloensis, Sinanthropus,* etc.) and partly through further local evolution. Such features as skin color, shape of the nose, etc., are largely the result of selective evolution, while such characteristics as height are simply the result of more favorable climatic and especially of better nutritional conditions.

All races of man known from the Old Testament belong to Homo sapiens; it is in the highest degree improbable that any other subspecies of man was still extant anywhere in the world—or had been for at least thirty thousand years. All known ancient races in the region which concerns us here belonged to the so-called "white" or "Caucasian" race, with the exception of the Cushites ("Ethiopians") who were strongly Negroid in type, as we know from many Egyptian paintings. The Near and Middle East has always been such a convenient cluster of bridges between the three continents of the Old World that pure races long since ceased to exist there. It is true that the Egyptians are proved by their skeletons to have developed a relatively standard type, which attained its present height during the fourth millennium B.C. and has ever since kept its anatomy, skin color, and average height with surprisingly little change. However, the Mesopotamians were of mixed long-headed (dolichocephalic) and broad-headed (brachycephalic) type as far back as the early third millennium. In Palestine we find prevailing dolichocephalism down to the second quarter of the second millennium; after that, brachycephalism gained the upper hand through the influx of peoples from the mountains skirting the Fertile Crescent. Language is not a criterion of race unless used with great caution and sustained by anatomical evidence from skeletons. Needless to say, the latter is seldom possible.

B. The Semites.—Scholars used to speculate about the possible origin of the peoples which historically spoke Semitic tongues (that is, languages closely related to Hebrew, Arabic, and Akkadian) in North Africa or somewhere in the regions north of the Fertile Crescent. More cautious students regarded Arabia as the cradle of the Semites, and some protagonists of this theory adopted the hypothesis that owing to periodic drying up, Arabia disgorged its hordes into the Fertile Crescent at regular intervals. However, archaeological evidence opposes this hypothesis of periodic desiccation in historical periods, so we may safely discard it. The facts are simple. In the third millennium B.C. we find the precursors of the later Semitic peoples living in North Arabia and the surrounding lands of the Fertile Crescent. At that time their languages were so closely related that we cannot speak of more than dialectical differences. The languages then spoken by Hamitic peoples (see below) were more closely related to one another than any of them were to Semitic. The difference between the earliest traceable Semitic and Hamitic is little greater than that existing between the oldest traceable Indo-European and Anatolian. The Hamitic peoples have occupied northern and northeastern Africa since not later than the fifth millennium B.C. Egyptian, while essentially Hamitic rather than Semitic, stands linguistically between the other Hamitic languages and Semitic, exactly where it should be if the peoples in question continued to occupy approximately their older homes. Moreover, the anatomical differences between the purest Egyptian and Cushitic (Bedja) types, on the one hand, and the purest Bedouin, on the other, are slight; both types show pronounced dolichocephaly, with delicate bony structure, as was first shown in detail by Felix von Luschan. It follows that the Semites had lived in North Arabia and the adjacent territories for thousands of years before the dawn of written history.

C. The Hamites.—The Hamites (named from Ham, son of Noah) include the Egyptians, the Libyans (Berbers), and the Cushitic tribes south of Egypt; in the third millennium B.C. they seem to have occupied all North Africa, extending farther south than they do today. Negro infiltration had not yet penetrated to any extent, it would appear, into Cush (Nubia). The Berbers were already as mixed a people as they are today; the Egyptians represented them consistently as blonds, presumably because of the high proportion of blonds among them. We have no way of knowing the source of this blond strain, but it can scarcely have been Indo-European at such a remote date. The Egyptians had probably occupied the Nile Valley for many thousands of years before they began to settle down and live in villages, as we may infer from the fact (see above) that they are linguistically intermediate between the Berbers and the Semites, and especially from the fact that men had the same reddish-brown color on the monuments of the Pyramid Age as they possess today, some 4,500 years later. Since this color is admirably adapted to the climate of the Nile Valley, it seems evident that they had acquired it through a long process of preadaptive selection. The one difference of consequence between the earliest Badarian village dwellers of Egypt and their descendants was in height; the former were almost pygmies, like the oldest known Semitic villagers of Byblos and Gezer, also from the fourth millennium B.C. Evidently the rapid development of agriculture in the Chalcolithic Age (see below, p. 241) was mainly responsible for the growth in height which then took place; nutritional factors have recently been found to be responsible for almost as striking changes in average stature in the United States.

D. Sumerians, Hurrians, Elamites, and Hittites.—In Old Testament times there were still many remnants, large and small, of old linguistic stocks which have since become extinct. The Semites, and especially the Indo-Europeans, were only beginning the vast expansion which has since overwhelmed so many other linguistic groups. First and most interesting among these extinct groups are the Sumerians, who created the civilization of Mesopotamia on which the Semitic Akkadians built an impressive superstructure. The Sumerian language does not resemble any known tongue, ancient or modern; its principal features were a tendency to agglutinate or to incorporate words and particles into a highly complex sentence structure and a tendency to phonetic breakdown which rivals that of Chinese. Thanks to the intensive research of Assyriologists, basing their work on the lexical and grammatical treatises of the Semitic Babylonians and the interlinear translations of Sumerian texts which they made, Sumerian is very well known today, though archaic Sumerian texts still offer much difficulty to the interpreter. The Sumerians were probably the bearers of the painted-pottery culture of the Mesopotamian Chalcolithic; it was certainly they who invented the cuneiform script and gave Sumero-Akkadian culture its characteristic features. Sumerian remained a sacred and learned language for many centuries after it ceased to be spoken, and it was still studied in Babylonian schools at the time of Christ.

Second in importance to Sumerian among these now-extinct groups were the Hurrians. The latter people, called "Horites" in the Bible, remained unknown to modern scholars until about 1919, though a specimen of their language had been published in 1889. Since 1925 new material in this language has turned up in many different places, and it is now certain that the Hurrians were the chief cultural intermediaries between the Babylonians on the one hand and the peoples of Asia Minor on the other. The Hurrian language was quite as complex structurally as the Sumerian, but paucity of documents in it makes its complete interpretation much more difficult. We owe to E. A. Speiser our best treatment of the language (1941). Its bearers certainly emerged from the mountains of Armenia and Kurdistan, and their dominant physical type was undoubtedly Armenoid (brachycephalic, with a tendency toward very large noses). Between the middle of the third millennium and the early first we find Hurrians in these regions, from which they pushed out at different times as far as the frontiers of Babylonia and Egypt. The Hurrian language was distantly related to Urartian and may be still more remotely akin to Georgian, though the evidence is tenuous.

The Elamites and Cossaeans (Kassites) flourished from very early times in the mountains and alluvial plains east of Babylonia. Elamite was simpler in structure than Sumerian or Hurrian; it has been plausibly connected with modern Brahui in Baluchistan, but the evidence is still inadequate. Our knowledge of Cossaean is much slighter.

The progress of archaeological discovery is bringing other new and strange extinct languages into the light of history. Among them may be mentioned the original Hittite language, called "Hittite" by the Hittites themselves, though they spoke and wrote a different language, which we call also by the same name. This "Proto-Hattic" was in any case a prefixing tongue not in the least like any other known language of this part of the world.

E. The Indo-Europeans.—With the Indo-Europeans we enter the full light of history. This group includes linguistically all Teutons, Celts, Latins, Greeks, Slavs, Iranians, and Hindus who speak offshoots of Sanskrit. Since English, French, Spanish, German, Russian, and most tongues of India belong to the Indo-European family of languages, the latter is now dominant in four continents, as well as in two thirds of Asia and in the southern part of Africa. The close kinship existing between Indo-Iranian and the European languages was not discovered by modern scholars until the end of the eighteenth century and was not established until even later; it was, however, known to the author of Gen. 10, who makes the Indo-Iranian Medes and Scythians children of Japheth, along with the Greeks, Cimmerians, and others. The true Indo-Europeans first appeared in southwestern Asia in the seventeenth century B.C., about the same time as their first invasion of India; they formed a curious partnership with the Hurrians in Mesopotamia, Syria, and Palestine. The Iranians migrated south into Iran toward the end of the second millennium B.C.; to this movement belonged the ancestors of the Medes and Persians.

In 1915 Friedrich Hrozný proved that cuneiform Hittite was closely related to Indo-European; since then this has also been shown to be true of other recently deciphered Anatolian languages such as Luyyan or Luvian, Palaic, and the Hittite of the hieroglyphic inscriptions. It is increasingly probable that Lycian and Lydian, both known from inscriptions of the Persian period, were younger members of the same group, and the same has recently been shown to be probable of Armenian (which is still a living language). Scholars are divided about the degree of relationship between Indo-European proper and Anatolian; but the most plausible view is that of Emil Forrer and Edgar H. Sturtevant, who hold that the Anatolian tongues in question stem from a sister of Indo-European. The relationship between Hittite and Greek would then be something like that existing between Hebrew and Egyptian, but somewhat closer in detail. At all events, the ancestors of the Anatolian peoples were certainly settled in Asia Minor before the middle of the third millennium B.C., at a time when the ancestors of the later Indo-Europeans can scarcely have expanded beyond Eastern Europe.

IV. The Beginnings of Sedentary Culture

A. The Neolithic Age.—Nowhere in southwestern Asia or neighboring regions can we trace the beginnings of settled village life beyond the Neolithic Age into the preceding Mesolithic. It is true that the beginnings of agriculture may now be carried back into the Mesolithic (Natufian) of Palestine and Iran, but the Palestinians of that day lived in caves and probably in small clusters of huts, which were moved each year, if not oftener. The Neolithic of the Near East has not yet been clearly and indisputably demarcated: it was a period of culture in which artifacts with ground edges and massive stone construction of the type known as "megalithic" had come into use; it was characterized by prepottery and pottery phases, and to it belong the oldest village sites yet discovered. The clearest neolithic stratification comes from the sites of Jericho in Palestine and Mersin in Cilicia, both excavated by John Garstang between 1935 and 1947. At Jericho a characteristic neolithic pottery-bearing level (Stratum IX) covered three earlier strata (X-XII) with the same types of artifacts but without any pottery. At Mersin twelve successive chalcolithic strata covered at least two and probably many more neolithic levels. Similar neolithic deposits, usually much thinner and less defined, have been found at the bottom of a number of other mounds in northern Mesopotamia and Syria. Further west there are neolithic cultures at several points in northwestern Egypt, but lack of stratification makes it still difficult to establish a clear chronology of this phase of culture.

Thanks to very recent finds we are now sure about the neolithic date of the constructions and tombs of megalithic masonry which are sprinkled over southwestern Asia and which are particularly abundant in Trans-Jordan. The dolmens of Trans-Jordan belong in the main to the fifth millennium B.C. Supporting this date are two sets of facts: (a) the dolmens practically never contain any pottery, and where vases or shards appear in previously opened dolmens, they may belong to any age; (b) the burial places of Middle and Late Chalcolithic and Early Bronze are well known to us, and only the most primitive of them show any resemblance in mode of construction to the dolmens. In northern and western Europe megalithic construction was introduced later and did not die out until well along in the second millennium B.C., but its cultural horizon was still characteristically neolithic.

B. The Chalcolithic Age.—The following Chalcolithic Age represents one of the greatest forward steps in the history of civilization. Our dates are now fixed by radiocarbon (carbon isotope 14) counts of organic matter found by archaeologists. In the course of the fifth and fourth millenniums B.C. the men of western Asia and Egypt ceased to be mere food gatherers and became food producers. In the river valleys and lowland plains they began systematic irrigation of crops, while villages sprang up everywhere. Many of these villages were well constructed and surrounded with fortifications, as a result of which the characteristic *tell* profile (a low truncated cone) became common. In the Chalcolithic Age we find four principal cultural areas: (a) the Mesopotamian and Iranian painted-pottery horizon, which extended westward into northern Syria and Cilicia; (b) the Anatolian and Aegean horizon, which superficially resembled the Neolithic of Cilicia and Syria-Palestine; (c) the horizon of Palestine and southern Syria, best known through the excavation of Tuleilat Ghassul near Jericho; (d) the Egyptian horizon, which differs sharply from all the Asiatic cultures in detail.

As a result of sedentary life there was a rapid acceleration of the learning process; the experience of previous generations became cumulative as special crafts and guilds began to be formed. Knowledge of food plants spread rapidly through trade and acculturation. Irrigation made it possible to cultivate fruit and vegetables systematically, in addition to the grain crops which had been introduced in the Mesolithic and Neolithic Ages. Through intensive cultivation of many food plants it became possible to improve individual diet and to increase the population greatly; average height and weight grew rapidly. In higher cultural life there was an extraordinary amount of mythmaking, as we know from the dominantly agricultural nature of the myths of the immediately following periods. The increasing complexity of life in the river valleys, where struggle for water rights and co-operation in building and maintaining irrigation works gave rise to organized states, was quickly followed by the development of highly differentiated societies and especially by the invention of writing. Higher culture developed along with this art.

1. Mesopotamia.—The Chalcolithic Age in Mesopotamia shows a greater flowering of civilization than anywhere else in that period. Because of intensive study of chalcolithic remains in this region since about 1930, the sequence of main cultural periods has been established stratigraphically. Following scanty remains of neolithic occupation with unpainted pottery, we find successively Hassunan, Samarran, Halafian, Obeidian, and Warkan cultures; the last of them brings us to the end of the fourth millennium. Occupation became relatively dense in the northern river valleys of Mesopotamia in the Halafian, about 4000 B.C. This phase of painted-pottery culture is characterized by extremely beautiful ware, often polychrome. There are so far no clear signs of village settlement in the Babylonian plain until the early fourth millennium. The building of towns in Babylonia may have begun somewhat earlier, but it took centuries to drain the swampy alluvium and create centers of urban life. Once men had mastered the Babylonian earth, its richness proved inviting to more and more tribes from the north and east. Population increased rapidly, and great urban centers were established at Ur, Erech, Eridu, and Nippur, around which were crystallized the most sacred traditions of Sumer. Between 3500 and 3000 B.C. we find great temples of mud brick being erected

241

on raised platforms in order to keep them beyond the reach of the devastating inundations which periodically flooded the new settlements. In and around these temples have been found our oldest clay tablets, inscribed in Sumerian with pictographic characters whose forms suggest that the invention of writing was still recent. Art made rapid advances under the propitious conditions brought into being by the concentration of wealth. Babylonian culture was so superior to that of surrounding lands that it spread rapidly, characteristic elements of it being adopted by the Egyptians of the latest predynastic and protodynastic periods.

2. *Palestine.*—As indicated above, the Chalcolithic of Mesopotamia extended westward into northern Syria and Cilicia as far as the Mediterranean, separating the contemporary culture of Anatolia from that of southern Syria and Palestine. In Palestine our record is still incomplete, but we already recognize a series of chalcolithic cultures, notably Jericho VIII, Ghassul IV (the earlier Ghassul levels are still too inadequately known to warrant any dogmatism), and a series of later cultures down to the beginning of the Early Bronze about the thirty-first century B.C. Of these the Ghassulian is by far the best known and the most interesting; its remains have been found in numerous places scattered through the country. The Ghassulians flourished before the middle of the fourth millennium, and they represent a well-developed stage of Chalcolithic, far from its neolithic origins. Arrowheads were no longer made of stone, and axheads were even being made of true bronze, that is, of copper with tin alloy (or perhaps of copper ore with an admixture of tin). The Ghassulians were buried in cists made of small stone slabs, arranged like miniatures of the older megalithic dolmens. Remarkable fresco paintings were found on some house walls; they show astonishing capacity for artistic expression, both along naturalistic and geometrical lines.

3. *Egypt.*—The Chalcolithic of Egypt is chiefly known from a chain of predynastic cemeteries, with occasional village sites, lining the Nile all the way from Ma'adeh near Cairo to Upper Egypt. In 1902 Flinders Petrie arranged all the predynastic graves then known in a typological series to which he gave the name "sequence dating"; though bitterly attacked at the time, it has proved a reliable guide to relative chronology. Since 1924 older chalcolithic cultures have been discovered, but there are still more serious gaps in our documentation than there are in Mesopotamia. The oldest of the cultures hitherto found in the Nile Valley proper, south of the delta, is Tasian. Next comes Badarian, in some respects the best known of all these early cultures; it was already a thoroughly char-

acteristic early chalcolithic assemblage. After we reach Petrie's sequence date "30" (*ca.* 3500 B.C.), we have a large number of cemeteries containing graves from two successive periods, Amratian and Gerzean. As we approach the First Dynasty we find a more and more complex culture, with rapid development of art hinting at a correspondingly rapid concentration of power, which reached its climax shortly before the First Dynasty (minimal date in the twenty-ninth century B.C.). Somewhere about the thirty-fourth century B.C. commerce sprang up with Asia, as is proved by the discovery of Palestinian pottery of Late Chalcolithic type, as well as by the growing popularity of motifs and objects of Mesopotamian origin. A vivid idea of simple town life at this time may be obtained from recent excavations of the Egyptian government at Ma'adeh, southeast of Cairo. From later traditions and myths it may be possible to reconstruct something of the political history of this age, but details will probably never be known.

V. The Empires of the Third Millennium

A. Mesopotamia. 1. The Classical Sumerian Period (ca. 2800-2360).—By the early part of the third millennium Babylonian civilization was already beginning to assume the characteristic Sumerian dress which it wore until the triumph of Sargon I of Akkad over his Sumerian enemies in the south. It is true that we can hardly as yet read the earliest tablets from the Jemdet Nasr Age, which followed the chalcolithic Warka period. Nor can we make much out of the earliest tablets from Ur, dating from Early Dynastic I, perhaps about 2800 B.C. But the Farah tablets, from about 2600, are intelligible in the main, and by the time of Ur-Nanshe of Lagash, about 2500 B.C., the inscriptions offer little difficulty. It was not until the twenty-fifth century that Sumerian script was developed to the point where verbal and nominal forms were as a rule spelled out phonetically. Practically all texts which we possess from this pre-Akkadian period are either royal inscriptions of stereotyped nature or administrative and economic documents. However, it is certain that most of the Sumerian literary and religious texts from the temple library at Nippur and other libraries of the early second millennium are copies of texts which were composed in the first three quarters of the third millennium and transmitted orally for some centuries before being put into writing.

The Sumerian literary texts bear witness to a remarkable flowering of higher culture around temples and scribal schools. We find a number of literary types well represented. Most interesting are the epic tales, based on legendary exploits of the early Sumerian heroes, included by later Sumerian historiographers among the kings of the first two postdiluvian dynasties at Kish and Ur. Among these heroes were a number who found places later in the Sumerian pantheon, such as Enmerkar, Lugalbanda, and Gilgamesh. There are many myths of the gods which, like the heroic epics, have been recovered in large part by the untiring efforts of S. N. Kramer. There are also hymns and lamentations, proverbs, and other didactic compositions. Only the future can provide more detailed information about the relative date of this rich new literature from a study of language and content, with the aid of occasional finds of literary fragments from earlier times. For the present we must be content to know that the already excavated Sumerian literature represents by far the largest early corpus of its kind in the world. Little that we possess in Egypt antedates the end of the third millennium, aside from the Pyramid Texts, which are almost entirely magical in content and provide no surrogate for the missing belles-lettres of the Egyptians, invaluable though they may be for the history of religion.

Some of the Sumerian mythological tablets from the third millennium, preserved in copies of the early second, parallel the early stories of Genesis. Thus we have accounts of creation preserved in bilingual Sumerian and Akkadian texts which probably go back to early times. However, none has yet turned up in the Sumerian tablets from the early second millennium. The so-called Dilmun Poem may refer to a kind of Sumerian Eden, but the text as a whole is very different from anything in Genesis. We possess a list of antediluvian kings dating in its present form about 2100 B.C., but going back earlier in its oldest parts; it runs:

When royalty descended from heaven, royalty was in Eridu. In Eridu Alulim (Alorus) was king, reigning 28,800 years. Alalgar reigned 36,000 years. Two kings reigned 64,800 years.

Eridu I leave; its royalty was brought to Badtibira. In Badtibira Enmenluanna reigned 43,200 years; Enmengalanna reigned 28,800 years; the god Dumuzi (Tammuz), a shepherd, reigned 36,000 years. Three kings reigned 108,000 years.

Badtibira I leave; its royalty was brought to Larak. In Larak Ensipazianna reigned 28,800 years. One king reigned 28,800 years.

Larak I leave; its royalty was brought to Sippar. In Sippar Enmenduranna became king and reigned 21,000 years. One king reigned 21,000 years.

Sippar I leave; its royalty was brought to Shuruppak. In Shuruppak Ubartutu became king and reigned 18,600 years. One king reigned for 18,600 years. These five cities, eight kings reigned there for 241,000 years. The flood then swept over.[1]

[1] Ancient texts are quoted in the author's own translation. Editors.

Another early Sumerian list differs considerably in detail and gives us ten antediluvian kings with a total of 456,000 years of reign. Still later, in the third century B.C. Berosus quotes the list of kings in a slightly different form, but still with ten kings, who rule 432,000 years. The only resemblance between the Hebrew list and the Sumerian lists lies in the number of items (reigns in one case, generations in the other) and their extension from the Creation to the Flood; there are no similarities in detail. However, the resemblance in framework is so close that an ultimate relationship cannot be doubted.

A Sumerian account of the Flood, following a narrative of antediluvian times, is preserved in a Nippur tablet published by Arno Poebel. In the first part we find a reference to the creation of animals, the descent of royalty from heaven, and the same list of five antediluvian cities, in the same order as in the Nippur list of antediluvian kings. Unhappily the text is preserved in a mutilated form, so we have only a few details about the Flood preserved:

The flood. . . . The goddess Nintu [wept] like a . . . , the pure goddess Inanna mourned for its (sic) people; Enki consulted with himself, Anu, Enlil, Enki, and Ninhursag . . . the gods of heaven and earth. . . . Then Ziusudra (Xisuthrus, the flood hero), the king . . . built huge. . . . "Stand at my left side . . . I will say a word to thee . . . hearken to my instruction . . . a flood . . . to destroy the seed of mankind . . . is the decision, the command of the assembly of the gods, the word decreed by Anu and Enlil."

After a long break the tablet continues:

All the mighty winds attacked together. At the same time the flood swept. . . . After seven days and seven nights while the flood swept through the land and the huge ship was tossed by the winds on the great waters, Utu (the sun-god) . . . the huge ship. Ziusudra, the king, bowed down before Utu, while the king butchered an ox, sacrificed a sheep. . . . Life like that of a god they gave him, eternal life like a god they . . . him. Then Ziusudra, the king, . . . of the seed of mankind, in the land of . . . the land of Dilmun, at the place where the sun rises, they caused to dwell.

A number of the Sumerian compositions were later adapted to Akkadian listeners; the differences between them are very instructive. Among the best known of such poems or poetic cycles are a number of compositions celebrating the deeds of Gilgamesh; they appear to form an epic of considerable length, but we lack conclusive evidence with regard to their relation and sequence.

Sumerian religion was organized into a pantheon much earlier than was true of Egypt, presumably because the Babylonian plain was much more compact than the Nile Valley, making possible much more rapid intercommunication and discouraging local isolation. Nippur in central Babylonia, where the storm-god Enlil held his terrestrial court, became recognized at an early date as the cultic center of the whole country, to which votive offerings were brought from all parts of Babylonia. As high cosmic deities of the presedentary Sumerians became settled in local temples, they often received new appellations and thus tended to split up into different figures. But the opposite tendency then began to operate: originally distinct deities which shared functions and attributes were identified, and thus the total number of widely recognized divinities seems to have remained about the same through historical times. Other leading Sumerian deities were An (Akkadian Anu), "Heaven," the titular father of the gods, whose chief city was Erech (Warka); Enki (Ea), lord of the fertilizing flood waters, and hence god of the subterranean fresh-water ocean, whose chief seat was at Eridu; the mother-goddess Inanna or Innin; Nanna, the moon-god, whose terrestrial residence was at Ur; Utu, the sun-god, whose favored abodes were Larsa in the south and Sippar in the north. Many of the deities which rose to prominent positions in the Akkadian pantheon had been relatively insignificant in Sumerian times, though they bear Sumerian names: to this group belonged Sin, the moon-god; Nergal, lord of the underworld; Ninurta, god of war; and many more. In part the rise and fall of deities resulted from the vicissitudes of the cities where they received special honor; thus Nanna, the moon-god of Ur, became replaced by Sin, the Sumerian god of Harran in the north; Ningirsu of Lagash faded out with the disappearance of his city and was replaced by Ninurta; Enlil's figure gradually dissolved into that of Marduk, lord of the new capital at Babylon.

2. The Sumero-Akkadian Period (ca. 2360-1960).

While the Sumerians were certainly the authors of the earliest sedentary Mesopotamian civilization that we can trace, the Semitic Akkadians, who received their later name from the city of Akkad (Gen. 10:10), were present both as seminomads and as settled folk at an exceedingly early date. At Kish we find tradition recognizing kings with Semitic names immediately after the Flood; at Mari excavations have disclosed a Semitic dynasty which antedated the Sumerian dynasty of Ur-Nanshe at Lagash. Semitic loan words, like *damgar*, "merchant," were adopted by the Sumerians in very early times. Akkadian was reduced to writing, using

Sumerian script, before the time of the oldest fully intelligible Sumerian texts which we possess. So we cannot be surprised to find the Akkadians displacing the Sumerians to such an extent, especially in northern Babylonia, that under the great Sargon of Akkad, in the twenty-fourth century B.C., Semitic dislodged Sumerian as the official language of royal inscriptions and business documents. The Dynasty of Akkad (ca. 2360-2180 B.C.) was probably larger than any of the ephemeral Sumerian empires which are vaguely reported by tradition; at its height it dominated the entire region of the Two Rivers, beyond which it extended northwest to control Syria and southeastern Asia Minor, east to control the Zagros region and Elam, and southeast to control the basin of the Persian Gulf. Trade was very active, extending, according to tradition, as far as central Asia Minor, and according to later copies of contemporary texts, as far as South Arabia. Recent finds of a fortified palace at Tell Ibraq and of archives of business documents at various points in northern Mesopotamia show that the administration of the Akkadian Empire must have been astonishingly well organized. Nineveh was a focal point of the empire in the north.

Less is now known about the art and literature of the Dynasty of Akkad than about its political and economic life. A few superbly executed monuments and small objects, including especially cylinder seals, prove that the art of the period was from our point of view immeasurably superior to that of the Sumerian centuries which immediately preceded it. We are just beginning to have some idea of the early Akkadian literature, thanks to stray finds. It would appear that there was an extensive religious literature in Old Akkadian, which was probably transmitted in the main through oral channels. Omen texts in Old Akkadian have been found at Mari, written in the script of the Third Dynasty of Ur. Characteristic grammatical peculiarities of Old Akkadian appear in archaizing prose and poetry of the First Dynasty of Babylon (see below), making it highly probable that the so-called Hymnal-Epic dialect goes back ultimately to the period of Akkad. For centuries thereafter the mighty power of Akkadian arms and civilization dominated the culture of the regions around Babylonia. The earliest heroes of Hurrian heroic saga, as transmitted to us by way of the Hittite libraries of Hattusa (Boğazköy), were kings of Akkad, not native warriors.

The naïve exuberance of this oldest preserved Semitic poetry may be illustrated by the following two quotations. The first represents the opening canto of the Hymn to the Lady of the

Gods (Beletili), copied on tablets from the early second millennium B.C.:

The song of the Lady of the Gods I will sing—
O comrades, attend,	O warriors, hearken!
I sing of Mama, whose song	
Is sweeter by far	Than honey and wine,
Sweeter than honey and wine,	
Sweeter it is	Than grapes and figs,
Sweeter it is than the purest cream,	
Sweeter it is	Than grapes and figs!

Secondly may be quoted two cantos of the epic poem of Agushaya, celebrating the prowess of Ishtar as goddess of battles. In its extant form it goes back only to the reign of Hammurabi, about 1700 B.C., but there can be no doubt that the content and form are centuries older:

Let me praise the Mighty one,	Most valiant of the gods,
The first-born of Nikkal,	Her might let me exalt!
Ishtar, the Mighty One,	Most valiant of the gods,
The first-born of Nikkal,	Her might let me recount!

. . . .

Her feast is the clash	Of those who dance into battle—
Ere the kindled fire flares up,	They are turned to ashes!
Ishtar's feast is the clash	Of those who dance into battle—
Ere the kindled fire flares up,	They are reduced to ashes!

After four generations the Akkadian Empire fell into anarchy, and was soon overwhelmed by an irruption of the Qutu (Gutium) barbarians from the Zagros region, who are said in the dynastic lists to have dominated Babylonia for more than a century. Under their loose control the central administration broke up and was replaced by numerous local states, especially in the south, where a Sumerian renascence began. The end of this period, about 2100 B.C., is brightly illuminated by the monuments and inscriptions of Gudea, viceroy (*ensi*) of Lagash, whose building operations and trading expeditions prove him to have been virtually autonomous. Shortly afterward the Qutu were defeated and driven out of Babylon by Utu-hegal, king of Erech, who claimed the distinction of "dragon-slayer" as token of his prowess. Then came Ur-Nammu, about 2070 B.C., who established a new organized empire with its capital at Ur. For over a century the Third Dynasty of Ur controlled most of the Mesopotamian Plain, apparently extending its control at different times well into the Zagros on the northeast and Syria on the northwest. Trade and commerce

flourished exceedingly during this century, but almost all of our scores of thousands of tablets are in Sumerian; it was only in the north that the Semitic tradition of Akkad continued to show vitality. However, the return of Sumer to power was brief; Sumerian names became rapidly fewer and finally disappeared entirely, Semitic Akkadian becoming the common language of all Babylonians early in the second millennium.

B. Egypt. 1. *The Protodynastic and Early Dynastic Periods (ca. 2850-2600).*—Somewhere in the twenty-ninth century (following the minimal chronology) the kings of Upper Egypt invaded the north and founded the first lasting union of the two parts of Egypt. It is highly probable that they were not the first rulers of united Egypt, since the Cairo fragment of the Palermo Stone seems to contain some obscure names of earlier kings wearing the double crown of the north and south. In any case, there was a remarkable flowering of art and architecture under the kings of the First Dynasty, especially under the two first and most powerful, Menes and Athothis (probably Narmer, as pointed out by G. A. Reisner). The arms and trade of Egypt pushed out into Nubia and Asia. Representations of Asiatics appear for the first time on Egyptian monuments, and Syro-Palestinian pottery of typical Early Bronze II type is found in the royal tombs of Adydos. The cedar emporium at Byblos was founded (or greatly developed), and it is probable that much of the coastal plain of Palestine and Syria was under Egyptian control. Mining operations at Sinai were commemorated by the seventh king of the dynasty.

Practically nothing is known about the literature of this period. Though hieroglyphs were written in ink even before Menes, there are no inscriptions which contain more than names and titles and brief formulas. Words were still written ideographically, as a rule. In art there was also a strange archaism, which seemed un-Egyptian to Egyptologists when its monuments were first discovered half a century ago. It was not until near the end of the Thinite period, in the twenty-seventh century (minimal chronology), that we see in statues and reliefs a definite stereotyping of forms and proportions along the lines which afterward became standard through twenty-four centuries of Egyptian life.

The religion of protodynastic Egypt may be approximately reconstructed from the Pyramid Texts (see below) and a few other early religious texts, such as the so-called Monument of Memphite Theology, since much of their content goes back into this period and some of it must go back to predynastic times. From personal names and inscriptions, especially from the Palermo Stone, it is possible to recognize the substantial identity of the gods and practices of the Thinite period with those of the Pyramid Age. Recent discoveries have gone far to prove that a considerable proportion of the beliefs and practices of later times goes back with little change into the earliest dynastic age, if not earlier. Just as among the Sumerians, when the Egyptians settled down in the Chalcolithic Age, the chief gods of their older pantheon were distributed among the districts into which the Nile Valley was divided. But Egyptian religion was far more conservative than Sumerian, on account of the isolation of the country and the regularity of its natural phenomena, which discouraged change. We find that most of the local deities were represented in animal or in half-animal form, and that a number were identified with trees and plants, while a few seem to have been embodied in inanimate objects of fetish nature. However, it would be a gross exaggeration to regard these zoomorphic gods as nothing but deified animals, since there is not a single name of such a god which can certainly, or even probably, be explained as a word for the animal in question. This wholesale combination of gods with animals illustrates rather the prelogical association of animals with the invisible dynamic entities of primitive man's imagination. These dynamic beings were active and possessed definite characteristics, but they remained, in general, invisible. What was therefore more natural than that they should be selectively associated with the mysterious visible beings which moved about and brought so much benefit and loss to mankind? It is probable that the zoomorphism of Egyptian religion was an inheritance from the food-gathering times of the Paleolithic and Mesolithic, though it appears never to have been crystallized into any form of totemism, as happened among other primitive food gatherers in different parts of the world. Whenever we are able to learn something about a specific early Egyptian pantheon, as is particularly true of Heliopolis, the religious center of Lower Egypt, the fundamentally cosmic nature of its deities becomes clear. The head of the Heliopolitan pantheon was the sun-god Re, who was identified with an old cosmic god Atum. The latter is never represented in any but human form. Atum created the air-god Shu and the latter's twin sister Tefnut by masturbation, since he had no consort to impregnate. Shu and Tefnut were the parents of the next pair, Geb and Nut, "Earth" and "Heaven," whose names illustrate the mixture of primitive belief and secondary speculation which created the framework of ancient mythology. To these five cosmic deities were added four more, all regarded as children of Geb and Nut: the famous deities Osiris and his sister-wife Isis,

Seth and his sister-wife Nephthys. The falcon-god Horus of Behdet (Damanhur), ancient sacred center of Lower Egypt, and the enigmatic Seth of Ombos in Upper Egypt became sworn foes, probably on both mythological and political grounds. But Horus was by no means restricted to Lower Egypt, since his cult was also popular in the south, while Seth became later closely associated with the history of a north Egyptian shrine at Tanis in the northeastern delta.

2. The Pyramid Age (ca. 2600-2150).—The protodynastic Thinite period was followed by a long period of Memphite ascendancy, during which Memphis, just south of Cairo, was the chief seat of royalty. This period, which included the Third, Fourth, Fifth, and Sixth Dynasties (minimal chronology: about 2600-2150), is known as the Pyramid Age. It was ushered in by the reign of Djoser, whose remarkable stone constructions at Sakkarah, probably designed by his chief minister, the famous Ii-em-hotep, reflect a very early stage of building in hewn stone. The following Fourth Dynasty lasted little over a century, but its chief members, Snefru, Cheops, Chephren, and Mycerinus, must be counted among the greatest kings of Egypt. Under them Egypt became a centralized absolutism, where everything was in theory owned and directed by the king. During the civil wars of the Thinite period the old local nobility had been practically annihilated, and their properties had been distributed among the friends and relatives of the king. Hence the high officials of the Fourth Dynasty appear as parvenus, owing little to their ancestors but everything to the king. Even though this situation may have been in part administrative fiction, the fact remains that the entire country was in the hands of a bureaucratically organized body of royal pensioners. The power and wealth of the state were concentrated on the construction of the royal pyramid, which was so planned that it could be finished quickly at the death of the king. The four mighty pyramids, which represent the tombs of the four greatest kings of this dynasty, give us a stupendous proof that belief in the incarnation of the sun-god in the person of the king was a living force in the Egypt of the day. Though the state was exhausted by the effort and the Fourth Dynasty was replaced by a line of humble origin, the concentration of forces on a task without utilitarian function may yet have contributed to the future unity and cultural momentum of the country.

The Fifth Dynasty shifted the focus of its interest somewhat to the south, and the reaction against the abuse of royal power led on the one hand to the substitution of temples of the sun-god for the great pyramids, and on the other to the breakup of the centralized bureaucracy, whose chief members became local nomarchs, each relatively autonomous within the limits of his district. In the Sixth Dynasty the feudal system grew in strength until the king became a mere figurehead.

To the late Fifth and the Sixth Dynasty belong the inscriptions carved on the walls of the pyramid chambers and corridors—the Pyramid Texts. Though their contents were copied from earlier sources which may have been handed down orally in some cases for nearly a thousand years, they bear witness to religious beliefs which were still current in the twenty-fourth and twenty-third centuries. Consisting largely of magical spells and incantations, with hymns and occasional myths interspersed, they were intended to insure the union of the king after death with the sun-god whom he embodied on earth. By a fusion with another chain of belief, it was thought that the king became Osiris as well as Re. However, these beliefs were in part already anachronistic; in the next phase of Egyptian history nobles were to partake in the hope of union with the god after death, and in the New Empire any commoner who could afford the price of a proper burial might expect the same reward.

The following selections from the Pyramid Texts well illustrate their primitiveness and their naïve belief in the union of Pharaoh with the sun-god Re or the Nile-god Osiris after death; the prelogical flavor of these dynamistic spells is evident:

An ascent to heaven is built for him (the reigning Pharaoh), in order that he may climb up it to heaven. He climbs up on the smoke of the great incense. He flies as a bird and alights as a beetle on an empty seat in the bark of Re. . . . He rows in heaven in thy bark, O Re; he punts in thy bark, O Re! When thou dost rise from the horizon, O Re, it is he who is the pilot of thy bark, with his staff in his hand!

. . . .

He who flies, flies! He flies away from you, O men; he is no longer on earth, he is in heaven. Thou who art his personal god, his genius is with thee (?). He has soared to heaven as a heron, he has kissed heaven as a falcon, he has leaped to heaven like a locust.

3. The First Intermediate Period (ca. 2150-1992).

—About 2150 Phiops II died after a reign of more than ninety years. Egypt then broke up into several small states, and at least three lines of rulers claimed the double crown. The Memphite claim was carried on by the Heracleopolites, who were after a long civil war crushed by the princes of Thebes. Toward the end of the twenty-first century Egypt became reunited under Mentuhotep II. This obscure age (ca. 2150-1992) is called the first Intermediate period.

C. Palestine. 1. The Early Bronze Age (ca. 3100-2100).

—From the thirty-first to the twenty-first century the archaeological history of Palestine has been conveniently divided by G. Ernest Wright into four phases: Early Bronze I (ca. 3100-2900), Early Bronze II (ca. 2900-2600), Early Bronze III (ca. 2600-2300), and Early Bronze IV (ca. 2300-2100). These dates are all based on our minimal chronology for Egypt, since archaeological synchronisms between the two countries are numerous and are increasing steadily in number. Thus Early Bronze I must be synchronized with the latest Predynastic Age; Early Bronze II was contemporary with the First Egyptian Dynasty; Early Bronze III was coeval with the Pyramid Age, especially the Third to Fifth Dynasties; Early Bronze IV was parallel with the Sixth Dynasty and the First Intermediate. The excavations at Megiddo and Bethshean, Jericho, Khirbet Kerak (Beth Yerah on the Sea of Galilee), and Tell el-Far'ah, northeast of Nablus, have established the stratigraphic succession of periods.

Palestine was far from being a primitive land in the Early Bronze Age; on the contrary, it was dotted with flourishing towns, especially in the river valleys and coastal plains but also in the hill country. The population must have been very small, scarcely over a hundred thousand at any time in the third millennium. It must be remembered that the number of towns which coexisted in any one period was small. A number of Early Bronze temples have now been excavated in whole or in part; the most remarkable group is formed by the sanctuaries of Ai and Megiddo, from Early Bronze I and II. A most extraordinary rectangular structure with circular pits has lately been discovered at Khirbet Kerak, dating from Early Bronze III; Benjamin Maisler plausibly conjectures that it represents an early public granary of a class known to have been in use among the Canaanites. Egyptian influence appears in constructions from Early Bronze III at Taanach and in a quantity of imported Egyptian alabaster bowls found in a shrine of about the twenty-sixth century at Ai.

2. The Precursors of the Canaanites.

—There can be no doubt that the Palestinians of the third millennium were Semites, presumably the linguistic precursors of the later Canaanites. This is proved by Canaanite loan words in Egyptian from the Second Dynasty on, by Egyptian mention of Canaanite place names, by the fact that all extant names of places known to have been occupied during this period are certainly or probably Semitic, and by the fact that the prevailing physical type of this age is shown by skeletal evidence to have been dolichocephalic. We may accordingly feel sure that their religion was of much the same type as the Canaanite religion of the following millennium (see below).

VI. The Middle Bronze Age (ca. 2100-1550)

A. Mesopotamia. 1. The Rise of Ashur and Mari (ca. 1960-1700).—At the beginning of the second millennium in Mesopotamia we find Babylonia divided between a number of petty states, one of which laid claim with some success to the kingship over Sumer and Akkad. The Third Dynasty of Ur had come to an end about 1960 B.C., when the Elamites destroyed the capital and took its last king, Ibbi-Sin, into captivity. Isin and Larsa, which had previously revolted, disputed the succession; other independent city-states were set up at Eshnunna in the extreme northeast of Babylonia and elsewhere. The nomadic Westerners (Amorites) swarmed into the country and were soon in control of the entire land (see below).

The political chaos into which Babylonia fell is reflected in the extraordinary decrease in the number of economic texts when compared to the century ending about 1960. On the other hand, there appears to have been much quiet scholarly activity on the part of the scribes of Nippur and elsewhere, who kept on copying Sumerian tablets and developing new sciences and pseudosciences. We may recall that literature flourished under the rump state at Heracleopolis, and may assume that much the same activity went on at Nippur under the protection of the kings of the rump state of Isin.

The weakness of Babylonia made it possible for former dependencies of Ur to break away and form new states in the north. Notable among these new states were Ashur on the Tigris and Mari on the Euphrates. For some unknown reason the princes of Ashur in this period did not claim the title "king," but called themselves simply "viceroy" (ishakkum) or "priest" (shangum). However, the same is attested of the Middle Assyrian kings who certainly held the title, and the Khorsabad List calls all of these rulers "king." It also designates the initial group of seventeen rulers, some of whom bore Northwest-Semitic names, as "tent dwellers": they were Semitic nomads. This group is followed by a line of ten kings, most of whom had characteristically Northwest-Semitic names. Then about 2000 B.C. came six with Akkadian or Hurrian names, last of whom was Ilushuma (about 1900 B.C.), who invaded Babylonia. During the next six reigns (ca. 1874-1748 B.C.) there was a tremendous expansion of Assyrian trade westward into Asia Minor, as we know from thousands of "Cappadocian Tablets," that is, Old Assyrian economic texts and letters excavated in various towns of Cappadocia. Most of these documents, which have been studied particularly by Julius Lewy, date from the end of the nineteenth and the beginning of the eighteenth century, about 1800 B.C. in round numbers. These tablets have already thrown a flood of light on the life of the early Patriarchal Age; and as work on them continues, they are likely to become of increasing importance, since they are about a century older than the Mari tablets (see below) and in general antedate the Amorite infiltration into northeastern Mesopotamia. The Assyrians entered Asia Minor and established trading posts outside the principal capitals by treaty with the native Anatolian princes, several of whom also appear in their own inscriptions copied by later Hittite scribes at Hattusa (Boğazköy). We have in these documents the oldest examples known so far of the commercial empires of later times, which formed a kind of symbiosis with surrounding states; none of the latter sacrificed any political power by encouraging reciprocally profitable trade through foreign channels.

2. The Amorite Infiltration (ca. 2000-1700).—For centuries after the Akkadians had settled down in Mesopotamia, their seminomadic successors continued to maintain a nomadic existence on the edges of the cultivated regions of the Fertile Crescent. In those days, before camels had been effectively domesticated, nomads had to keep much closer to a permanent water supply than their Bedouin successors. In a Sumerian hymn to the storm-god of the west, originally composed somewhere in the third quarter of the third millennium, we are told that the nomads were wild marauders who spent their time in fighting, ate raw food, did not live in houses, did not bury their dead, and so forth. Disregarding the exaggeration of their savagery by the civilized Sumerian, we may see in this a reflection of a state of society roughly intermediate between the modern Bedja and similar Hamitic groups in the eastern desert of the Sudan, on the one hand, and the modern sheep-raising seminomads of the Upper Euphrates Valley, on the other. The Akkadians, following Sumerian usage, called them "Westerners" (Amurru, whence "Amorite"). Periodically the Amorites gathered in larger hordes and raided the sown land; their pressure became so serious in the reign of Shu-Sin of Ur, early in the twentieth century, that the latter built a line of fortifications to which he gave the name "Western Wall Which Keeps the Didnu [read Di-id-ni-im] Far Away." These nomadic Didnu or Didanu (the word is identified with Amurru by contemporary Babylonian lexicographers)

had presumably migrated nearly six hundred miles from the region of the great oasis of el-'Ula in southern Midian, which was still called Dedan by the Israelites and South Arabians over a millennium later.

After the downfall of the Third Dynasty of Ur there was no longer any serious obstacle to Amorite immigration, and the infiltration of preceding generations became a flood. It is significant that an end also came to the relatively dense sedentary culture of southern and central Trans-Jordan in the course of the same twentieth century. Semitic nomads moved on beyond the barrier of the Tigris into the semiarid regions east and northeast of Babylonia, which became Amorite country, just as the same regions were later to fall to the seminomadic Aramaean tribes of the Assyrian Empire. By the middle of the eighteenth century Amorite dynasties were enthroned in large and small states all over Mesopotamia and Syria; among the most important of them were Larsa and Babylon (1930—), Mari on the Middle Euphrates (ca. 1950—), Yamkhad (Aleppo), Qatna (el-Mishrifeh), Ashur (1748—). Among the minor Amorite states were Abram's home at Harran (Haran) and Apum (the region of Damascus, later Opa).

Our knowledge of the Northwest-Semitic nomads, called "Amorites" by the Babylonians, was exceedingly tenuous until the discovery in 1935-36 of some twenty thousand tablets from the second half of the eighteenth century B.C. These documents were excavated at Tell el-Hariri (ancient Mari) on the Middle Euphrates by André Parrot; many hundreds of them have been published or described since then by Georges Dossin and others. Several thousand of them are letters which formed the official correspondence of successive princes of Mari, mostly of Zimri-Lim, older contemporary of Hammurabi. Since Mari lay in the geographical center of Amorite land and kept up close relations with the surrounding Amorite states, the tablets give us a comprehensive picture of conditions at the time. When all these priceless records have been published and digested it will be possible to have a clear idea of Amorite institutions and customs, which include many items of extraordinary interest such as the custom of sacrificing an ass to solemnize a pact, or the practice of rapid communication by means of fire signals. The natives of Mari, though their scribes wrote Akkadian, were themselves by this time almost solidly Northwestern Semites, as shown by innumerable names of "Amorite" type and by Northwest-Semitic words, expressions, and grammatical peculiarities which swarm in the letters. The ethnic and cultural background is very definitely that of the Hebrew patriarchs, a num-ber of whose names recur in the new texts. The religion of the Amorites now appears to have been a mixture of Mesopotamian and Northwest-Semitic elements; among the deities of Mari were Dagan (Dagon), Rasap (Resheph), the water-god Id (the 'ēdh of Gen. 2:6).

The following letters from Mari illustrate the close relationship existing between the life and culture reflected in them and the early traditions of Israel, especially from the Patriarchal Age. In the first we learn that the southern tribes of the Mari region were called "Benjamin" (Banu Yamin, literally, "Children of the Right Hand= South"; their opposite numbers were the Banu Sim'al, "Children of the Left Hand=North"). We also learn that the use of telegraphic fire signals was highly developed in that day. Of course there are many other letters which further illustrate these points.

To my lord say: Thus Bannum, thy servant. I departed yesterday from Mari and spent the night at Zuruban. All the Benjaminites raised fire signals. From Samanum to Ilum-Muluk (a name meaning literally, "Moloch Is God"), from Ilum-Muluk to Mishlan, all the towns of the Benjaminites in the district of Terqa raised fire signals in reply, but so far I have not determined the meaning of those signals. Now I shall ascertain their meaning, and I shall write to my lord [telling him] whether it is thus or not. Let the garrison of the city of Mari be ·strengthened and let my lord not go outside the gate.

Another letter throws light on the ecstatic seers of that time and their oracles, delivered presumably while they were in a trancelike state.

To my lord say: Thus Kibri-Dagan thy servant. The gods Dagan (biblical Dagon) and Ikrub-El are well; the city Terqa and the district are well. Further, on the very day in which I send this tablet of mine to my lord, the ecstatic seer (mukhkhum) of the god Dagan has come to me and has spoken to me as follows, "The god has commanded me, 'Write at once to the king in order that they may present funerary meals to the shade of Yakhdun-Lim (the deceased king of Mari, father of the reigning king, Zimri-Lim).'" This is what that ecstatic seer has said, and I write it to my lord in order that my lord may do what seems good to him!

In another letter we read:

And when the Benjaminites were at war with my lord, my lord wrote you asking you to furnish troops, but ye did not furnish troops to my lord. At the command of the gods Dagan and Itur-Mer my lord slew the chief (dawidum=Hebrew dāwîdh, "David") of his foes and turned their towns into mounds and ruin heaps.

Other letters often mention the 'Apiru, who were perhaps the Hebrew relatives of the patriarchs, then living in the region of Harran. One of the Hebrew towns mentioned in Genesis (24:10) , "the city of Nahor," appears frequently as Nakhur in the Mari tablets; it seems to have been located in the Balikh Valley, south of Harran.

3. The Age of Hammurabi (1748-1675).—The Age of Hammurabi may be conveniently defined as the period which began with the accession of Shamshi-Adad I, the Amorite conqueror of Assyria, about 1748 B.C., and which ended with the partial break-up of the Babylonian Empire in the reign of Samsu-iluna, about 1675 B.C. The great wealth of Babylonia and the vigor of its inhabitants, who had received a fresh transfusion of blood from the Amorite settlers, made it the leading center of civilization in the world of that day. Thanks to many thousands of published letters and economic texts, we possess a very clear picture of the life of the time. Of the greatest possible interest is the famous Code of Hammurabi, discovered at Susa, the capital of Elam, in 1901. This priceless document, now in the Louvre, dates from the closing years of Hammurabi's reign (1728-1686 B.C.) . It was not the first code of laws promulgated in Babylonia; in 1947 Francis R. Steele announced his discovery of a Sumerian law code from the Nippur Library, dated in the reign of Lipit-Ishtar of Isin, about 1885 B.C., nearly two centuries before the Code of Hammurabi; in 1948 Albrecht Goetze discovered a law code in Akkadian from the city of Eshnunna, also dating about two centuries before Hammurabi. Moreover, it reflects the established tradition of Akkadian law, not the customary law of the Amorites, as has sometimes been inferred from the fact that the country was then ruled by an Amorite dynasty. All three Babylonian codes already exhibit the same formulation and some of the same provisions as we find in the Hittite, Assyrian, and Israelite laws—especially the Book of the Covenant (Exod. 21–23) —all of which were compiled in their extant form centuries later.

The contents of these earliest Mesopotamian codes are of very great comparative value. Thus the Eshnunna Code contains exactly the same law which we find in Exod. 21:35: "If an ox gores an ox and causes its death, both the owners of the oxen shall divide the price of the live ox and also the equivalent of the dead ox." Among other interesting provisions is the following: "If a dog is mad and the authorities have informed its owner, but he does not cage it; if it then bites a man and causes his death, the owner of the dog shall pay two thirds of a mina [forty shekels] of silver." Still another law runs: "If a wall is about to fall and the authorities have informed its owner, but he does not consolidate

his wall; if it then collapses and causes the death of a free man, it is a capital offense and comes under the jurisdiction of the king."

The Code of Hammurabi is directly descended from the stream of legal decision and practice which produced the Code of Lipit-Ishtar, but it is very much fuller and more systematic; it was copied down into Neo-Babylonian times and seems, in fact, to have played something of the role in later Babylonian history that the Code of Justinian did in Byzantine jurisprudence. Antedating the Book of the Covenant (Exod. 21–23) by several centuries, it may be taken as the best extant representative of the class of customary and codified law from which the Israelite code arose. The following provisions illustrate both the cultural level and the stern justice of the time:

If a physician performs an operation on a freeman with a bronze knife and saves the freeman's life, or if he removes a cataract from a freeman and saves the freeman's eye, he shall receive ten shekels of silver.

If it is a plebeian, he shall receive five shekels.

If it is a freeman's slave, the owner of the slave shall pay two shekels of silver to the physician.

If a physician performs an operation on a freeman with a bronze knife and causes the freeman's death, or if he removes a cataract from a freeman and destroys the freeman's eye, they shall cut off his hand.

If a physician performs an operation on the slave of a freeman (!) with a bronze knife and causes his death, he shall replace slave for slave.

If he removes a cataract with a bronze knife and destroys his eye, he shall pay one half his value in silver.

If a physician sets a freeman's broken bone or cures an injured ligament, the patient shall pay the physician five shekels of silver.

If it is a plebeian, he shall pay three shekels of silver.

If it is a freeman's slave, the owner of the slave shall pay the physician two shekels of silver.

If a veterinary performs an operation on an ox or an ass and saves its life, the owner of the ox or ass shall pay the surgeon one sixth of a shekel of silver as his fee.

If he performs an operation on an ox or an ass and causes its death, he shall give to the owner of the ox or ass one fourth its value.

A more complex law of a type impossible in Mosaic law, where sorcery was not recognized legally, appears in the following:

If a freeman brings a charge of sorcery against a freeman but does not prove it, the one against whom the charge of sorcery is brought shall go to the river-god (for the ordeal) ; he shall throw himself into the river, and if the river overcomes him, his accuser shall take over his property. If the river shows that freeman to be innocent and he has accordingly emerged unharmed, the one who brought the charge of sorcery against him shall be put to death, while the one who threw himself into the river shall take the property of his accuser.

4. Babylonian Science.—To this general age belong the principal achievements of the Babylonian mind which have come down to us, including especially intellectual triumphs in the fields of mathematics, astronomy, and philology. In arithmetic and algebra the Babylonians developed a place value notation based on the sexagesimal numeration of the Sumerians. This notation, which recognized the existence of zero, was just as superior to the cumbersome Egyptian hieratic system of numbering as the Hindu-Arabic system was superior to the Greek and Roman methods of numbering. Thanks to their control of such a powerful tool, the early Babylonians were able to develop algebra to a level never quite reached by the Greeks. Tablets from the First Dynasty of Babylon, discovered by Otto Neugebauer, preserve elaborate tables of multiplication, division, reciprocal numbers, squares and square roots, cube roots, and even a kind of simple logarithms. With their place value notation, fractions offered no insuperable difficulties, and the solution of complex quadratic equations by the method of false position became relatively easy. Of course all these complex calculations were carried out without benefit of formal logic, and mathematicians had to follow the time-honored empirical way: trial and error, analogy, and systematic tabulation of all the details which had been learned.

The love of the Babylonian scholars of the early centuries of the second millennium for systematizing their learning led to an enormous amount of tabulated and classified knowledge. To be sure, much of the knowledge which was then put into great canonical tablet series was scarcely useful from our point of view, since it dealt largely with magic and divination, especially with omens of all kinds. However, this incredible industry in collecting knowledge led to very remarkable achievements in the field of philology. Owing to their familiarity with ideograms which no longer had any similarity whatever in form to the objects or ideas portrayed, and which possessed many equivalents in two languages, the Babylonian scholars of this age acquired a familiarity with abstract thinking which stood them in good stead throughout their intellectual activity and which contrasts strikingly with the comparative absence of abstract thinking in ancient Egypt. Thanks to their command of two languages of entirely different structure, they early acquired a surprising grasp of grammatical problems, impressively illustrated in the numerous grammatical texts of the period, designed for students of both Sumerian

and Akkadian. Nothing quite like it is known in the extant remains of the Alexandrian grammarians, and it was not until the medieval Arabic and Hebrew grammarians that the achievements of these Babylonian forerunners were surpassed. Moreover, they prepared exhaustive lists of cuneiform signs and their values, and elaborate dictionaries of words and their meanings, again unsurpassed in some respects before Byzantine times. For another millennium and a half these collections of philological material remained authoritative in Mesopotamia; they were copied by the Assyrian scholars of Nineveh and by the Aramaean cuneiformists of Erech in the Seleucid Age. Because of them modern Assyriologists have acquired a far deeper and more exact knowledge of Akkadian and Sumerian than Egyptologists have of Egyptian. From mathematics and philology Babylonian scholars turned to astronomy and religion, both of which were elaborately catalogued and recorded for the benefit of subsequent generations.

In literature also the First Dynasty of Babylon reached heights unsurpassed in most respects during the following fifteen hundred years of cuneiform writing. Best known are the great epics: the Epic of Creation and the Gilgamesh Epic. The former dates from the seventeenth century B.C. in approximately its extant form (found in Late Assyrian and Neo-Babylonian copies), but the framework which it employs and much of the content are Sumerian. There is no direct connection with the creation narratives of Genesis, but the story in Gen. 1 may preserve a reminiscence of the seven tablets of the Babylonian epic in its arrangement in seven days of creation. Both the stories in Gen. 1–2 preserve the characteristic Sumerian framework, "when . . . then." *Enuma elish* ("When Above," the Babylonian title of the poem, from its first two words) begins as follows:

When on high heaven had not been called by name,
The earth below a name had not received—
The primordial Nether Waters being their begetter,
The sovereign Sea she who bore them all,
While their waters were mingled together,
Not [yet] matted into reed lands, not appearing as reed marshes,
When no gods at all had come into existence,
Not [yet] called by name, not [yet] with their destinies fixed—
Then it was that the gods were created within them,
Lahmu and Lahamu came into being, they were called by name.
While they grew up and became big,
Anshar and Kishar were created, surpassing the others.
They prolonged the days, added the years;
Anu was the heir, rivaling his parents.
To Anshar did Anu make his first-born equal;
Anu begot in his image Nudimmud (Ea).

From this highly polytheistic version of the Creation we turn to the account near the end of the Creation Epic of the creation of man:

When Marduk heard the word of the gods,
His heart guided him to devise a cunning scheme.
Opening his mouth he addressed Ea,
Imparting the plan he had fashioned in his heart,
"Blood I will clot and make bones.
I will bring into existence humankind; 'man' shall be its name;
Verily humankind I will create.
It shall be charged with the service of the gods, that they may rest!
The ways of the gods I will cunningly change;
All shall be worshiped, but into two [classes] shall they be divided."
Ea answered him, speaking to him,
Telling him a plan for the relief of the gods,
"Let just one of their brethren be handed over;
He alone shall perish that mankind may be made!"

Ea goes on to suggest that the rebel Kingu, who was responsible for the revolt of the dragon Tiamat, be bound and executed:

> From his blood they formed mankind.

The Gilgamesh Epic, which contains some four thousand lines in twelve tablets, describes the adventures of the legendary king of Erech, whose historical prototype may have flourished about 3000 B.C., when the early city of Erech in southern Babylonia was at the height of its power. It is partly mythological, partly heroic saga, reaching its climax in the journey of the hero in search of his ancestor, the flood hero Utnapishtim, in the hope that the latter may teach him his own secret of living forever and thus escaping the dreaded fate of death. Utnapishtim tells the story of the great flood, which resembles the biblical account in many respects, but is shot through and through with the crassest polytheism. Nearly two hundred lines are devoted to this story, from which is quoted the passage describing the release of birds from the ark after the deluge had subsided and the following sacrifice to the gods (cf. Gen. 8:6-22):

When the seventh day arrived,
I sent forth and set free a dove;
The dove went and returned,
For there was no resting place, so it returned.
I sent forth and set free a swallow;
The swallow went and returned,
For there was no resting place, so it returned.
I sent forth and set free a raven;
The raven went forth and saw that the waters had fallen,
So it ate, waded (?), cawed, but did not return.
Then I released [the animals] to the four winds
And offered a sacrifice.
I poured out a libation on the peak of the mountain;

I set up incense stands, seven by seven,
And heaped sweet flag, cedar, and myrtle on their bowls.
The gods smelled the savor,
The gods smelled the sweet savor,
The gods swarmed like flies around the sacrificer.

The contrast between the polytheistic crudity of the Babylonian story and the simple monotheistic dignity of the biblical narrative is only too evident.

B. Egypt. 1. The Twelfth Dynasty (1992-1779).—The brief rule of the Theban kings of the Eleventh Dynasty over a united Egypt came to an end in 1992 B.C., when the chief minister Amenemmes I (Amenemhet) made himself king, founding the Twelfth Dynasty. This was in many respects the greatest family of kings in the history of Egypt; its members enjoyed long reigns, and by associating their successors with them on the throne, as a rule, they ensured continuity of succession. The old feudal chieftains were partly eliminated and partly reduced in power. There was much building activity, but instead of being limited to imposing royal monuments, it included drainage works in the Faiyum and fortifications for the protection of the delta against the Semitic hordes. Nor did the Pharaohs of this dynasty restrict themselves to internal action; they also reduced Nubia, Libya, Palestine, and Phoenicia to subjection. More than that, they kept some control through special Egyptian envoys over such remote lands as Ugarit on the coast of northern Syria and Qatna to the southeast, on the border of the Syrian Desert. The Execration Texts (see below, p. 254) enable us to fix the northern boundary of the territory claimed by Egypt in the nineteenth century B.C. north of Damascus and Byblos.

The Twelfth Dynasty was a period of intense literary and scholarly activity in Egypt, corresponding in this respect to the immediately following age in Babylonia. Between 2100 and 1800 were composed a large proportion of the most significant literary works, including such autobiographical narratives as the Story of Sinuhe (see below, p. 254), such fiction as the Story of the Shipwrecked Sailor, and King Cheops and the Wizard, such didactic literature as the Eloquent Peasant, the Teaching of Merikare, of Amenemhet, and of Sehetep-ib-re, such poems as the Debate Between a Man and His Soul, prophetic texts as the Prophecy of Neferrohu, and many others. While the extant copies of our oldest mathematical and medical texts come from the Hyksos Age (1720-1550), there is no reason to doubt that the originals go back to this same golden age of Egyptian culture. The Egyptians developed geometry and especially medicine beyond anything known in Babylonia, though in arithmetic and algebra, astronomy and the philological disciplines they remained far behind the Babylonians.

The most popular literary work of the Middle Empire was the Story of Sinuhe, purporting to describe the adventures in Asia of an Egyptian prince who had been forced to flee from Egypt about 1970 B.C. It was long believed to be fiction, but modern discoveries have confirmed details to such an extent that a solid historical nucleus is now probable. It may be a literary expansion of an autobiography inscribed in Sinuhe's tomb; our oldest hieratic manuscripts go back to within two centuries of Sinuhe's flight. It contains many interesting parallels to episodes in the early Hebrew tradition, for example, Moses' flight from Egypt and his kind reception by the nomads. After the introductory narrative we find Sinuhe about to escape across the Egyptian frontier:

I let my feet carry me northward and I reached the Wall of the Prince, built to keep away the Asiatics and to suppress the Sand dwellers. I crouched in the bush, fearing that a watchman whose turn it was to be on the wall might see me. When night fell I departed, and by daybreak I had reached Peten. I stopped at the Island of Kem-wer. I was overcome by thirst; I was parched and my throat became dry. I said, "This is the taste of death!" But I revived and gathered myself together after I heard the lowing of cattle and caught sight of Asiatics. A chief among them, who had been in Egypt, recognized me; he gave me water and boiled milk for me. I went with him to his encampment and they treated me well.

One foreign land led me to another. I left Byblos and went in the direction of Qedem (the East), where I spent a year and a half. Then Ammunenshi, chief of Upper Retenu, took me and said to me, "Thou wilt do well with me and wilt hear the speech of Egypt." This he said because he knew my ability and had heard of my cleverness, for Egyptians who were there with him had told him about me....

He put me in charge of his children and married me to his eldest daughter. He made me chief of a tribe in the best part of his land. . . . After I had spent many years [there] my children became strong men, each one keeping his tribe in order. A courier who went north or south to the [Egyptian] capital stopped with me; I showed hospitality to all men; I gave water to the thirsty; I guided those who were lost to their road; I saved the man who had been robbed.

In the following narrative we hear of Sinuhe's duel with a native champion whom he slew. Then Pharaoh invited him to return to Egypt, and the latter half of the composition is devoted to details of the negotiations and to the hero's happy return to his native country and the honors which he received in Egypt. This part of the story is extremely rhetorical, diverging widely from the narrative simplicity of the first part.

Out of the wealth of Egyptian didactic literature of the Middle Empire we may select a few passages from the Teaching of Ptahhotep:

Be not vain because of thy knowledge and rely not on the fact that thou art a wise man. Consult the ignorant as well as the learned, for there are no boundaries for skill and no skilled man is skillful in all respects. Good speech is better hidden than turquoise, yet it may be found among maidservants at their hand mills. . . .

If thou art sitting at the table of one who is greater than thyself, take what he gives when it is placed before thee. Look not on what is before him but look at what is before thee. Do not keep looking at him. . . . Look down until he greets thee and speak only after he greets thee. Laugh when he laughs, so that he will be happy and what thou doest will please him. No one knows what is in the heart.

If thou desirest to prolong friendship in a house to which thou hast access, either as lord, as brother, or as friend, in any place into which thou mayest enter, beware of approaching the women. A place where they are is not good.

2. The Age of the Hyksos (ca. 1720-1550).— After the flourishing Twelfth Dynasty, Egypt rapidly fell into a state of anarchy. The Thirteenth Dynasty continued to carry on the Theban tradition of learning, but art and literature languished. Within a space of less than fifty years (*ca.* 1778-1740) the Turin Papyrus lists twenty kings, and contemporary inscriptions add still others. Then came a brief renascence of the Theban Empire under Neferhotep, whose suzerainty was still recognized at Byblos in Phoenicia. About 1720 B.C. Lower Egypt was flooded with Asiatic invaders ("Hyksos") about whom practically nothing is known except the good Northwest-Semitic names of some of their chieftains, such as Ya'qub-har (Jacob), 'Anathar, Samuqena, Bablimma. Probably after 1690 a better organized Semitic group overran the country, penetrating into Nubia and making the weak Thebans their vassals. This group founded the Fifteenth Dynasty, which lasted 108 years (*ca.* 1690-1580), according to the Turin Papyrus. Brief inscriptions and scarabs of two of its kings have been found in Egypt and Palestine. These two, Apophis I and Khayana (whose monuments have been found even in Crete and Babylonia) reigned approximately sixty years (*ca.* 1650-1590); their combined reigns represent the Hyksos golden age, during which the Hyksos Empire extended from Nubia to Syria—possibly for short periods even beyond. There can be no doubt that this brilliant epoch left its mark on Egyptian culture and especially on its administrative organization; it was probably an age of close international relations between the Northwestern Semites of Egypt and their kindred in other parts of the Near East. At all events, it left a deep impress on Hebrew historical tradition.

C. Palestine and Syria. 1. The Egyptian Eclipse (1778-1720).—In the Middle Bronze Age (ca. 2100-1550 B.C.) Palestine and Syria developed a flourishing civilization. At the end of the third millennium we find the culture of the Early Bronze in decadent condition on both sides of the Jordan. In the anarchic period of the First Intermediate Age Egyptian control over the Asiatic dependencies vanished, and Egypt itself was invaded by Semitic nomads. The density of settlement decreased rapidly, and by the end of the twentieth century virtually all of Trans-Jordan had been abandoned, not to be reoccupied by sedentary populations until the thirteenth century. Even in western Palestine there are singularly few sites which continued to be occupied during the first phase of the Middle Bronze (the period of "caliciform" pottery, Tell Beit Mirsim H). This period is illustrated by the hieratic Story of Sinuhe and the Execration Texts from the late nineteenth century B.C., published by Kurt Sethe in 1926, which list Northwest-Semitic tribes and chieftains, but very few towns (among them Jerusalem and Ascalon). The following period saw the introduction of a new type of pottery, with carinated forms imitated from metallic originals (Tell Beit Mirsim G-F, Megiddo XIV-XIII, ca. 1850-1750 B.C.), which was used all over Phoenicia, southern Syria, and Palestine. There is not the slightest evidence that there was any ethnic change. With the Amorite blood transfusion and with Egyptian political and cultural domination, Canaan was more prosperous than it had been for a long time. This prosperity continued to increase, as we see from the rapidly increasing number of occupied sites and from the rich contents of tombs (Tell Beit Mirsim E[1], Megiddo XII). During the eighteenth century B.C. Byblos was ruled by a succession of wealthy princes, no longer more than nominally subject to Pharaoh; the best known of them is one Yantin'ammu or Enten (ca. 1740-1720), who was contemporary with Neferhotep in Egypt and with Zimri-Lim in Mari.

2. The Asiatic Invasions (ca. 1720-1550).—The beginning of the Hyksos Age in Palestine is not illumined by inscriptions. We know, however, that it was a time of steadily increasing wealth and material culture, during which there seem to have been tremendous historical developments. The horse-drawn chariot was just coming into use in the eighteenth century, but early in the following century there was a sudden change in dominant methods of fortification in order to accommodate chariots inside permanent fortifications. Great rectangular camps, surrounded by earthworks lined with beaten earth, suddenly make their appearance, together with extensive use of earthworks in protecting towns and fortresses. This new type of construction appears almost simultaneously in Syria, Palestine, and Egypt; it is mentioned in contemporary Babylonian inscriptions. The introduction of chariotry was accompanied by the widespread use of the composite bow, previously unknown in Egypt and little used in Canaan. With the coming of the horse-drawn chariot there came new ethnic elements, apparently carried into Mesopotamia and Syria on the crest of a mighty inundation which took the Hurrians and other northern peoples much farther south in both countries than they had ever been before. Palestine's earlier dolichocephaly was replaced by growing brachycephaly, a legacy from the mountain peoples who poured into the country in the seventeenth century.

VII. The Late Bronze Age (ca. 1550-1200)

A. Asia Minor. 1. The First Hittite Empire (ca. 1600-1500).—Through the light shed by the Cappadocian Tablets (see above, p. 248), we saw the emergence of previously unknown Anatolian states about 1800 B.C. Not long after this period, in the late seventeenth century, the town of Hattusa, on the strong natural site now called Boğazköy, became the capital of a rapidly growing state, called "Hittite" after its capital. Three powerful kings were responsible for signal triumphs; Labarnas unified central and eastern Asia Minor under Hittite domination, about 1600 B.C.; Hattusilis I extended the arms of Hattusa beyond the peninsula; Mursilis I conquered the kingdom of Aleppo and even raided distant Babylonia, destroying the city of Babylon (ca. 1550). Soon afterward internal strife brought the ephemeral Old Hittite Empire to an abrupt close, and for a good century and a half thereafter the Hittite kings do not seem to have ventured beyond the Taurus Mountains. The Hittites had originally been speakers of a strange prefixing language without demonstrable connection with any other known tongue, but practically all their native inscriptions were written in an Anatolian tongue of Indo-European type (see above, p. 240). Their religion, like their material culture, was a mixture of elements from different sources, but it was already characterized by the orgiastic cult of the Great Mother (Kubaba, Khepat), and the god Telibinus was fundamentally identical with the later Phrygian Attis. Eunuch priests (galli) formed an important element in the Hittite priesthood.

2. Hurrian Cultural Influence.

2. Hurrian Cultural Influence.—The Hurrians were drawn by their conquerors into the Hittite state, and it was probably at this time that the custom arose of associating a queen bearing a Hurrian name with a king bearing a Proto-Hittite name. Hurrian literature was copied and translated by the Hittite scholars, so we find nearly all the yet discovered fragments of Hurrian mythology preserved for us in Hittite translation. In 1946 H. G. Güterbock collected all the now available fragments of the "Song of Ullikummis," the myth of Kumarbis, father of the gods (like Anu, El, and the Greek Cronus), the myth of the dragon Khedammu, the myth of the rape of Ishtar by Mount Pisaisa, and so forth. Since the Hurrians also translated and adapted many Akkadian compositions like the Gilgamesh Epic, the resulting mixture of elements almost defies analysis.

B. Mesopotamia. 1. Mitanni (1500-1370).—After the downfall of the Old Hittite Empire a new power rose rapidly into a dominant position; this power was formed by a kind of symbiosis between the incoming Indo-Aryans and the older Hurrian population of the region. The Indo-Aryans, with good Sanskrit names of Vedic type, brought with them fast horse-drawn chariots which gave them tremendous prestige, probably quite out of proportion to their numbers. At all events, in Late Bronze Mesopotamia, Syria, and Palestine we find that princes and leading nobles very often have Indo-Aryan names, while their subjects bear Hurrian names. This was true, for example, in different parts of Syria, as at Ratna and Damascus, as well as at Taanach and elsewhere in Palestine.

2. Hurrian Documents.—The new power to which allusion was made above was Mitanni, which grew rapidly from its beginnings in the sixteenth century until the time of Saushshatar, about the middle of the fifteenth century, when it controlled most of Mesopotamia and northern Syria, as well as probably most of Armenia. A small but wealthy Hurrian town of this period has been located south of Kirkuk. This town, then called Nuzu or Nuzi, has yielded thousands of cuneiform tablets from the fifteenth century B.C., which have given us a remarkably clear picture of life and customs in northern Mesopotamia during the late Patriarchal Age. The resemblances between the practices mentioned in Genesis and the customs of the Nuzians are frequently so close that all scholars who have studied them are convinced that there is some connection.

One of the most remarkable documents from the fifteenth century which has yet come to light is the autobiography of Idrimi, king of Alalakh in northern Syria. Published by Sidney Smith in 1949, it contains some very striking parallels to the biblical story of Joseph and throws direct light on the background of Balaam. Idrimi may be dated about 1480-1450 B.C.; he was son of Ililimma, king of the lands of Mukishkhe, Ni'a, and 'Amau. The land of 'Amau is mentioned in a slightly later Egyptian inscription as being in northern Syria; it must obviously be identified with the land called by the same name in the Hebrew original of Num. 22:5. In the introductory lines of his inscription Idrimi describes a rebellion in the city of Khalab (Aleppo) in which his father appears to have been killed, and says that he and his brothers fled to the town of Emar, where they found asylum with his mother's sisters. He goes on:

My brothers, who were older than I, abode with me, but none of them thought the things which I thought. So I said, "Whoever hath his father's estate, let him live on it, but whoever hath not, from the children of Emar let him depart!"

I took my horses, my chariot, and my groom and fled. The wilderness I traversed and entered [a camp of] the Sutu (Semitic nomads). With them I spent the night in my chariot. The next day I departed and went to the land of Canaan (which appears here for the first time in ancient records, though it later became common). In the land of Canaan is situated the town of Ammiya; in Ammiya dwelt children of Aleppo, children of Mukishkhe, and children of 'Amau. They saw me and behold, I was the son of their lord, so they joined me. . . . And I dwelt in the midst of the 'Apiru people (perhaps the Hebrews) for seven years. I interpreted [the flight of] birds, I inspected [the intestines of] lambs, while seven years of the storm-god turned over (?) my head.

And I built ships. My troops did not tarry; I put them on the ships and traversed the sea to the land of Mukishkhe (valley of the lower Orontes); and I reached dry land in front of Mount Khazi (Casius). I went ashore and my land heard about me and brought oxen and sheep into my presence. And in a single day, as one man, the land of Ni'a, the land of 'Amau, the land of Mukishkhe, and the city of Alalakh, my capital, turned back to me. My brothers heard and came into my presence. When my brothers had been reconciled to me, I confirmed them [in the rank of] my brothers.

But Barattarna, the great king, king of the Horites (Gen. 36:20-21), had been hostile to me for seven years. In the seventh year I sent to Barattarna, king of the Umman Manda (literally: "Barbarian Hordes"), and I stated the conditions of peace of my fathers when my fathers had made peace with them and our words found favor with the Horite kings. . . . So I became king of the city Alalakh. Kings on my right hand (=south) and on my left hand (=north) came up against me, and when they heaped on the earth ruins beyond (?) the ruins of the fathers, I also caused ruins to be heaped (?) on the earth, and I made them stop fighting.

Idrimi then raided the land of the Hittites, dividing the rich spoil between the troops, the king's brothers, and his friends, while he himself took his share.

In subsequent sections of the long inscription the king tells of building a palace with the proceeds of the Hittite spoils and of furnishing it in the royal fashion of the day. He then organized the settlement and defense of his country and reorganized religious festivals and temple liturgies. Finally he handed over the reins of power to his son Adadnirari after he had reigned thirty years.

C. Egypt. 1. The Theban Renascence and the New Empire (ca. 1570-1370).—Under Hyksos suzerainty two dynasties of Theban princes continued the traditions of the Middle Empire in Egypt. The earlier of these has been identified and dated by H. E. Winlock, who calls it the Sixteenth Dynasty; the other represents the Seventeenth Dynasty of Manetho and followed its predecessor in the early sixteenth century. One of its princes revolted against the Hyksos, beginning a war of liberation which was completed by the founder of the Eighteenth Dynasty, Ahmose I (1570-1546 B.C.), shortly before the end of his reign. Ahmose even invaded Asia before his death, and the devastation wrought by Egyptian arms is witnessed by the destruction which befell a good many fortified towns of southern Canaan about the middle of the sixteenth century, immediately before the period of bichrome pottery. Though we know next to nothing about the wars of his son, Amenophis I, he must have been a great conqueror, since the Egyptian frontier in Nubia was pushed south as far as the region of the Fourth Cataract, while his successor, Thutmose I, claimed the Euphrates as his northern border at the beginning of his reign. These victories were followed by a rapid decline under Queen Hatshepsut, who seems to have lost most of the Egyptian empire in Asia. However, her young nephew Thutmose III, whom she had married and kept powerless, invaded Asia immediately after the death of his aunt and in a daring campaign regained the whole of Palestine (1468 B.C.), taking Megiddo after a siege of seven months. The king's further progress northward was considerably hampered by the fact that he had to fight against a powerful Mitanni, whereas his predecessors had begun their Syrian campaigns after the collapse of the Old Hittite Empire and before the expansion of Mitanni. The war with Mitanni continued under the reign of Amenophis II (1435-1414?), but the rise of the New Hittite Empire (see below, p. 261) induced his son Thutmose IV (1414?-1406) to make a treaty with Mitanni, which was renewed in the two following reigns, until Mitanni in its turn was finally conquered by the Hittites.

2. The Religious Reform (ca. 1370).—The following age was outwardly one of the most brilliant in the history of Egypt, but inwardly it was sown with the seeds of decay. During the thirty-six years of Amenophis III's reign (1406-1370) Egypt's foreign policy remained static, and the bureaucratic corruption which spread rapidly during all weak reigns began to undermine the administration at home and alienate the subject peoples abroad. Amenophis married a commoner named Teye, who exercised a dominant role in the affairs of state, as we see not only from native inscriptions but also from the Mitannian correspondence. Egypt had become prodigiously wealthy and the resulting luxury was eating like a cancer at its vitals. Under the New Empire the process of democratizing life after death which had begun in the Feudal Age, when nobles adopted the funerary rites which had belonged previously to the king alone (see above, pp. 246-47), was extended to any commoner who could afford the price. The new sacred book, which brought together spells and religious texts that were deemed efficacious in protecting the soul of the deceased from the dangers of the journey to the hereafter, is called by Egyptologists the "Book of the Dead"; its oldest copies go back to the fifteenth century B.C., before this work had become stereotyped. It is hard to think of any process which could so thoroughly demoralize the social conscience as the faith of that day in Egypt; in this faith all the sanctions of religion were marshaled to support the belief that a wicked rich man who spent money on magic and mummery could thereby assure for himself a splendid eternity. At the same time the temples and priesthood flourished as they apparently never had before, and the wealth of the nation was drawn almost irresistibly to them. Higher culture ceased to be productive; the language of literature was the extinct speech of the Middle Kingdom, and there is no evidence that a single literary masterpiece (from our point of view) was composed between 1600 and 1375 B.C.

The time was obviously overripe for revolution; it came in the shape of a new "teaching" (sbaye), which substituted solar monotheism for the complex polytheism of traditional religion, replaced the fossilized art of the past by a new art intended to reproduce nature, and made the speech of the court the new literary language of the country. It is impossible to believe that the weak Amenophis IV (1370-1353) was responsible for such a tremendous change in basic ways of thinking. Some unidentified genius, probably working through the young king's gifted mother Teye, is a far more likely candidate. The roots of the new religion go back to the Heliopolitan solar theology of the Pyramid Age (see above, pp. 245-47), and it is foreshadowed in texts from the reign of Amenophis III. It may have been in Heliopolis itself that this revolt against the powerful priests of Amun at Thebes was hatched. However this may be, the king and his courtiers took the revolution very seriously, and for some twelve years they tried to suppress the cult of Amun and of all other gods except the solar disk, in honor of which the king changed his name to Akhenaton (or Ikhnaton). Singularly beautiful hymns to the solar disk attest the high idealism of the revolution, but it had no foothold among the masses, and indeed seems to have made no effort to improve their wretched condition. Between the hatred of the old nobility and the apathy or aversion of the common people, the reform movement collapsed within a year or two after the death of the heretic king, and his new city of Akhetaton ("Horizon of the Solar Disk") was abandoned some twelve years after its foundation.

The monotheistic hymns to the Aton (solar disk) as the only god are of very great historical importance. Dating from the century immediately preceding Moses and the Israelite conquest of Palestine, they undoubtedly exerted some influence on the monotheism of early Israel, though the extent and character of the influence are naturally subject to debate. The following prayer from Amarna illustrates the "theology" of the Aton cult very well:

Fair is thy rising, O Harakhti ("Horus of the Two Horizons"), he who rejoices on the horizon in his name Shu, which is the sun, thou living sun-god besides whom there is none other; who strengthens the eye with its rays, who has created all that exists. Thou dost rise on the horizon of heaven in order to give life to whatever thou hast created, all men [all beasts], everything that flies and flutters, and all creeping things in the earth. They live when they see thee; they sleep when thou dost set.

In this prayer the Aton appears as the sole deity, without competitors, and the creator of everything, like Yahweh in early Israel.

In the famous hymn to the Aton, which in some ways strikingly resembles Ps. 104, we have emphasized the universality of Aton's sway:

Fair is thine appearance on the horizon of heaven,
Thou living Aton, who first lived!
When thou dost rise on the eastern horizon
Thou dost fill every land with thy beauty.
. . . .
All beasts are content with their herbage;
Trees and plants are green.
The birds fly from their nests,
Their wings praise thy spirit (literally, "thy ka");
All wild beasts leap on their feet,
Whatever flies and flutters,
It lives when thou dost rise for them.

Ships sail north and sail again south,
And every road is open because thou dost rise.
The fish in the river leap before thee;
Thy rays are in the interior of the sea.
. . . .
How much it is, what thou hast created,
O thou sole god, like whom there is no other!
Thou hast created the earth according to thy wish,
When thou wert alone:
All men, cattle, wild beasts,
Whatever is on earth, walking on its feet,
And whatever soars above, flying with its wings.
The lands of Syria and Nubia, the land of Egypt—
Every man dost thou put in his place,
Providing what they need.
Each one has his food and his allotted time of life;
Their tongues are separate in speech,
And so are their forms;
Their skin is different,
For thou makest the foreign peoples different.
. . . .
All remote foreign peoples, thou makest what sustains their life.
Thou hast placed the Nile in heaven,
That it may come down for them [in rain]
And break over the mountains like the sea,
To water the fields in their towns.

3. The Amarna Tablets.—Toward the end of 1887 an Egyptian peasant woman accidentally discovered the archives of cuneiform tablets from Akhetaton which we call "the Amarna Tablets." Since their initial publication in 1889 and 1892 many additional tablets and fragments have turned up in private hands or have been found in organized excavation at the site of Tell el-Amarna, until we now have nearly four hundred pieces. Most of them are letters written by the kings of Babylonia, Assyria, Mitanni, Hatti (the Hittites), Alashiya (Cyprus), Arzawa (Cilicia), as well as by many local princes in Syria and Palestine, to Pharaoh Amenophis III and his son, Akhenaton. The tablets which interest us most were written by local scribes on behalf of their Canaanite masters. Among them are letters from Byblos (Gebal), Ugarit, Sidon, Tyre, Berytus (Beirut), Damascus, Accho (Acre), Megiddo, Hazor, Shechem, Jerusalem, Hebron (probably the capital of Shuwardata), Gezer, Lachish, Ascalon (Ashkelon). Since the scribes had learned Akkadian in school from other Canaanite scribes, who had learned it in their turn from still others, the Akkadian which they wrote was a curious jargon, quite different in detail from contemporary Babylonian. This official language had developed from a more archaic stage of Akkadian about the seventeenth century B.C. and had acquired a strange grammar of its own, strongly influenced by the fact that the native tongue of most of these scribes was Canaanite. A few of the letters, notably one written from Shechem by Lab'ayu, are so full of

Canaanitisms that whole lines may be read as straight Canaanite.

These documents exhibit an extraordinary mixture of groveling before Pharaoh and of plotting and counterplotting against him. Different princes accuse each other and their Egyptian commissioners (assigned to watch them) of disloyalty. In the face of such intrigue it is obviously quite impossible for us to determine who, if any, was more honest than his fellows. The letters paint a depressing picture of corrupt administration and insecurity of life and property. Under the exactions of ruthless Egyptian tribute collectors, an increasing proportion of the people are said to be joining the "bandits," also called the 'Apiru, a name which may be the source of our "Hebrew." The references to them in the Amarna letters and other sources come from Syria as well as from Palestine; they appear as a separate group along with other ethnic groups, but the name is also used as a mere synonym for "brigand," or the like.

We now have about 350 Amarna letters, as well as about a score found in Palestine, Phoenicia proper, and southern Syria. Some 300 letters came from Semitic-speaking territory. In this article we can quote only two or three of them. Typical of the state of the country about 1370 B.C. is the following letter (one of six) from 'Abduheba, prince of Jerusalem (perhaps about 150 years before Joshua):

To the king, my lord, say: Thus 'Abduheba, thy servant. At the two feet of my lord the king seven times and seven times I fall. Behold Milkilu (prince of Gezer) does not break his pact with the sons of Lab'ayu and with the sons of Arzayu in order to acquire the land of the king for themselves. When a governor does such a deed as this, why does not my king call him to account? Behold Milkilu and Tagu (probably prince of Gath in Sharon)! The deed which they have done is this, that they have taken it, [namely] Rubutu. And now Jerusalem [itself]—if this land [really] does belong to the king—why is it as loyal to the king as Gaza (seat of the Egyptian resident)? Behold the land of Gath-carmel, it belongs to Tagu, and the men of Gath have a garrison in Bethshean (excavated by Alan Rowe). Or shall we do like Lab'ayu, who gave the land of Shechem to the 'Apiru (perhaps the Hebrews)? Milkilu has written to Tagu and the sons of [Lab'ayu] as follows: "Ye are allied with my house. Yield all the demands made by the men of Keilah, and let us break our pact with Jerusalem!" The garrison which thou didst send through (the Egyptian officer) Haya son of Miyare, Addaya (Canaanite in Egyptian service) has taken and has placed in his residence in Gaza, and he has sent twenty men to Egypt. Let my lord know that there is no royal garrison with me. So now, as my king lives, truly the master of the stable, Puwure, has taken leave of me and is in Gaza; so let my lord look out for him! And let the king send fifty men as a garrison for the land! The entire land of the king has rebelled. Send me Yanhamu and let him take care of the land of the king!

To the scribe of the king, my lord: Thus 'Abduheba, thy servant. Present eloquent words to the king. I am much inferior to thee; I am thy servant.

Of the names of towns mentioned in this letter six are biblical; the seventh—Rubutu—does not appear in the Bible but is found several times in other sources. Lab'ayu's capital was Shechem, later the second most important city of the northern kingdom. An Amarna letter from Lab'ayu is written in a Babylonian which is so full of Canaanite words and phrases that it might just as well have been written entirely in the native language of Bronze Age Palestine:

To the king, my lord, say: Thus Lab'ayu, thy servant. At the feet of my lord I fall. With respect to what thou hast written to me, "Are the men strong who have seized the town? How can the men be stopped?" [I reply] By hostile action was the town seized, despite the fact that I had taken an oath of conciliation and that, when I took the oath, an [Egyptian] officer took the oath with me. The town has been seized together with my god. I have been slandered/betrayed before the king, my lord.

Further, if even ants are smitten, they do not accept it [passively] but they bite the hand of the man who smites them. How can I hesitate this day when two of my towns have been seized?

Further, even if thou shouldst say, "Fall beneath them and let them smite thee!" I should still repel my foe, the men who seized the town and my god, the despoilers of my father, yea, I would repel them!

Note the curious tone of truculence which pervades this letter; Lab'ayu of Shechem was protected by the wooded mountains of central Palestine against the swift retaliation which might be expected by his servile brethren on the coastal plain. The otherwise unknown Canaanite proverb about the ant may be compared with two very ancient proverbs about the same insect found in Prov. 6:6 and 30:25.

A letter from the same general age, found at Shechem in 1926, throws a very interesting side light on education of boys in Canaanite Palestine:

Unto Birashshena say: Thus Baniti-[Ashirat(?)]. From three years ago until now thou hast caused me to be paid. Is there no grain nor oil nor [wine(?)] which thou canst send? What is my offense that thou dost not pay me? The boys who are with me continue to learn; their father and their mother every [day] alike am I. . . . Now [behold], whatever [there is] at the disposal [of my lord let him send] to me and let him inform me!

An interesting letter to the prince of Taanach in northern Palestine from his brother in the

Jordan Valley south of Bethshean has been recovered. The writer complains of having been ambushed and robbed, and asks for various parts of a chariot and weapons; at the end of the letter he says that he wants to be married:

To Rewashsha say: Thus Akhiyami. May the lord of the gods protect thy life. My brother art thou and there is no friend here (?). And thou wilt remember that I was ambushed in Gurra, so give me today two chariot wheels and an axle, also two . . . And when the making of the axle has been finished, send it to me by Purdaya. Further, charge thy towns that they do their work (*corvée*). Anyone who attacks the towns is responsible to me. Now behold me, that I do well by thee! Further, if there are copper arrows let them be given to me. Further, let Elrapi'i come to me at Rakhabu (south of Bethshean) or I will send my man to thee, for truly I wish to be betrothed.

D. Palestine and Syria. 1. The Ras Shamra Texts.—In 1929 C. F. A. Schaeffer began excavations at Ras Shamra on the coast of northern Syria, opposite Cyprus. In eleven campaigns he excavated a considerable area in the upper stratum and a much smaller part of the second level. The name of the city was found to be Ugarit, said in the Amarna Tablets to be proverbial for its wealth. His most important finds consisted of two large groups of tablets from the early fourteenth century B.C., one consisting mainly of religious texts in a new cuneiform alphabet, the other including several hundred tablets in the same script or in Akkadian, all of official and administrative character. Many individual tablets in both cuneiform scripts add materially to the cumulative effect of the principal finds. The religious texts have been found to consist mainly of large and small fragments of mythological epics, including parts of the texts of Baal and Anath, Keret, and Aqhat or Danel (Daniel). The new script was deciphered by Paul (Edouard) Dhorme and Hans Bauer almost immediately after Charles Virolleaud first published a sample of the texts. Ugaritic is a Northwest-Semitic dialect closely related to contemporary Phoenician and a little less closely to biblical Hebrew. The language of the epics is more like biblical Hebrew than is the language of ordinary letters and administrative documents; the content of the epics proves that they had originally been composed in Phoenicia proper, south of Ugarit. When we compare the new sources for early Canaanite literature with the Bible, we find extraordinarily close resemblances in diction and style with the oldest Israelite poetry (the Song of Moses, the Oracles of Balaam, the Song of Deborah, the Blessing of Moses, etc., as well as with the oldest psalms, such as Pss. 18; 29; 68). In archaizing Hebrew poetry we find similar resemblances, for ex-

ample, in the psalm of Habakkuk and in a few later psalms. The rich new data from Ugarit are rapidly revolutionizing our entire approach to the history of Hebrew literature, and everything written on this subject before the late 1930's is already in need of revision. However, it is difficult to exaggerate the difference between the ethical monotheism of the Old Testament and the brutal coarseness of many polytheistic narratives in the newly discovered Canaanite literature. Between the religion of early Israel and that of the Canaanites there is a wide and deep gulf.

The surviving fragments of the great Epic of Baal and Anath reflect a series of loosely connected myths in poetic dress, all of which probably go back centuries before the date of our extant copies (which precede the great earthquake of about 1360 B.C.). The following are some of the better preserved and more intelligible passages which deal with the mythical adventures of the great Canaanite storm-god Baal and his sister Anath. These selections follow the theoretical, but plausible, order proposed by H. L. Ginsberg.

Apparently the earliest episode extant is the conflict between Baal and the mighty water dragon called Prince Sea and Judge River. Sea and river figured in Hebrew allegory as primordial foes of Yahweh (e.g., Ps. 89:25; Hab. 3:8). Some deity is describing forthcoming events:

"Let words proceed from her (Anath's?) mouth,
From her lips her speech!
And as she raises her voice,
The foundations of the throne of Prince Sea will shake."
And Koshar-and-Khasis will reply,
"I have told thee, O Prince Baal,
I have repeated, O Cloud Rider—
Behold thine enemy, O Baal,
Behold thine enemy shalt thou smite,
Behold thou shalt destroy thy foe! [1]
Thou shalt take thine eternal kingdom,
Thine everlasting dominion."
Koshar will bring two maces
And will give them their names:
"Thy name is Yagrush—
Yagrush, drive Sea,
Drive Sea from his throne,
River from the seat of his dominion!
Thou shalt swoop in the hand of Baal,
Like an eagle from his fingers;
Strike the back of Prince Sea,
The breast of Judge River!"
It will strike the back of Prince Sea,
The breast of Judge River—
The mighty one, Sea, shall droop,
His pinnacles shall tremble,
His visage shall sink.
Koshar will bring two maces,
And will give them their names:

[1] Cf. Ps. 92:9.

"Thy name is Ayamur (?) —
   Ayamur (?), . . . Sea
. . . Sea from his throne,
   River from the seat of his dominion!
Thou shalt swoop in the hand of Baal,
   Like an eagle from his fingers;
Strike the skull of Prince Sea,
   The forehead of Judge River."
Sea will collapse
And will fall to the ground!

In another important section of the Baal Epic there is a long series of intrigues and actions on behalf of Baal, who wishes a temple like the other gods. His sister Anath supports him in this project, while El's consort, the biblical Asherah, seems to alternate between hostility and favor. Again we find ourselves in a typical prospective narrative, with a deity foretelling what is going to happen, or what ought to happen:

Then let her (Asherah) direct herself
   Toward El at the Source of the Two Rivers,
      In the midst of the Fountains of the Two Deeps.
She shall pass through the Field of El
   And shall enter the pavilion of the King, Father
      of Years,
At El's feet she will bow and fall down,
   Will prostrate herself and pay him obeisance.
As soon as El espies her,
   He will put away grief and will smile,
His feet on the footstool he will place,
   And he will entwine his fingers.
He will lift up his voice and will cry,
"Why has the Lady, Asherah of the Sea, come,
   Why has the Creatress of the Gods arrived?
Art thou indeed hungry . . .

   Or art thou indeed thirsty . . . ?
      Eat then and drink!
Eat bread from the tables,
   Drink wine from the vessels,
      From gold cups blood of trees.
Behold the love of El holds thee,
   The affection of the Bull sustains thee."
And the Lady, Asherah of the Sea, shall reply,
"Thy command, O El, is wise,
   Thy wisdom lasts forever,
      A life of good fortune is thy command!
Our king is Triumphant Baal,
   Our judge, above whom there is no one!
Each of us will bring his gift,
   Each of us will bring his purse;
Let the Bull, his father El, call ships,
   El, the king who brought him into being,
Let Asherah and her sons call,
   Elath and the band of her companions!"

In the next column we have further details about the extent of the projected preparations for building Baal's temple:

Call a caravan into thy temple,
   A trading company (?) into thy mansion;
The mountains shall bring thee much silver,
   The hills a treasure of gold,

They shall bring thee glorious gems (?).
So build a house of silver and gold,
   A house of pure lapis lazuli.

The following episode from the Baal Epic describes the sanguinary fury of the goddess Anath and her slaughter of men. Unfortunately, we do not know what occasioned such an outburst of vindictive cruelty:

The Seven Maidens (Pleiades) were hidden,
   The Propitious Ones and the Bees (?) were at rest,
      The gates of Anath's house were bolted,
When she met the youths on the slopes of the moun-
      tain.
And then Anath did battle,
   Mightily she hewed down the folk of the two
      cities;
Smiting the people of the Seacoast,
   Crushing the men of the Rising Sun.
Beneath her are heads like pellets,
   Above her are hands like locusts,
      Like . . . the hands of warriors.
She fastened the heads to her back,
   The hands she bound to her girdle;
Knee-deep she plunged into the blood of champions,
   Up to the throat (?) in the gore of warriors.

. . . .

Her liver swelled with laughter,
   Her heart filled up with joy,
      Anath's liver with success,
When she plunged knee-deep into the blood of
   champions.

. . . .

She washed her hands, did Maid Anath,
   Her fingers, did the . . . of the Peoples;
She washed her hands in the blood of champions,
   Her fingers in the gore of warriors.

Baal's death and subsequent resurrection form the theme of what was probably the largest portion of the epic. After Death (Mot) had conquered Baal in battle and had carried him down to the nether world, the bad news was brought to the gods:

"We two came upon Baal lying on the ground—
Dead is triumphant Baal,
   The Prince, lord of the earth, has perished!"
Then the Kindly One, God of Mercy (?),
   Came down from the throne, sat on the footstool,
   And from the footstool he sat on the earth;
He poured dust of mourning on his head,
   Earth of sorrow (?) on his skull.

After a certain lapse of time Anath overtook Death (Mot) and fought a mighty battle with him over her lost brother:

Like the heart of a wild cow for her calf,
   Like the heart of a wild ewe for her lamb,
      So was the heart of Anath for Baal.
She caught Death by the fold of his garment,
   Seized him by the hem of his robe

. . . .

She seized Death, son of the gods,
    She cleaved him with a sword;
She winnowed him with a fan,
    She burned him in the fire;
She ground him in a hand mill,
    She sowed him in the field;
That the birds might eat his remnants.

When we next reach an extant portion of the epic, Anath's exertions for Baal have been rewarded, and the great storm-god lives again:

"In a dream, O Kindly One, God of Mercy (?),
    In a vision, Creator of Creatures,
The heavens rained oil,
    The dry valleys flowed with honey;
So I know
That Triumphant Baal lives,
    That the Prince, Lord of Earth, is alive!"

.   .   .   .

The Kindly One, God of Mercy (?), rejoiced,
    His feet he placed on the footstool,
    He put away grief and he smiled.
He lifted up his voice and cried,
    "Now will I sit and rest,
    And my spirit shall be at rest in my breast."

2. The New Hittite Empire (ca. 1375-1200).—
The collapse of the Aton heresy was roughly synchronous with the rapid emergence of the New Hittite Empire, which under Suppiluliumas (*ca.* 1370-1335 B.C.) overran Mitanni as far as Lebanon, the Upper Tigris, and the frontiers of Babylonia. Egypt lost several of its Syrian provinces, which it apparently made no serious effort to recover during the forty years which followed the death of the heretic king. During this interval the Hittites were kept too busy resisting the expansion of the new Middle Assyrian Empire under its vigorous monarch, Ashuruballit (1356-1321 B.C.), to undertake the conquest of Egypt itself, which could otherwise scarcely have resisted a Hittite invasion. In 1309 a high military officer of Haremhab (who had himself been general of the army under the feeble successors of Akhenaton), named Ramses, made himself king with the help of his energetic son Seti I (1308-1290 B.C.). Ramses I died almost immediately after founding the Nineteenth Dynasty, but his son set about reorganizing the weakened Egyptian empire in Palestine and southern Syria. Since the Ramesside family came from the district later called Tanis, the new residence of the king was established there, and Seti's son Ramses II (1290-1224 B.C.) called it by his own name, "House of Ramses," or Raamses (Exod. 1:11) for short. The identification of the Ramesside capital with later Tanis (biblical Zoan) has been convincingly demonstrated by Edouard Montet as a result of his years of excavation there; occasional objectors forget the simple fact that if Ramses is moved

to an insignificant site in the neighborhood, the great city of Tanis, with all its Ramesside monuments, is left without any contemporary name! From their residence in the northeastern delta the kings of the Nineteenth Dynasty continued the war against the Hittites, which reached its climax in the Battle of Kadesh on the Orontes (1286 B.C.), but was finally brought to an end by a treaty (1270 B.C.), the text of which has been found in an Egyptian translation at Thebes and in an Akkadian rendering at Boğazköy. The reason for the cessation of hostilities between the Hittites and Egypt is not far to seek; Assyria was then continuing its steady encroachment on the Mitannian province of the Hittites, under two vigorous rulers, Adad-nirari I (1298-1266 B.C.) and his son, Shalmaneser I (1265-1236 B.C.), the second of whom liquidated the last Hittite holdings east of the Euphrates. Under Shalmaneser's son, Tukulti-Ninurta I (1235-1199), the Middle Assyrian Empire reached its climax with the conquest of Babylonia.

VIII. The Early Iron Age (ca. 1200-900)

A. The Eclipse of the Empires.—With the end of the Bronze Age and the rapid spread of the use of iron came also the end of the creative age of the ancient Near East. Original intellectual and artistic productivity came almost to an end in Egypt with the Ramesside Age; in Mesopotamia the influx of fresh Aramaean blood revivified the country and brought fresh life in the sphere of higher culture as well as in material affairs, but the religion of the country and its canonical literature remained virtually unchanged until the last days of Babylonia. On the other hand, new life was pulsing in the arteries of hitherto unknown peoples, such as the Israelites and the Hellenes.

1. The Inscription of Merneptah (ca. 1224-1216).—The first contemporary indications of the emergence of Israel are found in the blackened ruins of Canaanite towns of the thirteenth century B.C. and in the surprising couplet with which Merneptah (1224-1216 B.C.) ends an enumeration of conquered foes in the poem celebrating his triumph over the Libyans:

The people of Israel is desolate,   it has no offspring;
Palestine has become   a widow for Egypt!

2. The Peoples of the Sea (ca. 1175).—
The Hellenes appear dramatically, though briefly, in the history of Egypt and Palestine as one of the barbarian elements taking part in the invasion of the Peoples of the Sea. In the inscriptions of Merneptah and of Ramses III (*ca.* 1180-1149) a number of peoples from the northern shores of the Mediterranean are men-

tioned among the invaders who swarmed across to raid or to settle the coasts of Africa, Egypt, and Palestine; among them are the Aqiwasha (probably the Achaeans), the Tursha (certainly the Tyrsenians or Etruscans), the Shardina (certainly the Sardinians), the Pelast (certainly the Philistines), the Tjikal (probably the Sicilians, called "Sikel" in the *Odyssey*), and the Danuna (probably the Danaans, an archaic name for the Hellenes). Though the invading hosts were repelled, they occupied the coastland of Palestine. At the same time as these peoples attacked by sea, other barbarous peoples (including some of those just mentioned) flooded Asia Minor and Syria, destroying the Hittite Empire and razing many cities, Ugarit among them. There are a number of allusions, early and late, in the Old Testament to the great impression made on the Israelites and their neighbors by this inundation from the north (e.g., Num. 24:24).

B. The Rise of New Powers.—After the reign of Ramses III, who had briefly tried to restore the glories of his precursors, Egypt fell into a state of chronic disorder, and Phoenicia and Palestine gained complete autonomy after the middle of the twelfth century B.C. Since the Hittite Empire had collapsed under the blows of the northern barbarians, there was no power strong enough to dominate Syria and Palestine. After the great victories of Tukulti-Ninurta I, Assyria relapsed into a state of weakness and was unable to maintain its old boundaries. Under Tiglath-pileser I (1116-1078 B.C.) a brilliant series of victories restored much of Assyria's lost prestige: the Phrygians and other barbarians who had put an end to the Hittite Empire were forced back from their foothold in southern Armenia; Babylonia was reduced to a vassal state; the nomadic Aramaeans were checked, and northern Syria and Phoenicia were added for a short time to the Assyrian Empire. But Tiglath-pileser's successors did not possess his energy; the empire gradually lost ground, yielding its outposts on the Euphrates to the Aramaeans in the reign of Ashurrabi II (1012-972), and being finally pushed back to the borders of Assyria proper under the latter's grandson, Tiglath-pileser II (966-935 B.C.). There was thus no longer any power which offered a serious threat to the growing might of Israel under David and Solomon.

1. The Phoenicians.—Within a single century (1250-1150 B.C.) the Canaanites of Palestine, southern Syria, and Phoenicia suffered a series of terrific blows which sent them reeling back into Mount Lebanon and the narrow coastal strip which it protected. These blows came in the form of successive invasions of Canaan by the Israelites, the Sea Peoples, and the Aramaeans.

The few remaining Canaanite towns in Palestine and in Syria east of Lebanon were too weak to stand by themselves (cf. the account of the fall of Laish, Judg. 18:27-28) and gradually yielded. Phoenicia itself was devastated by the Sea Peoples; Ugarit was then destroyed and was never reoccupied; Tyre must have been peculiarly exposed, and Sidon, according to Timaeus, a very reliable Hellenistic historian who followed Phoenician tradition, seems to have fallen about 1194 B.C. Timaeus states that the Sidonians crossed over to Tyre and built it. Since Tyre was a famous Canaanite city in the Bronze Age, it had probably just been destroyed and was founded anew by the Sidonians, who still claimed Tyre as a colony on their coins of the early Hellenistic Age. According to the Tyrian tradition reported by Josephus on the authority of Menander of Ephesus, Tyre was founded about 1198 B.C.; both traditions agree with the fact that the attack by the Sea Peoples must be dated in the years just before their defeat by Ramses III (*ca.* 1175).

Thanks to the new art of digging and lining cisterns with waterproof lime plaster, the Phoenicians were able to build towns and villages where none had existed before, and Tyre was no longer dependent on fresh water from the mainland, as had been true in the Late Bronze Age. Moreover, the still more recent spread of iron, which followed the destruction of the Hittite monopoly by the Sea Peoples, soon made the felling of the great conifers of Lebanon and the construction of fleets of ships much easier than it had been. The use of iron nails made it possible to build much larger seagoing vessels. The Report of Wen-Amun, a narrative of the adventures of an Egyptian envoy to Byblos about 1060 B.C., gives us a vivid picture of the resulting state of affairs. The Byblians and the Sidonians were the two principal Phoenician maritime groups, but the former were still in the ascendancy under a King Zakarbaal. Owing presumably to the insecurity of the seas in the days of widespread piracy which followed the collapse of the Mycenaean thalassocracy (command of the seas) in the late thirteenth century B.C., the Phoenicians were organized into a system of *khubur*, or trading syndicates, which were closely allied with contemporary ruling personalities. The system is twice referred to in the Old Testament, with the use of the same term (Job 41:6; II Chr. 20:35-37). Not long afterward the Sidonians gained the ascendancy over the Byblians, who became a minor state. It seems to have been Hiram I of Tyre (969-936 B.C.) whose energy led to the first great step in the Phoenician exploitation of the Mediterranean: the partial colonization of Cyprus and the sending of Phoenician trading expeditions into the western Mediterranean. Quite aside from Greek and biblical evidence for the early date of Phoenician expansion is the fact that a recently published Phoenician inscription from Cyprus must be dated in the century following Hiram's death, and that there are several Phoenician inscriptions from Sardinia whose script places them also in the ninth century. One of them, a fragment of an edict from Nora in southern Sardinia, mentions Tarshish in connection with Shardin (Sardinia); Tarshish was almost certainly the name of the Phoenician mining colony on the island, where there had already been a great copper mining industry in the preceding centuries.

2. The Israelites.—In recent years excavations have thrown much light on the progress of the Israelite occupation of Palestine, as well as on the character of its material culture. Excavations at sites where an intensive Canaanite occupation in the Late Bronze Age was followed by Israelite reoccupation after the Conquest show that very little time elapsed before the resettlement. This is notably true of two sites at which I have excavated: Tell Beit Mirsim (probably Kiriathsepher) and Bethel. At other sites where there was no Late Bronze occupation, as at Tell en-Naṣbeh (Ataroth?) and Beth-zur, we find Israelite settlement beginning in the twelfth century, at the latest. This situation proves that the Israelites were not merely desert nomads, but were ready to settle down immediately after the Conquest. On the other hand, we find a striking decline in the quality of material culture at these sites, where the contrast between the excellence of Canaanite masonry and the crudeness of the Israelite masonry which replaced it is most extraordinary. We also find that Palestine was in a state of relative anarchy in the early part of the Iron Age. At Bethel, for example, there were no fewer than four successive phases of occupation in the twelfth and eleventh centuries, each followed by a destruction by fire. About the middle of the eleventh century a number of towns were destroyed, among them Shiloh, Tell Beit Mirsim, and Beth-zur; since Shiloh was certainly attacked by the Philistines after the capture of the ark (I Sam. 4:12-22) and was not reoccupied as a town for several centuries (Jer. 7:12, 14; etc.), we may safely credit the destruction of the other towns also to the Philistines.

Under the monarchy progress was rapid. Saul's citadel at Gibeah (Tell el-Ful), which I excavated, was still extremely simple in construction, though planned according to the patterns of its time and solidly built of hammer-dressed stones. The few constructions of David's time which can be identified with some plausibility were still simple, showing as yet no trace of Phoenician influence. Under Solomon all is changed, just as might be inferred from the chapters in Kings and Chronicles which describe his wealth and his building operations, emphasizing the part played in them by Phoenician craftsmen and enterprise. Excavations at Megiddo, Gezer, and Ezion-geber on the Red Sea have demonstrated the introduction of new techniques in building and decorative art. They have also demonstrated an extraordinary development of wealth and power. The stables at Megiddo and traces of contemporary stables at several other towns of tenth-century Palestine confirm the biblical statements about Solomon's interest in horses and chariots (I Kings 4:26-28; II Chr. 1:14; 8:6; 9:25). Nelson Glueck's work at Tell el-Kheleifeh illustrates what is said about metallurgy in I Kings 7:46. Above all, discoveries at Megiddo, Taʿyinat, and elsewhere have brought to light some of the northern models after which the temple of Solomon was planned and decorated.

3. The Aramaeans.—In the Late Bronze Age we have many references to the Semitic nomads of the Syrian Desert, then called the Ahlamu, who were scattered from the Persian Gulf to the Upper Euphrates basin. Tiglath-pileser I calls the Aramaeans, who are first mentioned in his inscriptions, the Aramaean Ahlamu, that is, the Aramaean Bedouin. From other sources it is clear that they occupied much of Syria after the collapse of the Hittite and Egyptian power there in the early twelfth century. We can, however, no more speak of a migration of Aramaic-speaking nomads from Central Arabia at this time than we can describe the Amorite inundation as coming from Central Arabia. Linguistic and other evidence make it clear that Aramaic developed as the local speech of some district of the Middle or Upper Euphrates basin, from which it spread among the seminomadic population in the oases and around the fringes of the Syrian Desert. As Aramaic spread, nomadic tribes which might better be described as Arab, joined Aramaean tribal groups. In later centuries this process was accelerated until Aramaic became the principal language of all Mesopotamia, Syria, and Palestine, and the secondary language of the entire Persian Empire. Having no urban culture of their own, the Aramaeans who settled eastern Syria and northwestern Mesopotamia adopted the Syro-Hittite culture which they found in the country. We recall that the Hittites had conquered Syria in the early fourteenth century B.C.; in the following two centuries they established a firm political organization, whose basic forms persisted into the following Iron Age. The monuments of Carchemish from Iron I illustrate the survival of Hittite art and religion. The partial decipherment of the Hittite hieroglyphic inscriptions from Syria shows even more strikingly how the old royal dynasties survived, continuing Hittite traditions down into the Aramaic period. Both the Assyrian inscriptions and the Old Testament allusions to Syria in this period call it "Land of the Hittites." In northern Mesopotamia the Hurrian tradition prevailed over the Hittite, but the difference between the Aramaean monuments of Gozan (Tell Halaf), from the tenth century, and those of Sam'al and Carchemish in Syria, from the same general period, is slight. As the Assyrians swept over the young Aramaean settlements in the ninth century, the Aramaeans lost no time in making necessary adjustments; from then on Aramaic culture became rapidly Assyrianized.

IX. The Middle Iron Age (ca. 900-600)

A. Egypt.—While Assyria was painfully awaking from its long lethargy, Egypt had re-entered the Asiatic stage under a vigorous new dynasty of Libyan origin. After the reign of Ramses III the Ramessides of the Twentieth Dynasty relapsed into helpless impotence, while the high priests of Amon at Thebes gained power steadily at the expense of the crown. Finally, about 1065 B.C., the high priest Hrihor took the title of king, and was followed by a line of Theban high priests, which was soon merged with the Tanite house founded by Smendes about the same time. This new dynasty, partly Theban and partly Tanite, is called the Twenty-first Dynasty (*ca.* 1065-935 B.C.). The richly adorned mummies of several of its later kings have been discovered at Tanis by Edouard Montet; the insignificance of their tombs illustrates the impotence to which they had been reduced by their powerful Libyan generals. The last of these generals, Shishak, founded the Twenty-second Dynasty, which had its seat at Bubastis, half way between Tanis and Heliopolis. On the walls of the temple of Amon at Karnak Shishak recorded the names of the Palestinian towns which his troops had taken in the fifth year of Rehoboam (I Kings 14:25); the list includes numerous north Israelite as well as Judahite names; most interesting, however, is a list of names of Edomite towns, several of which can still be identified. In the excavation of Megiddo a large fragment of a stele of Shishak came to light, confirming the inclusion of Megiddo in the Shishak list. The northward extension of Bubastite influence is further attested by the remains of two statues found at Byblos; one represents Shishak and bears an inscription of Abibaal, king of Byblos, and the other represents Shishak's son Osorkon I, with an inscription of Elibaal, king of Byblos. The increasing power of the Sidonians had endangered Byblos, which had evidently accepted nominal overlordship in return for aid against the common foe. However, the Bubastites in their turn relapsed into impotence, and there is no trace of any serious attempt on their part to intervene in the affairs of Asia after the reign of Osorkon II (middle of the ninth century).

B. Mesopotamia. 1. The Assyrian Renascence (883-826).—Tiglath-pileser II's son, Ashurdan II (934-912 B.C.), began the arduous process of recovering Assyria's lost empire. His son, Adadnirari II (911-891), was more successful, driving back the advancing Aramaean tribes and extending Assyrian power to the Habur River. The next king, Tukulti-Ninurta II, successfully continued the conquest of Mesopotamia, so when Ashurnasirpal II (883-859) became king, he found Assyria well organized and ready for new wars of conquest. His voluminous inscriptions heap up nauseating details about the suppression of the surrounding peoples. While the brutality of the Assyrians was proverbial (Nah. 2-3), no other king has left such descriptions of the harrowing details, in which Ashurnasirpal seems to have found sadistic pleasure. Captives were flayed alive, impaled, burned alive, buried alive; their skins were used to decorate walls and their heads were employed to construct triumphal pyramids. In spite of the bitter hostility which such savagery aroused, the organized might of Assyria was so great that resistance crumbled in all directions. Before the end of his reign he invaded Syria, reaching the coast and receiving the tribute of Phoenicia. We do not know whether he measured swords at that time with Benhadad of Damascus, who was easily the most powerful king in Syria. However, his successor, Shalmaneser III (858-824 B.C.), invaded Syria in 853; at Qarqar on the Orontes he met the coalition of Western princes, which included a strong contingent from Ahab of Israel and even a detachment from Egypt. Apparently the Assyrians won the decision but lost so heavily that they were unable to follow up their victory. However this may be, Shalmaneser returned again and again to Syria, and by 841 had obtained the submission of Israel, though without being able to force the new Syrian king, Hazael, to his feet. In 826 the Assyrian king's son rebelled against his father, and by the time the rebellion was suppressed by Shamshi-Adad V, at least six years later, Assyrian power had to be consolidated anew.

2. The Assyrian Expansion (825-745).—Shamshi-Adad had married an Aramaean princess, one Sammuramat, who seems to have been an exceptional woman. For the first four years of her son's reign, Adad-nirari III (810-783), she was queen regent. We know nothing of the details of her administration, but it made a tremendous impression among her Aramaean kinsmen, who remembered her in their tales of the past, calling her by her native name Shamiram, which the Greeks popularized as Semiramis. As soon as her son was free (806 B.C.), he invaded the West, which he claims to have overrun as far as Philistia. Damascus surrendered to Assyrian arms, paying heavy tribute. From early in Adad-nirari's reign until the death (745 B.C.) of the last of the three sons who followed him successively on the throne, there is no royal inscription to give us information about the state of the empire. The Eponymous Chronicle and some miscellaneous official documents indicate that the highly organized Assyrian administrative system continued its somewhat ponderous grinding, while the empire lost ground slowly on all sides. In the north the kings of Urartu (Ararat) steadily built up their own empire, which came to blows repeatedly with Assyria and gradually pressed southward. The Medes and Babylonians gained their independence, and so did most of Syria. Provincial Assyrian governors assumed autonomous powers and some of their inscriptions do not even mention their masters' names.

3. The Assyrian Apogee (744-630).—At this critical point in the history of Assyria there was a change of dynasty, and a man of unknown background adopted the famous name of Tiglath-pileser, becoming the third of that name (744-727 B.C.). He found the Assyrian Empire in a most precarious state, following some forty years of rule by the weak sons of Adad-nirari III. The Aramaean states of Syria were in rebellion; the kingdom of Urartu was slowly closing its pincers on the Assyrian homeland. The new king acted promptly: in 743 he smashed the might of Urartu and its Syrian allies; in 740 he captured Arpad, capital of the leading Aramaean state of that time in northern Syria. From then on the Assyrian advance was rapid; Philistia was invaded in 734, and the following two years were devoted to the conquest of Damascus, which became an Assyrian province. Palestine seems to have remained passive under the onerous Assyrian yoke for a number of years, but not long after the accession of Shalmaneser V (726-722), son of Tiglath-pileser III, Samaria revolted. Unfortunately there is a break in our information for several years, so we know little about details.

The next Assyrian king, Sargon II (721-705 B.C.), was again a usurper who assumed a famous name. He proved himself, like Tiglath-pileser III, to be much more energetic and successful than kings who were born to the throne. In the year of his accession Samaria fell. Sargon tells us succinctly about the fall of Samaria in his inscriptions, probably not enlarging on the event because it was really his predecessor's achievement. The following is the longest account, which can be restored almost completely from duplicates; phrases restored from parallel texts are not indicated as such in the translation:

> At the beginning of my reign, in my accession year (about January, 721 B.C.), Samaria I captured. . . . I carried away 27,290 of its inhabitants and levied fifty chariots from among them for my standing army. . . . The city I rebuilt, making it better than before, and I settled in it people from other countries which I had conquered. One of my officials I set over them as governor and I imposed tribute on them according to Assyrian practice.

Sargon continued the deportation policy which seems to have been inaugurated on a systematic basis by Tiglath-pileser III, and thenceforth rebellions were generally followed by removal of most of the rebellious population to some other region and importation of other conquered peoples into the depopulated areas. Before the end of the Assyrian Empire this practice had resulted in such complete shuffling of subject peoples that little local particularism was left. On the other hand, the amorphous mass of apathetic humanity over which the Assyrians now ruled proved to be the worst possible foundation on which to erect a dynamic state. When Assyria collapsed, the structure fell like a house of cards. During Sargon's reign numerous new provinces were set up; if he had been followed by a wise administrator, the Assyrian Empire might have become much stronger in the next generation. As it was, Sennacherib (704-681) proved to be a vindictive braggart, hated by his subjects and his own family. In 701 he invaded Palestine and defeated the Ethiopian and Egyptian army sent by Shabaka to oppose him. Hezekiah escaped loss of his throne only by paying heavy tribute and sacrificing territory.

In his famous inscription (Taylor Prism) Sennacherib tells at some length of his invasion of Judah in 701:

> In the course of my campaign I besieged Beth-dagon, Joppa, Bene-berak, Yazor (Azuru), towns belonging to Sidqia, who did not submit to me at once; I conquered and plundered them. The rulers, the notables, and the people of Ekron, who had thrown Padi, their king, into iron fetters since he remained loyal to his oath of allegiance to Assyria, and had turned him over to Hezekiah the Judahite —who imprisoned him unlawfully as an enemy— were afraid. They called for aid on the kings of Egypt and on the archers, the chariotry, and the cavalry of the king of Cush (Ethiopia)—a host without number—and they came to their help. In the environs of Eltekeh they were drawn up in battle array before me and they sought recourse to arms. Relying on Ashur, my lord, I fought with them and

defeated them; in the clash I captured the commander of chariotry and the royal sons of an Egyptian king together with the commander of chariotry of the Ethiopian king, all alive. The towns of Elteкeh and Timnah I besieged, captured, and plundered. . . .

As for Hezekiah, the Judahite, who did not submit to my yoke, forty-six of his strong fortified towns and the small towns in their environs without number I besieged and captured with ramps of trampled earth (aggers), with the onslaught of battering-rams, with the storming of shock troops, with tunnels and breeches in the wall and demolition. I brought out 200,150 people, young and old, male and female, together with horses, mules, asses, camels, cattle large and small without number, and counted them as spoil. Him I shut up in Jerusalem, his royal city, like a caged bird; I made a chain of forts around him and forced back those who escaped through the city gate to their doom (?). His towns, which I had plundered, I gave to Mitinti, king of Ashdod, Padi, king of Ekron, and Sillibel, king of Gaza; and I reduced his territory. I increased the tribute and the special gifts due my lordship, and imposed them upon them (the kings just listed).

As for Hezekiah himself, the terror and the splendor of my lordship overwhelmed him and he sent after me to my capital, Nineveh, the mercenaries and his elite troops, which he had brought in and had used as auxiliaries in order to strengthen the city of Jerusalem, his capital, together with thirty talents of gold, eight hundred talents of silver, precious stones, antimony, stibium, lapis lazuli in large chunks, ivory beds, ivory chairs (i.e., pieces inlaid with ivory), elephant skins, ivory, ebony, boxwood, and all kinds of valuable treasure, his daughters, palace women, male and female musicians. He also sent his courier to deliver the tribute and to make [formal] submission

In 689 Sennacherib, irritated by his constant wars with the Chaldeans who had infiltrated into Babylonia during the preceding three centuries, destroyed Babylon, apparently trying to erase it completely from the map. His son, Esarhaddon, was to be known for his great effort to rebuild the ancient capital. During his reign (680-669) he conquered Egypt and beat back the first attacks of the Cimmerian and Scythian hordes which were inundating Asia Minor and Armenia. Known to the biblical writers as Gomer and Ashkenaz, these barbarians destroyed the Phrygian monarchy of Midas and nearly conquered Lydia before they were checked.

The last great king of Assyria was Ashurbanipal, the Sardanapalus of the Greeks (668-631?), long remembered for the splendor of his reign and the catastrophe which followed his death. He was faced with difficult problems, which he solved in the Assyrian way by hammering at them with the whole might of the empire. Egypt rebelled and was subdued; the sack of Thebes in 663 made a great impression on the world of the day (Nah. 3:8). Esarhaddon had placed Ashurbanipal's uterine brother, Shamashshumukin, on the throne of Babylon; civil war broke out, dividing the empire. Finally Babylon was stormed in 648 and the rebels were savagely punished. Among the allies of Babylon had been Elam and the Arabs; both were crushed in a series of bitter campaigns which came to an end about 640 B.C. The stupid devastation of Elam removed a potentially valuable buffer state between Assyria and the growing power of the Iranians. The Arab tribesmen had taken advantage of the distraction of the Assyrian army during the civil war and had inundated eastern Syria and Palestine all the way from the Palmyrene to Mount Seir; the little states of Moab and Edom never recovered from this blow, but fell completely into Arab hands before a century had passed.

Ashurbanipal's reign represents the culmination of Assyrian civilization. The reliefs of his royal palaces are the best, from our modern Western point of view, of all the Assyrian monuments which have survived. His library at Nineveh, thousands of tablets from which are now in the British Museum, has saved for us many ancient literary and religious works which would otherwise have been lost, such as the Akkadian Poem of the Flood. The agents of the Assyrian king scoured Babylonia to collect or copy old tablets for the royal library. However, the royal inscriptions themselves were written in an ungrammatical Assyrian which cannot be compared with the language of the texts of Sargon and Sennacherib. The royal scribes already spoke Aramaic, and Akkadian was fast becoming a foreign tongue to them. As so often in history, the conquered Aramaeans had subdued their conquerors, and cuneiform Assyrian was almost completely displaced by alphabetical Aramaic as the language of commercial and administrative documents before the death of the great king himself.

4. The Assyrian Decadence (630-612).—The Assyrian Empire was tottering, and the surrounding nations were gathering for the kill. The first country to rebel and turn against its former master was Egypt. In the late eighth century the Libyan Bubastites had been conquered by the Nubian kings of Ethiopia, Kashta, and Piankhi. The Ethiopians founded the Twenty-fifth Dynasty, which lasted only a generation, from about 705 to 663; the last king Taharko, biblical Tirhakah (689-663), was driven out of Egypt by Esarhaddon in 671, and the efforts of the Ethiopians to regain control of the country proved unsuccessful. The son of a member of an old Bubastite family, who had taken the Assyrian side in the contest between would-be foreign masters, finally threw out the Assyrian officials while Ashurbanipal was busy with the war against his brother. About 650, Psammetichus, son of Necho of Sais, became king of independent Egypt, founding the Twenty-sixth, or Saite, Dynasty (which was officially dated from Necho's death in 663). When the power of Assyria began to collapse toward the end of the Pharaoh's reign, he was clever enough to take the Assyrian side against the still greater menace of the Medes, but he doubtless exacted stiff conditions from his erstwhile masters.

The second country to rebel against Assyria was Babylonia, which had now become solidly Chaldean; Nabopolassar declared his independence about 625 B.C., the date of his official accession. The Medes, under their king Cyaxares, made common cause with the Babylonians, and beneath the force of the blows from both south and east, the end could not be long delayed. In 612 Nineveh fell and the Assyrian king was killed. For a few years thereafter an Assyrian who assumed the famous old name of Ashuruballit maintained the fiction of empire at Harran, the old home of Abram, but with the fall of Harran, the Assyrians ceased to be a nation. Meanwhile their Egyptian allies annexed Palestine and Syria, having defeated Josiah of Judah in 609. But four years later the Egyptians were decisively beaten by the Chaldeans at Carchemish, and soon afterward they were ousted from Asia.

The events attending the downfall of Assyria are succinctly and accurately described, with precise dating, in a tablet belonging to the Babylonian Chronicle, which was published by C. J. Gadd in 1923. Previously it had been impossible to give anything but a very general picture of what may have happened, without exact dates or details. The value of this tablet for the interpretation of Kings and such prophetic books as Nahum is very considerable. Unfortunately, the tablet is badly broken in places. It begins in the tenth year of the Babylonian King Nabopolassar (616-615 B.C.) and closes in his seventeenth year (609-608). In 612 Nineveh was besieged and taken by storm; our chronicle describes the event as follows:

[In the fourteenth year] the king of Akkad (Babylonia) levied his army, and Cyaxares, king of the Manda Hordes, marched to meet the king of Akkad. . . . They met one another. The king of Akkad . . . and Cyaxares . . . he ferried across and they marched along the Tigris . . . against Nineveh. . . . From the month of Sivan until the month of Ab three battles (?) . . . a mighty assault against the city they made. In the month of Ab . . . there was a great massacre (?). At that time Sinsharishkun, king of Assyria. . . . Many captives from the city, beyond counting, they carried away. The city they turned into mounds and heaps of ruins.

C. Palestine and Syria.—Archaeology has thrown a great deal of light on the material culture of Palestine, Phoenicia, and Syria during Iron II (ninth-sixth centuries B.C.). The material culture of Phoenicia and Palestine long retained the pattern which had been developed in the tenth century. Recent excavations at Megiddo and Samaria show the survival of the Phoenician culture of the Solomonic Age well down into the eighth century B.C. This is illustrated by the buildings of the ninth and early eighth centuries, and especially by the ivory inlay from Samaria, which so closely resembles Phoenician and Syrian ivories from the same period previously discovered at Calah and Khadattu in Assyria as well as in various parts of the Mediterranean basin. In Syria excavations at Carchemish, Sham'al (Zinjirli), and elsewhere show that Syro-Hittite art was replaced during the late ninth and early eighth century by the Assyrian style. Palestine became Assyrianized somewhat later, in the course of the late eighth and early seventh centuries.

Our knowledge of the life of the common people comes principally from the excavation of Tell Beit Mirsim, where many well-preserved houses of the eighth and seventh centuries were cleared. From this site, supplemented by finds elsewhere, it has become clear that in Judah at the time of Isaiah and Jeremiah the ordinary citizen lived much better than had been supposed by previous archaeologists, working with inadequate material and sometimes (as at Gezer and Jericho) in an entirely different period. There was more room in a house than had been supposed, and hygienic conditions in particular were much better than had been assumed before the excavation of Tell Beit Mirsim. Most unexpected was the discovery of a surprising uniformity in the way of life in this representative town, with no indication of great wealth or poverty. Everything about the town of this period suggests freedom and relative equality, together with public security, all in sharp contrast to the situation in early periods. Evidently the prophets had not labored in vain—though much that was objectionable doubtless remained to vex the god-fearing man of Judah.

X. The Late Iron Age (ca. 600-331)

A. The Neo-Babylonian Empire (612-539).— We have a wealth of written material from the Neo-Babylonian Empire, but nearly all of it consists of business documents and private letters. During the years before 1914 the German excavators of Babylon discovered many administrative records, but very few of them have yet been published. The royal inscriptions are lengthy, but seldom go beyond accounts of building operations, following a tradition of many centuries which prevented the Babylonian kings (as distinguished from the Assyrian) from mentioning their wars.

Nabopolassar's son, the Chaldean King Nebuchadrezzar II, took the name of a famous predecessor and ruled forty-three years (604-562 B.C.). Under him the boundaries of the Neo-Babylonian Empire were fixed along the lines which it maintained until its downfall in 539 B.C. His empire included Babylonia and Susiana (Elam), Mesopotamia west of the Tigris, Syria and Palestine, together with considerable areas in North Arabia. His invasion of Egypt came late in his reign and did not succeed in establishing Chaldean domination in the Nile Valley.

Under Nebuchadrezzar the language of the empire became Aramaic. There was a revival of Babylonian culture, but cuneiform was used only for formal documents, and the Aramaic tongue displaced it for all practical affairs, just as we are told by the later author of Daniel. Commerce developed and craftsmen were brought in from all parts of the empire, as well as beyond it, for use in the colossal building operations of the king. Babylon and its temples and palaces were completely rebuilt (Dan. 4:30). Chief among these constructions was the great temple tower of Marduk, god of Babylon, called "House of the Foundation Platform of Heaven and Earth" (Etemenanki), which evoked the memory of the legendary Tower of Babel. Its length, breadth (both at the bottom) and height were each about three hundred feet.

We know little about the wars of Nebuchadrezzar except what we find in the Bible, for the reasons already indicated. However, excavations and surface surveys have established the accuracy of the biblical tradition of thoroughgoing devastation. Jerusalem and all other towns of any significance were demonstrably or probably destroyed and not rebuilt until after the Restoration. The savagery of the Chaldean invasion is amply illustrated by the results of the excavation of such towns as Tell Beit Mirsim (probably Debir) and Lachish (Tell ed-Duweir). These two towns were twice destroyed within a decade or two, thus illustrating the record of two destructions in 598 and 587 B.C. in Kings. Both pottery and inscriptional data agree on the chronology of the destruction, so there is no excuse for the skepticism sometimes heard about the validity of the evidence.

Evidence from inscriptions has been slowly accumulating. In 1948 an Aramaic papyrus found in a sixth-century deposit at Saqqarah near Cairo was published by André Dupont-Sommer; it contains part of an Aramaic letter, probably from the local prince of Ashkelon, telling his Egyptian suzerain about the advance of the Chaldean armies, perhaps in 603 B.C. At Lachish J. L. Starkey discovered numerous ostraca (potsherds inscribed in ink), which vividly portray the state of mind among local officials in the Lachish area just before the invasion of 589 B.C. Written in beautiful classical Hebrew of the type familiar from the prose sections of Jeremiah, these ostraca are of equal significance to the historian and the biblical philologist. Some administrative tablets from Babylon, published by E. A. Weidner, list rations distributed in or about the year 592 B.C. among royal pensioners of all kinds, among whom is Jehoiachin, king of Judah, together with five royal princes and several other Jews living in the capital city. It is interesting to note that his name is written *Yaukin*, with exactly the same abbreviated form of the name which we find on contemporary seal inscriptions from Judah itself.

After Nebuchadrezzar's death the Chaldean state lasted only twenty-three years longer. Its only important ruler was also its last, Nabonidus, who associated his son, the Belshazzar of Daniel, with him on the throne. Nabonidus came from an old family of Harran in northwestern Mesopotamia, and he showed a striking preference for Aramaean gods and ways, preferring the cult of Sin to that of Marduk of Babylon, and carrying on antiquarian researches for the purpose of recovering half-forgotten cults and temples. His excavations in order to find ancient foundation records endear him to the modern archaeologist, but since he rebuilt the sanctuaries which he had first probed for records of the past, his antiquarian activities cost the state dear. Hints in the records of Nabonidus show that he also fought a number of wars, especially, it would seem, for the control of the caravan routes from the spice lands of South Arabia. These caravan routes had been steadily increasing in importance for several centuries, and the spice trade reached a high point of prosperity at this time, as we know from archaeological discoveries in Arabia and Palestine. For some reason Nabonidus decided to make his home in the oasis of Tema (Teima) in North Arabia, and here he spent years, turning the administration of the empire over to his son Belshazzar. Through his religious and fiscal policy he bitterly antagonized the priests of Marduk in Babylon, who plotted against him and welcomed the Persian invasion when it finally came in 539 B.C. We possess a poetic composition denouncing Nabonidus and praising Cyrus, who was welcomed no less, it would seem, by the priests of Marduk than by the Jewish exiles.

B. The Persian Empire (539-331).—A new Indo-European power now created an empire more powerful than any previously known.

Many centuries after the irruption of the Indo-Aryans into Iran (Persia) and the countries to the east and west came a similar migration of the seminomadic Iranians from the plains of Turkestan into Iran. The date of this migration is still uncertain, but the indications are that it began about the twelfth century and was practically completed by the tenth century B.C. Probably about the ninth century B.C. arose the great Iranian prophet, Zoroaster, who undertook to replace the old polytheism by a new dualism between good and evil, truth and falsehood, light and darkness. The old high gods, which the Iranians had shared with their Aryan kinsmen in India, were replaced by angels, very much as in contemporary Israel. To judge from the Avesta, which transmits the hymns and ritual of Zoroaster, the dualism of Iran was, however, much more primitive in character than the religion of the prophets of Israel. His teachings gained ground slowly, sects arose, and there was so much fusion of Zoroastrian teachings with the old polytheism (forming a mixed faith known as Magianism) that it cannot be said that Zoroastrianism was adopted by the Persian people as their national faith until the Parthian period, before and after the Christian Era. The description of Persian religion which we find in the pages of Herodotus, who wrote in the middle of the Achaemenian period, has very little in common with what we find in the Avesta.

In the seventh century B.C. the Iranian settlers created two powerful kingdoms in western Iran, one in Media, south of the Caspian Sea, and another in Persis, east of Babylonia and Susiana. Inscriptional evidence indicates that the Persian state rose first to prominence, since inscriptions of Ashurbanipal mention Cyrus I, king of Persia about 640 B.C., whereas no kings of Media appear by name in the inscriptions of this Assyrian king. But soon afterward, the Median King Phraortes was succeeded by Cyaxares, under whom the Medes gained ground with extraordinary rapidity. Their conquest of Assyria proper after storming Nineveh in 612 B.C. made them the most powerful people of southwestern Asia. Cyaxares next attacked and conquered Armenia, after which he proceeded against the Lydian Empire in central and western Asia Minor. A long war between two well-matched adversaries was brought to an end by a treaty, after the solar eclipse of 585 B.C. (predicted by the Ionian philosopher Thales) had frightened both parties into a stalemate. The last independent king of Media, Astyages, was defeated by Cyrus II, king of Persia, in 550 B.C., after a revolt of the former's Iranian troops. Thereafter Media and Persia became a dual monarchy under the permanent rule of a prince of the Achaemenian line.

Cyrus climaxed his career of conquest by overrunning Lydia (546) and the Babylonian Empire (539), dying in 530. His moderation in victory gained him a great reputation for magnanimity, well known from the Bible and Xenophon's *Cyropaedia*. To judge from cuneiform inscriptions written on his orders or to honor him, he understood how to endear himself to the conquered peoples. In Babylon he befriended the aggrieved priests of Marduk, but he also helped other cities and restored their cults.

The Cyrus cylinder describes the Babylonian reaction to the Neo-Babylonian regime of Nabonidus and the triumph of the Achaemenian king very vividly:

The worship of Marduk he (Nabonidus) suppressed (?); he did evil to his city daily. . . . [Oppressing its people] with a yoke beyond relief, he destroyed them all. Because of their lamentation the Lord of the Gods became terribly angry . . . their boundaries. The gods dwelling in them left their abodes, angry because [Nabonidus] had brought them into Babylon. Marduk . . . turned again to all the settlements which had been laid waste and restored the people of Sumer and Akkad, who had become like corpses; . . . he had mercy on them. All of the lands he surveyed and inspected, searching for a just prince, one according to his heart, whose hand he might take. Cyrus, king of Anshan, he called by name, he announced his name for rule over the universe. . . .

When I entered into Babylon in peace and established the seat of rule in the princely palace amid rejoicing and jubilation, Marduk, the great lord, caused the generous heart of the Babylonians to . . . me, while I strove daily to worship him. My widespread troops walked in Babylon in peace, and I did not permit anyone to terrorize any part of the land of Sumer and Akkad.

All the kings enthroned on the royal dais in all parts of the world, from the Upper Sea to the Lower Sea, the dwellers in . . . , the kings of the land of the West, all of whom dwell in tents, brought their valuable tribute and in Babylon they kissed my feet. . . . As for the cities east of the Tigris, which had been founded in antiquity, I returned the gods who dwelt in them to their shrines, and caused them to inhabit dwellings forever. All of their people I gathered and restored to their settlements.

The decree of Cyrus restoring the old city of Jerusalem to the Jews and facilitating the building of the temple, though often called a forgery by biblical scholars, is thoroughly in keeping with what we know of his policy elsewhere, and the language suits both period and circumstances so well that most historians have recognized its substantial authenticity.

His son, Cambyses II (529-522), continued

his father's policy of expansion by the conquest of Egypt and Cyrene (525), but later tradition agrees that he was not equal to his father in ability. After a brief interruption during the Magian revolt, another branch of the Achaemenian house came to power with the victory of Darius I (521-486). Darius Hystaspis was perhaps one of the greatest organizers of history. Under him the Persian Empire attained its greatest extent, from the Indus Valley to Macedonia, and from central Asia to south Arabia. There is good reason to believe that he espoused Zoroastrianism, though in what precise form remains uncertain. Under Darius the system of provinces ruled by members of the leading families arose; these governors were called satraps, and their rule became hereditary. Darius understood how to curb their power, by establishing roads and couriers who carried the royal mails with a speed previously unknown in the ancient world. The statements of Greek authors about this postal system have been illuminated by the discovery of official letters written by a great satrap named Arsames, toward the end of the fifth century, to his officials in Egypt.

The administrative system of Darius is now being elucidated through the interpretation of the Elamite documents found at Persepolis and published by G. G. Cameron. Under Darius, Aramaic documents appear in Egypt, and Aramaic was increasingly used as the common speech of the empire. Darius also introduced a system of coinage in imitation of Greek precedents, since there had never been any coinage before his time east of the Greek cities of Asia Minor.

Unfortunately for the stability of Persia, both Darius Hystaspis and Xerxes I spent the energies and resources of the empire in an increasingly unsuccessful war against the Greeks. The subsequent history of the empire is largely a story of intrigue and open war between the powerful satraps, some of whom were equal to the king himself in wealth and prestige. This was certainly true of the satrap Arsames, already mentioned, since he ruled the entire southwestern part of the empire, including Babylonia, Syria, Palestine, Egypt, and adjacent territories.

Our knowledge of Achaemenian history must be pieced together from many sources, among which the data supplied by Greek historians continue to rank high. For reliable information regarding conditions of life in the Persian Empire we turn increasingly to the discoveries of archaeologists. Mention has been made of the administrative documents in Elamite cuneiform which have been discovered at Persepolis. In Babylonia proper many thousands of economic texts and private letters have been excavated, and many of them have been published. From Egypt we have papyri and leather documents in demotic Egyptian and Aramaic. The latter come mostly from the Jewish colony at Elephantine, near the southern frontier of Egypt at the First Cataract. Two large collections of papyri from Elephantine were published by Sayce-Cowley and Eduard Sachau, and many more papyri and ostraca from different parts of Egypt were subsequently added to the already large collection. Recent discoveries have added notably to this material. Dupont-Sommer is about to publish some three hundred ostraca which were excavated nearly fifty years ago. A large collection of papyrus rolls in the Brooklyn Museum is now being published by E. G. Kraeling. Another group of some eight rolls from Hermopolis in Middle Egypt is soon to be published by Murad Kamil. And finally there is the group of leather rolls belonging to the Arsames correspondence, which will be published by G. R. Driver. All these documents belong to the fifth century B.C., and the light which they have already shed and will continue to shed on the period of Nehemiah and Ezra promises soon to make this period one of the clearest in biblical history instead of one of the most obscure.

The Aramaic documents preserved in Ezra are written in the same language that we find in these documents, though they have been slightly modernized in spelling. The administrative and political picture which we have in the books of Ezra and Nehemiah is being illustrated in numerous details by the contemporary Aramaic documents which have been discovered. There can no longer be any doubt whatever in the mind of any scholar who takes the trouble to acquaint himself with these discoveries, with regard to the authenticity of the material contained in these two books. It has been said, for example, that the word *pithgam* is a Greek loan word, borrowed in the Hellenistic period, and therefore a proof that the Aramaic sections of Ezra are late forgeries. Now we find the same word, in the same meanings, in the correspondence of Arsames and elsewhere in the Aramaic documents of the fifth century B.C., contemporary with the period to which they refer. Another illustration is found in the word *darkemonim*, "drachmas," mentioned in Ezra and Nehemiah as a standard of coinage employed in the Persian period. Critical scholars have scoffed at the suggestion that the drachma might have become known to the Jews before the conquest of Alexander about 330 B.C. However, archaeological research has long since established the fact that the Athenian (Attic) drachma standard spread before the middle of the fifth century over Syria and especially Palestine. Moreover, a considerable number of Jewish coins imitating Attic originals have come to light; they are in part inscribed with the name "Judah," leaving no doubt as to their origin. These are only a few out of many striking examples which could be given. We are accordingly entirely justified in insisting on the historicity of the matter which we find in Ezra and Nehemiah, which yields a picture entirely consistent with our new knowledge of the period.

Thanks to these discoveries, as well as to the finds in Egypt and Babylonia, we can reconstruct a picture of an active and rapidly expanding Jewish Diaspora (Dispersion), centering in the temple of Yahweh at Jerusalem, and cultivating its sacred literature and traditions assiduously. During the last seventy years, more or less, of the independent existence of the Persian Empire, the high priests of Jerusalem enjoyed a considerable amount of autonomy, probably according to the model set by the contemporary high priests of Hierapolis (Bambyce) in northern Syria. These high priests were permitted to strike their own silver coins and levy their own taxes for the maintenance of the sanctuary. This was probably one of the most productive periods of Jewish scholarship, during which most of the canon of the Old Testament reached the standard form which we know. The Dead Sea scrolls of the last two centuries B.C. have confirmed the evidence from the Greek translation for early canonization of most of the literature of the Hebrew Bible. Hellenistic dating is no longer admissible for any of the Prophets or the Psalter, and has become very doubtful for the didactic writings—with the exception of Ecclesiastes and Daniel. The peaceful conditions which in general prevailed in Judah during the last decades of the Achaemenian Empire favored the burst of Jewish scholarly activity to which we owe the canonical form of many books of the Old Testament.

The Jews also took a very active part in the commerce and public life of their day. They played a leading role in the development of the Aramaic civilization of their day without which the later adaptation of Jewry to Hellenism would have been difficult. In the last two centuries of the Persian Empire normative Judaism was established throughout Jewry, and the first great step toward a future world Christianity was taken.

XI. Selected Bibliography

ALBRIGHT, W. F. *Archaeology and the Religion of Israel.* 2nd ed. Baltimore: Johns Hopkins Press, 1946. Complements the author's *From the Stone Age to Christianity.*

———. *Archaeology of Palestine.* Harmondsworth: Penguin Press, 1949. Cheap and up to date.

———. *From the Stone Age to Christianity.* 2nd ed. Baltimore: Johns Hopkins Press, 1946. A still further revised German edition appeared in 1949. Comprehensive but somewhat difficult to read.

BREASTED, J. H. *A History of Egypt from the Earliest Times to the Persian Conquest.* 2nd ed. New York: Charles Scribner's Sons, 1912. Still standard, but needs revision in detail.

BURY, J. B., COOK, S. A., and ADCOCK, F. E., eds. *The Cambridge Ancient History.* New York: The Macmillan Co., 1923-27. This important work is detailed but now out of date.

FINKELSTEIN, LOUIS, ed. *The Jews: Their History, Culture, and Religion.* New York: Harper & Bros., 1949. Contains chapters by W. F. Albright, E. J. Bickerman, Ralph Marcus, *et al.* on biblical history and literature in the light of the surrounding world. Up to date.

FRANKFORT, HENRI and H. A., WILSON, JOHN A., JACOBSEN, THORKILD, and IRWIN, W. A. *The Intellectual Adventure of Ancient Man.* Chicago: University of Chicago Press, 1946. Also reprinted in large part in a Pelican edition. The contributions of Frankfort, Wilson, and Jacobsen are particularly good.

McCOWN, C. C. *The Ladder of Progress in Palestine.* New York: Harper & Bros., 1943. Very good.

OLMSTEAD, A. T. *History of Palestine and Syria to the Macedonian Conquest.* New York: Charles Scribner's Sons, 1931. Comprehensive but already out of date.

PRITCHARD, JAMES B., ed. *Ancient Near Eastern Texts Relating to the Old Testament.* Princeton: Princeton University Press, 1950. A magnificently planned and executed volume containing an enormous mass of material from all lands of the ancient East, translated by the foremost authorities in the various fields. Recommended without reservation.

STEINDORF, GEORG and SEELE, KEITH C. *When Egypt Ruled the East.* Chicago: University of Chicago Press, 1947. Very good.

WRIGHT. G. ERNEST and FILSON, FLOYD VIVIAN, eds. *The Westminster Historical Atlas to the Bible.* Philadelphia: Westminster Press, 1945. Excellent.

The Biblical Archaeologist. A quarterly review of current archaeology relating to the Bible. Ed. G. Ernest Wright. Published by the American Schools of Oriental Research, New Haven, Connecticut. Cheap and excellent. Recommended without reservation.

THE HISTORY OF ISRAEL

by THEODORE H. ROBINSON

"Thy father was an Amorite, and thy mother a Hittite" (Ezek. 16:3). This was the judgment passed by a prophet early in the sixth century B.C. Such a statement may have been in a sense metaphorical, but there seems to be little doubt that it contains a large element of historical truth. Israel was a mixed people.

I. The Origins (ca. 1800-1500 B.C.)

There were three successive waves of "Semites" moving northward out of Arabia, in migrations which were separated by a millennium or more (see article "The Old Testament World," pp. 233-71). The earliest of the three, speaking an Akkadian language, occupied southern Mesopotamia, and spread up the great river valleys, subduing or dispossessing their Sumerian predecessors. The second wave, to which may be given the general title of "Amorite," seems to have broken out in two directions, moving into Mesopotamia in the east and into Syria-Palestine in the west. The third wave, which followed the second more closely than the second did the first, again took a double line, though it was stronger in the west than in the east. Its speech came under the general heading of Aramaic.

Probably all three waves started in their new areas as nomads, living at first on the borders of the cultivated land, and gradually, either by conquest or by peaceful penetration, settling down to agricultural life. The process was less complete in the case of the Aramaic-speaking group than in the other two, and till a comparatively late period Aramaean states were few,

though they played an important part in the carrying trade of the Fertile Crescent, and a form of Aramaic became the international language of the Near East, superseding Akkadian till it in turn gave way to Arabic.

These Semitic elements, however, were far from being the only sources of Israelite blood. Constant irruptions from without added their share to the physical ancestry of peoples dwelling in the Fertile Crescent, the most important being of Hurrian origin. It was this rather than any true Semitic group which gave to the Israelites—and, indeed, to the peoples of northern Mesopotamia—their characteristic physical appearance. The name "Hittite" applies to this element of the common ancestry.

Physical ancestry, however, plays only a secondary part in determining the sense of nationality. What counts is tradition, and it is a striking fact that the traditions of Israel nearly always refer to an Aramaean group which, invading Palestine early in the Iron Age, succeeded in imposing much of its religion and social theory on the country, though in some parts its contribution to the actual blood of the population was by no means the largest. It is to this group of Aramaean tribes that the term "Israel" properly applies.

This view of Israel's origins is confirmed by the evidence of philology. Classical Hebrew is a mixed language (see article, "The Language of the Old Testament," pp. 220-32), and the mixture is of a type found elsewhere in the case of a minority conquest. The history of the English language is a good parallel. For a fairly long period Anglo-Saxon and Norman-French remained apart, but in the end the tongue of the subject people retained its position, and that of the conquerors merely added to the vocabulary. In England the process took about

The dates proposed in this article are the same as those adopted in W. O. E. Oesterley and T. H. Robinson, *A History of Israel* (Oxford: Clarendon Press, 1932). Cf. another chronology in article, "The Old Testament World," pp. 233-71; cf. also article, "Chronology, Metrology, Etc.," pp. 142-52. Editors.

three centuries, but it may have been shorter in Palestine, since the Amorite and Aramaean languages are much nearer to one another than Anglo-Saxon is to Norman-French. The parallel still holds good, however, for classical Hebrew is basically the speech of pre-Israelite Canaan, with the addition of certain words from the Aramaean stock.

The actual traditions of Israel, as preserved in the book of Genesis, nearly all go back to the nomadic stage of the Aramaean tribes. Some of them made their way into Egypt during the Hyksos period (*ca.* 1800-1600 B.C.), where they were eventually reduced to slavery and put to forced labor. Thence they were rescued through Moses, and after a period of wandering in the wilderness to the south and east of Palestine, made their way into that country.

So much may be regarded as certain, but a number of questions as to details are still unsolved. Most of the narratives which have come down from pre-Mosaic days deal with individuals, the eponymous ancestors of the tribes which were eventually amalgamated into the nation of Israel. There is a strong feeling among scholars that these narratives should be interpreted as tribal rather than personal history, especially where they are concerned with marriages and other connections between individuals or groups. In the story of Jacob, for example, we are told that he had two wives, Leah and Rachel, and that he also had children by their maids, Zilpah and Bilhah. From Leah were descended six tribes, of whom the most prominent was Judah, and from Rachel the Joseph tribes, to which was attached that of Benjamin. The subordinate tribes grouped themselves around these. According to the interpretation just suggested, these narratives represent coalitions of tribes which united to constitute more or less close entities of a type similar to the Greek "amphictyony."

The important fact is that the Aramaeans not only contributed to the physical ancestry of Israel but also brought into the country, and to some extent retained, the social mentality of the nomad. This is marked by an intensely strong emphasis on the value of persons as compared with things, and by a passion for freedom. The nomad has little that can be called private property; his wealth consists in his cattle (camels, sheep, or more commonly, goats), and belongs to the tribe as a whole rather than to any individual. It follows that he is free from many problems which arise in a more complicated order of society. At the same time, he lays stress on matters which affect the life of his group as a whole, with the result that he usually holds to a high standard of sexual morality and insists on those laws and customs which are designed to protect tribal life; the most obvious of these is the principle of blood revenge. His religion is simple, at least in externals, and his deities are those which are bound up with community living. The gods worshiped by the ancestor of Israel may have been originally eponymous ancestors or semi-animistic spirits of the wilderness. But they are of little importance for the actual history of Israel, since all earlier cults were absorbed in or superseded by that of Yahweh, at least in the official religion of the united people.

The pre-Aramaean inhabitants of Palestine were of Amorite stock (to judge from their language), though with a very strong admixture of other blood, particularly Hurrian. Their political organization was that of the small "city-state," and in the period at which the history of Israel began, all Palestinian states were nominally subject to Egypt. But Egyptian control was incomplete and spasmodic, short periods of activity being interspersed with longer intervals of comparative neglect. The arts were well developed, especially that of architecture, and a number of sites which have been excavated reveal a fairly high degree of skill. The main occupations were agriculture and trade, the latter being stimulated by the geographical situation of Palestine, which forms the only land bridge between Africa and the Eurasian continent. A system of civil law was well established, and though it might vary in detail, it was generally of a type found elsewhere in western Asia. Religion was a somewhat complicated matter, centering around ancient sanctuaries and everywhere involving the worship of the fertility-powers. There was a regular calendar of agricultural festivals, and animal sacrifice was an essential part of the cultus. Human sacrifice seems to have been frequently practiced, and the ethical standard demanded by the religion was normally low—as is not uncommon in early agricultural communities. The whole order of society offered as strong a contrast as possible to that of the nomad, and the history of Israel as an independent people settled in Palestine is conditioned by the way in which these two types of organization and political theory reacted on one another.

II. *Moses and the Exodus (After 1500 B.C. [?])*

The history of Israel properly begins with Moses. Both in politics and in religion the nation owes to him its very existence as well as that character which made it unique among the peoples of the ancient world. He himself was endowed with an extraordinary personality, and legendary developments which may now color the traditions concerning him are an evidence of his magnitude. Curiously enough, there is practically no mention of his name outside the Pentateuch till the time of the Exile or later, but the earliest strata in the Law are full of him, and both prophets and poets frequently refer to the work that he accomplished.

Moses appeared among those Hebrew nomads who were subjected to forced labor in Egypt. The tribe to which he belonged is not known with certainty, although it is traditionally Levi (a name which in itself raises problems), but there are indications which suggest that the oldest tradition made him an Ephraimite. According to the Exodus narratives he was born during a period of oppression, when the very existence of his people was threatened. Adopted by an Egyptian princess, he was brought up at the royal court, though he seems to have been aware of his Hebrew descent. The time came when he was forced to leave Egypt, and he sojourned with a nomadic tribe, probably that of the Kenites (wandering smiths, the ancient equivalent of "tinkers") who were at the time making their home among some Midianites, probably in the Sinaitic Peninsula. There he married, and after forty years' absence from Egypt, received the divine commission to return and lead his people into freedom, that they might offer sacrifice to Yahweh, the God who had appeared to him. In Egypt he found the reigning Pharaoh unwilling to accede to the demands of Yahweh, in spite of a series of calamities which reinforced the deity's claims. Finally, as the Hebrews could not go to Yahweh's home to observe the Spring festival (Passover?), Yahweh came to Egypt, with disastrous consequences for the Egyptians. The Hebrews escaped in the confusion, and were pursued to the edge of the Sea of Reeds. Divine interference enabled them to cross this barrier in safety, while their pursuers were swallowed up by the returning waters. Then the people made their way to Sinai (Horeb?) where they entered into a "covenant" with Yahweh. In that act the nation was born.

Such is a rough outline of the story handed down to us in the Pentateuch. Many questions arise, some of them no longer soluble, and it is impossible here even to indicate them all (see Intro. to the book of Exodus, pp. 833-48). The account of Moses himself has been so shaped as to conform in many ways with the familiar pattern of the deliverer-hero, of whom we have several examples in the Ancient Near East and elsewhere. The figure of Moses combines Hebrew and Egyptian elements; his name is probably a hypocoristic modification of something like Ahmose, a form common in the royal houses of the Eighteenth and Nineteenth Dynasties.

The date and place of the Exodus are much disputed. The former has to be considered in connection with the conquest of Palestine, and the latter is closely linked with the situation of the sacred mountain. The *terminus a quo* is that of the expulsion of the Hyksos and the establishment of the Eighteenth Dynasty; on the other hand, a date so far down as the twelfth century has been suggested (see article, "The Old Testament World," p. 256). The two favorite dates are the middle of the Eighteenth Dynasty and the middle of the Nineteenth, i.e., roughly 1450-1400 B.C., and about a century later. In the former case the Pharaoh of the oppression was Tutmose III; in the latter, Ramses II. Strong arguments may be adduced for each, though in my opinion the balance of evidence is in favor of the earlier date.

The location of Sinai is also much disputed. The conventional identification of the site with the Jebel Musa in the Sinaitic Peninsula is due to a comparatively late tradition. The mention of Midianites has led some scholars to place the sacred mountain to the east of the Gulf of Aqaba, since that was the region assigned to the Midianites in the first century A.D. Others would find a clue in the name 'Ain Kadis, a spot lying midway between the Egyptian border and the most southerly of Palestinian sites, Beersheba. Still others suggest a place well to the north of Egypt, near the Mediterranean coast. If the first-named proposal were adopted, the "Red Sea" would be the northern end of the Gulf of Aqaba; the second would imply an ancient extension of the Gulf of Suez. According to some scholars, the accounts given in Exodus suggest that the mountain of the Law was an active volcano. This would have been a most useful clue if there had been any trace of volcanic activity in recent geological time anywhere near the Egyptian-Palestinian frontier, but none has been offered.

Of the two accounts describing the crossing of the Red Sea which have been interwoven in Exod. 14 (see Exeg.), the earlier seems to be that which depicts a withdrawal of the water, leaving a stretch of bare sand, which was first turned into a quicksand and then covered by the return of the sea. This may have been due to an earthquake, or it may have been the natural action of the tide, especially if the site lay between the present Bitter Lakes and the Gulf of Suez. To a people knowing only the tideless Mediterranean this would inevitably appear miraculous. We must admit that we know for certain neither where the sea was crossed nor where the sacred mountain stood.

But the exact location of Sinai matters little. What is important is the event. Somewhere the Hebrews made their escape in a fashion which proved to them that Yahweh was working for them, and somewhere they met him. It was then that the real work of Moses was accomplished; the rest was but a preliminary. What was done there was the making of a covenant between Yahweh and Israel.

The conception of a covenant is fundamental to the whole history of the people, and a clear understanding of its significance is needed. To the modern ear the word implies something like a bargain. Not so to ancient Israel. A covenant meant the union—indeed, the unification—of two parties who had previously been independent but were now to be regarded as a single entity. It might apply within a limited range of activity; there might be conditions imposed on both sides, or conditions imposed only on one side, or no conditions at all. In a sense, the Sinai covenant was one-sided. Israel undertook certain obligations; Yahweh undertook none, except to be the God of Israel. It has been plausibly conjectured that he was already accepted by Hebrew (or Kenite?) groups which had never been in Egypt, and which regarded the sacred mountain as his home and therefore their own religious center. What gods the others worshiped we do not know for certain, but there are enough references to "strange gods" to make it clear that they had a number of cult-objects among them. In the future they were to have only the one, and so found a unity not only with other groups but with a single God. The people Israel had come into existence, and what made them a people was their unification in Yahweh.

Two forms of covenant ritual are mentioned in Exod. 24 (see Exeg.). The first is simply a common meal, shared by the deity and by representatives of the people (vss. 1a, 9-11). The other (vss. 1b-8) is more elaborate. An "altar" represents the deity. Victims are killed and their blood drained into bowls. Half this blood is thrown over the altar. The terms to be observed by the people are read and accepted, and the remainder of the blood is thrown over them. Both forms point in the same direction. The two parties, originally separate, have now been united to one another through their union with a third party—the slaughtered victim—whose vital essence has entered into or includes all who have shared in the ritual. Henceforward they are *one*.

We can no longer state exactly what were the original terms imposed by the covenant on Israel. But we are certain that they included moral obligations, and that the standard of conduct indicated was much that was expressed in the familiar Ten Commandments, though it does not follow that these were then written down in the form in which we have them now.

Whatever the conditions, one important fact remains beyond dispute: Israel was a single people, a *nation*, and she had achieved her unity, indeed her existence, through union with Yahweh. This historical achievement was the work of Moses.

III. Entry into Palestine (ca. 1350 B.C. [?])

The narrative which describes the entry of Israel into Palestine is on the surface simple and straightforward. During the lifetime of Moses, after an unsuccessful attempt to enter the land from the south (Num. 14:40-45), the country to the east of Jordan and north of the Arnon was conquered and occupied (Num. 21: 21 ff.). Immediately after Moses' death the people were led by Joshua across the Jordan (Josh. 3). Jericho fell at once (Josh. 6), and the next conquest was that of Ai, in the central hills, not far from Bethel (Josh. 8). The people of Gibeon, in the same general region, submitted voluntarily, and became serfs to the Israelites (Josh. 9). A coalition of kings ruling in central Palestine was defeated, and most of their territory passed into Israelite hands (Josh. 10). This gave control of the center of the land, and from that point the Conquest proceeded north and south. When the whole was occupied, the tribes met and solemnly divided the land between them, having exterminated their predecessors, with some few exceptions such as the Gibeonites.

Further examination, however, shows that this story is an idealized presentation of history; in fact the Conquest was neither sudden nor complete. Many of the places listed in Judg. 1 were not subdued. In the fertile parts of the country, especially in the Esdraelon district, the old inhabitants remained, and relations between them and the Israelites were often strained, one side or the other subjecting their opponents to forced labor. Jerusalem remained a foreign city down to the time of David, and Gezer till the reign of Solomon.

The evidence of archaeology is also significant. One instance will suffice. The book of Joshua ascribes the fall of Jericho and that of Ai to the same period; indeed, we get the impression that the interval was not more than a few weeks. But certain archaeological data indicate that the two events were several centuries apart. Ai was destroyed early in the second millennium B.C., and not reoccupied till after 1200. Jericho appears to have fallen in the first half of the fifteenth century B.C., though some archaeologists would put the date as late as the thirteenth century. It seems clear that Israel was well established in the land before the arrival of the Philistines soon after 1200 B.C.

We have to face the probability that the actual conquest was spread over a period of several centuries, and that it was carried out spasmodically by different groups acting independently—some of them may even have settled before the descent into Egypt. Traditions have been handed down from a number of sources, giving details of conquest here and there. Such are the accounts of Kiriath-sepher and Bethel given in Judg. 1; in neither case is there any suggestion of united Israelite action, nor is Joshua mentioned. It seems clear that a collection of these traditions has been crystallized into the continuous narrative which we have before us in the book of Joshua, though even there we find signs of a variant tradition, and indications that the whole has been colored by a religious theory which is usually ascribed to a comparatively late period in the monarchy.

But allowing for all this, we can trace three main stages in the Israelite conquest of Palestine. The book of Numbers records an unsuccessful attempt made from the south, shortly after the making of the great covenant (Num. 14). There are, however, signs of its renewal (cf. Num. 21:1-3), and though elsewhere the narrative places the conquest of the southern area after that of central Palestine, and ascribes it to a southward movement, there is reason to suspect that the actual advance was made in the opposite direction. Here it will be enough to note two points. In the first place, Jerusalem and Gezer—possibly other strong places as well —long held out against the newcomers. One can best explain this by assuming a gap between the main Israelite settlements in the center and the south, which would have been unlikely if the movement had been in one direction only. The other is the fact that Judah (the chief element in the south) always stood a good deal apart from the central and northern tribes. There is a tradition, for example, which looks on Judah as permanently settled even in the patriarchal age (Gen. 38), and it is usual today to consider this tribe as one of those which never were subject to Egyptian slavery, or possibly as a Canaanite group absorbed into the Israelite whole only long after the general settlement. In the earliest times the southern members of the covenant people seem to have been rather nomads like Kenites and Jerahmeelites, perhaps even Amalekites. But whether the event came early or late, southern Palestine was occupied by a section of the Israelite people, and was included in the area covered by the Yahweh cult.

There is less uncertainty about the conquest of the country to the east of the Jordan. Biblical texts assign it to the lifetime of Moses, and there may be good ground for the tradition.

Archaeological evidence has not yet pronounced a verdict on the age of these conquests. Num. 21 mentions the overthrow of two kings to the east, Sihon king of the Amorites, and Og king of Bashan. The territory of the latter lay to the north, and stretched out to the desert, though it does not seem to have included any part of what later became the Damascus district, since the latter was still dominated by semi-nomad Aramaeans in David's day. Here, till the rise of Damascus in the reign of Solomon, there seems to have been no serious frontier question. But to the south the matter was different. The land between the Arnon and the Jabbok was always in dispute between Israel and Moab. The Moabites were held to be of Aramaean stock, though their language was Amorite (as that of Israel afterwards became). They may, then, have had an early history not unlike that of the Israelites, overcoming and subduing an older Amorite population. It is difficult to form a clear opinion of them; their only well-known literary monument—the Mesha (Moabite) stone—dates from the ninth century B.C. There is in Judg. 11 the argument that the disputed territory had been given to Sihon's people in the first instance, while in Num. 21:27 ff. there seems to be the remains of a song which commemorates the conquest of this area by Sihon. Israel claimed that, as Sihon's successors, she had a God-given right to all that he had possessed, no matter how he had acquired it. But whatever the actual rights of the position were, there was always the possibility of strife along the frontier, and the Moabite inscription was set up to record an advance of Moab into the country north of the Arnon. At the same time, it is clear that a considerable part of this east Jordan land remained genuinely Israelite, and the fact proved to be of the highest importance in the development of the Israelite religion and social theory.

The occupation of the central hills was carried out in the main by the Joseph group, and there is no reason to doubt the tradition which makes Joshua their leader. The Jordan was crossed easily, perhaps, on account of a heavy landslide near the mouth of the Jabbok, which dammed the stream for a time (Josh. 3), and Jericho fell almost at once (Josh. 6). Recent excavations have made it almost certain that the city walls collapsed as the result of an earthquake—perhaps one of a series which was also responsible for the stoppage in the river. The city was then burned. From this point an entry into the hills was comparatively easy, and with the fall of Bethel (which may have taken place only after the death of Joshua—cf. Judg. 1:22-26), the invaders were able to make their headquarters in the center of the land. They spread down toward the western coast, where they held their own till the advent of the Philistine migrants. The "hill country of Ephraim" was more thoroughly Israelite than any other part of the country. The earliest great national shrine was established at Shiloh, and archaeological research has shown that the Hebrews made far more use of the land than did any of their predecessors. In a large number of sites the first signs of occupation belong to the early Iron Age, in strong contrast to some other places whose relics can be traced back even beyond the Bronze Age. It follows that they were not occupied till the period of Israelite invasions.

It seems that the strong cities and fertile lands of the plain of Esdraelon long resisted any Israelite attacks. There may have been some penetration, but it is clear that in this area Israel was never in a commanding position till the time of David. Cities like Megiddo, Taanach, Jezreel, and Bethshean still continued to be directly under Egyptian rule. The last-named certainly had an Egyptian garrison till late in the period of the Judges, and there the Egyptian occupation was immediately followed by that of the Philistines. Standing as it did where it could cover one of the main fords of the Jordan, Bethshean was one of the key positions in Palestine, for it was traversed by one of the great routes of the ancient world. David was the first Israelite leader to hold it.

The fourth area of conquest was in the far north. Here Joshua is said to have overthrown a certain Jabin king of Hazor, in a battle fought by the "waters of Merom" (Josh. 11). This site was once identified as Lake Huleh, but modern opinion is inclined to locate it somewhere else in northern Galilee. It also seems clear, especially in view of the situation in the plain of Esdraelon, that the attack was delivered from the east and not from the south, and this military operation, like the southern invasion, was probably quite independent of Joshua. The Hebrews penetrated far up into the valleys which lie between the Lebanon and the Anti-Lebanon ranges. Their ideal frontier was "the entering-in of Hamath," and whether they always effectively occupied the whole or not, they certainly claimed as their own the land as far north as the watershed between the Litany and the Orontes.

So after a long and slow process the land was occupied. In many places the occupation remained incomplete, and the older inhabitants still held their position. There may have been much mingling of blood, and certainly, as the Israelites settled down, they tended to adopt the civilization, religion, and language of the more highly cultured peoples whom they dis-

placed. There was no unified political organization; each group was largely free to act as it saw fit and to remain independent even of its Israelite fellows. Some Hebrew clans, especially to the east of the Jordan, remained nomadic; others became sedentary farmers and city dwellers. But they were still conscious of their unity. The covenant mediated by Moses had given them the sense of a common life, and formed a far stronger bond of union than their traditions of a common ancestry. In their national cult of Yahweh they were one, and at his call became, at least for the time being, a single people who were compelled to work together for a common cause. The full effects of this awareness were not apparent in the earliest stages of the conquest, but in later times again and again the influence of Moses' work was manifest, to the salvation of Israel and to the development of her faith.

IV. The Judges (ca. 1300-1030 B.C. [?])

The establishment of Israel in Palestine did not mean that there was in any modern sense a Hebrew state. On the contrary, modern historians envisage a number of more or less isolated groups, each carrying on its own affairs normally without reference to its kinsmen, and uniting only when some great peril threatened them. For the most part they were in the middle of the larger masses of their predecessors, and gradually learned the operations of agriculture and city life. In doing so they naturally tended to take over Canaanite points of view and methods, both in secular and in religious matters—if it is possible to separate the two. Exceptions to this gradual absorption into the existing community are to be found only to the east of the Jordan and to the far south, where the land was not suited to agriculture or to the building of large cities, on account of the scanty water supply. To the east in particular there seems to have come a comparatively dry spell about the beginning of the Iron Age, since there are plenty of traces showing an earlier occupation of the land. But the evidence of the Old Testament points to a traditional maintenance of the shepherd life on a large scale in this area (cf. Num. 32). It seems probable also that Israelite blood and customs remained purer in the central hills, at least between the Jerusalem region and the plain of Esdraelon, though even there a certain amount of cultural syncretism took place, as the story of Gideon shows (cf. Judg. 8:31).

Throughout the period—roughly about two centuries—between the entry into Palestine and the unification of the people into a single political whole, Palestine was subject to attacks from the outside. In addition, there were conflicts from time to time with the earlier inhabitants, though such occurrences seem to have become exceptional as time went on.

Leaders against enemies from outside were found in the so-called "judges." The word *shôphēṭ*, as the use of its Phoenician cognate in Carthage shows (see the Latin *sufes*), meant to the Semitic mind far more than the administration of justice in the ordinary sense. "Judges" were men who felt themselves called to the leadership of their people in times of distress, and were able to send out a call in the name of the national God. At the same time, their activities do not seem as a rule to have covered a very wide range. They gathered about them the men of their own and neighboring districts, won their victories, and secured for themselves a real authority during their lifetime. In only one instance do we hear of an attempt to establish an actual kingdom with a hereditary dynasty, and that proved to be a failure.

The book of Judges presents a series of these rulers, and arranges them in a regular framework, involving also a chronological scheme. The latter has the appearance of being an artificial structure, with its repeated periods of twenty or forty years. The framework itself seems also to be based on a special theory of history, and runs somewhat as follows: The Israelites forgot Yahweh their God, and he sold them into the hands of a foreigner who oppressed them for some years; they repented and cried to Yahweh, who raised up for them a deliverer who "judged" Israel for a number of years; and Israel served Yahweh all the days of this hero, but after his death they forgot Yahweh and served the Baals. And then the whole cycle begins again. Now this pattern may have been due to a religious theory, but it embodies a sound philosophy of history. The independent communities of Palestine were seldom strong enough to repel invaders by themselves; it was only in combination that they could muster the necessary strength, and even then, as the narrative of Joshua testifies, they were liable to be overthrown by the battle fury of the hardy wilderness tribes. In the absence of help from Egypt (and the Tell el-Amarna documents show how difficult it might be to arouse the Egyptian court to activity), they had neither the will nor the power to oppose a united front to the raiders. Their religion, strongly corrupted by the cult of the Baals, or local fertility spirits, may have encouraged a village patriotism, but otherwise it was a disintegrating, not a uniting force. Whenever Israelites adopted Canaanite forms of worship, they too were disunited. But in Yahweh they had a unifying power which covered all the tribes, including those far away

from the scene of trouble; all were morally bound to answer a call sent out in the name of the covenantal deity. This religious factor made them formidable to enemies, and under the leadership of inspired judges they were often able to save their districts from plunder and slaughter. Surviving Canaanites profited by Israelite unity, and this fact, more than any other, enabled the Hebrews to impose on the whole land in large measure a Yahwistic pattern of living. It may be said that the Hebrews conquered Palestine not by destroying their predecessors, but by defending them.

The full list of the judges includes twelve names, counting Deborah and Barak together. Of these, six are generally regarded as minor, since little is said about their exploits; of the other six, tradition has fairly long accounts to give. Only in one instance is the enemy a Canaanite power. That is the case of Sisera, a local prince of the Esdraelon region, who clearly made life difficult for the Israelites in or near this part of the country. His defeat and death were celebrated in one of the finest pieces of ancient Hebrew poetry which have been preserved, the so-called "Song of Deborah" (Judg. 5). It is contemporary with the events which it records, and constitutes the best available witness to the conditions and ideas of the period. The little clans gathered in answer to the appeal sent out by an inspired prophetess. Some refused to help and ignored the summons; they were cursed. The rest were little more than a wild horde, collected on the slopes to the north of the Kishon Valley. They were not adequately armed as compared with their foes, who were well equipped with chariots. But as they looked out over the enemy crossing the plain, a thundercloud gradually rose in the south, and Israel saw in it the coming of Yahweh from his southern home. Panic fell on Canaanite horse and man, who turned at the breaking of the storm. Before they reached the farther banks of the swollen torrent of Kishon, beyond which lay their safety, they were drowned in large numbers. Sisera himself fled alone, and was murdered by a Kenite woman in whose tent he had sought refuge. This is regarded as the climax of the whole story; it is the death of the personal enemy which brings the real triumph.

The other enemies were all invaders from outside Palestine. One of the first to be mentioned is Moab, which apparently was not content with expanding into the disputed territory north of the Arnon, but crossed the Jordan River into central Palestine. The hero in this case was a Benjamite named Ehud, and he achieved the deliverance of Israel by assassinating the Moabite king, Eglon (Judg. 3:12-30).

One event, which belongs wholly to Trans-Jordan, introduces the story of Jephthah the Gileadite (Judg. 11), who is best known for the sacrifice of his daughter in performance of a vow. It is not quite clear who his enemies were; they are called Ammonites, but in arguing with them Jephthah seems to have been speaking to Moabites. Perhaps traditions from two different sources have been intertwined.

The most southern oppressor was a certain Cushan-rishathaim, who was king of Mesopotamia (Judg. 3:7-11). Here again the historical details are uncertain, for such an adversary would have naturally attacked from the north, but the deliverer was Othniel, the hero of southern Palestine, who was held to have been the son-in-law of Caleb (Judg. 1:13).

A good deal of space is given to Gideon, otherwise known as Jerubbaal (Judg. 6–8). Once more records of two distinct invasions appear to have been telescoped into a single narrative. The raiders came from the east, and were of that class of wilderness nomads to which Israel originally belonged. In one case the chiefs of the enemy are named Oreb and Zeeb—"Raven" and "Wolf"—and in the other Zeba and Zalmunna. The story of the latter involved trouble with the town of Succoth, to the east of the Jordan, and with the tribe of Ephraim, which was jealous of Manassite leadership. One significant feature of the story is the abortive attempt at the establishment of a monarchy, made by Gideon's son, Abimelech, who was partly of Canaanite descent (Judg. 9).

A far more serious enemy threatened the independence of Israel, and indeed of all Palestine. Extensive racial movements were taking place in the last quarter of the second millennium B.C., and one of the early cultures was coming to an end. Some of the ancestors of the Greeks were breaking into the region of the eastern Mediterranean, destroying or driving out those peoples generally known as the Aegeans. It was the era of the Trojan wars, and foreign pressure was driving the dispossessed Aegeans southward from Crete and the coasts of Asia Minor. They migrated by land and sea, heading toward Egypt. Naturally their route led them down the coast of Palestine, but early in the twelfth century they were checked on the borders of Egypt by Ramses III. They made their home in the coastal plain, and we have indications of the effect produced by their arrival on Israel. The first sufferers were the Danites, who had penetrated to the sea. Their resistance is best seen in the familiar stories of Samson, in whose day the Danite settlements seem to have been reduced to two small villages (Judg. 13–16). A narrative attached to the end of the book of Judges (chs. 17–18) tells of the way in which the remainder, including only six hundred fighting men, made their way to the north, and settled as far from the Philistines as they could, in a valley lying between the Lebanon and the Anti-Lebanon ranges. Here was the city to be known later as Dan, the most northern of the Israelite settlements.

Philistine pressure, however, was not yet spent. The complete political disunion of the Palestinian cities is exemplified in the story of the Benjamite war, which forms the second appendix to the book of Judges (chs. 19–21). Attempts to unite the people failed, and the Philistines made their way up into the hills, establishing military posts even on the eastern side of the central range, though they did not cross the Jordan. Farther north they put an end to the last remains of Egyptian occupation by the capture of Bethshean, and from that point southward they reduced the inhabitants to submission. One or two places, however, remained independent, apparently in some kind of alliance with the Philistines. Chief of these was Jerusalem, one of the strongest fortresses of the ancient Near East. The completeness of the Philistine conquest over a large part of Palestine is attested by the story of the battle fought at Ebenezer, where the Philistine booty actually included the ark (I Sam. 4). It seems highly probable that the one great shrine in Israel, that of Shiloh (cf. Jer. 7:12), was destroyed as a result of this crushing defeat.

So the period of the judges closed with the Philistines' supremacy in western Palestine. Comparatively small local combinations had sufficed to defeat and destroy other invaders, but the Philistines were cast in a different mold. They were a people of great skill and high culture, the survivors of long and heroic wars, and it is clear that some closer and stronger form of amalgamation was necessary if they were to be driven out of the central lands. The story of the period of the judges is the record of the way in which the isolated elements in western Palestine were gradually welded into a single whole by the hammer strokes of foreign invasion; the presence of the Philistines made a final unification imperative.

V. The United Monarchy (ca. 1030-936 B.C.)

The Philistine threat called for a far higher degree of centralization than was possible under the loose system (if it can be called a system at all) which prevailed through the period of the judges. With the need arose the man: Saul, son of Kish, a Benjamite. Like the judges, he was summoned to his task by direct inspiration; his office was in the first instance charismatic. He was indeed the typical "nabi," or ecstatic prophet, subject to strange psychological conditions which came upon him from time to time. The story of his anointing by Samuel is familiar (I Sam. 9:1–10:16). Samuel is presented alternately as a seer, a priest, and a judge, and once the term "prophet" is applied to him. It is as a seer that he played his part in the anointing of Saul, and the earlier strata of the numerous stories which have gathered about him do not give him any active military role in the course of events. There is, however, no reason to doubt his connection with Saul, or the very important place he took in the early days of the monarchy.

Saul's first great act was the relief of Jabesh-gilead, threatened by Ammonites (I Sam. 11:1-13). On this occasion he acted exactly as the older judges had done, and might have gone no farther than they did but for the pressure of the Philistines. This first exploit, however, gave Saul immense prestige and secured for him a base to the east of the Jordan, on which he could fall back if necessary. That connection remained throughout his life and that of his son.

The Philistines seem to have tolerated Saul, perhaps treating him as a local ruler under their authority. They had posts in various places among the central hills, and, at selected spots, government officials. War with the Philistines was started when Jonathan, Saul's son, killed an official (I Sam. 13:3), and Saul summoned the clans to gather to his standard. The most eastern garrison seems to have been at Michmash, looking down on the Jordan Valley. Saul lay a few miles away, but his force dwindled till Jonathan took advantage of a raid which the Philistine garrison was making to attack and destroy the few men left to hold the fort. The result was a general rising (I Sam. 14:1-46), which swept the Philistines from the hill country and confined them to the plains to the west and north. Saul's authority was practically complete over the central range and to the east of the Jordan, but he never occupied the Jerusalem area or the Plain of Esdraelon. All his life he was engaged in the struggle to keep the Philistines out of the central hills. As long as their main assaults were made from the west he was successful, probably because chariots were comparatively useless in the high and narrow valleys, but at last they moved from the north, since they were now in complete occupation of the plain of Esdraelon. Saul and most of his sons fell in battle on Mount Gilboa, which looks down on the plain, and the hill country once more fell under Philistine control (I Sam. 31).

Saul left a successor greater than himself. David the Bethlehemite had been a successful warrior in Saul's army, till the king's jealousy was aroused, and the young man took service with Achish, king of Gath (I Sam. 21:11-16). He thus had links with the Philistines, and may also have been connected with Moab through Ruth, an ancestress of his. He used his position with Achish to win for himself the enthusiasm of the extreme south of the country, and at the same time gathered about him a band of refugees from all Israel (I Sam. 27). After Saul's death he felt strong enough to act by himself, and selected Jerusalem as the first point of attack. The Philistines appear to have had some interest in the city, though nominally it was still in the hands of the Jebusites, for David had to fight a series of battles and sustained several setbacks before he succeeded in taking the place through an exploit of Joab, his captain (II Sam. 5:6-9).

Even before the capture of Jerusalem, the house of Saul had come to an end with the murder of Ishbosheth (II Sam. 4:1-8; called Esh-baal in I Chr. 8:33), and all Israel recognized David as king (II Sam. 5). He showed his genius as a statesman by making his new conquest the capital of the land. Apparently this decision was not reached at once, for he broke down the defenses to the north of the old city, the most vulnerable point, and had to restore them later. But his occupation of the place solved one of his problems: the "city of David" had belonged neither to Judah nor to northern Israel, and so was as independent of the various elements composing his dominions as Washington and Canberra are of their countries.

David's military efforts did not stop with the capture of Jerusalem. It is a curious fact that we have little record of his further activities against the Philistines; the battles recorded took place in the Jerusalem campaign for the most part. But he certainly drove the Philistines from the plain of Esdraelon, and established his authority far north into the valleys between the Lebanon and Anti-Lebanon ranges—the "entering-in of Hamath" was his traditional frontier.

The whole of western Palestine (except for the Philistine cities to the southwest) was thus for the first time in its history formed into a single political unit under a native ruler. But the land was still as exposed as ever to assault from the outside, and David's next care was to erect barriers around it. Edom (cf. II Sam. 8:14; I Kings 11:15-16), Moab (II Sam. 8:2), Ammon (II Sam. 10; 13:26-31), and the Aramaean tribes (II Sam. 10:6-19) to the northeast were defeated in battle and subdued. A close alliance of friendship was formed with the Phoenician powers (II Sam. 5:11; 8:9-10), and it is clear that this was to the advantage of both parties. To the southwest the Philistines were no longer formidable. Palestine was thus protected on every side, and the Israelite portion of the land was able to develop in security. It is no wonder that the reign of David was regarded in later times as the golden age in Israel's history.

These outer conquests were even more important from the economic point of view than from that of politics. Squeezed between the Great Sea and the Arabian Desert, Palestine formed a regular ganglion of trade routes. The caravans which came to the Phoenician ports or to Egypt had to pass through David's territories. Egypt could be reached by the rest of the world only through Palestine or the drier route to the east of the Jordan; both were now in David's hands. The occupation of Edom meant control of the ports at the head of the Gulf of Aqaba, and opened the door to sea traffic with the farther east; there is little doubt that in this period there was trade between Israel and India. It is possible, too, that there was some commerce with eastern Africa.

It is obvious that no trade passed through David's territories without leaving something to his advantage. He is reputed to have built up vast financial reserves, and Palestine in ancient times had little if any exportable products. International trade was still in the hands of the crown; the wealthy class mentioned by the literary prophets in the eighth and seventh centuries had not yet come into being. The commercial advantage was reaped by the king, and it was rendered possible by the possession of the great lines of international communication.

David did not neglect the affairs of his own country. As time went on it is clear that he developed a highly organized system of internal administration, although no allusion to such an organization is found in the record till the reign of Solomon (cf. I Kings 4:7 ff.). The various elements in the population were still far from being united, and at least twice in David's reign the mutual jealousies of north and south endangered his position. Some kind of secure control was indispensable.

In the two rebellions mentioned David owed his success largely to his military organization. For wars abroad he could rely on the national levies, a kind of militia in which every Israelite was bound to serve. At its head was the doughty old warrior Joab, who had followed David faithfully since the early days. As this force might well have proved insufficient in case of domestic trouble, the king maintained also a permanent military establishment composed of professional soldiers, many, if not most of them, recruited from outside Israel, and particularly from among the Philistines. Their leader, Benaiah, to judge from his name, was an Israel-

ite, and David seems to have instituted various orders of merit and distinction within the royal bodyguard. There can be little doubt as to David's organizing ability, and if his successors had been his equals, Israel might have risen to a commanding position among the nations.

At the same time, sociological changes were taking place which were destined to have a profound effect on the future of the people. It must never be forgotten that the population not only was mixed in blood, but also contained elements whose social practices were very different from one another. On the one hand there were the older peoples, long accustomed to agriculture and resigned to a more or less despotic rule. They had the normal Oriental outlook and regarded the king as a supreme person to whom all his subjects stood in the relation of slaves to their master, with no rights of person or of property against him. On the other side stood the free Israelite, clinging to the traditions handed down from Mosaic days, impatient of authority, and insisting on the rights of every free member of the community. It was to the latter element that David had owed his elevation, and those of his early comrades who survived into the period of his prosperity still clung to the old ideals. A striking instance of their influence is given in the story of Uriah and Bathsheba (II Sam. 11–12). Nowhere else in the ancient world would the king's conduct have been regarded as iniquitous or even abnormal; in all probability an Eastern monarch would not have troubled to put the husband to death. But the spirit of Israel arose against the adultery and the murder, and found expression in Nathan. It is a striking tribute to the strength of the tradition that not only was the protest made, but that David accepted it, and acknowledged the justice of the rebuke. We cannot imagine any other king in the ancient East behaving as David did.

At the same time, it appears that the other tendency was at work, and in his later days David was drifting into the position of an ordinary Oriental autocrat. The existence of his bodyguard is significant, and the revolts which the king had to meet may have hardened his outlook. Matters came to a climax in his old age, when a palace revolution put the young prince Solomon on the throne and overthrew the popular candidate, Adonijah (I Kings 1). The names of each side are revealing —Joab and Abiathar, companions of David's youth, are with Adonijah, and clearly the "democratic" principle might have found some support from him. But Solomon had been born in the purple, some time after the last of David's foreign wars, and knew little or nothing of the way in which the genuine Israelite spirit had raised his father to the throne. His accession was a victory for the principle of autocracy.

Even so, a wise man might have preserved and strengthened the new Israelite state, but Solomon was quite unfit for the task. Vain, ostentatious, shortsighted, selfish, and cowardly, he was unscrupulous in the attainment of his ends, and largely indifferent to the personal values which meant so much to the genuine Israelite. Nevertheless, he had certain mental abilities. If tradition is to be trusted, he was a clever judge (cf. I Kings 3:16 ff.) and had a pretty turn for epigram (cf. I Kings 4:32). It is to this fact that he probably owes his reputation for wisdom. His great passion was for building, and he has gone down in history as the founder of the temple. But this was not his only work. Jerusalem itself was enriched with magnificent structures on which no expense was spared. He established a force of chariotry, and modern excavation has revealed some of his stables; that at Megiddo, for example, had accommodation for two hundred chariots. It was also in his reign that the last of Canaanite strongholds, Gezer (I Kings 9:16-17), fell into Israelite hands.

It is to be noted that Solomon himself did not conquer Gezer. It was captured and sacked by his Egyptian father-in-law, probably one of the last Pharaohs of the Twenty-First Dynasty. In spite of his equipment, he did not undertake any war; he made no attempt to recover the outlying dependencies with which David had so carefully surrounded his proper kingdom. Edom fell away (I Kings 11:14-22), and the Aramaeans to the northeast revolted, setting up an independent state at Damascus (I Kings 11:23-25). These political events had an important bearing on Israel's domestic history.

For Solomon's aims involved considerable expense, and his temperament was far from frugal. He had to import all his best material, especially timber for his buildings and precious metals for their adornment. Horses, too, were not bred in Palestine, and had to be purchased in Egypt. It was not long before the treasure accumulated by David was exhausted, and the king had to find other sources of income. One method of reducing expense was to impose the corvée (I Kings 5:13-14; 9:15), that forced and unpaid labor which every true Israelite regarded as the final violation of human rights. Matters were not improved by the fact that a large part of the service had to be rendered as unskilled labor in the cedar forests of the Lebanon. Every Israelite peasant had to give one third of his year to the king's service, and for the purposes of this conscription the land was divided into twelve districts (I Kings 4:7-18). Judah, it seems, had preferential treatment, for

it is not included in the list. The loss of Edom and of the Damascus area meant that a large proportion of the royal income from trade disappeared, and in the end Solomon was forced to cede to the Phoenician king a portion of his territory in order to liquidate his debts (I Kings 9:11-13). There is also the darker suspicion that he was in the habit of selling his own subjects, particularly to Egypt; man power was the only exportable product of Palestine in the tenth century B.C. The reign which had begun in such brilliance closed in gloom, and it was already clear that David's ideals would never be realized in the political world.

VI. The Divided Kingdom (936-721 B.C.)

On the death of Solomon, his son Rehoboam was accepted by Jerusalem and Judah, which had suffered less than the north from royal oppression. But when the new king came to Shechem to take the covenant imposed on Israelite sovereigns (Solomon's coup d'état had apparently escaped this national custom), he was at once faced with a demand for the relaxation of the corvée. Rejecting the crafty advice of those councilors who recommended him to make promises which he did not need to keep, Rehoboam brusquely rejected the demand, and at once the northern tribes broke away. They accepted the leadership of Jeroboam, a former royal officer who had been under suspicion and had taken refuge at the court of Sheshonk, the founder of the Twenty-Second Egyptian Dynasty (I Kings 12:1-20). Naturally war followed, and Sheshonk interfered. It seems that Rehoboam had made some progress, for the list of cities Sheshonk claimed to have conquered included several from northern Israel. But the trained and organized forces of the south were unable to cope with an Egyptian army, and Rehoboam was forced to withdraw his troops and to pay a large indemnity, which exhausted even the last of his father's treasures (I Kings 14:25-26).

From this time onward there was no political unity in Israel, though the two parts continued to regard themselves as a single whole for many purposes. They had a common tradition and a common faith, and these often proved stronger than political divisions. Two centuries later, prophets like Amos and Isaiah were interested in the north as well as in the south, and the ideal Israel always included the full tale of twelve tribes. This did not prevent a century of rivalry, usually leading to war along an artificial frontier. Jeroboam did his best to keep the two parts separate; his most famous measure was the establishment of sanctuaries at Bethel and Dan to rival that of Jerusalem. Here Yahweh was worshiped under the form of a bull, possibly according to a type of cult adopted from earlier Canaan (I Kings 12:26 ff.). Little protest was heard against it until the time of Hosea, at the very end of the northern monarchy (cf. Hos. 8:5-6).

All the little western states became engaged in a desultory warfare, in which the most striking feature was the rise of Damascus to supremacy, a result no doubt due to her favorable position as a commercial center. While Assyria and Egypt remained in a state of weakness, these small principalities were free to quarrel among themselves without interference from the outside. In the south the house of David retained the throne, but there were frequent changes of dynasty in the north; only two royal houses lasted into a third generation. Slave raids, the plundering and destruction of farms near the frontiers, mutual jealousy and suspicion—these were the characteristic features of a period in which the strength of David's old realm was steadily drained away. Even in northern Israel there appears to have been disunion, and we hear of hostility between Ephraim and Manasseh. The whole area was in more or less permanent political confusion.

The rise of Omri (I Kings 16:23-26) in the early part of the ninth century brought a considerable change. More than any other Israelite king, he had something of the political genius of David. His first step was to erect a new capital at Samaria. He entered into an alliance with Phoenicia, and recovered the old authority over Moab. He so impressed his contemporaries that the Assyrians themselves for many years after him called Israel "the land of Omri."

Omri's son, Ahab, did not succeed in maintaining his father's dominions unimpaired, for Moab recovered its independence. But he was wise enough and strong enough to take a leading part in a coalition of the little western states which was formed to resist the growing power of Assyria. This country, under Shalmaneser III, was waking up after a long period of internal weakness, and in 853 B.C. made a determined effort to extend its dominions to the Mediterranean. About a dozen of the small peoples combined; the two leading powers were Damascus and Israel, the former stronger in infantry, the latter in chariotry. A great battle was fought at Karkar in the Orontes Valley, and though Shalmaneser claimed a great victory, he went no farther. Unfortunately, with the relaxation of external pressure, the coalition temporarily broke up, and Ahab himself fell in battle against the forces of Damascus. Nevertheless, when need arose, the same resistance was offered to Assyria as long as the house of Omri remained on the throne.

But at this point the course of foreign politics was gravely affected by events in Israel itself. The Phoenician alliance, in itself a fine stroke of policy, brought with it disaster. Ahab had married Jezebel, the daughter of Ethbaal, king of Sidon (I Kings 16:31), and the foreign princess was imbued with the normal ideas of Oriental monarchs—a complete absolutism (I Kings 21) such as had not been seen in Israel since the days of Solomon. Four outstanding figures deserve to be noted. First there was Naboth, the Israelite free peasant-farmer, independent and obstinate, and sure of rights on which he would insist, even against the king. Second, Ahab, who, with the old tradition behind him, saw no alternative to accepting Naboth's refusal. Third, the foreign queen, a much stronger character than her husband, who could not understand how it was possible for any subject to refuse a fair and perhaps even generous demand made by the king. It will be observed that Ahab himself apparently had no knowledge of what was happening till Naboth was actually dead. The fourth figure was that of Elijah, the most significant of all.

Among the groups which were at work all through Israelite history, striving to maintain the old standards and principles which the Aramaean invaders had brought into Palestine, the most conspicuous and successful were the prophets. As enthusiasts for the covenant God, Yahweh, they were concerned to see that the rights of free personality were respected, and that no authority, even that of the king, could override them. It will be remembered that the stern rebuke to David for his sin with Bathsheba came from this section of the community (II Sam. 12). The great disruption under Jeroboam had a prophet behind it (I Kings 11:29 ff.), and the spirit was not dead. While it survived in western Palestine, it was strongest in the cattle districts to the east and to the south, and it is not an accident that Elijah's home lay in the former region. To him and those who stood with him for the old Israelite theory of life, the death of Naboth was sheer murder, and the taint of blood attached to all that had been his. Though Ahab himself might have been guiltless of the actual crime, by taking the vineyard he assumed the load of sin, which must work itself out on him and his successors.

The crisis came within a dozen years of Ahab's death. Once again the prophets moved, and their nominee, Jehu, extinguished the whole house of Ahab, including Jezebel, in a frightful massacre (II Kings 9–10), which called for the condemnation of Hosea a century later (cf. Hos. 1:4). In all Israelite history only once again did a king attempt to ape Solomon, and that was Jehoiakim, who had been placed on the throne of Judah by a foreign power.

The prophetic revolution, however, had an important effect on foreign policy. To secure his position Jehu submitted to Assyria and paid tribute. This broke up the old coalition, and ensured the temporary success of Assyria. Damascus was the chief sufferer, and her weakness meant a relaxation of the pressure which she had exerted on Israel for nearly a century.

It was, then, under Jeroboam II, the grandson of Jehu, that Israel reached the highest prosperity she had known since the division of the monarchy. Even with the accession of the house of Omri the hostility between north and south had died away. Probably Judah occupied a subordinate position; the marriage of Athaliah to a Judean king points in that direction, and the list of the allies who fought at Karkar does not include the name of Judah. The narrative of I Kings 22 makes it clear that Jehoshaphat was not wholly a free agent. There was thus unity in foreign affairs between the two kingdoms. The further expansion in the age of Jeroboam II gave back to Israel much of the territory she had lost to the east of the Jordan, and in the far south the recovery of Elath by Judah (II Kings 14:22) opened once more the sea route to the south and east. It is significant that the writer of the pre-exilic record (preserved in II Kings 14:25-27) looked on Jeroboam as a divinely appointed savior of his people. Judged by purely material standards, the statement is sound.

VII. Fall of Northern Israel (721 B.C.)

Although the reign of Jeroboam II was a time of prosperity, greater than any since the days of Solomon, all was not well beneath the surface. It is true that little or nothing is said of royal exactions or tyranny, but a yet more serious peril threatened the nation. In earlier days it seems that commerce abroad, with the wealth which it brought into the country, was the king's prerogative. In the century which followed the death of Ahab, however, there grew up a class of wealthy subjects, who used their traditional liberty to amass fortunes for themselves. The genuinely "democratic" spirit of Israel, which had found expression in the prophetic movement, had won its victory over autocracy; it had now to face a deadlier enemy in plutocracy.

Between 850 and 760 B.C. a complete change had come over the social and economic structure of Israelite society. The old peasant of the Naboth type had almost entirely disappeared, and the land was now parceled out into large estates, worked by tenant farmers or serf labor. The prophetic reaction to the new order may be exemplified by such a passage as Isa. 5:8 ff. The absentee owner spent his time in one of the cities, giving himself up to a life of idle luxury such as is depicted in Amos 6:1 ff.; Isa. 5:11 ff. There was a great gulf between him and the actual workers, whose abject misery excited the pity of men like Amos and Isaiah, and called for their strong denunciations. Micah's language was even stronger, but seems to have been justified by the facts. His account of an eviction is classical (Mic. 2:9-10).

It is not hard to guess at the means whereby this result had been brought about. The laws of debt in the East always press heavily on the poor peasant. A bad harvest, a raid from across the border, a domestic calamity—and the poor fellow had to apply to the moneylender, a familiar figure in Israelite society (cf. II Kings 4:1 ff.), to enable him to live at all. His land was the only security he could offer, and when fresh trouble came the mortgage would be called in. The original owner might be retained as a tenant paying an enormous rent (cf. Amos 5:11), but he would be sure to need a fresh loan at some time, and then had only the persons of himself and his children to pledge. Next time they would become actual slaves, and it seems that the law which limited the period of slavery (cf. Exod. 21:2 ff.) was either unknown or disregarded. Probably the victims had only the choice between permanent slavery (cf. Exod. 21:5-6) and actual starvation, for the law which ordained the restoration of property does not appear to have been effective till the discovery of Deuteronomy in 621 B.C.

The process was possibly accelerated by judicial corruption. A rich man had only to bring a charge of debt against his neighbor, and a small bribe to the judge would secure a verdict. It was literally true that the poor could be bought for a pair of shoes (Amos 2:6; 8:6). Added to this was the general dishonesty in retail trade (cf. Amos 8:5), and it will be seen that the wealthy classes were building up for themselves a strong position at the expense of the workers.

The prophets understood that such a state of society could end only in ruin. History has abundantly justified their insight. The oppressed classes may still retain something of the human spirit, and an internal explosion follows. Or if they do not, then the land falls as easy prey to the first serious invader. So it was with Israel. The sturdy nation which had led successful resistance to Shalmaneser III in 853 B.C. had vanished, and when Assyria once more recovered her strength, the armies of Tiglath-pileser (who came to the throne in 745 B.C.) easily overran the western states, and incorporated a number of them in his empire.

In Israel the collapse was hastened by internal disunion. Zechariah, son of Jeroboam II, was murdered by a usurper named Shallum (II Kings 15:10), and Shallum by Menahem (II Kings 15:14), who paid tribute to Tiglath-pileser in 738 B.C. (II Kings 15:19). He was the last northern king to be succeeded by a son. Pekahiah fell to Pekah (II Kings 15:25), who, in concert with Rezin of Damascus, attempted to revive the old western alliance which had so firmly held its ground a century earlier. But Ahaz of Judah refused to join him (II Kings 16:5; Isa. 7:1-17) and called in the Assyrian king (II Kings 16:8-9). Within three years Tiglath-pileser had conquered a large part of the country (cf. II Kings 15:29). He organized the territory of Damascus and the northern part of Israel as provinces of his empire, appointing officials directly from the court. Samaria was left with a little brief independence, at least in name, though her new king, Hoshea, was compelled to pay a regular tribute to the Assyrians (II Kings 17:3).

Egypt in the meantime took alarm. She was no longer the power she had been, and was unable effectively to meet the Mesopotamian forces in the field. But she was an adept at intrigue, and stirred up all possible trouble. Hoshea revolted, and seems to have disappeared about 724. Tiglath-pileser had been succeeded by Shalmaneser V, who soon laid siege to Samaria. The city held out for three years, but in the end was captured and destroyed (II Kings 17:5-6). Hoshea's dominions, which seem to have been limited to the northern part of the central range, were organized as the province of Samaria by Sargon, who had succeeded Shalmaneser before the fall of the city. Of all the western states, Judah and some of the Philistine cities alone retained a nominal independence. Numbers of people from Israel were deported eastward, and their places taken by groups introduced from other conquered districts (II Kings 17:24). Assyria was never again troubled by disturbances in the newly occupied lands.

But the remaining free states were still liable to give trouble. Ashdod made a bid for complete independence in 711 B.C., and was ruthlessly suppressed. Hezekiah of Judah may have been implicated in the matter, but escaped severe punishment, remaining faithful to Assyria as long as Sargon lived. On Sargon's death in 705 B.C., however, his successor, Sennacherib, was faced with widespread revolt. The moving spirit was Marduk-appal-uddina, the subject king of Babylon, who fomented a general revolt. Sennacherib was at first occupied in securing his position against his nearest adversaries, but in 701 B.C. was able to turn westward. Only one prince had been faithful to him, Padi, king of Ekron, and he had been deposed by his people and handed over to Hezekiah. An attempt at a diversion was made by Egypt, and it seems that Sennacherib's army suffered from bubonic plague (cf. II Kings 19:35). Jerusalem was a very strong fortress, and Sennacherib was content to accept Hezekiah's surrender and leave him on the throne. The Judean king, however, was compelled to pay an enormous indemnity (cf. II Kings 18:13-16), and many of his people, including royal princesses, were taken prisoner. Padi, on the other hand, was rewarded for his fidelity by considerable grants of land from Judah's territories. But Jerusalem did not fall, and the house of David still sat on the throne. As a matter of fact, Judah was the only western state to outlive the kingdom of Assyria, and for the next three quarters of a century there is no hint of any further attempt to break loose from Assyrian dominance.

VIII. Fall of Judah (586 B.C.)

For the greater part of the seventh century the land of Judah was under Manasseh, the son of Hezekiah, a king more strongly condemned by the prophetic party than any of his predecessors (cf. II Kings 21:2 ff.). He was charged with apostasy of many kinds, and particularly with the practice of human sacrifice (II Kings 21:6). It seems clear also that foreign cults were freely introduced, some, no doubt, imposed by the Assyrian overlord. But to all appearance the country remained externally at peace.

The truth is that the two great world powers were not for the time in acute conflict. Egypt was passing through one of her recurrent periods of weakness and had actually been invaded by Esarhaddon, the successor of Sennacherib, who had organized the Delta as an Assyrian province. She began to recover under Psamtik (ca. 660 B.C.), but did not become again a serious military power till well on in the seventh century. Ashurbanipal succeeded Esarhaddon in 668 B.C., and became the last great king of Assyria. The empire had grown unwieldly, and was unable to resist the influx of wild tribes from the north (ca. 630 B.C.). Peoples known to Greek historians as Scythians and Cimmerians broke down the defenses and made their way into the Fertile Crescent. Though Ashurbanipal remained on the throne till 626 B.C., we have no official records of his reign later than 639. Egypt had regained her independence before 640 B.C., and when the Scythians moved down through Palestine (there may be references to these events in Jer. 4–6), she was able to check them on her borders. They failed to take Jerusalem or seriously to occupy Palestine, and in a few years they had vanished from western Asia.

The northern invaders had weakened Assyria

beyond recovery. Under Nebopolassar, the first king of the new Chaldean dynasty, Babylon recovered her independence in 626 B.C., and in a few years formed an alliance with the eastern power of the Medes. The final struggle was long, and its fortunes varied. But in 614 B.C. the combined armies of the Neo-Babylonians and of the Medes took and sacked Asshur, and two years later Nineveh itself fell. The Assyrians continued the struggle from Harran, but that city also was taken in 610 B.C. It seems that the final stand was made at Carchemish (cf. Jer. 46:1-2) where the last great Chaldean victory was won in 605 B.C. This last event was recorded in western documents. Necho, son and eventually successor of Psamtik in Egypt, hoped to revive the ancient glories of Egypt, and seeing that the real danger came no longer from Assyria but from Babylon, he came to the rescue of the dying empire of Nineveh. Year after year, from 616 B.C., onward, he led armies into Mesopotamia and, more often than not, achieved a certain amount of success. At Carchemish he was clearly the most important enemy the Chaldeans had to face, and that battle marks not only the end of Assyria, but the last attempt of Egypt to secure world domination.

It was inevitable that all these events should have profound effects on Judah. In 641 B.C. Manasseh was succeeded by his son Amon (II Kings 21:19 ff.), who was assassinated two years later; his successor was Josiah, then a child of eight (II Kings 22:1). The Scythian inroads of 626 B.C. laid the whole country waste, and five years later Josiah took a definite step toward independence. Its most striking aspect was a religious reform, which appears to have resulted from the discovery of a book of law (II Kings 22:8), commonly identified with Deuteronomy or a part of it. All foreign cults were eradicated, not only from Jerusalem, but also from the whole country, and it is interesting to note that records mention the shrine of Bethel (II Kings 22–23). The Assyrian province of Samaria was breaking up, and it seems that Josiah was able to claim at least a part of its territory for himself. But ultimately he came into contact with Necho, and was killed at Megiddo in 608 B.C. The book of Chronicles gives a circumstantial account of a battle (II Chr. 35:20-24), but the language used in the book of Kings implies that the Judean king was simply executed (II Kings 23:29), probably on some charge of conspiracy with the Assyrians.

Josiah has a better reputation than any other king of Judah since David. Naturally his purification of the cultus gave him a high position in the eyes of those biblical writers whose primary concern was with theology. But the evidence shows that he was also the true ideal of the democratic king, free from pomp and vanity, fair in the administration of justice, and friendly to all his people (cf. Jer. 22:15). It is no wonder that he was generally mourned by Judah.

Presumably Necho was on his way to make his annual expedition into Mesopotamia in 608 B.C. when Josiah met his death. The people chose as his successor his second son, Jehoahaz (II Kings 23:30), but three months later, probably on his return from the expedition, Necho deposed him and put Jehoiakim, the elder brother, on the throne (II Kings 23: 33-34). The new king was quite different from his father; if the one was a second David, the other was a second Solomon. He erected magnificent buildings, and was ostentatious in his parade of monarchy, but he put his people to forced labor and reintroduced the cults which Josiah had removed (cf. Jer. 22:13-19). As an Egyptian nominee, he probably was not compelled to take the normal covenant.

The battle of Carchemish meant that all the west passed under the authority of Babylon rather than that of Egypt. Jehoiakim accepted the new regime (II Kings 24:1) and for some years remained faithful to the court of Babylon. But even if the Egyptians could not fight, they could intrigue, and there was probably a strong party in Jerusalem which favored them. In 597 B.C. Jehoiakim came out openly on their side (II Kings 24:2-3). Nebuchadrezzar, the king of Babylon, was not the man to let this come to pass, but before his armies could capture Jerusalem, possibly even before they reached the city, Jehoiakim died, and was succeeded by his young son Jehoiachin, one of the most pathetic figures in Old Testament history. Three months after his accession Jehoiachin surrendered (II Kings 24:12 ff.) and was carried to Babylon, together with many of the best people in the land. Still Nebuchadrezzar did not take the extreme step of destroying the Judean state, and placed a third son of Josiah on the throne, Zedekiah (II Kings 24:18), who offers a strong contrast both to his father and to his elder brother. His intentions were good, but his character was weak. The new nobility, with one or two striking exceptions, were far inferior to the old in every way (cf. Jer. 24), and the country was in a constant state of unrest. The final revolt broke out in 588 B.C. Jerusalem was besieged, and after eighteen months of suffering, relieved only by a short interval during which an Egyptian army made a fruitless demonstration (Jer. 37:5), the city was taken by storm. It was laid in ruins, the temple was burned, and all but the poorest peasants were carried off to Mesopotamia as prisoners. Zedekiah himself made a futile effort to escape, but was captured. His eyes were put out after he had witnessed the execution of his sons, and he too was deported. Judah, as an independent political entity, had come to an end (II Kings 25:1-21).

IX. The Exile (586 B.C.) and the Return (After 538 B.C.)

The desolation of Judah was practically complete. The process of destruction, of which we have an illuminating flash in the Lachish letters, left only a semipastoral community, with few if any well-established sites. Archaeologically, the sixth century is almost a blank in southern Palestine. But small farmers still remained, and for their government the Chaldeans set up Gedaliah, a member of a Judean princely house, at Mizpah (II Kings 25:22 ff.). It seems that the land began to recover under this wise and chivalrous nobleman, and for a time there was hope. But Gedaliah was murdered by a certain Ishmael, a scion of the old royal house. Fearing Chaldean vengeance, most of the remaining people fled to Egypt, taking with them Jeremiah among others (II Kings 25:25-27; Jer. 41:1-43:7).

In Babylonia the exiles settled down and took their part in the life of their new home, but they were never wholly absorbed in the general population. On account of their distinctive religion they retained their identity in a remarkable fashion. They had been united by Moses at Sinai through their common bond with Yahweh, and this same power still held them together. This was a unique phenomenon in the ancient world. They began to develop the worship of the synagogue, a new form of cultus which has ever since made religious exercise possible for a scattered people. They also engaged in considerable literary activity, including the compilation of law, history, and prophetic utterances.

In the early years of the Exile the Jews did not seem to find the rule of their masters oppressive, but after the middle of the sixth century Nabunaid, who was not of the family of Nebuchadrezzar, appears to have had religious designs not unlike those of Ikhnaton in Egypt, seven centuries earlier, and to have attempted the establishment of a single cultus. Other gods were removed from their shrines, and it is possible that Jews and others were subjected to persecution. Certainly there is a strong contrast between the tone of Jeremiah and Ezekiel on the one hand and that of prophets who lived toward the end of the Exile on the other.

The Chaldean Empire, however, was short-lived. A new power arose in Persia, under the leadership of Cyrus, king of Anshan (cf. Isa. 44:28–45:6; etc.). He first conquered Asia Minor, and then turned on Babylon. Nabunaid himself was in retirement at the Oasis of Tema, but his son, Belshazzar, was defeated and killed in a battle at Opis, and Babylon opened its gates gladly to the conqueror. One of the first acts of Cyrus was to restore the cults which Nabunaid had suppressed—indeed, he claimed that it was for this purpose that the gods had summoned him to overthrow the Chaldean power. Among others, the shrine of Yahweh at Jerusalem was marked out for restoration (Ezra 1:1 ff.; cf. Isa. 40:1 ff.), and this necessarily involved the return of a certain number of his worshipers.

It cannot be too strongly emphasized that the restoration was in the first instance a religious movement. The great prophet of the period, Second Isaiah, predicted first of all the return of Yahweh to Jerusalem (Isa. 40:1 ff.); that of the people was a necessary corollary (cf. Ezra 1:3 ff.). Indeed, the initial phases of the event are unknown. A certain Sheshbazzar was the leader of the first group (Ezra 1:8), but for sixteen years nothing definite was done. According to the records, a fresh expedition was led by Zerubbabel (Ezra 2:2), a son or a grandson of the unfortunate Jehoiachin. With the support of two prophets, Haggai and Zechariah, he rebuilt the temple, and it is suspected that he attempted to achieve some kind of political independence. His end is wrapped in mystery, but it seems that Jerusalem itself remained an unwalled city till the middle of the fifth century, when it was rebuilt by another Jewish governor, Nehemiah (Neh. 3; etc.), who had probably two periods of office, one beginning in 444 B.C. (Neh. 2:1) and the other in 432. To him, more than to any other one man, is due the recovery of Israel as a national though not an independent entity. He was insistent on the purity of the Jewish blood, and came into conflict with his immediate northern neighbors of Samaria (cf. Neh. 2:10 ff.) where the population was believed to be more affected by an infusion of foreign blood. His enemies tried to represent his erection of the walls around Jerusalem as an act of rebellion against the Persian court, but he was able to maintain his position, and charges against him were not sustained.

Ezra the scribe completed the work of Nehemiah. He came to Jerusalem in the sixth year of Artaxerxes—probably Artaxerxes II, not Artaxerxes I, as was formerly supposed because of his reputed connection with Nehemiah. It was, then, in 398 (on the older view 458) B.C. that Ezra promulgated the law (Neh. 8), and in so doing made the Jewish community what it continued to be through its whole history, the "People of the Book." While his purpose was primarily religious, his action gave to the new Israel a unity which it has never lost.

The position remained practically unchanged

till the advent of Alexander the Great. The land of Judah was far from being wealthy or prosperous, and the first two centuries after the return from Babylon must have been a period of depression and struggle. The people had the nominal protection of their Persian overlords, but Susa was far away, and, as the story of Nehemiah shows, local administrators and neighbors took advantage of the little community. The Persian conquest of Egypt left the Jews untouched, except in so far as some of them were called on as soldiers to take part in the conflict, or to garrison Persian military posts in Egypt (remains of such a post have been found at Elephantine near Assouan). But steady progress was being made, and by the time the Persian empire came to an end, the Palestinian Jews were a fairly contented people, gaining gradually in strength and stability. We hear vaguely of a revolt under Artaxerxes Ochus, which resulted in the deportation of large numbers, but details are lacking.

The conquests of Alexander seem to have made little difference to the general situation of the Jewish communities in Palestine or elsewhere. The king himself favored Jewish merchants, and made use of them in the founding of his new cities, especially of Alexandria, where they formed a very important element in the population until the seventh century A.D. The measure of independence and self-government which had been allowed to them by the Persians was continued.

Even the death of Alexander brought no serious change in the position. His empire was broken up, and Palestine became again what it had been centuries before, the debatable ground between north and south, between Syria and Egypt. For a century and more the land remained within the dominions of the Ptolemies, and the Greek government of Egypt followed the old policy.

X. The Maccabean Age and After
(167 B.C–A.D. 70)

The conquest of Palestine by Antiochus II, king of Syria, had a serious effect on the history of the Jews. Even under the Ptolemies they had been exposed to Greek influences, which had tended to weaken in some quarters the sense of national and religious uniqueness. But the Seleucids were far more enthusiastic missionaries of Hellenism than the Ptolemies had been, and with the advent of Antiochus IV (Epiphanes), matters came to a head. By this time there were two distinct parties within Jewry, the "broadminded," who were ready to accept Greek culture with all that it involved, and those on the other hand who clung more tenaciously to the old national faith and way of life.

The spark which fired the train was the appointment by Antiochus of a certain Jason as high priest, after the deposition of Onias. Jason in turn was superseded by a man named Menelaus, who did not even belong to the high priestly family. Orthodox Jews refused to accept him, and so challenged the right to nominate the high priest, which was claimed by the king. Antiochus in 169 B.C. made an attempt to conquer Egypt, but was compelled by the Romans to withdraw from that country. During his absence Jason made a bid to recover his position, and when Antiochus returned, he wreaked his vengeance on the troublesome Jews by spoiling the temple. Supported by the Hellenizing party among the Jews, he seems to have felt that the root of his trouble with this people was to be found in their religion, and he determined to stamp it out. Heathen altars were set up all over the country, and worst of all a shrine of Zeus was erected in the temple itself. The attempt to secure religious uniformity led to a revolt; at a place named Modein one of the local elders killed the officer who was sent to impose acceptance of a heathen cult. This man, Mattathias, and his sons, became the focus of the national and religious movement. The father did not long survive his heroic deed, and the leadership devolved on his son Judas, known to history as Maccabaeus—"The Hammerer." It must be remembered that there was already a strong Hellenizing element among the Jews themselves, and that Judas had to face a party among his own people as well as the military power of Syria. But the stricter Jews had behind them the driving force of a great spiritual impulse, and the early successes of Judas strengthened his position, turning a sectional revolt into a national uprising. Antiochus had to control a large and heterogeneous empire, and could spare only small forces for Palestine. The rebels, too, had the advantage of knowing their ground thoroughly, and in Judas they had a guerrilla leader to whom history offers few equals.

The first armed clash was with a detachment under a certain Apollonius, who was defeated and killed. A second and rather larger force under Seron was surprised near Beth-horon, and met with no better fortune. The spot was already famous in Israel's history for one of Joshua's great victories. A third engagement also resulted in the defeat of a Syrian army. The king himself was busy fighting the Parthians on his eastern frontier, and the local governors, whose seat was at Antioch, were unable to prevent Judas from occupying Jerusalem.

In December, 164 B.C., the victorious Jewish leader carried out a solemn purification of the temple. The altar had been defiled by heathen sacrifice, and much else in the sacred building had been contaminated by Greek worship. All that could be moved was taken away, even the great altar, whose stones were left in a place by themselves "till a prophet should arise" who would give more exact instructions. A new altar was built in accordance with the prescriptions laid down in the law, and on it sacrifices were offered. The occasion is still celebrated in the Jewish winter festival of Hanukkah. There remained, however, a Syrian garrison in the citadel of Jerusalem, the so-called "Akra," and as long as these men held their ground, the Jewish nation could not regard herself as politically free.

The religious aim of the revolt, however, was now secured, provided that Judas and his followers could maintain what they had won. From this time onward within the national party a rift appears which in the course of years led to serious division. Many felt that they had now gained all that they were fighting for. Others, including Judas himself and his brothers, seem to have felt that their position was insecure till they had attained complete liberty, and gradually the conception of a growing territorial state took the place of the purely spiritual ideal with which the movement had begun. So the struggle was continued, and the Jews were aided by internal troubles within the Syrian kingdom. Antiochus IV died soon after the purification of the temple, and at once a struggle began among different claimants for his throne. From time to time a ruler who held the western portion of the empire was able to use force in Palestine, but the whole power of Syria was never again united against the Jews. Judas and his brothers were thus able to add Gilead and Galilee to the districts of Judah which they already controlled.

A determined effort was made by Lysias, the governor in Antioch, who very nearly recovered the ground which had been lost. But just as he seemed at the point of complete success, other dangers compelled him to make terms with Judas, granting complete religious liberty, though still asserting political sovereignty. The war was renewed, however, with the advent of a certain Demetrius, one of the pretenders to the Syrian crown, and though Judas won a great victory over a Syrian general named Nicanor, he himself was defeated and killed at Elasa in 159 B.C.

The leadership was then assumed by Judas' brother Jonathan. Mattathias had belonged to the priestly family of Hasmon (whence Judas and his successors are commonly called the Hasmonaeans), and Jonathan was therefore eligible for the Jewish high priesthood, an office which he assumed in 152 B.C. He was at first confronted with a difficult situation, for the Hellenistic Jews were now in the ascendant, and the national party dispirited and scattered by the death of Judas. Gradually Jonathan recovered his brother's position, skillfully taking advantage of the conflicts which separated rivals for the Syrian throne, and at last secured himself against interference from them. In 147 B.C. an attack was made by an army under a certain Apollonius, but Jonathan won a complete victory which still further strengthened his position. There were still two signs of Syrian domination: the Jews had to pay tribute to Syria and the garrison of the Akra was retained. Jonathan not only extended Jewish territory but also made a determined effort to get rid of the two emblems of subjection. He succeeded in getting the tribute abolished, but was unable to drive out the Syrians from the Jerusalem citadel. Jonathan himself was at length entrapped by the Syrian general Tryphon, and treacherously murdered (141 B.C.).

The last surviving son of Mattathias was Simon, who then succeeded to the high priesthood. He won a reputation among his contemporaries even higher than that of his brothers. Like Jonathan he made good use of the civil wars constantly carried on in the Syrian kingdom, and one of his first acts was to recover the citadel of Jerusalem. He continued to expand the borders of his territory in spite of an attempt made by the Syrians to overthrow him. His sons, however, won a complete victory in 137 B.C., and Simon's power was unimpaired when he was murdered by his own son-in-law, a man named Ptolemy, in 134 B.C.

Simon was succeeded in the high priesthood by his son John, commonly known as John Hyrcanus. For a time he was in serious difficulties, and even Jerusalem was occupied by the Syrian king, Antiochus VII (Sidetes). Unlike so many of his predecessors, however, Sidetes showed himself magnanimous and sympathetic. He was content with a nominal sovereignty, and it seems that Hyrcanus was even allowed to assume the title of king as well as that of high priest. He, like the other Hasmonaeans, was able to make good use of the dissensions in the Syrian kingdom, and broadened the territory of Judah. His most notable achievement was the conquest of Idumaea, the ancient Edom. He compelled all the inhabitants to accept the Jewish faith, and so to become members of the Jewish community. In later years many Jews found reason to regret that achievement of Hyrcanus.

It was during this reign that the two main sections of the Jewish people crystallized into the parties known as Pharisees and Sadducees. The latter were the consistent supporters of the

Hasmonaeans in their political as well as in their religious efforts. The Pharisees, on the other hand, felt that Judas had secured all that was necessary when he rededicated the temple and restored pure Jewish worship. They concentrated on the religious aspect of Judaism, and developed that strictness, even in small details, for which they are so well known. They went so far as to challenge the right of Hyrcanus to be high priest, on the ground that there was a possible doubt concerning the circumstances of his birth. They won a very large measure of popular sympathy, though they were seldom able to wield any political power.

John Hyrcanus was the last of the really great Hasmonaeans, and with his death in 103 B.C. began a period of conflict and decline. It was characteristic of Eastern dynasties that a few able men were liable to be succeeded by weaklings, and the death of a strong ruler might easily lead to civil war between rival claimants for his throne. In Judah there was also a marked lowering of the moral standard, and the later Hasmonaeans present a strong contrast to the first two generations. Lust of power and personal jealousies had their inevitable effect, and the last forty years of Jewish freedom tell a sad story.

John Hyrcanus left five sons. The eldest, Aristobulus (it is significant that the Hasmonaean names were now Greek rather than Hebrew), assumed the high priesthood, imprisoned three of his brothers and put the fourth to death. But his reign lasted barely a year, and on his death his widow secured both the high priesthood and the kingship for one of her brothers-in-law, Alexander Jannaeus. He continued the policy of his predecessors, taking advantage of the political confusion in Syria to extend his own dominions. His ambitions and his character awoke resentment and even hatred among his own people, especially among those elements which were influenced by the Pharisees. Civil war broke out in Judah itself, and Alexander nearly lost his throne. The danger seems to have made him realize that he must try to meet popular feeling, and it appears that in his later years he was inclined to show some favor to the party of the Pharisees.

Alexander died in 76 B.C., leaving behind his widow, Alexandra, and two sons, Hyrcanus and Aristobulus. Alexandra herself became queen, making Hyrcanus high priest. During the nine years of her reign the Pharisees became quite influential, and their conduct did little to reunite the nation. The Sadducees attached themselves to Aristobulus, and on Alexandra's death in 67 B.C. bitter fighting broke out between the brothers. Of the two, Aristobulus was the abler, but Hyrcanus had the support of a very clever and vigorous Idumaean named Antipater, who enabled him to maintain the struggle at least on equal terms.

The general confusion led at last to the interference of Rome. Nearly a century earlier communication with the senate had been established by Judas Maccabaeus, and the alliance had become traditional. In the course of a general settlement in the east Pompey established a Roman province of Syria, and then interfered in Jewish affairs. He entered Jerusalem in 63 B.C., and maintained Hyrcanus in the high priesthood, giving him a certain amount of authority in his own country, though Judea was nominally incorporated in the province of Syria. The brief spell of Jewish independence had come to an end.

From this time onward the history of the Jewish people is dominated by their relations with Rome. The natural feeling of hostility to any foreign government was enhanced by the action of Crassus, who in 54 B.C. robbed the temple at Jerusalem of its treasures. Julius Caesar, on the other hand, adopted a policy of conciliation, and at his death was nowhere more sincerely mourned than in Judea.

Hyrcanus had taken the side of Pompey in the Roman civil war, but had transferred his allegiance to Caesar after the battle of Pharsalus in 48 B.C. As a reward for Jewish help, Caesar bestowed on Hyrcanus the title, not indeed of king, but of ethnarch, which at least seemed to be a symbol of comparative independence. More practical were the remission of tribute to Rome, the assurance of religious liberty, and the rebuilding of the walls of Jerusalem which had been destroyed by Pompey.

All classes of Jews, however, were united in their abhorrence of Antipater, the true ruler of the land. In spite of his wise, vigorous, and beneficial government, he was hated as an Idumaean, and racial prejudice overrode all other considerations. He was assassinated in 43 B.C., and his place was taken by his son Herod, a man who was at least his father's equal in ability and in strength. But Roman affairs were still far from being settled, and in 40 B.C. Antigonus, son of Aristobulus, allied himself with Parthian invaders and deposed his uncle Hyrcanus. His rule, however, was short, for Herod won the support of the stronger party in Rome, and in 37 B.C. defeated and killed Antigonus, becoming himself the political ruler of Judea.

For centuries the name of Herod the Great has been held up to general execration. There are good grounds for this judgment. He was ruthless in taking the lives of those who stood in his way, or who seemed to be dangerous. It is remarkable, however, that the worst acts ascribed to him are domestic atrocities such as the judicial murder of his wife Mariamne and of her mother. But there is no doubt that the royal palace was a hotbed of intrigue, and Herod, who knew so well how to handle men, was no match for feminine arts. The air was full of plots and counterplots, charges and countercharges, and during the first twelve years of his reign, Herod could have had little peace in his own household. He was in a most difficult position, and his cruelty may be taken as evidence of a helpless bewilderment in face of a situation he could neither control nor understand. In such circumstances power as absolute as Herod's becomes a moral danger.

In other respects it seems clear that Herod earned the title of "The Great." While he had warmly espoused the cause of Antony against Octavius, he succeeded, after the destruction of the former, in making his peace with the new ruler of the world, and even of winning his favor. While his government was strict, it was not unjust, and he had a passion for adorning the cities of his kingdom with beautiful buildings, of which the best-known example is the temple at Jerusalem. During the middle period of his reign there seems to have been little in his conduct to which objection could be fairly taken, but his later years were clouded once more by domestic trouble, and when he died in 4 B.C. there were few if any to mourn him.

Rome did not recognize a hereditary kingship, and Herod's dominions were divided. Galilee fell to a son named Antipas, a district to the northeast to another son, Philip, while a third son, Archelaus, was placed over Judea proper. But the experiment was not a success. Antipas alone seems to have inherited his father's abilities and character, though in the end he failed to maintain his position and was driven into exile. The reign of Archelaus was short; he was quite unequal to the government of a people like the Jews. Procurators, subordinate officials under the proconsuls of Syria, were placed in charge of Judea. Their official residence was at Caesarea; it was rightly felt that their permanent presence in Jerusalem might be an unnecessary irritant. From time to time, however, they appeared in the city, where they had a regular palace. Of these governors the best known is Pontius Pilate, whose name will be forever remembered as that of the Roman governor who sent Jesus to the Cross. As a rule, these men were not the best type of Roman official, and the tension between them and the people steadily grew.

Caligula and Claudius tried another experiment by placing a grandson of Herod, named Agrippa, on the throne. He had been brought up in Rome, and was reputed to have spent a wild youth. But responsibility steadied him, and on his appointment as king of the districts formerly held by Philip and another tetrarch, he began to show himself a wise and skillful ruler. He, like others of his race, knew how to deal with the Roman authorities, and before he died in A.D. 44, he had become king of all the country ruled by Herod the Great. He also manifested real sympathy for and understanding of his Jewish subjects, and he lost no opportunity of displaying his Jewish behavior. Had he been succeeded by men of similar character, the Palestinian community might have survived much longer than it did. But Judea was never again under the rule of a native king; even Agrippa's son, Agrippa II, had to be content with a comparatively distant principality.

The method of government by procurator was resumed, and the hostility between Jews and Romans became more bitter. A new and violent nationalistic sect appeared, known as Zealots, who were constantly on the verge of rebellion, and shrank from no means of annoying the Roman authorities. Matters came to a head in A.D. 66, when the Zealots succeeded in arousing the whole people. The Romans were forced to take the matter seriously, and Vespasian, the general appointed by Nero, spent the whole year 67 in reducing Galilee. In 68 he turned his attention to Judea, but events in Rome, where Nero was overthrown, kept him comparatively inactive, and in the following year Vespasian himself became emperor, leaving his son Titus to finish the Judean campaign.

In Jerusalem itself the Jewish factions were constantly fighting among themselves, even while the Roman armies were besieging the city. In the circumstances only one end was possible; the legions broke down resistance, entered the city, and after taking a certain amount of booty, destroyed both temple and city with fire.

XI. Selected Bibliography

ALBRIGHT, W. F. *From the Stone Age to Christianity*. 2nd ed. Baltimore: Johns Hopkins Press, 1946.

LODS, ADOLPHE. *Israel from Its Beginnings to the Middle of the Eighth Century*. Tr. S. H. Hooke. New York: Alfred A. Knopf, 1932.

———. *The Prophets and the Rise of Judaism*. Tr. S. H. Hooke. New York: E. P. Dutton & Co., 1937.

OLMSTEAD, A. T. *History of Palestine and Syria to the Macedonian Conquest*. New York: Charles Scribner's Sons, 1931.

ROBINSON, H. WHEELER. *The History of Israel, Its Facts and Factors*. New York: Charles Scribner's Sons, 1938.

ROBINSON, THEODORE H., and OESTERLEY, W. O. E. *A History of Israel*. Oxford: The Clarendon Press, 1932.

THE HISTORY OF THE
RELIGION OF ISRAEL

by JAMES MUILENBURG

From the secular point of view the books of the Old Testament represent the classical religious literature of an ancient, Oriental people known as the Hebrews or as Israel; from the religious point of view, however, they comprise the sacred scripture of two of the world's great religions, Judaism and Christianity. Each religion views the Old Testament as more than merely a significant deposit of ancient writing.

The way in which the history of Israel's religion is written will depend upon our manner of viewing it. In the following discussion the Old Testament is interpreted from within a religious community which holds it to be sacred scripture.

I. Introduction

A. Faith and History.—In Judaism and Christianity history and faith are inextricably related.

292

The way in which faith is related to events provides a major disclosure into the meaning of the religion. In the Old Testament the nature of history is grasped in terms of the nature of the God of Israel. It is interpreted from the perspective of the initiative, revelation, sovereignty, and purpose of a covenantal God. History is therefore the area of maximum interest and concern. When we try to discern the character of Israel's religion in the light of the form in which it has been transmitted to us, we are confronted first of all not with doctrines or principles or even ideas, but with the activity of God in events. It is in the relation of the covenant God with a covenant history that the Old Testament is to be understood.

This historical orientation of the Old Testament is apparent in the earliest records; in them we witness the presence of a dynamic historical faith (Exod. 15:21; Judg. 5). When the early traditions are compiled and ordered into the extensive patterns of epic, as in the Yahwist and Elohist sources, or when the events of the early monarchy are related to a major historical continuity, as in the stories of Saul and David, the meaning of events is greatly deepened. Without the biblical point of view, Israel's history has only a minor importance. Viewed secularly, the uniqueness of this people does not emerge, for Israel's history cannot be understood in secular categories. It is only when faith and event meet that the situation is changed. Event without faith yields little illumination; it is faith that transforms the event and makes of it the reality which the Bible describes. And conversely, faith without event is not relevant faith; it is the event that gives to Israel's religion its form and character.

This is clearly seen in connection with the biblical personalities who appear in the course of Israel's history. Abraham and Jacob-Israel, Moses and Samuel and Elijah, Amos and Isaiah and Jeremiah are not significant apart from the faith which motivates and inspires them. It is in the immediacy of his own personal situation in history that the person hears "the word" spoken to him. To apprehend the significance of biblical persons, then, we must apprehend the nature of the religious faith which lies within and behind them. They cannot be understood without this faith. The one subject of the Bible is God, and it is only in relation to him that the Bible can be understood. This provides us with the first answer to the question, "How shall we read the Bible?"

B. Faith and Interpretation.—As it is faith that inspires the history of Israel and gives it content and meaning, so it is only through faith that the record can be understood. There is an interior approach to the history of Israel's religion, over and beyond the critical and analytical approach, which is assumed in any effort to recover what the faith was. This interior approach of participation or empathy opens up vistas and sounds depths that are undisclosed in any other fashion. For this approach it is necessary to identify oneself with the ancient writer, to stand where he stands. This does not mean that we read uncritically. It means that we must read with the eye of appreciation—in an interior way. It means that we must read with imagination, for it is the religious imagination that is at work throughout the Bible. It means that we must read with sympathy as though we ourselves are somehow involved in what is being written. We belong to it, and it belongs to us. We stand in community with it. It is Israel's story, Israel's life and thought and aspiration, and we do not read well or profoundly if we stand outside as spectators. It is only the poet in us which responds to great poetry. It is only the artist in us which helps us to see, really see, the work of the artist. For the kind of literature that the Bible presents to us, it is essential that we adopt an attitude and point of view of this sort. For an ancient Semitic literature which is at once imaginative and poetic and historical and personal and eventful, such an approach is indispensable.

C. Bible and Church.—The point of view and attitude which have just been described have particular force for those who stand in living continuity with the great tradition. We do not think of ourselves as detached and separated from it, but rather as belonging to it. Within the community of Israel, whether old or new, the Bible wears a different aspect from that which it has outside the community. Church and Bible belong together.[1] They are reciprocal realities. They depend upon each other. Within the church the Bible is confessed as scripture, and the church finds in its pages the record of the story of its deepest origins. The church cannot understand itself without the Bible. Similarly, the Old Testament is unintelligible outside of Israel, the living, historical community which passes through varying vicissitudes and through deep chasms of crisis and destruction. It is true that such language as this has peculiar force within the sacred community, that is, the faith of a Jew or Christian helps him to appropriate this language as something congenial and intelligible. But a good historical defense can also be made for this position, for from early times sanctuary and tradition exist together. The sanctuary is the place where the tradition is preserved, trans-

[1] See article "The Bible: Its Significance and Authority," pp. 3-31.

mitted, interpreted, and implemented into the life of the cult.

The history of the religion of Israel is not the chief among biblical disciplines. That distinction belongs to biblical theology. But the latter requires the reinforcement and concreteness of the former. The theology of the Old Testament cannot be rightly understood without the history of Israel's religion. Standing isolated by itself, Old Testament theology always involves a distortion of the faith of Israel.[2] It runs the danger of violating the historical character of the revelation as it is transmitted to us in the biblical records. The creation of a theology out of the kind of materials that the Old Testament presents us is always to do the religion of Israel some degree of violence. The revelation that comes to us is historical and existential, and so it is the historical approach that most accurately reflects and does greatest justice to the biblical records. It is here that historical criticism finds its highest justification. For Hebraic religion, above all others, it is essential that the records be subjected to careful criticism and evaluation. It is impossible to recover the nature of that historical revelation without placing the documents in their proper historical setting. What is spoken or written is spoken or written in a definite context, and the "word" is not rightly apprehended, that is, as it was meant to be apprehended, if we leave it hanging in the air. Word and event belong together, and this means concrete word and concrete event. Perhaps no contribution in modern times has been greater than the contribution of the scholars of the past century who have helped us to discern what this means. The prophets have come to life for us, and in our new appreciation of them as men of God to their own times they have spoken to us and our own times with a directness and force unprecedented in the history of Hebrew-Christian faith.

D. The Biblical Perspective.—When the whole of the Old Testament is read in this historical context and we get a picture of its movement from its earliest beginnings to its final end, we are in a position to understand the achievement of Israel, or rather, the nature of the divine activity in the Chosen People. We must evaluate and interpret the individual event and individual word, but we must move beyond this if we are to assess the true significance of Israel's religion. The context of biblical thinking is linear. It moves from beginning to end. The thought and mentality of Israel are keenly sensitive to beginning and end; they constantly play reflectively upon these two focuses. It is natural that beginning and end should be variously understood and interpreted,

but before the Old Testament comes to a close, these great focuses are comprehended at their final points of the primordial and the eschatological, of creation and redemption, of old covenant and new, of the word to Abraham (Gen. 12:1) and the realization of that word.

But what can be said of the history of Israel's religion itself? What is the nature of its movement as it presses beyond the limits of the Old Testament canon? Naturally, Judaism and Christianity will give divergent answers. The one will discern the most authentic culmination in the literature of rabbinical Judaism, while the other will see the Old Testament fulfilled in the New. The view we take as to the culmination of Israel's faith will inevitably influence our reading of the Old Testament. We cannot help being influenced by our understanding of its most authentic outcome. To be sure, both Jew and Christian will seek to read their scriptures in the light of the meaning of the original writers. But there will certainly be a difference in emphasis and evaluation, and there will be a difference in discerning where the deepest continuity really lies. Such writings as Deuteronomy, Jeremiah, Ezekiel, and the Priestly Code will be treated somewhat differently when their importance is assessed. But for both religions the Old Testament is indispensable to an understanding of their true character. For the Christian community the belief that the New Testament fulfills the Old is a major fact concerning the religion of Israel. It is the faith of Christians that the new Israel is the true continuation of the old. The confession of the people of the new covenant concerning Jesus of Nazareth can never be ignored completely. Such a confession has its grave perils when it comes to interpreting the Bible, for it is always our first task to learn what the text really means, and later developments must not be allowed to obscure the original meaning. At the same time, we do not read a passage in isolation only, but inquire into the subsequent development of its thought and into its use in other parts of the Bible or in rabbinical and other literature.

II. The Age of the Patriarchs
(ca. 2000-1500 B.C.)

A. Historical and Cultural Background.—The period covered by the Hebrew patriarchs was one of almost universal turbulence among the peoples of the ancient Near East.[3] There is a curious interruption in the flow of contemporary records toward the beginning of the Middle Bronze Age and extending to 1500 B.C. and beyond. Fortunately the discovery of the Mari archives in the region of the Upper Euphrates

[2] See article "The Faith of Israel," pp. 351-52.

[3] See article "The Old Testament World," pp. 233-71.

by André Parrot has made it possible for us to gain a fairly clear picture of the situation in the Euphrates region in the eighteenth century B.C. Following the brilliant Twelfth Egyptian Dynasty (2000-1750 B.C.) and the great age of Hammurabi in Babylon (1792-1747 B.C.) Hurrians from the Caucasian highlands pressed into the Fertile Crescent and spread throughout the entire region, both east and west, and even into Egypt. About 1750 B.C. the Hyksos, who were in all probability predominantly North Semites, invaded Egypt, where they remained for almost two centuries until they were driven out by Ahmose I (*ca.* 1550) to mark the beginning of the Eighteenth Dynasty and the New Empire. Not much later than the Hyksos conquest, the Hittites from Anatolia burst into the Euphrates region and brought the dynasty of Hammurabi to a decisive end. This invasion, in turn, prepared the way for the Kassites, who swept from their mountain home in the Zagros into Babylonia and retained control of the region for over four centuries.[4] Other groups were involved in the turbulence of this age, but enough has been shown to indicate that the period was one of great unrest. The documents from Mari and those which emerge after the period of silence all reflect the same situation. The Fertile Crescent, which was far from being racially homogeneous before these invasions, became much more complex in its racial composition. "It was amid this welter of diverse races rapidly commingling that the Hebrew people were born." [5] In many ways the most interesting and significant of all these movements was the Hurrian invasion, for our recent knowledge of these people provides almost certain proof that the origins of the Hebrew patriarchs are to be traced among these people who settled in the region of the Upper Euphrates later controlled by the Mitanni. The linguistic and cultural affinities that have been adduced from this region and the equally startling parallels between Genesis and the Nuzi materials go far to settle the issue as to the origin of the patriarchs. The biblical account of the sojourn from Harran has much to support it, and the general emphasis upon Aram and the Aramaeans in the accounts corroborates what is probable on other independent lines.[6] One

other name appears among the peoples of this era, the Habiru. The name appears almost everywhere in the ancient Near East, so it is certain that the Habiru were widely disseminated. The name bears no ethnic association, but the equation of Hebrew with Habiru is widely accepted.

It was in this period of international anarchy and ethnic diversity that the patriarchs lived—the period represented by the book of Genesis. The movement and pressure of various races and racial types were reflected in the Hebrews, and the complex picture of the culture and religion of the book of Genesis is consistent with what our recent knowledge has taught us concerning conditions of the whole of the ancient Near East during the period of the Middle Bronze Age. It is obvious that many forces and influences went into the making of the Hebrews. In any attempt to reconstruct the religion of this age these are the facts that must be borne in mind.

B. Sources.—The Bible contains no contemporary sources for the history of Israel's religion before the time of Moses. Our earliest literary documents come from a period centuries after the events they record. This situation combined with the highly legendary character of many of the materials, the indisputable presence of eponymous elements, a number of anachronisms, and obvious traces of the point of view of a much later age, has prompted many historians in the past to view the representations of the Pentateuch with great suspicion. There certainly was a long period of oral tradition in which the memories of Israel were transmitted from generation to generation, but many scholars have been skeptical whether these memories have been accurately preserved. Critical analysis has demonstrated the presence of two great epic works: the Yahwist epic, emanating from the time of the early monarchy (*ca.* the tenth century B.C.), the Elohist epic from the northern kingdom (some time in the eighth century B.C.).[7] There is no question that the theology which dominates these works in their present form represents the point of view of their authors and compilers. Until recent times, therefore, the

---

[4] W. F. Albright, *From the Stone Age to Christianity* (2nd ed.; Baltimore: Johns Hopkins Press, 1946), pp. 150 ff.

[5] Theophile J. Meek, *Hebrew Origins* (rev. ed.; New York: Harper & Bros., 1950), p. 6.

[6] Albright, *From Stone Age to Christianity*, p. 179. Here Albright is inclined to believe that the localization of Abraham's home at Ur was secondary (*a*) because it is without archaeological illustration, and (*b*) because the Greek translators nowhere mention Ur. In his article, "The Biblical Period," in *The Jews: Their History, Cul-*

ture, and Religion, ed. Louis Finkelstein (New York: Harper & Bros., 1949), I, 4, he appears to accept the historicity of the Ur tradition: "We shall probably never be able to fix the date of Terah's migration from Ur to Harran, but there can be no doubt that a date about the third quarter of the twentieth century B.C.E. would suit historical indications remarkably well."

[7] Two other sources of considerable scope and of major importance are present in the Pentateuch: the Deuteronomic, emanating from the seventh century B.C., though its sources in turn are often much earlier, and the priestly history and law, codified *ca.* 538-450 B.C., but containing a great amount of early and trustworthy material.

majority of scholars have felt impelled to treat the accounts in the Pentateuch as unreliable to a considerable degree for the historical period which they describe.

Our vastly enlarged knowledge of the ancient Near East has changed the situation appreciably, however. Today many scholars recognize a substantial amount of genuine historical material for such a period as the age of the patriarchs. Archaeology has revealed an extraordinary correspondence between the general social and cultural conditions portrayed in Genesis and those exposed by excavations. Discoveries from such sites as Nuzi, Mari, and elsewhere, provide the geographical, cultural, linguistic, and religious background against which the stories of the patriarchs are laid.[8] Many passages which were heretofore obscure have become clear. A large number of details which the spade has unearthed fit in with the details of Genesis. Moreover, today we attach greater credence to oral tradition than in earlier times. If the sanctuaries were repositories of many of the traditions, as seems likely, then we can understand more readily why the traditions remained as reliable as they now appear to be.[9] Again, the striking differences between the religion of Genesis and the religion of Exodus argue for the preservation of an authentic tradition.

Yet it is important not to exaggerate the situation as we meet it in the Pentateuch. It is obvious that the literary materials are of great complexity, that various sources have gone to their making, and that the point of view of the compilers has left its stamp upon their compilations. If we do not distinguish between the work and thought of the compilers and their sources we are in danger of throwing the history into confusion. In actuality we are confronted with a number of strata from different times, and these times are much later than the patriarchal age. The true historian will seek to avoid the Scylla of undue skepticism and the Charybdis of undue credulity. For such an undertaking we are in a better position today than ever before. It is not too much to say, however, that all the sources, late as well as early, preserve an appreciable amount of ancient and trustworthy tradition.

C. The Religion of the Patriarchal Age.— Pre-Mosaic religion has its home in Palestine. Only against the background of Canaanite religion are we able to make any estimate of the religion of the patriarchs. The biblical traditions of the book of Genesis do not suggest any sharp difference between the worship of the patriarchs and the worship of the Canaanites. The most telling witness of the inscriptions from widely separated places (Mari, Ras Shamra [Ugarit], Nuzi, Boğasköy, Tell el-Amarna, and elsewhere in Egypt) is in fundamental harmony with the Canaanite milieu and Canaanite character of pre-Mosaic religion. All this is amply reinforced by the later biblical record (such as Deut. 26; Ezek. 16; the Priestly Code, etc.). Complex and late as our literary sources may be in their present form, the background against which Mosaic religion came into existence is without question Palestinian and Canaanite.

The head of the Canaanite pantheon worshiped by the patriarchs was El. His presence is seen in such titles as El Elyon (Gen. 14:18-20, 22; Num. 24:16; Deut. 32:8), El Shaddai (Gen. 17:1; 28:3; 35:11; 48:3; 49:25; Exod. 6:3), El Olam (Gen. 21:33), El Roi (Gen. 16:13), El Berith (Judg. 9:46). In Gen. 14:19 Melchizedek, the king of Salem and priest of El Elyon, blesses Abram:

Blessed be Abram by El Elyon,
Maker of Heaven and Earth;
And blessed by El Elyon,
Who has delivered your enemies into your hand.

Such compounds are kin to Ugaritic compounds *tpn 'el dp'ed, 'el mlk, šr' el,* etc.[10] In the Ugaritic poems El is described as dwelling in a distant cosmic locale, the "Source of the Two Deeps" (cf. Hebrew *tehôm*). He was worshiped at Shechem, Jerusalem, Ugarit, and elsewhere. A developed cult of El Elyon which existed at Jerusalem has left its impress upon more than one Old Testament passage.[11] His cosmic character is affirmed in Melchizedek's blessing and is closely paralleled by the Ugaritic expression *qnyn 'El,* El our Creator. At Shechem, El Berith (El of the covenant) was worshiped, and while biblical evidence first appears in Judg. 13:33; 9:4, it is confirmed to a degree by the phrase "the terebinth of the lawgiver" in connection with the theophany to Abram upon his entrance into Palestine (Gen. 12:6 [J]). In the light of these considerations Joshua's covenant at Shechem, with its accompanying statute and ordinance, is most illuminating. That the cult at Shechem was somehow related to the cult at Jerusalem is suggested by the name Abimelech

[8] For detailed illustrations see Millar Burrows, *What Mean These Stones?* (New Haven: American Schools of Oriental Research, 1941), *passim.*

[9] Despite exaggeration in some quarters, it is the great merit of the contemporary Scandinavian school of traditio-historical criticism that it has called attention to the living process of the growth of traditions.

[10] Herbert G. May, "The Patriarchal Idea of God," *Journal of Biblical Literature,* LX (1941), 113-28.

[11] Aubrey R. Johnson, "The Role of the King in the Jerusalem Cultus," in *The Labyrinth,* ed. S. H. Hooke (London: Society for Promoting Christian Knowledge, 1935), pp. 71-111.

(Judg. 9), king of Shechem, and the name Melchizedek at Jerusalem. The component parts of these two names have good Ugaritic parallels. Another deity whose name is familiar to us from the second millennium B.C. is Bethel.[12] It will be recalled that the Old Testament records at least three references to theophanies to Jacob at Bethel (Gen. 28:10-22 [JE]; 31:13 [E]; 32:9-11 [J], "I am El-Bethel"). Philo of Byblos mentions Bethel as a deity along with El, Dagon, and Atlas,[13] and in the Elephantine papyri of the fifth century B.C. the name seems to appear again as that of a deity. The appellation El Shaddai is commonly employed by the priestly writer before the time of Moses (cf. Exod. 6:3). The inscriptions, together with an early biblical source (Num. 24:16) and the archaizing references in the book of Job, lead to the conclusion that El Shaddai was in actuality head of the Canaanite pantheon, and this is confirmed by his identification in Num. 24:16 with El Elyon. El Shaddai is evidently a mountain deity, "the Mountain" or "the One of the Mountain." [14] Among the Canaanites, as among other peoples of the Near East, the plural form Elohim was already applied to one god.

The chief interest in the cult represented by these various names was in nature. The mystery of life as it manifested itself in the fertility of soil was articulated in the worship on the *bâmôth* or high places. Here the most characteristic appurtenances were the *maccēbhāh* or sacred stone and the '*ashērāh*, perhaps the image of the god by that name (cf. "Ashirat of the Sea" in the Ugaritic inscriptions). Offerings and gifts were made on the high places and other sanctuaries, as at Bethel, Beersheba, Hebron, Shechem, and Jerusalem. Festivals were probably celebrated at certain seasons of the year, all of them nature celebrations, not very different from those celebrated at the vineyard dances at Shiloh (Judg. 21), or "the marriage festival of the fields" at Shechem, of the wailing for Jephthah's daughter "upon the mountains" (Judg. 11:38). The religion of the fathers was not the same as the worship of the thundering Yahweh of Sinai. The God pictured in Genesis is not like the God who reveals himself to Moses in the book of Exodus.

On the other hand, the biblical traditions present us with a religion which was much more than, and quite different from, Canaanite worship. A comparison of the stories of Genesis with the Ugaritic texts will reveal at once that we are moving in another world of thought. The Canaanites were agriculturists, and their interest was in nature and the fertility of the soil; the Hebrews were nomad shepherds and the interest in nature is quite secondary to the interest in history. This contrast is not to be explained as solely the work of the late compilers. The deities of Genesis are gods of the fathers. Albrecht Alt has subjected the sources to close scrutiny in the light of Palmyrene and Nabataean texts, and has drawn a picture of religious development which is not only consistent with the biblical traditions, but also in conformity with the situation as we encounter it in the revelation to Moses on Mount Sinai.[15] With each of the patriarchs there is associated a special theophany in which the deity reveals himself in a highly personal way. The names of the deities are directly connected with the patriarchs: the Shield of Abraham (Gen. 15:1), the Kinsman (*páḥad*) of Isaac (Gen. 31:42, 53), and the Mighty One of Jacob (Gen. 49:24). These were family or clan gods with family names and associations in which the intimate relationships of the family (father, brother, etc.) were applied to the deities, as is reflected in many of the biblical names.[16] They were personal gods and they bore the names of those to whom they first appeared: the God of Abraham, the God of Isaac, and the God of Jacob (Exod. 3:6). These were ancient tribal deities which later coalesced into one in the revelation to Moses. The view of Alt is not without its difficulties, but it has the merit of focusing upon the biblical traditions themselves and of being in harmony with the mentality of these traditions. Family kinship is of course prominent in all West Semitic religions, and the Hebrews employ exactly the same terms to describe it as their neighbors do. But in Genesis there is an historical germ which was not only original but also susceptible of further development.

III. The Age of Moses (ca. 1350-1250 B.C.)

A. Sources.—The biblical records which center in the life and work of Moses are the Yahwist (J) and Elohist (E) epics and the priestly (P) history and legal codes. It is significant that much of the most important material concerning Moses and the theophany on Sinai,

---

[12] J. P. Hyatt, "The Deity Bethel and the Old Testament," *Journal of the American Oriental Society*, LIX (1939), 81-98. Hyatt traces the origin of the god Bethel to the second millennium, possibly to Ugarit, but certainly "to the religion of the territory of Syria or Syria-Palestine which is best represented to us by the Rās Shamra documents" (p. 90).

[13] *Phoenicum Historia* II. 14.

[14] Cf. Albright, *From Stone Age to Christianity*, p. 186: "The mountain-deity in question is clearly . . . called Baal (lord) by the Canaanites, and often addressed as 'great mountain,' or the like, in Accadian invocations to Amurru, the 'Western One,' i.e., the storm-god of the West."

[15] *Der Gott der Väter* (Stuttgart: W. Kohlhammer, 1929).

[16] Albright, *From Stone Age to Christianity*, p. 185.

with its covenant events, come to us from E, although occasionally it is J which provides us with valuable information (e.g., Exod. 19:3b-8). The book of Deuteronomy witnesses to a recrudescence of Mosaic religion. The priestly sections of the Pentateuch, although they are late, often preserve important and early reminiscences, and even much of the legislation in its ultimate origin goes back to very early times. Of great value, too, are the not infrequent allusions to the Exodus and the wilderness sojourn in the Prophets and Psalms (Amos 2:10; 9:7; Hos. 11:1; 13:4; Mic. 6:4; Jer. 2:2-3, 5-7; Pss. 66:6; 78:18-53; 136:10-11). While we have no firsthand extrabiblical material corroborating the story of the Exodus, such materials as we may glean from the ancient Near East concerning the periodic invasion of Semitic tribes into Egypt, the reference to Israel in the Merneptah stele (ca. 1229 B.C.), the earlier witness of the Tell el-Amarna letters (fourteenth century B.C.), and the important results of excavations in Palestine (e.g., Bethel, Lachish, etc.) as well as extra-Palestinian sites, help us to see the events in a convincing context and setting. As to the historical existence of Moses there can no longer be any serious doubt. He is as well authenticated as the founder of any of the great world religions. The imaginative and folkloristic elements in the accounts do not deprive them of their general historicity.

B. Historical Background.—The beginnings of religions are characteristically obscure, and this is also true of the beginnings of Israel's religion. On such important questions as the time and circumstances of the entrance into Egypt, the number and identity of the tribes, the length of the Egyptian sojourn, the date of the Exodus, and the location of Sinai, we are not in a position to give any decisive answer. Yet archaeology has aided us enormously in recent years so that the obscurity is not nearly so great as it was even a generation ago.

There is good reason to suppose that the Hebrew clans entered Egypt during the period of Hyksos occupation (1750-1560 B.C.). It is not likely that all twelve tribes were present in Egypt, but neither is it likely that only one tribe (e.g., Levi) was there. The Exodus itself is to be dated in all probability in the early part of the thirteenth century B.C.

C. Moses and His Work.—While there has been much gratuitous speculation for centuries upon Egyptian influences in the records which deal with Moses, we are now in a better position to assess the true situation. The name of Moses is certainly Egyptian (cf. the Egyptian *mesu* as it appears in Ah-mesu [Ahmose], Ra-mesu [Ramses], Thut-mesu [Thutmose]). Other Egyptian names continue for several generations

after Moses. Some scholars have seen the influence of the solar monotheism of Amenhotep IV's reform movement upon Moses. It is certainly not impossible that Moses and his contemporaries came under this Egyptian influence, but nothing at all certain can be deduced from our present records, and there is very little to suggest any direct bearing of Akhenaton's lofty monotheism upon the mind of Moses.

The idyllic story of the birth of the child which has many parallels among other peoples, the daring stroke for justice, the flight to Midian, the romantic scene at the well, the theophany of the burning bush, Moses' mighty wrestling, and the great contest between Moses and Pharaoh all constitute a stirring prologue to the fateful events which follow. Oriental imagination is at work in all these accounts, but the figure of the personality which emerges from them is not inconsistent with sections which lay claim to greater credence. The theophany to Moses reveals a great psychological struggle which is not only consistent with later biblical "calls" but also in harmony with the kind of personality which the records describe Moses to have been.

D. The Exodus.—The central event upon which all the early stories converge is the Exodus from Egypt. In this event the Hebrews believed that their God had made himself known to them. He came to them in the hour of their deepest need and wrought a mighty liberation for them. At the Sea of Reeds (or Papyrus Marsh) he prepared a road that they might pass over dry-shod. In the moment of supreme crisis when the Egyptians pursued them, he came to their rescue from the pillar of cloud and fire (Exod. 14:24-25). From the midst of the gathered clans Miriam came forth with a tambourine, and in ecstatic joy sang a hymn of deliverance and redemption. No lines in the whole account lay greater claim to fact than these. In a profound sense they mark the beginning of the religion of Israel:

Sing to Yahweh, for he has triumphed mightily,
The horse and its rider he has hurled into the sea
(Exod. 15:21).

In a succession of events all the way from Egypt to the mount of convenanting, Yahweh came to the help of Israel. They needed a leader in the desert, and he came in pillar of cloud and fire to lead them. They suffered from thirst, and he healed the bitter waters of Marah with a branch of leafy foliage (Exod. 15:25 [J]). They hungered for the onions and garlic of Egypt, and he came with "bread from heaven" in the gift of manna and quail (Num. 11:4-10 [E]). In the supreme hour of their arrival at the mount, Israel encountered Amalek in internecine warfare, but in miraculous fashion Yahweh gave victory to his people (Exod. 17:8-16 [E]). Such was the God who had revealed himself to Moses: Deliverer, Leader, Physician, Provider, and Victor in war. Now he was to reveal himself to them as more than all these.

Israel saw in the series of events centering in the Exodus the living matrix of her faith. The thought and reflection of later periods focused again and again on this creative period, and our present Pentateuch is a major witness to it, just as the remaining portions of the Old Testament, and often of the New Testament, return again and again to them as the lodestar of the great tradition. It is common in modern accounts of this period to speak of "the work of Moses," and surely nothing should obscure the momentous proportions of his achievement. But it is by no means certain that this is the point of focus of the Bible; rather, it is Yahweh who is at work through Moses, his mediator, in every crisis and vicissitude. With grateful hearts the generations rehearsed the "righteous deeds" (צִדְקוֹת) of Yahweh.

E. The Covenant.—In the biblical accounts of the covenant the central features of the faith emerge with clarity. What is the significance of this event? The Scriptures are rightly called "the Old and the New Covenants," for it is the covenant that constitutes the cardinal fact underlying them. The historicity of the covenant at this early time has been challenged, but without success. Not only the contention of the narratives themselves, but the subsequent development of Israel's life from Sinai onward needs this basis to give it the meaning which it professes to have. It is a covenant God who speaks covenant words to a covenant people and consummates a covenant relationship in a fateful covenant act. The memories of Israel are memories which find their source and vitality in some such event as this. The absence of references to the covenant is often perplexing.[17] But many sections before Deuteronomy and Jeremiah (e.g., I Kings 19:10, 14; Amos 3:2; Hos. 1-3) demand the covenant to explain them. And as Israel treasured these covenantal memories in her communal life, so she looked forward to the covenantal promises which all versions of the covenant contain. Past, present, and future, all of history in fact, was read in terms of the reality of the covenantal event and revelation. In saying this it is important not to exceed our evidence by relying on sources which are inextricably intertwined with our present narratives (e.g., P), but which are nevertheless

late. At the same time, it is just as important to evaluate our earliest sources, late as they are, and to discern what is historically reliable and religiously significant in them. When the true place of the covenant in Israel's religion is once recognized and appreciated, we shall have to find an adequate source for such a momentous development as the Old and New Testaments present to us.[18]

The significance of the covenant for Israel in the age of Moses may be stated as follows:

(a) In the complex of events of which the covenant is the center it is Yahweh who takes the initiative and brings about the beginning of Israel's historical existence. There are horizontal elements in the account, such as Israel's slavery in Egypt, conditions under the New Empire, the influence of Akhenaton's reform, the reign of Ramses II, the Midianite or Kenite cult with Jethro as its priest on the mount of God, and many other similar factors. These forces are obviously of importance for an understanding of the account. But there is also a transcendent element here; at least Israel understands it so, and obviously understood it so from the beginning. Faith and history are interwoven in this account of Israel's beginnings, and faith does justice to the transcendent elements as historical and literary criticism seeks to do justice to the immanent elements. Both are present, and we must recognize both if we are to understand Israel's religion. The narrative is theocentric, and the theocentricity is marked by God's breaking into history in behalf of his people Israel.

(b) The initiative of God in delivering Israel and thus bringing her to self-consciousness was marked by his revelation, "God spake all these words, saying" (Exod. 20:1). When God takes the initiative by a great event he accompanies the event by his word. Yahweh speaks to Israel, who knows herself to be addressed. But the distinctive feature of this account is that Yahweh reveals what Israel needs above all things else to know. The first words are in the characteristic form of all theophanies, biblical and nonbiblical. But to Israel the word is "I am Yahweh" (Exod. 20:2). A relationship has been established. The name has been spoken, and Israel can know her God and call upon him and praise him.

(c) This God who speaks from the mountain does not speak to Israel as a God of nature. It is possible that he was a nature god originally,

[17] Gerhard von Rad, *Das formgeschichtliche Problem des Hexateuchs* (Stuttgart: W. Kohlhammer, 1938).

[18] For recognition of the Mosaic date of the covenant see Walther Eichrodt, *Theologie des Alten Testaments* (Leipzig: J. C. Hinrichs, 1933-39), where the covenant dominates the whole of biblical faith from beginning to end and in every area and phase of its life; cf. also the works of Ernst Sellin, Ludwig Köhler, Adolphe Lods, W. F. Albright, Theophile J. Meek.

the god of the Kenite clans of which Jethro was priest. The natural elements in the theophany are striking, but they are transcended and even deified. Israel understood her origins to be not animistic, but historical.

(d) The revelation of Yahweh meant that a relationship had been established. Later sources described it in the familiar words, "I will be your God, and ye shall be my people," but this idea is present from the beginning. It is not too much to say that the fundamental word of the Old Testament scripture is this expression of relationship: Yahweh the God of Israel, and Israel the people of Yahweh.[19] This is in reality the basis of Old Testament ethics as it is the basis of the cult; in it both priest and prophet find their task.

(e) The relationship between Yahweh and Israel is one that is understood and described in terms of history. "I am Yahweh who brought you out of the land of Egypt, out of the house of slaves" (Exod. 20:2). This is the prior and essential revelation of Yahweh; other revelations are subordinate to it and must be read in the light of it.

(f) The revelation of Yahweh in the covenant situation was one that confronted Israel with obligation and responsibility. The covenant is contingent: "If you will indeed heed my injunctions and keep my covenant" (Exod. 19:5). The account may reflect the views of a later period of composition, but the sources are unanimous in this fundamental and fateful representation of Israel's responsibility as expressed in a law. From the beginning Israel knows herself to be accountable. This must be recognized as an authentic contribution of Moses. At the heart of his own "call" throbs this imperious demand upon him, which he seeks to evade but cannot resist. If the Old Testament is a development from the covenant relationship, then this confrontation with an absolute demand belongs with it. There is no theophany without obligation, no meeting of God without meeting the urgency of a demand.

(g) Yahweh's revelation is to a people; it is not Moses who is "called," but Israel; Moses' call is a call to confront Israel with Yahweh's word of revelation and his deed of deliverance. Yahweh's purpose is to choose for himself a people. Every people has its god, and the gods have their peoples, but the historical character of Yahweh's choice of Israel and the series of events in which he has made himself known makes Israel a people in a unique sense.

(h) When Israel covenanted with Yahweh, they covenanted together. It was a voluntary

act of solidarity. Who were those who gathered at Sinai? We do not know, but they probably represented disparate tribal elements. Together they covenanted with Yahweh, and they were bound by one central loyalty, an exclusive loyalty to Yahweh alone. They were bound so surely because they were so surely bound to Yahweh, the Lord and initiator of the covenant. The covenant is the basis of Israel's consciousness of community.

(j) In the later religious development Israel reflected upon the motive of Yahweh in his election of her and in his entering into covenant with her. The later prophetic leaders could see nothing in Israel that merited such a choice and such a deed (Deut. 7:7-8). The final answer was that it was an act of Yahweh's unmerited love and in accordance with his oath to the patriarchs. This is not articulate in the earliest sources, but it is implicit in them. One might say that Yahweh's choosing of Israel was no different from Chemosh's relationship to Moab, or Rimmon's to Aram, or Marduk's to Babylon. But no careful reading of the relevant accounts substantiates such a view. There is elsewhere no living, personal, voluntary relationship in which the two parties are dynamically involved. In Israel choice and decision, loyalty and fidelity, obligation and accountability, and mutuality of response are writ large over the whole account. And Yahweh, who brought about the whole situation, is one who acts because it is his character to act and speak and make his claim. At least we may say that the later consciousness of an election love ('ahᵃbhāh) and a covenant love (ḥésedh) demanding mutuality and fidelity are adumbrated here. It was present enough for Israel to proceed upon its basis.

(k) The covenant relationship as the primary locus of Israel's loyalty and self-consciousness provides her with a perspective from which to view all the relativities of her history. What the covenant meant in relationship to the life of the nation could be apprehended only in the course of on-going history, but the oldest accounts clearly describe the commands which govern Israel's community life from the point of view of the covenant. The tendency in recent decades to find in the Elohistic Decalogue of Exod. 20:1-17 the original Mosaic deposit is not guided by this covenant consciousness necessarily, but it is the covenant relationship which gives this Decalogue another claim to authenticity alongside of other claims. To assume the general representation of J and E concerning the covenant to be substantially correct is to give a meaning to the whole Mosaic age which is in accord with the later representations of the Old Testament.

---

[19] For an admirable statement of this see Johannes Hempel, *Gott und Mensch im Alten Testaments* (2nd ed.; Stuttgart: W. Kohlhammer, 1936).

F. Yahweh and His Nature.—Almost the first question to come from the lips of Moses on the occasion of the theophany was, "What is his name?" (Exod. 3:13). This is an important question in all ancient religion, and the answer for ancient man is of supreme import. When the deity revealed himself to Israel, the first words were the communication of the name. The reply Moses received to his question seems to be cryptic or enigmatic, and it is the view of many scholars that it was meant to be so. That is not impossible. But most scholars have sought to find the meaning of the famous four letters, YHWH, for it is a natural assumption that the name was expected to mean something significant. Since the verb is most obviously from the Hebrew verb "to be" (better, "to become," "to befall," "to happen," "to come to pass"), it is natural that many explanations have started with what appears superficially to be the primary meaning. This has had at least one unfortunate effect, for it has encouraged metaphysical interpretations of being, which are certainly wide of the original meaning. Similarly, the rendering "Eternal," popularized by its employment in the Moffatt translation, must be rejected. The view taken here is also that adopted by T. J. Meek, "I that cause to be what comes to pass" [20] or "I who cause to happen what happens." [21] This translation is linguistically permissible and is in accord with the context of the revelation to Moses. The chief question is whether the name was thus understood by those who worshiped Yahweh before Moses. This is not likely. As in other biblical etymologies, the word is given a meaning to suit the Hebraic interests.

The view of the origin of the Yahweh cult set forth by Karl Budde [22] still commends itself as the most probable, although many details would have to be restated. According to that view, Yahweh was the God of the Midianite (Kenite) clans inhabiting Sinai-Horeb, "the mountain of God." Jethro was priest of this tribe, and was expert in the cult associated with it. When Moses married into the family of Jethro he was adopted covenantally as a member of the tribe whose God was Yahweh. The revelation to Moses was a revelation of Yahweh, perhaps at the sanctuary or sacred spot (before the cave?) where the god dwelt. Both the character and the wide range of evidence in the Old Testament, most important of which is found in the earlier and later associations of Israel with the Kenites, make it inherently probable.

But more important than the origins of Yahweh and the cult associated with his name is the character of the deity. What is most striking in his nature is his holiness. He is a zealous, jealous, mighty God who thunders with his voice and sends forth lightning and fire. There is something fearful, terrifying, even demonic in him. The whole mountain quakes at his descent, and the people tremble before the awfulness of the theophany. This utterly holy character of Yahweh makes him and everything associated with him taboo. Therefore Moses and Israel must engage in elaborate cultic acts in order that Yahweh may not burst upon them. Such a God is a "consuming fire." There is no suggestion of mysticism anywhere in these accounts; it would be unthinkable that any devotee, even Moses, should feel himself mystically united with him. This holy character of Yahweh appears at the beginning in primitive fashion, but it put its stamp upon the whole faith to our own day. Yahweh the God of Israel is a holy God.

It is this jealous, terrible aspect of Yahweh that lends such urgency to the first of the commands of the Elohistic Decalogue, "Thou shalt have no other gods before me" (Exod. 20:3). Yahweh tolerates no other God to be worshiped beside him. Yahweh stands alone. In contrast to the nature gods of the Semitic East, Yahweh has no consort, although in the Elephantine papyri of the fifth century B.C. there is more than a suggestion that in Egypt the Jews did recognize such a consort. But as the narratives are before us now, and indeed as the whole Old Testament now stands, Yahweh is without any connections of family. To be sure, Israel is his son (Exod. 4:23), but the relationship is one of adoption, not of nature. The later expression, "sons of El," is a poetic reminiscence of Canaanite provenance which refers to angelic beings and should not be taken literally. Yahweh permits no cleavage in Israel's piety; there is no separation between belief in God and belief in demons. He comprehends within his being both the divine and the demonic (Exod. 4:24-26; 19:21-22), the positive and the negative, light and darkness. Yahweh has no mother goddess at his side; he includes within his nature both husband and wife, both father and mother. The feminine attributes as well as the masculine are absorbed into his holy being. He forbids the perpetuation of beliefs and practices of the ancient folk religion such as the cult of the dead. Yahweh is in control over every area; there is no need for a special cult of the family, for he is Lord within the family and over the family. The family traditions associated with

---

[20] *Hebrew Origins*, p. 100.

[21] Even a hasty examination of the usage of the verb *hāyāh* in Francis Brown, S. R. Driver, C. A. Briggs, eds., *A Hebrew and English Lexicon of the Old Testament* (Boston: Houghton, Mifflin & Co., 1906) will reveal the active connotations of the word.

[22] *Religion of Israel to the Exile* (New York: G. P. Putnam's Sons, 1899).

the patriarchs are absorbed and taken over by the Yahweh cult (Exod. 3:15).

Yahweh admits no easy toleration of other divine beings. He demands an exclusive worship. Everywhere else in antiquity the belief is common that the more gods the better; the more diverse and manifold the pantheon, the greater the resources for every kind of need and every aspect of human life. The gods are as many as the needs of men. Not so in Mosaic religion. The demand that Yahweh makes of his people is monolatrous, however, not monotheistic. The existence of other gods is not denied; the command to worship him alone, "Thou shalt have no other gods before me," actually implies their existence. What is required is that Israel shall neither worship nor recognize these gods. The later formulation, Yahweh, and Yahweh only shall you serve (Deut. 6:10-15), is Mosaic through and through. But further, the urgency with which the demand of monolatry is made of Israel, and the power and holiness and jealousy of Yahweh which are associated with the demand, are such as to give it not only a peculiarly binding force but also an impulsion and impetus in the direction of something more than monolatry. In a continuing historical revelation, where the intense reality of Yahweh's holiness asserted itself in the movement of succeeding vicissitudes and events, and where his sovereignty was viewed in new contexts of ever more extensive range, monotheism was certain to emerge in the course of time. It is not too much to say, therefore, that monotheism is already implicit in the original command to Israel (Exod. 20:3). Not until we do justice to this feature of Mosaic religion are we prepared to measure the magnitude of Moses' work as the founder of Hebrew religion; not until we appreciate the implications of the command are we prepared to understand either the immediately subsequent religious development of Israel or the relative absence of fear among the Israelites in comparison with other peoples of the ancient Near East. Precisely because Yahweh is to be worshiped alone, because he demands everything and excludes nothing, life was destined to be grasped as a unity, the ethical demand was destined to have singular force, and the interpretation of history was destined to be grasped under a controlling unity as in Second Isaiah and the book of Daniel.

Consonant with the holiness of Yahweh and his status as the only God to be worshiped by his devotees is the command against the making of images: "Thou shalt not make unto thee any graven image, or any likeness" (Exod. 20:4a). Yahweh must not be represented by visual imagery of any kind, or at least by any imagery which bears the trace of human handiwork. The Yahweh whom Moses proclaims to Israel, and with whom Israel enters into living covenantal relationship, is invisible to human eyes. The intensity of the conviction that no man shall see God and live extended itself congenially into the whole area of God's nature. He was not such a God as could be adequately represented by the work of men's hands. The contrast of the cult of Yahweh with the cults of the ancient Near East was tremendous at this point, for visual imagery belonged to the very heart of the cult practices and the religious mentality associated with them. It is questionable whether Yahweh was ever represented in the form of animals, but in this period at least there is no suggestion that Yahwism permitted any kind of theriomorphism. Again, if we consider the wide currency of theriomorphism among the ancient Oriental cults, the Yahweh cult stands out conspicuously.

Yet the language of the Old Testament is strongly anthropomorphic, and it never ceased to be so. In nothing is the stirring quality of our sources more apparent than in their use of anthropomorphic and anthropopathic language, "I have seen the plight of my people, . . . and I have heard their cry, and I have come down to deliver them" (Exod. 3:7-8 [J]). "At the morning watch YHWH looked down toward the Egyptian army in the column of fire and cloud, and threw the Egyptian army into a panic. And he clogged their chariot wheels" (Exod. 14:24-25 [J]). It is the use of this vivid, living speech that opens a window into one of the most important features of Hebraic mentality, for parts of the body are bearers of psychical functions, and the physical becomes a remarkably powerful and significant agent of expressing psychical meanings.[23]

G. Law and Cult.—Through the mediation of Moses, Israel became the people of Yahweh. The covenant relationship between Yahweh and Israel demanded a mutuality of obligation. Yahweh agreed to be the God of Israel, and Israel agreed to accept the provisions upon which alone the covenant could be based. We have already observed that the relationship was contingent upon Israel's keeping the covenant, yet it is only God who can abrogate it. The sojourn at Kadesh (En Mishpat)[24] and the instructions of Jethro to Moses on the occasion

[23] On this very important subject see the following: H. Wheeler Robinson, "Hebrew Psychology," in *The People and the Book*, ed. A. S. Peake (Oxford: Clarendon Press, 1925), pp. 353-82; and especially Johannes Pedersen, *Israel, Its Life and Culture I-II, III-IV* (London: Oxford University Press, 1926, 1940).

[24] Adolphe Lods, *Israel from Its Beginnings to the Middle of the Eighth Century*, tr. S. H. Hooke (London: Kegan Paul, Trench, Trubner & Co., 1932), pp. 176-81.

of his attempts to adjudicate disputes and give decisions to the people (Exod. 18:13) certainly suggest the development of a body of social practice and law.

It is somewhat more difficult to decide how extensive this body of law was and to identify its original scope. At the present time the Pentateuch contains a vast body of elaborate law, but this is almost all the work of the priests in the exilic and postexilic periods of Israel's history. That this may contain much that is early is fairly certain, but it is impossible to distinguish early and late with any great degree of plausibility. For years the J Decalogue (Exod. 34), first isolated by Goethe in 1773, was considered the earliest, although it has always been recognized that this could scarcely be Mosaic in view of its agricultural interest. More recently, however, there has been a tendency to turn to the Elohistic Decalogue of Exod. 20:1-17, which follows the important interview of Jethro and Moses in Exod. 18 and the theophany to Israel in Exod. 19, and precedes the covenant act of Exod. 24 (reported by J in vss. 1-2, 9-11; E in vss. 3-8; and P in vss. 15-18a). To be sure, the Decalogue appears in an expanded form, and there is no universal agreement as to its exact contents. Without vouching for the historicity of every line, one may construct the passage somewhat as follows:

> God spoke all these words: I am Yahweh, your God, who brought you forth out of the land of Egypt, out of the house of slaves.
> 1. You shall have no other gods before me.
> 2. You shall not make for me any graven image or any likeness.
> 3. You shall not invoke the name of Yahweh your God in vain.
> 4. Remember the- sabbath day to keep it holy.
> 5. Honor your father and your mother.
> 6. You shall not commit murder.
> 7. You shall not commit adultery.
> 8. You shall not steal.
> 9. You shall not bear false witness against your neighbor.
> 10. You shall not covet your neighbor's house.

Paul Volz finds in the E Decalogue our only authoritative source for the real work of Moses, except for reminiscences outside the Pentateuch. Perhaps this is going too far, for there is much other material in the Pentateuch emanating from J, and especially from E, which has a claim to consideration. On the other hand, even the Elohistic Decalogue has its difficulties. The tenth command has often been suspected, and the command of sabbath observance in a no-

madic milieu is troublesome. The fifth through the ninth commandments should occasion no difficulty, for there is no good reason why they should be placed as late as the *florescat* of the prophetic movement. After all, other peoples in antiquity had long before recognized these basic demands of any stable social order.

The Covenant Code which follows the Elohistic Decalogue (Exod. 20:23–23:19) is in its present form not later than the ninth century, but the researches of Anton Jirku,[25] Albrecht Alt,[26] and W. F. Albright[27] have greatly added to our knowledge of this material. Alt distinguishes between the casuistic laws of Canaanite provenance found in the Covenant Code and the apodictic laws. The Decalogue and the curses of Deut. 27 illustrate the form and spirit of the Hebrew apodictic formulations. Albright says of these: "The most striking thing about the apodictic laws is their categorical character . . . ; the Israelites are commanded *not* to sin, *because Yahweh so wills.*"[28] Law and religion in ancient Israel belong together; ethics and religion are one and inseparable.

Of the institutions in the desert only two will demand our attention here. Circumcision is perhaps pre-Mosaic, so it need not deter us. First of all, the ark.[29] Controversy has raged for long concerning this sacred emblem. Whether its historical associations lie with the wilderness sojourn or with the later conquest of Palestine (I Sam. 4–7) has long been a major center of dispute, but the argument has gone with those who have defended the biblical representation of a desert palladium. The parallels among the nomad Arabs and the researches of Morgenstern and Klamroth are almost decisive. But what was the function of the ark, and what did it signify to those for whom it was a very sacred and holy object? Certainly it was closely connected with Yahweh himself. Rejecting older interpretations of W. Robertson Smith and those who follow him, we may say with assurance that in some way it mediated the presence

[25] *Das weltliche Recht im Alten Testament* (Gütersloh: C. Bertelsmann, 1927).

[26] *Die Ursprünge des israelitischen Rechts* (Leipzig: S. Hirzel, 1934).

[27] *Journal of Biblical Literature*, LV (1932), 164-69. The Canaanite casuistic laws of the Covenant Code belong in the same genre as the Sumerian Lipit Ishtar Code 150 years before Hammurabi, the Akkadian Eshnunna laws, which Albrecht Goetze thinks may be even older, the Code of Hammurabi of the eighteenth century B.C., the Hittite laws of the fourteenth century, and the Assyrian laws of the twelfth century. For a most important and illuminating discussion see Goetze, "Mesopotamian Law and the Historian," *Journal of the American Oriental Society*, LXIX (1949), 115-20.

[28] *From Stone Age to Christianity*, p. 204.

[29] For a brief though excellent discussion see Elmer A. Leslie, *Old Testament Religion* (New York: Abingdon Press, 1936), pp. 121-26.

and even the will of Yahweh. Some scholars have thought of the ark as the throne of the invisible Yahweh. Others have held that the ark contained some object or objects of a holy character. Its military associations are clear both in Numbers and I Samuel, and are classically formulated in the early songs of the ark:

Arise, O Yahweh, and let thine enemies be scattered;
Let those that hate thee flee before thee.
Return, O Yahweh, to the ten thousand thousands of Israel (Num. 10:35-36).

But there is no reason to believe that this was its only or even its chief function. It may well have been used for the consultation of the oracle, although our earliest sources connect the "inquiry of God" with the tent of meeting. On the basis of the Deuteronomic writings, such modern scholars as Ernst Sellin, Paul Volz, and Hans Schmidt have maintained that the ark contained the Sinaitic laws. Sellin argues:

If it was recognized at the very beginning that the source of the holy will of God—his words—was contained in a box, as the pledge of the conclusion of the covenant between him and the community, then it is most easily explained how there was erected for him the cult of prayer, of blessing, and of consultation of the deity.[30]

The direction of the cult was left to Yahweh, for at all times the word of God was considered to be the source of all directions, so that even in the land of Canaan, so remote from Sinai, where Israel came under the dominance of Canaanite religion, the presence of Yahweh was nevertheless in their midst and his will was known in the concreteness of his commandments. This is surely an attractive view and has more to commend it than the alternative view that it was some meteorite stone taken from the sacred mount. It is a daring conjecture that Sellin makes, for it runs the serious danger of reading back the situation of later times into the time of Moses, but it is coherent with the movement and progress of Israel's historical life. We may at least recognize that the ark was intimately associated with Yahweh himself, that it was in some fashion or other connected with the expression of his will, whether as an instrument of divination or as containing the sacred words enshrined in the Elohistic Decalogue. Finally, it is likely, as William R. Arnold maintained, that there were many arks in ancient Israel, perhaps one at each of the great sanctuaries, but that the Deuteronomists recognized only one ark and one place of worship.[31]

[30] *Israelitisch-Jüdische Religionsgeschichte* (Leipzig: Quelle & Meyer, 1933), p. 31.
[31] *Ephod and Ark* (Cambridge: Harvard University Press, 1917).

Although the report concerning the tent of meeting has been subjected to fanciful elaboration, the central representation of the early sources may be accepted as reliable. Quite certainly it was used already in the Mosaic period for the consultation of the oracle, the "inquiry of God" (Exod. 33:7-11 [E]). As so frequently in the Pentateuch, it is the Elohist who gives us information that appears to be authentic. In fact, the Yahwist does not mention the tent at all.

"Now Moses used to take the tent and pitch it outside the camp, at a distance from the camp. It was called the tent of meeting. If there was anyone who wanted to consult Yahweh he would go outside the camp." (Exod. 33:7.) It is doubtful whether the ark and the tent belong together; more likely they were separate from each other until the time that David brought the various sacred tribal emblems into the city of Jerusalem. As to the central importance of ark and tent of meeting, little need be said. As instruments for mediating the presence and the will of God they belong to the center of the cult.

Did the Israelites sacrifice to Yahweh in the desert? If one were to confine his attention to the representations of the prophets alone, the answer would in all probability be in the negative. Amos seems to deny categorically that Israel sacrificed to Yahweh in the desert, and Jeremiah confirms Amos' apparent denial. On the other hand, it is the uniform witness of all the major Pentateuchal sources that sacrifice was offered to Yahweh and on notable occasions (Exod. 18:12-13 [E]; 24:5-8 [E]). Moreover, the Covenant Code contains the fundamental command that no one shall come before Yahweh empty-handed (Exod. 23:15), prescribes the construction of altars for sacrifice (Exod. 20:24), and even enters into details which are probably very early (Exod. 23:18-19). It is significant that the Elohistic Decalogue has no word about sacrifice, since throughout the ancient Near East sacrifice is the natural expression of religion. The conclusion, then, will be that Israel did indeed offer sacrifices to Yahweh in the desert, but that they never assumed the central role in her religion which the Priestly Code, for example, suggests. In sacrifices Israel was brought into communion with Yahweh. They brought him into dynamistic relationship with his people, who became united with him by sharing with him in the sacrificial flesh. The priesthood nowhere assumes any place of importance in our earliest sources, although Moses himself functions as a priest in the great moment of the covenant relation (Exod. 24).

H. Conclusion.—The first great period of Israel's religion centers in the name of Moses, and if the picture here presented of the religion which he founded has not been overdrawn then the period may be designated as the age of Moses. The patriarchal age lies behind that epoch, to be sure, but it comes to us rather as prologue to Moses and the emergence of Israel. The period of great beginnings, the seminal age, was the time of Moses. The great act of redemption from slavery rehearsed in Miriam's song, the succession of mighty deeds culminating in the covenant on Sinai, the covenant itself with its tremendous demands of monolatry, imageless worship, and the elemental commands for the cohesion and purity of the social solidarity, all these stand as the pillars which uphold the faith. Behind all and within all is the historical consciousness of Yahweh's mighty deed in history; the personality of Moses, the servant of Yahweh; the chosen people with a great commission; the prospect toward a future in which the meaning of the covenant will articulate itself and Israel will trust and hope in its promises.

IV. The Period of the Conquest
(ca. 1250-1020 B.C.)

A. *Sources.*—The period of the Conquest is exceptionally well documented, both for the ancient Near East as a whole and for the international corridor of Palestine. If we may include the Late Bronze Age (1500-1200 B.C.) as an indispensable background for the understanding of this period, then we are confronted with almost an embarrassment of riches. First of all, there are the Egyptian records emanating from the New Empire, the Eighteenth (*ca.* 1550-1319 B.C.) and Nineteenth (1319-1200 B.C.) Dynasties. Of greatest importance are the famous Tell el-Amarna letters from the reigns of Amenhotep III (1413-1377 B.C.) and Amenhotep IV (Akhenaton; 1377-1360 B.C.). These letters are of inestimable value for the light they cast upon the international character of the age which J. H. Breasted has felicitously styled "The First Internationalism," and for the vivid picture they give of conditions in Palestine and the Near East as a whole. Of like value are the materials from ancient Ugarit. These inscriptions do for us culturally and religiously what the Tell el-Amarna tablets do politically. The language and culture reflected in the Ugaritic inscriptions show the same international outreach and cultural fusion of diverse elements from the ancient Near East as are suggested by the Tell el-Amarna letters. Of great interest and importance also are the Hittite archives from Hattusa (modern Boğazköy) in Asia Minor, the Nuzi texts from the Upper Euphrates, belonging to the fifteenth century B.C., which give us an amazingly vivid insight into the social conditions of an ancient city

from this period, and finally, the Assyrian Code of Laws.

The biblical sources for the period of the Conquest are the anticipations of the Conquest in the Pentateuch and the books of Joshua, Judges, and I Samuel. The biblical books must, of course, be subjected to criticism before they can be used by the historian. In its present form, for example, the book of Joshua has peculiar difficulties, and it is natural that there should be great diversity of opinion concerning its historical character and value. Albrecht Alt has subjected Josh. 1–12 to careful examination and has recovered the original etiological stories.[32] Used in conjunction with other sources, they are of great value. The highly compressed précis of "the lost J account of the Conquest" (Judg. 1:1–2:5) and the Song of Deborah (Judg. 5) are sources of the first importance, though the text is not always secure and the continuity of the former narrative is confused.[33] The stories of Judges both in the body of the book (3:7–16:31) and in the "appendix" (chs. 17–21) give us much good historical information for the period. The two early poems of the blessing of Jacob (Gen. 49) and the blessing of Moses (Deut. 33) preserve authentic memories. Even the late, conventionalized, editorial materials of Joshua and Judges confirm in their own stylized and exaggerated way what we learn in a different fashion from JE. We have come to have new respect for the priestly sections of Joshua too, for in recent years the lists have been subjected to critical examination by the Alt-Noth-Jirku-Albright school on the basis of the Gunkel method of *Gattungsforschung.*[34] It should be added that the results do not always present us with sources for the period of the Conquest but for later periods of Israel's history.[35]

B. *Historical Background.*—The historical problems for this period are even more acute than those of the Mosaic age, although here we are aided by the vast resources of archaeology. It would seem that not infrequently the name of Joshua has been adapted to the Pentateuch

[32] "Josua," in *Werden und Wesen des Alten Testaments,* ed. Paul Volz (Berlin: A. Töpelmann, 1936), pp. 13-29.

[33] R. H. Pfeiffer, *Introduction to the Old Testament* (New York: Harper & Bros., 1941), pp. 296-301. Pfeiffer concludes that J's account of the Conquest, "which survives in a meager and revised summary, without being strictly accurate in all details is our main source for a period of Israel's early history as obscure as it is important for the nation's later achievements."

[34] Albright, *From Stone Age to Christianity,* pp. 210 ff.

[35] Alt, "Judas Gaue unter Josia," *Palästinajahrbuch,* 1925, pp. 100-16; "Das System der Stammesgrenzen im Buche Josua," *Sellin-Festschrift* (Leipzig: A. Deichert, 1927), pp. 13-14; Martin Noth, *Das Buch Josua* (Tübingen: J. C. B. Mohr, 1938; "Handbuch zum Alten Testament").

at crucial moments; and that similarly the allusions to Moses in Joshua, besides being highly stylized, have been accommodated to the narrative. Even more troublesome is the presence of what seem to be conflations of the Moses and Joshua traditions. Such accounts as the crossing of the Jordan, the story of the spies, the circumcision at Gilgal, the passover at Gilgal, the extraordinary theophany to Joshua which culminates in exactly the same words as those addressed to Moses (Josh. 5:15), the law on Mount Ebal, and the covenant at Shechem cannot be cavalierly dismissed, for they raise the question of what is historical in the biblical tradition of this period and what is not.

Certain general conclusions may be derived from the sources which bear upon the religion of this period: (a) The period of Israel's emergence into history was one of great international activity. It was an age of many peoples, and Palestine was a land of many peoples—Hurrians,[36] Hittites,[37] Canaanites,[38] etc. (b) Almost throughout the period of the New Empire Palestine continued to be an Egyptian province.[39] (c) The conquest of Palestine extended over many decades. Indeed, the land was not securely in Hebrew hands until the time of David. National unity was hammered out under the successive blows of foes without and within. (d) Many competing peoples entered into the struggle for the corridor (Moabites, Ammonites, Philistines, and Canaanites), although the conflicts with the Canaanites were neither as fierce nor as extended as is wont to be believed. (e) The Conquest was the achievement of many leaders in different times and in different places and against different invading or resident foes. The narratives in Joshua, Judges, and Samuel which stand the test of historical inspection by no means tell the whole story. The uprising of the tribes under Deborah and Barak, the routing of the Midianites under Gideon of Manasseh, the repulsion of the Ammonites under Jephthah the Gileadite, the fabulous exploits of the Danite hero Samson,

the remarkable defeat inflicted by Joshua of Ephraim upon the Amorites, these are all part of the great period of the Conquest, but altogether they are far from being the whole of it. (f) It follows from this that the Conquest was not the work of united Israel standing embattled against the resident Canaanites to strike one fell blow against them, but rather the work of various tribes or groups of tribes. (g) Chief of all the foes to threaten Israel after her success in gaining at least a precarious foothold were the Philistines (ca. 1170), and it is against these that Israel launched her greatest strength under the leadership of Saul and David. (h) The leader responsible for securing the corridor for the Hebrews, for bringing the Conquest to an end, was David of the tribe of Judah. (j) Israel's prowess in war constitutes a dominant feature of the whole period. (k) In the larger perspective of history, however, it was not Israel's military power nor even her nomadic heritage that contributed most, but the religious vitality with which she was endowed. The meeting of Hebrew and Canaanite indeed represents a profound cultural phenomenon which was destined to stamp a large part of the Old Testament, to influence the character of the faith itself, and to give it powers of survival and stability which the less rigorous cults of the Baal could not ultimately withstand.

The period of the Conquest was one of profound transition: from the seminomadic life of the desert to the farming life of the Palestinian oasis, from the life of the desert to the great international corridor, the highway of the nations and what has been called "the political and geographical center of the world"; from relatively tribal organization to an organization of a more inclusive type, the amphictyony of tribes, and later to the monarchy itself under Saul and David; and finally, from an inferior culture to a superior one. On this latter point, however, it must be remembered that the invasion made a profound impress upon the land as the excavations eloquently show. The Hebrews were in the ascendant, the Canaanites in the descendant. The meeting of Hebrews and Canaanites represents the dominating feature of the second great age. The meeting involved a clash that transformed Hebrew religion for the age of transition itself and beyond it. The Yahweh who met Gideon as he was beating out wheat in the wine press, exacted the fulfillment of Jephthah's dreadful vow, and appeared to Samson's mother with assurance of a Nazirite son, was not in all respects the same as the Yahweh who had thundered forth amidst the fire of Sinai, yet had much in common with

[36] Albright, *From Stone Age to Christianity*, pp. 108-12; E. A. Speiser, "Ethnic Movements in the Near East in the Second Millennium B.C.," *Annual of the American Schools of Oriental Research*, XIII (1932), 13-54; *Mesopotamian Origins* (Philadelphia: University of Pennsylvania Press, 1930); "Hurrians and Subareans," *Journal of the American Oriental Society*, LXVIII (1948), 1-13; Albrecht Goetze, *Hethiter, Churriter und Assyrer* (Oslo: H. Aschehoug & Co., 1936).

[37] Emil Forrer, ed., *Geschichtliche Texte aus Boghazköi* (Leipzig: J. C. Hinrichs, 1926; "Die Boghazköi-Texte im Umschrift"); "The Hittites in Palestine," *Palestine Exploration Quarterly for 1937*, pp. 100-15.

[38] The literature is vast. For an excellent discussion, see Albright, "The Rôle of the Canaanites in the History of Civilization," *Studies in the History of Culture* (New York: Modern Language Association, 1942), pp. 11-50.

[39] Albright, *From Stone Age to Christianity*, p. 155.

the El of Genesis. What is left after the stories are told and retold is that Yahweh of the Exodus and the mount of covenanting remains (cf. Judg. 6:8 ff.). The God of history stands forth triumphant in battle. They who were "called" and commissioned by Yahweh were endowed with the urgency and unction of the charism of the Spirit.

C. The Religion of the Conquest. 1. Canaanites and Israelites.

Canaan, the "land of milk and honey," was in Baal's possession, and it was to Baal's land that Israel came.[40] Baal ensured fertility of the soil and thus guaranteed self-preservation. Baal was native to the land, and the Canaanites were Baal worshipers. Between gods and soil there was a deep, warm, psychic, even passionate relationship. To secure fertility one must therefore satisfy the pleasure of the Baal. He naturally withheld his gifts to those who refused to recognize his ownership of the land and denied him his due. Canaanite Baalism at this time was in a stage of decadence and degeneracy. The depth of the corruption is evidenced in the cult of ritualistic prostitution and sacrifice of infants.

How would Israel relate herself to the new land with its fertility cult? What would be most natural and simple and approved is that she would grant the fertility gods their due; this would be assumed throughout the ancient East. In Canaan one respected and honored the indigenous divinities of the land. Israel was leaving the desert and entering an oasis where farming was possible, where vineyards were cultivated, and the fig and the olive were nurtured. This was not the province of Israel's seminomadic Yahweh. It is likely that many Israelites took the easiest and most natural course: they recognized the Baal's prerogatives. Some, indeed, may have forgotten their covenant God of Sinai completely; many more simply recognized Baal for what Baal had to give, and Yahweh for what Yahweh offered in time of war and national crisis. Tolerance was a characteristic of ancient religions, and only the small minority, men like Samuel and Elijah and the band of their successors, understood the nature of Yahweh, the jealous, zealous god of Israel. Thus the worship of Yahweh and the Baal went on together with no intended mutual affront. On the other hand, there must have been a considerable body of Israelites, how many it is impossible to conjecture, who carried on the Mosaic tradition

and refused to "bow the knee to Baal."[41] The orgiastic cult of fertility, the highly sensuous symbols of the nude mother goddess, and the elaborate mythologies of springtime and harvest repelled the austere and simple nomadism of Yahweh's followers. If the picture here given of Mosaic religion is at all accurate, then there certainly must have been many who would not be so easily lured by Baalism.

Our crucial problem here is to discern the nature of the meeting of Hebrew with Canaanite. The problem is greatly complicated by the fact that different social strata reacted differently to the nature cults; groups like the Nazirites and Rechabites represented one extreme while many farmers represented another. What wrong could there be in acknowledging the agricultural divinities in agricultural territory? Neither of the extremes won the day. At times the nation would move toward Canaanite deities, but at other times under the urgency of some crisis they would turn to their own national God. The neat Deuteronomic framework of Judges is a theological stereotype, but it contains much historic truth. Israel did follow the Baals and Astartes, and only national crisis forced the tribes to recognize Yahweh as the God of their national life and destiny. Such reflections as the vintage festival at Shiloh (Judg. 21:19-23), Gideon's name of Jerubbaal and the idolatrous ephod, the annual festival of Jephthah's daughter, Jotham's fable with its interesting reminiscences of the Canaanite cult of nature, Shechem's Baal-berith, and many other similar instances give us too eloquent a witness to be ignored. In the time of Hosea there were those who looked to Baal as the giver of "the grain and the wine and the oil" (Hos. 2:8), and as late as the fifth century B.C. the Jewish community at Elephantine championing, evidently without any embarrassment, a religion into which Canaanite religious rites and conceptions of deity had made deep incursions.

2. Yahweh in Canaan.

The book of Judges contains several theophanies, each of which presents a revealing picture of Israel's view of Yahweh at this time. The angel of Yahweh (or Yahweh himself) appears to Gideon under the terebinth at Ophrah. When Gideon offers his sacrifice on the open rock, the angel touches the food, fire bursts forth from the rock, and the angel vanishes from sight. The theophany is memorialized by an altar called Yahweh-Shalom. Similarly in the theophany to the par-

---

[40] According to W. F. Albright the Canaanite Baals were all high gods in their own right: "The Baal *par excellence*, undoubtedly intended whenever the singular noun 'Baal' is mentioned, was the storm-god, who ruled over the world from his home in the northern heavens" (*Archaeology and the Religion of Israel* [Baltimore: Johns Hopkins Press, 1942], p. 116.

[41] Cf. Albright, *From Stone Age to Christianity*, pp. 217-18, for evidence that the Israelites' invasion of Palestine actually represented "a most abrupt break between the culture of the Canaanite Late Bronze Age and that of the Israelite Early Iron Age in the hill-country of Palestine."

ents of Samson, when the flame of the cereal offering rises from the rock, the divine being ascends in the flame on the altar. As in the Genesis story of Abraham and Sarah or of Rebekah's sterility, so here the woman is promised a son, who is to be a Nazirite to Yahweh. Over against these stories, which tell their own tale, we have the remarkable theophany of Deborah's militant song. When Yahweh came forth from Seir or marched from the fields of Edom,

The earth quaked, the heavens also shook,
The clouds too dripped water,
The mountains rocked at the presence of Yahweh,
At the presence of Yahweh, the God of Israel (Judg. 5:4-5).

The literary construction of the lines suggests Canaanite influence, but the theophany described is Hebraic or Mosaic. The reminiscence of Sinai is inevitable, though the reference to the mountains in vs. 5 is an obvious gloss.

The great command of the Decalogue for the exclusive loyalty to Yahweh resounds again and again throughout the period of the Conquest. The dynamic urgency of monolatry is shown nowhere more powerfully than in the call of the tribes to unity. In the name of Yahweh they are summoned to battle, and in the name of Yahweh they are extolled or cursed according to their participation or unwillingness "to come to the help of Yahweh" (Judg. 5:23). In the period of the Conquest Yahweh appears as the mighty man of war (cf. Exod. 14:14; 15:3). Israel's wars are Yahweh's wars. One of the earliest collections of poetry surviving in fragments here and there in the Old Testament was the book of the Wars of the Lord. The Conquest of Canaan was Yahweh's work, and he endued deliverers with the gift of the Spirit so that they might be supernaturally equipped to carry on the work of battle. Deborah, Barak, Gideon, Jephthah, Samson, and others are indeed charismatic leaders, men of war commissioned by Israel's God of war. The spoils of war must be devoted to him as a great holocaust (the *ḥérem*). Yahweh participates actively in Israel's historical life in order that his will for them may be done. But Yahweh is not bound to Israel in any coercive way. Israel's defeats are not Yahweh's defeats. Yahweh is not defeated. Israel is defeated because she has defied the will of her God.

The conviction arose during that period that Yahweh was Lord of the land of Canaan. The contention that the soil of Palestine belonged to Yahweh signified a change. The name "baal" appears for some time in theophorous names (Eshbaal, the son of Saul; Merib-baal, David's son, etc.). Yet it is not Baal who is absorbing Yahweh, but Yahweh who absorbs Baal. In the process the character of Yahweh was changed. *"Jahweh was the sole object of worship, but all the titles and attributes of the baals were transferred to him."* [42] For one thing, it meant a vast increase in the range of Yahweh's activity in nature. The story of the "dew" in the Gideon narrative had perhaps itself little significance, for it might easily be told in any desert oasis so far as the nomadic Yahweh was concerned, but in the context it is perhaps significant and belongs with that movement which declared Yahweh to be the giver of the rain as over against Baal (I Kings 18–19), the giver of grain and wine (Hos. 2), and finally Lord of all nature.

Yet Yahweh, the God of Israel's life, is not primarily a God of nature. He is first of all the covenant God, and however the two traditions of the Sinaitic and the Shechem covenants are ultimately explained, in Palestine as in Sinai, he is Lord of the covenant (El-berith). The Canaanite expression "Baal-berith" points clearly to the Canaanite background of Shechem and its life, and it is possible that the Canaanite casuistic laws of the Covenant Code have their ultimate origin here in the great covenant at Shechem (Josh. 24). Yahweh is also understood by the true Israelite to be sovereign over his people Israel. When his fellow tribesmen urge him to rule over them after his successful defeat of Midian, Gideon replies laconically, "I will not rule over you, nor shall my son rule over you, since Yahweh rules over you" (Judg. 8:23). Such a reply is authentically Hebraic, above all in its immediate context, and provides the major impulse to the motif of the divine sovereignty which runs through the history of Israel's religion from beginning to end. Yahweh is king, and he alone will rule over Israel.

The nature of Yahweh in this period is best revealed in the activity of his Spirit. The Spirit is never a pervasive, silent influence, but is rather invasive and dynamic. The spirit of Yahweh comes upon Jephthah (Judg. 11:29) so that he is able to launch an attack against the Ammonites; it rushes upon Samson (Judg. 14:19) so that he performs remarkable feats of physical strength.

3. Sanctuaries.—The religious life of Israel during the period of the Conquest is reflected in the sanctuaries. Most of these were simply taken over from the native inhabitants, and in the transfer much else was taken over. Indeed, these sacred places became major centers for the transfer of Canaanite traditions, rites, and ideology. A later age naturally adorned these places with etiological narratives, but in no

[42] Lods, *op. cit.*, p. 405.

case perhaps is the story pure fancy. The ancient associations with Hebron and Bethel and Beersheba made the transfer of such sanctuaries to the Israelites relatively simple, and wherever pre-Israelite Hebrews existed in the land we have reason to believe that the coalescence of the two groups progressed without much difficulty, especially in the light of the conditions prevailing in Palestine at that time and the decadence of Canaanite religion. It was little wonder that the worship of Yahweh suffered severe strains and stresses. But our sources point particularly to such sanctuaries as Dan in the far north near the sources of the Jordan, where Jonathan, the grandson of Moses, and his sons served as priests "until the day of captivity of the land"; to Gilgal, where twelve memorial stones were erected (Josh. 4:19 ff.), a sanctuary was established, the rite of circumcision observed etiologically, the Passover celebrated, a great theophany vouchsafed, and where the first king was crowned; to Ophrah in the fertile plain of Esdraelon, where the tensions between Canaanite and invading Israelite were more acute than elsewhere and the fertility cult was particularly strong; but above all, to Shechem and Shiloh, the two greatest of all the sanctuaries of the Conquest.

Shechem had long been Canaanite and doubtless the Israelites and Canaanites lived in close relationship to each other. On the one hand, Genesis tells how the first great Hebrew patriarch pitched his tent at Shechem upon his arrival in Canaan, where was "the terebinth of the lawgiver" (Gen. 12:6), and how Jacob-Israel after a succession of notable events (Gen. 32:22-32) arrived at Shechem, where he purchased a piece of ground from Hamor the father of Shechem, built an altar, and called it El-Elohe-Israel (Gen. 33:18-20). On the other hand, Joshua gives an account of another series of notable events at Shechem: the establishment of a covenant, the promulgation of laws, and the formation of an amphictyony of tribes. Here at Shechem the Canaanites worshiped their god, Baal-berith ("Lord of the Covenant"), in a temple. Both Genesis and Joshua show the intimate Canaanite associations with Shechem. Sellin suggests that the covenant described in Josh. 24 was a coming together of the pre-Israelite tribes in Canaan who had long before bound themselves into an amphictyony with the invading Hebrews, and that they were bound by their worship of El, the God of Israel. The laws which were promulgated there are sometimes thought to be preserved in Deut. 27, and this has much to be said for it; but in recent years, since the notable researches of Alt and Albright, the alternative view that the Covenant Code contains the original Shechemite laws

has gained in force. To be sure, the Covenant Code exists in two recensions, and some have proposed that the J Decalogue of Exod. 34, with its agricultural emphasis, is the original, but the majority of scholars who follow this line are inclined to hold that the casuistic Canaanite statutes present a much better case. If we can accept this view, then we are in a good position to describe the nature of the bond which united this early Israelite confederacy. Most interesting perhaps is the reference to the three agricultural festivals: the feast of Unleavened Bread, the feast of First Fruits or Weeks, and the feast of Ingathering (Exod. 23:14-19). Later these agrarian feasts were transformed by Hebrew thought and faith into festivals commemorating historical events, but here they clearly refer to nature. The present form of our Covenant Code is doubtless late.

Nowhere is the life at an ancient sanctuary during the period of the Conquest described with greater clarity than in the case of Shiloh. It was here that the tribe of Ephraim had erected a sanctuary in the middle of the thirteenth century. It was obviously well built and stationary, equipped with all the necessary paraphernalia for an elaborate cultus, provided with various chambers for the celebration of the cult and its continuance: the central shrine containing the sacred ark, rooms for the slaughter of the animals, for the preparation of the sacrifice, for the altars, and for the eating of the meal in the *lishkāh* or festal chamber. Besides, there were doubtless rooms for Eli and his sons and their families. One tiny glimpse gives us a vivid picture of the practice of the cult: "Whenever any man was about to sacrifice, an attendant of the priest would come, while the meat was still boiling, and with a three-pronged fork in his hand, he would thrust into the pot, or kettle, or cauldron, or vessel; all that the fork brought up the priest would take for himself. So they used to do to all the Israelites who came there to sacrifice in Shiloh" (I Sam. 2:13-14).

4. Cultic Personnel and Religious Groups.—
Eli was the head of the sanctuary at Shiloh, and thus of the religious focus for all the Israelite tribes of central Palestine. The prestige and dignity of his office is clearly reflected in the narrative itself and in the tradition which carries him back to Aaron and extends into the future for more than two centuries. Similarly, the sanctuary at Dan claims continuity with the Mosaic tradition. In this period the Levites emerge as a priestly class; Levites and priests tend to become partially synonymous terms. The importance of the priestly office is reflected in the story of the migration of Dan.

Shiloh contained the sacred ark, which in the stories of I Sam. 4–7 serves as a kind of palladium of war intimately associated with Yahweh's presence, so that when the Philistines hear of its presence in battle, they cry out in great fear, "Their God is come into the camp!" (I Sam. 4:7). When the wife of Phinehas hears the dreadful news that the ark is captured, she cries in her death agony, "The glory is departed from Israel, for the ark of God is taken" (I Sam. 4:21). It was in the presence of the ark that the child Samuel heard himself addressed, and finally heard the words of doom against the house of Eli. Sleeping in the presence of the ark was eminently suitable to divine revelation.

Both Samson and Samuel were Nazirites, according to the accounts, from their birth. They were not to drink strong drink and no razor was to come upon their head. The Nazirites long continued as a nomadic group within Israel, protesting against all syncretism with the indigenous Canaanite cults and calling Israel back to the seminomadic ways of the desert and Sinai. Other groups were closely associated with them at a somewhat later period: the Rechabites, who likewise fostered desert folkways and ideals in Palestine, and the "nebiim" or prophets, who recalled Israel to the days of "purity" in the desert, when Yahweh had made no such demands as their contemporaries assumed in their current cultic practices.

Finally, there were the "shophetim" or "judges," who may at times have adjudicated disputes, although their function was much wider than this. They included "heads of clans like Othniel, military leaders of humbler origin like Ehud, Barak, and Gideon, men of wealth like Jair, Ibzan, and Abdon, bastard adventurers like Jephthah, priests like Eli, prophets like Samuel, and even Canaanite chieftains like Shamgar of Beth-anath." [43] Max Weber, Albrecht Alt, and W. F. Albright all apply the term "charismatic" to these various leaders, and Albright has styled this period as "the charismatic age in Israel." Alt has gone so far as to suggest that it was through the judges that the Canaanite casuistic law was transferred to Israel. Perhaps it was the prowess, courage, and energy exhibited by these men which prompted their contemporaries to think of them as peculiarly endowed with charismatic powers.

5. Moral Standards.—The biblical books which report the Conquest present a vivid picture of the moral conditions prevailing in Israel. We may discount the Deuteronomic accounts of the subjection of the Canaanites to destruction, but there are obvious historical instances where Canaanite towns were subjected to the terrible *ḥérem*. This is viewed and accepted as the requirement of Yahweh, infringement of which produces such dreadful consequences as were visited upon Achan and all his blood relatives. The role of Yahweh as God of war assumes its most sinister aspects in accounts such as these. In the Song of Deborah the act of Jael is obviously recounted with great pride. More appalling is the incident at Gibeah reported in the narrative of Judg. 19–21. The crime itself sends a shock throughout the tribes, but their treatment of Benjamin and Jabesh-gilead is a dark reflection on this whole period. The sacrifice of Jephthah's daughter becomes tolerable only on one basis, that it is in fact an etiological cult story on the order of Agamemnon's sacrifice of Iphigenia, to account for the annual festival of Jephthah's daughter. Samson's amours and adventurous exploits, culminating in his prayer to Yahweh for revenge upon his foes, were evidently listened to with relish by the ancient Hebrews, and Gideon's polygamy is taken quite for granted. The account of the behavior of Samuel's sons at Shiloh is certainly not condoned, but it does afford us a glimpse of conditions in Israel. "At that time there was no king in Israel. Everyone used to do as he pleased" (Judg. 17:6 *et passim*).

How can this appalling picture of conditions in Israel be explained? Perhaps the following comments are in order: (*a*) The transition from the desert and seminomadic life to the situation existing among the Canaanites in this period would naturally produce a radical deterioration. One has only to remind himself of the conditions among soldiers and sailors when they are freed from the restraints of civilian life, and of course the contrast in the case of Israel and Canaan was much sharper. (*b*) The formative character of the period with its inevitably tentative organization and accompanying insecurity would produce the kind of lawlessness that is described. (*c*) In some instances the temptations of the new land were such as were associated with the very nature of agricultural, fertility worship and belief, and nomadic mores must have seemed to many to be peculiarly inapplicable to the changed situation.

V. The Early Monarchy (ca. 1020-922 B.C.)

A. Sources.—A new social and political self-consciousness naturally reflected itself in the production of historical documentation. Our sources grow both in variety and in authenticity. The books of Samuel are extraordinarily rich in the diversity of types of tradition. The dirges of David over Saul and Jonathan (II Sam. 1:19-27) and Abner (II Sam. 3:33-34) are universally recognized as the work of David. Similarly, the great narrative sequence on the history of

---

[43] Albright, *From Stone Age to Christianity*, p. 216.

David's reign in II Sam. 9–20 and I Kings 1–2 is unsurpassed not only in the Old Testament but in the historical archives of the ancient Near East, and it is possible that the traditions preserved in II Sam. 2–6; 8 are almost as reliable. Of great value, too, is the early source in I and II Samuel. Not a few of the stories are legendary in character as, for example, the call of Samuel (I Sam. 3) and the stories of the appendix (e.g., II Sam. 21:1-14; 24). On the other hand, the lists in the appendix have great historical value. The late source, associated chiefly with the name of Samuel but extending beyond him, is less trustworthy than the primary materials which have been mentioned, but it is valuable if carefully interpreted and evaluated. The ark stories seem to belong to a special source and may originally have been the continuation of Judg. 3:7–16:31. Hannah's Song (I Sam. 2:1-10) in its present form is postexilic.

B. Historical Background.—The Early Iron Age has not infrequently been known as "the age of small peoples." It is certainly true that during the period of the united monarchy none of the great "powers" like Egypt or Babylonia or Assyria was in a position to press its claims upon the corridor. The incursions of sea rovers upon the "New Empire" of Egypt and the Levantine region "were incidental effects of a Central European barbarian Völkerwanderung," and the Philistine invasion (*ca.* 1170) was the major threat to Israel for many decades, a superb illustration of Arnold J. Toynbee's "stimulus under blows." [44] During this period three cultural events of the first consequence emerge into our region: the coming of iron, the domestication of the camel as over against the ass, and the use of the horse. The destruction of Shiloh by the Philistines brought to an end the amphictyony of tribes in central Palestine, of which Shiloh was the chief sanctuary.

C. The Religion of the Early Monarchy. 1. Samuel.—The dominant interest of this period is political and social rather than religious. It is doubtful whether at any time during this period, despite advance in culture and social life, Israel achieved the religious vitality and "purity" of the age of Moses. To be sure, Samuel is a kind of Moses redivivus, but he seldom emerges with any historical distinctness. The story of the origin of his name (I Sam. 1:20) applies better to Saul (the name *shā'ûl* means "asked"), and his call is described in the form of a folk tale. In his relations to Saul he

[44] *A Study of History* (London: Oxford University Press, 1934), V, 290; cf. also I, 100-1 *et passim*. See also Albrecht Alt, *Die Staatenbildung der Israeliten in Palästina* (Leipzig: Alexander Edelmann, 1930); Leslie, *Old Testament Religion*, pp. 111 ff.; Burrows, *What Mean These Stones?* pp. 19-20, 97-98, 165-66.

appears as the embodiment of the tragic nemesis which pursues the afflicted king to his terrible doom. Nevertheless he stands as a giant monolith in the age of Conquest, and appears in the varying guise of seer, prophet, judge, itinerant justice, priest, and maker of kings. He is a veritable "man of God," so mighty indeed that the divine words which fall from his lips make and unmake kings and his prayers bring about a heavy hailstorm so that the Philistines no longer appear in the land. The two great movements which tower over everything else in his lifetime are the beginnings of the monarchy and the coeval beginnings of prophecy. The late B source in I Sam. 15:22-23 sounds the note of authentic prophecy and illustrates the kind of tradition which came to be attached to his name:

Has Yahweh as great delight in burnt-offerings and
    sacrifices
    as in obedience to the voice of Yahweh?
Behold, obedience is better than sacrifice,
    and hearkening than the fat of rams;
For rebellion is the sin of divination,
    and stubbornness the iniquity of teraphim.
Since you have rejected the word of Yahweh
    he has rejected you from being king.

2. Saul of Benjamin (ca. 1020-1004 B.C.).—If Samuel has been enshrouded in devotion and loyalty in the memories of Israel, then the historical Saul has been all but eclipsed by the Judean edition which preserved the story of his life. Historical criticism and modern psychology provide the two major instruments whereby we are able to recover Saul and to understand his true character. He was himself his own worst victim, and as the narratives succeed each other we see him caught in the coils of a destiny beyond his control and beyond his comprehension. Saul has his great historical importance as the first king of Israel, as the first to cope with the Philistine domination, and as the one to reveal the strange and baffling contradiction of prophet and king, the Lord's anointed, within the breast of a single man. Attractive, shy, sensitive, passionate in his rage and in his love, he was unable to deal with the cunning and capacity of one who was his superior. In religion he was the child of the times. He could invoke a terrible curse and was willing to allow its consequences to fall upon the head of his eldest son (I Sam. 14:24-30, 43-46). Yahweh was the God of battles, and Saul was a fit servant to him. In his name he practiced the *hérem*, and yet compassion could deflect him from this course. Samuel might slay Agag in pieces before Yahweh; not so the vacillating, mercurial, softhearted Saul (I Sam. 15:7, 32-33). He sought to be loyal and faithful to

Yahweh, erring and blind though he may have been in his understanding. He used the divining instrument of Benjamin, the ephod, to inquire of Yahweh, and employed the Urim and Thummim to determine who had violated his taboo on food. He built altars to Yahweh, and in an awful dilemma performed the sacrifice himself in the absence of Samuel. He exiled those with familiar spirits from the land, yet in his darkest hour was driven to consult the necromancer at Endor. The narratives which preserve his memory are cast in a remarkable framework showing how an evil spirit from Yahweh sends him to his inevitable ruin, whereas the spirit of Yahweh is upon David to exalt him to be king over Israel.

Our earliest source views the establishment of the kingdom with favor. It is the gift of Yahweh to his people. Yahweh sends Saul to Samuel to deliver Israel from the Philistines (I Sam. 9:16). The late theocratic source takes the opposite view. When this document was written the prophets had entered upon the scene, and the institution of the monarchy was viewed as an act of apostasy. He who would appraise the contradictions of historical existence does well to read both accounts and to understand their place within the tradition.

The prophet (נביא) is one who is "called"—called of God—to perform a special task in behalf of the people, to warn them of what God is about to do. The remarkable story in I Sam. 9:1–10:16 presents us with a vivid scene of a band of prophets coming from a high place, "the hill of God where is the garrison of the Philistines," playing various musical instruments, and prophesying ecstatically. The spirit of Yahweh comes mightily upon Saul (I Sam. 10:6), so that he prophesies with them and "is turned into another man." It is significant that the origins of the kingdom are so closely bound with the emergence of these prophetic bands. Always in times of great crisis the prophets came to declare the word and will and purpose of Yahweh, and this simple tale, so profoundly revealing in many respects, combines prophecy and politics in a way that was destined to be of great omen for Israel's future life in the world.

3. *David of Judah (ca. 1004-961 B.C.).*—The true greatness of the historical David lies more in the area of Israel's political history than in religion. But since it is impossible in the Old Testament to divorce history and faith, especially in relationship to the king, it is natural that his achievements bear directly on the history of Israel's religion. Not the least of David's achievements was the bringing of the ark to the city which he secured for the Hebrews, Jerusalem, the "city of David." It was he who gave Jerusalem the place it was to occupy in all subsequent history as the center of Israel's political life and the center of worship, first for the united kingdom and later for the kingdom of Judah. Whatever judgment one may finally pronounce on David's religion, there can be no question that he sought sincerely to be a faithful worshiper of Yahweh. His nature, with all its contrasts, is nevertheless basically consistent. For him, as for Saul and the judges, Yahweh was a God of war, and none served Yahweh as a God of battles more valiantly and successfully than he. At the height of his career he committed adultery with Bathsheba, the wife of a Hittite mercenary, and when he failed to escape the consequences of his act, he ordered the murder of her husband. Nathan, the prophet, confronted him with the word of Yahweh in the form of the parable of the little ewe lamb (II Sam. 12:1-6). The effect was not lost upon the king, and he repented bitterly for his crime. In this circumstance, as in all the circumstances of his life, David's relation with Yahweh seems to have been peculiarly close and intimate, though it was not without a deep-seated fear and reverence.

The tradition which associates him with the establishment of the temple cult has an authentic source in his life, as does indeed the tradition which connects him with the musical life and heritage of ancient Israel (cf. Amos 6:5). Yet his cruelty scarcely knew any bounds. His curses were violent and intemperate, and he believed in their terrible efficacy. He was willing to invoke blood revenge against the house of Saul in his slaughter of the sons of Rizpah and Michal. It is possible, indeed, to describe David as one who was motivated solely by ambition and self-interest. But this would not do justice to other forces in his nature, such as his devotion to and fear of God and his capacity for repentance.

The same logic of events which pursues Saul to his death now follows David the king after his adultery and murder. Event follows event in heartbreaking succession as the judgment of Yahweh follows him to a broken and ineffectual old age. His biographer can sketch the matchless narrative of the disintegration of his family, above all of Absalom's revolt, with such sympathy and restraint that the Orient has no close parallel to offer to it, and one is reminded only of the lament of Priam for his son Hector after he is dragged about the walls of Troy. David had other weaknesses also. Yet the final verdict is a merciful one, and tradition was not completely faithless to the facts of his life. The Deuteronomist could view him as the norm for the perfect king; the Chronicler could see in him the servant of the Lord, the priestly writers as the founder of the cult, and the editors of the Psalter as the author of many hymns, prayers, and liturgies, while those who looked for a deliverer found in him the prototype of the messiah or, as David redivivus, the messiah himself.

David became a king in the fashion of the western Semites. To what degree he was considered in any sense divine it is hard to say. Not a few passages suggest that he was believed to possess divine qualities. That his kingship was dynamically related to the life of the people with whom he stood in psychic rapport there can be little doubt. He was the protector of his people, and his battles were Yahweh's battles. His anointing equipped him with God's spirit (*rûah Yahweh*), and the following narratives vividly portray the effect of the spirit upon him. He dances ecstatically before the ark. In his old age the men about him swear to him, "You shall no more go out with us to battle, lest you quench the lamp of Israel" (II Sam. 21:17; cf. the perpetual light [*nēr tāmîdh*] of the temple). That he was subject to Canaanite influence is apparent not only from the language and style of his lament over Jonathan and Saul but from a number of other passages. He was the charismatic king par excellence in Israel, and such passages as II Sam. 7 in which Nathan's oracle speaks of his intimate relationship to Yahweh as that of a son to his father (late though it is in its present form) show the influence of this charismatic quality of David upon the thought of later times.[45]

4. Solomon (961-922 B.C.).—The importance of Solomon's reign belongs to the history of civilization and the development of culture rather than to the development of Israel's religion. Thanks to the amazing revelations from archaeology throughout the Fertile Crescent—Mesopotamia, Syria, Phoenicia, and Egypt—and more specifically to the excavations at Megiddo, Ezion-geber (Tell el-Kheleifeh), Lachish, and elsewhere, we are now in a position to evaluate its true character. But for religion it represented no advance. The account in I Kings 3–12 is devoted almost entirely to the construction of the Temple of Solomon. In composition and point of view the narrative is Deuteronomic, and the importance attached to it represents the attitude of another age than Solomon's. In

actuality the construction of the temple was only a part of Solomon's elaborate building program, and was motivated by political considerations fully as much as by religious interest. The temple was essentially a royal chapel. Without doubt it kindled the animosities and resentment of all who cherished the Mosaic tradition. In architecture, furnishings, cultic symbolism, and ritual, it was more Phoenician (Canaanite) and Syrian than Hebrew. As such it was alien to Israel, and it was only subsequent events like the destruction of the northern kingdom in 722 B.C., the miraculous preservation of Jerusalem during Sennacherib's campaign, and above all, the reformation of 621 B.C., which gave it the central place it later assumed in the history of Judah and Judaism. For an understanding of the religion of Israel in the tenth century it is not of the first importance.

And yet the temple bore witness to the incursion of foreign influence within the royal court.[46] The brazen sea, supported by twelve bulls, the universally recognized symbols of fecundity, three of them on each of the four sides, bears a cosmic significance, probably symbolic of the subterranean fresh-water stream, the source of all life and fertility comparable to the Babylonian Apsu. The two isolated pillars, Jachin and Boaz, standing before the entrance, the lions, the lavers, the shovels, and the basins and the four hundred pomegranates, the ten bases with their bronze frames, the great altar of burnt offering with its reflection of Mesopotamian cosmic ideas, together with all the other appurtenances of the temple and its cult were the work of Phoenicians and reflected the religious symbolism and ideology of the Semitic world. When after many decades and even centuries it became the central shrine for all Israel, the temple was accepted as the true center of worship for Yahweh of hosts, who dwells on Mount Zion where his "tabernacling presence" abode in the midst of the people.[47]

[45] For an extended treatment of this subject see Aubrey R. Johnson, "The Role of the King in the Jerusalem Cultus," in *The Labyrinth*, ed. Hooke, pp. 73-111. (The literature on this subject is extensive. In English it is represented by the school of Hooke in such books as the foregoing and in *Myth and Ritual* [London: Oxford University Press, 1933].) Cf. also Ivan Engnell, *Studies in Divine Kingship in the Ancient Near East* (Uppsala: Almquist & Wiksells, 1943). For an examination of the theory of divine kingship see Martin Noth, "Gott, König, Volk im Alten Testament," *Zeitschrift für Theologie und Kirche*, LVIII, 1950, Heft 2.

[46] Herbert Gordon May, "Some Aspects of Solar Worship at Jerusalem," *Zeitschrift für die Alttestamentliche Wissenschaft*, LV (1937), 269-81.

[47] Cf. the extremely early words of dedication in I Kings 8:12, which the LXX attributes to the book of Jashar:

"Yahweh has set the sun in the heavens [LXX, not in M.T.]
But has said that he would dwell in thick darkness.
I have indeed built thee a shrine of Zebul for you,
A fixed place for your seat forever."

May comments as follows: "It is not improbable that Solomon declared that he was building a house of Baal-Zebul for Yahweh, thus applying to Yahweh a title of deity which we know was current not only in the fourteenth century at Ugarit, but also in the ninth century in Palestine" ("Some Aspects of Solar Worship at Jerusalem," p. 270). Cf. I Kings 1:2 ff. where we should read "Baal-Zebul" instead of "Baal-Zebub."

The ascription of wisdom literature to the age of Solomon and even to Solomon himself doubtless has a historical basis. There is no good reason for doubting the tradition itself, but all the literature attributed to Solomon is clearly the work of a much later age. As law was attributed to Moses, psalmody to David, so sapiential writing was "Solomonic." But in the deeper sense of true wisdom, the wisdom of justice and mercy and of the word of the Lord, Solomon was far from wise. He might well have died with the words of another monarch on his lips, *Après moi le déluge.* The glory of Solomon remembered down the centuries was not a reflection of the glory on the face of Moses, or the glory of the mount of theophany, or the glory of the Presence in the simple "ark of the covenant" which he housed in the dark recesses of the temple *debhîr.* Yet despite the new direction in which Solomon and in only a lesser degree David turned the course of Israel's history, what lay deepest within Israel was the allegiance of the covenant people to Yahweh, her covenant Lord.

D. The Epic of the Yahwist.—The national self-consciousness and unity which David and Solomon had sought to achieve over against the inveterate tribalism of the disparate elements of the population reflected itself in a great literary awakening. The long reigns of David and Solomon quickened the pulse of the time as Elizabeth's reign stimulated the thoughts of Tudor England. It is significant that both David and Solomon are credited with literary activity, the former as a poet and the latter as a sage. Above all else, even the remarkable history of David's reign (II Sam. 9–I Kings 2), towers the dramatic epic of the Yahwist. Out of materials of great variety—stories of cultic "heroes," etiological stories recounting theophanies at sacred places, poems coming full-fledged out of the raw primitivity of oral tradition, historical pieces enshrining past memories, laws defining and regulating communal relations, genealogies preserving the continuity of the tradition in the guise of a family relationship (Abraham, Isaac, Jacob and his twelve sons)—out of all the complexity of tradition the Yahwist fashioned an epic of vast scope and remarkable unity. The individual narratives emerge in all their sharp identity like pieces of finely carved ivory or chiseled marble.[48] In them Oriental imaginative mentality and insight combine to produce a literature that has in turn fired the

imagination and haunted the memory of men throughout the ages. The inner conflicts and sharp tensions persist from beginning to end: man's creation and fall; his rebellion and defection which deserved death and extinction (Gen. 6:5-6) ; the promise to Abraham of a child who is born in the face of apparently insurmountable obstacles; the sojourn to Egypt and the long period of slavery; the hazards and harshness of the desert wanderings; the discontent, despair, and revolt of the people; the difficulties of the journey to Palestine; the long years of conquest and the indecisiveness of the invasion (Judg. 1:1–2:5) ; the choice and rejection of the first king, and David's tortuous rise to power. Yet despite the diversity of literary traditions, the possible presence of alien influences (Kenite and Canaanite), the conflict in cultural patterns, the numerous shifts of scene and circumstance, the Yahwist keeps before him the single goal of his dramatic narrative. This is succinctly stated in the promise to Abram, Israel's progenitor (Gen. 12:1-3), the man of obedience in whom Israel's true life is already dynamically and psychically existent. To it the J narratives of Gen. 1–11 are but prologue, a prologue which places the patriarch's emergence in a setting of universal scope and of a supremely revelatory theological context. Overarching all else is the "philosophy of history" in which the purpose and will and action of God are the factors which press time and event to their culmination.

In reading such an epic as this the reader recognizes the artistic composition of the individual literary units, but beyond this he sees how they are fashioned into a mighty work of literary art and theological insight. From the creation and fall of man to Babel's tower, from the call of Abraham to the birth of Jacob-Israel and his twelve sons, from Jacob-Israel to the Exodus, from the Exodus to the mount of the covenant, from Sinai to Palestine, from the travailing years of conquest to the possession of the land under David, the Yahwist moves on in sure-footed progress to the fulfillment of the divine promise to Abraham. It is a covenantal history in which the faith of Israel is recorded in the concreteness of many events. Creation and nature, sin and judgment and suffering, sin and ever-recurring supervening grace, the union of man and wife, the conflict of brother against brother, the coming of sinister powers of darkness in the fall of the angels, the fateful resort to culture and technology, the confusion of tongues, the Exodus from Egypt, the birth of the people of God, the giving of the law, the covenant relation, the gift of the good land as Yahweh's heritage to his people, the resort to a

[48] It is the great merit of the monumental commentary of Hermann Gunkel on Genesis that he has portrayed the quality and character of these separate units. Only in our time are we beginning to see the heterogeneity and number of the traditions in their total perspective and unity. See Gerhard von Rad, *Das erste Buch Mose* (Göttingen: Vandenhoeck & Ruprecht, 1949).

king and yet the deep-dyed apostasy of reliance upon him, the birth of the nation, and the creation of David's far-flung empire—these are the realities which lie within the matrix of the monumental epic of Israel's early life. The interpretation of history is grasped here for the first time by a mind of almost unsurpassed insight. Second Isaiah ascends a yet greater height and views the history of the covenant people at the end of the Semitic age when Cyrus the Great emerges into world history in the framework of beginning and end, but he builds on foundations laid by the Yahwist.[49] When in the decline of the Roman Empire Augustine wrote his *City of God,* he was the conscious heir of a tradition classically enshrined in this epic.[50] If the Yahwist narrative is read and understood from beginning to end in terms of the height and depth and breadth of its own categories, and if it is read with empathy and a sense of identification, that is, existentially, it becomes clear that here Hebraism has reached an understanding of itself that has seldom if ever been surpassed.[51]

VI. The Divided Kingdoms
(922-586 B.C.)

A. Historical Background.—From a purely political point of view the disruption of the united monarchy following the death of Solomon was disastrous for the life of Israel. But more than this, it reflected the general divisiveness of peoples in the Fertile Crescent. It meant that when "the Assyrian came down like the wolf on the fold," they were unprepared to withstand this fresh and incalculable vitality and finally fell before it. Periods of effective resistance there were indeed, as when Aram succeeded in enlisting the co-operation of the "Syriac states" at Qarqar in 853 B.C., but in the great perspective of the centuries it was the divisiveness of the nations of western Asia which finally brought about their disintegration and

---

[49] The eschatological poems of Second Isaiah incorporate within them all the main features of the Yahwist epic: e.g., the promise after the Flood (P elements are present here also); Abraham in whom all the nations will bless themselves; the redeemed, called, chosen, and covenanted people; the Yahwist "philosophy of history"; the significance of David; in fact, all the "beginnings" of the sacred history.

[50] Augustine deepened his view of Israel's sacred history by his profound conception of the place and significance of memory as the agency of the Holy Spirit.

[51] For valuable treatments of the nature of these Hebraic categories the following works may be consulted: Johannes Pedersen, *Israel, Its Life and Culture* (London: Oxford University Press, 1926-40); Artur Weiser, *Glaube und Geschichte im Alten Testament* (Stuttgart: W. Kohlhammer, 1931); H. Wheeler Robinson, "Hebrew Psychology," in *The People and the Book,* ed. Peake; *Inspiration and Revelation in the Old Testament* (Oxford: Clarendon Press, 1946).

---

collapse.[52] And yet the division of the monarchy into Israel in the north and Judah in the south had its important consequences for the future. It meant for one thing that two nations, separate and distinct, both worshiped the same God. Again, because of the division the north now lay more exposed to the world of nations. Israel could orient herself to Phoenicia or Aram, and in so doing would assimilate herself to the religious ideologies of these people.[53] Economic and political alliances inevitably involved religious recognition and *rapprochement.* The Phoenician Baal would be worshiped in Palestine, especially at a time when the countries were intimately bound by royal marriage. The presence of Phoenician merchants in Samaria and elsewhere would inevitably have its effect. Finally, it meant that Judah, while far from being isolated in the world, would orient itself more to its classical Yahweh tradition.[54] The nomadic tribes to the south and the nomadic groups of Nazirites and Rechabites within her borders would be free to exercise their influence without the constant hindrance of extraneous Baalistic influences to which the north was always more susceptible. However catastrophic the disruption of the monarchy may have been from a purely political point of view, for the religion of Yahweh its total effect was not calamitous. The conservative forces of the great tradition associated with Moses and that part of the cult which retained the memory of the Mosaic heritage could assert themselves and thus prevent the corrosive and debilitating effects of syncretism with Canaanite Baal and the later astral deities.

B. The Prophets of the Ninth Century.—The revolution of Omri brought to an end the fifty years' war between north and south and saved both kingdoms from complete exhaustion and collapse. The greatness of Omri belongs to Israel's history, but it is against the background of his achievements that we must read the religion of Israel during this period. Omri's policies and successes cannot be understood in isolation from the history of the ancient Near East, but in connection with it. It is possible, as Rudolf Kittel suggests, that it was determined by the rise of Assyria under the dynamic aggression of Ashurnasirpal II (883-859 B.C.).[55] More certainly it was determined by the conflicts be-

---

[52] Toynbee, *Study of History,* IV, 67-68.

[53] *Ibid.,* V, 535-36. The Baals mentioned by Toynbee are not the animistic baals but refer to the national Baal of the Ugaritic inscriptions.

[54] Martin Noth, *Geschichte Israels* (Göttingen: Vandenhoeck & Ruprecht, 1950), pp. 157-58.

[55] *Geschichte des Volkes Israel* (Gotha: Leopold Klotz, 1925), II, 234. The dates of the Assyrian monarchs here and elsewhere are based on Arno Poebel, "The Assyrian King List from Khorsabad," *Journal of Near Eastern Studies,* II (1943), 56-90.

tween an emerging Aram with its exceedingly crucial position in the Fertile Crescent and its pivotal situation in relation to the great commercial highways in the ancient East. The researches of Julian Morgenstern [56] and Nelson Glueck [57] have created for us a convincing background against which the prophetic movement of the whole ninth century may be understood. It is only against such a detailed and vivid picture that we are able to appreciate the significance of the relation of Israel's faith to history and of the profound problem which emerges from her trust in a covenantal God as determiner of her historical destiny. Concretely stated, how shall we interpret the position of the great proponents of classical Yahwism in relation to the practical exigencies of historical circumstance and the successes of Omri and his policy in preserving Israel from destruction?

Three prophets emerge from this period of Israel's history: Elijah the Tishbite, Micaiah ben Imlah, and Elisha ben Shaphat of Abel-meholah. It is striking that the tradition which preserves their memory comes to us in the form of story.[58] Narrative was more suited than any other literary mold to express Israel's consciousness of the initiative and activity and will and word of God. These stories were remembered in Israel and to a degree were transformed in the telling, though not nearly to the extent that is sometimes supposed. In the history of the Jewish-Christian tradition they have naturally occupied a place out of proportion to modern estimates, precisely because they preserve so faithfully the quality of the prophetic faith.

1. Elijah the Tishbite.—Legend has preserved a vivid picture of this mighty man. His very name proclaims his central message: "Yahweh is my God," "Yah is my El." His clothing, his home, his food and drink, his intimate relations with nature, his extremely dramatic and sudden appearances make him a fit subject for popular imagination. He is a veritable incarnation of nomadic Yahwism, fierce, unyielding, austere, and unafraid.

But if Elijah is so shrouded in the imaginative memory of those who revered and loved him, what can be said of him as a historical figure? It goes without saying that much of the material cannot pass the muster of careful historical examination. But what is more important to recognize is that he was the kind of

[56] *Amos Studies* (Cincinnati: Hebrew Union College Press, 1941), I, 258 ff.

[57] *The River Jordan* (Philadelphia: Westminster Press, 1946), pp. 169 ff.

[58] Many scholars assign the Yahwist epic to the ninth century. If this is correct, then the stories in this epic witness to the same kind of literary movement. However, the Yahwist should probably receive an earlier date.

person who inevitably elicited the tribute of stories, miracles and remarkable predictions. Memory preserved above all the great witness that the word of the Lord was in his mouth. It is this conviction that dominates the famous story of the drought and its dramatic end on the heights of Carmel's promontory. He was a prophet of Yahweh, a man of God, and he spoke the words of the Lord. He was the mediator of the divine revelation. Moreover, in the mighty conflict with the Phoenician Baal it was through Elijah that the issue was decisively drawn: Yahweh is God in Israel. All the machinations of an energetic mercantile civilization could not withstand the greater drive and dynamism of Yahweh, the covenant God of Israel, who thundered on Sinai and engaged as war God in behalf of his people. Here on Carmel the national Baal of Phoenicia was conquered by a mightier competitor.

At least two elements emerge out of the story of Elijah on Horeb. The great climax of the narrative falls not on the earthquake or the wind or the fire, but on the sound of a gentle whisper. Here is an advance we would not have anticipated. The narrator characteristically makes no comment. Another element in the Horeb account is the reference to the remnant which had not yet bowed the knee to Baal, the seven thousand worshipers of Yahweh. This is not the earliest mention of the remnant, but it is one of the most important and the fit prototype for all further speculation on the continuing community of the devoted, loyal pious who are not overcome by the strength and clamor of loud majorities. One might even suspect still another feature in the story, the command to Elijah to return to Palestine to foment a revolution. This demand is native to the Yahweh cult. It could never end in the quiet contemplation of the gentle whisper, valuable and important though that may be. The mighty prophet is confronted with three great commands upon him, and they have at least one level of historicity which cannot be doubted. They were all fulfilled, and fulfilled under the influence of Elijah: "Go, return on your way to the desert of Damascus, and when you arrive, anoint Hazael to be king over Syria; and Jehu the son of Nimshi you shall anoint to be king over Israel; and Elisha the son of Shaphat of Abel-meholah you shall anoint to be prophet in your place" (I Kings 19:15-16).

Finally, Elijah comes before us as the champion of the rights of the common man. In the story of Naboth's vineyard we see him standing stoutly against the king and the subtle intrigues of the shrewd and calculating Baal emissary who was his wife. When Ahab comes to take over his vineyard, Elijah confronts him with his terrible word of doom from Yahweh. The prophet stanchly supports the common peasant who has no friend in court against a king. There is little that can surpass a story like this for its sheer purity of heart, its unqualified urgency, its passionate, selfless, and fearless support of the little man. But the sources of such blazing passion lay deep in the religion of Yahweh. They went back as far as Moses, even to Yahweh who had revealed himself in such fashion on Sinai that this thing of Naboth's cruel and unwarranted death could never go by unnoticed. ·

Elijah's influence trailed on into the next century and beyond. The eighth-century prophets are under debt to him and to the tradition which he embodied with such purity. Israel looked forward to the return of the prophet (Mal. 4:5) and the New Testament preserves his memory in passages of crucial importance.[59] But when all is said, no "contributions" of Elijah can describe his work. "In lonely splendor this prophet towered above his time, a majestic figure of heroic stature, as no other in the Bible; legend could preserve a firm impression of him as history could not." [60] Not the least of these legends was that he was carried off to heaven in a whirlwind.

2. Micaiah ben Imlah.—Of the prophetic career of Elijah's contemporary, Micaiah ben Imlah, only a single narrative survives (I Kings 22). The kings of Israel and Judah are sitting in solemn conclave. To their inquiry whether they should attack Ramoth-gilead, the ecstatic Baal prophets of the court give an uncompromisingly optimistic answer. Jehoshaphat, the king of Judah, inquires significantly for a prophet of Yahweh. But Ahab hates Micaiah "for he never prophesies good concerning me, but evil" (I Kings 22:8). When Micaiah is brought in, he at first mimics the court prophets, but under pressure reveals the word of Yahweh which had come to him in a remarkable vision of a celestial council in which the historical crisis is under judgment. The decision is reported by Micaiah, "God has spoken evil concerning Ahab" (I Kings 22:23). Micaiah suffered for his outspoken fidelity to Yahweh's word, but history proved him right. The word of Yahweh had come to him, and the word was fulfilled in event. Micaiah, like Elijah, belonged to a long succession of which Amos and Jeremiah were notable members. They scorned the easy optimism of loud majorities, looked the bare realities of history in the face, and proclaimed the oracles of judgment that they had heard in the divine councils.

3. Elisha ben Shaphat.—Elisha ben Shaphat was another contemporary of Elijah and was in some ways a strong foil to him (cf. Amos and Hosea, Jeremiah and Ezekiel). Popular memory recalled many wonderful deeds wrought by the prophet. Numerous magical elements appear in the stories which are preserved concerning him (II Kings 2–9; 13:14-21), some of them strangely similar to those of Elijah, his prophetic master. One theme runs through all the prophet's activity, his kindness and sympathy for those in trouble. He is remembered not only as a prophet who spoke to the conditions of the times in the hours of Aramean crisis, but also as an understanding pastor who would spare no pains to help the needy and distressed.

C. The Prophets of the Eighth Century. 1. Amos of Tekoa.—The book of Amos is a source of incomparable value since it is not only contemporary with the man and message it describes, but is in the main the work of the prophet himself. The so-called "motto" of Amos 1:2 (cf. Joel 3:16) is possibly late. The oracles against Edom and Judah are certainly secondary in their present form. The doxologies come from a time later than Amos and reflect the theology of Second Isaiah (Amos 4:13; 5:8-9; 9:5-6). The optimistic liturgical appendix of 9:8b-15 is similarly the work of another time. The superscription (1:1) is the work of the editor. There are numerous minor additions.

The prophetic revolution responsible for the isolationist dynasty of Jehu (842-745 B.C.) did not improve material conditions. Jehu was himself forced to pay heavy tribute,[61] and Jehoahaz was compelled to subsidize the campaigns of Adad-nirari IV against Aram (806-803 B.C.). The bitter blow of Damascus' destruction in 805 B.C. was well-nigh fatal. Aram declined, but Assyria was not in a position to press her claims in the Fertile Crescent. Israel soon revived as a consequence. Jeroboam II (786-746 B.C.) extended his territories from Hamath to the sea of the Arabah (II Kings 14:23-29), and won back the Trans-Jordanic cities of Lodebar and Karnaim. Israel entered upon her last great period of prosperity. Her commerce was at flood tide, and her economy had become incontestably urban in keeping

---

[59] Mark 6:15; 8:28 (cf. Matt. 16:14); Matt. 11:14; Mark 9:4 ff. (Matt. 17:3 ff.; Luke 9:30 ff.); Mark 15:35-36 (Matt. 27:47-49); Luke 1:17; 4:25-26; 9:8, 19.

[60] Julius Wellhausen, *Israelitische und jüdische Geschichte* (3rd ed.; Berlin: G. Reimer, 1897), p. 74.

[61] On the Black Obelisk of Shalmaneser III (860-824 B.C) Jehu is pictured kneeling before the Assyrian monarch. Behind him stand the tribute-bearers. The inscription reads as follows: "Tribute of Jehu, son of Omri. Silver, gold, a golden bowl, a golden beaker, golden goblets, pitchers of gold, lead, staves for the hand of the king, javelins, I received from him." See Jack Finegan, *Light from the Ancient Past* (Princeton: Princeton University Press, 1946), pp. 172-73 and Fig. 73; A. T. Olmstead, *History of Assyria* (New York: Charles Scribner's Sons, 1923), Fig. 77.

with the traditional orientation of her life toward Phoenicia and the demands of the Phoenician merchants.[62]

Such would be the usual account of the history of this age in western Asia. But Amos tells another story. He sees the prosperity of the rich and also the grinding poverty of the poor. Houses of hewn stone and ivory, wine from bowls, silken cushions on luxurious couches, choice lambs from the stalls, generosity in tithes and sacrifices, hilarity and excitement at the great festivals witness to the prosperity of the land. But beneath the external show Amos exposes the gross dishonesty of the merchants, the exploitation of the poor, the corruption of justice both in ordinary relations of buying and selling and in the execution of justice in the courts; the gross insensateness of the leaders to "the affliction of Joseph"; the callousness and intemperance of the women—"cows of Bashan" Amos styles them in characteristic bluntness—and the complete unawareness of the deep insecurity that lurks in the shadows of Israel's political and social life. With almost brutal candor Amos exposes the rottenness of Israel's social and economic and religious life, exhibits it to the eyes of all, and goes to the very centers of corruption and entrenched power, the king's sanctuary and the royal palace (7:13), where his message will cut the deepest.

Amos' call to prophesy was a call to speak the divine oracles. The first "words" are addressed to the nations, to Syria and Philistia and Tyre (?), and Ammon and Moab, but above all, to Israel herself. From beginning to end they are words of judgment. They announce what Yahweh is about to do. "Thus saith Yahweh," they begin; and they end with the formula, "the oracle of Yahweh." Amos proclaims his oracles as divine revelations.

Yahweh speaks the language of history. He names names: nations, cities, kings, events, and the instruments men use to destroy each other. Nations can perform terrible deeds of power (Amos enumerates them), but Yahweh's fire is more terrible than all that nations can do. All the nations among whom Israel has lived are involved in the words of judgment. They fall under the same sovereignty as Israel does. Yahweh brought the Israelites from Egypt but also the hated Aramaeans from Kir and the Philistines of bitter memory from Caphtor (9:7). Israel is in the same category as the distant Ethiopians of Africa. It is true Yahweh had entered into particular relationship with Israel (3:2; 2:13-16), but this meant only greater responsibility and obligation. The chosen people are chosen for a purpose, and if that pur-

[62] Morgenstern, *Amos Studies*, I, 383-428.

pose is disobeyed, then the chosen people are to be rejected. Here we have a great advance in the history of religion, for this is the first appeal to an international morality. History is understood from the perspective of the sovereignty of a divine will and purpose. It is understood as a unity of transcendent significance and quality, for the God whose purpose and activity history reveals is a God of overwhelming demonic power, and at the same time a God of righteousness and justice. But if there is to all intents and purposes but one God who determines the course of history, then all peoples exist under a single sovereignty, and if that God is of the character of Yahweh, then this sovereignty is above all moral. Here we meet the major contribution of eighth-century prophecy.

This view of history naturally focused upon the issue or outcome of things. Amos is the first to refer to the "day of Yahweh." On this "day" Yahweh will reveal himself decisively. He will engage in battle and will come forth in triumph as victor over his foes. Contrary to popular expectations, Amos declares that Yahweh's appearing will be a time of darkness and deep gloom, a day of judgment against the covenant people Israel, a day when he will act in order to effect his will and purpose, and above all, a day that is near at hand (5:18-20). Judgment dominates the thought of the prophet. The early visions (7:1-6) still hold out hope, but the later ones (7:7-8; 8:1-3; 9:1-4) make it clear that "the end" has come (8:2) and Israel must be destroyed. Yet it is by no means absolutely certain that Amos could see no other possibility than doom. At least there is the one clear reference: "It may be that Yahweh, the God of hosts, will be gracious to the remnant of Joseph" (5:15). If this text is secure—and there is no good reason for rejecting its authenticity—then certain other passages gain greater force.

We have seen how trenchantly Amos exposed the social evils of his day, and how fiercely he denounced the inhumanities of his contemporaries. Every social wrong—profiteering at the expense of the poor, commercial dishonesty, intemperance, bribery, social callousness, distortion of justice, luxury, and extravagance—is an offense to Yahweh. Not all the exercises of the cult could avail anything in the light of such a situation. However elaborate the ritual, however pleasant and moving the music inherited from David (6:5), however generous the tithes and hilarious the festivals and costly the various kinds of sacrifices (5:21-27), however eagerly and loyally Israel streamed to the great sanctuaries—Bethel and Beer-sheba and Gilgal and Dan and all the others—Yahweh could take no notice. These are not the things he desired first of all, they could never be a substitute for righteousness ($ç^edh\bar{a}q\bar{a}h$) and justice ($mishp\bar{a}t$; 5:24). Amos' message is deeply rooted in the past. He is unintelligible outside the matrix of the historical revelation beginning with Moses. But he is the first to set the religious faith of Israel completely free of nationalism, and his message rises to a height not before attained. There is a fierce integrity in this prophet, a moral earnestness born of intense religious devotion, a consuming passion for the realization of Yahweh's will and purpose, and withal a perspicuity of vision and faith that place him in a position by himself. Yet he is not so much a spiritual monolith towering isolatedly into the sky as he is one of the loftiest among the many peaks that tower above the ranges of Israel's historic faith.

2. Hosea ben Beeri.—The book of Hosea is an excellent source for the social and political history of Israel in the middle years of the eighth century B.C. The book has certainly been edited, but the condition of the text often makes it hard to determine how far-reaching this process went. The superscription (1:1) has been expanded. The second verse serves as a summary of the prophet's message and is responsible for many of the difficulties of the first chapters. The final verse (14:9) is obviously very late. The majority of scholars hold that 1:7; 1:10–2:1, the greater part of 2:14-23 (e.g., vss. 16, 18, 21-23), and 3:5 are additions. It is possible that 14:1-8 is a late liturgical appendix, but we cannot be sure. In all probability, the prophet had a message of hope and restoration. The book does not make sense without this hope, and so 14:1-8 may be original, though this is doubtful.

Hosea was a younger contemporary of Amos. His writing reflects the disintegration and confusion which followed upon the death of Jeroboam II (786-746 B.C.) and the accession of Tiglath-pileser III (744-727 B.C.) to the throne of Assyria. Indeed, the entire book is as sensitive as a seismograph to the conditions in Palestine and the Near East. Assyria and Egypt are never absent from the prophet's mind, and his sense of imminent doom was probably evoked both by what he saw happening all about him and by the distant rumblings of new Assyrian advances. It is likely that Hosea belonged to the tribe of Benjamin, and if the references to Judah are original—which is by no means certain—he was in a good position to see the threat that lurked beneath both the northern and the southern kingdoms.

The prophecy of Hosea begins with a story of the infidelity of his wife Gomer. In this story we receive the deepest insight into the meaning of the book; actually the book is unintelligible without it. Only by an appreciation of the form and the substance of the story is it possible to understand the deeper "story" with which the book is occupied, the "story" of Yahweh's relationship to Israel and Israel's relationship to Yahweh. For the meaning of Gomer's faithlessness and whoredom is simply this: Israel, the chosen people, has broken the covenant. As the covenant dominates the life of Israel and provides it with its meaning, so the broken covenant constitutes the tragic matrix for the yet deeper revelation of God's reconciling and redeeming love. This it is which stirs the prophet and prompts his thought to range from the beginnings of Israel's history to the present, and from the present to that future when the starkness of the tragedy will somehow be caught up in pain and suffering into the heart of God himself.

To express the meaning of the covenant relationship in the catastrophic days of Israel's historical existence (745-722 B.C.), Hosea turns to the two most intimate areas of human life with an intensity that makes his little book quite *sui generis* in Scripture. The covenant on Sinai was Yahweh's marriage to Israel. Conjugal relationships were universal among the deities of the ancient Near East. But that Yahweh betrothed himself to a people, his people Israel, was a new insight, however deep the roots of the idea and the language might lie in the contemporary fertility cults. It is in the most profound and revealing of all man's intimate relationships that Hosea finds an expression of Yahweh's relation to his people. Yahweh is not only a husband; he is also a father, and Israel is his son. Yahweh's redemption from Egypt was a "calling" of his son (Hos. 11:1; cf. Exod. 4:22-23). What Gomer was to Hosea, Israel is to Yahweh.

When Hosea speaks of the relations between husband and wife and between parent and child, he does so because he finds in them an appropriate and revealing language to describe the relationship which exists between Yahweh and Israel. It was a love which only love can understand. This is why Hosea becomes so authentic an interpreter of Yahweh's love. He knew how love could suffer, and under its strains and in its violation he came to see its greater depth. He pointed again and again to the concrete evidences of this covenant love in the events of history. "I am Yahweh from the land of Egypt" (12:9); "by a prophet Yahweh brought Israel up out of Egypt" (12:13); "I found Israel like grapes in the wilderness" (9:10). Hosea has his own favorite word for this relationship, *hésedh*. This word may be rendered "devotion" or "covenant faithfulness." It is partly on account of Hosea himself that we find it so difficult to get precisely the right term. But he would be the first to say that we can understand it best by reading Israel's history through the eyes that *ḥéṣedh* gives us to see. As Adam C. Welch says,

What engrossed all his thoughts was the historic religion which had made his nation what it was, which had given it a different genius from all the other nations among which it lived, and the loss of which would mean the loss of a great thing from the world. He did not speak of a God who was Lord of heaven and earth, but of One who had come into contact with this people, who revealed Himself through the deeds which had made the people's history and through the institutions which moulded its life.[63]

But Israel had broken the covenant. She had gone after the Baals as the givers of fertility, or even worse, had identified Yahweh with Baal. Yahweh could not tolerate such easy syncretism. "She did not know that I gave her the grain, and the new wine, and the oil" (2:8). The Yahweh cult must be de-Canaanized. What this means is clear from Hosea's description of the new covenant in which Yahweh will betroth Israel to him in righteousness and in justice, and in fidelity, and in mercies, in faithfulness and in knowledge of Yahweh (2:19). Israel had violated the covenant in a second respect. She had organized herself into a monarchy with a king. But creation of the kingdom was an act of apostasy! The trouble all began at Gibeah whence Saul came, at Gilgal, where he was crowned king (10:9; 9:15; 10:3; 8:4; cf. also 7:3-7). Similarly, Israel's reliance on diplomacy, her periodic flirtation with the great nations of Egypt and Assyria, was infidelity, want of knowledge, apostasy. "Ephraim mixes among the peoples, and strangers devour his strength" (7:8-9); "She is a silly dove cooing to Egypt and then to Assyria" (7:11); "She is swallowed up among the nations, wandering off like a wild ass alone" (8:8-9). Again, Israel's resort to arms and defense measures will not avail her; her fortified cities and palaces are no security to her (8:14). Israel's infidelity to Yahweh is seen in her apostasy to the Baal cult of fertility, in her trust in the monarchy with its kings, in her trust in foreign relations, in her dependence upon material power and arms. All this shows that she does not know Yahweh. This is her cardinal sin. Just as the covenant meant that Yahweh knew Israel, and that Israel's acceptance showed she knew Yahweh, so all this infidelity shows that she does not know Yahweh. There is no knowledge of God in the land (4:1, 6, 11; 5:4; 6:6). Knowledge of God is not one quality

[63] *The Religion of Israel Under the Kingdom* (Edinburgh: T. & T. Clark, 1912), p. 111.

among others. All of Israel's relationship to Yahweh is gathered up in knowledge of God, and all her apostasy is seen in her failure to know Yahweh. Her infidelity shows her lovelessness to Yahweh; her lovelessness has blinded her to the covenant relation, and this blindness has brought about judgment.

The consequence of Israel's breaking of the covenant is her destruction. Yahweh has abandoned his people (5:6, cf. 4:6). He will love them no more (9:15); he is Israel's destruction (13:9 ff.); he will not be their God any more, "Ye are not my people, and I will not be your God" (1:9). The covenant made at Sinai is ended. Yahweh is like a lion to Israel (5:14), a leopard (13:7), a bear (13:8), a moth and rottenness (5:12). Israel has sowed the wind, but she will reap the whirlwind (8:7). Ephraim shall return to Egypt, and eat unclean food in Assyria (9:3).

Quite as vigorously as Amos, Hosea excoriates the existing cult. Even more plainly he shows how far it has gone in its syncretism with Baal worship. The flourishing cult of ritualistic prostitution at the high places and its association with the fertility of the soil (4:13-14), the worship of the bulls (13:1-3), the festivals of the Baals' days (2:13), the sacrificial meals (8:13), and the thoroughgoing depravity of the entire cult, all are denounced by Hosea in scathing rebuke. Hosea's scorn and contempt and ridicule and the definiteness of his characterizations are even more piercing than Amos' invective. He comes out flatly against the whole business of visual images in worship, so flatly, indeed, that many scholars believe him to be the first to launch this protest. On the matter of sacrifice, central as it was doubtless deemed by many to be, and not without some justification, Hosea is as outspoken as Amos, but his touchstone is not justice (*mishpáṭ*), though Hosea also knows what justice is, but mercy and covenant faithfulness (*ḥéṣedh*) and knowledge of God (*daʿath 'elóhîm*):

For *ḥéṣedh* I desire and not sacrifice;
and the knowledge of God more than burnt offerings (Hos. 6:6).

And yet this is not the end, not the final end. For Yahweh could no more reject Israel utterly than Hosea could cast off Gomer. That is the message of Hosea, the triumphant love of God, triumphant over wrath and judgment. What binds Israel and Yahweh is stronger than what separates them. Like Gomer, Israel will pass through a long period of discipline and purgation, "without king, and without prince, and without sacrifice, and without pillar, and without ephod or teraphim" (3:4), but there will be a new covenant, a new marriage in which they will live together on the basis of a covenant God and a covenant people in justice and righteousness and mercy and love, and in faithfulness. Then Israel will know Yahweh as Yahweh knows her. Hosea sees the reality of the divine judgment and he sees how deep and terrible Israel's infidelity is, but he sees even more clearly the covenant faithfulness that outlasts judgment and a mercy that reconciles and restores and redeems a wayward and faithless people.

> How shall I give thee up, O Ephraim!
>   how shall I cast thee off, O Israel!
> How shall I make thee as Admah!
>   how shall I set thee as Zeboim!
> My heart is turned against me,
>   my compassions are kindled together.
> I will not execute the fierceness of my anger,
>   I will not again destroy Ephraim;
> For I am God and not man;
>   the Holy One in the midst of thee;
> and I will not come in wrath (Hos. 11:8-9).

3. Isaiah of Jerusalem.—The original materials belonging to Isaiah of Jerusalem are found chiefly in chs. 1–12; 28–33, although there are authentic Isaiah materials outside these chapters. The prophet lived during the period of the most dynamic phase of Assyrian imperialistic aggression. The oracles of Isaiah gather about the chief crises of his day, although the entire period was one of international ferment. The reign of the usurper Tiglath-pileser III (745-727 B.C.) lies behind Isaiah's early ministry. This monarch's fateful policy of shifting conquered populations from one part of the empire to another, the death of Uzziah king of Judah, the Syro-Ephraimitic war, the decline and fall of the northern kingdom, and the campaigns of Sennacherib are but a few of the events which marked the career of Isaiah. Elijah, Elisha, Micaiah, Amos, and Hosea had directed their messages almost exclusively to the northern kingdom. Now on the eve of Israel's destruction Judah appears upon the scene in the person of one of the greatest of all the prophets, Isaiah of Jerusalem.

Isaiah seems to have come from the privileged class. He is pre-eminently a citizen of Jerusalem. He has the manner and speech of a city man. He possesses a kind of *savoir-faire*, a personal dignity and ease, and a sophistication which distinguishes him sharply from his prophetic predecessors in the north. He is supported by the stability of a social structure in which he has an instinctive trust and confidence. Institutions mean more to him than they do to any other prophet with the exception of Ezekiel. He is never quite able to break completely with the conservatism of Judah, and he has an innate and even profound regard for the house of David. Behind his call and through all the years of his preaching of judgment, and above all in the final crisis of Sennacherib's invasion, his patriotism and loyalty to Jerusalem and the monarchy are never lost. Deeply influenced by Amos, he nevertheless has so absorbed the herdsman-prophet's passion and message that he has made them to some degree his own. Amos can be brutal, unrestrained, ruthless, and impetuous; Isaiah's breeding and heritage and home life in Jerusalem transform the message of Amos into something more measured and grand and classical.

In the account of his inaugural vision all the major emphases of the prophet's teaching are present. "In the year that king Uzziah died," he begins simply, "I saw the Lord." The reality of this vision runs through all the oracles. He sees the Lord "high and lifted up," a phrase that keeps appearing in one form or other in his later messages. It is the holiness of God that is borne in upon him above all else. Holy, holy, holy! Hereafter this became his word for Yahweh, "the Holy One of Israel." It described Yahweh in his unapproachableness, his overwhelming majesty, his piercing glory. Overpowering and shattering in his awfulness, yet fascinating and compelling in his nearness, Yahweh was sublime and sinless and of purer eyes than to behold iniquity, before whom the seraphim hide their faces in reverence, cover their limbs in their awareness of the "holy," and poise their wings in flight to do his bidding. Isaiah in the utter authenticity of this final moment has but one word to speak, "Woe!" the woe of one who knows his own "uncleanness" and the uncleanness of the solidarity which he cherished so deeply. The threshold trembles, and the house is filled with smoke. Only Second Isaiah and, to a lesser degree, the psalmists inherit this great and central word of Isaiah's, "the Holy One of Israel." It is Isaiah more than any other who transforms the customary meaning of the word. He transforms it by seeing in God's justice and righteousness that which makes holiness the supreme reality that it is (Isa. 5:16). Intense as this realization is in the singing of the seraphim still, "the whole earth is full of his glory," or literally, "the fullness of the earth is his glory." But good Hebrew that he is, Isaiah presses on with utter economy of phrase: "For the King, Yahweh of hosts mine eyes have seen!" All the baffling relativities of history which have so much perplexed him now fade away as he sees who and what it is that is utterly sovereign. Yahweh is king. Amos would not have said it that way, and Hosea would have repudiated the expression for his own reasons. But not Isaiah. Then a seraph touches his lips with a glowing stone from off the altar, and the prophet knows in this "act" that the word he needs above all to hear has been spoken.

Lo! this has touched your lips;
Your guilt is removed; your sin is forgiven (Isa. 6:7).

Now Isaiah, standing within the council of God, can hear himself addressed, and it is the characteristic word of prophetic faith throughout the Old Testament, "Go!" Then follows the unbearable commission to which the prophet can only cry with dreadful poignancy, "How long?" The reply is even more terrible, but the last verse, corrupt as it is, may have some suggestion of hope in it, though the final sentence does not appear in the Greek text.

Isaiah's message, like that of Amos, is prevailingly one of judgment. In a series of magnificent strophes, disordered and mutilated as they now are in our text, he describes the imminent day of Yahweh. Yahweh has a day, final and decisive beyond all the other days of men. The pride of men has erected lofty structures of security and self-sufficiency but

the haughtiness of man will be humbled,
And the pride of man will be brought low;
And Yahweh alone will be exalted in that day (2: 17; cf. vs. 11).

"Yahweh has abandoned his people." This is the terrible word which Isaiah has to speak. Again and again he makes justice and righteousness the measuring rod to apply to Judah's life, and the verdict is always "destruction." The coming judgment of Assyrian conquest cannot be prevented; all the many resorts which men use to strengthen themselves are futile, as futile as the petty godlings, nonentities, which they worship:

For all this his anger is not turned away,
But his hand is stretched out still to strike (9:12, 17, 21; 10:4; cf. 5:25).

In the crisis of the Syro-Ephraimitic threat Isaiah appealed to one permanent and sufficient resource at the king's disposal—it is faith in Yahweh, the God of history.

If you will not have faith [tha'amînú]
You shall surely not be established [thē'āmēnú] (Isa. 7:9).

Isaiah had had his glorious vision, and such trust, such unreserved and single-minded confidence was for him the only possibility. But Ahaz could examine the water mains more closely! Then Isaiah presses the issue, but Ahaz

piously evades it. Nevertheless, Isaiah says, Yahweh will give a sign, the sign of a child about to be born who will bear the name Immanuel, "God with us." Before the child is grown, the king of Assyria will come to accomplish the will of Yahweh. The final and all-sufficient potency of faith was not the inspiration of a single moment. Yahweh had placed in Zion a stone, a well-tested stone, a precious stone, as the cornerstone of a sure foundation, and this is the great security, "He who believes will not be in haste" (28:16). Israel's strength lies in quietness and confidence (30:15). The waters of Shiloah that flow softly will outlast the waters of the great Euphrates. For the first time in history faith was appealed to in a moment of great destiny as man's supreme resource. For Christianity the child Immanuel is the symbol of that faith (Matt. 2:23).

Like Amos, Isaiah sees the activity of God's purpose in the history of his own times. The series of moving strophes in 9:7–10:5; 5:26-29 describe the sovereignty of the divine purpose. Stroke after stroke the judgment falls until men have lost every support and stay (cf. 3:1-12; 1:4-9; 31:1 ff.; etc.). Again like Amos, Isaiah denounces the false security of the cult. Yahweh despises sacrifices; their odor is an abomination to him. Amos could go no further. This fervid attendance at the sanctuary, why do you trample my courts? New moons and sabbaths and solemn gatherings, Yahweh cannot endure them. Even when you pray, he will not listen.

Your hands are full of bloodshed—wash yourselves clean;
Put away the evil of your doings from before my eyes;
Cease to do evil,
  learn to do good;
Seek justice,
  restrain the oppressor;
Uphold the orphan's rights,
  defend the widow's cause (1:16-17).

But despite the urgency and apparently unqualified character of Isaiah's oracles of judgment, he did not look forward to the future without hope. A remnant will survive the judgment, and the inconspicuous minority will become the community which is to be the bearer of the word of God.[64] Some of the passages which relate to the remnant are questionable.

[64] Sigmund Mowinckel, in his *Jesaja* (Oslo: Gyldendal, 1949) and other writings, sees in Isaiah the *fons et origo* of an extensive Isaiah tradition and school. To it he attributes the non-Isaiah, pre-exilic portions of the book of Isaiah, parts of Micah, Zephaniah, Nahum, Habakkuk, "The Song of Moses," and parts of the Deuteronomic laws; cf. G. W. Anderson, "Some Aspects of the Uppsala School of Old Testament Study," *Harvard Theological Review*, XLIII (1950), 242 ff.

The reference to Isaiah's older son, Shear-jashub, "the remnant shall return," more probably bears the meaning of judgment, not hope. More certain is the triumph of his faith to which he appealed at all times. For example, the prophet's stand on the occasion of Sennacherib's siege of Jerusalem has a consistency which is lost if one does not regard the totality of his message and views only the great number of oracles of doom. But standing above all are the lines from Isaiah himself on the occasion of his rejection during the Syro-Ephraimitic crisis: "I will bind up my testimony and seal my law [teaching] in the heart of my disciples. Then I will wait for Yahweh, who is hiding his face from the house of Israel; I will set my hope on him, while I and the children whom Yahweh has given me remain as signs and symbols in Israel from Yahweh of hosts who dwells on Mount Zion" (8:16-18). In the biblical perspectives the faithful community survived beyond all the din of empires and the machinations of kings. Signs and symbols from Yahweh of hosts!

Did Isaiah look forward to a messianic age governed by a messiah? If the great passages associated with his name (2:2-4; 9:1-6; 11:1-9; 32:1-8) are his, then of course no one in the whole range of biblical faith looked more steadily and confidently to the coming of such an age and such a deliverer than he. There are great difficulties in the way of accepting them, however. And yet it cannot be said to be impossible. Some of the passages have a greater claim than others to authenticity (e.g., 9:1-6); and our more recent studies of ancient Oriental literature put the problem in a new light. It is at least precarious to reject them. In certain respects they have an interior consistency with Isaiah's religious thought, his great concern for the monarchy, and above all, the house of David:

For to us a child is born,
  to us a son is given.
And the government will be on his shoulder,
  and his name will be called
Wonderful counsellor, Mighty God,
Everlasting father, Prince of peace.
Of the increase of his government, and of peace,
  there will be no end,
Upon the throne of David, and over his kingdom,
  to establish it and to uphold it,
  with justice and with righteousness,
  from henceforth and forever.
The zeal of the Yahweh of hosts will do this (9:6-7).

4. Micah of Moresheth-gath.—The prophetic oracles which most surely come from Micah are contained in the first three chapters of the book which bears his name, and of these 2:12-13 is probably a later addition. Mic. 4–7 may preserve isolated utterances of the prophet, but one cannot be certain. The famous controversy before the mountains in 6:1-8 comes a full half century after Micah lived and belongs to the reign of Manasseh. Of Micah himself the book tells us little, and yet he stands forth as clearly as any of his contemporaries. A peasant-farmer from the Shephelah, he knows the harsh and grudging life of the poor. He speaks out in bitter outrage at the injustices done to those who have neither power nor capacity to resist, but with deep compassion for those who suffer from the devices and machinations of shrewd and prosperous men.

The utterances that are preserved for us are nearly all invectives and threats. Yahweh is coming in great theophany to bring judgment upon the cities, for it is cities like Samaria and Jerusalem which embody the evil of the time (1:5). Across the book might be written *Jerusalem delenda est*. But Micah does not gloat over the divine judgment (1:8). His condemnation of the social injustices of his contemporaries falls particularly upon the landholders who devise ways in which to fleece the peasants of their holdings.

You are my people's foe,
You rise against those who are at peace,
For the sake of a mere trifle you take a heavy mortgage! (2:8.)

Next comes the rulers. "Is it not your place to know justice?" (3:1.) The priests demand fees for their oracles, and the prophets prophesy for cash. Micah cuts straight through the sham and pretense of the professional classes, not least of all his own. The thought of the insincere prophet evokes his apologia:

  But I am full of power,
  The spirit of Yahweh, justice, and strength,
  To declare to Jacob his transgressions,
  And to Israel its sins (3:8).

In one final and smashing threat he speaks his last and most remembered word against the city's leaders:

Therefore, because of you,
Zion shall be plowed like a field,
And Jerusalem shall become a ruin,
And the temple hill a high place in a forest (3:12).

The temple which Isaiah of Jerusalem had declared to be inviolate, Micah consigns to destruction. Jerusalem is no place for Yahweh's tabernacling presence!

Much of the remainder of his book comes from later times. In the heart of it stands the great controversy of Yahweh with his people (6:1-8). It is a mistake merely to repeat the great finale in vs. 8; the passage is a unit, and one must enter into the whole drama of the trial at law, and with the case each party has to make, before it can be really appreciated. Yahweh's case in vss. 3-4 is prophetic to the core. What is it that Yahweh has done for Israel? Israel must answer, for this is peculiarly her province. She must remember because it belongs to her nature to remember. She must remember Moses and Aaron and Miriam and the events that culminated at Gilgal, "that you may understand the righteous acts of Yahweh." Israel's defense is poignant. It is not sacrifices, not even those of her children, that Yahweh requires. This is a good summary of the prophetic message of Amos, Hosea, and Isaiah on the subject of sacrifice. And then the great commandment is flung before them. You have been told what is good!

> What does Yahweh require of you?
> To do justice, and to love ḥésedh,
> And to walk humbly with your God (6:8).

Not much is preserved for us from Manasseh's long and evil reign, but here the heritage of the great prophetic tradition of the ninth and eighth centuries has found a stirring and clamant voice. The little minorities who served as signs and symbols for Yahweh of hosts held firm and steady, and prepared the way for Josiah's great reform in 621 B.C.

D. The Reformation of 621 B.C. 1. Historical Background.—When Ashurbanipal, the last of the succession of great Assyrian kings, died in the year 633 B.C., the empire was in a state of rapid decline. The king had succeeded in meeting the revolt of Babylonia in 650-648 B.C., but it proved to be the handwriting on the wall. Soon after his death, Nabopolassar, a Chaldean prince, made himself king over Babylonia and became the founder of the neo-Babylonian kingdom. In a short time other powers became involved: [65] Egypt under Psamtik I, Media under Cyaxares, hordes of Scythians from beyond the Caucasus, and other lesser peoples. It is in this international setting that the history of Judah recounted in II Kings 22-23 should be interpreted. The tensions between nation and covenant, to both of which the reform movement of Josiah sought to do justice, constitute the major realities that make this reformation of such profound consequence in the history and religion of Israel.

Nowhere in the Old Testament is Israel's sensitiveness to history better illustrated than in her response to the momentous events between the death of Ashurbanipal and the destruction of Jerusalem in 586(7) B.C. Toynbee's theory of "challenge and response" is confirmed in the history of Israel in general, but there is one phase of this response that has special significance for us, the relation of history to the production of scripture. The great events of the seventh and sixth centuries left their literary precipitate in the form of such works as Zephaniah, Jeremiah, the Code of Deuteronomy, the original edition of I and II Kings, Nahum, Habakkuk, Ezekiel, and a number of psalms. No period of comparable extent is so rich in biblical writings of the first importance.

2. Source.—Among the more important of these sources is the Book of the Covenant contained in Deuteronomy. This document must be read and understood in the light of the narrative given in II Kings 22-23. It is prefaced by two extensive introductions (Deut. 1:1-4:43; 4:44-11:32), both of which are probably later than the code itself, although the second has a greater claim to originality than the first. The remaining chapters (27; 29-34) come from different times. Deuteronomy is a rhetorical book with a moving hortatory style, which has no adequate extrabiblical parallels. The materials within the Bible which have a similar style are the work of Deuteronomists. The code contains many ancient elements. The Covenant Code of Exod. 20:23-23:19, or its prototype (as is more probable), was in the hands of the authors.[66] Times as disturbed as those of the decline and fall of Assyria naturally inspired a great return to tradition. The writers of Deuteronomy doubtless intend to give a transcription of Mosaic faith, as they understood it, for their own times.

3. The Code of Deuteronomy.—Dominating all else in the code is the demand for an exclusive loyalty to Yahweh. This is stated with an urgency unmatched in the Scriptures. Its classical formulation appears in the Shema (Deut. 6:4-9). Translated literally, the opening words read as follows: "Hear, O Israel, Yahweh our God is one Yahweh. And you shall love Yahweh your God with all your heart [mind], and with all your life [néphesh], and with all your strength. These words which I am commanding you today shall be upon your heart. . . ." The code itself repeats the assertion of Yahweh's unity again and again and in different ways: historically, by applying the ḥérem to the whole period of the Conquest; practically, by the demand for complete extermination of all Canaanite and other alien elements from the

---

[65] In the case of Egypt and the Scythians, at least, the intervention into the international situation preceded their activity at this time; nevertheless it was Nabopolassar's revolt that gave the impetus to the final overthrow of the empire.

[66] See the excellent analysis of the materials in S. R. Driver, *Introduction to the Literature of the Old Testament* (9th ed.; Edinburgh: T. & T. Clark, 1913), pp. 73-75.

existing worship; cultically, by the reorganization of worship and the centralization of the sanctuary; ethically, by the insistence upon complete commitment to the will of God. "It is Yahweh your God that you must follow; of him you must stand in awe; his commands you must keep; his injunctions you must heed; him you must serve; and to him you must hold fast" (13:4).

Jerusalem is the place where men must worship. Heretofore the sanctuaries were near and accessible to all. Every slaughter was a sacrifice, every festival a festival to Yahweh. This new concentration of worship at Jerusalem actually produced an unprecedented separation between the secular and religious life. Secular slaughter was now permitted. Only the three great festivals of Passover, Weeks, and Tabernacles (16:1-15) must be celebrated. The centralization of the sanctuary now required going to Jerusalem, the national capital, with all its venerable associations with David, Solomon, Isaiah, and the Davidic dynasty. The cult with its various practices and its priesthood was rigorously controlled. Sacrifices were not only permitted but enjoined. Directions were given for their proper performance. Specific and elaborate instructions were issued for the care of the Levites. Distinctions between clean and unclean food were carefully set forth (14:3-20).

The book is addressed to the average man of Israel; it is a layman's book, and it has the style and content to which the layman would be the first to respond. One cannot help but sense throughout the urgent situation out of which such demands for control came. The inroads of the Canaanite fertility cult and Babylonian astral worship were so serious that rigor had to be applied if the religion of Israel, continuous with Moses, was to survive. Moreover, the emphasis upon rejoicing in all the celebrations of the cult is a particularly salutary and authentic element in the code.

The main characteristic of Deuteronomy is its strong emphasis upon love: Yahweh's love for Israel and Israel's loving response to Yahweh. Yahweh, the holy God, has chosen Israel to be a holy people (cf. Exod. 19:6). It was Yahweh's love, unmotivated and spontaneous, that prompted him to take the initiative (Deut. 7:6-8). But this love of Yahweh is interpreted in the light of the concrete historical evidence of Israel's own history. "You must remember all the experiences through which Yahweh your God has led you for the past forty years in the desert" (8:2). The future, too, lies within the providence and love of God. The prophets were the instruments of his continuing revelation so that Israel might always be guided by his word. "They have spoken well; from time to time I will raise up for them someone like you [Moses] from among their fellow countrymen to be a prophet; and I will put my words in his mouth, and he shall tell them all that I command him" (18:17-18). Past, present, and future, all are evidences of Yahweh's love for his people. Yahweh sent the law as his gift to Israel; his law was in fact revelation, revelation of what above all they needed to know. And so Yahweh's unmotivated love for Israel has as its corollary the demand for Israel's reciprocal love to God. After the great opening line of the Shema about the unity of Yahweh, there follows this cardinal demand of love from Israel, a love that will dominate all her life, a love of such intensity that it enlists the whole mind, the whole self (néphesh), the whole of one's energy. While the second command of the gospel appears in Lev. 19:18 and not here, yet it really appears everywhere in Deuteronomy also. For the writers would certainly agree that this was the motivation of all the ethical requirements laid upon Israel. To be sure, love does not have the universality that it has in the gospel, for it is circumscribed in various ways; but this circumscription needs to be understood in terms of the milieu which makes it central. Not only must Israelites love each other; they must love the resident alien (gêr) also, "for you were once aliens yourselves in the land of Egypt" (Deut. 10:19).

Israel is a holy, a chosen, and a covenant people. The holiness of Israel describes the character and meaning of its life. "For you are a holy people to Yahweh your God, and Yahweh has chosen you to be a people for his own possession out of all the peoples that are on the face of the earth" (14:2). The uniqueness of Israel is a constant stress of the Deuteronomist. This uniqueness is derived from the uniqueness of her God. She is granted this uniqueness by being made holy, chosen, and "covenanted." It is Israel's responsibility both in the practices of the cult and in acts of humanitarianism to live as a holy people. Her relations to other peoples are to be determined by her holy character. She must separate herself from the ways of other nations and maintain her religious purity. The holiness of Israel is closely related to two other dominant emphases in Deuteronomy: election and covenant. The belief in election gives a historical character to the idea of holiness. This event never ceases to excite the wonder of the Deuteronomic writers (7:6-8; 9:4-6; 10:14-15; 14:2; 26:18-19). Yahweh's choice of Israel is not explained by Israel's genius for religion, by her native endowment, by the purity of her ethical life, or by any merit in Israel at all, but rather by the divine mercy. Above all, in the covenant relationship Yahweh manifested his love and mercy to Israel. The nations of the Near East met the confusion and disintegration of their world in their own ways; Israel's major response was in terms of the return to the Mosaic covenant. But Deuteronomy gives new content and force to it by viewing its significance in the light of the conditions in western Asia in the late seventh century B.C. If the covenant receives remarkable emphasis, it is because the situation called it forth. The Deuteronomic writers contributed more than any others after Moses to center Israel's life in the covenant: a covenantal people, a covenantal book, a covenantal God.

The laws of love as they were understood by the prophets and priests who were responsible for the code are set forth in great detail. Love demands justice. Justice gathers into one all the requirements of Israel's social life. The influence of the eighth-century prophets is apparent in their formulation and content. As Yahweh is God of gods and Lord of lords, the great, the mighty, and the terrible God, who is never partial and never takes a bribe, executing justice for the fatherless and the widow, and loving the resident alien, and giving him food and raiment, so Israel must live and act in relation to her neighbors (10:17 ff.). What is required of Israel is determined by the character of God in his dealings with men. There must be no poor in the land. Poverty is forbidden (15:4-11). The Israelite, like Yahweh, must make no distinctions between important and unimportant people. Servants and slaves have their rights; even a runaway slave must not be turned over to his master. "He shall dwell with you in your midst" (23:15-16). No interest is to be exacted of the fellow countryman. Cities of refuge are to be set up throughout the land so that there may be no miscarriage of justice. Various aspects of family life are treated with sensitiveness for the persons involved (21:15 ff.; 22:5, 13 ff., 22 ff.). Not least important is the concern for animal life. The ox that treads the grain must not be muzzled (25:4). If one comes upon a nest with eggs in it or with the young, the mother bird must not be seized (22:6). In time of war or siege the fruit trees may not be cut down. "Are trees in the field to be besieged by you?" (20:19-20.)

The moral sense of the reformers reflects itself in another way in the moral logic of Deuteronomy. The same mind which insists upon the claims of the law of God views the consequences of good and evil in a perfectly simple way. The motivation for doing good was reward: "That it may be well with you in the land." This note is sounded again and again throughout the book. Justice demanded that good should produce good consequences and evil, evil conse-

quences. This simple view of the divine sovereignty dominates not only Deuteronomy, but the whole succession of books upon which the Deuteronomic school laid its hand.

This interpretation of history was one of the chief defects of Deuteronomy.[67] In many ways it was an evil legacy. The ultimately profound truth it embodied was in actuality obscured because of the immediate perspectives in which it asserted the divine justice. To our own day we are cursed with superficial constructions of the historical process in neat moral categories which history itself contradicts, precisely as the history of Israel contradicted the Deuteronomists and finally evoked the deeper interpretations of Second Isaiah, some of the psalmists, and all the apocalyptists. A theodicy which saw life in terms of rewards and punishments only could not cope with the realities of national tragedy; indeed, it was the simple moral logic of the Deuteronomists and their like that made the blow of 586 and the succeeding years all the more intolerable.

A second defect in Deuteronomy was the intensity of its nationalism. The attempt to take the prophets seriously and to apply the great ideals of justice and mercy and mutuality to the life of the nation was glorious enough, but not infrequently nationalism gained the upper hand. At the same time, it is important to read this nationalism in terms of the political climate which produced it. Again, the emphasis upon the written code was destined to produce important consequences. A book became the medium of a divine revelation. It was not the living voice of an Amos or an Isaiah proclaiming the will of God, but the letters and words of a book, and Deuteronomy set itself up as the criterion for orthodoxy. With Deuteronomy began the movement which was to make of Judaism the people of the Book. But if the written word had its consequences, so too did the emphasis upon the single sanctuary in Jerusalem. The absolutizing of the cult and its temple could not go unchallenged. This was not in the spirit of any of the great prophets, of Hosea or Amos or Micah, or even Isaiah. Such an emphasis led to superstitious veneration of the temple, and it needed the terrible castigations of a Jeremiah and later of Jesus of Nazareth to expose the dangers of exalting even the temple too highly.

E. The Prophets of the End of Judah. 1. Zephaniah.—This little book was inspired by

---

[67] A. C. Welch, in *The Code of Deuteronomy* (London: James Clarke & Co., 1924), attributes the nationalism and ecclesiasticism of the book to the work of the southern king and priests, not to the original form of the book, which he believes, perhaps correctly, to have its home in the north. For further discussion of the effects of this nationalism see his *Jeremiah: His Time and His Work* (London: Oxford University Press, 1928).

the threat of the invasion of Scythian hordes from beyond the Caucasus. The following passages are probably secondary: 2:7; parts of 2:8-11; 3:14-20. The book is valuable for its picture of conditions existing in Jerusalem in the years preceding the reform of 621 B.C.

A day of doom is to descend upon the world: "I will cut off mankind from off the face of the ground" (1:2-3). Judah and Jerusalem will be destroyed because of their worship of astral deities, the Canaanite Baal, and Milcom (1:4-6). Zephaniah seizes upon the day of Yahweh for his classical formulation of the terrible *dies irae* (1:7-13, 14-18). Because of the gross corruption of their worship of Yahweh in the temple, priests, princes, the rich, and the illustrious are singled out for bitter attack: "Yahweh will bring trouble upon mankind so that they will walk like blind men, because they have sinned against Yahweh" (1:17). From Judah and Jerusalem, Zephaniah turns to the nations. To the passionate demands of his predecessors for righteousness and justice and mercy Zephaniah adds his own great word of humility in a passage that echoes Amos 5:14-15:

Seek Yahweh, all you meek of the earth,
Who do his will,
Seek righteousness, seek humility;
Perhaps you may be hidden on the day of the anger
    of Yahweh (Zeph. 2:3).

One other feature for which this little book is memorable is its emphasis upon the remnant. Jerusalem will be purged of its proud and haughty leaders; Israel will be the holy nation it was destined to be from the beginning, a holy remnant:

And you shall no more be haughty in my holy
    mountain;
For I will leave in the midst of you a people humble and poor.
And in the name of Yahweh shall they seek refuge
    —the remnant of Israel (3:11b-13b).

2. Habakkuk.—The book of Habakkuk is one of the most appealing and important books in the Bible, as it is one of the most difficult. The critical problems are peculiarly troublesome. We cannot be certain even of its date. It is probable, however, that it was written in the year of the Battle of Carchemish (604 B.C.). Only chs. 1–2 belong to Habakkuk himself, as may be confirmed by the commentary on the book discovered among the Dead Sea scrolls. The problem which occupies the prophet is the righteousness of the divine sovereignty in history.

How long, O Yahweh, shall I cry for help,
    and thou wilt not hear,

Call out to thee, "Violence!"
    and thou wilt not save?
Why dost thou make me see wrongs
    and look upon trouble?
·   ·   ·   ·   ·   ·   ·   ·
For the wicked surround the righteous,
    so justice goes forth perverted (1:2-3b, 4cd).

Habakkuk is not satisfied with easy or conventional answers. The Babylonians are surely no worthy instruments of judgment upon Judah, evil as the latter may be. Finally Habakkuk determines to station himself upon a watchtower "to see what he will say to me." There he receives a word from Yahweh:

Write the vision,
Make it plain upon tablets,
So he may run who reads it.
For still the vision waits its time,
It hastens to the end—it will not fail;
If it tarry, wait for it;
It will surely come, it will not delay.
Behold, he whose soul is not upright in him shall
    fail,
But the righteous lives by his faithfulness (2:2-4).

Such a revelation in a time of darkness was destined to receive fresh formulations in other periods of history. Both the apostle Paul (Rom. 1:17; Gal. 3:11) and Martin Luther seized upon these words to express a meaning deeper than the prophet himself divined. Habakkuk belongs to the company in Israel who learned to wait (Isa. 8:16-18; 40:28-31; 64:4; Ps. 130:6). The righteous gets not a pat answer to his desperate query, but an answer which demands all the resources of his soul. He must walk and live by his trust and faithfulness to God.

Ch. 3 is an independent psalm, but it was placed here intentionally. The poem is one of the most vivid in the Old Testament.[68] Its description of the theophany has mythological echoes and contains reminiscences of the language of ancient Ugarit. But it is the closing lines that bind it securely to the rest of the book in its wonderful expression of unconquerable trust. If Habakkuk did not write them, he would certainly have wished to claim them for his own.

Though the fig-tree do not blossom
    nor fruit be on the vine,
The produce of the olive fail
    and the fields yield no food,
The flock be cut off from the fold
    and there be no herd in the stalls,
Yet will I exult in Yahweh,
    I will rejoice in the God of my salvation (3:17-18).

[68] See the reconstruction of the text by W. F. Albright, "The Psalm of Habakkuk," *Studies in Old Testament Prophecy*, ed. H. H. Rowley (Edinburgh: T. & T. Clark, 1950), pp. 1-18.

3. Jeremiah of Anathoth.—The prophetic activity of Jeremiah, the son of a priestly family at Anathoth, a village to the north of Jerusalem, is understood in the light of his own extraordinary personality and the international background against which he delivered his oracles. Called to be a prophet in 626 B.C., or possibly some years later, he felt himself to be predestined, set apart (lit., "made holy"), and appointed to match the events of his world with the word of God. His call, his confessions, and his oracular utterances reveal him as a person peculiarly endowed with the capacity for personal identification with the storm and stress of his age. His poetic temperament, his solitariness and sense of isolation, his profoundly interior sense of communion with God, and his constant preoccupation with the problem of the meaning of Israel's life and destiny fitted him uniquely to interpret the religious significance of the world-shaking events that were going on in the crucial period from 626 to 586 B.C.

In a series of early oracles (2:2–4:4) Jeremiah contrasts Israel's religion, as it had come down from Moses enshrined in the covenant relationship, with the current syncretistic versions which had undermined what the prophet believed to be the most distinctive elements in the inherited faith. Yahweh remembers Israel's past relationship with him in the desert, an elected, called, redeemed, and holy covenant people whose life was oriented to a historical revelation. But she and her leaders had corrupted the traditional faith into a grievous apostasy (2:4-8). They were skilled in doing evil, building cisterns that held no water (2:13), but they had no will or ability to do good. They exchanged their God for gods of their own making and their glory for vanity. The appetite grew on what it fed, and the lure of the fertility cults had tempted Israel to an insatiate lust so that her moral degradation grew apace into a fatal spot incarnadine (2:20-22, 23-29; 3:21-25). So Jeremiah calls for a profound inward transformation, a circumcision of the heart (4:1-4), in which men will really know Yahweh as they had once known him in covenantal devotion.

The subsequent poems deal with "the foe from the north." In their present form, at least, they refer to the Babylonians. In lyrical utterances of striking quality, in which the prophet's identification with the travail of his age is almost unmatched, Jeremiah says that the foe has been sent by the Lord as a judgment upon Judah. The deepening darkness and tragedy of the times are set forth in the powerful descriptions of the approaching foe, Jeremiah's own inward suffering (4:19-21), and the remarkable description of the returning chaos (4:23-26). The cry to repent, to return, sounds throughout these poems, "O Jerusalem, wash your heart of wickedness that you may be saved" (4:14). History is understood as the arena of a divine sovereignty, of a God whose will and purpose are revealed in the disaster and confusion of the times.

It is doubtful whether the book of Jeremiah contains any authentic utterances relating to the Deuteronomic reform of 621 B.C. It is possible that a nucleus of authentic material may be recovered, but the difficulties involved in such a recovery are so serious that it is better to leave the problem unsettled.[68a] In another group of passages we have a record of what is indubitably Jeremiah's personal confessions, perhaps the first of their kind in history (11:18-23; 12:1-6; 15:10-21; 17:9-10, 14-18; 18:18-23; 20:7-12, 14-18). There are no more "interior" words in the history of religion than these. The intimacy of the dialogue, the passionate outbursts of pain and deep travail, the urgency of prayer, and the way in which God conquers Jeremiah's own inveterate temptation to self-centeredness expose the depths of his agonizing struggle. The prophet is influenced by the devotional traditions of Israel preserved in the psalms, but there is a sovereign independence from them also, for his confessions express what is deepest within him. It was in part out of experiences such as these that the confessions record that Jeremiah's individualism is forged.

In the prophetic utterances connected with the Babylonian aggression Jeremiah's message to the nations and to his own people is dominated by the conviction of God's reign in history. In season and out, the prophet urges his people to surrender to the Babylonians. It is a mistake to call him a pacifist. He sees in the crisis of western Asia the working out of the divine purpose. The issues involve a choice between life and death (21:8-9). It is the business of the "house of David" to execute justice and relieve oppression (21:12). He rejects the easy optimism of his contemporaries, which sees the exile as short-lived. There is more than a suggestion that his hope for the future rested in those who had been carried away. Yet his purchase of a field from his cousin was a sign of a better time to come (32:1-15). That he looked forward to a messiah from David's house is problematical at best.

[68a] J. P. Hyatt, "Jeremiah and Deuteronomy," *Journal of Near Eastern Studies*, I (1942), 156-73; H. H. Rowley, "The Prophet Jeremiah and the Book of Deuteronomy," in *Studies in Old Testament Prophecy*. Rowley makes a strong case for the view that Jeremiah first supported the Deuteronomic reforms but later recognized the dangers implicit in them. On somewhat different lines Wilhelm Erbt (*Jeremia und seine Zeit* [Göttingen: Vandenhoeck & Ruprecht, 1902]) takes a similar view. This, after all, is the more common position taken by scholars and may be right.

The consistency of Jeremiah's prophetic message is admirably reflected in his attitude toward the great historical institutions of Israel. The temple was not inviolable as some had interpreted Isaiah as saying, but it was to be destroyed like Shiloh. The "law" had been turned into a lie by the scribes (8:8), and the circumcision which the Lord really required of his people was a radical change of heart (4:4). Even the intercession of a Moses or a Samuel would not avail to avert the impending judgment. The city of Jerusalem, with all its hallowed associations with the cult, with David and Isaiah and the Deuteronomic reforms, must be destroyed, and the nation was to go into exile as the verdict of God upon its apostasy. Above all, Yahweh will make a new covenant, not like the old one on tables of stone, but graven on the heart of man (31:31-34). The knowledge of God, which runs like a major strain in Jeremiah as in Hosea, is to be a new kind of inward relationship in which all men will know the Lord. For God "will forgive their iniquity and will no more remember their sin" (31:34; cf. Isa. 40:2). This is an eschatological utterance. It forms the culmination of the interior conflict within the prophet from his earliest days, crystallizes the meaning of Israel's life and destiny in the covenant relation, and prepares the way for its appropriation by his prophetic successors and the writers of the New Testament (Luke 22:20; I Cor. 11:25; II Cor. 3:6; Heb. 8:8-12).

4. Ezekiel.—The study of the book of Ezekiel presents problems as difficult as any in the whole Old Testament. The dominant critical view today is that it is highly composite. There can be little question that more than one hand has gone to its making. But radical disintegration of the book is peculiarly precarious in the case of Ezekiel because of the personal portrait which the book gives us of the prophet. For if Ezekiel was the kind of person there described, then it is likely that this reflected itself in his writings. Moreover, the literary argument is not disposed of simply. We are not in a position today to assert with any degree of certainty how much of the book comes from a time later than the prophecy. The position of R. H. Pfeiffer [69] seems on the whole the safest one to adopt. This assigns a substantial portion of the book to the prophet himself.

Ezekiel, son of a Jerusalem priest, was carried into captivity in the deportation of 597 B.C., together with King Jehoiachin. There, on the banks of the river Chebar, the great canal of the city of Nippur, in the year 592 B.C., he had an extraordinary vision of a throne-chariot above the firmament, and upon the "likeness of the throne . . . was the likeness as the appearance

of a man above upon it" (1:26). This was the appearance of the glory (*kābhôdh*) of Yahweh. The character of the vision suggests a priestly interest, although the imagery has been doubtless influenced by its Babylonian provenance. [70] The holiness of God, his transcendence, and his glory which the vision portrays, constitute the major features of the prophet's thought of God. Doubtless his own experience in the life of the cult, his close association with "the tabernacling presence" in the dim recesses of the sanctuary, his appreciation of symbolism, his profound sense of incommensurable dimensions in the reality of God, and his deep sense of Israel's guilt lie behind his description.

The message of the prophet before the fall of Jerusalem in 586 B.C. is prevailingly one of judgment. The guilt of Judah is so deep and dark that its doom cannot be averted. Ezekiel surpasses both Hosea and Jeremiah in his tragic portrait of the sin of his people. It is significant that he does not describe it in any metaphysical category, but rather in terms of Israel's origins and history. From birth Judah was corrupt, the offspring of an Amorite father and a Hittite mother. Historical reflection is present here, but it is not the historical datum which concerns him so much as the religious. The biography of Israel was one continuous story of infidelity and apostasy. Not even the presence of Noah, Daniel, and Job in the city could ward off its inevitable destruction. Cultic and ethical transgressions are put on the same level. The prophet characterizes the former as idolatry, the latter as murder, harlotry, rebellion, and apostasy. Jerusalem is worse than Samaria, the foreign peoples, and even Sodom. Worst of all, the temple has become the seat of pagan practice. Therefore it must be destroyed. The prophet resorts to every kind of symbolism and imagery to express the reality of judgment. Judah is responsible, and she will be held accountable for her breach of the covenanted bond.

The sin of Israel is terrible to Ezekiel because he profoundly apprehends the holiness of God. God manifests his holiness by his rule and sovereignty over Israel's history. The ever-recurring phrase, "in order that you may know that I am Yahweh," expresses the transcendent lordship of God, his sovereignty over all that is human. Before him man is as nothing, and the words with which the prophet is addressed, "son of man" or mortal man, express the vast distance which separates God and man. The nations are to be destroyed "for his name's sake." The divine honor and majesty must not be profaned. Throughout his prophecy Ezekiel

[69] *Intro. to O.T.*, pp. 518-65.

[70] Lorenz Dürr, *Ezechiels Vision von der Erscheinung Gottes* (Münster: W. Aschendorff, 1917).

seeks to vindicate the righteousness and holiness of God.

After the fall of Jerusalem the obdurateness and pride of the people turned to despair. On the one hand, they were burdened with the consciousness of their guilt: "Our transgressions and our sins are upon us and we pine away in them; how then can we live?" (33:10.) To this plaint the prophet replies with a divine oracle: "As I live, saith the Lord Yahweh, I have no pleasure in the death of the wicked; but that the wicked turn from his way and live: turn ye, turn ye from your evil ways; for why will ye die?" (33:11.) On the other hand, when the people complain of God's injustice (33:17), he vindicates God by asserting that the people have deserved what has befallen them and *mirabile dictu* he appeals to the principle of individual responsibility: everyone is judged according to his own way. To the ancient belief in the solidarity of guilt (Exod. 34:6-7 [J]; Exod. 20:5 [E]; II Kings 21:1-15; 22:15-20; etc.) Ezekiel replies with a strong assertion of the responsibility of the individual. In ch. 18 and 33:10-20 he appears as a pastor rather than a theologian. He is attempting in the first instance not to formulate a generalization, but to meet a critical need. He does so in a mechanical and rigid fashion, in contrast to the more profound message of Jeremiah (31:29-30); but his pronouncement ministered more effectually perhaps to the situation which he confronted.

With the destruction of Jerusalem and its temple, Ezekiel becomes a prophet of hope. God will not allow his honor to be profaned among the nations. His holy people will be vindicated before the eyes of all the world. In an ecstatic vision the prophet sees a valley filled with dry bones. He is commanded to prophesy, "O ye dry bones, hear the word of the LORD" (37:4). As the word is spoken the bones assume sinews and flesh, and they become living beings again. So it will be with Israel, which now lies dead and buried in Exile. God will bring her out of her grave and restore her to the Holy Land. All Israel will be reunited into one, both the northern and the southern kingdoms. God will put his Spirit into his people, and they shall live and know that he has spoken and performed his purpose. It is the Spirit of God that gives life to the nation.

This radical transformation appears in another form in the condemnation of the false shepherds, the rulers who feed themselves and not the sheep. God himself becomes the good shepherd, as in Ps. 23, and on a day of clouds and thick darkness he goes out to deliver the sheep and restore them to their fold. "I myself will be the shepherd of my sheep" (34:15). "I will feed them in justice" (34:16). Land and

people will both be transformed. God will make a new covenant, a covenant of peace, and an eternal covenant with his people; he will bless them and multiply them, and set his sanctuary in the midst of them, and the new covenant will be ratified by the ancient covenant formula, "I will be their God, and they shall be my people."

Finally, the prophet envisages an ecclesiastical restoration. Only the first section of chs. 40-48 is genuine. Here (Ezek. 43:1-4) the prophet returns with consistency to the opening vision of the glory of the Lord. A new temple will be built, and Israel will become a temple community. The nation will be transformed into a church. The glory of the Lord will return to its ancient abode and will fill it with its radiance. Israel will at last be a holy people, not by her own work but by the gracious act of her holy God (cf. Exod. 19:6 and Deuteronomy, *passim*).

Ezekiel and Jeremiah were almost contemporaries. The influence of Jeremiah is apparent in Ezekiel's book. Both prophets reflect within their minds the deep hurt of their times. Ezekiel is more versatile than Jeremiah; he is poet, pastor, priest, prophet, apocalyptist, and theologian. The tragedy of his time cuts deeper into his soul. He is more terribly wounded even than Jeremiah by the word of the Lord. Yet he has a deeper sense of the structure of Israel's community life in history. He understands the necessity for institutions as Jeremiah does not. He is more disheveled than Jeremiah, and yet he finds a shelter and a fortress within the temple as Jeremiah evidently could not. Jeremiah and Ezekiel belong together as Amos and Hosea do. They both plumb the deepest depths of Israel's faith and heritage, and together form a mighty witness to the meaning of the decline and fall of the nation in an international world.

VII. The Babylonian Exile (586-538 B.C.)

A. The Significance of the Fall of Jerusalem (586 B.C.).—The fall of the southern kingdom in 586 B.C., which involved the destruction of the temple where dwelt in mystery and splendor the tabernacling glory of Yahweh; the cessation of the cult, above all, of sacrificial offerings; the termination of the royal line of David after more than four hundred years of continuous rule; and the deportation of substantial elements of the population into exile had the most profound consequences for the religion of ancient Israel. The nation as the bearer of the people's history was gone. To be sure, the covenant had always stood from the time of Moses as the community in which Israel's truest life was expressed, but the covenant gained its relevance precisely because it existed in relation to the life of the nation and its king. Whether the king bore any divine associations or not, he was "the anointed of the Lord," and as such was the protector and supporter and guarantor of the nation's prosperity and welfare. But now the kingdom was destroyed, and Zedekiah and his family suffered the most ignominious humiliation and torture (cf. Lam. 4:20; cf. also Pss. 20:6; 28:8; 89:51; 132:10, 17). When on the ninth of Ab the Babylonians entered the holy city, a new period was inaugurated in the history of biblical religion. The traditional faith had then to be read in the light of an event, catastrophic for Israel's political life and consequently supremely fateful for the quality of faith enshrined in the sacred history. Faith in a historical revelation was seriously threatened, and not a few came to conclusions of hopelessness that the facts of history seemed only too eloquently to warrant.

The literature following 586 B.C. bears witness to the character of the transformation that took place. To be sure, there was real continuity with the past, but profoundly altered conditions called into being new emphases and more penetrating reflections. In the books of Deuteronomy, Ezekiel, and Jeremiah we detect powerfully seminal forces which were destined to bear fruit. In a radical fashion the writers of these books respond to the stress and malaise of the age. The most significant of these forces we may record as follows:

Pessimism and Beyond. The immediate effect of the nation's fall is vividly described in the much-neglected book of Lamentations. Jerusalem sits in the ashes of mourning. She finds no resting place among the nations. Her glory has passed away. She knows that doom has befallen her for her rebellions. She recalls the past, and sees in it the meaning of the present. This meaning is twofold: judgment and grace. Despite all that has happened, "the LORD is good to those who wait for him. . . . It is good that one should wait quietly for the salvation of the LORD." (Lam. 3:19 ff.)

Revision of History. The problem of history raised by the fall of Judah impelled historians to view the past in the light of the primary presuppositions regarding moral coherence within history. The theologians who represented the Deuteronomic school undertook to revise and edit the whole of Israel's past history from Moses to the present (Deuteronomy to II Kings) in order to reconcile the actual, tragic history of the past in the light of a moral sovereignty within history. This simple moral logic had vast repercussions for the future of religion.

Deepening Sense of Sin. The strong sense of responsibility which marked Israel's religious life and the consciousness of purpose and destiny involved in her redemption from Egypt, her call, her election, and her covenant relationship combined to kindle within the hearts of the faithful a strong sense of guilt. The proclamation of the prophets and the cultic ministrations of the priests served to emphasize in season and out that Israel had broken the covenant, that the land had been taken from her, and that sin required a deeper expiation than even the pre-exilic prophets had seen. In this Jeremiah and Ezekiel prepared the way for their successors (Lamentations, Psalms, Zechariah, etc.).

Individualism. The constant preoccupation of Jeremiah and Ezekiel with the character of the covenant people, especially in relation to the national solidarity by which they understood themselves, prompted them to discover within the individual person the source of hope and meaning. That is, what could not be easily explained in terms of the solidarity of the community might be more readily understood in the life of the individual. Out of such experiences as are recorded in his confessions Jeremiah came to grasp the reality of fellowship with God, and thus personal religion received a new and profound emphasis. Ezekiel, on the other hand, focused upon the responsibility of the individual. Again, both prophets prepared for their successors in the Psalter and the wisdom literature.

The Revival of Tradition. The confusion and chaos of the period following 626 B.C., and more particularly 586 B.C., prompted certain of Israel's prophets and priests to view the present in the more spacious and more revealing context of the great tradition stemming from the Exodus, and before that, to Abraham, the Flood, and even the creation of the world. Among these was the priestly historian who gave not only a new continuity to history, but also a structure which was destined to influence later thinkers not a little.

Reflection on Cosmogony. To the historian of religion it is astonishing to see how relatively little preoccupation there is with creation in the Old Testament compared, for example, to the great neighboring peoples. After 586 B.C. this cosmogonic interest asserts itself in many ways, for example, in Second Isaiah, the priestly history, the Psalms, and the wisdom literature. A profound eschatology inevitably evoked speculation about the beginning, and in a period when historical categories were under grave threat or suspicion, it was deemed necessary to find a perspective from which the emergence of history might be understood. In this speculation Babylonian and Ugaritic influences are apparent.

The Ecclesiastical Community. Ezekiel had prepared the way for the Jewish church. Particularly in the Persian period, when the Achaemenides ruled their world in the stable organization of the satraps, the Jewish community became a church and came to govern its life increasingly in the terms of a church organization. The books of Chronicles offer a vivid picture of the interests and character of the temple community.

The Life of Worship and Devotion. The disappearance of the external features of religion made possible a greater emphasis on its inward aspects, above all the life of prayer. It is possible that Jeremiah was a major influence here. When the foundations of national and cultic life were shaken, men could seek God in the intimate communion of prayer.

The Problems of Theodicy. The decline and fall of Judah and the rise of new empires stirred the prophets and others to new thought concerning the ways of God with men. Habakkuk (*ca.* 604 B.C.) had already raised the problems of the righteousness of the divine sovereignty in history in acute form, and had come to the conclusion that "the righteous man lives by his faithfulness" (Hab. 2:4); the Deuteronomists gave the orthodox reply to contemporary queries, and both Jeremiah and Ezekiel gave their own characteristic answers to the same problem. Above all, the Second Isaiah discerned in the earth-shaking events of his day a depth of meaning in suffering and pain which no one before him had divined. This preoccupation with the moral government of history and nature runs like an unbroken cord through all the centuries between 626 B.C. and the Christian Era. Historians, apocalyptists, wisdom writers like the author of the book of Job, psalmists, and prophets reveal the same great concern for this problem. The thought of Israel plumbs its deepest depths in relation to the most baffling and disturbing problem of philosophy and religion.

The Transformation of Prophecy. With the loss of the political matrix of the nation and the conventional features of political life, the message of the prophets was changed. In Second Isaiah we see the prophetic spirit overcoming its limitations. The prophet has a perspective of Israel's tradition, of her past and future, unmatched by any other writer of the old covenant and perhaps of the new, with the exception of the apostle Paul. Here is prophecy on a new level. But there is another change in the prophetic message, such as we see in Haggai and Zechariah. The prophets were always associated with the cult in one way or another, but here there is an interest in the cult which is far removed from anything that we find in such pre-exilic prophets as Amos, Hosea, Micah, or Jeremiah. Again, we find prophecy transformed by a greater emphasis on transcendence, a readier appeal to cosmic categories, a more persistent pessimism concerning any resolution of the divine will within history, and a more passionate and intense faith in the coming of the divine kingdom. In other words, prophecy develops into apocalyptic, which sees more deeply into the tragic perplexities of history.

The Quest for Authority. The sense of insecurity induced by the fall of the nation and the destruction of the temple with its priestly ministrations aroused a widespread hunger for authority and certainty. In a previous age, as we have seen, the decline of Assyria and the widespread dislocation and confusion that followed in its wake were major forces behind the great reformation of 621. This reform had been conceived as a renaissance of Mosaic religion, and in the book which gave classical formulation to the fundamental realities of the faith in Yahweh, "Moses" addressed Israel with an emotional appeal and urgency seldom equaled elsewhere in the Bible. Deuteronomy, which contains the "Book of the Covenant," became sacred par excellence. It was the first book to become authoritative, and the movement toward canonicity finds in it its *fons et origo.*

Later the two epics of the south and the north, already amalgamated into one (JE), were combined with it, and later still the priestly history and law provided the general framework for the whole mass of tradition. The result was the first major division of the canon of the Torah. The Former Prophets (Joshua, Judges, Samuel, Kings) and the Latter Prophets (Isaiah, Jeremiah, Ezekiel, and the Twelve) received canonical status and authority in due time, probably under the stress of the crisis of the Maccabean period, and finally, in A.D. 90, at the famous Council of Jamnia, the third section of the Writings or Ketubim completed the Old Testament canon.

Life Under the Law. The law gave form and structure to life. To the constant query, "What must we do?" the reply came in terms of the revealed Torah. The large mass of legislation which goes under the name of the Priestly Code is in reality a codification of material that is in many instances very ancient. It was the ideal of the legalist that the whole of life should conform to the divine statutes. There is not much evidence in the Old Testament that it was a grievous burden. Quite the contrary! The book of Psalms is an eloquent witness to what the law meant to the pious Israelite (Pss. 1; 19; 119). The Torah was more than a mass of legal precepts. It was teaching and it was susceptible of vastly extended elaboration and interpretation.

A Holy People. The central command for Israel was often expressed in terms of the Holiness Code (Lev. 17–26): "Be holy even as I am holy." Deuteronomy and Ezekiel had stressed the peculiar relation of holiness that existed between the holy God and the holy people, and in the Holiness Code we have a superb expression of what this holiness involved, both for the body and for the soul. Israel's uniqueness was expressed in her holiness as a people.

Particularism and Universalism. One of the strange phenomena of the Old Testament is that particularism and universalism often exist together, as in Deuteronomy and Second Isaiah. The recognition that there was but one God, even one covenant God, for all peoples, did not necessarily imply the forfeiture of the uniqueness of Israel. On the other hand, we do find such narrowly nationalistic books as Esther, and such catholic and warmhearted and compassionate books as Jonah and Ruth. It was of supreme importance for the religious life of the world that Israel did not easily capitulate her uniqueness and evanesce into an undiscriminating universalism. Indeed, universalism gains its force and relevance only by appealing to the so-called particularistic categories by which Israel construed her covenant life.

Life After Death. There are not a few adumbrations of life after death. To be sure, there was the abode in Sheol, but it was not a significant existence, not one to look forward to. Only Isa. 26:19 and Dan. 12:2 present us with clear statements, and in both of these we have resurrection of the body. The Old Testament knows nothing, of course, of immortality of the soul. But to state the case so is to state it too simply, for again and again we stand at the borderline of a personal survival in which man enters into fuller fellowship with God.

Expectation and Hope. The primary orientation of the Old Testament as a whole is toward the future, not toward the past. To be sure, the experience of the past is invoked again and again, but the very nature of biblical thinking, whether in the form of story and history or in the nature of the bonds of election and covenant, was such that men looked forward to an outcome or issue of the dilemma and uncertainties of the present. In times of stress this expectation grew very strong (cf. Isa. 8:17; Hab. 2:1-4). Isa. 40:28-31 puts an emphasis on waiting in a context which is all embracing. The psalmists (e.g., Pss. 25:3, 5, 21; 27:14; 37:34; 39:7; 42:6; 69:6; 130:5-7) sense in the inner life of devotion the profound reality of the life of faith which anticipates the coming of the dawn of a great redemption. The supreme expectation for Christians is of course the messianic. It is essential to distinguish, however, the messianic age and the messiah. That is, more often than not the future period of felicity is without the messiah. Moreover, it must be borne in mind that the messiah, in many passages, is not the kind of deliverer which appears in the New Testament. Yet when every reservation has been made, we have such messianic passages as Isa. 9:1-6; 11:1-9; 32:1 ff.; Mic. 5:2-5a, and perhaps some of the psalms. The messianic hope is part of Israel's great expectations which made of her increasingly, at least among remnants, the waiting people.

B. Second Isaiah.—The sequence of poems which appear in Isa. 40–55 represents the supreme contribution of the Hebrew mind to the religious history of the world. The poet, like his prophetic predecessors, has appropriated within him the nature of the times in which he lives. He stands at the turning point of world history, between two ages, at the point which Toynbee describes as "the end of the Syriac Time of Troubles." The period of internationalism which began with the death of Ashurbanipal comes to its focus in his time, and Second Isaiah stands in lineal succession to the writers of Deuteronomy, Jeremiah, and Ezekiel. Yet there is also a sovereign independence from them.

The thought of the prophet is eschatological. The end of Israel's historical "warfare" has come. "The glory of the LORD shall be revealed, and all flesh shall see it together" (40:5). A new exodus, greater than the first, will usher in the kingdom of God (40:10; 52:7-10). Zion, the herald of the gospel, is to proclaim to all the world,

> Behold your God,
> Behold the Lord Yahweh comes in power
> And his arm shall rule for him,
> Behold his reward is with him (40:10).

Reflection upon the "end" prompts the prophet to turn to the various dynamic beginnings in which Israel's life was enshrined: the Exodus, the sojourn in the desert, the promise to Abraham, the waters of Noah, the creation of the world. What is happening in Cyrus' meteoric career is to be understood in the light of these seminal moments of the past.

The conception of the word of the Lord assumes new dimensions and forms in Second Isaiah. On the one hand, it must be understood in the light of the whole conception of the word in biblical thought,[71] with all its dynamistic associations; but on the other, it must be understood as the eschatological word. "The word of our God shall stand for ever" (40:8).

[71] Pedersen, *Israel, Its Life and Culture, I-II,* pp. 167-68 *et passim.*

It has a power and reality like the creation (45:18-19). The servant knows his unique character because Yahweh's words have been whispered in his ear. The oracular formula, "Thus saith the Lord," nearly always appears in relation to such categories as creation, redemption, election, sovereignty. It has a universal range. Event and word belong together, but for our prophet the event and the word are eschatological. God accomplishes his purpose in the word (55:10-11).

The thought of imminent redemption is matched by God's creation of the world. But creation never stands by itself. It stands in relation to other ideas and gains its significance by this association. God's creation is described as a source of comfort for Israel (40:27-31). Behind and within the world of history stands the Creator (40:15, 17, 23-24, 29-31). Moreover, creation is related to eternity: "Yahweh is an everlasting God, Creator of the ends of the earth" (40:28). He is incomparable. The idols are as nothing before him, like chaff which the wind drives away. The prophet's vision of God is so intense that he spares no words to denounce the making of all representations (40:18-20; 41:6-7; 44:9-20). Between creation and redemption lies the whole span of history which gains its meaning from the life of Israel (cf. 41:1–42:4). The nations cannot reply to historical questions like the coming of Cyrus, but Israel has a unique history beginning with the call of Abraham and her election and all the sacred events from that time in which Yahweh was guiding the destinies of his people (41:8-10; 51:1-2). Yahweh is Israel's King, and he is about to appear as King before all the nations of the world (52:7-10). He is Israel's Holy One. He has fashioned her from the womb to be his servant. He has redeemed, called, chosen her, revealed himself to her, and entered into covenant relation with her. He is the only God, a thought which the prophet never wearies of repeating. But his monotheism always stands in relation to other ideas like creation, history, redemption, eternity, and so forth, and never appears as an independent generalization. Second Isaiah is profoundly convinced that the meaning of history—of past, present, and future—is seen in the purpose of God, a purpose which he interprets and elaborates in the concrete terms of Israel's sacred history and the imminent *eschaton*.

The thought of the prophet is both universal and particular. Yahweh is God of all the earth, Lord of history and of nature, but he is also the covenant God of Israel. His redemption is not confined to his own people. All nations are to be included within the covenant relation (ch. 55). The redemption does not come as a result of Israel's merits, for her persistent blindness and infidelity deserve only judgment. Israel's great suffering (40:2) is not sufficient to bring about the redemption. Rather, God works for his own sake (43:25; 48:9, 11). The time of his coming to usher in his kingdom is a time of forgiveness (43:25; 44:22; 54:8-10); it is the inauguration of the new covenant.

Throughout the poems there appears the figure of the servant of the Lord. While many scholars follow Duhm in separating the passages 42:1-4; 49:1-6; 50:4-9; 52:13–53:12 from the rest of the poems, the literary relationships of these passages are so intimate with the rest that it is precarious to do so. But who is this servant? A decisive answer is impossible, but the balance of the evidence probably favors Israel rather than an individual. Wheeler Robinson's discussion of the idea of corporate personality in the Old Testament helps to make this view plausible.[72] But more important than the identity of the servant is his task and mission. Over all the poems stands the divine asseveration, "Thou art my servant." These words must be read in the light of the whole of the sacred tradition, as is true of the prophet's whole eschatology. Israel was fashioned in the womb to be Yahweh's, she was called and chosen to be servant. She has been endowed with the charism of the Spirit to perform her unique task of bringing judgment to the nations. She is appointed to be God's witness, that men may know and believe and understand that he is the one God (43:10-12; 44:8). She is the light of the nations so that God's salvation may reach to the ends of the earth (44:6). Through her all the nations of the world will be forgiven and redeemed. Through her the covenant will be mediated to all men. But above all, the servant is a vicarious sufferer for the transgressions of the nations. The orthodox view was that men suffered for their own sins: "we did esteem him stricken, smitten of God" (53:4). But it was God's purpose that he should be so afflicted. By the servant's suffering the nations were healed. He bore the sin of many, and made intercession for the transgressors. He goes to his death like a criminal (so the text seems to read). Yet dominating the whole of this supreme passage is the vindication and exaltation of the servant.

The history of Israel does not suffice to account for this description.[73] Israel is present surely, but there is more than Israel here. The portrait is eschatological and must so be under-

[72] H. Wheeler Robinson, "The Hebrew Conception of Corporate Personality," *Werden und Wesen des Alten Testaments*, ed. Paul Volz, pp. 49-62.

[73] H. H. Rowley, *The Re-Discovery of the Old Testament* (Philadelphia: Westminster Press, 1946), pp. 198 ff.

stood. It is flung into the future. A shroud of the unknown hangs over the passage, in the manner of many other eschatological passages. Many elements have gone to its making, both historical and mythological. It must not be read by itself, but in the light of the whole of the sacred tradition. It was destined to stir the minds of the prophet's successors, in the Old Testament and in the intertestamental literature. In the gospels the servant passages appear in contexts of central and decisive importance, and in the early church at least, if not in the thought of Jesus himself, our Lord is identified with him.

VIII. Postexilic Judaism (538–ca. 150 B.C.)

A. The Priestly Edition of the Pentateuch.— The exilic and postexilic periods of Israel's religious history reproduced the ancient traditions associated with the patriarchs and Moses in a fashion corresponding to the interests and point of view of the emerging of Judaism. The Yahwist epic was the precipitate of the nationalism of the united monarchy; the Elohist epic assumed written form during the great reign of Jeroboam II; and the Deuteronomic discourses and regulations were the expression in part of the national revival under Josiah. Each had its distinct point of view, but in all of them the prophetic impetus was primary, although in Deuteronomy it was qualified by concern for a legitimate and proper cult. The priestly historians and lawgivers (P) sought to give form and structure to the tradition. For this purpose they gathered together many ancient sources which had not yet found a place in J or E or D, some of them doubtless in already codified form. In this they reflected the point of view of the Judaism of the Persian period (538-333 B.C.). They were the custodians, teachers, and learned experts of Israel's religious heritage. It was they, more than any other group, who were responsible for preserving and perpetuating the tradition. But the nature of the times required a formulation of the tradition which would set forth the faith of Israel more succinctly and clearly, and which would also describe what the content of the revelation was and what ought to be believed. A theological work was required in which the central institutions of Israel would be given adequate grounding, the law produced in ordered fashion, the period of the beginnings articulated into periods, and the significance of the fathers properly understood. The result was priestly writing. Instead of the vivid stories which embodied the interior meaning of prophetic faith, we have priestly teaching; instead of the intimate psychological portraiture of the Yahwist, we have individuals whose meaning for religion is their

connection with institutions like the prohibition of blood (Gen. 9:1-7) and circumcision (Gen. 17:9-14) ; instead of a dramatic account of conflict and resolution, we have a fixed scheme into which are fitted in predestined fashion both history and human personality. History is subordinated to priestly faith and belief.

The creation of the world culminates in the institution of the sabbath. The prohibition of blood follows the Deluge. Circumcision began with Abraham, the Hebrew progenitor. The period of primeval beginnings and of the patriarchs is prologue to the appearance of Moses and the institution of the theocracy. In this theocracy the whole life of Israel is regulated. The cultic regulations are enumerated in ordered fashion. Service at the sanctuary is the only valid worship. The meaning of holiness is interpreted in the conduct of life, above all, of course, in the cult. Clean and unclean are sharply separated. Always the priests attempt to order and regulate life in fixed patterns. This is clearly seen not only in the way the priestly narratives are written (indeed, there is little narrative) but also in the self-consciousness of the chronological data, in the extensive genealogies, in the division of the pre-Mosaic traditions into fixed molds, in the succession of covenants, and in the rigid care to center everything in the theocracy.

The priestly source was added to JED and constituted the framework for the whole. The result was exceedingly impressive. The grandiose perspectives of the priestly writers; the great sense of structure and form, doubtless influenced by the struggle for maintaining the "purity" of Judaism in the presence of Persian power; the subordination of the flux and fluidity of history; and the elimination of the vivid personal qualities of the patriarchs in order that God might thereby be exalted—these features made the priestly source a pre-eminently suitable means for gathering the vast diversity, complexity, and heterogeneity of the literary materials into a work of colossal amplitude and theological significance. The redactors who were responsible for the fusion of the sources into an ordered whole were men of genius, men guided and directed of God. They saw profoundly into the needs of their times. Judaism demanded such an imposing edifice of revelation, and succeeding centuries have amply vindicated their work by the place that the Torah has assumed in the subsequent development of the religion. The opening account of the Creation (Gen. 1:1–2:4a), a liturgy of surpassing dignity and elevation, even of sublimity, was a fit introduction to the complete work. For the modern student the sources must be recognized, studied, and pondered. But his task is not complete until the Pentateuch is seen and read as a whole, until it is understood in the spirit of those who fashioned it into one. For these great compilers and editors and theologians deserve a place in the development of Judaism which may surpass even that of their great predecessors. Indeed, when the Pentateuch is seen in its diversity and its unity, we have before us one of the loftiest achievements of the human race, and for faith, a holy Scripture; it is a history of Israel's religion; it is the Torah of Israel, the revelation of God.

B. The Religion of the Psalms.—In the book of Psalms we meet Israel at worship. Without it we should have a one-sided view of Israel's religious life. To be sure, the prophetic and historical literature gives us more than a glimpse of the temple and the practices of the cult, but in the Psalter we are taken within the sacred precincts of the sanctuary itself to listen to Israel's hymns, laments, and thanksgivings.

Ancient Israel was endowed with the gift of music, both vocal and instrumental. The Psalter witnesses to the place that music served in her worship. The last psalm, for example, is a tumultuous finale of exultant praise, but it is more than that. It is a superb expression of the musical activities of the worshiping community. When the Babylonian captors demanded of the exiles, "Sing us one of the songs of Zion" (137:3), they were calling upon them to express themselves in their wonted fashion. For singing was more typical of the average Israelite than the prophetic gift and, together with narration, constituted a most natural response to God's goodness and grace.

The Psalter is a book of great variety. It comes from many different authors and many different occasions. Various literary types appear throughout the collection: hymns, prayers, songs of thanksgiving, laments, blessings and curses, royal psalms, and others. The streams of prophecy, law, wisdom, history, reflection on nature, and mythology meet in the Psalter. More important is the fact that most of the psalms are liturgical and find their life situation in the part that they play in the active cult. It is difficult to assign a precise date to most, if not all, of the psalms, but it has become possible to describe something of their place in the rituals of the Jewish church.

The uniqueness of the Psalter as devotional literature must not obscure its affinities with other literatures, however. Many of the poems remind one of the Babylonian penitential and other hymns.[74] Others recall the Egyptian songs

of thanksgiving.[75] More important, however, is the kinship of many of the psalms with the Ugaritic materials.[76] Among the most important of these are Pss. 18; 29; 45; 68; 78; 89; and the "enthronement hymns" (47; 93; 95–100).

The Psalter throbs with the worshiper's passionate devotion to the temple, a devotion even more intense than that to the law. There he came to "seek Yahweh's face," to dwell in the tabernacles of the Most High. He called upon the gates to lift up their heads that the King of glory might come in (24:7, 9) to join the procession to the altar. His soul longed, even fainted, for the courts of Yahweh. With jubilation he joined the throng of those who went to the house of God. His one consuming desire was that he might "dwell in the house of Yahweh all the days of [his] life, to behold the beauty of Yahweh, and to inquire in his temple" (27:4). In the offering of sacrifices and in participation in the liturgical responses he found comfort and joy. Through the ministrations of the priests, and alone also, he could unburden himself of his weight of sorrow, trouble, and guilt.

The presence of God was an intense reality in the temple, and the experience was infinitely deepened by the character of Israel's God. For Yahweh was personal. He entered into relationship with those who called upon him. He was one whose will and purpose were decisive for human life. His compassion, kindness, devotion, covenant-faithfulness, justice, goodness, and truth were available to all who called upon him in sincerity. The nearness and reality of God's presence and personality are set forth in numerous anthropomorphic and anthropopathic expressions. God remembers and forgets, chides and rewards, searches the heart, ascends his royal throne, sees with his eyes, hears with his ears, calls with his voice, and loves his children. He is judge, king, keeper, shepherd, and redeemer. In all these ways and in many others God is near to those who seek him with their whole heart. Yet it is characteristically within the covenant bond that the psalmist calls upon his God, and within this bond the covenant God answers (25:10, 14; 50:16; 74:20; 78:10, 37; 89:3, 28, 34; 103:18; 105:8; 106:45; 111:5, 9). The Psalter is pre-eminently a covenant book.

We should not expect much stress on monotheism in a devotional literature of this kind,

[74] G. R. Driver, "The Psalms in the Light of Babylonian Research," in *The Psalmists*, ed. D. C. Simpson (London: Oxford University Press, 1926), pp. 109-75. Driver comes to a negative conclusion as to the influence

of the Babylonian poems on the Psalter. See also Geo. Widengren, *The Accadian and Hebrew Psalms of Lamentation as Religious Documents* (Uppsala: Almquist & Wicksells, 1937).

[75] Hermann Gunkel, *Reden und Aufsätze* (Göttingen: Vandenhoeck & Ruprecht, 1913), "Aegyptische Danklieder," pp. 141-49.

[76] John Hastings Patton, *Canaanite Parallels in the Book of Psalms* (Baltimore: Johns Hopkins Press, 1944).

and yet it does emerge more than once, though the existence of other gods is not infrequently recognized (86:8; 89:6; 95:3; 135:5). One of the most distinctive emphases is upon God as creator. Like Job and Second Isaiah, the psalmist uses the ancient myth of the chaos-dragon (74:13-16; 89:9-12; 104:6-9). The heavens recount the glory of God, and the firmament shows his handiwork. This is the mysterious secret that is passed on from day to day and night to night (19:1-4). In the face of the wonder of the heavens the psalmist feels his smallness and yet, strangely, his uniqueness also (8:1-9). By his word God creates the heavens (33:6), an idea that was susceptible of future development (Ben Sirach, Philo, John). Every event in nature, whether rain or hail or snow or storm or flood or earthquake, is the express deed of his will.

The psalmist never wearies of speaking of God's eternity. It is a favorite device of his to bring the psalm to a climax on this note. His thought is not the result of philosophical speculation. Eternity is a very great extension of time, perhaps even an infinite extension, though one must be cautious in affirming this (90:1-2; 102:11-12). "The eternity of Jahveh did not consist in His ability to transcend the category of time." [77] Eternity is ascribed to human actions also. The pious Israelite will praise God forever and ever, and he longs to dwell in the Lord's house "to length of days."

An even more constant note is the goodness and love of God. What goodness and love are is made known in concrete events.

The psalmist trusts in the goodness of God. "Thou art good, and doest good" (119:68). The ordinances of God are good (119:39) as are his justice and knowledge (119:66). The remarkable poem dealing with the problem of theodicy, Ps. 73, begins by affirming, "Surely God is good to Israel." "The Lord is good; his covenant faithfulness [ḥéṣedh] is everlasting" (100:5). Ps. 136 is completely devoted to the ḥéṣedh of God. It recounts God's wonders in creation and in history in a great succession of lines, but each is followed with the emphatic affirmation, "for his ḥéṣedh is everlasting." Here too it would seem that covenant faithfulness is the appropriate word.

In four psalms God's revelation in nature is described (8; 19:1-6; 29; 104). They are among the most magnificent of the poems, and yet it is significant that precisely these psalms have the greatest affinities with the literature of the ancient Near East. The modern conception of nature is alien to the Psalter, as to the whole Old Testament. God reveals his majesty in the

[77] T. H. Robinson, "The God of the Psalmists," in *The Psalmists*, ed. D. C. Simpson, p. 37.

processes of nature: in the rising of the sun, the waxing and waning of the moon, and the myriad stars; in the stormy sea, the thundercloud, and in the thunderstorm. Every "natural" event occurs by his will and purpose. Most striking is the way in which nature and history are combined (78; 136).

The history of Israel is intimately drawn into the center of the cult. In the experiences of worship and devotion the psalmists recall the wonderful works of the Lord in the past, and they are fond of recounting these events in great detail. One of the central words of the Psalter is the verb "to remember." The piety of Israel is kindled by the things that are remembered. Out of these memories Israel forges her expectations. She grounds her trust in the future in the concreteness of past covenant events.

Not only history but also prophecy influences the devotional life of Israel. The prophetic polemic against sacrifice which we have seen in Amos, Hosea, Micah, Isaiah, and Jeremiah has left its stamp on more than one psalm.

Sacrifice and offering thou dost not desire,
But thou hast given me an open ear to hear.
Burnt offering and sin offering thou hast not required;
So I said, "Lo, I come,"
For in the roll of the book it is written of me:
I delight to do thy will, O my God;
Thy law is within my heart (40:6-8).

Ps. 50:8-13 is a devotional paraphrase of Isa. 1:10-17, and Ps. 51:16-17 is brought into the inner citadel of the worshiping heart. The conditions for fellowship with God are ethical, as is illustrated by the little decalogue of Ps. 15 and the similar requirements for entrance into the sanctuary of Ps. 24:

Who may ascend into the hill of the LORD?
And who may stand in his holy place?
He who has clean hands and a pure heart,
And does not lift up his soul to what is false (24:3-4).

The law also makes its appearance in the Psalter, though not frequently. This is remarkable in view of the fact that so many of the psalms are believed to have been composed in the time when legalism was regnant in Israel. Moreover, we should expect the Torah to be more fully represented in the sanctuary. But there are not many psalms in praise of the law (1; 19:7-14; 119).

Nature, history, prophecy, and law, all form part of the texture of Israel's worship. Still another force was the thinking of the Deuteronomist. That God punished sin and rewarded righteousness was the foundation of Israel's religious ethic. So when affliction and sorrow and pain came, when the unjust persecutor got the better of his victim, when the dark spells of uncanny forces laid the sufferer low on his death bed, the mind endured tortures deeper than any physical pain. Many a cry breaks forth out of the night of despair. The large number of such psalms illustrates how real this problem was, as real as it was to Habakkuk and Jeremiah and Job. In Ps. 73, the greatest of all the psalms on this subject, a lonely man reveals the depth and the stress of the problem which tortures him, yet he finally comes to think and live by his faith and his awareness of the presence and fellowship of God:

Whom have I in heaven but thee?
Having thee, I desire naught else on earth;
Though my flesh and my heart waste away,
God is the rock of my heart and my portion forever
  (73:25-26).

Such an affirmation gains added force by the fact that the psalmist could not envisage the possibility of a significant personal survival beyond death. A number of the psalms seem to stand on the very frontier of this possibility, but nowhere is it stated with any absolute clarity.

The consciousness of sin is present throughout the Psalter. God is the judge of all men and all nations, and to him they are accountable. Yet the awareness of sin is seldom so deep as in Ezekiel. The most moving of the psalms which center in man's sin are the so-called penitentials (6; 32; 38; 51; 102; 130; 143). Here the awareness of sin is very deep indeed, and the psalmist sees no hope for escape from his sore dilemma except in the forgiving mercy and love of God. He sees the terrible effect that sin has in alienating man from God's presence. That is the most grievous of all his ills. And so he prays for an event from God as great within the interior recesses of the heart as the redemption from Egyptian bondage in history.

It was out of experiences such as these that the psalmist came to know the great resources of comfort and joy. When all is said and done, what remains after the psalms have been read again and again is the sense of joy and triumph and interior peace. Often such gifts of grace came after the storm and stress of pain and travail, after a night of utter darkness with no answer but the echo of a lonely cry.

Weeping may tarry for the night,
But joy comes with the morning (30:5; cf. 130:5-7).

But there is another kind of joy in the Psalter, one that appears much more consistently throughout, the joy that breaks from a heart kindled by praise. The psalms have been called "the praises of Israel." "Hallelujah, praise the Lord" rings like an exultant shout of triumph again and again. The spontaneity, exuberance, and full-throated abandon of the worshiper shows that here his deepest self is being revealed. No history of the religion of Israel is either complete or reliable which does not assign a central role to Israel's praise of her God. For to him belongs praise, and praise befits his sanctuary. The Psalter moves in its closing poems into a magnificent crescendo, a universal and ecstatic paean of praise, "Let everything that has breath praise the Lord."

C. The Religion of the Wisdom Literature.— The wisdom literature calls attention to the great diversity of the religious thought of ancient Israel. One and the same people produced history, prophecy, law, psalmody, didactic romance, apocalypse, and wisdom. Each of these developed in many different literary types and forms, and each continued throughout a substantial period of time. They cannot be read or understood in isolation. They represent different facets and emphases of the same fundamental mentality. More than any other mode of literary expression, the wisdom literature of Israel was intimately connected with the wisdom literatures of other peoples, above all of Egypt.[78] Yet like the nature psalms of the Psalter, which have striking affinities with extrabiblical literature, the wisdom of Israel transforms what it borrows and sets the stamp of what is peculiarly Israelite upon it.

The chief features of Israel's wisdom thought may be summarized briefly as follows:

(a) In all wisdom there is a strong emphasis upon human experience. Here the individual emerges with a clarity scarcely equaled anywhere else in the Old Testament. The many experiences and vicissitudes of ordinary everyday life are observed with close and realistic scrutiny. The sage was a keen observer of the ways of man and beast. Man bears a moral responsibility, and this is atomized in concrete and realistic detail. Family relationships such as those of a husband to his wife and a wife to her husband, of parent to child and child to parent, are reflected upon with common sense and shrewdness. The books of Proverbs and of Ben Sirach (Ecclesiasticus) are guidebooks for practical living. Observe the father's counsels to his son, for example, in Prov. 4; the warnings against the wiles of the adulteress in 6:20–7:27; the praise of the "good wife" in 31:10-31; or

[78] Paul Humbert, *Recherches sur les sources égyptiennes de la littérature sapientale d'Israël* (Neuchâtel: Secrétariat de l'Université, 1929); Johannes Fichtner, *Die altorientalische Weisheit in ihrer israelitisch-jüdischen Ausprägung* (Giessen: A. Töpelmann, 1933); W. O. E. Oesterley, *The Book of Proverbs* (London: Methuen & Co., 1929; "Westminster Commentaries").

such illuminating passages as the following from Ecclesiasticus: 7:24; 13:3-24; 19:4-12; 25:13-26; 26:1-4, 13-18; 29:1-10, 11-13; 31:12 ff.; 38:1-15.

(b) With sagacity and morality belongs piety. "The fear of Yahweh is the instruction of wisdom" (Prov. 15:33); it is "the beginning of knowledge" (1:7) as "of wisdom" (9:10).

Every way of a man is right in his own eyes,
But the weigher of hearts is Yahweh (Prov. 21:2).

All conduct is thus brought under the surveillance of God; all human motives and intentions and desires are determined by his will. In this connection it is important to observe the close relationship of wisdom and law. Obedience to the law is Israel's first duty (Ecclus. 9:15; 10:19; 32:15-24). Law and wisdom are identified (15:1; 19:20; 21:11; 34:8). The root meaning of "righteousness" (çĕdheq) was congenial to wisdom, for righteousness meant to conform to a certain standard and norm. "To gain wisdom, keep the commandments" (Ecclus. 1:26; cf. 24:23).

(c) To the persistent questions raised by the presence of suffering in human life the wisdom writers gave no single or consistent answer. Greek influence was destined to make its impress upon Israel, especially in the Hellenistic Judaism of Alexandria, just as Iranian influence was destined to alter the prophetic point of view and perspective of history. As is to be expected, the conventional view of Hebrew orthodoxy that suffering was a result of sin asserted itself in the greater part of wisdom thought: Proverbs, Ben Sirach, Koheleth (Ecclesiastes), the speeches of the friends of Job, and elsewhere. With this view the writer of the book of Job could not rest content. The dialogue as a whole culminates in the remarkable speeches of Yahweh out of the whirlwind, and Job responds to the vast mystery of natural existence which those speeches reveal:

I had heard of thee by the hearing of the ear,
But now mine eye has seen thee (Job 42:5).

The problems of theodicy represent an inscrutable mystery, and Job makes his confession before God, retracts his precipitate words, and repents in dust and ashes. But there is another answer in the prologue. Here Job demonstrates that there is such a thing as disinterested religion. He vindicates God before the thrusts and taunts of Satan. Job trusts where he does not see. By his suffering he becomes a witness for God, a martyr to God's purpose and righteous rule which are hidden from him. Like the writer of Ps. 73, the poet of Job places this great affirmation of trust at the head of his writing. The scene in the heavenly council gives the context for the whole book, and it is not without significance that it ends with Job's intercession for his friends.

Koheleth cuts the Gordian knot of the problem by denying outright the moral government of the world. The final development of the problem is seen in the late book, the Wisdom of Solomon (ca. 50 B.C.), which shows much Greek influence. The writer believes that righteousness is immortal (1:15), that the souls of the righteous are in the hands of God (3:1), that the righteous shall live forever and in the Lord is their reward (5:15). There are many other elements in the book, and different points of view are not always easily harmonized. Nowhere, significantly, does the wisdom literature deal with suffering as sacrificial. The martyr witness of Job is not remote from the suffering servant of Isa. 53, but the latter is on a different level and in a much more spacious context.

(d) The nature of wisdom itself ranges all the way from simple sagacity to the wisdom of vision, which borders on apocalyptic wisdom. This latter wisdom has not infrequent affinities to the wisdom of the sages. What is most interesting, however, is the movement of wisdom from personification to hypostasis. Prov. 8:22 ff. pictures wisdom as the first of God's created works, the beginning of his deeds; wisdom is present at the creation and serves God as his "master workman" or artificer (8:28 ff.). In Ben Sirach the personification is less universal than in Prov. 8:22 ff., and is closely related to Israel, with whom wisdom first finds rest (Ecclus. 24:6-8), to the holy tabernacle on Zion (24:10), and to the law of Moses (24:23). Yet she comes forth from the mouth of the Most High, and covers the earth as a mist, fixing its throne in the cloud and compassing the circuit of heaven (24:3-5). Finally, the Wisdom of Solomon brings the development to its culmination. The central passage is Wisd. Sol. 7:22-8:1. Wisdom "pervades and penetrates all things by reason of her pureness"; she is "a clear effluence of the glory of the Almighty" (7:25), a "reflection of the everlasting light," and "the image of the goodness of God" (7:24-26).

Though being [but] one she can do all things,
. . . .
And from generation to generation passing into holy souls,
She maketh men friends of God and prophets.
For nothing doth God love save him that dwelleth with wisdom. (Wisd. Sol. 7:27-28.)

D. The Religion of Apocalyptic.—The development from prophetic to apocalyptic thought was influenced to a degree by forces from without, but it does not represent an aberrant movement in Israel. On the contrary, the theology of the apocalypses may be accounted for by elements deeply embedded in prophecy itself. An examination of the prophetic books reveals a number of "apocalyptical" passages, and these cannot be always simply ascribed to later writers (cf., e.g., Mic. 1:3-4). Apocalyptic actually represented a deepening of Israel's prophetic consciousness in the light of the destruction of the nation and the somber years of suffering and tragedy which followed.

The book of Daniel is the most familiar of the apocalyptic sections of the Old Testament, but such books as Joel, Zechariah, Ezekiel, Isaiah (chs. 24–27; 34–35; etc.), contain much of the same kind of thought. The Apocrypha, and especially the pseudepigraphical writings, contain not a few apocalypses, and these should be included in any study of apocalyptic, especially for an apprehension of the meaning of some passages in the New Testament. To understand this strange literary genre it is essential to observe (a) that apocalypses stand in relation to their own historical times and reflect the conditions of crisis behind them; (b) that the imagery is not infrequently drawn from mythology and that the thought is itself often of a mythological character; (c) that Iranian influences of dualism, angelology and demonology, and so forth, as well as Hellenistic influences have left their impress upon this work; and (d) that the apocalypses are by their nature made up of a great variety of materials and must not be reduced too quickly to a collection of sources and fragments.

The major elements in apocalyptical thought may be stated briefly:

(a) God is all-wise and all-powerful. He is God of gods, Lord of lords, and King of heaven. He works great signs and wonders in the earth. He breaks through the orderliness of the natural world to bring about his will and purpose among men. In the book of Daniel the "assurance of supernatural deliverance . . . rests on the doctrine that Jehovah is the only God and that his power is irresistible." [79]

(b) The time of God's coming to effect his final purpose in the world is near at hand. In this as in so many of his ideas the writer of Daniel is indebted to his prophetic predecessors. Different apocalypses construe this coming in various ways, but they are one in their conviction that it is a time in which the justice and sovereignty of God will be vindicated in history.

(c) To the supernatural world view and the belief in God's imminent parousia is to be added the theological dualism of the apocalyptists. This was stated later in a pronounced form by IV Ezra (II Esdras), "The Most High

[79] Pfeiffer, Intro. to O.T., p. 774.

has made not one world, but two" (7:50). There are two ages, and it is the general view of these writers that one age is coming to an end and a new one is about to dawn.

(d) The book of Daniel represents the imminent coming of the kingdom of God as the shattering of the great image, which represents four pagan empires (Babylonia, Media, Persia, Greece) and by "one like the son of man," who pronounces sentence against the four beasts and inaugurates an eternal and universal rule. Both symbols represent Israel, "the people of the saints of the Most High" (Dan. 7:27). Thus we have no personal messiah in Daniel, though it is important to add that Israel is here conceived as the messianic people, performing the function of the messiah. Dan. 7:13, the central passage in question, was susceptible of future elaboration in which the idea of a personal messiah was set forth (Enoch 46:1-6; 48:2-10; II Esdras 13:3, cf. vs. 6; Mark 13:26=Matt. 24:30; Acts 7:56; Mark 14:61-62=Matt. 26:63-64).

(e) When God comes to judge the earth the righteous will receive their reward and the wicked their punishment. The nature of the judgment and the reward varies greatly. Most important here is the belief in the resurrection of the dead. Dan. 12:2-3, together with Isa. 26:19, is the *locus classicus* for this doctrine: "And many of those who sleep in the dust of the earth shall awake, some to everlasting life, and some to shame and everlasting contempt. And those who are wise shall shine like the brightness of the firmament; and those who turn many to righteousness, like the stars forever and ever."

(f) History is ordered according to the divine plan. God both knows and determines the course of history. He reveals his "secrets" in visions of the end of things to his servants, the apocalyptic seers. Such representations as Dan. 2 and 7 (cf. also chs. 10–12) portray the writer's dramatic conception of history. With the deterioration of history reaching its climax in the time of Greece a new reality enters in—the kingdom of God "which shall never be destroyed" (Dan. 2:44-45).

And the kingdom, the dominion, and the greatness
   of the kingdoms under the whole heavens
Shall be given to the people of the saints of the
   Most High;
Their kingdom shall be an everlasting kingdom,
And all kingdoms shall serve and obey them (Dan
   7:27).

IX. The Function of the Cult in Israel's Religion

There is a danger within Protestantism of giving such undue emphasis to the prophetic religion that the worship of the sanctuary and the work of the priests are greatly obscured. Even a hurried analysis of the biblical materials will reveal that an exclusive emphasis upon prophecy distorts the meaning of the Old Testament. It is true that prophecy has a special meaning for Christians, but today we see, as we did not see for many decades, that even the prophets cannot be studied in isolation from the cult.

Foreign influences asserted themselves in the worship of the temple and the sanctuaries. The fertility interests of the Canaanite nature cult found expression in rites and rituals and even in the persons active within the cult. like the *qedheshîm* and *qedheshôth* (lit., "holy ones"). In the heyday of Mesopotamian power astral elements found their way into Israel's worship. While the syncretistic forces within the cult must be recognized, it is also necessary to recognize the degree to which the cult perpetuated realities that belonged to the heart of Israel's religion. The best indication of this is the function of the cult as the repository of Israelite memory, whether the memories of the cult legends of the patriarchal period or, more strikingly, the ministrations and ministry of the prophets.

Divine revelation evokes human response. The firm basis of Old Testament faith is that God has taken the initiative in behalf of his chosen people. In the practices and rituals of the cult we observe Israel's response to Yahweh, who has already made himself known in event and word. The covenantal people seek to draw near to their covenantal God through rites and ceremonies. The cult is instituted, created, and performed by Israel, although it is under the constant direction and supervision of God. Because the cult is man's work, it is subject to the radical criticism of the word of God through the prophets.

The forms and characteristics of the cult undergo constant change in the light of new situations and new cultural environments. It cannot be understood therefore as a static reality, as a fixed phenomenon which endures throughout all time unaltered. The experience of worship is not for Israel the contemplation of the timeless, infinite Reality. The worshiper does not lose himself in mystical absorption; he does not unite himself with God so that the separation between the divine and the human is overcome. On the contrary, the man of Israel knows that he worships as a member of a particular covenantal community, whose character is stamped deep upon his soul. He understands this community in the light of the particular history which describes its life. Therefore cult and history are closely related, and the best interpretation of the former is in terms of the latter. An adequate study of the cult demands a historical description. The Mosaic cult, the cult of the time of the judges and more especially of the Israelite amphictyony whose center was the sanctuary at Shiloh, the cult of Solomon's temple, and the cult which the prophets of the eighth century observed were not identical, but each reflected in some ways its own time. Similarly, the representations of the Covenant Code (Exod. 20:23–23:19), the Deuteronomic Code (Deut. 5–26), the Holiness Code (*ca.* 550 B.C.), and the Priestly Code, while they have much in common, constitute different strata and formulations, though, it is important to add, not necessarily of the temporal periods to which they are customarily assigned. There is a third reason why Israel's cult cannot be understood statically. All personal and historical life is precarious, and in Israel's practice of the cult the precariousness of personal and historical living is drawn into the very center of its observance.

There was a certain distinctiveness, then, in the development of the cult in ancient Israel, but this must not be affirmed at the expense of the wide scope of community which Israel's modes of worship shared with those of neighboring peoples. In no area of Israel's religion are the affinities with the religions of other peoples more clear than in the cult. In the construction of the sanctuaries—above all, of Solomon's temple—in the observance of sacrifice and the celebration of the festivals, in the liturgies and hymns, and even in fundamental attitudes like man's view of nature, Israel had much in common with contemporary peoples.

The basic and underlying reality of the cult common to all Semitic and other peoples was the holiness of God. In the cult the holy and profane enter into relationships with one another. In his sense of "the holy" the worshiper is made aware of the presence of the "otherness" of the divine. This otherness is a present reality, but it is also incomprehensible, imponderable, and "beyond." The deity cannot be approached cavalierly or without fear. He is unapproachable, full of zeal and uncanny power. The presence of the divine means the presence of holiness. It is with holiness that the worshiper has to do, but he must know what is holy and what is not. Woe betide him who does not regard the distinction!

It is because God is holy that the cult is necessary. To enter into the presence of God one must "cleanse" himself lest the deity be offended. Therefore all sorts of ablutions, abstinences, and other apotropaic actions are necessary. In the pursuit of war, for example, the soldier must make himself ritually "clean," for war is a holy undertaking, and Yahweh, who leads the battalions, is present in the midst of the camp as "man of war." Again, certain objects have numinous qualities and associations, and they must be approached with great caution. There are holy places, holy times, holy objects, holy persons, and holy actions or observances. For Israel, Yahweh's name and his glory are all-holy. To call upon the name of the Lord is to invoke the holy God, and to worship in the temple where his glory dwells is to enter into the reality of his holiness.

A. Holy Places.—God is present where he has revealed himself. To such places the Israelite may repair either in pilgrimage or indeed in any time of need. Many theophanies are described in the Old Testament: at Hebron, where Yahweh appeared to Abraham (Gen. 18 [J]) ; at Bethel, where he appeared to Jacob-Israel in a dream (Gen. 28:10-22 [JE]), at Shechem, where he appeared to both patriarchs (Gen. 12:6-7 [J]; 33:18-20 [J]), at Gilgal, where he appeared to Joshua (Josh. 5:13-15) ; and at other places. The holiness of the sacred place is strongly emphasized in the theophany granted to Moses: "Do not come near, take your shoes from your feet, for the place on which you are standing is holy ground" (Exod. 3:5). Centuries later Elijah makes a pilgrimage to Horeb to receive another theophany. Finally, Jerusalem becomes a sanctuary by the theophany at the floor of Araunah the Jebusite (II Sam. 24:16b-17a), and David makes it not only his political capital but also the central sacred place of his kingdom.

It is clear from the Genesis accounts that the patriarchs appropriated the Canaanite shrines. Likewise Canaanite legends and traditions were adopted and transformed according to the nature of "the god of the fathers." Before the time of the Deuteronomic reformation in 621 B.C., no protest is raised against worship at the high places (*bâmôth*). On the contrary, in a very early source God says to Moses: "At every place [sanctuary] where I record my name I will come to you and bless you" (Exod. 20:24). There is no doubt that these country sanctuaries were the seats of extensive syncretism with the Canaanite fertility cults. Here Baal, the high god of the Canaanites, was worshiped along with Yahweh, or indeed identified with him. The sanctuary at Bethel obviously carried this syncretism to an advanced stage.

With the reformation of 621 B.C. the tide was stemmed for a time. In the Deuteronomic Code Yahweh is to be worshiped at a single sanctuary, the one at Jerusalem, and the high places, with their ancient Canaanite associations and their current Canaanite practices and rituals, are to be destroyed. Such debased practices as sacred prostitution are to be wiped out,

and the cult is to be under the supervision of the custodians and officials of the Jerusalem temple, itself the creation of a radical syncretizing process.

The typical shrine had an altar, a *maççēbhāh* or sacred stone, and an Asherah, in all likelihood the image of the goddess by that name, as we know from the Ugaritic inscriptions.[80] The altar is older than the "house of God," which can be authenticated only after the Conquest (Exod. 23:19; 34:26). Jacob's anointing of the *maççēbhāh* at Bethel with oil (Gen. 28:17 ff. [E]) and perhaps also at Shechem (Gen. 33:20 [E]) suggests that it served the function of an altar. In the story of Gideon and in the account of Samson's mother (Judg. 6:19-22; 13:19-20) we have an extremely primitive offering of a sacrifice upon a rock. This mode of offering has been confirmed archaeologically. The altar, as the Hebrew word makes clear, was used for the slaughter of animal sacrifices. Notable among all the altars mentioned in the Old Testament, including those in Jerusalem, was the great rock which served as the altar in Solomon's temple. The altar was the place par excellence where Yahweh had caused his name to be remembered. Theophanies are characteristically memorialized by the erection of the altar, even when Genesis makes no mention of any sacrifice being offered on them.

B. Holy Objects.—David sought to center the religious loyalties of the tribes by transporting the various cultic symbols to the city of Jerusalem. Abiathar, of the tribe of Benjamin, came to the city with the divining ephod; Levi's serpent was sent for, and the tent of meeting was lodged within the City of David. Chief among all the symbols, however, was the ancient ark of Yahweh Sabaoth. Originally it was a nomadic shrine which represented the presence of Yahweh in the midst of Israel. It was associated with the desert wandering (Num. 10:35-36), and in the period of the Conquest it was lodged for a considerable period in the central sanctuary of the Israelite amphictyony at Shiloh. According to Josh. 6 it had wrought great wonders in connection with the conquest of Jericho. But what was the nature of this shrine? Was it a palladium of war? If so, how was it conceived? A positive answer is impossible. We cannot be certain, for example, what its contents were, but according to Deut. 10:1-5, two tables of stone inscribed with the Decalogue were placed within it. The suggestion of Martin Dibelius [81] that it was a portable shrine without any image of the deity is the one that commends

[80] William L. Reed, *The Asherah in the Old Testament* (Fort Worth: Texas Christian University Press, 1949).
[81] *Die Lade Jahves* (Göttingen: Vandenhoeck & Ruprecht, 1906).

itself as most likely. Yet Yahweh's presence and power were associated with it in a peculiarly intense fashion, as many accounts bear witness. When the Israelites carry the ark into battle, the Philistines cry that their God has come against them. When the ark is captured, the Philistine cities are stricken with a deadly pestilence, and when the report of its capture reaches the wife of Phineas, she cries out in her death throes, "The glory [*kābhôdh*] is departed from Israel." Later when David seeks to convey it to Jerusalem, Uzzah is struck dead by touching it. At the building of the temple, Solomon places the portable ark in the holy of holies. It is possible, as Arnold has attempted to show, that there were a number of arks in ancient Israel for various sanctuaries.[82]

C. Holy Times and Seasons.—God reveals himself at particular times as well as at special places. From the Canaanites Israel took over three great agricultural festivals: the feast of Unleavened Bread (*maççôth*), the feast of Harvest (*qāçîr*), and the feast of Ingathering (*'āsîph* or *teqûphāh;* Exod. 23:14-17 [E]; 34:18, 22-23 [J]). The first of these was celebrated at the beginning of the barley harvest. Unleavened cakes were used so that the produce of the new year might be eaten with fresh leaven. First fruits were brought forward, and the priest waved a sheaf of these toward and away from the altar, a symbol of the gift to Yahweh, the giver of the grain, and the acceptance from him again of "that sustenance of earth which He had caused to grow."[83] The feast of Harvest or of Weeks was celebrated seven weeks later when the barley harvest was over and the wheat harvest began. During the feast of Ingathering the Israelites lived in booths for seven days (Lev. 23:39-43). This festival was the great day of thanksgiving, when the fruits of the year had been gathered and especially the harvest of the vineyards. It was also the time of the celebration of the New Year festival. That this latter festival profoundly influenced Israel's life is quite certain. Under the inspiration of Sigmund Mowinckel, many scholars find the origin of eschatology in a celebration of the enthronement of Yahweh. Appeal is made to the parallel celebration of the Babylonian New Year or *akitu* festival. A number of scholars have discovered the basic patterns of the latter within

the Old Testament, above all in the so-called enthronement psalms (47; 93; 95-99). It is very doubtful whether the *akitu* festival had the degree of influence that Mowinckel claims for it, and we cannot even be certain that there ever was such an enthronement festival in Israel, but such psalms as Ps. 47 certainly seem to suggest something of the sort. The most that can be said, however, is that the imagery and language of these psalms has been influenced by the patterns of thought associated with the celebration of the New Year. The references to creation, the chaos-dragon myth, the primeval combat of Yahweh, and the enthronement of the king are all described with great vividness. The use of Ps. 47 in the modern celebration of the feast of Tabernacles and of the New Year supports the view.

Our sources for the Passover are relatively late, the earliest authentic witness appearing in the late seventh century. But while the most extended descriptions occur in the priestly source (Exod. 12:1-20, 43-49), there is no reason to question the essential accuracy of its representations. What the nature of the original festival was we do not know; many theories have been proposed.[84] A common view and one that seems most plausible is that it was the day on which the first born of the flock was sacrificed. Later it became associated with the Exodus and the last night of Israel's sojourn in Egypt when the first born of the Egyptians were slain but the destroying angel passed over the homes of the Israelites on the lintels of whose doorposts had been placed the prophylactic blood. The outstanding features of the festival are threefold: (*a*) the sacrifice of a sheep or goat, a sacrificial meal celebrated in the homes of the participants; (*b*) a night celebration between sunset and sunrise; and (*c*) the application of the blood of the animal on the doorposts. The original meaning of the details of the celebration is obscure. In Deuteronomy the Passover is most clearly associated with the Exodus from Egypt, and this is the association which it has in most of the subsequent history. As such it relates to the greatest of all the events of Israel's history. It was a memorial of the night of Israel's redemption from bondage. Christian faith has made its own use of the Passover and refers it to the death of Christ "our Passover." One feature of these festivals needs special attention: all of them were originally connected with the phenomena of nature and fertility, but eventually they were transformed into memorials of historical events.

The observance of the sabbath goes back to an early time. Its connection with the new

[82] *Ephod and Ark.* W. C. Graham and H. G. May (*Culture and Conscience* [Chicago: University of Chicago Press, 1936], pp. 261-67; cf. also H. G. May, "The Ark— A Miniature Temple," *American Journal of Semitic Languages and Literature,* LII [1936], 215-34) hold that the ark probably existed in the form of a miniature temple, such as the one discovered at Megiddo, and that such miniature temples were present in other sanctuaries.

[83] Norman H. Snaith, "Worship," in *Record and Revelation.* ed. H. Wheeler Robinson (Oxford: Clarendon Press, 1938), p. 259.

[84] Lods, *Israel from Its Beginnings to Middle of Eighth Century,* p. 291, n. 4.

moon (Amos 8:5) and its weekly observance suggest that it was a lunar day. According to early accounts (II Kings 4:23; Amos 8:5; Hos. 2:11), it is a holy day. Deuteronomy appeals to humanitarian grounds for its observance, calling to mind the days of Israel's slavery in Egypt and the need for rest for every person in Israel, whether native or resident alien, and for domestic animals also. The E Decalogue has been expanded in the light of Gen. 1. Here the reason is given in terms of God's own sabbath rest. In the exilic and postexilic period, and in later Judaism, the sabbath became one of the chief institutions of Israel. With circumcision it became a distinctive mark of Judaism.

The day of Atonement is described in detail in Lev. 16. For Judaism it became the most important of all holy seasons. It expressed a profound awareness of sin and a longing for restoration to holiness and cleanness. Through the mediation of the high priest, their representative, the Jews seek to approach their holy God. On this day the high priest, after changing his usual garb and going through appropriate ablutions, enters into the holy of holies. He there makes atonement for all Israel (Lev. 16:17). The word rendered "atone" (*kipper*) properly means here "to wipe away" in the sense of expiation.[85] The central concern of the cult with the holiness of God and man's relation to this holiness here reaches its culmination. The tragedy of 586 and the following decades greatly deepened Israel's sense of guilt (Ezekiel, Lamentations, Psalms, Zechariah) so that restoration to holiness became the supreme quest of her cultic life. In the day of Atonement unholy Israel is made holy.

D. Holy Acts.—To the fundamental question of the cultic community, "How shall I come before God?" (Mic. 6:6) Israel, like other ancient peoples, had a ready reply: "Through sacrificial gifts." By the offering of sacrifices the cleavage between the holy and unholy was overcome. From the world of the profane, man entered the area of "the holy." Sacrifice is the holy act. As a holy act it possessed the numinous and mysterious and sacramental associations of all holiness. As the conception of holiness undergoes development in the history of Israel's religion, so the conceptions of sacrifice change in different periods. There are many varieties of sacrifice, and to the varieties correspond different situations and occasions and different attitudes and points of view. In times of relative peace and prosperity the mood and mode of sacrifice are quite different from those in times of distress and darkness. Thus during the Exile and in postexilic times certain sacrifices

receive a greater prominence and emphasis than theretofore. The wide diversity of sacrifice illustrates both the fluidity and the large scope of Israel's cultic life. Yet it is difficult to write a history of sacrifice. The discovery of the Ugaritic materials, which mention nearly all of the Old Testament sacrifices, warns us against a too simple construction of Israel's cult.[86] The Old Testament gives its most ample descriptions of sacrifice in the Priestly Code. Much of this material is drawn from ancient ordinances and regulations, but it also reflects the conditions of its own time (*ca.* 550-450 B.C.). On the other hand, it is possible to exaggerate these difficulties, for the Bible contains numerous illuminating accounts of sacrificial practice outside the priestly documents. In all of them, however, it is with the conception of holiness that we have to do. As has already been said, sacrifice constituted the major response to the major question of the worshiper in connection with his approach to God. Three basic elements entered into this response: (*a*) communion, (*b*) gift, and (*c*) impartation of life and vitality. The opposition between the sacred and the profane was broken by the act of communion. The alienation between worshiper and the divine was overcome through gifts of propitiation and expiation. The need for strength and vitality and blessing was satisfied by the infusion of fresh life in the soul of the devotee.

Israel was influenced by her Canaanite (Hebrew) forebears in her sacrificial offerings and rituals, but here, as elsewhere, she transformed what she borrowed according to the presuppositions and history of her covenantal life with Yahweh. Sacrifice was a covenantal act, and through it the covenantal bond was restored (Ps. 50:5). It is not sufficient merely to record the various kinds of sacrifice, for the concrete meaning of the sacrifice may thereby be obscured. The sacrifice must be apprehended in its situation and context, and these may be of an extremely great diversity. Here again history enters deeply into the cult, as is shown, for example, by the celebration of the festivals or by the offering of sacrifices in times of social crisis. With this in mind we may refer to the more important sacrifices which appear in the pages of the Old Testament.

The Burnt Offering (*'ōlāh*): This sacrifice is

---

[85] George Buchanan Gray, *Sacrifice in the Old Testament* (Oxford: Clarendon Press, 1925), pp. 67 ff.

[86] René Dussaud, *Les origines cananéennes du sacrifice israélite* (Paris: Ernest Leroux, 1921); Theodor H. Gaster, "The Service of the Sanctuary: a Study of Hebrew Survivals," *Mélanges syriens* (Paris: P. Geuthner, 1939), II, 577-82. Gaster's estimate of the nature of the influence is, however, well taken: "The Israelites did not *borrow* their institutions on Canaanite soil from the inhabitants of the country, but . . . both *inherited* them independently from that common Hebrew stock from which they were alike descended" (p. 578).

described in detail in Lev. 1 (P). It is an animal offering, whether ox, sheep, or goat, and it must be a male. The Yahwist describes Noah's burnt offering after the Flood. Through it the curse of God on the soil was expiated, his anger appeased (Gen. 8:20-22).

The Tribute or Gift Offering (*minḥāh*): In early times the word could apply to an offering of any kind. Cain and Abel both offer a *minḥāh* to Yahweh, one of agricultural produce, the other of an animal. As late as Malachi it is still used in this general sense (Mal. 1:10-11, 13). On the other hand, it is often considered as a cereal offering, invariably so in P. Burnt offering and tribute offering are also used together in distinction from each other (II Kings 16: 12 ff.; Amos 5:22; Isa. 1:13). In I Kings 18:29, 36 the word is used in connection with the evening oblation of Elijah on Mount Carmel, more often, however, with the morning offering. It is also used in connection with both the morning and the evening oblation (Exod. 29:41; Num. 28:8 [P]; I Kings 18:29, 36).

Slaughter Sacrifice (*zébhah*): This is the most common term for sacrifice in the Old Testament; the word for altar (*mizbēªh*) has the same root. The rite consisted of consuming the flesh of the victim in which the deity was believed to participate by receiving the blood and fat pieces. *Zébhah* is the name applied to all the sacrifices eaten at the festivals. It is used, together with burnt offerings, of the covenant sacrifice at Sinai (Exod. 24:5 [E]), of the Passover (Exod. 34:25 [JE]), of the annual sacrifice (I Sam. 20:29), in connection with thank offerings (Lev. 7:13; Ps. 107:22). In the rituals of the Holiness Code and the priestly writer they are defined by the word *shelāmîm* (Lev. 3; 7:28 ff.), that is, complete sacrifice. With this sacrifice are associated three other kinds of offerings: the thank offering (*tôdhāh*), which was an expression of thankfulness for God's goodness and help (Amos 4:5; Lev. 22:18; Pss. 50:14, 23; 116:17); the freewill or voluntary offering (*nedhābhāh*), which included gifts to the sanctuary (Exod. 35:27-29 [P]) and the sacrifices for festival meals at the feasts (Deut. 16:10; Ezra 3:5); and the vow (*nédher*), which was an offering that had been promised in recognition of the fulfillment of a request.

Sin Offering (*hattā'th*) and Guilt Offering (*'āshām*): Both are animal offerings, though not exclusively so, for in II Kings 12:4-5 they are used of a payment of money to the priests. The sin offering is holy. It was especially important in postexilic times, though it was offered before the Exile also. Like so many of the words for sacrifice, it appears in the Ugaritic inscriptions. Related to the sin offering is the guilt or

trespass offering. The chief significance was restitution or compensation. The offering was customarily a ram, together with restitution and a penalty of one fifth its value. The blood and fat pieces were for the altar, the skin and flesh for the priests. Although the term appears relatively late in the Bible (Ezek. 40:39 and later), its origin is doubtless much earlier. It appears in the Ugaritic texts and is there differentiated from the sin offering. In Second Isaiah the servant of the Lord offers himself as an *'āshām* in substitution for the sins of the nations (Isa. 53:10).

Many other kinds of sacrifices were offered in ancient Israel. They were usually occasions of rejoicing, sometimes in the mood of festal celebration, at other times in the mood of reconciliation and peace. In other situations they were the expression of a stricken conscience. For an appreciation of their significance one must read not only the detailed provisions of the Priestly Code and the references in Chronicles, but also the earlier historical passages and, above all, the Psalter. Many of the liturgies of the book of Psalms are doubtless to be understood in connection with sacrificial offerings of the temple.

E. Holy Persons.—In modern times the importance and function of the priesthood in Israel have been somewhat obscured, especially by the modern recognition of the great importance of the prophets. But the Old Testament contains almost as much "priestly" literature as prophetic, and we are only now coming to grasp something of the stature of the priest as theologian.[87] The priest is the holy person through whom the Israelite seeks to approach God in the cult. He is "set apart" to serve as the representative of the people before God. He stands in peculiar relation to the institutional side of Israel's religion. He remembers the traditions of the past, preserves their continuity with the present, and treasures them for the future. The priest appears from the earliest days of Israel's history to its close. The opposition between prophet and priest has been grossly exaggerated in modern times, and we now see that they had a fundamental relation to each other and that both of them performed their services to the cult. Prophetic criticism of the cult must certainly be taken seriously, but it must be understood in its total framework. Many of the cultic prophets were doubtless "false prophets" according to the standards of a Micah or a Jeremiah, but surely not all of them. Moreover, we have abundant evidence to show that the prophets did not divorce them-

[87] Gerhard von Rad, *Die Priesterschrift im Hexateuch* (Berlin: W. Kohlhammer, 1934); Pfeiffer, *Intro. to O.T.*, pp. 190-200.

selves from the life of the sanctuary as has been sometimes supposed.[88]

The most difficult problem in connection with "holy persons" is the place and function of the Levite. In the blessing of Jacob (Gen. 49) Levi is a tribe without any sacerdotal connections, but in the blessing of Moses (Deut. 33:8-11) he is in charge of the divinatory Urim and Thummim. Mowinckel thinks that the tribal association of Levi was a development from his priestly status, that is, a tribal origin was assigned him to explain his existence. But this view runs against serious obstacles. It is not possible to take up this problem here, but reference may be made to Theophile Meek's discussion.[89]

In the early period of Israel's history the priest served the function of a diviner. As we have seen, the blessing of Moses puts him in charge of the Urim and Thummim, and his casting of the sacred lot points in the same direction (Josh. 18:6). In this Joshua passage the verb "to cast" is the root for the word *tôrāh*. An examination of the employment of the verb *yārāh* confirms the judgment concerning the priestly divinatory function. It is the task of the priest to ascertain the divine will through techniques and instruments of which he is an expert. His is a learned craft, whereas the "word of the Lord" comes to the prophet. From lowly beginnings developed the whole *tôrāh*, usually translated "law" but rendered frequently quite as plausibly by "revelation." There were prophetic *tôrôth* also, but it was the task of the priest, above all, to give *tôrāh* (Jer. 18:18). The history of the development of the *tôrāh*, from original single words of "Yes" or "No" in response to the priestly query of the divining instrument to the vast corpus of priestly literature in the Pentateuch with its successive codes, gives one some notion of the importance of the priest in the history of Israel's religion.

Closely associated with the priest's original function as revealer of the will and decision of God is his teaching office. In perhaps the majority of instances the word *tôrāh* should be rendered "teaching" or "instruction." The sages of Israel, whose work is preserved in the wisdom literature, were teachers also, as in the case of the writers of our book of Proverbs and Ecclesiasticus. But the priest had a special teaching to promulgate, one which stood in intimate relationship to the continuity of tradition. It is likely that the sanctuaries preserved ancient records. Not only the temple archives at Jeru-

salem, but the archives of such sanctuaries as Hebron, Bethel, Gilgal, Samaria, and others included accounts of their original founding set forth in etiological stories, such as are preserved for us in Genesis; legends of the prophets like those concerning Elijah and Elisha (I Kings 17–II Kings 9) ; legal records of great variety and extent like the decalogues, the Covenant Code (Exod. 20:23–33:33), and similar formulations; and even liturgical compositions such as are represented by Pss. 15 and 24. The priest was master of all this treasure, it may be supposed, and it was his task to teach it. Two books of the Old Testament in quite different ways point to such a conclusion: Deuteronomy, the teaching book par excellence, and Ezekiel, the work of a priest who gives us an admirable impression of the nature of the teaching materials of the sanctuary (cf. also Hos. 4:6; Lev. 10:11; Mal. 2:6).

Finally, the priest was in charge of the sacrificial cult. He was not always exclusively charged with this function since the king and others could perform the sacred act quite as well. With the development of the cult, however, the responsibility and prerogative were increasingly his. Moreover, the many different kinds of sacrifices for many different kinds of occasions and situations and the great increase of their number in the postexilic period inevitably demanded a high degree of specialization. The priest does not appear before us in the striking manner that the prophets do, and that alone says a great deal. For the priest was devoted to the life of the institution, and he stood daily in the presence of the Glory whose will and work in Israel was preserved in the records of which he was custodian. Yet we do have the traditions about Aaron, and the portraits of men like Eli, Zadok, Ezekiel, and Ezra. If the priest was not the central figure in ancient Israel, he was essential to her life, and it is chiefly to him that we owe the canon in all its great variety and extent. In more than one sense he prepared the way for the new covenant and for the fuller glory to be revealed.

F. The Synagogue.—With the dispersion of Israel throughout the Mediterranean Basin, the destruction of the Holy City, and the Exile, it was inevitable that sooner or later some institution should arise to take the place of the temple and of its worship if Israel's religion was to survive. The loss of the external vehicle for the practices of worship, above all, of sacrifice, was destined to affect profoundly the whole subsequent development of the religion. The preexilic prophets by their trenchant criticism of the cult prepared the way for such an institution. Jeremiah and Ezekiel, each in his own way, contributed to the inner forces which made

---

[88] Adam C. Welch, *Prophet and Priest in Old Israel* (London: Student Christian Movement Press, 1936); Aubrey R. Johnson, *The Cultic Prophet in Ancient Israel* (Cardiff: University of Wales Press Board, 1944).

[89] *Hebrew Origins*, pp. 119-47.

worship beyond the confines of Israel possible and effective. The institution which arose to satisfy Israel's needs and aspirations was the synagogue.

The origins of the synagogue are wrapped in obscurity. Our earliest certain witness to its existence comes from the reign of Ptolemy III (247-222 B.C.). In the Roman period it is a flourishing institution, not only in the Diaspora but in the city of Jerusalem as well.[90] Some scholars attribute its origin to the period of the Exile. Paul Volz, for example, thinks that Second Isaiah was a synagogue teacher in the sixth century B.C. At any rate, we may be confident that the synagogue was the creation of the Dispersion. It is difficult to exaggerate its importance. It influenced the spiritual commonwealth of Israel, the nature and form of Christian worship, and the later religion of Islam.

It is not necessary to pause to describe the architecture, physical characteristics, and interior of the synagogue.[91] Most important is the connection of the synagogue with the teaching of the Law. Indeed, it is not too much to say that it was the Law which was the primary force behind the creation of the synagogue. Originally it was read at the great festivals, but later it became the regular practice at the weekly assemblies of the sabbath. In the course of time the Torah was divided into 150 sections and was read through completely in three years.[92] The Prophets came to be included in the synagogical readings. The haphtarah, or prophetical lesson, began as illustration to the torah passages read at the festivals, but later grew both in length and in importance so that in New Testament times the practice is recognized at the weekly assemblies (Acts 13:15; 15:21; cf. also Luke 4:16-19). An exposition or interpretation followed the reading of the scripture. From this developed the paraphrases of the Targums and the sermon. The New Testament vividly illustrates the use of the "preaching of the word."

The Shema, which in its liturgical use was first limited to Deut. 6:4 ("Hear, O Israel: The LORD our God is one LORD") but later developed into its present form (Deut. 6:4-9; 11:13-21; Num. 15:37-41), was foremost among the declarations of faith and came to be regarded as embodying the central "creed" of Judaism. Of great importance was the practice of prayer. Like the reading of the Law, the gathering for prayer goes back to the Old Testament itself.

The earliest of the great synagogue prayers is the Eighteen (Shemoneh Esreh) Benedictions, sometimes referred to as Tephillah ("The Prayer") or Amidah ("Standing").[93]

The singing of hymns and spiritual songs, some of them from the old temple liturgies and others of original composition, was part of the synagogue service. The Psalter doubtless contributed greatly to the spiritual life of the community. Life under the law and the joyful praise of God in singing were expressions of the same religious devotion.

X. Conclusion

When one surveys the religion of Israel as a whole and contemplates the course of its movement from its earliest beginnings, certain features and characteristics stand out with striking clarity. First of all is the colossal scope of tradition and the extensive range of the historical revelation. From the simple family and tribal religion of the patriarchs to the highly developed cult of Judaism we advance through a period of over a thousand years. It must be remembered that the literary deposit is made up almost throughout of relatively small literary units. When these are viewed in their totality and in the almost infinite diversity of circumstance and occasion, two things emerge: the concreteness and the extent of tradition. Again, one is impressed with the constant interaction of Israel's religion with the religions of other peoples: Canaanite, Assyrian, Babylonian, Persian, and Greek. The polemic and struggle of Israelite mentality with the mentalities of other peoples account in no small measure for the vitality and power of the Bible. Again, one stands in wonderment before the number and character of unique personalities: patriarchs, judges, prophets, kings, priests, and psalmists. Even more significant is the conscious solidarity of "the people," the redeemed, called, chosen, holy, covenant people, with the praises of God on their lips and the divine Torah in their hearts. One cannot read through the Old Testament without constantly asking the question which Israel itself seems to be asking constantly: who and what is this people, and what is the meaning of its life in history? When this question is taken seriously, the significance of Israel both for the Old Testament and for the New Testament begins to dawn upon the mind. Further, the historical character of the divine revelation is a major feature of the Bible as a whole and of the Old Testament in particular. The sense of continuity pervades much of the Old Testament in its present form, but the compilers and canonizers did not do funda-

[90] W. O. E. Oesterley, The Jewish Background of the Christian Liturgy (Oxford: Clarendon Press, 1925), p. 97.

[91] See Herbert Gordon May, "Synagogues in Palestine," The Biblical Archaeologist, VII (1944), 1-20.

[92] H. St. John Thackeray, The Septuagint and Jewish Worship (London: British Academy, 1923), p. 45.

[93] Oesterley, op. cit., pp. 53 ff.

mental violence to the religious mentality of the people. The movement from the past to the present and into the future is an expression of Israel's self-understanding. In her history and in the world at large God is making his will and purpose known. The promises made to the patriarchs, to Moses and Israel, to the prophets and the Deuteronomists, implied some issue, some outcome or resolution of Israel's existence. The movements of prophecy and apocalyptic were no capricious phenomena; rather, they lay inherent in the character of the faith already revealed to Moses. Yahweh called his son out of Egypt, a holy God made for himself a holy people, a covenantal God chose an "elect" people, a righteous God called a responsible people, and a faithful God fulfilled his promises to a waiting people. To this people was vouchsafed a revelation, a "holy book." Such a book could be accepted only on its own terms. It required for its proper understanding a faithful appropriation. Through faith the Jew and each Christian in his own way identifies himself with the people of God, shares in its history and the living record of the sacred events, participates in the covenantal reality in the midst of a world where nations exist and struggle for power and pre-eminence, grasps the meaning of his life under the awareness of the sovereign, redemptive God of Israel, and finally, expects and waits for the fulfillment of his purpose from the foundation of the world. Yet for the Christian the reality of the people of God finds its complete fulfillment and living expression in the church, the new Israel. The major categories of Old Testament faith therefore undergo a kind of transformation, for they are apprehended in the light of the Christ. Violence is not done to these categories. On the contrary, the New Testament understands them as receiving their final meaning and ultimate illumination in the teachings, the life, the suffering and death, and the resurrection of its Lord. Fulfillment is not understood without a profound awareness of that which is fulfilled. The Christian Bible is divided into two covenants: old and new. The relations and the tensions between the two constitute a revelation of the meaning of the Bible as a whole. It is Paul the Christian apostle who bears a witness (cf. Rom. 9:1 ff.) the church can dismiss only at the cost of its life and gospel: "They are Israelites, and to them belong the sonship, the glory, the covenants, the . . . law, the worship, and the promises; to them belong the patriarchs, and of their race, according to the flesh, is the Christ. God who is over all be blessed forever. Amen."

XI. Selected Bibliography

ALBRIGHT, W. F. *From the Stone Age to Christianity.* 2nd ed. Baltimore: Johns Hopkins Press, 1946.

————. *Archaeology and the Religion of Israel.* Baltimore: Johns Hopkins Press, 1942.

BUDDE, KARL. *Religion of Israel to the Exile.* New York: G. P. Putnam's Sons, 1899.

ELMSLIE, W. A. L. *How Came Our Faith.* Cambridge: Cambridge University Press, 1948.

HÄNEL, JOHANNES. *Die Religion der Heiligkeit.* Gütersloh: C. Bertelsmann, 1931.

HÖLSCHER, GUSTAV. *Geschichte der israelitischen und jüdischen Religion.* Giessen: Alfred Töpelmann, 1922.

HOOKE, S. H., ed. *The Labyrinth.* London: Society for Promoting Christian Knowledge, 1935.

————. *Myth and Ritual.* London: Oxford University Press, 1933.

JAMES, FLEMING. *Personalities of the Old Testament.* New York: Charles Scribner's Sons, 1946.

LESLIE, ELMER A. *Old Testament Religion.* New York: Abingdon Press, 1936.

MEEK, THEOPHILE J. *Hebrew Origins.* Rev. ed. New York: Harper & Bros., 1950.

OESTERLEY, W. O. E., and ROBINSON, T. H. *Hebrew Religion, Its Origin and Development.* 2nd ed. rev. New York: The Macmillan Co., 1937.

————. *The Jewish Background of the Christian Liturgy.* Oxford: Clarendon Press, 1925.

PEDERSEN, JOHANNES. *Israel, Its Life and Culture, I-II, III-IV.* London: Oxford University Press, 1926-40.

PHYTHIAN-ADAMS, W. J. *The People and the Presence.* London: Oxford University Press, 1942.

ROBINSON, H. WHEELER. *Inspiration and Revelation in the Old Testament.* Oxford: Clarendon Press, 1946.

————. *The Religious Ideas of the Old Testament.* London: Duckworth, 1934.

SELLIN, ERNST. *Israelitisch-jüdische Religionsgeschichte.* Leipzig: Quelle & Meyer, 1933.

WELCH, ADAM C. *The Religion of Israel Under the Kingdom.* Edinburgh: T. & T. Clark, 1912.

THE FAITH OF ISRAEL

by G. Ernest Wright

As we approach the study of Old Testament faith, it is important that we consider first the central contents of the Bible and the place of the Old Testament within it. When this has been done, we shall be in position the better to understand the special nature of the word "theology" when applied to the faith of the Bible and as well the task of the biblical theologian.

I. Introduction

A. The Christian Approach to the Old Testament.—In the earliest Christian preaching as recorded in the book of Acts it is significant that the Old Testament is used as the clue to the meaning of the life, death, and resurrection of Jesus Christ. Equally significant is the fact that in Jesus Christ the apostles have been given a fresh and impelling key to the meaning of the Old Testament.

How was the new age in Christ to be explained, except that it was the day of salvation long promised by God through the prophets of Israel? And could the primary meaning of the history of Israel be anything other than the record of God's mighty acts of grace and of the promises contained in them? In Christ this scripture was seen fulfilled, and in him the new community was the heir of the promises. It is true that Jesus as the Christ was rejected and crucified, but this again should occasion no surprise, it is said, since the scriptures are filled with the story of the people's sin and rebellion against God, of which these last events are the crowning example.

The new credo, or confession of faith, is succinctly presented by the apostle Paul in his sermon at Antioch of Pisidia (Acts 13:16 ff.). It contains the following articles of faith: (*a*) the God of Israel chose the fathers (patriarchs); (*b*) with uplifted arm he delivered their seed from Egyptian slavery, and suffered them in the wilderness; (*c*) he gave them their land as an inheritance; (*d*) in the course of time he

349

raised up David as their king, (e) of whose seed he brought unto Israel a Savior, Jesus, as he had promised.

It will be noted that this is a typical biblical statement of faith, cast not in the form of theological abstractions, but in terms of historical events which are seen as the acts of God. Furthermore, the particular history of Israel which Paul here reviews begins with the patriarchs and ends with David; from that point he passes immediately to Jesus Christ. He thus suggests that the period from Abraham to David is the most significant history of the former times, and that Christ is the continuation, the clarification, and the fulfillment of the redemptive purpose of God within it.

From the study of such passages as this it becomes obvious that the primary element which holds the two testaments together is a confessional proclamation or kerygma of certain great redemptive acts of God which have taken place in one particular history, the climax and fulfillment of which is Jesus Christ.[1] The history of Israel thus is seen directed not to the Law as its end, but to Jesus Christ in whom the forgiveness of sins is effected (Acts 13:38-39) and the purpose and promise of God in the call and election of Israel are fulfilled.

It is from this perspective, then, that the Christian begins the detailed study of the Old Testament. He does not begin with the Law because the priority belongs to the proclamation of the redemptive action of God which furnishes the context in which the Law is to be understood. Taking his clue from the New Testament, he turns to the first part of the Old Testament and there discovers that the core of Israel's proclamation is precisely that which the preaching of Acts affirms. Through the roughhewn conglomerate of material of which the Hexateuch, or first six books, is composed there runs one central theme: God, the creator of the world, chose the fathers of Israel and promised them a goodly heritage in the land of Canaan. When Israel became numerous and was enslaved in Egypt, God delivered them by the most remarkable proofs of his power and grace; and after a long wandering, he provided them with the Promised Land, the gift of an inheritance.

This theme is the Israelite credo, the Hebrew confession of faith. In its oldest and simplest forms it can be found in certain cultic recitations which must go back in their essential elements to a very early period of Israel's his-

tory. An old cultic law preserved in Deut. 26:1-9 is an example. When the Israelite had arrived in the land of Canaan, he was to present a basket of firstfruits at the sanctuary, presumably each year. When he did so, he was to recite a confession as follows: "A Syrian ready to perish [wandering or lost—ASV mg.] was my father; and he went down into Egypt, and sojourned there with a few, and became there a nation . . . : And the Egyptians . . . laid upon us hard bondage. . . . And the LORD brought us forth out of Egypt with a mighty hand. . . . And he hath brought us into this place, and hath given us this land" (Deut. 26:5-9) .

The dominant references here are to God's deliverance in the Exodus and to his gift of the land. A similar confessional statement or credo is to be found in Deut. 6:20-24, where the same great saving acts which brought the Israelite community into being are emphasized. Much more elaborate is the sermon of Joshua in the covenant ceremony at Shechem (Josh. 24:2-13) . The present form of this passage is to be dated between the ninth and seventh centuries B.C., but its basic form is not a new literary creation. It bears the stamp of the old cultic credo, here elaborated with some freedom of expression. It is the Hexateuch in miniature, in which the confessional elements emphasized are (a) God's choice of Abraham, (b) his deliverance at the Exodus, and (c) his gift of the land.[2]

The conglomerate nature of the first six books of the Old Testament in their present form is the result of a long and complicated history, during which Israel's traditions were compiled and edited around this basic theme. We probably owe the first written edition of our present Hexateuch to one who is called the Yahwist (J) writer. He was a collector of old traditions from every available source, and in his arrangement and editing of a variety of materials he constructed a great confessional history, using the old stories to present a profound theological base for the credo. It was probably he who collected and put into writing the earliest traditions about the prehistorical period in Gen. 2–11, using them as the setting for the history of Israel. In so doing he employed his material in such a way as to analyze the problem of universal man. Man lives no longer in the paradise God provided, because

---

[1] Cf. the words with which Jesus began his ministry, "The time is fulfilled" (Mark 1:15). This "time" is the special, particular time of God, beginning with Abraham and climaxed in Christ, in which the establishment of God's kingdom and his salvation have been accomplished.

[2] See Gerhard von Rad, Das erste Buch Mose (Göttingen: Vandenhoeck & Ruprecht, 1949), pp. 7 ff.; and more fully his Das formgeschichtliche Problem des Hexateuchs (Stuttgart: W. Kohlhammer, 1938). For an evaluation and qualification of von Rad's view concerning the manner in which the Hexateuch was built up from such old cultic confessions see Artur Weiser, Einleitung in das Alte Testament (Göttingen: Vandenhoeck & Ruprecht, 1949), pp. 66-79.

he has rebelled against his creator and repeatedly has rejected the conditions of his creation. The answer to man's problem is seen by the Yahwist to lie in the call or election of Abraham, in whose seed the nations of the earth shall find a blessing (Gen. 12:1-3). The old credo is thus given a new and deeper dimension, for the election of Israel is set within the universal redemptive purpose of God.[3]

The election promises and the gracious guidance of God were the theme around which the various cycles of patriarchal traditions were collected, while Exodus presents the first stage in the fulfillment of the promises. The traditions concerning the Sinai covenant (Exod. 19–24), which once seem to have circulated separately from those narrating the great saving acts of God, were built into the over-all theme as the immediate goal and purpose of the deliverance from Egypt. Having rescued Israel from slavery, God bound the people to him in a solemn compact and thus formed them into a nation. Together with the good news of the old confession there was now the reminder of the obligation for unconditioned obedience to the will of the Lord. This joining of the Exodus and Sinai traditions gave the needed undergirding to the recital of God's saving acts in the credo; together they presented the basic elements of the biblical proclamation, the gospel and the law of God. Deuteronomy expanded the covenant theology in this framework, giving a summary of the faith in an earnest, homiletical appeal to remember the great things God had done, to fear, obey, and love him with a wholehearted devotion. In it the confessional story and the covenant law are brought together in a series of solemn sermons, in which the redemptive love of God and the whole duty of man in God's service are nobly proclaimed.[4]

The greatest contribution of the priestly editors (P) to the older Yahwist and Elohist material was the detailed description of the tabernacle, with the forms and offices of worship associated with it (Exod. 25–31; 35–40; Leviticus; and parts of Numbers). The tabernacle was the seal of God's real presence in the midst of the people; and the priesthood and sacrificial rites were the means ordained by him through which he might be approached and worshiped, forgiveness of sins secured, and atonement effected.

The Hexateuch as compiled around its central theme is thus a great confessional history based upon the saving acts of God, his sover-

eignty over the life of man, and the temporal means by which he was to be worshiped. It contained the promises of God to and through Israel, and as well the proclamation of his lordship with the requirement of human obedience. It thus held the Israelite credo, in the light of which the remainder of the Bible was composed and interpreted. Yet to be added, however, was the office of kingship, David being its typical representative. Israel in Palestine, in possession of the old credo and its early cultic institutions, was promptly faced with the problem of security among hostile neighbors. Kingship was granted and the promise of justice and salvation was conferred with it. But the central theme of the remainder of the history and of the prophets was that of God's controversy with his people for their failure to live by their credo, his destruction of the nation by successive stages, to the end that he might revive and fulfill his promises. Their complete fulfillment, however, was not accomplished within the period of the Old Testament, though it was ardently awaited. Small wonder, therefore, that the early church seized so confidently upon the Old Testament kerygma as the explanation of God's work in Jesus Christ! In him the meaning of the whole was perfectly clear, for it was now possible to penetrate within the roughhewn accumulation of material and behind the law with its multitudinous ramifications, and to do so with clarity, certainty, and boldness unknown since the days of the prophets.

B. The Task of Biblical Theology.—The purpose of this brief review of the central content of the Bible as seen through the perspective of the New Testament is to make clear at the outset what the chief task of biblical theology must be. That task is simply to expound the meaning and implications of the biblical credo in its various forms. This must be done in as coherent, reflective, and relevant a manner as possible, to the end that the gospel may be proclaimed in and by the church with clarity and power. It must further be stated that the Christian in approaching the Old Testament inevitably does so with certain presuppositions which he must confess. These involve the conviction that Jesus Christ is both the destination of and the guide to the Old Testament's basic content. This does not mean that the Christian is entitled to betray the Old Testament by reading into it meanings which are not there, nor that he can neglect the most rigid use of the tools of scholarship. Yet it does mean that he performs his scholarly and exegetical work in the knowledge of God's fulfilled "time," and with the conviction that Israel's faith in its deeper dimensions is an integral part

---

[3] See further, von Rad, *Das erste Buch Mose*, pp. 15-16, 132-34.

[4] The various aspects of the completed credo are beautifully treated in the poetry of the psalms; cf. especially Pss. 78; 104; 105; 106; 136.

of his own faith through the new Israel of which he is a member by faith in Jesus Christ.

Such a definition of our task and of its presuppositions is, however, far too simple unless it recognizes the many difficulties which lie in the way of a biblical theology or of a theology of either Testament. By its very nature theology involves an attempt to systematize and generalize by means of abstract language. Yet biblical religion is a living faith which can never be confined in simple generalizations nor in an abstract system. It is based upon an anthropomorphic vocabulary which, when translated into abstractions, loses its creative power. Its central content is a historical credo, the ramifications of which are many and various in the complexities of a long history and of various schools of thought within that history. Yet the task of the church demands that we must make the attempt to organize the central articles of the faith, to penetrate behind them in order to discover their foundations, and to portray as well as we can their historical developments and ramifications. This the church has done repeatedly, as it was done in each generation of biblical history itself. Thus while at times our gait may be a bit unsteady, we must proceed in the faith that God himself will verify and validate his truth, even though our own attempts to express and expound it are incomplete and historically conditioned.

II. The God of Israel

A. God and People.—It would be an injustice to the faith of Israel if we were to begin our discussion with an abstract analysis of God's nature and attributes. God was known to Israel because he had revealed himself, his purpose, and his nature through dramatic historical acts. The Old Testament as a religious literature is basically a historical narration because the description of the faith was primarily the story of what God had done, how the people had responded or should respond, and what God was yet to do. Our point of beginning, therefore, must be with the phrase "the God of Israel," or, in other words, with the doctrine of election.

1. The Election of Israel.—How had Israel come to have such faith in the Lord Yahweh that she owed her very existence as a nation to him, that she saw him engaged through her in a unique redemptive work in history, that thus she could say, "What great nation is there that hath a god so nigh unto them as is Yahweh our God whenever we call upon him" (Deut. 4:7)? Such faith cannot be explained solely in terms of an evolutionary process wherein a social organism gradually evolved from polytheism through the interplay of a variety of environmental and sociological factors. A descriptive study of this type can explain many things, but by its intrinsic limitations it cannot explain how Israel became the people of Yahweh. In a presentation of Old Testament theology, therefore, it is necessary to take seriously the doctrine of Israel's special election by God, to see that doctrine as the primary article of the faith, and to understand the significance of the Exodus as the only historical event in which such a conception could have originated, or at least been confirmed as an integral part of the faith of the nation.

At the center of that faith lay the joyful proclamation that the God of the fathers had heard the cry of an oppressed people in Egypt, and by mighty acts of power had delivered them from slavery and made them a nation. They were a weak, dispirited, and helpless people whom the world's justice had passed by. Yet they were freed; and to them this miracle of deliverance could not be explained on simple naturalistic grounds. It was a sign, a wonder; as such it revealed a God who was more powerful than the greatest temporal power of the age (i.e., Pharaoh), a God who could make the forces of nature serve him, a God who for some gracious reason had set his pity on this defenseless people and had chosen them for his own.

Israel's doctrine of God, therefore, was not derived from speculative thought; it was derived from the sole interpretation of historical events possible to them. Their God was the one who had met and chosen them in their weakness and had shown his power over all human and natural powers in delivering them from oppression. Accordingly, in all subsequent events they could but recognize and acknowledge the one deity who had chosen and saved them. Wherever they were, or in whatever condition, he was to be found in their midst. In Canaan it was he, not Baal, who made "the hinds to calve" (Ps. 29:9), who sent the rain and the dew from heaven, the fresh water from the earth, and the blessings of beast and womb (Gen. 49:25; Deut. 33:13-16). Yet even in the earliest poetry he was no mere storm or fertility deity; he was the great Lord whose righteous acts in Israel's behalf men shall rehearse (Judg. 5:11). In the international crises of the subsequent history it was none other than Yahweh, the God of Israel, who was directing the wars of conquest to his own ends. The Assyrian was "the rod of [his] anger" (Isa. 10:5); Nebuchadrezzar was his "servant" (Jer. 25:9); and Cyrus was his "anointed" (Isa. 45:1). Even in the captivity of Israel and Judah he was seen at work for his own name's sake. As the God of Israel who had met this people in a historical event, he thus was recognized as the Lord of all events who was directing the whole course of history to his own ends, for nothing happened in either nature or history in which his power was not acknowledged.

The problem of Israelite monotheism, how it is to be defined and when it was achieved, is left for subsequent discussion (see pp. 359-62). The point emphasized here is that Israel's knowledge of God cannot in the first instance be described in theological abstractions. God was known in Israel because events were interpreted as his handiwork. Israel learned of him because he had chosen them from all the nations of the earth, because he had set his love upon them to deliver, to guide, and to govern them. The theological language used of him was inevitably concrete, historically conditioned, and based upon human analogy; to confess him thus meant to describe what he had done. The deepening of the language in the direction of the abstract was only gradually and partially accomplished when through the succession of historical events he revealed himself more clearly.

Such is the conception implicit in the phrase "the God of Israel." This God was known because he had revealed himself as Savior and Lord of one particular people whom he had chosen out of all the peoples of the earth. But why had God chosen Israel? A typical modern explanation is to assert that the Hebrews were an extraordinarily gifted people with a special genius for religion. Natural endowment is thus used to explain Israel's consciousness of being an elect people. Yet this is not the emphasis of the Old Testament. There God's election is not based on special considerations of human power or righteousness. Israel was seen by the leaders of the faith to have been a hardhearted and rebellious people from the earliest times.[5] The election was rooted in the mystery of divine grace. It was not and could not be explained; it could only be accepted in faith and in gratitude.

2. *The History and Problems of Election.—* In presenting the various traditions about the fathers of Israel in Genesis, it was inevitable that even the earliest historians should project the election faith back into that period as the occasion for the patriarchal migration from Mesopotamia into Canaan.[6] God selected and called each patriarch, repeating to Isaac and Jacob the promises made in the call of Abraham

[5] This is especially emphasized by the prophets and Deuteronomy (e.g., Jer. 7:21-26; Ezek. 16; Hos. 11; Deut. 7:7-8; 9). The stories of the murmuring and rebellion in the Sinai wanderings, preserved even in the oldest sections of Exodus and Numbers, were the source from which these writings drew their emphasis.

[6] For a detailed analysis of the two different emphases in the literature as to the origin of election (the Exodus and Abrahamic traditions), see especially Kurt Galling, *Die Erwählungstraditionen Israels* (Giessen: Alfred Töpelmann, 1928).

(Gen. 12:1-3). The theme of the Yahwist document is precisely the election with its glorious promises and the successive stages in which those promises were fulfilled. Furthermore, election is presented as furnishing the central spiritual problem which the fathers had to face. Abraham had no sooner received the promises than he was caught lying about his wife in Egypt (Gen. 12:10-20). Having been promised a son, Sarah could not believe. Taking matters into her own hands, she immediately involved the family in turmoil over Hagar and Ishmael (Gen. 16). God promised to give Israel an inheritance of land; but lacking the faith and courage to take it, the people were consigned to a generation of fruitless wandering in the wilderness (Num. 13–14). Faith meant the acceptance of God's election promises and the belief that he would do what he had promised. Sin was born in the doubt which was nourished by anxiety.

The knowledge of God's special election was so deeply rooted in the Israelite religious consciousness that we must presume it to have arisen in a very early period of the people's history, long before the earliest documents now preserved were written down. It furnished the context in which Israel's conception of God's nature was evolved, in which the significance of history was understood, and in which the meaning of the people's life and destiny was interpreted. While no answer could be given as to why God chose Israel rather than some other nation, yet this particularism in the exercise of the divine favor seems early to have been understood as in some way set within God's purpose of universal salvation. As pointed out on pp. 350-51, it was the Yahwist writer who first seems to have given the doctrine of election this wider context, thus delivering it from the dangers involved in a conception of divine favoritism. However dimly this conception of the crucial role which Israel was to play in a divine drama of universal salvation may have been understood in the early days of the nation's history, it certainly became most explicit in Isaiah 40–55, in the book of Jonah, and in prophetic eschatology as a whole (e.g., Isa. 2:2-4; Zech. 2:11; 8:22-23; 14:16). God's purpose was to establish his redemptive sovereignty over all the earth, and he had chosen Israel as his special agent through whom this aim was to be accomplished.

Since the days of Celsus in the second century A.D., biblical faith has been subjected to constant criticism for this particularism in the operation of divine grace. Yet the election of Israel was not for selfish or self-centered privilege. God had his own purposes which Israel was continually struggling to understand. He was no objectification of a people's natural desires; he was an external point of reference, one who set his course and required that his people follow, one whose will was in constant conflict with that of the nation. Actually, the story told by this elect people about itself is in its total scope a sordid, terrible tale. Contemporary gods of nature and culture perished in the very tragic events which confirmed to a remnant of Israel both the sovereignty and the election of Yahweh. Such an election can scarcely be conceived as the objectification of the egotism of a small nation. It demanded more than the people would normally give; its violation involved the destruction of the nation's political life; and it had such a purifying effect upon the national consciousness that its historians and prophets told the truth about their people as have the patriots of no other nation. The greatest heroes of Israel were at one and the same time both sinners and heroes of faith.

B. The God of the Covenant.—The particular vocabulary which expressed most clearly the meaning and implication of the doctrine of election for Israelite life was drawn from the realm of jurisprudence—that is, from the conception of covenant. In covenant the sense of law and legal obligation was given concrete form and theological setting; responsibility and obedience were interpreted as the proper human response to the grace of God as shown in his saving acts and election promises. The priority thus belongs to God's grace in election, apart from which there would have been no covenant.[7] The apostle Paul in the books of Galatians and Romans was correct in his attempt to prove from the early Old Testament material that the proper order is gospel and law, not the reverse as was emphasized in Judaism. The setting of law in the grace of God meant that at least in the deeper reaches of Israelite faith human righteousness in the law could never be completely identified with the righteousness of God nor in any way confine or circumscribe divine grace.

The sense of covenant was rooted in the nomadic, patriarchal society which formed the ideal background of Israelite community life. The basis of society, its harmonious nature, its freedom from bloodguiltiness, its inner and outer wholesomeness or peace, all these were derived from the various levels of sacred compact or covenant in which men lived and moved and had their being. Covenant created the community which gave meaning to the individual; it supplied the norms of right and wrong; it

was rooted in legal compact, but went deeper than modern legal forms of covenant in that it basically involved a psychical, wholesome union of souls wherein there was an intermingling, a mutuality of life. It was usually consecrated by sacrificial rites, and the deity or deities of the respective parties were members and guarantors of the union (cf. Gen. 31:44-54; Josh. 9:3-21; I Sam. 18:1-4). The dissolution of covenant meant the disintegration of society; violation of covenant as in murder meant that the individual was deprived of the community's protection and blessing—the worst curse which could befall anyone (cf. Gen. 4:10-14).[8]

From this background in the people's common life the conception of covenant was borrowed as the means of expressing the special relationship existing between Yahweh and Israel. In this sense it no longer referred to a legal compact between human beings, sanctioned by deity; instead it furnished the language with which the relationship of God and people was described.

1. The Ceremonies of the Covenant.—A number of covenant ceremonies are recorded. For example, Ezra returned to Jerusalem with the law of God, presumably the complete Pentateuch, in his possession and with the royal commission to reform religious affairs on the basis of this law (Ezra 7:14, 25-26). An eight-day ceremony was held, during which the law was read by Ezra and expounded by the priests and Levites so that the people understood what they had heard. This was followed by a solemn public confession of sin and a formal vow to keep the law, written and sealed in the people's behalf by the leaders (Neh. 8-10). A similar ceremony before an official assembly was conducted by Josiah in 621 B.C., on the basis of the Deuteronomic law, at the inauguration of a great religious reform (II Kings 23:1-3).[9] In Josh. 24 a great covenant ceremony at Shechem was conducted by Joshua. In this case the law was not read. Instead, the confessional history which forms the theme of the Hexateuch was rehearsed, and in response the people formally vowed to serve Yahweh and no other.[10] Deuteronomy preserves the tradition of a covenant

---

[7] Cf. H. Wheeler Robinson, *Inspiration and Revelation in the Old Testament* (Oxford: The Clarendon Press, 1946), pp. 150-55; Galling, *Die Erwählungstraditionen Israels*, p. 37.

[8] See Johannes Pedersen, *Israel, Its Life and Culture I-II* (London: Oxford University Press, 1926), 263-310.

[9] Cf. also II Chr. 23:16-21 for the covenant between priest, people, and king "that they should be Yahweh's people," after the slaying of Jezebel's daughter, Athaliah, in Jerusalem.

[10] The significance of the Shechem covenant is that in this ceremony the Sinai compact was probably accepted as binding upon all the tribes, some of which had not participated in the Exodus under Moses. In this way the tradition of Sinai became normative for all twelve tribes; see Martin Noth, *Das Buch Josua* (Tübingen: J. C. B. Mohr, 1938; "Handbuch zum Alten Testament"), pp. 108-9.

ceremony in Moab, in which the law was expounded by Moses and the people vowed to keep it (cf. Deut. 29). Basic to all of these ceremonies, however, was the tradition of an original solemn rite at Sinai. There the "book of the covenant" was read by Moses, the people vowed to keep the law, and the vow was sealed with the sacrificial blood (Exod. 24:4-8; cf. 19:5-8).

2. The Vocabulary of the Covenant.—Covenant thus bound the chosen people to God in a solemn relationship of obligation and obedience. Its ratification was one of the most holy and sacred rites in the nation's life.[11] It was based upon a political anthropomorphism, that of kingship applied to God, which furnished the central metaphors by means of which God was apprehended and the basic religious terminology by which the nation's life, its meaning and aim, its institutions and officials, were described.[12] Since national law was the duty of kings to provide and administer in the ancient world, the God of Israel was first apprehended as *King* and *Lord,* who rescued a people, formed them into a nation, and bound them to him in a relationship of *servant*s to a ruler. He did not force them into this relationship; he offered it to them as a gracious act. He promised to be their king who would provide justice for them, together with salvation and security from those who would oppress them. When they accepted this offer, they in turn made their promises to *obey* and *serve* their ruler.[13] They were to *hearken* and to *be obedient* to his will. He gave them the law as the constitution of the society, which to keep meant life and peace within the nation. He governed them directly, though he chose leaders for specific tasks and gave these leaders the power to perform them (Moses, Joshua, the judges). Later, in response to the people's necessity, he gave them the institution of kingship; the human king, like the priest, was anointed with oil as to a holy office, and he was to rule as God's earthly vicegerent or "son." Yet the divine King did not confine his will to any one institution. He also called his

[11] That there was a yearly festival in the central sanctuary commemorating the conclusion of the covenant, and at the same time renewing it, is considered a probability in the light of the evidence derived from studies in form criticism and in the history of tradition; see Martin Noth, *Überlieferungsgeschichte des Pentateuch* (Stuttgart: W. Kohlhammer, 1948), p. 64.

[12] See G. Ernest Wright, "The Terminology of Old Testament Religion and Its Significance," *Journal of Near Eastern Studies,* I (1942), 404-14; cf. also Wright, *The Challenge of Israel's Faith* (Chicago: University of Chicago Press, 1944), ch. iii.

[13] The one word which more than any other comprehends these covenant promises and obligations is the Hebrew *ḥeṣedh*, frequently translated "lovingkindness": see Nelson Glueck, *Das Word ḥesed im alttestamentlichen Sprachgebrauche* (Giessen: Alfred Töpelmann, 1927).

prophets, who were his *heralds,* his *messengers,* who knew his heavenly counsel and who proclaimed it directly to the people and to their ordained leaders. Such metaphors as "judge" and "shepherd" as applied to God were also drawn from the office of kingship. They were commonly used of kings in the ancient world and indicated different aspects of the royal office. The marriage metaphor, introduced by Hosea, in which God is the husband of the faithless wife, Israel, was a fresh way of describing the covenantal relationship existing between God and people; it was one which made Israel's faithlessness vividly clear (cf. Ezek. 16). The father-son terminology was largely avoided between the tenth and sixth centuries B.C. because of the merely physical use made of it in paganism.[14]

The covenant, based as it was on a terminology derived from a monarchial form of government, thus involved an interpretation of the meaning and significance of Israel's life. In ideal form it provided the structure of the nation's social and political organization, with the result that a tension continually existed between it and the political actualities. It furnished the Deuteronomic historian (Joshua-II Kings) and the Chronicler (I Chronicles-Nehemiah) with the chief clue to the interpretation of the national history between the conquest of Canaan and the reformation of the postexilic community under Nehemiah and Ezra. The special interests of the Deuteronomist centered in the political affairs of the nation, while those of the Chronicler lay in ecclesiastical matters. Yet both saw the succession of events as the story of the divine King's acts of judgment and of grace in ruling a people who had solemnly promised to be his loyal subjects but who had repeatedly rebelled against his sovereignty. Indeed, to Israel the whole course of history was to be viewed in terms of God's purpose to establish his kingship over all peoples of the earth. The term "kingdom of God" in this sense does not occur in the Old Testament, but the conception behind it is a theme which becomes increasingly explicit and is particularly evident in prophetic eschatology and the psalms which celebrated God's enthronement as universal king (e.g., Pss. 47; 93; 96–99).

3. The Covenant Law.—It is also significant that the covenant furnished the setting for both the common and the cultic law. Much of the social law was adapted from ancient Near Eastern common law; in its typical formulation it

[14] It was known, however, and used particularly to emphasize Israel's special election rather than the covenant (cf. Exod. 4:22; Hos. 11:1-4; Mal. 1:6; see further, Wright, *Challenge of Israel's Faith;* Johannes Hempel, *Gott und Mensch im Alten Testaments* [Stuttgart: W. Kohlhammer, 1926], pp. 131 ff.).

was introduced by a conditional clause in which the case is carefully defined but the person addressed left indefinite.[15] The type of legal formulation peculiar to Israel, however, is that in which the case is not defined with care but in which each member of the community was addressed directly by the divine Ruler, "Thou shalt," or "Thou shalt not." [16] This command or apodictic type of law is the characteristic law of the covenant relation. Yet regardless of origin or type, all law was taken into the covenant as the expression of the will of God.

From this fact certain important inferences are to be drawn: (a) Israel conceived of the law not as a penal burden to be borne, but as a special gift of God that a people who had been without law might now have it and in it find justice and security. (b) Israel's law as God's special gift was thus not a *natural* law. Of the latter there are intimations (e.g., Gen. 2:23-24; Amos 1–2; Isa. 1:3; Jer. 8:7), but they are never collected together into what might be called a doctrine. The law instead was rooted in the grace of God and conceived as a special revelation. (c) For Israel totalitarian rule was lifted from the earthly to the cosmic sphere. The law of the covenant meant that the people had an association with the divine King which was prior to political organization. Thus the human king could not take credit for the law; he could only administer it and be subject to it.[17] (d) The covenant law was given by God to the community as a whole, for the covenant was made with the nation. Yet in the law the individual was singled out of the group and addressed directly with God's "Thou shalt." Man as man was not lost in tribal or mass society, but was given his place and function within it. Individuality and community were thus held in proper balance. In the covenant with the nation each man was bound to God in the realm of will; he was called upon to obey his Lord. As a result, life assumed a meaning and a dignity unknown elsewhere.[18] The great gods of polytheism were aristocrats inaccessible to the common man. Yet the covenant God of Israel was not a respecter of persons; he would hearken to the prayer of the most humble for he had dignified each one with his personal address.

4. The History of the Covenant.—Old Testament scholarship has shown a tendency to regard the special covenant between God and Israel as a conception which arose late in Israel's history, perhaps in Hosea at the earliest and more probably in the Deuteronomic reform of the seventh century.[19] Recent study, however, makes it increasingly difficult to give credence to this point of view. In the period of the judges Israel was distinguished from other peoples of the day by her peculiar organization. While other nations had a monarchial form of government, Israel was an amphictyony—that is, an association of tribes, bound together by sacred compact around a central sanctuary.[20] The association of the tribes was thus not a natural or secular one; it was a religious "assembly" or "congregation" (Hebrew, *mô'ēdh,* *'ēdhāh; qāhāl*) composed of those who were partners in the compact. The antiquity of this tribal covenant is further certified by the results of form criticism,[21] by the fundamental nature of the ruler-servant terminology described above, and by the legal terms so basic to the Israelite religious vocabulary and so clearly illustrated in the prophetic proclamation of God's controversy (i.e., legal case) against his chosen nation (e.g., Isa. 1:2; Jer. 2:1-13; 25:31; Hos. 4:1-3; Mic. 6:1-5).

It can thus be affirmed that election and covenant are so closely related in Israelite faith that they cannot be separated. Together they furnish one of the central themes of the Bible, the gracious acts and promises of God together with the binding relationship and obligation to God on the part of the believer who has accepted the promises. It was natural, therefore, that covenant should be projected into the patriarchal period as the only means of explaining the relationship of Abraham to God. This was done by J and E in Gen. 15; and the priestly edition of JE elaborates the conception into a framework for all of history. In the covenant with Noah the rainbow is the "token" of

---

[15] Cf. Exod. 21:18: "And if men strive together, and one smite another. . . ."

[16] For an analysis of this distinction in legal formulation see Albrecht Alt, *Die Ursprünge des israelitischen Rechts* (Leipzig: S. Hirzel, 1934).

[17] Cf. Deut. 17:14-20: Henri Frankfort, *Kingship and the Gods* (Chicago: University of Chicago Press, 1948), pp. 337-44.

[18] Cf. Walther Eichrodt, *Das Menschenverständnis des Alten Testaments* (Basel: Heinrich Majer, 1944), pp. 7-11.

[19] E.g., Julius Wellhausen, *Prolegomena to the History of Israel,* tr. J. Sutherland Black and Allan Menzies (Edinburgh: Adam & Charles Black, 1885), pp. 418-19; Adam C. Welch, *The Religion of Israel Under the Kingdom* (Edinburgh: T. & T. Clark, 1912), p. 263; Richard Kraetzschmar, *Die Bundesvorstellung im Alten Testament* (Marburg: N. G. Elwert, 1896).

[20] See Martin Noth, *Das System der zwölf Stämme Israels* (Stuttgart: W. Kohlhammer, 1930); Albrecht Alt, *Die Staatenbildung der Israeliten in Palästina* (Leipzig: Alexander Edelmann, 1930).

[21] See Martin Noth, *Überlieferungsgeschichte des Pentateuch,* pp. 272-77. For an excellent review of the arguments concerning the importance and age of the covenant see Walther Eichrodt, *Theologie des Alten Testaments* (3rd ed.; Berlin: Evangelische Verlagsanstalt, 1948), I, 6-11.

God's eternal covenant with all mankind (Gen. 9) ; the election covenant with Abraham was sealed by the rite of circumcision; and the great covenant with all Israel at Sinai had as its "token" or "sign" the sabbath (Exod. 31:12-17) . Thus in priestly circles the relationship of God to man was conceived under these forms of covenant as possessing an eternal and universal character.

Covenant, as the dominant language in which the election relationship of God to Israel was expressed, could, however, be misused by too great a narrowing of its rich meaning. Instead of pointing first and foremost to the gracious and marvelous acts of God in saving and binding the nation to himself, it came to be interpreted among many in an external, legalistic way, so that attention was drawn more to the covenant ordinances than to their Giver. This tendency reached expression in Deuteronomic circles, where the very word "covenant" could be used as the name for the Decalogue (Deut. 4:13, 23; I Kings 8:21) . But to identify covenant with a law to be kept is so to emphasize the external, statutory nature of the compact as to push the spiritual bond and communion between God and people into the background. Deuteronomy attempted to preserve a balance between the two,[22] but among the people as a whole this was not done. Covenant as a purely juridical institution encouraged them to keep the outward forms of legal decency while neglecting the spiritual nature of their relationship with God, which alone could produce a worthy fruit.

It was perhaps for this reason that the prophets did not make more use of the term, but frequently employed other metaphors drawn from human analogy to express the relationship of God to Israel. Thus Hosea used the figures of marriage (chs. 1–3) and of fatherly love (ch. 11) , both of which appear again in Jeremiah (chs. 3; 31) . Ezekiel speaks of the foundling, reared, loved, and married by God (ch. 16) ; Second Isaiah, of the mother who has not forgotten her child (49:15) and of the acts of the redeemer (gô'ēl) who because of a close family relationship saves his relative from slavery (43:1, 14; etc.) . Through such pictures the prophets present the warm, personal love and fidelity of God, which seek a response from the heart, but which stand in contrast to the faithlessness and disloyalty of the people. "In this battle against all *opus operatum* the covenant thought could not help them." [23] Yet later prophecy employs the thought anew in depicting the relationship with God which the future will bring. In the days to come God will renew his relationship with his people in an "everlasting covenant" (Isa. 55:3; 61:8; Jer. 32:40; Ezek. 37:26) , a "covenant of peace" (Isa. 54:10; Ezek. 34:25; 37:26) , a "new covenant" written upon the heart (Jer. 31:31-34) . The servant of Second Isaiah is even to be the mediator of the covenant for all people and as such the agent of their salvation (Isa. 42:6; 49:8) . In these cases there is no longer any question about the nature of the covenant as an external, legal compact. It is based upon the pure grace of God which shall create in man a new heart and new spirit to receive it.

It is in this last sense that the covenant conception is carried over into the church of the New Testament. The Christian as a member of the new covenant in the blood of Christ becomes the true and actual heir of the election promises made to Israel. Yet in a sense the basic conflict between the apostle Paul and Judaism lay in the conception of the meaning of God's relationship and revelation to his people as established in election and covenant. Judaism had identified covenant solely with the Mosaic law, with the result that Paul was no more able to use its terminology in his struggle than were the prophets—except to oppose it. Thus in the Bible as a whole there are two lines of development in the theological use of a legal compact for expressing the relationship between God and people. In one the movement was "from covenant through covenant relationship, covenant statute, statutory order to religion, cult, and covenant people." In the other it was from covenant through the institution of the nation, relationship of grace and revelation "to redemptive order, saving decree, and world consummation." Two opposing conceptions thus stand over against one another. Yet they of necessity must be taken together, though held in tension, for on the one hand they point to the legal ordering of human life under God in our present existence, and on the other to the eschatological fulfillment of that life in the promise of the kingdom which is to come.[24]

C. God and the Gods.—It has been assumed by many scholars during the first part of the twentieth century that the most significant thing about Israel's faith was its development from very primitive beginnings to the "ethical monotheism" of the prophets. In seeking to explain the nature of the earliest stages of the faith and of the development to "higher" beliefs, the pagan environment was studied intensively for

---

[22] For the background of Deuteronomy in the old amphictyonic circles of North Israel see Gerhard von Rad, *Deuteronomium-Studien* (Göttingen: Vandenhoeck & Ruprecht, 1947).

[23] Eichrodt, *Theologie des Alten Testaments*, I, 15; cf. also A. B. Davidson, "Covenant," in James Hastings, ed., *A Dictionary of the Bible* (New York: Charles Scribner's Sons, 1898), I, 512.

[24] Eichrodt, op. cit., I, 23.

parallel conceptions, and the idea of progress was used as the clue to the significance of Israel's achievement.[25] This type of study has been exceedingly fruitful in showing Israel's dependence upon her environment and in demonstrating the fact that the Old Testament cannot be treated as a static literature without regard for its history. It is highly questionable, however, whether such study has succeeded in *explaining* the nature of the faith or in proving that the clue to Israel's achievement is to be found in *development*. From our present knowledge of the nature of polytheism it must rather be affirmed that the faith of Israel, even in the earliest days of the nation's history in Palestine, was so radically different from its environment that one has difficulty in seeing how it could have evolved by a gradual process from pagan religion. It can only be interpreted as a new creation, a mutation. It owed much to its environment, and in the successive crises of history it was refined and deepened. Yet its basic affirmations, in the framework of which the development took place, are so unique that a radical discontinuity with the environment rather than a simple continuity must be acknowledged.

1. The Contrast Between Pagan and Israelite Faith.—Contemporary religions were all natural religions—that is, the problem of human life was seen over against nature and the divine forces which personified the powers of nature. The realm of the gods was the realm of nature, and in the latter the life of man and society was embedded. The aim of human endeavor, therefore, was to achieve an integrated harmony with the natural powers of the universe on which man's life is utterly dependent. Even by the time of the Hebrew patriarchs the ancient world had left the stage of "primitive" religion far behind, and had achieved a highly developed and sophisticated polytheism. The belief in many gods was occasioned by the fact that the forces which man met in nature, and to which he had to adjust, were many. Yet the great achievement of polytheism was in its reduction of this plurality into a cosmic order, one in which there was coherence and meaning. The universe was seen to be organized into a cosmic state in which the various powers assumed the respective duties decreed for them in primordial time. Complementary forces were paired as male and female, and derivative powers were

interpreted as their offspring. The opposing or contradictory forces of nature were believed to be in yearly combat with one another, yet so balanced that at the end of the annual cycle of events life could begin afresh.[26]

The life of the gods was thus the life of nature, and within this cosmic rhythm man adjusted or integrated his own existence. In Babylon man was believed to have been created as the slave of the gods because those among the latter whose duty it was to look after the earthly economy were wearied by the onerous tasks of irrigation, seedtime, and harvest. The good life for man thus consisted in the obedience which a slave owed to his master. He showed this obedience by fitting himself willingly into the hierarchy of authority with which he was surrounded, beginning with his elders within the family. The bad man was the active, self-willed person who disrupted the authoritarian harmony, and the evil society was one in which the authorities, who were always right, were not respected or obeyed.[27] Polytheism with its emphasis upon harmony and integration was thus pre-eminently a religion of the *status quo,* in which sin was basically an aberration to be abhorred because it disrupted the natural integration and rhythm of the universe. Consequently, in no country has such a religion ever been the cause of a revolution in the social structure to provide justice for the common man. The ancient polytheisms were so tied to the political and social orders which they buttressed that they inevitably perished in the decline and fall of their nations.

In Israel religious faith was based upon an entirely different theological foundation. The God of Israel was not a natural god. Nature was his handiwork, and no force in it was more characteristic of him than another. As the Lord of nature he transcended it and thus transcended the whole realm of the pagan gods. He was one (cf. Deut. 6:4), not many; he possessed no consort and no offspring. The family principle was unneeded as a means of ordering the cosmic forces, because Yahweh himself was that order and the source of all power and creativity.

As indicated in pp. 349-51, Yahweh was known to Israel because of his great historical acts. The dominant themes of Israel's faith centered in the God who had vanquished Pharaoh by the use of natural signs and wonders, who

[25] For a well-written summary of this viewpoint as it was elaborated in nineteenth- and early twentieth-century scholarship see especially Harry Emerson Fosdick, *A Guide to the Understanding of the Bible* (New York: Harper & Bros., 1938); cf. also W. O. E. Oesterley and Theodore H. Robinson, *Hebrew Religion* (2nd ed.; New York: The Macmillan Co., 1937); I. G. Matthews, *The Religious Pilgrimage of Israel* (New York: Harper & Bros., 1947).

[26] See further H. and H. A. Frankfort, John A. Wilson, Thorkild Jacobsen, and William A. Irwin, *The Intellectual Adventure of Ancient Man* (Chicago: University of Chicago Press, 1946), chs. i-vii, xii.

[27] Cf. Jacobsen, in Frankfort, *et al., Intellectual Adventure of Ancient Man,* pp. 202-3; Henri Frankfort, *Ancient Egyptian Religion* (New York: Columbia University Press, 1948), ch. iii.

had chosen this people for himself, bound them to him in covenant, led them through the wilderness and into the Land of Promise. Israel's faith was thus grounded in what God had done and was yet to do in the sphere of human history. There was no primary interest in nature as such, except as it revealed God's creative power and as it was used by him to further his purposes in history. To think of him as originally a mountain god or fertility deity is simply to overlook the clear implications of the earliest poetry and confessional statements which indicate that Yahweh's primary sphere was history, nature playing a secondary role. It is true that the theophany on Mount Sinai traditionally was of such a character that Yahweh's appearances were frequently described in the categories of the storm (Exod. 19; Judg. 5; Hab. 3; etc.), together with many expressions which once were used of Baal in Canaan (e.g., Deut. 33:26; Ps. 68:4, 33). It is also true that Yahweh was seen as the power in nature's fertility and as the dispenser of her good things, even as was Baal (e.g., Gen. 49:25; Deut. 33:13-17; Ps. 29:9). Yet such language was used only to exalt his cosmic power; it was not the basic language of the faith.

In polytheism precisely the opposite was the case. There the original and primary metaphors by means of which the divine was apprehended were derived from nature. Metaphors drawn from society, such as king, lord, father, mother, judge, or craftsman, were important in the historical period but were nonetheless secondary and imposed on earlier forms. As a result, there was little stability in the conception of the outward form of the gods, theriomorphic and anthropomorphic forms abounding in mixed confusion. In Israel, by contrast, anthropomorphism was central because the polytheistic integration of the divine, natural, and human worlds was broken. Metaphors drawn from nature were secondary, not indigenous. In other words, the basic language of the Bible and of the Christian religion is an anthropomorphic language, drawn from the categories of personality and community. Confusion with metaphors drawn from other realms should be avoided because there is a basic relatedness and kinship between God and human life which does not exist in the same sense between God and nature.

Israel's knowledge of God was not based, therefore, on a numinous awareness of nature as in polytheism. It was founded in historical event and in special relationship with human existence. As a result, the problem of life was seen to be grounded in the realm of the will of man as it was related to the will of God. The polytheistic notion of the rhythmic harmony existing between nature, man, and deity was done away. Instead, a tension continually existed between the will of God and the will of man. Revolution in history was expected because God was at work mightily to effect his historical purposes. The religious literature of polytheism was accordingly of little use to Israel, because its mythology was essentially the description of the workings of nature, the powers of which were immanent and personified. In Israel religious literature took many forms, but its core was an interpreted history. Thus it was that biblical faith produced that conception of human history as a meaningful process en route to a goal which has exerted such a profound influence upon Western culture. Such a conception could never arise in polytheism with its concentration on the cyclical rhythm of nature and on the function of human existence as integration in this rhythm.

2. The Nature of Biblical Monotheism.—The transcendence of Yahweh over the realms of history and nature and thus over the sphere of the pagan gods meant, however, that the problem of the one in relation to the many forces of the cosmos was raised to a degree of acuteness unknown elsewhere. Polytheism by its very nature was as tolerant as the philosophies and mysticisms which later developed out of it. Travelers and sojourners from Canaan in Egypt, for example, found it comparatively easy to identify the chief gods of their homeland with certain of those in the new land and thus to acclimate themselves in the new religious environment. Beliefs, rites, and customs circulated with ease from one polytheistic sphere to another, particularly in those times when political conquest opened the avenues for cultural interchange. Yet in Israel from as early as the time of the conquest of Canaan one of the most important aspects of Yahweh was his "jealousy." This meant that he was intensely and zealously concerned for his own prerogatives. To him alone belonged all authority and power. No other deity was associated with him in his great acts (e.g., Deut. 32:12); no other deity was to be compared with him or placed on his level; no images whatsoever were to be made of him; nothing in the universe was worthy to be worshiped except him and him alone. He would not put up with a religious tolerance on the part of his people but insisted on their exclusive and undivided loyalty to him. As time passed and the issues were clarified, these assertions became increasingly explicit. The worship of man-made images was derided as foolish and dangerous; the gods of the nations were ridiculed as "no gods," until Second Isaiah forthrightly exclaimed that before Yahweh there was no god; neither shall there be after him. Besides him there is no savior; he will work and none can hinder it (Isa. 43:10-13).

Such claims for the exclusive prerogatives of one deity are unique and astonishing. In the vast sea of a tolerant polytheism this jealousy of Yahweh was such a new and startling conception that it is small wonder the Israelite common people sought to compromise it and numerous kings to qualify it. In the past most scholars have assumed that the greatest danger to Israelite faith lay in the temptation to identify Yahweh with Baal of Canaan. It can be shown, however, that a far greater danger lay in another direction. Of course, as in every religion, numerous pagan intrusions among the common people are to be traced to magical rather than to theological reasons. An illustration is the widespread use of figurines made in the image of the Canaanite fertility or mother goddess.[28] Yet this was not a danger to normative Yahwism. The real peril lay in the conception of the divine assembly—that is, in the heavenly host associated with Yahweh in his rule of the world.

References to this heavenly assembly are numerous. One need only recall the vision of the prophet Micaiah in I Kings 22:19-22, and the scene in Job 1–2. In this assembly Yahweh was enthroned as king and judge, presiding over the deliberations. The divine members of the council were called "angels" (properly "messengers"), "ministers," "servants," "holy ones," and "sons of God" (a borrowed Canaanite term meaning simply "divine beings"). That this conception of a divine assembly or council was present in early as well as in late Israel is evident from passages in the earliest strata of the Pentateuch and in early poetry.[29] Whether the meetings of the council were held only once a year on New Year's Day, as some scholars believe,[30] we have no certain knowledge, but it can be inferred from the evidence that at least one of the purposes of the meetings was to pronounce judgment upon sin and rebellion. The true prophet was one who heard the divine sentence and commission (cf. Isa. 6:8), whereas the false prophet did not (cf. Jer. 23:16-18).

The danger to Israel in this conception of the divine assembly lay in its similarity to divine assemblies in Canaan and in Babylon.[31] In Israel the undefined nature of the council's membership left the door open for a large amount of syncretism. While the exalted position of Yahweh himself was not changed, pagan deities could be introduced as members of his heavenly host. That this happened during the seventh century, for example, is clear from the statement that Manasseh erected altars to the host of heaven, meaning the sun, moon, and stars, in the very courts of the house of Yahweh (II Kings 21:3-5). Jeremiah refers to the people's burning incense on the housetops to all the host of heaven and pouring out drink offerings to other gods (Jer. 19:13). While the Deuteronomists and Jeremiah denounce such paganizing of the faith (e.g., Deut. 4:19), the heavenly bodies continued as members of the assembly in postexilic Judaism (cf. Neh. 9:6; Ps. 148:1-3), though it was not permitted to give them independent worship as had been done in the time of Manasseh.

Ps. 82 goes a step further by assuming that the gods of the nations are actually members of the host. This psalm pictures a heavenly assize in which God calls the gods to account for their misdeeds. He indicts them for their failure to provide justice for the poor and the oppressed (vss. 2-4). In an aside (vs. 5) he exclaims that they so wander about in the darkness of their understanding that the foundations of the universal order are shaken. As a result, he sentences them to die like a mortal (vss. 6-7). The final verse is the poet's prayer that God will arise and assume direct control over all the earth. We infer from this that the psalmist takes for granted the membership of pagan deities in the assembly; to them Yahweh has delegated authority over the nations. This recalls the reference in Deut. 32:8-9 which, according to the correct text preserved by the Septuagint, speaks of God's apportioning the nations and establishing the boundaries of the peoples according to the number of the divine beings, but has retained Israel as his special possession.[32] From such a conception it was but a step to the later belief in the patron angels whom God placed in charge of the nations (cf. Dan. 10:20).

The Israelite seems not to have conceived of an inanimate nature any more than did the polytheist. The prophets, for example, in proclaiming the divine indictment against the people called heaven, earth, and the everlasting

[28] See further, G. Ernest Wright, "How Did Early Israel Differ from Her Neighbors?" *The Biblical Archaeologist*, VI (1943), 16.

[29] Observe not only the frequent mention of angels but such a passage as Gen. 3:22: "Behold, the man is become as one of us," i.e., he has asserted himself to possess a knowledge like that possessed by a member of the heavenly council; cf. also Exod. 15:11 (LXX); Deut. 32:8-9 (LXX); 33:2-3; Pss. 29; 89:5-8.

[30] See especially Julian Morgenstern's articles in *Hebrew Union College Annual*, VI (1929), 1 ff.; XII-XIII (1937-38), 1 ff.; XIV (1939), 40 ff.

[31] Cf., Jacobsen in Frankfort, *et al.*, *Intellectual Adventure of Ancient Man*, chs. v-vi.

[32] Cf. also Deut. 33:3, the first phrase of which probably is to be rendered, "Yea, the ones who care for the peoples," i.e., the guardians of the peoples: see Frank M. Cross, Jr., and David Noel Freedman, "The Blessing of Moses," *Journal of Biblical Literature*, LXVII (1948), 193, 200.

mountains as witnesses (e.g., Mic. 6:2). It seems improbable that this is simply poetic language with nothing concrete behind it. Much more probable is the assumption that the heavenly court of Yahweh included the whole host of powers in heaven and earth. The ambiguity between such a conception and that of polytheism is one which many in Israel did not escape. Yet the difference is much more phenomenal. In normative Yahwism these powers were left undefined and not clearly distinguished from one another. Not one of them received any special attention. None were to be worshiped or provided with temple, altar, or cultus. Yahweh alone is the source of all power, authority, and creativity. All other heavenly beings owe their existence and functioning solely to him. They possess no independent validity and thus are not the focus of religious attention. It is a dangerous waste of time to give them heed, when all direction of life, of history, and of nature is in the hands of Yahweh, who demands exclusive worship. Israel's solution of the problem of the one in relation to the many was thus an intense, unswerving monolatry, any deviation from which was rebellion and idolatry.

During the last century the German scholar Max Müller invented the term "henotheism," which since that time has been widely used to designate the faith of early Israel. It means the worship of one god who is confined to one geographical area, yet an exclusive worship which does not deny the existence of other gods. The value of this term is that it prevents the interpretation of Israel's faith in terms of a philosophical monism. Yet actually it is an exceedingly poor term because it does not do justice to the cosmic power and rulership of Yahweh and to the complete devaluation of all other superhuman powers. Furthermore, it is impossible to trace a development in the Old Testament from "henotheism" to "monotheism"; indeed, if one were forced to contest the issue he might argue that the movement was in precisely the reverse direction, since the composition of the divine assembly undeniably grew more complex and syncretistic with the passing centuries. Either the whole of the Old Testament is "henotheistic" or else none of it is. Even Second Isaiah was no "monotheist" in the unitarian sense, for he believed in the heavenly host (i.e., the stars) as superhuman beings created and appointed to their work by Yahweh.[33]

On the other hand, the term "monotheism" places the emphasis upon that unique and astonishing feature of Israelite faith: the unity of all power and authority in Yahweh, who is so exalted that even the heavenly powers are called upon to praise him (cf. Pss. 103:20-21; 148:1-6), and who if he wills can destroy these powers (Ps. 82). Yet at no point in the Bible can "monotheism" be applied in a unitarian or Greek monistic sense. The word must be defined by the actual phenomena in Judaism, Christianity, and Islam, for it is intended to designate that which these three religions have in common over against all other religions. That is the transcendence of one God over nature and history; who is the giver and sustainer of all life; who is without sexuality or mythology; whose holiness does not permit images to be made of him; whose jealousy does not allow any worship except that directed to him alone; and whose superiority over all powers in the host of heaven and earth, including demons and false gods, is such as to make him completely unique and *sui generis*.[34]

If we are deprived of the use of "monotheism" for describing the faith of Israel in even its early stages, then we shall experience considerable difficulty in finding the exact point at which it can be used. The divine world grew steadily more complex in conception, including the elaboration of a considerable mythology of angels and demons in later Judaism. In the New Testament it is affirmed that God the Father as the ultimate authority in the universe has exalted Christ to his right hand and put all things, including the angels and host of heaven, in subjection to him (cf. Heb. 1–2). Such heavenly powers are to receive no independent worship, for this would spoil the "simplicity that is in Christ" (cf. Col. 2:18). There is yet another realm of the superhuman, however, composed of Satan together with the principalities and powers of darkness against which we wrestle (cf., e.g., Eph. 6:12), though the victory is assured through Christ. The attitude of the apostle Paul toward the pagan deities indicates that one cannot force a philosophical monism on him any more than on the Israelite of old. In I Cor. 10:19-21 the existence of such deities is not altogether denied; they are simply degraded to the rank of demons. With the development of the host of Satan there was no longer any need to conceive of the gods as members of Yahweh's assembly with whom he was displeased, as in Ps. 82. If their existence was not completely ignored, one might, if

[33] See Charles Cutler Torrey, *The Second Isaiah* (New York: Charles Scribner's Sons, 1928), pp. 309, 376-77 (on Isa. 40:26; 48:13).

[34] The greatest defense of the use of the term "monotheism" in this sense for even the earliest religion of the nation of Israel is that of W. F. Albright, *From the Stone Age to Christianity* (Baltimore: Johns Hopkins Press, 1940), chs. iv-v; cf. also his *Archaeology and the Religion of Israel* (Baltimore: Johns Hopkins Press, 1942), p. 116.

pressed, assume them to be members of Satan's host. It is surely obvious that no dictionary ever intended to exclude early Christianity from its definition of monotheism in favor of an abstract monism as conceived in later philosophy. Indeed, the trinitarian Christian has always and will ever resist the attempt so to exclude it.[35]

Yet we must beware that such a discussion as the foregoing does not lead us to a betrayal of the real nature of biblical faith. The significance of the latter does not lie in a developing human conception of deity or in an "ethical monotheism." It is a confessional proclamation of the sovereignty of God and of his saving acts in man's behalf, a proclamation which demands of its hearers that they make a decision as to where they stand in relation to this sovereignty. For God is to be known not in the first instance as the power in nature's rhythmic cycle, nor as the absolute of metaphysical speculation, but as the "Lord" who "chose" Israel for himself and as the "Father" of our "Lord" Jesus Christ.

D. The Being of God. 1. The God Who Acts. —The dominant impression given by the Old Testament about God is the concreteness, definiteness, and energy of his being. His ever-present power is to be seen and felt in all movement of nature and history. His dynamic moving vigor stands in complete contrast to the Greek "unmoved Mover," to the mystic's Source of illumination and beatification, and to every form of deism or philosophical abstraction. He is "the *living* God" in contrast to the dying-rising deities of the natural cycle in polytheism. The idols of the nations know nothing and can do nothing; Yahweh alone is the source of both creative and destructive activity. Baal may be away on a journey or asleep (I Kings 18:27), but Yahweh never sleeps (cf. e.g., Ps. 121); his directing presence is the comfort of the faithful, the terror of the wicked, and the problem for which Job seeks an answer (Job 7:17-21).

The existence of God was never doubted in Israel; but this powerful, direct, energetic, and pervasive activity of God was and has always been the chief source of men's difficulty with biblical faith. The fool who says there is no God (Pss. 14:1; 53:1) was actually calling God's works, not his existence, into question. He was in the same position as those of whom Jeremiah speaks, "It is not he; neither shall evil come upon us; neither shall we see sword nor famine" (Jer. 5:12). The tension which God's ever-seeing eye places at the heart of existence led men to attempt an escape into deistic idolatry. The practical atheism of the sinner who claims

[35] For a more detailed review of the point of view outlined in this section see G. Ernest Wright, *The Old Testament Against Its Environment* (Chicago: Henry Regnery Co., 1950), ch. i.

to believe that God does not see him and does not act directly in the affairs of this earth has always been the simplest means of escape from this biblical conception of the active, living God.

In the philosophies and mysticisms of Greece and India, time and history are without significance except as they are the source of evil and misery from which man must escape to find the good life. Deity cannot be involved in the corroding movement of earthly life; if it were, it could be neither absolute nor good. The Bible in the most daring fashion asserts by contrast the meaningfulness of history and the dynamic working of God within it. Man in history has betrayed his destiny by sin; but God's purpose in his earthly creation is not defeated. His directing presence is the ground of man's hope, for his redemptive activity is never ceasing. He adjusts that activity to the contingencies of earthly need, yet never compromising his being, his holiness, his sovereignty, his righteousness.

2. The Anthropomorphism of God.—The Old Testament makes no attempt to define God's being. Throughout he is simply depicted as a person by means of a free and frank use of anthropomorphic language. To be sure, there are various levels of anthropomorphism; a difference exists between the simple story form of Gen. 2–3 and the more abstract and theologically self-conscious presentation of Gen. 1 and Ezekiel. Yet this difference is actually a minor one of degree. In general, God is depicted as possessing practically all the characteristics of a human being, including bodily form and personality, though excluding sex.

In the past there has been a tendency to assume that this aspect of the Old Testament indicates a fairly primitive level of religious conception; growth to a "higher" level of thought, it has been claimed, came with the increasing emphasis on the spirituality of God. This is an exceedingly doubtful assumption. Nowhere in the Bible can there be said to be a *doctrine* of God's spirituality, unless one were to except John 4:24. The spirit of God is not to be identified with God himself. The latter is conceived in personal, even corporeal terms, and perhaps the most vivid example and the climax of this anthropomorphism is to be found in the doctrine of the Incarnation. In pp. 358-59 something of the significance of this vocabulary drawn from human analogy was suggested. God is not to be depicted by a mixture of metaphors drawn from nature as in polytheism; he is not conceived as an abstract idea or principle; he cannot be apprehended primarily by means of an undefined analogy drawn from wind or breath (hence "spirit"). He is a living, active, forceful personality whom men can meet, know, and worship, before whom they can bow in confession of sin and not be broken as before an inexorable law of fate, but in whom there is both justice and forgiveness.

To be sure, anthropomorphism has its limits which many in Israel transgressed. The second commandment (Exod. 20:4; cf. Deut. 4:15-19) thus forbids all attempts to confine or materialize God's being. He cannot be seen by human eye, and thus in theophany his presence is hidden by a blinding brilliance, called his "glory," or by a cloud or smoke (Exod. 19:9; 24:15-18; Num. 10:11, 34; I Kings 8:10-11; Isa. 6:4; Ezek. 1:26-28). He does not lie or change his mind as does man (Num. 23:19; I Sam. 15:29; Mal. 3:6). The contrast between the weakness of man and the strength of God can be said to be the same as that between flesh and unconfined spirit (Isa. 31:3). Indeed, God is God and not man (Hos. 11:9), but he reveals himself as a personality whom men can know and describe as being known in the language familiar to them.

3. The Holiness of God.—The conception of holiness was that which most distinguished the divine from the human. It is exceedingly difficult to define, and the etymology of the Hebrew word, even if certainly known—which it is not—could not provide much assistance. It is rooted in man's knowledge of *mysterium tremendum* and of the "numinous," to use the terms of Rudolf Otto.[36] As such it defies a completely rational analysis. It is that which makes God deity and without which he would not be deity. Thus it is the essence of the divine which separates him from the human. In primitive religion and in polytheism it is at the center of religious attention and known as the mysterious, positive power which breaks into the world, often in the most unexpected ways. It produces awe, wonder, and fear. It leads men to elaborate devices which are thought to control this awesome dynamism. Certain things are taboo; care must be taken to separate clean and unclean, pure and impure, the holy and the profane.

The basis of holiness is thus quite different from morality; this is true both in paganism and in Israel. In the latter, relics of the primitive, nonmoral dynamism survived in the priestly cultus and in the popular interpretation of certain mysterious events (cf. I Sam. 5–6). Yet holiness as the essence of God's being was qualified by the other attributes of his character, and thus differed from pagan holiness primarily as the total being of Yahweh differed from that of the gods. Yahweh's holiness possessed a con-

[36] *The Idea of the Holy,* tr. John W. Harvey (London: Oxford University Press, 1923).

sistency unknown elsewhere because his character and purpose were consistent. As in paganism, anything especially separated and related to God derived its holiness from him. In the case of cultic objects, rites, persons, and places of worship this derived holiness seems to have differed only in the sense that the total meaning of the cultus in Israel had a different meaning than in paganism (see pp. 375-87). Yet in the case of the people as a whole, holiness expressed both the relatedness to Yahweh as known in election and the obedience which the Lord required of his servants as made clear in the covenant. To be holy as God is holy was thus the reason for obedience to God's law in the Holiness Code (Lev. 17–26); and from this viewpoint the whole aim of Israel's existence was to be as a kingdom of priests, a holy nation (Exod. 19:6), sharing in a measure God's holiness because they were faithful to his covenant. Hence in Israel the dominant conception of holiness was no longer that of an irrational, impersonal dynamism in nature; instead it was controlled by the knowledge of God's personal and consistent character and imparted by God to those things in creation which he chose to separate to himself. His being was holy and the source of holiness, and thus distinct from anything in creation; yet he was also personal, and holiness was the mystery of his personality wherein he willed to be Lord and Lord alone.

4. The Name and Attributes of God.—The revelation of God's name was a further sign of his personality, and a warning against all mystical and philosophical misunderstanding of his being. That this revelation occurred at the time of the Exodus is the historical assumption of the Elohist and priestly writers (Exod. 3:13-15; 6:3). The pronunciation of the name was probably "Yahweh," but its meaning has been much debated. At the present time, however, by far the best linguistic arguments have been marshaled in favor of the view that the word is the causative of the verb "to be," meaning "he causes to be," that is, he is the creator.[37]

In possession of the name of God, the Israelite worshiped with confidence in God's knowableness. He used the name in prayers and oaths, in blessing and cursing in war and triumph. It was not to be used lightly or in false swearing (Exod. 20:7). Places of worship bear the name, and the worshiper trusts that God will hear and answer prayer when offered

[37] See Albright, *From Stone Age to Christianity,* pp. 197-99; and Albright's review of B. N. Wambacq, *L'épithète divine Jahvé Seba'ôt, Journal of Biblical Literature,* LXVII (1948), 379-80. The phrase in Exod. 3:14 ("I AM THAT I AM") in its original form in the third person would mean, according to this view, "He causes to be that which is," i.e., "He brings what exists into being."

in his name and directed toward the sacred sanctuary (cf. e.g., I Kings 8:28 ff.). The close connection between God's name and being can be understood only in the light of the religious thought of the ancient world, wherein the name of a deity or even of his temple often possessed independent mythological significance and could be used in multitudinous ways, especially in the realm of magic. In Israel magic dropped into the background; and while the name continued to play a vital role in cultic activity, it was primarily conceived as the gracious revelation of the covenant Lord whereby he could be definitely worshiped.[38] The large number of epithets and appellations used in addition to the proper name served the same purpose, most of them emphasizing certain particular aspects of God's being or activity.[39]

The so-called attributes of God, such as his justice, love or grace, jealousy, anger, wrath and vengeance, are also drawn from the category of personality. As the living personal God engaged in a creative, historical work, his active pleasure and displeasure were vividly expressed by the language of human analogy. The one word which more than any other summarizes the totality of God's attributes is "righteousness"; Yahweh pre-eminently is the "righteous God" ($'el\hat{o}h\hat{i}m$ $\c{s}add\hat{i}q$). The term was derived from the realm of jurisprudence; it is the "right" to which one is legally entitled. Yahweh is righteous, therefore, because he helps his people to their "right." Conversely, he is righteous because he actively shows his "wrath" and his judgment upon the wicked who are his enemies and who thwart his purposes. In the deliverance from Egypt God's righteousness was known as his saving power directed to a weak and de-

[38] Cf. Eichrodt, *Theologie des Alten Testaments*, I, 96-97.

[39] A number of them were borrowed from Canaanite religion, e.g., *Elohim*, the most general and abstract of all names used for God (for its Canaanite background see G. Ernest Wright, "The Significance of the Temple in the Ancient Near East, Part III: The Temple in Palestine-Syria," *The Biblical Archaeologist*, VII [1944], 69), *El* (both the general Semitic word for "god" and the name of the head of the Canaanite pantheon), *Elyon* ("exalted"), *Adon* ("Lord") and *Baal* ("Lord"). The last mentioned does not appear in the Pentateuch; it came to be used as the common surrogate for the Canaanite storm-god, Hadad, only after about the sixteenth century B.C. It was used in Israel of Yahweh during the early centuries of the nation's life in Palestine, but after the Elijah-Elisha movement in the ninth century it dropped rapidly from use because of its dangerous connotations (cf., e.g., Hos. 2:17). *Shaddai*, commonly translated "almighty," was derived from a Mesopotamian word and evidently meant originally "mountaineer." It is unknown in Canaanite religion and was probably brought by the patriarchs to Palestine as an epithet of the "god of the fathers" (so P in Gen. 17:1; Exod. 6:3; see Albright, *From Stone Age to Christianity*, pp. 184-85; also, "The Names Shaddai and Abram," *Journal of Biblical Literature*, LIV (1935), 180-93).

fenseless people. Consequently, throughout Israel's history God was looked upon as zealously concerned with the poor, the weak, the outcast, who had nothing else to depend upon than his righteousness. Thus salvation and righteousness in many passages are synonyms.[40] Yet the work of salvation is not conceived apart from God's active warfare against evil, and this also is his righteousness. The word "vengeance" has the same double meaning. When applied to God, it does not refer to an unjust vindictiveness. On the one hand, it is his salvation (cf. Isa. 35:4; 61:2); on the other, his just retribution for the wicked (cf. Isa. 59:17; Jer. 46:10; 51:6).

Perhaps the best description of the personal character of God as known from his historical acts is to be found in an old liturgical confession embedded in Exod. 34:6-7 and quoted at least in part in many subsequent passages (e.g., II Chr. 30:9; Neh. 9:17, 31; Joel 2:13; Jonah 4:2; Ps. 86:15; etc.); "Yahweh, Yahweh, a compassionate and gracious God, slow to anger, abundant in *hésedh* [gracious loyalty to his covenanted promises] and fidelity, keeping *hésedh* for thousands, forgiving iniquity and rebellion and sin, though by no means acquitting [the guilty], visiting the iniquity of the fathers upon the children and upon the children's children unto the third, even the fourth [generation]." We should note here the emphasis upon the gracious, loyal, and forgiving nature of God, an emphasis which stands at the center of the Old as well as of the New Testament. Yet this divine grace is a two-edged sword which appears in the human scene as the power working both for salvation and for judgment, that salvation may be accomplished. Thus the man of faith worships a gracious and righteous God who responds to human need in a personal way. To the penitent he offers forgiveness and a new chance to accept his commission. Yet he will never rest in his warfare against the wicked; his righteous and gracious holiness permits of nothing else. Were it not so, man's hope of earth would indeed be futile.

E. God and the World. 1. The Relationship Between Creator and Creation.—The God who formed Israel into a nation, through it to establish his sovereignty over the lives of all men, stood in a completely free and independent relationship to human history. At the same time he was the creator of the world and stood in the same unconfined and unlimited relationship to the universe. The unity of his will and being was the ground of the world's unity and, therefore, of the inner relationship between

[40] This is especially true in Second Isaiah; cf. Isa. 41:10; 42:6; 45:8; 51:5-6; but see also Isa. 11:4; 32:17; Mic. 6:5.

nature and history. In Israel, accordingly, the conception of a universal theogony or dualism of opposing forces was excluded as a necessary means of explaining the origin and movement of the world. So also was every form of pantheism in which God and the world are in some measure identified, or in which the divine is believed to be immanent in the evolving process, a principle, whether personalized or impersonal, pulsating through the movement of nature and giving it form and coherence. By New Testament times, it is true, a dualistic element had been introduced through the development of the doctrine of Satan in intertestamental Judaism. But this was a cosmic projection of the inner spiritual and moral struggle of man. Satan was not conceived as a natural power in the sense that the opposition forces of polytheism were; he is allowed his temporary opportunities and victories, but his kingdom is not eternal. Yet in the Old Testament even this amount of dualism is not present; the few references to Satan belong to postexilic literature in which he is still a member in good standing of God's heavenly council, a tester and tempter of man (I Chr. 21:1; Job 1-2; Zech. 3:1-2).

Israel's conception of the universe was so closely related to the ancient conceptual world that the creation of matter *ex nihilo* was not a question which yet was raised. When the subject became an issue under the influence of Greek thought, it was promptly settled (II Macc. 7:28 is the first such reference). For the most part, God's creation is described by the use of very simple, anthropomorphic words (e.g., "to make," "form," "establish"), though the priestly author of Gen. 1 does attempt a more abstract presentation by using the term *bārā'* and the conception of the divine creative *word*.

The Israelite view of the world was essentially that of the other peoples of the time. Heaven was not a limitless space. It was erected as a vault over the earth; it was a solid substance, a "firmament," which kept out the primeval waters and thus left a clear space for the sky and the dry earth (Gen. 1:6-10; Isa. 40:22). There was evidently a series of heavens (Deut. 10:14; I Kings 8:27; Ps. 148:4); the number of them is not mentioned, though in Babylon and in Judaism seven were distinguished. In the highest heaven was the palace (temple) and throne of God. Both heaven and earth were believed to be supported on pillars or mountains; those supporting the earth reached down into the waters of the underworld ocean, so that in poetry the earth could be said to have been founded on the seas (Pss. 24:2; 136:6). Below the earth, yet still associated with it, was the underworld, Sheol, the home of the "shades" of the dead.

The whole of this universe was God's creation, and its stability was due to his continuing and sustaining power. Life was possible because God created and preserved a space for it in the midst of the primeval waters, a space which could be done away at any moment were it not for his gracious will to preserve it (cf. Gen 6-9). The utter dependence of all life upon the creative will and sustaining energy of God was thus the Hebrew emphasis.

In Israel, however, God as creator cannot be understood apart from the conception of God as "Lord." As the originator of the universe and all its life, he was its sovereign. The life of the creature was not conceived to exist by its own natural resources; it lived in relationship to the divine Person and the events of its existence had significance only in the context of this dependent relationship. Thus creation bore a close connection to history; it was the starting point of history. There was no pessimism regarding the worth of God's work such as is so frequently encountered in other religions; it was all "good" (Gen. 1). Accordingly, it was a proper setting for the "good" life. The material nature of man was not an evil thing which separated him from God; man's trouble lay in the realm of the mind and the emotions, in his refusal to accept or remain in his dependent relationship. Consequently, God's creative work is felt to imply a teleology in the world order which gives the clue to the meaning of its history. The words "in the beginning" involve a conception of "the end of days," [41] and thus a meaningful historical process directed by the divine Sovereign. In prophetic theology the original creation was conceived to have been so marred by human sin that God's judgment would take the form of a destruction of the world order (Isa. 2:21; 34:4; 51:6; Jer. 4:23-26; Amos 7:4; Zeph. 1:15), though not a complete return to the original chaos. Beyond this will come God's erection of a new heaven and a new earth (Isa. 11:6-9; 51:6; 60:20; 65:17; 66:22; Ezek. 47; Amos 9:13). God the creator, the judge, and the redeemer are one and the same God, as will become perfectly clear in the new creation. Creation and history, therefore, are involved in one another because God is the Lord of both.

2. The Revelation of God in the World.—If, however, the Israelite conception set a gulf between God and his creation, if God's being was in no way confined in or a part of nature, how did he make himself and his will known upon the earth? One means, of course, was through

[41] Cf. Ps. 102:26-27; see Eichrodt, *Theologie des Alten Testaments*, II, 53.

his steady support of the cycle of nature; but that which received most emphasis were the "signs" and "wonders." Any spectacular happening in history, but particularly in nature, was a "sign," a revelation of God. We today are inclined to define miracle as an event which contravenes natural law, and we have diligently sought to reduce this element in the Bible by means of our new knowledge of nature. Yet in the Bible a miracle is something quite different. It is any spectacular happening or "wonder" which is a "sign" of God's working. Most of these "wonders" are capable of a double explanation (cf. John 12:28-32), but from the biblical viewpoint they cannot be explained away. The "signs" and "wonders" of God in nature are significant revelations and as much the normal language of God as the dependable order of nature. The reason is that nature is not only the arena of history but the instrument of history and thus of God's historical work.[42]

The gulf which separated God and creation was bridged, however, in an even more important way by God himself. That was his direct communication and intercourse with human life. The language of revelation was simple and concrete. For the most part God "spoke" or revealed himself (the reflexive of the verb "to see," i.e., he permitted himself to be seen), and men "heard" or "saw." Thus Yahweh spoke to Abram and Abram obeyed "as the LORD had spoken unto him" (Gen. 12:4). So also God spoke directly to the prophet, his messenger, and the latter proclaimed, "Thus saith the Lord." Dreams and visions were regarded as important mediums of revelation and were emphasized by those who were more self-conscious about the problem of immediacy and manner of God's communication (cf. especially the Elohist writer in Gen. 15:1; Num. 12:6).

Yet in whatever manner God appeared, he did so in order to speak and to have his "word" heard and obeyed. God's "word" was one of the most general terms used by Israel for revelation. This word came to all the great leaders of Israel; in legal circles it was the law, the commands of God; in Deuteronomic circles it was the clue to the meaning of Israel's history, for as proclaimed by the succession of prophets it was the means whereby God directed the course of his people's life (Deut. 18:15-19; cf. Jer. 7:13, 25-26). In the psychology of the ancient world a person's word was an extension of his personal presence, and this was the case with the word of Yahweh in Israel. It was endowed with the personal power and planned activity of God himself (Isa. 45:23; 55:10-11). He sends his

word and the afflicted are healed or delivered (Ps. 107:20), the prophet's heart burns as with fire (Jer. 20:9), yet with joy and rejoicing (Jer. 15:16), the people despise it to their own hurt (Isa. 5:24), whereas it should be hidden in the heart (Ps. 119:11), obeyed and praised (Ps. 56:10). Yet there is no clear hypostatization of the word in Israel; it was not so separated from God as to be an independent being, though in the later Jewish Targums it seems to have been so used in order to avoid the frank anthropomorphism of the sacred narratives.

The gulf between God and his creation was further bridged by the conceptions of God's presence, his angel, his spirit, and his wisdom. The idea of God's presence or face (*pānîm*) originated in paganism wherein it was a concrete reality in the deity's statue in his temple. In Israel, while there was no such materialization of the divine being, yet his presence was still to be met in the sanctuary (see pp. 378-79), and his face would shine or be lifted up upon the sincere and contrite worshiper (cf. Num. 6:24-26). To be sure, no one could see God's being; it was always hidden by his glory (see above, p. 363). Yet in the context of the *pānîm* it could be said that one might see God "face to face," though such an expression could not be taken in a materially literal sense, unless the case of Moses was in some measure an exception (Exod. 33:11; Deut. 34:10; but cf. Num. 14:14; Deut. 4:12; 5:4; Ezek. 20:35). In other words, the use of the term "presence" does not explain, it simply affirms the present reality of God with his people.

God's angel, spirit, and wisdom were separate entities which he created, though as such they must largely be considered in function as extensions of his active personality. The angel as his messenger did not possess an independent personality. God "appeared" to Abraham (Gen. 18:1), but the following verse speaks of the three angelic visitors who were evidently considered as the mediums of that "appearance." Throughout Gen. 18–19, verses in which the visitors are said to speak and to carry out the destruction of Sodom and Gomorrah alternate with verses in which God speaks and himself destroys the cities. After Jacob's nocturnal wrestling with the heavenly messenger, he believed he had seen God himself "face to face" (Gen. 32:22-30). Thus God's word and action are so completely identical with those of the angel that the independent personality of the latter fades into insignificance. Only during the intertestamental period do the personalities of separate angels, such as Gabriel, Michael, and Raphael appear to have been distinguished. Consequently, the conception of angel must be said to be nothing more than a theological

---

[42] See Paul S. Minear, *Eyes of Faith* (Philadelphia: Westminster Press, 1946), pp. 183-97; Robinson, *Inspiration and Revelation in O.T.*, pp. 34-48.

means of relating God to his world and of describing how that relation was achieved.

The spirit of God was another such means, though appearing much more frequently than angel. Unlike the latter, it was not conceived in anthropomorphic terms. It was primarily the means whereby the empowering activity of God *within* man was expressed. Consequently, it was conceived after the analogy of wind (the primary meaning of the Hebrew *rûah*), rather than of the human body. It was God's agent acting within man, and thus by simple extension it could be conceived also as the life-producing energy in man. On the one hand, when the spirit entered the prophet, he prophesied (cf., e.g., Num. 11:24-29; cf. I Sam. 10:10; Joel 2:28); when it entered the man of valor, or any servant of God, he was empowered to do the work God meant him to do (Judg. 6:34; cf. 14:6, 19; Isa. 42:1); indeed its presence in the midst of Israel had led and saved the people in the days of old and would do so yet again (Isa. 63:11; Hag. 2:5). On the other hand, it is God who gives man his breath or spirit (Isa. 42:5; Zech. 12:1; Job 27:3), that is, the mysterious principle of life, which, if God takes away, means death for a man (Job 34:14; Ps. 104:29-30). Consequently, in the new aeon to come God's spirit will be poured out on creation and make all things new, including a new spirit in man (Isa. 32:15; 44:3; Ezek. 11:19; 36:26-27).[43]

The personification of wisdom as that by which God created and ordered the world seems to have been a subject of importance only to a small group in later Israel (Prov. 8:22-31; cf. Job 28; Ps. 104:24). Yet in Jewish and Christian theology it played a significant role; among other things, it was identified with the spirit of God (Dan. 5:11; Wisd. Sol. 9:17) and with the Word or law of God (Ps. 111:10; 119:97-104; Ecclesiasticus: Prologue; Baruch 3:9–4:4). As such, it formed an important bridge between the biblical and Hellenic worlds, especially in the doctrine of the logos. Thus John 1 could adopt the form of the latter but fill it with the meaning derived from the pre-existent wisdom-word and identify it with Christ.

In the Old Testament, therefore, and in the New as well, the problem of transcendence and immanence in the relationship of God to his creation was not keenly felt. Consequently, it was not a major issue to the faith in the sense that it was later to become in Judaism and Christian philosophy. The independent, personal, and creative activity of God was so conceived as to combine his transcendence with his lordship over the world. An unbridgeable gulf existed between his being and his creation, but it was one which formed no barrier to the exercise of his sovereignty. He bridged it as he himself chose and in ways which permitted men to employ a variety of conceptual language in depicting it.

F. God and Man. 1. Man in the Image of God.—The central fact about the place of man in creation according to the Old Testament is the dignity and honor accorded him by God. As Ps. 8 affirms, God has made man almost like a divine being ("a little lower than the angels"), has given him the insignia of royalty ("crowned him with glory and honor"), and has placed the whole of the earthly creation under his rule. This teaching is precisely that of Gen. 1, in which man is said to be formed "in the image of God," a phrase in some measure equivalent to "a little lower than the angels" in Ps. 8:5, and in which he is commanded by God "to have dominion" over all creatures, indeed actively "to subdue" the earth. In Gen. 2 the centrality and lordship of man in creation are likewise affirmed, though in a different manner, by a story in which all the animals are brought to man that he may give them names; yet among them there is none which can be "a help meet for him." Thus man, though a part of creation and made from "the dust of the ground" with the mysterious life principle "breathed" into him by God, is nevertheless separate and distinct from all other creatures of God. He alone, according to Gen. 1, is made "in the image of God."

This phrase, though it occurs elsewhere in the Old Testament only in Gen. 5:1-3 and 9:6, has rightly been considered in Christian theology as an excellent statement of the biblical conception of man. Yet its precise meaning in the biblical setting is by no means easy to define. The Hebrew word "image" means primarily a definite material object which is made to look like or to represent something else; it is the customary word for an idol. How can man be an "image" of God in this sense? Does it mean that man physically resembles the corporeal form of God? Or is the word given an extended meaning and intended to convey only a spiritual resemblance? A moment's reflection on the nature of man, as the Bible conceives it, will make it evident that we are not permitted to phrase the problem in this way.

For the most part, we are accustomed to think of man in the dualistic terms derived from Greek philosophy, in which the spiritual and material natures are sharply distinguished. In the Bible no such dualism exists. Man is a vital unity composed of various interdependent elements. To be sure, we read of the "flesh," "soul," and "spirit" of man, but these are not

43 See further, Eichrodt, *Theologie des Alten Testaments*, II, 18-31; Robinson, *Inspiration and Revelation in O.T.*, pp. 50-53, 74-77.

independent, clearly distinguishable or definable entities. The word "flesh" does denote properly the material nature of man's being. The word *néphesh*, translated "soul," is most commonly used to designate a person's vitality, the total self as a self-conscious unit which is activated by the mysterious principle of life; thus it does not have reference to the "soul" at all in the Greek sense of the term. The "spirit" of man refers to the immaterial part of man's being. It is the breath, the source of which is God; it also is used of the psychical aspects of life, including the whole range of man's emotional and mental life. There are many other words, however, particularly the various parts of the body, which are credited with psychical functions. Chief among them may be mentioned the "heart," which is the seat or instrument of mind and will and thus the center of psychical activity, and the bowels or kidneys, among the most sensitive parts of the body in which the emotions were believed to be concealed.

It is obvious from the above that most of these terms which depict human psychology overlap considerably and defy clear definition. Man was conceived as a unified psycho-physical organism, and thus nearer to the point of view of modern psychology than to that of the Greeks. The psychical functions of the ego were conceived as finding expression in the various parts of the body and to be located in them. Thus we may say with H. Wheeler Robinson, "The Hebrew conceived man as an animated body and not as an incarnate soul." [44]

Man "in the image of God" means, therefore, that there is a correspondence between the total being of God and the total being of man. The thought cannot be confined to physical resemblance; indeed, it is improbable that the physical is in the center of attention. Instead, the emphasis must lie on the self-conscious, self-directing vitality which constitutes the sum of personal being. This, of course, does not exclude the corporeal because the Hebrews did not conceive of pure being in spiritual terms apart from material form. Yet it does mean that the "image" in man must primarily be concerned with the deeper aspects of personal being and not merely with the superficial. [45]

This is made quite clear in Gen. 1 and Ps. 8,

[44] *Inspiration and Revelation in O.T.*, p. 70. For a treatment of Hebrew psychology see especially Aubrey R. Johnson, *The Vitality of the Individual in the Thought of Ancient Israel* (Cardiff: University of Wales Press, 1949); cf. also H. Wheeler Robinson, *The Christian Doctrine of Man* (Edinburgh: T. & T. Clark, 1911), ch. i; Eichrodt, *Theologie des Alten Testaments*, II, 58-77; Pedersen, *Israel, Its Life and Culture I-II*, 99 ff.

[45] Contrast, e.g., Hermann Gunkel, *Genesis* (5th ed.; Göttingen: Vandenhoeck & Ruprecht, 1922; Göttinger Handkommentar zum Alten Testament"), pp. 110-12; but cf. von Rad, *Das erste Buch Mose*, pp. 44-47.

where as a consequence of the divine resemblance in man the latter is enabled to assume the lordship of the earthly creation. As God is Lord of the universe, so man is lord of the created earth, crowned with glory and honor as befits his lordship. This implies a consciousness of the radical difference existing between the animals and man as personal being. Man is endowed with a freedom and capacity for self-direction which enable him to plan and execute his plans. Furthermore, as personal being he can respond to the personal direction of God and assume office as God's steward or vicegerent on earth. Implied in Gen. 1 and made perfectly clear in Gen. 2–3 is the dependent and responsible relationship existing between man and God. Man's lordship is to be exercised in the context of God's lordship and in the understanding of the dependent relationship. Thus God has the right to command, while man must obey. This places a limit upon man's freedom, yet only within this limitation can man find the meaning of his freedom and of life itself.

The freedom given man by God, therefore, is a freedom to rule the earth. The capacity which makes it possible for him to do this is, at least in part, the "image" of God in him. Yet the freedom accorded man was meant by God to be used properly. It is a positive, not a negative attribute. For each order of human freedom in the Bible there exists a corresponding order of responsibility. Each area of freedom exists *in order that* the corresponding responsibility can be assumed. Thus freedom is limited by the responsibility conferred with it. Each area of freedom has its law, its order, its divine command. Consequently, freedom and election or calling go together. The first witnesses to the mystery of creation in God's "image"; the second, to the mystery of communion and dependence.

2. Man as Sinner Against God.—The dignity, nobility, and freedom of man constitute one of the Bible's primary assumptions. It should be pointed out, however, that these human attributes are not the focus of the Bible's attention. The peculiar worth of man is taken for granted, and occasionally God is praised for it (cf., e.g., Ps. 8) ; but the *problem* of man is the Bible's central concern. Why is this noble creature of God confronted with so much misery, trouble, and sorrow? He owes his life to God and his continued existence is wholly dependent upon the continued activity of God's spirit (cf. Job 10:12; 12:10; Ps. 104:29-30; Ezek. 37:14; Zech. 12:1) which, when taken away, leaves him without his vitality so that he dies (cf., e.g., Job 17:1; Eccl. 12:7; cf. Deut. 32:39; I Sam. 2:6) . His greatest desire should be to be "bound in the bundle of life with the LORD" (I Sam. 25:

29). If he is so bound, then he will walk with Yahweh in fullness of life, experiencing good health and material prosperity. Yet he lives so much of his existence apart from this fullness of life. The reason is that "walking with God" involves both an inner and outer obedience in which man's total being finds its true unity, happiness, and fulfillment. Apart from this obedience there is no communion; and apart from communion there is only disintegration, misery, and death (the loss of vitality). It is the mystery of the freedom given man that by it he is enabled to find both true life in communion with God and also his own disintegration and destruction. On the one hand, man wants to obey and to live in communion with God, but on the other, he desires to be "like God" (Gen. 3:5, 22). But the self-assertion in the latter is a denial of the former and thus one of the chief roots of sin. Furthermore, man wants to "walk with God," but to do so demands a firm belief in God's promises at times when such faith is difficult. Thus Sarah, having heard the promise of a son, could not believe but attempted to take matters into her own hands (Gen. 16). Sin is thus born in the doubt, nourished by anxiety, which leads to a self-assertion that does not wait on God.

Man's problem is further complicated by the fact that he does not exist in isolation before God. He has been placed by God in a community, apart from which he is not his true self. In Gen. 1:27-28 this is made clear by the use of the term "man" for the species, which is divided into male and female, to whom the command to "be fruitful, and multiply" is given. In Gen. 2:18-24 the life of the individual man is seen to be incomplete apart from woman, and the two in marriage are to be "one flesh"—that is, as one person. In the order of creation, therefore, the individual is seen to exist in the context of the family and in relation to the "thou" of the opposite sex. Such a conception immediately cuts the ground from under a whole realm of later asceticism wherein sex is considered as in its very nature a primary source of evil. Yet the freedom of man is limited by the necessity laid upon him in creation to live in the context of the family relationship and in obedience to the will of God governing it.

Furthermore, the family unit does not exist in isolation but is set within the larger groupings of society and nation. God's law in the covenant thus further delimits the freedom of the individual in the interests of peace and harmony within the group. Yet man must live in society for apart from it his life has no meaning. "Walking with God" involves, therefore, a type of obedience which involves the twofold love of God and the neighbor. Man's problem in this case is to love both as himself, and his sin is the self-assertion in which self-love denies and betrays the other two.

Thus the roots of sin in the Old Testament appear to be numerous. In Gen. 3; 11; Isa. 10:13-16; Ezek. 28:2-10; etc., we see the picture of man striving to be "like God," exhibiting his lordly power without relation to God. In Genesis, Exodus, and Numbers numerous incidents illustrate the lack of faith in God's promises on the part of the elect, with the result that anxiety becomes the root of sin. In the Deuteronomic and prophetic writings sin is the violation of God's covenant law, both as regards worship and the common life. Its cause in this case is, on the one hand, a "spirit of whoredom" or infidelity, and, on the other, a "hard heart" and a "stiff neck" which destroy community peace and well-being.

Yet in all cases the significance of sin is seen to be violation of God's command and rebellion against his authority. The Yahwist writer in Gen. 3 presents this rebellion as the cause of man's trouble on earth. By disobeying God man has violated communion, has been expelled from paradise, and has brought on himself and on the earth God's curse. Thus in this life he can expect nothing else but struggle with temptation (Gen. 3:15), with childbirth (vs. 16), and with nature for his food (vss. 17-19). This "fall" of man from God's gracious communion, a conception which has played such an important role in Christian theology, does not, however, separate him completely from God's grace. The election of Israel is the most signal proof of this grace (Gen. 12:3), as is also the salvation of a remnant in the Flood. Furthermore, to the priestly editor the "fall" does not mean that God's image has been effaced from man (cf. Gen. 9:6). Yet it does mean that man can expect no simple peace or security in this life apart from God's judgment, known both in natural and historical tragedy, and apart from God's gracious salvation.

It is in this perspective that the whole Bible sees the life of man and earthly society. The focus of attention is not on the worth of man. It is rather on man's sin, God's judgment, his gracious promises of salvation and their fulfillment.

G. The Hope of Man.—Man's creaturely existence, involved as it is in the problems of finitude, self-will and sin, is nevertheless not without hope. This hope is emphatically not a natural optimism based upon an illusory faith in the native capacity of man for self-salvation. Instead, it rests entirely upon the knowledge of God, whose revelation of himself has broken through man's finitude and sinful state and has disclosed the divine purpose through the medium of both past and future. The known activity of God thus becomes the guarantee that man may hope; indeed, it *creates* the hope and establishes the conditions and the bases in which and on which the hope may exist. Time, therefore, becomes significant as the arena of God's redemptive action; it ceases to be static or cyclical as it is in paganism.

The central theological theme of the Old Testament is that of the sovereign and redeeming activity of God, who is engaged for his own name's sake in establishing his kingdom over the whole earth. What happens in history is thus to be interpreted in this context, and when the day of final victory comes, the peace and perfection of the original creation will have been re-established. In all that God does, even in the most tragic and terrible of historical events, his ultimate redemptive purpose is understood. The reason for his action at any one moment may not be entirely clear (cf. the problems of Habakkuk and Job), but the man of faith need not despair. His hope is grounded in the over-all purpose and direction of God's work.

1. The Problem of Death.—The one area which this redemption-faith of Israel had most difficulty in penetrating was that of the suffering and death of the individual man. The views of Israel regarding death were so strongly conditioned by those of her pagan neighbors, excepting Egypt, that the invasion and transformation of this realm by the new and unique theology of Israel was a slow process, completed in the intertestamental period long after the classic age had come to an end. At death man's unity of being is destroyed and he loses vitality. The *néphesh* or "soul" (see above, pp. 367-68) thus does not continue to exist. It disintegrates, or as in the case of the suffering servant, it is said to be "poured out" as an offering to death (Isa. 53:12). The dead are like "water spilt on the ground, which cannot be gathered up again" (II Sam. 14:14).

This does not mean, however, that existence ceases. Man continues to live, though in a very weak state, in the underworld of Sheol, together with those who have passed into this realm before him. There he subsists in darkness (Job 10:21-22), in a kind of sleep (Nah. 3:18), in weakness (Isa. 14:10), in forgetfulness (Ps. 88:12). Existence in Sheol thus was conceived as the opposite of life. Earth is the land of light; Sheol is filled with the primordial darkness (cf. Gen. 1:2). Life means vitality and energy; death is weakness, inaction, a mere shadow of life. Since God is pre-eminently the giver of life and Lord of the living, it was something of a question to the Israelite as to what

relation he had with the dead. Is not death the separation from life and thus from the God of life? Consequently, the psalmist questions whether God will show his wonders to the dead, whether his lovingkindness and his righteousness will be known in the land of forgetfulness (Ps. 88:10-12; cf. Isa. 38:18). He prays the more earnestly, therefore, to be delivered from death's power. Many of the psalmists lived in great danger of their lives or in grave illness; and any form of weakness which robbed them of the free exercise of their powers was to them a form of death, though as yet the gates of Sheol had not closed finally upon them. Their prayers were for God to save them and to bring them back from the "pit" or from the waves of the deep through which they have been forced to go in the journey to the underworld (cf. Jonah 2:2-6). In God's hands are the issues of life and death, for it is he who "killeth, and maketh alive; he bringeth down to Sheol and bringeth up" (I Sam. 2:6; cf. Deut. 32:39).

The dominant emphasis in the prayers of sick and troubled individuals was thus on the redemptive power of God to save them from death. The greatest boon in life is to walk with God and to dwell in his presence, for there is "fulness of joy" and "pleasures for evermore" (Ps. 16:11). The faithful man was certain, therefore, that God would redeem his life (*néphesh*) from Sheol's power (Ps. 49:15; Hos. 13:14). Does this mean that death will be abolished? Such a passage as Ps. 23:6 ("I will dwell in the house of the LORD for ever") is somewhat ambiguous and unclear. There is no doubt, however, that during the postexilic period some believers began to answer the question in the affirmative. In God's new age there shall be no more death, and tears shall be wiped away from all faces (Isa. 25:8; cf. I Cor. 15:26, 54; Rev. 21:4). The chief difficulty which the man of faith had with death was that it separated him from life with God. Consequently, it was inevitable that sooner or later he would assert that the cause of this separation would be removed (cf. Ps. 139:8), for God in life will guide him with his counsel and afterward receive him with glory (Ps. 73:24). Illustration of the thought in the last passage was at hand in the cases of Enoch and Elijah, neither of whom suffered death but was taken directly to God's heavenly abode (Gen. 5:24; II Kings 2:11). This made it easier for some to believe that God would send Elijah back to earth again as the forerunner of the new age (Mal. 4:5; cf. Mark 9:11-13).

Yet if death is to be abolished by God in the new age so that redeemed man need never be separated from him, what about those who have died before that time? Two late passages affirm their resurrection: Isa. 26:19 and Dan. 12:2. In keeping with the unitary view of man, this doctrine of the resurrection of the dead is the only one which would be congenial to the biblical point of view. Many people under the ultimate influence of Greek thought have felt it simpler to believe in the immortality of the soul, though from the standpoint of reason this separation of soul from body appears as difficult as the belief in the resurrection of the body, i.e., of the complete person. The latter view, however, excludes all thought of a *natural* immortality and focuses attention upon the gracious miracle of God to raise the departed into fellowship with himself in the new age on earth. It was in this context that the doctrine became widespread in the intertestamental period, though there continued to be those who retained the position of the earlier literature of the Old Testament and who thus did not believe it (cf. Eccl. 3:20-21; and the Sadducees of the New Testament time, Matt. 22:23). Yet for the majority of the Jews the faith in God's redemptive power had finally won its victory over death.[46]

2. God's New Age.—It is characteristic of the resurrection faith which developed in Judaism, however, that for the most part it was closely related to the fulfillment of God's aims in the earthly creation. The resurrection was usually conceived as taking place in order that the dead might participate in God's new age on earth. There is no thought whatsoever of a salvation *from* the earth to an ethereal existence. God had a purpose in creation and that purpose he would fulfill. The world is in need of redemption, to be sure, but in its original creation it was good and it shall be good once again. God had a purpose in the election of Israel, and while Israel's sin has complicated the process of universal redemption, God will not be defeated. His purpose in election will be fulfilled. The primary concern in the faith of Israel, therefore, was not with the problem of the individual in death, but with the re-creation of earth and of Israel, that the original intention of God might be carried out in this earth. To know God is to know both past and future;

46 For a very succinct review of the eschatology of the apocryphal literature see article, "The Literature and Religion of the Apocrypha," pp. 391-419; also R. H. Charles, "Eschatology of the Apocryphal and Apocalyptic Literature," in James Hastings, ed., *A Dictionary of the Bible*, I, 741-49. See also the interesting treatment of Johnson, *Vitality of the Individual in the Thought of Ancient Israel*, pp. 88-107, with references there cited, including Christoph Barth, *Die Errettung vom Tode in den individuellen Klage- und Dankliedern des Alten Testaments* (Zürich: Zollikon, 1947); Pedersen, *Israel, Its Life and Culture I-II*, 453-96; Eichrodt, *Theologie des Alten Testaments*, II, 112-19; III, 148-68.

the past reveals his intention and will, the future will see their fulfillment.

The Israelite's knowledge of God, then, did not allow him to give up his hope of earth. The goods of this earth are not evil in themselves; they were meant by God for man's enjoyment. Consequently, the future will see the re-establishment of the peace, harmony, and material abundance of the original creation. Prophetic eschatology is quite explicit on this point. The new age will be one in which conflict and bloodletting of every sort will be done away. The weapons of war will be converted into agricultural tools (Isa. 2:4; Mic. 4:3). All animals will become domesticated so that the lion, the wolf, the bear, the viper will be at peace with the lamb, the cow, and the child. There shall be no hurting nor destroying "for the earth shall be full of the knowledge of the LORD" (Isa. 11:6-9). The seasons will be done away so that earth's productivity will never cease: "The plowman shall overtake the reaper, and the treader of grapes him that soweth seed; and the mountains shall drop sweet wine, and all the hills shall melt" (Amos 9:13). The divine curse on the ground which the Yahwist writer conceives as the reason for man's material hardship (Gen. 3:17-19) will no longer exist in the new age. All elements of nature will become exceedingly fertile. Indeed, Palestine will be so remade, according to Ezek. 47–48, that the poorest sections of the country will be as fertile as the best. The divine blessing will be so poured out upon the earth that sun and moon will no longer be needed for light because God himself will be the everlasting light (Isa. 60:19-20).

It is of course impossible to construct these various prophetic pictures into an exact blueprint for the age to come. Yet their essential meaning is that the goodness and abundance of the earth will be created anew. There is nothing intrinsically wrong with material abundance. Man was not created for poverty and hardship; he was intended by God to enjoy the marvelous abundance of nature, and this he *shall* enjoy in the time to come. Why does he not enjoy this abundance now? The whole implication of prophetic teaching, and the explicit statement of the Yahwist (Gen. 3:17-19), is that the sin of man has marred the peaceful harmony of the world so that the whole earth and all its life has experienced the divine judgment. Consequently, the transformation of nature must be accompanied by the transformation of man. God will give him a new heart and a new spirit so that he can enjoy the earthly abundance without self-destruction, without rebellion, and therefore without divine judgment. Since Israel is God's agent whereby the transformation is to be brought about among the nations, the saving grace of God will first be known in Israel. But it was prophetic insight which saw that the salvation would be known through and beyond judgment, not apart from it.

According to the early account of the call of Abram as given by the Yahwist writer, three divine promises were made: (a) that Israel would become a great nation (Gen. 12:2), (b) in possession of the land (Gen. 12:7), and (c) the recipients of a blessing with which all nations shall bless themselves (Gen. 12:3). The first two of these promises were fulfilled in the Conquest and in the reign of David. The third was unfulfilled at the time of the writing, but in all probability was continued as the anchorage of Israel's hope. When oppression and the loss of independent national existence came in the years between 733 and 586 B.C., the first two promises were again remembered and became an integral part of the future hope.

Amos 5:18 is the first reference to a popular expectation of a "day of the Lord." It is unexplained, but we can presume that it involved in some way the third of the divine promises referred to above, namely, that it would be a time when God's sovereignty would be extended over all the world with the resultant glorification of Israel. But Amos warns that the day expected will be the opposite of that hoped for. It will be a day of judgment, taking the form of a captivity "beyond Damascus" (Amos 5:27). In the succeeding prophecies of the next three centuries the day assumed various forms, depending upon historical circumstances. The book which presents the clearest outline of eschatological events is that of Ezekiel. We cannot presume that this outline was dogmatically fixed, and therefore accepted in detail by all Judean circles of the pre- and postexilic periods. Yet it does present a coherent picture of the main lines of expectation. First, God's terrible judgment will fall on the chosen people, destroying both state and temple (Ezek. 4–24). While the agency of the destruction is the Babylonian army, a vision depicts it as actually an angelic visitation (Ezek. 9). In keeping with the priestly theology which pervades the book, God's glory, the shining, refulgent brilliance which surrounds his being, is then seen to leave both temple and city (Ezek. 10–11). Since the wilderness period, the fullness of Israel has been God's tabernacling presence in the people's midst; but now the nation is deserted, alone, shortly to be destroyed and scattered. The second stage is the divine visitation on Israel's pagan neighbors in Egypt, Palestine, and southern Syria (Ezek. 25–32). Virtually the whole civilized world has thus come under the terrible judgment of God, the chief exception being the agent, Babylon, which is unmentioned perhaps because it *is* the agent and God's purpose in its regard is as yet unclear.[47]

From this picture of the judgment of God, first against the chosen nation and then against the pagan nations, one must affirm that no support or comfort for any existing order of society can be derived from the Old Testament. In the day of the Lord all shall be overthrown. The chief sin of the chosen people was that of rebellion against the God who had chosen them and bound them to himself. The chief sin of the nations was that of inordinate ambition and self-deifying pride which their power, wealth, and idolatry made possible. Thus they felt themselves able to say, "I am, and there is none else besides me" (Isa. 47:10; cf. Ezek. 28:2).

After the judgment will come the restoration of the remnant (Ezek. 33–37). God's purpose in his terrible visitation was to destroy the self-deifying pride of man and the institutions which man used for a security rooted in them instead of in God himself. A new heart and a new spirit will now be given, not because the remnant of Israel deserves such consideration, but because God works for his own name's sake and is determined to bring into being that which he had promised (Ezek. 36:22-23). Neither the original election nor the salvation is based on merit, but solely on the grace which is the ultimate and glorious mystery of God's being.

Before the era of peace is completely established, however, there will occur the final, terrible war with the barbarous, unrepentant forces of evil from the distant places of the world (Ezek. 38–39; Joel 3; Zech. 14; cf. also Matt. 24; Rev. 19:11–20:15). Only after this battle will the world be completely purified and ready for the new Jerusalem, to which the glory of God shall return (Ezek. 40–48; cf. Rev. 21–22).

Prophetic eschatology was thus based on an interpretation of the meaning of the great historical events of the time and on the certain faith that God would fulfill his promises. National tragedy did not mean that God is defeated or that he has wearied of his earthly task and gone off in search of greener pastures; it is instead the very proof of his determination to make his will known and operative in his earthly creation. The gods of the nations were unstable and without real power to direct the

---

[47] Cf. Isaiah's treatment of the agent, in this case Assyria, in Isa. 10:5-19; and that of Jeremiah in Jer. 25:12; 50–51. Under similar circumstances to those of Ezekiel, Second Isaiah makes no mention of the ultimate fate of God's agent of restoration, Cyrus.

course of events; consequently, they perished in the very disasters which continually proved the lordship of Yahweh (cf. Isa. 41:21-24; 46: 1-7). Yet the salvation of God, even for the elect people, is to be found *through* judgment, not *apart* from it. Man's hope for security amidst the goods of this earth is not fulfilled except through God's radical and searing treatment of sin. Such a juxtaposition of judgment and salvation is in direct contrast to the hope of the natural man, but it is precisely that to be found in the New Testament's view of the Cross and the Resurrection. For this reason the Christian understands that the Cross is the only adequate symbol of biblical faith. In the Old Testament it is the social aspect of salvation which receives the emphasis, while in the New the problem of the individual is finally resolved. Yet both are integral aspects of the full Christian hope, which is concerned with nothing less than the redemption of the whole of creation (cf. Rom. 8:19-23).

The central and unresolved problem of Old Testament eschatology, however, is the precise relationship between the salvation of the one and the many, of the restored Israel and the people of the nations. In the latter days all nations shall stream to Jerusalem and acknowledge the sovereignty of God and of his law (Isa. 2:2-4; Mic. 4:1-3). In the midst of the world darkness the light of God shall illumine Jerusalem, and to it the Gentiles shall come and shall name the walls "Salvation" and the gates "Praise" (Isa. 60). People will lay hold on the garments of the Jew and say, "We will go with you: for we have heard that God is with you" (Zech. 8:23). Thus the problem of universal man as first envisaged by the Yahwist writer in Gen. 2–11 will receive its resolution in accordance with the promise in Gen. 12:3. But under what conditions? Will the new age in which God's blessing and sovereignty are extended to the world mean the political supremacy and enrichment of Israel? In the figure of the suffering servant of the Lord in Isa. 53 the meaning of Israel's suffering is seen in a deeper dimension than anywhere else in the Old Testament. This suffering is more than a punishment for sin; it is a vicarious atonement for the sins of the world, through which the world will be brought to the knowledge of God. What relation exists between the redemptive function of Israel and her political and national aspirations? This is a question which the Christian must pose, and it is one which was not solved, except in the affirmation of the identity of the two seeming opposites. The problem stands out clearly in the conception of the Messiah.

3. The Messiah.—Messianic thought in Israel was rooted in the theology of the office of king-ship. In the circles of the Jerusalem royal court, beginning in the time of Saul and David, an elaborate attempt was made to fit the royal office into the older theology of the covenant. The king was anointed with holy oil, hitherto reserved for the office of priest. The anointing oil was especially prepared and none was to be made like it (Exod. 30:22-32). It was holy and to be used only for sacred purposes. When poured on the priests and the paraphernalia of worship, these were "cleansed" and readied for the cultic service (Exod. 40:9-15; Lev. 8:10 13, 30). Anointing and hallowing thus went together. When taken over for use at the coronation of the king, the anointing signified the consecration and the hallowing of the king's person for a divinely appointed office. His person was thus separated from the persons of ordinary people; for this reason David refused to harm a hair of Saul's head (cf. I Sam. 24:6, 10; 26:9-23; II Sam. 1:14-16). With the anointing, as with the baptism of Christ, went the special gift of the spirit; at least this was the case when Saul and David were anointed (I Sam. 10:1, 10; 16:12-13).

The king as God's Anointed (Messiah) was chosen by God; that is, the office was divinely instituted and its personnel was considered especially elect. Accompanying the election of the king, as in the election of Israel, were the divine promise and covenant (II Sam. 7:8-29; 23:5; I Kings 8:22-26; Ps. 89:3-4, 19-37). God would grant enduring power and stability to the throne; in return the ruler was expected to fulfill the purposes for which his office was established, namely, to provide both inner and outer justice and security for the people. He should not misuse his power in order to violate the law of his office and of his relationship to God. He could not presume too much; he could not claim credit for the law or violate it; he could only administer it in justice (cf. Deut. 17:14-20).

In the "royal psalms"[48] the function of the king and his relationship to God are seen even more clearly. These psalms are messianic, but not in the customary usage of this term. Originally they probably did not refer to a future king in the new age. Instead, it is likely that they were hymns composed for religious ceremonies in which the king played a prominent role (e.g., at a coronation, a royal marriage, and perhaps at a New Year's service in which Yahweh's enthronement as king of the world was celebrated). From Ps. 110, for example, we

[48] Especially Pss. 2; 18; 20; 21; 45; 72; 89; 101; 110; 132; see Hermann Gunkel and Joachim Begrich, *Einleitung in die Psalmen* (Göttingen: Vandenhoeck & Ruprecht, 1933; "Göttinger Handbuch zum Alten Testament"), pp. 140-71.

infer that in ideal the king was God's vice-gerent, endowed with his power; he would rule until all enemies in the earth are subdued. He was a "son," "begotten" of God (Ps. 2:7; II Sam. 7:14), an extension of God's power, who was to subdue and rule the world with and for God.

It is quite clear that the pretensions of this royal theology were not accepted by all elements of the community (e.g., the Deuteronomic movement). This was especially true when the office of kingship was so badly misused that few of the rulers could be said to be faithful to their consecration. In the new age depicted in Ezek. 40-48 this theology scarcely appears, and an old tribal term of "prince" was applied to the ruler instead of "king." [49] Yet the theology of kingship was taken over by certain of the prophets in Judah who were familiar with the royal court and with the priestly circles. In so doing, however, these prophets shifted its basic reference from the current king to a ruler whom God himself would provide from the Davidic line in the new age about to dawn. In him will lie complete security and justice, for he will be a mighty warrior, an everlasting father of his people, a prince of peace (Isa. 9:6-7), endowed with the spirit of Yahweh to rule the world according to the justice of God rather than of men (Isa. 11:1-5). His name shall be "Yahweh our Righteousness" (Jer. 23:6); under his rule Judah shall be saved, dwell in safety (Jer. 33:15-16), and be reunited into one kingdom under a new and everlasting covenant of peace (Ezek. 37:21-28). He shall "be great" over the whole world (Mic. 5:4); and "his dominion shall be from sea even to sea, and from the river [Euphrates] even to the ends of the earth" (Zech. 9:10).

It is perfectly clear from an analysis of the above-mentioned material that the suffering servant of Second Isaiah is not drawn from the royal theology, and is therefore not messianic in the proper sense of the term. Everything about the servant is the antithesis of royalty. He is not endowed with the kingly insignia; he has no glory or honor; he is given no power and no political role to play in the sense that the king will play it. To Second Isaiah, Cyrus has been given the power to function as Yahweh's anointed king (cf. Isa. 45:1-4). Though Cyrus has not known Yahweh, yet it is he who shall do Yahweh's work, using the power given him to make the crooked straight, to break the bars of iron, and to open the treasures of secret places. The servant, on the other hand, has a redemptive, vicarious, prophetic, and pacific role to fill. His is a salvation apart from the wielding of

[49] See, e.g., Noth, *Das System der zwölf Stämme Israels*, pp. 151-62.

power, and it will mean the pouring out of his "soul" unto death, though in so doing God will divide for him a portion with the strong and the great (Isa. 53:12).

Second Isaiah thus comes nearer than any other Old Testament writer to resolving the problem of the relation between the political hope and the spiritual redemption involved in Israel's election. Yet this writing stands apart from the main stream of Judaism's eschatology. For this reason nationalism and racial consciousness were never clearly distinguished or separated from the redemptive mission of Israel in the world. It is small wonder, then, that Judaism's future hope has been something of a theological problem, since it is difficult to understand how God's salvation of the world can be accomplished in the nationalistic framework of the chosen instrument. Consequently, it should be no surprise that Judaism increasingly through the centuries has become a religion without a missionary zeal and has persisted largely on a nationalistic basis.

At this point the Christian understands the impasse of Israel's hope to have been broken in Christ, so that the hope became genuinely universal. The pages of the New Testament were written under the triumphant assurance of the risen Lord, who has ascended into heaven and is seated on the right hand of God (cf. Ps. 110:1; Mark 16:19; Acts 2:33-36). Christ is the king to whom all power has been given in heaven and earth, for he is indeed the Christ, the Anointed One and the Son of God from the seed of David. Thus the royal theology of Israel was seen to be fulfilled in him, for he was and is the hope of Israel, the mediator of the new covenant, of the new kingdom, of the new age.

The rule of Christ, however, is from his heavenly, not an earthly, throne. Thus we must note that the messianic theology of Israel has been transformed, that the kingdom is at this moment a spiritual one which is missionary in its essence and universal in scope. It is most difficult to explain this transformation unless one assumes that Jesus himself made a profound, novel, and daring bit of scriptural interpretation. He accepted the messianic faith of Israel but he interpreted it by means of Isa. 53. Thus God's king of the new age is precisely the suffering Redeemer. He was despised and rejected of men, yet he bore the sins of the world, was exalted by God and crowned with glory and honor. Henceforth the citizens in Christ's kingdom are the children of Abraham by faith and adoption, heirs of the promises, and members of the new covenant, who live in the assured hope of the consummation of all things in the final redemption of the world.

III. The Worship and Service of God

A. The Spiritual Basis of Worship.—When one looks beneath the surface of pagan religion, he finds a dark, mysterious world, comparable in its complexity to the depths of unconscious life laid bare by modern psychoanalysis. That is the world of magic, divination, and demons. To be sure, the higher forms of paganism, such as Greek philosophy and Eastern mysticism, are relatively free from this world of the occult. Yet the philosophical and mystical mediums of salvation are at best available only to the few, whereas the common man is left in his superstitions. Both the Israelite and the pagan were vitally concerned with the discovery of the divine will and with the proper worship and service to be accorded deity, but to the polytheist there was available an elaborate and mysterious methodology from which Israel was largely excluded. Though there is always grave danger in oversimplification, yet the difference may perhaps be stated as follows: In polytheism the basis of worship was for the most part in magic; in the faith of Israel the basis of worship lay in historical memory and in spiritual communion and obedience.

1. Pagan Magic, Divination, and Demons.—Illustrations of ancient magic abound from every country of the Near East, but from Mesopotamia come the most detailed and numerous records. In almost every collection of tablets a large number have to do with omens of various sorts. Astrology was highly developed, and the profession of deducing omens from the movements of the stars and planets reached such importance that a system of periodic reports to the king came into being.[50] When the omens were unfavorable, a substitute king could be placed on the throne, while the real king went into hiding.[51] Far more common was divination by a variety of humbler means, one of which was the inspection of the liver of animals. The Babylonian diviner was an extremely important person, and it was unsafe to make any major decision without his aid. From the tablets of Mari on the middle Euphrates we learn that each section of troops had its own diviner and no campaign could be undertaken without the proper omens (cf. Ezek. 21:21-22). Balaam is the best known of these ancient experts, and the Israelite writers who tell about him (Num. 22–24) do so with high good humor, for to them it was absurd to assume that magic could in any way thwart the purpose of Yahweh. Instead, Yahweh turned the divination to his own purpose and made a prophet out of the pagan

specialist, greatly to the disgust of the Moabite king who quite naturally refused to pay Balaam the promised fee.

Even more disturbing was the vast world of demonology, in which sickness and every form of trouble were believed to be caused by lesser deities who were pictured in the most fantastic combination of animal, bird, and human bodies. To secure release from the power of these demons the help of a priestly magician had to be secured, who could conjure up the proper incantation and by exorcism drive off the offending beings.[52]

2. Israel's Rejection of Pagan Magic and Demonology.—The attitude of the Old Testament is very explicit on this type of approach to the divine world. In both law and prophecy it is directly forbidden as a part of the abominations of the nations from which Israel must separate herself (cf. Exod. 22:18; Lev. 20:6, 23, 27). Isaiah derides the people who seek out spiritualists and diviners that "chirp and mutter" their incantations, when God's direct revelation should be sought (8:19-22). Diviners, dreamers, spiritualists, necromancers, and soothsayers continually make the people believe lies, but the power of salvation is not in them (Jer. 27:9-10; Ezek. 13:17-23; cf. Isa. 47:12-15). The clearest elaboration of the law together with the reason for it is given in Deut. 18:9-15. There the whole pagan world of magic and divination is forbidden as incompatible with the worship of Yahweh. The God of Israel cannot be tricked, influenced, or coerced into revelation by occult means. He will make his will known when, where, and how he chooses. When he does so, it will not be by magic. His word will be heard directly, clearly, and understandably through his prophet to whom he has revealed his counsel. In Israel God's mediums of revelation undercut the world of pagan superstition.

This does not mean that Israel could or did so separate herself from the cult of magic that no remnants remained. The law would have had no reason to exist had not the forbidden practices been well known and used among the people. Furthermore, Israel shared in the common separation of clean and unclean, in ceremonial purifications, in recognizing the importance of dreams. The rod of Moses was a magical device (Exod. 7–8). There is one very mild example, though only one, of trial by ordeal (Num. 5:11-31). Saul inquired of the witch of Endor, who conjured up the ghost of Samuel for him (an example of necromancy or spiritualism), though this act was felt to be a

[50] See R. Campbell Thompson, *The Reports of the Magicians and Astrologers of Nineveh and Babylon* (London: Luzac & Co., 1900).

[51] Cf. Frankfort, *Kingship and the Gods*, pp. 262-65.

[52] Cf. R. Campbell Thompson, *The Devils and Evil Spirits of Babylonia* (London: Luzac & Co., 1903-4), and *Semitic Magic* (London: Luzac & Co., 1908).

terrible thing, an act of desperation on the part of a sinful man who should have used other means to reconcile himself to God in order to secure God's forgiveness. David frequently inquired of Yahweh by Urim and Thummim, the sacred dice carried by the chief priest, though there is no reference to the practice after that time. Closely related was the effort to determine God's choice by the casting of lots (e.g., I Sam. 10:17-24; 14:36-45; cf. Acts 1:26). Throughout Israel's history in Palestine the problem of discerning true prophecy from a pagan type of divination was acute (cf. I Kings 22; Jer. 23:9-32; Ezek. 13). For this reason Jeremiah classed the prophets of his day with the diviners, soothsayers, and magicians (Jer. 27:9-10).

This situation should occasion no surprise, since the relics of magic exist in many forms to this day. The important thing to observe is that the worship of God in Israel actually cut the ground from beneath the magical approach to deity, so that the world of the occult was no longer the center or basis of worship. This is equally clear in the study of demonology. The Old Testament contains few references to demons (cf. Deut. 32:17; Isa. 13:21; 34:14; and the mysterious Azazel in the wilderness, mentioned in the ceremonies of the day of Atonement, Lev. 16:8, 10, 26). Israel had no abstract or reasoned position regarding the existence or nonexistence of demons; they simply were unimportant and played no role whatever at the center of religious attention. The source of the psalmist's trouble is never personified as a demon. Sickness is not caused by a malevolent spirit, but by God himself (cf. Ps. 38). So radical was the wholehearted exaltation of and concentration on Yahweh that the realm of lesser beings dropped from conscious sight. If a person were afflicted or appalled by the terror of night or the destruction of noonday, he needed only to turn in faith to God, who would be with him in trouble, deliver him, and show him his salvation (Ps. 91). Sigmund Mowinckel[53] and Alfred Guillaume[54] believe that the penitential psalms were composed as prayers, comparable to those in Babylonia, the purpose of which was to ward off the evil effects of magical spells. The imprecatory psalms are also thought to have had the prophylactic purpose of slaying the sorcerer at his evil work. As in the case of the "terror by night" in Ps. 91:5-6, this view has some evidence to commend it, but both scholars, especially the first, are generally felt to have carried the argument much too far. In any case, it is most improbable that these psalms were composed as ritual in-

[53] *Psalmenstudien I* (Kristiania: Jacob Dybwad, 1921).
[54] *Prophecy and Divination* (New York: Harper & Bros., 1938), pp. 272-89.

cantations against sorcerers. They are simply prayers to the God who alone can and will deliver a person from all danger, but who will not permit the chirping and muttering of ritual incantations and exorcisms to have any effect whatever on his decisions. Faith, not incantation, is what he demands.

Furthermore, the true prophet as God's spokesman was no soothsayer in possession of numerous ritual incantations. He was possessed by God, and there existed between him and his Lord a fellowship of understanding and conscious communion which is the very antithesis of the attitude of the magician whose ritual has an automatic efficacy when properly performed. In other words, the worship of God in Israel had a far deeper basis than that in paganism. In Israel, spiritual attitude was all important. God's first requirement is a holy fear or reverence. Unless man can bow in humble contrition and reverence before God, there can be no such thing as worship. But the second requirement is one of faith, trust, and love, which means to believe God, to accept his promises with grateful heart, and to act obediently in love without anxiety. The man possessed of such fear and faith has nothing whatever to be afraid of, except sin. That faith was a remarkable and unique thing in the ancient world. It was rooted in a knowledge of the divine nature and purpose which through Christ has become the basis of man's faith and worship.

By New Testament times the doctrine of Satan with his principalities and powers of darkness had altered the situation which existed in Israel. The realm of Satan had opened the door to pagan demonology, with the result that the use of spells and exorcism became common among the Jewish people, as did an elaborate mythology of angels and demons. The New Testament world was thus one of demon possession. Yet the essential faith of Israel was carried over into the church by Christ and the apostles. In the cures effected by them little is said about incantations. To Christ, God has given complete power over the demons. Consequently, Christ could command the demons and they would obey him, and his disciples could accomplish the same cures by the use of his name. But faith was necessary, and without faith there was no cure (cf., e.g., Mark 2:5; 3:15; 5:34, 36; 6:5-6).

3. Israelite and Pagan Festivals.—The significance of Israel's conception of worship is further clarified when we examine the nature of the religious festivals. In polytheism the great cultic festivals centered in three major celebrations: (a) the New Year's festival in which the divine creation battle was refought, rewon, and the security of society in nature re-established for the ensuing year; (b) the marriage rite in the spring between the rain and vegetation god and the goddess of fertility; and (c) the rites incident to the revival of this god in the fall after his death in the summer's drought. These festivals cannot be conceived merely as celebrations, however, nor were they occasions for the reverent worship of deity in the biblical sense. Basic to them was the conception of sympathetic magic. In them man acted ritually, taking on the form or identity of the gods. By acting out the divine events mimetically, man by a willed exercise achieved what he desired, security and integration within nature. Like produces like; man in a drama taking the part of a god became that god temporarily, and his actions became the actions of the god. He thus created anew the orderly world in the battle against chaos, and he secured the revival of nature in spring and fall.[55]

In Israel, by contrast, the official festivals of normative Yahwism betray no hint whatsoever of sympathetic magic. In the cultic laws the primary attention is focused on three annual festivals (Deut. 16:16): (a) the Passover and associated feast of Unleavened Bread in the spring; (b) the feast of Harvest or Pentecost, fifty days later; and (c) the feast of Ingathering or Tabernacles in the fall.[56]

The original setting of the festivals, like that of our own Christmas and Easter, was within paganism, but the meaning was transformed in the religious environment of Israel. The harvest festival was a time of rejoicing when gifts of the first fruits were presented to the divine owner of the land. Only with the remarkable events recounted in Acts 2 was it completely historicized in the Christian community. From the earliest times in Israel, however, Passover and Unleavened Bread were together the great commemorative festival of liberation from Egyptian bondage (Exod. 13:8-9; Deut. 16:3). The feast of Ingathering lost much of its original significance and became the feast of Tabernacles, commemorating the booths in which Israel had to live in the wilderness after the Exodus (Lev. 23:43).

The new moon, marking a natural calendar division, was a holy day which was difficult to historicize. Similarly, the day of Atonement (Lev. 16) had a special signification since its central concern was with the sin of the nation. Yet the sabbath, which to the priestly writers was the token of the Sinai covenant (Exod.

31:12-17), was observed as a holy day commemorating the rest of God after the six days of creation (Exod. 20:8-11), though Deuteronomy connects it with the Exodus (Deut. 5:15) as also the harvest festival (Deut. 16:12).

Thus while the Hebrew festivals had behind and in them a variety of motives, yet the dominating and most significant tendency was that toward historical commemoration. Thus the later festivals of Purim and Hanukkah were solely commemorative, while in the Roll of Fasting, dating from the first or second century A.D. and evidently intended as a supplement to Lev. 23, practically every festival listed was given a historical background of which it was a memorial.[57] Nowhere is there the slightest hint that the primary purpose of a festival was the re-enactment of a drama, in which by sympathetic magic and the identification of man with the divine the harmonious integration of nature and society was thought to be achieved. The basis of Israelite worship was on an utterly different foundation.

In modern times a great deal of work has been done in the attempt to reconstruct a New Year's festival in Israel, in which the king took the role of God in acting out the original drama of creation. This reconstruction is based upon a number of psalms which are considered as ritual for the festival.[58] While the results of this investigation are by no means certain, in any case the festival would have been sponsored solely by the royal court in Jerusalem on a theological basis completely different from that of the Babylonian New Year's festival. The enemies to be annihilated were not the chaos monsters, but historical forces which must be done away before God's universal reign can be established. If such a festival existed, it was actually a celebration of God's rulership over the whole world and of the king's position as God's vicegerent. Sympathetic magic in the Babylonian sense could have played no prominent role whatever.

Perhaps the most significant differentiation between Israelite and Christian worship on the one hand, and that of pagan religion on the other, is to be found at this point. In the worship of the Israelite and the Christian, primary attention is focused upon the great redeeming acts of God. In worship these historical events are rehearsed and the worshiper joins himself by sympathetic imagination with the original participants and understands that these acts

---

[55] See Jacobsen in Frankfort, et al., Intellectual Adventure of Ancient Man, pp. 198-200.

[56] For Passover and Unleavened Bread see Exod. 12-13; 24:15; 34:18; Lev. 23:4-8; Num. 28:16-25; Deut. 16:1-8. For the harvest and ingathering festivals see Exod. 23:16; 34:22; Lev. 23:15-21, 34-36; Num. 28:26-31; 29:12-38; Deut. 16:9-15.

[57] G. B. Gray, Sacrifice in the Old Testament (Oxford: Clarendon Press, 1925), pp. 277-84.

[58] See especially Mowinckel, Psalmenstudien II; Aage Bentzen, Messias, Moses redivivus, Menschensohn (Zurich: Zwingli, 1948); Elmer A. Leslie, The Psalms (New York and Nashville: Abingdon-Cokesbury Press, 1949) pp. 62-130.

were done for him also (cf. Deut. 5:3; 26:3-11). He then gives thanks and praise to God for what God has done, and solemnly renews his covenanted vows. The spiritual process which biblical worship entails thus involves a combination of historical narration with participation by means of memory and imagination, with illumination derived from the continued working of God's spirit, with praise and thanksgiving, and with solemn renewal of covenant as the worshiper again faces his own life. Much more than this is involved, depending upon the occasion and the type of worship, yet illumination from historical memory and participation remain central and primary. As such, the worship avoids the pitfalls of magic and mysticism, but combines the historical past, present, and future in the conception of God's gracious and continuous direction of human life.

B. The Forms and Places of Worship. 1. Tabernacle and Temple.—In ancient paganism, while there was no stability or uniformity in the manner in which the outward form of the gods was represented, the inner structure of all of them was personal, with the result that they could be met and addressed by human beings. The most spectacular witness to this anthropomorphism was the conception of the deity's house or palace. In western Asia no word corresponding to our term "temple" seems to have existed; the god's dwelling was designated by the same terms as those used for the residence of king or other important person. The temple was conceived as a manor house in which a god resided with his family and servants, both divine and human. Food (sacrifices and offerings) and drink (oblations) had to be provided for the daily needs of the god and his attendants; in the larger temples, at least, the human task of providing the needed sustenance was very great. The amount of food consumed by the court of Solomon in one day (I Kings 4:22-23) seems unreasonably luxurious; but it appears to have been only slightly more than that provided in the four daily meals for the god Anu and his family in the Babylonian city of Uruq. The original and basic meaning of the sacrificial cultus, therefore, was simply to provide for the needs of the gods who lived as the human aristocracy in palaces of varying degrees of luxury, depending upon the available wealth. In most cases the great temples owned large amounts of land and were thus the centers of large commercial transactions. From this land the basic requirements of the god were met, though supplementation was continually available from the gifts of suppliants who came to the home of the divine lord for assistance.

The existence of rival temples for the same god seems to have caused no intellectual difficulty. As a king or noble might have more than one palace, so could a god. A real danger existed, however, in the numerous temples for one deity; that was the danger of the splitting up of the divine personality. Consequently, the god might be worshiped under various manifestations. That this happened with regard to the goddess Ishtar of Mesopotamia and to the god Baal of Canaan is quite clear. In the Old Testament we hear of many Baals, though in reality Baal was one, the cosmic god of the storm and the executive king of the divine and human worlds.

The problem of transcendence and immanence in regard to the temple seems also to have been no problem. A cosmic god could be immanent in an earthly temple because that building was erected as a microcosm of the deity's limitless world. Thus all ancient temples were filled with cosmic symbolism. Since in the conceptual world of paganism like makes like, the temple as a representation of the universe could in a sense be the universe; and the gods who inhabited the universe, whose proper home was in the heavens or on the cosmic mountains, could thus live also in an earthly abode.[59]

It is in this pagan setting that the forms and places of worship in Israel, so foreign to our own religious life, may best be comprehended. The meaning and nature of the Israelite cultus differed radically from that of polytheism, though the outward forms were directly borrowed. Before the Deuteronomic reform in 621 B.C. (II Kings 22–23) the particular places where Yahweh revealed himself and was worshiped were numerous. Many of those places were Canaanite holy sites before the time of Israel, but none of them were conceived as dwelling places of Yahweh. Rather, they were simply places where he revealed himself. There never was serious danger of the divine personality's being split into various local manifestations. Wherever his chosen people were, there he also could be found. Yahweh's dwelling was properly in heaven from which he could be said to "come down" to earth (Gen. 11:5; 18:21; 28:12-17; Exod. 19:11, 18, 20).

Yet the tabernacle and the temple were also conceived as his dwelling. The latter was simply entitled "the house" or "the house of Yahweh." The cosmic symbolism in the temple of Solomon indicates that in all probability under Canaanite influence it was conceived to be the abode of God in the sense that it was the earthly representation of his heavenly dwelling. In other

[59] See Harold H. Nelson, "The Egyptian Temple," *The Biblical Archaeologist*, VII (1944), 44-53; Thorkild Jacobsen, "Temples, Mesopotamian," in Vergilius Ferm, ed., *An Encyclopedia of Religion* (New York: Philosophical Library, 1945), pp. 770-71; Frankfort, *et al.*, *Intellectual Adventure of Ancient Man*, pp. 186-91.

words, the problem of transcendence and immanence was resolved by means of a rich, sacramental symbolism.[60]

Yet the important thing to observe is that Israelite theology found it difficult to accommodate itself to this theology of the temple, closely dependent as it was on pagan conceptions. The first clear reaction against it is to be observed in the Deuteronomic writings. For example, in the Deuteronomic edition of the Solomonic prayer of dedication of the temple, the question is asked directly as to whether God really dwells on earth at all. Since not even the heaven of heavens can contain him, how much less this earthly building! Yet while the temple does not actually contain God's being, nevertheless God has seen fit to place his *name* there and to hear and answer the prayers directed toward it (I Kings 8:27-30; cf. Deut. 12:5). Thus the temple is God's gracious accommodation to human need. When prayer is directed toward the temple, either by an Israelite or a stranger, God will hear it in his dwelling place in heaven and answer. Consequently, the temple is important not because it is his palace—indeed, he has no need of a palace—but because he has consented to place his name there in response to humble prayer (cf. Isa. 56:7).[61]

The Israelite priests were likewise aware of the problem of the transcendent God in any sense being localized in an earthly abode. Consequently, they carefully avoided using the ordinary word for "dwell" (*yāshabh*) when speaking of God's presence on earth. Instead, they employed an archaic term meaning "to tent" or "to tabernacle" (*shākhan*). Yahweh never "dwells" on earth as does man; he "tabernacles" in the midst of his people. The technical term for the tabernacle was drawn from the same root and properly means "tent" (*mishkān*), but not "dwelling" in the ordinary sense. The center of priestly theology was the conception of God's covenant-presence in the midst of the people for the purposes of revelation and atonement. The tabernacle was thus conceived primarily as a tent of revelation (Exod. 25:22; 29:42-43; 30:36), where God had graciously allowed his presence, hidden by his "glory," to "tabernacle" and there be met.[62]

It is thus significant that Israelite thinkers found the conception of the temple a theological problem demanding careful treatment. Both the Deuteronomic and priestly circles carefully avoided the literalism of paganism, and their views prepared the way for the later conception of synagogue and church as places where God may be worshiped, though his physical being is in no way permanently resident there. Yet it must be confessed that Israel's attachment to God in election and covenant demanded a spiritual type of worship and obedience for which the temple was no primary symbol or adequate means of expression. Consequently, both the prophets and Jesus could envisage God's actual destruction of the temple precisely in order that a proper worship might be ordained (cf. especially Jer. 7:1-15;[63] Mark 13:1-2; 14:58; John 2:19). In polytheism the temple was the all-important link between heaven and earth, and the welfare of society was utterly dependent upon the integration with the world of nature and deity, established by its cultic rites. But in Israel the temple could play no corresponding role, and when destroyed left no irreparable damage to the faith. Even in the economic life of the nation it could not achieve the importance of the pagan temple. It could own no land, but had to be supported solely by the gifts of the worshipers. Instead of grants of land, the law prescribed a system of tithes (Lev. 27:30-33; Deut. 14:28-29) which meant that its priests could never achieve a measure of control over the economy, as happened in Egypt and Mesopotamia.

2. The Meaning of Sacrifice.—Equally important and unique was the conception of the meaning of sacrifice in Israel. In polytheism the idea that sacrifices were the needed food and drink of the gods was never completely spiritualized. Yet in Israel there is no thought whatever of God's need of physical sustenance; anthropomorphism in the Old Testament had its distinct limits. To be sure, some of the sacrifices continued to be prepared as food, including the addition of salt, but there is never the slightest suggestion of God's eating them. There is reference to God's smelling the "sweet savor" of the burning sacrifice (Gen. 8:21), but the phrase had been spiritualized and meant little more than that God found the offering acceptable. Indeed, in Levitical terminology the words "sweet savor unto the LORD" were a technical expression referring to an offering's acceptability unto God (Lev. 1:9, 13, 17; 2:2, 9, 12; etc.).

In other words, the theological basis of the sacrificial cultus was shifted to a different foun-

---

[60] See Albright, *Archaeology and the Religion of Israel*, pp. 142-55; G. Ernest Wright, "Solomon's Temple Resurrected," *The Biblical Archaeologist*, IV (1941), 17-31.

[61] Cf. von Rad, *Deuteronomium-Studien*, pp. 25-30; G. Ernest Wright, "The Temple in Palestine—Syria," *The Biblical Archaeologist*, VII (1944), 74-76.

[62] This technical vocabulary of P was first discerned by Frank M. Cross, Jr.; see his brief review of the evidence in "The Tabernacle," *The Biblical Archaeologist*, X (1947), 65-68; cf. also von Rad, *loc. cit.*

[63] On this passage and its significance see especially Walther Eichrodt, "The Right Interpretation of the Old Testament: a Study of Jeremiah 7:1-15," *Theology Today*, VII (1950), pp. 15-25.

dation from that on which it rested in paganism. The whole cultus was conceived as God's special revelation to Israel, a means which he provided and accepted whereby he could be worshiped. There is no thought whatever of God's personal need of the sacrifices or that somehow they were of benefit to him. The setting is thus prepared for the amusing apocryphal tale in Bel and the Dragon, relating Daniel's exposure of the false claim of the pagan priests about the idol's consumption of the offerings, and as well the statement of the apostle Paul that the Creator does not dwell in man-made temples to be worshiped with men's hands as though he needed anything (Acts 17: 24-25).

Furthermore, as the course of Israel's history moved on, we observe particularly in Ezekiel and the priestly writings an increasing atmosphere of somber seriousness. The prophetic indictment of the nation had been validated, and as a result there existed a heavy feeling of sin. The priestly writers, no less than the prophets, emphasized the persistent and perennial sin of Israel and the conditional nature of the covenant. Israel was unclean and the holiness of the "tabernacling" God would not mix with uncleanness. Consequently, both state and temple, which in polytheism were the sole foundation of human existence, were destroyed. The primary meaning of the sacrificial cultus was that God had given it as a means of atonement. By making atonement the breach of the covenant could be repaired and the problem of sin resolved.

Behind the Hebrew expression for atonement (kipper) there seems to have been the metaphor of "covering." While the etymology and derivation of the word are not certainly known, the basic metaphor involved is clear from a careful study of the contexts in which it occurs. In a number of cases it is used in parallelism with words properly meaning "to cover" (kāṣāh), or "to hide" (ṣāthar), or the latter are used in place of it. For example, Nehemiah prays that God would not atone ("cover," kāṣāh) the iniquity of his enemies and that their sin might not be blotted out from before him (Neh. 4:5). The psalmist (Ps. 32:1-2) says: "Blessed is he whose transgression is forgiven [borne away], whose sin is covered (kāṣāh); blessed is the man unto whom the LORD imputeth not iniquity" (Ps. 32:1-2; cf. 85:2-3). In Ps. 51 the psalmist prays that God will "blot out" his transgressions, wash and cleanse him, and "hide" his face from his sins (vs. 9). In Prov. 10:12 are the words, "Hatred stirreth up strifes; but love atones for (covers, kāṣāh) all sins" (cf. Prov. 17:9). A noun from the same root as kipper ("to atone") means "bribe"

(kōpher), and the function of a bribe, it is said, is "to cover" (kāṣāh) or "to blind the eyes" of the offended party or the righteous or the judge (cf., e.g., Gen. 20:16; Exod. 23:8; Deut. 16:19). Indeed, the purpose of Jacob's present to Esau is "to cover" (kipper) his face so that Jacob may see him (Gen. 32:20).

In other words, the trouble with sin is that it is an act of disloyalty which breaks off personal communion. The offended one in his injury has the just desire to remove the offender from his sight. The problem of the sinner is thus one of reconciliation; something must be done to appease or propitiate the anger of the one sinned against, whether it is one's neighbor, the human judge, or God himself. The sacrificial cultus was a means which God graciously provided whereby reconciliation and atonement (or "covering") were effected. Man's sacrificial act of worship atoned for sin in the sense that it "covered" him, his sin, or the eyes of the divine Judge so that the latter no longer saw the sin. God's holiness was a consuming fire in the midst of uncleanness. In the presence of that holiness no mortal, sinful man could exist. But God has provided a "covering" of which man can avail himself, and with the aid of which the broken, personal relationship can be reconstituted. To comprehend Israel's conception of atonement, therefore, one must keep in mind the metaphor behind it, and relate it closely with the more abstract conception of forgiveness and reconciliation.[64]

The difficulty with all outward acts of atonement, however, is that they may become mechanical, conceived as automatically effective, ex opere operato. Consequently, the Israelite cultus of temple, priesthood, and sacrifice did not escape the prophetic censure any more than did the institution of kingship. To the prophets sacrifice could make no atonement for a people who, while multiplying their offerings and thronging the religious festivals, engaged in the most elemental violation of God's laws. God would not accept a mechanical sacrifice; he despised it. His purpose is not fulfilled by an elaborate ceremonial, but by a humble, righteous life, filled with the knowledge of himself (Isa. 1:10-17; Jer. 6:20; 7:22-23; Hos. 6:6; Amos 5:21-24; Mic. 6:6-8).

So forthright and wholehearted is the prophetic condemnation that many have assumed that the prophets would like to have seen the sacrificial system abandoned entirely. More cautious scholars, however, believe that the

[64] The above treatment of the word kipper is dependent upon an unpublished monograph which breaks new ground in the investigation of the subject of atonement: Sidney O. Hills, "The Meaning of Kaphar in the Old Testament," a B.D. thesis submitted to the faculty of McCormick Theological Seminary, Chicago, in 1948.

prophets were merely condemning the misuse of the cultic system. In doing so they naturally used the language of hyperbole, but they had no intention of doing away with sacrifice. Such an argument about what the prophets might have done, had they been in official charge of worship, is actually rather futile. We do not know what they might have done, and it is doubtful whether they themselves knew. They were not religious legislators. They were given God's word to proclaim, and their task was completed when God's message was uttered.

Nevertheless, it was under the influence of the prophetic proclamation that Pss. 50 and 51 do imply a spiritualization of the term "sacrifice." Ps. 50, more than any other passage in the Old Testament, points out the incongruity of offering animals as food to the God who owns the whole of creation. The purified worship envisaged is composed of thanksgiving, the payment of vows, and prayer. In Ps. 51:17 it is said that the only sacrifices God does not despise are a broken spirit and a contrite heart. It is doubtful that we should take these psalms as indicative of a clearly conceived movement in Israel for the revision of the sacrificial system. Yet Ps. 51:17 does show a spiritualization of the term "sacrifice," one which was carried over into the New Testament and into the church. This was possible because God's primary desire in the covenant was a personal relationship and communion, centered in the realm of that which we term "the spiritual life." It was this personal attachment alone which made true and willing obedience possible and the cultic worship acceptable. Consequently, when the people debased temple and sacrifice into a type of fetish which operates automatically, they actually were conceiving of God in terms of a pagan idol whose power one exploits for himself. God's word to the prophets thus condemned the whole cultic institution because it was used to validate the people's security when the true relationship between man and deity, which alone can give security, had been violated. The ground is thus prepared for the Christian church to move out into the world as the body of Christ, who replaces the temple and whose sacrifice of himself brought an end to the ancient cultus.

C. The Common Life.—Man's treatment of his neighbor has been subject to some measure of social control since the dawn of history. In order to live in society at all man has had to have an ethical law. Consequently, one may assume with Amos 1-2 and Rom. 1 that the will of God in social relations is so deeply rooted in his creation that peoples who do not acknowledge his sovereignty are nevertheless responsible for a proper ethical life. The true distinctiveness of a religious faith or of a people's ethic is thus

not to be determined solely by a detailed comparison of ethical injunctions. While such comparison must be made, the real nature of a given social morality is to be discovered within the context of the world view and theological framework in which the moral law is placed.

1. Israelite Wisdom.—This fact is clearly illustrated by Israel's wisdom movement. The wise men were evidently a special class in the community, as distinct from priests and prophets, whose function was to give practical advice on the conduct of affairs in the community (Jer. 18:18; Ezek. 7:26). They came under the same prophetic condemnation as the priests and popular prophets. Nevertheless, they were considered an important source of knowledge by the people and three of their books—Job, Proverbs, and Ecclesiastes—were retained in the canon. The anthology of epigrams in Proverbs seems to have been typical of their work. The primary source of their insight in such proverbs seems to have been observation, experience, and common sense. The teaching is chiefly practical, prudential, and utilitarian, much of it beautifully phrased, easily quoted, and exhibiting a profundity of observation. Like many sermons on character education in the past three generations, however, they represent for the most part the type of thing which any man of good will can say, regardless of his theological affiliation or lack of it. Consequently, the close relation between Israelite wisdom and that particularly of Canaan and of Egypt is by no means surprising. In fact, the wisdom type of interest and of epigram existed in those countries before it did in Israel, and many of Israel's proverbs undoubtedly were borrowed from the international collections. It is well that this is the case, for the proverbs indicate that a prudential, common-sense ethic, based upon broad experience, is by no means excluded from Israelite faith.

Yet it is important to notice that the new theological setting in Israel has altered the inner meaning of the ethic. A basic pattern in proverbial writing was to make clear what the good man should do by giving in contrast the manner of the bad man. In Egyptian wisdom the contrast was between the silent and the passionate man. The former is the self-disciplined, patient, modest person who is master of himself at all times. The latter is the self-assertive, grasping, arbitrary person who disturbs the existing order and destroys the harmonious integration of society.[65] In Israel proverbs similar to those in Egypt were used, but the basic contrast is between the righteous or upright man and the wicked or foolish man. This presupposes an entirely different kind of judgment between the

[65] See Frankfort, *Ancient Egyptian Religion*, ch. iii.

good and the bad from that which existed in Egypt. The righteous and the wicked are evaluated according to a given standard, which can only be the revealed law of Yahweh. Thus the wisdom ethic in Israel cannot be conceived as unrelated to revelation; on the contrary, it rests squarely upon the peculiarly Israelite understanding of what constitutes good and evil. This is the more clear when we observe that the motto of the wisdom movement in Israel seems to have been "the fear of Yahweh," which is the beginning of knowledge and wisdom (Prov. 1:7; 9:10). It is this holy reverence for Yahweh which is strength to the upright (Prov. 10:29), which produces righteousness (Prov. 14:2), which is a fountain of life (Prov. 14:27; cf. 19:23; 22:4). Thus Yahweh is in truth the source of wisdom (cf. Job 28) and the author of prudential morality. It is he who rewards the righteous and punishes the wicked.[66]

Yet the extremely individualized perspective of the wisdom movement's doctrine of divine reward and punishment furnished the setting for theological controversy. The book of Job was written to deny that this doctrine is sufficient to explain all human suffering. The prophetic teaching concerning the judgment of God upon human sin is not necessarily rejected by the author. Rather, the subtle inversion of that doctrine is combated, wherein the presence of suffering in the life of an individual may be assumed to be proof of God's judgment upon his gross sin. There is a deeper dimension in life than this; in the economy of God there is a mystery in the divine dealing with men which must be accepted humbly without loss of faith in God's providence.

On the other hand, Ecclesiastes represents a development in another direction toward a denial of the whole belief in individual rewards and punishments in this life or hereafter. God's moral government of the world, if it exists at all, is beyond our comprehension. The ordinary pursuits of man are vanity, emptiness, and weariness; they achieve no good end. God's administration of the world cannot be understood by man, for whether one is righteous or wicked, wise or foolish, death is the great leveler in which both good and evil, love and hatred, perish (Eccl. 8:16–9:6). Yet wisdom is indeed better than folly, and the proper life is one which enjoys the simple pleasures here and now in the fear of God. The portion which God has given every man is the enjoyment of his labor and of eating and drinking, while avoiding

[66] Cf. Robinson, *Inspiration and Revelation in O.T.,* chs. xviii-xx; contrast in part J. Coert Rylaarsdam, *Revelation in Jewish Wisdom Literature* (Chicago: University of Chicago Press, 1946).

self-assertive folly, pride, and rashness of spirit and action.

The wisdom movement is deficient insofar as its theological base and intellectual interest are too narrowly fixed. It represents an extreme individualism in ethics and theology without a doctrine of society. In this respect Proverbs remains near the pagan source of wisdom in which society played no important theological role. In the canon of scripture Proverbs has the important function of supplying an explication of the meaning of the law for individual life. But to survive as a living force in Judaism, the wisdom movement had to undergo a more thorough acclimation to the doctrines of election and covenant. This was done, on the one hand, in the apocryphal Wisdom of Solomon, wherein eschatology is employed to overcome the difficulties of the writer of Ecclesiastes. On the other hand, the book of Ecclesiasticus exalts the Mosaic law, the study of which is actually the source of wisdom, and therefore is of universal validity.[67]

2. The Covenant Law.—In Israelite law and prophecy, as distinct from wisdom, individual and social ethics were held together within the framework of covenant theology. If a man would act aright in the exercise of his social responsibility, he was immediately confronted with the will of the sovereign Lord of the covenant, which meant that he looked back to God's formation of the nation at Sinai and forward to the final redemption in the future. Precisely because of this faith the Israelite attained an understanding of his work and of his use of earthly goods which hitherto was unknown. The common law of the nation was part and parcel of the international law of the day, but in its adaptation to the needs of the covenant society a change of interior meaning occurred which necessitated also numerous changes in specific laws.

God's law in the covenant was not conceived as a penal burden to be borne. It was God's gracious gift to Israel that the nation, which previously had lived outside the benefits of law, might now know the security which is derived from justice. It was not an invention of men; it was the expression of the authoritative will of the covenant God. The king of Israel, unlike Hammurabi of Babylon, could not take credit for the law; it was not God's special gift to him alone. He was as subject to it as was the nation as a whole. Totalitarianism was lifted from the earthly to the heavenly sphere. The law thus envisaged a security and a freedom for the individual, who was not to be unrighteously oppressed by human power. To be sure, the individual person found meaning in life within the

[67] See further Rylaarsdam, *ibid.*, pp. 27-46.

context of the covenant society, but his individuality was not lost in the society. God's command to the people of Israel was addressed also to him personally. The election of Israel included within it his own election, and for the first time in history work became a sacred and responsible vocation.

Consequently, the covenant theology meant that the Near Eastern common law in Israel had to be revised in such a way as to provide for the equality of all citizens before the court of law. The limitation of revenge and the institution of a just penalty on the principle of "an eye for an eye, and a tooth for a tooth," was also a part of Babylonian law, but there it applied only to free men; for others compensation in money was sufficient. In Israel, however, all classes of society, no matter what their social status may have been, were included in the provision (Exod. 21:23-25; Lev. 24:19-22). The death penalty for embezzlement no longer obtained in Israel, and the mutilation of the body as a legal penalty was abolished.

Since Israel was once in slavery in Egypt, from which God had redeemed her, the righteousness of God in the law was seen to be especially solicitous of the poor and the weak in society. The sojourner who does not have full civil rights, and the widow and orphan who are defenseless against the powerful, must not be oppressed in any way (Exod. 22:21-24). The poor man has the same right in court as the rich, and his justice must not be wrested from him (Exod. 23:6). In Israel alone in the ancient world is there a prohibition against the taking of interest on a loan. The man of property should freely make loans to those in need, but he must not make the practice into an income-producing business. The poor man's need must not become the occasion for profit. If he gives his clothing as a pledge of repayment, it should be returned to him before sundown because it is all he has to wear. When the poor man cries to God, the latter will hear him for he is gracious (Exod. 22:21-27). In Israel alone there was for the first time an interest in the victims of slavery. In the covenant law there was registered "an open denial of the right of man to own man in perpetuity. This denial of the right of possession of man by man is as yet restricted to Hebrews only (cf. Neh. 5:8), but it is a step which no other religion had taken before." [68]

In Lev. 19 we have an excellent summary of Israelite social legislation, together with the motive behind it. There we find instructions concerning gleaning that the poor and the sojourner may get food; against stealing, false swearing, oppression; about wages, gossip, impartiality in court; about honoring the aged, helping the deaf and the blind, caring for trees, cattle, and crops, forbidding sexual irregularities, mutilation of the body, unjust weights and measures, and so forth. The reason for all these specific regulations is given in vss. 17-18: "Thou shalt not hate thy brother in thine heart. . . . Thou shalt not avenge, nor bear any grudge against the children of thy people, but thou shalt love thy neighbor as thyself: I am the LORD." In vs. 34 the law is extended also to the sojourner. The whole meaning of economic and social life in Israel is thus seen to be the service of one's neighbor. The Israelite is commanded by God to love every member of his community, and he is to do so regardless of any attitude of love or hate exhibited toward himself (Lev. 19:17b; Exod. 23:4-5, where the enemy is specified; cf. Prov. 25:21). Though cast in legal form, the law of love is obviously not an ordinance which can be enforced in a human court of law. Yet since both lawgiver and judge are God, all of his commands are legally phrased to make one's duty vividly clear. Before the divine Judge every member of the community has an equal status; and God's requirement of the people who acknowledge him as their Lord is that they treat each other with a mutual respect and concern which transcend legal duty, but are rooted in the recognition of their common Lord, who has made them members together in the covenant community. Of course nothing is here said about love for those who are not members of the Israelite community. Yet the law of the covenant was not given originally for the government of the world, but solely for the one people. The wider reaches of the law of love could be faced only when decisions were being made regarding the relevance of the whole law for the governance not of a political, but solely of a spiritual and universal community (cf. Mark 12:31; Gal. 5:14; Jas. 2:8).

The Israelite attitude toward earthly goods is also determined by the theology. Property belongs to God, who gives it to his people as a loan (cf. Lev. 25:23). Land as the primary source of profit cannot be bought and sold at will. It belongs to God, who has given it to the community. There is no such thing as a natural and private right to the exploitation of property. Since the freedom and security of every community depended upon the land as the basis of its existence, each clan had the right to redeem any property that was sold. If this were not done, the property would automatically revert to the clan or family in the fiftieth or jubilee year (Lev. 25:13-17). While the jubilee may never have been observed, it nevertheless illustrates the aim of Israel's economy, which

[68] I. Mendelsohn, "Slavery in the Ancient Near East," *The Biblical Archaeologist*, IX (1946), 88.

was to protect its citizens from every form of economic slavery.[69]

The conception of God and the covenant faith thus brought about astonishing changes in the ancient common law when it was adapted as the basis for the Israelite economy. The prophetic protest against social iniquity was based squarely on the old covenant law in the attempt to see to it that this law was unconditionally enforced. In the great development of commerce and trade which occurred between the tenth and seventh centuries B.C. the danger of the misuse of economic power was vastly increased. The government, faced with the problem of taxation and armament, found it expedient to be lenient with those in possession of the new wealth. The landed peasantry found itself in difficulty: debt slavery increased; interest rates were charged; land was purchased at cheap prices, until great estates were formed and the old order of justice was completely overturned. Indeed, justice was at times destroyed entirely through the bribery of the courts. At the same time, the sanctuaries prospered with a worship which seemed to be sincere. Yet to the prophets every acknowledgment of the God of the fathers which led to a purely personal piety and a moral quietism was a dangerous and terrible idolatry. Obedience to the will of God involved more than an individual piety; it meant that one must hate the evil and love the good, and this involved the whole of man's social life in both its inner and outer manifestations. Israel was indeed the elect nation, but her calling and the success of her fulfillment of that calling were dependent upon the way in which her service of God bore witness to his mighty action in choosing a people from among the nations and binding them to himself in covenant.

D. Sin and Forgiveness.—The worship and service of God failed to bring to the Israelite the comfort, security, and peace which he so deeply desired and which God promised to the nation in election and covenant. The good life was to be found in a close personal relationship of communion and fellowship, in which man's proper attitude and activity were based on trust, love, and loyalty, on humility, integrity, and generosity. The desired and promised life did not exist when the communion was violated by

the failure of proper attitude or action. This violation was sin which brought guilt and judgment. Thus the conception of sin was rooted deep within the spiritual life of man and in the knowledge of life's relatedness to God. The Israelite could not atomize his misdeeds entirely and seek to repair their damage by making an outward atonement for this or that specific act, assuming thereby that the covenant relationship was re-established. One's whole being was involved, and the spiritual sins of pride and hardness of heart were more serious than the outward breach of a law. There was no way by which the tension within life between the will of God and the spirit of man could be removed except by the humble surrender of one's whole being to the gracious sovereignty of God.

1. The Conception of Sin.—The Old Testament abounds with portrayals of character in which the spiritual problem is always central and in which heroism is conceived in terms of faith and obedience. The frequent contrasts make this clear, as for example between Abram and Lot, Moses and the people, Samuel and Saul, Elijah and Ahab, Isaiah and Ahaz, Jeremiah and Zedekiah. The first name in each case is that of a man who possessed a wholeness and soundness of character. The close relationship existing between him and God was unimpaired by irresolution in faith and obedience. It is not that he was sinless (e.g., Abram and Moses), but that he possessed a wholesome relationship to God, with the result that through him God's work was done. This is what the Hebrew called *tāmîm*, inadequately rendered as "perfect" in English translations. The second parties in the above pairs are not "perfect"; a barrier exists between them and God. Therefore they are not spiritually whole; they are weak, and their weakness issues in overt acts of sin.[70]

It is this aspect of the conception of sin in the Bible which so differentiates it from the conceptions of wrongdoing in other religions. Sin as the personal violation of one's relationship with God, as the involvement of one's whole being in a haughty and rebellious act, and as the destruction of one's normal, healthy, and dependent integrity—such an analysis of the meaning of man's evil is completely unknown elsewhere. In Egypt there were many words denoting evil acts, but none of them are properly rendered "sin" in the biblical sense.

The Egyptian viewed his misdeeds not as sins, but as aberrations. They would bring him unhappiness because they disturbed his harmonious in-

[69] See further Bruno Balscheit und Walther Eichrodt, *Die soziale Botschaft des Alten Testaments für die Gegenwart* (Basel: Friedrich Reinhardt, n.d.); Eichrodt, "The Question of Property in the Light of the Old Testament," *Biblical Authority for Today*, ed. Alan Richardson and W. Schweitzer (Philadelphia: Westminster Press, 1952), pp. 257-74; Millar Burrows, *An Outline of Biblical Theology* (Philadelphia: Westminster Press, 1946), ch. xvii; Charles L. Taylor, Jr., "Old Testament Foundations," *Christianity and Property*, ed. Joseph F. Fletcher (Philadelphia: Westminster Press, 1947), ch. i.

[70] For the significance of *tāmîm* in Hebrew psychology and ethics see Ludwig Köhler, *Theologie des Alten Testaments* (Tübingen: J. C. B. Mohr, 1936), p. 155; Pedersen, *Israel, Its Life and Culture*, I-II, 336-77.

tegration with the existing world. . . . It is especially significant that the Egyptians never showed any trace of feeling unworthy of the divine mercy. For he who errs is not a sinner but a fool, and his conversion to a better way of life does not require repentance but a better understanding. . . . Man is not seen in rebellion against the command of God nor does he experience the intensity and range of feelings from contrition to grace which characterize the main personages of the Old and New Testaments. By the same token the theme of God's wrath is practically unknown in Egyptian literature; for the Egyptian, in his aberrations, is not a sinner disciplined and corrected.[71]

The above remarks about the conception of sin, or lack of it, in Egypt seem capable of being applied to other religions, ancient and modern. In no nonbiblical faith does there occur such a radical, profound, and penetrating view of human error as that occasioned by the doctrine of God in the Bible. The Mesopotamians understood themselves as subject to the divine will and decree, but they knew nothing of the righteousness of God in the biblical sense and the question of sin did not enter their minds. "Hence their penitential psalms abound in confessions of guilt but ignore the sense of sin; they are vibrant with despair but not with contrition—with regret but not with repentance." [72] The problem of man in worship was to isolate and identify the particular offense which had angered the gods and to make the specific penance prescribed for its expiation. Human error was thus atomized and its remedy mechanistic.

For a chosen people conformance with the will of God can be a source of joy. For the Mesopotamians the divine decrees merely circumscribed man's servitude. Religious exaltation fell, for them, outside the sphere of ethics; it sprang from the awareness that they lived in conformity with the rhythm of divine life. This is what we have called "living in harmony with nature"—for in nature the life of the gods was manifest.[73]

Yet while pointing to the central meaning of sin in the Bible, we should not infer that Israel had completely liberated herself from the ancient conceptual world. The remnant of an amoral, dynamistic view of holiness in the cultus, particularly in the earlier stages of life in Palestine, meant that the priests knew of a ritualistic, amoral view of sin as ceremonial uncleanness, for which expiatory rites were necessary. Furthermore, we infer from the teaching of the prophets that many of the people,

especially in the middle and upper classes, found a purely cultic understanding of the nature of sin as extremely desirable and convenient because it left them free to divorce God's "thou shalt" from the newly arisen complexities of economic and political life. It was a mission of the prophets to denounce this divorce, and to indicate that the area of responsible obedience included every phase of human existence. No matter what the complexities and ramifications of the law may be, God's primary demand is a spiritual "perfection" (*tāmîm*, wholesome wholeness, innocence, and integrity) which issues in just dealing, loyalty to one's covenant vows, and humility of attitude and action before God (Mic. 6:6-8) .

2. Atonement and Forgiveness.—In priestly theology it would appear that the efficacy of the sacrificial cultus for the atonement of sins was limited. Leviticus, at any rate, makes no provision for sins done with a high hand, that is, with premeditation in a proud, arrogant, and rebellious spirit. The provisions of the levitical law appear to be confined to those sins committed unwittingly and without arrogant premeditation. In other words, sacrificial worship was efficacious in healing the breach in communion between the "tabernacling" God and his covenant community only when the sins were committed by sincere and law-abiding members of the community. In theory, at least, those who sinned with a high hand were to be deprived of membership in the theocratic society. In any event, such sinners could appeal only in repentance to God directly; their sacrifice could not make atonement for them.

For comparatively minor sins, therefore, in the committing of which no serious rebellion or haughty attitude was involved, an atonement rite performed in a spirit of worship was deemed acceptable to God. The latter would accept the offering as a "covering" for the sin. Where there are gross sins, the occasion for which is a hard or "uncircumcised" heart, a stiff neck, a "spirit of whoredom"—that is, where man is clearly rebelling against the covenant presence of God—then the sacrificial law which was given to the covenant community was no longer efficacious. The laws for worship were given to the "church," the community of the faithful. If one cut himself off from the "church" by flagrant sins, either of an interior or overt nature, or both, then he must not expect the law to cover his situation.

Does the gross sinner, then, have no hope? Israel's knowledge of the gracious nature of God was so deep that she possessed an extraordinary understanding of his forgiveness. Before the holiness and covenant presence of God the gross sinner stands condemned. Yet to him God ex-

[71] Henri Frankfort, *Ancient Egyptian Religion* (New York: Columbia University Press, 1948), pp. 73, 77. Used by permission.

[72] Frankfort, *Kingship and the Gods*, p. 278.

[73] *Ibid.*, p. 279.

tends his redeeming mercy. The plight of the highhanded sinner is that he stands alone, his communion severed—the most terrible fate of which the Old Testament can conceive (cf. Cain as murderer in Gen. 4). God's forgiveness means that he desires to repair the communion and to restore the offender into the sacred fellowship with himself and his fellows in the congregation (*qāhāl*) of Israel. Other religions of that day and later knew of divine holiness and goodness, as also of divine grace to those whom the gods deemed worthy of it. But this biblical conception of a redemptive, forgiving love, the purpose of which was to create community and to repair the breach between it and God, is as phenomenal as it is unique. It is radically different from the subtle, modern idolatry in the church which assumes that of course God will forgive because it is his primary business to do so (Voltaire).

The vocabulary for divine forgiveness in the Old Testament is almost as extensive as that for sin. In Ps. 51, for example, the following expressions appear: "blot out my transgressions" (vss. 1, 9), "wash me," "cleanse me," "purge me" (vss. 2, 7), and "hide thy face from my sins" (vs. 9). When God does these things, the petitioner will possess a "clean heart" and a "right spirit" (vs. 10). The difficulty of the sinner is that he is "cast away" from God's presence and removed from the working of his spirit; but in forgiveness there is restoration unto "the joy of thy salvation" (vss. 11, 12). A very common expression for forgiveness is "to take away" or "to carry away" sin, employing the common Hebrew verb *nāsā'* which means simply "to bear" or "to carry" (e.g., Exod. 34:7, translated above, p. 364). Also common is the conception of sin as a sickness which God "heals" (forgives), e.g., "I will heal their backsliding, I will love them freely" (Hos. 14:4); "LORD, be merciful unto me; heal my soul; for I have sinned against thee" (Ps. 41:4); "He was wounded for our transgressions . . . , and with his stripes we are healed" (Isa. 53:5). Sickness and injury being so frequently conceived as God's judgment upon sin, his forgiveness could be expressed in terms of healing, usually accompanied by deliverance from the trouble.

All of the above are figurative expressions derived from various phases of the cultic and conceptual life (e.g., washing or wiping away, from lustration rites; "hiding the face," from atonement conceptions; etc.). The only abstract term for forgiveness is the verb *ṣālaḥ,* a brief examination of which will indicate some of the conceptions involved. In thirteen (or possibly fourteen: Lev. 5:6 LXX?) cases in Leviticus and Numbers it is used for the declaration of forgiveness when the proper sacrificial rite is performed (cf., e.g., Lev. 4:20, 26, 31, 35). More frequently, however, it is used in a broader context (in thirty-two cases), which may be divided into four categories.

(*a*) In the Solomonic prayer at the dedication of the temple the structure is conceived as a place toward which prayer should be directed. When God hears the prayer, he will forgive (I Kings 8:30). When the person praying is in any kind of trouble, the forgiveness will be accompanied by a deliverance from the difficulty (I Kings 8:34, 36, 39, 50).

(*b*) As later in Christianity, the relationship between intercessory prayer and the operation of divine grace was very close. Only by virtue of the intercession of Moses was God prepared to pardon Israel in the wilderness wanderings (Exod. 34:9; Num. 14:19-20). Similarly, at the intercession of the prophet God forgave and removed the pestilence (Amos 7:2-3). The context of thought in this case has to do with the divine "repentance." The Hebrew word used for this repentance (*nāham*) has as its basic meaning the conception of compassion, pity, and sorrow. Intercessory prayer furnished the condition in which God could show his compassion; thus he "repents," not in the sense that he changes his mind, but in the sense that the changed situation permits him to change his action from punishment to redemption.

(*c*) God's forgiveness is also granted when a human being or a people repents. This is implicit in Jer. 5:1-7 and explicit in Jer. 36:3. The most common Hebrew expression for repent was the word "to turn" (*shûbh*). Even in the midst of the gross sin of Jehoiakim's time, if the people will "turn, every man from his evil way," God will forgive their sins (cf. also Isa. 55:7).

(*d*) Yet finally there is a forgiveness which God will grant at the end of the present era in the eschatological time when the conflicts of the present will be resolved. In this case the forgiveness is a free and unmerited act of God, independent of human repentance. Man will be given a "new heart" so that his rebellion will cease, and God will forgive the sins of the past (Jer. 31:34; 33:8; 50:20; cf. Isa. 40:2; Ezek. 36:25-38). These passages portray the reconstitution of God's people as a sacred community in fellowship with himself. Forgiveness is both an integral part and a consequence of this future redemption.[74]

The conception of a personal reconciliation with God thus prevented the deepest ranges

[74] See Johann Jakob Stamm, *Erlösen und Vergeben im Alten Testament* (Bern: A. Francke A.-G., 1940), pp. 47-86; cf. J. Philip Hyatt, *Prophetic Religion* (New York and Nashville: Abingdon-Cokesbury Press, 1947), ch. x.

of Old Testament faith from conceiving of forgiveness solely as a cultic matter for which mechanical rites of atonement were considered magically effective. It also prevented an impersonal and purely legalistic conception of sin from taking a position at the center of religious attention. This does not mean, however, that these tendencies toward the misunderstanding of the free operation of the divine grace in the context of the total sin of man were eradicated. On the contrary, they survived and were developed in seemingly rigid and doctrinaire forms in Judaism. Indeed, the same thing has happened repeatedly in the history of Christianity. Yet in the latter there is no excuse for misunderstanding. In Jesus Christ the riches of Israel's faith are brought together into a clear focus and the elements unharmonized are either harmonized or set aside. The forgiving and redemptive love of God is seen in Christ's ministry to the sinners for whom Judaism had no message except through adherence to a formal and stultifying legalism. But this love was demonstrated most vividly in the vicarious suffering of Christ and in the creation of the redeemed fellowship, the new Israel, in his risen body.

In the final analysis the promise of life to Israel, conditioned as it was upon the proper worship and service of God, was an eschatological promise, because the love and the wrath of God could not be resolved into harmony in the midst of the persistent violation of the covenant. In the atoning work of Christ the Christian sees God's forgiveness in a more radical form than was possible in Judaism, because the eschatological salvation for which Israel hoped was rescued from the limbo of embarrassment and re-created at the center of the new faith.[75]

IV. The Faith of Israel

A. Biblical Faith and Biblical Theology.—In conclusion, what was said in the introduction must be reaffirmed—that the faith of Israel was not anchored in abstract, propositional statements of the type to which we have become accustomed in dogmatic theology. Indeed, if we define "theology" solely as propositional dogmatics, or as the systematic presentation of a series of religious ideas about God and man, then we shall be forced to conclude that the Bible cannot truly be exhibited in a "theological" manner. Those who insist on retaining the term "biblical theology" do so because they refuse to surrender the term "theology" entirely to the systematic dogmatician. Biblical faith can be expressed only by a different type of theology, one which is based on the confessional

[75] See further, Eichrodt, Theologie des Alten Testaments, III, 81-141.

recital of the great acts of God. The unity of the Bible is to be found, therefore, neither in the realm of systematically presented ideas nor in the naturalistic development of a human organism in the evolving social process. Various levels of unity exist, to be sure, in both these spheres, but the basic unity lies in the intense awareness of the redemptive purpose of God as expressed in his historical activity.

It is for this reason that any discussion of Old Testament theology must begin not with God alone, but with God in relation to his elect people (see pp. 352-54). To do so means that the historical events of the Exodus and the wilderness wandering have to be taken seriously as primary data for theological reflection. The knowledge of God in the Old Testament was not formulated philosophically or abstractly; it was an inference drawn from what he had done in saving and constituting a people. Election and covenant thus became the means by which the true meaning of the patriarchal period was comprehended and by which the subsequent history was interpreted. From these events both before and after the Exodus the particular Israelite understanding of the nature of God came into being. What God had done revealed his lordship over history and his purposive action in history. He thus transcended both history and nature, and in so doing revealed the utter difference between himself and the gods of the nations (pp. 357-62). In the same light also his being and his relationship to the world and to man were comprehended (pp. 362-67). He is the living, active God whose relationship to man and to history can be depicted only by means of an anthropomorphic vocabulary. None of his attributes are understood as static qualities like the Greek conceptions of the transcendent good, truth, and beauty. The biblical attributes express, for the most part, the nature of God's activity: his love and grace, his righteousness and justice, his jealousy and wrath. His relationship to the world was therefore an active rather than a static one, so that the gulf which his holiness set between himself and his creation was constantly bridged by his own mediums of revelation. The conception of man as a creature made in God's image, but also as a sinner, was derived ultimately from the nature of God's action, for the doctrines of creation, election, and judgment lie at the root of Israel's anthropology. Moreover, the knowledge of God's lordship over history and his purpose within it was the source of the biblical hope, and furnished the setting in which that hope unfolded as the successive crises revealed the more clearly the nature of God's intention and method of working in history (pp. 367-74).

The worship and service of God (as described

in pp. 375-87) was the response of man to the God who had revealed himself in historical events. Pagan magic was excluded from worship since its occult and mysterious nature did not correspond to the open, clear, and definite means by which God chose to reveal himself. Most of the chief festivals of worship became historical commemorations of God's saving acts. Temple and sacrifice were shifted from the theological base on which they rested in paganism, and the conceptions of good and evil were tied into the covenant faith in which man met God as a sovereign Person.

In the churches which trace their lineage to the Reformation it is especially common to speak of the Bible as "the Word of God." When this phrase is interpreted to mean that the center of the Bible is a series of divinely given teachings, then it is certainly a serious misconception. The Bible is indeed filled with the words of God, but they are not the type of "words" which in themselves constitute a propositional theology. They are always definitely related to historical events. The law was rooted in the covenant at Sinai and was thus historically conditioned. The "word" which came to the prophets was at least in large part inferential in the sense that it was based upon the knowledge of God as known from past events which was used to interpret present happenings. If a prophet was accused of proclaiming a false "word" he could only rely upon his inner certainty and upon the future action of God for confirmation. New Testament theology is of a similar type to that of the Old. In the forefront stand the Synoptic Gospels, which are confessional histories of the life and death of Jesus Christ, written in the light of his resurrection. To speak of the divine work in Christ as "the Word of God" is to betray the faith except as we reinterpret the meaning of this "Word" as one which became flesh, in accordance with John 1 (that is, the Word is a Person, not a system of ideas). The theology of the epistles is not of a systematic nature, but an explication of the meaning of the event of Christ in the light of the whole biblical history of God's works and in the light also of particular situations which the letters were written to confront.

The word, the promise, and the law of God were thus not static abstractions in their original setting; they were an integral part of the historical work of God. A law or a word which accompanied one act might not fit precisely the historical situation and purpose of God in a subsequent event some centuries later. Furthermore, God taught his people by his acts, so that theological understanding was deepened with the passing centuries. Consequently, variety in biblical theology must be expected. Yet that variety does not constitute a series of different theologies; it witnesses to the unity of God, his purpose, and his saving acts which transcend the whole and keep all variety together in one unique book, the Bible.

The belief that historical events reveal the action, the purpose, and the will of God is of course a faith which, though not unreasonable, is nevertheless not subject to complete rational proof. Biblical theology as primarily an explication of God's unique historical work among one people in one particular epoch is thus more than an objective description of the historical process by which the people arrived at their conceptions. It is the attempt to put into communicable language the basis and implications of the faith. Thus a tension will always exist between the faith itself and our attempts to communicate it in rational language at a given historical period. The faith is greater than our attempts to express it and deeper than any one individual can conceive in his historical finitude. There is thus a sense in which every essay on biblical theology must inevitably be partial and unsatisfactory. Furthermore, the creeds of the church which preserve our historical continuity with the original revelation and discipline our tendencies toward pagan idolatry are not in themselves a substitute for the Bible. They are not sacrosanct in the sense that they bear the same authority as the Bible itself. The faith of the church must constantly be reformed and illumined on the basis of a fresh study of the biblical record. A relatively static authoritarianism, either of the Roman Catholic or fundamentalist type, so confuses the authority of the church and its creeds with the authority of the biblical faith that the tension which God places between himself and our human understanding is removed. And the removal of this tension is the first step in opening the doors of the church to idolatry.

B. The Faith of Israel and the Faith of the Church.—Implicit in all that has been written above is the assumption that the faith of Israel is an integral and vital part of the faith of the church. For the Christian the Old Testament is at once independent of the New and yet without significance apart from the New. It is independent in the sense that we must study it on its own merits as the historical witness to the faith by which a people once lived. Yet its manifest incompleteness, its unreconciled hopes, and its nationalistic framework make it impossible for any subsequent people to live within it alone. Judaism and Christianity are two very different religions precisely because they have seen the Old Testament fulfilled in different ways. Judaism took the specific formulations of the law seriously as the guide to proper life in the interval before the dawn of the new age. The Talmud actually fulfills the law in the sense that the latter is made applicable to the changing situations of Jewish life. The New Testament, on the other hand, emphasizes instead the historical work of God which is climaxed in Jesus Christ. In his person are fulfilled the purposes and promises of God in the Israelite offices of prophet, priest, and king. With him God ushers in the new age which was the goal of Old Testament history and its hope. God's purpose and promise in the election and covenant of Israel are fulfilled in Christ's kingship over the elect and the world. Nationality is broadened in scope so that the elect are the new Israel who are not necessarily the sons of Abraham after the flesh but by adoption according to faith.

Thus both Judaism and Christianity possess the Old Testament and both believe it to be a unique, once for all, revelation of God. But Judaism in thinking of the Old Testament thinks first of the Pentateuch as the law of God and of the Talmud as its exposition. The primary attention of the Jew is thus given to the law and especially to the Talmud. Christianity, on the contrary, refuses to see the law as the center of the Old Testament. The redemptive activity of God is the primary content of the Pentateuch, not the law, and that activity continues through the remaining historical books. Consequently, the Pentateuch cannot be separated as a legal literature from the prophetic histories which follow, for all bear witness to the work of God which leads directly to Jesus Christ. In Christ the essentials of the law are retained, though in a nonjuridical setting, while the specific cultic and national laws which served their divinely given purpose at a given time are set aside and seen to be meaningful only as illustrations of the manner in which the will of God was made applicable then and of the way in which we also must make the same will applicable to our own situation. God's salvation is thus to be conceived not in a forensic or juridical manner, but in the terms of the new covenant of grace in Christ.

The church affirms, therefore, that Christ is the key to the central meaning of the Old Testament; but at the same time it must be emphasized that the Old Testament is the clue to Christ. The church has received an enlightenment from the faith of Israel which has enabled it to see that entrance into the kingdom of Christ cannot be found among the religions of this world, but solely in the faith of Abraham's seed of which we are heirs in the church by Christ Jesus. It is the Old Testament which has always been one of the chief bulwarks of the church against paganism because in Israel the revolutionary faith was first established over against paganism and the theological basis on which we stand was achieved. When the New Testament is separated from the Old, it is a superstructure hanging in midair, a small torso of a literature filled with presuppositions which can be misunderstood and perverted. Without the Old Testament there could be little conception of God's purposive work in and through history, which reaches its climax in Christ. When separated from that perspective, Christ can be conceived only as another in the series of mankind's prophets and martyrs, or else as a new God, or on a par with the old, displacing the old. The whole Bible is needed for a trinitarian theology. By itself the New Testament contains insufficient material for a doctrine of creation, of justice and the responsible society, and of man in relation to his world and people. The New Testament presupposes Old Testament faith, while correcting, deepening, and fulfilling it, so that in Christ that faith becomes a new creation for a new Israel which is the body of Christ. In other words, the fathers of the church in the second and third centuries A.D. had the very best of reasons for rejecting Marcionism, the view that the God of the Old Testament was a different God from that of the New. Neither Testament possesses its full significance in the church apart from the other. Both together constitute the Christian Bible; separate one from the other and the theology of the church will be torn asunder.

V. Selected Bibliography

ALBRIGHT, W. F. *From the Stone Age to Christianity.* Baltimore: Johns Hopkins Press, 1940.

BAAB, OTTO J. *The Theology of the Old Testament.* New York and Nashville: Abingdon-Cokesbury Press, 1949.

BURROWS, MILLAR. *An Outline of Biblical Theology.* Philadelphia: Westminster Press, 1946.

DAVIDSON, A. B. *The Theology of the Old Testament.* New York: Charles Scribner's Sons, 1904.

EICHRODT, WALTHER. *Theologie des Alten Testaments.* Vol. I, 3rd ed.; Vols. II-III, 2nd ed. Berlin: Evangelische Verlagsanstalt, 1948.

FRANKFORT, H. and H. A.; WILSON, JOHN A.; JACOBSEN, THORKILD; and IRWIN, WILLIAM A. *The Intellectual Adventure of Ancient Man.* Chicago: University of Chicago Press, 1946.

KNUDSON, ALBERT C. *The Religious Teaching of the Old Testament.* New York: Abingdon Press, 1918.

KÖHLER, LUDWIG. *Theologie des Alten Testaments.* Tübingen: J. C. B. Mohr, 1936.

ROBINSON, H. WHEELER. *Inspiration and Revelation in the Old Testament.* Oxford: The Clarendon Press, 1946.

SCHULTZ, HERMANN. *Old Testament Theology,* tr. J. A. Paterson. Edinburgh: T. & T. Clark, 1892.

WRIGHT, G. ERNEST. *The Old Testament Against Its Environment.* Chicago: Henry Regnery Co., 1950.

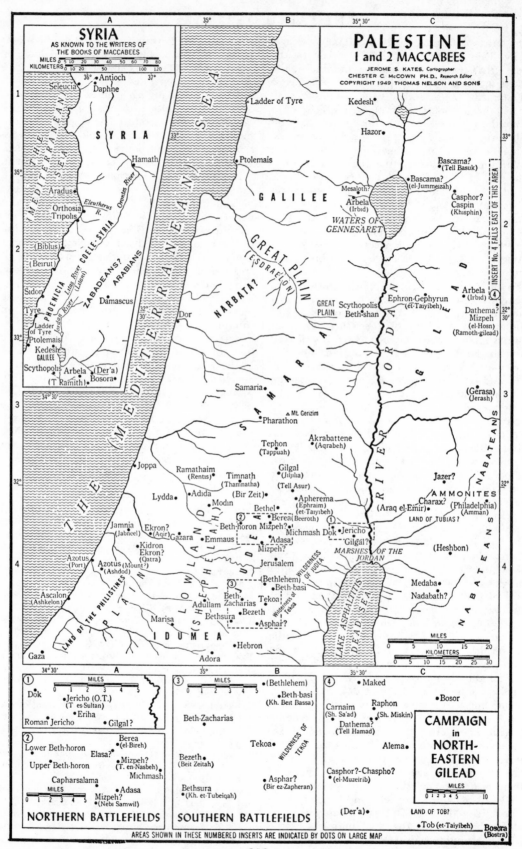

SYRIA
AS KNOWN TO THE WRITERS OF THE BOOKS OF MACCABEES

MILES 0 5 10 20 30 40 50 60 70 80
KILOMETERS 0 10 20 50 100 120

PALESTINE
1 and 2 MACCABEES
JEROME S. KATES, *Cartographer*
CHESTER C. McCOWN PH.D., *Research Editor*
COPYRIGHT 1949 THOMAS NELSON AND SONS

Antioch
Daphne
Seleucia

SYRIA

THE MEDITERRANEAN SEA

Hamath

Aradus
Orthosia
Tripolis
Eleutherus R.
ZABADEANS?
ARABIANS
Damascus

(Biblus)
(Beirut)

Sidon
PHOENICIA
Tyre
Litas River (Litani)
Jordan River
COELE-SYRIA

Ladder of Tyre
Ptolemais
Kedesh
GALILEE
Scythopolis
Arbela (Der'a)
(T Ramith) Bosora

Ladder of Tyre

Kedesh

Hazor

Ptolemais

GALILEE

Bascama? (Tell Basuk)
Bascama? (el-Jummeizah)
Mesaloth?
Arbela (Irbid)
WATERS OF GENNESARET
Casphor? Caspin (Khisphin)

Arbela (Irbid)
Dathema? Mizpeh (el-Hosn) (Ramoth-gilead)

GREAT PLAIN (ESDRAELON)

NARBATA?

GREAT PLAIN
Scythopolis
Beth-shan
Ephron-Gephyrun (et-Taiyibeh)

RIVER JORDAN
GILEAD

Dor

SAMARIA

Samaria
△ Mt. Gerizim
Pharathon

(Gerasa) (Jerash)

Joppa

Tephon (Tappuah)
Akrabattene (Aqrabeh)

Ramathaim (Rentis)
Timnath (Thamnatha)
Gilgal (Jiljilia)
(Tell Asur)

Jazer?

AMMONITES
Charax? (Araq el-Emir) (Philadelphia) (Amman)
LAND OF TUBIAS?

Lydda
Adida
Modin
(Bir Zeit)
Bethel
Apherema (Ephraim) (et-Taiyibeh)
Berea (Beeroth)

Jamnia (Jabneel)
Ekron? (Aqir)
Gazara
Emmaus
Beth-horon Mizpeh?
Michmash Dok
Adasa
Mizpeh?
Jericho
Gilgal?

Kidron
Ekron? (Qatra)
MARSHES OF THE JORDAN

(Heshbon)

Azotus (Port)
Azotus (Mount) (Ashdod)
Jerusalem
WILDERNESS OF JUDEA

Medaba
Nadabath?

Ascalon (Ashkelon)
(Bethlehem)
Beth-basi
Beth Zacharias
Tekoa
Bezeth
Wilderness of Tekoa
Adullam
Bethsura
Asphar?
LAKE ASPHALTITIS DEAD SEA

NABATEANS

Marisa

IDUMEA
Hebron

MILES 0 5 10 15 20
KILOMETERS 0 5 10 15 20 25 30

Gaza
Adora

INSERT No. 4 FALLS EAST OF THIS AREA

---

① NORTHERN BATTLEFIELDS
MILES 0 1 2 3 4 5
Dok
Jericho (O.T.) (T es-Sultan)
Eriha
Roman Jericho
Gilgal?

②
Berea (el-Bireh)
Lower Beth-horon
Elasa?
Upper Beth-horon
Mizpeh? (T. en-Nasbeh)
Michmash
Capharsalama
Adasa
MILES 0 1 2 3 4 5
Mizpeh? (Nebi Samwil)

③ SOUTHERN BATTLEFIELDS
MILES 0 1 2 3 4 5
(Bethlehem)
Beth-basi (Kh. Beit Bassa)
Beth-Zacharias
Tekoa
WILDERNESS OF TEKOA
Bezeth (Beit Zeitah)
Asphar? (Bir ez-Zapheran)
Bethsura (Kh. et-Tubeiqah)

④ CAMPAIGN in NORTH-EASTERN GILEAD
Maked
Raphon (Sh. Miskin)
Bosor
Carnaim (Sh. Sa'ad)
Dathema? (Tell Hamad)
Alema
Casphor?-Chaspho? (el-Muzeirib)
(Der'a)
LAND OF TOB?
Tob (et-Taiyibeh)
MILES 0 1 2 3 4 5 10
Bosora (Bostra)

AREAS SHOWN IN THESE NUMBERED INSERTS ARE INDICATED BY DOTS ON LARGE MAP

THE LITERATURE AND RELIGION
OF THE APOCRYPHA

by ROBERT H. PFEIFFER

The term "Apocrypha," a Greek word meaning "hidden, spurious (books)," denotes noncanonical books. Apocrypha (of the Old Testament) in its Roman Catholic meaning—attested in the writings of Origen and Augustine—refers to the books which are here called the "Pseudepigrapha." In its Protestant meaning adopted here, "Apocrypha" is the collection of the Jewish writings included in the Septuagint and in the Vulgate, but not in the Hebrew Old Testament. Catholics call these Apocrypha "deuterocanonical books"; Jerome called them "ecclesiastical books," using "apocrypha" in the sense of *all* noncanonical books. The contents of the Septuagint and the Vulgate Old Testaments differ slightly. Some Septuagint manuscripts include III-IV Maccabees and Ps. 151, never found in the Vulgate. The standard editions of the Vulgate print in an appendix at the end of the New Testament the following books: The Prayer of Manasses (in some manuscripts of the Septuagint and in some printed editions of the Septuagint it is placed among the Odes or Cantica which follow the Psalms), III Esdras (I Esdras in the Greek and English Bibles), and IV Esdras (lost in the Greek version, except for a few citations in Barn. 12 and Clement of Alexandria *Stromata* III. 16. 100; it is called II Esdras or Esdras Apocalypse in English).

According to common usage, the following books are here included among the Apocrypha: I Esdras, II Esdras, Tobit, Judith, the Rest of the Book of Esther, the Wisdom of Solomon, Ecclesiasticus, Baruch (ch. 6 of which is the Epistle of Jeremy), additions to Daniel (the Song of the Three Holy Children, the History of Susanna, the History of the Destruction of Bel and the Dragon), the Prayer of Manasses, I-II Maccabees.

In the Greek and Latin Bibles, however, the Apocrypha are scattered throughout the Old Testament, and nothing indicates that they are of debatable canonicity. In the following list of the contents of the Septuagint Old Testament (according to the order of Codex B, Vaticanus) the Apocrypha are *italicized:* The Pentateuch; Joshua, Judges, Ruth, I-IV Kings (i.e., I-II Samuel, I-II Kings), I-II Chronicles, *I Esdras,* II Esdras (i.e., Ezra-Nehemiah); Psalms, Proverbs, Ecclesiastes, Song of Songs, Job, *Wisdom of Solomon, Ecclesiasticus,* Esther (with the *Rest of the Book of Esther*), *Judith, Tobit,* the Book of the Twelve (Minor Prophets), Isaiah, Jeremiah, *Baruch,* Lamentations, *Epistle of Jeremy,* Ezekiel, Daniel (with the *Song of the Three Holy Children,* the *History of Susanna,* and *Bel and the Dragon*); (*I-II Maccabees* are not in the Codex Vaticanus). In the Vulgate, Tobit and Judith follow II Esdras and in turn are followed by Esther, Job, Psalms, etc.; the Book of the Twelve follows Daniel and precedes I-II Maccabees.

I. The Apocrypha in Judaism

All the books of the Apocrypha were written by Jewish authors whose names, with the sole exception of Jesus the son of Sirach (Ecclus. 50:27), are unknown (II Maccabees is the summary of a five volume history of Jason of Cyrene). Biblical authors likewise wrote their books anonymously or using as a nom de plume the name of an ancient renowned leader, such as Moses, David, or Solomon: only the prophetic books (Amos, Hosea, Isaiah, etc.) bear the name of their real authors because the prophets, being primarily preachers, could not conceal their identity. Sirach likewise was convinced that he was writing prophecy (Ecclus. 24:33), and his book contains to a great extent the rewriting of material delivered orally in the form of classroom lectures. Pride of authorship was unknown among the Israelites, and interest in the name of the writers of biblical books arose only in connection with their divine inspiration.

The books of the Apocrypha (except I-II Esdras) were written presumably during the last two centuries B.C., and certainly before the Council at Jamnia (*ca.* A.D. 90), where the Jewish scriptural canon was fixed for all time; later rabbinical discussions on the canonicity of certain books were purely academic. Before that time the Hebrew Bible had consisted of "the Law and the Prophets" (II Macc. 15:9; Matt. 5:17; etc.). The third division, the Writings or Hagiographa, was in a fluid state between 200 B.C. and A.D. 90, although we may surmise that at least Psalms, Proverbs, and Job had attained a more or less official canonical status by 100 B.C. During this period there must have been great differences of opinion in regard to what books were to be accepted as canonical. We may well imagine that some Jews preferred Judith to Esther, Wisdom to Ecclesiastes, I Maccabees to Chronicles, Ecclesiasticus to Proverbs—and vice versa. What were the criteria by which the rabbis at Jamnia distinguished inspired from human books? In view of the prevailing confusion and of the circulation of Christian books, drastic steps had to be taken—and they could be taken only on the basis of arbitrary standards and a priori principles. It so happens that two sources contemporary with the council at Jamnia *ca.* A.D. 90 (Josephus *Against Apion* I. 8; II [IV] Esdras 14:45-46), besides later rabbinical ones (Seder 'Olam Rabba 30; Baba Bathra 14b-15a; Tosefta Yadaim 3:5), have recorded for us the basic principle of selection.

At least as early as *ca.* 250 B.C., as we see from the writings of the Chronicler, the shadowy figure of Ezra—whose historical role seems to have been insignificant compared with that of Nehemiah—was growing in importance until he became almost a second Moses. The Chronicler had merely claimed that Ezra was the founder of the guild of the scribes and came from Babylonia with God's law in his hand (Ezra 7:11-12, 25); but according to II (IV) Esdras, Ezra had, through divine inspiration, dictated to five scribes the twenty-four books of the Hebrew Bible, besides seventy esoteric (apocalyptic) works, in forty days. Josephus likewise, and manifestly the rabbis at Jamnia, were convinced that the Old Testament canon was complete and closed forever in the time of Ezra because the Lord ceased at that time to reveal himself to prophets: after Artaxerxes I (465-424), during whose reign Ezra was active, "the exact succession of prophets no longer existed" (Josephus *Against Apion* I. 8). Consequently no book written after the time of Ezra could be regarded as inspired and canonical scripture. Incidentally, this is why no Jewish apocalypse was attributed to an author later than Ezra. On the basis of this principle some of the Apocrypha were automatically excluded from the canon: I-II Maccabees, because they dealt with a later period of Jewish history; Ecclesiasticus, because Jesus ben Sirach committed the error of naming himself as the author, and was known to have lived long after Ezra.

The other books, which were not manifestly too recent for canonization, were excluded for other reasons. Some of the Apocrypha were *ipso facto* excluded because they had been written in Greek: Wisdom of Solomon, II Macc. 2:19–15:39, III-IV Maccabees. The following books were written in Hebrew: Ecclesiasticus, Baruch, I Maccabees, Judith, Prayer of Manasses, additions to Daniel. The others were written in Aramaic: II Macc. 1:1–2:18, I Esdras 3:1–4:47 (the rest was for the most part written in Hebrew), Tobit, Epistle of Jeremy.

Thus we have some books (Judith, Tobit, Baruch, Epistle of Jeremy) which had every qualification for inclusion into the canon: the ostensible early date, Hebrew or Aramaic language, sound orthodox teaching, and the literary quality of these books—all of these are on a par with (if not superior to) the latest parts of the canonical Old Testament. Why were they excluded? *Habent sua fata libelli.* In every case the primary condition for canonization at Jamnia was survival, which depended on popularity. Popular taste is unpredictable, irrational, and often at variance with expert opinion. The success of certain books, plays, and paintings, or the failure of better ones, has baffled the best of the critics. All that we can say is that, with the exception of Ecclesiasticus (which is quoted three times as scripture in the Talmud and survived in Hebrew until the twelfth century), the Hebrew and Aramaic Apocrypha did not strike the popular fancy and therefore ceased to be copied soon after their translation into Greek. Thus they were lost in the original language. Except for Ecclesiasticus, it seems probable that no copies of the Apocrypha in Hebrew or Aramaic were readily available to the rabbis at Jamnia, and that there was no popular demand—such as is apparent in the case of Esther, Song of Songs, and Daniel—for their canonization. At least since the beginning of our era the interest in these books has been at low ebb. In the reorganization of Judaism after the destruction of Jerusalem in A.D. 70, works such as the Apocrypha and the apocalypses soon ceased to be written and copied (II Esdras 3–14 and the Apocalypse of Baruch, ca. A.D. 90, are among the last), and existing copies of earlier noncanonical books may have been systematically destroyed. Henceforth the Scriptures alone were searched by the Jews for inspired truth, guidance, illumination, and the edification of congregations or individuals. Other literature was either useless or dangerous, and Jews were warned against it: "Whoever brings together in his house more than twenty-four books [the Hebrew Old Testament] brings confusion" (Midrash Qoheleth 12:12). Rabbi Akiba (died ca. 132) even declared that readers of apocryphal literature had no part in the future world (Jerusalem Talmud, Sanhedrin X. 1, folio 28a; Babylonian Talmud, Sanhedrin 100b). The survival of the Apocrypha and of the Pseudepigrapha is due entirely to the Christian Church.

II. The Apocrypha in Christianity

A. Before the Reformation. 1. The Septuagint.—While the Bible of Jesus was "the Law and the Prophets" in Hebrew, the Old Testament of Paul and of his Gentile converts was—and remained, at least in principle, until the Reformation—the Septuagint (LXX), the Greek version begun in Alexandria ca. 250 B.C. and continued by various hands during more than one century.

Except for a few ancient scraps of papyrus, all extant manuscripts of the Septuagint are Christian. Nevertheless it is commonly assumed that the Septuagint (including the Apocrypha) was the Bible of the Alexandrian Jews before the Christians adopted it. If such was the case, as seems probable, what was the canonical status of the Apocrypha among the Alexandrian Jews? Opinions vary, and even the evidence is ambiguous. Flavius Josephus (died ca. A.D. 100) in his use of the Septuagint as a source for his

Jewish Antiquities regarded I Maccabees, I Esdras, and the additions to Esther (omitting the first and last, A and F) as no less authentic and canonical than the Hebrew Bible. Philo of Alexandria (died ca. A.D. 50), however, adhered strictly to the Hebrew canon, ignoring the Apocrypha *in toto,* and like the Palestinian rabbis regarded the Pentateuch as the central and supreme revelation of the Lord. But the Hellenistic Jews were not all as strict as Philo. In Palestine sacred and profane literature were both circulating in Hebrew and Aramaic, but in Alexandria all profane literature was in Greek, while all sacred literature was translated into Greek from Hebrew or Aramaic. Consequently it was natural to regard as holy writ all Palestinian books translated into the Greek vernacular. Thus, for instance, the translator of the second half of Jeremiah also translated the book of Baruch, at least in part, as if it were no less canonical. Moreover, it is difficult to explain how the Christians could have regarded the Apocrypha as an integral part of their Greek Bible—the Septuagint which they received from Alexandria—if the Hellenistic Jews had not so done before them.

2. The New Testament.—Eighty per cent of the Old Testament quotations in the New Testament reproduce the Septuagint, although by no means always verbatim. The New Testament writers never quote from the Apocrypha, but allusions to certain passages in the Apocrypha occur: Ecclus. 5:11 (in Jas. 1:19; James has many other reminiscences of Ecclesiasticus); II Macc. 6–7 (in Heb. 11:35-36); echoes from the Wisdom of Solomon in Paul's epistles (Rom. 1:20-32; 9:21; II Cor. 5:4; Eph. 6:14; etc.), in Heb. 1:3 (ἀπαύγασμα, "effulgence, reflection"; Wisd. Sol. 7:26), and in Matt. 27:43 (Wisd. Sol. 2:18). References to some of the Pseudepigrapha are even more direct: Assumption of Moses (Jude 9; according to Origen), the book of Jannes and Jambres (II Tim. 3:8; according to Origen), Martyrdom of Isaiah (Heb. 11:37, "they were sawn asunder"), and Enoch (Jude 14, 15).

3. Church Fathers and Councils.—Allusions to passages in the Apocrypha occur in the earliest Christian writings outside of the New Testament beginning with the Didache or Teaching of the Twelve Apostles (cf. Did. 4:5 with Ecclus. 4:31). The Epistle of Barnabas in chs. 6, 12, and 19 quotes Wisdom, Ecclesiasticus, and II Esdras. I Clement quotes the Wisdom of Solomon. Tertullian praises Judith, cites Ecclesiasticus as scripture, and attributes Wisdom to the pen of Solomon. Irenaeus quoted Baruch as a work of Jeremiah, and Susanna (as also Bel and the Dragon) as part of Daniel; Hippolytus paraphrased Susanna and wrote a commentary on the Song of the Three Children. Clement of Alexandria, Origen, and Cyprian not only quoted passages in the Apocrypha, but they specifically regarded them as scripture. Athanasius reports that catechumens were taught parts of the Apocrypha, which he freely cites as scripture. The same point of view prevails in Chrysostom, Ambrose, Augustine, and other church fathers.

This acceptance of the Apocrypha as canonical scriptures in the early church was frowned upon by some of the most learned of the church fathers, beginning with Origen. As a churchman (see above) Origen followed the general practice, but as a scholar he clearly and definitely limited the canonical Old Testament to the Hebrew Bible, without the Apocrypha. Similarly, Cyril of Jerusalem exhorted the catechumens to hold fast to the twenty-two books and to disregard the Apocrypha; he distinguished between recognized and questionable scriptures, but in practice he could not deviate from the general usage. Such is also the attitude of Jerome: in theory he made a sharp distinction between *libri canonici* and *libri ecclesiastici,* declaring categorically that books which were outside the Hebrew canon should be placed *inter apocrypha* (among the apocryphal writings) ; but in practice he overcame his scruples and included the Apocrypha in his Latin version of the Bible, the Vulgate, which is still the official Roman Catholic Bible. He even cited Ecclesiasticus as scripture.

Thus the two divergent points of view, the canonicity of the Apocrypha in Roman Catholicism and their relegation outside the scriptural canon prevailing in Protestantism (together with controversies on the matter), reach back to the early church, if not indeed to the difference between the Palestinian and Alexandrian Jewish canons. In 238, Julius Africanus of Emmaus wrote to Origen of Alexandria expressing amazement at his quotation of the story of Susanna as canonical scripture. Origen, being unable to defend his position with scholarly arguments, merely appealed to the authority of the church, which is not derived from the Jews, and quoted the verse, "Remove not the ancient landmark, which thy fathers have set" (Prov. 22:28).

But only a few scholars expressed some qualms about the tacit canonization of the Apocrypha. Jerome reports that the Council of Nicaea (325) reckoned Judith among the Scriptures; but this information is not confirmed otherwise. Local synods, however, issued decisions on the matter. The African Council of Hippo (393), attended by Augustine, recognized the canonicity of Wisdom of Solomon, Ecclesiasticus, Tobit, Judith, I-II Maccabees,

and, presumably, I Esdras, Baruch, Epistle of Jeremy, and the additions to Daniel and Esther, which did not need to be specifically mentioned, being considered parts of canonical books. The third (397) and the sixteenth (419) Councils of Carthage, likewise attended by Augustine, confirmed the decision of the Council of Hippo. The Council of Trent (April 8, 1546), confirmed by the Vatican Council (1870), both of which Roman Catholics alone regard as ecumenical, pronounced the anathema against whoever did not regard as "sacred and canonical" all the books contained in the Vulgate. The Sistine edition of the Vulgate (1590) had omitted I-II [III-IV] Esdras and the Prayer of Manasses, but in the Clementine edition (1592), which became official and was followed in later editions, these books were printed in smaller type as an appendix to the New Testament, with the statement that they are not included in the list of canonical books decreed at the Council of Trent.

In the Greek Church, despite some objections, the Apocrypha were recognized as canonical, and the second Trullan Council (692) followed the African councils in recognizing the canonicity of the Apocrypha. The Council of Jerusalem (1672), however, limited the Old Testament to the Hebrew canon (probably with the tacit assumption that I Esdras, and the additions to Esther and Daniel were included therein) and to only four books of the Apocrypha (Tobit, Judith, Ecclesiasticus, and Wisdom of Solomon).

The Syriac Church, which in the early period was greatly influenced by the Jews, at first read only the books of the Hebrew Old Testament (omitting Chronicles, Ezra-Nehemiah, and Esther) and Ecclesiasticus, in the Peshitta ("simple") version. Eventually, however, the influence of the Septuagint became dominant (except among the Nestorians). The Syro-Hexaplaric version made by Paul of Tella (in 616-17) from the Septuagint column in Origen's Hexapla, preserved for the most part in the Ambrosian Manuscript published by A. M. Ceriani (1874), contained Wisdom of Solomon, Ecclesiasticus, Baruch, Epistle of Jeremy, and the additions to Daniel. The Codex Ambrosianus of the sixth century, also published by Ceriani (1876-83), contains the Apocrypha (omitting I [III] Esdras, Prayer of Manasses, Tobit, and the additions to Esther) scattered in part among the canonical books, and also III-IV Maccabees, II [IV] Esdras, and Josephus *Jewish War* VII.

In the *Instituta regularia divinae legis (ca.* 550), Junilius Africanus has preserved for us in a Latin translation the course on biblical introduction given at the theological school of

Nisibis (northern Mesopotamia) by Paul the Persian. The critical liberalism and rational scholarship of the school of Antioch survived for a while at Nisibis and through this volume became known to the Western Church. Theodore of Mopsuestia (died in 428) not only rejected the Apocrypha, but also Ezra-Nehemiah, Esther, and Job from the Old Testament canon. Paul the Persian, in the *Instituta* attributed to Junilius, taught that the following books were of unquestionable canonicity: the books of the Hebrew Bible, except those mentioned in the next two groups, and also Ecclesiasticus. He added that the following books, which many placed in the first group, possessed only limited authority: Job, Chronicles, Ezra-Nehemiah, Esther, Tobit, Judith, I-II Maccabees. Finally he ascribed no authority whatever to all other books, although some regarded Wisdom of Solomon and Song of Songs as canonical. He did not mention Ecclesiastes at all.

All the other ancient churches in Africa and western Asia used vernacular translations of the Greek Bible (Septuagint), and consequently accepted the Apocrypha as a matter of course; some of them even added one or more of the Pseudepigrapha to their Bible, and have thus preserved in Oriental translations some books that would otherwise have utterly perished.

A few ancient lists of canonical books may also be mentioned. Melito, bishop of Sardis (*ca.* 180), according to Eusebius (*Church History* IV. 26), omitted from his list not only the Apocrypha, but also Lamentations and Esther (which may, however, have been included in Jeremiah and Ezra). Origen (Eusebius *Church History* VI. 25) lists the books in the Hebrew canon, adding Τὰ Μακκαβαϊκά (I-II Maccabees) outside their number at the end. The Muratorian Fragment (*ca.* 180) is confined to the New Testament, except that it curiously places Wisdom of Solomon before Revelation. Epiphanius, in one of his lists, adds Wisdom of Solomon and Ecclesiasticus after the New Testament, but in another he places them after the Old Testament, on a lower plane. A third-century list in the Codex Claromontanus (sixth century, Paris) includes the Apocrypha (except the Prayer of Manasses) in the list of canonical books.

The principal uncial Greek manuscripts contain the Apocrypha, but with some variations. The Codex Vaticanus (fourth century) omitted I-II Maccabees and the Prayer of Manasses; the Codex Sinaiticus (end of fourth or beginning of fifth centuries) in its extant portions contains the Prophets, Esther, Judith, Tobit, I and IV Maccabees; the Codex Alexandrinus (fifth century) contains, in addition to the standard Apocrypha, also III-IV Maccabees and the

Prayer of Manasses (among the Odes, supplementing the Psalms).

B. Since the Reformation.—After the Apocrypha had thus enjoyed almost undisputed canonicity during the Middle Ages, two factors contributed to their relegation outside the Scriptures in the majority of the Protestant churches: the polemic against Roman Catholic doctrines, and the study of Hebrew.

The basic principle of the Reformation was, "The just shall live by faith" (Rom. 1:17; Gal. 3:11; Heb. 10:38; cf. Hab. 2:4)—not by works. The Roman Catholic doctrine of justification by works was supported by proof texts in the Apocrypha (Ecclus. 3:3, 14-15, 30; Tob. 4:7-11; 12:9; 14:11; etc.), but had been vigorously attacked by Paul (Rom. 3:20, 28; Gal. 3:2). Equally, if not more distasteful to the Reformers was the Roman Catholic doctrine of the merits of the saints, for which likewise the Apocrypha furnished confirmation (Song of the Three Holy Children 12; contrast Luke 3:8).

The revival of classical learning, humanism, the Renaissance, and the invention of printing —all had contributed to a renewal of interest in the study of Hebrew (which had been in abeyance since Jerome) among Christians, before Martin Luther nailed his Ninety-Five Theses to the door of the Wittenberg castle church (October 31, 1517). Nicholas of Lyra (died *ca.* 1340), a Franciscan of Jewish parentage, wrote an important commentary on the Old Testament, omitting the Apocrypha. Thoroughly familiar with Hebrew, he interpreted the Scriptures accurately, with the help of the famous Jewish commentaries; regarding Wisdom of Solomon, Ecclesiasticus, Judith, Tobit, and I-II Maccabees as noncanonical, he interpreted them later in a separate work. He even published in 1333 a pamphlet on the differences between the Vulgate and "Hebrew Truth" (i.e., the Hebrew Bible). Lyra's influence may have induced Luther to study Hebrew, but in any case is apparent in his biblical interpretation. The first Hebrew grammars written by Christians were those of Konrad Pellicanus (1503) and especially of Johann Reuchlin (1506). Christian students of the Hebrew Bible would naturally conclude with Jerome that it alone—the *hebraica veritas* (Hebrew truth) without the Apocrypha—constituted the canonical Old Testament.

The determination of the exact contents and wording of the Scriptures was of primary importance to the Reformers. Having refused to recognize the authority of the Papacy, they made the Scriptures the supreme guide and norm in matters of faith and conduct. Since the Vulgate was no longer regarded by the Protestants as the correct transcript of God's word, it became imperative to publish vernacular translations made from the "inspired" original texts in Hebrew (Old Testament) and Greek (New Testament). As a result, the canonicity of the Apocrypha could no longer be maintained.

The first to draw the natural conclusions from the Protestant principles was Andreas Rudolf (Bodenstein) Karlstadt, who in his *De canonicis scripturis libellus* (Wittenberg, 1520) divided the Old Testament scriptures into canonical writings (the Hebrew Old Testament), hagiographic apocrypha (Wisdom of Solomon, Ecclesiasticus, Judith, Tobit, I-II Maccabees), and worthless apocrypha (the other books, not listed). Luther accepted these conclusions (to some extent) when in his German version of the whole Bible (1534) he relegated those six books of the Apocrypha, together with the additions to Daniel and Esther, and the Prayer of Manasses (but without I-II Esdras) to an appendix at the end of the Old Testament, with the following superscription, "Apocrypha, these are books which are not held equal to the sacred Scriptures, and yet are useful and good for reading." Luther's example was immediately followed by Coverdale, who in accordance with the Latin Bible omitted the Prayer of Manasses and added I-II Esdras to the books placed at the end of the Old Testament under the title The Apocrypha (1535). Wycliffe's Bible (*ca.* 1382, revised 1388) had failed to segregate the Apocrypha. All English editions of the Bible prior to 1629 contained the Apocrypha, either with the canonical books or relegated to an appendix: "Thomas Matthew" (1537, in which the Prayer of Manasses appeared for the first time in English), the Great Bible (1539), the Geneva Bible (1560, in which for the first time in English some of the Apocrypha were translated from the Greek instead of the Latin), the Bishop's Bible (1568), and the King James Bible or Authorized Version (1611, made from the Hebrew and Greek, in which the Apocrypha are scattered among the canonical books). But as early as 1629 the Apocrypha were omitted in some editions of the English Bible and, following some bitter controversies, the British and Foreign Bible Society has excluded them since 1827 from all printings of the Bible (except some pulpit Bibles).

The Church of England, in the sixth of the Forty-Two Articles of Religion (1553; Thirty-Nine in 1563), declared: "The other Books (as Hierome saith [see Jerome's *Preface to the Books of Solomon*]) the Church doth read for example of life and instruction of manners; and yet doth it not apply them to establish any doctrine."

In conclusion, there are three attitudes toward the Apocrypha in Christendom: they are fully canonical (Roman Catholicism); they are not God's word but are edifying (Lutheran, Anglican, and Zurich Reformed churches); they should be rejected (Calvinistic and other Protestant churches).

III. The Books of the Apocrypha

A. I Esdras. 1. I Esdras and Its Canonical Parallels.—This book—or rather this torso of an edition of Chronicles-Ezra-Nehemiah—is called I Esdras in the Septuagint, Old Latin, and Syriac versions; II Esdras in Lucian's recension of the Septuagint; III Esdras in the Vulgate (where it is relegated outside the canonical Bible, after the New Testament). It relates the Jewish history from Josiah's celebration of the Passover to the reading of the Law in the time of Ezra. Except for some changes in order (Ezra 4:7-24 here precedes Ezra 2:1), some omissions (Ezra 4:6; Neh. 1:1–7:5; 8:13*b*–13: 31), and the addition of 1:23-24 and of the Story of the Three Youths (I Esdras 3:1–5:6), the book is merely an older, more idiomatic, freer, and better translation of the following portions of the canonical Chronicles-Ezra-Nehemiah: II Chr. 35:1–36:21 (I Esdras 1); Ezra 1:1-11 (I Esdras 2:1-15); Ezra 2:1-67=Neh. 7:6-69 (I Esdras 5:7-43); Ezra 2:68–4:5; 4:24–6:22 (I Esdras 5:44–7:15); Ezra 7:1–8:36 (I Esdras 8:1-67); Ezra 9:1–10:44 (I Esdras 8:68–9:36); Neh. 7:73–8:13*a* (I Esdras 9:37-55).

A comparison of the Greek I Esdras with the canonical Hebrew-Aramaic parallels listed above will show that our Greek Esdras was translated from a text which differed only in minor variants from the canonical text. Thus I Esdras 1:11 ("before [*liphnê*] the people") is a better reading than II Chr. 35:12 ("of the children [*libhnê*] of the people"); similarly "and he lodged" (וילן, I Esdras 9:2) is preferable to "and he went" (וילך, Ezra 10:6), which the King James Version mistranslates "and *when* he came" in order to make sense.

The Greek Ezra is not a revision of the Septuagint of Chronicles-Ezra-Nehemiah. It is true that at times the same Hebrew or Aramaic words are given a very different meaning in the two Greek texts: "being arrayed in their vestments" (I Esdras 1:2) corresponds to "and he encouraged them" (II Chr. 35:2, LXX). Moreover, at times the two Greek texts agree in the use of unusual words, and even in vocalizing the Hebrew otherwise than in our Masoretic text (לבקר is vocalized to mean "in regard to the oxen" in II Chr. 35:12: the two Greek versions, however, read it as "in the morning"). But the differences are more significant than the agreements. I Esdras is idiomatic and free, not pedantically literal and obscure like the Septuagint version of the canonical books. It correctly renders "beyond the river" (i.e., west of the Euphrates) with "Coelesyria and Phoenicia"; "according to the hand of the LORD his God upon him" (Ezra 7:6) becomes "having found favor in his sight" (I Esdras 7:6). The stylistic superiority of the Greek of I Esdras over that of the Septuagint of Ezra appears from the following exact English version of unintelligible Greek jargon, "And they performed the Feast of Tents according to the written, and burnt offerings day in day in number like the judgment, a word of the day in its day" (Ezra 3:4, LXX). Contrast the lucidity of I Esdras 5:51, rendering the same Hebrew text, "And they celebrated the Feast of Tabernacles, as it is commanded in the law, and sacrifices daily, as it was proper." Of course the rendering in I Esdras is not always correct: erroneous renderings occur in 5:7; 8:62; 9:4, 37; etc. Occasionally when the translator does not know the meaning of a word, he simply omits it (e.g., 2:19, 27; 4:13; 8:22; etc.). But generally he attains a notable clarity, distinction, and freshness of diction which are far superior to the Septuagint translator of the canonical parallels. In some twenty instances I Esdras reveals a better Hebrew-Aramaic text than the Masoretic one.

It has been plausibly surmised that I Esdras is a surviving fragment of the oldest Greek translation of Chronicles-Ezra-Nehemiah which, exactly as in the case of Daniel (where the original Septuagint survives solely in the Chigi Manuscript, while all others give Theodotion's version), was eventually discarded in favor of Theodotion's by the Christians. Flavius Josephus used I Esdras exclusively, ignoring the Theodotion text of the canonical parallels, which probably did not yet exist at the time.

The differences in contents and in sequence between I Esdras and the canonical parallels are best explained by supposing that both represent two revised editions of the Chronicler's work (Chronicles-Ezra-Nehemiah), for it is hardly possible to derive one from the other. The first edition of the Chronicler's work apparently still lacked the genuine Memoirs of Nehemiah (Neh. 1:1–7:5, which is lacking in I Esdras), as also the Story of the Three Youths (I Esdras 3:1–5:6). It was primarily the popularity of this story among Christians that saved the fragment of the old version of the Chronicler's work, which we call I Esdras, from being lost and forgotten.

2. *The Story of the Three Youths (I Esdras 3:1–5:6).*—In brief the narrative runs as follows.[1] Each of three young pages or guardsmen

[1] Cf. Josephus *Antiquities* XI. 3.

of Darius I, king of Persia, wrote what he considered the strongest thing in the world and placed the sealed slips under the pillow of the sleeping king, with the expectation that the winner in the contest would be richly rewarded (3:1-12). In the morning the king, after summoning his courtiers, invited the youths to expound and defend their opinions (3:13-17). The first one maintained that wine was the strongest because it affected so deeply the mind of all men, from slave to king (3:18-24). The second asserted that the king was the strongest (4:1-12). The third one (identified with Zerubbabel in a gloss), after recognizing that woman dominated over man (4:13-32), concluded that "great is truth, and stronger than all things" (4:35). "And all the people shouted, Great is truth, and mighty above all things" (4:41; 4:33-41). This famous utterance is usually quoted from the Vulgate—with the present *praevalet* changed into the future ("will prevail"); *Magna est veritas, et praevalebit.* As his reward, Zerubbabel requested that Darius rebuild Jerusalem and its temple, and return thither the temple vessels (4:42-46). Darius complied and also allowed the Jewish exiles to return (4:47-57). Zerubbabel praised God (4:58-60) and led back the exiles (4:61–5:6).

The original story (3:1–4:41), manifestly translated from the Aramaic, was a popular Gentile tale. In its earliest form the three strongest things were wine, the king, and women; its tone was humorous if not sarcastic. It was moralized by adding that truth was strongest of all. The story was probably Persian, and as the mention of truth (Avestan *Asha*, Vedic *Rta*) may indicate, it was moralized under Zoroastrian influence. By identifying the third youth with Zerubbabel (note the gloss in 4:13), and connecting the tale with the return of the exiles and the rebuilding of the temple (4:42–5:6), Jewish editors incorporated it into the work of the Chronicler. It seems probable that the authors of Daniel and Esther were acquainted with the Aramaic original, and the author of the Wisdom of Solomon with the Greek version (which was probably made in the second or first century B.C.). The date of the original Persian tale may go back to the fifth century and the Aramaic version may have been made in the fourth; the Jewish edition was probably added to the Chronicler's work about 200 B.C. or soon after. The excellent style, the irony, and the vivid scenes from actual life give to the three speeches a strong sense of reality. The praise of Truth is really eloquent. All in all, this is one of the best surviving ancient tales. The high quality of the style and thought may be illustrated through the following extracts from the three speeches of the youths.

> O ye men, how exceeding strong is wine! it causeth all men to err that drink it; . . . it turneth also every thought into jollity and mirth, so that a man remembereth neither sorrow nor debt. . . . And when they are in their cups, they forget their love both to friends and brethren, and a little after draw out swords. . . . O ye men, is not wine the strongest, that enforceth to do thus? (3:18-24.)

O ye men, do not men excel in strength, that bear rule over sea and land, and all things in them? But yet the king is more mighty. . . . If he bid them make war the one against the other, they do it. . . . They slay and are slain, and transgress not the king's commandment. . . . Likewise for those that are no soldiers, . . . but use husbandry, when they have reaped again that which they had sown, they bring it to the king (4:2-6).

Women have borne the king and all the people that bear rule by sea and land. Even of them came they: and they nourished them up that planted the vineyards, from whence wine cometh. . . . Yea, and if men have gathered together gold and silver, or any other goodly thing, do they not love a woman which is comely in favour and beauty? And letting all those things go, do they not gape, and even with open mouth fix their eyes fast on her . . . ? Do ye not labour and toil, and give and bring all to the woman? (4:15-22.)

Wine is wicked, the king is wicked, woman are wicked, all the children of men are wicked, . . . and there is no truth in them. . . . As for the truth, it endureth, and is always strong. . . . Neither in her judgment is any unrighteousness; and she is the strength, kingdom, power, and majesty, of all ages. Blessed be the God of truth (4:37-40).

B. II Esdras.—The gloomy Ezra Apocalypse (II Esdras in English; IV Esdras in Latin) reflects the tragic aftermath of the destruction of Jerusalem in A.D. 70 and was written about twenty years later. The Latin text in the Vulgate (the Greek is lost except for two or three verses) and its translation in the King James Version and the English Revised Version contain, besides the Jewish apocalypse (II Esdras 3–14), four additional chapters (1–2; 15–16) of Christian origin which are missing in the Syriac, Ethiopic, Arabic, and Armenian versions; they are sometimes called V or V-VI Esdras. Chs. 1–2 are a Christian apocalypse (ca. A.D. 150) culminating in a vision of the Son of God and his martyrs (ch. 2 seems to have been used in the Roman breviary and missal); chs. 15–16 (ca. A.D. 250) are a dismal description of future woes in the vein of certain Old Testament prophecies and the apocalypses in the Gospels: not only the wicked and the heathen, but also the believers will be robbed and sorely afflicted by strangers before their final deliverance. "For yet a little, and iniquity shall be taken away out of the earth, and righteousness shall reign

among you" (16:52). "The days of trouble are at hand, but I will deliver you from the same. Be ye not afraid, neither doubt, for God is your guide" (16:74-75). The seven visions of II Esdras 3–14, of which the first six (3:1–13:53a, 57-58, omitting the references to Ezra in 3:1; 6:10; 7:2, 25; 8:2, and "there I sat three days" in 13:58) are revelations to Salatiel (Hebrew, Shealtiel; cf. Ezra 3:2; 5:2; Neh. 12:1) and the seventh (ch. 14) is a report of the rewriting of the Scriptures through a revelation to Ezra, may be summarized as follows:

(a) The first vision (3:1–5:20). Thirty years after Nebuchadrezzar destroyed Jerusalem, Shealtiel complains in Babylon over the misery of the Jews. God did not remove the evil impulse resulting from Adam's sin, so that his descendants might observe the law revealed to Moses (3:4-22); as a punishment for its sins, Jerusalem was delivered into the hands of God's enemies (3:23-36). The angel Uriel replies that man cannot understand God (4:1-11). Shealtiel objects that it would have been better for man never to have been created (4:12). Uriel says that nature's laws cannot be defied and what lies outside of one's experience cannot be understood (4:13-21). Israel is ruined because an evil seed produces an evil fruit (4:22-32). The evil age will come to an end when the abode of the righteous dead is completely filled (4:33-43). The time that is past is longer than the time to come (4:44-50). Cosmic upheavals will indicate the imminence of the end (4:51–5:13). Shealtiel, awakening from his trance, weeps and mourns (5:14-20).

(b) The second vision (5:21–6:34). Why was Israel delivered up? Man is incapable of comprehending God (5:21-40). Why could not all generations have lived when the new age will begin? Because they must follow one another (5:41-49). Generations now living on this aged mother earth are inferior to the first ones (5:50-55). Alone God created, alone God will dissolve the world (5:56–6:6): the age to come will follow the present one without an interval (6:7-10), after the signs of the end (6:11-24; cf. 4:51–5:13) and the time of salvation (6:25-34).

(c) The third vision (6:35–9:25). Since God created the world in six days for the benefit of Israel, should not the Jews be masters of the earth (6:35-59)? Owing to Adam's sin, the Jews must reach the future world, which belongs to them, through narrow and difficult paths; then they will leave the corruptible world to the heathen (7:1-16). Is the future bliss only for the Jews? Yes, despite their sins (7:17-25). At the end of this world the Messiah ("My Son," omitting "Jesus" in the Vulgate) will rule four hundred years; then he and all living will die and silence will reign during seven days (7:26-

30). The age to come begins with the resurrection, the final judgment, and the revelation of Paradise and Gehenna (7:31-44).[2] The seer laments the fact that only a few among all men will be saved (7:45-74): the wicked after death will wander about and be tortured, while the righteous are happy in their chambers (7:75-101). The righteous cannot intercede for the wicked (7:102-115). Through his sin Adam brought perdition to the human race; nevertheless, says the angel, everyone is responsible for his eternal lot (7:116-131) and consequently few are saved (7:132–8:3). Why should God create men, and especially his people, in order to destroy them (8:4-19a)? Like God, the seer should rejoice with the saved and forget the wicked (8:19b-62). The vision closes with another description of the signs of the end (8:63–9:13) and another explanation of the paucity of the saved (9:14-25).

(d) The fourth vision (9:26–10:60). While the seer complains that Israel must perish though his divine law is eternal (9:26-37), he sees a woman (i.e., Zion) mourning for her son and preparing to fast unto death (9:38–10:4). When the seer rebukes her for not mourning for Zion (10:5-24), she vanishes and a city appears (10:25-28). The angel explains that the woman is Zion, her son is Jerusalem in ruins, and the city is the New Jerusalem (10:29-60).

(e) The fifth vision (11:1–12:51). In a dream an eagle rises from the sea. It has twelve wings, three heads, and eight winglets with contrary feathers. The twelve wings and two winglets rule in succession; two winglets remain under the head on the right, two are devoured by the heads; the latter rule next; finally two winglets rule (11:1-35). A lion announces the end of the eagle (11:36-46), which is then burned (12:1-3a). As the angel explains, the eagle is the fourth of Daniel's kingdoms (Dan. 7:7-8, 23), now understood to be the Roman Empire (not the Seleucid Kingdom, as in Daniel); heads and wings are twenty-three Roman rulers (the first and second wings are Caesar and Augustus; the three heads are Vespasian, Titus, and Domitian; the book was written in the

[2] The ordinary MSS and editions of the Vulg., and therefore also the KJV, lack the verses which are here numbered 7:36-105. Vss. 36-70 of the Vulg. and of the KJV are consequently numbered 106-140 here, in accordance with the ERV. The omission of these verses is the result of the removal of one sheet from the Codex Sangermanensis (written in 822, now in the Bibliothèque Nationale in Paris). Bensly published the Latin missing fragment, which he discovered in Amiens, France, in 1875. In English the missing fragment (7:36-105) is found in R. H. Charles, The Apocrypha (Oxford: Clarendon Press, 1913), and in E. J. Goodspeed, The Apocrypha: An American Translation (Chicago: University of Chicago Press, 1938).

reign of Domitian [81-96]). The lion is the Messiah (12:3b-51).

(f) The sixth vision (13:1-58). In a dream a man (i.e., the Messiah) rises from the depths of the stormy sea and flies with the clouds of heaven (cf. Dan. 7:13); he annihilates his foes and gathers a harmless throng (13:1-13), that is, the ten tribes of Israel and the remnants of Judah in Palestine (13:14-58).

(g) Ezra dictates the text of the Scriptures (14:1-48). Before Ezra is to be taken into the invisible world (14:1-17), he withdraws from Israel with five scribes for forty days (14:18-26), admonishes his people (14:27-36), and dictates ninety-four books to his scribes: twenty-four (the Hebrew Bible) he is to publish, seventy (the apocalypses) are esoteric (14:37-48). Then he ascends to heaven (14:49-50).

It is clear from this synopsis that the seventh section (ch. 14), explaining in imaginary fashion the restoration of the Scriptures, is an appendix loosely attached to the book and presumably the work of another author. The six preceding visions are an apocalyptic drama in two acts: the "tying of the knot," in the present age (visions 1-3 [3:1–9:25]); and the "denouement" in the world to come (visions 4-6 [9:26–13:58]). The first part is an impassioned discussion of the problem of God's love and justice in this world filled with sin and woe; the second is a solution of the problem, on the basis of faith and hope, in the world to come. But the solution fails to satisfy the disheartened and pessimistic author, writing about A.D. 90, during the tragic years following the destruction of Jerusalem by Titus (A.D. 70).

The problem of theodicy, or how to prove the justice and love of God in a world where there seems to be no relationship between man's behavior and man's lot, is treated both in its national and in its personal aspects.

The misery of Israel after A.D. 70 (bitterly contrasted to the prosperity of Babylon [i.e., Rome], 3:2, 29) is tearfully described: "Our sanctuary is laid waste, our altar broken down, our temple destroyed ["our cult is abolished"— Syriac version], our psaltery is laid on the ground, our song is put to silence" (10:21-22). Does God no longer care for his beloved chosen people (5:23-30), for whom he created the world and to whom he promised the dominion of the earth (6:55-59)? True, sinfulness is universal: "What is man, that thou shouldest take displeasure at him? Or what is a corruptible generation, that thou shouldest be so bitter toward it? For in truth there is no man among them that be born, but he hath dealt wickedly; and among the faithful [Jews] there is none which hath not done amiss" (8:34-35; cf. 3:35; 7:46, 68 [missing fragment]; contrast 3:36). The sorrow and travail in the world is the result of this sinfulness, which had its origin in Adam's sin (7:11-12): as a result of this fall the world has been filled with iniquity, death, and misery (3:7-18; cf. Rom. 5:12). "Alas, Adam, what have you done! When you sinned, the fall was not yours alone, but ours likewise, who are your descendants" (7:48 [118]). The root of all evil is the *cor malignum*, the wicked mind or evil impulse which passed from Adam to the human race (3:21-22, 26). "A grain of evil seed was sown in the heart of Adam from the beginning, and how much ungodliness has it produced and will yet produce until the threshing floor comes!" (4:30; cf. 4:31-32; 7:92 [missing fragment].) Since God alone created the world and Adam (3:4-6), whence comes the evil impulse (4:4)? The author reverently refrained from giving the obvious answer—namely, that the evil impulse was created in Adam by God, who "left him in the power of his impulse" (Ecclus. 15:14). Early rabbinical sources not only answered the question, but cited biblical proof texts in support of this doctrine.[3] The author could merely recognize the inability of man to understand God's ways (4:2-21 [containing a fable]; 5:36-40) and look forward to the coming of the future world (4:26-50).

But the realization that very few will participate in the bliss of the world to come (7:49-61; 8:1, 3; cf. Matt. 22:14; Luke 13:23-24; etc.) raises the problem of theodicy—in its individual aspect—to a tragic pitch. For the mass of mankind and even of Israel is doomed to eternal perdition after death, following the tribulations and trials of this life: how can this dreadful lot of the creature be harmonized with the justice and love of the Creator (chs. 7-8)? Why did not God take away from men the evil impulse (3:20)? Would it not have been better for God not to create man at all (4:12)? Neither the author nor any thinker since his day has been able to answer such questions rationally.

The eschatology of II (IV) Esdras resembles that of contemporary apocalypses (Syriac Baruch Revelation). The coming of the future age will be proclaimed by the signs of the end of the world, cosmic and national upheavals (4:51–5:13; 6:11-24; 8:63–9:13; cf. Matt. 24:6-8, 29-30; Mark 13:7-8, 12, 24-25; Luke 21:9-11, 25-26). After the end of the world, following the reign of the Messiah and his death (7:26-29), and seven days of silence (7:30), the new world will appear (7:31), the dead shall rise (7:32) when the trumpet is blown (6:23; cf. Matt. 24:31; I Cor. 15:52; I Thess. 4:16; etc.) and the Lord (6:6; 7:87, missing fragment) will

sit in the final judgment (7:33-35). Already after death and before the Last Judgment the souls of the wicked are tormented in seven ways and those of the righteous enjoy seven kinds of bliss (7:75-99, missing fragment). On the day of the Last Judgment (described in 7:39-42, missing fragment) the books will be opened (6:20): there will be no mercy for the wicked (7:33), but only justice (7:34); for intercession in their behalf is futile (7:102-115, missing fragment). The pit of torment, the furnace of Gehenna (where the wicked suffer pain, thirst [8:59] and burning [7:38, missing fragment]) will be manifested over against the place of refreshment, the paradise of delight (7:36, missing fragment); according to 7:92 (missing fragment) and 8:38, death and destruction are the fate of at least some of the wicked. After the judgment, creation will be renewed (7:75, missing fragment) and changed (6:16; cf. II Pet. 3:13; Rev. 21:1): evil and sin will be abolished (6:27-28; 7:113-114 [43-44]), death will be gone and forgotten (8:53). Paradise (7:36, missing fragment; 8:52) and the New Jerusalem (7:26; 8:52; 10:54-55; 13:36) have been prepared in heaven by God from the beginning of time (3:6; cf. 6:2). Beautiful flowers (6:3) are in the paradise, and the tree of life (7:52), whose incorruptible fruit produces delight and healing (7:123, missing fragment). Hell is near paradise (7:36, 38, missing fragment) so that the saved might enjoy the spectacle of the torments of the damned (7:36, 38, missing fragment; on this proximity cf. Luke 16:22-26).

We thus see that in II (IV) Esdras (as also in Syriac Baruch and in the Jewish substratum of Rev. 19:11–21:8) the messianic age is no longer the final culmination of world history, as in earlier apocalypses, but a limited period (four hundred years in II Esdras; a thousand, or the millennium, in Rev. 20:2, 7) preceding the manifestation of the new heavens and the new earth, the pit of torment and the paradise of delight, which will endure for all eternity.

The following passages illustrate the style and thought of II (IV) Esdras.

For the first Adam bearing a wicked heart transgressed, and was overcome; and so be all they that are born of him (3:21).

A city is builded, and set upon a broad field, and is full of all good things: the entrance thereof is narrow, and is set in a dangerous place to fall, like as if there were a fire on the right hand, and on the left a deep water: and one only path between them both, even between the fire and the water, so small that there could but one man go there at once (7:6-8).

O thou earth, wherefore hast thou brought forth, if the mind is made out of dust, like as all other

[3] See G. F. Moore, *Judaism* (Cambridge: Harvard University Press, 1927), I, 480-81.

created things? For it were better that the dust itself had been unborn, so that the mind might not have been made therefrom. But now the mind groweth with us, and by reason of this we are tormented, because we perish and know it (7:62-64, missing fragment).

For in this, O Lord, thy righteousness and thy goodness shall be declared, if thou be merciful unto them which have not the confidence of good works (8:36).

For unto you is paradise opened, the tree of life is planted, the time to come is prepared, plenteousness is made ready, a city is builded, and rest is allowed, yea, perfect goodness and wisdom. The root of evil is sealed up from you, weakness and the moth is hid from you, and corruption is fled into hell to be forgotten: sorrows are passed, and in the end is shewed the treasure of immortality (8:52-54).

C. Tobit.—The book of Tobit was written in Aramaic soon after 200 B.C. (probably 190-170 B.C.). The original text is lost, as is that of all the Palestinian Apocrypha except parts of Ecclesiasticus; but the three extant Greek translations, and their versions in other languages, testify of its great popularity among the Jews until the first century of our era, and among the Christians thereafter. The first (and best) text is that of Codex Sinaiticus (א) of about A.D. 400, and of the Old Latin, Armenian, Vulgate, and Hebrew translations. The second is the Codex Vaticanus (B) of the fourth century, and the Alexandrinus (A) of the fifth: this is found in the ordinary editions of the Septuagint (but Rahlfs gives also the text of the Sinaiticus), in the King James Version and the English Revised Version, and in some Oriental versions (Syriac, Ethiopic, Sahidic, and Armenian). The third text is partially preserved in some Greek manuscripts, and is later than the others. The content of the book, in brief, is as follows:

(a) The misfortunes of Tobit (1:1-3:17). Tobit, of the tribe of Naphtali, observed punctiliously the prescriptions of the law of Moses in Nineveh, where he had been exiled, even though he was the purchasing agent of Shalmaneser (1:1-14). He incurred the wrath of Sennacherib by burying the bodies of executed Jews (1:15-20), but returned to Nineveh under Essarhaddon (1:21-22). One night, after the burial of a corpse, he slept outdoors on account of his impurity, and was blinded by birds' dung (2:1-10). A quarrel with his wife so increased his misery (2:11-14) that he begged God to end his life (3:1-6).

(b) The misfortunes of Sara (3:7-15). At the same moment in distant Ecbatana (Hamadan, Media) Sara, daughter of Raguel, also begged God to release her from this life; for not only had the demon Asmodeus killed her seven hus-

bands on successive wedding nights, but she was even accused of murdering them (3:7-15).

(c) Divine intervention (3:16-17). God, hearing both, sent Raphael to help Tobit and Sara (3:16-17).

(d) Tobias sent to Rages (4:1-5:22). Tobit told his son Tobias that he had deposited with Gabael in Rages (Media) ten talents of silver, or more than $20,000 (4:1-2; cf. 1:14). Then he gave him moral counsel (4:3-21). Raphael, under the guise of Azarias, was hired to accompany Tobias to Media (5:1-16a), and so they took their leave and departed (5:16b-22).

(e) The journey to Media (6:1-9:6). Tobias caught a fish in the Tigris and, upon the advice of Raphael, took along its gall, heart, and liver (6:1-8). Raphael told Tobias the story of Sara and predicted that he would marry her after driving away Asmodeus (6:9-17). And so it happened: Asmodeus, nauseated by the "fishy fume" (Milton, *Paradise Lost*, Bk. IV) produced when Tobias burned the liver and heart of the fish, fled and was bound by Raphael in Upper Egypt (7:1-8:3). So the wedding was celebrated with festivities lasting two weeks (8:4-21), while Raphael brought the ten talents, and even Gabael himself, from Rages (9:1-6).

(f) The return to Nineveh (10:1-11:19). Tobit and Anna in Nineveh awaited anxiously the arrival of their son Tobias (10:1-7a), who refused to delay his departure from Ecbatana, in the company of Sara and Azarias (10:7b-11:1). Near Nineveh, Azarias and Tobias went ahead of the rest, bearing the gall of the fish, with which they restored Tobit's sight (11:2-13). The wedding celebration was then repeated (11:14-19).

(g) Raphael's departure (12:1-22). Offered a large sum, Azarias made himself known as Raphael (12:1-15), and ascended unto heaven (12:16-22).

(h) Tobit sang a psalm of thanksgiving (13:1-18).

(j) Epilogue (14:1-15). Before his death Tobit predicted to Tobias the destruction of Nineveh (14:1-7), and advised him to leave the doomed city and to observe the law of Moses (14:8-11a). Before Tobias died in Ecbatana he heard the glad tidings of Nineveh's destruction (14:11b-15).

Few scholars now defend the historical reality of the story of Tobit, which is generally regarded as an excellent example of ancient Aramaic fiction. The supernatural elements would alone class it as such:

Raphael, the sociable spirit, that deigned
To travel with Tobias, and secured
His marriage with the seven-times-wedded maid

[4] Milton, *Paradise Lost*, Bk. V.

The author knew the Law, the Prophets, and some of the Hagiographa (at least Psalms, Proverbs, and Job). He refers specifically to the story of Ahikar (1:21-22; 2:10; 11:18; 14:10); he utilizes folkloric motifs (the healing power of the entrails of the fish) and plots (the "grateful dead" and the "dangerous bride" cycles are here combined). It is possible that the glaring anachronisms and historical errors in the tale (the tribe of Naphtali was exiled by Tiglath-pileser, not by Shalmaneser [1:2], whose successor was Sargon, not Sennacherib [1:15]; Nineveh was not captured by Nebuchadrezzar and Ahasuerus [14:15]; etc.) were made deliberately to warn the alert reader that the story was pure fiction, although the pedantically official title (1:1-2) and the use of the first person, after the manner of Nehemiah's autobiography, in 1:3–3:6 (where, however, the Vulgate uses the third person), seem to give the book a genuinely historical tone.

Like other Jewish short stories in the Old Testament, and in the Apocrypha, Tobit inculcates the principles of Judaism both by example and by precept. The *national* aspect of Judaism appears in the pilgrimages to Jerusalem and the payment of tithes to the temple (1:6-8; 5:13; the Codex Sinaiticus gives the earlier practice), which is the object of the deepest reverence (1:4) and toward which one turned in prayer (3:11-12; cf. Dan. 6:10). Negatively, nationalistic religion stresses the utter separation of the Jews in the Dispersion from the heathen, particularly in regard to food (1:10-12) and marriage (1:9; 3:15; 4:12-13; 6:11; 7:12-13), although without the bitterness noticeable in books (Daniel, Judith, Esther) written after the persecutions of Antiochus Epiphanes in 168-165. Tobit still expects the future conversion of the heathen (13:11; 14:6), not their extermination.

Personal religion and morality (as in Ecclesiasticus) are, however, more prominent than national institutions. "My son, be mindful of the Lord our God all thy days, . . . and follow not the ways of unrighteousness" (4:5). Prayer of petition (3:1-6, 11-15) ascended to God (3:16; 12:12) and was answered; after deliverance from trouble, hymns of praise were sung in God's honor (8:15-17; 11:14-15; 12:6-7, 22; ch. 13).

The negative precepts of morality are summarized thus: "Do that to no man which thou hatest" (4:15; for the positive form of the Golden Rule see Matt. 7:12). Among the active duties, summarized in 12:7 ("Do that which is good and no evil shall touch you"), the burial of the pious dead and almsgiving are especially stressed (1:17-18). "Give alms of thy substance; and when thou givest alms, let not thine eye be envious, neither turn thy face from any poor [but: "give nothing to the wicked" (4:17)], and the face of God shall not be turned away from thee. If thou hast abundance, give alms accordingly: if thou have but a little, be not afraid to give according to that little: for thou layest up a good treasure for thyself against the day of necessity" (4:7-9).

Bless God, praise him, and magnify him, and praise him for the things which he hath done unto you in the sight of all that live. It is good to praise God, and exalt his name, and honourably to shew forth the works of God; therefore be not slack to praise him. It is good to keep close the secret of a king, but it is honourable to reveal the works of God. Do that which is good, and no evil shall touch you. Prayer is good with fasting and alms and righteousness. A little with righteousness is better than much with unrighteousness. It is better to give alms than to lay up gold: for alms doth deliver from death, and shall purge away all sin. Those that exercise alms and righteousness shall be filled with life: but they that sin are enemies to their own life (12:6-10).

Although there is still no trace of Daniel's doctrine of the resurrection (Dan. 12:2; cf. Tob. 3:6), the book of Tobit (like Ecclesiasticus) is a good record of the life and faith of those pious Jews out of whom were eventually developed the Pharisees and the rabbis of the Talmud.

D. Judith.—The story of Judith (the Greek form of the Hebrew word meaning "Jewess") has been celebrated in painting and verse.

> Judith, a woman, as he lay upright
> Sleeping, his hed of smote, and fro his tente
> Ful prively she stale from every wight,
> And with his hed unto here town she wente.[5]

The original book, now lost, was written in Hebrew somewhere in Palestine about 150 B.C., after the victories of Judas Maccabaeus (168-161) and before the patriotic fervor of the Maccabean rebellion had abated. We have a good Greek translation of the book in the Septuagint; all extant versions render the Greek text.

The Book of Judith is divided into two parts describing Holofernes' war against the Jews (chs. 1–7) and Judith's deliverance of her people (chs. 8–16). It may be summarized as follows:

(*a*) The victory of Nebuchadrezzar [Nabuchodonosor] over Arphaxad (1:1-16). In the twelfth year of his reign Nebuchadrezzar, "who ruled over the Assyrians at Nineveh" (*sic!*), attacked Arphaxad (cf. Gen. 10:22) king of Media (1:1-5) and summoned the troops of the various parts of his empire, but some re-

[5] Chaucer, *The Monk's Tale*, XIV. 489-92.

fused to come (1:7-11). After his complete victory five years later, Nebuchadrezzar feasted 120 days (1:12-16).

(b) Holofernes subjected the western nations, but not the Jews (2:1–3:10). Nebuchadrezzar sent Holofernes to destroy the nations which had not furnished troops (2:1-13). At the head of an immense army (2:14-20), Holofernes won victory after victory (2:21-27); the cities of the Mediterranean coast quickly surrendered (2:28–3:6). Henceforth Nebuchadrezzar alone was to be worshiped as god (3:7-9).

(c) The Jews alone defied Holofernes (4:1–7:32). The Jews who had returned from the exile and had rebuilt the temple (in the time of Nebuchadrezzar!) prepared to bar the Assyrian advance from the north against Jerusalem (4:1-8), and invoked God's intervention (4:9-15). When Holofernes asked information about the Jews from the chieftains of neighboring nations (5:1-4), the Ammonite Achior, after summarizing the history of Israel (5:5-19), declared that the Jews were invincible unless their God was wroth at them (5:20-21). After declaring that only Nebuchadrezzar was god (6:1-4), Holofernes, instead of killing Achior (5:22-24), had him brought bound to the Jews besieged in Bethulia (6:5-13). Achior reported to Ozias and the other Jewish leaders what had happened and was welcomed by them (6:14-21). Holofernes cut off the food and water supplies of Bethulia (7:1-18). After thirty-four days the besieged Jews began to lose heart, but reluctantly agreed with Ozias to resist five more days before surrendering (7:19-32).

(d) Judith's reproach of the Jewish leaders (8:1-36). Judith, still mourning her husband Manasses after more than three years (8:1-6), was comely and pious (8:7-8). She declared to the elders of Bethulia that they had tempted God by promising surrender in five days unless he intervened (8:9-16); God might nevertheless deliver them (8:17-24), after testing them through affliction (8:25-27). Ozias said that he would keep the promise made to the people (8:28-31). Judith assured him that God would save the city (8:32-36).

(e) Judith's prayer (9:1-14). She begged the God of justice and power to prevent the Assyrians from defiling his temple (9:1-8), and to enable her to destroy their might through deceit (9:9-13), thus proving himself the defender of Israel (9:14).

(f) Judith's preparations (10:1–11:23). Removing her mourning garments, Judith dressed alluringly (10:1-4), and with a maid went to the Assyrian camp (10:5-10). She was taken to Holofernes (10:11-19), who assured her that she had nothing to fear (10:20–11:4). Judith promised Holofernes her help (11:5-8): although Achior's words (cf. 5:5-21) were true (11:9-10), Holofernes would triumph because the Jews had incensed their God by their decision to eat the animals and vegetable offerings which had been sanctified for the temple (11:11-16). She would pray in the valley every night until Bethulia's transgression was revealed to her; then she would guide Holofernes to victory (11:17-19). Holofernes agreed, and assured her of Nebuchadrezzar's appreciation (11:20-23).

(g) Judith's deed (12:1–13:10). Obedient to the law of Moses, Judith ate only of her own victuals (12:1-4), and for three days went into the valley at the morning watch for ablutions and prayer (12:5-9). On the fourth day Holofernes invited Judith to a private banquet (12:10-14). Attired in her finery, Judith attended it, but partook of her own food (12:15-19). Holofernes was so charmed by her that he drank to excess (12:20). Alone with him, Judith prayed (13:1-5), cut off his head while he was asleep, gave it to her maid, and with her walked to Bethulia (13:6-10).

(h) Judith's triumph (13:11–15:13). After entering Bethulia (13:11-13), Judith showed the elders and the people the head of Holofernes and his canopy, for which they praised God (13:14-20). Judith arranged for an attack on the morrow (14:1-4), and summoned Achior, who at once became a proselyte (14:5-10). In the morning the Assyrians fled in panic as far as Damascus (14:11–15:5), and their camp was sacked (15:6-17). Joakim, the high priest, and the Sanhedrin came to bless Judith (15:8-10), to whom the people donated the tent of Holofernes (15:11). She led the maidens in a dance (15:12-13).

(j) Judith's praise of the Lord (16:1-17). God destroyed the Assyrians through the charms of Judith (16:1-12); the almighty Creator is merciful and demands piety rather than offerings (16:13-16); he dooms eternally nations attacking Israel (16:17).

(k) Judith lived quietly ever after (16:18-25). While the people worshiped in Jerusalem, Judith dedicated to God the tent and canopy of Holofernes (16:18-19), and returned to Bethulia after three months of festivities (16:20-21). She refused to remarry (16:22), freed her maid, and was mourned at her death. She bequeathed her estate to her own and her husband's relatives (cf. Num. 27:11). No enemy troubled Israel until long after her death (16:23-25).

The story of Judith is no longer regarded as a record of actual happenings, at least among Protestants, although the supernatural is not the factor bringing about a happy ending, as in Tobit. Already Martin Luther regarded the story as an allegory of God's help to the Jews, and acutely observed that the false chronology and names were used to warn the reader that this is a holy parable. The anachronisms are even more glaring than in Tobit: Nebuchadrezzar (605-561 B.C.) ruled *after* the Assyrian Empire and Nineveh had ceased to exist (contrast 1:1; 2:1, 4, 14, 21; etc.) in 612 B.C., but long before the return of the Babylonian exiles and the rebuilding of the temple (contrast 4:2-3; 5:19; cf. 11:13; 16:18-20). The high priest Joakim (4:6, 8, 14; 15:8) presumably belongs to the time of Nehemiah (Neh. 12:10, 26), unless Baruch 1:7 is regarded as historical; and the Persian names of Bagoas (12:11; 13:1, 3; 14:14) and Holofernes are known only at an even later period. Moreover, it seems probable that, as in Daniel, Nebuchadrezzar is merely the symbol of the detested Antiochus IV Epiphanes (175-164 B.C.), who actually proscribed Judaism and persecuted the Jews. The passionate hatred of the heathen; the beginnings of Pharisaic Judaism, evidenced in the punctilious observance of the law (4:9-14; 8:5-6; 10:5; 11:10-15; 12:2, 5-9; 16:16-17), in the rise of the "tradition of the ancients" or oral law (8:6), in the doctrine of the final judgment and eternal punishments (16:17); and the authority of the high priest and the Sanhedrin (4:6-8, 11, 14; 15:8) over the Palestinian Jews, all preclude a date earlier than the third or second centuries for the historical background and consequently exclude the historicity of the events narrated. It is hardly necessary to adduce other evidence, such as impossible occurrences (a troop movement of three hundred miles in three days, 2:21), and confused geography (2:23-27) abounding with unknown localities, such as Bethulia (which C. C. Torrey, however, identifies with Shechem).

The value of this edifying short story is not to be found in elusive historical information about a Jewish victory, but rather in its literary and religious qualities. The working out of the details of a well-known plot (suggested, for instance, by Judg. 5:24-27), the sharp delineation of the situations and the characters, and the fairly good style (in spite of occasional prolixity and ostentation not to be found in Esther, apparently written a few years later), testify to the skill of the author. From the religious and ethical point of view, Judith and Esther reflect, not the highest ideals of the prophets, but the intense nationalism during the wars for independence, when deceit, falsehood, and assassination seemed justified if advantageous to the nation. In this milieu God is conceived primarily as the champion of Israel (as generally before Amos), the almighty Creator able to destroy the mightiest empires of this world, the God who determines all events in advance:

For thou [O God] hast wrought not only those things, but also the things which fell out before, and which ensued after; thou hast thought upon the things which are now, and which are to come. Yea, what things thou didst determine were ready at hand, and said, Lo, we are here: for all thy ways are prepared, and thy judgments are in thy foreknowledge (9:5-6).

He is, however, also a god of justice and mercy with respect to Israel, testing and warning his people through minor misfortunes (8:25-27) and defending it only if it avoids wickedness (5:21). Trust in God's immense power and infinite mercy is expressed in the following verses:

For thy power standeth not in multitude, nor thy might in strong men: for thou art a God of the afflicted, an helper of the oppressed, an upholder of the weak, a protector of the forlorn, a saviour of them that are without hope (9:11).

I will sing unto the Lord a new song: O Lord, thou art great and glorious, wonderful in strength, and invincible. Let all creatures serve thee: for thou speakest, and they were made, thou didst send forth thy spirit, and it created them, and there is none that can resist thy voice. For the mountains shall be moved from their foundations with the waters, the rocks shall melt as wax at thy presence: yet thou art merciful to them that fear thee. For all sacrifice is too little for a sweet savour unto thee, and all the fat is not sufficient for thy burnt offering: but he that feareth the Lord is great at all times (16:13-16).

We have thus side by side in Judith some of the noblest tenets of Judaism and some of the chauvinistic attitudes which are often brought to the surface in times of national emergency.

E. The Rest of the Chapters of the Book of **Esther.**—The popularity of the Book of Esther among the Jews forced its admission into the canon of scriptures in spite of the misgivings of some ancient rabbis. They were presumably disturbed by the lack of any allusion to Judaism in the book, and by the rather boisterous and convivial celebration of Purim, which moreover was not ordained by Moses—although eventually, through subtle and ingenious exegesis, allusions to Purim were discovered in all three divisions of the Hebrew canonical scriptures.

It was inevitable that such a well-liked book would eventually be edited with the addition of pious edifying matter. This is the usual explanation of the expanded editions in Greek (containing 270 verses, while the canonical Hebrew has only 163), and in Aramaic (two Targums, dated about A.D. 700 and 800). C. C.

Torrey,[6] however, claims that sections A, C, D, and F (omitting the colophon) were part of the Aramaic book which was translated in 114 (cf. the colophon), while B and E were written in Greek, presumably by the translator. These supplements were paraphrased by Josephus, with the exception of A and F, but were not in the Hebrew Bible in the time of Origen. In the Septuagint these supplements are located in their right context as follows: A (before 1:1), B (after 3:13), C (after 4:17), D (after C), E (after 8:12), F (at the end). But Jerome removed them *in toto* outside of the canonical book (leaving F where it was), with the result that, following Jerome's Vulgate, the English Apocrypha not only gives six disconnected sections but places the last one (F) first (including the final colophon in the Greek!), so that the interpretation of Mordecai's dream (F) precedes the account of the dream itself (A). In their proper order, and with the chapter and verse references of the Vulgate, which are printed in the English Apocrypha, these sections may be summarized as follows:

(a) Sec. A. Mordecai's dream (11:2–12:6; cf. F). Mordecai, in the second year of Artaxerxes, saw two dragons ready to fight, nations preparing for war, the Jewish nation threatened until a spring became a river, the sun came up, and the humble Jews triumphed over the mighty. While pondering the prophetic meaning of the dream, Mordecai heard Gabatha and Tharra plotting to assassinate Artaxerxes; he informed the king, who had them executed. Haman sought to avenge the two eunuchs.

(b) Sec. B. The edict against the Jews (13:1-7). Artaxerxes wrote to the governors of his 127 provinces that, in behalf of his subjects, the Jews should be exterminated on the fourteenth of Adar because they were opposed to all other men.

(c) Sec. C. The prayers of Mordecai (13:8-18) and Esther (14:1-19). God knows that Mordecai did not bow down before Haman because he prostrates himself before God alone; the Lord should now save his people from destruction. Queen Esther, dressed in mourning, prayed to God, her only help; he chose Israel, and exiled his people. Let God now prevent the abolition of Judaism in behalf of idolatry, let him save the Jews through Esther, who dislikes being married to a heathen and being a queen, and whose only joy is to serve the Lord.

(d) Sec. D. Esther's appearance before the king (15:1-16). In fine attire but filled with fears, Esther came to the king, and at his angry look fainted. God changed the king's disposition, but Esther fainted again in speaking of her terror.

(e) Sec. E. The edict in favor of the Jews (16:1-24). Some men seek to hurt their benefactors, and kings may be misled by deceitful ministers. Kings must rely on justice. Haman, for instance, taking advantage of the king's favor, plotted against the king and the queen (together with her people), with the intention of furthering the Macedonian conquest of the Persian Empire [Alexander's!]. The Jews, sons of the living God, observe just laws. The late Haman's decree is abrogated, and the Jews should be helped to take vengeance against their foes on the thirteenth of Adar—a future annual festival. Cities violating this decree will be destroyed.

(f) Sec. F. Interpretation of Mordecai's dream (10:4-13; cf. A) and colophon (11:1). Mordecai recognized God's hand in the Jewish triumph because it fulfilled his dream, which is thus interpreted: the spring is Esther; the two dragons are Mordecai and Haman; the nations are the enemies of the divinely rescued Jews. God's lots for the Jews and the Gentiles were both fulfilled, and the fourteenth and fifteenth of Adar were joyfully celebrated (10:4-13). The Epistle of Phrurai (Purim), or Greek Esther, was brought to Egypt by Dositheus in the fourth year of Ptolemy and Cleopatra (probably 114 B.C.), after being translated by Lysimachus (11:1).[7]

The Greek version containing these additions was thus made either in 114 or in 78 B.C., not long after the writing of the Hebrew book (probably about 125; cf. Intro. to the book of Esther, Vol. III of this Commentary). While Jewish hostility to the Gentiles is apparent in both the Hebrew and in the Greek texts, the first bases it primarily on intrigues and personal dislikes at the Persian court, while the Greek Esther seems to regard the conflict between Jews and Gentiles as eternal and divinely approved, for God made two lots (10:10). Anti-Semitism was strong at Alexandria about 100 B.C., and our Greek book (prepared by an Alexandrian Jew who settled in Jerusalem and became a citizen of that city) was welcomed there as an anti-Gentile tract in which the partiality of the universal Creator for the Jews and his hostility against the Gentiles was not in the least questioned.

The following passages from the prayers of Mordecai and Esther illustrate this religious attitude:

O Lord, Lord, the King Almighty: for the whole world is in thy power, and if thou hast appointed

---

[6] "The Older Book of Esther," *Harvard Theological Review*, XXXVII (1944), 1-40.

[7] See, on this colophon, Elias J. Bickerman, "The Colophon of the Greek Book of Esther," *Journal of Biblical Literature*, LXIII (1944), 339-62; cf. Ralph Marcus, "Dositheus, Priest and Levite," *Journal of Biblical Literature*, LXIV (1945), 271. Bickerman's date for it is not 114 B.C., but 78-77 B.C.

to save Israel, there is no man that can gainsay thee: for thou hast made heaven and earth, and all the wondrous things under the heaven (13:9-10).

And now, O Lord God and King, spare thy people: for their eyes are upon us to bring us to nought; yea, they desire to destroy the inheritance, that hath been thine from the beginning (13:15).

Hear my prayer, and be merciful unto thine inheritance: turn our sorrow into joy, that we may live, O Lord, and praise thy name (13:17).

Remember, O Lord, make thyself known in time of our affliction, and give me boldness, O King of the nations, and Lord of all power (14:12).

O thou mighty God above all, hear the voice of the forlorn, and deliver us out of the hands of the mischievous, and deliver me out of my fear (14:19).

F. The Wisdom of Solomon.

—The Wisdom of Solomon resembles a Greek diatribe, or popular ("soapbox") address on some philosophical or religious theme. It was placed into the mouth of Solomon, but composed in Alexandria, in Greek, during the period 100-50 B.C. The imaginary audience of the author includes Jews (good and bad, rich and poor) and Gentiles. The "evangelistic" preacher strives to bring back into the fold the worldly and apostate Jews (chs. 1-5), to strengthen the faith and loyalty of the pious Jews (chs. 10-12; 16-19), and to prove to the heathen both the truth of Judaism (chs. 6-9) and the folly of idolatry (chs. 13-15). The contents of this important and original book may be summarized as follows:

(a) How wisdom determines the destiny of pious and wicked Jews (1:1–5:23). Wisdom is attained through righteousness (1:1-5). God created man for immortality, but blasphemy brings death (1:6-15). The ungodly Jews devote their lives to worldly pleasures and to oppression of the humble and pious Jews (1:16–2:20). The latter's hope "is full of immortality": for God "created man to be immortal," but "through envy of the devil came death into the world" (2:21-24). After death "the souls of the righteous are in the hand of God" (3:1-9); and in this life, in spite of afflictions, childlessness, and premature death, the lot of the righteous is preferable to that of the wicked (3:10–4:19). In the final judgment, seeing the bliss of the righteous, the wicked will repent and admit their folly (4:20–5:16). Eventually God will put on his "panoply," using the whole creation as his weapons, and destroy the ungodly (5:17-23; cf. Eph. 6:11-17).

(b) The nature of wisdom and how it is attained (chs. 6-9). Heathen kings need wisdom (6:1-11), which is accessible (6:12-16). Those who gain wisdom reign over a kingdom (6:17-21). Solomon will share the mysteries of wisdom with the other kings for the good of mankind (6:22-25). Solomon attained wisdom from God through prayer (7:1-7; cf. ch. 9; I Kings 3:9-12), preferring wisdom to worldly goods, but obtaining both (7:8-12). Wisdom confers on man not only friendship with God, but also the knowledge of all sciences (7:13-21). Wisdom, which has twenty-one qualities (7:22-23), is "more moving than any motion"; she is "the breath of the power of God," an emanation of his glory (7:24-26; cf. Heb. 1:3; 4:12-13); she renews all things, inspires the prophets, and rules the world (7:27–8:1). Solomon loved wisdom for what she is and for what she gives (8:2-8; the four Stoic cardinal virtues are listed in 8:7; cf. IV Macc. 1:2-4, 18; 5:23-24). So Solomon wished to have wisdom as his life companion (8:9-16), and sought to win her for himself (8:17-18) through the following prayer (8:19-21): May God grant wisdom to Solomon (9:1-4), for he needs her to reign and to build the temple (9:5-12). Men's "corruptible body presseth down the soul, and the earthly tabernacle weigheth down the mind that museth upon many things" (9:15); consequently, they can hardly understand visible things—and much less God—unless he gives them wisdom (9:13-18).

(c) Wisdom's activity in Israel's history (10:1–12:27). The heroes of wisdom from Adam to Moses are contrasted with the wicked in their days (10:1–11:1). The Israelites are contrasted with the Egyptians (11:2-14, continued in 16:1–19:22) at the time of the plagues and of the Exodus, "For by what things their enemies were punished, by the same they in their need were benefited" (11:5). God's punishment is mild, "Wherewithal a man sinneth, by the same also shall he be punished" (11:16), as in the case of the Egyptians (11:15–12:2) and the Canaanites (12:3-11). God is particularly just and merciful in dealing with Israel (12:12-22). The heathen have disregarded God's minor warning afflictions, "therefore came extreme damnation upon them" (12:23-27).

(d) The folly of idolatry (13:1–15:19). The foolishness of paganism appears in the adoration of the phenomena of nature or of the heavenly bodies instead of their Creator (13:1-9); in the worship of idols (13:10–14:11); in the divinization of human beings, such as a young son after his death on the part of his father (14:12-16), or of an inaccessible living king on the part of his remote subjects (14:17-21; Euhemerus, who died ca. 290 B.C., had previously regarded the Greek gods as divinized rulers). Idolatry produces moral decay (14:22-31; cf. Rom. 1:19-32), while knowledge of the true God keeps Israel from gross sins (15:1-5). Makers and worshipers of idols are guilty, notably the potter who makes cheap reproductions of expensive idols (15:6-14), and the Egyptians who, besides foreign images (15:15-17), worship the most horrible beasts (15:18-19; cf. 11:15; 12:24).

(e) Contrasts between the Israelites and the Egyptians (16:1–19:22, concluding 11:2-14 after two intervening digressions; introduced by 11:15; 15:18-19). While the Egyptians were plagued by small beasts (frogs?), the Israelites enjoyed well-cooked quails in the desert (16:1-4). While the Egyptians were killed by locusts and flies, the Israelites were reminded of the observance of the Law by the bites of snakes (16:5-14; cf. Num. 21:6-9). While the Egyptians were vexed by terrific rain and hail and wondrous thunderbolts, God rained on the Israelites heavenly manna which tasted like every kind of delicious food (16:15-29). While total darkness and dreadful apparitions frightened the Egyptians (17:1-21), the Israelites enjoyed brilliant light in Egypt and were guided by the pillar of fire in the desert (18:1-4). While the Egyptians, determined to slay the Israelite infants, had their own firstborn slain and perished in the Red Sea, the Israelites in Egypt celebrated the Passover and in the desert were saved from the plague (18:5-25; cf. Num. 16:41-50). While the Egyptians drowned in the Red Sea, the Israelites crossed it safely (19:1-9). Thus does nature, under God's control, punish the wicked and reward the pious: the Egyptians were plagued while the Israelites were saved; the Sodomites were punished for being unfriendly to strangers; and miracles transformed the natural elements at the time of the Exodus (19:10-21). "For in all things, O Lord, thou didst magnify thy people" (19:22).

While it is clear that the various parts of the book present great differences in style and thought, it does not seem necessary to suppose, as some modern critics do, that part of the book was translated from the Hebrew, and part written in Greek; or that more than one author was responsible for the composition of separate parts. It seems preferable to follow Jerome and to regard the book as a unit entirely composed in Greek, for "the very style gives forth the aroma of Greek eloquence."

The author is a precursor of Philo of Alexandria (a contemporary of Paul) in combining the Jewish religion with Greek philosophy. His knowledge of the teaching of Plato and the Stoics (echoed in 7:22, 24, 26-27; 8:7, 19-20; 9:15; 11:17; 14:3; 16:21; 17:2; 19:17) is however much more superficial than Philo's (on the Logos see 18:15-16; 16:12), and is derived more from dwelling in a Hellenistic center like Alexandria than from actual study of Greek philosophical texts.

It is particularly in the author's notions about eschatology that his attempt to amalgamate Jewish and Greek ideas is manifest, and that his originality and influence are perhaps the greatest. From the Hebrew Bible he derives: the hope of the messianic kingdom (3:8; without a Messiah); the doctrine of divine retribution of human deeds in this life, either for the nation (10:17–11:14; chs. 16–19) or the individual (10:1-16); the notion of the underworld or Sheol (called Hades, following the Septuagint), which the ungodly regarded as the eternal abode of all the dead (2:1; cf. 2:5), but which was exclusively reserved, in the author's opinion, for the wicked (16:13; 17:14); and the Lord's future onslaught against the heathen (5:17-23). Incongruously the author connects this Armageddon with the Last Judgment (cf. ch. 5). The Judgment, however, is not merely the prelude of the triumph of Israel over the Gentiles, as in Joel and in 5:17-23, but primarily a final verdict on individual Jews, pious or wicked (4:20–5:16).

The teaching about the retribution of individual Jews after death is more Greek than Hebrew. Logically—but (alas!) not generally—notions about the future life should be based on the ideas of the elements constituting a human being, as in Eccl. 12:7, which refers to Gen. 2:7. In attempting to combine this Hebrew notion of man (body and spirit, Gen. 2:7) with the Greek notion (body, soul, and spirit; cf. I Thess. 5:23), the author on the one hand asserted that man consists of a physical and a spiritual element (1:4; 2:3; 15:8), but on the other used indiscriminately the Greek terms *pneuma*, *psyche*, and *nous* (mind) which presupposed the Greek anthropology. Moreover, he recognized with Plato that the souls are pre-existent (8:20) and pressed down by the corruptible body (9:15). In principle souls are immortal (1:13; in 2:23 the Platonic notion is derived from Gen. 1:26-27!), and death came into the world through the envy of the devil: in 2:24, for the first time, the serpent of Gen. 3 is identified with Satan (as later in III Baruch 9:7; Rev. 20:2)—unless Satan merely used the serpent. This excludes the Pharisaic doctrine of bodily resurrection (cf. Dan. 12:2), which was absurd in the eyes of the Greeks (Acts 17:32)—at least for the pious. The soul's return some time after death into the "earthly tabernacle" (9:15; cf. II Cor. 5:1, 4; the figure is common in Greek writings) would have been the worst of punishments. On the contrary, "the souls of the righteous" (3:1) *without their bodies* abide with God after death (3:9). Of course there is no way of reconciling logically (as the author attempts to do in chs. 1–5) the Jewish doctrine of the Last

Judgment with the Greek idea that souls are rewarded or punished immediately after death. This inconsistency concerning the end of this life corresponds to an inconsistency about the beginning of this world. If the world (13:1-5), man's soul (2:23), and wisdom (i.e., the cosmic soul [7:26]), were created in the image of God, whence come evil and death? Either, according to Judaism, they are the result of the envy of the devil (2:24), or, according to Plato, of the base and corruptible quality of matter (9:15).

The author is particularly effective in describing the opposite fates of the righteous and of the wicked after their death. The following passages are among the most beautiful in the Apocrypha:

But the souls of the righteous are in the hand of God, and there shall no torment touch them. In the sight of the unwise they seemed to die: and their departure is taken for misery, and their going from us to be utter destruction: but they are in peace. For though they be punished in the sight of men, yet is their hope full of immortality. And having been a little chastised, they shall be greatly rewarded: for God proved them, and found them worthy of himself. As gold in the furnace hath he tried them, and received them as a burnt offering. And in the time of their visitation they shall shine, and run to and fro like sparks among the stubble. They shall judge the nations, and have dominion over the people, and their Lord shall reign forever (3:1-8).

We wearied ourselves in the way of wickedness and destruction: yea, we have gone through deserts, where there lay no way: but as for the way of the Lord, we have not known it. What hath pride profited us? or what good hath riches with our vaunting brought us? All those things are passed away like a shadow, and as a post that hasted by; and as a ship that passeth over the waves of the water, which when it is gone by, the trace thereof cannot be found, neither the pathway of the keel in the waves; or as when a bird hath flown through the air, there is no token of her way to be found, but the light air being beaten with the stroke of her wings, and parted with the violent noise and motion of them, is passed through, and therein afterwards no sign where she went is to be found; or like as when an arrow is shot at a mark, it parteth the air, which immediately cometh together again, so that a man cannot know where it went through: even so we in like manner, as soon as we were born, began to draw to our end, and had no sign of virtue to shew; but were consumed in our own wickedness. For the hope of the ungodly is like dust that is blown away with the wind; like a thin froth that is driven away with the storm; like as the smoke which is dispersed here and there with a tempest, and passeth away as the remembrance of a guest that tarrieth but a day. But the righteous live for evermore; their reward also is with the Lord, and the care of them is with the most High. Therefore shall they receive a glorious kingdom, and a beautiful crown from the Lord's hand: for with his right hand shall he cover them, and with his arm shall he protect them (5:7-16).

The Wisdom of Solomon, one of the earliest extant witnesses to Hellenistic Judaism, did not exert a lasting influence on Judaism; but it is one of the sources of the Greek (and especially Platonic) strain in Christian theology, which begins with Paul and the Epistle to the Hebrews.

G. The Wisdom of Jesus the Son of Sirach (Ecclesiasticus).—Aside from the prophetic books and Nehemiah, Ecclesiasticus is the only book in the Septuagint whose real author is named (50:27). Jesus the son of Sirach had a school in Jerusalem (51:23, 29, Hebrew text). He was one of the early scribes (cf. 38:24–39: 11). About 180 B.C. he turned his classroom lectures into Hebrew verse and collected them in two books (chs. 1–23 and 24–50). Almost two thirds of the original Hebrew text have been published from manuscripts of the eleventh and twelfth centuries, found in a genizah (storage room for worn-out books) at Old Cairo in Egypt in 1896 and the following years. Although some scholars have suggested that this Hebrew text is a translation from the Syriac or Greek, its authenticity is generally admitted in spite of its many textual errors. The Hebrew book was translated into Greek soon after 132 B.C. by a grandson of the author, who wrote a prologue to the Greek version (the second prologue in the English version). The only other version made from the Hebrew is the Syriac. These three basic texts (from which all other versions are derived) differ occasionally in a very drastic way; none of them reproduces in all details the original Hebrew text, which as early as 132 must have been circulating in several recensions.

In general, Ecclesiasticus resembles the book of Proverbs, although longer sections are more numerous in it. The chief topics treated by Ben Sirach are the following:

(a) Part I (1:1–23:27). Introduction (1:1-30). Wisdom comes from God (1:1-10) and is identical with the fear of the Lord (1:11-21). Wisdom is attained through self-control (1:22-25) and obedience to God's commandments (1:26-30).

(i) On patience in affliction (2:1-18), respect for parents (3:1-16), humility (3:17-31), and courtesy in helping the poor (4:1-10).

(ii) On wisdom's tests and rewards (4:11-19), false shame (4:20-28), arrogance (4:29-30), cupidity (4:31–5:8), wrong talk (5:9–6:4), friendship (6:5-17).

(iii) On the search after wisdom (6:18-37). "Do no evil" of any sort (7:1-17), but be just and kind with all (7:18-34); avoid association with certain people (8:1-4), but be considerate and sympathetic (8:5-7).

(iv) On discrimination in social intercourse (8:8–9:16).

(v) Advice for rulers and men of wealth (9:17–14:19).

(vi) The blessing of wisdom (14:20–15:10). God is not responsible for human sin (15:11-20). On godlessness and its disastrous results (16:1-10). On God's just rule (16:11-23); and on his creation of the world (16:24-30) and of man (17:1-24). A psalm on divine mercy and forgiveness (17:25–18:14).

(vii) Miscellaneous counsel on kindness (18:15-18), on foresight (18:19-29), and self-control (18:30–20:26).

(viii) Contrast between the wise and the fool (20:27–22:18). On sins of speech and of lust (22:19–23:27).

(b) Part II (24:1–50:29). Introduction (24:1-34). Wisdom personified introduces herself (24:1-22), and is identified by the author with the Pentateuch (24:23-29), from which he has drawn so much instruction that, since it overflowed the first volume (1:1–23:27), he has prepared a second (24:30-34).

(i) A contrast between good and bad wives (25:1–26:27).

(ii) On the risks and sins besetting men of wealth and prominence (26:28–27:10); on the various kinds of sins of the tongue (27:11–28:26); on financial assistance to neighbors (29:1-20); on the vexations of travel abroad: "it is a miserable life to go from house to house" (29:21-28).

(iii) On strict discipline in bringing up children (30:1-13). Health is better than wealth (30:14–31:2);[8] the worship of mammon (so the Hebrew text in 31:8; cf. Matt. 6:24; Luke 16:9, 11, 13) is fatal to the soul (31:3-11). On table manners, moderation in drinking, and the correct behavior of dinner guests (31:12–32:13).

(iv) On good and bad teachers (32:14–33:6). God has exalted some men (Israel) and debased others (33:7-15). The author has labored for all those that seek learning (33:16-18).

(v) On the authority of the head of the family (33:19-31); on true and false dreams (34:1-8). Practical experience and travel increase wisdom, as the author can testify (34:9-17). True piety does not consist in ritual acts, but in righteousness and mercy (34:18–35:3), although offerings must be presented in obedi-

[8] On account of the accidental transposition of two leaves in the prototype from which the Greek version and translations thereof (except the Old Slav) were made, in Greek manuscripts (and most printed editions of the LXX) the section 30:25–33:16a (33:13b–36:16a in the Greek) follows 33:16b–36:13a (Greek: 30:25–33:13a).

ence to the law (35:4-11), remembering however that God cannot be bribed through offerings obtained dishonestly (35:12-20). A psalm of petition in behalf of Israel's deliverance from foreign oppressors (36:1-17).

(vi) On helpful persons: the wife (36:18-26), the friend (37:1-6), the counselor (37:7-18), the wise (37:19-26), the physician (37:27–38:15). On moderation in mourning (38:16-23).

(vii) On the value of a good education and on the unsurpassed position of the scribe (or scholar) in the community (38:24–39:15). A hymn to God the creator (39:16-35).

(viii) Suffering and death are the lot of all men, but there are compensations for the pious (40:1–41:13).

(ix) Concealed wisdom is useless (41:14-15; identical with 20:30-31). "Instruction Concerning Shame," as the Hebrew heading reads (41:16–42:8). Daughters occasion much worry to their fathers (42:9-14).

(x) A hymn praising God for the magnificence of his creation (42:15–43:33); "Praise of the Fathers of Old" (Hebrew title) or "Hymn of the Fathers" (Greek title), extolling biblical characters from Adam to Nehemiah (44:1–49:16; cf. Heb. 11); praise of the high priest Simon (50:1-24). Three hateful peoples: Edomites, Philistines, and Samaritans (50:25-26). Colophon (50:27-29).

(c) Appendix. A hymn praising God for his help in trouble (51:1-12); a liturgy with the refrain, "Give thanks unto the Lord, for he is good; for his mercy endureth forever" (in the Hebrew, after 51:12; cf. Ps. 136); alphabetic acrostic poem on how the author gained and passes on wisdom (51:13-30). Final doxology and colophon (in the Hebrew and Syriac only, following 51:30).

In depicting the ideal scribe (38:24–39:11) Sirach has given us an insight into his varied experiences and into his life's goal. He summed up what he sought and what he taught in one word, wisdom, the *summum bonum* which combined practical matters (ranging all the way from etiquette to ethical and religious standards of conduct ordained in the law of Moses), as also learned research in the Scriptures and in the sciences.

Sirach occasionally stressed the national aspects of Judaism, notably the temple services (50:4-24) —for there is only a vague allusion to the synagogue service (39:6) —as a reaction against the tendency of the aristocracy in Jerusalem to adopt Greek manners and customs. But he believed that sacrifices and offerings should be presented merely because the law prescribed them (35:4-5), and, like Amos, he condemned offerings unaccompanied by honesty and mercy for the poor (34:18-26). Religion consists in observing the law, almsgiving, and avoiding wickedness: these practices are the equivalent of sacrifices and offerings (35:1-3). Sirach's ideas on personal piety are inspired by the Prophets and by the Psalms (stressing morals and prayer), but also by the Pentateuch (stressing righteousness, or obedience to God's law). He was convinced that God rewarded piety on this earth (for he still believed that at death men's ghosts gathered in Sheol: 14:16; 17:27-28; 41:4); but in view of the misery of many pious people he concluded that the highest rewards were of the spirit, such as communion with God (2:7-11; 34:13-17), and, after death, continued remembrance (44:8, 13-15).

The most original and interesting parts of Ecclesiasticus deal with practical matters: observations on human life and counsels for attaining happiness and success. Man's life is a mixture of woes and joys. Sirach is both a pessimist and an optimist. Man is endowed with freedom of choice (15:11-20), but what happens to him is determined inexorably by God (11:2-28; 18:6; 42:21). Men were created in God's image (17:3), but all are sinful (8:5; 17:31-32) since Eve's fall (25:24); all are dust (33:10) and return thereto (17:1). Notably vivid are Sirach's sketches of family life (educating sons, worrying about daughters, good and bad wives and servants); and his reflections about social intercourse with friends (good and bad), dinner parties, conversation (as in James, much attention is given to the sins of the tongue), professional activities, the advantages and dangers of wealth and poverty, and the like. It is in dealing with these subjects that Sirach is at his best as a writer and pens his wittiest and most striking aphorisms, such as the following:

Water will quench a flaming fire;
And alms maketh an atonement for sins (3:30).

Let not thine hand be stretched out to receive,
And shut when thou shouldest repay (4:31).

Be in peace with many:
Nevertheless have but one counsellor of a thousand (6:6).

Strive not with a man that is full of tongue,
And heap not wood upon his fire (8:3).

A new friend is as new wine;
When it is old, thou shalt drink it with pleasure (9:10b).

As the wild ass is the lion's prey in the wilderness:
So the rich eat up the poor (13:19).

Like a drop of water in the sea or a grain of sand,
So are [man's] years in eternal time (18:10, Hebrew).

As the climbing up a sandy way is to the feet of the aged,
So is a wife full of words to a quiet man (25:20).

The stroke of the whip maketh marks in the flesh:
But the stroke of the tongue breaketh the bones (28:17).

Better is the life of a poor man in a mean cottage,
Than delicate fare in another man's house (29:22).

Where no hedge is, there the possession is spoiled:
And he that hath no wife will wander up and down mourning (36:25).

Neither consult with a woman touching her of whom she is jealous:
Neither with a coward in matters of war (37:11).

All that are of the earth shall turn to earth again:
So the ungodly shall go from a curse to destruction (41:10).

A good life hath but few days:
But a good name endureth forever (41:13).

The longer sections which follow illustrate the more profound views of Sirach concerning God, and man's right attitude toward his Maker:

For the Lord is full of compassion and mercy, long-suffering, and very pitiful, and forgiveth sins, and saveth in time of affliction. Woe be to fearful hearts, and faint hands, and the sinner that goeth two ways! Woe unto him that is fainthearted! for he believeth not; therefore shall he not be defended. Woe unto you that have lost patience! and what will ye do when the Lord shall visit you? (2:11-14.)

Say not thou, It is through the Lord that I fell away: for thou oughtest not to do the things that he hateth. Say not thou, He hath caused me to err: for he hath no need of the sinful man. The Lord hateth all abomination and they that fear God love it not. He himself made man from the beginning, and left him in the hand of his counsel; if thou wilt, thou canst keep the commandments and perform acceptable faithfulness. He hath set fire and water before thee: stretch forth thy hand unto whether thou wilt. Before man is life and death; and whether him liketh shall be given him. For the wisdom of the Lord is great, and he is mighty in power, and beholdeth all things: and his eyes are upon them that fear him, and he knoweth every work of man. He hath commanded no man to do wickedly, neither hath he given any man licence to sin (15:11-20).

The number of a man's days at the most are an hundred years. As a drop of water unto the sea, and a gravelstone in comparison of the sand; so are a thousand years to the days of eternity. Therefore is God patient with them, and poureth forth his mercy upon them. He saw and perceived their end to be evil; therefore he multiplied his compassion. The mercy of man is toward his neighbour; but the mercy of the Lord is upon all flesh: he reproveth, and nurtureth, and teacheth, and bringeth again, as a shepherd his flock (18:9-13).

The most High is not pleased with the offerings

of the wicked; neither is he pacified for sin by the multitude of sacrifices. Whoso bringeth an offering of the goods of the poor doeth as one that killeth the son before his father's eyes. The bread of the needy is their life: he that defraudeth him thereof is a man of blood. He that taketh away his neighbour's living slayeth him and he that defraudeth the labourer of his hire is a bloodshedder (34:19-22).

H. Baruch.—Of several books attributed to Jeremiah's secretary, Baruch son of Neriah, this one alone was included in the Septuagint and in the Vulgate. In the King James Version (following the Vulgate) the Epistle of Jeremy is attached to it as the sixth chapter. The book, though brief, is generally attributed to more than one author: one writer composed 1:1–3:8 in prose; one or two other writers are held responsible for the two poetic sections, 3:9–4:4 and 4:5–5:9. We may summarize Baruch (sometimes referred to as "I Baruch") as follows:

(a) Repentance after the fall of Jerusalem (1:1–3:8). Baruch is said to have written and publicly read the book in Babylonia, in the fifth year (after 586?); his audience fasted and prayed, and sent a collection to Joakim, the high priest in Jerusalem (1:1-7), together with silver temple vessels (1:8-9). The priests should pray for Nebuchadrezzar and *his son* (an error reproduced from Dan. 5:2, 13, 18, 22) Balthasar (i.e., Belshazzar son of Nabonidus) for the benefit of the exiles (1:10-12); they should also pray for the forgiveness of the exiles (1:13) and read Baruch's book on feast days (1:14).

The Jewish community in Jerusalem confesses its sins since the Exodus, notably the service of other gods, which have brought upon it the threats of Deut. 28:15-68; nevertheless, the Jews have not observed the Lord's commandments (1:15–2:10). The exiles implore the divine mercy on Israel (2:11-13) for the sake of his honor (2:14-19). Despite God's warnings, Judah rebelled against Nebuchadrezzar and was savagely punished (2:20-26). In accordance with Deut. 28:62 the Lord exiled his stiff-necked people, but in their captivity they will repent and will be brought back to Zion (2:27-35). Praying for their salvation, the exiles beg for divine mercy because, having repented, they are now punished for the sins of their fathers (3:1-8).

(b) A poem on wisdom (3:9–4:4). "Hear, Israel, the commandments of life: give ear to understand wisdom" (3:9), for Israel was exiled for failing to do so (3:10-12). Life and peace are with wisdom (3:13-14), which neither ancient and modern kings, nor the sages of Edom were able to find (3:15-23). In God's immense house, the universe (3:24-25), primeval giants "were destroyed because they had no

wisdom" (3:26-28). God alone has found wisdom, and he gave it to Israel (3:29-37): it is the law of Moses (4:1), in whose light Israel should walk (4:2-4).

(c) "Be of good cheer, my people" (4:5–5:9; cf. Isa. 40–55). Jerusalem in her desolation weeps (4:5-8) over her children in Judea (4:9-16) and in exile (4:17-20). Before long the Lord will bring back the exiles (4:21-26), who should now seek their God (4:27-29).

Babylon's "pride shall be turned into mourning" (4:30-34). "O Jerusalem, . . . Lo, thy sons come, whom thou sentest away" (4:35-36). "Put off, O Jerusalem, the garment of thy mourning" (5:1), for thou shalt be called "The peace of righteousness" (5:2-4). Stand on the mountain to behold thy returning children (5:5) brought back by God (5:6-9).

Few, if any, Protestant critics would now attribute the book, or any of its parts, to Baruch, the secretary of Jeremiah. Neither of them, as far as we know, ever was in Babylonia (as 1:1 and some Jewish writings assert; in the Septuagint, for instance, Ps. 137 is attributed to Jeremiah). The book is considerably later than "the Exile." The first part (1:1–3:8) may date from 150-100 B.C. and was obviously written in Hebrew (as the extant Greek version clearly indicates).

The poem on wisdom (3:9–4:4) discloses echoes of Jer. 49:7; Obad. 8; Job 28; Prov. 8 (all passages of uncertain date) and like Ecclus. 24, identifies wisdom with the law of Moses; Wisd. Sol. 7:1–8:1 was however unknown to the author. We may therefore infer that this poem was composed in the period 180-100 B.C., possibly to counteract the heresies of Ecclesiastes; the Palestinian character of the teaching indicates that its author wrote it in Hebrew (hardly in Aramaic).

Another poet wrote 4:5–5:9 in order to counteract the despairing mood of 1:1–3:8, drawing his inspiration from the Second Isaiah (and also from Isa. 56–66). This passage was likewise originally penned in Hebrew, presumably about 100 B.C., although some critics have detected in it the aftermath of the destruction of Jerusalem by Titus in A.D. 70.

The religious teaching of the poem on wisdom (3:9–4:4) differs from that of the rest of the book, although the presumably secondary introduction (3:9-13) and conclusion (4:2-4) strive to harmonize this poem with the rest of the book, and with the destruction of Jerusalem in 586. Here God is primarily the universal creator, whose attribute is wisdom (not justice and mercy, as elsewhere in the book). Wisdom is conceived as the mysterious plan of creation (cf. Job 28), as the counselor of man (as in

Prov. 8), and as the law of Moses (cf. Ecclus. 24):

Who hath gone up into heaven, and taken her [Wisdom], and brought her down from the clouds? Who hath gone over the sea, and found her, and will bring her for pure gold? No man knoweth her way, nor thinketh of her path. But he that knoweth all things knoweth her, and hath found her out with his understanding: he that prepared the earth for evermore hath filled it with fourfooted beasts: he that sendeth forth light, and it goeth, calleth it again, and it obeyeth him with fear. The stars shined in their watches, and rejoiced: when he calleth them, they say, Here we be; and so with cheerfulness they shewed light unto him that made them. This is our God, and there shall none other be accounted of in comparison of him. He hath found out all the way of knowledge, and hath given it unto Jacob his servant, and to Israel his beloved (3:29-36).

The rest of the book pictures the Lord's people in exile and in misery on account of its rebellion against its God, imploring divine forgiveness and salvation, not on account of Israel's merits, but to safeguard God's covenant with Abraham, Isaac, and Jacob (2:34), and his honor among the Gentiles (2:14; 3:5). The usual messianic and eschatological comforts for the despairing Jews (the Messiah and his kingdom, the resurrection, etc.) are entirely lacking; the two future blessings are those promised by the Second Isaiah: the return of the exiles, and the destruction of Babylon.

J. The Epistle of Jeremy.—This little tract against idolatry is found in the Vulgate and in the King James Version as ch. 6 of Baruch. It is said to be (vs. 1) a copy of Jeremiah's epistle to the exiles (cf. Jer. 29). During seven generations or about 280 years (*not* seventy years, Jer. 25:11; 29:10; nor seventy weeks of years, Dan. 9:2, 24-27) the exiles will remain in Babylonia: in those days they must refrain from worshiping Babylonian idols (vss. 2-7). The sarcastic attack on the folly of idolatry (vss. 8-73) following this introduction may be summarized thus:

Ornaments do not save idols from rust, moths, and dust (vss. 8-14); scepters and swords do not turn them into living judges and warriors (vss. 15-16). Insensitive to dust in the eyes, helpless against thieves, idols cannot see the lamps that illuminate them; they cannot prevent worms from devouring them, nor smoke from blackening them, nor animals from alighting on them (vss. 17-23); they are inactive, must be shined, were once molten into shape and felt nothing, have no breath, and cannot move by themselves; offerings placed before them benefit only the priests (vss. 24-29). Even priestesses minister in temples, as also priests in mourning garb moaning as in a funeral; priests take the idols' garments; idols cannot reward nor punish, crown nor set aside a king, grant wealth, demand payment of a vow, save a life, protect the oppressed, restore human sight, help the needy (vss. 30-40a). Chaldeans deal disrespectfully with idols; the dumb are brought before Bel (Marduk), as if he could make them talk; women wait by the road to be seduced by men passing by (vss. 40b-44; cf. Herodotus *History* I. 199). Being the work of men's hands, fashioned in accordance with a sculptor's whim, they perish with their makers; in time of war they must be hidden (vss. 45-52). Being helpless, idols cannot produce rain, judge, redress wrongs, save themselves in a fire or in a battle (vss. 53-56). They are useless: they are less capable than a king, less useful than a vessel, a door, a pillar, less impressive than heavenly bodies and atmospheric phenomena, less alive than beasts (vss. 57-69). Idols are like a scarecrow, a thorn, a corpse; not being gods, they will rot away, bringing shame to their country; therefore the righteous, having no idols, will not be put to shame (vss. 70-73).

This polemic tract, denouncing heathen religions after the sarcastic manner of Isa. 40:18-20; 44:9-20; Jer. 10:2-5, 9, 14-15; etc. neither is an epistle, nor was it written by Jeremiah (as Jerome recognized). Composed as a warning of Jeremiah to the Babylonian exiles, it is really an attack against paganism, penned originally in Aramaic, although only a Greek version is extant, in the Hellenistic period (presumably 300-100 B.C.) to strengthen the faith of the Jews and their horror for paganism. Beholding the multitudes worshiping idols, the Jews should say in their hearts, "O Lord, we must worship thee [alone]" (vss. 5-6). The author wished perhaps to convey this message to the Gentiles even more than to the Jews.

K. The Song of the Three Holy Children.—The superscription in the King James Version reads as follows: "The Song of the Three Holy Children, which followeth in the third Chapter of DANIEL after this place,—*fell down bound into the midst of the burning fiery furnace,*—verse 23. That which followeth is not in the Hebrew, to wit,—*And they walked*—unto these words,—*Then Nebuchadnezzar,*—verse 24."

This is the first of the additions to Daniel in the Septuagint and the Vulgate. All of them have come down to us in two Greek recensions: the Septuagint text (in the Codex Chisianus alone), and Theodotion's revision of the Septuagint, which became standard in the Christian Bibles (Greek, Latin, Syriac, Coptic, Ethiopic, Arabic, Armenian, King James Version, English Revised Version, etc.). The other additions to

Daniel are the stories of Susanna, Bel and the Dragon. The Song of the Three Children comprises three parts, summarized as follows:

(a) The Prayer of Azarias (vss. 1-22; LXX and Vulg.=Dan. 3:24-45). Ananias, Misael, and Azarias praised God in the fiery furnace, and Azarias offered the following prayer (vss. 1-2). Even when the Lord brought calamity on the Jews by destroying Jerusalem, he was just (vss. 3-10); but for his name's sake, and on account of his covenant and his love for the patriarchs, he should not annihilate his people (vss. 11-13). Having no state and temple like other nations, the Jews beg God for deliverance (vss. 14-22).

(b) The heating of the fiery furnace (vss. 23-28; LXX and Vulg.=Dan. 3:46-51). The abundance of fuel sent the flames forty-nine cubits above the furnace and destroyed the Chaldeans near it (vss. 23-25). An angel removed the flames from inside the furnace, substituting a cooling breeze; [9] so the three youths were unharmed (vss. 26-27) and sang the following hymn (vs. 28):

(c) The Song of the Three Children (vss. 29-68; LXX and Vulg.=Dan. 3:52-90). "Blessed art thou, O Lord God of our fathers: and to be praised and exalted above all for ever" (vss. 29-34). All creation should bless the Lord, notably the heavens and their contents, the earth with what is on it—inanimate things, animals, mankind, and primarily Israel (vss. 35-65, the Benedicite [Bless ye!] of the Prayer Book). Ananias, Azarias, and Misael should bless the Lord, as also all pious Jews (vss. 66-68).

Azarias (vss. 1-22) did not request his deliverance from the fiery furnace—the three youths had already been saved from the flames —but (like Baruch 1:15–3:1-8, which our author may have known) he confessed Israel's sins and begged God's forgiveness. Like the Song of the Three Children, the Prayer of Azarias was written in Hebrew, the language of hymns and prayers. Like the rest of Dan. 3, the narrative section (vss. 23-28) was presumably in Aramaic, and may well have been written by the editor who inserted the two poems in Dan. 3, adding an introductory verse to each (vss. 2, 28), and the conclusion of the second (vss. 66-68), in order to adapt these poems to the story of the fiery furnace. The poems could very well have been quoted from an anthology or a hymnal (as I Sam. 2:1-10; Isa. 38:9-20; Jonah 2:1-9). These texts were added to Daniel soon after it was written in 164 B.C., and before the so-called Septuagint version of Daniel was made. These two poems, Susanna, Bel and the

Dragon, were therefore composed in Hebrew and translated into Greek ("Septuagint" text) between 160 and 100 B.C.

The second poem is a liturgy in praise of God like Ps. 148 (cf. Ps. 150), in which the second half of the line is an identical refrain: "and to be praised and exalted above all for ever" (vss. 29-34); "praise and exalt him above all for ever" (vss. 35-65); a similar repetition of a refrain occurs in Ps. 136 ("for his mercy endureth for ever"). In antiphonal singing the congregation may have sung the refrain. The similarity between this song and Ps. 148 is such that one hymn was probably derived from the other (our song, being much longer, may be the later one of the two), and both may have been inspired by Ecclus. 43. Although the Benedicite is thus far from original, it achieved a place in Christian liturgy.

Here are brief selections from the Prayer of Azarias and from the Benedicite:

> Blessed art thou, O Lord God of our fathers: thy name is worthy to be praised and glorified for evermore: for thou art righteous in all the things that thou hast done to us: yea, true are all thy works, thy ways are right, and all thy judgments truth. In all the things that thou hast brought upon us, and upon the holy city of our fathers, even Jerusalem, thou hast executed true judgment: for according to truth and judgment didst thou bring all these things upon us because of our sins (vss. 3-5).

> And now we follow thee with all our heart, we fear thee, and seek thy face. Put us not to shame: but deal with us after thy lovingkindness, and according to the multitude of thy mercies (vss. 18-19).

> Blessed art thou, O Lord God of our fathers: and to be praised and exalted above all for ever. And blessed is thy glorious and holy name: and to be praised and exalted above all for ever (vss. 29-30).

> O all ye works of the Lord, bless ye the Lord: praise and exalt him above all for ever (vs. 35).

L. Susanna.—This short story—fictitious, of course—is one of the earliest detective stories known (cf. the following story of Bel), although much later than the other one in I Kings 3:16-27. The superscription in the King James Version reads, "The History of Susanna, Set apart from the beginning of Daniel, because it is not in the Hebrew, as neither the Narration of Bel and the Dragon." The following summary (like those of Bel and the Dragon) is based on the Greek text of Theodotion, the Vulgate, and the King James Version (as also the English Revised Version and E. J. Goodspeed, Apocrypha); but the text of the Septuagint, which differs from Theodotion here and there, is older and better (parallel English versions of the Septuagint and of Theodotion are printed in R. H. Charles, Apocrypha). Susanna is placed

---

[9] Remember how God made the fierce fire seem
To those three children like a pleasant dew.
—Tennyson, Queen Mary, Act IV, scene 3.

at the beginning of Daniel in the Septuagint and appears as Dan. 13 in the Vulgate.

Susanna was the beautiful and pious wife of Joakim, a wealthy Babylonian Jew (vss. 1-3). Among the visitors to their home, which was surrounded by a park, were two aged judges, of whom the Scriptures (cf. Jer. 29:21-23?) spoke saying "that wickedness came from Babylon from ancient judges" (vss. 4-6). They saw Susanna walking in her park and they became inflamed for her (vss. 7-9). They hid their passion from each other (vss. 10-12), but one day they returned separately in secret and thus discovered one another's infatuation (vss. 13-14). One day while they were hidden in the park Susanna prepared to bathe in the garden pool (vss. 15-17). The elders demanded that she lie with them or they would accuse her of adultery with a young man (vss. 18-21); but she preferred a false accusation to sin (vss. 22-23), and shouted for help; the elders charged her with adultery when servants came from the house (vss. 24-27). On the following day, in the presence of the visitors in Joakim's house, the elders asserted that they had surprised Susanna with a young man who escaped (vss. 28-40). The assembly condemned Susanna to death (vs. 41), but God heard Susanna's appeal (vss. 42-44). While Susanna was being led to execution, Daniel was inspired by God and accused the elders of false testimony (vss. 45-49). In the new trial Daniel questioned the elders separately (vss. 50-51): the first declared that Susanna had committed adultery under a mastic tree (vss. 52-55), while the second said it was a holm oak (vss. 56-59).[10] In accordance with Deut. 19:18-19 (which, in 105-79 B.C., the Pharisees interpreted as requiring the death sentence for false witnesses, even if the defendant was still alive), the two elders were executed (vss. 60-62). Susanna's family praised God (vs. 63), while the people praised Daniel (vs. 64).

The tale of Susanna (the name means "lily" in Hebrew) may well have been pagan in origin and have been rewritten by a Jew to glorify the prophet Daniel. Two folkloric motifs are combined in its plot: the "Genoveva" motif of a chaste wife accused by a rejected suitor; and the motif of the young judge or friend who delivers a person falsely accused from death. The motif of trees giving testimony in trials is known in Oriental fiction. By adding the Jewish

background and religious teaching (which is similar to that in Tobit and Judith), and by slight retouching, an editor changed a detective tale into an edifying instance of God's vindication of innocence falsely accused, and gave us the proverbial figure of "a Daniel come to judgment," "a second Daniel." [11]

The religious lesson of the book is expressed in the following verses:

Then Susanna cried out with a loud voice, and said, O everlasting God, that knowest the secrets, and knowest all things before they be: thou knowest that they have borne false witness against me, and, behold, I must die. . . . And the Lord heard her voice (vss. 42-44).

M. Bel and the Dragon.—These two stories are placed at the end of Daniel in the Septuagint and in the Vulgate (ch. 14, Vulg.). They not only exhibit Daniel's detective brilliance, as does the story of Susanna, but also ridicule Babylonian paganism. They may be summarized as follows, according to Theodotion's version (the text used in Christian Bibles):

(*a*) The Story of Bel (vss. 1-22). Cyrus followed Astyages on the throne and honored Daniel greatly (vss. 1-2). The Babylonians offered daily to the idol of Bel (Marduk) twelve measures of flour, forty sheep, and six vessels of wine (vs. 3). Daniel refused to worship Bel, a hand-made idol, and assured Cyrus that it never did eat or drink anything (vss. 4-7). The king summoned Bel's seventy priests: unless they proved that Bel consumed the food they would be put to death; but if they did so, Daniel would be executed (vss. 8-10). The priests had no fear when the king placed the food before Bel and sealed all the temple's doors, for they could enter through a trap door under the table (vss. 11-13). But on Daniel's instructions ashes had been secretly scattered over the floor of the temple (vs. 14). In the night the priests and their families came to eat the food (vs. 15), and in the morning the king praised Bel—for the seals were intact and the food was gone (vss. 16-18). But Daniel showed him the footprints in the ashes (vs. 19); the priests were forced to disclose the trap door and were slain with their families (vss. 20-21). Daniel destroyed the idol and the temple (vs. 22).

(*b*) The Story of the Dragon (vss. 23-42). When the king asked Daniel to worship the Babylonian dragon, which was alive and really ate, Daniel refused (vss. 23-25). He received permission to slay the dragon without sword or staff (vs. 26). The dragon burst asunder when he ate a concoction of pitch, fat, and hair which Daniel had prepared (vs. 27). The Babylonians

---

[10] Daniel punned the names of the trees in announcing the elders' doom: *schinos, schizein* (mastic, to cut asunder); *prinos, prinein* (holm oak, to saw asunder). The puns do not prove, as Africanus thought in his letter to Origen (*ca.* A.D. 240) that Susanna was written originally in Greek, for the Hebrew could have coined similar puns with other trees; cf. in English pine, pine away; ash, turn to ashes; etc.

[11] Shakespeare, *Merchant of Venice*, Act IV, scene 1.

accused the king of having become a Jew (vss. 28-29); Daniel was cast into the den of hungry lions (vss. 30-32). In Judea, Habakkuk was instructed by an angel to bring to Daniel the food intended for the reapers (vss. 33-34), and was carried to the lions' den by an angel (vss. 35-36). Daniel praised the Lord for this dinner, and Habakkuk was instantly brought back (vss. 37-39). On the seventh day the king found Daniel alive and, having praised God, cast Daniel's enemies to the lions (vss. 40-42).

Jerome called these two stories "fables," and few would regard them as history. Bel's story is a sample of Jewish polemic against idolatry (inaugurated by the Second Isaiah; cf. the Epistle of Jeremy, above) in narrative form. The great temple of Marduk (Bel), built by Nebuchadrezzar—one of the seven wonders of the ancient world—was found in ruins by Alexander (332 B.C.), and our author attributed its destruction to Daniel.

While the Bel story has thus a meager historical background, the Story of the Dragon is purely mythical, for no living dragon (and probably not even a living serpent) was ever worshiped by the Babylonians. The author may have been inspired by the Babylonian myth of Marduk's slaying of the dragon Tiamat (as Hermann Gunkel asserted), but if so, changed it entirely. Both tales, dating from 150-100 B.C., lack religious significance, and merely illustrate the popular Jewish literature of the time, which is almost completely lost.

N. The Prayer of Manasses.—This penitential psalm, composed with reference to II Chr. 33:11-13, is placed among the Odes or Cantica which follow the Psalms in some manuscripts of the Septuagint, and after the New Testament in the printed editions of the Vulgate (late manuscripts of the Vulgate place it after II Chronicles). In brief, its contents are as follows:

The almighty Creator in his infinite mercy has appointed repentance for sinners like Manasses, not for the righteous. Having committed numberless transgressions, the King is bound in fetters, oppressed by his sins, and he humbly confesses them, begging for forgiveness. After God in his mercy has saved him—unworthy as he is—he will praise the Lord as long as he lives; for, as the angels proclaim, his is the glory forever.

Although there is no reference to this prayer before the third century of our era, when its Syriac text is included in the *Didascalia,* there is no reason for regarding it as a Christian work, nor for doubting that it was composed in Hebrew, shortly before the beginning of our era, and accidentally escaped oblivion.

As is usually the case in Babylonian penitential psalms, both the awareness of sin and the agonizing cry for forgiveness result from sudden illness or other calamity: "I am bowed down with many iron bands, that I cannot lift up mine head, neither have I any release." Although Ps. 51 is on a higher spiritual level, the note of repentance rings true here also:

Now therefore I bow the knee of mine heart, beseeching thee of grace. I have sinned, O Lord, I have sinned, and I acknowledge mine iniquities: wherefore, I humbly beseech thee, forgive me, O Lord, forgive me, and destroy me not with mine iniquities.

O. I Maccabees.—Of the four books entitled "Maccabees"—from the title given to Judas Maccabaeus, usually interpreted as "the Hammerer"—the first is historically the most valuable, giving us the best account of Jewish history from 175 to 135 B.C. Its contents may be summarized as follows:

(a) Introduction. After the death of Alexander (323 B.C.), his empire was divided among his successors (1:5-9).

(b) The causes of the Maccabean rebellion (1:10-64). Early in the reign of Antiochus IV Epiphanes (175-164 B.C.), some Jews, eager to imitate the Greeks, built a gymnasium in Jerusalem and "submitted to uncircumcision" (1:10-15). After Antiochus returned from his victorious campaign in Egypt (171), he plundered the temple in Jerusalem (1:16-24). The Jews lamented and mourned (1:25-28, in verse). In 168, Antiochus sent a tax collector to Jerusalem; he plundered part of the city (1:29-32), and placed a garrison on Zion (1:33-36). New indignities were suffered by Jerusalem (1:37-40, in verse). Antiochus prescribed Greek cults for his subjects and forbade the practice of Judaism; but the faithful Jews went into hiding (1:41-53). On the twenty-fifth of Chislev (about December) of 168, the "abomination of desolation" (i.e., an altar dedicated to the Olympian Zeus) was placed upon the altar in Zion, books of the law were burned, circumcision was forbidden, and faithful Jews (Hasidim) were put to death (1:54-64).

(c) The beginnings of the Maccabean rebellion (2:1-70). Mattathias (the father of John, Simon, Judas, Eleazar, and Jonathan; 2:1-5) lamented the pollution of the sanctuary (2:6-14; vss. 8-13 are in verse) and started the rebellion at Modin by slaying an apostate Jew and the king's officer (2:15-28). Some of the Hasidim refused to fight on the sabbath and were slaughtered (2:29-38). Mattathias and the Hasidim decided to fight defensively on the sabbath (2:39-41), and having collected an army proceeded to enforce the law of Moses (2:42-48). On his deathbed Mattathias urged his sons to observe the law and fight the heathen under the leadership of Judas (2:49-70).

(d) A poem in praise of Judas Maccabaeus (3:1-9).

(e) Judas' wars for religious liberty (3:10–4:61). Judas defeated and slew Apollonius (3:10-12), and forced the retreat of Seron (3:13-26). Antiochus Epiphanes went on a campaign in Persia, and placed Lysias in command (3:27-37). Judas defeated Gorgias (3:38–4:25) and Lysias (4:26-35). He then rededicated the desecrated temple on the twenty-fifth of Chislev, 165 B.C., which became an annual holiday (Hanukkah or Dedication, cf. Ps. 30 and John 10:22), and fortified Bethsura (4:36-61).

(f) Judas' wars against the pagan enemies of the Jews (5:1-68). Stirred by pogroms (5:1-2), Judas defeated the Idumeans (5:3), the "children of Bean" (5:4-5), and the Ammonites (5:6-8). Appeals for help came from Jews in Gilead and in Galilee (5:9-15). Judas sent Simon to Galilee, and went to Gilead with Jonathan (5:16-17); he instructed Joseph and Azarias, whom he left in charge of Judea, not to wage war (5:18-19). Simon brought the Galilean Jews to Judea (5:20-23). East of the Jordan, Judas reassured the Nabataeans (5:24-27), and after some victories slew Timotheus at Karnaim (5:28-44). On the way back he destroyed Ephron (5:45-51), and returned to Jerusalem by way of Bethshean (5:52-54). But meanwhile Joseph and Azarias (cf. 5:18-19) were routed by Gorgias when they attacked Jamnia, for they were not "of the seed of those [the Hasmonaeans], by whose hand deliverance was given unto Israel" (5:55-64). Judas fought successfully against Hebron in Idumea (5:65), was checked at Marisa (Samaria in KJV; 5:66-67), and destroyed the idols of Azotus (5:68).

(g) The death of Antiochus Epiphanes and the campaign of Lysias against the Jews (6:1-63). Ill after his failure to plunder a temple in Persia and after hearing of the success of Judas, Antiochus died after having appointed Philip as regent; but Lysias set up Antiochus V Eupator as king (6:1-17). When Judas besieged the Syrian garrison in the Acra on Zion (6:18-27), Lysias marched against him from the south, besieging Bethsura (6:28-31). Judas was defeated at Beth Zacharias (6:32-47), Bethsura fell (6:48-50), and the garrison in the temple was unable to resist (6:51-54). Lysias and Antiochus V signed a peace treaty with Judas, allowing the Jews full religious freedom (6:55-61), and defeated Philip (6:62-63; cf. 6:14).

(h) The wars against Demetrius I, and the death of Judas (7:1–9:22). Demetrius I Soter slew Lysias and Antiochus V in 161 (7:1-7), and sent Bacchides against Judas in order to support the Hellenists in Jerusalem, headed by Alkimus (7:8-20). Judas defeated Nicanor at Adasa, a victory celebrated annually on the thirteenth of Adar (7:21-50). Judas signed a treaty of friendship with Rome (8:1-32), but fell at Elasa (in 161), fighting against Bacchides (9:1-22).

(j) Jonathan and Bacchides (9:23-73). Acclaimed as the successor of his brother Judas (9:23-31), Jonathan withdrew east of the Jordan (9:32-34), where he met Arabian hostility (9:35-42). Defeated at the mouth of the Jordan by Bacchides (9:43-49), Jonathan, after the death of Alkimus (9:50-56), signed a peace treaty with Bacchides (9:57-73).

(k) Jonathan and Alexander Balas (10:1–11:19). Alexander Balas, a pretender, forced Demetrius I to make concessions to Jonathan (10:1-14), but gained the latter's support by appointing him high priest (10:15-21). In vain did Demetrius promise the Jews virtual independence (10:22-45): Jonathan luckily supported Balas (10:46-47), for Demetrius fell in battle (10:48-50). Jonathan attended the wedding of Balas with Cleopatra, the daughter of Ptolemy VI (10:51-66). Demetrius II Nicator sent Apollonius against Jonathan (10:67-73), but Jonathan defeated him at Azotus (10:74-89). But when Ptolemy VI allied himself with Demetrius II, Alexander Balas was doomed (11:1-19).

(l) Jonathan and Demetrius II (11:20–12:53). Demetrius, having become king, confirmed and increased the territory and authority of Jonathan (11:20-37). Jonathan helped Demetrius fight against Tryphon, who set up Antiochus VI, son of Balas, as king (11:38-51); but Demetrius failed to keep his promises to Jonathan (11:52-53). So Jonathan gave his support to Antiochus VI and Tryphon, fighting against the forces of Demetrius (11:54-74); he made alliances with the Romans and the Spartans (12:1-23), and continued his successful campaigns (12:24-38). But Tryphon deceitfully captured Jonathan (12:39-53).

(m) Simon's support of Demetrius II (13:1–14:3). Elected leader in place of Jonathan (13:1-11), Simon sent tribute and hostages to Tryphon for the liberation of Jonathan, but Tryphon attacked him, executed Jonathan (13:12-30), and made himself king (13:31-32). Demetrius II granted political independence to the Jews in 141 (13:33-42). Simon conquered Gazara (13:43-48) and the Acra on Zion (13:49-53). Demetrius, however, was captured by the Parthians (14:1-3).

(n) Simon's rule (14:4-49). Simon is praised in prose (14:4-5) and poetry (14:6-15). Romans and Spartans renewed their treaties with him (14:16-24; cf. ch. 8; 12:1-23; 15:15-24). On the eighteenth of Elul, 140 B.C., a grateful nation appointed Simon and his descendants as high priests and rulers in perpetuity (14:25-49).

(*o*) Simon and Antiochus VII Sidetes (15: 1–16:24). Antiochus VII, brother of Demetrius II, confirmed Simon's authority (15:1-9), and in 138 besieged Tryphon in Dor (15:10-14). The Romans wrote to various rulers reaffirming their friendship for the Jews (15:15-24). Antiochus VII, not needing Simon's help, sent him an ultimatum imposing conditions that Simon refused (15:25-37). Cendebeus, on orders of Antiochus, attacked Simon, but was defeated (15:38–16:10). Together with two sons, Simon was assassinated by his son-in-law Ptolemy (16:11-18), but Simon's son John Hyrcanus escaped death (16:19-22) and succeeded his father: his deeds are recorded in the (lost) chronicles of his rule (16:23-24).

While I Maccabees deals with the period 175-135 B.C., II Maccabees begins one year earlier, but closes with the death of Nicanor in 161. There are however great differences in the treatment of the period 175-161, which they have in common, quite apart from the fact that I Maccabees was written in Hebrew, in a style patterned after Samuel and Kings, while II Maccabees was written in Greek and exhibits the ornate rhetorical style of romantic Hellenistic prose. The two books differ in contents (each having some exclusive material), in the order of the stories (the death of Antiochus IV in I Macc. 6:1-16 correctly follows the first campaign of Lysias in 4:26-35, but in II Macc. 9 precedes this campaign; see ch. 11), and in many details. The two books were written independently of one another. The first book on the whole is better history, but in some matters may be advantageously supplemented by the second. Many events are dated in I Maccabees (1:10, 20, 54; 2:70; 3:37; 4:52; etc.) in accordance with the Seleucid era, which in Palestine probably began in March-April, 311 B.C.

I Maccabees was certainly written after 135 B.C. (16:14) and, if 16:23-24 is genuine, soon after 104 B.C. (when John Hyrcanus died): presumably about 100 B.C. The author admired the Maccabean leaders, notably Judas and Simon, regarding them as God's instruments for the deliverance of Israel (5:62), which is not merely the nation but also God's holy congregation. Israel's enemies are God's enemies, and therefore doomed (7:41-42). The ideal Israelite is Mattathias, whose motto is, "Yet will I and my sons and my brethren walk in the covenant of our fathers. God forbid that we should forsake the law and the ordinances" (2:20-21). Although the author reverently avoids naming God (he uses the substitute "heaven"; cf. "the kingdom of heaven" in Matthew), he detects God's

hand in the historical events, even the most tragic (1:64; 2:49), and in prayers and speeches from his pen expresses his indomitable faith in God's help for Israel in distress (2:19-22, 27, 34, 37; 3:18-22; 4:8-11, 30-33; 7:37-38, 40-42; 16:3). This faith may be shown in the following:

Then said Judas to the men that were with him, Fear ye not their multitude, neither be ye afraid of their assault. Remember how our fathers were delivered in the Red sea, when Pharaoh pursued them with an army. Now therefore let us cry unto heaven, if peradventure the Lord will have mercy upon us, and remember the covenant of our fathers, and destroy this host before our face this day: that so all the heathen may know that there is one who delivereth and saveth Israel (4:8-11).

P. II Maccabees.—According to II Macc. 2:23, this book is the summary of a history in five volumes written (in Greek) by Jason of Cyrene. All we know of the contents of this work is what the epitomist tells us in 2:19-22. In all probability the letters in 1:1–2:18 (translated from the Aramaic) were neither in the book of Jason nor in the first edition of II Maccabees (in which 2:19-32 and 15:37-39 were contributed by the epitomist). This book, written in Greek in Alexandria about 50 B.C., may be summarized as follows:

(*a*) Two letters to the Egyptian Jews (1:1–2:18). (i) The first letter (1:1-10*a*), allegedly written in 123 B.C. (1:10*a*). After the salutation (1:1-6), the Palestinian writers recall a letter written in 142 about the tribulation which began in Judea with the persecutions of Jason (cf. 4:7-22), and report that now the temple worship has been restored and the Egyptian Jews should therefore celebrate the feast of Dedication (1:7-9).

(ii) The second letter (1:10*b*–2:18). It was allegedly written in 164, before the rededication of the temple, to Aristobulus and the Egyptian Jews. Antiochus IV was killed in Persia (1:10*b*-17); the rededication is imminent and should be celebrated in Egypt (1:18*a*). When Nehemiah inaugurated anew the temple service, he searched for the sacred fire hidden by the priests of Jerusalem (1:18*b*-20*a*), and found a black liquid which the sun ignited (1:20*b*-22) so that the sacrifices were consumed while the priests prayed (1:23-30). Some of the liquid burned on stones (1:31-32). The place where the liquid was found was sanctified (1:33-35). Nehemiah called the liquid νεφθαρ (cleansing [?]), the people, νεφθαι, that is, naphtha (1:36). Jeremiah not only had given instructions for hiding the sacred fire, but urged the exiles to keep the law which he gave them (2:1-3); he hid the tabernacle, the ark, and the altar of incense on Mount Nebo (2:4-5); they

417

would remain concealed until "God gather his people again together" (2:6-8). As in the days of Moses, so when Solomon dedicated the temple, fire from heaven consumed the sacrifices (2:9-12). Nehemiah founded a library, and Judas collected books (2:13-15). Let the Egyptian Jews celebrate the dedication of the temple, for God has delivered the Jews and may soon gather them together again (2:16-18).

(*b*) The epitomist's preface (2:19-32). The five books of Jason of Cyrene have been condensed into one book for the general reader (2:19-32).

(*c*) Intrigues in the temple (3:1–4:50). Simon's accusations against Onias III under Seleucus IV (187-175 B.C.) brought Heliodorus to Jerusalem to seize the funds in the temple (3:1-21), but heavenly beings assailed him and almost killed him (3:22-40). When Onias went to Seleucus to exculpate himself (4:1-6), his brother Jason displaced him and became high priest (4:7-10), introducing Greek customs and institutions into Jerusalem (4:11-22). But Menelaus took Jason's place (4:23-26) and gained the favor of Andronicus (4:27-32), inducing him to kill Onias (4:33-38). The Jews protested in vain against the plunder of the temple (4:39-50).

(*d*) Antiochus Epiphanes persecutes the Jews (5:1–7:42). During the second Egyptian campaign of Antiochus (5:1-4), Jason occupied Jerusalem for a while (5:5-10). Antiochus plundered the temple, oppressed the Jews (5:11-27), and forbade the practice of Judaism on penalty of death (6:1-17). The aged Eleazar (6:18-31) and a mother with her seven sons (7:1-42) preferred to be tortured unto death rather than partake of swine's meat.

(*e*) The first victories of Judas Maccabaeus (8:1-36). With an army of six thousand Judas defeated Nicanor (8:1-29), and slew twenty thousand of the men of Timotheus and Bacchides (8:30-36).

(*f*) The death of Antiochus Epiphanes (9:1-29). After attempting to rob a temple in Persepolis, Antiochus was stricken in Ecbatana (9:1-10). He vowed to become a Jew (9:11-17), urged the Jews to be loyal to Antiochus V (9:18-27), and was buried in Antioch (9:28-29).

(*g*) The rededication of the temple (10:1-9). The temple was cleansed (10:1-5) and the feast of Dedication was celebrated (10:6-9).

(*h*) Judas' first victory over Lysias (10:10–11:38). After the appointment of Lysias (10:10-13), Judas attacked the Idumeans (10:14-23), routed Timotheus (10:24-38), and through his victory forced Lysias to offer favorable terms (11:1-15), stated in various official documents (11:16-33) and approved by the Romans (11:34-38).

(*j*) Various campaigns of Judas (12:1-45). Judas fought the heathen at Joppa (12:1-9), and the Arabs in its vicinity (12:10-12); he conquered Kaspis (12:13-16), Charax, Karnaim, and Ephron (12:17-28), but spared Bethshean (12:29-31). Gorgias was routed at Jamnia (12:32-37), where local idols were discovered on the corpses of wicked Jews (12:38-45).

(*k*) Judas' second victory over Lysias (13:1-26). Menelaus was executed (13:1-8). Judas attacked Lysias at Modin (13:9-17). Antiochus V was defeated at Bethsura and forced to accept the peace terms dictated by the Jews (13:18-26).

(*l*) Judas' victory over Nicanor (14:1–15:36). Demetrius I appointed Alkimus as high priest and Nicanor as governor (14:1-13). Nicanor made peace with Judas (14:16-25), but upon the accusations of Alkimus was ordered to send Judas to Antioch (14:26-30). In spite of his threats against the priests, Nicanor could not lay hands on Judas (14:31-36). Razis disemboweled himself to escape arrest (14:37-46). Nicanor was unable to attack Judas in Samaria on a sabbath (15:1-5). Judas encouraged his men by relating a dream (15:6-21), and after a prayer (15:22-25) defeated Nicanor, exhibiting his head on the citadel (15:26-35); then he proclaimed an annual festival on the day preceding Purim (15:36).

(*m*) Epilogue (15:37-39). Jerusalem was thus permanently freed from the heathen after Nicanor's death in 161 (15:37). To please his readers the epitomist has blended actual facts and fanciful style (15:38-39).

The temple is the focus of interest in II Maccabees (and presumably in the five lost books of Jason of Cyrene), while the congregation is of paramount significance in I Maccabees. The epitomist deals with his subject dramatically: the temple is desecrated or threatened twice—first by Antiochus Epiphanes, then by Nicanor—but is twice saved by God through Judas Maccabaeus (3:1–10:9; 10:10–15:36); an annual festival (Dedication, Day of Nicanor) is instituted to celebrate each deliverance. Thus the book's theme is expressed, with apt poetic justice, by Heliodorus who failed to desecrate the temple: "He that dwelleth in heaven hath his eye on that place [the temple], and defendeth it; and he beateth and destroyeth them that come to hurt it [like Heliodorus, Epiphanes, and Nicanor]" (3:39). The actual desecration by Epiphanes receives theological explanation (5:17-20; 6:12-17; 7:18, 32-33).

This passionate interest in the earthly abode of the sole God in existence (14:35), which is characteristic of the Diaspora Jews like Jason of Cyrene, explains the far greater religious and theological contents of II Maccabees, as compared to the simple faith in the background of

I Maccabees. Among characteristic doctrines in II Maccabees may be mentioned the poetic justice in God's punishments, which are made to conform with the transgression (4:38, 42; 5:9-10; 8:33; 9:8-10, 28; 13:5-8; 15:31-35) ; miraculous interventions (14:15) in behalf of the temple (3:25-26, 33-34, 38-39) and of Israel (10:29-30; 11:8; 13:17; cf. 5:2-4) on the part of God, "the wonder worker" (15:21) ; the reward of Jewish martyrs through their *bodily* (7:11; 14:46) resurrection (7:9, 14, 23, 29, 36; 12:43-45) ; nothing is said, as in Dan. 12:2, of a resurrection of the apostate Jews unto everlasting contempt. This Pharisaic doctrine contrasts sharply with the Platonic doctrine of the immortality of the spirit in Wisdom of Solomon and IV Maccabees. The book has left its mark on Christian literature: the stories about the martyrs (6:18–7:42; 14:37-46), beginning with Heb. 11:35-38, furnished encouragement and example to Christians in times of persecution; it has also provided proof texts for the creation *ex nihilo* (7:28), the intercession of the saints (15:14), eternal death of the wicked (7:9, 14), resurrection of the flesh (7:11; 14:46), intercession for the dead (12:43), deliverance of the dead from purgatory (12:43-45, possibly annotated), and the doctrine of angels (3:24-28; 10:29-30; 11:8).

IV. Selected Bibliography

CHARLES, R. H. *Religious Development Between the Old and New Testaments.* New York: Henry Holt, 1914.

——. *The Apocrypha and Pseudepigrapha in English.* Oxford: Clarendon Press, 1913.

GOODSPEED, EDGAR J. *The Apocrypha: An American Translation.* Chicago: University of Chicago Press, 1938.

——. *The Story of the Apocrypha.* Chicago: University of Chicago Press, 1939.

HUGHES, H. MALDWYN. *The Ethics of Jewish Apocryphal Literature.* London: Robert Culley, 1910.

OESTERLEY, W. O. E. *An Introduction to the Books of the Apocrypha.* New York: The Macmillan Co., 1937.

PFEIFFER, ROBERT H. *History of New Testament Times, with an Introduction to the Apocrypha.* New York: Harper & Bros., 1949.

SCHÜRER, EMIL. *A History of the Jewish People in the Time of Jesus Christ.* Tr. John Macpherson, Sophia Taylor, and Peter Christie. Edinburgh: T. & T. Clark, 1885-1890.

TORREY, C. C. *The Apocryphal Literature: A Brief Introduction.* New Haven: Yale University Press, 1945.

WACE, HENRY, ed. *The Apocrypha* ("Speaker's Commentary"). London: John Murray, 1888.

WICKS, HENRY J. *The Doctrine of God in the Jewish Apocryphal and Apocalyptic Literature.* London: Hunter & Longhurst, 1915.

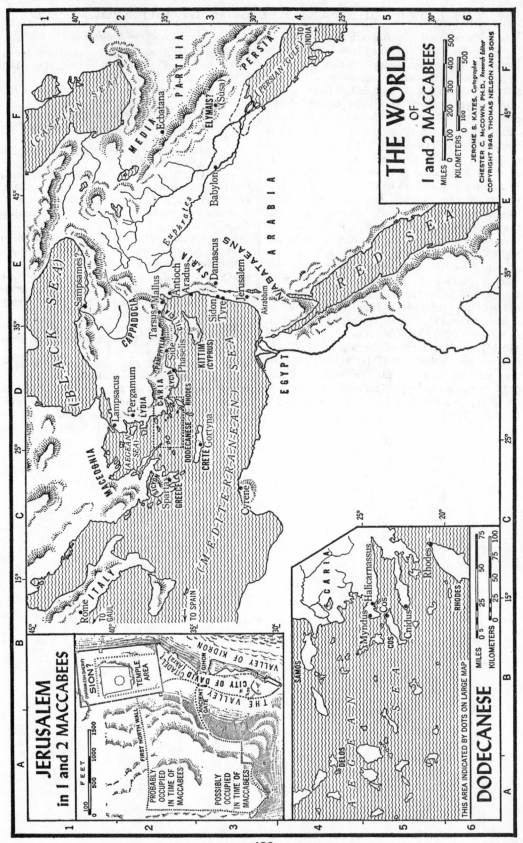

THE WORLD OF 1 and 2 MACCABEES

JEROME S. KATES, Cartographer
CHESTER C. McCOWN, PH.D., Research Editor
COPYRIGHT 1949, THOMAS NELSON AND SONS

MILES 0 100 200 300 400 500
KILOMETERS 0 100 500

JERUSALEM in 1 and 2 MACCABEES

FEET 0 100 500 1000 1500

(QARAM ESH-SHERIF) SION?

TEMPLE AREA

FIRST NORTH WALL

PROBABLY OCCUPIED IN TIME OF MACCABEES

POSSIBLY OCCUPIED IN TIME OF MACCABEES

ANCIENT GIHON

CITY OF DAVID CITADEL (Acra)

THE VALLEY OF KIDRON

DODECANESE

MILES 0 5 25 50 75
KILOMETERS 0 25 50 75 100

THIS AREA INDICATED BY DOTS ON LARGE MAP

SAMOS
DELOS
CARIA
Myndus Halicarnassus
Cos COS
Cnidus
RHODES Rhodes
A E G E A N   S E A

CASPIAN SEA
MEDIA
Ecbatana
PARTHIA
PERSIA
ELYMAIS?
Susa
Babylon
Euphrates
ARABIA
PERSIAN GULF
TO INDIA
NABATAEANS
RED SEA
EGYPT
Jerusalem
Akrabbim
Damascus
SYRIA
Sidon
Tyre
Aradus
Antioch
Mallus
Tarsus
CAPPADOCIA
CILICIA
PAMPHYLIA
Side
Phaselis
CARIA
LYDIA
Pergamum
Lampsacus
RHODES
DODECANESE
KITTIM (CYPRUS)
Cortyna
CRETE
(MEDITERRANEAN SEA)
Cyrene
MACEDONIA
GREECE
Sparta
(AEGEAN SEA)
COS
SICON?
ITALY
Rome
TO GAUL
TO SPAIN
BLACK SEA
Sampsames?

THE LITERATURE AND RELIGION
OF THE PSEUDEPIGRAPHA

by ROBERT H. PFEIFFER

The term "pseudepigrapha" means literally writings attributed to fictitious authors, and in this sense would apply to some books in the canonical Old Testament and in the Apocrypha, as for instance, all the books attributed to Solomon. But in a technical—originally Protestant—sense the term is applied to Jewish writings of the period from 200 B.C. to A.D. 200, outside of the Old Testament and the Apocrypha (excluding, however, most of the Alexandrian-Jewish writings, and the works of Philo and Josephus), which were for a time popular in certain branches, notably Oriental, of the ancient Christian church. There is consequently no recognized fixed limit to the Pseudepigrapha. Thus, for instance, R. H. Charles[1] has added to the standard list some writings entirely unknown to the ancient Christians (The Sayings of the Fathers, The Story of Ahikar, and the Fragments of a Zadokite Work); while Charles Cutler Torrey[2] omits these three works, but adds the Lives of the Prophets and the Testament of Job. Moreover, the extant Pseudepigrapha are merely a few among similar books now lost (or almost so), but mentioned in patristic literature, for which the reader is referred to M. R. James, *The Lost Apocrypha*

[1] *The Apocrypha and Pseudepigrapha in English* (Oxford: Clarendon Press, 1913), Vol. II.
[2] *The Apocryphal Literature: A Brief Introduction* (New Haven: Yale University Press, 1945).

of the Old Testament: Their Titles and Fragments.[3]

Since there is no standard order in the arrangement of the Pseudepigrapha, as for the Apocrypha, they will be grouped here as Palestinian (originally in Hebrew or Aramaic) and Alexandrian (originally in Greek) and subdivided according to their literary genre.

I. Palestinian Pseudepigrapha

A. Legends About Biblical Characters. 1. The Testaments of the Twelve Patriarchs.— This work was written in Hebrew about 140-110 B.C., probably late in the time of John Hyrcanus (135-104). The whole work is extant in a Greek translation (and versions thereof). In addition to Jewish interpolations (notably those attacking the high priesthood of the late, worldly Hasmoneans; see Judah 21:6–23:5; Levi 14:5–16:5; etc.; cf. the Psalms of Solomon), the Greek text contains Christian glosses (some missing in the Greek book from which the Armenian text was translated) announcing the Incarnation: "Honor Levi and Judah; for from them shall arise [unto you the Lamb of God who takes away the sins of the world, the one who saves all the Gentiles and Israel]" (Joseph 19:11; the Armenian instead of the Christian words in brackets reads, "the salvation of Israel"; see also Benjamin 3:8; 9:3-5;

[3] New York: The Macmillan Co., 1920.

10:7-10; in 11:1-5 there are allusions to Paul). Reuben 2:3–3:2 is a Hellenistic (Stoic) interpolation.

The author was inspired by Gen. 49 and Deut. 33 to write the spiritual testament of the twelve sons of Jacob. Each patriarch recalls first of all his life, and in particular the sin or sins which he had committed and the consequences thereof; then, drawing lessons from his experience, he warns his descendants against such sins and urges them to practice the virtues and avoid temptations; and at last he predicts the future vicissitudes of his tribe. Reuben naturally deals with unchastity (cf. Gen 35:22; 49:4); Simeon with his jealousy of Joseph and his wrath against Judah, for which he was detained in Egypt (Simeon 2; cf. Gen. 42:24). Levi (6:4; cf. Gen. 34:25-27) had been a cutthroat, but as ancestor of the high priests stands at the head of his brothers, whose descendants are repeatedly urged to revere Levi and Judah, the priesthood and the kingdom; but God "set the kingdom beneath the priesthood" (Judah 23:3). On the basis of legendary embellishments to the Genesis stories, Judah warns against wine, women, and greed; but he also predicts the coming of the Messiah from his seed. Issachar (chs. 3–5; cf. Gen 49:15 [LXX], "he became a husbandman") is the type of the honest and hard-working farmer. Zebulun was the first sailor (6:1-3; cf. Gen. 49:13). Dan warns against anger and almost like Jesus (Matt. 22:37-39) sums up the law in these words, "Love the Lord throughout your life, and one another with a true heart" (Dan 5:3). Naphtali is as swift as a hind (2:1; cf. Gen. 49:21) and studies the divine order in the human organism and in nature. Gad hates Joseph and warns against hatred. Asher notes the two ways, the two inclinations, the two issues—good and bad; he warns against duplicity. Joseph dwells at length on his refusal to yield to Potiphar's wife and urges mutual love which hides one another's faults. Benjamin's counsel is to have "a good mind," such as Joseph's when he forgave his brothers.

Throughout the book the moral law is stressed, rather than the ceremonial, and the ethical teaching is consistently noble (comparable to that of Ecclesiasticus). Sin results from the "evil impulse" in man, which is personified in Beliar, the prince of evil, and his seven false spirits (evil tendencies rather than demons): lust, greed, hostility, hypocrisy, arrogance, falsehood, and injustice (Reuben 3:3-6). Repentance receives considerable attention: sinners impose upon themselves a penance in the form of long abstinence from meat and wine (Reuben 1:9-10; Judah 15:4), and fasting (Simeon 3:4); "For true, godlike, repentance drives away the darkness, illuminates the eyes, gives knowledge to the soul, and leads the mind to salvation" (Gad 5:7; cf. II Cor. 7:10).

2. The Book of Jubilees.—This enlarged Targum or Midrash of Gen. 1:1–Exod. 12:47 was probably composed in Aramaic (although many critics regard Hebrew as the original language) near the end of the reign of John Hyrcanus (135-104), shortly after the Testaments of the Twelve Patriarchs. The Greek translation is lost except for a few quotations in Christian writings, but the full text of the Ethiopic version made from the Greek is extant, and over one fourth has come to light in a Latin translation.

The book is named after its exact, but fictitious, system of dating events (from the Creation to the eve of the Exodus) by forty-nine-year "jubilee" periods (cf. Lev. 25:8-12), and their subdivision into seven weeks of years. For instance, "And in the first year of the first week of the forty-fifth jubilee [or the year 2157 (44×49=2156+1=2157) since the Creation] Rebecca called Jacob . . ." (35:1). The book purports to be a revelation made to Moses by the angel of the presence, holding the tables of the divisions of the years in his hand (1:29–2:1).

In dealing with the canonical text of Genesis and Exod. 1–12 the author uses three different procedures: he follows the text very closely (e.g., 3:1-7, cf. Gen. 2:18-25; Jubilees 7:6-12, cf. Gen. 9:21-27 [LXX]), or he adds to it many legendary details, or he omits entirely the stories (but not all; see 33:1-9, cf. Gen. 35:21-22; etc.) which are not to the credit of the patriarchs or are otherwise objectionable to the author, as those in Gen. 30:14-16, 31, 33-38, 40-42; 31:5-9, 14-18, 25-42. The most important part of the book consists of the additions which are of two kinds, narrative and juristic (in technical language, haggadic and halakic).

The author supplies much information, genealogical and historical, lacking in Genesis. Adam and Eve gave birth not only to nine sons (4:10), but also to daughters, so that Cain could marry his sister Awam (4:9) and Seth his sister Azura (4:11). In general the names of the wives of the patriarchs are supplied whenever they are not given, and their ancestry is given; for example, "Methuselah took unto himself a wife, Edna the daughter of Azirai" (4:27). Geographical names are also supplied: the ark rested on "Lubar, one of the mountains of Ararat" (5:28; 7:1, 17; 10:15); see also the remote localities named in 8:12-29 (including the Urals, the Don, Africa, the Atlantic [?], Cadiz, the Celts, Phrygia). The author explains puzzling features of the canonical narratives: the angels loaded the animals into Noah's ark

(5:23); the apparently unfulfilled threat of death in Gen. 2:17b was realized literally (4:30); Rebecca loved Jacob more than Esau on the advice of Abraham (19:16-31). Like the Jewish apologists at Alexandria, the author attributes to the patriarchs some technical inventions and cultural contributions: Enoch invented the art of writing (4:17) and wrote the book of Enoch (4:18-20); Kainam, son of Arpachshad, was the first archaeologist and paleographist (8:3); the angels taught Noah medicine, and he wrote the first medical treatise (10:10-13); Abraham invented a plow having a deep seeder attached to it (11:19-24), and learned Hebrew (12:26-27). The books of Enoch and Noah were transmitted to their descendants (21:10), down to Levi (45:16).

This tendency to carry back to Israel's early ancestors the institutions of culture is also apparent in the juristic parts of the book. Antediluvian patriarchs are said to have observed the law of Moses in all its details, including the prescriptions of the oral law. For the law was written on heavenly tablets and observed in heaven (cf. 2:18; 3:10; 4:5; 6:17; etc.); angels were created circumcised (15:27) long before the creation of Adam. Accordingly, the festivals (except for the Passover; 49:1-23) were observed long before Moses, whereas in the Pentateuch only the sabbath is traced back to Adam (cf. 2:17-21; 50:6-13). The feast of Weeks was instituted by Noah (6:17-22); that of Tabernacles by Abraham (16:20-31; 18:18-19) —and Jacob, who added an eighth day (32:27); the day of Atonement by Jacob (34:17-19). The sacrificial ritual in all its details is performed in the time of Noah (7:3-5; cf. Num. 29:2, 5), although the priesthood was unknown before Levi's solemn ordination (32:1-15). The legal prescriptions about the various kinds of sacrifices which Abraham ordained to Isaac (21:7-25; cf. Test. Levi 9) include some rules unknown before the Hellenistic period, like the list of the trees whose wood may be used for fuel on the altar (21:12-15) —a list which is stricter than the regulation in the Mishnah (Tamid 2:3) —allowing any kind of wood except the olive and the vine. Other examples of early halakah indicate a notable development of the oral law: the recipe for incense (16:24), regulations about tithes and offerings (7:36; 32:15 [cf. Tob. 1:6, Codex Sinaiticus]), the dating of the feast of Weeks on the fifteenth of Sivan, the third month (15:1; 16:13; 44:4-5). Other laws given in some detail, in accordance with their text "on the heavenly tablets," are: purification after childbirth (3:8-14), cursing a murderer (4:5; cf. Deut. 27:24), circumcision (15:11-34), the older daughter to be married before the younger (28:6), intermarriage between Israel and heathen forbidden (30:7-17), incest forbidden (33:10-20). Even the most radical innovation proposed in the book, the substitution of a solar year of fifty-two weeks (364 days), divided into four quarters of thirteen weeks each (6:29-38; cf. Enoch 72–75; 78), was allegedly inscribed on the heavenly tablets.

The reform of the calendar and many of the laws have the purpose of separating Israel from the heathen. The nations are ruled by angels, Israel by God (15:31-32). The Jews should avoid eating with Gentiles (22:16-18), intermarriage (22:20; 25:9; 30:7-17), idolatry (11:4; 20:7-9; 21:3-5), pagan funeral rites (22:17). Philistines (24:28-33; cf. Ecclus. 50:26; hated in the Maccabean wars: I Macc. 5:68; 10:84; 16:10), Edomites or Idumeans (26:34; chs. 37–38; John Hyrcanus forced the Idumeans to be circumcised; see Josephus *Antiquities* XIII. 9. 1; *Jewish War* I. 2. 6), and the Amorites (34:1-9, possibly an echo of Maccabean campaigns) are particularly detested.

Some doctrines in the book have parallels in the New Testament. Human sinfulness is traced to demonic inducement to sin (7:27; 10:1-15; 11:4-5; 12:20); Beliar (from Belial) also ensnares men (1:20; cf. 15:33; the Testament of the Twelve Patriarchs; II Cor. 6:15). The chief of the demons is called Mastema (Aramaic, "the enmity," "the enemy"; cf. Satan), "the chief of the spirits" (10:8-9; cf. Mark 3:22). "And prince Mastema . . . sent forth other spirits, those which were put under his hand, to do all manner of wrong and sin, and all manner of transgression, to corrupt and to destroy, and to shed blood upon the earth" (11:5). He sent ravens and birds to eat the seed (11:11), and suggested to God (as Satan did in Job's case) to test the faith of Abraham (17:16; similarly, in I Chr. 21:1 Satan, not God as in II Sam. 24:1, induced David to take a census), but was put to shame by God (18:12); likewise Mastema, and not God (Exod. 4:24), sought to kill Moses (48:2), hardened the heart of the Egyptians (48:16-17; contrast Exod. 14:17; etc.), and slew the firstborn of the Egyptians (49:2). Men sacrifice to demons as if these were gods (22:17; cf. I Cor. 10:20). But in the messianic age, following the Last Judgment (23:11), men will live one thousand years without becoming old and "there shall be no Satan nor evil destroyer" (23:27-30; 50:5; cf. Rev. 20:2-3). The spirits of the righteous will then rejoice while their bones rest in the earth (23:31: immortality apparently *without* resurrection).

3. The Martyrdom of Isaiah.—The Martyrdom of Isaiah is the first part of the Ascension of Isaiah, which according to R. H. Charles was put together by a Christian editor out of three separate works, the Martyrdom, the Testament of Hezekiah, and the Vision of Isaiah; the Martyrdom (1:1-2a, 6b-13a; 2:1–3:12; 5:1b-14; omitting 2:9) was Jewish in origin; the Testament (3:13b–4:18) and the Vision (6:1–11:40) were written by Christians. The contents, according to the Ethiopic version which alone preserves the whole text of the Ascension (the two Latin versions contain 2:14–3:18; 7:1-19, and 6:1–11:19 respectively), may be summarized as follows:

(a) The Martyrdom of Isaiah. The prophet Isaiah predicted to Hezekiah that Manasseh would serve Beliar instead of God and would saw Isaiah asunder (ch. 1; cf. Heb. 11:37). After Hezekiah's death, the devil (Sammael or Beliar) entered into Manasseh, who introduced every abomination into Jerusalem including the worship of Satan; so Isaiah and the true believers withdrew to the wilderness (2:1-11). A man of Samaria (a Samaritan) named Belchira, Bechira, or Melchira (a name of the devil in 1:8), accused Isaiah of prophesying against king and nation, so Manasseh had him arrested (2:12–3:12). [Christian section: Beliar detested Isaiah because he had predicted the redemption through Jesus Christ, the growth of the church until the Neronian persecution, and the final judgment (3:13–5:1a)]. Then Manasseh ordered Isaiah to be sawed asunder with a "wooden saw"—a mistranslation of "wood saw" (5:1b-14).

(b) The Vision of Isaiah (Christian). In the twentieth year of Hezekiah, Isaiah had a vision and related it to the king and his courtiers (ch. 6). An angel led Isaiah in spirit through the firmament and six heavens up to the seventh heaven (chs. 7–8), where Isaiah saw the deceased saints from Adam and Abel on, and God himself (ch. 9). Having heard that God would send his son down to earth, Isaiah returned to the firmament (ch. 10), where he saw in a vision the birth of Jesus Christ, his life and passion, his resurrection, and his return to the seventh heaven. While the angel ascended to heaven, Isaiah's spirit returned to his earthly body; it was on account of this vision that Satan had Isaiah sawed asunder by Manasseh (ch. 11).

The Christian parts of the book probably date from the second century of our era. In 4:2–5:1a the Antichrist, the incarnation of Beliar, is clearly identified with Nero (A.D. 54-68): his sway is to last three years, seven months, and twenty-seven days or, with a slight correction, 1,335 days as in Dan. 12:12.[4]

[4] See H. H. Rowley, The Relevance of Apocalyptic (London: Lutterworth Press, 1944), pp. 135-36.

If, as is generally supposed, there is a Jewish "Martyrdom" in the first part of the Ascension, we may conjecture that it was written originally in Aramaic in the last century B.C., perhaps in its second half. C. C. Torrey,[5] however, regards the Ascension in its entirety as a Christian work.

4. Paralipomena of Jeremiah.—These "remaining words of Jeremiah" (or "of Baruch"), like the preceding work, may well be Christian in toto, although the Paralipomena stress the duty of Jews to keep apart from the heathen, particularly from pagan women (6:13-14; 8:2), in contrast with the New Testament, which opposes divorces even when one of the parties is heathen (I Cor. 7:12-13; I Pet. 3:1). The last chapter is manifestly Christian; the rest may contain a Jewish kernel. The contents, in brief, are as follows:

The Lord announced to Jeremiah the destruction of Jerusalem through the Chaldeans, and ordered him to bury the sacred vessels of the temple and to go to Babylonia in exile, leaving Baruch in Jerusalem; and so it happened (chs. 1–4). Before the disaster, Jeremiah had sent the eunuch Abimelech to pick figs in the orchard of Agrippa: Abimelech fell asleep there and awoke sixty-six years later; an old man informed him of what had happened (ch. 5). Baruch was ordered by God to write to Jeremiah that he should remove all foreigners from the midst of Israel; only then would God bring the people back to Zion. This letter of Baruch, together with some of the figs still fresh after sixty-six years, was brought to Babylonia by an eagle (ch. 6). The eagle raised a dead man to life and persuaded Jeremiah to bring the people back; the prophet refused to let the men who would not divorce their Babylonian wives enter Jerusalem; since Babylonia would not admit them, they founded the city of Samaria and thus organized the Samaritan sect (chs. 7–8). [Jeremiah fainted while offering sacrifice in Jerusalem, and coming back to life after three days he praised God for the redemption through Jesus Christ. The Jews were able to stone the prophet to death only after he gave his permission (ch. 9).]

The Greek text has been edited by James Rendel Harris.[6] The reference to Agrippa (Agrippa I died in A.D. 44; Agrippa II in A.D. 100) dates the book after A.D. 50; it was probably written in the second century. If chs. 1–8 are of Jewish origin, they were probably written in Aramaic and translated into Greek. Ethiopic,

[5] The Apocryphal Literature (New Haven: Yale University Press, 1945), pp. 133-35.

[6] The Rest of the Words of Baruch: A Christian Apocalypse of the Year 136 A.D. (London: C. J. Clay & Sons, 1889).

Armenian, and Slavic versions from the Greek have been published.

5. The Lives of the Prophets.—This series of biographical sketches was probably written in Hebrew in the first century of our era. It is preserved in Greek among the writings of Epiphanius, bishop of Salamis in Cyprus (ca. 315-403), in a longer and briefer recension; among the writings of Dorotheus of Tyre; and in the Codex Marchalianus or Q of the Prophets. We also have Syriac, Latin, and Ethiopic versions of the work which is now available in a critical edition of the Greek text with an English translation.[7]

The biographies of the four major and of the twelve minor prophets are followed by those of Nathan, Ahijah of Shiloh (I Kings 14:1-18), Joed (Neh. 11:7; identified with Jedo of II Chr. 9:29 and the anonymous prophet of I Kings 13:23-32), Azariah (II Chr. 15:1-15), Zachariah son of Jehoiada (II Chr. 24:20-22; his assassination seems to be referred to in Matt. 23:35; Luke 11:51), Elijah, and Elisha. The biblical data on these prophets are condensed very briefly, and legendary stories are added, notably in the lives of Isaiah, Jeremiah, Ezekiel, Daniel, Jonah, Habakkuk; the other lives are brief, but usually supply some information not found in the Bible.

The life of Jeremiah, according to Torrey, was furnished to the Palestinian author by a man from Egypt. He had been told this story by "the children of Antigonus and Ptolemy, aged men." This story is the only one in the original form of the Lives which contained Christian elements (Christian additions are found in the main Epiphanius recension). Jeremiah told the Egyptian priests that "their idols would be shaken and their gods made with hands would all collapse, when a virgin bearing a child of divine appearance [Jesus] would arrive in Egypt. Therefore even to this day they honor a virgin mother, and placing a babe in a manger they bow down to it" (Lives of the Prophets, Jeremiah §§ 7-8). The prophet had hidden the ark of the covenant in a sealed cave (cf. II Macc. 2:5) until the coming of the Lord "when all nations worship a piece of wood [i.e., the cross]." The rest of the Jeremiah legend is Jewish: he destroyed the poisonous snakes in Egypt (ἐφώθ, Hebrew "vipers") through the snake-killing argolai (Hebrew ḥargōl, locust [Lev. 11:22], a term used by the Egyptian Jews for the ichneumon or mongoose [cf. Lev. 11:22, LXX: "snake killer"]).[8]

A few details from some of the other lives may be mentioned here. Isaiah, immediately before Manasseh had him sawed asunder, received water from the spring (Greek: "oak," reading 'ēṣ [tree] instead of 'ēn [spring]) of Rogel, which was therefore called Siloah, "sent" (cf. John 9:7). He had formerly caused the waters of Siloah to flow only for the Hebrews. Ezekiel was killed in Babylonia by a Jewish exile. In time of famine Ezekiel had saved the people through fish from the Kebar canal which on another occasion miraculously dried up for the Jews but drowned the Chaldeans pursuing them. Daniel interceded for Nebuchadrezzar, who had been changed into an animal having the fore parts of a bull and the hind parts of a lion. Amos was killed with a cudgel by a son of Amaziah, the priest of Bethel. Jonah was the son of the widow of Zarephath (I Kings 17:8-24). Habakkuk fed Daniel in the den of lions (cf. Bel and the Dragon). When Elisha was born "the golden calf bellowed so loudly that the shrill sound was heard in Jerusalem."

6. The Testament of Job.—This Aramaic midrash to the book of Job, written probably in the last century B.C., is extant in a Greek translation first published by Angelo Cardinal Mai in 1833 and republished, with an English translation by Kaufmann Kohler;[9] a slightly different Greek text was published, with a critical introduction, by M. R. James.[10] See also the accounts of the book by Kohler[11] and C. C. Torrey.[12] Some of the material of the book has found its way into the Septuagint of the canonical Job (following 2:9), the long colophon of which (42:18), translated from the Aramaic, could have stood in a variant recension of the Testament of Job.

Job's first wife, Sitidos (from Ausitidos, the woman of Ausitis [Uz], Job's land), defends her husband, though harassed by Satan, who is finally driven away by Job. She witnesses Job's vindication and dies comforted after seeing her dead children in heaven. Job marries Dinah after his restoration to health and riches, and she is the mother of his seven sons (whose curious Greek and Egyptian names were supplied by the Greek translator) and three daughters. Job's spirit was taken up by a heavenly chariot.

7. The Life of Adam and Eve (Apocalypse of Moses).—This imaginative haggadah was ap-

[7] C. C. Torrey, The Lives of the Prophets (Journal of Biblical Literature, Monograph Series, Vol. I; Philadelphia: Society of Biblical Literature and Exegesis, 1946).

[8] See Torrey, Lives of the Prophets, pp. 49-52; Apocryphal Literature, p. 140.

[9] Semitic Studies in Memory of Rev. Dr. Alexander Kohut, ed. George Alexander Kohut (Berlin: S. Calvary & Co., 1897), pp. 264-338.

[10] Apocrypha Anecdota, 2nd Ser. (Cambridge: The University Press, 1897).

[11] Jewish Encyclopaedia (New York: Funk & Wagnalls, 1906), VII, 200-2.

[12] Apocryphal Literature, pp. 140-45.

parently composed in Aramaic in the first century of our era, before the destruction of Jerusalem in A.D. 70. It has been reworked by Christian hands and has been reconstructed with fair probability out of remnants and recensions in various versions, primarily the Greek (erroneously entitled "Apocalypse of Moses") and Latin texts. In the English version of L. S. A. Wells [13] the two texts (and occasionally the Slavonic) supplement one another. The story, in brief, runs as follows:

Adam and Eve repented and did penance after their expulsion from the Garden of Eden (Latin text, §§ 1-5). Adam stood forty days in the Jordan up to his neck in the water (§§ 6-8), while Eve, after standing in the Tigris eighteen days, was tempted by Satan, in the guise of an angel, to come to Adam (§§ 9-11). Satan related the story of his fall (§§ 12-17). Eve gave birth to Cain (§§ 18-21). After the birth of Abel, Eve had a premonition of Cain's murder in a dream, and gave birth to Seth after Abel's death (Latin, §§ 22-24; Greek, §§ 1-4). Adam told Seth his vision: he was translated to paradise, where God granted his seed the privilege of serving God; then Michael froze the waters around paradise and led Adam back to earth, where Adam predicted to Seth the history of the Jews to the Last Judgment (Latin, §§ 25-29). Adam was in great pains, so Eve and Seth went to the gate of Eden to entreat God, but a wild beast bit Seth; Michael announced the future resurrection and golden age (Latin, §§ 30-44; Greek, §§ 5-14). Eve related in great detail the story of her fall (Greek, §§ 15-34). Adam died (Latin, §§ 45-48; Greek, §§ 35-41), and Eve, knowing that her life was near its end, gave instructions about preserving a record on stone tablets of Adam's and her lives (Latin, §§ 49-50), and after her death Michael told Seth to mourn six days but to rejoice on the seventh (Latin, § 51; Greek, §§ 42-43).

B. Hymns and Psalms. 1. The Cantica.—The canonical book of Psalms did not include all Hebrew hymns in existence when it was finally limited to 150 compositions about 100 B.C. The Hebrew psalms in Ecclesiasticus (39:12-35; 42:15-43:33; 51:1-12; and the liturgy which appears in the Hebrew text between 51:12 and 51:13), Tobit (ch. 13; in Aramaic), Judith (ch. 16), and Baruch (4:5-5:9), as also the hymns and prayers in Exodus, Deuteronomy, Samuel, Jonah, Habakkuk, Chronicles, Nehemiah, Daniel, etc., were in existence but were excluded. In some Greek manuscripts a collection of hymns (Cantica or Odes) follows the Psalter, supplementing it. The Codex Alexandrinus, for instance, contains the Cantica in the following chapters: Exod. 15; Deut. 32; I Sam. 2; Isa. 26; Jonah 2; Hab. 3; Isa. 38; the Prayer of Manasses; Dan. 3 (LXX); Luke 1:46-55; 2:29-32; 1:68-79; and the Morning Hymn.

2. The Psalms of Solomon.—Aside from the Cantica prepared for the Christians, the church has preserved the Greek translation (and a Syriac version from the Greek) of eighteen Hebrew psalms of the Pharisees, known as the Psalms of Solomon, not to be confused with the five Christian Odes of Solomon included in the gnostic book entitled *Pistis Sophia*. The Greek and English text of these psalms was published by H. E. Ryle and H. R. James.[14]

In contrast with the Psalms of David, which express timeless religious emotions and therefore cannot be dated, some of the Psalms of Solomon indicate by clear historical allusions the time of their composition in the first century B.C. The seventeenth of these psalms expresses the violent hostility of the Pharisees against the Hasmonaean rulers, which began in the time of Alexander Jannaeus (103-76 B.C.): they illegally usurped the throne of David, until God cast them down through an alien (Pompey; he placed the Jews under Roman rule in 63 B.C.) who carried Aristobulus and his sons to Rome (17:1-15). When God brought a mighty one [Pompey] from the ends of the earth, the princes of the land foolishly welcomed him and opened the gates of Jerusalem to him (8:15-20). So Gentiles trod on God's altar [Pompey in 63 B.C.], but before long (48 B.C.) the conqueror was slain in Egypt and left unburied (2:2, 29-31). If all the Psalms of Solomon are the work of a single author, as the uniformity of style and thought seems to indicate, they were composed after 48 B.C., and presumably before the beginning of our era. Ps. Sol. 11 bears a close resemblance to Baruch 4:36-5:9 and was manifestly influenced by it.

The religious teaching of these psalms is typically Pharisaic. Israel, as already in the Psalter, is divided between the righteous poor who fear the Lord, and the sinners or transgressors, who are chiefly the Hasmonaeans and the priestly or Sadducean aristocracy—wealthy and arrogant hypocrites (especially Ps. Sol. 4). The pious, or Hasidim, are humble and poor (16:12-15), quiet souls seeking peace (12:6), enduring patiently the chastisement of the present distress (14:1; 16:11). They look forward to a reward after death (13:9-11; 14:3; 15:15; 16:1-3), and to the coming of the messianic Son of David (17:23-51; 18:6-10). The following

[13] In Charles, *Pseudepigrapha*, pp. 134-54.

[14] ΨΑΛΜΟΙ ΣΟΛΟΜΩΝΤΟΣ: *Psalms of the Pharisees, Commonly Called the Psalms of Solomon* (Cambridge: Cambridge University Press, 1891); there is also a translation by G. Buchanan Gray in Charles, *Pseudepigrapha*, pp. 631-52.

426

lines are a summary of the teaching of the early Pharisees:

Our works are subject to our own choice and power
To do right or wrong by the works of our hands;
And in thy righteousness thou visitest human beings.
He who does righteousness lays up life for himself with the Lord;
And he who does wrongly forfeits his life to destruction (9:7-9).

Thus human freedom and responsibility are maintained, in spite of the fact that man's fate is determined by God (5:4-6).

C. Apocalypses.—A number of Jewish revelations of future events, reaching to the end of the present age and the coming of God's kingdom on earth, were written in the period intervening between the Jewish and the Christian canonical apocalypses—Daniel (164 B.C.) and Revelation (ca. A.D. 90). All of them are attributed to prophets living before divine inspiration was said to have ceased in the time of Ezra and Nehemiah. The latest of these fictitious authors was Ezra. Such revelations are often visions which an angel interprets for the seer and for us; at times the seer is taken through the recondite and remote parts of the universe, notably through the seven heavens. In the predictions, the point at which the author ceases to be historically accurate and explicit, becoming vague and either fanciful or historically wrong, marks the date of the work. While the following works written in Palestine between 164 B.C. and A.D. 100 are grouped here as "apocalypses," it should always be remembered that apocalyptic sections occur in other writings (cf. above, the Life of Adam and Eve, and the Psalms of Solomon, for instance) and that these writings contain parts which have nothing to do with eschatology.

1. The Book of Enoch.—This book is sometimes called Ethiopic Enoch or I Enoch, to distinguish it from other books ascribed to the imaginary pen of the intriguing patriarch who, after walking with God a mere 365 years, "was not; for God took him" (Gen. 5:23-24). I Enoch is a vast encyclopedic work comprising a number of separate books of various dates and authorships, written in Aramaic during the period 163-80 B.C. The whole work has survived only in an Ethiopic version based on the Greek translation, which is lost except for 1:1-32:6; and chs. 97-104; 106-107. R. H. Charles, who has published the text and translation of Enoch,[15] has detected interpolations from a book of Noah (indicated below by brackets)

[15] The Book of Enoch (London: Society for Promoting Christian Knowledge, 1925).

in chs. 6-11; 54:7-55:2; 60; 65:1-69:25; 106-107 (as also in Jubilees 7:20-39; 10:1-15).

The book may be divided in its various parts as follows:

(a) Introduction (chs. 1-5; ca. 150-100 B.C.). The angels reveal to Enoch God's imminent appearance in judgment.

(b) The fall of the angels (chs. 6-16), and Enoch's two remote journeys (chs. 17-20; 21-36; ca. 100 B.C.). The fallen angels taught to the giants their sons (cf. Gen. 6:1-4) the impious arts of civilization (chs. 6-8), but soon they will be punished and then the Golden Age will come (chs. 9-11). Enoch is not allowed to intercede for the fallen angels, but must announce their ruin (chs. 12-16). In his first journey Enoch visits the angels' place of punishment (chs. 17-20); in the second, he sees the underworld, the tree of life, the holy mountain, and the four ends of the earth (chs. 21-36).

(c) The three parables or similitudes of Enoch (chs. 37-71; ca. 100-80 B.C.). Introduction (ch. 37). (i) The judgment of the wicked (ch. 38), the abode of the righteous (ch. 39), the angels and the four archangels (ch. 40), the mysteries of astronomy (chs. 41-44).

(ii) The fate of the unbelievers (ch. 45), the Son of man (or the Elect One) and his wisdom (chs. 46-49; cf. Dan. 7:13), the glory of the elect manifested to induce others to repent (ch. 50). Finally,

The earth will restore what was committed to it
And Sheol what it has received
And hell will surrender what it owes.
And [God] will select the righteous and holy in their midst,
For the day in which they shall be saved is at hand.
The Elect One in those days shall sit upon my throne,
And all secrets of wisdom will pour forth from the counsels of his mouth,
For the Lord of Spirits has given them to him and has glorified him (51:1-3).

Then the whole earth, and particularly the righteous, will rejoice (51:4-5). The seven metal mountains (symbolizing the heathen empires; cf. Dan. 2) shall melt in the presence of the Elect One (ch. 52). Vision of the valley of judgment (ch. 53), the valley of fire for the punishment of kings, and the chains for the fallen angels (54:1-6; cf. Rev. 20:1-2); [the Flood was the first judgment, 54:7-55:2]; the judgment of the fallen angels (55:3-56:4). Then the heathen powers (Parthians and Medes) will attack Israel but will be devoured by the underworld (56:5-8; cf. Ezek. 38-39; Rev. 20:7-9); the dispersed Jews will come back (ch. 57).

(iii) The bliss of the saints (ch. 58), the mysteries of lightning and thunder (ch. 59), [Behemoth and Leviathan, other mysteries; ch. 60], preparations for the judgment of the righteous by the Elect One (ch. 61); he will triumph over the kings of the earth (ch. 62), whose repentance avails nothing (ch. 63). The place of punishment of the fallen angels (ch. 64) [the flood and Noah's rescue, 65:1–67:3] in the burning valley (67:4-7; cf. 54:1-6) where the kings will be tormented (67:8-13); the final judgment (chs. 68–69). Enoch's translation (chs. 70–71).

(d) The astronomical book (chs. 72–82). The sun (ch. 72), the moon (ch. 73), the lunar and solar years; the substitution of a solar year of 364 days for a lunar year of twelve months amounting to 354 days and an intercalary month, totaling 384 days (chs. 74–75, cf. ch. 78 and Jubilees 6:29-38). The twelve winds (ch. 76), and four quarters of the world (ch. 77), the solar and lunar calendars (ch. 78), summary (79:1–80:1). Cosmic disturbances resulting from human sin (80:2-8), the heavenly tablets (81:1-4), Enoch's return (81:5-10), the new calendar (ch. 82).

(e) Two visions (chs. 83–90; ca. 163-130 B.C.). (i) The vision of the Flood (chs. 83–84). (ii) Sketch of the history of Israel under the figure of oxen, sheep, shepherds, and wild beasts (chs. 85–90): Adam and Eve, Cain and Abel, Seth (ch. 85); the fall of the angels (ch. 86), and their punishment through the seven archangels (chs. 87–88); Noah (89:1-9) and the history until the Exodus (89:10-27); Moses and Joshua (89:28-40); the judges and the kings down to the building of the temple (89:41-50); the decay of the kingdoms to the destruction of Jerusalem in 586 B.C. (89:51-67). Four periods of foreign rule over Israel: twelve shepherds: the Exile (89:68-71); twenty-three shepherds: from Cyrus to Alexander (89:72-77); twenty-three shepherds: from Alexander to Antiochus Epiphanes (90:1-5); twelve shepherds: the Maccabean rebellion and the rule of the Hasmonaeans to the Last Judgment (90:6-19). The condemnation of the wicked rulers and of the fallen angels (90:20-27); the New Jerusalem, the resurrection, and the messianic age (90:28-42).

(f) Enoch's book of exhortation (92:1-5; 91:1-11, 18-19; ca. 100-80 B.C.).

(g) The Apocalypse of Weeks (93:1-10; 91:12-17; ca. 163 B.C.; [93:11-14]). These are the ten weeks of human history: Enoch (93:3), Noah (93:4), Abraham (93:5), Moses (93:6), the building of the temple (93:7), Elijah and the destruction of the temple (93:8), an apostate generation (93:9-10); [who can understand God and the universe? (93:11-14)]; the righteous will prevail over the wicked and the temple will be built (91:12-13); judgment will be revealed (91:14); the Last Judgment and the age to come (91:15-17).

(h) The Last Judgment (chs. 94–105; ca. 100-80 B.C.). Let the righteous avoid the paths of wickedness (94:1-5), for the Lord will destroy the sinners (94:6–95:7). "Be hopeful, ye righteous, for the sinners will suddenly perish before you!" (Ch. 96.) Woe to sinners and to those who acquire wealth dishonestly (ch. 97)! Man himself is responsible for sin, such as the self-indulgence of the wealthy (98:1-4); sins are recorded in heaven (98:5-8); woe to fools and sinners (98:9-16), to the godless and lawless (ch. 99). At the end of this age the sinners will destroy one another (100:1-3); then the Lord will sit in judgment against the fallen angels and the sinners (100:4-13). Fear God, for he is the Lord of all creation (ch. 101). The horrors preceding the Day of Judgment should not terrify the righteous (ch. 102); for "all goodness, joy, and glory are prepared for them," while the souls of the sinners "will be wretched in their great tribulation" (chs. 103–105).

(j) Appendixes (chs. 106–108; ca. 100-80 B.C.). The birth of Noah (chs. 106–107). The final fate of the sinners and of the righteous (ch. 108).

This meager summary indicates that there is no uniform teaching about the events at the end of this age and in the future world: we must therefore sketch the eschatological teaching of the several parts, in their chronological order, omitting those parts like the astronomical book (chs. 72–82) which do not touch upon eschatology.

The Apocalypse of Weeks (93:1-10; 91:12-17) was written soon after Daniel (164 B.C.), and under its influence. Like Daniel, it combines the ancient hope of national restoration (without a Messiah) with the newer expectation of individual rewards or punishments after the end of this age, although the resurrection (Dan. 12:2) is not specifically mentioned. Purely national is the expectation that in the eighth week, following the seven weeks of history which were completed by the time of the author (who lived in the time of the seventh week's Hellenizing apostasy, 180-168 B.C.), the hosts of the heathen would attack the Jews (91:12; cf. 90:13-19; Joel 3:1-3; Ezek. 38–39; Obad. 15; Mic. 4:11; Zeph. 3:8; Zech. 12:2-3, 9; 14:1-2) and be defeated and destroyed (Zech. 12:4; 14:12-15; Mic. 7:16-17; Ezek. 38–39; Rev. 20:8-9; etc.). With the rebuilding of the temple and the piety and prosperity which follow (91:13) the national goal is fully attained, but there are two more weeks. In the ninth and tenth weeks attention is focused on the individual: the final judgment, revealed in the ninth week and fulfilled in the tenth (91:14-17), will eliminate the wicked from the new heavens and new earth (cf. Rev. 21:1-5).

Of the two visions in chs. 83–90 only the second (chs. 85–90) concerns us here. Again, as in the Apocalypse of Weeks, we note the influence of Daniel, and we see the panorama of world history unrolling before our eyes, from Adam and Eve to the Hasmonaeans, but under the allegory of animals. Here also the national and individual aspects of the final events are both presented and are separated by the final judgment, and here also the righteous live forever without having been specifically raised from the dead (90:33 is usually interpreted as a reference to the resurrection, but without sufficient reasons). In Palestine the Lord sits in judgment, the books are opened; the fallen angels, the seventy shepherds, and the renegade Jews ("the blinded sheep") are found guilty and are cast into the fiery abyss (90:20-27). To the New Jerusalem and its temple the scattered Jews and the converted Gentiles will come together (90:28-33). But here, in contrast with Daniel and the Apocalypse of Weeks, the Messiah appears. Indeed, according to C. C. Torrey [16] the wild ox or buffalo (emending the text of 90:38, where the Ethiopic "word" is meaningless) with great black horns (cf. Deut. 33:17) is the Messiah son of Ephraim or of Joseph; all admit that the white bull (90:37) is the Messiah, son of David.

In the Introduction to the book (chs. 1–5), the final judgment is a cosmic upheaval rather than a court scene (ch. 1): the resurrection is not mentioned, the ungodly are destroyed by God (1:9), and their names become an eternal execration (5:6); "and there shall be bestowed upon the elect wisdom, and they shall all live and never again sin" (5:8).

In the first of his two journeys to the ends of the earth (chs. 17–20; 21–36) Enoch sees the four Hades rivers of Greek mythology (Pyriphlegethon, Styx, Acheron, and Cocytus, 17:5-6) the mountain of God in the north (18:8), the fiery abyss (18:11), the seven stars which transgressed God's orders and are to be punished ten thousand years (18:12-16), and the future place of punishment of the angels who seduced women (Gen. 6:1-4)—these women become evil spirits, that is, sirens (ch. 19). In the second journey (chs. 21–36) he sees again the seven stars and the fiery abyss in which the fallen angels are to be imprisoned forever (ch. 21), the deep smooth hollows in a great mountain in the west (22:1), where the souls of the dead

Jews are imprisoned until the final judgment: one, for the righteous, is bright and has a fountain (22:2, 9); the three others are dark and house spirits of sinners: those who have not been judged in their lifetime (22:10) and are now in torment until they will be bound forever in the Last Judgment (22:11); those who like Abel were unjustly slain in the days of the sinners (22:5-7, 12); and the godless sinners who consorted with the heathen, who will not be punished nor be raised in the Day of Judgment, but are apparently to be left eternally in their present condition (22:13). The final fate of the heathen is not considered here: the righteous Jews and some of the sinners, it would seem, will be raised from the dead at the time of the final judgment.

Continuing on his journey westward, Enoch reached a river of fire (23:2, cf. 17:4-6), and a fiery mountain range (24:1), seven beautiful mountains (24:2), the seventh of which is the seat of God's throne in the north and contains the tree of life (24:3–25:7). Passing through Jerusalem and the valley of Jehoshaphat, where the Lord will judge the wicked (chs. 26–27), Enoch went eastward to the lands of aromatic and fragrant trees (28:1–32:1), passed over the Erythraean Sea (32:2), coming to the Garden of Righteousness, the earthly paradise with the tree of wisdom (32:3-6), strange animals, and the heavenly gates of the stars (ch. 33). Going northward, he saw the three northern heavenly gates (chs. 34–35), and then three southern ones in the extreme southern end of the world (ch. 36). It will be noted that national features are completely missing in these accounts of Enoch's journeys: there is no Messiah, no attack of the heathen on the Jews, no Jewish kingdom; but only the final separation, even before the Last Judgment, between individual Jews, the saved and the damned. Of the latter there are three categories destined to suffer different eternal punishments. For the first time in a Jewish writing we have here a classification of the damned, as also the Greek names of the rivers of Hades: has our author been influenced by Hellenistic notions? The fate of the saved may remind us likewise of the Elysian fields, although the author utilized biblical materials for his description. The tree of life will be placed next to the temple, far from its present location on the inaccessible mountain; the saved will partake of its fruit and live long lives on the earth, like Methuselah; "and in their days shall no sorrow or plague or torment or calamity touch them" (25:4-6). Perhaps even the fruit of the tree of knowledge or wisdom may then be granted to the saved (cf. 32:3-6).

[16] *Apocryphal Literature*, p. 112; "The Messiah Son of Ephraim," *Journal of Biblical Literature*, LXVI (1947), 253-77.

The so-called parables or similitudes of Enoch (chs. 37–71), and the end of the book (chs. 91–108, omitting the much earlier Apocalypse of Weeks [93:1-10; 92:12-17]), are the latest sections of Enoch. The second of the similitudes (chs. 45–57) is of particular interest to New Testament students for its messianic teaching. The expression "his Messiah" (God's anointed) occurs only in 48:10 (cf. Ps. 22:2) and 52:4 (cf. Ps. 72); Messiah is usually called "that Son of man" or "the Elect"; only once "Son of woman" (62:5). The author takes not only the term "Son of man" but also the person itself from Dan. 7:13-14. The expression "son of man" in its literal meanings of "gentleman" and "minor" occurs in Hammurabi's Code; later, in Hebrew (ben-'ādhām, common in Ezekiel) and Aramaic (bar 'enāsh, "a son of man"; bar nāshā', "the son of man"), it means "a human being," a member of the human race, as the expression "sons of the prophets" means members of the prophetic fraternity, and "sons of God," divine beings. As in Dan. 7:9-14, the Son of man in 46:1-6 appears in the presence of "the Ancient of days [God]"; "And there I saw One who had a head of days [i.e., an aged head], and his head was white as wool, and with him was another being whose countenance was like the appearance of a man, and his face was full of graciousness, like that of one of the holy angels" (46:1). In later passages this being is referred to as "that [or "this"] Son of man" (except in 62:7; 69:27, "the Son of man"): this is the natural Ethiopic rendering of the Greek "the Son of man" (as in the Gospels). Daniel's human figure, symbolizing "the people of the saints of the Most High" (Dan. 7:27)—God's saints ruling over his kingdom, in contrast with the heathen empires [the beasts]—becomes here a messianic ruler. The congregation of Daniel becomes an individual in Enoch, where the beasts have disappeared. This messianic interpretation of Daniel's "Son of man" may well be older than the similitudes; we find it in Sibylline Oracles Bk. V, l. 414 (cf. Bk. III, ll. 46-50, 652), and later, about A.D. 90, in II (IV) Esdras 13:3. In any case such an interpretation was current in the time of Jesus (Mark 13:26; 14:61-62; Matt. 24:30; 26:63-64; Luke 22:67-68; cf. Acts 7:56; Rev. 1:13).

Unlike the Messiah son of David of earlier days, still presented in Pss. Sol. 17, Enoch's Son of man is not a human being: he appears with God in the Last Judgment (46:1-6; 48:8-9; 49:2-4) and sits on God's throne (51:3; cf. 45:3; 61:8), ruling on this earth over the righteous (cf. 62:13-16). Moreover, long before his revelation to the elect, the Son of man had been hidden by God: he had existed before the

creation of the world (48:3, 6; 62:7), "his dwelling place [was] under the wings of the Lord of Spirits" (39:7). In contrast with the bliss of the saved, Enoch contemplated the valley of fire into which the evil rulers are cast, and the enormous chains prepared for Azazel and his hosts on the Day of Judgment (54:1-6; 55:3-4; 56:1-4). The onslaught of the heathen hordes and their end (56:5-8), and the return of the scattered Jews (ch. 57), complete the picture of the future events. In the two other similitudes (chs. 38–44 and 58–71) we have likewise a vision of the judgment and of the places of bliss or torment. Similar descriptions are found in chs. 94–108, except for the greater attention given to the signs of the end and the condemnation of the fallen angels.

2. The Assumption of Moses.—This book was written in Aramaic during the lifetime of Jesus (a few years after the death of Herod the Great in 4 B.C. and not later than A.D. 28), but survives only partially in a Latin version, made from the Greek rendering of the original, which is quoted in Jude 9. Its contents may be summarized as follows:

In the year 2500 after the Creation, Moses, perceiving that his end was near, appointed Joshua as his successor and gave him his final instructions (1:1-9). Moses had been appointed before the creation of the world to be the mediator of God's covenant; now he entrusts the holy books to Joshua (1:10-18). Moses predicts briefly the history of Israel from the invasion into Canaan to the end of the kingdoms of Israel and Judah (ch. 2). Nebuchadrezzar will destroy Jerusalem and exile two tribes (586 B.C.), while the other ten will mourn for them; all of them will remember that Moses had predicted this calamity, which will last seventy-seven years (ch. 3). Through the intercession of Daniel, God will induce Cyrus to let the Jewish exiles go back; the two tribes will hold fast to their faith, but will be unable to offer sacrifice (ch. 4). Punishment on the Jews will come through their Seleucid kings (198-141 B.C.); Hellenizing priests will pollute the altar, scribes and judges will pervert justice (ch. 5). Then Hasmonaean kings (141-37 B.C.) will call themselves priests of the Most High while working iniquity in the holy of holies, but Herod the Great (37-4 B.C.), "an insolent king," will destroy them, punishing the Jews for thirty-four years; his children shall rule for shorter periods [Archelaus, 4 B.C.–A.D. 6; Antipas, 4 B.C.–A.D. 39; Philip, 4 B.C.–A.D 34; the author wrote before it became clear that Antipas and Philip would rule longer than Herod]; the cohorts of Varus (4 B.C.) will crucify some (about two thousand) insurgent Jews (ch. 6). Then the end of time will come:

certain impious men, claiming to be just (probably the hypocritical Pharisees), will rule—treacherous, gluttons, despoilers of the poor in the name of piety, who being unclean say, "Do not touch me lest you pollute me" (ch. 7). In a second visitation the king of kings (Antiochus IV Epiphanes, 175-164 B.C.) will crucify the Jews who confess their circumcision, will force their boys to conceal it, and oblige them to wear heathen idols (ch. 8). But when this edict will be proclaimed, a man of the tribe of Levi named Taxo (presumably Mattathias, as suggested by C. C. Torrey; cf. I Macc. 2) will exhort his seven sons (only five sons of Mattathias are known) to die rather than transgress the commandments of the Lord (ch. 9). Then the kingdoms of God will be revealed and "Satan shall be no more"; the Lord will come to avenge the Jews, while the earth trembles, the sun is darkened, and the horns of the moon are broken. God will punish the heathen and Israel will rejoice. Joshua is to keep this book (ch. 10). Joshua lamented and Moses comforted him (ch. 11). Moses urged Joshua never to doubt the future of Israel; for God would punish the sinners, but never root out the people (ch. 12; the manuscript breaks off in the middle of a sentence).

In the Latin manuscript, which alone preserves the first part of this book (the "assumption" of Moses to heaven, in the second part, quoted in Jude 9, is lost), chs. 8–9 have accidentally been displaced, and should be restored to their right context, between chs. 5 and 6. The chronological order will then be correct, as follows: 1200-586 B.C. (ch. 2); 586-538 B.C. (ch. 3); 538-444 B.C. (ch. 4); 332-170 B.C. (ch. 5; cf. II Macc. 4:7-20); 170-164 B.C. (ch. 8); 168 (ch. 9); 164-4 B.C. (ch. 6); after 4 B.C. (ch. 7).

Like Daniel, the book attributes to God alone the establishment of his kingdom on earth, in which Israel will be glorified and the Gentiles humbled (ch. 10); human participation in the struggle is not mentioned. The vindication of Israel takes place on this earth (unless 10:9 is understood literally); no Messiah appears; there is no heathen onslaught; the advent is dated 250 "times" (or 1,750 years if a "time" is a week of years) after the death of Moses (10:12). The future hope seems to be nationalistic rather than personal: there is no resurrection. Even if the future world consists merely of Paradise and Gehenna (as some interpreters believe on the basis of 10:8-10), the first is the abode of Israel, the second of the Gentiles, without any moral discrimination. The attack on Pharisaic hypocrisy in ch. 7 may be compared with the indictment of Jesus (Matt. 23; Mark 12:38-40; Luke 11:39-52; etc.).

3. The Apocalypse of Baruch.—This book was written in Aramaic shortly after II (IV) Esdras, between A.D. 90 and 100, and shows the influence of that apocalypse. It is extant only in a Syriac version made from the Greek translation of the original. Only parts of chs. 12–14 survive in Greek. Both Syriac Baruch (or II Baruch) and II Esdras raise the question of God's justice, in view of Israel's misery and Babylon's prosperity (i.e., the distress of the Jews after Titus destroyed Jerusalem in A.D. 70, and Rome's prosperity and invincible power); both fail to find a sufficient explanation in Adam's fall and its repercussions through the generations of men. Since II (IV) Esdras is the work of a man of genius, and II Baruch the product of a clever imitator, the priority of Esdras (confirmed by numerous comparisons of parallel passages) is manifest. Baruch may be summarized as follows:

(a) The destruction of Jerusalem in 586 B.C. (1:1–12:4). The Lord announces to Baruch the imminent fall of Jerusalem on account of the people's sins (chs. 1–5). On the morrow the Chaldeans besiege the city, but it is destroyed by four angels after they have buried the holy vessels of the temple; then the Chaldeans take possession of the ruined city (chs. 6–8). While Jeremiah goes into exile, Baruch remains in Jerusalem and sings a lamentation (9:1–12:4).

(b) Divine answers to Baruch's doubts (12:5–20:6). After a fast, Baruch receives a divine revelation (12:5–13:12). Baruch cannot understand why the righteous in Jerusalem are not spared since the world was made for them (ch. 14). God answers that men sin deliberately; the future world belongs to the righteous (chs. 15–17); men are free to choose light or darkness (chs. 18–19); Zion's destruction will hasten the coming of the future world (ch. 20).

(c) The final woes (chs. 21–34). In reply to Baruch's disconsolate prayer (ch. 21) the Lord assures him that the divine promises will be fulfilled in due time (ch. 22), after all souls have been born (ch. 23). Before the Last Judgment (chs. 24–26), twelve woes are to come (ch. 27), but Palestine will be spared (chs. 28–29); then will come the Messiah and the resurrection (ch. 30). Baruch urges the people to prepare for future woes (chs. 31–34).

(d) The allegory of the cedar (chs. 35–46). After another lament for Zion (ch. 35), Baruch sees in a vision a vine growing over a spring in front of a forest; the spring roots out the forest except for one cedar, which is finally consumed by flames; but the vine flourishes (chs. 36–37). The forest is the Roman Empire (the fourth world kingdom after the Chaldean, the Persian, and the Hellenistic), the cedar is its last king, executed by "My Messiah" (the vine), whose dominion is symbolized by the spring (chs. 38–40). Baruch, in obedience to God's command, warns and comforts the people (chs. 41–46).

(e) The future world (chs. 47–52). After Baruch fasts (ch. 47) and prays (48:1-24), God announces new afflictions (48:25-50), reveals the character of the resurrection bodies, and the final fate of the righteous and the wicked (chs. 49–52).

(f) The vision of the cloud (chs. 53–76). A great cloud rises from the sea and covers the earth; twelve outpourings of alternately black and clear waters; after an additional outpouring of black waters, lightning illuminates the earth (ch. 53). In answer to Baruch's prayer (chs. 54–55) the following interpretation of the vision is given: the cloud is the present age, the twelve outpourings are alternating evil and good periods of history, namely: Adam (ch. 56); Abraham (ch. 57); the Egyptians (ch. 58); Moses, Aaron, and Joshua (ch. 59); the Amorites (ch. 60); David and Solomon (ch. 61); Jeroboam I and Jezebel (ch. 62); Hezekiah (ch. 63); Manasseh (chs. 64–65); Josiah (ch. 66); destruction of the temple (ch. 67); rebuilding of the temple (ch. 68). The additional black outpour represents the woes at the end of the world (chs. 69–71), and the lightning is "My Messiah" (chs. 72–74). Baruch praises the Lord (ch. 75) and is ordered to teach the people and to be ready to be translated from this earth (ch. 76).

(g) Baruch's letters to the nine-and-a-half and to the two-and-a-half tribes of Israel (chs. 77–87). After addressing his final admonitions to the people in Judea (77:1-16), Baruch writes to the Judean exiles in Babylonia and to the northern Israelites in exile (77:17-26). Only the text of the second letter, which is sent through an eagle (ch. 87), is given in full (chs. 78–86).

Both II (IV) Esdras and II Baruch are concerned with the misfortunes of Israel as a whole, and of individuals, and they seek to find comfort in visions of the world to come; but the national aspect is stressed more in Baruch, where little or no prominence is given to what seems to trouble Esdras most: Why are so few human beings destined to be saved? This question is still unanswered.

II. Alexandrian Pseudepigrapha

A. Jewish Propaganda Attributed to Gentiles. 1. The Letter of Aristeas.—The unknown Jewish author of this book pretends to be Aristeas, an official of Ptolemy II Philadelphus of Egypt (285-245 B.C.), writing to his brother Philocrates an account of the origin of the Greek version of the Pentateuch (the Septuagint [LXX] in its original sense, before the term

included the whole Old Testament). The story is merely a pretext for the glorification of the Jews and their religion; the events narrated are legendary or fictitious, although there is no reason to doubt that the Pentateuch was translated into Greek about 250 B.C. The book, written in Greek at Alexandria about 100 B.C., may be summarized as follows:

(a) Introduction on the purpose of this epistle (vss. 1-8).

(b) Preparations for the translation of the Pentateuch (vss. 9-50). When Demetrius of Phalerum induces Ptolemy II to have the Jewish law translated (vss. 9-11), Aristeas obtains a royal decree emancipating the Jewish slaves in Egypt (vss. 12-27). After Demetrius prepares a memorandum (vss. 28-32), the king requests the high priest Eleazar to send from Jerusalem seventy-two translators, six from each tribe (vss. 33-40). Eleazar answers favorably (vss. 41-50).

(c) The royal gifts to Eleazar (vss. 51-82): a sacred table (vss. 51-72), gold and silver bowls (vss. 73-78), and golden vials (vss. 79-82).

(d) Jerusalem (vss. 83-106) and Palestine (vss. 107-20). Aristeas describes the temple and its water supply (vss. 83-91), the priestly (vss. 92-95) and high priestly (vss. 96-99) rites, the citadel (vss. 100-4), the city of Jerusalem (vss. 105-6), and the rest of Palestine (vss. 107-20).

(e) The translators prepare to leave for Egypt (vss. 121-27), and Eleazar eloquently extols the nobility and reasonableness of the Jewish law (vss. 128-71).

(f) Ptolemy receives the translators with unusual deference (vss. 172-86) and, at banquets on seven successive days, is delighted with their replies to his seventy-two questions (vss. 187-300).

(g) On the island of Pharos the seventy-two translators finish the translation in seventy-two days (vss. 301-7). The Jewish population (vss. 308-11) and the king (vss. 312-17) approve the translation, and the translators return to Jerusalem with costly gifts (vss. 318-22).

The apologetic purpose of the work is clear from the eulogy of the Jewish law (vss. 128-69), in which puzzling ordinances are interpreted allegorically (vss. 146-62); from the plea for the emancipation of the Jews, who are said to worship Zeus under another name (vss. 15-16, 19); from the admiration for the temple services (vs. 99); and particularly from the soundness of the answers given by the translators to the king's questions (vss. 187-294).

2. The Sibylline Oracles.—The sibyls were the pagan counterpart of the Hebrew prophets: like the prophets they pronounced and supposedly wrote down divine oracles. The Sibyl-

line Oracles enjoyed great prestige in the Greco-Roman world, and were even consulted officially by the government of the Roman Republic. The official collection of oracles in Rome was destroyed by fire in 82 B.C., but a new collection was prepared. These oracles were generally in Greek hexameter verses, imitating the meter of the *Iliad* and *Odyssey*.

The popularity of such oracles induced a Jew in Alexandria to fake sibylline verses for purposes of propaganda among the heathen: about 140 B.C. he composed the bulk of Bk. III of the extant collection. This series of Greek oracles in fifteen books (of which Bks. IX, X, and XV are lost) is in a state of chaotic confusion. The Jewish oracles are contained in Bks. III, IV, and V; the rest of the books are mostly of Christian origin: the Jewish oracles date from about 140 B.C. to about A.D. 125; the Christian parts come down to the fifth century; the final edition was prepared in the sixth century. The Jewish oracles at times incorporate purely pagan material, with or without slight retouches (as Bk. III, ll. 110-154), and have passed through the hands of Christian editors, who have generally refrained from introducing specifically Christian ideas.

The main topics in the Jewish parts of the Sibylline Oracles are the following:

Bk. III (*ca.* 140 B.C.). Introduction (preserved by Theophilus of Antioch) on the superiority of Jewish monotheism over pagan idolatry and animal worship. Bk. III, ll. 1-92 (which may belong to Bk. II) deals with monotheism, idolatry, the Last Judgment, the ruin of Beliar from Samaria (Simon Magus?), and the world conflagration during the rule of a widow. In Bk. III, ll. 93-96 a Christian (?) longs for the coming of the Savior. Bk. III, ll. 97-294 outlines the history of the world from the Tower of Babel, and the rule of Cronos, Titan, and Japetus, down to Ptolemy VII, who ruled alone from 145 to 116. In Bk. III, ll. 295-572, the sibyl predicts woes for Babylon, Egypt, Gog and Magog, and Lybia; a comet will presage the travails at the end of this age, to be followed by the messianic age; Alexander, and later Antiochus IV Epiphanes, will devastate Asia; Homer plagiarized the sibyl in the *Iliad* and the *Odyssey;* many cities and countries are doomed. In Bk. III, ll. 573-651, Israel is praised and the heathen are denounced. The messianic age (Bk. III, ll. 652-808) will bring peace and wealth to the Jews, but judgment against the heathen. In the colophon (Bk. III, ll. 809-29), the sibyl identifies herself as having come from Babylon, although the Greeks call her the Erythraean; she is the daughter-in-law and blood relation of Noah.

Bk. IV was composed about A.D. 80, for it refers to the eruption of Vesuvius in A.D. 79 (Bk. IV, ll. 130-36). The sibyl utters the oracles of the true God (Bk. IV, ll. 1-23). The Jews will not go to hell like the heathen (Bk. IV, ll. 35-46). The summary of world history in Bk. IV, ll. 47-139 begins with the Assyrian, Medic, and Persian kingdoms, and comes down to the mythical return of Nero redivivus (soon after his death in A.D. 68) from Parthia and the destruction of Pompeii in A.D. 79. The book concludes with a series of woes against various localities (Bk. IV, ll. 140-61), an exhortation to repentance lest fire consume the world (Bk. IV, ll. 162-78), and the Last Judgment (Bk. IV, ll. 179-195).

Bk. V dates from about A.D. 125, since it refers favorably to Hadrian (A.D. 76-138; see Bk. V, ll. 46-50) before his war against the Jews in 132-35 (the reference to his successor Marcus Aurelius in Bk. V, l. 51 is probably spurious). The book opens with a history of Rome, in which the emperors from Julius Caesar to Marcus Aurelius are cryptically mentioned (Bk. V, ll. 1-51). A series of woes against Egypt, Asia, India, Ethiopia, Greece, etc. (Bk. V, ll. 52-227) is followed by a curse on *hybris* or violence (Bk. V, ll. 228-46), and a eulogy of the Jews (Bk. V, ll. 247-85, in which ll. 256-59 are a Christian interpolation). The woes against nations are resumed (ll. 286-343). Cosmic upheavals, the return of Nero redivivus, the resurrection, and war are the signs of the end of the world, followed by the golden age for the Jews only (Bk. V, ll. 344-85). Roman immorality (Bk. V, ll. 386-93; cf. Rom. 1:24-31) and the destruction of Jerusalem by Titus (ll. 394-413) are denounced. The Messiah will exterminate the heathen and make Jerusalem more radiant than the sun (Bk. V, ll. 414-33). A denunciation of Babylonia (Bk. V, ll. 434-46), cosmic upheavals in the eastern Mediterranean (Bk. V, ll. 447-57), the peaceful rule of Octavian Augustus (Bk. V, ll. 458-63), the invasion of the Gauls into Asia Minor (Bk. V, ll. 464-75), a total darkness for the heathen but not for the Jews (Bk. V, ll. 476-83). Egypt will forget Isis and Serapis; it will worship instead the Lord in the temple built by Onias at Leontopolis (Bk. V, ll. 484-503; cf. Isa. 19:18-21). Egypt will eventually be destroyed (Bk. V, ll. 504-11). Stars and constellations will fight until the heavens will cast them into the ocean and they will kindle the earth (Bk. V, ll. 512-30).

B. *Legendary History. III Maccabees.*—This book, written in Greek by an Alexandrian Jew shortly before or after the beginning of our era, has nothing to do with the Maccabees and was placed in the group of the books dealing with the Maccabean rebellion merely because it is a story—entirely fictitious—of an unsuccessful persecution of the Jews, like that of Antiochus Epiphanes. As in II Maccabees, Esther, and Judith, the triumph of the Jews is celebrated by a festival. The author was influenced by these books, particularly II Maccabees, and also by the Greek Daniel with its additions (6:6); his pseudoclassical Greek style is rhetorical and bombastic. In *Against Apion* II. 5, Josephus relates a similar tale, manifestly without direct knowledge of III Maccabees: placing it in the time of Ptolemy VII [IX] Physkon (145-116 B.C.), instead of Ptolemy IV Philopator (221-203 B.C.): in both cases drunken elephants, instead of trampling the Jews, turn against their enemies. In addition to the annual celebration of the day there are other parallels. Since neither story has the slightest historical foundation, it is unprofitable to attempt to determine whether both versions are derived from an earlier one, or whether Josephus merely reproduced an incorrect echo of III Maccabees. The tale of the latter book runs as follows:

Ptolemy IV Philopator was saved by Dositheus (a converted Jew) from a deadly plot (1:1-3) and defeated Antiochus III the Great (223-187 B.C.) at Raphia in 217 (1:4-5); he then visited neighboring shrines (1:6-7). After sacrificing to the Lord in Jerusalem, Ptolemy decided to enter the holy of holies in spite of the warnings of all Jews (1:8-29). But in answer to the ardent prayer of the high priest Simon (2:1-20), God smote Ptolemy senseless to the ground (2:21-23). Returning to Egypt unrepentant (2:24), the king had slanders against the Jews spread by his friends (2:25-26); he degraded them to serfs (2:27-28) and had them branded with an ivy leaf as worshipers of Dionysus (2:29); only those few who were initiated into the Dionysiac mysteries would retain civic rights (2:30). The king then ordered that provincial Jews be brought to the capital to be put to death (3:1), in spite of the fact that the Jews were faithful to the king and had many friends among the Greeks (3:2-10). Ptolemy issued a royal decree as follows: the peoples of Coelesyria and Phoenicia welcomed the king (3:11-15), except the Jews who prevented him from entering their temple (3:16-20); forgiving the Jews, he offered them Alexandrian citizenship and participation in the worship (3:21), but they contemptuously refused (3:22-23); convinced that they were traitors, he ordered that all be brought to Alexandria for execution (3:24-30). This decree provoked the jubilation of the heathen and the wailing of the Jews (4:1-3), who were carried away without mercy (4:4-10) to Schedia and imprisoned in the hippodrome (4:11); soon the Alexandrian Jews were added to their number (4:12-13). The listing of this multitude of Jews by name was interrupted on account of the lack of writing material (4:14-21). Then the king ordered Hermon to intoxicate his five hundred elephants and let them kill the Jews (5:1-5). But in answer to the prayer of the Jews the king overslept, and the massacre was postponed to the next day (5:6-22). But on the morrow the king, having forgotten his instructions (through divine intervention), ordered that the Jews be freed (5:23-35). During the banquet, however, having reprimanded Hermon for not having killed the Jews, the king again gave orders for their execution on the morrow (5:36-42) and decided to destroy the temple in Jerusalem (5:43). At dawn heathen throngs, the king, and the elephants proceeded to the hippodrome for the Jewish massacre (5:44-47), while the Jews appealed to God (5:48-51). The aged priest Eleazar reminded God of his former deliverance in the Exodus from Egypt, and begged for help (6:1-15). As the king arrived, the Jews cried out loudly (6:16-17), and two angels filled king and troops with terror (6:18-20). The elephants destroyed the armed men (6:21). The king's anger now turned against the heathen, and he set free the Jews (6:22-29), giving them a seven-day banquet (6:30-31). The Jews praised God (6:32), and the king celebrated with a feast (6:33). The enemies of the Jews were put to shame (6:34), while the Jews made the day an annual festival (6:35-37). The king allowed the Jews to return to their homes (6:38-41), and published a decree in their behalf (7:1-9). Before their departure the Jews asked and obtained permission to execute their apostate brethren (7:10-14), and perpetrated the killing of three hundred of them (7:15); then they returned home (7:16). In Ptolemais they again celebrated with a banquet (7:17-18), erected there an inscribed stele and a shrine (7:19-21), and recovered all their property without trouble (7:22-23).

C. Popular Philosophy: IV Maccabees.—This book has more or less the form of a diatribe, or popular speech on philosophical and religious matters, after the manner of the Cynics and the Stoics. The author was an Alexandrian Jew who wrote the book in Greek two or three decades before or after the beginning of our era: he thus lived not long before Philo of Alexandria. This sermon is addressed to Jews (18:1) and has for its theme the supremacy of devout reason (ὁ εὐσεβὴς λογισμός) over the passions (a Stoic principle): "whether devout reason is supreme ruler over the passions" (1:1); the stories of the Maccabean martyrs in II Macc. 6:18–7:41 are used as evidence to prove his thesis. We may summarize the book as follows:

(a) The introduction (1:1-12) gives a synopsis of the theme and the plan of the book.

(b) The philosophical exposition (1:13–3:18). Reason is the mind's choice for the life of wisdom; wisdom (according to the Stoic definition) is the knowledge of human and divine things, as well as of their causes, and (according to Judaism) is acquired through the law of Moses (1:13-17), manifesting itself in the four (Stoic) cardinal virtues: prudence, justice, courage, temperance (1:18). The several passions or emotions spring from pleasure and pain. Regular sequences are to be observed in the passions: desire precedes, and satisfaction follows, pleasure (1:19-27). Reason, through prudence and temperance, is the guide of virtues and the master of passions (1:28-35): it controls covetous desires, passions opposed to justice, and the more aggressive or violent impulses (2:1-24); all passions, in fact, with the exception of forgetfulness and ignorance, are restrained, but not extirpated, by reason (3:1-18).

(c) The demonstration of the thesis (1:1) through historical evidence (3:19–17:24). Historical introduction (3:19–4:26). The events preceding the Maccabean rebellion, notably the attempt of Apollonius [Heliodorus in II Macc. 3] to enter the temple (3:19–4:14), and the efforts of Antiochus Epiphanes to abolish Judaism (4:15-26; cf. II Macc. 4–6). The martyrdom of Eleazar, and its philosophical and religious lessons (chs. 5–7; cf. II Macc. 6:18-31). The martyrdom of the seven brothers (chs. 8–12; cf. II Macc. 7). Edifying reflections suggested by the same (13:1–14:10). Considerations about the fortitude of the mother (14:11–16:25) and her death (17:1-7). Closing reflections on the martyrs (17:8-24): text of a fitting epitaph for these heroic figures (17:8-10) who fought a holy war in the arena as athletes of the law and were amply rewarded (17:11-24).

(d) Peroration (ch. 18). The Israelites should follow the example of the martyrs (18:1-2), who won the admiration of mankind, obtained eternal bliss with God, national restoration, and triumph over the tyrant Antiochus (18:3-5). Exhortation of the mother to her seven sons (18:6-19); contrast between the tyrant and the Jews (18:20-24).

As a writer and a thinker, the author of this book is superior to the author of II Maccabees, and notably better than the pretentious Atticist who wrote III Maccabees. He is an ardent and orthodox Jew, in spite of the fact that he does not teach the Pharisaic doctrine of the resurrection of the body (II Macc. 6:26; 7:9, 11, 14, 23, 29, 31, 36; 12:43-45), but the Platonic doctrine of the immortality of every human soul (5:37; 9:8; 10:11; 12:12; 13:15; 14:5-6; 16:13, 25; 17:5, 12, 18; 18:3, 23; cf. Wisd. Sol. 3–5). As in Wisd. Sol. 2:24, the serpent in Eden (Gen. 3) is identified with Satan (18:8; cf. Rev. 12:9; 20:2). Another characteristic doctrine is found in 6:28 and 17:21-22: the martyrs' punishment is to be a satisfaction in behalf of Israel; their lives a ransom for their souls; their blood the people's purification; their death a propitiation; here the author (perhaps under the influence of Isa. 53) goes beyond II Macc. 7:18, 32-33, 37-38, where the torments of the martyrs are a punishment for their own sins, a confession that the Lord is the only God, and the means for bringing to an end God's just wrath against Israel.

D. Apocalypses. 1. Slavonic Enoch.—This book, also called II Enoch, or The Book of the Secrets of Enoch, was written at Alexandria in Greek during the first half of the first century of our era, but is extant only in Slavic versions. That the book was written in Greek is shown, for example, by the author's discovery that the initials of the Greek words which designate the four points of the compass spell out the four letters of the name *ADAM* (30:13; cf. Sibylline Oracles Bk. III, ll. 24-26); the initials of the corresponding English words would spell *NEWS*. The contents, briefly, are as follows:

(a) Introduction (chs. 1–2). In his 365th year Enoch announced to his sons his impending assumption into heaven.

(b) Enoch's ascension through the seven heavens (chs. 3–21); the mention of the eighth, ninth, and tenth heavens (20:3; 21:6; 22:1) is secondary. In the first heaven he saw the angels ruling over the stars (chs. 3–4), and the storehouses of snow and dew (chs. 5–6). In the second he saw the angels who sinned through ambition, chained in total darkness (ch. 7). In the third was paradise (cf. II Cor. 12:2-4) prepared for the righteous (chs. 8–9), and a hell of fire and ice (ch. 10). In the fourth Enoch saw the sun and its elements (Phoenixes and Chalkydri), and the moon (chs. 11–17). In the fifth are the Grigori or Watchers, and their prince, Satanail, who rebelled against God; their brothers are chained in the second heaven (ch. 18; cf. ch. 7). The archangels, the angels of nature, and others are in the sixth heaven (ch. 19). Archangels, forces, dominions, orders and governments, cherubim and seraphim, thrones, and many-eyed ones are in the seventh heaven, where the Lord is enthroned in the distance (chs. 20–21).

(c) God's revelations to Enoch (chs. 22–38). Clad in heavenly garments, Enoch stood before God (ch. 22), and under Pravuil's (or Vretil's) dictation, wrote 366 books (ch. 23). The Lord himself revealed to Enoch how he planned a visible creation (ch. 24), and created the world from pre-existing elements (ch. 25; cf. Wisd. Sol. 11:17) in six days (chs. 26–30; cf. Gen. 1). Adam and Eve were placed in the Garden of Eden until the devil seduced Eve (chs. 31–32). God also revealed to Enoch the history of the world down to his own time (ch. 33): the deluge to punish the idolaters (ch. 34), the survival of one family (ch. 35), the return of Enoch to earth for thirty days to tell them everything (chs. 36–38).

(d) Enoch's admonitions to his sons (chs. 39–66). In his books Enoch has described the secret things of nature (chs. 39–40); he has seen the forefathers beginning with Adam (ch. 41), the key holders of the gates of hell (ch. 42); he has discovered that nothing is greater than he who fears God (ch. 43). Man is God's creature, and should never be reviled (ch. 44). God requires pure hearts, not sacrifices (chs. 45–46). Enoch's books describe the Lord's works (ch. 47), including the sun's passage through the seven circles (ch. 48). Enoch's sons should not swear (ch. 49), nor take vengeance (ch. 50); they should give alms (ch. 51), glorify the Lord and be merciful (ch. 52), and not believe in the intercession of the saints (ch. 53). The books should be handed on to others (ch. 54). Enoch must now return to heaven (ch. 55), and he refuses food (ch. 56). Having summoned the whole household (ch. 57), he warns them not to harm beasts (chs. 58–59), not to injure any man (ch. 60), but to help the needy (chs. 61–63). Then two thousand people come to kiss Enoch (ch. 64); he describes God's creative work, the Last Judgment, and paradise (chs. 65–66). In total darkness he is translated to the highest heaven (chs. 67–68).

2. **Greek Baruch.**—This book, also called III Baruch, is preserved in a Greek condensation, and a Slavic abridgment of the original book written in Greek early in the second century of our era and known to Origen. Our extant book has been edited by a Christian who added 4:9-15, and extensively revised chs. 11–17. The contents of the book, in brief, are as follows:

(a) Introduction (ch. 1). While Baruch was weeping over the ruin of Jerusalem, an angel came to reveal to him the mysteries of God.

(b) The five heavens (chs. 2–16). The first heaven (ch. 2) houses the builders of the Tower of Babel. The second heaven (ch. 3) houses those who directed the building of the Tower of Babel. In the third heaven (chs. 4–9) Baruch saw a great dragon who devoured the bodies of the wicked (4:1-7), and the vine which Adam was forbidden to touch, but whose fruit the devil (cf. Gen. 3; Wisd. Sol. 2:24; II Enoch 31:3; IV Macc. 18:8; Rev. 20:2) tempted him to eat (4:8); God changed the bitterness of the vine into sweetness through Jesus Christ's redemption (4:9-15; wine being used in the Eucharist: Christian interpolation). As Adam was condemned through the vine, so are drunkards (4:16-17). Hades is the belly of the dragon (ch. 5). Baruch then saw the phoenix, a bird which flies with the sun (chs. 6–8), and the chariot of the moon (ch. 9). In the fourth heaven the souls of the righteous in the shape of birds sang the praises of God (ch. 10). In the fifth heaven Michael received the prayers of men and the merits of the righteous brought by angels (chs. 11–12). The angels assigned to the wicked, having brought no good works, wished to be transferred to others (ch. 13; the reference to the church in 13:4 is Christian). Michael distributed rewards for men in proportion to their good works (chs. 14–16; 15:4 quotes Matt. 25:21 and is Christian).

(c) Conclusion (ch. 17). Without ascending to the sixth and seventh heavens, Baruch is brought back to earth (ch. 17; the original ending has probably been omitted by the editor).

Of interest for the study of Christian doctrines are the Jewish views about the seven heavens (five of which are described in the extant book), the mediation of angels bearing human merits to Michael and returning with appropriate rewards (chs. 11–16; cf. Enoch, the Testament of Levi, and the Testament of Abraham; Rev. 8:3; contrast II [IV] Esdras 7:102-15, where intercession is excluded), and the notions about Adam's fall (4:8, 16-17).

III. Selected Bibliography

See the list at the end of the article, "The Literature and Religion of the Apocrypha," and, more in detail:

PFEIFFER, R. H. *Introduction to the Old Testament.* New York: Harper & Bros., 1941. Pp. 876-77, 881-84 (the latter pages were omitted in the new edition, 1948); *History of New Testament Times.* New York: Harper & Bros., 1949. Pp. 531-33, 538-41.

ROWLEY, H. H. *The Relevance of Apocalyptic.* London: Lutterworth Press, 1944.

The Book of

GENESIS

Introduction and Exegesis by Cuthbert A. Simpson
Exposition by Walter Russell Bowie

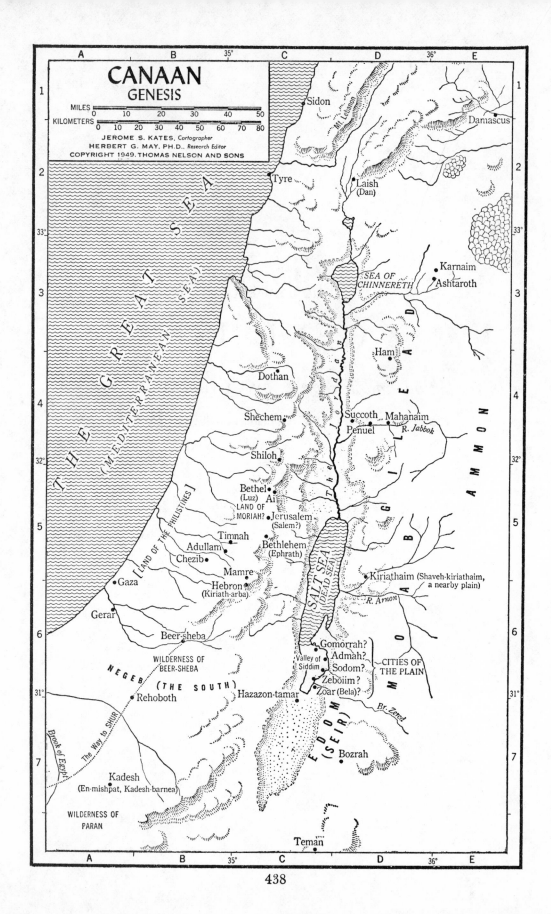

CANAAN
GENESIS

MILES
0   10   20   30   40   50

KILOMETERS
0   10   20   30   40   50   60   70   80

JEROME S. KATES, *Cartographer*
HERBERT G. MAY, PH.D., *Research Editor*
COPYRIGHT 1949. THOMAS NELSON AND SONS

A   B   35°   C   D   36°   E

Sidon

Mt. Lebanon

Damascus

Tyre

Laish
(Dan)

Karnaim
Ashtaroth

SEA OF
CHINNERETH

THE GREAT SEA

(MEDITERRANEAN SEA)

Ham

Dothan

Shechem

Succoth   Mahanaim
Penuel   R. Jabbok

Shiloh

Bethel
(Luz)   Ai
LAND OF
MORIAH?   Jerusalem
(Salem?)

Timnah

Adullam
Chezib

Bethlehem
(Ephrath)

Mamre

Hebron
(Kiriath-arba).

Kiriathaim (Shaveh-kiriathaim,
a nearby plain)

Gaza

Gerar

Beer-sheba

R. Arnon

SALT SEA
(DEAD SEA)

Gomorrah?
Admah?
Valley of
Siddim   Sodom?
Zeboiim?
Zoar (Bela)?

CITIES OF
THE PLAIN

WILDERNESS OF
BEER-SHEBA

NEGEB   (THE SOUTH)

Rehoboth

Hazazon-tamar

Br. Zered

The Way to SHUR

Brook of Egypt

Kadesh
(En-mishpat, Kadesh-barnea)

Bozrah

WILDERNESS OF
PARAN

Teman

[LAND OF THE PHILISTINES]

The Jordan

G I L E A D

A M M O N

M O A B

E D O M   (S E I R)

A   B   35°   C   D   36°   E

438

GENESIS

INTRODUCTION

Genesis means "beginning." The title comes through the Vulgate from the Septuagint, where it is dependent on the Hebrew superscription— simply the first word of the text, berē'shîth, "In the beginning."

I. Composition and Authorship

Genesis is the first book of the Pentateuch. The Pentateuch, ending with the death of Moses (Deut. 34), is, in turn, the first part of a continuous history extending from the creation of the world (Gen. 1) to the middle of the Babylonian exile (II Kings 25:30). At what point in the literary development this first part of the history was divided into five books it is impossible to say; but since the division appears in the Septuagint, it was before its translation into Greek, ca. 250 B.C. As has been shown in the article "The Growth of the Hexateuch" (pp. 185-200), the book is the result of a conflation, first of two originally separate documents, J and E, to form a narrative, JE, which some centuries later was itself conflated with a third document, P. Neither the J nor the E

439

document was in its original form when the two were combined; each had been subjected to elaboration of various kinds; and the P document had received similar though less extensive treatment before being conflated with JE. That is, the tradition underlying each of the documents remained a living tradition, and so capable of adaptation to changing conditions and responsive to new needs, until it was crystallized by deliberate fusion with another tradition.

It is thus impossible to speak in any strict sense of the author of Genesis. The redactor—RP—who conflated JE and P has the best claim to be so regarded, for he determined the form of the book. Yet even his work received certain additions, for it was not until the Pentateuch was canonized, that is, recognized as scripture, that the process of elaboration and adaptation came to an end.

II. Purpose

Underlying and finding expression in this variegated narrative is Israel's consciousness of standing in a unique relationship to God, the creator, the controller of history, the source of all righteousness, the foundation of all meaning. The purpose of the book is to account for this sense of uniqueness, to establish its validity, to show that it originated not in what today would be called wishful thinking, but in God's free act of choice.

A. Relationship Between Yahweh and Israel.
1. Beginning of Israel's Faith.—Historically this unique relationship began not with the response of one man, Abraham, to an explicit divine call, but in a collective response by the group, then or later known as the sons of Israel, to external reality manifesting itself in the thunderstorm and in the volcano [?] of Sinai. These phenomena the Israelites attributed to the activity of a god to whom they or others had long since given the name of Yahweh. The significance of their response lay in the fact that it was characterized not by a self-regarding fear of the appalling destructiveness of the storm and the volcano, but by a self-surrendering acceptance of that destructiveness as the strange, majestic manifestation of a power apprehended, however inarticulately, as a part of the nature of things, existing independently of them, but to which they must relate themselves if they were to discern the meaning of life and realize its potentialities.[1]

[1] For a more detailed analysis of the initial response of Israel to the self-revelation of God in the storm, see Cuthbert A. Simpson, *The Early Traditions of Israel* (Oxford: Basil Blackwell, 1948), pp. 419-25; *Revelation and Response in the Old Testament* (New York: Columbia University Press, 1947), pp. 3-22.

2. Growth of Israel's Faith.—This response, emotional rather than volitional, was first made in the desert, long before Israel's movement into Palestine. It resulted in a heightened awareness of the nature of the reality which was making its impact upon them, and drew their imagination outward from preoccupation with self to a recognition of the rights and the independence of the other-than-self. And this awareness, thus heightened, grew richer and more acute as they maintained and deepened their response. By the time of the settlement they had already come to feel that they stood in a unique relationship to Yahweh the God of the storm. He had become the God of Israel, as is clear from the song now preserved in Judg. 5, generally recognized as having been composed within a few years of the Conquest.

B. The Call of Abraham.—According to Genesis, however, the unique relationship between Yahweh and Israel began with the call of Abraham. What is the reason for this?

1. Desire for Concreteness.—It would have been difficult for an Israelite at any period in biblical times to have depicted concretely and convincingly the experience from which the national consciousness of having been chosen by Yahweh had arisen. It would have been difficult for him to give a reasoned account of why his people were convinced that Yahweh had singled them out, and had moved toward them in the storm to evoke from them the response which had intensified their relationship to him. It would have been difficult for him to show how this intensification quickened his people's perceptions so that they were able to apprehend ever more adequately the character of Yahweh and heightened their powers so that they were able to make an ever more adequate response to him; it would have been difficult for him to explain how they had, with each successive response, reached a new vantage point from which a further advance in the knowledge of God had been made. The Israelite thought in the terms of what Abraham Kuenen has called the law of religious historiography:

In ancient time and specifically in Israel, the sense of historical continuity could only be preserved by the constant compliance on the part of the past with the requirements of the present, that is to say its constant renovation and transformation. This may be called the law of religious historiography. At any rate it dominates the historical writings alike of the Israelites and of the early Christians.[2]

[2] "The Critical Method," *The Modern Review*, I (1880), 705, quoted by Stanley A. Cook, "Notes on Old Testament History," *Jewish Quarterly Review*, XVIII (1906), 739.

2. Influence of the Traditions of Palestine.—

The native tendency to this kind of thinking was, however, but one of the factors that determined the form in which Israel's religious history is written in Genesis and, indeed, in the Hexateuch as a whole. Equally if not more decisive was the need for relating the religious traditions of Palestine, with which Israel first came into contact following the settlement, to the historical tradition which they had brought with them from the desert.

C. Component Documents.—It was J¹ who made the first systematic attempt to meet this need.[8] His work was later expanded by J², and J²'s narrative was in turn revised and rewritten by E. In the course of time the J² and E documents were conflated, and the resultant narrative was eventually fused, after the Exile, with the P document. Therefore, for any clear understanding of the purpose of the book, there must be an examination of the purposes and methods of the authors of these its component documents.

III. The J¹ Document

A. The Elements of J¹. 1. Origins.—Interest in origins is a mark of J¹ and furnishes a convenient starting point for the analysis of the original J material in chs. 2–4. This narrative tells of how man was expelled from the garden, in which he had lived a carefree life, "to till the ground from which he was taken" (3:23), of his subsequent reduction, following the crime of Cain—in the mind of the author the sole representative of the human race as it was then constituted—to the cultureless life of "a fugitive and a wanderer on the earth" (4:12), and of the origins of nomadism, music, and metalworking (cf. 4:20-22), the beginning of civilization.

Furthermore (see Exeg.), underlying the not too clear statement in 9:20 is a notice that "Noah was the first tiller of the soil," that is, agriculture originated with him.

In marked contrast to the extraordinary skill with which the garden story is told and the concise simplicity of the account of the rise of nomadism, music, and metalworking (4:20-22), is the awkwardness of the movement of man here depicted, from the garden, through agriculture, to the cultureless life of a fugitive and a wanderer on the earth, through nomadism to agriculture again—an awkwardness which suggests the presence of the work of more than one hand.

It will be noted in the Exegesis (a) that the Cain story is from the same hand as the story of man's life in, and expulsion from, the garden, and (b) that the account of the rise of nomad-

[8] On the symbols J¹, J², E, and P, see article "The Growth of the Hexateuch," pp. 189-92.

ism, and so forth, knows nothing of the Flood. The story of the Flood contains certain stylistic indications that it is from the same hand as the garden story. The inference to be drawn is that the garden story, and so the story of Cain and Abel, are from another hand than the account of the rise of nomadism. When these two stories are placed to one side a very simple narrative is left, telling of the birth of the first child, Seth (4:25), and of his son Enosh, who originated the cult of Yahweh (4:26); of the birth of his son Cain (4:1), and of five succeeding generations to Lamech (4:17-18), whose three sons originated, respectively, nomadism, music, and metalworking (4:20-22). And the possibility has been suggested that Lamech's daughter Naamah (4:22b) was represented as the mother of Noah, the originator of agriculture (cf. 5:29b as emended, and 9:20).

This simple narrative—allowing for the possibility of some expansion, e.g., 4:18—is from J¹.

The reference to "the man"—to be read for "Adam" in 4:25 (see Exeg.)—in the opening sentence of the extant J¹ material suggests that this narrative began with an account of the creation of man, if not of the universe as a whole—an account which, if it ever existed, was dropped by J² in favor of his more elaborate myth. J¹ then told of the origins of Yahwism (4:26b); of nomadic civilization (4:20-22); of agriculture (5:28b-29abα); of viticulture (9:20)—attaching to this a tale intended to account for the superiority of Israel over the Canaanites (9:21-25); of the mighty ones (10:8); of the Nephilim (6:2); and of diverse peoples and languages (11:4-6, 8a).

2. Contact of Yahwism with the Religion of Canaan.—For this, the introduction to his history of Israel, J¹ for the most part had drawn upon the traditions of the seminomadic society on the edge of Palestine, between the desert and the sown. He now turned his attention to the legends of Canaan proper. His methods can best be discerned and appreciated through a consideration of the situation which confronted Yahwism in Hebron. The Israelites who settled there quite naturally began to worship the local deity from whom the fertility of the land and of the flocks was believed to derive. At first the question as to the relationship of this deity to Yahweh would scarcely be raised, but it soon became pressing. For the felt relationship between Israel and Yahweh was, because of its character, inimical to polytheism, as the so-called Song of Deborah shows (Judg. 5). This hymn of thanksgiving to Yahweh for his victory in battle is remarkable in many ways, not least because it speaks of his defeat of the Canaanites but never mentions their gods. It might have been expected that the author would have sought to enhance Yahweh's prestige by claiming for him a triumph over beings of his own rank, yet he makes no such claim. The meaning of this strange silence is suggested by the ecstatic character of the song. The exclusion of the gods of Canaan was the spontaneous expression of an immediate awareness of the sole deity of Yahweh.

That is to say, in those moments when Yahweh was apprehended as immediately and catastrophically present—when he was manifesting himself in the raging storm or, as the God of war, had seized upon his people to use them as the agents of his wrath against his enemies—Israel's experience was one of possession, so intense that all thought of other deities faded out in a momentary, emotional monotheism. Because of this experience there was implicit in Yahwism almost from the first a tendency, indeed a drive, toward monotheism.

3. The God of Hebron Identified with Yahweh.—When therefore the question as to the relationship of Yahweh to the god of Hebron became pressing, it was all but inevitable that the local deity should come to be identified with Yahweh, and this is what happened. The local sanctuary was taken over. The primary legend of the sanctuary, telling of the theophany which had occasioned its founding (18:1-8), was incorporated into the Yahwist tradition. The values which its religion enshrined were related to the values of Yahwism.

4. The Abraham Tradition.—The central human figure in the tradition of Hebron was Abraham, venerated as the founder of the sanctuary and as the father of the community. Entering into the life of the community, the Israelites who settled there came to claim him as their father too. But Israel had come from the desert, and the memory of their desert origin could not be ignored. Nor did they wish to ignore it, for it marked them off from the Canaanite element in the population, from whose immoral behavior they recoiled in horror (see Exeg. on 9:20-27; 19:30-38). The contradiction was resolved by having Abraham come from the desert (see Exeg. on 12:1-4a; 13:18; 29:1-14).

5. Lot and the Legend of Sodom.—With him came Lot, his nephew, who was identified with the man who, according to another legend current in the vicinity of Hebron, had been delivered from the overthrow of Sodom (13:2, 5, 7, 11a, 13; 19:1-28), and also with the somewhat dubious character who, a third legend related, had entered into an incestuous union with his daughters in a certain cave in the mountains of Moab (19:30-38).

6. Isaac of Beer-sheba Made the Son of Abraham.—To these three originally independent legends of Hebron, Sodom, and the cave, J[1] now related the tradition of the sanctuary of Beer-sheba. There Isaac had filled much the same role as that filled by Abraham at Hebron. So long as the communities of Hebron and Beer-sheba had remained separate and distinct, with no consciousness of a common past, the fact that they had different fathers would cause no difficulty. But once Isaac came to be venerated as father by the Israelites who settled in the vicinity of Beer-sheba, the question of his relationship to the father of the Israelite community at Hebron was bound to be raised. This question J[1] answered by making Isaac the son promised to Abraham as a reward for his hospitality to Yahweh when he visited Hebron incognito (18:1-9; 21:1a, 2a, 6b).

7. The Isaac Tradition.—But the tradition also connected Isaac with Beer-lahai-roi. J[1] accordingly represented his birth as occurring there (see Exeg. on 20:1a), told of his living there upon attaining manhood (25:11b), and then described his movement northward to Beer-sheba, incorporating into the narrative at this point a derisive tale concerning the Philistines (26:1-11), and some material dealing with the origin and ownership of certain wells in the desert (26:12-33).

8. Primacy of Abraham.—It is significant that in this process of unification of the traditions of the two sanctuaries Abraham of Hebron emerged as the father of Isaac of Beer-sheba. Doubtless the custodians of the latter shrine would have preferred to have their hero made the father of his rival. That the articulated tradition took the form it did can be due only to the power and prestige of the priesthood of Hebron, to which J[1] may well have belonged, and which could maintain the position of its patron against all claimants.

9. The East-Jordan Tradition.—The legends of Abraham, Isaac, and the destruction of Sodom are all rooted in the south. That of the man and his daughters living in the cave in the mountains of Moab, on the other hand, belongs to the land east of the Jordan. So, too, does the figure of Jacob (see Exeg. on 25:21-26), whom J[1] now linked with the southern tradition.

The fact that J[1] not only included in his narrative legends which had taken their rise across the Jordan, but gave them a marked prominence, is of considerable significance. His primary interest was certainly in the south, and indeed, as has been seen, in Hebron. The southern clans had been under the immediate influence of Moses, and had entered Palestine by a movement northward from Kadesh, bringing with them the concept of Yahweh as the transcendent God of righteousness. Yet J[1], articulating the local legends of the south with the tradition which the clans had brought from the desert, felt it necessary to relate the legends of the land east of the Jordan to this unified tradition. This indicates not only that there must have been considerable coming and going between the south and the east,[4] but also that the east had been influenced by Mosaism to such an extent that it was, in the mind of J[1], of equal importance with the south with which, indeed, it formed practically one religious community.[5]

10. The Jacob Tradition.—It was therefore necessary for Jacob, who had already come to be known as the father of the east-Jordan Israelite community (see Exeg. on 29:31–30:24), to be made the son of Isaac. But according to the legend (25:21-26) Jacob was not the first-born of his father; that role was filled by Esau, his twin; and Esau was traditionally the father of the Edomites. To account for the fact that not Esau but Jacob had inherited the divine promise to Abraham, J[1] adapted a folk tale to make it an account of how Esau sold his birthright to Jacob (25:27, 29-34).

11. Tribal Traditions.—The way was now clear for the linking with Jacob of the eponymous ancestors of such Israelite tribes as were known to J[1]. But two of these eponyms, Simeon and Levi, had long been regarded as the sons of one Leah (see Exeg. on 29:16), and a third, Joseph, was already known as the son of Rachel (see Exeg. on 29:1-14). Furthermore, Jacob was already associated, in the east-Jordan legend, with Laban the Aramaean (see Exeg. on 31:44-55). To unify these diverse traditions J[1] made Leah and Rachel the daughters of Laban, whom Jacob married (29:9-12, 26) when visiting the land of the people of the east in the North Arabian desert (29:1).

The narrative then recorded the birth of four sons to Leah: Reuben, the eponym of the east-Jordan tribe of that name, and Simeon, Levi, and Judah, the eponyms of three southern groups (29:31-35). Dinah, who played a leading role in a Simeon-Levi tradition (see Exeg. on ch. 34), was made Leah's daughter. By making Joseph, the Shechemite figure from whom the tribes of Ephraim and Manasseh had come to trace their descent (see Exeg. on 47:27–48:22),

the son of Rachel, J[1] both preserved a tradition which had already taken form in the north, and at the same time accounted for the fact that these tribes, though Yahwist, were, in his time, in many ways still alien to the southern confederacy.

12. Folklore.—Before recording Jacob's return to Palestine J[1] incorporated into his narrative a humorous tale of one shepherd overreaching another, adapting it so that it would show the cleverness of the Israelites in comparison with the dull-witted, though grasping, Aramaeans (30:27-43)—the dubious morality of Jacob's conduct does not appear to have troubled him (cf. Exeg. on 26:1-11; 25:29-34). The account of Jacob's departure was also enlivened by the inclusion of the incident of the stolen teraphim—another example of Israelite cleverness and of Aramaean stupidity (see Exeg. on 31:17-43). This led up to the traditional material of the covenant by which Mount Gilead had been fixed as the boundary line between the east-Jordan Israelites and the desert Aramaeans (see Exeg. on 31:44-55).

13. Jacob Identified with Israel.—At this point in his narrative J[1] found a place for what may well have been the primary legend of Jacob—his wrestling with the numen of the river Jabbok (32:24-31). To this he added the incident of the change of Jacob's name to Israel (32:27-28). In this way he furnished an explanation of the fact that the Yahwist tribes whose varied traditions he was articulating were known not as the sons of Jacob but as the sons of Israel.

14. Rise of Judah.—J[1]'s representation of the eponym of the unimportant tribe of Reuben as Jacob's first-born was in all probability due to the fact that this east-Jordan tribe was the first Israelite group to claim Jacob as an ancestor. Similarly Simeon and Levi were represented as the second and third sons respectively because they alone were traditionally the sons of Leah (see Exeg. on 29:31–30:24). Historically, leadership among the clans with which J[1] was concerned was exercised by none of these three, but by Judah, whom J[1] had placed as the fourth of Jacob's sons. To account for this J[1] made use of two tribal legends: that of Reuben's violation of his father's concubine (35:22a), and that of the treachery of Simeon and Levi (the Horite story in ch. 34). Whatever the original significance of these tales may have been, for J[1] they explained how Reuben had lost the privilege and prestige belonging to the first-born, which then devolved upon Simeon. But Simeon and Levi also disgraced themselves, and the rights of leadership passed to Judah.

15. Joseph and the Descent into Egypt.—With the story of Tamar, accounting for the

---

[4] In this connection it may be noted that of the stories belonging to the J[1] stratum in the book of Judges, two record events occurring east of the Jordan (Judg. 8:4-21; 11:30-40), and a third is located at the Jordan near Jericho (the basic material in Judg. 3:12-30). J[1] also records Saul's deliverance of Jabesh-gilead (I Sam. 11:1-11).

[5] The early spread of Mosaism east of the Jordan is a fact which may have considerable bearing upon the question as to why the Deuteronomic movement selected the land east of the Jordan as the scene of the second, and, from their point of view, the definitive, lawgiving by Moses.

presence of a Canaanite element in the tribe of Judah (see Exeg. on ch. 38), J¹ completed his articulation of the various local legends of Palestine. This material had now to be linked with the historic Israelite tradition of the Exodus. This was accomplished by means of the story of Joseph, Jacob's fifth son. While J¹ may have been aware of some tradition associating the Shechemite hero Joseph with Egypt, he for the most part depended in this section of his narrative upon his own imagination. He told how Joseph was sold into slavery by his brothers (37:26-27, 28aγ), and was taken to Egypt (39:1), where he rose to a position of power which enabled him to bring his father and his family to Egypt in a time of famine (46:1aα). Their descendants remained there even after Joseph's death (50:24abα, 26aα), and the stage was set for the Exodus.

B. Religion and Theology of J¹. 1. Uniqueness of Yahweh.—The J¹ narrative was thus composed of legends of diverse origin which the author brought together and ordered in such a way as to relate them to the desert tradition of Yahwism and to make them a vehicle for the preservation both of the ancient values of that tradition and of the values with which it had been enriched through its understanding and generous contact with the religion of Canaan. That is, his accomplishment was much more than a literary tour de force. The narrative he produced has a note of authenticity which bears witness to the fact that he really believed the events he recorded were due to the activity of Yahweh, not to the activity of some other god or gods whom he had, by a kind of literary device, identified with Yahweh. In other words, J¹ was religiously a monotheist. Whatever he may have thought of other gods—there is, it should be noted, no mention of them in his narrative—he certainly did not take them seriously. Yahweh was the only supernatural being who counted for anything, and he counted for everything. He was the sole source of power, the arbiter of man's destiny, the fountain of justice. For this reason J¹ was aware of a unity underlying all life and making for order. To the realization of this order, which had its source in Yahweh's will, he dedicated himself, and because of this self-dedication he was able to discern the often hidden meaning of the material lying before him and to weld it into an ordered and meaningful unity.

2. Significance of Human Activity.—And yet in this narrative Yahweh is rarely represented as intervening directly in human affairs. He does so at the dispersal of peoples (11:8), and at the destruction of Sodom (19:1-28), but in both of these stories J¹ was dependent upon previ-

ously existing legends which he was adapting to Yahwism. In his representation that the conception of Isaac was miraculous he was probably dependent upon the inaugural legend of the sanctuary of Hebron (see Exeg. on 18:1-33), for tales of this kind not infrequently ended with the miraculous birth of a son to the couple who had showed hospitality to the visiting stranger.[6] In three other passages (25:21; 29:31; 30:22) dealing with the rise of the second and third generations of Abraham's descendants, he simply follows the pattern laid down in the notice of the conception of Isaac.

The only other case of direct divine intervention is in the call of Abraham (12:1-4a). Here there is no dependence upon an earlier source. The author, as has already been suggested, is giving expression in simple, concrete form to the conviction of his people that they had been chosen by Yahweh. His representation thus rests upon an actual historical experience of divine action.

It may therefore be maintained that J¹ where he is writing freely, not under the necessity of preserving a salient point in an already existing legend, keeps his narrative on a very human level. His consciousness of the will of God as a decisive force in history has not led him to underestimate the importance of human action. Israel is superior to Edom because Jacob, however unscrupulous, was more provident than Esau (25:27, 29-34). Jacob increased his flocks and herds not through a special blessing, but because he was clever enough to outwit Laban (30:29-43). Judah rose to a position of leadership not by divine appointment, but because his three older brothers, Reuben, Simeon, and Levi, in turn forfeited their privileges through lack of respect for another's rights (35:22a; ch. 34; cf. Exeg. on 49:3-8).

The history of Reuben, Simeon, and Levi shows that J¹ did not simply subscribe to the dictum that God helps those who help themselves. On the other hand, he did not believe that divine protection released a man from the necessity of protecting himself and his own interests. It was in these terms, inadequate though they were, that he apprehended the truth that the supernatural does not in its operation displace or destroy the natural, but heightens its capacity.

3. Uniqueness of Israel.—This throws light upon another characteristic of his narrative—an apparently naïve sense of the superiority of Israel to all foreigners. Two of the stories just cited—Jacob's outwitting of Esau (25:27, 29-34)

---

[6] See John Skinner, *A Critical and Exegetical Commentary on Genesis* (rev. ed.; New York: Charles Scribner's Sons, 1925; "International Critical Commentary"), pp. 302-3.

and his successful overreaching of Laban (30:29-43)—illustrate this. In these tales the cleverness of the Israelite Jacob is contrasted with the stupidity of the Edomite Esau and the Aramaean Laban. Other instances of this attitude are the story of Isaac's hoaxing of the Philistines (see Exeg. on 26:1-11), the derisive tale of the stolen teraphim (see Exeg. on 31:17-43),[7] and the account of Jacob's encounter with the shepherds at the well (29:1-12) with its implicit contrast between the hard-working, careful Israelite and the shiftless Aramaean. This however represents something more than a kind of childish, nonmilitary jingoism. Rather, it voices the conviction of J[1] that Israel's prosperity and sense of security were due to a heightening of a native shrewdness through supernatural illumination and endowment. Doubtless his illustrations were not altogether happy. But it should be remembered that he was here making use of folk material. He was aware of what his public wanted, and may well have felt that the inclusion of these stories in his narrative would help toward the popular acceptance of the great truths he was presenting. However that may be, he was on firmer ground when he contrasted Israelite with Canaanite in the tale of Noah's drunkenness (9:20-25) and—though possibly unfairly—Israelite with Moabite and Ammonite in the story of Lot's daughters (19:30-38). Yahwism did make for morality.

4. Definitive Character of Work of J[1].—J[1]'s work was definitive. It is indeed probable that the diverse material contained in his narrative had already been reduced to some kind of order by the priesthood of Hebron before he wrote. If so, then his story when it appeared will have been to some extent a familiar one. Yet the very process of writing it down inevitably involved a considerable degree of editing to provide a smooth transition from one legend to another and to weld them more firmly into a unity. It is, of course, impossible to distinguish J[1]'s own contributions to the unification of the tradition from the work, unwritten, of his predecessors. Nor is there any need here to attempt to do so. What is important is the fact that his narrative both preserved the tradition of the community to which he belonged and, at the same time, established its form and determined the lines of its future development. He secured for all time the position of Abraham as the father of the faithful. Hebron was already in decline when he produced his history, but the prestige of its patron saint remained undiminished because the legend had been reduced to writing, and had been made the legend not of one locality only, but of the community as a whole.

So Abraham of Hebron came to be accepted by the north which had known nothing of him. So Isaac of Beer-sheba—a shadowy figure at best—remained as the second member in the hierarchy of the nation's ancestors. So Jacob retained his role as the father of Joseph of Shechem, despite the latter's commanding position in the tradition of the powerful tribes of Ephraim and Manasseh. The scheme of relationships devised by J[1] became the pattern for all future historians of Israel's beginnings until modern times.

IV. The J[2] Document

A. Purpose and Methods of J[2].—J[1] had been prompted to write his history by the crisis in the fortunes of Hebron occasioned by David's move to his new capital, Jerusalem. It was another and more serious crisis which was responsible for the literary activity of J[2]—the disruption of the kingdom of David and Solomon. J[2] was concerned to counter the blow which this event had administered to the unity of Israel. He set about providing a history which would show that this unity inhered not in the political framework in which it had for a time found partial expression, but in the relationship of the people to Yahweh. He took as the foundation of his new narrative the work of J[1], adding to it myths and legends of various kinds of which J[1] had known nothing, probably because they formed no part of the pastoral tradition of the south.

1. Babylonian Myths.—The first of these tales was, it seems probable,[8] a Canaanite version of the Babylonian creation myth, *Enuma eliš.* The second was the saga of Eden, the garden of God (see Exeg. on ch. 3), also current in Palestine, presumably in Jerusalem and its vicinity. Both of these, it will be seen, J[2] drastically revised to render them more compatible with Yahwism. The revision was carried through with consummate artistry. When the secondary material has been excised from 2:4b-3:24, the narrative which remains is all but flawless. It concludes with the expulsion of the man and his wife from the garden to wrest a living from the ground. Thus, according to J[2], man's first occupation was agriculture. This representation was inconsistent with the scheme of J[1], according to whom man had risen from a cultureless existence first to nomadism (4:20) and only later to agriculture (see Exeg. on 5:29). To resolve this contradiction J[2] made use of the story of Cain and Abel, according to which Cain—in the J[2] context the sole representative of the human race—had been condemned to live the life of "a fugitive

[7] With these may be compared the earliest stratum of the Samson cycle (Judg. 13–16).

[8] See the article "The Growth of the Hexateuch," pp. 194-95, also Exeg. on 1:1–2:4a; 2:4b-25.

and a wanderer on the earth" (4:12), that is, to a life without security and without culture.

At this point J[2] caught up the narrative of his predecessor and told of man's rise through nomadism to agriculture again. The material added by J[2] to his predecessor's simple narrative is then the nucleus of 2:4b–3:23; 4:2-12, 16; and possibly some of the names in 4:18, 26. J[2] also inserted a third myth of Babylonian origin, the story of the Flood, purging it of all suggestion of polytheism and divine caprice, and representing the catastrophe as sent by Yahweh to punish human wickedness (see Exeg. on 6:5–9:19). To tie this in with the earlier narrative he identified the hero of the Flood with Noah, the discoverer of agriculture and viticulture in the J[1] tradition. Then, following the tale of Canaan's impiety (9:20-25) taken over from the document of his predecessor, he gave a brief list of the descendants of the three sons of Noah (see Exeg. on 10:1-32) —thus revealing an interest in the world outside of Israel considerably greater and more objective than that of J[1]. This was followed by the stories of the dispersal of peoples (11:2-8), and of the origin of the Nephilim (6:1-4), both taken over with some elaboration from the earlier narrative.

2. Literary Skill of J[2]—Up to this point J[2] has simply expanded the J[1] narrative by adding to it material chiefly of Babylonian origin. His treatment of the history of the patriarchs is more varied. First of all may be noted the passages by which the transition from legend to legend was made more smooth and the narrative as a whole more carefully articulated. The outstanding instance is the tale of Jacob's deception of Isaac (the earlier strand of 27:1-45), with which belongs the story of his meeting and reconciliation with Esau (the earlier strand of 32:3-23; 33:1-15). To bring Jacob into contact with Laban, J[1] had simply stated that he went to the land of the people of the east (29:1). J[2] provided a motive for his journey—his fear of his brother whom he had defrauded—being careful later, artist that he was, to tell how the feud between them was resolved. At the same time he elaborated the tale of Jacob's meeting with Rachel so as to explain how Jacob had recognized her as his cousin (29:3-6) —a point which J[1] had left unexplained.

Again, J[1] had linked the legend of Hebron and Sodom by making the man saved from the overthrow of the city Abraham's nephew, and by identifying the strangers whom he had protected with the three visitors to Hebron, who had gone from there directly to Sodom. J[2], by inserting 18:16, 20-21, 33b, tightened this connection: the Lord and his companions had been on their way to Sodom when they stopped at Hebron.

Once more J[1], to identify the son promised to Abraham with Isaac, had simply recorded Abraham's journey to Beer-lahai-roi (see Exeg. on 20:1a) and Sarah's words at the child's birth, "every one who hears will laugh over me" (21:6b). J[2] added the story of Sarah's incredulous laughter when she overheard the promise made to Abraham by his as yet unrecognized guest (18:10-15).

3. Activity of Yahweh in History.—This little story provides an instance also of J[2]'s care to stress the often hidden activity of the Lord which J[1] had been content to take for granted. For it is to be noted that in 18:10-15 it is explicitly stated that the Lord himself is the speaker. In contrast to this is the consistent use of the plural in vss. 2, 4-9. That is, J[1], after prefixing vs. 1a to the old Hebron saga, had made no distinction between the three visitors and had preserved the traditional representation that Abraham had not had the slightest idea that they were divine, let alone that one of them was the Lord. J[2], concerned lest the point of the J[1] story should be missed—that the birth of the heir to the promise had been made possible only by the intervention of the Lord himself—cast 18:10-15 in the singular. At the same time he added to Abraham's greeting of his guests the words in vs. 3—the use of the singular distinguishes between the Lord and his companions—to underline the fact of the Lord's presence.

Another instance of J[2]'s concern that the will of God should be recognized as the determining factor in life is provided by his treatment of the story of the birth of Esau and Jacob (25:21-26a). J[1] had explained the fact that Israel, not Edom, had inherited the divine promise by the tale of Esau's selling his birthright (25:29-34). His explanation was thus on a purely human level, to say nothing of its dubious morality. J[2], by inserting 25:22-23, represented the relative positions of the two peoples as having been determined and divinely revealed before the birth of their respective ancestors. Esau's surrender of his rights at Jacob's heartless insistence was thus emptied of any significance. So, too, was the story of the deception of Isaac (27:1-40), which J[2] was to include for reasons already noted, and which ascribed Israel's favored position to a father's blessing, however fraudulently obtained.

This desire to stress the part played by the Lord in human affairs underlies the occasional, smaller additions which J[2] made to the earlier narrative. Examples of this kind of material are: the words "the Lord being merciful to him" in 19:16; "and the Lord has blessed you wherever I turned" (30:30), explicitly ascribing the increase of Laban's wealth not to Jacob's work, but primarily to divine favor; and 31:3, representing Jacob's decision to return home as being due not to his realization that he would be safer out of Laban's reach, but to God's command.

4. Moral Sensitivity of J².—Of a character similar to this theological editing are the additions which J² made to five of J¹'s stories which he found morally disturbing. In three of these—the story of Jacob's outwitting of Laban (30:27-43), that of Rachel's theft of the teraphim (31:19-35), and that of Judah and Tamar (ch. 38)—his purpose is to mitigate the very dubious conduct of the two patriarchs. In the fourth—that of the seduction of Dinah (the earlier strand of ch. 34—his concern is to correct what appeared to him to be the too lenient judgment of J¹ as to the seriousness of the sexual offense. This he does by justifying to some extent the conduct of Simeon and Levi. In the fifth—the story of Joseph's rejection of the advances of his master's wife (ch. 39)—he emphasizes the virtue of his hero. Allied with these additions is the revision to which J² subjected the tale of Jacob's wrestling at the Jabbok (32:24-31).

5. Uniqueness of Israel.—Another notable addition by J² to the document lying before him was the story of Isaac's marriage (the earlier strand of 24:2-67; note also the implications in 22:20; 24:1; 25:5). Its significance lies in the fact that it bears witness to an increased concern, over that shown by J¹, for the purity of Israelite blood. It may indeed be questioned whether J¹ had been concerned with this at all. True, he tells of Jacob going to the land of the people of the east, where he falls in with his kinsfolk and takes as his wives the two daughters of Laban. But, as has been suggested above, his primary reason for having Jacob make this journey was to bring him into contact with Laban so that the east-Jordan tradition of the covenant of Gilead (the earlier strand of 31:44-55) might be recorded. His identification of Leah and Rachel as Laban's daughters appears to have been made for the purpose of unifying his narrative; at any rate, he nowhere stresses the fact that they were Aramaean, not Canaanite, as he would presumably have done had he attached any importance to this supposed fact.

But though J¹'s representation of Jacob's wives as of nomad origin thus seems to have been merely an accidental result of the necessity he was under to unify the diverse material he was using, it appears to have taken on a significance of its own as time passed: Jacob's wives were not Canaanites; they were of the same stock as Abraham. This gave rise to a self-conscious concern to maintain the purity of that stock, and from this developed the tale in ch. 24, which is thus dependent on that in 29:1-14, 26—a dependence which manifests itself further in the motif of the meeting at the well (a prominent feature in both tales).

6. The Tradition of Beer-sheba.—In the J² narrative this account of the marriage of Isaac is immediately preceded by a story which ascribes to Abraham the founding of Beer-sheba (the earlier strand of 21:22-33, with which belongs the secondary harmonizing material in 26:12-33). J¹ had not associated Abraham with that sanctuary. According to him Beer-sheba was founded by Isaac (26:31-33). In assigning this role to Abraham (21:33), J² was presumably dependent upon a development in the local tradition which had occurred in the course of the century intervening between J¹ and himself. This development was, it may be assumed, due to the activity of the priesthood of Hebron in its endeavor to preserve and to establish the unity of Yahwism. This, as has been seen, had led to the representation of Abraham as the father of Isaac. Apparently such a representation had not accomplished its purpose, so a further modification was introduced: Abraham himself was made the founder of Beer-sheba. This was in effect to claim that Beer-sheba—and its priesthood—stemmed from, and so was subject to the control of, Hebron. How far the priesthood of Hebron succeeded in implementing the claim it is impossible to say. The fact that J² included in his narrative another, less creditable, story which had been carried over from Isaac to Abraham—that of his representing his wife as his sister (12:10–13:1; cf. 26:1-12)—is significant in this connection. It is in the highest degree improbable that J² would have tolerated this very questionable tale. He can only have included it because of popular pressure. That such pressure was brought to bear at this point would seem to indicate that the claim of the priesthood of Hebron had been effective to this extent, that Abraham had supplanted Isaac in the popular mind as the hero of Beer-sheba.

It would thus appear that J², concerned to have the J¹ tradition of the south accepted in the north, found himself compelled to take full account of the tradition then current at Beer-sheba. The reason for this can only be surmised. It is possible that the claim of Hebron to ecclesiastical pre-eminence (see Exeg. on 12:6-8) was offensive to the northerners. If so, the unique position of that sanctuary in the J¹ narrative will have militated against their acceptance of that tradition. By representing Beer-sheba as of equal rank with Hebron, J² deprived the latter sanctuary of its uniqueness and undercut its claims. At the same time he enlisted Beer-sheba on his side. Now Beer-sheba at a later date had some special connection with the north: witness the statement in I Kings 19:3—in itself quite unnecessary to the narrative as a whole—that Elijah stopped there on his way to Horeb; the mention of the sanctuary along with Bethel, Gilgal, Samaria, and Dan in Amos 5:5; 8:14; and the references to Isaac in Amos 7:9, 16. It is impossible to say whether at the time J² wrote Beer-sheba was already held in special reverence in the north. If it was, then J²'s respect for its tradition is explained.

7. *Ishmael.*—Another story added by J² to the work of his predecessor was that of the birth of Ishmael (16:1b-2, 4-8, 11-12). This tale obviously originated among the Ishmaelites. The facts (*a*) that J² included it in his narrative, (*b*) that in so doing he associated Ishmael with Abraham—no feature of the tale in its primary form (see Exeg. on 16:11-16)—and so with Isaac, and (*c*) that the Ishmaelites lived in the desert to the south of Palestine in which Beer-sheba was situated, suggest that the story formed part of the tradition of that sanctuary. If so, then its preservation by J² provides further evidence of the weight he attached to that tradition. It is also an additional indication of his interest in the non-Israelite world, already revealed by his listing of the descendants of Noah.

8. *The Tradition of the North.*—The remaining material which J² added to the patriarchal narrative was inserted to bring it into closer agreement with the traditions of the north. His story of Jacob at Bethel (28:13-16, 19) reflects the legendary association of the patriarch with that sanctuary. His additions to the chronicle of the birth of Jacob's children (the earlier strand of 30:1-30) account for certain Israelite tribes of which J¹ had known nothing. So, too, does his story of the birth of Benjamin. Only a fragment (35:17) of this survives, but it may safely be assumed—in view of the parallel E narrative (35:16, 18-20), and of the reference to Rachel's grave in a later part of the J document (I Sam. 10:2)—that J² here told of Rachel's death in childbirth and of her burial. The story thus not only accounts for the tribe of Benjamin; it also preserves the local tradition of Ephrath.

9. *Joseph and the Tradition of Shechem.*—One of the sacred places of Shechem was the grave of Joseph. Of this J¹ appears to have known nothing, tacitly assuming that he was buried in Egypt. J², having recorded Jacob's purchase of a piece of ground at Shechem (33:19), tells of the dying Joseph's directions as to the ultimate disposal of his body (50:25, 26b),

and later records their fulfillment (Exod. 13:19; Josh. 24:32).

The Shechemite tradition of Joseph appears to have placed the misadventure which had brought him to Egypt at Dothan (see Exeg. on ch. 37). Of this also J¹ seems to have been ignorant, for he located the event in the south. J² therefore corrected the apparent error (37:15-17). At the same time he greatly elaborated his predecessor's account of Joseph's dealings with his brothers. In this he was motivated by his concern that his narrative should be accepted by the great tribes of Ephraim and Manasseh (cf. especially the earlier strand of ch. 48). He was also availing himself of an opportunity to allow his literary powers full expression; for here, scarcely hampered by already existing traditions, he could at last write freely.

B. *Additions to the J² Document.*—Except for the material in ch. 15 and the poem in ch. 49, only minor additions were made to that part of the J² document now preserved in Genesis before it was conflated with a new history which was written in the north some two hundred years later, early in the seventh century, the E document (see article "The Growth of the Hexateuch," pp. 196-97).

V. The E Document

A. *Purpose and Methods of E.*—There is no trace of E in chs. 1–11. Since it is unlikely that RJE would have thus completely ignored his treatment of the prepatriarchal period had such existed, it may safely be assumed that this part of the J narrative created no difficulty in the north, and so was tacitly accepted. It was only with the story of Abraham that difficulties first made themselves felt; and it was with Abraham that the E narrative began.

1. *The Horeb Tradition.*—Its most notable divergence from the J tradition is its consistent use of "Elohim" instead of "Yahweh" in the stories of the patriarchs and up to the point of the explicit revelation of the divine name to Moses (Exod. 3:13-15). What the author here had in mind it is difficult to say. The fact that in the narrative of the Exodus he designates Horeb, not Sinai, as the mount of God, suggests that he is depending in part upon the traditions of a group in the north of another origin than the tribes which had come from Sinai.

It is of course possible that Yahweh, the storm god, had come to be identified with the deity of Horeb while the ancestors of this group were still ranging the desert in the vicinity of that mountain—that is, that the identification made at Sinai was duplicated at Horeb. It is also possible that the god of Horeb was identified not directly with the storm god but with the god of

Sinai—that is, that one mountain deity was identified with another. But the acceptance of either of these possible explanations would demand the further acceptance of a somewhat remarkable coincidence. For it would mean that the identification of the god of Horeb with the god of Sinai, whether directly or indirectly, had been followed by the movement, quite independently, of the worshipers of both deities to Palestine. It seems therefore more probable that the god of Horeb was first identified with Yahweh the God of Sinai subsequent to the settlement of his devotees in Palestine. If this is the case, then Exod. 3:13-15 will have been E's justification of the identification, and his use of "Elohim" up to this point will have been merely incidental.

2. Yahweh and the Deities of Canaan.—There is another possibility: that E was aware of and wished to stress the fact that many of the legends concerning the patriarchs had once been associated with deities other than Yahweh. The memory of this fact may have lingered longer in the north than in the south, where it had grown dim—if it had not, indeed. completely disappeared—as a result of the literary activity of J[1] and J[2], whose tacit identification of these deities with Yahweh had been thoroughly accepted. In the north, where the J document was not well known, the popular mind may well have been still in the same uncertainty as to the relationships between Yahweh and the ancient local deities as the southern mind had presumably been before J[1] wrote. A third consideration may have influenced E, namely his realization that the work of Moses had so profoundly affected Yahwism as to make it almost a new religion. E, it seems likely, would have been more acutely aware of this fact than J[2] had been. For J[2] was presumably a southerner, and the Yahwist tradition of the south had been, not only since but even before the entry into Palestine, a Mosaic tradition. That is, for J[2] Mosaic Yahwism was normal Yahwism. E's background was different. He was a northerner, and for some hundreds of years after the Conquest the Yahwism of the north had remained, predominantly at least, crisis Yahwism, and had not been enriched by the ideas of Mosaism until the time of David.

3. Importance of Beer-sheba.—E's most notable departure from J[2] in the Abraham stories is his omission of all reference to Hebron. Beersheba was the patriarch's only dwelling place in Palestine. While this omission may have been polemic in its intent, it seems more likely that E was simply recording the Abraham tradition as it was current in the north. The connection between Beer-sheba and the north has already been noted. It will have been through Beer-sheba that Abraham had come to be known in the north at all: the legends regarding him had been carried back there by pilgrims returning from the southern sanctuary. Thus, E's silence may reflect a certain rivalry between Hebron and Beer-sheba as well as northern hostility to Hebron.

E followed J[2] in associating Isaac, and through him Abraham, with Beer-lahai-roi (see Exeg. on 16:13-14), and in recording Abraham's imperiling of his wife (20:1*b*-16). This event he located not in Egypt, as J[2] had done (12:10-20), but, following the parallel story of Isaac (26:1-11), in Gerar. This change appears to have only a literary significance in that it is the result of a fusing of the two stories, both of which E found in the J narrative lying before him.

4. Concern for the Reputation of the Patriarchs.—Much more significant is his attempt to provide some justification for Abraham by his representation that Sarah was indeed his half sister (20:12). This is the first instance of E's consistent endeavor to rehabilitate the moral reputation of the patriarchs, whose conduct at certain points still remained somewhat dubious in J[2]'s narrative despite his efforts, noted above, to mitigate the effects of J[1]'s earthy appreciation of a good story told at a foreigner's expense. Other instances of this kind of revision on the part of E are his attributing to Rebekah the major role in the deception of Isaac (see Exeg. on 27:1-40); his drastic rewriting of the Jacob-Laban story so that it no longer told of one rogue trying to outwit another but depicted Jacob as the innocent victim of Laban's duplicity, from the full consequences of which he was protected only by divine intervention (see Exeg. on 29:15–31:55); his representation that Joseph was kidnaped by a passing caravan of traders, not deliberately sold by his brothers (37:28*a*α*β*); and his omission of what seemed to him to be the needlessly cruel incident of the placing of Joseph's cup in Benjamin's sack.

5. Dislike of the Sex Motif.—Similarly motivated was his omission of the stories of the destruction of Sodom (19:1-28), of Lot and his daughters (19:30-38), of Reuben's impiety (35:22*a*), of the seduction of Dinah (the earlier strand of ch. 34), of Judah and Tamar (ch. 38), and of the temptation of Joseph by his master's wife (39:1-20), in all of which sex provided the dominant motif. The tale of Jacob's wrestling at the Jabbok was dropped, doubtless because of the theological difficulties it occasioned.

6. Humanism.—The only story of Abraham peculiar to E is that of the testing of his faith when he was commanded by God to sacrifice Isaac (22:1-14, 19). It will be argued in the

Exegesis on the passage that E was here making use of the inaugural legend of the sanctuary of the oak of Moreh near Shechem. He has, however, told it in such a way that his own awareness of the place of human relationships in religion shines through it. The love of a father for his son was not a matter of no concern to God. So, too, into his version of the Hagar-Ishmael story (21:8-21) he has introduced a note of tenderness which was lacking in the more rugged narrative of J². Both these tales thus reflect the sense of the humane, of the value of the natural virtues, the claim of which could not be ignored. Such other minor changes as E introduced into the narrative were designed either to bring it more into accord with the popular thinking of the north or to underline certain of the theological ideas to which J² had given expression.

B. Conflation of the J and E Documents.—Very few additions were made to the E patriarchal narrative—the more important of them are noted in the Exegesis—before it was combined with the J document. As to the work of the redactor R^JE, responsible for this conflation, little need be added to what has been said in the article "The Growth of the Hexateuch" (see p. 197). His method was, clearly, to preserve the salient points of both narratives so as to secure the acceptance of his composition by both the south and the north, upon whose traditions J and E respectively depended.

VI. The P Document

A. Purpose and Methods of P.—That the P document was a rewriting of the tradition of the south is indicated by the fact that it associates Abraham exclusively with Hebron, and that in the Exodus narrative it places the great revelation to Moses at Sinai, not at Horeb.

1. Creation and Flood Stories.—The author drastically revised the J story of Creation, purging it of certain mythological elements which J² had apparently found it necessary to retain. The result—whether immediately or after some further redaction (see Exeg. on 1:1–2:3)—was the narrative, austere in its grandeur, with which the book opens.

That the story in 1:1–2:3 is in some way dependent upon the Babylonian creation myth *Enuma elis* [9] becomes apparent when a comparison is made of the two documents.

The Babylonian tale begins with a description of primeval chaos, personalized as Apsu and Tiamat, and of the evolution therefrom of several generations of deities, culminating in the supreme triad of the Babylonian pantheon, Anu, Bel, and Ea, and the sun-god Marduk. The powers of chaos attempting to destroy the heavenly deities, Apsu is subdued, and Tiamat, renewing the struggle, is slain by Marduk, who splits her carcass in two, making one half into a covering for the heavens and the other half the earth. He then creates the stars to regulate time, and the moon to rule the night. Finally, after declaring his intention to Ea, he creates man, taking for this purpose his own blood. In the hymn of praise to Marduk with which this recension closes the creation of vegetation is ascribed to him, but it is impossible to say at what point in the process this occurred owing to the illegibility of some parts of the tablets upon which the epic is preserved.

The points at which the narrative of 1:1–2:3 most clearly echoes this epic may be briefly noted. (a) The notion of a primeval watery chaos as the substance of which the earth was made (cf. 1:2), and the etymological equivalence of the Babylonian *ti'āmat* and the Hebrew word *tehôm*—"the deep." There is in Genesis, however, no reference to Apsu, perhaps because of the relative insignificance of the role played by him in the parent myth. On the other hand, it is possible that the representation of "the Spirit of God . . . moving over the face of the waters" (1:2) may be dependent upon the reference to Apsu's mingling his waters with those of Tiamat to beget heaven and earth.[10] (b) The representation that the firmament—the covering for the heavens—is a solid substance (cf. 1:6-7). (c) The purpose of the heavenly bodies —to regulate time and, in the case of the moon, to rule the night (cf. 1:14-18). (d) The representation that Marduk before making man, using his own blood, took counsel with Ea, which finds an echo in "Let us make man in our image" (1:26).

In view of the fact that the P Code was written in Babylonia during, and in the years immediately succeeding, the Exile,[11] it is difficult to believe that an author as Jewish as its author was would deliberately have made use of foreign material derived from the polytheistic environment in which he was living. It would seem, therefore, that the Babylonian epic which echoes throughout his story of Creation must earlier have become a part of Israel's cultural and religious heritage.

Now it is significant that 2:4b, derived from J, simply assumes, without describing, the making of "earth and heaven"—so the Hebrew, literally, not "the earth and the heavens"

---

[9] The parts of this document most relevant to our purpose are given in a translation in Skinner, *Genesis*, pp. 43-47. Skinner also reproduces (pp. 41-42) two Greek versions—by Berossus and Damascius—of this cosmogony.

[10] See Skinner, *Genesis*, p. 43.

[11] See article "The Growth of the Hexateuch," pp. 198-200.

(KJV, RSV)—an expression which, it may be noted, indicates that the half verse is from another source than 1:1–2:3, in which "the heavens and the earth" (1:1, RSV; 2:1) is used.

Since this can scarcely be all that J had to say about the origin of the universe, it may reasonably be assumed that 2:4b was preceded in his narrative by a saga of Creation—which has been completely suppressed by RP in favor of the P story now under consideration. What the content of J's saga was can only be conjectured, but Karl Marti,[12] commenting on Isa. 51:9, has argued cogently that, in view of Deutero-Isaiah's use of J,[13] it was a version of the Babylonian myth and told of God's destruction of the chaos monster, personalized, it would appear, as Rahab.[14]

Since the J document was written in the tenth or the ninth century B.C., before Israel had had any direct contact with Babylonia, it must be assumed that the myth had earlier found its way to Palestine and formed part of the culture of the land into which Israel entered at the Conquest. J, writing in the interest of Israelite monotheism, was compelled to take account of it and to relate it to Yahwism.

Consideration will be given to J's adaptation and revision of the myth in the Exegesis on 2:4b-25. Before this is undertaken, however, some further attention must be given to P's use of the story, now lost, which it is assumed he found at the beginning of the J narrative.

It is probable that 1:2 is not from P's hand (see Exeg.). That is, he seems to have carefully omitted any explicit reference to a primeval chaos from which the world was created and to have limited himself to an extremely cryptic allusion to it in 1:1, 4, 6, 9. The fact that 1:2 was later inserted indicates that the older form of the tale died hard.[15]

[12] *Das Buch Jesaja* (Tübingen: J. C. B. Mohr, 1900; "Kurzer Hand-Commentar zum Alten Testament"), pp. 338-39.

[13] Cf. Isa. 41:8; 43:16-20; 51:1-2; and see Bernhard Duhm, *Das Buch Jesaia* (4th ed.; Göttingen: Vandenhoeck & Ruprecht, 1922; "Göttinger Handkommentar"), *ad loc.*

[14] References to the monster Rahab in the O.T. are Job 26:12; Ps. 89:10; Isa. 51:9; possibly also Job 9:13; the name is used referring to Egypt in Ps. 87:4, and cryptically in Isa. 30:7.

[15] That the myth of the conquest of chaos had a remarkable hold upon the Israelite mind is evidenced by (a) the allusions to Yahweh's subjection of the monster in Ps. 74:13-15—according to Isa. 27:1, a feat which will be repeated at the time of the end; (b) the references to the monster in Job 3:8; 7:12; 41:1-8; Ps. 104:26; Amos 9:3; (c) the use of the motif in Ezek. 29:3-7; 32:2-10; (d) the references to God's ordering of the waters in Job 38:10-11; Pss. 18:15; 33:6-7; 65:7; 104:5-9; Prov. 8:29; Jer 5:22; Nah. 1:4; Hab. 3:10; Ecclus. 43:23; Prayer of Manasses; (e) the representation of the time of the end as a resurgence of chaos in Ps. 46 (cf. Isa. 27:1); and (f) the similar depiction of the last unrest

But not only did P omit any reference to chaos; by his representation that the world was created by simple fiat—"And God said 'Let there be. . . .' And it was so" (1:3, 6, 7b, 9, 11, 14a, 15b, 20, 24)—he eliminated any suggestion of physical activity on the part of God. That this austere record of command and realization was for the average reader too far removed from the colorful myth is suggested by the fact that into it a later writer intruded vss. 7a, 12a, 16a, 17a, 18a, 21abα (without "the great sea monsters and"), 25a—a significant reminder of the need for anthropomorphism in religion. Certainly the material with which the account of the making of the heavenly bodies—vss. 14b, 15a, 16b, 17b—was subsequently elaborated is drawn from the earlier form of the myth, as is the mention of "the great sea monsters" in vs. 21.

A further point to be noted is the compression of eight creative acts into six days.[16] This, of course, was to make possible the representation that God rested on the seventh day, hallowing it as the sabbath, which is thus presented as his final creative act.

Finally the notice in 1:29-30, the evidence for the secondary character of which is noted in the Exegesis, was added to the P narrative, possibly, as is there suggested, to supply a reference, however faint, to the J story of man's blissful life in the garden.

Omitting the story of the Fall, P revised and elaborated the J genealogical list of the descendants of the first man to fill in the period extending from the Creation to the Flood (5:1-28a, 30-32). The account of the Flood he likewise revised, heightening the element of the miraculous and reducing the role of Noah to one of little more than automatic obedience to a succession of divine commands (see Exeg. on 6:5–9:19). He then listed the descendants of Noah (the late strand of ch. 10) and traced the line through the first-born in each generation from Shem, Noah's eldest son, to Terah, the father of Abram.

2. *The Patriarchs.*—In his account of the patriarchs P omitted all reference to sanctuaries and their altars. According to his schematization of the history of Israel, no sacrifice was offered to Yahweh until Moses received directions

of the nations in Isa. 5:30; 17:12-14; on these passages see Hermann Gunkel, *Genesis* (5th ed.; Göttingen: Vandenhoeck & Ruprecht, 1922; "Göttinger Handkommentar"), pp. 121-22.

[16] This perhaps raises the question whether the narrative which forms the nucleus of the present story, and which has been taken above as the work of the author of the P Code in its primary form, may not be rather an earlier revision of the myth as it appeared in J, which was then taken over by P, elaborated as noted above, and made into an account of creation not in eight days but in six.

thereto at Sinai. He did not argue the case for a single sanctuary, much less fulminate against those who opposed it. His polemic took the form of the implied assertion that the patriarchs could not have erected altars—and that therefore the claim of any sanctuary to have been founded by one of the fathers was false. He also omitted all stories reflecting unfavorably upon the moral character of his heroes as well as other legends and folk tales which had been included in the J document because of their popular appeal. P was not interested in this kind of thing. Consequently he reduced the rich and varied narrative of the J document to a bare skeleton outline, expanding it only to provide divine sanction for the custom of circumcision (ch. 17), and to assert the people's claim to the sepulcher of their ancestors at Hebron (ch. 23). Except at these two points his narrative is dry as dust. Everything that happened happened by plan. His characters are little more than lay figures making certain necessary motions in preparation for the great revelation to come at Sinai. Abraham comes to Palestine, begets two sons, and dies. Ishmael is retired from the scene, and Isaac begets two sons and dies. Esau moves to Edom, and Jacob begets twelve sons and in course of time goes down into Egypt, where he dies. The Exodus follows.

The only additions of importance made to this narrative before its conflation with JE were the story of the covenant with the Shechemites (see Exeg. on ch. 34) and the notices stating the ages of the patriarchs at certain points in their respective careers. The former seems to have been in the nature of an overture to the leaders of the still embryonic Samaritan schism. The notices reveal an interest in chronology which possibly developed in compensation for the lack of the interest in places—the sanctuaries—which had characterized the earlier documents.

B. Completion of the Book.—The P document is the framework of the present narrative of Genesis. Into it the redactor RP fitted the older JE history, making occasional adaptations to reconcile his sources. Subsequently the story of the war of the kings (ch. 14) was added, and the book as it now exists was substantially completed. It stands as a monument to the piety, the wisdom, and the ability of a long line of writers, unknown to us by name, who in successive generations accepted the task of bearing witness to, and explaining, the unshakable conviction of Israel that she had, by a divine act of choice, been brought into a unique relationship with the God whom she had come to apprehend as the one and only God, the creator,

the redeemer, the ultimate controller of history, just, righteous, and loving, ever working to make men just, righteous, and loving in all their dealings, and to bring them to offer themselves to him in worship. Only through the worshipful acknowledgment of God's majesty and love could men be freed from pride and self-concern and receive the "power to become children of God" (John 1:12).

VII. Importance of Documentary Analysis

In the Exegesis considerable attention is paid to the sources from which the stories in their present form have been built up. The purpose of this is not merely to satisfy the academic interest of the commentator. It is to show how the religious and moral conscience of Israel developed in response to her deepening apprehension of the being and character of God. This development has been to some extent obscured by the redactors who combined the source documents, with the result that at certain points in the present narrative the impression is conveyed that the sometimes extremely dubious conduct of the patriarchs has been accepted without misgivings. But as the Exegesis of the Jacob-Esau and Jacob-Laban stories, for example, shows (25:21–33:16), both J² and E were often gravely disturbed at the moral implications of the traditions with which they were dealing.

Had the three documents, J¹, J², and E, been preserved intact, it would have been much less difficult to detect the concern of J² as regards certain of the details in the J¹ tradition, and to discern the drastic character of the measures taken by E to free the patriarchs from the charge of moral laxity. The method adopted here of breaking the narrative down into its component sources will, it is hoped, make more clear the way in which the religious and moral insight of the leaders of Israel deepened as they grew in the knowledge of God.

It need not be supposed that the moral sensitivity of the redactors was less than that of J², E, and P. RJE was faced with the necessity of combining two documents, J and E, in such a way as to secure the acceptance of his work by the two groups whose traditions they respectively embodied. This demanded the construction of a unified narrative in which, nevertheless, the salient points of each tradition would be preserved. That is, RJE conceived of the task as primarily a literary one, and he accomplished it with extraordinary skill. It may be doubted whether, engrossed as he was in reconciling the contradictions and inconsistencies presented by the two documents lying before him, he was aware of the occasionally unfortunate ethical implications of his own narrative. However that may be, the limitations imposed upon him by the historical situation in which he was working made it impossible for him entirely to avoid this consequence of the method he necessarily employed. And the same thing is true, *mutatis mutandis,* of R^P.

VIII. Theological Significance of Genesis

In what sense can it be claimed that the authors who contributed to the building up of the present book of Genesis were inspired?

In the search for an answer to this question—and it is a question of fundamental importance—this fact must be borne in mind: that it is only in the Bible as a whole, not in any part of it, let alone in any one of its books, that we find the Word of God in its fullness. That word came "at sundry times and in divers manners" (Heb. 1:1) to a long succession of men. It came with power—with power to deal with certain concrete, historical situations, to judge them and to shape them so that they would contribute to the fulfillment of God's purpose. That purpose was not clear for centuries. To each of the biblical writers was revealed just so much as he needed to know to achieve the work God was calling him to do. Indeed, it may be doubted whether with fuller knowledge he could have accomplished his work.

That is to say, inspiration was historically conditioned. Consequently, to answer the question stated above, "In what sense can it be claimed that the authors who contributed to the building up of the present book of Genesis were inspired?" full account must be taken of the historical situation in which each of them worked, and with which he was called to deal.

A. Work of J^1.—J^1 was called to relate the Yahwism of the desert, with its drive toward monotheism, to the life of Palestine. He was inspired to recognize the values of that life and the insights of its religion. He was inspired to draw out the implications of his own inarticulate monotheism, and to identify the deities worshiped at the local sanctuaries with Yahweh. He was inspired to see that Yahwism was something greater than a wilderness religion, that it was the religion which alone could give meaning to the new life into which Israel had entered. He was inspired to lead Yahwism to take the first of the steps by which it ceased to be the religion of one people and became a religion for all men. He was inspired to begin the fashioning of the national community of Israel into a world-wide community in which all nations would find their true meaning.

It is clear from the Bible as a whole that the fashioning of such a community was necessary to the process of man's redemption. The individual is to be redeemed from the self-centeredness which issues in sin, through membership in a saving community. And a saving community is a community which finds its meaning not in itself but in God, and which recognizes that the reason for which it exists is not its own aggrandizement but the furthering of God's purpose of redemption. J^1, by his recognition of the values of Canaanite religion and culture, and by his simple, unaffected appropriation of those values for Yahwism, fructified the tough desert mentality of the community of Israel and helped to create that attitude of receptivity to new ideas without which it could never have transcended the limitations of its origins to become a community of world-wide significance. There can be no doubt that the work of J^1 furthered the process of redemption.

B. Work of J^2.—So, too, did the work of J^2. His concern, as has been seen, was for the spiritual unity of Israel, and he did much to preserve, strengthen, and deepen it. In his taking over of the Babylonian myths current in Palestine and his adaptation of them to Yahwism, he carried further the work begun by J^1 when he had identified the local deities of Canaan with Yahweh: Yahweh was active not only in the desert and in Palestine, but also far to the east in Mesopotamia.

Little need be added here to what has already been said regarding J^2's insistence upon the activity of Yahweh in history, his moral sensitivity, and his conviction as to the uniqueness of Israel.[17] In all this he was underlining and clarifying the meaning, vocation, and experience of the saving community to which he belonged. Outside the Bible inspiration need not have been claimed for him. Within the Bible the fact of his inspiration is so obvious that it need only be mentioned. Even his literary skill noted above is relevant in this connection. The fact that writing of this kind is found nowhere in ancient literature outside the literature of the Hebrews warrants the claim that J^2's artistry derived from his religion—that is, that it was the fruit of inspiration—for it was its religion and only its religion which distinguished the culture of Israel from that of the surrounding peoples. This being so, the skill of J^2 reveals something of the meaning of life and the meaning of redemption. The redeemed life must be an ordered life, sensitive to beauty. Oafishness and ugliness are not attributes of redemption.

[17] By his use later in his document (Exod. 34:10) of the idea of the covenant, he gave concrete expression to the faith of the religious leaders of the community that the significance of Israel was to be found in its relationship to God, and that it was not simply one national community among many, but that from its beginning it had had a supranational vocation.

C. Work of E.—The same considerations apply to E as applied to J¹ and J², especially if, as is suggested in the article "The Growth of the Hexateuch" (see pp. 196-97), E wrote for the benefit of the northern community during the period of its reconstruction following the fall of Samaria.

D. Work of RJE.—The redactor RJE, who conflated the J and the E documents, was, as has been noted in the article just mentioned, concerned with building into a unity the northern and southern groups in Palestine during the Exile. His aim was to remove the hazard to unity presented by variant traditions. How great the hazard was, how tenaciously the two groups clung to their respective traditions, is shown by the fact that RJE found it necessary to preserve certain features of the J document which must have been morally repugnant to him. This reveals in turn how crucially important he believed a unified community to be. To claim inspiration for him, therefore—and the claim must be made in view of the place of the community in the biblical scheme of salvation—is to recognize by implication the evil of schism—For RJE the unity of the people of God must be maintained, even at the cost of the formal retention of dubious traditions. It might be hoped that these could later be corrected; in the meantime, the tares must be allowed to grow with the wheat.

E. Work of P.—The concern of the writer of the P document for the community needs no stressing. In this he stands in line with his predecessors. In his tacit insistence upon the sole legality of one sanctuary—by implication, Jerusalem—he affirms the need for unity. A world-wide community could have only one center. Doubtless he was influenced by his concern for the prestige of Jerusalem and its priesthood. Nevertheless, it would be doing him an injustice to assert that it was nothing more than ecclesiastical jealousy that prompted him to reject the traditions which ascribed to the patriarchs the founding of certain ancient sanctuaries outside of Jerusalem. He may well have believed that these traditions must be false; in any case, he regarded them as harmful. And unlike RJE he felt that the time had come to root out the tares from the wheat.

But there is another aspect to this part of his work. So long as the ancient traditions associating the patriarchs with the local sanctuaries remained living traditions, just so long the tendency to regard Israel as primarily a national community would persist. For P, however, Israel was a world-wide community, and it had come into being not as the result of historical circumstance but by an act of God. The Palestinian community of the fifth century B.C. was informed by the spirit of Deuteronomy.[18] And Deuteronomy, for all its recognition of the mighty acts of God in the founding of the community, is far more nationalist in its overtones than is P. The leaders of the Deuteronomic school, never having lived in a foreign land, were far less sensitive to the problem of Israel's relationship and mission to the Gentiles than was P. It was to fit Israel to deal with this problem, and eventually to accept its mission to the Gentiles, that P entered the lists against localism and nationalism, even the sanctified nationalism of Deuteronomy. His meticulous insistence upon the proper performance of the cult—not found, of course, in Genesis—was no mere expression of an arid ritualism. It was his way of driving home to his contemporaries the fact that Israel was a worshiping community, a holy community, a community standing in a unique relationship to God. It could discern and implement its own meaning and mission only when it recognized its uniqueness, and accepted its unique responsibilities.

Again, in view of the total biblical attitude toward the Gentiles, and as regards the nature and purpose of the community of Israel—both the Old Israel and the New—it is possible to deny inspiration to P only if the concept of inspiration is rejected on a priori grounds. It is true that this inspiration was historically conditioned, but this, as has been argued above, is always so. P was inspired to deal with a concrete crisis in the life of the community. The action he advocated was what was required at the moment to bring Israel to a deeper consciousness of its vocation. When that goal had been achieved it would be time enough to raise the question whether his drastic treatment of the ancient traditions might not be modified.

F. Work of RP.—It was such a modification that was in effect accomplished by RP. There can be little doubt that the conflation of the P document with the composite document JED was undertaken in response to popular pressure. The members of the community showed themselves unwilling to accept P's relentless proscription of the old stories of the patriarchs. Nor can this be dismissed as mere hidebound conservatism. It was rather that the people came to realize, however inarticulately, that these stories embodied a truth of fundamental importance—namely, that the holy community had been fashioned out of the natural community of Israel. In this fashioning the natural community had not been destroyed. Natural interests and natural ties had not been cut away as irrelevant. On the contrary those interests and

[18] See article "The Growth of the Hexateuch," pp. 197-98.

ties had been sanctified and their true meaning had been revealed. The holy community was not composed of professional ecclesiastics. It was composed of human beings with human affections, living in the world, who were called to establish a pattern of natural relationships within the community which would inform their relationships outside the community, to the ultimate transformation—not the elimination—of all human relationships. Israel could be a supranational community only in a world of nations with local interests. It must be sympathetic with those interests, recognize their values, discern their possibilities for good as well as their possibilities for evil. This it could not do if its religion treated them by implication as irrelevant.

To say all this is not to suggest that the community reasoned articulately along these lines. Such a suggestion would be absurd. What is postulated is a kind of restless misgiving on the part of the more sensitive members of the community as regards P's lack of concern for human values. To this group RP belonged, and he was inspired to deal with the situation. This he did, employing the well-tried [19] method of conflation. In this way he maintained almost intact the ancient patriarchal tradition as it had been embodied in JE, and P's drastic revision of it. He thus preserved the values of both his documents and at the same time related them in such a way that each set of values interpreted and enriched the other.

To break down Genesis into its component parts is accordingly not to deny inspiration. On the contrary, the use of the method of documentary analysis—reversing as it does the process by which the book was laboriously built up—makes possible a clearer apprehension of the way in which the Word of God came to Israel. It came in the context of successive historical situations, judging them and interpreting them, indicating the action required from the community to deal with them, so that its vocation might be fulfilled.

G. The Book as a Whole.—It was to the Word of God thus mediated that the authors of the component documents, each in his own age, responded. The book they have given us presents in summary form the Old Testament doctrine of God and man. Whether 1:1 is a sentence complete in itself or, as is suggested in the Exegesis, is the protasis of vs. 3, it implies that God himself is the uncreated, transcendent source of all being and all existence (cf. Isa. 44:6b; 45:5a, 7). Nevertheless, his relationship

with the world he has created is close and personal, for the austere grandeur of the narrative of ch. 1 is balanced and enriched by the more homely story in ch. 2, according to which God "formed man of the dust of the ground" (vs. 7aα). Originally the meaning of this was that God fashioned man with careful hands, as a potter molds his clay. But the placing of the two chapters in juxtaposition has rendered this meaning forever impossible. In their present context the words speak of the intimacy of the essential relationship between God and man, without in any way weakening the idea of the divine transcendence.

This intimacy is further stressed by the statement that having formed man, God "breathed into his nostrils the breath of life; and man became a living soul" (2:7aβb). This was J2's account of the mystery of human personality—an account so concrete that it seemed dangerous to P. Nevertheless, there is a warmth to the words which is lacking in the statement in ch. 1 that "God created man in his own image" (vs. 27aα). Each statement is needed to complete the other.

Similarly, the two accounts of the creation of woman, 1:27b and 2:18, 21-24, are complementary. In the former, woman stands beside man as his equal; in the latter, the essential character of their mutual relationship, their dependence each on the other, is movingly depicted. In 1:28a, the man and the woman are commanded to "be fruitful, and multiply, and replenish the earth." In its cold formality this command is far removed from the narrative in chs. 3-4, in which the mystery of sex, its intimacy and its perils, its power for good and for evil, find such poignant expression. Here the family is a society of persons; the author is cruelly aware of the tensions to which relationships within that society are subject. But the tensions are endurable, and must be endured if man is to remain man. The story of Cain is fraught with significance. His demonic individualism (cf. 4:7) had driven him to murder his brother, and thus to threaten the very existence of society. So he is condemned to be "a fugitive and a wanderer on the earth" (4:12), that is, to a life on a subhuman level, without culture and without friends.

The fundamental thesis of chs. 3-4 is that man from the very beginning has been in revolt against God, and Lamech's song (4:23-24) dramatically portrays the social disintegration this has caused, and must cause. Nor can this be corrected by punishment, even by the punishment of the Flood. The malady of sin remained, to break out again in the impiety of one of Noah's own sons (9:20-25). Further, the un-

---

[19] Well tried, for it was used not only by the redactor who conflated the J and E documents but by other redactors as well, whose work is to be found, for instance, in II Sam. 9–20, and in Jer. 40:7–41:18.

changed, demonic character of man's arrogance was revealed in the attempt to build a tower which should reach to heaven. The sole result of this blasphemy was that human society was broken into fragments, each one unable to understand, and so hostile to, all the others (11:1-9).

It was then that the process of redemption began in the call of Abraham, symbolizing God's covenant choice of a people. It was in relation to this people, Israel, and through Israel to God, that the nations of the world would eventually find their true meaning and be saved (cf. 12:1-3). Nevertheless, Abraham and his family remained intensely human, themselves involved in and contributing to the situation which made redemption necessary. The stories of the patriarchs drive this point home. Called though they were to perfection (cf. 17:1), to be the instruments of God's saving power, they were sinful men, feuding, lusting, and lying. But God, ever active in history, made the wrath of man to praise him (cf. Ps. 76:10), overruling his evil designs for good, "to save much people alive" by a great deliverance (cf. 45:5, 7-8; 50:20).

The book thus foreshadows the salvation to be wrought by God, in which, however, man would have his indispensable part to play. This salvation would not involve the negation of the desires and longings divinely planted in man. Rather, it would through suffering illumine them and discipline them, and at last fulfill them.

IX. Outline of Contents

X. Selected Bibliography

DRIVER, S. R. *The Book of Genesis* ("Westminster Commentaries"). 15th ed. London: Methuen & Co., 1948.

GORDON, ALEXANDER R. *The Early Traditions of Genesis.* Edinburgh: T. & T. Clark, 1907.

GUNKEL, HERMANN. *Genesis* ("Göttinger Handkommentar"). 5th ed. Göttingen: Vandenhoeck & Ruprecht, 1922.

MEYER, EDUARD. *Die Israeliten und ihre Nachbarstämme.* Halle: M. Niemeyer, 1906.

PROCKSCH, OTTO. *Die Genesis.* 2nd & 3rd eds. Leipzig: A. Deichert, 1924.

SKINNER, JOHN. *A Critical and Exegetical Commentary on Genesis* ("International Critical Commentary"). Rev. ed. New York: Charles Scribner's Sons, 1925.

GENESIS

TEXT, EXEGESIS, AND EXPOSITION

The Book of Genesis.*—In the parlors of houses a generation or two ago, on a center table, one would often find what for a long period became unfamiliar, but later in improved form has come back into use—a stereoscope. Lying beside it was a stack of cardboard mounted photographs. Each photograph was a double one of the same scene or group of figures, one picture having been taken at a slightly different angle from the other. Seen together through the two lenses of the stereoscope, the two pictures coalesce in one impression, with the figures and objects not flat as in the photograph itself, but standing out distinct and three-dimensional as in their actuality.

The method of *The Interpreter's Bible* is like that of the stereoscope. On the one side is the picture of biblical facts as seen by the exegete; on the other, the picture as seen by the expositor. These are different, but they are not separate. They register the truth from two perspectives, that the ultimate perception may have a depth and vividness greater than either one alone could give.

With such a book as Genesis the synthesis may not be immediately apparent. Exegetical scholarship has explored the problems involved with such extraordinary patience and devotion that an immense number of technical details come into view. But the perspective of critical analysis is not enough. The multitude of people who come to the Bible to seek primarily not exhaustive acquaintance with its minutiae, but an over-all perception of its meaning, will want to see the facts also from another angle. It can be a matter of fascinating interest to trace who wrote this verse and that, but men and women will ask further: "Why did they write as they did? What was the ultimate purpose they had at heart? What have they given us to believe in and to live by?"

Here enters the possible value of the Expos. It must not ignore what the Exeg. has revealed, nor be finally inconsistent with it. But neither will it necessarily highlight the same points. The great events and figures of Genesis—the

*Pp. 458-65 include the expositor's introduction. Text and Exegesis begin on p. 465. Editors.

story of Eden, the Flood, Abraham, Isaac, Jacob, Joseph, and the rest—may from one angle be results of legends interwoven by the ancient writers; but from another angle they appear as embodiments of spiritual realities more vital and inescapable than much of our contemporary life. The personalities portrayed in the Bible have lived in the thought of many generations and have powerfully affected the ideals and judgments of innumerable people. Whether or not objective history can validate the details of some of the lives and some of the incidents of which the Bible tells is of secondary importance. The important matter is that these figures are immortal representatives of man. They focus the conceptions of many ages as to what life is in its struggle of good with evil, of courage with cowardice, and of the glory of God entering in through human experience to transform the things of earth.

The conjunction of the Exeg. and the Expos. should give us therefore a sense of having seen truth in the round and a feeling that in the persons of the patriarchs it walks out of the pages of a book to touch our present lives.

The comments should be taken not as ends but as beginnings. They are to be considered not as expositions finished, but as incitements and provocations to larger ones that should be developed. It will be noted that frequently there is mention of a book or a poem or some prose passage recommended to be read. It is not meant that these should be incorporated bodily into what may be said by the preacher or teacher or leader of a Bible study group. They are to be the deeper and wider ground for the foundation thinking that may not expressly appear in the finished exposition, but upon which that exposition may securely rest.

The Beauty of the Book of Genesis.—The Expos. will deal of course with particular passages and particular words; but before going forward chapter by chapter, it is well to think of certain aspects of Genesis as a whole.

The first and plainest of these is its sheer beauty of expression. Genesis, like so much of the rest of the Bible, belongs among the supreme works of human literature. Of course it is more than that, for a Spirit higher than human is speaking through it. But considered at the outset only in comparison with other writings which have come by way of human hands, this book has a nobility all its own.[1]

What is the reason for the literary power of Genesis? There is, to begin with, the sublimity of its theme. It deals with God and man and destiny. It makes our thought confront the fundamental questions, stand in the presence of the ultimate mysteries, look up to the skies of an infinite faith. As Dinsmore has put it:

Religion of itself, because it brings man face to face with the Eternal, and includes life's most significant experiences, is a powerful incentive to elevated and emotional expression. Religion by deepening the soul of man has been the prolific and fostering mother of music, architecture, letters, drama, and all the arts. Atheism writes no hymns; agnosticism does not burst into song; skepticism constructs no institutions. The singing and building eras of the world are periods of stalwart belief.[2]

Genesis is great literature also because of its realism and its honesty. It does not evade facts. It describes life as it is, people as they are. This realism and truthfulness which the O.T. writers aimed at had its instrument in the extraordinary concreteness of the Hebrew mind. The Hebrew was not instinctively a philosopher. He was not at home in abstract ideas. His thinking was vivid and pictorial, and so put truth into pictures, not into wordy generalizations or nebulous expression. The language itself was fitted for this even by its limitations. Hebrew words and constructions did not readily set forth subtle shadings of cerebration, but Hebrew did have a sinewy directness that was admirably adapted to graphic narrative. And the English language, though of much wider compass than the Hebrew, matches Hebrew in its particular strength. It also has the virility which can express the flesh-and-blood concreteness of action and event. So it results that the translations in which the English-speaking world is accustomed to read the book of Genesis have lost nothing of the force of the original. The company of scholars who finished the King James Version in 1611 had back of them the work of Wycliffe, Tyndale, and Coverdale, whose heroic devotion to the dangerous adventure they dared to undertake gave a moral earnestness and passionate vigor to everything they wrote. The noble English which was the native speech of men who belonged to the age of Shakespeare, and the influence of which is never lost, has made the translated narrative of Genesis as

living and powerful as the first writers could ever have desired.

Genesis, as the book has come down to us, is made up of many strands; and as the Exeg. repeatedly points out, those who wove them had their different ways of writing. The divine Spirit does not operate mechanically. It takes men's separate gifts and uses these. There is a dignity of the individual and of that individual's manner of apprehending and expressing truth which inspiration does not destroy but rather heightens. It takes the human ability and gives it wings. So of the writers of the book of Genesis it may be said essentially what George Eliot said of the supreme maker of violins:

'Tis God gives skill,
But not without men's hands: He could not make
Antonio Stradivari's violins
Without Antonio.[3]

Similarly, the Word of God was written through the instrumentality of human hands.

Though the styles of the parts of Genesis vary they represent the handiwork of men who obviously were sensitive to beauty. There is the organ roll of the majestic account of the Creation in the opening chapter; the childlike imagination which lies back of the story of the Garden of Eden, but to which there has been brought also a grave awareness of the willfullness in the soul of man which rebels against God, and of the tragic consequence of that rebellion: the somber tale of Cain and Abel, and the deepening course of human sin that comes to its crisis in the Flood; lovely simplicities of limpid narrative, like the description of Rebekah at the well; never-to-be-forgotten presentments of persons, such as Abraham and Lot and Jacob and Esau; and at the climax the superbly sustained drama of Joseph that began in what seemed disaster and ended on a viceregal throne.

The Great Portrayals of Character.—Nor is it of course only a general beauty of expression that makes Genesis notable. The book is masterful in substance and particularly in its portrayal of human character in its wide gamut of good and bad and in-between. For evidence one needs call only a partial roll: Abraham, the adventurer; Isaac, the quiet man; Esau, with his lusty appetites; Jacob, so strangely mixed of earthly craft and yet of stubborn would-be consecration; Joseph, the mighty dreamer; Sarah, with her fierce affection; Rebekah and Rachel and the wife of Potiphar. Some of them are heroes, but they are never presented with false heroics. In even the best of them their failures and faults are portrayed as surely as

---

[1] See Charles A. Dinsmore, *The English Bible as Literature* (Boston: Houghton Mifflin Co., 1931); A. C. Deane, *How to Enjoy the Bible* (New York: George H. Doran Co., 1925).

[2] *Op. cit.*, pp. 58-59.

[3] "Stradivarius."

their virtues. It is as though the far-off writers to whom we owe the book of Genesis had obeyed a charge such as Oliver Cromwell gave to the painter of his portrait, "Paint me as I am, wart and all."

Yet there is a question which necessarily will rise—the question as to whether we have a right to treat these figures in Genesis as though they were men and women who actually lived and breathed and struggled in this real world as the stories say they did. Obviously the book begins in that misty region of tradition and transmitted myth in which imagination precedes knowledge. Few will suppose that Adam and Eve and the Garden of Eden belong to factual history. Cain and Abel and Lamech and Nimrod and Methuselah and Noah—these also come down to us as legends rather than as persons identifiable in the literal history of a particular time. And what of even the later figures in the book, Abraham and the three generations following him? Preachers and commentators have long assumed as a matter of course that Abraham and the other patriarchs were clear-cut historical figures. Many would still maintain that in essential outline they were such. But others question whether there was an actual Abraham or Isaac or Jacob, and hold instead that they are heroes of tribal tales and personifications of tribal characteristics (see Exeg. on 11:28).

Between the differing judgments there can be no wholly categorical and dogmatic conclusion. No present knowledge can positively prove or disprove that this or that character in the book of Genesis lived upon our definite human scene. But assuming the most radical possibility, what then? Suppose that many of the great portraits in the book of Genesis are products of imagination. Is their worth thereby diminished, or their long-cherished place in the records of religious inspiration disturbed? Here in these descriptions is the inspired reflection of a people's experience as to what life is and what it ought to be. The great fact is that such descriptions should have been born out of the mind and heart of the Hebrew race. In such forms this people expressed their sense of what the human soul is and of how it is related in good or evil to its world. The truth they saw was truth alive, and it has been alive and will be till the end of time. Therefore the preacher or teacher of the Bible need have no timid hesitancy about drawing lessons for himself and others from the motives and the actions of the characters whom the pages of Genesis make so intimately real. They *are* real—real with the everlasting certainties of right and wrong, of conscience and character, of human shadows and of the heavenly light.

Here then is material richly to be used, provided one is in earnest to use it rightly. That means, first of all, sincerity. It is not necessary to thrust into a sermon or lesson all the opinions of critical scholarship; but certainly no man, for the cheap purpose of standing in with what is no more than unenlightened traditionalism, ought to say anything that flies in the face of what he genuinely believes to be the established conclusions which a reverently fearless search for truth has reached. It is a poor business, and ultimately a self-defeating one, to enroll among those who are willing to be "orthodox liars for the glory of God."

But the other side of the fact is immediately and equally important. Biblical interpretation is of very little use—and sometimes worse than of no use at all—unless it is constructive. A congregation of people who come to church or to a Bible class to worship and to listen to some word that may help them to live better do not want to hear what an expositor can say to depreciate the importance of some character in the Bible; they want to hear what vital lesson he has learned and can pass on to them, so helpful that the Bible will seem more important than it ever did before.

That sort of interpretation calls for a man's complete alertness. To sleepy minds even the Bible can seem dull; and for the interpreter who reads familiar passages mechanically, as though he were threshing out old straw, nothing new will spring forth. But to the expectant mind the Bible proves itself unendingly productive. The living message of it communicates itself wherever the mind and spirit are alive. Figures that had never been noticed in the background of some story suddenly stand out significant; and some great figures, about whom one supposes that he has already said everything he could think of that would be interesting, show a new relevance to the very problems of behavior which history has pushed into the forefront of contemporary life. So much, indeed, is this true of the figures in Genesis that for the lessons to be learned from them it might well be said of Genesis what William Lyon Phelps said of the Bible as a whole:

Western civilisation is founded upon the Bible; our ideas, our wisdom, our philosophy, our literature, our art, our ideals, come more from the Bible than from all other books put together. . . . I thoroughly believe in a university education for both men and women; but I believe a knowledge of the Bible without a college course is more valuable than a college course without the Bible.[4]

Those Whom the Spirit Used.—The greatness of Genesis, both as literature and as

---

[4] *Human Nature in the Bible* (New York: Charles Scribner's Sons, 1923), p. ix.

religion, is the more remarkable in that its authorship can be only dimly guessed. "J1," "J2," "E," and "P"—such are the symbols that the exegetical scholars have made familiar. So the men who wrote can be represented only by signs and labels. What they did remains, but their identities have long since disappeared. Who were "J" and "E" and "P," and where exactly did they live, and what manner of men were they, and what regard, if any, did their contemporaries give to them? Such questions we ask and cannot answer. Whoever they were, they have influenced the thought of many centuries and have affected the lives and characters of men in a way they could not have conceived and that no historian even now can fully measure. Like the nameless soldier who is buried in the nave of Westminster Abbey they are "known only to God."

They are among those whose achievements are more significant than the accident of fame or lack of fame. Nor are they alone in that company of the great unknowns. Who wrote the chapters at the end of the book of Isaiah, and who was it that drew the picture of the suffering servant that found its fulfillment in Christ himself? Who wrote those passionate outpourings of praise and petition, of joy and hope and self-abasement and repentance, of confession of the sins of men and of adoration of the glory of God, which make up the Psalter? Once it was supposed that David wrote them; but if he wrote any at all, it was certainly not by him that most of them were written. Instead, they have come out of the minds and hearts of men whose names may be written in heaven but are inscribed nowhere on the earth.

See the same fact reflected in the N.T. The Gospels of Matthew and Luke are believed to have drawn much of what they have recorded of the teachings of Jesus from the source called "Q." Who first brought those sayings together? Who searched his own memory, or turned with his questioning to others, to recall the accounts of the Master? We may never know. But beyond all measurement is the debt of gratitude which all Christendom owes to him.

Thus J and E and P have given us this scripture. That is a vital fact in the history of Israel, for Judaism has been pre-eminently a religion of the Book. It was not left to shifting standards. In the Scripture, once its writings had come to embody men's sifted and proven convictions about God and his will for human life, there was guidance that seemed as sure as the everlasting stars. The immense tenacity and steadfastness of the people of Israel have been due to the fact that they could turn always to the Scripture and reassure themselves there of the explicit covenant God had made with them. The most sacred object in the synagogue is "the rolls" from which the law is read. To the devout, God has spoken, and what he has said is written there for the ages to understand. And J and E and P were his instruments for the writing.

But what they wrote does not tell the whole story of their importance. The record they set down was life before it was scripture. Their minds were wide open to new truths about God, even when these came to them in partial understandings. When minds are no longer thus open, then even the most sacred scripture can be so used as to smother the spirit rather than to give it life and breath. Revelation considered as comprehended and wholly completed in the Book can make religion rigid. So there have developed the unbending formalities of the orthodox Jew and the literal dogmas of the Christian fundamentalist.

On the contrary, there is needed always what J and E and P actually represented so long ago, "a living tradition . . . capable of adaptation to changing conditions and responsive to new needs." There is truth in the Roman Catholic insistence that the Bible must not stand alone, but must be read and interpreted in the light of the faithful and continuing tradition of the church. But the stultifying error in that has been the claim that pronouncement of what the tradition is must come from a hierarchy that holds itself to be infallible. So the tradition is no longer flexible, but pontifically fixed, and in place of what should be the living truth there is offered again a hardened stereotype. The real tradition is a more vital and inspiring power. It is the *consensus fidelium,* the expanding consciousness of God's meaning for life, which grows from the insights of innumerable humble and devoted souls; for wherever men in reverent simplicity have tried to understand and to reflect the way and the will of God, God's truth has been—and is—conveyed through them. Here is the holy meaning of the church—the church of Israel and the church of Christ. It is to be the continuing fellowship of worship and experience which transmits all that is most sacred in the past, but at the same time kindles for every generation a clearer understanding by which contemporary life is to be illumined with the light of God.

God's meaning for life—that is the great theme with which Genesis deals. Looked at from one angle, this book might seem to be a mosaic of many traditions fitted together gradually and sometimes also with what appear to be overlappings and inconsistencies. But looked at from another and a higher perspective, it will be seen that this book, as it was ultimately shaped, has a noble unity. In it, perhaps for the first time in any ancient writing, there emerges a conception of history that is lofty and far-seeing and grandly unified. It is history not as the chance actions of men, but as the unfolding will of God. There is no flat monotony in it. It recognizes the shadows as well as the lights in human destiny. Yet through them all and beyond them all it sees the assurance of a heavenly plan. God creates the universe and says it is good. God makes man in innocence and sets before him the open doors of spiritual opportunity. Next come the fact of human perversity and disobedience and the descending story of sin and evil until there has to be the great cleansing of the Flood. Yet over that catastrophe shines the rainbow of promise and hope. Then comes the story of the redeeming acts of God: the call of Abraham, the covenant with him and his descendants, the development, generation by generation, of those who would carry on the great commission of a family and a nation whom the Most High will use for his witness among the peoples of the earth.

Thus far, then, we have thought of the values of Genesis, which are clear and great. But there is another side to the picture.

The Difficulties in the Book.—1. The Account of the Creation. Everyone whose mind is at all open to modern facts has realized some of the perplexities which have beset readers of Genesis. For assumptions which used to be taken for granted have been flatly challenged. The first and most acute focus of those perplexities has been the opening chapter of the book. There stands an account of the Creation which for many centuries men regarded as infallible. According to it, the universe was made by God in six days. The earth was shaped, the sun and the moon and the stars were hung in the heavens, birds and animals appeared, and then a man and a woman were made. Thus, before God rested on the seventh day, which he made into the sabbath, everything was finished. Moreover, it is clear from later pages that the writers of the O.T. thought the earth was the center of everything and over its flat surface the sun and the moon obediently rose and set.

Against that finished picture came the new and disturbing ideas of Copernicus and Galileo, with their assertion that the earth is not the center of the universe but a little satellite that goes round the sun; and of the geologists and the paleontologists, with their evidence that the earth had not been made in six days but slowly formed through almost unimaginable time; and of Darwin with his theory of evolution, which pictured man as emerging slowly out of an ancestry that went back to subhuman life. If one would realize again the shock which

these ideas produced when they were new let him read Andrew D. White's *A History of the Warfare of Science with Theology in Christendom.*[5] Or turn to the account of the denunciation of Darwinism by Samuel Wilberforce, bishop of Oxford, in 1860, as it is vividly described in Leonard Huxley's *Life and Letters of Thomas Henry Huxley.* In a gathering of which one who was present wrote, "I never saw such a display of fierce party spirit," the bishop, in an "open clash between Science and the Church," first ridiculed the new teachings and then "asserted, in a solemn peroration, that Darwin's views were contrary to the revelation of God in the Scriptures."[6]

That collision between the new teachings and the old tradition seemed at first as shattering as an earthquake. Multitudes of men and women reacted in panic or in defiance, supposing that if their confidence in the literal exactitude of the first verses of Genesis should go, then their whole religious faith would be gone with it.[7] Yet the new teachings had come not to blight religion but to stimulate it to new growth. If they seemed at first to break up old patterns of belief, the result was to lift men's eyes to mightier perspectives of the majestic works of God.

If this world is not God's world, even the most frenzied arguments could not make it so. But if it is God's world, we do not need to be afraid of anything it actually reveals. All life is growth, and in growth there are often growing pains. But these are profitable. It is not the man of faith but the man of secret doubts, which he is trying to smother, who will be afraid of unfamiliar facts and will try to drown them out with clamor. Whoever really believes that he is moving in God's world will go forward steadily to meet even its dismaying revelations. The right attitude is expressed by William Newton Clarke, who inspired many students. He wrote of his own change of thought from old traditionalism to a wider understanding:

I know that in my case the change has been an honest one, and am equally sure that it has been a legitimate one, which I could not have refused to make without being false to the true light. . . . I shall hope that my experience may lead many a man to commit himself without fear to the journey that I have been led to make, assured that the good hand of his God will be upon him as he moves out into the broader country.[8]

[5] New York: D. Appleton & Co., 1925.

[6] New York: D. Appleton & Co., 1901, I, 203, 194, 200.

[7] See Harry Emerson Fosdick, *The Modern Use of the Bible* (New York: The Macmillan Co., 1924); *A Guide to Understanding the Bible* (New York: Harper & Bros., 1938).

[8] *Sixty Years with the Bible* (New York: Charles Scribner's Sons, 1912), pp. 7, 10.

2. The Element of Myth. The noise and tumult of what was called "the warfare between science and theology," so far as they had to do with the account of the Creation, have died down. But there is another and a newer concern that may perhaps have risen for readers of the Intro. and Exeg. to this particular book. Is there danger that the whole of Genesis may seem to lose its substance? Frequently in the analysis and description of its elements one encounters the word "myth," and that word has a disturbing sound, for it is assumed that myth is only an ancient fairy tale, a haunting mirage conjured up in men's imaginations and dissolving into nothing when it collides with actual fact. What becomes of the authority of the Bible if any part of it can be described as myth? These are questions that some cannot refrain from asking. They are fair questions which deserve an answer. And there is an answer—an answer that growingly appears as one studies Genesis and reflects upon the distinction between vehicles of truth and the truth itself. In any age our means of expression are imperfect; we feel realities which cannot with any mathematical rigidity be defined or described. So the poet arises, and the artist, gifted with divine inspiration to suggest by symbolic words and forms the truths which no flat prose or scientific measurement can represent. Shakespeare wrote of the forest of Arden that in it one could find

tongues in trees, books in the running brooks,
Sermons in stones, and good in every thing.[9]

Is that truth? The literal-minded could say that it is only nonsense. Whoever saw a tongue in a tree, or a sermon in a stone? And what would happen to a book if it did get into a running brook? The pompously dull-witted might argue —as someone has wittily suggested—that somebody printed Shakespeare's words askew, and that what he must have written was "sermons in books, stones in the running brooks," which is where they obviously belong. But he wrote no such utter dullness. He wrote the beautiful lines as we have them. In terms of raw fact they are not true; in terms of the living meaning they convey they are true to the point of inspiration. Similarly, it has been suggested that if anyone should want to know what Venice is like, he could get a *Baedeker* and read there the exact detail of every point of important interest in the city; but if he should look at one of Turner's paintings, though not a single detail in it might be exact, he would *feel* the wonder of Venice more certainly than any guidebook could enable him to do. So all imaginative

stories, including the element of myth, which form part of the early chapters of the Bible are the efforts of men to put truth into pictures. Some of the creation stories of the Babylonians or of other ancient peoples (influencing, as the Exeg. has shown, the stories in Genesis) are primitive to the point of seeming now fantastic; but even in them a great fact was breaking through into expression. These wondering thinkers were sure of this: that man is not the first or greatest reality in existence. There was and is Something or Someone greater than he. Granted that their ideas of what that Something or Someone was like were crude, nevertheless it was what they thought about and tried to interpret that really counted. And the distinction of the Bible as a whole is this: not that it moved completely away from language that is imaginative and even mythical and put everything into scientific prose, for it did not; but rather that it took the imaginative forms which had come down in traditions, and by a sure instinct purged these of their cruder features and made them more sensitive reflections of spiritual truth. The Something or Someone is seen now to be the God who is known not only in the physical creation, but most of all in what he has put into good men's hearts, the God concerning whom it can be said:

Speak to Him, thou, for He hears, and Spirit with
  Spirit can meet—
Closer is He than breathing, and nearer than hands
  and feet.[10]

When we have thus learned to judge truth, it is a very subordinate matter that some of the conceptions of how God once worked have long since been outgrown. The important point is that the Bible brings us face to face with One who is at work now, and where it matters most, viz., in human hearts that give themselves to his control. What difference then does it make that old descriptions of his ways were mythical, if the God of whom men in their poor way were trying to tell has been brought to us as a mighty fact?

3. The Conception of "Yahweh." One more matter may disturb. It is not so difficult to see, someone may say, that men in the O.T. times may naturally have reflected some of the naïve ideas of other religions. But what of the origin of Israel's own religion? Doubtless the statement in the Intro. (see p. 440), "Historically this unique relationship began . . . in a collective response by the group, then or later known as the sons of Israel, to external reality manifesting itself in the thunderstorm . . . of Sinai," will seem to many both startling and unwel-

---

[9] *As You Like It*, Act II, scene 1.

[10] Tennyson, "The Higher Pantheism."

come. Could anything so wonderful as the faith of Israel have begun in such a way as that? Was the God of the patriarchs and the prophets first felt as men shrank before a terror in the sky? How could a supreme religion of the inner soul and conscience derive from a primitive fear? Such are the objecting questions which may instinctively arise. But as one begins to meditate, vistas open into a larger meaning.

The first of these is the realization that God does not disdain humble processes. The more we study the history of religions, including the religion of Israel that led up to Christ, the more we see that their roots were in untutored instincts that were simple but very deep. A missionary to Africa at the end of the nineteenth century told of a message that came to a missionary post from a distant African village, asking that the village might have someone to teach its people of the white man's God. For a considerable while no one could go; and when at last a missionary managed the journey through the jungle and arrived, as it chanced, at the edge of the village on a Sunday morning, he was startled to see it apparently deserted. Passing by one hut after another, he found each one empty as though a pestilence had swept the village. But going on until he reached the central space, he halted in a different amazement. For there on this first day of the week, which they had somehow heard was the white man's day of worship, stood all the people silent, lifting up their hands in dumb petition to a God they did not know. If the pathos of ignorance was there, so also was there the dignity of aspiration. Wherever and whenever that aspiration has existed and been expressed the first reality of religion has been present. Men's wordless prayers, their groping ritual, their crudest shrines, must all have been of worth in the eyes of God. Thus of primitive fear he may be saying, as he said to Simon Peter at Joppa, that we must not call any outreach of the soul of man common or unclean.

There is a second reassuring fact. The awareness of God at the mountain bears witness to the predominance of awe in Israel's religion. Perhaps because of revulsion from pagan corruptions like those of Baalism the serene or soft aspects of nature did not attract the Hebrew mind, nor did nature ever seem the "gentle nurse" which long afterward she was to seem to Wordsworth. There was no sense of mystic companionship with her such as one finds in the Romantic poets. Some of the psalms celebrate the natural world by which we are environed, but (except for grateful reference to its production of food) it is its grandeur or its austerity that provokes the song. Ps. 8 ranges from the moon and the stars to "whatsoever passeth through the paths of the seas." Ps. 19 imagines the sun as a giant about to run his race. Ps. 97 sees God in clouds and lightnings above the hills that "melted like wax at the presence of the Lord." Ps. 104 celebrates also the beneficent aspects of the earth, the springs in the valleys, the grass for the cattle, the vegetation for the use of men, but only as derived from the majesty of God "who maketh the clouds his chariot: who walketh upon the wings of the wind." The men of Israel were free from the vanity of those who imagine themselves to be self-sufficient. They bowed before a power that held them in the hollow of his hand. This fear in its origin may seem only an abasement before the terrible power of the unknown. But even at Sinai there was more than that. The clouds and lightning and all the other dreadful aspects of creation belonged to the Creator; men themselves belonged to him, and he to them.

So, paradoxically but unmistakably, these men who bowed most before the sublimity of God, instead of being enfeebled, became of heroic moral fiber. Because they feared God altogether, they feared men not at all. That was true in Israel, and the religious heritage which began in Israel made it true for Martin Luther, for the men of Geneva, for the Covenanters in Scotland, for the Pilgrims to New England, and for all the rest of the heroic succession of men who have been bold in their religion because they knew that

> A mighty fortress is our God,
> A bulwark never failing.

In the words of Isaiah, they could proclaim that there was no reason to be "afraid of a man that shall die, and of the son of man which shall be made as grass" as long as they remembered "the Lord thy Maker, that hath stretched forth the heavens, and laid the foundations of the earth" (Isa. 51:12-13).

The Spirit of the Interpreter.—So—to summarize—Genesis has in it rich meanings charged with immediate interest and inspiration; and it has also elements that may provoke perplexity and unrest. A brave and true interpretation will make sure that honest questions shall never be evaded. Many persons in every religious group, old and young, will already have been made uneasy by them. They will have heard them raised, often by flippant people who like to disparage the Bible; and if the preacher or teacher is silent, they will wonder whether the reason is that he has no answer. Unmistakably he must show that he recognizes alertly and sympathetically whatever genuine disturbance has been caused. Yet he must show that he himself is not disturbed, because he has

1 In the beginning God created the heaven and the earth.

2 And the earth was without form, and void; and darkness *was* upon the face of

1 In the beginning God created*a* the heavens and the earth. 2 The earth was without form and void, and darkness was upon the face of the deep; and the Spirit*b*

a Or *When God began to create*
b Or *wind*

I. THE CREATION (1:1–2:4a)

Chs. 1–2 contain two accounts of the creation of the world by God. According to the first (1:1–2:4a), man was created, male and female (1:26-27), after the creation of plants (1:11-12) and animals (1:20-25); according to the second (2:4b-25), man was created first (2:7), then the trees (2:9), then the animals (2:19), and finally woman (2:21-22). In view of these discrepancies, to say nothing of the differences of style and feeling so obvious as to need no detailed enumeration here, the two stories cannot come from the same hand. The first is basically from P, the second from J2; both of them bear the marks of having been elaborated by writers other than their original authors.

something to say that is confident and constructive. Not to be disturbed because he is ignorant and bumptious is one thing; not to be disturbed because he possesses—and shows that he possesses—a larger integrating knowledge is another.

How then shall he shape his message? First, by bringing the facts out fearlessly. If he sees that some of the biblical writers reflected primitive traditions which had come from the naïve thinking of various peoples in the human family, let him say so, and not wait for it to be said first by some snickering detractor of the Bible who thinks he is being devastatingly smart and new. Religious people will feel a great sense of relief if the man they trust, and whose essential reverence for the Word they are sure of, can pick up questions which they thought were deadly serpents and then before their eyes perform what seems to them the miracle of showing that the supposed serpents are not serpents at all, but tendrils of a living vine of fruitful truth. People like to be taught something, and they like it all the more if what they learn is a happy surprise. It may be a happy surprise in the first place to discover that their minister or other church leader is not afraid of new knowledge which they imagined would make orthodox and proper people quake; and it will be more gratifying if he can go on to show why he is not afraid, and why they also need not be.

Always, of course, he must be reverent. That is the heart of the matter. It fundamentally distinguishes the religious man from the mere flippant debater in the arena of ideas. The Bible deals with the profoundest matters and concerns man's most vital hopes and longings. Therefore no study of it should ever be pursued with shallowness or conceit. Biblical criticism is worse than useless if it is an arrogant exhibition of what a man does not believe. It is useful only

when it is positive, i.e., when it is bent not only on taking away the broken stones of inadequate conceptions, but on showing where the rock foundations of the sure convictions stand.

Such interpretation, finally, makes faith secure. The reality of God does not need to be bolstered up by us. It vindicates itself. Many particular ideas about the ways of God's working may be changed, but through these changes the consciousness of God as a power to penetrate and inspire living can grow continually more sure. Religion in the end is not a matter of argument, but of experience. One can say: "I know whom I have believed" (II Tim. 1:12). Consider the great souls in all ages whose lives have reflected that confidence. They could not be thrown into a panic merely because they had to reconstruct their conceptions of the ways in which God works. They felt him working in themselves. They saw him working wherever good men went about their duty. Faith is an anvil which has worn out many hammers, and the great faith in the living God which the O.T. proclaims is more enduring than any noise of controversy. To read Genesis is to have one's conscience recognize the revelation which the whole O.T. expands—that there is an eternal Righteousness to which all human souls must be accountable. It is to recognize also that this Righteousness is not something impassive and aloof, but is the quality of him who is equally the God of mercy, and who offers to men in their individual and in their corporate life the covenant of his redemption. So of Genesis there may be said what an old Mohave Indian chief said of all the Bible, "I know this must be the Word of God because it pulls my heart."

1:1a. The Priority of God.—These great words with which the Bible opens, In the beginning God, . . . express the Hebrew faith in the foundation of all life. The universe and everything in

A. In the Beginning (1:1-2)

1:1. Does this verse speak of creation *ex nihilo?* Yes, if the rendering of the RSV (cf. KJV) is correct: **In the beginning God created the heavens and the earth.** But the Hebrew *berê'shith* seems to mean "in the beginning of" rather than **in the beginning,** and this requires that vs. 1 should be taken with vs. 3—on vs. 2 see below—and rendered, "In the beginning of God's creating the heavens and the earth, God said, etc." With this rendering the meaning is less clear. Vss. 4, 5, indeed, imply that when God said, "Let there be light" (vs. 3), there was already darkness in existence, and vss. 6, 9 presuppose the existence of waters with land already formed beneath them. But this may be due to the author's dependence upon an earlier myth in which creation consisted in imposing order upon an already existing chaos.

But whence came the chaos? Vs. 1 cannot be taken as an account of its origin, for **the heavens and the earth** is a description of the organized universe, not of chaos (see Hermann Gunkel, *Genesis* [5th ed.; Göttingen: Vandenhoeck & Ruprecht, 1922; "Göttinger Handkommentar"], p. 102; John Skinner, *A Critical and Exegetical Commentary on Genesis* [rev. ed.; New York: Charles Scribner's Sons, 1925; "International Critical Commentary"], p. 14). Vs. 2, indeed, speaks of a chaos which God began to reduce to order. It must be noted, however, that this verse stands apart from the rest of the chapter in that (*a*) it represents **the Spirit of God,** not the uttered word, as the agent of creation; and (*b*) the reference to the Spirit "brooding upon"—the literal meaning of the word rendered **moved upon** or **was moving over,** in the English versions—the chaos has underlying it the idea of a cosmic egg which was hatched by the brooding Spirit, as by a bird, to produce the universe, an idea which is foreign to the story as a

---

it depend upon a divine conception and can be understood only in the light of a divine plan.

Does the universe have a meaning? The Bible is sure it does, and that the meaning is a heavenly one; cf. this account of the Creation with the Babylonian story and with the stories imagined by other peoples. Very crude and mythological some of those cosmogonies are. It is a dark and doubtful welter of forces from which the world and human life emerge. Later philosophies are more intellectual, but they may be equally arid for great hope and faith to grow in. The universe is the product of no guiding will at all, but only of mechanical chance; or, if a will is back of it, it is the will of a blind weaver or the capriciousness of one who is cruelly indifferent to the human fates he deals with in the dark. Read Thomas Hardy's *The Dynasts,*[11] and see the tragic climax of his *Tess of the D'Urbervilles.* After the black flag goes up over the prison walls to indicate the execution of the girl who was caught in the complex of disaster for which she was not originally to blame, Hardy summarizes thus: "'Justice' was done, and the President of the Immortals (in Æschylean phrase) had ended his sport with Tess. And the D'Urberville knights and dames slept on in their tombs unknowing."[1] Against such bleak and somber fatalism humanity needs continually to turn to the life-giving reassurance of the faith of Genesis. The Hebrew mind, like

the Greek mind which Thomas Hardy reflected, was aware of tragedy, as chs. 2–4 profoundly show. Over life there is the shadow of the darkest of all tragedies—that of human sin. But that is not the final word because it was not the first word. Since the universe began in God's beneficent purpose, all existence can be viewed not tragically but with trust: "This is my Father's world."[2] Essentially all creation is such that a man may look at it rejoicingly and believe that it is framed to let him live and grow. Sun and moon, seedtime and harvest, earth and ocean, beasts and birds, do not belong to hostile demigods, but to the God who makes himself known within the heart and soul of man.

If men can trust that life began in goodness (vs. 31), they can go forward into it with courage and gallant expectation. The evil in the world is not due to some relentless fate; it is a contradiction of the Creator's purpose, and so can be redeemed. Creation is not a finished story. As there was the beginning in God, so there can be new beginnings. In some hymns the hymn that stands first is

> New every morning is the love
> Our waking and uprising prove.

And it carries the promise

> New mercies, each returning day,
> Hover around us while we pray.[3]

[11] New York: The Macmillan Co., 1936.
[1] New York: The Modern Library, 1919, p. 457.

[2] Maltbie D. Babcock, *Thoughts for Every-Day Living* (New York: Charles Scribner's Sons, 1901), p. 180.
[3] John Keble.

whole. Vs. 2 thus appears to be an intrusion into the narrative as it left the hand of P. It was added presumably to supply what seemed to be a lack in P's account, viz., an explicit reference to the primeval chaos, of which **without form and void** was a traditional description (cf. Jer. 4:23; Isa. 34:11; see Gunkel, *Genesis*, p. 103). The Hebrew word *tehôm*, rendered **the deep**, is the philological equivalent of Tiamat, the name borne by the personified chaos monster in the Babylonian creation myth (on the relation between the Babylonian myth and the P story see Intro., p. 450).

The cumulative effect of the considerations just enumerated seems to warrant the conclusion that P was endeavoring to present the idea of a creation *ex nihilo*, at least in so far as he could conceive of it. But he was not only dependent upon some version of the Babylonian creation myth; he was also—as will be argued below—under the necessity of retaining its representations in a recognizable form. This accounts in part for the idea of an already existing darkness, implicit in vs. 4, and of an already existing chaos, under which lay the land, in vss. 6 and 9. But, to counter any suggestion that the chaos did not derive its existence from God, he prefaced his account with the phrase "in the beginning of God's creating the heavens and the earth." What P intended to

---

1b. Our Security in God.—In the one strong word **created** there throbs the virile Hebrew faith in the unconditioned creatorship of God. The universe did not come into existence by chance. It did not advance by the blind gropings of unconscious energies. It was not some dark welter of lifelessness inexplicably evolving into life. On the contrary, it was the purposeful creation of him who is the fount of life. Therefore in God all things belong to some consistent pattern. The universe was made to fit together and to have meaning.

Without that faith by which the O.T. is illumined the whole framework of existence would not have as much sense as a jigsaw puzzle. The pieces of a puzzle may be scrambled and bewildering, but they were shaped by intelligence, and intelligence can find the clue by which every fragment can be fitted into the intended picture. On the contrary, a universe that had no divine Creator—the universe assumed in the theory of mechanistic evolution—never could make complete sense, because it never would have been designed to have any. One element in the total is the human being, with mind and conscience, with longings and hopes and aspirations, with an instinct of the spirit that makes him say:

Thou wilt not leave us in the dust:
Thou madest man, he knows not why;
He thinks he was not made to die;
And thou hast made him: thou art just.[4]

But this human being is set in an environment that physically is far vaster than himself. Often it would seem that this titanic setting has no concern for him and is indifferent to his notion that "he was not made to die." Man is an insignificant accident, the willing atheist or the

unwilling skeptic may feel compelled to say. He has no necessary relationship to the huge frame of things, nor it to him. He is

Rolled round in earth's diurnal course,
With rocks, and stones, and trees,[5]

and whether at any given moment they sustain him or crush him makes no difference to any except himself. But with faith in a divine Creator the entire scene and its suggestion change. Then there is coherence in the whole fabric of existence, and an unfolding purpose in history and in life. For a holy will created it, and supreme intention holds within itself the

one far-off divine event,
To which the whole creation moves.[6]

How did the men of the O.T. know that? How do we know it now? Those are questions which wistful folk in every time will ask. In religious understanding there are many who think of themselves as retarded souls. How can other people seem so sure of God when they themselves feel anything but sure? If they could see God at work and speak about him as confidently as the writers of Genesis did, then they would not feel so uncertain and so troubled. But must they just assume that the certainty the Bible voices is different from any conviction that ever can be theirs?

No, that is not true. The faith that is expressed in ch. 1 is not different from the faith that can come to any and every honest and humble soul. The conviction expressed there in the Bible did not come from sight. The men who wrote about the Creation were not standing by when the Creation happened. God is not an object to be perceived like other objects in the

[4] Tennyson, *In Memoriam*, Prologue, st. iii.

[5] Wordsworth, "A Slumber Did My Spirit Seal."
[6] Tennyson, *op. cit.*, Conclusion, st. xxxvi.

the deep. And the Spirit of God moved upon the face of the waters.

3 And God said, Let there be light: and there was light.

of God was moving over the face of the waters.

3 And God said, "Let there be light";

---

imply was that the first step in the creation of the organized universe was the creation of chaos—*bārā'*, "to create," is used in the O.T. exclusively of divine activity—which God then proceeded to reduce to order. In this way P was able to reconcile those features in the myth he was revising which were dualistic in their implications with his conviction, arrived at on religious grounds, that the universe owed its existence to God, a conviction to which, it may be noted, the Second Isaiah had already given utterance, "I [God] form the light, and create darkness" (Isa. 45:7).

B. The First Day (1:3-5)

3. And God said: The representation that the divine word was the agent of creation is found in the Babylonian, Egyptian, and Indian cosmogonies; but, as Gunkel points out (*ibid.*, pp. 104-5), in these myths the word is a magic word—the correct formula which, being uttered, released the power to bring order out of the chaos. In Genesis, however, the word is the expression of God's will, "He spake, and it was done; he commanded, and it stood fast" (Ps. 33:9).

---

world, and therefore no man ever saw him. But there is a "conviction of things not seen," as the Epistle to the Hebrews puts it; and those who contemplate the ways and works of God are given by him an intuition of who he is and what he must be like. Out of a reverent regard for the facts of life within, and of the world without, arises faith. And if we ask how we may know faith to be something altogether different from wishful fantasy, this is the answer: Faith is validated when it proves to be a key that opens the gates to road after road of freedom and fulfillment. Walking on those roads of actual life to which faith has given entrance, a man knows within himself that this must be the reality which was intended all along. The record that runs through the O.T., and all the religion represented there, rose from the faith that back of everything are the hands of God. If God was the creator then nothing in creation can put a veto on his purposes. Men whom he has fashioned as living souls can be sure that all the forces of this universe are working with them when they are trying to become what the voice of God has told them they are meant to be. The humblest human spirit can say nothing truer, and the most learned philosopher nothing wiser than this: God made me, and God made the world I live in. Therefore, as long as I am faithful, I need have no fear of circumstances. God can make conditions work together to finish whatever is the best that he means to create in me.

2. The Life-Giving Spirit.—In this verse, as in the verse preceding, one feels again the sublimity of thought and expression to which

the Hebrew writers have lifted the conception of the Creation. The Babylonian story, with which they must have been familiar, moves on a level that is here transcended. According to the Babylonian myth, the chaos which lay back of the created universe was ruled over by the god Apsu and the goddess Tiamat. Apsu was conquered by the higher gods; but not until Marduk, the highest of all, was called upon could the more dreadful Tiamat be slain. Then it was out of the body of Tiamat that the solid frame of things was shaped. Split in two, one half of her was made into the earth and the other half into the firmament above it. Thus creation emerged out of the dark welter of mythological strife.

But to the biblical writers there are no half-gods. There could be chaos and darkness, but in these were no malignant forces of such kind that God had to use them as materials for his creation. "The high and lofty One that inhabiteth eternity" alone is God. Over whatever is waste and void his Spirit moves—moves broodingly and creatively according to a holy purpose which nothing can be strong enough to turn aside. That is good to remember when life seems empty within, or when over the life of the world around us darkness seems to descend. The brooding Spirit has not vanished from our universe. Not only did he bring forth the world from "chaos and old night," but by God's mercy he may yet bring forth a fairer world from new darknesses that beset us.

3-4. Light and Darkness.—The Exeg. has made it plain that this chapter is no scientific treatise. Labored effort to make it appear that

4 And God saw the light, that *it was* good: and God divided the light from the darkness.

and there was light. 4 And God saw that the light was good; and God separated the light

---

Let there be light; and there was light: The representation that light was the first creation, found also in the Indian, Greek, and Phoenician cosmogonies (*ibid.*, p. 105), may be a somewhat subtle refinement of the Babylonian myth which ascribes the creation of the world to the sun-god Marduk. It also reflects the thought of P that without light there could be no life, no order. Light was therefore created before even the sun—one of the features of the story which renders impossible all attempts to bring it into line with modern scientific knowledge. Indeed, it must be said that where the story does correspond with scientific fact, the correspondence is purely accidental. The author's main purpose was to set forth his conviction and that of his people—a conviction arrived at on religious, not on scientific, grounds—that the universe and all that is in it had its origin solely in the will of God. At the same time he was trying to give an ordered and reasonable account of the way in which it came into being. To this extent he was trying to be "scientific," as were those responsible for the other creation myths of the ancient world.

4. And God saw the light, that it was good, viz., that it was the perfect reflection of his thought. This is not said of the antecedent darkness, for though it had been created by God, it was, so to speak, an incomplete creation, still lacking order and meaning. God now **separated the light from the darkness.** "To separate" means to put into different places (cf. Job 3:6; 38:19-20). In this act God imposed some degree of order upon the

---

its picture of creation does parallel here and there the conclusions of physical science is misconceived and misdirected. Those who wrote this beginning to the book had none of the long process of detailed discovery slowly and laboriously pursued by which science has pushed its way into the unknown; they had to use the daring of the poet to imagine where they could not see. Like the unborn science which they could not dream, they too wanted an answer to the riddle of the universe, but the kind of answer they were seeking was different from that in which science may be content to rest: Not primarily "How was the universe created?" but "Who created it?" Not "What was the process?" but "What was the purpose?" In such terms they sought to express the one truth which to them was all-important, viz., that before all and in all is God.

So in each aspect of the creation story, as in the whole of it, it is the spiritual insight that matters. As to vss. 3-4, the Exeg. has pointed out that the thought of the one who wrote them had not quite emerged from the shadowlands of ancient and dim ideas. Probably his own conception was not clear as to what existed before the world was made. Was there nothing at all? Or was there a raw chaos which God did not make but found and had to work from? This latter thought is in most of the mythologies of the other Eastern peoples. But if the writers of this prelude to Genesis at first reflected it, as the Exeg. has shown, they moved beyond it.

They said God made the **light,** and they hesitated at first to say he made the **darkness;** but gradually they believed that darkness too belongs to him.

Consider the spiritual suggestions in this double fact. God's first creation is the light. Here first occurs the phrase that echoes grandly through all ch. 1. God saw **that it was good.** Among many peoples the soul of man has instinctively thought of light as the supreme symbol of God, the perfect reflection of his thought. Consider the role of Marduk in the myths of Babylon, which were known to the writers of Genesis; the worship of Re, the sun-god in ancient Egypt, Zoroastrianism, and Ormazd, the lord of light; the sacred fire of the Parsis. It is no wonder that light did thus seem to be the most nearly perfect symbol of the meaning of God.

For light is life. The simplest man knew that. It was the sun that brought forth the harvest after the inundations in the valley of the Nile. So in the great plains by the Tigris and the Euphrates it was when the sun came back from the darkness of winter that the seed sprouted and the flocks and herds brought forth their young. And light is guidance. In the night men grope and stumble. What they think is the path may be only the blind bewilderment of the forest. Till light comes they cannot be sure where they are or which way to go. So therefore light is safety and assurance. The fear of the dark, which is rooted deep in primitive man

5 And God called the light Day, and the darkness he called Night. And the evening and the morning were the first day.

from the darkness. 5 God called the light Day, and the darkness he called Night. And there was evening and there was morning, one day.

---

darkness and gave it meaning—a meaning which finds tender expression in Ps. 104:20, "Thou makest darkness, and it is night: wherein all the beasts of the forest do creep forth."

5. He also gave it a name, **Night.** The name is "that by which the thing is summoned into the field of thought" (Skinner, *Genesis,* p. 20), and is necessary for its full existence; cf. the first line of the Babylonian creation myth, "heaven was not named," i.e., did not yet exist. The thought underlying the statement that God named the darkness is that he thereby endowed it with complete existence, setting in motion the ordered alternation

---

who never knew what dangers might be lurking in the night, is still instinctive. The little child may be afraid to go to bed alone; and what grown man or woman, at some time of illness or acute anxiety, has not felt the darkness lie like a dreadful weight and longed desperately for the breaking of the day? With the dawn the place where they were was the same, yet not the same: no longer haunted, but pervaded by the inexpressible comfort of the light. And finally, the light brings beauty. All color vanishes in the dark, but the day brings back the blue of the sky, the green of trees and meadows, the kaleidoscope of gardens. What light thus brings to the physical earth God brings to the soul: life, guidance, assurance, beauty. So the psalmist sang of God, "Who coverest thyself with light as with a garment" (Ps. 104:2); and so believed that "light is sown for the righteous, and gladness for the upright in heart" (Ps. 97:11).

But observe also the other aspect of the profound truth which in vs. 4 begins to appear. Here, as the Exeg. has said, the author is approximating the position of Isa. 45:6-7: "I am the LORD and there is none else. I form the light, and create darkness." All aspects of the universe belong to God: therefore no aspects of man's experience can be without his presence: "If I make my bed in hell, behold, thou art there. . . . If I say, Surely the darkness shall cover me; even the night shall be light about me. . . . The darkness and the light are both alike to thee" (Ps. 139:8, 11-12). Consider how noble is the faith which is here emerging. It is not easy to believe that God is near and that he has not forgotten when life walks in the dark. The writers of Genesis could not bring themselves to say that darkness was good. The soul in darkness wants to get out of it. But the O.T. moves on to a more heroic confidence. Hear the instinctive cry of Pss. 88:12; 102:11. Note the awful loneliness of Job. Not only has God at great moments of deliverance brought men out of darkness (Ps. 107:14), he reveals

himself in the darkness and robs it of its terror (Ps. 91:5). "Unto the upright there ariseth light in the darkness" (Ps. 112:4). Thus not only the sunny but also the shadowed side of life is made the realm of faith. The tragic can be transfigured. See this again and again in the Psalms. See it in Jeremiah. See it at last in Jesus. No trial or disaster can be so dark as to eclipse the redeeming presence of God. Through the night as well as through the day the road of his benignant purpose runs. As a great modern Christian wrote to a friend in the darkness of affliction: "You cannot understand, or explain, but you know as well as I, that back of everything is God, and God is light,—we shall see. And God is love—we shall be satisfied. It may be a long while, but it will be worth waiting for." [7]

5. *Life's Goings Out and Comings In.*—Here is not the order of words our usual thought would frame. Why the evening first? When sunset comes, we do not say that the day begins, but rather that it is drawing to its close. When we think of the day's beginning, we think of dawn.

Yet all through the Bible, and in Jewish reckoning still, the day begins at evening. That conception may have its roots in times far back beyond the Bible, before stable civilization developed, when the earliest tribes were nomads of the desert. In the heat of the desert sun they kept in their tents. In the cool of the evening life could actively begin. Those times had long gone by when the priestly author wrote ch. 1, but he inherited and instinctively expressed the ancient thought. Was there in his mind also a deeper consideration? The night is the time of mystery, and out of the night therefore came the first creative act of God. The primary fact was darkness, and it is against the background of darkness that God appears. Here, at any rate, there is stimulus for our own meditation. The new experience, the moment when the day of life begins, may not be in sudden brightness,

[7] Babcock, *Thoughts for Every-Day Living,* p. 152.

of day and night which the author sees as a manifestation of the power of God (cf. 8:22). With the naming of light and darkness the night came, followed by the dawn; the first day was over, the second day had begun.

There can be no question but that by **Day** the author meant just what we mean— the time required for one revolution of the earth on its axis. Had he meant an aeon he would certainly, in view of his fondness for great numbers, have stated the number of millenniums each period embraced. While this might have made his account of creation less irreconcilable with modern science, it would have involved a lessening of God's greatness, one sign of which was his power to do so much in one day.

---

much less in the glare of noon. It may come when we are most conscious of the shadows and the silence. It may come in the hushed mystery of the twilight before the stars appear.

But however the beginning and the sequence are conceived, there is the double fact of day and night; and the message of the Bible is that God gave them both. Life has its beautiful and blessed rhythm. There is a time for action and a time for rest. There is a time when all the ways of the world are clear and open, and a time when the shadows fall and we must wait. And the promise is that as the Lord made both day and night, so "the Lord shall preserve thy going out and thy coming in" (Ps. 121:8).

The truly religious life must have its "going out," i.e., it must reflect the spirit of the day in which man "goeth forth . . . to his labor until the evening" (Ps. 104:23). Religion can have no partnership with laziness. "One of the facts most creditable to human nature," as has been wittily said, "is that it gets up in the morning." The steady dependability of human beings in the familiar duties of every day constitutes the moral fiber of the world's affairs. Martin Luther understood this relationship between the responsibility of the day's demands and religion when he declared:

What you do in your house is worth as much as if you did it up in Heaven for our Lord God. . . . It looks like a small thing when a maid cooks, and cleans, and does other housework. But because God's command is there, even such a lowly employment must be praised as a service of God.[8]

And so did George Herbert when he wrote:

A servant with this clause
Makes drudgery divine;
Who sweeps a room, as for Thy laws,
Makes that and th' action fine.[9]

Some of the religions of the Orient have paralyzed the nerve of action by offering a

counsel of quiescence which leads to moral passivity and surrender. But the religion of the O.T. and the N.T. has no such inertness. Just because it never forgets that man is the servant of God and subject to him, it can declare that man need never be subject to the forces of this world but can be their sovereign. Each one of us is to say like Jesus, "I must work the works of him that sent me, while it is day" (John 9:4), even as we pray, "Thy will be done."

So equally the "coming in" must be part of all true life. Religion is not to be a hectic activism devoid of meditation. Here a dangerous one-sidedness of the West needs to be corrected by the deeper penetration of the East; there must be a time to be quiet and to receive.

The truth in all this may sometimes be perverted. It is perverted when what ought to be refreshment of body and spirit becomes a flabby indolence. Certainly we are not to imitate the subject of a skillful artist's drawing in a current magazine—a drawing of a stout and well-to-do dowager of middle age, lying in a hammock on a lawn, and saying to an equally well-padded caller drinking tea and eating sandwiches: "You would just *love* my Dr. Baxter. His prescription is rest, rest, rest." John of Damascus' hymn "Those eternal bowers" can make us know that we are not to

Dream away the light,
When he bids you labor,
When he tells you, "Fight."

And the purpose of the night is perverted too when so-called recreation means only jazz music and liquor in a round of night clubs which make a man or woman more spent and jaded than all the activities of the day.

But underneath the falsities this fact remains: God who blessed the day has also blessed the night. He gave it for the kind of rest that genuinely restores—rest of body, rest of mind, and rest of soul. It would be a good thing to learn by heart some of the lovely evening hymns and to learn from those who wrote them that the "coming in" at the end of the day can be a coming in to God.

[8] Arthur C. McGiffert, *Martin Luther, the Man and His Work* (New York: The Century Co., 1911), pp. 177-78.

[9] "The Elixir," st. v.

6 ¶ And God said, Let there be a firmament in the midst of the waters, and let it divide the waters from the waters.

7 And God made the firmament, and divided the waters which *were* under the firmament from the waters which *were* above the firmament: and it was so.

8 And God called the firmament Heaven. And the evening and the morning were the second day.

9 ¶ And God said, Let the waters under the heaven be gathered together unto one place, and let the dry *land* appear: and it was so.

6 And God said, "Let there be a firmament in the midst of the waters, and let it separate the waters from the waters." 7 And God made the firmament and separated the waters which were under the firmament from the waters which were above the firmament. And it was so. 8 And God called the firmament Heaven. And there was evening and there was morning, a second day.

9 And God said, "Let the waters under the heavens be gathered together into one place, and let the dry land appear." And it

C. The Second Day (1:6-8)

6. In the conception of the **firmament** as a solid substance (cf. Job 26:11) there is a distinct reminiscence of the Babylonian myth, according to which the sun-god Marduk split the slain chaos monster in two and used one half of the carcass as a firmament, the other half as the earth. But it is a reminiscence only. For this author the firmament was called into being by divine fiat. Above it was the heavenly sea referred to in Pss. 29:10; 148:4; Rev. 4:6; etc.

7. And it was so, appearing in the Hebrew at the end of this verse, comes in the LXX at the end of vs. 6. This raises the question as to whether vs. 7a may not be an addition to the original narrative. There is nothing corresponding to it after vss. 3 and 9. To be noted further is the absence from vs. 8 of the formula of approval, "and God saw that it was good," found in vss. 10, 12, 18, 21, 25 (cf. vss. 4, 31). If its omission is intentional on the part of the author, it is probably due to the fact that the business of bringing the waters to order was not yet completed. This would seem to suggest that the creative acts of vss. 6 and 9—the separation of the upper waters from the lower, and that of the lower waters from the land—were originally more closely associated than is now the case, and that the representation that they occurred on successive days is simply a feature of the author's ordering of the material with which he was working.

D. The Third Day (1:9-13)

9. The third day, like the sixth, was marked by two acts of creation. The first—the gathering together of the waters under the heavens—is, as has already been noted, more closely associated with the preceding act than with that which follows it. For **place** the

6-10. *The Loftier Perception.*—Here, as at many other points in ch. 1, we may perceive how some of the religious conceptions of Israel could have their roots in primitive ideas and yet lift the flower of their ultimate thought high above that old dark ground. In its fundamental elements this description of the creation of the firmament and the waters above it, of the earth and the waters beneath it, and of the seas upon the earth, is like the creation epic that came from Babylon. The physical picture is the same: a flat earth with mountains round its rim, on which the dome of the firmament rested as on pillars; in the firmament, windows through which the waters above could come down in rain; and in the earth, the hidden channels

through which the waters of the underlying deep could flood to make the seas. But to the Hebrew mind the physical picture had a spiritual interpretation which belonged to another level altogether. In the Babylonian epic a palace was built above the firmament for a pantheon of gods; and in the firmament the stars were other gods that men were to worship. In the biblical account all lesser powers that might compel men's superstitious homage and make them afraid have vanished before the transcendent majesty of God. This, then, is the greatness of the prologue to Genesis: not that it has any authoritative word of scientific fact concerning the physical earth men live upon, but rather that it leads men on to faith that the one power

10 And God called the dry *land* Earth; and the gathering together of the waters called he Seas: and God saw that *it was* good.

11 And God said, Let the earth bring forth grass, the herb yielding seed, *and* the fruit tree yielding fruit after his kind, whose seed *is* in itself, upon the earth: and it was so.

was so. 10 God called the dry land Earth, and the waters that were gathered together he called Seas. And God saw that it was good. 11 And God said, "Let the earth put forth vegetation, plants yielding seed, and fruit trees bearing fruit in which is their seed, each according to its kind, upon the

---

LXX reads "mass," probably correctly in view of the occurrence of the same word rendered **gathered together** in vs. 10. **And let the dry land appear** implies, as has been noted, that the land was already in existence beneath the waters (cf. Ps. 104:6-9, rendering vs. 6 "the deep covered it [the earth] as with a vesture," with Bernhard Duhm, *Die Psalmen* [Freiburg: J. C. B. Mohr, 1899; "Kurzer Hand-Commentar zum Alten Testament"] p. 242) ; on this see Exeg. on vss. 1-2.

10. God called the dry land Earth, and the waters that were gathered together he called Seas. The creation of the organized universe, "the heavens and the earth" (vs. 1), is thus advanced another step; both **the dry land** and what remains of the primeval chaos are "named" (cf. vs. 5). **Seas** embraces more than the waters upon the face of the earth; it includes also the (supposed) subterranean waters upon which the earth was believed to rest (cf. Ps. 24:2), to which P refers in 7:11, and the circumfluent ocean (cf. Ps. 139:9), upon which the pillars of the firmament (cf. Job 26:11) stood.

11. A literal rendering of **Let the earth put forth vegetation** would be "Let the earth vegetate vegetation." The growth is then classified into plants bearing seed, and trees bearing fruit in which the seed is—the same classification is implicit in the distinction between "herbs" and "trees" in Exod. 9:25; 10:15—a curious piece of "science." Of more significance is the emphasis on **seed**, i.e., on the reproductive activity of nature. This the author sees to be a continuing manifestation of the creative power of God.

---

under which they live is God in whose sovereignty and sure purpose they can trust (see also Expos. on vss. 2, 14).

11-13. The Good Earth.—There is no act of creation for which it is more instinctive to thank God than for this one. Here is the blessing of the fertile ground, with its productivity of growth—the everlasting miracle of "the good earth." Human existence depends upon the earth's fertility. Bread is rightly called "the staff of life." The cave men did not till the ground or make bread, they ate meat and gnawed bones; but there would have been no meat for the cave men to eat if animals had not fed on the grass the earth produced. And civilization began when men got past the cave, past the life of nomad hunters, and began to settle on the land and plant seed in it and cultivate the grain. Facts so familiar that they are taken casually may be of all facts the most wonderful because they lie at the foundation of life. Consider the miracle of any seed when the earth receives it, the root going down for nourishment in the darkness, the stalk pushing up into the light. Multiply that by all the grainfields of the world and their

total harvest, which in one year amounts to billions of bushels, and nearly one billion bushels in the United States alone. The strength of a nation may be closely linked to the soundness of its agriculture.[1] Consider what men's love for the land has meant in the history of England. Her fierce attachment to the earth she had inherited was the one thing admirable in Scarlett O'Hara of *Gone with the Wind.* Not only economic stability but also social health depend upon the blessings of the land. Where the soil is impoverished the whole level of life is low. Schools, roads, sanitation, medical care, all are poor. The rural church languishes or is abandoned altogether when the people have no roots of ownership in worth-while land and begin to drift.

To sin against the land is to sin against the good life which God has put within the reach of men. The Christian church therefore, and every intelligent individual in it, has a concern for the forces that destroy the land. Greedy

[1] See V. G. Simkhovitch on "Rome's Fall Considered," a chapter in *Toward the Understanding of Jesus* (New York: The Macmillan Co., 1921), pp. 84-139.

12 And the earth brought forth grass, *and* herb yielding seed after his kind, and the tree yielding fruit, whose seed *was* in itself, after his kind: and God saw that *it was* good.

13 And the evening and the morning were the third day.

14 ¶ And God said, Let there be lights in the firmament of the heaven to divide the day from the night; and let them be for signs, and for seasons, and for days, and years:

earth." And it was so. 12 The earth brought forth vegetation, plants yielding seed according to their own kinds, and trees bearing fruit in which is their seed, each according to its kind. And God saw that it was good. 13 And there was evening and there was morning, a third day.

14 And God said, "Let there be lights in the firmament of the heavens to separate the day from the night; and let them be for signs and for seasons and for days and years,

---

12. The first sentence is unnecessary after **and it was so** (vs. 11*b*), which records the fulfillment of the command of vs. 11*a*. It may well be part of the systematic elaboration (cf. vss. 7*a*, 16*a*, 21*a*, 25*a*) to which the original narrative of P was subjected, possibly to bring the account of the other acts of creation into line with vss. 26-27.

E. THE FOURTH DAY (1:14-19)

14-15. The purpose of the **lights in the firmament**, according to vs. 14*a*, is **to separate the day from the night**, i.e., they are not to give light—for light has existence independent of the sun (cf. vs. 3)—but to determine when day shall give way to night. When the sun rises, then it is day; when it sets, it is night. In vs. 14*b* a further purpose is stated:

---

exploitation is one. Whole mountainsides of timber in the United States and in other countries have been so ruthlessly and carelessly cut that the possibility of new growth has been destroyed. Oil wells have been drilled in such blind haste of competition that millions of gallons have been wasted. Constantly there must be watchfulness against private interests that try to possess the resources which ought to belong to a whole people.

In addition to deliberate exploitation there is the more widespread fact of ignorance. Great sections of the earth are robbed of their fertility because farmers have not been taught the necessity for rotation of crops and of contour plowing. Precious topsoil is washed away by rains and floods, or blown off in dry years, so that what had been rich farming regions becomes a "dust bowl." The appalling poverty of whole provinces in China, and the continual recurrence of famines, is due in large part to centuries of erosion of the soil. These are not merely technical problems. They have their immense spiritual implications and their social repercussions. As inhabitants of this planet we are stewards of what might be the limitless bounty of God. There could always be an answer to the petition "Give us this day our daily bread." But if public indifference to the waste and destruction of the earth's resources should continue, it can blight God's promise of a fertility that is meant to bring forth abundantly for the needs of men.

Another thought comes from this text. God created not only the trees and the grain for practical necessities. He made the flowers also. Consider the function of beauty for the human soul. Remember Wordsworth's "Daffodils." Unbridled industrialism and commercial moneymaking can destroy the beauty on which men's souls should feed, and throw away the "things unmerchantable, that cannot be purchased with the finest of fine gold." Note how the borders of the highroads have been defaced and defiled by billboards, and note in any legislative session the lobbies that resist any regulation of the interests that despise public enjoyment where private profit can be made. See on the other hand the slow advance of enlightened policies that create national parks and make sanctuaries of natural beauty. Here is a chance for the aroused activity of a citizenship which is not only socially responsible but also religiously sensitive; for the preservation of the earth's fertility and its beauty is a duty both to man and to God.

14. *The Consecration of Time.*—The sun and moon have a purpose more august than that of giving light; they set the times and seasons that make up life. The sun and moon are not independent forces, as early mythologies supposed, but they are God's handiwork and belong to him; and as the writer perceived that, so also he was sure that time, which these heavenly instruments mark out, likewise belongs to God.

15 And let them be for lights in the firmament of the heaven to give light upon the earth: and it was so.

15 and let them be lights in the firmament of the heavens to give light upon the earth."

---

they are to be **for signs and for seasons and for days and years. Signs** has a certain astrological significance; the luminaries will provide on occasions **signs** such as those referred to in Isa. 7:11 and II Kings 20:8-11. At the same time, in ascribing this sign-giving power to God's endowment the author seems to be guarding against the kind of thing condemned in Jer. 10:2. With the reference to **seasons** cf. Ps. 104:19, "He [God] appointed the moon for seasons." **For days and years** simply repeats and extends the thought of vs. 14a.

Vs. 15a is in direct contradiction to vs. 3. The confused character of this description of the functions of the heavenly luminaries (cf. Heinrich Holzinger, *Genesis* [Freiburg: J. C. B. Mohr, 1898; "Kurzer Hand-Commentar zum Alten Testament"], pp. 8-9; Gunkel, *Genesis*, p. 109; Skinner, *Genesis*, pp. 26-27) suggests that it may be the work of more than one hand. Possibly the narrative as it left the hand of P contained only vss. 14a, 15b; i.e., P was content to affirm that the heavenly bodies were the creation of God and that therefore, by implication, they had no power beyond that with which God had endowed them. So absurd was it to think that they were gods, and so objects of worship, that P

That of course was to him no abstract idea, but a most vital and controlling fact. Perhaps he was remembering specifically what happened when men had no clean and reverent conception that all times and seasons do belong to God—remembering the orgiastic feasts of Baal worship, the pagan celebrations of the nature cycle, and other practices rooted in ancient superstition which were oftentimes corrupt. What he wanted men to understand was that in all the gamut of their experience and their emotions they ought to be directed by those signs that come to them from the hand of God.

Nor is that some distant notion unrelated to ourselves. On the contrary, it is a truth of which we constantly need to be reminded. What gives their actual meaning to our times and seasons? Consider the facts and see. Note how often the days that ought to be sacred are profaned: Sunday secularized, Christmas commercialized, Easter cheapened into an hour's outward show.

And in a larger and more inclusive way men may forget that life with its times and seasons belongs to God. They ignore the fact that there are any such things as heavenly directions which should control what they are and do. Charles Dickens put the truth in his own unforgettable way in the first chapter of *Dombey and Son.* Mr. Dombey had no doubt whatever that the affairs of the commercial house of which he was the head were more important than anything else imaginable—more important than private affection or public concern.

Dombey and Son. . . . Those three words conveyed the one idea of Mr. Dombey's life. The earth was made for Dombey and Son to trade in, and the sun and moon were made to give them light. Rivers and seas were formed to float their ships; rainbows gave them promise of fair weather; winds blew for or against their enterprises; stars and planets circled in their orbits to preserve inviolate a system of which they were the centre. . . . A.D. had no concern with anno Domini, but stood for anno Dombei—and Son.

That sort of blind arrogance comes sooner or later to its fall. Only if a man is looking to something higher than his own self-interest or his pride and passion for the signs that shall control his seasons and days and years will he know at last truly how **to divide the day from the night.**

14-19. Sun, Moon, and Stars.—The sun and the moon are such immense and obvious facts in the universal experience of the human race that it is natural that they should have entered often into religion. Solar myths are numerous. In Egypt particularly the worship of the sun was the center of religious thought and spiritual imagination. Among some of the peoples of Asia, especially the desert peoples who because of the heat of daytime did their journeying mostly by night, the moon was the influence to which they gave the more awesome regard. The winter and summer solstices especially were associated with worship and appeal because they represented the withdrawal or the coming again of life-bringing light. Eclipses of the sun struck primitive man with inevitable terror; and the moon also, in some phases, was feared as baleful. Note our words "moonstruck" and "lunatic." Here in these verses of Genesis is one of the many instances in which the Hebrew writer lifted instinctive conceptions of earlier peoples up into

16 And God made two great lights; the greater light to rule the day, and the lesser light to rule the night: *he made* the stars also.

17 And God set them in the firmament of the heaven to give light upon the earth,

And it was so. 16 And God made the two great lights, the greater light to rule the day, and the lesser light to rule the night; he made the stars also. 17 And God set them in the firmament of the heavens to give

---

would not even deny it. A later commentator, feeling vs. 14a to be an inadequate statement of the functions of the luminaries, will then have added vss. 14b and 15a, though it is possible that vs. 15a, which has no astrological implications, is from another hand than vs. 14b.

16-19. These verses, except for vss. 18b, 19, also seem to be an addition to the primary narrative of P. **And God made the two great lights** is, strictly speaking, unnecessary after vs. 15b and, like vss. 7a, 12a, may be a part of a systematic elaboration of P's work. With it belongs **the greater light to rule the day, and the lesser light to rule the night. . . . And God set them in the firmament of the heavens . . . , to rule over the day and over the night, and to separate the light from the darkness** (vss. 16aβγ, 17a, 18a). Indicative

---

a nobler faith. To the Hebrews the sun and moon are no longer independent forces. They also are the handiwork of the one living God whose final work is man.

In an age when there was no such thing as a telescope the sun and the moon seemed, of course, the mightiest creations in the sky. Nevertheless, the seer who wrote this prelude of Genesis did not stop with them. He looked at the innumerable lights that glittered in the heavens, and he said that God had **made the stars also.** He did not know the immensity he added with that **also.** He could not have guessed that what seemed to him as little twinkling pin points against the darkness were planets and constellations that witnessed to the glory of God to a degree of wonder inconceivably greater than the witness of the sun and moon. But if he had been able to be aware of all that he was saying, he still would have said it. For the wings of his faith went out to whatever might be the fullness of the universe. All that was belonged to God.

The stars also. The solar system shrinks to a small thing as measured by the majesty of the stars and the fathomless depths of space in which they move. The sun is estimated to be a little less than ninety-three million miles distant from the earth. But the distance to Alpha Centauri, one of the nearest of the stars, is twenty-five million millions of miles. Arcturus, the star to which the handle of the Dipper points, and which shines in the northern sky hardly bigger to human eyes than the golden flicker of a candle, has a diameter of ten million miles. In 1933, through a photo-electric cell which had caught the light of Arcturus through the telescope of the Yerkes Observatory and actuated electric relays, the lights were turned on to open the Chicago World's Fair. It was esti-

mated then (though these calculations have since been slightly revised) that these beams from Arcturus reaching the earth in 1933 had left that star in 1893, when the first Chicago World's Fair was opened. The beams had taken forty years to reach the earth; and the distance traveled by light in one year is six trillion miles.

As we contemplate these facts, what is brought home to our awareness? First, a sense of awe before the majesty and mystery of God. The men of the O.T. felt this (see Pss. 8; 19; 104; 148; Isa. 40). Who can contemplate without a hushed and humbled reverence in mind and soul the universe which modern knowledge has unfolded? If men instinctively recognized the reality of God and bowed down before the grandeur of the Creator as they looked up at the firmament of their contracted thought, what of the compulsion to a more immense religious awe which reaches out from the infinity of the skies as they are now perceived? Recall Joseph Addison's hymn "The spacious firmament on high," and Oliver Wendell Holmes's, "Lord of all being, throned afar."

True, there is a difficulty here. For some there is a frightening bewilderment in the new conceptions of the universe. God seems lost in its immensity. Their faith would feel safer in a smaller framework.[2] But here is the everlasting necessity for that stretching of the mind which religious maturity requires. Greater understanding can lead through greater wonder to the grown man's faith. Willard L. Sperry has written of an old minister in a New England mill town to whom he was assistant, who once every year preached a sermon on the latest discoveries in astronomy. When Sperry expostulated and

[2] See the first chapters of Walter Lippmann, *A Preface to Morals* (New York: The Macmillan Co., 1929).

18 And to rule over the day and over the night, and to divide the light from the darkness: and God saw that *it was* good.

19 And the evening and the morning were the fourth day.

light upon the earth, 18 to rule over the day and over the night, and to separate the light from the darkness. And God saw that it was good. 19 And there was evening and there was morning, a fourth day.

---

of the secondary character of this material is: (*a*) **to rule** over day and night is an advance on the thought of vs. 14*a*, and (*b*) **to separate the light from the darkness** differs, in view of vs. 4*b*, somewhat significantly from vs. 14*a*. To this was later added vs. 17*b*, **to give light upon the earth,** possibly by the same hand as vs. 15*a*, and vs. 16*b*, to include **the stars** with the sun and moon. Vss. 18*b*-19 are from the hand of P and complete his description of the work of the fourth day.

The elaboration to which the originally simple account of the creation of the heavenly bodies (vss. 14*a*, 15*b*, 18*b*, 19) has been subjected is not only more extensive than that which other parts of the narrative have received, but also differs from it somewhat in character. Elsewhere the secondary material really adds nothing to what has already been said. In this section, however, not only vss. 14*b*, 15*a* and 17*b*, but even the material referred to above as "systematic elaboration" (vss. 16*a*, 17*a*, 18*a*), has a certain didactic intent, which, indeed, it may be noted, characterizes even the primary vs. 14*a*, for only here does the author state the purpose of what was being created **to separate the day from the night.** The systematic elaboration adds that the lights are **to rule over the day and over the night** (vs. 18*a*), and the later commentators that they are **to give light upon the earth** (vss. 15*a*, 17*b*), and are to be **for signs and for seasons and for days and years** (vs. 14*b*). The intent of vss. 15*a* and 17*b* is clear enough: they seem to be from the hand of one who realized, as P had not, that light derives from the sun. The other material would seem to be combating current astrological ideas. The intent of vss. 16*a*β*γ*, 18*a* may well be to emphasize that the rule over the day and the night popularly

---

wanted to know what possible use such a sermon preached in such a place could have, the older man answered, "My dear boy, of course it is of no use at all, but it greatly enlarges my idea of God." Then, says Sperry:

That stray remark lighted up a whole area of which I had been until that time utterly unaware. . . . From that day to this I have known that "greatly enlarged ideas of God" are supremely necessary to religion and that in the long run you cannot make good cotton cloth or sell it honestly in want of such ideas.[3]

And if contemplation of the stars enlarges one's thoughts of God, so it wakes the realization that there is order in the universe which needs to be matched by disciplined order in life. Consider the majestic rhythm of the stars, the unswerving certainties of movement because of which may be foretold the exact path of a star's progression or the exact instant when the shadow of an eclipse begins. Said Immanuel Kant, "Two things fill the mind with ever new and increasing admiration and awe . . . : the starry heavens above me and the moral law within me."[4] Read Wordsworth's "Ode to

Duty," and consider how God, who "dost preserve the stars from wrong," speaks from the example of the heavens this lesson to the human heart: that it is not by license or chaotic so-called freedom, but only by obedience to everlasting laws of righteousness that the great energies of life are swung into their harmonious orbits. That is so within the personality in the control of impulses by ideals. It is so in all relationships: of friendship, of marriage, of the citizenship that sees a community in the light of the kingdom of God.

Thus the stars speak of God. But they speak also of man. What they first seem to say is devastating. "When I consider thy heavens, . . . what is man?" If the psalmist could ask that, how much more crushing might the question seem now? Beside what we know of this majestic and immeasurable universe, what is man but a speck of restless protoplasm, crawling on this little earth? Listen to Theodore Dreiser: "As I see him, the unutterably infinitesimal individual weaves among the mysteries a floss-like and wholly meaningless course—if course it be. In short, I catch no meaning from all I have seen, and pass quite as I came, confused and dismayed."[5]

[3] *"Yes, But ———"* (New York: Harper & Bros., 1931), p. 127.

[4] *Critique of Practical Reason,* Conclusion.

[5] *Living Philosophies* (New York: Simon & Schuster, 1931), p. 74.

20 And God said, Let the waters bring forth abundantly the moving creature that hath life, and fowl *that* may fly above the earth in the open firmament of heaven.	20 And God said, "Let the waters bring forth swarms of living creatures, and let birds fly above the earth across the firmament of heaven.

attributed to the sun and the moon was merely figurative, as they were not gods, not even living beings, but merely lights. And the author of vs. 14*b* may be saying that if the heavenly bodies did give signs, as was commonly supposed, they did not do so independently, in their own power, but as the agents of God who had created them to reveal his will. But for all their methodical classification of the tasks supposedly performed by the sun, moon, and stars—indeed, perhaps because of such classification—neither P nor his commentators rose to the height attained by the author of Ps. 19:1, "The heavens declare the glory of God; and the firmament showeth his handiwork."

F. The Fifth Day (1:20-23)

20. Like the earth in vs. 11, the **waters** are now endowed with productive powers. A literal rendering of this verse would be, "And God said, 'Let the waters swarm with

Against the profundities of time and space which astronomy explores, what conceivable significance has man? Well—as has been truly said—the answer is that man is the astronomer. Man has the intellect, the intuition, and the power of ordered thought to master the secrets of the universe. To him has been given to think God's thoughts after him. How much can this fact mean for further mastery of what God intends us to understand? If man has gone so far in intellectual grasp, what of the moral conquests that ought to be possible?

In a time of pessimism and of possible frustration that is the crucial question. Too many influences disparage human possibilities; who will dignify them? Thomas Mann wote:

Who cannot embroider upon the depravity of this strange creature called man, who does not often despair over his future? . . . And yet it is a fact—more true today than ever—that we cannot allow ourselves, because of so much all too well-founded scepticism, to despise humanity. Despite so much ridiculous depravity, we cannot forget the great and the honourable in man, which manifest themselves as art and science, as passion for truth, creation of beauty and the idea of justice; and it is also true that insensitiveness to the great mystery which we touch upon when we say "man" or "humanity" signifies spiritual death.[6]

Let this emphasis be carried forward to our generation, and in a difficult time. When many representations already confront us with what seems a pitch-dark night, the thing to do is not to splash it with the black paint of added pessimism. Rather, the need is to carry into it the lighted candle of a better faith in human possi-

bilities when these are kindled by the flame of God.

20-21. *The Treasures of the Waters.*—Thank God for fish! If one should begin with those words he might startle his hearers, but he would be saying something worth their listening to, all the same. In the beautiful old *Benedicite,* which is sung in many church services, there is the echo of man's gratitude for what the record in Genesis tells that God created on the fifth day—not only fish in general, but the great sea-monsters too. "O ye Whales, and all that move in the waters, bless ye the Lord: praise him, and magnify him for ever."

The whaling ships that went out from the seaports of New England and from other harbors of the world established an industry that in its day was as full of economic profit as it was of romance. Everyone who has read Melville's *Moby Dick* will understand that, but not everyone may realize the whole immensity of the fisheries of the world. Before the outbreak of World War II, the fisheries were producing thirty-seven billion pounds of fish products annually, valued at almost a billion dollars. Some countries owe their very existence to their fishing fleets, e.g., Japan before 1941 controlled nearly a third of the fishery harvest of the world. As the United States Department of the Interior has stated:

The high nutritive quality and digestibility of fish proteins class fish among the more desirable food products. . . . Much of the yield of the fisheries may be consumed directly as human food, while the remainder may be converted into such essential by-products as vitamin oils, livestock and poultry feeds, fertilizers, and industrial oils.[7]

[6] *The Coming Victory of Democracy* (New York: Alfred A. Knopf, 1938), pp. 20-21.

[7] Fish and Wild Life Service, Fishery Leaflet 109; February, 1945.

swarming things, living creatures, and let birds fly, etc.'" **Living creatures** thus appears to be a gloss, a reflex probably of vs. 21a. The conjunction of fishes and birds in one creative act would seem to be due to P's schematization of his material to bring the whole work of creation into six days. The LXX and the Vulg. render, "and birds that may fly." On the basis of this William Henry Bennett (*Genesis* [Edinburgh: T. C. & E. C. Jack, n.d.; "The New-Century Bible"], p. 81) suggests that the author may have been influenced by some ancient tradition that birds as well as fishes were produced by the water. Against this interpretation is the fact that the verb above rendered "swarm with"

Nor is the supply of fish left to chance. The governments of all progressive countries have their hatcheries that not only stock the streams, but are concerned also with the ocean. A Japanese scientist wrote after 1945: "The ocean and the seas contain inexhaustible treasures; in order to utilize them fully we must be guided by scientific methods of fishing." And he went on to urge the cultivation of "sea-farms," in which, "as we fertilize the rice fields, we should fertilize the sea-weeds which are rich in iodine and serve as food both for man and fish." [8]

But it is not only that fish are caught for food and for innumerable other purposes; the catching of them has made a special breed of men. Among Jesus' disciples at least the first four, and the leaders of them all, were men straight from the fishing boats. For their occupation, with its rough chance of wind and water, a man must be of virile stuff; and such men can be the mainstays of church and nation. They may look like crude material in the beginning, but so does iron; and like iron, they can be forged and hammered into heroic strength. After he had sailed with the men of the North Sea fishing fleets of England, Wilfred Grenfell wrote: "They . . . never thought of deprivation or danger. . . . In efficiency and for their daring resourcefulness in physical difficulties and dangers, they were absolutely in a class by themselves. . . . Whatever they did, they did hard." [9] Men inured like that to the sea have made the greatness of England as they have manned her navies and her fleets of exploration since the days of Raleigh and Drake. And much of the vigor of France would not have belonged to her if she had not had the fishermen of Brittany.

In gentler ways, also, fish have played a part in the widening of human experience and in the development of human character. They have been the lure to lead men to the rivers where they learn much more than the delicate skill of casting with rod and line. They learn to know the spell of silence and the long, slow restfulness of being alone with their own thoughts. The classic description of the fisherman's pursuits as leading mind and spirit to happy exer-

cise is old Izaak Walton's *The Complete Angler, or the Contemplative Man's Recreation.* Even if the fisherman takes nothing, he says, "Yet he enjoyeth a delightful Walk by pleasant Rivers, in Sweet Pastures, among odoriferous Flowers, which gratifie his Senses and delight his Mind," all of which "composeth the Soul to that calmness and sincerity which give a man the fullest possession and fruition of himself." [1] An earlier writer, Gervase Markham, in 1614, had celebrated the spiritual fruits of angling in a still more specific way, and in his quaint listing of what a fisherman learns there is a suggestion as to what all men in all pursuits might well decide to achieve; for the list begins with patience and ends with fortitude, which "inableth the minde to undergoe tne travaile and exchange of Weathers with a delightful ease, and not to despaire with a little expence of time, but to persevere." [2]

For Izaak Walton, however, the fisherman's contact with the quiet loveliness of the outdoors was more than an incitement to serene philosophy. It was a wide open door through which religious reverence entered into a larger world. Here is a revealing fact for thought to dwell upon: the simple things which in themselves are insignificant may become the avenues to God. The gentle old Walton was one of the first in England to learn to catch from nature a message of the divine. Just by being a fisherman he became a more discerning Christian. He remembered:

When God intended to reveal any future events or high notions to his prophets, he then carried them either to the deserts or the sea-shore, that having so separated them from amidst the press of people and business, and the cares of the world, he might settle their mind in a quiet repose, and there make them fit for revelation. [3]

And he ends his book thus:

So when I would beget content, and increase confidence in the power, and wisdom, and Providence of Almighty God, I will walk the meadows by some gliding stream, and there contemplate the lilies

---

[8] Fishery Leaflet 288; March, 1948.

[9] *A Labrador Doctor* (Boston: Houghton Mifflin Co., 1919), pp. 91, 94.

[1] New York: John Wiley & Son, 1866, pp. li, lii.

[2] *Ibid.,* p. xliii.

[3] *Ibid.,* pp. 25-26.

21 And God created great whales, and every living creature that moveth, which the waters brought forth abundantly, after their kind, and every winged fowl after his kind: and God saw that *it was* good.

ment of the heavens." 21 So God created the great sea monsters and every living creature that moves, with which the waters swarm, according to their kinds, and every winged bird according to its kind. And God saw

---

seems to mean not "produce a swarm," but rather "be a place where swarming things abound"; it cannot, therefore, govern **birds** as an object (Skinner, *Genesis*, pp. 27-28). It may be noted that there is no suggestion that only a single pair of each kind was produced, but rather that the whole species appeared in considerable numbers. At the end of vs. 20 the LXX has "and it was so," correctly it would seem (cf. vss. 7*b*, 9*b*, 12*b*, 15*b*).

21. The first sentence is probably secondary (cf. vss. 7*a*, 12*a*, 16*a*, 17*a*, 18*a*); not only is it necessary after "and it was so"; it also ascribes the "swarming things" to an immediate creative act of God, not to the productive power with which he had endowed **the waters.** The sudden introduction of **the great sea monsters** suggests that these words, with the following **and,** are still later, an addition by one who was concerned with the thought

---

that take no care, and those very many other various little living creatures, that are not only created, but fed, man knows not how, by the goodness of the God of Nature, and therefore trust in him. This is my purpose; and so "Let every thing that hath breath praise the Lord."[4]

If to any persons it should seem a long way from vs. 20 to the thoughts that culminate in Izaak Walton's words, let it be remembered that indeed they are linked by an everlasting truth. As the ancient writers contemplated the waters and the living things therein, and counted that work of God as good, so those who walk by quiet rivers may behold the goodness of God again. As the unnamed American editor of *The Complete Angler* wrote:

I trust that I have drunk enough of the old angler's spirit not to let such pastime break in upon better things; but, on the other hand, I have worked the harder from thankfulness to HIM who taught the brook to wind with musical gurglings, as it rolls on to the Great Sea.[5]

21-23. The Wonder of Birds.—Here is a possibility for a meditation or sermon, at least to a particular group and at a special time. **God created . . . every winged bird according to its kind.** So the Creation had another aspect in its manifold fascination. Looking at the birds, men may well echo the words of Genesis concerning this work of God, **that it was good.** Granted that not all people are equally enthusiastic about all birds. As Uncle Remus might have said, "Dey comes different." Farmers have no liking for some of them, e.g., crows and hawks. But most birds are the friendly allies of men's pursuits; and in their own lives they give

to the universe a fresh element of variety and wonder. They wake the poetry in human minds and souls. Read Shelley's "To a Skylark," Keats's "Ode to a Nightingale," Wordsworth's "To a Skylark" and "To the Cuckoo," and Henry Vaughan's "The Bird."

God may be thanked for birds because they open up an avenue of happy interest to everyone who chooses to pursue it. John James Audubon devoted his life to the study of birds. He wrote of his boyhood:

During all these years there existed within me a tendency to follow Nature in her walks. Perhaps not an hour of leisure was spent elsewhere than in woods and fields, and to examine either the eggs, nest, young, or parents of any species of birds constituted my delight.[6]

To Henry David Thoreau, who withdrew from towns and people and lived alone in his cabin by Walden Pond, the song of the wood thrush was

cool bars of melody from the atmosphere of everlasting morning or evening. . . . There is the liquid coolness of things that are just drawn from the bottom of springs. . . . Whenever a man hears it, he is young, and Nature is in her spring. Wherever he hears it, it is a new world and a free country, and the gates of heaven are not shut against him.[7]

Not many people will be lifetime naturalists like Audubon or will live in the woods like Thoreau, but people busy in many ordinary ways can get out of dull ruts and find the expansiveness of a new delight because they look at birds. In his *Twenty-five Years 1892-*

[4] *Ibid.*, p. 248.
[5] *Ibid.*, p. ii.

[6] Maria R. Audubon, *Audubon and His Journals* (New York: Charles Scribner's Sons, 1897), I, 15.
[7] *The Heart of Thoreau's Journals*, ed. Odell Shepard (Boston: Houghton Mifflin Co., 1927), pp. 139-40.

22 And God blessed them, saying, Be fruitful, and multiply, and fill the waters in the seas, and let fowl multiply in the earth.

23 And the evening and the morning were the fifth day.

that it was good. 22 And God blessed them, saying, "Be fruitful and multiply and fill the waters in the seas, and let birds multiply on the earth." 23 And there was evening and there was morning, a fifth day.

---

that these mythological beings (cf. Ps. 74:13; Isa. 27:1; 51:9; Job 7:12), the existence of which was doubtless still believed in, derived their being from God.

22. The fishes and birds are now endowed with reproductive powers by a specific creative act (contrast vs. 11). The reason for this would seem to be that, whereas the bearing of seed by the plants was automatic, reproduction of their species by the fishes and the birds demands from them a certain degree of co-operation—this presumably on the analogy of the mammals, unless it is to be supposed that the author was aware, whether by personal observation or otherwise, of the behavior of the fishes and the

---

1916, Sir Edward Grey, British secretary of state for foreign affairs, has this to tell of Theodore Roosevelt:

While Roosevelt was still President, Bryce had written to me to say that after Roosevelt's term of office was over he intended to travel, and among other places to visit England. He had not heard the songs of British birds, and would time his visit so as to be in England at the time of the singing of birds. He would like it to be arranged that someone, who knew the songs of birds, should spend a day walking with him and naming the songs as they were heard.[8]

Then Lord Grey goes on to recount how Roosevelt, although he had gone first to British East Africa, the Sudan, and Europe, tenaciously held to his purpose, and when he had arrived in England, insisted that a whole day should be set aside from the crowded schedule of public events so that he and Lord Grey might spend it listening to the songs of English birds. It was this sort of vivid interest and enjoyment over and above the engrossment of practical things that made Roosevelt the scintillating person he was.

As the contemplation of birds feeds the sense of beauty, so also it does more. It wakes a spiritual wonder. Consider the instincts which birds follow—instincts which no knowledge of ours can analyze or explain: the skill and adaptation in the building of nests; the unerring certainty of flight over great distances of land and water in migration.

Ponder the analogy which may be offered here concerning the elements of our human guidance: analytical knowledge on the one hand; a more profound instinctive feeling on the other. A brittle intellectualism may argue that nothing should be taken seriously that cannot be rationalized completely; that a religion

that reaches into mystery is superstition; that trust in God is nothing but credulity unless the proof of it can be set down in arithmetic as flatly obvious as that two and two make four. But great living goes beyond such squinting calculation. It follows profounder impulses in the soul. As Augustine wrote in his *Confessions*, "Thou hast made us for thyself, and our hearts are restless till they rest in thee." Birds that did not follow the instinct telling them where to fly would perish. What of human souls? Has God put into us the instinct of spiritual migration that bids us trust the great wings of faith and far obedience by which alone we may fulfill our living and come home?

A final thought: God's providence. Consider the words of Jesus in Matt. 6:26; 10:29; Luke 12:6. We look at life and say that its necessities must be met by forethought. We read Paul's words to the Thessalonians, "Study . . . to do your own business, and to work with your own hands, . . . that ye may have lack of nothing" (I Thess. 4:11-12). It seems obvious that we are not meant to sit down with folded hands and expect the ravens to feed us. Nothing comes to irresponsibility. But when that is seen, there is a deeper fact to which the tension we build up in ourselves may make us blind. It is the fact which Jesus in his great steadiness perceived: that there are fundamental reliances for which we do not have to be responsible. In God's world there are unmeasured resources of strength and a sustenance which he has provided for all those who approach life with a direct expectancy. So comes the assurance which makes a man serene.

One evening when Luther saw a little bird perched on a tree, to roost there for the night, he said, "This little bird has had its supper, and now it is getting ready to go to sleep here, quite secure and content, never troubling itself what its food will be, or where its lodging on the morrow. Like

[8] New York: Frederick A. Stokes Co., 1925, II, 90.

24 ¶ And God said, Let the earth bring forth the living creature after his kind, cattle, and creeping thing, and beast of the earth after his kind: and it was so.

25 And God made the beast of the earth after his kind, and cattle after their kind, and every thing that creepeth upon the earth after his kind: and God saw that *it was* good.

26 ¶ And God said, Let us make man in our image, after our likeness: and let them have dominion over the fish of the sea, and

24 And God said, "Let the earth bring forth living creatures according to their kinds: cattle and creeping things and beasts of the earth according to their kinds." And it was so. 25 And God made the beasts of the earth according to their kinds and the cattle according to their kinds, and everything that creeps upon the ground according to its kind. And God saw that it was good.

26 Then God said, "Let us make man in our image, after our likeness; and let them

---

birds. The fact, however, that no similar blessing follows vs. 25 may indicate that vs. 22 is from an even later hand than vs. 21.

G. The Sixth Day (1:24-31)

24. The animals, like the plants (cf. vs. 11; also, as regards the production of fishes by the waters, vs. 20), are represented as having been produced by the earth. They are given a threefold classification: **cattle**—domesticated animals, roughly Herbivora; **creeping things**—reptiles, insects, and very small quadrupeds; and **beasts of the earth**—wild beasts, roughly Carnivora.

25. The first half of the verse in which it may be noted there is no mention of "cattle" (which therefore seem to be subsumed under **the beasts of the earth**) is probably secondary (cf. vss. 7a, etc.).

It has already been noted that there is no blessing of the animals similar to that of the fishes and the birds in vs. 22. Three explanations of this are possible: (*a*) vs. 22 is even later than vs. 21a, as has been suggested above—and so, later than vs. 25a, from the same hand as vs. 21a; or (*b*) the author of vs. 25a—and of vs. 21a—did include a blessing of the animals which has disappeared by accident; or (*c*) he deliberately omitted it because the account of what happened on the sixth day was already rather long. In any case, it seems likely that only man was blessed in the original narrative of P, and that the blessing of the fishes and birds—and of the animals if one was recorded—is a reflex of vs. 28.

26. The creation of man is invested with a special solemnity. God first consults with divine beings other than himself, **Let us make man.** **Let us** could indeed be taken simply as a plural of majesty, for the custom of rulers speaking in the plural appeared with the Persians (see Gunkel, *Genesis*, p. 111; cf. Holzinger, *Genesis*, p. 10). Although

---

David, it 'abides under the shadow of the Almighty.' It sits on its little twig content, and lets God take care."[9]

Likewise, for every life it may be true as Sidney Lanier wrote in "The Marshes of Glynn":

As the marsh-hen secretly builds on the watery sod,
Behold I will build me a nest on the greatness of God.[10]

24-25. See Expos. on vs. 31.

26. *The Purpose in Human History.*—Out of this verse might naturally come a consideration

[9] Quoted by Mary W. Tileston, *Daily Strength for Daily Needs* (Boston: Little, Brown & Co., 1900), p. 84.
[10] *Poems*, ed. by his wife (New York: Charles Scribner's Sons, 1904), p. 17. Used by permission.

of how the human race got to be upon this earth. There might be a review of what was once the startling conflict between the doctrine of evolution and the ancient faith of creation at the hands of God. That has been touched upon in the Expos., p. 462, and also in the Expos. on 37:24. Here, then, thought may center especially on **let them have dominion.**

To read the Bible is to know that creation does not remain in the past tense. The Hebrew conviction was of a God who acted, who acts, and who will act. His purposes for life go on enlarging. As Isaiah was to say: "Hast thou not known? hast thou not heard, that the everlasting God, the LORD, the Creator of the ends of the earth, fainteth not, neither is weary?

over the fowl of the air, and over the cattle, and over all the earth, and over every creeping thing that creepeth upon the earth.

have dominion over the fish of the sea, and over the birds of the air, and over the cattle, and over all the earth, and over every creep-

P nowhere else alludes to angels, it is evident from 3:22; 11:7; I Kings 22:19; Isa. 6:8, all of which passages are earlier than the Persian period, that Hebrew religious thought was familiar with the idea of a heavenly host with whom God took counsel. Reference may also be made to the representation of the Babylonian creation epic that Marduk, before creating man, declared his intention to Ea (see Skinner, *Genesis,* p. 45).

There is thus an echo of polytheism here, but it is only an echo. What seems to be significant is the idea that for the creation of man it was fitting, if not necessary, that there should be something like co-operation on the part of the whole company of heaven. A further possibility should be considered: whether there is not here an attempt, however inarticulate, to give expression to the feeling that God could not be adequately represented as just a bare unity. At any rate, some such idea as this seems to underlie the apparent hypostatization of the divine attributes in such passages as Pss. 43:3; 89:14; 147:18.

After our likeness, more abstract than **in our image,** may well be a gloss on the latter phrase, especially in view of the absence of "after his likeness" in vs. 27. For **over all the earth** should be read, with the Syriac, "over every beast of the earth." God thus gives man dominion over all life as it has been enumerated in its species in vss. 20 and 24.

. . . He giveth power to the faint; and to them that have no might he increaseth strength." (Isa. 40:28-29.)

How is God's continuing creativity expressed? He raises up new men. Note the stirring repetition of that fact in Hebrew history. Out of Ur of the Chaldeans, from among the miscellaneous and now-forgotten crowd, comes Abraham to be the pioneer of a new civilization of the spirit. Out of a group of ordinary brothers emerges Joseph; and a psalmist, remembering what God wrought in him for the generations following, wrote, "He sent a man before them" (Ps. 105:17). When Israel was in bondage, Moses came to lead the Exodus. When Moses was old, came Joshua; and after him, in hours of crisis, the long line of men of destiny, Gideon and Jephthah, Samuel and Saul, Jonathan and David, Elijah, Amos, Isaiah, Nehemiah—to name no more. To be sure not in the Bible only but all down the course of history the coming of the great leader has changed the current of events. This appearance of the right man at the critical time is often like a miracle. No law of averages produces him. No characteristics of the crowd show what he is to be. The qualities he brings may be unique. He is like a fresh gift from the hands of God.

But God's creativity is not only in raising up the new man. It is in taking a man who is already there and making him over so that his significance is new. Moses would never have led the Exodus unless the spirit of God had first laid hold of him in the vision of the burning bush and challenged and corrected him and compelled him to conquer his own self-distrust. Hosea became the passionate prophet of the love of God because he learned through his suffering. The revolution wrought in Saul of Tarsus, the conversion of Augustine, the transformation of the careless young Francis of Assisi into the saint—all these are examples of the way God creates something different out of what had seemed to be of a fixed mold. Added to those are the uncounted instances, familiar to every generation, of persons who at first seemed altogether ordinary, but who by steady obedience to the moving of the Spirit became great servants of God. To those who of themselves would have had no might, he increased strength.

Futhermore, God's creativity is in the shaping of events. Often in critical issues, even though it is never possible completely to analyze or ascribe the forces which determine history, men do at least begin to realize that the tilting of the balance comes from something other than the human weights that have been thrown into the scales. Victor Hugo in *Les Misérables* gave the supreme expression of this sense that into the shaping of our human events there comes a power higher than this earth. He was writing of the Battle of Waterloo and the defeat of Napoleon, a defeat which might have seemed to have its immediate explanation in the fact that the reinforcements which might have saved him were misdirected, and did not arrive in time—or in Hugo's words, "Because on the afternoon of a certain summer's day, a shepherd said to a Prussian in the forest, 'Go this way

27 So God created man in his *own* image, in the image of God created he him; male and female created he them.

ing thing that creeps upon the earth." 27 So God created man in his own image, in the image of God he created him; male and

---

27. To emphasize further the solemnity of the event a specific act of creation is recorded—in metrical form it may be noted, three lines of four beats each; i.e., the author was not content at this point with the representation that God said, "Let there be, etc.," and it was so. Possibly the influence of 2:7 is operating here; nevertheless, it does not seem fanciful to discern in vss. 26-27 the beginnings of that doctrine of man, congruent with the O.T. doctrine of God, which was to be developed in the wisdom literature.

The idea of man being created **in the image of God** is probably dependent on Babylonian mythology. "Before proceeding to the creation of Ea-bani, Aruru forms a mental image (*zikru* . . .) of the God Anu . . . ; and similarly, in the Descent of Ištar, Ea forms a *zikru* in his wise heart before creating Aṣūšunamir" (*ibid.*, pp. 31-32). In the mind of P, there can be little doubt, bodily form was to some extent at any rate involved in the idea of the divine **image**; cf. the numerous references in the O.T. to God's hands, feet, mouth, etc. (e.g., Pss. 119:73; 33:6; Isa. 60:13; Zech. 14:4, to cite only late passages). The incorporeality of God was too abstract a thought for an Israelite even of the fifth century (cf. Gunkel, *Genesis*, p. 112). Nevertheless, it caused always a certain tension which manifests itself, e.g., in the prophetic polemic against images (cf. Deut. 5:8; Isa.

---

and not that.'" But the real cause, as Victor Hugo saw it, was more majestic.

End of the dictatorship. A whole European system crumbled away. . . .
Was it possible that Napoleon should have won that battle? We answer No. Why? Because of Wellington? Because of Blucher? No. Because of God. . . .
Napoleon had been denounced in the infinite, and his fall had been decided on.
He embarrassed God.
Waterloo is not a battle; it is a change of front on the part of the Universe.[1]

27. In the Image of God.—Those religious conceptions which first come into sight at primitive levels may be the root of greater adult faith; and the greatness of developed faith must not be disparaged because its origin was in crude ideas. That is the double truth which emerges from this verse, and from the Exeg. on it. It is a truth which presents itself repeatedly in these first chapters of Genesis, and it is one that needs to be brought home often to our recognition—for we may not readily accept it. Our tendency may be to suppose that high beliefs lose their dignity if their origins are humble.

That is one error; and William James has illumining comments on certain aspects of that error in the first chapter of his famous *The Varieties of Religious Experience.*[2] In our individual experience we may recapitulate the experience of the race. The early thinkers about God thought of him as corporeal (cf. Exeg.).

[1] "Cosette," Bk. I, chs. xviii, ix.
[2] New York: Longmans, Green & Co., 1917.

So does the child. There is an instinctive yearning for Someone whom we can see and touch. A little girl whose mother was kissing her good night and about to go downstairs clung to her and did not want to let her go. "But, darling," said her mother, "you have your doll, and God is with you." "Yes," said the little girl, "I know I have my doll and that God is with me, but I want somebody with a skin face."

We are creatures of flesh as well as of spirit, and we want reality to manifest itself in terms of the flesh. As the Exeg. has said, "In Hebrew thought, the body was a part of the whole man and was necessary to his complete being"; and so not only in Hebrew thought but in all humanity there is the feeling that something outside us is made certain to us only when we apprehend it in bodily terms.

But of course there is the equally important fact that we are more than bodies; and the danger is that if we never get beyond the bodily conceptions we forfeit the development of our spirits. All true growth depends upon the gradual lifting of our awareness above the limits of our physical sensations. To the baby nothing is real except what satisfies his elementary and instinctive appetites. Keep him warm and feed him and let him sleep, and he is satisfied. Nothing beyond that matters. What his father and mother may be saying and what they may have in their minds for him are completely outside his recognition. But as he grows, his world enlarges. The time will come—unless morally he still is infantile—when the best that his father and mother are, with their hopes, their princi-

28 And God blessed them, and God said unto them, Be fruitful, and multiply, and | female he created them. 28 And God blessed them, and God said to them, "Be fruitful

---

40:19-20; 44:9-20), in the silence of Isaiah as to the appearance of God (Isa. 6:1), and in the insistence that man could not see God's face (Exod. 33:20-23). And in the present passage P does not represent God as saying, "Let us make man in my image," but **in our image**—the image of us, the divine beings. A sentence of Skinner's may be quoted, "That P retained the idea [of a heavenly council] in spite of his silence as to the existence of angels is due to the fact that it was decidedly less anthropomorphic than the statement that man was made in the image of the one incomparable Deity" (*Genesis*, p. 31).

In view of the fact, however, that in Hebrew thought the body was a part of the whole man and was necessary to his complete being, and that it was furthermore the outward manifestation of the reality of which it was a part, the representation that man was made **in the image of God** meant much more than that man looked like God or like the divine beings which formed his retinue. The **image** included likeness to them in spiritual powers—the power of thought, the power of communication, the power of self-transcendence. No doubt these concepts remained to some extent inarticulate in the author's mind; nevertheless they were there. He was trying to state in concrete terms— the only terms with which he, being a Semite, was familiar—what could only be stated, however inadequately, in abstract terms.

To be noted is the fact that the male and the female are created at the same time, with which the representation of the older J story (2:21-22) should be contrasted. As to whether P believed that a single pair only had been created at this time, or whether he thought of the creation of men and women in numbers, it is difficult to say. Skinner (*ibid.*, p. 33), noting that the great majority of commentators favor the former possibility, points out that there is nothing in the narrative to bear out this view, and cites with approval the opinion of the minority that the analogy of the marine and land animals is, on the whole, against it.

28. The power of procreation is given to man, with a special blessing, immediately upon his creation. With this should be contrasted the motif of the older story—that the man and his wife attained consciousness of sex only as a result of eating the fruit of the

---

ples, and their purposes, will become his heritage. Not only physically, but now in this more important inner way, he is being fashioned in their image.

It is no reproach to religion if it also begins where the infant begins. The only reproach is if it stays there. God is sensed first just as the outside power that controls the things we want. Primitive worship is thus the method of trying to persuade or placate this sort of God. If the worshiper can go away from the shrine believing that he will get the particular favor he has asked for, that is all he wants. There is not much meaning yet in the idea of being made in God's image. Rather, he makes his god according to his own image, as a small child's mind makes his father into a big something moving about that may be useful if he can be made to listen. But here in ch. 1 a greater conception is breaking through. As the Exeg. has pointed out, this Hebrew writer expressed himself in concrete fashion, for the Semitic mind worked instinctively with pictures, not with abstractions. But when he spoke of man as in the image of God,

he was considering not so much man's body as his spirit. Man was like God because he had "the power of thought, the power of communication, the power of self-transcendence" (see Exeg.).

If man had lived in the beginning, and had continued to live, on that level, then he would have fulfilled God's purpose in creation. But as ch. 2 goes on to show, a demonic element entered into his history. He turned away from obedience to God to follow his own rebellious impulses. So the image of God in him was blurred and broken and could be restored only by a long process of redemption. But the O.T. never loses sight of the ideal which was there in the beginning. It keeps reminding every man that he is never true to himself, and that he can never really be content, until he is brought back to the great thoughts and the lofty impulses which were planted in him as his heritage from God.

28-30. *A Projected Longing.*—Man is to have dominion over all other living things on earth, and that dominion has often seemed a merciless

replenish the earth, and subdue it: and have dominion over the fish of the sea, and over the fowl of the air, and over every living thing that moveth upon the earth.

29 ¶ And God said, Behold, I have given you every herb bearing seed, which is upon the face of all the earth, and every tree, in the which is the fruit of a tree yielding seed; to you it shall be for meat.

and multiply, and fill the earth and subdue it; and have dominion over the fish of the sea and over the birds of the air and over every living thing that moves upon the earth." 29 And God said, "Behold, I have given you every plant yielding seed which is upon the face of all the earth, and every tree with seed in its fruit; you shall have

---

forbidden tree. As is noted below, this representation reflects J's melancholy attitude toward sex which, it is suggested, was a result of his contact with Baalism. P's matter-of-fact point of view was possible because by his time Baalism, its values having been assimilated by Yahwism, had ceased to be a threat to its integrity.

29-30. It is now divinely ordained that man shall have for his food **every plant yielding seed . . . , and every tree with seed in its fruit;** with this may be compared the classification in vs. 11. The wild beasts, the birds and the creeping things (cf. vs. 24), on the other hand, are to subsist on the green herbage (vs. 30). Man is thus to be a vegetarian. This is something of a contradiction to vs. 26, according to which he was to **have dominion over** all living creatures. Furthermore, there are in the Hebrew certain significant differences of style (for the details see Skinner, *Genesis*, p. 35) from the preceding section, and no reference is made to the domestic animals which, as in vs. 25, are subsumed under **every beast of the earth.** To be noted finally is the senseless **and it was so** at the end of vs. 30, suggesting a somewhat wooden imitation of an existing form. For these reasons vss. 29-30 may well be an addition to P's original narrative (cf. Richard Kraetzschmar, *Die Bundesvorstellung im Alten Testament* [Marburg: N. G. Elwert, 1896], pp. 193-94, referred to by Gunkel, *Genesis*, p. 114). Gunkel, however, retains vss. 29-30 as part of P's original narrative, and accounts for the inconsistency between them and vss. 26-28 by holding that P was combining two originally independent traditions—that of the Creation, and that of the peace of the primeval age. The question as to whether this combination was made by P or by some later commentator is not of primary importance.

The point of vs. 29 is not what man may eat, but rather that he may not eat flesh (contrast 9:2-3). It thus echoes the idea—found in Persian and Greco-Roman mythology (see Gunkel, *Genesis*, p. 113)—of a primitive golden age when men were at peace with the beasts, an idea which had already found expression among the Hebrews in the J story of the Garden of Eden (2:18-20). Vs. 29 may therefore have been added in order to supply some allusion to this—especially in view of Isa. 11:6-8; 65:25; Hos. 2:18, all of

---

one. Fish and fowl and animals have been his food. It would seem that the priestly writer of this account of the Creation had a sensitiveness to all life and a pity for the lower creatures which made him believe that such dominion was not in God's ordaining. His picture here is of men living on fruit and on grain; neither are there any carnivorous animals, but they have instead every green herb for meat. This vision of an idyllic world in which there is no fear and no taking of life appears again in the prophecy of Isaiah. "The wolf also shall dwell with the lamb, and the leopard shall lie down with the kid; and the calf and the young lion and the fatling together: and a little child shall lead them" (Isa. 11:6).

And Hosea too dreams of a time when all creatures shall "lie down safely" (Hos. 2:18). Later in Genesis the picture presented in this chapter changes. Man may have the other creatures for his food, "even as the green herb have I given you all things" (9:3). But the reluctance to feed on life persists, and so it is enjoined (and the Jewish laws of kosher food keep that injunction to this day) that "flesh with the life thereof, which is the blood thereof, shall ye not eat" (9:4). And lest the sense of sacredness of human life should be cheapened by the permission to feed on animals, there is added the emphatic warning, "Whoso sheddeth man's blood, by man shall his blood be shed; for in the image of God made he man" (9:6).

30 And to every beast of the earth, and to every fowl of the air, and to every thing that creepeth upon the earth, wherein *there is* life, *I have given* every green herb for meat: and it was so.

31 And God saw every thing that he had made, and, behold, *it was* very good. And

them for food. 30 And to every beast of the earth, and to every bird of the air, and to everything that creeps on the earth, everything that has the breath of life, I have given every green plant for food." And it was so. 31 And God saw everything that he had made, and behold, it was very good.

---

which reveal an interest in the myth, in that they predict that this idyllic peace between man and beast will be a condition of the restored golden age in the future.

---

31. God's Good World.—This verse is a gladdening thought on which to meditate whenever life seems drab or shadowed. For times come when men are inclined to pessimism. They have reasons for personal depression; they may look out on their world and see it involved in tragic shadows. Nevertheless this verse exalts the truth that the universe as God made it, and the life which God meant to be lived within it, are beautiful. God looked at everything and saw that **it was very good.** In the light of that we may well remember the words of Bishop Jeremy Taylor, "He that hath so many causes of joy, and so great, is very much in love with sorrow and peevishness, who loses all these pleasures, and chooses to sit down upon his little handful of thorns." [3]

Consider some of the aspects of God's creation which can lift and inspire the spirit. There is first the majestic framework of the universe itself. "When I consider thy heavens, the work of thy fingers, the moon and the stars, which thou hast ordained . . ." is the preface to a psalmist's meditation (Ps. 8:3). Because he had been considering those, his thoughts were enlarged with a sense of the glory of God and the wonder of life as in his presence. To stand in silence on a hilltop and watch the sun rise, or to walk out under the immense silence of the stars, is one simple avenue into that mood of awe and wonder which is the forecourt of religion. Read the little book *Silex Scintillans* of the seventeenth-century poet Henry Vaughan, and among his poems especially "The World," that begins:

I saw Eternity the other night,
Like a great ring of pure and endless light,
All calm as it was bright.

Nor is it only in the great aspects of the universe, but in the beautiful little things, that one may understand why it is written that God looked at all that he had made and found it good. In *The Life of Alice Freeman Palmer,*[4]

by her husband, George Herbert Palmer, there is the account of a club she had for little girls in one of the dreariest tenement sections of Boston. It was called "The Happiness Club." It had three rules, and one of them was that each child must see something beautiful every day. That, in the drab streets and houses to which they were accustomed, was the hardest rule of all to follow, but with childish eagerness they did live up to it—even when the "something beautiful" they could report they had looked at was nothing more than a sparrow shaking his feathers in the rain gutter, or a glint of sunlight on a baby's hair. What Mrs. Palmer wanted her children to understand was that beauty may be everywhere for those whose eyes and hearts alike are open to perceive it; whereas to one who has gone on his way with a preoccupied mind and unawakened interest

A primrose by a river's brim
A yellow primrose was to him,
And it was nothing more.[5]

A man may so plod through his existence as to see only the dusty road, or he may see also the flower growing there beside it. He may see only the hard street with its noise and clamor, or he may see the blue sky between the canyons of the crowded buildings and the white clouds floating above the city's smoke. He may notice in the life around him only its ugliness and greed, or he may recognize with quick eye the little glimpses of courage and beauty which break like sunlight through the common fog.

Consider, likewise, the world of animate things. Earlier than the creation of man was the creation of the birds and animals. According to Genesis, man is to have dominion over these. But it is not to be a brutal dominion. He can delight in them as God did. To observe and study birds, to mark their comings and goings in spring and fall, to look for them in meadow and wood and to know their songs is endless fascination. Read the life of Edward Grey of Fallodon. Think of the comradeship men have

[3] *The Rule and Exercises of Holy Living* (Cambridge: E. P. Dutton & Co., 1876), p. 155.
[4] Boston: Houghton Mifflin Co., 1908.

[5] Wordsworth, "Peter Bell," Part I, st. xxi.

the evening and the morning were the sixth day.

2 Thus the heavens and the earth were finished, and all the host of them.

2 And on the seventh day God ended his work which he had made; and he rested on the seventh day from all his work which he had made.

And there was evening and there was morning, a sixth day.

2 Thus the heavens and the earth were finished, and all the host of them. 2 And on the seventh day God finished his work which he had done, and he rested on the seventh day from all his work which he had

---

The absence of a verb—supplied in the English translations, **I have given**—from vs. 30 suggests that this verse may be even later than vs. 29, a suggestion which is strengthened by the fact that there is little significant difference between the food allowed to man and that allowed to the beasts. The affinity, already noted, of the verse to vs. 25 makes it likely that the two verses are from the same hand, i.e., that vs. 30 is a part of what has been called above the systematic elaboration of P's narrative.

H. The Seventh Day: The Sabbath (2:1-4a)

2:1. All the host of them: Nowhere else in the O.T. is "the host of the earth" referred to, either explicitly or by allusion. The author has thus compressed the statement that the heavens and their host and the earth and all that was in it were finished.

2. The repetition of **finished**, already used in the passive in vs. 1, is infelicitous. Furthermore, according to the narrative as a whole, God finished the world not on the **seventh** but on the sixth day. Samar., LXX, and the Syriac, indeed, read here, "on the sixth day," but the harder reading, **on the seventh day**, is certainly to be preferred.

---

had with horses and dogs. For those who have a right perception there may be an almost mystical relationship to wild life. Remember Francis of Assisi and the birds. Dhan Gopal Mukerji, who wrote his books in the West but who grew up in India, has told of going into the jungle and sitting perfectly still to watch the great beasts come to the water holes. As long as the human being has no fear, he says, they have no fear or hostility toward him. Read Rudyard Kipling's "My Lord the Elephant."

Again, in the goodness of God's universe there is the goodness of people. The emphasis on the sinfulness of man which has been so dominant after two world wars must not blind us to the virtue and winsomeness of multitudes of actual people. The relationships of life often are determined by what we look for. To a considerable degree people become what we expect them to be. Read William Saroyan's *The Human Comedy*.[6] Better still, reread Charles Dickens. When we do, "we are filled," as Gilbert Chesterton wrote, "with the first of all democratic doctrines, that all men are interesting."[7] That is not only a democratic doctrine. It is a religious one. The man who looks at life with the eyes of God will be finding some worth in even the worst people and some goodness everywhere.

[6] New York: Harcourt, Brace & Co., 1943.
[7] *Charles Dickens* (New York: Dodd, Mead & Co., 1934), p. 15.

2:1-3. The Lord's Day.—There is need for much thought and reflection concerning the sabbath, which for most Christians is now Sunday. Secularists ignore it; and many supposedly religious people treat it with indifferent forgetfulness of what should be its priceless value.

The origins of the sabbath as it was observed in Israel, as the Exeg. indicates, are not wholly clear. Its roots may go far back to the dimly remembered days of desert life when the Israelites, as nomads, marked the changes of the moon. But whatever may have been the first observance of the seventh day, the nobility of the development of sabbathkeeping is a towering fact in the long history of Judaism. It was set apart as a day of rest, and held to be such not by any human ordinance but by the will of God that was part of the very nature of creation. Here the priestly writer lifts the ordinances of Judaism to a universal validity when he records the sabbath as part of the primal constitution of nature as it comes from the hands of God. Nor was the sabbath rest something to be claimed only by individuals. Great conceptions of mercy and corporate responsibility and social concern and kindness entered into it. "Six days thou shalt do thy work, and on the seventh day thou shalt rest: that thine ox and thine ass may rest, and the son of thy handmaid, and the stranger, may be refreshed" (Exod. 23:12). "The seventh day is the sabbath of the Lord thy God: in it thou shalt not do any

3 And God blessed the seventh day, and sanctified it: because that in it he had rested from all his work which God created and made.

done. **3** So God blessed the seventh day and hallowed it, because on it God rested from all his work which he had done in creation.

Skinner (*Genesis,* p. 37) maintains that the rendering here should be not **finished,** but "desisted from"; this, however, would not help the stylistic difficulty of the Hebrew. Gunkel (*Genesis,* p. 114) regards vs. 2a as a variant to vs. 2b. It is more probably a gloss on vs. 2b—with **finished** meaning "desisted from"—by one to whom the idea of God resting caused a certain difficulty; cf. Isa. 40:28, where it is stated that God is never weary—and so in no need of rest—and Ps. 121:3b, 4. With its omission, "God" must be restored as the explicit subject of **rested** in vs. 2b.

3. The final clause, lit., "which God had created to make"—note the unnecessary repetition of **God**—is probably an explanatory gloss on **work.** The verse, together with vs. 2b, is an etiological myth accounting for the sabbath. It invests the sabbath with all the reality of creation itself, and represents its observance as a fundamental law of the world order.

This exalted idea of the sabbath was one of the results of the Exile. The origin of the observance is still in dispute but it seems reasonable to suppose, in view of the juxtaposition of new moon and sabbath in, e.g., II Kings 4:23; Isa. 1:13, that it stemmed from the feast of the full moon. If this is the case then it may be inferred that in the course of time two subordinate feasts came to be kept between these two major observances, so that there was a moon festival roughly every seven days. We may assume further that when Israel settled down to agriculture and abandoned the worship of the moon-god, which had formed part of their religion when as nomads they had moved about the desert at night, convenience suggested that the occurrence of these holy days be regularized by divorcing them from the changes of the moon, and the sabbath every seven days was the result—the feast of the new moon being retained independently of it. Apparently the sabbath in pre-exilic times called for a minimum of cultic observance, a fact which made possible its continuance in Babylonia. However that may be, it was there that the keeping of the sabbath became one of the three great marks of the Jews— the others being the refusal to eat blood (cf. 9:4) and the practice of circumcision (cf. 17:10)—and its observance took on a new and central significance until it ultimately came to involve abstention from work. It was to provide a rationale for this that P told of God resting on the seventh day and hallowing it.

The fact that P thus connects the origin of the sabbath not with some event in the life of one of the patriarchs—as he connected circumcision in ch. 17—or in the history of Israel, but with Creation itself, is of some significance. For the implication of this passage is that observance of the day—actually a peculiarly Jewish institution—is really binding upon all mankind. P thus claims that Judaism is no merely national religion, but is rather of universal validity, the only religion which is in accordance with the true nature of things.

---

work, . . . that thy manservant and thy maidservant may rest as well as thou" (Deut. 5:14).

With the rise of the synagogue, the sabbath was made pre-eminently a day also of worship, instruction, and meditation upon God and his laws for life. Thus the significance of the sabbath grew to fullness. It was to be the day of rest and refreshment for the bodies and also for the souls of men.

As so often happens with institutions, there grew a danger also. The form could eclipse the spirit. The commandment against work, con-

ceived at first with living imagination, tended to become a harsh and rigid orthodoxy; e.g., see what it had become to the scribes and Pharisees in the days of Jesus. Its prohibitions were so sacrosanct that life was cramped within them. To such a point did the sabbath regulations against work or any kind of physical effort go that, as Emil Schürer describes in his *History of the Jewish People in the Time of Jesus Christ,*[8] rabbis solemnly debated whether a crip-

[8] Tr. S. Taylor and P. Christie (New York: Charles Scribner's Sons, 1855), Div. II, Vol. II, sec. 28.

4 ¶ These *are* the generations of the heavens and of the earth when they were created, in the day that the LORD God made the earth and the heavens,

4 These are the generations of the heavens and the earth when they were created. In the day that the LORD God made the

---

The idea of separation, division, is a dominant motif throughout P's story of Creation. Light is separated from darkness (1:4; cf. 1:14), waters are separated from waters (1:6), the waters under the firmament from the land (1:9); and, by implication, species is separated from species in 1:11, 20, 24. Underlying the ordaining of the sabbath is the same motif, in that a distinction is made between times. The significance of this becomes apparent when it is recalled how later P, in accepting the idea of a central sanctuary, distinguishes between place and place and ascribes the distinction to God's command. The universe was for him hierarchical in its structure and thus gave expression to the divine attribute of order. It was a universe of relatedness, in which everything had its place and its purpose. **God blessed the seventh day and hallowed it,** making it sacred in itself and a constant source of well-being to man. Through blessing it was endowed permanently with beneficial qualities, and through its hallowing placed in a special relationship to God (cf. Skinner, *Genesis*, p. 38).

4a. This clause is a redactional insertion to bind the foregoing account of Creation with the J narrative following. It seems more probable that it is from the hand of RP, imitating 5:1; etc. (*ibid.*, pp. 40-41), than that it originally stood before 1:1, as some commentators think (e.g., Gunkel, *Genesis*, p. 101), and so was the opening sentence of P.

---

ple must be condemned as guilty if in case his house caught fire on the sabbath he should carry out his wooden leg.

That excessive literalism in the keeping of the sabbath came down in some of the streams that influenced Christian history. The Puritans of New England were as inflexible as the first-century Jewish scribes in their conception and enforcement of the sabbath laws. It was this excess that has been one cause of the modern reaction. When the iron pattern of the sabbath laws was clamped upon life in a way that seemed beyond all reason, there was disaffection and gradual disobedience, and at last wide repudiation. So "puritanical" was turned into a word of scorn, and many people have supposed that to get away as far as possible from puritanical ideas, especially about the sabbath, is a mark of emancipation.

Nevertheless, the essential meaning and message of the sabbath are indestructible. Human life can become dwarfed and mean if provision is not constantly made for rest and for worship. The general intelligence of society is beginning to see again at least the first half of that truth. It is realized that monotonous and unbroken toil is killing. There must be a rhythm of work and rest. Hence the rapid growth of laws that protect laborers from week-long exploitation. But that has not kept the sabbath, whether the Jewish seventh day or the Christian Sunday, from being largely secularized. Men have knocked off work, but too often not that they might worship.

Here is the point at which the great truth ought to be proclaimed. Men and women need to get beyond the shallow satisfaction of being free to do on Sunday what the old sabbatarianism once forbade; they need to think of what the sabbath everlastingly is for. Said Jesus, "The sabbath was made for man, and not man for the sabbath" (Mark 2:27). Yes, and what he said there was that the sabbath is meant for man's free and glad advantage; it is not meant for man to ignore and lose. It is to be a day, as it was for him, when all beautiful aspirations and energies are to find their full expression. He rejoiced to do on the sabbath whatever would help anyone who needed him most; and one of the sources of his strength was that "as his custom was, he went into the synagogue on the sabbath day" (Luke 4:16). In modern words, he went to church.

For the Christian, Sunday should have an even more radiant value than the seventh-day sabbath ever had in Israel. The day of rest and worship has been transferred to the first day of the week to commemorate the rising again on Easter morning of the crucified Christ. So the great conception is that Sunday should be for all Christian men and women a day of resurrection: resurrection from the dust of earthiness, in which life so often may be buried, into the morning sunlight of the soul's awakening consciousness of new life as a child of God.

2:4–3:24. *Primitive Insights That Were Profound.*—"You have too much curiosity" is sometimes said as an impatient rebuke; and one

II. The Creation of Man (2:4b-25)

Reasons have been advanced in the Intro. (see pp. 450-51) for holding that the J story of Creation in part consisted of an account of the destruction of the chaos monster by Yahweh. The fact, to be established below, that a later writer intruded into the second part of this J creation narrative—the story of the creation of man—vss. 5, 9, and 19, telling of the making of plants and animals, suggests that the first part had contained no explicit notice of their appearance on the earth. If this was the case, there are grounds for holding that the Canaanite version of the Babylonian myth, upon which J was drawing, itself represented a fusing together of two recensions of the original. For in addition to the recension already outlined, there has been discovered another recension, differing from it to a considerable degree (see Skinner, *Genesis*, pp. 47-48). It tells of a movement in the primeval chaos, designated impersonally *tāmtu* (cf. and contrast the personalized *ti'āmat* of the first recension), from which emerged the gods. Then, no reference being made to his conflict with the monster, it records how Marduk made man out of dust, then beasts, rivers, vegetation, and various kinds of animals. If the myth in its Canaanite form thus preserved from the first recension the feature of Marduk's conflict with the chaos monster, and from the second the representation that he made man from the dust, and then the beasts, etc., then J's use of it was economical in the extreme.

It can be taken as certain that he made no use whatever of the representation that the gods had emerged from chaos—he was too firm a monotheist for that. And it may also be assumed that the preservation of the story of the conflict with the chaos monster

---

definition of curiosity in Webster's *Dictionary* is "disposition to inquire into anything, . . . often implying meddlesomeness." But the first definition is "careful attention." In this sense curiosity is one of the great distinctions that make a man more than an animal. The animal—so far as we can tell—does not wonder and reflect. But a little three-year-old child begins to ask questions. He wants to have an explanation of things he does not understand. He keeps his elders busy with his constant "Why?" Those elders may have no better sense than to grow irritated and try to hush him up. We may do the same with grown people's questions too when they become disturbing. Much conservatism may be just the annoyed resistance of sluggish minds to the questions and challenges that compel supposed knowledge or settled opinion to explain itself. A desire to know is the yeast of life. The human mind and the human spirit ought to ask questions, and the more a person grows, the bigger questions he will ask.

The story of the Garden of Eden grew out of questions. As the Exeg. has pointed out, back of the biblical story are folklore and traditions that were woven out of more primitive imagination. The questions that were earliest asked were elemental ones. Here is this world full of living things. How did they come to be? Who made them? Why do people have to live the way they do? When it would be so pleasant to walk in the shade and have fruit drop into men's hands from the trees, why do men have to go out and sweat in the sun with backbreaking

digging of the soil? And what about women? Why do animals have their young so easily, and why must women suffer? And the stealthy, slithering things that men are afraid of—why were they made like that? Especially snakes.

Those ancient questions which the writer of ch. 2 remembered were not profound ones about man's soul. They had to do with men's physical experiences and feelings, and especially their discomforts and unrest. Why was life often so hard? Why was it painful? Why was it dangerous? Men knew it to be so, and the sting of that fact made them wonder and think. Does thinking always come from something in life that stings us out of sleepiness and acquiescence?

But if the first questions were primitive, they had in them the germ of something more profound. Study Rodin's great statue, "The Thinker." That low-browed naked man with the gnarled fist pressed against his lips yet has huge dignity—the dignity of mind awakening. So with the questions that grope toward their answers in the dim period that antedates the writing of Genesis. A great and significant thrust toward knowledge had been made in the fact that struggling human minds had flung out this interrogation: "Why is life not better than it is?"

The greatness of the opening chapters of the Bible is that they take the elemental questions and give them a new dimension. If the primal concern had been with men's bodies—hard work, the travail of women, and the risks

was, in part at least, due to his realization that the myth had to be related in a recognizable form to Yahwism, if the truth that Yahweh and Yahweh only—not Marduk—was the creator of earth and heaven was to be secured in Israel. Having recorded the conflict, he presumably passed at once to the making of man and to the account of his life in the garden, leading up to the story now preserved in ch. 3, which explains man's tragic sense of alienation from his Creator.

A. From the Dust of the Ground (2:4b-7)

4b. On the designation of the Deity as "Yahweh-Elohim" see on 4:26. It may, however, be noted here that in Genesis the use of "Yahweh"—rendered **the Lord** in both the KJV and the RSV, is, except for a few places where it is redactional, an indication of J. J used "Elohim" throughout the story which follows, though there is no doubt whatever that he meant "Yahweh" (see below). As it left the hand of J, the narrative told of God forming man from the ground (vs. 7) in the day he made earth and heaven (vs. 4), and of his placing him in a garden which he had planted (vs. 8). The garden was watered by a mist which rose from the earth (vs. 6), i.e., it did not have to be tended. God then decided to create a companion for the man (vs. 18), which he did by making a woman from one of the man's ribs (vss. 22-24). God then told the man and the woman that they might eat of the fruit of all the trees except one—that growing in the midst of the garden (vss. 16-17). This part of the story then closed with the statement in vs. 25 that "the man and his wife, were both naked, and were not ashamed," i.e., they were without consciousness of sex—leading up to the second part, now contained in ch. 3.

This simple account of the creation of man and woman, of their lack of sex consciousness, and of their happy, carefree life in the garden was later elaborated by the intrusion of vss. 5, 9, 10-14, 15, 19, 20. The grounds for regarding this material as secondary will be made clear as the chapter is considered verse by verse.

---

men run in the physical world—now in Genesis the concern has shifted. What is the reason for the unrest in man's soul? Why is he troubled and torn within by a sense of estrangement from that to which his life belongs? Even if he could answer all the perplexities about his physical existence and could not answer that ultimate question about his spirit, man would be unsatisfied. Men in the O.T. knew that; men likewise know it now. Alexander Whyte, of Edinburgh, was remembering with gratitude the enlightenment that had come to him from men of science; from the geologists, the paleontologists, the biologists, and the students of evolution who have interpreted the history of the earth and of life upon it. But he wrote:

I always miss in them . . . a matter of more importance to me than all else that they tell me. For, all the time . . . I still feel . . . a disorder and a dislocation that my scientific teachers neither acknowledge nor leave room for its acknowledgment and redress. . . . When I come to the end of my reading—Is that all? I ask. . . . To speak out the whole of my disappointment and complaint in one word, What about sin? What is sin? When and where did sin enter in the evolution of the human race and seize in this deadly way on the human heart? Why do you all so avoid and shut your eyes to sin? [9]

[9] *Bible Characters* (New York: Fleming H. Revell Co., 1896) I, 11-12.

Obviously the story of the Garden of Eden does not answer all the questions that the mind and soul of man will ask. Some of these questions which are as old as human thinking may baffle us till the end of time—the reason for human hardships, the origin of evil, the everlasting contradiction of the serpent in the paradise. But the supreme contribution of the Genesis story is that it lifted up the one concern that supremely matters—Why has man lost touch with God? It was not the kind of world that Adam and Eve had around them, but the kind of behavior they showed in it, that was the decisive issue. It is man's soul, not his circumstances, that needs redemption. So there is a sense in which every woman is Eve and every man is Adam, and the cardinal question for every soul is how it can find the grace to keep it from a continual repetition of the Fall.

4-15. The Meaning of a Garden.—The two accounts of the Creation in chs. 1-2 reflect conceptions which have come down from the far-off dawn of human thinking; and they are different because of the different environments in which their life and thought began. According to the account with which Genesis begins, the raw material of the universe was "darkness" and "the deep." Does this picture go back perhaps to the minds of the earliest men in the lands of Babylonia who, wandering southward, gazed

5 And every plant of the field before it was in the earth, and every herb of the field before it grew: for the LORD God had not caused it to rain upon the earth, and *there was* not a man to till the ground.

6 But there went up a mist from the earth, and watered the whole face of the ground.

7 And the LORD God formed man *of* the dust of the ground, and breathed into his nostrils the breath of life; and man became a living soul.

earth and the heavens, 5 when no plant of the field was yet in the earth and no herb of the field had yet sprung up — for the LORD God had not caused it to rain upon the earth, and there was no man to till the ground; 6 but a mist*c* went up from the earth and watered the whole face of the ground — 7 then the LORD God formed man of dust from the ground, and breathed into his nostrils the breath of life; and man be-

c Or *flood*

5. The statement that **no plant of the field was yet in the earth and no herb of the field had yet sprung up** demands a subsequent notice of the later appearance of vegetation (cf. Gunkel, *Genesis,* p. 28; it should be noted, however, that Gunkel's explanation of the inconsistencies of the present narrative differs from that offered here). This notice is missing, since vs. 9 and 3:18, which might be so construed, are as will be seen also secondary.

Similarly the next statement, that **the LORD God had not caused it to rain upon the earth,** demands a subsequent notice of the eventual appearance of rain, also lacking. The final statement in the verse implies that man's natural occupation was **to till the ground**—a representation which is inconsistent with 3:23, according to which man's lot as a tiller of the ground was the result of his disobedience.

For these reasons no part of vs. 5 appeared in the original J narrative. The fact that some author was moved to add vs. 5a would seem to suggest that in his now-missing account of the making of "earth and heaven" (cf. vs. 4b) J had, for whatever reason, omitted any reference to the creation of plants; it may have been to supply this lack that the clause was intruded. Vs. 5bα appears to be a gloss on the **mist** mentioned in vs. 6. Vs. 5bβ can only be a gloss by one for whom tilling the ground was man's natural occupation and who therefore was concerned to soften the implication of 3:23.

6. This verse came originally after vs. 8 and read, "and a mist used to go up from the earth and water the garden" (Johannes Meinhold, "Die Erzählung vom Paradies und Sündenfall," in *Beiträge zur alttestamentliche Wissenschaft,* ed. Karl Marti [Giessen: Alfred Topelmann, 1920; "Beihefte zur Zeitschrift für die alttestamentliche Wissenschaft"], pp. 122-31; cf. Otto Eissfeldt, *Hexateuch-Synopse* [Leipzig: J. C. Hinrichs, 1922], p. 255*). This is a statement to the effect that the garden was irrigated supernaturally—the word rendered **mist** has probably a mythological connotation (see Skinner, *Genesis,* p. 55)—not by human labor. (On the land watered by the Baal, as against that artificially irrigated, see W. Robertson Smith, *Lectures on the Religion of the Semites* [3rd ed.; London: A. & C. Black, 1927], p. 97.) The verse was placed here and adapted to its new position by the author who added vss. 10-14.

7. This originally followed immediately on vs. 4b, the sequence being "on the day that the LORD God made earth and heaven he formed, etc." **The dust of,** spoiling the wordplay in the statement that *'ādhām,* **man,** was formed from *'adhāmāh,* **ground,** is a

out first in dread upon the sea, or who somewhere in the low-lying valleys of the Euphrates were caught in a waste of flooding inland waters? Water thus was to them the symbol of primeval chaos; and the real creation began, they thought, when the dry land first appeared.

But for other men, moving through other regions, there were different forces which shaped the imagination out of which arose their ancient

myths. Not any dim tradition of a dark abyss of waters, but the constant presence around them of the desert, was the fact that pressed most inescapably upon their consciousness. Nomads whose life was largely bounded by the desert, moving in precarious existence amid the vast aridity of its sands, might well conceive the desert as the primeval emptiness which preceded the habitable earth. For what redeemed

8 ¶ And the Lord God planted a garden eastward in Eden; and there he put the man whom he had formed.

9 And out of the ground made the Lord God to grow every tree that is pleasant to the sight, and good for food; the tree of life also in the midst of the garden, and the tree of knowledge of good and evil.

10 And a river went out of Eden to water the garden; and from thence it was parted, and became into four heads.

came a living being. 8 And the Lord God planted a garden in Eden, in the east; and there he put the man whom he had formed.

9 And out of the ground the Lord God made to grow every tree that is pleasant to the sight and good for food, the tree of life also in the midst of the garden, and the tree of the knowledge of good and evil.

10 A river flowed out of Eden to water the garden, and there it divided and be-

gloss dependent on 3:19b. The verb rendered **formed** is that used in the O.T. (e.g., Isa. 29:16; Jer. 18:4) of a potter molding clay. The word *néphesh,* rendered **soul** (KJV) or **being** (RSV), denotes here "a complete person" (for the rich content of the word *néphesh* see Johannes Pedersen, *Israel, Its Life and Culture I-II* [London: Oxford University Press, 1926], pp. 99-181).

B. The Garden of Eden (2:8-15)

8. In Eden is an addition to harmonize the story with the fragments of the older Eden saga (cf. 3:22, 24; cf. Eissfeldt, *Hexateuch-Synopse,* pp. 254*-55*), which, it will be seen, had been intruded into it. With the deletion of the words, **eastward** (KJV) should be rendered **in the east** (RSV). In the narrative as it left the hand of J this verse, as has been noted above, was followed by vs. 6 in its original form.

9. That this verse is secondary is suggested by: (a) The explicit statement that God caused the trees to grow **out of the ground** seriously weakens the force of one of the main points (cf. 3:19, 23b) of the original narrative, that man was formed from the ground. (b) The statement that every tree was **pleasant to the sight and good for food** weakens the force of 3:6, which implies that one reason the woman succumbed to the serpent's temptation was that the tree in the midst of the garden was "good for food" and "a delight to the eyes." (c) The verse refers to **the tree of life . . . in the midst of the garden,** and follows this with a reference to **the tree of the knowledge of good and evil.** Consideration of ch. 3 will show that J said nothing of **the tree of life**—3:22 is, as will be seen, secondary. Furthermore, in 3:3 the woman refers to the forbidden tree simply as "the tree which is in the midst of the garden." It is the serpent who says that its fruit will convey knowledge of "good and evil"—falsely, for it brought only awareness of sex.

The cumulative effect of these considerations is compelling and warrants the excision of this verse as an addition by the same hand, and for the same reason, as vs. 5a.

10. The **river** had its source outside the garden through which it flowed and then divided into four.

the desert for nomadic men was its oases. Here and there oases did exist; and when across the sun-scorched sands their green and living beauty met the eye, men knew that refreshment and life were waiting there for themselves and for their flocks. No wonder then that their conception of creation out of primal nothingness should have taken the form it did. The miracle of miracles, the thing of all things most wonderful, was an oasis. That was the ultimately imagined paradise. So in ch. 2 we see the instinctive picture grow: a great emptiness of sand and dust, then a mist and rain, springs bubbling from the earth, and the wonder of grass and

trees growing up under the hand of God. The eager imagination saw it as no little spot of ground, but rather as a region wide and rich enough to be the fertile source of all the rivers of the world, where its green spaces led to vistas of great trees. Such was the Garden of Eden.

The imagination that pictured it and the symbol which it contains of ancient men's religion belong to the childhood of the race; but there are lovely suggestions in it which come down undimmed by time. The Lord God would be "walking in the garden." Taken literally and put in prose, that is childlike and naïve, but as poetry it is immortal. In the miracle of

11 The name of the first *is* Pison: that *is* it which compasseth the whole land of Havilah, where *there is* gold;

12 And the gold of that land *is* good: there *is* bdellium and the onyx stone.

13 And the name of the second river *is* Gihon: the same *is* it that compasseth the whole land of Ethiopia.

14 And the name of the third river *is* Hiddekel: that *is* it which goeth toward the east of Assyria. And the fourth river *is* Euphrates.

came four rivers. 11 The name of the first is Pishon; it is the one which flows around the whole land of Hav'i-lah, where there is gold; 12 and the gold of that land is good; bdellium and onyx stone are there. 13 The name of the second river is Gihon; it is the one which flows around the whole land of Cush. 14 And the name of the third river is Hid'de-kel, which flows east of Assyria. And the fourth river is the Eu-phra'tes.

---

11. The **Pishon** is mentioned in Ecclus. 24:25 as an illustration of abundance, but not elsewhere in the O.T. It is identified here as **the one which flows around the whole land of Havilah. Havilah** is used in 10:7, 29; 25:18, of a district apparently somewhere in Arabia. Here, **the whole land of** may indicate a larger region, as is indeed suggested by the note about its **gold** and the further information in vs. 12, obviously an attempt at identification which would perhaps hardly be necessary if the reference was merely to Arabia. In the mind of the author, whose geographical ideas were not only vague but mythically colored, it may even have included India, conceived as an eastward extension of Arabia. If so, then by the **Pishon** he may have meant the Ganges; but there can be no certainty (for an excellent summary of the possible identifications of the Pishon and the Gihon, see Skinner, *Genesis*, pp. 62-66).

13. **Cush** is used in the O.T. of (*a*) Ethiopia (e.g., Ezek. 29:10); (*b*) Midian (e.g., Num. 12:1; cf. Cushan, Hab. 3:7) in Arabia; and (*c*) *Kaššû*, the country of the Kassites (cf. Gunkel, *Genesis*, p. 89). Which of the three is meant here cannot be determined; if it is (*a*) then the **Gihon** would seem to be the Nile, the headwaters of which the author thus represented as being near those of the Tigris and the Euphrates; (*b*) would place the **Gihon** somewhere near the Pishon, as would (*c*), *Kaššû* being conceived of as extending indefinitely eastward from Babylonia.

14. The **Hiddekel** is the Tigris. This, together with the mention of the **Euphrates,** indicates that the author located Eden somewhere near the sources of these two rivers, in the vicinity of Armenia—and this regardless of the identity of the Pishon and the Gihon.

Vss. 10-14 contradict vs. 6 and reveal an interest in the locality of Eden which is foreign to the rest of the narrative. The passage is accordingly to be regarded as secondary elaboration (*ibid.*, p. 9), dependent upon another form of the Paradise myth.

---

nature God always does appear. Man can fashion many things, but only God creates that on which all life depends. In the meadows and the forest he still is walking. Even in the little places of fertility and growth he will appear.

Whether then in the great spaces of the earth or in the familiar spots which men make their own, a garden and the thought of God come close together. For a garden, to begin with, is a place of beauty especially—as that instinctive sense of wonder repeated in the ancient story saw it—"in the cool of the day." Who that has walked in a garden has not had moments when he felt a mightier Presence walking there when sunset fades, and the soft air of evening is sweet with the scent of grass and flowers, and the dew begins to fall, and the stars are born out of the

still mystery of the oncoming night? Read Francis Bacon's "Of Gardens." One of the sins which the so-called civilization of our modern cities commits against the souls of people is that in their drab deserts of brick and stone so often there have been no gardens; and one of the signs of our awakening is the increasing movement to make space for parks and to plant trees and flowers there. The best in man's nature cannot live without beauty. At Christmas in a year of widespread unemployment and financial disaster an organization which exists to minister to the poor and the hard-pressed of a certain city printed a letter from a woman on behalf of a family once prosperous and then destitute. In the family, shut now in dreary rooms, was a little girl who once had known

15 And the LORD God took the man, and put him into the garden of Eden to dress it and to keep it.	15 The LORD God took the man and put him in the garden of Eden to till it and keep it. 16 And the LORD God commanded the man, saying, "You may freely eat of every tree of the garden; 17 but of the tree of the knowledge of good and evil you shall not eat, for in the day that you eat of it you shall die."
16 And the LORD God commanded the man, saying, Of every tree of the garden thou mayest freely eat:	
17 But of the tree of the knowledge of good and evil, thou shalt not eat of it: for in the day that thou eatest thereof thou shalt surely die.	

15. The verse in part repeats vs. 8*b* and, like 5*b*β, contradicts 3:23 in regarding the tilling of the ground as man's natural occupation. It is redactional, and its purpose is to link vss. 10-14 to what follows.

C. THE FORBIDDEN TREE (2:16-17)

16-17. These verses are neither in their original form nor in their original position. (*a*) The forbidden tree is called **the tree of the knowledge of good and evil**; contrast 3:3 (some commentators, e.g., Gunkel, *Genesis,* pp. 10-11, emend vs. 17 to agree with 3:3), and see the Exeg. on vs. 9 above. (*b*) They contain no prohibition against touching the tree; contrast 3:3. (*c*) The command is given before the making of the woman, who is nevertheless cognizant of it when the serpent speaks to her.

In its original form the command came after vs. 23; i.e., the story in its primary J form told of the man being placed in the garden (vs. 8), and followed this immediately with vss. 18, 21-23, recording the provision of "a helper fit for him" (vs. 18). Then came the command—now preserved in altered form in vss. 16-17—reading probably, "And God commanded them, saying, 'Of every tree of the garden you may freely eat, but of the tree which is in the midst of the garden you shall not eat, neither shall you touch it; for in the day that you eat of it you shall surely die.'" The intrusion of vs. 9, telling of the making of the trees, and of vss. 19-20 (on the secondary character of these see below), telling of the making of the animals, retarded the tempo of the story, and gave rise to the possibility that the man might have eaten of the fruit of the tree before it was forbidden. To meet this difficulty some editor shifted the prohibition to its present position, and at the same time, since the mention of the tree of life in vs. 9 had introduced an element of confusion into the story, made it apply explicitly to the tree, the fruit

a home that had a garden. Send her this and that necessity, if you can, the letter pleaded, but, "Oh, above all, send her one red rose."

If in a garden there is beauty, so there also is the miracle of growth. It is good to have something remind us anew and repeatedly of that miracle. Remember how often Jesus was aware of it. "Consider the lilies . . . how they grow" (Matt. 6:28). "The kingdom of heaven is like to a grain of mustard seed" (Matt. 13:31). "Behold, a sower went forth to sow" (Matt. 13:3). One danger in our urban civilization is that men may lose their consciousness of the elemental realities on which life depends and with which it must co-operate if it is to endure. In a garden the everlasting facts are plain; there truth walks and may be heard as the voice of God was heard in Eden when he walked among the trees. Reflect upon what that voice is

telling: that what ultimately appears, of beauty or of ugliness, depends upon the seed, and that the heart of man, like the ground, can produce nothing unless it has received from God, and planted in itself, those influences which have in them the miracle of life; that the responsibility of every man is like the gardener's, to know that though he creates nothing he is responsible to cultivate what God has given; that growth cannot be forced by any human haste and that the silent process of the divine unfolding must be trusted; and that those who have grown most in grace, like men who must have their gardens grow in sun and rain and changing seasons, will be most humble in themselves and most reverent before the unfolding mysteries of God.

16-17. See Expos. on 2:4–3:24; 3:1-24.

18 ¶ And the LORD God said, *It is* not good that the man should be alone; I will make him a help meet for him.

18 Then the LORD God said, "It is not good that the man should be alone; I will

---

of which the serpent was to claim would give knowledge of good and evil, but which, in the event, awakened only the knowledge of sex.

A further point in support of this argument, that the prohibition of vss. 16-17 originally came after vs. 23, may be noted here, and that is the resulting juxtaposition with vs. 25; 3:1-7: eating of the fruit of the tree in the midst of the garden is prohibited. No reason is given, but there follows immediately the notice that the man and his wife were without consciousness of sex, and the tragic account of how they acquired it. This, one of the main points of the story, is obscure as the material is now ordered; it is crystal clear if the prohibition immediately precedes vs. 25.

For the implication of the warning **on the day that you eat of it you shall die** see Exeg. on 3:3.

D. MAN NEEDS A COMPANION (2:18-20)

18-20. The grounds for regarding vss. 19-20 as secondary are: (*a*) The statement that the beasts were formed **out of the ground**—see above on vs. 9.

---

18. *The Consecration of Relationships.*— Genesis, which starts with the beginning of the universe, goes on to tell of other particular beginnings. Its wide-reaching message is that every aspect of existence finds its right interpretation only when it is related first to God. It is wise enough to know that what ought to be is not accomplished suddenly, and that man's understanding of his life must grow through early ignorance and much blundering; but its great truth is that every relationship must begin with a recognition of God's meaning for it if it is ever to have meaning and worth.

So in ch. 1, and again in the story of the Garden of Eden, there is a spiritual note in the account of the beginning of marriage. "God created man in his own image," and "male and female created he them" (vs. 27). It was God who said, **It is not good that the man should be alone,** and God who commanded that a man "shall cleave unto his wife: and they shall be one flesh" (2:24)—or, as the strong Hebrew words imply, one personality. They shall "be fruitful and multiply." Thus marriage and the conception of children are lifted up above blind instinct and endowed with sacredness; and although the kind of marriages and the kind of family life among the patriarchs which Genesis goes on to portray have the imperfections of a primitive society, there is goodness in them, and that goodness is directly related to the measure of loyalty and faithfulness which religion put there.

And as Genesis sets the beginning of the earth, and the beginnings of man and of marriage and of the family, in the light of God, and thus makes human beings responsible to him for

the right development of these, so it brings the same suggestion for society and for civilization. A new nation begins with Abraham, and its glory is that it begins with God (12:1-4). The nation that was to be appeared at first only as a little clan dwelling in tents, heirs of a promise that seemed a long way off. But their greatness was that they "looked for a city which hath foundations, whose builder and maker is God" (Heb. 11:10).

What of modern nations? How far has all that is best in them been due to religious faith and religious purpose in the men who helped to make them? Look at the declared ideals and reflect upon the prayers of some of the great statesmen of England; of Washington and Lincoln and others who helped to make the United States. What deliberate effort is being made by us to share and transmit the high conceptions which only religion can preserve? The future of civilization depends on that. In many regions of the earth civilization had not advanced far in the times portrayed in Genesis, but the qualities of character which undergird it and advance it—honesty, idealism, social-mindedness, imagination, intelligent devotedness—are all suggested in the concluding chapters of this book as it comes to its climax in the story of Joseph.

And the whole sequence of beginnings—for the individual, for the family group, and for the community—which Genesis includes is dependent upon the two other and supreme beginnings which are recorded there: the beginning of conscience and the beginning of communion with God.

19 And out of the ground the Lord God formed every beast of the field, and every fowl of the air; and brought *them* unto Adam to see what he would call them: and whatsoever Adam called every living creature, that *was* the name thereof.

20 And Adam gave names to all cattle, and to the fowl of the air, and to every

make him a helper fit for him." 19 So out of the ground the Lord God formed every beast of the field and every bird of the air, and brought them to the man to see what he would call them; and whatever the man called every living creature, that was its name. 20 The man gave names to all cattle,

---

(*b*) The loose style of the writing (see Skinner, *Genesis*, pp. 67-68; cf. the emendations proposed by Holzinger, *Genesis*, pp. 28-29; Gunkel, *Genesis*, p. 11; Eissfeldt, *Hexateuch-Synopse*, p. 255*).

(*c*) The fact that the verses are a *non sequitur* to vs. 18. Gunkel and others, indeed, hold that J is representing God as making a number of unsuccessful attempts to provide a suitable companion for the man; against this it may be argued either (i) that J would scarcely have tolerated such an implication, even if it had been in the material he was using—in this connection his drastic revision of the Eden saga, considered below, may be noted; or alternatively (ii) that he would have made his meaning more clear than is here the case.

(*d*) Whereas the naming of the woman in vs. 23 is etiological—explaining, wrongly, the similarity between the Hebrew words for "man" and "woman"—the naming of the animals is without significance, so that vss. 19*aβb*, 20*a* seem to be a mere reflex of vs. 23.

(*e*) The use of the word "made" in 3:1, in contrast to **formed** (vs. 19), is a further indication, though slight, of diverse authorship.

(*f*) The narrative in its present form fails to account for the existence of beasts outside the garden, since there is no suggestion that they were driven out with the man. With the deletion of these verses, together with vss. 5 and 9, this difficulty vanishes, for

---

In the story of the Garden of Eden there is revealed the eternal truth that there is right and wrong, a true choice and a false choice; an obedience to the voice that represents the highest, and a willful disobedience; and that when man has sinned, no matter with what plausible excuse, there is that within him which shrinks away and hides, naked and ashamed before the light. But there is another and redeeming revelation in Genesis, a promise of what can be the way of life. Weak and imperfect though he is, and prone to sin, man can yet "walk with God," as Enoch did, and Abraham, and others in the Bible's long succession of aspiring souls. So the book points forward to a gradual fulfillment— and to the ultimate fulfillment that should come in Christ.

19-20a. The Animals.—There is a delightfully childish quality about this picture. God makes all the animals, and they march obediently past Adam in review. It was an earlier and greater Noah's ark parade. Then, according to engravings in old picture books of the Bible, all these animals, elephants and rhinoceroses and lions and tigers and the rest, walk about or lie down in a sort of purring cheerfulness, a universal happy family.

It is part of an ancient tale which some writer

long unknown put here into the scriptural narrative. One might feel hard pressed to find in it a specifically religious message; yet by analogy and imagination there is one. **Whatsoever Adam called every living creature, that was the name thereof.** "The name is that by which the thing is summoned into the field of thought, and is necessary for its full existence" (Exeg. on 1:5). That, to the mind of the ancients, was the power of a name. When Adam named the animals he determined what they should be like and how they should behave.

We cannot manage as conveniently as that. Lions and tigers and leopards and wolves do not become tame because we tell them to. Not in the physical world, nor in the moral one either. There are some forces surrounding every man which are like wild beasts that stay wild. We cannot change them by pretending that this is not the way they are. These hearts of ours are not innocent gardens of Eden where nothing dangerous intrudes. There are appetites and passions against which we have to be on watch as actually as a man at night would have to be on watch against a tiger or a wolf. There are qualities in ourselves as undesirable as the boar and the ape. We had better call them by their right names. Someday, by God's grace, they

beast of the field; but for Adam there was not found a help meet for him.

21 And the LORD God caused a deep sleep to fall upon Adam, and he slept; and he took one of his ribs, and closed up the flesh instead thereof.

22 And the rib, which the LORD God had taken from man, made he a woman, and brought her unto the man.

23 And Adam said, This *is* now bone of my bones, and flesh of my flesh: she shall be called Woman, because she was taken out of man.

and to the birds of the air, and to every beast of the field; but for the man there was not found a helper fit for him. 21 So the LORD God caused a deep sleep to fall upon the man, and while he slept took one of his ribs and closed up its place with flesh; 22 and the rib which the LORD God had taken from the man he made into a woman and brought her to the man. 23 Then the man said,

"This at last is bone of my bones and flesh
of my flesh;
she shall be called Woman,*d*
because she was taken out of Man."*e*

d Heb *ishshah*
e Heb *ish*

---

the story is seen to be an account not of the creation of the world as a whole, but simply of the making of man and of his life in the garden.

(*g*) Vs. 20*b* has no connection with vs. 20*a*, and practically repeats vs. 18*b*.

Vss. 19-20*a* are thus an elaboration of the original story, made for the same reason, and probably by the same hand, as vs. 9. The author may, of course, have been dependent on a feature of the earlier saga not preserved by J. Vs. 20*b* resumes the thread of the story after the intrusion of vss. 19-20*a*; **Adam** (KJV) should be read **the man** (RSV).

E. THE MAKING OF WOMAN (2:21-25)

21-23. These verses are thus the original continuation of vs. 18. In vs. 23 for **out of man** should be read "out of her man," following the Samar. and the LXX.

---

may be different; but in the meantime we had better be sure that we are different, if we have been foolish enough to suppose that they can be idly played with.

20*b*-24. Man and Woman.—In the minds of those to whom we owe the several elements woven in Genesis, there are different attitudes toward sex (cf. Exeg. on 1:28; 2:16-17, 24; 3:1, 22, 23; 34). There is that which regards it simply and wholesomely as the fundamental of existence. And there is that which looks at it with doubt and distress because of the strange complexities of good and evil which it brings.

This difference need arouse no wonder, for this double appraisal of sex runs through all history. Many of the fiercest human passions and the darkest crimes come out of it. But loyalty and love and the deepest and most enduring human relationships also are rooted in it. The drama of the everlasting conflict between its good and evil has inspired much of the world's immortal poetry, poetry that reflected not only the throbbing impulses of the body, but the inextricable web of power and pathos and pitifulness that makes up human souls. Remember Helen of Troy and Hector and Paris, Ulysses and Penelope, Antony and

Cleopatra, Paolo and Francesca, Tristram and Iseult, Lancelot and Guinevere.

Sex is fundamental. It cannot be got rid of or forgotten. It may be sublimated into adorations that are separate from the flesh. There is a kind of desire for saintliness that will deliberately choose celibacy. Sometimes whole groups have attempted this, as the Essenes did in the first century and as other little communities in many lands since have sought to do. But that cannot be normative. There was good reason for the writer of 1:27-28 to say of God's creation of humanity that "male and female created he them," and to ascribe to God the words, "Be fruitful, and multiply, and replenish the earth."

Therefore, since sex is of divine ordaining, it must be related religiously to life. As the slowly maturing experience of the people of Israel learned, and as the whole Bible expresses, the way in which this becomes possible is through monogamous marriage.

But how may the marriage of one man and one woman be of such a kind that in it the best that God has meant for them may flourish? The answer of course is wider than any few words can cover. It requires devotion and many disciplines. But there is one word that may mean

24 Therefore shall a man leave his father and his mother, and shall cleave unto his wife: and they shall be one flesh.

24 Therefore a man leaves his father and his mother and cleaves to his wife, and they

---

24. This verse cannot, in view of the statement in vs. 25, be a continuation of the man's speech recorded in vs. 23. Commentators generally treat it as an explanatory comment by J. In view of the fact, however, that the note obscures one of the main points of the narrative—that the man and the woman were still without consciousness of sex—it may be doubted that such a finished writer as J would have inserted it here. For this reason the verse seems to be an addition by a later writer who, reflecting upon the desire of man for his wife, found an explanation of it in the—supposed—fact that woman by her very origin was bone of man's bones and flesh of his flesh. Because of this he **leaves his father and his mother,** of whose bone and flesh he was formed, and **cleaves to his wife,** to become in the marriage act **one flesh.**

The verse was not originally an affirmation that marriage was from the beginning, by divine intention, monogamous. Such an affirmation would indeed have been impossible at that time. Only when it had come to be recognized, however inarticulately, that woman was a person in her own right was it possible to discern the true meaning of the sexual desire of man which the verse seeks to explain. Nevertheless, its author has said more than he knew. For in his very affirmation that sexual desire is part of the divinely ordered nature of things, he was in effect affirming that its true meaning would unfold with the unfolding of the meaning of the universe as a whole. Consequently his words had in them a meaning which would likewise unfold, so that the interpretation placed upon them in Mark 10:6-9 (cf. Matt. 19:4-6) ; I Cor. 6:16; Eph. 5:31 is ultimately valid.

---

more than any other single one. It is companionship: the companionship of two personalities each developing to its fullest and giving and receiving the utmost that both can share. When marriage does not have that mutuality it fails to reach its highest possibility. "It is not good that the man should be alone." That is true in a much larger way than the physical, and the true divine commandment that **a man shall cleave unto his wife** has to do with far more than the flesh. Nor is it enough that the woman should be a **help meet,** if that is taken to mean one who is subordinate to the male. In many societies and in many times, including periods of the O.T., woman has been regarded as a chattel, a household drudge, a servant of man's appetites. Influences from that inheritance remain. But true marriage, the marriage on which Christian blessing may be invoked, is a marriage between a man and woman who bring their different gifts in equal honor and in equal exercise. The greater opportunities for women to which Christian civilizations have at last moved forward not automatically will, but can, lift marriage nearer to the divine intention. For then there can be a partnership not only in the body, but of two minds furnished with quickening ideas and of two spirits who both know something of the wider reality of life to which they ought to be adjusted.

G. A. Studdert-Kennedy, a great interpreter of truth in his generation, wrote a book called *The Warrior, the Woman, and the Christ.* In it he said this:

Love is the joyous conflict of two or more free self-conscious persons who rejoice in one another's individualities and . . . through the clash of mind on mind and will on will work out an ever-increasing but never finally completed unity. . . . And the primary school of this vital and vitalising love is the home.[1]

But "the home" as such will not produce and keep that unity. It must be a home which is held together by something larger than itself. The great attraction of the remembrance of God must permeate it and hold its individuals harmoniously together, as the sun holds the planets in their course. Many a home that started with romance has ended in recriminations and wretchedness because neither husband nor wife had a loyalty higher and more controlling than his or her desires. But when they both look up to the beauty of holiness which worship has taught them to behold in God, affections are purified and selfishness is transcended in devotion to ideals that endure.

[1] Garden City: Doubleday, Doran & Co., 1929, pp xiii-xiv.

25 And they were both naked, the man and his wife, and were not ashamed.

3 Now the serpent was more subtile than any beast of the field which the LORD God had made. And he said unto the woman, Yea, hath God said, Ye shall not eat of every tree of the garden?

become one flesh. 25 And the man and his wife were both naked, and were not ashamed.

3 Now the serpent was more subtle than any other wild animal that the LORD God had made. He said to the woman, "Did God say, 'You shall not eat of any tree of

---

25. Following vs. 23, as has been argued above, came in its original form the prohibition now preserved in vss. 16-17, to be followed in turn by the statement, implicit in the words **the man and his wife were both naked, and were not ashamed,** that they were without consciousness of sex.

III. Man's Alienation from God (3:1-24)

The story in this chapter of man's disobedience to God's command and of his expulsion from the garden to a life of toil is dependent upon an ancient myth which J drastically revised. A fragment of this myth is now preserved in vs. 22. That this verse is an intrusion into the main narrative of ch. 3 is generally recognized. Here it need only be noted that the reason it gives for man's expulsion from the garden is quite other than that implied in vss. 17, 19, 23.

From this verse it is possible to recover the salient features of the earlier form of the tale. It told not of one only, but of two magic trees in Eden, the garden of God (cf. Ezek. 28:13; 31:8-9, 16), the tree of life and the tree of the knowledge of good and evil. Man was forbidden on pain of death to eat of them, the reason for the prohibition being God's fear that man, acquiring knowledge of good and evil, might become like him and, approaching too near his throne, might endanger his supremacy. But the serpent, a demon hostile to God, told man the truth. He was thus no subtle tempter but, in intention at least, a benefactor of the human race. Man, thus enlightened, ate of the tree and became like God, **knowing good and evil** (vs. 22). The potential threat to God's supremacy had thus become actual, so God, acting decisively and at once, drove him from the garden lest he should **put forth his hand and take also of the tree of life, and eat** (vs. 22), and so make the threat permanent.

A. Temptation and Sin (3:1-8)

3:1. Revising the myth, J represented the serpent not as a demon whose origin, whatever it may have been, owed nothing to God, but as a **beast of the field which . . .**

---

25. The Innocence that Did Not Last.—Adam and Eve were **naked, . . . and were not ashamed.** But presently "they knew that they were naked; and they sewed fig leaves together, and made themselves aprons" (3:7). And later the Lord God made "coats of skins, and clothed them" (3:21). Two strands of thought may be woven into the ideas which these verses express. First may be the recollection of what had actually happened in the long development of human groups. In the dim past people wore no clothes at all. Then came girdles of leaves or grass, as among some primitive tribes today; and then, as the human race moved on toward civilization, the sewing and weaving of clothes. But if these facts were in the minds of the writers of these chapters, their interest was not in the facts as

such but in what they symbolized. Once men could stand unembarrassed before the gaze of God. Then when they had sinned they had guilty shame both before God and in the presence of one another. But the flimsy devices they sewed together were not enough. Ultimately God himself must clothe them in that which represented pain and blood and sacrifice.

3:1-24. Changing Theories and Unchanging Truth.—In the entire range of the world's writings it would be difficult to find any passage so brief which has had such immense influence upon human thought as ch. 3. Paul made it a foundation stone of his theology: "By one man sin entered into the world" (Rom. 5:12); "By the offense of one judgment came upon all men to condemnation" (Rom. 5:18); "By one man's

God had made. Nor was he, even in intention, a benefactor of the human race, but a **subtle** liar. He deliberately misled the woman in telling her that by eating of the forbidden tree she and her husband would **be like God, knowing good and evil** (vs. 5),

disobedience many were made sinners" (Rom. 5:19). What happened in Adam and to Adam was for Paul the awful fact by which all human destiny was originally determined. Augustine enlarged the first structure of the doctrine which Paul had begun to build. Calvin fortified it with his relentless logic. So it has happened that the mind of nearly the whole of Christendom has dwelt for generations within the structure of thought that took its architecture from this one conception of the sin of Adam.

In modern times there have been two contrasting reactions to the whole doctrine of Adam's sin and the condemnation which is said to have fallen on the whole human race through him. The first of these has been repudiation. Christian thinkers here and there began to say that orthodox theology had become a monstrous exaggeration. Biblical criticism dissolved the literal authority of the story of the Fall. Here is an ancient myth, men said, which has been treated as actual history. The whole structure built upon it is illusion; and worse than that, it is an illusion which has done bitter harm to human spirits. The vast walls of thought which Paul and Augustine and Calvin raised above the dark ground of the ancient story, so it is declared, have been the walls of a prison house in which generations have had to dwell among false shadows of fear and guilt and condemnation. Get rid of the phobia which has grown out of a fable that never was a fact, and let the spirit of man go free!

This new representation had wide welcome in the nineteenth century and on into the beginning of the twentieth. The thought of man as fallen was to become a discredited superstition. The intelligent and informed were to cast off the old robes of self-depreciation. The mother of Charles William Eliot, who was to be one of the great presidents of Harvard University and a powerful influence upon all education in his time, exclaimed to a friend who had gone into the Episcopal Church and presumably, therefore, would say the old prayer of the General Confession, "Eliza, do you kneel down in church and call yourself a miserable sinner? . . . Neither I nor any of my family will ever do that!" [2] The theology of the Unitarians, and of many liberal thinkers in other groups, glorified man's powers and potentialities. He was not fallen; he had only begun to rise. Presently religion tended to change to humanism. God was no longer a

sovereign power before whose holiness men stood under judgment; God was the goodness resident in men themselves. Set men free from the belief of the old falsehood and their inherent virtues would be enough to bring in the millennium.

This tendency of thought has been powerfully reinforced by the school of psychoanalysis which began with Freud. The guilt complex has been arraigned as Public Enemy No. 1. G. B. Chisholm, deputy minister of health of Canada, a psychiatrist of wide recognition, delivered in 1945 the William Alanson White Memorial Lectures in Washington. In the first of these lectures he said:

We have been very slow to . . . recognize the unnecessary and artificially imposed inferiority, guilt and fear, commonly known as sin, under which we have almost all labored and which produces so much of the social maladjustment and unhappiness in the world. . . . Misguided by authoritarian dogma, bound by exclusive faith, stunted by inculcated loyalty, . . . bewildered by invented mystery, and loaded down by the weight of guilt and fear . . . , the unfortunate human race, deprived by these incubi of . . . its reasoning power and its natural capacity to enjoy the satisfaction of its natural urges, struggles along under its ghastly self-imposed burden. The results, the inevitable results, are frustration, inferiority, neurosis, and inability to enjoy living, to reason clearly or to make a world fit to live in.[3]

So the vehement claim is that intelligent people must get free from dogmatic definitions of "good" and "evil," and above all, from obsession with the notion of "sin."

There are those who like to think themselves intelligent and welcome that conclusion. And there are many others who, on a different ground, will join them in repudiating the story of "the fall" of Adam, and the fall of the whole human race in him. They repudiate it not only because they consider it an unsubstantial myth, but also because they hold that the traditional theology which has been built upon it is full of error and distortion. They doubt that anyone can actually believe what the *New England Primer* taught,

> In Adam's fall
> We sinned all.

No matter what traditional authority lies back of that, no matter if Paul is claimed for its sup-

[2] Henry James, *Charles W. Eliot* (Boston: Houghton Mifflin Co., 1930), I, 33.

[3] "The Psychiatry of Enduring Peace and Social Progress," *Psychiatry*, IX (1946), 7-8.

2 And the woman said unto the serpent, We may eat of the fruit of the trees of the garden:

the garden'?" 2 And the woman said to the serpent, "We may eat of the fruit of the

---

for he knew all the time that the sole result would be consciousness of sex with, in the thought of J, its consequent misery.

---

port! Paul—great though his mind was—worked within the limitations of his inheritance and his times. Taking the Jewish scriptures too literally, he gave to this chapter of Genesis a kind of categorical authority it did not possess. As a Jew he believed instinctively also in the corporate solidarity which was a central conviction in the early religion of Israel, and so it was possible for him to think that if Adam sinned and was condemned, then all his human descendants were condemned because of him. But we recognize no such conclusion, many sincere men today will say; and they go on to say further that the whole story of the fall of Adam leads to such twisted suggestions that it had better be got rid of once for all.

That then is—or has been—one attitude toward what is written in ch. 3—the attitude of repudiation. But the pendulum is swinging. There grows another and more profound perception which turns back to the ancient story with the realization that there are meanings in it which never must be lost. The truth of the wonderful old drama of Eden is not that we are accounted evil because somebody before us did evil. The truth dramatized there is this: Human nature, made to go God's way, has an inveterate tendency to listen to the temptation to go its own way, and this rebellious way must have an evil end—evil not only for the individual who has sinned but, in that solidarity of human nature and human destiny which Paul perceived, evil that may involve many generations in its long entail. For there are laws as old as creation which we are meant to obey; and as sure as creation, if we disobey them, we shall be in trouble. No circumstances outside us can outweigh that inner fact. No blessings of environment or material opportunity can guarantee a happy life, not even though they should be as complete as those of the Garden of Eden. The disobedience of Eve and Adam is the symbol of a fatal truth: We human beings are continually disobeying and rejecting the law of life; only when our wills are kept in accord with the higher will of God can life be blessed. The instant we yield to the rebellious self-importance which establishes our own ungoverned desires as controlling, that instant life breaks up into little egocentric fragments doomed to irrational discord and collision. D. R. Davies, in his book

with the wholesomely sardonic title, *Down Peacock's Feathers*, has put the reality well.

Now in history we have to face the fact . . . that the human race through the individuals composing it, has willed itself out of the subordinate relation to God, with the fatal result that every individual becomes his own centre. . . . Since we are all alike in wanting to be our own centre, we are irrevocably divided from one another. United in Sin, we become disunited in everything else. This is the brilliant mess in which humanity finds itself, especially the progressive civilized humanity of to-day.[4]

It follows naturally therefore that the same author, referring to the General Confession and its abasement of human pride, should say for himself and for many others:

I believe its truth absolutely. Especially do I subscribe to its more offensive clauses—offensive, that is, to the modern, progressive mind [such as, "There is no health in us"]. . . . That is the part which I believe with the utmost conviction. I am for clouting the secularized mind—hard.[5]

How the secularized and self-sufficient mind may be redeemed is not answered in the story of the Fall. But that answer begins in the O.T. record of the covenant which God made with the saving faith of Abraham and reaches forward through the long hope of patriarchs and prophets to the "Second Adam" whose coming the N.T. reveals.

1-5. *The Serpent.*—When these words were written men told stories simply as children do. They were concerned chiefly not with laborious prose fact but with imagination; and through that imagination they had instinctive intuitions of the truth. They saw great realities of life and saw them in pictures which are more vivid than any careful pedantry. The description of the serpent is a serious reckoning with the fact of sin. Evil enters into the world, and once here it is dangerous and may be deadly. Moreover, as the writer of this Genesis story knew, it may be more deadly than it seems. Observe that in this account the serpent is not at first repulsive. He comes with plausible argument. He comes with a kind of insinuating grace.

At the beginning of the story the man and the woman are content. They have all they

[4] New York: The Macmillan Co., 1946, pp. 10, 11.
[5] *Ibid.*, p. viii.

3 But of the fruit of the tree which *is* in the midst of the garden, God hath said, Ye shall not eat of it, neither shall ye touch it, lest ye die.

trees of the garden; 3 but God said, 'You shall not eat of the fruit of the tree which is in the midst of the garden, neither shall

---

3. Lest you die: God had warned the man and the woman that if they should eat of the fruit of the forbidden tree, the consequence would be death. There can be little doubt that this was a feature of the earlier myth. There it was, it would seem, a mere threat, impossible of fulfillment. In the event, the best that the offended deity could do was to prevent man's access to the tree of life (cf. vs. 22). J could not tolerate the idea that God would threaten what he could not perform, nor could he, without defeating the purpose of his narrative (see Exeg. on vs. 23), have the warning put into effect. At the same time he was under the necessity of preserving the salient points of the original tale (cf. Exeg. on vs. 22), of which the warning of immediate death was one.

It is hardly possible that J intended the sentence in vs. 19, "you are dust, and to dust you shall return," to be taken as the implementation of the warning. For in the first place it is difficult to suppose that he, artist that he was, would have been content to leave unexplained the awkward fact that action had been thus delayed. And secondly there is no suggestion in vs. 19*aβb* that man's "return to the ground" was a consequence of his disobedience; the implication is rather that this was his natural end.

The inference would seem to be unavoidable that for J not death itself but man's attitude toward death as the final frustration of a frustrated life was the last consequence of the alienation from God which his rebellion had caused. And, as will be shown below (see Exeg. on vs. 7), this attitude was the inevitable result of the radical disordering of human relationships which was the immediate consequence of his act. Thus J has here again revised the original myth. Facing the problem of how to deal with the threat which was not fulfilled, he was brought to a new understanding of man's fear of death— "the king of terrors" (Job 18:14)—in which all other fears are bound up. No magic tree of life could cure this malady, let alone give immortality, so J omitted all mention of it from his narrative.

---

need, though they do not have everything. God has given them the garden, with the exception of the fruit of one tree. They were told to let that fruit alone, and they did leave it alone, until. . . . Until the suggestion came sliding in with a serpent's subtlety: "Why not have everything? Why not know more about life? Why not take possession of the tree of the knowledge of good and evil? Why not try the taste of sin?" It is thus that the seductions of sin do present themselves: in the glass of liquor to the boy who thinks he will know what it is to be a man, in the temptation of quick gain that makes the gambler, in the short cut that promises success.

Eve knew that the fruit of the one tree was forbidden. **Of the fruit of the tree which is in the midst of the garden, God hath said, Ye shall not eat of it, neither shall ye touch it, lest ye die.** But the serpent was quick with a convenient doubt: "Did God really say that? Perhaps you only thought he said so. And if he did say it, why did he? The fruit is good. What sense can there be in not enjoying it? Why listen to unreasonable commands of God that

fence you off from full experience?" The serpent suggested that to Eve, and Eve adopted the suggestion after a little manipulation of her conscience. When she had passed the idea on to Adam, he adopted it too.

The serpent that managed such adroit persuasion was not only in the Garden of Eden. It comes plausibly up to every one of us, presenting the idea that we can know better than God. Are there appetites we have been commanded to control? Well, what are they for if not to indulge them? Are there desires just out of our reach that look more inviting than any we have already satisfied? Well, why not find some hook or crook by which to grasp them? Does the moral law put certain "thou shalt nots" in our way? Yes, but the fruit on the other side is not only pleasant to the eyes, but also is something **to be desired to make one wise.** Why not "see life," and follow the impulse to try everything once? Suppose we do seem to remember that God's word was different? Perhaps that is just a notion that we ought to outgrow. And besides, how can we take seriously anything so extreme as **In the day**

4 And the serpent said unto the woman, Ye shall not surely die:

5 For God doth know that in the day ye eat thereof, then your eyes shall be opened, and ye shall be as gods, knowing good and evil.

6 And when the woman saw that the tree *was* good for food, and that it *was* pleasant to the eyes, and a tree to be desired to make *one* wise, she took of the fruit thereof, and did eat, and gave also unto her husband with her; and he did eat.

you touch it, lest you die.' " 4 But the serpent said to the woman, "You will not die. 5 For God knows that when you eat of it your eyes will be opened, and you will be like God, knowing good and evil." 6 So when the woman saw that the tree was good for food, and that it was a delight to the eyes, and that the tree was to be desired to make one wise, she took of its fruit and ate; and she also gave some to her husband, and

---

4-5. The account of the temptation of the woman in vss. 1-6 is written with superlative skill, and reveals further the psychological penetration of the author. The serpent appeals to the human desire to be **like God.** This is a right and reasonable desire. The later command, "ye shall be holy; for I the LORD your God am holy" (Lev. 19:2; cf. Matt. 5:48), makes it clear that man is possessed of the potentiality to become **like God—** in character. This likeness is to come through submission to God's will. The serpent in telling the woman that likeness to God is to be achieved by defiance of his command tacitly suggests that the likeness which is within human reach is likeness not in character but in power. He suggests that man can make himself the equal of God.

6. The woman sees that the tree is **good for food and . . . a delight to the eyes.** Deceived by the serpent, she is now deceiving herself. All that she wants to do, she tells herself, is to satisfy two legitimate desires, for food and for beauty. By what right has God forbidden their satisfaction? Her real desire, however, is for power. It is difficult to say whether or not this same self-deception is implicit in the next clause, **that the tree was to be desired to make one wise.** Both the fact that this was not something which could actually be seen and the explicit subject **the tree,** unnecessary after the preceding clause, suggest that this clause is a gloss (cf. Gunkel, *Genesis,* p. 17). If this is the case,

---

that thou eatest thereof thou shalt surely die? If God really said that, either he did not altogether mean it or we can get around it somehow.

But the fact is that we are in a universe which God controls, not we. When he put us here to learn our lessons and to grow up spiritually he did not intend that we should take over the school and change the requirements to suit ourselves. We have to meet conditions and meet them none the less when we are not grown up enough to know the reasons why they have been set. That is hard for human pride to learn, but it must be learned regardless. Psychologically and religiously one mark of maturity is to know that we live in a universe where we must square with facts and not suppose that we can indulge every vagrant fancy. Only incorrigible children think they must cry and complain when they do not get everything they want. There are some things we are not to have, some prizes we shall not win, some ambitions that the wisdom of God will not let us gratify. And when conscience tells us, as it told Eve, that some particular fruit is not for

us, we had better not rationalize our curiosity or our appetite into an alleged justification for reaching out to take it.

The temptation that comes to individuals comes also to nations. Reinhold Niebuhr once began a lecture with these words: "Our question is, Does the state belong to God or to the devil? And the answer is that the state belongs to God, but it is in danger of becoming the devil by imagining that it is God." In the words of the serpent, **You will be like God, knowing good and evil;** i.e., every nation, in its pride and lust for power, is apt to deify its own interests and make definitions of good and evil that have nothing to do with universal moral law. Stephen Decatur's toast, "Our country, . . . may she always be in the right; but our country, right or wrong!" plausible and patriotic though it sounds, can be another echo of the serpent's suggestion to let our own enlarged selves be God.

6-13. *The Emptiness of Excuses.*—It would appear that this account represents a man's idea. Adam and Eve were both involved in the wrongdoing, but it is Eve who is described as

7 And the eyes of them both were opened, and they knew that they *were* naked; and they sewed fig leaves together, and made themselves aprons.	he ate. 7 Then the eyes of both were opened, and they knew that they were naked; and they sewed fig leaves together and made themselves aprons.

the glossator may simply be carrying J's description of the woman's thought a little further: the desire for wisdom, too, is a legitimate desire which God has no right to thwart. On the other hand, his reference may be to a wisdom which is not of God, the wisdom of magic, an instrument of power. If so, it would seem that J in describing the woman's self-deception had been careful to tell only how she had consciously justified her action to herself, thus suggesting that she had refused to admit her real motive. The glossator then, feeling that this was too subtle to be grasped by the ordinary man, added the clause to make explicit what J in his sensitivity had left implicit.

7. The perfidy of the serpent was immediately apparent on the eating of the fruit. Far from becoming **like God, knowing good and evil** (vs. 5), they knew only **that they were naked.** The concreteness of the statement is characteristically Semitic. The nakedness of which they hitherto "were not ashamed" (2:25) becomes an intolerable indecency, demanding that it be covered now that the consciousness of sex has sprung to life within them. It must not be supposed that J regarded the sexual relationship as in itself evil. Having been ordained by God (cf. 2:18, 21-23), this could only be good. But it had been infected with evil when man in his desire for power had disobeyed God. This had impaired the relationship between man and God and so had thrown the relationship between the man and his wife into disorder.

Whatever the context of the earlier myth may have been, in the present form of the story the actors, the first man and the first woman, constitute the whole human race. The relationship between them thus symbolized all human relationships. It is difficult to say whether J would have consciously subscribed to the statement that the sexual relationship is the basic human relationship. It is unlikely that he thought in such terms. Nevertheless in view of the psychological penetration which marks the story as a whole there can be little doubt that he was, however inarticulately, aware of the definitive character of this relationship. The representation that the awakening of sex consciousness was accompanied by a consciousness of guilt thus contains a recognition of the fact that all human relationships are disordered. Alienation from God has brought with it alienation from man. Loneliness is the specter which haunts unredeemed humanity.

starting it. It is always convenient to have somebody else to blame when trouble comes. Observe Adam's double excuse. The woman tempted him, and he ate. Eve was responsible, not he; for Eve presented the temptation and all he did was to respond. That was the first excuse: temptation comes, and when it comes, of course it is natural to follow it. Oscar Wilde said once, "I can resist everything except temptation"; and underneath the wry humor of that there is sober fact. Many people act as though no one could reasonably be supposed to resist temptation. But stop the sentence in the middle. The woman tempted me, and. . . . And what? There is the crux of human character. Temptation is an element in every life and comes to everybody. But it is always possible to end the sentence another way. This and that tempted me, but I was not persuaded. That is the sort of answer made by souls who are not paper to be scorched by fire but iron to be

purified and hardened by it. The fact that evil is possible is no alibi for choosing it.

The second element in Adam's excuse was to throw the blame one stage farther back. **The woman whom thou gavest to be with me, she gave me of the tree, and I did eat.** So neither Eve nor Adam was really responsible; God was. If God did not want Adam to sin, why had he given Eve to him, and why had he made Eve the sort of person she was in the first place? If Adam said that, his descendants have often said it too. We did not make our own environment, nor the people with whom we have to live. God created them; and if trouble somehow comes to us through them, God ought to have prevented it. Thus without being offensively personal, we can still satisfy ourselves with the assumption that we have transferred our fault by passing it on to the general scheme of things. No other person may have been worse than we, but then all of us were turned

8 And they heard the voice of the LORD God walking in the garden in the cool of the day: and Adam and his wife hid themselves from the presence of the LORD God amongst the trees of the garden.

9 And the LORD God called unto Adam, and said unto him, Where *art* thou?

10 And he said, I heard thy voice in the garden, and I was afraid, because I *was* naked; and I hid myself.

8 And they heard the sound of the LORD God walking in the garden in the cool of the day, and the man and his wife hid themselves from the presence of the LORD God among the trees of the garden. 9 But the LORD God called to the man, and said to him, "Where are you?" 10 And he said, "I heard the sound of thee in the garden, and I was afraid, because I was naked; and

---

8. The idea that God, like a man of substance, strolled in his garden in the evening was presumably derived from the earlier myth. In the statement that **the man and his wife hid themselves** from God the author, again in concrete terms, records their sense of guilt.

B. Discovery (3:9-13)

10. The economy of the narrative should be noted. Nothing is said of what the culprits thought when God called to them, or of how they emerged from their hiding place and stood guiltily at a distance (*ibid.*, p. 19). And yet there is no loss of effect. The concrete directness of the writing gives the narrative strength and clarity.

---

out originally as a poor lot. Our inheritance is poor. Our circumstances are depressing. The world we were born into has made us what we are; and if God expects us to be different, he ought to have made a different world.

Sometimes that general concept is translated into a whole people's philosophy. Consider some aspects of Hinduism. Individual effort is smothered by the heavy pressure of belief that everything is fated. Why should men struggle when indifferent gods have made the handicap too heavy? From another quarter comes "The Rubáiyát of Omar Khayyám" expressing that same defeatism in its picture of men as shadow-shapes which to the "Master of the Show" are

But helpless Pieces of the Game He plays
Upon this Chequer-board of Nights and Days;
  Hither and thither moves, and checks, and slays,
And one by one back in the Closet lays.[6]

But our Western thought, because it has inherited the virile assumptions of the O.T., has never been able to lull itself into the belief that we can blame the gods for our shortcomings. When all is said and done, we know that the God who means us to grow has put us into a risky world, surrounded by influences both better and worse, and that we cannot shift responsibility but must make our own creative choice. We know as well as Adam did that alibis will not work. The God we must meet at the end of the day will not be put off by references to other people's sins or by com-

[6] St. lxix.

plaints about the universe. When he speaks it will not be in terms of they, or it, but you.

8-11. The Reckoning with God.—Self-will and rebelliousness sooner or later confront the sovereign fact. Adam and Eve had Someone bigger than themselves to reckon with. They had to meet God; and they did meet him, **walking in the garden in the cool of the day.** Childlike as the form of the story is, note how dramatic and spiritually deep is its suggestion. The Eternal Righteousness moves in a great peace and calm; but Adam and Eve, with their guilty consciences, are hot and embarrassed when they meet him. For the first time they are uneasy with one another: "They knew that they were naked."

Thus always the confusion of conscious wrongdoing is confronted by the steady truth that is inescapable. Eat forbidden fruit against our better knowledge, and it turns out to be not the tree of life but the tree that is deadly to self-respect and peace of mind. Try to know better than God, to break the laws of life, to imagine that our cleverness and our clutching after power can say the final word, and we stand at the end of the day dumb before the quietness of God. "The tumult and the shouting dies." The excitement of the short cut we tried to take, the smart evasion we thought we could get away with, look cheap and futile. Then at length we find—in the words again of "Recessional"—that the only thing to save us is a "humble and a contrite heart." So in the end we may attain to the great hope expressed by Paul, that we may "put off the old man with

11 And he said, Who told thee that thou *wast* naked? Hast thou eaten of the tree, whereof I commanded thee that thou shouldest not eat?

12 And the man said, The woman whom thou gavest *to be* with me, she gave me of the tree, and I did eat.

13 And the LORD God said unto the woman, What *is* this *that* thou hast done? And the woman said, The serpent beguiled me, and I did eat.

14 And the LORD God said unto the serpent, Because thou hast done this, thou *art* cursed above all cattle, and above every beast of the field; upon thy belly shalt thou go, and dust shalt thou eat all the days of thy life:

I hid myself." 11 He said, "Who told you that you were naked? Have you eaten of the tree of which I commanded you not to eat?" 12 The man said, "The woman whom thou gavest to be with me, she gave me fruit of the tree, and I ate." 13 Then the LORD God said to the woman, "What is this that you have done?" The woman said, "The serpent beguiled me, and I ate." 14 The LORD God said to the serpent,

"Because you have done this,
cursed are you above all cattle,
and above all wild animals;
upon your belly you shall go,
and dust you shall eat
all the days of your life.

11. The impression conveyed by the record of the questioning which follows is not that God had to make an inquisition to find out what had happened, but rather that he at once knew the cause of man's shame and was compelling him and his wife to convict themselves. This is in agreement with the clear though implicit representation in the account of the sentencing of the serpent, the woman, and the man—that God was in complete and enduring control of the situation which confronted him. With this vs. 22 may again be contrasted: there God fears that man may put himself permanently beyond his control by attaining immortality. Vss. 9-19, 23 thus provide a further example not only of the skill with which J has revised the earlier myth, but also of his unshakable conviction of the omnipotence and omniscience of God and of man's inescapable dependence upon him.

C. THE CURSE (3:14-19)

14-15. The curse pronounced upon the serpent explains etiologically: (*a*) why serpents have no legs—the myth seems to imply that formerly they had walked like other animals—and (*b*) why, as was supposed, they ate dust. Thus in vs. 14 two physical characteristics—one real, the other imaginary—of the animal are accounted for. Vs. 15, on the other hand, deals with a psychological characteristic, not only of the serpent but also of man—the ineradicable hostility between them. The verse is accordingly on another level than vs. 14. This may suggest that it is secondary, a suggestion which perhaps receives a certain support from the fact that its meaning is not altogether clear. It is a matter of dispute as to whether the author thinks of the serpent's attack upon man as fatal, causing man's death by striking at his heel as surely as man causes the serpent's death by crushing his head. To this question Gunkel (*ibid.*, p. 21) gives an affirmative

his deeds," and "put on the new man, which is renewed in knowledge after the image of him that created him" (Col. 3:9-10).

14-15. *When the Nature of Evil Is Disclosed.* —After evil has had its way its real nature begins to be revealed. It is not clear what the serpent is supposed to have looked like at first, but evidently its looks were pleasant. Then it turned into something different. **Upon thy belly shalt thou go, and dust shalt thou eat all the days of thy life.** The serpent now is obviously the snake. In our world of physical

experience there is nothing from which men have a more natural revulsion than from the snake. It is secret and stealthy. It strikes without warning and its bite has poison in it. Only a fool will walk carelessly where snakes lurk. Many men have come to their senses when God has intervened to show the nature of sin, for then its reality is unmistakably abhorrent.

The evil that somehow is in our world cannot be whistled off. It shall bruise man's heel. A man cannot think he will escape the fact of sin by acting as if it were not there. It will

15 And I will put enmity between thee and the woman, and between thy seed and her seed; it shall bruise thy head, and thou shalt bruise his heel.
 	
16 Unto the woman he said, I will greatly multiply thy sorrow and thy concep-
	15 I will put enmity between you and the woman,
	    and between your seed and her seed;
	he shall bruise your head,
	    and you shall bruise his heel."
	16 To the woman he said,
	    "I will greatly multiply your pain in child-
	        bearing;

answer, Skinner (*Genesis,* p. 80) a negative, and with this agrees the messianic interpretation placed upon the verse by Targ. Jonathan, Targ. Jerusalem, the medieval Christian exegetes, and Calvin (see *ibid.,* pp. 80-82, for an outline of this development and for a summary of the allegorical interpretation the verse has received).

There is, furthermore, the difficulty that the Hebrew verb *shûph,* rendered **bruise,** adequately describes the effect of man's action against the serpent but scarcely that of the serpent's action against man. It may be, as Gunkel suggests (*Genesis,* p. 21), that the use of *shûph* is due to a scribal error, and that *shā'aph,* which seems to have the required double meaning of "crush" and "aim at," was original (see, however, Skinner, *Genesis,* pp. 79-80). Finally, it is perhaps not without significance that the verse reveals a certain reflectiveness not unlike that which informs 2:24, the J authorship of which has already been called into question on independent grounds.

16. Thy sorrow and thy conception (KJV) is a more literal rendering of the Hebrew than **your pain in childbearing** (RSV). Since, however, for a Hebrew woman **conception** was not a burden but a joy, the word can scarcely be original here. Instead, "thy grief" should be read; cf. the LXX, "thy groaning."

strike at him and wound him. When it does wound him the effect must be dealt with drastically, as with the bite of a snake. There may be need of quick, sharp, moral surgery to keep the poison of sin from spreading. Much contemporary religious thinking has emphasized anew the fact of sin and man's vulnerability to it. See the writings of Karl Barth and Emil Brunner and of most of the continental theologians and others deeply affected by the brutal aspect of our civilization in the twentieth century. Neither life nor civilization is an easy process. A generation ago some churches had on their bulletin boards a statement of belief which included belief in "the progress of man onward and upward forever." We are not so shallow now as to believe in automatic progress. Humanity has a hard struggle if its good hopes are to prevail. There is need of vigilance, courage, and moral combativeness.

But if the first suggestion is of the fact of sin, there is a second great suggestion also. It is the call to the kind of moral conflict which promises victory. The serpent may bruise man's heel, but ultimately man is meant to crush the serpent's head. The religion of the O.T. has in it always a virile optimism. It is not blind to the tragedy of life, but all the while it looks forward to triumph. Men and nations in their struggles against temptation and in their warfare against evil are meant not to surrender but to prevail. Phillips Brooks had a great sermon which he entitled "The Giant with the Wounded Heel." In it he expressed, as all of us ought to express, the essential dignity and greatness of man. Man is subject to the poisonous fangs of sin but he can crush sin if he is so determined.

What every soul needs to learn is that it is in a constant battle, but a battle which ought to be and may be a winning one. As it was written of Thomas Arnold, the great headmaster of Rugby School, he so preached that to every young boy who heard him there was brought home "for the first time, the meaning of his life; that it was no fool's or sluggard's paradise into which he had wandered by chance, but a battlefield ordained from of old, where there are no spectators but the youngest must take his side, and the stakes are life and death." And Charles Kingsley wrote, "O, be at least able to say in that day,—Lord, I am no hero. . . . But a traitor I have never been; a deserter I have never been. . . . I have tried to do the duty which lay nearest me; and to leave whatever Thou didst commit to my charge a little better than I found it." [7] To do that is to stand at last, wounded perhaps, but crushing the head of evil.

16-18. See Expos. on 2:4–3:24.

[7] Quoted by Mary W. Tileston in *Daily Strength for Daily Needs,* pp. 164, 181.

tion; in sorrow thou shalt bring forth children; and thy desire *shall be* to thy husband, and he shall rule over thee.	in pain you shall bring forth children, yet your desire shall be for your husband, and he shall rule over you."
17 And unto Adam he said, Because thou hast hearkened unto the voice of thy wife, and hast eaten of the tree, of which I commanded thee, saying, Thou shalt not eat of it: cursed *is* the ground for thy sake; in sorrow shalt thou eat *of* it all the days of thy life;	17 And to Adam he said, "Because you have listened to the voice of your wife, and have eaten of the tree of which I commanded you, 'You shall not eat of it,' cursed is the ground because of you; in toil you shall eat of it all the days of your life;
18 Thorns also and thistles shall it bring forth to thee; and thou shalt eat the herb of the field:	18 thorns and thistles it shall bring forth to you; and you shall eat the plants of the field.

The first half of the verse provides an etiological explanation of the pain suffered by women in childbirth, the agony of which is frequently referred to in the O.T. (cf. e.g., Isa. 13:8; Jer. 4:31). It is a question whether the second half,

> yet your desire shall be for your husband,
> and he shall rule over you,

speaks of sexual desire in woman, or whether it alludes to her natural desire for children—in which case **thy desire shall be to thy husband** (KJV) would perhaps be the better rendering. In either case the reference is to the wife's dependence upon her husband and so to the necessity she was under to endure the arbitrary treatment customary in the age in which the story was written. Most significant is the fact that J, far in advance of his time, sees that this domination of woman by man is an evil thing. The implication is that the relationship between husband and wife was intended by God to be a mutual and complementary relationship of love and respect, not a relationship in which one dominates the other. And the further implication is that all human relationships were intended to be mutual relationships—though the expression of this mutuality would necessarily differ with the character of the relationship; i.e., the mutuality between friend and friend differs from that between parent and child, for instance. Thus all attempts at domination, so characteristic of human conduct, are a consequence of the disorder which has infected the relationship of man to man, and at the same time make for further disorder and for the further alienation of man from God.

This being the case, J2's melancholy attitude as regards sex (in contrast to the matter-of-fact attitude of J1; see Exeg. on 34:1-31) becomes understandable. On all sides he was confronted by Baalism. This, being a fertility religion, was concerned above all else with the reproductive powers of nature, and this concern had issued in sexual license. To the temptation of this religion the Israelite peasant only too easily succumbed, and this led to further alienation from Yahweh. It is not surprising therefore that J2 reveals a tendency to regard the sexual relationship as the focal point of evil, the center of the tragic infection which blasts human hopes and reduces life to dust.

17. The penalty laid upon the man (read "the man" for **Adam**; in the J narrative *'ādhām*, "man," is not elsewhere a proper name; see vss. 9, 12, etc.) is that of expulsion from the garden "to till the ground from which he was taken" (vs. 23). This involved toil—for **you shall eat of it** should be read "you shall till it," required by vs. 23—as unremitting as it was frustrating—the word rendered **toil** (RSV) also has the meaning "pain" or **sorrow** (KJV). The frustration is the result of God's curse, **cursed is the ground because of you.** Man's relationship with nature, like his relationships with God and with his fellow men, is in disorder.

18. That this verse is not from the same hand as vs. 19a is shown by the awkward double occurrence of **eat** (cf. Holzinger, *Genesis*, p. 35; Rudolf Smend, *Die Erzählung*

19 In the sweat of thy face shalt thou eat bread, till thou return unto the ground; for out of it wast thou taken: for dust thou *art,* and unto dust shalt thou return.

19 In the sweat of your face
  you shall eat bread
till you return to the ground,
  for out of it you were taken;
you are dust,
  and to dust you shall return."

---

des Hexateuch [Berlin: Georg Reimer, 1912], p. 19) and by the fact that it breaks the connection between vss. 17 and 19. It is a gloss by one who presumably felt that J's meaning was not sufficiently clear: it might be thought that he was representing the simple necessity of tilling the ground as the punishment for man's disobedience. This was indeed for J part of the punishment; it was not the whole of it. For (as has been pointed out in the Exeg. on vs. 17; see also that on vs. 19) he regarded the sense of frustration which dogged the peasant—and every man—in his work as the more terrible consequence of man's sin. It is this point which the glossator is concerned to stress in vs. 18*a*. Vs. 18*b*, noting the contrast between man's present food and the fruit of the garden, may be from a still later hand, as is suggested by Holzinger (*Genesis,* pp. 35-36), who, however, retains vs. 18*a* as part of the original narrative.

19. Till you return to the ground: The reference is to the burial of the dead. **For out of it you were taken** refers back to 2:7, and stresses one of the salient points, of the story. **You are dust, and to dust you shall return** would seem to have been taken

---

19. *Work: a Curse or a Blessing?*—Work is represented as the curse laid upon Adam and his descendants. To have to work, instead of getting the fruits of life without working, seemed to the human instinct to be the mark of punishment, a fate from which ideally life should have escaped. It was a natural way of thinking. But is this part of a divine revelation, or is it one of man's misreadings of the heavenly truth? The men who shaped the traditions which have come down in Genesis were here trying to interpret experience and the good and bad they found in it. The necessity of labor was something they did not like; so they regarded it as evil. It felt like punishment, so they concluded that it was punishment. Yet the ideas reflected here, as elsewhere in the early strata of the O.T., may not be infallible. In a green landscape one may come upon outcroppings of rough primeval rock, interrupting the fertile plowland. So in the rich productive ground of the O.T. there may be an outcropping of primitive conceptions in which the seeds of larger life will not take root. It is not necessary to accept and try to make use of everything which far-off men believed when they listened first to the telling of the story of the Garden of Eden.

Is work a curse? Yes and no. No and yes. It depends on circumstances and the kind of work. It is a curse when it is meaningless. Then it becomes an intolerable tedium, deadening the mind and embittering the spirit, like the labor of convicts in a chain gang set to breaking rocks all day. It is a curse when it is done under compulsion for ends which the worker hates and against which he inwardly rebels, like the labor of prisoners of war made to work in the enemy country for the enemy's advantage. It was a curse in the days of slavery (remember the haunting notes of prayer for release and rest in many of the Negro spirituals), and it is a curse now in those places where weaker people like farm workers in some southern parts of the United States are exploited in ways not much short of slavery. Study the facts as to peonage and the practice of keeping share croppers, particularly Negroes, so hopelessly in debt to the owners that they can never get out from under the load that holds them on the land. Consider the poverty and ignorance linked with that in a vicious circle. Similarly, the whole development of the economic and industrial system of the last century has tended to make labor seem a curse by creating conditions that become almost intolerable. Ostensibly the workers in the modern industrial system who are the hired hands of the owners of factories and mills are free to go and come as they please and to live or not live where they choose, but in fact the necessity to earn enough to live on forces them to work in hateful places which they would not willingly have chosen but which they cannot change. (Read the life of Lord Shaftesbury,[8] and note the almost incredible cruelties which marked the beginnings of mechanized production in England.) Consider in the United States the history of child labor

[8] J. L. Hammond and Barbara Hammond, *Lord Shaftesbury* (2nd ed.; London: Constable & Co., 1923).

by J from an independent poem, for it says that man was made not from the ground but from dust—which led to the intrusion of "the dust of" in 2:7.

It has already been noted that there is no suggestion here that man would have lived forever had he not eaten of the forbidden fruit (cf. Gunkel, *Genesis*, pp. 22-23; Skinner, *Genesis*, p. 83). Rather the implication is (see Exeg. on vs. 3) that man would have regarded death not as the last fearful frustration but as his natural end. The fear of death is a consequence of the disorder in man's relationships, as a result of which they are no longer characterized by mutuality but by domination. Man, aware of his need for others, attempts to compel them to fill his need that he may be secure. In this he may even be successful for a time. But he is always haunted by the fear that those whom he dominates will free themselves from him, and he tries to quiet this fear by further aggression. In this, too, he may be temporarily successful. From the fear of death, however, he cannot escape. For in the depths of his soul he knows that the structure of relationships which he has erected to protect himself is fundamentally without

---

in cotton mills, the springing up of the drab and shoddy industrial towns with the crowded tenements to which people were lured from the villages and the wholesome open country; and the danger and degradation of the coal mines and of the huddled shacks which often have been all that wives and children of the miners had for homes. Consider what sort of existence the migratory workers endure. (Read John Steinbeck, *The Grapes of Wrath*,[9] and Carey McWilliams, *Factories in the Field*[10] and *Ill Fares the Land*.[1])

Furthermore, even when grosser handicaps have been removed, work may still seem to many people at least in part a curse when it exhausts the energies and leaves the worker too tired to enjoy his life. Observe how many protests and strikes among industrial workers are concerned not primarily with wages but with hours and conditions of work: against "the speed-up," for a shorter working week, for holidays. Let Christian people consider their responsibility as citizens for what industry exacts from millions of the working population. Labor unions have their excesses, and often they are uncritically blamed and their contribution to human well-being ignored. Yet what would have happened to workers in the last hundred years but for the amelioration the unions have brought?

Thus work may be a curse. But it need not be. In the long run men would not be better off for having no work to do. The picture of the Garden of Eden is a childlike picture of human happiness, and in mature people the hidden instinct which turns back with a child's nostalgic longing for irresponsibility and undiscipline still thinks of freedom from work as a kind of paradise. But the human race would never have amounted to much, and

parts of it do not amount to much now, in conditions which require no exception. In the tropics men do live in a kind of Garden of Eden on the fruit that drops from trees. But the virile races are not developed there. It is in the other and sterner zones, where men are compelled by nature to win their livelihood by hard effort and in the face of danger, that the great human stocks have been produced. Compare the peoples of Europe with those of Central Africa. Compare the hardihood of the men of New England, wrestling with a rocky soil and developing the courage and initiative that sent the trains of covered wagons to pioneer the West, with the tribes in the green jungles of Brazil. Men who have worked hard are usually the happiest men. Said Le Baron R. Briggs, once the beloved dean of Harvard College, "There is always somebody or something to work for; and while there is, life must be, and shall become, worth living."[2]

What are the factors necessary in order that work may be a blessing? Freedom, so that a man feels that the best in himself has a chance to find expression instead of being frustrated by the compulsion that drives him to uncongenial tasks. It is one of the indictments against a totalitarian system such as that of Soviet Russia that it regiments its workers. But in a so-called free society the pressure of economic dependence may make men equally unfree.

Training and education enough to release his best capacities. Here is a moral responsibility for every individual—for the boy or girl at school, and for the adult, to make intelligent pursuit of further information; and for society to see to it that schools and other influences of enlightenment are actually accessible to all the people.

Something to work for. The pouring out of energy becomes not exhausting but inspiring

[9] New York: The Modern Library, 1939.
[10] Boston: Little, Brown & Co., 1939.
[1] Boston: Little, Brown & Co., 1942.

[2] *Routine and Ideals* (Boston: Houghton Mifflin Co., 1904). p. 22.

| 20 And Adam called his wife's name Eve; because she was the mother of all living.

21 Unto Adam also and to his wife did the Lord God make coats of skins, and clothed them. | 20 The man called his wife's name Eve,*ƒ* because she was the mother of all living. 21 And the Lord God made for Adam and for his wife garments of skins, and clothed them.

ƒ The name in Hebrew resembles the word for *living* |

substance. In the end it will crumble and he will be compelled to face the fact which he had always tried to deny—that he is man and not God. Man's disordered relationships and his fear of death are inextricably bound up together, the consequence of his alienation from God.

D. Expulsion from Eden (3:20-24)

20. In view of the fact that nowhere in his narrative does J record the naming of man, it is unlikely that this verse is from his hand. In any case it would not belong here, between the sentence passed upon the man and its execution, and before the woman had become **the mother** of anything **living.** It is, however, scarcely a casual gloss, for the name "Hawwah" **(Eve)** seems to be traditional; it is therefore probably an insertion from the Eden saga which thus (cf. also vss. 21, 22, and 24 in part) appears to have remained extant for some time after J had produced his revision of it.

The fact that the verse was intruded here, rather than after the notice of man's expulsion from the garden, would seem to suggest that in this earlier recension of the myth children had been born to the man and his wife while they were still in Eden. If this is so, then the awareness which J reveals of the distortion in human nature, reaching down to its very depths and manifesting itself in all man's relationships, owes little to the original myth. It derives from Yahwism, the religion which Israel had brought from the desert and which threw light upon the religion of Canaan, discerning its values and rejecting its errors, and in the process relating itself to the peasant culture into which Israel had entered.

21. This verse also, scarcely necessary though not impossible after vs. 7, is probably from the Eden story. If, as has been suggested, that recension regarded sex consciousness as a natural attribute of man, the notice in its original context will have followed immediately upon the account of the making of the man and the woman. If the verse is not from J it is not necessary to emend **Adam** to "the man."

---

when it is related to some large benefit which it can produce—for those closest to the worker first, but also for everybody. Christian people cannot be content without an ideal for individuals and a growing will and program in society for the kind of creative labor that may make human beings fellow workers with God. When work does not seem to be creative of anything worth while it can become drab to the point of degradation. Too many men and women are forced to earn their living in ways which do not bring benefit to anybody, and there is nothing to give them pride or satisfaction in what they do. On the other hand, all honest work which by its product increases the well-being of society can enable those who do the work to feel that they are carrying out some part of God's good purpose for his world. To organize our actual society so that this shall

be true for workers generally is a far goal, but all Christian economists and all men of influence in industry must be aiming at nothing less.

20. *Motherhood.*—Here for the first time in the Bible occurs the rich word **mother.** In theological disquisitions Eve has generally been represented as the mother of the woes of mankind. Yet in all motherhood there is a deep and divine wonder. By the woman all life is conceived and transmitted; and to the woman's nurture and her understanding most that is tenderest and best is due. One remembers Hannah, the mother of Samuel; the vicarious motherhood of the daughter of Pharaoh; and the one who has become for so many Christians the reverent symbol of the holiest motherhood, Mary the mother of Jesus. Nor would one forget the lovely reference of Paul when, with his message to one of his fellow Christians, Rufus,

22 ¶ And the LORD God said, Behold, the man is become as one of us, to know good and evil: and now, lest he put forth his hand, and take also of the tree of life, and eat, and live for ever:

23 Therefore the LORD God sent him forth from the garden of Eden, to till the ground from whence he was taken.

22 Then the LORD God said, "Behold, the man has become like one of us, knowing good and evil; and now, lest he put forth his hand and take also of the tree of life, and eat, and live for ever" — 23 therefore the LORD God sent him forth from the garden of Eden, to till the ground from

---

22. The reasons for supposing that this verse is an intrusion from the Eden myth upon which J based his story of the garden have already been stated and need not be repeated here. It was presumably inserted in part to supply some reference to the tree of life which J had chosen to ignore, in part because he regarded as intolerable and morally dangerous the implication that immortality could be attained apart from, not to say in spite of, God; and also because he could not permit the suggestion that the disorder in human relationships, springing from man's alienation from God and giving rise to the fear of death, could be healed by external means. But the very fact that the addition was made suggests that J had been more drastic in his revision of the original myth than popular acceptance would allow—a significant, interesting indication of the extent to which he, writing to maintain and strengthen the unity of Israel, was limited in his treatment of non-Yahwist material.

While the verse obscures the thought of J, it is far from being without value. For in its total biblical context it affirms that man, for all his fantastic self-deception, cannot make himself the equal of God; that not **knowing good and evil** but knowing the only true God, and Jesus Christ whom he has sent (cf. John 17:3) is eternal life; and that the love of God is so great that man cannot make permanent and irremediable the tragic frustration which he has brought upon himself.

But the Eden saga was drawn upon not only to supply the missing reference to the tree of life. The other insertions from this recension (vss. 20, 21, together with 2:24) seem to reveal a certain uneasiness concerning J's tendency noted above (see Exeg. on these verses) to regard the sexual relationship as the focal point of evil. It was to correct this that these verses were inserted by one who had been reflecting upon the great story lying before him, who recognized in its tragic verdict on sex a certain validity but who nevertheless could not accept it without qualification. This was provided, to a slight degree, by vss. 20-21 which by implication reaffirmed the older representation that sex consciousness was a natural human attribute; and, more clearly, by the affirmation of the naturalness and sanctity of the marriage act in 2:24.

Finally, it should be noted that in the creation narrative as a whole (chs. 1–3) the melancholy pessimism of J² as regards sex is qualified by the relatively optimistic attitude of P: "So God created man in his own image, in the image of God created he him; male and female created he them. And God blessed them, and God said unto them, Be fruitful, and multiply, and replenish the earth, and subdue it. . . . And God saw every thing that he had made, and, behold, it was very good" (1:27-28a, 31a). And it is the narrative as a whole which has the finality of the Word of God.

23. With the excision of vss. 20-22 this verse is left as the immediate and original continuation of vs. 19. The initial **therefore** must accordingly be rendered "and," no change being involved in the Hebrew. **Of Eden** is redactional linking with the Eden fragments which have been inserted into the story.

This verse concludes the original J story. It is a story written to account for man's tragic experience of alienation from God, and neither the fact that it is based upon and is a drastic revision of an older myth, nor the fact that it is one-sided in its judgment as to the meaning of sex, nor the fact that it regards the necessity of work as a result of disobedience should be permitted to obscure this truth. It is not a historical account of "the Fall," nor is the doctrine of original sin based upon it. Indeed, it may be said that

24 So he drove out the man: and he placed at the east of the garden of Eden cherubim, and a flaming sword which turned every way, to keep the way of the tree of life.

which he was taken. 24 He drove out the man; and at the east of the garden of Eden he placed the cherubim, and a flaming sword which turned every way, to guard the way to the tree of life.

without the experience of alienation from God, of which that doctrine is the metaphysical explanation, the story would never have been written. Starting from that experience, the author voices his conviction—a conviction rooted in his knowledge of God—that man's sense of alienation from God springs from his own act, that it is not natural, that it would never have arisen had man been obedient.

24. This verse has suffered in transmission and must be restored, with the LXX, "And he drove out the man, and caused him to dwell to the east of the garden of Eden; and he stationed the cherubim and a flaming sword [lit., in Hebrew, "the flame of the sword"], which turned every way to guard the way to the tree of life." The reference to **Eden** and to **the tree of life** indicates that the verse is another insertion from the Eden saga—**the garden of** being redactional harmonization—made at the same time as vs. 22 to explain why it was that the man, being banished, could never get back to **the tree of life.** The role of **the cherubim** here is that of guardians of a holy place, as it is in Exod. 37:7-9 and I Kings 6:23-27 (cf. "covering cherub" in Ezek. 28:16; also Exod. 26:31; I Kings 6:29, 32). In II Sam. 6:2; Ps. 18:10; Ezek. 1, they are represented as the supporters of Yahweh's throne. They were winged beings with two faces (cf. Ezek. 41:18-19)—of a man and of a lion—or with four (cf. Ezek. 1:10)—of a man,

---

he speaks of "his mother and mine" (Rom. 16:13).

24. *After Failure.*—So the past was to be irrevocable. The man and his wife must turn from all they had known to a future that was unknown. The gate was shut, and the angel with the flaming sword kept them from ever going back. The ancient story has its continually repeated parallels. Many lives have their lost Edens. Knowing the better, men have chosen the worse. Curious to know the taste of evil, they have eaten of its fruit, and from that time on they must face the bitter consequence.

What then? Nothing is suggested in the Scriptures as to what Adam thought and felt. Yet Adam standing outside the Eden to which he could not return is a symbol of what may happen to every man. Some deliberate sin, or some stupid carelessness as of the foolish virgins in the parable of Jesus, has destroyed our finest opportunity; and when we turn too late to that which might have been ours the door is shut. There is bitter finality in that fact. Yet even so the whole story of life is not then finished. What happens to the modern Adam excluded from the Eden of his lost innocence depends upon the attitude he adopts toward that which now he cannot change.

Sometimes that attitude may be only weakly reminiscent. Many a man at some critical turning point of life will not face reality but lets himself be paralyzed by a dull remorse that has in it no brave element of moral renewal. Or he

may try to figure out some explanation of his failure that lays the blame on something or somebody else. Fate has been against him, and what is the use then of struggling against fate? Gamaliel Bradford wrote of Henry Adams: "He needed not to think, but to live. But he did not want to live. It was easier to sit back and proclaim life unworthy of Henry Adams than it was to lean forward with the whole soul in a passionate, if inadequate, effort to make Henry Adams worthy of life." [3] The modern Adam may try to persuade himself that his world is one which by its very nature gives a man no chance of making good, in which there is nothing left but fatalistic acceptance of moral defeat.

But there can be another and better spirit— the spirit which recognizes the inexorable deprivations which because of its blunders it must suffer and yet has the will not to let these say the last word. The old story does not attempt to tell what, if anything, Adam made up his mind to do, but the whole Bible makes this plain: all that is best in the history of the human race has come from those who did not surrender to defeat but went ahead to try to correct disastrous beginnings and to put something better together out of the pieces of broken hopes and plans. Yet not by themselves! For far above what men can do is what God does in and for them. The Adam in every man that may be standing outside the Eden which

[3] *American Portraits* (Boston: Houghton Mifflin Co., 1922), p. 56.

4 And Adam knew Eve his wife; and she conceived, and bare Cain, and said, I have gotten a man from the LORD.	4 Now Adam knew Eve his wife, and she conceived and bore Cain, saying, "I have gotten[g] a man with the help of the
	[g] Heb qanah, get

a lion, an ox, and an eagle (cf. Rev. 4:7). With them may be compared the sphinx in Egypt and the hybrid figures stationed before Assyrian temples and palaces. "The flame of the sword"—it can scarcely have been conceived as in the hand of one of the cherubim—is an independent symbol, a representation of lightning (Skinner, *Genesis,* p. 89). It is possible that originally this only was mentioned and that the cherubim, and is a gloss (cf. Gunkel, *Genesis,* pp. 24-25, who, however, derives the cherubim and the flame from parallel sources).

In its present context the verse makes explicit what had been implicit in vs. 23—that man could never redeem himself. Redemption would be possible only when God by his own act once again opened the way to the tree of life.

IV. BEGINNINGS OF CIVILIZATION (4:1-26)

That ch. 4 as a whole is derived from J is indicated by the use of the LORD in vss. 1-16, of which vss. 17-24 are obviously the continuation, and in vs. 26. The material is, however, not in its original order. According to vs. 26, men did not begin to call upon the name of the LORD—i.e., to worship the Lord—until the time of Enosh; yet Cain and Abel are represented as offering sacrifice to him.

This inconsistency is the result of the redactional activity of RP. Other solutions of the difficulties presented by chs. 4–5 are proposed by, e.g., Gunkel (*Genesis,* pp. 40-41), who postulates two independent strands in J, as does Skinner (*Genesis,* pp. 98-101). On the solution offered here cf. Bernhard Stade, "Beiträge zur Pentateuchkritik (1) Das Kainszeichen," *Zeitschrift für die alttestamentliche Wissenschaft,* XIV (1894), 264-65. According to this solution, RP had before him two genealogies beginning with the first man: (*a*) That of P, now preserved in 5:1-28*a*, 30-32—vss. 28*b*-29 are from J and have been substituted for P's simple statement, "he became the father of Noah." The first names in this genealogy were Adam (=the Man), Seth, and Enosh (cf. 5:3-6). (*b*) That of J, the first three names of which were likewise the Man (=Adam), Seth, and Enosh (cf. 4:25-26*a*). From that point, however, the two lists diverged, P continuing with the names Kenan, Mahalalel, etc., to Lamech, the father of Noah (cf. 5:9-31); J with Cain—another, and in Hebrew, very similar form of the Kenan of P—Enoch, Irad, etc., to Lamech the father of Jabal, Jubal, and Tubal-cain (cf. 4:17-22).

RP, seeking not only to preserve but to unify the traditions of J and P, could not because of these divergences simply place these genealogies in juxtaposition unaltered. At the same time he was unwilling to omit either list of names; concrete detail attached to those in J (vss. 2-16, 17-24) demanded the preservation of that material, and P's highly schematized list would not stand mutilation.

RP accordingly changed the order of J. He made Cain, whom J had listed as the son of Enosh, the son of the first man and then, following the story of the murder of Abel (vss. 3-16), continued with the J genealogy from Cain to Lamech and his sons

his sin has forfeited can learn that there is a Second Adam through whose new nature his past can be redeemed. Knowing now good and evil, but having chosen the evil in some disastrous disobedience, he cannot yet know the full meaning of the tree of life. But the Bible which begins with Genesis goes on to Revelation, with its promise of "that great city, the holy Jerusalem, descending out of heaven from God" (Rev. 21:10), in the midst of which shall

be "the tree of life," the leaves of which are for "the healing of the nations" (Rev. 22:2).

4:1-8. *The Murderer.*—The instant the name of Cain is spoken one association follows it as inescapably as a man's shadow follows a man. That name has become proverbial as the name of the first murderer. Yet everyone who reads the whole narrative must note this fact: there is no indication that Cain intended to commit murder. Thus far in the narrative of Genesis

2 And she again bare his brother Abel. And Abel was a keeper of sheep, but Cain was a tiller of the ground.

LORD." 2 And again, she bore his brother Abel. Now Abel was a keeper of sheep, and

---

(vss. 17-24). Then, reverting to the beginning of the J genealogy, Man, Seth, Enosh (vss. 25-26) and adding a few harmonizing words to vs. 25, he placed this immediately before the P material with which it agreed, so that it had the effect of being a brief anticipation of P's elaborate scheme.

The order of the J material in ch. 4 as it lay before RP was vss. 25 (in its original form, see below), 26, 1-24.

A. CAIN AND ABEL (4:1-16)

4:1. In this verse, therefore, "Enosh" originally stood in place of **Adam,** and **Eve** is an intrusion of RP. The use of **knew**—frequent in the O.T.—referring to the marriage act is a significant indication of the character of the relation between the knower and the known in the Hebrew mind; it involved always a surrender of the self, though the degree of that surrender and the action it demanded necessarily varied with the object or the person known. The implications of this for the prophets', especially Hosea's, concept of the knowledge of God are far reaching in their importance.

Cain seems originally to have been the ancestor of the Kenites. The implications of his appearance in this tale will be considered below. The meaning of the name is "metalworker" or "smith"; here, however, it is represented as a derivation of a word meaning "acquire," "get"—one of the popular etymologies frequent in Genesis—hence the mother's words **I have gotten a man. From the LORD** (KJV) is a rendering, following the LXX and the Vulg., of *'eth Yahweh,* which is lit., "with Yahweh," and so unintelligible here **(the help of** [RSV] is not in the Hebrew). It seems probable that *'eth* should be *'ōth*—so, "the mark of Yahweh"—and that the words are a gloss referring either to the new Yahweh cult mentioned in vs. 26*b*, which immediately preceded this verse in J, or to the mark set on Cain (vs. 15).

2. And again, she bore his brother Abel may indicate that the brothers were twins, as is further suggested by the repeated **my brother, your brother,** throughout the narrative.

The secondary character of vs. 2*b*, which attempts to explain why the brothers offered different kinds of sacrifice, is indicated by (*a*) the mention of Abel before Cain; (*b*) the statement that Cain was **a tiller of the ground,** unnecessary for the reason that according to J (cf. 3:23) this was at the time the common occupation of all men; and (*c*) the fact that it breaks the close connection between vss. 2*a* and 3.

---

there has been no such thing as death, and therefore no way by which anyone could clearly imagine what death might be. Cain strikes Abel in the instinctive reflex of his anger, but who can say that he had any deliberate purpose to end his brother's life? When Abel fell, Cain may have been astonished that he lay so long, so still. Why did he not get up again? Only little by little, and incredulously, did Cain grow conscious that something had happened beyond the framework of his previous imagining. This motionless body on the ground that did not speak or stir—what did that mean? He may have seen a sheep die, but never a man. Was it really possible that he had killed his brother?

The tragedy of that first murder lay in a fact which may be repeated in every ungoverned sin. The result outruns what the will intended. How

often do we hear the cry, "But I didn't mean to do it!" Anger gets loose and before we know it has gone beyond all bounds. We may commit murder before we have fully grasped what murder is.

Not physical murder, perhaps, though there is an appalling amount of that. But that is not the whole story, nor is it for most of us the crucial part of it. We may commit murder in subtler ways than physical. We retail some poisonous gossip, not out of direct malice, but for the relish of saying something that will be exciting; and then are startled to read in the newspapers that the man we helped to slander has committed suicide, or that the husband and wife we smeared have been divorced. But the moral murder of which we may be guilty may begin nearer home. Oscar Wilde, who in spite

3 And in process of time it came to pass, that Cain brought of the fruit of the ground an offering unto the LORD.

4 And Abel, he also brought of the firstlings of his flock and of the fat thereof. And the LORD had respect unto Abel and to his offering:

5 But unto Cain and to his offering he had not respect. And Cain was very wroth, and his countenance fell.

6 And the LORD said unto Cain, Why art thou wroth? and why is thy countenance fallen?

7 If thou doest well, shalt thou not be accepted? and if thou doest not well, sin lieth at the door: and unto thee *shall be* his desire, and thou shalt rule over him.

Cain a tiller of the ground. 3 In the course of time Cain brought to the LORD an offering of the fruit of the ground, 4 and Abel brought of the firstlings of his flock and of their fat portions. And the LORD had regard for Abel and his offering, 5 but for Cain and his offering he had no regard. So Cain was very angry, and his countenance fell. 6 The LORD said to Cain, "Why are you angry, and why has your countenance fallen? 7 If you do well, will you not be accepted? And if you do not do well, sin is couching at the door; its desire is for you, but you must master it."

---

5. It is not stated why the Lord had **no regard** for Cain and his offering. The same silence may have marked the legend in its original form before it was adapted by J to its present context. It is possible, however, that a reason was there given, and that its omission by J was a piece of polemic against the peasant custom of bringing **the fruit of the ground** as **an offering** to the Lord (vs. 3), instead of the time-honored nomad offering of an animal.

7. The text is corrupt; if its meaning is, as Skinner (*Genesis*, pp. 106-7) suggests, that the cause of Cain's dissatisfaction lies within himself, the verse, together with vs. 6, may be an addition seeking to answer the question left unanswered in vs. 5a.

---

of his spotted record had often a piercing discernment of the truth, wrote in his *Ballad of Reading Gaol*:

> Yet each man kills the thing he loves,
>   By each let this be heard,
> Some do it with a bitter look,
>   Some with a flattering word,
> The coward does it with a kiss,
>   The brave man with a sword! [4]

Those mordant lines may go beyond the facts, but they are close enough to reality to stab attention wide awake. Who can be sure that he may not give mortal wounds by cold unconcern, kill joy by sullenness, and gradually destroy devotion by gestures of affection which have become perfunctory?

Damage goes back beyond any obvious deed. A famous criminal lawyer is reported to have said in a newspaper interview: "Everybody is a potential murderer. I have not killed anyone, but I frequently get satisfaction out of the obituary notices." Trouble begins with a twisted thought in the mind and a grudge hidden in the heart. Jesus made that plain in the Sermon on the Mount. It is not clear why Cain hated Abel: perhaps not for anything that Abel did, but perhaps because of what he was. All Cain

thought of was what Cain himself was not. He had the idea that Abel was preferred to him and he resented that. Similarly, many of us today may nurse some dark feeling of inferiority which can burst out one day in cruel disparagement or violent injury toward the one who seems to us to have gotten a better break from life than we have.

It was a strange contradiction that the first murder came with an act of worship. It was while he was approaching God that Cain knew how much he hated his brother. He felt frustrated because he felt somehow that God's truth ranked Abel higher than himself; and if he knew within himself that this was what he deserved, he struck out all the more blindly and bitterly against the superiority that shamed him. This is the explanation of the vindictive hostility that men may express toward those whose achievements they envy—the hostility of the citizen to a great political leader or the dislike which a minister may feel for a more honored brother minister.

But when Cain had done his worst to Abel he could not get away from God. To a guilty conscience came the question: **Where is Abel thy brother?** And the bravado of his answer, **Am I my brother's keeper,** could not hide the truth that this was exactly what he **must be.**

[4] Part I, st. vii.

8 And Cain talked with Abel his brother: and it came to pass, when they were in the field, that Cain rose up against Abel his brother, and slew him.

9 ¶ And the LORD said unto Cain, Where *is* Abel thy brother? And he said, I know not: *Am* I my brother's keeper?

8 Cain said to Abel his brother, "Let us go out to the field."[h] And when they were in the field, Cain rose up against his brother Abel, and killed him. 9 Then the LORD said to Cain, "Where is Abel your brother?" He said, "I do not know; am I my brother's

[h] Sam Gk Syr Compare Vg: Heb lacks *Let us go out to the field*

---

8. The Hebrew of the first half of the verse is truncated: **Cain said to Abel his brother.** As is noted in the RSV mg., **Let us go out to the field** has been supplied from the versions. This is, however, a not particularly happy anticipation of **when they were in the field.** Possibly the Hebrew *wayyŏ'mer*, "and [he] said," is a corruption of *wayyishmōr*, "and [he] eyed," or "lay in wait for" (Holzinger, *Genesis*, p. 48) —a change of one letter only in the consonantal text—and that the sentence originally read "And Cain eyed Abel his brother." If so, there is a subtle wordplay in Cain's defiant **Am I my brother's keeper** [watcher]? (vs. 9), for the verb *shāmar* means not only "to eye" or "to lie in wait for" (cf. I Sam. 19:11), but also "to watch," and so "to keep."

The field means the open country, where Cain thought he would be safe from observation.

9-10. But the Lord saw him and the damning inquisition (vss. 9-12, 16) follows— reminiscent of, and from the same hand as, 3:9-19, 23; note, "What is this that you have done?" (3:13) and **What have you done?** (vs. 10), the use of the word **ground** (3:17, 19, 23; and vss. 10, 11, 12), and of the word "till" (3:17—as emended—3:23; and vs. 12).

Nor is blood brotherhood the only authoritative bond. Sooner or later men must recognize that any cruelty to any human being, yes, any careless or flippant unkindness, brings them face to face with the judgment of God. When the large-hearted William H. Taft was governor of the Philippine Islands, he made public reference to "our Filipino brothers," and was answered in a derisive song by somebody who thought himself better than any Filipino:

> He may be a brother of William H. Taft,
> But he ain't no brother of mine.[5]

All the same, he is; and whoever looks at the Orient in the aftermath of World War II is bound to see that whenever brotherhood is violated the blood of the victims will cry out from whatever ground the victor treads.

9. *Acknowledgment of Guilt.*—Where is . . . thy brother? That was the question that Cain wanted to evade. The unrepentant guilty always will try to evade it. But the need of souls is to face it squarely and to accept deliberately the consequences of confession and repentance. Who is there that has not hurt some other human being, if not with such a mortal stroke as that which Cain gave to Abel, yet in some way that has left some part of that other one's happiness and well-being lying dead? It may

[5] Cf. Francis McHall, *President and Chief Justice, the Life and Service of William H. Taft* (Philadelphia: Dorrance & Co., 1931), p. 71.

have been through hot passion: through lust that has defiled another life, through sudden anger that has lashed out against some supposed offense, through violence of word or act that satisfied revenge. It may have been through a colder cruelty: a sneer, a contemptuous look, a sinister disparagement that struck home like a poisoned arrow. Where are they now, those victims of the evil that we did? To what grave of undeserved suffering or sorrow have we brought them down? Or suppose that we never deliberately intended evil: are there no hurts we have given just because we were too stupid to understand? Read Edward Rowland Sill's "The Fool's Prayer." Remember that it is not only by malicious wrong but by our blundering folly that we can give to others, and especially to those we love, wounds that may be too deep for healing. The clumsy word, the careless indifference, the self-absorption that can treat a soul hungering for affection as though it were no more than a thing for our convenience, are enough to make us guilty. We recoil from admitting that, but the voice of God cannot be escaped. **Where is . . . thy brother?** it asks; and "Where are you, and why is your back turned to him? What will you do now? In deep contrition go to him and see whether by God's mercy that which you struck down can be restored?"

It may be also that God's voice will ask what seems a more drastic question than he asked of

10 And he said, What hast thou done? the voice of thy brother's blood crieth unto me from the ground.

11 And now *art* thou cursed from the earth, which hath opened her mouth to receive thy brother's blood from thy hand.

12 When thou tillest the ground, it shall not henceforth yield unto thee her strength; a fugitive and a vagabond shalt thou be in the earth.

13 And Cain said unto the LORD, My punishment *is* greater than I can bear.

keeper?" 10 And the LORD said, "What have you done? The voice of your brother's blood is crying to me from the ground. 11 And now you are cursed from the ground, which has opened its mouth to receive your brother's blood from your hand. 12 When you till the ground, it shall no longer yield to you its strength; you shall be a fugitive and a wanderer on the earth." 13 Cain said to the LORD, "My punishment is greater

---

Vss. 9-10 imply that a man is indeed his brother's keeper; this statement of a moral principle is probably J's contribution to the legend which in its original popular form is not likely to have risen to this height.

11. "The idea cannot be that the earth is a monster greedy of blood; it seems rather akin to the primitive superstition of a physical infection or poisoning of the soil, and through it of the murderer, by the shed blood" (Skinner, *Genesis*, p. 108; cf. Deut. 21:1-9).

12-15. Cain, hitherto like his father a tiller of the ground, is now condemned to **be a fugitive and a wanderer on the earth.** This is not a description of nomadism, for the nomad was no fugitive or aimless wanderer (cf. Theodor Nöldeke, "Amalek" in *Encyclopaedia Biblica,* ed. T. K. Cheyne and J. Sutherland Black [New York: The Macmillan Co., 1899], I, 130). Rather, it describes a completely cultureless existence from which Cain's descendants began to rise again only some generations later in the time of Jabal (vs. 20). Vss. 19-22 embody, however, as will be shown below, a tradition quite independent of this tale; i.e., in its origin the story of the crime of Cain was told with reference to the existence of some subnomad group, regarded—whether correctly or not—as so squalid that it was understood as being the result only of some heinous crime committed by one of their ancestors. The fact that this ancestor bears the name of Cain suggests that the group was of Kenite extraction. Eduard Meyer (*Die Israeliten und ihre Nachbarstämme* [Halle: M. Niemeyer, 1906], pp. 389-99) has cogently argued that the Kenites were in origin a clan of Israel's hated enemies, the Amalekites, and suggests, it would seem fairly, that the story in vss. 3-12 reflects Israel's opinion of them.

The mark which the Lord put on Cain (vs. 15) is, however, a protective mark, not the mark of a murderer, as the popular phrase, "the mark of Cain," implies. In vss. 13-15, therefore, Cain appears as the representative ancestor of a group under special divine protection and known for its custom of exacting sevenfold vengeance upon an aggressor. J would scarcely have dignified in this way the group against which he was directing his polemic. This suggests that vss. 13-15 are secondary, a suggestion which is supported by the facts: (a) **The face of the ground** in vs. 14 obviously means a certain

---

Cain, particularly of those who have responsibility in and for the fellowship of the Christian church: he may ask not only concerning those we may have hurt, but concerning those also whom we have neglected. Where are they whom we ought to have shepherded? Into what harm have they fallen because we were not diligent to keep them safe? Before that challenge, who will not need to bow down and confess his fault?

10-17. *The Entail of Evil.*—These verses are perplexing. According to the narrative up to

this point, Adam and Eve and Cain and Abel were the only human beings on the earth. Abel now is dead, and so the population would seem to be reduced to three. Yet suddenly the picture changes to a world in which Cain is apprehensive that at any moment he may encounter other persons who will try to kill him, in which he finds a wife and marries, and presently builds a city. It would appear that here is a separate old story of Cain, perhaps a legend connected with the tribe of Kenites, which originally had nothing to do with the

14 Behold, thou hast driven me out this day from the face of the earth; and from thy face shall I be hid; and I shall be a fugitive and a vagabond in the earth; and it shall come to pass, *that* every one that findeth me shall slay me.

15 And the LORD said unto him, Therefore whosoever slayeth Cain, vengeance shall be taken on him sevenfold. And the LORD set a mark upon Cain, lest any finding him should kill him.

16 ¶ And Cain went out from the presence of the LORD, and dwelt in the land of Nod, on the east of Eden.

17 And Cain knew his wife; and she conceived, and bare Enoch: and he builded a city, and called the name of the city, after the name of his son, Enoch.

than I can bear. 14 Behold, thou hast driven me this day away from the ground; and from thy face I shall be hidden; and I shall be a fugitive and a wanderer on the earth, and whoever finds me will slay me." 15 Then the LORD said to him, "Not so!*i* If any one slays Cain, vengeance shall be taken on him sevenfold." And the LORD put a mark on Cain, lest any who came upon him should kill him. 16 Then Cain went away from the presence of the LORD, and dwelt in the land of Nod,*j* east of Eden.

17 Cain knew his wife, and she conceived and bore Enoch; and he built a city, and called the name of the city after the name

i Gk Syr Vg: Heb *therefore*
j That is *Wandering*

---

tract of territory—possibly Palestine—whereas **the ground** in vss. 10-12 means the ground and nothing else. (*b*) An inconsistency is involved in the representation that there were at the time hostile strangers in existence of whom Cain stood in fear. (*c*) The passage breaks the close connection between vs. 12, in which Cain is condemned to be a **wanderer,** and vs. 16, which states that Cain **dwelt in the land of Nod,** i.e., the land of **Wandering.** Vss. 13-15 thus being secondary, they may well have been added under pressure from the Kenite element in the tribe of Judah (cf. I Sam. 27:10; 30:29). Taking exception to the treatment of their eponymous ancestor in the original story, they secured the inclusion of this passage in mitigation. The tradition it embodies, that the descendants of Cain bore a special "mark"—cf. "the mark of Yahweh," vs. 1 as emended above—may well have originated among the Kenites subsequent to their adoption of Yahwism and their incorporation into the tribe of Judah. And the reference to the custom of sevenfold vengeance may well be authentic and so an indication that the Kenites were not—all of them at any rate—so depressed a group as vs. 12*b* implies.

16. This verse was thus in its original context the immediate continuation of vs. 12, and concluded the story of Cain. **East of Eden** is a gloss, possibly from the hand of the redactor who inserted the fragments of the Eden saga in ch. 3, certainly in dependence on those fragments.

B. CAIN'S DESCENDANTS (4:17-19)

17. This section continues the J genealogy begun in vss. 25-26, which had been interrupted by the story of Cain and Abel. The second half of the verse, depicting Cain as the originator of urban civilization, is obviously an intrusion, for J would never have represented city life as anterior to the rise of nomadism (vs. 20). Furthermore, the

---

story of Adam and Eve but was linked by a later compiler with the narrative that began with the Garden of Eden. In that case, the chief purpose seems to have been to bring accumulating emphasis to the tragedy of human sin and its consequences. The disobedience of Adam and Eve in regard to the forbidden fruit is followed by the more deadly sin of Cain in the murder of his brother; and as the sin was worse, so was the punishment. Adam and Eve are expelled from Eden; Cain is driven from all the

land that he had known, and doomed—as he himself sees his fate—to be **a fugitive and a vagabond . . . in the earth.** But the last part of vs. 14 and vs. 15 strike another note. Perhaps there is here an echo from dim old days of tribal feuds and vengeance, when one tribe let it be known that any killing of one of its members would have multiple retaliation. And conceivably there is the beginning of the instinct which led later to the establishment among the Israelites of the "cities of refuge," the purpose

18 And unto Enoch was born Irad: and Irad begat Mehujael: and Mehujael begat Methusael: and Methusael begat Lamech.

19 ¶ And Lamech took unto him two wives: the name of the one *was* Adah, and the name of the other Zillah.

20 And Adah bare Jabal: he was the father of such as dwell in tents, and *of such as have* cattle.

of his son, Enoch. 18 To Enoch was born Irad; and Irad was the father of Me-hu'-ja-el, and Me-hu'ja-el the father of Me-thu'sha-el, and Me-thu'sha-el the father of Lamech. 19 And Lamech took two wives; the name of the one was Adah, and the name of the other Zillah. 20 Adah bore Jabal; he was the father of those who dwell

notice itself presents a certain difficulty in that Cain does not call the city after his own name, as would be expected, but after the name of his son. Thus, while the half verse echoes a tradition of the origin of city life independent of the tradition of the rise of nomadism, it is impossible to say whether it was primarily associated with Cain or with Enoch.

18. The figures listed here were presumably of some importance in the tradition upon which J was depending, but the role they played apparently had no bearing upon the origin and development of civilization, with which he is here concerned. He accordingly includes their names without comment.

19. He is similarly silent as to the original significance of **Adah, Zillah,** and **Lamech** —mentioned in the ancient poem preserved in vss. 23-24.

C. RISE OF NOMADISM (4:20-24)

20. According to this verse, nomadism—the life of **those who dwell in tents and have cattle**—was the first step in the development of civilization from the cultureless

of which was to prevent the hasty and passionate putting to death of even the suspected criminal.

18-24. *The Spirit of Lamech.*—It is a curious fact that in this narrative the progress of the race from primitivism toward civilization is attributed to the descendants of Cain. Jabal is said to have been **the father of those who dwell in tents.** So begins the free movement of the nomad peoples. Jubal is **the father of all those who play the lyre and pipe.** So the arts begin with music. And Tubal-cain was **the forger of all instruments of bronze and iron,** and thus opened the way for the mastery of man over his environment. All this is described as done by men who were alienated from God, as though "the children of this world are in their generation wiser than the children of light" (Luke 16:8). And the accomplishments of Lamech's sons lead to the arrogant and boastful self-sufficiency of Lamech himself. As Marcus Dods puts it:

Lamech has no need of God for any purpose; what his sons can make and his own right hand do is enough for him. This is what comes of finding enough in the world without God—a . . . man . . . dangerous to society, the incarnation of the pride of life. In the long run separation from God becomes isolation from man and cruel self-sufficiency.[6]

[6] *The Book of Genesis* (New York: A. C. Armstrong & Son, 1895; "The Expositor's Bible"), pp. 50-51.

It seems that to the mind of the Yahwist from whom this part of Genesis comes the whole course of history lay under the shadow of the evil that began in the Garden of Eden and that grew to more deadly expression in the sin of Cain. After the period of original innocence the progress of what might have been called civilization appeared to him as a moral declension that went on deepening until it was checked by the crisis and cleansing of the Flood. Cain was a murderer, but at least he had remorse; Lamech, his descendant, not only could kill but could celebrate the killing in the fierce triumph of his taunting song. It would be a gloomy conclusion if it had to be believed that all the development of man's material life as the race "spread itself abroad, made itself now more at home on the earth, and was able in its way to ease life of its burdens and to beautify it by advance in discoveries and accomplishments"[7] had to be associated with godlessness. Yet there is ground for serious meditation on the fact that the great resources of human knowledge and ability can be perverted by passion and pride. The freedom of the nomad can be turned into the warfare of predatory peoples long after the nomad stage has passed; and arts and scientific skill can be destructive forces in

[7] August Dillmann, *Genesis Critically and Exegetically Expounded,* tr. W. B. Stevenson (Edinburgh: T. & T. Clark, 1897), I, 174.

21 And his brother's name *was* Jubal: he was the father of all such as handle the harp and organ.

22 And Zillah, she also bare Tubal-cain, an instructor of every artificer in brass and iron: and the sister of Tubal-cain *was* Naamah.

21 His brother's name was Jubal; he was the father of all those who play the lyre and pipe. 22 Zillah bore Tubal-cain; he was the forger of all instruments of bronze and iron. The sister of Tubal-cain was Na'amah.

---

existence of the human race since the time of Cain. Since historically nomadism was not anterior to agriculture, this account of the origins of human culture comes from a nomadic group.

21. Jubal is represented as the originator of music. There is no suggestion here that his supposed descendants, the musicians, were in any way inferior to the full-blooded Bedouin that have cattle (vs. 20), or that they formed a separate "caste"; i.e., J is simply recording the origin of one of the skills which seemed to him to be important.

22. This verse should be emended, with Gunkel (*Genesis*, p. 53), to agree in form with vss. 20, 21, "He was the father of all forgers of bronze and iron," i.e., he was the originator of metalworking. Again, there is no suggestion that metalworkers formed a separate caste, such as is formed by the Solubby (Charles M. Doughty, *Travels in Arabia Deserta* [new and definitive ed., New York: Random House, 1946], I, 324-27)—a group who lived "partly by hunting, partly by coarse smith-work and other gipsy labor in the Arab encampments; they are forbidden by their patriarch to be cattle-keepers, and have no property save a few asses; they are excluded from fellowship and intermarriage with the regular Bedouin, though on friendly terms with them" (Skinner, *Genesis*, p. 113). If, however, as is suggested by Otto Procksch (*Die Genesis* [2nd and 3rd ed.; Leipzig: A. Deichert, 1924; "Kommentar zum Alten Testament"], p. 55), **-cain** is taken as a gloss on **Tubal**—its omission restores the name of Lamech's third son to the same form as the other two—by one who knew Cain (=smith) as the ancestor of the smiths, then in view of vs. 12*b* it may have been intended as a suggestion of their low-caste status.

The verse is silent as to the role filled by **Naamah**. In view of this, and of the fact that in the extant J material nothing is said of Noah's parentage—it is P who makes

---

the hands of any human group that has lost its obedience to God.

One can remember that music has often been used to let the passions loose. The most primitive tribes had their tom-toms, and their hypnotic rhythms were devised to arouse the instincts of fear and retaliation and revenge that lurk in the jungles of the human heart. To read Vachel Lindsay's "The Congo," or to remember the terrible weird beating of the voodoo drums in Eugene O'Neill's *Emperor Jones* is to feel again the aboriginal savagery that music can express. Nor have the old appeals lost their power to evoke response. In times of mass excitement, is it not true that peaceful men and women may feel themselves moved to an irrational war hysteria by the marching music of brass bands?

To say that and to say no more would be of course to libel the meaning of music. It is written that "the morning stars sang together," as though in God's music of creation. The psalms are the singing of the human heart,

sometimes—it is true—in bitterness and anger, but also in confession, praise, and adoration. And from the time of Palestrina on, who can measure the purifying and ennobling influence of great music in orchestras and choirs, in symphonies and chorales?

But all the same, does not the old shadow of Cain still represent an influence that we need to be aware of? Whether or not Cain's children started music, they seem too often to get hold of it. The primitive creeps back and seizes again what the higher genius of man has been trying to perfect. The blaring of jazz, the horrible croonings of advertisements on the radio, the reversion of "civilized" dances to the rhythms of African bushmen, have outdone Macbeth, who "murdered sleep." They are in the way of doing to death the higher appreciation, which prefers great music to miscellaneous noise.

And what of man's use of metals? The long story of human inventiveness is a thrilling record. The mastery of man over his physical

23 And Lamech said unto his wives, Adah and Zillah, hear my voice; ye wives of Lamech, hearken unto my speech: for I have slain a man to my wounding, and a young man to my hurt.

24 If Cain shall be avenged sevenfold, truly Lamech seventy and sevenfold.

23 Lamech said to his wives:
"Adah and Zillah, hear my voice;
    you wives of Lamech, hearken to what
      I say:
I have slain a man for wounding me,
    a young man for striking me.
24 If Cain is avenged sevenfold,
    truly Lamech seventy-sevenfold."

---

him the son of Lamech (5:28) —it is not impossible that she was traditionally Noah's mother.

It may be noted here that the implication of vss. 20-22a is that Jabal, Jubal, and Tubal (-cain) were the "fathers" of the nomads, musicians, and metalworkers existing at the time of writing; i.e., that the author of this account of the origins of civilization knew nothing of the Flood.

23-24. These verses are, as Stade ("Beiträge zur Pentateuchkritik," pp. 295-96) and Eissfeldt (*Hexateuch-Synopse,* p. 255*) have argued, a secondary addition to the J narrative: (a) They are irrelevant to the purpose of that narrative, which is to describe the beginnings of civilization. (b) They are inconsistent with vss. 1-22, in which Cain is represented as an individual and an ancestor of Lamech; here he stands for a people and is a contemporary and rival of Lamech. (c) They refer to the Cain not of vs. 12b, but of vss. 13-15 already seen to be secondary. (d) The reappearance of Lamech after the mention of his sons is awkward in the extreme.

The poem, of great antiquity and so valuable for the reconstruction of cultural development, comes from a Cain-Lamech tradition. It may have been inserted as polemic against the secondary vss. 13-15.

24. Probably for **is avenged** should be read, with Gunkel (*Genesis,* p. 53, following Karl Budde, *Die biblische Urgeschichte* [Giessen: J. Ricker, 1883], p. 133), "avenges himself." This involves only a change in the vocalization of the Hebrew, which is in any case suspicious here (cf. E. F. Kautzsch, *Gesenius' Hebrew Grammar,* tr. A. E. Cowley [2nd English ed.; Oxford: The Clarendon Press, 1910], sec. 29 g).

---

environment has come through his use of tools. We tend to take for granted what we have inherited, but the amazing facts of our mechanized civilization are due to the nameless men who ages ago first conceived the wheel, forged instruments of bronze and then of iron, and thus laid the groundwork for all that inventive human genius has since accomplished (see Lewis Mumford, *Technics and Civilization* [8]). The O.T. was right when it thought of craftsmanship as one of the gifts of the Spirit of God (Exod. 31:2-3), for it has lifted the level of human life from a brutish struggle for existence to the possibility of abundance and beauty.

But here again there is the shadow of Cain. The prophet Isaiah dreamed of a day when men should "beat their swords into plowshares" (Isa. 2:4), but our world is in danger of reversing that process and beating its plowshares into swords. If mounting tensions between the nations continue, most of the fruits of human productivity will be sucked into military pre-

paredness or into the immeasurable ruin of another world war for which we will have been so frenziedly prepared.

"I will give thee two thousand horses, if thou be able on thy part to set riders upon them" (Isa. 36:8). That was the taunt of Rabshakeh the Assyrian to the officers of Hezekiah king of Judah. The same ironic challenge is being given to the human race by destiny. We have already that which makes two thousand horses insignificant—the gigantic energy of machines which represent horsepower not by the thousands but by the billions. What riders can we set upon these horses? Can we train sufficient intelligence and enlist enough good will to master and direct their fearful forces? Or will our positive controls, being too feeble or too late, be shoved aside by other horsemen—the four horsemen of the Apocalypse, war and famine and pestilence and death? There is fateful need that Christian teachers and preachers shall make all people they can reach consider that!

[8] New York: Harcourt, Brace & Co., 1934.

| 25 ¶ And Adam knew his wife again; and she bare a son, and called his name Seth: For God, *said she,* hath appointed me another seed instead of Abel, whom Cain slew. | 25 And Adam knew his wife again, and she bore a son and called his name Seth, for she said, "God has appointed for me another child instead of Abel, for Cain slew |

D. WORSHIP OF THE LORD (4:25-26)

25. As has been argued above, this verse was in its original form the immediate continuation of 3:23. For **Adam** there stood in J "the man." **Again, another,** and **instead of Abel, for Cain slew him** are redactional harmonization by RP. Thus in the J tradition, as in that of P (5:3), **Seth** was the first child born into the world.

God has appointed for me, the first of the usually fanciful etymologies of the names of the heroes provided by J, derives **Seth**—lit., *Shēth*—from *shîth,* appoint. Its real etymology is unknown. In this connection it may be noted that in Num. 24:17 "the sons of Sheth" refers to the Moabites, which indicates the existence of another tradition concerning *Shēth,* apparently familiar to J2 since the words occur in the oracle he puts in the mouth of Balaam. However, the Balaam oracle seems to be an adaptation of an independent poem which J2 has incorporated into his narrative at that point. It has been argued in the Intro. that vs. 25, now under consideration, is from J1.

25-26. To God Through Children.—What is the meaning of then? It is not possible to know exactly what was in the mind of the one who wrote the clause beginning with that word, but there is room for much meditation here. It is after the reference to children being born that we come upon this: **then began men to call upon the name of the Lord.** It was a right time to do so. It always is and will be.

People who have not been much conscious of God before may well seek him when their children come. It is instinctive then to feel grateful to a Goodness which has given the miracle of life. "For this child I prayed," said Hannah (I Sam. 1:27). "My soul doth magnify the Lord," sang Mary (Luke 1:46). In every generation parents have felt that way. God has seemed more real; and suddenly they have known that he was more needed. It is one thing to manage—or suppose to manage—one's own life. It is another thing to face the responsibility for guiding the life of a little child. Every person worth speaking of would like to have then more wisdom and a purer will than he or she possesses. So a father and mother may call upon God—at least in seeming. Perhaps in seeming only. The child may be taught a prayer or two, though their own praying falls back into perfunctoriness or is forgotten altogether. Presently the child may be sent to Sunday school, for somebody else to teach him, while they stay at home. That sort of calling on God is hollowness, if not hypocrisy. But what if their calling is not that sort? What if they really want God? Then because of a child they can be led a long way.

Thoughtful parenthood can give a new sense of the nature of God. It is through the heart that God may be most surely faced and known. Many adults have grown up with nothing warmer than ideas about God; they have never been aware of him in any deep perception. But the coming of a little child may awaken an instinct that lies at a profounder level, for the best there is in a man and woman comes to expression when they take a baby in their arms. Then, if ever, they have a love that is outgoing and unselfish; and because they do have that they may find unfolding in themselves a new faith in a love that is greater than their own. For this truth expressed with the beauty of the poet's insight, read George MacDonald's lines beginning, "O Lord, I sit in Thy wide space," and Coventry Patmore's "The Toys."

When the thought of God is thus brought into parenthood, wide-reaching influences come with it. The first is the feeling that life is bigger than it ever seemed before. Whether a man or woman is religious or not, there may be a kind of biological exultancy in parenthood, but the one whose thoughts have turned to God has much more than that. This much more is the realization that one has been entrusted by the Creator of souls with a child's soul, not just with a child's body. Women often realize that more wonderingly than men, and that is the reason why mothers have again and again achieved the immense joy of walking in companionship with a child on an advancing road of consecration. Read the lives of John Wesley and of Phillips Brooks and see what their mothers meant to them. A father may have

26 And to Seth, to him also there was born a son; and he called his name Enos: then began men to call upon the name of the LORD.

him." 26 To Seth also a son was born, and he called his name Enosh. At that time men began to call upon the name of the LORD.

---

26. The second half of the verse should read, following the LXX, "He was the man who began to call upon the name of the LORD." J thus reveals for the first time his interest in origins, here the origin of the cult of Yahweh. In vss. 20-22, as has been seen, he tells of the origins of nomadism, music, and metalworking; 6:2 is a fragment of his account of the origin of the Nephilim; 9:20, in its original form, told of the origin of viticulture, and back of it, as will be seen, is a lost passage ascribing the origin of agriculture also to Noah; 10:8 tells of the first of the Gibborim; and the nucleus of 11:1-9 is J's account of the origin of diverse languages.

J's narrative thus began with a story of some length in which, unlike the rest of the document, the name of Yahweh, the Lord, was not used; for J2—in this probably following J1; cf. the use of "God" in the J1 verse, 4:25—had refrained from employing it until after the notice now contained in 4:26b (cf. Budde, *Biblische Urgeschichte,* pp. 232-33), thus leaving open the possibility of the misconception that some deity other than Yahweh was the creator. It was to obviate this that some redactor inserted "the LORD"—Yahweh—before "God" wherever it occurred in the narrative. When, however, "God" occurred in a speech (3:1b, 3, 5; 4:25b) he did not insert "the LORD," in order to avoid contradicting the implication of 4:26b that the name of the Lord was unknown to man until the time of Enosh. It should be noted that Gunkel, *Genesis,* pp. 1-4 (where other proposed solutions are noted; cf. Skinner, *Genesis,* pp. 52-53), accounts for the double name "the LORD God" as resulting from the combination of two independent strands in the J material, one of which used "the LORD," the other, "God." Sigmund Mowinckel, *The Two Sources of the Predeuteronomic Primeval History (JE) in Gen. 1-11* (Oslo: J. Dybwad, 1937), pp. 44-61, maintains that there is an E strand in chs. 1-11, and ascribes the form to RJE.

---

this experience too. Every father might well write in his heart a prayer like this:

O God, who art our Father, take my human fatherhood and bless it with thy Spirit. Let me not fail this little son of mine. Help me to know what thou wouldst make of him, and use me to help and bless him. Make me loving and understanding, cheerful and patient and sensitive to all his needs, so that he may trust me enough to come close to me and let me come very close to him. Make me ashamed to demand of him what I do not demand of myself; but help me more and more to try to be the kind of man that he might pattern after. And this I ask in the name, and by the grace, of Christ. Amen.[9]

The thought of God when children come can create also self-discipline and self-sacrifice. There is enough of the divine innate in parenthood to create that on some level at least. At the end of World War II some of the illustrated magazines had a vivid article describing the American prisoners of the Japanese in Manila after they were released by MacArthur's

[9] W. R. Bowie, *Lift Up Your Hearts.* Copyright 1939. Used by permission of The Macmillan Co., publishers.

armies from their long and bitter imprisonment. The men and women were emaciated, but they had managed to keep their children fed. A similar article describing German families two years after Germany's defeat and occupation showed how parents had lost weight and strength, but the rations which they denied themselves had kept the children relatively well. In ordinary times and places also there is an inspiring amount of everyday and unheralded nobility of sacrifice among the poor. Look at the innumerable men and women working for small wages who give to their children better clothes, more amusements, more small luxuries than they themselves ever have.

That is on the physical plane; but there is another level of life which religiously sensitive men and women will remember. Influenced by the thought of God, a father and mother can achieve a further and more constant kind of discipline and self-mastery. Careless habits of indulgence, dissipations that adults might take for granted but would be disillusioning to a child, begin to look ugly when a parent whose religious conscience has been awakened asks himself what these would do to his child's

5 This *is* the book of the generations of Adam. In the day that God created man, in the likeness of God made he him;

2 Male and female created he them; and blessed them, and called their name Adam, in the day when they were created.

5 This is the book of the generations of Adam. When God created man, he made him in the likeness of God. 2 Male and female he created them, and he blessed them and named them Man when they

---

V. Descendants of Adam (5:1-28)

This chapter is derived from P, with the exception of vss. 28*b*-29 which, taken from the J document, have been substituted by RP for "he became the father of Noah." In constructing the genealogy P seems to have been dependent on that of J (cf. 4:1, 17-18, 25-26), from which he has however departed, for reasons now irrecoverable, by transposing Mehujael=Mahalalel and Enoch. The ages assigned to each figure may depend upon some Babylonian tradition, though it should be noted that the figures given differ markedly in the M.T., Samar., and LXX. With this genealogy P bridged the period from the Creation to the Flood.

5:1. Adam: In this use of the word for man as a proper name P may be dependent, however remotely, upon the Eden saga (cf. 3:20).

---

standards and his child's ideals. "These things have not hurt me too much," a parent might argue, and so keep on in habits which he knows are questionable; but when the coming of his child has made him think of God and ask himself whether these things will do hurt to God's possibilities in him, then many a man has called **upon the name of the Lord** for a new personal reformation, and has got it.

From the same source may come a larger wisdom. Most decent men and women would like to do what is advantageous for their children, but often they have a poor idea of what advantageous means. They may take the easy road of giving their children what they want, or what will cause least trouble, or what the general fashion says. If they have not faced life's great realities in the light of God they will not have learned that "the fear of the LORD is the beginning of wisdom" (Ps. 111:10), and the love of the Lord is the fulfillment of it.

That kind of shallow worldliness leads to nothing that is great. It is only when the thought of God is brought to bear upon the facts and the choices of life that one sees what things are mean and cheap, and what things are worth desiring. Love for a child can lead a man and woman to understand that only that which is true to the spirit of God is completely blessed, and that only God can make their devotion wise.

5:1-32. The Lineage of the Chosen People.— In this long chapter there is indicated the ruling purpose of the priestly writers to whose influence is due so much of the ultimate structure of Genesis. They desired to show that the history of Israel was no human accident, but that from the beginning it had been shaped by the sure and sovereign will of God. Out of humanity in general God had been sifting a particular people who should embody his plan, with whom he would make his covenant, and through whom he would give his special revelation. That is why the genealogies are set forth in such meticulous detail. To the modern reader they may seem to be a dull catalogue; but to those who wrote them, and to those who understood their purpose, they were the cardinal guarantee of Israel's divine preferment. The line which begins with Adam is channeled through Seth and his descendants down to the righteous Noah (vss. 30-32), through Noah's son Shem to Abraham (11:10-26), through Abraham to Isaac and Jacob. The overruling directness of God's choice is emphasized by the fact that repeatedly the elder son is set aside in favor of the younger one whom God had chosen. So Ishmael must give place to Isaac (17:18-21), and Esau is supplanted by Jacob; and Joseph, next to the youngest among twelve brothers, becomes the greatest among Jacob's sons.

Thus the priestly writers, both in direct expression and by incorporating the older narratives of J and E into their pattern, held to their unswerving aim of maintaining that the one controlling purpose which has given meaning to history from the moment of the Creation is God's shaping of a people fit to become a theocracy. The great prophets, beginning with Amos, had exalted the conception of God from that of the jealous deity of one people to that of the Lord of impartial justice and of universal sway. At the height of the prophetic vision the little bounds of race and particularity were transcended. But the priestly writers

3 ¶ And Adam lived a hundred and thirty years, and begat *a son* in his own likeness, after his image; and called his name Seth:

4 And the days of Adam after he had begotten Seth were eight hundred years: and he begat sons and daughters:

5 And all the days that Adam lived were nine hundred and thirty years: and he died.

6 And Seth lived a hundred and five years, and begat Enos:

7 And Seth lived after he begat Enos eight hundred and seven years, and begat sons and daughters:

were created. 3 When Adam had lived a hundred and thirty years, he became the father of a son in his own likeness, after his image, and named him Seth. 4 The days of Adam after he became the father of Seth were eight hundred years; and he had other sons and daughters. 5 Thus all the days that Adam lived were nine hundred and thirty years; and he died.

6 When Seth had lived a hundred and five years, he became the father of Enosh. 7 Seth lived after the birth of Enosh eight hundred and seven years, and had other

---

had a more intense and specialized concern. As R. H. Pfeiffer has described it:

The aim of the Priestly Code is to show how the only God in existence became the invisible sovereign of the Jewish community. From the moment when God created heaven and earth, his one purpose, according to P, was to separate Israel from the other nations, reveal his Law, give his covenant, and provide a country for it.[1]

Ten times occurs the introductory phrase, or its equivalent, "These are the generations of" (vs. 1; 2:4; 6:9; 11:10, 27; 25:12, 19; 36:1; 37:2; 35:22b) ; and as Pfeiffer puts it:

The racial history of Israel in P is like a funnel comprising ten rings of decreasing size, down to the extremely small but all-important tube at its bottom—the theocratic community. This racial history is purely genealogical and chronological— nothing else matters in vital statistics.[2]

This was a lofty belief. For any people to hold the faith that God has given it an immortal destiny is to lift its life up above the common considerations of this earth. Such a people can rise superior to delays and disappointments because they trust in him with whom a day is as a thousand years and a thousand years as one day. They have that within their soul which can sing, in the words of a modern hymn:

O beautiful for patriot dream
That sees, beyond the years,
Thine alabaster cities gleam,
Undimmed by human tears! [3]

Through their conviction that the future, like its present, would be held in the hands of God,

Israel has had the unconquerable fortitude which has enabled it to outlast persecution and disaster; and it was in large part the priestly writers who gave that conviction. Similarly, for any people today, it is only as men arise who can give to their nation a comparable sense of religious meaning and religious mission that the nation's flame of life will burn so bright that the winds of time cannot extinguish it.

Yet it must also be said that there is a reverse side to the picture of what the priestly writers did for Israel—and what men of the same intensity of purpose may do for any people. The danger was that they could make the thought of Israel hard and narrow. It is a glorious thing to believe in a great destiny, but only when that destiny is conceived with generous imagination. To think of destiny in terms of a nation's own exaltation, and of that alone, is to bring abasement. That was the risk which Israel would run—and which every nation runs when its pride supposes that it has conscripted God to be its exclusive ally, instead of committing itself to be the instrument of God's grace for all mankind.

5. *Death.*—Eight times in this chapter the words **and he died** occur. They represent that recognition of the inevitability of death which sounds through all history like the strokes of an iron bell. There is a double element in human nature which makes the fact of death so tragic. Man is akin to all animal existence in that every individual dies. He is different from the animal in that he is conscious of dying, foresees it, and feels its contradiction of his insatiable hunger for life. Nor does the universality of death dull its poignancy:

That loss is common would not make
My own less bitter, rather more.
Too common! Never morning wore
To evening, but some heart did break.[4]

---

[1] *Introduction to the Old Testament* (New York: Harper & Bros., 1941), p. 191.
[2] *Ibid.*, p. 197.
[3] Katharine Lee Bates, "America the Beautiful."
[4] Tennyson, *In Memoriam*, Part VI, st. ii.

8 And all the days of Seth were nine hundred and twelve years: and he died.

9 ¶ And Enos lived ninety years, and begat Cainan:

10 And Enos lived after he begat Cainan eight hundred and fifteen years, and begat sons and daughters:

11 And all the days of Enos were nine hundred and five years: and he died.

12 ¶ And Cainan lived seventy years, and begat Mahalaleel:

13 And Cainan lived after he begat Mahalaleel eight hundred and forty years, and begat sons and daughters:

14 And all the days of Cainan were nine hundred and ten years: and he died.

15 ¶ And Mahalaleel lived sixty and five years, and begat Jared:

16 And Mahalaleel lived after he begat Jared eight hundred and thirty years, and begat sons and daughters:

sons and daughters. **8** Thus all the days of Seth were nine hundred and twelve years; and he died.

9 When Enosh had lived ninety years, he became the father of Kenan. **10** Enosh lived after the birth of Kenan eight hundred and fifteen years, and had other sons and daughters. **11** Thus all the days of Enosh were nine hundred and five years; and he died.

12 When Kenan had lived seventy years, he became the father of Ma-hal'alel. **13** Kenan lived after the birth of Ma-hal'alel eight hundred and forty years, and had other sons and daughters. **14** Thus all the days of Kenan were nine hundred and ten years; and he died.

15 When Ma-hal'alel had lived sixty-five years, he became the father of Jared. **16** Ma-hal'alel lived after the birth of Jared eight hundred and thirty years, and had other

---

How have men tried to deal with death in their efforts to overcome it? There is the belief that existence here may somehow be prolonged. The stories of the patriarchs with their immense longevity are a sort of wistful reflection of what men have liked to believe might be. But later in the O.T. the imaginary hope has faded. "The days of our years are three score years and ten" (Ps. 90:10). In the twentieth century there has actually been a new prolongation of life. In the United States at the halfway mark of the century there were six million persons over seventy years of age, and the expectancy is that this will increase to ten million in fifteen years and to fifteen million not long afterward. The average age is lengthening. Nevertheless there comes the inescapable end. "Though men be so strong that they come to fourscore years, yet is their strength then but labour and sorrow; so soon passeth it away, and we are gone" (Book of Common Prayer, Ps. 90:10).

Or men may attempt to ignore the coming of death by steeping themselves in material satisfactions. Optimism imagines a life and an age so comfortable and rich that its transiency can be forgotten. Consider Jesus' parable of the rich man and his stored-up barns, who thought he had "much goods laid up for many years" (Luke 12:19). Compare with that the weary cynicism of the book of Ecclesiastes.

Or men have tried to drown death in dissipation. The emptiness of that effort also is reflected in Ecclesiastes. As a parable of the

failure of men thus to drown the fear of death, read Edgar Allan Poe's "The Masque of the Red Death."

Again, men may grasp the hope that though they themselves die they somehow live on in the lives of their children or their nation. This was the hope that grew up in Israel. Its negative aspect is seen from the time of the patriarchs onward in the dread of being childless. Its positive side appears in the noble devotion to the future of Israel which the prophets represent.

But in the end there is the longing of the individual soul for life which cannot be put off with any substitute. It is not a mere selfish wish for continued existence. It represents the instinctive faith that the highest values we know of in this universe, the life and loving loyalty which are expressed in particular human souls, ought not to be extinguished.

Consider what this faith rests upon and how it may be strengthened and assured. The finer a life is in moral purpose, the more it keeps its spirit sensitive to goodness and to truth, the more is faith in the indestructibility of a soul will grow. Remember the lines of *In Memoriam:*

> A warmth within the breast would melt
> The freezing reason's colder part.[5]

So the fire of brave and generous emotions can burn away the fog and chill of doubt.

The more one is related to some great cause, the more one feels that life has too great a dignity to be destroyed by death. See the last

[5] Part CXXIV, st. iv,

17 And all the days of Mahalaleel were eight hundred ninety and five years: and he died.

18 ¶ And Jared lived a hundred sixty and two years, and he begat Enoch:

19 And Jared lived after he begat Enoch eight hundred years, and begat sons and daughters:

20 And all the days of Jared were nine hundred sixty and two years: and he died.

21 ¶ And Enoch lived sixty and five years, and begat Methuselah:

22 And Enoch walked with God after he begat Methuselah three hundred years, and begat sons and daughters:

23 And all the days of Enoch were three hundred sixty and five years:

24 And Enoch walked with God: and he *was* not; for God took him.

---

sons and daughters. 17 Thus all the days of Ma-hal'alel were eight hundred and ninety-five years; and he died.

18 When Jared had lived a hundred and sixty-two years, he became the father of Enoch. 19 Jared lived after the birth of Enoch eight hundred years, and had other sons and daughters. 20 Thus all the days of Jared were nine hundred and sixty-two years; and he died.

21 When Enoch had lived sixty-five years, he became the father of Methu'selah. 22 Enoch walked with God after the birth of Methu'selah three hundred years, and had other sons and daughters. 23 Thus all the days of Enoch were three hundred and sixty-five years. 24 Enoch walked with God; and he was not, for God took him.

---

pages of Wilfred Grenfell, *What Life Means to Me.*[6]

Companionship with lovely persons is the highest human fortification to faith. Looking at ourselves, we might doubt our worthiness to go on living. Looking at some others whom we love, we know that death could not destroy them unless the whole universe were irrational. See the last chapter in George Herbert Palmer, *Life of Alice Freeman Palmer,* his wife. Read the chapter "Bereavement" in W. R. Inge, *Personal Religion and the Life of Devotion.*[7]

Finally, there is the fact of Jesus. The nearer one comes to him in thought and spiritual companionship the stronger is the faith that the cross and the grave could not and did not conquer him, and that we can trust his promise, "Because I live, ye shall live also" (John 14:19).

22-24. *The Man Who Walked with God.*— Is there a re-enforcement of the thought suggested by 4:26 (see Expos.) in the statement that **Enoch walked with God** after he begat **Methuselah**? Whether or not the ancient writer explicitly meant to say so, certainly it is true that often the first real turning of a man's heart toward God comes as the result of some deep experience that awakens in him new emotions: a great joy, a blessed responsibility, a sorrow, a relationship that stirs the profundities of his soul. The description of Enoch shines like a single brilliant star above the earthy record of this chapter. The significance of many men may perish with their bodies. Their achievements have to do only with material things. They may sew their tents, raise

their cattle, make their musical instruments, and work in brass and iron (4:20-22). But the man who towers in meaning above all the others is the man who walks with God.

Enoch walked with God: and he was not; for God took him. Note, as the Exeg. has stated, that this chapter comes from P. Therefore it is much later than the parts of the book which have come from J and E and may reflect conceptions not existing in their day. In the early history of Israel there seems to have been no expectation of personal immortality. The only way in which a man's spirit might survive would be in his children or in the clan and nation. Or if he did survive, it would be only as a shadowy wraith in Sheol. But gradually there grew the increasing sense of the dignity and enduring worth of the individual human soul. Life on earth might be so linked with Spirit that it would go on beyond the gates of death. That belief seems to be shining here.

What a haunting phrase it is: **He was not; for God took him!** There is no effort to elaborate upon the mystery of death or to presume in human terms to define what lies beyond it. Only the one great conception: when the good man dies God takes him and he goes to be with God. He goes to be with God because he has learned to be with God already. See what limitless suggestions there are in the brief and simple words, he **walked with God.** Hubert L. Simpson has a lovely paragraph concerning Enoch:

One day Enoch's place upon earth was empty, and the people who had known him drew their own conclusions. He had been known as the inti-

[6] Boston: Pilgrim Press, 1910.

[7] New York: Longmans, Green & Co., 1924, pp. 87-96.

25 And Methuselah lived a hundred eighty and seven years, and begat Lamech:

26 And Methuselah lived after he begat Lamech seven hundred eighty and two years, and begat sons and daughters:

27 And all the days of Methuselah were nine hundred sixty and nine years: and he died.

28 ¶ And Lamech lived a hundred eighty and two years, and begat a son:

29 And he called his name Noah, saying, This *same* shall comfort us concerning our work and toil of our hands, because of the ground which the LORD hath cursed.

25 When Methu'selah had lived a hundred and eighty-seven years, he became the father of Lamech. 26 Methu'selah lived after the birth of Lamech seven hundred and eighty-two years, and had other sons and daughters. 27 Thus all the days of Methu'selah were nine hundred and sixty-nine years; and he died.

28 When Lamech had lived a hundred and eighty-two years, he became the father of a son, 29 and called his name Noah, saying, "Out of the ground which the LORD has cursed this one shall bring us relief from our work and from the toil of our

---

VI. BEGINNING OF AGRICULTURE (5:29-32)

29. For bring us relief the LXX reads "cause us to rest"—a translation of the Hebrew *yenîḥēnû*—a reading which is to be accepted as providing a more satisfactory etymology for **Noah** than does the M.T. Now *yenîḥēnû* can also bear the meaning "cause us to settle down" (cf. Deut. 3:20). In view of J1's representation of Noah as the first husbandman, it seems likely that "this one shall cause us to settle down" was the explanation given of the name Noah in that document. For J2 the first man, not Noah, was the originator—however unwilling—of agriculture. He accordingly added **from our work and from the toil of our hands,** thus taking *yenîḥēnû* to mean "cause us to rest." In the Hebrew the clause rendered **out of the ground which the LORD has cursed** comes after **from the toil of our hands;** furthermore there is a certain awkwardness in the use of the preposition *min* with different meanings—**out of** and **from**—in the two parts of the sentence. These facts may indicate that the clause, clearly dependent on 3:17, was added by a later hand (Holzinger, *Genesis,* p. 60) to relate the notice more closely

---

mate of God; and what more natural than that, when night fell, he should have gone home with his Friend? A little girl was telling the story of Enoch in her own way. "Enoch and God," she said, "used to take long walks together. And one day they walked further than usual; and God said, 'Enoch, you must be tired; come into My house and rest.' " [8]

Thought may dwell further upon the analogy of walking together, for it has much to say concerning the life of prayer and communion which must be the prelude to the immortal hope. To walk together with a human friend has clear meanings which have their reverent expansions in what it means to walk with God. It is to have the same goal and so to be moving in the same direction. It is to have the serene and happy sense of companionship upon the way. And it is to have unforced, spontaneous conversation as one goes along: sometimes to keep silence and just feel the other's presence, sometimes to speak out what is in one's mind and heart, sometimes to listen to what the

[8] *Altars of Earth* (London: James Clarke & Co., 1922), p. 136. Used by permission.

greater Friend will tell us of the road, what to look for on it, and the goal to which we go.

27. *The Dimensions of Life.*—Everybody who has read the Bible or studied the old catechisms remembers Methuselah as the oldest man. "Old as Methuselah" has become a byword. Yet a physician, commenting humorously, once said that even Methuselah might have lived longer. Consider the dates in chs. 5 and 7: Methuselah, 187 years old when Lamech was born; Lamech, 182 years when Noah was born; Noah, 600 years when the Flood came. Add together 187, 182, and 600, and the total is 969. And Methuselah was 969 when he died. So, asks the physician, was he drowned in the Flood? Did even Methuselah die prematurely? But for the Flood, might he have been living yet? At any rate, according to the story, he lived longer than anybody else. He has become the symbol of longevity.

There is beauty and blessing in long life. One of the promises in the psalms is "with long life will I satisfy him" (Ps. 91:16). All normal people want to live long. This earth is not "a

30 And Lamech lived after he begat Noah five hundred ninety and five years, and begat sons and daughters:

31 And all the days of Lamech were seven hundred seventy and seven years: and he died.

32 And Noah was five hundred years old: and Noah begat Shem, Ham, and Japheth.

hands." 30 Lamech lived after the birth of Noah five hundred and ninety-five years, and had other sons and daughters. 31 Thus all the days of Lamech were seven hundred and seventy-seven years; and he died.

32 After Noah was five hundred years old, Noah became the father of Shem, Ham, and Japheth.

---

to the tragic story in ch. 3. The reading of the M.T., **bring us relief,** is thus a further change in the same direction.

It may be noted that the verse in the form it held in J[2] implies that the speaker is eventually to share in the blessings of the new life to be inaugurated by Noah. This suggests that J[2] may have included Noah's parents in his "house" (7:1) which went with him into the ark.

---

vale of tears," but a place of interest, activity, rich experience. Good reason, therefore, to preach and teach the kind of thoughtful common sense and consideration that makes for physical health and vigorous life. Dissipation shortens life. Carelessness shortens it. The gift of long life which God has intended can be thrown away by those who let their bodies become so flabby that they have no physical resistance. The toll of automobile smash-ups and needless accidents also is terrific. (What is the actual number of them in whatever year these words are read?) Nor is this only an individual problem. It is a social one. What about the multitudes with substandard incomes who cannot afford medical care? What about workers inadequately insured against maiming and crippling in industries? There is a social duty to assure a man that he shall not be robbed of God's gift of life and soundness. But longevity is not all. **All the days of Methuselah were nine hundred sixty and nine years: and he died.** That is all that could be said of him. His life was long, but thin as a string.

There is another dimension which life needs. It must have not only length but breadth. Though, in Robert Louis Stevenson's words, "the world is so full of a number of things," some people let their minds sink into narrow grooves. Preoccupied with petty things, they do not cultivate new interests. Therefore life grows unnecessarily cramped and drab. William Lyon Phelps wrote, "The happiest man is the man who has the most interesting thoughts." In our actual world, with its newspapers, its periodicals and magazines in reach of everybody, its libraries, its museums, its crowding opportunities for new ideas and new interests, there is no reason why any life should lack intelligent breadth. Some of the men who have most in-

tense and exacting responsibilities are those whose interests range out with happiest spontaneity. Broadening one's interests is not primarily dependent upon having more time—or less—than somebody else. It is a matter of being alert and alive. Consider the value of hobbies: Franklin D. Roosevelt collecting and studying stamps, Winston Churchill painting. See Arnold Bennett, *How to Live on 24 Hours a Day.*[9]

If the range of thought can broaden, so also can the range of sympathy. The man who makes many friends has breadth. The man who looks out on the world with generous human understanding can create the public mood which will keep nations from falling into grooves of jealous self-interest and instead will make their policies broaden toward world co-operation and peace.

Length and breadth—but there is a third dimension needed. It is the vertical one. In some aspects that may be called depth, in others, height. The shallow lake, no matter how long or wide it is, may stagnate. It needs the depth of new inflowing water to keep it vital. A landscape that is all flat plain may be depressing. Men who have ever known the mountains want to see them again. There is an instinct in human souls that needs to reach down to great convictions and to reach up to great hopes and faiths. A horrible punishment in some of the medieval dungeons was to put men in cells where they could not stand erect. Yet some of us condemn ourselves spiritually to an existence like that. We live confined in ideas and insights so low-ceilinged that the soul cannot stand up. We must get out under the open skies and stars.

A life may be great without great length. It may still be significant even if it has not had a

[9] New York: George H. Doran Co., 1910.

6 And it came to pass, when men began to multiply on the face of the earth, and daughters were born unto them,

2 That the sons of God saw the daughters of men that they *were* fair; and they took them wives of all which they chose.

6 When men began to multiply on the face of the ground, and daughters were born to them, 2 the sons of God saw that the daughters of men were fair; and they took to wife such of them as they chose.

VII. Sons of God and Daughters of Men (6:1-4)

The nucleus of this tale is a brief notice of the origin of the Nephilim, a mythical race of giants referred to again in Num. 13:33. It is preserved in part in vs. 2, which originally concluded with some such sentence as "and they conceived and bare the Nephilim" (cf. Budde, *Biblische Urgeschichte,* p. 38; Skinner, *Genesis,* p. 146). The Nephilim were thus represented as semidivine, the offspring of the sons of God and the daughters of men.

The interest in origins (cf. 4:20-22) suggests that the notice is from the hand of J[1], in whose narrative it probably occurred immediately before the account of the origin of diverse peoples (11:4-8; cf. Julius Wellhausen, *Die Composition des Hexateuchs* [2nd ed.; Berlin: Georg Reimer, 1889], p. 14).

Having inserted, as will be seen, the story of the Flood into the narrative of his predecessor, J[2] placed this notice after the account of how the Lord had "scattered [the descendants of Noah] abroad . . . over the face of all the earth" (11:8), prefixing to it vs. 1, in which **the face of the ground** (cf. vs. 7; 7:4, 23; 8:8, 13) is an indication of his hand; "the face of all the earth" in 11:8 is, as will be seen, from J[1].

It is to be noted that there is in vss. 1-2 no suggestion of reprobation of the conduct of the sons of God and the daughters of men; the passage is simply a "scientific" notice of origins, an objective statement of "fact."

The beliefs that among the early inhabitants of the earth were men of great stature and that marriages of the gods with mortals frequently occurred are found in other ancient literatures (see Skinner, *Genesis,* p. 140, for references). And in the O.T. there are numerous references to the one-time existence of giants (e.g., Num. 13:33, already cited; cf. Josh. 15:14; Deut. 1:28; 2:10, 11, 21; 9:2; Amos 2:9).

For R[P] this marriage of divine and human beings was infamous and demanded punishment. He accordingly placed the story in its present position, omitted the sentence with which the notice in vs. 2 had originally concluded, and added the groundwork of vss. 3-4, later expanded. The episode thus became in his composition—the Pentateuch, practically in its present form—the culminating act of human wickedness before the Flood.

6:2. The sons of God—not, be it noted, "the sons of Yahweh"—is the designation of the heavenly host in Job 1:6; 2:1; 38:7 (cf. also Pss. 29:1; 89:6; see ASV mg.).

---

chance to broaden much. But it cannot be true life unless it has depth and height. Against a life like that of Methuselah stand the infinite dimensions of the life of Christ. By the world's calendar, it was only some thirty years long. But it was wide as the needs of man, and deep and high as the love of God.

6:1-3, 4b. Out of the Past.—No one can say surely what these verses mean. They come from some period of primitive thought which is dim to our perception. Were **the sons of God** rebellious and fallen angels, as Milton conceived them in *Paradise Lost?* Were they deities like the Greek gods who came down from Mount Olympus to consort with **the daughters of men?** In either case there is the projection here of an ancient fantasy that is inconsistent with the higher faith of Genesis. Apparently the compilers included this fragment of an ancient myth because it was too familiar to be ignored. But though it has a likeness to the traditions of other lands, there is a difference. In the Homeric epics the love-making of the gods is simply a dramatic tale that is unconcerned with any moral judgments; but here in the biblical account there is the judgment of the Lord. Be-

3 And the LORD said, My Spirit shall not always strive with man, for that he also *is* flesh: yet his days shall be a hundred and twenty years.

4 There were giants in the earth in those days; and also after that, when the sons of

3 Then the LORD said, "My spirit shall not abide in man for ever, for he is flesh, but his days shall be a hundred and twenty years." 4 The Nephilim were on the earth in those days, and also afterward, when the

---

3. The first half of the verse is from RP. Its secondary character (cf. Smend, *Erzählung des Hexateuch,* p. 26; Eissfeldt, *Hexateuch-Synopse,* pp. 255*-56*) is indicated by the abruptness of its beginning and by the fact that it is a *non sequitur,* since there is no indication in vss. 1-2 that the Lord's **Spirit** was in any way involved in the action of the sons of God. **But his days shall be a hundred and twenty years** is a gloss either to the effect that the Flood would occur in a hundred and twenty years' time, thus placing the action of the sons of God before the birth of Noah's sons (cf. 5:32; 7:6), or perhaps making some cryptic reference to the age of Moses.

4. In the statement that **there were giants in the earth in those days** RP denies that **the Nephilim** were a semidivine race wiped out by the Flood; they were simply

---

cause of the sin of **the daughters of men** the life span of human beings is reduced.

Yet if there is value in these verses it is not in anything they directly say, but in something which by contrast they suggest. In the old mythology, when the gods came down to earth, they came for their own gratification. They used human beings for their transient purposes and left them behind when they went back to their Olympus. The story of the Bible comes to its climax in the record of One "who, though he was in the form of God, did not count equality with God a thing to be grasped, but . . . taking the form of a servant, . . . humbled himself and became obedient unto death, even death on a cross" (Phil. 2:6-8); and who, when he went home to his Father, said to those on earth to whom he had brought his redeeming love, "In my Father's house are many mansions. . . . I go to prepare a place for you" (John 14:2).

4a. The Twisted Judgments of Fear.—To imagination there always are **giants.** Distant facts grow legendary and larger, like mountains capped with clouds. With men of the time of Genesis, belief in giants was entirely literal. They listened to stories about them with the same unquestioning and fascinated wonder that children have when they hear of a giant in their fairy tales. They were not thinking merely of men larger than ordinary men but still somewhere within the reach of normal measurements, not merely of huge persons like Goliath, who was said to have been more than nine feet tall. They meant giants as the credulous and unspoiled imagination sees them—huge portentous creatures beside whom the human being is like a midget.

In later and more sophisticated times the conception of giants is no longer literal, but it may be no less significant. Men hear of forces which they do not yet know, or begin to descry them dimly in the distance, and their imagination makes them look tremendous. They are not quite delivered from the shadow of the ancient fear—fear of the unknown which seems to them gigantic. Men in the time of Caleb still were haunted by it, and their blood could chill at what somebody else told them had been seen. Read the vivid story of the spies in Num. 13–14. Moses sends them out to scout the land in advance of the people of Israel, to see what the opportunities are and also what obstacles may have to be encountered. Ten out of the twelve men come back in panicky excitement, "All the people that we saw . . . are men of a great stature. And there we saw the giants, . . . and we were in our own sight as grasshoppers, and so we were in their sight" (Num. 13:32-33). That is what they thought, or thought they thought, and the more they told their tale the more it was magnified. But the proof that what they said they saw was no such thing is in the fact that two other better-balanced men who saw exactly what they saw came back completely cool and undismayed. They had seen no giants. Instead, what they saw was a delectable land they ought to occupy, with no difficulties too great for them to overcome.

The old facts can be a modern parable. In moral and spiritual matters men may move in the old shadowland of fearful apprehension where they will think that they are seeing giants. Or they may look instead at reality with steady eyes, seeing it for what it is, neither less nor more, and going out to meet it as brave

God came in unto the daughters of men, and they bare *children* to them, the same *became* mighty men which *were* of old, men of renown.

sons of God came in to the daughters of men, and they bore children to them. These were the mighty men that were of old, the men of renown.

---

mighty men of great stature whose prowess was in no way due to their parentage. And **also afterward** points ahead to Num. 13:33.

---

men should. Reflect upon the examples in history and the instances in everyday experience of those who see giants where no real giants exist. Scan the whole record of the people of Israel in the march through the wilderness toward the Promised Land as recorded in Exodus and Numbers. They were continually magnifying difficulties, hesitating, balking, and complaining. Note Num. 14:1. See John Mark turning back at Perga (Acts 13:13). Consider in the history of the War Between the States the failure of McClellan through overcaution and apprehensive exaggeration of the strength of the forces arrayed against him. Read in D. S. Freeman's *R. E. Lee* [10] of the similar failure of Longstreet at Gettysburg. Think of men and women now whose first impulse in the face of a hard assignment is to tell themselves that it cannot be carried through. Think also of those who discourage every program for social advance and betterment, seeing all the old evils in successive generations, slavery, peonage, economic exploitation, degrading poverty, imperialism, war, as giants which there is no sense trying to cope with.

What produces that defeatist spirit? A clinging to the past, its habits of thought and its associations; a self-indulgent craving for former satisfactions and the unwillingness to leave these as part of the price for the greater possibilities that lie ahead; halfheartedness in a task which requires men wholeheartedly committed; and out of these emotional faults and failures, a rationalization of the entire fact which creates alleged good reasons for doubting and avoiding what there is not will to do. On the other hand, who are the men that, like Caleb and Joshua, will face the untried confidently, appraise difficulties without distortion, and scorn the superstitious fear that dangers a little greater than the usual may prove to be gigantic? What makes this kind of men? A purpose that fills their minds and masters positively their imaginations; the courage that comes from complete commitment; and, in all religious men, the dominating faith in the divine assistance which makes them sure that there can be no insuperable obstacles in their way. In the war for the liberation of

the Netherlands, after the dreadful siege and fall of Haarlem, the Prince of Orange wrote in 1573 to Diedrich Sonoy, lieutenant governor of the province of North Holland:

You ask if I have entered into a firm treaty with any great king or potentate, to which I answer, that before I ever took up the cause of the oppressed Christians in these provinces, I had entered into a close alliance with the King of kings; and I am firmly convinced that all who put their trust in Him shall be saved by his almighty hand.[1]

4b. The Glamour of Yesterday.—If the thought of giants (see Expos. on vs. 4a) carried an aura of dread, here in the **mighty men, . . . men of renown** there is a note of human pride; yet it is pride in reverse, as though the writer of the words turned from contemplation of contemporary life, as small and common, to imagination of a time when it was great. The **mighty men . . . were of old.** How familiar that sounds! Again and again we hear the suggestion that in other times there were men of lofty stature in mind and morals, whereas now there are no great men, but only such as are ordinary and inadequate. That may sound like reverence for the past, but actually it may be a weak pretext by which an indolent cynicism avoids the responsibility which the recognition of present greatness would impose upon choice and action. To complain that there are no commanding leaders is a convenient excuse for not arousing oneself to any positive allegiance. But it is a poor self-deception. Seldom in any generation have the majority of the people acknowledged the greatness of the great. Martin Luther was treated with contempt by most of those who might have seen his immense significance; so were John Wesley, and Lord Shaftesbury, and Wilberforce. Washington was vilified, so was Lincoln, so was Franklin Roosevelt. It is easier and more comfortable to build the tombs of dead prophets than to recognize the challenging authority of present greatness. But to let imagination be sluggish and the will contemptuous can prevent the appearance in any era of the **mighty men . . . of renown** who might bring their magnificent contribution, and can leave

[10] New York: Charles Scribner's Sons, 1934-37.

[1] John Lothrop Motley, *The Rise of the Dutch Republic* (New York: E. P. Dutton & Co., 1906), II, 381.

5 ¶ And G\Od saw that the wickedness of man *was* great in the earth, and *that* every imagination of the thoughts of his heart *was* only evil continually.

5 The L\Ord saw that the wickedness of man was great in the earth, and that every imagination of the thoughts of his heart was

---

VIII. THE FLOOD (6:5–9:19)

This section is from the hand of RP, who conflated the J recension of the flood story with that of P, using the latter, which he has preserved intact, as the groundwork of his narrative and fitting into it, with certain omissions and with some dislocation, the material of J. RP's narrative has been subjected to some slight elaboration, but the additions are for the most part of little importance.

The J Recension.—Contradicting as it does the implications of 4:20-22, noted above, the J recension is from J². It told of the Lord's distress at the wickedness of man (cf. 6:5-7) and of his decision to **blot out** [all life] **from the face of the ground** (6:7) — **the face of the ground** is a characteristic expression of J in this story (cf. 7:4, 23; 8:8, 13) —saving only Noah (6:8) and his household. He therefore commanded Noah to build an ark; the account of this and of Noah's fulfillment of the command has been dropped by RP in favor of the elaborate version of P (6:14-22). Only when the ark had been finished did the Lord tell Noah of his intention to cause forty days' rain upon the earth which would begin in seven days' time, and command Noah and his household to enter the ark with seven of each kind of clean animal—i.e., of each kind of animal used in sacrifice—and one pair of each kind of unclean (cf. 7:1-5). Thus, according to J², Noah built the ark in faith, not knowing its purpose but simply obeying the Lord's command. During the seven days intervening between the announcement of the coming rain and its beginning he was busy, it is implied, assembling the animals.

The next section of the J narrative has been broken up by RP to make it fit into the representation of P. In its original order it seems to have told how at the end of seven days the Flood began (7:10). Noah and his household thereupon entered the ark (7:7), **and the** L\Ord **shut him in** (7:16*b*). The rain lasted forty days and forty nights (7:12) and floated the ark (7:17*b*), and every living thing died except Noah and those with him in the ark (7:22). The waters then began to disappear (8:3*a*), and the ark came to rest—the J notice of this is now missing, having been dropped in favor of 8:4 (P). Following the threefold sending out of the dove (8:6, 8-12) Noah left the ark—the J notice of this is also missing—and offered a sacrifice to the Lord, who resolved—**said in his heart**—never again to destroy all life (8:20-22).

The Babylonian Flood Story.—It is generally recognized that this story is ultimately based upon the Babylonian myth preserved in the Gilgamesh Epic (see Skinner, *Genesis,* pp. 175-76). According to this, the gods decided to send a flood upon the earth. One of them, Ea, resolved to save his favorite, the mortal Utnapishtim and, without divulging the gods' capricious intention, commanded him to build a ship of definite dimensions to preserve his life. Utnapishtim, discerning the reason for this command, complied—

---

the field open to the imagined giants of fatalistic evil. Which type of men shall religious people believe in and thus help create?

5-13. When Man Revolts Against God.—God who created man for goodness, but evil rampant on the earth: that is the contradiction recognized in the ancient narrative and still recurring. In the play *The Green Pastures* [2] one may read a graphic suggestion of the kinds of evil God had to contemplate as he regarded his world; and what with the general rowdiness and miscellaneous irresponsibility, it was no

[2] Marc Connelly, New York: Farrar & Rinehart, 1929.

wonder that impatient Gabriel was always begging the Lord that he might blow his trumpet for the Judgment. What would Gabriel say now? **The wickedness of man was great in the earth, and . . . every imagination of the thoughts of his heart was only evil continually; . . . and the earth was filled with violence.** If that was true in the days of Noah what of the century which has seen the brutal violence of two world wars, the extermination camps of Buchenwald and Belsen and Oswiecim, the massacre of millions of Jews, murder, starvation, mass cruelty beyond imagination? "What is the

compare the representation of J that Noah built the ark in faith, not knowing its purpose (cf. 7:4-5)—and entered the ship with his family and dependents, taking with him a number of animals. The storm raged for six days and all mankind was destroyed. On the seventh day Utnapishtim sent out three birds in succession (cf. 8:8-12). The first two, a dove and a swallow, returned to him, but the third, a raven, did not. Whereupon Utnapishtim released the animals and, leaving the ship, offered sacrifices, and "the gods smelt the goodly savor" (cf. 8:21).

Legends of a universal flood are found in almost every part of the world (see Gunkel, *Genesis,* pp. 74-76; Skinner, *Genesis,* pp. 174-75). There can be little doubt that where they have not been borrowed from alien traditions they go back to some natural event, local in its extent. A universal flood such as J² describes, to say nothing of P's account, would of course be a physical impossibility. The Babylonian myth is presumably based upon a particularly devasting inundation of the Euphrates Valley (cf. Harold Peake, *The Flood* [New York: R. M. McBride & Co., 1930]).

J's Revision.—The myth of the Flood, it may be assumed, was, like the creation myth, ultimately carried to Palestine—the Babylonian element in the civilization of Palestine before the Israelite conquest is witnessed to by the Amarna letters which are written in cuneiform. There it became a part of the cultural tradition into which the Israelites entered when they settled in the land. This J², writing in the interests of Israelite monotheism, related to Yahwism. The most significant feature of his adaptation of it is, of course, his representation that the Flood was not the result of malicious divine caprice—an impossible idea for him, holding as he did the Mosaic concept of the Lord as the God of righteousness—but was sent by the Lord in punishment for man's wickedness (6:5-8). Congruent with this is the reason given for the saving of Noah. He **found favor in the eyes of the LORD** (6:8), not through capricious choice, such as governed Ea's favoring of Utnapishtim, but because he was righteous (7:1).

This adaptation, it may be noted, was not too skillfully made, for in J²'s narrative 6:5 followed immediately upon 5:29 which seems to have been, with 5:28b, the continuation of 4:20-22; i.e., he nowhere suggested before 6:5 that wickedness was increasing on the earth—the crime of Cain was several generations back. This is a significant indication of J²'s hierarchy of values. Artist though he was and a master of style, literary values were for him always subordinate to moral considerations. There could be no tampering with the idea of the righteousness of God.

The P Recension.—It has been argued above that P in writing his creation story was dependent on J's revision of the Babylonian myth *Enuma eliš.* It seems probable

shape of the earth?" asked a schoolteacher, and one small pupil replied, "My Daddy says the shape of the earth is a mess."

A world revolting not only against God's ideals but against the most elemental decencies: that has been the fact. And the root of it? One phrase suggests it: **Every imagination of the thoughts of his heart was only evil continually.** What men are and what the world is depend upon the conceptions they set up for their inward eyes to see and obey. As a man "thinketh in his heart, so is he" (Prov. 23:7). Imagination creates its images, and images may become idols that take the place of God. The surest way to keep them out is to be sure that God comes in. The guarantee against corrupting thoughts is to fill the mind and heart with wholesome ones. Remember Jesus' parable of the house swept and garnished and left empty, and invaded then by seven devils worse than the one that

had been driven out (Luke 11:24-26). Psychology reinforces what religion had always instinctively perceived, that evil cannot be overcome by argument; evil must be overcome by good. Consider the critical significance for the individual of prayer, since prayer at its purest is not words of ours, but waiting—the waiting of the open soul for God to enter. Consider the immense social problem and opportunity of right programs of public education, in order that accepted ideals of the sacredness of human personality, of justice, generosity, and brotherhood, may be strong enough to block the entrance or re-entrance of perversions such as fascism or a Marxism that is wholly materialistic; that the kind of democracy which has been the British ideal of liberty and "the American dream" may have its own antitoxin to dictatorship; that the religion which the fathers followed may keep the loyalty of their

therefore that here again he was drawing not immediately on the Gilgamesh Epic but on J²'s adaptation of it. The reason for the Flood, of course, remained the same—human wickedness (6:9-22). There is a departure however from J in the representation that Noah, when commanded to build the ark, was at the same time apprised of the disaster which was coming (6:13, 17). Whether, in the mention of **pitch**—bitumen— (6:14) and in the representation that God, in giving the command, specified the dimensions of the ark (6:14-17), P was drawing on the earlier myth, or whether, as seems more probable—compare the reference to the window of the ark in 8:6 (J²)— these details were in some form included by J² it is impossible to say, since the J parallel is lacking. J²'s distinction between clean and unclean animals he ignored, for in his theory this distinction was first made by divine precept at Sinai (Lev. 11:1-30), and two only of each kind were taken into the ark (6:19). For J² the Flood was the result of forty days' rain. P, perhaps realizing that this could not account for such a catastrophe as the tale depicted, told of the unleashing of the subterranean waters and of the opening of the windows of heaven so that the waters above the firmament (cf. 1:6) poured down (7:11) for one hundred and fifty days (7:24). Then the waters began to subside, and the ark came to rest upon the mountains of Ararat (8:1, 2a, 3b, 4), but it was not until a year and ten days had elapsed since the beginning of the Flood that the earth was dried (8:5, 13a, 14) and Noah was commanded to leave the ark (8:15-19). The sending out of the dove was omitted—for according to P Noah did nothing without explicit divine command. J²'s representation of him as acting independently is thus more in accordance with the Babylonian original in which Utnapishtim is designated the "superlatively clever one" (Skinner, *Genesis,* p. 176). All reference to Noah's sacrifice was also omitted in accordance with P's theory that no sacrifice was ever offered until God commanded it at Sinai (Lev. 1). Instead it is recorded that God now made a covenant with Noah never again to destroy all flesh by the waters of a flood (9:8-11) and made the rainbow the sign of the covenant (9:12-17; on 9:1-7 see Exeg.).

A. Making of the Ark (6:5-22)

5. The word rendered **imagination** is *yēçer*. Although it is used with this meaning in only five other places in the O.T. (8:21; Deut. 31:21; I Chr. 28:9; 29:18; Isa. 26:3), the word came to be of extraordinary significance in Jewish thought. It is used in Ecclus. 15:14, "He [God] himself made man from the beginning, and left him in the hand of his counsel [*yēçer*]." This verse is part of Ben Sirach's explanation of the presence of moral evil in God's creation. Its origin is within man—a thought to which the author gives further sardonic expression in Ecclus. 21:27, "When the ungodly curseth Satan, he curseth his own soul." Sin is the result of man's fixing his imagination on himself, or on some other person or thing short of God. With this thought may be compared that of Isa. 26:3, "Thou wilt keep him in perfect peace [i.e., unharmed, or in welfare], whose mind [*yēçer*] is stayed on thee; because he trusteth in thee" (see George Buchanan Gray, *A Critical and Exegetical Commentary on the Book of Isaiah I–XXXIX* [New York: Charles Scribner's Sons, 1912; "International Critical Commentary"], p. 439). In rabbinical literature *yēçer* is used with the meaning of "impulse," the (good or evil) "tendency" in man (*A Hebrew and English Lexicon of the Old Testament,* ed. Francis Brown, S. R. Driver and C. A. Briggs [Boston: Houghton Mifflin Co., 1906], p. 428).

sons. It is when imagination ceases to dwell upon the great convictions that debasing paganisms overcome us.

A second truth: The world in revolt against God brings retribution. The ancient story of the Flood is partly myth; yet it is also a parable of what is no myth but terrible reality. There can be a point in the disintegration due to evil when something has to break. Then the

forces of decency left on earth are not strong enough to hold back the pressure of moral consequence. It will rain upon the earth not only for forty days, as in the story of Noah, but for four years as in World War I, and more than four years, as in World War II; and the wash and welter of it may prevail not only "a hundred and fifty days," but through dragging decades in which the aftermath of war still

6 And it repented the LORD that he had made man on the earth, and it grieved him at his heart.

7 And the LORD said, I will destroy man whom I have created from the face of the earth; both man, and beast, and the creeping thing, and the fowls of the air; for it repenteth me that I have made them.

8 But Noah found grace in the eyes of the LORD.

9 ¶ These *are* the generations of Noah: Noah was a just man *and* perfect in his generations, *and* Noah walked with God.

10 And Noah begat three sons, Shem, Ham, and Japheth.

11 The earth also was corrupt before God; and the earth was filled with violence.

12 And God looked upon the earth, and, behold, it was corrupt; for all flesh had corrupted his way upon the earth.

13 And God said unto Noah, The end of all flesh is come before me; for the earth is filled with violence through them; and, behold, I will destroy them with the earth.

only evil continually. **6** And the LORD was sorry that he had made man on the earth, and it grieved him to his heart. **7** So the LORD said, "I will blot out man whom I have created from the face of the ground, man and beast and creeping things and birds of the air, for I am sorry that I have made them." **8** But Noah found favor in the eyes of the LORD.

9 These are the generations of Noah. Noah was a righteous man, blameless in his generation; Noah walked with God. **10** And Noah had three sons, Shem, Ham, and Japheth.

11 Now the earth was corrupt in God's sight, and the earth was filled with violence. **12** And God saw the earth, and behold, it was corrupt; for all flesh had corrupted their way upon the earth. **13** And God said to Noah, "I have determined to make an end of all flesh; for the earth is filled with violence through them; behold, I will de-

---

In vs. 5, J2 to a certain degree anticipates the thought of Ben Sirach by some seven hundred years. In his recognition of the deep-rooted tendency to evil in the human heart, however, he shows himself to be much more realistic in his estimate of man than was Ben Sirach, for J2 could scarcely have written Ecclus. 15:15.

7. Whom I have created is a gloss; J does not elsewhere use the word rendered "create." **Man and beast and creeping things and birds of the air** is a pedantic gloss in the style of P. Consequently in the original "made him" was read for **made them.**

---

spreads its slime of bitterness and suffering. And the flood is not of water only; it is, and in every recurring judgment it must be, of blood and tears.

8-13. Noah and His Neighbors.—The old story which here begins of Noah setting to work to build his ark is much more than a story. It has actual modern parallels. There are more arks needing to be built than Noah's. Noah is described as building that ark of his because a crisis was at hand. Most people around him did not know it; and if Noah or anybody else warned them they only shrugged their shoulders and passed on. This is what the majority generally will do. "In the days that were before the flood," said Jesus, "they were eating and drinking, marrying and giving in marriage, . . . until the flood came, and took them all away" (Matt. 24:38-39). "Woe to them that are at ease in Zion," cried the prophet (Amos 6:1) to the arrogant civilization of Israel which did not believe that its destruction by Assyria was coming—as it actually was coming—in less than

a generation. "I set watchmen over you," Jeremiah declared in the name of God, "saying, Hearken to the sound of the trumpet. But they said, We will not hearken" (Jer. 6:17)—no, not even when the Babylonian terror was at their gates. "My people are destroyed for lack of knowledge," cried Hosea (4:6). They lacked the knowledge because they were too grossly satisfied to want to know.

So in many times there are men who stare so hard at what they want to see that the critical realities are not seen. They can tell all about the way the winds blow in their little world, but they are oblivious of the forces that may be breaking in to smash their world to bits. "You know how to interpret the appearance of the sky," said Jesus, "but you cannot interpret the signs of the times" (Matt. 16:3). Noah's neighbors looked at the ordinary skies that seemed to promise ordinary weather; they did not see in the skies of moral facts the signs that betokened imminent disaster. At the halfway point of the twentieth century there was

14 ¶ Make thee an ark of gopher wood; rooms shalt thou make in the ark, and shalt pitch it within and without with pitch.

15 And this *is the fashion* which thou shalt make it *of:* The length of the ark *shall be* three hundred cubits, the breadth of it fifty cubits, and the height of it thirty cubits.

16 A window shalt thou make to the ark, and in a cubit shalt thou finish it above; and the door of the ark shalt thou set in the side thereof; *with* lower, second, and third *stories* shalt thou make it.

stroy them with the earth. 14 Make yourself an ark of gopher wood; make rooms in the ark, and cover it inside and out with pitch. 15 This is how you are to make it: the length of the ark three hundred cubits, its breadth fifty cubits, and its height thirty cubits. 16 Make a roof[k] for the ark, and finish it to a cubit above; and set the door of the ark in its side; make it with lower,

[k] Or *window*

---

15. A cubit is about eighteen inches. The dimensions of the ark, according to P, were thus about 450 by 75 by 45 feet.

16. And finish it to a cubit above is unintelligible. Skinner lists the suggestions which have been made as to its original meaning (*Genesis,* pp. 161-62).

---

danger that peoples of the Western world, especially in the United States, who suffered comparatively little from the first and second world wars, might be—and still may be—more like Noah's neighbors than like Noah. They could eat and drink and rise up to play (I Cor. 10:7) while the portents gathered.

In the arresting suggestion of the biblical story, how did Noah perceive what others were blind to? **God said unto Noah, The end of all flesh is come before me.** The dramatic simplicity of the old narrative presents the truth concretely, as though God stood face to face with Noah and spoke to him alone. As a matter of fact, God was speaking through the unmistakable signs of the times to everybody. But Noah was the one who could hear, because he was **a just man and walked with God.** How many leaders of the nations in the critical present century have walked with God? How many of us, the people, are keeping alive within ourselves those conceptions of justice and judgment which will help us see the evils of godless pride and power, and make us know that if they keep building up they will bring some new flood of dreadful retribution?

14, 22. *Knowing Plus Doing.*—Remembering Noah again, we observe that he not only foresaw the crisis; he also did something about it, and he did it ahead of time. He began to build his ark before there was any obvious evidence that it would be needed. The fateful developments of history often come about because men's imaginations are lazy, as in *Pilgrim's Progress,* Presumption says, "I see no danger"; and Sloth says, "A little more sleep." Winston Churchill, in the somber retrospect of *The Gathering Storm,* wrote, with reference to the

careless failure in the 1930's of England and the other democratic countries of Europe to see the fateful portents of the times: "Counsels of prudence and restraint may become the prime agents of mortal danger."[3]

The dull apathy which has made great people stupid in matters of national safety can have even more deadly consequences in regard to world safety. For the time is past when there can be any such thing as national safety, or any continuingly decent human existence whatever, without a means of rescue for the whole world's peace. How clearly do God's people see this, and as citizens and creators of public opinion and action, what are we setting to work to do? Longfellow in his "Ship of State" set forth an ideal for the nations so fervent that Franklin D. Roosevelt quoted it in one of his messages when the issue of World War II was still hanging in the uncertain balances.

> Sail on, O Ship of State!
> . . . .
> Humanity with all its fears,
> With all the hopes of future years,
> Is hanging breathless on thy fate!

But it is more than a ship of state that must be built now. Rather it is the ark of a new hope, big enough to shelter all humanity.

14-22. *The Divine Specifications.*—Noah built the ark according to the specifications which God gave him. In the quaint picture as Genesis presents it, that ark must have seemed to the onlookers fantastically big. It was none too big for what had to go into it if life on the earth was to be saved from destruction and to get a fresh start. In the ultimate suggestion for us

[3] Boston: Houghton Mifflin Co., 1948, p. 18.

17 And, behold, I, even I, do bring a flood of waters upon the earth, to destroy all flesh, wherein *is* the breath of life, from under heaven; *and* every thing that *is* in the earth shall die.

18 But with thee will I establish my covenant; and thou shalt come into the ark, thou, and thy sons, and thy wife, and thy sons' wives with thee.

19 And of every living thing of all flesh, two of every *sort* shalt thou bring into the ark, to keep *them* alive with thee; they shall be male and female.

20 Of fowls after their kind, and of cattle after their kind, of every creeping thing of the earth after his kind; two of every *sort* shall come unto thee, to keep *them* alive.

21 And take thou unto thee of all food that is eaten, and thou shalt gather *it* to thee; and it shall be for food for thee, and for them.

22 Thus did Noah; according to all that God commanded him, so did he.

7 And the LORD said unto Noah, Come thou and all thy house into the ark; for thee have I seen righteous before me in this generation.

2 Of every clean beast thou shalt take to thee by sevens, the male and his female: and of beasts that *are* not clean by two, the male and his female.

second, and third decks. **17** For behold, I will bring a flood of waters upon the earth, to destroy all flesh in which is the breath of life from under heaven; everything that is on the earth shall die. **18** But I will establish my covenant with you; and you shall come into the ark, you, your sons, your wife, and your sons' wives with you. **19** And of every living thing of all flesh, you shall bring two of every sort into the ark, to keep them alive with you; they shall be male and female. **20** Of the birds according to their kinds, and of the animals according to their kinds, of every creeping thing of the ground according to its kind, two of every sort shall come in to you, to keep them alive. **21** Also take with you every sort of food that is eaten, and store it up; and it shall serve as food for you and for them." **22** Noah did this; he did all that God commanded him.

7 Then the LORD said to Noah, "Go into the ark, you and all your household, for I have seen that you are righteous before me in this generation. **2** Take with you seven pairs of all clean animals, the male and his mate; and a pair of the animals that

---

B. THE FLOOD COMES (7:1-24)

7:2. Both occurrences of **the male and his mate** are redactional additions depending on 6:19*b*; for **seven pairs** should then be read **by sevens** (*ibid.*, p. 152, referring to Kautzsch, *Gesenius' Hebrew Grammar*, sec. 134 *q*) ; i.e., according to J, seven of each

---

it was not big enough. Nearly all through the O.T. there is the tendency to think that a particular group could claim special favor with God and preference in his salvation. But that particularism disappears in the limitless pity which was revealed in Christ. The ark of the greater society which men must set themselves to build now must have its heavenly specifications, as Noah had his: but they will be such specifications as are received from the heaven that arches over the N.T., not only over the O.T. The wideness of God's mercy will be in them. The ark will be not for one family or blood or nation, not for descendants of Noah only, but—as in Jesus' parable of the good Samaritan—for the neighbors too who are in **need.**

7:1-24. *The Saved and Saving Remnant.*— According to the story, it was upon Noah and his family that the continuation of life on the earth should depend. Everybody else was drowned, and they alone were left. One may find here the foretokening of a great theme which comes into clear light later in the O.T., viz., the saving significance of the remnant. The physical flood and the physical drowning pictured here do not recur, but there is a kind of spiritual drowning that does. Repeatedly it is as though the great mass of people were caught in the disastrous consequences of an evil life so that they must lose their place in God's enduring plans. In the story of the Exodus most of those who first started out

3 Of fowls also of the air by sevens, the male and the female; to keep seed alive upon the face of all the earth.

4 For yet seven days, and I will cause it to rain upon the earth forty days and forty nights; and every living substance that I have made will I destroy from off the face of the earth.

5 And Noah did according unto all that the LORD commanded him.

6 And Noah *was* six hundred years old when the flood of waters was upon the earth.

7 ¶ And Noah went in, and his sons, and his wife, and his sons' wives with him, into the ark, because of the waters of the flood.

8 Of clean beasts, and of beasts that *are* not clean, and of fowls, and of every thing that creepeth upon the earth,

9 There went in two and two unto Noah into the ark, the male and the female, as God had commanded Noah.

10 And it came to pass after seven days, that the waters of the flood were upon the earth.

11 ¶ In the six hundredth year of Noah's life, in the second month, the seventeenth day of the month, the same day were all the fountains of the great deep broken up, and the windows of heaven were opened.

12 And the rain was upon the earth forty days and forty nights.

13 In the selfsame day entered Noah, and Shem, and Ham, and Japheth, the sons of Noah, and Noah's wife, and the three wives of his sons with them, into the ark;

14 They, and every beast after his kind, and all the cattle after their kind, and

are not clean, the male and his mate; 3 and seven pairs of the birds of the air also, male and female, to keep their kind alive upon the face of all the earth. 4 For in seven days I will send rain upon the earth forty days and forty nights; and every living thing that I have made I will blot out from the face of the ground." 5 And Noah did all that the LORD had commanded him.

6 Noah was six hundred years old when the flood of waters came upon the earth. 7 And Noah and his sons and his wife and his sons' wives with him went into the ark, to escape the waters of the flood. 8 Of clean animals, and of animals that are not clean, and of birds, and of everything that creeps on the ground, 9 two and two, male and female, went into the ark with Noah, as God had commanded Noah. 10 And after seven days the waters of the flood came upon the earth.

11 In the six hundredth year of Noah's life, in the second month, on the seventeenth day of the month, on that day all the fountains of the great deep burst forth, and the windows of the heavens were opened. 12 And rain fell upon the earth forty days and forty nights. 13 On the very same day Noah and his sons, Shem and Ham and Japheth, and Noah's wife and the three wives of his sons with them entered the ark, 14 they and every beast according to its kind, and all the cattle according to

---

kind of clean animal were taken into the ark—possibly three pairs, and an extra male intended for sacrifice.

3. **To keep their kind alive** is the only authentic part of this verse. The preceding sentence is redactional harmonization. **Upon the face of all the earth** is a gloss; J in this narrative consistently uses "upon the face of the ground."

---

of Egypt died in the wilderness. In the days of Elijah the apostates from God seemed to be so overwhelmingly in the majority that Elijah could cry out, "I, even I only, am left" (I Kings 19:10). Eager though he was to see the whole nation redeemed, the prophet Isaiah was forced to conclude that only a few would be found fit to be the seed of the future. Later still there had to be the winnowing of the captivity and

the Exile before Jerusalem that had been destroyed should be built again.

So the ark has become the symbol of the church. The family of Noah had at least enough consciousness of God to become the nucleus of his mercy and his redeeming purpose. Granted that the church is still most lamentably human and, like the ark, in its human aspects still a crude and unlovely thing. William War-

every creeping thing that creepeth upon the earth after his kind, and every fowl after his kind, every bird of every sort.

15 And they went in unto Noah into the ark, two and two of all flesh, wherein *is* the breath of life.

16 And they that went in, went in male and female of all flesh, as God had commanded him: and the LORD shut him in.

17 And the flood was forty days upon the earth; and the waters increased, and bare up the ark, and it was lifted up above the earth.

18 And the waters prevailed, and were increased greatly upon the earth; and the ark went upon the face of the waters.

19 And the waters prevailed exceedingly upon the earth; and all the high hills, that *were* under the whole heaven, were covered.

20 Fifteen cubits upward did the waters prevail; and the mountains were covered.

21 And all flesh died that moved upon the earth, both of fowl, and of cattle, and of beast, and of every creeping thing that creepeth upon the earth, and every man:

22 All in whose nostrils *was* the breath of life, of all that *was* in the dry *land,* died.

23 And every living substance was destroyed which was upon the face of the ground, both man, and cattle, and the creeping things, and the fowl of the heaven; and they were destroyed from the earth: and Noah only remained *alive,* and they that *were* with him in the ark.

24 And the waters prevailed upon the earth a hundred and fifty days.

their kinds, and every creeping thing that creeps on the earth according to its kind, and every bird according to its kind, every bird of every sort. 15 They went into the ark with Noah, two and two of all flesh in which there was the breath of life. 16 And they that entered, male and female of all flesh, went in as God had commanded him; and the LORD shut him in.

17 The flood continued forty days upon the earth; and the waters increased, and bore up the ark, and it rose high above the earth. 18 The waters prevailed and increased greatly upon the earth; and the ark floated on the face of the waters. 19 And the waters prevailed so mightily upon the earth that all the high mountains under the whole heaven were covered; 20 the waters prevailed above the mountains, covering them fifteen cubits deep. 21 And all flesh died that moved upon the earth, birds, cattle, beasts, all swarming creatures that swarm upon the earth, and every man; 22 everything on the dry land in whose nostrils was the breath of life died. 23 He blotted out every living thing that was upon the face of the ground, man and animals and creeping things and birds of the air; they were blotted out from the earth. Only Noah was left, and those that were with him in the ark. 24 And the waters prevailed upon the earth a hundred and fifty days.

---

23. The enumeration **both man . . . air** is redactional harmonization by RP.

---

burton, bishop of Gloucester in eighteenth-century England, put the truth in blunt words when under date of June 13, 1751, he wrote to a friend:

The Church, like the Ark of Noah, is worth saving; not for the sake of the unclean beasts and vermin that almost filled it, and probably made most noise and clamour in it, but for the little corner of rationality, that was as much distressed by the stink within, as by the tempest without.[4]

If the church is to be a saving remnant, it needs continual inside cleansing; and that cleansing must begin not with general complaint and

4 *Letters from a Late Eminent Prelate* (New York: E. Sargeant, 1809), p. 84.

with miscellaneous raising of dust, but with individual consecration: "O Lord, reform thy church, beginning with me." The church is purified by individuals (think of Francis of Assisi, Martin Luther, John Wesley); and individuals are given power to become their best selves by the fellowship of the church. The company in the ark might well have become discouraged if they had not had one another to depend on; and men and women who morally and spiritually may be near discouragement are often kept steady by the fact that there are other would-be Christians-in-the-making who face up every day to the same difficulties they face.

8 And God remembered Noah, and every living thing, and all the cattle that *was* with him in the ark: and God made a wind to pass over the earth, and the waters assuaged.

2 The fountains also of the deep and the windows of heaven were stopped, and the rain from heaven was restrained.

3 And the waters returned from off the earth continually: and after the end of the hundred and fifty days the waters were abated.

4 And the ark rested in the seventh month, on the seventeenth day of the month, upon the mountains of Ararat.

5 And the waters decreased continually until the tenth month: in the tenth *month,* on the first *day* of the month, were the tops of the mountains seen.

6 ¶ And it came to pass at the end of forty days, that Noah opened the window of the ark which he had made:

8 But God remembered Noah and all the beasts and all the cattle that were with him in the ark. And God made a wind blow over the earth, and the waters subsided; 2 the fountains of the deep and the windows of the heavens were closed, the rain from the heavens was restrained, 3 and the waters receded from the earth continually. At the end of a hundred and fifty days the waters had abated; 4 and in the seventh month, on the seventeenth day of the month, the ark came to rest upon the mountains of Ar'arat. 5 And the waters continued to abate until the tenth month; in the tenth month, on the first day of the month, the tops of the mountains were seen.

6 At the end of forty days Noah opened the window of the ark which he had made,

---

C. The Waters Recede (8:1-12)

8:6. In J **at the end of forty days** preceded vss. 2b, 3a; the present position of the clause is of course due to RP. Before the notice of Noah opening the window of the ark, J must have told of him waiting seven days, as is indicated by **another seven days** in vs. 10.

8:1-5. *The Faithfulness of God.*—**And God remembered Noah.** Few words and simple ones, yet a world of meaning for the souls of men is in them. Even when we seem lost to everything else we are not lost to God. Visualizing the story of the ark as the graphic pages of Genesis set it forth, one might well suppose that Noah may have thought himself forgotten. Though he could tell himself that God had once spoken to him and given him his promise of protection, nevertheless, where was God now—now when the gray days and black nights went by and wherever he looked there were only the empty waters and the sky that seemed to hold no hope?

So, many men in many times have found themselves cut loose from all moorings, with the familiar landmarks gone, adrift in a world from which God himself, so far as they can see, has vanished. The flood which has carried them away is sorrow, or loneliness, or moral perplexity, or the sense that some great adventure to which they were committed has meant only long disappointment which will end perhaps in despair. Then they will be saying, like the psalmist, "I am so troubled that I cannot speak," and "Is his mercy clean gone for ever? doth his promise fail for evermore?" (Ps. 77:4, 8.)

But the noble story in Genesis does not end on a note of hopelessness. The Flood did at last abate. The mountaintop of hope appeared, and then one day the earth was habitable. Similarly, religious men in every generation have discovered at last that God did remember and that his purposes would not fail. They have sung with Whittier:

> I only know I cannot drift
> Beyond His love and care.[5]

Or in William Cowper's hymn, "Hark, my soul! it is the Lord," they take comfort in the verse that tells how even though a mother toward the child she bare

> may forgetful be,
> Yet will [He] remember thee.

The reasons for that faith may not appear when the days are dark; but even then the heart may have its intuition that somehow God's Providence is there; and as life goes on to its unfolding, it justifies that faith.

6-12. *Encouragement in Little Things.*— After the Flood had begun to abate there were still days when Noah had to continue to be

[5] "The Eternal Goodness," st. xx.

7 And he sent forth a raven, which went forth to and fro, until the waters were dried up from off the earth.

8 Also he sent forth a dove from him, to see if the waters were abated from off the face of the ground.

9 But the dove found no rest for the sole of her foot, and she returned unto him into the ark; for the waters *were* on the face of the whole earth. Then he put forth his hand, and took her, and pulled her in unto him into the ark.

10 And he stayed yet other seven days; and again he sent forth the dove out of the ark.

7 and sent forth a raven; and it went to and fro until the waters were dried up from the earth. **8** Then he sent forth a dove from him, to see if the waters had subsided from the face of the ground; **9** but the dove found no place to set her foot, and she returned to him to the ark, for the waters were still on the face of the whole earth. So he put forth his hand and took her and brought her into the ark with him. **10** He waited another seven days, and again he sent forth

---

7. This is an intrusion into the J narrative, doubtless to bring it into closer agreement with the Babylonian original.

---

patient; and the last days of waiting may be the hardest. **Noah opened the window** and sent out a raven and a dove, but at first there was only disappointment. The raven vanished; and when the dove came back to shelter in the ark he knew that it meant the waters were too deep for her to find **rest for the sole of her foot.** More waiting, and more weariness of postponed hope. Seven days went by and he sent the dove out again. This time **the dove came in to him in the evening, and, lo, in her mouth was an olive leaf plucked off.**

One leaf might not have seemed of much significance, but it meant a lot to Noah. He could not eat it and he could not do anything else with it that was useful; but it made the whole world look different. It was a sign **that the waters were abated from the earth** and that out of death and destruction life was again emerging. That is a good thing to remember in times of crisis. For instance, in the crisis—like that through which Noah had passed—of human sin and God's judgment upon it. There are times when everything that is familiar seems to have come to an end. When the Flood was at its height, Noah might well have wondered whether God's endurance was exhausted, the final doom pronounced, and the very basis of man's existence upon the earth forever gone. To some of the peoples in Europe after World War II that might well have seemed to be true. More than two years after the war had ended an experienced observer wrote from Germany: "All Germans are completely pessimistic. At best, they are fatalists whose only care is to get through the day. They have lost . . . will and hope." If there should be another war, and with atomic weapons, the impression would be still more overwhelming. Is human civilization to be not only devastated but wiped out altogether? In the face of such a possibility men may well thank God for one leaf, for one small but certain sign that there are living and recreative forces which God has not allowed wholly to be swept away. When the contrary signs seem so much more prevailing it takes courageous faith to believe in the little signs of promise—the little new shoots of youth and energy and budding effort that may push out from roots that had seemed to disappear. But in the strength of these humanity, like Noah, must take heart and ride out the rest of the storm.

The description of the dove coming back with the one leaf may be linked with vs. 1, which begins, "And God remembered Noah." Perhaps it was hard for Noah to think so. With the wild emptiness of the waters around him, shut in by the gray curtains of the pitiless rain, waiting day after day while nothing happened, it might well have seemed to him that God had forgotten. So men are often tempted to think. They suppose that they are left to face impossible conditions which God created and about which—and about them—God no longer seems to care. So Moses in the midst of the Exodus cried out, "Wherefore hast thou afflicted thy servant? . . . I am not able to bear all this people alone" (Num. 11:11, 14). "O Lord, how long shall I cry, and thou wilt not hear!" exclaimed Habakkuk (1:2). And from the Psalms comes this, "Wherefore hidest thou thy face, and forgettest our affliction?" (44:24). But the ultimate message of the Bible, of the prophets, the psalmists, and all the great figures of its history, is that God does not forget. "God remembered Noah," and the hand of his ultimate deliverance would not be slack. Here

11 And the dove came in to him in the evening, and, lo, in her mouth *was* an olive leaf plucked off: so Noah knew that the waters were abated from off the earth.

12 And he stayed yet other seven days, and sent forth the dove, which returned not again unto him any more.

13 ¶ And it came to pass in the six hundredth and first year, in the first *month*, the first *day* of the month, the waters were dried up from off the earth: and Noah removed the covering of the ark, and looked, and, behold, the face of the ground was dry.

the dove out of the ark; 11 and the dove came back to him in the evening, and lo, in her mouth a freshly plucked olive leaf; so Noah knew that the waters had subsided from the earth. 12 Then he waited another seven days, and sent forth the dove; and she did not return to him any more.

13 In the six hundred and first year, in the first month, the first day of the month, the waters were dried from off the earth; and Noah removed the covering of the ark, and looked, and behold, the face of the

---

11. The olive does not grow at great altitudes, hence the **freshly plucked olive leaf** was an indication that the waters had considerably receded. Gunkel, however, suggests that the dove and the olive leaf may originally have had some mythological significance (*Genesis,* p. 65) .

---

is the message of reliance through grim times for every man who has once had the conviction that God had a purpose for him. A great Christian wrote once to a friend who was undergoing tragic suffering: "Trust God now in the dark, when it means something." The floods of danger and delay and disappointment may seem dismaying, but

> There's a wideness in God's mercy,
> Like the wideness of the sea.[6]

The symbol of the leaf may suggest another thought which is not directly related to the Noah story but does belong in the wide inconclusiveness of life. Not only in circumstances of sin and judgment but in circumstances of moral victory there may be great meaning in a single leaf. When Charles William Eliot, president of Harvard University and one of the great personalities of his time, was being honored at the climax of an illustrious career he referred to various tributes that had been paid him, and he said that one message which had come to him had meant more than all the rest. It was from a beloved citizen of Boston, a lifelong friend. "When I opened the envelope addressed to me," he said, "I found in it no written word, not one. Instead, there was a single leaf. But that leaf was a laurel."

It was the symbol of a victorious life; and such a symbol may well be prized more than many tangible rewards. To some it may come late; but it is worth waiting for. Here is a woman who as wife and mother waits long and wistfully for those she loves best to want what she wants for them. Her husband may be in-

terested only in making money, while she knows how much deeper and finer the values are that go into the making of life. Her sons may wander recklessly, uninfluenced by her religion. She does not grudge anything she does for them, and certainly she is not looking for any material gift. What she does yearn for is the sign that her long faith has been justified, that the ark of the hopes she has cherished can see ahead of it the promise of a world restored. It is enough for her when the one new leaf appears—the one first word or token that those she has lived for are ready to rise up and call her blessed. Or here is a man whose character and career have been involved in a community which resisted and at first perhaps even laughed at his ideals. With clear prevision he may have seen the forces of moral retribution gather, and yet not have been able to persuade his contemporaries that they were coming. But he has gone on unswervingly to fulfill the duties laid on him. He has believed in life's ultimate promise and kept his faith in God. Then at length from the quarters he cares for most there comes the recognition that goes closest to his heart. He has the sign which vindicates at last what he had trusted. The full unveiling of his world is not yet before him, but he has the evidence of what has certainly begun. The one leaf brought to him is like Noah's, the olive leaf of peace; but it is also the laurel leaf of victory.

13-19. *Every Living Thing.*—The Flood was over, and the hour of release from the ark had arrived. Noah and his wife and his sons and his sons' wives come out to start life on the earth anew. But it is not these alone that God has in mind. **Bring forth with thee,** he says to

6 Frederick W. Faber.

14 And in the second month, on the seven and twentieth day of the month, was the earth dried.

15 ¶ And God spake unto Noah, saying,

16 Go forth of the ark, thou, and thy wife, and thy sons, and thy sons' wives with thee.

17 Bring forth with thee every living thing that *is* with thee, of all flesh, *both* of fowl, and of cattle, and of every creeping thing that creepeth upon the earth; that they may breed abundantly in the earth, and be fruitful, and multiply upon the earth.

18 And Noah went forth, and his sons, and his wife, and his sons' wives with him:

19 Every beast, every creeping thing, and every fowl, *and* whatsoever creepeth upon the earth, after their kinds, went forth out of the ark.

20 ¶ And Noah builded an altar unto the Lord; and took of every clean beast, and of every clean fowl, and offered burnt offerings on the altar.

21 And the Lord smelled a sweet savor; and the Lord said in his heart, I will not again curse the ground any more for man's sake; for the imagination of man's heart *is* evil from his youth: neither will I again smite any more every thing living, as I have done.

ground was dry. 14 In the second month, on the twenty-seventh day of the month, the earth was dry. 15 Then God said to Noah, 16 "Go forth from the ark, you and your wife, and your sons and your sons' wives with you. 17 Bring forth with you every living thing that is with you of all flesh — birds and animals and every creeping thing that creeps on the earth — that they may breed abundantly on the earth, and be fruitful and multiply upon the earth." 18 So Noah went forth, and his sons and his wife and his sons' wives with him. 19 And every beast, every creeping thing, and every bird, everything that moves upon the earth, went forth by families out of the ark.

20 Then Noah built an altar to the Lord, and took of every clean animal and of every clean bird, and offered burnt offerings on the altar. 21 And when the Lord smelled the pleasing odor, the Lord said in his heart, "I will never again curse the ground because of man, for the imagination of man's heart is evil from his youth; neither will I ever again destroy every living crea-

---

D. Noah's Sacrifice (8:13-22)

20. And of every clean bird is an intrusion by RP.

21. I will never again curse the ground because of man, for the imagination of man's heart is evil from his youth is a reversal of the sentence found in 3:17 and can only be an addition by the hand of one who misunderstood the significance of the garden story. It may be noted that in the Hebrew another word is used for **curse** than that in 3:17; and further, that the second clause is strictly a *non sequitur* to the first. With the sentence belongs the initial and—included in **neither**—of vs. 21*b*, which therefore read in J, continuing **said in his heart,** "I will never again destroy, etc."

Noah, **every living thing that is with thee**—creeping things and fowl and cattle and animals of every kind. Recollection goes back to the account of the sixth day of the Creation, on which God made all living creatures, as well as man, and then "saw that it was good." So in this story of life renewed imagination awakens to consider what gratitude is owing to God for all his handiwork—for the fowl of the barn-yard, for the cattle on the farm, for sheep and shepherd dogs and horses and all patient beasts of burden, for the birds of the air, and all the magnificent wild things of the forest and the

plain. Rightly may we sing, in the words of Mrs. C. F. Alexander's hymn,

> All things bright and beautiful,
> All creatures great and small,
> All things wise and wonderful:
> The Lord God made them all.

20-21. God's Long-Suffering.—Few sentences in Genesis reflect thought so naïve as this. God is pleased with the smoke of sacrifice, and he begins to feel more warmly disposed. Like "de Lawd" in *The Green Pastures,* he resigns himself to recognize that the heart of man is just

22 While the earth remaineth, seedtime and harvest, and cold and heat, and summer and winter, and day and night shall not cease.

ture as I have done. 22 While the earth remains, seedtime and harvest, cold and heat, summer and winter, day and night, shall not cease."

22. J² here gives fine expression to the truth he has apprehended—there is nothing similar to this in the Babylonian epic—that the orderly processes of nature are no less a manifestation of the power of God than is the catastrophic, destructive event. An indication of the not-too-happy effect of Baalism on J²'s thinking has been discerned in his melancholy attitude toward sex revealed in the garden story. In this verse such an attitude is to some extent balanced. The sequence of **seedtime and harvest** at least had long been attributed to the baal. Now it is claimed for the Lord, together with the ordered alternation of **cold and heat, summer and winter, day and night.** The Mosaic concept of Yahweh as a God of order has been enriched through contact with Baalism, as has the primitive concept of him as the God of those forces of nature which are

about hopeless. It has been **evil from his youth.** So the only thing to do is to accept the situation and not put any dependence upon the possibility of correcting matters by another flood. There is something to the credit of humanity in the person of Noah, and that perhaps is all God can expect.

As theology, that is childlike; yet there is a strange instinctive wisdom in it, just as there is sometimes in the pictures that children draw. There is the recognition that human sin is incredibly stubborn, that only a patient God could put up with it, that in spite of everything he will not visit upon us our deserts. The vision of what God's infinite compassion actually went out to do in Christ is a long way off, but even so the window of instinctive trust is open in that direction.

22. *The Dependableness of the Seasons.*— Rightly these alternations of nature are reckoned as the beneficent gifts of God. The great aspects of nature are not monotonous, but neither are they capricious. One can know what is coming next. The longest day will be followed by the restful quiet of the dark, and every night can look forward to another dawn. When winter comes the spring and summer will be not far behind. If there is seedtime, there will be harvest too. There are beauty and stimulus in this unfailing rhythm. Life must respond in different ways to the ebb and flow of light and darkness, cold and heat. Robert Louis Stevenson knew the exhilaration of it when he wrote:

To make this earth, our hermitage,
A cheerful and a changeful page,
God's bright and intricate device
Of days and seasons doth suffice.[7]

Thank God, then, that his creation is so various and yet in its essential forces so dependable.

But a larger thought emerges than that which has to do only with the earth. For human

life, in its moral and spiritual aspects, there needs likewise to be a rhythm that swings from one fact toward another and different fact necessary to its fulfillment. Men need to have the double experience of darkness and light, the wintry chill of difficulty and the expansive summer of life released, the sowing of seed on barren ground and the reaping of the harvest. Especially these last. For the dependable rhythm of **seedtime and harvest** is one of God's supreme gifts to human life, as it obviously is to the earth. The trouble is that the value of the first part is not so easy to recognize. If the farmer went by appearances, he might never sow. The earth at the end of winter is empty and barren. To buy seed costs money, and plowing and harrowing, digging, and weeding, are heavy work. Suppose nothing should come of it. The sowing of intellectual and moral seed may also be uninviting. The boy in school and college may be bent on something that gives quicker enjoyment and so waste the springtime of his opportunity in idleness or in frivolous amusement. The seed of vital interest sown then can grow up into rich results: the sowing neglected then can never wholly be recovered. Many who have wasted the early chance will never try to make it up, for the ground of their minds has been left too resistant for seeds of later curiosity to get in.

On the other hand, seedtime for the intellectually alert does not depend on the calendar. Some part of a man's mind can always be ready for new planting. Consider the immense increase of knowledge possible in adult years for men who have the continuing will for the deep plowing of hard study and determined thought. Read the description of Charles Evans Hughes in Bruce Barton, *The Man Nobody Knows.*[8] Recall Thomas Edison, Charles P. Steinmetz, Ernest Bevin, Alfred E. Smith (see

[7] "The House Beautiful."

[8] Indianapolis: Bobbs-Merrill Co., 1925.

9 And God blessed Noah and his sons, and said unto them, Be fruitful, and multiply, and replenish the earth.

2 And the fear of you and the dread of you shall be upon every beast of the earth, and upon every fowl of the air, upon all that moveth *upon* the earth, and upon all the fishes of the sea; into your hand are they delivered.

9 And God blessed Noah and his sons, and said to them, "Be fruitful and multiply, and fill the earth. 2 The fear of you and the dread of you shall be upon every beast of the earth, and upon every bird of the air, upon everything that creeps on the ground and all the fish of the sea; into your hand

---

destructive in their effect, the storm and the volcano. In those days it was perhaps easier for men to see the hand of God in the catastrophic and the sudden than it was in the ordered quiet of the succession of the seasons. Nor can it be claimed that man's realization of God's activity is generally more adequate even in this age. For the tendency is still to take for granted the ordered, stable elements in life, and to say "Thy will be done" only in the face of the catastrophic.

E. The Noachian Laws (9:1-7)

9:1-7. It has been seen that 1:29-30, prescribing a vegetarian diet for man, is a secondary addition to the creation story—whether from the hand of P making use of an earlier version of the story, or from a redactor working on P's narrative. Vss. 1-7, presupposing 1:29-30 as a background, are from the same hand; to be noted is the fact that obedience to the command here given—not to eat blood nor to shed the blood of man—is not made a condition of the covenant following (vss. 8-17). The passage is intended to bring out both the cultural and the religious significance of the Flood in the mind of the priestly writers:

(*a*) It marked the end of the golden age (see Exeg. on 1:29-30) in which men lived in harmony with the beasts.

(*b*) It was the occasion of the prohibition of eating blood, a prohibition which, it is implied, is binding not only on Israel but on all mankind; hence the requirement that it be observed by "proselytes of the gate"; cf. also Acts 15:20; 21:25 where, according

---

his biography by Henry F. Pringle [9]). And if the blessing of springtime should be captured for the mind, so it must be also for the moral nature. "Keep thy heart with all diligence; for out of it are the issues of life" (Prov. 4:23). The responsibility of parents is critical here. The seeds of early suggestion will take root in a child and produce the good grain of sound impulses or the weeds of worse than useless ones. Note here the problem and opportunity of schools and churches for the moral and spiritual education imperatively called for if democracy is to endure. Without right principles individuals grow up irresponsible, and public policy is ignorant and corrupt. What are Christian citizens doing to safeguard our society in this crucial respect? What ways are there of making sure that clean thoughts and wholesome purposes are implanted in boys and girls before the springtime has gone by?

For the harvest inevitably follows the sowing. That is one of the facts of God that is full of blessing, but which, like all blessings abused, can be dark with judgment. The process of

development cannot be reversed and is not likely to be interrupted.

> Sow a Thought, and you reap an Act;
> Sow an Act, and you reap a Habit;
> Sow a Habit, and you reap a Character;
> Sow a Character, and you reap a Destiny. [10]

If we sow weeds, we get weeds; and if we want to get something better we must do more than want it. We must follow in the inner life the discipline which the farmer follows in his dealing with the earth: faith in the possibilities of empty ground, courage to risk good seed even though it is costly, intelligent labor, and the willingness to keep on weeding and working until the harvest is secure. Through it all there shines the truth of God's proclamation that life's processes will be dependable. If unfaithfulness ends in sterility, with equal sureness faithfulness will be blessed. Sobering therefore, but still more inspiring is that promise that **While the earth remaineth, seedtime and harvest . . . shall not cease.**

9:1-7. See Expos. on 1:29.

[9] New York: Vanguard Press, 1927.

[10] Author unknown.

3 Every moving thing that liveth shall be meat for you; even as the green herb have I given you all things.

4 But flesh with the life thereof, *which is* the blood thereof, shall ye not eat.

5 And surely your blood of your lives will I require: at the hand of every beast will I require it, and at the hand of man; at the hand of every man's brother will I require the life of man.

6 Whoso sheddeth man's blood, by man shall his blood be shed: for in the image of God made he man.

7 And you, be ye fruitful, and multiply; bring forth abundantly in the earth, and multiply therein.

8 ¶ And God spake unto Noah, and to his sons with him, saying,

9 And I, behold, I establish my covenant with you, and with your seed after you;

they are delivered. 3 Every moving thing that lives shall be food for you; and as I gave you the green plants, I give you everything. 4 Only you shall not eat flesh with its life, that is, its blood. 5 For your lifeblood I will surely require a reckoning; of every beast I will require it and of man; of every man's brother I will require the life of man. 6 Whoever sheds the blood of man, by man shall his blood be shed; for God made man in his own image. 7 And you, be fruitful and multiply, bring forth abundantly on the earth and multiply in it."

8 Then God said to Noah and to his sons with him, 9 "Behold, I establish my covenant with you and your descendants

to the present context, it is imposed upon all Gentile converts to Christianity. The prohibition is found again in Lev. 7:27; 17:10, 14; 19:26, though it antedates the priestly legislation (cf. Deut. 12:16, 23; 15:23; also Ezek. 33:25). Originally it may have been directed, in part at least, against the superstition that by eating the blood in which is the life of the totem animal the worshiper appropriated the life of the god (for an example of this practice see W. Robertson Smith, *Religion of Semites*, p. 338). In any case the ancient narrative in I Sam. 14:31-34 indicates that the practice was abhorrent and forbidden by Yahwism as early as the rise of the monarchy.

(c) It was the occasion of the divine prohibition of the taking of human life (vs. 5); for human life was sacred since man was made in the image of God (vs. 6). The poetic form of vs. 6 suggests that the author has here incorporated into his narrative an ancient judicial formula which had become proverbial—especially since nothing is said as to who had the power and the responsibility to take vengeance for murder.

The three provisions of these so-called Noachian laws are in a way interdependent. The writer developing here his theory of the end of the golden age (a) was led by association of ideas to the prohibitions of (b) and (c): animals could be killed for food, but the blood must not be eaten; though the life of animals might be taken, human life was sacred.

F. THE COVENANT WITH NOAH (9:8-19)

The covenant is unconditional: no requirement is laid upon man. This raises the question whether, since the Noachian laws are in some sense secondary, the original narrative did not pass from vss. 1, 2a—the command to "be fruitful and multiply, and fill the earth" (vs. 2a)—to vss. 9, 11-17. In this case, the fulfillment of the command of vs. 2a would be the implicit condition of the covenant; vs. 8 will thus be the redactional resumption of the main narrative following the intrusion of vss. 2b-7, and vs. 10 will be an addition by the same hand.

8-11. *The Enduring Universe.*—Here, as in 8:22, there is the promise of God's mercy undergirding the life of men. In primitive times there were recurrent hours of dread. The tremor of an earthquake, a flooding river, a volcano, the **darkness of an eclipse,** seemed more than

dangers that would pass; rather, they were terrifying portents that threatened an end to everything. Men might grovel hopeless in what appeared to be a hostile earth. But here is the Hebrew faith that God the creator is also God the sustainer. Notwithstanding the ignorance

10 And with every living creature that *is* with you, of the fowl, of the cattle, and of every beast of the earth with you; from all that go out of the ark, to every beast of the earth.

11 And I will establish my covenant with you; neither shall all flesh be cut off any more by the waters of a flood; neither shall there any more be a flood to destroy the earth.

12 And God said, This *is* the token of the covenant which I make between me and you, and every living creature that *is* with you, for perpetual generations:

13 I do set my bow in the cloud, and it shall be for a token of a covenant between me and the earth.

after you, 10 and with every living creature that is with you, the birds, the cattle, and every beast of the earth with you, as many as came out of the ark.*l* 11 I establish my covenant with you, that never again shall all flesh be cut off by the waters of a flood, and never again shall there be a flood to destroy the earth." 12 And God said, "This is the sign of the covenant which I make between me and you and every living creature that is with you, for all future generations: 13 I set my bow in the cloud, and it shall be a sign of the covenant between me

l Gk: Heb repeats *every beast of the earth*

13. The symbolism of the **bow**—the Hebrew word is always used of a weapon, never of an arc—goes back to the idea that the lightnings are the Lord's arrows (cf. Pss. 7:13; 18:14; Hab. 3:11), shot from his bow (cf. Ps. 7:12; Hab. 3:9), which is laid aside when his wrath is sated. (The idea of the rainbow as a divine weapon is found in many mythologies; see Skinner, *Genesis,* p. 173.) For P, however, the lightnings are no longer God's arrows shot from the bow. The bow is permanently **in the cloud,** a perpetual reminder to God of his promise. Presumably P, knowing nothing of the laws of refraction and reflection of light, thought that the rainbow had never appeared before the Flood. A possible source of his imagery is the representation of the Babylonian creation myth—

and folly of men—a demonic folly which in an age of atomic power might itself unloose destruction—God's great patience will not destroy.

12-17. *The Rainbow of Hope.*—In the well-known painting by G. F. Watts, Hope is depicted as a woman with a bandage over her eyes, sitting bowed in what looks like an empty universe, trying to make music on one string of a broken lyre. But there is a better and a braver symbol here in Genesis: at the end of catastrophe, a rainbow shining in the sky.

The times come when there is great need of a rainbow. In the twentieth century, with two world wars, civilization has passed through crises almost as dreadful as the Flood. In the aftermath many people, including theologians, are shadowed by black memories and fearful of the clouds that still hang in the sky. If there is any rainbow, they do not see it. But it is only when people do see a rainbow, or something like it, that they can, like Noah, take up life again. Noah lived a long time before the world had ever heard of Christianity, but the old story about him nevertheless can have its parable for Christians.

"To hope" is defined by Webster as "to cherish a desire with expectation," i.e., it is more than a blind and feeble wish. To desire is joined a creative expectation—expectation that can

arouse the energy of the will. To reach what is desired may be difficult, and the trouble is that in dark times men may see nothing but the difficulties until these grow paralyzing. But belief in what lies beyond the barrier of difficulty is the rainbow. In the great old story Noah did not make the rainbow. God put it there. So the ground for hope always is in God; and the man who will most certainly have hope in God for the future is the man who has been conscious of God in the past. Furthermore, the man who is conscious of God, and who therefore can face the present and the future bravely, is the man who has been doing the duty in which he could feel God's help. That was true of Noah. He might not have seen the rainbow or trusted what it meant unless he had learned through obedience that God was carrying him on.

The moral theologians have pointed out that there are two great enemies to a right Christian hope.[1] One enemy is presumption. That is the sin of the man who lightly or impudently assumes that he is good enough as he is, or that if perhaps he might desirably be a little better he can make himself so by his own ability whenever he gets ready. He is blind to

[1] See R. C. Mortimer, *The Elements of Moral Theology* (London: A. & C. Black, 1947).

14 And it shall come to pass, when I bring a cloud over the earth, that the bow shall be seen in the cloud:

15 And I will remember my covenant, which *is* between me and you and every living creature of all flesh; and the waters shall no more become a flood to destroy all flesh.

16 And the bow shall be in the cloud; and I will look upon it, that I may remember the everlasting covenant between God and every living creature of all flesh that *is* upon the earth.

17 And God said unto Noah, This *is* the token of the covenant, which I have established between me and all flesh that *is* upon the earth.

18 ¶ And the sons of Noah, that went forth of the ark, were Shem, and Ham, and Japheth: and Ham *is* the father of Canaan.

and the earth. **14** When I bring clouds over the earth and the bow is seen in the clouds, **15** I will remember my covenant which is between me and you and every living creature of all flesh; and the waters shall never again become a flood to destroy all flesh. **16** When the bow is in the clouds, I will look upon it and remember the everlasting covenant between God and every living creature of all flesh that is upon the earth." **17** God said to Noah, "This is the sign of the covenant which I have established between me and all flesh that is upon the earth."

18 The sons of Noah who went forth from the ark were Shem, Ham, and Japheth.

---

which may even have been preserved in some form in the creation story of J2—that Marduk's bow which he had used against Tiamat was set in the heavens as a constellation.

18-19. These verses are redactional (RP) linking—note especially vs. 18*b* and cf. vs. 22—the foregoing story of the Flood with the tale following.

---

the weakness or corruption in his own nature and to his absolute need of God. It is the menace of this sort of presumption which has made Christian theology so fearful of Pelagianism, and which makes contemporary theology denounce so vehemently the sin of pride and emphasize the tragic frustration of all mere human strength. There is the kind of presumption also which thinks it can take every advantage of the goodness of God; which shrugs its shoulders in the face of moral distinctions, and says, "I may as well be hanged for a sheep as for a lamb"; or, having sinned, postpones amendment because it supposes that there is plenty of time before God's patience will come to an end.

The other and the opposite enemy of hope is despair. Modern theologians who sound so continually the note of tragedy, as though it must be the dominant chord in Christian orthodoxy, may well remember that Thomas Aquinas declared despair to be the deadliest of all sins because it sinks a life in moral torpor. Once begin to doubt that God wills good, or that future good is possible, and the nerve of moral effort may be cut. The medieval theologians wrote much of the sin they called "acedia," the kind of creeping and gradual despair which has been described as a "sad dejection of spirit, in which a man feels out of sorts with God, the world, and himself. It is an acute and universal

boredom. Nothing is any good. Nothing gives any pleasure." [2] The children of Israel complaining in the wilderness (Exod. 17:3) showed what acedia could do; and so does the Christian who "laden with the gifts of God and brought on his way to the promised land of eternal happiness cries in disgust, 'My soul loatheth the means of grace and is sick of this hard and stony pilgrimage.' " [3]

But the great souls are those who yield neither to presumption nor despair, who know that the good they aim at is too difficult for complacent human strength, but not beyond the divine attainment, and who therefore believe in the rainbow because the rainbow has been given by God. That rainbow is not an accident or a fleeting hope. It is a sign of the covenant made by God's eternal goodness that will not fail.

18-27. The Drunkenness of Noah.—Drunkenness is as old as history, and as unpredictable. Noah was a good man; but as the blunt unvarnished truthfulness of the O.T. admits, Noah got drunk. Conceivably he might have got drunk earlier. In the childlike naïvete of the picture in *The Green Pastures* [4] Noah is presented as pleading with "de Lawd" to be allowed to take some whisky with him on the

[2] *Ibid.,* p. 134.
[3] *Ibid.*
[4] Part I, scene 8.

19 These *are* the three sons of Noah: and of them was the whole earth overspread.

Ham was the father of Canaan. **19** These three were the sons of Noah; and from these the whole earth was peopled.

---

ark—two kegs of it. Why two kegs? According to Noah, to put one keg on each side to balance the boat. He is told he can take only one keg and put it in the middle. But a keg of whisky, whether on the side or in the middle, will not keep either an ark or a man on an even keel, and it is certain that if Noah had had a keg of whisky on board, the inhabitants of the ark, man and beast, would have had reason to regret it.

Why did Noah get drunk? Suppose he had done his duty on the ark; why did he act so differently on land? The answer introduces us to one of the deepest reasons for drunkenness. There are many reasons; some of them real and some of them rationalizations of actual reasons which men would rather not admit. But with Noah—and with many since his time whose drunkenness is not only of the body but of the mind and spirit—the root of the matter may be a desire for escape. Noah wanted to escape from what he remembered, and he wanted to escape from what he realized he had to do.

Noah might have pleaded some excuse for the first half of that desire. The weeks in the ark were something a man might well want to forget. To be shut up inside it with a whole menagerie of animals to take care of may have been too much for Noah's nerves. Noah had got out of drab surroundings in body; he wanted to get out of them in mind. That is a natural impulse, but it can take degrading forms of satisfaction. When the Allied troops first entered Paris in 1944 after the occupying Germans had retreated, there were wild orgies in the streets. So were there also in other capitals on the days of the ending of the war. People wanted to wash out the taste of ugly years, and for many of them liquor seemed the quickest way to do it.

But the desire for escape is not only from the past but from the future. Memories of the ark were bad enough, but after all, they were only memories. The more troublesome matter was to make a new adjustment when the ark was left behind. Even hated things can become a habit which a man cannot let go. Remember Dr. Manette, in *The Tale of Two Cities*, clinging to his prison room. Men have hated war, but it has had a sort of concentrated simplicity, like Noah's existence in the ark; and the complexities of peace and of reconstruction may seem to them worse than war. The size of their new opportunity dismays them. In their sober minds they are bound to feel responsible; but they do not want to feel responsible, and their escape is to get drunk.

Individual drunkenness is bad enough, but drunkenness of society is worse. Consider the situation of the victorious nations in World War II. Immediate danger was over. The ark had ridden out the Flood. Tension could be relaxed and discipline let down. The first delusion was to think that everything would be easy; but the long business of rebuilding a civilization emerging from a flood, not of water but of blood, is far from easy. Yet if the hard fact is there, perhaps it can be forgotten. Why not everybody get pleasantly drunk on other ideas and interests?

There is the wine of feeling prosperous. Noah had to get to work and plant his vineyard, but the vineyard grew with gratifying promptness. Some of the peoples in the mid-twentieth-century world have been as Noah would have been if he had come back from the Flood to find his little pet corner of the earth undamaged and his vineyards richer than before. The United States was like that; and the first thing the nation tended to do was to get drunk on indulgence: scrap wartime controls, spend more money, eat more food, buy more luxuries.

There is also the wine of power. Military victory always is intoxicating. To drink of that may inflame pride, breed a false sense of permanent security, dull the mind to the harder tests which no military strength but only moral strength can meet. Danger is ahead

If, drunk with sight of power, we loose
Wild tongues that have not Thee in awe.[5]

Fumes from this heady wine of power may fog a nation's estimate of the picture it presents to others, making it feel, as the man who is drinking feels, so pleased with itself and so important that it is sure it must be universally pleasing and popular. But that drunkenness of power, which at first may be good natured, may have malignant influences poured into its wine so that presently it may become truculent and cruel. Poisoned editorials and news distortions in the "gutter press" have frequently been designed—and in moments of decision will be designed again—to intoxicate the mind of a nation with self-sufficiency.

[5] Rudyard Kipling, "Recessional," from *The Five Nations.* Used by permission of Mrs. George Bambridge; Methuen & Co.; The Macmillan Co., Canada; and Doubleday & Co.

| 20 And Noah began *to be* a husband- man, and he planted a vineyard: | 20 Noah was the first tiller of the soil. |

IX. LAST DAYS OF NOAH (9:20-29)

A. FARMER AND VINEGROWER (9:20)

20. The present Hebrew text of this verse, best rendered "And Noah the husbandman was the first to plant a vineyard" (Gunkel, *Genesis,* p. 78; Skinner, *Genesis,* p. 182), is the result of J2's treatment of a J1 notice that **Noah began to be a husbandman** (cf. 4:26*b* [LXX]; 10:8*b*). This recorded the fulfillment of the prediction made at Noah's birth, "this one shall cause us to settle down" (see Exeg. on 5:29). For J1 Noah was thus the originator of agriculture as the sons of Lamech had been the originators of nomadism, etc. (4:20-22). Presumably J1 had then continued with the present vs. 20*b*, **and he planted a vineyard**—so the Hebrew literally. The rendering of both KJV and RSV is thus the translation of the J1 form of the verse—reached by ignoring the definite article prefixed to *'adhāmāh.*

J2 found it impossible to retain the notice that Noah was the first husbandman because of his garden story, which represented husbandry as man's occupation from the time of his expulsion from the garden until his degradation when Cain was made a fugitive and a wanderer on the earth (cf. 4:12). He therefore dropped it, and in compensation prefixed to J1's statement, **he planted a vineyard**, the present vs. 20*a*, "and Noah the husbandman began"; this demanded that J1's **and he planted** be taken as meaning "to plant" (for the construction see Kautzsch, *Gesenius' Hebrew Grammar,* sec. 120 *d*). J2 thus made explicit what had been implicit in J1: that Noah, the first husbandman, was also the first vinegrower.

Or again, there is the drugged wine of an idle optimism. Why worry with effort if things may somehow work out themselves? After the first explosion of the atomic bomb and the announcement of its terrific meaning the popular mood was shocked into a new realization of the desperate need of safeguarding the world against another war; but the slow disintegration of this impulse has been called by one of the atomic experts a tragedy of errors for which the world may have to pay a heavy price unless measures are taken in time to counteract them. It is no time to be drunk with indulgence, or with the pride of power, or with foolish optimism. The word for our time is "Be sober, be vigilant" (I Pet. 5:8).

20-23. The Man Who Sins, and Those Who Judge Him.—There is another way of considering this incident, which has in it a double suggestion: one is as to a man's lapse, the second is as to the attitude of others toward it.

Noah is described originally as a righteous man, and not without cause. He stood out conspicuous for integrity in a corrupt generation. Moreover, his virtue was not merely in avoidance of prevailing sins but in positive act. In the scene, as the old story paints it, it took stubborn courage to start building the ark and to keep on building it when everybody else thought it was nonsense; and it took resolution to manage that ark and what was in it through the dark weeks of the Flood. Noah had to be

dead in earnest in those days, a man of purpose and a man of prayer. One would have expected that he would prove always admirable. Actually he did not—a fact which has something to say about human life in general. Moral self-mastery is never something that can be taken for granted. Because the fight has gone successfully up to a point is no guarantee against sudden humiliation if a man leaves himself unguarded.

Duly, daily, needs provision be
For keeping the soul's prowess possible.[6]

Moreover, the worst defeats may take place in the area which the man may think is relatively unimportant. When Noah was engrossed in conspicuous responsibilities, with everybody's eyes upon him, there was plenty of stimulus to do his best. To be the one on whom depended in a time of crisis the lives and safety of all those he cared for most called out heroic qualities. But when the immediate danger was over it did not seem to matter so much what he did. Having coped with the immense fact of the Flood outside him, why should he bother much with what might happen from an insignificant thing like a feeling inside? If suddenly he wanted to drink, what business was that of anybody else, and what harm could it do? This inner arena of a man's personal actions,

[6] Robert Browning, "A Death in the Desert."

21 And he drank of the wine, and was drunken; and he was uncovered within his tent.

22 And Ham, the father of Canaan, saw the nakedness of his father, and told his two brethren without.

He planted a vineyard; 21 and he drank of the wine, and became drunk, and lay uncovered in his tent. 22 And Ham, the father of Canaan, saw the nakedness of his father,

---

B. THE CURSE ON CANAAN (9:21-25)

The nucleus of vss. 21-25 is a tale which would seem to have taken its rise among the newly settled nomadic Israelites. It reflects their recoil from the drunkenness, sexual perversion, and filial impiety which confronted them in Palestine, and by implication attributes their own success in subduing the inhabitants of the land to the social disintegration resulting from these practices. It is thus not necessarily a story of the first vinegrower, but rather of any vinegrower who had partaken too freely of the fruits of his labors. This tale J1, with some expurgation as will be seen, attached to the figure of Noah.

This story of the cursing of Canaan is, like the record of the rise of nomadism (4:20-22), fundamentally irreconcilable with the story of the Flood. Here Noah's sons, since they are living with their father, are represented as still unmarried; although the J flood material nowhere mentions them explicitly—its reference is consistently to Noah's "household" (7:1; the enumeration in 7:7, basically J, is as has been seen redactional) —it may reasonably be assumed in the light of P that "household" included the sons and their wives. If it is suggested that in the J document the story came before the Flood, and was shifted to its present position by RP—for no apparent reason—then the difficulty arises that among those present with Noah in the ark was a man under a curse. It may therefore be assumed that this tale is from J1 and, as has already been argued, the flood story from J2.

The primary role of Noah in the J tradition was thus that of the first husbandman and, by implication, the first vinegrower. J2, in his adaptation of the Babylonian Gilgamesh epic to Yahwism, simply identified the hero of the Flood with Noah, the first husbandman. It may be noted that the alternative to such an identification would have been the postponement of the event recorded in 9:21-25 to a much later date, after the earth had been repopulated. This, however, would have made the relative positions of Israel and the Canaanites less fundamental in the nature of things. It would also have involved the necessity of somehow relating the hero of the Flood to the basic genealogical structure which J2 had taken over from J1.

22. Since the curse in vs. 25 is laid not on **Ham** but on **Canaan, Ham, the father of** is redactional harmonization by RP; i.e., in the J narrative Noah's sons were named Shem, Japheth, and Canaan. In P they were Shem, Ham, and Japheth (5:32; 7:13).

---

where his own impulses and appetites move, does often seem thus unimportant; and the same man who has been magnificent in public affairs may fall into ignominy in his private life. Samson was invincible against the Philistines, but he had no defense against Delilah. Antony had an empire in his grasp, but he lost it in the snares of Cleopatra. As Marcus Dods has put it, "Noah is not the only man who has walked uprightly and kept his garment unspotted from the world so long as the eye of man was on him, but who has lain uncovered on his own tent-floor." [7]

Also, the tendency of a man to regard some

[7] *Genesis*, p. 76.

areas of moral decision as unimportant may be due to the complacent assumption that resistance there is unnecessary, because he imagines he is safe at that point anyway. There is no suggestion in the story that Noah had ever been drunk before. He might have thought therefore that whatever might happen to somebody else, nothing of consequence was going to happen to him. A dangerous assumption always! There is a virile self-respect and self-confidence which may rightly belong to a man because of the honor of his previous record, but it can be justified only when he uses it as a shield held to guard him. When Nehemiah said, "Should such a man as I flee?" (Neh. 6:11), he was

23 And Shem and Japheth took a garment, and laid *it* upon both their shoulders, and went backward, and covered the nakedness of their father; and their faces *were* backward, and they saw not their father's nakedness.

24 And Noah awoke from his wine, and knew what his younger son had done unto him.

and told his two brothers outside. 23 Then Shem and Japheth took a garment, laid it upon both their shoulders, and walked backward and covered the nakedness of their father; their faces were turned away, and they did not see their father's nakedness. 24 When Noah awoke from his wine and knew what his youngest son had done

---

The reason for this change would seem to have been P's desire to bring the genealogical material of J2 in ch. 10, in which Mizraim (Egypt) had been represented as a son of Japheth, into accord with another scheme which made Egypt a descendant of Ham (cf. "the tents of Ham," referring to Egypt, in Ps. 78:51; "the land of Ham," Pss. 105:23, 27; 106:22). RP, having accepted P as definitive in this connection (cf. vs. 18), harmonized the two narratives by the insertion of **Ham, the father of** here.

In the primary, popular form of the story there probably occurred here—as shown by the reference in vs. 24 to **what his youngest son had done to him**—an account of an indecent attack by Canaan on his father. This J1 omitted from motives of delicacy.

23. If the names of the other two sons of Noah had been given in J1's version of the tale, they would presumably have occurred at the first mention of **his two brothers** (vs. 22). **Shem and Japheth** are accordingly secondary here—from a hand even later than that of J2 who, as will be seen, mentions them as for the first time in ch. 10; i.e., this story for J1 was primarily a story of Canaan and he did not name these two subordinate characters.

24. Noah is part of J1's adaptation of the popular story in which the drunken father had probably been nameless.

---

using his proven and conscious integrity exactly as it ought to be used, viz., as a fact that held him inflexible against temptation. When Noah said—as in effect he did—"Should such a man as I fall?" he was using his self-assurance recklessly as an alibi for letting in temptation.

A man's worst lapses may come exactly at the point where, after he has put forth great effort, he wants recognition and reward which he thinks he has deserved. Noah may have let himself get plain tired of having everybody assume that it was easy for him to keep on being heroic. Why didn't they all see how much he had borne, and that he had a right to relax? That kind of reaction is dangerously apt to come. Many a man and woman, long conspicuous in the service of others, may begin to be irritated because the family or the community seems to take it all for granted. So they begin to claim for themselves with silent indignation the indulgence that others—so they think—do not have the decency to give. They may nourish the germ of self-pity. Irascibly they are inclined to show that they have the right to do what they choose, and the melancholy result is that they may spoil a great record by conduct not much better than that of the common crowd. It takes a great soul to keep on

being his best when the incentives to a brave life have for the moment lost their old intensity.

Now as to the conclusion of the story which has to do not with Noah but with Noah's sons. Their actions were diametrically different. When one of them came upon Noah in the ignominy of his drunkenness all he did was to go out and spread the tale. But the other two **took a garment, . . . and went backward, and covered the nakedness of their father.** Not only would they prevent others from seeing him at the moment of his discredit; they would try to make it possible for him to think they had not seen it themselves.

So always there are two kinds of attitudes to the failures of those who need to be protected. One is the crude and cruel impulse that snickers at the disclosed weakness in one supposed to be strong, the gossiping satisfaction in knowing and telling that somebody else is no better than ourselves. Or it is the impudent pleasure in belittling and discrediting what had formerly been authority, the quick exploiting of the chance to announce that what had commanded respect in an older generation is really not entitled to any respect at all. But loyalty and truth know better. They see and judge what may be a single failure in the light of the whole long

25 And he said, Cursed *be* Canaan; a servant of servants shall he be unto his brethren.

26 And he said, Blessed *be* the LORD God of Shem; and Canaan shall be his servant.

to him, 25 he said,
"Cursed be Canaan;
    a slave of slaves shall he be to his brothers."
26 He also said,
"Blessed by the LORD my God be Shem;[m]
    and let Canaan be his slave.

[m] Or *blessed be the* LORD, *the God of Shem*

---

25. The words purport to explain the success of Israel in subduing the Canaanites, whose eponymous ancestor had been cursed for an act of filial impiety. They may also reflect the free nomad's contempt for what seemed to him to be their subservient acceptance of a social organization necessarily more hierarchical than that which obtained in the desert. Vs. 25—containing the point of the matter—concluded the story as it left the hand of J[1].

C. Blessing of Shem and Japheth (9:26-27)

26. This verse, the secondary character of which is indicated by the unnecessary introduction, **he also said,** was added by a later writer who felt not only that some recognition should be made of the piety of **Shem** but also that there should be some positive accounting for the success of Israel, his supposed descendants (cf. 10:21, 25 J[2]), represented in vs. 25 as a mere consequence of Canaanite viciousness.

---

affirmative fact. They understand, forgive, and forget. "Charity shall cover the multitude of sins" (I Pet. 4:8).

From Genesis one's thought widens out to consider the message of the whole Bible concerning the forgiveness of sin. The first reaction to another's fault ought to be not cruel condemnation but self-examination and humility; "considering thyself, lest thou also be tempted" (Gal. 6:1).

The good man will not consider only his own possible weakness; he will identify himself with the weakness he sees, and try to help. Remember Barnabas, "the son of consolation." Reflect upon the compassion to which Paul was moved. "My heart's desire and prayer to God for Israel is, that they might be saved. . . . I could wish that myself were accursed . . . for my brethren" (Rom. 10:1; 9:3). Only that sort of sympathy which goes and makes itself at one with the guilty can be redeeming. Among the prophets the greatest were those who did more than condemn. See the faces in Sargent's frieze in the Boston Public Library. Some of the prophets there depicted stood at a distance to pronounce their woes; others of them drew near with the yearning that could melt men's hearts. That is why Hosea was greater than Amos, and the message of Isaiah of the Exile more eternal than the denunciations of Elijah.

So one is led to contemplate the divine forgiveness. It does not blunt the edge of truth. The evil of sin is never evaded or palliated. It is made all the more shameful as it is set against the purity of God's purpose which the sinner has defiled; but through it all there is his everlasting pity. That pity, and God's ultimate forgiveness, are summed up in the inexhaustible meaning of the Cross. "While we were yet sinners"—and because we were sinners, and to keep us from remaining sinners— "Christ died for us" (Rom. 5:8).

25. *Race Prejudice.*—Here is an early expression of race prejudice. Through a long period of history the people of Israel hated the Canaanites. In this story of Noah and his sons is an explanation devised to justify it. But the fact was older and deeper than the story. Popular tradition is rationalizing here what was instinctive and not always rational. It is an ironic fact that this Jewish expression of hatred for another people has been reversed in later centuries, so that the Jews themselves have been the victims of race prejudice and persecution. Unregenerate human impulses may have calamitous conclusions.

What are the reasons for race prejudice? On the first level of instinct there is the dislike of difference. The animal herd is suspicious of any individual who does not have the herd traits. The human herd is suspicious of the stranger. To be different is to be suspect. We often feel toward one another as the old Quaker said to his friend, "All the world is peculiar except thee and me, and sometimes I think thee is a little peculiar." Race prejudice is accentuated by a feeling of superiority. The race that plumes itself on its own excellence,

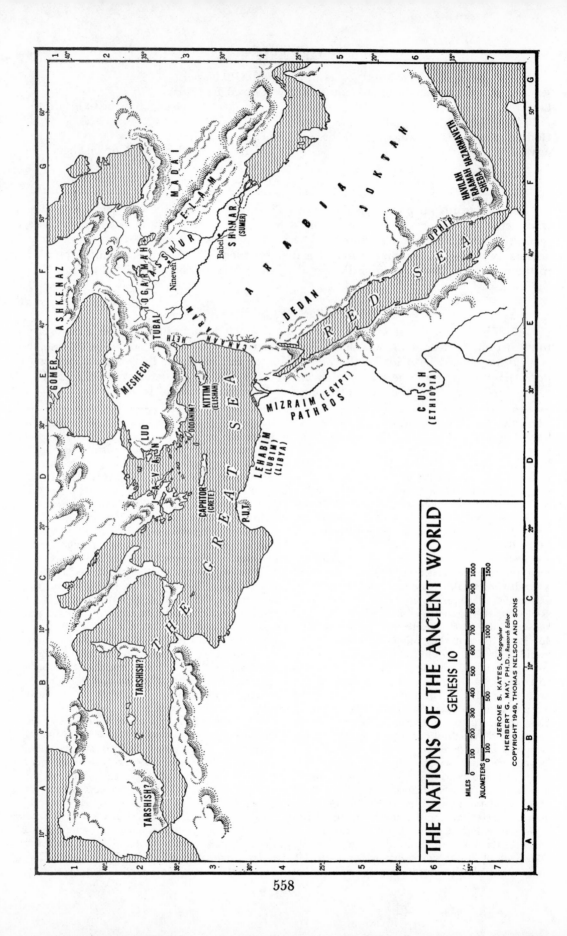

THE NATIONS OF THE ANCIENT WORLD

GENESIS 10

MILES 0 100 200 300 400 500 600 700 800 900 1000

KILOMETERS 0 100 500 1000 1500

JEROME S. KATES, Cartographer
HERBERT G. MAY, PH.D., Research Editor
COPYRIGHT 1949, THOMAS NELSON AND SONS

27 God shall enlarge Japheth, and he shall dwell in the tents of Shem; and Canaan shall be his servant.	27 God enlarge Japheth,
	    and let him dwell in the tents of Shem;
	    and let Canaan be his slave."

28 ¶ And Noah lived after the flood three hundred and fifty years.	28 After the flood Noah lived three hundred and fifty years. 29 All the days of Noah were nine hundred and fifty years; and he died.
29 And all the days of Noah were nine hundred and fifty years: and he died.	
10 Now these *are* the generations of the sons of Noah; Shem, Ham, and Japheth: and unto them were sons born after the flood.	**10** These are the generations of the sons of Noah, Shem, Ham, and Japheth; sons were born to them after the flood.

27. The continuation of vs. 26, also secondary. **Japheth** in the J[2] tradition (see below on ch. 10) was the ancestor, and so the representative of Cush and Mizraim; Cush here meaning not Ethiopia, but *Kaššû*, the Kassites who were from the seventeenth to the middle of the twelfth century the overlords of Babylonia (cf. Gunkel, *Genesis*, p. 89). Just as Israel continued to be known to the Assyrians as the land of the house of Omri long after the fall of the Omri dynasty, so Cush may well have continued to be the popular designation in Israel of the great power to the east for some time after its fall. So Japheth here represents the empires flanking Israel on either side; and the words **let him dwell in the tents of Shem** are perhaps best understood as reflecting the—doubtless negative—friendship shown by them to Israel before Assyria renewed its march westward in the ninth century.

D. Noah's Death (9:28-29)

28-29. These verses are the conclusion of the P story of Noah.

X. Descendants of Noah (10:1-32)

The material in this chapter is the result of the conflation of the tables of the descendants of Noah as they appeared in the final forms of the J and P documents

real or supposed, is apt to despise others. Superiority in opportunity and privilege may lead to the unconscious hypocrisy of believing that one has been born to dominate. Kipling's "Take Up the White Man's Burden" became a cloak of self-satisfied imperialism. Note the Nazi philosophy of- the master race. Race prejudice may be at its worst when religion enters into it, for fanaticism can become "sanctified." Consider the campaigns of Islam with the alternative of conversion or the sword. Consider the religious wars in Europe, and particularly in France, with the Massacre of St. Bartholomew and the expulsion of the Huguenots. Note how hostility toward Russia has been inflamed by the interests of the Vatican.

The O.T. describes people as they actually are, including the Jewish people. In Judges and I Samuel we can see the kind of race passion of which the Jews, like other peoples, can be guilty. But the great significance of the O.T. is the reverse of this. Its glory is not in the alloy of human passions but in the gold of a divine perception. Its ultimate message is of the universal purpose of God which destroys race pride and passion. Hitler recognized the con-tradition the O.T. presented to his new paganism of race and blood and soil, so he banned the O.T. and tried to destroy Judaism.

The supreme message of the whole Bible, O.T. and N.T., is the universality of human destiny. It may be outlined and considered as follows: the recognition of the rights of strangers, and mercy and compassion to the weak, as expressed in Deuteronomy; the accountability of all nations equally to the one moral judgment of God as expressed in the prophets and summed up in such passages as Amos 1:1–3:2; the recognition of Israel's responsibility to the Gentiles and to the kinship of all humanity as expressed in parts of the book of Isaiah, in the book of Ruth, and in the book of Jonah; finally, the culmination in the teaching of Jesus as represented in his parable of the good Samaritan, in his declaration that men should come from the east, the west, the north, and the south and sit down with Abraham, Isaac, and Jacob in the kingdom of God, and in his death as a sacrifice for the sins of all men and his risen life as redemption offered to all.

10:1-32. See Expos. on 5:1-32.

2 The sons of Japheth; Gomer, and Magog, and Madai, and Javan, and Tubal, and Meshech, and Tiras.

3 And the sons of Gomer; Ashkenaz, and Riphath, and Togarmah.

4 And the sons of Javan; Elishah, and Tarshish, Kittim, and Dodanim.

5 By these were the isles of the Gentiles divided in their lands; every one after his tongue, after their families, in their nations.

6 ¶ And the sons of Ham; Cush, and Mizraim, and Phut, and Canaan.

7 And the sons of Cush; Seba, and Havilah, and Sabtah, and Raamah and Sabtecha: and the sons of Raamah; Sheba, and Dedan.

8 And Cush begat Nimrod: he began to be a mighty one in the earth.

2 The sons of Japheth: Gomer, Magog, Madai, Javan, Tubal, Meshech, and Tiras. 3 The sons of Gomer: Ash'kenaz, Riphath, and Togar'mah. 4 The sons of Javan: Elis'hah, Tarshish, Kittim, and Do'danim. 5 From these the coastland peoples spread. These are the sons of Japheth[n] in their lands, each with his own language, by their families, in their nations.

6 The sons of Ham: Cush, Egypt, Put, and Canaan. 7 The sons of Cush: Se'ba, Hav'i-lah, Sabtah, Ra'amah, and Sab'teca. The sons of Ra'amah: Sheba and Dedan. 8 Cush became the father of Nimrod; he was the first on earth to be a mighty man.

[n] Supplied from verses 20, 31. Heb lacks *These are the sons of Japheth*

---

respectively. Because of the disagreement of the two documents as to the names of the sons of Noah—Shem, Japheth, and Canaan in J; Shem, Ham, and Japheth in P—the redactor, RP, who conflated the traditions was compelled to make certain adaptations. The P material is contained with some later additions in vss. 1a, 2-7, 20, 22-23, 31-32.

The primary form of the J tradition appears to have been: "And Canaan became the father of Sidon his first-born, and Heth. And to Japheth, the elder brother of Canaan, to him also were born Cush and Mizraim. And Cush became the father of Nimrod; he began to be a mighty one in the earth. The beginning of his kingdom was Babel. And to Shem, the elder brother of Japheth, to him also was born Eber. To Eber were born two sons: the name of one was Peleg (for in his days the earth was divided), and his brother's name was Joktan." (For details of the analysis see Cuthbert A. Simpson, *The Early Traditions of Israel* [Oxford: Basil Blackwell, 1948], pp. 65-67.)

The identification of Japheth as the elder brother of Canaan and of Shem as the elder brother of Japheth indicates that this was the first mention of them by name in the J document (cf. Exeg. on 9:23).

The table is from J2. It may be noted that it traces back to the sons of Noah the origin not only of the Hebrews, the descendants of Eber, but that of the nonnomadic peoples affecting the fortunes of Palestine. The nomad Aramaeans were, according to the J document, of the same stock as Abraham, Laban being his nephew.

The interest underlying vs. 8, which tells of the origin of the *gibbôrîm*, the tyrants, suggests that for this verse J2 was dependent on J1. As to how far he was dependent on other traditions for the rest of the material it is impossible to say. In any case the scheme is obviously artificial since the Sidonians and the Hittites were certainly not offshoots of the Canaanites (cf. vs. 15), nor were the Babylonians (see Exeg. on 9:27) and the Egyptians derived immediately from a common stock.

J2 used this material to provide a background of world history, however rudimentary, for the history of Israel, which was to begin with Abraham; i.e., he saw that Israel made no sense in isolation. The tables are thus evidence of an incipient universalism which was to develop in the succeeding centuries until it issued in the statement of Israel's vocation as a light to lighten the Gentiles (cf. Isa. 49:6).

J2's simple table of nations was expanded and elaborated in the years that followed, to make it a supposedly more inclusive record of the origins of the various nations with which Israel came into contact. It was thoroughly revised by P, and finally the two lists were conflated by RP to produce the present tables.

9 He was a mighty hunter before the LORD: wherefore it is said, Even as Nimrod the mighty hunter before the LORD.

10 And the beginning of his kingdom was Babel, and Erech, and Accad, and Calneh, in the land of Shinar.

11 Out of that land went forth Asshur, and builded Nineveh, and the city Rehoboth, and Calah,

12 And Resen between Nineveh and Calah: the same *is* a great city.

13 And Mizraim begat Ludim, and Anamim, and Lehabim, and Naphtuhim,

14 And Pathrusim, and Casluhim, (out of whom came Philistim,) and Caphtorim.

15 ¶ And Canaan begat Sidon his firstborn, and Heth,

16 And the Jebusite, and the Amorite, and the Girgasite,

17 And the Hivite, and the Arkite, and the Sinite,

18 And the Arvadite, and the Zemarite, and the Hamathite: and afterward were the families of the Canaanites spread abroad.

19 And the border of the Canaanites was from Sidon, as thou comest to Gerar, unto Gaza; as thou goest unto Sodom, and Gomorrah, and Admah, and Zeboim, even unto Lasha.

20 These *are* the sons of Ham, after their families, after their tongues, in their countries, *and* in their nations.

21 ¶ Unto Shem also, the father of all the children of Eber, the brother of Japheth the elder, even to him were *children* born.

22 The children of Shem; Elam, and Asshur, and Arphaxad, and Lud, and Aram.

23 And the children of Aram; Uz, and Hul, and Gether, and Mash.

24 And Arphaxad begat Salah; and Salah begat Eber.

25 And unto Eber were born two sons: the name of one *was* Peleg; for in his days was the earth divided; and his brother's name *was* Joktan.

9 He was a mighty hunter before the LORD; therefore it is said, "Like Nimrod a mighty hunter before the LORD." 10 The beginning of his kingdom was Babel, Erech, and Accad, all of them in the land of Shinar. 11 From that land he went into Assyria, and built Nin'eveh, Reho'both-Ir, Calah, and 12 Resen between Nin'eveh and Calah; that is the great city. 13 Egypt became the father of Ludim, An'amim, Leha'bim, Naphtu'him, 14 Pathru'sim, Caslu'him (whence came the Philistines), and Caph'torim.

15 Canaan became the father of Sidon his first-born, and Heth, 16 and the Jeb'usites, the Amorites, the Gir'gashites, 17 the Hivites, the Arkites, the Sinites, 18 the Ar'vadites, the Zem'arites, and the Ha'mathites. Afterward the families of the Canaanites spread abroad. 19 And the territory of the Canaanites extended from Sidon, in the direction of Gerar, as far as Gaza, and in the direction of Sodom, Gomor'rah, Admah, and Zeboi'im, as far as Lasha. 20 These are the sons of Ham, by their families, their languages, their lands, and their nations.

21 To Shem also, the father of all the children of Eber, the elder brother of Japheth, children were born. 22 The sons of Shem: Elam, Asshur, Arpach'shad, Lud, and Aram. 23 The sons of Aram: Uz, Hul, Gether, and Mash. 24 Arpach'shad became the father of Shelah; and Shelah became the father of Eber. 25 To Eber were born two sons: the name of the one was Peleg,[o] for in his days the earth was divided, and

[o] That is *Division*

10:9. **Nimrod** is one of the two figures in the lists of which anything concrete is recorded. The notice that he was the first tyrant (vs. 8) is, as has been seen, from J[1]. To this J[2] added the statement (vs. 10), based perhaps on some floating tradition, that he was the founder of **Babel**, viz., Babylon. The rest of vs. 10 is later than J[2]. A subsequent hand recorded that **he was a mighty hunter before the LORD**. Skinner, referring to Delitzsch, remarks that "the union of a passion for the chase with warlike prowess makes

26 And Joktan begat Almodad, and She-leph, and Hazarmaveth, and Jerah,

27 And Hadoram, and Uzal, and Diklah,

28 And Obal, and Abimael, and Sheba,

29 And Ophir, and Havilah, and Jobab: all these *were* the sons of Joktan.

30 And their dwelling was from Mesha, as thou goest unto Sephar, a mount of the east.

31 These *are* the sons of Shem, after their families, after their tongues, in their lands, after their nations.

32 These *are* the families of the sons of Noah, after their generations, in their nations: and by these were the nations divided in the earth after the flood.

11 And the whole earth was of one language, and of one speech.

2 And it came to pass, as they journeyed from the east, that they found a plain in the land of Shinar; and they dwelt there.

---

his brother's name was Joktan. 26 Joktan became the father of Almo'dad, Sheleph, Hazarma'veth, Jerah, 27 Hador'am, Uzal, Diklah, 28 Obal, Abim'a-el, Sheba, 29 Ophir, Hav'i-lah, and Jobab; all these were the sons of Joktan. 30 The territory in which they lived extended from Mesha in the direction of Sephar to the hill country of the east. 31 These are the sons of Shem, by their families, their languages, their lands, and their nations.

32 These are the families of the sons of Noah, according to their genealogies, in their nations; and from these the nations spread abroad on the earth after the flood.

11 Now the whole earth had one language and few words. 2 And as men migrated in the east, they found a plain in

---

Nimrod a true prototype of the Assyrian monarchs" (*Genesis*, p. 208). Skinner also (p. 209) summarizes the suggestions which have been made as to the original of the biblical Nimrod.

XI. The Confusion of Tongues (11:1-9)

The nucleus of this story is a tale by J[1], telling how **the children of men** (vs. 5), still undivided into peoples, decided to build a tower with its top in the heavens, to make a name for themselves (vs. 4). For this act of arrogance **the Lord scattered them abroad . . . over the face of all the earth** (vs. 8). Gunkel (*Genesis*, pp. 92-94; cf. Skinner, *Genesis*, pp. 223-24) accounts for the unevennesses in the present form of the story by postulating, here as elsewhere, two independent strands in the J narrative.

The interest in origins—here the origin of diverse peoples and by implication of diverse languages—suggests that the author is J[1]. Support for this suggestion is furnished by the fact that J[2], having already accounted for the diversity of peoples in the genealogical material in ch. 10, would have no need of this tale. He retained it simply because it was already in the document lying before him.

With this story J[1] brought the introductory part of his narrative to a close, to take up, with Abraham, the history of Israel—one of the diverse peoples whose origin he had accounted for.

11:1-9. The Sin of Pride.—Men may fail to find the right answer to some question that intrigues their minds, and yet in this process be led unwittingly into the presence of some great truth that concerns their souls. The early Hebrews, like all other early peoples and like children in every generation, have wanted to know how the world began. Genesis opened with such questions: how were the heavens made, and the earth and the sea, and who made them; and who made man, and if he was made to be good, why then is he so often evil? Here in ch. 11 is another reflection of old

wondering. How did it happen that there are so many languages that peoples cannot understand each other? The account of the Tower of Babel is the story-answer.

It is a naïve answer. The facts were not so simple. Differences of language developed over long periods of time as various groups of the human race went through the separate phases of their existence. They did not come all in a moment by God's descending from the sky to confound them by his immediate rebuke. But back of the ancient story there is a profound insight. Differences of language are a source of

This J¹ material is now preserved in vss. 4a, 5 (omitting in both **a city, and**), 6, 8a. Vs. 4a is obviously not the original beginning of the tale. This has been dropped by J² who, having prepared for the tale by the note regarding Peleg in 10:25 that "in his days the earth was divided," substituted for it vs. 2, making the actors the early descendants of Noah and locating the tower in **a plain in the land of Shinar** which they had reached as they "migrated" from the east—**from the east** (KJV) is at least as valid a rendering as **in the east** (RSV), if indeed it is not preferable (cf. Skinner, *Genesis*, p. 225).

This, it may be noted, presupposes that J² had recorded that Noah's ark had come to rest on a mountain in the east (cf. Gunkel, *Genesis*, pp. 95-96). This part of the J flood story was, as has been seen, suppressed by RP in favor of the P representation that "the ark came to rest upon the mountains of Ararat" (8:4), which are not east but north of Palestine.

Whence J¹ derived the tale it is difficult to say. It would seem, however, that the problem of diverse peoples and languages would have been of more interest to the inhabitants of Palestine than to the nomad, whom it affected more remotely. It may accordingly be inferred that J¹ found the myth current in Palestine and incorporated it, possibly in a shortened form (see below), into his narrative, changing the name of the deity originally appearing therein to the Lord.

It is unlikely however that a myth representing the building of a ziggurat—undoubtedly the original of the tower—as a defiance of God took its rise among the Babylonians themselves. It is more probable that some ruined or never-finished tower was explained as the result of divine action against human arrogance, perhaps by nomads who later moved to Palestine, where over the years they came to associate it with the confusion of tongues, possibly because of the similarity between Babel, the site of the ruin, and *bālal*, "to confuse."

If this is the case, then some light is thrown upon the later elaboration which the J story received, making it the account of not only the building of a tower but also of a city (cf. vss. 4-5) which was then called Babel because of the babble of tongues which had broken out there when the Lord confused men's speech (vs. 9). This may be dependent on certain features of the still-current myth which J¹—who would have had no particular interest in Babylon—and J² after him had ignored; cf. the intrusion into the J² garden story of fragments from the Eden saga (3:20-22) which, it may be noted, contains the same motif of divine action against human arrogance.

11:1. This is from RP, linking the tale following to the material in ch. 10.

2. Men (RSV) is not in the Hebrew, but **they** (KJV), i.e., the descendants of Noah listed in the J² material in ch. 10. **The land of Shinar** is Babylonia; the **plain** is the

---

trouble, the symbol and accentuation of division, strangeness, suspicions, and hostility. And by profound insight, again, this fact was linked with the overweening spirit by which men are always trying to make themselves bigger than they are. In other words, one of the primary roots of trouble in human history is human pride. The nomads had seen the ziggurats of great Babylon. They had seen also ruined towers. Hence came the symbolism of the story of Babel, where men said, **Let us build us a city, and a tower, whose top may reach unto heaven;** and they began to build out of bricks and slime. That is a picture of what people have always been trying to do. They have thought that by their own devices they could reach the pinnacle of coveted importance and sit triumphantly on top of their world.

The Egyptian Pharaohs thought they could

do that. They were thirsty for everlasting fame and so they carved gigantic statues of themselves, raised the obelisks which were chiseled with the record of their honors, and harnessed innumerable slaves to the task of building the colossal pyramids that should preserve their bodies forever and lift their glory to the stars. But the tombs are long since rifled, and the pyramids stand among the empty sands of a civilization that slowly drifted to decay.

Greece sought to achieve its eminence with building blocks of a different kind. It would make an earthly heaven out of knowledge. If men knew enough and had a taste for beauty sufficiently exalted, then that would be all that was required to make life complete; and the gods could be relegated to the world of pretty myths. But "the glory that was Greece" is a memory now, not a potent fact.

3 And they said one to another, Go to, let us make brick, and burn them thoroughly. And they had brick for stone, and slime had they for mortar.

4 And they said, Go to, let us build us a city, and a tower, whose top *may reach* unto heaven; and let us make us a name, lest we be scattered abroad upon the face of the whole earth.

5 And the LORD came down to see the city and the tower, which the children of men builded.

6 And the LORD said, Behold, the people *is* one, and they have all one language; and this they begin to do: and now nothing will be restrained from them, which they have imagined to do.

7 Go to, let us go down, and there confound their language, that they may not understand one another's speech.

the land of Shinar and settled there. 3 And they said to one another, "Come, let us make bricks, and burn them thoroughly." And they had brick for stone, and bitumen for mortar. 4 Then they said, "Come, let us build ourselves a city, and a tower with its top in the heavens, and let us make a name for ourselves, lest we be scattered abroad upon the face of the whole earth." 5 And the LORD came down to see the city and the tower, which the sons of men had built. 6 And the LORD said, "Behold, they are one people, and they have all one language; and this is only the beginning of what they will do; and nothing that they propose to do will now be impossible for them. 7 Come, let us go down, and there confuse their language, that they may not understand

---

Tigris-Euphrates Valley. In the J narrative it was to the east of this that the ark had come to rest.

3. The representation that the men first made **bricks** and then cast about for a use to put them to is naïve in the extreme—too naïve for J[2], who in any case would not have been guilty of placing the notice here. It is probable that the narrative was first glossed with vs. 3b—a learned note by one who knew there was no building stone in Babylonia— and when this found its way into the text vs. 3a was prefixed to it.

4. A city, and—here and in vs. 5—is an intrusion from the hand of the writer who added to the tale the etymology of Babylon in vs. 9. The ziggurat, the most conspicuous feature of a Babylonian sanctuary, is described by Skinner as "a huge pyramidal tower rising, often in 7 terraces, from the centre of the temple-area, and crowned with a shrine at the top. . . . These structures appear to have embodied a half-cosmical, half-religious symbolism: the 7 stories represented the 7 planetary deities as mediators between heaven and earth; the ascent of the tower was a meritorious approach to the gods; and the summit was regarded as the entrance to heaven." (*Genesis*, p. 226.)

The military empires all down the ages have built with ruder and more defiant stuff. Their bricks were veined with iron. Assyria, Babylon, Persia, Rome, all set themselves in the pride of power to build on earth a structure that would match whatever authority there might be in the sky. If there was a throne of God, they would climb up and occupy it. Other peoples of the modern world have followed, and will yet be tempted to follow, their example. Immense material resources, scientific inventiveness, the mobilization of unprecedented military might, economic mastery, the control of atomic energy—are not these at last the bricks out of which the tower may be built that will enable a nation to supplant the sovereignty of God? "The Third Reich will last for a thousand years"; "There will always be an England"; "America, God's country"—is there not in all

of these an element of that same blind pride of power which became obsessed with building the tower that ultimately must be confounded? The picture of the Tower of Babel still confronts us with its prophecy.

Crude in form as the legend is, it embodies a truth of permanent validity—the futility and emptiness of human effort divorced from the acknowledgment and service of God: hæc perpetua mundi dementia est, neglecto cœlo immortalitatem quærere in terra, ubi nihil est non caducum et evanidum (Calv.).[7]

According to the story in Genesis, the punishment for the attempted building of the tower was the destruction of human solidarity. There-

[7] John Skinner, *A Critical and Exegetical Commentary on Genesis* (New York: Charles Scribner's Sons, 1910; "International Critical Commentary"), pp. 229-30.

8 So the LORD scattered them abroad from thence upon the face of all the earth: and they left off to build the city.

9 Therefore is the name of it called Babel; because the LORD did there confound the language of all the earth: and from thence did the LORD scatter them abroad upon the face of all the earth.

10 ¶ These *are* the generations of Shem: Shem *was* a hundred years old, and begat Arphaxad two years after the flood:

11 And Shem lived after he begat Arphaxad five hundred years, and begat sons and daughters.

12 And Arphaxad lived five and thirty years, and begat Salah:

one another's speech." 8 So the LORD scattered them abroad from there over the face of all the earth, and they left off building the city. 9 Therefore its name was called Babel, because there the LORD confused*ᵖ* the language of all the earth; and from there the LORD scattered them abroad over the face of all the earth.

10 These are the descendants of Shem. When Shem was a hundred years old, he became the father of Arpach'shad two years after the flood; 11 and Shem lived after the birth of Arpach'shad five hundred years, and had other sons and daughters.

12 When Arpach'shad had lived thirty-five years, he became the father of Shelah;

ᵖ Compare Heb *balal*, confuse

---

9. The name **Babel**=Babylon—a transliteration of the Hebrew rendering of *Bāb-ili,* "gate of God"—is here fancifully derived from the polpal of *bālal,* "to mix," "to confuse," a form not found in Hebrew but occurring in Aramaic and Arabic. The verse, together with vs. 8*b,* is from a hand later than J²; the fact that the concluding sentence repeats vs. 8*a* indicates its secondary character.

XII. DESCENDANTS OF SHEM (11:10-26)

10-26. This material is from P, who, having listed the descendants of the three sons of Noah (ch. 10), now reverts to the line of Shem, the ancestor of Abraham, and traces

---

fore is the name of it called Babel; because the LORD did there confound the language of all the earth: and from thence did the LORD scatter them abroad upon the face of all the earth. Never mind if that is only a childlike explanation of the physical differences in languages and in racial life. More important is the fact that here is a true suggestion of the reason for that moral and spiritual confusion of tongues which now afflicts the earth. "They do not speak our language" is a saying that implies something much more critical than difference in syntax and vocabulary; it implies a sense of alienation in thought, a gulf cut across the whole area of instinctive feelings on which men and nations need to stand on common ground.

Consider the need in our imperiled world for understanding: through the spread of accurate and sympathetic knowledge in each nation of the human needs and aspirations in another; through suppression of the half-truths or whole lies by which other peoples and governments are misrepresented in irresponsible newspapers by columnists or commentators; through increase in the international cooperation which prevents epidemic diseases and promotes universal health, encourages economic development and unhindered trade, and

builds up gradually the mutual confidence which is the only effective antidote to war. Above all, reflect upon the fact that our world can be brought from its confusion into closer and more confident life only by a spiritual humility which will stop men from trusting in their towers of Babel. God's truth and God's judgment are still on high, and no human pride or power can climb above them or bring them down. There are eternal moral principles which cannot be defied. That is what all nations alike must learn if there is to be a human family instead of a planetary failure. There is a common language of the human spirit that will be recovered only when men trust less in the bricks of their own building and turn more toward God. And if that hope seems distant because some nations in theory are atheistic, then there is the more need that those nations which claim to be Christian should show what better life a reverence for God can in fact create.

10-26. *The Generations of Shem.*—From the story of Babel, with its picture of the folly and blunder of men, the compilers of Genesis have recourse again to the record of the priestly writers and their genealogy of a part of the human family which God had destined for better things (see Expos. on 5:1-32).

13 And Arphaxad lived after he begat Salah four hundred and three years, and begat sons and daughters.

14 And Salah lived thirty years, and begat Eber:

15 And Salah lived after he begat Eber four hundred and three years, and begat sons and daughters.

16 And Eber lived four and thirty years, and begat Peleg:

17 And Eber lived after he begat Peleg four hundred and thirty years, and begat sons and daughters.

18 And Peleg lived thirty years, and begat Reu:

19 And Peleg lived after he begat Reu two hundred and nine years, and begat sons and daughters.

20 And Reu lived two and thirty years, and begat Serug:

21 And Reu lived after he begat Serug two hundred and seven years, and begat sons and daughters.

22 And Serug lived thirty years, and begat Nahor:

23 And Serug lived after he begat Nahor two hundred years, and begat sons and daughters.

24 And Nahor lived nine and twenty years, and begat Terah:

25 And Nahor lived after he begat Terah a hundred and nineteen years, and begat sons and daughters.

26 And Terah lived seventy years, and begat Abram, Nahor, and Haran.

13 and Ar-pachsh'ad lived after the birth of Shelah four hundred and three years, and had other sons and daughters.

14 When Shelah had lived thirty years, he became the father of Eber; 15 and Shelah lived after the birth of Eber four hundred and three years, and had other sons and daughters.

16 When Eber had lived thirty-four years, he became the father of Peleg; 17 and Eber lived after the birth of Peleg four hundred and thirty years, and had other sons and daughters.

18 When Peleg had lived thirty years, he became the father of Re'u; 19 and Peleg lived after the birth of Re'u two hundred and nine years, and had other sons and daughters.

20 When Re'u had lived thirty-two years, he became the father of Serug; 21 and Re'u lived after the birth of Serug two hundred and seven years, and had other sons and daughters.

22 When Serug had lived thirty years, he became the father of Nahor; 23 and Serug lived after the birth of Nahor two hundred years, and had other sons and daughters.

24 When Nahor had lived twenty-nine years, he became the father of Terah; 25 and Nahor lived after the birth of Terah a hundred and nineteen years, and had other sons and daughters.

26 When Terah had lived seventy years, he became the father of Abram, Nahor, and Haran.

---

his descendants through eight generations to Terah, Abraham's father. Whence P derived these names it is impossible to say; some are geographical. The figures in the Samar., LXX, and the Book of Jubilees are not the same as those in the M.T.

---

26. *The Character of Abraham.*—Terah . . . begat Abram. Thus into a long list of inconsequential names there is slipped, as it were indifferently, the name of one who was destined to be great. So it may often be. In the endless succession of human births one birth may seem at first not to be distinguished from another. In circumstance and appearance it is like the rest. But the mysterious and initially hidden qualities of the spirit will presently lift the one personality above the crowd. Abraham (for the two forms of the name, Abram and Abraham, see Exeg. on 11:29; 17:5) would become one of the supreme figures in religious history. The people of Israel regarded him as the father of

their race, and the more proudly because of the manner of man he was described as having been.

He was not perfect. None of those portrayed in Genesis were. Once, at least, Abraham was skeptical of God (17:17). Also there is told of him a discreditable incident (12:11-20). But these facts did not lessen the inspiration that men drew from Abraham; they made his total example seem more real and relevant because not separated from ordinary human nature by some unbridgeable gulf. The significance of this was expressed in unusual fashion by a greathearted Christian who has been a city missionary of his church. With a happy devotion he goes

27 ¶ Now these *are* the generations of Terah: Terah begat Abram, Nahor, and Haran; and Haran begat Lot.

28 And Haran died before his father Terah in the land of his nativity, in Ur of the Chaldees.

27 Now these are the descendants of Terah. Terah was the father of Abram, Nahor, and Haran; and Haran was the father of Lot. 28 Haran died before his father Terah in the land of his birth, in

---

XIII. GENEALOGY OF ABRAHAM (11:27-32)

This section is a conflation of P and J. The P material, vss. 27, 31-32, is the conclusion of the genealogy in vss. 10-26. The J material, vss. 28-30, is the conclusion of a genealogy, the beginning of which has been suppressed by RP in favor of vss. 10-26. It may be assumed that the J genealogy began with Peleg, in whose days "the earth was divided" (10:25), and came after the account of how the Lord had "scattered [the human race] abroad . . . over the face of all the earth" (11:8a). The abrupt mention of Lot in 12:4a (J) indicates that his name, not found in the previous extant J material, was mentioned in this genealogy, presumably as Abraham's nephew, since it is unlikely that P would, without the pressure of existing tradition, have dignified the supposed ancestor of Moab and Ammon by making him a close relative of the father of the faithful.

28. Ur of the Chaldeans is the city of Uru in southern Babylonia, the remains of which have been discovered in the mounds of *'el-Muḳayyar* on the right bank of the Euphrates, 125 miles from Babylon (C. Leonard Woolley, *Ur of the Chaldees* [New York: Charles Scribner's Sons, 1930], pp. 13-14).

The J[1] material in 29:1-14 represents Abraham's kinsfolk as living in "the land of the people of the east" (29:1). This was presumably the earliest written form of the Israelite tradition of Abraham's "country" (12:1). According to J[2], Abraham's people lived in Haran (24:10; cf. 29:4-6) —the reason for this change of representation will be considered in connection with ch. 24. In the meantime, it may be noted that neither J[1] nor J[2] ascribe a Mesopotamian origin to Abraham. As to whether or not the J document in its final form represented him as coming from **Ur of the Chaldeans** it is impossible to say; 15:7, coming from the late sixth or early fifth century B.C. (see Simpson, *Early Traditions of Israel*, pp. 73-75), gives this as the place of his origin, but it may be a substitution by RP for a less definite original (cf. Eissfeldt, *Hexateuch-Synopse*, p. 20). However that may be, **in Ur of the Chaldeans** here is an addition to the notice as it left the hand of J[2], as is indeed suggested by the phraseology of the verse. Had **in Ur of the Chaldeans** been authentic, it would have come before **in the land of his birth**.

The representation that Abraham came from Mesopotamia, whether it first appeared in a later stratum of the J document or in P, is a concrete embodiment of an authentic

---

about his ministry to orphanages, old people's homes, hospitals, and jails. His sure and cheerful faith caught from the Bible is so much a part of his nature that he can express it altogether naturally. One day when he was preaching to the convicts in the state penitentiary, he put his message in a way that might have startled the conventional—if any conventional hearers had been there. He said that, what with polygamy and slavery and occasional lying and deception, even the patriarchs, if they were living today, might have been in the penitentiary. But God, he said, regards a man's times and circumstances and his opportunity or lack of opportunity for full knowledge. The important thing is that a man's face should be turned in the right direction—toward goodness

when he sees what that is, and away from sin when he knows what that is. The convicts understood what he was telling them—that the mercy of God reaches out not only to the good man but to the man who is trying to be better.

Indeed, with regard to Abraham, the first great fact about him is that he constantly suggests the future. Here is correction for a blunder into which thought too often falls. Religion is sometimes interpreted as though it were tied up with the past—a satisfaction with something achieved, a life without risk. Preachers have frequently represented goodness as negative and dull, and they have made belief a tame and passive matter. They have urged people "to guard the faith," warned them against too much questioning, proclaimed strict

29 And Abram and Nahor took them wives: the name of Abram's wife *was* Sarai; and the name of Nahor's wife, Milcah, the daughter of Haran, the father of Milcah, and the father of Iscah.

30 But Sarai was barren; she *had* no child.

Ur of the Chal'deans. 29 And Abram and Nahor took wives; the name of Abram's wife was Sar'ai, and the name of Nahor's wife, Milcah, the daughter of Haran the father of Milcah and Iscah. 30 Now Sar'ai was barren; she had no child.

---

memory of a migration from Mesopotamia preserved by some group of non-Israelite origin in Palestine. This group had, in the course of time, come to form a part of the Israelite community and to accept Abraham as its father, and a place was thus found for its tradition, which included no doubt the myths underlying chs. 1–3, in the national history (cf. Exeg. on ch. 24).

29. Abram and **Sarai** are the forms in which P introduced the father of the faithful (cf. vs. 27) and his wife. He records the change of their names to Abraham and Sarah in 17:5, 15. There is no parallel in the extant J material. This is, of course, not in itself an indication that J[1] and J[2] knew nothing of such a change, for their account of it might have been completely suppressed by R[P] in favor of ch. 17. Nevertheless, the fact that there is nothing in the J narrative which seems to presuppose or to demand it rather suggests that the forms Abraham and Sarah were used in this tradition from the beginning.

In its present context the statement that Nahor married **Milcah, the daughter of Haran** represents him as marrying his niece. As to whether or not this was the representation of the J document, it is difficult to say. J, as has been seen, appears to have regarded Lot as Abraham's nephew, and so presumably as the son of Haran. But was this Haran of J supposed to be the same as the father of Nahor's wife? The explanatory **the father of Milcah and Iscah** is possibly an indication that he was not. Nothing further is known of Iscah. Milcah appears again in 22:20 and ch. 24.

Sarai seems to be an archaic form of *sārāh*, meaning "princess." **Milcah** means "queen." In the Babylonian the relations are reversed, *sharratu* being the queen and *malkatu* the princess. In the pantheon of Haran (cf. vs. 32) Sharratu was the title of

---

dogmas lest all religion should be swept away. They have regarded religion as a sort of title deed to be locked up in a safe of cautious orthodoxy. Such conceptions fossilize faith. Faith is essentially an adventure. See Moffatt's translation of Heb. 11:1, "Now faith means that we are confident of what we hope for, convinced of what we do not see." Faith is not the anchor but the hoisted sail. It is not the ship in the harbor but the ship that puts out to sea. It is not holding on to something that already is but exploration and adventure toward something vaster that lies ahead. This kind of faith Abraham typifies, and this is the life of all great religion.

Observe also that Abraham went on believing in God's purpose, even when doors were shut in his face. He would try to go down into Egypt, which was a natural thing to do. It was the rich land, the land apparently of abundant opportunity; but he was turned back to the relatively barren land of Canaan, which nevertheless was to be the way of his life's fulfillment. In Egypt he would have been lost among a

people whom he could not have affected; in Canaan he became the founder of a nation. The empty ground of unsought opportunity became a new world of significance for the history of men. See the same truth in the career of Moses, who left his place of privilege in Pharaoh's house to lead his people through a desert.

Note that the justification of a man's life is not in any immediately disclosed accomplishment but in the fact that he has followed his vision until his trust in God is vindicated. Consider the example of Columbus. He set out to discover a new way across the ocean to the Indies. He hoped, and the old world coveted, that he should bring back the Orient's spices and gold. He never got to the Indies, and all that he brought back were a few curiosities and a tale of strange people in almost empty lands. But in Columbus' seeming failure was the way of colossal success. He had found a new continent more important to the future of the world than all the treasures of the East. So Abraham opened new continents of spiritual possibility for all the generations afterward to enter and

31 And Terah took Abram his son, and Lot the son of Haran his son's son, and Sarai his daughter-in-law, his son Abram's wife; and they went forth with them from Ur of the Chaldees, to go into the land of Canaan; and they came unto Haran, and dwelt there.

32 And the days of Terah were two hundred and five years: and Terah died in Haran.

31 Terah took Abram his son and Lot the son of Haran, his grandson, and Sar'ai his daughter-in-law, his son Abram's wife, and they went forth together from Ur of the Chal'deans to go into the land of Canaan; but when they came to Haran, they settled there. 32 The days of Terah were two hundred and five years; and Terah died in Haran.

---

the moon-goddess, the consort of Sin, and Malkatu a title of Ishtar, also worshiped there. This would certainly seem to indicate that the tradition of Hebron, centering on Abraham, was in some way related to, if not dependent on, that of Haran and explains in part the J2 representation of Haran as the place of Abraham's origin. Needless to say, neither J1 nor J2 were aware that Sarah was in any way associated with the moon-goddess or Milcah with Ishtar.

In view of the information as to the parentage of Milcah, a less important figure than Sarah, it is probable that the J document also gave the name of Sarah's father. If so, it was dropped, presumably by RJE, because it contradicted the statement of Abraham in 20:12 (E) that Sarah was his half sister, the daughter of his father, but not the daughter of his mother.

31. Haran—in Hebrew a different form from "Haran," Abraham's brother—was located in northwest Mesopotamia, some sixty miles east of Carchemish. It was one of the great centers of the worship of the moon-god and, at the time the J2 document was

---

explore. Let men remember that when they are apt to grow boastful about what they have done or discouraged about what they have not done. It is not what man does that exalts him, but what man would do (see Robert Browning's "Saul"). The man who is ultimately vindicated in God's eyes is the man who has followed his best light and has kept on believing in it, whatever the temporary results might or might not be.

31-32. When Old Age Is Gallant.—A brilliant American preacher, using the second of these verses as a text, once preached an arresting sermon on the idea that the only good thing Terah did was to die. He was represented as a type of the stodgy, complacent person who sits down short of achievement and holds everybody else back. Only when Terah died, and Abraham had him off his hands, could Abraham go ahead to the Promised Land. Yet that seems doubtful exegesis and less than fair to Terah. Note that **Terah took Abram his son, . . . and they went forth . . . from Ur of the Chaldees, to go into the land of Canaan.** Apparently, then, the original impulse came from Terah. Here was an old man who had a vision of the future. Age does not have to be complacent or backward-looking. Terah had his eyes toward a new country, just as Moses had, up to his dying moment. New ideals and inspirations may often come from men of ripe years. Walter B.

Pitkin wrote a book entitled *Life Begins at Forty*.[8] It is possible to maintain the *élan* of youth long after the physically youthful years. An elderly man, making a speech at a public gathering, began by saying: "According to the calendar I am an oldish man, but a few days ago I played baseball with some boys and I made a two-base hit. When I got to second, my breath was on first, but my heart was on third." Bishop William Lawrence of Massachusetts, who lived to be over ninety, wrote at seventy-six in his *Memories of a Happy Life*: "To me the surprising feature of life is that it becomes more interesting as one grows older. And a lifelong Christian faith suffuses the later years with serenity and hope." [9]

It is true that Terah died in Haran, a long way short of the goal of Canaan, but there is no evidence that Terah deliberately settled down there to die. He had got that far even if he could get no farther. Partial achievements are not wasted. They represent an impulse in the world that has its permanent effect. Read Robert Louis Stevenson's "Aes Triplex," with its message that all who have begun a worthwhile work have done good work, even if they have not lived to sign it. Read Browning's "Rabbi Ben Ezra" and "A Grammarian's Funeral."

[8] New York: Whittlesey House, 1932.
[9] Boston: Houghton Mifflin Co., 1926, preface.

12 Now the LORD had said unto Abram, Get thee out of thy country, and from thy kindred, and from thy father's house, unto a land that I will show thee:

12 Now the LORD said to Abram, "Go from your country and your kindred and your father's house to the land that I

---

written, a center of Aramaean culture (cf. Meyer, *Israeliten und ihre Nachbarstämme,* p. 248; Gunkel, *Genesis,* p. 168; Skinner, *Genesis,* p. 334). In representing Abraham as settling in Haran on his journey from Ur of the Chaldeans to Palestine, P would seem to be attempting to reconcile the J² tradition of Haran as his place of origin with the later tradition which brought him from Ur of the Chaldeans.

XIV. THE CALL OF ABRAHAM (12:1-8)

The section is a conflation of J and P. The P material is vss. 4b-5, the immediate continuation of 11:32. Vs. 4b, giving Abraham's age at the time, may be, with the other notices of ages in the history of the patriarchs, an addition to the original P narrative as Smend suggests (*Erzählung des Hexateuch,* p. 12); certainly the notice would better follow than precede vs. 5, but the present order may be due to RP, fusing P with J. It may be noted that P simply records without comment Abraham's journey from Haran to Canaan.

The J material is from J¹, with some elaboration from J². This narrative is more detailed. The Lord commands Abraham to leave his country to go to an as yet undesignated land, promising him that he will make of him a great nation and a blessing to all peoples, and Abraham goes in faith (vss. 1-4a). Since vs. 1 is from J¹, his **country** was "the land of the people of the east" (29:1), in the north Arabian desert. Now, in the primary, pre-Israelite form of the tradition concerning him Abraham was (see Intro., p. 442) a purely Hebron figure, the patron saint, so to speak, of the sanctuary there and the father of the community. Following the settlement in Hebron the Israelite clans made the sanctuary a sanctuary of the Lord. This was no mere appropriation of a place of sacrifice or the expulsion of one god and the enthronement of another. The Israelites took over the traditions cherished at the sanctuary, in which its religion found concrete

---

Furthermore, not all of Terah died and was buried in Haran. It was he who first stirred Abraham to start with him from Ur of the Chaldeans, and in a real sense Terah went on with Abraham and in Abraham the rest of the way. Life, as the writer of the Epistle to the Hebrews pointed out, is like a relay race. The impulse of struggle and partial success goes through all the way from the beginning to the end; and the runners who are not physically present at the finish line nevertheless have part in the victory if they have helped to speed the one who runs the final lap.

12:1. The Greatness of the Adventurer.—The glory of human history is in its pioneers. Webster defines a pioneer as "one who goes before, as into the wilderness, preparing the way for others to follow." The pioneer may be moved by one of many motives: inner restlessness, ambition, a thirst for the new and undiscovered. Whatever it is that sends him forward, he is often a creative force in the destiny of mankind. Think of Columbus sailing from Spain over untraveled oceans to find a new world. Think of the explorers of this Western continent, of

the colonists at Jamestown and the Pilgrims in New England; and of those in many regions who have blazed new paths over land and sea. In every case stodgy men thought the adventures foolish. But the great man goes out ahead to follow that which claims him, in the lonely heroism of a conviction that had not been expressed before. Many of us contract, as William James expressed it, "the habit of inferiority to our full self," and as a result, "the human individual thus lives usually far within his limits; he possesses powers of various sorts which he habitually fails to use. He energizes below his *maximum,* and he behaves below his *optimum.*" [10] But the pioneer, whether in the physical or the mental realm, shows what a life's optimum can be.

In this sense Abraham was a pioneer, but more than a pioneer. He belonged to the company of the daring; but his daring came from a higher force and with a more inspired consciousness than most of the adventurers have known. Let it be recognized, indeed, that in

[10] *Memories and Studies* (New York: Longmans, Green & Co., 1911), p. 238.

expression, and made them their own, entered into them in such a way that that religion became an integral part of Yahwism.

In this way Yahwism, instead of remaining an alien religion thrust into but scarcely related to a new setting, became the religion of the community at Hebron, preserving its own values and insights of which Abraham was the symbol. Both sets of values thus took on a new meaning: those of Hebron by being brought into the context of the living awareness of the transcendence and the centrality of God which characterized desert Yahwism; those of Yahwism by being related to the soil and to a community which, having its roots in the soil and being conscious of itself as belonging to a certain place, was more aware than the nomad could ever be of the continuity of history and of life as a process, and so more able to apprehend the fact of the divine purpose.

Abraham, the father of the community of Hebron, thus became the father of the Israelite clans which had entered into and transformed that community. But the Israelites could not forget their desert origin and sought to preserve, and to give expression to, the memory of it in the national tradition which was taking form. It was for this reason that J¹ represented Abraham as having come from the desert to Palestine and eventually as having settled at Hebron.

Thus in vss. 1-4 Abraham is less an individual than a symbol or personification of the Israelite clans which had moved from the desert into Palestine and had settled at Hebron.

Now this migration of the nomad clans from the desert to the sown land had been historically the result of various forces such as pressure by other desert groups and the need for more abundant pasturage. It certainly was not undertaken, at least consciously,

---

every great advance in history the divine will, whether known or unknown, has been moving; yet not always has that completely transcended human impulse and human act. With Abraham, as he stands in the mighty record of O.T. faith, it did so. God's purpose laid hold of him and sent him forth. If we could imagine Abraham being asked how he knew that God had called him, doubtless he could hardly have put the answer into words. No great soul completely can; but he knows and obeys his urge, whereas the little man may never know that such an urge exists but sits in his Ur of the Chaldeans safe and comfortable.

Always the pioneer will have discouragements. The way of any man who goes out ahead is not easy. Abraham must have had his wistful moments when he looked back and wondered why he had ever come to Canaan. He was seeking the Promised Land. But often the land seemed more full of disappointments than of promise. The Epistle to the Hebrews says that he sojourned there "as in a foreign land, living in tents" (11:9). A tent is an unstable thing. It is pitched here today; tomorrow it may have to be moved on. So it often is with the spiritual pioneers. They may seem never to reach their journey's end or have any proof of hopes fulfilled. Think of William Tyndale translating the Bible into English, persecuted and killed before he knew its immense effect; John Bunyan, writing *The Pilgrim's Progress*, and having as his reward twelve years in jail;

Woodrow Wilson giving his life to create the League of Nations but watching his ideal flung aside. Yet the greatness of the pioneer is that he goes on in spite of uncertainty and unfulfillment. He does not need assurance of quick results, if only he is satisfied that his direction is right. He does not have to perceive the end from the beginning, for he is confident that beside and above him is the reality of God who sees what he cannot see.

And the results? The dour eyes of immediate calculation might not see any. The Epistle to the Hebrews says that Abraham "looked for a city which hath foundations, whose builder and maker is God" (11:10). But where was any such city in Abraham's so-called Land of Promise when he died? Apparently nowhere. But the fact was mightier than the appearance. Spiritually Abraham had built a city, a dwelling place for new hope, new purpose, new ideals, for history, and for the human race. Every great pioneer has done that. Every ordinary man who thinks he is not great but who follows as best he can the spiritual light and leading that takes him out from Ur of the Chaldeans, out from the stodginess of accepted habit, out from laziness and complacency of soul, into some difficult obedience at the call of God—he too is helping to create the spiritual city in which human life can find a larger home.

1-5. *The Cost of Obedience.*—To follow a call from God may be a costly matter, particularly when it leads on a lonely road. **Get thee**

in response to a specific divine command, however mediated. To say this is not to deny that it was in accordance with God's unfolding purpose and contributed to its fulfillment. Rather, it may reasonably be maintained that the movement at this time into Palestine, the crossroads of the ancient world, of a people whose religion was already characterized by a drive toward monotheism, was a necessary step toward the redemption of mankind through Christ, and so was divinely planned. But it does not follow from the recognition of this fact *post eventu* that the Israelite clans, as they made this move, had any conception of its cosmic significance. To all outward appearances it was just another of the many migrations of peoples which occurred in the ancient world, and was so regarded by the Israelites, in the unlikely event that they gave the matter any thought whatever.

But the settlement of the clans in Palestine resulted, as has been noted above, in an extraordinary deepening and enrichment of Yahwism, the religion they had brought with them from the desert. The more sensitive minds among them, reflecting on this at a later date, reasoned that the movement which had made this possible must have been divinely

---

out of thy country, and from thy kindred, and from thy father's house. Those prepositions have the sharpness of a sword. It is no longer to be in and with, but out and from. Abraham must turn his back on what had been the familiar and the friendly and go out to the unwelcome and unknown. That contradiction may often recur. There are human relationships so instinctively dear that they seem surely God-given; yet a voice that also surely comes from God may cut across them. When is this true, and why should it be so?

Note the rightness of the instinct that holds relationships dear. God has set men in families. Every human individual owes his life to some sort of family nurture and protection. Not only his physical, but his mental and moral self also, is largely shaped by the influence of others. No man can lightly tear himself from the web of social thoughts and feelings into which he has been woven. He belongs to its pattern; separated from it, he seems to himself like a torn strip with raw edges and loose threads. All through the O.T. runs the conviction of family solidarity. In every household there was a group responsibility. Virtue in one person might bring blessedness to all; crime in one, punishment upon all. The whole nation also was thought of as a single family—the family of the sons of Israel. Observe the passionate devotion to the people of Israel and to the homeland expressed in present-day Zionism. For both ancient and modern Jewry, to hold together has been exalted as a supreme end.

Consider the Fifth Commandment. Consider also the need of modern life for the ideal there set up: for loyalty as against individualistic license, for reverent defense of proven standards as against the moral recklessness which despises and destroys. Does not the modern picture seem to point to exactly the opposite conclusion from that in this story of Abraham? When so many men lightly forsake their inherited loyal-

ties, when families disintegrate and parental authority is a shadow and there are fewer and fewer bonds of continuing homes, when communities lose their accepted standards, when old codes of morals disappear and individuals become a law to themselves and the prevailing tendency is to cast adrift from old moorings, it might well be said that there is urgent need for a voice whose word is not "from" but "with," that says not "Go out," but "Stay in."

What then is the other truth? It is this: that often the group can move forward only as the individual breaks the path ahead. On every level of life there must be the pioneer. Reflect upon the facts of evolution. Individuals are born who differ from the average of the species. They have the qualities that are fit for the new environment of an expanding life, and they reach upward to possess it. So in moral and spiritual advance. The lonely adventure may be the only way to higher life. Kipling wrote, "The race is run by one and one and never by two and two." [1] Joseph had to dream dreams that went beyond what his brothers wanted. Jesus had to go out to a greatness of conceptions which all his former friends in Nazareth would hate. Remember the sternness of his words: "If any man come to me, and hate not his father, and mother, and wife, and children, and brethren, and sisters, yea, and his own life also, he cannot be my disciple" (Luke 14:26). Read the first pages of *The Pilgrim's Progress* and see there the realization that sometimes the imperative quest of the soul for God requires that all who refuse to answer it may have to be left behind. Albert Schweitzer in *Out of My Life and Thought* [2] wrote of those who could not or would not understand the compulsion he felt to dedicate his life to an unheard-of new service in French Equatorial Africa. So in ways less conspicuous but essentially as real, other

[1] "Tomlinson."

[2] New York: Henry Holt & Co., 1933.

| 2 And I will make of thee a great nation, and I will bless thee, and make thy name great; and thou shalt be a blessing: | will show you. 2 And I will make of you a great nation, and I will bless you, and make your name great, so that you will be a bless- |

---

willed, and this story of Abraham's coming to Palestine is but one of the many passages in the O.T. in which this conviction has found expression. It has, moreover, been told with extraordinary skill.

The representation that Abraham left his own country "not knowing whither he went" (Heb. 11:8) preserves something of the element of contingency in the actual movement of the clans. The faith ascribed to him is not only a reflection of the developed faith of the author—the result of his experience and the experience of his people—in

---

men and women, and particularly the young, may have to pay the price of estrangement from those most near if they are to follow the choices which they know are highest: the young man whose aims cannot be satisfied by the easy and profitable position in the family fortune to which his father wants him to succeed; the girl who must resist a worldly-minded mother who urges her to a marriage for social prestige and wealth; the mature man in community affairs or in public life who refuses to "play the game" when he sees that the playing of it is crooked, and must endure the cynical hostility of the crowd that considers him an alien. That sort of loneliness may be inevitable for all great spirits. Read Frederick W. Robertson's sermon on "The Loneliness of Christ." [3] Reflect upon the beautiful story of the magi who came from their distant land to look for Christ, yet in the eyes of the world found nothing significant at all. How scornful must their neighbors have been concerning so fantastic a quest! But they were right, as Abraham was right. Only when men are brave enough to rise above the crowd opinion do they follow the roads of freedom for their souls.

Yet the two truths do not stand permanently separated. The instinct of relation, the terrible compulsion to be true to one's own soul— these two may meet at last. Loyalty to the highest in one's self is loyalty to the highest that ought to be and the highest which someday may come to pass in the family and the group. The bonds which Abraham broke may have been renewed on a higher level (cf. 24:4); for it is to his own kindred that he turns again when he seeks a wife for Isaac. One at least of the brothers of Jesus became a leader in his church. In the second part of The Pilgrim's Progress Christian's family sets out to follow him on the road which in such desperate devotion he had first walked alone. As was said of Thomas Arnold, so it may be said at last of every man of unreckoning consecration, that

he comes to the end of what was at first a lonely road not alone, but as one to whom it is given

> Many to save with thyself;
> And, at the end of thy day,
> O faithful shepherd! to come,
> Bringing thy sheep in thy hand.[4]

2. False and True Desires.—What is most worth a life's desiring? There are many possible answers among which men actually make choices.

Some want more than anything else to be left alone. What they emphatically do not want is to be provoked to anything effortful or difficult. They may be belligerent in that avoidance or they may be merely irresolute and procrastinating, but the ultimate fact is largely the same. They prefer to stay where they are and as they are rather than to try hard to arrive at something different. Men of this type appear all through the Bible—men who might have made their lives significant but never wanted to put their energies in motion as much as they wanted to stand still and take things easy. Think of Lot, of Esau, of the rich young ruler, of Nicodemus. Their failure was not generally in aiming at anything bad; it was in the fact that they did not aim strongly enough at anything. They and their successors in every time would rather sit comfortably on the grass than to be called up to pull a bowstring taut and to speed an arrow to its mark.

Others are not so indifferent or indolent, but they have positive desires of a kind. They want to live luxuriously. Read in Exodus what most of the Israelites were thinking about in the long march through the wilderness. To get to the Promised Land was what they were supposed to want, but what they did want and what they vociferously clamored for was to get back to the good food of Egypt. Demas forsook Paul because he "loved this present world" (II Tim. 4:10), i.e., he had a hankering after its relative comforts and conveniences. Sometimes that rul-

[3] *Sermons Preached at Brighton* (New York: E. P. Dutton & Co., 1894), pp. 168-77.

[4] Matthew Arnold, "Rugby Chapel."

3 And I will bless them that bless thee, and curse him that curseth thee: and in thee shall all families of the earth be blessed.

ing. 3 I will bless those who bless you, and him who curses you I will curse; and by you all the families of the earth will bless themselves."*q*

q Or in you all the families of the earth will be blessed

---

the wisdom and power of God. It is also an indication of the way in which Israel's response to the divine initiative, in its beginning emotional to the point of a frenzied

---

ing desire for food and drink and the pleasurable indulgence of fastidious appetite is unashamedly expressed, as in *The Rubáiyát* of Omar Khayyám. More often it is not so avowed, but may be none the less controlling. Among members of churches which actually comes out ahead—an appeal for some vital opportunity in the church's missions and for relief of some desperate human need, or the pull of habitual self-interest that sees to it that our own tastes are not disturbed?

Some are not so concerned with self-indulgence; what they want is self-aggrandizement. In their eyes the one thing most desirable is power. Saul was consumed by that ambition; so was Jezebel; so was Herod. But the desire for power is not confined to exemplars so fanatical. Consider in the modern world how many there are who in ways quite legal and often quite polite pursue their appetite for power: in public office; in positions of control in industry, whether among employers or among those who can dominate a union; in the church. Such men and women may get what they want. Their lives may seem rich with many benefits. But that does not mean that they are among the blessed.

For a life that is blessed and that feels blessed must come to its blessedness by another way. That may include some of the same satisfactions which ordinary lives have, yet not as main interests but rather as secondary accompaniments. Every human life, including the blessed ones, is lived in this world and is subject to this world's necessities. Therefore it legitimately seeks its livelihood and a reasonable provision for its material wants. Part of God's favor to Abraham was that his flocks and herds increased. Jesus included in his prayer, "Give us this day our daily bread." No social order or economic system can claim justification unless it makes available to all men the physical basis of decent living. The possession of power may also be wholesome if there is honest recognition that a life has influence and that the right exercise of it must not be shirked. But no life wins blessedness by seeking possessions or power for their own sake. Neither does it win blessedness by wanting to be left alone.

What therefore is blessedness? It is first the

recognition of a divine relationship. Abraham's inner strength and happiness never came from worldly things; they came from his sense of a purpose above this world that was controlling. The last thing he wanted was to be left to his own devices; instead, he wanted to know his God-appointed destiny. Consequently, he was a man of prayer, which is the antithesis of a man who wants to be let alone. True prayer becomes a benediction precisely because it lifts a soul out of itself.

> A spark disturbs our clod;
> Nearer we hold of God.[5]

Blessedness is also a sense of sufficiency for whatever life may bring. Some suppose that the most blessed good fortune they could think of would be to have life made smooth. But that is a false notion. Complacency may come that way, but never the kind of completeness of life which makes the soul exultant. Beginning with Abraham and going on through the long succession of great souls—like Joseph, Moses, Joshua, the prophets, Stephen, and Paul—the Bible makes clear that a man knows himself to be blessed not when he has managed to get rid of dangers and risks and burdens but when he has been given great and gallant strength to bear them.

Finally, blessedness is in the knowledge that one may be a blessing. That is not an easy truth at first for either individuals or nations to believe in. Jacob at Bethel tried to make a bargain with God as to benefits which might surely come to him—that was his idea of being blessed—but Jesus prayed for his disciples that they might be blessed through him, "For their sakes I sanctify myself" (John 17:19). The Jewish people often had a narrow and selfish concern for their own interests; but the highest vision of the prophets was of a suffering servant of mankind. Whatever the selfishness of men might prefer to think, in God's universe blessedness comes no other way.

3. *Nationalism and the Larger Outlook.*—As one reads this promise, one has a sense of curious contrast between its two halves. Its climax is that the lineage of Abraham will bring

[5] Browning, "Rabbi Ben Ezra."

4 So Abram departed, as the Lord had spoken unto him; and Lot went with him: and Abram *was* seventy and five years old when he departed out of Haran.

4 So Abram went, as the Lord had told him; and Lot went with him. Abram was seventy-five years old when he departed

---

fanaticism, had deepened into a response which involved the intellect and the will, i.e, a response of the whole being.

Finally, in the statement in vs. 3*b* that **by you all the families of the earth will bless themselves,** the author has voiced his conviction as to the significance of Israel for mankind and has thus given further expression to the incipient universalism which, it has been seen, informs however rudimentarily the J material in ch. 10.

12:4. In mentioning **Lot,** J[1] prepares for the story in 13:5-13, which in turn not only sets the stage for the originally independent legends of the destruction of Sodom and of

---

a blessing to the whole earth; but its beginning seems to reflect an unregenerate nationalism. This was what some in early Israel thought that God would promise to those who felt themselves to be his chosen people—a blessing for their friends and a curse upon their enemies. The family consciousness within the nation was an extraordinarily close and vital fact and altogether concrete in what it represented. "For the Israelite it is a matter of course that common flesh makes common character. Therefore family, *mishpāhā,* is the designation of those who are of the same kind, have the same essential features." [6] There is a kind of herd instinct which makes a people hostile to all those who are not "of the same kind" and do not have "the same essential features." Many Israelites did not want a God who would be equally the God of all the nations of the earth. They did not want one who would be impartial Holiness. They wanted a God who would be partial to them. So we read in Deuteronomy of demands for a complete extermination of all the non-Israelitish peoples of Palestine: "And when the Lord thy God shall deliver them before thee; thou shalt smite them, and utterly destroy them; thou shalt make no covenant with them, nor show mercy unto them" (Deut. 7:2). And as to the carrying out of that injunction, read the harsh sentences of Deut. 20:10-17. In the twentieth century millions of Jews were exterminated by the savage fanaticism of Hitler. It is one of the tragic ironies of history that the motive for that slaughter could be expressed in terms like those which Israel itself in ancient times did not scruple to proclaim: the right of the preferred people to life and victory, the will-to-power of the master race.

In basic instincts Israel was intensely human, and its history might have been no better than the rest of human history except for one immeasurable fact. This people had the tremendous consciousness that they had been laid hold upon by God. They belonged to him, and his invincible purposes would be worked out through them. That conceivably might have added only a religious fanaticism to their fierce tribal self-assertion. But as a matter of fact it did what was far greater and more wonderful: it led them on from nationalism toward universalism. It made the great souls among them understand that "the glory of thy people Israel" must be to become "a light to lighten the Gentiles." The inspired prophets looked forward to a day when "many people shall go and say, Come ye, and let us go up to the mountain of the Lord, to the house of the God of Jacob" (Isa. 2:3); in that day it could indeed be said of the seed of Abraham, **in thee shall all families of the earth be blessed.**

That ideal was never fully grasped even by the prophets. Certainly it has never yet been fulfilled. The emergence of a universal family in God still waits to come true in history. But the power that may someday establish it did come into clear and final light in Christ, who lived and died not to be the Savior of one nation only, but by his sacrifice to make "of one blood all nations of men for to dwell on all the face of the earth" (Acts 17:26). It is this family of mankind, become obedient to a sovereignty which is mightier than the decrees of dictators or of any other rulers of this earth, which in spite of war and tragedy and destruction must ultimately emerge out of the travailing experience of our human race.

4-5. Vision and Deed.—As a small surface of still water can mirror the immensity of the sky, so these few words reflect a truth that overarches all life and time. It is the truth that the great idea must lead to action. Spiritual opportunity is spiritual obligation. Religion must be obedience. But though that is true, men do not always accept the truth.

So it might have been with Abraham. Instead of responding to the voice in his conscience,

---

[6] Johannes Pedersen, *Israel, Its Life and Culture I-II* (London: Oxford University Press, 1926), p. 48.

| 5 And Abram took Sarai his wife, and Lot his brother's son, and all their sub- | from Haran. 5 And Abram took Sar'ai his wife, and Lot his brother's son, and all |

the origin of Moab and Ammon in ch. 19, but also articulates them with the legend of Hebron in 18:1-16.

which he felt to be the voice of God, he might have refused to heed it for various reasons which were so plausible that they well might have seemed convincing. How did he know that the disturbing and difficult new urging was the voice of God? What practical sense was in it? What proof was there that what it suggested would work out right? Why should any sensible man pay such a price as the breaking up of the whole basis of his life just because of something uncomfortable in his soul? "There is no sense in it," Abraham might have said, just as many men have said. The rich young ruler heard a voice that called him to a complete new commitment, and he refused. So did Nicodemus. So, less conspicuously but not less actually, men and women are doing every day: smothering the voice that speaks of some new movement of the will, of moral courage, of uncalculating loyalty to a far ideal. What has happened, or is happening, in our own souls?

Or the voice may not be refused, but insincerely responded to. Abraham might have accepted the divine message with the momentary enthusiasm of the man who is proud to feel that he has been singled out for special notice, but whose enthusiasm quickly cools when he finds where he must go. Consider the son in Jesus' parable who, when his father bade him go into the vineyard, said, "I go, sir; and went not" (Matt. 21:30). It is one thing to have religious emotion; it is another thing to set the whole life actually in motion on the roads of God. What of church members who can be "just thrilled" by a beautiful service or a sermon, who like to think they are much affected, who will say the Creed and sing the hymns with fervor, but who, as soon as they get outside the church's atmosphere, let their spiritual temperature drop to exactly what it was before.

Again, the voice may be responded to sincerely, but with a sincerity that has shallow roots, i.e., the soul may really mean to obey the heavenly voice, and may begin to do so; it makes a new commitment, starts on some road of honest progress. But the road proves longer and harder than was thought. There are interruptions which stop the first impetus and make it that much more of an effort to start again. Think of what Abraham might have said to himself. The voice had come to him first in Ur of the Chaldeans. He had listened to it, accepted it, started on his way. But through

circumstances beyond his control he had had to stop in Haran. He was there long enough to get accustomed to it. He had set out for Canaan, but Canaan was still a long way off and the original impulse could have cooled. Now that he was in Haran, why not stay? Why not let that much of a new venture be enough? Thus many might have asked; thus many might have concluded. Most failures in relation to the road of the ideal are not because of complete unfaithfulness but because faithfulness is not complete. Men who have put their hand to the plow look back, get tired, sit down, and go to sleep.

But Abraham represents a different example. He had the quality of desire, in the first place, which kept him from being disobedient to the heavenly voice; and that kind of desire is not produced in a moment but is present with effective strength at the critical hour if and because a man in the long course of routine days has been cultivating the kind of thoughts and the kind of emotion that make high desires controlling. How did he know the voice was the voice of God? Because there had been developed in himself the kind of responsive conscience which alone can recognize the reality of that voice. So he understood through experience what he repeated in action: that the proof of religious intuition runs not through speculation but through action. The way to be sure whether or not a moving in the soul is the voice of God is to answer it, and see. Jesus said, "If any man will do his will, he shall know" (John 7:17). Read Frederick W. Robertson's sermon on "Obedience as the Organ of Spiritual Knowledge." [7] James Strachan wrote:

True religion is a willing, cheerful obedience to God. It is only when the will, the controlling faculty, is called into play that religion is actualised. Thomas Fuller more than two centuries ago divided mankind into three classes, intenders, endeavourers, and performers, these making an ascending scale. . . . If we bravely advance through the darkness, we shall have the whole way of life illumined. [8]

So, though Abraham could not foresee the end of his adventure, he had the ready courage to begin. Like Newman, he did not ask to see "the

[7] *Sermons Preached at Brighton*, 4th ser. (New York: E. P. Dutton & Co., 1882), pp. 300-7.
[8] *Hebrew Ideals* (Edinburgh: T. & T. Clark, 1906), I, 31.

stance that they had gathered, and the souls that they had gotten in Haran; and they went forth to go into the land of Canaan; and into the land of Canaan they came.

6 ¶ And Abram passed through the land unto the place of Sichem, unto the plain of Moreh. And the Canaanite *was* then in the land.

their possessions which they had gathered, and the persons that they had gotten in Haran; and they set forth to go to the land of Canaan. When they had come to the land of Canaan, 6 Abram passed through the land to the place at Shechem, to the oak[r] of Moreh. At that time the Canaanites

[r] Or *terebinth*

---

6. Abraham is represented as making his first stop in Palestine at **the place of Shechem**, the sanctuary of the famous **oak of Moreh** (cf. 35:4; Deut. 11:30). Shechem, the modern Balâṭah, is some twenty-seven miles north of Jerusalem. The note regarding the presence of the **Canaanites . . . in the land** is a gloss to underline Abraham's faith.

---

distant scene—one step enough." How many a life needs to learn this truth, that what God asks of any soul is not self-assurance that it can go a long way, but only the humble obedience that makes a start in the right direction. The man who has begun courageously in his heart is no failure.

Moreover, the right spirit in beginning can produce, as in Abraham, the resolution to carry through. He did not stop in Haran because his purpose was too clear and strong for that. The vision of the Promised Land in Canaan neither faded out nor was destroyed by delay; on the contrary, the energy he had put into following it made it dominant. He and those he took with him **went forth to go into the land of Canaan; and into . . . Canaan they came.** What a challenge is in those words for those whose temptation is to let their best ambitions stop short in moral compromise. How great a thing it would be to say at last like Abraham, like Paul, "I have finished my course" (II Tim. 4:7).

6-8. When Men Worship.—It is told of Abraham not once but repeatedly that he **builded an altar unto the LORD.** Wherever he was, he worshiped. With his altars he was a representative of man's deepest instinct, the instinct to draw near to God. Worship is independent of time and place. There has been no age and no race in which worship has not appeared. Skeptics, it is true, may deny the value of this fact. Even if worship seems universal, has it not often expressed ideas so primitive and crude as to repel intelligence? But imperfect expressions of a great reality do not destroy the reality itself. It would be stupid to conclude that there is no such thing as medical science because a century and a half ago the search for medical truth had arrived at no better idea than to bleed George Washington to death because he had a cold. It would be stupid to conclude that art has no true validity in its quest for beauty because sometimes it has turned out chromos. It would be stupid likewise to conclude that there

is no reality in man's eternal approach to God because men have sought him in forms and rituals which we would not practice now. In religion, as in other areas of experience, the race moves from partial conceptions toward larger fulfillments of the truth which it has felt.

If the search for God is thus instinctive, what does communion with God result in? First, it gives to life a sense of meaning. If existence were only a maze, devoid of any intelligible clue, sooner or later it would become intolerable. Life cannot be lived with any satisfaction unless it falls into patterns which we can understand. The deepest need of every living being is to discover the relationship between himself and the universe in which he moves. Consider a child's growth into awareness and adjustment. Not to make right adjustments is to be forever immature. One person may become a crabbed introvert; another may be interested in other persons, but interested in them only as they serve his selfish interests and ends. But a full development of personality in its human relationships comes only when one discovers the meaning of life in friendship and in love. Without great loyalties and deep emotions life is cramped and mean. But the human spirit cannot stop with mortal satisfactions. Are we only unaided human beings, lighting here under indifferent skies a little flame which tomorrow will be extinguished? If so, then there might be justification of what was written by the father of a brilliant young student in an American university who killed himself. "My son saw no reason in life and so none for it. We do not understand life, and so, not understanding life, we say, some of us, let's end it." That may be the tragic consequence when existence has no meaning and life is

> a tale
> Told by an idiot, full of sound and fury,
> Signifying nothing.[9]

[9] Shakespeare, *Macbeth*, Act V, scene 5.

7 And the LORD appeared unto Abram, and said, Unto thy seed will I give this land: and there builded he an altar unto the LORD, who appeared unto him.

8 And he removed from thence unto a mountain on the east of Bethel, and pitched his tent, *having* Bethel on the west, and Hai on the east: and there he builded an altar unto the LORD, and called upon the name of the LORD.

were in the land. 7 Then the LORD appeared to Abram, and said, "To your descendants I will give this land." So he built there an altar to the LORD, who had appeared to him. 8 Thence he removed to the mountain on the east of Bethel, and pitched his tent, with Bethel on the west and Ai on the east; and there he built an altar to the LORD and

---

7. At Shechem the Lord appeared to Abraham and told him that he had reached the land which, it was now promised, was to be given to his descendants. This promise is the first rudimentary expression of the idea of the covenant between the Lord and Israel. The fact that J[1], from whom this verse comes, locates this at Shechem suggests that even he, who as will be seen was not familiar with the details of the tradition of Shechem, was aware of the covenant idea which dominated that tradition (see article "The Growth of the Hexateuch," p. 195).

In recording that Abraham **built there an altar to the LORD, who had appeared to him,** J[1] ascribes to Abraham, the patron of Hebron, the founding of the sanctuary of the oak of Moreh. This was in effect a claim on the part of the Israelite priesthood of Hebron to primacy over the great shrine of the north. This claim should not be dismissed offhand as merely an overt expression of the lust for power and prestige, often supposed, not entirely without justification, to be a dominant characteristic of organized priesthoods. No doubt this element entered into it. But it was also a manifestation of the drive in Yahwism toward a unification of life. Historically, it is probable that there was in this case some ground for the claim, for the sanctuary of Hebron in the time of J[1] would seem to have been controlled by the Levites, the priesthood of Kadesh, which had for whatever reason accompanied the Israelite clans when they moved thence to Palestine. Hebron would thus be the center from which that priesthood infiltrated through Palestine to take over sanctuary after sanctuary for Yahweh, whether by expelling the local priesthood or by incorporating it by a kind of legal fiction into the Levitical caste. If this is the case, then the Israelite priesthood of the oak of Moreh—undoubtedly Levitical when Deut. 27 received its present form—presumably stemmed from Hebron, though having established themselves in Shechem they may well have been unwilling to acknowledge the continued primacy of the parent center which is claimed here.

8. Here the same claim is made as regards **Bethel.** If the sanctuary referred to was the Aaronite sanctuary of the golden calf, the claim was made with less historical justification than had been the case as regards Shechem, for the Aaronite priesthood of Bethel

---

But the witness of Abraham is part of the eternal witness that life does signify something. Life had a meaning for him because the divine voice spoke in his conscience and a divine purpose directed him from day to day.

As it is only God who can give life sufficient meaning, so it is only God who can give a happiness which is dependable. Consider the unhappiness of so much contemporary life: with everything to amuse it, not amused; with everything to distract, yet never fully distracted from a sense of hollowness at its heart; with the feet of men and women dancing to jazz, but their souls not dancing, rather moving heavily, knowing that there is nothing adequate to

which they could be in tune. Read *The Story of My Life,* by Clarence Darrow, the brilliant lawyer who called himself an atheist. "Emotionally," he wrote, "I shall no doubt act as others do to the last moment of my existence. With my last breath I shall probably try to draw another, but, intellectually, I am satisfied that life is a serious burden, which no thinking human person would wantonly inflict on some one else."[1] Contrast with that drab disillusionment the highhearted courage of the great men of the O.T. Listen also to Paul's words to the elders of Ephesus, "None of these things move me, neither count I my life dear unto myself, so

[1] New York: Charles Scribner's Sons, 1932, p. 395.

9 And Abram journeyed, going on still toward the south.

called on the name of the LORD. 9 And Abram journeyed on, still going toward the Negeb.

---

seem to have remained outside of, and indeed opposed to, the Levitical caste (see Simpson, *Early Traditions of Israel*, pp. 625-26, 631, 635-36). It is possible, however, that the detailed location of the altar is intended to distinguish it from the more famous shrine.

Ai refers to the ruin of a city, burned to the ground between 2200 and 2000 and remaining unoccupied until about 1200 B.C. (see W. F. Albright [describing Mme. Judith Krause-Marquet's excavations at Ai, 1933-35], "Archaeological Exploration and Excavation in Palestine and Syria, 1935," *American Journal of Archaeology*, XL [1936] 157-58).

It may be noted that in contrast to vs. 7 no theophany is here recorded, so that no reason is provided for Abraham's building of an altar there. This silence is probably the result of the work of J2 who, as is indicated by the story in 28:13, 15-16, 19, represented Jacob as the real founder of the sanctuary at Bethel. Unwilling, however, to ignore altogether the linking by J1 of the shrine with Abraham, he simply struck out here the reference to the theophany.

XV. ABRAHAM IN EGYPT (12:9–13:1)

There are two other recensions of this story in Genesis: one in ch. 20, telling how Abraham represented Sarah as his sister to Abimelech, king of Gerar; the other in 26:1-11, in which Isaac makes the same representation as regards his wife, also to Abimelech. That in ch. 26 is from J1; that in ch. 20 is from E; the recension in this chapter is accordingly from J2, as is further indicated by the fact that Lot is not mentioned in the tale, suggesting an author other than the writer responsible for the groundwork of vss. 1-8.

The story in its earliest Israelite form (J1) was thus told concerning Isaac. In the development of the southern (J) tradition it was carried over to Abraham—an instance of the tendency to make him, not Isaac, the hero of the legends preserved at Beer-sheba. This tendency, it may be noted, reflects the prestige of the priests of Hebron,

---

that I might finish my course with joy" (Acts 20:24). Watch Francis of Assisi making riches out of deprivation and glory out of loss, so winsome that the very birds would cluster around his hands, so joyous that men honored him as the troubadour of God.

Moreover, it is only through finding God that a life is saved from wavering between skepticism on one side and superstition on the other. It has often been supposed that skepticism would give a satisfying sense of freedom. Get rid of all beliefs and enjoy the irresponsibility of being bound by no convictions! Shrug off all loyalties and devotions! Believe in nothing definite and be bound to nothing! But the terse fact is that though men may think they like this, they do not like it long. When the mind is homeless it grows as unhappy as a homeless body. It must find some sort of shelter in which to rest. Deprived of ancient and august loyalties, men begin instinctively to create new ones which they will adopt. Deprived of one temple, they make another and set up new gods, even in the moment when they think that all gods have been denied. Mark the veneration of the tomb of Lenin in the midst of Soviet Russia,

which theoretically has no use for God or for religion. Note the tragic result in Germany when the inherited religion of Christendom was repudiated and in its place came the barbaric new superstitions of race and blood and soil.

Abraham building his altars is back in the dawn of the Bible's history of man's approach to God. But he had his face toward the true light. He was seeking him whom afterward the prophets interpreted and Jesus revealed—God in whom alone life finds meaning and happiness and assurance.

9-10. Egypt and Israel.—Abraham and Egypt —a suggestive contrast emerges. How insignificant Abraham and all he represented appeared to be as compared with Egypt! On the one hand, an unimportant wanderer; on the other hand, a proud civilization, ancient and deep-rooted. At the time when Abraham conjecturally came within its borders the history of its life already went back more than two thousand years. From the rich valley of the Nile and from their conquests beyond it the Pharaohs drew the wealth to build the magnificence of Memphis and Thebes and the colossal temples at Karnak; and the pyramids were even then cen-

who were thus able to associate with their patron saint the traditions of other sanctuaries which originally had known nothing of him.

Not only has Abraham been substituted for Isaac in this recension, but the scene has been changed from Gerar to Egypt. This again magnified the importance of Abraham who is thus represented as having had contacts not merely with the Philistines and other neighboring peoples, but even on one occasion with Egypt, where he was received as an equal by the Pharaoh himself.

There may also be here a reminiscence of the exodus tradition, as though the story of how Jacob went down into Egypt, where his descendants ultimately triumphed over the Pharaoh, was thought not to be sufficient. Popular legend weaving therefore evolved this tale—basing it on the story now preserved in 26:1-11—that Abraham himself had anticipated all this. Because of famine he had gone down to Egypt (vs. 10; cf. chs. 41–45), where he was deprived of his wife (vs. 15; cf. the persecution of Exod. 1:11-22); nevertheless he grew wealthy (vs. 16; cf. Exod. 1:9), the Pharaoh was plagued (vs. 17; cf.

---

turies old. What did it matter to Egypt or to history that this Hebrew should exist? To Egypt, nothing; to history, more than Egypt itself would ultimately mean. Egypt represented material pride and power and possessions, and all these would crumble. Abraham represented a new spiritual impulse, and this would be creative long after Egypt should have ceased to count. A lesson is here in the relative values which history reveals; a lesson, too, specifically for those who forget or belittle the contribution to history of the Jews. Abraham is the symbol and the foreshadowing of something immeasurable that was to come: a nation that should influence the world to a degree that outstripped every seeming probability. Ponder the mystery of the forces that may emerge through some great personality or from some limited human group. Thus God enters and re-enters history, not by outward acts, but by the new dynamic he has put within human instruments.

So much for the general fact. What specifically are the contributions that have come to human life through the family of Abraham, and what therefore is the debt that humanity owes to the Jews? First, the imprint of the moral law. Every people has had its codes of conduct, but the Jewish perception of what the right life ought to be attained a singular loftiness and dignity. It was crystallized in the Ten Commandments. Consider the immense influence which the Ten Commandments have exerted through centuries of history. They have reflected the absolute distinction which exists between the basic rights and wrongs—an absoluteness which needs to be continually reasserted against the relativism of morals by which individuals and nations may be corrupted. Family disloyalty, adultery, stealing, lying, killing, are outrages against an eternal order which men disobey only at their peril and can never with impunity defy: that is the truth which the Jewish people through the Ten Commandments

have handed down. As Henry C. Link, psychologist, has written in *The Rediscovery of Morals:* "Times and customs may change, but the basic moral laws are just as changeless as the law of gravity or the axioms of mathematics." [2]

Outrages against an eternal order—let the mind linger upon the significance of those words. In the Ten Commandments the standards held up for human conduct are not shifting calculation and expediency; they are the recognition of the higher Will to which the human conscience must be sensitive if it is to steer straight. The six commandments which have to do with "our duty to our neighbor" are not the first six, but the second; they follow the four commandments which have to do with "our duty to God." Thus, morality must be grounded in religion. It is only when men hold themselves accountable to an everlasting Righteousness that they will keep on dealing rightly with one another. Consider what happened to Germany when Nazi leaders, in the insolence of their imagined power, thought they could get rid of the God of the Ten Commandments. Consider the nemesis that certainly lurks in any other atheistic system which makes the end justify the means and holds traditional morality in contempt. The conscience which Judaism has put into so much of our civilization knows better. "Sin is a reproach to any people" (Prov. 14:34); and, in the end, it is ruin too.

As the Jews gave to humanity its clearest recognition of the moral law, so they gave the enlarging interpretation of law and of life which was voiced by the prophets. Law may become fossilized. It has its codes of duty which may be sufficient for one age but may be too narrow for the needs of the next. Religion may become identified with a conservative priestcraft which is obsessed with ritual and regularity and has no vision for new ways of

[2] New York: E. P. Dutton & Co., 1947, p. 25.

10 ¶ And there was a famine in the land: and Abram went down into Egypt to sojourn there; for the famine *was* grievous in the land.	10 Now there was a famine in the land. So Abram went down to Egypt to sojourn there, for the famine was severe in the land.

Exod. 7-10). At this point, however, the parallel breaks down, for the implication of vss. 19b-20 is that Abraham was expelled from the country in disgrace (contrast Exod. 14:8b). It is not impossible that this, together with the Pharaoh's stern rebuke, is due to a revision to which the story was subjected by J² who, compelled by the popularity of the tale—evidenced by the fact of its three recensions—to include it in his narrative, was nevertheless not too happy about it.

Gunkel maintains that the story implies that the Pharaoh actually entered into marital relations with Sarah (*Genesis*, pp. 173, 225). However, had J² intended such a representation he would have stated the fact explicitly by saying, e.g., at the end of vs. 15, that Pharaoh lay with her. Furthermore, it is impossible to suppose that in adapting the original Isaac legend to Abraham, popular imagination—to say nothing of J²—would have gratuitously (26:10 is specific in its statement that Rebekah had escaped the possible consequences of Isaac's deception) represented the wife of Abraham as having suffered such an indignity. Rather, all three recensions imply that the woman involved was divinely protected from this.

The moral implications of the story will be considered in the Exeg. on ch. 26.

obedience into which God means a people to move forward. There was priestcraft in Israel, just as there has been everywhere (remember Amaziah at Bethel); but the unique contribution of Israel was that it produced the prophets. No such inspired succession of clear-seeing men has appeared in any other nation. They simplified religion and at the same time expanded it. "What doth the LORD require of thee, but to do justly, and to love mercy, and to walk humbly with thy God?" asked Micah (6:8); "I will put my law in their inward parts, and write it in their hearts," said Jeremiah (31:33) in the name of God. Religion thus simplified as the contact of the human heart with the living God has the endless expansiveness of an overflowing fountain. What God wanted in men was not little pools of segregated piety; he wanted them to be the channels through which his redeeming purpose would flow to every area of life. "Let judgment run down as waters, and righteousness as a mighty stream" (Amos 5:24). So wherever the heritage of Judaism has entered into it, religion can never stagnate. It will always be prophetic for the higher and better life that ought to be.

Again, the gift of Judaism is the note of promise. Even in the darkest times it had indomitable hope. Men should yet see "the Sun of righteousness arise with healing in his wings" (Mal. 4:2). Messiah would come. And from the Jewish race and out of a Jewish home he did come.

10-20. The Supremacy of God.—In this unvarnished story there are several points that are significant. Conspicuous—to begin with—is the fact that here, as elsewhere, the O.T. is written with an unhesitating realism. The faults of even its greatest figures are not disguised. What Abraham is described as having done when he went into Egypt would throw discredit on any man. Being afraid that the Egyptians would covet Sarah, and thinking that if they knew she was tied to him as her husband they would kill him to get possession of her, he persuaded Sarah to pose as his unmarried sister; and as such she was taken to the house of Pharaoh. In the climax of the story the Egyptian stands in a much better light than Abraham, the man of the covenant; for he denounced indignantly the lie that Abraham had told him, gave Sarah back to him, and let him go out of the country with the rich possessions which had been bestowed upon him when Sarah was first taken. **What is this that thou hast done unto me?** he demanded of Abraham when he learned of Abraham's deception. So, as Frederick W. Robertson has written:

The man of God was rebuked by the man of the world: a thing singularly humiliating. It is common to find men of the world whose honor and integrity is a shame to every Christian; and common enough to find men of religious feeling and aspiration, of whom that same world is compelled to say that whenever they are tried in business there is always a something found wanting. . . . Morality is not religion; but unless religion is grafted on morality, religion is worth nothing.[8]

[8] *Notes on Genesis* (New York: E. P. Dutton & Co., 1877), p. 53.

11 And it came to pass, when he was come near to enter into Egypt, that he said unto Sarai his wife, Behold now, I know that thou *art* a fair woman to look upon:

12 Therefore it shall come to pass, when the Egyptians shall see thee, that they shall say, This *is* his wife: and they will kill me, but they will save thee alive.

13 Say, I pray thee, thou *art* my sister: that it may be well with me for thy sake; and my soul shall live because of thee.

14 ¶ And it came to pass, that, when Abram was come into Egypt, the Egyptians beheld the woman that she *was* very fair.

15 The princes also of Pharaoh saw her, and commended her before Pharaoh: and the woman was taken into Pharaoh's house.

16 And he entreated Abram well for her sake: and he had sheep, and oxen, and he asses, and menservants, and maidservants, and she asses, and camels.

17 And the LORD plagued Pharaoh and his house with great plagues, because of Sarai, Abram's wife.

18 And Pharaoh called Abram, and said, What *is* this *that* thou hast done unto me? why didst thou not tell me that she *was* thy wife?

19 Why saidst thou, She *is* my sister? so I might have taken her to me to wife: now therefore behold thy wife, take *her,* and go thy way.

20 And Pharaoh commanded *his* men concerning him: and they sent him away, and his wife, and all that he had.

11 When he was about to enter Egypt, he said to Sar'ai his wife, "I know that you are a woman beautiful to behold; 12 and when the Egyptians see you, they will say, 'This is his wife'; then they will kill me, but they will let you live. 13 Say you are my sister, that it may go well with me because of you, and that my life may be spared on your account." 14 When Abram entered Egypt the Egyptians saw that the woman was very beautiful. 15 And when the princes of Pharaoh saw her, they praised her to Pharaoh. And the woman was taken into Pharaoh's house. 16 And for her sake he dealt well with Abram; and he had sheep, oxen, he-asses, menservants, maidservants, she-asses, and camels.

17 But the LORD afflicted Pharaoh and his house with great plagues because of Sar'ai, Abram's wife. 18 So Pharaoh called Abram, and said, "What is this you have done to me? Why did you not tell me that she was your wife? 19 Why did you say, 'She is my sister,' so that I took her for my wife? Now then, here is your wife, take her, and be gone." 20 And Pharaoh gave men orders concerning him; and they set him on the way, with his wife and all that he had.

---

11. The representation that Sarah was a beautiful woman and still physically desirable is of course at variance with vss. 4b, according to which Abraham was at the time seventy-five years old, and Sarah therefore (cf. 17:17) sixty-five, and is an outstanding indication of the use of different source documents.

That this story, so unflattering to Abraham, should have a place in Genesis is one of many evidences that for those who compiled the book the supreme focus of interest was not any man, however great, but God. Though the pages are full of vivid human characters the essential drama is not human but divine. We see what Abraham did when he went down into Egypt, but that was not the decisive factor. The natural consequence of his acts would have been disaster, but God prevented that disaster. Even in the times when Abraham failed, God's purpose for him would not fail. That is the mighty faith which is here expressed, and that same faith

shines like a great shaft of light down all O.T. history. In the confidence it gave, the people of Israel went ahead on their eternal road, unshakably convinced that

> behind the dim unknown,
> Standeth God within the shadow keeping watch
> above his own.[4]

When a people believes thus in a divine will that shapes its destiny, it will have—as Israel has had through all its generations—incredible tenacity to face the future, no matter what it may be.

[4] James Russell Lowell, "The Present Crisis," st. viii.

13 And Abram went up out of Egypt, he, and his wife, and all that he had, and Lot with him, into the south.

2 And Abram *was* very rich in cattle, in silver, and in gold.

3 And he went on his journeys from the south even to Bethel, unto the place where his tent had been at the beginning, between Bethel and Hai;

13 So Abram went up from Egypt, he and his wife, and all that he had, and Lot with him, into the Negeb.

2 Now Abram was very rich in cattle, in silver, and in gold. 3 And he journeyed on from the Negeb as far as Bethel, to the place where his tent had been at the begin-

---

13:1. And Lot with him is an incorrect gloss, as the absence of mention of Lot in 12:9-20 indicates. J2 represented him as having remained at Bethel during Abraham's absence.

The section 12:9-10*a* implies that Abraham had remained for some time in the Negeb before entering Egypt. This verse brings him back to the Negeb again, thus suggesting that the J2 document included here a story connected with some southern sanctuary. This story is now found in ch. 16, and the sanctuary was, in the original form of the tradition, probably Beer-sheba. The present position of the tale is due to RP who, influenced by the P representation that Abraham's only dwelling place in Palestine was Kiriath-arba, i.e., Hebron (23:2), placed it after the notice of his arrival there (13:18).

XVI. ABRAHAM AND LOT (13:2-18)

2-18. Vs. 2 was the original continuation in J1 of 12:8 and was followed by vs. 5. Vss. 3-4 are from J2—with some glossing—to bring Abraham back to Bethel where he had left Lot. Vss. 5-18 are a conflation of J and P, the P material being vss. 6, 11*b*, 12*ab*α —probably the immediate continuation of 12:5. P thus omitted the notices that Abraham built altars at Shechem and Bethel, for on his theory there were no sacrifices and so no altars until the law had been given at Sinai. He also omitted all reference to Abraham's sojourn in Egypt and, in accordance with his usual practice in the history of the patriarchs, reduced the detailed narrative of vss. 7-11*a* to the bare notice of vs. 6.

The J story sets the stage for the tale of the destruction of Sodom (19:1-28) which was originally quite independent of that in 18:1-16, the nucleus of the Abraham cycle.

So in the accounts of individuals in the O.T. the emphasis is always on a level different from ordinary biographies. On the stage of the vast O.T. story no mortal persons, not even the most important, determine its action and its meaning. The cosmic drama centers not in what they do but in what Another does. Abraham or some other human figure may be for the moment in the foreground; but always back of him and above him, as here particularly in Abraham's undeserved deliverance, is the majesty of God. Within the framework of O.T. faith, therefore, the final significance of the story of Abraham in Egypt is not that Abraham failed to be a hero; rather, it is in the fact that God's will is in control, whether those who are his instruments are for the moment worthy or unworthy. As in Christian doctrines of the sacraments, faith believes that God's grace comes to the worshiper even though the ministrant is not free from sin, so long ago the men of the O.T. saw God's grace unfailingly at work according to his covenant. A man like Abraham might fall into dishonor. That was a shadow upon the course of history; but no shadow of human dereliction could obscure the light of the heavenly purpose that was building a road of redemption which went on through every obstacle, undefeated by any sin.

13:1-4. Dedication Renewed.—In 12:8 there was the first mention of the name that was to be sacred in the history of Israel henceforth— the name of **Bethel.** At Bethel Abraham set up his first altar in the Land of Promise, to which by God's moving he had come from Ur. Since then he had been down into Egypt, where through a lapse in courage and in honesty he ran into a danger which, except for God's saving mercy, might have been disastrous. He was coming back now with the rewards which, without deserving them, he had had from Pharaoh, **very rich in cattle, in silver, and in gold.** That might have turned his head and made him imagine that his own cleverness and good luck could get him all he wanted. But what he did was to go back to the altar of his

4 Unto the place of the altar, which he had made there at the first: and there Abram called on the name of the LORD.

5 ¶ And Lot also, which went with Abram, had flocks, and herds, and tents.

6 And the land was not able to bear them, that they might dwell together: for their substance was great, so that they could not dwell together.

7 And there was a strife between the herdmen of Abram's cattle and the herdmen of Lot's cattle: and the Canaanite and the Perizzite dwelt then in the land.

ning, between Bethel and Ai, 4 to the place where he had made an altar at the first; and there Abram called on the name of the LORD. 5 And Lot, who went with Abram, also had flocks and herds and tents, 6 so that the land could not support both of them dwelling together; for their possessions were so great that they could not dwell together, 7 and there was strife between the herdsmen of Abram's cattle and the herdsmen of Lot's cattle. At that time the Canaanites and the Per'izzites dwelt in the land.

To give unity to his narrative, J[1] first identified the hero of the Sodom saga with the father of Moab and Ammon, and then made him the nephew of Abraham who had come with him from the desert. This story explains how he came to be living in Sodom instead

---

first dedication, and there again he **called on the name of the LORD.** What was symbolized here in the case of Abraham can be a saving fact in every life. Suppose at the beginning of each chapter of new experience a man sets up the altar of a new consciousness of God, his own Bethel where he perceives and acknowledges his need of heavenly light and guidance. Suppose then that like Abraham he moves on to something that outwardly may seem to have been successful but which inwardly he knows he should be ashamed of. It is well for him that he has that first altar to which he can go back in humility and penitence for renewal of his dedication.

5-8. *The Good and the Bad in Strife.*—The words **Let there be no strife . . . between me and thee** have to do with a personal relationship. Abraham and Lot were kinsmen, and between them there was the further bond of a long-shared experience. It is easy to understand that Abraham, being the sort of man he was, wanted to prevent any strife with Lot and would go a long way to avoid it. But the words suggest a larger thought. To what extent is it a desirable and possible ideal that there should be no strife between human beings?

On the one hand, peace seems unrealistic. Life appears to be largely a process of strife. Through the long course of biological evolution the unfit have had to give way to the fit. Organisms capable of adapting themselves to environment have survived; those incapable have perished. Stronger types thus have developed. On the human level, as well as on lower ones, the creative results of struggle can be seen. The more energetic and resourceful individuals, families, and nations have outstripped inferior

ones, and in so doing have been the pioneers of advancing civilization. And within civilization an element of strife seems still to be necessary if life and character are not to deteriorate. The individual who is relieved from any necessity to strive grows flabby. "Rich folk's children," said Martin Luther, "seldom turn out well. They are complacent, arrogant, and conceited, and think they need to learn nothing because they have enough to live on anyway." [5]

It is a familiar maxim that "competition is the life of trade." Unless men are pitted against one another in some way that excites their efforts and stimulates their wits the whole possibility of accomplishment is apt to stagnate. Consider the ultimate failure of utopian experiments—like Brook Farm and the Oneida Community—where people were segregated from the provocative currents of the general life, and competition was renounced in a little society where everybody was to take care of everybody else. All the eager idealism invested there could not make what was supposed to be a strifeless society endure.

Still more surely do human arrangements seem to stagnate when competition is removed for other and less worthy reasons. All vested interests which stifle competition become inefficient and frequently also corrupt. Consider the sections where there is some dominant economic power, or only one political party, or organs of opinion such as newspapers which have bought out all opposition. One of the worst features of the United States Congress is the flabby principle of seniority, which automatically gives powerful committee chairmanships to the old men. The stodgy rule of precedence is

[5] McGiffert, *Martin Luther*, p. 4.

8 And Abram said unto Lot, Let there be no strife, I pray thee, between me and thee, and between my herdmen and thy herdmen; for we *be* brethren.

8 Then Abram said to Lot, "Let there be no strife between you and me, and between your herdsmen and my herdsmen; for we

---

of at Hebron with Abraham. It is free composition on the part of J[1], depending upon no local tradition.

---

substituted for the test of excellence. Totalitarian governments set themselves to destroy domestic strife altogether by clamping down an iron uniformity, but the forces of life will either revolt or be paralyzed. There would be peril in world government if it fell into the control of one or two of the great powers. Inequities within a nation and injustices between nations seem to require for their correction some sort of strife. Can the component parts of any society ever successfully therefore say to one another, **Let there be no strife . . . between me and thee?**

Yet on the other hand, the evils that may come from strife are plain: the devil-take-the-hindmost principle in business competition, ruthless inequalities of rewards, international trade rivalries with exploitation of weak people and the weapons of tariffs and embargoes used against one another by the strong, growing antagonisms which break out at last into war.

Thus, though the element of strife cannot and perhaps ought not to be eliminated from the general life, there is sharp necessity to correct the evils associated with it. The problem is to adjust it and to make it wholesome.

Steps toward that end may begin with the elimination, by private conscience and by public control, of unfairness. In too many human relationships there are intolerable handicaps laid upon many for the advantage of the few. A century ago the farm laborer or tenant in the country and the worker in the industrial towns were at the mercy of landlords and employers. Some still are. Minority races, such as the Negro in the United States, meet barriers put across the road of their advancement. Children of the poor, no matter how great may be their inherent abilities, are condemned to menial opportunities if they grow up under conditions which leave them physically undernourished and intellectually untrained. In the necessary competition for livelihood there is always struggle, but struggle in which every individual has a fair start and a square deal is different from the crooked fight which is decided by a foul. In every civilized country there is progress in the public opinion, crystallized in law and public policy, which requires a decent chance for health and education for all children, pro-

tection of weak groups from exploitation, the right of working people to organize collectively —in short, provision everywhere for making competition fair.

The criterion of excellence is the positive side of the removal of unfairness. Wherever advantage is gained by favor and pull individuals are corrupted and social good retarded. The kind of competition in which men advance according to demonstrated character and ability brings benefit all around. An example of its perversion is the cheap political patronage on which the government of many American cities is built.

And excellence should be in service. The International Rotary Club has the motto "He profits most who serves best." That might be piety commercialized, but it may be instead a genuine glimpse of a great truth: that in the long run society, and the individual members of it, can prosper only as men honestly strive to produce what is for the general good.

The next step away from unhealthy strife is co-operation. If natural selection governed the early stages of evolution, mutual aid may govern the climactic stages. Note the vital importance of the commissions of the United Nations which are trying to promote for universal benefit, world-wide agreements on access to raw materials, unhampered commerce, the safeguarding of public health, economic and social progress—a kind of co-operation which may remove the tensions that otherwise build up to the insane strife of war.

Finally, through such educative processes of mutual benefit the peoples of the world may learn on the great scale of humanity what Abraham remembered in his relationship with Lot: the bond of kinship. For in the supreme desires all men are akin: in the desire for a decent existence, for freedom from fear and freedom from want, for the chance for themselves and their children to pursue their various ways in peace. And to the extent that the Christian message is not only preached but believed in and put increasingly into practice, we may approach that religious kinship in which men everywhere will be quicker to recognize their own sins and more magnanimous to others who with them are of the one family of "Our Father."

9 *Is* not the whole land before thee? separate thyself, I pray thee, from me: if *thou wilt take* the left hand, then I will go to the right; or if *thou depart* to the right hand, then I will go to the left.

10 And Lot lifted up his eyes, and beheld all the plain of Jordan, that it *was* well watered every where, before the Lord destroyed Sodom and Gomorrah, *even* as the garden of the Lord, like the land of Egypt, as thou comest unto Zoar.

are kinsmen. **9** Is not the whole land before you? Separate yourself from me. If you take the left hand, then I will go to the right; or if you take the right hand, then I will go to the left." **10** And Lot lifted up his eyes, and saw that the Jordan valley was well watered everywhere like the garden of the Lord, like the land of Egypt in the direction of Zo'ar; this was before the Lord de-

---

A. Abraham's Magnanimity (13:2-9)

9. The magnanimity of Abraham should be noted; Lot is given first choice.

B. Lot Moves to Sodom (13:10-13)

10. By **the plain of Jordan** (KJV) is meant the lower part of **the Jordan valley** (RSV), beginning about twenty-five miles north of the Dead Sea and including apparently the basin of the Dead Sea itself, i.e., the author believed that the Dead Sea had come into existence at the time of the destruction of Sodom (cf. 14:3). This was of course quite erroneous. "Geological evidence proves that that amazing depression in the earth's surface had existed for ages before the advent of man on the earth, and formed, from the first, part of a great inland lake whose waters stood originally several hundred feet higher than the present level of the Dead Sea" (Skinner, *Genesis,* p. 273).

9-13. The Mean Man's Folly.—Lot was a man who made what seemed to be a clever choice but which turned out to be a wrong one. He set the example which has been followed by innumerable people since his time who have reached out for what they thought was easy gain and instead have got disaster. The story of Lot is the more arresting because it might have been so different. When we first see him, everything is optimistic. He is disposed to be a good man, at least to the extent of Mr. By-ends in *The Pilgrim's Progress,* who said:

It is true we somewhat differ in religion from those of the stricter sort, yet but in two small points: first, we never strive against wind and tide; secondly, we are always most zealous when Religion goes in his silver slippers; we love much to walk with him in the street, if the sun shines, and the people applaud him.[6]

Lot had associations of the kind that can keep a man up to what he ought to be. He was Abraham's nephew and Abraham's friend; and even when he did not deserve it Abraham stood by him and never let him down. If he had stayed with Abraham he would have kept out of trouble. But when their interests split, he thought he saw a chance to get the better of a deal, and he went off to live in Sodom, even

[6] Part I, ch. vii.

though any man of sense would have known that Sodom was a place to be avoided like the plague.

Note how the facts develop. Abraham and Lot with their respective families and retainers are moving here and there through Canaan, according to where they find pasture for their flocks. The herdsmen of the two begin to quarrel. That distresses Abraham, though it does not seem to have troubled Lot. The one thing Abraham is most bent upon is that friendship should not be embittered; personal loss is to him a secondary matter. So when it seems necessary to separate he offers the advantage wholeheartedly to Lot. Let Lot say whichever part of the land he wants for his own flocks. He can have first choice and Abraham will take what he has left. A right-spirited man would have refused an offer so one-sided, but this man snapped it up. Lot's only concern was to make sure that he used his advantage to the limit. That was his first step in the wrong direction.

The next one followed naturally. The man who had the essential meanness that made him interested only in himself had therefore a moral nearsightedness that kept him from intelligently estimating his own interest. He looked about the land and chose what pleased the eye. All the country in the valley of the Jordan was green and well watered; it was as inviting as a garden but in its human aspect it was no

11 Then Lot chose him all the plain of Jordan; and Lot journeyed east: and they separated themselves the one from the other.

12 Abram dwelt in the land of Canaan, and Lot dwelt in the cities of the plain, and pitched *his* tent toward Sodom.

13 But the men of Sodom *were* wicked and sinners before the LORD exceedingly.

stroyed Sodom and Gomor'rah. 11 So Lot chose for himself all the Jordan valley, and Lot journeyed east; thus they separated from each other. 12 Abram dwelt in the land of Canaan, while Lot dwelt among the cities of the valley and moved his tent as far as Sodom. 13 Now the men of Sodom were wicked, great sinners against the LORD.

The verse has been extensively glossed; **in the direction of Zoar** (cf. 19:22) is connected with **everywhere;** all that intervenes is secondary. **Like the garden of the LORD** refers to 2:10; **the land of Egypt** is also irrigated by a river.

12. Moved his tent as far as Sodom seems to imply that Lot did not at this time take up residence in Sodom but continued to live as a nomad or seminomad in the plain outside the city. On the other hand, in ch. 19 he is living in Sodom and there is no notice in the extant intervening J material of his having changed his mode of life.

13. The verse is not in condemnation of Lot's indifference, but simply part of J¹'s preparation for ch. 19. With this verse may be contrasted 18:20-21 (J²).

---

garden. It was the territory adjacent to Sodom, and **the men of Sodom were wicked and sinners before the LORD exceedingly.** A fine country to make fat sheep, but a poor place for a man to risk his fate. Once he got to Sodom, Lot had an unhappy conscience. He did not like the corrupt things that went on there but his dislike was never virile enough to make him get up and leave. Instead, he stayed in Sodom, complaining but also compromising (cf. ch. 19) until the wickedness of Sodom led to its destruction and he lost all his possessions and barely got away with his life.

Abraham, meanwhile, who had given generously when Lot was concerned only to grab, had gone into paths that God could bless. When Lot took the low road because it was the easy one, he took the high road. And he had gone where Lot had no steady will to go, viz., through the choices day by day which a man makes by asking not "Will it pay?" but "Is it right?"

Note that there are always two classes of men; and regarding them, every man needs to consider which one he is tending to belong to: the men like Lot or the men like Abraham. It is a distinction that confronts every young man who first surveys his world and determines what kind of "success" he will aim at. It confronts every mature person in the recurring decisions where conscience would go one way and the temptation to experiment in Sodom points another. The danger of becoming like Lot is in the fact that a man gets there by degrees. Lot began as a decent person; yet he ended not only in disaster, but caught in a debacle which the environment he had chosen for his family and the influences he had thus created for them

brought about (read ch. 19). It is not only the risks a man runs directly but the risks that indirectly he produces which may be decisive. The steps by which Lot came to the end he reached have been well suggested by James Strachan in *Hebrew Ideals:*[7]

First, Lot looked toward Sodom (vs. 10). That was partly accident. He was looking all about to make what he thought would be a shrewd decision, and Sodom happened to be among the possibilities. He was not responsible for its existence; what he was responsible for was the appeal he let its existence make to him. Second, he **pitched his tent toward Sodom** (vs. 12). He had not decided yet to go into it, but he was led closer to its attraction because the prosperity he wanted seemed to lie in its environment. When later he had been sucked into the life of Sodom he might have offered the excuse that he had not originally intended that. But the answer he got might have been like the answer of a father to his son who was caught in an act he should have been ashamed of. Said the boy, "But I didn't mean to." "That is not enough," was the reply. "You should have meant not to." Lot did not positively mean not to.

And so—third—he "dwelt in Sodom" (14:12). Having got that far in his descending choices, it is not surprising that when the critical hour came and the society he shared was ripe for judgment he could not bring himself to break with Sodom. "He lingered" there (19:16). In the same gradual fashion many a life may lose the chance to take the high road with Abraham, and instead will take the low road with Lot.

[7] I, 50.

14 ¶ And the LORD said unto Abram, after that Lot was separated from him, Lift up now thine eyes, and look from the place where thou art northward, and southward, and eastward, and westward:

14 The LORD said to Abram, after Lot had separated from him, "Lift up your eyes, and look from the place where you are, northward and southward and eastward

C. ABRAHAM SETTLES IN HEBRON (13:14-18)

14-17. These verses, breaking the connection between vss. 13 and 18 and lacking concreteness in that no theophany is recorded, are secondary, inserted into the J2 narrative

14-17. The Fallacy of Bigness.—There is an almost invincible human tendency to think that greatness is a matter of size. A small boy brags that he is taller than another boy or, if the other boy has something, that he has something bigger and better than that. Chambers of commerce advertise their cities' populations or the amount of bank clearings and commercial profits. Nations embark on policies of expansion. In its interpretation of the promise that God made to Abraham and to the nation whose father he should be even Genesis partially reflects the idea that to be bigger is to be better. That nation should possess unbounded lands. It should grow to infinite numbers.

But greatness is not a matter of size. Bulk and bigness are not decisive. The huge reptiles which once dominated the earth, the dinosaurs and the brontosaurs, were enormous. So was the mammoth. But they have all become extinct. Notwithstanding their size and seeming strength they could not adapt themselves to a changing world. Similarly, great empires have perished in spite of their physical dimensions. Ponder the history of Assyria, of the kingdoms of Alexander the Great, of the Roman Empire, of sixteenth-century Spain. Remember the lines in Kipling's "Recessional,"

> Lo, all our pomp of yesterday
> Is one with Nineveh and Tyre! [8]

Mussolini might well have reflected upon that before he proclaimed, as he did again and again in flamboyant speeches, that the power of a nation is rooted in its ability to expand, and that unless Italy embarked on the adventures of expansion she was living a useless national existence; and Hitler likewise might well have paused before he launched Nazi Germany upon its program of ruthless conquests and boasted that the Third Reich would "last for a thousand years."

So there is a fallacy of bigness. Wherein does this fallacy lie? To begin with, bigness arouses

[8] From *The Five Nations*. Used by permission of Mrs. George Bambridge; Methuen & Co.; The Macmillan Co., Canada; and Doubleday & Co.

fear. In all life there is instinctive resistance to physical domination. In the measure that a nation appears able to impose its will the antagonism of others begins to be organized against it. At the same time, while bigness is provoking opposition without, it may be producing inefficiency within. That was the trouble with the Roman Empire. It spread so far that there was not sufficient intelligence and clear purpose at the center to maintain it. Bigness not only in a military but in an economic and industrial sense is subject to the same dangers. In the United States the very vastness of the nation's resources raises the question as to whether sufficient intelligence and moral force can be mobilized to prevent huge energies from passing through domestic conflict into chaos. The more dominant one class becomes within a nation, or the more dominant one nation becomes upon the earth, the greater may be its danger. As Lord Acton wrote, "All power corrupts. Absolute power corrupts absolutely." Finally, the fact of bigness and the boastful satisfaction which it brings may make a nation as well as an individual blind to the day of crisis. Consider Jesus' parable of the man who built his greater barns and was sure that he had an unlimited time in which to eat, drink, and be merry. Yet that night his soul was required of him. The life of a nation, like the life of every man, stands ultimately accountable to the judgments of God. No amount of material possessions can save it unless it maintains its soul.

14-17. What Makes a Nation Great?—There is, as we have seen, a fallacy of bigness. It is true that in the case of a nation this does not mean that material elements have no importance. The nation with the large population and with great resources can play an additionally powerful role in history, but great power misused can no less surely provoke disintegration and doom. The ultimate determinant is not in mass but quality. Athens was great, though physically she was small; so was medieval Florence; so has been the Jewish nation. Like other nations, it has had its sins

15 For all the land which thou seest, to thee will I give it, and to thy seed for ever.

16 And I will make thy seed as the dust of the earth: so that if a man can number the dust of the earth, *then* shall thy seed also be numbered.

17 Arise, walk through the land in the length of it and in the breadth of it; for I will give it unto thee.

18 Then Abram removed *his* tent, and came and dwelt in the plain of Mamre, which *is* in Hebron, and built there an altar unto the LORD.

and westward; **15** for all the land which you see I will give to you and to your descendants for ever. **16** I will make your descendants as the dust of the earth; so that if one can count the dust of the earth, your descendants also can be counted. **17** Arise, walk through the length and the breadth of the land, for I will give it to you." **18** So Abram moved his tent, and came and dwelt by the oaks[s] of Mamre, which are at Hebron; and there he built an altar to the LORD.

[s] Or *terebinths*

by one who presumably felt that Abraham's magnanimity should receive some immediate recognition.

18. For oaks should be read with the LXX and Syriac, "oak"; cf. the reference to "the tree"—singular—in 18:4, 8; also "the oak of Moreh," in 12:6. The statement that Abraham immediately upon his arrival at Hebron **built an altar to the LORD** divorces his founding of the sanctuary there from the theophany recorded in 18:1-8, with which it was originally connected. In both J[1] and J[2] the story in ch. 18 followed at once upon this verse, but the altar had already been built, and by implication the cult was inaugurated by Abraham before "the LORD appeared to him" (18:1).

and blunders, but it has also pointed the way to realities which in God's eyes make a nation great.

What are these elements of greatness? First, a sense of spiritual destiny. Israel always had that. Read the farewell address attributed to Moses in Deut. 8. Consider the hope of the great prophets, such as appears in Isa. 11. In the times when any nation has had claim to moral and spiritual greatness, it has been because that nation had a sense of destiny infused with a religious passion. Reflect upon the struggles of the Netherlands for freedom against Spain. Think of the best elements in the British Empire as it develops into a commonwealth of nations, inspired by a common ideal of democracy. As concerns the United States, read James Truslow Adams, *The Epic of America*,[1] and Ralph Barton Perry, *Puritanism and Democracy*.[2]

A nation's greatness may be tested by the quality of the men it exalts and honors. See in the O.T. how the great figures are chiefly those not of military conquerors but of men whose conquests were in the arena of the soul: Abraham, Joseph, Moses, Elijah, and all the prophets. The hero David, it is true, was in some measure a conqueror, but even he was exalted mostly because he was believed to have been chosen by God as "a man after his own heart" (I Sam.

[1] Boston: Little, Brown & Co., 1932.
[2] New York: Vanguard Press, 1944.

13:14). The souls of nations will be tested today by the type of men they really honor.

The greatness of a nation depends also upon its ability to endure. A notable pageant which dramatized Jewish history was entitled *The Eternal Road,* and it showed through the centuries Israel's loyalty and devotion moving on in spite of persecution and disaster. No nation can last if it has not suffered. Consider the immense patience and courage of China's people through World War II. Read the speeches of Winston Churchill when he said in the House of Commons on June 18, 1940, the most desperate moment of England's danger, that the nation must so bear itself that "if the British Commonwealth and Empire last for a thousand years, men will still say 'This was their finest hour.' "

The great nation looks forward and not backward. There comes a time in many so-called patriotic organizations when they lose the spirit which they claim to represent and become mere stubborn guardians of a fossilized past. The message of the prophets in Israel was something greater that was always beckoning, a messianic purpose for the nation and the world. The great nation must have a consciousness of "the living God," and so must know that its conception of its own destiny is to be continued and renewed and extended.

18. See Expos. on 12:8.

14 And it came to pass in the days of Amraphel king of Shinar, Arioch king of Ellasar, Chedorlaomer king of Elam, and Tidal king of nations;

14 In the days of Am′raphel king of Shinar, Ar′ioch king of Ella′sar, Ched-or-lao′mer king of Elam, and Tidal king of

---

XVII. THE WAR OF THE KINGS (14:1-24)

This narrative is an isolated unit belonging to none of the main documents of the Hexateuch (cf. Gunkel, *Genesis*, pp. 288-90; Skinner, *Genesis*, pp. 271-76), and comes from an age which "admires military glory all the more because it can conduct no wars itself; . . . an age in which, in spite of a certain historical erudition, the historic sense of Judaism had sunk almost to zero" (Skinner, *Genesis*, p. 274, quoting from the second edition [p. 255] of Gunkel's commentary). It is thus of much the same character as the book of Judith and the Chronicler's accounts of military exploits.

The tale itself provides evidence of its unhistorical character: (*a*) The representation that four great rulers of the east themselves moved westward to curb the revolt of five petty kings in Palestine (vss. 5-9) and that they came by the circuitous route outlined in vss. 5-7. (*b*) The representation that Abraham with 318 retainers defeated the combined armies of the eastern kings (vss. 14-16). In this connection it may be noted that nowhere else in the tradition is Abraham represented as living in such state. In ch. 23 (P), for instance, he is a lone stranger among the Hittite inhabitants of Kiriath-arba. (*c*) The representation that the Dead Sea was not yet in existence (cf. 13:10). It should be said, however, that the words in vs. 3, **that is, the Salt Sea,** may be a gloss, and so may not reflect accurately the thought of the original author.

Nevertheless, the author may have been, and probably was, piecing together fragments of different historical traditions. The names of the four kings in vs. 1 may be historical, though it does not follow that they acted together as the narrative depicts, or even that they were contemporaries. Vss. 5-7 may preserve an authentic though distorted tradition of an Elamite subjugation of southern Palestine—not of a punitive raid upon recalcitrant vassal kings. And the story of Abraham's pursuit and defeat of the kings may echo an actual event, such as a surprise attack by a band of Palestinians upon a raiding force which would, however, have been much smaller than is represented here.

A. THE WAR (14:1-16)

14:1. On the identification of the kings see Skinner, *Genesis, ad loc.,* who notes the attempt which has been made to identify **Amraphel** with the well-known Hammurabi

---

14:1-16. *The Ancient Evil: War.*—Here in the Bible we come upon its first glorification of war. It will be followed by many chronicles of the same spirit: in Exodus, in Joshua, in Judges, and so through a long line. The proudest literature of other peoples, from Homer's *Iliad* on, is full of the sound of war. The reason for this is plain enough. Human existence has always been a struggle. Man fought first for survival against the beasts, then for hunting grounds and food. Individual fighting expanded into the mutual ferocity of tribes. The deep primal instinct of self-preservation was at the root of it. In part of his nature man expressed, and still expresses, the inheritance of the jungle and a demonic element that is in his humanity itself.

That would make him take war for granted. But it was something more that made him glorify it. War has been the most vivid expres-sion of qualities that he held as noble. It represented physical hardihood, discipline, and uncalculating courage. It involved the willingness of the individual to risk his life, and if necessary to lose it, for the sake of the group. In its romantic development war was clothed with the mantle of chivalry and provided a symbol of gallantry and heroic greatness. Because war thus embodied so many of humanity's ideals it became almost identified with the supreme ideal. It grew to seem synonymous not only with romance but with religion. The wars of the O.T. are the wars of the Lord. Christian civilizations—or those that think themselves to be such—like to call their wars "crusades."

So it is true that this story of Abraham the warrior has been a welcome passage for many preachers. So have the many other accounts of

2 *That these* made war with Bera king of Sodom, and with Birsha king of Gomorrah, Shinab king of Admah, and Shemeber king of Zeboiim, and the king of Bela, which is Zoar.

3 All these were joined together in the vale of Siddim, which is the salt sea.

4 Twelve years they served Chedorlaomer, and in the thirteenth year they rebelled.

5 And in the fourteenth year came Chedorlaomer, and the kings that *were* with him, and smote the Rephaim in Ashteroth Karnaim, and the Zuzim in Ham, and the Emim in Shaveh Kiriathaim,

6 And the Horites in their mount Seir, unto El-paran, which *is* by the wilderness.

7 And they returned, and came to En-mishpat, which *is* Kadesh, and smote all the country of the Amalekites, and also the Amorites, that dwelt in Hazezon-tamar.

Goi'im, 2 these kings made war with Bera king of Sodom, Birsha king of Gomor'rah, Shinab king of Admah, Sheme'ber king of Zeboi'im, and the king of Bela (that is, Zo'ar). 3 All these joined forces in the Valley of Siddim (that is, the Salt Sea). 4 Twelve years they had served Ched-or-lao'mer, but in the thirteenth year they rebelled. 5 In the fourteenth year Ched-or-lao'mer and the kings who were with him came and subdued the Reph'aim in Ash'te-roth-kar-na'im, the Zuzim in Ham, the Emim in Sha'veh-kir-iatha'im, 6 and the Horites in their Mount Se'ir as far as El-paran on the border of the wilderness; 7 then they turned back and came to Enmish'pat (that is, Kadesh), and subdued all the country of the Amal'ekites, and also the Amorites who

---

(*ca.* 2100 B.C.) of the First Babylonian Dynasty, and is extremely dubious as to its validity (cf. W. F. Albright, "A Revision of Early Hebrew Chronology," *Journal of the Palestine Oriental Society,* I [1920], 70-71; "Shinar-Šangar and Its Monarch Amraphel,"

---

fighting under the banner of "the God of the armies of Israel." There is much satisfaction when what old instincts press upon us can be linked with piety and the stirring of our blood can be indulged as a fulfillment for our souls.

But the arresting fact is that in this twentieth century there has been a break in the ancient thinking. Always of course a minority of seers and prophets have recognized war to be a thing of darkness and evil, and have proclaimed it so; but the great chorus of human voices glorified it. Now that chorus begins to stammer, especially among the preachers. To be sure, there is not in religious circles, as there is not in the general world, any majority of pacifists. Most people as they read history maintain that wars have sometimes been the only means by which great principles could be defended and that the same may be true today. But the tone is different. War may be justified as a grim necessity, but there is reluctance to try to make it seem religious. It is not God, but the long complex of human sin in its revolt from God, that compels us to devote reason and science and culture to the service of death and stupidity. . . . Can anything be more utterly idiotic, *e.g.*, than civilised communities depriving themselves of food in order to utilise the materials and energies saved in this way to blow one another to hell? [3]

[3] Davies, *Down Peacock's Feathers,* pp. 10-11.

Most Christian interpreters today would be embarrassed to say what good men said a generation ago with robust good conscience. James Strachan of the Church of Scotland published in 1906 his *Hebrew Ideals,* and through it his sturdy faith and his religious insight have given rich meaning to much of Genesis. But in it, as he dealt expansively with the story of Abraham's defeat of the five kings, he wrote: "Abram the Hebrew left his people an ideal of noble warfare and high chivalry. He is the type of all . . . heroes of faith, mighty men of valour animated by the spirit of God. . . . The appropriate limits of the Holy Land—Dan and Beersheba—were a battlefield and a shrine." [4] And later, referring to Melchizedek as he met Abraham fresh from his fighting, he wrote: "He blessed the hero whose good sword was wet with the blood of tyrants. Before the dulcet notes of peace there must often be heard the trumpet tones of war for righteousness." [5]

How many now would write or think in quite those terms? We are not so much at ease in equating "the trumpet tones of war" with righteousness and battlefields with shrines. We recognize that war may be a good way to worship Moloch but that it is a poor way to worship the God of the prophets and of Jesus Christ. War may employ many of the ideals

[4] I, 54-55.
[5] *Ibid.,* I, 63.

8 And there went out the king of Sodom, and the king of Gomorrah, and the king of Admah, and the king of Zeboiim, and the king of Bela, (the same *is* Zoar;) and they joined battle with them in the vale of Siddim;

9 With Chedorlaomer the king of Elam, and with Tidal king of nations, and Amraphel king of Shinar, and Arioch king of Ellasar; four kings with five.

10 And the vale of Siddim *was full of* slime pits; and the kings of Sodom and Gomorrah fled, and fell there; and they that remained fled to the mountain.

11 And they took all the goods of Sodom and Gomorrah, and all their victuals, and went their way.

12 And they took Lot, Abram's brother's son, who dwelt in Sodom, and his goods, and departed.

13 ¶ And there came one that had escaped, and told Abram the Hebrew; for he dwelt in the plain of Mamre the Amorite, brother of Eshcol, and brother of Aner: and these *were* confederate with Abram.

dwelt in Haz′azon-ta′mar. **8** Then the king of Sodom, the king of Gomor′rah, the king of Admah, the king of Zeboi′im, and the king of Bela (that is, Zo′ar) went out, and they joined battle in the Valley of Siddim **9** with Ched-or-lao′mer king of Elam, Tidal king of Goi′im, Am′raphel king of Shinar, and Ar′ioch king of Ella′sar, four kings against five. **10** Now the Valley of Siddim was full of bitumen pits; and as the kings of Sodom and Gomor′rah fled, some fell into them, and the rest fled to the mountain. **11** So the enemy took all the goods of Sodom and Gomor′rah, and all their provisions, and went their way; **12** they also took Lot, the son of Abram's brother, who dwelt in Sodom, and his goods, and departed.

13 Then one who had escaped came, and told Abram the Hebrew, who was living by the oaks[s] of Mamre the Amorite, brother of Eshcol and of Aner; these were allies of

[s] Or *terebinths*

American Journal of Semitic Languages, XL [1924], 125-33) . In any case, in view of the unhistorical character of the present narrative, no light is thrown by this verse upon the

---

of the human spirit, but it also prostitutes them. If it calls men to be brave, it also deforms them into killers. It breeds hatreds which spread like poison everywhere. In the long run no people can win in war, but everyone can lose. And the evils that war is supposed to destroy are like the heads of the Hydra. Cut off one and a hundred grow in its place. Consider the malignant forces that multiplied after 1918, when "the war to end war" was supposed to have been won, and look at those which were released in the late 30's and 40's. With the fatal secret of atomic energy now as an instrument for men's passions, another war would have no room for "high chivalry" in its beastly and indiscriminate annihilation. General Omar Bradley spoke on Armistice Day, 1948, to the Boston Chamber of Commerce and said:

With the monstrous weapons man already has, humanity is in danger of being trapped in this world by its moral adolescents. Our knowledge of science has clearly outstripped our capacity to control it. We have many men of science; too few men of God. We have grasped the mystery of the atom, and rejected the Sermon on the Mount. Man is stumbling blindly through a spiritual darkness while toying with·the precarious secrets of life and

death. The world has achieved brilliance without wisdom, power without conscience. Ours is a world of nuclear giants and ethical infants. We know more about war than we know about peace, more about killing than we know about living. This is our twentieth century's claim to distinction and progress.

So the true interpreter today will not be disposed to consider that Abraham gave the "ideal of noble warfare" most signally in the glamorously remembered battle with the kings. He gave it more eternally in the other warfare that he waged prevailingly in his own soul, the warfare exemplified in his relationship with Lot: the warfare whose victory was of magnanimity over mean interest, of patience over irritation, of greatness in service over narrow self-regard.

13. *Life's Great Decisions.*—The name **Hebrew,** as the Exeg, has pointed out, may mean "the crosser." In any case, the thought of the Hebrew people was steeped in the tradition that back in their history was a momentous crossing. Their fathers had come from beyond the river.

Rivers are one of the chief aspects of geography and one of the most formative in the history of the human race. Civilization

14 And when Abram heard that his brother was taken captive, he armed his trained *servants,* born in his own house, three hundred and eighteen, and pursued *them* unto Dan.

Abram. 14 When Abram heard that his kinsman had been taken captive, he led forth his trained men, born in his house, three hundred and eighteen of them, and went in

---

began in the river valleys, as in the valley of the Nile.[6] For the civilization that spread to Europe, north of the Mediterranean, the rivers of Mesopotamia had supreme importance. There in the valleys of the Tigris and the Euphrates developed the society from which Abraham came. In the fertile lands which the rivers watered, men could comfortably live. To leave the river and go out into the untamed regions that lay beyond was a hazardous adventure.

A river is a natural boundary. To cross a river, or some other dividing water, or to turn one's back upon the region determined by it, may be a decisive event in the affairs of men: Abraham leaving the valley of the Euphrates; the Israelites, led by Moses out of Egypt, crossing the Jordan; Caesar crossing the Rubicon; Paul, the torch-bearer of a new gospel, crossing the Hellespont into Greece. To stand irresolute on the near side of the dividing water and flinch from crossing over may be to stop the march of destiny. Only beyond the accustomed and long accepted barrier may lie the greatness of life.

The physical waters over which the adventurers have passed are parables of the barriers which must be crossed in the world of the mind and of the spirit. There are rivers of complacency and prejudice so wide and staggering that to most men it seems unthinkable that there could be anything on the other side that belongs to them. What rivers of self-satisfaction, of pride of race and color, of stubborn selfishness of class or nation, must we cross if life is to go forward?

Are we great enough of mind and spirit, furthermore, to launch out upon those currents of the unpredictable to the edge of which the fateful hours of history bring us? In the twentieth century we have arrived at such a place and hour. The splitting of the atom and the awful possibilities which that unfolds have brought us to the end of one world and to the brink of an unexplored ocean beyond which lies another; for atomic fission, as scientists who know it most have reiterated, is "not just another weapon against which our military minds will find a defense, but the greatest cataclysmic force ever released on earth." The Emergency Committee of Atomic Scientists, headed by Albert Einstein, has declared: "If war breaks

out, atomic bombs will be used, and they will surely destroy our civilization. There is no solution to this problem except international control of atomic energy and, ultimately, the elimination of war." [7]

To all but the ignorant and the shallow it will be plain that those words are not rhetoric but terrible reality. Mankind has been pushed to the edge of its old continent of ideas and of existence. It has got to take possession of a new one or perish. Both individuals and nations must be ready to be crossers—crossers from the constriction of complacency and imagined local immunity to the moral and spiritual advances which humanity must make together if it would survive. The human race must lay hold upon the Hebrew heritage. The dividing waters can be crossed.

But the great crossings cannot be made by the careless. The seizing of the Remagen Bridge and the crossing of the Rhine to end the war against Nazi Germany in 1945 was not made by accident. Such a crossing had been imagined, the possibility of it foreseen and prepared for. General Dwight D. Eisenhower had ordered every one of his commanders to look for it. He sent his forces instantly ahead when the opportunity came. So it must be with the moral and spiritual crossings. The one thing that would be fatal would be indifference or fumbling irresolution at the critical hour. Public opinion and public action cannot halt at the banks of the Rhine of universal destiny and think that there is no necessity to make a critical advance. The issue for civilization is life or death. Or let us turn the two words to put the greater at the climax and say that the issue is death or life. Atomic energy does not have to spell doom. On the contrary it can give into human hands the power to create a more abundantly furnished and happier society than the earth has ever known.

Here is where the force of Christian ideals and Christian faith can enter. David E. Lilienthal, chairman of the United States Atomic Energy Commission, in an address at the University of Rochester, voiced the conviction which needs to be echoed everywhere: "The foundation of our strength and amazing vitality is not in material things at all but . . . in the faiths we cherish. . . . If we live with faith I deeply believe that these great discoveries of

[6] See James H. Breasted, *The Dawn of Conscience* (New York: Charles Scribner's Sons, 1933).

[7] *New York Times,* Nov. 18, 1946.

15 And he divided himself against them, he and his servants, by night, and smote them, and pursued them unto Hobah, which *is* on the left hand of Damascus.

pursuit as far as Dan. **15** And he divided his forces against them by night, he and his servants, and routed them and pursued them to Hobah, north of Damascus.

our time can be made to better the lot of mankind and further the kingdom of God." [8] Christian people and the Christian church may be able to cast into the scales the weight which will bring about that vast result; for in order that humanity may now cross the river on the way to the Promised Land there will be needed supremely what Christianity can give—reverence for life, belief in a divine destiny, inspired imagination, and the courageous practical dedication that comes from faith in God.

13. The Better Possibilities.—Consider further the qualities suggested above that make possible advance of the general human life:

Reverence for life itself. The savage has no compunction against killing, whether he is the savage of prehistoric times or the savage emerging again under the veneer of civilization. But wherever there is a developing conscience there is an enlarging respect for life, including subhuman life. See the relationship of a man to his horse or his dog. Note the rise and spread of such organizations as the Society for the Prevention of Cruelty to Animals, and the enactment of laws for the protection of wild life. Formerly there was miscellaneous slaughter of whatever hunters chose to kill or people could be found to buy. Women wore stuffed songbirds as ornaments on their hats; and the beautiful egret was almost exterminated in the United States to satisfy the greedy vanity that wanted the plumes made from its feathers. The Audubon societies represented the conscience which has brought that particular cruelty to its end.

As society has become more sensitive to the worth of life in its subhuman forms, so it has become more sensitive in its treatment of human life even in its subnormal aspects. Witness the changing conscience as to the treatment of criminals, of the insane, of the feeble-minded, and the revulsion of the general conscience against the "removal of the unfit" which went on in Nazi Germany. All these are signs of the central recognition that any society emerges from brutishness in direct proportion to its sense of a sacredness in life and its gradual enlightenment as to those values by which life must be estimated. All life is of worth, yet not of equal worth. The pantheism of India, with its sacred cows and cobras, can sink into ethical stagnation. The highest life, as reason and revelation agree in telling, is the life of the

[8] *Ibid.*, Jan. 16, 1948.

human soul that is conceived as a child of God. Reverence for personality therefore is the mainspring of social progress. Without that, the relationship of employer and employee, of landlord and tenant, of banker and borrower, can be nothing but a wolfish struggle in which nothing matters but money. Without that, the relationship of nations will sink inevitably through insensate rivalry, suspicion, and hostility to "the next war." How great therefore is the responsibility of Christian churches and Christian citizens to try to create so deep an understanding and appreciation of human souls as such, whatever their class or color or nation, that the binding social forces may be stronger than the disruptive ones.

Belief in a divine destiny. It is true that this belief is subject to perversion. Classes and nations may falsely assume a kind of divine prerogative and privilege. "Economic royalists" have sometimes asserted a supposed right to dictate the conditions under which lesser men must live and work for them. Nations have set up their philosophies of "the master race" (see the writings of Nietzsche). Note the brutal self-assertion of Nazism, which in its repudiation of real religion went back to an atavistic religion of pagan gods which gave license to a blind worship of race and blood and soil; yet note more importantly that this is no unparalleled phenomenon, but only the ultimate expression of a cruel arrogance which may be in part in every people. See the smug use of such a phrase as "God's country," and the tendency of every country in a crisis to think that God must properly be on its side. Hebrew history was not free from this. But there is a great belief which is not only positive but also pure and redeeming. It is the belief that a group or a nation is meant to be and may be an instrument in the hands of God, so that "the glory of Israel" is also in moral quality "a light to lighten the Gentiles" (Luke 2:32). The great liberal statesmen of England have seen that ideal. So did the men who lighted the burning convictions of American democracy. What is our thought of destiny today, and in that thought are the convictions that come from God made dominant?

Inspired imagination. Both words are important. Social advance does not come from dull and dead adherence to tradition. "It was said of old time" is not enough. There must be the explosive power of new ideas, as the prophets of Israel understood, and as Jesus supremely

| 16 And he brought back all the goods, and also brought again his brother Lot, and his goods, and the women also, and the people. | 16 Then he brought back all the goods, and also brought back his kinsman Lot with his goods, and the women and the people. |

date of Abraham—or upon the chronology of the period preceding the Exodus in "Israel's history."

exemplified. Neither can the great power be unloosed by any plodding arithmetic which assumes that in the world of moral creativity, as in mathematics, two and two can never make more than four, nor the whole ever be greater than its parts. In the life of the spirit, when old men and young men alike see visions and dream dreams, there are mighty emergent possibilities. The supreme movements in social advances, the breakup of the gladiatorial shows, the abolition of slavery, the humanizing of prisons, the protection of children, the lifting of the status of women, have come to pass because men of imagination looked away from dead precedent and beyond demonstrable probability to the hopes they saw on the horizon and dared believe could be attained. Only imagination has given—and for the critical human needs of today and tomorrow can give—substance to things hoped for and create its own antecedent evidence of things not seen. And such imagination must be inspired. The fire does not kindle from any dull combustion of ordinary calculations. It comes as something given by God, the coal from off the altar, which can be communicated only to those who have drawn near enough to the altar to receive it.

A courageous practical dedication. It is only those who are dedicated who can be completely courageous. Human strength and confidence waver, but the dedicated man knows he is not alone. The cause he is pledged to is his reinforcement; God's strength is at his back. Over and beyond the ranks of the enemy he sees the chariots of the hosts of God (read II Kings 6; see A. H. Clough's poem "It fortifies my soul to know"). And the right sort of dedication is not a mystical absorption; it is the application of the ideal to practical and pressing needs. Consider the striving toward a Christian conviction made relevant to the real world, as in the program of the World Council of Churches. Faith without works is dead; faith with works is like a fire that renews itself with its own spreading power.

13. The Final River.—The great progressions of life are made by those who, like Abraham, cross over the rivers. Past the dividing lines and barriers that bind the old, they go forward to new adventure. If that is true in life, it is true also at the end of life. With this difference:

there is a final river which everyone must cross, whether he will or no. On the banks of that river there can be no refusal. It is not a question of crossing or not crossing; it is a question of how one regards the river, and of the spirit in which he goes over. For that river is death.

The fact of it is sure. But the recognition of it is not. One of the marks of modern times is its effort to obscure and forget the fact of death and to hide all signs that the years move on toward it. Women with dyed hair and fantastic make-up try pathetically to look young. Neither women nor men like to talk of death or to have it talked about. How many sermons deal directly with it? Yet all this is a complete reversal of the attitude of earlier generations. In St. Paul's Cathedral, London, as the only monument saved from the burning of the older cathedral, is a statue of John Donne, the famous dean, made by his direction while he was living, but made of him dressed in his shroud. See his "Hymn to God My God, in My Sickness" and "A Hymn to God the Father." The old graveyards of New England are full of unflinching proclamations of the imminence of death. On numberless tombstones is cut the same inscription to arrest whoever passes by:

> As you are now, so once was I;
> As I am now, you soon will be;
> Prepare to die and follow me.

The literature of the seventeenth and eighteenth centuries in England and the United States had the remembrance of death ringing through it like a solemn bell. So with the great preaching. Observe the sermons of John Donne, of Jonathan Edwards, of George Whitefield, and John Wesley. That was morbid? The sharp reaction from it is the mark of our more normal and more wholesome age? We like to think so. But the truth may be different. Is our age better balanced, or is it only unbalanced, toward a shallow carelessness instead of the forefathers' grave concern? Is the taboo we have put on talk of death a mark of fearlessness, or is it only evasion and a nervous mechanized means of escape? Certainly we do not dispose of death by disregarding it. Whether we want to face it or not, it faces us. The fact is there.

What is the nature of that fact? There have been many answers in the course of human

17 ¶ And the king of Sodom went out to meet him, after his return from the slaughter of Chedorlaomer and of the kings that *were* with him, at the valley of Shaveh, which *is* the king's dale.

18 And Melchizedek king of Salem brought forth bread and wine: and he *was* the priest of the most high God.

17 After his return from the defeat of Ched-or-lao′mer and the kings who were with him, the king of Sodom went out to meet him at the Valley of Shaveh (that is, the King's Valley). 18 And Mel-chiz′edek king of Salem brought out bread and wine;

B. Melchizedek (14:17-20)

17-20. The Melchizedek section, although it may be secondary as Gunkel suggests (*Genesis*, pp. 284-85), is probably the more significant part of the story. Melchizedek is introduced as the priest-king of Salem, i.e., Jerusalem (cf. Ps. 76:2). That his name is traditional is suggested by its occurrence in Ps. 110:4 and by the fact that the root *çdq*—usually transliterated *zdk*—"righteousness," is found repeatedly in the O.T. in connection

---

thought. Death may be conceived of as extinction. But the human spirit is seldom able to believe that for long. Wrote Browning:

Just when we are safest, there's a sunset-touch,
A fancy from a flower-bell, some one's death,
A chorus-ending from Euripides,—
And that's enough for fifty hopes and fears
As old and new at once as nature's self,
To rap and knock and enter in our soul,
Take hands and dance there, a fantastic ring,
Round the ancient idol, on his base again,—
The grand Perhaps! [9]

The river of death has been conceived as the river Styx, where a grim ferryman takes the traveler over into a land of shades. Has the modern mind drifted back to an unconscious paganism which looks at death therefore instinctively in that drab pagan way—the obsession with material realities being so masterful that the immaterial, the invisible, the spiritual, can seem nothing but unsatisfying shades? Let the individual reflect upon what may be the involvement of his own thoughts and affections. Some are carnal; some are careless; many lie only in the things of sense and time. How can the realities beyond the river seem real if the heart has never been fastened upon those interests in life which can be carried over there? But in the great thought of the Hebrew-Christian heritage death has been regarded as the river Jordan, beyond which lies the Promised Land. To pass over it is not a thing of fear but the achievement of the ends of faith. Some of the early Negro spirituals are the naïve but beautiful expression of an everlasting vision. But a vision which is only a dream of undeveloped human children? No. For the same conception of death as the boundary beyond which lies all the best that this life has been reaching for is reflected in men and women whose minds and wills are most mature. Read Browning's "Prospice." It is a delusion to suppose that the so-called realism which satisfies only a material appetite is practical. Seen in the final light, "realism" may be as infantile as the play of children who think that castles in the sand will last. But the growing soul can leave its sand castles for something better. With a great expectancy it can pass over Jordan.

How is this expectancy created? By a lengthening perspective of those whose spirits have reached on and up toward God, who has reached down to them. "Where your treasure is, there will your heart be also" (Matt. 6:21). An otherworldliness that makes a person unrelated and irresponsible to the duties of every day is wrong; but there is an otherworldliness which introduces the meaning of the beyond into the here and now. Some attachments are so rooted in the flesh that they are bound to die when the body dies, but the great loyalties lead on. Stonewall Jackson, wounded at Chancellorsville, said in his last words, "Let us cross over the river and rest in the shade of the trees." That was in the moment of dying. Peace was there, but beyond the peace is progress for such souls as his. Those who have learned to live for causes greater than themselves, and in the spiritual comradeship of the good and great, know the immortality of that with which their life is linked. "So faith, hope, love abide" (I Cor. 13:13). Read also Paul's letter to the Philippians. To him, because of what he had learned of Christ, there was a high calling to which death is the open door.

17-24. Melchizedek.—In the picture dimly outlined here the figures move against a background of immense and mystical remoteness. The king of Sodom belonged to the city that would be doomed. And Melchizedek—who was he? In Ps. 110:4 it is declared of the hoped-for Deliverer, "The LORD hath sworn, and will not

[9] "Bishop Blougram's Apology."

19 And he blessed him, and said, Blessed be Abram of the most high God, possessor of heaven and earth:

20 And blessed be the most high God, which hath delivered thine enemies into thy hand. And he gave him tithes of all.

he was priest of God Most High. 19 And he blessed him and said,

"Blessed be Abram by God Most High,
   maker of heaven and earth;
20 and blessed be God Most High,
   who has delivered your enemies into
   your hand!"

---

with Jerusalem: e.g., (*a*) Isa. 1:21, 26; Jer. 33:16; (*b*) Josh. 10:1, 3, where the king of Jerusalem bears the name Adoni-zedek; (*c*) II Sam. 8:17—"the son of Ahitub" is secondary—the first mention of the priest Zadok, significantly just after David's capture of Jerusalem; cf. II Sam. 15:24; (*d*) Hag. 1:1, where the name of the father of Joshua the high-priest is Jehozadak; (*e*) Ezek. 40:46. In this connection it is significant that in Ezek. 40:46; 44:15 (cf. 43:19) the Jerusalem priests are designated "the sons of Zadok," who are contrasted with "the Levites" in Ezek. 48:11, indicating that "from among the sons of Levi" in Ezek. 40:46 (ASV) and "the Levites" in Ezek. 44:15 are secondary. The Zadokite priesthood were thus not of Levitical origin but seem rather to have been the ancient priesthood of Jerusalem which accepted Yahwism when David captured the city and were, through their great prestige, able to maintain themselves as the custodians of its sanctuary up to the Exile and to refuse to have dealings with the Levitical priesthood, the custodians par excellence of the Mosaic tradition; cf. Ezek. 48:11, noted above, and the feud between Zadok and Abiathar ending in the latter's expulsion (I Kings 1:7-8; 2:27, 35). Following the Exile they were forced to come to terms with the Aaronite priesthood of Bethel which had, presumably, established itself in Jerusalem during the enforced absence of the Zadokites in Babylonia (cf. R. H. Kennett, "The Origin of the Aaronite Priesthood," *Journal of Theological Studies,* VI [1905], 161-86; VII [1906], 620-24).

It was in connection with this settlement that the fiction of Zadok's descent from Aaron (I Chr. 6:1-8) was devised. This was to base the exclusive claims of the Jerusalem priesthood, thus reconstituted through a fusion of Aaronites and Zadokites, upon the fiction that Aaron had been divinely chosen at Sinai as the first high priest—one of the major themes of the P code—and to ignore the historical fact of the age-old prestige of Jerusalem and its sanctuary.

The sudden appearance of Melchizedek in Ps. 110:4 and in the passage now under consideration suggests that in the course of time this Jerusalem tradition began to reassert itself. This suggestion receives further support from the title '*ēl* '*elyôn,* rendered **God Most High** in vss. 18, 19, 20, 22, by implication ascribed to Yahweh. '*Ēl* is the component rendered "God" in the compound names "God Almighty" (17:1), "the

---

repent, Thou art a priest for ever after the order of Melchizedek." In the Epistle to the Hebrews that phrase is repeated of Christ, except that he is called high priest as well as priest (5:6, 10; 6:20). And in Heb. 7:1-3, the name of "this Melchisedec, king of Salem, priest of the most high God" is interpreted as "King of righteousness, and after that also King of Salem, which is, King of peace; without father, without mother, without descent, having neither beginning of days, nor end of life."

With the king of Sodom Abraham deals majestically. He recognizes no right of that king to offer him anything, and he will take no gain from his deliverance of Sodom. Neither that city nor its representative shall be

allowed the opportunity to say, **I have made Abram rich.** But from Melchizedek Abraham accepted blessing. The significance of this was that Salem meant Jerusalem, and so Abraham is linked already with what was to be the Holy City that should become the center of his people's life. The naked fact that no mention is made of Melchizedek's ancestry or origin is transformed by the writer to the Hebrews into superhuman mystery. That is fanciful; but there is great suggestion in his thought that this prototype of the ideal priest and ruler is both king of righteousness and king of peace. Often in history there has been the tragic perversion of attempts not by the righteous but by the self-righteous to enforce what they chose to

21 And the king of Sodom said unto Abram, Give me the persons, and take the goods to thyself.

22 And Abram said to the king of Sodom, I have lifted up mine hand unto the LORD, the most high God, the possessor of heaven and earth,

23 That I will not *take* from a thread even to a shoe-latchet, and that I will not take any thing that *is* thine, lest thou shouldest say, I have made Abram rich:

24 Save only that which the young men have eaten, and the portion of the men which went with me, Aner, Eshcol, and Mamre; let them take their portion.

15 After these things the word of the LORD came unto Abram in a vision, saying, Fear not, Abram: I *am* thy shield, *and* thy exceeding great reward.

And Abram gave him a tenth of everything. 21 And the king of Sodom said to Abram, "Give me the persons, but take the goods for yourself." 22 But Abram said to the king of Sodom, "I have sworn to the LORD God Most High, maker of heaven and earth, 23 that I would not take a thread or a sandal-thong or anything that is yours, lest you should say, 'I have made Abram rich.' 24 I will take nothing but what the young men have eaten, and the share of the men who went with me; let Aner, Eschol, and Mamre take their share."

15 After these things the word of the LORD came to Abram in a vision, "Fear not, Abram, I am your shield; your

---

Everlasting God" (21:33), "God, the God of Israel" (33:20), and "God of Bethel" (35:7), and is the oldest Semitic appellation for God. '*Elyôn* is used frequently in the O.T. of the Lord (with '*ēl* in Ps. 78:35), notably in psalms referring clearly to Jerusalem and its temple—Pss. 9:2; 21:7; 46:4; 50:14; 87:5. A possible inference is that '*ēl 'elyôn* was the ancient name of the deity of the sanctuary at Jerusalem, which was later carried over to Yahweh; and in this connection it is significant that the Maccabees are called "priests of the Most High God" in the Assumption of Moses 6:1 (cf. Carl Siegfried, reviewing Gesenius' *Hebräisches und aramisches Handwörterbuch*, in *Theologische Literaturzeitung*, XX [1895], 304).

C. ABRAHAM'S DISINTERESTEDNESS (14:21-24)

21-24. Abraham's refusal to accept a reward from the king of Sodom may be a protest against a postexilic concern for material wealth. Abraham, the author implies, was more high-minded than his descendants.

XVIII. THE COVENANT WITH ABRAHAM (15:1-21)

The use of **the LORD** throughout this chapter indicates that it is derived from the J document. Gunkel (*Genesis*, pp. 177-78) regards it as a conflation of J and E. Skinner (*Genesis*, pp. 276-77) is dubious as to the validity of Gunkel's analysis, and inclines to the hypothesis that the groundwork is from E and that it has been recast by a J or a D redactor. (The analysis outlined here is argued in detail in Simpson, *Early Traditions*

---

think was peace. Arrogance of power can cloak itself in a "holy war." Not in that way can the ends of God be reached. Peace can be achieved only through that righteousness which begins in every heart and cleanses it of pride, self-assertion, and whatever deliberately sets itself against the love of God.

15:1. Our Strength in God.—Set with this verse the words in Ps. 71:3, "Be thou my strong habitation, whereunto I may continually resort." That prayer is answered by God's promise. To Abraham and to others life in God will be both strength and hope.

Considered more specifically, God can be to human lives as a strength beneath us. Willa Cather describes the great mesa on which the Ácoma Indians live. "The Ácomas, who must share the universal yearning for something permanent, enduring, without shadow of change, . . . had their idea in substance. They actually lived upon their Rock; were born upon it, and died upon it." [1] For human souls there can be rocklike certainties at their backs. "O thou, who changest not, abide with me." Read

[1] *Death Comes for the Archbishop* (New York: Alfred A. Knopf, 1927), p. 99.

2 And Abram said, Lord GOD, what wilt thou give me, seeing I go childless, and the steward of my house *is* this Eliezer of Damascus?

3 And Abram said, Behold, to me thou hast given no seed: and, lo, one born in my house is mine heir.

4 And, behold, the word of the LORD *came* unto him, saying, This shall not be thine heir; but he that shall come forth out of thine own bowels shall be thine heir.

reward shall be very great." 2 But Abram said, "O Lord GOD, what wilt thou give me, for I continue childless, and the heir of my house is Elie'zer of Damascus?" 3 And Abram said, "Behold, thou hast given me no offspring; and a slave born in my house will be my heir." 4 And behold, the word of the LORD came to him, "This man shall not be your heir; your own son shall be

---

of Israel, pp. 73-75.) The chapter falls into two parts: (*a*) vss. 1-6, promising an heir to Abraham; (*b*) vss. 8-21, promising him the land of Palestine, connected with vss. 1-6 by vs. 7.

Of these two parts, vss. 8-21 is the earlier, and once followed upon 13:17 which, it has been noted above, is secondary elaboration of the J2 narrative; i.e., Abraham, having been promised the land in 13:17, is now made to ask, **How am I to know that I shall possess it?** (Vs. 8.) In response the Lord makes a covenant with him (vss. 9-12, 17-18). Vss. 13-16 are a later intrusion maintaining, possibly against those who claimed that Jewish title to the land—or certain parts of it—had been forfeited through absence during the Exile, that temporary absence from the land had been permitted in the original deed of gift and therefore could not affect the title. Vss. 19-21 are a gloss.

To this covenant narrative another writer prefixed vss. 1-6 together with vs. 7 to effect a transition to vs. 8, insisting that Abraham's heir shall be his own son. This may well be further polemic against claims by non-Israelite groups after the Exile.

Neither J2 nor E use the word "covenant" to describe the relationship of Israel to God before the inauguration of the covenant at Sinai (J), or Horeb (E). In this late J passage the covenant idea is carried back to the time of Abraham.

15:1. Fear not, . . . I am your shield, implying that Abraham is in need of protection, possibly alludes to the danger he faced in obeying God's command to "walk through the length and the breadth of the land" (13:17). The **reward** is presumably for his magnanimity toward Lot.

2. Of Damascus is a gloss on the Hebrew word rendered here **heir,** with Procksch (*Genesis,* p. 295); it is itself probably corrupt.

---

in *The Life, Letters, Lectures and Addresses of Frederick W. Robertson* his description of the crisis through which he passed in his struggle for faith. In his darkest moments he knew that some great principles at least must be certain. "It is better to be generous than selfish, better to be chaste than licentious, better to be true than false, better to be brave than to be a coward." [2] The convictions which the thought of God can build as the foundations beneath a life give it a stronghold to which it may resort. Collapse of faith which represents itself as intellectual doubt is often really something different from that. It is lack of will to build life resolutely upon those sure realities, even if they are partial ones, which God has revealed to conscience.

God is not only a strength beneath us. He is a meaning above us. Life without meaning would be like walking on an eternal prairie,

with never a landmark anywhere. With nothing to which the eyes can be lifted up, existence is indeed "flat, stale, and unprofitable." The visitor to London sees the dome of St. Paul's Cathedral rising dominant out of the city's center, and the cross surmounting it suggests that in which life finds its focus and its meaning. Read at the end of H. G. Wells's novel, *Mr. Britling Sees It Through,* the letter of Mr. Britling beginning, "Religion is the first thing and the last thing, and until a man has found God and been found by God, he begins at no beginning, he works to no end." [3] It is necessary to have some beginning and some clearly desired end to give life happy unity. This kind of meaning does not depend upon clever thoughts. It depends upon the clean heart that is trying to be loyal to the highest it can be aware of.

As the thought of God gives a strength be-

[2] New York: Harper & Bros., n.d., p. 86.

[3] New York: The Macmillan Co., 1916, p. 442.

5 And he brought him forth abroad, and said, Look now toward heaven, and tell the stars, if thou be able to number them: and he said unto him, So shall thy seed be.

6 And he believed in the LORD; and he counted it to him for righteousness.

your heir." 5 And he brought him outside and said, "Look toward heaven, and number the stars, if you are able to number them." Then he said to him, "So shall your descendants be." 6 And he believed the LORD; and he reckoned it to him as righteousness.

---

6. Skinner (*Genesis, ad loc.*) rightly refers to this verse as a "remarkable anticipation of the Pauline doctrine of justification by faith" (Rom. 4:3, 9, 22; Gal. 3:6). **Righteousness** is here a right relationship to God, and it was conferred by the divine sentence of approval in response to Abraham's trust in God's character. In Deut. 6:25; 24:13 this righteousness is attained by obedience to the law. Here Abraham, who had no law to

---

neath us and a meaning above us, so it gives a sense of the majesty of life beyond us. The religious man knows that he is not an isolated individual. He belongs to the past and he belongs to the future. The little moment can have a great significance because of the inheritance from which it can draw and the heritage to which it can contribute. With God a day is as a thousand years, and a thousand years as one day. Remembrance of the past, of the long line of witness-bearers for the faith, of the communion of saints, can strengthen life and hold it steady in the face of temporary discouragement. Thought of the life ahead to which we can contribute can give inspiration to efforts which if bounded by their immediate effect might seem trivial. As the Epistle to the Hebrews suggests, the course of religion is like a relay race. The energy which any one of us puts into the running of his own lap of the relay speeds those who take up the race where we leave off.

6. *The Power of Faith.*—It is this passage that lies back of one of the great proclamations of the N.T.—the infinite power of faith: "By faith Abraham, when he was called . . . went out" (Heb. 11:8). We must "walk in the steps of that faith of our father Abraham," wrote Paul (Rom. 4:12). The heart of the whole gospel that Paul preached is beating here, the gospel that it is not what a man is but what a man trusts God to do that saves him.

Note the fact that in the life of Abraham it was when he trusted most that he was strongest and when he stopped trusting that he was weak. He trusted the voice of God that called him out of Ur and out of Haran, and he went forward on the road that was to open up a new world in spiritual history. He trusted the heavenly voice that told him he could find a blessing in the barren lands when he gave up the richer lands to Lot (ch. 13). He trusted that the purpose of God which had begun to work through him would be carried on through

a son whom God would give him (ch. 15). He trusted that between his soul and the Almighty there was a covenant which God would never break (ch. 17); and remembering that, he was capable of great physical daring (ch. 14) and heroic sacrifice (see Expos. on ch. 22). When sometimes he forgot that covenant and looked at facts which faced him as if he had to deal with these by himself, then he could lapse into timidity and weakness as ignominious as other men's (read 12:10-20). But if Abraham had in himself the same alloy of moral limitations that all human nature has, he had also something else: he had the fire of a faith in God which, when he kept it burning, could separate the dross and make his whole thought and will pure metal for God's use. Thus a man becomes good not because he is born so or because he lifts himself to goodness, but because he lets the goodness of God take hold of him and have its way. **He believed** and it was **counted . . . to him for righteousness:** the inspired intuition of Genesis saw that profound truth. The spiritual genius of Paul caught hold of it and put it at the forefront of his preaching of salvation.

It is a gospel that begins in humility. The first necessity for any soul's progress is to see how far it is from where it wants to go. Abraham had no illusion of self-importance. He knew well enough that left alone he would fall into sin. Before the glory of God he saw himself as "dust and ashes" (18:27). The only thing that can block God's purpose of redemption is the stubbornness of pride. Consider the terrible condemnation of the Pharisees by Jesus: "Now ye say, We see; therefore your sin remaineth" (John 9:41). Note, by contrast, Jesus' exaltation of a little child as the symbol of the kingdom of heaven. A child has no illusions of grandeur and no hard shell of satisfied pretense. It will often do wrong, but its heart is soft, and before the face of love it can be ashamed and sorry. Only from that sort of sorrow before the face

7 And he said unto him, I *am* the LORD that brought thee out of Ur of the Chaldees, to give thee this land to inherit it.

8 And he said Lord GOD, whereby shall I know that I shall inherit it?

9 And he said unto him, Take me a heifer of three years old, and a she goat of three years old, and a ram of three years old, and a turtledove, and a young pigeon.

10 And he took unto him all these, and divided them in the midst, and laid each piece one against another: but the birds divided he not.

11 And when the fowls came down upon the carcasses, Abram drove them away.

7 And he said to him, "I am the LORD who brought you from Ur of the Chal'deans, to give you this land to possess."
8 But he said, "O Lord GOD, how am I to know that I shall possess it?" 9 He said to him, "Bring me a heifer three years old, a she-goat three years old, a ram three years old, a turtledove, and a young pigeon."
10 And he brought him all these, cut them in two, and laid each half over against the other; but he did not cut the birds in two.
11 And when birds of prey came down upon the carcasses, Abram drove them away.

fulfill, was nevertheless made righteous because of his inner attitude, a position which is approximated in Ps. 24:5 and to a lesser degree in Ps. 106:31.

7. Ur of the Chaldeans: See Exeg. on 11:28.

of God do souls, like seeds watered by the rain, begin to grow.

It is a gospel of hope. As long as a man relies upon himself he is doomed to bitter moral disappointment. Read in Romans Paul's self-disclosure of his own unavailing struggle to win a sense of righteousness. Ponder what he meant by the impossibility of being saved by works or by any mechanical process of the law. Read also the passionate confession of Martin Luther concerning the early period of his personal efforts and his impotence and near despair. But hope comes when the man turns from looking in to looking up. "That I may apprehend that for which also I am apprehended," cried Paul (Phil. 3:12). "A mighty fortress is our God," sang Luther when his soul caught the eternal truth that he did not stand unaided. "The submission of man's nothing-perfect to God's all-complete" [4] is the way out of weakness into strength. Look at the ship lying stranded in the estuary when the tide is low. What human strength could push it out to sea? But the man who trusts to the certainty of the incoming tide will see his ship lifted and set free. So he who

throws himself on God, and unperplexed
Seeking shall find him.[5]

Then, out of the great leadings of the hope which is kindled as the soul looks up to God, comes happiness. Observe how the men whose virtue has been that they had great beliefs and were brave enough to follow them have been radiant men—not always, it is true, for no

earthly experience is perfect, but prevailingly. They have known that "the joy of the LORD is your strength" (Neh. 8:10). Mark how often the letters of Paul are starred with "joy" and "rejoice." Read the life of John Wesley, and note how he passed from shadow into sunlight when he learned to find his righteousness not in anything he could achieve but in the grace that God through Christ had freely given. In a world beset by many fears and frustrations and often at the verge of cynical unfaith in the attainment of any general righteousness, consider the need for the kind of inner glow that belongs to souls in whom God's assurance shines. Their strength is not primarily in what they do. It is in the happy courage they reflect, because a long faithfulness in following their best beliefs has given them an unlimited confidence in what God can do. That sort of faith can wipe out many human failings. It is not only reckoned as righteousness; more than anything else it can bring righteousness to pass in an unrighteous world.

7-21. *The Retrospect of Faith.*—In this chapter, drawn from the E document, the historian of probably the eighth century is thinking back to the long story of Israel's guidance by God. He sees all that has happened as no succession of chance events nor the result of human choices; it has been due from the first to God's ordaining. He is so sure that what has come to pass was enfolded in the covenant made with Abraham that he thinks of it as foretold in explicit words to Abraham himself. The captivity in Egypt (vs. 13) and the Exodus (vs. 14) of course were centuries later than the time when Abraham lived and died. Still more time

12 And when the sun was going down, a deep sleep fell upon Abram; and, lo, a horror of great darkness fell upon him.

13 And he said unto Abram, Know of a surety that thy seed shall be a stranger in a land *that is* not theirs, and shall serve them; and they shall afflict them four hundred years;

14 And also that nation, whom they shall serve, will I judge: and afterward shall they come out with great substance.

15 And thou shalt go to thy fathers in peace; thou shalt be buried in a good old age.

16 But in the fourth generation they shall come hither again: for the iniquity of the Amorites *is* not yet full.

17 And it came to pass, that, when the sun went down, and it was dark, behold a smoking furnace, and a burning lamp that passed between those pieces.

12 As the sun was going down, a deep sleep fell on Abram; and lo, a dread and great darkness fell upon him. 13 Then the LORD said to Abram, "Know of a surety that your descendants will be sojourners in a land that is not theirs, and will be slaves there, and they will be oppressed for four hundred years; 14 but I will bring judgment on the nation which they serve, and afterward they shall come out with great possessions. 15 As for yourself, you shall go to your fathers in peace; you shall be buried in a good old age. 16 And they shall come back here in the fourth generation; for the iniquity of the Amorites is not yet complete."

17 When the sun had gone down and it was dark, behold, a smoking fire pot and a flaming torch passed between these pieces.

---

17. **A smoking fire pot and a flaming torch** is symbolic of the God of fire (cf. Exod. 3:2; 13:21; 19:18). On the ceremony of passing between the pieces cf. Jer. 34:18-19, the only other allusion to it in the O.T.

---

would intervene before the conquest of Canaan (the Amorites of vs. 16); and not until the reign of Solomon would it be possible to say that the descendants of Abraham possessed the land **from the river of Egypt unto the great river, the river Euphrates** (cf. I Kings 4:21, 24). But the historian who looked back and saw these things as facts beheld them as the fulfillment of what God had let Abraham foresee. The way in which Abraham is described as having sought a revelation from God, and the way in which that revelation came, is remote from modern thought, but as late as the time of Jeremiah it was familiar (Jer. 34:18). Animals and birds were slain in sacrifice and their bodies divided; then between the pieces the two parties to a covenant advanced and met and sealed agreement. Here in the midst of the sacrifice which Abraham had made, as the wondering awe of the eighth-century historian imagines it, God's presence came in the darkness after sundown, like **a smoking furnace, and a burning lamp**—a light that shone, and yet was veiled in cloud and mystery. Did Abraham have an experience such as that, and did he hear the voice of God telling him what would be in centuries unborn? Literalism answers "No"; but none the less there is spiritual suggestion in the picture through which the historian of Israel projected his exalted faith. The way by which Israel had been led was the way God had chosen from the be-

ginning. Its achievements and successes were part of the blessing that God had promised Abraham. But so were its tribulations. Seen in the restrospect of faith even the captivity in Egypt was not a calamity. It too was part of God's redeeming plan. When the seeming disasters of the past could be viewed in that light the future also, whatever it might hold, could be faced with steady confidence.

12. *Through Darkness to Light.*—Dreams often seem so illogical as to be fantastically irrelevant. Why should Abraham, the good man, have had **a horror of great darkness?** One might have supposed that what came up out of his unconscious would have been serene and bright. Instead, this description shows what may sometimes be the fact, no matter how little the surface indications hint of it. Under the career which outwardly appears to be altogether prosperous there may be deeper levels of apprehension and unrest. When we begin to reflect we can see that Abraham had had his heavy disappointments. The sorest of them was expressed in his cry to God, "Behold, to me thou hast given no seed: and, lo, one born in my house is mine heir" (vs. 3). The years were passing by, and he was childless. And now and then forebodings of a different kind may have come to him. It is not necessary to take literally the words of vs. 13. Abraham could hardly have had explicit foreknowledge of the captivity in

18 In that same day the LORD made a covenant with Abram, saying, Unto thy seed have I given this land, from the river of Egypt unto the great river, the river Euphrates:

19 The Kenites, and the Kenizzites, and the Kadmonites,

20 And the Hittites, and the Perizzites, and the Rephaim,

21 And the Amorites, and the Canaanites, and the Girgashites, and the Jebusites.

18 On that day the LORD made a covenant with Abram, saying, "To your descendants I give this land, from the river of Egypt to the great river, the river Eu-phra'tes, 19 the land of the Kenites, the Ken'izzites, the Kad'monites, 20 the Hittites, the Per'izzites, the Reph'aim, 21 the Amorites, the Canaanites, the Gir'gashites and the Jeb'usites."

18. **Covenant:** It has been argued in the article, "The Growth of the Hexateuch" (p. 195), that the covenant idea was derived by Israel from the cult of Baal-berith at Shechem. Whatever may have been the supposed relative standing of the two parties to the covenant in this cult, in the Israelite tradition it was no agreement between equals. The terms of the covenant were not the result of negotiation; they were imposed by the Lord (cf. Exod. 34:10-11; 24:7); and the covenant was inaugurated at the foot of the flaming mountain (cf. Exod. 19:18). Israel in taking over the covenant idea from the cult of Shechem made it the vehicle of their faith in the dependability of God. He was no capricious despot but a God of righteousness and order who respected human personality. He would not change; his favor was sure. But Israel would benefit by that favor only in so far as they were obedient to the divine will.

In this passage, stating God's promise to Abraham in covenant terms, no conditions are imposed. But the implication of the narrative in its present and final form would seem to be that the covenant would stand so long as Abraham's descendants continued to follow the example set by him when **he believed the LORD** (vs. 6). Originally, before vss. 1-6 had been prefixed to this section of the story, the reference would have been to the faith shown by Abraham when "he went out [from his own country], not knowing whither he went" (Heb. 11:8), and to the magnanimity with which he had treated Lot.

In the J document as it lay before RJE—the redactor who combined it with E—the order of the material in chs. 13–16 was: 13:1; the story in ch. 16 (see below); 13:2-17; 15; 13:18. RJE preserved this order, inserting only two verses from E in ch. 16. RP, who combined the JE narrative with P, placed the Hagar story (ch. 16) in its present position to bring Abraham to Hebron before the birth of Ishmael. The writer who inserted ch. 14, which represents Abraham as living at Hebron, necessarily moved the notice now preserved in 13:18 to its present position to record Abraham's arrival there before the war of the kings.

Egypt and of how long it would last. But Abraham's descendants did learn what was symbolized here in Abraham's dream, viz., the double truth that life which is guided by God may nevertheless have its times of darkness and delay, but that the end result will be not worse but better because of these. It may be that "we must through much tribulation enter into the kingdom of God" (Acts 14:22).

Therefore we must not be in a hurry to define the significance and worth of any part of life. One's estimate may be impatient and unseeing. Abraham Lincoln, when he was defeated for the senate by Stephen Douglas, could not have known that in the process of that defeat he was learning lessons which would make him fit for

a far greater role in his country's service. Phillips Brooks, who was to become one of the greatest preachers of his age, could not have known that it was the hand of God that shut a lesser door for him when he found himself in his first choice of a career marked an ignominious failure as a teacher. Those who look back upon any life may see in it great moments of overruling destiny which the man himself at the moment could not see. Therefore it is worth while to take the long look ahead. The climax of the book is not written in the first chapter.

As one needs to look farther, so he needs to look deeper. The value of any experience or of any period in life is not represented by what is obvious. If one's ambitions are selfish and

16 Now Sarai, Abram's wife, bare him no children: and she had a handmaid, an Egyptian, whose name *was* Hagar.

2 And Sarai said unto Abram, Behold now, the LORD hath restrained me from bearing: I pray thee, go in unto my maid; it may be that I may obtain children by her. And Abram hearkened to the voice of Sarai.

3 And Sarai, Abram's wife, took Hagar her maid the Egyptian, after Abram had dwelt ten years in the land of Canaan, and gave her to her husband Abram to be his wife.

16 Now Sar'ai, Abram's wife, bore him no children. She had an Egyptian maid whose name was Hagar; 2 and Sar'ai said to Abram, "Behold now, the LORD has prevented me from bearing children; go in to my maid; it may be that I shall obtain children by her." And Abram hearkened to the voice of Sar'ai. 3 So, after Abram had dwelt ten years in the land of Canaan, Sar'ai, Abram's wife, took Hagar the Egyptian her maid, and gave her to Abram her

XIX. ABRAHAM AND HAGAR (16:1-16)

Vss. 1*a*, 3, 15-16, are from P and presumably followed upon a notice of Abraham's arrival at Kiriath-arba (=Hebron, cf. 23:2), dropped by RP in favor of 13:18.

The rest of the chapter, except for some redactional material noted below, is from J[2] who inserted the story, together with that of Abraham in Egypt, into the J[1] narrative, placing it after the notice now preserved in 13:1. Abraham was thus, according to J[2], in the Negeb at the time of Ishmael's birth, the notice of which was dropped by RP in favor of vss. 15-16.

A. SARAH'S JEALOUSY (16:1-6)

16:1. It is probable that **an Egyptian** is an insertion by RP to harmonize the J story with the representation of P (vs. 3); in J, Hagar is characteristically a woman of the desert, not an Egyptian.

2. The custom of a barren wife giving her handmaid to her husband in order that she might **obtain children by her** is further attested by 30:3, according to which the childless Rachel gave her maid Bilhah to Jacob; and by 30:9 where Leah, who had

shallow, so that the satisfactions he wants are those which are most easily and quickly picked up, he will never be possessed by the unfolding purposes of God. In George Eliot's *Romola* the boy Lillo says:

I should like to be something that would make me a great man, and very happy besides—something that would not hinder me from having a good deal of pleasure.

And Romola, remembering the great-souled Savonarola, who has just gone to his martyrdom, replies:

That is not easy, my Lillo. It is only a poor sort of happiness that could ever come by caring very much about our own narrow pleasures. We can only have the highest happiness, such as goes along with being a great man, by having wide thoughts, and much feeling for the rest of the world as well as ourselves; and this sort of happiness often brings so much pain with it, that we can only tell it from pain by its being what we would choose before everything else, because our souls see it is good.[6]

[6] Epilogue.

Finally—yet also first and continuingly—there is the fact that those who are to fulfill God's purposes must trust that a divine purpose does exist, and that if we are faithful to the best we know in the plain duties of every day we shall find that purpose—or in deeper truth be found by it.

16:1-16. *Hagar and Ishmael.*—The story in this chapter has close resemblances to the one which is to follow in ch. 21 (see Expos.), but they are not identical. In both stories Hagar is driven out from Abraham's tent by Sarah's angry jealousy. In both the angel of the Lord comes to Hagar in her desolation and sends her back to Abraham. But in this first story Ishmael has not yet been born; whereas in the second he is a lad old enough to arouse Sarah's indignation because she thinks he is "mocking" Isaac, who is himself old enough to be weaned. The inclusion in Genesis of both stories, so nearly alike and yet sufficiently different to be inconsistent, is one of the many instances of the reluctance of the compilers to sacrifice any of the traditions which had become established in Israel.

4 ¶ And he went in unto Hagar, and she conceived: and when she saw that she had conceived, her mistress was despised in her eyes.

5 And Sarai said unto Abram, My wrong *be* upon thee: I have given my maid into thy bosom; and when she saw that she had conceived, I was despised in her eyes: the LORD judge between me and thee.

6 But Abram said unto Sarai, Behold, thy maid *is* in thy hand; do to her as it pleaseth thee. And when Sarai dealt hardly with her, she fled from her face.

7 ¶ And the angel of the LORD found her by a fountain of water in the wilderness, by the fountain in the way to Shur.

8 And he said, Hagar, Sarai's maid, whence camest thou? and whither wilt thou go? And she said, I flee from the face of my mistress Sarai.

husband as a wife. 4 And he went in to Hagar, and she conceived; and when she saw that she had conceived, she looked with contempt on her mistress. 5 And Sar'ai said to Abram, "May the wrong done to me be on you! I gave my maid to your embrace, and when she saw that she had conceived, she looked on me with contempt. May the LORD judge between you and me!" 6 But Abram said to Sar'ai, "Behold, your maid is in your power; do to her as you please." Then Sar'ai dealt harshly with her, and she fled from her.

7 The angel of the LORD found her by a spring of water in the wilderness, the spring on the way to Shur. 8 And he said, "Hagar, maid of Sar'ai, where have you come from and where are you going?" She said, "I am

"ceased bearing," gave him Zilpah. The children born of such a union were thus reckoned as the children not of the handmaid, but of the wife, by adoption, the slave girl being delivered on the knees of her mistress (cf. 30:3).

5. Sarah, however, is unable to go through with this arrangement, Hagar's contempt for her childlessness (vs. 4) being more than she can stand. Unreasonably she blames Abraham. The verse throws a significant light upon the tensions inevitable in a polygamous household.

6. She fled from her: Hagar is here depicted as the sturdy independent Bedouin woman who will brook no restraint. With this may be contrasted the tender tone of the E recension of her expulsion in 21:9-21.

B. HAGAR IN THE DESERT (16:7-10)

7. The spring on the way to Shur identifies the spring just named with Beer-lahai-roi. In J (25:11*b*; cf. 20:1*a*) this spring is associated with Isaac; it is probable, therefore, that this phrase, associating it with Ishmael, is from RJE (see Exeg. on vss. 13-14).

In the story as it is here recounted there is a double interest. The first has to do with the relationship of Israel to the Ishmaelite tribes of the desert. Manifestly there was a kinship of blood. In the thought of Israel that was something to be acknowledged and yet qualified. Granted that there was a common ancestry, nevertheless it was not to be admitted that there was equality; and in the story of Hagar both these emphases appear. Ishmael, like Isaac, is a descendant of Abraham; but Isaac is the child of ultimate promise, born of Sarah the true wife, while Ishmael is born of the slave girl. According to the customs of the time it was right and generous of Sarah to be willing— since she seemed to be barren herself—to allow her maidservant to bear a child to her husband;

and it was fully within her rights to send that servant off when it seemed to Sarah that the servant had become arrogant and overweening, so that Sarah was despised in her eyes. Thus the status of Hagar's son is made plain. Though he came of the stock of Abraham, yet it was right that he should be separated from the legitimate son. So the partial bond between Israelites and Ishmaelites, and yet their deeper alienation, was accounted for. From the story of the way Ishmael was born it followed naturally that he should be "as a wild ass among men" (ASV), and that his hand should be against every man, and every man's hand against him.

That emphasis in the story is the expression of a human instinct which is as old as history. Every tribe and every nation has liked to believe

9 And the angel of the Lord said unto her, Return to thy mistress, and submit thyself under her hands.

10 And the angel of the Lord said unto her, I will multiply thy seed exceedingly, that it shall not be numbered for multitude.

11 And the angel of the Lord said unto her, Behold, thou *art* with child, and shalt bear a son, and shalt call his name Ishmael; because the Lord hath heard thy affliction.

12 And he will be a wild man; his hand *will be* against every man, and every man's hand against him: and he shall dwell in the presence of all his brethren.

fleeing from my mistress Sar'ai." 9 The angel of the Lord said to her, "Return to your mistress, and submit to her." 10 The angel of the Lord also said to her, "I will so greatly multiply your descendants that they cannot be numbered for multitude." 11 And the angel of the Lord said to her, "Behold, you are with child, and shall bear a son; you shall call his name Ish'mael;[t] because the Lord has given heed to your affliction. 12 He shall be a wild ass of a man, his hand against every man and every man's hand against him; and he shall dwell over against

[t] That is *God hears*

9. There can be no doubt that J represented Ishmael's birth as occurring in the wilderness by the spring referred to in vs. 7a, and said nothing of Hagar's returning to Abraham's encampment. This verse is accordingly secondary, an insertion by RJE to prepare for the E recension of the tale. It may be noted that the command is inconsistent with "the Lord has given heed to your affliction" in vs. 11.

10. This is also secondary, as is indicated both by **the angel of the Lord also said to her,** unnecessary after vs. 9—also is a rendering of a simple "and" in the Hebrew—and by the fact that the promise it contains, if an original part of the narrative, would have followed the promise of a son.

C. Birth of Ishmael (16:11-16)

There can be no doubt that the story was first told of their eponymous ancestor by the Ishmaelites, a group of Bedouin tribes which ranged the desert to the south of Palestine (cf. 25:18). The historical event reflected here in their association with the Hagarenes (cf. Ps. 83:6) is irrecoverable. That the tale had originally nothing to do with Abraham, the hero of Hebron, is suggested by **Behold, you are with child,** unnecessary after vs. 4, and indicating that the oracle to which it belongs is independent of its present context. J2, incorporating the tale into his narrative, identified the deity concerned with the Lord.

It is likely that in the development of the tradition Ishmael was first associated with Isaac, the hero of Beer-sheba, and that it was because of this association that J2 made him the son of Abraham.

11. This verse is thus the original continuation of vs. 8. To be noted is the fact that the second component of Ishmael is 'ēl, indicating that the deity in the original saga was not Yahweh but the numen of the spring of vs. 7a.

12. This verse describes and accounts for the intractable isolationism of the Ishmaelites. It was followed in J2 by a notice of the naming of the spring, dropped by RJE in favor of vss. 13-14, and an account of the birth and naming of Hagar's son, dropped by RP in favor of vss. 15-16.

itself superior to some rival tribe or nation and in its traditions has sought to dramatize that belief. So there is an element in the story of Hagar which is narrow and exclusive. But woven in with that there is another and more beautiful conception. Though Hagar has been driven **out by Sarah, with Abraham's consent, yet the** angel of God follows her. She is to go back again to Sarah's tent. Her child will be born, and from him shall spring those who **shall not be numbered for multitude.** Through the tangled human relationships the divine mercy does not fail. And as so often happens with the inspired language of the Bible, the words with

13 And she called the name of the LORD that spake unto her, Thou God seest me: for she said, Have I also here looked after him that seeth me?

14 Wherefore the well was called Beer-lahai-roi: behold, *it is* between Kadesh and Bered.

15 ¶ And Hagar bare Abram a son: and Abram called his son's name, which Hagar bare, Ishmael.

16 And Abram *was* fourscore and six years old, when Hagar bare Ishmael to Abram.

all his kinsmen." 13 So she called the name of the LORD who spoke to her, "Thou art a God of seeing"; for she said, "Have I really seen God and remained alive after seeing him?"*u* 14 Therefore the well was called Beer-la'hai-roi;*v* it lies between Kadesh and Bered.

15 And Hagar bore Abram a son; and Abram called the name of his son, whom Hagar bore, Ish'mael. 16 Abram was eighty-six years old when Hagar bore Ish'mael to Abram.

u Cn. Heb *have I even here seen after him who sees me?*
v That is *the well of one who sees and lives*

---

13. That this verse, together with vs. 14, is not the original continuation of vss. 7-12 is suggested by the fact that its dominant idea is **seeing,** whereas the story up to this point has stressed the fact of the Lord's hearing Hagar; and by its association of Ishmael with Beer-lahai-roi, suggesting a source other than 25:11*b* (J). LORD is here impossible, and can only be a redactional substitution for an original "God." **Thou art a God of seeing** is awkward because of the occurrence of **thou** in the name; furthermore, it does not explain Beer-lahai-roi of vs. 14. What is required is "the living God of seeing."

The second half of the verse is unintelligible. Wellhausen (*Prolegomena to the History of Israel,* tr. J. Sutherland Black and Allan Menzies [Edinburgh: A. & C. Black, 1885], p. 326) suggests an emendation which would give, "Have I actually seen God and lived after my vision?" (see RSV)—an allusion to the belief that seeing God is followed by death (cf. Exod. 33:20; Judg. 6:23; 13:22).

14. The etymology of **Beer-lahai-roi** is fanciful. Probably its real meaning is "The Well of the Antelope's Jawbone" (*ibid.,* p. 326).

In view of the fact that RJE has attached vss. 13-14 to the J² story of an event occurring during Abraham's first sojourn in Negeb, it may reasonably be assumed that the E story, of which they were the conclusion, also came near the beginning of the Abraham cycle. It is, however, unlikely that the tale had anything to do with Ishmael, since E would scarcely have considered him of sufficient importance to warrant the inclusion of a story concerning him in addition to that now preserved in 21:9-21.

The fact that it is Isaac who is traditionally associated with Beer-lahai-roi suggests that the verses may be the conclusion of the E story of the promise of a son to Sarah, who would then be the speaker in vs. 13. In this case the tale would be the E parallel to the J² narrative in 18:10-15, and E accounted for the traditional association of Isaac with both Beer-lahai-roi and Beer-sheba by representing the former as the place where his mother received the divine promise of a son and the latter as the place of his birth (cf. 21:31, which originally preceded the E narrative of Isaac's birth of which 21:6*a* was the conclusion).

---

which Hagar responded to that mercy have come down across the centuries with a length and profundity of suggestion which the ancient writer could not have foreseen: **Thou God seest me.** In old houses of the stern Puritan tradition those words embroidered could be seen framed upon the wall, and usually they were taken to mean the watchful eye of God's unceasing judg-

ment. But that is not their meaning in the story of Hagar. Rather, they are the glad acknowledgment of the heavenly grace that beholds our human needs. As the psalmist sang, "He that keepeth Israel shall neither slumber nor sleep" (Ps. 121:4); and many a lonely soul for whom the world seemed desolate, as it seemed to Hagar, has been able to take comfort in the

17 And when Abram was ninety years old and nine, the LORD appeared to Abram, and said unto him, I *am* the Almighty God; walk before me, and be thou perfect.

17 When Abram was ninety-nine years old the LORD appeared to Abram, and said to him, "I am God Almighty;[w]

[w] Heb *El Shaddai*

XX. THE COVENANT OF CIRCUMCISION (17:1-27)

This chapter, derived from the P document, falls into four parts: (*a*) the covenant with Abraham, vss. 1-8; (*b*) circumcision the sign of the covenant, vss. 9-14; (*c*) the promise of a son, vss. 15-22; and (*d*) the fulfillment of the divine command, vss. 23-27.

A. THE COVENANT (17:1-8)

The covenant with Abraham is the P parallel to 12:2-3, 7*a* (J²; cf. ch. 15).

17:1. This is the only occasion on which **the LORD appeared to Abram,** according to P, who is very sparing of theophanies. **The LORD** is a redactional substitution for the original "God" (cf. vs. 4 and throughout the chapter). El Shaddai (RSV mg.) was probably the name of a Canaanite deity, like 'ēl 'elyôn (14:18), ultimately identified with the Lord. The meaning of Shaddai is uncertain (see Skinner, *Genesis*, pp. 290-91). On the significance of the verse for the critical analysis of the Hexateuch, see article "The Growth of the Hexateuch," pp. 189-90.

---

faith that there was One who saw its sorrow and would come with compassion and with help.

17:1. *A Man Bound to God.*—Abraham is an example of a man whose life had an inner unity. He had something stronger than himself that gave him certainty and strength. The most characteristic element of modern life is that it is at loose ends. People are at loose ends in their own personalities. Observe the realization of this in the immense contemporary interest in psychology and psychoanalysis. Men and women know that they are full of inner friction and dislocations, with jangled and discordant energies. They cannot tie themselves together in one effective whole.[7] People are at loose ends in their most intimate relationships. Marriage is ideally the full union of a man and woman, body and soul; yet often there is no union, but instead only a superficial meeting of appetite and physical attachment. Note the appalling modern divorce rate, and note that the proportion of divorces for couples who have no strong background of religious interests is far greater than for those who have. For a happy and enduring marriage there is needed a loyalty to something big enough to produce a bond of union that can overcome the temporary irritations of individual selfishness.

We are at loose ends in industrial relationships. During the period of World War II the immense energies within each of the warring nations were tied together by the pressure of danger. After the war they began to fall apart.

Reflect upon the postwar industrial strife in many countries, the waste of productivity, the bitter collisions of class with class. The world is at loose ends in its international relationships. The United Nations was launched as an effort to tie the interests of the world together, but by itself it cannot be enough. The full co-operation which is needed for human welfare can be achieved only as men recognize a divine imperative and obey it.

As against life at loose ends it is necessary to find a great faith. Without God, life flies apart. With God, its elements are held together like the stars in the immense harmony of the heavens. A soul's response to the will of God is like the spiritual gravitation that keeps the different parts of us from flying off at tangents. So the inner life of great exemplars of religion reveals an otherwise unattainable stability and strength. Religious sensitiveness can save marriages from destruction. The kind of conscience which is created in men aware of God can give the understanding justice which is necessary for the solution of industrial disputes. And only this conscience in statesmen and the public opinion of common men can ultimately create world co-operation and world peace. Education integrated around the sought meanings of God can give wisdom instead of disjointed bits of information, and produce a personality "profoundly integrated and profoundly energized."[8]

This faith is fortified by a great fellowship. For the individual at any moment the problems of life may seem overwhelming, but the Bible

[7] See C. G. Jung, *Modern Man in Search of a Soul* (New York: Harcourt, Brace & Co., 1933).

[8] Winifred Kirkland, *Portrait of a Carpenter* (New York: Charles Scribner's Sons, 1931), p. 60.

2 And I will make my covenant between me and thee, and will multiply thee exceedingly.

3 And Abram fell on his face: and God talked with him, saying,

4 As for me, behold, my covenant *is* with thee, and thou shalt be a father of many nations.

5 Neither shall thy name any more be called Abram, but thy name shall be Abraham; for a father of many nations have I made thee.

walk before me, and be blameless. 2 And I will make my covenant between me and you, and will multiply you exceedingly."

3 Then Abram fell on his face; and God said to him, 4 "Behold, my covenant is with you, and you shall be the father of a multitude of nations. 5 No longer shall your name be Abram,ˣ but your name shall be Abraham;ʸ for I have made you the father

ˣ That is *exalted father*
ʸ Here taken to mean *father of a multitude*

4. God's first promise is that Abraham shall be **the father of a multitude of nations.** The reference is not only to Israel but also to the Ishmaelites, the Edomites, and the nations whose eponymous ancestors are listed in 25:2-4, all of whom the J document had claimed as descendants of Abraham.

5. The change of name from **Abram to Abraham**—the two forms seem to have the same meaning despite the fanciful etymology provided here—may be a reflex of the Jewish custom of naming a child at circumcision, when he was brought into the covenant of which circumcision was the sign. If so, then it would seem that the use of the form

can widen our perspective. God has made a covenant with many souls, and those souls have not been disappointed. There is a communion of the saints, living and dead. When any man tries to be worthy of that, his life is lifted up into a spiritual companionship which gives it dignity. He can no longer be at loose ends.

2-6. The Covenant of God.—Here is the ultimate guarantee of a life that shall be significant. The profound Hebrew understanding knew well the limitations and frailties of man, but it had been gripped by the amazing faith that man in his weakness can yet have behind him the infinite strength of God. A man is not to be made more confident in himself; he can be confident because he has a covenant with Another.

Note how this thought of the covenant runs through all the O.T. Here it begins with Abraham. It comes again with Moses (Exod. 34:27). It echoes in the words of the great prophets. In its whole instinctive recognition the religion of the Hebrew race was objective. The Hebrew mind and heart reached up to a transcendent Reality, and knew that the springs of life were not in the shallowness of human souls but in the illimitableness of God.

Mark the contrast with some of our diluted modern thinking as exemplified by the Ethical Culture Society. Earnest people of good will belong to it; its purposes are all beneficent. But how thin and substanceless it sounds, a skeleton of religion, dry bones of behavior, all rightly held in place but with no heart of heavenly certainty beating in its midst. By

mechanical processes men can carry on the habitual attitudes of inherited character, but the O.T. seers knew that character was first created, and can be long sustained, only through a life-giving consciousness of God. That God is, that he enters into relationship with human souls, that all worth-while inspiration comes from him—this was the Hebrew faith. The glory of that inheritance should not be lost.

Note a second fact. The covenant with God is initiated by God. Religion is not a human notion, a pathetic projection of human wishes which may or may not find a divine response. On the contrary, it is God moving toward man and giving to the bond between them therefore the eternal assurance of his own purpose. God spoke first to Abraham, not Abraham first to God. So to Moses, to Isaiah, to Jeremiah, to all the inspired souls. Great religious experience always rests in the certainty that the soul has not gone out into an empty universe where all that it would hear would be the echo of its own cry, but that the Lord of the universe has come into the soul itself and spoken there. That is the eternal truth which was trying to voice itself in the doctrine of predestination: the truth of the priority of God. The aspirations of human hearts are not just the pathetic smoke of a self-kindled fire; they are the answering flame that has been lighted by the fire that has come down from on high. Consider the difference this makes for moral and spiritual courage. To say "I want God and I am willing to try to draw near to him if only he will let me" is

6 And I will make thee exceeding fruitful, and I will make nations of thee, and kings shall come out of thee.

7 And I will establish my covenant between me and thee and thy seed after thee

of a multitude of nations. 6 I will make you exceedingly fruitful; and I will make nations of you, and kings shall come forth from you. 7 And I will establish my covenant between me and you and your de-

---

Abram was a device of P's, and its occurrence in the J material up to this point in the narrative will have been due to RP, as has already been suggested (cf. 11:29).

7. God's second promise is **to be God to you and to your descendants after you.** It is to be noted that the correlative "and they shall be to me a people" (cf. Jer. 7:23; 11:4; etc.) is missing here as always in P (Exod. 6:7 is secondary, and Lev. 26:12 is H).

---

one thing; and there is only feeble influence in it. To hear it promised that God himself draws near is something else, and in it there is assurance that nothing can upset.

A third fact. As the covenant comes from God, so it must be remembered that it is in him and not in our unenlightened selves that we must look for its interpretation. Men who started out to be religious can go wrong if they begin to think they know where north is better than the North Star knows; or if they reason that God's covenant means that he has agreed to be a passenger on the ship of which we are the pilot. Reflect upon how often this distorting pride may take possession of individuals and institutions: the men and women who want God to bless designs which they choose to think are most desirable; the churches which salute God with elaborate aesthetic worship and then expect to be prospered in a narrow parochialism that does not relate religion to the great needs of the general life; the statesmen who invoke God's name in patriotic eloquence but do not bow before the ultimate question of what his will is for a nation's highest mission in the world. The true ideal is expressed in the words attributed to Abraham Lincoln when a self-confident delegation waited upon him, presented their case, said they had prayed about it, and felt sure that God was on their side. Said Lincoln: "I am not so much concerned to ask whether God is on my side. What I am concerned with is to try to be sure that I am on God's side." A very different and much more important matter.

A fourth fact. The covenant with God makes some other covenants unthinkable and all other covenants subordinate. Through O.T. history the people of Israel are revealed as constantly tempted to make degrading covenants—with pagan practices in Canaan, with the gods of Tyre, with the plausible power of Assyria or Egypt. They were always thinking that in a shifting world smart stratagems would most help them to survive, instead of believing that

the true necessity was to hold hard to that integrity of life which God had taught them and which could make them deserve survival. "In quietness and in confidence shall be your strength," said Isaiah (30:15). In every age those who have kept faith with the best they have believed have found that the covenant did not fail, but that in ways they could not have predicted God proved to be their final strength. It is still given to religious faith not to make a covenant with any lesser reliance, but to accept the covenant which God himself offers and in which alone there is the promise of triumphant life.

7-9. The Consecration of the Family.—The covenant was made by God with Abraham, but not with Abraham alone. **I will establish my covenant between me and thee and thy seed after thee in their generations. . . . Thou shalt keep my covenant, therefore thou, and thy seed.** In Hebrew thought a man and his children were no casual aggregation. They were bound together under God by a spirit stronger than individual caprice. Family consciousness, family constancy, family cohesiveness, built on loyalty to something in itself but larger than itself—that stands out through all the O.T., and it stands out likewise in the entire story of the Jewish people down to this day. (Nor is that truth set aside—indeed, the inspiration of it is thrown into stronger light—by the fact that the "acids of modernity" have partly disintegrated the old sacredness of the family among those Jews who have drifted into secularism and lost the holding power of a great religion.) Characteristically, Jewish marriages have been faithful, Jewish divorces exceedingly few. The sense of family solidarity has been strong enough to reach out beyond the intimate household group and make the whole people in actual ways a family. Note the extraordinary efficiency of organized Jewish charities, the immense response of Jews to needs of their persecuted peoples in Europe during World War II and its aftermath, the passionate persistence of the Zionist move-

in their generations, for an everlasting covenant, to be a God unto thee and to thy seed
after thee.

8 And I will give unto thee, and to thy
seed after thee, the land wherein thou art a

scendants after you throughout their generations for an everlasting covenant, to be
God to you and to your descendants after
you. 8 And I will give to you, and to your
descendants after you, the land of your

Skinner remarks that the covenant is thus "conceived as a self-determination of God
to be to one particular race all that the word God implies." His further statement, "a
reciprocal act of choice on man's part being no essential feature of the relation" (*Genesis*,
p. 293), needs modification, for the imposition of the condition of circumcision certainly
implies that some response is demanded from Israel.

8. God's third promise is that Abraham and his offspring will possess **all the land
of Canaan, for an everlasting possession**. With this cf. Ps. 105:44-45, where the possession
of the land is regarded as necessary if Israel is to keep God's statutes and observe his laws.
The chosen people was no abstract idea. Israel was a concrete reality, a people, however
unique, among the peoples of the earth. To be itself and to achieve its destiny it needed
its own land, in which would be the center of its religion—the temple—and within
which it could freely order its life in accordance with the divine law.

---

ment to make a homeland again in Palestine. If
the Jews have been called "the eternal people,"
enduring through such a succession of bitter
trial, exile, and cruelty as few races have ever
known, it is their family solidarity that has kept
the flame of mutual confidence and courage
burning in spite of every wind that blew.

What has been true pre-eminently in Jewish
history is corroborated among other peoples.
The strength of Rome in the great times of
the republic was in the strength and integrity
of its family ideals; it was when these were
corrupted that Rome sank to its decline and fall.
Consider the example of China, outlasting other
civilizations because in spite of huge general upheavals the tough core of family cohesion was
never penetrated. The Jewish witness to the
importance of the family is thus not unparalleled, but in its conception of what makes and
keeps the family it is supreme. Religion of
some sort has been woven into the loyalty of
family in every nation where that loyalty was
great. It was so in Rome, in China. But back
of the O.T. idea of which all Christian faith is
the heir there lay the surpassing religious consciousness and unequaled revelation which
were given to the Jewish people. The God of
Abraham is he whom the highest instincts of the
human race are led to acknowledge as the
Lord of life. Therefore from the Bible come the
surest suggestions of the truth for life.

Note then, in the text, the elements out of
which family integrity, and therefore all sound
community relationships, are made.

First, personal example. It was not what
Abraham knew, nor what he had, that made him
fit to be the creator of a great inheritance. His

possessions at the most were simple: a tent, a
few flocks and herds. By modern reckoning he
had no conspicuous education. But he had
moral earnestness, a sense of high responsibility,
and the will to be obedient to the best he knew.
There is a description by old Ephraim Peabody
of the insights of the man who is technically
unlearned, but is schooled by character in the
ways of God.

> A good conscience sometimes seems almost identi-
> cal with wisdom. Who has not seen ignorant men,
> quite incompetent to defend their opinions, pos-
> sessing an almost fatal certainty of judgment,
> especially in regard to the moral character both
> of ends and men? The secret of it was that they
> were seeking only what was right, and in seeking
> what was right they have taken the shortest road
> to what is wise.[9]

What the head of a family talks about and tells
his children because he theoretically thinks it
advisable or convenient is gone with the wind.
What he actually is will be impressed upon them
unforgettably: "What you are speaks so loud
that I cannot hear what you say." The good
man sets up a living ideal of goodness that is
powerful forever. Normally it will make his
children follow it. When they do not follow it,
it still persists as an inward protest against their
own rebellious way.

Second, the transmission of ideals. Teaching
alone will not get far. It must be certified by
the substance of what a man is. Yet given character, the parent not only can but ought to
make his convictions articulate. The strength

[9] Quoted in Francis G. Peabody, *Reminiscences of
Present-Day Saints* (Boston: Houghton Mifflin Co., 1927),
p. 16.

stranger, all the land of Canaan, for an everlasting possession; and I will be their God.

9 ¶ And God said unto Abraham, Thou shalt keep my covenant therefore, thou, and thy seed after thee in their generations.

sojournings, all the land of Canaan, for an everlasting possession; and I will be their God."

9 And God said to Abraham, "As for you, you shall keep my covenant, you and your descendants after you throughout

---

This insistence on the part of P was in part an expression of the natural love of a people for its home. It was in part a consequence of the fact that Israel had as yet no adequate belief in life after death, so that God's promise had to be realized, if at all, here and now on this earth. Nevertheless, in insisting upon the importance of the natural community he was on sure ground for, without this insistence, belief in the supernatural becomes little more than a world-escaping piety.

---

of the religious tradition of the O.T. was linked directly with the explicit charge to teach it. "These words, which I command thee this day, shall be in thine heart" (Deut. 6:6). "In thine heart" first. But not to be hidden there in silence. "Thou shalt teach them diligently unto thy children" (Deut. 6:7). When? In some formal and occasional fashion, like a father perfunctorily showing his child the lesson he is supposed to learn for Sunday school? No, but in all the familiar conversation and the loving watchful counsel of the home in which religious ideals are made familiar. "Thou . . . shalt talk of them when thou sittest in thine house, and when thou walkest by the way, and when thou liest down, and when thou risest up" (Deut. 6:7). That parental duty expressed in Deuteronomy is echoed in the Psalms, in the Proverbs, in the Prophets; not as precept only but as something greatly practiced. When Jesus was born to be the little boy entrusted to a home in Nazareth, that fact was still true. How much of the influence that under God shaped the growing consciousness of Jesus was due to the education in the Scriptures that the father of a Jewish family was explicitly responsible to give, and which Joseph gave? Was it because of the warmth and loveliness of the first conceptions of God which came to him that way that Jesus so instinctively thought of God always as "my Father"?

Third, authority. There is an authority that is arbitrary. There is another authority that is right. A parent may be moved by nothing more than the irritable whim of his own selfishness and yet impose his will because he has the power. That authority is degrading both to the one who asserts it and to the one who suffers from it. But the authority that comes from character and from ripened knowledge is the rich gift that makes for human progress. Read John Fiske, *The Destiny of Man*,[1] on the significance

[1] Boston: Houghton Mifflin Co., 1897.

of human infancy. Ponder the danger in modern educational theories of letting children wait to learn and choose until they do it on their own motion. Those theories have inspiring value in so far as they encourage initiative and spontaneity, but often they accompany and are used to rationalize a flabby evasion of the constructive task to give children solid foundations for knowledge and character. Teachers in schools, directors and counselors in summer camps for boys and girls, are increasingly confronted with the problem of children who have come from homes where parents have let them grow up undisciplined and intractable and who therefore are disruptive influences in any group. The real cause of that is parental feebleness, or the moral indolence of men and women more interested in cocktail parties and night clubs than in their children's nurture; but the salve to conscience may be some formula such as, "It is better for children not to be repressed."

There was a man who had the same idea, that convictions should not be implanted in children until they came to years of discretion. A friend of his recounted: "I showed him my garden, and told him it was my botanical garden. 'How so?' said he; 'it is covered with weeds.' 'Oh,' I replied, 'that is only because it has not yet come to its age of discretion. The weeds you see have taken the liberty to grow, and I thought it unfair in me to prejudice the soil toward roses and strawberries.' " But the great harvests in human life, like the harvests of the earth, come, as was thus well understood, from those who have sense enough to "prejudice the soil" by right planting. That is the creative wisdom of all true authority: the authority of the sower, the authority of the teacher who makes it plain that two and two do make four, the authority of the guide who knows the right way up the mountain, the authority of the parent who humbly but certainly can say to his children of

10 This *is* my covenant, which ye shall keep, between me and you and thy seed after thee; Every man child among you shall be circumcised.

11 And ye shall circumcise the flesh of your foreskin; and it shall be a token of the covenant betwixt me and you.

12 And he that is eight days old shall be circumcised among you, every man child in your generations, he that is born in the house, or bought with money of any stranger, which *is* not of thy seed.

their generations. 10 This is my covenant, which you shall keep, between me and you and your descendants after you: Every male among you shall be circumcised. 11 You shall be circumcised in the flesh of your foreskins, and it shall be a sign of the covenant between me and you. 12 He that is eight days old among you shall be circumcised; every male throughout your generations, whether born in your house, or bought with your money from any for-

---

B. The Sign (17:9-14)

10. Circumcision was widely practiced in primitive religion. It was a custom of the western Semites and the Egyptians, among others. In this connection the epithet "uncircumcised" applied to the non-Semitic Philistines is significant (cf. I Sam. 17:26, 36; II Sam. 1:20; also I Sam. 18:25-27). Originally the rite was performed at puberty as a ceremony of initiation into the full religious and civil status of manhood. In the J

---

a great truth God has given him, "This is the way, walk ye in it" (Isa. 30:21).

10-14. Circumcision.—Thus is described the beginning of the rite which was to play an immense part in the history of Israel and in the life and thought of the early Christian church that grew out of it. As the Exeg. points out, circumcision may go back to older and more general origins which now can be traced only dimly; but there is no doubt of the way in which Israel conceived it. It was linked with the direct and definite ordaining of God. This was his own sign and seal that Israel was a chosen people.

For a people to regard itself as chosen by heaven, and marked thus for a superior destiny, may be dangerous. It was dangerous for Israel when it meant a fierce separateness and fanatical intolerance. Yet it put at the core of the people's life a sureness and tenacity of conviction which could be magnificent strength—strength that continually needed to be chastened and corrected and led toward higher understanding of why God had chosen this people and what he had chosen it for—but strength, all the same. And the rite of circumcision made that strength corporate. It was the mark which made a man belong to the whole body of the nation whose dignity and consequence he thereby shared. Since Israel was chosen and called of God, so was he. Since God's promises had been given to Israel, he himself was a child of promise. Therefore the rite of circumcision, like every sacrament, was more than an external act. It conveyed something vital to the man within. As the catechism of the Book of Com-

mon Prayer defines a sacrament, it is "an outward and visible sign of an inward and spiritual grace." Circumcision was in that true sense a sacrament to all believing Jews. Through it a man's life was linked with a great fellowship whose dignity was its high consciousness that it must fulfill the purposes of God.

Thus a rite like that of circumcision can be a vast power for good. It brings the individual into the magnetic field of suggestions and influences greater and more significant than his lonely self. So with the sacraments of all religions. But the trouble is that the rite may lose its inspiration. It may become only a traditional form from which the meaning has evaporated. Or its supposed meaning may become so hard and self-assured that it paralyzes all growth and expansion of the spirit. That is what tended to happen in later Judaism. Men assumed that because they had been circumcised, therefore *ipso facto* they were saved. That was the reason for the blazing words of John the Baptist, "Do not presume to say to yourselves, 'We have Abraham as our father'; for I tell you, God is able from these stones to raise up children to Abraham" (Matt. 3:9).

The problem and the opportunity of religion always meet in this, viz., in the need so to interpret and to use the rite and sacrament that they shall minister to a growing life. The outward form cannot be discarded as though it had no use. That is to forfeit the corporate power of religion and to take away from individuals what can be their steadying strength. But the old form must forever be charged with living meaning, or sometimes a new form must unfold

13 He that is born in thy house, and he that is bought with thy money, must needs be circumcised: and my covenant shall be in your flesh for an everlasting covenant.

14 And the uncircumcised man child whose flesh of his foreskin is not circumcised, that soul shall be cut off from his people; he hath broken my covenant.

15 ¶ And God said unto Abraham, As for Sarai thy wife, thou shalt not call her name Sarai, but Sarah *shall* her name *be*.

eigner who is not of your offspring, 13 both he that is born in your house and he that is bought with your money, shall be circumcised. So shall my covenant be in your flesh an everlasting covenant. 14 Any uncircumcised male who is not circumcised in the flesh of his foreskin shall be cut off from his people; he has broken my covenant."

15 And God said to Abraham, "As for Sar'ai your wife, you shall not call her name Sar'ai, but Sarah shall be her name.

---

strand of ch. 34 it is taken for granted as an Israelite practice. The basic E material in Josh. 5:2-3, 8*b*-9 represents it as having been instituted in Israel by Joshua. The fact is that the origin of the rite is lost in the mists of antiquity. The curious story in Exod. 4:24-26 (J[1]) suggests that the circumcising of infants was a custom that obtained at Kadesh, whence Israel adopted it.

Deut. 10:16; 30:6, neither of which is dependent on P, show that circumcision had, quite apart from the P tradition, come to be regarded as a sign of allegiance to the Lord, but the idea is found in germ in the J narrative of ch. 34, and more clearly in Exod. 4:24-26, where the implication of "and touched Moses' feet" (Exod. 4:25)—"feet" being a euphemism for "genitals"—is that Moses was saved from the wrath of the Lord by vicarious circumcision. This tale is of Kadesh provenance, and would seem to indicate that an uncircumcised man was thought to be in grave danger from the numen of that sanctuary. When the Israelites took over the sanctuary they adopted many of its beliefs and legends, attaching them to Yahweh, so that it is by no means impossible that the origin of the developed Israelite theory of circumcision as the mark of the covenant is to be found there.

However that may be, there is no doubt that during the Exile the rite took on a new importance and became, with the keeping of the sabbath and abstention from blood, one of the marks of the Jew. Just as in 2:2-3 P had claimed divine authority for the sabbath and in 9:4 for the practice of abstaining from blood, so here he ascribes circumcision to God's explicit command. It is indeed "placed above the Mosaic ritual, and second in dignity only to the Sabbath" (Skinner, *Genesis*, p. 297).

C. PROMISE OF A SON (17:15-22)

15. The change of name from **Sarai** to **Sarah** probably reflects the change from Abram to Abraham.

---

out of the chrysalis of the old. That was what the experience of Paul had taught him, and what he proclaimed with passionate conviction in his letters to the Romans and to the Galatians. "In Christ Jesus neither circumcision availeth any thing, nor uncircumcision; but faith which worketh by love" (Gal. 5:6). Christian baptism meant to Paul, and must mean to us, the sacrament of initiation into the new Israel which, like circumcision of old, should create in the soul the conviction that it is chosen and sealed by God's own grace to be one of those through whom his purpose in life shall be revealed. When baptism is allowed to become a perfunctory fashion, or at the other extreme re-

garded as a kind of automatic magic of salvation, its meaning is degraded; but truly sought, it can become the mystical gateway into the fellowship of the redeemed. The right prayer is that which is contained in the Prayer Book's ancient collect for the feast of the Circumcision of Christ: "Almighty God, who madest thy blessed Son to be circumcised, and obedient to the law for man; Grant us the true circumcision of the Spirit; that, our hearts, and all our members, being mortified from all worldly and carnal lusts, we may in all things obey thy blessed will."

15-22. *Again the Covenant.*—To the priestly writers whose voice speaks here through the

16 And I will bless her, and give thee a son also of her: yea, I will bless her, and she shall be *a mother* of nations; kings of people shall be of her.

17 Then Abraham fell upon his face, and laughed, and said in his heart, Shall *a child* be born unto him that is a hundred years old? and shall Sarah, that is ninety years old, bear?

18 And Abraham said unto God, O that Ishmael might live before thee!

19 And God said, Sarah thy wife shall bear thee a son indeed; and thou shalt call his name Isaac: and I will establish my covenant with him for an everlasting covenant, *and* with his seed after him.

20 And as for Ishmael, I have heard thee: Behold, I have blessed him, and will make him fruitful, and will multiply him exceedingly; twelve princes shall he beget, and I will make him a great nation.

21 But my covenant will I establish with Isaac, which Sarah shall bear unto thee at this set time in the next year.

22 And he left off talking with him, and God went up from Abraham.

16 I will bless her, and moreover I will give you a son by her; I will bless her, and she shall be a mother of nations; kings of peoples shall come from her." 17 Then Abraham fell on his face and laughed, and said to himself, "Shall a child be born to a man who is a hundred years old? Shall Sarah, who is ninety years old, bear a child?" 18 And Abraham said to God, "Oh that Ish'mael might live in thy sight!" 19 God said, "No, but Sarah your wife shall bear you a son, and you shall call his name Isaac.[z] I will establish my covenant with him as an everlasting covenant for his descendants after him. 20 As for Ish'mael, I have heard you; behold, I will bless him and make him fruitful and multiply him exceedingly; he shall be the father of twelve princes, and I will make him a great nation. 21 But I will establish my covenant with Isaac, whom Sarah shall bear to you at this season next year."

22 When he had finished talking with

[z] That is *he laughs*

---

16. The P parallel to 18:10 (J[2]), and possibly to the E story of which the fragmentary 16:13-14 was the conclusion.

17. Laughed purports to explain the name Isaac—meaning **he laughs**— (cf. vs. 19), and is a parallel to 21:6*b* (J[1]); 18:12 (J[2]); 21:6*a* (E). The origin of the Isaac tradition will be discussed below.

In vss. 18, 20-21 Ishmael is set aside as the inheritor of the covenant. The fact that the (supposed) elder son of Abraham did not become the heir to the divine promise is accounted for in J[2] by Hagar's flight before the child's birth (ch. 16), and in E by her expulsion with the child (21:9-21), a simple variant to the J[2] story in ch. 16. P, having discarded this story, was compelled to provide another explanation.

---

history of Genesis no degree of emphasis could be too great for the conviction that God had chosen Israel for his people. In vss. 1-21 the word **covenant** occurs thirteen times, and every sentence reinforces it. Sarai's name is changed to Sarah, which means "princess"; she should be **a mother of nations; kings of people shall be of her.** In this more stately and formal priestly narrative there is no rebuke to Abraham for the fact that he **fell upon his face, and laughed** when he heard the promise that a son should be born to Sarah—though in the more dramatic narrative of J, which follows in the next chapter, Sarah is rebuked when she laughs. Here the whole light is turned upon the astonishing

greatness of the promise itself, so that it need not seem strange that Abraham should laugh at its incredible wonder. The special covenant centering in Isaac and God's sovereign action in it are accentuated by Abraham's instinctive plea for Ishmael, **O that Ishmael might live before thee!** There is the cry of affection from the father's heart for his son who is already born. In answer to that, God does promise blessing to Ishmael, **Twelve princes shall he beget, and I will make him a great nation.** But the people of Israel who would be the descendants of Isaac should be greater than the Ishmaelites. **My covenant will I establish with Isaac.**

23 ¶ And Abraham took Ishmael his son, and all that were born in his house, and all that were bought with his money, every male among the men of Abraham's house; and circumcised the flesh of their foreskin in the selfsame day, as God had said unto him.

24 And Abraham *was* ninety years old and nine, when he was circumcised in the flesh of his foreskin.

25 And Ishmael his son *was* thirteen years old, when he was circumcised in the flesh of his foreskin.

26 In the selfsame day was Abraham circumcised, and Ishmael his son.

27 And all the men of his house, born in the house, and bought with money of the stranger, were circumcised with him.

18 And the LORD appeared unto him in the plains of Mamre: and he sat in the tent door in the heat of the day;

him, God went up from Abraham. 23 Then Abraham took Ish'mael his son and all the slaves born in his house or bought with his money, every male among the men of Abraham's house, and he circumcised the flesh of their foreskins that very day, as God had said to him. 24 Abraham was ninety-nine years old when he was circumcised in the flesh of his foreskin; 25 and Ish'mael his son was thirteen years old when he was circumcised in the flesh of his foreskin. 26 That very day Abraham and his son Ish'mael were circumcised; 27 and all the men of his house, those born in the house and those bought with money from a foreigner, were circumcised with him.

18 And the LORD appeared to him by the oaks[a] of Mamre, as he sat at the

[a] Or *terebinths*

D. GOD'S COMMAND FULFILLED (17:23-27)

23-27. It is impossible to say what P had in mind in recording the circumcision of Ishmael. He may have regarded the Ishmaelites—and presumably the Edomites and other supposed descendants of Abraham—as somehow participating in the Abrahamic covenant; or he may simply have been accounting for the fact that these groups practiced circumcision.

XXI. THE LORD'S VISIT TO HEBRON (18:1-33)

This chapter is from the J document. The story was included by J[1] in his narrative, elaborated by J[2], and added to by a late J editor. Its nucleus is contained in vss. 1b-3a, 4-8, telling of the appearance of three men, divine beings incognito, to Abraham and of his hospitality to them.

This was the description of the theophany which inaugurated the pre-Yahwist cult of Hebron. The motif of a man entertaining strangers, unaware that they were divine, is a common one in ancient literature (see Gunkel, *Genesis,* pp. 193-94; Skinner, *Genesis,* pp. 302-3). The hospitality usually, if not always, resulted in a blessing. As to whether

---

23-27. See Expos. on vss. 10-14.

18:1-15. *The Unrecognized Visitation.*—This passage manifestly must come from a very early and ingenuous stage of thought. One remembers the vivid picture in the story of the Garden of Eden of "the LORD God walking in the garden in the cool of the day" (3:8). Here the conception that underlies the narrative is still more primitive. Not only one but three divine beings appear to Abraham, and in the form of men. Then, in the story as the compilers have left its interwoven strands, one of the three is revealed as the Lord himself, who talks directly with Abraham and tells him what he plans to do.

Here therefore, as often in Genesis, one

recognizes that the framework of a story belongs to a far-off time. Yet there are values in it which do not disappear. There is the opening picture of the hospitality of Abraham. From the door of his tent he sees three figures coming toward him through the heat of the day—figures whom he has no reason to believe are other than ordinary men who have chanced to come his way. Instantly he goes out to meet them and to offer to them his utmost hospitality; and the men, thus welcomed, bring to Abraham a reward of which he had not dreamed. It was not the last time that a generous spirit has found that he has "entertained angels unaware" (Heb. 13:2). When anyone receives another human being with warm-

2 And he lifted up his eyes and looked, and, lo, three men stood by him: and when he saw *them,* he ran to meet them from the tent door, and bowed himself toward the ground,

door of his tent in the heat of the day. 2 He lifted up his eyes and looked, and behold, three men stood in front of him. When he saw them, he ran from the tent door to meet them, and bowed himself to the earth,

---

this was a feature of the original Hebron form of the tale it is impossible to say, or whether, if it was, the blessing was the promise of a son. It may be assumed, however, that the story ended with an account of how Abraham ultimately realized that his visitors were divine beings and offered sacrifice—cf. the realization of Gideon (Judg. 6:22), and of Manoah and his wife (Judg. 13:20-21), that they had seen the angel of the Lord; also Jacob's response to the theophany at Bethel (28:18).

This legend was probably current at Hebron when the Israelites appeared upon the scene, and when they took over the sanctuary for the Lord, they necessarily took over the legend. J¹, incorporating it into his history, prefixed to it the opening words of vs. 1, "and the LORD appeared to him by the oak of Mamre" (reading "oak" for "oaks" with the LXX and Syriac; cf. 13:18). He did not, however, distinguish the Lord as one of the three visitors; i.e., having said it was a theophany of the Lord, he was content to tell the tale presumably as it was told in Hebron, preserving the plural throughout vss. 4-6. The speech in vs. 3, in which Abraham addresses one of the visitors only, is an addition by J², implying that they were the Lord and two attendants; see further on vss. 10-15 below.

A. ABRAHAM'S HOSPITALITY (18:1-8)

18:2. The implication of **and behold, three men stood in front of him** is that they suddenly appeared; they had not been seen approaching. Abraham does not at once realize the significance of this. The statement that he **bowed himself to the earth** does not mean that he recognized his visitors as divine beings. The act was an expression of the self-deprecating courtesy of the Orient (cf. 23:7; I Sam. 24:8; II Sam. 14:4, 22; I Kings 1:31).

---

hearted kindness he may be nearer than he knows to a divine experience. Although it is a long way from Genesis to the Gospels, in the story of Abraham there is at least a foregleam of the promise of Christ, "Inasmuch as ye have done it unto one of the least of these my brethren, ye have done it unto me" (Matt. 25:40).

From the visit to Abraham comes the promise to him and to Sarah that Isaac shall be born. To both Abraham and Sarah that seemed almost unthinkable (as to Sarah's incredulous laughter, see Expos. on vs. 12). But the divine voice spoke to them, **Is anything too hard for the LORD?** To that question the faith of the O.T. answered "No." It was sure that always a heavenly purpose was at work and that those who trusted it would not be disappointed.

12. *Laughter.*—There are various kinds of laughter. There is a happy laughter like that of carefree children in their play. Zechariah's vision of the redeemed society was of a city "full of boys and girls playing in the streets thereof" (Zech. 8:5). Was that also one of the reasons why Jesus made little children the symbol of

the kingdom of God? There is a beauty in God's creation and an exhilaration in existence which can give to all life an essential joyousness. A lovely, simple hymn in the Church of England's *Songs of Praise* begins, "Glad that I live am I." In the good world which God has made we ought to be able to say with the psalmist, "Then was our mouth filled with laughter, and our tongue with singing" (Ps. 126:2). Too often religion is supposed to be represented by severity and somberness and a dour face. It is better represented by a Francis of Assisi, who was called the "troubadour of God"; or by such a gay and gallant modern saint as "Dick" Sheppard, the beloved vicar of St. Martin's-in-the-Fields, London. There is the laughter that comes from seeing the little absurdities of life, including especially our own. That also is a laughter that goes hand in hand with real religion. The egocentric man who must act as though he were a focus of creation looks at everything with a kind of suspicious grimness. He is too self-important to recognize that life may be ridiculous, and especially he can never take a joke on himself.

3 And said, My Lord, if now I have found favor in thy sight, pass not away, I pray thee, from thy servant:

4 Let a little water, I pray you, be fetched, and wash your feet, and rest yourselves under the tree:

5 And I will fetch a morsel of bread, and comfort ye your hearts; after that ye shall pass on: for therefore are ye come to your servant. And they said, So do, as thou hast said.

6 And Abraham hastened into the tent unto Sarah, and said, Make ready quickly three measures of fine meal, knead *it,* and make cakes upon the hearth.

7 And Abraham ran unto the herd, and fetched a calf tender and good, and gave *it* unto a young man; and he hasted to dress it.

8 And he took butter, and milk, and the calf which he had dressed, and set *it* before them; and he stood by them under the tree, and they did eat.

3 and said, "My lord, if I have found favor in your sight, do not pass by your servant. 4 Let a little water be brought, and wash your feet, and rest yourselves under the tree, 5 while I fetch a morsel of bread, that you may refresh yourselves, and after that you may pass on — since you have come to your servant." So they said, "Do as you have said." 6 And Abraham hastened into the tent to Sarah, and said, "Make ready quickly three measures[b] of fine meal, knead it, and make cakes." 7 And Abraham ran to the herd, and took a calf, tender and good, and gave it to the servant, who hastened to prepare it. 8 Then he took curds, and milk, and the calf which he had prepared, and set it before them; and he stood by them under the tree while they ate.

[b] Heb *seahs*

3. The verse, except for the introductory **and said,** is, as has been noted, from J[2].

4. **The tree** is the sacred oak of Mamre.

5. The length of Abraham's speech, suggesting a certain nervousness, is to be noted, especially in contrast to the dignified **Do as you have said.** In these ancient tales the greater person is always succinct in utterance, the lesser person inclined to garrulousness; cf. the meeting of Obadiah with Elijah (I Kings 18:7-15). **Since you have come to your servant** implies that to be thus entertained is only to be expected by those who come to his tent. J[1] thus unobtrusively stresses once more Abraham's generosity and magnanimity (cf. 13:9).

6. **Three measures of fine meal**—about four pecks—not only indicates Abraham's prodigal generosity but, in the telling of the story in its original form, would be the first subtle suggestion to the hearers that the visitors were divine beings.

8. In view of the fact that Hebron was the center of a grape-growing country (cf. 49:11-12) it seems likely that the tale in its pre-Yahwist form included wine in the repast. If so, its absence here will be due to J[1] who, being aware of its abuses (cf. 9:21-25), was unwilling to represent the Lord as partaking of it.

But men who are conscious of the greatness of God can be simplehearted enough to laugh at what might be the exaggerated pretensions of their own littleness. It is a sign of a wholesome spirit when any individual or nation is capable of that kind of laughter. Shakespeare and Milton reveal the strength of England, and so does *Punch.* When a nation can laugh at itself it is saved from delusions of grandeur and is ready to face the challenge of each new time with the stripped sincerity of truth and the courage of good humor. This does not depend upon some accidental racial quality. It can have a deeper and surer root. In one part of himself the Anglo-Saxon has plenty of instinctive arro-

gance; but in another part of him he has his long-inherited Christian consciousness which makes him see himself as measured against the majesty of God and so keeps him ultimately from being an unregulated fool.

But there are other kinds of laughter which are not wholesome. There is the laughter which, the more it is careless, the less it is carefree—the loud, coarse laughter of men and women whose feverish efforts to amuse themselves still leave them miserable. They are looking for escape from thinking, escape from themselves. If they can laugh loud enough, perhaps they can drown out the inner voice which tells them that their life can have some satisfying purpose and that

9 ¶ And they said unto him, Where *is* Sarah thy wife? And he said, Behold, in the tent.

10 And he said, I will certainly return unto thee according to the time of life; and, lo, Sarah thy wife shall have a son. And Sarah heard *it* in the tent door, which *was* behind him.

11 Now Abraham and Sarah *were* old *and* well stricken in age; *and* it ceased to be with Sarah after the manner of women.

12 Therefore Sarah laughed within herself, saying, After I am waxed old shall I have pleasure, my lord being old also?

9 They said to him, "Where is Sarah your wife?" And he said, "She is in the tent." 10 He said, "I will surely return to you in the spring, and Sarah your wife shall have a son." And Sarah was listening at the tent door behind him. 11 Now Abraham and Sarah were old, advanced in age; it had ceased to be with Sarah after the manner of women. 12 So Sarah laughed to herself, saying, "After I have grown old, and my hus-

---

B. Sarah Laughs (18:9-15)

9. This is the conclusion of the extant J[1] material, since the change to the singular (cf. vs. 3) in the following verses indicates J[2]. The sudden revelation by the strangers that they knew the name of the host's wife is one of the finer points of the story. It was designed to quicken the interest of the listeners: "How did they know this? They must be divine." And the unspoken suggestion is that Abraham himself was startled by this strange display of knowledge.

The question and its answer were, it may be assumed, followed by a simpler form of a promise of a son to Sarah. Whether or not J[1] continued this by recording that Abraham then offered sacrifice—presumably the conclusion of the story in its pre-Yahwist form—it is impossible to say. If he did, the incident was dropped by J[2], who in this case will be responsible for the statement in 13:18 that Abraham immediately upon his arrival at Hebron "built an altar to the Lord."

10-15. These verses are, as the use of the singular suggests, from J[2], who here identifies the son promised to Sarah with Isaac, the patron of Beer-sheba (see Exeg. on 21:1-7). J[1] had, in view of 21:6b, apparently postponed this identification until he recorded the child's birth. J[2] may himself be responsible for the incident here recorded, or he may have been dependent upon a tradition which had taken form at Hebron subsequent to the time of J[1]. In either case the little narrative is superbly told as it describes Sarah listening, laughing, and lying.

11. The implication is that some considerable period had elapsed since Abraham had taken Sarah to Egypt.

12-15. Sarah had **laughed to herself** (vs. 12), i.e., silently. Yet the stranger—whom she and her husband had not yet recognized as the Lord—cf. his reference to himself in the third person in his next speech in vs. 14—at once knew that she had done so. This was another indication of his supernatural character. Its effect upon Sarah is brought out in **for she was afraid** (vs. 15).

---

they should be finding it. For the moment, it is easier and seems less painful to let everything be covered up by the kind of laughter that can be got out of a bottle of gin or out of the coarse humor of a night club show; but that laughter has nothing in it to warm the heart. In the words of Eccl. 7:6, it is like "the crackling of thorns under a pot."

There is the laughter of disbelief. Such was Sarah's laughter. And indeed, Abraham had once been guilty of this same disbelieving

laughter also (17:17). The promise that was supposed to be from God seemed to her to be absurd. To have a general pious belief in God's existence was one thing; to trust that his power and grace could come directly into her life with a wonderful blessing was another. Why should she be simple-minded enough to believe that? Why should people in any time believe? The worldly wise will always be around to say that faith is nothing but credulity; and inside ourselves there is a vanity which is deathly afraid

13 And the LORD said unto Abraham, Wherefore did Sarah laugh, saying, Shall I of a surety bear a child, which am old?

14 Is any thing too hard for the LORD? At the time appointed I will return unto thee, according to the time of life, and Sarah shall have a son.

15 Then Sarah denied, saying, I laughed not; for she was afraid. And he said, Nay; but thou didst laugh.

band is old, shall I have pleasure?" 13 The LORD said to Abraham, "Why did Sarah laugh, and say, 'Shall I indeed bear a child, now that I am old?' 14 Is anything too hard^e for the LORD? At the appointed time I will return to you, in the spring, and Sarah shall have a son." 15 But Sarah denied, saying, "I did not laugh"; for she was afraid. He said, "No, but you did laugh."

^e Or wonderful

The idea of God reflected in this kindly Hebron story is very different from the primitive idea of the Lord as the God who manifested himself in the destructive forces of nature—the storm (cf. Pss. 18:7-15; 29), the fire (cf. Exod. 19:18), the earthquake (cf. I Kings 19:11)—and whose activity in human relationships was that of the God of war (cf. Exod. 15:3; Judg. 5). This primitive idea had been enriched through the work of Moses at Kadesh before the southern clans settled in and about Hebron, and the Lord had come to be known to them as the God of righteousness and justice, concerned with the ordinary, everyday relationships between man and man. Nevertheless, at Kadesh the people were still nomads and the Lord was still a desert deity, as austere as the hard land through which they ranged.

At Hebron the Israelite clans came into contact with another kind of religion— the religion symbolized by Abraham and finding partial expression in the story now under consideration. This religion was rooted in a locality; it cherished the values of a settled community, a community which was more stable and more aware of the beneficence and kindliness of nature than a nomad community could be. The identification of the god of Hebron with the Lord meant that these values came to be associated with him and with the values and beliefs which the clans had brought from the desert. This resulted in an increased unification of life as it came to be seen that the creative power of nature—the power which made things grow, which gave increase to the flocks and herds, which even quickened the barren womb—and the destructive power of nature— the power which reminded men of their littleness and dependence—came from the same transcendent source. At Hebron the process begun at Kadesh was advanced. The Lord took over the functions of a tribal god without being regarded as himself a member of the tribe and, as such, committed to the protection of its material interests regardless of the moral problems involved.

of being laughed at. So like Sarah, we may try to hide our most eager longings behind a laugh that tries to say, "You cannot fool me."

In the story as it developed, God's promise was fulfilled in spite of her derisive skepticism, and Sarah herself could cry out in a great and wonderful happiness, "God hath made me to laugh, so that all that hear will laugh with me" (21:6). But it is not always so. Those who would like to trust in God may be overawed by those who sit in the seat of the scornful. They meet fresh opportunities for their souls with an embarrassed smirk instead of with independent courage. Or they surrender to the thought that great hopes which God has kindled in them are too good to be true. That way lies frustration and the soul's defeat.

Once more: There is the laughter of delib-

erate evil when it has won malignant victory over what is better than itself. Remember the picture of the laughing Hitler, dancing his demonic jig in the Forest of Compiègne on the day of the surrender of France. Evil laughter does not have to be as dramatic as it was in him to be a fact. Each one of us may sometimes exhibit it: in a cruelly triumphant satisfaction in a rival's failure; in the discrediting of someone we do not like; in the reversal of Paul's great appeal to love, by which we rejoice in evil instead of rejoicing in the truth. That may wake the most awful laughter of which the Bible speaks. God's infinite holiness looks in annihilating judgment upon our petty human rancors. "He that sitteth in the heavens shall laugh: the Lord shall have them in derision" (Ps. 2:4).

16 ¶ And the men rose up from thence, and looked toward Sodom: and Abraham went with them to bring them on the way.	16 Then the men set out from there, and they looked toward Sodom; and Abraham went with them to set them on their way.
17 And the LORD said, Shall I hide from Abraham that thing which I do;	17 The LORD said, "Shall I hide from Abraham what I am about to do, 18 seeing that Abraham shall become a great and mighty
18 Seeing that Abraham shall surely become a great and mighty nation, and all the nations of the earth shall be blessed in him?	nation, and all the nations of the earth shall bless themselves by him?ᵈ 19 No, for I have chosenᵉ him, that he may charge his
19 For I know him, that he will command his children and his household after him, and they shall keep the way of the LORD, to do justice and judgment; that the LORD may bring upon Abraham that which he hath spoken of him.	children and his household after him to keep the way of the LORD by doing righteousness and justice; so that the LORD may bring to Abraham what he has promised

ᵈ Or *in him all the families of the earth shall be blessed*
ᵉ Heb *known*

C. DEPARTURE FOR SODOM (18:16-22)

16-22. These verses effect a transition from the legend of Hebron to the originally independent saga of the destruction of Sodom. To the simple statement of J¹, preserved in vs. 22a, J² added vss. 16, 20-21, together with vs. 33b, and into this narrative vss. 17-19 were later intruded.

The text of vss. 20-21 is in disorder (Wellhausen, *Composition*, pp. 27-28; Gunkel, *Genesis*, p. 202; Skinner, *Genesis*, p. 304). Its primary form would seem to have been: "And the LORD said, 'An outcry against Sodom and Gomorrah is come to me, that their sin is great; I will go down now and see whether they have done altogether according to

---

The blessed laughter is that of the man who rejoices in the goodness of God's world, who keeps his spirit humble and his heart sensitive to whatever is lovely and of good report, and of whom it can be said at the end that

E'en as he trod that day to God so walked he from his birth,
In simpleness and gentleness and honour and clean mirth.[2]

19. Handing on the Faith.—To meditate upon the O.T. is to live in two worlds—the ancient, yet also the contemporary. The customs and the ways of speech of Abraham could not be ours; but the central values of life reflected from his relationship to God are independent of time. The words of the Lord to him were that he should **command his children and his household after him**, in order that they might **keep the way of the LORD, to do justice and judgment.** There is a charge that belongs to every parent for every family as surely in the twentieth century as in Abraham's far-off age. Abraham would have to fulfill it according to the knowledge of his time. The vital question for us is how we can best fulfill it now. If there-

fore we ask what are the principles of understanding which today should guide those who look upon their children as a trust from God, answers may be such as these:

Intelligent sympathy. Note both words. Sympathy is a matter of emotion and imagination. In all normal parents there is an instinctive tenderness and brooding love for a baby. The baby begins to grow into the little child who has characteristics of his own, and that is where the need for sympathy begins; for sympathy means imaginative understanding by the adult of what the child thinks and feels. That sort of sympathy is not easy. On the contrary, it takes a warm purpose and an outgoing spirit. When Jesus set a child in the midst of the disciples and said that men must become as children to enter the kingdom of God, that was and is in some ways a hard saying. For a child is a biological primitive, self-centered and mostly self-assertive. In some of his outbreaks he may seem less a type of the kingdom of heaven than a proof of original sin. Why then did Jesus say what he did? Because a child is infinitely expectant, trustful, forgiving, innocent in impulse even when he is most blundering in act. Unpredictable possibilities are there in the sensitive nature that has not yet been hurt or disillusioned. Remembrance of that will warm the hearts of every right-minded

---

[2] "Barrack Room Ballads," Dedication, st. vii. From *Rudyard Kipling's Verse,* Definitive Edition. Used by permission of Mrs. George Bambridge; Methuen & Co.; The Macmillan Co., Canada; and Doubleday & Co.

20 And the Lord said, Because the cry of Sodom and Gomorrah is great, and because their sin is very grievous,

21 I will go down now, and see whether they have done altogether according to the cry of it, which is come unto me; and if not, I will know.

22 And the men turned their faces from thence, and went toward Sodom: but Abraham stood yet before the Lord.

him." **20** Then the Lord said, "Because the outcry against Sodom and Gomor'rah is great and their sin is very grave, **21** I will go down to see whether they have done altogether according to the outcry which has come to me; and if not, I will know." **22** So the men turned from there, and went toward Sodom; but Abraham still

---

the outcry concerning them or not; I must know.' " Thus J2 represents the Lord as going to investigate conditions at Sodom and Gomorrah (contrast 13:13 J1). The reason for this addition was presumably to avoid any possible suggestion of divine caprice in the coming catastrophe.

It may be noted further that Gomorrah is here mentioned for the first time. The actual story has to do only with Sodom, though the tradition upon which J1 depended seems, in view of the references elsewhere in the O.T. (see below), to have bracketed Gomorrah with it. Possibly Gomorrah was added to the J1 recension by J2 for this reason.

---

father and mother. They will want to be compassionate and to be sensitive to understand. Read Coventry Patmore's "The Toys." But they will need to have an intelligent understanding and an intelligent sympathy. Hardness can hurt a child, as one can see in the irritable uncontrol of selfish and callous people; but the softness of haphazard indulgence can hurt him equally. A child's nature can be helped to its right development only by those who take much thought, inform themselves, and so have not only a right will but also an effective wisdom.

A purposeful ideal. The tragedy with many people is that they have no clear aim and no fixed standards for themselves, and so none for their children. They drift here and there in ideas and notions, according to the shifting winds of casual or convenient impulse, like ships with no compass and no chart. The result is that their children are never given the moral and spiritual certainties that would make them sure of themselves and of their direction. "The way of man is not in himself: it is not in man that walketh to direct his steps" (Jer. 10:23). It is the way of God that needs to be made inviting and made plain.

Patience. It is reverence for human souls that makes patience possible. Consider the example of Jesus. The disciples thought that he and they had much too important matters on hand to be bothered with children, but Jesus said, "Let the children come to me, do not hinder them" (Mark 10:14). Mothers instinctively knew that he would welcome them: and the same Jesus who "steadfastly set his face to go to Jerusalem" (Luke 9:51) was the Jesus

who stopped to take children up into his arms. Observe likewise his patience with all the lonely or distressed people who, like children, needed someone who cared and took time to understand (read Matt. 8:17; Mark 10:46-52; Luke 8:41-56; 19:1-10; John 4:5-29; 9:1-38).

Then last—yet also first, for it is the beginning and end of all—a continuing trust and faith of the father himself that is directed where he would have his son look. George MacDonald has expressed it in four lines:

> Lo! Lord, I sit in thy wide space,
> My child upon my knee;
> She looketh up into my face,
> And I look up to thee.[3]

20-33. The Great Soul's Mercy.—In Genesis the wickedness of Sodom is set forth so emphatically that its name has become proverbial —"a very Sodom." Yet here is Abraham interceding for Sodom. The good man pleads for mercy for the wicked.

Who is most likely to come to the help of the wicked? Can bad men in trouble expect help more certainly from other bad men? No. Men who are thoroughly bad are as merciless to others of their kind as a wolf pack is merciless to the wounded wolf. But "bad" and "good" may be misleading labels. There are so-called "good" men who are as hard as flint, the self-righteous and pharisaical, such as those whom Jesus confronted one day with his withering indignation when they brought to him the woman taken in adultery; and there are so-

[3] "The Father's Hymn for the Mother to Sing." Used by permission of the author's executors.

23 ¶ And Abraham drew near, and said, Wilt thou also destroy the righteous with the wicked?

24 Peradventure there be fifty righteous within the city: wilt thou also destroy and not spare the place for the fifty righteous that *are* therein?

25 That be far from thee to do after this manner, to slay the righteous with the wicked; and that the righteous should be as the wicked, that be far from thee: Shall not the Judge of all the earth do right?

stood before the LORD. 23 Then Abraham drew near, and said, "Wilt thou indeed destroy the righteous with the wicked? 24 Suppose there are fifty righteous within the city; wilt thou then destroy the place and not spare it for the fifty righteous who are in it? 25 Far be it from thee to do such a thing, to slay the righteous with the wicked, so that the righteous fare as the wicked! Far be that from thee! Shall not

---

D. ABRAHAM'S INTERCESSION (18:23-33)

23-33. In vss. 20-21 the fate of Sodom still hangs in the balance. Vss. 23-33a imply that it has already been determined, and tell of Abraham's endeavor to persuade the Lord to stay his hand. This alone would suggest that the passage, with which vs. 22b belongs, is secondary. Furthermore, both J[1] and J[2], concrete in their thinking, would have told of Abraham interceding for Lot and for any other righteous people there

---

called "bad men," such as saloonkeepers and the neighborhood leaders of corrupt political machines, who have a bighearted compassion for all human beings, no matter how reprobate they are. But it is the consistent badness in the bad and the inconsistent badness in the hypocritically good which make them cruel, and the generosity of those whom the respectable may class as bad men is due to the great warm fact that there is so much actual goodness in them. So also the highest generosity and compassion are in those who are neither all bad, nor half bad, nor half good, but who, like Abraham, come as near to thoroughgoing goodness as human nature can. The most merciful men all through the Bible are the best men— Joseph, Moses, David, Stephen, Barnabas. Supremely so was Jesus, who in his perfect righteousness could be the friend of publicans and sinners. There is no more corrupting sin than censoriousness and self-righteousness. Let church members examine their own hearts.

The truth which applies to individuals applies to nations also. How can a world which has been torn and ravaged by the cruelty of war be healed? Only by the merciful. At the peace conference in Paris in August, 1946, Alcide de Gasperi, representative of the new government of defeated Italy, pleaded for "the universal aims of Christianity," for "a lasting and constructive peace which you are also seeking, and that co-operation between nations which it is your task to accomplish." Tragically, he was listened to for the most part in stony silence. "You would think," wrote Dorothy Thompson, "that men who had failed to prevent a world war and now fail to create a peace would be

humble of heart, but they are not. . . . Perhaps all must be vanquished to learn the first law of human life—that we are all members of one another." It is easy for the proud and for those who are drunk with power to consider the enemy as men of Sodom, deserving of nothing but destruction. They like to arrogate to themselves a supposed right to the favor of God and to act as though fanatical revenge had the merit of religion. If Abraham had been like them he would have gloated over Sodom. Being the man he was—an example sorely needed—he was moved with pity.

A second truth stands out: the sacred worth of individuals, and the evil of involving the innocent minority in a judgment visited on the mass. The deepest depravity and moral perversion of war lies there; and war with modern weapons makes this evil more monstrous than ever before. Obliteration-bombing of cities, economic blockade, miscellaneous death, whether coming suddenly or through slow starvation, strike women and children impartially with men, the guiltless of a nation's sins as surely as the guilty.[4] It is a grievous fact that even good people may grow callous to these things. Atrocities which at first shocked the conscience may come to be accepted with only lukewarm questioning or with none at all. But a world in torment will begin to have a better hope only when there shall be many men like Abraham. Sodom did deserve punishment, he knew. But what if in wicked Sodom there were fifty who were righteous; what if there were not fifty, but yet were forty-five, or forty, or thirty, or twenty,

[4] Cf. John Hersey, *Hiroshima* (New York: Alfred A. Knopf, 1946).

26 And the LORD said, If I find in Sodom fifty righteous within the city, then I will spare all the place for their sakes.

27 And Abraham answered and said, Behold now, I have taken upon me to speak unto the Lord, which *am but* dust and ashes:

28 Peradventure there shall lack five of the fifty righteous: wilt thou destroy all the city for *lack of* five? And he said, If I find there forty and five, I will not destroy *it*.

29 And he spake unto him yet again, and said, Peradventure there shall be forty found there. And he said, I will not do *it* for forty's sake.

the Judge of all the earth do right?" 26 And the LORD said, "If I find at Sodom fifty righteous in the city, I will spare the whole place for their sake." 27 Abraham answered, "Behold, I have taken upon myself to speak to the Lord, I who am but dust and ashes. 28 Suppose five of the fifty righteous are lacking? Wilt thou destroy the whole city for lack of five?" And he said, "I will not destroy it if I find forty-five there." 29 Again he spoke to him, and said, "Suppose forty are found there." He answered, "For the

---

might be in the city instead of representing him as pursuing a discussion of abstract principles. It was not, indeed, until an age much later than that of J[2] that the problem of the righteous individual in an evil community began to trouble the religious conscience of Israel. Even the great prophets of the eighth and following centuries scarcely raise the question as to the fate of the righteous in the national calamity, the certain approach of which they were proclaiming.

To say that the passage is late is not, of course, in any way to lessen its significance. It reflects a realization that the Lord cares for the individual who is not, so to speak,

---

or even only ten? Should those ten also be caught in the general destruction and given no chance to escape? To Abraham it seemed to be intolerable that this should be allowed to happen.

So much for the instincts which made Abraham the type of a great soul. But observe the further and more important fact: Abraham believed that what was highest in his own heart was his right clue to the nature of God. That which to his own conscience seemed lifted above all doubt must be divine in its authority. That is the meaning of the vivid story of Abraham in the dialogue with God and of his question which he was sure could have only one answer, **Shall not the Judge of all the earth do right?** Compare this approach to truth with the danger present in some twentieth-century theology, especially Barthianism, when pushed to an extreme. To make God "wholly other," the unknowable, save as he draws near in supernatural revelations that have no direct relationship to the natural awareness of human minds and hearts, is to blunt the belief of men that in their best selves they can know God and feel his near direction.

But the final suggestion of the story of Sodom—though certainly not the final suggestion of the Bible or the O.T.—is a somber one. Not even five righteous persons were left in Sodom to justify its being spared destruction. Here is an eternal picture of the corrosive possibilities

of a bad environment. Those who accustom themselves to the ways of an evil society may themselves at last be evil. What is happening now to people who make no effective protest against the wrongs they live with every day?

27. Out of the Dust.—Here is a message which belongs particularly to the generations which have been caught in two world wars. The words of Abraham may be the words of twentieth-century mankind, for to Abraham too it looked as though his world would go up in flames. Pleading for the mercy of God, he recognized on the one hand his human unworthiness; on the other hand he knew the dignity of a man who dares to converse with God.

I . . . am but dust and ashes. Much of the heritage of human civilization has been forced to say that. Note the scars of London and the destruction of historic edifices in England, the devastation of towns and cities in Holland, in Italy, in the countries of middle Europe, and in Germany. Consider the near obliteration of Hiroshima and Nagasaki and Tokyo. Shadowing the future, there is for every nation the menace of the atomic bomb, with its possibility of turning not merely a few cities but all civilization into dust and ashes.

There is a mood in individual spirits like the picture of our earth, a waning in confidence, a sense of frustration, of moral failure. There are lives which are like spiritual dust bowls. Old springs of refreshment from which our fathers

30 And he said *unto him,* Oh let not the Lord be angry, and I will speak: Peradventure there shall thirty be found there. And he said, I will not do *it,* if I find thirty there.

31 And he said, Behold now, I have taken upon me to speak unto the Lord: Peradventure there shall be twenty found there. And he said, I will not destroy *it* for twenty's sake.

32 And he said, Oh let not the Lord be angry, and I will speak yet but this once: Peradventure ten shall be found there. And he said, I will not destroy *it* for ten's sake.

sake of forty I will not do it." **30** Then he said, "Oh let not the Lord be angry, and I will speak. Suppose thirty are found there." He answered, "I will not do it, if I find thirty there." **31** He said, "Behold, I have taken upon myself to speak to the Lord. Suppose twenty are found there." He answered, "For the sake of twenty I will not destroy it." **32** Then he said, "Oh let not the Lord be angry, and I will speak again but this once. Suppose ten are found there." He answered, "For the sake of ten I will

---

swallowed up in the community, for the community is a community of persons. It indicates that at the time it was written thought was being given to the matter of vicarious righteousness—the city might be saved because of the righteousness of a few. This surely reflects at least the beginning of a realization of the organic relationship of Israel—and

---

drew seem to be no longer flowing. Life for many of their sort is like those arid stretches in the western United States where the forests have been cut down, where the rain does not fall, and the earth which ought to grow the harvest blows away in dust. There are other lives which have turned into dust and ashes in another way. A sign on a railroad which ran through forests read, "Do not let fires start. They are hot, and run faster than you can." But many persons have let fires start in the field of their own passions—physical passions or passions of hot ambition, and the moral freshness and vitality of their spirits have been scorched and burned. Or lives may be turned to ashes in still another way. The kind of fires which ought to have been there, the altar fires of idealism and hope and courage, may have burned down until there is next to nothing left. One may see this unhappy tendency in much of the literature of the mid-twentieth century. W. H. Auden has written of the weakening of moral responsibility:

It is only lately that in novel after novel one encounters heroes without honor or history; heroes who succumb so monotonously to temptation that they cannot truly be said to be tempted at all; heroes who, even if they are successful in a worldly sense, remain nevertheless but the passive recipients of good fortune; heroes whose sole moral virtue is a stoic endurance of pain and disaster.[5]

Thus the mood of the middle and later twentieth century is not one of smooth vanity or bravado. We voice more readily the General

Confession with its summary, "and there is no health in us."

But consider the other reality as expressed in the words of Abraham. Dust and ashes though he was he had taken upon himself to speak to the Lord. If we are not to think too largely of ourselves neither must we believe too little. The revulsion from overconfidence must not turn into moral cowardice. Note the danger today of pessimism, not only in secular thought but also in some theology. To guard against that danger two facts should be pondered. First is the fact of God's judgment. We may think we want a pliable and soft universe which would yield to human wish and convenience; yet we know that there could be no growth in a universe that had no moral certainties. God's judgment corrects, but also it fortifies. Alongside the judgment of God stands the mercy of God. Consider Abraham's conviction that even a few righteous in Sodom constituted a sufficient plea for God's mercy. In every continent there may be the saving remnant, the obscure men and women who are true and decent, the salt that can preserve. Belief in the goodness that may be somewhere in every human community is the antidote to moral pessimism and defeat. As that great Christian of the twentieth century, Albert Schweitzer, wrote:

However much concerned I was at the problem of the misery in the world, I never let myself get lost in broodings over it; I always held firmly to the thought that each one of us can do a little to bring some portion of it to an end. . . . Because I have confidence in the power of truth and of the spirit, I believe in the future of mankind.[6]

[5] "Henry James and the Artist in America," *Harper's Magazine,* CXCVII (1948), 37.

[6] *Out of My Life and Thought,* pp. 280-81.

33 And the LORD went his way, as soon as he had left communing with Abraham: and Abraham returned unto his place.

19 And there came two angels to Sodom at even; and Lot sat in the gate of Sodom: and Lot seeing *them* rose up to meet them; and he bowed himself with his face toward the ground;

not destroy it." 33 And the LORD went his way, when he had finished speaking to Abraham; and Abraham returned to his place.

19 The two angels came to Sodom in the evening; and Lot was sitting in the gate of Sodom. When Lot saw them, he rose to meet them, and bowed himself with

---

still more, of the Christian church—to the world. And in the question in vs. 25, **Shall not the Judge of all the earth do right?** we have a moving affirmation of Israel's faith in the essential righteousness of the God who demanded righteousness from men—all men, not Israel only. The universalism should be noted.

XXII. DESTRUCTION OF SODOM AND GOMORRAH (19:1-29)

Vss. 1-28 are from J1, with some slight elaboration by J2 and more extensive additions by later editors. Vs. 29 is from P, and is all that writer had to say about the event. It may have been the immediate continuation of 13:12abα. It may have been followed by a genealogy of Lot, dropped by RP in favor of the J narrative in vss. 30-38.

This story—belonging to a widely diffused class of tales having possibly a mythological background (see Skinner, *Genesis*, pp. 311-12) —of the destruction of a city which had once stood in the vicinity of the Dead Sea, probably at its southern end, was presumably current in Hebron when the Israelites settled there. The fact that the tale in the form it has here suggests a volcanic upheaval makes it likely that it was carried over to this region from some other locality—there is no volcanic matter near the Dead Sea—to explain the disappearance of the city. Had it been indigenous, it seems probable that it would have told of the city being overwhelmed by the waters forming the Dead Sea, especially as Genesis, as has been seen, seems to hold that the Dead Sea did not come into existence until after this event (cf. 13:10; 14:3, 10).

The tale was thus non-Yahwist in its origin. J1, unifying the various local traditions by relating them to Yahwism, took it over and linked it to the saga of Hebron by identifying the supernatural visitants with those whom Abraham had entertained, and by making the man who was saved from the disaster Abraham's nephew, who had come with him from the desert (12:4a) and who had settled in, or in the vicinity of, Sodom (13:7-11a, 12bβ).

19:1. This verse was in J2 the immediate continuation of 18:33b and, it may be assumed, recorded that "the men" **came to Sodom in the evening.** The intrusion of 18:22b-33a resulted in the representation that the Lord's two companions proceeded to Sodom alone. Hence the reading **the two angels;** it is to be noted that nowhere else in chs. 18–19 are they designated as **angels.** The author who inserted this material states simply that "the LORD went his way, when he had finished speaking with Abraham" (18:33a). He does not represent him as following the **angels** to Sodom, an omission which was doubtless due to his horror at the thought that the Lord should have been subjected to the shocking insult recorded in vss. 4-9.

19:1-25. The City of Sodom.—In this chapter Lot appears in a better light than in his previous relationships with Abraham, yet at the same time the sordid folly of his selfish choice to live in Sodom appears all the darker as seen in its results. Compared with the general population of Sodom, Lot was a decent person. The writer of II Peter could even think of him as "just

Lot, vexed with the filthy conversation of the wicked." The moments came when, as in the vile events described in this chapter, he was more than vexed. He tried to resist the extreme outrage which the lustful gang in Sodom were about to perpetrate upon the men who had harborage in his house. He would go to great lengths to fulfill the obligation of hospitality—

2 And he said, Behold now, my lords, turn in, I pray you, into your servant's house, and tarry all night, and wash your feet, and ye shall rise up early, and go on your ways. And they said, Nay; but we will abide in the street all night.

3 And he pressed upon them greatly; and they turned in unto him, and entered into his house; and he made them a feast, and did bake unleavened bread, and they did eat.

4 ¶ But before they lay down, the men of the city, *even* the men of Sodom, compassed the house round, both old and young, all the people from every quarter:

5 And they called unto Lot, and said unto him, Where *are* the men which came in to thee this night? bring them out unto us, that we may know them.

6 And Lot went out at the door unto them, and shut the door after him,

7 And said, I pray you, brethren, do not so wickedly.

8 Behold now, I have two daughters which have not known man; let me, I pray you, bring them out unto you, and do ye to

his face to the earth, 2 and said, "My lords, turn aside, I pray you, to your servant's house and spend the night, and wash your feet; then you may rise up early and go on your way." They said, "No; we will spend the night in the street." 3 But he urged them strongly; so they turned aside to him and entered his house; and he made them a feast, and baked unleavened bread, and they ate. 4 But before they lay down, the men of the city, the men of Sodom, both young and old, all the people to the last man, surrounded the house; 5 and they called to Lot, "Where are the men who came to you tonight? Bring them out to us, that we may know them." 6 Lot went out of the door to the men, shut the door after him, 7 and said, "I beg you, my brothers, do not act so wickedly. 8 Behold, I have two daughters who have not known man; let

A. Lot's Hospitality (19:1-3)

2. With this cf. 18:2-5. The men's initial refusal to accept the proffered hospitality may be intended merely as a piece of Oriental politeness, or it may be that the author had in mind the fact that they had come to investigate conditions in the city.

3. The sin of Sodom was unnatural vice. Lot therefore knew only too well what remaining in the street all night would have meant, and **urged them strongly** to come to his house.

B. The Sin of Sodom (19:4-11)

The text of vss. 4-10 is confused on account of successive glossings, but what is recorded as having happened is clear enough. The men of the city demanded that Lot hand over his guests to them that they might gratify their unnatural lust. Lot, horrified at the mere thought of such a breach of hospitality, goes so far as to offer to deliver his daughters to them—an offer which was angrily refused. At this point the visitors, who had been listening to the conversation—this suggests that **shut the door after him** (vs. 6), and so vs. 9bβ, are secondary—intervened, drew Lot back into the house, shut the door, and smote the men outside with blindness.

8. This is recorded to Lot's credit as one who was concerned at all costs to fulfill the sacred obligation of a host to protect his guests. At the same time, such treatment of

an obligation which in his world and time was one of the supreme laws of honor. But he had got himself into a place where there could be no decent way out of the crisis that had caught him. All he could think of was the desperate and shameful alternative of sacrificing his own daughters. Even this would not avail. The gang

that assaulted his house wanted the men who were his guests there—wanted them for sodomy, the vileness to which the city of Sodom gave its name. In the day when Lot made what he thought was his smart decision to select the neighborhood of Sodom in the choice Abraham offered him he did not foresee that the place

them as *is* good in your eyes: only unto these men do nothing; for therefore came they under the shadow of my roof.

9 And they said, Stand back. And they said *again,* This one *fellow* came in to sojourn, and he will needs be a judge: now will we deal worse with thee than with them. And they pressed sore upon the man, *even* Lot, and came near to break the door.

10 But the men put forth their hand, and pulled Lot into the house to them, and shut to the door.

11 And they smote the men that *were* at the door of the house with blindness, both small and great: so that they wearied themselves to find the door.

12 ¶ And the men said unto Lot, Hast thou here any besides? son-in-law, and thy sons, and thy daughters, and whatsoever thou hast in the city, bring *them* out of this place:

13 For we will destroy this place, because the cry of them is waxen great before the face of the LORD; and the LORD hath sent us to destroy it.

14 And Lot went out, and spake unto his sons-in-law, which married his daughters, and said, Up, get you out of this place; for the LORD will destroy this city. But he seemed as one that mocked unto his sons-in-law.

me bring them out to you, and do to them as you please; only do nothing to these men, for they have come under the shelter of my roof." 9 But they said, "Stand back!" And they said, "This fellow came to sojourn, and he would play the judge! Now we will deal worse with you than with them." Then they pressed hard against the man Lot, and drew near to break the door. 10 But the men put forth their hands and brought Lot into the house to them, and shut the door. 11 And they struck with blindness the men who were at the door of the house, both small and great, so that they wearied themselves groping for the door.

12 Then the men said to Lot, "Have you any one else here? Sons-in-law, sons, daughters, or any one you have in the city, bring them out of the place; 13 for we are about to destroy this place, because the outcry against its people has become great before the LORD, and the LORD has sent us to destroy it." 14 So Lot went out and said to his sons-in-law, who were to marry his daughters, "Up, get out of this place; for the LORD is about to destroy the city." But he seemed to his sons-in-law to be jesting.

---

the daughters would have been abhorrent to Hebrew morality. The incident was doubtless a part of the story as it lay before J[1] and he included it in his narrative, possibly with the implication that the sin of Sodom was so great that a righteous man living there inevitably found himself confronted with such a moral predicament that he could choose only between the two evils—an instance of the realism of J[1]'s thinking—and he chose the lesser. In this connection, however, the story of Abraham's surrendering of Sarah to the Pharaoh (12:11-20), and that of Isaac's surrendering of Rebekah to the king of Gerar (26:7-11), should be noted. It is unlikely that either J[1] or J[2] approved of this conduct, so that the inclusion of the stories in their collections provides an indication that the populace in general still regarded the wife as the chattel of her husband. Similarly, an unmarried daughter was the property of her father (cf. Deut. 22:13-21, 28-29).

9. The meaning of this verse is that Lot, a mere sojourner in the city, had no right to interfere.

C. GOD DESTROYS THE CITIES (19:12-29)

12-29. Vss. 12-26 have also been extensively glossed. Vs. 28 indicates that by sunrise the destruction was complete; this contradicts the implication of vs. 15 that the men waited all night—the attempt against them had been made early in the evening (cf. vss. 4)—before taking action. The narrative following vs. 11 must originally have told how the men announced their intention to destroy the city, how they got Lot and his daughters out—perhaps miraculously, cf. **and set him outside the city** (vs. 16)—and urged him to

15 ¶ And when the morning arose, then the angels hastened Lot, saying, Arise, take thy wife, and thy two daughters, which are here; lest thou be consumed in the iniquity of the city.	15 When morning dawned, the angels urged Lot, saying, "Arise, take your wife and your two daughters who are here, lest you be consumed in the punishment of the city." 16 But he lingered; so the men seized

15 ¶ And when the morning arose, then the angels hastened Lot, saying, Arise, take thy wife, and thy two daughters, which are here; lest thou be consumed in the iniquity of the city.

16 And while he lingered, the men laid hold upon his hand, and upon the hand of his wife, and upon the hand of his two daughters; the LORD being merciful unto him: and they brought him forth, and set him without the city.

17 ¶ And it came to pass, when they had brought them forth abroad, that he said, Escape for thy life; look not behind thee, neither stay thou in all the plain; escape to the mountain, lest thou be consumed.

18 And Lot said unto them, Oh, not so, my Lord:

19 Behold now, thy servant hath found grace in thy sight, and thou hast magnified thy mercy, which thou hast showed unto me in saving my life; and I cannot escape to the mountain, lest some evil take me, and I die:

20 Behold now, this city *is* near to flee unto, and it *is* a little one: O, let me escape thither, (*is* it not a little one?) and my soul shall live.

21 And he said unto him, See, I have accepted thee concerning this thing also, that I will not overthrow this city, for the which thou hast spoken.

22 Haste thee, escape thither; for I cannot do any thing till thou be come thither. Therefore the name of the city was called Zoar.

15 When morning dawned, the angels urged Lot, saying, "Arise, take your wife and your two daughters who are here, lest you be consumed in the punishment of the city." 16 But he lingered; so the men seized him and his wife and his two daughters by the hand, the LORD being merciful to him, and they brought him forth and set him outside the city. 17 And when they had brought them forth, they*f* said, "Flee for your life; do not look back or stop anywhere in the valley; flee to the hills, lest you be consumed." 18 And Lot said to them, "Oh, no, my lords; 19 behold, your servant has found favor in your sight, and you have shown me great kindness in saving my life; but I cannot flee to the hills, lest the disaster overtake me, and I die. 20 Behold, yonder city is near enough to flee to, and it is a little one. Let me escape there — is it not a little one? — and my life will be saved!" 21 He said to him, "Behold, I grant you this favor also, that I will not overthrow the city of which you have spoken. 22 Make haste, escape there; for I can do nothing till you arrive there." Therefore the name of

f Gk Syr Vg: Heb *he*

flee to the hills (vs. 17), and how they rained on Sodom . . . brimstone and fire from the LORD out of heaven" (vs. 24).

The representation that Lot went out in vs. 14 is out of keeping with the desperate situation depicted in vss. 6-11, and indicates that the verse is secondary—inserted possibly to answer the question how it was that Lot's two daughters of marriageable age (cf. vs. 31) were still unmarried. Its intrusion retarded the tempo of the narrative in its primary form and this led to the addition of vs. 15.

Vss. 18-22, accounting for the survival of the city of Zoar, possibly at the south end of the Dead Sea, in a region represented by the tale as having been completely devastated, are also secondary. So too is vs. 26, as is indicated by the fact that his (KJV) syntactically

would prove so evil. But because he did not care enough to consider that, he took the chance and he reaped the consequences. Like many another man since, he learned that early choices which seem clever when they smother conscience must pay their heavy reckoning.

There is no guarantee of limited liability for a wrong act.

Yet Lot does not fully share the fate of Sodom. There was worth in his recognition that the city was at the point of destruction and in his effort to save his family. But when all is

23 ¶ The sun was risen upon the earth when Lot entered into Zoar.

24 Then the LORD rained upon Sodom and upon Gomorrah brimstone and fire from the LORD out of heaven;

25 And he overthrew those cities, and all the plain, and all the inhabitants of the cities, and that which grew upon the ground.

26 ¶ But his wife looked back from behind him, and she became a pillar of salt.

the city was called Zo'ar.ᵍ 23 The sun had risen on the earth when Lot came to Zo'ar.

24 Then the LORD rained on Sodom and Gomor'rah brimstone and fire from the LORD out of heaven; 25 and he overthrew those cities, and all the valley, and all the inhabitants of the cities, and what grew on the ground. 26 But Lot's wife behind him looked back, and she became a pillar of salt.

ᵍ That is Little

refers to the subject of the preceding sentence (vs. 25). The verse explains a curiously shaped salt formation in the terrain. Its insertion led to the earlier mention of Lot's wife in the tale.

By vss. 27-28 J¹ completes his articulation of the story with the Hebron saga of ch. 18.

The frequent allusions to the legend in the O.T. indicate the impression it made upon the Israelite mind. The overthrow of the cities is referred to as an outstanding instance of the operation of the divine judgment in Deut. 29:23; Isa. 1:9; 13:19; Jer. 49:18; 50:40; Amos 4:11; Zeph. 2:9. The two cities are mentioned as examples of appalling wickedness—with the implication that those who imitate them will meet the same fate— in Deut. 32:32; Isa. 1:10; Jer. 23:14; and Sodom alone in Isa. 3:9; Lam. 4:6; Ezek. 16:46-55. In Deut. 29:23 Admah and Zeboiim, mentioned alone in Hos. 11:8, are

said and done, his deliverance was not due to his deserts. The climax of the story is in the LORD being merciful unto him.

26. *When Regrets Are Ruinous.*—The woman caught in the whirlwind of fire from doomed Sodom because she was still too reluctant to leave the wicked city has become proverbial: "Remember Lot's wife" (Luke 17:32).

The deadliest looking back is that of the imagination which has become entangled in sinful associations which it cannot willingly let go. Lot's wife was not only accustomed to Sodom; apparently she liked it and did not want to leave. In that she was representative of all those in every time who are caught in the consequences of the evil they cannot quite let go. It is not enough to turn the back tentatively upon old temptations; there must be a clean, full break. The man for whom drink may be ruin must make himself resolute to escape it. Unless he genuinely wants to, nobody else can save him. So is it also with other sins, particularly those sins of the flesh, with regard to which the permitted backward thought can so quickly light again the instinctive passions. If a lighted candle is blown out, a column of smoke will rise from the quenched wick. Touch a lighted match to the smoke, even if an inch or two from the candle, and the fire will run down the smoke and set the wick aflame again. Lot's wife held her hot desires too close to Sodom, and the result was disastrous.

There is another kind of looking back which may not be associated with sinfulness, but which may also be destructive of the great possibilities of life. It is the looking back which is obsessed with the memory of old failures and lets wholehearted energy be paralyzed because the forces of personality are split. Half of them are pulling back to yesterday, and what remains of imagination is too feeble to go forward. This may be a danger for men who essentially are good—or want to be. They realize that in certain critical moments and matters they have failed. If only they could go back and live life over, they say to themselves, how different the present then would be. That of course is a natural and almost inevitable movement of the mind, and it has in it this good element: it testifies to a sensitive conscience. Nevertheless, the imagination must be disciplined and turned another way. The past must be faced, acknowledged, and written off with unflinching recognition of the red ink on the ledger; but then the page must be resolutely turned to a new one where another and more positive record can begin. That is the lesson which brave souls have to learn. Many a man told of in the Bible had to overcome original blunders and defeats. Remember Jacob, Joseph, Moses, David. Paul the apostle is the great witness to that truth. Looking back on his earlier life, he might have been sucked down into a quicksand of vain regrets; but, as he wrote to the Philippians, he had learned instead to be as one who, "forgetting those things

27 ¶ And Abraham gat up early in the morning to the place where he stood before the LORD:	27 And Abraham went early in the morning to the place where he had stood before the LORD; 28 and he looked down toward
28 And he looked toward Sodom and Gomorrah, and toward all the land of the plain, and beheld, and, lo, the smoke of the country went up as the smoke of a furnace.	Sodom and Gomor'rah and toward all the land of the valley, and beheld, and, lo, the smoke of the land went up like the smoke of a furnace.
29 ¶ And it came to pass, when God destroyed the cities of the plain, that God remembered Abraham, and sent Lot out of the midst of the overthrow, when he overthrew the cities in the which Lot dwelt.	29 So it was that, when God destroyed the cities of the valley, God remembered Abraham, and sent Lot out of the midst of the overthrow, when he overthrew the cities in which Lot dwelt.
30 ¶ And Lot went up out of Zoar, and dwelt in the mountain, and his two daughters with him; for he feared to dwell in Zoar: and he dwelt in a cave, he and his two daughters.	30 Now Lot went up out of Zo'ar, and dwelt in the hills with his two daughters, for he was afraid to dwell in Zo'ar; so he dwelt in a cave with his two daughters.

bracketed with Sodom and Gomorrah, suggesting perhaps that another variant of the tale was once current in Israel.

XXIII. ORIGIN OF MOAB AND AMMON (19:30-38)

The section is from the J[1] narrative, except for the references to **Zoar** in vs. 30, which are from the hand of the writer responsible for vss. 19-23.

The legend was derived by J[1] from the east Jordan tradition—his familiarity with which is indicated by his inclusion of other tales from that region in his narrative. It was independent of the sagas of Sodom and Hebron with which J[1] has linked it, was presumably current in some form among the Moabites and the Ammonites, and was associated with a certain cave in the mountains of Moab. In vs. 30 the Hebrew should be rendered "the cave" (Gunkel, *Genesis*, p. 218) or "a certain cave," not **a cave.**

There is not a man on earth to come in to us (vs. 31) presupposes that the background of the tale was a world-wide disaster, such as the Flood, which had wiped out the human race. The action of the two women was thus in its original setting heroic, and the story was doubtless told with pride by their supposed descendants. It may be doubted, however, whether J[1] shared this admiration. He seems rather to have regarded the story as a reflection upon Moab and Ammon. (This is certainly the intention of Deut. 32:32 where "their"—"our enemies" vs. 31—refers to Ammon and Moab.) Their origin was incestuous, and the implication may have been that this kind of thing was still prevalent among them (cf. Exeg. on 9:20-25).

which are behind," must be "reaching forth unto those things which are before" (Phil. 3:13).

27-29. The Power of Intercession.—Moffatt translates vs. 27, "In the morning when Abraham rose and went to the spot where he had stood before the Eternal"; and that standing "before the Eternal" was the event described in 18:22-33 when Abraham pleaded with God not to destroy Sodom if even ten righteous men were there. Now Abraham goes back to that place of his intercession, as though prayer were his first instinctive morning act; and he sees the burning city, for not even ten righteous men were there. But Lot is **sent . . . out of the midst of the overthrow.** And why? Because **God re-**membered Abraham. There was not much to remember about Lot that would have deserved his saving. But Abraham's devotion had thrown a protection around him. So in ways deeper and wider than we know the prayer of the good man may avail to save. Who can set limits to intercessory prayer and to vicarious mercy? The declaration of Lot as saved because **God remembered Abraham** may stand as a little foregleam of the faith in the salvation of mankind because God remembers Jesus and the atonement he made upon the Cross.

30-38. Lot's Daughters.—As the Exeg. has pointed out, this story is of obscure origin and purpose. Its inclusion in the total narrative is another evidence of the unwavering solicitude

31 And the firstborn said unto the younger, Our father *is* old, and *there is* not a man in the earth to come in unto us after the manner of all the earth:

32 Come, let us make our father drink wine, and we will lie with him, that we may preserve seed of our father.

33 And they made their father drink wine that night: and the firstborn went in, and lay with her father; and he perceived not when she lay down, nor when she arose.

34 And it came to pass on the morrow, that the firstborn said unto the younger, Behold, I lay yesternight with my father: let us make him drink wine this night also; and go thou in, *and* lie with him, that we may preserve seed of our father.

35 And they made their father drink wine that night also: and the younger arose, and lay with him; and he perceived not when she lay down, nor when she arose.

36 Thus were both the daughters of Lot with child by their father.

37 And the firstborn bare a son, and called his name Moab: the same *is* the father of the Moabites unto this day.

31 And the first-born said to the younger, "Our father is old, and there is not a man on earth to come in to us after the manner of all the earth. 32 Come, let us make our father drink wine, and we will lie with him, that we may preserve offspring through our father." 33 So they made their father drink wine that night; and the first-born went in, and lay with her father; he did not know when she lay down or when she arose. 34 And on the next day, the first-born said to the younger, "Behold, I lay last night with my father; let us make him drink wine tonight also; then you go in and lie with him, that we may preserve offspring through our father." 35 So they made their father drink wine that night also; and the younger arose, and lay with him; and he did not know when she lay down or when she arose. 36 Thus both the daughters of Lot were with child by their father. 37 The first-born bore a son, and called his name Moab; he is the father of the Moabites to

---

The fact that the two daughters are unnamed suggests that in the original tale their named father had played the more important part and that the initiative had been with him. In view of the references to the wine of Moab in Isa. 16:7-10; Jer. 48:11-12, 32-33 (cf. Deut. 32:32), it is possible that among the Israelites the tale had already been embellished by the addition of the feature that he had been drunk when he committed incest. However that may be, the representation here that his daughters deliberately made him drunk will be the work of J[1], endeavoring to preserve something of his reputation, for J[1], articulating this tale with the sagas of Sodom and Hebron, had identified him with the nephew of Abraham who had come with him from the desert and had been delivered from Sodom.

The fact that the man in the cave appears to have been named suggests that the name Lot was carried back from him to the hero of Sodom and thence to Abraham's nephew. In this connection 36:20 should be noted, where Lotan, another form of Lot, appears as a son of Seir the Horite. Lot thus had a place in the tradition of Edom.

37. **Moab** is taken as the equivalent of *mē'ābh,* meaning "from a father" or "from my father." The true etymology of the word is uncertain.

---

of the compilers of Genesis to preserve every fragment of tradition that had come down to them. It was as though they felt that everything that was told as having happened must have had some part in the plan of God, and therefore must be recorded. It may be that here the purpose was to show the superiority of the line of Israel that descended through Abraham over that of the Moabites and Ammonites, who are

described as of incestuous birth. It may be, on the other hand, that this is a more ancient story from some lost setting, not to slur but to honor women who at a crisis in their world's existence allowed themselves to conceive thus in order that life might not be extinguished. Such an act would have its special appeal in an age when the corporate interest of the clan or tribe outranked concern for the individual.

38 And the younger, she also bare a son, and called his name Ben-ammi: the same *is* the father of the children of Ammon unto this day.

20 And Abraham journeyed from thence toward the south country, and dwelt between Kadesh and Shur, and sojourned in Gerar.

this day. 38 The younger also bore a son, and called his name Ben-ammi; he is the father of the Ammonites to this day.

20 From there Abraham journeyed toward the territory of the Negeb, and dwelt between Kadesh and Shur; and he

---

38. Ben-ammi, taken as meaning "son of my kinsman," is represented as the father of the Ammonites, always called in the O.T. "sons of Ammon," except in the M.T. of I Sam. 11:11—where the LXX, Syriac, and three Hebrew MSS also have "sons of Ammon" —and Ps. 83:7. The RSV renders **Ammonites** here and elsewhere. The true etymology of '*Ammôn* is also uncertain.

XXIV. Abraham and Isaac (20:1–21:7)
A. Abraham Leaves Hebron (20:1*a*)

20:1*a*. And dwelt between Kadesh and Shur is a doublet to **and he sojourned in Gerar** (cf. Procksch, *Genesis,* p. 113; Smend, *Erzählung des Hexateuch,* p. 43; and Eissfeldt, *Hexateuch-Synopse,* p. 259*, who hold that the verse has been shortened by RJE). The latter, belonging to the story following, is from E; the former, accordingly, from J.

Between Kadesh and Shur was, as 16:7, 14 indicates, the location of Beer-lahai-roi. The association of Isaac with Beer-lahai-roi (cf. 24:62; 25:11*b*) is certainly traditional, for there would otherwise have been no reason for mentioning the place alongside of Beer-sheba, with which he is elsewhere associated (cf. 22:19; 26:33; 28:10, the continuation of ch. 27; also 21:14, suggesting that Abraham was living there at the time Isaac was weaned). It may accordingly be assumed that the first half of this verse, recording Abraham's move to Beer-lahai-roi, is from J[1], and that the purpose of the notice was to bring him to that place for Isaac's birth.

The Beer-lahai-roi figure, Isaac, was not originally connected with Abraham of Hebron. The Israelites who settled in the vicinity of Beer-lahai-roi, in taking over that sanctuary for the Lord, necessarily took over its legends. Isaac thus became their patron saint, the father of the community, as Abraham had come to fill this role for the Yahwists who settled at Hebron.

The Israelites at Hebron and those at Beer-lahai-roi were, however, conscious of the interclan unity which existed between them, and which, being Semites, they expressed in genealogical terms. It was necessary, therefore, that Isaac, the father of Beer-lahai-roi, should be related to Abraham, the father of Hebron. This necessity was met by making Abraham the father of Isaac. Whether the two traditions had already been thus articulated before J[1] wrote it is impossible to say. J[1], at any rate, accepted the articulation and possibly strengthened it by adding the detail that Abraham had been at Beer-lahai-roi when Isaac was born.

The probability has already been noted in connection with 16:13-14 that E took account of the Beer-lahai-roi element in the Isaac tradition by placing the promise of a son to Sarah there. In J this occurred at Hebron (18:9-14). As will be seen below, E located the birth of the child at Beer-sheba.

20:1-18. Abraham in Gerar.—(See Expos. on 12:11-20.) This chapter incorporates from the E document what seems to be a parallel story to that which had come from J in ch. 12. Essentially the two stories are the same—in the danger and dilemma Abraham faces when he goes with his wife into another country, in the discreditable device by which he tries to protect himself, in the actions of the foreign ruler, and finally in Abraham's undeserved deliverance at the hands of God. Only at two points does the second story have any important difference from

2 And Abraham said of Sarah his wife, She *is* my sister: and Abimelech king of Gerar sent, and took Sarah.

3 But God came to Abimelech in a dream by night, and said to him, Behold, thou *art but* a dead man, for the woman which thou hast taken; for she *is* a man's wife.

4 But Abimelech had not come near her: and he said, LORD, wilt thou slay also a righteous nation?

5 Said he not unto me, She *is* my sister? and she, even she herself said, He *is* my brother: in the integrity of my heart and innocency of my hands have I done this.

6 And God said unto him in a dream, Yea, I know that thou didst this in the integrity of thy heart; for I also withheld thee from sinning against me: therefore suffered I thee not to touch her.

7 Now therefore restore the man *his* wife; for he *is* a prophet, and he shall pray for thee, and thou shalt live: and if thou restore *her* not, know thou that thou shalt surely die, thou, and all that *are* thine.

8 Therefore Abimelech rose early in the morning, and called all his servants, and told all these things in their ears: and the men were sore afraid.

sojourned in Gerar. 2 And Abraham said of Sarah his wife, "She is my sister." And Abim'elech king of Gerar sent and took Sarah. 3 But God came to Abim'elech in a dream by night, and said to him, "Behold, you are a dead man, because of the woman whom you have taken; for she is a man's wife." 4 Now Abim'elech had not approached her; so he said, "Lord, wilt thou slay an innocent people? 5 Did he not himself say to me, 'She is my sister'? And she herself said, 'He is my brother.' In the integrity of my heart and the innocence of my hands I have done this." 6 Then God said to him in the dream, "Yes, I know that you have done this in the integrity of your heart, and it was I who kept you from sinning against me; therefore I did not let you touch her. 7 Now then restore the man's wife; for he is a prophet, and he will pray for you, and you shall live. But if you do not restore her, know that you shall surely die, you, and all that are yours."

The two documents J and E, which lay before R^JE, thus differed at these two points. R^JE solved the difficulty by taking a fragment of the E story of the promise of a son to Sarah and attaching it to the Hagar-Ishmael legend (ch. 16), and followed J in his representation that the promise to Sarah had been given at Hebron. He then favored E by placing Isaac's birth at Beer-sheba—cf. 21:31, which originally preceded the E account of Isaac's birth (see below)—and made the J notice of Abraham's journey to Beer-lahai-roi, **between Kadesh and Shur,** a mere preliminary to his further move to Gerar.

The Beer-sheba element in the Isaac tradition is discussed in the Intro., p. 442.

B. Abraham at Gerar (20:1b-18)

This is a parallel to the stories in 12:10-20 (J²) and 26:6-11 (J¹). It is accordingly from E, as the use of God (*'elōhîm*) throughout the narrative—except in vs. 18, which is a gloss on vs. 17—and the revelation in a dream (vs. 3) indicate. It is thus the latest of the three recensions. As in the J¹ version the episode is located at Gerar. To be noted are: (*a*) the explicit statement in vs. 4 that Abimelech had not entered into marital relations with Sarah, and (*b*) the partial justification of Abraham in vs. 12—both instances of E's concern, to be noted below, for the moral reputation of the patriarchs.

4. **People** is a scribal error; "man" should be substituted for it (Holzinger, *Genesis*, p. 159).

7. **A prophet** here means little more than a man of God. In Israel the prophet was originally an ecstatic, but the title came eventually to be applied to men who were regarded as the exponents of God's word and the agents of his will, with special powers

9 Then Abimelech called Abraham, and said unto him, What hast thou done unto us? and what have I offended thee, that thou hast brought on me and on my kingdom a great sin? thou hast done deeds unto me that ought not to be done.

10 And Abimelech said unto Abraham, What sawest thou, that thou hast done this thing?

11 And Abraham said, Because I thought, Surely the fear of God is not in this place; and they will slay me for my wife's sake.

12 And yet indeed she is my sister; she is the daughter of my father, but not the daughter of my mother; and she became my wife.

13 And it came to pass, when God caused me to wander from my father's house, that I said unto her, This is thy kindness which thou shalt show unto me; at every place whither we shall come, say of me, He is my brother.

14 And Abimelech took sheep, and oxen, and menservants, and womenservants, and gave them unto Abraham, and restored him Sarah his wife.

15 And Abimelech said, Behold, my land is before thee: dwell where it pleaseth thee.

16 And unto Sarah he said, Behold, I have given thy brother a thousand *pieces* of silver: behold, he is to thee a covering of the eyes, unto all that are with thee, and with all *other:* thus she was reproved.

17 ¶ So Abraham prayed unto God: and God healed Abimelech, and his wife, and his maidservants; and they bare *children*.

8 So Abim'elech rose early in the morning, and called all his servants, and told them all these things; and the men were very much afraid. 9 Then Abim'elech called Abraham, and said to him, "What have you done to us? And how have I sinned against you, that you have brought on me and my kingdom a great sin? You have done to me things that ought not to be done." 10 And Abim'elech said to Abraham, "What were you thinking of, that you did this thing?" 11 Abraham said, "I did it because I thought, There is no fear of God at all in this place, and they will kill me because of my wife. 12 Besides she is indeed my sister, the daughter of my father but not the daughter of my mother; and she became my wife. 13 And when God caused me to wander from my father's house, I said to her, 'This is the kindness you must do me: at every place to which we come, say of me, He is my brother.'" 14 Then Abim'elech took sheep and oxen, and male and female slaves, and gave them to Abraham, and restored Sarah his wife to him. 15 And Abim'elech said, "Behold, my land is before you; dwell where it pleases you." 16 To Sarah he said, "Behold, I have given your brother a thousand pieces of silver; it is your vindication in the eyes of all who are with you; and before every one you are righted." 17 Then Abraham prayed to God; and God healed Abim'elech, and also healed his wife and female slaves so that they bore children.

---

as intercessors (cf. vs. 17), whether they were ecstatics or not. For E, with his northern affinities, the prophet rather than the priest was the accredited representative of the Lord. It should be noted, however, that vs. 7aβ together with vs. 17 which belongs with it are probably secondary: nothing is said before vs. 17 about Abimelech being stricken—a difficulty recognized by the glossator who added vs. 18—and vs. 7aβ makes the forgiveness of Abimelech dependent on the prayer of Abraham who had wronged him, not on his obedience to God's command.

9. And my kingdom is an addition, the result of **people** in vs. 4.

---

the first: the scene is changed; and there is an evident concern to palliate Abraham's actions by suggesting that he did not completely lie, since Sarah, although she was his wife, was also his half sister. Notwithstanding these differences in details, the purpose of the two narratives remains identical. It was to express the faith, sometimes as it may seem to us uncritical in its analysis of particular circumstances but always greatly convinced, that God's protection of his people of the covenant would never fail.

18 For the LORD had fast closed up all the wombs of the house of Abimelech, because of Sarah, Abraham's wife.

21 And the LORD visited Sarah as he had said, and the LORD did unto Sarah as he had spoken.

2 For Sarah conceived, and bare Abraham a son in his old age, at the set time of which God had spoken to him.

3 And Abraham called the name of his son that was born unto him, whom Sarah bare to him, Isaac.

4 And Abraham circumcised his son Isaac being eight days old, as God had commanded him.

18 For the LORD had closed all the wombs of the house of Abim'elech because of Sarah, Abraham's wife.

21 The LORD visited Sarah as he had said, and the LORD did to Sarah as he had promised. 2 And Sarah conceived, and bore Abraham a son in his old age at the time of which God had spoken to him. 3 Abraham called the name of his son who was born to him, whom Sarah bore him, Isaac. 4 And Abraham circumcised his son Isaac when he was eight days old, as God

C. Birth of Isaac (21:1-7)

This section is a conflation of J, E, and P, with some redactional elaboration. The J material is the continuation of 20:1a, and places Isaac's birth at Beer-lahai-roi. E locates it at Beer-sheba, for, as will be shown below, the story in ch. 20 was in that document followed immediately by the account of Abraham's dispute with Abimelech over certain wells and by the naming of Beer-sheba, i.e., the E recension of 21:22-34. According to P, Isaac was born at Kiriath-arba, i.e, Hebron, Abraham's only Palestinian dwelling place in that document.

21:1-8. *Father and Son.*—The picture drawn in Genesis of Abraham and Isaac and the other patriarchs may have curious and complex origins, as the Exeg. indicates: yet the fact remains that here are figures which represent with imperishable vividness the likenesses and contrasts in human character.

Abraham's son is a very different person from his father. The great man's son is seldom great. This should be surprising, but actually it has become almost a truism. When there do appear two men of eminence in successive generations, as "the Elder Pitt" and "the Younger Pitt," or as in the Adams family of Masachusettts, it is a conspicuous exception in the course of history. Isaac was no exception. He was the ordinary son of the extraordinary father. Abraham's life moved through a wide orbit, Isaac's in a narrow one. The story of Abraham began in far-off Ur of the Chaldeans, where he left what had been his home and kindred and an old environment to follow an unpredictable adventure, and once went as far as Egypt; but Isaac never moved out of his little circle in Palestine. Abraham broke new paths; Isaac trod in those marked for him. Abraham was the adventurer; Isaac fitted himself into a pattern already set. Abraham was a dominant personality; Isaac was for the most part a passive one. Abraham is pictured as a commander of men, while Isaac avoided collisions. See the picture of Abraham

as drawn in ch. 14, and note the contrast between Abraham reproving Abimelech in 21:25 and Isaac moving away from the disputed wells in 26:22.

Yet Isaac had qualities which have their place in human life. Most men cannot play a role like Abraham's. Neither the characteristics born in them by the strange variations of inheritance nor outward opportunity enable them to do so. They will not create, but they can conserve. Isaac was a link between the new life which had been begun and the expanding life which was destined to be. He had an instinctive recognition of what made his father's greatness, and a reverence for it. He saw that the best thing in Abraham was his religion, and he reflected and transmitted that. He himself was not built on a superlative scale; nevertheless he had a hold on something bigger than himself. Observe the quiet confidence with which he faced the strife about the wells in ch. 26. If he avoided the conflict, it was not because of any cowardice (see in 26:28-29 the impression he is shown as having made on Abimelech) but because of a trust that what he needed would be given him from God. Measured by the standards of his time, his family life had a faithfulness and concentration of affection which made it notable. He was no King Arthur, but nevertheless he anticipated one standard of the good man's life

5 And Abraham was a hundred years old, when his son Isaac was born unto him.

6 ¶ And Sarah said, God hath made me to laugh, *so that* all that hear will laugh with me.

7 And she said, Who would have said unto Abraham, that Sarah should have given children suck? for I have borne *him* a son in his old age.

8 And the child grew, and was weaned: and Abraham made a great feast the *same* day that Isaac was weaned.

9 ¶ And Sarah saw the son of Hagar the

had commanded him. 5 Abraham was a hundred years old when his son Isaac was born to him. 6 And Sarah said, "God has made laughter for me; every one who hears will laugh over me." 7 And she said, "Who would have said to Abraham that Sarah would suckle children? Yet I have borne him a son in his old age."

8 And the child grew, and was weaned; and Abraham made a great feast on the day that Isaac was weaned. 9 But Sarah saw the

---

21:6. God has made laughter for me is E's explanation of the name Isaac—a parallel to 17:17 (P) and 18:12 (J²). **Every one who hears will laugh over me,** a doublet to the preceding sentence, is from J¹.

XXV. Hagar and Ishmael (21:8-21)

This is the E recension of the J² story in ch. 16. The main difference between the two recensions is that in J Hagar left Abraham's tent before the birth of her son because, sturdy Bedouin that she was, she would not put up with the harsh treatment meted out to her by Sarah, chagrined by her maid's pregnancy and her own barrenness and angered by the former's lusty contempt for her. In E Sarah, seeing Ishmael playing with Isaac (see RSV), demands that Hagar and her son be sent away in order that Isaac may be the sole heir of Abraham. E thus makes Sarah's jealousy a little more respectable. He also records Abraham's reluctance to let the child go (vs. 11; contrast 16:6). There is accordingly a tenderness in E, absent from J, which finds further expression in his account of the anguish of the mother—no longer the self-reliant figure of J—at her child's weeping in the desert.

A. Sarah's Jealousy (21:8-10)

8. A child was **weaned** at about the age of three. The **feast** was the customary family feast on the occasion of the weaning of a child.

9. The Egyptian may be harmonization by RP (cf. 16:3). According to E, Ishmael was at this time a mere babe (cf. vss. 14, 17, and see below). The words **with her son Isaac**

---

which Tennyson put into the words of the king:

> To speak no slander, no, nor listen to it,
> . . . .
> To lead sweet lives in purest chastity,
> To love one maiden only, cleave to her.[7]

In our modern world, with its restlessness and strife, its instability and its temptations to unfaithfulness, we could do worse than to regard the example of Isaac:

What was fine in him developed because he had the wisdom and grace to welcome the best that he had inherited. Fortunate is the man who when he has looked at his father has seen in him a real religion, so that his father's goodness is to him not a perfunctory thing but a winsome fact. Not all men have that inheritance,

and that may be the father's fault. But some men who do have it turn their backs indifferently upon what can be their greatest riches. They go after gods of their own, with the shallow and impatient notion that to recognize the "God of Abraham thy father" would abridge their independence. This is more likely when the son knows that neither his own temperament nor his career will parallel his father's. He is afraid that the same religious loyalties might cramp his individuality. That—whenever it occurs—is a frustrating delusion. The inspiration which comes from the ever-living God can make each generation more characteristically itself and more sure to bring its own contribution to the value of life, as Isaac brought his.

6-8. See Expos. on 18:12.

9-21. *A Developing Humaneness.*—With this passage there should be read also ch. 16 (cf.

[7] "Guinevere," *Idylls of the King.*

Egyptian, which she had borne unto Abraham, mocking.

10 Wherefore she said unto Abraham, Cast out this bondwoman and her son: for the son of this bondwoman shall not be heir with my son, *even* with Isaac.

11 And the thing was very grievous in Abraham's sight because of his son.

12 ¶ And God said unto Abraham, Let it not be grievous in thy sight because of the lad, and because of thy bondwoman; in all that Sarah hath said unto thee, hearken unto her voice; for in Isaac shall thy seed be called.

13 And also of the son of the bondwoman will I make a nation, because he *is* thy seed.

son of Hagar the Egyptian, whom she had borne to Abraham, playing with her son Isaac.[h] **10** So she said to Abraham, "Cast out this slave woman with her son; for the son of this slave woman shall not be heir with my son Isaac." **11** And the thing was very displeasing to Abraham on account of his son. **12** But God said to Abraham, "Be not displeased because of the lad and because of your slave woman; whatever Sarah says to you, do as she tells you, for through Isaac shall your descendants be named. **13** And I will make a nation of the son of the slave woman also, because he is your offspring."

[h] Gk Vg: Heb lacks *with her son Isaac*

---

were dropped by some scribe who either felt that Ishmael, now seventeen years old (cf. 17:25) according to the present narrative, would not be playing with a three-year-old, or he wished to provide some further justification for Sarah's conduct by giving the participle *meçaḥēq*—a wordplay on "Isaac"—the meaning **mocking.**

B. Expulsion of Hagar (21:11-14)

11. Abraham's reluctance to accede to Sarah's demand is **on account of his son.** There is no concern for the mother. With this may be compared Abraham's reply to Sarah's bitter charge in 16:6. In that recension Hagar's child had not yet been born, and Hagar herself, as here, was little more than a chattel.

12. In view of the absence of reference to the mother in vs. 11 it is probable that **and because of your slave woman** is an addition by a later writer who had come to recognize that a woman was a person. **For through Isaac shall your descendants be named** makes explicit one of the reasons for the inclusion of the tale: to explain why it was that the divine promise to Abraham had passed to his second son Isaac instead of to Ishmael (cf. 17:18, 20-21).

Exeg. of both passages). The narrative here is from a later source than the one which precedes it in the book.

From the parallel forms of the story of Hagar two facts emerge. One is common to both tellings of the story, viz., the low estimate in which the woman was held in the times to which the account of Abraham belongs. Little or no dignity was accorded her as a person. She could be treated as a chattel, a mere instrument of convenience for the man and for the family he headed. Concubinage was taken as a matter of course and appears without any special sense of inconsistency in the old writers' pictures of the patriarchs. So with Abraham here, and so similarly with Jacob in 30:3-5, 9-13. Hence comes a reminder of what must frequently be borne in mind in reading Genesis, viz., that the religious consciousness which was to have so noble a growth in Israel had its subsoil in the same life and the same ideas as those of other

peoples of ancient times. Consequently the examples of the patriarchs must not be taken indiscriminately and slavishly as though they were God's permanent patterns for human behavior. Their greatness was in what they were growing toward, not in the primitive conceptions to which some of their roots went down. Remembrance of that would have saved the history of religion from some of the shadows of ignorance and misinterpretation which have lain upon it, e.g., saved it from such dark errors as defense of slavery as an ordinance of God, and the burning of women accused of being witches, because both of these could be buttressed by examples in the Bible.

The other fact which emerges from the Hagar stories is brighter and happier. It is a growing humaneness and compassion. Abraham had an instinctive fondness for his child, even if it was not his real wife's child—"O that Ishmael might live before thee!" (17:18.) But in the first form

14 And Abraham rose up early in the morning, and took bread, and a bottle of water, and gave *it* unto Hagar, putting *it* on her shoulder, and the child, and sent her away: and she departed, and wandered in the wilderness of Beer-sheba.

15 And the water was spent in the bottle, and she cast the child under one of the shrubs.

16 And she went, and sat her down over against *him* a good way off, as it were a bowshot: for she said, Let me not see the death of the child. And she sat over against *him,* and lifted up her voice, and wept.

17 And God heard the voice of the lad; and the angel of God called to Hagar out of heaven, and said unto her, What aileth thee, Hagar? fear not; for God hath heard the voice of the lad where he *is.*

18 Arise, lift up the lad, and hold him in thine hand; for I will make him a great nation.

14 So Abraham rose early in the morning, and took bread and a skin of water, and gave it to Hagar, putting it on her shoulder, along with the child, and sent her away. And she departed, and wandered in the wilderness of Beer-sheba.

15 When the water in the skin was gone, she cast the child under one of the bushes. 16 Then she went, and sat down over against him a good way off, about the distance of a bowshot; for she said, "Let me not look upon the death of the child." And as she sat over against him, the child lifted up his voice[i] and wept. 17 And God heard the voice of the lad; and the angel of God called to Hagar from heaven, and said to her, "What troubles you, Hagar? Fear not; for God has heard the voice of the lad where he is. 18 Arise, lift up the lad, and hold him fast with your hand; for I will

[i] Gk: Heb *she lifted up her voice*

14. The original reading of **putting it on her shoulder, along with the child**—the Hebrew of which is awkward—was "and put the child upon her shoulder." The present text is due to R^P, attempting to harmonize the story with the representation of P that Ishmael was fourteen years old when Isaac was born (17:24-25; 21:5). The reference to **Beer-sheba** as a known place is an indication that the story to which vs. 31, recording its naming, belongs preceded this tale in E.

C. GOD'S PROMISE TO HAGAR (21:15-21)

16. The Hebrew **she lifted up her voice** (RSV mg.) is further harmonization of the same character as that in vs. 9, by a later hand than R^P. The picture of the mother helplessly awaiting the death of her baby in the desert is a further instance of the tenderness of the E recension.

17. **And God heard the voice of the lad** indicates that the LXX of vs. 16 is correct. **Where he is** is an allusion to the site of the **well** mentioned in vs. 19, a sacred spot among the Ishmaelites. As to whether E included in his story a notice of its naming it is impossible to say; if he did, it has been dropped by R^{JE}, possibly because of his manipulation of the J recension by which he had identified Hagar's well with Beer-lahai-roi (cf. 16:7b, 13-14). On the other hand E, not being particularly interested in the Ishmaelites, may simply have ignored this feature of the tale.

This verse must have been followed in E by a notice of the naming of the child Ishmael; cf. **God heard** (vs. 17), and note that the name does not appear in the story itself up to this point.

of the story neither Sarah nor Abraham is represented as having any compassion toward Hagar. When Sarah turned bitterly against her, Abraham replied, "Behold, thy maid is in thy hand; do to her as it pleaseth thee" (16:6); and what seemed good to Sarah was to deal "hardly with her," so she fled into the desert. Later on, however, one who pondered that story was troubled by its harshness, and in the later narrative of

this ch. 21 a new note of tenderness appears. **The thing was very grievous in Abraham's sight**—first, it is true, **because of his son,** but also, it is added, because of Hagar. And more important than what is represented concerning Abraham is what is suggested of the compassion of God. The picture of Hagar here in this second story has a greater pathos and pitifulness than in the first; and above the mother's

19 And God opened her eyes, and she saw a well of water; and she went, and filled the bottle with water, and gave the lad drink.

20 And God was with the lad; and he grew, and dwelt in the wilderness, and became an archer.

21 And he dwelt in the wilderness of Paran: and his mother took him a wife out of the land of Egypt.

22 ¶ And it came to pass at that time, that Abimelech and Phichol the chief captain of his host spake unto Abraham, saying, God *is* with thee in all that thou doest:

23 Now therefore swear unto me here by God, that thou wilt not deal falsely with me, nor with my son, nor with my son's son: *but* according to the kindness that I have done unto thee, thou shalt do unto me, and to the land wherein thou hast sojourned.

24 And Abraham said, I will swear.

25 And Abraham reproved Abimelech because of a well of water, which Abimelech's servants had violently taken away.

26 And Abimelech said, I wot not who hath done this thing: neither didst thou tell me, neither yet heard I *of it,* but to-day.

make him a great nation." 19 Then God opened her eyes, and she saw a well of water; and she went, and filled the skin with water, and gave the lad a drink. 20 And God was with the lad, and he grew up; he lived in the wilderness, and became an expert with the bow. 21 He lived in the wilderness of Paran; and his mother took a wife for him from the land of Egypt.

22 At that time Abim'elech and Phicol the commander of his army said to Abraham, "God is with you in all that you do; 23 now therefore swear to me here by God that you will not deal falsely with me or with my offspring or with my posterity, but as I have dealt loyally with you, you will deal with me and with the land where you have sojourned." 24 And Abraham said, "I will swear."

25 When Abraham complained to Abim'elech about a well of water which Abim'elech's servants had seized, 26 Abim'elech said, "I do not know who has done this thing; you did not tell me, and I have not

20. **And became an expert with the bow** may be an allusion to a special skill of the Ishmaelites; more probably it is a softening of 16:12, due perhaps to a decline in Ishmaelite truculence in the period intervening between J² and E.

XXVI. Abraham's Dispute with Abimelech (21:22-34)

This section is a conflation of J² and E. Both documents had an account of a dispute between Abraham and the servants of Abimelech king of Gerar over certain wells—in vs. 25 "wells" should be read with the LXX for **a well** (RSV)—which the former had dug. Abraham and Abimelech succeeded in reaching an agreement and swore to abide by it. The place was then named **Beer-sheba,** meaning lit., **Well of seven** (RSV mg.; cf. the **seven ewe lambs** in vss. 28-30), here interpreted as **well of the oath** (RSV mg.); the Hebrew word for **oath** is a derivative of that meaning **seven.**

anguish over what she thought was her dying child is a God who understands and pities what is in the mother's heart. **Hagar, fear not; for God hath heard the voice of the lad where he is. Arise, lift up the lad, and hold him in thine hand.** Thus, as so often in the O.T., out of the primitive and undeveloped, new vistas open. From human instincts which at first were harsh and might be cruel the divine spirit was leading men forward to a larger and more sensitive conception of the dignity and worth of every human life.

22-32. Beer-sheba.—A striking fact in Genesis is the frequency of reference to wells. One's

thought is carried back to another age and another world—to a nomadic world in which access to wells was vital to existence. In this narrative of Abraham and Abimelech the ancient chroniclers were registering what they desired to have regarded as the title deeds of Abraham's descendants to the wells at Beersheba. In the account as they give it there is a double emphasis. There is stress upon the personal dignity and strength of Abraham, who speaks to Abimelech with authoritative forcefulness (vs. 25). But as always in this book the greater stress is not upon the inherent qualities of a person but upon his significance

27 And Abraham took sheep and oxen, and gave them unto Abimelech; and both of them made a covenant.

28 And Abraham set seven ewe lambs of the flock by themselves.

29 And Abimelech said unto Abraham, What *mean* these seven ewe lambs which thou hast set by themselves?

30 And he said, For *these* seven ewe lambs shalt thou take of my hand, that they may be a witness unto me, that I have digged this well.

31 Wherefore he called that place Beer-sheba; because there they sware both of them.

32 Thus they made a covenant at Beer-sheba: then Abimelech rose up, and Phichol the chief captain of his host, and they returned into the land of the Philistines.

33 ¶ And *Abraham* planted a grove in Beer-sheba, and called there on the name of the LORD, the everlasting God.

34 And Abraham sojourned in the Philistines' land many days.

heard of it until today." 27 So Abraham took sheep and oxen and gave them to Abim'elech, and the two men made a covenant. 28 Abraham set seven ewe lambs of the flock apart. 29 And Abim'elech said to Abraham, "What is the meaning of these seven ewe lambs which you have set apart?" 30 He said, "These seven ewe lambs you will take from my hand, that you may be a witness for me that I dug this well." 31 Therefore that place was called Beer-sheba;*j* because there both of them swore an oath. 32 So they made a covenant at Beer-sheba. Then Abim'elech and Phicol the commander of his army rose up and returned to the land of the Philistines. 33 Abraham planted a tamarisk tree in Beer-sheba, and called there on the name of the LORD, the Everlasting God. 34 And Abraham sojourned many days in the land of the Philistines.

j That is *Well of seven* or *Well of the oath*

---

33. Abraham is here represented as the founder of the sanctuary at Beer-sheba and the inaugurator of its cult. It may be inferred that the deity of the place was known as 'ēl 'ôlām, **the Everlasting God,** i.e., that the sanctuary was originally non-Yahwist. From the J1 recension (26:19-33)—the oldest of the three—it is clear that its founder was traditionally Isaac. J2, followed by E, now ascribes it to Abraham—another example of the way in which the priesthood of Hebron reached out and claimed for its patron the founding of other sanctuaries (cf. 12:6, 8).

For both J2 and E this was the first introduction of **Beer-sheba.** This indicates that the E recension of the story preceded the story of the expulsion of Hagar—in which (vs. 14) Beer-sheba is mentioned as a known place—and indeed followed upon the tale in ch. 20 (cf. the order of events in ch. 26). E thus, as has been noted, placed Isaac's birth at Beer-sheba, in this way preserving his traditional association with that sanctuary (cf. Exeg. on ch. 26). Vs. 22 (E), which begins this story, must have been preceded by a notice of Abraham's moving from Gerar (cf. 26:17). The present position of the story is due to RJE, who preferred the J2 order of events, according to which the dispute about the wells followed upon the birth of Isaac.

---

as a servant of God. Abimelech himself must testify to Abraham that **God is with thee in all that thou doest;** it was because of this recognition that Abimelech wanted Abraham to make a covenant with him. And the covenant thus represented to have been made gives a reason for the traditional significance of the border point of Beer-sheba.

33-34. *Trees.*—In Beer-sheba **Abraham planted a grove.** Far older than Abraham was the belief among ancient peoples that awesome or grand objects of nature might be dwelling places of the divine. Some mighty oak or other

majestic tree could suggest the numinous. That could be superstition: but it can also be the symbolic poetry of worship. Joyce Kilmer lent wings to imagination when he wrote of

A tree that looks at God all day,
And lifts her leafy arms to pray. [8]

And Abraham may have been led to larger thoughts of **the LORD, the everlasting God,** within the grove he planted at Beer-sheba.

[8] From *Trees and Other Poems.* Copyright 1914 by Doubleday & Co., Inc. Used by permission.

22 And it came to pass after these things, that God did tempt Abraham, and said unto him, Abraham: and he said, Behold, *here* I *am*.

2 And he said, Take now thy son, thine only *son* Isaac, whom thou lovest, and get thee into the land of Moriah; and offer him there for a burnt offering upon one of the mountains which I will tell thee of.

3 ¶ And Abraham rose up early in the morning, and saddled his ass, and took two of his young men with him, and Isaac his son, and clave the wood for the burnt offering, and rose up, and went unto the place of which God had told him.

4 Then on the third day Abraham lifted up his eyes, and saw the place afar off.

22 After these things God tested Abraham, and said to him, "Abraham!" And he said, "Here am I." 2 He said, "Take your son, your only son Isaac, whom you love, and go to the land of Mori'ah, and offer him there as a burnt offering upon one of the mountains of which I shall tell you." 3 So Abraham rose early in the morning, saddled his ass, and took two of his young men with him, and his son Isaac; and he cut the wood for the burnt offering, and arose and went to the place of which God had told him. 4 On the third day Abraham lifted up his eyes and saw the place afar off.

XXVII. Testing of Abraham (22:1-19)

The story, except for vss. 15-18 and a few minor additions, is from E. It is one of the most beautifully told and most moving of the stories in Genesis, and indicates that E, at his best, is artistically on a level with J2. There is a note of human sympathy here, as in the E Hagar story (21:9-21), a feeling for the relationship between father and child which finds expression again in the E recension of Laban's farewell to Jacob (31:43-55).

22:2. Moriah is the name of the temple mount in II Chr. 3:1. Thus in its present form the story claims for Abraham the founding of the great sanctuary in Jerusalem. That this is secondary, however, is clear from the text of the narrative. For **upon one of the mountains of which I shall tell you** is contradicted by **the place of which God had told him** (vs. 3).

3. Nor was this place a mountain, for a mountain would have been visible from a much greater distance than is implied by vss. 4-6.

4. *Mērāḥōq*, rendered **afar off**, does not mean a great distance away, as is indicated by 37:18, where it is used of the distance at which his brothers could recognize Joseph, and Exod. 2:4, where it refers to the distance at which Moses' sister stood to watch the ark in which he was.

22:1-19. What Abraham Learned.—Here is a chapter of the O.T. which shows the need of reading with discretion and discrimination. There is truth before which one will stand with reverence; but there are vestiges also of old ideas which the developing conscience has long since outgrown. It is as though in some green and fruitful field where harvests ripen one should come upon the fossil bones of strange, dismaying creatures which once walked the earth. Here in the story of Abraham and Isaac there is imbedded the fact that once men not only practiced human sacrifice, but did it at what they thought was divine command. Suppose they did that now? Any man who thought of it, if his thoughts were detected, would be put in a mental hospital. Any man who actually carried it out would be convicted of murder and executed. So the story of Abraham going

out to sacrifice Isaac may seem either incredible or else profoundly disturbing to children in Sunday school or to adults who hear it read in church, unless they know what to sift out of it in order that the real truth may appear.

Why did this story of what was planned to be a human sacrifice get into the Bible? Because it was desired to show that Abraham's devotion to the God he worshiped was capable of going to the farthest point religion could reach. Human sacrifice was an actual custom among some of the Canaanite tribes. It was practiced for centuries. In the time of Elisha, *ca.* 800 B.C., in a crisis of battles for his capital, the king of Moab "took his eldest son . . . and offered him for a burnt offering upon the wall" (II Kings 3:27). If men worshiping pagan deities could carry their religion to that terrific cost, how could Abraham show that his religion

5 And Abraham said unto his young men, Abide ye here with the ass; and I and the lad will go yonder and worship, and come again to you.

6 And Abraham took the wood of the burnt offering, and laid *it* upon Isaac his son; and he took the fire in his hand, and a knife; and they went both of them together.

7 And Isaac spake unto Abraham his father, and said, My father: and he said, Here *am* I, my son. And he said, Behold the fire and the wood: but where *is* the lamb for a burnt offering?

8 And Abraham said, My son, God will provide himself a lamb for a burnt offering: so they went both of them together.

9 And they came to the place which God had told him of; and Abraham built an altar there, and laid the wood in order, and bound Isaac his son, and laid him on the altar upon the wood.

10 And Abraham stretched forth his hand, and took the knife to slay his son.

11 And the Angel of the LORD called unto him out of heaven, and said, Abraham, Abraham: and he said, Here *am* I.

5 Then Abraham said to his young men, "Stay here with the ass; I and the lad will go yonder and worship, and come again to you." 6 And Abraham took the wood of the burnt offering, and laid it on Isaac his son; and he took in his hand the fire and the knife. So they went both of them together. 7 And Isaac said to his father Abraham, "My father!" And he said, "Here am I, my son." He said, "Behold, the fire and the wood; but where is the lamb for a burnt offering?" 8 Abraham said, "God will provide himself the lamb for a burnt offering, my son." So they went both of them together. 9 When they came to the place of which God had told him, Abraham built an altar there, and laid the wood in order, and bound Isaac his son, and laid him on the altar, upon the wood. 10 Then Abraham put forth his hand, and took the knife to slay his son. 11 But the angel of the LORD called to him from heaven, and said, "Abraham, Abraham!" And he said, "Here am I."

---

5. **If the place of which God had told him** (vs. 3) had been a mountain Abraham would, in accordance with general O.T. usage, have said not that he would **go,** but that he would "go up."

8. *'elōhīm-yīreh,* **God will provide,** is the first of the three wordplays on *'ēl yīreh*—the original of **Jehovah-jireh**—in vs. 14; see below.

11. **The angel of the LORD** is redactional for "God"; cf. "from me" (vs. 12).

---

meant as much to him? Only by being willing to go as far as they did. So, in representing what went on in the mind of Abraham, the story has a deep and dramatic authenticity. Here was a great soul living in a crude age. He saw people around him offering up their children to show their faith and their obedience to false gods. In spite of the torment to his human love he could not help hearing an inward voice asking him why he should not do as much; and because that thought seemed to press upon his conscience he thought it was the voice of God. The climax of the story is the revelation that what the voice of God would ultimately say was something completely different from what Abraham in his first agony of acceptance had supposed. The climax is not the sacrifice of Isaac but the word from God that Isaac shall not be sacrificed. The story that began with threatened tragedy ends in a perfect oneness between the heart of God and the heart of man.

So the immortal story has a double aspect. The first is what it reveals of God. William Cowper's hymn beginning, "God moves in a mysterious way" has in it these lines:

Behind a frowning providence
He hides a smiling face.

That phrase has a repellent crudeness. Who can imagine God smirking behind a mask? But a truth is seeking expression there: the ways of God are sometimes hidden and at first not understood; but ultimately his will is found to be not contradictory to the purest emotions planted in human souls. God is not a dark authority who requires the immolation of instinctive human emotions. The Bible read in its great sweep and progress is the story of the revelation of God as love—a love vaster and more profoundly wise than human souls can always immediately recognize, but in the end such as will satisfy all that is highest in those

12 And he said, Lay not thine hand upon the lad, neither do thou any thing unto him: for now I know that thou fearest God, seeing thou hast not withheld thy son, thine only *son*, from me.

13 And Abraham lifted up his eyes, and looked, and behold behind *him* a ram caught in a thicket by his horns: and Abraham went and took the ram, and offered him up for a burnt offering in the stead of his son.

14 And Abraham called the name of that place Jehovah-jireh: as it is said *to* this day, In the mount of the LORD it shall be seen.

12 He said, "Do not lay your hand on the lad or do anything to him; for now I know that you fear God, seeing you have not withheld your son, your only son, from me."

13 And Abraham lifted up his eyes and looked, and behold, behind him was a ram, caught in a thicket by his horns; and Abraham went and took the ram, and offered it up as a burnt offering instead of his son. 14 So Abraham called the name of that place The LORD will provide;[k] as it is said to this day, "On the mount of the LORD it shall be provided."[l]

[k] Or *see*
[l] Or *he will be seen*

---

12. *Yere' 'elōhîm,* **you fear God,** is the second wordplay on *'ēl yīreh.*

13. *Wayyar' . . . 'ayil,* **and looked . . . a ram,** is the third.

14. *Yhwh yīreh,* **Jehovah-jireh,** is impossible in E, who never uses the name Yahweh before the revelation to Moses (Exod. 3:14-15). Originally *'ēl yīreh,* "God will see" or **provide** (RSV), must have stood here.

The second half of the verse, Skinner remarks, yields "no sense appropriate to the context" (*Genesis,* p. 330). The emendation suggested by Procksch (*Genesis,* p. 318) is perhaps the most satisfactory: to insert "this" before **mount;** the reference to the **mount,** however, indicates that the sentence is secondary, so Procksch's further emendation of **the LORD** to "God" is unnecessary. The half verse as reconstructed may be rendered: "As it is said to this day, 'On this mount one sees the LORD.' "

There can be little doubt that this recurring motif *'ēl yīreh* is a wordplay on the name of the sanctuary of which the tale was originally told. Procksch (*ibid.,* p. 316), noting the probability that a story such as this peculiar to E would, in view of his northern affinities, have to do with some northern sanctuary, has argued cogently that this was the sanctuary of the oak of Moreh—*'ēlôn Môreh*—at Shechem. (Gunkel, *Genesis,* pp. 240-42, argues for Jeruel [II Chr. 20:16]. Against this is the improbability that E would be preserving the legend of a southern sanctuary as obscure as Jeruel was.) If Procksch's argument is sound, then for **the land of Moriah,** in vs. 2, originally stood "the oak of Moreh." (Wellhausen, *Composition,* p. 21, suggests "the land of the Hamorites" [cf. the reference to Hamor in 33:19]; Skinner, *Genesis,* p. 329, mentions "the land of the Amorites" as a possibility. In both cases the suggestion seems to be that the corruption of the present text is accidental. In favor of the proposed "Moreh" may be noted the LXX, τὴν γῆν τὴν ὑψηλήν; cf. 12:6, where τὴν δρῦν τὴν ὑψηλήν renders "the oak of Moreh.") The change to the present text will then be due to some writer, possibly R^P, who (*a*) finding no saga concerning Jerusalem in Genesis wished to provide

---

souls. The O.T. is continually lifting the conception of God out of the irrationality and arbitrariness of pagan superstitions. Reflect upon the consistent message of the prophets. "For I desired mercy, and not sacrifice; and the knowledge of God more than burnt offerings" (Hos. 6:6). "What doth the LORD require of thee?" they asked, and answered as Micah did (Mic. 6:8). Read Ps. 103:13, "Like as a father pitieth his children, so the Lord pitieth." And beyond the O.T. lies the revelation of God in Jesus. Ponder the eternal significance of the

Incarnation and the Atonement. See how in the Gospels and the Epistles all that is most tender and loving in human hearts is identified with God and made a sign of God. "If you, then, who are evil, know how to give good gifts to your children, how much more will your Father who is in heaven give" (Matt. 7:11). So the Almighty is revealed to be not inscrutable fate, nor some cruel Moloch, but our Father.

The other aspect of the story has to do with man. Its message is that only an all-out religion is supremely real. As long as Abraham believed

15 ¶ And the Angel of the LORD called unto Abraham out of heaven the second time,

16 And said, By myself have I sworn, saith the LORD, for because thou hast done this thing, and hast not withheld thy son, thine only *son,*

17 That in blessing I will bless thee, and in multiplying I will multiply thy seed as the stars of the heaven, and as the sand which *is* upon the seashore; and thy seed shall possess the gate of his enemies;

18 And in thy seed shall all the nations of the earth be blessed; because thou hast obeyed my voice.

19 So Abraham returned unto his young men, and they rose up and went together to Beer-sheba; and Abraham dwelt at Beer-sheba.

---

15 And the angel of the LORD called to Abraham a second time from heaven, 16 and said, "By myself I have sworn, says the LORD, because you have done this, and have not withheld your son, your only son, 17 I will indeed bless you, and I will multiply your descendants as the stars of heaven and as the sand which is on the seashore. And your descendants shall possess the gate of their enemies, 18 and by your descendants shall all the nations of the earth bless themselves,*m* because you have obeyed my voice." 19 So Abraham returned to his young men, and they arose and went together to Beer-sheba; and Abraham dwelt at Beer-sheba.

m Or *be blessed*

---

one, and (*b*) possibly was not averse to eliminating the close association of Abraham with the Samaritan center at Shechem. **Upon one of the mountains of which I shall tell you** (vs. 2) is part of the same redaction. If, as seems likely, the story was traditional at Shechem, then it was originally told of another hero than Abraham of Hebron, and its association with him and Isaac will be the work of E.

The primary intent of the tale was presumably to explain why it was that human sacrifice was no longer offered at the sanctuary at which it was told. In E it has a deeper significance: human sacrifice has no place in the worship of the Lord the God of Israel (cf. Mic. 6:6-8).

15-18. These verses are an addition of some writer, possibly RJE, who felt that Abraham's faith was deserving of explicit commendation here.

---

that the sacrifice of his own son was right he was ready to walk even the road of that awful obedience. That is what is expressed in **God did tempt Abraham,** or in truer phrase, "did put him to the test"; i.e., there came a moment in the life of Abraham, as there may come to every man, when it must be discovered whether he is willing to pay the utmost price for what his conscience tells him ought to be compelling. The faith of the Bible is that God at last can prevent the necessity for that sacrifice; or if he permits it, as with Jesus in Gethsemane and his sacrifice on the cross, will so enter into and identify himself with human suffering that it will become redeeming.

15-19. *Unlimited Devotion.*—Those today who read the Bible reverently, but with reverence that is discriminating, cannot take this passage as simply and uncritically as earlier generations did. It used to be held that to question the authority of any part of Holy Writ was close to blasphemy. Who were we that we should "pick and choose"? If it was written that Abraham's blessing was confirmed because he was

ready to slay his son in sacrifice, then that was God's truth, and the matter ended there. But it could not end there. Religious thinkers who humbly and truly wanted to think God's thoughts after him began to perceive that his thoughts are higher even than some of the O.T. interpreters understood. Those early interpreters sometimes saw truth in a limited perspective and ascribed to God convictions which had come to them out of an environment where they saw "through a glass darkly." It was not the will of God that Abraham should sacrifice Isaac; the nature of God was revealed in the moment when he stayed Abraham's hand and prevented the sacrifice. Abraham was not blessed for correctness in conception of God's will; he was blessed because when he thought he knew God's will he was willing to obey it to the limit.

That sort of spirit always does mean greatness. When everything a man has is committed to what he believes, he can go far. Those who wrote of Abraham were right when they recognized the power of such all-out commitment.

20 ¶ And it came to pass after these things, that it was told Abraham, saying, Behold, Milcah, she hath also borne children unto thy brother Nahor;

21 Huz his firstborn, and Buz his brother, and Kemuel the father of Aram,

22 And Chesed, and Hazo, and Pildash, and Jidlaph, and Bethuel.

23 And Bethuel begat Rebekah: these eight Milcah did bear to Nahor, Abraham's brother.

24 And his concubine, whose name *was* Reumah, she bare also Tebah, and Gaham, and Thahash, and Maachah.

23 And Sarah was a hundred and seven and twenty years old: *these were* the years of the life of Sarah.

20 Now after these things it was told Abraham, "Behold, Milcah also has borne children to your brother Nahor: 21 Uz the first-born, Buz his brother, Kemu'el the father of Aram, 22 Chesed, Hazo, Pildash, Jidlaph, and Bethu'el." 23 Bethu'el became the father of Rebekah. These eight Milcah bore to Nahor, Abraham's brother. 24 Moreover, his concubine, whose name was Reumah, bore Tebah, Gaham, Tahash, and Ma'acah.

23 Sarah lived a hundred and twenty-seven years; these were the years of

XXVIII. Descendants of Nahor (22:20-24)

20-24. The nucleus of this list (vs. 20) is from J[2], preparing for the story in ch. 24. This was elaborated by a later J hand to connect Israel with certain Bedouin tribes in the desert east of Palestine—another instance of the tendency toward universalism in the J school. In vs. 22 **Bethuel** is a substitution by R[P] for an original "Laban." R[P] also added vs. 23*a* to harmonize the list with the representation of 28:5 (P).

XXIX. Burial of Sarah (23:1-20)

Only here and in ch. 17 does P expand the history of the patriarchs to something more than a dry chronicle. It has been noted that the expansion of ch. 17 was made to

There are loyalties which deserve all that a man can give, and in that giving he is blessed. Not only the story of Abraham but history in general witnesses to the instinctive belief that this is true. Consider what men have done and will do for their clan or their country. They give their sons to die in battle, to "make the supreme sacrifice." Though they themselves are bereaved, they trust that their nation may be blessed, because through the dedication of young lives the nation may hear the promise which was spoken to Abraham, **thy seed shall possess the gate of his enemies.**

How shall the two facts that seem contradictory be brought into unity: the fact that God prevented the sacrifice of Isaac, and the fact that Abraham was ready to make that sacrifice? It is in the truth that the dedication God desires is not to death but to life. There is such a thing as a sovereign loyalty which must overrule the ordinary reservations of affection, and it is a higher call than the patriotic passion which may be the strongest loyalty the secular world understands. God may have some great purpose to which he would have a man see his son dedicated—a purpose in which that son's life is not lost but enlarged. Yet the father may

not want to give him up. Perhaps it is that the boy shall turn aside from the profitable opportunity of his father's business to choose some career of service which the world will never reward. Perhaps it is to go as a missionary to some difficult and lonely place. In church they may be singing, "Give of thy sons to bear the message glorious," [9] but the father shuts his lips to words like those. Nevertheless, it is only when human love is lifted up and consecrated to the love of God that life can be on the road to its redemption. That is the mighty truth which shines in the story of Abraham, as a great light which glorifies whatever else was limited in the thoughts of those who told it.

23:1-20. *The Poignancy of Sorrow.*—Sarah's death is recounted briefly, but the description of the arrangements for her burial is long. From time immemorial the burial of the dead has had a vast solemnity. Human sorrow has tried to immortalize the names and to perpetuate the memory of those whom it has lost. Witness the pyramids of Egypt. So Abraham, though he could have no great monument for Sarah, is represented here as paying a lavish price for

[9] Mary Ann Thomson, "O Zion, haste, thy mission high fulfilling."

2 And Sarah died in Kirjath-arba; the same *is* Hebron in the land of Canaan: and Abraham came to mourn for Sarah, and to weep for her.

3 ¶ And Abraham stood up from before his dead, and spake unto the sons of Heth, saying,

4 I *am* a stranger and a sojourner with you: give me a possession of a buryingplace with you, that I may bury my dead out of my sight.

the life of Sarah. 2 And Sarah died at Kir'-iath-ar'ba (that is, Hebron) in the land of Canaan; and Abraham went in to mourn for Sarah and to weep for her. 3 And Abraham rose up from before his dead, and said to the Hittites, 4 "I am a stranger and a sojourner among you; give me property among you for a burying place, that I may

provide explicit divine authority for the rite of circumcision, which had taken on a special importance for Israel because of the circumstances of the Exile. No such institutional interest informs this chapter. Here P is affirming Israel's claim that the cave of Machpelah at Hebron, the sepulcher of Abraham and Sarah (25:10), of Isaac and Rebekah (49:31), and of Jacob (50:13) and Leah (49:31) belonged to them. This affirmation was presumably made against the Edomites, who had taken possession of Hebron when its former inhabitants had been carried into exile or had moved northward into lands left vacant by war and deportation.

23:2. The implication is that Abraham had moved from Beer-sheba (22:19) back to Hebron. **Kiriath-arba:** Josh. 14:15 (cf. Judg. 1:10) states, probably correctly, that this was the former name of Hebron. P's use of it is an archaism. The name means "City of Four." The significance of the component "four" cannot be recovered. Gunkel (*Genesis*, p. 273) suggests that it refers to four roads which met there. Another possibility is that it is reminiscent of the four characters of the legend preserved in ch. 18—the three supernatural visitants and Abraham. In Josh. 15:13 (cf. Josh. 21:11) Arba is personalized as the father of Anak, i.e., the ancestor of the Anakim, the pre-Israelite inhabitants of Hebron, according to Num. 13:28; Josh. 15:14 (cf. Judg. 1:20).

3. The Hittites: A people whose center was in the central part of Asia Minor—the modern Turkey. In the fourteenth century B.C. their empire reached as far as, and included part of, Palestine (G. Ernest Wright and Floyd Vivian Filson, eds., *The Westminster Historical Atlas to the Bible* [Philadelphia: Westminster Press, 1945], pp. 29-30). Hence the presence of a Hittite strain in the population there in O.T. times, evidenced by, e.g., 15:20; Exod. 3:8, 17; 23:23, 28; Deut. 7:1; I Sam. 26:6; II Sam. 11:3; also Ezek. 16:3. P is the only document in which they are definitely located in the south (cf. 26:34; 36:2). The representation here that they formed the population of Hebron in the time of Abraham is quite impossible as the kingdom did not become powerful until the sixteenth century.

4. Abraham, merely **a stranger and a sojourner,** had no right to own land. Here he asks that he may be given this right.

the cave in which to bury her. In the customary formula of Oriental bargaining, Ephron the Hittite declares magniloquently that he gives the cave to Abraham, but in the same breath parades the fact that it is **worth four hundred shekels of silver.** As the picture is presented here, Abraham does not even attempt to reduce the exaggerated price. He weighs out the silver, **current money with the merchant,** and calls all the Hittites who are near to bear witness to the transaction. So the cave of Machpelah belonged irrevocably to him and to his family— **the cave in which he himself would ultimately**

be buried, and Isaac, and Jacob, and others after them; and over which a Mohammedan mosque would rise, to guard to this day what are maintained to be the patriarchs' graves. The importance of the record for the people of Israel was that the land to which Abraham had come was thus certified forever as belonging sacredly to them.

Such is the formal aspect of this chapter. But the sentences with which it opens are more personal and poignant. Here is the voice of human sorrow which is as old as the world, and as new as the most recent heartbreak. **Abraham**

5 And the children of Heth answered Abraham, saying unto him,

6 Hear us, my lord: thou *art* a mighty prince among us: in the choice of our sepulchres bury thy dead; none of us shall withhold from thee his sepulchre, but that thou mayest bury thy dead.

7 And Abraham stood up, and bowed himself to the people of the land, *even* to the children of Heth.

8 And he communed with them, saying, If it be your mind that I should bury my dead out of my sight, hear me, and entreat for me to Ephron the son of Zohar,

9 That he may give me the cave of Machpelah, which he hath, which *is* in the end of his field; for as much money as it is worth he shall give it me for a possession of a buryingplace amongst you.

10 And Ephron dwelt among the children of Heth: and Ephron the Hittite answered Abraham in the audience of the children of Heth, *even* of all that went in at the gate of his city, saying,

11 Nay, my lord, hear me: the field give I thee, and the cave that *is* therein, I give it thee; in the presence of the sons of my people give I it thee: bury thy dead.

bury my dead out of my sight." 5 The Hittites answered Abraham, 6 "Hear us, my lord; you are a mighty prince among us. Bury your dead in the choicest of our sepulchres; none of us will withhold from you his sepulchre, or hinder you from burying your dead." 7 Abraham rose and bowed to the Hittites, the people of the land. 8 And he said to them, "If you are willing that I should bury my dead out of my sight, hear me, and entreat for me Ephron the son of Zohar, 9 that he may give me the cave of Mach-pe'lah, which he owns; it is at the end of his field. For the full price let him give it to me in your presence as a possession for a burying place." 10 Now Ephron was sitting among the Hittites; and Ephron the Hittite answered Abraham in the hearing of the Hittites, of all who went in at the gate of his city, 11 "No, my lord, hear me; I give you the field, and I give you the cave that is in it; in the presence of the sons of my people I give it to you; bury your dead."

5-20. P may wish to imply that the generosity of the burghers had an ulterior motive —an unwillingness to permit an alien to own land. If so, then the remainder of the narrative is intended to show that it was despite this reluctance that Abraham obtained legal possession of the cave of Machpelah (vss. 17-18, 20), paying for it **four hundred shekels of silver, according to the weights current among the merchants** (vs. 16).

It should be noted that P is making no claim to Israelite possession of Hebron or of its sanctuary by the oak of Mamre. The relative location in Hebron of the cave of

---

came to mourn for Sarah, and to weep for her. As Genesis portrays her, Sarah had been a person whose passing, like the fall of some tall tree, must leave an empty space against the sky. As Abraham's wife and comrade she had gone through many experiences with him, and always in fidelity. She, with him, had made the choice to leave the rich civilization of Ur of the Chaldeans, and to go out to the long adventure of the spirit. She, with him, had known the uncertain life of Canaan, sojourning "in a foreign land, living in tents" (Heb. 11:9). She, with him, had lived through the wistful and sometimes bitter disappointment of the years of childlessness. She, with him, had shared the joy and pride of Isaac's birth. According to the portrayal of Genesis, she was very beautiful. She had her obvious faults, but she had char-

acter and great distinction—a woman who could be jealous, but who had passionate devotion to those she loved. There is a tender imaginative touch in one of the naïve religious dramas of medieval England. In the Brome play, *Abraham and Isaac*, when Abraham has led Isaac out to sacrifice him, and Isaac has just learned what his father's purpose is, he cries:

Now I wold to God my moder were her on this hyll!
Sche woold knele for me on both hyr kneys
To save my lyffe.[10]

She was dead now, and Abraham mourned and wept for her. Then he **stood up from before his dead,** i.e., he had to go out and meet the

[10] John Matthews Manly, *Specimens of Pre-Shakespearean Drama* (Boston: Ginn & Co., 1897), I, 47.

12 And Abraham bowed down himself before the people of the land.

13 And he spake unto Ephron in the audience of the people of the land, saying, But if thou *wilt give it,* I pray thee, hear me: I will give thee money for the field; take *it* of me, and I will bury my dead there.

14 And Ephron answered Abraham, saying unto him,

15 My lord, hearken unto me: the land *is worth* four hundred shekels of silver; what *is* that betwixt me and thee? bury therefore thy dead.

16 And Abraham hearkened unto Ephron; and Abraham weighed to Ephron the silver, which he had named in the audience of the sons of Heth, four hundred shekels of silver, current *money* with the merchant.

17 ¶ And the field of Ephron, which *was* in Machpelah, which *was* before Mamre, the field, and the cave which *was* therein, and all the trees that *were* in the field, that *were* in all the borders round about, were made sure

12 Then Abraham bowed down before the people of the land. 13 And he said to Ephron in the hearing of the people of the land, "But if you will, hear me; I will give the price of the field; accept it from me, that I may bury my dead there." 14 Ephron answered Abraham, 15 "My lord, listen to me; a piece of land worth four hundred shekels of silver, what is that between you and me? Bury your dead." 16 Abraham agreed with Ephron; and Abraham weighed out for Ephron the silver which he had named in the hearing of the Hittites, four hundred shekels of silver, according to the weights current among the merchants.

17 So the field of Ephron in Mach-pe'lah, which was to the east of Mamre, the field with the cave which was in it and all the trees that were in the field, throughout its

Machpelah and the sacred oak cannot be determined. According to vs. 19, the cave was **east of Mamre.** In modern times Ḥārām Rāmet el Ḥalīl, some two miles north of Hebron, is represented as the site of the oak. The cave is in the famous sanctuary el Ḥārām (Gunkel, *Genesis,* p. 273).

P, of course, had no interest in the oak or its sanctuary. For him there were no Yahwist sanctuaries, places of sacrifice, until the tabernacle was erected in the desert (Exod. 40:17) pursuant to a divine command. He may indeed be maintaining by implication here that the so-called holy place at Hebron was really profane—a burying ground.

The significance of the story lies in the fact that it provides evidence that P, for all his ecclesiasticism, was, however dimly, aware of the importance of Israel as a natural

world and its sad responsibilities. In every age human beings have had to do that. There is the everlasting poignancy of human pain: bereavement, and then the fact that one must go on in loneliness to face what life requires. As a modern Jewish rabbi has written:

The first law . . . which should be followed in the loss of a loved one is: *express as much grief as you actually feel.* Do not be ashamed of your emotions.[1]

It may be either a cold heart, or one unnaturally frozen by some inhibition, that does not at some time like Abraham mourn and weep. Yet there is another truth which Abraham also

represented. It is not right that grief should be allowed to become a paralyzing bondage. According to ancient rabbinical tradition,

Rabbi Joshua said . . . : "My sons, I know that it is impossible not to mourn, but to mourn excessively is forbidden." Why? Because that great Jewish sage felt that we human beings must think not only of the past but of the future. We are commanded by our religion to be the servants of life as long as we live.[2]

So Abraham is identified with us, and we with him. Yet not altogether. There is a grayness in the picture of Abraham that need not always exist. So far as the evidence in Genesis

[1] Joshua Loth Liebman, *Peace of Mind* (New York: Simon & Schuster, 1946), p. 113.

[2] *Ibid.,* p. 116.

18 Unto Abraham for a possession in the presence of the children of Heth, before all that went in at the gate of his city.

19 And after this, Abraham buried Sarah his wife in the cave of the field of Machpelah before Mamre: the same *is* Hebron in the land of Canaan.

20 And the field, and the cave that *is* therein, were made sure unto Abraham for a possession of a buryingplace by the sons of Heth.

24 And Abraham was old, *and* well stricken in age: and the Lord had blessed Abraham in all things.

whole area, was made over 18 to Abraham as a possession in the presence of the Hittites, before all who went in at the gate of his city. 19 After this, Abraham buried Sarah his wife in the cave of the field of Mach-pe′lah east of Mamre (that is, Hebron) in the land of Canaan. 20 The field and the cave that is in it were made over to Abraham as a possession for a burying place by the Hittites.

24 Now Abraham was old, well advanced in years; and the Lord had

---

society stemming from Abraham. With this may be compared his insistence upon the necessity of the possession of Palestine; see Exeg. on 17:8.

XXX. CHOICE OF A WIFE FOR ISAAC (24:1-67)

This chapter is a conflation of J[2] and E. R[P] has added the name of Bethuel throughout as Rebekah's father (cf. 22:22*b*, 23*a*); in the older sources Laban, and so Rebekah, are the children of Nahor (29:5), the husband of Milcah (11:29; 22:20).

The two recensions of the story were in general agreement. R[JE], conflating them, used that of J[2] as the basis of his narrative, inserting into it certain features from E:

(*a*) According to the J[2] recension the servant was commissioned to obtain any woman of Abraham's kindred as a wife for Isaac (vss. 4, 49); according to E, the girl desired by Abraham was definitely named, as is indicated by "the woman" (vss. 5, 8). This difference between the two versions is something more than a literary variation. Underlying it is a certain difference in the theory of revelation. In J[2] the natural is given full scope; the servant is to use his discretion, though he will be guided by the angel whom God will send before him (vs. 7). In E, Abraham, with the heightened

---

goes, no belief in immortality was attributed to Abraham or to his contemporaries. Of such it might be said, in Whittier's words:

> Alas for him who never sees
> The stars shine through his cypress-trees!
> Who, hopeless, lays his dead away,
> Nor looks to see the breaking day
> Across the mournful marbles play! [8]

But the O.T. moves forward to the N.T., in which the message is: "That ye sorrow not, even as others which have no hope" (I Thess. 4:13); and, "Death is swallowed up in victory . . . through our Lord Jesus Christ" (I Cor. 15:54, 57).

24:1-3. The Individual and the Group.—The Oriental custom here assumed as a matter of course seems strange now in some of our Western lands. When the time had come for Isaac to marry it was not Isaac who was to choose his bride. His father, the head of the family, would find the right one for him. Isaac was not a detached individual. His individuality

[8] "Snow-Bound."

was not even a decisive consideration. He was part of the family, with its solidarity of inheritance, of character, and of destiny; and what should be legitimate for him in even his most personal affairs was conditioned by those facts.

Through a great part of the O.T. the corporate consciousness is dominant. The person is subordinate to the group. A whole family could be punished for the sins of its members. When Achan appropriated the forbidden spoils of Jericho, "his sons, and his daughters, and his oxen, and his asses, and his sheep, and his tent, and all that he had" were seized together with Achan himself and put to death (Josh. 7:24-25). When Ezekiel prophesied, he knew that this conception of the responsibility of all for each and each for all was woven into every thread of Jewish thinking. The family and the nation made the faith of the individual. If the children's teeth were set on edge, it was because the fathers had eaten sour grapes (Ezek. 18:2).

Plainly, there was strength and virtue in this solidarity of the group. It gave to the Jewish race a pre-eminent tenacity. Filial piety knit the

supernatural powers of a man on his deathbed (see below), specifically designates the
woman, and the servant has no discretion; the natural is thus restricted, if not distrusted.
And connected with this is E's realistic admission of the possibility that "the woman
may not be willing" (vs. 5; cf. vs. 8) to accept her divine vocation.

(b) In the J² recension Laban and Milcah grant the servant's request for Rebekah
without consulting her (vss. 50a, 51-54); in E Rebekah herself makes the decision (vss.
50b, 57-58, 60; also vs. 5). Here again there is something more than a literary variation.
Rebekah is a person, with rights; with this may be compared the implications of "because
of your slave woman" (21:12). The ingenuity with which the redactor has combined
these two diverse representations may be noted: Rebekah's assent has become an assent
to the servant's desire to leave for Palestine at once instead of waiting for a few days.

(c) According to J² Abraham's kinsfolk lived in "the city of Nahor" (vs. 10), i.e.,
Haran (cf. 29:4-5); according to E they lived in Mesopotamia (vs. 10).

It has already been noted that J¹ represented Abraham as having come from "the
land of the people of the east" (29:1) in the north Arabian desert. J², in making Haran
his place of origin, may have been motived, as Meyer suggests (Israeliten und ihre
Nachbarstämme, p. 248; cf. Gunkel, Genesis, pp. 168, 325; Skinner, Genesis, p. 334), by
the fact that in his time that city had become the chief seat of Aramaean culture. But
a further factor may have influenced him if, as has been suggested above, the names
Sarah and Milcah point to a Haran element in the traditions of Hebron and Beer-sheba.
For this, in turn, would point to a pre-Israelite migration from Haran to Palestine,
and J² may well have been giving concrete expression to that tradition. In this case
Abraham is for the moment the personification not of the Yahwist clans who settled in
Hebron but of this group from Haran.

The significance of J²'s concern to relate this pre-Israelite migration to the Yahwist
tradition of the desert should not be overlooked. It indicates that the Israelite settlement
in Palestine had issued not merely in the appropriation and adaptation of the cult
legends of certain Canaanite sanctuaries. It had resulted in the incorporation of the
communities which had worshiped at those sanctuaries not only into Yahwism but also
into Israel—so completely that account was taken of their cultural as well as of their
religious traditions.

E, representing Abraham as having come from Mesopotamia, would seem to be
preserving the tradition of still another group of non-Israelite origin which had come
from there; and he has made Abraham for the moment the personification of this group.

members of a family together, and the proud
belief that they were a chosen people preserved
the purity of their blood. They held the Fifth
Commandment in unquestioned reverence, and
with good reason believed that a nation which
knew how to honor its fathers and mothers
would be long in the land.

The Jewish conviction of responsibility to the
group has its tonic suggestion still, especially
in marriage. The Roman Catholic Church takes
a stand in this matter which can be offensively
arrogant and narrow, but which can be respected at least for the clearness of its purpose.
It believes that it is the custodian of a saving
faith which must be handed on uncompromised,
and therefore it insists that marriage shall be on
its own terms, and that the children of every
marriage shall be brought up in its own nurture. It has built up a distorted doctrine of
Christian inheritance, but it is right in seeking
to make sure that the inheritance is not lost. It

is wise enough to know that a rich married life
cannot be built on passion and unthinking
impulse, but only on principles bigger than
individuals, to which they must be true. Protestants, on the other hand, are often too complacent and flabby in this matter. The Protestant
young man or woman about to be married may
treat religious loyalties as inconsequential for
both sides of the marriage or may yield indifferently to the emphatic Roman Catholic
claims. But marriages without religious conviction, and mixed marriages in which those
convictions are incompatible, may lack the
fortifying strength which the men and women
of the Bible understood. Among Christians outside Romanism there is an awakening realization that our young people must be helped to
know more clearly and to feel more deeply the
preciousness of their own heritage and toler-
antly but with unswerving loyalty to maintain
it. That there should be division within the

2 And Abraham said unto his eldest servant of his house, that ruled over all that he had, Put, I pray thee, thy hand under my thigh:

3 And I will make thee swear by the LORD, the God of heaven, and the God of the earth, that thou shalt not take a wife unto my son of the daughters of the Canaanites, among whom I dwell:

4 But thou shalt go unto my country, and to my kindred, and take a wife unto my son Isaac.

5 And the servant said unto him, Peradventure the woman will not be willing to follow me unto this land: must I needs bring thy son again unto the land from whence thou camest?

6 And Abraham said unto him, Beware thou that thou bring not my son thither again.

blessed Abraham in all things. 2 And Abraham said to his servant, the oldest of his house, who had charge of all that he had, "Put your hand under my thigh, 3 and I will make you swear by the LORD, the God of heaven and of the earth, that you will not take a wife for my son from the daughters of the Canaanites, among whom I dwell, 4 but will go to my country and to my kindred, and take a wife for my son Isaac." 5 The servant said to him, "Perhaps the woman may not be willing to follow me to this land; must I then take your son back to the land from which you came?" 6 Abraham said to him, "See to it that you do not

---

Both recensions of the story insist that the pure Israelite stock, symbolized by Abraham, had not been contaminated by the marriage of Isaac. But the meaning of the tale goes deeper than that. It reflects Israel's consciousness of the authentic values of primitive Yahwism and a concern for their preservation. These values had, historically, been apprehended in the desert. In making Abraham originally an Aramaean from the city of Haran, J2 obscured this fact—the fact of the ineradicable influence of the desert upon Israel's thinking, an influence which had early set them on the path toward transcendent, ethical monotheism. That J2 himself had not lost sight of this is, however, indicated by his later insistence upon Sinai as the original center of Israel's religion.

But though J2, and E after him, had a purpose in writing the tale, he at the same time allowed his artistry full play in its composition. The story moves freely, is finely concerned with human values, and provides us with a trustworthy picture of the conditions of the age in which it took form.

A. Abraham's Directions to His Servant (24:1-10)

24:2. Put your hand under my thigh: A reference to an oath by the genital organs, emblems of the life-giving power of deity, though this ancient significance of the act had doubtless been forgotten by the time of J2.

3-10. I will make you swear by the LORD: The implication is that Abraham is on his deathbed, and so is himself unable to ensure that his wishes will be carried out. The same implication attaches to vs. 6, derived from E. The notice of Abraham's death must

---

whole church which ought to be one in Christ is a tragic fact, and though it is necessary now to live within that limitation, it ought to be transcended in spirit as much as possible. The great thing is to try to make sure that according to our best lights the supreme loyalties are preserved. The soundness of individual life and the stability of marriage and the home depend upon that which has been given by God. As Abraham knew, so we should know, that the

great traditions of a family and a religious culture must be treated by successive generations as a holy trust.

1-9. *Abraham's Desire.*—The story begins on a note of thankfulness. Abraham recognizes that he has been blessed in all things. He has prospered in his possessions, and above all, he has a son. Now his most commanding hope is that Isaac should be rightly married and thus the family and the inheritance be carried on. Then

7 ¶ The Lord God of heaven, which took me from my father's house, and from the land of my kindred, and which spake unto me, and that sware unto me, saying, Unto thy seed will I give this land; he shall send his angel before thee, and thou shalt take a wife unto my son from thence.

8 And if the woman will not be willing to follow thee, then thou shalt be clear from this my oath: only bring not my son thither again.

9 And the servant put his hand under the thigh of Abraham his master, and sware to him concerning that matter.

10 ¶ And the servant took ten camels of the camels of his master, and departed; for all the goods of his master *were* in his hand: and he arose, and went to Mesopotamia, unto the city of Nahor.

11 And he made his camels to kneel down without the city by a well of water at the time of the evening, *even* the time that women go out to draw *water*.

take my son back there. **7** The Lord, the God of heaven, who took me from my father's house and from the land of my birth, and who spoke to me and swore to me, 'To your descendants I will give this land,' he will send his angel before you, and you shall take a wife for my son from there. **8** But if the woman is not willing to follow you, then you will be free from this oath of mine; only you must not take my son back there." **9** So the servant put his hand under the thigh of Abraham his master, and swore to him concerning this matter.

10 Then the servant took ten of his master's camels and departed, taking all sorts of choice gifts from his master; and he arose, and went to Mesopota'mia, to the city of Nahor. **11** And he made the camels kneel down outside the city by the well of water at the time of evening, the time when

thus have followed upon vs. 9 in both recensions. The addition to the J2 narrative of the material now preserved in 25:1-4, 6 necessitated the postponement of this notice, and also of that in 25:5, telling how Abraham disposed of his goods. This originally followed vs. 1 in J2 (cf. vs. 36*b*) and was in turn followed by 25:11*b* (cf. vs. 62), which J2 had taken over from J1. Its present position is due to RP, who separated it from 25:5 because of 25:7-10 (P).

B. The Servant Meets Rebekah (24:11-27)

11. In placing the servant's meeting with Rebekah at a **well of water**, J2 makes use of a theme apparently not uncommon in shepherd folklore. It was at a well that Moses met his future wife (Exod. 2:16-17), and that Jacob met Rachel (29:2-12). It may be noted that the well here, just outside the city and open, is not the same as that in ch. 29,

appear that intense consciousness of kindred and that recoil from alliance with the uncovenanted stranger which pervade Hebrew thought in all Genesis. Isaac must not marry one of the Canaanites. It is the father's concern (see also Expos. on 18:16-19) to find for him a bride of his own blood and lineage. Therefore Abraham will send his devoted servant to seek for one in the land from which Abraham had come and in which his kindred dwelt. But equally imperative it is to make sure that Isaac shall not go there himself to live. The servant suggests that possibility (vs. 5) and Abraham rejects it with utmost emphasis. As the servant has sworn a most solemn oath to try to find a bride for Isaac, so now Abraham has him take another oath that, even at the cost of failing to bring a bride, he shall not take Isaac there.

Abraham recalls God's promise, **Unto thy seed will I give this land.** Here is the consciousness of destiny which shines through all the history of Abraham. And with it is an equally shining faith that God who has purposed great ends for a human life will also make sure the way by which those ends shall be achieved. Eliezer, the servant, will be guided in his search. **The Lord God of heaven, which took me from my father's house, and from the land of my kindred, . . . shall send his angel before thee, and thou shalt take a wife unto my son from thence.**

10-20. *The Double Guidance.*—A lovely description is this—so serene, so gentle, so marked by purity of purpose and the sweetness of right response! In Eliezer's prayer (vs. 12) there is the same instinctive piety that had already been manifest in the prayer of Abraham. The mas-

12 And he said, O LORD God of my master Abraham, I pray thee, send me good speed this day, and show kindness unto my master Abraham.

13 Behold, I stand *here* by the well of water; and the daughters of the men of the city come out to draw water:

14 And let it come to pass, that the damsel to whom I shall say, Let down thy pitcher, I pray thee, that I may drink; and she shall say, Drink, and I will give thy camels drink also: *let the same be* she *that* thou hast appointed for thy servant Isaac; and thereby shall I know that thou hast showed kindness unto my master.

women go out to draw water. 12 And he said, "O LORD, God of my master Abraham, grant me success today, I pray thee, and show steadfast love to my master Abraham. 13 Behold, I am standing by the spring of water, and the daughters of the men of the city are coming out to draw water. 14 Let the maiden to whom I shall say, 'Pray let down your jar that I may drink,' and who shall say, 'Drink, and I will water your camels' — let her be the one whom thou hast appointed for thy servant Isaac. By this I shall know that thou hast shown steadfast love to my master."

---

where it is located in the field, i.e., the open country, and is covered with a stone which required a number of men to move it (see Exeg. on ch. 29).

12. The servant, standing outside the city of Nahor, Abraham's brother, has now reached a critical point in his mission. According to the J2 recension, from which the prayer following is derived, Abraham had left the choice of a wife for his son to his discretion. In the exercise of that discretion his concern must be that he should act in accordance with the Lord's will and choose the woman whom the Lord had already appointed for Isaac (vs. 14). Thus with great sensitivity J2 presents the problem of the interaction of the human and the divine.

---

ter's spirit had communicated itself to the servant; and to Eliezer the thought of God had a surer meaning because he was the LORD God of . . . Abraham. How greatly the relationships of men would be enriched if the religion of the employer were always such as to win the heart of the man employed!

So Eliezer prayed. That was his first way of seeking guidance. He had an errand on which he could invoke God's blessing, and he trusted that a wisdom higher than his own would light his way. But he did not assume that this guidance would be arbitrary. It would enlist his own intelligence and his consecrated common sense. Presently the girls of the countryside would be coming to draw water from the well where he had halted with his camels. If there should be one among them whom God intended as the bride of Isaac, how should he, Eliezer, know her? By something that she wore? By some particular feature of her looks? No. There was a more important criterion than that—the criterion of her spirit. The girl who should be the quickest in discernment, the kindest, the swiftest to help—that was the girl he would be seeking. So his prayer was that God would bring it to pass that the girls who came would so naturally reveal themselves, and that he

might so clearly observe, that he would know without doubt which one was meant to be the bride of Isaac. Exactly thus his prayer was answered. To the well at evening came Rebekah, a **damsel . . . very fair to look upon,** and when Eliezer asked her that he might drink a little from her pitcher, she not only gave him what he asked **but hasted, and emptied her pitcher into the trough, and ran again unto the well to draw water, and drew for all his camels.** Eliezer knew then that he had received his sign. May it not be that God's signs are often given through this same combination of prayer and the use of human faculties which have been offered for God to guide?

It might have been said of Eliezer, as was said of David Livingstone by his biographer who was interpreting the reason for Livingstone's clear perception of his course of duty:

How did he get this? First, his singleness of heart, so to speak, attracted the light: "If thine eye be single, thy whole body shall be full of light." Then, he was very clear and very minute in his prayers. Further, he was most careful to scan all the providential indications that might throw light on the Divine will.[4]

[4] W. Garden Blaikie, *The Personal Life of David Livingstone* (New York: Fleming H. Revell Co., 1880), p. 132.

15 ¶ And it came to pass, before he had done speaking, that, behold, Rebekah came out, who was born to Bethuel, son of Milcah, the wife of Nahor, Abraham's brother, with her pitcher upon her shoulder.

16 And the damsel *was* very fair to look upon, a virgin, neither had any man known her: and she went down to the well, and filled her pitcher, and came up.

17 And the servant ran to meet her, and said, Let me, I pray thee, drink a little water of thy pitcher.

18 And she said, Drink, my lord: and she hasted, and let down her pitcher upon her hand, and gave him drink.

19 And when she had done giving him drink, she said, I will draw *water* for thy camels also, until they have done drinking.

20 And she hasted, and emptied her pitcher into the trough, and ran again unto the well to draw *water,* and drew for all his camels.

21 And the man wondering at her held his peace, to wit whether the Lord had made his journey prosperous or not.

15 Before he had done speaking, behold, Rebekah, who was born to Bethu'el the son of Milcah, the wife of Nahor, Abraham's brother, came out with her water jar upon her shoulder. 16 The maiden was very fair to look upon, a virgin, whom no man had known. She went down to the spring, and filled her jar, and came up. 17 Then the servant ran to meet her, and said, "Pray give me a little water to drink from your jar." 18 She said, "Drink, my lord"; and she quickly let down her jar upon her hand, and gave him a drink. 19 When she had finished giving him a drink, she said, "I will draw for your camels also, until they have done drinking." 20 So she quickly emptied her jar into the trough and ran again to the well to draw, and she drew for all his camels. 21 The man gazed at her in silence to learn whether the Lord had prospered his journey or not.

15-27. The explicit naming of Rebekah and her parents here—**Bethuel the son of** is an intrusion by RP—anticipates and destroys the effect of vs. 24. It is accordingly

15-16. *The Character of Rebekah as a Girl.*—Here begins one of the most winsome passages in Genesis. In most early societies, including the society of Israel, men were dominant and women were generally obscure. But in the O.T. there are women who were significant, and one of them is Rebekah. She is, in the words of the Exeg., "a person, with rights." And note what an extraordinarily attractive person she at first appears to be as Abraham's servant meets her at the well (see Expos. on vss. 10-20). After she had drawn water for Eliezer she tells him who her father is and that she knows her father will want to give this stranger and his camels shelter. Presently at her father's house Abraham's servant tells his story: who had sent him, why he had come, his prayer that God would bless his coming. So will Rebekah go with him? Yes, she will go. It is all innocent, fresh, and simplehearted, and everything about Rebekah has been winsome. Abraham's servant had good reason to think he saw in her spontaneous actions at the well the finest grace of womanhood: the fearlessness of a pure and unspoiled spirit, friendliness, and a quick and generous impulse to be kind. So it would come about that he would take Rebekah home with him to be the bride of Isaac.

If then or later the servant whose mission was to win Rebekah for Isaac's bride had wished to particularize what was admirable in her, he could have set these facts within his list: Her natural charm and winsomeness (vs. 16); her swift and kindly friendliness (vs. 18); the happyheartedness which made her do not only what was asked of her but more (vs. 19); her quick and sure decisiveness (vs. 58); her ability to command a great devotion. Isaac loved her when he first saw her (vs. 67), and apparently he loved no other woman but Rebekah all his life. Here, in an age and in a society where polygamy was familiar, is monogamous marriage. So in the marriage service of the Book of Common Prayer through many generations there was the petition that "as Isaac and Rebekah lived faithfully together, so these persons may surely perform the vow and covenant betwixt them made."

21-49. *Rebekah's Family.*—Eliezer's **wondering** (vs. 21) could not have been due to any uncertainty about Rebekah. What he had seen in her gave no room for doubt on her account as to whether the Lord had made his journey prosperous or not. He gave her the rich token jewels which he had brought. But there remained her family to be considered. In Hebrew

22 And it came to pass, as the camels had done drinking, that the man took a golden earring of half a shekel weight, and two bracelets for her hands of ten *shekels* weight of gold;

23 And said, Whose daughter *art* thou? tell me, I pray thee: is there room *in* thy father's house for us to lodge in?

24 And she said unto him, I *am* the daughter of Bethuel the son of Milcah, which she bare unto Nahor.

25 She said moreover unto him, We have both straw and provender enough, and room to lodge in.

26 And the man bowed down his head, and worshipped the Lord.

27 And he said, Blessed *be* the Lord God of my master Abraham, who hath not left destitute my master of his mercy and his truth: I *being* in the way, the Lord led me to the house of my master's brethren.

28 And the damsel ran, and told *them of* her mother's house these things.

29 ¶ And Rebekah had a brother, and his name *was* Laban: and Laban ran out unto the man, unto the well.

30 And it came to pass, when he saw the earring, and bracelets upon his sister's hands, and when he heard the words of Rebekah his sister, saying, Thus spake the man unto me, that he came unto the man; and, behold, he stood by the camels at the well.

31 And he said, Come in, thou blessed of the Lord; wherefore standest thou without? for I have prepared the house, and room for the camels.

32 ¶ And the man came into the house: and he ungirded his camels, and gave straw and provender for the camels, and water to wash his feet, and the men's feet that *were* with him.

33 And there was set *meat* before him to eat: but he said, I will not eat, until I have told mine errand. And he said, Speak on.

34 And he said, I *am* Abraham's servant.

35 And the Lord hath blessed my master greatly, and he is become great: and he hath given him flocks, and herds, and silver, and gold, and menservants, and maidservants, and camels, and asses.

36 And Sarah my master's wife bare a son to my master when she was old: and unto him hath he given all that he hath.

22 When the camels had done drinking, the man took a gold ring weighing a half shekel, and two bracelets for her arms weighing ten gold shekels, 23 and said, "Tell me whose daughter you are. Is there room in your father's house for us to lodge in?" 24 She said to him, "I am the daughter of Bethu'el the son of Milcah, whom she bore to Nahor." 25 She added, "We have both straw and provender enough, and room to lodge in." 26 The man bowed his head and worshiped the Lord, 27 and said, "Blessed be the Lord, the God of my master Abraham, who has not forsaken his steadfast love and his faithfulness toward my master. As for me, the Lord has led me in the way to the house of my master's kinsmen."

28 Then the maiden ran and told her mother's household about these things. 29 Rebekah had a brother whose name was Laban; and Laban ran out to the man, to the spring. 30 When he saw the ring, and the bracelets on his sister's arms, and when he heard the words of Rebekah his sister, "Thus the man spoke to me," he went to the man; and behold, he was standing by the camels at the spring. 31 He said, "Come in, O blessed of the Lord; why do you stand outside? For I have prepared the house and a place for the camels." 32 So the man came into the house; and Laban ungirded the camels, and gave him straw and provender for the camels, and water to wash his feet and the feet of the men who were with him. 33 Then food was set before him to eat; but he said, "I will not eat until I have told my errand." He said, "Speak on."

34 So he said, "I am Abraham's servant. 35 The Lord has greatly blessed my master, and he has become great; he has given him flocks and herds, silver and gold, menservants and maidservants, camels and asses. 36 And Sarah my master's wife bore a son to my master when she was old; and to him

37 And my master made me swear, saying, Thou shalt not take a wife to my son of the daughters of the Canaanites, in whose land I dwell:

38 But thou shalt go unto my father's house, and to my kindred, and take a wife unto my son.

39 And I said unto my master, Peradventure the woman will not follow me.

40 And he said unto me, The LORD, before whom I walk, will send his angel with thee, and prosper thy way; and thou shalt take a wife for my son of my kindred, and of my father's house:

41 Then shalt thou be clear from *this* my oath, when thou comest to my kindred; and if they give not thee *one*, thou shalt be clear from my oath.

42 And I came this day unto the well, and said, O LORD God of my master Abraham, if now thou do prosper my way which I go:

43 Behold, I stand by the well of water; and it shall come to pass, that when the virgin cometh forth to draw *water*, and I say to her, Give me, I pray thee, a little water of thy pitcher to drink;

44 And she say to me, Both drink thou, and I will also draw for thy camels: *let* the same *be* the woman whom the LORD hath appointed out for my master's son.

45 And before I had done speaking in mine heart, behold, Rebekah came forth with her pitcher on her shoulder; and she went down unto the well, and drew *water:* and I said unto her, Let me drink, I pray thee.

46 And she made haste, and let down her pitcher from her *shoulder,* and said, Drink, and I will give thy camels drink

he has given all that he has. 37 My master made me swear, saying, 'You shall not take a wife for my son from the daughters of the Canaanites, in whose land I dwell; 38 but you shall go to my father's house and to my kindred, and take a wife for my son.' 39 I said to my master, 'Perhaps the woman will not follow me.' 40 But he said to me, 'The LORD, before whom I walk, will send his angel with you and prosper your way; and you shall take a wife for my son from my kindred and from my father's house; 41 then you will be free from my oath, when you come to my kindred; and if they will not give her to you, you will be free from my oath.'

42 "I came today to the spring, and said, 'O LORD, the God of my master Abraham, if now thou wilt prosper the way which I go, 43 behold, I am standing by the spring of water; let the young woman who comes out to draw, to whom I shall say, "Pray give me a little water from your jar to drink," 44 and who will say to me, "Drink, and I will draw for your camels also," let her be the woman whom the LORD has appointed for my master's son.'

45 "Before I had done speaking in my heart, behold, Rebekah came out with her water jar on her shoulder; and she went down to the spring, and drew. I said to her, 'Pray let me drink.' 46 She quickly let down her jar from her shoulder, and said, 'Drink,

---

from the other recension (E) and suggests that in that document the servant's petition had been that the woman named by Abraham—obviously Rebekah—might appear upon the scene and make herself known. This suggestion finds confirmation in vs. 21—obviously from another source than vss. 17-20, telling of the fulfillment of the sign asked for in vs. 14—which indicates further that the E narrative at this point differed from that of J[2].

---

thought it was not possible that a girl alone should decide whether she should be married. He must go and confer with her kinsmen. The first member of her family he met was her brother Laban, and Laban hurried to greet Eliezer with what seemed to be a warmth equal

to Rebekah's. But a wry thought suggests itself as one notes the exact words of the story. It was when Laban **saw the earring, and bracelets upon his sister's hands** that he was lavish with hospitality. Whether the narrator deliberately meant to or not, he has given a hint here of

also: so I drank, and she made the camels drink also.

47 And I asked her, and said, Whose daughter *art* thou? And she said, The daughter of Bethuel, Nahor's son, whom Milcah bare unto him: and I put the earring upon her face, and the bracelets upon her hands.

48 And I bowed down my head, and worshipped the Lord, and blessed the Lord God of my master Abraham, which had led me in the right way to take my master's brother's daughter unto his son.

49 And now, if ye will deal kindly and truly with my master, tell me: and if not, tell me; that I may turn to the right hand, or to the left.

50 Then Laban and Bethuel answered and said, The thing proceedeth from the Lord: we cannot speak unto thee bad or good.

51 Behold, Rebekah *is* before thee; take *her,* and go, and let her be thy master's son's wife, as the Lord hath spoken.

52 And it came to pass, that, when Abraham's servant heard their words, he worshipped the Lord, *bowing himself* to the earth.

53 And the servant brought forth jewels of silver, and jewels of gold, and raiment, and gave *them* to Rebekah: he gave also to her brother and to her mother precious things.

and I will give your camels drink also.' So I drank, and she gave the camels drink also. **47** Then I asked her, 'Whose daughter are you?' She said, 'The daughter of Bethu'el, Nahor's son, whom Milcah bore to him.' So I put the ring on her nose, and the bracelets on her arms. **48** Then I bowed my head and worshiped the Lord, and blessed the Lord, the God of my master Abraham, who had led me by the right way to take the daughter of my master's kinsman for his son. **49** Now then, if you will deal loyally and truly with my master, tell me; and if not, tell me; that I may turn to the right hand or to the left."

50 Then Laban and Bethu'el answered, "The thing comes from the Lord; we cannot speak to you bad or good. **51** Behold, Rebekah is before you, take her and go, and let her be the wife of your master's son, as the Lord has spoken."

52 When Abraham's servant heard their words, he bowed himself to the earth before the Lord. **53** And the servant brought forth jewelry of silver and of gold, and raiment, and gave them to Rebekah; he also gave to her brother and to her mother costly orna-

---

C. The Marriage Is Arranged (24:28-60)

49. The Lord had indeed revealed his choice of Rebekah, but the possibility remained that her people might not consent to her marriage. In this case the servant would have to go farther.

50. Laban and Milcah—**Bethuel** is RP's substitution for "Milcah"—recognizing that **the thing comes from the Lord** give their consent without (vs. 51) consulting Rebekah.

Laban's characteristic—the characteristic which he was to show later in his dealings with Jacob, a quick eye for profit.

Anyhow, Eliezer was welcomed; and as he recites the whole story of his mission, there shines in it again his high sense of heavenly guidance. Abraham had told him, he said, that the Lord . . . will send his angel with thee, and prosper thy way, and he thanked God that this had been true. What he said to Rebekah's family echoed what he had already said to her: **Blessed be the Lord God of my Master Abraham, who hath not left destitute my master of**

his mercy and his truth: **I being in the way, the Lord led me to the house of my master's brethren.** Note the bright meaning in those words. Eliezer was **in the way** and so the angel of the Lord went with him. So it may often be. The divine guidance does not come to those who idly sit and speculate; nor to those who evade an obligation; nor to those who, having started, hesitate and stop. It comes to those who, knowing they are on the road of duty, have only the one purpose to pursue it to the end.

50-60. *The Giving of Rebekah.*—Once again, in vss. 50-51, there sounds the dominant note

54 And they did eat and drink, he and the men that *were* with him, and tarried all night; and they rose up in the morning, and he said, Send me away unto my master.

55 And her brother and her mother said, Let the damsel abide with us *a few* days, at the least ten; after that she shall go.

56 And he said unto them, Hinder me not, seeing the LORD hath prospered my way; send me away that I may go to my master.

57 And they said, We will call the damsel, and inquire at her mouth.

58 And they called Rebekah, and said unto her, Wilt thou go with this man? And she said, I will go.

59 And they sent away Rebekah their sister, and her nurse, and Abraham's servant, and his men.

60 And they blessed Rebekah, and said unto her, Thou *art* our sister; be thou *the mother* of thousands of millions, and let thy seed possess the gate of those which hate them.

61 ¶ And Rebekah arose, and her damsels, and they rode upon the camels, and followed the man: and the servant took Rebekah, and went his way.

62 And Isaac came from the way of the well Lahai-roi; for he dwelt in the south country.

ments. 54 And he and the men who were with him ate and drank, and they spent the night there. When they arose in the morning, he said, "Send me back to my master." 55 Her brother and her mother said, "Let the maiden remain with us a while, at least ten days; after that she may go." 56 But he said to them, "Do not delay me, since the LORD has prospered my way; let me go that I may go to my master." 57 They said, "We will call the maiden, and ask her." 58 And they called Rebekah, and said to her, "Will you go with this man?" She said, "I will go." 59 So they sent away Rebekah their sister and her nurse, and Abraham's servant and his men. 60 And they blessed Rebekah, and said to her, "Our sister, be the mother of thousands of ten thousands; and may your descendants possess the gate of those who hate them!" 61 Then Rebekah and her maids arose, and rode upon the camels and followed the man; thus the servant took Rebekah, and went his way.

62 Now Isaac had come from[n] Beer-la'-hai-roi, and was dwelling in the Negeb.

[n] Syr Tg: Heb *from coming to*

---

57. This was in its original context (E) the reply of Laban and Milcah to the servant's request for Rebekah; i.e., the decision was left with the girl herself, who (vs. 58) consents to go.

D. ISAAC MARRIES REBEKAH (24:61-67)

62. The mention of **Beer-lahai-roi** in association with Isaac indicates a J source. J[2], as has been seen, had already stated in the notice now preserved in 25:11*b*, but which came in his narrative after 24:1*b*; 25:5, that "Isaac dwelt at Beer-lahai-roi." He must

---

that echoes through all the narrative like the motif of a symphony—the note of the guidance of God. **The thing proceedeth from the LORD**, say Laban and Bethuel; Rebekah must go to be Isaac's wife, **as the LORD hath spoken.** Then Eliezer thanked God that his quest was completed, and he was eager to turn home. **Hinder me not**, he urged, **seeing the LORD hath prospered my way.** When Rebekah's family wanted to keep her with them a little longer, Rebekah herself was called—doubtless with the hope that she would surely shrink from going so very quickly. But instead of that she answered simply, **I will go.** And so the story comes to its

climax as though to say that God's purpose for Isaac was achieved through no arbitrary compulsion, but with the free consent of this girl's heart. A dignity is accorded to her womanhood which was unusual for the ancient Orient. Finally, with a characteristic blessing (vs. 60), they send her on her way.

61-67. *Rebekah Comes to Isaac*.—The centuries succeed one another, customs change, and the center of life shifts from old lands to new; but the primal realities abide. Rebekah comes to marry a man she has never seen; and when she realizes that he is near she immediately veils herself that he may not yet see her. To modern

63 And Isaac went out to meditate in the field at the eventide: and he lifted up his eyes, and saw, and, behold, the camels *were* coming.

64 And Rebekah lifted up her eyes, and when she saw Isaac, she lighted off the camel.

65 For she *had* said unto the servant, What man *is* this that walketh in the field to meet us? And the servant *had* said, It *is* my master: therefore she took a veil, and covered herself.

66 And the servant told Isaac all things that he had done.

67 And Isaac brought her into his mother Sarah's tent, and took Rebekah, and she became his wife; and he loved her: and Isaac was comforted after his mother's *death*.

63 And Isaac went out to meditate in the field in the evening; and he lifted up his eyes and looked, and behold, there were camels coming. 64 And Rebekah lifted up her eyes, and when she saw Isaac, she alighted from the camel, 65 and said to the servant, "Who is the man yonder, walking in the field to meet us?" The servant said, "It is my master." So she took her veil and covered herself. 66 And the servant told Isaac all the things that he had done. 67 Then Isaac brought her into the tent,[o] and took Rebekah, and she became his wife; and he loved her. So Isaac was comforted after his mother's death.

[o] Heb adds *Sarah his mother*

---

accordingly have told how the servant brought Rebekah to him there. The author who inserted 25:1-4, 6 and transferred the notice of Abraham's death, originally coming after 24:9, naturally represented the servant as returning to Abraham at Beer-sheba (cf. 21:33 [J²]; 22:19 [E]). This necessitated a change in the wording of the original of vs. 62 to its present form. Originally it read, "And they came to the entrance of Beer-lahai-roi" (cf. Gunkel, *Genesis*, p. 259; Skinner, *Genesis*, p. 347).

67. **His mother Sarah's** (KJV) is a gloss; the words are syntactically impossible in the Hebrew. The concluding phrase originally read "his father's death"; the **mother's** of the present text is due to the intrusion of 25:1-4, 6.

Western thought that belongs to a bygone time; but what has time to do with these four words, **And he loved her?** Here is the fountain of the wonder of life. A man has his links with the past, as Isaac did. He has grown up as a little boy under the wing of his mother, but a new knowledge of what a woman gives him comes when he finds his wife. **He loved her.** In its primitive expression that might mean only sexual union, with no great meaning for the spirit. But in the scene of Rebekah's coming to Isaac there is a simplicity and sweetness that creates another atmosphere. Through it vistas of contemplation open far beyond what actually happened with Isaac and Rebekah, vistas into all that the love of man and woman has meant and can mean in human life—for reverence toward one another's personality, for romance, for richness of mutual devotion. If sordid stories of infidelity make the headlines in the news, it is because they are exceptional; back of them are the numberless men and women who have the deep and quiet comfort of their certainty of love—and in that certainty are most sensitive to God. Not many husbands and wives could express in words what Elizabeth Barrett Brown-

ing wrote for Robert Browning, but, in a love which God has blessed, many besides herself have said within their hearts:

How do I love thee? Let me count the ways.
I love thee to the depth and breadth and height
My soul can reach, when feeling out of sight
For the ends of Being and ideal Grace.
I love thee to the level of everyday's
Most quiet need, by sun and candle-light.
I love thee freely, as men strive for Right;
I love thee purely, as they turn from Praise.[5]

63a. Meditation.—"To meditate" is defined by Webster as "to dwell in thought." Multitudes of people physically and intellectually are transients. They do not dwell in anything, least of all in thought. Isaac is not the greatest of O.T. figures, but he appears here as an example of a quality greatly needed. We see in him the contemplative man, and this twentieth century needs contemplation. People scurry here and there, worried, hurried, tense. Look at the crowds on the subway. One of the most notable sociological reports made in many years was the thorough analytic study of a small American

[5] *Sonnets from the Portuguese*, XLIII.

25 Then again Abraham took a wife, and her name *was* Keturah.

2 And she bare him Zimran, and Jokshan, and Medan, and Midian, and Ishbak, and Shuah.

25 Abraham took another wife, whose name was Ketu'rah. 2 She bore him Zimran, Jokshan, Medan, Mid'ian, Ishbak.

XXXI. Sons of Keturah (25:1-6)

25:1-6. Vss. 1-4, 6, are, as has already been noted, a late insertion in the J document. They affirm Israel's relationship with certain Arabian tribes (cf. 22:21-24; also the expansion of the J2 material in ch. 10). Vs. 5 is from J2 and originally followed 24:1*b*.

city which "was selected as having many features common to a wide group of communities." This report, which had to do with the whole field of life in that representative city, its businesses, its homes, the education and recreation of its young people, its leisure, and its community activities, was published under the generic name of *Middletown*.[6] A review of the book summed up its picture of contemporary facts as follows:

In Middletown, everybody is busy. Idleness is a vice. To be continually busy, to fill one's days with exacting engagements, to rush from one organized activity to another—in brief, to keep going—this is the supreme virtue in Middletown. . . . There is no spirit of leisure in Middletown, . . . no time to read, no time to think, no time . . . for serenity and balance.

Or note the description of Dodsworth in Sinclair Lewis' novel of that name. Back from Europe and passing through Grand Central Terminal in New York,

he stood contemplatively (he who a year ago would never have stood thus, but would have rushed with the most earnest of them) on the balcony overlooking the shining acres of floor. . . . Why, he wondered, was it that the immensity of Notre Dame or St. Paul's did not dwarf and make ridiculous the figures of the worshippers as this vastness did the figures of travelers galloping to train-gates. Was it because the little people, dark and insignificant in the cathedrals, were yet dignified, self-possessed, seeking the ways of God, whereas here they were busy with the ludicrous activity of insects?[7]

Much of our modern life is like children riding on a merry-go-round, exultant as the hobbyhorses move up and down and the music plays, and then when the whole thing wheezes to a stop, climbing down a little dizzily, exactly where they got on, having gone nowhere. We need more Isaacs, men who know how to meditate, "to dwell in thought."

What ought meditation to be? Not idle daydreaming, not the drifting of the mind away from the day's reality. Rather it should be the deliberate relating of life to a high pattern. The noblest figures of the Bible are men with that gift. Nothing specifically is said about meditation in the case of Abraham, but the fact that he came out of Ur of the Chaldeans shows that he had been thinking great thoughts to which his whole life was to be related. Moses dwelt with such thoughts in exile, and saw the vision of the burning bush. David meditated in the silence of the pastures of Bethlehem. Paul went off into Arabia. Jesus himself withdrew into the wilderness after his baptism in the Jordan. In every case meditation had to do with the vital pattern of God's purpose to which life was to be related. To that purpose everything should belong, including the inner and the intimate. Isaac was meditating on the eve of his marriage. Was that the reason why in an age of polygamy he kept one loyalty all his life? Friendship, love, family life, right citizenship, all depend upon setting them contemplatively in relation to ideals and great ends. Moreover, meditation should look forward. The best meditation is not the passive recollections of people grown old in spirit, but the looking forward of those whose purpose is always young (see Isa. 40:31).

How shall the right meditation be made possible? For one thing, a man must get apart from the crowd. There is a "strife of tongues" from which one must be separated. "Religion is what the individual does with his own solitariness."[8] Partial truth, but a truth. Unless a man is sometimes alone, he may be so deafened that he cannot hear God. Moreover, for the right meditation a man must seek the right surroundings. Isaac goes out into the fields at eventide—the serenity of wide spaces, the silence of sunset, the mystery of the slowly descending dark. See Jesus going apart into the hills, spending whole nights in prayer. He knew what it was to dwell in thoughts great enough for God.

25:1-18. Mostly Genealogies.—As the Exeg. has indicated, the first part of this chapter is

[6] Robert S. Lynd and Helen Merrell Lynd (New York: Harcourt, Brace & Co., 1929).

[7] New York: Harcourt, Brace & Co., 1929, pp. 163-64.

[8] A. N. Whitehead, *Religion in the Making* (New York: The Macmillan Co., 1926), p. 16.

3 And Jokshan begat Sheba, and Dedan. And the sons of Dedan were Asshurim, and Letushim, and Leummim.

4 And the sons of Midian; Ephah, and Epher, and Hanoch, and Abidah, and Eldaah. All these *were* the children of Keturah.

5 ¶ And Abraham gave all that he had unto Isaac.

6 But unto the sons of the concubines, which Abraham had, Abraham gave gifts, and sent them away from Isaac his son, while he yet lived, eastward, unto the east country.

7 And these *are* the days of the years of Abraham's life which he lived, a hundred threescore and fifteen years.

8 Then Abraham gave up the ghost, and died in a good old age, an old man, and full *of years;* and was gathered to his people.

9 And his sons Isaac and Ishmael buried him in the cave of Machpelah, in the field of Ephron the son of Zohar the Hittite, which *is* before Mamre;

10 The field which Abraham purchased of the sons of Heth: there was Abraham buried, and Sarah his wife.

11 ¶ And it came to pass after the death of Abraham, that God blessed his son Isaac; and Isaac dwelt by the well Lahai-roi.

12 ¶ Now these *are* the generations of Ishmael, Abraham's son, whom Hagar the Egyptian, Sarah's handmaid, bare unto Abraham:

and Shuah. 3 Jokshan was the father of Sheba and Dedan. The sons of Dedan were Asshu'rim, Letu'shim, and Le-um'mim. 4 The sons of Mid'ian were Ephah, Epher, Hanoch, Abi'da, and Elda'ah. All these were the children of Ketu'rah. 5 Abraham gave all he had to Isaac. 6 But to the sons of his concubines Abraham gave gifts, and while he was still living he sent them away from his son Isaac, eastward to the east country.

7 These are the days of the years of Abraham's life, a hundred and seventy-five years. 8 Abraham breathed his last and died in a good old age, an old man and full of years, and was gathered to his people. 9 Isaac and Ish'mael his sons buried him in the cave of Mach-pe'lah, in the field of Ephron the son of Zohar the Hittite, east of Mamre, 10 the field which Abraham purchased from the Hittites. There Abraham was buried, with Sarah his wife. 11 After the death of Abraham God blessed Isaac his son. And Isaac dwelt at Beer-la'hai-roi.

12 These are the descendants of Ish'mael, Abraham's son, whom Hagar the Egyptian,

---

XXXII. DEATH OF ABRAHAM (25:7-11)

7-11. Vss. 7-10 are from P. To be noted is the fact that Ishmael is represented as present at his father's burial, indicating that P retained nothing of the story preserved in ch. 16 (J²) and 21:9-21 (E). Vs. 11*b*, as has been noted, came in the J² narrative following 24:1*b*; 25:5. RP transferred it to this point, and supplied vs. 11*a* as the connecting link.

XXXIII. DESCENDANTS OF ISHMAEL (25:12-18)

12-18. Vss. 12-17 are from P. The names in vss. 13-15 indicate that P thought of the Ishmaelites as inhabiting the Syro-Arabian desert, east of Edom and Moab. According

---

made up of many strands. Its main concern is to enlarge the details of relationships within which the central life of Israel is to be exactly framed. The list of the children of Keturah establishes that relationship with some of the Arabian tribes, as to whom it is made plain (vss. 5-6) that they were dismissed with only

secondary tokens from Abraham, while the real inheritance went to Isaac. Similarly in vss. 12-18 there is recorded the lineage of the Ishmaelites, who may have been a powerful tribe of the desert in the centuries just before the first narratives now woven into Genesis were written. Then in vss. 19-20 there is part of the

13 And these *are* the names of the sons of Ishmael, by their names, according to their generations: the firstborn of Ishmael, Nebajoth; and Kedar, and Adbeel, and Mibsam,

14 And Mishma, and Dumah, and Massa,

15 Hadar, and Tema, Jetur, Naphish, and Kedemah:

16 These *are* the sons of Ishmael, and these *are* their names, by their towns, and by their castles; twelve princes according to their nations.

17 And these *are* the years of the life of Ishmael, a hundred and thirty and seven years: and he gave up the ghost and died, and was gathered unto his people.

18 And they dwelt from Havilah unto Shur, that *is* before Egypt, as thou goest toward Assyria: *and* he died in the presence of all his brethren.

19 ¶ And these *are* the generations of Isaac, Abraham's son: Abraham begat Isaac:

Sarah's maid, bore to Abraham. 13 These are the names of the sons of Ish'mael, named in the order of their birth: Neba'ioth, the first-born of Ish'mael; and Kedar, Adbeel, Mibsam, 14 Mishma, Dumah, Massa, 15 Hadad, Tema, Jetur, Naphish, and Ked'emah. 16 These are the sons of Ish'mael and these are their names, by their villages and by their encampments, twelve princes according to their tribes. 17 (These are the years of the life of Ish'mael, a hundred and thirty-seven years; he breathed his last and died, and was gathered to his kindred.) 18 They dwelt from Hav'i-lah to Shur, which is opposite Egypt in the direction of Assyria; he settled*p* over against all his people.

19 These are the descendants of Isaac, Abraham's son: Abraham was the father of

p Heb *fell*

to the J document, from which vs. 18 is derived, they ranged as far as the border of Egypt. There can be little doubt that of the two representations J's is the more authentic.

The Ishmaelites have left practically no mark in history. From the fact that they are mentioned in neither the Egyptian nor the Assyrian records Meyer (*Israeliten und ihre Nachbarstämme,* p. 324) infers that they flourished from the twelfth to the ninth centuries B.C. After that, "Ishmaelite" may have become more or less synonymous with "Bedouin" (cf. Judg. 8:24). This may be the explanation of the conflict between vss. 13-17 and vs. 18.

18. Following the LXX and the Vulg., "he dwelt" should be read for **they dwelt**. **In the direction of Assyria** is either a gloss, or possibly from RP harmonizing the verse with vss. 13-17. The verse is from J2 and originally formed the conclusion of the story in ch. 16. RJE presumably transferred it to follow 21:21. RP placed it here as the final notice regarding Ishmael.

XXXIV. JACOB AND ESAU I (25:19-34)

A. PORTENTS AT THEIR BIRTH (25:19-26)

Vss. 19-20, 26*b* are from P. Vs. 20 is all that P had to say of Isaac's marriage; contrast the detailed narrative of J2 and E in ch. 24.

formal record of the priestly writers, whose main concern was to show the unbroken and sure succession of the family of Abraham.

Of warmer suggestion are vss. 7-11. Abraham, at a ripe old age, **was gathered to his people.** This cannot mean that he was buried with his ancestors, since their graves must have been in far away Chaldea. Does it reflect perhaps a hope, desirous though dim, of life beyond this life? Vss. 9-10 add sacredness to the associations of Machpelah, where Sarah already had been

buried (see Expos. on ch. 23; 35:29). But thought may linger most on these words of vs. 11, **It came to pass after the death of Abraham, that God blessed his son Isaac.** Here again is the great Hebrew conviction of religion binding a family together. It was not a transient thing for one man to be related to God. The covenant which enfolded father and son bound the generations in a continuing benediction.

19-26. *The Foreordaining of Israel.*—To the Hebrew sense of the preciousness of the family,

20 And Isaac was forty years old when he took Rebekah to wife, the daughter of Bethuel the Syrian of Padan-aram, the sister to Laban the Syrian.

21 And Isaac entreated the Lord for his wife, because she *was* barren: and the Lord was entreated of him, and Rebekah his wife conceived.

22 And the children struggled together within her; and she said, If *it be* so, why *am* I thus? And she went to inquire of the Lord.

23 And the Lord said unto her, Two nations *are* in thy womb, and two manner of people shall be separated from thy bowels; and *the one* people shall be stronger than *the other* people; and the elder shall serve the younger.

Isaac, 20 and Isaac was forty years old when he took to wife Rebekah, the daughter of Bethu'el the Aramean of Paddan-aram the sister of Laban the Aramean. 21 And Isaac prayed to the Lord for his wife, because she was barren; and the Lord granted his prayer, and Rebekah his wife conceived. 22 The children struggled together within her; and she said, "If it is thus, why do I live?"*q* So she went to inquire of the Lord. 23 And the Lord said to her,

"Two nations are in your womb,
  and two peoples, born of you, shall be divided;
- the one shall be stronger than the other,
  the elder shall serve the younger."

q Syr: Heb obscure

Paddan-aram is P's equivalent of the Haran of J[2] and the Mesopotamia of E. Just what it designates is uncertain. It may be equivalent to "the field of Aram" mentioned in Hos. 12:12—"field" meaning "open country"—or, since the Assyrian *padanu* and *ḫarrânu* (Haran) both mean "a way," it may mean simply Haran.

The remaining material in the section, vss. 21-26*a*, is from J. Originally it followed the tale in 26:1-33—also from J—as is indicated by the fact that there Isaac and Rebekah are obviously still childless. Its present position is due to R[P], who substituted it for the colorless statement (cf. vs. 13) of the names of Isaac's sons with which P had continued vs. 20.

Basically the narrative is from J[1]. It has however been elaborated by J[2], as is indicated by the facts: (*a*) The name Rebekah is given not at the first mention of Isaac's wife, vs. 21, where it would be expected, but in vs. 22. (*b*) **Behold** in vs. 24 suggests that this is the first mention of the twins. It may accordingly be inferred that vss. 22-23, together with **Rebekah his wife** in vs. 21, are from J[2]. This suggests that in the J[1] tradition Isaac's wife was unnamed. The J[1] tradition is basically that of Hebron. This J[2] supplemented, in the stories of the patriarchs, with material derived in part from the tradition of Beer-sheba which, it may be inferred, included the detail that Isaac's wife was named Rebekah.

22. The Hebrew of **struggled together** is lit., "crushed one another." Rebekah took this as a portent, and **went to inquire of the Lord**, i.e., she consulted the oracle at the sanctuary, presumably (cf. 26:33) at Beer-sheba.

23. The poem may well have had independent currency. Its inclusion here ascribes the superiority of Jacob to Esau, i.e., of Israel to Edom, not to the cold-blooded calculation of Jacob recorded in vss. 27-34, but to divine decree. J[2] thus again affirms his faith in God's control of history.

and especially to the faith that every family which stemmed from Abraham was part of the covenant of God, barrenness was the supreme calamity; and no act of God could be a more direct blessing than the reversal of a woman's barrenness. God's answer to prayer in the case of Rebekah is only one instance of the recorded belief of Israel that he had intervened. So it had been with Sarah (15:2-6; 18:12-14). So also it would be with Rachel (29:31; 30:22-23),

with the mother of Samson (Judg. 13:2-7), with Hannah (I Sam. 1:2-20), and so at the beginning of the N.T. with Elizabeth, of whom John the Baptist should be born (Luke 1:7-13).

But it is not only in Rebekah's fertility that the O.T. accents here its belief in the special act of God. The children struggling together in the womb represent the rivalry between Israel and the desert Ishmaelites, a rivalry in which the descendants of Abraham should pre-

24 ¶ And when her days to be delivered were fulfilled, behold, *there were* twins in her womb.

25 And the first came out red, all over like a hairy garment; and they called his name Esau.

26 And after that came his brother out, and his hand took hold on Esau's heel; and his name was called Jacob: and Isaac *was* threescore years old when she bare them.

27 And the boys grew: and Esau was a cunning hunter, a man of the field; and Jacob *was* a plain man, dwelling in tents.

24 When her days to be delivered were fulfilled, behold, there were twins in her womb. 25 The first came forth red, all his body like a hairy mantle; so they called his name Esau. 26 Afterward his brother came forth, and his hand had taken hold of Esau's heel; so his name was called Jacob.[r] Isaac was sixty years old when she bore them.

27 When the boys grew up, Esau was a skilful hunter, a man of the field, while Jacob was a quiet man, dwelling in tents.

[r] That is *He takes by the heel* or *He supplants*

---

25. Red, *'adhmônî*, is a gloss, playing on Edom, *'edhôm*. **Hairy**, *sē'ār*, provides the etymology not of **Esau** but of "Seir"; the word alludes to Esau's traditional role as the father of the Edomites who dwelt in Mount Seir. The name Esau thus appears to be a secondary feature in the tradition upon which J¹ was drawing, i.e., at some point in its development Seir came, for whatever reason, to be identified with Esau, who may be connected, or identical, with the Phoenician *Ousōos*, a hero of the chase (cf. vs. 27).

26. This feature of the tale is referred to in Hos. 12:3. The name **Jacob—He takes by the heel** or **He supplants** (RSV mg.)—appears as a component of a Palestinian place name, Jacob-el, in the lists of Thutmose III, dating from the fifteenth century, some time before the entry of Israel into the land. Whether Jacob-el means "God overreaches" or "Jacob is God" is uncertain. In any case, there can be no doubt that the name Jacob is derived from the pre-Israelite tradition of Canaan. That he was an east Jordan figure is indicated by the fact that the scene of each of the two legends concerning him which are inseparably bound up with a certain locality· is laid in that region—the covenant with Laban in Mount Gilead (31:44-48; cf. 31:25), and the wrestling at the Jabbok in the vicinity of Penuel (32:24-31).

The east Jordan figure was taken up into the tradition of the Israelite tribes which settled east of the Jordan and, in the process of unification, was related to Abraham and Isaac of Hebron and Beer-sheba by being made the son of the latter. As to whether this occurred gradually as the result of popular speculation or whether it was part of J¹'s schematization of his material it is impossible to say. Similarly there can be no decision as to whether Jacob's twin, Esau, came to be regarded as the ancestor of Edom before or after Jacob had been connected with Israel.

The birth story in vss. 19-26 thus originally had nothing to do with Isaac and Rebekah, but was independently current east of the Jordan. The motif of the prenatal struggle of twins may have been fairly widespread; cf. the story of Acrisius and Proetus, sons of Abas, king of Argos (Apollodorus *The Library* II. 2. 1), and the Polynesian myth of the twins Tangaroa and Rongo (T. K. Cheyne, *Traditions and Beliefs of Ancient Israel* [London: Adam and Charles Black, 1907], p. 356).

B. Jacob Acquires Esau's Birthright (25:27-34)

This story is from J¹, with some minor additions by later hands. It is a tale of the kind that would be told among peasants living on the edge of the desert to express their

---

vail. Here again is set forth the conviction which echoes so often in Genesis—that the people who looked back to Jacob as their forefather were destined to greatness not through any chances of human history, but because of the sovereign purpose of God. Nothing that should happen to Jacob or through Jacob could

be explained by contingent or superficial factors of time and place. What he was to be was predestined; and that predestination is seen as active even before he came out of the womb.

27-34. The Character of Esau.—Esau is an example of how a man with a bad reputation can be more attractive than another who has

contempt for what they thought to be the nomad's lack of care for the future. J¹ used it to account for the fact that not Esau, traditionally the first-born of his father, but Jacob, his younger brother, was the heir to the divine promise of Abraham; i.e., it explains away, so to speak, that feature—the priority of Esau—in the birth story in vss. 21-26 which was inconsistent with the historical situation in J¹'s time. It was true that Esau's supposed descendants, the Edomites, had attained national organization earlier than

---

managed to acquire a good one. In the O.T. estimates Esau has a black mark, while his brother Jacob has all the marks of favor. Jacob is listed as a prince in Israel, and the father of the twelve tribes of the chosen people: but the Edomites, whom the Jews hated, were called sons of Esau. Yet notwithstanding all that, in the choice of a companion as between Esau and Jacob, almost anyone would have chosen Esau.

Thus there was a plus side to his ledger. What were the assets on it? The first asset was his physical vigor. Esau was an outdoorsman, a cunning hunter, a man of the field, a contrast to Jacob who seemed a paler sort of creature, his mother's favorite, and generally to be found about her tent. Esau was rough but he was virile, and his old father Isaac turned to him instinctively because he knew that if there was anything he wanted done, Esau could do it; and as he grew old he leaned increasingly on Esau's strength. It is true, of course, that the best man, and the bravest, is not necessarily the man with the biggest body and the strongest muscles. The frail man may be the spiritual giant: consider the apostle Paul. Nevertheless, physical soundness and vigor are greatly to be desired, and every man has the duty of making his body as fit an instrument as it possibly can become. A body neglected may make the whole personality seem anemic, while the deliberate purpose to bring the body to its highest pitch adds power inwardly as well as outwardly. Remember Theodore Roosevelt, born a delicate boy, yet setting out persistently to develop—as he did develop—a physique of astonishing resilience and tough endurance. Although he is no saint in the biblical calendar, Esau may well stand as an example in this first point.

Nor was physical vigor his only virtue. He was a warmhearted man. Evidently he loved his father, as his father loved him. When Isaac was old and blind, the rough Esau was gentle with him and quick to respond to everything he wanted. If Isaac had a wish for something special to eat, it was Esau who would go and get it. If Esau was careless about the particular advantages of the birthright, he was not careless about his father's blessing. He wanted that, whatever else was lost. And his bigheartedness was shown not only in relation to one he loved: he could be generous and magnanimous even to Jacob, who had defrauded him of his birthright.

At first his hot blood flared into such anger that Jacob got away fast and far: but in the end, when Jacob came cautiously home, with timid stratagems to placate Esau by gifts sent out in advance, Esau made all those look cheap by his own magnanimity as he "ran to meet [Jacob], and embraced him, and fell on his neck, and kissed him" (35:4). He was not the kind of man who could keep a grudge. He would rather be fond of people than to go on hating, even when he had a right to hate. In any time or place a man like Esau will be lovable. He may be easygoing and careless and lacking in any strenuous principles or fixed aims, so that he may be set down in public records as a poor sort of citizen, and yet have such impulsive lovingkindness that he is immensely attractive. Note how in some sentimental movies the villain may be more appealing than the hero, or the bootlegger and the gambler more companionable than the caricature set up to be a clergyman. Note what it is that makes unprincipled political machines powerful in many cities. They hand out public assets for private gain, and play fast and loose with the birthright of civic honor, and every genuine observer knows that they are bad; but they hold power because the district leaders and the workers in the wards are so often men who love people and get them what they think they want. Life at its best must keep away from the faults and failures of Esau, but it is also true that life will not reach its best unless it has an infusion of Esau's virtue. Programs of social reform will not succeed if their spirit is

> scrimped and iced,
> In the name of a cautious, statistical Christ.[9]

Men in public office will not win the heart of the people and make them follow willingly on the road of some new adventure unless they have the human touch.

What then was the matter with Esau? Why did he not play a great role in Israel's spiritual history? Because he was a man who lived only in the immediate moment, and by the light only of what was obvious. He was heir to the birthright, and the birthright meant a great deal if you looked far enough. It meant the privilege someday of being the family's representative,

[9] John Boyle O'Reilly, "In Bohemia."

28 And Isaac loved Esau, because he did eat of *his* venison: but Rebekah loved Jacob.

29 ¶ And Jacob sod pottage: and Esau came from the field, and he *was* faint:

30 And Esau said to Jacob, Feed me, I pray thee, with that same red *pottage;* for I *am* faint: therefore was his name called Edom.

28 Isaac loved Esau, because he ate of his game; but Rebekah loved Jacob.

29 Once when Jacob was boiling pottage, Esau came in from the field, and he was famished. 30 And Esau said to Jacob, "Let me eat some of that red pottage, for I am famished!" (Therefore his name was called

---

Israel, as is indicated by the list of Edomite kings preserved in 36:31-39 (see below), but culturally they had remained stationary while Israel had passed from nomadism to peasantry, and were furthermore conscious that they stood in a unique relationship to Yahweh, the powerful God of Sinai, who had given them the land of Palestine.

Why had leadership passed from Edom to Israel? J[1] had given one answer to this question in his story of Abraham's obedience to the divine call (12:1-4a, 6-7). Here he provides another answer, one which was doubtless more in accord with popular thinking. It was because the Israelites, like their father Jacob, were cleverer, more provident, and more self-controlled than the Edomites, represented by their father Esau.

28. An addition by J[2], preparing for the story in ch. 27.

29. The word translated **pottage** is from the same root as that translated **boiling.** The sentence might therefore be rendered, "Jacob once was boiling something."

30. A literal rendering of the Hebrew is, "Pray let me swallow of the red stuff—that red stuff there—for I am famished." The fact that the statement that the stuff which

---

and especially its priestly representative to guide it in the ways of God. It may have been an exaggeration to say that Esau **despised his birthright** (vs. 34); but he did disregard it. Its benefits were intangible and seemed a long way off. They did not fill the stomach when it was hungry. So when one day Esau came in from a long hunting, so famished that he was almost faint, and smelled some food that Jacob had been cooking, the birthright seemed very insubstantial in comparison with the steaming pottage that Jacob offered. What he wanted right then was something to eat; **I am at the point to die,** said he, **and what profit shall this birthright do to me?** So he made the deal. Possibly he thought the whole transaction did not amount to anything, since who could ever get Isaac to consent? But in any case he had lost his right to protest against such deprivation as might subsequently come to him. He had showed that he did not care enough for life's great possibilities to pay the price of present discipline. He must have what he wanted when he wanted it, and consequences could go hang. That was the critical weakness of Esau and that was his condemnation. He lost tomorrow because he snatched so greedily at today.

Consider his descendants in every generation, including ours: the young men who cannot let any long-range dedication stand in the way of appetite; the frivolous girl who says of something trivial, "I'll die if I do not get it"; the

mature people for whom comfort always comes first and for whom anything like religious responsibility is ruled out if it is hard; the men in public office who will sell a birthright of great ideals to satisfy immediate clamor. Attractive traits will not save such people from ultimate dishonor.

28. *The Character of Rebekah as a Woman.* —A character study of Rebekah is significant more in the questions it provokes than in the answers. The O.T. writers do not often draw a neat moral at the end of a description. They give the facts even though they may be inconsistent and confused, and leave us to interpret them as best we can. Thus is suggested an enduring truth: there is rarely any sure clue to any life. Any personality, ancient or modern, has elements that baffle analysis. We move toward true appraisal only when we are undogmatic. Honestly and patiently we seek for partial certainties, and are frank to recognize that no picture of another soul will ever be complete.

The story of Rebekah had an idyllic beginning (cf. Expos. on 24:15-16). But what followed was not idyllic. It was the uncomfortable realization of this that made the revisers of the American Book of Common Prayer omit in the 1920's the reference to the mutual faithfulness of Isaac and Rebekah which had been in the inherited book for centuries. That reference was put there originally because Isaac and Rebekah were the one notable pair among

| 31 And Jacob said, Sell me this day thy birthright. | Edom.⁵) **31** Jacob said, "First sell me your birthright." **32** Esau said, "I am about to |
| 32 And Esau said, Behold, I *am* at the point to die: and what profit shall this birthright do to me? | die; of what use is a birthright to me?" |

⁵ That is *Red*

Jacob was boiling was red occurs here, rather than at the first mention of it in vs. 29, suggests that it was not a feature of the tale in its primary, popular form, but is part of J¹'s adaptation of it to make it refer to Israel and Edom. **Therefore his name was called Edom** is an explanatory gloss; neither J¹ nor J² would have been guilty of thus breaking into the narrative. Gunkel remarks that the name Edom is "a memento of the greed and stupidity of [the Edomites'] ancestor" (*Genesis*, p. 297).

31. The term **birthright** denotes the advantages and rights normally enjoyed by the eldest son. These included natural vigor of body and character (cf. 49:3; Deut. 21:17), a position of honor as head of the family (cf. 27:29), and a double share of the inheritance (Deut. 21:15-17). When applied to tribes or nations it conveys the notion of political and material superiority. This is what it means here, i.e., the story is definitely nonreligious and, as has been suggested above, reflects the earthy ideas of the peasantry, not the religious insight of J¹.

the patriarchs who were monogamous. But the fact that a man or woman has only one mate does not of itself make a marriage successful. Divorce is not the only thing that destroys a marriage; there may be a gradual divergence so wide and deep that the essential marriage is destroyed even though the shell of it remains. It takes more than staying together to keep a man and woman "faithful." To be faithful they must create and cherish mutual sympathies, mutual convictions, mutual aims. They will not do that if their individual desires and preferences get out of hand. Faith in one another and faithfulness toward one another depend upon a bond secured by something higher than either one. What minister has not heard the shabby story of the recriminations between a man and woman whose marriage has become a bitterness because one or both was selfishly obsessed to have his or her own way? The only road of faithfulness is when both are humbly and truly trying to walk God's way. Any preparation for marriage is hollow unless it is filled with that conviction.

The divergence between Isaac and Rebekah came out of their different regard for their two sons. **Isaac loved Esau . . . but Rebekah loved Jacob.** For that divided favoritism perhaps both Isaac and Rebekah were to blame, but Rebekah more aggressively so than Isaac. Her love for Jacob was so fiercely jealous that it broke loose from any larger loyalty. As between her twin sons, she wanted Jacob to have the best of everything, no matter how he got it; and to that end she would not scruple at trickery and unfairness both toward her husband and her son Esau. There was something of the tigress in

Rebekah, instinctively protecting the cub that by physical comparison was inferior. So she could come to the point of saying to Jacob even this: "Upon me be thy curse, my son: only obey my voice" (27:13).

Thus the Rebekah-of-the-well has become an altogether different woman: scheming for Jacob to steal the birthright, pushing both Esau and Isaac for the moment out of her regard, unscrupulous because one purpose only obsessed her. It was not that she wanted to hurt anybody, she might have said. It was just that she was so determined to do what she thought would help Jacob that she was blind to anything or anybody that might get hurt. And all the while what she was doing was in the name of love.

A study in character here, and of the way in which an emotion essentially beautiful may become perverted. It is instinctive and right that a woman should love passionately. But the greatest love must always be subject to a greater loyalty: loyalty to truth, to honor, to the relationship of life to God. Rebekah forgot that, and she corrupted Jacob as she tried to cherish him. As it is the passion of her love that can make a woman wonderful, so it is the failure to keep that love purified by the light of God that can make love ruinous. Jezebel is pictured as one of the evil women of the Bible, but it may be that originally she was not deliberately evil. She loved Ahab, proudly, fiercely, but with blind disregard for everything except what Ahab wanted; and see what she did to Ahab. Consider Lady Macbeth; read the story of Steerforth and his mother in *David Copperfield*. In every congregation there is a woman who is repeating the story of Rebekah—a mother

33 And Jacob said, Swear to me this day; and he sware unto him: and he sold his birthright unto Jacob.

34 Then Jacob gave Esau bread and pottage of lentils; and he did eat and drink, and rose up, and went his way. Thus Esau despised *his* birthright.

26 And there was a famine in the land, besides the first famine that was in the days of Abraham. And Isaac went unto Abimelech king of the Philistines unto Gerar.

33 Jacob said, "Swear to me first."[t] So he swore to him, and sold his birthright to Jacob. 34 Then Jacob gave Esau bread and pottage of lentils, and he ate and drank, and rose and went his way. Thus Esau despised his birthright.

26 Now there was a famine in the land, besides the former famine that was in the days of Abraham. And Isaac went to Gerar, to Abim'elech king of the

[t] Heb *today*

Nevertheless J¹, in including the tale in his narrative, was again insisting upon the values of the natural through which the supernatural works. Indeed, it may be said that this discernment of the values of the natural was one of the factors which enabled the spiritual leaders of Israel to raise their people from the level reflected in this tale to the conscious awareness of themselves as a holy nation.

34. Esau rose and went his way: With these words J¹ dismissed Esau from his narrative. J² had further stories to tell about him, however, and gave to **went his way** the meaning that he went about his business, not that he left Isaac's tent for good.

XXXV. Isaac, Rebekah, and Abimelech (26:1-33)

This story is basically from J¹ and is the earliest Israelite recension of the tale which appears also in 12:11-20 (J²) and in 20:1*b*-17 (E). It was thus originally told not of Abraham, but of Isaac. It boasts of the cleverness of Isaac in outwitting Abimelech and takes pride in the beauty and desirability of Isaac's wife. Like the tale in 25:27-31, it reflects a certain lusty nationalism in which considerations of morality had little place.

---

who secretly encourages her son in self-indulgence and extravagance, or presses her unworthy schemes in order that her daughter may be "a social success." She is expressing what she thinks is her devotion, but that does not make it the less demoralizing. What ought to be great qualities of heart can end in deadly hurtfulness if love is not purified and disciplined by principles that have come from God.

Yet even out of the unlovely chapter of Rebekah's life there emerges something fine. Why did Rebekah prefer Jacob? Was it because of a woman's insight which can be more sensitive to unseen values than a man is likely to be? Isaac preferred Esau, the bluff and virile son, the full-blooded and physically more attractive man. But Jacob, in spite of limitations and glaring faults, had something which Esau did not have. In the Hebrew family the birthright was at least in part a spiritual privilege. It meant that the holder of it would be a shaper of ideas and ideals. Esau, who lived mostly by the lusty dictates of his body, was indifferent to these; not so Jacob. He had a belief in spiritual destiny, dim and distorted at first, but nevertheless so stubborn that ultimately it would pre-

vail. Rebekah saw this, and she was determined to protect it.

Thus the thought of Rebekah ends like an unsolved equation. She represents the woman's greatest contribution to the race, viz., the ability to recognize and to cherish those qualities in her child by which the future may be shaped. In that primitive family she advanced her purpose by the stratagems of a relentless shrewdness that laid other loyalties aside. How can the relationship between husband and wife in this Christian Era be so developed that the insights of Rebekah may not have to stoop to dishonesty in order to be expressed?

26:1-6. *The Divine Overruling.*—Here again recurs the emphasis, so constant in Genesis, upon God's guidance of events, often not perceived, but always present. To Isaac it seemed as though the obviously sensible thing was to go down to Egypt. In the land where he found himself there was famine; in Egypt there would be food. Why stay where he was and be hungry, when he could go to Egypt and be satisfied? But in the crowded civilization of Egypt he and all that he represented would have been lost. God's purpose was that the

2 And the Lord appeared unto him, and said, Go not down into Egypt; dwell in the land which I shall tell thee of.

3 Sojourn in this land, and I will be with thee, and will bless thee; for unto thee, and unto thy seed, I will give all these countries, and I will perform the oath which I sware unto Abraham thy father;

4 And I will make thy seed to multiply as the stars of heaven, and will give unto thy seed all these countries; and in thy seed shall all the nations of the earth be blessed:

5 Because that Abraham obeyed my voice, and kept my charge, my commandments, my statutes, and my laws.

Philistines. 2 And the Lord appeared to him, and said, "Do not go down to Egypt; dwell in the land of which I shall tell you. 3 Sojourn in this land, and I will be with you, and will bless you; for to you and to your descendants I will give all these lands, and I will fulfill the oath which I swore to Abraham your father. 4 I will multiply your descendants as the stars of heaven, and will give to your descendants all these lands; and by your descendants all the nations of the earth shall bless themselves: 5 because Abraham obeyed my voice and kept my charge, my commandments, my statutes, and my laws."

Whether or not J[1] approved of the tale it is difficult to say—J[2] and E both reveal their uneasiness about it. The stories he tells about Jacob in his dealings with Laban rather suggest that, however insistent he may have been on the moral necessity of justice and decency between Israelite and Israelite, he was less concerned about moral standards in Israel's relations with other peoples. And, since in the tale Isaac's wife was never really in peril, he may have overlooked the possible consequences of Isaac's deception— another point at which the moral thinking of J[2] and E had advanced beyond that of J[1].

A. Deception of Abimelech (26:1-11)

26:1. Beside the former famine that was in the days of Abraham is an addition by J[2] to harmonize the story with his own recension. Isaac's starting point must have been Beer-lahai-roi (cf. 25:11*b*).

The **Philistines,** coming from the islands of the Aegean and the coasts of Asia Minor, were the leading people in a great invasion of Syria, *ca.* 1175 B.C., in the reign of Ramses III (Wright and Filson, *Westminster Atlas,* pp. 45-46). They established themselves on the coast of Palestine to the south and were still powerful at the time of J[1]. The mention of them here indicates that the present story is not an ancient legend current at Beer-sheba or Beer-lahai-roi in pre-Israelite times, i.e., before the advent of the Philistines, but is Israelite in its origin. It jeers at the supposed stupidity of the Philistines, just as the tale in 25:27-34 jeers at the nomad neighbors of Israel. It may be noted further that the relationship of Israel with the Philistines is again the theme of the Samson stories, which also contrast Israelite cleverness with Philistine stupidity though in a more somber vein.

To Gerar is an erroneous gloss—dependent perhaps on ch. 20—contradicting vs. 17, which records Isaac's arrival at Gerar after he had left Abimelech.

---

people of whom Isaac should be a progenitor must develop its destiny in a more rugged land. If Abraham's descendants had not stayed in Canaan, Israel as a people might never have emerged.

There is suggestion here for lives in every generation. Often there is the threat of some kind of famine. Sometimes it is physical famine; sometimes it is the subtler famine of what seems a lack of opportunity for ambition. Men may flinch from either, but some high purpose

in history would be frustrated if they do. The first pioneers of English civilization in the western continent were tempted to leave the hardships and dangers of Jamestown Island, and the Pilgrims at Plymouth were tempted to abandon their adventure after the dreadful winter when they laid the bodies of a large part of their company in the graves on Burial Hill; but history would have been different and poorer if they had not endured. So it may be also with individuals. Here is one in some post

6 ¶ And Isaac dwelt in Gerar.

7 And the men of the place asked *him* of his wife; and he said, She *is* my sister: for he feared to say, *She is* my wife; lest, *said he,* the men of the place should kill me for Rebekah; because she *was* fair to look upon.

8 And it came to pass, when he had been there a long time, that Abimelech king of the Philistines looked out at a window, and saw, and, behold, Isaac *was* sporting with Rebekah his wife.

9 And Abimelech called Isaac, and said, Behold, of a surety she *is* thy wife: and how saidst thou, She *is* my sister? And Isaac said unto him, Because I said, Lest I die for her.

10 And Abimelech said, What *is* this thou hast done unto us? one of the people might lightly have lain with thy wife, and thou shouldest have brought guiltiness upon us.

6 So Isaac dwelt in Gerar. 7 When the men of the place asked him about his wife, he said, "She is my sister"; for he feared to say, "My wife," thinking, "lest the men of the place should kill me for the sake of Rebekah"; because she was fair to look upon. 8 When he had been there a long time, Abim'elech king of the Philistines looked out of a window and saw Isaac fondling Rebekah his wife. 9 So Abim'elech called Isaac, and said, "Behold, she is your wife; how then could you say, 'She is my sister'?" Isaac said to him, "Because I thought, 'Lest I die because of her.'" 10 Abim'elech said, "What is this you have done to us? One of the people might easily have lain with your wife, and you would

---

6. The mention of **Gerar** is again secondary. It may have displaced the name of another locality, but more probably J¹ contented himself with the statement that **Isaac went . . . to Abimelech king of the Philistines** (vs. 1*b*).

7. In the first half of the verse Isaac's wife is not named. Since this is the first reference to her in J¹, the inference (cf. 25:21*a*) is that in that document her name was not given. The second half of the verse, awkward because of the use of the first person—**thinking** is not in the Hebrew—is an addition, dependent on 12:12. Thus, in this recension Isaac represented his wife as his sister simply to find out how stupid the Philistines might be.

8. The Hebrew of the word rendered **fondling** is from the same root and so is a wordplay on **Isaac. Rebekah** is an intrusion by J².

10. What is this you have done to us? is an expression of indignation which comes too late in the recorded conversation. Furthermore, Isaac's explanation in vs. 9 depends

---

where conscience tells him he ought to be, but he is beginning to grow dissatisfied. He looks across the borders of his life and sees other men more comfortable and prosperous than he. Why not pull up stakes and try his fortune in their Egypt? In the immediate calculations of common sense, that might seem to be the thing to do. So at moments it has seemed to many a man or woman working in a settlement in some discouraging city slum; to a teacher in an ill-equipped country school; to the minister in what might be called an unimportant parish; to the missionary in a lonely post. They may be developing in themselves and communicating to others qualities of character which will enrich the whole future of the community they serve. They cannot see that now. It is hard to believe

that there is any reality except the reality of famine. Yet they stay where they are, their hearts held by a compulsion which is the unseen hand of God. Like a great man and schoolmaster of the nineteenth century, they may say at last: "How strange life is! How little one knows what is best! Life is best, the living the day manfully, truly, and humbly. Not what we plan, but how we live. Not what we aim at doing, but how we do what we have to do—that is God's life." [1]

6-17. *God's Watchfulness.*— (See Expos. on 12:11-20; ch. 20.) In these verses there seems to be another variant of a traditional story that had to do first with Abraham, but now is at-

[1] G. R. Parkin, *Edward Thring* (London: Macmillan & Co., 1900), p. 366.

11 And Abimelech charged all *his* people, saying, He that toucheth this man or his wife shall surely be put to death.

12 Then Isaac sowed in that land, and received in the same year a hundredfold: and the Lord blessed him.

13 And the man waxed great, and went forward, and grew until he became very great:

14 For he had possession of flocks, and possession of herds, and great store of servants: and the Philistines envied him.

15 For all the wells which his father's servants had digged in the days of Abraham his father, the Philistines had stopped them, and filled them with earth.

16 And Abimelech said unto Isaac, Go from us; for thou art much mightier than we.

have brought guilt upon us." 11 So Abim'elech warned all the people, saying, "Whoever touches this man or his wife shall be put to death."

12 And Isaac sowed in that land, and reaped in the same year a hundredfold. The Lord blessed him, 13 and the man became rich, and gained more and more until he became very wealthy. 14 He had possessions of flocks and herds, and a great household, so that the Philistines envied him. 15 (Now the Philistines had stopped and filled with earth all the wells which his father's servants had dug in the days of Abraham his father.) 16 And Abim'elech said to Isaac, "Go away from us; for you are much mightier than we."

---

upon the secondary material in vs. 7. Vss. 9*b*, 10*a* thus have the appearance of being an insertion to bring this recension of the tale more into line with those of J² and E. With their removal the somewhat raucous tone of the narrative is recovered.

11. As a result of his cleverness Isaac now receives special protection.

It would thus appear that the theme of this, the original recension of this tale, was Israelite cleverness. Isaac was not trying to save himself at the cost of danger to his wife; he was simply showing up the gullibleness of the Philistines. The story hangs together loosely as though the narrator were in a hurry to reach the point and go on. Abimelech himself is not involved and, indeed, seems to have been brought in for the sole purpose of providing undeserved protection for Isaac so that he could proceed to amass wealth, as described in the section following.

J², not understanding that he was dealing with an earthy piece of humor on a somewhat low level and taking too seriously the startled remonstrance of Abimelech, **One of the people might easily have lain with your wife** (vs. 10), was troubled by the story. Apparently he could not ignore it because of its popularity—witness the fact that it was carried over to Abraham. He accordingly tried, not too successfully, to mitigate the conduct of the patriarch. Nevertheless, he represents Abraham as being expelled from Egypt for it.

E was less sensitive. Possibly he was nearer to J¹ than he was to J², thinking that foreigners were fair game. He does make a feeble attempt to maintain that Abraham had not really lied because Sarah was actually his half sister. Apart from this, however, he reveals no moral concern; instead, Abraham is materially benefited as a result of the affair (cf. 20:14-15). Indeed, E's attitude toward the story is one of the more puzzling problems in Genesis. The fact that, apart from the fragment preserved in 16:13-14, the story in ch. 20 is the beginning of the extant E material tempts one to speculate whether E may not have represented the episode as having occurred before Abraham's call.

B. Dispute Concerning the Wells (26:12-31)

12-31. This section is basically from J¹. The J² and E recensions of the story—in both of which Abraham, not Isaac, is the hero—are preserved, conflated, in 21:22-33.

Vss. 15, 18 are from J² or RJE, harmonizing the story with 21:25. In vs. 23 the mention of **Beer-sheba** is awkward in view of the notice in vs. 33 that the place received

17 ¶ And Isaac departed thence, and pitched his tent in the valley of Gerar, and dwelt there.

18 And Isaac digged again the wells of water, which they had digged in the days of Abraham his father; for the Philistines had stopped them after the death of Abraham: and he called their names after the names by which his father had called them.

19 And Isaac's servants digged in the valley, and found there a well of springing water.

20 And the herdmen of Gerar did strive with Isaac's herdmen, saying, The water *is* ours: and he called the name of the well Esek; because they strove with him.

17 So Isaac departed from there, and encamped in the valley of Gerar and dwelt there. **18** And Isaac dug again the wells of water which had been dug in the days of Abraham his father; for the Philistines had stopped them after the death of Abraham; and he gave them the names which his father had given them. **19** But when Isaac's servants dug in the valley and found there a well of springing water, **20** the herdsmen of Gerar quarreled with Isaac's herdsmen, saying, "The water is ours." So he called the name of the well Esek,ᵘ because they con-

ᵘ That is *Contention*

---

its name only after Isaac had dug a well there. J¹ must therefore have given a less explicit designation of the locality. For this J², for whom Beer-sheba had already been

---

tached to Isaac. The apparent purpose in the other versions, to set forth God's watchfulness over and blessings upon those who were his own, is less clearly evident here, though it is suggested in vss. 12-14.

18. The True Conservatism.—Here is more than a particular incident. Here is an enduring parable. In what sense did Isaac's action illustrate the meaning and the value of the conservative spirit? Isaac was turning back to what were proven wells. There might be other oases if he looked for them, but here were those he knew. So in the field of religion there are some things which have been proved. Life does not begin anew with any generation. We are heirs of a long past: in culture and experience; in lessons learned about life, man, God, and duty; in knowledge of which experiences lead to soundness and which to sickness of the soul. The rebellion of immaturity which turns away from the old springs of knowledge and faith may be dangerous. As Jowett of Baliol said, "We are none of us infallible, not even the youngest." Isaac had sense enough to know that what his father had found to be good would be good for him.

The wells of Abraham were not only proven wells: they would be easier to draw from than new wells would. It is true that the Philistines had done their worst to spoil them by flinging in them earth and stones. Yet it would take less labor to clear these wells than to dig wells in hard, new ground. So it is in uncovering the waters from which faith has already drunk. Sometimes a new generation comes to the old wells and is annoyed because they seem to be

uselessly choked. The living waters of religious meaning seem blocked by old dogmas and disputes. Some people desert the church because they find it cluttered up with petty things. But the waters of God can flow again where they used to flow. The sensible thing is to come with honesty and patience to help clear away the stodgy ideas and the inconsistencies which have got into religious institutions and let the waters of God flow free again.

The wells of the fathers are the wells which are rich in sentiment. When Isaac went back to where he had been with Abraham, old memories awoke. The water he drank there slaked the thirst not only of his body but of his spirit. Old associations may awake again those emotions which belonged to life when it was most sensitive and pure. "The old oaken bucket that hung in the well" can mean more than the shiniest new faucet (see II Sam. 23:15-17, with its story of David longing for the water that was by the gate of Bethlehem). So the best men in their best moments will turn back yearningly to recapture the faith they learned from their mothers, the principles ingrained in a religious home, the everyday goodness of men and women who were their neighbors in some little town, the first response to the reality of religion which some simple man of God in a village church aroused in them. Life may make many experiments and excursions, but it can never dispense with the conservative instinct that comes back to drink again from the father's wells.

19-22. Peace After Strife.—From the portrayal in Genesis, Isaac appears as a milder and more pacific man than most of the O.T. figures. For

21 And they digged another well, and strove for that also: and he called the name of it Sitnah.

22 And he removed from thence, and digged another well; and for that they strove not: and he called the name of it Rehoboth; and he said, For now the LORD hath made room for us, and we shall be fruitful in the land.

23 And he went up from thence to Beer-sheba.

tended with him. 21 Then they dug another well, and they quarreled over that also; so he called its name Sitnah.ᵛ 22 And he moved from there and dug another well, and over that they did not quarrel; so he called its name Reho'both,ʷ saying, "For now the LORD has made room for us, and we shall be fruitful in the land."

23 From there he went up to Beer-sheba.

ᵛ That is Enmity
ʷ That is Broad places or Room

named (21:31), substituted Beer-sheba and added vss. 24-25aαβ. The original author would scarcely have recorded that Isaac **built an altar** before he **pitched his tent** (vs. 25).

anyone who had to move his flocks here and there in a land where water was scarce, wells were vital. Patiently Isaac had dug again Abraham's old wells which the Philistines had tried to destroy. The herdsmen of Gerar twice disputed his possession of them, and twice Isaac moved away. As he left the first well, he named it **Esek**, which means **Contention**; and as he left the second, he named it **Sitnah**, which means **Enmity**. To the third well the herdsmen of Gerar did not follow, and he named that **Rehoboth**, which means **Enlargement**, and he said, **For now the LORD hath made room for us, and we shall be fruitful in the land.**

The earth is more crowded than it was in the days of Isaac. We live in the time of "the vanished frontier." It is not so possible to move magnanimously from one place of opportunity that someone else may have it, and find another one farther on. Nevertheless, there is a sense in which every good man's life must seek to be like that of Isaac, in that it does not want stubbornly to maintain itself at the place of contention or strife, but will seek the place where not only possessions but all peaceful happiness can be enlarged. It is interesting to note that later verses of this same chapter tell of a visit to Isaac of Abimelech with the chief captain of his army, but they did not come to fight. On the contrary, they came to say: "We saw certainly that the Lord was with thee: and we said, Let there be now an oath betwixt us, even betwixt us and thee, and let us make a covenant with thee" (vs. 28). There was long time and far space of understanding between Isaac at his well and the Teacher by the Sea of Galilee; but in the spirit of Isaac one may see a foregleam of him who said, "Whosoever shall compel thee to go a mile, go with him twain" (Matt. 5:41); and also a hint of the promise that "the meek . . . shall inherit the earth" (Matt. 5:5).

23-24. The Faith a Man Inherits.—Here for the first time appear the words which are to echo and re-echo in the Bible—**the God of Abraham**. The full reality of God no language can describe. "I AM THAT I AM." But the meaning of God for any generation may be largely determined by what the preceding generation has known. Isaac's consciousness of God did not have to wait to grow out of his own unhelped experience. His father had made the thought of God a fact in life since as far back as he could remember. Religion had been part of the atmosphere he breathed, and worship would have for him always the living warmth of its association with his father.

This is not an indispensable condition for the growth of religious consciousness. God can and does reveal himself directly and anew to an individual human soul, and no revelation avails unless the individual accepts it for himself. But knowledge of God and love of him have a long start when they come warm and living through the example of some person whom a younger one has looked up to and loved. Here is the high and solemn responsibility of parenthood. It is a hollow business when all that a father gives his son is perfunctory acknowledgment of the supposed worth of religion which is not real to him.

Think on the other hand of the enrichment which comes to a son when God is to him first of all "my father's God." **The God of Abraham:** from the beginning the Jewish people understood that and built their life upon it. Religious instruction of a son was not left to chance. In early and formative years it was the clear and definite duty of his father. At best of course it is more than duty; it is desire and devotion. Think of some of those who have exemplified what a father can do to give his son a spiritual inheritance for which he will

24 And the Lord appeared unto him the same night, and said, I *am* the God of Abraham thy father: fear not, for I *am* with thee, and will bless thee, and multiply thy seed for my servant Abraham's sake.

25 And he builded an altar there, and called upon the name of the Lord, and

24 And the Lord appeared to him the same night and said, "I am the God of Abraham your father; fear not, for I am with you and will bless you and multiply your descendants for my servant Abraham's sake." 25 So he built an altar there and called upon the

---

In vs. 26 **from Gerar** is redactional, cf. vs. 1*b*. For J[1], Abimelech was not king of Gerar, but simply king of the Philistines. Abimelech's statement in vs. 29, **We . . . have done to**

---

be forever thankful. Religious inheritance which is transmitted first through individuals and through families may become embodied in a nation. Consider the immeasurable results in history of the fact that for the Jewish race the God to be worshiped and obeyed was **the God of Abraham**—the God reflected in a great soul whose quality was righteousness. Because the God of Israel was the God interpreted by a man like that, the religion that stems from the O.T. has always had a singular loftiness of ethical ideals and tenacity of moral principle. Consider the contrast between **the God of Abraham** and the adulterous deities of the Greek Olympus, or the gods represented in the degrading images of Hindu temples. Modern nations which owe the best of their moral substance to the Judaeo-Christian heritage have critical need to consider whether that substance is being dissipated by laxity and carelessness. A nation which no longer has such principles to stand by will disintegrate; and only as it passes on great convictions to its children and its children's children is it strong. The psalmists understood that (Ps. 105). Remember too the words in the Litany of the Book of Common Prayer, "O God we have heard with our ears, and our fathers have declared unto us, the noble works that thou didst in their days, and in the old time before them."

As the O.T. goes on, the words **the God of Abraham** are expanded. In the record of Moses' vision of the burning bush (Exod. 3:15) it is written that "God said moreover unto Moses, Thus shalt thou say unto the children of Israel, the Lord God of your fathers, the God of Abraham, the God of Isaac, and the God of Jacob, hath sent me unto you." Prophets of Israel, seeking to proclaim God with most majestic and comprehensive meaning, would name his name with a wider reference than this first one in Genesis. Elijah in his contests with the priests of Baal calls upon the "Lord God of Abraham, Isaac, and of Israel" (I Kings 18:36).

The significance of God is not only that he

inspired one great man; he inspired and inspires men of different sorts, and the greatness of his godhood is that it can thus be a power on many levels of life. Abraham the heroic man, Isaac the inconspicuous man, Jacob the inconsistent man—all had their part in revealing the many-faceted light of the divine as it shines into human souls. There are not many Abrahams. They have their priceless worth—the spiritual pioneers, the channels of new revelation, the great men of vision and of action, and history is ennobled because of them. But by themselves they can never constitute society. God must manifest himself in the quiet men like Isaac, who make up the great majority. He must manifest himself, too, in the men of warring impulses, like Jacob—the men for whom it is not easy to be good but who let the purifying forces so work upon them that they grow better. The God who is seen in Abraham *and* Isaac *and* Jacob is a God who brings to human hearts more assurance and more comfort than one who might have been known only as **the God of Abraham.**

Here is a truth which has rich application to every group of would-be religious people, and here is happy stimulus for those whose privilege it is to minister to them. Often when people listen to what is preached about God they may be left wistful. They begin to think that perhaps only specially endowed persons can hope to be in touch with God. But the great truth is otherwise. The reflection of God is never finished. The glory of his manifested meaning can be increased by all the little growing goodnesses inspired in the humble men and women of every ordinary congregation.

25. The Essentials of Life.—This single sentence has a larger suggestion than is contained in the facts so tersely stated. Here is only the bare catalogue of what Isaac did on a particular day. But note the deeper implications in the three nouns: **an altar, a tent,** and **a well**—and the altar first. With Isaac, as with Israel in all its history, God was no afterthought. A stage in

pitched his tent there: and there Isaac's servants digged a well.

26 ¶ Then Abimelech went to him from Gerar, and Ahuzzath one of his friends, and Phichol the chief captain of his army.

27 And Isaac said unto them, Wherefore come ye to me, seeing ye hate me, and have sent me away from you?

28 And they said, We saw certainly that the LORD was with thee: and we said, Let there be now an oath betwixt us, *even* betwixt us and thee, and let us make a covenant with thee;

name of the LORD, and pitched his tent there. And there Isaac's servants dug a well.

26 Then Abim'elech went to him from Gerar with Ahuz'zath his adviser and Phicol the commander of his army. 27 Isaac said to them, "Why have you come to me, seeing that you hate me and have sent me away from you?" 28 They said, "We see plainly that the LORD is with you; so we say, let there be an oath between you and us, and

---

you nothing but good and have sent you away in peace refers to vss. 1-17 and ignores vss. 19-21, indicating that for J¹ the Gerarites were not even subjects of Abimelech.

The original narrative thus tells of Isaac's moving from the realm of Abimelech to Gerar (vs. 17). There he had trouble with the Gerarites over certain wells (vss. 18-21), and moved to Rehoboth—probably the modern er-Ruhaibeh, about twenty miles

---

a journey, a place of abiding, must be linked with a new commitment of life. Existence was not secular, but lifted up always to a religious reference. Isaac was expressing here the inherited impulse which he had received from his father Abraham and which gave to Abraham his greatness. The careers of many men, ancient and modern, judged by this world's measurements, might seem immensely more important and impressive than that of either Abraham or Isaac. They deal with more intricate affairs, have more possessions, play their parts in a vastly more elaborate civilization. They have so much that they tend to think they are self-sufficient, and that their own immediate ambitions are enough to give direction to every day. God may be only occasionally in their consciousness. How different is the O.T. picture! Here are men with whom prayer comes ahead of their own particular devices. If any part of life was to be worth something, it must begin with worship.

And Isaac pitched his tent. Within that the life of a family was sheltered. In one aspect, all that went on there was commonplace enough. Everyday human needs had to be provided for through the routine of ordinary work. The building of an altar could not obviate that, nor contact with the spiritual world take men out of this one. But what Israel remembered was that family life—its duties, loyalties, and affections—needed always to be under the protection of the altar. Consider further the significance of what it was that Isaac dwelt in. He had no house, solid and comfortable, such as men today normally desire. He lived in a tent.

That contrasting fact suggests a consciousness possessed by men of the O.T. which modern life may lack. They were not rooted in material things, but "confessed that they were strangers and pilgrims on the earth" (Heb. 11:13). In the civilization of today, complex and materially rich, there is danger that men may be so satisfied with what they already possess that they do not reach forward to that spiritual communion which pilgrim souls would seek to gain. Yet in the scale of the eternal values the great man is he who knows that life is a pilgrimage, and for whom the words of the old hymn are commanding:

> Yet nightly pitch my moving tent,
> A day's march nearer home.[2]

The third thing related to Isaac was the **well.** The well was essential for existence. Out of it must come the water to slake the thirst of men and cattle; and because of it there could be an oasis of growth and shade. Without water, physical life would end. But all through the Bible water is a symbol for the satisfaction of a deeper thirst. "As the hart panteth after the water brooks, so panteth my soul after thee, O God" (Ps. 42:1). And the promise of the Bible is that as God has given the wells for men's physical needs, so he gives to those who seek them the wells of the spirit. "Ho, every one that thirsteth, come ye to the waters" (Isa. 55:1). "The water that I shall give him shall be in him a well of water springing up into everlasting life" (John 4:14).

26-33. See Expos. on vss. 19-22.

[2] James Montgomery, "Forever with the Lord."

29 That thou wilt do us no hurt, as we have not touched thee, and as we have done unto thee nothing but good, and have sent thee away in peace: thou *art* now the blessed of the LORD.

30 And he made them a feast, and they did eat and drink.

31 And they rose up betimes in the morning, and sware one to another: and Isaac sent them away, and they departed from him in peace.

32 And it came to pass the same day, that Isaac's servants came, and told him concerning the well which they had digged, and said unto him, We have found water.

33 And he called it Shebah: therefore the name of the city *is* Beer-sheba unto this day.

let us make a covenant with you, **29** that you will do us no harm, just as we have not touched you and have done to you nothing but good and have sent you away in peace. You are now the blessed of the LORD." **30** So he made them a feast, and they ate and drank. **31** In the morning they rose early and took oath with one another; and Isaac set them on their way, and they departed from him in peace. **32** That same day Isaac's servants came and told him about the well which they had dug, and said to him, "We have found water." **33** He called it Shibah; therefore the name of the city is Beer-sheba to this day.

---

southwest of Beer-sheba—where his possession of the well he dug was not disputed (vs. 22). Thence he moved northward again (vs. 23, 25aγb), and came once more into contact with Abimelech, with whom he made a covenant (vss. 26-31). The same day his servants found water, and he named the place Beer-sheba (vss. 32-33).

It is probable that J¹, following vs. 33, recorded that Isaac built an altar and called upon the name of the Lord, thus explicitly crediting him with the inauguration of the cult of Beer-sheba. If so, the notice was dropped by J² when he inserted vss. 24-25aαβ.

The story voices an Israelite claim to Rehoboth (vs. 22), if not to ownership of two other wells, Esek (vs. 20), and Sitnah (vs. 21), and reflects the continual concern for water in the desert. The account of the covenant with Abimelech may well echo an actual agreement between the inhabitants of Beer-sheba and the neighboring Philistines.

C. ISAAC AT BEER-SHEBA (26:32-33)

32-33. With vss. 1-11 the account of the covenant with Abimelech also records Isaac's migration from Beer-lahai-roi to Beer-sheba. In this way J¹ accounted for the fact that Isaac was connected with two sanctuaries. Such a dual association would seem to indicate that some clans actually did migrate from Beer-lahai-roi, carrying with them certain of its traditions, including that of Isaac, to Beer-sheba. (It is of course possible that these clans were not Israelite, i.e., that the association of Isaac of Beer-lahai-roi with Beer-sheba antedated the Israelite occupation.) The memory of the move was part of the tradition of Beer-sheba which J¹, it has been noted, related to the tradition of Hebron by making Isaac of Beer-lahai-roi and Beer-sheba the son of Abraham.

In J², as has been seen, the process is carried a step further in that Abraham, not Isaac, is represented as the founder of Beer-sheba (21:33); and the other stories told about Isaac in this chapter are transferred to Abraham (12:11-20; and the J² strand of 21:22-33). This may have been the work of J² himself; more probably, however, it reflects the development of the tradition of Beer-sheba in the century which elapsed between J¹ and J².

It may be noted once again that J¹'s relating of Isaac to Abraham was no mere manipulation of diverse traditions. Rather it reflects the unifying power of Yahwism and was a necessary step in the direction of a monotheism which was something more than an affirmation about God. Israelite monotheism, religious rather than speculative, aimed always at, and achieved to a remarkable degree, unification of life under the one God, Yahweh.

34 ¶ And Esau was forty years old when he took to wife Judith the daughter of Beeri the Hittite, and Bashemath the daughter of Elon the Hittite:
35 Which were a grief of mind unto Isaac and to Rebekah.

27 And it came to pass, that when Isaac was old, and his eyes were dim, so that he could not see, he called Esau his

34 When Esau was forty years old, he took to wife Judith the daughter of Be-e'ri the Hittite, and Bas'emath the daughter of Elon the Hittite; 35 and they made life bitter for Isaac and Rebekah.

27 When Isaac was old and his eyes were dim so that he could not see, he

---

XXXVI. JACOB AND ESAU II (26:34–28:9)

A. ESAU'S MARRIAGES (26:34-35)

34-35. The section is from P, leading up to 28:1-9. The implication is that Esau did not inherit the promise because he had taken foreign wives. The verses are thus the P parallel to 25:21-26a; 25:27-34; 27:1-40.

B. JACOB SECURES HIS FATHER'S BLESSING (27:1-40)

This is a conflation of the J² and E recensions of a story telling how Jacob secured for himself the blessing which his father had intended to bestow upon his first-born and favorite son Esau.

The purpose of the story is, like that in 25:27-34, to explain the relative positions of the Israelites and the Edomites. It further resembles the earlier story in that it is probably based upon a piece of crass folk humor, a tale showing the ease with which the clever seminomad could outwit the simple desert dweller. By the introduction of the

---

34-35. *Xenophobia.*—When Esau married two Hittite girls, what offended Isaac and Rebekah was not that they were two, but that they were Hittites. Plural marriages were neither uncommon nor unacceptable to the standards of the time, but to marry outside the clan was to mix its blood and to break its solidarity. That is why these Hittite daughters-in-law **were a grief of mind unto Isaac and to Rebekah.**

Determination to maintain what is called the purity of a people's blood may spring only from an arrogant and arbitrary sense of superiority, and may be put forward with fantastic claims—such as in Houston Stewart Chamberlain's defense of German megalomania in *The Foundations of the Nineteenth Century,*[3] or in Madison Grant's diatribe against those who would tolerate the weakening of the Anglo-Saxon empire, in *The Passing of the Great Race.*[4] Unreasoning instinct may be at the root of the **grief of mind** which accompanies any idea of alliance with aliens. So in part it was with Isaac and Rebekah, and with the people of Israel through its later history; e.g., consider the feelings which underlie the book of Esther. But there was another factor in Israel which tended to lift what might have been only a fierce instinctive separatism to a higher level of emotion. That was the passionate conviction

[3] Tr. from the German by John Lees (London: J. Lane, 1911).
[4] New York: Charles Scribner's Sons, 1923.

that Israel was meant to be not only a nation, but a theocracy. To maintain its racial integrity therefore was to maintain the religious institution of covenant and law and holy faith. That purpose shines through what otherwise would have seemed the inflexible and cruel judgment of Nehemiah against those in Jerusalem who had married out of Jewry, when he "contended with them, and cursed them, and smote certain of them," and compelled them to put away their alien wives (Neh. 13:25). It shines more nobly through the heroic struggle of the Maccabees, who fought to the death against the foreigners who defiled the temple and threatened all that was distinctive of the Jewish soul. But there was a still higher level to which the thought of Israel was to rise. Not only could it give to its exclusiveness a religious meaning; at its highest it could transcend exclusiveness. Read the story of Jonah; consider the lovely outreach of the book of Ruth; and meditate upon the conception of a saving remnant in Israel that should be the suffering servant, of whom it might be said that "he hath poured out his soul unto death; . . . he bare the sin of many, and made intercession for the transgressors" (Isa. 53:12).

27:1-4. *Dignity in Age.*—In Isaac's words there is a curious blending of the earthy and the spiritual. Isaac is thinking of something that he particularly wants to eat, and his affection for Esau is linked with the fact that Esau

names of Isaac, Jacob, and Esau, J2—or the tradition upon which he depended—gave it an ethnographical significance.

The story does not advance in any way the earlier J1 account of the relations between Jacob and Esau. J2's inclusion of it in his narrative can be due only to its popularity, and is a further indication of the extent to which he was responsive to the tastes of those for whom he was writing. There is in his recension no shadow of condemnation of Jacob's action, and the only possible indication that he was at all uneasy about it is the role played by Rebekah (see below). It is not until the account of Jacob's meeting with Esau is reached in ch. 33 that we find signs of his disapproval.

But if he included the tale under necessity, he put it to good use. J1, when he told of Jacob's going to "the land of the people of the east" (29:1), had left his journey unmotivated. In J2's narrative it is motivated by Jacob's fear that Esau would revenge himself upon him for the trick recorded in this story.

Though the two recensions of the tale are in absolute agreement in that both represent Jacob as deceiving his dying father and obtaining his blessing, they differ, sometimes significantly, at certain points:

(a) J2 speaks of **game**, E of **savory food** (vs. 3); this may be due merely to the fact that the word rendered **game**—literally, "that which is hunted"—is used in a slightly different form in other parts of E, with the meaning "provisions" (cf. 42:25; 45:21; Exod. 12:39; Josh. 1:11; 9:11).

(b) J2 has Jacob carry through the deception by wearing Esau's **best garments** (vs. 15)—the derisive implication being that Esau "smelled to high heaven," so that even his best clothes were odoriferous. E makes use of another motif: Esau was hairy—a wordplay on Seir (cf. 25:25)—like a goat; Jacob therefore put goat skins on his hands and neck so that his blind father, feeling him, thought he was Esau. This difference, it may be assumed, represents the embellishment the tale had received in the north in the two centuries which elapsed between J2 and E.

(c) Both recensions represent Rebekah as the real author of the plan to deceive Isaac (cf. vss. 5a, 15 [J2]; vss. 8-14, 16-17 [E]), but E is at special pains to stress Jacob's unwillingness to fall in with the scheme. This suggests that by E's time the tale had come to be regarded as morally objectionable, so an attempt was made to lessen the embarrassment it caused by shifting the blame from Jacob to Rebekah, who, being a woman, might be expected to act in a questionable manner, and whose reputation, for the same reason, was of less concern to her descendants. This, it may be noted, is one of the many attempts—significant in that they reflect a heightening of moral sensitivity—made by E to rehabilitate the reputations of the patriarchs: cf. his partial justification of Abraham in 20:12, and his treatment of the whole Jacob-Laban story, discussed below.

(d) J2 represents the deception as being carried through without difficulty; Isaac asks no questions, he smells the clothes Jacob is wearing, and blesses him (vss. 25-27, 29aαβb); only when Esau appears upon the scene does Isaac bewilderedly realize that he has been deceived (vss. 32-33a). E is more appreciative of the difficulties involved. He has Jacob raise the question as to the feasibility of his mother's plan (vss. 11-12). depicts Isaac as suspicious from the first (vss. 21-22), and represents him as realizing what had happened immediately after Esau came in (vs. 35).

---

is the one who can get it for him. Thus far he was like many human beings, whose interests seem to center in the body; but he was different in that he had no illusions about that body. He did not try to ignore the fact that he was growing old and that he must prepare to die. Numberless people do try to ignore both—or try to hide what grows impossible to ignore. Witness the women obsessed with all the pitiful modern devices which they try to think will disguise their age. And as for facing the end of life, a director of the British Broadcasting Corporation has remarked that he had listened to over six hundred radioed sermons, and only one of them had had anything to say about death. Often one may read with surprise that some person he knows has died without leaving a will, or with a will that is obviously out of date; but it need not be surprising, for it is only one more evidence of the fact of men's reluctance to come

eldest son, and said unto him, My son: and he said unto him, Behold, *here am* I.

2 And he said, Behold now, I am old, I know not the day of my death:

3 Now therefore take, I pray thee, thy weapons, thy quiver and thy bow, and go out to the field, and take me *some* venison;

4 And make me savory meat, such as I love, and bring *it* to me, that I may eat; that my soul may bless thee before I die.

5 And Rebekah heard when Isaac spake to Esau his son. And Esau went to the field to hunt *for* venison, *and* to bring *it*.

6 ¶ And Rebekah spake unto Jacob her son, saying, Behold, I heard thy father speak unto Esau thy brother, saying,

7 Bring me venison, and make me savory meat, that I may eat, and bless thee before the LORD before my death.

8 Now therefore, my son, obey my voice according to that which I command thee.

9 Go now to the flock, and fetch me from thence two good kids of the goats; and I will make them savory meat for thy father, such as he loveth:

10 And thou shalt bring *it* to thy father, that he may eat, and that he may bless thee before his death.

called Esau his older son, and said to him, "My son"; and he answered, "Here I am." 2 He said, "Behold, I am old; I do not know the day of my death. 3 Now then, take your weapons, your quiver and your bow, and go out to the field, and hunt game for me, 4 and prepare for me savory food, such as I love, and bring it to me that I may eat; that I may bless you before I die."

5 Now Rebekah was listening when Isaac spoke to his son Esau. So when Esau went to the field to hunt for game and bring it, 6 Rebekah said to her son Jacob, "I heard your father speak to your brother Esau, 7 'Bring me game, and prepare for me savory food, that I may eat it, and bless you before the LORD before I die.' 8 Now therefore, my son, obey my word as I command you. 9 Go to the flock, and fetch me two good kids, that I may prepare from them savory food for your father, such as he loves; 10 and you shall bring it to your father to eat, so that he may bless you be-

---

(*e*) According to J2, Esau received no blessing; his request for one (vs. 34) was received by his father in silence, as is indicated by the words "and Isaac was silent" occurring in some LXX MSS at the end of vs. 38*a*. J2 thus reflects the complete subservience of Edom to Israel at the time the story took form (cf. II Sam. 8:14). By the time E wrote, Edom was again independent (cf. II Kings 8:20-22), so he tells of Isaac blessing Esau, though in somewhat ambiguous terms (vss. 39-40).

27:1. Isaac's blindness is of course crucial to both recensions of the story. The close connection of the blessing and the eating, insisted on in both recensions, rests upon some religious notion—possibly as Holzinger (*Genesis,* p. 180) suggests, that the desired prophetic utterance would be induced by the physical stimulus (cf. I Sam. 10:5-6; II Kings 3:15-17); possibly that of a sacrificial meal establishing communion with the Deity (Gunkel, *Genesis,* p. 309).

4. The implication of **that my soul may bless thee before I die** (KJV) is that Isaac is on his deathbed. *Néphesh,* soul, here bears the meaning of the totality of the person's power (Pedersen, *Israel I-II,* pp. 99-112; see RSV). Strengthened by the meal, the soul

---

to grips with the uncertainty and shortness of life. And when men do make their wills, what is generally the substance of their testament? Property. They specify what is to be the division of their money, their real estate, and other material assets; and beyond that they may have no more to say. But the words of Isaac have a larger suggestion. The end of what he had to say to Esau was **that my soul may bless thee**

before I die. How many fathers have a spiritual testament which above all else they want to pass on to their sons?

5-17. *Rebekah and Jacob.*—When Jacob had managed to bargain Esau out of his birthright, he had acted alone; now his mother is the moving spirit. Where Jacob's interests were at stake, she had a cleverness and a determination that rose completely to meet the occasion. When

11 And Jacob said to Rebekah his mother, Behold, Esau my brother *is* a hairy man, and I *am* a smooth man:

12 My father peradventure will feel me, and I shall seem to him as a deceiver; and I shall bring a curse upon me, and not a blessing.

13 And his mother said unto him, Upon me *be* thy curse, my son: only obey my voice, and go fetch me *them*.

14 And he went, and fetched, and brought *them* to his mother: and his mother made savory meat, such as his father loved.

15 And Rebekah took goodly raiment of her eldest son Esau, which *were* with her in the house, and put them upon Jacob her younger son:

16 And she put the skins of the kids of the goats upon his hands, and upon the smooth of his neck:

17 And she gave the savory meat and the bread, which she had prepared, into the hand of her son Jacob.

fore he dies." 11 But Jacob said to Rebekah his mother, "Behold, my brother Esau is a hairy man, and I am a smooth man. 12 Perhaps my father will feel me, and I shall seem to be mocking him, and bring a curse upon myself and not a blessing." 13 His mother said to him, "Upon me be your curse, my son; only obey my word, and go, fetch them to me." 14 So he went and took them and brought them to his mother; and his mother prepared savory food, such as his father loved. 15 Then Rebekah took the best garments of Esau her older son, which were with her in the house, and put them on Jacob her younger son; 16 and the skins of the kids she put upon his hands and upon the smooth part of his neck; 17 and she gave the savory food and the bread, which she had prepared, into the hand of her son Jacob.

is to pour out all its dynamic force in one last prophetic act. The belief in the peculiar efficacy of the utterance of a dying man finds frequent expression in the O.T. (48:10-20; 49:1-28; 50:24; Deut. 33; Josh. 23; II Sam. 23:1-7; I Kings 2:1-4; II Kings 13:14-19). It approximated the divine word which carried in it the power of its own fulfillment (cf. Isa. 55:11; Jer. 23:29) —such was the solemnity of death.

13. A dying man's curse would be as efficacious as his blessing, but such an utterance as Rebekah's **upon me be your curse,** spoken beforehand, had the power to deflect it. Such a belief is on a level with that implied throughout the narrative that the blessing uttered over Jacob would benefit him even though it was intended for Esau.

she overheard Isaac's words to Esau, indicating that he was about to give Esau his final blessing, she acted instantly. Calling Jacob and telling him what she had heard, she said to him, **Now therefore, my son, obey my voice according to that which I command thee.** The authority of a mother's affection may turn a man to goodness; misused, it may involve him in evil for which he will pay a heavy price. Rebekah could make a decision for Jacob; but notwithstanding her readiness (see Expos. on vs. 13), she could not take upon herself the debt of retribution which it would entail. As a strange example of the way in which lofty ideas may be made a motive for low acts, it may be that Rebekah told herself she was carrying out the will of God. Had not the divine voice said to her, before Esau and Jacob were born, that the elder shall serve the younger? Why, then, should she not act now, by whatever stratagem was necessary,

to appropriate Isaac's blessing for Jacob rather than for Esau? So she framed and carried out her stratagem of disguising Jacob, which the narrative so vividly describes. The end, she thought, must justify the means. But she was wrong. If she had dealt openly and honestly with Isaac, she might have persuaded him to give willingly to Jacob that which was predestined to be his. But instead she incited a deceit which made Jacob look contemptible, brought bitterness to Isaac, roused Esau's justified fury, and led to Jacob's exile and to a breach in the family which not in her lifetime would be healed.

13. *Emotion Evilly Used.*—Frederick W. Robertson was among the greatest of English-speaking preachers, and one of his notable sermons was on "Isaac Blessing His Sons." In it, as he touched upon these words of Rebekah, **Upon me be thy curse, my son,** he set forth unforgettably the truth that even the most pas-

18 ¶ And he came unto his father, and said, My father: and he said, Here *am* I; who *art* thou, my son?

19 And Jacob said unto his father, I *am* Esau thy firstborn; I have done according as thou badest me: arise, I pray thee, sit and eat of my venison, that thy soul may bless me.

20 And Isaac said unto his son, How *is it* that thou hast found *it* so quickly, my son? And he said, Because the LORD thy God brought *it* to me.

21 And Isaac said unto Jacob, Come near, I pray thee, that I may feel thee, my son, whether thou *be* my very son Esau or not.

22 And Jacob went near unto Isaac his father; and he felt him, and said, The voice *is* Jacob's voice, but the hands *are* the hands of Esau.

23 And he discerned him not, because his hands were hairy, as his brother Esau's hands: so he blessed him.

24 And he said, *Art* thou my very son Esau? And he said, I *am*.

25 And he said, Bring *it* near to me, and I will eat of my son's venison, that my soul may bless thee. And he brought *it* near to him, and he did eat: and he brought him wine, and he drank.

18 So he went in to his father, and said, "My father"; and he said, "Here I am; who are you, my son?" 19 Jacob said to his father, "I am Esau your first-born. I have done as you told me; now sit up and eat of my game, that you may bless me." 20 But Isaac said to his son, "How is it that you have found it so quickly, my son?" He answered, "Because the LORD your God granted me success." Then Isaac said to Jacob, 21 "Come near, that I may feel you, my son, to know whether you are really my son Esau or not." 22 So Jacob went near to Isaac his father, who felt him and said, "The voice is Jacob's voice, but the hands are the hands of Esau." 23 And he did not recognize him, because his hands were hairy like his brother Esau's hands; so he blessed him. 24 He said, "Are you really my son Esau?" He answered, "I am." 25 Then he said, "Bring it to me, that I may eat of my son's game and bless you." So he brought it to him, and he ate; and he

---

sionate human devotion, if unprincipled, will not bless but destroy. In her ambition for Jacob, Rebekah stopped at nothing. If evil means seemed necessary, she would assume the consequences. Said Robertson:

Here you see the idolatry of the woman: sacrificing her husband, her elder son, high principle, her own soul, for an idolized person. . . . Do not mistake. No one ever loved child, brother, sister, too much. It is not the intensity of affection, but its interference with truth and duty, that makes it idolatry. Rebekah loved her son more than truth, *i.e.* more than God. . . . The only true affection is that which is subordinate to a higher. . . . Compare, for instance, Rebekah's love for Jacob with that of Abraham for his son Isaac. Abraham was ready to sacrifice his son to duty. Rebekah sacrificed truth and duty to her son. Which loved a son most?—which was the nobler love? [5]

Though Rebekah was ready to take the consequences of the wrong entirely upon herself, she could not do it. They involved Jacob—as the

[5] *Sermons on Bible Subjects* (New York: E. P. Dutton & Co., 1906; "Everyman's Library"), pp. 27-28.

punishment of the evil which Lady Macbeth prompted involved Macbeth. The sin of deception was not originally Jacob's, but when he acquiesced in his mother's suggestion, it became his too. So he went on to increasingly gross and deliberate falsehood until he became capable of the blasphemous lie of telling his father, Isaac, when the old man asked how he could so quickly have secured the venison which he, Jacob, was offering under the pretense that he was Esau, "The LORD thy God brought it to me" (vs. 20). So the lesson of Jacob's relationship to Rebekah is summed up in Robertson's vivid words, "Beware of that affection which cares for your happiness more than for your honor."

18-40. Jacob and Isaac and Esau.—How dramatic and moving Genesis can be! Where in prose literature can this passage be surpassed in portrayal of human emotions, and in the poignancy and pathos of its conclusion? In the first place there is Jacob, following his mother's craftily suggested trick with an unscrupulous thoroughness that could make him descend to claiming the help of God (vs. 20) in making his lie successful. There is Isaac, pitiful in his

26 And his father Isaac said unto him, Come near now, and kiss me, my son.

27 And he came near, and kissed him: and he smelled the smell of his raiment, and blessed him, and said, See, the smell of my son *is* as the smell of a field which the LORD hath blessed:

28 Therefore God give thee of the dew of heaven, and the fatness of the earth, and plenty of corn and wine:

29 Let people serve thee, and nations bow down to thee: be lord over thy brethren, and let thy mother's sons bow down to thee: cursed *be* every one that curseth thee, and blessed *be* he that blesseth thee.

30 ¶ And it came to pass, as soon as Isaac had made an end of blessing Jacob, and Jacob was yet scarce gone out from the presence of Isaac his father, that Esau his brother came in from his hunting.

31 And he also had made savory meat, and brought it unto his father, and said unto his father, Let my father arise, and eat of his son's venison, that thy soul may bless me.

32 And Isaac his father said unto him, Who *art* thou? And he said, I *am* thy son, thy firstborn, Esau.

33 And Isaac trembled very exceedingly, and said, Who? where *is* he that hath taken venison, and brought *it* me, and I have eaten of all before thou camest, and have blessed him? yea, *and* he shall be blessed.

brought him wine, and he drank. 26 Then his father Isaac said to him, "Come near and kiss me, my son." 27 So he came near and kissed him; and he smelled the smell of his garments, and blessed him, and said,

"See, the smell of my son
  is as the smell of a field which the LORD
    has blessed!
28 May God give you of the dew of heaven,
  and of the fatness of the earth,
  and plenty of grain and wine.
29 Let peoples serve you,
  and nations bow down to you.
Be lord over your brothers,
  and may your mother's sons bow down
    to you.
Cursed be every one who curses you,
  and blessed be every one who blesses
    you!"

30 As soon as Isaac had finished blessing Jacob, when Jacob had scarcely gone out from the presence of Isaac his father, Esau his brother came in from his hunting. 31 He also prepared savory food, and brought it to his father. And he said to his father, "Let my father arise, and eat of his son's game, that you may bless me." 32 His father Isaac said to him, "Who are you?" He answered, "I am your son, your first-born, Esau." 33 Then Isaac trembled violently, and said, "Who was it then that hunted game and brought it to me, and I ate it all[x] before you came, and I have blessed him? — yes,

x Cn. Heb *of all*

---

27. The opening words of the blessing given in J[2]—its continuation is the first two and the last two lines of vs. 29—allude to the fact that Jacob was wearing Esau's garments. This indicates that the utterance J[2] ascribed to Isaac was his own composition, from the first a part of the tale.

29. The third and fourth lines, preceded by vs. 28, constitute the E blessing. The reference to **your mother's sons** indicates that this poem had an independent existence

---

troubled eagerness, trying to assure himself that this son before him is Esau whom he loves. Then the blessing wrongly given—wrongly, so far as Isaac's desire was concerned, and yet in accord with destiny. Isaac's heart was wrapped up in Esau, and his anguish was as deep as Esau's anger when he knew that Esau had been defrauded. But the tragedy was that he could not reverse what he had done. **What shall I do now unto thee, my son?** he cried. He would give to Esau all the blessing that rested in him to confer, a blessing that had love in it like the **dew of heaven from above,** and had fierceness

in it, in the hope that although Jacob should have the pre-eminence, Esau should someday **break his yoke from off thy neck.** But the tragedy was that he must see this son of his chief devotion sacrificed to facts which he could not cancel. The method which Rebekah and Jacob had contrived happened only to be the particular means through which the blessing passed away from Esau. In Esau's earlier limitations that loss was predetermined. It was written in his character that he could not have the birthright blessing; and though Isaac might have cried out in such words as would come

34 And when Esau heard the words of his father, he cried with a great and exceeding bitter cry, and said unto his father, Bless me, *even* me also, O my father.

35 And he said, Thy brother came with subtilty, and hath taken away thy blessing.

36 And he said, Is not he rightly named Jacob? for he hath supplanted me these two times: he took away my birthright; and, behold, now he hath taken away my blessing. And he said, Hast thou not reserved a blessing for me?

37 And Isaac answered and said unto Esau, Behold, I have made him thy lord, and all his brethren have I given to him for servants; and with corn and wine have I sustained him: and what shall I do now unto thee, my son?

38 And Esau said unto his father, Hast thou but one blessing, my father? bless me, *even* me also, O my father. And Esau lifted up his voice, and wept.

39 And Isaac his father answered and said unto him, Behold, thy dwelling shall be the fatness of the earth, and of the dew of heaven from above;

40 And by thy sword shalt thou live, and shalt serve thy brother: and it shall come to pass when thou shalt have the dominion, that thou shalt break his yoke from off thy neck.

and he shall be blessed." 34 When Esau heard the words of his father, he cried out with an exceedingly great and bitter cry, and said to his father, "Bless me, even me also, O my father!" 35 But he said, "Your brother came with guile, and he has taken away your blessing." 36 Esau said, "Is he not rightly named Jacob? For he has supplanted me these two times. He took away my birthright; and behold, now he has taken away my blessing." Then he said, "Have you not reserved a blessing for me?" 37 Isaac answered Esau, "Behold, I have made him your lord, and all his brothers I have given to him for servants, and with grain and wine I have sustained him. What then can I do for you, my son?" 38 Esau said to his father, "Have you but one blessing, my father? Bless me, even me also, O my father." And Esau lifted up his voice and wept.

39 Then Isaac his father answered him:
"Behold, away from^y the fatness of the
    earth shall your dwelling be,
    and away from^y the dew of heaven on
    high.
40 By your sword you shall live,
    and you shall serve your brother;
  but when you break loose
    you shall break his yoke from your
    neck."

^{y} Or of

---

before being incorporated into the narrative. In none of the documents do Isaac and Rebekah have more than two sons.

39. The blessing of Esau begins with a couplet which refuses—the rendering of the KJV is incorrect—to him what had been granted to Jacob in the E recension, **the fatness of the earth** and **the dew of heaven.**

40. The first line refers to Edomite raids on the territory of their neighbors and to their plundering of caravans. The second line alludes to Edom's subjugation to Israel from the time of David to that of Joram (II Kings 8:20-22) . The metrical difficulty of the last two lines, reversing the blessing given to Jacob, makes it probable that they have been added by E to make the oracle agree with the course of events.

---

from the lips of Othello concerning Desdemona, "Oh, the pity of it!" not all the pitifulness within the fact could change it.

34. *The Inexorableness of Judgment.*—**Bless me.** So Esau cried, but for the blessing he wanted now it was too late. His father would have given it to him if he could, but his father also was helpless. The wheels of moral destiny had turned too far. Esau had despised his birthright at one critical moment of choice, and he himself had made possible the success of Jacob's

plot. He had been weighed in the balances of divine judgment and had let himself be found wanting. Now when the verdict had been sealed, no human emotions could reverse it. So moral causes—what a man does or fails to do—go on to their implacable conclusions. Esau was never a bad man; but he was a man careless and contemptuous of unseen values. Heb. 12:16 calls him a "profane person." To be profane is not primarily a matter of coarse speech, but a half-contemptuous irreverence that treats the holiest

41 ¶ And Esau hated Jacob because of the blessing wherewith his father blessed him: and Esau said in his heart, The days of mourning for my father are at hand; then will I slay my brother Jacob.

42 And these words of Esau her elder son were told to Rebekah: and she sent and called Jacob her younger son, and said unto him, Behold, thy brother Esau, as touching thee, doth comfort himself, *purposing* to kill thee.

43 Now therefore, my son, obey my voice; and arise, flee thou to Laban my brother to Haran;

44 And tarry with him a few days, until thy brother's fury turn away;

41 Now Esau hated Jacob because of the blessing with which his father had blessed him, and Esau said to himself, "The days of mourning for my father are approaching; then I will kill my brother Jacob." 42 But the words of Esau her older son were told to Rebekah; so she sent and called Jacob her younger son, and said to him, "Behold, your brother Esau comforts himself by planning to kill you. 43 Now therefore, my son, obey my voice; arise, flee to Laban my brother in Haran, 44 and stay with him a while, until your brother's fury turns away;

C. Esau's Hatred of Jacob (27:41-45)

41-45. This section is a conflation of J[2] and E, both of whom represent Jacob as leaving his home for fear of Esau. To be noted are Rebekah's words in vss. 44-45 (E), where she sends her favorite son away for a short time. In the event, Jacob's absence lasted for more than twenty years because of her brother Laban's fraudulent dealing with him. The E narrative never refers to Rebekah from this point on, for she died without ever seeing her son again, the victim, in a sense, of her own duplicity. Both the J[2] and E narratives recorded Isaac's death at this point and R[JE] retained the notice here. It was later dropped by R[P] in favor of the material in 35:27-29 (P).

---

possibilities of life as though they were cheap and did not matter. Joseph's older brothers were profane persons. The Herod of the Gospels was profane (Luke 23:9-12). So was Herod Agrippa who said mockingly to Paul, "Almost thou persuadest me to be a Christian" (Acts 26:28).

Note that though the profane man may show what he is in one recklessly decisive moment, it is not that moment which has made him what he is. The birthright which should have belonged to Esau had material advantage (Deut. 21:17), but it was not the material benefit that was most important. The first-born was the representative of the family in its relationship to God, its priestly intercessor. But Esau cared little for that. Someday perhaps he might get around to being interested in it, but actually he had too many other things that came first—like the men in the N.T. parable of the wedding feast who had excuses why they could not come (Luke 14:16-24), Esau could not bother yet to fit himself for a religious role; and what was neglected came to seem more and more negligible.

Note also that the final tossing away of his right to the blessing was for an inducement that would have seemed ridiculous had he not grown so casually indifferent to the birthright's value. To barter away his highest privilege for a mess of pottage was something nobody could have

done unless his imagination had been for a long time in process of being dulled. But since it was dulled, the sudden impulse to get some trivial thing he wanted met no great resistance. It may happen again! A boy is born into a family of high inheritance. He has the chance to be a spiritual influence in his generation. But he is not interested. He ignores his privilege, or laughs it off—not finally, he thinks, but until he feels more seriously inclined to take it up. Then one day by some uncalculated word or act he once for all sells out his destiny—for a fleshly appetite, for money, for popular applause, thinking that this betrayal of his better self would be incidental, like so many former ones, and not dreaming that this time it would be fatal. For the tragic lesson of the O.T. story is that some lapses are fatal. Isaac could give to Esau, when Esau woke in bitter realization, the blessing of his affection; but he could never give now the full blessing of the destiny which Esau had denied. Esau had laid a judgment on his life which Isaac could not alter. In how many other lives may the moral fates be sealed by the long carelessness that culminates in one word that cannot be unsaid, in one deed that cannot be undone! So Heb. 12:17 says that Esau, when afterward he desperately wanted the birthright he had held so lightly, "was rejected," and

45 Until thy brother's anger turn away from thee, and he forget *that* which thou hast done to him: then I will send, and fetch thee from thence: why should I be deprived also of you both in one day?

46 And Rebekah said to Isaac, I am weary of my life because of the daughters of Heth: if Jacob take a wife of the daughters of Heth, such as these *which are* of the daughters of the land, what good shall my life do me?

45 until your brother's anger turns away, and he forgets what you have done to him; then I will send, and fetch you from there. Why should I be bereft of you both in one day?"

46 Then Rebekah said to Isaac, "I am weary of my life because of the Hittite women. If Jacob marries one of the Hittite women such as these, one of the women of the land, what good will my life be to me?"

D. Jacob Leaves for Paddan-aram (27:46–28:5)

Vs. 46 is from RP, to effect a transition from the foregoing JE material to the P account of Jacob's departure, 28:1-5, originally the immediate continuation of 26:34-35. P, following his scheme of recording nothing unfavorable about the patriarchs, omitted entirely the story of Jacob's deception of his father and of his consequent flight from his brother's fury. Jacob left home at his father's express command to take a wife from his mother's family (vs. 2)—here P is dependent upon the motif of ch. 24; and he went with his father's blessing, freely bestowed, which designated him as the heir of the divine

---

"found no place of repentance, though he sought it carefully with tears." As in the *Rubáiyát,*

The Moving Finger writes; and, having writ, Moves on.[6]

In the N.T. there is another figure who was profane, as Esau was. It is the younger son in Jesus' parable who was contemptuous of his sonship and almost threw it away (Luke 15). Observe however that in the merciful teaching of Jesus the profane and reckless lad does find room to repent, and by grace is restored in his father's home.

41-45. The Long Consequence of Evil.—It was no wonder that Rebekah was fearful for Jacob when she learned of the threat that Esau had made. She knew well enough that Esau had reason to be enraged. He had been deceived by his brother at his mother's instigation, and he had lost irrevocably the blessing that might have been his. Now that he declared he would kill Jacob, he might surely do it. But if Rebekah was alarmed, she did not lose her self-command. She thought she could take care of this situation as she had managed the former one. **Now therefore, my son, obey my voice,** she said to Jacob. He had obeyed her before, and had succeeded in tricking Esau out of the birthright; let him listen to her again, and he could get himself with equal success out of the consequence of Esau's anger. He could go off to her own brother, where presumably he would be safe

and comfortable. It would be necessary just to **tarry with him a few days.** Then when Esau's gusty anger had blown by, she would send Jacob a message and tell him to come home. It was all as smooth and simple as that—so she imagined. But the consequences of evil may be longer and graver than the one who has instigated the evil can foresee. Rebekah had hoped that after a temporary tumult everything would settle down peacefully, and this favorite son of hers would be with her as the head, after Isaac, of the family. But her slow and silent punishment was still to come. The son she had sent off for **a few days** was to stay in exile for more years than her life could bridge. The message that she said she would send him presently either she did not dare to send, or Jacob did not dare to answer. There is no sign in the following narrative that the mother and the son ever met again. When Jacob did at last come back, Rebekah apparently was dead; and if so, she carried to her grave the frustration of her own life which had grown out of the false act by which she had tried to lift her preferred child into favor.

46. The Daughters of Heth.— (See Expos. on 26:34-35.) George Hodges, in his bright and affectionate O.T. stories for children called *The Garden of Eden,* has Rebekah say, "Those Heth girls worry me almost to death." [7] Thus with gentle humor he puts it; but there was no humor, only strict seriousness, in the thought of the priestly writers that above everything Israel must be kept separate from alien people and alien ideas.

---

[6] St. lxxi.

[7] Boston: Houghton Mifflin Co., 1909, p. 27.

28 And Isaac called Jacob, and blessed him, and charged him, and said unto him, Thou shalt not take a wife of the daughters of Canaan.

2 Arise, go to Padan-aram, to the house of Bethuel thy mother's father; and take thee a wife from thence of the daughters of Laban thy mother's brother.

3 And God Almighty bless thee, and make thee fruitful, and multiply thee, that thou mayest be a multitude of people;

4 And give thee the blessing of Abraham, to thee, and to thy seed with thee; that thou mayest inherit the land wherein thou art a stranger, which God gave unto Abraham.

5 And Isaac sent away Jacob: and he went to Padan-aram unto Laban, son of Bethuel the Syrian, the brother of Rebekah, Jacob's and Esau's mother.

6 ¶ When Esau saw that Isaac had blessed Jacob, and sent him away to Padan-aram, to take him a wife from thence; and that as he blessed him he gave him a charge, saying, Thou shalt not take a wife of the daughters of Canaan;

7 And that Jacob obeyed his father and his mother, and was gone to Padan-aram;

8 And Esau seeing that the daughters of Canaan pleased not Isaac his father;

28 ¹ Then Isaac called Jacob and blessed him, and charged him, "You shall not marry one of the Canaanite women. ² Arise, go to Paddan-aram, to the house of Bethu'el your mother's father; and take as wife from there one of the daughters of Laban your mother's brother. ³ God Almighty[z] bless you and make you fruitful and multiply you, that you may become a company of peoples. ⁴ May he give the blessing of Abraham to you and to your descendants with you, that you may take possession of the land of your sojournings which God gave to Abraham!" ⁵ Thus Isaac sent Jacob away; and he went to Paddan-aram to Laban, the son of Bethu'el the Aramean, the brother of Rebekah, Jacob's and Esau's mother.

6 Now Esau saw that Isaac had blessed Jacob and sent him away to Paddan-aram to take a wife from there, and that as he blessed him he charged him, "You shall not marry one of the Canaanite women," ⁷ and that Jacob had obeyed his father and his mother and gone to Paddan-aram. ⁸ So when Esau saw that the Canaanite women

ᶻ Heb *El Shaddai*

promise to Abraham (vss. 3-5). Thus Jacob's marriages to his cousins, which in both J² and E had been an unforeseen result of his journey to Laban, became in P the reason for it—an interesting example of P's treatment of history.

28:3. God Almighty (El Shaddai RSV mg.) : See Exeg. on 17:1.

E. ESAU'S THIRD MARRIAGE (28:6-9)

6-9. These verses, recording Esau's third marriage, are from P. They depend upon a tradition preserved in 36:10 (J²).

28:1-9. *For Proper Marriages.*—This passage is not part of the description from the Yahwist document which makes up 27:1-45. Together with 27:46, these verses link up directly with 26:34-35, and are as though 27:1-45 had not been written. The beginning of ch. 28 resumes the terse summary of the priestly writers, whose main interest was to show the certified and unbroken lineage through which the inheritance from Abraham was preserved and passed on. There is no hint here of conflict between Jacob and Esau, nor any suggestion that the reason for Jacob's journey to the east was trouble at home. He is not in flight; he is going peacefully and expressly to get married. And it is a different

picture of Esau that is presented. He is as amenable as Jacob. When he saw that his first marriage grieved his parents, he determined to marry in a circle they would be more likely to approve. So he married a granddaughter of Abraham. She was the daughter of Ishmael, and thus not of the preferred legitimate line; whereas Jacob is to marry from among the kinspeople of Rebekah, as to whom there was no doubt of proper blood and status. Thus within the framework of genealogy, with which the priestly writers were constantly concerned, the descendants both of Esau and Jacob have their assured place, with those of Jacob being put satisfactorily on a higher level.

9 Then went Esau unto Ishmael, and took unto the wives which he had Mahalath the daughter of Ishmael Abraham's son, the sister of Nebajoth, to be his wife.

10 ¶ And Jacob went out from Beer-sheba, and went toward Haran.

did not please Isaac his father, 9 Esau went to Ish′ma·el and took to wife, besides the wives he had, Ma′ha·lath the daughter of Ish′ma·el Abraham's son, the sister of Neba′-ioth.

10 Jacob left Beer-sheba, and went to-

XXXVII. Jacob at Bethel (28:10-22)

This account of the inauguration of the, or a, sanctuary at Bethel is a conflation of J² and E, both of which placed the incident at this point in the narrative. The J² recension is much less concrete than the E. It tells of the Lord appearing to Jacob and bestowing upon him the blessing of Abraham and Isaac (vss. 13-15), and of Jacob's offering of the inaugural sacrifice, the account of which is, however, only fragmentarily preserved in vss. 16 and 19.

The E recension is more detailed and colorful, telling of Jacob's vision of the angels of God ascending and descending on a ladder reaching from the earth to heaven (vss. 11-12), and of how the pillar, standing at Bethel in the writer's own day, was set up there as a memorial by Jacob, who also inaugurated the custom of anointing it (vss. 17-18). This was followed by the vow in vss. 20-22, concluding presumably with an explicit notice of the naming of the place Bethel (cf. vs. 19 [J²]).

It is thus E who has preserved the ancient legend current at Bethel, with which J² was apparently unfamiliar. He must, however, have known of the tradition associating Jacob with the sanctuary there and embodied it as best he could.

Now the belief and ideas finding expression in the older legends which J² incorporated into his narrative are the beliefs and ideas of the people among whom the legends took form. They are not necessarily those of J² himself. This story is, however, his own free composition, and as such reflects his own ideas. It is therefore a fact of highest importance for an understanding of his point of view that he here attributes Jacob's inheritance of the promise to Abraham not to his own heartless cunning, as in the tales preserved in 25:27-34 and 27:1-40, but to the Lord's free choice of him (vss. 13-14). In this he is neither voicing his approval of Jacob's earlier conduct nor suggesting that the Lord approved of it. He is rather tacitly emptying the two older tales of their significance and so revealing his own inner feeling regarding them.

The E story, on the other hand, is traditional and reflects certain beliefs held at Bethel, beliefs in which E doubtless shared, for they were in no way inconsistent with his idea of the character of God and his ways with men.

10-15. *Jacob's Dream.*—Now it is from the vivid materials of the J and E traditions that the narrative is woven; and few passages in all the O.T. have equaled these six particular verses in their influence upon religious thought. Jacob's vision of the ladder and the angels—how numberless are the souls who have kindled at the thought of that! It echoes in Christian prayers and hymns. Philip Doddridge invokes the

> God of Bethel, by whose hand
> Thy people still are fed.

One of the beautiful Negro spirituals goes, "We are climbing Jacob's ladder." And worshipers beyond counting have sung, and will sing, "Nearer, my God, to Thee," through which the

wistful seeker after God identifies himself with "the wanderer," when, "the sun gone down," darkness was over him and his "rest a stone"; and from that background comes the prayer:

> Yet in my dreams I'd be
> Nearer, my God, to Thee,
> Nearer to Thee!

In the Genesis story Jacob was a wanderer; that is the first fact which makes his story so poignant for many a heart. Men and women often feel themselves in spiritual exile—not pilgrims, for there is no clear quest before their eyes; but just poor, lonely travelers through what often seems an empty land. They long for an experience like Jacob's, to show that in the most desolate place there can be a shin-

11 And he lighted upon a certain place, and tarried there all night, because the sun was set; and he took of the stones of that place, and put *them for* his pillows, and lay down in that place to sleep.

12 And he dreamed, and behold a ladder set up on the earth, and the top of it reached to heaven: and behold the angels of God ascending and descending on it.

ward Haran. 11 And he came to a certain place, and stayed there that night, because the sun had set. Taking one of the stones of the place, he put it under his head and lay down in that place to sleep. 12 And he dreamed that there was a ladder set up on the earth, and the top of it reached to heaven; and behold, the angels of God were

---

11. The rendering **a certain place** does not preserve all the connotations of the Hebrew. The meaning is rather "the well-known place," "the place we are talking about," i.e., the sanctuary at Bethel. The word translated **place** also has the meaning "sanctuary."

The implication of the verse is thus that the place was already holy—according to Semitic ideas, a spot at which man could come into effective contact with the divine. Of this, however, Jacob knew nothing. He simply happened to stop there for the night, as Moses happened to stop at a holy place in the desert (Exod. 4:24-26).

Jacob slept, his head upon a stone he found there. This is probably a reference to a practice of incubation at Bethel in which dream oracles were sought by sleeping with the head against the sacred stone. The stone, later the ceremonial pillar of the sanctuary (cf. vs. 18), will have been of considerable size, which suggests an earlier form of the tradition in which the hero—whether Jacob or another figure—was a giant.

12. The **ladder** may call to mind the similar idea which underlies the story of the tower whose top was to reach to heaven, by means of which men hoped to approach the gods (11:1-9). Something of this kind would seem anciently to have been behind this story, though E, of course, intended no such suggestion. It has been conjectured that the image of the ladder was suggested by the "huge stones [which] seem to be piled one upon another to make columns nine or ten feet or more in height" (John P. Peters, *Early Hebrew Story* [New York: G. P. Putnam's Sons, 1904], p. 111) near the summit of the slope north of the modern Beitin, the site of the ancient Bethel.

This verse and 32:1-2 are the only references in the Hexateuch to companies of angels. The angel of the Lord, or of God, in such passages as 16:7 and 21:17, is simply the representative of God, even God himself in self-manifestation. Indeed, it is probable that in an earlier form of these and similar stories it was the Lord, or God, himself who appeared. Later God was represented as sending one of his retinue to reveal his will. The idea of a numerous retinue, reflected here and in 32:1-2, is the product of men's deeper apprehension of the majesty of God to which they gave expression by depicting

---

ing something which bridges the gap between earth and heaven so that henceforth all the horizons of hope and trust are lifted and enlarged. And the promise that lies in the story of Bethel becomes the more touching when it is remembered that Jacob was not only a wanderer, but a guilty and burdened and remorseful one. He had not deserved a vision of God. But he needed it; and all his life in his groping and unworthy way he had desired it. The reason he wanted the birthright was because he had at least an instinct for spiritual realities. The birthright did not mean inheritance of money; it meant the headship of the family in its covenant with God. He could not be content with the things of the flesh, as Esau was; and even when he was most guilty of the sins of earth, he

knew that there was a higher Righteousness to which he was accountable. To such a man, unworthy but in a deep sense wistful, the vision came—and comes:

But (when so sad thou canst not sadder)
Cry;—and upon thy so sore loss
Shall shine the traffic of Jacob's ladder
Pitched betwixt Heaven and Charing Cross.[8]

Thus it was in beauty and benediction that the vision came to Jacob. Notwithstanding all that he had done, communication between earth and heaven was not broken. The Lord God of Abraham, and the God of Isaac—the

[8] Francis Thompson, "The Kingdom of God." Used by permission of Sir Francis Meynell and The Newman Press, publishers.

13 And, behold, the LORD stood above it, and said, I *am* the LORD God of Abraham thy father, and the God of Isaac: the land whereon thou liest, to thee will I give it, and to thy seed;

14 And thy seed shall be as the dust of the earth; and thou shalt spread abroad to the west, and to the east, and to the north, and to the south: and in thee and in thy seed shall all the families of the earth be blessed.

15 And, behold, I *am* with thee, and will keep thee in all *places* whither thou goest, and will bring thee again into this land; for I will not leave thee, until I have done *that* which I have spoken to thee of.

16 ¶ And Jacob awaked out of his sleep, and he said, Surely the LORD is in this place; and I knew *it* not.

ascending and descending on it! 13 And behold, the LORD stood above it[a] and said, "I am the LORD, the God of Abraham your father and the God of Isaac; the land on which you lie I will give to you and to your descendants; 14 and your descendants shall be like the dust of the earth, and you shall spread abroad to the west and to the east and to the north and to the south; and by you and your descendants shall all the families of the earth bless themselves.[b] 15 Behold, I am with you and will keep you wherever you go, and will bring you back to this land; for I will not leave you until I have done that of which I have spoken to you." 16 Then Jacob awoke from his sleep and said, "Surely the LORD is in this place; and

[a] Or *beside him*
[b] Or *be blessed*

---

him as surrounded by a mysterious court, far greater than that of any earthly monarch. In view of these considerations it is probable that the E story, in the form in which it was originally told at Bethel, told not of angels but of gods ascending and descending the ladder.

God of his fathers and of all the inheritance of his home—was with him still, and would go with him on the way ahead. In that experience of Jacob is expressed what the Hebrew people felt about their whole contradictory history: in the midst of ignorance and evil there is still the possibility of a saving revelation. Even on the rocky slopes where Jacob was alone there rose the shining stairway that brought the heavenly glory, with angels going up like prayers of men to God and angels coming down like the grace of God to men. That vision epitomizes the whole wonder of the Hebrew faith and hope as they move on through the O.T. to their culmination in Christ.

16. *God's Unexpected Presence.*—Hear the surprise in Jacob's cry as he awakened from his sleep: Surely the LORD is in this place; and I knew it not. What less likely place and time—so it had seemed to him—could there be for God to manifest himself? He had come to one of the bleakest and most forbidding spots a man could have chanced upon. It was no pleasant meadow, no green oasis, no sheltered valley. It was a hilltop of barren rock; and its barrenness seemed to represent at that moment Jacob's claim on life. He was a fugitive, and he was afraid. His mother had told him to go off for "a few days," and then she would send and bring him home. But Jacob may have had a better idea of the truth: that it would be no "few days" but a long time of punishing exile

before he could ever dare to return. There was good reason to feel that he was alone with emptiness. When he had lain down to sleep, he was a long way off from the place of his clever and successful schemes. There was nothing to measure his own little soul against except the silent and dreadful immensities he saw from the height of Bethel: the empty earth, the sky, the stars. Yet the strange fact was that there existed in Jacob's soul something to which God could speak (see Expos. on vss. 10-15). Unprepossessing though he was, he was capable of response to more than the things of flesh and sense. He had not despised or ignored his inheritance. He knew that it was faith in God that had given dignity to Abraham and Isaac, and he had a hunger—even if mixed with baseness—to get his own life into touch with God. When such a man is confronted in his solitariness with the sublimity of the hills and the awful mystery of the marching stars, he may be capable of great conceptions which begin to take shape in his subconscious. In his dreams he sees not only nature, but the gates of heaven. Yet how many there are who fall short of Jacob in this—men in whom solitariness produces nothing, who fall asleep but will not dream, who when they are forced to be alone are either bored or frightened. Out of the aloneness they dread they get nothing, because they have not kept the seed of religion that in their hour of need and crisis might have quickened in their souls.

17 And he was afraid, and said, How dreadful *is* this place! this *is* none other but the house of God, and this *is* the gate of heaven.

I did not know it." 17 And he was afraid, and said, "How awesome is this place! This is none other than the house of God, and this is the gate of heaven."

17. Jacob's emotion upon waking from his dream—**awoke from his sleep** in vs. 16 is from the J recension—is one of awe, and he utters the name of the place *bēth-'ēl*, **house of God**.

---

17. *Reverence as the Root of Religion.*—In the words here written Jacob expresses a realization in which he was the representative of what made the Hebrew people great. To him, and to them, there could be a **gate of heaven,** because in the first place there was a heaven. To the Hebrew mind this world was never all: something vaster overarched it. The supernatural enfolded the natural, and the numinous was as real as everyday events. The existence of this other world might seem dreadful; the emotion it first produced might be awe, and even fear. But it was never despised and seldom forgotten or ignored. So there was always an element of nobility in the Hebrew character and in Hebrew history, because there was reverence before an Eternal One who was increasingly recognized as just and holy. However forgetful, rebellious, or unworthy men might be, they could never be irresponsible, because they were conscious of an authority high and lifted up which it was their destiny to obey. Life could not be aimless, because there was a star of truth to steer by; nor small and mean, because there were infinite horizons. The reason the Bible is in a class apart from other ancient history is because through all its human record there is this overtone of reference to the reality of the divine; and the reason why the Jews have lasted while other ancient peoples perished is because this tenacity of faith gave them endless fortitude.

What does this fact suggest, by contrast, concerning nations of today? Consider the perilous secularism which is exhibited too often in contemporary "culture," and particularly in the relatively rich United States: the smug assumption that prosperity is natural; the belief that "money talks"; the lax standards in "society"; the everlasting "Let's have a drink"; the obsession with sex in books, plays, and movies, and the exploitation of it in advertisements to commercialize suggestiveness; the cheap ridicule of self-control and chastity among the young. What clear code of conduct is there? What recognition of principle, so firm and commanding that violation of it would be counted as dishonor? If history means anything, it is certain that a nation which is not conscious of standing at the gate of any heaven, and lifts its eyes no

higher than the level of its impulse, is moving toward disintegration. Subject to none of the great imperatives reflected in the Bible, its life becomes cheap and flabby.

There is no beginning, no movement, no peace and no end
But noise without speech, food without taste.

. . . .

And the wind shall say: "Here were decent godless people:
Their only monument the asphalt road
And a thousand lost golf balls." [9]

17. *Religious Dread.*—When Jacob woke from his vision and felt that he had stood at the gate of heaven, there was first the sense of wonder and thanksgiving at the revelation of God's mercy; but then there swept over him an overwhelming awe. **How dreadful is this place!** he cried. When a man is made to know that God has not forgotten him, even though he has been a moral failure, there is the moment of rapturous exaltation such as Jacob had when he saw the shining ladder and the angels; but when he remembers the holiness of God, he turns his face away from its intolerable light. The vision must be more than the immediate emotion: it calls him to account. Who can contemplate the distance between himself and God, even when the angels of God's forgiveness throw a bridge across it, and not bow down in agonized unworthiness? So it was with Jacob. The consciousness of guilt in him made him shrink from the revelation of God even when he craved it. He had done wrong, and he was trying to escape its consequences. His brother's anger was formidable enough; but there was something more formidable which he wanted to forget but which confronted him. His conscience was shocked into the certainty that he could not get away from God. The dread of that perception was on him now. Before he could ever be at peace with himself and with his world, he would have to come to grips with the facts of his past experience—and with the invisible power of the righteousness he had violated—and wrestle with

[9] T. S. Eliot, *The Rock* (New York: Harcourt, Brace & Co.; London: Faber & Faber, 1934), pp. 11, 30. Used by permission.

| 18 And Jacob rose up early in the morning, and took the stone that he had put *for* his pillows, and set it up *for* a pillar, and poured oil upon the top of it. | 18 So Jacob rose early in the morning, and he took the stone which he had put under his head and set it up for a pillar |

18. *Maççēbhāh,* **pillar,** is the technical name of the sacred monolith which stood, apparently, in every Canaanite sanctuary. Originally the supposed abode of the deity—there are traces of this idea here, cf. vs. 22—these came to be regarded as symbols of the Lord's presence. By a later refinement they became memorials of some theophany or other important event, and this is the meaning E always attaches to them (31:13, 45; 33:20, as emended, see below; 35:14; Exod. 24:4; cf. Josh. 24:26). J never mentions them

---

them for his life, as he would one day at Peniel. It was well for Jacob that his awareness of God did not end with the vision of the ladder, but went on to realize the purification through which he must go before he could take the blessings which the angels of the ladder might bring to him. For Jacob, and for all men, there can be no flippant self-assurance. In relation to their sins the inexorable love of God must first seem dreadful before it can be redeeming.

18. *The Primitive in Religion.*—When Jacob took the stone on which he had pillowed his head and set it up as a sacred thing, he followed an impulse which is as old and deep as man's religious consciousness. When a man has had a spiritual experience it is natural for him to think that the place where he had it and the thing associated with it are in themselves holy. He wants to make a shrine at which the particular experience he has had may be not only remembered but repeated. The danger is that afterward the shrine may represent not a repetition of the real experience, but only a superstition. In Canaan and among the early Hebrews the land was dotted with shrines made sacred because some natural object had laid its spell upon imagination and created a sense of the supernatural: some huge old oak, a cave, a rock, a well. Consider the later history of the O.T., with its long conflict between the prophets and the stubborn crudities and corruptions that characterized the "high places" and the sacred groves. Once those hilltops and the darkness of those forests had been the sign to men of Something greater than themselves; now they had sunk to be excuses for what was most undeveloped and unmoral in themselves. A localized God could be satisfied with localized honors; prayers and sacrifices at the shrines were the worshiper's obligation, but with these his obligation ended. When he wanted to worship, he must go back and perform the proper ritual where the divine was supposed to dwell. Think of the woman of Samaria and her belligerent assertion that "our fathers worshiped on this mountain" (John 4:20). Reflect upon the way

in which primitive religion survives in modified but still recognizable forms: in the strange dark carry-over from plain paganism which has turned a black image of ancient Mexico into the Virgin of Guadaloupe; in the unreasoning attachment to particular customs and conditions simply because they are traditional; in the preservation of relics, "a fragment of the true cross," the "holy blood," a bone of some dead saint—in which material thing a supernatural healing and sanctifying power is supposed to dwell; in the crowd contagion raised by some excited vision and reported miracle which turns the grotto at Lourdes into a shrine to which streams of pilgrims come, convinced that the Virgin Mary visibly appeared there and in miraculous presence dwells there now. The danger of localized religion is that it so emphasizes locality and related ritual that religion drifts back toward the shadowland of magic.

18. *Consecrating the Commonplace.*—It would be well to read Hubert L. Simpson's *Altars of Earth* in connection with this passage. His thesis is that the altars of men's approach to God are built upon our common ground. He is referring primarily to Exod. 20:24, "An altar of earth thou shalt make unto me." He writes:

The essential characteristic of all spiritual worship is that it should spring out of a sense of man's weakness [and be thus] an altar of earth, raised from the dust of the ground to which the mortal part of man bears kin, and yet smoking with the flame of imperishable things.

And of this altar raised by Jacob from the loose stones, he writes:

Let permanence, if you will, be an element in the expression of your religious experience, so far as you are able to secure it; but above all let the predominant characteristic be simplicity and immediacy. The stones at Bethel, the boulders from the river-bed at the crossing of Jordan; to-day's temptation, to-day's trouble, to-day's triumph—through these things we rise to God.[1]

[1] London: James Clarke & Co., 1922, pp. 25, 26. Used by permission.

19 And he called the name of that place Bethel: but the name of that city *was called* Luz at the first.

and poured oil on the top of it. 19 He called the name of that place Bethel;[c] but the name of the city was Luz at the first.

[c] That is *The house of God*

---

except in connection with Canaanitish worship (Exod. 34:13). The polemic of Deuteronomy against them, however, indicates that E was in advance of his time and that they still retained their idolatrous associations in the popular mind.

"Immediacy" and "simplicity"—those are good key words. A man's contact with God can begin wherever he is and whenever his need reaches up to find the heavenly answer. Abraham lived in tents, pitching them here today and there tomorrow, but it was never as though he had left God behind. Moses found God in the desert before the burning bush. Gideon had his call to God's service when he was threshing wheat. The first disciples were called by Jesus from their fishing boats. And that blessedly unpretentious saint, Brother Lawrence, who was a cook in a monastery kitchen, declared: "It is not necessary for being with God to be always at church. We may make an oratory of our heart wherein to retire from time to time to converse with Him in meekness, humility and love." [2] It was observed of him "that in the greatest hurry of business in the kitchen he still preserved his recollection and heavenly-mindedness"; for, said he: "The time of business does not with me differ from the time of prayer, and in the noise and clatter of my kitchen, while several persons are at the same time calling for different things, I possess God in as great tranquility as if I were upon my knees at the Blessed Sacrament." [3]

With immediacy, simplicity. Always there is danger that real religion may be lost in the complexity of its forms. What begins as a living spring of spiritual experience may lose its freshness in the elaborate reservoirs which men may think they must establish to contain its waters. So the inspiration of the great pioneers of Israel was choked in the intricate channels of the law. So the quickening message of the prophets was turned into the ornate ritual of the temple, and what had been a surge of the spirit slowed into a ceremonial form. Remember what Amos found at Bethel; and what Jesus said as he saw the way the priests and Pharisees made much of ostentatious worship, but inwardly gave no glory to God. They needed—he told them—to recall what Hosea had said long before, "I desired mercy, and not sacrifice; and the knowledge of God more than burnt offerings" (Hos. 6:6).

Is there not equal danger in our Christian churches that real religion, which is the swift and simple impulse of the heart, may be smothered by elaborations which are supposed to lead men to God, but instead may only hide him? Great architecture, beautiful music, art and color, may ennoble worship, but they may also become an overpowering obsession that leads to nothing beyond itself. Who has not seen congregations that are less interested in drawing near to God than they are in drawing up plans for a more elegant church building; that will raise money enthusiastically for a new steeple or for tiles and marble and stained glass, but have not put their heart into raising their own life and the life of their communities closer to the purposes of Christ? "The pure in heart shall see God." However much more those words may mean, they surely mean this: only those who have kept unspoiled the simplicity of their desire for God can perceive how and where he comes into life.

19. *The New Name*.—This note about the names of the place may seem on the surface only a passing matter of nomenclature. People in the region near which Jacob had his vision would have said that they lived at Luz; but afterward the name Jacob gave to the spot which had become for him a shrine overshadowed that earlier routine name. In the tradition which came down from Jacob, this neighborhood was no longer merely what men had called it; it was what God had made it. Bethel means **The house of God.** So the whole suggestion widens. One's imagination dwells upon the fact that frequently in the O.T., and in history generally, a place which originally was ordinary has become exalted because some great spiritual experience was associated with it. Jerusalem was at first only the rocky hilltop where Araunah the Jebusite had his threshing floor, but after the temple had been built there it became the Holy City which should be the symbol of God's presence on the earth. One undistinguished house in that same city, that of John Mark's mother, if it existed today, would be as a shrine of the Holy Grail, because the Last Supper was held in its upper room. And less likely places have become for the moment a house of God. Paul made the prison at Philippi into such when he and Silas

[2] *The Practice of the Presence of God*, Seventh Letter.
[3] *Ibid.*, Fourth Conversation.

20 And Jacob vowed a vow, saying, If God will be with me, and will keep me in this way that I go, and will give me bread to eat, and raiment to put on,

21 So that I come again to my father's house in peace; then shall the LORD be my God:

20 Then Jacob made a vow, saying, "If God will be with me, and will keep me in this way that I go, and will give me bread to eat and clothing to wear, 21 so that I come again to my father's house in peace, then

---

20. It is unlikely that this and the two following verses belong to the old story; they are rather from E himself, to effect a transition to the story of Jacob and Laban. The bargaining tone of the **vow** may be a subtle indication of what E thought of Jacob's character as it had hitherto developed.

21. The LORD shall be my God cannot be from E, who does not use **the LORD** before Exod. 3:14-15, and in any case could not have represented Jacob as going as far as this in dictating his terms of service. It is either an explanatory—and somewhat erroneous—gloss on vs. 22a or, less likely, an insertion by RJE.

"prayed, and sang praises unto God" (Acts 16:25). So did John Bunyan, writing *The Pilgrim's Progress,* transform Bedford jail. Everywhere it is possible for a **Luz** to become a **Bethel.** There is a story of two simple folk who lived in a fisherman's cottage in a little village by the sea. When the man came home at the end of a day, his wife said to him, "The new minister came here today, and he asked a question I couldn't answer." "What did he ask?" "He asked me," said she, " 'Does Jesus Christ live here?' " "And what did you say?" the husband demanded. "I didn't know what to say." "Well, why couldn't you tell him that we are respectable people?" "But he didn't ask me that." "Well, why didn't you tell him we go to church when we feel like it?" "But he didn't ask me that either." "Then you could have told him that we read the Bible—sometimes." "But he didn't ask me *that.* What he asked me was 'Does Jesus Christ live here?' " It is a question which goes far. In what home or place of daily business are those who dwell there desiring to make it a **Bethel, the house of God?**

20-22. *Conceptions of Prayer.*—What Jacob prays is certainly not an inspiring prayer, or even a creditable one. No wonder the man who made it stands at that moment as an unattractive figure. Jacob has just deceived his father and defrauded his brother, and in fear of Esau's anger all he can do is guiltily to run away. He has had his dream of the ladder of angels that reminded him of God. Yet now the only thing it suggests to him is that perhaps he can persuade God to make a bargain by offering to do great things—on condition. If God will save his skin and also make him prosperous, then he will give back to God a tenth of what God may have given him. A cheap prayer, if ever there

was one! Yet how sure are we that we have outgrown it—or even come up all the little way to Jacob's level? Are there none so shallow as to think that all they need to do is to pay God lip service, hoping in return to claim rich benefits; to say, as Jacob did, **then shall the LORD be my God,** but never feel obliged to bring back even 1 per cent, much less 10 per cent as Jacob promised, of God's blessings to the service of God?

In what Jacob said there is much room for reflection on the meaning of prayer. Here is an expression of religious primitiveness, a primitiveness not surprising in the record of early times, but all too often repeated in the religion of a generation remaining infantile even though it is supposed to be adult. The first instincts of human nature have to do with the material and tangible—the physical instincts to keep alive and be comfortable. God is the Power off somewhere who controls what we want and do not have, who might give it to us if we can make him well disposed. If we can contrive what he likes, perhaps he will answer with what we like. That is the primitive idea— an idea no less primitive when it is found in modern sophistication, as in the paltry religious approaches of men who think they can treat the majesty of God as they might treat—in Harry Emerson Fosdick's vivid phrase—"a cosmic bell-hop" who can be persuaded by a tip.

From this crude idea, as symbolized in the prayer of Jacob, we may follow in the Bible the growing consciousness of the meaning of prayer. First there is the expanding recognition of what God is: the Spirit of truth and holiness, and of deep-reaching as well as far-reaching mercy. He is the source from which comes indeed the answer to our everyday needs: life itself, sustenance and safety, daily bread, the

22 And this stone, which I have set *for* a pillar, shall be God's house: and of all that thou shalt give me I will surely give the tenth unto thee.	the Lord shall be my God, 22 and this stone, which I have set up for a pillar, shall be God's house; and of all that thou givest me I will give the tenth to thee."

22. The initial **and** belongs with the preceding clause. This being eliminated, the terms of Jacob's vow are that if God protects him then Bethel will be a sanctuary and the stone its **pillar**. The second half of the verse is secondary, as the change to the second person indicates. It claims that the custom of tithing at Bethel also originated with Jacob.

23. In view of the antagonism which E shows elsewhere in his narrative toward the Aaronite priesthood of Bethel (cf. Smend, *Erzählung des Hexateuch,* pp. 354, 358-59), and of the fact that the inaugural legend of the cult of the golden calf appears to have attributed the founding of that sanctuary to Aaron (Exod. 32:1-6; Simpson, *Early Traditions of Israel,* pp. 625-26), the question presents itself as to what sanctuary it was that E was referring to in this story.

It may be noted that the location of the sanctuary at Bethel referred to in 12:8 is somewhat carefully defined. The verse 12:8 is from the J document. As to whether its present form is that in which it left the hand of J[1] or J[2], or whether it has been elaborated by a later hand—cf. also the labored attempt to define the location of the place in the redactional 13:4—it is impossible to say. In any case it would seem to represent an attempt to distinguish between sanctuary and sanctuary at Bethel, a fact which may be relevant here.

materials for the clothes we wear, the houses we live in, the tools for an existence more abundant. But these are only the beginning of what he is and what he has to offer. He is the One to whom men turn to

> keep us in His grace,
> And guide us when perplexed,
> And free us from all ills
> In this world and the next.[4]

He is the creator not only of men's bodies but of their souls; and his nature and purpose are understood only when men remember this. See in the psalms and in the prophets the recognition of God as the High and Holy One, to be approached with awe and reverence and adoring wonder. There is also the corresponding development in men's recognition of what they themselves are meant to be. Since God has created them not only as bodies but as souls, it is in their souls supremely that they must grow. This awareness too can be traced all through the O.T. as it expands. The great voices in Israel go a long way beyond bargaining or the desire only for earthly benefits. They cry out for purity of heart, for the spirit of holiness, for attunement of man's will to the redeeming will of God. See this at least emerging in the prayer of Solomon (I Kings 3) who confesses, "I am but a little child; I know not how to go out or come in"; and who pleads therefore for "a wise and an understanding heart." Read Jer. 1; Ps. 51.

So gradually there comes the perception that prayer is the relationship between the best that man has discovered in himself and the infinite goodness of God. Prayer then no longer moves on the level of small preoccupations. It can put the petition for the needs of the body into one swift phrase, as Jesus put it in the Lord's Prayer, and leave it there with trustfulness; and then look up and on to larger matters—to God's cleansing mercy for the soul's faults and his strength for the soul's purposes, to loyalty to his kingdom and its coming. Not anything that comes from God, but God himself, is the concern of prayer at its highest. "Man's chief end is to glorify God, and to enjoy him forever." Think of Jesus. Meditate upon the message which comes from the words of innumerable great souls, both among the mystics and among the militant saints—a message expressed anew by a contemporary exponent of the mystical life, Thomas R. Kelly:

> There is . . . no need for fret when faithfully turning to Him, if He leads us but slowly into His secret chambers. If He gives us increasing steadiness in the deeper sense of His Presence, we can only quietly thank Him. If He holds us in the stage of alternation we can thank Him for His loving wisdom, and wait upon His guidance through the stages for which we are prepared. . . . Here is not ecstasy but serenity, unshakableness, firmness of life-orientation. We are become what Fox calls "established men." [5]

[4] Martin Rinkart, tr. Catherine Winkworth, "Now thank we all our God."

[5] *A Testament of Devotion* (New York: Harper & Bros., 1941), p. 42.

29 Then Jacob went on his journey, and came into the land of the people of the east.

2 And he looked, and behold a well in the field, and, lo, there *were* three flocks of sheep lying by it; for out of that well they watered the flocks: and a great stone *was* upon the well's mouth.

29 Then Jacob went on his journey, and came to the land of the people of the east. 2 As he looked, he saw a well in the field, and lo, three flocks of sheep lying beside it; for out of that well the flocks were watered. The stone on the well's mouth was

---

XXXVIII. Jacob at Paddan-aram (29:1–31:55)

The fact that the J¹ document, which embodies the tradition of the south, claims Jacob as one of the ancestors of the group that centered at Hebron indicates that there was some close connection between that group and the clans east of the Jordan. It is only reasonable to assume that Jacob, himself an east Jordan figure (cf. Exeg. on 25:26), was first adopted as an ancestor by the eastern clans and, indeed, that it was pressure from the east which led to his incorporation into the southern tradition.

The E story of Bethel, together with the association of Jacob with the Ephrathite figure Rachel (see Exeg. on 29:1-14) and with the Shechemite figure Joseph (see Exeg. on 29:1-14; ch. 37), would seem to indicate that he was similarly and independently adopted by the northern tribes.

A. Jacob's Meeting with Rachel (29:1-14)

29:1-14. The nucleus of this story is from J¹. It told how Jacob met Rachel, the daughter of Laban, at a well in **the land of the people of the east** (vs. 1), i.e., in the north Arabian desert. It seems probable that the east Jordan figure Jacob had been associated with Laban, the representative of the nomad Aramaeans, before he was brought into the southern tradition, which J¹ systematized and reduced to writing, for the contact with the Aramaeans which this story reflects would naturally have been established in the first instance by the clans east of the Jordan, which had first claimed Jacob as their ancestor. It also seems probable that Jacob's association with Rachel antedated his incorporation into the tradition of the south.

Rachel appears to have been in origin the central figure in the tradition of Ephrath in Benjamin, the site of her sepulcher (35:19, in which "that is, Bethlehem" is a gloss; cf. I Sam. 10:2). The fact that a pillar (cf. Exeg. on 28:18) stood beside the sepulcher (35:20) indicates that it was a sanctuary of which, it may be inferred, Rachel was the patron saint—possibly of totemistic origin, for Rachel means "ewe."

It is this Ephrathite figure who fills the role of the mother of Joseph (30:23-24) in the J¹ tradition—and in J² and E. Joseph was, as will be seen, a figure in the tradition of Shechem, the site of his grave (Josh. 24:32). It is unlikely that this association of these two figures was the work of the southerner, J¹. It seems rather to be the result of a process of unification which had begun in the north, similar to that going on in the south.

Now it has been noted in connection with the Exeg. of 28:10-22 that the appearance of Jacob in the role of the founder of the sanctuary at Bethel points to a fusing of the

---

Thus the true prayer ends in dedication. It has passed beyond the controlling thought, like Jacob's, of what a man can get; for, having been in touch with God, it has caught the joy of wondering what one can give. No man can commune with the love of God without becoming more loving. Read the epistles of John. Reflect upon what Paul learned of God from his Master. See in his letters, as at the end of Romans, what he knew and wanted all Chris-

tians to understand of that dedication in service by which men present their whole selves as a "living sacrifice, holy, acceptable unto God" (Rom. 12:1).

29:1-11, 18, 20. *Jacob: Another Aspect.*—Jacob at first was not attractive, but in the glimpses of him here he is revealed in a brighter light. Of the two brothers, Esau had appeared as the virile one. Beside Esau's outdoor energies and his swift, bold strength, Jacob seemed passive

3 And thither were all the flocks gathered: and they rolled the stone from the well's mouth, and watered the sheep, and put the stone again upon the well's mouth in his place.

4 And Jacob said unto them, My brethren, whence *be* ye? And they said, Of Haran *are* we.

5 And he said unto them, Know ye Laban the son of Nahor? And they said, We know *him*.

6 And he said unto them, *Is* he well? And they said, *He is* well: and, behold, Rachel his daughter cometh with the sheep.

7 And he said, Lo, *it is* yet high day, neither *is it* time that the cattle should be gathered together: water ye the sheep, and go *and* feed *them*.

8 And they said, We cannot, until all the flocks be gathered together, and *till* they roll the stone from the well's mouth; then we water the sheep.

large, **3** and when all the flocks were gathered there, the shepherds would roll the stone from the mouth of the well, and water the sheep, and put the stone back in its place upon the mouth of the well.

4 Jacob said to them, "My brothers, where do you come from?" They said, "We are from Haran." **5** He said to them, "Do you know Laban the son of Nahor?" They said, "We know him." **6** He said to them, "Is it well with him?" They said, "It is well; and see, Rachel his daughter is coming with the sheep!" **7** He said, "Behold, it is still high day, it is not time for the animals to be gathered together; water the sheep, and go, pasture them." **8** But they said, "We cannot until all the flocks are gathered together, and the stone is rolled from the mouth of the well; then we water the sheep."

---

tradition of the north with that of the land east of the Jordan, quite independent of the movement by which Jacob had been taken into the tradition of the south. Jacob had, so to speak, moved in two directions—south to Hebron and west to Bethel and Shechem, where he had become the father of Joseph and the husband of the Ephrathite Rachel.

In this story J[1] dramatizes Jacob's association with Rachel, making use of one of the favorite motifs current among nomad shepherds, that of the meeting at a well (cf. 24:11-23; Exod. 2:15-21; also the reference to the gatherings at the "places of drawing water" [Judg. 5:11]).

Jacob, in the desert, came to a well covered with a stone, so great that it took a number of men to move it, thus ensuring that no one person would be able to take more than his fair share of the precious water. He found some shepherds with their flocks (vss. 2-3) and asked them why they were loitering there. He was told that they had to wait for enough men to gather to move the stone (vss. 7-8)—in vs. 8 "shepherds"

---

and pale. But now in the new country he is anything but that. **A great stone** was over the well where the sheep were watered, and the men who were there were waiting for other shepherds to come and help them roll it aside; but Jacob went and rolled it aside himself. Why? Because he had met Rachel; and in contact with Rachel, Jacob from the first moment was a different man. He kissed her first as his kinswoman, but quickly he fell in love with her. He said to Laban, her father, that he would serve seven years for her; **and they seemed unto him but a few days, for the love he had to her.** In the light of words like these, Jacob's remoteness in time and place passes like a shadow, and he is at one with all lovers of every age in the timeless wonder of the meeting of man and maid. Moreover, Jacob showed himself to be

an individual to a degree that was notable in that period when family pressure was generally so controlling. His father, Isaac, had had his bride picked out for him. Laban tried to foist upon Jacob the daughter he wanted Jacob to take; but in spite of that deception, Jacob would not be turned from the girl to whom his heart went out. He served for her not only the first seven years of his agreement, but seven years more; and Rachel was henceforth the center of his life's devotion. In the whole story of his career, which sometimes was far from beautiful, this relationship with Rachel shines like a shaft of sunlight, sifting with a lovely radiance through a broken, cloudy sky.

4-6, 12-14. *Welcome from One's Own.*— "Blood is thicker than water" is not an ancient phrase, but the fact which it seeks to express

9 ¶ And while he yet spake with them, Rachel came with her father's sheep: for she kept them.

10 And it came to pass, when Jacob saw Rachel the daughter of Laban his mother's brother, and the sheep of Laban his mother's brother, that Jacob went near, and rolled the stone from the well's mouth, and watered the flock of Laban his mother's brother.

11 And Jacob kissed Rachel, and lifted up his voice, and wept.

12 And Jacob told Rachel that he *was* her father's brother, and that he *was* Rebekah's son: and she ran and told her father.

13 And it came to pass, when Laban heard the tidings of Jacob his sister's son, that he ran to meet him, and embraced him, and kissed him, and brought him to his house. And he told Laban all these things.

14 And Laban said to him, Surely thou *art* my bone and my flesh. And he abode with him the space of a month.

---

9 While he was still speaking with them, Rachel came with her father's sheep; for she kept them. 10 Now when Jacob saw Rachel the daughter of Laban his mother's brother, and the sheep of Laban his mother's brother, Jacob went up and rolled the stone from the well's mouth, and watered the flock of Laban his mother's brother. 11 Then Jacob kissed Rachel, and wept aloud. 12 And Jacob told Rachel that he was her father's kinsman, and that he was Rebekah's son; and she ran and told her father.

13 When Laban heard the tidings of Jacob his sister's son, he ran to meet him, and embraced him and kissed him, and brought him to his house. Jacob told Laban all these things, 14 and Laban said to him, "Surely you are my bone and my flesh!" And he stayed with him a month.

---

must be read for **flocks** with the LXX and the Syriac. At this moment Rachel appeared with her father's sheep (vs. 9), whereupon Jacob himself, without assistance, removed the stone for her and watered her flock (vs. 10). He then told Rachel who he was and she ran to tell her father, who came and welcomed him (vss. 12-13). Jacob then remained with him for a month (vs. 14*b*).

This was the J[1] version of the story and it was not too skillfully related to its context, for it does not explain how Jacob, fresh from Beer-sheba, recognized Rachel. It was to correct this that J[2], a more finished writer than J[1], inserted vss. 5-6. That these verses are secondary is suggested by the fact that vs. 6*b* anticipates vs. 9; furthermore, Jacob's speech in vs. 7 not only is an awkward reply to vs. 6*b*, but would come better as the first remark of an enterprising young man to a group of seemingly idle shepherds. J[2] also inserted vs. 4, to locate Laban at Haran (cf. 24:10-11). It should be noted, however, that the well described here is certainly not that of the tale in ch. 24.

J[2] is further responsible for the three references to Laban as **his mother's brother** in vs. 10, and for the words **and that he was Rebekah's son** in vs. 12; i.e., according to J[1], who never mentions the name of Rebekah, Jacob's relationship with Laban was through Abraham only, not through his mother (cf. **kinsman** in vs. 12 [RSV]; this is lit., **brother** [KJV], but the word bears another meaning than that which it has in vss. 10-11— suggesting diversity of authorship). In vs. 13 **his sister's son** is also from J[2], as is vs. 14*a*.

And embraced him and kissed him (vs. 13) is all that is left of the E account of Jacob's arrival at Laban's.

The stage is now set for the story of Jacob's marriage. It should, however, be noted that in neither J[1], J[2], nor E is it stated that Jacob had gone to the east for the purpose of marrying Laban's daughters. This feature appears only in P (28:1-5). J[2] and E both represent Jacob as fleeing from Esau (27:41-44), while J[1] leaves the journey quite unmotivated. But there can be no doubt that both J[2] and E, though perhaps not J[1], intended to imply that the course of events was determined by the guiding hand of God.

15 ¶ And Laban said unto Jacob, Because thou *art* my brother, shouldest thou therefore serve me for nought? tell me, what *shall* thy wages *be?*	15 Then Laban said to Jacob, "Because you are my kinsman, should you therefore serve me for nothing? Tell me, what shall

The purity of Israelite blood was being divinely preserved. This should not be taken as indication of racism. Desert blood stands for desert values (cf. Exeg. on ch. 24) —the values of Yahwism—which, these authors are concerned to insist, are and must remain dominant in Israel's religion and culture.

B. Jacob's Marriages (29:15-30)

This section is from E, except vss. 24, 26, 28*b*, and 29. Vss. 24, 28*b*, and 29 are from P —all that remains of his matter-of-fact notice of Jacob's marriages, which presumably followed on 28:9; cf. 28:5, according to which Jacob had already arrived at Paddan-aram.

Vs. 26 is from J, probably J¹. It should be noted that Laban's words here have a certain dignity not altogether suitable in their present setting. This suggests that they were originally not a defense—somewhat irrelevant—against Jacob's arraignment of him for his duplicity, but rather a simple reply to Jacob's request for the hand of his younger daughter, **It is not so done in our country, to give the younger before the first-born.**

From this, and from the fact that there is no trace of J elsewhere in vss. 15-30, it may reasonably be inferred that neither J¹ nor J² knew anything of Jacob's serving fourteen years for his two wives. (Cf. Eissfeldt, *Hexateuch-Synopse,* pp. 262*-63*. It should be noted, however, that Eissfeldt, postulating three independent pre-Deuteronomic narratives [see article "The Growth of the Hexateuch," p. 192], maintains that it was only the first of them—his L document—which placed Jacob's marriages early. On this see Simpson, *Early Traditions of Israel,* pp. 99-100, 592-93.) Instead they represented Jacob's marriages as occurring shortly after his arrival at Laban's. Their chronology accordingly differed considerably from that of E, a fact which the J material in ch. 34 and certain features in the Joseph story (see Exeg. on 37:3; also on chs. 42–44), in any case, suggest.

In support of this reconstruction a further point is to be noted: the unlikelihood of either J¹, the exponent of the southern tradition, or of J², whose sympathies lay in the south, representing Leah, the mother of the southern tribes, as having been foisted off on Jacob by fraud. This story of Laban's deception of Jacob is thus a northern tradition, developed over the years, to explain why it was that Rachel, the "mother" of the powerful Joseph tribes, was not Jacob's first wife but his second. It was because Jacob had been tricked by his father-in-law; his love was given to Rachel and he served

is as old as the heart of man. There is the everlasting impulse to find security, and to feel the warmth of it, within the circle of those to whom one belongs by birth and blood, within the tribe, the clan, the family. At the end of his lonely journey Jacob's heart leaped up to know that he had come to his kinsmen. When he first met Rachel and told her who he was, **she ran and told her father. And . . . Laban . . . ran to meet him, . . . and kissed him, and brought him to his house.** Association with Laban was to prove later on to have its drawbacks, but Jacob did not know it then. What he did know, and what Laban also knew, was that kinship meant

hospitality. When a man came to his own people, he was coming home. Human life would be a chilled and lonely thing if that were not true— if, instead, every individual had to shift utterly for himself, and never know that there are those with whom he has a oneness that can make him sure of welcome. As Robert Frost has put it:

Home is the place where, when you have to go there,
They have to take you in. I should have called it
Something you somehow haven't to deserve.[6]

[6] "The Death of the Hired Man." From *Complete Poems of Robert Frost.* Copyright 1930, 1949 by Henry Holt & Co. Used by permission.

16 And Laban had two daughters: the name of the elder *was* Leah, and the name of the younger *was* Rachel.

17 Leah *was* tender eyed; but Rachel was beautiful and well-favored.

18 And Jacob loved Rachel; and said, I will serve thee seven years for Rachel thy younger daughter.

19 And Laban said, *It is* better that I give her to thee, than that I should give her to another man: abide with me.

20 And Jacob served seven years for Rachel; and they seemed unto him *but* a few days, for the love he had to her.

21 ¶ And Jacob said unto Laban, Give *me* my wife, for my days are fulfilled, that I may go in unto her.

22 And Laban gathered together all the men of the place, and made a feast.

23 And it came to pass in the evening, that he took Leah his daughter, and brought her to him; and he went in unto her.

24 And Laban gave unto his daughter Leah Zilpah his maid *for* a handmaid.

25 And it came to pass, that in the morning, behold, it *was* Leah: and he said to Laban, What *is* this thou hast done unto me? did not I serve with thee for Rachel? wherefore then hast thou beguiled me?

your wages be?" 16 Now Laban had two daughters; the name of the older was Leah, and the name of the younger was Rachel. 17 Leah's eyes were weak, but Rachel was beautiful and lovely. 18 Jacob loved Rachel; and he said, "I will serve you seven years for your younger daughter Rachel." 19 Laban said, "It is better that I give her to you than that I should give her to any other man; stay with me." 20 So Jacob served seven years for Rachel, and they seemed to him but a few days because of the love he had for her.

21 Then Jacob said to Laban, "Give me my wife that I may go in to her, for my time is completed." 22 So Laban gathered together all the men of the place, and made a feast. 23 But in the evening he took his daughter Leah and brought her to Jacob; and he went in to her. 24 (Laban gave his maid Zilpah to his daughter Leah to be her maid.) 25 And in the morning, behold, it was Leah; and Jacob said to Laban, "What is this you have done to me? Did I not serve with you for Rachel? Why then have

---

seven years for her, and then the crafty Laban had substituted weak-eyed, unattractive Leah for her beautiful younger sister. Rachel was really Jacob's first choice.

16. The fact that Rachel is here introduced as for the first time indicates that E retained nothing of the story in vss. 1-12. It has been suggested above that the association of Rachel with the Aramaean figure Laban is the result of the interaction between the northern and east Jordan Israelite traditions. Leah's position as Laban's daughter seems to be a reflex of this, for Leah appears to have been first the traditional mother of the tribe of Simeon—and possibly of Levi. When Simeon came to be reckoned as a son of Jacob, his mother of necessity came to be regarded as Jacob's wife. The fact that the pre-exilic tradition nowhere mentions her grave is a slight indication that she was not a Palestinian figure, and furnishes support of Meyer's suggestion (*Israeliten und ihre Nachbarstämme*, pp. 426-27; cf. Simpson, *op. cit.*, pp. 465-66) that she originated in the desert, far to the south. The meaning of her name, "wild cow," points to a totemistic milieu. (P, indeed, records that she was buried in the cave of Machpelah [49:31]. It is unlikely, however, that he is preserving an authentic tradition. For P, the cave of Machpelah was the sepulcher of all the patriarchs, and he deliberately set aside, as will be seen [50:11-13], the earlier tradition that Jacob had been buried east of the Jordan.)

18. The custom of serving for a bride was known among the ancient Arabs, and was still met with in recent times (John Lewis Burckhardt, *Travels in Syria and the Holy Land* [London: John Murray, 1822], pp. 297-98).

23. The deception was possible because of the custom of bringing the bride to the bridegroom veiled (cf. 24:65).

26 And Laban said, It must not be so done in our country, to give the younger before the firstborn.

27 Fulfil her week, and we will give thee this also for the service which thou shalt serve with me yet seven other years.

28 And Jacob did so, and fulfilled her week: and he gave him Rachel his daughter to wife also.

29 And Laban gave to Rachel his daughter Bilhah his handmaid to be her maid.

30 And he went in also unto Rachel, and he loved also Rachel more than Leah, and served with him yet seven other years.

31 ¶ And when the LORD saw that Leah *was* hated, he opened her womb: but Rachel *was* barren.

you deceived me?" 26 Laban said, "It is not so done in our country, to give the younger before the first-born. 27 Complete the week of this one, and we will give you the other also in return for serving me another seven years." 28 Jacob did so, and completed her week; then Laban gave him his daughter Rachel to wife. 29 (Laban gave his maid Bilhah to his daughter Rachel to be her maid.) 30 So Jacob went in to Rachel also, and he loved Rachel more than Leah, and served Laban for another seven years.

31 When the LORD saw that Leah was hated, he opened her womb; but Rachel

---

27. Complete the week of this one: The seven days of the marriage festivity (cf. Judg. 14:12; Tob. 11:19).

28-30. At the end of the week Jacob is given Rachel, for whom he then proceeds to serve another seven years.

C. JACOB'S FAMILY (29:31–30:24)

This section is a conflation of J and E, with some minor additions by R^P. P apparently had no equivalent birth chronicle but was content simply to list the sons of Jacob (35:22b-26). J1 recorded the births of five sons only: Reuben, Simeon, Levi, and Judah, sons of Leah; and Joseph, the son of Rachel. To these he added Dinah, preparing for the story in ch. 34. The J1 material in the section is thus contained in 29:31-35; 30:21-24.

Reuben's position as first-born seems to have been due to the fact that the east Jordan tribe bearing this name had been the first to claim Jacob as ancestor; there is no historical evidence that it ever held a position of leadership among the other tribes (cf. Judg. 5:15b-16).

Simeon appears as the second son, possibly because Leah had been reckoned as his mother before coming to fill that role for the other clans (cf. Meyer, *Israeliten und ihre Nachbarstämme*, pp. 426-27).

Levi is represented as the third son. When J1 wrote, he was regarded as the ancestor of the Levitical priesthood (cf. Deut. 33:8-11) centering at Hebron. There is evidence (49:5-7; cf. also ch. 34), however, of the one-time existence of a secular tribe of Levi which had, as a result of some violence, been so nearly exterminated (49:7b) that only

---

26. Tradition.—The words of Laban find their echo in every century. They are what conservatism always says. **It must not be so done in our country.** New ideas, new choices, are taboo; if something has not been before, it is not to be now. There is value in that. Long established customs are not likely to have grown up without reason. Instead, they represent the slowly matured consciousness of a social group as to what gives soundness to the general life. To challenge such conviction may invite deserved rebuke. In Great Britain, where the accepted code of morals and manners has a sturdiness which often seems unique, the person who

inclines to violate it may not be met with any expostulating argument but be told, "It simply is not done." There does come a point, however, when that is not a sufficient answer. Some customs need to be challenged and changed. The instinct of the individual may perceive that what was meant to be a benefit, and long had seemed so, has become a bondage of the spirit. When Laban asserted that Jacob must marry Leah whether he wanted to or not, because it was the custom that the older daughter should be married first, Jacob protested in every way he could. No matter what sanction the custom had, he knew that a more vital reality for him

its priesthood survived. The close association of this tribe with Simeon—note "Simeon and Levi are brothers" (49:5) —may well account for Levi's position in the list.

Judah, the fourth son, was the eponym of the most powerful group in the south which was, even when J¹ wrote, in process of welding together certain other groups, such as the Simeonites, who had shared in the disaster which decimated Levi (49:7b; ibid., p. 411), the Jerahmeelites, and the Kenites (I Sam. 27:10; 30:29), to form with it the tribe of Judah.

The fact that the grave of Joseph—the first and only son of Rachel in J¹—was one of the ancient monuments at Shechem (33:19; cf. Josh. 24:32) suggests that he was in origin a Shechemite figure, who had come to be regarded as their ancestor by the northern tribes of Ephraim and Manasseh (see Exeg. on 29:1-14; also on ch. 48), which formed "the house of Joseph" (Judg. 1:22).

J¹'s chronicle is thus a schematization in genealogical terms of the relationships of those tribes which were known to him—the southern group, the east Jordan Reuben, and the house of Joseph. The representation of Reuben as a son of Leah, despite the fact that historically the tribe appears to have been a member, however inactive, of the northern confederacy (Judg. 5:15b-16), suggests that it was culturally closely connected with the south—as indeed J¹'s familiarity with legends rooted east of the Jordan further indicates (cf. 32:24-31; also Judg. 8:4-21; 11:34-39, both of which belong to the earliest stratum of J).

J² knew of seven other tribes. Of these, Issachar and Zebulun were apparently regarded as of pure Israelite stock, and their eponyms were reckoned as sons of Leah (cf. 30:17-20). This is basically E, but the inclusion in it of a fragment from J² (vs. 20aβγb), and the clear allusion to the birth of Issachar in vs. 16aγ, indicate that there was a parallel in J². The tribes of Dan, Naphtali, Gad, and Asher, on the other hand, seem to have been of mixed origin; accordingly, the eponyms of the first two were represented as sons of Bilhah, Rachel's handmaid (cf. 30:1-8), and those of the other two as sons of Zilpah, Leah's handmaid (30:9-13). On the seventh, Benjamin, see 35:16-20.

E's chronicle agrees substantially with that of J², though he provided variant etymologies for some of the names as the doublets in 30:13, 20, 23, 24 indicate. He also differed from J² in placing the birth of Issachar before Zebulun—the order accepted by RJE (cf. 30:17-20). The implication of 30:14-16, 22-24, is that in J² Issachar was

---

and for Rachel was being sacrificed to it. In his partial way Jacob was the forerunner of a new emphasis on the value of the individual. In the growing understanding of life and man and God which the O.T. expresses, the individual begins to emerge with an increased importance. Jeremiah, Ezekiel, and many of the psalms bring a message of the responsibility of all persons for their own choices and character. Where in our own time culture has been most deeply affected by the Judaeo-Christian heritage, especially in its Protestant form, as in the British Commonwealth and the United States, there has been ascribed to the individual a worth such as the ancient world did not know. So it is proclaimed that all men have rights God-given and inalienable, among which are "life, liberty, and the pursuit of happiness." Herbert Hoover, speaking on his seventy-fourth birthday in the little Iowa town where he was born, referred to the Quaker Meetinghouse where he had gone as a boy, "with its deep roots in religious faith, its tolerance and devotion to the liberty of the

individual"; and to his conception of the United States, where are "the open windows through which pours the sunlight of the human spirit," and where human dignity is "not a dream, but an accomplishment." The human dignity which is the gift of God is not idiosyncrasy or license. Its freedom must be conditioned by all that is wisest and best in what society has learned. But there is invincible truth in what Jacob intuitively felt and Laban resisted—that

The old order changeth, yielding place to new,
And God fulfils himself in many ways.[7]

29:21–30:24. Jacob's Family.—We have remembered Jacob's love for Rachel, and there was beauty in it (see Expos. on 29:1-11, 18, 20). But Jacob lived within the framework of his time. He had polygamous relationships and these did not seem strange to the writers of Genesis. By that means the family was preserved and enlarged. To modern readers the status of

[7] Tennyson, Idylls of the King, "The Passing of Arthur."

32 And Leah conceived, and bare a son; and she called his name Reuben: for she said, Surely the LORD hath looked upon my affliction; now therefore my husband will love me.

33 And she conceived again, and bare a son; and said, Because the LORD hath heard that I *was* hated, he hath therefore given me this *son* also: and she called his name Simeon.

34 And she conceived again, and bare a son; and said, Now this time will my husband be joined unto me, because I have borne him three sons: therefore was his name called Levi.

35 And she conceived again, and bare a son; and she said, Now will I praise the LORD: therefore she called his name Judah; and left bearing.

30 And when Rachel saw that she bare Jacob no children, Rachel envied her sister; and said unto Jacob, Give me children, or else I die.

was barren. 32 And Leah conceived and bore a son, and she called his name Reuben;[d] for she said, "Because the LORD has looked upon my affliction; surely now my husband will love me." 33 She conceived again and bore a son, and said, "Because the LORD has heard[e] that I am hated, he has given me this son also"; and she called his name Simeon. 34 Again she conceived and bore a son, and said, "Now this time my husband will be joined[f] to me, because I have borne him three sons"; therefore his name was called Levi. 35 And she conceived again and bore a son, and said, "This time I will praise[g] the LORD"; therefore she called his name Judah; then she ceased bearing.

30 When Rachel saw that she bore Jacob no children, she envied her sister; and she said to Jacob, "Give me chil-

[d] That is *See, a son*
[e] Heb *shama*
[f] Heb *lawah*
[g] Heb *hodah*

born about the same time as Joseph, and so after Zebulun; cf. also the order of Zebulun-Issachar in Deut. 33:18.

31. Cf. the circumstances in I Sam. 1:2-5. The belief that the Lord protects the less favored wife and makes her fruitful is an expression of the concern for the family which marks the religion of Israel.

32. The true derivation of **Reuben** is uncertain. The original form of the name may have been *Re'ûbhēl*, which possibly means "lion"; this would point to an original totemistic significance.

33. Simeon: Possibly also totemistic, denoting the offspring of a hyena and a wolf.

34. Levi may be the gentilic of Leah, "wild cow." There is also the possibility (Meyer, *Israeliten und ihre Nachbarstämme*, p. 426) that both **Levi** and Leah are derivatives of a word meaning "serpent," from which "leviathan" (Job 3:8; Pss. 74:14; 104:26; Isa. 27:1; also Job 41:1) is also derived.

35. Judah: The derivation is uncertain. Meyer suggests it is derived from *hôdh*, meaning "he [God or people?] is majestic" (*ibid.*, p. 441).

the wives, and of the maids who were treated as wives, seems pathetic. For the most part they appear as instruments of a group purpose rather than as independent persons. It is as though they were bearing the burden of Eve as it is written in the story of the Garden of Eden, "Thy desire shall be to thy husband, and he shall rule over thee." In primitive societies women are thus the creatures of a man, and that stage had not altogether passed for Israel. Children, and especially male children, were needed for the strength of the family and the tribe; and so a childless woman felt disgraced, and to have children was the chief blessing she could desire. In the record given here in Genesis it is not the

women who are of most importance, but rather the roll of the children born of them. The genealogy of the twelve tribes is being established, with its climax in the birth of Joseph; and their origin is being set in the light of the particular purpose of God.

30:1. *The Gift of Children.*—Give me children, or else I die! Here in supremely poignant phrase is the expression of a longing that throbs through all the O.T. To the people of Israel childlessness was the ultimate calamity; and to the woman it meant not only sorrow but humiliation and shame. Note the affliction of Abraham and Sarah when for so long they had no heir born of their own flesh (15:2-3; 16:2).

2 And Jacob s anger was kindled against Rachel; and he said, *Am* I in God's stead, who hath withheld from thee the fruit of the womb?

3 And she said, Behold my maid Bilhah, go in unto her; and she shall bear upon my knees, that I may also have children by her.

4 And she gave him Bilhah her handmaid to wife: and Jacob went in unto her.

5 And Bilhah conceived, and bare Jacob a son.

6 And Rachel said, God hath judged me, and hath also heard my voice, and hath given me a son: therefore called she his name Dan.

7 And Bilhah Rachel's maid conceived again, and bare Jacob a second son.

8 And Rachel said, With great wrestlings have I wrestled with my sister, and I have prevailed: and she called his name Naphtali.

dren, or I shall die!" 2 Jacob's anger was kindled against Rachel, and he said, "Am I in the place of God, who has withheld from you the fruit of the womb?" 3 Then she said, "Here is my maid Bilhah; go in to her, that she may bear upon my knees, and even I may have children through her." 4 So she gave him her maid Bilhah as a wife; and Jacob went in to her. 5 And Bilhah conceived and bore Jacob a son. 6 Then Rachel said, "God has judged me, and has also heard my voice and given me a son"; therefore she called his name Dan.[h] 7 Rachel's maid Bilhah conceived again and bore Jacob a second son. 8 Then Rachel said, "With mighty wrestlings I have wrestled[i] with my sister, and have prevailed"; so she called his name Naph'tali.

[h] That is *He judged*
[i] Heb *niphtal*

30:3. **Bilhah:** Probably connected with the Horite clan Bilhan (36:27). **That she may bear upon my knees:** In cases of this kind the slave girl seems to have been delivered upon the knees of her mistress, to whom the child was reckoned to belong; cf. **even I may have children through her.** It is uncertain, however, whether this is the origin of the ceremony of adoption alluded to in 50:23. Both customs may be derived from the practice by which the child of a lawful marriage was actually brought forth on its father's knees (see Skinner, *Genesis*, pp. 386-87).

7. **Dan:** The etymology given here is probably correct, the name being an abbreviation of a theophoric form such as Abidan (cf. Num. 1:11), meaning "My father [God] is judge."

8. Rachel with two sons had not yet **prevailed** against her sister. The original idea was that she had **wrestled** with God. **With my sister** is a gloss by one to whom this was distasteful. **Naphtali**, Meyer suggests (*op. cit.,* p. 539), is derived from the word *naphtal*—not found in the O.T.—denoting the northern highlands, west of the upper Jordan (cf. Isa. 9:1).

Now it is Rachel who cries out in unbearable distress that her sister has children and she has none.

The longing for parenthood which the O.T. continually reflects was the natural human instinct, and it was something more. It represented the deep desire for the continuance of one's own life and character. In the records of the earliest patriarchs there is little or no evidence of belief in personal immortality. The one way in which what had been real in a man could survive would be through his descendants. Children therefore were the greatest gift that could be asked of God. "Lo, children are a heritage of the LORD: and the fruit of the womb is his reward. As arrows are in the hand of a

mighty man; so are children of the youth. Happy is the man that hath his quiver full of them." So sang one of the psalmists (Ps. 127:3-5), and Proverbs went on to say: "Children's children are the crown of old men" (Prov. 17:6). All through Jewish history the family tie has been tenacious and dear. This has been one of the great reasons for the amazing power of survival which the race has shown in spite of persecution and all the other alien forces that threatened its disintegration. In the Fifth Commandment family solidarity is made the ground of God's own assurance of the people's life.

In modern days there has grown up a movement undreamed of in ancient times—that of birth control. Essentially it is the effort to adjust

9 When Leah saw that she had left bearing, she took Zilpah her maid, and gave her Jacob to wife.

10 And Zilpah Leah's maid bare Jacob a son.

11 And Leah said, A troop cometh: and she called his name Gad.

12 And Zilpah Leah's maid bare Jacob a second son.

13 And Leah said, Happy am I, for the daughters will call me blessed: and she called his name Asher.

14 ¶ And Reuben went in the days of wheat harvest, and found mandrakes in the field, and brought them unto his mother Leah. Then Rachel said to Leah, Give me, I pray thee, of thy son's mandrakes.

15 And she said unto her, *Is it* a small matter that thou hast taken my husband? and wouldest thou take away my son's mandrakes also? And Rachel said, Therefore he shall lie with thee to-night for thy son's mandrakes.

9 When Leah saw that she had ceased bearing children, she took her maid Zilpah and gave her to Jacob as a wife. 10 Then Leah's maid Zilpah bore Jacob a son. 11 And Leah said, "Good fortune!" so she called his name Gad.*j* 12 Leah's maid Zilpah bore Jacob a second son. 13 And Leah said, "Happy am I! For the women will call me happy"; so she called his name Asher.*k*

14 In the days of wheat harvest Reuben went and found mandrakes in the field, and brought them to his mother Leah. Then Rachel said to Leah, "Give me, I pray, some of your son's mandrakes." 15 But she said to her, "Is it a small matter that you have taken away my husband? Would you take away my son's mandrakes also?" Rachel said, "Then he may lie with you

j That is *Fortune*
k That is *Happy*

9. **Zilpah** may mean "abundance."

11. **Gad** is the name of an Aramaean and Phoenician god of luck or fortune, referred to in Isa. 65:11. A hybrid tribe like Gad may well once have claimed descent from this deity.

13. *Asaru* appears in the inscriptions of Seti I and Ramses II (*ca.* 1400 B.C.) as the name of a region in the west of Palestine (*ibid.*, p. 540). If **Asher** is derived from this, then the tribe took its name from the locality it occupied. Holzinger (*Genesis,* pp. 197-98), however, connects the name with the Canaanite goddess *'Ashērāh.*

14-16. These verses contain a piece of folklore according to which the eating of mandrakes—a plumlike fruit—was an aid to conception. The implication is that Rachel's pregnancy was due to this. J2's dislike of the idea is evident from his explicit statement in vs. 22 that Rachel conceived because God **remembered Rachel, . . . and opened her womb.** RJE has further obscured the implication of the tale by following E in placing the birth of Zebulun between those of Issachar and Joseph.

the size of families to the economic resources of parents, and to give to children the nurture they need. It has been resisted by one fanaticism, and by another dogmatism which can be fanatical. Militaristic leaders have seized upon the slogan to increase and multiply, and have issued it by an authority which has no concern for biblical or religious sanctions. Mussolini and Hitler, in the heyday of their pretension to enduring power, used every persuasion and compulsion to increase the birth rate, whether legitimate or illegitimate. They were not interested in families as such; they were interested in more children so that in the next generation there could be more soldiers. Obviously that sort of production of children not for any sacredness of personal

worth but as pawns for the purposes of the state —cannon fodder for another war—is a perverted evil. A multiplication of children encouraged by an institution for other and less openly avowed ends may also be an evil. Roman Catholicism opposes birth control with a rigid dogmatism that may be passionately conscientious; but mixed with this is the motive of producing more Roman Catholics, and not less willingly when the many children keep the population—as in Roman Catholic Quebec—at a low economic level and in a relative illiteracy which makes the people more amenable to the direction of the priests. But if the indiscriminate propagation of children is wrong, this is not to say that birth control is necessarily right.

16 And Jacob came out of the field in the evening, and Leah went out to meet him, and said, Thou must come in unto me; for surely I have hired thee with my son's mandrakes. And he lay with her that night.

17 And God hearkened unto Leah, and she conceived, and bare Jacob the fifth son.

18 And Leah said, God hath given me my hire, because I have given my maiden to my husband: and she called his name Issachar.

19 And Leah conceived again, and bare Jacob the sixth son.

20 And Leah said, God hath endued me *with* a good dowry; now will my husband dwell with me, because I have borne him six sons: and she called his name Zebulun.

21 And afterward she bare a daughter, and called her name Dinah.

22 ¶ And God remembered Rachel, and God hearkened to her, and opened her womb.

23 And she conceived, and bare a son; and said, God hath taken away my reproach:

24 And she called his name Joseph; and said, The LORD shall add to me another son.

tonight for your son's mandrakes." 16 When Jacob came from the field in the evening, Leah went out to meet him, and said, "You must come in to me; for I have hired you with my son's mandrakes." So he lay with her that night. 17 And God hearkened to Leah, and she conceived and bore Jacob a fifth son. 18 Leah said, "God has given me my hire*l* because I gave my maid to my husband"; so she called his name Is'sachar. 19 And Leah conceived again, and she bore Jacob a sixth son. 20 Then Leah said, "God has endowed me with a good dowry; now my husband will honor*m* me, because I have borne him six sons"; so she called his name Zeb'ulun. 21 Afterwards she bore a daughter, and called her name Dinah. 22 Then God remembered Rachel, and God hearkened to her and opened her womb. 23 She conceived and bore a son, and said, "God has taken away my reproach"; 24 and she called his name Joseph,*n* saying, "May the LORD add to me another son!"

l Heb *sakar*
m Heb *zabal*
n That is *He adds*

---

18. Issachar probably does mean "man of hire" (Meyer, *op. cit.*, p. 536; Gunkel, *Genesis,* p. 331); 49:15 refers to the tribe as being "a slave at forced labor." The name would thus seem to have been that given to its members by their Canaanite overlords.

20. Zebulun is probably derived (Meyer, *op. cit.*, p. 538) from the personal name Zebul (cf. Judg. 9:28), possibly the name of the leader under whom the group first attained tribal status.

21. Dinah is included in preparation for ch. 34. It is a personal name, and it is highly improbable that she was the eponym of a clan.

24. For the origin of the figure **Joseph** see above, and Exeg. on 29:1-14. The name, here explained as a derivative of the Hebrew verb **add,** may be a contraction of *Yôṣeph-ēl.* Whether or not it is identical with the *Yṣp'r* of the list of Thutmose III is uncertain.

With some persons and some motives it may be what its bitter enemies say it is, "a gospel of unrestrained lust sure to result in grave physical and moral disorders." [8] Techniques for preventing conception may be seized upon as a cover for sexual license outside of marriage, and in marriage birth control may be used as a means of deliberately evading the responsibility of children. The only birth control that has dignity and sacredness is what is better called "planned parenthood," which is not the prevention of

parenthood, but the thoughtful and conscientious use of knowledge to provide that children are brought into the world at such times and in such spacing as will make the whole family grow up in fullest health and happiness.

In other words, the emphasis should always be positive and creative. The instinctive cry of Rachel has in it an eternal truth—**give me children, or else I die.** Married persons who deliberately deny themselves children, or have only one child or two, solely because they are more interested in their own luxurious irresponsibility, destroy in themselves the possibility

[8] *The Catholic Encyclopedia* (New York: Encyclopedia Press, Inc., 1922, XVII, 593.

25 ¶ And it came to pass, when Rachel had borne Joseph, that Jacob said unto Laban, Send me away, that I may go unto mine own place, and to my country. 26 Give *me* my wives and my children, for whom I have served thee, and let me go: for thou knowest my service which I have done thee. 27 And Laban said unto him, I pray thee, if I have found favor in thine eyes, *tarry: for* I have learned by experience that the Lord hath blessed me for thy sake. 28 And he said, Appoint me thy wages, and I will give *it*. 29 And he said unto him, Thou knowest how I have served thee, and how thy cattle was with me. 30 For *it was* little which thou hadst before I *came*, and it is *now* increased unto a multitude; and the Lord hath blessed thee since my coming: and now, when shall I provide for mine own house also?	25 When Rachel had borne Joseph, Jacob said to Laban, "Send me away, that I may go to my own home and country. 26 Give me my wives and my children for whom I have served you, and let me go; for you know the service which I have given you." 27 But Laban said to him, "If you will allow me to say so, I have learned by divination that the Lord has blessed me because of you; 28 name your wages, and I will give it." 29 Jacob said to him, "You yourself know how I have served you, and how your cattle have fared with me. 30 For you had little before I came, and it has increased abundantly; and the Lord has blessed you wherever I turned. But now when shall I provide for my own household

---

D. Jacob Outwits Laban (30:25-43)

25-43. The section is a conflation of J[1], slightly elaborated by J[2] and E.

The J[1] narrative told of the proposal of Jacob, who had hitherto been working for Laban, to set up an establishment for himself (vss. 29-30). Laban, unwilling to lose his services, thereupon offered to allow him to fix his own wages. Jacob replied that he wanted nothing at the moment, but proposed that Laban should remove from his flocks all the **speckled and spotted** animals—vs. 32, in which the imperative "pass" is to be read for **let me pass**, with the Vulg., and "and remove" for **removing**, with the LXX and the Vulg. (Smend, *Erzählung des Hexateuch*, p. 76). These were to be set apart by themselves (cf. vs. 36). Jacob would then care for the rest of the flock and would receive as his wages any speckled and spotted that might be born to these normally colored animals in the future. To this Laban promptly agreed (vss. 34-36) —indeed, why would he not accept a proposal so favorable to himself? If Jacob was such a fool as to suggest it, let him take the consequences!

---

of their richest growth. It is in homes where there are a number of children that the happiest and fullest human character can flower. It is out of such homes that there may come the qualities of understanding, co-operation, and mutual affection which are sorely needed if society is to be lifted toward a divine ideal. Now, as truly as in the O.T. times, the opportunity of parenthood must be recognized as the high and holy gift of God.

25-43. *Jacob Outwits Laban.*—The chronicler must have set down this account with a very human and perhaps unregenerate pleasure. Here was Jacob, the progenitor of Israel, outsmarting the uncovenanted Laban. From a natural point of view that seemed eminently appropriate. More than once Laban had deliber-

ately cheated Jacob. He had promised him Rachel to wife, and after Jacob had served seven years for her he withheld Rachel and gave him Leah instead. According to Jacob, Laban had also changed his wages ten times (31:7). Jacob had good reason therefore to be suspicious when Laban tried to persuade him to stay and work for him further (vs. 27), and all the more so when Laban added unctuously, **for I have learned by experience that the Lord hath blessed me for thy sake.** Anybody would have said that if Laban could now be cheated in his turn, it would be what he thoroughly deserved.

As a matter of fact, Jacob does not cheat him. He carries through exactly the terms of an agreement which he had proposed to Laban, and which Laban explicitly accepted. He was not

31 And he said, What shall I give thee? And Jacob said, Thou shalt not give me any thing: if thou wilt do this thing for me, I will again feed *and* keep thy flock.

32 I will pass through all thy flock to-day, removing from thence all the speckled and spotted cattle, and all the brown cattle among the sheep, and the spotted and speckled among the goats: and *of such* shall be my hire.

33 So shall my righteousness answer for me in time to come, when it shall come for my hire before thy face: every one that *is* not speckled and spotted among the goats, and brown among the sheep, that shall be counted stolen with me.

34 And Laban said, Behold, I would it might be according to thy word.

35 And he removed that day the he goats that were ring-streaked and spotted, and all the she goats that were speckled and spotted, *and* every one that had *some* white in it, and all the brown among the sheep, and gave *them* into the hand of his sons.

also?" 31 He said, "What shall I give you?" Jacob said, "You shall not give me anything; if you will do this for me, I will again feed your flock and keep it: 32 let me pass through all your flock today, removing from it every speckled and spotted sheep and every black lamb, and the spotted and speckled among the goats; and such shall be my wages. 33 So my honesty will answer for me later, when you come to look into my wages with you. Every one that is not speckled and spotted among the goats and black among the lambs, if found with me, shall be counted stolen." 34 Laban said, "Good! Let it be as you have said." 35 But that day Laban removed the he-goats that were striped and spotted, and all the she-goats that were speckled and spotted, every one that had white on it, and every lamb that was black, and put them in charge of

---

But Jacob, though he may have been a knave, was no fool. He placed rods upon which he had peeled white streaks before the eyes of the stronger animals in the flocks at rutting time, with the result that the young born to them were **striped, speckled, and spotted,** and so belonged to him (vss. 37-39, 42*a*). Thus his substance increased rapidly (vs. 43), and Laban was left with the feebler animals (vs. 42*b*).

This story of one knave outwitting another—doubtless another piece of shepherd lore—is of a piece with that in 25:27-34 (cf. also 26:1-11; 27:1-40), and it was told by J[1] with unfeigned delight; clever Jacob had outwitted the dull nomad Aramaean.

J[2] was less enthusiastic, but there was not much he could do about it. The popularity of the story made it necessary for him to include it in his enlarged edition of the J[1] narrative. He did, however, prefix to it vss. 25, 27, to suggest that if Jacob had had his way he would have returned to Palestine at this point. Furthermore, the implication is, Laban having admitted that his present prosperity was due to the Lord's blessing on Jacob (vs. 27)—underlined in vs. 30*aγ*, also J[2]—his willingness to take advantage of Jacob's seeming simplicity was the more reprehensible and went far to justify the latter in his sharp practice.

---

false like Laban; he was simply more inventive and adroit. When he had proposed to Laban that all he asked in the way of wages was that little fraction of the flock which might be odd in color, that seemed to Laban a highly desirable bargain, especially since he, Laban, took the opportunity then and there to remove from the flock all the sheep and goats that might breed the type that would belong to Jacob. The trouble was that he did not foresee the extraordinary device by which Jacob would be able to make the flock breed according to his interest—a device not ruled out by the bargain.

So by every secular standard Jacob was entitled to his triumph. But the interest of the O.T. story lies in the fact that the narrator was not judging by secular standards. He believed that Jacob's triumph was directly linked to his religion. He describes Jacob as saying to Rachel and Leah, "God hath taken away the cattle of your father, and given them to me" (31:9). Moreover, an angel appears to Jacob and gives him God's message thus: "I have seen all that Laban doeth unto thee. I am the God of Bethel, . . . where thou vowedst a vow unto me" (31:12-13). In other words, Jacob's clever

36 And he set three days' journey betwixt himself and Jacob: and Jacob fed the rest of Laban's flocks.

37 ¶ And Jacob took him rods of green poplar, and of the hazel and chestnut tree; and pilled white streaks in them, and made the white appear which *was* in the rods.

38 And he set the rods which he had pilled before the flocks in the gutters in the watering troughs when the flocks came to drink, that they should conceive when they came to drink.

39 And the flocks conceived before the rods, and brought forth cattle ring-streaked, speckled, and spotted.

40 And Jacob did separate the lambs, and set the faces of the flocks toward the ring-streaked, and all the brown in the flock of Laban; and he put his own flocks by themselves, and put them not unto Laban's cattle.

his sons; 36 and he set a distance of three days' journey between himself and Jacob; and Jacob fed the rest of Laban's flock.

37 Then Jacob took fresh rods of poplar and almond and plane, and peeled white streaks in them, exposing the white of the rods. 38 He set the rods which he had peeled in front of the flocks in the runnels, that is, the watering troughs, where the flocks came to drink. And since they bred when they came to drink, 39 the flocks bred in front of the rods and so the flocks brought forth striped, speckled, and spotted. 40 And Jacob separated the lambs, and set the faces of the flocks toward the striped and all the black in the flock of Laban; and he put his own droves apart, and did not put them

The E narrative at this point was very different. J²'s additions, both here and later, to the J¹ story of Jacob and Laban had done little to change the character of the tale. It remained a lusty account of rogue competing with rogue. E revised it thoroughly, to represent Laban as repeatedly endeavoring to defraud Jacob. (Gunkel is in error in maintaining that E also told of Jacob using the peeled-rod device [*Genesis,* pp. 336-40]; also Skinner [*Genesis,* p. 390]. Holzinger [*Genesis,* p. 201] holds that the material is from J, with some harmonization by Rᴶᴱ.) E's account of the agreement between the two can be reconstructed with little difficulty from the fragments which Rᴶᴱ inserted into the J narrative—thus to some extent obscuring its point—vss. 26, 28, the words in vs. 32 **and every black lamb, such shall be my wages,** and vs. 33; and from his condensation of the rest of it in 31:8-12. Laban first agreed that Jacob should receive the spotted and speckled young of the goats and the black of the sheep and then, as each arrangement worked out favorably for Jacob, changed his wages ten times (cf. 31:7*a*). God, however, intervened to protect Jacob from being victimized (31:7*b*).

37-39. A note by S. R. Driver may be quoted for what it is worth: "The physiological principle involved is well established, and, as Bochart shewed (*Hieroz.* II. c. 49: I. p. 619 ff.,

stratagem and the success it brought him are the result of the commitment he believed God had given to him at Bethel to make him prosperous. A curious blending of the earthy and the heavenly—a blending which one must recognize to exist in part of the O.T. and in influences which have flowed from it! The people of Israel were convinced that there is an intimate relationship between favor with heaven and material well-being in this world. The positive aspect of that was to give powerful sanction to keen-wittedness and commercial sagacity, so that the Jew in many practical matters has exhibited an intelligence greater than that of his non-Jewish rival. As with Jacob in his contest with Laban, he can show that he deserves to win.

The negative aspect is of course the implication that prosperity ought to be the concomitant of religion. That is not confined to Judaism. John Calvin, who was greatly influenced by the O.T., tended to make it appear that the Christian citizen, sturdy and self-reliant, would be more evidently a man of God if he was a success in business. It is true that there are qualities inspired by religion—integrity, diligence, faithfulness in familiar duties—which may bring this world's goods as their result. But to look toward these as a necessary reward of religion is to dishonor the love of God, which must be sought for itself, by trying to make it an instrument of our selfishness. It is not in Jacob's outwitting Laban that we see the true end of worship. It

41 And it came to pass, whensoever the stronger cattle did conceive, that Jacob laid the rods before the eyes of the cattle in the gutters, that they might conceive among the rods.

42 But when the cattle were feeble, he put *them* not in: so the feebler were Laban's, and the stronger Jacob's.

43 And the man increased exceedingly, and had much cattle, and maidservants, and menservants, and camels, and asses.

31 And he heard the words of Laban's sons, saying, Jacob hath taken away all that *was* our father's; and of *that* which *was* our father's hath he gotten all this glory.

2 And Jacob beheld the countenance of Laban, and, behold, it *was* not toward him as before.

3 And the Lord said unto Jacob, Return unto the land of thy fathers, and to thy kindred; and I will be with thee.

4 And Jacob sent and called Rachel and Leah to the field unto his flock,

5 And said unto them, I see your father's countenance, that it *is* not toward me as before; but the God of my father hath been with me.

6 And ye know that with all my power I have served your father.

with Laban's flock. 41 Whenever the stronger of the flock were breeding Jacob laid the rods in the runnels before the eyes of the flock, that they might breed among the rods, 42 but for the feebler of the flock he did not lay them there; so the feebler were Laban's, and the stronger Jacob's. 43 Thus the man grew exceedingly rich, and had large flocks, maidservants and menservants, and camels and asses.

31 Now Jacob heard that the sons of Laban were saying, "Jacob has taken all that was our father's; and from what was our father's he has gained all this wealth." 2 And Jacob saw that Laban did not regard him with favor as before. 3 Then the Lord said to Jacob, "Return to the land of your fathers and to your kindred, and I will be with you." 4 So Jacob sent and called Rachel and Leah into the field where his flock was, 5 and said to them, "I see that your father does not regard me with favor as he did before. But the God of my father

ed. Rosenm.), was known to the ancients, and was applied, for instance, for the purpose of obtaining particular colours in horses and dogs (Oppian, *Kynegetica*, i, 327 ff., 353-6). According to an authority quoted by Delitzsch, cattle-breeders now, in order to secure white lambs, surround the drinking-troughs with white objects." (*The Book of Genesis* [15th ed.; London: Methuen & Co., 1948], p. 279.)

E. Jacob's Decision to Return Home (31:1-16)

31:1-16. Except for vss. 1 and 3, the section is from E. Vs. 1 is J[1] and was immediately followed by vss. 19, 21aα; i.e., in J[1] Jacob's departure was motivated simply by his recognition of the fact that he had about reached the limit: Laban's sons were getting restless. J[2], concerned here as elsewhere to make more explicit the providential element in Jacob's career, added vs. 3.

is rather in Jesus, who, "though he was rich, yet for your sakes . . . became poor" (II Cor. 8:9).

31:1-29. *The Purpose and Providence of God.* —For the intricate composition of this passage, with its overlappings and inconsistencies, see the Exeg. For the expositor it is not particularly fruitful, since it deals mostly with the sharpening disagreement between Laban and Jacob, and their mutual recriminations. Yet through it all

it is impressive to see how the narrators are moved by their central conviction that everything in Jacob's life, no matter how small and ordinary, was overarched by the high purpose and providence of God. It must not be only annoyance with Laban that determines Jacob to go home; his going must be another chapter in the divine ordaining. So **the Lord said unto Jacob, Return unto the land of thy fathers, and to thy kindred; and I will be with thee** (vs. 3).

7 And your father hath deceived me, and changed my wages ten times; but God suffered him not to hurt me.

8 If he said thus, The speckled shall be thy wages; then all the cattle bare speckled: and if he said thus, The ring-streaked shall be thy hire; then bare all the cattle ring-streaked.

9 Thus God hath taken away the cattle of your father, and given *them* to me.

10 And it came to pass at the time that the cattle conceived, that I lifted up mine eyes, and saw in a dream, and, behold, the rams which leaped upon the cattle *were* ring-streaked, speckled, and grizzled.

11 And the angel of God spake unto me in a dream, *saying*, Jacob: and I said, Here *am* I.

12 And he said, Lift up now thine eyes, and see, all the rams which leap upon the cattle *are* ring-streaked, speckled, and grizzled: for I have seen all that Laban doeth unto thee.

13 I *am* the God of Bethel, where thou anointedst the pillar, *and* where thou vowedst a vow unto me: now arise, get thee out from this land, and return unto the land of thy kindred.

has been with me. 6 You know that I have served your father with all my strength; 7 yet your father has cheated me and changed my wages ten times, but God did not permit him to harm me. 8 If he said, 'The spotted shall be your wages,' then all the flock bore spotted; and if he said, 'The striped shall be your wages,' then all the flock bore striped. 9 Thus God has taken away the cattle of your father, and given them to me. 10 In the mating season of the flock I lifted up my eyes, and saw in a dream that the he-goats which leaped upon the flock were striped, spotted, and mottled. 11 Then the angel of God said to me in the dream, 'Jacob,' and I said, 'Here I am!' 12 And he said, 'Lift up your eyes and see, all the goats that leap upon the flock are striped, spotted, and mottled; for I have seen all that Laban is doing to you. 13 I am the God of Bethel, where you anointed a pillar and made a vow to me. Now arise, go forth from this land, and return to the land

The E narrative has been to some extent dislocated by RJE, who intruded material harmonizing the passage with the preceding J account of Jacob's sharp practice and summarizing the omitted E parallel to this (vss. 8-12). It must have recorded at the beginning the theophany—probably in a dream (cf. vs. 11)—mentioned by Jacob in vs. 13, in which God explicitly commanded him to return to Palestine and fulfill the vow he had made at Bethel (28:20-22a) twenty years before. Jacob then summoned his two wives, reminded them of the shifty treatment their father had given him, and told them of the command he had now received in the theophany (vss. 4-7, 13). Rachel and Leah aligned themselves unreservedly against their father—another point in E's rehabilitation of Jacob's character; he had treated them "as foreigners" and had, with incredible meanness, kept for himself the dowry (Exod. 22:17) or purchase price which Jacob had paid for them, i.e., the fourteen years' service which Jacob had given him had not benefited the daughters in the slightest. They were accordingly more than willing that Jacob should return home (vss. 14-16).

The stage was now set in both the J2 and E narratives for Jacob's flight.

Jacob says to Rachel and Leah, **the God of my father hath been with me** (vs. 5). It is through God's express favor that he has got the best of Laban; and the angel of the Lord, he tells them, has come to him in a dream and said to him: **I am the God of Bethel, where thou anointedst the pillar, and where thou vowedst a vow unto me; now arise, get thee out from this land, and return unto the land of thy kindred** (vs. 13).

Moreover, God warns Laban against any violence to Jacob, so that he has to say: It is in **the power of my hand to do you hurt: but the God of your father spake unto me yesternight, saying, Take thou heed that thou speak not to Jacob either good or bad** (vs. 29). Also Laban's concern for his little idol gods which he accused Jacob of having stolen is so pictured as to put him on the level of primitive superstition,

14 And Rachel and Leah answered and said unto him, *Is there* yet any portion or inheritance for us in our father's house?

15 Are we not counted of him strangers? for he hath sold us, and hath quite devoured also our money.

16 For all the riches which God hath taken from our father, that *is* ours, and our children's: now then, whatsoever God hath said unto thee, do.

17 ¶ Then Jacob rose up, and set his sons and his wives upon camels;

18 And he carried away all his cattle, and all his goods which he had gotten, the cattle of his getting, which he had gotten in Padan-aram, for to go to Isaac his father in the land of Canaan.

19 And Laban went to shear his sheep: and Rachel had stolen the images that *were* her father's.

20 And Jacob stole away unawares to Laban the Syrian, in that he told him not that he fled.

21 So he fled with all that he had; and he rose up, and passed over the river, and set his face *toward* the mount Gilead.

22 And it was told Laban on the third day, that Jacob was fled.

23 And he took his brethren with him, and pursued after him seven days' journey; and they overtook him in the mount Gilead.

24 And God came to Laban the Syrian in a dream by night, and said unto him, Take heed that thou speak not to Jacob either good or bad.

25 ¶ Then Laban overtook Jacob. Now Jacob had pitched his tent in the mount: and Laban with his brethren pitched in the mount of Gilead.

of your birth.' " 14 Then Rachel and Leah answered him, "Is there any portion or inheritance left to us in our father's house? 15 Are we not regarded by him as foreigners? For he has sold us, and he has been using up the money given for us. 16 All the property which God has taken away from our father belongs to us and to our children; now then, whatever God has said to you, do."

17 So Jacob arose, and set his sons and his wives on camels; 18 and he drove away all his cattle, all his livestock which he had gained, the cattle in his possession which he had acquired in Paddan-aram, to go to the land of Canaan to his father Isaac. 19 Laban had gone to shear his sheep, and Rachel stole her father's household gods. 20 And Jacob outwitted Laban the Aramean, in that he did not tell him that he intended to flee. 21 He fled with all that he had, and arose and crossed the Eu-phra'tes, and set his face toward the hill country of Gilead.

22 When it was told Laban on the third day that Jacob had fled, 23 he took his kinsmen with him and pursued him for seven days and followed close after him into the hill country of Gilead. 24 But God came to Laban the Aramean in a dream by night, and said to him, "Take heed that you say not a word to Jacob, either good or bad."

25 And Laban overtook Jacob. Now Jacob had pitched his tent in the hill country, and Laban with his kinsmen encamped

---

F. Jacob's Flight from Laban (31:17-43)

17-43. The section is a conflation of J (J¹+J²) and E, except for vs. 18aβγb, from P.

The J¹ story is of the same character as his account of Jacob's outwitting of Laban. It is built around the incident of the theft of the teraphim. While Laban was away at sheepshearing, Rachel stole the images (vs. 19) and Jacob fled (vs. 21aα). The implication of this recension is that Jacob was involved in, or at least knew of, the theft (contrast vs. 32b, J²).

Laban, hearing that Jacob had gone, went after him, and came up with him at the mountain (vss. 22, 23a, 25abα), shortly to be named Galeed, a wordplay on Gilead (vs. 48), and immediately charged him with having stolen his gods (vss. 26aα, 30b). Jacob knowing the trick Rachel had planned—in J¹, vs. 34 followed vs. 30b—embarked upon a brazen piece of bluff, and replied, **Any one with whom you find your gods shall not live** (vs. 32a). Laban then searched Leah's tent (vs. 33a—the mention of the tent of the maidservants is secondary), and then went into Rachel's tent. There Rachel, despite

26 And Laban said to Jacob, What hast thou done, that thou hast stolen away unawares to me, and carried away my daughters, as captives *taken* with the sword?

27 Wherefore didst thou flee away secretly, and steal away from me; and didst not tell me, that I might have sent thee away with mirth, and with songs, with tabret, and with harp?

28 And hast not suffered me to kiss my sons and my daughters? thou hast now done foolishly in *so* doing.

29 It is in the power of my hand to do you hurt: but the God of your father spake unto me yesternight, saying, Take thou heed that thou speak not to Jacob either good or bad.

30 And now, *though* thou wouldest needs be gone, because thou sore longedst after thy father's house, *yet* wherefore hast thou stolen my gods?

in the hill country of Gilead. 26 And Laban said to Jacob, "What have you done, that you have cheated me, and carried away my daughters like captives of the sword? 27 Why did you flee secretly, and cheat me, and did not tell me, so that I might have sent you away with mirth and songs, with tambourine and lyre? 28 And why did you not permit me to kiss my sons and my daughters farewell? Now you have done foolishly. 29 It is in my power to do you harm; but the God of your father spoke to me last night, saying, 'Take heed that you speak to Jacob neither good nor bad.' 30 And now you have gone away because you longed greatly for your father's house, but why did

---

the way of women (vs. 35) which rendered her ceremonially unclean (cf. Lev. 15:19-23), was sitting on the gods. She apologized for not rising when her father entered, pleading her condition. Laban accordingly searched in vain (vss. 33*b*, 35).

The teraphim were probably, as the RSV translation indicates, **household gods.** J[1]'s scorn for them is clear. Rachel in her uncleanness even sat on them, and nothing happened to her. In contrast with this is Laban's concern for his gods which, despite their supposed divinity, could be insolently stolen. And in the background is the derisive figure of Jacob, playing his last wanton stroke against his father-in-law.

The relish with which J[1] told the tale is obvious. That J[2], on the other hand, found it morally offensive is evident from the revision to which he subjected it. By inserting vs. 32*b* and shifting the notice in vs. 34 to its present position, he represented Jacob as

---

upon which the events of the story pour a sardonic scorn.

30-35. Rudiments of Worship.—Probably it is true, as the Exeg. suggests, that the main purpose for the mention of the images is to disparage Laban for the superstitious value he put on them, and by contrast to indicate that Jacob was superior to such things. In that case, Rachel's sitting upon them would be only another stroke in the picture of the idols' degradation. But there is another road on which imagination travels. Suppose that Rachel sat upon the images not to make her father's search for them ridiculous, but because she craved to keep them for herself. Then that might be taken as evidence simply of pathetic superstition on her part; but it is possible to see in it something more than that. Suppose that on her way to an unfamiliar country and to a strange new relationship, Rachel wanted to carry with her what had been significant at home. That can be a wholesome human instinct. None of us is iso-

lated and self-sufficient. The meaning of life is bound up with the complex of associations of the family or the group. If these are altogether left behind, the human being will be lonely and lost. The immigrant is for witness. A stream of peoples came, e.g., to the United States from the old countries of Europe. They brought their picturesque costumes, their music, their folk dances, and their folkways. Often the communities into which they went have been too crass and too stupidly self-satisfied to see the worth of what these newcomers brought. They have ridiculed the manners and the customs that differ from their own; too frequently with the result that the immigrants themselves have grown embarrassed and ashamed. In the process of being Americanized they have discarded the inheritance and hidden the particular gifts by which the culture of American communities might have been colored and enriched. One of the obligations owed to sensitive leaders in some neighborhood settlements is that they have

31 And Jacob answered and said to Laban, Because I was afraid: for I said, Peradventure thou wouldest take by force thy daughters from me.

32 With whomsoever thou findest thy gods, let him not live: before our brethren discern thou what *is* thine with me, and take *it* to thee. For Jacob knew not that Rachel had stolen them.

33 And Laban went into Jacob's tent, and into Leah's tent, and into the two maidservants' tents; but he found *them* not. Then went he out of Leah's tent, and entered into Rachel's tent.

34 Now Rachel had taken the images, and put them in the camel's furniture, and sat upon them. And Laban searched all the tent, but found *them* not.

35 And she said to her father, Let it not displease my lord that I cannot rise up before thee; for the custom of women *is* upon me. And he searched, but found not the images.

you steal my gods?" 31 Jacob answered Laban, "Because I was afraid, for I thought that you would take your daughters from me by force. 32 Any one with whom you find your gods shall not live. In the presence of our kinsmen point out what I have that is yours, and take it." Now Jacob did not know that Rachel had stolen them.

33 So Laban went into Jacob's tent, and into Leah's tent, and into the tent of the two maidservants, but he did not find them. And he went out of Leah's tent, and entered Rachel's. 34 Now Rachel had taken the household gods and put them in the camel's saddle, and sat upon them. Laban felt all about the tent, but did not find them. 35 And she said to her father, "Let not my lord be angry that I cannot rise before you, for the way of women is upon me." So he searched, but did not find the household gods.

---

being ignorant of the theft. At the same time he endeavored to shift the emphasis from the fact that the teraphim had been stolen by stating (vs. 20, cf. vs. 26aβγ) that "Jacob stole the heart of Laban"—rendered in the RSV, **outwitted Laban**—and by having Jacob defend himself against a general charge of dishonesty (vs. 32aβ) which, in fact, had not been made; with this is allied Jacob's outraged protest in vss. 37-40. These last verses, it may be noted, are a moving description of a faithful shepherd, in which the artistry of J² appears at its best.

The only other addition made by J² to his predecessor's narrative is the geographical note in vs. 21aβ, necessitated by his having changed the location of Laban's home from the desert to Haran. It may be noted that the representation that Mount Gilead was from seven to ten days' journey (cf. vss. 22-23) from Laban's starting point fits only with J¹'s location of him. Both Haran and the vague Mesopotamia of E (cf. 24:10) are much farther away, Haran some 350 miles as the crow flies. J² had, however, to tolerate the inconsistency.

E dealt with the story by rewriting it completely, preserving only the feature that Jacob had departed secretly (vss. 17-18aα, 27). Since the covenant following was made at Mizpah, E refers quite naturally to the hill country of Gilead as a known place (vss.

---

actively encouraged the foreign people to preserve and contribute the unique values which have been their own.

So far, then, perhaps so good. But what exactly, it may be asked, has this to do with Rachel and her images? Rachel was bringing not gracious aspects of human culture, musical and artistic, but the representations of primitive religion. Ought they not to have been promptly despised and left behind? To that question one may give a too-quick dogmatic answer. Get rid of the childlike and the crude; get rid of it even when tendrils of all the worship we

have known are wrapped about it, and we have not yet found what will take its place! In the days of slavery the Negroes conceived the poignant words and haunting music of the spirituals. Later, in the advancing years of freedom and new opportunity and knowledge, many were ashamed of the associations of the spirituals and wanted to forget them; but the truer interpreters of the genius of the race knew that they were too precious to let go. Rachel's images are far from standing on a level of religious truth and beauty with the spirituals; but nevertheless they are a symbol of that instinct of

36 ¶ And Jacob was wroth, and chode with Laban: and Jacob answered and said to Laban, What *is* my trespass? what *is* my sin, that thou hast so hotly pursued after me?

37 Whereas thou hast searched all my stuff, what hast thou found of all thy household stuff? set *it* here before my brethren and thy brethren, that they may judge betwixt us both.

38 This twenty years *have* I *been* with thee; thy ewes and thy she goats have not cast their young, and the rams of thy flock have I not eaten.

39 That which was torn *of beasts* I brought not unto thee; I bare the loss of it; of my hand didst thou require it, *whether* stolen by day, or stolen by night.

40 *Thus* I was; in the day the drought consumed me, and the frost by night; and my sleep departed from mine eyes.

36 Then Jacob became angry, and upbraided Laban; Jacob said to Laban, "What is my offense? What is my sin, that you have hotly pursued me? 37 Although you have felt through all my goods, what have you found of all your household goods? Set it here before my kinsmen and your kinsmen, that they may decide between us two. 38 These twenty years I have been with you; your ewes and your she-goats have not miscarried, and I have not eaten the rams of your flocks. 39 That which was torn by wild beasts I did not bring to you; I bore the loss of it myself; of my hand you required it, whether stolen by day or stolen by night. 40 Thus I was; by day the heat consumed me, and the cold by night, and my sleep

---

21*b*, 23*b*). When Laban came up with Jacob he did not question his honesty, the implication being that on such a point there could be no dispute. Instead, he reproached him for carrying off his daughters without giving him an opportunity to say farewell to them, and Jacob replied in kind (vss. 26*b*, 28, 31). There is a lacuna in the extant E material at this point, but apparently Laban made some further complaint, Jacob's reply to which is preserved in vss. 36*b*, 41-43.

Into this narrative a later hand, E², inserted vs. 24—awkward in its representation that Laban delayed a whole night before arraigning Jacob—to emphasize God's care for him. From the same hand comes the related vs. 42*b*.

---

worship which is deeper than its poor forms. The wisest missionaries of the Christian gospel have learned to look with a reverent understanding upon even the crudest religious expressions of pagan people, and never to despise these but to lead through them to the larger truth. It would be well if all Christian teachers should meet with the same patience ideas that seem to them childish and grotesque. The words of Thomas Carlyle are worth remembering:

You take wheat to cast into the Earth's bosom: your wheat may be mixed with chaff, chopped straw, barn-sweepings, dust and all imaginable rubbish; no matter: you cast it into the kind just Earth; she grows the wheat,—the whole rubbish she silently absorbs, shrouds *it* in, says nothing of the rubbish. The yellow wheat is growing there; the good Earth is silent about all the rest.[9]

36-42. *Jacob's Indignation.*—Here in the midst of what is mostly an unattractive story is a flash of beauty. In the first place, there is a

[9] *On Heroes, Hero-Worship, and the Heroic in History,* "The Hero as Prophet."

ring of honest indignation in Jacob's words to Laban. He, Jacob, had certainly been no perfect example in his dealings; but it was true that at the beginning, and by his own initiative, he had been completely faithful to the agreement between Laban and himself. It was Laban who began deceit; and in comparison with Laban, Jacob's own original honesty of purpose gave him some reason for his passionate claim: **Except the God of my father, the God of Abraham, and the fear of Isaac, had been with me, surely thou hadst sent me away now empty. God hath seen my affliction and the labor of my hands, and rebuked thee yesternight.**

Then there is the stirring description of the shepherd in vss. 38-40—of the shepherd so devoted to his flock and so careless of his own advantage that no risk or cost was too great for him to incur for his sheep. Reading Jacob's words, even if Jacob's own career was not always consistent with them, one is reminded of David in the upland pastures defending his sheep against the lion and the bear; and of the one supreme Shepherd who "calleth his own sheep

41 Thus have I been twenty years in thy house: I served thee fourteen years for thy two daughters, and six years for thy cattle; and thou hast changed my wages ten times.

42 Except the God of my father, the God of Abraham, and the fear of Isaac, had been with me, surely thou hadst sent me away now empty. God hath seen mine affliction and the labor of my hands, and rebuked *thee* yesternight.

43 ¶ And Laban answered and said unto Jacob, *These* daughters *are* my daughters, and *these* children *are* my children, and *these* cattle *are* my cattle, and all that thou seest *is* mine: and what can I do this day unto these my daughters, or unto their children which they have borne?

44 Now therefore come thou, let us make a covenant, I and thou; and let it be for a witness between me and thee.

45 And Jacob took a stone, and set it up *for* a pillar.

46 And Jacob said unto his brethren, Gather stones; and they took stones, and made a heap: and they did eat there upon the heap.

fled from my eyes. 41 These twenty years I have been in your house; I served you fourteen years for your two daughters, and six years for your flock, and you have changed my wages ten times. 42 If the God of my father, the God of Abraham and the Fear of Isaac, had not been on my side, surely now you would have sent me away empty-handed. God saw my affliction and the labor of my hands, and rebuked you last night."

43 Then Laban answered and said to Jacob, "The daughters are my daughters, the children are my children, the flocks are my flocks, and all that you see is mine. But what can I do this day to these my daughters, or to their children whom they have borne? 44 Come now, let us make a covenant, you and I; and let it be a witness between you and me." 45 So Jacob took a stone, and set it up as a pillar. 46 And Jacob said to his kinsmen, "Gather stones," and they took stones, and made a heap; and

---

G. Jacob's Covenant with Laban (31:44-55)

44-55. According to J, the purpose of the **covenant** between Jacob and Laban was to define the boundary between the Israelites east of the Jordan and the nomad Aramaeans. As a witness to the agreement, a **heap** of **stones** was made, which was given the name **Galeed,** meaning **The heap of witness** (RSV mg.), intended to provide an etymology for Gilead. The extant material of this recension is found in vss. 44*b*, 46 (reading "Laban" for "Jacob" with the O.L.; note that it is Laban, not Jacob, who explains the meaning of the heap in vs. 51), 51-52, 48; in vss. 51-52 the references to the pillar are redactional harmonization. The meal referred to in vs. 46 is the sacred feast preceding the covenant ceremony. Vs. 47 is a learned gloss. Nowhere else in the Jacob-Laban cycle of stories is there the slightest suggestion that the two spoke different languages.

This is probably the primary Palestinian tradition of Laban: he was the representative of the nomad Aramaeans. And Jacob stands opposite him representing the people living immediately east of the Jordan. In all likelihood it was this association of the two which led to Laban's being given the role of the father of Leah and Rachel, Jacob's wives.

The tale itself was presumably preserved in the vicinity of a certain cairn in the hill country of Gilead, which was originally believed to be the abode of some god, who ever stood on guard to enforce the provisions of the agreement. For J[1], however, it was simply a memorial and the agreement was without supernatural sanctions. These J[2]

---

by name, . . . for they know his voice" (John 10:3-4).

43-55. *Jacob's and Laban's Covenant.*—Here the tumultuous story of Jacob and Laban comes to its more peaceful and pleasant conclusion. It *is* like a day that had been marked by noon-

time heat and sudden clouds and thunderstorm, drawing now toward a quiet evening. It is characteristic of the O.T. that all human relationships are lifted up into the larger relationship with God. Laban and Jacob make a covenant with one another, and when they call upon God

47 And Laban called it Jegar-sahadutha: but Jacob called it Galeed.

48 And Laban said, This heap is a witness between me and thee this day. Therefore was the name of it called Galeed,

49 And Mizpah; for he said, The LORD watch between me and thee, when we are absent one from another.

50 If thou shalt afflict my daughters, or if thou shalt take *other* wives beside my daughters, no man *is* with us; see, God *is* witness betwixt me and thee.

51 And Laban said to Jacob, Behold this heap, and behold *this* pillar, which I have cast betwixt me and thee;

they ate there by the heap. 47 Laban called it Je'gar-sahadu'tha:[o] but Jacob called it Galeed.[p] 48 Laban said, "This heap is a witness between you and me today." Therefore he named it Galeed, 49 and the pillar[q] Mizpah,[r] for he said, "The Lord watch between you and me, when we are absent one from the other. 50 If you ill-treat my daughters, or if you take wives besides my daughters, although no man is with us, remember, God is witness between you and me."

51 Then Laban said to Jacob, "See this heap and the pillar, which I have set be-

[o] In Aramaic *The heap of witness*
[p] In Hebrew *The heap of witness*
[q] Cn. Compare Sam: Heb lacks *the pillar*
[r] That is *Watchpost*

provided by inserting vs. 53a, in which **the God of their father**—awkward in the Hebrew —is a gloss.

It is impossible to identify the site of the cairn. All that can be said is that J[1] located it somewhere in the hill country of Gilead, between the Syro-Arabian desert and the river Jabbok, the next place mentioned in his account of Jacob's journey home.

In the J narrative of Jacob's flight there is no real connection between the theft of the household gods and the covenant with Laban which followed. The two incidents are simply placed side by side—a fact which suggests that the tale of the theft was in its origin independent of the Jacob-Laban tradition.

The E story of the covenant, on the other hand, is organically related to his story of Jacob's flight. There, as has been seen, Laban had reproached Jacob for not allowing him to say farewell to his daughters. Vs. 43, in which Laban voiced his concern for their future safety, leads directly to the covenant (vs. 44a) in which Jacob promised that he would not ill-treat Leah and Rachel or take wives in addition to them (vs. 50). As a memorial of the covenant, Laban sets up a pillar (vs. 45—"Laban" should be read for "Jacob"; in vs. 49 it is Laban, not Jacob, who explains its significance). The pillar is called **Mizpah** (vs. 49). In the present form of the text it stands simply as a symbol of the Lord's watching between Laban and Jacob (vs. 49). **The LORD** is impossible in E; the LXX reads more correctly "God." Even this, however, is probably a substitution for an original "this pillar" (cf. Holzinger, *Genesis*, pp. 206-7). If so, then E preserves something of the ancient idea of the pillar (*maççēbhāh*) as an abode of deity (cf. vs. 48 [J]), though he empties the allusion of any real significance by the words in vs. 50, **God is witness between you and me**, and by the statement that **Jacob swore by the Fear of his father Isaac** (vs. 53b). For E, **the Fear of his father Isaac** undoubtedly meant the God worshiped and feared by Isaac. Originally it probably had a more mythological significance (Meyer,

to confirm that covenant it is characteristic of the O.T. again that they think of him first not as the God of the individual only, but as the God of their fathers. Laban invokes **the God of Abraham, and the God of Nahor,** and Jacob swears **by the fear of his father Isaac.** Here is that sense of a corporate and continuing loyalty which made the religion of Israel so tenacious and so strong. To the heap of stones which they set up as a token of their covenant they gave the name **Mizpah,** which means **Watchpost;** and the meaning was that they were

calling God to witness that they must keep their agreement, after they had parted.

It is significant also that the cairn of stones and the pillar described as thus set up by Jacob and Laban were thought of in the later tradition of Israel as the boundary line between the land of Israel and the land of Syria—a boundary line which should not be transgressed by the descendants of Jacob and of Laban. Certainly the purpose suggested there has meaning and importance for every time. "Good fences make good neighbors," wrote Robert Frost in "Mend-

52 This heap *be* witness, and *this* pillar *be* witness, that I will not pass over this heap to thee, and that thou shalt not pass over this heap and this pillar unto me, for harm.

53 The God of Abraham, and the God of Nahor, the God of their father, judge betwixt us. And Jacob sware by the fear of his father Isaac.

54 Then Jacob offered sacrifice upon the mount, and called his brethren to eat bread: and they did eat bread, and tarried all night in the mount.

55 And early in the morning Laban rose up, and kissed his sons and his daughters, and blessed them: and Laban departed, and returned unto his place.

32 And Jacob went on his way, and the angels of God met him.

2 And when Jacob saw them, he said, This *is* God's host: and he called the name of that place Mahanaim.

tween you and me. 52 This heap is a witness, and the pillar is a witness, that I will not pass over this heap to you, and you will not pass over this heap and this pillar to me, for harm. 53 The God of Abraham and the God of Nahor, the God of their father, judge between us." So Jacob swore by the Fear of his father Isaac, 54 and Jacob offered a sacrifice on the mountain and called his kinsmen to eat bread; and they ate bread and tarried all night on the mountain.

55ˢ Early in the morning Laban arose, and kissed his grandchildren and his daughters and blessed them; then he departed and returned home.

32 Jacob went on his way and the angels of God met him; 2 and when Jacob saw them he said, "This is God's army!" So he called the name of that place Mahana'im.ᵗ

ˢ Ch 32.1 in Heb
ᵗ Here taken to mean *Two armies*

Israeliten und ihre Nachbarstämme, pp. 254-55). Vss. 54—in which again "Laban" is to be read for "Jacob"—and 55abα conclude the E recension.

In this tale E claims that **Mizpah** received its name from the *maççēbhāh* erected there by Laban to watch between him and Jacob. Mizpah means **Watchpost** (vs. 49 RSV mg.), or "outlook point." A number of Mizpahs, or Mizpehs, are mentioned in the O.T. (e.g., Josh. 11:3; 15:38; Judg. 10:17; 20:1; I Sam. 22:3); the name might be given to any high point.

It is impossible to say whether E is here preserving the local tradition of one such place east of the Jordan or whether he invented the story because, having located Laban in Mesopotamia, the J story of a boundary agreement between him and Jacob was no longer relevant. In any case, he has given a unity of theme—Laban's concern for his family—to the account of Jacob's separation from his father-in-law, which is lacking in the J parallel. In so doing he records effectively the final defeat of Laban. At the same time, he has done something to redeem the character of the man whom, in his effort to rehabilitate the character of Jacob, he had made into a shifty, most unattractive figure.

XXXIX. Jacob and Esau III (32:1–33:16)
A. Jacob Prepares to Meet Esau (32:1-23)

32:1-23. A conflation of J—J2 plus some later material—and E.

According to J2, after Laban had departed, Jacob sent messengers to the land of Seir, i.e., Edom, in the hope of making friends with Esau, from whose anger he had fled

---

ing Wall." But more than good fences are needed for that. There must be a consciousness of God as stabilizing the relationships of men by a righteousness that at last may prove stronger than human rivalry and passion. One remembers, with desire that its ideal might be both actual and universal, the "Christ of the Andes," the majestic figure set up on the border between Argentina and Chile as a symbol of

commitment to peace between the two countries.

32:1-2. *Mahanaim.*—How often we meet this mention of angels in the story of Jacob's life! Angels on the ladder in the vision at Bethel; the dream of an angel that told him to leave the country of Laban; angels now before him on his way; the memory of an angel at the last when he laid his hands upon the sons of Joseph, and said, "The Angel which redeemed me from

3 And Jacob sent messengers before him to Esau his brother unto the land of Seir, the country of Edom.

4 And he commanded them, saying, Thus shall ye speak unto my lord Esau; Thy servant Jacob saith thus, I have sojourned with Laban, and stayed there until now:

5 And I have oxen, and asses, flocks, and menservants, and womenservants: and I have sent to tell my lord, that I may find grace in thy sight.

6 ¶ And the messengers returned to Jacob, saying, We came to thy brother Esau, and also he cometh to meet thee, and four hundred men with him.

7 Then Jacob was greatly afraid and distressed: and he divided the people that *was* with him, and the flocks, and herds, and the camels, into two bands;

3 And Jacob sent messengers before him to Esau his brother in the land of Se'ir, the country of Edom, 4 instructing them, "Thus you shall say to my lord Esau: Thus says your servant Jacob, 'I have sojourned with Laban, and stayed until now; 5 and I have oxen, asses, flocks, menservants, and maidservants; and I have sent to tell my lord, in order that I may find favor in your sight.' "

6 And the messengers returned to Jacob, saying, "We came to your brother Esau, and he is coming to meet you, and four hundred men with him." 7 Then Jacob was greatly afraid and distressed; and he divided the people that were with him, and the flocks and herds and camels, into two com-

---

some twenty years before (vss. 3-5). The messengers returning with the word that Esau was coming to meet him with four hundred men, Jacob's fear increased, and he divided his family, servants, and animals into two companies, hoping that if Esau attacked one of them the other might escape (vss. 6-8). Both companies he sent on ahead of him while he himself remained beside a certain stream—the Jabbok, cf. vs. 22 (E)—for the night (vss. 24a, 13a).

At this point J2 broke into his Jacob-Esau narrative by inserting the story of Jacob's wrestling at the Jabbok, taken over from J1, vss. 24b-29, 31, to be considered presently. In the meantime, it may be noted that J2 represents Jacob as relying on his own cleverness to extricate himself from a difficult situation, which, it will be seen, he manages to do, though at some cost to himself (cf. 33:1-16). There is no suggestion that he relied on divine assistance—indeed, J2 seems purposely to be avoiding such a suggestion. He is showing how Jacob at long last had to pay for the deception by which he had deprived Esau of his father's blessing, and also for his tricky dealings with Laban; i.e., J2 in this story, which is his own free composition, is drawing the sting of the morally difficult

---

all evil, bless the lads" (48:16). There had been much earthliness and evil in Jacob, and certainly it was too bold a phrase to say that he had been redeemed from all of it. But the striking fact is the repeated association of angels with the name of this imperfect man. The one great characteristic which gradually refined him was his desire—which from the beginning he possessed—for nearer knowledge of God. May it be therefore that the angels of God come, even though in invisible presence, to every man who has that saving eagerness? Not only in the case of Jacob, but in that of many another, those who look at the man's life and what is happening in it and around it may be able to say that as he went on his way the angels of God met him.

3-23. *Old Fears Returning.*—This long passage is a vivid picture of a man who could not

get away from the consequences of an old wrong. Many years before, Jacob had defrauded Esau. He had got away to a safe distance and he had stayed there a long time. Doubtless he had tried to forget about Esau, or at any rate to act as if Esau's oath to be avenged could be forgotten. While he was in Laban's country he could feel comfortable. But the time had come when he wanted to go back home; and though the thought of it drew him, it appalled him too. There was the nostalgia of early memories, but there was the nightmare of the later one, and it overshadowed all the rest. Esau was there; and what would Esau do?

As a matter of fact, Esau would not do anything. If he had not forgotten what Jacob had done to him, he had stopped bothering himself about it. Hot tempered and terrifying though he could be, he was too casual to carry a grudge.

8 And said, If Esau come to the one company, and smite it, then the other company which is left shall escape.

9 ¶ And Jacob said, O God of my father Abraham, and God of my father Isaac, the LORD which saidst unto me, Return unto thy country, and to thy kindred, and I will deal well with thee:

10 I am not worthy of the least of all the mercies, and of all the truth, which thou hast showed unto thy servant; for with my staff I passed over this Jordan; and now I am become two bands.

11 Deliver me, I pray thee, from the hand of my brother, from the hand of Esau: for I fear him, lest he will come and smite me, *and* the mother with the children.

12 And thou saidst, I will surely do thee good, and make thy seed as the sand of the sea, which cannot be numbered for multitude.

panies, 8 thinking, "If Esau comes to the one company and destroys it, then the company which is left will escape."

9 And Jacob said, "O God of my father Abraham and God of my father Isaac, O LORD who didst say to me, 'Return to your country and to your kindred, and I will do you good.' 10 I am not worthy of the least of all the steadfast love and all the faithfulness which thou hast shown to thy servant, for with only my staff I crossed this Jordan; and now I have become two companies. 11 Deliver me, I pray thee, from the hand of my brother, from the hand of Esau, for I fear him, lest he come and slay us all, the mothers with the children. 12 But thou didst say, 'I will do you good, and make your descendants as the sand of the sea, which cannot be numbered for multitude.' "

---

material—whether derived from J[1] or elsewhere—which circumstances had compelled him against his will to include in his narrative. Here Jacob does not emerge as a hero. A later J writer, to ameliorate this unfavorable picture, inserted the prayer in vss. 9-12.

The E narrative differed from that of J[2] to a very considerable extent. It locates Jacob's preparations for meeting Esau at Mahanaim (vss. 1-2), preserving what may be only a fragment of the tradition of that place. The implication would seem to be that the vision of angels deepened Jacob's moral sensitivity. At any rate, when he heard that Esau was coming—to be inferred from what follows; the E notice is missing, having been dropped by RJE in favor of vs. 6 (J)—he at once resolved to make handsome amends for the past. Taking from his own vast flocks and herds a large number of animals, he made up five droves—of goats, sheep, camels, cows, and asses. He then sent them on ahead of him, a drove at a time, carefully spaced, instructing the servant in charge of each to tell Esau that it was a gift from his brother who was coming along behind. In this way Jacob hoped that Esau would be prevailed upon to forget the past (vss. 13b-21a). The implication is that Jacob would himself meet Esau shortly after the fifth drove; i.e., E, having dropped the story of the wrestling at the Jabbok, had no need to have Jacob remain behind alone.

As ch. 33 tells, he would meet Jacob presently with the bluff generosity of the big man who lets bygones be bygones. But not only did Jacob not know that; what he supposed he knew was the exact opposite. Esau would confront him as a deadly threat.

Consequently, he begins to plan how he can placate him. He will send an ingratiating message. He will pretend to trust what he does not really dare believe, **that I may find grace in thy sight.** He waits for his messengers to come back; and when they do come and tell their tidings, he is panic-stricken. For they tell him that Esau is coming—not only Esau, but Esau with four hundred men. To Jacob's imagination they all

had swords in their hands. Certainly it looked as though punishment was on the march, and that seemed the more certain because he knew that there was nothing better that he had merited. It was a time for desperate devices. He divided his flocks and herds and everything he possessed into two companies, and he told his servants that if Esau attacked one, the other at least should try to escape. Meanwhile, Esau had no idea of attacking anybody; but "the wicked flee when no man pursueth" (Prov. 28:1).

At this point Jacob said his prayers. After that he felt less afraid. He thought of another plan to protect himself against Esau's coming. He distributed his camels and cattle into nu-

13 ¶ And he lodged there that same night; and took of that which came to his hand a present for Esau his brother;

14 Two hundred she goats and twenty he goats, two hundred ewes and twenty rams,

15 Thirty milch camels with their colts, forty kine and ten bulls, twenty she asses and ten foals.

16 And he delivered *them* into the hand of his servants, every drove by themselves; and said unto his servants, Pass over before me, and put a space betwixt drove and drove.

17 And he commanded the foremost, saying, When Esau my brother meeteth thee, and asketh thee, saying, Whose *art* thou? and whither goest thou? and whose *are* these before thee?

18 Then thou shalt say, *They be* thy servant Jacob's; it *is* a present sent unto my lord Esau: and, behold, also he *is* behind us.

13 So he lodged there that night, and took from what he had with him a present for his brother Esau, 14 two hundred she-goats and twenty he-goats, two hundred ewes and twenty rams, 15 thirty milch camels and their colts, forty cows and ten bulls, twenty she-asses and ten he-asses. 16 These he delivered into the hand of his servants, every drove by itself, and said to his servants, "Pass on before me, and put a space between drove and drove." 17 He instructed the foremost, "When Esau my brother meets you, and asks you, 'To whom do you belong? Where are you going? And whose are these before you?' 18 then you shall say, 'They belong to your servant Jacob; they are a present sent to my lord Esau; and

RJE, putting these two recensions together, placed that of J first, intact. Then he told of Jacob stopping where he was for the night—making use of the notice with which J2 had introduced the Jabbok story (vs. 13a) —and continued with the E account of Jacob's preparations. He then in vss. 21b-24a—in part derived from J2—represented Jacob as sending on his immediate family late at night while he remained behind alone. The stage was thus set for the Jabbok story.

It has already been noted that in the story in ch. 27, E placed the blame for the incident therein related upon Rebekah—thus to a considerable degree clearing Jacob of responsibility—and that he implied that Rebekah paid the price for her duplicity by never seeing her favorite son again. It has further been noted that in the E recension of the Laban stories, Jacob is consistently the innocent victim of his father-in-law's grasping unscrupulousness. In this story the same point of view is manifest. Jacob, though not himself responsible, recognizes the justice of Esau's anger, and takes steps to effect a reconciliation; i.e., in the E material read in isolation, Jacob's character is morally unobjectionable. One of the effects of the conflation of E with J2 is that in the resultant

merous groups, and he sent them out at intervals in the direction from which Esau would be approaching. When Esau should encounter the first of these, he was to be told that they were a present from his brother Jacob; so with the second group, and the third, and all down the line until Esau should be appeased. Then he sent off his handmaids and their children, and Leah and her children, and last of all he and Rachel followed. The irony of it was that all these precautions were unnecessary. When Esau finally appeared, and Jacob bowed himself to the ground seven times before him, "Esau ran to meet him, . . . and fell on his neck, and kissed him" (33:4).

Jacob had passed through a humiliating process. He had been thoroughly afraid, and this was the more galling because he thought of himself as somebody who ought not to have had to be afraid. In his possessions he was a person of consequence. He had tried to suggest that to Esau in his first messages. But none of his possessions fortified him when his conscience let him down. Even when Esau met him with such astonishing magnanimity, Jacob was not yet at ease. He still kept on his guard, with unhappy apprehension lest Esau might change his mind (see 33:12-17). Knowing that he had not deserved Esau's brotherliness, he could not believe that he could trust it.

19 And so commanded he the second, and the third, and all that followed the droves, saying, On this manner shall ye speak unto Esau, when ye find him.

20 And say ye moreover, Behold, thy servant Jacob *is* behind us. For he said, I will appease him with the present that goeth before me, and afterward I will see his face; peradventure he will accept of me.

21 So went the present over before him; and himself lodged that night in the company.

22 And he rose up that night, and took his two wives, and his two womenservants, and his eleven sons, and passed over the ford Jabbok.

23 And he took them, and sent them over the brook, and sent over that he had.

24 ¶ And Jacob was left alone; and there wrestled a man with him until the breaking of the day.

moreover he is behind us.'" 19 He likewise instructed the second and the third and all who followed the droves, "You shall say the same thing to Esau when you meet him, 20 and you shall say, 'Moreover your servant Jacob is behind us.'" For he thought, "I may appease him with the present that goes before me, and afterwards I shall see his face; perhaps he will accept me." 21 So the present passed on before him; and he himself lodged that night in the camp.

22 The same night he arose and took his two wives, his two maids, and his eleven children, and crossed the ford of the Jabbok. 23 He took them and sent them across the stream, and likewise everything that he had. 24 And Jacob was left alone; and a man wrestled with him until the breaking of the

---

narrative J²'s disapprobation of Jacob on moral grounds is obscured, and it seems as though his conduct, as it is represented in J², were condoned.

The analysis of the JE narrative into its component documents thus helps to make clear the fact that there was a distinct advance in moral sensitivity. It is only J¹ who manifests any delight in the more than questionable conduct of his hero, and it was not long before the moral austerity of Yahwism asserted itself and in one way or another condemned his duplicity.

B. Jacob's Wrestling at the Jabbok (32:24-32)

24-32. Except for vs. 30 (E), this section is from J—J¹ revised by J², with vs. 32 added. (Gunkel, *Genesis*, pp. 359-60, and Procksch, *Genesis*, pp. 193, 372 [cf. Skinner, *Genesis*, p. 407] regard it as a conflation of J and E. Smend, *Erzählung des Hexateuch*, p. 86, and Eissfeldt, *Hexateuch-Synopse*, p. 264*, ignoring the inconsistencies in the story, derive it from J¹ [L].)

J¹ appears to have taken over practically unchanged the legend of the Jabbok—the word *'ābhaq*, **wrestled**, occurring only here in the O.T., is a wordplay on "Jabbok"—

The barrier in the way of forgiveness may lie not in unreadiness of the wronged to give, but in the inability of the one who has done wrong to receive. Jacob had to be humbled and chastened before he could be made clean. The wrestling by the Jabbok would be the beginning of that. He had to admit down deep that he did not deserve anything, and he had to get rid of the pride that thought he could work out his peace by his own wits. Only so could he ever feel that the relationship with Esau had really been restored. More importantly, it is only so that men can believe in and accept the forgiveness of the love of God.

24-32. *The Reckoning with God.*—Primitive myth, Jewish particularism, the light of lofty

spiritual understanding—all these are blended in this story of Jacob's wrestling. Once it was believed that every conspicuous natural object had its particular spirit, and a river might have its river-god who resented any crossing of the river. Such a myth may have influenced the form of the story here. The impulse to explain the Jewish taboo upon eating the muscle of the thigh, the proud desire to link the name of Israel with a heroic origin, may be the reasons for other elements in the story, such as vss. 25, 28. But out of the mixed material emerges one dominant picture. It is that of the man who, in spite of many faults, had an indomitable desire to have his life rightly related to God, but who must be disciplined and chastened before that desire

25 And when he saw that he prevailed not against him, he touched the hollow of his thigh; and the hollow of Jacob's thigh was out of joint, as he wrestled with him.

26 And he said, Let me go, for the day breaketh. And he said, I will not let thee go, except thou bless me.

day. **25** When the man saw that he did not prevail against Jacob, he touched the hollow of his thigh; and Jacob's thigh was put out of joint as he wrestled with him. **26** Then he said, "Let me go, for the day is breaking." But Jacob said, "I will not let

---

according to which some supernatural being, presumably the numen of the place, wrestled with Jacob all night (vs. 24) to prevent him from crossing the stream. In the course of the struggle Jacob dislocated the other's thigh (vs. 25a). As the dawn approached the mysterious wrestler—the implication is that he was a night demon who must not be abroad in the daytime—urged Jacob to let him go, but Jacob, possibly realizing now for the first time the supernatural character of his antagonist, refused to comply until the other blessed him (vs. 26). The original, pre-Israelite form of the tale, it may be assumed, then recorded that **there he blessed him** (vs. 29b), continued with the sentence in vs. 31a, which noted the narrow escape of the demon, **the sun rose upon him as he passed Penuel,** and concluded in all probability with a notice that Jacob named the stream Jabbok.

---

could be fulfilled. A very different experience is the one here described from the one at Bethel. There the vision of the ladder and the angels of God had come to Jacob as a benediction—as God does come, in some first wondering spiritual experience, to the young. Now the reality of God had to be encountered in another and more awful way. The soul must wrestle with the dreadful mystery of existence. It must learn the full meaning of the ultimate power to which it is constrained to give account. On his way home Jacob had prayed to God for protection against Esau (vss. 10-11), but he well knew he did not deserve it. "I am not worthy of the least of all the mercies, and of all the truth, which thou hast showed unto thy servant." And now he was left alone. No human helper could be at his side in the agonizing struggle which presently he had to face. No props of former confidence or conceit could sustain him. His own character would be put to its determining proof.

24-25. *The Struggle in the Dark.*—Who was the antagonist coming out of the darkness to seize Jacob for a struggle that would last **until the breaking of the day?** Not Esau, as in the first fearful moment of surprise Jacob might have imagined. Not any human foe, however terrible. Not a river-god. No; but the Almighty God of Righteousness, forcing him to make his reckoning. The O.T. story is dramatizing here the consequence that comes to every soul that has tried too long to evade the truth about itself. Thus far Jacob's life had seemed successful. By one stratagem and another he had outwitted Esau, Isaac, and Laban. Coming home prosperous, all the outward circumstances might

have made him boastful. But his conscience saw something else. He saw his world shadowed by his guilt. Old memories awakened, old fears rose up from the past in which he had tried to bury them. He had to face these memories and submit to their bruising recollection. Now that he was to meet Esau, he knew that he was not the masterful person he had liked to imagine he was. He had made his smooth way ahead among people who had not known him; now he had to encounter people who did know him, and would remember him as a liar and a coward. He was brought up short to a reckoning with himself, which was a reckoning with God. He could ignore the prospect of that in the busy daytime, but now it was night, and he was alone; and when a man is alone, then least of all can he get away from God. When the mysterious antagonist touched the hollow of Jacob's thigh, **and the hollow of Jacob's thigh was out of joint,** it was a symbol of the fact that Jacob was in the grip of a power which his self-assurance could not match. Jacob knew that henceforth he could never walk in lofty arrogance again.

26. *Holding On.*—Another strange mingling of elements is in the picture here. The exclamation of the unnamed wrestler, **Let me go, for the day breaketh** seems to have its origin in the dim old belief that spirits could walk the earth only during the darkness, and that when the day began to break they had to go back to the place of shadows from which they had come. But the timeless meaning is in the words of Jacob, **I will not let thee go, except thou bless me.** In the good and evil that made up Jacob there were two factors of nobility that saved

27 And he said unto him, What *is* thy name? And he said, Jacob.

you go, unless you bless me." 27 And he said to him, "What is your name?" And he said,

---

This story, the antiquity of which is obvious, is probably the basic Jacob legend in the O.T. Jacob prevailed over his supernatural opponent; cf. Hos. 12:3-4, "In his [Jacob's] strength he strove with God: yea he struggled with the angel, and prevailed" (ASV mg.). A point to be noted is the superhuman strength ascribed to Jacob; with this may be compared the implications of 28:18, according to which Jacob himself set up the pillar at Bethel, and of 29:10, where he alone and unaided moved a stone which normally could be moved only through the combined efforts of a number of men (cf. 29:8). All three passages seem to echo the representation of Jacob as a giant.

---

him. The first was his awareness that life has a divine meaning above its material fact—the awareness that made him seek the birthright and made possible his vision at Bethel. The second quality, revealed here in his wrestling, was his determination. He had struggled all night until he was lame and agonized; but when his antagonist wished to separate himself, Jacob desperately held on. When a man is forced to wrestle with moral reality and its consequences, he may try to get rid of them as quickly as he can. But Jacob's quality was otherwise. Caught in the grip of judgment, his prevailing desire was not for escape. He would hold on until something decisive happened. In punishment, as in prosperity, he would not let the experience go until he had wrung a blessing from it. The shallow man may ignore his sins; the cowardly man may try to evade their consequences; but Jacob now was neither one. Hurt and humiliated though he was, and needing to repent, he still dared believe that his great desire could prevail. In Charles Wesley's hymn one can hear his cry:

> Yield to me now, for I am weak,
> But confident in self-despair;
> Speak to my heart, in blessing speak;
> Be conquered by my instant prayer.[1]

Frederick W. Robertson has given a further interpretation to Jacob's answer to the demand of his antagonist, Let me go:

Jacob held Him more convulsively fast, as if aware that the daylight was likely to rob him of his anticipated blessing: in which there seems concealed a very deep truth. God is approached more nearly in that which is indefinite than in that which is definite and distinct. He is felt in awe, and wonder and worship, rather than in clear conceptions. There is a sense in which darkness has more of God than light has. . . . In sorrow, haunted by uncertain presentiments, we feel the infinite around us. The gloom disperses, the world's joy comes again, and it seems as if God were gone—the Being who had touched us with a withering hand, and

[1] "Come, O Thou Traveler unknown."

wrestled with us, yet whose presence, even when most terrible, was more blessed than His absence. . . . Yes, in solitary, silent, vague darkness, the Awful One is near.[2]

27-28. The Significance of a Name.—There is a little book by Charles R. Brown entitled *What Is Your Name?* [3] and its first chapter deals with this same Genesis story. A new name is given to Jacob. There is profound significance in the names of God (see Expos. on vs. 29). What of the significance of the name of a man? At first a particular name may mean nothing. But what is "at first"? A child is given a name when he is born. But that is not the beginning of his name. He is somebody's son. His "given name" may be new with him, but part of his name belongs to his family. That family name is never altogether colorless. It may have the nearly neutral tint of average respectability; it may be dark with discredit; or it may shine with the purple and gold of accumulated honor. A man cannot help his heredity? No, but to an important degree he can determine which part of his heredity he appropriates. Many tendencies are born in him. It will be easier to follow some than others, but there is room for choice and courage to determine which will be dominant in the end.

Jacob was a mixed character if ever there was one. He had in him some of Rebekah's quick, unscrupulous wit, but also some of Isaac's loyalty. He had some of Sarah's jealousy, but some of Abraham's farseeing faith. What he would make out of his family inheritance would depend on which part of it he seized and sanctified. In ch. 30 there is the curious tale of how Jacob got the sheep to produce lambs "ringstreaked, speckled, and spotted" by arranging when the sheep conceived that they had ringstreaked, speckled, and spotted things to look at. In relation to the ring-streaked possibilities he was born with, it was possible for Jacob, if he looked with enough desire at the white streaks

[2] *Sermons on Bible Subjects*, pp. 17-18.
[3] New Haven: Yale University Press, 1924.

28 And he said, Thy name shall be called no more Jacob, but Israel: for as a prince hast thou power with God and with men, and hast prevailed.

"Jacob." **28** Then he said, "Your name shall no more be called Jacob, but Israel,[u] for you have striven with God and with men, and

[u] That is *He who strives with God* or *God strives*

J[1], including this legend in his narrative, gave it a new point of extraordinary importance. By vss. 27-28 he unified the tradition brought from the desert, that his people were the sons of Israel, with the various local traditions of Canaan, in assimilating which they had come to claim Abraham, Isaac, and, finally, Jacob as their ancestors. As to whether at the same time he dropped the notice of the naming of the Jabbok, or whether this was deleted later by R[JE] when he inserted vs. 30, it is impossible to say.

J[2], taking this story over from J[1], rejected the representation that Jacob had prevailed over God (cf. vs. 28) by laming him. He added vs. 25*b*—thus changing the

---

and looked away enough from the black ones, to become a man patterned according to the better rather than the worse elements in his inheritance. To some degree at least that was what he did.

It would make a big difference if not only individuals but nations set themselves to do the same. Germany of the twentieth century had a double inheritance; Goethe, Schiller, Beethoven, and Bach were on the one side; Nietzsche, Bernhardi, and the Prussian *Junkers* on the other. Its doom was that it repudiated the part of its inheritance that was born of the spirit, and chose to incarnate what was brutal. The United States also has a double inheritance: from Washington and Lincoln and the world ideals of Woodrow Wilson on the one hand, and from pinchbeck politicians and profiteers and economic pirates on the other. Read Russell Davenport, *My Country*.[4] Read—as related to England—*Our Threatened Values*, by Victor Gollancz.[5] Destiny is determined not mechanically by the so-called "human nature that never changes," but by the part of its inherited nature which it chooses to value and promote.

A name, however, is more than an inheritance. It is the mark of an individual who can create something new: new not only in relation to the ancestral past, but new also in relation to the stages of his own development. Jacob's name, when he first appears, makes a poor impression. Read "Jacob" in ch. 27, and all that the name suggests is the self-interest and mean spirit of "the supplanter." His name was never wholly divested of its first unattractiveness, but by the grace of God associations were added to it which made the final balance different. The One who wrestled with him there by the ford of Jabbok said he should be called Israel; and strange as it might seem, it was thus as Israel, "a prince of God," that succeeding generations thought of him.

[4] New York: Simon & Schuster, 1944.
[5] Hinsdale, Ill.: Henry Regnery Co., 1947.

Why? Because he had shown another side of himself to which God could give a different name. At his worst he had been something better than a sensualist. He was not ruled by the appetite of his body, as Esau—so much more immediately attractive but so easygoing and therefore so inconsequential—generally was. His ambitions were on a higher level than the physical. He wanted the birthright because the one who held it should be the representative of the family not only toward men but toward God—a fact which interested Esau not at all. That Jacob could have had his dream at Bethel showed that he was sensitive to the unseen. And when he had once fixed the goal of this desire, he had unlimited determination in moving toward it. Consider the long years he served Laban before he reached the end which inflexibly he had pursued. It was this tenacity of purpose which was his essential strength, and this that made the mysterious wrestler say to him that he had **power with God and with men** and had prevailed.

Moreover, the name of Jacob is lighted at the end by a ray of beauty not often met with in Genesis. At first he seemed to love nobody but himself; but when he met Rachel he showed that love for her and for all that belonged to her could become the ruling power of his life. The man whose name in the beginning is synonymous with one contemptible deed identifies that name at last with a great devotion. Far better it is of course if a man can make his name winsome from the outset. "Wherewithal shall a young man cleanse his way? by taking heed thereto according to thy word" (Ps. 119:9). But many a man may need the encouragement which comes from the story of Jacob to believe that a name which has once been shadowed by discredit can be lifted to honor. Recall what Jesus helped Simon son of Jonas to believe about himself (John 1:42). Read the baptismal office in the Book of Common Prayer, and the promise which stands back of the

29 And Jacob asked *him,* and said, Tell *me,* I pray thee, thy name. And he said, Wherefore *is it that* thou dost ask after my name? And he blessed him there.

29 Then Jacob asked him, "Tell me, I pray, your name." But he said, "Why is it that you ask my name?" And

meaning of the preceding sentence so that it was Jacob who was lamed—and vs. 31*b,* so that vs. 31*a* now referred to Jacob passing Penuel. In this way any suggestion that God had to get away at dawn was removed from the tale. Vs. 29*a* is also from J², and is evidence of popular speculation as to who Jacob's opponent was. J² implies (cf. Judg. 13:17-21) that he was the angel of the Lord. **And with men** in vs. 28, alluding to Jacob's discomfiture of Laban, is from a later hand than J², who would not thus have commended Jacob's duplicity.

A further purpose of J²'s additions becomes clear when it is recognized that he represents the event recorded in the story as the occasion of an extraordinary change in Jacob. Prior to this his character had left much to be desired. From now on he appears in a new light. There is a vast difference between the depiction of him—however softened by J²—as a crafty rogue in the Laban stories and the patient old man of chs. 37; 42-45.

J² has implicitly given a profound significance to the blessing of vs. 29. What was originally a crass piece of mythology has become in his hands a parable. Jacob, congratulating himself on his final besting of Laban, is brought down to earth by the news of Esau's approach. His reaction is remorse, not penitence, and this determines the preparations he makes to extricate himself from what seems to be a difficult situation.

Christian name. Remember what the Spirit said to "him that overcometh": "I . . . will give him a white stone, and in the stone a new name written" (Rev. 2:17). As Charles R. Brown wrote:

The ideals you cherish, the purposes you hold, the capacity you feel for something finer than anything as yet attained—all these are contained in that new name written upon the white stone which every man is privileged to wear upon his breast.[6]

29. The Names of God.—In Jacob's question, **Tell me, I pray thee, thy name,** there is the echo of an ancient superstition, but there is also the reaching out toward an everlasting truth. Men used to think there was a sort of magical potency in a name. A name was much more than a label of identification; it belonged to the essence of a personality. Know a name and you had a way open to the secret of the person. You could use the name not only for invocation but as a spell of incantation. So it was believed in relation not only to human beings but also to beings who were divine. Jacob felt himself in the grip of a supernatural power. He needed above everything to know that power's name.

But beyond the element in Jacob's desire that reflects old superstition there is the greater truth. The Bible is a history of man's discovery, by God's revealing, of nobler names of God. The

character of religion is determined by the name and therefore by the nature of the God men worship. That was so all through the O.T. and into the N.T.; and it is true now. God could be thought of as the Elohim, the power in many ways inscrutable, with whom one came into contact in the forces of nature, in the resurrection of light in the springtime, or in the waning of the sun in winter; in the nameless terror of an eclipse, in earthquakes and volcanoes and thunder and lightning and the wild fury of storms. His presence was suggested by the dark mystery of the forest or by some vast old tree and some strangely shaped stone. Modern men may think of God in terms superficially altered but essentially the same. Consider how many there are to whom God is real only when they are confronted by something that mystifies them or shocks them and makes them afraid; a mortal illness, a pestilence, a storm at sea that threatens shipwreck. The name of God may be Yahweh, which signified originally the god of the tribe. Consider the twentieth-century obsession of nationalism which again may make religion the worship of a tribal god, until in its perverted forms patriotism becomes—in Samuel Johnson's words—"the last refuge of a scoundrel." The name of God may be "the God of Sabaoth," the god of war, whose chief function is to lead the fighting men. Read the Song of Moses in Exod. 15, the prayer of Joshua in Josh. 10, the Song of Deborah in Judg. 5, the imprecatory psalms; and consider how in all

[6] *What Is Your Name?* p. 9.

30 And Jacob called the name of the place Peniel: for I have seen God face to face, and my life is preserved.

there he blessed him. 30 So Jacob called the name of the place Peni'el,ᵛ saying, "For I have seen God face to face, and yet my life

ᵛ That is *The face of God*

But then, at last, he has to reckon with God. He emerges from the conflict physically lamed but spiritually regenerated. Nevertheless, as will be seen, the penalty for his past treatment of Esau has to be paid, and in this section of the tale (33:1-16) the old self-centeredness reappears momentarily for a final purging. And it may well be that in the mind of J² Jacob's suffering at the loss of Joseph was in expiation of the past.

Vs. 32, referring to a custom not elsewhere mentioned in the O.T., is a later addition. The significance of the taboo is uncertain. Robertson Smith (*Religion of Semites*, p. 380) explains it from the idea that the thigh was sacred as the seat of life. Wellhausen (*Reste arabischen Heidentums* [2nd ed.; Berlin: Georg Reimer, 1897], p. 168) calls attention to a trace of it in ancient Arabia.

Vs. 30, as has been noted above, is from E, a fragment of the story which he substituted for the J story of the wrestling, shrinking from its stark anthropomorphism. As to whether he drew upon the legend of the founding of the sanctuary at **Penuel**— of which **Peniel** is simply another form—it is impossible to say. The site of Penuel has not been identified. All that is known is that it was east of the Jordan, not far from Succoth (cf. 33:17; Judg. 8:5-8).

---

generations even the church has invoked God for the ends of violence.

But a truer perception of God breaks through the long record of the Bible. His name becomes "the Holy One of Israel." It is seen that his supreme revelation is not in the awesomeness of nature, but in the heart of man; and that his most essential working is not in what the forces of his universe do to man, but in what his spirit achieves within man. Consider the immense significance of the ethical insight of the prophets, beginning with Elijah, and their inflexible message that the Holy One of Israel could not be approached with empty rituals but only through righteousness of life. Later it was perceived that even the name "the Holy One of Israel" was not enough. God's holy purpose was not limited to one people. Read the first chapters of the prophecy of Amos, and see how passionately he makes it clear that all nations alike must become the instruments of the Holy One, in whose hands are the destinies of all mankind. Hosea and Second Isaiah take another step in understanding: with them the sternness of Amos is suffused by a new appreciation of God as redeeming love. And so the O.T. stands at the threshold of the N.T., and over that threshold came Jesus, teaching us to say "Our Father." Which name then interprets God to us? The Lord who is encountered only as the author of the unpredictable emergencies which insurance policies rule out as "acts of God"; the God of the tribe; the God who marches with flags and drums? Or the God of conscience, the God of the growing heart, the

God who is seen in the face of him to whom was given "the name which is above every name"?

30. The Encounter with God.—Jacob got no verbal answer to his question. In his demand to know God's name there may have been reflected the primitive belief that to know a name was to have the key word to control (see Expos. on vs. 29). Men have outgrown that idea, but may substitute for it another equally fallacious. Knowledge about God may still seem the important thing; and if some glib theological phrase is learned, we may suppose that we have caught the reality of religion. There is a sense, of course, in which the name of God is decisive for life and hope. Is he fate, or Father? Is he an indifferent force that moves on its blind and cruel way, or can we call upon him as one who has compassion on his children? In that sense to know his name, ultimately revealed as the God and Father of our Lord Jesus Christ, is to have life undergirded by joyful trust. But that sort of knowing does not come through formulas. Jacob could never have got his real answer through a word or phrase. Such may be husks for the intellect, while the soul is left unfed. Jacob had to feel the truth of God—to feel in his own experience an actual contact with the Infinite, to know the awful power of God's holiness that may have to blast and burn our petty human confidence before it can fully bless. That is why Jacob called the place of his struggle **Peniel**, and said that he had **seen God face to face**. He did not need to be told anything. Ineffably he knew that his soul was not only

727

31 And as he passed over Penuel the sun rose upon him, and he halted upon his thigh.

32 Therefore the children of Israel eat not *of* the sinew which shrank, which *is* upon the hollow of the thigh, unto this day; because he touched the hollow of Jacob's thigh in the sinew that shrank.

is preserved." 31 The sun rose upon him as he passed Penu'el, limping because of his thigh. 32 Therefore to this day the Israelites do not eat the sinew of the hip which is upon the hollow of the thigh, because he touched the hollow of Jacob's thigh on the sinew of the hip.

How closely E associated his Penuel story with the account of Jacob's meeting with Esau is apparent from the frequent wordplays on Penuel—**The face of God** (RSV mg.) — in the latter; cf. vs. 20*b*, in which "see his face" occurs, and in which the Hebrew expressions rendered "appease," "before," and "accept," all have "face" as one of their constituents; cf. also 33:10.

---

preserved but expanded because he had encountered the terrible but transforming spirit of the Lord.

31. From Darkness into Sunrise.—In the wrestling with his dread antagonist, Jacob's thigh had been thrown out of joint, and henceforth he was lame. But the lame Jacob was to be a better man than the Jacob who had not been lame. It often takes hurts to make better men. A man's conceit and self-sufficiency may have to be humbled before he is fit to play his right role. Jacob as he first appeared dislocated relationships and disturbed society. The only person he cared about was Jacob. He had been possessed by the idea that the best ought properly to belong to him; and if it did not belong to him already, he reached out to take it. He was quicker witted than most people, and so when he used unscrupulous means to get what he wanted, he generally succeeded. Prompted by his mother, he had carried out the conspiracy that had won from blind old Isaac the birthright that should have gone to Esau. Then he had escaped Esau's anger, and got away to a safe place where he could begin to build up his fortunes. In Laban he encountered one who could be crafty too, but in the end he got the best of Laban. He started out poor and came back rich. What else could he be, then, but aggressive and cocksure? He had taken it for granted that in any group he would come out on top. Such qualities may make for what seems success, but they make intolerable men. Something had to happen to Jacob to bring down his self-assurance, and it had happened when the touch of the mysterious antagonist withered his thigh. In his own soul's recognition he was lame. So a new humility begins to appear in him. He will confess his wrong to Esau, ask forgiveness, seek re-entrance into the relationship he knows he has abused. In the home country he seemed a smaller man than when he had been away with Laban. But inwardly he had grown to be a bigger one. He was ready to stop pretending that he was somebody more dominant than he was fit to be.

Consider the enduring relevance of this truth that a man becomes his better self only when he is forced to lay aside his pride. Trace the career of Simon Peter: impulsive and self-assertive, boasting that though other men might fail, he would not fail (Matt. 26:33); brought to confess himself so sinful that he was not fit to stand in Jesus' presence (Luke 5:8); abjectly disgraced at a crucial hour, so that he went and wept in bitter shame (Matt. 26:75); but through these experiences chastened so that afterward he would be faithful. Trace the career of Saul of Tarsus made into the apostle Paul: his pride as a Pharisee, his confidence in his learning and his Hebrew birthright, his cold fanaticism of self-assurance as he watched the death of Stephen; then his conversion, his repudiation of his imagined worth (Phil. 3:8), his recognition of the weakness of all human strength (Rom. 7:9-23), and his emergence into the man who by confession and humility was exalted.

Consider this same truth in relation to classes and nations. Ponder those economic and social groups in history that have failed because they would not recognize their defects as revealed by the truth of God. And must a nation's prosperity and seeming success blind it to the fact that self-sufficiency will bring it to a moral reckoning with God by which it may be not only lamed, but so broken that it will be at the end of its road?

The story of Jacob's wrestling ends on a brighter note. **As he passed over Penuel the sun rose upon him.** At the very hour when he might have been most discouraged about himself, a new day dawned. Being ready now to recognize his shortcomings, he could begin to pass beyond them. He knew he was lame and so had stopped thinking of himself as a person of unlimited fitness and unlimited deserts. Instead, he was

33 And Jacob lifted up his eyes, and looked, and, behold, Esau came, and with him four hundred men. And he divided the children unto Leah, and unto Rachel, and unto the two handmaids.

2 And he put the handmaids and their children foremost, and Leah and her children after, and Rachel and Joseph hindermost.

3 And he passed over before them, and bowed himself to the ground seven times, until he came near to his brother.

4 And Esau ran to meet him, and embraced him, and fell on his neck, and kissed him: and they wept.

5 And he lifted up his eyes, and saw the women and the children, and said, Who *are* those with thee? And he said, The children which God hath graciously given thy servant.

6 Then the handmaidens came near, they and their children, and they bowed themselves.

33 And Jacob lifted up his eyes and looked, and behold, Esau was coming, and four hundred men with him. So he divided the children among Leah and Rachel and the two maids. 2 And he put the maids with their children in front, then Leah with her children, and Rachel and Joseph last of all. 3 He himself went on before them, bowing himself to the ground seven times, until he came near to his brother.

4 But Esau ran to meet him, and embraced him, and fell on his neck and kissed him, and they wept. 5 And when Esau raised his eyes and saw the women and children, he said, "Who are these with you?" Jacob said, "The children whom God has graciously given your servant." 6 Then the maids drew near, they and their chil-

---

C. Jacob's Meeting with Esau (33:1-16)

33:1-16. This section is basically from J². Into it RJE has inserted from the parallel E recension the words **and embraced him . . . and kissed him** in vs. 4, and vss. 5, 10*b*, 11*a*. For **Jacob,** vs. 1 and throughout this narrative, and in vs. 17 and in the story in ch. 34, J², having recorded the changing of Jacob's name (32:28), probably had "Israel" (cf. 35:21; 37:13; etc.). The present use of **Jacob** is due to RP, who preferred not to anticipate 35:10 (P).

---

willing to learn what God might do with a man who confessed that he was lame. To learn that may be the last and greatest lesson for many a human soul.

33:1-17. *Jacob and Esau Meet and Part.*—In this chapter the long and fascinating story of the relationship between Esau and Jacob comes to its conclusion. Here, as earlier, the curious contrast between the characters of the two brothers is manifest. Esau is impetuous and outgoing, moved by the impulse of the moment; Jacob is cautious and calculating. Jacob has just been depicted in his all-night wrestling, struggling in the darkness until he had won "power with God" and had been given his great new name of Israel. Yet here, after all that, one sees again some of the traits of the same old Jacob who had schemed Esau out of his birthright. What is the explanation of these inconsistent pictures? Perhaps it must be found in a recognition that the O.T. writers, along with their extraordinary spiritual insights, had also the limited estimates which belonged to their racial inheritance, their environment, and

their time. On the one hand, they had caught the supreme truth of the overruling grace of God. On the other hand, as they thought of Jacob, ancestor of the Israelites, as against Esau, ancestor of the Edomites, they never wholly escaped the impulse to take a very human pride in Jacob's superior shrewdness and skill; and they do not seem to have been troubled by the fact that—as they portray him—he was not guileless. They had not begun to reach the understanding of the One who would ultimately say, "Whosoever shall not receive the kingdom of God as a little child, he shall not enter therein" (Mark 10:15).

So it comes about that in this chapter, as in some of the earlier ones, Esau seems at first the better of the two brothers. Jacob is full of inhibitions; Esau has none, and lets himself go wherever the flood of his emotion turns. Jacob makes his elaborate plans to placate what he thinks will be Esau's long-cherished wrath. Esau has dismissed that long ago, and the instinct uppermost in him is just the old one of kinship. So he ran to meet Jacob, **and fell on his**

7 And Leah also with her children came near, and bowed themselves: and after came Joseph near and Rachel, and they bowed themselves.

8 And he said, What *meanest* thou by all this drove which I met? And he said, *These are* to find grace in the sight of my lord.

9 And Esau said, I have enough, my brother; keep that thou hast unto thyself.

10 And Jacob said, Nay, I pray thee, if now I have found grace in thy sight, then receive my present at my hand: for therefore I have seen thy face, as though I had seen the face of God, and thou wast pleased with me.

11 Take, I pray thee, my blessing that is brought to thee; because God hath dealt graciously with me, and because I have enough. And he urged him, and he took *it*.

12 And he said, Let us take our journey, and let us go, and I will go before thee.

13 And he said unto him, My lord knoweth that the children *are* tender, and the flocks and herds with young *are* with me; and if men should overdrive them one day, all the flock will die.

dren, and bowed down; **7** Leah likewise and her children drew near and bowed down; and last Joseph and Rachel drew near, and they bowed down. **8** Esau said, "What do you mean by all this company which I met?" Jacob answered, "To find favor in the sight of my lord." **9** But Esau said, "I have enough, my brother; keep what you have for yourself." **10** Jacob said, "No, I pray you, if I have found favor in your sight, then accept my present from my hand; for truly to see your face is like seeing the face of God, with such favor have you received me. **11** Accept, I pray you, my gift that is brought to you, because God has dealt graciously with me, and because I have enough." Thus he urged him, and he took it.

12 Then Esau said, "Let us journey on our way, and I will go before you." **13** But Jacob said to him, "My lord knows that the children are frail, and that the flocks and herds giving suck are a care to me; and if they are overdriven for one day, all the

---

It will be recalled that in the J² narrative Jacob, preparing to meet Esau, had divided his flock and herds into two companies for the sake of their safety (32:7-8). The irony with which J² recorded the sequel has been obscured by RJE by his insertion of vss. 10*b*, 11*a*. According to J², when Esau inquired why it was that Jacob's caravan was traveling in two divisions Jacob, still terrified, did not dare give the true explanation but, to save his face, gave half of his possessions to Esau (vss. 8-9, 11*b*) —which he had not had the slightest intention of doing. And J²'s sardonic humor finds further expression

---

neck, and kissed him. He is unconcerned with all the presents Jacob tries to urge upon him; he does not want them. And note the difference in the way each of the two speaks to the other. Jacob, fearful and anxious, says of the presents he is offering, **These are to find grace in the sight of my lord.** But Esau waves them aside, because he has enough, and because Jacob is **my brother.**

How strange are the mingled elements in human characters! Esau was to be reckoned as the "profane" man; and in the end, of the two he was the failure. Yet in immediate ways he seemed often so much more attractive; for he was vigorous, warmhearted, and too essentially good-natured to carry a grudge. One can see men like him in every generation—impulsive, friendly men who seem to like everybody, and whom it is easy for everybody to like. Yet their fatal weakness may be, as with Esau, that they

are too easygoing to care greatly about the values in life that matter most.

Consider, on the other hand, Jacob. Even yet he has not finished with the consequences of old wrongs. He is distrustful of Esau because he knows that he has not deserved kindness at his hands. That is always one of the possible penalties of wrongdoing. A man projects into the imagined feelings of others the condemnation he inwardly visits upon himself. He dares not assume their good will, or even take the risk of believing in it when it is made plain. So Jacob not only tried anxiously to buy Esau's favor, but when Esau showed that he had it without any price, Jacob was still incredulous; and the one thing he wanted to do was to separate from Esau as soon as he plausibly could (vss. 12-15). And yet, and yet—this Jacob is the one who at Peniel had "prevailed," had "seen God face to face," and who would prevail. The

14 Let my lord, I pray thee, pass over before his servant; and I will lead on softly, according as the cattle that goeth before me and the children be able to endure, until I come unto my lord unto Seir.

15 And Esau said, Let me now leave with thee *some* of the folk that *are* with me. And he said, What needeth it? let me find grace in the sight of my lord.

16 ¶ So Esau returned that day on his way unto Seir.

17 And Jacob journeyed to Succoth, and built him a house, and made booths for his cattle: therefore the name of the place is called Succoth.

flocks will die. 14 Let my lord pass on before his servant, and I will lead on slowly, according to the pace of the cattle which are before me and according to the pace of the children, until I come to my lord in Se'ir."

15 So Esau said, "Let me leave with you some of the men who are with me." But he said, "What need is there? Let me find favor in the sight of my lord." 16 So Esau returned that day on his way to Se'ir. 17 But Jacob journeyed to Succoth,[w] and built himself a house, and made booths for his cattle; therefore the name of the place is called Succoth.

w That is *Booths*

---

in Jacob's nervous rejection of his brother's proposal that they continue their journey together (vss. 13-15). Jacob's sigh of relief when the other set out for his home in Seir (vs. 16) is almost audible.

The E recension simply told of Esau's acceptance of Jacob's gift and of the brothers' reconciliation.

XL. Jacob and His Family (33:17–35:26)
A. Jacob Comes to Shechem (33:17-20)

17-20. This section is a conflation of J², E, and P. J² told of Jacob proceeding to **Succoth** (vs. 17*a*α) —the site of Succoth is unknown—and there crossing the Jordan en route to Shechem, where **from the sons of Hamor . . . he bought for a hundred pieces of money the piece of land on which he had pitched his tent** (vs. 19; **Shechem's father** is from R^P, harmonizing the notice with ch. 34). The sons of Hamor were, it may be inferred from Judg. 9:28, historically one of the leading clans of Shechem. The piece of land Jacob purchased from them was the site of Joseph's grave (cf. Josh. 24:32). J¹, whose familiarity with the details of the Joseph tradition of Shechem was of the slightest, appears to have known nothing of this. J², on the other hand, is concerned to assert the Israelite claim to the shrine there (cf. ch. 23 [P]), the ownership of which thus appears to have been in dispute at the time he wrote. This was one of the reasons for which he brought Jacob to Shechem. For in having Jacob cross the Jordan at Succoth J² was departing radically from the J¹ narrative.

As Meyer (*Israeliten und ihre Nachbarstämme*, pp. 275-76; cf. Skinner, *Genesis*, pp. 414, 427) has shown, in the J narrative in its primary form Jacob's route from the Jabbok to Hebron lay east of the Jordan. Thus it was in the territory of the tribe bearing his name that Reuben's violation of his father's concubine occurred (35:22*a*). It was because of this shocking act of impiety, J¹ implies, that Reuben lost the prerogatives belonging to him as first-born (Meyer, *op. cit.*, p. 276; Eissfeldt, *Hexateuch-Synopse*, pp. 23-24).

J², by having Jacob cross the Jordan to Shechem and proceed from there to Hebron, necessarily transferred the scene of Reuben's impiety to some undefined point between Shechem and Hebron. More important, however, is his change in the Joseph story. J¹, as will be seen, located the sale of Joseph to the Ishmaelites in the south. J², possibly in dependence upon a detail of the Joseph tradition unknown to his predecessor, transferred it to the north. This was indeed the second reason for which he brought Jacob to Shechem.

The E parallel narrative is very different from this account of Jacob's peaceful arrival at Shechem. He first told of Jacob building himself a **house**, possibly at the place where he had met Esau, and making **booths for his cattle**, for which reason the place

18 ¶ And Jacob came to Shalem, a city of Shechem, which *is* in the land of Canaan, when he came from Padan-aram; and pitched his tent before the city.

19 And he bought a parcel of a field, where he had spread his tent, at the hand of the children of Hamor, Shechem's father, for a hundred pieces of money.

20 And he erected there an altar, and called it El-Elohe-Israel.

18 And Jacob came safely to the city of Shechem, which is in the land of Canaan, on his way from Paddan-aram; and he camped before the city. 19 And from the sons of Hamor, Shechem's father, he bought for a hundred pieces of money[x] the piece of land on which he had pitched his tent. 20 There he erected an altar and called it El-El'ohe-Israel.[y]

[x] Heb *a hundred qesitas*
[y] That is *God, the God of Israel*

received the name of **Succoth** (vs. 17aβb) . The implication of the house building is that Jacob remained there for some considerable time. E would here seem to be echoing the northern tradition that the invading Israelites had occupied the country there for some time before moving west (cf. W. F. Albright, "Archaeology and the Date of the Hebrew Conquest of Palestine," *Bulletin of the American Schools of Oriental Research,* No. 58 [1935], p. 15) . This tradition also underlies the account—peculiar to E—of the conquest of the Amorite kingdom of Sihon (Num. 21:21-31) .

The E notice of how long Jacob remained at Succoth and of his departure therefrom has been dropped by RJE, who preferred at this point the J2 representation that Jacob settled down quietly near Shechem, buying the land where he had spread his tent. E, having had Jacob remain at Succoth long enough for his family to grow up and for himself to acquire a considerable retinue, had told of Jacob taking the place by storm. This is indicated by Jacob's dying reference to the event in 48:22, where the wordplay on Shechem is to be noted (cf. RSV mg.) . The beginning of this narrative is found in vs. 18*b,* **and he camped before the city,** where **camped before** in its original content had a hostile significance (cf. Isa. 29:3) . The conclusion of it is in vs. 20, in which "a pillar" (*maççēbhāh*) is to be read for **an altar,** with Wellhausen (*Composition,* p. 50; Wellhausen is followed by most modern commentators; see Holzinger, *Genesis,* pp. 212-13; Gunkel, *Genesis,* p. 369; Skinner, *Genesis,* p. 416) . The Hebrew word rendered **erected** is from the same root as *maççēbhāh,* and is not elsewhere used of the building of an altar.

The pillar thus referred to, it may be inferred, was still standing at Shechem when E wrote. Originally it was, no doubt, the ceremonial *maççēbhāh* of some sanctuary, but in the course of time it had come to be regarded as the memorial which Jacob had erected following his capture of Shechem (cf. Exod. 17:15; I Sam. 15:12) . The name it bore, **El-Elohe-Israel** (vs. 20) , was also ascribed to Jacob. It may be noted that this is E's introduction of the name Israel. As to whether or not he recorded a changing of Jacob's name, as in 32:28 (J) , it is impossible to say. In either case, he continued to use the name Jacob in his narrative (cf. 35:20, and see further below) .

Vs. 18aαβ is from P. **On his way from Paddan-aram** (vs. 18aγ) is from RP, inserted because of his transposition of 35:9, 11—occurring in P before this, see below—to their present context.

reason was in the fact which the earlier chapters already have prefigured, that this man in spite of his faults never lost the consciousness that his life must try to relate itself to God.

18-20. Jacob's Altars.—In these final verses there is symbolized what has been suggested in connection with the preceding verses, viz., why it was Jacob and not Esau who, notwithstanding many contrary indications, was to become the decisive figure in the history of Israel. There is no record that Esau ever built an altar. His in-

terests moved casually and, in the main, contentedly upon the level of this earth. But for Jacob life had another dimension. As he had done at other times and places, so now upon his return home **he erected there an altar. And he called it El-Elohe-Israel.** It was dedicated to God, as God's chastening yet redeeming power had been revealed to him at Peniel. Not by any virtue of what he was, but by the purpose of God which would work through him, his life would be significant.

34 And Dinah the daughter of Leah, which she bare unto Jacob, went out to see the daughters of the land.

2 And when Shechem the son of Hamor the Hivite, prince of the country, saw her, he took her, and lay with her, and defiled her.

34 Now Dinah the daughter of Leah, whom she had borne to Jacob, went out to visit the women of the land; 2 and when Shechem the son of Hamor the Hivite, the prince of the land, saw her, he seized her and lay with her and humbled her.

B. Seduction of Dinah (34:1-31)

34:1-31. This chapter is a conflation of J and a narrative from a secondary strand of P. (Gunkel, *Genesis*, pp. 369-74; Smend, *Erzählung des Hexateuch*, pp. 93-94; Eissfeldt, *Hexateuch-Synopse*, pp. 23-25, regard the chapter as a conflation of J [J¹, L] and E. Skinner, *Genesis*, pp. 417-18, with considerable hesitancy, makes it a conflation of supplementary narratives attached respectively to J and E. Procksch, *Genesis*, pp. 199-200, 543-44, holds that it is a conflation of J and P. An analysis of the chapter, substantiating in detail the position advanced here, will be found in Simpson, *Early Traditions of Israel*, pp. 116-21.) The two narratives, as will be seen, differed markedly from each other so that RP, who conflated them, had to provide considerable harmonizing material.

It has already been noted that in 35:22a J¹ accounts for the fact that the tribe of Reuben, supposedly descended from the first-born of Jacob, was not the leader of the tribes of Israel: Reuben had forfeited the prerogatives and privileges of his position by his shocking act of impiety. These prerogatives would have then passed to Simeon, Jacob's second son. But his putative descendants were also historically of little importance. J¹ accounts for this fact by the present story. Simeon, by an act of treachery, lost the leadership which had come to him; and since Levi, the third son of Jacob, was involved with Simeon, the rights and privileges of the first-born passed to Judah (cf. Eissfeldt, *op. cit.*, pp. 23-24; see also Simpson, *op. cit.*, pp. 132, 471), the eponymous ancestor of the most powerful group in the south, and for J¹ the leading tribe of Israel.

This story of how Simeon and Levi lost their rights must therefore in the J¹ document have followed the account of Reuben's downfall and have been located in the south. Nor would there be any reason for J² to change this order of events. The J narrative thus had nothing to do with Shechem, where the P narrative, on the other hand, was firmly rooted. RP, conflating the two stories, necessarily retained Shechem as the scene of the outrage.

Support for the position that in the J narrative the incident was located in the south is provided by the reading of several LXX MSS of "the Horite" for **the Hivite** in vs. 2, the correctness of which has been argued by Meyer (*Israeliten und ihre*

34:1-31. *Provocation and Revenge.*—A dark and turbulent old tale is this, with good and evil strangely mingled. There is the pathos of a girl's betrayal; the wild passion of a young man who was not corrupt at heart; the fierce, unbridled vengeance let loose upon him. It is life in the raw, as it was lived in a primitive society; and yet its essential emotions are common to human beings always.

Jacob's daughter, Dinah, goes out to see the daughters of the land—the innocent venture of a young girl wanting to find friends. To her there came the tragedy which has come to some girls in every age and place—the tragedy which Thomas Hardy has made timeless in *Tess of the d'Urbervilles*. A young man sees her, covets her, violates her. Yet what he meant and what he did

were not completely evil. It was not a trivial affection that Shechem felt for Dinah. Of the warmth with which he loved her it was written that **his soul clave** to her. He begged his father, Hamor, to secure her for his wife. So much for Shechem. But now others come into the picture. Jacob heard what had happened to Dinah and held his peace until his sons came in from the field. When he told them they were furious that Shechem had defiled their sister, and **wrought folly in Israel, . . . which thing ought not to be done.** How charged with meaning the old words are! **Which thing ought not to be done.** So speaks a moral conscience which is as old as history. As long as men have been human they have had a sense of ought and ought not, and have known that they were held accountable

3 And his soul clave unto Dinah the daughter of Jacob, and he loved the damsel, and spake kindly unto the damsel.

4 And Shechem spake unto his father Hamor, saying, Get me this damsel to wife.

5 And Jacob heard that he had defiled Dinah his daughter: now his sons were with his cattle in the field: and Jacob held his peace until they were come.

3 And his soul was drawn to Dinah the daughter of Jacob; he loved the maiden and spoke tenderly to her. 4 So Shechem spoke to his father Hamor, saying, "Get me this maiden for my wife." 5 Now Jacob heard that he had defiled his daughter Dinah; but his sons were with his cattle in the field, so Jacob held his peace until they came.

Nachbarstämme, p. 331). The O.T. consistently locates the Horites in the south (14:6; 36:20-21, 29-30; Deut. 2:12, 22; cf. Num. 13:5; I Chr. 1:39).

The name of Dinah's suitor in the J narrative here cannot therefore have been **Shechem** (vs. 2). The reference to him as **the young man** in vs. 19 (J) suggests that he may well have been designated simply as "a young man, a Horite"; with this may be compared I Sam. 30:13, where "a young man of Egypt" is a rendering of the Hebrew "a young man, an Egyptian."

The J[1] story told of how this young man fell in love with Dinah (vs. 3), of his cohabitation with her (vs. 2bα)—apparently with her consent; the representation of the act as a rape is from J[2]; the word rendered **seized** (vs. 2 RSV) does not necessarily have a stronger connotation than **took** (KJV); see below. Her father, hearing of this, told his sons about it when they returned from the field (vss. 5aαγ, 7aαβ). The young man, however, agreed to undergo circumcision (cf. vss. 11-14), the implication being that this would satisfy the girl's family so that marriage would follow. But Simeon and Levi, despite the agreement, killed the young man and took Dinah out of his house. It may be assumed that J[1]'s version of the tale concluded with an explicit condemnation of their action by Jacob.

This story J[2] took over from J[1], adding to vs. 2 the words **and humbled her,** and to vs. **7, and very angry, because he had wrought folly in Israel.** He also substituted for the condemnation of Simeon and Levi which, it is assumed, J[1] had put in the mouth of Jacob, the somewhat colorless vs. 30 and the brothers' indignant justification of their act (vs. 31).

J[2] thus reveals an attitude toward sex more rigorous than that of J[1]. The latter's horror of sexual perversion is indicated by his expurgation of the story in 9:21-25, and by his comment in 13:13. The revulsion with which he regarded the incestuous action of Lot's daughters (19:30-35) has been noted. And his abhorrence of adultery is implicit in 35:22a; 39:11-12. On the other hand, he records without condemnation Dinah's yielding to the Horite, and, as will be seen, describes with evident admiration the heroic measures taken by Tamar to ensure the realization of her right to bear children (ch. 38). In both these narratives the women concerned were either unmarried or widowed, so there was no infraction of the marital rights of a third party; nor is there in the stories any suggestion of promiscuity. J[1]'s attitude toward sex, where perversion, incest, or the rights of a third party were not involved, was thus essentially matter of fact.

For J[2] the matter was less simple. It was doubtless his contact with Baalism that made him more aware than his predecessor had been of the lurking dangers in the relationships of men and women. As a result, there is a certain note of melancholy in his treatment of the problem of sex—already noted in the Exeg. of ch. 3—and this led to his revision of the J[1] narrative here.

It may be noted that since both J[1] and J[2] had placed Jacob's marriages to Leah and Rachel soon after his arrival at Laban's, according to J[2] more than twenty years before (cf. 31:38), there is no difficulty as regards the ages of Simeon, Levi, and Dinah in fitting the story into their narratives.

It is hard to say what the historical event was upon which the J[1] tale was based. It was probably some act of treachery toward the Horites on the part of the clans of Simeon

6 ¶ And Hamor the father of Shechem went out unto Jacob to commune with him.

7 And the sons of Jacob came out of the field when they heard *it:* and the men were grieved, and they were very wroth, because he had wrought folly in Israel in lying with Jacob's daughter; which thing ought not to be done.

8 And Hamor communed with them, saying, The soul of my son Shechem longeth for your daughter: I pray you give her him to wife.

9 And make ye marriages with us, *and* give your daughters unto us, and take our daughters unto you.

10 And ye shall dwell with us: and the land shall be before you; dwell and trade ye therein, and get you possessions therein.

11 And Shechem said unto her father and unto her brethren, Let me find grace in your eyes, and what ye shall say unto me I will give.

12 Ask me never so much dowry and gift, and I will give according as ye shall

6 And Hamor the father of Shechem went out to Jacob to speak with him. 7 The sons of Jacob came in from the field when they heard of it; and the men were indignant and very angry, because he had wrought folly in Israel by lying with Jacob's daughter, for such a thing ought not to be done.

8 But Hamor spoke with them, saying, "The soul of my son Shechem longs for your daughter; I pray you, give her to him in marriage. 9 Make marriages with us; give your daughters to us, and take our daughters for yourselves. 10 You shall dwell with us; and the land shall be open to you; dwell and trade in it, and get property in it." 11 Shechem also said to her father and to her brothers, "Let me find favor in your eyes, and whatever you say to me I will give. 12 Ask of me ever so much as marriage present and gift, and I will give according as

and Levi, and this may well have been a contributing cause to their near annihilation reflected in 49:5-7.

The P story contained nothing of any dishonoring of Dinah, but told of the desire of Shechem, the son of Hamor, to have her as his wife, and of Hamor entering into negotiations with Jacob for a general treaty permitting marriage between their respective families. To this Jacob agreed, provided the Shechemites would undergo circumcision, a condition which was immediately accepted.

This story, coming from P2, may well represent an attempt—somewhat liberal in its outlook (cf. Isa. 56:2)—to deal with the problem of mixed marriages which troubled the postexilic Palestinian community.

RP, finding in the documents with which he was working two stories in which circumcision was laid down as the condition on which a foreigner could marry an Israelite woman, combined them, identifying "the young man" of the J narrative with Shechem the son of Hamor. The process of conflation was accomplished with little difficulty up to the point at which the young man in the J narrative, and all the Shechemites in the P narrative, were circumcised. Then to provide an ending to his new narrative congruent with that of J, RP supplied vss. 25*b*, 27-29. The awkward confusion of these verses, noted by all commentators, is an indication of their redactional character.

7. Wrought folly in Israel: This striking phrase is again used of acts of sexual immorality in Deut. 22:21; Judg. 20:6, 10; II Sam. 13:12-13; Jer. 29:23; cf. Judg. 19:23, 24.

to its judgment. And there is the other word, the significance of which the sons of Jacob did not stop to ponder. Shechem's act was to them an insult and an outrage, a crime to be avenged. But it was also folly. With Shechem, and with many a man in every time, some evil deed has come to pass not through deliberate viciousness, but through the hot impulse and the lack of

self-control which makes the man morally a fool. As Edward Rowland Sill has put it:

'Tis not by guilt the onward sweep
  Of truth and right, O Lord, we stay;
'Tis by our follies that so long
  We hold the earth from heaven away.[7]

[7] "The Fool's Prayer."

say unto me: but give me the damsel to wife.

13 And the sons of Jacob answered Shechem and Hamor his father deceitfully, and said, because he had defiled Dinah their sister:

14 And they said unto them, We cannot do this thing, to give our sister to one that is uncircumcised; for that *were* a reproach unto us:

15 But in this will we consent unto you: If ye will be as we *be,* that every male of you be circumcised;

16 Then will we give our daughters unto you, and we will take your daughters to us, and we will dwell with you, and we will become one people.

17 But if ye will not hearken unto us, to be circumcised; then will we take our daughter, and we will be gone.

18 And their words pleased Hamor and Shechem Hamor's son.

19 And the young man deferred not to do the thing, because he had delight in Jacob's daughter: and he *was* more honorable than all the house of his father.

20 ¶ And Hamor and Shechem his son came unto the gate of their city, and communed with the men of their city, saying,

21 These men *are* peaceable with us; therefore let them dwell in the land, and trade therein; for the land, behold, *it is* large enough for them; let us take their daughters to us for wives, and let us give them our daughters.

22 Only herein will the men consent unto us for to dwell with us, to be one people, if every male among us be circumcised, as they *are* circumcised.

you say to me; only give me the maiden to be my wife."

13 The sons of Jacob answered Shechem and his father Hamor deceitfully, because he had defiled their sister Dinah. 14 They said to them, "We cannot do this thing, to give our sister to one who is uncircumcised, for that would be a disgrace to us. 15 Only on this condition will we consent to you: that you will become as we are and every male of you be circumcised. 16 Then we will give our daughters to you, and we will take your daughters to ourselves, and we will dwell with you and become one people. 17 But if you will not listen to us and be circumcised, then we will take our daughter, and we will be gone."

18 Their words pleased Hamor and Hamor's son Shechem. 19 And the young man did not delay to do the thing, because he had delight in Jacob's daughter. Now he was the most honored of all his family. 20 So Hamor and his son Shechem came to the gate of their city and spoke to the men of their city, saying, 21 "These men are friendly with us; let them dwell in the land and trade in it, for behold, the land is large enough for them; let us take their daughters in marriage, and let us give them our daughters. 22 Only on this condition will the men agree to dwell with us, to become one people: that every male among us be

---

In Josh. 7:15 it refers to Achan's act of impiety in taking plunder for himself at the capture of Jericho, thus breaking God's command that the city and everything in it was to be utterly destroyed.

The word *nebhālāh,* here translated **folly,** and its cognate *nābhāl,* "fool," are difficult to render in English. " 'Fool,' and 'folly' . . . are inadequate, and suggest wrong associations. The fault of the *nābāl* [*nābhāl*] is not weakness of reason, but moral and religious insensibility, a rooted incapacity to discern moral and religious relations, leading

---

So Shechem had committed **folly,** and was guilty for that fact. He deserved punishment, and Jacob's sons were determined to make themselves the agents of it. But what they did was worse than the original offense, more cruel, more hateful, and more ruinous. Its ugly details

are written in the story, and they include the smooth advances of calculated deceit, then treachery, then pitiless slaughter. The whole action of Jacob's sons was an example of the way in which men can make the pretense of administering justice become an excuse for fero-

23 *Shall* not their cattle and their substance and every beast of theirs *be* ours? only let us consent unto them, and they will dwell with us.

24 And unto Hamor and unto Shechem his son hearkened all that went out of the gate of his city; and every male was circumcised, all that went out of the gate of his city.

25 ¶ And it came to pass on the third day, when they were sore, that two of the sons of Jacob, Simeon and Levi, Dinah's brethren, took each man his sword, and came upon the city boldly, and slew all the males.

26 And they slew Hamor and Shechem his son with the edge of the sword, and took Dinah out of Shechem's house, and went out.

27 The sons of Jacob came upon the slain, and spoiled the city, because they had defiled their sister.

28 They took their sheep, and their oxen, and their asses, and that which *was* in the city, and that which *was* in the field,

29 And all their wealth, and all their little ones, and their wives took they captive, and spoiled even all that *was* in the house.

30 And Jacob said to Simeon and Levi, Ye have troubled me to make me to stink among the inhabitants of the land, among the Canaanites and the Perizzites: and I *being* few in number, they shall gather themselves together against me, and slay me; and I shall be destroyed, I and my house.

circumcised as they are circumcised. 23 Will not their cattle, their property and all their beasts be ours? Only let us agree with them, and they will dwell with us." 24 And all who went out of the gate of his city hearkened to Hamor and his son Shechem; and every male was circumcised, all who went out of the gate of his city.

25 On the third day, when they were sore, two of the sons of Jacob, Simeon and Levi, Dinah's brothers, took their swords and came upon the city unawares, and killed all the males. 26 They slew Hamor and his son Shechem with the sword, and took Dinah out of Shechem's house, and went away. 27 And the sons of Jacob came upon the slain, and plundered the city, because their sister had been defiled; 28 they took their flocks and their herds, their asses, and whatever was in the city and in the field; 29 all their wealth, all their little ones and their wives, all that was in the houses, they captured and made their prey. 30 Then Jacob said to Simeon and Levi, "You have brought trouble on me by making me odious to the inhabitants of the land, the Canaanites and the Per'izzites; my numbers are few, and if they gather themselves against me and attack me, I shall be

---

to an intolerant repudiation in practice of the claims which they impose. . . . *Senseless* and *senselessness* may be suggested as fair English equivalents, it being understood that the defective 'sense' which they predicate shows itself particularly in acts of impiety, profligacy, and churlishness, and that it is, in fact, the latter ideas which the two words, in actual use, really connote." (S. R. Driver, *A Critical and Exegetical Commentary on Deuteronomy* [New York: Charles Scribner's Sons, 1895; "International Critical Commentary"], p. 256.) I.e., the fool is one who refuses to recognize his obligations to the community to which he belongs. Folly, the action of a fool, is thus action which is criminally irresponsible, making for social, and so for personal, disintegration.

---

cious violence. In modern society that is no longer so possible for individuals. The modern area where it is possible is in war. The massed and impersonal violence of a nation against another nation can be almost as brutal as the work of Jacob's sons. The nation which has no

restraining principle in its world contacts may be—to use our common phrase—"in bad odor" among decent peoples. Jacob had a stronger word for it. Using that, men of conscience within a nation could say to those who would dishonor the whole national membership by militaristic

31 And they said, Should he deal with our sister as with a harlot?

35 And God said unto Jacob, Arise, go up to Bethel, and dwell there: and make there an altar unto God, that appeared unto thee when thou fleddest from the face of Esau thy brother.

2 Then Jacob said unto his household, and to all that *were* with him, Put away the strange gods that *are* among you, and be clean, and change your garments:

3 And let us arise, and go up to Bethel; and I will make there an altar unto God, who answered me in the day of my distress, and was with me in the way which I went.

4 And they gave unto Jacob all the strange gods which *were* in their hand, and *all their* earrings which *were* in their ears; and Jacob hid them under the oak which *was* by Shechem.

destroyed, both I and my household." 31 But they said, "Should he treat our sister as a harlot?"

35 God said to Jacob, "Arise, go up to Bethel, and dwell there; and make there an altar to the God who appeared to you when you fled from your brother Esau." 2 So Jacob said to his household and to all who were with him, "Put away the foreign gods that are among you, and purify yourselves, and change your garments; 3 then let us arise and go up to Bethel, that I may make there an altar to the God who answered me in the day of my distress and has been with me wherever I have gone." 4 So they gave to Jacob all the foreign gods that they had, and the rings that were in their ears; and Jacob hid them under the oak which was near Shechem.

C. Jacob's Return to Bethel (35:1-15)

35:1-15. This section is a conflation of E and P. From E are derived vss. 1-5, 6*b*, 7-8, 14*a*α, telling how Jacob at God's command left Shechem for Bethel to fulfill the vow he had made (28:20) twenty years before. In vss. 2-4 there is an echo of a local tradition—the motif recurs in Josh. 24:14-18—accounting for the imageless character of the worship at Shechem (cf. Meyer, *Israeliten und ihre Nachbarstämme*, p. 559). The fact that nowhere in the preceding narratives is there the slightest suggestion that Jacob's family had been practicing idol worship would seem to indicate that in its primary form the tradition had no connection with Jacob. It had simply said that **under the oak which was near Shechem** (vs. 4)—probably identical with the oak at Moreh (12:6; Deut. 11:30) —there were buried images of gods that had once been worshiped by Israel's ancestors. This tradition E now associated with Jacob. He thus not only drew the sting of the J story of the theft of Laban's household gods; he also represented Jacob as the person

---

savagery, You make me to stink among the inhabitants of the earth.

35:1-7. *Belated Obedience.*—Let the mind linger upon this chapter's first three words, **And God said.** They are not new. In Genesis one comes upon them again and again. They are so short and seem so simple that it is possible to pass over them almost without notice. Yet in those three syllables sounds a supreme motif of this whole book. **And God said. . . . God said** the words that made creation. **God said** what Adam and Eve should hear in Eden. **God said** to Cain, "Thou art cursed from the earth"; and to Noah, "With thee will I establish my covenant." He spoke to Abraham, and to Isaac, and now to Jacob. In the actual issues of life, and to all sorts of men, the good and the bad and the in-between, God makes his purpose known. That is the continual message of Genesis,

and nothing in the book is more important than that. If we ask haggling questions about the how of revelation, we shall find no answer. What we do find is simply the plain, straight statement of the fact. The old writers knew nothing of our "psychology," but they knew a great deal about what happens in human souls. One thing they knew was that every man has a conscience, and that God in his own way will make that conscience recognize truth it cannot pretend it does not hear.

So much for the general fact. Consider now the special suggestion of the words as they have to do with Jacob. God said to him, **Arise, go up to Bethel, and dwell there.** It was at Bethel in the days of his worst distress that he had seen his vision of the ladder reaching up to heaven and the angels of God ascending and descending. He had set up an altar there that day and

5 And they journeyed: and the terror of God was upon the cities that *were* round about them, and they did not pursue after the sons of Jacob.

6 ¶ So Jacob came to Luz which *is* in the land of Canaan, that *is*, Bethel, he and all the people that *were* with him.

7 And he built there an altar, and called the place El-beth-el; because there God appeared unto him, when he fled from the face of his brother.

8 But Deborah Rebekah's nurse died, and she was buried beneath Bethel under an oak: and the name of it was called Allon-bachuth.

5 And as they journeyed, a terror from God fell upon the cities that were round about them, so that they did not pursue the sons of Jacob. 6 And Jacob came to Luz (that is, Bethel), which is in the land of Canaan, he and all the people who were with him, 7 and there he built an altar, and called the place El-bethel,[z] because there God had revealed himself to him when he fled from his brother. 8 And Deb'orah, Rebekah's nurse, died, and she was buried under an oak below Bethel; so the name of it was called Al'lon-bacuth.[a]

[z] That is *God of Bethel*
[a] That is *Oak of weeping*

who had established monolatry in Israel, and so claimed for him a place of much greater significance in the development of Yahwism than had ever been suggested by J[2].

The reference in vs. 5 is to Jacob's storming of Shechem. The implication is that Jacob spent little time there after taking the city. Vs. 7 records Jacob's actual fulfillment of his vow. Vs. 8, curious because of its sudden introduction of Rebekah's nurse as a member of Jacob's caravan, may be secondary, a fragment of the tradition of the sanctuary **Allon-bacuth.** This may be identical with the Bochim mentioned in Judg. 2:5. Vs. 14aα was originally the continuation of vs. 8, and told of Jacob erecting a pillar on Deborah's grave. The verse in its present form is from RP, equating the pillar with that mentioned in 28:18.

sworn a vow of dedication. But that was many years ago. Early intentions had grown dim. He had lived in Laban's country, and if he had held on supposedly to his own faith, he did not hold it so importantly as to be troubled by the fact that his household had its idols. And when he came back to the home country, he did not go to Bethel; he went to Shechem, a softer place.

He did not intend what happened there: but what did happen came about because that was where he took his family. Dinah, his daughter, "went out to see the daughters of the land" (34:1). It was the natural thing for any young girl to do—to look for companionship. She found it, and the result was tragic, as the story in ch. 34 has recounted. Whose fault was it? Dinah's? If hers in part, certainly not hers wholly; and indeed the story gives no sign that she anticipated the evil in which she was caught. Whose fault, then? Jacob's conscience knew well enough. What had he done to give this daughter any conception of the God with whom he had once made a covenant? How had he helped fortify her for the temptations she might meet? Who but himself had brought her to where temptations were? So Jacob had to ask himself, and it was a remorseful answer that he had to make. Now he would try to give his family the

religious dedication which they should have had at first: he would go with them to Bethel and renew there the sense of the presence of God which he ought to have sought before.

8. *The Humbly Great.*—A name, a single descriptive word, and one bare statement; that is all. Meager information, but a spark for the imagination. For why should Deborah's death find place in the narrative at all unless there was one clear reason, viz., her loss was grievous to somebody? It had no importance in history, but there was somebody whose heart was feeling what another would one day put into words:

> But she is in her grave, and, oh,
> The difference to me! [8]

Deborah was the nurse of Jacob's mother, and perhaps two generations of the family had depended upon her loving faithfulness. Later in the same chapter it is told that Rachel, the wife whom Jacob loved above all other human beings, died when Benjamin was born. If Deborah had been with her, conceivably she might have lived.

So the humble person may play a part in human affections and needs that will never be

[8] Wordsworth, "She Dwelt Among the Untrodden Ways."

9 ¶ And God appeared unto Jacob again, when he came out of Padan-aram, and blessed him.

10 And God said unto him, Thy name *is* Jacob: thy name shall not be called any more Jacob, but Israel shall be thy name; and he called his name Israel.

11 And God said unto him, I *am* God Almighty: be fruitful and multiply; a nation and a company of nations shall be of thee, and kings shall come out of thy loins;

12 And the land which I gave Abraham and Isaac, to thee I will give it, and to thy seed after thee will I give the land.

9 God appeared to Jacob again, when he came from Paddan-aram, and blessed him. 10 And God said to him, "Your name is Jacob; no longer shall your name be called Jacob, but Israel shall be your name." So his name was called Israel. 11 And God said to him, "I am God Almighty:[b] be fruitful and multiply; a nation and a company of nations shall come from you, and kings shall spring from you. 12 The land which I gave to Abraham and Isaac I will give to you, and I will give the land

[b] Heb *El Shaddai*

The rest of the material in the section is from P or RP. Part of it, vss. 6a 11-13a, 15, occupied in P the same position as the Bethel saga (28:11-22) in JE (Gunkel, *Genesis*, p. 387; cf. Skinner, *Genesis*, pp. 425-26) ; i.e., P followed JE in the representation that it was at Bethel on his way to visit Laban that Jacob was appointed heir to the divine promise first made to Abraham. Thus the command, **be fruitful and multiply** (vs. 11), in its original context had an appropriateness quite lacking at this point in the narrative, following the chronicle of the birth of Jacob's family. RP, perhaps because he felt it would be too difficult to conflate it with 28:11-22, placed it here and, by changing the E

accounted for in public records. Who can measure all that nurses have given to those they loved and served? The formal definition in the dictionary is only a cold form of words, but "my nurse" may say something immensely more. Robert Louis Stevenson prefaced his *Child's Garden of Verses* with a dedication "To Alison Cunningham, from Her Boy," a dedication which begins:

> For the long nights you lay awake
> And watched for my unworthy sake,

and ends with a prayer that every child may hear

>   as kind a voice
> As made my childish days rejoice!

Similarly, though they cannot put it so fittingly into words, many may remember the nurse that has been a second mother; and when she dies, the place where she is buried may well have such a name as Deborah's **Allon-bacuth**, the **Oak of weeping**.

In modern times the word "nurse" has come also to have a broader association. Nurses are not only the simple and unlearned persons who have charge of children. There is also the "trained nurse." Something new in history began with Florence Nightingale. The care of the sick has been revolutionized, and the incalculable ministry of modern hospitals made possible by the trained nurse. Then Lillian Wald in New York established the "visiting nurses," and

sent their gentleness and skill into the homes of the poor to be a benediction to whole communities.

Yet always it is the spirit rather than the institution which is vital. Professional nursing, with its new dignity of status and unlimited possibilities for good, can be spoiled if it is separated from its original root of warm compassion. Who has not seen and felt the difference between a nurse who really cares, and the perfunctory one who is interested only in drawing her pay and watching the clock? Much has rightly been done by organized nurses in self-protection, in improving working conditions and establishing reasonable hours. But with nursing, as with every other profession, if it becomes commercialized its finest meaning is corrupted. A decisive difference comes through the contribution made by a warm human heart. To care enough for people to be sensitive to suffering, to want so much to help that the thought of self can disappear, is a more priceless thing even than technical ability. That makes nursing a dedication, and exalts the nurse into an instrument of the spirit for whom many men and women may thank God.

9-15. The Name Israel: Another Record.— The compiler of Genesis in its ultimate form has already included the vivid stories, drawn from J and E and woven together, of Jacob's wrestling by the brook Jabbok with the awesome antagonist who said to him at last, "Thy name

13 And God went up from him in the place where he talked with him.

14 And Jacob set up a pillar in the place where he talked with him, *even* a pillar of stone: and he poured a drink offering thereon, and he poured oil thereon.

15 And Jacob called the name of the place where God spake with him, Bethel.

16 ¶ And they journeyed from Bethel; and there was but a little way to come to Ephrath: and Rachel travailed, and she had hard labor.

to your descendants after you." 13 Then God went up from him in the place where he had spoken with him. 14 And Jacob set up a pillar in the place where he had spoken with him, a pillar of stone; and he poured out a drink offering on it, and poured oil on it. 15 So Jacob called the name of the place where God had spoken with him, Bethel.

16 Then they journeyed from Bethel; and when they were still some distance from Ephrath, Rachel travailed, and she had

---

verse referring to the pillar on Deborah's grave, made the pillar a memorial of the theophany.

P placed the incident recorded in vss. 9-10 not at Bethel but on the border of Palestine; i.e., the change of Jacob's name to Israel occurred in that document in relatively the same position as in J (32:24-30).

D. Birth of Benjamin (35:16-20)

16-20. This section is a conflation of J[2] and E. In vs. 19 **that is, Bethlehem** is a gloss, erroneously identifying this **Ephrath** with the "Ephrathah" of Ruth 4:11; Mic. 5:2. It is clear from I Sam. 10:2 (cf. Jer. 31:15) that Rachel's grave was situated in Benjamin not far from Ramah.

The fact that there was **a pillar** standing beside it (vs. 20) suggests that it was a **cult** center. Of this J[1] appears to have been ignorant, despite his knowledge of the tradition representing Rachel as Jacob's wife. J[2], more familiar with the traditions and legends of the north than his predecessor had been, knew of its existence, and therefore included in his narrative the account of Rachel's death and burial. Indeed, the necessity of bringing Jacob to Ephrath was one of the reasons which led him to abandon the representation of J[1] that Jacob had proceeded from the Jabbok to Hebron by an east Jordan route.

In locating the birth of Benjamin in Palestine, J[2] recorded in genealogical terms the fact that the Benjamites, though long quasi-independent (cf. Judg. 5:14), had attained tribal status only after the Conquest. J[1], though aware of them as a group (cf. Judg. 3:15aγ), appears to have tacitly included them in the house of Joseph.

---

shall be called no more Jacob, but Israel" (32:28). But he chooses to include also the more formal record which had come to his hand from the priestly writers, and which is inserted here in these verses (with the exception of vs. 14, which comes apparently from one of the older sources). In their precise and emphatic way the priestly writers are underscoring the proclamation of the mighty destiny of the Israelitish people as this had been for many generations established in the people's faith. From God Almighty had the promise come that not only should the Promised Land be theirs, but that **kings shall come out of thy loins.** Already there had been kings whom tradition glorified: Saul, David, Solomon. Bravely—even if in the light of later events wistfully—they believed that other kings and conquering leaders would arise.

In the outward form of their expectation they were to be disappointed. Yet in a deeper sense the truth would be greater than they had dreamed; for out of the line of Israel was to come the King of kings.

16-20. Rachel's Death.—Full of pathos is this brief description. Jacob's love for Rachel had been the brightest element in his character; now she dies, and he must make her grave. There had been sadness in her life before: her father's trick of having Leah married first, the bitter years when she was barren. Then joy had come with the birth of Joseph (30:22-24). But now the coming of her hoped-for second son must cost her life. At first, when she had no children, she had cried, "Give me children, or else I die" (30:1); now when her sons had been born, she should die and leave them. It is not

17 And it came to pass, when she was in hard labor, that the midwife said unto her, Fear not; thou shalt have this son also.

18 And it came to pass, as her soul was in departing, (for she died,) that she called his name Ben-oni: but his father called him Benjamin.

19 And Rachel died, and was buried in the way to Ephrath, which is Bethlehem.

20 And Jacob set a pillar upon her grave: that is the pillar of Rachel's grave unto this day.

21 ¶ And Israel journeyed, and spread his tent beyond the tower of Edar.

22 And it came to pass, when Israel dwelt in that land, that Reuben went and

hard labor. 17 And when she was in her hard labor, the midwife said to her, "Fear not; for now you will have another son." 18 And as her soul was departing (for she died), she called his name Ben-o'ni;[c] but his father called his name Benjamin.[d] 19 So Rachel died, and she was buried on the way to Ephrath (that is, Bethlehem), 20 and Jacob set up a pillar upon her grave; it is the pillar of Rachel's tomb, which is there to this day. 21 Israel journeyed on, and pitched his tent beyond the tower of Eder.

22 While Israel dwelt in that land

[c] That is Son of my sorrow
[d] That is Son of the right hand or Son of the South

The name **Benjamin**, meaning **Son of the right hand**, suggests that they were so designated because of their geographical position to the right, i.e., the south, of Ephraim. The designation almost inevitably gave rise to the claim that they were descended from one Benjamin, who, on their achievement of independence, naturally came to be regarded as the youngest son of Jacob.

As has already been noted (see further below), J[2] located the sale of Joseph to the Ishmaelites in the vicinity of Shechem. In his narrative, accordingly, the birth of Benjamin occurred after this event. E, who placed Joseph's kidnaping by the Midianites in the south, necessarily transposed the order of the two events. RJE, conflating the two narratives, adopted at this point the representation of E.

E. Reuben's Impiety (35:21-22a)

21-22a. This section is from J[1], who located the event east of the Jordan in the territory occupied by the tribe of Reuben. It seems likely that J[1] is here dependent upon some local tradition having its origin in that region. Some confirmation of this is furnished by the abrupt appearance of Jacob's concubine, not previously mentioned by J[1]. The identification of the concubine with Bilhah is the work of J[2].

In view of the characterization of Reuben in the ancient oracle in 49:3-4, the historical event underlying the tale may well have been some rash act of aggression on the part of the Reubenites against a neighboring tribe. However that may be, J[1] used the story to account for the fact that although Reuben was traditionally the first-born of Jacob, the tribe claiming him as ancestor was comparatively insignificant (cf. Judg. 5:15b-16). The tale, it may be assumed, in its primary form ended with a curse pronounced by his father on Reuben—"and Israel heard of it" (vs. 22b) is certainly not the original conclusion. This was dropped, so as not to anticipate 49:4a, when the blessing of Jacob (49:2-27) was added to the J narrative.

J[2] having, as has been noted above, abandoned the representation of J[1] that Jacob had journeyed from the Jabbok to Hebron east of the Jordan, was compelled to change

strange therefore that she became in the thought of Israel a symbol of wistfulness and sorrow, so that Jeremiah (31:15) would say concerning the desolation of Jerusalem, "A voice was heard in Ramah, lamentation, and bitter weeping; Rachel weeping for her children." She named her child, **Benoni, Son of my sorrow.** But a happier fact was expressed in the name that Jacob gave him, **Benjamin, the Son of the right**

hand. For the tribe of Benjamin was to play its signal part in history, since from it came Saul, the first king (I Sam. 9:1-2), and that greater Saul of Tarsus, who was to be the apostle Paul (Phil. 3:5).

21-22a. See Expos. on 49:4.

22b-26. Another item in the genealogical tables which the priestly writers were bent upon making complete.

lay with Bilhah his father's concubine: and Israel heard *it*. Now the sons of Jacob were twelve:

23 The sons of Leah; Reuben, Jacob's firstborn, and Simeon, and Levi, and Judah, and Issachar, and Zebulun:

24 The sons of Rachel; Joseph, and Benjamin:

25 And the sons of Bilhah, Rachel's handmaid; Dan, and Naphtali:

26 And the sons of Zilpah, Leah's handmaid; Gad, and Asher. These *are* the sons of Jacob, which were born to him in Padan-aram.

27 ¶ And Jacob came unto Isaac his father unto Mamre, unto the city of Arba, which *is* Hebron, where Abraham and Isaac sojourned.

28 And the days of Isaac were a hundred and fourscore years.

29 And Isaac gave up the ghost, and died, and was gathered unto his people, *being* old and full of days: and his sons Esau and Jacob buried him.

Reuben went and lay with Bilhah his father's concubine; and Israel heard of it.

Now the sons of Jacob were twelve. **23** The sons of Leah: Reuben (Jacob's firstborn), Simeon, Levi, Judah, Is'sachar, and Zeb'ulun. **24** The sons of Rachel: Joseph and Benjamin. **25** The sons of Bilhah, Rachel's maid: Dan and Naph'tali. **26** The sons of Zilpah, Leah's maid: Gad and Asher. These were the sons of Jacob who were born to him in Paddan-aram.

27 And Jacob came to his father Isaac at Mamre, or Kir'iath-ar'ba (that is, Hebron), where Abraham and Isaac had sojourned. **28** Now the days of Isaac were a hundred and eighty years. **29** And Isaac breathed his last; and he died and was gathered to his people, old and full of days; and his sons Esau and Jacob buried him.

---

the scene of Reuben's outrage to a point west of the Jordan. This change could be made with little difficulty. The Hebrew *mighdal 'ēdher,* rendered **the tower of Eder** (vs. 21), means simply "a flock tower"—one of the many such towers which must have existed in a pastoral country. A *mighdal 'ēdher,* probably in the neighborhood of Jerusalem, is mentioned in Mic. 4:8.

F. Sons of Jacob (35:22*b*-26)

22*b*-26. This section is from P—apparently all that was contained in that document on the birth of Jacob's sons; contrast the detailed JE material in 29:31–30:24. The original position of the list was probably immediately after 37:2aα, "This is the history of the family of Jacob."

XLI. Death of Isaac (35:27-29)

27-29. This section, originally the continuation of vs. 10, is from P. Both the J and the E narratives represent Isaac as being on his deathbed when he blessed Jacob (27:1-40; cf. 27:41), and so imply that he died shortly after Jacob's departure to visit Laban.

27-29. *The Solemnity of Death.*—In vs. 29 there comes a haunting echo of an earlier passage: 25:8-9. Except for the names, the two are identical. Isaac dies, and his sons Esau and Jacob come to bury him. Abraham died, and his sons Isaac and Ishmael came and buried him. In each case there had been bitterness between the two sons. Isaac was the cherished one; Ishmael had been driven out because of Sarah's jealousy for Isaac. So in the next generation also the two sons had been divided by Jacob's crafty trick that stole the birthright and Esau's resulting furious anger. But both times the two

sons meet at a father's funeral—the one thing that after long separation could reunite them.

The verses are more than bare records of events. They suggest a deep instinct that runs through all the history of Israel—the instinct of family loyalty. Whatever might drive individuals apart, something still stronger held them, and would keep them from complete estrangement. Not in word only, but in fact the people of Israel accepted the commandment, "Honor thy father and thy mother: that thy days may be long upon the land which the Lord thy God giveth thee." Obedience to that commandment

36 Now these *are* the generations of Esau, who *is* Edom.

2 Esau took his wives of the daughters of Canaan; Adah the daughter of Elon the Hittite, and Aholibamah the daughter of Anah the daughter of Zibeon the Hivite;

3 And Bashemath Ishmael's daughter, sister of Nebajoth.

4 And Adah bare to Esau Eliphaz, and Bashemath bare Reuel;

5 And Aholibamah bare Jeush, and Jaalam, and Korah: these *are* the sons of Esau, which were born unto him in the land of Canaan.

36 These are the descendants of Esau (that is, Edom). 2 Esau took his wives from the Canaanites: Adah the daughter of Elon the Hittite, Oholiba'mah the daughter of Anah the son[e] of Zibeon the Hivite, 3 and Bas'emath, Ish'mael's daughter, the sister of Neba'ioth. 4 And Adah bore to Esau, El'iphaz; Bas'emath bore Reu'el; 5 and Oholiba'mah bore Je'ush, Jalam, and Korah. These are the sons of Esau who were born to him in the land of Canaan.

[e] Sam Gk Syr: Heb *daughter*

The chronological difficulties to which vs. 28 gives rise have been noted in the article "The Growth of the Hexateuch" (see p. 187).

XLII. Descendants of Esau (36:1-43)

36:1-43. This chapter is a conflation of J and P, with considerable redactional harmonization.

A. The Edomites (36:1-19)

1-19. The first section contains valuable information regarding the Edomites (see Skinner, *Genesis,* pp. 436-37), some of it, doubtless, derived from Edomite records.

---

is one reason why the Jewish race has had such tenacity and toughness of survival. It has honored and protected the family. It has chastened and corrected selfish irresponsibility by putting into the hearts of each generation a sense of duty to the group.

A funeral is not the place or time at which to begin a family loyalty, nor the occasion at which to express it best, but it may be a symbol of the loyalty that is or ought to be. Among all sorts of people there are reunions like those of Isaac and Ishmael, and of Esau and Jacob— reunions of living persons long estranged brought together at least for that hour in the presence of the dead. For a funeral breaks through the crust of the present and revives the past. It stirs half-forgotten memories—memories of childhood, of innocence, of happy, unconscious acceptance of life as good. Such memories may be joy and blessing if they have been woven into life; but even if they have been overlaid instead by "barren gain and bitter loss," they may still be a blessing if they make us more sensitive to our shortcomings, more charitable to others, more ready to let new and better emotions grow from ground watered by tears. So it is when there has been estrangement, or estrangement partially made up, as Esau's and Jacob's had been. Something older and stronger

than the rift may rise in the presence of the dead to speak of unity.

But what when there has been no division, and nothing deeply calling for repentance? Suppose Isaac and Ishmael, and Esau and Jacob, had brought to their father's funeral a devotion to one another and to him that had never been breached. Then they need have had—as many men do have when they stand at the funeral of one they have loved—no deep bitterness in grief, but a great thankfulness and pride for that which God had given them in the relationships to which they had belonged. A noble gentleman, Sir Edward Grey, British secretary of state for foreign affairs in the early 1900's once wrote: "I was thinking the other day what a secure possession the past is. The happiness and beauty that it had cannot now be spoiled or impaired: having had it one cannot be pessimistic either about this life or another."[9] Out of personal loyalties and family loyalties such convictions can come; and the Bible more than any other book has shown men what loyalty can mean, and especially has made plain that loyalty to family and to people is sweet only when it is lifted up into the thought of God.

36:1-43. *More Family History.*—See Expos. on ch. 5. Here again the chroniclers, particularly

[9] George M. Trevelyan, *Grey of Fallodon* (Boston: Houghton Mifflin Co., 1937), p. 177.

6 And Esau took his wives, and his sons, and his daughters, and all the persons of his house, and his cattle, and all his beasts, and all his substance, which he had got in the land of Canaan; and went into the country from the face of his brother Jacob.

7 For their riches were more than that they might dwell together; and the land wherein they were strangers could not bear them because of their cattle.

8 Thus dwelt Esau in mount Seir: Esau *is* Edom.

9 ¶ And these *are* the generations of Esau the father of the Edomites in mount Seir:

10 These *are* the names of Esau's sons; Eliphaz the son of Adah the wife of Esau, Reuel the son of Bashemath the wife of Esau.

11 And the sons of Eliphaz were Teman, Omar, Zepho, and Gatam, and Kenaz.

12 And Timna was concubine to Eliphaz Esau's son; and she bare to Eliphaz Amalek: these *were* the sons of Adah Esau's wife.

13 And these *are* the sons of Reuel; Nahath, and Zerah, Shammah, and Mizzah: these were the sons of Bashemath Esau's wife.

14 ¶ And these were the sons of Aholibamah, the daughter of Anah the daughter of Zibeon, Esau's wife: and she bare to Esau Jeush, and Jaalam, and Korah.

15 ¶ These *were* dukes of the sons of Esau: the sons of Eliphaz the firstborn *son* of Esau; duke Teman, duke Omar, duke Zepho, duke Kenaz,

16 Duke Korah, duke Gatam, *and* duke Amalek: these *are* the dukes *that came* of Eliphaz in the land of Edom: these *were* the sons of Adah.

17 ¶ And these *are* the sons of Reuel Esau's son; duke Nahath, duke Zerah, duke Shammah, duke Mizzah: these *are* the dukes *that came* of Reuel in the land of Edom: these *are* the sons of Bashemath Esau's wife.

18 ¶ And these *are* the sons of Aholibamah Esau's wife; duke Jeush, duke Jaalam, duke Korah: these *were* the dukes *that came* of Aholibamah the daughter of Anah, Esau's wife.

19 These *are* the sons of Esau, who *is* Edom, and these *are* their dukes.

6 Then Esau took his wives, his sons, his daughters, and all the members of his household, his cattle, all his beasts, and all his property which he had acquired in the land of Canaan; and he went into a land away from his brother Jacob. 7 For their possessions were too great for them to dwell together; the land of their sojournings could not support them because of their cattle. 8 So Esau dwelt in the hill country of Se'ir; Esau is Edom.

9 These are the descendants of Esau the father of the Edomites in the hill country of Se'ir. 10 These are the names of Esau's sons: El'iphaz the son of Adah the wife of Esau, Reu'el the son of Bas'emath the wife of Esau. 11 The sons of El'iphaz were Teman, Omar, Zepho, Gatam, and Kenaz. 12 (Timna was a concubine of El'iphaz, Esau's son; she bore Am'alek to El'iphaz.) These are the sons of Adah, Esau's wife. 13 These are the sons of Reu'el: Nahath, Zerah, Shammah, and Mizzah. These are the sons of Bas'emath, Esau's wife. 14 These are the sons of Oholiba'mah the daughter of Anah the son[f] of Zib'eon, Esau's wife: she bore to Esau Je'ush, Jalam, and Korah.

15 These are the chiefs of the sons of Esau. The sons of El'iphaz the first-born of Esau: the chiefs Teman, Omar, Zepho, Kenaz, 16 Korah, Gatam, and Am'alek; these are the chiefs of El'iphaz in the land of Edom; they are the sons of Adah. 17 These are the sons of Reu'el, Esau's son: the chiefs Nahath, Zerah, Shammah, and Mizzah: these are the chiefs of Reu'el in the land of Edom; they are the sons of Bas'emath, Esau's wife. 18 These are the sons of Oholiba'mah, Esau's wife: the chiefs Je'ush, Jalam, and Korah; these are the chiefs born of Oholiba'mah the daughter of Anah, Esau's wife. 19 These are the sons of Esau (that is, Edom), and these are their chiefs.

f Gk Syr: Heb *daughter*

20 ¶ These *are* the sons of Seir the Horite, who inhabited the land; Lotan, and Shobal, and Zibeon, and Anah,

21 And Dishon, and Ezer, and Dishan: these *are* the dukes of the Horites, the children of Seir in the land of Edom.

22 And the children of Lotan were Hori and Hemam; and Lotan's sister *was* Timna.

23 And the children of Shobal *were* these; Alvan, and Manahath, and Ebal, Shepho, and Onam.

24 And these *are* the children of Zibeon; both Ajah, and Anah: this *was that* Anah that found the mules in the wilderness, as he fed the asses of Zibeon his father.

25 And the children of Anah *were* these; Dishon, and Aholibamah the daughter of Anah.

26 And these *are* the children of Dishon; Hemdan, and Eshban, and Ithran, and Cheran.

27 The children of Ezer *are* these; Bilhan, and Zaavan, and Akan.

28 The children of Dishan *are* these; Uz, and Aran.

29 These *are* the dukes *that came* of the Horites; duke Lotan, duke Shobal, duke Zibeon, duke Anah,

30 Duke Dishon, duke Ezer, duke Dishan: these *are* the dukes *that came* of Hori, among their dukes in the land of Seir.

31 ¶ And these *are* the kings that reigned in the land of Edom, before there reigned any king over the children of Israel.

32 And Bela the son of Beor reigned in Edom: and the name of his city *was* Dinhabah.

33 And Bela died, and Jobab the son of Zerah of Bozrah reigned in his stead.

34 And Jobab died, and Husham of the land of Temani reigned in his stead.

20 These are the sons of Se'ir the Horite, the inhabitants of the land: Lotan, Shobal, Zib'eon, Anah, 21 Dishon, Ezer, and Dishan; these are the chiefs of the Horites, the sons of Se'ir in the land of Edom. 22 The sons of Lotan were Hori and Heman; and Lotan's sister was Timna. 23 These are the sons of Shobal: Alvan, Man'a-hath, Ebal, Shepho, and Onam. 24 These are the sons of Zib'eon: A'iah and Anah; he is the Anah who found the hot springs in the wilderness, as he pastured the asses of Zib'eon his father. 25 These are the children of Anah: Dishon and Oholiba'mah the daughter of Anah. 26 These are the sons of Dishon: Hemdan, Eshban, Ithran, and Cheran. 27 These are the sons of Ezer: Bilhan, Za'avan, and Akan. 28 These are the sons of Dishan: Uz and Aran. 29 These are the chiefs of the Horites: the chiefs Lotan, Shobal, Zib'eon, Anah, 30 Dishon, Ezer, and Dishan; these are the chiefs of the Horites, according to their clans in the land of Se'ir.

31 These are the kings who reigned in the land of Edom, before any king reigned over the Israelites. 32 Bela the son of Be'or reigned in Edom, the name of his city being Din'habah. 33 Bela died, and Jobab the son of Zerah of Bozrah reigned in his stead. 34 Jobab died, and Husham of the land of the Te'manites reigned in his stead.

B. The Horites (36:20-30)

20-30. The Horites are the Hurrians, a non-Semitic people from the highlands east of Mesopotamia; in the fifteenth and fourteenth centuries they spread so widely over Syria and Palestine that one of the Egyptian names for Canaan was *Khûru* (see Wright and Filson, *Westminster Atlas,* p. 29; also W. F. Albright, *From the Stone Age to Christianity* [2nd ed.; Baltimore: Johns Hopkins Press, 1946], pp. 109-10) .

C. The Kings of Edom (36:31-43)

31-43. Of particular interest are vss. 31-39. The first king of Edom, **Bela the son of Beor,** is probably to be identified with "Balaam the son of Beor," whom the king of Moab hired to curse Israel (Num. 22:5; cf. Meyer, *Israeliten und ihre Nachbarstämme,* pp. 376-80) . In vs. 39, "Hadad" should be read for **Hadar,** with some MSS and version

35 And Husham died, and Hadad the son of Bedad, who smote Midian in the field of Moab, reigned in his stead: and the name of his city *was* Avith.

36 And Hadad died, and Samlah of Masrekah reigned in his stead.

37 And Samlah died, and Saul of Rehoboth *by* the river reigned in his stead.

38 And Saul died, and Baal-hanan the son of Achbor reigned in his stead.

39 And Baal-hanan the son of Achbor died, and Hadar reigned in his stead: and the name of his city *was* Pau; and his wife's name *was* Mehetabel, the daughter of Matred, the daughter of Mezahab.

40 And these *are* the names of the dukes *that came* of Esau, according to their families, after their places, by their names; duke Timnah, duke Alvah, duke Jetheth,

41 Duke Aholibamah, duke Elah, duke Pinon,

42 Duke Kenaz, duke Teman, duke Mibzar,

43 Duke Magdiel, duke Iram: these *be* the dukes of Edom, according to their habitations in the land of their possession: he *is* Esau the father of the Edomites.

37 And Jacob dwelt in the land wherein his father was a stranger, in the land of Canaan.

35 Husham died, and Hadad the son of Bedad, who defeated Mid'ian in the country of Moab, reigned in his stead, the name of his city being Avith. 36 Hadad died, and Samlah of Masre'kah reigned in his stead. 37 Samlah died, and Shaul of Reho'both on the Eu-phra'tes reigned in his stead. 38 Shaul died, and Ba'al-ha'nan the son of Achbor reigned in his stead. 39 Ba'al-ha'nan the son of Achbor died, and Hadar reigned in his stead, the name of his city being Pau; his wife's name was Mehet'abel, the daughter of Matred, daughter of Me'zahab.

40 These are the names of the chiefs of Esau, according to their families and their dwelling places, by their names: the chiefs Timna, Alvah, Jetheth, 41 Oholiba'mah, Elah, Pinon, 42 Kenaz, Teman, Mibzar, 43 Mag'diel, and Iram; these are the chiefs of Edom (that is, Esau, the father of Edom), according to their dwelling places in the land of their possession.

37 Jacob dwelt in the land of his father's sojournings, in the land of

support (cf. I Chr. 1:50). There is little doubt that this Hadad was the king subdued by David (cf. I Kings 11:14-18; see *ibid.,* pp. 355-63). On the assumption that each of the eight kings mentioned in the present list reigned on an average for twenty years—"a reasonable allowance in early unsettled times" (Skinner, *Genesis,* pp. 434-35)—the foundation of the Edomite monarchy may be dated about 150 years before the rise of the monarchy in Israel, a circumstance which is reflected in the representation of Esau as the elder brother of Jacob.

XLIII. JOSEPH COMES TO EGYPT (37:1-36)

37:1-36. The P material in this chapter is limited to vs. 1 and part of vs. 2: **This is the history of the family of Jacob. Joseph, being seventeen years old, was . . . with the sons of Bilhah and Zilpah, his father's wives; and Joseph brought an ill report of them to their father.** Apart from this, the chapter is a conflation of J[2] and E.

the priestly ones, are at their congenial task of trying to put not only the direct but the collateral lines of the Israelitish family into a firm frame of history.

37:1-3. *Jacob's Blunder.*—Jacob is dwelling now in a land where his father was a stranger. So the chronicler suggests what the people of Israel constantly desired to emphasize—that the country to which Abraham had come with his lonely mandate from God had now become the

home of his descendants. Jacob has the chance to establish his family in peace and happiness. But he begins with a serious blunder. He shows the same sort of favoritism which his mother had shown to him. Plenty of trouble grew up from that, and may grow up in other instances from roots not of conscious wrongdoing but only of mistakes.

Observe the mixed emotions which were at work in Jacob. Always he had been a person of

The J[2] narrative began by recording Jacob's love for Joseph, because of which he made him **a long robe with sleeves** (vs. 3)—the KJV rendering **a coat of many colors** depends upon the LXX—and the brothers' consequent hatred of their father's favorite, a hatred which was increased by Joseph's dream of the sheaves (vss. 5a, 6-8). It then told how it happened that Joseph fell into his brothers' hands at Dothan (vss. 12-13a, 14b-17), and of their selling him to a caravan of Ishmaelites after stripping him of his coat (vss. 19-21, 25-27, 23b, 28aγ). This they dipped in blood and brought to their father, convincing him that Joseph had been killed by a wild beast (vss. 31-33, 34b-35).

Underlying this narrative is a much briefer story by J[1]—fragments of which are preserved in vss. 3a, 4aαγ, 26-27, 28aγ—which located Joseph's misadventure not at Dothan near Shechem in the north, but in the desert to the south of Hebron.

It is important to note that J[1] had now completed his articulation of the various local traditions of the south and east. These he had related to Yahwism and brought together into a connected narrative. He was now confronted with the necessity of getting the family of Jacob into Egypt in preparation for the second and more historical part of his work, the account of the Exodus and the Conquest. This he accomplished by telling how Jacob's fifth son was sold by his brothers to the nomad Ishmaelites, who in turn sold him into slavery in Egypt. There he rose to a position of great power. This made it possible for him to bring his father and his brothers from Palestine to Egypt in a time of famine. The stage was thus set for the Exodus.

This tale of a boy being kidnaped and sold into slavery may be based upon nothing more than what was doubtless a not infrequent occurrence in the desert near Hebron; i.e., J[1], having exhausted his store of local traditions, may have here resorted to free composition. However, it is not impossible that he was drawing upon a tradition which associated the Shechemite figure, Joseph, with Egypt. There is, of course, no way of determining whether or not the pre-Israelite tradition of Joseph associated him with Egypt from the beginning. It may have done so. But it is perhaps more likely that the Egypt motif was a later accretion drawn from the career of Yanhamu, the Semitic minister of Amenhotep IV (cf. Skinner, *Genesis*, pp. 441, 501-2; Gunkel, *Genesis*, pp. 398-99, 437-38), to whom reference is made in the Tell-el-Amarna letters (J. A. Knudtzon, ed., *Die El-Amarna-Tafeln* [Leipzig: J. C. Hinrichs, 1907-15], II, 1169-72).

However that may be, it would seem that if there was a tradition associating Joseph with Egypt, it was only vaguely known in the south, with the result that J[1]'s version of it differed markedly from the form in which it was current in the north. J[2], concerned to have his predecessor's narrative as a whole accepted by the powerful tribes of Ephraim and Manasseh, was therefore at special pains to revise the story of Joseph, whom they had come to claim as their ancestor, so that it would conform more closely in its details to the legend of Shechem. It was for this reason that he changed the location of the sale of Joseph from the southern desert to the vicinity of Shechem—a very considerable alteration, since it involved changing Jacob's route from the Jabbok to Hebron from the east to the west of the Jordan. Indeed, it is likely that the local tradition explicitly placed the event at Dothan. Nothing else seems to account for the otherwise pointless vss. 16-17.

---

conflicting impulses. There was good in him, even if sometimes it seemed hard to find; and one element that was most surely good was the love he had had for Rachel. For seven years he served her father Laban for the promise that then he might marry her, "and they seemed unto him but a few days, for the love he had to her" (29:20); and when Laban broke his promise, he set himself to face with inflexible persistence seven years more. In an age when polygamy was the custom, Jacob had more than one wife, but that was with him more a matter of accepted rule than of his own moving. Apparently the one and only woman he really loved was Rachel. He had other children, but Rachel's children only were close to his heart. Joseph was her first-born. Then, when she gave birth to Benjamin, she died; and when Jacob buried her, his heart was buried with her, except for the sons she left behind. Of these two Joseph, who had been born first, still stood first in his affection. Great traits of human nature are

2 These *are* the generations of Jacob. Joseph, *being* seventeen years old, was feeding the flock with his brethren; and the lad *was* with the sons of Bilhah, and with the sons of Zilpah, his father's wives: and Joseph brought unto his father their evil report.

Canaan. 2 This is the history of the family of Jacob.

Joseph, being seventeen years old, was shepherding the flock with his brothers; he was a lad with the sons of Bilhah and Zilpah, his father's wives; and Joseph brought an

---

Another feature of J²'s elaboration was the introduction of the motif of the coat with long sleeves (vss. 3*b*, 23*b*, 31-33). This, it may be inferred from II Sam. 13:19— II Sam. 13:18 seems to be gloss—was a royal garment (cf. Gunkel, *op. cit.*, p. 404). J² is thus acknowledging the claim of the Joseph tribes to a royal authority independent of the tribe of Judah.

The dream of the sheaves (vss. 5-8) is a third feature from J². The implication of this is that Joseph's future thus revealed—note the subtle allusion to the agrarian policy which brought about his rise to power—had already been determined by God. Despicable as his brothers' action was in selling him into slavery, they were the unwitting agents of divine Providence. History was in God's control.

J²'s elaboration of the earlier narrative thus included (*a*) the provision of details of the tradition which had been unknown to J¹; (*b*) the recognition of the right of the northern tribes to have their own king; and (*c*) an emphasizing of the religious and theological significance of the story. At the same time he allowed his imagination and his literary skill to have free play. His account of Joseph's brothers bringing his cloak to their father and of the old man's grief has rarely been surpassed. Up to this point in his narrative he has for the most part been under certain restrictions in that he has had to take account of the traditions lying before him, to expurgate those which J¹ had not used, and to adapt them to Yahwism. Even under these limitations he has shown an extraordinary skill—witness, e.g., his narrative in chs. 2–3. Here, however, he has been able to write freely, and he shows himself to be an artist of the first rank.

The E recension, while it followed the story of J² in its main outline, differed from it in certain details:

(*a*) It omitted all reference to the coat with long sleeves which the brothers had callously brought to their father as evidence that Joseph was dead. This scene E rejected because of his concern, here as elsewhere, for the moral reputation of the patriarchs.

(*b*) For J²'s dream of the sheaves (vs. 7) it substituted that of the sun, moon, and stars bowing down to Joseph (vs. 9). This is more mythological in character than that of the sheaves in which J² had pointed ahead to Joseph's agrarian policy, and may have been derived from a tradition originally having nothing to do with Joseph, as the reference to Joseph's mother (vs. 10), already dead according to E (35:19), suggests. E's motive for substituting this for the more homely allegory of J² may have been his desire to provide a symbol more suggestive of the splendor of Joseph's future career.

(*c*) It represented Reuben as intervening to save Joseph's life (vss. 22, 29). This change was made presumably because the historic rivalry between the north and the south

---

independent of time. The romance of many a modern story has its prototype in Jacob—the romance of a man who never moves out from the influence of a supreme devotion. To Jacob, Joseph represented not only himself; he represented Rachel. Jacob would give to the living the devotion he had given to the dead. Jacob would take the place of the dead, and be to Joseph mother as well as father. There was pathos in that, and beauty, as there always is in a parent's prodigal emotion toward a child.

But was there also another impulse? As Jacob tried to satisfy a broken affection, so perhaps he was trying to fulfill an unfinished picture of himself. He had always been ambitious. He could not bear to be under the shadow of Esau. He had wanted to be the first in the family— recognized to be the first indisputably. By craftiness and patience he seemed to have succeeded, but inwardly he was never sure. Often he felt inferior, even when his fortunes were superior. Now he would compensate for that. In this son

3 Now Israel loved Joseph more than | ill report of them to their father. ³ Now
all his children, because he *was* the son of | Israel loved Joseph more than any other of
his old age: and he made him a coat of | his children, because he was the son of his
many colors. | old age; and he made him a long robe with

---

had made difficult of acceptance J²'s portrayal of Judah as Joseph's protector (vss. 21, 26; in vs. 21 "Judah" must be read for "Reuben." Practically all modern commentators recognize the necessity of this emendation; see Holzinger, *Genesis,* p. 224; Gunkel, *Genesis,* p. 401; Skinner, *Genesis,* p. 447; Driver, *Genesis,* p. 324.) Furthermore, E had dropped as morally offensive the story in which J² had told of Reuben's forfeiture of his position as first-born through his violation of his father's concubine (35:22a). In the E document, therefore, Reuben was still by right and in fact the leader of his brothers.

(d) It told of Joseph being kidnaped by Midianites (vss. 28aαβ, 29-30), not sold to an Ishmaelite caravan by his brothers (vs. 28aγ). This not only greatly lessened the brothers' guilt—in line with E's general treatment—but also made less difficult the subsequent interpretation of the event as a providential act of God (45:8; cf. 45:7 [J²]). The substitution of the Midianites for the Ishmaelites was doubtless made because the story in 21:9-21, according to which Ishmael was the brother of Isaac, had rendered awkward the representation that his descendants in the third generation already formed an ethnological group. J² was of course, because of the story in 16:1-12, involved in the same difficulty. But he apparently found it impossible to abandon the J¹ tradition that Joseph had been sold to the Ishmaelites. J¹ does not relate Ishmael to Israel. It may be noted further that E does not relate Midian to Israel; 25:2 is from a late stratum of J.

(e) It located the kidnaping in the wilderness (vs. 22), i.e., in the desert near Beer-sheba where, according to E (cf. 46:5), Jacob was living. This departure from the J² tradition is especially significant in view of the fact that J² seems to have placed Joseph's misadventure at Dothan to meet the requirements of the tradition of Shechem, of which E, a northerner, was certainly aware and so was deliberately disregarding.

Now it has already been argued in connection with 33:19 that J²'s affirmation of the Israelite ownership of Joseph's grave suggests that at the time he wrote this claim was in dispute. There can be little doubt that Joseph's grave was a cult center. J²'s claim that the site belonged to Israel was in effect an assertion of the right of the Levitical priesthood to control the shrine. If the Levites failed to establish their claim, one result will have been the survival of a non-Levitical priesthood at Shechem functioning at the shrine of Joseph, and a deep-rooted antagonism between them and the Levitical priesthood at the sanctuary of the oak of Moreh (cf. 12:6; Deut. 11:30; Josh. 24:26). The Levites, it may safely be assumed, would be at pains to minimize the importance of the shrine of their rivals. E's interest in the sanctuary beside the oak of Moreh is evidenced both by the story in 22:1-14, and by the circumstance with which he describes the institution of the covenant there by Joshua (Josh. 24:1-25; 8:30-34). The absence of any allusion in his narrative to Joseph's grave at Shechem (50:25; Exod. 13:19; Josh. 24:32 are all from J²; see Simpson, *Early Traditions of Israel, ad loc.*) may thus be not an oversight, but rather due to E's deliberate policy of ignoring the association of Joseph with Shechem. If this is the case, then E's changing of the scene of Joseph's misadventure from the vicinity of Shechem to the south is perhaps explained: it was designed to undermine the prestige of the priesthood of the shrine of Joseph by tacitly rejecting the traditional association of their patron with Shechem.

A. JOSEPH HATED BY HIS BROTHERS (37:1-11)

3. The phrase **the son of his old age** implicitly ignores Benjamin, whom J² refers to in the same words in 44:20. It may be noted further that in the chronicle of the birth of Jacob's children, in both J² and E, there was little difference in the ages of Joseph and of the younger children of Leah. J¹, on the other hand, knew of only five children of Leah, born in close succession, and it may be inferred, represented Joseph as being born

4 And when his brethren saw that their father loved him more than all his brethren, they hated him, and could not speak peaceably unto him.

5 ¶ And Joseph dreamed a dream, and he told *it* his brethren: and they hated him yet the more.

6 And he said unto them, Hear, I pray you, this dream which I have dreamed:

7 For, behold, we *were* binding sheaves in the field, and, lo, my sheaf arose, and also stood upright; and, behold, your sheaves stood round about, and made obeisance to my sheaf.

8 And his brethren said to him, Shalt thou indeed reign over us? or shalt thou indeed have dominion over us? And they hated him yet the more for his dreams, and for his words.

9 ¶ And he dreamed yet another dream, and told it his brethren, and said, Behold, I have dreamed a dream more; and, behold, the sun and the moon and the eleven stars made obeisance to me.

10 And he told *it* to his father, and to his brethren: and his father rebuked him, and said unto him, What *is* this dream that thou hast dreamed? Shall I and thy mother and thy brethren indeed come to bow down ourselves to thee to the earth?

sleeves. 4 But when his brothers saw that their father loved him more than all his brothers, they hated him, and could not speak peaceably to him.

5 Now Joseph had a dream, and when he told it to his brothers they only hated him the more. 6 He said to them, "Hear this dream which I have dreamed: 7 behold, we were binding sheaves in the field, and lo, my sheaf arose and stood upright; and behold, your sheaves gathered round it, and bowed down to my sheaf." 8 His brothers said to him, "Are you indeed to reign over us? Or are you indeed to have dominion over us?" So they hated him yet more for his dreams and for his words. 9 Then he dreamed another dream, and told it to his brothers, and said, "Behold, I have dreamed another dream; and behold, the sun, the moon, and eleven stars were bowing down to me." 10 But when he told it to his father and to his brothers, his father rebuked him, and said to him, "What is this dream that you have dreamed? Shall I and your mother and your brothers indeed come to bow our-

considerably later. The fact that J² retained the words **the son of his old age** is one indication that in his narrative Joseph was still Jacob's youngest son, and that the birth of Benjamin occurred after Joseph had been sold to the Ishmaelites.

10. The first clause, difficult after **and told it to his brothers** (vs. 9), must originally have been "and his brethren told his father," a reading suggested by Jacob's question,

who had traits so like his own—his ambition and his thirst for life—he would enact more brilliantly the role he had always wanted to play. The **coat of many colors** which he put on Joseph was a symbol of that desire. Joseph should be what Jacob had always wanted to be; in Joseph he would see himself as the admiration and envy of all. In the present day there are many who may recognize themselves in that mirror of Jacob: parents who try to satisfy their own frustrated dreams by putting a child into a pattern in which their thwarted pride vicariously is fed. But such a fact is planted thick with unhappy consequences, such as those which in the case of Jacob were quickly to appear.

4-28. The Older Brothers.—The sons of Leah and Bilhah and Zilpah saw that Joseph was their father's favorite, the petted child of his

too-obvious partiality. Human nature being as it is, it was not strange that they were irritated. They could justify among themselves the anger they felt by charging that their father was unjust. But there was a subtler and less conscious reason for their resentment. They must have recognized that Joseph, with his bright, imaginative spirit, was more attractive than they were. Perhaps there was real cause why his father should prefer him; but that was exactly what they did not choose to admit.

If they had been men of more magnanimous spirit, they would have thought and felt differently. If they could not share Jacob's fondness for the little brother, they could have treated it with amusement; there was nothing in it that did them too serious harm. On the contrary, Joseph could have done them good if they had

11 And his brethren envied him; but his father observed the saying.

12 ¶ And his brethren went to feed their father's flock in Shechem.

13 And Israel said unto Joseph, Do not thy brethren feed *the flock* in Shechem? come, and I will send thee unto them. And he said to him, Here *am I*.

14 And he said to him, Go, I pray thee, see whether it be well with thy brethren, and well with the flocks; and bring me word again. So he sent him out of the vale of Hebron, and he came to Shechem.

15 ¶ And a certain man found him, and, behold, *he was* wandering in the field: and the man asked him, saying, What seekest thou?

selves to the ground before you?" 11 And his brothers were jealous of him, but his father kept the saying in mind.

12 Now his brothers went to pasture their father's flock near Shechem. 13 And Israel said to Joseph, "Are not your brothers pasturing the flock at Shechem? Come, I will send you to them." And he said to him, "Here I am." 14 So he said to him, "Go now, see if it is well with your brothers, and with the flock; and bring me word again." So he sent him from the valley of Hebron, and he came to Shechem. 15 And a man found him wandering in the fields; and the man asked him, "What are you seeking?"

What is this dream that you have dreamed? which implies that the content of the dream had not been related to him by Joseph himself.

B. Joseph Is Sold into Slavery (37:12-28)

12. There can be little doubt that according to the document from which this verse derived—J²—Jacob was still living in the vicinity of Shechem, for the representation that the brothers went from the pastoral south to Shechem to pasture their flocks is an impossible one.

14. From the valley of Hebron is thus redactional harmonization. RJE, in conflating the J² and E narratives, chose to follow the former in locating Joseph's misadventure in the north, and the latter in placing the birth of Benjamin (35:16-19) before the event. He recorded Jacob's move from Shechem to Bethel (35:1-6) and from Bethel southward (35:16) before beginning the story of Joseph. He favored J², however, in that he represented Jacob as settling not at Beer-sheba (cf. 46:5a, and see below), but at Hebron. It may be noted further that it is highly improbable that either J² or E would have told of Jacob sending his favorite son alone from the south to Shechem.

---

not dourly shut their eyes to what his temperament suggested. Their natural disposition was to settle down into the groove of dull ideas and of drab routine. They were the sort of men who did not readily think or do anything different—commonplace men who, left to themselves, will keep everything around them commonplace. But the fact that Joseph was around meant that they could not be left to themselves. His character broke in on their complacency. His restless imagination was always suggesting that life could have an exciting wideness if anyone were not too dull or lazy to explore it. So what must happen? One of two things. Either they would respond to his provocation, or they would get rid of it and if necessary get rid of him.

Observe the parallels to that in other families: the tendency of brothers and sisters who are stodgy, and want to stay so, to ridicule and

repress the boy or girl who has ambitions. Consider how nearly frustrated Moses was by Aaron and Miriam. Think of the family of Jesus, and of his brothers' antagonism when he first went out from Nazareth. They also were the sort who let the youthfulness of the spirit die—men already old in prejudice though in years still in their prime. In *Family Portrait*,[1] James the brother of Jesus, annoyed by the disturbing purpose of that uncomprehended brother of his, is commenting bitterly on what he thinks are the fantastic ideas with which Jesus has been allowed to grow up. "When *I* was a young boy"— he begins; and then Mary Cleophas interrupts him. "Get out, James! You were *born* middle-aged." Consider the families today in which one child, unusually dowered by God, wakes only the hostility of others in the family because

[1] Lenore Coffee and William J. Cowan (New York: Random House, 1939), Act I, scene 1.

16 And he said, I seek my brethren: tell me, I pray thee, where they feed *their flocks.*

17 And the man said, They are departed hence; for I heard them say, Let us go to Dothan. And Joseph went after his brethren, and found them in Dothan.

18 And when they saw him afar off, even before he came near unto them, they conspired against him to slay him.

19 And they said one to another, Behold, this dreamer cometh.

20 Come now therefore, and let us slay him, and cast him into some pit, and we will say, Some evil beast hath devoured him; and we shall see what will become of his dreams.

21 And Reuben heard *it,* and he delivered him out of their hands; and said, Let us not kill him.

22 And Reuben said unto them, Shed no blood, *but* cast him into this pit that *is* in the wilderness, and lay no hand upon him; that he might rid him out of their hands, to deliver him to his father again.

16 "I am seeking my brothers," he said, "tell me, I pray you, where they are pasturing the flock." 17 And the man said, "They have gone away, for I heard them say, 'Let us go to Dothan.' " So Joseph went after his brothers, and found them at Dothan. 18 They saw him afar off, and before he came near to them they conspired against him to kill him. 19 They said to one another, "Here comes this dreamer. 20 Come now, let us kill him and throw him into one of the pits; then we shall say that a wild beast has devoured him, and we shall see what will become of his dreams." 21 But when Reuben heard it, he delivered him out of their hands, saying, "Let us not take his life." 22 And Reuben said to them, "Shed no blood; cast him into this pit here in the wilderness, but lay no hand upon him" — that he might rescue him out of

---

17. **Dothan,** the modern Tell Dôthā, is some fifteen miles north of Shechem.
21. As is noted above, **Reuben** is an error or a redactional substitution for "Judah."

---

they do not want to grow. But lest this should seem the only way in which human nature can act, observe the opposite reality. In the presence of persons more brilliant than themselves men do not have to recoil into sullen resentment lest they should seem to be outshone. On the contrary, the less brilliant man may so generously and ungrudgingly identify himself with the other one that his own life attains a happy expansiveness which it would never have had alone. It is as possible to be magnanimous as it is to be mean. Think of Jonathan's relationship to David, of Andrew's relationship to Peter, of Barnabas' relationship to Paul. Let the members of every Christian family ponder and heed. To stifle and distort another personality is a deadly wrong; to help it to expand is divine. Remember the words of Jesus: "Whosoever shall offend one of these little ones . . . it is better for him that a millstone were hanged about his neck, and he were cast into the sea" (Mark 9:42) ; and "Whosoever shall not receive the kingdom of God as a little child, he shall not enter therein" (Mark 10:15) . Hearing that, let each one who is a father ask himself whether by any blunder he is jeopardizing his son's devel-

opment, and every brother ask himself whether another brother is being hurt by him.

21-30. *Reuben or Judah?*—In this description of what went on between the brothers in regard to Joseph two strands are woven without any particular attempt to make them harmonize—another instance of the will of the ultimate compilers of Genesis not to let any part of the tradition go. In one breath it is Reuben who says of Joseph, **Let us not kill him;** in the next it is Judah who demands, **What profit is it if we slay our brother, and conceal his blood?** Then presently it is Reuben again who returns to the pit where Joseph had been left and, not finding him, rends his clothes because he supposes Joseph to be dead. Perhaps in both the tribes of Reuben and of Judah men wanted to believe that their own ancestor had been better than the other sons of Jacob. At any rate, it is good to find in the dark story these gleams of human compassion set against so much that was cruel and malevolent. But even at its best, the action of the brothers was an ugly witness to what men can descend to in any time. The value of a human being, to say nothing of the bond of brotherhood, was cheap to them. For twenty pieces of silver they sold Joseph as a slave. One

23 ¶ And it came to pass, when Joseph was come unto his brethren, that they stripped Joseph out of his coat, *his* coat of *many* colors that *was* on him;

24 And they took him, and cast him into a pit: and the pit *was* empty, *there was* no water in it.

25 And they sat down to eat bread: and they lifted up their eyes and looked, and, behold, a company of Ishmaelites came from Gilead, with their camels bearing spicery and balm and myrrh, going to carry *it* down to Egypt.

26 And Judah said unto his brethren, What profit *is it* if we slay our brother, and conceal his blood?

27 Come, and let us sell him to the Ishmaelites, and let not our hand be upon him; for he *is* our brother *and* our flesh: and his brethren were content.

their hand, to restore him to his father. 23 So when Joseph came to his brothers, they stripped him of his robe, the long robe with sleeves that he wore; 24 and they took him and cast him into a pit. The pit was empty, there was no water in it.

25 Then they sat down to eat; and looking up they saw a caravan of Ish'maelites coming from Gilead, with their camels bearing gum, balm, and myrrh, on their way to carry it down to Egypt. 26 Then Judah said to his brothers, "What profit is it if we slay our brother and conceal his blood? 27 Come, let us sell him to the Ish'maelites, and let not our hand be upon him, for he is our brother, our own flesh." And his

---

24. The E narrative at this point must, in view of vs. 29, have gone on to say that the brothers moved away from the pit. This notice was dropped by RJE in favor of vss. 25-27.

25. In the J1 narrative, which located the event in the desert to the south of Hebron, the presence of the Ishmaelites did not have to be accounted for: they lived there. J2, to account for their appearance near Shechem, tells of **a caravan of Ishmaelites coming from Gilead.**

27. Note **the Ishmaelites,** instead of "these Ishmaelites," to be expected after vs. 25— an indication that the verses are from different hands.

---

thinks ahead to Israel in the time of Amos, greedy and merciless in its exploitation of the poor and helpless, and remembers the blazing wrath of the prophet against those who were "not grieved for the affliction of Joseph" (Amos 6:6). And the **twenty pieces of silver** which the sons of Jacob received when they sold their brother have a tragic echo in the fact that human loyalty can be so corrupted that a Judas for thirty pieces of silver will sell the Christ himself.

24. *Into the Pit, and Out of It.*—Joseph is thrown by his brothers into a pit—a dreadful physical fact. But morally and spiritually, too, it may often seem that the soul of man is in a pit. The realization of this may come with shocking suddenness. Joseph at one moment walked in the sunlight in his coat of many colors; the next moment he was down in stifling darkness. One moment he seemed to have no need of anything; the next moment he had agonized need of everything. So with human souls. From self-sufficiency they may be plunged into paralyzing helplessness and desperate need of God. Yet at Joseph's worst moment there were unsuspected

forces moving for his release. God's purpose working through its own instruments would carry his life on to deliverance and great destiny. Beyond this verse in Genesis comes the sound of Ps. 40:2, "He brought me up also out of a horrible pit, out of the miry clay, and set my feet upon a rock."

In what sense may the soul of humanity seem to be in a pit? First, in its history and its inheritance. Life on this earth has developed from primeval forms. Note H. G. Wells's words in *The Outline of History:*

If a disembodied intelligence with no knowledge of the future had come to earth and studied life during the early Palæozoic age, he might very reasonably have concluded that life was absolutely confined to the water, and that it could never spread over the land. It found a way. In the Later Palæozoic Period that visitant might have been equally sure that life could not go beyond the edge of a swamp.[2]

When life did go beyond the edge of the swamp, it was represented first by the great reptiles. Then came the age of the great beasts. Then

[2] New York: The Macmillan Co., 1920, I, 39-41.

28 Then there passed by Midianites merchantmen; and they drew and lifted up Joseph out of the pit, and sold Joseph to the Ishmaelites for twenty *pieces* of silver: and they brought Joseph into Egypt.

29 ¶ And Reuben returned unto the pit; and, behold, Joseph *was* not in the pit; and he rent his clothes.

30 And he returned unto his brethren, and said, The child *is* not; and I, whither shall I go?

brothers heeded him. **28** Then Mid'ianite traders passed by; and they drew Joseph up and lifted him out of the pit, and sold him to the Ish'maelites for twenty shekels of silver; and they took Joseph to Egypt.

29 When Reuben returned to the pit and saw that Joseph was not in the pit, he rent his clothes **30** and returned to his brothers, and said, "The lad is gone; and I, where

---

28. RJE, by attaching the J2 sentence, **and sold him to the Ishmaelites for twenty shekels of silver,** to the preceding E account of Joseph being taken out of the pit by the Midianites, and by tacitly identifying the Ishmaelites with the Midianites, has skillfully fused together the J2 story of the sale of Joseph and the E story of his being kidnaped.

---

appeared man. It was a long way by which he had to come, through an evolution from crude beginnings. Pessimists and moral cynics belittle the difference between what man was and what he is and may be. They think of human nature as still essentially most kin to the reptile, the ape, the wolf, or the tiger. But the great fact is that man is different. The reptile was content to stay in the swamp; man wanted to climb out of it. He had and still has primitive instincts against which he must struggle, for he began on the plane of the animal; but he has not been content to dwell there. Admittedly such progress as he has made has been painful, and woefully imperfect; for as his consciousness developed there developed with it an inner area of possible evil choice which the animal never knew. But nevertheless a divine influence has been urging him. Read James Henry Breasted, *The Dawn of Conscience,* especially this:

In the life of the prehistoric hunter, struggling to survive among the fierce and terrible mammals about him, it was a profound change, a fundamental advance, when he first began to hear whispers from a new world which was dawning within him. Here was a new trumpet call which, unlike the tug of hunger or the panic call of self-preservation, did not stir one impulse alone while leaving all the others cold, but for the first time marshalled all the battalions of the human soul.[3]

See William Herbert Carruth's "Each in His Own Tongue," with the concluding lines of its first verse:

[3] New York: Charles Scribner's Sons, 1933, pp. xxiii-xxiv.

Some call it Evolution,
And others call it God.[4]

So the religious man today in his interpretation of human life and of its possibilities must believe in a power whose purpose is to lift the human spirit out of the pit of frustration or pessimism or despair.

Not only humanity in general, but individuals, may seem to be in the pit. Men get into terrifying situations. Why? Partly because they may be caught in the net of irrational human evil. That was partly the fact with Joseph. He was in the pit because his brothers put him there, and because they had in them a malevolence which he could not have expected. So sometimes there seems to be a malevolence in human relationships which can be explained only by the profound old doctrine of original sin. But it was only partly because of the evil of others that Joseph was in the pit. He had been wrong himself: conceited, self-absorbed, exasperating in his assurance. When any man is like that, God's sternly merciful providence may need to put him into a pit to show him that he is no colossus bestriding the earth, but a poor shamed thing, muddy, ignominious, and inadequate.

But Joseph did not belong in the pit. There was essential goodness in him. Reuben had recognized that, and Reuben would be God's instrument for his deliverance. The Lord had a purpose with Joseph, and through being cast into a pit Joseph was started on a road on which he would understand God as never before —understand him as the truth which was to search him, the judgment which was to chasten

[4] Used by permission of Mrs. William Herbert Carruth.

31 And they took Joseph's coat, and killed a kid of the goats, and dipped the coat in the blood;

32 And they sent the coat of *many* colors, and they brought *it* to their father; and said, This have we found: know now whether it *be* thy son's coat or no.

33 And he knew it, and said, *It is* my son's coat; an evil beast hath devoured him; Joseph is without doubt rent in pieces.

34 And Jacob rent his clothes, and put sackcloth upon his loins, and mourned for his son many days.

35 And all his sons and all his daughters rose up to comfort him; but he refused to be comforted; and he said, For I will go down into the grave unto my son mourning. Thus his father wept for him.

36 And the Midianites sold him into Egypt unto Potiphar, an officer of Pharaoh's, *and* captain of the guard.

shall I go?" 31 Then they took Joseph's robe, and killed a goat, and dipped the robe in the blood; 32 and they sent the long robe with sleeves and brought it to their father, and said, "This we have found; see now whether it is your son's robe or not." 33 And he recognized it, and said, "It is my son's robe; a wild beast has devoured him; Joseph is without doubt torn to pieces." 34 Then Jacob rent his garments, and put sackcloth upon his loins, and mourned for his son many days. 35 All his sons and all his daughters rose up to comfort him; but he refused to be comforted, and said, "No, I shall go down to Sheol to my son, mourning." Thus his father wept for him. 36 Meanwhile the Mid'ianites had sold him in Egypt to Pot'i-phar, an officer of Pharaoh, the captain of the guard.

C. Jacob's Grief (37:29-36)

35. A literal rendering of the last sentence is "and his father wept for him." This notice is somewhat redundant after vss. 34a (E) and 34b-35a (J²). It is possible that the original was, "and his mother wept for him," for in the J² narrative Rachel was still alive at the time. If so, the present text is from RJE. Some support for this conjecture is perhaps furnished by the moving figure in Jer. 31:15, of Rachel weeping for her exiled children. Note also the alteration of the original "father's" to "mother's," in 24:67, by a late J hand.

Sheol: The underworld, whither it was believed a man's shade went at death to continue an existence colorless and without significance because it was separated from God (cf., e.g., Ps. 115:17; Eccl. 9:10b). Jacob, wearing sackcloth until the day of his death, would appear in Sheol as a mourner, and then Joseph would know the depth of his grief.

him, the strength which was to lift him, the hope which was to lead him on.

31-36. Evil After Evil.—The consequences of wrongdoing cannot be cut short. One sin creates a situation where it seems necessary to commit another in order to try to hide the first. The sons of Jacob had been guilty of a crime against their brother. Though they did not mind hurting him, they had no direct desire to hurt their father. The fact of what they had done would certainly hurt him enough; but now in order to protect themselves and to cover up their guilt, they had to hurt him worse by a lie that enlarged his grief. They could not dare to tell him what they had actually done with Joseph, which at least had left him alive; they made up the cruel tale that a wild beast had torn him, and that he was dead. They even refined their

father's anguish by showing him Joseph's precious coat which they had smeared with blood. Before the tragic depth of their father's sorrow they felt perhaps a shamed remorse; but the words with which they pretended to comfort him could be only hypocrisy. Henceforth their relationship to their father, as well as their relationship to Joseph, was poisoned. Suppose Jacob should find out what they had done. Suppose one brother should betray the others. Because that was possible, there could be no confidence any more. The lie, once it had been let loose, infected every association in the family. Their effort to make their situation with their father secure through falsehood had only added to their risks. So it always is with a lie. "For the lie is but an artificial attempt to prop up an inverted pyramid which becomes more top heavy with every lie, while truth, like a pyramid

38 And it came to pass at that time, that Judah went down from his brethren, and turned in to a certain Adullamite, whose name *was* Hirah.

38 It happened at that time that Judah went down from his brothers, and turned in to a certain Adullamite, whose

---

XLIV. JUDAH AND TAMAR (38:1-30)

This section is from J¹, with some minor additions by J², to be noted below. The story is built up around three motifs. The first is that of the woman who slays her lovers—the theme which is basic to the book of Tobit (cf. Tob. 3:8). It finds expression here in the words "For he feared that he would die, like his brothers" (vs. 11), in which Judah by implication lays the deaths of Er and Onan, actually the consequence of their own wickedness (vss. 7-10), to the sinister power of Tamar. This motif appears to have been introduced simply to provide a background to the main part of the story. In view of the fact, however, that the names Tamar and Sarah—the heroine of Tobit—are both connected with Ishtar (cf. Skinner, *Genesis*, p. 452), there may be here an echo of a myth which was perhaps still current in Palestine in J¹'s time.

The second motif is that of heroic incest (vss. 13-26), and the third that of the birth struggle of twins for priority (vss. 27-30). Both of these occur elsewhere and separately in the J¹ narrative, the former in the story of Lot's daughters (19:30-36), the latter in that of the birth of Esau and Jacob (25:24-26).

Since these two legends were derived from Canaanite sources they are necessarily of earlier origin than this obviously Israelite story of Judah, which would therefore appear to be dependent upon them. This dependence would seem to be due to conscious and deliberate appropriation, for it is difficult to suppose that the recurrence in one story of two originally separate and independent motifs is due to chance.

The tale appears to have a twofold purpose. First, it justifies the possibly recent incorporation into the tribe of Judah of three clans which had hitherto been regarded as of alien stock, and whose presence in the land had long antedated the Israelite conquest. It is now claimed that they were Judahite in origin: their eponyms, Shelah, Perez, and Zerah, were sons of Judah by Canaanite women, and, it is implied, had remained with their Canaanite kinsfolk in Palestine when their father migrated to Egypt.

Second, the story accounts for an increase in the prestige of the clan of Perez—historically due, in all probability, to the fact that David was a member of the clan (cf. Ruth 4:18-22).

These two points could certainly have been made even if Judah had not been cast in such a dubious role—as indeed the clan of Shelah was accounted for. (Eissfeldt, *Hexateuch-Synopse*, pp. 29-30, maintains that in this story J¹ was explaining why tribal leadership had passed from Judah to Joseph. But if the suggestion advanced above is sound, that J¹ wrote in the reign of David, then Eissfeldt's interpretation can hardly be valid.) Since it is unlikely that J¹ would himself have deliberately put Judah in such an unfavorable light—witness his uneasiness regarding the story of Lot's daughters (see Exeg. on 19:30-38)—it would seem that he has simply incorporated into his narrative a popular tale which was already in circulation when he wrote. At the same time, as has been noted above in the Exeg. of ch. 34, his attitude toward sex was essentially matter of

---

broadly based on reality, cannot be overturned." [5]

38:1-30. Judah and Tamar.—To many readers of the Bible, it must seem strange that this story is inserted in the midst of the narrative of Joseph. It is like an alien element, suddenly and

arbitrarily thrust into a record which it serves only to disturb. Certainly few people would choose this chapter as a basis for teaching or preaching. Then why is this dark old tale preserved? Apparently because it is the expression, under the names and figures of individual persons, of traditions as to how certain minglings and intermarryings of tribes occurred. This **part**

[5] Ella Lyman Cabot, *Everyday Ethics* (New York: Henry Holt & Co., 1906), p. 280.

2 And Judah saw there a daughter of a certain Canaanite, whose name *was* Shuah; and he took her, and went in unto her.

3 And she conceived, and bare a son; and he called his name Er.

4 And she conceived again, and bare a son; and she called his name Onan.

5 And she yet again conceived, and bare a son; and called his name Shelah: and he was at Chezib, when she bare him.

6 And Judah took a wife for Er his first-born, whose name *was* Tamar.

7 And Er, Judah's firstborn, was wicked in the sight of the LORD; and the LORD slew him.

8 And Judah said unto Onan, Go in unto thy brother's wife, and marry her, and raise up seed to thy brother.

name was Hirah. 2 There Judah saw the daughter of a certain Canaanite whose name was Shua; he married her and went in to her, 3 and she conceived and bore a son, and he called his name Er. 4 Again she conceived and bore a son, and she called his name Onan. 5 Yet again she bore a son, and she called his name Shelah. She*g* was in Chezib when she bore him. 6 And Judah took a wife for Er his first-born, and her name was Tamar. 7 But Er, Judah's first-born, was wicked in the sight of the LORD; and the LORD slew him. 8 Then Judah said to Onan, "Go in to your brother's wife, and perform the duty of a brother-in-law to her, and raise up offspring for your

g Heb *He*

fact. He shows no misgivings about the story. The heroism of Tamar was the important thing. The behavior of Judah was indeed deplorable, but J[1] may have felt that it would do the Judahites no harm to have their tribal pride punctured. Certainly he had been even more merciless with Reuben (cf. 35:22*a*) and Simeon and Levi (cf. 34:25*a*, 26*a*).

J[2], more concerned about the reputations of the patriarchs, and indeed more sensitive as regards moral issues than J[1] had been—witness his treatment of the J[1] stories of Jacob and Laban, and of Simeon and Levi—made a somewhat desperate effort to lessen Judah's guilt. He inserted the note in vs. 12 that Judah's wife had died. This fact, he implies, explained, though it did not justify, Judah's behavior with Tamar. He also added vss. 21, 22*b*. In these verses the word used of Tamar signifies a **cult prostitute** (RSV mg.), not a common **harlot** (cf. vs. 15). The implication of this is that Judah's relationship with her had been something more than a mere vulgar adventure. It had had religious overtones, however abhorrent to J[2] the religion in question may have been. And this representation was strengthened by the note in vs. 12 that Judah was accompanied by his friend. That this note is an addition to the original tale is indicated by the fact that the friend does not appear in the narrative in vss. 13-20, the clear implication of which is that Judah was alone.

In the J[1] narrative the story presumably followed those of Reuben (35:22*a*), and of Simeon and Levi (ch. 34), and preceded that of Joseph (ch. 37). The present sequence of events is due to J[2], whose transfer of the sale of Joseph to the north necessitated some reordering of the J[1] material.

A. TAMAR, ER, AND ONAN (38:1-11)

38:1. It happened at that time is part of J[2]'s dealing with the chronological difficulties arising from his relocation of the story of the sale of Joseph and his introduction of that of the birth of Benjamin into the J[1] narrative. Nothing is recorded of **Hirah** beyond the fact that he was a native of Adullam, the modern Tell esh-Sheikh Madhkûr (Wright and Filson, *Westminster Atlas*, p. 107; Félix Marie Abel, *Géographie de la Palestine* [Paris: Gabalda, 1938], II, 239), some twelve miles southwest of Bethlehem in the territory of the tribe of Judah.

5. Chezib—Achzib in Josh. 15:44; Mic. 1:14, probably the modern Tell el-Beidā (Wright and Filson, *op. cit.*, p. 107; Abel, *op. cit.*, II, 90), southwest of Adullam—was, it may be inferred, the center of the clan of Shelah.

8. The custom of levirate marriage, presupposed here, was widespread in primitive **times.** Its motive was to prevent the extinction of a family, for it was deemed a disaster

9 And Onan knew that the seed should not be his; and it came to pass, when he went in unto his brother's wife, that he spilled *it* on the ground, lest that he should give seed to his brother.

10 And the thing which he did displeased the LORD: wherefore he slew him also.

11 Then said Judah to Tamar his daughter-in-law, Remain a widow at thy father's house, till Shelah my son be grown: for he said, Lest peradventure he die also, as his brethren *did*. And Tamar went and dwelt in her father's house.

12 ¶ And in process of time the daughter of Shuah Judah's wife died; and Judah was comforted, and went up unto his sheepshearers to Timnath, he and his friend Hirah the Adullamite.

13 And it was told Tamar, saying, Behold, thy father-in-law goeth up to Timnath to shear his sheep.

14 And she put her widow's garments off from her, and covered her with a veil, and wrapped herself, and sat in an open place, which *is* by the way to Timnath; for she saw that Shelah was grown, and she was not given unto him to wife.

brother." 9 But Onan knew that the offspring would not be his; so when he went in to his brother's wife he spilled the semen on the ground, lest he should give offspring to his brother. 10 And what he did was displeasing in the sight of the LORD, and he slew him also. 11 Then Judah said to Tamar his daughter-in-law, "Remain a widow in your father's house, till Shelah my son grows up" — for he feared that he would die, like his brothers. So Tamar went and dwelt in her father's house.

12 In course of time the wife of Judah, Shua's daughter, died; and when Judah was comforted, he went up to Timnah to his sheepshearers, he and his friend Hirah the Adullamite. 13 And when Tamar was told, "Your father-in-law is going up to Timnah to shear his sheep," 14 she put off her widow's gaments, and put on a veil, wrapping herself up, and sat at the entrance to Enaim, which is on the road to Timnah; for she saw that Shelah was grown up, and she had not been given to him in marriage.

---

if a man should be left without a descendant to perpetuate his name. That the responsibility tended to be evaded is suggested not only by this tale, but also by Deut. 25:5-10 and Ruth 4:1-8 (see further, Driver, *Deuteronomy*, pp. 280-82).

9. The verbs in the second and third clauses of the verse are in the frequentative and should be translated, "whenever he went, etc." Vs. 10, however, seems to refer to a single act. It is therefore highly probable that vs. 9*b* is a substitution, made on grounds of delicacy by J2 or another hand, for an original, more detailed account of Onan's offense.

B. TAMAR'S RELATIONS WITH JUDAH (38:12-23)

12. **Was comforted** is a conventional phrase for the effect of the mourning ceremonies (cf. Jer. 16:7). Sheepshearing was the occasion of an important festival in ancient Israel (cf. I Sam. 25:4-11; II Sam. 13:23-28). In view of **went up,** the **Timnah** referred to can hardly be the Danite city of that name (Judg. 14:1), which is on lower ground than Adullam. It is probably the Timnah of Josh. 15:57, the modern Tibne, some ten miles west of Bethlehem.

14. A widow wore mourning garments all her life (cf. Judith 8:5; 10:3; II Sam. 14:2). According to Prov. 7:10, a harlot was known by her attire. Here **put on a veil**

---

of the tradition had attained a kind of authority which made the final compiler of the materials of Genesis hesitate to discard it. So he let it remain, crude and unedifying though it might appear, just because it was too deeply imbedded in the transmitted stories of Israel to be got rid of. It is like the outcropping through some green and fertile landscape of ancient geologic

strata in which are fossils of forms of life we would not want to see walking upon our earth today.

Even so, in the unlovely narrative there are at least some elements of right purpose emerging like flowers from rank ground. One can see here—twisted though its manifestation may be—the powerful and generally wholesome instinct

15 When Judah saw her, he thought her *to be* a harlot; because she had covered her face.

16 And he turned unto her by the way, and said, Go to, I pray thee, let me come in unto thee; (for he knew not that she *was* his daughter-in-law:) and she said, What wilt thou give me, that thou mayest come in unto me?

17 And he said, I will send *thee* a kid from the flock. And she said, Wilt thou give *me* a pledge, till thou send *it?*

18 And he said, What pledge shall I give thee? And she said, Thy signet, and thy bracelets, and thy staff that *is* in thine hand. And he gave *it* her, and came in unto her, and she conceived by him.

19 And she arose, and went away, and laid by her veil from her, and put on the garments of her widowhood.

20 And Judah sent the kid by the hand of his friend the Adullamite, to receive *his* pledge from the woman's hand: but he found her not.

21 Then he asked the men of that place, saying, Where *is* the harlot, that *was* openly by the wayside? And they said, There was no harlot in this *place.*

22 And he returned to Judah, and said, I cannot find her; and also the men of the place said, *that* there was no harlot in this *place.*

23 And Judah said, Let her take *it* to her, lest we be shamed: behold, I sent this kid, and thou hast not found her.

15 When Judah saw her, he thought her to be a harlot, for she had covered her face. 16 He went over to her at the road side, and said, "Come, let me come in to you," for he did not know that she was his daughter-in-law. She said, "What will you give me, that you may come in to me?" 17 He answered, "I will send you a kid from the flock." And she said, "Will you give me a pledge, till you send it?" 18 He said, "What pledge shall I give you?" She replied, "Your signet and your cord, and your staff that is in your hand." So he gave them to her, and went in to her, and she conceived by him. 19 Then she arose and went away, and taking off her veil she put on the garments of her widowhood.

20 When Judah sent the kid by his friend the Adullamite, to receive the pledge from the woman's hand, he could not find her. 21 And he asked the men of the place, "Where is the harlot[h] who was at Enaim by the wayside?" And they said, "No harlot has been here." 22 So he returned to Judah, and said, "I have not found her; and also the men of the place said, 'No harlot has been here.' " 23 And Judah replied, "Let her keep the things as her own, lest we be laughed at; you see, I sent this kid, and you could not find her."

ʰ Or *cult prostitute*

and **wrapping herself up** are doublets. The former may be from J², implying that Tamar was representing herself as a temple prostitute. The veiling of the prostitute may have originally signified her dedication to Ishtar, the veiled goddess; the veiling of Ishtar may be a reflex on the veiling of her votaries, which rested upon a primitive sexual taboo. This taboo accounts for the bridal veil (cf. 24:65) and the implications of 29:23, 25. Jer. 3:2 and Ezek. 16:25 allude to the custom of the harlot sitting by the wayside.

18. **Signet, cord,** and **staff** were apparently the insignia of a man of rank among the Israelites.

21. Sacred prostitution was widely practiced at Canaanite sanctuaries. The prostitute was dedicated to Ishtar or some other deity. Commerce with her was believed to ensure, through sympathetic magic, the fertility of the land, the flocks and herds, and the family.

of the Jewish people that family heritage must be continued. One may see also in Tamar the wistful and pathetic yearning of the woman for motherhood.

But with this said, the fact remains that the significance of this story is not in any positive

content, but in the perspective it suggests for a whole reading of Genesis. It reminds us anew that in the midst of those parts of the O.T. through which there shines a right understanding of God and of his will for human life, there are other parts which are the cloudy medium of

24 ¶ And it came to pass about three months after, that it was told Judah, saying, Tamar thy daughter-in-law hath played the harlot; and also, behold, she *is* with child by whoredom. And Judah said, Bring her forth, and let her be burnt.

25 When she *was* brought forth she sent to her father-in-law, saying, By the man, whose these *are, am* I with child: and she said, Discern, I pray thee, whose *are* these, the signet, and bracelets, and staff.

26 And Judah acknowledged *them,* and said, She hath been more righteous than I; because that I gave her not to Shelah my son. And he knew her again no more.

27 ¶ And it came to pass in the time of her travail, that, behold, twins *were* in her womb.

28 And it came to pass, when she travailed, that *the one* put out *his* hand: and the midwife took and bound upon his hand a scarlet thread, saying, This came out first.

29 And it came to pass, as he drew back his hand, that, behold, his brother came out: and she said, How hast thou broken forth? *this* breach *be* upon thee: therefore his name was called Pharez.

30 And afterward came out his brother, that had the scarlet thread upon his hand: and his name was called Zarah.

24 About three months later Judah was told, "Tamar your daughter-in-law has played the harlot; and moreover she is with child by harlotry." And Judah said, "Bring her out, and let her be burned." 25 As she was being brought out, she sent word to her father-in-law, "By the man to whom these belong, I am with child." And she said, "Mark, I pray you, whose these are, the signet and the cord and the staff." 26 Then Judah acknowledged them and said, "She is more righteous than I, inasmuch as I did not give her to my son Shelah." And he did not lie with her again.

27 When the time of her delivery came, there were twins in her womb. 28 And when she was in labor, one put out a hand; and the midwife took and bound on his hand a scarlet thread, saying, "This came out first." 29 But as he drew back his hand, behold, his brother came out; and she said, "What a breach you have made for yourself!" Therefore his name was called Perez.[i] 30 Afterward his brother came out with the scarlet thread upon his hand; and his name was called Zerah.

[i] That is *A breach*

C. Tamar Is Exonerated (38:24-30)

24. Death by burning is the punishment imposed by the Code of Hammurabi (157) for incest with a mother. This passage suggests that it was in ancient Israel the usual punishment for adultery. Later the penalty of stoning was substituted (Deut. 22:23-24; cf. Ezek. 16:40), except in the case of a priest's daughter turned prostitute (Lev. 21:9).

---

human ignorance and passion. In the story of Judah and Tamar the human instincts and ancient customs set forth with such startling realism should certainly not be confused with lives redeemed. Yet even when its realism is most stark, and least accompanied by any spiritual illumination, the O.T. record can still, as was said in II Tim. 3:16, be "profitable for . . . reproof, for correction, for instruction in righteousness." Just because of the seeming inconsistency and inappropriateness of this story of Judah and Tamar as compared with the main message of Genesis, we are helped to remember that the road of revelation to the final height of spiritual understanding is a long road and an uneven one. Often it has to "slope through darkness up to God."

27-30. *The Birth of Perez.*—A strange pendant to an unlovely story, so this seems; and it still may seem so, even when its purpose is perceived. At the end of the book of Ruth we read, "These are the generations of Perez"; and the following list of his descendants ends thus: "And Obed begat Jesse, and Jesse begat David." In other words, Perez was the ancestor of the hero-king David, who came from the tribe of Judah. But why should the chronicler have wished to record the fact that David's ancestor was born of such a one as Tamar? Because, here as elsewhere, the emphasis is not on human worth, but on the will and saving work of God. As Rahab the harlot, who received the spies at Jericho, was exalted in memory as an instrument in God's long purpose of deliverance (Heb. 11:31), so Tamar, through her pitiful desire for a child,

39 And Joseph was brought down to Egypt; and Potiphar, an officer of Pharaoh, captain of the guard, an Egyptian, bought him of the hands of the Ishmaelites, which had brought him down thither.

39 Now Joseph was taken down to Egypt, and Pot'i-phar, an officer of Pharaoh, the captain of the guard, an Egyptian, bought him from the Ish'maelites

---

XLV. JOSEPH IN EGYPT (39:1–41:57)

Ch. 39 is basically from J—J¹ with some additions—who continued his story of Joseph by telling how the Ishmaelites who had bought him from his brothers took him down with them to Egypt, and sold him to an unnamed Egyptian. This was followed by the account of his rejection of the advances of his master's wife. The story seems to be based upon the Egyptian "Tale of the Two Brothers" (see, among others, Skinner, *Genesis*, p. 459), to which, however, there are numerous parallels in other literatures (see Andrew Lang, *Myth, Ritual and Religion* [new ed.; London: Longmans, Green & Co., 1899] II, 318-26). According to the Egyptian tale, Bata, unmarried, lives with his older brother Anubis, is tempted by the latter's wife, exactly as Joseph was by his mistress, and rejects her advances in horror. When Anubis returns home in the evening his wife, covered with self-inflicted wounds, falsely accuses Bata. Anubis, believing her, plans to kill him, but finally convinced of his innocence slays his wife instead.

This story J perhaps adapted, changing its conclusion. Joseph was thrown into prison. There he was able to help two of the Pharaoh's servants, and this led eventually to his release and to his meeting with the Pharaoh.

J's purpose was thus not only to present Joseph as an honorable and competent young man (39:2b, 4b), but also to set the stage for his rise to power in Egypt.

E, disliking the sex motif, omitted the story of Joseph's temptation entirely; cf. his omission of the stories of Reuben's incest (35:22a), of the seduction of Dinah (ch. 34), and of Judah's relations with Tamar (ch. 38). Instead he had the Midianites who had kidnaped Joseph sell him to "Potiphar, an officer of Pharaoh, the captain of the guard" (37:36; cf. 39:1). Joseph attended him (39:4a), i.e., he became his personal servant. When two of the officers of the court fell into disfavor with the Pharaoh, they were put under arrest in the house of the captain of the guard, and Joseph was assigned the duty of attending them until their case was decided (cf. 40:3aα, 4). From that point, as will be seen, E's narrative of Joseph's rise to power parallels that of J.

R^JE combined these two narratives (*a*) by identifying the unnamed Egyptian of J with Potiphar, the captain of the guard; (*b*) by representing Joseph, following his imprisonment, as being given a position of responsibility by the keeper of the prison (39:21-23); and (*c*) by interpreting the phrase, **in custody in the house of the captain of the guard** (40:3aα), as meaning **in the prison where Joseph was confined** (40:3aβb).

A. JOSEPH CAST INTO PRISON (39:1-23)

39:1. The word rendered **officer** is literally "eunuch." This creates no difficulty, however, when it is realized that Joseph's temptress was the wife, not of Potiphar the

---

was used by God's mercy to play a part in history.

39:1-6. The Turn of the Road.—Here was the beginning of the discipline by which Joseph's character was put to the proof and his possibilities fulfilled. Potiphar **bought him of the hands of the Ishmaelites.** He was a slave now in a foreign land. That might have meant for him nothing but discouragement and disintegration. But he met this situation with a courage and fidelity which were to turn evil

into incalculable ultimate good. He **served** Potiphar in such a way that he not only **found grace in Potiphar's sight, but that the LORD blessed the Egyptian's house for Joseph's sake; and the blessing of the LORD was upon all that he had in the house, and in the field.**

As a boy at home Joseph had had serious faults. Unquestionably he liked the favoritism that his father showed him. He had strutted in his coat of many colors. He had been vain and self-assertive. What saved him now? Two things,

2 And the LORD was with Joseph, and he was a prosperous man; and he was in the house of his master the Egyptian.

3 And his master saw that the LORD *was* with him, and that the LORD made all that he did to prosper in his hand.

4 And Joseph found grace in his sight, and he served him: and he made him overseer over his house, and all *that* he had he put into his hand.

5 And it came to pass from the time *that* he had made him overseer in his house, and over all that he had, that the LORD blessed the Egyptian's house for Joseph's sake; and the blessing of the LORD was upon all that he had in the house, and in the field.

who had brought him down there. 2 The LORD was with Joseph, and he became a successful man; and he was in the house of his master the Egyptian, 3 and his master saw that the LORD was with him, and that the LORD caused all that he did to prosper in his hands. 4 So Joseph found favor in his sight and attended him, and he made him overseer of his house and put him in charge of all that he had. 5 From the time that he made him overseer in his house and over all that he had the LORD blessed the Egyptian's house for Joseph's sake; the blessing of the LORD was upon all that he had, in

---

eunuch, but of the unnamed Egyptian of the J narrative. It should nevertheless be noted that cases of eunuchs being married are not unknown. Procksch (*Genesis*, pp. 231, 391), noting indications of more than one hand in vss. 7-20, accordingly maintains that E also told of Joseph's being tempted. The unevennesses in vss. 7-20 are, however, to be accounted for as the result of J2's elaboration of J1's simpler narrative (see Simpson, *Early Traditions of Israel*, pp. 131, 355).

2. The LORD was with Joseph: The words are intended to explain not only the fact that **Joseph found favor** with his master and was put in charge of the household (cf. vs. 4), but also his subsequent rise to power over the whole of Egypt.

---

under God: an influence that went far back in his family tradition, and a change of environment that human calculations would not have been wise enough to choose. From the time of Abraham there had been bred in this family a consciousness of God that laid hold of Joseph and would ennoble him. A child's character cannot be shaped by sudden accidents or by extemporized advice. The inherent quality in the sons of one generation traces back to the family's convictions; and what a present generation believes in will affect children yet unborn. But his inherent possibilities would not alone have been enough to change Joseph from a spoiled child into a great man. He had to have what his father would never have chosen for him: adversity, hardship, and affliction. He had to be tried in the furnace in order that the dross in him might be burned away. So the overruling facts of life, shaped by the unseen hand of God, ordained.

> For the love of God is broader
> Than the measure of man's mind.[6]

Yet how many parents flinch from stern conditions for their children, and induce in them

[6] Frederick W. Faber, "There's a wideness in God's mercy."

self-pity instead of the courage that can meet hard tests! When Joseph disappeared, Jacob thought he was dead and so found nothing to do but to lament; but if he had known that Joseph was alive in Egypt and could have communicated with him, would he have had the wisdom to help him meet the hard new facts affirmatively and bid him resolve—as Joseph by God's grace did resolve—that no disaster should dismay him and no bludgeoning of events should beat him down?

In that crucial matter Joseph had no human help. He had to work out, under God, his own salvation. He had to be willing to learn, and above all to learn the truth about himself. The disasters which had come upon him were partly his own fault, but that is the hardest thing for a man ever to admit. It would have been more agreeable to say that if his father had petted him, he should also have been able to protect him, that if his brothers hated him, it was only because they were hateful men. As a matter of fact, he had been an irritating person: vain, self-absorbed, oblivious to the offense he gave. If he had failed to face that fact, he would have continued not only an egotist but a whimpering one. But he did face it. After he had been sold into Egypt, he had to begin to think—to think honestly about Joseph and about what was

6 And he left all that he had in Joseph's hand; and he knew not aught he had, save the bread which he did eat. And Joseph was a goodly person, and well-favored.

7 ¶ And it came to pass after these things, that his master's wife cast her eyes upon Joseph; and she said, Lie with me.

8 But he refused, and said unto his master's wife, Behold, my master wotteth not what *is* with me in the house, and he hath committed all that he hath to my hand;

9 *There is* none greater in this house than I; neither hath he kept back any thing

house and field. 6 So he left all that he had in Joseph's charge; and having him he had no concern for anything but the food which he ate.

Now Joseph was handsome and good-looking. 7 And after a time his master's wife cast her eyes upon Joseph, and said, "Lie with me." 8 But he refused and said to his master's wife, "Lo, having me my master has no concern about anything in the house, and he has put everything that he has in my hand; 9 he is not greater in this house

---

7. Cf. Prov. 2:16-17; 5:3-6, 20; 6:24-35; 7:4-27; 9:13-18.

9. **Sin against God:** The reference is to Yahweh. J, here as elsewhere, does not permit his characters to use the sacred name of the God of Israel when speaking to foreigners. But he represents Joseph as conscious of the Lord's presence even in a strange land. Any sin is a sin against him (cf. 20:6; II Sam. 12:13; Pss. 41:4; 51:4).

---

wrong with him. He must have been learning to pray most of all not "change facts" or "change other men," but "change me." That is what all who climb to moral greatness have to pray. "I acknowledge my transgressions: . . . cleanse me from my sin" (Ps. 51:3, 2). The overconfident Simon Peter had to be brought to such a cry. So did Paul, who was at first the Pharisee. "O wretched man that I am! who shall deliver me?" (Rom. 7:24.) "I know how to be abased," he said (Phil. 4:12). That was what Joseph had to come to know. It is what every man needs to know. The true abasement is not merely accepting the hard things that happen; it is the painful humbling of a man's own pride to admit the reasons in himself that helped to make them happen. Then for the first time, as with Joseph, his soul is free and fit to be exalted.

7-9. *The Basis of Moral Integrity.*—Here in less than a hundred words is revealed the reinforcement which a man may call upon in a moment of fierce temptation. Note first the intensity of the temptation. There was the appeal to the passions of the body, which a young man may feel with such hot instinct that he can tell himself the response is "only natural." There was the appeal also of the seemingly romantic, which can set before a young man a lure that is the more seductive because it may appear that it is the ideal in him rather than the evil that is being appealed to. Potiphar's wife was unsatisfied with her own husband. She could whisper that she not only wanted Joseph, but that she needed him. If she was not older than Joseph, she was certainly more experienced; and there is a kind of feminine experi-

ence that has the sinuous fascination of the serpent. Joseph was assailed with the flattery of her affection, and this could have had an added power if he had let it touch another possible emotion in himself, viz., self-pity. He had been cruelly battered about by hostility in his own family, and here was someone whose softness would compensate for that. Here was healing for his inner hurt. Furthermore, here was incitement for ambition, and a prospect for pride. This woman, powerfully placed, if he encouraged her devotion to him might carry his interests far. And all the while he could excuse his conscience by the plain fact that whatever might be questionable, he had not provoked it. He could have repeated the old words of the Garden of Eden. The woman tempted me, "and I did eat." Put all those things together—sex-passion, romance, a man's secret hunger for a woman's solace, calculations of advantage, an alibi for conscience—and there was a net of temptation that took great moral strength to break. Yet what Joseph faced can essentially be repeated in every generation. Names are different, scenes are modernized, the exact pattern shifts, but the same test tries men's fiber. It is easy to find excuses for defeat, not so easy to find strength to win. A virile old priest whose ministry was mostly among sailors met one day a man in public life who had got himself involved in a corrupt entanglement. "But, Father," the man said to his rebuke, "you don't know what the outside pressure was." "Outside pressure," came the indignant answer, "outside pressure! Where were your inside braces?"

from me but thee, because thou *art* his wife: how then can I do this great wickedness, and sin against God?

10 And it came to pass, as she spake to Joseph day by day, that he hearkened not unto her, to lie by her, *or* to be with her.

than I am; nor has he kept back anything from me except yourself, because you are his wife; how then can I do this great wickedness, and sin against God?" 10 And although she spoke to Joseph day after day, he would not listen to her, to lie with her or

---

In the experience of Joseph, what were the "inside braces"? There was first a decent sense of human fairness which made him a man of honor. The baby is an individualist, and little children are anarchic. They are conscious only of their own wants and they reach out to get these satisfied. Human growth is a growth into relationships. The child must learn to adjust himself to others, for only so can there be any tolerable society. Petulant and demanding self-assertion must be controlled. But morally some men never grow up from being babies. Men of mature souls do—as Joseph did. That maturity does not come automatically; it must be achieved. It must feed on straight thoughts and on right feelings responsibly cultivated. Deprived of these the moral character, like an unfed body, has the rickets and cannot stand up under press. Neglect in little choices, irresponsibility in what seems unimportant conduct, will have disastrous results when the heavy test comes.

What lay back of Joseph when he was confronted with the sudden and wholly unforeseen temptation in Potiphar's house? Hidden facts, but real facts and decisive ones, somewhere in the earlier years. From something good in his inheritance, from something faithful in his own accumulating attitudes, from mindfulness of God, he had built up subconsciously the moral reserves he would need. He had produced a nature that was incompatible with knavery. Behold, he said, **my master wotteth not what is with me in the house, and he hath committed all that he hath to my hand.** He might have argued that he could sin against Potiphar without Potiphar's ever knowing it, but he could not sin without knowing it himself. "Character is what a man is in the dark." Joseph had built up inside himself the sense of honor which has respect for other men's honor and therefore cannot be mean enough to disgrace both himself and them. **How . . . can I do this great wickedness?** he cried. "How can I not do it?" the weak man will plead. It takes a long integrity to make the kind of man whose inability is to do wrong, whose compulsion is to do right.

This leads to a further truth. A man's integrity in the world of men is not the result of human motives only. Joseph made that clear in the full sentence of which only half just now was quoted: **How . . . can I do this great wickedness, and sin against God?** Only in relation to God are other human souls seen in their full dignity, and duty toward them made compelling. Humanitarianism alone is a structure of morals built on sand. Unless men are regarded as of eternal worth, human obligations become reduced to passing whim or shifting calculation. "Men have no Father, and therefore they should all act as brothers": the flimsiness of humanistic ethics is laid bare in that sardonic saying. Consider how in Nazi Germany all decent respect for human beings disappeared with repudiation of religion. Without accountability to God, human relationships can degenerate into a crafty manipulation of advantage. What ultimate reason then is there for not treating human beings as pawns to be pushed off the board as part of a winning game? What reason unless there is the ultimate authority of truth and righteousness, and magnanimity and mercy, as established in the character of God? The dependably good man is the godly man. Reflect upon the convictions which must be inculcated in a child if there is to be any moral certainty. There must be a steady star to steer by if the course is to be held true through changing winds and across a changing sea.

10. Continuing Resistance.—Potiphar's wife kept on in her passionate allurement. Failing to persuade Joseph the first time, she pursued him **day by day.** Temptation thus renewed may be harder to resist than was the first suggestion. A decent man can be shocked by the bold suddenness of evil, and his conscience may recoil. But the shock wears off and presently the suggestion seems not so strange. Then comes a new time of danger. As a steel bridge which can resist a heavy blow may be endangered by the successive shocks that come from the tread of marching men, so a man's moral resistance may disintegrate beneath the impact of temptation that comes relentlessly on and on. Joseph had sense enough to know that he must not be where the feet of temptation continually walked. He must not depend upon the fact that he had said "No" to Potiphar's wife. Henceforth he must take care not **to be with her.**

11 And it came to pass about this time, that *Joseph* went into the house to do his business; and *there was* none of the men of the house there within.

12 And she caught him by his garment, saying, Lie with me: and he left his garment in her hand, and fled, and got him out.

to be with her. 11 But one day, when he went into the house to do his work and none of the men of the house was there in the house, 12 she caught him by his garment, saying, "Lie with me." But he left his garment in her hand, and fled and got out of

---

11-12. *Defenses Against Temptation.*—Sexual immorality in present-day society is so general, and sometimes so unashamed, that the preacher and teacher of the truths of God will have it on their hearts continually to guard those they care for from that sin. Vss. 7-9 have suggested one message; these suggest a further one.

Face at the outset the discreditable fact: many men today, if tempted less dramatically than Joseph, may yet be tempted oftener. "Sex appeal" is everywhere; and there is less restraint, either by good manners or by accepted modesty. Principles of conduct which once were powerful have been eaten into by the "acids of modernity." From Freudian psychiatrists, from the snickering suggestiveness of decadent novels, from scraps of salacious conversation, adolescent boys and girls have been infected with the idea that sexual control is nothing but outdated superstition. Why resist their impulses when not resisting them is the mark of grown-up men and women? So they think they know; and who is responsible for that corrupting pseudo knowledge? A great network of influences, some of them represented by gentlemen of most polite demeanor and personal respectability, who sit perhaps in the pews of churches: writers who turn out erotic stuff because there is a market greedy for it; owners or executives of magazines that in text and illustrations make license look alluring; businessmen who advertise products by linking them with sex attraction; and all the multitude of lesser folk who throw their weight into the sinking scale by the kind of books they buy, the plays they go to see, and the general laxness they encourage. Meanwhile, right-minded men and women may be timid or confused. They have no clear moral yea and nay to speak, because their religious loyalties have grown too vague and weak to furnish sure convictions. Therefore it is not so much particular and personal wickedness as a want of principles which an older generation should have passed on to them that has made innumerable people act as if there were no such thing as principle in sex.

Note what Joseph did. When temptation reached out for him, he tore himself away quickly and decisively. He **fled, and got him out.** "Flee . . . youthful lusts," says II Tim. 2:22.

The first necessity with the allurement of sexual sin is to see it for what it is, to call it by its right name. Miscellaneous sex relationships, illicit so-called love affairs, are not love; they are only lust. Sex is part of the divine ordaining and in its right use it is sanctified. But sex impulse undisciplined degrades the personality into an instrument of low passion. It has no loyalty and therefore its "romance" is rottenness. It may corrupt the body—it does corrupt the soul. Read Prov. 7. Those who have let themselves go in sexual license can become so carnal, cynical, and callous that it will be hard for them to love one woman truly or to bring to any marriage a whole heart. The high imperatives of religion which keep a man clean, and not any perverted philosophy which justifies philandering, are the road to happiness. Many a man has thanked God that he did "flee . . . youthful lusts." Where is the one who is sorry that he did?

Turning again to Joseph—what enabled him to flee? Influences which the narrative makes plain: his innate moral integrity, his sense of honor in human relationships, his reverence toward God (see Expos. on vss. 7-9). These were linked together, and the first two depended on the third. They were the great factors in his resistance, but less conspicuous factors may be noted. He was occupied and interested. He found himself faced with the suddenly seductive woman at the moment when he was going about his responsible business. If he had had a lazy or an empty mind, it would have been more open to what she was trying to put into it; but being neither lazy nor empty its wholesome occupancy resisted the push of the unexpected and uncongenial. Work which enlists a man's energies and gives him contented self-expression is always a safeguard against sensuality. It is those who lounge about in uselessness, the "playboys," who have nothing to do with imagination but let the doors to it swing open the easiest way, that are like ramshackle houses into which every disreputable guest can find an entrance. Joseph, busy with the trust which Potiphar had given him, was a different sort. Furthermore, it seems evident that he was being made a different sort from the beginning. The positive con-

13 And it came to pass, when she saw that he had left his garment in her hand, and was fled forth,

14 That she called unto the men of her house, and spake unto them, saying, See, he hath brought in a Hebrew unto us to mock us; he came in unto me to lie with me, and I cried with a loud voice:

15 And it came to pass, when he heard that I lifted up my voice and cried, that he left his garment with me, and fled, and got him out.

16 And she laid up his garment by her, until his lord came home.

the house. **13** And when she saw that he had left his garment in her hand, and had fled out of the house, **14** she called to the men of her household and said to them, "See, he has brought among us a Hebrew to insult us; he came in to me to lie with me, and I cried out with a loud voice; **15** and when he heard that I lifted up my voice and cried, he left his garment with me, and fled and got out of the house." **16** Then she laid up his garment by her until his master came

---

14. Insult: The word is the same as that rendered "fondling" in 26:8, except that here it is followed by a preposition suggesting a certain aggressiveness.

---

tent of his mind was no momentary accident. His habitual thinking had been positive—positive with purpose and with clean resolve.

> My strength is as the strength of ten,
> Because my heart is pure.[7]

Back of what the man will do lies what the boy was thinking—the thoughts let in and the thoughts kept out. Purity which can stand great tests is not come by passively. It must be wanted and be hardly won. Tests come early and must be bravely met. Wrote Milton, "I cannot praise a fugitive and cloistered virtue, unexercised and unbreathed."[8] Something must have been striven for if there is to be honor at the end. A man must have prayed in earnest the psalmist's prayer, "Create in me a clean heart, O God; and renew a right spirit within me" (Ps. 51:10).

13-23. Through Disaster.—Here is the event which must have seemed to Joseph the bitterest and most undeserved blow which fate could deal him, but which nevertheless he met with a faith in God and a fidelity that brought good in the end. The test he faced was the more crucial because it seemed so contradictory. In Canaan he had not been without fault, and there was some reason why his brothers had turned against him; but in any moral order of life, what reasonableness could there be in what happened now? He was betrayed by a vile woman's treachery. He was punished and imprisoned not because he had been evil but because he had been innocent. In the face of such sardonic injustice as that, he might have been tempted to curse both man and God. But stripped of all human comradeship though he was, Joseph yet

believed that the Lord was with him; and because he bore himself as a man accountable to God, he had the quality that gave him favor in the sight of the keeper of the prison.

A young artist who had been through a cruel period of poverty, loneliness, and seeming failure said: "If I could write a book, I would call it by this title—*From Ashes to God*. It is only when you have been burned to ashes that you completely find God. Then when everything in you seems to have been extinguished, a new little flame is somehow lighted, which grows and grows and can never be put out. That flame is God." Joseph was obviously a man who had to find God out of ashes if he was to find God at all—and know that God had found him and held him all the while. The same is true of other great figures of the Bible: Elijah, crying out in his loneliness and despair, "Now, O LORD, take away my life" (I Kings 19:4); Peter, looking at Jesus and saying, "Depart from me; for I am a sinful man" (Luke 5:8); Paul the apostle crying, "Who shall deliver me from the body of this death?" (Rom. 7:24). Religious experience thus may begin with stark realism, but it need not so end. It can end with redemption. In place of mourning, it can bring the oil of joy; in place of a spirit of heaviness, the garment of praise.

Consider two aspects of life in which a soul can rise from ashes to God. First, there is deliverance from defeat. This defeat may be in the realm of material circumstances, as with the artist whose words were quoted. Many other persons similarly have had legitimate hopes and ambitions apparently destroyed, eager and creative purposes frustrated. How can such lives emerge into victory? The answer is a strange one, but it is true. The way to overcome defeat may

[7] Tennyson, "Sir Galahad."
[8] *Areopagitica*.

17 And she spake unto him according to these words, saying, The Hebrew servant, which thou hast brought unto us, came in unto me to mock me:

18 And it came to pass, as I lifted up my voice and cried, that he left his garment with me, and fled out.

19 And it came to pass, when his master heard the words of his wife, which she spake unto him, saying, After this manner did thy servant to me; that his wrath was kindled.

20 And Joseph's master took him, and put him into the prison, a place where the king's prisoners *were* bound: and he was there in the prison.

home, 17 and she told him the same story, saying, "The Hebrew servant, whom you have brought among us, came in to me to insult me; 18 but as soon as I lifted up my voice and cried, he left his garment with me, and fled out of the house."

19 When his master heard the words which his wife spoke to him, "This is the way your servant treated me," his anger was kindled. 20 And Joseph's master took him and put him into the prison, the place where the king's prisoners were confined,

---

20. Death would be the usual punishment for such conduct as that with which Joseph was charged (cf. "The Tale of the Two Brothers" referred to above). J obviously had to ignore this fact.

---

be to accept defeat. When a man enters most completely into defeat, disguises nothing, avoids nothing, accepts the full consequences of life as life really is, then he may be on the threshold of larger triumph. So it was with Joseph. Sold as a slave by the vindictiveness of his brothers, accused now falsely of a crime, thrown into prison, what does he do? He does not sit down idly and bemoan his lot. He meets his disasters with a spirit that grows increasingly intelligent, self-critical, steadfast, and determined. Looking back presently on his darkest hours, he will see that it was not human agency that shaped his life, but God. **The LORD was with Joseph, and showed him mercy. . . . The LORD was with him. . . . The LORD made it to prosper** (vss. 21-23). Listen to that threefold repetition of the LORD.

Nor is it only in the Bible that we see men who move through ashes up to God. Read the life of Edward L. Trudeau, caught in the prime of life and doomed, as it seemed at first, to a useless invalidism, but becoming the pioneer of the modern treatment of tuberculosis. He said:

I have learned that the conquest of Fate is not by struggling against it, not by trying to escape from it, but by acquiescence; that it is often through men that we come to know God; that spiritual courage is of a higher type than physical courage; and that it takes a higher type of courage to fight bravely a losing than a winning fight.[9]

As defeat in outward circumstances may need to be met by recognizing that defeat, so it is also

as concerns the inner life. An individual has sinned. Or irrespective of personal guilt, one recognizes himself to be a member of a sinful society. The blight of moral mistakes lies on us in our world. That defeat must be met with open eyes. Our world can be delivered from its increasing perils only if we are honest enough to realize our need for moral understanding, repentance, and regeneration.

Second, there is deliverance from seeming victory. That may sound like a paradox, but it is plain fact. Often we find God only when we stop thinking that we have already found him, and win our spiritual victories only when we reject the thought that we have already won. Consider the symbolic meaning in some great churches of laying on the altar on Ash Wednesday, the beginning of the penitential time of Lent, the ashes got from burning palms used on the festival Palm Sunday the year before. So the religious man must be continually offering up his early and partial achievements as only so much ashes in the sight of God. Read Phil. 3. Think of Paul counting everything that once had been his pride as being nothing in comparison with Christ; and now, forgetting the things behind, pressing forward to the things ahead.

Will it be claimed that this discounting of partial victories dooms life to discouragement? No, for the soul's progress is like climbing up a mountain. There are many lesser heights that must be scaled before the summit can be reached. To halt on any one of these is to be defeated. It is necessary to keep going down into intervening valleys in order to climb up out of them to higher ground ahead. Energy

[9] *An Autobiography* (Garden City, N. Y.: Doubleday, Page & Co., 1916), pp. 318-19.

21 ¶ But the LORD was with Joseph, and showed him mercy, and gave him favor in the sight of the keeper of the prison.

22 And the keeper of the prison committed to Joseph's hand all the prisoners that *were* in the prison; and whatsoever they did there, he was the doer *of it.*

23 The keeper of the prison looked not to any thing *that was* under his hand; because the LORD was with him, and *that* which he did, the LORD made *it* to prosper.

40 And it came to pass after these things, *that* the butler of the king of Egypt and *his* baker had offended their lord the king of Egypt.

2 And Pharaoh was wroth against two *of* his officers, against the chief of the butlers, and against the chief of the bakers.

3 And he put them in ward in the house of the captain of the guard, into the prison, the place where Joseph *was* bound.

and he was there in prison. 21 But the LORD was with Joseph and showed him steadfast love, and gave him favor in the sight of the keeper of the prison. 22 And the keeper of the prison committed to Joseph's care all the prisoners who were in the prison; and whatever was done there, he was the doer of it; 23 the keeper of the prison paid no heed to anything that was in Joseph's care, because the LORD was with him; and whatever he did, the LORD made it prosper.

40 Some time after this, the butler of the king of Egypt and his baker offended their lord the king of Egypt. 2 And Pharaoh was angry with his two officers, the chief butler and the chief baker, 3 and he put them in custody in the house of the captain of the guard, in the prison where

---

B. INTERPRETER OF DREAMS (40:1-23)

Ch. 40 is a conflation of J and E, the E narrative being the basic element in the composition. This recorded that the Pharaoh, being angry with two of his officers, the chief of the butlers and the chief of the bakers, placed them under house arrest with the captain of the guard (vss. 2, 3aα), who detailed his personal servant (cf. 39:4aβ), Joseph, to attend them (vs. 4). One night each of them had a strange dream (vs. 5a). These Joseph interpreted for them (vss. 7-14a, 15a, 16-19): that of the chief butler as auguring his restoration to office, that of the chief baker as an omen of his coming execution. In each case Joseph's interpretation was fulfilled (vss. 20aα, 21-22), but the chief butler, whom Joseph had asked to plead for him to the Pharaoh, did not remember him (vs. 23a).

The J narrative was similar. Here, however, the royal establishment is thought of as less elaborate: the king of Egypt had but one butler and one baker (vs. 1), who were incarcerated in the same prison as Joseph (vs. 3aβb). Their dreams seem to have been identical (see Exeg. on vs. 5) and Joseph interpreted them as presaging their release from prison, asking them to speak to the Pharaoh on his behalf (vss. 14b, 15b); but when they were freed, on the occasion of the Pharaoh's birthday (vs. 20aβγ), they forgot about him (cf. vs. 23b). This story is from J[1], with some elaboration by J[2].

40:1. The title **the king of Egypt** is an indication of the earliest narrative of the Hexateuch, J[1] (Meyer, *Israeliten und ihre Nachbarstämme,* p. 25).

3. R[JE] identifies **the house of the captain of the guard** (E) with **the prison where Joseph was confined** (J).

---

and effort must be given to the utmost, burned down to the ashes of complete commitment, before the victory is won. So it is always with the soul's ascent to God. It is only when we are through with self-saving that we are saved. Joseph could not have stopped and said that he had already done enough when he had won his victory over temptation in Potiphar's house. He could not plead that he must not go down into the darkness of a still worse trial. Out of that

darkness came new light. And all the way from Joseph to our own time it has been true that then is lighted the flame which "can never be put out. That flame is God."

40:1-22. *Joseph's Fellow Prisoners.*—From primitive savages all the way to present-day psychologists, dreams and the meaning of dreams have had a haunting fascination. In strange ways they mirror events, and sometimes they seem to foreshadow them. But what of the life

4 And the captain of the guard charged Joseph with them, and he served them: and they continued a season in ward.

5 ¶ And they dreamed a dream both of them, each man his dream in one night, each man according to the interpretation of his dream, the butler and the baker of the king of Egypt, which *were* bound in the prison.

6 And Joseph came in unto them in the morning, and looked upon them, and, behold, they *were* sad.

7 And he asked Pharaoh's officers that *were* with him in the ward of his lord's house, saying, Wherefore look ye *so* sadly to-day?

8 And they said unto him, We have dreamed a dream, and *there is* no interpreter of it. And Joseph said unto them, *Do* not interpretations *belong* to God? tell me *them,* I pray you.

9 And the chief butler told his dream to Joseph, and said to him, In my dream, behold, a vine *was* before me;

10 And in the vine *were* three branches: and it *was* as though it budded, *and* her blossoms shot forth; and the clusters thereof brought forth ripe grapes:

Joseph was confined. 4 The captain of the guard charged Joseph with them, and he waited on them; and they continued for some time in custody. 5 And one night they both dreamed — the butler and the baker of the king of Egypt, who were confined in the prison — each his own dream, and each dream with its own meaning. 6 When Joseph came to them in the morning and saw them, they were troubled. 7 So he asked Pharaoh's officers who were with him in custody in his master's house, "Why are your faces downcast today?" 8 They said to him, "We have had dreams, and there is no one to interpret them." And Joseph said to them, "Do not interpretations belong to God? Tell them to me, I pray you."

9 So the chief butler told his dream to Joseph, and said to him, "In my dream there was a vine before me, 10 and on the vine there were three branches; as soon as it budded, its blossoms shot forth, and the

---

5. The awkwardness of the verse is due to the fact that RJE is here combining two different representations—that of J, according to which the dreams were identical, and that of E, that they were different. From J comes **and one night they both dreamed;** from E, **each his own dream, and each dream with its own meaning.** The clause referring to **the king of Egypt** is, of course, from J. The Israelites shared in the belief, held by the Egyptians and by other peoples in that age, in divinely inspired dreams (for references see Skinner, *Genesis,* p. 461). But generally in the O.T. the dream either contains the revelation (e.g., 20:3; 28:13, 15; I Kings 3:5-15), or its significance is plain (e.g., 28:11-12; 37:5-10). The art of interpreting dreams is ascribed only to Joseph and to Daniel. It may be that this was a feature of the Shechem tradition of Joseph. The story of Daniel is modeled on that of Joseph.

8. Since they were under arrest they could not consult a professional interpreter, as they would have done had they been at liberty. Joseph implies that a professional is not needed: God can reveal the meaning of their dreams to whom he will.

---

they foreshadow? That is where the deeper mystery lies. In the story here two men are condemned to prison by Pharaoh's sudden anger. One is taken back into favor, the other put to death. For what reason? Perhaps there was no reason, but only a ruler's irresponsible caprice. Yet life was as dear to one man as to the other, and the dreadful sequel to his dream all the more bitter and irrational by the side of the other man's deliverance. Who shall interpret the tragedy of life's contradictions? Joseph could

not do that. Only God can reveal at last the pattern on the other side of what seems to human eyes the tangled skein.

For the writer of this chapter the fellow prisoners of Joseph have a secondary interest. They concern him only because of the relationship they happen to have with Joseph. And that relationship does throw added light on Joseph's character. In prison, as in Potiphar's house, he was the direct opposite of the sort of man whom George Bernard Shaw satirically characterized

11 And Pharaoh's cup *was* in my hand: and I took the grapes, and pressed them into Pharaoh's cup, and I gave the cup into Pharaoh's hand.

12 And Joseph said unto him, This *is* the interpretation of it: The three branches *are* three days:

13 Yet within three days shall Pharaoh lift up thine head, and restore thee unto thy place; and thou shalt deliver Pharaoh's cup into his hand, after the former manner when thou wast his butler.

14 But think on me when it shall be well with thee, and show kindness, I pray thee, unto me, and make mention of me unto Pharaoh, and bring me out of this house:

15 For indeed I was stolen away out of the land of the Hebrews: and here also have I done nothing that they should put me into the dungeon.

16 When the chief baker saw that the interpretation was good, he said unto Joseph, I also *was* in my dream, and, behold, *I had* three white baskets on my head:

17 And in the uppermost basket *there was* of all manner of bakemeats for Pharaoh; and the birds did eat them out of the basket upon my head.

18 And Joseph answered and said, This *is* the interpretation thereof: The three baskets *are* three days:

19 Yet within three days shall Pharaoh lift up thy head from off thee, and shall hang thee on a tree; and the birds shall eat thy flesh from off thee.

clusters ripened into grapes. 11 Pharaoh's cup was in my hand; and I took the grapes and pressed them into Pharaoh's cup, and placed the cup in Pharaoh's hand." 12 Then Joseph said to him, "This is its interpretation: the three branches are three days; 13 within three days Pharaoh will lift up your head and restore you to your office; and you shall place Pharaoh's cup in his hand as formerly, when you were his butler. 14 But remember me, when it is well with you, and do me the kindness, I pray you, to make mention of me to Pharaoh, and so get me out of this house. 15 For I was indeed stolen out of the land of the Hebrews; and here also I have done nothing that they should put me into the dungeon."

16 When the chief baker saw that the interpretation was favorable, he said to Joseph, "I also had a dream: there were three cake baskets on my head, 17 and in the uppermost basket there were all sorts of baked food for Pharaoh, but the birds were eating it out of the basket on my head." 18 And Joseph answered, "This is its interpretation: the three baskets are three days; 19 within three days Pharaoh will lift up your head — from you! — and hang you on a tree; and the birds will eat the flesh from you."

---

11. The implication seems to be that just as the natural process of the growth of the grapes had been miraculously accelerated, so the juice fermented as it was being pressed into the cup.

14. For **house** the LXX reads "prison," rightly.

15. The first half of the verse alludes to Joseph's kidnaping by the Midianites (E); the second half to the injustice done to him by his master's wife (J).

17. **The birds were eating it:** The implication is that he could not drive them away. This is the ominous feature of the dream, and determines its meaning.

---

as one who "will never miss a chance to lose an opportunity." Joseph never failed to seize each opportunity; and this he seemed to do not by any selfish calculation but by the moving of God's Spirit in him which made him meet every turn of life magnanimously. When Joseph was put in charge of the two new prisoners, **he served them.** And he did more. He had the sensitiveness and the instinctive sympathy which made him observant of these men's faces so that

he could read their feelings underneath; and what they felt, he cared about. One morning he looked at them, **and, behold, they were sad.** Why were they sad? he asked them. That question led to the story of their dreams; that story to his interpretation; and as a sequel to that came the release of the chief butler, and through him—though tardily—the release of Joseph himself. So far as Joseph was concerned, there was nothing he could do for the two men that he

20 ¶ And it came to pass the third day, *which was* Pharaoh's birthday, that he made a feast unto all his servants: and he lifted up the head of the chief butler and of the chief baker among his servants.

21 And he restored the chief butler unto his butlership again; and he gave the cup into Pharaoh's hand:

22 But he hanged the chief baker: as Joseph had interpreted to them.

23 Yet did not the chief butler remember Joseph, but forgat him.

20 On the third day, which was Pharaoh's birthday, he made a feast for all his servants, and lifted up the head of the chief butler and the head of the chief baker among his servants. 21 He restored the chief butler to his butlership, and he placed the cup in Pharaoh's hand; 22 but he hanged the chief baker, as Joseph had interpreted to them. 23 Yet the chief butler did not remember Joseph, but forgot him.

---

20. As Smend (*Erzählung des Hexateuch*, p. 103) observes, Pharaoh's birthday would not be the occasion of the punishment of the chief baker. The words **which was Pharaoh's birthday, he made a feast for all his servants** are from J. They suggest that according to this narrative both men were released.

23. But forgot him: Lit., "and forgot him," a doublet to the preceding sentence, is from J. The verb was therefore probably in the plural originally. Though nothing is said of the slow withering of Joseph's hopes for release, his sad figure casts its shadow over the conclusion of the story, another instance of J's literary skill.

---

had not done; and he comes through the prison experience increasingly revealed as having qualities that would make him great.

23. The Sin of Forgetfulness.—Joseph had already suffered two betrayals: through the jealous violence of his brothers and through the twisted passion of Potiphar's wife. Now comes another injury less malicious but hardly less disillusioning than the others. Here is a man he had befriended and helped. The chief butler did not set out to do him any harm; he simply did nothing at all. He just went off casually and **forgot**. But to Joseph, in prison, that was as hurtful as if it had been a deliberate wrong.

The sins of omission often are our worst discredit. In the Book of Common Prayer the General Confession acknowledges that "we have done those things which we ought not to have done," but rightly first it confesses that "we have left undone those things which we ought to have done." It is not enough to say to a friend, "I did not mean to hurt you." The test of friendship is how truly did you mean to help? The chief butler doubtless meant to help Joseph; he may have been voluble with promises. But all the same, he **forgot**. Forgetfulness in matters of this kind is no accident. It represents a deeper moral failure of unfaithfulness. Shallow-spoken gratitude, hollow loyalty professed but not put into practice, can convict a man's whole character of being sham, not substance.

"But I did intend to help Joseph," the chief butler might have argued in his own excuse. "I would have helped him sooner if I had remembered. But how could I help it if I forgot?"

So too often say the rest of us. Any day may see its best possibilities spoiled not by gross evil but by small neglect, by the errand not carried out, the letter stuck in the pocket and not posted, the responsibility accepted and then let drop out of mind. "How can I be blamed if I did not remember?" may be smoothly asked. But the answer is that failure to remember is no unavoidable bad luck. It is bad management of the mind which, because of its irresponsibility, can be immoral. When what ought to be dependable and solid becomes only a "frustrate ghost," then that is not mere unfortunate circumstance. It is sin.

Why is it possible to pledge trust and then forget? First, because of lack of intention and lack of attention. A promise may be so glibly made that it does not register. A person says he will do something and he thinks he means to do it, but the intention will wither as surely as a flower with no roots if he does not pay enough attention to plant it positively in his mind. Second, because of defective association paths. Memory depends upon the network of contacts established in the brain. Some of them form into a complex so strongly charged by habitual emphasis that there is little chance that anything linked with it can be lost from consciousness. With many persons that dominant complex is self-interest. Anything which has to do with that, and which is energized by that, is remembered. So we can always remember what we really want to do. But something that mainly affects somebody else is like an uncharged wire in the mind of the person who is self-absorbed.

41 And it came to pass at the end of two full years, that Pharaoh dreamed: and, behold, he stood by the river.

2 And, behold, there came up out of the river seven well-favored kine and fat-fleshed; and they fed in a meadow.

3 And, behold, seven other kine came up after them out of the river, ill-favored and lean-fleshed; and stood by the *other* kine upon the brink of the river.

4 And the ill-favored and lean-fleshed kine did eat up the seven well-favored and fat kine. So Pharaoh awoke.

41 After two whole years, Pharaoh dreamed that he was standing by the Nile, 2 and behold, there came up out of the Nile seven cows sleek and fat, and they fed in the reed grass. 3 And behold, seven other cows, gaunt and thin, came up out of the Nile after them, and stood by the other cows on the bank of the Nile. 4 And the gaunt and thin cows ate up the seven sleek and fat cows. And Pharaoh awoke.

C. Joseph's Rise to Power (41:1-57)

This chapter is a conflation of J and E, with some additions from P: vss. 44, 46-47, 54b, 57, and possibly 45aα.

The J story told of the Pharaoh's dream of the ears of grain (vss. 5-7), of Joseph's interpretation of it (vss. 14aβ, 22-24a, 21a, 26aβ, 27aβ, 31, 32bβ), of his advice to the Pharaoh to appoint overseers who would gather up all the food of the seven plenteous years and store it in the cities against the coming famine (vss. 34a, 35abβ, 36a), of the Pharaoh's appointment of Joseph himself (vss. 38, 41, 43a), of Joseph's marriage (vs. 45aβ), of how he carried out his policy (vss. 45b, 48a, 49bα), of the birth of Joseph's sons (cf. vs. 51bβ), and of the beginning of the famine (vss. 53-54a, 55-56a).

For the J dream of the ears of grain E substituted that of the cows (vss. 1-4), less fantastic, but at the same time less apt in its imagery of the famine. He recorded Joseph's interpretation of it (vss. 8-14aα, 14b-20, 21b, 24b-26aα, 27aαb, 28-30, 32bα) much as J had done, but changed Joseph's advice to the Pharaoh to appoint a number of overseers to make it agree with the action taken, the appointment of one man who would store up not all the yield of the years of plenty—which was obviously impossible—but only one fifth of it (vss. 33, 34b, 35bα, 36b). He then recorded the appointment of Joseph (vss. 37, 39-40, 42, 43b, 49a), the birth of his sons (vss. 50a, 51abα, 52), and the coming of the famine (vs. 56b). The E narrative is thus little more than a revision of that of J.

RJE, in weaving the two accounts together, was careful to preserve the salient points of each. Such statements as **the dream of Pharaoh is one** (vs. 25) are part of his harmonization.

There is no electric energy of interest to make it come alive. The thought of Joseph was only an unnoticed flicker on the edge of the chief butler's thought. No recollection concentrated there because he did not really care. It is the self-absorption which similarly does not care that makes so many of us guilty of the sin of forgetting. But sometimes the forgetting may be more directly purposeful. It is due to deliberate repression. Consider what modern psychology has revealed of the secret operation of the subconscious. The mind buries what it does not want to remember. Perhaps the chief butler's impulse was to banish the whole humiliating incident of his imprisonment, to wipe it from his recollection as though it had never been. This involved forgetting Joseph too, though no doubt the chief butler never could forget him

wholly; but he stifled the memory so far as any effective consciousness was concerned, because he did not want to arouse the other painful memories connected with it. How many of us forget the gratitude we owe, the faithfulness we promised, the help we were going to render, because pride does not want to recall the circumstances in which our obligation rose?

41:1-8. Pharaoh's Dream.—The symbolism of Pharaoh's dream grew out of conceptions deep-rooted in Egyptian thought. The Nile, out of which the fertility and the very life of Egypt came, was anciently venerated as the father of the gods. In Egyptian carvings the male ox represented it, and sometimes the ox was accompanied by seven cows. So in that labyrinth of the subconscious out of which dreams arise, some premonition of disaster took shape for

5 And he slept and dreamed the second time: and, behold, seven ears of corn came up upon one stalk, rank and good.

6 And, behold, seven thin ears and blasted with the east wind sprung up after them.

7 And the seven thin ears devoured the seven rank and full ears. And Pharaoh awoke, and, behold, *it was* a dream.

8 And it came to pass in the morning that his spirit was troubled; and he sent and called for all the magicians of Egypt, and all the wise men thereof: and Pharaoh told them his dream; but *there was* none that could interpret them unto Pharaoh.

9 ¶ Then spake the chief butler unto Pharaoh, saying, I do remember my faults this day:

10 Pharaoh was wroth with his servants, and put me in ward in the captain of the guard's house, *both* me and the chief baker:

11 And we dreamed a dream in one night, I and he; we dreamed each man according to the interpretation of his dream.

5 And he fell asleep and dreamed a second time; and behold, seven ears of grain, plump and good, were growing on one stalk. 6 And behold, after them sprouted seven ears, thin and blighted by the east wind. 7 And the thin ears swallowed up the seven plump and full ears. And Pharaoh awoke, and behold, it was a dream. 8 So in the morning his spirit was troubled; and he sent and called for all the magicians of Egypt and all its wise men; and Pharaoh told them his dream, but there was none who could interpret it*j* to Pharaoh.

9 Then the chief butler said to Pharaoh, "I remember my faults today. 10 When Pharaoh was angry with his servants, and put me and the chief baker in custody in the house of the captain of the guard, 11 we dreamed on the same night, he and I, each having a dream with its own meaning.

j Gk: Heb *them*

The J material in this chapter seems to be the free composition of J2 based in part perhaps, as has already been suggested, upon the career of Yanhamu. Under what circumstances J1 recorded Joseph's release from prison it is impossible to say, as there is a lacuna in his narrative between 40:14*b*β and 43:11 (see further below).

41:5. Were growing (RSV) is a translation of the same word as that rendered **came up** in vs. 2. This use of the word with two different meanings is an indication of a difference of source.

8. The magicians of Egypt and all its wise men are mentioned in order to show the inferiority of heathen magic and the occult art as practiced in Egypt to the true religion of Israel (cf. Exod. 8:18-19*a*; 9:11; Dan. 2:2-19; 5:8, 15-28).

Pharaoh in these symbolic pictures of the fat cows and the lean cows—adumbrations of forces that could in fact make the stark difference of good or ill for Egypt, the fertilizing inundations of the river, or no water and paralyzing drought. But though dreams come thus from hidden mental associations which have rational relationship, the conscious mind cannot always recognize the relationship which the symbols express. All that Pharaoh knew was that he was under the shadow of a portent which perplexed and depressed him. The portent was worse when the dream shifted its imagery, but with the same calamitous suggestion. He awoke, and found it was a dream, but the effect of it was so inescapable that he was convinced it was more than a dream. No wonder **he sent and called for all the magicians of Egypt, and all the wise men thereof.** But they could not interpret what he told them. To the writers of Genesis this was

a matter of course. Only an understanding given by God could interpret the realities of today and tomorrow.

9-15. Joseph Is Remembered.—Now comes another vivid link in the whole close-woven drama of the Joseph story. (One thinks wishfully, and with wonder, of what Shakespeare might have done with it if his attention had turned that way!) The chief butler, who had been helped by Joseph in prison and, when set free, had promptly forgotten, now recalled his benefactor. **I do remember my faults this day,** he exclaimed. He had certainly been at fault, and it was perhaps no credit to him that the divine plan for Joseph was to be no longer frustrated. Why did he remember? Was it because he suddenly saw advantage for himself in being able to give to Pharaoh this report of the sort of man Pharaoh was seeking? Was his confession of his fault merely the cringing self-

12 And *there was* there with us a young man, a Hebrew, servant to the captain of the guard; and we told him, and he interpreted to us our dreams; to each man according to his dream he did interpret.

13 And it came to pass, as he interpreted to us, so it was; me he restored unto mine office, and him he hanged.

14 ¶ Then Pharaoh sent and called Joseph, and they brought him hastily out of the dungeon: and he shaved *himself,* and changed his raiment, and came in unto Pharaoh.

15 And Pharaoh said unto Joseph, I have dreamed a dream, and *there is* none that can interpret it: and I have heard say of thee, *that* thou canst understand a dream to interpret it.

16 And Joseph answered Pharaoh, saying, *It is* not in me: God shall give Pharaoh an answer of peace.

17 And Pharaoh said unto Joseph, In my dream, behold, I stood upon the bank of the river:

18 And, behold, there came up out of the river seven kine, fat-fleshed and well-favored; and they fed in a meadow:

19 And, behold, seven other kine came up after them, poor and very ill-favored and lean-fleshed, such as I never saw in all the land of Egypt for badness:

20 And the lean and the ill-favored kine did eat up the first seven fat kine:

21 And when they had eaten them up, it could not be known that they had eaten

12 A young Hebrew was there with us, a servant of the captain of the guard; and when we told him, he interpreted our dreams to us, giving an interpretation to each man according to his dream. 13 And as he interpreted to us, so it came to pass; I was restored to my office, and the baker was hanged."

14 Then Pharaoh sent and called Joseph, and they brought him hastily out of the dungeon; and when he had shaved himself and changed his clothes, he came in before Pharaoh. 15 And Pharaoh said to Joseph, "I have had a dream, and there is no one who can interpret it; and I have heard it said of you that when you hear a dream you can interpret it." 16 Joseph answered Pharaoh, "It is not in me; God will give Pharaoh a favorable answer." 17 Then Pharaoh said to Joseph, "Behold, in my dream I was standing on the banks of the Nile; 18 and seven cows, fat and sleek, came up out of the Nile and fed in the reed grass; 19 and seven other cows came up after them, poor and very gaunt and thin, such as I had never seen in all the land of Egypt. 20 And the thin and gaunt cows ate up the first seven fat cows, 21 but when they had eaten

---

16. Cf. 40:8.

21. The word rendered **eaten them** is literally "come into their midst." This is an extraordinary circumlocution for the eating up of the cows, but is apt enough as a descrip-

---

blame which might prevent angry punishment from Pharaoh? Or was he genuinely sorry and honestly ashamed? Whatever the outward event, the answer to that question would make a crucial inward difference with the man himself. A fault may be remembered only with the purpose of squirming out of its consequences, and in that case it remains as a hidden corruption to the conscience. Or it may be remembered with the emphasis on **my faults,** in which case the stabbing memory may mean repentance and a new turn on the moral road.

16. *Not Man, but God.*—How characteristic of the whole book of Genesis are the words of this sentence: **It is not in me: God shall give Pharaoh an answer of peace!** *Non nobis,*

Domine! The O.T. writers understood the dignity that could belong to a man, but always that dignity was derived. It was not in anything that a man could boast about as his own endowments. It was in the fact that he could be an instrument in the hands of God. Conspicuously that was true of Joseph, both in what happened to him and in his own awareness. He was not depending now on his own cleverness. He would use all the discernment he had, but it was God who must direct it and illumine it. Not he, but God, would give Pharaoh his answer; and because the answer would come from God, it could turn Pharaoh's perplexity into peace.

17-33. *The Dream Retold and Interpreted.*—(For the dream itself see Expos. on vss. 1-8.)

them; but they *were* still ill-favored, as at the beginning. So I awoke.

22 And I saw in my dream, and, behold, seven ears came up in one stalk, full and good:

23 And, behold, seven ears, withered, thin, *and* blasted with the east wind, sprung up after them:

24 And the thin ears devoured the seven good ears: and I told *this* unto the magicians; but *there was* none that could declare *it* to me.

25 ¶ And Joseph said unto Pharaoh, The dream of Pharaoh *is* one: God hath showed Pharaoh what he *is* about to do.

26 The seven good kine *are* seven years; and the seven good ears *are* seven years: the dream *is* one.

27 And the seven thin and ill-favored kine that came up after them *are* seven years; and the seven empty ears blasted with the east wind shall be seven years of famine.

28 This *is* the thing which I have spoken unto Pharaoh: What God *is* about to do he showeth unto Pharaoh.

29 Behold, there come seven years of great plenty throughout all the land of Egypt:

30 And there shall arise after them seven years of famine; and all the plenty shall be forgotten in the land of Egypt; and the famine shall consume the land;

31 And the plenty shall not be known in the land by reason of that famine following; for it *shall be* very grievous.

32 And for that the dream was doubled unto Pharaoh twice; *it is* because the thing *is* established by God, and God will shortly bring it to pass.

33 Now therefore let Pharaoh look out a man discreet and wise, and set him over the land of Egypt.

them no one would have known that they had eaten them, for they were still as gaunt as at the beginning. Then I awoke. 22 I also saw in my dream seven ears growing on one stalk, full and good; 23 and seven ears, withered, thin, and blighted by the east wind, sprouted after them, 24 and the thin ears swallowed up the seven good ears. And I told it to the magicians, but there was no one who could explain it to me."

25 Then Joseph said to Pharaoh, "The dream of Pharaoh is one; God has revealed to Pharaoh what he is about to do. 26 The seven good cows are seven years, and the seven good ears are seven years; the dream is one. 27 The seven lean and gaunt cows that came up after them are seven years, and the seven empty ears blighted by the east wind are also seven years of famine. 28 It is as I told Pharaoh, God has shown to Pharaoh what he is about to do. 29 There will come seven years of great plenty throughout all the land of Egypt, 30 but after them there will arise seven years of famine, and all the plenty will be forgotten in the land of Egypt; the famine will consume the land, 31 and the plenty will be unknown in the land by reason of that famine which will follow, for it will be very grievous. 32 And the doubling of Pharaoh's dream means that the thing is fixed by God, and God will shortly bring it to pass. 33 Now therefore let Pharaoh select a man discreet and wise, and set him over the land of Egypt.

---

tion of what happened to the first seven ears of grain, and suggests that vs. 21 belongs to J and so stood originally after vs. 24*a*.

Now Joseph justifies the faith he had expressed in vs. 16. The symbolism of Pharaoh's dream resolves itself in his enlightened understanding, and he tells Pharaoh the meaning of the seven fat cows and seven full ears of corn, and the seven sinister cows and seven blasted ears— and the meaning is that there shall be seven seasons of plenty, then seven years of famine

when all the plenty shall be forgotten. What Pharaoh needs to do is to find a man discreet and wise, whom he shall set over all the land to provide against the coming calamity.

Is that only an ancient story, or is it a solemn warning that needs to ring like an iron bell for the hearing of modern times? In the nineteenth century and in the early part of the twentieth,

34 Let Pharaoh do *this,* and let him appoint officers over the land, and take up the fifth part of the land of Egypt in the seven plenteous years.

35 And let them gather all the food of those good years that come, and lay up corn under the hand of Pharaoh, and let them keep food in the cities.

36 And that food shall be for store to the land against the seven years of famine, which shall be in the land of Egypt; that the land perish not through the famine.

37 ¶ And the thing was good in the eyes of Pharaoh, and in the eyes of all his servants.

38 And Pharaoh said unto his servants, Can we find *such a one* as this *is,* a man in whom the Spirit of God *is?*

34 Let Pharaoh proceed to appoint overseers over the land, and take the fifth part of the produce of the land of Egypt during the seven plenteous years. 35 And let them gather all the food of these good years that are coming, and lay up grain under the authority of Pharaoh for food in the cities, and let them keep it. 36 That food shall be a reserve for the land against the seven years of famine which are to befall the land of Egypt, so that the land may not perish through the famine."

37 This proposal seemed good to Pharaoh and to all his servants. 38 And Pharaoh said to his servants, "Can we find such a man as this, in whom is the Spirit of God?"

---

38. The thought of **the Spirit of God** as the enduring source of inward illumination and intellectual power finds expression elsewhere in the O.T. only in later writings, e.g., Exod. 31:3; Num. 27:18; Ezek. 36:27. Earlier the Spirit appears as a catastrophic force, seizing upon a man and empowering him to feats of physical prowess, as, e.g., in Judg.

---

in many countries of the world and more particularly in Great Britain at the proud zenith of the Victorian era and in the United States rising rapidly to world power, there was prosperity, **fat-fleshed and well-favored,** such as was not seen on the earth before. But what of the years to follow—years which come from horizons dark with the clouds of confusion and the threat of war? Those years can be like the devouring cows and blasted corn. Where is there a statesman **discreet and wise** enough to discern the signs of the times, and great enough to mobilize under God the physical and moral resources of the earth sufficiently to avert disaster?

34-49. *Executing the Idea.*—It is sometimes supposed that the religious man will be only a visionary. He may see what is desirable, but he will have no practical ability to get it done. Goodness, yes; but what about his gumption? Joseph had both, and Pharaoh intuitively recognized that fact. He saw at once not only that Joseph had the right idea; he perceived that here was also the man who could carry it out. So there follows the gorgeous pageant of Joseph's investiture with viceregal power; his progress through the land in Pharaoh's chariot while the people bow before him; and the swift translation into action of his plan to gather in the years of plenty the food that would be needed for the famine that was to come. Thus Joseph the man of prayer was the man who could also perform. So it should always be. One of Phillips Brooks's great sermons is on "Visions and

Tasks." "It is a terrible thing," he said, "to have seen the vision, and to be so wrapped up in its contemplation as not to hear the knock of needy hands upon our doors." And he said also, "It is a terrible thing to hear the knock and have no vision to declare to the poor knocker."[1] Egypt would have faced a grim future if Joseph had been lacking in either way. So will other lands and later civilizations if there are no new Josephs. With Joseph a vision of the great forces moving in his world was linked with compassion for people, and his compassion for people was made effective because he understood the forces with which he had to deal.

38. *The Meaning of Inspiration.*—What the Exeg. suggests here as to the developing conceptions of **the Spirit of God** may have a practical and present message. There is still the idea that the more authentic gifts of God come as inexplicable miracles. Even more frequent and familiar are the ideas that religion when it is real must show itself in exciting ways, and as a corollary that unless a man is moved by conspicuous emotions there must be something the matter with his religion.

Hidden in both assumptions is an element of truth, crude and groping though the expression of it may be. Special energies do come from God to give men unwonted strength. The old chronicler was right when in Judges he re-

[1] *Visions and Tasks* (New York: E. P. Dutton & Co., 1886), p. 19.

39 And Pharaoh said unto Joseph, Forasmuch as God hath showed thee all this, *there is* none so discreet and wise as thou *art:*

40 Thou shalt be over my house, and according unto thy word shall all my people be ruled: only in the throne will I be greater than thou.

41 And Pharaoh said unto Joseph, See, I have set thee over all the land of Egypt.

42 And Pharaoh took off his ring from his hand, and put it upon Joseph's hand, and arrayed him in vestures of fine linen, and put a gold chain about his neck;

39 So Pharaoh said to Joseph, "Since God has shown you all this, there is none so discreet and wise as you are; **40** you shall be over my house, and all my people shall order themselves as you command; only as regards the throne will I be greater than you." **41** And Pharaoh said to Joseph, "Behold, I have set you over all the land of Egypt." **42** Then Pharaoh took his signet ring from his hand and put it on Joseph's hand, and arrayed him in garments of fine linen, and put a gold chain about his neck;

6:34; 14:19; I Sam. 11:6. Allied with this idea is that of the Spirit as the cause of ecstasy, found, e.g., in Num. 11:25; I Sam. 10:6; Joel 2:28. With this development may be compared Paul's insistence that the most excellent gift of the Spirit is not speaking with tongues or working miracles, but the enduring quality of love (I Cor. 12:30–13:13).

41. Joseph is put in charge not only of the royal household but of the whole administration. The reference would seem to be to the coveted office of *T'ate*, "the second after the king in the court of the palace" (Adolf Erman, *Life in Ancient Egypt*, tr. H. M. Tirard [London: Macmillan and Co., 1894], p. 87). Syrian slaves were frequently elevated to such dignities (*ibid.*, pp. 106-7, 517-18).

It is evident from this verse that J2 had a certain knowledge of Egyptian customs and institutions. This can scarcely be attributed to the remembered experience of the sojourn in Egypt, at least 250 years before he wrote. It will have been acquired from Egyptian merchants and other travelers in Palestine. Indeed, it is not impossible that he himself had visited Egypt.

42. The **signet ring**, used in sealing documents (cf. Esth. 3:12; 8:8; also I Kings 21:8), is given as a token of authority (cf. Esth. 3:10; 8:2). The weaving of **fine linen**

---

ported Gideon's victory as due to something supernatural which filled Gideon with a force he would not have had alone. It is a plain fact which every physiologist confirms that when some new stimulus enters a man's mind it may be answered by the release of glandular energies within him which lift his whole self to a higher pitch. The religious man knows that the supreme stimulus is the one which comes when he is in touch with God. Henry M. Stanley, in the journal he kept concerning his hazardous search in central Africa for the lost Livingstone, wrote:

On all my expeditions, prayer made me stronger, morally and mentally, than any of my non-praying companions. It did not blind my eyes, or dull my mind, or close my ears; but, on the contrary, it gave me confidence. It did more: it gave me joy, and pride, in my work, and lifted me hopefully over the one thousand five hundred miles of Forest tracks, eager to face the day's perils and fatigues. You may know when prayer is answered, by that glow of content which fills one who has flung his cause before God, as he rises to his feet.[2]

[2] *Autobiography*, ed. Dorothy Stanley (Boston: Houghton Mifflin Co., 1909), p. 519.

It would be an unhappy thing if we should be too sophisticated to see any value in the belief—no matter how primitive have been some of its expressions—that the Spirit may appear "as seizing upon a man and empowering him to feats of physical prowess." Christian Science and similar cults ought not to be allowed to appropriate and exploit the faith which is as old as time that the spirit of God can work divine results in human bodies.

Error comes when the crudity rather than the deeper and holier content of the agelong belief is preserved. That God can give men strength is true; that this strength comes as a sort of arbitrary marvel apart from moral meaning is superstition. In our modern times, when money is often accounted a surer instrument of strength than muscle, thousands who want to make religion a short cut to prosperity flock to hear self-appointed leaders promise that if we expect it hard enough, God will give us whatever we want. Religion slides back then into the realm of magic, which may be no less magic when its formulas are those of New Thought instead of tribal thaumaturgy.

43 And he made him to ride in the second chariot which he had; and they cried before him, Bow the knee: and he made him *ruler* over all the land of Egypt.

44 And Pharaoh said unto Joseph, I *am* Pharaoh, and without thee shall no man lift up his hand or foot in all the land of Egypt.

45 And Pharaoh called Joseph's name Zaphnath-paaneah; and he gave him to wife Asenath the daughter of Poti-pherah priest of On. And Joseph went out over *all* the land of Egypt.

46 ¶ And Joseph *was* thirty years old when he stood before Pharaoh king of Egypt. And Joseph went out from the presence of Pharaoh, and went throughout all the land of Egypt.

47 And in the seven plenteous years the earth brought forth by handfuls.

48 And he gathered up all the food of the seven years, which were in the land of Egypt, and laid up the food in the cities: the food of the field, which *was* round about every city, laid he up in the same.

49 And Joseph gathered corn as the sand of the sea, very much, until he left numbering; for *it was* without number.

43 and he made him to ride in his second chariot; and they cried before him, "Bow the knee!"[k] Thus he set him over all the land of Egypt. 44 Moreover Pharaoh said to Joseph, "I am Pharaoh, and without your consent no man shall lift up hand or foot in all the land of Egypt." 45 And Pharaoh called Joseph's name Zaph'enath-pane'ah; and he gave him in marriage As'enath, the daughter of Poti'phera priest of On. So Joseph went out over the land of Egypt.

46 Joseph was thirty years old when he entered the service of Pharaoh king of Egypt. And Joseph went out from the presence of Pharaoh, and went through all the land of Egypt. 47 During the seven plenteous years the earth brought forth abundantly, 48 and he gathered up all the food of the seven years when there was plenty[l] in the land of Egypt, and stored up food in the cities; he stored up in every city the food from the fields around it. 49 And Joseph stored up grain in great abundance, like the sand of the sea, until he ceased to measure it, for it could not be measured.

[k] *Abrek*, probably an Egyptian word similar in sound to the Hebrew word meaning *to kneel*
[l] Sam Gk: Heb *which were*

was an Egyptian art (*ibid.*, p. 448). The **gold chain** (cf. Dan. 5:7) may contain an allusion to the Reward of the Gold, an Egyptian decoration often conferred in recognition of eminent service to the crown (*ibid.*, p. 118). E thus evinces a knowledge of Egyptian customs, similar to that of J and doubtless similarly acquired.

43. Bow the knee: A rendition, based on the Vulg. *ut genuflecterent,* of the Hebrew *'abhrēk,* an obscure word of uncertain meaning (cf. RSV mg.).

45. The conferring of a new name was common with promotions such as that of Joseph (*ibid.*, pp. 106, 517; cf. p. 144). The meaning of **Zaphenath-paneah** is uncertain. **Potiphera** is another form of "Potiphar," who appears in the E document not as the priest of On, but as the captain of the guard, Joseph's master (37:36). **On** is Heliopolis, seven miles northeast of Cairo, anciently a center of the worship of the sun-god Re.

But more serious, because more likely to trouble people who are both simple and sincere, is the other tendency to identify religion with ecstasy. Here again truth is at the heart of what may become distortion. Of course religion does have deep ties with the emotions. It can lift men into an exalted state which expressed itself in the O.T. in religious dances and in the frenzied utterances of bands of wandering prophets in the time of Saul, and similarly today in the hysteria of camp meeting evangelism and among the sects which consider that men and women have more fully arrived at holiness when they fall down in excitement and roll on the floor. Most people will not be attracted to these extremes, but numbers of earnest souls are troubled by this question: "What if my religion seems to have no ecstasy at all?" "Surely," they think, "if we are in touch with God, something ought to happen. Why do we not have new feelings of superhuman happiness? And if no experience has come, how do we really know that we are Christians? Other people have passed through great crises of conversion; and some, like Paul, have felt themselves lifted up to the third heaven. That unmistakably would be to know the Holy Spirit. But when we are so different, and when our religious life seems to move along on level ground, have we missed the Spirit al-

50 And unto Joseph were born two sons, before the years of famine came: which Asenath the daughter of Poti-pherah priest of On bare unto him.

51 And Joseph called the name of the firstborn Manasseh: For God, *said he,* hath made me forget all my toil, and all my father's house.

52 And the name of the second called he Ephraim: For God hath caused me to be fruitful in the land of my affliction.

50 Before the year of famine came, Joseph had two sons, whom As'enath, the daughter of Poti'phera priest of On, bore to him. 51 Joseph called the name of the first-born Manas'seh,[m] "For," he said, "God has made me forget all my hardship and all my father's house." 52 The name of the second he called E'phraim,[n] "For God has made me fruitful in the land of my affliction."

[m] That is *Making to forget*
[n] From a Hebrew word meaning *to be fruitful*

51. **Manasseh** appears among the Babylonians as a personal name, *Mannašu* (Meyer, *Israeliten und ihre Nachbarstämme,* p. 515), a fact which suggests that the historic tribe of Manasseh was called by the name of the leader under whom it emerged as an independent entity. As to when this occurred it is difficult to say. The tribe is not mentioned in the Song of Deborah (Judg. 5), which does, however, refer to Machir (Judg. 5:14), later reckoned as a son, i.e., as a clan, of Manasseh (50:23). This may indicate one of two things: either (*a*) that the Manassites entered Palestine at a date subsequent to that of the defeat of Sisera (*ca.* 1200 B.C.), and that the clan of Machir eventually attached itself to them; or (*b*) that they were in Palestine at the time the song was composed, but had not yet attained tribal status. In favor of the former alternative is the fact, evidenced by the E document, that there was among the northern tribes a group which looked not to Sinai but to Horeb as the desert center of Yahwism. The entry of this group into the land will presumably have been independent of that of the Sinai group. The concern of the E document with Shechem, the capital of Manasseh, suggests that the Manassites belonged to the Horeb group from which that document emanated.

However that may be, Manasseh cannot have come to be regarded as a son of Joseph until after the settlement. It was the necessity of reconciling the tribal tradition with that of the Shechemite figure Joseph which led ultimately to the representation. The etymology provided in this verse is, as is usually the case, fanciful—a device to clinch the linking together of two originally independent figures.

52. **Ephraim** is primarily a place name, from the same root as Ephrathah, situated in the center of the territory of the tribe (*ibid.,* p. 514); i.e., the tribe took its name from the land it occupied in Palestine. Like Manasseh, and for the same reason, its eponym

together?" No. There is no ground for that discouragement, as the Exeg. has reminded us; Paul himself insisted "that the most excellent gift of the Spirit is not speaking with tongues or working miracles, but the enduring quality of love."

This does not mean that religious experience need be flat. We may not be temperamentally emotional; the important matter is not intensity of emotion, but honesty of obedience. So far as concerns Joseph, there is no indication in the narrative of how he felt, nor any indication that Pharaoh chose him because he looked excited. The evidence that the Spirit of God was in him had to do with deeper aspects than that. Here was a man who showed in his controlled but unmistakable authority that there was a spirit in him not present in ordinary men—the

spirit of truth to see what needed to be done, and the spirit of faithfulness to go and do it.

50-52. *Joseph Names His Sons.*—By the favor of Pharaoh, Joseph has been married to a daughter of a priest of Re, the sun-god, at Heliopolis, and has been given the name which represented the profound impression he had made on Pharaoh—the name which seems to have meant "God, the living one, hath spoken" (vs. 45). Thus Joseph was highly exalted in Egypt, although as the developing drama will show, he was never to lose his controlling loyalty to his own people. Now he gives to his two sons names which are significant of his reflection upon his life. The name **Manasseh** symbolized the fact that God had made him forget his hardships and his father's house, i.e., forget them not in the sense of their being wiped out of

53 ¶ And the seven years of plenteousness, that was in the land of Egypt, were ended.

54 And the seven years of dearth began to come, according as Joseph had said: and the dearth was in all lands; but in all the land of Egypt there was bread.

55 And when all the land of Egypt was famished, the people cried to Pharaoh for bread: and Pharaoh said unto all the Egyptians, Go unto Joseph; what he saith to you, do.

56 And the famine was over all the face of the earth: and Joseph opened all the storehouses, and sold unto the Egyptians; and the famine waxed sore in the land of Egypt.

57 And all countries came into Egypt to Joseph for to buy *corn;* because that the famine was *so* sore in all lands.

53 The seven years of plenty that prevailed in the land of Egypt came to an end; 54 and the seven years of famine began to come, as Joseph had said. There was famine in all lands; but in all the land of Egypt there was bread. 55 When all the land of Egypt was famished, the people cried to Pharaoh for bread; and Pharaoh said to all the Egyptians, "Go to Joseph; what he says to you, do." 56 So when the famine had spread over all the land, Joseph opened all the storehouses,*º* and sold to the Egyptians, for the famine was severe in the land of Egypt. 57 Moreover, all the earth came to Egypt to Joseph to buy grain, because the famine was severe over all the earth.

º Gk Vg Compare Syr: Heb *all that was in them*

---

came eventually to be represented as a son of Joseph. The etymology provided is less fanciful than that of Manasseh, for the land from which the tribe of Ephraim derived its name seems to have been so called because of its fertility (cf. Skinner, *Genesis,* p. 471).

55. This verse, derived from J, was in its original context followed by 47:15aβγδ, 16a, 17a (see below).

56. The clause in 47:17a was followed by the first half of this verse, **And the famine was over all the face of the earth** (J), leading up to the account of the coming of Joseph's brothers from Canaan to buy food in Egypt. The second half is from E. This was, in its original context, followed by the primary material in 47:14, 18-21 (see below), and the account of the coming of Joseph's brothers.

---

thought or canceled from experience, but rather in the sense that what had been bitter in them was transcended. His was the resolve which Paul was afterward to glorify when he wrote of "forgetting those things which are behind, and reaching forth unto those things which are before" (Phil. 3:13). His other son he named **Ephraim: For God hath caused me to be fruitful in the land of my affliction.** How deep and rich is the suggestion of that! The land of affliction is often the fruitful land—fruitful of patience, faith, courage, fortitude, victory. The times when the soul of Israel rose to its noblest heights were often the times when outward events were darkest: Moses in the wilderness, Elijah coming back from Horeb, Isaiah and Jeremiah in besieged Jerusalem. The psalmist understood the truth when he sang of those who "going through the vale of misery use it for a well" (Ps. 84:6 Book of Common Prayer). And Paul could lift that same truth to heroic purpose when he wrote concerning what he chose to stay and face in Ephesus, "A great door and effectual

is opened unto me, and there are many adversaries" (I Cor. 16:9).

53-57. The Coming of the Famine.—According to Joseph's interpretation of Pharaoh's dream, so the facts proceeded. After the years of plenty, the distress which he had prophesied began. At first the dearth was **in all lands;** soon it was worse than dearth, and **famine was over all the face of the earth.** Because of Joseph's inspired foresight, there was food in Egypt; and people from everywhere began to come and try to buy the food they could not get in their own countries. Such was the plainly recounted physical fact; but in it one may catch the gleam of a suggestion that has to do with a higher realm than the physical. Often in regions of our earth and of our life there can be a spiritual dearth that can deepen into spiritual famine. Yet by the mercy of God there may be a place where there is food, if men know where to turn to seek it. And the mark of that place will be the presence in it of some great man inspired by God to know the needs of his time and to consecrate himself to meet them.

42 Now when Jacob saw that there was corn in Egypt, Jacob said unto his sons, Why do ye look one upon another?

42 When Jacob learned that there was grain in Egypt, he said to his sons,

---

XLVI. JOSEPH AND HIS BROTHERS IN EGYPT (42:1–45:28)

This section is a conflation of J and E, except for 42:5-6a which come from P. The two narratives followed along the same lines. They told of Jacob's sending his sons to Egypt, while he kept Benjamin with him at home; of Joseph's recognition of his brothers when they appeared before him, and of their failure to recognize him; of his charging them with being spies; of their defense of themselves by insisting that they were brothers; of their mention of Benjamin; of Joseph's providing them with grain; of his warning them that they would not see him on another visit unless they brought Benjamin with them; of their return to Palestine; and of their second journey to Egypt, accompanied by Benjamin.

Within the framework of the tale there are some interesting differences, especially in the development of the motif of Joseph's desire to see Benjamin, his full brother, the son of Rachel. It may be recalled here that according to the J document it was not until after Joseph had been sold to the Ishmaelites that Benjamin was born, at Ephrath on the way from Shechem to Hebron. Joseph thus knew nothing of his existence—or of his mother's death—until the facts emerged in his questioning of his brothers (cf. 43:7; 44:19-20). The J account of the actual cross-examination is missing, together with his description of Joseph's reaction to the news, RJE having preferred the E recension (42:13-16) at this point. However it is clear from 43:3-7 that, knowing the famine would continue for another five or six years, Joseph had no doubt that his brothers would have to come to Egypt again for grain. Therefore all he had to do to ensure that his desire to see Benjamin would be fulfilled was to tell them that he would not see them unless they had the boy with them—an excellent example of J's literary artistry.

E is less sensitive. He has Joseph, ostensibly on the ground of his suspicions as to their good faith, demand that they send one of their number back to Palestine to get Benjamin, while the rest of them are held in custody. He then puts them in prison for three days to convince them of the seriousness of their situation. On the third day, however, he relents a little. He will hold only one of them as a hostage. The others are to return home and bring Benjamin down to Egypt at once.

E further represents the brothers as recognizing that whatever was happening to them was in retribution for their treatment of Joseph seven or eight years before. Possibly there was a parallel to this in J, though it is unlikely, in view of the fact that there is no trace of it in RJE's compilation. It would rather seem that here again J so contrived his narrative that its overtones would suggest the truth to those who had ears to hear (cf. 42:38; 44:19-29, and see below).

Underlying the J material in chs. 42–45 is a simpler narrative by J[1] which told of only one journey of Joseph's brothers to Egypt (cf. Gunkel, *Genesis*, p. 441), and knew nothing of Benjamin (cf. Hugo Gressmann, "Ursprung und Entwicklung der Joseph-Sage," ΕΥΧΑΡΙΣΤΗΡΙΟΝ, ed. Hans Schmidt [Göttingen: Vandenhoeck & Ruprecht, 1923], I, 11). Fragments of this are preserved in 43:11, 13bα, 15b-17, 24b, 26aαb (see Simpson, *Early Traditions of Israel*, pp. 144-46).

42:1-5. *The Quality of Decision.*—Here in vss. 1-2 is one of those extraordinary O.T. sentences which with a handful of words lights up a whole scene. There they all are, Jacob and the full circle of his sons, so sharply outlined that it is as though we could see their attitudes and mark the expression on each face. The crucial fact is what everybody knows. There is famine in the land. The little that they have to eat is running low, and there is no hope of getting any more from their own fields. What is there to do then? The brothers have no answer. They only stare at one another helplessly. Nobody gives a lead. But it was different with Jacob. He was an old man now, but energy still could kindle in him like a fire. He said he had heard

2 And he said, Behold, I have heard that there is corn in Egypt: get you down thither, and buy for us from thence; that we may live, and not die.

3 ¶ And Joseph's ten brethren went down to buy corn in Egypt.

4 But Benjamin, Joseph's brother, Jacob sent not with his brethren; for he said, Lest peradventure mischief befall him.

5 And the sons of Israel came to buy *corn* among those that came: for the famine was in the land of Canaan.

6 And Joseph *was* the governor over the land, *and* he *it was* that sold to all the people of the land: and Joseph's brethren came, and bowed down themselves before him *with* their faces to the earth.

7 And Joseph saw his brethren, and he knew them, but made himself strange unto them, and spake roughly unto them; and he said unto them, Whence come ye? And they said, From the land of Canaan to buy food.

"Why do you look at one another?" 2 And he said, "Behold, I have heard that there is grain in Egypt; go down and buy grain for us there, that we may live, and not die." 3 So ten of Joseph's brothers went down to buy grain in Egypt. 4 But Jacob did not send Benjamin, Joseph's brother, with his brothers, for he feared that harm might befall him. 5 Thus the sons of Israel came to buy among the others who came, for the famine was in the land of Canaan.

6 Now Joseph was governor over the land; he it was who sold to all the people of the land. And Joseph's brothers came, and bowed themselves before him with their faces to the ground. 7 Joseph saw his brothers, and knew them, but he treated them like strangers and spoke roughly to them. "Where do you come from?" he said. They said, "From the land of Canaan, to buy

A. JOSEPH'S BROTHERS COME TO EGYPT (42:1-6)

42:1. The abrupt change of scene is remarkably effective. Skinner notes that "the energy and resourcefulness of the father is set in striking contrast to the perplexity of the sons" (*Genesis*, p. 474).

6. An official in such a responsible position as that assigned to Joseph in the story would scarcely himself have interviewed foreigners coming to buy grain. The representation that he did so was, of course, demanded by the story as a whole. It seems probable, however, that if J had had any real awareness of the administrative problems involved in such an office as Joseph's he would have taken pains to account more adequately for the brothers' contact with him.

B. JOSEPH'S TREATMENT OF HIS BROTHERS (42:7–44:34)
1. JOSEPH'S BROTHERS IN PRISON (42:7-17)

7. Joseph's treatment of his brothers from this point until the disclosure of his identity (45:1) is, in the present combined narrative, a strange mixture of harshness

that there was grain in Egypt. Doubtless his sons had heard so too, but apparently they took it just as empty information, not as something to be translated into instant action. They were ready to give up, but Jacob said, **Get you down.** Get down, as it were, to earth—to the good earth of Egypt, where there might be an answer to their need.

Jacob was no ideal character. But he shows now as earlier one great quality of strength: he could decide, and he could act. His sons at this moment were in danger of being unable to do either. They stared at one another as though to say, "Somebody ought to think of something"; and then they shifted irresolutely as though

they were also saying, "It's up to somebody to do something—but not me." Jacob, on the other hand, took command. To him the report about food in Egypt meant something and must lead to something. The authority of his perception and his purpose was great enough to arouse his sons to action. It is as though they had been waiting for the masterful word. Men often are: individuals and families get by their crises only when there is some person here and there who, notwithstanding imperfections, has this quality of decisive strength.

6-38. *Joseph's Brothers Come to Egypt.*—Here begins the long and somewhat repetitious story of the re-establishment of Joseph's rela-

8 And Joseph knew his brethren, but they knew not him.

9 And Joseph remembered the dreams which he dreamed of them, and said unto them, Ye *are* spies; to see the nakedness of the land ye are come.

10 And they said unto him, Nay, my lord, but to buy food are thy servants come.

11 We *are* all one man's sons; we *are* true *men;* thy servants are no spies.

12 And he said unto them, Nay, but to see the nakedness of the land ye are come.

13 And they said, Thy servants *are* twelve brethren, the sons of one man in the land of Canaan; and, behold, the youngest *is* this day with our father, and one *is* not.

food." 8 Thus Joseph knew his brothers, but they did not know him. 9 And Joseph remembered the dreams which he had dreamed of them; and he said to them, "You are spies, you have come to see the weakness of the land." 10 They said to him, "No, my lord, but to buy food have your servants come. 11 We are all sons of one man, we are honest men, your servants are not spies." 12 He said to them, "No, it is the weakness of the land that you have come to see." 13 And they said, "We, your servants, are twelve brothers, the sons of one man in the land of Canaan; and behold, the youngest is this day with our father,

---

and magnanimity. There is first the charge that they are spies—an opinion which he is represented as maintaining with all the obstinacy of a government official—culminating in their imprisonment for three days (42:9-17). This is followed by an apparently unmotivated change of heart, and the brothers, all except Simeon, are released, provided with grain, and sent back to Palestine to get Benjamin (42:18-26). Their money is, however, placed in the mouth of their sacks (42:25) apparently out of generosity (cf. 43:23), though, as might have been expected, it has the effect of striking terror into them (cf. 42:28*b*). Similarly, Joseph's treatment of them when they came to Egypt the second time (43:16-34) appears to have been kindly intentioned, though again it aroused their fears (cf. 43:18). This kindly treatment was, however, at once offset by the placing of the cup in Benjamin's sack (44:2), and Joseph's insistence that the boy should be left with him as a slave (44:17).

The impression of heartless capriciousness is to a considerable degree due to the fact that the narrative as we have it is the result of the conflation of two documents. Neither of these source documents taken by itself represents Joseph as thus playing with his brothers. The E document told simply of their imprisonment for three days and of their release to bring Benjamin down to Egypt. The fact that nothing except 43:23*b* has been preserved of E's account of Joseph's reception of them on their second visit suggests that it contained nothing striking, and warrants the inference that 43:23*b* was in its original context followed almost immediately by 45:2-3.

Thus Joseph's harshness in the E narrative was limited to his temporary imprisonment of his brothers and to his retaining of Simeon in custody. Nor is there in it the slightest suggestion of caprice, for the implication of 42:21-24 is that he acted as he did for the purpose of bringing them to recognize the cruelty of their own conduct to him some eight years before.

---

tionship with his family, leading up to the disclosure of his identity to his astonished brothers, and finally to the bringing down of old Jacob into Egypt. The contrasts in Joseph's extraordinary career mount now toward their climax. When the brothers, driven by the famine in Canaan, come to Egypt to try to buy food, Joseph recognizes them; but they do not know him in this awesome man in the seat of Pharaoh's power. Joseph remembers (vs. 9) the dreams which he had had long ago in Canaan concerning them—the dreams in which under

the symbols of sheaves standing in the field they all bowed down to him. Now the dreams were mightily fulfilled. Here were these brothers who had sold him into slavery, suing abjectly to him for food with which to keep alive. If the rest of the picture of Joseph were not of a completely different tone, it might seem that he is moved by the very human impulse to make their punishment bitter. He speaks roughly to them (vs. 7) ; he declares, **You are spies**. But as the narrative proceeds, it appears that Joseph has another purpose. He is develop-

14 And Joseph said unto them, That *is it* that I spake unto you, saying, Ye *are* spies:

15 Hereby ye shall be proved: By the life of Pharaoh ye shall not go forth hence, except your youngest brother come hither.

16 Send one of you, and let him fetch your brother, and ye shall be kept in prison, that your words may be proved, whether *there be any* truth in you: or else by the life of Pharaoh surely ye *are* spies.

17 And he put them all together into ward three days.

18 And Joseph said unto them the third day, This do, and live; *for* I fear God:

and one is no more." 14 But Joseph said to them, "It is as I said to you, you are spies. 15 By this you shall be tested: by the life of Pharaoh, you shall not go from this place unless your youngest brother comes here. 16 Send one of you, and let him bring your brother, while you remain in prison, that your words may be tested, whether there is truth in you; or else, by the life of Pharaoh, surely you are spies." 17 And he put them all together in prison for three days.

18 On the third day Joseph said to them, "Do this and you will live, for I fear God:

The J document, after telling of Joseph's initial charge against them, simply recorded the stipulation he then laid down that they would not be permitted to see him should they return without Benjamin. The placing of the money in their sacks was thus in its original context a thoughtful act of generosity (cf. 43:23a). Their terror when they found it (42:28b) was, J would imply, no fault of Joseph's; it represented the first slight stirring of conscience as regards an action done years before, which had that very day been called out of the past by Joseph's seemingly undesigned questioning. Joseph's hospitable reception of them when they came the second time was thus quite genuine. It failed, however, to elicit from them any explicit recognition of their past treachery (contrast 42:21-22 [E]). Joseph therefore resorted to the device of charging Benjamin with the theft of his divining cup. Not only did the confession of guilt follow (44:16) but Judah's moving plea (44:18-34), showing his concern for his old father, revealed that a deep change of heart had occurred.

15. By the life of Pharaoh: In Egypt the Pharaoh was honored as a god. This oath is thus analogous to "as the LORD liveth" (cf. Judg. 8:19; I Sam. 14:39, 45; I Kings 17:1, 12; II Kings 2:2; etc.).

2. THE ORDER CONCERNING BENJAMIN (42:18-25)

18. The words **I fear God** in this context postulate by implication the existence of a standard of international morality of which God is the guardian (cf. Gunkel, *Genesis,*

---

ing a plan by which he can keep control of his brothers' movements, inform himself continuously about his father and his younger brother, and ultimately bring them into Egypt. That, of course, is the reason for the device of the money put into the sacks of grain.

The older brothers are uneasy and fearful as they stand before the powerful "Egyptian." They would have been still more fearful had they known that he was Joseph. The fact stated in vs. 23 is simple and obvious, but it suggests an intriguing if accidental spiritual parallel. The thoughts and speech of guilty men are disclosed in ways they do not guess. There is a curious suggestion also in vs. 13: **Thy servants are twelve brethren,** they say. They supposed that Joseph was dead, but they still speak of the twelve as though he were one of them. Perhaps there is a reflection here of the Hebrew

sense of unbreakable family solidarity; and one remembers Wordsworth's "We Are Seven."

18, 35. *The Noble and the Ignoble Fear.*—To **fear,** and to be **afraid;** it may sound as though they meant the same, but they are as wide apart as the world. One word had to do with Joseph, the other with his brethren; the emotions on one side and the other were as different as day and night.

I fear God, said Joseph. Reviewing his life, we can see what that phrase, used so often in the Bible, means. It has nothing to do with fright. It is not abject. It is the reverent awe of a soul, at the highest point of its own awareness, before the infinite greatness and glory of God. It is watchfulness, intent and serious, against any disloyalty to God's righteousness and truth. The man who in this sense "fears God" is not afraid of any mortal danger:

19 If ye *be* true *men,* let one of your brethren be bound in the house of your prison: go ye, carry corn for the famine of your houses:

20 But bring your youngest brother unto me; so shall your words be verified, and ye shall not die. And they did so.

19 if you are honest men, let one of your brothers remain confined in your prison, and let the rest go and carry grain for the famine of your households, 20 and bring your youngest brother to me; so your words will be verified, and you shall not die."

---

p. 444). The same thought underlies 20:11 and, less immediately, the closing words of 39:9.

20. **And they did so,** senseless here, is a variant to vs. 25*b* **This was done for them** and should be deleted.

---

the only thing he could be afraid of is unfaithfulness. He is like a sentry put at a post of guard by an authority which he completely accepts and trusts. He is vigilant against any hostile forces that may be moving in the dark, but he has no fear of them. Lesser fears are dwarfed and lost in one supreme concern; that he shall not be unfaithful to God who has trusted him.

So it was with Joseph. In the hot assault made upon his moral integrity when he was first a slave in Egypt, he was saved from wickedness because he shrank from outraging the conscience God had given him. When the long frustration and unfairness in which his life had seemed to be caught might have tempted him in Pharaoh's prison to act like a criminal since he was treated like one, he still kept not only his integrity but also his disciplined intelligence. When his brothers came into Egypt, he had the chance to satisfy the natural impulse to revenge after what he had suffered at their hands; but an authority more commanding spoke to his heart. **I fear God,** he said. That kind of fear always has the magnificent moral astringency which a great life needs. It scorches the mean choice by the fire of the divine choice. See how true that was in all the noblest figures of the O.T.—in Moses, Elijah, Isaiah, Nehemiah. See the reflections of the same truth in other lives down the long course of history—Joan of Arc, John Huss, John Wycliffe, Abraham Lincoln, Robert E. Lee. Souls who have bound themselves to a great commitment, and whose only fear is lest they fail to be loyal, are lifted out of all lesser fears to walk on the heights of courage.

Observe now the contrast of Joseph's brothers. They had not feared God. They thought they did not need to fear anything. They had followed their ungoverned impulses of jealous hatred, anger, and calculating cruelty. When they got rid of Joseph they thought that was the end of the matter. But it was only the beginning. Murder will out, and no evil can be successfully buried. Having started with one

kind of evil, they had to adopt another kind to try to protect it. They had to lie to Jacob. Thus their relationship to their father was poisoned. So was their relationship to one another. How did they know that one of them might not betray the secret? They were like men who had to walk henceforth with the haunted sense that something was following them. "Our fatal shadows that walk by us still." [3] So it always is with hidden guilt. Macbeth and Lady Macbeth could not forget the blood of Duncan, and even in the midst of a feast Macbeth sees Banquo's ghost. Remember Hawthorne's description of Arthur Dimmesdale in *The Scarlet Letter.* The most terrible nemesis of guilt may be that its ghosts arise even in the moments when there seems least likelihood. The moment here, when it was said of Joseph's brothers that **they were afraid,** was the finding of the money in their sacks. That might naturally have been a moment for happy excitement and delighted gratitude. They knew they had not stolen the money. Their hands in this instance were clean. Why could they not assume therefore that this was an amazing act of generosity which they could accept with rejoicing? The reason was that they knew they did not deserve generosity and so they could not believe in it. Even if they were innocent in this matter they could not think of themselves as innocent, or suppose that others would so consider them. Their record had its foundation in rottenness, and therefore they were fearful that any accident might bring the structure of life tumbling down. So **they were afraid,** as men always will be when they have flaunted God's moral realities. Because they have not had a holy and a saving fear they dwell continually in a shameful fear—the fear that their flimsy pretenses will collapse. The foolish and the flippant sometimes argue that religion is weakening because men then depend no longer on themselves. They had better not! A house rests on its foundations; and a life that is to stand stanch and

[3] John Fletcher, *Upon an Honest Man's Fortune.*

21 ¶ And they said one to another. We *are* verily guilty concerning our brother, in that we saw the anguish of his soul, when he besought us, and we would not hear; therefore is this distress come upon us.

22 And Reuben answered them, saying, Spake I not unto you, saying, Do not sin against the child; and ye would not hear? therefore, behold, also his blood is required.

23 And they knew not that Joseph understood *them;* for he spake unto them by an interpreter.

24 And he turned himself about from them, and went; and returned to them again, and communed with them, and took from them Simeon, and bound him before their eyes.

25 ¶ Then Joseph commanded to fill their sacks with corn, and to restore every man's money into his sack, and to give them provision for the way: and thus did he unto them.

And they did so. 21 Then they said to one another, "In truth we are guilty concerning our brother, in that we saw the distress of his soul, when he besought us and we would not listen; therefore is this distress come upon us." 22 And Reuben answered them, "Did I not tell you not to sin against the lad? But you would not listen. So now there comes a reckoning for his blood." 23 They did not know that Joseph understood them, for there was an interpreter between them. 24 Then he turned away from them and wept; and he returned to them and spoke to them. And he took Simeon from them and bound him before their eyes. 25 And Joseph gave orders to fill their bags with grain, and to replace every man's money in his sack, and to give them provisions for the journey. This was done for them.

---

21. See Exeg. on vs. 7 above.

25. This verse is from E, except the clause **and to replace every man's money in his sack.** Thus, according to this document, the men were given **provisions for the journey.** They would therefore not open their sacks until they reached home.

---

unafraid against all the winds that blow must be founded on that deep adjustment to the everlasting facts of truth and righteousness which the Bible calls "the fear of the Lord."

21. *Nemesis.*—Here is a picture of the fact that buried guilt will not stay buried, but rises again as a terrifying ghost. These brothers of Joseph had done an evil thing, and they knew it, but had tried to forget it. People looking on them from the outside might not suspect the guilt that festered within. Their father did not know, and perhaps no one else knew, that they had sold their brother into slavery and to what might have been death. But because *they* knew, they could not kill their uneasiness. Even when no consequence had caught up with them, they always secretly feared it would. Now they thought it had. **Therefore is this distress come upon us.**

What was the sin of these brothers, and in what way does it represent a continually recurring human sin? Essentially it was the sin of betraying those right relationships of life which are ordained by God. They were all sons of one father, and they lied to him, betrayed him, and committed a cruelty that had broken his heart. They were brothers to Joseph and they treated him not as a brother but as an enemy. Their own particular impulses of anger,

jealousy, and self-assertion had torn relationships in pieces.

There is no ultimate meaning in life without right relationships. Consider the illustration of a symphony orchestra. Suppose the violinists in angry petulance or jealousy insisted upon playing on one string, or the cornetist blasted on his horn, or the man at the kettledrum banged it when he felt inclined. Here would be individual license turning what ought to be co-operation into ugly chaos. So in the larger facts of life. The man who begins to drink too much cannot co-ordinate, either physically or morally. He may argue that as an individual he is free to do as he pleases. But engrossed in one appetite, he loses increasingly his intelligent human contacts, responsibilities, and loyalties. A man and woman falling in love establish a new relationship, but selfishness on the part of either one, or unwillingness for mutual adjustment, will destroy it. In the business and industrial world the gravest evils come from failure in relationship: a hard employer treating men as impersonal tools; the employee shrugging off responsibility for honest work. In international affairs the repudiation of relationships lies at the root of war and its world-wide wreckage. Consider the Nazi philosophy, which scoffed at any relationship to the rest of the world except

26 And they laded their asses with the corn, and departed thence.

27 And as one of them opened his sack to give his ass provender in the inn, he espied his money; for, behold, it *was* in his sack's mouth.

28 And he said unto his brethren, My money is restored; and, lo, *it is* even in my sack: and their heart failed *them,* and they were afraid, saying one to another, What *is* this *that* God hath done unto us?

29 ¶ And they came unto Jacob their father unto the land of Canaan, and told him all that befell unto them; saying,

30 The man, *who is* the lord of the land, spake roughly to us, and took us for spies of the country.

31 And we said unto him, We *are* true *men;* we are no spies:

32 We *be* twelve brethren, sons of our father; one *is* not, and the youngest *is* this day with our father in the land of Canaan.

33 And the man, the lord of the country, said unto us, Hereby shall I know that ye *are* true *men;* leave one of your brethren *here* with me, and take *food for* the famine of your households, and be gone:

26 Then they loaded their asses with their grain, and departed. 27 And as one of them opened his sack to give his ass provender at the lodging place, he saw his money in the mouth of his sack; 28 and he said to his brothers, "My money has been put back; here it is in the mouth of my sack!" At this their hearts failed them, and they turned trembling to one another, saying, "What is this that God has done to us?"

29 When they came to Jacob their father in the land of Canaan, they told him all that had befallen them, saying, 30 "The man, the lord of the land, spoke roughly to us, and took us to be spies of the land. 31 But we said to him, 'We are honest men, we are not spies; 32 we are twelve brothers, sons of our father; one is no more, and the youngest is this day with our father in the land of Canaan.' 33 Then the man, the lord of the land, said to us, 'By this I shall know that you are honest men: leave one of your brothers with me, and take grain for the famine of your households, and go your

---

3. The Brothers' Return to Canaan (42:26-38)

27. This verse and vs. 28*a* are from J (see vs. 25), who (cf. 43:21) went on to tell how all the brothers at once opened their sacks. This notice was dropped by RJE because of vs. 35 (E).

28. What is this that God has done to us? See Exeg. on vs. 7. J regularly uses **God** instead of "the Lord" (Yahweh) in the Joseph story after ch. 39.

30-37. This passage is from E. Thus, according to that document, the brothers told Jacob immediately upon their arrival home of Joseph's demand to see Benjamin; and the second journey was undertaken at once in order to secure the release of Simeon. The J narrative ran somewhat differently. Nothing was said by the brothers of Joseph's demand until, when the grain was exhausted, Jacob asked them to go to Egypt again

---

to master it. Consider isolationism in the United States with its mean indifference to constructive international accord. In every case the violation of human relationships is due to the breaking of men's obedient relationship to the remembered will of God.

How are men saved from the sin and guilt of wrong relationships? Through recognition of their sin and through repentance. But repentance often cannot come directly out of the heart which sin has hardened. The saving element may need to be made possible through the forgiveness of the one who has been injured. So with the brothers of Joseph. Because he treated them as brothers, they at last could be his

brothers again. Thus we gain a glimpse into salvation through Christ. He, the Elder Brother, can relieve human souls from the burden of their guilt and bring them back to right relationships in the Father's family. It is the restoration of right relationships therefore which all followers of Christ must strive for. Consider the Christian's duty to rise like Joseph above personal injury and prejudice into a larger magnanimity.

Only such a spirit can redeem industrial relationships. Read the life of William Henry Baldwin, Jr., one of the most distinguished railroad executives of the early twentieth century. "Ignorance, arrogance and tyranny rise to the

34 And bring your youngest brother unto me: then shall I know that ye *are* no spies, but *that* ye *are* true *men*: so will I deliver you your brother, and ye shall traffic in the land.

35 ¶ And it came to pass as they emptied their sacks, that, behold, every man's bundle of money *was* in his sack: and when *both* they and their father saw the bundles of money, they were afraid.

36 And Jacob their father said unto them, Me have ye bereaved *of my children:* Joseph *is* not, and Simeon *is* not, and ye will take Benjamin *away:* all these things are against me.

37 And Reuben spake unto his father, saying, Slay my two sons, if I bring him not to thee: deliver him into my hand, and I will bring him to thee again.

38 And he said, My son shall not go down with you; for his brother is dead, and he is left alone: if mischief befall him by the way in the which ye go, then shall ye bring down my gray hairs with sorrow to the grave.

way. 34 Bring your youngest brother to me; then I shall know that you are not spies but honest men, and I will deliver to you your brother, and you shall trade in the land.' "

35 As they emptied their sacks, behold, every man's bundle of money was in his sack; and when they and their father saw their bundles of money, they were dismayed. 36 And Jacob their father said to them, "You have bereaved me of my children: Joseph is no more, and Simeon is no more, and now you would take Benjamin; all this has come upon me." 37 Then Reuben said to his father, "Slay my two sons if I do not bring him back to you; put him in my hands, and I will bring him back to you." 38 But he said, "My son shall not go down with you, for his brother is dead, and he only is left. If harm should befall him on the journey that you are to make, you would bring down my gray hairs with sorrow to Sheol."

to replenish their supply (43:2). Only then did they break the news to him that Benjamin must accompany them. Jacob's reply to this is now contained in 42:38, which was placed in its present position by RJE when he combined the two narratives. Judah's words in 43:3-5 were thus in their original context his reply to his father's refusal to permit Benjamin to go (42:38).

35. This verse awkwardly breaks the connection between vss. 34 and 36. It cannot be from J, in view of vss. 27-28. It is probably a secondary elaboration of the E narrative.

36-37. Me and upon me are both emphatic. Jacob reminds them that it is his children, not their own, that they are disposing of one by one. Reuben's reply in vs. 37 is thus to the point.

38. On the grave or Sheol (RSV) see Exeg. on 37:35.

top in organized labor," he said, "whenever such organization is opposed by tyranny and arrogance, and in my experience I have seen as much of these qualities of human nature in the employer as in the employee." [4] Carroll D. Wright, United States Commissioner of Labor, said of him; "If you could get Baldwin's capacity, sympathy, and moral interest into all our big employers, there would be an end to all really serious labor trouble within two years." [5]

So in politics, a great man is not the narrow partisan but an Abraham Lincoln, "with malice toward none, with charity for all."

[4] John Graham Brooks, *An American Citizen* (Boston: Houghton Mifflin Co., 1910), p. 164.
[5] *Ibid.*, p. 148.

35. See Expos. on vss. 18, 35.

36-38. *Jacob's Grief.*—The shadow of what threatens to be a new calamity falls on the old man. The partiality which he had had for Joseph has been transferred to Benjamin; and now there is danger that he may lose him. Simeon may be lost too; and for all these afflictions he blames the other brothers. But there is one brighter element in what his words disclose about himself. At least his sense of values is higher than it once was. When he was with Laban his mind was much on how he could get more sheep and cattle. He knows more surely now that life for him is in his children. (In connection with the words of Reuben [vss. 22, 37] see Expos. on 38:21-22, 29-30.)

43 And the famine *was* sore in the land.

2 And it came to pass, when they had eaten up the corn which they had brought out of Egypt, their father said unto them, Go again, buy us a little food.

3 And Judah spake unto him, saying, The man did solemnly protest unto us, saying, Ye shall not see my face, except your brother *be* with you.

4 If thou wilt send our brother with us, we will go down and buy thee food:

5 But if thou wilt not send *him,* we will not go down: for the man said unto us, Ye shall not see my face, except your brother *be* with you.

6 And Israel said, Wherefore dealt ye *so* ill with me, *as* to tell the man whether ye had yet a brother?

7 And they said, The man asked us straitly of our state, and of our kindred, saying, *Is* your father yet alive? have ye *another* brother? and we told him according to the tenor of these words: Could we certainly know that he would say, Bring your brother down?

8 And Judah said unto Israel his father, Send the lad with me, and we will arise and go; that we may live, and not die, both we, and thou, *and* also our little ones.

9 I will be surety for him; of my hand shalt thou require him: if I bring him not unto thee, and set him before thee, then let me bear the blame for ever:

10 For except we had lingered, surely now we had returned this second time.

11 And their father Israel said unto them, If *it must be* so now, do this; take of

43 Now the famine was severe in the land. 2 And when they had eaten the grain which they had brought from Egypt, their father said to them, "Go again, buy us a little food." 3 But Judah said to him, "The man solemnly warned us, saying, 'You shall not see my face, unless your brother is with you.' 4 If you will send our brother with us, we will go down and buy you food; 5 but if you will not send him, we will not go down, for the man said to us, 'You shall not see my face, unless your brother is with you.'" 6 Israel said, "Why did you treat me so ill as to tell the man that you had another brother?" 7 They replied, "The man questioned us carefully about ourselves and our kindred, saying, 'Is your father still alive? Have you another brother?' What we told him was in answer to these questions; could we in any way know that he would say, 'Bring your brother down'?" 8 And Judah said to Israel his father, "Send the lad with me, and we will arise and go, that we may live and not die, both we and you and also our little ones. 9 I will be surety for him; of my hand you shall require him. If I do not bring him back to you and set him before you, then let me bear the blame for ever; 10 for if we had not delayed, we would now have returned twice."

11 Then their father Israel said to them,

43:1-14. *Jacob's Appeal.*—Swiftly and vividly there is given the tense conference between Jacob and the older brothers, with Judah as their spokesman. With a heavy heart Jacob agrees at last to their insistence that he allow Benjamin to go down with them this time to Egypt. He supposes that their errand may have its way to the Egyptian's favor smoothed by gifts, and so he bids his sons to take of the best fruits in the land, . . . and carry down the man a present, a little balm, and a little honey, spices, and myrrh, nuts and almonds: and take double money in your hand. It was a natural supposition, and seemingly a wise one. He did not know that the man in Egypt was one who had no desire for presents, and that already his heart was reaching out to him. Unconsciously

Jacob was enacting here a parable of the mistake men make in a far higher relationship. The mercy of God is often as unrealized as Joseph's mercy was by Jacob. God may be thought of as someone off at a distance, holding in his hand the issues of life and death, but with his disposition hidden from our knowledge. Therefore he must be placated with material gifts and sacrifice. But all the while God's goodness needs no buying. As with Joseph and Jacob, his compassion foreruns our appeal.

I sought the Lord, and afterward I knew
He moved my soul to seek him, seeking me.[6]

8. See Expos. on 37:26-27.

[6] Author of this hymn is unknown.

the best fruits in the land in your vessels, and carry down the man a present, a little balm, and a little honey, spices and myrrh, nuts and almonds:

12 And take double money in your hand; and the money that was brought again in the mouth of your sacks, carry *it* again in your hand; peradventure it *was* an oversight.

13 Take also your brother, and arise, go again unto the man:

14 And God Almighty give you mercy before the man, that he may send away your other brother, and Benjamin. If I be bereaved *of my children,* I am bereaved.

15 ¶ And the men took that present, and they took double money in their hand, and Benjamin; and rose up, and went down to Egypt, and stood before Joseph.

16 And when Joseph saw Benjamin with them, he said to the ruler of his house, Bring *these* men home, and slay, and make ready; for *these* men shall dine with me at noon.

17 And the man did as Joseph bade; and the man brought the men into Joseph's house.

"If it must be so, then do this: take some of the choice fruits of the land in your bags, and carry down to the man a present, a little balm and a little honey, gum, myrrh, pistachio nuts, and almonds. **12** Take double the money with you; carry back with you the money that was returned in the mouth of your sacks; perhaps it was an oversight. **13** Take also your brother, and arise, go again to the man; **14** may God Almighty*p* grant you mercy before the man, that he may send back your other brother and Benjamin. If I am bereaved of my children, I am bereaved." **15** So the men took the present, and they took double the money with them, and Benjamin; and they arose and went down to Egypt, and stood before Joseph.

16 When Joseph saw Benjamin with them, he said to the steward of his house, "Bring the men into the house, and slaughter an animal and make ready, for the men are to dine with me at noon." **17** The man did as Joseph bade him, and

p Heb *El Shaddai*

4. The Brothers' Second Journey to Egypt (43:1-15)

43:14. The reference to the **other brother,** Simeon, indicates that this verse is from E, as is vs. 23*b*. Apart from these two fragments, chs. 43–44 are from J. On **El Shaddai** (RSV mg.) see Exeg. on 17:1.

5. Joseph's Meeting with Benjamin (43:16-34)

16. The mention of **Benjamin** is awkward in view of vs. 29 and is probably a gloss, the original reading being "Now when Joseph saw them."

14. See Expos. on 42:36-38.

15-34. *Brotherly Love.*—Ch. 42 began to sound a new note in the story of Joseph—his yearning for his younger brother (see 42:4, 15-16, 20, 34). This note now becomes predominant. Benjamin appears before Joseph (vs. 15). Joseph orders a feast of welcome; he releases Simeon, with **Peace be to you, fear not;** and when he looks at Benjamin again and cries out a blessing in the name of God upon him, he is so moved that he cannot control himself and goes out where he may weep. Nor is it only in the story of Joseph that this note of the love of brother for brother is new. It is new for the whole of Genesis. Other human relationships have been emphasized and made beautiful: the love of man and woman, as between Abraham and Sarah, Jacob and Rachel; the love of father

and son, as with Abraham and Isaac, Jacob and Joseph; the love of mother to child, as with Hagar and Ishmael, Rebekah and Jacob. But a brother has not yet been pictured as devoted to another brother; not Ishmael and Isaac, not Esau and Jacob; not the older sons of Jacob among themselves. But Joseph's love for Benjamin is deep and passionate. Those other relationships are perhaps easier to achieve than this love of Joseph for Benjamin. The bond between father and son may involve no rivalry, for each one can give expansion to the other's life. The love of a man for a woman has the binding power of the two complementary sexes. But two brothers in a family may seem only to get in each other's way. They are on the same level and may become rivals. In the early chapters of Genesis the instances of the relationship

18 And the men were afraid, because they were brought into Joseph's house; and they said, Because of the money that was returned in our sacks at the first time are we brought in; that he may seek occasion against us, and fall upon us, and take us for bondmen, and our asses.

19 And they came near to the steward of Joseph's house, and they communed with him at the door of the house,

20 And said, O sir, we came indeed down at the first time to buy food:

21 And it came to pass, when we came to the inn, that we opened our sacks, and, behold, *every* man's money *was* in the mouth of his sack, our money in full weight: and we have brought it again in our hand.

22 And other money have we brought down in our hands to buy food: we cannot tell who put our money in our sacks.

23 And he said, Peace *be* to you, fear not: your God, and the God of your father, hath given you treasure in your sacks: I had your money. And he brought Simeon out unto them.

24 And the man brought the men into Joseph's house, and gave *them* water, and they washed their feet; and he gave their asses provender.

25 And they made ready the present against Joseph came at noon: for they heard that they should eat bread there.

26 ¶ And when Joseph came home, they brought him the present which *was* in their hand into the house, and bowed themselves to him to the earth.

27 And he asked them of *their* welfare, and said, *Is* your father well, the old man of whom ye spake? *Is* he yet alive?

28 And they answered, Thy servant our father *is* in good health, he *is* yet alive. And they bowed down their heads, and made obeisance.

brought the men to Joseph's house. 18 And the men were afraid because they were brought to Joseph's house, and they said, "It is because of the money which was replaced in our sacks the first time, that we are brought in, so that he may seek occasion against us and fall upon us, to make slaves of us and seize our asses." 19 So they went up to the steward of Joseph's house, and spoke with him at the door of the house, 20 and said, "Oh, my lord, we came down the first time to buy food; 21 and when we came to the lodging place we opened our sacks, and there was every man's money in the mouth of his sack, our money in full weight; so we have brought it again with us, 22 and we have brought other money down in our hand to buy food. We do not know who put our money in our sacks." 23 He replied, "Rest assured, do not be afraid; your God and the God of your father must have put treasure in your sacks for you; I received your money." Then he brought Simeon out to them. 24 And when the man had brought the men into Joseph's house, and given them water, and they had washed their feet, and when he had given their asses provender, 25 they made ready the present for Joseph's coming at noon, for they heard that they should eat bread there.

26 When Joseph came home, they brought into the house to him the present which they had with them, and bowed down to him to the ground. 27 And he inquired about their welfare, and said, "Is your father well, the old man of whom you spoke? Is he still alive?" 28 They said, "Your servant our father is well, he is still alive." And they bowed their heads and made

---

27. The question as to whether Jacob was **still alive** indicates that some time had elapsed since the brothers' first journey.

---

of brothers are anything but admirable. Cain becomes so sullen and bitter against his brother Abel that he kills him. Jacob is so envious of the opportunity of Esau that he defrauds him of his birthright. But here in the story of Joseph and Benjamin the beauty that can be in brotherhood comes into the light. Joseph had

loved Benjamin with all the complex of affection associated with his feeling for his father and mother. He loved him as the companion of his boyhood (but see Exeg. on 42:1–45:28), and with a protectiveness which he had never lost. Thought lingers upon this picture of a brother's devotion; and then turns forward to

29 And he lifted up his eyes, and saw his brother Benjamin, his mother's son, and said, *Is* this your younger brother, of whom ye spake unto me? And he said, God be gracious unto thee, my son.

30 And Joseph made haste; for his bowels did yearn upon his brother: and he sought *where* to weep; and he entered into *his* chamber, and wept there.

31 And he washed his face, and went out, and refrained himself, and said, Set on bread.

32 And they set on for him by himself, and for them by themselves, and for the Egyptians, which did eat with him, by themselves: because the Egyptians might not eat bread with the Hebrews; for that *is* an abomination unto the Egyptians.

33 And they sat before him, the first-born according to his birthright, and the youngest according to his youth: and the men marveled one at another.

34 And he took *and sent* messes unto them from before him: but Benjamin's mess was five times so much as any of theirs. And they drank, and were merry with him.

44 And he commanded the steward of his house, saying, Fill the men's sacks *with* food, as much as they can carry, and put every man's money in his sack's mouth.

obeisance. **29** And he lifted up his eyes, and saw his brother Benjamin, his mother's son, and said, "Is this your youngest brother, of whom you spoke to me? God be gracious to you, my son!" **30** Then Joseph made haste, for his heart yearned for his brother, and he sought a place to weep. And he entered his chamber and wept there. **31** Then he washed his face and came out; and controlling himself he said, "Let food be served." **32** They served him by himself, and them by themselves, and the Egyptians who ate with him by themselves, because the Egyptians might not eat bread with the Hebrews, for that is an abomination to the Egyptians. **33** And they sat before him, the first-born according to his birthright and the youngest according to his youth; and the men looked at one another in amazement. **34** Portions were taken to them from Joseph's table, but Benjamin's portion was five times as much as any of theirs. So they drank and were merry with him.

44 Then he commanded the steward of his house, "Fill the men's sacks with food, as much as they can carry, and put each man's money in the mouth of his

---

32. An interesting glimpse of Egyptian custom. J scarcely intends to suggest that Joseph's isolation was due to his being a Hebrew, but rather to his exalted position and perhaps to his having been admitted to the priestly caste (cf. 41:45).

6. BENJAMIN IN JEOPARDY (44:1-34)

44:1. And put each man's money in the mouth of his sack may be regarded as an inept addition. With it belongs **with his money for the grain** (vs. 2).

---

the lovely story of the spiritual brotherhood between Jonathan and David, and to the words of Jesus, "One is your Master, even Christ; and all ye are brethren" (Matt. 23:8). This is the basis of all ultimate brotherliness.

32. *Joseph's Loyalty.*—Obviously Joseph, with his identity as yet undisclosed, could not sit at the table with his brothers. But neither did he eat with the Egyptians. Why not? To eat with ordinary Hebrews was **an abomination unto the Egyptians;** but it is hardly likely that anyone at Pharaoh's court would have dared to treat Pharaoh's viceroy as an ordinary Hebrew. Indeed, need he have been considered a Hebrew at all? In his lofty status could he not have been held to outrank in Egyptian citizenship

the others in Pharaoh's court? Why then did he not eat with the Egyptians? Was it because he deliberately refrained from incorporating himself into the life of the more privileged people, and, as Moses was afterward to do, kept his devoted loyalty to his own? (But see Exeg.)

44:1-5. *The Discerning Spirit.*—Whether or not Joseph—according to the story—actually used his **cup** for divining is not certain, but it is obvious that the Egyptians thought he did. Among the Egyptians, as among many other ancient peoples, it was a familiar matter to seek supernatural guidance by signs. In Exod. 7 appear "the wise men," "the sorcerers," and "the magicians" of the court of Pharaoh. Repeatedly in the O.T. it is evident that the Israelites also took for granted this efficacy of magic and necromancy (see Num. 22:7; Judg. 6:21; I Sam. 9:18; 14:41-42; 28:7). Nor does belief in seers, magicians, medicine men, and all the paraphernalia of the mysterious belong only to primitive periods. Thousands of present-day people, sometimes at first sheepishly but sometimes then with a credulity that grows slavish, go peering into the shadow world where they think mysterious forces move. Joseph's divining cup was supposed to give guidance according to the patterns in which little pieces of gold and silver dropped into it were seen to fall. So people today will give at least a half belief to the fortuneteller who announces what will happen to them according to the pattern of tea leaves in a cup. Multitudes give much more than a half belief to other kinds of occult knowledge. Note the numbers in any community who will be drawn to the seances of a medium who is well advertised. Note the still more conspicuous fascination of astrology.

What do these facts suggest? A truth which the crudities mixed with it must not eclipse, viz., that there is a realm of genuine mystery that lies outside and around our ordinary comprehension. In the words of Hamlet,

There are more things in heaven and earth, Horatio,
Than are dreamt of in your philosophy.[7]

The realities in the midst of which life moves cannot be bounded by any brash definition. A sense of wonder is a spring of the expansion of the soul. To feel that there is something in our universe greater than our easy understanding, something to be sought after with humility and awe—that is what makes man different from the animal, and that is the beginning of religion. Therefore it is right to respect all gropings of men's souls toward what is to them the Great Unknown. From the perspective of a larger revelation many primitive religions, and much in some contemporary religions, may seem to be only superstition. But in that alloy of ignorance may be recognized the thread of gold. By recognition of this truth Christian missions to non-Christian lands have gained the effective wisdom of a new sympathy.

But on the other hand, it is equally a duty to separate the truth from the crude alloy, with gentleness for others, in resolute devotion to the truth itself. Often there is resistance to this, such as the resistance of Roman Catholicism in willingness to compromise with paganism among ignorant multitudes, and thus to exploit their loyalty to priestcraft and to an obscurantist ecclesiastical domination. We dare not forget the words of Jesus, "Thou shalt love the Lord thy

[7] Act I, scene 5.

God . . . with all thy mind" (Matt. 22:37). The majesty and mystery of God will always have its widths and depths that cannot be put into any glib rationalizations; but his reality is reflected only as one approaches it with a mind made clean from any lazy ignorance.

Here is the glory of that freedom of thought which the Protestant Reformation brought back into Christianity—a freedom which is not irresponsibility, but on the contrary is the realization that only when every faculty of a man is released for fearless following of the truth do we find him who has made, not part of us only, but all of us for himself.

So we are led to the real meaning of prayer. In even the dim beginnings of religion, where it has not crossed the border from the shadowland of superstition, there is the living germ of prayer. Genuinely even when gropingly, souls in their religious childhood have tried—and many such still are trying—to climb the

altar-stairs
That slope thro' darkness up to God.[8]

Because of the darkness, they have reached out for all sorts of signs to assure them that they were moving toward something or Someone real. But religion which has gained the mature enlightenment which comes from what the O.T. progressively teaches knows that the real signs are not in outward portents, but within. Read ch. i of Harry Emerson Fosdick's The Meaning of Prayer [9] and ch. iii of George A. Buttrick's Prayer.[1] In order to divine the guiding truth that is beyond our immediate ken we do not need Joseph's divining cup; what we need is what we have—a conscience that turns deliberately toward God's light, and prays that he may "take the dimness of my soul away."[2]

1-13. Benjamin Is Brought Back.—Here Joseph has his servants repeat, with partial alteration, the device which he had used earlier to bring the older brothers back into his presence. As money had been put secretly into all their sacks before, now his own cup is sent off with them; but this time it is in the sack of Benjamin. In the story, as the narrator develops it, the suspense and tension keep increasing. It seemed acute enough when the older brothers were in danger of being accused of being thieves, but now Benjamin is involved: Benjamin the beloved of his father, Benjamin of whom Judah had promised his father, "I will be surety for him. . . . If I bring him not unto thee, . . . then

[8] Tennyson, In Memoriam, part lv.
[9] New York: Association Press, 1915.
[1] New York and Nashville: Abingdon-Cokesbury Press, 1942.
[2] George Croly, "Spirit of God, descend upon my heart."

2 And put my cup, the silver cup, in the sack's mouth of the youngest, and his corn money. And he did according to the word that Joseph had spoken.

3 As soon as the morning was light, the men were sent away, they and their asses.

4 *And* when they were gone out of the city, *and* not *yet* far off, Joseph said unto his steward, Up, follow after the men; and when thou dost overtake them, say unto them, Wherefore have ye rewarded evil for good?

5 *Is* not this *it* in which my lord drinketh, and whereby indeed he divineth? ye have done evil in so doing.

6 ¶ And he overtook them, and he spake unto them these same words.

7 And they said unto him, Wherefore saith my lord these words? God forbid that thy servants should do according to this thing:

8 Behold, the money, which we found in our sacks' mouths, we brought again unto thee out of the land of Canaan: how then should we steal out of thy lord's house silver or gold?

9 With whomsoever of thy servants it be found, both let him die, and we also will be my lord's bondmen.

10 And he said, Now also *let* it *be* according unto your words: he with whom it is found shall be my servant; and ye shall be blameless.

11 Then they speedily took down every man his sack to the ground, and opened every man his sack.

12 And he searched, *and* began at the eldest, and left at the youngest: and the cup was found in Benjamin's sack.

13 Then they rent their clothes, and laded every man his ass, and returned to the city.

14 ¶ And Judah and his brethren came to Joseph's house; for he *was* yet there: and they fell before him on the ground.

sack, 2 and put my cup, the silver cup, in the mouth of the sack of the youngest, with his money for the grain." And he did as Joseph told him. 3 As soon as the morning was light, the men were sent away with their asses. 4 When they had gone but a short distance from the city, Joseph said to his steward, "Up, follow after the men; and when you overtake them, say to them, 'Why have you returned evil for good? Why have you stolen my silver cup?*q* 5 Is it not from this that my lord drinks, and by this that he divines? You have done wrong in so doing.'"

6 When he overtook them, he spoke to them these words. 7 They said to him, "Why does my lord speak such words as these? Far be it from your servants that they should do such a thing! 8 Behold, the money which we found in the mouth of our sacks, we brought back to you from the land of Canaan; how then should we steal silver or gold from your lord's house? 9 With whomever of your servants it be found, let him die, and we also will be my lord's slaves." 10 He said, "Let it be as you say: he with whom it is found shall be my slave, and the rest of you shall be blameless." 11 Then every man quickly lowered his sack to the ground, and every man opened his sack. 12 And he searched, beginning with the eldest and ending with the youngest; and the cup was found in Benjamin's sack. 13 Then they rent their clothes, and every man loaded his ass, and they returned to the city.

14 When Judah and his brothers came to Joseph's house, he was still there; and

q Gk Compare **Vg:** Heb lacks *Why have you stolen my silver cup?*

let me bear the blame for ever" (43:9), Benjamin whom, without realizing it (vs. 9), they had specified when they said that if anyone should be found with the cup, **Let him die, and we also will be my lord's bondmen.** No wonder **they rent their clothes.** It seemed that the meshes of old guilt had entangled them in inexorable punishment now, even in a matter of which they knew that they were innocent. But actually it

would be only a part of the mounting drama which was to lead in a few hours to the disclosure of Joseph and his forgiveness, and would give Joseph the occasion to keep Benjamin and send back to old Jacob the glad news of the welcome waiting for them all in Egypt.

14-34. Judah's Plea.—Not many prose passages in any literature can compare in beauty and poignancy with this writing of an ancient

15 And Joseph said unto them, What deed *is* this that ye have done? wot ye not that such a man as I can certainly divine?

16 And Judah said, What shall we say unto my lord? what shall we speak? or how shall we clear ourselves? God hath found out the iniquity of thy servants: behold, we *are* my lord's servants, both we, and *he* also with whom the cup is found.

17 And he said, God forbid that I should do so: *but* the man in whose hand the cup is found, he shall be my servant; and as for you, get you up in peace unto your father.

18 ¶ Then Judah came near unto him, and said, O my lord, let thy servant, I pray thee, speak a word in my lord's ears, and let not thine anger burn against thy servant: for thou *art* even as Pharaoh.

19 My lord asked his servants, saying, Have ye a father, or a brother?

20 And we said unto my lord, We have a father, an old man, and a child of his old age, a little one; and his brother is dead, and he alone is left of his mother, and his father loveth him.

21 And thou saidst unto thy servants, Bring him down unto me, that I may set mine eyes upon him.

they fell before him to the ground. 15 Joseph said to them, "What deed is this that you have done? Do you not know that such a man as I can indeed divine?" 16 And Judah said, "What shall we say to my lord? What shall we speak? Or how can we clear ourselves? God has found out the guilt of your servants; behold, we are my lord's slaves, both we and he also in whose hand the cup has been found." 17 But he said, "Far be it from me that I should do so! Only the man in whose hand the cup was found shall be my slave; but as for you, go up in peace to your father."

18 Then Judah went up to him and said, "O my lord, let your servant, I pray you, speak a word in my lord's ears, and let not your anger burn against your servant; for you are like Pharaoh himself. 19 My lord asked his servants, saying, 'Have you a father, or a brother?' 20 And we said to my lord, 'We have a father, an old man, and a young brother, the child of his old age; and his brother is dead, and he alone is left of his mother's children; and his father loves him.' 21 Then you said to your servants, 'Bring him down to me, that I may

16. **The guilt** is, of course, that of their treatment of Joseph years before. (Skinner, *Genesis*, p. 485, it may be noted, denies this, though without giving his reasons.)

18-34. Judah's speech in these verses is one of the best pieces of writing found in J, and indeed in the O.T.

and unnamed Hebrew as it has come down to us in the KJV. For here is no artifice of wording. Here instead are the fundamental emotions of human life, expressed with a simplicity so immediate and spontaneous that they find their echo in hearts of every generation.

The brothers of Joseph had originally seemed to be a sorry lot—narrow-minded, jealous, and vindictive. But it may be that the experience of life, and especially the lesson of hard years, had begun to change them. It is a happy fact to have it suggested thus early in the O.T. that men who have been evil may repent. Whether this was wholly true or not of all the brothers, Judah at any rate appears as different; and Judah is the spokesman for the others. What he says is what they all have at least begun to feel. They had begun to understand that one of the worst of human sins is hardheartedness. They had been cruel because they did not care. Note how that sin and the retribution of it re-echo in the pages of the Bible. Nathan is standing before

David and telling him the shattering story of the rich man who took the poor man's lamb; and he makes David condemn himself with the indignant cry, "As the LORD liveth, the man that hath done this thing shall surely die . . . because he had no pity" (II Sam. 12:5-6). Amos is pronouncing judgment and doom upon the ruthless people of his time, summing up their evil in this, that they were "not grieved for the affliction of Joseph" (Amos 6:6). Consider Jesus' terrible arraignment of the Pharisees in Matt. 23. He could forgive the weak and erring, but his anger blazed at men who had no pity for the little people. Read the parable of the unmerciful servant in Matt. 18, to whom the final devastating question was, "Shouldest not thou also have had compassion?"

Joseph's brothers had begun to learn what the real values of life are. See them reflected in the matchless plea which Judah makes to Joseph. He does not know who Joseph is, but he understands the emotions which every decent man

22 And we said unto my lord, The lad cannot leave his father: for *if* he should leave his father, *his father* would die.

23 And thou saidst unto thy servants, Except your youngest brother come down with you, ye shall see my face no more.

24 And it came to pass when we came up unto thy servant my father, we told him the words of my lord.

25 And our father said, Go again, *and* buy us a little food.

26 And we said, We cannot go down: if our youngest brother be with us, then will we go down: for we may not see the man's face, except our youngest brother *be* with us.

27 And thy servant my father said unto us, Ye know that my wife bare me two *sons:*

28 And the one went out from me, and I said, Surely he is torn in pieces; and I saw him not since:

29 And if ye take this also from me, and mischief befall him, ye shall bring down my gray hairs with sorrow to the grave.

30 Now therefore when I come to thy servant my father, and the lad *be* not with us; seeing that his life is bound up in the lad's life;

31 It shall come to pass, when he seeth that the lad *is* not *with us,* that he will die: and thy servants shall bring down the gray hairs of thy servant our father with sorrow to the grave.

32 For thy servant became surety for the lad unto my father, saying, If I bring him not unto thee, then I shall bear the blame to my father for ever.

33 Now therefore, I pray thee, let thy servant abide instead of the lad a bondman to my lord; and let the lad go up with his brethren.

set my eyes upon him.' 22 We said to my lord, 'The lad cannot leave his father, for if he should leave his father, his father would die.' 23 Then you said to your servants, 'Unless your youngest brother comes down with you, you shall see my face no more.' 24 When we went back to your servant my father we told him the words of my lord. 25 And when our father said, 'Go again, buy us a little food,' 26 we said, 'We cannot go down. If our youngest brother goes with us, then we will go down; for we cannot see the man's face unless our youngest brother is with us.' 27 Then your servant my father said to us, 'You know that my wife bore me two sons; 28 one left me, and I said, Surely he has been torn to pieces; and I have never seen him since. 29 If you take this one also from me, and harm befalls him, you will bring down my gray hairs in sorrow to Sheol.' 30 Now therefore, when I come to your servant my father, and the lad is not with us, then, as his life is bound up in the lad's life, 31 when he sees that the lad is not with us, he will die; and your servants will bring down the gray hairs of your servant our father with sorrow to Sheol. 32 For your servant became surety for the lad to my father, saying, 'If I do not bring him back to you, then I shall bear the blame in the sight of my father all my life.' 33 Now therefore, let your servant, I pray you, remain instead of the lad as a slave to my lord; and

responds to: the sorrow of a man's heart over a lost son, the wistfulness of old age, the memory of a dead mother, the protective love for a youngest child. In the name of these Judah pleads, because he knows instinctively that such a plea ought not to be in vain. And his feeling is not a matter of words only: he is ready to act in a spirit exactly opposite from the spirit he had earlier followed. Once he had helped to sell a brother into slavery; now (vs. 33) he is asking to be put in prison himself in order that another brother may go free.

A chance for the searching of our own hearts

is here. What has life done to us, and what do we respond to? Has life made us callous, so that we are ashamed lest somebody should call us "sentimental"? Or have we learned, like Judah, even if it is by the hard way as was the case with him, that a man can begin to live with himself only when he knows that the great affections are beyond all other things supremely worth preserving? The man who is hard to others turns his own soul into stone, and the whole ground of his life's best possibility for happiness grows barren. In I Pet. 3:8 there are two beautiful words: "Be pitiful." They make a summary

34 For how shall I go up to my father, and the lad *be* not with me? lest peradventure I see the evil that shall come on my father.

45 Then Joseph could not refrain himself before all them that stood by him; and he cried, Cause every man to go out from me. And there stood no man with him, while Joseph made himself known unto his brethren.

2 And he wept aloud: and the Egyptians and the house of Pharaoh heard.

3 And Joseph said unto his brethren, I *am* Joseph; doth my father yet live? And his brethren could not answer him; for they were troubled at his presence.

let the lad go back with his brothers. 34 For how can I go back to my father if the lad is not with me? I fear to see the evil that would come upon my father."

45 Then Joseph could not control himself before all those who stood by him; and he cried, "Make every one go out from me." So no one stayed with him when Joseph made himself known to his brothers. 2 And he wept aloud, so that the Egyptians heard it, and the household of Pharaoh heard it. 3 And Joseph said to his brothers, "I am Joseph; is my father still alive?" But his brothers could not answer him, for they were dismayed at his presence.

C. JOSEPH REVEALS HIS IDENTITY (45:1-28)

This chapter is a conflation of J and E. These two narratives varied only in minor details. To be noted especially is the philosophy of history presented in vss. 7, 8*a*. The former of these is from J, who thus maintains that the brothers, in selling Joseph to the Ishmaelites, had unwittingly been carrying out God's will. That J was not entirely oblivious of the difficulty involved in this interpretation of the event is indicated by the preceding section of this narrative—the account of the way in which Joseph labored to bring his brothers to acknowledge their guilt. Nevertheless, the moral difficulty remains that a deliberately sinful act is represented as having been practically caused by God.

---

of what Judah had learned, and of what he tried to say.

45:1-5. *God Turns Evil to Good.*—Joseph's remark to his brothers (vs. 5) seems at first like strange and indefensible counsel. Joseph's brothers not to be distressed or angry with themselves? Why was that not exactly what they should have been? Earlier in the story (see Expos. on 42:21) we hear what they themselves had been driven to confess. "We are verily guilty concerning our brother," they said to one another, "in that we saw the anguish of his soul, when he besought us, and we would not hear. Therefore is this distress come upon us," they concluded, as they looked around at the walls of an Egyptian prison and wondered whether they would ever get out. Retribution had caught up with them and they knew it was deserved. If anything at this moment appeared certain, it was that they ought to be angry with themselves—and to wish that they had been angry and disgusted a long time before.

For now they were facing something worse than punishment. They were facing the final exposure of their own souls to themselves, and they found that revelation sickening. They had evaded that acknowledgment before, stifled whatever stirring of conscience they had, and

gone on with bravado. But now the outward disaster cracked the inward repression. All the stifled foulness of their past spilled out where they could see and smell it. They were guilty men, guilty of the kind of sin that offends the elemental decencies. They had not only conceived an outrageous evil against their own brother, but had carried it out with ruthless unconcern for his desperate pleading. They could never be wicked enough to keep from wincing at that recollection. These brothers of Joseph, with the moral consequences overwhelming them at last, were ready to recognize that the Lord did live, and that fact seemed to promise nothing good for them.

But the words of Joseph strike another note. These brothers of his were to look away from themselves to something greater. They were to consider the inexhaustible goodness and grace of God, which could bend even the worst facts to his ultimately redeeming purpose. For men still hardened in their sin that thought would be impossible; or if it were partly laid hold of, it would be perverted. It would be a license for more evil if God was thus so little to be feared. But Joseph knew these men were beginning to be repentant. For the first time they had looked squarely into their own hearts and had recoiled.

4 And Joseph said unto his brethren, Come near to me, I pray you. And they came near. And he said, I *am* Joseph your brother, whom ye sold into Egypt.

5 Now therefore be not grieved, nor angry with yourselves, that ye sold me hither: for God did send me before you to preserve life.

6 For these two years *hath* the famine *been* in the land: and yet *there are* five years, in the which *there shall* neither *be* earing nor harvest.

4 So Joseph said to his brothers, "Come near to me, I pray you." And they came near. And he said, "I am your brother, Joseph, whom you sold into Egypt. 5 And now do not be distressed, or angry with yourselves, because you sold me here; for God sent me before you to preserve life. 6 For the famine has been in the land these two years; and there are yet five years in which there will be neither plowing nor harvest.

It was to meet this difficulty that E, as has already been suggested, told not of Joseph's being sold by his brothers to a passing caravan, but of his being kidnaped before his brothers had finally decided what to do with him.

Henceforth they would not think of the greatness of God as something to be taken advantage of, but as terrible—yet also healing—in its contrast and rebuke. They would see that his purpose was not to destroy life but to preserve it; that to those who defied his purpose he stood as with a drawn sword across their path, but that to those who were ready to learn their lesson he was like a beckoning hand.

Reflect upon the career of Joseph and see how he had exemplified this truth. He had been sensitive to the values of life, not only physical but spiritual also. In Potiphar's house he might have destroyed what was more important than physical existence—destroyed a man's home and chance for happiness; but whatever else was dark to him at that moment, he knew clearly enough that God had meant him for something better than that. When he himself was unjustly put in prison, he again was proof against demoralization because God kept him sensitive to life. His relationships with the other prisoners, and particularly with Pharaoh's former chief butler and chief baker, were not accidental. He was generously interested in other people, and never so much obsessed with his own fate and fortune as to lack a quick imagination for their needs. He had the instinctive sympathy which could read men's trouble in their faces. "Why do you look so sad today?" he said to Pharaoh's officers one morning—the morning after they had had their cryptic dreams. He wanted to help them as far as he could in their difficulties; and there is no sign that he let his feelings rankle when one of them was released to freedom and honor while he himself was left behind forgotten. When the opportunity came to interpret the dream of Pharaoh, he was thinking again of life in an area much larger than his own. He was not reaching out for personal recognition. "It is not in me," he said to Phar-

aoh; "God"—and notice the emphasis on that first word—"God shall give Pharaoh an answer of peace." And the answer that Joseph interpreted, and of which later he was to become the instrument, was possible because the chance to preserve life summoned up his immediate energy and ability. As Pharaoh recognized, he was "discreet and wise"; and his wisdom came from the deep fact which Pharaoh also reflected when he called him "a man in whom the Spirit of God is." If he had not had a divine concern for the fate of a whole people, Joseph might not have had either the foresight or the long patience to become the agent of salvation for Egypt through the years of famine. Let laymen whose business is in practical affairs reflect here upon how high a thing it is to use that opportunity not predominantly for personal advantage but in some far-reaching sense "to preserve life." Which of us, man or woman, does not need the spirit of Joseph as it is expressed at the end of the story: when in spite of reasons he had for returning hurt for hurt, his affection for his family is so clean and true that the one thing he is concerned with is to forgive and to restore. What he wanted to know most was, "Doth my father yet live?" And to the men who had wronged him he did not say, "I am the authority who can break you"; he said, "I am Joseph your brother."

6-8. *Life's Ultimate Perspectives.*—Looking back, Joseph could say that the whole long course of his life had been shaped by God. It was God who had brought him where he was, not chance, nor men's choices, good or evil. But if it seemed that way now, it had certainly not always seemed so. God had not appeared concerned when his brothers put him in the pit, when the caravan took him into slavery in Egypt, when a woman's lies got him undeserved disgrace, when he lay in Pharaoh's prison. Note

7 And God sent me before you to preserve you a posterity in the earth, and to save your lives by a great deliverance.

8 So now *it was* not you *that* sent me hither, but God: and he hath made me a father to Pharaoh, and lord of all his house, and a ruler throughout all the land of Egypt.

7 And God sent me before you to preserve for you a remnant on earth, and to keep alive for you many survivors. 8 So it was not you who sent me here, but God; and he has made me a father to Pharaoh, and lord of all his house and ruler over all the land

---

45:7. It is not impossible that the words **to save your lives by a great deliverance** not only refer to the preservation of Jacob and his family from death by famine, but also point ahead to the deliverance at the Red Sea. If so, then J is representing this event—the greatest in the history of his people—not as historically conditioned but as having been determined by God from the beginning. It thus falls into the category of the supra-temporal.

8. A father to Pharaoh may have been an honorific title of the chief minister (cf. I Macc. 11:32).

---

then the fact that the long reality may be very different from the first appearance, and that God's hand may be moving long before it is revealed. Plainly that was true with Joseph. The very things that seemed at the moment the blindest and most cruel strokes of fate had brought his life to its fulfillment. Think also of the trials of Moses, the development of David's character by the persecution of Saul, the enlargement of the soul of Paul the apostle through the afflictions in which he had learned to glory because he could say at last, "When I am weak, then am I strong" (II Cor. 12:10). As a modern instance, would Franklin D. Roosevelt have attained the degree of power and public influence that he did attain but for the self-mastery he learned in the long months of meditation when infantile paralysis seemingly had ended his career? God's purposes, like grain, can grow in the dark as well as in the day, under rain as well as under sun. See Francis Thompson, "The Hound of Heaven":

Is my gloom, after all,
Shade of His hand, outstretched caressingly?

Note further that the hidden working of God's hand may be frustrated by refusal to trust and wait. Obviously that might have been true with Joseph. He could have grown cynical. The disappointed and disillusioned dreamer is often the man who does react into the most bitter cynicism. Are there no instances that come to mind of contemporary men who began as idealists in political life or in social service, but turned into reactionaries, disillusioned and sometimes corrupt?

Joseph could have become defiant. Men who have supposed themselves to be sincerely religious do sometimes become defiant if they have considered their relationship with God as a kind of contract, to be angrily repudiated if it does not work out quickly according to their wish. Job's wife said to him, "Curse God, and die" (Job 2:9). Joseph in the pit and Joseph in the prison—and any modern parallel to Joseph —may be tempted to say the same.

Or he might have been revengeful. If he had not blamed God, he still could have blamed his brothers and made up his mind to get even with them if ever he had the chance. He could have been vindictive in his heart, like Joab (II Sam. 4); like Mme. LeFarge in *A Tale of Two Cities*. There is the fierce pleasure of a terrible intoxication in the spirit of revenge, but it paralyzes the better self. If Joseph had spent his time and energy nursing his grievance against his brothers, he would not have had the clear-eyed and controlled perception to recognize the new possibilities that God put in his way.

But even if he had become neither cynical, nor rebellious, nor revengeful, he still might have become discouraged. The ordinary man can stand reverses and disaster up to a certain point, but after that he cannot take it. The real greatness is to be able to say, as Winston Churchill said in the darkest hours of England's destiny and his own, long before there was any sign of victory, "We shall not flag or fail. We shall go on to the end; . . . we shall fight with growing confidence . . . whatever the cost may be. . . . We shall never surrender." [3]

Why then did Joseph prevail? How did he attain to conquest over himself and over his destiny? Because he clung to his invincible instinct that God had a purpose for him worth believing in and pursuing; and because he followed at each turn of the way the partial light that showed the road ahead. Like Christian in

[3] Speech in the House of Commons, June 4, 1940.

9 Haste ye, and go up to my father, and say unto him, Thus saith thy son Joseph, God hath made me lord of all Egypt: come down unto me, tarry not:

10 And thou shalt dwell in the land of Goshen, and thou shalt be near unto me, thou, and thy children, and thy children's children, and thy flocks, and thy herds, and all that thou hast:

11 And there will I nourish thee; for yet *there are* five years of famine; lest thou, and thy household, and all that thou hast, come to poverty.

12 And, behold, your eyes see, and the eyes of my brother Benjamin, that *it is* my mouth that speaketh unto you.

13 And ye shall tell my father of all my glory in Egypt, and of all that ye have seen; and ye shall haste and bring down my father hither.

of Egypt. **9** Make haste and go up to my father and say to him, 'Thus says your son Joseph, God has made me lord of all Egypt; come down to me, do not tarry; **10** you shall dwell in the land of Goshen, and you shall be near me, you and your children and your children's children, and your flocks, your herds, and all that you have; **11** and there I will provide for you, for there are yet five years of famine to come; lest you and your household, and all that you have, come to poverty.' **12** And now your eyes see, and the eyes of my brother Benjamin see, that it is my mouth that speaks to you. **13** You must tell my father of all my splendor in Egypt, and of all that you have seen. Make haste and bring my father down here."

---

10. You shall dwell in the land of Goshen is inconsistent with 47:6b, according to which the settlement in Goshen was made at Pharaoh's order on the ground that Joseph's brothers were shepherds. The clause here can only be a gloss, since E nowhere mentions Goshen (on the locality of Goshen see Exeg. on 46:28–47:12).

The Pilgrim's Progress, he obeyed the guidance that was given him. To Christian at the outset of his journey came Evangelist, and said,

pointing with his finger over a very wide field, "Do you see yonder wicket gate?" The man said, "No." Then said the other, "Do you see yonder shining light?" He said, "I think I do." Then said Evangelist, "Keep that light in your eye, and go up directly thereto, so shalt thou see the gate; at which, when thou knockest, it shall be told thee what thou shalt do."

Joseph let the invitation of the generous interests God kindled in him lead him out of what could have been a cramped and corroding self-concern. Note the imaginative interest which made him able to interpret Pharaoh's perplexity, and the readiness to identify himself with a whole people's need, so that he could meet the crisis of Egypt in the time of famine. Read the story of Nehemiah and consider what it was that made him say, "Should such a man as I flee?" (Neh. 6:11). Remember Washington at Valley Forge. In World War I Lord Haldane was cruelly maligned and driven from office in England because it was falsely supposed that his numerous visits to Germany and his interest in German philosophy made him sympathetic with the enemy. Instead of yielding to self-pity, he devoted himself anew to generous labors, and he said afterward to a friend, "When things

seem darkest for a man's self, let him get a cause to serve, and then he need never despair."

It was not you that sent me hither, but God. That can be said at last by many a man who has come out of seeming frustration into fulfillment: *ad astra per aspera.* That great fact can be trusted when skies are clouded and visibility obscure—the great fact that God's hand is on the helm. But that fact must be answered by another one: the brave and faithful readiness of the man himself not to

> bate a jot
> Of heart or hope, but still bear up and steer
> Right onward.[4]

9-15, 25-26. *The Vindicated Dream.*—So the great story comes to its splendid climax. Through long years Jacob had thought of his son Joseph as dead. Actually he was alive; not only that, but his life had been lifted up to heights of unbelievable achievement. There in Egypt he occupied the seat of viceregal power. He could send back to his father now what once would have been the incredible message: **God hath made me lord of all Egypt. . . . And ye shall tell my father of all my glory** (vss. 9, 13). Turn back and recall the beginning of the story. When Joseph first came upon the scene in what was to prove the brilliant drama of his

[4] Milton, "To Cyriack Skinner."

14 And he fell upon his brother Benjamin's neck, and wept; and Benjamin wept upon his neck.

15 Moreover he kissed all his brethren, and wept upon them: and after that his brethren talked with him.

16 ¶ And the fame thereof was heard in Pharaoh's house, saying, Joseph's brethren are come: and it pleased Pharaoh well, and his servants.

14 Then he fell upon his brother Benjamin's neck and wept; and Benjamin wept upon his neck. 15 And he kissed all his brothers and wept upon them; and after that his brothers talked with him.

16 When the report was heard in Pharaoh's house, "Joseph's brothers have come," it pleased Pharaoh and his servants well.

---

career, he was greeted with no applause. On the contrary, his brothers had looked at him with derision. They were in the fields with the sheep, and as they saw him coming toward them they pointed to him angrily, "Behold, this dreamer cometh" (37:19). To their minds he was a person who went mooning about with nonsensical ideas. Ordinary people often have similar prejudice against the so-called dreamer. They sneer at him as impractical. Even in more kindly ways the dreamer may be suspected. Charles Kingsley wrote, "Do lovely things, not dream them all day long."

Nevertheless Joseph was great, and great not in spite of being a dreamer but because of it. He would not be stifled by the commonplace. He had large thoughts and large ambitions. Only from such impulses can greatness emerge. Scan the O.T. and consider other significant figures who played a supreme part in history because they had great thoughts and bold imagination: to some degree Jacob, Moses, David, Nehemiah. Note instances of the same truth in secular history.

But Joseph was not yet fit for success. His dreams originally were self-centered (37:5-10). He was thinking about himself and his supposed pre-eminence. His dreams were about the honors that should come to him. He might have developed into only a vain self-seeker. Therefore in God's providence the story of his life had to enter into another and different chapter—a dark chapter before his possibilities could be fulfilled. Sold by his brothers into slavery, exiled into Egypt, beset by circumstances humiliating and almost hopeless, what would happen now? Would he turn bitter and cynical? Would he say that destiny had played him a dirty trick? Would he let both his hopes and his character disintegrate?

Here is the test of a man faced by difficulty and disaster. These might destroy him. On the other hand, it was possible that they might strengthen him. It depended upon the qualities inside. What actually happened was that Joseph met his tests with a courage that made him steadily a bigger man. Remember how in the midst of the apparent wreck of his life's hopes Joseph kept his moral integrity (see Expos. on 39:7-9). Remember the enlargement of his sympathies which came to him when he was shut up in Pharaoh's jail. Remember, too, how the field for the exercise of ambition became larger and nobler in Joseph's thought (see Expos. on vss. 6-8). He learned to be concerned not simply about himself, but about the fate of a nation. So he was capable of becoming Pharaoh's servant in the salvation of Egypt from threatened famine. Thus spiritually he had won the right to have his life go forward into its final shining chapter. His brothers coming down to Egypt, desperately seeking food, were ushered into the presence of an official who would hold their fate in his hands. That official was Joseph, but they were unaware that it was he. They, like their father, supposed that he was dead.

In one sense the Joseph they had known was dead. Here was a new man—the lad grown now into a man of such dimensions that he seemed a different person. In crucial ways he was different. He had become no longer a self-seeker, but a servant. He had let himself be used by the purposes of God, and so he had become great— great enough no longer to be conceited, great enough not to be inflated by success. It was said once sardonically: "When a man is elected a bishop he never remains the same. He either grows or he swells." Joseph, as one who had gone far in eminence, might have attributed his eminence verbally to God and yet really all the time have been preening himself upon his own achievements. He might have been a swollen man, but instead he was a man who in a very solid sense had grown. He had grown because he dared believe in his dreams through all dark days. In the beginning it was with contempt that his brothers said, "Behold, this dreamer." At the end they beheld the dreamer on a throne.

16-24. *Pharaoh's Welcome.*—Another stroke in the picture of Joseph's greatness. Not only is he himself exalted in Pharaoh's favor, but that favor is so sure that it extends to all who belong to him. That Joseph should have rediscovered his family **pleased Pharaoh well.** So the

17 And Pharaoh said unto Joseph, Say unto thy brethren, This do ye; lade your beasts, and go, get you unto the land of Canaan;

18 And take your father and your households, and come unto me: and I will give you the good of the land of Egypt, and ye shall eat the fat of the land.

19 Now thou art commanded, this do ye; take you wagons out of the land of Egypt for your little ones, and for your wives, and bring your father, and come.

20 Also regard not your stuff; for the good of all the land of Egypt *is* yours.

21 And the children of Israel did so: and Joseph gave them wagons, according to the commandment of Pharaoh, and gave them provision for the way.

22 To all of them he gave each man changes of raiment; but to Benjamin he gave three hundred *pieces* of silver, and five changes of raiment.

23 And to his father he sent after this *manner;* ten asses laden with the good things of Egypt, and ten she asses laden with corn and bread and meat for his father by the way.

24 So he sent his brethren away, and they departed: and he said unto them, See that ye fall not out by the way.

25 ¶ And they went up out of Egypt, and came into the land of Canaan unto Jacob their father,

26 And told him, saying, Joseph *is* yet alive, and he *is* governor over all the land of Egypt. And Jacob's heart fainted, for he believed them not.

27 And they told him all the words of Joseph, which he had said unto them: and when he saw the wagons which Joseph had sent to carry him, the spirit of Jacob their father revived.

28 And Israel said, *It is* enough; Joseph my son *is* yet alive: I will go and see him before I die.

17 And Pharaoh said to Joseph, "Say to your brothers, 'Do this: load your beasts and go back to the land of Canaan; **18** and take your father and your households, and come to me, and I will give you the best of the land of Egypt, and you shall eat the fat of the land.' **19** Command them[r] also, 'Do this: take wagons from the land of Egypt for your little ones and for your wives, and bring your father, and come. **20** Give no thought to your goods, for the best of all the land of Egypt is yours.' "

21 The sons of Israel did so; and Joseph gave them wagons, according to the command of Pharaoh, and gave them provisions for the journey. **22** To each and all of them he gave festal garments; but to Benjamin he gave three hundred shekels of silver and five festal garments. **23** To his father he sent as follows: ten asses loaded with the good things of Egypt, and ten she-asses loaded with grain, bread, and provision for his father on the journey. **24** Then he sent his brothers away, and as they departed, he said to them, "Do not quarrel on the way." **25** So they went up out of Egypt, and came to the land of Canaan to their father Jacob. **26** And they told him, "Joseph is still alive, and he is ruler over all the land of Egypt." And his heart fainted, for he did not believe them. **27** But when they told him all the words of Joseph, which he had said to them, and when he saw the wagons which Joseph had sent to carry him, the spirit of their father Jacob revived; **28** and Israel said, "It is enough; Joseph my son is still alive; I will go and see him before I die."

r Cn. Compare Gk Vg: Heb *you are commanded*

---

narrative recounts the lavishness of Pharaoh's preparations for bringing Jacob and his sons into Egypt and establishing them there. They shall have **the good of the land.** With rich provision for them all, and most for Benjamin, the brothers set out for Canaan to carry the amazing message to their father.

25-28. Light at Eventide.—So it must have seemed to Jacob, the news concerning Joseph

breaking like the glory of an ineffable sunset through parted clouds at the end of a long, dark day. The latter part of his life, since Rachel died and Joseph disappeared, had been gray and sad. No wonder that he could not believe what his sons came now to tell him, and that his **heart fainted.** No wonder, either, that when he saw the wagons which Joseph had sent to carry him, his spirit revived. Nor was it the wagons

46 And Israel took his journey with all that he had, and came to Beer-sheba, and offered sacrifices unto the God of his father Isaac.

2 And God spake unto Israel in the visions of the night, and said, Jacob, Jacob. And he said, Here *am* I.

3 And he said, I *am* God, the God of thy father: fear not to go down into Egypt; for I will there make of thee a great nation.

4 I will go down with thee into Egypt; and I will also surely bring thee up *again:* and Joseph shall put his hand upon thine eyes.

5 And Jacob rose up from Beer-sheba: and the sons of Israel carried Jacob their father, and their little ones, and their wives, in the wagons which Pharaoh had sent to carry him.

6 And they took their cattle, and their goods, which they had gotten in the land of Canaan, and came into Egypt, Jacob, and all his seed with him:

7 His sons, and his sons' sons with him, his daughters, and his sons' daughters, and all his seed brought he with him into Egypt.

46 So Israel took his journey with all that he had, and came to Beer-sheba, and offered sacrifices to the God of his father Isaac. 2 And God spoke to Israel in visions of the night, and said, "Jacob, Jacob." And he said, "Here am I." 3 Then he said, "I am God, the God of your father; do not be afraid to go down to Egypt; for I will there make of you a great nation. 4 I will go down with you to Egypt, and I will also bring you up again; and Joseph's hand shall close your eyes." 5 Then Jacob set out from Beer-sheba; and the sons of Israel carried Jacob their father, their little ones, and their wives, in the wagons which Pharaoh had sent to carry him. 6 They also took their cattle and their goods, which they had gained in the land of Canaan, and came into Egypt, Jacob and all his offspring with him, 7 his sons, and his sons' sons with him, his daughters, and his sons' daughters; all his offspring he brought with him into Egypt.

XLVII. Jacob in Egypt (46:1–48:22)

The passages in 46:6-27; 47:5aβb, 6a, 7-11, 27b-28; 48:3-6 are from P, some being secondary. The rest of the material is a conflation of J and E, with J predominating.

A. Jacob Comes to Egypt (46:1-7)

46:1. The implication of vss. 1b-4 is that it was the theophany there described which decided Jacob to go to Egypt; vs. 5a then records his departure. Vs. 1aα is thus from another hand than vss. 1b-5a; the use of the name **Israel** in vs. 1aα indicates its J derivation. J must accordingly have represented Jacob as being at some place other than Beer-sheba (vs. 5a). This place is nowhere mentioned in the extant J material of the Joseph stories, but there can be no doubt that it was Hebron, in view both of the

---

and their contents that thrilled him. It was the fact that they came from Joseph, and that to Joseph he would go. **Joseph my son is yet alive.** That was enough. He would see him again before he died, and his life would go on in Joseph's. Here could be his *nunc dimittis.*

46:1-7. *Israel Comes to Egypt.*—Who can forecast the mysterious events that make up history? A boy is sold as a slave to a caravan. By developments which seem incredible he becomes a great man in the land of Egypt to which he had been taken. His family follow him there. That family and clan grow to be a numerous people; and from their sojourn in Egypt, at first beneficent and afterwards bitter and tragic, come Moses, the Passover, the Exodus, and the road

to the Promised Land. No wonder the Israelitish chroniclers, holding the tradition of all this to have been true, believed that when Jacob went on his way he heard the very voice of God assuring him of what would happen. **Fear not to go down into Egypt; for I will there make of thee a great nation: I will go down with thee . . . and I will also surely bring thee up again.** It is significant too that Jacob's vision of the future is grounded in the faith which had come to him from the past. The divine voice said to him, **I am God, the God of thy father;** and it was **unto the God of his father Isaac** that Jacob offered sacrifices at Beer-sheba. According to the narratives in Genesis, Beer-sheba had been made sacred by both Abraham and Isaac. There Abra-

8 ¶ And these *are* the names of the children of Israel, which came into Egypt, Jacob and his sons: Reuben, Jacob's firstborn.

9 And the sons of Reuben; Hanoch, and Phallu, and Hezron, and Carmi.

10 ¶ And the sons of Simeon; Jemuel, and Jamin, and Ohad, and Jachin, and Zohar, and Shaul the son of a Canaanitish woman.

11 ¶ And the sons of Levi; Gershon, Kohath, and Merari.

12 ¶ And the sons of Judah; Er, and Onan, and Shelah, and Pharez, and Zarah: but Er and Onan died in the land of Canaan. And the sons of Pharez were Hezron and Hamul.

13 ¶ And the sons of Issachar; Tola, and Phuvah, and Job, and Shimron.

14 ¶ And the sons of Zebulun; Sered, and Elon, and Jahleel.

15 These *be* the sons of Leah, which she bare unto Jacob in Padan-aram, with his daughter Dinah: all the souls of his sons and his daughters *were* thirty and three.

16 ¶ And the sons of Gad; Ziphion, and Haggi, Shuni, and Ezbon, Eri, and Arodi, and Areli.

17 ¶ And the sons of Asher; Jimnah, and Ishuah, and Isui, and Beriah, and Serah their sister: and the sons of Beriah; Heber, and Malchiel.

18 These *are* the sons of Zilpah, whom Laban gave to Leah his daughter; and these she bare unto Jacob, *even* sixteen souls.

8 Now these are the names of the descendants of Israel, who came into Egypt, Jacob and his sons. Reuben, Jacob's firstborn, 9 and the sons of Reuben: Hanoch, Pallu, Hezron, and Carmi. 10 The sons of Simeon: Jemu'el, Jamin, Ohad, Jachin, Zohar, and Shaul, the son of a Canaanitish woman. 11 The sons of Levi: Gershon, Kohath, and Merar'i. 12 The sons of Judah: Er, Onan, Shelah, Perez, and Zerah (but Er and Onan died in the land of Canaan); and the sons of Perez were Hezron and Hamul. 13 The sons of Is'sachar: Tola, Puvah, Iob, and Shimron. 14 The sons of Zeb'ulun: Sered, Elon, and Jah'leel 15 (these are the sons of Leah, whom she bore to Jacob in Paddan-aram, together with his daughter Dinah; altogether his sons and his daughters numbered thirty-three). 16 The sons of Gad: Ziph'ion, Haggi, Shuni, Ezbon, Eri, Aro'di, and Are'li. 17 The sons of Asher: Imnah, Ishvah, Ishvi, Beri'ah, with Serah their sister. And the sons of Beri'ah: Heber and Mal'chiel 18 (these are the sons of Zilpah, whom Laban gave to Leah his daughter; and these she bore to Jacob —

---

prominence of that city in the J document and of the P notice in 35:27, which has displaced the equivalent notice of J. **And came to Beer-sheba** is RJE's harmonization of the two narratives.

B. JACOB'S FAMILY (46:8-27)

8-27. A tradition, preserved in Deut. 10:22, represented the number of Israelites who settled in Egypt as seventy. These the compiler of this list desired to enumerate. To this

---

ham was said to have made a covenant with Abimelech (21:31). There he went to dwell after the Lord had turned aside his proffered sacrifice of Isaac (22:19). It was in the wilderness of Beer-sheba that Hagar was wandering when the angel of God came to show her the well of water which would save the life of Ishmael (21:14-19). According to another tradition, the servants of Isaac dug wells there (26:32-33). And it was from Beer-sheba that

Jacob himself had started out on the journey that was to be marked by his never to be forgotten vision at Bethel (28:10). With Jacob, as with many men in other times, the renewal of associations such as those gave him the spiritual sensitiveness which enabled him to believe that the voice of God was speaking to him again.

8-27. *More Genealogy.*—Once more, as often in the preceding chapters, we meet the favorite and familiar purpose of the priestly writers to

19 The sons of Rachel Jacob's wife; Joseph, and Benjamin.

20 ¶ And unto Joseph in the land of Egypt were born Manasseh and Ephraim, which Asenath the daughter of Poti-pherah priest of On bare unto him.

21 ¶ And the sons of Benjamin *were* Belah, and Becher, and Ashbel, Gera, and Naaman, Ehi, and Rosh, Muppim, and Huppim, and Ard.

22 These *are* the sons of Rachel, which were born to Jacob: all the souls *were* fourteen.

23 ¶ And the sons of Dan; Hushim.

24 ¶ And the sons of Naphtali; Jahzeel, and Guni, and Jezer, and Shillem.

25 These *are* the sons of Bilhah, which Laban gave unto Rachel his daughter, and she bare these unto Jacob: all the souls *were* seven.

26 All the souls that came with Jacob into Egypt, which came out of his loins, besides Jacob's sons' wives, all the souls *were* threescore and six;

27 And the sons of Joseph, which were borne him in Egypt, *were* two souls: all the souls of the house of Jacob, which came into Egypt, *were* threescore and ten.

28 ¶ And he sent Judah before him unto Joseph, to direct his face unto Goshen; and they came into the land of Goshen.

29 And Joseph made ready his chariot, and went up to meet Israel his father, to Goshen, and presented himself unto him; and he fell on his neck, and wept on his neck a good while.

sixteen persons). 19 The sons of Rachel, Jacob's wife: Joseph and Benjamin. 20 And to Joseph in the land of Egypt were born Manas'seh and E'phraim, whom As'enath, the daughter of Poti'phera the priest of On, bore to him. 21 And the sons of Benjamin: Bela, Becher, Ashbel, Gera, Na'aman, Ehi, Rosh, Muppim, Huppim, and Ard 22 (these are the sons of Rachel, who were born to Jacob — fourteen persons in all). 23 The sons of Dan: Hushim. 24 The sons of Naph'tali: Jahzeel, Guni, Jezer, and Shillem 25 (these are the sons of Bilhah, whom Laban gave to Rachel his daughter, and these she bore to Jacob — seven persons in all). 26 All the persons belonging to Jacob who came into Egypt, who were his own offspring, not including Jacob's sons' wives, were sixty-six persons in all; 27 and the sons of Joseph, who were born to him in Egypt, were two; all the persons of the house of Jacob, that came into Egypt, were seventy.

28 He sent Judah before him to Joseph, to appear[s] before him in Goshen; and they came into the land of Goshen. 29 Then Joseph made ready his chariot and went up to meet Israel his father in Goshen; and he presented himself to him, and fell on his neck, and wept on his neck a good

[s] Sam Syr Compare Gk Vg: Heb *to show the way*

---

end he drew upon some census record—originally having nothing to do with the migration into Egypt—of the leading Israelite clans (cf. Num. 26:5-50), which traditionally numbered seventy (cf. Exod. 24:1, 9; Num. 11:16).

C. Jacob Settles in Goshen (46:28–47:12)

46:28–47:12. The nucleus of this is a simple account of Jacob's meeting with Joseph, of Joseph's presenting five of his brothers to the Pharaoh, and of the latter's decision that, being shepherds by occupation, they should settle in Goshen.

The statement that the Israelites were settled apart by themselves in Goshen is first found in J[2]. J[1] knows nothing of it; his account of the Exodus has the Israelites living

---

certify the whole genealogy of the people of Israel (see Expos. on ch. 5).

46:28–47:6. *The Arrival in Goshen.*—The narrative at this point deals tersely with the meeting of Joseph and his father; it is more concerned with the question of where the family of Israel

shall settle. After the munificent welcome decreed by Pharaoh in ch. 45, the last words in ch. 46 have a surprising sound in their suggestion that the Israelites were **an abomination unto the Egyptians.** As a matter of fact, however, herdsmen seem to have been represented on

30 And Israel said unto Joseph, Now let me die, since I have seen thy face, because thou *art* yet alive.

31 And Joseph said unto his brethren, and unto his father's house, I will go up, and show Pharaoh, and say unto him, My brethren, and my father's house, which *were* in the land of Canaan, are come unto me;

32 And the men *are* shepherds, for their trade hath been to feed cattle; and they have brought their flocks, and their herds, and all that they have.

33 And it shall come to pass, when Pharaoh shall call you, and shall say, What *is* your occupation?

34 That ye shall say, Thy servants' trade hath been about cattle from our youth even until now, both we, *and* also our fathers: that ye may dwell in the land of Goshen; for every shepherd *is* an abomination unto the Egyptians.

47 Then Joseph came and told Pharaoh, and said, My father and my brethren, and their flocks, and their herds, and all that they have, are come out of the land of Canaan; and, behold, they *are* in the land of Goshen.

2 And he took some of his brethren, *even* five men, and presented them unto Pharaoh.

3 And Pharaoh said unto his brethren, What *is* your occupation? And they said unto Pharaoh, Thy servants *are* shepherds, both we, *and* also our fathers.

while. **30** Israel said to Joseph, "Now let me die, since I have seen your face and know that you are still alive." **31** Joseph said to his brothers and to his father's household, "I will go up and tell Pharaoh, and will say to him, 'My brothers and my father's household, who were in the land of Canaan, have come to me; **32** and the men are shepherds, for they have been keepers of cattle; and they have brought their flocks, and their herds, and all that they have.' **33** When Pharaoh calls you, and says, 'What is your occupation?' **34** you shall say, 'Your servants have been keepers of cattle from our youth even until now, both we and our fathers,' in order that you may dwell in the land of Goshen; for every shepherd is an abomination to the Egyptians."

47 So Joseph went in and told Pharaoh, "My father and my brothers, with their flocks and herds and all that they possess, have come from the land of Canaan; they are now in the land of Goshen." **2** And from among his brothers he took five men and presented them to Pharaoh. **3** Pharaoh said to his brothers, "What is your occupation?" And they said to Pharaoh, "Your servants are shepherds, as our fathers were."

---

among the Egyptians (cf. Exod. 1:15-19; 3:22). (The additions to the J² narrative of the Exodus similarly have the two peoples living side by side [cf. Exod. 12:23], as do E and P.) It is unlikely, therefore, that J²'s representation rests upon anything more substantial than speculation, in the light of a more adequate knowledge of the geography of Egypt than had been possessed by J¹, as to the precise scene of the events which, according to the J¹ narrative, had preceded the Exodus.

Goshen has been identified as the Wadi Ṭumilat, "a long narrow valley leading 'straight from the heart of the Delta to a break in the chain of the Bitter Lakes,' and therefore marking a weak spot in the natural defences of Egypt" (Skinner, *Genesis*, p. 488).

The earliest tradition appears to have represented the Exodus as a flight (cf. Exod. 14:5a). Although this feature became less prominent as the story was more and more elaborated, it would seem to have remained in the background of Israelite thinking. The location of the Israelites in Goshen was therefore a point of some importance in the J² narrative of the Exodus.

The J² nucleus of this section thus represents the Pharaoh as all unwittingly helping to set the stage for the "great deliverance" (45:7; cf. Exeg. on that verse, and on ch. 45 as a whole). This was too subtle a thought for some later writer of the J school: the assignment of Goshen to the Israelites could not have been made so casually as 47:3, 5a, 6b

4 They said moreover unto Pharaoh, For to sojourn in the land are we come; for thy servants have no pasture for their flocks; for the famine *is* sore in the land of Canaan: now therefore, we pray thee, let thy servants dwell in the land of Goshen.

5 And Pharaoh spake unto Joseph, saying, Thy father and thy brethren are come unto thee:

6 The land of Egypt *is* before thee; in the best of the land make thy father and brethren to dwell; in the land of Goshen let them dwell: and if thou knowest *any* men of activity among them, then make them rulers over my cattle.

7 And Joseph brought in Jacob his father, and set him before Pharaoh: and Jacob blessed Pharaoh.

8 And Pharaoh said unto Jacob, How old *art* thou?

4 They said to Pharaoh, "We have come to sojourn in the land; for there is no pasture for your servants' flocks, for the famine is severe in the land of Canaan; and now, we pray you, let your servants dwell in the land of Goshen." 5 Then Pharaoh said to Joseph, "Your father and your brothers have come to you. 6 The land of Egypt is before you; settle your father and your brothers in the best of the land; let them dwell in the land of Goshen; and if you know any able men among them, put them in charge of my cattle."

7 Then Joseph brought in Jacob his father, and set him before Pharaoh, and Jacob blessed Pharaoh. 8 And Pharaoh said to Jacob, "How many are the days of the

---

might seem to imply. He therefore elaborated the story to represent Joseph as somewhat deviously contriving to have his brothers placed there, adding 45:10aα (see Exeg.), 46:28aβb, the words in **Goshen** in vs. 29, vss. 31-34, 47:1b, 4.

Egyptian monuments as rough and uncouth, of lower caste than the dwellers in Egyptian cities, and therefore despised. It is a fact too, of course, that in the succeeding narrative of Exodus the Egyptians are represented as hostile to the Israelites. So perhaps here the more stark reality crops up through the lavish colors which the chronicler has used in depicting the attitude of Pharaoh in ch. 45, and which for the most part are used in the first part of ch. 47—especially vs. 6a.

7-10. Retrospect.—*Few and evil have the days of the years of my life been.* That may be only an Oriental manner of speech, the fashion in which the ordinary person represents himself as insignificant in order to show his humble deference to the greater man. But it may also be an expression of what Jacob actually felt about his own life, and life in general. Even the longest life may seem desperately short. Every man as he grows older feels that the years go by at a faster pace. In the unlikely event that his age should be **a hundred and thirty years,** as Jacob said his was, still the whole span telescopes itself in memory so that it becomes almost incredible that it has been so long. Measured by the greatness of desires, longings, regrets, and hopes and ambitions unfulfilled, it seems as fleeting as a candle flame about to be blown out by the unpitying wind. And if it seems short, so also it may seem evil, in that disaster has dogged it and that in the end it goes down to decay. It may be symbol-

ized by Hamlet standing in the graveyard holding in his hand a skull. Many literary and philosophical interpreters in the twentieth century have agreed with Jacob's appraisal.

But it is obvious that life need not be regarded with such mordant pessimism. Jacob sounded as though he were ready to creep out of existence, beaten. But a man can say, instead, in the words of J. B. S. Haldane, "I hope that I shall find time to think as I die, 'I am glad that I lived when and where I did. It was a good show.' " [5] Why then to Jacob had life come to seem so sour and shriveled; and why may men in every generation suffer the same disillusionment? Because, first, of self-seeking. That was the fundamental defect in Jacob. Conspicuously, in his youth, and more or less always, he was bent on getting something for himself. Every human being, of course, has selfish instincts, and biologically could not exist without them; but the difference between the man who makes life mean and the one who makes it magnanimous is in whether or not he has let the leading of God turn that self-seeking into imaginative sympathy for the interests of others. When self-seeking becomes habitual, the man simply does not see the human facts around him which at least might arouse his vivid interest in life's "good show." Jacob's own son, Joseph, began with impulses almost as obviously selfish as his father's, but nobler interests drew him out beyond himself:

[5] *Living Philosophies,* p. 330.

9 And Jacob said unto Pharaoh, The days of the years of my pilgrimage *are* a hundred and thirty years: few and evil have the days of the years of my life been, and have not attained unto the days of the years of the life of my fathers in the days of their pilgrimage.

10 And Jacob blessed Pharaoh, and went out from before Pharaoh.

11 ¶ And Joseph placed his father and his brethren, and gave them a possession in the land of Egypt, in the best of the land, in the land of Rameses, as Pharaoh had commanded.

12 And Joseph nourished his father, and his brethren, and all his father's household, with bread, according to *their* families.

13 ¶ And *there was* no bread in all the land; for the famine *was* very sore, so that the land of Egypt and *all* the land of Canaan fainted by reason of the famine.

years of your life?" 9 And Jacob said to Pharaoh, "The days of the years of my sojourning are a hundred and thirty years; few and evil have been the days of the years of my life, and they have not attained to the days of the years of the life of my fathers in the days of their sojourning." 10 And Jacob blessed Pharaoh, and went out from the presence of Pharaoh. 11 Then Joseph settled his father and his brothers, and gave them a possession in the land of Egypt, in the best of the land, in the land of Ram'eses, as Pharaoh had commanded. 12 And Joseph provided his father, his brothers, and all his father's household with food, according to the number of their dependents.

13 Now there was no food in all the land; for the famine was very severe, so that the land of Egypt and the land of Canaan

This elaboration thus throws an interesting side light upon the J philosophy of history.

D. Joseph's Agrarian Policy (47:13-26)

47:13-26. This section is a conflation of J and E (for a detailed analysis see Simpson, *Early Traditions of Israel,* pp. 148-49). The E material, vss. 14, 18, 20-21 (allowing for

the distress of fellow prisoners, the problem of Pharaoh's dream, the plight of Egypt. But outside of some special family affections there is no evidence that Jacob was interested in anybody else. The nemesis of that sort of self-absorption is nearly always self-pity. Note the tone of Jacob's laments in 37:35; 43:6, 14. "He refused to be comforted" sounds suspiciously like deliberately nursing his grief. Of course he had reason to grieve, but not to make a virtue of it— nor to be a prototype for succeeding persons who, like Mrs. Gummidge in *David Copperfield,* insist on being "a lone, lorn creetur," and on having everybody else admit that they "feel things more than other people." But apparently Jacob had sunk so deep in that emotional groove that even in what might have been the moment of complete rejoicing he still could not get out of his thought that life was short and evil.

The unhappy Jacobs in every generation, shut within their self-seeking, self-absorption, and self-pity, need to learn what Albert Einstein wrote, "The ideals which have always shone before me and filled me with the joy of living are goodness, beauty, and truth." [6] Or let them listen to a great Englishman of the nineteenth

century, Edward Thring, headmaster of Uppingham School, who, when he looked back on a life that often had been marked by bitter difficulties and disappointments, declared: "I cannot even now bear to think of living it over again, yet year by year, aye, day by day, I felt the warrior joy of life and the conqueror's joy of getting the mastery. . . . My positive creed is an absolute, unfaltering certainty of life triumphant." [7]

Jacob was not the sort who could feel that life had been triumphant. But even in his most pessimistic and self-depreciatory hours, he had hold of something greater and more important than his estimate of himself. Whatever happened to Jacob, still there was God. Notwithstanding his own unworthiness, God could be declared through him. Therefore he blessed **Pharaoh,** not with his blessing but with God's.

11-26. *Joseph the Administrator.*—This whole passage may well provoke curious reflection. It is obviously a panegyric upon Joseph. Here is recounted his foresight, his acumen, his clearly calculated and unswerving purpose. He had determined exactly how he would execute Phar-

[6] *Ibid.,* p. 4.

[7] Parkin, *Life and Letters of Edward Thring,* p. 462.

14 And Joseph gathered up all the money that was found in the land of Egypt, and in the land of Canaan, for the corn which they bought: and Joseph brought the money into Pharaoh's house.

15 And when money failed in the land of Egypt, and in the land of Canaan, all the Egyptians came unto Joseph, and said, Give us bread: for why should we die in thy presence? for the money faileth.

16 And Joseph said, Give your cattle; and I will give you for your cattle, if money fail.

17 And they brought their cattle unto Joseph: and Joseph gave them bread *in exchange* for horses, and for the flocks, and for the cattle of the herds, and for the asses; and he fed them with bread for all their cattle for that year.

18 When that year was ended, they came unto him the second year, and said unto him, We will not hide *it* from my lord, how that our money is spent; my lord also hath our herds of cattle; there is not aught left in the sight of my lord, but our bodies, and our lands:

languished by reason of the famine. **14** And Joseph gathered up all the money that was found in the land of Egypt and in the land of Canaan, for the grain which they bought; and Joseph brought the money into Pharaoh's house. **15** And when the money was all spent in the land of Egypt and in the land of Canaan, all the Egyptians came to Joseph, and said, "Give us food; why should we die before your eyes? For our money is gone." **16** And Joseph answered, "Give your cattle, and I will give you food in exchange for your cattle, if your money is gone." **17** So they brought their cattle to Joseph; and Joseph gave them food in exchange for the horses, the flocks, the herds, and the asses: and he supplied them with food in exchange for all their cattle that year. **18** And when that year was ended, they came to him the following year, and said to him, "We will not hide from my lord that our money is all spent; and the herds of cattle are my lord's; there is nothing left in the sight of my lord but our bodies and our lands.

---

some necessary redactional harmonization; vs. 22 is a learned gloss), is a unity and followed 41:56b. It told how Joseph sold grain to the Egyptians until their money was exhausted, after which, in the second year of the famine, they surrendered the ownership of their land to Pharaoh, thus being reduced to slavery, since the only basis of personal freedom in a state like ancient Egypt was the possession of land.

The J parallel to this was in two sections: (a) Following 41:55, the account of the Egyptians giving their flocks and their herds to Joseph in exchange for food—vss. 15-17a, with allowance for redactional harmonization. (b) Following 47:12, the account of the

---

aoh's authority, and how he would go about enabling Egypt to survive the famine. But note how he did it. During the seven years of plenty he collected a rich proportion of the grain. The record does not say he bought it; more probably he levied upon the crops a tax in the name of Pharaoh. But when the lean years came, it is specifically recorded that the people who came to beg for it had to buy it—to buy back what they had produced. They paid so heavily for it that **Joseph gathered up all the money that was found in the land of Egypt.** When the people had no more money, he took their cattle (vss. 16-17). When they had no more cattle, he took title to their land (vs. 20). With all the land in his possession and the people therefore wholly subject to him, he even shifted some of them from one area to another (vs. 21). Only the priests were treated differently. Everybody else's land came into the grip of Pharaoh, but

not the lands of the priests (vs. 22). Meanwhile the impoverished and landless people were represented as grateful that they were still in existence. They said, **Thou hast saved our lives: let us find grace in the sight of my lord, and we will be Pharaoh's servants.**

Because this chapter is in the Bible, and because it deals with Joseph who rightly is one of the Bible heroes, it is often taken for granted and passed by without remark. If one happens to see the dubious element in it, and the question arises as to why the Bible should praise a proceeding which seems so ruthless, some commentators are driven to extraordinary answers. Observe what even so great and good a man is Marcus Dods could write. When the people of Egypt had

yielded to [Joseph] both their lands and their persons . . . the result . . . was that the people who

19 Wherefore shall we die before thine eyes, both we and our land? buy us and our land for bread, and we and our land will be servants unto Pharaoh: and give *us* seed, that we may live, and not die, that the land be not desolate.

20 And Joseph bought all the land of Egypt for Pharaoh; for the Egyptians sold every man his field, because the famine prevailed over them: so the land became Pharaoh's.

21 And as for the people, he removed them to cities from *one* end of the borders of Egypt even to the *other* end thereof.

22 Only the land of the priests bought he not; for the priests had a portion *assigned them* of Pharaoh, and did eat their portion which Pharaoh gave them: wherefore they sold not their lands.

23 Then Joseph said unto the people, Behold, I have bought you this day and your land for Pharaoh: lo, *here is* seed for you, and ye shall sow the land.

19 Why should we die before your eyes, both we and our land? Buy us and our land for food, and we with our land will be slaves to Pharaoh; and give us seed, that we may live, and not die, and that the land may not be desolate."

20 So Joseph bought all the land of Egypt for Pharaoh; for all the Egyptians sold their fields, because the famine was severe upon them. The land became Pharaoh's; **21** and as for the people, he made slaves of them[t] from one end of Egypt to the other. **22** Only the land of the priests he did not buy; for the priests had a fixed allowance from Pharaoh, and lived on the allowance which Pharaoh gave them; therefore they did not sell their land. **23** Then Joseph said to the people, "Behold, I have this day bought you and your land for Pharaoh. Now here is seed for you, and you

[t] Sam Gk Compare Vg: Heb *he removed them to the cities*

permanent tax of one fifth laid upon the Egyptians in return for the provision of seed at the end of the famine—vss. 19*b*, 23-26*a*. RJE, combining these three passages, was compelled, in view of the seed motif, to place the resultant narrative here.

Both the J and the E narratives are etiological, the former to explain the rate of taxation in Egypt, and the latter to account for the system of land tenure which differed from that in force in Palestine. As to whether the authors were drawing upon Egyptian

would otherwise have perished were preserved. . . . The people ceased to be proprietors of their own farms, but they were not slaves with no interest in the soil, but tenants sitting at easy rents—a fair enough exchange for being preserved in life.

Dods has not confronted the fact that people supposedly "sitting at easy rents" were picked up and relocated here and there, for this is what he says:

Modern experience supplies us with instances in which, by such a policy, a country might be regenerated and a seven years' famine hailed as a blessing if, without famishing the people, it put them unconditionally into the hands of an able, bold, and beneficent ruler.[8]

He does not tell us what "modern experience" he is thinking of. Obviously he was not thinking of the totalitarianisms of the twentieth century, for he was writing long before those times. But Hitler and Stalin would have found his words entirely to their liking.

The truth is, of course, that this chapter is

[8] *Genesis*, pp. 375-76.

an illustration of the fact that the actions of even the best men of the O.T. are not to be praised indiscriminately, as though they were sacrosanct, but must be set in the perspective of the Bible's growing revelation. In ancient times autocracy was taken for granted, and only gradually did any recognition of the rights of the common man arise. That Joseph should have been an autocrat in Egypt did not surprise anyone: people were simply grateful for his efficiency. Also, the men of Israel who wrote the story of Joseph were accustomed to the unconditional rule of kings. Most of them believed in autocracy. An increasing number believed in a particular form of it, theocracy, which is rule in the name of God administered by the church. So the biographers of Joseph thought it was quite proper that he had the people in his power and even that he should take their land; and equally proper that he should not take the lands of the priests.

From this two considerations emerge. The first is as to the conception of the worth of human beings, and the right conception therefore of society and government which the O.T. as a

24 And it shall come to pass in the increase, that ye shall give the fifth *part* unto Pharaoh, and four parts shall be your own, for seed of the field, and for your food, and for them of your households, and for food for your little ones.

25 And they said, Thou hast saved our lives: let us find grace in the sight of my lord, and we will be Pharaoh's servants.

26 And Joseph made it a law over the land of Egypt unto this day, *that* Pharaoh should have the fifth *part;* except the land of the priests only, *which* became not Pharaoh's.

27 ¶ And Israel dwelt in the land of Egypt, in the country of Goshen; and they had possessions therein, and grew, and multiplied exceedingly.

28 And Jacob lived in the land of Egypt seventeen years: so the whole age of Jacob was a hundred forty and seven years.

shall sow the land. 24 And at the harvests you shall give a fifth to Pharaoh, and four fifths shall be your own, as seed for the field and as food for yourselves and your households, and as food for your little ones." 25 And they said, "You have saved our lives; may it please my lord, we will be slaves to Pharaoh." 26 So Joseph made it a statute concerning the land of Egypt, and it stands to this day, that Pharaoh should have the fifth; the land of the priests alone did not become Pharaoh's.

27 Thus Israel dwelt in the land of Egypt, in the land of Goshen; and they gained possessions in it, and were fruitful and multiplied exceedingly. 28 And Jacob lived in the land of Egypt seventeen years; so the days of Jacob, the years of his life, were a hundred and forty-seven years.

tradition or were relying upon Israelite imagination working on the material of the Joseph legend it is impossible to say.

E. Jacob's Last Words to Joseph (47:27–48:22)

Of the P material in this section 47:27b-28 is the continuation of 47:11, and 48:3-6, accounting for the tribal status of Ephraim and Manasseh, parallels 48:8-20. The verse 48:7 is an addition based on 35:16-19 and supplementing 49:31.

The rest of the material is from J and E. RJE was apparently desirous of preserving both his sources in substantial entirety. He was therefore compelled in conflating them to dislocate one of them (E) to produce a unified narrative. (A detailed analysis will be found in Simpson, *Early Traditions of Israel*, pp. 150-52.) The dislocations are noted below.

J recorded, first, Jacob's charge to Joseph to bury him in Palestine (47:27a, 29-31) — preparing for the narrative in ch. 50. He then told of his blessing Joseph's two sons (48:2b, 9b, 10a, 13-14, 17-19, followed by "and he blessed them"). This tale was designed to explain two facts: (a) that the house of Joseph was composed of two divisions, each of tribal status, and each claiming Joseph as ancestor, though not as the tribal eponym;

whole inspired, but which Genesis only partially suggests. The O.T. moves forward to larger and wider understanding. When the great prophets rose they proclaimed the rights of common men to justice and opportunity and laid the deep religious foundation upon which democratic civilizations were afterward to be built. The second consideration is as to the priests. Through numberless centuries priests and ecclesiastics of many names have been given special privileges and emoluments. A right impulse was being expressed in that—the impulse to safeguard in human society the status of those who were supposed to bring into it the atmosphere of the divine. But that impulse can hold

danger. The fierce reaction in many European countries to ecclesiastical establishments is the embittered protest against ecclesiastical privilege and power that in many instances had grown overweening and corrupt. Though it had not come true in Joseph's Egypt, it has come true now, that religious hierarchies will no longer be given unconditional privilege. Not by smooth claims, but by character and the actual contribution of their service, they must justify their place in the community.

27-31. *Jacob Faces His Death.*—The O.T. looks with a straight gaze at the facts of human existence. The people of whom it tells did not deceive themselves with illusions or evasions.

29 And the time drew nigh that Israel must die: and he called his son Joseph, and said unto him, If now I have found grace in thy sight, put, I pray thee, thy hand under my thigh, and deal kindly and truly with me; bury me not, I pray thee, in Egypt:

30 But I will lie with my fathers, and thou shalt carry me out of Egypt, and bury me in their buryingplace. And he said, I will do as thou hast said.

31 And he said, Swear unto me. And he sware unto him. And Israel bowed himself upon the bed's head.

48 And it came to pass after these things, that one told Joseph, Behold, thy father is sick: and he took with him his two sons, Manasseh and Ephraim.

29 And when the time drew near that Israel must die, he called his son Joseph and said to him, "If now I have found favor in your sight, put your hand under my thigh, and promise to deal loyally and truly with me. Do not bury me in Egypt, 30 but let me lie with my fathers; carry me out of Egypt and bury me in their burying place." He answered, "I will do as you have said." 31 And he said, "Swear to me"; and he swore to him. Then Israel bowed himself upon the head of his bed.

48 After this Joseph was told, "Behold, your father is ill"; so he took with him his two sons, Manas'seh and E'phraim.

and (b) that the tribe of Manasseh which had once ranked first in importance—a fact reflected in the representation of him as Joseph's first-born—had later yielded place to Ephraim. The implication of the story is that Jacob in blessing the two boys had given them a status equal to that of his own sons; and that by laying his right hand on the head of the younger he had set in motion the train of events by which Ephraim had risen to precedence over Manasseh. It may be assumed that the legend took its rise among the Ephraimites. The tale reflects the belief—finding expression also in ch. 27—that the words of a dying man had in them the power to ensure their own fulfillment.

E told of Jacob's prediction of the Exodus (48:1-2a, 21), of his giving to Joseph a double portion of land (vs. 22), of his blessing of Ephraim and Manasseh (vss. 8-9a, 10b-11, 15—reading "them" for **Joseph**—16, 12a), and finally of his blessing of Joseph himself (vss. 12b, 20a—reading "him" for **them**). The E narrative thus parallels that of J in that it accounts for the fact that the house of Joseph was composed of two tribes. On the other hand, it evinces little concern regarding the relative positions of Ephraim and Manasseh; it simply represents Jacob as mentioning Ephraim first (vs. 20a). A later writer, possibly R[JE], added vs. 20b to call attention to this.

29. With put your hand under my thigh cf. 24:2.

30. Their burying place is a substitution by R[P] for an explicit designation of the site of Jacob's grave. This, according to J, was east of the Jordan (see Exeg. on 50:10-13).

If there was life, so certainly there would be death. As old age came upon them they recognized the inevitable nearness of the end and made ready for it. Our modern generations often flinch from that unvarnished honesty. There is an effort to act as though if death were kept out of mind, it could be kept off the horizon altogether. Sometimes its prospect is pushed away with flippant speech; more often the attempt is made to hide the fear of it in an uneasy silence. The men of the O.T. were of sterner stuff. They did not ask that death should bandage their eyes, and bid them "creep past." They met it as it was. It does not appear that faith in an eternal life had dawned for Jacob. Yet even without that, he could keep his spirit steady. How much more ought that to be true of those who are heirs of all the Christian hope that was born with the Resurrection.

48:1-7. *Life's Eternal Lessons.*—It is true, of course, that this chapter cannot be read too literally. It may be, as the Exeg. has previously suggested, that Jacob is more the personification of tribal ideals than a person; and if he was a person, it would remain to be questioned whether we have more than a legendary tradition of words spoken by him when he was drawing near his death. Nevertheless, here is the expression of the Hebrew belief as to what one like Jacob would have said. Here is a mirror in which one may see a people's conception of the meaning of life.

What was the supreme heritage that Jacob would hand on to his descendants? Not posses-

2 And *one* told Jacob, and said, Behold, thy son Joseph cometh unto thee: and Israel strengthened himself, and sat upon the bed.

3 And Jacob said unto Joseph, God Almighty appeared unto me at Luz in the land of Canaan, and blessed me,

4 And said unto me, Behold, I will make thee fruitful, and multiply thee, and I will make of thee a multitude of people; and will give this land to thy seed after thee *for* an everlasting possession.

5 ¶ And now thy two sons, Ephraim and Manasseh, which were born unto thee in the land of Egypt, before I came unto thee into Egypt, *are* mine; as Reuben and Simeon, they shall be mine.

6 And thy issue, which thou begettest after them, shall be thine, *and* shall be called after the name of their brethren in their inheritance.

7 And as for me, when I came from Padan, Rachel died by me in the land of Canaan in the way, when yet *there was* but a little way to come unto Ephrath: and I buried her there in the way of Ephrath; the same *is* Bethlehem.

2 And it was told to Jacob, "Your son Joseph has come to you"; then Israel summoned his strength, and sat up in bed. 3 And Jacob said to Joseph, "God Almighty[u] appeared to me at Luz in the land of Canaan and blessed me, 4 and said to me, 'Behold I will make you fruitful, and multiply you, and I will make of you a company of peoples, and will give this land to your descendants after you for an everlasting possession.' 5 And now your two sons, who were born to you in the land of Egypt before I came to you in Egypt, are mine; E'phraim and Manas'seh shall be mine, as Reuben and Simeon are. 6 And the offspring born to you after them shall be yours; they shall be called by the name of their brothers in their inheritance. 7 For when I came from Paddan, Rachel to my sorrow died in the land of Canaan on the way, when there was still some distance to go to Ephrath; and I buried her there on the way to Ephrath (that is, Bethlehem)."

[u] Heb *El Shaddai*

sions. Not worldly shrewdness, craftiness in bargaining, smart stratagems by which to outwit and outmaneuver rivals. Not pride or supposed success. No, none of these, but one thing only: his tested experience of the guidance of God. A life which has nothing to say concerning that is a spiritual failure, no matter what else it has; and no life which can bequeath that has altogether failed.

3-7. *Two Factors in Salvation.*—Note the two events which stand pre-eminent in Jacob's retrospect while all lesser matters fade. One is his vision at Bethel (vs. 3); the other is the death of Rachel (vs. 7). They represent the two influences which had taken this man, whose life began so meanly, and had made him a person fit to have part in the purposes of God. One was his faith, the other was his love. To speak of his faith is to use the great word with qualifications, for Jacob's first conception of God (cf. vs. 4) was cramped into the pattern of his own original selfishness. Nevertheless he had, as Esau did not have, a sense of being apprehended by the Unseen. He believed that life had a larger destiny than any immediate circumstances showed. That was his faith, and little by little it led him to larger understanding. Also, in the midst of inconsistent relationships he

had one great love which never lost its primacy, a love not of the flesh only but of the spirit. These two, faith and love, were everlasting facts when everything else should sink to insignificance. When any man comes to die, these alone will stand by him. Without these, the whole record will seem empty. With these and for these the final consciousness can be full of gratitude to God. And that gratitude can be not the less but the more profound when love has known the shadow of loss. As William R. Inge has written:

Bereavement is the deepest initiation into the mysteries of human life, an initiation more searching and profound than even happy love. Love remembered and consecrated by grief belongs, more clearly than the happy intercourse of friends, to the eternal world; it has proved itself stronger than death.[9]

Jacob remembered Rachel who had died on the way home to Canaan, and whom he had buried near Bethlehem; and her grave symbolized emotions without which his life would have been impoverished. The name of Bethlehem, which means "House of Bread," was given to it

[9] *Personal Religion and the Life of Devotion* (New York: Longmans, Green & Co., 1924), pp. 88-89.

8 And Israel beheld Joseph's sons, and said, Who *are* these?	**8** When Israel saw Joseph's sons, he said, "Who are these?" **9** Joseph said to his father,
9 And Joseph said unto his father, They *are* my sons, whom God hath given me in this *place*. And he said, Bring them, I pray thee, unto me, and I will bless them.	"They are my sons, whom God has given me here." And he said, "Bring them to me, I pray you, that I may bless them." **10** Now the eyes of Israel were dim with age, so that
10 Now the eyes of Israel were dim for age, *so that* he could not see. And he brought them near unto him; and he kissed them, and embraced them.	he could not see. So Joseph brought them near him; and he kissed them and embraced them. **11** And Israel said to Joseph, "I had
11 And Israel said unto Joseph, I had not thought to see thy face: and, lo, God hath showed me also thy seed.	not thought to see your face; and lo, God has let me see your children also." **12** Then Joseph removed them from his knees, and
12 And Joseph brought them out from between his knees, and he bowed himself with his face to the earth.	he bowed himself with his face to the earth. **13** And Joseph took them both, E'phraim in
13 And Joseph took them both, Ephraim in his right hand toward Israel's left hand, and Manasseh in his left hand toward Israel's right hand, and brought *them* near unto him.	his right hand toward Israel's left hand, and Manas'seh in his left hand toward Israel's right hand, and brought them near him. **14** And Israel stretched out his right
14 And Israel stretched out his right hand, and laid *it* upon Ephraim's head, who *was* the younger, and his left hand upon Manasseh's head, guiding his hands wittingly; for Manasseh *was* the firstborn.	hand and laid it upon the head of E'phraim, who was the younger, and his left hand upon the head of Manas'seh, crossing his hands, for Manas'seh was the first-born.

48:10. In this source (J) Jacob is blind; contrast vss. 8, 11, both E, despite the use of the name "Israel," usually a mark of J.

12. The allusion to the fact that the boys had been on or between Jacob's **knees** suggests an adoption ceremony; cf. 30:3*b*α; 50:23.

---

for other reasons; but in it is the everlasting suggestion that for all human souls life will be in a profounder way the House of Bread if sorrow, as well as joy, dwells in it.

8-14. Jacob's Choice.—Joseph had brought his two sons to his father that they might receive his blessing; and he presented them with Manasseh, the first-born, before Jacob's right hand, so that the chief blessing might be given to him. But Jacob crossed his hands, **guiding his hands wittingly,** so that his chief blessing might fall upon the head not of Manasseh, but of Ephraim, the younger son. It seemed an arbitrary act. But to those who made the record of Genesis it was not arbitrary. A mightier choice than Jacob's was back of what he did. The choice was God's. **The eyes of Israel were dim for age, so that he could not see;** but as he embraced the boys, a discerning impulse moved him, and he followed this inward moving as against what Joseph had supposed he would do.

Back of the record doubtless lies the *ex post facto* influence of Ephraim's actual greatness among the tribes. The chroniclers rooted this in the story of Jacob's blessing. But whether or not the story is completely factual, it represents a profound perception. The chroniclers read history in the light of a divine purpose which they believed was moving there. As is repeatedly evidenced in Genesis, they saw the destiny of Israel shaped not by human intentions, but by the long, sure purpose of God. The accidents of birth and circumstance were not controlling. Cain was older than Abel, but Abel's sacrifice was preferred. Ishmael was Abraham's first-born son, but the voice of God said to Abraham, "in Isaac shall thy seed be called" (21:12). Esau was the elder of Isaac's twin sons, but to Jacob, not to Esau, was the promise given. In every instance, as men looked back, it appeared to them that the unseen Hand had been at work. That interpretation of the past gave dignity to history. It gave steadiness to the present, and tenacious courage to face the future, which has always been characteristic of the people of Israel.

15 ¶ And he blessed Joseph, and said, God, before whom my fathers Abraham and Isaac did walk, the God which fed me all my life long unto this day,

15 And he blessed Joseph, and said,
"The God before whom my fathers Abraham and Isaac walked,
the God who has led me all my life long to this day,

15-16. *The God of the Fathers.*—Nothing is more characteristic of Genesis than the way in which the thought of God is always linked with something larger than the individual. He is the God who claims the particular person's loyalty, but he is his God because he has been also the God of his fathers. God's promise to Abraham was, "I will establish my covenant between me and thee and thy seed after thee in their generations, for an everlasting covenant, to be a God unto thee and to thy seed after thee" (17:7). God's voice came to Isaac, saying, "I am the God of Abraham thy father: fear not, for I am with thee, and will bless thee, and multiply thy seed for my servant Abraham's sake" (26:24). Isaac said to Jacob, "God Almighty bless thee . . . and give thee the blessing of Abraham" (28:3-4); and to Jacob himself as he dreamed at Bethel came the voice of God, "I am the LORD God of Abraham thy father, and the God of Isaac" (28:13). All this Jacob remembers as he invokes now the **God, before whom my fathers Abraham and Isaac did walk.** That was the God who had fed him all his **life long unto this day.** This consciousness of the bond of faith that ran from generation to generation was the power that made the spiritual stanchness of the people of Israel.

Kipling wrote, "The race is run by one and one and never by two and two." [1] There is truth in that, but it is partial truth; and like all half-truths, it can be overbalanced into falsehood. Each man spiritually must run his own race, but in a larger sense he does not run alone. It is like a relay race in which each man must meet his own responsibility, but in which his opportunity and the victory in which he would share depend also upon the impetus which is handed on to him by those who have run before. In our modern world, with its atomistic tendencies, we are too apt to forget the mighty truth which the men of the O.T. knew. Inherited faith and old convictions may be casually laid aside; and the result is that we are in danger of losing the superb transmitted strength which Israel had. Yet history holds up before us examples of what the continuity of a great tradition can give to a people's life. Consider the British Commonwealth. What is it that has made, and that still makes, that little isle of England so sovereign a force among the civilizations of the earth? The heart of it is not so much in physical

[1] "Tomlinson."

as in spiritual power; and that spiritual power has come down as the accumulating heritage from unforgotten centuries. The pageantry, the long-kept ancient customs, the stately public manners, might seem to a stranger only queerness; but as a matter of fact they are the expression of the abiding character to which all the generations have contributed. Justice, fair opportunity, the love of freedom as surely for commoner as for king, private morals and public honor—these are the qualities which have come down to the British people through an unbroken history of constancy and courage; and because they honored that inheritance they were able to reveal in the dark and disastrous days of the twentieth century such reserves of steady strength and unbreakable tenacity as newer and less tried peoples might hardly dare think they could achieve. Nor can that spirit be accounted for on secular grounds. Back of all that is noble in its civic expression is the religious heritage—that Judaeo-Christian heritage of God-fearing men which in its essential loyalties goes back all the way to Abraham, and which in its N.T. fulfillment has been lifted up before the thought of the English generations as dominantly as the dome and cross of St. Paul's are lifted up against the London sky. It is the God in whose light the **fathers . . . did walk** who is needed by all the families of the earth today, as Jacob knew he was needed for the family of Joseph.

15. *The Agelong Blessing.*—Note the way in which Jacob describes what God had been to him. First, he recognized God in the light of all the best he had seen in his father and his father's father (cf. Expos. on 26:24). Then God was to him the one by whom his own experience had been enriched. He **fed me all my life long unto this day.** The word translated **fed** means "shepherded," and here for the first time we come upon the beautiful metaphor so characteristic of the Bible. God's protecting goodness had the intimate watchfulness of a shepherd for his flock. Isa. 40:11 proclaims, "He shall feed his flock like a shepherd." In Jer. 31:10 and Ezek. 34:12 there is the same promise. Still more personal is Ps. 23, "The LORD is my shepherd," and this figure of the lovingkindness of God is lifted up to its supreme expression in Jesus' parable of the shepherd going out to rescue his lost sheep (Luke 15:4). A man like Jacob, with his imperfect nature, was not large enough of soul to

16 The Angel which redeemed me from all evil, bless the lads; and let my name be named on them, and the name of my fathers Abraham and Isaac; and let them grow into a multitude in the midst of the earth.

17 And when Joseph saw that his father laid his right hand upon the head of Ephraim, it displeased him: and he held up his father's hand, to remove it from Ephraim's head unto Manasseh's head.

18 And Joseph said unto his father, Not so, my father: for this is the firstborn; put thy right hand upon his head.

19 And his father refused, and said, I know it, my son, I know it: he also shall become a people, and he also shall be great: but truly his younger brother shall be greater than he, and his seed shall become a multitude of nations.

20 And he blessed them that day, saying, In thee shall Israel bless, saying, God make thee as Ephraim and as Manasseh: and he set Ephraim before Manasseh.

21 And Israel said unto Joseph, Behold, I die; but God shall be with you, and bring you again unto the land of your fathers.

22 Moreover I have given to thee one portion above thy brethren, which I took out of the hand of the Amorite with my sword and with my bow.

16 the angel who has redeemed me from all evil, bless the lads;
and in them let my name be perpetuated, and the name of my fathers Abraham and Isaac;
and let them grow into a multitude in the midst of the earth."

17 When Joseph saw that his father laid his right hand upon the head of E′phraim, it displeased him; and he took his father's hand, to remove it from E′phraim's head to Manas′seh's head. 18 And Joseph said to his father, "Not so, my father; for this one is the first-born; put your right hand upon his head." 19 But his father refused, and said, "I know, my son, I know; he also shall become a people, and he also shall be great; nevertheless his younger brother shall be greater than he, and his descendants shall become a multitude of nations." 20 So he blessed them that day, saying,
"By you Israel will pronounce blessings, saying,
'God make you as E′phraim and as Manas′seh' ";
and thus he put E′phraim before Manas′seh. 21 Then Israel said to Joseph, "Behold, I am about to die, but God will be with you, and will bring you again to the land of your fathers. 22 Moreover I have given to you rather than to your brothers one mountain slope[v] which I took from the hand of the Amorites with my sword and with my bow."

[v] Heb *shekem*, shoulder

20. **Them** is RᴶE's substitution for the "him" of E. The singular **thee** indicates that the formula is a blessing of one person. (The LXX rendering of **thee** in the plural represents an attempt to smooth the text.)

22. A reference to Jacob's conquest of Shechem by military action. This event must have been recorded in E before 33:20, which, as has been suggested above, tells of the erection of a monument to commemorate the victory. This account of the battle was

know the full meaning of his own faith, but for that very reason the faith he did experience can come with closer relationship to us. For here was a man who certainly was no saint and whose life, had it been guided by nothing but first impulses, would have been hardly better than contemptible. Yet he became aware that no human life has to depend upon itself alone. There is a divine Love which has us in its keeping, and values us beyond our deserving. God does not overlook us, although we seem unprepossessing and obscure. He will be following us even when in our ignorance or our willfulness we wander away. And if we listen, even imper-

fectly like Jacob, we hear the Shepherd's voice which will lead us from the barren ground of our foolish impulse to those fields of life where our souls can grow.

16. *The Redeeming Angel.*—Jacob speaks of the Angel which redeemed me from all evil. He had been acquainted with evil: evil as meaning outward circumstances which threatened harm, such as the anger of Esau which he had deserved, and the trickery of Laban which he had not deserved; evil as meaning the sins which were in himself. He was typical in that he was more concerned to be delivered from that first group of evils than from the second; but he had learned

49 And Jacob called unto his sons, and said, Gather yourselves together, that I may tell you *that* which shall befall you in the last days.

2 Gather yourselves together, and hear, ye sons of Jacob; and hearken unto Israel your father.

49 Then Jacob called his sons, and said, "Gather yourselves together, that I may tell you what shall befall you in days to come.

2 Assemble and hear, O sons of Jacob, and hearken to Israel your father.

---

dropped by R^JE, who preferred the J representation that Jacob came peacefully to Shechem and bought a piece of ground there (33:19). It should be noted that the natural implication of Jacob's words here is that he was, when he spoke, in actual and enduring possession of the territory he had conquered (cf. Gressmann, "Joseph-Sage," EYXAPIΣTHPION, I, 7-8; Gunkel, *Genesis*, pp. 474-75; Meyer, *Israeliten und ihre Nachbarstämme*, pp. 110, 227, 414, etc.). Since there can be no doubt that the E document, even in its earliest form, told of Jacob's descent into Egypt and of his death there, this verse would seem to be a fragment of a story of Jacob's last will and testament, antedating the acceptance by the north of the southern tradition of the Egyptian sojourn.

XLVIII. Jacob Blesses His Sons and Dies (49:1-33)

The foundation of this section is P's account of Jacob's final charge to his sons and his death (vss. 1a, 28bβ-32, 33aαb). Into this R^P inserted from J vs. 33aβ, **he drew up his feet into the bed,** from the account of Jacob's death, and the poem, vss. 2-27, linking it to the P source material with vss. 1b and 28abα.

A. The Blessing of Jacob (49:1-28)

The poem, the so-called Blessing of Jacob, has been built up from a number of originally independent tribal oracles. These were brought together by a writer who, making the necessary redactional alterations, treated the collection as an utterance of the dying Jacob, and so as a definitive prediction (cf. Exeg. on 27:4) of the character and destiny of the several tribes. It was later added to the J narrative.

---

enough at least to know where the emphasis ought to lie. Not even an angel could make much of Jacob's life until he had made more of Jacob.

Jacob's words are true to a deep fact, viz., what God does in a man's life is as much beyond what he himself could accomplish as though an actual angel were walking always at his side. The redemption of a life does not come about accidentally, nor by force of circumstances. There is a misleading translation in the KJV which the RSV corrects. The KJV reads, "We know that all things work together for good to them that love God" (Rom. 8:28). But "things" do not work. The revealing form of the RSV is this, "We know that in everything God works for good with those who love him." God works; and he alone can resolve all contradictions and turn evil into good. The pious blessing which Jacob wanted to hand on to those he left was this faith that God's help is close and real and can be redeeming. It is the blessing which all men need.

49:1-28. The Scales of Judgment.—Genesis begins with the creation of the universe that culminates in man, and here at its climax suggests how the human beings whom God created had accepted or spoiled his creation. "God created man in his own image," says ch. 1; but life in many instances has marred the image. Here in ch. 49 is a portrait gallery of human types, good, bad, and indifferent. Here is what individuals and peoples can do to the original purpose of God. What is written is often called "the blessing of Jacob"; but much of it is no blessing; it is scathing rebuke and blame. Furthermore, as the Exeg. has shown, it does not come from Jacob. It is impassioned poetry written long after Jacob's time but ascribed, in the poet's high imagination, to that great remembered figure. These matters of date and authorship are interesting but not vitally important. What is important is the truth of the picture of life. The writer dramatizes his message in terms of vivid single persons. He has the individual Jacob speak to his individual sons. Actually he is speaking to the tribes who bore those names. He is showing the characteristics, noble or ignoble, which can come to be predominant in a human group. All that we need do to make his

3 ¶ Reuben, thou *art* my firstborn, my might, and the beginning of my strength, the excellency of dignity, and the excellency of power:

4 Unstable as water, thou shalt not excel; because thou wentest up to thy father's bed; then defiledst thou *it:* he went up to my couch.

5 ¶ Simeon and Levi *are* brethren; instruments of cruelty *are in* their habitations.

6 O my soul, come not thou into their secret; unto their assembly, mine honor, be not thou united: for in their anger they slew a man, and in their self-will they digged down a wall.

7 Cursed *be* their anger, for *it was* fierce; and their wrath, for it was cruel: I will divide them in Jacob, and scatter them in Israel.

3 Reuben, you are my first-born,
 my might, and the first fruits of my strength,
 pre-eminent in pride and pre-eminent in power.
4 Unstable as water, you shall not have pre-eminence
 because you went up to your father's bed;
 then you defiled it — you[w] went up to my couch!
5 Simeon and Levi are brothers;
 weapons of violence are their swords.
6 O my soul, come not into their council;
 O my spirit,[x] be not joined to their company;
 for in their anger they slay men,
 and in their wantonness they hamstring oxen.
7 Cursed be their anger, for it is fierce;
 and their wrath, for it is cruel!
 I will divide them in Jacob
 and scatter them in Israel.

[w] Gk Syr Tg: Heb *he*
[x] Or *glory*

49:3. The word rendered **pride** (RSV) can have either a good (cf. **dignity** [KJV]) or an evil connotation, and that rendered **power** also means "fury." Probably the author intended the words to be suggestive of both meanings.

4. The Hebrew original of **unstable** is a noun meaning "wantonness" or "recklessness." The allusion in the first line of the verse is thus to the violent instability of the tribe of Reuben, and Reuben's action, recorded in 35:22aβ, is cited as a particularly disastrous expression of this wanton recklessness. The historical event underlying the story of Reuben's relations with his father's concubine would thus seem, as has already been suggested, to have been some rash act of aggression against another tribe which resulted in a serious loss of prestige and power by Reuben.

It has already been noted that the addition to the J narrative of this oracle on Reuben was the cause of the omission of the curse with which the tale in 35:22 originally ended.

7. In view of the otherwise unnecessary reference to Simeon and Levi as brothers in vs. 5, this verse seems to attribute the all but complete disappearance of the tribes

ancient message modern is to change tribe to nation. Here is a mirror in which a nation may look at its particular reflection, and consider whether it is satisfied with what it sees there.

3-7. *Condemnation of the Violent.*—All twelve sons of Jacob pass in review, so there are twelve descriptions. But they sift out into three general groups. The first is those who fall under devastating judgment. Of such is Reuben, and his condemnation is the more tragic because of the contrast with what ought to have been his destiny. He was his father's first-born, **the beginning of my strength**—type of the nation

therefore long established, endowed with leadership, confident and proud. But Reuben, for all his proud position, had sunk into insignificance. Think of the nations in history that have done the same. The reason is linked with the ugly reference to Reuben in 35:22, which may be a dramatic way of indicating that sexual licentiousness had become conspicuous in the Reuben tribe. **Unstable as water** means not merely restless, like the restlessness of the sea; the picture is of passions that cannot be contained, as dammed up waters, once their barriers are broken, spill out wildly everywhere. The

| 8 ¶ Judah, thou *art he* whom thy brethren shall praise: thy hand *shall be* in the neck of thine enemies; thy father's children shall bow down before thee. | 8 Judah, your brothers shall praise you; your hand shall be on the neck of your enemies; your father's sons shall bow down before you. |

bearing their names to fratricidal warfare between them. Simeon, in historical times, was simply a clan of Judah (cf. Meyer, *Israeliten und ihre Nachbarstämme*, p. 411); and of Levi only the priesthood remained. (For an attempted reconstruction of the history of the tribe of Levi see Simpson, *Early Traditions of Israel*, pp. 442-43.)

8. An allusion to the achievement of David, leading to the shortlived pre-eminence of Judah over the northern tribes.

---

historian might read in the fall of imperial Rome a re-enactment of the tragedy of Reuben, when the old moral virility of the republic had changed to unstable and ungoverned impulses. As Reuben was condemned, so also were Simeon and Levi, for reasons equally as strong and relevant in every generation. **Cursed be their anger, for it was fierce; and their wrath, for it was cruel** (vs. 7). So it was written of them, with reference particularly to the ferocity described in ch. 34. Note the significant fact that Simeon and Levi would have argued that their violence was virtue. Did they not do what they had done for the glory of Israel and for its right to dominate? Were they not defending the family honor? So modern nations have perpetrated outrageous evils in the name of manifest destiny, and let themselves loose in the lust of conquest. They have built their colonies by cruelty; and like Simeon and Levi have slain with the edge of the sword and "spoiled even all that was in the house" (34:29). So also men with blind herd instinct have gone out, as they claimed, to protect the purity and predominance of their blood, as mobs in some of the United States have done and still do, in brutal lynchings. But Jacob was right when he cried out (34:30), "Ye have troubled me to make me to stink among the inhabitants of the land." Right-thinking men in every country know that a nation's real glory is not exalted but debased whenever its roads of expansion have gone forward through foul acts of cruelty. What can truth say to those who commit such abominations as lynching but, "You have made me to stink among the decent people of the world"? In any nation when men grow drunk with power and let violence loose, there may recur the deadly sin of Simeon and Levi, which must be denounced, and which if unrepented is bound to lead to doom.

13-21, 27. Qualified Commendation.—The second group among the twelve is of those condemned less drastically; and of some who won a blessing which had some value, even if it was

not complete, e.g., Issachar. One wonders whether the judgment here is faintly contemptuous, or whether it is a tolerant and kindly commendation. **Issachar is a strong ass couching down between two burdens.** An ancient Israelite may have meant nothing derisive when he compared a man or a people to an ass. The ass was the animal most depended upon for service. And Issachar was **a strong ass.** But he is **couching down between two burdens.** Does that mean that he is patiently ready to be laden with them, or that he is lying down so that he will not carry them at all? If the latter, then he is the people that shirks responsibility. If the former, he is the people without much ambition who yet deserves honor because he carries the humdrum burdens of the world; for he sees that at least there are mild rewards in obedience and subordination, and so he bows **his shoulder to bear.** Such are some of the humble peoples of the earth, like the black men of Africa who carried the loads of David Livingstone on the great explorations which would not have been possible without them; like the patient Chinese coolies that built the Burma Road; like the humble people everywhere who represent none of the brilliant achievements of civilization, but on whose shoulders much of its fundamental structure rests. Along with Issachar are other tribes to whom at least a qualified blessing belongs. There is Zebulun, which **shall dwell at the haven of the sea; and he shall be for a haven of ships**—the people that represented thus adventure and the energies of far-reaching commerce. There are Gad and Dan and Benjamin, each of which represents in its particular way the elemental courage of the little people that maintains its independence against larger forces by which it is surrounded. And there are Asher and Naphtali, representing the contentment of peoples who settle down peacefully to cultivate a fruitful land.

8-12, 22-26. The Source of Greatness.—But the great blessings are reserved for two tribes only—Judah and Joseph. The reason is plain:

9 Judah *is* a lion's whelp: from the prey, my son, thou art gone up: he stooped down, he couched as a lion, and as an old lion; who shall rouse him up?

10 The sceptre shall not depart from Judah, nor a lawgiver from between his feet, until Shiloh come; and unto him *shall* the gathering of the people *be*.

11 Binding his foal unto the vine, and his ass's colt unto the choice vine; he washed his garments in wine, and his clothes in the blood of grapes:

12 His eyes *shall be* red with wine, and his teeth white with milk.

13 ¶ Zebulun shall dwell at the haven of the sea; and he *shall be* for a haven of ships; and his border *shall be* unto Zidon.

14 ¶ Issachar *is* a strong ass couching down between two burdens:

15 And he saw that rest *was* good, and the land that *it was* pleasant; and bowed his shoulder to bear, and became a servant unto tribute.

9 Judah is a lion's whelp;
  from the prey, my son, you have gone up.
He stooped down, he couched as a lion,
  and as a lioness; who dares rouse him up?
10 The scepter shall not depart from Judah,
  nor the ruler's staff from between his feet,
until he comes to whom it belongs;*y*
  and to him shall be the obedience of the peoples.
11 Binding his foal to the vine
  and his ass's colt to the choice vine,
he washes his garments in wine
  and his vesture in the blood of grapes;
12 his eyes shall be red with wine,
  and his teeth white with milk.
13 Zeb'ulun shall dwell at the shore of the sea;
  he shall become a haven for ships,
  and his border shall be at Sidon.
14 Is'sachar is a strong ass,
  crouching between the sheepfolds;
15 he saw that a resting place was good,
  and that the land was pleasant;
so he bowed his shoulder to bear,
  and became a slave at forced labor.

y Syr Compare Tg: Heb *until Shiloh comes* or *until he comes to Shiloh*

9. The first line refers to the youthful vigor of the tribe. The second line would be better rendered, "On prey, my son, you have grown up"; it elaborates the thought of the preceding statement. The last two lines are almost verbally identical with Num. 24:9*a* and are probably a quotation from another poem.

10. **To whom it belongs:** The Hebrew original, *shîlōh*, is cryptic in the extreme. On this rendering it refers to **the scepter.** Another possible rendering is "he who is his"—i.e., he who is pre-eminently the representative of Judah. In either case the verse has a messianic significance and is probably later than its present context.

11. A fragment of an old poem on Judah's land.

12. A later addition, taunting the tribe with decadence (cf. Prov. 23:29).

13. Refers to the advantageous geographical position of Zebulun.

14. The meaning of the second line is uncertain.

15. A gibe at Issachar's comfortable submission to foreign domination at the price of his own freedom.

to these tribes the greatest men belonged. In the one case, Joseph himself; in the other, David. Joseph as the hero from whom one tribe originated, David as the hero whom the other produced, gave a quality of spirit which seemed in retrospect to permeate a whole people. Therefore to the poet's vision **the scepter shall not depart from Judah,** and the blessing of Joseph shall be better than the blessings of this earth,

a glory from God that shall be **unto the utmost bound of the everlasting hills.** Here we touch one of those deep, sure insights which make the O.T. incomparable among ancient writings, and full of truth which no modern conditions can outgrow. The great nation will be the one which has for its hero the highest type of man. It was the instinct which felt this that made Israel unique. The history it cared for and the

16 ¶ Dan shall judge his people, as one of the tribes of Israel.

17 Dan shall be a serpent by the way, an adder in the path, that biteth the horse heels, so that his rider shall fall backward.

18 I have waited for thy salvation, O LORD.

19 ¶ Gad, a troop shall overcome him: but he shall overcome at the last.

20 ¶ Out of Asher his bread *shall be* fat, and he shall yield royal dainties.

21 ¶ Naphtali *is* a hind let loose: he giveth goodly words.

22 ¶ Joseph *is* a fruitful bough, *even* a fruitful bough by a well; *whose* branches run over the wall:

23 The archers have sorely grieved him, and shot *at him,* and hated him:

24 But his bow abode in strength, and the arms of his hands were made strong by the hands of the mighty *God* of Jacob; (from thence *is* the shepherd, the stone of Israel;)

25 *Even* by the God of thy father, who shall help thee; and by the Almighty, who

---

16 Dan shall judge his people
   as one of the tribes of Israel.

17 Dan shall be a serpent in the way,
   a viper by the path,
   that bites the horse's heels
   so that his rider falls backward.

18 I wait for thy salvation, O LORD.

19 Raiders[z] shall raid Gad,
   but he shall raid at their heels.

20 Asher's food shall be rich,
   and he shall yield royal dainties.

21 Naph'tali is a hind let loose,
   that bears comely fawns.[a]

22 Joseph is a fruitful bough,
   a fruitful bough by a spring;
   his branches run over the wall.

23 The archers fiercely attacked him,
   shot at him, and harassed him sorely;

24 yet his bow remained unmoved,
   his arms[b] were made agile
  by the hands of the Mighty One of Jacob
   (by the name of the Shepherd, the
     Rock of Israel),

25 by the God of your father who will help
   you,
  by God Almighty[u] who will bless you
  with blessings of heaven above,

[z] Heb *gedud*, a raiding troop
[a] Or *who gives beautiful words*
[b] Heb *the arms of his hands*
[u] Heb *El Shaddai*

---

16. An allusion to Dan's attainment of tribal status; contrast "the family of the Danites" (Judg. 13:2; 18:11).

17. A reference to the kind of warfare by which the Danites grew in power.

18. An ejaculatory gloss.

19. An allusion to the frequent raids from the desert upon Gilead, east of the Jordan, where the tribe of Gad was settled.

20. An allusion to the fertility of Asher's land, north of Carmel.

21. A possible rendering of this is "Naphtali is a spreading terebinth, producing comely tops" (cf. LXX). This will refer to the territorial expansion of the tribe (cf. Deut. 33:23).

22-26. The text of these verses is uncertain. The original oracle, limited possibly to vs. 22, has been elaborated by a succession of writers to stress the pre-eminence of the

---

history it recorded, from Abraham on through patriarchs, kings, and prophets, was the history of men who walked not in the light of this world only, but in the light of heaven. Israel has endured because of that inheritance. Few in numbers, scattered, persecuted often, it has maintained its existence because it kept in its soul the memory of men who obeyed God.

In the long run the permanence of any nation will depend upon the quality of its heroes. Does it exalt only its men of glittering so-called

success, its creators of material wealth, its generals and admirals who by any means whatever have won their victories? Or does something deep within its soul acknowledge a greater inheritance? Does it feel the upward pull upon its character and conduct of a Robert Bruce, a Joan of Arc, a Washington, or of some other hero of the spirit concerning whom it could be said, as of Charles George Gordon, that he gave "his strength to the weak, his substance to the poor, his sympathy to the suffering, and his

shall bless thee with blessings of heaven above, blessings of the deep that lieth under, blessings of the breasts, and of the womb:

26 The blessings of thy father have prevailed above the blessings of my progenitors unto the utmost bound of the everlasting hills: they shall be on the head of Joseph, and on the crown of the head of him that was separate from his brethren.

27 ¶ Benjamin shall raven *as* a wolf: in the morning he shall devour the prey, and at night he shall divide the spoil.

28 ¶ All these *are* the twelve tribes of Israel: and this *is it* that their father spake unto them, and blessed them; every one according to his blessing he blessed them.

29 And he charged them, and said unto them, I am to be gathered unto my people: bury me with my fathers in the cave that *is* in the field of Ephron the Hittite,

30 In the cave that *is* in the field of Machpelah, which *is* before Mamre, in the land of Canaan, which Abraham bought with the field of Ephron the Hittite for a possession of a buryingplace.

31 There they buried Abraham and Sarah his wife; there they buried Isaac and Rebekah his wife; and there I buried Leah.

32 The purchase of the field and of the cave that *is* therein *was* from the children of Heth.

33 And when Jacob had made an end of commanding his sons, he gathered up his feet into the bed, and yielded up the ghost, and was gathered unto his people.

blessings of the deep that couches beneath,
blessings of the breasts and of the womb.

26 The blessings of your father
are mighty beyond the blessings of the eternal mountains,[c]
the bounties of the everlasting hills;
may they be on the head of Joseph,
and on the brow of him who was separate from his brothers.

27 Benjamin is a ravenous wolf,
in the morning devouring the prey,
and at even dividing the spoil."

28 All these are the twelve tribes of Israel; and this is what their father said to them as he blessed them, blessing each with the blessing suitable to him. 29 Then he charged them, and said to them, "I am to be gathered to my people; bury me with my fathers in the cave that is in the field of Ephron the Hittite, 30 in the cave that is in the field at Mach-pe'lah, to the east of Mamre, in the land of Canaan, which Abraham bought with the field from Ephron the Hittite to possess as a burying place. 31 There they buried Abraham and Sarah his wife; there they buried Isaac and Rebekah his wife; and there I buried Leah — 32 the field and the cave that is in it were purchased from the Hittites." 33 When Jacob finished charging his sons, he drew up his feet into the bed, and breathed his last, and was gathered to his people.

c Compare Gk: Heb *of my progenitors to*

Joseph tribes. In this its final form it contradicts vs. 8, according to which Judah has the leadership of the nation.

27. Benjamin is praised for its predatory habits and its zest for war. The difference between this characterization (which finds support in Judg. 19–21) and the conception of Benjamin in the Joseph stories may be noted. In the last line there seems to be an allusion to the prowess of Saul (cf. II Sam. 1:24).

B. JACOB'S DEATH (49:29-33)

29. According to P, Jacob was buried in the cave of Machpelah at Hebron. With this representation should be contrasted that of J; see Exeg. on 50:10.

---

heart to God"? With lesser ideals a nation may seize for itself many temporary benefits, but on no lower terms can it win the lasting greatness which depends upon the blessing of God.

49:29–50:13. *Jacob's Death and Burial.*—There is an instinct which seems almost universal for men to desire to be buried with their

people. It is as though the loneliness of death were in this measure overcome, and the bond with one's own still preserved. So there is a sacrosanctity to the place of graves. One may see in the midst of a great city some obscure corner, with modern buildings overlooking it, where old tombs stand dusty but undisturbed; or by

50 And Joseph fell upon his father's face, and wept upon him, and kissed him.

2 And Joseph commanded his servants the physicians to embalm his father: and the physicians embalmed Israel.

3 And forty days were fulfilled for him; for so are fulfilled the days of those which are embalmed: and the Egyptians mourned for him threescore and ten days.

4 And when the days of his mourning were past, Joseph spake unto the house of Pharaoh, saying, If now I have found grace in your eyes, speak, I pray you, in the ears of Pharaoh, saying,

50 Then Joseph fell on his father's face, and wept over him, and kissed him. 2 And Joseph commanded his servants the physicians to embalm his father. So the physicians embalmed Israel; 3 forty days were required for it, for so many are required for embalming. And the Egyptians wept for him seventy days.

4 And when the days of weeping for him were past, Joseph spoke to the household of Pharaoh, saying, "If now I have found favor in your eyes, speak, I pray you, in the

XLIX. Burial of Jacob (50:1-21)

Vss. 12-13 are from P. The rest of the material is a conflation of J and E.

J² recorded Joseph's grief at his father's death (vs. 1), the embalming of Jacob's body (vs. 2a), and the national mourning in Egypt (vs. 3b). He then told of Joseph's securing permission from the Pharaoh to bury his father in Palestine (vss. 4-6), of the burial in Palestine (vss. 7-11), of Joseph's return to Egypt (vs. 14), and of his reassuring his brothers of his continued good will toward them (vss. 18, 21abβ).

This narrative is an elaboration of a slightly simpler tale which goes back to J¹. As has already been noted J¹, having completed his articulation of the various local traditions of Canaan into a unified whole, had been faced with the necessity of getting the supposed ancestors of the Israelite tribes into Egypt, in order that he might continue his narrative and set down in writing the historical tradition of the Exodus and the Conquest. It was for this reason that the story of Joseph was told. Having thus recorded Jacob's death as occurring in Egypt, it was necessary for J¹ to reconcile this representation with the fact that his grave was one of the famous sites of Palestine. This he probably did by means of this tale.

Only fragments of the E narrative have been preserved: vss. 2b-3a, telling of the embalming, and vss. 15-17, 19-20, 21bα, telling in more detail than J had done of the brothers' fears that Joseph would now take vengeance on them for their harsh treatment of him years before. This incident was recorded in E as occurring during the forty days mentioned in vs. 3a, i.e., before the burial. The present position of the material is of course due to RJE, who here preferred the representation of J² that Joseph's brothers had not expressed their misgivings until after their return to Egypt (vs. 18).

Although nothing has been preserved of E's account of the actual burial, it seems reasonable to assume that he followed the J narrative in this respect. If so then E, like J, by this narrative reconciled the representation that Jacob died in Egypt with the fact of his grave in Palestine. At the same time he seized the opportunity to emphasize once more the providential element in Joseph's career (vss. 19-20).

50:2. The first occurrence of **the physicians** is a redactional addition to harmonize the J representation (vs. 2a) that Joseph's servants embalmed the body of Jacob with the more sophisticated statement of E that this was done by **the physicians.**

some country lane a little burying ground still preserved, though the property surrounding it may have changed hands many times. Men do not readily violate what seem the title deeds of the dead. To Jacob the cave of Machpelah was holy ground, for there had been buried Abra- ham and Sarah, Isaac and Rebekah, and there he had buried Leah. When he expressed his wish to be carried there, he knew that Joseph would fulfill it—as he did, with Egyptian pomp and pageantry. But the story of Jacob's burial as told in these two chapters has another ref-

5 My father made me swear, saying, Lo, I die: in my grave which I have digged for me in the land of Canaan, there shalt thou bury me. Now therefore let me go up, I pray thee, and bury my father, and I will come again.

6 And Pharaoh said, Go up, and bury thy father, according as he made thee swear.

7 ¶ And Joseph went up to bury his father: and with him went up all the servants of Pharaoh, the elders of his house, and all the elders of the land of Egypt,

8 And all the house of Joseph, and his brethren, and his father's house: only their little ones, and their flocks, and their herds, they left in the land of Goshen.

9 And there went up with him both chariots and horsemen: and it was a very great company.

10 And they came to the threshingfloor of Atad, which is beyond Jordan; and there they mourned with a great and very sore lamentation: and he made a mourning for his father seven days.

11 And when the inhabitants of the land, the Canaanites, saw the mourning in the floor of Atad, they said, This is a grievous mourning to the Egyptians: wherefore the name of it was called Abel-mizraim, which is beyond Jordan.

12 And his sons did unto him according as he commanded them:

13 For his sons carried him into the land of Canaan, and buried him in the cave of the field of Machpelah, which Abraham bought with the field for a possession of a buryingplace of Ephron the Hittite, before Mamre.

ears of Pharaoh, saying, 5 My father made me swear, saying, 'I am about to die: in my tomb which I hewed out for myself in the land of Canaan, there shall you bury me.' Now therefore let me go up, I pray you, and bury my father; then I will return." 6 And Pharaoh answered, "Go up, and bury your father, as he made you swear." 7 So Joseph went up to bury his father; and with him went up all the servants of Pharaoh, the elders of his household, and all the elders of the land of Egypt, 8 as well as all the household of Joseph, his brothers, and his father's household; only their children, their flocks, and their herds were left in the land of Goshen. 9 And there went up with him both chariots and horsemen; it was a very great company. 10 When they came to the threshing floor of Atad, which is beyond the Jordan, they lamented there with a very great and sorrowful lamentation; and he made a mourning for his father seven days. 11 When the inhabitants of the land, the Canaanites, saw the mourning on the threshing floor of Atad, they said, "This is a grievous mourning to the Egyptians." Therefore the place was named ·A'bel-mizraim;[d] it is beyond the Jordan. 12 Thus his sons did for him as he had commanded them; 13 for his sons carried him to the land of Canaan, and buried him in the cave of the field at Mach-pe'lah, to the east of Mamre, which Abraham bought with the field from Ephron the Hittite, to possess

[d] That is meadow (or mourning) of Egypt

---

10. The explicit statement that the cortege **came to the threshing floor of Atad**, east of the Jordan, suggests that the J narrative located the burial there. This suggestion is supported by the fact, noted in the Exeg. on 25:26, that Jacob was originally an east Jordan figure, i.e., the monument known as Jacob's grave was located at **the threshing floor of Atad** (cf. Meyer, *Israeliten und ihre Nachbarstämme*, pp. 280-81; Skinner, *Genesis*, p. 538) near **Abel-mizraim** (vs. 11), east of the Jordan.

The J notice of the burial there was later dropped by R^P in favor of the P representation (vss. 12-13) that Jacob was buried with Abraham and Isaac (49:31) in the cave of Machpelah at Hebron. The journey to the east of the Jordan was thus rendered quite purposeless.

11. The real meaning of **Abel-mizraim** is **meadow of Egypt**. The name doubtless commemorates some incident of the Egyptian occupation of Palestine. For other place names with the component "meadow" see Num. 33:49; Judg. 7:22; 11:33; II Sam. 20:15; II Chr. 16:4. The consonants of the Hebrew words for **meadow** and **mourning**, '*bl*, are identical.

14 ¶ And Joseph returned into Egypt, he, and his brethren, and all that went up with him to bury his father, after he had buried his father.

15 ¶ And when Joseph's brethren saw that their father was dead, they said, Joseph will peradventure hate us, and will certainly requite us all the evil which we did unto him.

16 And they sent a messenger unto Joseph, saying, Thy father did command before he died, saying,

17 So shall ye say unto Joseph, Forgive, I pray thee now, the trespass of thy brethren, and their sin; for they did unto thee evil: and now, we pray thee, forgive the trespass of the servants of the God of thy father. And Joseph wept when they spake unto him.

18 And his brethren also went and fell down before his face; and they said, Behold, we *be* thy servants.

19 And Joseph said unto them, Fear not: for *am* I in the place of God?

20 But as for you, ye thought evil against me; *but* God meant it unto good, to bring to pass, as *it is* this day, to save much people alive.

21 Now therefore fear ye not: I will nourish you, and your little ones. And he comforted them, and spake kindly unto them.

as a burying place. 14 After he had buried his father, Joseph returned to Egypt with his brothers and all who had gone up with him to bury his father.

15 When Joseph's brothers saw that their father was dead, they said, "It may be that Joseph will hate us and pay us back for all the evil which we did to him." 16 So they sent a message to Joseph, saying, "Your father gave this command before he died, 17 'Say to Joseph, Forgive, I pray you, the transgression of your brothers and their sin, because they did evil to you.' And now, we pray you, forgive the transgression of the servants of the God of your father." Joseph wept when they spoke to him. 18 His brothers also came and fell down before him, and said, "Behold, we are your servants." 19 But Joseph said to them, "Fear not, for am I in the place of God? 20 As for you, you meant evil against me; but God meant it for good, to bring it about that many people should be kept alive, as they are today. 21 So do not fear; I will provide for you and your little ones." Thus he reassured them and comforted them.

---

19. **Am I in the place of God**: To judge and to punish at my pleasure?
20. Cf. 45:7-8.

---

erence besides that which had to do with Jacob's own desire. The last verses of ch. 49 and 50:12-13 are the work of the priestly writers; and the formal record of the purchase of the cave by Abraham, which had been meticulously given in ch. 23, is here twice repeated (49:30; 50:13). Thus it was to be certified beyond doubt that this burying place belonged to Israel, and that the land in the midst of which the dust of the fathers rested was also destined to be Israel's possession.

50:14-21. *Joseph's Ultimate Forgiveness.*— Sometimes it is harder for men who have sinned to believe that they are forgiven than it is for one who has been wronged to forgive. Joseph had shown to his brothers the most moving and unmistakable evidence of the magnanimity with which he could put the past behind him, and of the old affection which not all the wrong they had done to him could quench. Yet now

that Jacob was gone, they fell into a panic. What if Joseph had spared them only because he did not want to distress his father? What if he had no real concern for them? Those were questions which could have been asked only by men into whose hearts the consciousness of guilt had entered so deeply that hardly anything could wash it clean. That may be the deepest tragedy of evil. It so affects the outlook of guilty men that it may become almost impossible for them to look at goodness and see it cleanly and clearly for what it fully is. Even now the brothers thought they did not dare to plead directly for forgiveness. They had to claim that Jacob before he died had sent a plea on their behalf.

And Joseph wept. Why?—we ask. Was it from sheer disappointment that these brothers of his had so little understood him? Was it from sudden pity for their torment of fear? Was it some

22 ¶ And Joseph dwelt in Egypt, he, and his father's house: and Joseph lived a hundred and ten years.	22 So Joseph dwelt in Egypt, he and his father's house; and Joseph lived a hundred and ten years. 23 And Joseph saw E'phraim's children of the third generation; the children also of Machir the son of Manas'seh were born upon Joseph's knees. 24 And Joseph said to his brothers, "I am about to die; but God will visit you, and bring you up out of this land to the land which he swore to Abraham, to Isaac, and to Jacob."
23 And Joseph saw Ephraim's children of the third *generation:* the children also of Machir the son of Manasseh were brought up upon Joseph's knees.	
24 And Joseph said unto his brethren, I die; and God will surely visit you, and bring you out of this land unto the land which he sware to Abraham, to Isaac, and to Jacob.	

L. Death of Joseph (50:22-26)

Vss. 22*b*, 26*a*β, stating that **Joseph lived a hundred and ten years,** are from RP, based doubtless on P. The rest of the section is a conflation of J and E.

From E come vss. 22*a*, 23, telling of Joseph's long life and of his adoption of the children of his grandson Machir. As Judg. 5:14 indicates, the Machirites once formed an independent unit in the northern confederacy. Possibly E is here reflecting a claim of theirs, perhaps revived in the closing days of the northern kingdom, to tribal status, or to quasi-tribal status within Manasseh.

---

foregleam of the sort of tragic sorrow with which Jesus would look at Jerusalem and grieve that sin could be so hard to reach? Whatever the reason for his weeping, the words Joseph spoke showed him at his noblest. **Fear not: for am I in the place of God?** How different the world's history would have been in many times and places if there had been more men like Joseph whose purpose toward those who had wronged them was to steady and restore, not to terrify and punish. Too many suppose that they are in the place of God: that at all costs they must "see justice done," make sure that the sinner is humiliated, implacably "balance the account," when what they actually do is to tilt the scales the other way—to vengeance that calls itself disinterested virtue. Joseph looked at the events of life from a point of view so high that it rose above the thick atmosphere of human passion. He saw that what had been meant as evil God had turned to good. Therefore he could be the instrument of God's goodness now. **Fear ye not,** he said, **I will nourish you, and your little ones. And he comforted them, and spake kindly unto them.** From such a picture it is not a great distance to the standards proclaimed in the Sermon on the Mount.

24. The Inevitability of Death.—That is the reminder that rings most unmistakably from these words: **And Joseph said, . . . I die.** As against all the infinite variety of men's lives stands the fixed fact of the appointed end. From all separate ways, and across the changing centuries, the many roads of their existence converge upon the single gate. As a generality, all

know that. Yet no recognition that death is inevitable and universal can keep a particular death from seeming unique. The moment comes when the individual is saying something much more poignant than "all men are mortal." He is saying, **I die.**

Note in the example of Joseph the marks of a good man's death. There is no distress or fear. Instead, there is a simplicity of acceptance that is at once childlike and mature. **I die.** In these serene monosyllables there is the response of the soul that with a child's obedience answers to the roll call: like Thackeray's Colonel Newcome, of whom it was written that as the chapel bell began to toll, he lifted his head with a sudden smile, and quickly said, *"Adsum,"* and fell back upon his pillow. "It was the word we used at school, when names were called; and lo, he, whose heart was as that of a little child, had answered to his name, and stood in the presence of The Master."

There is also a trustfulness that is more than the child's surrender: a confidence that has in it not only the instinct of early innocence but an assurance woven out of long obedience to God. So in all ages men who like Joseph have tried to walk with God may say, as Mr. Standfast said in *The Pilgrim's Progress:* "I see myself now at the end of my journey; my toilsome days are ended. . . . My steps hath He strengthened in His way." And he can go on to say, like "Stonewall" Jackson dying at Chancellorsville when his duty had been done, "Let us cross over the river, and rest in the shade of the trees." Serenity in death is not accidental. It

25 And Joseph took an oath of the children of Israel, saying, God will surely visit you, and ye shall carry up my bones from hence.

25 Then Joseph took an oath of the sons of Israel, saying, "God will visit you, and you

---

Vss. 24-25, 26aαb are from J. Vs. 24b points ahead to the Exodus (cf. Exeg. on 45:7). In vss. 25, 26b, J² prepares further for his reconciliation of the representation of J¹ that Joseph died in Egypt with the fact—apparently unknown to J¹—of Joseph's grave in Shechem (cf. 33:19; Exod. 13:19; Josh. 24:32). This is another indication that

---

comes, as it came to Joseph, out of the dedication of the preceding years. Consider the words of the often sung hymn of which the climactic prayer is,

> God be at mine end,
> And at my departing.

Leading up to that are the prayers which justify the final one: prayers that

> God be in my head,
> And in my understanding;
> God be in mine eyes,
> And in my looking;
> God be in my mouth,
> And in my speaking.[2]

The death of Joseph suggests further that the good man in his death can be not only serene but also hopeful. Often it seems, unhappily, that this is not true. Many men when they die have no hope or inspiration to hand on to those who follow; and such men may include by no means only those whose lives have been evil or indifferent. They may include those who have been called good, but whose goodness was of a passive and unventuresome kind. They have invested nothing in the future. They have failed to keep themselves allied with what was young and brave and new. Consequently, when their own strength wanes and they feel the pathos of old age, it is as though all the flame of life had burned low and begun to flicker. Their dying, and not a greater living, is what seems to them overwhelmingly real. But for spirits like that of Joseph—and in every generation there are spirits like his—the whole outlook is different. They have loved children, and made companionship with the young. They have invested their sympathy and strength in large and generous causes that reach far beyond themselves. So, like Joseph, they have the happy confidence that God will lead their children and their children's children on great ways of fulfillment. And more than that: their hearts will say in the words that Henry van Dyke put into the mouth of

old Abgarus when "the other wise man" was starting on his search "I am too old for this journey, but my heart shall be a companion of the pilgrimage day and night, and I shall know the end of the quest." [3]

25-26. To the Homeland at Last.—Beyond these few words that record the burial of Joseph in Egypt there looms a background of magnificent suggestion. More than any other people known to history the Egyptians surrounded death with pomp and grandeur. Witness the pyramids, the colossal temples and statues at Thebes and Karnak, the tombs in the valley of the kings. Among them the incredibly costly splendor of the recovered tomb of Tutankhamon, with his coffin beaten out of gold, gives probably only a partial revelation of the riches in the tombs of the greater Pharaohs, which were rifled long ago.

Here is witness to the agelong hunger of man for survival. Distorted and futile though some of the efforts to satisfy that hunger may have been, can one fail to reverence the instinct itself, or fail to see in it a promise that anything so deeply implanted in the human spirit must at last find fulfillment? Yet what is it that can justify that hope? Certainly, not the ostentation of tombs in which the dead are laid—either in ancient Egypt or in the fantastic modern "Forest Lawn" of California's Hollywood. "In what way shall we bury you?" asked Crito of Socrates just before he drank the fatal hemlock. "In any way that you like," answered Socrates, "you are burying my body only." [4] What is real is that which no one can bury. If Joseph was embalmed in Egypt and put into a coffin, even a coffin of gold, that would not have guaranteed that Joseph still was there, nor made him more significant. Only the revelation of something immortal in the quality of the life that has been lived can be the token that a soul goes on.

"The souls of the righteous are in the hands of God." Also their influence is in the world,

[2] From the Sarum Primer of 1558.

[3] *The Story of the Other Wise Man* (New York: Harper & Bros., 1896), p. 29.

[4] *Phaedo, The Dialogues of Plato*, tr. B. Jowett (London: Oxford University Press, 1892), II, 263-64.

26 So Joseph died, *being* a hundred and ten years old: and they embalmed him, and he was put in a coffin in Egypt.

shall carry up my bones from here." **26** So Joseph died, being a hundred and ten years old; and they embalmed him, and he was put in a coffin in Egypt.

J² was much more familiar with the local traditions of Shechem than J¹ had been. On E's silence regarding Joseph's grave see Exeg. on 37:1-36.

26. The book, the overture to the Exodus, ends on a muted note.

---

and it is indestructible. Shakespeare made Mark Antony say in his oration over the dead Caesar:

> The evil that men do lives after them,
> The good is oft interred with their bones.[5]

That is a distortion of the full reality. In the solemn responsibility of life nothing that a man is and does can be limited to himself. It is true that the evil he does lives after him; but it is not true that the good is buried with his bones. Every man of morally heroic stature in the Bible or anywhere in history has set in motion a noble influence that moves in blessing down the years. As Emerson truly wrote, "We may say great men exist that there may be greater men." [6]

But the last verse of the book, which tells that Joseph **was put in a coffin in Egypt,** is not the verse of greatest significance. More important is the one that precedes it, for it is here that Joseph exacts the promise that his body shall not have its final resting place in Egypt. He would have it taken back to Canaan. It might have seemed that he had little reason to desire that: his memories of Canaan were short and clouded, and they ended in pictures which he might well wish to forget—of the pit into which his brothers threw him, his sale to the slavers, his being carried off from his home. Most of his life had been spent in Egypt, and this part of his life, unlike the other, had come to a climax of great achievement. He might have had his final burial there with pomp and honor. Why, then, did he not desire this? And why did he strictly charge that his body should be taken back to

Canaan to be buried there? It was because still in his heart there was loyalty to the land where he had been born and to the spirit and hopes it represented. In him was that nostalgia for the scenes of childhood which is in the heart of every man. Not that a man wants to go back and be a child again; but what he does want is to recapture the fresh wonder of those days when all his world was new. Across the years he sees it "appareled in celestial light." Although he was to die in Egypt, Joseph still belonged to a dearer country—like Rupert Brooke, dying at Skyros in the Aegean, but with the echo of these words which he had written:

> If I should die, think only this of me:
> That there's some corner of a foreign field
> That is for ever England.[7]

So Joseph in his death expressed the everlasting faithfulness of a man's devotion to the country and the people and the purpose of God to which it was given him first to belong, and with the ongoing life of which, beyond all other attachments of the world, he wanted at last to be identified.

Thus Genesis ends with the record of a great man desiring to go back at last to what was to him the homeland. But Genesis means "The Book of the Beginnings"; and we remember the One who was not only the beginning but the ending, not only the Alpha but the Omega too. In him for lives like that of Joseph there can be the ultimate Homeland of the soul's desire.

---

[5] *Julius Caesar,* Act III, scene 2.

[6] "Uses of Great Men," *Representative Men* (Boston: Houghton Mifflin Co., 1876), p. 38.

[7] "The Soldier." From *Collected Poems of Rupert Brooke.* Copyright 1915 by Dodd, Mead & Co., Inc., and Sidgwick & Jackson, Ltd., publishers. Used by permission.

The Book of
EXODUS

Introduction and Exegesis by J. Coert Rylaarsdam
Exposition by J. Edgar Park

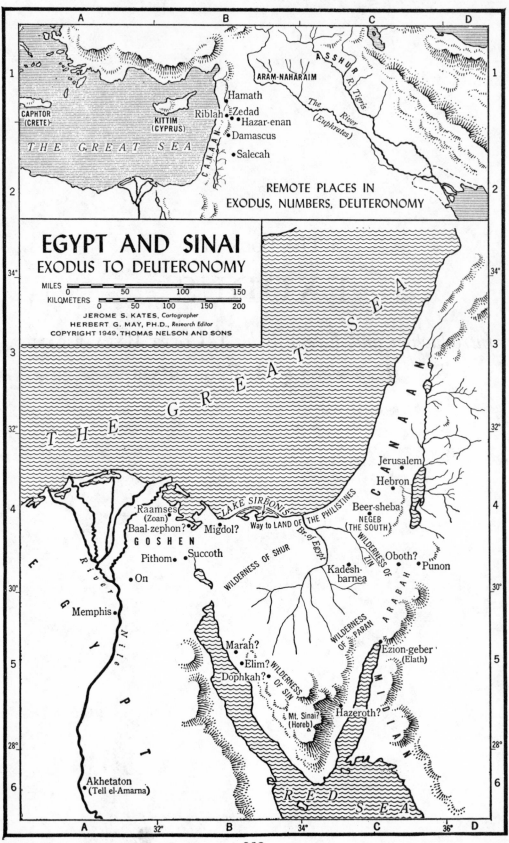

REMOTE PLACES IN
EXODUS, NUMBERS, DEUTERONOMY

EGYPT AND SINAI
EXODUS TO DEUTERONOMY

MILES
0   50   100   150
KILOMETERS
0   50   100   150   200

JEROME S. KATES, *Cartographer*
HERBERT G. MAY, PH.D., *Research Editor*
COPYRIGHT 1949, THOMAS NELSON AND SONS

EXODUS

INTRODUCTION

Biblical religion rests on a historical faith that affirms revelation. The Bible assumes throughout that God has revealed himself in unique events that attest both his freedom and his gracious initiative. But these events are nevertheless conditioned by the dimensions of time and space. They are organically related to the processes of nature and history of which they are also a part and in whose context they occur. Consequently every book of the Bible must be studied and understood in terms of its uniqueness as over against its general Oriental environment. But it must likewise be studied and understood in terms of its affinity with and dependence upon this environment. This is notably true of a book such as Exodus, of which the explicit and immediate concern is the interpretation of that historic event of revelation on which the faith and community of Israel rested. The apparently heterogeneous and unrelated list of topics discussed in this Introduction actually have a common rationale in this double concern involved in all Bible study. The object of the Introduction is only in the first instance to correlate the result of critical literary and historical studies; its ultimate purpose is to show how our knowledge of the God who reveals himself as "the Lord of history" is, nevertheless, historically mediated.

I. Title, Subject, and Motif

The Hebrew title for the second division of the Pentateuch is *we'ēlleh shemôth*, "Now these are the names of," the initial words of the document. This is commonly abbreviated as *shemôth*, "Names." It offers no clue to the contents of the book.

"Exodus" is a naturalized English word resting on the Septuagint title. It denotes the marching out en masse of a large company.

This title may have suggested itself to the translators by their use of the word in 19:1, or by their estimate of the book as a whole, notably chs. 1–15. But it does not do full justice to the subject matter. Nor does it disclose the central motif. Less than half of the book deals with Israel's departure from Egypt. The larger part is concerned with the institution and ordering of its common life. Further, God rather than Moses, the leader and lawgiver, or Israel, the elect and redeemed, stands at the heart of the document. The controlling motif is the revelation of God's power in his victory over the Pharaoh which for the writers is a disclosure of his universal lordship.

The book of Exodus is comparable to a drama. The action consists of God's preparation for the deliverance of the enslaved Hebrews, his victory over Pharaoh, which accomplishes their rescue, and his establishment of Israel as his people. The action and triumph of God is the center from which the whole book proceeds. Not simply Israel's escape from bondage but also the meaning of its establishment as a community, the significance of its laws, and the efficacy of its cultus depend upon this divine action.

II. History of the Sources

Exodus belongs to "the five books of Moses." These, together with Joshua, are the outcome of a single process of development. Since Exodus is not an independent literary unit, the story of its production is a special aspect of the history of the larger complex to which it belongs.[1]

Like the Hexateuch, Exodus is a record with both an oral and a literary history. These two aspects of its history are closely interrelated.

[1] See article "The Growth of the Hexateuch," pp. 185-200.

They are two features of a single process. One can be understood only in the light of the other. It was the great accomplishment of Pentateuch research in the nineteenth century to establish the hypothesis that four primary documents— J, E, D, and P—are embodied in the present record. These are all found in Exodus, and their special features will be mentioned presently. What the hypothesis did not settle was the problem of the prior history of these documents, especially of J and E. In the twentieth century this whole issue has been greatly illumined by the growing recognition that these documents owe their character and form not so much to older literary units that may have gone into each of them as to the nature and history of Israel's oral tradition from which the documents, including antecedent literary forms, were derived.

Exodus is crucially important in the study and reconstruction of the oral history of the Hexateuch. It provides us with the most explicit historical memories we have of the actual events that gave rise to and continued to nurture the community of Israel and its distinctive tradition. Martin Noth [2] specifies five main "themes" which for him sum up the oral and written tradition that culminated in the Pentateuch. Three of these—the escape from Egypt, the nomadic period, and the Sinai covenant—have their point of departure enshrined in Exodus.

The ancient Song of Miriam (15:21) is a "hymn" evoked by the actual experience of the escape and served as the nucleus of an evergrowing series of forms, cultic and "secular," which helped to keep alive that historic event as a living experience. The accounts of the plagues and of the Red Sea, as well as many episodes in the Moses saga, were among the elements that began to cluster about this original core of the theme of the escape from slavery. All of them were the outcome of the dialogue between history and present experience in which Israel's faith characteristically expressed itself.

Similarly, the "oath" against Amalek (17:16) serves as at least one of the nucleuses for the nomadic theme to which chs. 16–18 are related. It probably had its inception in the struggle in which Israel established its nomadic center at Kadesh.

Noth is possibly correct in assuming that the Sinai theme constitutes a development in the tradition which rests on no such primary actualities in Israel's past as do the other two.[3] It is not impossible that this Sinai theme, featuring at its core the covenant (24:1, 2, 9-11), is an adaptation by Israel of the yearly renewal of the

social bonds which was a constituent of the Canaanite autumn festival. What is certain is that in its Sinai theme the tradition reflects Israel's perennial internalization of the meaning of its history as this was exhibited in "the great deeds" of the Lord, notably in the exodus motif. Artur Weiser [4] stresses the interrelated common development, at the same centers, of these divergent dimensions in Israel's tradition. Through the cultus the revelation of the divine nature, which is the concern of the themes that celebrate "the great deeds of Yahweh," is translated into the revelation of the divine will, which is the concern of the Sinai theme. Each depended upon the other. Sinai provided the Exodus with enduring relevance. But the historical basis provided by the Exodus was indispensable to the founding of the Sinai theme and, indeed, of Israel itself. The Decalogue and the laws of the covenant (chs. 20–23) constitute the oldest extant evidence for the internalizing process which was the peculiar function of the Sinai theme. They also attest the assimilative capacity of Israel's faith.

Modern students believe that the oral tradition was mediated and ordered by a cultic context which was essentially the same in all Israel. The "themes" of the tradition thus understood were everywhere available as "sources" for the literary documents embedded in Exodus. However, some of the earliest essays in the history of oral tradition did not think of it as thus integrated and ordered by a single cultic context. They were premised on the view that there was a variety of oral "traditions," popular and local in character. They presupposed all sorts of local etiological tales, provincial histories, and tribal or hero sagas. In his commentary,[5] Hugo Gressmann maintained that such sagas, with Moses as hero, formed the basis of Exodus. The early chapters of Exodus dealing with the birth and youth of Moses make such an assumption very plausible. The written documents J and E are indeed continuous. But one is left with the impression that they utilize in Exodus a very different source from that used in Genesis. There seems to be a conscious effort to tie together the sources as part of a single story (cf. 1:1-7). Noth would describe this phenomenon as a variation in the themes of a single common source. One may discuss the extent to which the possible existence of such independent oral units as Gressmann contemplated can be reconciled with the notion that there was a single dominant tradition, bound by the ordering implicit in a cultic context. It may be that such

[2] *Überlieferungsgeschichte des Pentateuch* (Stuttgart: W. Kohlhammer, 1948).

[3] *Ibid.*, p. 64.

[4] *Einleitung in das Alten Testament* (Göttingen: Vandenhoeck & Ruprecht, 1949), p. 73.

[5] *Mose und seine Zeit* (Göttingen: Vandenhoeck & Ruprecht, 1913).

noncultic and "local" oral traditions were gradually absorbed with their themes by the more formally controlled universal tradition. Or as Noth [6] feels, it is possible that the originally minor role of Moses was developed wholly within the context of the oral tradition. In either case it is safe to say that Moses is not the "hero" of Exodus.

The scope, character, and vitality of the oral tradition greatly determine the nature, history, and distinctiveness of the written sources in Exodus, notably J and E. Let us assume that all Israel possessed one main tradition, a series of sacred themes which remained normative for all, even after the political division of the kingdom.[7] If oral and written tradition developed for a long time in the same cultic context, then J and E have one common foundation. It also becomes hazardous to assign "authors" to these documents. The Yahwist and the Elohist are better thought of as selective artists who, each in his own time and situation, set down the living tradition as they experience it and as it interprets the situation they face. Furthermore, with the possible exception of legal materials, it becomes more difficult (and less important) to differentiate between the oral and written items utilized by J and E. Finally it becomes extremely difficult to separate out from one another the original contents of these documents, insofar as they are now preserved in Exodus.

The oral tradition from which both J and E were abstracted does not deny their significance as independent documents. But it does qualify this significance and set it in a wider context. In the Exegesis no new systematic separation of the basic documents will be attempted. As far as J and E are concerned, we shall follow the classical separation itemized in S. R. Driver, *The Book of Exodus.*[8] To some extent this will be qualified by comparison with the separation made in George Beer's more recent commentary, *Exodus, mit einem Beitrag von Kurt Galling.*[9] Beer was more hesitant than Driver about assigning every part of the text of JE to a specific source (cf. 2:1-10; 5:1-6:1). On the other hand, unlike Driver, he subdivided both J and E into separate documents, J[1], J[2] and E, E[1]. Only a few of the distinctive features of J and E can be cited here. A study of the Exegesis will reveal the multitude of the peculiarities of each.

With respect to vocabulary, the most significant feature is the name for God. This name, יהוה, which the Yahwist has used throughout,

[6] *Op. cit.,* pp. 172-73.
[7] *Ibid.,* p. 78.
[8] Cambridge: Cambridge University Press, 1911; "The Cambridge Bible."
[9] Tübingen: J. C. B. Mohr, 1939; "Handbuch zum Alten Testament."

the Elohist first introduces in 3:15, having previously used the common noun "Elohim." Further, whereas for J the holy mountain is called Sinai (19:11, 18, 20, 23; 34:2, 4), in E it is Horeb (3:1; 17:6; 33:6). Again, only E designates Moses' father-in-law as Jethro (3:1; 4:18; 18:1, 2, 5, 6, 9, 10, 12). J does not give his name in Exodus but seems to have known him as Hobab (Num. 10:29).

The lines which in Exodus separate the documents J, E, and P are most sharply illustrated in the account of the plagues (cf. pp. 838-39). There, and throughout, the theocentric emphasis and the simple and unreflective naturalness of J become apparent. The plagues are sent by God directly, Moses simply announcing them (9:1-7). At the same time "natural causes" are recognized in them (10:13). Likewise, at the crossing of the sea it was the "east wind" that removed the water (14:21).

In Exodus the E document shows a tendency to exalt Moses. To him the divine name is revealed (3:15). He wields the "rod of God" by which God accomplishes the wonders (7:15, 20; 9:23; 10:13; 14:16). In P Aaron has this honor. Further, in E Moses is recognized as a great leader by the Egyptians (3:21-22; 11:1-3). And for Israel he is the great intercessor and mediator (32:11-13, 30-34; 33:7-11).

The Deuteronomic editorial notes in Exodus are relatively few and for the most part easily distinguishable (10:1-2; 12:24-27a; 13:3-16; 15:25b-26; 17:14; 19:3b-8; 23:23-25a; 34:11-13, 16, 24; also in 20:1-17).

The Priestly document is easily separated from the others. The chief problem about it in Exodus concerns the integrity of chs. 25–31; 35–40. A. H. McNeile [10] and others have held that these sections consisted of a single basic narrative supplemented by one or two layers of editorial additions. More recently Gerhard von Rad [11] has separated them into two basically independent sources, P[A] and P[B], supplemented by a layer of editorial additions, P[S]. Though the hypothesis must be treated with reserve, especially as applied in details, it seems to constitute a genuine advance in the interpretation of the tabernacle accounts.

III. Exodus and the History of Israel

Exodus is not a history of early Israel in any strict sense. It is rather an exposition of the meaning of that history for Israel. It is an interpretation of Israel's faith. In the light of our understanding of the history of Israel's tradition (cf. pp. 833-35) this interpretation of the faith

[10] *The Book of Exodus* (London: Methuen and Co., 1908; "Westminster Commentaries"), p. xxxvii.
[11] *Die Priesterschrift im Hexateuch* (Berlin: W. Kohlhammer, 1934).

of Israel represents the cumulative result of centuries of organic development. Exodus deals seriously with the fact that Israel's faith rests on a historic revelation. It assumes that the faith is rooted in and illustrated by a particular historical occurrence. Therefore there are embedded in Exodus memories of the actual historical circumstances and events in which by faith the Hebrews first saw the decisive disclosure of God and became the people of Israel.

This interpretation of the great initial "act of God" was not produced all at once when J or later documents were composed. Exodus takes up into itself the entire tradition of the faith from the first. Exodus is not only, as is sometimes assumed, a one-sided attempt to impute to Moses and the nomads he led the ideas—religious, cultic, historical, and ethical—of the ninth, eighth, or sixth centuries. It is also a significant exposition of a remembered history and of the faith that culminated in the ideas it contains. In Exodus the event of revelation in its initial meaning, and all subsequent interpretations of it down to the sixth century, are woven together into a single literary fabric.

Israel's early history as remembered in Exodus has little substantiating corroboration in ancient records. There is no account of a company of slaves that escaped from Egyptian slavery and that was established as a racial and religious community by a man named Moses. The external evidence, such as it is, is circumstantial. The migration of the Hebrews to Egypt and their manner of life in that land as portrayed in Genesis and Exodus correspond to a role played for centuries by a class of seminomadic people, the Habiru or 'Apiru. The etymological relatedness of the names warrants the conjecture that the biblical Hebrews derived from that class. In the thirteenth century an Egyptian Pharaoh referred to "Israel" (cf. below). Aside from such particulars, it can be said that the general outline of Israel's life and experience in Egypt and in the desert is in harmony with the conditions of life and population movements typical of the Near East until recent times. This is notably true in respect to the perennial tendency of nomadic and seminomadic groups to infiltrate into the sown lands of Egypt and Palestine.[12]

Since Exodus is an interpretation of Israel's faith rather than a genetic account of the people who hold it, or of the forms in which it was expressed, it raises many questions of historical, geographical, and cultic import which it does not fully clarify. This creates a series of special problems for the modern student.

IV. The Pharaoh of the Exodus

From the time of the Egyptian historian Manetho (250 B.C.) until quite recently the Exodus was placed early in the sixteenth century. The violently anti-Jewish Manetho insisted that the Israelites were expelled along with the Hyksos. Actually the date can be reconciled neither with 1:11 nor with the admittedly artificial framework of chronology in 12:40 (cf. I Kings 6:1).

For a considerable time modern scholars debated the relative merit of the fifteenth and thirteenth centuries.[13] Increasingly the balance falls in favor of the thirteenth century.[14] This date takes 1:11 at face value. Scholars who accept the thirteenth century date have usually recognized Ramses II (1301-1234) as the oppressor, and his son Merneptah (1234-27) as the Pharaoh of the Exodus. But some feel that Seti I (1319-1301) was the oppressor and that the Exodus occurred under Ramses II.[15] These feel certain that Israel was in Palestine by the third quarter of the thirteenth century. Their conviction rests especially on the line of the Merneptah inscription [16] which reads, "Israel is desolated, her seed is not." The assumption is that the Israel mentioned by Merneptah consisted of the sons of the slaves who came out of Egypt. There is no explicit evidence for this. However, there is archaeological evidence that Seti I began the building program in which the Hebrews were impressed as slaves. It is thus possible that Seti I rather than Ramses II was the "new king . . . who did not know Joseph" (1:8).

V. The Location of Sinai

There is no single clear testimony about the location of the mountain. Uncertainty developed perhaps because the mountain lay in territory later occupied by Israel's foes and because Israelites fixed their attention on Jerusalem.

The Bible has two names for the mountain, Horeb and Sinai. E and the Deuteronomist seem to use Horeb exclusively (3:1; 17:6; 33:6; Deut. 1:2, 6, 19; 5:2; 9:8; 18:16; 29:1). J uses Sinai. So does P, and this usage becomes the more prominent. Sinai and Horeb are usually considered to refer to one place. But this has been

---

[12] For a fuller development see Theophile J. Meek, *Hebrew Origins* (rev. ed.; New York: Harper & Bros., 1950); W. F. Albright, *From Stone Age to Christianity* (2nd ed.; Baltimore: Johns Hopkins Press, 1946).

[13] A full discussion can be found in W. O. E. Oesterley and Theodore H. Robinson, *A History of Israel* (Oxford: The Clarendon Press, 1932), I, 71-80.

[14] Cf. Meek, *op. cit.*, pp. 33-34; Albright, *op. cit.*, p. 194.

[15] E.g., G. E. Wright and F. V. Filson, *The Westminster Historical Atlas to the Bible* (Philadelphia: Westminster Press, 1945), p. 37b.

[16] Robinson, *op. cit.*, I, 75.

seriously questioned by McNeile and others.[17] However, McNeile's carefully stated position has not been widely accepted.

Assuming that Sinai and Horeb are two different designations of the same place, there are three sites that are currently given serious consideration:

(a) *Jebel Musa.* This is the traditional site near the apex of the Sinai peninsula. Since late in the fourth century A.D. this mountain, eight thousand feet high, has been designated as Mount Sinai. Justinian (A.D. 527-65) officially recognized it as such. The statement of Deut. 1:2, that it was eleven days' journey from Sinai to Kadesh, favors this location. Moreover, the site is near the ancient Egyptian copper and turquoise mines which, in the days of Merneptah, were not worked as much as had been the case earlier. The Midianite clan with which Moses was associated was that of the Kenites (Judg. 4:11) who, according to their name, were smiths. Midianites therefore might well have settled at this mining center. It is largely on the basis of this proximity to the copper mines that Wright and Filson accept this traditional site as the location of Mount Sinai.[18] To some extent they also lean on the locations of the stations of the journey from Egypt to Sinai which Flinders Petrie and other archaeologists have identified. But the evidence for these identifications is not generally accepted as conclusive. Moreover, the copper deposits in Midian proper are richer than those in the Serabit el Khadim region; and it was also mined in the 'Arabah. The Kenite smiths need not have been in the lower part of the peninsula to ply their trade.

(b) *Midian.* A second group of scholars led by such men as Eduard Meyer, Hugo Gressmann, and Alois Musil, have sought to locate Mount Sinai to the east of Aqabah. They proceed from the assumption that at the sealing of the covenant the mountain was an active volcano in eruption (19:16-25). Since there are no volcanic mountains on the peninsula it has seemed necessary to locate a site farther east where extinct volcanoes are found. But the biblical evidence for the thesis is not very convincing. Besides, it is by no means certain that the mountain described was actually a volcano in eruption. It seems more probable that the notion of the presence of God, represented by the pillar of the cloud and of fire, has been augmented and made more awesome by metaphors drawn from earthquake, storm, and perhaps volcanic activity.

(c) *Paran.* According to a third view, Sinai was situated in the wilderness of Paran, south-west of Edom. This seems more probable than the other two. In Num. 10:12 the wilderness of Sinai is a synonym for that of Paran. And when Moses invited his father-in-law to march with them from there, he protested that he must return to his own land (Num. 10:29-30). Had they been coming up from the lower part of the peninsula they could have traveled together to the head of the Gulf of Aqabah. In the blessing of Moses (Deut. 33:2) Sinai and Paran, plus Seir, are tied together as the site of the mountain. Hab. 3:3 links Paran and Teman. And Judg. 5:4-5 combines Sinai and Seir. Further, it seems that the holy mountain was near Kadesh-barnea, where Israel encamped for a long time (Num. 13:26; 20:1-14; 27:14; 33:36). In Num. 20:16 Kadesh is said to be at the outer border of Edom. Edom, according to the archaeological investigations of Nelson Glueck, was perhaps the only region in which there were permanent settlements at this time. Ezion-geber, Elath, and Kadesh-barnea ('Ain el-Qudeirat) were not made permanent settlements until the tenth century. It seems most probable, therefore, that the mountain at which Moses met God and at which the covenant was sealed is located somewhere northwest of the head of the Gulf of Aqabah, just across the "'arabah from Edom."

VI. Origin of Israel's Name for God

In the postexilic period it became customary to read, "Adonai," LORD, wherever the tetragrammaton occurred in the text. This practice, based on reverence, became standard and has persisted in the synagogue until today. The pronunciation of YHWH had thus fallen into disuse long before the Hebrew text was provided with vowel signs, and was therefore long in doubt. However, with the aid of Greek transcriptions and other resources, scholars have gradually come to agree that it was pronounced Yahweh. In poetry and as a part of personal names in the Bible we find the related forms Yah and Yahu (Yah: 15:2; 17:16; II Kings 1:3; Pss. 68:10; 104:35; 105:45; 106:1, 48; etc.; Yahu: I Kings 17:1, 16, 18, 22, 24; etc.). For long it was the dominant view that Yahweh was a relatively late Israelite expansion of these shorter forms. Consequently, in the mighty efforts that were put forth to discover the antecedents of the God of Israel in the cultures of the Near East that were older than the Hebrew, the brief forms of Yah and Yahu naturally served as cues. A brief summary of this effort, which still continues, together with helpful bibliographical suggestions is provided by Meek, who himself shares its point of departure.[19] It seems, however, that this effort has largely failed.

[17] *Exodus*, pp. cii-cvi.
[18] *Op. cit.*, pp. 38b, 39a.
[19] *Hebrew Origins*, pp. 82-118.

That is, it has not resulted in any agreement as to the antecedent location or nature of the God of the Israelites. While this search continues, there is a drift today toward the view that Yah and Yahu are forms derived from Yahweh. Beer's confession of a personal change of view on this matter well points up a general tendency.[20] In the English-speaking world this current tendency is given momentum by the work and influence of William F. Albright.[21]

Once the priority of Yahweh over Yah and Yahu is granted, the possibilities are sharply limited. Three may be cited: (a) In Hebrew the root הוה has the meaning of "to be" or "to become." But this is a derived meaning. The primary meaning of this ancient Semitic root was "to fall" or "to blow." The name Yahweh should probably be understood in terms of the ancient meanings of this verb from which it is derived. Yahweh is "the falling one," or causatively, "the one who causes [lightning] to fall"; or he is "the blower," or causatively, "the one who causes [wind] to blow." The storm and nature attributes associated in the Bible with Yahweh are called in to fortify this hypothesis. But the view suffers from want of actual evidence that Yahweh was really abstracted from this root הוה when it possessed its primitive meaning. The best argument in favor of this view is a negative one: that the interpretations resting on the later Hebrew meaning of the root הוה seem too abstract, while this one is more material and dynamic. (b) There is next the view that Yahweh must be the causative form of the Hebrew verb היה or הוה, "to be," "to become," and so forth. Yahweh is the creator, "He causes to be." This is Albright's view. He scorns the objection that this was too abstract for the ancient mind, and cites comparable definitions from Babylonian, Canaanite, and Egyptian sources. On the basis of similar parallels he simultaneously makes sense of the formula in 3:14. Yahweh, "He causes to be," is an abbreviated form of a longer litany, "He causes to be what comes into existence." This "retransposition" of the formula includes changing its first verb to a causal form. Albright justifies this on the ground that the original transposition into the first person was made when the causative form of הוה was no longer used in Hebrew. This raises the question whether even at that time Israelites could still understand the meaning of Yahweh as Albright presents it. (c) The third view differs from Albright's chiefly in that it considers the 'eheyeh of 3:14 as the basis for interpreting Yahweh. Consequently, the meaning is not causative. Yahweh is made to mean "being," "he who is or will be,"

20 Exodus, p. 31.
21 From Stone Age to Christianity, pp. 196-99.

'Ο ὤν (LXX), "the Eternal" (Moffatt). It seems that this interpretation gives too much importance to 3:14.

It must be pointed out that by assuming the priority of Yahweh over Yahu or Yah, one is not reduced to looking for the antecedents of Moses' God in Israel alone. The first view mentioned above illustrates this position. Further it must be remembered that whether Yahweh was an abbreviation of the formula changed by the patriarchs, as Albright holds, or whether his name was the enlarged form of the name of a Canaanite deity, his decisive meaning for Israel was determined not by his antecedents, but by the revelation to Moses and his manifestation to Israel in the Exodus. This novelty and not the name is the element that is distinctive and crucial.

VII. The Plagues of Egypt

The "Plagues of Egypt" are variously designated as מגפות, "plagues" (9:14; 12:13); אותות, "signs" (7:3; 8:23; 10:1-2); מופתים, "portents" (7:3; 11:9-10); and נגע, "stroke," "visitation," or "plague" (11:1). In this general context these terms are synonymous; together they are God's "great acts of judgment" (7:4). All of the episodes are signs and portents, tokens of God's power and harbingers of his imminent conquest of Pharaoh. This is the way in which P refers to them exclusively. But all of the episodes likewise stress the calamity suffered by Pharaoh and his people. These ten plagues constitute the sanctions for God's demand on Pharaoh and they document the outcome of disobedience.

Our record is a narrative carefully constructed from the three literary traditions, J, E, P. To some extent the present literary form enables us to discern the growth of these stories, both following and preceding their first composition. At present J's hand is discernible in seven of the plagues, the fourth and fifth being wholly from his hand. P is present in five accounts, the third and sixth being by him alone. The account of the first plague well illustrates P's tendency to make the calamity more severe when he supplements either J or E. Five items show the hand of E and the ninth plague is perhaps entirely his. Since the third and sixth plagues are accounts by P alone and since the calamities they report seem analogous to the calamities in the fourth and fifth plagues (J) respectively, it has been suggested that these two are simply P's duplicates for four and five. Whatever may be the merit of that suggestion, it seems very likely that no single tradition or cycle originally counted ten plagues.

On account of the highly stylized and repetitious character of the entire literary unit it is relatively easy to distinguish the three literary strands. Thus, in P God always gives Moses the command, "Say to Aaron" (7:19; 8:5, 16), Aaron uses the rod, the plagues are always signs and portents, there is no interview with Pharaoh nor demand on him, there is a relation of God's demonstration to the powers of Egypt's magicians, and the closing formula is "and he would not listen to them; as the LORD had said" (7:22; 8:15b, 19; 9:12; cf. 7:3). In J Moses alone goes before Pharaoh (7:14-16; 8:1, 9-10, 20, 26, 29; 9:1, 13, 29; 10:1, 9, 25; 11:4-8; cf. 4:10-16). The demand formula is "let my people go, that they may serve me" (7:16; 8:1, 20; 9:1, 13; 10:3; cf. 4:23). God himself sends the plague and, sometimes at the intercession of Moses requested by Pharaoh, God himself removes it. At the end Pharaoh makes his heart "heavy," כבד (7:14; 8:15, 32; 9:7, 34; 10:1), in distinction from "strong," חזק, as in P and E. The most distinctive feature of the less fully represented tradition of E is that Moses uses the rod to produce the plague (7:15b, 17b, 20b; 9:23a; 10:13a). E ends a plague with the formula "and he did not let the children of Israel go" (9:35; 10:20, 27). The movement toward a climax and the premonition of Pharaoh's rout, which P communicates in Yahweh's contest with the magicians, J and E indicate by Pharaoh's increasingly generous efforts at striking a bargain with Moses.

There have been many efforts to rationalize these fantastic stories. Modern scholars have sought to provide a natural explanation at least for the core of each sign. McNeile even seeks to provide a natural explanation for the first six plagues in sequence, and likewise for the last four.[22] Thus the fetid river, with its decaying fish, bred a crop of frogs. Whereupon the decomposing frogs caused the swarms of insects in the third and fourth plagues. These again lead to the fifth and sixth plagues. This is a highly dubious and conjectural procedure. More seriously, it causes one to forget the real purpose of the stories in their total context. It betrays a concern for historical veracity or congruity at the cost of meaning and truth. To be sure, many of these stories reflect something of the natural conditions and hazards of life in Egypt. Furthermore, some of them probably rest on actual events that facilitated the escape of the Israelites, and in which they saw the hand of God. But the text now presents a series of piously decorated accounts, woven together in an elaborate and artistic sequence of narratives. The significance and value of this total complex is symbolic rather than historical. The mosaic as a whole attests Israel's faith, resting on the

[22] *Exodus*, pp. 44-46.

historic experience of its escape from slavery; it aims at showing that not Pharaoh or the gods of Egypt but the living God of Israel makes nature serve man—or rather, makes nature serve his purposes for man's fulfillment.

For those who developed the literary sequence, the quasi-deterministic processes that make up nature and history, whether seen as laws and scientific categories or as a multiplicity of gods and demons, met at single point which was neither fate nor chaos. For them the point of meeting was the freedom of the living God who seeks men's allegiance and redemption. For biblical faith these quasi-deterministic processes of nature and history are seen as actually the vehicles and means of God's purpose. This faith is rooted in a series of climactic events—Exodus, Return, Resurrection, Pentecost—in which God's creative and redemptive freedom becomes palpable. These are the events of the "history of salvation" (*Heilsgeschichte*), the miracle which all "miracles" seek to illustrate.

VIII. The Kenite Hypothesis

The burden of the Kenite hypothesis is that not only the name of Yahweh, the God of Israel, but many aspects of Israel's cultus and social life were derived from the Kenite clan of Midianites to which Jethro belonged (Judg. 4:11). This hypothesis, first stated nearly a century ago by Ghillany, has had a persistent attraction for biblical scholars, though it has not won undisputed acceptance.

The best-known and most conspicuous bit of evidence offered in behalf of the hypothesis consists of an interpretation of 18:10-12 to the effect that Yahweh was the God of Jethro and that he brought him a sacrifice, Aaron and the elders of Israel being invited. The actual merit of this interpretation of these verses must be evaluated on the basis of our estimate of the nature of the whole cycle of accounts to which this chapter belongs.

Hugo Gressmann,[23] who sought to work out the implications of this hypothesis in a most radical manner, insisted that the cycle of stories in chs. 16–18, and continued in Num. 10:29 ff., was originally oriented towards Kadesh. For this cycle, he held, Kadesh was the place at which Israel became a community. There the Exodus received its implementation in terms of cultus and social organization, and this implementation took place by means of the appropriation of Kenite models.

This fundamentally separate tradition of

[23] *Die Anfänge Israels* (Göttingen: Vandenhoeck & Ruprecht, 1922; "Die Schriften des Alten Testaments in Auswahl"), pp. 86-94.

Kadesh, as Gressmann saw it, is now interrupted by the long account of the tradition focused upon Sinai (Exod. 19:1–Num. 10:28). According to that inserted account, mostly of later provenance, the implementation of the Exodus in the birth of the Israel community or influence takes place without any reference to surrounding cultural forms. Chs. 16–18 are now simply the account of a pilgrimage that terminates at Sinai. Sinai is the focus of their significance. But Gressmann felt that this impression was first created by the latest editorial harmonists of the Pentateuch. He contended that chs. 16–18 formed the first part of an independent tradition, parallel to and older than the Sinai cycle. The focus of this tradition was Kadesh; and its concern was to give an account of the origin of Israel's cultic and social forms.

In its present form ch. 18 has the flavor of an idyllic family party. Gressmann held that originally it reported more explicitly than now the establishment at Kadesh of the cultus of Yahweh. The present flavor was given to the account by the later editors who wanted to excise from it explicit references to the taking over of cultic forms by Israel from non-Israelites. Assuming this editorial tendency, Gressmann sought to reconstruct the original account to indicate what cultic forms had been taken over at Kadesh. In this reconstruction he combined Num. 10:29-36 and 11:11-17, 24-30 with Exod. 18. From his effort he concluded that this Kadesh cycle originally reported Israel's appropriation of three Kenite forms at Kadesh: sacrifice, the sacred lot, and the ark.

It may never be possible to establish or to refute the Kenite hypothesis conclusively, let alone the specific and detailed account of it which Gressmann offered. But its persistent existence, as well as the persistence of attacks upon it, dramatizes a very important feature about the nature of the biblical record. The hypothesis draws attention to the fact that the Old Testament reveals, at least implicitly, that the forms of Israel's life as the community of Yahweh were genetically related to the cultural forms in the midst of which Israel arose. On the other hand, the opposition to the hypothesis draws attention to the fact that at least in its latest strata the Pentateuch insists on the uniqueness, not only in spirit but also in form, of the cultus and law of Israel, and considers them to be the work and gifts of the Lord of Israel, owing nothing to environment. An honest interpreter must deal realistically with all the data, implicit and explicit. When this is done with respect to the Old Testament he will be challenged by a question: What is the nature and meaning of a faith the modes of whose cultus,

and even possibly the name of whose deity, may have been appropriated from the Midianites (and whose temple was constructed by Phoenician engineers), but whose adherents nevertheless claimed throughout in word and practice that their cultus and culture were the unique work of the living God? It becomes clear that in its forms of expression—cultic, social, intellectual—biblical faith is always conditioned by and genetically related to its general setting and environment. It also becomes clear that its really distinctive feature is a center of experience and life, particular and historical in character, which is accepted in faith as the revelation of God. Proceeding from this "discontinuous" center the community assimilates and appropriates for itself the forms of the conditioning environment.

The strongest arguments for the Kenite hypothesis are: (a) the materials relevant to it are, on the whole, older than those of the Sinai cycle; (b) historically there is every reason to suppose that, because of perennial enmity, the writers would have wanted to emasculate any account in which Israelites were presented as debtors to Midian; and (c) the Midianites were actually distant kin of Israel, so that Israel under Moses may have recovered what was originally part of a common possession.

The hypothesis, however, has serious weaknesses: (a) For want of explicit evidence it is highly subjective, notably in its efforts at reconstruction; (b) the oldest written document of the Old Testament (J) does not hold that Moses first introduced a God to Israel as Yahweh, which is at least an aspect of the hypothesis; and (c) it is improbable that Moses would have won the confidence of the Israelites by coming to them in the name of a God they had not hitherto known. Meek[24] makes much of these last two objections, and insists that Yahweh was originally the God of Judah. H. H. Rowley, who accepts the Kenite hypothesis, ingeniously disposes of Meek's objections by incorporating his counterproposal in the hypothesis itself.[25]

IX. The Exodus and the Covenant of Sinai

For Israel the core of revelation was the Exodus, an objective historical fact. The climax of God's self-disclosure is reached in the crossing of the sea. By faith Israel sees the meaning of existence laid bare in this objective historical occurrence. Interpreted by Moses, the event becomes the basis for and the primary illustration of the peculiar apprehensions of the nature

24 *Hebrew Origins*, pp. 82-118.
25 *The Re-discovery of the Old Testament* (Philadelphia: Westminster Press, 1946), pp. 116-19.

of the God in whom Israel places its faith. This is attested in the ancient Song of Miriam (15: 21). This historical occurrence is the cornerstone of Israel's existence as the people of God.

Revelation has taken place in the Exodus, and joyful and spontaneous testimony is borne to the God who has made himself known. Sinai stands for the systematic interpretation and implementation of the faith which is the gift of revelation. Sinai symbolizes the establishment of Israel as the church. It is the locus for the covenant that sets forth the relationship in which Israel stands to the God of its deliverance, and for the laws and ordinances in which this relationship receives its concrete expression, both in society and cultus.

Sinai stresses the organic and living relationship that exists between the social and religious institutions of Israel and the exodus revelation. It may well be, as has been held by many responsible scholars, that the section entitled "The Pilgrimage to Sinai" (15:22–18:27) was originally an account of Israel's settlement at Kadesh and of its adoption there of cultic institutions of foreign origin. Certainly there can be no doubt that in cultic forms as well as in the forms of social institutions and laws Israel was a debtor to the wider environment in which it developed. We may take Kadesh as the symbol of this indebtedness. But Sinai is the symbol that Israel could assimilate cultural forms so as to transform their inner meaning. Forms might be of foreign origin and yet express the nature and will of Yahweh. Under "Sinai," whenever or wherever they may actually have been promulgated, the laws of common life and the ordinances for common worship are presented as the expression of Yahweh's will for his people, mediated directly through Moses.

Sinai is also the symbol of the covenanted relationship in which Israel stands to Yahweh. It is the reminder that the whole of Israel's community life is organically and integrally conceived as the implementation of the exodus revelation. Its central meaning is neither a mystical fellowship nor a set of moral demands. It rests on the Exodus (19:4-7; 20:2). Later tendencies to treat law as revelation obscured this fact.

The covenant is central in the implementation of the faith which constituted Israel's response to the Exodus. It is the symbol that describes the relationship in which Yahweh and his people stand to one another. In various parts of the Old Testament different aspects of this relationship are stressed. Sometimes the covenant is seen mainly in the historic actuality of revelation at the Exodus and in the founding of Israel as the people of God. Sometimes the

abiding and even the unbreakable character of the relationship is stressed. At still other times the demands conceived by Israel to be incumbent upon it in this relationship—the laws, the statutes, and ordinances—are made virtually synonymous with the covenant (Deut. 4:13). In general the prophets, when they utilize the metaphor to describe the relation of God to Israel, stress the theocentric, dynamic, and personal aspects of the relationship. Legal and priestly movements, however, stress its institutional, statutory, and static aspects. The eighth-century prophets, with the possible exception of Hosea, do not utilize the concept at all, probably because the notion that Israel has a claim upon God, which they combated, was too closely associated with the idea of the covenant at that time.

The Hebrew word for covenant, *berîth,* has the significance of bond or agreement. The etymology of the word is not certain. The meanings of "cutting," "binding," and "eating"—all associated with covenant making—show the variety of opinions as to the primitive meaning of the word. For the religious purpose it served in Israel the term was borrowed from social usage. In social practice covenants were of two general kinds. There were covenants between equals, in which the obligations and privileges under the agreement were equally shared. It seems that under the foreign influence of the nature mysticism, so central in Canaanite religion, Israelites increasingly conceived of their covenant with Yahweh as such a covenant between equals, in which God was as dependent upon Israel as Israel was upon him. Thus in the covenant relationship Yahweh had in effect forfeited his own freedom. This was a growing assumption against which the prophets protested. But in social relationships there were also agreements, known as covenants, between partners not equal: for example, between a king and his subjects, or between a lord and his servants (cf. II Sam. 5:3). In such a covenant the core of the agreement is really a promise or gift made by the stronger party. This is, however, normally conditioned upon certain demands or obligations to be met by the weaker party. In any case, the promise, central in such a covenant, does not destroy the freedom of him who gives it. Such is the form of the covenant of Sinai. The essence of the covenant is the promise of God, backed by the gift of deliverance already given, that Israel will be his special possession and instrument. The promise depends on the faithfulness and obedience of Israel.

The account of the theophany, the offer of the covenant to the people, and the final sealing of the agreement in a sacred meal is given in chs. 19 and 24. Two units of legal material break the continuity of this account: the Decalogue (20:1-17) and the Covenant Code (20:22–23: 33). The position of these two items seems to indicate that those who placed them in the middle of the account of the covenant-making ceremony intended that these laws be understood as the specific obligations laid upon Israel as a part of the covenant relationship. It is improbable that any of these items in their present form was the original statement of Israel's obligation in the relationship. Certainly it is virtually impossible that all could have been integrally a part of the covenant from the first. But their present position stresses the fact that it is characteristic of large sections of the Old Testament, notably the Deuteronomic, to conceive of the covenant as a law. Whether Israel's obligations under the covenant were specified from the first is disputed. Martin Buber,[26] for example, takes the view that, originally, stipulated conditions formed no part of the covenant at all. In any event, it becomes impossible to say with certainty what the first detailed form of Israel's obligation as a covenant member may have looked like. The ordinances for the regulation of the cultus, beginning at ch. 25, are presented as having been communicated to Moses, but stand outside the account of the forming of the covenant. This is characteristic of the P strand to which they belong. P seems to have thought of the Sinai covenant as only a renewal of the Abrahamic covenant. Further, the law was not an integral part of the covenant but rather a sign of it and a means of entering into it. The so-called ritual decalogue (34:10-26), though not placed in this major account of the sealing of the Sinai covenant, is nevertheless thought of as integral to it.

X. The Decalogue

The growing conviction among critical scholars that Moses was actually a historic figure of heroic proportions, who not only delivered the Israelites from slavery but founded them as a self-conscious community of Yahweh, has reached virtual unanimity. That Israel's obligations under the covenant promulgated by Moses were specified from the first, probably in written form, is also generally recognized as possible, or even probable. Moses may have produced a "book of the covenant" even though, as we have seen above, such a law did not originally bulk so large in the total significance of the covenant relationship as was true in the later Deuteronomic period. But with this, agreement ends.

[26] *Moses* (Oxford: East & West Library, 1946), p. 103.

There is no agreement that we possess today, in specifiable form, whatever legislation Moses may have promulgated or interpreted as representing Israel's social or cultic obligation under the covenant. Those who do think we possess this Mosaic legislation disagree as to where it is to be found. Until a relatively recent date it was most commonly looked for in the so-called "ritual decalogue" (34:10-26). Today it is more commonly felt that it is to be found in a larger or smaller "core" of the Decalogue (20:1-17). And all along there have been some, not many, who have maintained that the Covenant Code (20:22–23:33), or some part of it, must constitute the original Mosaic legislation.[27]

If anywhere, the specific forms of Moses' legislative work will be found in the Decalogue. But while it is possible that actual formulations of Moses are still preserved there, it does not seem probable. And as matters now stand, it seems virtually impossible that we shall ever be able to demonstrate conclusively any hypothesis about this problem. It is certain that the abiding structure of Israel's faith, resting on the historic exodus revelation, was provided through the work of Moses; but it does not seem likely that we shall ever be sure about the social or cultic prescription in terms of which that structure was given its precise definition and content in worship and society during the first centuries of Israel's existence.

Both the Covenant Code (20:22–23:33) and the Decalogue give the impression of having been inserted in the JE document. This is especially true of the Decalogue. Since in it God addresses the people directly, one would expect it to begin after 20:21. Even so it would interrupt the narrative. Conceivably, a briefer form of the Covenant Code is an original part of the JE narrative.[28] But both on text-critical grounds and in terms of the history of Israel's religious development one is almost forced to

[27] A picture of this uncertainty, and of some of the efforts to get beyond it, can be obtained by consulting and comparing such books as Beer, *Exodus*, pp. 96-125; Aage Bentzen, *Introduction to the Old Testament* (Copenhagen: G. E. C. Gad, 1948), II, 52-59; Julius Bewer, *The Literature of the Old Testament* (rev. ed.; New York: Columbia University Press, 1940), pp. 30-42; Driver, *Exodus*, pp. 191-251, 413-17; Walther Eichrodt, *Theologie des Alten Testaments* (3rd ed.; Berlin: Evangelische Verlagsanstalt, 1948), I, 25-39; Otto Eissfeldt, *Einleitung in das Alte Testament* (Tübingen: J. C. B. Mohr, 1934), pp. 240-51; McNeile, *Exodus*, pp. xxxviii-lxiv; Meek, *Hebrew Origins*, pp. 49-81; Sigmund Mowinckel, *Le décalogue* (Paris: Félix Alcan, 1927; "Études d'histoire et de philosophie religieuses"); R. H. Pfeiffer, *Introduction to the Old Testament* (New York: Harper & Bros., 1941), pp. 210-32; Rowley, *Re-discovery of O.T.*, pp. 116-23; Ernst Sellin, *Introduction to the Old Testament*, tr. W. Montgomery (New York: George H. Doran, 1923), pp. 40-48.

[28] McNeile, *Exodus*, p. lxii.

the conclusion that the insertion of these units occurred in the Deuteronomic era. This does not mean that they are therefore of Deuteronomic provenance; indeed, this is certainly not true in the case of the Covenant Code. But it does destroy the presumption in favor of their great age. It is not possible to say that the burden of proof is upon those who hold that the Decalogue is *not* of Mosaic origin. The whole matter is open.

We must also notice that the Decalogue differs greatly from the Covenant Code both in form and function. The Covenant Code, like its successor the Deuteronomic Code, is an instrument for the concrete and comprehensive regulation of a society in its civil and religious dimensions. Its so-called profane laws are in the form of case law. They rest on concrete precedents. They can be applied and/or expanded to cover new situations. The cultic sections of the code are in the nature of regulative rubrics. They too are concerned with details and specific problems. The Decalogue is different. It is rather a statement of general principles in terms of which such laws as one finds in the Covenant Code are to be understood and administrated. The "ten words" are not the outcome of or applicable to any concrete social or cultic situation. The Decalogue has something of the flavor of a "bill of rights" in which, in general terms, the prerogatives of all—God, parents, fellow Israelites—are recognized. The Decalogue cannot function in a society except indirectly, by means of an instrument such as the Covenant Code. The Decalogue, whenever it may have been devised, presupposes the existence of such an instrument. It is actually a summary and interpretation of it. And, as authoritative summary and interpretation, it provides the spiritual climate in which the actual social instrument is administered and continues to develop. It is in this respect, rather than in its "ethical emphasis," that the Decalogue plays an entirely different role from that of the "ritual decalogue" (34:10-26). The latter, whether it is envisioned as a fragment of the Covenant Code,[29] or whether it is held to be the nucleus from which the Covenant Code grew,[30] is of the same genre as that code. The Decalogue is different. It is not a social instrument concerned with details; it is a comprehensive epitome seeking to set forth the inner meaning and purposes of all actual laws.

If the Decalogue is the interpretation of the Code of the Covenant as we now have it, it cannot be of Mosaic origin. Even those most anxious to find in this code a nucleus of Mosaic

origin[31] agree that both in its cultic and civil preoccupations the Covenant Code is the instrument of a settled agricultural community. If the Mosaic authorship of the Decalogue is to be seriously proposed it must be on the assumption that it is the epitome of a social and cultic legal instrument now no longer extant. As judge Moses may have had a hand in the development of such an instrument, and the Decalogue would represent his reorientation of it. But he would hardly have composed such a common custom *de novo,* for such a comprehensive social instrument is a slow growth, deeply rooted in the mores of the people. McNeile[32] has shown that there is an affinity between the Decalogue and the Covenant Code which would make it possible to treat the former as an epitome of the latter. But the connection is too general to make this necessary. That Moses actually summarized and interpreted whatever laws and customs by which under him Israel ordered its life seems highly probable, for such summarization would represent a reorientation of the inner meaning of the common life in terms of the covenant. But whether this probable interpretation of Moses is actually preserved in the Ten Commandments remains an open question. As Gressmann[33] said, "the demands of the religion of Yahweh were at various times summarized in a variety of decalogues." He felt that 20:1-17 was the first in this series and was done by Moses. Perhaps it is safer to say that Moses began the series. That the Decalogue of 20:1-17 represents that beginning must be admitted as possible, despite some serious difficulties (cf. Exeg. on 20:4, 8); but it cannot be admitted as certain or even very probable.

It should be added that the slightly different duplicate of the Decalogue in Deut. 5:6-21 offers no real help in arriving at the problem of dating the unit in its original form, for the variations all concern acknowledged additions. This is also true in the case of the Nash Papyrus, a Hebrew text of the Ten Commandments and the Shema, which is probably older than the second century A.D.

XI. The Laws of the Covenant

The Covenant Code is the Hebrew cultic and social code in its most primitive extant form. As has been noted above, 34:14-26 is probably a fragment of this code. All subsequent "codes," beginning with Deuteronomy, are expansions of it. It is called the Covenant

---

[29] Eichrodt, *Theologie des A.T.,* I, 25.

[30] Pfeiffer, *Introduction to O.T.,* p. 211.

[31] Rudolf Kittel, *Gestalten und Gedanken in Israel* (Leipzig: Quelle & Meyer, 1925), pp. 334-40.

[32] *Exodus,* pp. lxi-lxii.

[33] *Mose und seine Zeit,* p. 473.

Code because it is set within the context of the account of the sealing of the covenant.

Though we call it a code, it is not a single structure: 20:21-26 and 23:13-19 consist of cultic provisions, and it is generally felt that the latter section is more recent than the former or than the rest of the code.[34] Further, 23:20-33 does not consist of laws but of a hortatory farewell address emphasizing the rewards that will come from observing the laws. This leaves a central block of "civil" and "criminal" law (21:1–23:12), which must also be divided into two sections. The latter (22:20–23:12) shows a strong religious orientation which is missing in the former. This has led some to conclude that 21:1–22:19 is the oldest section of the code and that 22:20–23:12 stands under prophetic influence.

It is almost certain that the code was developed in Palestine. Behind it lies the social practice of an agricultural society. As they settled down in Palestine, the Israelites incorporated these forms of social control into their own pattern of life. They also assimilated them to the covenant relationship in which Israel stood to Yahweh. The Covenant Code is an excellent illustration of the assimilative capacity of Israel's faith.

The Covenant Code, as a separable unit in the book of Exodus, was first isolated by Goethe. Of all the codes of the early Near East it is the only one that has played until today a continuous role in the cultural process. Less than a century ago it was the only one known to exist. Then the discovery of others—the Code of Hammurabi of ancient Babylon, the Assyrian Code, the Hittite Code, and the Hurrian laws—demonstrated that in the development of its social institutions and laws ancient Israel was organically related to the whole process of cultural forces in the midst of which it grew up. The meaning of the assertion that biblical religion is historical in character was given a much fuller significance when it was discovered that the social forms of the religious community which enshrined a unique faith were, sociologically speaking, of a piece with the forms of every other culture.

The relation between the Covenant Code and the Hammurabi and other ancient codes is an indirect one. There are no verbally parallel laws. Not a single law in the Covenant Code is an exact duplication of a law in the older Code of Hammurabi. The Hebrew legislators were unconscious of their dependence upon their Babylonian predecessors. The Covenant Code developed in Palestine in an environment long permeated by Babylonian cultural influ-

[34] Eissfeldt, Einleitung in das A.T., p. 245.

ences. At least in so far as its Israelite history is concerned, this development took place after the Babylonian Code as such, which had made its impression on Palestinian society, had disappeared from the scene. There was a time, shortly after the discovery of the Code of Hammurabi, when comparisons of it with the Covenant Code were made chiefly for the purpose of establishing points of literal dependence. Today there is a more comprehensive and constructive tendency which seeks to treat each code, including also the Hittite and Assyrian, as the index to the spirit and structure of a whole society, thereafter comparing the full impression that emerges from each. When this is done we soon discover that the Code of Hammurabi was the instrument of a much more complex society than the Covenant Code. It indicates a society in which the commercial interests far outstripped the agricultural, in which society was rigidly stratified, the professions highly self-conscious and controlled by a completely centralized government. A complex economy had been carefully standardized and was under state control. The Covenant Code talks about a pastoral and agricultural society, still largely tribal in its structure. There is a lack of differentiation based on social caste or professional calling. The family and the local community have not yet given way to an all-pervasive central government. The possibility that this code was initially sealed by Joshua at Shechem (Josh. 24:25), as has been frequently suggested, can hardly be ruled out. Its provisions may have served Israel's society at least until the rise of the Davidic empire.[35]

XII. Religious Significance of the Tabernacle

The priestly ordinances for the cultus stand outside the context of the promulgation account of the covenant at Sinai. This is significant, for it points to the very distinctive theological outlook of the priestly writers. The account of the sealing of the covenant is provided by JE. The Covenant Code and the Decalogue stand within the context of this account as the conditions for its maintenance undertaken by Israel. The Deuteronomists probably set them in this context (see pp. 842-43), for it was with the Deuteronomists that the correlation of covenant and law reached its climax. The law became the substance of the covenant and bore its title. The tradition that the two tables of stone on which the laws were inscribed were placed in the ark

[35] See English translations of the Code of Hammurabi and of the Hittite and Assyrian codes in J. M. Powis Smith, The Origin and History of Hebrew Law (Chicago: University of Chicago Press, 1931); Ancient Near Eastern Texts, ed. James B. Pritchard (Princeton: Princeton University Press, 1950).

was perhaps of Deuteronomic origin; at least it was most strongly emphasized by Deuteronomists. For them the ark, especially as the receptacle of the law, was the heart of Israel's cultus.

In Solomon's Temple, as earlier in Shiloh, and probably in the wilderness, the ark had been the symbol of God's constant presence with his people. It was the mark of his nearness and immanence. At times this seems to lead almost to an identification of Yahweh and the ark (Num. 10:35-36; I Sam. 4:5-11). Solomon built his temple because, as he put it, God resolved to dwell in a place of utter darkness (I Kings 8:12-13), and the ark was established in the most holy place as the heart of Solomon's Temple. It and the temple itself stressed the immanent and abiding presence of Yahweh in Israel's midst. The Deuteronomists refine and moralize this Presence by equating it with the law. They also conceptualize the notion of God's presence by coining for it the phrase "the name of Yahweh." Thus the temple was no longer the dwelling for Yahweh but for his "name" (I Kings 8:17; etc.). The actual Presence of an earlier era is thus attenuated. Nevertheless, the ark and the first temple remain throughout the symbols of the divine immanence, summed up in the covenant, the tables of the law (I Kings 8:21).

The priestly writers did their creative work during and immediately after the Exile. The movement they called forth lost its ascendancy to the rabbinical movement initiated by Ezra. Its day was brief. But these priestly writers offered a radically different central focus for the interpretation of Israel's cultus from that of the Deuteronomists who preceded them or the rabbis of "normative Judaism" who followed them. It is possible to sum up the original and distinctive contribution of the priestly movement to Israel's religious history by saying that the starting point for its interpretation of the cultus was not the immanence of God but his majestic transcendence.[36]

In Exodus this priestly interpretation of the faith and its cultus is given in the accounts of the instructions for and the erection of the tabernacle and its equipment. Ever since the days of Wellhausen it has been commonly recognized that the tabernacle of Exodus is an ideal structure. The temple of Solomon was its structural model. But was the temple also the primary source of inspiration for the concern which moved the priestly writers with respect to the meaning of the cultus? What, religiously speaking, was the point of this imagined tabernacle? Was it simply, as Wellhausen supposed, designed to establish the notion that the cultus as practiced in the first temple had been so ordained by Moses and had been performed in substantially the same way from the first? Or did these priestly writers have a more forward-looking constructive concern? They probably did. They wished to combine the meaning of the tent (33:7-11) with the very different symbolic significance of the ark of the first temple. Thus, in terms of its religious significance, the tabernacle represents an attempt at a synthesis of the experience of the God of Israel as transcendent and as immanent. The ancient tent was primarily a symbol of the experience of Yahweh in his transcendent majesty. Since this attempt at a synthesis is in part a reaction against the immanentist and legalistic-moralistic tendencies in Deuteronomy, the priestly movement stresses strongly both God's sovereign transcendence and the redemptive character of the relationship in which he stands to his people. While the first temple serves as a structural model for the tabernacle and its equipment, the ancient tent of meeting was the primary source for its inspiration and meaning.

As in the temple, the ark in the tabernacle stands at the very heart of the structure; in the instructions for the erection of the tabernacle (chs. 25–31) the ark is treated first, despite the fact that the historical ark probably no longer existed when the account was written. This is characteristic of the effort to absorb everything in the new interpretation. That the novelty is very real becomes apparent as soon as we compare the role of the ark in the tabernacle with that of the ark in the temple or in Deuteronomy. In the tabernacle it is no longer the tables of the law in the ark, or even the ark as such, but the mercy seat with the attached cherubim *on* the ark that is the significant feature. The ark is indeed "the ark of the testimony," the symbol of the law; but it is from above the ark and its mercy seat that the majestic God of Israel, the transcendent ruler of all existence, will meet with and commune with the priestly representative of Israel, even as he communicated with Moses in the tent (25:22). It is, moreover, not by means of Israel's observance of the law but through the atonement wrought by the annual sacrificial blood on the mercy seat that Israel's relation to God is maintained. In contrast to the moralistic legalism of both Deuteronomy and the later "normative Judaism," the priestly movement develops Israel's faith as a religion of grace. All too soon this priestly emphasis was eclipsed in its public influence

[36] Gerhard von Rad, "Zelt und Lade," *Neue Kirchliche Zeitschrift*, LXII (1931), 476-98, is a pioneer in this modern rediscovery; cf. Eichrodt, *Theologie des A.T.*, I, 197-221.

by the book-centered moralism of the rabbis. The latter retained the cultus in its priestly forms, but more and more reduced its meaning to a legal observance.

In P's interpretation of the cult the covenant of Sinai becomes insignificant. The laws committed to Moses are the testimony; they no longer constitute the covenant (25:21). For P the covenant is no longer "a mutual relationship between Israel and Yahweh, albeit not between equals" (see p. 841). The covenant consists of God's eternal decree disclosed in creation and in Israel's election. The latter P associates with Abraham rather than with Moses and Sinai. The relationship in which all mankind and Israel, each in its own way, stand to Yahweh is a preordained and lasting relationship. God sets up the covenant; it is his covenant (Gen. 17:7). Man's freedom, also Israel's freedom, is seemingly limited by this rather static apprehension of the transcendent role of God. The relationship tends to become trans-historical and mystical in character.[37] The cultus of the tabernacle, with emphases of separation, continuity, symmetry, and perpetual identity, sets forth the stable relationship presupposed by the P writers who developed it. The cultus as well as the laws are not the substance of the relationship, but a means of declaring it. The nature of the relationship Yahweh alone can determine.

XIII. Place of Exodus in the Bible and in Christian Faith

In the Old Testament Exodus has a role comparable to that of the Gospels in the New Testament. Its focus is the historic event on which the community of Israel was built. It is a book of faith. It assumes that Israel's escape from slavery, and its establishment as a people, is *the* event of revelation. It assumes that God's disclosure of himself in this event was decisive and definitive. Consequently, it treats Israel's experience of the meaning of this event as the key to the meaning of all existence. All of this is true of the entire Old Testament. What is distinctive about Exodus is that it focuses upon this event of revelation in terms of its historical actuality by recounting the remembered incidents of the emancipation of Israel and its establishment as a community, at the same time exalting the revelation which, to faith, was mediated through these.

The central moment in God's activity disclosed in the exodus event as attested in Exodus is power. Yahweh is Lord. He vanquishes the Pharaoh and the gods he represents, as well as the powers that can dispose of demonic forces.

This notion of power, freedom, and sovereignty, first illustrated in this book and in the event it celebrates, becomes a persistent apprehension in the framework of biblical faith. Later interpretations of God's nature and will which stress his justice, forgiveness, love, and compassion always do so on the prior assumption of his power. However, already in Exodus this power of God is affirmed as expressing itself in responsible and moral intention. The God of Exodus has a purpose, a plan. The content of this plan scarcely rises above the limits of Israel's possession of Canaan in Exodus. But the apprehension of God's activity as intentional persists to express itself finally in the most comprehensive expositions of Christian eschatology. The moral character of this intentional activity Exodus illustrates by treating the social-moral standards of Israel's common life, the Decalogue and the Covenant Code, as an expression of God's own moral activity.

Exodus is not a history in the modern sense. It is the history of the birth and establishment of a historic faith. It combines historic memory, notably remembered aspects of the primary event of revelation, with Israel's present living experience. Thus it seeks to bear witness to the faith by which Israel lives. It is not concerned to provide the facts relating to the Exodus and to Israel's establishment as a community for the purpose of a scientific reconstruction of the past. Its real concern is not with the past but with the present. But this "present" contains Israel's whole history and has its roots in a very particular past. It was at a certain time and in a certain place that God revealed himself and that Israel became his people. Exodus assumes that through this particular event, and the community of faith it evokes, there is mediated the saving insight into the meaning of existence. The whole Bible affirms this historic particularity in respect to revelation. In the New Testament this particularity is moved to the Christ event, and yet retained. The whole Bible insists with Exodus that the meaning of creation is seen by the light of redemption. It is the unique role of Exodus to deal directly with those historic incidents in relation to which this faith was first expressed.

Exodus has inextricably interwoven the affirmation that the character of God was disclosed in the historic exodus with the belief that his intention and will were expressed in the founding of the Israelite community. This corresponds to the apprehension, characteristic of the whole biblical view, that the revealing activity of God, in its decisive and saving depth, is both historical and elective in nature. "Historical revelation," in the biblical sense, entails a church. It can be affirmed only from within this church in

[37] Eichrodt, *op. cit.*, I, 206-9.

which it expresses itself, for it is affirmed in faith. On the other hand, this church or community of faith is not held together simply by a common life or by common principles and practices. It is held together by the remembrance and celebration of the particular historical event which it affirms as the event of revelation. In Exodus Israel is "a kingdom of priests and a holy nation" (19:6) only in the context of the living experience that God had led it out of Egypt. So also in the New Testament and in Christianity the church cannot be "the community of the faithful" unless it is also "the body of Jesus Christ." In the Old Testament it is primarily the book of Exodus that provides, celebrates, and insists on this historical basis which is both the distinctive feature and the offense of the Bible and of Christian faith. Exodus serves especially as a shield which protects the biblical community from being swallowed up by some nonhistorical, universal system, whether mystical or rational. Exodus provides a record of the framework of faith in which the prophets spoke and in relation to which they must be understood. This is true even though parts of Exodus as literature are chronologically postprophetic.

XIV. Outline of Contents

XV. Selected Bibliography

ALBRIGHT, W. F. *From the Stone Age to Christianity.* 2nd ed. Baltimore: Johns Hopkins Press, 1946.

BEER, GEORG. *Exodus, mit einem Beitrag von Kurt Galling.* Tübingen: J. C. B. Mohr, 1939.

BUBER, MARTIN. *Moses.* London: East & West Library, 1946.

DRIVER, S. R. *The Book of Exodus* ("The Cambridge Bible"). Cambridge: Cambridge University Press, 1911.

GRESSMANN, HUGO. *Mose und seine Zeit.* Göttingen: Vandenhoeck & Ruprecht, 1913.

MCNEILE, A. H. *The Book of Exodus* ("Westminster Commentaries"). London: Methuen & Co., 1908.

MEEK, THEOPHILE J. *Hebrew Origins.* Rev. ed. New York: Harper & Bros., 1950.

EXODUS

TEXT, EXEGESIS, AND EXPOSITION

The Book of Exodus.*—Some books can be read in half a dozen different ways. Books are like music. One can listen to a symphony idly or technically or sentimentally or religiously; while thinking of something else, or while attempting to re-create the mood of the composer. In great books the riches remain inexhaustible, ready for another reading. Such books grow in meaning with the growth of one's own powers of perception. One can read Exodus for the stories it contains, or for its hidden meanings. One can try to unravel its many threads, and guess at its varied authors or ages. One can even read it homiletically in search of good texts, though this method is apt to defeat its own end. Good texts are generally suggested to one who reads for the interest of the material rather than to one who is on a search for texts.

Exodus is one of the most complicated books in the Bible when one begins trying to distinguish between the different versions of the stories and the corrections and amplifications of old material by later hands. It has been said of England that it is to the visitor really a picture book. It is old now, and some of its pages are missing, and many of those that are left are torn and spoiled. Some of its ancient monuments have been restored by later hands in accordance with what they considered better ideas, and much that we would have treasured has been allowed to disappear by those who did not think it was important or interesting.

When you read Exodus you are listening to many voices of people in different places and times, retelling, correcting, misunderstanding, or inserting material which would give historical precedent for their doctrines and which they would like to believe recorded events which must have taken place. You sit around a kind of campfire listening to the evening storytellers. As one finishes his tale, another says, "Well, that is not exactly the way my grandmother told the story. She said. . . ." You sit beside the old scribe who tries for the first time to reduce into a semblance of unity what has passed from

mouth to mouth for centuries. You sympathize with the godly priest who sees as he writes that this story does not give credit enough to Aaron or the priests of the day, and so adds a touch of what he feels certain must have occurred. This is true of all history. Christopher Lloyd wrote of Napoleon: "I fancy . . . that more books have been written about Napoleon than about any other single person in history. . . . History is rewritten to suit the needs of the age. . . . Facts become overlaid with commentary." [1]

Some people have not faith enough to believe that God could reveal so much of his wisdom and truth through folk who were often as fallible and biased as we are. But to see how it happens, and with what grand result, is very comforting to us who do not consider ourselves perfect and yet hope that in some way we too may "fain be to the Eternal Goodness, what his own hand is to a man." [2] For the glory of the gospel is that it manifests itself in every life except in that which claims to be inerrant and literally inspired in every detail (cf. Luke 13:24-27). We see in Exodus how much of the goodness and glory of God shines through the very fallible men whose work it is.

There are those who will ask, "How can one stand up and proclaim, 'Thus saith the Lord,' if the Bible is full of mistakes?" This is exactly what the Lord in Exodus knew Pharaoh would say. It is the heathen point of view which prompts the question. The answer to the question which the Lord anticipated Pharaoh would ask, "Can you show a miracle to prove you are speaking for your God?" would be, "Your own heart should bear testimony enough to you that no one has any right to treat fellow human beings as you are treating my people." But there was no use talking to Pharaoh like that. He would not understand such language. The Egyptians were much impressed by what seemed to be strange and supernatural phenomena as evidence of divine power (as long as they could not understand how they were produced). So

*Pp. 849-51 include the expositor's introduction. Text and Exegesis begin on p. 851. Editors.

[1] *The Listener,* XLV (1951), 495.
[2] *Theologia Germanica* (Boston: J. P. Jewett & Co., 1856), p. 29.

the Lord taught Moses and Aaron some "signs" in order to get the attention of the ignorant man.

It is one of the relics of our heathenism, this longing we have for some tangible evidence that will clearly indicate the will of God. We would like an infallible church, or an inerrant book, to tell us just exactly what we should do. But "this kind goeth not out but by prayer and fasting" (Matt. 17:21). God works now as he did in the composition of the Bible—through fallible men. He has made us so that we can clearly recognize his voice when we hear it. That is the long lesson taught by moral effort and religious devotion. How did Moses know it was the voice of God that spoke to him out of the burning bush? He knew because it had in it the same accent of the Holy Ghost which he had as a child learned to recognize in the lives of the great saints of the past, Abraham, Isaac, and Jacob. He knew because it voiced the same deep sympathy which he himself had felt for downtrodden people. He knew because it called him to give himself on their behalf. It needed no voucher to prove that it was the voice of God. "I am the God of thy father"; "I know the sorrows of my people"; "Come now, therefore, and I will send thee." So can one stand up and say, "Thus saith the LORD." The proof that a Bible text is the word of God is that it is the testimony of all the saints of all ages, that it appeals to the deepest and best in every hearer's heart, and that it assigns each one his post in the army of the Lord.

When a prophet declares, "Thus saith the LORD," we find sometimes (as is also the case with the Supreme Court of the United States, or both houses of Parliament assembled) that he is wrong, and that he is corrected by some later and more considered decision. "Ye have heard that it was said by them of old time, . . . but I say unto you" (Matt. 5:21-22). This is one of the reasons why the Bible seems so alive as we read it: the understanding of God in it grows with the centuries. After the caste of professional clergymen or priests had come into being, we frequently find that they were apt to confuse the will of God with the particular ritual which they happened to favor. Customs which had the sanction of long usage were often declared to be of divine origin and given the same pious emphasis as were the weightier matters of the law, justice, mercy, and faith. Every religion gathers such accretions which are apt to be regarded as being equally important with religion itself, if not more so. There is a famous story of an old Scottish Presbyterian elder who, hearing that burglary, arson, and murder had taken place in a neighboring parish, said, "Things are going from bad to worse; if we do not repent, we shall have sabbathbreaking next."

The Decalogue, to cite but one example, is given in Exodus in two forms, that in ch. 34 being concerned with ritual matters entirely. Note the Tenth Commandment: "Thou shalt not seethe a kid in his mother's milk" (34:26). This commandment is perhaps due to the ancient belief that milk drawn from a cow remains in such vital connection with the animal that any injury done the milk will sympathetically be felt by the cow. James C. Frazer [3] gives many instances among many peoples of such a belief. To the priest who framed this Decalogue, such a prohibition may have seemed as important as that about stealing or killing. It is therefore put directly into the mouth of God.

Nor have we rid ourselves even yet of this type of confusion. Turn on the radio some Sunday and hear voices proclaiming in God's name similar commands. If any one should insist on making some inquiry into them, he would be deemed an enemy of God. They must be accepted. Many churches have at least one such rule, viz., "We are the true church. God has spoken to us. We represent him on earth."

But a conviction is valid only if it tolerates public discussion. In Exodus one sees how the ancient rules and regulations, believed in one generation to be given by the direct voice of God, were in another generation discussed and discarded and replaced by more vital, more humane, more religious precepts. Compare the Decalogue in ch. 34 with that in ch. 20. One contribution which democratic ways of thinking have made to religion is the conviction that the pronouncements of religion, even those which are said to be divine commandments, are subject to modification in view of man's growing knowledge of God. Much of the power of ritual seems to lie in its antiquity, perhaps rightly so; but it is also true that ritual precepts are the first to come under the scrutiny of each succeeding generation. The question as to whether or not Christ gave certain exclusive religious powers to a historic caste of self-perpetuating officials for all time, entirely independent of their Christian character, is in our view subject to free discussion; even as most of the ritual commands of Exodus must justify themselves to us on grounds other than that of their supposed divine origin.

Ritual is a means, not an end. One has to discover what the people who framed it were aiming at. Some writers, for instance, explain the commandment against seething a kid in its mother's milk by showing that flesh boiled in

---

[3] *Folk-lore in the Old Testament* (London: Macmillan & Co., 1918), Part IV, ch. ii.

1 Now these *are* the names of the children of Israel, which came into Egypt; every man and his household came with Jacob.

2 Reuben, Simeon, Levi, and Judah,

3 Issachar, Zebulun, and Benjamin,

4 Dan, and Naphtali, Gad, and Asher.

1 These are the names of the sons of Israel who came to Egypt with Jacob, each with his household: 2 Reuben, Simeon, Levi, and Judah, 3 Is'sachar, Zeb'ulun, and Benjamin, 4 Dan and Naph'tali, Gad and

---

I. Preamble (1:1-22)

If, as noted above (see Intro., p. 833), the book of Exodus is comparable to a drama, this first chapter may be likened to the biographical notes and explanations of scenes that introduce a play.

A. Israel in Egypt (1:1-7)

1:1-4. Now these are the names is the phrase by which the book is designated in Hebrew. The late priestly editors regularly use genealogies and name lists as a device for providing the history of Israel and of mankind with an explicit chronological framework. This list has the same order as that given in Gen. 35:23-26. The names of the

---

milk was considered a great dainty, and that wandering bands of boys, finding a kid and its mother on their excursions into the waterless wilderness, would often satisfy their appetites by cooking the kid on the sly, using the mother's milk for want of other liquid, not realizing that they were jeopardizing the existence of the whole tribe, and that the enormity of their act injured the herds which were food and prosperity for all. Such a sin seemed to the folk of that day more heinous than simple stealing, more heinous even than murder. Whether the command had some such moral ground or was simply a ritual injunction, we have not only the right but the duty to inquire if its grounds are still valid for us. It has been compellingly said that every class interest in all history has defended itself from examination by putting forth claim to absoluteness. And we ourselves are no exception. We seem to have advanced but little from the technique of the various groups who worked over the material in Exodus and inserted a "Thus saith the Lord" before their pet prohibitions. We will go to any length to avoid the intolerable effort of conscious thought. We let our columnists and commentators do our thinking for us. We capitulate to slogans. We need to be reminded constantly of the fact that what was a valid "Thus saith the Lord" to a band of nomads in the wilderness may not be pertinent now. Much of what was real and vital to them is today like the drinking troughs which the benevolent have endowed in perpetuity for horses in the very centers of our motorized cities —though such monuments do have much to teach us of the kindness and thoughtfulness of the human heart. So when people speak of the

inexorable law of supply and demand, of the duty of all men to be content in the lot to which God has called them, of the absolute character of national sovereignty, of the superior importance of individual initiative over social justice, we have a duty to discover for ourselves whether we are listening to the runes droned from the rocking chair of use and wont, or whether we are hearing the authentic voice of God. Foreign missions were not established on the basis of Exod. 22:20, "He that sacrificeth unto any god, save unto the Lord only, he shall be utterly destroyed."

Yet surely it needs to be said that when this book is read in a religious rather than in an idolatrous spirit, it is full of inspiration, wisdom, tenderness, shrewdness, and devotion. Augustine writes: "Blessed are they who know which are Thy commands. For the thing was all done by Thy servants; either to show something needful for the present, or to foreshow things to come." [4] Another ancient writer adds, where God speaks, there it is all God; here where man understands it, it is God and creature.[5]

1:1-6. *The Names of the Sons of Israel.*—An interest in one's own genealogy is often the preliminary symptom of old age. With nations it is the preliminary symptom of the sense of nationalism. These names are repeated many times in the Bible, every time in the order in which they were remembered. They occur in more than twenty different arrangements in the O.T. and the N.T. There is nothing extraordinary about that. Every nation has its list of founders, of

[4] *Confessions* III. 9. 17.

[5] Franz Pfeiffer, *Meister Eckhart,* tr. C. de B. Evans (London: John M. Watkins, 1924-31), I, 164.

5 And all the souls that came out of the loins of Jacob were seventy souls: for Joseph was in Egypt *already*.

6 And Joseph died, and all his brethren, and all that generation.

Asher. 5 All the offspring of Jacob were seventy persons; Joseph was already in Egypt. 6 Then Joseph died, and all his

---

sons of the wives, Leah and Rachel, precede those of the sons of the concubines. The **sons of Israel** means the sons of Jacob. The patriarchal stories in Genesis and the account of Moses and the Exodus originally belonged to different themes and may have circulated independently. Biblical writers and editors emphasize the ethnic tie between the descendants of the patriarchal heroes and the Israelites delivered from bondage. Thus they make Genesis and Exodus part of a single sequence. Also, they interpret the meaning of the nomadic Hebrew wandering into Egypt in the light of the deliverance of Israel and its establishment as the people of God.

5. Seventy souls: The word נפש here means **persons,** as it commonly does in P. The names of the seventy male descendants are given in Gen. 46:8-27. Deut. 10:22 also mentions seventy persons as having gone into Egypt, without specifying that they went down with Jacob. In each case the LXX tells us that there were "seventy and five" souls (cf. also, Codex Alexandrinus on Deut. 10:22). This larger total is justified by the LXX's insertion (Gen. 46:20) of the names of two sons and a grandson of Ephraim and a son and grandson of Manasseh. In Acts 7:14 the number given is also seventy-five. The LXX wants to include **all the offspring of Jacob.** The Hebrew text limits itself to those **who came to Egypt with Jacob.** In either case the number is symbolic. The P writer is not primarily concerned to offer a census statistic but a genealogy that symbolizes Israel's unity under God. The earliest writers of the Bible were content to be vague about numbers (e.g., 12:37; Gen. 16:10; Josh. 11:4). The story of Joseph suggests that the people of Exodus did not all enter Egypt at one time. Nor must this list be taken to mean that every tribe which later became a part of Israel in Canaan had once been enslaved in Egypt. The list is a symbol to attest that the event of deliverance is basic in the whole national and religious consciousness of Israel in Canaan, just as the American Revolution is basic to the national consciousness of all Americans wherever their ancestors may have been when it occurred.

6. Then Joseph died seems to have been the phrase by which the J historian introduced the traditions recorded in Exodus. It can be read as a continuation of Gen. 50:21, the probable close of the J strand in that book.

---

original tribal chiefs. The Nazis tried to make use of their own Germanic pantheon as the basis for a national religion. In the pulpits of Scotland, when to read the Scripture without comment was illegal lest one fall into the error of "vain repetitions," it was often the custom to illustrate this list in the first few verses of Exodus by a recitation of the names of Scottish heroes. Logically it would seem that other nations ought to be able to do what the Jews did and provide a list of their own national figures as a substitute in such religious litanies. But nothing of the sort has ever been a success. There is about Christianity a sense of universalism, illustrated by the fact that Abraham, Isaac, and Jacob, or the names in this list, such as Reuben, Simeon, Levi, and Judah, have come in the course of the

centuries to represent to all men the human race itself. Nationalism is a poor substitute for Christianity. Pride of lineage based on covenant or blood must manifest itself in accordance with the French phrase, *noblesse oblige*—"much given, much expected" (Luke 12:48).

6-8. *A New King . . . Which Knew Not Joseph.*—Death, which seems so tragic as an individual incident, is the condition of all progress. Joseph died, as did all the rich memories of the service he had rendered. **A new king** arose **which knew not Joseph,** nor anything at all that he had stood for and achieved. Joseph's ripe experience which could have counseled the people, "You must not try that; we did, years ago, and it would not work," was no longer available. A ruler unpracticed in the policies of co-operation

7 ¶ And the children of Israel were fruitful, and increased abundantly, and multiplied, and waxed exceeding mighty; and the land was filled with them.

8 Now there arose up a new king over Egypt, which knew not Joseph.

9 And he said unto his people, Behold, the people of the children of Israel *are* more and mightier than we:

brothers, and all that generation. 7 But the descendants of Israel were fruitful and increased greatly; they multiplied and grew exceedingly strong; so that the land was filled with them.

8 Now there arose a new king over Egypt, who did not know Joseph. 9 And he said to his people, "Behold, the people of Israel are too many and too mighty for us.

---

7. **Were fruitful and increased greatly** is the P phrase. It continues vs. 5. The Hebrew for **increased greatly** means to teem or to swarm. It is used of marine life (Gen. 1:20) and of insects of all sorts (Gen. 7:21). Here the emphasis is upon the extraordinarily rapid increase of Israel. Even in a foreign land the promise to Abraham was being fulfilled (Gen. 12:2). The command and the promise made to mankind at creation (Gen. 1:28) were now the prerogative of Israel. The phrase that follows means essentially the same thing; it is probably a J remnant. **The land was filled with them** hints at the reason for the repressive measures instituted by the Pharaoh. The slaves were on the way to becoming a cultural and political force, as well as an economic asset. The Egyptians were faced with the problem of exploiting the economic asset without risking political security and cultural integrity. **The land** refers to "the land of Rameses" (Gen. 47:11), that part of Egypt in which later on Ramses II built cities. It is the equivalent of what J called "the land of Goshen" (Gen. 47:1). E, however, seems to assume that the Israelites lived everywhere in Egypt rather than in a special section. This seems implied in his account of the midwives (vss. 15-22) and also in the story of the discovery of Moses and his adoption by the princess (2;1-10).

B. ISRAEL ENSLAVED (1:8-14)

8. Who was this **new king over Egypt?** The "Pharaoh of the oppression" and, on the basis of 2:23; 4:19, the immediate predecessor of the Pharaoh of the Exodus (cf. Intro., p. 836). The **new king** could not possibly have known Joseph personally. But what is implied is that he launched a new policy with respect to the Israelites. He chose to ignore the past services of Joseph (cf. Judg. 2:10). As the first strong ruler of the Nineteenth Dynasty, Ramses II was more than another ruler: he embodied a new era.

9. The RSV reading, **too many and too mighty for us**, is an adequate rendering of the Hebrew (cf. I Kings 19:7, where the Hebrew structure is the same). The tiny

---

and friendship which Joseph had so laboriously built up was on the throne. So often death seems to cancel all that life has learned. It was as if nobody was left who knew how this situation or that had come to pass, how reverently this tradition should be treated, what idea, born of experience, lay back of having this transaction done in just this way. It is these impieties of progress that shock the conservative.

And yet—without the cemetery in every village and town and country, how could any progress at all ever have been possible? This good man dies, and with him dies much hard-won knowledge; but with him dies also much prejudice and blind confidence and prudent paralysis. The new generation tries what the old genera-

tion has proved to be impossible—and does it. The present has to meet conditions undreamed of by the statesmen of the past. The only good that can outlast men's hands is the good they have so kneaded into life that it is able to operate without them.

7-12. *The Would-be Master Race.*—Here we find the Egyptians faced with the same problem which has worried many a national leader since. It is the eternal joke which unconscious biology plays at the expense of conscious culture. The "other people" are increasing faster than we are! The Germanic peoples multiplied faster than the French, the Slavs faster than any of them, the Japanese faster than the Europeans. We are always under the threat of having

10 Come on, let us deal wisely with them; lest they multiply, and it come to pass, that, when their falleth out any war, they join also unto our enemies, and fight against us, and *so* get them up out of the land.

11 Therefore they did set over them taskmasters to afflict them with their burdens. And they built for Pharaoh treasure cities, Pithom and Raamses.

12 But the more they afflicted them, the more they multiplied and grew. And they were grieved because of the children of Israel.

10 Come, let us deal shrewdly with them, lest they multiply, and, if war befall us, they join our enemies and fight against us and escape from the land." 11 Therefore they set taskmasters over them to afflict them with heavy burdens; and they built for Pharaoh store cities, Pithom and Ra-am'-ses. 12 But the more they were oppressed, the more they multiplied and the more they spread abroad. And the Egyptians were in

Israelite minority was one of many similar groups in Egypt. In retrospect our historian, who assumes that the Israelite slaves in Egypt lived out of the "promise" which was for him in process of fulfillment, asserts that they alone constituted a threat to Egypt's security. He does not say that the Israelites outnumbered the Egyptians, but that they were "too much" for them and made them afraid.

10. The king decides to **deal shrewdly** with the Israelites. His aim is to retain the people as an economic asset and yet avoid a threat to Egypt's security. He hopes that hard labor will break their spirit and check their rapid growth. We have a hint here of the dramatic action that is to come: the "fruitfulness" of the Israelites is the mark of divine promise. In seeking to destroy it the king enters into conflict with the God of Israel. He is determined that Israel shall not **escape from the land.** The literal meaning is "go up from the land," perhaps to the higher ground of Canaan.

11. To carry out their shrewd, two-pronged plan the Egyptians conscripted the Israelites into labor battalions. This was the *maṣ* or *corvée,* which was very common in the ancient world, as in the twentieth century. The great building programs of Egypt were executed by this type of slave labor and Solomon, who was under Egyptian influence, introduced it in the united kingdom (I Kings 5:13-14; 9:15), thus hastening the dissolution of his empire (I Kings 12:18). The **taskmasters,** general supervisors, were probably Egyptians, but the foremen seem to have been Israelites (5:14). The slaves **built for Pharaoh,** i.e., for the state; the title at this time was a synonym for public authority. Later, in the Twenty-second Dynasty, it became a personal title of the ruler. They built the **store cities, Pithom and Raamses.** Pithom was situated in the Wadi Tumilat, which connects the Nile and Lake Timsah. For a generation Tell el-Maskhuteh, excavated by Naville, was unanimously accepted as its site. This has now been given up and Pithom is located at Tell er-Retabeh, eight miles farther east in the same valley. Raamses was once located at Tell er-Retabeh, but its site is now generally identified with Tanis. Ramses II built more in this area than the two cities here mentioned; that has made it more difficult to be certain about the location of these two.

12. Here we turn from chronicle to poesy. The shame and honor of the facts just cited are raised to the theme of a folklore which is a prelude that introduces the story

"others," in the words of the text, become too many and too mighty to suit our convenience. It is a condition which has been one of the causes of war throughout history and threatens to be the cause of wars to follow. No one seems to know just why one nation should be possessed of so much more vitality than another; why

the Germans were able to recover in twenty-five years after their disastrous defeat in 1918, and to such an extent that they came within an ace of conquering the world. Perhaps they had more thyroid! At least we have begun to see that though wars never seem fatal, they are never won. That much is gain. Meanwhile the biolog-

13 And the Egyptians made the children of Israel to serve with rigor:

14 And they made their lives bitter with hard bondage, in mortar, and in brick, and in all manner of service in the field: all their service, wherein they made them serve, *was* with rigor.

dread of the people of Israel. 13 So they made the people of Israel serve with rigor, 14 and made their lives bitter with hard service, in mortar and brick, and in all kinds of work in the field; in all their work they made them serve with rigor.

---

of the Exodus and creates a proper mood for it. The greater the oppression, the greater the signs of the "promise." This historian is a man of faith for whom the story of Israel's enslavement and release are parts of a divine comedy. The efforts of the Egyptians must have made God smile! More than ever the Egyptians were **in dread . . . of Israel.** The Hebrew word conveys an element of awe; there was something eerie and unnerving about this people.

13-14. These two verses were added by P. They are motivated by the same faith that underlies the preceding verse. The hardness of the oppression is driven home; the term **rigor** is repeated; so is the verb **serve,** which means the toiling of slaves. **Hard bondage** (KJV) is perhaps preferable.

---

ical problem is as great a mystery to us as it was to this new Pharaoh. He found that these despised people were increasing more rapidly than the master race. And so he **afflicted** them. But as often happens, the more they were oppressed, the more they multiplied. He forced them to build store-cities for him, one of which —**Pithom**—has been identified with a moderate amount of certainty and found on excavation to contain the remains of large granaries.

People sometimes say that the only lesson learned from history is that it does not teach any lesson. It does seem to be generally true, however, that within certain limits hard times are apt to breed a stronger people than easy times; and that as difficulty tends to develop stamina, so prosperity tends to result in degeneration. When the pursuit of happiness is regarded as synonymous with the pursuit of comfort, the population begins to dwindle and discontent looks out of the eyes of the people. The Israelites in Egypt did not find life easy; but they became "too many and too mighty" for their masters.

13-14. *The Recognition of the Common Man.* —Because historians have generally come from the upper classes, history usually has been written about the doings of the masters. It is filled with the exploits of kings and queens, of politicians and financiers, of nobles and generals, and the movements of the lower classes have been labeled "rebellions" or "insurrections" which had to be "quelled." Tacitus speaks of the operations of Spartacus as shameful and humiliating.[6] No Roman writer recognizes his greatness. Labor leaders are "robbers," "public enemies," or "agitators." Their followers are

"mobs." People who work with their hands are apt to be looked upon as bad. In 1769, John Wilkes was thrice elected to Parliament, and thrice refused admission by the "masters." On the last occasion he won by a large majority; whereupon the House of Commons passed a solemn motion that the rival candidate "ought to have been returned," and installed his defeated opponent.[7] Only in recent years has an attempt been made to write the history of the people, of the workers, as well as of their masters.

The one notable, unexpected, astonishing exception to this tradition among ancient historians is Exodus. It is the sympathetic account of a great strike, a total walkout of oppressed laboring people, under a valiant leader. Comfortable church people, sitting in cushioned pews, have preferred to hear it expounded from the pulpit solely as the account of a supernatural episode, illustrating the favor shown by God to his chosen people, not for any merit or worthiness in them, but "out of his mere good pleasure." They lose sight too readily of the seething restlessness underneath. It is significant that Moses is portrayed not from Pharaoh's point of view as a rebel and an anarchist, not from the employers' point of view as an ambitious and self-seeking rabble-rouser, but from the people's point of view as the resourceful leader of the oppressed and exploited masses. "Up from slavery" is the crest of an honorable tradition, far more honorable than that of the masters. The Negro, who has more reason than most white men to be proud of his ancestry, has appreciated the truth of the

[6] *Annals* III. 73; see also Horace *Odes* III. 14. 19.

[7] J. R. Green, *A Short History of the English People,* ed. Mrs. J. R. Green and Miss Kate Norgate (New York: Harper & Bros., 1893-95), ch. x, sec. 2.

15 ¶ And the king of Egypt spake to the Hebrew midwives, of which the name of the one *was* Shiphrah, and the name of the other Puah;

16 And he said, When ye do the office of a midwife to the Hebrew women, and see *them* upon the stools, if it *be* a son, then ye shall kill him; but if it *be* a daughter, then she shall live.

17 But the midwives feared God, and did not as the king of Egypt commanded them, but saved the men children alive.

18 And the king of Egypt called for the midwives, and said unto them, Why have ye done this thing, and have saved the men children alive?

15 Then the king of Egypt said to the Hebrew midwives, one of whom was named Shiph'rah and the other Pu'ah, 16 "When you serve as midwife to the Hebrew women, and see them upon the birthstool, if it is a son, you shall kill him; but if it is a daughter, she shall live." 17 But the midwives feared God, and did not do as the king of Egypt commanded them, but let the male children live. 18 So the king of Egypt called the midwives, and said to them, "Why have you done this, and let the male children

---

C. PRELUDE TO MOSES (1:15-22)

15. The aim of the enslavement, aside from economic exploitation, was to curb the growth of the Israelites. This story stresses the king's fixed purpose. Since oppression did not impair their fertility, the king would destroy Israel's sons. The king did not know that God was his real protagonist. Because those who told or heard the story did know, the outcome of the new measure is never in doubt. The story is not so much a chronicle of fact as a testimony to the faith that God is free. It also sets the stage for the birth of Moses.

The **king of Egypt** is personally in charge and the Israelites rub elbows with the Egyptians. This is typical of E, through whom the story has come down to us. The writer probably thought of the **midwives** as Egyptian (cf. Josephus *Antiquities* II. 9. 2). By changing the initial vowel point of the Hebrew phrase to a *hîreq*, we can translate it "to the midwives of the Hebrew women" (Georg Beer, *Exodus mit einem Beitrag von Kurt Galling* [Tübingen: J. C. B. Mohr, 1939], pp. 16-17). **Hebrew** in this story is a synonym for Israelite; originally it had a wider reference. Israelites were one group of Hebrews (G. E. Wright and F. V. Filson, *The Westminster Historical Atlas to the Bible* [Philadelphia: Westminster Press, 1945], p. 35*b*).

17. For the midwives, humaneness was an obligation that outranked national duty. The story calls this common human pity their fear of God, an expression of true religion that had its reward. The story affirms that God has revealed himself universally, in man's creation, as well as particularly, in man's redemption.

---

point of view of Exodus. Many of his spirituals are adaptations of the story of Exodus to his own race's history.

15-22. Cruelty and Its Limits.—Before 1914, a preacher might have commented complacently enough on the words **If it be a son, then ye shall kill him**, as showing that human nature does make progress, pointing out that such brutality is impossible in days like these. But we have lived to see history repeat itself, and these and other such horrors recur. A false creed can be used to "justify" any brutality. "We have to get rid of these people if the master race is to have its place in the sun." But the easy method of extermination does not gain for the masters their desired end. For there is a limit beyond

which even the most subservient human nature will not go. The midwives took their orders, but could not bring themselves to carry them out. Good will, mercy, and kindness keep creeping into even the most brutal scheme of power. The aroused conscience of the world, like the waves of the Red Sea in our narrative, ultimately overwhelms the persecutors.

There are flashes of humor in the eyes of the narrator as he looks around his listening circle and tells them how Yahweh outwitted Pharaoh; how bright the midwives were in their reply to Pharaoh; and later, as he tells them how the departing Israelites "borrowed" treasures from their Egyptian neighbors, and how Moses' mother got paid for taking care of her own child.

19 And the midwives said unto Pharaoh, Because the Hebrew women *are* not as the Egyptian women; for they *are* lively, and are delivered ere the midwives come in unto them.

20 Therefore God dealt well with the midwives: and the people multiplied, and waxed very mighty.

21 And it came to pass, because the midwives feared God, that he made them houses.

22 And Pharaoh charged all his people, saying, Every son that is born ye shall cast into the river, and every daughter ye shall save alive.

2 And there went a man of the house of Levi, and took *to wife* a daughter of Levi.

live?" 19 The midwives said to Pharaoh, "Because the Hebrew women are not like the Egyptian women; for they are vigorous and are delivered before the midwife comes to them." 20 So God dealt well with the midwives; and the people multiplied and grew very strong. 21 And because the midwives feared God he gave them families. 22 Then Pharaoh commanded all his people, "Every son that is born to the Hebrews[a] you shall cast into the Nile, but you shall let every daughter live."

2 Now a man from the house of Levi went and took to wife a daughter of

a Sam Gk Tg: Heb lacks *to the Hebrews*

19. The excuse of the midwives is a clever use of fact to avoid the real issue at stake. This species of smart humor is quite typical of Israelite stories (cf. Gen. 29:26).

20. The king is made to look like a fathead; he is taken in by the excuse. God wins another round; the "promise" moves on in his design: **the people multiplied.**

21. This is an editor's gloss that almost ruins a good story. It tries to answer the pedantic question, How did God reward the midwives? Obviously, thinks the glossator, with motherhood, the best thing any woman could wish for.

22. This is really a third phase of the oppression and sets the stage for the Moses stories. The RSV wisely includes the phrase **to the Hebrews** on the basis of its occurrence in the Samar. and the LXX. The Hebrew word translated **Nile** is an adopted Egyptian word meaning "river" (cf. Dan. 12:5).

II. Preparation for Deliverance (2:1-7:13)

A. God Provides for a Leader (2:1-25)

The action continues to presuppose the conflict between God and Pharaoh, even though God is in the background. The accounts of Moses' birth and survival are intended as testimony to the faith that, despite Israel's troubles, the God who is its redeemer always has the initiative.

1. Birth and Adoption of Moses (2:1-10)

2:1. As with all great men, the story of Moses' birth did not begin to be told until after he was famous. Actual recollections were scanty. The form was largely determined by two other factors: (*a*) an ancient literary pattern, exemplified by the legend of Sargon of Agade, which was the standard form for relating the birth of a deliverer; and

There is another kind of humor, not so harmless, in Aaron's excuse to Moses about the golden calf—the people were partly to blame, and partly the fire, and partly it just happened to happen, "I cast it into the fire, and there came out this calf" (32:24), as if he were as much astonished as anybody.

2:1-10. *The Child in the Ark.*—One is sometimes tempted to say that a national idol should arrange to be born in a log cabin, or in some

very small cottage in the country; when he leaves home for the city, he should have no more than fifty cents in his pocket; then to get on his feet he should sell papers in the street—at least for a few days.

There is certainly in the human heart a demand for such stories about the early life of its heroes. Romulus and Remus were exposed on the hillside and suckled by a she-wolf. Sargon, the Babylonian king (*ca.* 2850 b.c.), was born

2 And the woman conceived, and bare a son: and when she saw him that he *was* a goodly *child,* she hid him three months.

Levi. 2 The woman conceived and bore a son; and when she saw that he was a goodly

---

(*b*) the tendency to impute to the hero connections and activities considered desirable or normative by those who transmit the tradition. This may account for Moses' designation as a member of a priestly family of **the house of Levi.** According to one line of evidence Levi was an Israelite tribe which, along with Simeon, was virtually annihilated (Gen. 34:25; 49:5-7). The remnant thereafter gave its energies to priestly concerns (Theophile J. Meek, *Hebrew Origins* [rev. ed.; New York: Harper & Bros., 1950], pp. 119-47). Another line of evidence has led some to conclude that the Levites always were an order and not a tribe (32:26-29; Deut. 10:8-9; Num. 18:21; Judg. 17:7; 18:3, 14-31; cf. Paul Volz, *Die biblischen Altertümer* [Stuttgart: Calwer Vereinsbuchhandlung, 1914], p. 57). It seems possible to do justice to all the evidence if we hold that very early in Israel's history this tribe became a priestly class. Both the Sargon legend and the predilections of the Israelite writers make it almost imperative that the story should associate Moses with Levi.

2. Here Moses is clearly the first-born, though immediately below he has an older sister, and for the P genealogist Aaron was an older brother (6:20; Num. 26:59). The

---

in the Armenian mountains of unknown parents. His mother put him in a basket, closed up the opening with pitch, and set him afloat on the Euphrates. He was picked up by the gardener Akki, and in the garden met the goddess Ishtar who loved him and made him king of Babylonia. The Japanese story is that the first child born of the divine parents of the human race was set adrift in an ark of reeds.

Thus the great man who is to lead his people through a sea baffles his enemies in his infancy when he is so small that reeds and rushes hide him. The feeling the author succeeds in conveying is the sense of the loving guardianship of the heavenly Father over the fortunes of his people. Every nation has known moments when its destiny seemed to tremble in jeopardy like the tiny ark among the reeds, watched by the loving eyes of one little girl, following it on the bank as it threaded its perilous way through the bulrushes. The fate of the centuries hung once on the life of another tiny babe, pursued and harried by those who sought its life (Matt. 2:13-23). One thinks also of Franklin in the Cockpit in London in 1774; or of Lincoln in the White House in 1864; or of Churchill in the winter of 1940-41, when he quoted the verse just sent him by President Franklin D. Roosevelt:

> Sail on, O Ship of State!
> Sail on, O Union, strong and great!
> Humanity with all its fears,
> With all the hopes of future years,
> Is hanging breathless on thy fate! [8]

The impression which Churchill wished to convey to the Houses of Parliament was exactly

[8] Longfellow, "The Building of the Ship."

that which our author felt as he told with such deep feeling the story of the ark on the waters of the Nile. Some call it coincidence, and some call it God, that the king's daughter should have just happened to come down to the river to bathe at the moment when the tiny ark with its precious freight was entangled among the flags at her feet. **She sent her maid to fetch it.** One might read in the papers that "stern measures have had to be taken to prevent the inordinate increase of the Jewish people, lest they become a menace to our security." But what woman could resist the tears of the little creature in the ark, so lovingly covered in by a mother's care? **She had compassion on him,** though she recognized that **this is one of the Hebrews' children** (vs. 6). Then the watchful little person who has been in charge comes up with her innocent question, **Shall I go and call . . . a nurse of the Hebrew women, that she may nurse the child for thee?** (Vs. 7.) This is good storytelling. It is the "patterns" of life that are cruel, as Amy Lowell says. People as a rule are kind. Here we see human nature breaking through the stern pattern of cruelty to save the great hero's life and give him a chance at an education as "the son" of Pharaoh's daughter, nursed by the best nurse a child ever had, his mother. The Quakers re-enacted the story for tens of thousands of lost children all over the world after the first and second world wars.

It all seems to hang upon coincidence, to depend upon chance, that Pharaoh's daughter happened to want to bathe at that particular time, that she happened to come to the very inlet of the river at which the tiny ark happened to be. Pious folk have always hailed chance as the

3 And when she could not longer hide him, she took for him an ark of bulrushes, and daubed it with slime and with pitch, and put the child therein; and she laid *it* in the flags by the river's brink.

4 And his sister stood afar off, to wit what would be done to him.

5 ¶ And the daughter of Pharaoh came down to wash *herself* at the river; and her maidens walked along by the river's side: and when she saw the ark among the flags, she sent her maid to fetch it.

child, she hid him three months. 3 And when she could hide him no longer she took for him a basket made of bulrushes, and daubed it with bitumen and pitch; and she put the child in it and placed it among the reeds at the river's brink. 4 And his sister stood at a distance, to know what would be done to him. 5 Now the daughter of Pharaoh came down to bathe at the river, and her maidens walked beside the river; she saw the basket among the reeds and sent

suggestion has been made that Aaron and Miriam were children by an earlier marriage (15:20; Num. 12:1). That is an *ad hoc* solution which ignores the dynamic tendencies in the development of the story. Jewish legend tried to solve the problem by maintaining that, because of the king's edict, Moses' parents had been officially separated for a number of years before his birth. The confusion possibly indicates that Moses was originally not a Levite (4:14).

3. The birth story of Sargon of Agade (Robert William Rogers, ed., *Cuneiform Parallels to the Old Testament* [2nd ed.; New York: Abingdon Press, 1926], p. 136) shows a common literary structure:

> My vestal mother conceived me, in secret she brought me forth.
> She set me in a basket of rushes, with bitumen she closed my door;
> She cast me into the river, which rose not over me.
> The river bore me up, unto Akki, the irrigator, it carried me.
> Akki, the irrigator, with . . . lifted me out,
> Akki, the irrigator, as his own son . . . reared me,
> Akki, the irrigator, as his gardener appointed me.

5. **The daughter of Pharaoh** herself discovers the basket. She is presumably in the water. The reeds hid the basket from attendants on the bank. According to Jewish

personal pleasure ground of the God of Law, where he is free from official legality and can at times waive such principles as those of cause and effect and act with arbitrary kindliness and favor. This popular conception satisfies and comforts a great many people. It becomes dangerous when devout students feel that God will see to it that the examination paper will contain the very few questions to which they happen to know the answers, so that toilsome study of the subject is unnecessary. We are very ignorant on such subjects as the relation of God to his own laws, but it is probably safe to say: (*a*) Without a law of some kind, nothing can exist. Nothing happens by chance. There are laws that determine the timing of a sneeze, the sudden impulse, the idle half-conscious act. (*b*) Some of these laws are so complicated, layer upon layer, wheels within wheels, that no one has been able to unravel them, and things seem to happen by chance. But one can never count upon such chance events occurring in his favor.

To do so is superstitious. God operates, by laws we have not been able to analyze, at the utmost bounds of human effort when we have done all we can to attain the desired end. (*c*) Our real acquaintance with God is shown in the way we meet and deal with such seemingly fortuitous events. Skill and virtue have an affinity for luck. Whatever happens to anybody may be turned to beautiful results.[9]

4. *The Little Sister Afar Off.*—This is a good illustration of what Milton was talking about in his sonnet "On His Blindness," when he wrote, "They also serve who only stand and wait." The experience is harrowing when one feels, as in Matt. 26:58, that he is in great part responsible for a situation. The key is to be found in Lam. 3:26: not fear and worry, but hope and prayer.

No one knows much about the laws which operate in prayer. Every minister and doctor is

[9] For a mystical fantasy on chance see the conclusion of the story "Reunion in Paris," by Alexander Woollcott, *While Rome Burns* (New York: Viking Press, 1934).

6 And when she had opened *it*, she saw the child: and, behold, the babe wept. And she had compassion on him, and said, This *is one* of the Hebrews' children.

7 Then said his sister to Pharaoh's daughter, Shall I go and call to thee a nurse of the Hebrew women, that she may nurse the child for thee?

8 And Pharaoh's daughter said to her, Go. And the maid went and called the child's mother.

9 And Pharaoh's daughter said unto her, Take this child away, and nurse it for me, and I will give *thee* thy wages. And the woman took the child, and nursed it.

her maid to fetch it. 6 When she opened it she saw the child; and lo, the babe was crying. She took pity on him and said, "This is one of the Hebrews' children." 7 Then his sister said to Pharaoh's daughter, "Shall I go and call you a nurse from the Hebrew women to nurse the child for you?" 8 And Pharaoh's daughter said to her, "Go." So the girl went and called the child's mother. 9 And Pharaoh's daughter said to her, "Take this child away, and nurse him for me, and I will give you your wages." So the woman took the child and nursed him.

---

tradition the maids refused to fetch the basket on account of the king's edict. So the princess herself procured it (cf. vs. 10, **I drew him**). A mural in the ancient synagogue excavated at Dura-Europos portrays this tradition (see M. I. Rostovtzeff, *Dura-Europos and Its Art* [Oxford: Clarendon Press, 1938], pp. 112, 114, Pl. XXIII). Jewish legend further adds that when she touched the basket, the princess was instantly healed of leprosy.

6. She took pity on him: The humaneness of the midwives is also a gift of the princess. There is a delicate sensitiveness here not found in the Sargon legend. It is at once humane and religious. The pagan princess too fears God. With the survival of Moses the slaughter of the innocents is a failure. This is stressed by Josephus (*Antiquities* II. 9. 2). The birth stories of Jesus and John the Baptist owe much to the stories of Moses' infancy. The princess who disobeys her father and the magi who ignore Herod play the same role.

9. The Hebrew mother nursed him. The point is that Moses was a real Israelite. In ancient Hebrew as in current Arabic thinking, ethnic solidarity is established by the suckling of the infant. Israelites took equal pride in the notion that the child was nursed by his Hebrew mother and that he was adopted by a princess of Egypt. As a deliverer he must belong to Israel as well as to Egypt; and the bond with Israel is more profound.

---

acquainted with families where there seem always to be disaster and sickness. These "birds of a feather flock together." Where the symptoms of the family's ills are served regularly at breakfast, where everyone dies a hundred times before his death in imagination and fear, where the worst is always expected, there is the soil on which disaster grows. We hope that this little girl was looking out to see that somebody nice picked baby brother up, not expecting to see a crocodile get him. For there is some kind of a connection between the state of mind of a person and the things that happen to him and to those dear to him. In the present state of our knowledge no clear blueprint or plan of operation is available as to the connection between our minds and others' minds, or between our inner life and the workings of nature. Often we cannot see any rhyme or reason in the way things happen to other people, but as we grow older we begin to see a kind of providence in the way things have happened to ourselves. For

the net result of any event is sometimes a long time clearing up. We are too spiritually adolescent to attain to the faith in faith which Jesus possessed, but we do realize that there is something there which we can follow afar off. One has to prepare himself for what is to happen. "Good" things cannot happen to "bad" people, and someday we may come to see that "bad" things cannot happen to "good" people, that "all things work together for good to them that love God" (Rom. 8:28). It is a tremendous faith, and so we are left wondering if the hope of the little girl and the love of the mother weeping at home had anything to do with the sudden impulse of the princess to take a bath. All we know is that real prayer is the preparing of the whole life for the occurrence of great events. Let no one tell us that it is ridiculous to pray to a loving Father for the things we have done our utmost to attain, and desire with all that is best in our lives. Look more closely, and perhaps we shall see the lips of the maiden mov-

10 And the child grew, and she brought him unto Pharaoh's daughter, and he became her son. And she called his name Moses: and she said, Because I drew him out of the water.

10 And the child grew, and she brought him to Pharaoh's daughter, and he became her son; and she named him Moses,[b] for she said, "Because I drew him out[c] of the water."

[b] Heb *Mosheh*
[c] Heb *mashah*

---

10. The adoption of Moses and his Egyptian education are never alluded to in his later conflict with Pharaoh. But it seems that he originally had an Egyptian name, *Mes*, meaning son or child. The Hebraic form of the name was *Môsheh* which could be the active participle of the Hebrew root, *mâshâh*, "to draw out." If the Hebrew form of his name is to have any meaning, it must be "the one who draws forth," i.e., he was *môsheh* 'ammô (Isa. 63:11), the drawer forth of his people. The statement of the princess is not a translation of *Môsheh*. Possibly it means that she, like Moses, is one who draws out.

---

ing in such a prayer, learned at her mother's knee.

Think not it is with God as with a human carpenter, who works or not as he chooses, who can do or leave undone at his good pleasure. It is not thus with God; but finding thee ready he is obliged to act, to overflow into thee; just as the sun must needs burst forth when the air is bright and clear, and is unable to contain itself. . . . Every good thing communicates itself to whatever is able to receive it.[1]

10. The Royal Adoption.—According to Acts 7:22, Moses was educated in the schools of Egypt and was learned in all their wisdom. So also says Philo. Schiller popularized this view in a beautifully written thesis [2] in which he described how the peoples of that time and subsequent centuries were sunk in the errors of polytheism and idolatry. There was however one exception —a small circle of Egyptian sages, students of the mysteries, who had arrived at the truth of God's unity. Moses, says Schiller, was a member of this small circle of scholars, and felt he was justified in breaking the vow of secrecy and revealing to the world the new truth of monotheism. The students of the mysteries had arrived at this conclusion by prolonged intellectual effort. Moses realized that no such process would be possible for his nomad people and had to demand from them blind faith, supported by miracle. Yet his courage in breaking his vow and telling the world the truth about God ranks with the greatest deeds of history. There is probably no truth in Schiller's beautiful hypothesis. The mysteries of Isis and their exercise of reason in the field of religion did not exist in Egypt in the time of Moses. All attempts to find any connection between the religion of

[1] Pfeiffer, *Meister Eckhart*, I, 23, 337.
[2] "Die Sendung Moses," *Sämmtliche Werke* (Stuttgart: Cotta, 1847), X, 401.

Egypt and that promulgated by Moses have failed. Egypt was still polytheistic in his time. It represented its gods with the heads of animals, and its essence was in the worship of the dead. Moses on the other hand was monotheistic, allowed no representations of the deity, and had little or nothing to say about the dead.

10. And She Called His Name Moses.—How far the stories of this book are founded on fact is a question which we cannot answer. Those who know most about the history of the period differ in their views as to the extent to which the writers had access to traditions going back to early times. There does seem to be evidence that there was a great leader called Moses in the early history of the Jewish people, and that some of the tribes of Israel were for a time in bondage in the land of Egypt. The etymology of the name Moses (see Exeg.) raises many questions, and all derivations have been disputed by some scholars. The question of the historical foundations of the narrative is so involved and requires such accumulated erudition and a lifetime of research that the ordinary man had better let it alone. "Literal inerrancy" is an idol in the temple of the false gods by whom men are deceived. The full name and street address of the good Samaritan are as irrelevant to faith as the birth certificate of Moses. God in Jesus revealed himself most fully in parables. But it is much easier to preach alleged facts than it is to enter into the faith of a prophet proclaiming his experience of God's guidance in story and parable. Everyone writes history from a point of view, as he must select the facts to be recorded from among millions of others. Much of Christian theology has depended on the idea that there took place in history nonrecurring official transactions between God and man on which our salvation depends. So we have come to believe that faith is the blind acceptance of historic facts by those who do not

11 ¶ And it came to pass in those days, when Moses was grown, that he went out unto his brethren, and looked on their burdens: and he spied an Egyptian smiting a Hebrew, one of his brethren.

12 And he looked this way and that way, and when he saw that *there was* no man, he slew the Egyptian, and hid him in the sand.

11 One day, when Moses had grown up, he went out to his people and looked on their burdens; and he saw an Egyptian beating a Hebrew, one of his people. 12 He looked this way and that, and seeing no one he killed the Egyptian and hid him in

2. Moses Discovers His People (2:11-15)

11. In many allusive and authentic ways the historic character of Moses is revealed in these stories of his first public acts. His readiness to sacrifice himself for his people, his passionate sense of justice, his capacity for flaming anger, his prudent recklessness, and his courageous audacity; these are the real traits of the hero in all the materials that bear on him. Here they are embodied in an incident. In a profound way Moses impressed these traits upon his people so that, as fact and ideal, they survive until now. Like many a later exempt "court Jew," he chose to share "ill-treatment with the people of God" (Heb. 11:25). In Israel ethnic responsibility and religious faithfulness are virtually inseparable. Moses was dismayed at the suffering, and when he saw a sadistic overseer kill a slave his anger rose to make him act. The translation **beating a Hebrew** is quite inadequate in this context.

12. Moses struck back; "life for life" (21:23). An outrageous combination of recklessness and prudence: he acts wholly on his own authority. This type of audacity was a common key to leadership in Israel; see, e.g., the stories of the judges, and especially of Saul (I Sam. 11).

trouble themselves to make sure that the evidence for them is sound. It may be, however, that such facts are only of value to us in so far as we have tested their underlying validity in our own experience (see Gal. 2:20).

The proof of the inspiration of the documents is not in the documents; it is in us, as Meister Eckhart says:

Ask a good man, "Why dost thou love God?"—He says: "I know not; for God's sake."—"Why dost thou love the truth?"—"For the truth's sake."—"Why dost thou love right?"—"For righteousness' sake."—"Why dost thou love good?"—"For good's sake."—"Why dost thou live?"—"'I' faith, I know not! I like living." [3]

11-12. *Moses Kills an Egyptian Taskmaster.*— In stories of this kind the hero as a rule accidentally discovers the secret of his birth and lineage. This incident may have been lost in editing the various stories which are woven into the Bible narrative. We are left to wonder how Moses learned that he was a Hebrew and not a genuine Egyptian prince. We are inclined to speculate, on the basis of other such stories, about a necklace left around his neck by his mother, or the little garment in which he was found by the princess in the river, preserved

throughout the years in the palace, or a chance meeting with his sister, or personal appearance different from other Egyptians. Whatever it was that raised his suspicions that he was not Egyptian, the phrase **he went out unto his brethren** indicates that he had come to know the secret of his birth. Such a discovery is a test of character. The author of the book of Hebrews recognizes the fine caliber of the man who is willing to renounce all his special privileges for the sake of his "ain folk" [4]: "Moses . . . refused to be called the son of Pharaoh's daughter" (Heb. 11:24). The greatest men of history have been those who have identified themselves with the oppressed, and have heard and understood those great words, "Never send to know for whom the bell tolls; it tolls for thee." [5] The supreme example in Christian theology has been our Lord, "who, being in the form of God, . . . made himself of no reputation, and took upon him the form of a servant, . . . and became obedient unto death: even the death of the cross" (Phil. 2:6-8). When this great act of renunciation takes place, it is only effective if it is not an act of condescension, but a proclamation of fact. Moses was a Hebrew and God was hu-

[3] Pfeiffer, *Meister Eckhart*, I, 42.

[4] Walter White, "Why I Remain a Negro," *Saturday Review of Literature*, XXX (1947), 13.
[5] John Donne, *Devotions* XVII.

13 And when he went out the second day, behold, two men of the Hebrews strove together: and he said to him that did the wrong, Wherefore smitest thou thy fellow?

14 And he said, Who made thee a prince and a judge over us? intendest thou to kill me, as thou killedst the Egyptian? And Moses feared, and said, Surely this thing is known.

the sand. **13** When he went out the next day, behold, two Hebrews were struggling together; and he said to the man that did the wrong, "Why do you strike your fellow?" **14** He answered, "Who made you a prince and a judge over us? Do you mean to kill me as you killed the Egyptian?" Then Moses was afraid, and thought,

---

13. Having discovered his people in their suffering, Moses cannot rest. He goes out to see them again **the next day.** He comes upon two Hebrews fighting each other. In such a fight death was the object and the typical outcome (II Sam. 14:6). Moses turns to the guilty party, perhaps the one who began the fight, and asks, **Why do you strike your fellow?** The social and psychological disintegration of the enslaved, sadly documented in our own century, troubles Moses (6:9).

14. The Hebrew looks on Moses as a troublemaker who will make the bitter life of the slaves even more unbearable. He reflects the servile and submissive pattern of the enslaved Israelites (Acts 7:25). Also, he is the type of those Israelites who challenged Moses' authority throughout his career. The historian would agree with the challenge at this point in Moses' career; obviously, for he has not yet received his vocation. He is not yet **a prince and a judge,** i.e., one who can make ethical decisions because he embodies authority. The core of justice, *mishpāṭ* in the O.T., is neither positive knowledge nor a metaphysical principle, but the living power of God.

---

man from all eternity, as has been expressed in the phrase "the Christhood of God."

Aflame with indignation at the mistreatment and torture of his brethren, Moses **looked this way and that, . . . and when he saw that there was no man, he slew the Egyptian, and hid him in the sand.** Under similar circumstances David Livingstone, according to the *Encyclopaedia Britannica,* had "the impression that he was in hell" as he saw in the crowded market place the Arab slavers, without warning or provocation, commence shooting the women, hundreds being killed or drowned in trying to escape. His "first impulse was to pistol the murderers," but he knew that would be futile. He acted more wisely than Moses, because it was the account of that incident which aroused indignation in England to such a pitch that the sultan was in great part forced by the British to suppress the trade.

Every detective story is proof of the futility of looking **this way and that.** Someone always sees, some clue is always left. Violence seems sometimes inevitable, but is generally a mistake. Deeds that seem glorious are done, but they do not help the cause. Remember Bernard Shaw's remark that one should always spank his children when in a violent temper, otherwise he misses the only good result which accrues to the spanking, the satisfaction it gives himself. John Brown, who thought he had "letters of marque from God" and expressed his ideas by

acts of violence rather than by words, had a soul that goes marching on in courage and heroism. Yet the *Encyclopaedia Britannica* has to add this postscript to his glorious deeds: "It now seems that this policy aided very little in making Kansas a free State, and that the attack on Harper's Ferry, while creating much feeling at the moment, had very little effect on the subsequent course of events." Though most men may still feel that organized national violence is sometimes inevitable, they are nevertheless more conscious than formerly of the evils which such violence brings in its train, and are less sure than formerly that the good done outweighs the evil. The race is preparing itself to resolve that mass violence must be restricted to some kind of international police force, and used for the good of all by the will of a body representing all men.

13-14. *The Ingratitude of the Oppressed.—* There is always disappointment when youth discovers that its first altruistic deeds are not met with appreciation and gratitude. Aflame to help the downtrodden, the young man finds they neither understand nor bless their benefactor. One of the first lessons in the good life is not to expect applause. The farseeing reformer is nearly always opposed by his nearsighted beneficiaries. A statesman who tries to save the capitalistic system will have most employers against him, and a real labor leader is apt to lose his job. Moses here learned the first

15 Now when Pharaoh heard this thing, he sought to slay Moses. But Moses fled from the face of Pharaoh, and dwelt in the land of Midian: and he sat down by a well.

16 Now the priest of Midian had seven daughters: and they came and drew *water*, and filled the troughs to water their father's flock.

"Surely the thing is known." 15 When Pharaoh heard of it, he sought to kill Moses.

But Moses fled from Pharaoh, and stayed in the land of Mid'ian; and he sat down by a well. 16 Now the priest of Mid'ian had seven daughters; and they came and drew water, and filled the troughs to water their

---

15. Moses discovers that his deed of the previous day is known and fears that his own people, in servile self-defense, will betray him to the Egyptians. Prudence tells him he must leave. Indeed, the Pharaoh is said to know already and to be seeking his life. For the writer this enforced departure is not so much the defeat of an abortive effort to emancipate Israel as a step in God's preparation for deliverance through the vocation of a leader. Moses hid **in the land of Midian.** The Midianites were seminomadic people who were encountered east of the Jordan (Num. 22:4), and who on occasion invaded Edom (Gen. 36:35) and Canaan (Judg. 6–8). But their center seems to have been near the Gulf of Aqabah, perhaps to the east of it (I Kings 11:18). It is not improbable, however, that the eastern part of the Sinai Peninsula can also be called **the land of Midian** as used here. The traditional location of Mount Sinai would demand this hypothesis.

3. MOSES IN EXILE (2:16-23a)

16. The story is reminiscent of Jacob's arrival in Haran (Gen. 29). Jacob was seeking refuge among known kinsmen, while Moses is among strangers who are nevertheless distant kinsmen (Gen. 25:2). "Moses came back to his forefathers by way of his flight. . . . A man of the enslaved nation, but the only one not enslaved together with

---

lesson of a leader—that he cannot work *for* people; he must humble himself and work *with* people.

We begin now to understand something of the character of the future lawgiver of Israel. Vss. 11-15 illustrate his passion for justice, his impatience with wrong, a hot temper of which his future life gives us many illustrations, and his wise prudence in not unnecessarily exposing himself to danger.

15-22. Moses Takes Refuge in Midian.—The composite material which constitutes Exodus can be appreciated when one honestly tries to discover from the text where the land of Midian was supposed to be or what the name of Moses' father-in-law really was. The Midianites were apparently an Arab people who lived south of the Edomites. The Nabataeans were probably their successors in this land, and it was they who built the famous city of Petra, the ruins of which show Egyptian influence. As to the name of the priest of Midian, one finds that he was probably nameless in the original narrative (see Exeg.) and that later versions of the story added various names: Reuel, Jethro, Hobab, Jether, and perhaps Cain (see vss. 16, 18; 3:1; 4:18; Num. 10:29; Judg. 4:11; and Judg. 1:16, where he is either a Kenite or, as some scholars read the text, had the name Cain).

The Arab background of the story centers upon the rare and precious well of water in the desert land. This incident reminds us of 15:27; Gen. 29; 24:11; Num. 33:9; John 4:6. Says Charles M. Doughty:

Sweet and light in these high deserts is the uncorrupt air, but the water is scant. . . . Hirfa doled out to me . . . hardly an ounce or two of the precious water every morning, that I might wash "as the townspeople." She thought it unthrift to pour out water thus when all day the thirsty tribesmen have not enough to drink. Many times between their waterings, there is not a pint of water left in the greatest sheykhs' tents; and when the good-man bids his housewife fill the bowl to make his guests' coffee, it is answered from their side, "We have no water."[6]

Jethro's encampment is this time not too far from the well, and his daughters (as may be seen today in that country) are in charge of the flocks. They have made the journey, let down the skin pails to the deep springs and filled the drinking troughs, when a gang of herdsmen come rushing over the desert and try to steal the water for their own beasts. It meant that the poor girls would have to go through the

[6] *Wanderings in Arabia* (New York: Charles Scribner's Sons, 1908), I, 72.

17 And the shepherds came and drove them away: but Moses stood up and helped them, and watered their flock.

18 And when they came to Reuel their father, he said, How *is it that* ye are come so soon to-day?

19 And they said, An Egyptian delivered us out of the hand of the shepherds, and also drew *water* enough for us, and watered the flock.

20 And he said unto his daughters, And where *is* he? why *is it that* ye have left the man? call him, that he may eat bread.

father's flock. 17 The shepherds came and drove them away; but Moses stood up and helped them, and watered their flock. 18 When they came to their father Reu′el, he said, "How is it that you have come so soon today?" 19 They said, "An Egyptian delivered us out of the hand of the shepherds, and even drew water for us and watered the flock." 20 He said to his daughters, "And where is he? Why have you left the man? Call him, that he may eat bread."

---

them, had returned to the free and keen air of his forebears" (Martin Buber, *Moses* [London: East and West Library, 1946], p. 38). The M.T. says that **he sat down by a well,** the definite center of a clan or tribe. The name of the **priest of Midian** is not given here in the Hebrew, but the LXX adds the phrase "tending the sheep of Jethro their father." The name of Reuel in vs. 18 is probably a gloss. There seem to be two names for the priest, Jethro and Hobab. The E tradition is consistent in calling him Jethro (3:1; 4:18; 18:1, 2, 5, 6, 9, 10, 12). In Num. 10:29 the J tradition says that "Moses said to Hobab the son of Reuel the Midianite, Moses' father-in-law. . . ." Reuel is apparently the father-in-law's father. It appears that Reuel in vs. 18 is the result of a glossator's misreading of Num. 10:29. The evidence may be construed to mean that Hobab was Moses' brother-in-law, but with more doubtful results (cf. RSV, Num. 10:29; Judg. 4:11; also Kittel, *Biblia Hebraica,* 3rd ed., *ad loc.*). In the KJV "Raguel" (Num. 10:29) comes from the LXX. The Hebrew רעואל (Reuel) was transliterated into Greek as ʽΡαγουήλ. Inasmuch as since the days of Gideon Israelites and Midianites were enemies, the probability that Moses was actually connected with them is very strong. Tradition could hardly have produced the account.

17-19. Other shepherds coming up did not simply deprive the sisters of their position in the queue; they appropriated the water they had drawn for **their father's flock.** Sitting by the well, Moses had seen the whole episode. He was aroused. His passionate sense of justice made him act in behalf of the wronged. The rendering, "Moses went to their rescue" (Amer. Trans.), aptly captures the flavor of the Hebrew verb here. It is intimated that he made the shepherds "back down" and then replenished the water they had unfairly used. Hence, to their father's surprise, the women arrived home much earlier than usual. They reported the benevolence of **an Egyptian** who delivered them from the shepherds. The real concern of the narrator is to present Moses. This is the character of the young man (Acts 7:23) whom God had designed for leadership.

20-22. Jethro was distressed because his daughters had not brought Moses with them. The sacred duty of hospitality demanded that he should entertain him. Besides,

---

hard labor of hauling up and pouring all over again; and it was probably already growing late in the evening. Our hero intervenes and, like all heroes, is more than able to drive off the whole crowd of rowdies. As they water the flock, and then take their way over the sandy miles back to their father's tents, the girls look kindly at the Egyptian stranger who has rescued them, especially one of the daughters whose name was Zipporah ("Little Bird"). Moses sees them safely home, and is about to leave when Jethro asks them how they had got back so soon.

(Usually they had had to draw water both for the herdsmen and for themselves.) They tell about the (handsome) stranger, and their father does just what they had been hoping he would do. He bids them invite the young man for supper. Out of such chance happenings comes romance, and we see Moses **content to dwell with the man.** He becomes one of the household, and everything turns out as perhaps Zipporah had planned and hoped when she first saw him standing in the shade of the palm tree by the well. The wedding takes place and soon

21 And Moses was content to dwell with the man: and he gave Moses Zipporah his daughter.

22 And she bare *him* a son, and he called his name Gershom: for he said, I have been a stranger in a strange land.

23 ¶ And it came to pass in process of time, that the king of Egypt died: and the children of Israel sighed by reason of the bondage, and they cried, and their cry came up unto God by reason of the bondage.

21 And Moses was content to dwell with the man, and he gave Moses his daughter Zippo'rah. 22 She bore a son, and he called his name Gershom; for he said, "I have been a sojourner[d] in a foreign land."

23 In the course of those many days the king of Egypt died. And the people of Israel groaned under their bondage, and cried out for help, and their cry under bondage

[d] Heb *ger*

---

he sensed that Moses was no ordinary guest. The girls returned to the well to call him. Moses, finding the priest's home congenial, became a part of it. Many centuries later, in the days of the P writers, this marriage with **Zipporah** would have been condemned (Num. 25:6-9). Zipporah is probably the "Cushite woman" whom Aaron and Miriam rebuke Moses for having married (Hab. 3:7; Num. 12:1). The narrator interprets the name of Moses' son, **Gershom,** as though it were Gersham, i.e., "sojourner there." There is no agreement on the actual meaning of Gershom.

23a. According to later chronology the many days that Moses dwelt in Midian totaled about forty years. **The king of Egypt died** while Moses was in exile.

4. THE COVENANT WITH ABRAHAM (2:23b-25)

23b. The P editor sets the stage for the call of Moses in his own way. The death of the king, whether Seti I or Ramses II, brought no relief to the slaves. Their cries were

---

the baby who is called Gershom ("Far from Home") is born.

One can see from Num. 25:6-18; 12:1 ff. (where Zipporah is certainly referred to; cf. Hab. 3:7), that this marriage with a woman of another nation was not entirely acceptable to the Hebrews.

2:23b–4:17, 20b, 27-31; 6:2–7:7. The Call of Moses.—The story of the call of Moses to the leadership of his people is a good example of the way in which various accounts have been intertwined in this book and edited by later writers.

The linguistic and historical learning and sagacity of many scholars have been able after many years of hard work to suggest some of the strands out of which the present narrative was woven. The result shows us the development of the religion of the Israelites over almost a thousand years. No better sample of the texture of the tapestry could be given. Here are the stories of at least four periods, as we try to disentangle them after studying the words and characteristic style and ideas of each contributor. (For fuller discussion of sources and variant views see Exeg. The words are as far as possible those of existing translations, though naturally there was some compression of each tale in the process of welding them together.) We call the authors of the original narratives the Yahwist

(J), the Elohist (E), the priestly writer (P), and the editor.

Even in translation, when the different accounts are disentangled, one can feel the difference in spirit and point of view. The oldest story is contained in the first five sentences of the Yahwist's narrative. It tells how Moses discovered the dwelling place of Yahweh in a sacred tree. The fact that the Hebrew word for "thornbush" is *seneh* reminds one of Sinai, but the mountain is not mentioned. Yahweh's presence is manifested by flames in the tree, which burn but do not consume. The god of the tree, the god of fire, is identified in the rest of this story with the God of the fathers, the God of Israel. From a place-god he becomes a race-god. The cult and ritual of tree and fire and sacred ground recede into the background, and historical and political circumstances take their place. This God whom Moses has discovered in the tree now calls him to be the leader of Israel's deliverance from Egypt; God knows of the people's hardships before he is told. Signs are given to Moses which he is to perform in order to convince the people that God has appeared to him. As for his own distrust of his powers of speech, God will inspire him to eloquence. The people believed the words and signs and worshiped.

The Elohist's story tells not of an Egyptian

prince, but of a humble shepherd, feeding his flocks, to whom the idea of going to Pharaoh was incredible. It tells not of a god of a tree and of flame, but of a god of a mountain, a god without a name. Horeb is probably Sinai under another name. The Elohist account is given us only in part. The sacred tree has become a sacred rod which is God's own staff or scepter and is handed to Moses by God himself. The great advance in the Elohist's thinking about God centers on the question of God's name, for he seems to have realized that a god had a personal name only when there were more gods than one. God has no personal name when he is God. He is the one that is: I AM. The God of Sinai is the one God, the only God. Other gods do not exist. Man finds God whom he seeks: God finds the man he needs. This man is his staff; he gives his old one to him (cf. Judg. 6:21) . In Babylonia, Shamash, the sun-god gives his scepter to Hammurabi, and in Greece, Hermes, to Pelops. It is not a matter of putting off his shoes in ritual form; Moses in spiritual awe hides his face.

The editorial additions come next in time. Sections 3:18-22; 4:9; 4:21-23, have not been included in the stories, as they seem to have been added by a later scribe from the succeeding narrative, with the purpose of showing that Yahweh knew exactly in advance how things were going to turn out. The insertion in the Elohist's story after the giving of the answer, I AM, seems to be concerned with the identity of God and Yahweh. In the Yahwist's story the passage about Moses being replaced by Aaron is the work of one of the priestly class who felt that Aaron and the priests were not given enough honor in the early story.

Next in time comes the narrative of the priestly writer. The charming picturesqueness of the earlier narratives vanishes. We are not told even where the interview takes place; there is no mention of sacred trees or mountains, or of magic tricks.

God here is a spirit who is making a covenant with the people, who has a plan in history. God's new name, Yahweh, takes the place of the old name by which he was known to the fathers. There is more of the spirit of religion than of nationalism in P. But contrary to the other stories, the people here will not obey, do not fall upon the ground and worship. Yet Moses and Aaron are to go forward, and God will fulfill his purposes in history.

J's Story.—Yahweh once appeared to Moses in a flame of fire out of the midst of a bush. He saw that the bush burned with fire, but was not consumed. And Moses said, "I will now turn aside, and see this great sight, why the bush is not burned." When Yahweh saw that Moses turned aside to see, he called out of the bush, "Draw not nigh hither: put off thy shoes from off thy feet; for the place whereon thou standest is holy ground." And Yahweh said, "I have surely seen the affliction of my people in Egypt, and have heard their cry, by reason of their taskmasters; for I know their sorrows. And I am come down to deliver them out of the hand of the Egyptians, and to bring them up out of that land unto a land flowing with milk and honey. Go, and gather the elders of Israel together, and say unto them, Yahweh, the God of your fathers, appeared unto me, saying, I have surely visited you, and seen that which is done to you in Egypt; and I have said, I will bring you up out of the affliction of Egypt unto a land flowing with milk and honey."

And Moses answered and said, "They will not believe me, nor hearken unto my voice, but say, Yahweh hath not appeared unto thee." Yahweh answered him, "What is that in thy hand?" And he said, "A rod." And he said, "Cast it on the ground." And he cast it on the ground, and it became a serpent; and Moses fled from it. And Yahweh said unto Moses, "Put forth thy hand, and take it by the tail." And he did so, and it became a rod in his hand: that they may believe that Yahweh, God of their fathers, hath appeared unto thee. And Yahweh commanded him again, "Put now thy hand into thy bosom." And he did so, and when he took it out, behold, his hand was leprous, as white as snow. And he said, "Put thy hand into thy bosom again." And he did so, and when he took it out, it was turned again as his other flesh. "And it shall come to pass, if they will not believe thee, neither hearken to the voice of the first sign, that they will believe the voice of the second sign." And Moses said unto Yahweh, "O Lord, I am not eloquent, neither heretofore, nor since thou hast spoken unto thy servant: for I am slow of speech, and of a slow tongue." And Yahweh said unto him, "Who hath made man's mouth? or who maketh a man dumb, or deaf, or seeing, or blind? Is it not I, Yahweh? Now therefore go, and I will be with thy mouth, and teach thee what thou shalt speak." And Moses went and gathered together all the elders of the children of Israel, and spake all the words the Lord had spoken unto him, and did the signs in the sight of the people. And the people believed: and when they heard that Yahweh had visited the children of Israel, and seen their affliction, then they bowed their heads and worshiped.

E's Story.— Now Moses was keeping the flock of Jethro, his father-in-law: and he led the flock to the back of the wilderness, and came to the mountain, Horeb. And God called to him and said: "Moses, Moses." And he said, "Here am

I." And God said, "I am the God of thy father, the God of Abraham, the God of Isaac, and the God of Jacob." And Moses hid his face; for he was afraid to look upon God. And God said, "Now, behold, the cry of the children of Israel is come unto me: moreover I have seen the oppression wherewith the Egyptians oppress them. Come now, therefore. I will send thee unto Pharaoh, that thou mayest bring forth my people Israel out of Egypt." And Moses said unto God, "Who am I, that I should go unto Pharaoh, and bring forth Israel out of Egypt?" And he said, "Certainly I will be with thee: when thou hast brought forth the people out of Egypt, ye shall serve God upon this mountain." And Moses said unto God, "Behold, when I come unto the children of Israel, and say unto them, The God of your fathers hath sent me unto you; and they say unto me, What is his name? what shall I say unto them?" And God said unto Moses, "I AM THAT I AM." And he said, "Thus shalt thou say unto the children of Israel, I AM hath sent me unto you. And thou shalt take in thy hand this rod, wherewith thou shalt do signs." And Moses took the rod of God in his hand.

Editorial Additions.—In J's story after the words "and teach thee what thou shalt speak" (4:12), this passage has been inserted:

And he said, "O Lord, send whom thou wilt send." And the anger of Yahweh was kindled against Moses, and he said, "Is there not Aaron thy brother the Levite? I know that he can speak well. And also, behold, he cometh forth to meet thee: and when he seeth thee, he will be glad in his heart. Thou shalt speak unto him, and put the words in his mouth: I will be with thy mouth, and with his mouth, and will teach you what ye shall do. He shall be thy spokesman unto the people. He shall be to thee a mouth, and thou shalt be to him as God." And Yahweh had said to Aaron, "Go and meet Moses in the wilderness." And he went, and met him in the mountain of God and kissed him. And Moses told Aaron all the words of Yahweh wherewith he had sent him, and all the signs wherewith he had charged him.

In E's story after the words, "I AM hath sent me unto you" (3:14), this passage has been inserted:

And God said moreover unto Moses, "Thus shalt thou say unto the children of Israel, Yahweh, the God of your father, the God of Abraham, the God of Isaac, and the God of Jacob, hath sent me unto you: this is my name forever, thus shall I be known for all generations."

P's Story.—And God spake unto Moses, and said unto him, "I am Yahweh, I appeared unto Abraham, unto Isaac, and unto Jacob as El-

Shaddai, but by my name Yahweh I was not known to them. And I also established my covenant with them, to give them the land of Canaan, the land in which they sojourned as strangers. And I have also heard the groaning of the children of Israel, whom the Egyptians keep in bondage; and I have remembered my covenant. Wherefore say unto the children of Israel, I am Yahweh, I will bring you out from under the burdens of the Egyptians, and I will rid you out of their bondage, and I will redeem you with a stretched out arm and with mighty deeds. I will take you for my people and will be your God: and ye shall know that I am Yahweh, your God, who bringeth you out from under the burdens of the Egyptians. And I will bring you in unto the land, which I swore to give to Abraham, to Isaac, and to Jacob; and I will give it you for an heritage, I Yahweh!" And Moses spake so unto the children of Israel; but they hearkened not unto Moses, for there was no spirit in them by reason of their cruel bondage. And Yahweh spake unto Moses, saying, "Go in, speak unto Pharaoh, king of Egypt, that he let the children of Israel go out of his land." But Moses answered Yahweh, saying, "Behold, the children of Israel have not hearkened unto me; how then shall Pharaoh hear me, for I am not skilled in speech?" And Yahweh said unto Moses, "See, I have made thee a god to Pharaoh; and Aaron thy brother shall be thy prophet. Thou shalt tell all that I command thee: and Aaron thy brother shall speak unto Pharaoh, that he let the children of Israel go out of his land. And I will harden Pharaoh's heart, and I will work many wonders and signs in Egypt. But Pharaoh will not hearken unto you, and I will lay my hand upon the Egyptians, and bring forth my hosts, my people Israel, out of Egypt by mighty deeds. And the Egyptians shall know that I am Yahweh, when I have stretched forth my hand against the Egyptians, and brought out the children of Israel from among them." And Moses and Aaron did so; as Yahweh commanded them, so they did. Moses was fourscore years old, and Aaron fourscore and three years old, when they spake unto Pharaoh.

When each story is read thus by itself we feel that we are following the history of the growth of the religious sense not only in Israel, but in mankind. There is no absolute certainty about the details of the allocation of the material to its different sources, but the general impression made by reading the stories as given is clear.

Man seems to begin to think of God as the god of a place, the tree god, the mountain god, or the fire god, or as the god of miracles; then as the god of a race; till at last in the priestly writer's story trees, mountains, fire, miracles fall

so great that God noticed them and remembered his ancient promise. Neither the P editor nor the earlier narrators have thus far hinted that the Hebrews cried to God. They seem to avoid this purposely, to point up the initiative of God in Israel's deliverance. But what strikes us here is that the P editor seems to have missed the implicit assumption of the narrative throughout that God was aware all along of what was going on; indeed, that he was the chief actor in it.

out of the picture and we have a god working in history for the downtrodden against the oppressor, giving strength to the weak in their struggle against injustice.

Every new insight in religion is apt to dismiss the old ideas as false, just as each denomination with unconscious humor is sure its own is the true religion and manifests its charity by saying to other faiths, "Let us not try to unite, but continue to work for Christ, you in your way and we in his." But religion is the growing part of man's nature, his probing out from the known into the not fully known. All our insights about it are imperfect. This is true both of our own ideas and of the ideas of other times and other faiths. But religious men are men at their best, and there is very apt to be a kernel of truth in the old and the other's ideas. The priestly writer's story is typical of religious reformations which try to cleanse the old faith from all superstitious matters and in so doing are apt to pour out the baby with the bath; it was a purer faith, but one can imagine that it lost much of its popular appeal. Puritans destroying the lovely paintings and statues of medieval churches, "liberal" Christians trying to substitute "the white light of the ideal" for the warm love of the believer for Jesus, are of the same school of thought. These people have a very good time enjoying a rarefied sense of truth, and they can never understand how their halls are apt to be empty, while apparently sensible people continue to worship in the presence of beauty and the saints.

The poet in religion comes back, after all, to find God in places—Gen. 28:16; Exod. 3:4; "Only God can make a tree"; in the fire of aureoles around the heads of the saints; or in the spirit and mission of a race of men; or in the miracles of autumn foliage, burning but not burned; or in the unexplained great miracle, the spark of genius in the mind of Einstein, or in the speeches of Churchill that seemed to save the world in one of its darkest hours.

The Yahwist and the Elohist may have been mistaken and ignorant, but they too had their moments of insight, such as come to unspoiled minds in a simple world. Must the priestly writer's ideas also be dismissed as superstitious by modern man? Is there any scientific evidence for the presence in history of a supernatural guiding power such as he supposed? While we

do not express ourselves in the way in which these biblical writers did, we do have an underlying faith of this kind. We believe that certain public policies are for the good of all the people, and that these decisions are certain in the end to triumph over special interests as opposed to the general good. We attribute this certainty to the good will in the majority of men. As to how this good will happens always to come eventually to the surface in the majority of men, we are not apt to speculate. Our faith lies in the operation not of fires and war and earthquakes to accomplish the hoped-for results, but in the spirit of man based on the best scientific knowledge of his day. This power in man must theoretically be accounted for by philosophers. The weakness of the old "liberal" religious view, sometimes called humanism, is well expressed by F. H. Bradley in his criticism of Matthew Arnold's *Literature and Dogma:*

"Is there a God?" asks the reader. "Oh yes," replies Mr. Arnold, "and I can verify him in experience." "And what is he then?" cries the reader. "Be virtuous, and as a rule you will be happy," is the answer. "Well, and God?" "That is God," says Mr. Arnold; "there is no deception, and what more do you want?" I suppose we do want a good deal more. Most of us, certainly the public which Mr. Arnold addresses, want something they can worship; and they will not find that in a hypostasized copy-book heading, which is not much more adorable than "Honesty is the best policy."[7]

The godless, automatically disintegrating view of human history is most ably given by Oswald Spengler;[8] the creative, God-implicit view, by Arnold J. Toynbee.[9]

But for the ordinary man, the picture language of a loving father working out his plans in human history, using the men he needs to do his work, is fundamentally sound. It would take a very profound thinker to make an intricate diagram showing the exact relationship of man to nature, and of man to this heavenly Father, and no one knows enough yet to get

[7] Quoted in T. S. Eliot, *For Lancelot Andrewes* (Garden City, N. Y.: Doubleday, Doran, & Co., 1929), pp. 81-82.

[8] *The Decline of the West* (New York: Alfred A. Knopf, 1926-28). The word "God" does not even appear in the index to this encyclopedic work.

[9] *A Study of History* (New York: Oxford University Press, 1934; Abridgement, 1947).

24 And God heard their groaning, and God remembered his covenant with Abraham, with Isaac, and with Jacob.

25 And God looked upon the children of Israel, and God had respect unto *them*.

3 Now Moses kept the flock of Jethro his father-in-law, the priest of Midian: and he led the flock to the back side of the

came up to God. 24 And God heard their groaning, and God remembered his covenant with Abraham, with Isaac, and with Jacob. 25 And God saw the people of Israel, and God knew their condition.

3 Now Moses was keeping the flock of his father-in-law, Jethro, the priest of

---

24. For P the **covenant with Abraham, with Isaac, and with Jacob** (Gen. 17:7-8, 19) is the motive for the deliverance from Egypt. The earlier writers also know of a covenant or promise to Abraham but do not use it as a sanction for the Exodus. As over against P, through whom the Abrahamic covenant becomes prominent in the Bible, they stress the radical novelty of the revelation of God in the deliverance of Israel from Egypt. For P revelation consists essentially of oracles; for his predecessors it consists first of all of God's action in history.

B. The JE Account of the Call and Commission of Moses (3:1–6:1)

The account of the call and commission of Moses comes to us through the J and E historians. The scene of the vocation is **the mountain of God** in Midian. There is a

---

all the lines and delimitations correctly; yet we are getting nearer the truth about such profound matters. Wiser than any that has hitherto appeared would be the theologian who could work out the myriad ways in which God is fitly described as our Father, and the ways in which the figure does not apply exactly. But we are on our way. When the Roman Catholics, after being horribly shocked by the tendency of Abelard to adopt the doctrines of Aristotle, were guided years afterward by Albertus Magnus and Thomas Aquinas to adopt those very doctrines as their own, and when the Protestant church tried to learn from the best scientific thought of its day, we see in such changes of doctrine the attempt being made to think out correctly the relationship of man to God. Some of this work can be preached with edification, but much of it must be the background of knowledge in the mind of the preacher, and must be expressed for the congregation by implication or in picture language. Most of us understand next to nothing about how the radio works, yet we can use it. "The knowledge of the priest is the eighth sacrament of the church," said St. Francis of Sales, and the preacher's task is to see that his figures, illustrations, and presuppositions are fitting symbols of the profound truth. As the sun, which is not of this world at all, is the source and sustainer of all the life of nature, so God is to the life of man. Humanism, which gives up as hopeless the attempt to justify the ways of God to man, which refuses to ask ultimate questions, is spiritual isolationism, as dangerous to man as national isolationism.

The study of these different stories of the

call of Moses will help the reader to understand what one man who spent his whole life in Bible scholarship meant when he said:

Bible, wonderful book, teacher of mankind, foundation of our spiritual being! Thou art like that serene City of God, set upon earth's towering mountain tops, touching the heavens. The peoples of the world look to thee and drink of the living waters of thy streams. Whole generations may turn from thee and think nought of thee, because they know thee not; but mankind ever turns back again to thee.

For more than two centuries man has striven to understand the Scriptures; but who dare say that he has plumbed those deeps. Every century has seen them in new light. To our forefathers they were one, a single word out of the mouth of God. To us it has been given to read the manifold history of which they are the record. Those who came before us have dipped impartially into these writings, and have found again in them what was deepest and best in themselves. We who come after them strive with care to catch the spirit of the various times in which they were written, and to discover what the authors themselves meant to say; and in no wise do we yield to our forefathers in our reverence and love for this majestic book. In fact the story, so human, so divine, as we begin to be able to see it in the Bible, is deeper and more precious than anything our forefathers thought they found therein.[1]

3:1. *Moses Keeps the Flock of Jethro.*—Mohammed said, "He will never be a prophet who

[1] Hermann Gunkel, *Die Urgeschichte und die Patriarchen* (Göttingen: Vandenhoeck & Ruprecht, 1921; "Die Schriften des Alten Testaments in Auswahl"), p. v.

desert, and came to the mountain of God, *even* to Horeb.

2 And the Angel of the Lord appeared unto him in a flame of fire out of the midst of a bush: and he looked, and, behold, the bush burned with fire, and the bush *was* not consumed.

3 And Moses said, I will now turn aside, and see this great sight, why the bush is not burnt.

Mid'ian; and he led his flock to the west side of the wilderness, and came to Horeb, the mountain of God. 2 And the angel of the Lord appeared to him in a flame of fire out of the midst of a bush; and he looked, and lo, the bush was burning, yet it was not consumed. 3 And Moses said, "I will turn aside and see this great sight, why the bush

---

second P account of the vocation of Moses (6:2–7:7). Because the P writer assumed that Moses received his call in Egypt rather than in the desert his account does not immediately follow this one. Rather, it is inserted at a point in the JE narrative where Moses has already returned to Egypt and begun his work.

Moses was the greatest of the prophets (Deut. 34:10). Some considered him more than a prophet (Num. 12:6-7). As prophet he is called. The call symbolizes the prophet's endowment with the living authority of God. As prophet Moses was God's spokesman, the interpreter of the divine power by virtue of which he has the prerogative of judgment. There are recognized literary forms in which biblical writers set forth a prophet's call. A vision in which God is depicted in historical or natural activity, in cultic ceremonial, or in mythological metaphor, is followed by a response of the candidate in which awe and receptiveness commingle. Then God declares his purpose. Finally the prophet is instructed in the ways and means of declaring God's "word" or purpose. The literary form of the call of Moses corresponds very closely to that of the call of Isaiah (Isa. 6).

1. The Vision (3:1-6)

3:1. Moses had adjusted himself to the shepherd's life. Perhaps in search of better grazing, **he led his flock to the west side of the wilderness.** The suggestion of Gunkel and Gressmann that the sheep were "divine guides" to the holy mountain (cf. I Sam. 6:7) does not seem to fit. Moving westward, probably out of the Arabah depression, he **came to Horeb, the mountain of God** (cf. "The Location of Sinai," Intro., pp. 836-37).

2. The angel of the Lord was actually the Lord himself (vs. 4). Angel means messenger; angels in this early period are not personal entities, as later, but people or things that temporarily embody deity (Gen. 21:15-19; Deut. 33:16; Judg. 6:11, 14; Ps. 104:4). The word Lord stands for YHWH, probably Yahweh, which in Hebrew is read as "Adonai," meaning Lord (cf. vss. 13-15 below). Flame indicates the bodily manifestation of God, his actual presence (19:18; Ezek. 1:27; I Tim. 6:16). We have a remnant of it in the halo of the saints. The other metaphor of the vision (the bush) has its origins in animism. The whole picture is drawn to make the point that Moses was visited by the living God.

3. Moses is awed but also receptive. He responds to the mystery. He is a seeker, a discoverer.

---

was not first a herdsman." The incubation of a great soul takes place in solitude and quietness. The man who is to forge a nation out of a slave gang, the man who is to codify a new law and found a new religion, spends his years keeping a flock in the wilderness. The number of years implied in 7:7 may be symbolic, but we can assume that years were so spent by Moses as a young man after his marriage. While history may not literally be the lives of its great men, yet it does seem to take the push of a great

personality to bring to a head the slow gathering forces of a new age.

2-3. *The Gaze of Wonder.*—Clement of Alexandria quotes Matthew as saying, "Look with wonder at that which is before you."[2] One of the sayings of Jesus discovered by the explorers of the Egypt Fund reads: "Let not him who seeks . . . cease until he finds, and when he finds he shall be astonished; astonished, he shall reach the kingdom, and having reached the

[2] *Miscellanies* II. 9.

4 And when the Lord saw that he turned aside to see, God called unto him out of the midst of the bush, and said, Moses, Moses. And he said, Here *am* I.

5 And he said, Draw not nigh hither: put off thy shoes from off thy feet; for the place whereon thou standest *is* holy ground.

6 Moreover he said, I *am* the God of thy father, the God of Abraham, the God of Isaac, and the God of Jacob. And Moses hid his face; for he was afraid to look upon God.

is not burnt." 4 When the Lord saw that he turned aside to see, God called to him out of the bush, "Moses, Moses!" And he said, "Here am I." 5 Then he said, "Do not come near; put off your shoes from your feet, for the place on which you are standing is holy ground." 6 And he said, "I am the God of your father, the God of Abraham, the God of Isaac, and the God of Jacob." And Moses hid his face, for he was afraid to look at God.

4-6. At his response the presence speaks his name, **Moses, Moses!** When the vision breaks out in speech the presence of deity is confirmed (Isa. 6:3). In Isaiah and some of the other prophets there occurs at this point a confession of sin and an absolution. This is significantly missing here. In the exodus event God is disclosed as power, rather than either as justice or love. Moral demand and forgiveness of sin play scarcely any role. It must be noted that this emphasis on power and authority remains basic in the Bible. The moments of judgment and forgiveness are predicated upon it. Moses is in the presence of power; **the place whereon thou standest is holy ground.** The distance between God and man is here indicated. Its measure is power. **Moses hid his face**, not in shame but in fear. He was not repentant but awed. In Luke 20:37 Moses is credited with the next word of the vision, **I am the God of thy father** (cf. 15:2; 18:4). This formula draws together the ethnic and religious past of the Hebrews and their existence as the Israel of the exodus covenant. Under it the God revealed in Israel's deliverance is the cue for the reinterpretation of all tribal traditions, even of universal history, so that history hitherto is seen as having consisted of a series of "covenants" (Adam, Noah, Abraham). Under it also the religious, ethnic, and cultural values antecedent to the Exodus, however difficult it may be for us to describe these, are affirmed to have been a preparation for the revelation of the Exodus, a conditioning element in it, and thereafter subsumed under it. The formula implies that creation and redemption are one process, but in this context of the exodus event, it also implies that creation is known in the light of redemption.

kingdom he shall rest." [3] There are two impulses in man: one is to accept and take for granted; the other is to look with inquiry and wonder. Out of the latter impulse religion is born. Instead of saying, "A tree on fire," and passing on, Moses turns aside, and to his astonishment notices that it is not immediately reduced to ashes. It is burning but not burned. That is mysterious. Out of wonder and mystery spring all philosophy and science and art. "Why?" Moses asks; and in that "Why?" the mind and the soul of man are born.[4]

4-5. The Symbol of Reverence.—As in the Mohammedan mosque today, a sign of reverence and awe: **Put off thy shoes from off thy feet**

(cf. Josh. 5:15). This mingled sense of wonder, reverence, and awe is what distinguishes religion from morals. It is the idea of the Holy about which Rudolf Otto writes.[5] There are essential elements in religion which cannot be comprised in any intellectual system, nor wholly exhausted in practice and conduct, and which are only faintly suggested by symbolism and sacrament. Ritual is only justified when words cannot exactly explain what it means. It is an attempt to say something which cannot otherwise be wholly expressed. "Now a thing was secretly brought to me, and mine ear received a little thereof" (Job 4:12). In a land where the heat and rays of the sun may be deadly, it would seem to be a safer gesture of reverence to remove the shoes than to remove the hat. Rites

[3] *Oxyrhynchus Papyri*, ed. Bernard P. Grenfell and Arthur S. Hunt (London: Egypt Exploration Fund, 1903), Pt. IV, p. 4.

[4] See William H. Davies' poem "Leisure."

[5] *The Idea of the Holy*, tr. J. W. Harvey (New York: Oxford University Press, 1929), ch. x.

7 ¶ And the LORD said, I have surely seen the affliction of my people which *are* in Egypt, and have heard their cry by reason of their taskmasters; for I know their sorrows;

8 And I am come down to deliver them out of the hand of the Egyptians, and to bring them up out of that land unto a good land and a large, unto a land flowing with milk and honey; unto the place of the Canaanites, and the Hittites, and the Amorites, and the Perizzites, and the Hivites, and the Jebusites.

9 Now therefore, behold, the cry of the children of Israel is come unto me: and I have also seen the oppression wherewith the Egyptians oppress them.

10 Come now therefore, and I will send thee unto Pharaoh, that thou mayest bring forth my people the children of Israel out of Egypt.

11 ¶ And Moses said unto God, Who *am* I, that I should go unto Pharaoh, and that I should bring forth the children of Israel out of Egypt?

7 Then the LORD said, "I have seen the affliction of my people who are in Egypt, and have heard their cry because of their taskmasters; I know their sufferings, 8 and I have come down to deliver them out of the hand of the Egyptians, and to bring them up out of that land to a good and broad land, a land flowing with milk and honey, to the place of the Canaanites, the Hittites, the Amorites, the Per'izzites, the Hivites, and the Jeb'usites. 9 And now, behold, the cry of the people of Israel has come to me, and I have seen the oppression with which the Egyptians oppress them. 10 Come, I will send you to Pharaoh that you may bring forth my people, the sons of Israel, out of Egypt." 11 But Moses said to God, "Who am I that I should go to Pharaoh, and bring

---

2. THE AUDIENCE (3:7–4:17)

God has made himself known to Moses. Now he reveals his plan and assigns Moses his role in it.

a) THE LORD'S PLAN (3:7-10)

7-8. The slaves did not have to call on the Lord. Here, for the J tradition, as in 2:23-25, the Lord hears before men call. And he has **come down to deliver** the slaves (cf. 19:18; Gen. 11:5). This emphasis upon God's actual intrusion into the historical scene is not found in the P document. The plan of the Lord is described after it was carried out, by a writer who shares in its beneficent results. He here attests his faith that Israel possesses Canaan by the grace of God and for his purpose. He sets out his understanding of God's attitude and relationship to Israel in Palestine—an attitude and relationship that are rooted in the Exodus.

10. It is "the fullness of time." God will reveal himself as the great destroyer and the great deliverer. Moses is to be his instrument to bring Israel **out of Egypt**. This is the point of his appearance. God will endow with authority and harness to his purpose the natural audacity, courage, and sense of justice, so strong in this man (2:11-15).

b) GOD INSTRUCTS MOSES (3:11-22)

11. God must instruct Moses before he can serve. Not only must he be told what to do in Egypt; more basically, he must be taught his relationship to the Lord in this mission. The cry **Who am I?** is not the pure *Domine non sum dignus* of humble faith (cf. Jer. 1:6). The cry shows indeed that Moses, the confident hero of 2:11-15, now knows

---

suitable and beautiful in one land seem artificial and strained in another. (The church once had to decide as to the legality of a baptism performed with sand in the waterless desert; the professional and artificial mechanics of some

modern methods of safeguarding our communion service are apt to destroy the symbolism and mar its ancient loveliness.) Reverence is the response of body and soul to lofty mysteries, deeply felt and only partially understood.

12 And he said, Certainly I will be with thee; and this *shall be* a token unto thee, that I have sent thee: When thou hast brought forth the people out of Egypt, ye shall serve God upon this mountain.

13 And Moses said unto God, Behold, *when* I come unto the children of Israel, and shall say unto them, The God of your fathers hath sent me unto you; and they shall say to me, What *is* his name? what shall I say unto them?

14 And God said unto Moses, I AM THAT I AM: and he said, Thus shalt thou say unto the children of Israel, I AM hath sent me unto you.

the sons of Israel out of Egypt?" 12 He said, "But I will be with you; and this shall be the sign for you, that I have sent you: when you have brought forth the people out of Egypt, you shall serve God upon this mountain."

13 Then Moses said to God, "If I come to the people of Israel and say to them, 'The God of your fathers has sent me to you,' and they ask me, 'What is his name?' what shall I say to them?" 14 God said to Moses, "I AM WHO I AM."*e* And he said, "Say this to the people of Israel, 'I AM has sent me

e Or I AM WHAT I AM or I WILL BE WHAT I WILL BE

---

he cannot impress Israel. He is modest. But his modesty partakes of faithlessness and frustration (4:10-14). God must transform it into the humility of faith.

12. Thus, God says, **I will be with you.** This must be read in the light of vss. 7-10. Moses is not divinely assured of helpful assistance on a project essentially his. He is told again that this is God's project. God is at the center of it and Moses is only a unit in his work. The following clause, **this shall be the sign for you,** carries through this instruction. The **sign** differs from those that follow. It is the pledge of God, not as proof but as promise (cf. I Sam. 2:34; 14:10; Isa. 7:14; Jer. 44:29). The promise can be relevant to Moses only if he believes God is the deliverer. And the content of the promise seeks to elicit this faith. It stresses the theocentric character or cosmic significance of the Exodus. God is not merely going to fulfill Moses' defeated hopes or ease the burden of slaves; he is going to establish a people for himself. The covenant will be sealed at this very mountain. This deliverance is God's work.

13-15. Moses responds in faith and proceeds to a practical question. How shall he convince the Israelites that God has really spoken to him? In the Bible a name, whether of man, angel, or deity, sets forth the character of its bearer. If the plan Moses presents to the elders is to impress them as God's revelation and not Moses' own idea, he must be able to give the name of God, a new name that goes with the new revelation.

13-15. *The Mystery of God's Name.*—Although his name is too sacred to be pronounced, we begin to see from the narrative what kind of a God this was who revealed himself to Moses. He was a mysterious power, in whose presence one must put off the shoes from one's feet and cover one's face; he had a dwelling place in nature, in mountain and tree and fire; he knew all that was happening among men; he hated injustice, helped the oppressed to freedom, and punished the tyrant; he could endow men with seemingly miraculous powers; he needed the help and co-operation of men to carry out his ends; he knew the heart of man, so as to choose the right man as his minister; he was the God of the fathers, even when known by them under a different name; he was omnipotent in directing the course of history through men and nature toward his own ends.

This citation reads something like our own

conception of God; we might define the miraculous powers somewhat differently, but wonder just as much at the greatness of great men in the world's crises; we are somewhat more hazy in our ideas about the connection between God and nature, and are more skeptical about what express companies call in their bills of lading "acts of God." We are inclined to think that earthquakes, tempests, epidemics, and droughts are sent not so much as punishments as for the purpose of goading sluggish man on to discover ways of understanding and controlling his environment. Yet God in nature for us is always one of the great sources of inspiration. In fact, all nature seems to us in moments of insight to be what it was for Jesus, a primer of the ways of God.

14. *I Am That I Am.*—"I am that I am, was his own definition unto Moses; and it was a short one, to confound mortality, that durst

15 And God said moreover unto Moses, Thus shalt thou say unto the children of Israel, The LORD God of your fathers, the God of Abraham, the God of Isaac, and the God of Jacob, hath sent me unto you: this *is* my name for ever, and this *is* my memorial unto all generations.

to you.' " **15** God also said to Moses, "Say this to the people of Israel, 'The LORD,*f* the God of your fathers, the God of Abraham, the God of Isaac, and the God of Jacob, has sent me to you': this is my name for ever, and thus I am to be remembered through-

f The word LORD when spelled with capital letters stands for the divine name, *YHWH,* which is here connected with the verb *hayah,* to be

---

Vss. 13-15 belong to the E document. Its view is that the divine name YHWH (**LORD**), in vs. 15, was given to Moses at Sinai, along with the plan of deliverance. It differs in this respect from the J document. What new name, if any, the J tradition associated with Sinai can no longer be determined. Consequently, the E document uses this name for the first time here, **this is my name for ever, and thus I am to be remembered.**

It is possible to read vs. 15 as the immediate continuation of vs. 13. **Moreover** may indicate that this reply of God is in addition to the one given in vs. 12. What we have in vs. 14 is a parenthetical statement, or interpretation, that analyzes the name YHWH. The analysis treats the name as a verb derived from the root *hāyāh* ("to be"). Since God is the speaker, the name is "transposed" to the first person of the verb. But as the RSV mg. shows, this etymological interpretation can be translated in various ways. "I AM, BE-CAUSE I AM" (ASV mg.) represents a further possibility. It seems possible that the interpreter wanted to stress the fullness and mystery of God and therefore purposely left his analysis open to a wide range of interpretations. He concludes by offering only the first verb of his interpretation, *'eheyeh,* "I am," or better, "I will be" (cf. Intro., pp. 837-38).

---

question God, or ask him what he was. Indeed he only is; all others have been and shall be." [6] The Atta Nimsa, one of the Jewish prayers for feast days, is the answering voice to this tremendous name:

> Thou art!
> The hearing of the ear,
> The seeing of the eye
> Cannot reach Thee;
> No How or Why or Where
> Can lead us to Thee.
>
> Thou art!
> Hidden is Thy secret,
> Who may fathom it!
> Deep, so deep,
> Who can find it! [7]

But there is a very practical application of the meaning of this mysterious name. If the name of the God I worship is I AM, it seems to follow that only through what I am can I worship him aright. God and the archangel Michael were in one of the anterooms of heaven. In a continuous torrent all the prayers, oral and sung, of mankind were ascending from earth. It was a babel of sound in all tongues, and on all sides of every question, hurricanes of passionate de-

mands, winds of speech whining with wheedling words, gusts of insistent requests for special favors. Overwhelmed with it all, Michael said to God, "If you will allow me, Sire, I would say that you made a great mistake when you let man learn to talk. If he was not able to talk, it would be possible then for you to know what he was really praying for." And God said, "I do not listen to their words. I listen only to their lives." He closed the window and opened the door, and all the tempest of words stopped. Instead from the earth came up clearly another prayer. Most of it was distressing, but a weak, wavering voice did arise also from the lives of men to heaven: "O Lord, if it does not cost us too much, we sometimes would like to be just and courageous and kind. Amen." For the only prayer of mine that rises above the roof is the prayer of what I am.

In this affirmation also is the pledge and proof of our existential unity with God and with one another, as the Swedish poet Runeberg puts it: "It is strange that, though we all say our 'I am,' we nevertheless fancy ourselves to be so far, so essentially, separated from one another. Is not the same spirit in all of us which from our thousand mouths says his 'I am,' thus proving himself and us true?" [8]

3:15-21. See Expos. on 2:23*b*-4:17.

---

[6] Thomas Browne, *Religio Medici,* Part I, ch. xi.

[7] Michael Sachs, *Festgebete der Israeliten* (Breslau: Koekner, 1898), Part III.

[8] Gunnar Tideström, *Runeberg* (Helsingfors: Mercators tryckeri, 1941), p. 395.

16 Go, and gather the elders of Israel together, and say unto them, The LORD God of your fathers, the God of Abraham, of Isaac, and of Jacob, appeared unto me, saying, I have surely visited you, and *seen* that which is done to you in Egypt:

17 And I have said, I will bring you up out of the affliction of Egypt unto the land of the Canaanites, and the Hittites, and the Amorites, and the Perizzites, and the Hivites, and the Jebusites, unto a land flowing with milk and honey.

18 And they shall hearken to thy voice: and thou shalt come, thou and the elders of Israel, unto the king of Egypt, and ye shall say unto him, The LORD God of the Hebrews hath met with us: and now let us go, we beseech thee, three days' journey into the wilderness, that we may sacrifice to the LORD our God.

19 ¶ And I am sure that the king of Egypt will not let you go, no, not by a mighty hand.

20 And I will stretch out my hand, and smite Egypt with all my wonders which I will do in the midst thereof: and after that he will let you go.

21 And I will give this people favor in the sight of the Egyptians: and it shall come to pass, that, when ye go, ye shall not go empty:

22 But every woman shall borrow of her neighbor, and of her that sojourneth in

out all generations. 16 Go and gather the elders of Israel together, and say to them, 'The LORD, the God of your fathers, the God of Abraham, of Isaac, and of Jacob, has appeared to me, saying, "I have observed you and what has been done to you in Egypt; 17 and I promise that I will bring you up out of the affliction of Egypt, to the land of the Canaanites, the Hittites, the Amorites, the Per'izzites, the Hivites, and the Jeb'usites, a land flowing with milk and honey." ' 18 And they will hearken to your voice; and you and the elders of Israel shall go to the king of Egypt and say to him, 'The LORD, the God of the Hebrews, has met with us; and now, we pray you, let us go a three days' journey into the wilderness, that we may sacrifice to the LORD our God.' 19 I know that the king of Egypt will not let you go unless compelled by a mighty hand.[g] 20 So I will stretch out my hand and smite Egypt with all the wonders which I will do in it; after that he will let you go. 21 And I will give this people favor in the sight of the Egyptians; and when you go, you shall not go empty, 22 but each woman shall ask of her neighbor, and of her who sojourns in

g Gk Vg: Heb *no, not by a mighty hand*

16-17. Yahweh instructs Moses to go to the people with the message. The writer, after the manner of ancient narrators, repeats the content of the message (cf. vss. 7-8).

18. The prediction about the receptivity of the elders prepares the way for Moses' exhibition of faithlessness (4:1-16). It also illustrates J's view that all the relations between Moses and the Israelites and between Moses and the Egyptians were first of all communicated by God to Moses (4:31). The strategy will be to ask for permission to go into the wilderness to sacrifice to **the LORD, the God of the Hebrews.** The phrase implies the worship of one God. The story of the contest between God and the Pharaoh develops a dramatic tension by having Israel increase its demand whenever the ruler grants the previous demand (10:9-11). God will demonstrate his omnipotence over Pharaoh; only under the compulsion of God's mighty hand will the people go free.

21-22. The spoliation of the Egyptians, here commanded by God, is reported to have been carried out by the people (12:35-36) at the order of Moses (11:2-3). The E writer

---

22. *Legitimate Spoils.*—Augustine's use of the metaphor of spoiling the Egyptians referred to in the Exeg. has had many applications during the centuries. The underlying idea is that good people can profit by rifling the stores of the ungodly of their material treasures, their worldly

wisdom, canny ways, and bright ideas. In the First Gospel it seems to be one of the favorite ideas of Jesus. The children of the kingdom can learn much from the children of the world. "If ye then, being evil, know, . . . how much more shall your Father?" (Matt. 7:11.) They can

her house, jewels of silver, and jewels of gold, and raiment: and ye shall put *them* upon your sons, and upon your daughters; and ye shall spoil the Egyptians.

4 And Moses answered and said, But, behold, they will not believe me, nor hearken unto my voice: for they will say, The LORD hath not appeared unto thee.

2 And the LORD said unto him, What *is* that in thine hand? And he said, A rod.

3 And he said, Cast it on the ground. And he cast it on the ground, and it became a serpent; and Moses fled from before it.

4 And the LORD said unto Moses, Put forth thine hand, and take it by the tail.

her house, jewelry of silver and of gold, and clothing, and you shall put them on your sons and on your daughters; thus you shall despoil the Egyptians."

4 Then Moses answered, "But behold, they will not believe me or listen to my voice, for they will say, 'The LORD did not appear to you.'" 2 The LORD said to him, "What is that in your hand?" He said, "A rod." 3 And he said, "Cast it on the ground." So he cast it on the ground, and it became a serpent; and Moses fled from it. 4 But the LORD said to Moses, "Put out your hand,

---

indicates in this way his approval of the reported occurrence. Note again that for him Israelites and Egyptians lived together. The "spoliation of the Egyptians" became a metaphor in early Christianity for the new faith's appropriation of the cultural heritage of the Greek world (Augustine *On Christian Doctrine* II. 40).

c) MOSES TAUGHT MAGIC (4:1-9, 17)

4:1. The problem of authenticating to the elders God's appearance to Moses, which in E was answered by the disclosure of the divine name, is here raised by J, who tells how God instructed Moses as a sage versed in Egyptian magic (cf. Acts 7:22). Actually, and despite vs. 5, the text implies that Moses shall ply the magicians' craft before the Egyptians rather than before the elders (vs. 21; 7:8-13). The writer seems to have confused the two problems: how to evoke faith in Moses, and how Moses was to impress the Egyptian priests and destroy their faith. The **signs** he is taught here relate to the latter. It is rewarding to read the dramatic account of the plagues as the record of the contest in which Yahweh vanquishes the enchanters and magicians of Egypt (8:19; 9:11). The theme is paralleled in the N.T. by Christ's defeat of the powers of darkness. As God's servant Moses is taught some of the occult knowledge, but not enough to accomplish the defeat of the Egyptians (7:11), for God is the deliverer, not Moses.

2-4, 17. In vs. 2 the rod is Moses' own cane. In vs. 17 (E) God gives it to Moses. In the latter it is also a wand with which Moses shall **do the signs**, whereas in the former only one sign is implied. It is not impossible that we have here the garbled account

---

learn from farmers (Matt. 13:3, 24); builders (Matt. 7:24); tailors (Matt. 9:16); bottlers (Matt. 9:17); weather prophets (Matt. 16:3); children (Matt. 18:2); shepherds (Matt. 18:12); idle questioners (Matt. 21:24); householders (Matt. 24:43); wedding guests (Matt. 25:1). From the Communists the Christian church can learn much by seeing how a comparatively small number of people can revolutionize a state because of their intent purposefulness. The modern church has profited much from following some of the practices of the business world. The Roman Catholic Church in the past has borrowed from the antecedent paganism of its converts, so the adoration of the Blessed Virgin filled the gap left in the minds of former

heathen who had always been familiar with female deities. The names of the saints took the place of the pagan gods in magic spells. Many old love songs were transformed into hymns; in fact, there was a word in medieval times used for such transformed songs, *contrafacta,* which means "things made over." The children of light are always learning from the children of darkness. Reading Exodus as Augustine did, his use of this episode must have been connected in his mind with ch. 25, and 35:22, which would indicate to him how the rich loot of the unbelievers became *contrafacta,* made over for the service and glory of the true God (see also Expos. on 13:16).

4:1-9. See Expos. on 2:23*b*-4:17.

And he put forth his hand, and caught it, and it became a rod in his hand:

5 That they may believe that the Lord God of their fathers, the God of Abraham, the God of Isaac, and the God of Jacob, hath appeared unto thee.

6 ¶ And the Lord said furthermore unto him, Put now thine hand into thy bosom. And he put his hand into his bosom: and when he took it out, behold, his hand *was* leprous as snow.

7 And he said, Put thine hand into thy bosom again. And he put his hand into his bosom again; and plucked it out of his bosom, and, behold, it was turned again as his *other* flesh.

8 And it shall come to pass, if they will not believe thee, neither hearken to the voice of the first sign, that they will believe the voice of the latter sign.

9 And it shall come to pass, if they will not believe also these two signs, neither hearken unto thy voice, that thou shalt take of the water of the river, and pour *it* upon the dry *land:* and the water which thou takest out of the river shall become blood upon the dry *land.*

10 ¶ And Moses said unto the Lord, O my Lord, I *am* not eloquent, neither heretofore, nor since thou hast spoken unto

and take it by the tail" — so he put out his hand and caught it, and it became a rod in his hand — 5 "that they may believe that the Lord, the God of their fathers, the God of Abraham, the God of Isaac, and the God of Jacob, has appeared to you." 6 Again, the Lord said to him, "Put your hand into your bosom." And he put his hand into his bosom; and when he took it out, behold, his hand was leprous, as white as snow. 7 Then God said, "Put your hand back into your bosom." So he put his hand back into his bosom; and when he took it out, behold, it was restored like the rest of his flesh. 8 "If they will not believe you," God said, "or heed the first sign, they may believe the latter sign. 9 If they will not believe even these two signs or heed your voice, you shall take some water from the Nile and pour it upon the dry ground; and the water which you shall take from the Nile will become blood upon the dry ground."

10 But Moses said to the Lord, "Oh, my Lord, I am not eloquent, either heretofore

---

of an Egyptian snake charmer's trick. By mesmerism he makes straight and rigid like a staff the body of a serpent; then he breaks the spell by grasping its tail. Serpent magic was common in Egypt and was associated with the gift of healing (Num. 21:9).

6-8. It is not reported that Moses practiced the second sign in Egypt.

9. Moses is taught the manner of the third sign, but does not attempt it. The first of the ten plagues, in which water is turned into blood, was not accomplished in this fashion. The form and content of these individual stories is foreign to us, but their point is perennially relevant: the God of biblical faith is master in the world he himself has made. The God who controls even the demons is not one who can or will be cajoled by men; rather he puts man under responsibility and calls him to commitment.

d) Aaron as Spokesman (4:10-16)

10-13. Moses again (see vs. 2; 3:11) complains that he cannot be a hero, not comprehending that God has called him to be a servant. "Please [*bî*]," he says, "I am not eloquent;

10-12. Man's Weakness and God's Power.— More than fifty years ago a student was lying very ill and weak in a back room in Edinburgh. Suddenly he dimly saw standing at the foot of his bed a tall, white-haired man, who closed his eyes and said, "O Lord, Thou givest the victory unto the weak! We give it to the strong and to the talented, but Thou givest it unto the

weak. Amen." These words of Alexander Whyte of Free St. George's Church have remained living in the life of that man ever since. In them was the seed idea God was trying to plant in the mind of Moses. The best work is done by people who do not think they are fitted for it. The man with all the advantages and gifts and assurance misfires; somehow he is too glib a

thy servant; but I *am* slow of speech, and of a slow tongue.

11 And the LORD said unto him, Who hath made man's mouth? or who maketh the dumb, or deaf, or the seeing, or the blind? have not I the LORD?

12 Now therefore go, and I will be with thy mouth, and teach thee what thou shalt say.

13 And he said, O my Lord, send, I pray thee, by the hand *of him whom* thou wilt send.

14 And the anger of the LORD was kindled against Moses, and he said, *Is* not Aaron the Levite thy brother? I know that he can speak well. And also, behold, he cometh forth to meet thee: and when he seeth thee, he will be glad in his heart.

15 And thou shalt speak unto him, and put words in his mouth: and I will be with thy mouth, and with his mouth, and will teach you what ye shall do.

or since thou hast spoken to thy servant; but I am slow of speech and of tongue." 11 Then the LORD said to him, "Who has made man's mouth? Who makes him dumb, or deaf, or seeing, or blind? Is it not I, the LORD? 12 Now therefore go, and I will be with your mouth and teach you what you shall speak." 13 But he said, "Oh, my Lord, send, I pray, some other person." 14 Then the anger of the LORD was kindled against Moses and he said, "Is there not Aaron, your brother, the Levite? I know that he can speak well; and behold, he is coming out to meet you, and when he sees you he will be glad in his heart. 15 And you shall speak to him and put the words in his mouth; and I will be with your mouth and with his mouth, and will teach you what

I cannot be a leader." Jeremiah made a similar protest (Jer. 1:6). The man of God must recognize his own poverty but must further learn to live in God's riches. Moses points out that his natural endowments were not greater by virtue of revelation. After God made himself known to him, his speech was the same as before. God replies that he knows what he is about; he himself is the creator of the men who are to serve him in his redeeming work. God's assurance, **I will be with your mouth,** does not mean that in crises Moses will suddenly become fluent. Rather since Moses' God will be the master in these crises, Moses' stammering as God's faithful servant will be adequate enough. God is equal to his own purposes and he knows how to make his creatures serve his ends. The adequacy of resources that seem futile in themselves draws attention to the power and centrality of God. This theme of the sufficiency of the weak for God is constantly played upon in the Bible (cf. I Cor. 1:27). In this instance, perhaps in order to serve the narrator's purpose of bringing Aaron onto the stage, Moses remains faithless.

14-16. Moses' unbelief arouses divine anger; he is then told of another human resource, **Aaron, your brother, the Levite.** The motive of the narrator (probably E or an editor of JE) is to establish the priesthood of Israel as a divinely ordained and authoritative institution in Israel's covenanted relationship with God. The passage seems to reflect strained relations between priest and prophet in the writer's own day. The narrator is irenic. He assumes the priority of the prophet in age and station. The priest **is coming out to meet** the prophet, Moses, who is already commissioned; and for his sake Aaron must

speaker, too easy socially, too efficient, too robust, too sure of himself (see 32:21-24). Every great thing was done in spite of something. Excuses are the unconscious humor of the unwilling. God would probably never have made Moses facile with words, but would have seen to it that his stammering voice rang with a sincerity and power which is more than eloquence. The best teachers and persuaders are a priori the most unexpected persons. It may be true, especially in politics, that God is not urg-

ing you to run for office at all; but when he really is, when your better self says, "You ought" —then dare to try, and you will find that the humble man with the help of God can always do better than he thought (II Cor. 12:9; I Cor. 1:27; Ps. 118:22), almost as well as God hoped (Gen. 18:14; Matt. 19:26).

15. *Through Thy Mouth Will I, the Lord, Speak.*—The good sermon is always better than the preacher had written, better than all his meditation. Something happens in the pulpit

16 And he shall be thy spokesman unto the people: and he shall be, *even* he shall be to thee instead of a mouth, and thou shalt be to him instead of God.

17 And thou shalt take this rod in thine hand, wherewith thou shalt do signs.

18 ¶ And Moses went and returned to Jethro his father-in-law, and said unto him, Let me go, I pray thee, and return unto my brethren which *are* in Egypt, and see whether they be yet alive. And Jethro said to Moses, Go in peace.

19 And the LORD said unto Moses in Midian, Go, return into Egypt: for all the men are dead which sought thy life.

you shall do. 16 He shall speak for you to the people; and he shall be a mouth for you, and you shall be to him as God. 17 And you shall take in your hand this rod, with which you shall do the signs."

18 Moses went back to Jethro his father-in-law and said to him, "Let me go back, I pray, to my kinsmen in Egypt and see whether they are still alive." And Jethro said to Moses, "Go in peace." 19 And the LORD said to Moses in Mid'ian, "Go back to Egypt; for all the men who were seeking

---

depend on the work of the prophet. But the priest rejoices in this arrangement; therefore, **when he sees you he will be glad in his heart.** On the other hand, the prophet needs the priest to implement, institutionally, the will of God revealed to him; therefore **he can speak well**—the LXX adds "for thee." The older writers are essentially prophetic in spirit. Aaron calls Moses "my lord" (32:22; Num. 12:11). Priestly rebellion against the prophet is condemned (Num. 12:1 ff.). And Aaron makes the golden calf (ch. 32). Yet they recognize both prophet and priest as the legitimate and active instruments of God in the ministry of the covenant.

The P writers exalt Aaron. Aaron, the priest, is older (6:20) than Moses, and Aaron wields the sacred rod that accomplishes the wonders (7:9-10, 19-20; 8:5-6, 16-17). Aaron is to give the word of the prophet, Moses, to Pharaoh (7:2). In P the prophet does retain the primacy over the priest in the sense that the latter would never act except on the basis of the prophet's word. But the prophet is shorn of an active role. He is in the background. He is the sanction for the program of the priest. This corresponds precisely to the role assigned to the prophets in the postexilic era when the written records of earlier prophets were accepted as normative but the outbreak of contemporary prophecy was discouraged.

17. See Exeg. on vss. 2-4, 17, pp. 877-78.

3. Moses Returns to Egypt (4:18-31)
a) Departure from Midian (4:18-23)

18, 20. Moses asks his father-in-law for permission to leave. The Hebrew text here reads "Jether" for **Jethro.** The assumption is that Moses had accepted God's commission; he did not, however, disclose the revelation to Jethro, a fact which seems to militate against a popular view that Moses was a convert of Jethro. The will of God, before its execution, is declared only to the prophet. According to this writer, **Moses took his wife and his sons.** Only one son (2:22) has been reported thus far. That Zipporah accompanied Moses is also assumed in vs. 25. On the other hand, 18:5 implies that Moses left his wife

---

which goes beyond all that he had prepared to say. The eloquence of the congregation blends subtly with the thinking of the leader to produce an occasion,

And the emulous heaven yearned down, made effort to reach the earth,
　As the earth had done her best, in my passion, to scale the sky.[9]

　[9] Browning, "Abt Vogler."

All suddenly realize that God is speaking, saying things deeper and more wonderful than either pulpit or pew had conceived. "This kind goeth not out but by prayer and fasting," but when it does happen, when the veil that hides God's glory from mortal eyes begins to tremble and grow thin, then listen to the people sing the closing hymn as though God's presence had indeed broken through into lives that could never be the same again.

20 And Moses took his wife and his sons, and set them upon an ass, and he returned to the land of Egypt: and Moses took the rod of God in his hand.

21 And the LORD said unto Moses, When thou goest to return into Egypt, see that thou do all those wonders before Pharaoh, which I have put in thine hand: but I will harden his heart, that he shall not let the people go.

22 And thou shalt say unto Pharaoh, Thus saith the LORD, Israel *is* my son, *even* my firstborn:

23 And I say unto thee, Let my son go, that he may serve me: and if thou refuse to let him go, behold, I will slay thy son, *even* thy firstborn.

your life are dead." 20 So Moses took his wife and his sons and set them on an ass, and went back to the land of Egypt; and in his hand Moses took the rod of God.

21 And the LORD said to Moses, "When you go back to Egypt, see that you do before Pharaoh all the miracles which I have put in your power; but I will harden his heart, so that he will not let the people go. 22 And you shall say to Pharaoh, Thus says the LORD, 'Israel is my first-born son, 23 and I say to you, "Let my son go that he may serve me"; if you refuse to let him go, behold, I will slay your first-born son.' "

and two sons behind; 18:2-4 seems to represent an effort to reconcile the discrepancy. There we are told that upon his arrival in Egypt "Moses had sent her away": i.e., back to Jethro. The passage also takes pains to introduce Eliezer, the second son. Consequently, it is not impossible that we should here read **sons** in the singular. Moses carries the cane or rod which is the sign of his endowment with God's power and commission.

21. The author assumes that the Lord gave Moses a preview of the course of the conflict between God and the Pharaoh. It is a part of God's purpose that the Egyptians will reject Moses' plan. The testimony of Moses will be the means of bringing the wickedness and pretension of the Pharaoh to maturity (cf. Isa. 6:10). God's design in deepening the ruler's stubbornness, which necessitates a multiplication of wonders, is frequently defined to show that (*a*) the Egyptians may know Yahweh is God (7:5, 17; 8:10; 9:14, 30); (*b*) Israel may know him as a great God (10:2); (*c*) Yahweh is Israel's God (11:7); and (*d*) Yahweh is free in the midst of all magic (7:11, 22; 8:7, 18; 22:18). The central moment in the exodus revelation is that of God's freedom and power. He makes even the wrath of man to praise him (cf. Ps. 76:10). The problem of divine and human freedom is implicit here. The interpretation of man's stubbornness as a part of God's design is not to deny man freedom and responsibility but to attest that the result of wickedness can be used by God for his own ends, a view which leads to the prophetic doctrine of the divine judgment (cf. I Thess. 5:9).

23. The anticipation of the death of the first-born is here limited to the first-born of the Pharaoh (cf. 11:5; 12:29-34). This is due punishment for his enslavement of

20*b*. See Expos. on 2:23*b*–4:17, 20*b*.

21-23. *Man's Will and God's Mastery.*—The whole narrative is arranged from its different sources so as to dramatize the great battle of wits between Moses and Pharaoh. It is especially made clear that all the details of the struggle were in the hands of a higher power. Nothing in the world occurs apart from the will of God (Ps. 76:10). Things all arrange themselves so that God can display his full power, even to the point noted in Isa. 6:10. So we find the ancient problem of divine grace and human freedom in the unsolved condition in which it has always remained. The biblical authors emphasize first one side and then the other, but

make no attempt to reconcile them. Calvin felt that unless God had a blueprint of every detail exactly as it was going to happen there could be no meaning in history—all would be the prey of chance. If God did not harden Pharaoh's heart, how then did it happen? The only answer seems to be that it happened contrary to the will of God. In that case, God has lost control of things and chance rules. On the other hand, Pharaoh knew that he was free to do as he wanted, and the guilt of his sin was his alone. Like two poles of an arc light, these two opposites stand across from one another, and the light of common sense shines between.

24 ¶ And it came to pass by the way in the inn, that the LORD met him, and sought to kill him. 25 Then Zipporah took a sharp stone, and cut off the foreskin of her son, and cast *it* at his feet, and said, Surely a bloody husband *art* thou to me. 26 So he let him go: then she said, A bloody husband *thou art*, because of the circumcision.	24 At a lodging place on the way the LORD met him and sought to kill him. 25 Then Zippo′rah took a flint and cut off her son's foreskin, and touched Moses' feet with it, and said, "Surely you are a bridegroom of blood to me!" 26 So he let him alone. Then it was that she said, "You are a bridegroom of blood," because of the circumcision.

Israel for, **says the LORD, Israel is my first-born son** (cf. Hos. 11:1). This statement refers to Israel's election by God; Israel is not only God's first-born, but his only son. Both Hos. 11:1 and the metaphor of Israel as the bride imply this (Jer. 2:1-3; Ezek. 16:1-15; Hos. 2:2-13). The corollary of Israel's sonship is God's fatherhood (Isa. 63:16; 64:8). This elective relationship of father and son in redemption the Bible distinguishes sharply from the fatherhood of God and the sonship (and brotherhood) of man in creation. In the account of the plagues this phrase **Let my son go** becomes the theme of Moses' demand upon the Pharaoh; the term **son,** however, is there changed to "people."

b) CIRCUMCISION OF MOSES (4:24-26)

24-26. As it stands this is an etiological story which gives a different account of the origin of circumcision in Israel from that in Gen. 17 (P). A flint knife is used, indicating the ancient practice of the rite (Josh. 5:2). Jewish tradition says it is the younger son of Moses who is circumcised; at any rate infant circumcision is indicated, though in the beginning it was performed at puberty or at the time of marriage. There are, however, difficulties connected with the story in its present form: the demonic element implied by Yahweh's attempt to slay Moses; the incongruity of addressing Moses, father of two children, as a bridegroom; and the fact that Zipporah herself performs the rite. Beer, following Gressmann, offers an interpretation which seems best to account for these problems (*Exodus*, pp. 37-39). Zipporah the Midianite performed the circumcision to indicate that the practice came to Israel from the Midianites. In an earlier version of the story she circumcised Moses, not his son; and the occasion was their bridal night. Her object was to save Moses' life from destruction by a demon who denied Moses the possession of his bride. Zipporah touches the demon with the foreskin and addresses to him the words, **Surely you are a bridegroom of blood to me!** Thus the demon is appeased. The second use of the phrase is perhaps to be understood as addressed to Moses and seems to hint at the ancient practice of adult circumcision. In Tobit we have such a demonic tale (Tob. 6:13–8:17). It is also probable that a similar demonic attack is implied in the statement in Gen. 38:7; by a quick-witted presence of mind Zipporah here avoids what happened there. To those who reworked the story into its present form its original demonic character had been lost; thus the name Yahweh has replaced that of the demon.

Man is free within certain limits. God lets him act as he wishes within them, but is able to control the results to his own glory. He hardens Pharaoh's heart in the sense that the laws which determine the progressive degeneration of a self-willed personality, and make it the prisoner of its evil past, are laws of God. **24-26.** *A Bridegroom of Blood.*—This incident, which seems to have no relation to its context in the narrative, may be an early legend	concerning the fateful dangers and importance of the bridal night (see Exeg.). It appears to refer to the ancient idea that a demon asserted the *jus primae noctis* and that adult circumcision was in part for the purpose of appeasing the spirit and saving the life of the bridegroom. Probably included from a mass of similar discarded material because it seemed to the editor to give the origin of the rite of circumcision, it is of value to us in that it emphasizes the jungle

27 ¶ And the Lord said to Aaron, Go into the wilderness to meet Moses. And he went, and met him in the mount of God, and kissed him.

28 And Moses told Aaron all the words of the Lord who had sent him, and all the signs which he had commanded him.

29 ¶ And Moses and Aaron went and gathered together all the elders of the children of Israel:

30 And Aaron spake all the words which the Lord had spoken unto Moses, and did the signs in the sight of the people.

31 And the people believed: and when they heard that the Lord had visited the children of Israel, and that he had looked upon their affliction, then they bowed their heads and worshipped.

5 And afterward Moses and Aaron went in, and told Pharaoh, Thus saith the Lord God of Israel, Let my people go, that they may hold a feast unto me in the wilderness.

27 The Lord said to Aaron, "Go into the wilderness to meet Moses." So he went, and met him at the mountain of God and kissed him. 28 And Moses told Aaron all the words of the Lord with which he had sent him, and all the signs which he had charged him to do. 29 Then Moses and Aaron went and gathered together all the elders of the people of Israel. 30 And Aaron spoke all the words which the Lord had spoken to Moses, and did the signs in the sight of the people. 31 And the people believed; and when they heard that the Lord had visited the people of Israel and that he had seen their affliction, they bowed their heads and worshiped.

5 Afterward Moses and Aaron went to Pharaoh and said, "Thus says the Lord, the God of Israel, 'Let my people go, that they may hold a feast to me in the wil-

c) Aaron Meets Moses (4:27-31)

27. The statement that Aaron met Moses **at the mountain of God** comes from a hand other than that which has given us the account of his journey to Egypt.

28. Moses communicates to Aaron **all the words of the Lord**, i.e., God's plan of redemption previously kept secret from Jethro (vss. 18).

29, 31. The name Aaron is perhaps a gloss here. The verb is in the singular. The people accept the call and commission of Moses as authentic and give thanks for the prospect of deliverance. The passage serves as a transition to a new phase of the drama.

4. Moses Confronts the Facts (5:1–6:1)

This chapter alludes to the difficulties and forces which operate in the process of the deliverance that is to come. In the rejection of Moses' request and in the retaliatory measures that follow we have a taste of the Pharaoh's idolatry and despotism. The failure of the appeal by the foremen arouses their resentment against Moses. To obtain deliverance even slaves must suffer "the loss of all things" (Phil. 3:8). The slaves have not yet grasped this mystery; Moses has not grasped it either, but with pity for his people and faith in God he seeks the answer.

a) The Pharaoh Scorns Yahweh (5:1-5)

5:1, 3. E and J here respectively report on the first visit to the Pharaoh. E stresses the demand God asked Moses to make (4:23), reports that Moses and Aaron were

of primitive superstitions out of which the religion of Yahweh was developed.

27-31. See Expos. on 2:23b–4:17, 20b, 27-31.

5:1-2. Who Is Yahweh?—Pharaoh has never heard of the god Yahweh; he does not seem to doubt that there is such a god, but the condition of the god's followers does not, in his opinion as a polytheist, seem to indicate that he

is a very important god. The modern analogy is the conflict between Locke's idea as imbedded in the American Constitution, that the sole justification for the existence of any government is the protection of private property, and the humanitarian doctrine that human welfare is more important than property rights. The domestic and foreign policy of the United States

2 And Pharaoh said, Who *is* the LORD, that I should obey his voice to let Israel go? I know not the LORD, neither will I let Israel go.

3 And they said, The God of the Hebrews hath met with us: let us go, we pray thee, three days' journey into the desert, and sacrifice unto the LORD our God; lest he fall upon us with pestilence, or with the sword.

derness.' " 2 But Pharaoh said, "Who is the LORD, that I should heed his voice and let Israel go? I do not know the LORD, and moreover I will not let Israel go." 3 Then they said, "The God of the Hebrews has met with us; let us go, we pray, a three days' journey into the wilderness, and sacrifice to the LORD our God, lest he fall upon us

---

spokesmen, and that they sought a permit to feast in the wilderness. J stresses the revelation of God as such, says that the elders (**they**) were spokesmen (3:18), and that the request was for permission to sacrifice. The oldest type of sacrifice in Israel consisted essentially in a common festal meal "before the LORD" (I Sam. 1:1-21; 9:11-24). The request to return to their ancestral haunts for a solemn occasion was perfectly natural and reflects a universal tendency. "Man is most conservative where he reverences most." But implicit in the request is the desire to exchange the service of Pharaoh for that of Yahweh.

2. Presumably Pharaoh knows all gods that matter (H. and H. A. Frankfort, John A. Wilson, Thorkild Jacobsen, and William A. Irwin, *The Intellectual Adventure of Ancient Man* [Chicago: University of Chicago Press, 1946], p. 81). But of the Hebrew God he says, **Who is the LORD?** It is preposterous that he should surrender Israel to a deity he does not even know. The irony of the drama that follows is that this is the very God who progressively strips Pharaoh of everything.

---

is the story of the struggle between the worship of these two gods. We are still undecided as to whether, in considering American oil rights in a foreign country, the matter should be decided on the basis of the rights of property or of the welfare of the people of that country. As in Egypt, the property owners seem to be so much more respectable and solid and cultured than the workers in the oil fields, mines, and factories, that, like Pharaoh, the courts still are inclined to ask, "Who is this new god, Human Welfare?"

Even the most elementary attempt upon the part of the Mexican Government to establish economic justice within its own country by regaining some of its natural resources would appear to the United States and Great Britain, as it did to Woodrow Wilson in 1916, as a breach not merely of traditional international law but also of the elementary principles of political morality.[1]

Pharaoh saw only property rights in the labor of slaves; Moses saw the right of his people to freedom and happiness. The authors of Exodus were in sympathy with Moses yet, as the book shows, were willing to enslave other peoples to their own profit. Among the Hebrews the mas-

ter's right of property in his slaves of foreign origin was unlimited.

3. *The Dread of the Divine.*—It is a common belief among ancient peoples that gods avenge themselves upon their followers for omitting their required rites by sending pestilence or war upon them. The pestilence may be the clue to the story of the death of the first-born of the Egyptians; perhaps originally it was supposed to start among the unsanitary quarters of the slums which housed the Hebrew slaves. Carlyle's incident is apposite:

A poor Irish Widow, her husband having died in one of the Lanes of Edinburgh, went forth with her three children, bare of all resource, to solicit help from the Charitable Establishments of that City. At this Charitable Establishment and then at that she was refused; referred from one to the other, helped by none; . . . till her strength and heart failed her: she sank down in typhus fever; died, and infected her Lane with fever, so that "seventeen other persons" died in consequence. . . . Very curious. The forlorn Irish Widow applies to her fellow-creatures, as if saying, "Behold I am sinking, bare of help: ye must help me! I am your sister, bone of your bone; one God made us: ye must help me!" They answer, "No; impossible; thou art no sister of ours." But she proves her sisterhood; her typhus fever kills *them*: they actually were her brothers, though denying it! Had human creature ever to go lower for a proof?[2]

---

[1] F. S. C. Northrop, *The Meeting of East and West* (New York: The Macmillan Co., 1946), p. 43.

[2] *Past and Present*, Bk. III, ch. ii.

4 And the king of Egypt said unto them, Wherefore do ye, Moses and Aaron, let the people from their works? get you unto your burdens.

5 And Pharaoh said, Behold, the people of the land now *are* many, and ye make them rest from their burdens.

6 And Pharaoh commanded the same day the taskmasters of the people, and their officers, saying,

7 Ye shall no more give the people straw to make brick, as heretofore: let them go and gather straw for themselves.

8 And the tale of the bricks, which they did make heretofore, ye shall lay upon them; ye shall not diminish *aught* thereof: for they *be* idle; therefore they cry, saying, Let us go *and* sacrifice to our God.

9 Let there more work be laid upon the men, that they may labor therein; and let them not regard vain words.

with pestilence or with the sword." 4 But the king of Egypt said to them, "Moses and Aaron, why do you take the people away from their work? Get to your burdens." 5 And Pharaoh said, "Behold, the people of the land are now many and you make them rest from their burdens!" 6 The same day Pharaoh commanded the taskmasters of the people and their foremen, 7 "You shall no longer give the people straw to make bricks, as heretofore; let them go and gather straw for themselves. 8 But the number of bricks which they made heretofore you shall lay upon them, you shall by no means lessen it; for they are idle; therefore they cry, 'Let us go and offer sacrifice to our God.' 9 Let heavier work be laid upon the men that they may labor at it and pay no regard to lying words."

4. Pharaoh has disposed of Yahweh; now, as despot, he turns to Yahweh's spokesmen. He assumes they are slaves who have left their work and tells them, **Get to your burdens.** In Egypt under the Ramessides it was normal practice for slaves with complaints to appeal directly to the court, by-passing the intricate system of *corvée* superintendents. The records show that occasionally, under threat of strikes, the complaints were met in part. But here the king is adamant. He treats Israel's spokesmen as agitators without a cause or a following. He implies that Moses and Aaron were charged with causing the people to refrain from work.

5. In J's account Pharaoh's response is similar. The **people of the land** are the Hebrews (cf. 1:7). Instead of **are now many,** Meek (Amer. Trans.) has "are lazy as it is." This reading demands a slight textual emendation but seems more to the point, especially in view of vss. 8, 17.

b) PHARAOH RETALIATES (5:6-14)

6-9. This is a specific instance of a general policy (1:8-14). Pharaoh will stop the agitation by breaking the spirit of the slaves. If they are utterly exhausted they will **pay no regard to lying words.** He orders the taskmasters and foremen to stop the provision of straw (*tebhen*) needed in making bricks.

4-5. *Those Common People!*—If the RSV reading is accepted (but see the Exeg.), the meaning apparently is that "there are already more of them than of the native population," which sounds as if it had been overheard today in the lounge of some exclusive men's or women's club. It is an agelong problem that "the right people" do not have the largest families. Boston of the later nineteenth century, shocked at the growth of the Irish immigrants; Germans of the 1930's, horrified at the brains and prosperity of the Jews in their midst; the South, alarmed at the number of Negro children—they all used the same words Pharaoh used.

They all longed for Pharaoh's power to deal with the situation with a high hand.

6-9. *Let Them Get to Work.*—Pharaoh's first remedy for the situation was to give the Hebrews longer hours and harder labor (see Exeg. on the gathering of stubble). One of the modern arguments against an eight-hour day was that if the workers had more leisure they would have time to think up dangerous thoughts. Give them more work to do, and at the end of the day they will be too tired to think of organizing and making trouble: this is the logic of the Pharaohs of all times. In the mills of Lowell, Massachusetts, in 1845, the average length of the working

10 ¶ And the taskmasters of the people went out, and their officers, and they spake to the people, saying, Thus saith Pharaoh, I will not give you straw.

11 Go ye, get you straw where ye can find it: yet not aught of your work shall be diminished.

12 So the people were scattered abroad throughout all the land of Egypt to gather stubble instead of straw.

13 And the taskmasters hasted *them,* saying, Fulfil your works, *your* daily tasks, as when there was straw.

14 And the officers of the children of Israel, which Pharaoh's taskmasters had set over them, were beaten, *and* demanded, Wherefore have ye not fulfilled your task in making brick both yesterday and to-day, as heretofore?

15 ¶ Then the officers of the children of Israel came and cried unto Pharaoh, saying, Wherefore dealest thou thus with thy servants?

16 There is no straw given unto thy servants, and they say to us, Make brick: and, behold, thy servants *are* beaten; but the fault *is* in thine own people.

10 So the taskmasters and the foremen of the people went out and said to the people, "Thus says Pharaoh, 'I will not give you straw. 11 Go yourselves, get your straw wherever you can find it; but your work will not be lessened in the least.' " 12 So the people were scattered abroad throughout all the land of Egypt, to gather stubble for straw. 13 The taskmasters were urgent, saying, "Complete your work, your daily task, as when there was straw." 14 And the foremen of the people of Israel, whom Pharaoh's taskmasters had set over them, were beaten, and were asked, "Why have you not done all your task of making bricks today, as hitherto?"

15 Then the foremen of the people of Israel came and cried to Pharaoh, "Why do you deal thus with your servants? 16 No straw is given to your servants, yet they say to us, 'Make bricks!' And behold, your servants are beaten; but the fault is in your

10-14. The officers implement the order. The slaves had to go into the fields to gather stubble (*qash*) for straw (*tebhen*). *Tebhen* consisted of that portion of the cut grain which remained after threshing; *qash* in this case seems to refer to the uncut stubble left on the root in the field. *Qash* was sometimes used for fuel. To make it serve the purpose of *tebhen* in brickmaking the slaves not only had to cut it in the fields but perhaps crush it as well, for *qash* was much coarser than *tebhen*. Nevertheless, the same tally of bricks was demanded. When it was not forthcoming the Egyptian taskmasters beat the Hebrew foremen. These foremen anticipate the trying role of the Jewish representatives or taxgatherers who in later ages were responsible to all sorts of hostile and nefarious foreign rulers.

c) THE FOREMEN APPEAL TO PHARAOH (5:15-21)

15-16. The slaves and their foremen assumed that even slaves have certain rights. Thinking that the impossible order was the word of some capricious underling, and trusting in responsible communication, they appeal to the king. They report the beating and point to the unreasonableness of the demand that led to it.

day varied from eleven hours and twenty-four minutes in January and December to thirteen hours and thirty-one minutes in April; when "agitators" protested, the committee appointed by the state government reported that they were "fully satisfied" that things "could not be improved by any suggestion of theirs, or by any act of the legislature." The *New York Journal of Commerce* added that "to work only ten

hours in summer and eight in winter is to waste life." [3]

5:10–6:1. *When Trust in God Seems Disappointed.*—Moses has no answer for the enraged foremen of the Hebrew slaves. What must have

[3] Arthur M. Schlesinger, Jr., *The Age of Jackson* (Boston: Little, Brown & Co., 1945), pp. 271 ff. gives the story of the struggle at that time in American life between the god of property and the Son of man.

17 But he said, Ye *are* idle, *ye are* idle: therefore ye say, Let us go *and* do sacrifice to the Lord.

18 Go therefore now, *and* work; for there shall no straw be given you, yet shall ye deliver the tale of bricks.

19 And the officers of the children of Israel did see *that* they *were* in evil *case,* after it was said, Ye shall not minish *aught* from your bricks of your daily task.

20 ¶ And they met Moses and Aaron, who stood in the way, as they came forth from Pharaoh:

21 And they said unto them, The Lord look upon you, and judge; because ye have made our savor to be abhorred in the eyes of Pharaoh, and in the eyes of his servants, to put a sword in their hand to slay us.

22 And Moses returned unto the Lord, and said, Lord, wherefore hast thou *so* evil entreated this people? why *is* it *that* thou hast sent me?

23 For since I came to Pharaoh to speak in thy name, he hath done evil to this people; neither hast thou delivered thy people at all.

own people." 17 But he said, "You are idle, you are idle; therefore you say, 'Let us go and sacrifice to the Lord.' 18 Go now, and work; for no straw shall be given you, yet you shall deliver the same number of bricks." 19 The foremen of the people of Israel saw that they were in evil plight, when they said, "You shall by no means lessen your daily number of bricks." 20 They met Moses and Aaron, who were waiting for them, as they came forth from Pharaoh; 21 and they said to them, "The Lord look upon you and judge, because you have made us offensive in the sight of Pharaoh and his servants, and have put a sword in their hand to kill us."

22 Then Moses turned again to the Lord and said, "O Lord, why hast thou done evil to this people? Why didst thou ever send me? 23 For since I came to Pharaoh to speak in thy name, he has done evil to this people, and thou hast not delivered thy people at

---

17, 19. But now they learn that the Pharaoh himself is capricious. Here is the insecure despot, the idol with feet of clay, who is haunted by the neurotic fear that despite all his efforts his slaves may break loose. He cannot weigh this complaint. His mind is obsessed by the need of maintaining his security. So he yells at the foreman, **You are idle, you are idle** ("You are lazy" Amer. Trans.; cf. vs. 5) and repeats the order which is the cause of the complaint. The foremen see that they are in evil plight. They would have to report the failure of the appeal to their fellow slaves. What is more, the impossible order was a sign of complete helplessness. The last shred of dignity, security, and hope was gone. Life had lost its meaning.

20-21. Moses and Aaron were interested in the outcome of the appeal. They may have helped to plan it. But now, in their fear and dismay, the foremen turn on the leaders.

d) The Surrender of Faith (5:22–6:1)

22. The foremen did not view the deprivation of their lost security as an aspect of the battle waged by God against Pharaoh on their behalf. Moses did believe this was all

---

been his feelings when he found how hard a task it was that Yahweh had given him! The people thought that he had just made things worse by his interference. He feels his outraged prayer to Yahweh is well justified. But Yahweh is not annoyed with him. He knows how difficult it is for his servant. His answer to the prayer is **Now shalt thou see what I will do.** It is cold comfort for us all when this is the answer to our prayers. As the Prayer Book version of Ps. 27:14 says, we have to "tarry . . . the Lord's leisure."

When we pray, we generally want quick action, but the mills of God grind slowly. Trollope humorously says:

Those who offend us are generally punished for the offence they give; but we so frequently miss the satisfaction of knowing that we are avenged! It is arranged, apparently, that the injurer shall be punished, but that the person injured shall not gratify his desire for vengeance.[4]

4 *The Small House at Allington,* ch. 1.

6 Then the LORD said unto Moses, Now shalt thou see what I will do to Pharaoh: for with a strong hand shall he let them go, and with a strong hand shall he drive them out of his land.

2 And God spake unto Moses, and said unto him, I *am* the LORD:

3 And I appeared unto Abraham, unto Isaac, and unto Jacob, by *the name of* God Almighty; but by my name JEHOVAH was I not known to them.

6 all." [1] But the LORD said to Moses, "Now you shall see what I will do to Pharaoh; for with a strong hand he will send them out, yea, with a strong hand he will drive them out of his land."

2 And God said to Moses, "I am the LORD. [3] I appeared to Abraham, to Isaac, and to Jacob, as God Almighty,[h] but by my name the LORD I did not make myself

[h] Heb El Shaddai

a part of the Lord's purpose, but he could not understand it. He had still to learn that if his people were to be the possession of the Lord rather than of Pharaoh, there must be a complete end to Pharaoh as a resource for them. Moses was discovering that if his people were to be delivered by God, they could have only God as a resource. The unreasonableness of Pharaoh furthers this discovery.

6:1. Yahweh teaches Moses that this defeat of the delegation of foremen is actually the beginning of God's victory over Pharaoh and of a security for Israel in which there is no caprice.

C. THE P ACCOUNT OF THE CALL AND COMMISSION OF MOSES (6:2–7:13)

The priestly editors supplement the story of the call and commission of Moses (3:1–6:1) by means of a brief parallel account of their own. In it they include only those episodes of the larger cycle which from their viewpoint need further clarification and comment and make them conform to the convictions or serve the purposes that are their own. The P account must be compared to the preceding one to learn that, despite radical alterations in concern and emphasis, these editors lived by the same faith as the people whose work they supplemented. The account assumes that God appeared to Moses in Egypt, not at Sinai. Therefore it is inserted at the point at which Moses had already returned to Egypt and introduced himself to the people and to the Pharaoh.

1. GOD DISCLOSES HIS PLAN (6:2-9)

2-3. God said to Moses: There is no hint of a vision (cf. 3:1-6). For P, God does not "come down" as in the older stories. God tends more and more to be separated from the realm of history and human life. But on occasion men do still hear his voice.

This is but one very human instance of our frustration in not being able to get God to act just as we would like to have him do. He says, **Now shalt thou see what I will do.** In the end things will be made clear; now we must go on and trust him. Religion consists in trusting God after we have come to the outermost bound of our human effort. There is no use praying till we have done our utmost for the end we desire. The airplane does not start from the spot where we idly sit on our doorstep; we must, by our own effort, get out of the city of circumstance to the place where the plane starts. Then we are justified in trusting to the air of the heavens. Moses had done his best, and was discouraged by the results, but it was his best; God said that there might seem to him to be needless delay, but he had only to trust God to operate when

the best time should come. As John Flavel said, "Man's extremity is God's opportunity." The proof of such a religious truth as this is not a talking theory, but a silent practice. "For sharp or acute searching alone doth it not; but to will and do well." [5]

6:2–7:7. See Expos. on 2:23b–4:17, 20b, 27-31; 6:2–7:7.

2-13. *God of the Covenant.*—This section is the work of the writer whom we call P. It is much later than the other accounts of the call of Moses. P is inclined to omit the elements of folklore in the stories, and tries to write world history at least as far as underlying principles go. As in the case of the ancient historians of Greece, we see in Exodus the technique of giving two or three accounts of the same episode,

[5] Jacob Boehme, *Epistles*: To C. B., Sept. 12, 1620.

4 And I have also established my covenant with them, to give them the land of Canaan, the land of their pilgrimage, wherein they were strangers.

5 And I have also heard the groaning of the children of Israel, whom the Egyptians keep in bondage; and I have remembered my covenant.

6 Wherefore say unto the children of Israel, I *am* the LORD, and I will bring you out from under the burdens of the Egyptians, and I will rid you out of their bondage, and I will redeem you with a stretched out arm, and with great judgments:

known to them. 4 I also established my covenant with them, to give them the land of Canaan, the land in which they dwelt as sojourners. 5 Moreover I have heard the groaning of the people of Israel whom the Egyptians hold in bondage and I have remembered my covenant. 6 Say therefore to the people of Israel, 'I am the LORD, and I will bring you out from under the burdens of the Egyptians, and I will deliver you from their bondage, and I will redeem you with an outstretched arm and with great

I am the LORD: Thus God begins his revelation. As E implies (3:15), P says explicitly that the patriarchs had not known this name. Their specific name for God, he adds, was **El Shaddai** (RSV mg.). This name was an archaic title in P's day. Job uses it thirty-one times (5:17; etc.). Its meaning was no longer very specific; probably the word **Almighty** well represents what it did mean in this later era. The word seems to derive from the root *shādhēdh,* which signifies power expressing itself in destructive violence. This may be reflected in Joel 1:15. In Deut. 32:17 the term refers to foreign gods or demons.

4-8. The phrase **my covenant** is characteristic of the entire later period (Gen. 17:2, 4, 7, 10; Lev. 26:9, 15, 42, 44; Mal. 2:4-5). Sometimes it refers to the law of Sinai (Lev. 26:15), but here and elsewhere it signifies the promise made to Abraham. The late period makes this covenant much more prominent than it was in the days of the prophets, treating it as a warrant for the Exodus and the possession of Canaan. For the P writers,

as if to say that the reader must decide how to harmonize the details (Herodotus does the same) and attempt to get a framework of meaning around the incidents related. Thus P seems to divide ancient history into epochs, each characterized by a special covenant and a new name for God. Each time there is a special ritual sign which seals the covenant forever. He thinks of four eras: from Adam to Noah; from Noah to Abraham; from Abraham to Moses; from Moses to the end of the world. Noah's sign is the rainbow; Abraham's is circumcision; Moses' is the sabbath. For Adam the name is God; for Abraham, El Shaddai; for Moses, Yahweh. This early attempt to begin the writing of world history can best be appreciated when P discards the old idea that different names always mean different gods, and asserts that the same God revealed himself at different times by different names; he also feels deeply the relationship between land, race, and religion.

The sign of the rainbow in the sky over the Promised Land, the sign in the flesh of the chosen people, the weekly sign of sabbath rest and worship of the true religion—these signs are constant reminders to the deity of his merciful engagements. With P, a covenant is a gracious act on the part of God, by which he binds himself to keep his part of a common agreement. The history of a nation is not an accidental growth, but the realization of the plans of a higher will.

The idea of a "chosen people" with a "promised land" and "special covenant" has been the source of much good and much evil in history. In the mid-twentieth century we have come to a point where the bad results of this belief seem to outweigh the good. It has proved to be one cause of the unpopularity of the Jews among the nations; it has been reduced to absurdity by Kipling's "White Man's Burden," and to unspeakable horror by the Nazi doctrine of the hierarchy of races, one a master race, the others slave peoples; even in democratic nations it appears in the tendency to act as missionaries to, rather than as brothers of, other peoples.

The good in the idea can be savored only by those who believe also that *every* nation has its own covenant, and is God's chosen people, and shares in a true religion; and that the differing contributions of all nations go to make up the ultimate discovery of that which is true for all.

4. Participation in the Covenant.—The master word in whose understanding alone many diffi-

7 And I will take you to me for a people, and I will be to you a God: and ye shall know that I *am* the LORD your God, which bringeth you out from under the burdens of the Egyptians.

8 And I will bring you in unto the land, concerning the which I did swear to give it to Abraham, to Isaac, and to Jacob; and I will give it you for a heritage: I *am* the LORD.

9 ¶ And Moses spake so unto the children of Israel: but they hearkened not unto Moses for anguish of spirit, and for cruel bondage.

10 And the LORD spake unto Moses, saying,

11 Go in, speak unto Pharaoh king of Egypt, that he let the children of Israel go out of his land.

12 And Moses spake before the LORD, saying, Behold, the children of Israel have not hearkened unto me; how then shall Pharaoh hear me, who *am* of uncircumcised lips?

13 And the LORD spake unto Moses and unto Aaron, and gave them a charge unto the children of Israel, and unto Pharaoh king of Egypt, to bring the children of Israel out of the land of Egypt.

acts of judgment, 7 and I will take you for my people, and I will be your God; and you shall know that I am the LORD your God, who has brought you out from under the burdens of the Egyptians. 8 And I will bring you into the land which I swore to give to Abraham, to Isaac, and to Jacob; I will give it to you for a possession. I am the LORD.' " 9 Moses spoke thus to the people of Israel; but they did not listen to Moses, because of their broken spirit and their cruel bondage.

10 And the LORD said to Moses, 11 "Go in, tell Pharaoh king of Egypt to let the people of Israel go out of his land." 12 But Moses said to the LORD, "Behold, the people of Israel have not listened to me; how then shall Pharaoh listen to me, who am a man of uncircumcised lips?" 13 But the LORD spoke to Moses and Aaron, and gave them a charge to the people of Israel and to Pharaoh king of Egypt to bring the people of Israel out of the land of Egypt.

people, country, and faith are bound up together. God had "lifted up his hand" as a sign of an oath that Israel would possess Canaan.

9. In contrast to the earlier accounts (3:18; 4:31) the people **did not listen to Moses** when he came to them. P uses this as a device to introduce the leader's doubts and fears.

2. THE INADEQUACY OF MOSES (6:10-13, 28-30)

10-13, 28-30. The purpose of this jumbled section is to prepare the way for the selection of Aaron as the partner of Moses (7:1-7). Vss. 10-12 are substantially repeated in vss. 28-30. Moses, not having been welcomed by the slaves (vs. 9), tells God that he lacks the necessary fluency for the assignment. In the earlier account of this objection (4:10-16) God spoke of the adequacy for his purposes of men whom he himself has created. The theocentric emphasis of JE does not interest P, who prefers to stress the indispensability of Aaron. In vs. 13 this appointment is already assumed. That verse is really a summary of 7:1-7. In an earlier form of the text it probably preceded immediately 7:1. After the insertion of the new genealogy, vss. 28-30 were added to remind the reader of what had gone before. Unfortunately vs. 13, preceding the genealogy, had actually carried the story farther than the addition does.

cult antinomies find their solution is the word "participation." Authority and freedom, revelation and reason, God and man—all are through this conception understood and reconciled. Authority is rational in which both sides, the ruler and the ruled, participate. Revelation is a

priceless gift when it becomes real by the participation of reason, as commentary, interpreter, and infusing spirit, rather than as an antagonistic substitute. In the Incarnation God participates in man, man in God, precluding the oppressive idea of a totalitarian deity. The spir-

14 ¶ These *be* the heads of their fathers' houses: The sons of Reuben the firstborn of Israel; Hanoch, and Pallu, Hezron, and Carmi: these *be* the families of Reuben.

15 And the sons of Simeon; Jemuel, and Jamin, and Ohad, and Jachin, and Zohar, and Shaul the son of a Canaanitish woman: these *are* the families of Simeon.

16 ¶ And these *are* the names of the sons of Levi according to their generations; Gershon, and Kohath, and Merari: and the years of the life of Levi *were* a hundred thirty and seven years.

17 The sons of Gershon; Libni, and Shimi, according to their families.

18 And the sons of Kohath; Amram, and Izhar, and Hebron, and Uzziel: and the years of the life of Kohath *were* a hundred thirty and three years.

19 And the sons of Merari; Mahali and Mushi: these *are* the families of Levi according to their generations.

20 And Amram took him Jochebed his father's sister to wife; and she bare him Aaron and Moses: and the years of the life of Amram *were* a hundred and thirty and seven years.

21 ¶ And the sons of Izhar; Korah, and Nepheg, and Zichri.

14 These are the heads of their fathers' houses: the sons of Reuben, the first-born of Israel: Hanoch, Pallu, Hezron and Carmi; these are the families of Reuben. 15 The sons of Simeon: Jemu'el, Jamin, Ohad, Jachin, Zohar, and Shaul, the son of a Canaanite woman; these are the families of Simeon. 16 These are the names of the sons of Levi according to their generations: Gershon, Kohath, and Merar'i, the years of the life of Levi being a hundred and thirty-seven years. 17 The sons of Gershon: Libni and Shimei, by their families. 18 The sons of Kohath: Amram, Izhar, Hebron and Uzzi'el, the years of the life of Kohath being a hundred and thirty-three years. 19 The sons of Merar'i: Mahli and Mushi. These are the families of the Levites according to their generations. 20 Amram took to wife Joch'ebed his father's sister and she bore him Aaron and Moses, the years of the life of Amram being one hundred and thirty-seven years. 21 The sons of Izhar: Korah,

---

3. The Genealogy of Aaron and Moses (6:14-27)

14-16. The genealogy begins with the three oldest sons of Jacob: Reuben, Simeon, and Levi. It lists the names of the sons of each. Thus far it duplicates the genealogy of all the sons of Israel in Gen. 46:9-27.

17-27. But its real concern is with the priestly tribe of Levi. Of the three sons of Levi, Kohath is the bearer of the line. Two of Kohath's sons are considered significant: Izhar, who becomes the father of Korah; and Amram, who becomes the father of Aaron and Moses. Through Aaron the line carries to Eleazar, and through him to Phinehas. In Num. 3 the same pattern is elaborated to show the role of various branches of the family

---

itual religion of the O.T. is an eternal **covenant** between God and man (see the words of Runeberg quoted in Expos on 3:14).

14-27. Priestly Pedigrees.—These lists of clans or families have been compiled from various sources with omissions and additions (see Num. 3:17-20; 26:59). Any attempt to harmonize the lists and ages with other information in the Bible is beset with many difficulties (see Ruth 4:18-20; I Chr. 2:4-10; etc.). The ages given for Moses, Aaron, and others have probably symbolic meaning rather than literal truth. Some have seen a connection with the forty years' wandering in the wilderness. It should be noted that his priestly friends have made Aaron this

time the first-born (7:7), contradicting 2:1-2. At the same time, no reference is made to the family of Moses, while full information is given about the wives and children of Aaron and Eleazar. Every royal or priestly hereditary line has to see to it that history backs up its claims to a clear pedigree. It is best to make no mention of rival families (see Exeg.).

The ages given for the various characters in the O.T. have resulted in much curious speculation, and much sacred mathematics for the purpose of proving the theories of inspiration fashionable in the day. *The Great Historical, Geographical, Genealogical and Poetical Dictionary,* published in London in 1694, seeks to

22 And the sons of Uzziel; Mishael, and Elzaphan, and Zithri.

23 And Aaron took him Elisheba, daughter of Amminadab, sister of Naashon, to wife; and she bare him Nadab and Abihu, Eleazar and Ithamar.

24 And the sons of Korah; Assir, and Elkanah, and Abiasaph: these *are* the families of the Korhites.

25 And Eleazar Aaron's son took him *one* of the daughters of Putiel to wife; and she bare him Phinehas: these *are* the heads of the fathers of the Levites according to their families.

26 These *are* that Aaron and Moses, to whom the LORD said, Bring out the children of Israel from the land of Egypt according to their armies.

27 These *are* they which spake to Pharaoh king of Egypt, to bring out the children of Israel from Egypt: these *are* that Moses and Aaron.

28 ¶ And it came to pass on the day *when* the LORD spake unto Moses in the land of Egypt,

Nepheg, and Zichri. 22 And the sons of Uzzi'el: Mi'sha-el, Elza'phan, and Sithri. 23 Aaron took to wife Eli'sheba, the daughter of Ammin'adab and the sister of Nahshon; and she bore him Nadab, Abi'hu, Elea'zar and Ith'amar. 24 The sons of Korah: Assir, Elka'nah, and Abi'asaph; these are the families of the Korahites. 25 Elea'zar, Aaron's son, took to wife one of the daughters of Pu'ti-el; and she bore him Phin'ehas. These are the heads of the fathers' houses of the Levites by their families.

26 These are the Aaron and Moses to whom the LORD said: "Bring out the people of Israel from the land of Egypt by their hosts." 27 It was they who spoke to Pharaoh king of Egypt about bringing out the people of Israel from Egypt, this Moses and this Aaron.

28 On the day when the LORD spoke to

---

in the service of the tabernacle. Aaron and Moses are four generations removed from Jacob. It is significant that the line does not carry on through Moses but through Aaron. The genealogist is concerned to show that the priest has played an active role in the founding of the nation; his list symbolizes the legitimacy and authority of the priesthood in his own day. Moses is the prophet by whom God spoke in the foundation of the nation, and who instructed the priests. But he has no extant continuation. The priests build on the foundation he laid long ago. The genealogy reflects the spirit of the postexilic period in conceptions of order and authority. Without attacking the priority of Moses it asserts the present priority of Aaron, the first-born of Amram.

28-30. See Exeg. on vss. 10-13, 28-30, p. 890.

---

show that Moses might have had word-of-mouth reports of the creation of the world. It says:

Here I add a curious observation concerning the manner how Moses could easily and certainly know the history from the creation of the world, by the help of eight persons only . . . : Adam, Methuselah, Sem, . . . Abraham, Isaac, Jacob, Levi . . . and Amram. [Moses] might know from [his father Amram] what he had learned from Levi, and so on to Adam.[6]

The book is written by "several learned men," and the man who writes this article goes on to show by computation of ages how this is possible. But even these calculations leave it a mystery how Adam could have been an eyewit-

ness of the happenings of the first five days before he himself was created.

26-27. *And Their Climax.*—W. H. Bennett says, "These verses explain the object of the preceding genealogy. We might paraphrase, 'Please observe that the preceding section gives the family history of Aaron and Moses, the deliverers of Israel.' "[7] But (see Num. 26:9) someone with a historical conscience has added a note or correction at the end of vs. 27, in order to restore Moses to his proper pre-eminence. One can still feel the satisfaction with which he added this "last word."

6:28–7:13. *The Miraculous: Material or Moral?*—The only unanswerable and omnipo-

[6] Article, "Moses."

[7] *Exodus* (Edinburgh: T. C. & E. C. Jack, n.d.; "The Century Bible"), p. 78.

29 That the LORD spake unto Moses, saying, I *am* the LORD: speak thou unto Pharaoh king of Egypt all that I say unto thee.

30 And Moses said before the LORD, Behold, I *am* of uncircumcised lips, and how shall Pharaoh hearken unto me?

7 And the LORD said unto Moses, See, I have made thee a god to Pharaoh; and Aaron thy brother shall be thy prophet.

2 Thou shalt speak all that I command thee; and Aaron thy brother shall speak unto Pharaoh, that he send the children of Israel out of his land.

3 And I will harden Pharaoh's heart, and multiply my signs and my wonders in the land of Egypt.

4 But Pharaoh shall not hearken unto you, that I may lay my hand upon Egypt, and bring forth mine armies, *and* my people the children of Israel, out of the land of Egypt by great judgments.

Moses in the land of Egypt, 29 the LORD said to Moses, "I am the LORD; tell Pharaoh king of Egypt all that I say to you." 30 But Moses said to the LORD, "Behold, I am of uncircumcised lips; how then shall Pharaoh listen to me?" 7 And the LORD said to Moses, "See, I make you as God to Pharaoh; and Aaron your brother shall be your prophet. 2 You shall speak all that I command you; and Aaron your brother shall tell Pharaoh to let the people of Israel go out of his land. 3 But I will harden Pharaoh's heart, and though I multiply my signs and wonders in the land of Egypt, 4 Pharaoh will not listen to you; then I will lay my hand upon Egypt and bring forth my hosts, my people the sons of Israel, out of the land of Egypt by great acts of judg-

4. THE APPOINTMENT OF AARON (7:1-7)

7:1. Moses is to be **as God to Pharaoh.** In 4:16 he had a role such as this in relation to Aaron, meaning that he would give to Aaron the words to speak. The implication here probably is that in the struggle with Pharaoh Moses will possess the authority of God but will not himself speak. A prophet is one who expresses the will of God in words; he is God's spokesman.

2. In 4:16 Aaron was to be the spokesman of Moses to the people. Both Moses and Aaron were to address Pharaoh (5:1). Here Aaron is made sole spokesman.

3-5. Pharaoh's stubbornness is again anticipated (3:19; 4:21). The point of it is indicated in vs. 5, **The Egyptians shall know that I am the LORD** (cf. Exeg. on 4:21). The defeat of Pharaoh would constitute the defeat of the gods of Egypt for he was their executive embodiment. The terms **signs** (אות) and **wonders** (מופת) are synonymous here. Both refer to the special display of God's power, detailed in the plagues, which will attend the deliverance and manifest God's concern for Israel. In addition to this, a sign

tent miracle that the forces of righteousness can use effectively against evil is goodness itself. Complete reasonableness and honesty mystify philosophers and politicians alike. Evil can produce by its enchantments a reasonable facsimile of everything. Even when Moses did something (as in 8:18) which was not in their bag of tricks, the magicians were unable to convince Pharaoh that it was the finger of God. He saw that it was just the same kind of thing as had been done before, and that it could be matched by his own men, given a little more time. Jannes and Jambres (II Tim. 3:8) shall proceed no further when it comes to resisting the truth. Even at their own game Aaron was brighter than they were, and **Aaron's rod swallowed up their rods,** which, while it did not seem to prove anything,

was highly satisfactory, as Pharaoh saw. There are all kinds of minor virtues and skills which have no high moral validity, yet are of immense value in convincing ordinary people that the prophet is a "regular fellow." Holy Cross and Notre Dame are chiefly known to the American public as football teams—a far cry from the original meaning of their names; but this very fact disabuses the mind of the public of the idea that there is something unnatural and otherworldly about all religious folk. The athletic minister who plays good baseball with his boys and beats all the old golfing reprobates of his town on the links has a more responsive audience when he speaks out on religion or righteousness than has the old mufffered bookworm who shuffles over the parish in galoshes; yet the latter

5 And the Egyptians shall know that I *am* the LORD, when I stretch forth mine hand upon Egypt, and bring out the children of Israel from among them.

6 And Moses and Aaron did as the LORD commanded them, so did they.

7 And Moses *was* fourscore years old, and Aaron fourscore and three years old, when they spake unto Pharaoh.

8 ¶ And the LORD spake unto Moses and unto Aaron, saying,

9 When Pharaoh shall speak unto you, saying, Show a miracle for you: then thou shalt say unto Aaron, Take thy rod, and cast *it* before Pharaoh, *and* it shall become a serpent.

10 ¶ And Moses and Aaron went in unto Pharaoh, and they did so as the LORD had commanded: and Aaron cast down his rod before Pharaoh, and before his servants, and it became a serpent.

11 Then Pharaoh also called the wise men and the sorcerers: now the magicians of Egypt, they also did in like manner with their enchantments.

12 For they cast down every man his rod, and they became serpents: but Aaron's rod swallowed up their rods.

13 And he hardened Pharaoh's heart, that he hearkened not unto them; as the LORD had said.

ment. 5 And the Egyptians shall know that I am the LORD, when I stretch forth mv hand upon Egypt and bring out the people of Israel from among them." 6 And Moses and Aaron did so; they did as the LORD commanded them. 7 Now Moses was eighty years old, and Aaron eighty-three years old, when they spoke to Pharaoh.

8 And the LORD said to Moses and Aaron, 9 "When Pharaoh says to you, 'Prove yourselves by working a miracle,' then you shall say to Aaron, 'Take your rod and cast it down before Pharaoh, that it may become a serpent.' " 10 So Moses and Aaron went to Pharaoh and did as the LORD commanded; Aaron cast down his rod before Pharaoh and his servants, and it became a serpent. 11 Then Pharaoh summoned the wise men and the sorcerers; and they also, the magicians of Egypt, did the same by their secret arts. 12 For every man cast down his rod, and they became serpents. But Aaron's rod swallowed up their rods. 13 Still Pharaoh's heart was hardened, and he would not listen to them; as the LORD had said.

---

may be a token such as the rainbow (Gen. 9:12-13), circumcision (Gen. 17:11), or a pledge (3:12). The last of these is synonymous with the predictive element sometimes carried by wonders (I Kings 13:3, 5; Isa. 20:3). The **great acts of judgment** are the **signs and wonders** just mentioned. In Israel's deliverance it is not so much Yahweh's moral character as his power and dominion that will be vindicated.

7. Moses' life was divided into three equal periods of forty years each (Deut. 34:7; cf. Acts 7:23). The third period of his life corresponds to the forty years Israel spent in the wilderness, the tradition of which reaches back at least into the eighth century (Amos 2:10).

5. THE EQUIPMENT OF MOSES AND AARON (7:8-13)

8. In P God commissions both Moses and Aaron and equips them with magic powers (cf. 3:11–4:9). These powers are not to be displayed before the people (4:1, 30-31), but before Pharaoh.

9. The rod now is Aaron's, but he will use it when Moses commands. When Aaron casts it "upon the earth" (LXX), it becomes a **serpent**. The serpent (*tannîn*) is a dragon or primeval monster. In 4:3 another Hebrew word (*nāḥāsh*) is used. That word may also designate a monster (Amos 9:3) but commonly refers to a mere snake. The element of wonder has grown.

10-13. Before Pharaoh, Moses and Aaron carry out the command. But the **magicians of Egypt**—i.e., the custodians of the powers of the Egyptian gods—match the demonstration. Every man's rod becomes a dragon! However, Aaron's dragon devours all the other

14 ¶ And the LORD said unto Moses, Pharaoh's heart *is* hardened, he refuseth to let the people go.

14 Then the LORD said to Moses, "Pharaoh's heart is hardened, he refuses to let

---

dragons, just as Yahweh will vanquish all the foreign powers and gods. Here a fanciful imagination has produced an illustration for a very genuine faith in the sovereignty of Israel's God. The Pharaoh remains obdurate as anticipated (vs. 3). The small measure of the divine power Moses and Aaron possess is inadequate. God remains the chief actor in the drama.

III. GOD REVEALS HIS POWER (7:14–18:27)

The first act in the drama of Israel's deliverance has indicated the issue and dimensions of the conflict. Yahweh and Pharaoh, as chief protagonists, prepared for the real contest of strength to come. Obsessed by fear (5:15-21), Pharaoh discarded all reasonableness in pursuing his policy of oppression and extermination designed to keep Israel in his power. In the birth of Moses, with his peculiar natural gifts, and in his religious vocation and commission as the divine instrument in redemption, Yahweh prepared for Israel's deliverance.

Now in a new act the decisive disclosure of power begins. It becomes clear again that whatever Israel's fears or Pharaoh's hopes, from God's point of view the outcome is never in doubt; this is a divine comedy, not a tragedy. In the account of the plagues we see Yahweh take the initiative and, with dramatic suspense, ever more intensely display his might and press his advantage. The situation of the Pharaoh, cornered by a god he did not know (5:1-5), becomes ever more grim. P illustrates this by means of the rout of the proud magicians; the other writers by noting that Pharaoh is willing to make ever greater concessions, even though in the nature of the case these can never be sufficient. This is a struggle between Pharaoh and Yahweh for the establishment of absolute lordship. In the death of the first-born, the institution of Passover, and the departure of the slaves, the furious action reaches its climax. Yahweh takes possession of Israel. Pharaoh is utterly unable to prevent him. Finally, in a desperate effort at a comeback, Pharaoh tries once more to repossess the Hebrew people. At the crossing of the sea, which is the border, Yahweh makes good his victory. Israel is free and knows its God is Lord, the only ruler, and the redeemer of enslaved humanity.

A. GOD MULTIPLIES SIGNS, WONDERS, AND PLAGUES (7:14–11:10)

For an analysis of the literary structure of this section and for an interpretation of the plagues as miracle see Intro., pp. 838-39.

1. THE POLLUTION OF THE NILE (7:14-25)

In its present form this account shows the hands of J, E, and P. According to J (vss. 14, 16, 17a, 18, 24-25) Yahweh killed the fish in the Nile and as a result the water became undrinkable. Pharaoh was relentless, even though the water famine set the Egyptians to dig water holes along the bank. According to E (vss. 15, 17b, 20b, 23[?]) Moses struck the Nile waters with his rod, changing them to blood. For P (vss. 19, 20a, 21b, 22)

---

may be the better man. Lincoln wore a muffler and Einstein is never seen on the tennis courts of Princeton. Still it is good to know a few things in life besides being good; wisdom needs familiarity with more than one realm of thought. God is interested in other things besides religion. Though a man's main interest in life may be the freeing of folk from slavery, it is good also to know something about such frivolities as are represented by Lincoln's stories.

It is a strange fact that piety without intellect or skill does not make a good preacher; but intellect and skill without piety sometimes seem to.[8]

7:14–12:30. *The Ten Plagues.*—The compiler had at his hand a number of different accounts of the plagues which he has combined into the narrative as it now stands (see Intro., pp. 838-

[8] See C. E. Montague, *Disenchantment* (New York: Brentano's, 1922), pp. 84-102.

15 Get thee unto Pharaoh in the morning; lo, he goeth out unto the water; and thou shalt stand by the river's brink against he come; and the rod which was turned to a serpent shalt thou take in thine hand.

16 And thou shalt say unto him, The LORD God of the Hebrews hath sent me unto thee, saying, Let my people go, that they may serve me in the wilderness: and, behold, hitherto thou wouldest not hear.

17 Thus saith the LORD, In this thou shalt know that I *am* the LORD: behold, I will smite with the rod that *is* in mine hand upon the waters which *are* in the river, and they shall be turned to blood.

18 And the fish that *is* in the river shall die, and the river shall stink; and the Egyptians shall loathe to drink of the water of the river.

19 ¶ And the LORD spake unto Moses, Say unto Aaron, Take thy rod, and stretch out thine hand upon the waters of Egypt, upon their streams, upon their rivers, and upon their ponds, and upon all their pools of water, that they may become blood; and *that* there may be blood throughout all the land of Egypt, both in *vessels of* wood, and in *vessels of* stone.

the people go. 15 Go to Pharaoh in the morning, as he is going out to the water; wait for him by the river's brink, and take in your hand the rod which was turned into a serpent. 16 And you shall say to him, 'The LORD, the God of the Hebrews, sent me to you, saying, "Let my people go, that they may serve me in the wilderness; and behold, you have not yet obeyed." 17 Thus says the LORD, "By this you shall know that I am the LORD: behold, I will strike the water that is in the Nile with the rod that is in my hand, and it shall be turned to blood, 18 and the fish in the Nile shall die, and the Nile shall become foul, and the Egyptians will loathe to drink water from the Nile." ' " 19 And the LORD said to Moses, "Say to Aaron, 'Take your rod and stretch out your hand over the waters of Egypt, over their rivers, their canals, and their ponds, and all their pools of water, that they may become blood; and there shall be blood throughout all the land of Egypt, both in vessels of wood and in vessels of stone.' "

Aaron did the wonder, and not only the water of the Nile but every bit of water in Egypt was changed to blood. Since the magicians also did the sign—with what water we are not told—Pharaoh **hardened** his heart.

14. This verse continues 6:1. For **hardened** J uses כבד while E and P use חזק. The Amer. Trans. preserves the distinction by translating the two words as "stubborn" and "obstinate" respectively.

15. The provision to meet Pharaoh at the Nile may reflect the fact that the river was worshiped as a deity and that the ruler personally officiated at the great festivals in its honor, notably at the annual inundation. In the presence of Pharaoh, Yahweh smites Egypt's god of life, the Nile.

16. Let my people go is J's formula. An earlier interview is presupposed by the phrase **not yet obeyed** (cf. 5:1-5).

17. As it stands, this verse leaves the impression that Yahweh would strike the river with the rod. J and E have been telescoped: for the former, God acts directly; for the latter, through Moses by means of the rod.

19. In P there are no interviews with Pharaoh.

---

39). For the curious student there are many interesting questions to be solved: Was all the water of a river 3,473 miles long turned into blood? What did Pharaoh and his servants in the palace do without water for seven days? Where did the magicians get the water to turn into blood, since all of it was already blood? It is stated that **all the cattle of Egypt died** (9:6), yet a little later (9:19) some seem to be alive!

But each story of the composite whole has more consistency, e.g., the plagues in J's story all cease naturally, the Egyptians dig around the Nile to find fresh water, the frogs die, the cattle also, the hailstorm ceases, the wind blows the flies and the locusts away.

While the compiler looks upon them as miraculous, there are analogies for them all in the known natural phenomena of Egypt. The words

20 And Moses and Aaron did so, as the LORD commanded; and he lifted up the rod, and smote the waters that *were* in the river, in the sight of Pharaoh, and in the sight of his servants; and all the waters that *were* in the river were turned to blood.

21 And the fish that *was* in the river died; and the river stank, and the Egyptians could not drink of the water of the river; and there was blood throughout all the land of Egypt.

22 And the magicians of Egypt did so with their enchantments: and Pharaoh's heart was hardened, neither did he hearken unto them; as the LORD had said.

23 And Pharaoh turned and went into his house, neither did he set his heart to this also.

24 And all the Egyptians digged round about the river for water to drink; for they could not drink of the water of the river.

25 And seven days were fulfilled, after that the LORD had smitten the river.

8 And the LORD spake unto Moses, Go unto Pharaoh, and say unto him, Thus saith the LORD, Let my people go, that they may serve me.

2 And if thou refuse to let *them* go, behold, I will smite all thy borders with frogs:

3 And the river shall bring forth frogs abundantly, which shall go up and come into thine house, and into thy bedchamber, and upon thy bed, and into the house of thy servants, and upon thy people, and into thine ovens, and into thy kneadingtroughs:

4 And the frogs shall come up both on thee, and upon thy people, and upon all thy servants.

20 Moses and Aaron did as the LORD commanded; in the sight of Pharaoh and in the sight of his servants, he lifted up the rod and struck the water that was in the Nile, and all the water that was in the Nile turned to blood. **21** And the fish in the Nile died; and the Nile became foul, so that the Egyptians could not drink water from the Nile; and there was blood throughout all the land of Egypt. **22** But the magicians of Egypt did the same by their secret arts; so Pharaoh's heart remained hardened, and he would not listen to them; as the LORD had said. **23** Pharaoh turned and went into his house, and he did not lay even this to heart. **24** And all the Egyptians dug round about the Nile for water to drink, for they could not drink the water of the Nile.

25 Seven days passed after the LORD had struck the Nile. **8** **1**ⁱ Then the LORD said to Moses, "Go in to Pharaoh and say to him, 'Thus says the LORD, "Let my people go, that they may serve me. **2** But if you refuse to let them go, behold, I will plague all your country with frogs; **3** the Nile shall swarm with frogs which shall come up into your house, and into your bedchamber and on your bed, and into the houses of your servants and of your people,ʲ and into your ovens and your kneading bowls; **4** the frogs shall come up on you and on your people and on all your servants." ' "

ⁱ Ch 7. 26 in Heb
ʲ Gk: Heb *upon your people*

---

20. The opening formula is P but the remainder is E. Only the Nile is changed to blood. Therefore he who **lifted up the rod** is Moses. The fact that the Nile takes on a reddish color at certain stages in its rise possibly lies at the basis of this story.

21b-22. For P the dramatic progress of Yahweh's battle is presented as a contest with the magicians.

24-25. The Egyptians themselves seek to make good the failure of their god.

2. FROGS (8:1-15 = Hebrew 7:26–8:11)

The characteristic demand formula, the manner of the plague's accomplishment as proposed by Yahweh, and the account of Moses' interview with Pharaoh, including the latter's request for Moses' prayer in his behalf, show that this account is mainly from J. But P has replaced J's account of the plague with his own characteristic version (vss. 5-7). The final conclusion is also a P formula (vs. 15b).

8:3-4. Yahweh tells Moses to warn Pharaoh that unless he surrenders **the Nile shall swarm with frogs.** The intimation seems to be that the Nile slime will spontaneously

5 ¶ And the LORD spake unto Moses, Say unto Aaron, Stretch forth thine hand with thy rod over the streams, over the rivers, and over the ponds, and cause frogs to come up upon the land of Egypt.

6 And Aaron stretched out his hand over the waters of Egypt; and the frogs came up, and covered the land of Egypt.

7 And the magicians did so with their enchantments, and brought up frogs upon the land of Egypt.

8 ¶ Then Pharaoh called for Moses and Aaron, and said, Entreat the LORD, that he may take away the frogs from me, and from my people; and I will let the people go, that they may do sacrifice unto the LORD.

9 And Moses said unto Pharaoh, Glory over me: when shall I entreat for thee, and for thy servants, and for thy people, to destroy the frogs from thee and thy houses, *that* they may remain in the river only?

10 And he said, To-morrow. And he said, *Be it* according to thy word; that thou mayest know that *there is* none like unto the LORD our God.

11 And the frogs shall depart from thee, and from thy houses, and from thy servants, and from thy people; they shall remain in the river only.

5ᵏ And the LORD said to Moses, "Say to Aaron, 'Stretch out your hand with your rod over the rivers, over the canals, and over the pools, and cause frogs to come upon the land of Egypt!' " 6 So Aaron stretched out his hand over the waters of Egypt; and the frogs came up and covered the land of Egypt. 7 But the magicians did the same by their secret arts, and brought frogs upon the land of Egypt.

8 Then Pharaoh called Moses and Aaron, and said, "Entreat the LORD to take away the frogs from me and from my people; and I will let the people go to sacrifice to the LORD." 9 Moses said to Pharaoh, "Be pleased to command me when I am to entreat, for you and for your servants and for your people, that the frogs be destroyed from you and your houses and be left only in the Nile." 10 And he said, "Tomorrow." Moses said, "Be it as you say, that you may know that there is no one like the LORD our God. 11 The frogs shall depart from you and your houses and your servants and your people;

ᵏ Ch 8. 1 in Heb

generate frogs. The belief that the river mud possesses this power persists until today and was widely accepted in the past (John A. Wilson in *Intellectual Adventure of Ancient Man*, pp. 50-51) .

5-7. For P, as in the first plague, every body of water in Egypt is affected. Aaron's rod causes the **frogs to come upon the land.** The magicians continue to match the power of Yahweh.

8. In asking Moses to **entreat the LORD,** Pharaoh recognizes him as the authentic spokesman of an actual deity. He no longer scorns Yahweh.

9-11. Moses asks Pharaoh to set the time for the prayer that will stop the scourge so that, at the disappearance of the frogs, Pharaoh will have another "sign" that **there is no one like the LORD our God.** Such concern for coincidence is common in the Bible (cf. Matt. 8:13; 15:28) .

"red water" are still used in Egypt of the waters of the Nile during the period of the year when the red soil of the Abyssinian mountains tinges it during its annual rise, and during July and August the presence of algae in the water tints it red. Plagues of frogs occur not infrequently in Egypt. Egypt, especially the Delta, suffers much (after the recession of the overflow of the Nile) from insects of all sorts. It has been called "The Eldorado of Flies." It is true that cattle in Egypt suffer less from epidemic diseases than elsewhere, yet when the herds are let out to graze such diseases do occur. Although the judgment of the Exeg. is that these facts should not be given weight, yet the details seem so true to life that one can imagine that the dynasty of the Pharaohs was weakened by a series of pestilences, epidemics, and plagues to the point of loosening its hold on its slave population. The part played by such scourges in the history of the world is astonishing (see the index of any popular world history such as that of H. G. Wells) .

The stories of the plagues are told with considerable literary art, like the succeeding con-

12 And Moses and Aaron went out from Pharaoh: and Moses cried unto the Lord because of the frogs which he had brought against Pharaoh.

13 And the Lord did according to the word of Moses; and the frogs died out of the houses, out of the villages, and out of the fields.

14 And they gathered them together upon heaps; and the land stank.

15 But when Pharaoh saw that there was respite, he hardened his heart, and hearkened not unto them; as the Lord had said.

16 ¶ And the Lord said unto Moses, Say unto Aaron, Stretch out thy rod, and smite the dust of the land, that it may become lice throughout all the land of Egypt.

17 And they did so; for Aaron stretched out his hand with his rod, and smote the dust of the earth, and it became lice in man, and in beast; all the dust of the land became lice throughout all the land of Egypt.

18 And the magicians did so with their enchantments to bring forth lice, but they could not: so there were lice upon man, and upon beast.

they shall be left only in the Nile." 12 So Moses and Aaron went out from Pharaoh; and Moses cried to the Lord concerning the frogs, as he had agreed with Pharaoh.[1]

13 And the Lord did according to the word of Moses; the frogs died out of the houses and courtyards and out of the fields. 14 And they gathered them together in heaps, and the land stank. 15 But when Pharaoh saw that there was a respite, he hardened his heart, and would not listen to them; as the Lord had said.

16 Then the Lord said to Moses, "Say to Aaron, 'Stretch out your rod and strike the dust of the earth, that it may become gnats throughout all the land of Egypt.' " 17 And they did so; Aaron stretched out his hand with his rod, and struck the dust of the earth, and there came gnats on man and beast; all the dust of the earth became gnats throughout all the land of Egypt. 18 The magicians tried by their secret arts to bring forth gnats, but they could not. So there

[1] Or which he had brought upon Pharaoh

15. But Pharaoh misreads the "sign." He thinks he detects "softness" in Yahweh. He is more impressed by his own relief than by the power of God, and he forgets his promise.

3. Gnats (8:16-19=Hebrew 8:12-15)

The account of this plague is entirely by P and without interruption exhibits all the features of this writer with respect to the plagues discussed above.

16. The insects have been understood as **lice** (KJV; ASV), mosquitoes (Amer. Trans.), sand flies or fleas (ASV mg.), and **gnats** (RSV). The term "gnat" seems best, but it must probably be understood as referring to the sand fly, an insect which carries dengue fever and is a scourge in all the Near East. The LXX adds "on man and beast" after **gnats**, which, in view of vss. 17-18, seems probable.

17. The phrase **And they did so** is lacking in the LXX. It must refer to Moses and Aaron (cf. 7:20). Assuming that in **all the land of Egypt** the dust would produce gnats, P concludes that **all the dust of the earth became gnats!** In a country as dusty as Egypt this is an exaggeration that defies all understanding.

18-19. For the first time Yahweh's power outstrips that of the magicians. Another power, **the finger of God** (Ps. 8:3), works through Moses and Aaron. But Pharaoh, who

tests of some great tournament. The sympathy, patience, and ingenuity of Yahweh are emphasized; and if some of the ill will felt by the authors against the oppressors of their people has crept into the character of the God they portray, one can understand and forgive. One can read the list of the plagues like a tragic his-

tory of the troubles of life. Starting with general unpleasantness, like the lack of good water and the stink of dead fish; followed by unpleasant company, hopping and croaking around everywhere; then stinging flocks of minor irritations, lice and flies; till in full earnest comes real sickness of man and beast, boils and blains and

19 Then the magicians said unto Pharaoh, This *is* the finger of God: and Pharaoh's heart was hardened, and he hearkened not unto them; as the LORD had said.

20 ¶ And the LORD said unto Moses, Rise up early in the morning, and stand before Pharaoh; lo, he cometh forth to the water; and say unto him, Thus saith the LORD, Let my people go, that they may serve me.

21 Else, if thou wilt not let my people go, behold, I will send swarms of flies upon thee, and upon thy servants, and upon thy people, and into thy houses: and the houses of the Egyptians shall be full of swarms of flies, and also the ground whereon they *are*.

22 And I will sever in that day the land of Goshen, in which my people dwell, that no swarms of flies shall be there; to the end thou mayest know that I *am* the LORD in the midst of the earth.

23 And I will put a division between my people and thy people: to-morrow shall this sign be.

24 And the LORD did so; and there came a grievous swarm of flies into the house of Pharaoh, and *into* his servants' houses, and into all the land of Egypt: the land was corrupted by reason of the swarm of flies.

were gnats on man and beast. 19 And the magicians said to Pharaoh, "This is the finger of God." But Pharaoh's heart was hardened, and he would not listen to them; as the LORD had said.

20 Then the LORD said to Moses, "Rise up early in the morning and wait for Pharaoh, as he goes out to the water, and say to him, 'Thus says the LORD, "Let my people go, that they may serve me. 21 Else, if you will not let my people go, behold, I will send swarms of flies on you and your servants and your people, and into your houses; and the houses of the Egyptians shall be filled with swarms of flies, and also the ground on which they stand. 22 But on that day I will set apart the land of Goshen, where my people dwell, so that no swarms of flies shall be there; that you may know that I am the LORD in the midst of the earth. 23 Thus I will put a division[m] between my people and your people. By to-morrow shall this sign be." ' " 24 And the LORD did so; there came great swarms of flies into the house of Pharaoh and into his servants' houses, and in all the land of Egypt the land was ruined by reason of the flies.

[m] Gk Vg: Heb *set redemption*

has already recognized that he is in conflict with an actual deity (8:8), does not relent. In vs. 19*b* we have the regular concluding formula of P and, consequently, the pronoun **them** must refer to Moses and Aaron rather than to the magicians.

4. FLIES (8:20-32=Hebrew 8:16-28)

This account is entirely by J and it clearly shows his pattern for relating the plagues. It seems probable that the third plague is simply P's duplicate version for this one.

21. J's announcement of a plague is conditional. Pharaoh is given a chance to repent (cf. vss. 2; 9:2). In Hebrew "the swarm" is the term for our **swarms of flies** (cf. Ps. 78:45). A moving mass of insects is indicated. Flies and insects were so thick in Egypt that they were synonymous with the country as such (Isa. 7:18; 18:1).

22. This is the first time Israel's relation to Egypt's plagues is mentioned. Its exemption from this plague will be a "sign" that Yahweh is God. We are reminded of the sign of Gideon's fleece (Judg. 6:36-40).

murrain; followed by storms, lightning and hail; and real enemies in battalions, locusts, the first inventors of the scorched earth policy; then terror in darkness; and death.

One can almost hear the pathetic voice of Pharaoh in later life, telling the story of how he lost all his valuable slaves. "What could I do?" one can hear him say. "Everything was against me." We can be sure that sooner or later he

would repeat again, "But the root of all the trouble was that man Moses. He was an agitator. If he had not stirred them up, they would be contentedly with us today." Or if you listen closely, it is George III of England who is speaking, before madness overtook him, telling again to some favorite the tragic story of how he lost his American colonies. "Everything was against me," one can hear him say. Then sooner or later

25 ¶ And Pharaoh called for Moses and for Aaron, and said, Go ye, sacrifice to your God in the land.

26 And Moses said, It is not meet so to do; for we shall sacrifice the abomination of the Egyptians to the LORD our God: lo, shall we sacrifice the abomination of the Egyptians before their eyes, and will they not stone us?

27 We will go three days' journey into the wilderness, and sacrifice to the LORD our God, as he shall command us.

28 And Pharaoh said, I will let you go, that ye may sacrifice to the LORD your God in the wilderness; only ye shall not go very far away: entreat for me.

29 And Moses said, Behold, I go out from thee, and I will entreat the LORD that the swarms of flies may depart from Pharaoh, from his servants, and from his people, to-morrow: but let not Pharaoh deal deceitfully any more in not letting the people go to sacrifice to the LORD.

30 And Moses went out from Pharaoh, and entreated the LORD.

31 And the LORD did according to the word of Moses; and he removed the swarms of flies from Pharaoh, from his servants, and from his people; there remained not one.

32 And Pharaoh hardened his heart at this time also, neither would he let the people go.

25 Then Pharaoh called Moses and Aaron, and said, "Go, sacrifice to your God within the land." 26 But Moses said, "It would not be right to do so; for we shall sacrifice to the LORD our God offerings abominable to the Egyptians. If we sacrifice offerings abominable to the Egyptians before their eyes, will they not stone us? 27 We must go three days' journey into the wilderness and sacrifice to the LORD our God as he will command us." 28 So Pharaoh said, "I will let you go, to sacrifice to the LORD your God in the wilderness; only you shall not go very far away. Make entreaty for me." 29 Then Moses said, "Behold, I am going out from you and I will pray to the LORD that the swarms of flies may depart from Pharaoh, from his servants, and from his people, tomorrow; only let not Pharaoh deal falsely again by not letting the people go to sacrifice to the LORD." 30 So Moses went out from Pharaoh and prayed to the LORD. 31 And the LORD did as Moses asked, and removed the swarms of flies from Pharaoh, from his servants, and from his people; not one remained. 32 But Pharaoh hardened his heart this time also, and did not let the people go.

25-26. Pharaoh makes a concession; Israel may sacrifice in Egypt. God's real plan compels Moses to refuse but he justifies the refusal by a clever use of fact (cf. 1:19). The Elephantine Papyri show that Egyptians of a later era actually did react violently to Israel's worship (A. E. Cowley, *Aramaic Papyri of the Fifth Century B.C.* [Oxford: Clarendon Press, 1923], pp. 108-22). Most of Israel's animal sacrifices would have offended Egyptians.

27-32. To Moses' demand for a three-day journey Pharaoh replies vaguely that they must **not go very far away.** But he is desperate to have the plague stopped and begs Moses to intercede with the God into whose hand he is more and more falling. Despite Moses' warning, he again confuses with his own power the respite Yahweh gives him.

he would sum it all up again, "If it had not been for that man Franklin, everything would be well. It was he who stirred up all the trouble." Yet back of all the plagues, the catastrophes, and mischances, was the real cause of the trouble: the hardness of a tyrant heart. The story is sad from Pharaoh's point of view throughout history; **just when everything is comfortable, and the**

treasure cities, Pithom and Raamses, are being built at last, just then somebody like Moses comes along stirring up discontent among the brickmakers or the coal miners, and we have to go through another "period of unrest"; the rules of the game which made life so pleasant for the few have to be revised again. But the happy side of the story is that after each revision the few

9 Then the Lord said unto Moses, Go in unto Pharaoh, and tell him, Thus saith the Lord God of the Hebrews, Let my people go, that they may serve me.

2 For if thou refuse to let *them* go, and wilt hold them still,

3 Behold, the hand of the Lord is upon thy cattle which *is* in the field, upon the horses, upon the asses, upon the camels, upon the oxen, and upon the sheep: *there shall be* a very grievous murrain.

4 And the Lord shall sever between the cattle of Israel and the cattle of Egypt: and there shall nothing die of all *that is* the children's of Israel.

5 And the Lord appointed a set time, saying, To-morrow the Lord shall do this thing in the land.

6 And the Lord did that thing on the morrow, and all the cattle of Egypt died: but of the cattle of the children of Israel died not one.

9 Then the Lord said to Moses, "Go in to Pharaoh, and say to him, 'Thus says the Lord, the God of the Hebrews, "Let my people go, that they may serve me. 2 For if you refuse to let them go and still hold them, 3 behold, the hand of the Lord will fall with a very severe plague upon your cattle which are in the field, the horses, the asses, the camels, the herds, and the flocks. 4 But the Lord will make a distinction between the cattle of Israel and the cattle of Egypt, so that nothing shall die of all that belongs to the people of Israel." ' " 5 And the Lord set a time, saying, "Tomorrow the Lord will do this thing in the land." 6 And on the morrow the Lord did this thing; all the cattle of the Egyptians died, but of the cattle of the people of Israel not

5. Cattle Plague (9:1-7)

This account of a plague by J is abbreviated. Pharaoh does not send for Moses to make his confession and ask for intercession. No hint is given on the end of the plague.

9:1-3. The announcement of the plague is again conditional. But this time Pharaoh receives a brief twenty-four hour ultimatum (vs. 5) ! It is impossible to specify the disease that constitutes the plague; the common view that it was anthrax is not demonstrable. **All the cattle** were struck, **camels** among others. The reference to camels in thirteenth-century Egypt seems anachronistic, for it is not likely that this animal was domesticated in Egypt as early as that. Even in the seminomadic area of the Midianites and elsewhere the domestication of the camel, though earlier than in Egypt, had hardly begun at this time. The references to camels in the patriarchal stories are almost surely anachronistic. The facts of this much discussed question seem well stated by W. F. Albright: "In the thirteenth century B.C. the domestication of the camel had not yet progressed to a point where it could have any decisive effect upon nomadism; no traces of domestic camels have been yet discovered in any contemporary record or excavation. It is not until the eleventh century that camel-riding nomads first appear in our documentary sources." (*Archaeology and the Religion of Israel* [Baltimore: Johns Hopkins Press, 1942], p. 96.)

4-7. Pharaoh notices the sign of Yahweh in the exemption of Israel, but remains unmoved.

who get something out of life become a few more, and the people as a whole pitch their tents one stage nearer the land which flows with milk and honey. The Bible believes that God has made a covenant with men to bring them at last to that promised land.

But why does God not do something quickly? In days of wicked oppression this question perplexes the humble believer. It is one of the difficulties about which thoughtful parishioners are always asking their pastors, and they are

seldom satisfied with the answers. In 9:14-16 there is an interpolation which gives in its different versions two answers. The RSV and the Hebrew text imply that God delays action in the hope of converting Pharaoh, **that you may know, . . . to show you my power.** The LXX and the KJV suggest that God is using Pharaoh, letting him do his worst, in order that in his ultimate downfall God's glory may be manifest, **to show in thee my power.** It must be admitted that both explanations will seem to the victims

7 And Pharaoh sent, and, behold, there
was not one of the cattle of the Israelites
dead. And the heart of Pharaoh was hardened, and he did not let the people go.

8 ¶ And the Lord said unto Moses and
unto Aaron, Take to you handfuls of ashes
of the furnace, and let Moses sprinkle it
toward the heaven in the sight of Pharaoh.

9 And it shall become small dust in all
the land of Egypt, and shall be a boil
breaking forth *with* blains upon man, and
upon beast, throughout all the land of
Egypt.

10 And they took ashes of the furnace,
and stood before Pharaoh; and Moses
sprinkled it up toward heaven; and it became a boil breaking forth *with* blains
upon man, and upon beast.

11 And the magicians could not stand
before Moses because of the boils; for the
boil was upon the magicians, and upon
all the Egyptians.

12 And the Lord hardened the heart of
Pharaoh, and he hearkened not unto them;
as the Lord had spoken unto Moses.

13 ¶ And the Lord said unto Moses, Rise
up early in the morning, and stand before
Pharaoh, and say unto him, Thus saith the
Lord God of the Hebrews, Let my people
go, that they may serve me.

one died. 7 And Pharaoh sent, and behold,
not one of the cattle of the Israelites was
dead. But the heart of Pharaoh was hardened, and he did not let the people go.

8 And the Lord said to Moses and Aaron,
"Take handfuls of ashes from the kiln, and
let Moses throw them toward heaven in the
sight of Pharaoh. 9 And it shall become
fine dust over all the land of Egypt, and
become boils breaking out in sores on man
and beast throughout all the land of Egypt."
10 So they took ashes from the kiln, and
stood before Pharaoh, and Moses threw
them toward heaven, and it became boils
breaking out in sores on man and beast.
11 And the magicians could not stand before
Moses because of the boils, for the boils
were upon the magicians and upon all the
Egyptians. 12 But the Lord hardened the
heart of Pharaoh, and he did not listen to
them; as the Lord had spoken to Moses.

13 Then the Lord said to Moses, "Rise
up early in the morning and stand before
Pharaoh, and say to him, 'Thus says the
Lord, the God of the Hebrews, "Let my

6. Boils (9:8-12)

This account departs from the normal P type in two ways: Moses performs the
wonder in Pharaoh's presence, and a form of magical action of the sympathetic type
replaces the use of the miraculous rod.

9. The nature of this plague is reminiscent of the one preceding it. This may represent
the P version of the same incident. However, Hugo Gressmann felt that **the fine dust
over all the land** pointed to the darkness of the ninth plague (*Mose und seine Zeit*
[Göttingen: Vandenhoeck & Ruprecht, 1951], p. 92).

10. Some sort of malignant pustule constituted the plague. Skin diseases were
prominently associated with Egypt (Deut. 28:27, 35). In the previous plague all the
cattle had died (vs. 6). If these accounts were to be understood as a sober recital of
fact, it would be difficult to know what beast was left to suffer this disease.

11. The magicians had already given up the struggle against Yahweh (8:19). Now
they can no longer protect even themselves. The contest moves on to the full victory of
the Lord.

7. Hail (9:13-35)

The core of this account is from J (vss. 13, 17-18, 23b-24, 26-30, 33-34). In vss. 22, 23a,
25, 35 we seem to have bits of E, with a conclusion from P in vs. 35. Three novel items
that do not fit the literary pattern of the plague accounts attract our attention (vss. 14-16,
19-21, 31-33). They seem to be features introduced by a redactor's hand to interpret and
harmonize the plague accounts.

14 For I will at this time send all my plagues upon thine heart, and upon thy servants, and upon thy people; that thou mayest know that *there is* none like me in all the earth.

15 For now I will stretch out my hand, that I may smite thee and thy people with pestilence; and thou shalt be cut off from the earth.

16 And in very deed for this *cause* have I raised thee up, for to show *in* thee my power; and that my name may be declared throughout all the earth.

people go, that they may serve me. 14 For this time I will send all my plagues upon your heart, and upon your servants and your people, that you may know that there is none like me in all the earth. 15 For by now I could have put forth my hand and struck you and your people with pestilence, and you would have been cut off from the earth; 16 but for this purpose have I let you live, to show you my power, so that my name may be declared throughout all the earth.

14. The phrase **upon your heart** gives no real meaning. It seems best to emend the Hebrew text (ה[אלה בך] for אל לבך) and read "I will send all these my plagues upon you." It is impossible to be sure whether the **plagues** refer to the variety of calamities J combines in this seventh plague (vss. 23b-24) or to all the plagues, especially those still to come. If, as it seems, we have here an interpolation by an editor who seeks to explain why the destruction of Pharaoh was such a long process, the vagueness is natural, though his concern is with the plagues as a whole.

15. The question discussed in the interpolation (vss. 14-16) is why Yahweh does not dispose of self-styled gods and tyrants—Pharaoh or any other—more quickly than he does. It is not a lack of capacity on God's part. He could have **cut off** Pharaoh **from the earth** at a single stroke. This writer insists that this slowness of the "mills of God" is actually a demonstration of his power.

16. God has maintained Pharaoh for his own purpose. The belief that God **raised ... up** (KJV; cf. Rom. 9:17) tyrants was prevalent in Israel too but is not explicitly stated here. The RSV follows the Hebrew text in **to show you my power,** and this is in harmony with vs. 14, **that you may know.** But the LXX, followed by the KJV, says that it is God's purpose **to show in thee my power.** Thus, Pharaoh is not just to learn about Yahweh but is actually the means by which God makes himself known in the world. This appears to be the real concern of the editor. For this interpreter these plagues are not just God's futile effort to "convert" Pharaoh; they are an illustration of the view that God makes himself known in his power in the midst of and in conformity with the characteristic processes of nature and history, even as these are exemplified in a tyrant. God could no doubt have disposed of Pharaoh at a single stroke, but God does not work that way (cf. Matt. 26:53); and the interpreter's reason for saying so is that history is not like that. Once established, tyrants and oppressions have a sort of natural life of their own which must be lived out. But in the midst of this process which opposes him, and by means of it, God manifests his power. This writer's faith is tough and realistic; it became deeply imbedded in Jewish tradition. His words are used by Paul (Rom. 9:17) to illustrate that in the succession of the covenant of Moses by that of Christ there is likewise a vindication of God's freedom.

of totalitarian butchery but as vacant chaff, well meant for grain. The fact is that as long as God is looked upon as a benevolent dictator, committed to the efficacy of force in cleaning up bad situations, there is no satisfactory reply to this poignant question. Only when one has grasped the fact that God works through men in human affairs, does one come to understand something of the answers given to this question by the incarnation and the agony on the cross. The

wished-for short cut of miraculous intervention would bring all human history to an end and destroy life's greatness and meaning. Pharaoh was allowed to proceed on his way partly to give him a last chance, partly that opportunity might be given to the oppressed people to find a triumphant way out of captivity and into the Promised Land, thus demonstrating the power and wisdom of God.

The early writer (J) has a direct story to tell

17 As yet exaltest thou thyself against my people, that thou wilt not let them go?

18 Behold, to-morrow about this time I will cause it to rain a very grievous hail, such as hath not been in Egypt since the foundation thereof even until now.

19 Send therefore now, *and* gather thy cattle, and all that thou hast in the field; *for upon* every man and beast which shall be found in the field, and shall not be brought home, the hail shall come down upon them, and they shall die.

20 He that feared the word of the LORD among the servants of Pharaoh made his servants and his cattle flee into the houses:

21 And he that regarded not the word of the LORD left his servants and his cattle in the field.

22 ¶ And the LORD said unto Moses, Stretch forth thine hand toward heaven, that there may be hail in all the land of Egypt, upon man, and upon beast, and upon every herb of the field, throughout the land of Egypt.

23 And Moses stretched forth his rod toward heaven: and the LORD sent thunder and hail, and the fire ran along upon the ground; and the LORD rained hail upon the land of Egypt.

24 So there was hail, and fire mingled with the hail, very grievous, such as there was none like it in all the land of Egypt since it became a nation.

25 And the hail smote throughout all the land of Egypt all that *was* in the field, both man and beast; and the hail smote every herb of the field, and brake every tree of the field.

17 You are still exalting yourself against my people, and will not let them go. 18 Behold, tomorrow about this time I will cause very heavy hail to fall, such as never has been in Egypt from the day it was founded until now. 19 Now therefore send, get your cattle and all that you have in the field into safe shelter; for the hail shall come down upon every man and beast that is in the field and is not brought home, and they shall die." ' " 20 Then he who feared the word of the LORD among the servants of Pharaoh made his slaves and his cattle flee into the houses; 21 but he who did not regard the word of the LORD left his slaves and his cattle in the field.

22 And the LORD said to Moses, "Stretch forth your hand toward heaven, that there may be hail in all the land of Egypt, upon man and beast and every plant of the field, throughout the land of Egypt." 23 Then Moses stretched forth his rod toward heaven; and the LORD sent thunder and hail, and fire ran down to the earth. And the LORD rained hail upon the land of Egypt; 24 there was hail, and fire flashing continually in the midst of the hail, very heavy hail, such as had never been in all the land of Egypt since it became a nation. 25 The hail struck down everything that was in the field throughout all the land of Egypt, both man and beast; and the hail struck down every plant of the field, and

19-21. There is an "underground" at Pharaoh's court which presages the imminent breakup of the tyrant's resistance to Yahweh.

23b-24. Violent storms of this sort are indeed unknown in Egypt (cf. vs. 18). The description probably owes something to a later observation of them in Palestine, where they do occur. J here speaks of thunder and flood as well as hail (cf. vss. 22, 24 [E]).

of quick results, but the later accounts were written by those who had more dramatic instincts and thought that greater capital could be made out of the material by emphasizing the supernatural and delaying the outcome by suspense. Success came too quickly in the early narrative. The material has been disarranged, but something like the following was intended: The Egyptians promised nothing after the first

plague, because they were able to reproduce it themselves. The effect of the next plagues is greater and, in order to get rid of them, Pharaoh promises to let the people go. But as soon as the scare is over, he cannot bring himself to keep his promise. After the second plague (frogs) he simply refuses to keep his promise. After the other plagues he shifts his ground. The third plague (vermin) forces him to give the people

26 Only in the land of Goshen, where the children of Israel *were,* was there no hail.

27 ¶ And Pharaoh sent, and called for Moses and Aaron, and said unto them, I have sinned this time: the LORD *is* righteous, and I and my people *are* wicked.

28 Entreat the LORD (for *it is* enough) that there be no *more* mighty thunderings and hail; and I will let you go, and ye shall stay no longer.

29 And Moses said unto him, As soon as I am gone out of the city, I will spread abroad my hands unto the LORD; *and* the thunder shall cease, neither shall there be any more hail; that thou mayest know how that the earth *is* the LORD's.

30 But as for thee and thy servants, I know that ye will not yet fear the LORD God.

31 And the flax and the barley was smitten: for the barley *was* in the ear, and the flax *was* bolled.

32 But the wheat and the rye were not smitten: for they *were* not grown up.

33 And Moses went out of the city from Pharaoh, and spread abroad his hands unto the LORD: and the thunders and hail ceased, and the rain was not poured upon the earth.

shattered every tree of the field. 26 Only in the land of Goshen, where the people of Israel were, there was no hail.

27 Then Pharaoh sent, and called Moses and Aaron, and said to them, "I have sinned this time; the LORD is in the right, and I and my people are in the wrong. 28 Entreat the LORD; for there has been enough of this thunder and hail; I will let you go, and you shall stay no longer." 29 Moses said to him, "As soon as I have gone out of the city, I will stretch out my hands to the LORD; the thunder will cease, and there will be no more hail, that you may know that the earth is the LORD's. 30 But as for you and your servants, I know that you do not yet fear the LORD God." 31 (The flax and the barley were ruined, for the barley was in the ear and the flax was in bud. 32 But the wheat and the spelt were not ruined, for they are late in coming up.) 33 So Moses went out of the city from Pharaoh, and stretched out his hands to the LORD; and the thunder and the hail ceased, and the rain no longer poured upon the earth.

27-30. Moses is again summoned by Pharaoh to be asked to intercede with the Lord. Pharaoh admits he is beaten: **I have sinned.** He makes a more generous promise.

31-32. The connection between vss. 30 and 33 is interpreted by an explanatory note. A harmonist wanted to make clear that the hail had left some herbage for locusts (10:15) ! Flax and barley mature a full month before wheat and spelt in Egypt. The reading **for they are late in coming up** (RSV) is too free and misleading. The KJV and the ASV are preferable. The Hebrew word means "concealed." Since only a month intervenes between the maturation of the earlier and later crops, we must conclude that the wheat and spelt had not yet "headed out" at the time of the storm. The ears were still "concealed" in the young growing plants. Hail can do little damage to a grain crop at that stage. Even if the pliable young stems are somewhat shattered, they will grow out again.

---

the right to sacrifice to their God, but inside the land of Egypt. Moses rejects this compromise on the ground that the sacrificial ceremonies of the Hebrews would be so different from those of the Egyptians as to cause bigoted riots among the Egyptians. The result of the fourth plague (pestilence) was that Pharaoh said they could go, but not as far from the border as they desired. But Moses holds to his requisite of three days' journey. The fifth plague of hail brings the further concession on the part of Pharaoh

that the men could go, but no one else. Moses rejects this suggestion, as the sacrifice requires the presence of all. Pharaoh, after the sixth plague (locusts), goes a little further and permits men, women, and children to go, but would keep their flocks and herds in Egypt; Moses answers that this would enrage Yahweh more than anything, as the flocks and herds are needed for the sacrifice. Thus everything is now ready for Moses to play his trump card, and proclaim the last plague which will free the people.

34 And when Pharaoh saw that the rain and the hail and the thunders were ceased, he sinned yet more, and hardened his heart, he and his servants.

35 And the heart of Pharaoh was hardened, neither would he let the children of Israel go; as the LORD had spoken by Moses.

10 And the LORD said unto Moses, Go in unto Pharaoh: for I have hardened his·heart, and the heart of his servants, that I might show these my signs before him:

2 And that thou mayest tell in the ears of thy son, and of thy son's son, what things I have wrought in Egypt, and my signs which I have done among them; that ye may know how that I *am* the LORD.

34 But when Pharaoh saw that the rain and the hail and the thunder had ceased, he sinned yet again, and hardened his heart, he and his servants. 35 So the heart of Pharaoh was hardened, and he did not let the people of Israel go; as the LORD had spoken through Moses.

10 Then the LORD said to Moses, "Go in to Pharaoh; for I have hardened his heart and the heart of his servants, that I may show these signs of mine among them, 2 and that you may tell in the hearing of your son and of your son's son how I have made sport of the Egyptians and what signs I have done among them; that you may know that I am the LORD."

---

8. LOCUSTS (10:1-20, 24-26, 28-29)

J is the chief source for the account of this plague also. Bits of E are discernible in Moses' use of the rod to bring the plague (vss. 12-13a), and the conclusion (vs. 20) is also E. After Moses has warned Pharaoh of the coming plague, and before it strikes, some of the court nobles compel the ruler to recall Moses for the purpose of arbitrating the conflict (vss. 7-8) but this inevitably fails since in a struggle with Yahweh for lordship a truce is unthinkable. He alone is God. But this attempt at negotiation before a plague strikes is a new feature in this series of accounts. After the plague has come Pharaoh, as usual in J, sends for Moses to ask him to intercede. But here an attempt at negotiation is conspicuously absent. One inevitably gets the feeling that this characteristic bit of J must have been transferred to some other location. Is it perhaps the interview that now precedes the actual coming of the plague? Or is it, as Beer suggests (*Exodus*, pp. 55-57), the account of the interview that now forms a part of the next plague (vss. 24-26, 28-29)? That interview, which ends in a violent scene at which Pharaoh sentences Moses to death if he dares to appear before him again, is the natural conclusion of the whole series of plagues leading up to the death of the first-born. It shows unmistakably the hand of J and seems to fit the note of finality introduced by Pharaoh in vs. 17, where he asks for forgiveness **only this once**. It is also strange that in its present position this interview of Moses with Pharaoh, in which the latter offers concessions, is not accompanied by his request for Moses' intercession to stop the plague. Previously such a request occurs without the offer of concessions as a bribe. This is a strong argument for transferring these verses to the account of the eighth plague. Such a transfer reduces the next plague to a mere skeleton, all from E. It was perhaps to fill out this skeletal account and provide it with dramatic force appropriate to its place in the series that the hypothetical transfer was originally made.

10:1-2. The instruction to **Go in to Pharaoh** is in the familiar J pattern. But this is at once followed by a commentary in the spirit of Deuteronomy. This is perhaps an

---

10:1-2. *The Beginning of the End: Locusts.*[9]— One swarm of locusts which crossed the Red Sea in 1889 was estimated to be two thousand square miles in extent. In Cyprus in 1881 official reports state that 1,300 tons of locust eggs were

[9] See G. A. Smith, *The Book of the Twelve Prophets* (London: Harper & Bros., 1928; "Expositor's Bible"), II, 390-408; Joel 1:6-10.

destroyed. Swarms have been seen at sea 1,200 miles from land. The Arabs today are losers every year by swarms bred in the land or carried to them by winds. They wrap the spring clusters of dates around with wisps of dry foliage for protection, and afterward avenge themselves on the ravenous hordes by beating down the insects with palm branches, then toasting, and eating

3 And Moses and Aaron came in unto Pharaoh, and said unto him, Thus saith the LORD God of the Hebrews, How long wilt thou refuse to humble thyself before me? let my people go, that they may serve me.

4 Else, if thou refuse to let my people go, behold, to-morrow will I bring the locusts into thy coast:

5 And they shall cover the face of the earth, that one cannot be able to see the earth: and they shall eat the residue of that which is escaped, which remaineth unto you from the hail, and shall eat every tree which groweth for you out of the field:

6 And they shall fill thy houses, and the houses of all thy servants, and the houses of all the Egyptians; which neither thy fathers, nor thy fathers' fathers have seen, since the day that they were upon the earth unto this day. And he turned himself, and went out from Pharaoh.

7 And Pharaoh's servants said unto him, How long shall this man be a snare unto us? let the men go, that they may serve the LORD their God: knowest thou not yet that Egypt is destroyed?

8 And Moses and Aaron were brought again unto Pharaoh: and he said unto them, Go, serve the LORD your God: *but* who *are* they that shall go?

9 And Moses said, We will go with our young and with our old, with our sons and with our daughters, with our flocks and with our herds will we go; for we *must hold* a feast unto the LORD.

10 And he said unto them, Let the LORD be so with you, as I will let you go, and your little ones: look *to it;* for evil *is* before you.

3 So Moses and Aaron went in to Pharaoh, and said to him, "Thus says the LORD, the God of the Hebrews, 'How long will you refuse to humble yourself before me? Let my people go, that they may serve me. 4 For if you refuse to let my people go, behold, tomorrow I will bring locusts into your country, 5 and they shall cover the face of the land, so that no one can see the land; and they shall eat what is left to you after the hail, and they shall eat every tree of yours which grows in the field, 6 and they shall fill your houses, and the houses of all your servants and of all the Egyptians; as neither your fathers nor your grandfathers have seen, from the day they came on earth to this day.'" Then he turned and went out from Pharaoh.

7 And Pharaoh's servants said to him, "How long shall this man be a snare to us? Let the men go, that they may serve the LORD their God; do you not yet understand that Egypt is ruined?" 8 So Moses and Aaron were brought back to Pharaoh; and he said to them, "Go, serve the LORD your God; but who are to go?" 9 And Moses said, "We will go with our young and our old; we will go with our sons and daughters and with our flocks and herds, for we must hold a feast to the LORD." 10 And he said to them, "The LORD be with you, if ever I let you and your little ones go! Look, you have

---

editor's addition. In contrast to J (8:15, 32; 9:34) he tells us that God has hardened Pharaoh's heart. The purpose of this is to make Yahweh great in Israel. It creates an occasion for the Lord to manifest his power; and so Israelites will be able to tell their sons and grandsons, forever after, how God **made sport of the Egyptians.** Far from being a sign of weakness, this long series of plagues is the ironical dallying of Yahweh (cf. 9:14-16).

3-6. The usual twenty-four hour warning is issued. **Locusts** are a scourge even more frequent in Palestine than in Egypt.

7-16. The forces in Egypt ready to submit to Yahweh (9:20) now appear strong enough to compel the stubborn Pharaoh to recall Moses for the purpose of negotiation. Moses raises the demand for a complete surrender, except for the plunder which the Israelites will presently demand of the Egyptians (3:22; 12:35-36). This absolute demand Pharaoh bitterly rejects. In sarcasm he gives his "blessing" (vs. 10); he hopes that the divine protection on the journey may be as nonexistent as his permit to go. He offers

11 Not so: go now ye *that are* men, and serve the LORD; for that ye did desire. And they were driven out from Pharaoh's presence.

12 ¶ And the LORD said unto Moses, Stretch out thine hand over the land of Egypt for the locusts, that they may come up upon the land of Egypt, and eat every herb of the land, *even* all that the hail hath left.

13 And Moses stretched forth his rod over the land of Egypt, and the LORD brought an east wind upon the land all that day, and all *that* night; *and* when it was morning, the east wind brought the locusts.

14 And the locusts went up over all the land of Egypt, and rested in all the coasts of Egypt: very grievous *were they;* before them there were no such locusts as they, neither after them shall be such.

15 For they covered the face of the whole earth, so that the land was darkened; and they did eat every herb of the land, and all the fruit of the trees which the hail had left: and there remained not any green thing in the trees, or in the herbs of the field, through all the land of Egypt.

16 ¶ Then Pharaoh called for Moses and Aaron in haste; and he said, I have sinned against the LORD your God, and against you.

17 Now therefore forgive, I pray thee, my sin only this once, and entreat the LORD your God, that he may take away from me this death only.

18 And he went-out from Pharaoh, and entreated the LORD.

19 And the LORD turned a mighty strong west wind, which took away the locusts, and cast them into the Red sea; there remained not one locust in all the coasts of Egypt.

some evil purpose in mind.[n] **11** No! Go, the men among you, and serve the LORD, for that is what you desire." And they were driven out from Pharaoh's presence.

12 Then the LORD said to Moses, "Stretch out your hand over the land of Egypt for the locusts, that they may come upon the land of Egypt, and eat every plant in the land, all that the hail has left." **13** So Moses stretched forth his rod over the land of Egypt, and the LORD brought an east wind upon the land all that day and all that night; and when it was morning the east wind had brought the locusts. **14** And the locusts came up over all the land of Egypt, and settled on the whole country of Egypt, such a dense swarm of locusts as had never been before, nor ever shall be again. **15** For they covered the face of the whole land, so that the land was darkened, and they ate all the plants in the land and all the fruit of the trees which the hail had left; not a green thing remained, neither tree nor plant of the field, through all the land of Egypt. **16** Then Pharaoh called Moses and Aaron in haste, and said, "I have sinned against the LORD your God, and against you. **17** Now therefore, forgive my sin, I pray you, only this once, and entreat the LORD your God only to remove this death from me." **18** So he went out from Pharaoh, and entreated the LORD. **19** And the LORD turned a very strong west wind, which lifted the locusts and drove them into the Red Sea; not a single locust was left in all the

[n] Heb *before your face*

---

to let the men go; if worship in its outer forms were the sole object, that would suffice (23:17; 34:23). What Pharaoh cannot see is that the God of Israel, who is the Lord of all the earth, must wholly possess those who worship him. Their possessions too belong to him.

13. The sirocco wind from the Arabian Desert carries the locusts. This natural explanation corresponds to the facts.

16-17. Pharaoh called Moses and Aaron in haste: He has increasingly ceased to rely on his own divine status in times of trouble. At such times he tries to make use of God to carry him through to better times.

20 But the Lord hardened Pharaoh's heart, so that he would not let the children of Israel go.

21 ¶ And the Lord said unto Moses, Stretch out thine hand toward heaven, that there may be darkness over the land of Egypt, even darkness *which* may be felt.

22 And Moses stretched forth his hand toward heaven; and there was a thick darkness in all the land of Egypt three days:

23 They saw not one another, neither rose any from his place for three days: but all the children of Israel had light in their dwellings.

24 ¶ And Pharaoh called unto Moses, and said, Go ye, serve the Lord; only let your flocks and your herds be stayed: let your little ones also go with you.

country of Egypt. 20 But the Lord hardened Pharaoh's heart, and he did not let the children of Israel go.

21 Then the Lord said to Moses, "Stretch out your hand toward heaven that there may be darkness over the land of Egypt, a darkness to be felt." 22 So Moses stretched out his hand toward heaven, and there was thick darkness in all the land of Egypt three days; 23 they did not see one another, nor did any rise from his place for three days; but all the people of Israel had light where they dwelt. 24 Then Pharaoh called Moses, and said, "Go, serve the Lord; your children also may go with you; only let your flocks

---

24-26. This interview takes up where the one preceding the plague (vss. 7-11) left off. Pharaoh will now let the women and children go but wants to hold the cattle as a pledge of the people's return. In the spirit of Israel's theocracy Moses says, in effect, that all the cattle belong to the Lord (cf. Ps. 50:10). His objection that only upon arrival at the place of sacrifice will they know what is wanted is not just a ruse; it is also, and more significantly, an explication of what it means to be the people of God. In Israel all of life is held in trust under a *single* trusteeship. The God of Israel is *one* Lord.

28-29. Now that the comprehensive and absolutist character implied in the formula **Let my people go** has been stated, the negotiations are at an end. Pharaoh threatens to slay Moses. He can tolerate a partial allegiance such as was implicit in his concessions hitherto, but he will not deny himself or his own understanding of himself. Moses, in anticipation, answers for Israel the question Elijah was to ask centuries later (I Kings 18:21). He trusts Yahweh absolutely now. His reply, **I will not see your face again,** is not just the close of a conference; it is the foundation of monotheism and of freedom (cf. Josh. 24:14-24).

9. Darkness (10:21-23, 27)

This brief account by E is at present augmented by a section from J (vss. 24-26, 28-29) which, as suggested above, may originally have formed a part of the preceding plague.

21. Perhaps while holding the rod Moses **is to stretch out** [his] **hand toward heaven** to bring about the plague (cf. vs. 12). The phrase **a darkness to be felt** rests on an uncertain Hebrew text. The Syriac renders it, "and the darkness will become dark." Whatever its precise meaning, the statement intends to convey the notion of an awesome darkness, perhaps one in which the spirits of darkness, always dreaded in Egypt, are dangerously active.

22-23. The **thick darkness** which falls is, lit., "a darkness of darkness," a complete gloom making movement impossible. Only in the dwellings of Israel was there light.

---

as many as they can. "Good and fat," they cry as they bring in their catch for a feast.

21-29. *The Darkness.*—The story here differs from the other stories. There are no divine instructions, no interview with Pharaoh. Very early in the study of the text, even when the

Greek translation of the Hebrew was made, this darkness was connected with khamsin, the wind that blows in the spring and brings with it clouds of sand and dust, darkening the sun. For a poetical description of it (for the Egyptians this terror would be the more frightful because

25 And Moses said, Thou must give us also sacrifices and burnt offerings, that we may sacrifice unto the LORD our God.

26 Our cattle also shall go with us; there shall not a hoof be left behind; for thereof must we take to serve the LORD our God; and we know not with what we must serve the LORD, until we come thither.

27 ¶ But the LORD hardened Pharaoh's heart, and he would not let them go.

28 And Pharaoh said unto him, Get thee from me, take heed to thyself, see my face no more; for in *that* day thou seest my face thou shalt die.

29 And Moses said, Thou hast spoken well, I will see thy face again no more.

11 And the LORD said unto Moses, Yet will I bring one plague *more* upon Pharaoh, and upon Egypt; afterward he will let you go hence: when he shall let *you*

and your herds remain behind." 25 But Moses said, "You must also let us have sacrifices and burnt offerings, that we may sacrifice to the LORD our God. 26 Our cattle also must go with us; not a hoof shall be left behind, for we must take of them to serve the LORD our God, and we do not know with what we must serve the LORD until we arrive there." 27 But the LORD hardened Pharaoh's heart, and he would not let them go. 28 Then Pharaoh said to him, "Get away from me; take heed to yourself; never see my face again; for in the day you see my face you shall die." 29 Moses said, "As you say! I will not see your face again."

11 The LORD said to Moses, "Yet one plague more I will bring upon Phar-

---

Since E does not refer to Goshen as a separate area for Israelites, the exemption must be limited to the individual homes.

24-26, 28-29. See Exeg. on vss. 24-26, 28-29, p. 910.

10. DEATH OF THE FIRST-BORN ANNOUNCED (11:1-10)

Vss. 1-3 (E) are a continuation of 10:27 and consist mainly in a repetition of God's command to Israel to take booty from the Egyptians. Vss. 4-8 (J) must be read as the conclusion of the last interview of Moses with Pharaoh (10:29), the announcement of the death of the first-born being God's answer to Pharaoh's threat on Moses' life. The concluding verses are by P.

11:1-3. The final plague is entirely God's work. Moses need only instruct Israel that the end is near and tell them what to do. In complete defeat Pharaoh will actually

---

they believed that evil spirits were abroad in the darkness), see Wisd. Sol. 17:1–18:4: "For well did the Egyptians deserve to be deprived of light and imprisoned by darkness; they who had kept in close ward thy sons, through whom the incorruptible light of the law was to be given to the race of men" (18:4).

11:1–12:30. Death.—In every home in Egypt at midnight the eldest son dies, from the heir apparent in the king's palace to the son of the wretched felon in the cell (12:29); the poor maid sitting grinding corn behind the hand mill loses her boy too (11:5). As in Matt. 2:18, there was "a voice heard, lamentation, and weeping, and great mourning, Rachel weeping for her children, and would not be comforted, because they are not." It was a night of horror: Pharaoh rose up, **he, and all his servants, and all the Egyptians; and there was a great cry in Egypt: for there was not a house where there was not one dead** (12:30). Then Moses was sent for and, without conditions, was granted every-

thing he had asked. The wonderful picture he had painted for the people's imagination by his faith in Yahweh (11:8) had actually come true. Everything was done to get the now unwelcome guests out of Egypt as soon as possible. Costly gifts were pressed upon them, if only they would leave at once; for the Egyptians were urgent upon the people, to send them out of the land in haste. In spite of the story in 12:1-20, we find the writer here represents the people as absolutely unprepared for the sudden realization of all their hopes. They were not ready for a journey. They had to take the dough (which they had set out in the evening for bread) before it was leavened; and on the way they had to bake matzoth, unleavened cakes. So we have seen the strokes of Yahweh strike like lightning, each bolt more terrifying than the last. We have held our breath each time to see if Pharaoh will not yield to the inevitable. Now at last, long after his advisers had seen his case was hopeless, Pharaoh capitulated. The great duel between

| go, he shall surely thrust you out hence altogether. | aoh and upon Egypt; afterwards he will let you go hence; when he lets you go, he will |

welcome the departure of Israel and seek its expulsion. We are led to believe that the "underground" in Egypt had become a majority.

Pharaoh and Moses was over, and Moses had won. Pharaoh had everything—armies of soldiers, cities filled with treasure, a rich land; Moses had nothing but a disorganized gang of slaves—and Yahweh—on his side. But it is better to have nothing and God on one's side than to have everything except God.

In spite of all the tragedy in Egypt, it was a great day for the lonely man who had communed with his God in solitary prayer, who had had to go on in spite of the discontent and murmuring of his own people, who had seen one attempt after another fail, who had at times even doubted if God had treated him fairly. One is reminded of the words of Woodrow Wilson, who knew all about the loneliness of leadership, at the dedication in 1916 of the memorial built over the log cabin birthplace in Hodgensville, Kentucky, the Lincoln home:

It was a very lonely spirit that looked out from underneath those shaggy brows and comprehended men without fully communing with them, as if, in spite of all its genial efforts at comradeship, it dwelt apart, saw its visions of duty where no man looked on. There is a very holy and very terrible isolation for the conscience of every man who seeks to read the destiny in affairs for others as well as for himself, for a nation as well as for individuals. That privacy no man can intrude upon. That lonely search of the spirit for the right perhaps no man can assist.[1]

But one has also to remember the interview which Lincoln had on September 13, 1862, with a group of clergymen urging immediate and universal emancipation. Lincoln said:

I am approached with the most opposite opinions and advice, and that by religious men, who are equally certain that they represent the Divine will. . . . I hope it will not be irreverent for me to say that, if it is probable that God would reveal his will to others on a point so connected with my duty, it might be supposed He would reveal it directly to me; for, unless I am more deceived in myself than I often am, it is my earnest desire to know the will of Providence in this matter. And if I can learn what it is, I will do it! These are not, however, the days of miracles, and I suppose it will be granted that I am not to expect a direct revelation. I must study the plain physical facts of the case, ascertain

what is possible, and learn what appears to be wise and right. The subject is difficult, and good men do not agree.[2]

Lincoln was speaking against the background of the ideas of revelation of his day. We believe that God's best revelations come in the course of that study and learning of which he speaks in his last sentences. Inspiration does not come to the slothful soul but is the miraculous "more" that is added to the best one can do. Beethoven says:

You ask me where I get my ideas. That I cannot tell you with certainty. They come unsummoned, directly, indirectly—I could seize them with my hands—out in the open air, in the woods, while walking, in the silence of the nights, at dawn, excited by moods which are translated by the poet into words, by me into tones that sound and roar and storm about me till I have set them down in notes.[3]

Being inspired is hard work. Inspiration is not an isolated phenomenon to be found only in the specific sphere of religion. It is very closely related to inspiration in all the creative arts. When Virgil, in Dante's *Inferno*, silences objections to the possibility of certain achievements with this hell-conquering formula, "Thus it is willed in that place where what is willed can be done; ask no more," he is as near as human language can come to expressing the secret of inspiration. Fontane gives us a secular expression of the same mystery:

The first dawn of the idea comes of itself; working it out and getting it right afterwards means much toil. Yet the old story that one becomes just the mouthpiece of a higher power has some truth in it; and the sense of being so inspired leaves one with but two emotions: those of humility and thanksgiving.[4]

For the religious leader of today, it is well to remember the secret toil which is the price of public leadership. *Maledictus est qui facit opus Dei negligenter,* which, being put into a figure, means "A study that is a lounge makes a pulpit that is an impertinence."

---

[1] *The Public Papers of Woodrow Wilson,* ed. Ray S. Baker and William E. Dodd (New York: Harper & Bros., 1926), II, 295.

[2] John T. Morse, Jr., *Abraham Lincoln* (Boston: Houghton, Mifflin Co., 1893), II, 110.

[3] J. Lindsay, *Inspiration* (London: Fanfrolico Press, 1928), p. 88.

[4] Conrad Wandrey, *Theodor Fontane* (München: C. H. Beck, 1919), p. 267.

2 Speak now in the ears of the people, and let every man borrow of his neighbor, and every woman of her neighbor, jewels of silver, and jewels of gold.

3 And the LORD gave the people favor in the sight of the Egyptians. Moreover, the man Moses *was* very great in the land of Egypt, in the sight of Pharaoh's servants, and in the sight of the people.

4 And Moses said, Thus saith the LORD, About midnight will I go out into the midst of Egypt:

drive you away completely. 2 Speak now in the hearing of the people, that they ask, every man of his neighbor and every woman of her neighbor, jewelry of silver and of gold." 3 And the LORD gave the people favor in the sight of the Egyptians. Moreover, the man Moses was very great in the land of Egypt, in the sight of Pharaoh's servants and in the sight of the people.

4 And Moses said, "Thus says the LORD: About midnight I will go forth in the midst

---

4. In response to Pharaoh's threat (10:29) Moses tells him, in God's name, that Yahweh will go through Egypt as the angel of death. Each night, according to Egyptian mythology, the sun fought and overcame the snake, Apophis, who symbolized the hostile darkness. As a god, Pharaoh was the incarnation of the sun, and the hostile darkness was his enemy also. The force of Moses' announcement is that the night is at hand when this customary victory, on which the autonomous existence of Egypt depends, will not take place (H. and H. A. Frankfort, in *Intellectual Adventure of Ancient Man*, p. 24).

---

2. *Reparations.*—As promised in 3:21-22, the people are not to "go empty." However the word is translated—**borrow, ask,** or "ask as a loan"—it seems to be implied that ostensibly the loan is for the three days' absence at the religious festival. Whether the neighbors ever expected to see their things returned or not, the fact seems to be that in the midst of the epidemic they were willing to give anything to get rid of the unwelcome guests. Jewish writers have justified the action in various ways. "She rendered unto holy men a reward for their toils" (Wisd. Sol. 10:17). "They plundered the Egyptians to make up for the years of slavery into which they had been forced" (Jubilees 48:18). One writer suggests that they had to leave their houses and much which they would be unable to move on so short notice and that these things would recoup the Egyptians for their loss of jewelry.

The question of reparations for injuries done by one race to another in time of war has always been a difficult question to solve honestly. The method these people took certainly saved a great deal of time lost in endless reparation conferences! The attempt to exact reparations in accordance with the principle of chs. 21–22 has never been very successful, as the Roman general in G. B. Shaw's play *Caesar and Cleopatra* indicates, "I do not try to think things out. I only act from instinct." Most attempts at reparation are instinctive reactions which reduce the injured to the moral level of the injurer; a reading of this play and *Androcles and the Lion* will give one the other side of the case from that usually maintained by the disciples of that great idol, abstract justice.

4. *The Cost of Folly and Sin.*—The original and oldest account of the last plague as told by J (vss. 4-8; 12:29-39) should be read by itself, as various interpolations have been inserted into it. Some scholars think that the whole story of the last plague was invented to account for the custom of slaying the first-born lamb at the Passover feast. But it seems more likely that there was some historical basis for this last terror. Egypt was notorious as a land of pestilences and epidemics, and one can well believe that the Hebrews escaped during one of these visitations. The epidemic happened to occur during the Passover feast, and was therefore looked upon as punishment sent by Yahweh for the neglect of the sacrifice he had ordained in the wilderness of Sinai. The key of the situation is that because Pharaoh did not spare the first-born of Yahweh (Israel), Yahweh did not spare the first-born of Egypt, even Pharaoh's eldest son (4:23).

Symbolically, the last plague illustrates the historic curse of war. The first-born in all races were considered the choicest and best, whether among man or beast. War destroys the cream of every race engaged in it—the boldest, bravest, most self-sacrificing young men. Any biography of any great man born about the time that made him eligible to partake in World War I is proof of this truth. Read such a book as John Buchan's *Pilgrim's Way*,[5] and see in his chapter on Oxford what happened to the most brilliant men of his youth. Over and over again, after glowing eulogies of incipient greatness, comes a sentence such as, "When our troops advanced

[5] Boston: Houghton Mifflin Co., 1940, pp. 65, 60, 50.

5 And all the firstborn in the land of Egypt shall die, from the firstborn of Pharaoh that sitteth upon his throne, even unto the firstborn of the maidservant that *is* behind the mill; and all the firstborn of beasts.

6 And there shall be a great cry throughout all the land of Egypt, such as there was none like it, nor shall be like it any more.

7 But against any of the children of Israel shall not a dog move his tongue, against man or beast: that ye may know how that the LORD doth put a difference between the Egyptians and Israel.

of Egypt; 5 and all the first-born in the land of Egypt shall die, from the first-born of Pharaoh who sits upon his throne, even to the first-born of the maidservant who is behind the mill; and all the first-born of the cattle. 6 And there shall be a great cry throughout all the land of Egypt, such as there has never been, nor ever shall be again. 7 But against any of the people of Israel, either man or beast, not a dog shall growl; that you may know that the LORD makes a distinction between the Egyptians

---

5. The death of the first-born therefore symbolizes God's defeat of Egypt through the conquest of its gods. In Israelite thought the first-born represent the whole. The dominion of Egypt as an independent entity is at an end. Its gods are dead.

6. The **great cry** is indeed unique, for it is the cry of idols and idolaters at the Last Judgment. The writer sees the historical Exodus as an illustration of the eschatological victory of Yahweh. The Lord reigns (Ps. 97:1).

7-8. In the midst of this upheaval those who belong to the living God are safe, for it is he who is taking possession of the whole earth. No one shall even think of

---

to victory in the autumn of 1918, they found his grave," or "But on the fifteenth that fatal fire from the corner of Ginchy village brought death to many in the gallant division, and among them was Raymond Asquith. . . . One gift only was withheld from him—length of years." A visitor to Russia tells how he inquired concerning one outstanding genius after another whom he had met in the interval between the wars, and received always the same answer, "Killed in the war." War would be far from being such a curse if international law permitted only those over sixty-five to engage in it. But the embarkation parade would not be so impressive. "The last plague" which robs us periodically of the coming leaders of the next generation, and leaves us with the politicians only, can never come to an end, the Bible teaches us, unless after a tremendous upheaval men dare to escape out of this bondage which is slavery to what they call instinct.

The story of the last plague, reflecting attitudes toward Egypt like those found in Isaiah, Jeremiah, and Ezekiel, illustrates the hatred felt by Israel for the Egyptians, due partly to the national tradition of enslavement by the hated foreigner and partly to the religious intolerance which was one of the Semitic characteristics transmitted in some measure to Christianity. The first step toward religious and international unity must be to remove from each group the notion that nothing but its own theory is correct. No pious pretense can be a substitute for that.

When Fénelon and Bossuet had said every mean thing they could think about each other, they were apt to announce publicly that they were praying for each other's conversion. Perhaps one of the brightest signs of the times is the growth of a new spirit in the missionary enterprise which is not concerned with the "nothing-but-our-way" conception, but realizes that the religion of the East has much to teach the religion of the West; and that John Locke, who formulated the underlying philosophy of the American Constitution, may have something to learn even from Karl Marx, while at the same time the West has much to teach the East, and the Western democracies much to add to and correct in the Russian ideology. Impatience with another's viewpoint is a barren sentiment. Lily Langtry, when asked about history, is reported to have said that she felt it was better to let bygones be bygones. The same thing is true of ancient wrongs. Sir Horace Plunkett said, "The history of England's attempted domination of Ireland is for Englishmen to remember and for Irishmen to forget."

Of course Pharaoh had his point of view, and till recently it is conceivable that supreme courts would have upheld it as legal. Apparently he had acquired his property by due process of conquest. Moses proposed to rob him of it. At this early stage in history the same problem is presented as when a foreign government of our time proposes to cancel leases held in their land by our citizens, in order to better the condition

8 And all these thy servants shall come down unto me, and bow down themselves unto me, saying, Get thee out, and all the people that follow thee: and after that I will go out. And he went out from Pharaoh in a great anger.

9 And the Lord said unto Moses, Pharaoh shall not hearken unto you; that my wonders may be multiplied in the land of Egypt.

10 And Moses and Aaron did all these wonders before Pharaoh: and the Lord hardened Pharaoh's heart, so that he would not let the children of Israel go out of his land.

12 And the Lord spake unto Moses and Aaron in the land of Egypt, saying,

2 This month *shall be* unto you the beginning of months: it *shall be* the first month of the year to you.

and Israel. 8 And all these your servants shall come down to me, and bow down to me, saying, 'Get you out, and all the people who follow you.' And after that I will go out." And he went out from Pharaoh in hot anger. 9 Then the Lord said to Moses, "Pharaoh will not listen to you; that my wonders may be multiplied in the land of Egypt."

10 Moses and Aaron did all these wonders before Pharaoh; and the Lord hardened Pharaoh's heart, and he did not let the people of Israel go out of his land.

12 The Lord said to Moses and Aaron in the land of Egypt, 2 "This month shall be for you the beginning of months; it shall be the first month of the year for

---

harming them. Even the court of Pharaoh will acknowledge the lordship of Yahweh and bow before his people. Moses leaves in **hot anger.** One is reminded of the direction given the apostles with respect to the towns that did not heed their message (Matt. 10:14; Luke 9:5). The action of God in signs and powers has reached its climax. He will now take possession of Israel.

B. Yahweh Takes Possession of Israel (12:1–13:16)

Before the final blow falls in the dramatic conflict between Yahweh and the powers of Egypt there occurs, as it were, an interruption. The narrators introduce a series of laws covering three of Israel's socio-cultic observances. Each of these three rites—Passover, Unleavened Bread, and the Dedication of the First-Born—are said to derive their meaning from the event that is about to take place. In all probability the history of all three rites goes back to a time before the Exodus, whether among the Hebrews or among other groups. But in Israel, in all the biblical accounts, they attain a new meaning. All three commemorate the exodus revelation. They all attest that Israel belongs to Yahweh because of his redemptive action at the Exodus.

The primitive meaning of these rites differed greatly from the significance they acquired in the context of the exodus faith. In each case the alteration in meaning was more radical and rapid than the change in phenomenological form. Consequently, aided by a recovered knowledge of the general religious and cultural history of the ancient Near East, it is possible up to a point to reconstruct the nature and meaning of these rites in their pre-Mosaic setting by studying the phenomena that clung to them after they became testimonies to the Exodus. Further, it is also clear, and for our purposes even more significant, that these observances *continued to alter*, both in form and meaning, even after they had become festivals of Yahweh. The variety of laws and descriptions for each rite, provided by successive schools or periods, is actually a record of this continuous alteration in the midst of which the rites continue to attest the redeeming power of Yahweh in the exodus event. Thus literary and historical criticism provides us not only with a truer factual account of tradition, but simultaneously shows the role of tradition in relation to faith in the Bible itself.

A long period may have intervened between the Exodus and the production of even the oldest extant regulation for some or all of these rites. The process of recasting the form and content of each rite never ceased. In adapting the forms to Israel's faith by

3 ¶ Speak ye unto all the congregation of Israel, saying, In the tenth *day* of this month they shall take to them every man a lamb, according to the house of *their* fathers, a lamb for a house:

you. 3 Tell all the congregation of Israel that on the tenth day of this month they shall take every man a lamb according to their fathers' houses, a lamb for a house-

---

"purifying" the meaning, the prophetic leadership in Israel was normally ahead of general practice. Whatever pagan echoes may have continued to cling to them, it can be assumed that each of these three rites was kept in honor of the God of the Exodus long before the laws we now have about it were written down. This seems especially true in the case of Passover. We cannot rule out the possibility that Moses himself instituted it as Israel's feast in honor of the event of deliverance.

Since both here and in Deut. 15:19–16:8 the laws of these rites are published as a single block, some conclude that two or all three of them are different aspects of one basic rite which maintained itself from the beginning. Thus Beer says that "Passover is the feast of the offering of the first born" (*Exodus,* p. 71). Deuteronomy, indeed, offers real support for the view that attempts were made to make a single observance out of the three. It integrates Passover and Unleavened Bread and makes the Passover victim and the first-born appear as identical sacrifice. But this may not have been true from the first. Nor did the Deuteronomists' attempt to integrate them succeed any more completely than their concern to concentrate the observances wholly in Jerusalem. Neither originally nor ultimately was Passover just the sacrifice that Deuteronomy makes of it. If it had been, it could not well have survived until today. Here the contiguous location of the laws for the three rites is simply due to the fact that all three commemorate the Exodus.

1. Passover (12:1-14, 43-49 [P])

12:1. The prescriptions of P for the observance of Passover are introduced with the standard priestly formula, that God revealed his will also in this matter to Moses and Aaron.

2. Passover takes place in the spring. It is here said to occur in **the first month of the year.** Before the Babylonian exile Israel's year began in the autumn (34:22). In exile Israel began to conform to the Babylonian custom of beginning the year in the spring. In older accounts the month of Passover and Unleavened Bread is Abib, month of growing ears (13:4; 23:15; 34:18; Deut. 16:1). In the time of this writer it was known by the Babylonian name Nisan (Esth. 3:7). P is here concerned to stress the lasting significance of the Exodus celebrated by the Passover; it ushers in a new age.

3. The Passover is a family observance and the lamb is its central feature. In Deuteronomy the family character of the feast had disappeared, and instead of the lamb

---

of their own nationals. In its most general form the problem is whether wealth is essentially social and therefore subject in all points to control in the interests of society as a whole. Pharaoh insisted on his legal rights in his own property. Moses contended for the common good of society as a whole. Today he would raise the question as to whether or not an economic system which produces unemployment, slums, and poverty can be justified by the property rights inherent in the system of individual enterprise. In recent years we have at least dared to experiment with methods for alleviating some of the scandals of our system. Pharaoh would have justified himself by pointing to the great public buildings, the high standard of living in Egypt

under his administration, and the comparatively low cost of construction now that the state was no longer under the necessity of providing straw for the bricks; while Moses would have pointed with his magic staff to the epidemics, flies, lice, decaying fish, and frogs, about which nothing was done, and to the shameful condition of the workers' homes. This controversy goes on today.

> In front, the sun climbs slow, how slowly,
> But westward, look, the land is bright.[6]

12:3-27. *The Meaning of the Passover.*—The whole section about the institution of the Pass-

[6] Arthur Hugh Clough, "Say Not, the Struggle Nought Availeth."

there was an offering from "the flock or the herd" (Deut. 16:1-8). The Deuteronomic effort to change Passover into a temple sacrifice was at least partly successful and continued as long as the temple stood (Ezek. 45:21-25; Lev. 23:5; Ezra 6:19-20; Jubilees 49; II Chr. 30; 35:1-19). Nevertheless, as the character of the documents emphasizing it indicates, this effort remained to a large degree an ideal prescription rather than an actual realization. Since it was never fully transformed into a temple sacrifice Passover could continue when Jerusalem and the temple were lost. The provisions of the P writer, while ostensibly designed only for the first Passover in Egypt as opposed to all later observances, "the Passover of the generations" (Pesahim 9:5), seem to imply that the family character of the feast, with the lamb as its feature, was still a fact in his day. In speaking of the **congregation of Israel, . . . according to their fathers' houses,** he is, to be sure, influenced by the organization of society among the returned exiles in Jerusalem.

---

over is composed of annotated and supplemented narrative and laws from J and P. There are repetitions and inconsistencies, and the story of the actual Exodus is confused by the introduction into the narrative of these laws. The theory of the editor is that all laws as to the first-born, the Passover, and the feast of Unleavened Bread, were given to Israel at the same time the people were departing from Egypt. The attempt to carry out this theory, which is not supported by other parts of the Pentateuch, leads to much necessary annotation (see Exeg. on 12:1–13:16).

A communal feast reminiscent of some great national deliverance, in the presence or in the company of God as participant, is an inspiring religious custom. Only a few nations have been able to carry out through the ages such a tradition. Western peoples have tried it over and over again, but have found that it degenerates soon into an individualistic and often vulgar holiday, without national or religious meaning. The Jews and some Oriental peoples have succeeded through centuries in preserving the national and religious significance of such festivals. The President of the United States still issues Thanksgiving proclamations, but a bird's-eye view of the country on Thanksgiving Day would not lead the observer to conclude that any national or religious festival was in progress. Open-air services at dawn on Easter morning are attempts to revive the idea of a religious festival, if they are not allowed to become theatrical shows. The Roman Catholic Church has been much more successful than the Protestant churches in perpetuating such religious festivals. Most citizens of Western countries suffer from a fear of making a show of themselves, and do not have as a matter of fact any aspirations or sentiments which they cannot adequately express in words. We have got far enough in our development as human beings to honor our spectacularly great men by processions and ticker tape, but the idea of thanksgiving to God for a great deliverance seems to most people to be a pious pose, participating in which would make them

feel awkward. The Passover is a grand example of more mature national and religious thought and feeling, with its reminiscences of the story of the national past in unleavened bread, bitter herbs, and sacrifice, observed while the participants are dressed for a journey, shoes on their feet and a staff in their hands.

Much of the sentiment and feeling connected with it has passed into the Christian sacrament of the Holy Communion: it, too, should be a feast in the presence of God, filled with grateful remembrances of past deliverances by God. It should not be allowed to be emptied of its original meaning by theological obsessions or by ecclesiastical trappings, or by the modern inventions of silversmiths, glass and tinware merchants. If custom demands that these dominate the rite, there is something to be said for the Roman custom of a Communion breakfast following the rite, which will perpetuate more of the friendly, family feeling of the Passover. The participants are called upon to remember that they have had a past, filled with the mercies of God, that they owe much that is most precious in life to the sacrifice of others, that the flavor of life is in the mingling of the bitter and the sweet, and that they should not sit at their ease, but should be dressed and ready for the journey, the hard journey they have to make together with their friends and neighbors into the Promised Land where there will be milk and even some honey for all.

3-7. The Belief in Salvation by the Blood.— From the earliest records of primitive sacrifice man has been obsessed by the efficacy of innocent blood to save from disaster. Both the Roman Catholic and the Protestant churches have perpetuated this primitive tradition in all their ritual, in their hymns and sacred books. Realistically, shed blood is horrible beyond words; imaginatively, it has been used as a symbol of the omnipresence of sacrifice in human life. The scene when the priest carries the struggling little animal in his arms, takes it to the edge of the altar, or rock, or lintel, and

4 And if the household be too little for the lamb, let him and his neighbor next unto his house take *it* according to the number of the souls; every man according to his eating shall make your count for the lamb.

5 Your lamb shall be without blemish, a male of the first year: ye shall take *it* out from the sheep, or from the goats:

hold; 4 and if the household is too small for a lamb, then a man and his neighbor next to his house shall take according to the number of persons; according to what each can eat you shall make your count for the lamb. 5 Your lamb shall be without blemish, a male a year old; you shall take it from the

---

According to the Mishnah the requirement to select the lamb on the tenth day, as well as the sprinkling of blood on the doorposts and the hasty consumption, applied *only* to the first observance (Pesahim 9:5). Such provisions must perhaps be interpreted as efforts at reform or justifications of disuse, in this instance probably the former.

4. According to Josephus ten was the minimum number for a **household** (*Jewish War* VI. 9. 3), the number required to this day for the organization of a Jewish congregation. Whenever two "households" had to use the same room scrupulous care was taken in their separation; they were seated with their backs to one another.

5. The lamb must be "perfect" (cf. the P regulations governing sacrifices in Lev. 22:19-25). Burnt offerings also consisted of males. The provision that the lamb must be "the son of a year" is traditionally interpreted to mean that the lamb is in its first year, one of the current crop. As such it would be only a few weeks old at most. Most modern interpreters, backed by the LXX, take the view that the lamb was fully a year old,

---

draws a knife across its throat, letting the jet of blood spurt from its throat and fall on the stains made by blood shed before—for "the colour of spilt blood is not properly a colour, it is in itself discoloured, it is a visible display of putrescence" [7]—the horror of the scene is forgotten because of the sense of the preciousness of the life that is offered for sin. Added to a subsconscious delight in gore, there is also an ancient superstition that there is some magic efficacy in the murder of the innocent. Man's vileness is in essence cruelty, and it has been felt that only by cruelty can it be atoned for. Murdering goodness must be paid for by murdering goodness. The fact rather is that it is not possible to kill goodness: there is always more of it. In times of peace, writers of blood and gore have been popular, but every war has demonstrated that shed blood cannot be idealized. It is pure horror.

To Paul and Augustine, both men with cruel pasts, both men living among scenes of sacrificial cruelty, the slaying of the lamb could become the central picture of their faith. We are not as heroic figures as they, but we are more able to distinguish between the more and less noble elements in their imagery. We begin to see that the idea of suffering as the price for all good is only a splendid half-truth; that it is even nobler and often harder to live one's faith

[7] Rebecca West, *Black Lamb and Grey Falcon* (New York: Viking Press, 1940), p. 823. For a vivid description of the ritual killing of a lamb see pp. 820-31.

than to die for it; that a satisfactory theory of atonement for murder by murder can be reached only by sophisticated and theological ruses inacceptable to fair minds today. We need a new statement of Christian doctrine which will discard outworn imagery and concentrate upon the fact that religious truth cannot be expressed in even the most deftly chosen words, but only in the lives of humble folk; that a Christian philosophy of life or theology must savor less of excessively speculative otherworldliness and give more help in deciding what things are most worth while in daily life and how they may be attained. A genuine theology grows its own ritual. The man who was asked how his new car worked and answered, "I do not know; nothing has gone wrong with it yet," gives us the cue to much of the understanding of how our human minds work. We learn a great deal as to how healthy minds operate by studying morbid conditions. In the process of editing hymns for use in hospitals for the insane, much of the usual material is found to savor too much of the morbid and unhealthy to make it possible to use as an instrument of mental healing.

Truth never wears out, but symbols do. The time has come when we can discard some of the imagery of blood which was entirely satisfactory to Paul and Augustine, as it was to Moses. There are already nobler methods of expressing the importance of sacrifice, and we can guard against evil in more rational ways than by painting our doorposts with the blood of innocent

6 And ye shall keep it up until the fourteenth day of the same month: and the whole assembly of the congregation of Israel shall kill it in the evening.

7 And they shall take of the blood, and strike *it* on the two side posts and on the upper doorpost of the houses, wherein they shall eat it.

sheep or from the goats; 6 and you shall keep it until the fourteenth day of this month, when the whole assembly of the congregation of Israel shall kill their lambs in the evening.*o* 7 Then they shall take some of the blood, and put it on the two doorposts and the lintel of the houses in which

o Heb *between the two evenings*

---

belonging to the previous year's crop. It seems doubtful, however, that this was the original meaning of the phrase which among Semitic peoples to this day signifies one who is "in his first year." All of these cultic regulations applied to the Passover by P are conspicuously lacking in J's account (vss. 21-28).

6. The postexilic celebration of the Passover is again in the writer's mind as he presents a picture of the heads of "households" all gathered in a single place for the slaying. The Mishnah understands that three groups of families successively entered the temple court for the killing of the lambs. Hence the pleonasm: **assembly, congregation, Israel.** The heads of families killed the animals, and the priests formed a "bucket brigade" to catch the blood in basins and toss it against the base of the altar, in lieu of the ancient threshold ceremony (Pesahim 5:5-6). In Jewish orthodoxy the time of the slaughter, **between the two evenings,** is specified as in the afternoon, before sunset; especially, the time of approaching sunset. The Mishnah implies that any time after noon was valid for the slaying (Pesahim 5:3). Samaritans, Karaites, and Sadducees specify the time as after sunset and before darkness. The latter probably designates the more archaic practice.

7. A very ancient part of the rite is here recognized as a legitimate aspect of the first Passover. The P writer has modified J's account as to the manner in which the blood is to be applied to the doorposts and lintel (cf. vs. 22). The application of the blood to the threshold in all probability is an aspect of the Passover that antedates its observance by Israel in memory of the Exodus. Indeed, it is possible that this points to the originally central meaning of the rite, i.e., that it was a ceremony designed to appease the spirit of the threshold or, perhaps more likely, to protect the inhabitants of a

---

lambs. For in the "fountain filled with blood" idea there is undoubtedly much of the mistakenly mystical justification and glorification of war.

The symbolism of shed blood is still very precious to many Christians, and will ever remain so in the Holy Supper, where its mysticism means participation in the very life of Jesus, his real presence in the daily life of the communicant. But in our days wholesale shedding of blood in war has actually been seen most horribly by too many of us. Its precious mystical meaning has been swallowed up in our common sense of guilt that such things can be.

All early races have been persuaded that there was something mystically potent about blood. Most deaths in those days were violent deaths. Blood was the symbol both of life and of death. The disease germ of our time had not yet taken its place as the symbol of death in peacetime. It is a curious commentary on the infantilism of human nature that Christian ritual has centered so much on the momentary heroism of war rather than on the continuous heroism of peace,

on dead blood, blood that has been shed, and has not been able to frame equally appealing symbols of live blood, blood throbbing in warm heroic life.[8] Those who feel most at home with the blood of the martyrs today would have felt anything but comfortable with the living men. People seek to find their solace in tableaux of legal transactions imagined to have taken place in heaven. They fall back on arbitrary commands supposed to have been issued by God, which must be blindly obeyed, long after the reasons why such commands were supposed to have come from God have become invalid. We seem in much theological dogmatism to be overhearing the conversation between two infants in adjacent cribs: "It is so!" "It isn't so!" "Mother says it is so, and if mother says it is so, it is so, even if it isn't so!" A deeper, fairer, more accurate theology, founded on accepted scien-

[8] For the hope of a religious ritual language really commensurate with our understanding of Christianity, see the later work of Paul Tillich, and Arnold J. Toynbee, *Christianity and Civilization* (Wallingford, Pa.: Pendle Hill, 1947), pp. 28, 32-34, 44.

| 8 And they shall eat the flesh in that night, roast with fire, and unleavened bread; *and* with bitter *herbs* they shall eat it. 9 Eat not of it raw, nor sodden at all with water, but roast *with* fire; his head with his legs, and with the purtenance thereof. | they eat them. 8 They shall eat the flesh that night, roasted; with unleavened bread and bitter herbs they shall eat it. 9 Do not eat any of it raw or boiled with water, but roasted, its head with its legs and its inner |

home or tent from attack by demons or spirits from without by barring their entrance. The lamb may well have been the symbol also of the bond that united the group protected by its blood, and thus it served as the sign of a covenant. The efforts to transform Passover into a priestly offering never really uprooted this communal quality. Originally the slaying of the lamb seems to have taken place on the threshold of the door to which the blood was applied (cf. vs. 22).

8. The roasting of the lamb is emphasized in the later period. The ordinance in Deut. 16:7 seems to prescribe boiling rather than roasting (cf. I Sam. 2:13). In the earliest periods the lamb was very probably consumed raw. The frequent prohibitions of blood and raw meat in Israel's legislation seem to point to an earlier use of both. According to the Mishnah, the lamb was roasted on a skewer of pomegranate wood thrust through the carcass from end to end (Pesahim 7:1). Metal skewers or grills were prohibited. The bitter herbs, symbolic of Israel's bitter suffering (Pesahim 10:5), could, according to the Mishnah, consist of lettuce, chicory, peppermint, snakeroot, or dandelion (Pesahim 2:6). When eaten, these were dipped into a sauce (*ḥarôseth*) of pounded nuts and fruit sprinkled with vinegar. This sauce was not accepted as obligatory by all (Pesahim 10:3). While in the biblical accounts the bitter herbs commemorated the hardness of bondage in Egypt, the original significance must have been something very different. Beer feels that this was originally a separate pre-Israelite rite which, like Passover, was assimilated to Israel's faith (*Exodus*, p. 65). It is the intention of P to distinguish Passover from Unleavened Bread as separate observances. Nevertheless, even where this was true, the removal of all leaven from homes had to be completed on the fourteenth day of the month, usually by noon (cf. Num. 28:16-17).

9. There were long and inconclusive debates in later Judaism as to whether the **legs** were to be folded inside the carcass while the lamb was being roasted, or left on the outside.

tific facts and on the highest human aspirations, may grow out of that common, humble silence around the grave of the unknown soldier, and bring with it its own ritual for the inspiration of all; for this experience speaks to all of every creed of the deep mystery of religion, of "God . . . the great companion—the fellow-sufferer who understands." [9] In all this imagery of blood man has been feeling after a true picture of death as the fulfillment of life. Great and princely death in each man's life is the fruit around which all else is flower and leaf; our dying is a part of and grows out of our living. Dreaded by itself, death hangs anticipated in each man's life, green and without sweetness like an unripened fruit. But "ripeness is all"

and when the moment comes, we find it the mellow consummation of a long process that has been continually maturing, that always has been dying to the old self in order to put on the new. "It is not death that kills but a more powerful life which, concealed behind the form of death, is bursting forth into a new phase of being." [1]

8. *Unleavened Bread.*—Originally Matzoth, the feast of Unleavened Bread, was distinct from the Passover; the editor, however, has identified them and explains the absence of leaven as due to the haste of the departure. Leaven, in the opinion of all antiquity, represents a process of corruption and putrefaction in the mass of the dough. (Cf. its use in the N.T.; Matt. 16:6; Mark 8:15; Luke 12:1; I Cor. 5:6;

[9] A. N. Whitehead, *Process and Reality* (New York: The Macmillan Co., 1929), p. 532.

[1] See "The Vocation of Man," in *The Popular Works of Johann Gottlieb Fichte*, tr. William Smith (4th ed.; London: Trübner & Co., 1889), I, 321 ff.

10 And ye shall let nothing of it remain until the morning; and that which remaineth of it until the morning ye shall burn with fire.

11 ¶ And thus shall ye eat it; *with* your loins girded, your shoes on your feet, and your staff in your hand; and ye shall eat it in haste: it *is* the Lord's passover.

12 For I will pass through the land of Egypt this night, and will smite all the first-born in the land of Egypt, both man and beast; and against all the gods of Egypt I will execute judgment: I *am* the Lord.

13 And the blood shall be to you for a token upon the houses where ye *are:* and when I see the blood, I will pass over you, and the plague shall not be upon you to destroy *you,* when I smite the land of Egypt.

14 And this day shall be unto you for a memorial; and ye shall keep it a feast to the Lord throughout your generations: ye shall keep it a feast by an ordinance for ever.

parts. 10 And you shall let none of it remain until the morning, anything that remains until the morning you shall burn.

11 In this manner you shall eat it: your loins girded, your sandals on your feet, and your staff in your hand; and you shall eat it in haste. It is the Lord's passover. 12 For I will pass through the land of Egypt that night, and I will smite all the first-born in the land of Egypt, both man and beast; and on all the gods of Egypt I will execute judgments: I am the Lord. 13 The blood shall be a sign for you, upon the houses where you are; and when I see the blood, I will pass over you, and no plague shall fall upon you to destroy you, when I smite the land of Egypt.

14 "This day shall be for you a memorial day, and you shall keep it as a feast to the Lord; throughout your generations you shall observe it as an ordinance for ever.

---

10. The nocturnal nature of Passover is emphasized by the provision to burn any Passover meat that remained until morning (Isa. 30:29).

11. The people ate Passover as though outside. **Staff** and **sandals** are not taken indoors, nor does one indoors tie his long robe about his waist as when on the march. According to later tradition this eating in haste and fear applied only to the first Passover (Pesahim 9:5). The word "Passover" was probably a derivative of the verb meaning to limp or to leap (cf. II Sam. 4:4; I Kings 18:21, 26). But here it is clearly treated as a derivative from an identical root that means "to pass over." It refers to the passing by of Yahweh. To the P writer this signifies God's protection of the community. Originally, however, the emphasis was one in which the blood was a means of protecting one's group from some outside evil power.

12-13. The Passover was thus the sign of the covenant and of the people's safety under it. When in a "last judgment" Yahweh displayed his power over Egypt and over its gods (cf. 6:6; 7:4) by destroying them, Israel would be safe. The rite of the first-born in Israel sets forth its acknowledgment of God's rule while Passover celebrates Israel as the community of the covenant.

14. The **memorial day** seems to conclude the account of the Passover. But it is possible that the remainder of the verse really is a form of transition in which Passover and Unleavened Bread are associated together.

43-49. The supplementary laws of the Passover by P remind us strongly that in Israel social unity rested on the foundation of a common faith. A sign of this faith in P's day was circumcision. All that belongs to Israel, like Israel itself, belongs to Yahweh. Hence slaves are circumcised. But a foreigner can also voluntarily become a member of the community by conversion to Israel's faith. This conversion is made effective by circumcision and transcends whatever ethnic or other differences may exist; hence, **one law for the native and for the stranger** (vs. 49). The blessings of the Passover are for the children of the covenant.

The provision not to carry the Passover outside or break a bone of it is perhaps best understood as intended to uproot ancient superstitions. Originally bones were perhaps

15 Seven days shall ye eat unleavened bread; even the first day ye shall put away leaven out of your houses: for whosoever eateth leavened bread from the first day until the seventh day, that soul shall be cut off from Israel.

16 And in the first day *there shall be* a holy convocation, and in the seventh day there shall be a holy convocation to you; no manner of work shall be done in them, save *that* which every man must eat, that only may be done of you.

17 And ye shall observe *the feast of* unleavened bread; for in this selfsame day have I brought your armies out of the land of Egypt: therefore shall ye observe this day in your generations by an ordinance for ever.

18 ¶ In the first *month,* on the fourteenth day of the month at even, ye shall

15 Seven days you shall eat unleavened bread; on the first day you shall put away leaven out of your houses, for if any one eats what is leavened, from the first day until the seventh day, that person shall be cut off from Israel. 16 On the first day you shall hold a holy assembly, and on the seventh day a holy assembly; no work shall be done on those days; but what every one must eat, that only may be prepared by you. 17 And you shall observe the feast of unleavened bread, for on this very day I brought your hosts out of the land of Egypt: therefore you shall observe this day, throughout your generations, as an ordinance for ever. 18 In the first month, on the fourteenth

broken to obtain the marrow. Bits of the meat and the marrow may have been used as magic means to insure fertility in field and flock or to insure against calamity. Hence P's prohibitions.

2. UNLEAVENED BREAD (12:15-20; 13:3-10)

15. Originally the feast of Unleavened Bread was a festival celebrated on the occasion of the barley harvest. As in the case of the other great festivals assimilated to Israel's faith, it was transformed from a nature festival to a historical feast, commemorating the historic event of Israel's deliverance by Yahweh. It became bound up with Passover. Walther Eichrodt suggests that when the two became known under one name, the term "Mazzoth" was used in the agricultural north and the term "Passover" in the pastoral south (*Theologie des Alten Testaments* [Berlin: Evangelische Verlagsanstalt, 1948], I, 52). That might explain why we have no reference to Passover in the E narrative. Here the feast is not separated by name from the Passover that precedes it. This does occur in Lev. 23:6. In Num. 28:17 we are told that it began on the fifteenth day of the month. Here the **first day,** on which leaven is removed, must mean the fourteenth (cf. vs. 18).

16. Thus **the first day** is in all likelihood the fifteenth, following the Passover night. There is to be rest from work except that, unlike on the sabbath, food may be prepared. On this and the seventh days burnt offerings in addition to those made daily were a central feature of the observance. The combination of the Unleavened Bread observance with Passover seems to have tended to make of the whole a more sacrificial rite.

Gal. 5:9; and in the Talmud, "Rabbi Alexander, when he had finished his prayers, said, 'Lord of the universe, it is clear to thee that it is our will to do thy will; what hinders that we do not thy will? The leaven which is in the dough!'") On the eve of the Passover Jewish households still scrupulously and joyfully search the house with lighted candle for any scrap of dough containing leaven; it must be burned before the feast. It is curious that Jesus uses it, however, as a figure of the slow growth of the kingdom (Matt. 13:33). Phillips Brooks's famous sermon, "The

Mystery of Iniquity," emphasizes the fact that badness seems to be a more contagious ferment than goodness, that a good little boy in a bad neighborhood is more likely to be depraved by his surroundings than to regenerate them. However, Jesus consciously used the very figure commonly employed to describe the contagious power of evil to illustrate the contagious power of good; but negative goodness does not so operate, as a comparison between the life of Jesus and the life of most of us, "good little boys," demonstrates.

eat unleavened bread, until the one and twentieth day of the month at even.

19 Seven days shall there be no leaven found in your houses: for whosoever eateth that which is leavened, even that soul shall be cut off from the congregation of Israel, whether he be a stranger, or born in the land.

20 Ye shall eat nothing leavened; in all your habitations shall ye eat unleavened bread.

21 ¶ Then Moses called for all the elders of Israel, and said unto them, Draw out and take you a lamb according to your families, and kill the passover.

22 And ye shall take a bunch of hyssop, and dip it in the blood that is in the basin, and strike the lintel and the two side posts with the blood that is in the basin; and none of you shall go out at the door of his house until the morning.

23 For the LORD will pass through to

day of the month at evening, you shall eat unleavened bread, and so until the twenty-first day of the month at evening. 19 For seven days no leaven shall be found in your houses; for if any one eats what is leavened, that person shall be cut off from the congregation of Israel, whether he is a sojourner or a native of the land. 20 You shall eat nothing leavened; in all your dwellings you shall eat unleavened bread."

21 Then Moses called all the elders of Israel, and said to them, "Select lambs for yourselves according to your families, and kill the passover lamb. 22 Take a bunch of hyssop and dip it in the blood which is in the basin, and touch the lintel and the two doorposts with the blood which is in the basin; and none of you shall go out of the door of his house until the morning. 23 For

19-20. The prohibition of **leaven** was eventually to become the most scrupulously observed regulation. Careful search had to be made to see that all of it had been removed. One who did not conform was "cut off," i.e., excommunicated from the family of Israel. This meant, as Mekilta observes (*ad loc.*), that he ceased to exist, either for Israel or for God (Lev. 22:3).

13:3-10. A Deuteronomic editor, who identifies himself by means of characteristic phrases (vss. 5, 9), provides the law of Unleavened Bread with a homiletic supplement. He assumes (vs. 4) that Moses published the law on the very day of the departure (cf. 12:2-3). He calls the month of the Exodus by its pre-exilic name Abib (cf. 12:2). The observance of the rite is a sign, comparable to the wearing of phylacteries and the memorized Torah (vs. 9; cf. Deut. 6:4-9).

3. PASSOVER (12:21-28 [J])

21. Here, as elsewhere in J (4:29), Moses speaks to the **elders**. This account pre-supposes neither the postexilic organization of society nor the Deuteronomic and priestly laws about Passover, as do vss. 1-14.

22. The **bunch of hyssop** was also used in purification ceremonies (Lev. 14:4, 6; Num. 19:6, 18). It consisted of the foliage of the marjoram plant which grew in the clefts of walls and between stones (I Kings 4:33). Some magical powers may originally have been attributed to it. Analogous features occur in nearly all religions. The hyssop has its Christian continuation in the holy water sprinkled from the aspergillum or in that brush itself. In Hebrew the words for "basin" and "threshold" are the same. There is every reason to suppose that the latter is intended here. It is so understood in the LXX and in Mekilta (*ad loc.*), where it is pointed out that Rabbi Akiba dissociated himself from this common understanding. The lamb was slaughtered on the threshold and its blood spilled into a hollow place probably made for this very purpose. H. Oort reports on Armenian miniatures that depict the slaying in this manner ("Oud-Israëls Paaschfeest," *Theologisch Tijdschrift,* XLII [1908], 489-90).

23. The judgment upon Egypt is God's work, but his activity is personified as **the destroyer**. It is possible that the assimilation of pre-Israelite demonology under the aegis of the Lord's rule is reflected in the form of this account.

smite the Egyptians; and when he seeth the blood upon the lintel, and on the two side posts, the LORD will pass over the door, and will not suffer the destroyer to come in unto your houses to smite *you.*

24 And ye shall observe this thing for an ordinance to thee and to thy sons for ever.

25 And it shall come to pass, when ye be come to the land which the LORD will give you, according as he hath promised, that ye shall keep this service.

26 And it shall come to pass, when your children shall say unto you, What mean ye by this service?

27 That ye shall say, It *is* the sacrifice of the LORD's passover, who passed over the houses of the children of Israel in Egypt, when he smote the Egyptians, and delivered our houses. And the people bowed the head and worshipped.

28 And the children of Israel went away, and did as the LORD had commanded Moses and Aaron, so did they.

29 ¶ And it came to pass, that at midnight the LORD smote all the firstborn in the land of Egypt, from the firstborn of Pharaoh that sat on his throne unto the firstborn of the captive that *was* in the dungeon; and all the firstborn of cattle.

30 And Pharaoh rose up in the night, he, and all his servants, and all the Egyptians; and there was a great cry in Egypt: for *there was* not a house where *there was* not one dead.

31 ¶ And he called for Moses and Aaron by night, and said, Rise up, *and* get you forth from among my people, both ye and

the LORD will pass through to slay the Egyptians; and when he sees the blood on the lintel and on the two doorposts, the LORD will pass over the door, and will not allow the destroyer to enter your houses to slay you. 24 You shall observe this rite as an ordinance for you and for your sons for ever. 25 And when you come to the land which the LORD will give you, as he has promised, you shall keep this service. 26 And when your children say to you, 'What do you mean by this service?' 27 you shall say, 'It is the sacrifice of the LORD's passover, for he passed over the houses of the people of Israel in Egypt, when he slew the Egyptians but spared our houses.' " And the people bowed their heads and worshiped.

28 Then the people of Israel went and did so; as the LORD had commanded Moses and Aaron, so they did.

29 At midnight the LORD smote all the first-born in the land of Egypt, from the first-born of Pharaoh who sat on his throne to the first-born of the captive who was in the dungeon, and all the first-born of the cattle. 30 And Pharaoh rose up in the night, he, and all his servants, and all the Egyptians; and there was a great cry in Egypt, for there was not a house where one was not dead. 31 And he summoned Moses and Aaron by night, and said, "Rise up, go forth

---

24-28. The statement that **the people bowed their heads and worshiped** (cf. 4:31) probably once concluded this brief J account. The remainder consists mostly of a didactic effort to make the people realize the importance of keeping the Passover in terms of its historic meaning for Israel. It has a Deuteronomic flavor.

4. DEATH OF EGYPT'S FIRST-BORN (12:29-32)

29-30. This account reports the fulfillment of the "last judgment" upon Egypt, as anticipated in 11:4-8. It follows immediately upon the account of the institution of the Passover, which, as vs. 27 implies and vs. 28 (P) makes explicit, was actually kept. The **great cry** of anguish (cf. 11:6) symbolizes the complete disintegration of human pride at the appearance of the day of wrath (cf. Isa. 2:12-22; Joel 2:6). Israel is safe by virtue of the covenant of God celebrated in Passover, under which it belongs to him.

31-32. According to J, Moses had vowed not to see Pharaoh again (10:29). This is another source of the story. Pharaoh begs Israel to leave, and thus the stubborn ruler recognizes the lordship of Yahweh.

the children of Israel; and go, serve the Lord, as ye have said.

32 Also take your flocks and your herds, as ye have said, and be gone; and bless me also.

33 And the Egyptians were urgent upon the people, that they might send them out of the land in haste; for they said, We *be* all dead *men*.

34 And the people took their dough before it was leavened, their kneadingtroughs being bound up in their clothes upon their shoulders.

35 And the children of Israel did according to the word of Moses; and they borrowed of the Egyptians jewels of silver, and jewels of gold, and raiment:

36 And the Lord gave the people favor in the sight of the Egyptians, so that they lent unto them *such things as they required:* and they spoiled the Egyptians.

37 ¶ And the children of Israel journeyed from Rameses to Succoth, about six hundred thousand on foot *that were* men, beside children.

from among my people, both you and the people of Israel; and go, serve the Lord, as you have said. 32 Take your flocks and your herds, as you have said, and be gone; and bless me also!"

33 And the Egyptians were urgent with the people, to send them out of the land in haste; for they said, "We are all dead men." 34 So the people took their dough before it was leavened, their kneading bowls being bound up in their mantles on their shoulders. 35 The people of Israel had also done as Moses told them, for they had asked of the Egyptians jewelry of silver and of gold, and clothing; 36 and the Lord had given the people favor in the sight of the Egyptians, so that they let them have what they asked. Thus they despoiled the Egyptians.

37 And the people of Israel journeyed from Ram'eses to Succoth, about six hundred thousand men on foot, besides women

---

5. Sudden Departure (12:33-36)

33. The Egyptians shared the attitude of Pharaoh at the victory of Yahweh. They urged the people to depart. *Ca.* 250 b.c. Manetho wrote a history in which he insisted that the ancestors of the Jews were so undesirable that they had been driven out of Egypt. A garbled account of this verse may have suggested his assertion.

34. This is an etiological note which explains the custom of eating unleavened bread in commemoration of the Exodus in a very natural and incidental manner. It did not rest on a divine command but came about as an incident of the sudden departure. The assumption is that the people had to leave long before daybreak: they had not mixed leaven in the dough from which they were to make bread in the morning. The explanation leaves Passover untouched by the custom. The suddenness of the departure is the beginning of the ever-recurrent theme in the Bible that God comes unexpectedly and that his people must always be ready.

35-36. The spoliation of the Egyptians (3:21-22; 11:2-3) is reported as having been carried out according to plan.

6. Israel Sets Out from Egypt (12:37-42)

37. The slaves pulled up stakes. The first leg of their sudden journey from Rameses to Succoth crossed the much-traveled coastal road to Palestine (13:17). Tell-el-Maskhuta is the site of ancient Succoth. Just to the east lies Lake Timsah and north and south of it the marsh across which the Israelites made their way into Asia and freedom. The adult men "alone" numbered **six hundred thousand.** It is plausible that this impossible number rests on a numerical interpretation of the Hebrew letters in the phrase "sons of Israel" (cf. Beer, *Exodus,* p. 69). That the figure has no basis in fact is clear from almost every point of view. Such a large number could not have lived in Egypt or survived in the desert. Nor could they have found room in Canaan. The actual situation is intimated by 23:29-30; Judg. 5:8.

38 And a mixed multitude went up also with them; and flocks, and herds, *even* very much cattle.

39 And they baked unleavened cakes of the dough which they brought forth out of Egypt, for it was not leavened; because they were thrust out of Egypt, and could not tarry, neither had they prepared for themselves any victuals.

40 ¶ Now the sojourning of the children of Israel, who dwelt in Egypt, *was* four hundred and thirty years.

41 And it came to pass at the end of the four hundred and thirty years, even the selfsame day it came to pass, that all the hosts of the Lord went out from the land of Egypt.

42 It *is* a night to be much observed unto the Lord for bringing them out from the land of Egypt: this *is* that night of the Lord to be observed of all the children of Israel in their generations.

43 ¶ And the Lord said unto Moses and Aaron, This *is* the ordinance of the passover: There shall no stranger eat thereof:

44 But every man's servant that is bought for money, when thou hast circumcised him, then shall he eat thereof.

45 A foreigner and a hired servant shall not eat thereof.

46 In one house shall it be eaten; thou shalt not carry forth aught of the flesh abroad out of the house; neither shall ye break a bone thereof.

47 All the congregation of Israel shall keep it.

48 And when a stranger shall sojourn with thee, and will keep the passover to the Lord, let all his males be circumcised, and then let him come near and keep it; and he shall be as one that is born in the land: for no uncircumcised person shall eat thereof.

49 One law shall be to him that is home-

and children. 38 A mixed multitude also went up with them, and very many cattle, both flocks and herds. 39 And they baked unleavened cakes of the dough which they had brought out of Egypt, for it was not leavened, because they were thrust out of Egypt and could not tarry, neither had they prepared for themselves any provisions.

40 The time that the people of Israel dwelt in Egypt was four hundred and thirty years. 41 And at the end of four hundred and thirty years, on that very day, all the hosts of the Lord went out from the land of Egypt. 42 It was a night of watching by the Lord, to bring them out of the land of Egypt; so this same night is a night of watching kept to the Lord by all the people of Israel throughout their generations.

43 And the Lord said to Moses and Aaron, "This is the ordinance of the passover: no foreigner shall eat of it; 44 but every slave that is bought for money may eat of it after you have circumcised him. 45 No sojourner or hired servant may eat of it. 46 In one house shall it be eaten; you shall not carry forth any of the flesh outside the house; and you shall not break a bone of it. 47 All the congregation of Israel shall keep it. 48 And when a stranger shall sojourn with you and would keep the passover to the Lord, let all his males be circumcised, then he may come near and keep it; he shall be as a native of the land. But no uncircumcised person shall eat of it. 49 There shall

38. If the **mixed multitude** is to be understood historically it most probably consisted of non-Israelite Semitic elements in Egypt.

39. One is left with the impression that not until they reached Succoth, about twenty-five miles away, did the fugitives stop to bake the unleavened dough (vs. 34).

40-42. The **four hundred and thirty** years compares with four hundred in Gen. 15:13 (cf. Acts 7:6; Gal. 3:17). The LXX here adds the phrase "and in Canaan," possibly to harmonize the discrepancy. This was the night of Israel's birth. Yahweh stood guard to protect it. Therefore Israel must guard the memory of this night. The reference is to the observance of Passover.

43-49. See Exeg. on vss. 43-49, pp. 921-22.

born, and unto the stranger that sojourneth among you.

50 Thus did all the children of Israel; as the Lord commanded Moses and Aaron, so did they.

51 And it came to pass the selfsame day, *that* the Lord did bring the children of Israel out of the land of Egypt by their armies.

13 And the Lord spake unto Moses, saying,

2 Sanctify unto me all the firstborn, whatsoever openeth the womb among the children of Israel, *both* of man and of beast: it *is* mine.

3 ¶ And Moses said unto the people, Remember this day, in which ye came out from Egypt, out of the house of bondage; for by strength of hand the Lord brought you out from this *place:* there shall no leavened bread be eaten.

4 This day came ye out in the month Abib.

5 ¶ And it shall be when the Lord shall bring thee into the land of the Canaanites, and the Hittites, and the Amorites, and the Hivites, and the Jebusites, which he sware unto thy fathers to give thee, a land flowing with milk and honey, that thou shalt keep this service in this month.

6 Seven days thou shalt eat unleavened bread, and in the seventh day *shall be* a feast to the Lord.

7 Unleavened bread shall be eaten seven days; and there shall no leavened bread be seen with thee, neither shall there be leaven seen with thee in all thy quarters.

8 ¶ And thou shalt show thy son in that day, saying, *This is done* because of that

be one law for the native and for the stranger who sojourns among you."

50 Thus did all the people of Israel; as the Lord commanded Moses and Aaron, so they did. 51 And on that very day the Lord brought the people of Israel out of the land of Egypt by their hosts.

13 The Lord said to Moses, 2 "Consecrate to me all the first-born; whatever is the first to open the womb among the people of Israel, both of man and of beast, is mine."

3 And Moses said to the people, "Remember this day, in which you came out from Egypt, out of the house of bondage, for by strength of hand the Lord brought you out from this place; no leavened bread shall be eaten. 4 This day you are to go forth, in the month of Abib. 5 And when the Lord brings you into the land of the Canaanites, the Hittites, the Amorites, the Hivites, and the Jeb'usites, which he swore to your fathers to give you, a land flowing with milk and honey, you shall keep this service in this month. 6 Seven days you shall eat unleavened bread, and on the seventh day there shall be a feast to the Lord. 7 Unleavened bread shall be eaten for seven days; no leavened bread shall be seen with you, and no leaven shall be seen with you in all your territory. 8 And you shall tell your

---

7. Dedication of First-Born (13:1-2, 11-16)

13:1-2. This is a summary statement by P of the law of the first-born. More complete statements of this law, as P understands it, are found in Num. 3:11-13, 40-51; 18:15-16. The rite's central meaning is that Israel and its possessions belong to God. Its institution was associated with the death of the first-born in Egypt, but it seems more probable that, whatever calamity may be the historical basis of that story, the present form of it owes much to God's customary claim of Israel's first-born. The P writer taught that at Sinai the Levites became the possession of God in lieu of all the first-born of Israel a month old and more, except that the number of Levites was not sufficient to cover all (Num. 3:40-51). The remainder were redeemed for five shekels of silver each (*ca.* three dollars). This also was the redemption fine, at the age of one month, of all the subsequent first-born. In 22:29*b*-30 (E) the redemption takes place on the eighth day.

3-10. See Exeg. on 13:3-10, p. 923.

which the Lord did unto me when I came forth out of Egypt.

9 And it shall be for a sign unto thee upon thine hand, and for a memorial between thine eyes, that the Lord's law may be in thy mouth: for with a strong hand hath the Lord brought thee out of Egypt.

10 Thou shalt therefore keep this ordinance in his season from year to year.

11 ¶ And it shall be when the Lord shall bring thee into the land of the Canaanites, as he sware unto thee and to thy fathers, and shall give it thee,

12 That thou shalt set apart unto the Lord all that openeth the matrix, and every firstling that cometh of a beast which thou hast; the male *shall be* the Lord's.

13 And every firstling of an ass thou shalt redeem with a lamb; and if thou wilt not redeem it, then thou shalt break his neck: and all the firstborn of man among thy children shalt thou redeem.

14 ¶ And it shall be when thy son asketh thee in time to come, saying, What *is* this? that thou shalt say unto him, By strength of hand the Lord brought us out from Egypt, from the house of bondage:

15 And it came to pass, when Pharaoh would hardly let us go, that the Lord slew all the firstborn in the land of Egypt, both the firstborn of man, and the firstborn of beast: therefore I sacrifice to the Lord all that openeth the matrix, being males; but all the firstborn of my children I redeem.

son on that day, 'It is because of what the Lord did for me when I came out of Egypt.' 9 And it shall be to you as a sign on your hand and as a memorial between your eyes, that the law of the Lord may be in your mouth; for with a strong hand the Lord has brought you out of Egypt. 10 You shall therefore keep this ordinance at its appointed time from year to year.

11 "And when the Lord brings you into the land of the Canaanites, as he swore to you and your fathers, and shall give it to you, 12 you shall set apart to the Lord all that first opens the womb. All the firstlings of your cattle that are males shall be the Lord's. 13 Every firstling of an ass you shall redeem with a lamb, or if you will not redeem it you shall break its neck. Every first-born of man among your sons you shall redeem. 14 And when in time to come your son asks you, 'What does this mean?' you shall say to him, 'By strength of hand the Lord brought us out of Egypt, from the house of bondage. 15 For when Pharaoh stubbornly refused to let us go, the Lord slew all the first-born in the land of Egypt, both the first-born of man and the first-born of cattle. Therefore I sacrifice to the Lord all the males that first open the womb; but

---

11-16. The same Deuteronomic editor who supplied the homiletic supplement (vss. 3-10) for the feast of Unleavened Bread seems to have provided this one for the law of the dedication of the first-born. He qualifies the basic requirement by stipulating that the first-born males of animals only are to be handed over. He quotes a provision of J (34:20) relating to the donkey and to the redemption of man. It is intimated that the redemption of Israel's sons is founded on the death of the first-born in Egypt (vs. 15).

13:1-10. See Expos. of 12:8.

14-16. *Sign or Substance?*—The tokens of remembrance commanded in vs. 16 were a metaphorical way of saying, "You must keep these things in mind." But that would be difficult to do; it would be much easier to carry out the injunction literally, as was done. Two leather capsules were each fastened to a band, one so tied that it was over the heart, the other between the eyebrows. In these were written certain words of the law (vs. 16; see Deut. 6:4-9; 11:13-21). Jesus refers to them in Matt. 23:5 as

examples of the way men love external acts of worship and the vain display of piety while neglecting the spiritual discipline of which they were intended to be a symbol.

The custom arose in antiquity from the desire to ward off evil spirits, and frontlets were habitually worn by many ancient tribes for this purpose. As missionaries have found, it is a sound practice to turn an ancient superstitious custom to a good use instead of trying fruitlessly to forbid it. Albert Schweitzer tells that, when asked to give a newborn baby its taboo, he

16 And it shall be for a token upon thine hand, and for frontlets between thine eyes: for by strength of hand the LORD brought us forth out of Egypt.

17 ¶ And it came to pass, when Pharaoh had let the people go, that God led them not *through* the way of the land of the Philistines, although that *was* near; for God said, Lest peradventure the people repent when they see war, and they return to Egypt:

all the first-born of my sons I redeem.' **16** It shall be as a mark on your hand or frontlets between your eyes; for by a strong hand the LORD brought us out of Egypt."

17 When Pharaoh let the people go, God did not lead them by way of the land of the Philistines, although that was near; for God said, "Lest the people repent when

---

C. YAHWEH'S VICTORY EMANCIPATES ISRAEL (13:17–15:21)
1. FROM SUCCOTH TO ETHAM (13:17-22)

17. God leads Israel by a way of his own choosing, a way that differs from the accustomed route of man's caravans and armies. But he does so for reasons that have a basis in natural processes; in this case the reasons are psychological and strategic. The people must not change their mind because of unexpected difficulties. In Israel's

---

solemnly pronounced the words to the African mother, "He must never touch alcohol."

All religious emotion tends to use metaphor, and prosaic people will always afterward try to interpret the metaphor literally; so we have sectarianism and theological controversy. A flag is a symbol, but it is much easier to wave it than to suffer and fight for the ideals for which it stands. Thus the people of Moses' day, instead of keeping these things in mind, put them in capsules, tied them around their necks, and so felt pious.

Much patriotism and much piety remind one of Lewis Carroll's lines:

> "I weep for you," the Walrus said:
> "I deeply sympathize."
> With sobs and tears he sorted out
> Those of the largest size,
> Holding his pocket-handkerchief
> Before his streaming eyes.[2]

17-22. The Leading of God.—As is usual in Exodus, the editor has combined a number of varying accounts of the adventure, but the occurrence has impressed itself on the human mind as one of the great symbolic scenes of humanity. Sir Walter Raleigh says:

Orusius, in his first book and tenth chapter against the Pagans, tells us, that in his time, who lived some four hundred years after Christ, the prints of Pharaoh's chariot wheels were to be seen at a low water on the Egyptian sands; and though they were some time defaced by wind and weather, yet soon after they appeared again. But hereof I leave every man to his own belief.[3]

The hurrying feet of a liberated people, the outstretched rod of the great leader, the banked-up seas at either side, the prints of dragging chariot wheels, the enemy corpses floating on the returning flood—no wind and weather can fully efface the image of these events from the sands of human history. They have been comfort and inspiration to all ages. When in 1776 the mistreated colonies in America took their courage in their hands and resolved to burn their bridges behind them and declare their independence, they faced tremendous perils. Franklin suggested for the reverse of the official seal of the United States:

Pharaoh sitting in an open chariot, a crown on his head and a sword in his hand, passing through the divided waters of the Red Sea in pursuit of the Israelites. Rays from a pillar of fire in the cloud, expressive of the Divine presence and command, beaming on Moses, who stands on the shore and, extending his hand over the sea, causes it to overflow Pharaoh. Motto: "Rebellion to Tyrants is obedience to God." [4]

And no one can read the life of Lincoln, in a later stage of American history, without being struck again and again by resemblances to the life of Moses. "Up from Slavery" would have been a good title for the book of Exodus. Lincoln, like Moses, was a man of humble birth, the son of a poor woman. Both men were trained in the knowledge of the laws of the land. Both men were struck by the horror of slavery in a dramatic instance of its cruelty: the one in Egypt, when Moses spied an Egyptian taskmaster

[2] *Through the Looking-Glass*, ch. iv.
[3] *History of the World*, Bk. II, ch. iii, sec. 9.

[4] Carl Van Doren, *Benjamin Franklin* (New York: Viking Press, 1938), p. 553.

18 But God led the people about, *through* the way of the wilderness of the Red sea: and the children of Israel went up harnessed out of the land of Egypt.

they see war, and return to Egypt." 18 But God led the people round by the way of the wilderness toward the Red Sea. And the people of Israel went up out of the land of

---

deliverance, and throughout, the Bible reports Israel's history as the record of God's leadership. This is the central tenet, the correlation of which, with its affirmation of human responsibility and the realities in the processes of nature and history, is the key to the Bible's interpretation of existence. The **land of the Philistines** was first occupied by Philistines *ca.* 1175 B.C., after the Exodus. Clearly the Israelites did not travel *on* the coastal highway. Beer (*Exodus*, p. 75), adopting a view of Eissfeldt, thinks that Lake Sirbonis, on the Mediterranean side of that highway, was the scene of the Egyptian disaster. The view rests mainly on the attempt to locate the places Pi-ha-hiroth, Migdol, and Baal-zephon (14:2, 9) at Lake Sirbonis. Unless this attempt succeeds beyond dispute the general theory will not gain wide acceptance, for most of the other biblical evidence, including this paragraph, militates against it.

18. For his people God chose **the way of the wilderness,** i.e., the way via the Sea of Reeds. This sea was in all probability the marshy area north or south of Lake Timsah, across which this way led into Asia. The term **Red Sea** rests on the LXX and indicates

---

smiting a Hebrew; the other in New Orleans, when Lincoln saw a mulatto girl put up to auction. Both men delivered a race from slavery, the one by ten terrible plagues, the other by a still more terrible war in which many of the first-born all over the land were slain. The signing of the Emancipation Proclamation was the crossing of the Red Sea into a new land of promise and opportunity, even if miles of wilderness had to be crossed first. Both men died just as they came to stand on the peak of Pisgah, looking out afar at the dim outlines of the Promised Land they themselves were not permitted to enter. Both men lived and died that they might give to a whole race the "bread of heaven," which is freedom.

In his story of the crossing of the Red Sea by a people fleeing hazardously through this dividing line from the dictatorship and tyranny of Pharaoh to seek for liberty, the writer seems to say, as Philippe de Coulanges said to an excited audience, "Do not imagine you are listening to me; it is history itself that speaks." For it is the faith of good men that progress in the direction of organized and assured freedom is the hand of God in human history. There always have been many, and there are many still, who do not share this faith, who hold that greater things are done for man by power concentrated than by power balanced and dispersed, and that to imagine that the ruler derives his power from the people is rebellion against the divine will all down the stream of time, that our business is to preserve, not to improve. One hears ad-

vanced today under many guises the ideas that precautions against abuses obstruct progress, that enlightened virtue is dethroned for the benefit of the ignorant mob, placing the capable at the mercy of the incapable. Indeed, the children of Israel, with all their rebellions and murmurings and errors in the forty years of the wilderness wanderings, learned all about the graduality of the process of attaining freedom. Just as one cannot learn to think all at once, but has to come to it gradually, so freedom of the will is not born overnight, but has to be progressively achieved. There are certain indications by which one can test the presence of the leaven of freedom in the body politic, e.g., the adequacy of the checks held by the people upon the action of their rulers or managers in political life and business affairs; the extinction of slavery; the security of weaker groups; the power of public opinion; the availability of facts on all questions; liberty of conscience. Israel fell down badly in such tests, as its subsequent history shows, just as the Pilgrims did when they were free to erect their own state in Plymouth; but in both cases the leaven of freedom was working, for the experiment of free government is not one which can be tried once for all. Every generation must try it for itself. As each generation grows up to manhood it has to launch afresh its ship of liberty on its experimental voyage. Apostles of freedom will also do well to remember the pertinent remark of Artemus Ward: "I believe we are descended from the Puritans, who nobly fled from a land of despotism to a land of freedom, where they

19 And Moses took the bones of Joseph with him: for he had straitly sworn the children of Israel, saying, God will surely visit you; and ye shall carry up my bones away hence with you. 20 ¶ And they took their journey from Succoth, and encamped in Etham, in the edge of the wilderness. 21 And the LORD went before them by day in a pillar of a cloud, to lead them the way; and by night in a pillar of fire, to give them light; to go by day and night. 22 He took not away the pillar of the cloud by day, nor the pillar of fire by night, *from* before the people.	Egypt equipped for battle. 19 And Moses took the bones of Joseph with him; for Joseph had solemnly sworn the people of Israel, saying, "God will visit you; then you must carry my bones with you from here." 20 And they moved on from Succoth, and encamped at Etham, on the edge of the wilderness. 21 And the LORD went before them by day in a pillar of cloud to lead them along the way, and by night in a pillar of fire to give them light, that they might travel by day and by night; 22 the pillar of cloud by day and the pillar of fire by night did not depart from before the people.

the sea we know by that name, also the Indian Ocean. It seems best here not to think of a wilderness in Egypt, as most interpreters do, but the wilderness to which the route leads, i.e., "the wilderness of Shur" (15:22; Num. 33:8), or more probably the right fork of the route leading toward the wilderness of Paran. The statement that Israel marched out **equipped for battle** rests on a term which sometimes means armed for war. The Hebrew word is probably the plural of the number five; thus, by fives or fifties. This also helps account for the LXX reading "in the fifth generation" (cf. 6:14-27).

19. The departure is again reported to have been anticipated by Joseph (Gen. 50:24-25) and the patriarchs. In the Bible God visits his people either in judgment or in redemption. The latter is assumed here.

20. **Etham** was apparently just across the Sea of Reeds from the wilderness of Shur or Etham (15:22; Num. 33:8).

21-22. The **pillar of cloud** and the **pillar of fire** set forth in mythical language the statement of vs. 17 that God led Israel. These are symbols of the divine presence. We must not so much think of them as religious adaptations of natural phenomena as of an experience of the divine presence set forth in images which may in part be derived from natural scenes.

could not only enjoy their own religion but prevent everybody else from enjoying his." [5] 19. *The Bones of Joseph.*— (See Gen. 50:25; Josh. 24:32.) The king of Egypt may not remember the great figure of the past (1:8), but the Hebrew people can never forget. One pictures the mummified figure of Joseph, borne on the shoulders of the new generation, going back to his "boyhood's home," to be buried near the well of Jacob, his father, and the sacred oak (Gen. 35:4). 20-22. *The Pillar of Cloud and the Pillar of Fire.*—This designation, which is an accurate description of a volcano, has led some to see in the tidal flood in the Red Sea and in the experiences at Sinai ancient memories of volcanic disturbances taking place at the time of the Exodus. Hugo Gressmann adduces several experiences with volcanic eruptions which coin-	cide with the descriptions of the pillars of cloud and fire, of the flames of Sinai, and of the recession of the sea and its sudden return, as so eloquently pictured in the Song of Miriam. The similarity of the phenomena described, and the possibility that Mount Sinai was near the sea, leave the reader free to indulge his imagination on the matter as he will. Actually, these things took place so long ago that it is impossible now to be certain whether the tidal wave, the cloud of fire, and the burning mountain were originally religious symbols or literally volcanic fact (but see Exeg.).[6] Certain it is that to primitive man no material phenomenon seemed to be so plainly divine as fire. This is seen in the flaming sword at the gate of paradise, in the sacrificial fire on the altar, in the burning bush, and in the refiner's fire (Isa. 48:10; Mal. 3:2).[7]

[5] From the fifth of his letters in *Punch*, published in 1866.

[6] See further Hugo Gressmann, *Die Anfänge Israels* (Göttingen: Vandenhoeck & Ruprecht, 1922; "Die Schriften des Alten Testaments in Auswahl"), pp. 55-56.

[7] See Homer *Iliad* V. 1-5 *et passim*.

14 And the LORD spake unto Moses, saying,

2 Speak unto the children of Israel, that they turn and encamp before Pi-hahiroth, between Migdol and the sea, over against Baal-zephon: before it shall ye encamp by the sea.

3 For Pharaoh will say of the children of Israel, They *are* entangled in the land, the wilderness hath shut them in.

4 And I will harden Pharaoh's heart, that he shall follow after them; and I will be honored upon Pharaoh, and upon all his host; that the Egyptians may know that I *am* the LORD. And they did so.

14 Then the LORD said to Moses, 2 "Tell the people of Israel to turn back and encamp in front of Pi-ha-hi'roth, between Migdol and the sea, in front of Ba'al-zephon; you shall encamp over against it, by the sea. 3 For Pharaoh will say of the people of Israel, 'They are entangled in the land; the wilderness has shut them in.' 4 And I will harden Pharaoh's heart, and he will pursue them and I will get glory over Pharaoh and all his host; and the Egyptians shall know that I am the LORD." And they did so.

---

2. CRISIS AT THE FRONTIER (14:1-14)

14:1-2. At the Lord's command Moses tells Israel to turn back and encamp by the sea. From where? By what sea? From Succoth-Etham *up* toward Lake Sirbonis on the Mediterranean Sea, says Eissfeldt, recalling that Israel had come *down* from Rameses. No, say more conventional interpreters, from north of Lake Timsah, where an attempt to cross may have failed (Wright and Filson, *Westminster Atlas*, p. 38b), back to its Egyptian or western shore.

3-4. There is no support in the text for the view that the return was occasioned by defeat. The writer accounts for the order by describing it as a ruse that would evoke an attack by Pharaoh's troops, an attack calculated to fail. That the Egyptians took the chance is, for the writer, another instance of the blindness of Pharaoh who could still

---

14:1-9. *Pharaoh's Returning Fury.*—The plagues were gone. There were no more flies or frogs than usual at this time of the year. The weather was bright and sunny, children well, flocks flourishing. "What fools we were to let our property go! Who is to finish building our grand treasure cities? There are rumors in the papers that Egyptian citizens will have to be sent to the brickyards to work like slaves. There was probably, after all, nothing in the idea that Yahweh was responsible for the plagues that happened to crowd in upon us. It would not surprise us if in after ages some scholar should discover that they were all due to perfectly natural causes; and anyway, the gods of Egypt are more powerful than the god of a gang of illiterate slaves. It was our hysterical bureaucrats who got us into this mess. Our Pharaoh was ill-advised by that crowd at the palace. We must have our slaves back if Egypt is to take her place among the great powers. What is our army for? There were six hundred chosen chariots in the last parade. And we know more about the country than they do; they must be entangled in the land; the wilderness must have shut them in. It will be easy to surround the mob and bring them back." So might it have been said in Egypt; and Pharaoh's heart was hardened

again. It had gone through that process so many times that it must have become pretty hard by then. He did not need much persuading. The repentance of a scared man is worth very little. When "the Devil was sick,—the Devil a monk would be." [8] In Boston a prison superintendent led a visitor around the "tombs," the cells in which the night's prisoners are confined, awaiting the opening of the morning court. It was "the morning after," before the opening of the court. Through almost every barred gate hands were thrust to seize the superintendent's sleeve with the words, "If you get me off this time, I promise to God that I'll never be here again!" It was the fourth, fifth, and in one case the tenth, appearance behind those same bars. In the same way in every modern war it is possible to cheer those going into battle with the slogan "A war to end war"; men in great depressions resolve to mend their ways, as we all remember. But Prov. 26:11 tells the whole story with horrible truth. Real repentance is not the resolve that if you do not catch it this time you will never do it again, that if the plagues let up you will be good. For you will not be able to preserve your present mood when you are tempted next time, any more than Pharaoh was.

[8] Rabelais, *Works*, Bk. IV, ch. xxiv.

5 ¶ And it was told the king of Egypt that the people fled: and the heart of Pharaoh and of his servants was turned against the people, and they said, Why have we done this, that we have let Israel go from serving us?

6 And he made ready his chariot, and took his people with him:

7 And he took six hundred chosen chariots, and all the chariots of Egypt, and captains over every one of them.

8 And the LORD hardened the heart of Pharaoh king of Egypt, and he pursued after the children of Israel: and the children of Israel went out with a high hand.

9 But the Egyptians pursued after them, all the horses *and* chariots of Pharaoh, and his horsemen, and his army, and overtook them encamping by the sea, beside Pi-hahiroth, before Baal-zephon.

5 When the king of Egypt was told that the people had fled, the mind of Pharaoh and his servants was changed toward the people, and they said, "What is this we have done, that we have let Israel go from serving us?" 6 So he made ready his chariot and took his army with him, 7 and took six hundred picked chariots and all the other chariots of Egypt with officers over all of them. 8 And the LORD hardened the heart of Pharaoh king of Egypt and he pursued the people of Israel as they went forth defiantly. 9 The Egyptians pursued them, all Pharaoh's horses and chariots and his horsemen and his army, and overtook them encamped at the sea, by Pi-ha-hi′roth, in front of Ba′al-zephon.

---

not see that his real protagonist was Yahweh. The success of Israel's strategy, as interpreted by faith, provided Yahweh with an occasion to clinch his victory over Pharaoh and set Israel free. Beer and Eissfeldt rightly stress the calculated strategy involved in the movement.

5. The text assumes that the pursuit was organized at the court. It may be, however, that the incident was the result of independent action taken by troops stationed at some frontier fort. The first half of the verse implies an escape without permit, while the last half seems to imply just the opposite.

6. The LXX says specifically that it was Pharaoh who prepared his chariot and such is the meaning.

7. Officers rests on a Hebrew word meaning "third" or "three." Our term "crew" may describe the intention of the writer. Actually Egyptians manned chariots with only two men, the driver and the fighter. (In later times the Israelites, following Assyrian and Hittite custom, had a crew of three for each chariot, including also an armor-bearer.)

8. The statement of the RSV that the Israelites went out **defiantly** is an interpretation of the Hebrew idiom, ביד רמה, rendered **with a high hand** in the KJV. It seems best to translate "by means of a high hand," meaning the hand or powerful act of God. The people were under God's protection (cf. vs. 31; 3:19; 6:1).

9-12. When Pharaoh approached panic shook the people. They **cried out to the LORD** in fear rather than in faith. Here begins a series of scenes in which the firm faith of

---

Reading articles and books on repentance, one is struck with the difficulty of distinguishing between a Pharaoh willing to let the people go because he is afraid of more plagues and a Pharaoh who has really repented of his tyrannical cruelty in the depths of his being and could be addressed in the language of the Book of Common Prayer: "Ye who do truly and earnestly repent you of your sins, and are in love and charity with your neighbours, and intend to lead a new life, following the commandments of God, and walking from henceforth in his holy ways." J. Ellis McTaggart

suggests that one can test oneself to see if one is only in a scared mood, or really repenting, by noting one's changed attitude toward God. The scared man has the feelings of a mouse toward a cat; the repentant, the feelings of a child toward its father. J. G. Fichte, in his latest stage, describes real repentance this way: "The inclinations which I have to sacrifice are not really my inclinations, but are enemies within the camp plotting against my real self." Paul puts it in a similar way, "It is no more I that do it, but sin that dwelleth in me" (Rom. 7:17). One other test of real repentance is that

10 ¶ And when Pharaoh drew nigh, the children of Israel lifted up their eyes, and, behold, the Egyptians marched after them; and they were sore afraid: and the children of Israel cried out unto the LORD.

11 And they said unto Moses, Because *there were* no graves in Egypt, hast thou taken us away to die in the wilderness? wherefore hast thou dealt thus with us, to carry us forth out of Egypt?

12 *Is* not this the word that we did tell thee in Egypt, saying, Let us alone, that we may serve the Egyptians? For *it had been* better for us to serve the Egyptians, than that we should die in the wilderness.

10 When Pharaoh drew near, the people of Israel lifted up their eyes, and behold, the Egyptians were marching after them; and they were in great fear. And the people of Israel cried out to the LORD; 11 and they said to Moses, "Is it because there are no graves in Egypt that you have taken us away to die in the wilderness? What have you done to us, in bringing us out of Egypt? 12 Is not this what we said to you in Egypt, 'Let us alone and let us serve the Egyptians'? For it would have been better for us to serve the Egyptians than to die in the

---

Moses is contrasted with the vacillation of his people (16:3; 17:3; Num. 11:4-5; 14:3; 16:13; 20:3-4; 21:5). It should be noted that the prophet Jeremiah (2:1-3) conspicuously dissociated himself from the tradition of murmuring and rebellion in the desert. But even though it is assumed that this series of accounts rests on historical fact we may find in them some echoes of the religious struggle which took place between prophets and people from the days of Elijah and onward.

---

the repentant man stands ready for any remedial task, however great, for any service, however distasteful. Repentance is the first sign of the operation of the law of growth within you, and this law is more potent than that of cause and effect. It is the interest of God in you, and as Meister Eckhart says, "Man goes far away or near, but God never goes far off; he is always standing close at hand, and even if he cannot get within he goes no further away than the door." [9]

10-12. The Weakness of Human Nature.—
Taking into account all that Moses had done for them, all he had had to go through, and the courage and resourcefulness he had shown, what the people said now was downright mean. It is true that with the sea in front of them and Pharaoh's hosts behind them they were frightened, but they had been frightened before, and Moses, under the guidance of Yahweh, had brought them through in safety. Where was their faith now?

Everyone sooner or later meets with similarly mean remarks about himself and his work. How should one act in such cases? The natural reaction is extreme indignation and assumed astonishment that anyone could say such things. In fact some people go through life in a continual state of astonishment that other people are not archangels. Every cowardly act or sweet gossipy slander leaves them speechless with apoplectic resentment. "Did you hear what they said, what they have done?" And bloodshot eyes

seek in one's face answering astonishment. What can one say? The calm answer, "Yes, that is the way people are," seems not to be sympathetic enough for the occasion; yet it is all that one can say in cases of plain meanness like this. There would be no problem, no great challenge in life, if people were all saints. Read Kipling's poem "If." It is important that Moses should not descend to their level and begin to argue that they never had said in Egypt that which they now said they had (vs. 12). Probably the farthest he went was vs. 14, which seems to mean, "You will stop talking like that when you see what is going to happen." No, Moses apparently said to himself, "That is the way people are. They are scared, poor folk. They need a little encouragement." So he said not one word in self-defense or recrimination but, omitting to notice their personal remarks, went on with the business in hand: **Fear ye not, stand still, and see the salvation of the LORD.** Until you have met real injustice in life, you cannot tell whether you are a man or a mouse. The mouse gets all worked up; the man ignores the personal slander and goes on to do the best he can for his folk. Moses was a man. "And there arose certain, and bare false witness against him, saying, We heard him say, I will destroy this temple. . . . And the high priest stood up in the midst, and asked Jesus, saying, Answerest thou nothing? . . . But he held his peace, and answered nothing" (Mark 14:57-58, 60-61).

[9] Pfeiffer, *Meister Eckhart*, II, 23.

13 ¶ And Moses said unto the people, Fear ye not, stand still, and see the salvation of the LORD, which he will show to you to-day: for the Egyptians whom ye have seen to-day, ye shall see them again no more for ever.

14 The LORD shall fight for you, and ye shall hold your peace.

15 ¶ And the LORD said unto Moses, Wherefore criest thou unto me? speak unto the children of Israel, that they go forward:

wilderness." 13 And Moses said to the people, "Fear not, stand firm, and see the salvation of the LORD, which he will work for you today; for the Egyptians whom you see today, you shall never see again. 14 The LORD will fight for you, and you have only to be still." 15 The LORD said to Moses, "Why do you cry to me? Tell the people of

---

13-14. In the crisis Moses issues orders: **Fear not, stand firm, and see. Salvation** does not effect the same result for men in every part of the Bible, but throughout God reveals himself as a savior. Salvation does not rest finally on the ethical value men have discerned as implicit in the working of God, but on his power of redemption. The Samar. text and Targ. seem sufficient warrant for changing **whom** to "as." The real point is not that these Egyptians are about to perish in the flood but rather that this is an eschatological event. The historic victory of God will establish his lordship beyond dispute. Egyptians will never again contend with Yahweh "as" they are doing now. God will establish his rule. Let men be silent. Moses does not just ask Israel to stop complaining; he proclaims here the transcendence of God.

3. ISRAEL CROSSES THE SEA (14:15-22)

The crossing was an event which lay wholly within the nexus of nature and history as these are scientifically understood. But for Israel this was God's "time" (John 7:8), and became a revelatory event which compelled those who saw it to reinterpret the meaning of both nature and history. It was the redemptive event which became the foundation of Israel's existence as the people of God. It was for Israel not simply a source of objective meaning, but also of abiding wonder (Buber, *Moses*, pp. 75-76). The event is for the O.T. what Jesus as Christ is for the N.T.—the normative redeeming and revealing act of God.

13-18. God's Answer to Man's Extremity.— In one of his critical days Abraham Lincoln wrote, "Whatever He designs, He will do for me yet. 'Stand still and see the Salvation of the Lord' is my text just now." [10] The best commentary on vs. 15 is that of George Meredith, "The soul's one road is forward."

When one is convinced that he is upon God's errand, how far can he expect natural forces to obey his will? Two religious answers have been given to this question. Through all history there have been some saints who have believed that under God's inspiration they are at times enabled to overcome and change nature's course; and in all ages there have been those who believe that no exceptions are made for the best or the worst, even in the most critical emergencies, that the laws of nature must be taken by the saint and the sinner as constant. "Do good to them that hate you, . . . that ye may be the children of your Father which is in

heaven: for he maketh his sun to rise on the evil and on the good, and sendeth rain on the just and on the unjust" (Matt. 5:44-45). Dwight D. Eisenhower, commander in chief of the Allied forces in the Normandy landings, issued to his men a noble call for D-Day: "The free men of the world are marching together to victory. . . . Good luck and let us all beseech the blessing of Almighty God upon this great and noble undertaking." [11] Never before in history were so many men so confident of the divine leadership. Yet just before June 5, the original D-Day, the worst June gale in forty years suddenly struck along the Channel, sweeping away the laborious preparations of many months' toil. When the landing hour came, two unpredictable things combined to make the situation critical. One was the weather, which swamped the boats, concealed the obstacles, and made the infantry sick; the other seemed to the Allies a stroke of the worst luck, for the

[10] Bryan Binns, *Abraham Lincoln* (New York: E. P. Dutton & Co., 1907), p. 77.

[11] H. S. Commager, *The Story of the Second World War* (Boston: Little, Brown & Co., 1945), p. 411.

16 But lift thou up thy rod, and stretch out thine hand over the sea, and divide it: and the children of Israel shall go on dry *ground* through the midst of the sea.

16 Lift up your rod, and stretch out your hand over the sea and divide it, that the people of Israel may

Israel to go forward.

By means of a process of communal embellishment the account was gradually altered and the event lifted out of its setting in the context of natural process. This process of providing the account with a "supernatural" dress continued after the O.T. canon was closed, but we can see it taking place in the development of the contents of the canon also. In this brief passage we detect three stages. The first is entirely natural: God uses an east wind to drive back the water, enabling the Israelites to cross over safely (vss. 15, 19a, 21aβbα, 22a). The second account (vss. 16, 19b, 20, 21aαbβ) attributes the disappearance of the water to Moses' use of the magic rod and hints that the cloud was a "supernatural" phenomenon. In the third account (vss. 17-18, 22b) the waters are so separated by the rod as to stand like walls.

15. It is assumed that Moses had cried to God, perhaps in intercession (32:32; Num. 21:7); this the Syriac text says explicitly. The command **to go forward** is an admonition to assume responsibility in faith. Men under grace will behave as creatures made in the divine image; only *they* will be able to do so. Let Israel "pull up stakes" and move toward its goal.

16. The dividing of the water by the rod (E) leads on to the later embellishment (P) that the water stood up as walls!

enemy moved to the coast during the night. "The landing went wrong from the beginning. The engineers' commanding officer and his second-in-command were killed a few minutes after they reached the beach." [1]

Yet many religious people would agree that it was better to pay this terrible price rather than have it said that it was not a fair fight because supernatural powers were interfering on behalf of one side. Perhaps there will always be the two schools of thought, for the story of God causing the sea to divide to save his people and drown his enemies appeals to the childish hope for an easy, wondrous way out of our difficulties—a story crooned at the cradle of all religious faith.

Most of us perhaps rejoice in the old story of King Canute:

He did one thing to the shame of Court-Flatterers, which is worth our taking notice of: While the Tide was coming in, he caused his Royal Seat to be put on the Shore; and, with all the State that Majesty could put into his Countenance, said thus to the Sea: "Thou Sea, . . . I charge thee come no further upon my Land, neither presume to wet the Feet of Thy Sovereign Lord." But the Sea, as before, came rowling on, and without reverence did both wet and dash him: Whereat the King quickly rising, wished all about him to behold and consider the weak and frivolous Power of a King.[2]

[1] *Ibid.*, p. 422.
[2] *Great Historical Dictionary*, article "Canute."

For every great religious leader and every great church are surrounded by flatterers who tell them they possess from God powers over nature or history or the fate of the dead. Few such leaders or churches would dare to do what King Canute did and demonstrate how helpless they are to change the powers of nature, the facts of history, or to interfere in the world beyond. For the child in us all likes to read in Thomas Fuller how

the Dutch escaped . . . the hostility of the Turks, who waited for them on the other side of Meander. The river was not fordable; ship or bridge the Christians had none: when, behold, Conrade the emperor adventured an action, which, because it was successful, shall be accounted valiant, otherwise we should term it desperate. After an exhortation to his army, he commanded them all at once to flounce into the river. Meander was plunged by their plunging into it: his water stood amazed, as unresolved whether to retreat to the fountain, or proceed to the sea, and in this ecstasy afforded them a dry passage over the stream. . . . The affrighted Turks, on the other side, thinking there was no contending with them that did teach nature itself obedience, offered their throats to the Christians' swords, and were killed in such number, that whole piles of dead bodies remain there for a monument; like those heaps of the Cimbrians slain by Marius, near Marseilles, where afterwards the inhabitants walled their vineyards with sculls, and guarded their grapes with dead men.[3]

[3] *The History of the Holy War*, Bk. II, ch. xxviii.

17 And I, behold, I will harden the hearts of the Egyptians, and they shall follow them: and I will get me honor upon Pharaoh, and upon all his host, upon his chariots, and upon his horsemen.

18 And the Egyptians shall know that I *am* the LORD, when I have gotten me honor upon Pharaoh, upon his chariots, and upon his horsemen.

19 ¶ And the Angel of God, which went before the camp of Israel, removed and went behind them; and the pillar of the cloud went from before their face, and stood behind them:

go on dry ground through the sea. 17 And I will harden the hearts of the Egyptians, so that they shall go in after them and I will get glory over Pharaoh and all his host, his chariots, and his horsemen. 18 And the Egyptians shall know that I am the LORD, when I have gotten glory over Pharaoh, his chariots, and his horsemen."

19 Then the angel of God who went before the host of Israel moved and went behind them; and the pillar of cloud moved from before them and stood behind them,

---

17. The momentarily resurgent Pharaoh will suffer a defeat that will establish the rule of God beyond cavil. With respect to the will of God it is not possible to hold "free elections"! Men vote "Yes" or they are destroyed.

19. The **angel of God** (E) and the **pillar of cloud** (J) are synonyms: both symbolize the protecting presence of Yahweh (13:21-22). As on the Passover night (12:42), God stood guard over his people.

Josephus also supports the credibility of our narrative by telling his readers that "for the sake of those that accompanied Alexander, king of Macedonia, who yet lived comparatively but a little while ago, the Pamphylian Sea retired and afforded them a passage through itself, when they had no other way to go." [4] W. H. Bennett adds a citation from another writer who says that "the Pamphilian Sea did not only open a passage for Alexander, but, by rising and elevating its waters, did pay him homage as its king." [5]

To childish minds miracles seem necessary lest man should ascribe his escape to his own ingenuity. But the mystics speak of "God thinking in me"; Jacob Boehme tells of "what God knew in him"; these are profound suggestions of the relation that all human thinking bears to the divine mind. As we grow more mature we begin to see that God's love and power are manifested in a still greater degree when he inspires people to think up for themselves some ingenious way of outwitting their Pharaoh and getting across their Red Sea; this was the way the American colonies escaped from their taskmasters in 1774-76. [6]

But the great scene at the Red Sea still survives as a metaphorical expression of the faith that God does stand on the side of the unjustly downtrodden and helps them to victory in ways

[4] *Antiquities* II. 16. 5.
[5] *Exodus*, pp. 126-27.
[6] Van Doren, *Benjamin Franklin*, pp. 336-52, 462-63, *et passim*.

that seem mysterious to both them and their oppressors.

19-22. The Protecting Angel.—The story in our text consists of sections taken from J, E, P, and an editor, R. In E's account there is apparently an "angel" rather than a "pillar." The Egyptians could not attack when they caught up with the children of Israel, owing to the change in position of the spiritual obstruction which conducted and, in this case, protected the people. The miracle of invisibility is commonly made use of by the deity in Arabian folklore and in primitive folklore generally. Everyone has dreamed at times of how much good or harm he could do if only he were invisible. The smoke screens of modern warfare are the scientific fulfillment of these dreams. Our writers here use the figure as symbol of the protecting care of God over his own. This kind of protection by God corresponds to something very deep and real in human experience. A prominent man once told of how as a boy he joined a Methodist country church, and how those good people unconsciously formed a kind of spiritual phalanx around him during the most dangerous period of his boyhood, protecting him both before and behind from dangers he knew little of at the time. Another man, one of a family of sons whose parents were absent from them as missionaries in the Orient during their boyhood, said: "We have all turned out pretty well, and this is due to the letters we used to receive from our mother; what could you do but be good, when you got letters with

20 And it came between the camp of the Egyptians and the camp of Israel; and it was a cloud and darkness *to them,* but it gave light by night *to these:* so that the one came not near the other all the night.

21 And Moses stretched out his hand over the sea; and the Lord caused the sea to go *back* by a strong east wind all that night, and made the sea dry *land,* and the waters were divided.

22 And the children of Israel went into the midst of the sea upon the dry *ground:* and the waters *were* a wall unto them on their right hand, and on their left.

23 ¶ And the Egyptians pursued, and went in after them to the midst of the sea, *even* all Pharaoh's horses, his chariots, and his horsemen.

24 And it came to pass, that in the morning watch the Lord looked unto the host of the Egyptians through the pillar of fire and of the cloud, and troubled the host of the Egyptians,

20 coming between the host of Egypt and the host of Israel. And there was the cloud and the darkness; and the night passed[p] without one coming near the other all night. 21 Then Moses stretched out his hand over the sea; and the Lord drove the sea back by a strong east wind all night, and made the sea dry land, and the waters were divided. 22 And the people of Israel went into the midst of the sea on dry ground, the waters being a wall to them on their right hand and on their left. 23 The Egyptians pursued, and went in after them into the midst of the sea, all Pharaoh's horses, his chariots, and his horsemen. 24 And in the morning watch the Lord in the pillar of fire and of cloud looked down upon the host of the Egyptians, and discomfited the

[p] Gk: Heb *and it lit up the night*

---

20. The point of this is that the cloud (i.e., the divine presence) and the darkness of night kept the two groups hidden from each other. The Hebrew **and it lit up the night** (RSV mg.) rests on a corrupt text and the RSV has wisely followed the LXX reading.

21-22. Since the wind is from the east we must assume that the crossing took place somewhere near the *eastern* shore of the sea or lake, probably Lake Timsah. In flat marshy districts large areas are often intermittently covered by shallow water or laid dry by the action of the wind; e.g., almost annually in the spring high winds off the Persian Gulf blow in waters at high tide to cover all the area lying south of Zobeir in Iraq, a distance of about twenty-five miles.

4. God Destroys His Enemies (14:23-31)

23. The final scene in the dramatic act in which God reveals his power is now presented. The heavily armed Egyptians follow Israel in a path that is less treacherous for the Israelites fleeing on foot. In Palestine, for generations, Israelites in war were guerrilla fighters who were canny in turning the technological superiority of their foes to their own advantage (Judg. 4:13; 5:19-23; Josh. 11:1-9; I Kings 20:22-30).

24. The **morning watch** is probably the period from 2 to 6 A.M. Here and in vs. 27 we are left with the impression that the successful crossing of the Israelites and the destruction of the Egyptians were all over as morning broke. We are reminded of the nocturnal defeat of the gods of Egypt (11:4-5). This statement about a crossing by night must somehow be harmonized with the statement in vs. 20 that they did not come

---

sentences in them like this, 'I thank my God that I do not have to worry about any of my boys' "? That mother was a protecting angel or pillar before and behind and all around her children. One compares her with the worrying mother of whom her student son said, "I can't work at home, for I know that she is sitting there at the other side of the door worrying about me." Religion, like science, takes the forces in life that are running to waste and

turns them into power. It turns worry into prayer, depression into humility, pride into thanksgiving; it turns the destructive smoldering fires and smoke into protective pillars or even, as our friend E would prefer to say, into guardian angels.

23-31. *The Hour of Vengeance.*—It is very seldom in real life that one finds all the rats caught in one trap. Such scenes as this at the Red Sea or in Nuremberg courtroom in 1946

25 And took off their chariot wheels, that they drave them heavily: so that the Egyptians said, Let us flee from the face of Israel; for the LORD fighteth for them against the Egyptians.

26 ¶ And the LORD said unto Moses, Stretch out thine hand over the sea, that the waters may come again upon the Egyptians, upon their chariots, and upon their horsemen.

27 And Moses stretched forth his hand over the sea, and the sea returned to his strength when the morning appeared; and the Egyptians fled against it; and the LORD overthrew the Egyptians in the midst of the sea.

28 And the waters returned, and covered the chariots, and the horsemen, *and* all the host of Pharaoh that came into the sea after them; there remained not so much as one of them.

host of the Egyptians, 25 clogging*q* their chariot wheels so that they drove heavily; and the Egyptians said, "Let us flee from before Israel; for the LORD fights for them against the Egyptians."
27 So Moses stretched forth his hand over the sea, and the sea returned to its wonted flow when the morning appeared; and the Egyptians fled into it, and the LORD routed*r* the Egyptians in the midst of the sea. 28 The waters returned and covered the chariots and the horsemen and all the host*s* of Pharaoh that had followed them into the sea; not so much as one of them remained.

q Or *binding.* Sam Gk Syr: Heb *removing*
r Heb *shook off*
s Gk Syr: Heb *to all the host*

near each other **all night** and with the statement in vs. 21 that the strong east wind blew **all night.** For cultic reasons, notably on account of the Passover ritual, the historic incident may have been crowded into a single night. The normal meaning of the Hebrew word translated **host** is "camp." It is possible that in this verse we have a statement about a confusion in the enemy camp during the night, a confusion caused by the divine presence (vss. 19-20). This verse seems to continue vs. 20 and to interrupt vss. 23-25.

25. As frequently in the account of the plagues, the Egyptians recognize that Yahweh is their real enemy. Nowhere in the account is the prowess or leadership of Moses intruded upon what is presented as wholly the work of the Lord.

26. Israel is already safely across; not the turning of the wind but Moses' hand makes the waters come back.

28-31. It is not specifically said that the Pharaoh was drowned. Later tradition inferred this on the basis of vss. 5-10. In terms of the relativities of historical process, even the utter destruction of Pharaoh's forces was an event of very minor import. It did not alter the fortunes of the empire of Egypt. The writers and editors of this account may have been under no illusions about this, for Egypt was frequently a threat to Israel's political security. Yet this insignificant event was in Israel the key that transformed the meaning of all history. Egypt was the same Egypt. But for the community of faith that sprang from this event it no longer bore the same meaning as heretofore. They had seen "the great hand" of God. What is of moment is the victory of God, not the drowning of the Egyptians.

are exceptional. It usually takes years, and generally it is never wholly accomplished. Did Pharaoh himself perish in the inundation? What happened to Hitler? These questions remain unanswered for years and perhaps forever. Life never seems to have as neat an edge as any theory of life presupposes. Although the point is not labored, the writers seem to imply that the drowning of the Egyptians was a just punishment for the killing of the newborn Hebrew boys (1:16). Wholesale extermination of

the enemy has always been the vindictive dream of persecuted peoples. Here there was justification for gloating over the corpses, for only the pursuing army was destroyed. It was left for our age at Hiroshima to come within sight of the realization of that agelong dream of the depraved human heart in its most horrible form. There is always justification to produce in the court; but inevitably history judges the use of power. How shall the virtuous triumphant of 1945 stand on this count at the bar of the ages?

29 But the children of Israel walked upon dry *land* in the midst of the sea; and the waters *were* a wall unto them on their right hand, and on their left.

30 Thus the LORD saved Israel that day out of the hand of the Egyptians; and Israel saw the Egyptians dead upon the seashore.

31 And Israel saw that great work which the LORD did upon the Egyptians: and the people feared the LORD, and believed the LORD, and his servant Moses.

15 Then sang Moses and the children of Israel this song unto the LORD,

29 But the people of Israel walked on dry ground through the sea, the waters being a wall to them on their right hand and on their left.

30 Thus the LORD saved Israel that day from the hand of the Egyptians; and Israel saw the Egyptians dead upon the seashore.

31 And Israel saw the great work which the LORD did against the Egyptians, and the people feared the LORD; and they believed in the LORD and in his servant Moses.

15 Then Moses and the people of Israel sang this song to the LORD, saying,

---

5. Hymns in Praise of Yahweh (15:1-21)

Two victory hymns in honor of Yahweh follow immediately after the account of Israel's deliverance: the Song of Moses and the Song of Miriam. Very probably the latter

---

29. Dry Land in the Midst of the Sea.—This is one of the great poetically descriptive verses of the Bible, symbolic of a life lived in the spirit of Ps. 2. **Dry land in the midst of the sea.** Mud is the obstacle to all true progress. How it clutters up our inner lives—words, words, words; inexact thinking; unsatisfied and unsublimated desires; moods of gloomy worry. Dante places all the sad, sullen, and slothful deep in mud in hell. It is a picture of an inner experience, this scene when Moses stretches forth the magic rod and all the mud dries up and there is suddenly before the people a fair way to walk upon. It is a very simple experience.

Hence you may see why our Saviour, who, though he had all Wisdom, and came to be the Light of the World, is yet so short in his Instructions, and gives so small a Number of Doctrines to Mankind, whilst every Moral Teacher, writes Volumes upon every single Virtue.[7]

The pearl of great price is the fact that

all the Holy Nature, Spirit, Tempers, and Inclinations of Christ, lie as in a Seed in the Centre of thy Soul.[8]

It was a kind of "walking faith" when Moses held up the staff of God's promise and then began walking into the sea. One has to do both in order to find the mud drying up and the sea of troubles becoming as a protective wall on his right hand and on his left. Every new morning one has to practice, through the best thinking of which he is capable, the sincerest detestation of the slum within him, the most imaginative and realistic picture in his mind of

[7] William Law, *The Spirit of Prayer.* Part II, Dialogue 2.
[8] *Ibid.*, Part I, ch. ii.

the promises of God, and a forward motion, committing himself irrevocably to the new way miraculously being opened up for him as he goes along.

To provide the figure some wider reference, it is only when sitting in cushioned seats that denominations disagree; in such triumphant experiences as that at the Red Sea, all dissensions and murmurings are forgotten and the church of Christ is one and victorious because it is engaged in its proper business of victory over sin. Hear again what William Law wrote in 1756:

Under this Light, I am neither Protestant, nor Papist, according to the common Acceptation of the Words.—I cannot consider myself as belonging only to one Society of Christians, in separation and distinction from all others.—It would be as hurtful to me, if not more so, than any worldly Partiality. And therefore as the Defects, Corruptions, and Imperfections, which, some way or other, are to be found in all Churches, hinder not my Communion with that, under which my Lot is fallen, so neither do they hinder my being in full Union, and hearty Fellowship with all that is Christian, Holy, and Good, in every other Church Division.[9]

A common war for a common cause has been heretofore the only method of uniting nations; churches will become one only in the ranks of one army fighting sin in themselves. As soon as the danger was over, the Israelites had time to dissent and murmur again, but when they were in peril together, they had no time but to fight, march forward, and sing together songs of victory.

15:1-19. The Song of Moses.—The O.T. contains three songs attributed to Moses: this one;

[9] *A Collection of Letters on the Most Interesting and Important Subjects,* Letter I.

and spake, saying, I will sing unto the LORD, for he hath triumphed gloriously: the horse and his rider hath he thrown into the sea.	"I will sing to the LORD, for he has triumphed gloriously; the horse and his rider[t] he has thrown into the sea.

[t] Or *its chariot*

actually originated at the rejoicing in Israel on the occasion of its escape. Therefore, though it may have had cultic perpetuation, it belongs in this context simply on the basis of chronological sequence in history. But the Song of Moses originated later. It recounts God's protection of Israel during its pilgrimage in the desert (vss. 13-16) and assumes the establishment of the temple and its worship in Jerusalem (vs. 17). Its earliest possible date, therefore, is the era of the united kingdom. It may be much later. This song had probably a place in the cultus, and may have been used liturgically for a feast at which God's victory at the sea was especially stressed. Thus it has been suggested (Beer, *Exodus,* p. 84) that the song was a Passover cantata composed for, and presented on the occasion of, the great celebration of the feast in Jerusalem attending the reformation of Josiah. Many scholars who are identified with the "myth and ritual school" of interpretation look upon 12:1–15:21 as, for the most part, a block of liturgical material of which the song is an integral part. Those among them who hold to the idea of an annual enthronement festival of Yahweh in Jerusalem claim that this song was a hymn used on that occasion (Aage Bentzen, *Introduction to the Old Testament* [Copenhagen: G. E. C. Gad, 1948] I, 163). In any case, it is not on the basis of chronological sequence in history but for the sake of stressing the meaning of a specific event in history that the editors have included this song in their book.

Deut. 31:22; Ps. 90. A study of the vocabulary style, and subject matter of this song shows that it is an expression of the sentiments and feelings of Moses as they were conceived by a writer at a much later time. Like the conversations in Eden in Milton's *Paradise Lost,* or the aspirations of John Brown by a modern poet, this song tells how Moses must have felt after the victory at the Red Sea, as a later writer tries to understand and appreciate his spirit. This poet looks before and after and sees the occasion in view of subsequent events. The poem probably was taken from a book of patriotic and religious songs in common use by the people at the close of the monarchy or in postexilic times. One sees Israel developing toward a true monotheism. The gods of other nations are still conceived of as existing, but Yahweh proves himself mightier than they. This is a real step toward the faith that there is but one God (vs. 11). Like all patriotic songs, this poem tells of national triumphs without mentioning the reverses sustained. Vss. 14-19 represent easier going than that related in 13:17; Num. 20:18; but few nations can stand any reference to their defeats and mistakes. Franklin was much criticized when he wrote, "During the course of a long life in which I have made observations of public affairs, it has appeared to me that almost every war between the Indians and the whites has been occasioned by some injustice of the latter towards the former." [1] The early American settlers acted much as the children of Israel did toward the original inhabitants of the lands they wished to occupy:

Under Captain John Mason, [they] fell upon the encampment with fire, sword, blunderbuss, and tomahawk. Only a handful escaped, and few prisoners were taken. Flames consumed almost all, and it was a fearful sight, said the Pilgrims in phrases quoted with delight . . . by Cotton Mather, "to see them thus frying in ye fyer, and ye streams of blood quenching ye same, and horrible was ye stinck and sente thereof; but ye victory seemed a sweete sacrifice, and they gave prayse thereof to God." [2]

Such was the end of the proud Pequot nation.

Winthrop informed Bradford that he had taken personal charge of the wife of a Pequot sachem, a woman "of a very modest countenance and behavior," whose only request was that the English "not abuse her body." [3]

How much religious value there is in the fact that Moses' song and the Pilgrims' thanksgiving ascribe the victories to God rather than to their own prowess remains a question. This Red

[1] Albert H. Smith, *The Writings of Benjamin Franklin* (New York: The Macmillan Co., 1905-7), IX, 625.
[2] George F. Willison, *Saints and Strangers* (New York: Reynal & Hitchcock, 1945), p. 306
[3] *Ibid.*

a) Song of Moses (15:1-18)

The song is a splendid example of biblical poetry. Spontaneous, even fiery, it nevertheless displays a highly developed and meticulously applied sense of literary form. Its dynamic and exuberant power is communicated rather than stymied by its studied construction. There is here all of the exhilaration but little of the "rugged" obscurity of older pieces (cf. Judg. 5). The concern, the mood, and to some extent the structure make it proper to classify this poem as a "hymn" in the sense applied to that term by the Gunkel-Eissfeldt school of literary analysis which studies the literary forms of poetry according to cultic usage. The song praises Yahweh for his goodness to Israel. **The LORD shall reign for ever and ever:** This exclamation is typical of the "hymns" of praise (Pss. 47:9; 96:10; 97:1). The quotation of the Song of Miriam provides the song with an introduction typical of the "hymn." It is also characteristic that the Lord is the principal character throughout, though he appears only in the third person, and that there should be a recital of God's power and of his care for Israel, past and present. However the contents of this description are in some respects nontypical. In the normal type of hymn descriptions are not specifically historical. They are more general, and reflective of Near Eastern mythology in their account of God as creator and ruler of his people. Vss. 2-3, 6-7, 11-12 well illustrate this character of the hymn, but they are interspersed by bits of what one may describe as a historical ballad (vss. 4-5, 8-10, 13-17), possibly not all from one source. This historical material has been beautifully fitted into and harmonized with the materials of the purer hymn type. Bentzen (*Intro. to O.T.*, I, 163) feels that the main subject of the hypothetical enthronement festival was Yahweh's victory at the sea. This assimilative process, by which more and more the historical was fitted into the form of the erstwhile mythological, illustrates a very general and profoundly significant phenomenon in Israel's religious history. The mythological heritage is always in process of being historicized until finally, as in Christianity, the liturgical year is essentially a "historical" year rather than a natural year, without, however, losing sight of the natural cycle. The hymn, as a cultic form, was gradually transformed from praising a God whose victory was mythological to one whose victory took place in a certain month on a certain day at the Sea of Reeds.

Since the poet's account of Israel's history stops with the era of Solomon (970-930), this poem may date from that time. Yet such a consideration is not decisive, for the poem's concern is not Israel's history but Yahweh's rule in Jerusalem. Those who see in the song a hymn used at an annual enthronement festival for Yahweh in the temple tend to date it rather early, since this festival is conceived to have had a long history in the era of the monarchy. The buoyancy and power of the poem fit well in the heroic age of David (cf. II Sam. 1:19-27). But power and literary artistry continued long after his era (cf. Hab. 3). Until it became associated with the liturgy of a hypothetical enthronement festival of Yahweh the poem was most commonly associated with the Deuteronomic period. A. H. McNeile (*The Book of Exodus* [London: Methuen & Co., 1908; "Westminster Commentaries"], p. 88) pointed out that the poem draws on the prose account as it now stands rather than on any one source present in it, but our recovery of a sense of the role of oral tradition must qualify the weight of that evidence. The vocabulary, however, also belongs to the period beginning *ca.* 600 B.C. Beer decided for this later date on the ground that the song teaches the universal rule of Yahweh from Jerusalem, a teaching characteristic of the Deuteronomists (Deut. 26:19; 28:1, 13; Isa. 2:2-4) but not attested in the documents of the Davidic age.

15:1. As characteristic of the "hymn," the song is sung by the entire community and concerns the life of the entire assembly of Israel. The Song of Miriam serves as introduction. The LXX, both here and in vs. 21, gives the first verb as a cohortative, "Let us sing." The "hymn" style argues for the imperative present in vs. 21. God has "risen up" in his majesty. The idea of "pride" is carried by the Hebrew root; Yahweh had displayed his true divinity. The chariots rather than the riders were lost in the water. There was no cavalry.

2 The Lord *is* my strength and song, and he is become my salvation: he *is* my God, and I will prepare him a habitation; my father's God, and I will exalt him.

3 The Lord *is* a man of war: the Lord *is* his name.

4 Pharaoh's chariots and his host hath he cast into the sea: his chosen captains also are drowned in the Red sea.

5 The depths have covered them: they sank into the bottom as a stone.

6 Thy right hand, O Lord, is become glorious in power: thy right hand, O Lord, hath dashed in pieces the enemy.

7 And in the greatness of thine excellency thou hast overthrown them that rose up against thee: thou sentest forth thy wrath, *which* consumed them as stubble.

8 And with the blast of thy nostrils the waters were gathered together, the floods stood upright as a heap, *and* the depths were congealed in the heart of the sea.

---

2 The Lord is my strength and my song,
  and he has become my salvation;
this is my God, and I will praise him,
  my father's God, and I will exalt him.

3 The Lord is a man of war;
  the Lord is his name.

4 "Pharaoh's chariots and his host he cast
  into the sea;
  and his picked officers are sunk in the
  Red Sea.

5 The floods cover them;
  they went down into the depths like a
  stone.

6 Thy right hand, O Lord, glorious in
  power,
  thy right hand, O Lord, shatters the
  enemy.

7 In the greatness of thy majesty thou overthrowest thy adversaries;
  thou sendest forth thy fury, it consumes them like stubble.

8 At the blast of thy nostrils the waters
  piled up,
  the floods stood up in a heap;
  the deeps congealed in the heart of
  the sea.

---

2. The first half of this verse is quoted in Isa. 12:2; Ps. 118:14. Yahweh has saved the poet and Israel. In this liturgical contest the content of the salvation is the material and social security of the community of Israel in its own land. The phrase **my father's God** simply underscores the phrase **this is my God** in the manner characteristic of parallelism in Hebrew poetry.

3. The central moment in the revelation of God at the Exodus is power, a moment which is here presented in a military metaphor: Yahweh is a warrior.

4-5. This is a specified historical reference. Vs. 4 describes the deed of Yahweh. In terms of meaning the phrase **and his host** is redundant; the chariots and their "crews" (14:7) constituted the host of Egypt at the incident in question. In terms of meter the phrase does not fit. In vs. 5 the shallow Sea of Reeds becomes an abyss like the "great deep" of mythology.

6-7. In this more strictly "hymn" section of the song the references to Yahweh's power to overthrow his enemies are general. He who displayed his power at the sea is always powerful.

8-10. The poet's account of the scene at the sea combines the natural movement of the water by the wind (14:21) and the report (14:22) that the waters stood like walls or, as here, **in a heap** (cf. Josh. 3:13, 16). The breath of Yahweh is the wind (cf. vs. 10). **The deeps congealed in the heart of the sea:** This phrase refers most probably to the fountains connecting the sea with the mythological ocean to which the ancients thought

---

Sea hymn has been quoted often in succeeding wars. The Latin version of vs. 10, *Afflavit Deus et dissipati sunt,* was the motto used by the English in their celebrations over the sinking of the Spanish Armada in 1588. The hymn is a celebration of the triumphal march of Yahweh

to the center of his eternal world kingdom in Jerusalem (Ps. 146:10).

1. *I Will Sing Unto Yahweh.*—J. G. von Herder, speaking of the drama of his day, says, "An ancient Greek coming into one of our performances would say, 'Is it a decorated grave?

9 The enemy said, I will pursue, I will overtake, I will divide the spoil; my lust shall be satisfied upon them; I will draw my sword, my hand shall destroy them.

10 Thou didst blow with thy wind, the sea covered them: they sank as lead in the mighty waters.

11 Who *is* like unto thee, O Lord, among the gods? who *is* like thee, glorious in holiness, fearful *in* praises, doing wonders?

12 Thou stretchedst out thy right hand, the earth swallowed them.

13 Thou in thy mercy hast led forth the people *which* thou hast redeemed: thou hast guided *them* in thy strength unto thy holy habitation.

14 The people shall hear, *and* be afraid: sorrow shall take hold on the inhabitants of Palestina.

15 Then the dukes of Edom shall be amazed; the mighty men of Moab, trembling shall take hold upon them; all the inhabitants of Canaan shall melt away.

9 The enemy said, 'I will pursue, I will overtake,
I will divide the spoil, my desire shall have its fill of them.
I will draw my sword, my hand shall destroy them.'

10 Thou didst blow with thy wind, the sea covered them;
they sank as lead in the mighty waters.

11 "Who is like thee, O Lord, among the gods?
Who is like thee, majestic in holiness, terrible in glorious deeds, doing wonders?

12 Thou didst stretch out thy right hand, the earth swallowed them.

13 "Thou hast led in thy steadfast love the people whom thou hast redeemed,
thou hast guided them by thy strength to thy holy abode.

14 The peoples have heard, they tremble;
pangs have seized on the inhabitants of Philistia.

15 Now are the chiefs of Edom dismayed;
the leaders of Moab, trembling seizes them:
all the inhabitants of Canaan have melted away.

the seas to be connected. In vs. 9 six brief clauses, tense with action, effectively communicate the eager confidence and greedy desire with which the enemy entered the fray. The last verb does not simply signify destruction but basically carries the idea of taking possession. Egypt again wishes to claim Israel as its own. But as vs. 10 emphasizes, the power of Yahweh is so much greater as to make this utterly impossible.

11-12. This bit of the hymn is in the form of the "negative question," a common liturgical device (cf. Pss. 35:10; 71:19; 89:7-9; 113:5-6). The verses reveal how faith generalized the event on which it rests. Because Yahweh had shown himself Lord over Pharaoh, he is above all gods. In the phrase **majestic in holiness** the poet compares Yahweh and the other gods. He is in a class apart, unapproachable: his freedom and power, rather than his ethical character, here determine this distinction. The LXX renders **in holiness** as "among the holy ones," i.e., "among the gods." The Hebrew says that Yahweh is feared in respect to or on account of "praises," i.e., the deeds for which he is praised (cf. Ps. 78:4; Isa. 63:7).

13. God led his people as pilgrims after setting them free. The **holy abode** may here refer to the entire holy land (Jer. 10:25; 25:30), but in vs. 17 Mount Zion seems unmistakably singled out. *Ḥéṣedh* is the Hebrew word translated **steadfast love**. The LXX gives it not as ἔλεος but as δικαιοσύνη. The parallelism suggests "faithfulness" or "power."

14-16. The writer is deeply convinced of the actuality and adequacy of Yahweh's providential care for Israel. He illustrates his faith by suggesting that Israel's career was always smooth, which it was not. Edom and Moab made Israel avoid their territories (Num. 20:18-21; 21:13). **The inhabitants of Canaan** did not melt away but, with the Philistines, troubled Israel until the era of David (Judg. 2:21-23). This glossing over of the hard realities of history does not vitiate the sincerity or the truth of the poet's faith,

16 Fear and dread shall fall upon them; by the greatness of thine arm they shall be *as* still as a stone; till thy people pass over, O LORD, till the people pass over, *which* thou hast purchased.

17 Thou shalt bring them in, and plant them in the mountain of thine inheritance, *in* the place, O LORD, *which* thou hast made for thee to dwell in; *in* the sanctuary, O LORD, *which* thy hands have established.

18 The LORD shall reign for ever and ever.

19 For the horse of Pharaoh went in with his chariots and with his horsemen into the sea, and the LORD brought again the waters of the sea upon them; but the children of Israel went on dry *land* in the midst of the sea.

20 ¶ And Miriam the prophetess, the sister of Aaron, took a timbrel in her hand;

16 Terror and dread fall upon them;
　　because of the greatness of thy arm,
　　　they are as still as a stone,
till thy people, O LORD, pass by,
　　till the people pass by whom thou hast
　　　purchased.
17 Thou wilt bring them in, and plant them
　　on thy own mountain,
　　the place, O LORD, which thou hast
　　　made for thy abode,
　　the sanctuary, O LORD, which thy hands
　　　have established.
18 The LORD will reign for ever and ever."

19 For when the horses of Pharaoh with his chariots and his horsemen went into the sea, the LORD brought back the waters of the sea upon them; but the people of Israel walked on dry ground in the midst of the sea. 20 Then Miriam, the prophetess, the

---

but it does convey to later generations an unrealistic impression of the relationship of revelation to nature and history.

18. This exultant cry of faith, the heart and focus of the hymn, expresses the current meaning of the historic rescue at the sea. The two are ineradicably bound together.

b) SONG OF MIRIAM (15:19-21)

19. The editor's introduction connects the song with the prose account of the deliverance (ch. 14).

20-21. Miriam leads a chorus of women who perform a victory dance. It is because of such activity that she is called a **prophetess.** The chorus repeated the hymn that Miriam

---

You stride and sigh and rant, move the arms, arrange the features, reason and declaim! But voice and feeling never burst into song, do you not miss this accent of the true Voice of God?' " [4] A Welsh woman, after hearing an eloquent preacher, said, "Ah, yes, but he ought to have sung the last part of the sermon!" Great sermons seem to be at least on the verge of breaking into song: John Donne, preaching at St. Paul's on Christmas Day, 1626, at Communion:

And then to come from that table . . . with a bosom peace in thine own conscience in that seal of thy reconciliation, in that Sacrament; that so, riding at that anchor, and in that calm, whether God enlarge thy voyage by enlarging thy life, or put thee into the harbour, by the breath, by the breathlessness of death, either way, east or west, thou mayest depart in peace according to his word, that is, as he shall be pleased to manifest his pleasure upon thee.

When read aloud, when spoken as in the pulpit, such speech is nigh unto song, song like that

into which the people of Israel broke spontaneously in their day of triumph and tragedy.

20-21. *Miriam's Response.*—Just why Miriam should be called the sister of Aaron, who is hardly mentioned in this narrative, rather than the sister of Moses is a mystery. Perhaps E did not consider Moses and Aaron to be brothers, or, as no learned critic seems to suggest, perhaps Aaron and Miriam were twins. Stanley A. Cook suggests that Miriam and Aaron may have been only stepsister and stepbrother of Moses.[5] She was probably the sister spoken of as watching the baby's ark in the Nile (2:4). The name appears as Mary in the N.T.; among Semitic women it was considered desirable to be plump, which is probably the derivative meaning of the name. Miriam is also mentioned in Num. 12:1-15; 26:59; 20:1; Deut. 24:9; Mic. 6:4.

The form in Hebrew is that of a victory dance song. Jewish women were accustomed to celebrate victories in this manner (see Judg. 5:1 ff.; 11:34; I Sam. 18:6). Every age reads the Bible,

⁴ *Sämmtliche Werke*, ed. Bernhard Suphan (Berlin: Wiedmann, 1885), XXIII, 347.

⁵ Article "Miriam," in T. K. Cheyne and J. Sutherland Black, eds., *Encyclopaedia Biblica* (New York: The Macmillan Co., 1902), Vol. III, col. 3152.

and all the women went out after her with timbrels and with dances.

21 And Miriam answered them, Sing ye to the LORD, for he hath triumphed gloriously: the horse and his rider hath he thrown into the sea.

22 So Moses brought Israel from the Red sea, and they went out into the wilderness of Shur; and they went three days in the wilderness, and found no water.

sister of Aaron, took a timbrel in her hand; and all the women went out after her with timbrels and dancing. **21** And Miriam sang to them:

"Sing to the LORD, for he has triumphed gloriously;
     the horse and his rider he has thrown into the sea."

22 Then Moses led Israel onward from the Red Sea, and they went into the wilderness of Shur; they went three days in the

---

sang out. The introductory statement that Miriam took a timbrel reminds us that liturgical "hymns" frequently cite the instruments used in their performance (Pss. 33; 92; 98; 150).

D. The Pilgrimage to Sinai (15:22–18:27)

The deliverance at the sea was the climax of the Exodus. Taught by Moses, Israel saw the whole process that led to it as the work of Yahweh in which he disclosed his power and lordship. The permanent meaning of this event for Israel, however, is still to be made clear. There is a momentary exaltation, but this must give way to a response in which, in cultus and social institutions, Israel lives out the meaning of the revelation in its own communal and historical existence. Eventually Sinai becomes the focus for the implementation of the faith of the Exodus. The Exodus and Sinai become inextricably bound together. Every tendency in Israel's life castigated in the Bible as faithless and sinful is, in one way or another, determined by an outlook that denies or ignores the bond of Exodus-Sinai. Whether the cycle of episodes in 15:22–18:27, continued in Num. 10:29 ff., was originally oriented to Sinai is an open question. It has been persuasively argued that this cycle was actually focused on Kadesh and that the Sinai tradition (Exod. 19:10–Num. 10:28) now interrupts it (see "The Kenite Hypothesis," Intro., pp. 839-40).

In relating the journey from the sea to Sinai the writers show little concern with the empirical facts of geography or history. The harshness and risk of life in the barren desert are pointed up, but there are few details. The general picture is put to the service of the writers' main purpose: to show that Israel, despite the existential character of its deliverance, was still subject to the moral and physical conditions of struggle that all

---

omitting to notice those things in it of which it does not approve. The place of the dance in O.T. worship has been ignored and the importance of solemn assemblies has been underlined. But most scholars and saints are middle-aged before they become scholars or saints. So the example of Miriam and the exhortations of the author of Pss. 149; 150 have been forgotten. "The principal occasions of dancing are, in an ancient community, religious. . . . Dancing, then, was of the essence of a primitive religious festival." [6] "The use of dancing as a social pastime is comparatively modern." [7] Worship, however,

has become too sedentary; indeed almost the only remnant left in some Protestant churches of the ritual dance is in the processional. Dancing, divorced from the church, has tended in modern times to take one of two lines, either popular degeneracy into vulgarity, or a professional revival of the ancient inspiration by which it becomes one of the supreme artistic forms for the expression both of ideas and emotion.

22-25. The Bitter Waters.—The murmuring begins as soon as the crisis and imperative demand for common action ends. It happens after every victorious war. Smaller discomforts are felt again when the great danger is over. Many of us would feel more at home with J than E or P; notice how he likes to find natural causes for events the others ascribe to miracle. J has a

[6] See article on "Dance" in Cheyne and Black, *Encyclopaedia Biblica*, Vol. I, cols. 998-99.

[7] A. E. Crawley, "Processions and Dances," in James Hastings, ed., *Encyclopaedia of Religion and Ethics* (New York: Charles Scribner's Sons, 1919), X, 362.

23 ¶ And when they came to Marah, they could not drink of the waters of Marah, for they *were* bitter: therefore the name of it was called Marah.

24 And the people murmured against Moses, saying, What shall we drink?

25 And he cried unto the LORD; and the LORD showed him a tree, *which* when he

wilderness and found no water. 23 When they came to Marah, they could not drink the water of Marah because it was bitter; therefore it was named Marah.ᵘ 24 And the people murmured against Moses, saying, "What shall we drink?" 25 And he cried to the LORD; and the LORD showed him a tree,

ᵘ That is *Bitterness*

men meet in history, though with the difference that the revelation gave meaning and direction to the struggle. The desert pilgrimage with its fears and crises is made to convey the writers' teaching that Israel's fulfillment of life at the Exodus is a fulfillment *in faith*. Hence it must live responsibly in history.

1. THE CRISES (15:22–17:16)

Yahweh had destroyed Pharaoh and the gods of Egypt, but life for Israel was still the same. Thirst, hunger, and enemies remained inescapable facts. Security was, it seemed, no greater than before. This whole series of incidents makes it plain. But those who relate it are likewise attesting that in the midst of this relentless process of nature and history God is as free and active as he was in the dramatic escape. And Yahweh is represented as "trying" Israel to see if it will live by this faith which can give significance to its historical pilgrimage.

a) MARAH (15:22-27)

22. The **wilderness of Shur** is the same as "the wilderness of Etham" (Num. 33:8). The way of Shur was a familiar caravan route that approached Kadesh-barnea as it led to Beer-sheba. Shur was familiar to the patriarchs (Gen. 16:7; 20:1; 25:18). This route of the **wilderness of Shur** is one possible route taken by the Israelites to Sinai-Horeb. Another possibility, perhaps more probable, is the present pilgrim route that leads toward the head of the Gulf of Aqabah. On the basis of the biblical evidence that tends to the conclusion that Sinai-Horeb is located in the Edom-Paran region (cf. 3:1-5), either one of these routes is more probably the way traveled by Israel than the route predicated upon the traditional Sinai site near the apex of the peninsula. A three-day journey by a mixed caravan was perhaps no more than fifty miles.

23. Brackish pools and wells are frequent in many desert areas. The account here has an etiological form, i.e., the Israelites are said to have given **Marah** its name. It is impossible definitely to locate the site.

24-25a. This incident may have parallel accounts in Massah-Meribah (17:1-7; Num. 20:1-12). The metaphor of "striving" (*merîbhāh*) is not introduced here. The people "murmur" (cf. 16:1-12) against Moses. Moses does not show the irritation he does in the other accounts, nor are the people condemned for their fear. Yahweh, to whom Moses appeals, is the central actor in the healing (cf. II Kings 2:21; Ezek. 47:8) of the water. It may be that an originally independent allusion to a magic ritual, in which a bitter wood made bitter water sweet, has been recast with this theocentric concern. The Samar. text says that Yahweh "caused [Moses] to see" the wood. In the M.T. the root is ירה, "to point."

more scientific mind; he wants to know why and how. The Lord showed Moses a tree which he could throw into the bitter waters and make them sweet. Various plants are used in different parts of the world for this purpose. E. F. K. Rosenmüller mentions Nellimaran in Coromandel, Sassafras in Florida, and Yerva Caniani in Peru. Ferdinand de Lesseps was told by Arab chiefs that they used in this way a certain

bitter thorn, growing in the desert, but nothing is known about it.

Treating the incident symbolically, we wonder if there is any tree which, thrown into the bitter waters of life, will make them sweet. The ancient philosopher said that a wise and good man could be perfectly happy even on the rack; the modern philosopher, Benjamin Jowett, when asked if he believed that was possible,

had cast into the waters, the waters were made sweet: there he made for them a statute and an ordinance, and there he proved them,

26 And said, If thou wilt diligently hearken to the voice of the LORD thy God, and wilt do that which is right in his sight, and wilt give ear to his commandments, and keep all his statutes, I will put none of these diseases upon thee, which I have brought upon the Egyptians: for I *am* the LORD that healeth thee.

and he threw it into the water, and the water became sweet.

There the LORD[v] made for them a statute and an ordinance and there he proved them, 26 saying, "If you will diligently hearken to the voice of the LORD, your God, and do that which is right in his eyes, and give heed to his commandments and keep all his statutes, I will put none of the diseases upon you which I put upon the Egyptians; for I am the LORD, your healer."

[v] Heb *he*

25*b*-26. Yahweh, having healed the water, is presented as the healer of Israel (Deut. 32:39; Ps. 103:3). The vocabulary of this section and its preoccupation with the diseases of Egypt (cf. Deut. 7:15; 28:27, 60) mark it as the work of a Deuteronomic editor. The phrase **there he proved them** associates the incidents with the Massah-Meribah accounts. The testing or proving is presented as something lying in the future. God challenges Israel to express its faith in his constant protection and power by keeping his law. In later ages rabbis used this verse as a prayer in the blessing of the sick.

---

replied, "Perhaps—a *very* good man on a *very* bad rack." This is about as far as we can go. The waters of life are sometimes bitter, and no art or religion can make them sweet. But religion can help us to drink bitter waters without being embittered ourselves. The highest point personal religion can reach is when it is possible for us to add the second clause to the first in the great text, "O my Father, if it be possible, let this cup pass from me: nevertheless, not as I will, but as thou wilt" (Matt. 26:39).

26. *The Ultimate Fact of God.*—Both the O.T. and the N.T. give much attention to bodily health in its relation to religious faith. This is true also of the religions of Greece, Egypt, and Babylonia, and indeed of most primitive faiths. Generally, as can be seen in Homer, external injuries and affections were treated by common-sense and often wise methods. But epidemics and obscurer complaints left the people helpless, and they had recourse to what seem to us superstitious religious rites such as spells, processions, or magical mixtures.

The history of the art and science of medicine has been largely the transfer of one type of ailment after another from treatment by superstitious or hit-and-miss methods to treatment by experimental knowledge. This general movement is typified by the shift in popular faith from solemn processions with sacred images in case of epidemics to modern methods of sanitation, etc.

The shift has largely been a salutary one, but in the process something has been lost. Montaigne's remark, "Whence proceeds the subtilest

folly, but from the subtilest wisdom?" [8] is really inscribed, though few scientists can see it, around the base of the image of the Great God Science, which stands by the boulevard of modern life opposite the Great God Mammon. The two idols are mighty, but they have feet of clay, for there are whole regions of human experience which they do not understand and have therefore ignored. They reign supreme, each over a section of human life. One must make friends with mammon to live at all (see G. B. Shaw's *Major Barbara*). Father Neville Figgis once acknowledged that after he had joined a monastic order, given to it all his worldly possessions, and taken the vow of poverty, he found he was as much dependent upon the present evil economic system as ever. A. J. Carlson, one of the high priests in the holy temple of science, said:

No matter how high in state, church, society or science the individual may be who makes pronouncement on any subject, the scientist always asks for the evidence. When no evidence is produced other than personal dicta, past or present "revelations" in dreams, or the "voice of God," the scientist can pay no attention whatsoever, except to ask: How do they get that way? [9]

This is a very superstitious statement, founded on the unproved idea that truth can be reached only by scientific methods. One can imagine Carlson buttonholing people coming out of a

[8] *Essayes*, Bk. II, ch. xii.
[9] "Science and the Supernatural," *The Scientific Monthly*, LIX (1944), 85. See comments on this article, *ibid.*, LIX (1944), 321-24.

27 ¶ And they came to Elim, where *were* twelve wells of water, and threescore and ten palm trees: and they encamped there by the waters.

16 And they took their journey from Elim, and all the congregation of the children of Israel came unto the wilderness of Sin, which *is* between Elim and Sinai, on the fifteenth day of the second month after their departing out of the land of Egypt.

27 Then they came to Elim, where there were twelve springs of water and seventy palm trees; and they encamped there by the water.

16 They set out from Elim, and all the congregation of the people of Israel came to the wilderness of Sin, which is between Elim and Sinai, on the fifteenth day of the second month after they had departed

27. **Elim** is a word meaning "gods" and "terebinths." The place must have been an oasis which was likewise a sacred site. It is possible that it is the site of Elath (Deut. 2:8; II Kings 16:6) at the head of the Gulf of Aqabah, but this suggestion, resting mainly on etymological affinity, must not be pressed.

b) THE MANNA (16:1-36)

16:1. The chronological note, **on the fifteenth day of the second month** (cf. 12:1), and the characteristic phrase, **all the congregation of the people of Israel** (vss. 1, 2, 9, 10), show that the bulk of this narrative is by the P writer. The **wilderness of Sin** is mentioned elsewhere only in 17:1; Num. 33:11-12. Nothing definite is said or known about it. The wilderness of Zin, however, can be quite definitely located to the immediate south of Judah (Num. 13:21; 20:1; 27:14; 33:36; 34:3; Deut. 32:51; Josh. 15:1, 3). It included Kadesh-barnea (Num. 20:1). One version of what may have been the single Marah-

music hall in an endeavor to find scientific evidence for their "pronouncements" that it was a good concert. He is right as far as verifiable facts are concerned, but he forgets that the poetry and faith of today sometimes become the scientific fact of tomorrow, and that to live wisely man has to make up his mind on more things than science can verify. We know very little about how things grow; we know more about disease than we do about health; there are strange powers of recovery in man which religion calls God. We can all help or hinder, but God does the growing in the garden and the healing in the hospital. "Lo, these are parts of his ways; but how little a portion is heard of him? but the thunder of his power who can understand?" (Job 26:14.)

27. *The Immediate Blessing.*—A pleasant interlude amid many miseries—this chance to camp by **twelve wells of water, and threescore and ten palm trees.** Some people seem to be so intent on getting on so as to be suitably ensconced in a final grave that they have no time to enjoy the passing day. They rush by Elim with its springs and palm trees because they have to reach some promised land. They do not enjoy their wedding because of fear that they may miss the scheduled train for the honeymoon; they do not enjoy their children as they grow up because they have to be so busy laying by for their education; they always have

to be "after" doing something. If they ever get to heaven, which one may doubt, they will be annoyed when no answer is given to their repeated question, "Well, then, where do we go from here?" It is the happiness of going on together that is the fragrance of life; taste is in chewing slowly, not in swallowing. "Well, thank God, I have got here safely at last," said the hustler on his deathbed.

Sometimes we do as these people did and encamp **there by the waters.** All art and all literature and all music are the catching and holding of the best and happiest moments of the best and happiest minds. "Stop! Look! Listen!" No matter where you are, you will find that

All places that the eye of heaven visits
Are to a wise man ports and happy havens.[1]

Some of the most moving scenes in Tolstoy's *War and Peace* (perhaps of all modern books most like the O.T.) are descriptions of people simply being happy. Clifton Fadiman, in a foreword to the book, says the ability to describe such scenes has died out in our time because the simple glow of happiness seems so much less common than it was a century ago.

16:1-31. *The Manna from God.*—Religion does not exist anywhere as an essence: it is always mixed up with other things. In no scientist's,

[1] Shakespeare, *King Richard II*, Act I, scene 3.

2 And the whole congregation of the children of Israel murmured against Moses and Aaron in the wilderness:

3 And the children of Israel said unto them, Would to God we had died by the hand of the LORD in the land of Egypt, when we sat by the fleshpots, *and* when we did eat bread to the full; for ye have brought us forth into this wilderness, to kill this whole assembly with hunger.

4 ¶ Then said the LORD unto Moses, Behold, I will rain bread from heaven for you; and the people shall go out and gather a certain rate every day, that I may prove them, whether they will walk in my law, or no.

5 And it shall come to pass, that on the sixth day they shall prepare *that* which they bring in; and it shall be twice as much as they gather daily.

from the land of Egypt. 2 And the whole congregation of the people of Israel murmured against Moses and Aaron in the wilderness, 3 and said to them, "Would that we had died by the hand of the LORD in the land of Egypt, when we sat by the fleshpots and ate bread to the full; for you have brought us out into this wilderness to kill this whole assembly with hunger."

4 Then the LORD said to Moses, "Behold, I will rain bread from heaven for you; and the people shall go out and gather a day's portion every day, that I may prove them, whether they will walk in my law or not. 5 On the sixth day, when they prepare what they bring in, it will be twice as much as

---

Massah-Meribah episode is located there (see Num. 20:1-13). When the traditional location of Sinai at the southern point of the peninsula is given up, it becomes difficult to avoid the conclusion that the two wildernesses are the same. This identification is actually made in the LXX transliteration.

2-3. The cause of murmuring, merely cited in 15:24, is here specified. Similar specifications are given in Num. 11:5-6, in an account that separates the coming of the quails from the gift of manna; and in Num. 20:3-5 where the people deplore the absence of fruit and water in the desert. Death by **the hand of the LORD** must refer to death from natural causes in contrast to the rigors of the desert. The people have lost faith in Yahweh's leadership and therefore denounce those who represent it.

4. This word of the Lord to Moses is an older, brief statement of the developed account of P in the midst of which it appears. The word to Moses in vss. 9-12 must originally have preceded vss. 6-8 which tell of the report Moses and Aaron gave of it to the people. The displacement was probably caused by the presence of vss. 4-5. The **day's portion** is not specified as in vs. 16. By providing food for only a day at a time Yahweh will test the people to see if they will live by faith in his power and deliverance. The petition in the Lord's Prayer, "Give us this day . . . ," probably derives from this verse.

5. The note about **the sixth day** may be an old, undeveloped provision about the sabbath, later expanded to the account in vss. 22-30. More probably it is a preface to that account by the same writer.

---

psychologist's, or even professor of religious education's laboratory can the investigator take down a tiny flask and, holding it to the light, say, "This is the pure essence of religion." Metaphors, legends, incidents, human lives, all contain the essence of religion. The perfect religious symbol should be founded on an actual incident which has been retold, enjoyed, mulled over, and enriched by one generation after another, till it comes to enshrine the combined religious experience of thousands of different people who have added new point and application to it in the retelling. Manna is an

almost perfect example of such a religious symbol, making its way through the lives of generations, changing them and being changed by them. Founded upon an actual experience, it has been used by one school of thought after another to give texture, picturesqueness, and substance to their religious teaching. The historical element gives to the common man what seems to him a firm foundation, while the root idea is deep, rich, and flexible enough to apply neatly to the new problems and conceptions of different kinds of ages and different types of people. Ethical pellets, scientifically pure, ad-

6 And Moses and Aaron said unto all the children of Israel, At even, then ye shall know that the LORD hath brought you out from the land of Egypt:

7 And in the morning, then ye shall see the glory of the LORD; for that he heareth your murmurings against the LORD: and what *are* we, that ye murmur against us?

8 And Moses said, *This shall be,* when the LORD shall give you in the evening flesh to eat, and in the morning bread to the full; for that the LORD heareth your murmurings which ye murmur against him: and what *are* we? your murmurings *are* not against us, but against the LORD.

9 ¶ And Moses spake unto Aaron, Say unto all the congregation of the children of Israel, Come near before the LORD: for he hath heard your murmurings.

10 And it came to pass, as Aaron spake unto the whole congregation of the children of Israel, that they looked toward the wilderness, and, behold, the glory of the LORD appeared in the cloud.

they gather daily." 6 So Moses and Aaron said to all the people of Israel, "At evening you shall know that it was the LORD who brought you out of the land of Egypt, 7 and in the morning you shall see the glory of the LORD, because he has heard your murmurings against the LORD. For what are we, that you murmur against us?" 8 And Moses said, "When the LORD gives you in the evening flesh to eat and in the morning bread to the full, because the LORD has heard your murmurings which you murmur against him — what are we? Your murmurings are not against us but against the LORD."

9 And Moses said to Aaron, "Say to the whole congregation of the people of Israel, 'Come near before the LORD, for he has heard your murmurings.' " 10 And as Aaron spoke to the whole congregation of the people of Israel, they looked toward the wilderness, and behold, the glory of the LORD

6-8. Moses and Aaron report the word of God to the people. The manna, actually a natural phenomenon in the desert, will be the mark of the presence of God: **you shall see the glory.** The leaders teach the people that their complaints against them (vs. 2) are actually complaints against Yahweh. He, not Moses and Aaron, is the object of their faith: he is their Lord. This reflects the growing tendency in later Judaism to make a wide separation between God and men. God is indeed *with* his people but not *in* their leaders.

9-12. In this section, originally preceding vss. 6-8, Moses asks Aaron to summon the congregation so that in their presence he may present the complaint to God. The appearance **before the LORD** points to a place at which God's will was communicated. The ark or the tent seems implied. Even though this account now stands before the Sinai ordinance of these appointments, they seem to be assumed (cf. vs. 33). In Num. 16:42 (Hebrew 17:7) the cloud and the glory were visible above the tent. The statement here that **they looked toward the wilderness** to behold the glory must be taken as an editor's attempt to harmonize the account with the pre-Sinai economy of worship.

The glory of the LORD is the mark of God's presence. It is not the presence itself. In the Judaism of the Targums the actual presence of God, in a localized manner, is

ministered by enlightened professionals, do not nourish people as well as this natural food with all its irrelevancies.

The historical foundation: A sweet, sticky, honeylike juice exudes in heavy drops in May or June from a shrub found in the desert near which the people were wandering. It melts in the heat of the sun, after falling on the earth in grains. It has the flavor of honey. It is the natural juice of the shrub, but the Arabs believed that it fell from heaven with the dew. Samuel Johnson in his dictionary says: "It is

but lately that the world were convinced of the mistake of manna being an aërial produce, covering a tree with sheets in the manna season, and the finding as much manna on it as on those which were open to the air" (see also Josephus *Antiquities* III. 1. 6).

It was something new which the children of Israel had not seen before (vs. 15); the account in Num. 11 does not seem to indicate that there was anything supernatural about it, but our story surrounds it with mystical qualities. The suggested derivation from *mān hŭ',* **What is it?**

11 ¶ And the LORD spake unto Moses, saying,

12 I have heard the murmurings of the children of Israel: speak unto them, saying, At even ye shall eat flesh, and in the morning ye shall be filled with bread; and ye shall know that I *am* the LORD your God.

13 And it came to pass, that at even the quails came up, and covered the camp: and in the morning the dew lay round about the host.

14 And when the dew that lay was gone up, behold, upon the face of the wilderness *there lay* a small round thing, *as* small as the hoar frost on the ground.

appeared in the cloud. 11 And the LORD said to Moses, 12 "I have heard the murmurings of the people of Israel; say to them, 'At twilight you shall eat flesh, and in the morning you shall be filled with bread; then you shall know that I am the LORD your God.' "

13 In the evening quails came up and covered the camp; and in the morning dew lay round about the camp. 14 And when the dew had gone up, there was on the face of the wilderness a fine, flakelike thing, fine

---

indicated by the term "Shekinah," but the biblical phrase **the glory of the LORD** is not equated with that term; it remains the mark or sign of the presence. In this case the cloud and the glory are perhaps the same in the sense that the former is the mark that constitutes the latter (cf. Num. 16:19, 42).

12. The quails are here associated with the gift of manna, though the narrative is exclusively preoccupied with the latter. The extensive account of the quails in Num. 11:1-35 assumes that the manna preceded the coming of the quails (vs. 5) and that the latter were a curse rather than a blessing (vs. 33). The Israelite meal that included meat was eaten in the evening. The purpose of the provision of the food is to confirm the people in their faith: **then you shall know.**

13. The quail is still a well-known migratory bird in the Egypt-Palestine region. In Num. 11:31 it is reported that the wind blew the birds in from the sea. They began coming in the evening and by morning they surrounded the camp at the distance of a day's journey. Here they are represented as flying over the camp. The quails are easily exhausted and the ease with which the Israelites are reported to have gathered them (Num. 11:32) is explained from that fact.

14. In the early summer several types of desert trees and shrubs, notably the tamarisk, exude a sweet sticky substance such as this appears to have been. It drips to the ground, crystallizes and turns white. The comparison which likens the manna to hoarfrost and the observation that it tasted "like wafers made with honey" (vs. 31) show that this material substance was the origin for the manna story. Instead of describing it as a **flakelike thing** the LXX here compares it to the coriander seed (cf. vs. 31), which is small, flat, and white.

---

is a popular sound-likeness (like the popular derivation of "sirloin" from the story that Henry VIII was so pleased with a loin of beef that he knighted it on the spot). Out of this historical incident the story has developed to become a religious symbol for many ages (see Exeg. on vs. 15). The mental and spiritual life of all who have used it has precipitated and crystallized in it. In vs. 4 it is said to be a test by which Yahweh is to prove the people, **whether they will walk in my law, or no.** The points which were progressively noted were that it must be gathered every day—it would not keep overnight; that in some way not clearly explained it was rationed, like food in wartime,

so that the grasping individual could not get more than his share; though at the time, according to our story, neither the law of the sabbath, the Ark, nor the tables of the law existed, yet we are given the later additions to fit the story into the later institutions and regulations. So we see how the priestly writer has used the old story, modified it, and added to it in order to enforce the regulations of his day.

Some applications of the symbol of manna in later days may be noted:

(*a*) The petition in the Lord's Prayer, "Give us this day our daily bread." It is particularly evident in the case of food that we are not as a race self-sufficient, since the operations of sun

15 And when the children of Israel saw *it,* they said one to another, It *is* manna: for they wist not what it *was.* And Moses said unto them, This *is* the bread which the LORD hath given you to eat.

16 ¶ This *is* the thing which the LORD hath commanded, Gather of it every man according to his eating, an omer for every man, *according to* the number of your persons; take ye every man for *them* which *are* in his tents.

17 And the children of Israel did so, and gathered, some more, some less.

18 And when they did mete *it* with an omer, he that gathered much had nothing over, and he that gathered little had no lack; they gathered every man according to his eating.

as hoarfrost on the ground. 15 When the people of Israel saw it, they said to one another, "What is it?"ʷ For they did not know what it was. And Moses said to them, "It is the bread which the LORD has given you to eat. 16 This is what the LORD has commanded: 'Gather of it, every man of you, as much as he can eat; you shall take an omer apiece, according to the number of the persons whom each of you has in his tent.'" 17 And the people of Israel did so; they gathered, some more, some less. 18 But when they measured it with an omer, he that gathered much had nothing over, and he that gathered little had no lack; each gathered according to what he could eat.

ʷ Or *It is manna.* Heb *man hu*

15. The question **"What is it?"** is a translation of הוּא מָן. It could be translated "Is it *mān?*" or "It is *mān."* But it is unlikely that the pilgrims historically knew enough about natural life in the desert to make such statements. Besides, if such a translation were adopted, the following clause, **for they did not know what it was,** would have to be understood as meaning that the desert food had no relation to *mān,* the natural edible substance described in vs. 14. The question must be understood as another "popular etymology" which professes to explain how the food came to be called *mān* in Israel (vs. 31). The chief difficulty is that the word מָן means "what" only in late Aramaic and Syriac. The normal Hebrew word for "what" is מָה. The best conclusion is that the term *mān,* probably of Egyptian origin, was fitted into a popular etymological scheme by the use of an unusual pronoun. In Num. 11:5, 6, the LXX reads μάννα instead of μάν (Exod. 16:31, 33, 35). That is the basis for the English word "manna." The account lifts the natural phenomenon to the level of a sign confirming Israel's faith: **It is the bread which the LORD has given.** Beginning here and throughout the Bible and in Christian tradition "manna" becomes a metaphor for God's grace and providence.

16. An **omer** was about two quarts, one tenth of an ephah or bushel. It seems that **as much as he can eat** was estimated at about an omer per person.

17-18. The amazing thing was that despite the greed and fear of some, all had the same amount, just enough (cf. vs. 4). In II Cor. 8:15 Paul uses this account as a warrant for Christian sharing.

and rain are not in our hands. Our lives depend upon God. All bread is bread from heaven.

(b) Spiritual food, as in the sacraments, is as necessary to man's life as material food. "I have meat to eat that ye know not of" (John 4:32; see also John 6:31-35). So in secular life it is a wonder to see the peasants of Mexico, with hardly pesos enough to buy the bare necessities, save a few at the end of their day at the market to buy some flowers to bring home.

(c) There must be some regulations to prevent grasping individuals or nations from getting more than their share of the good things of this life. In wartime's scarcity, the poor family is able to get as much food at the store as the

chauffeur sent down by the dowager duchess on the hill. War ration coupons are of divine origin, according to vss. 17-18.

(d) Filing systems have their defects: the used word is stale. The editor of a chain of trade papers was asked if he did not have huge stores of illustrations, references, stories, paragraphs in his office so that he could fill up every page of all these journals from them. He replied, "I have none; my motto is 'Every day the manna fell.'" He found, as every preacher finds sooner or later, that articles or sermons of scraps preserved in files lack the spontaneity of the fresh inspiration, the newly suggested illustration, the passing incident which God sends to

19 And Moses said, Let no man leave of it till the morning.

20 Notwithstanding they hearkened not unto Moses; but some of them left of it until the morning, and it bred worms, and stank: and Moses was wroth with them.

21 And they gathered it every morning, every man according to his eating: and when the sun waxed hot, it melted.

22 ¶ And it came to pass, *that* on the sixth day they gathered twice as much bread, two omers for one *man:* and all the rulers of the congregation came and told Moses.

19 And Moses said to them, "Let no man leave any of it till the morning." 20 But they did not listen to Moses; some left part of it till the morning, and it bred worms and became foul; and Moses was angry with them. 21 Morning by morning they gathered it, each as much as he could eat; but when the sun grew hot, it melted.

22 On the sixth day they gathered twice as much bread, two omers apiece; and when all the leaders of the congregation came

---

19-21. The command not to leave any of the manna until morning fits in with the Oriental custom of baking fresh bread each day. The statement that what was kept over became spoiled is in general harmony with conditions in a tropical climate. But the real purpose of the command is to remind the people that this daily gift of food is Yahweh's means of testing Israel and of teaching it to live in the constant dependence of faith (vs. 4). As in the case of the account of the plagues and of life in Egypt, this narrative is in general harmony with desert conditions, but its real concern is to attest God's universal freedom and power. To do this the narrators "develop" certain aspects of natural life until they seem "grotesque" when considered as sober fact. All the tamarisk trees in the entire wilderness could not possibly have provided such amounts of manna so regularly for "forty years" (vs. 35) as this account implies. Even if they had known this the narrators would not have been disturbed, for their concern is to drive home the point that God keeps Israel safe. As compared to Num. 11:6-9 (JE), this account has increased the element of fantasy, but the point is the same.

(1) INSTITUTION OF THE SABBATH (16:22-30)

The sabbath was an ancient institution in Israel (Gen. 29:27; Judg. 14:12; II Kings 4:23; 11:5-7; Isa. 1:13; Amos 8:5). It was in all probability observed also by pre-Mosaic Hebrews. The term may be a cognate of the Babylonian *šapattu*. On the Babylonian sabbath there was a cessation of activity. Sabbath days were considered to be days of evil. Originally the sabbath was an integral part of a lunar cultus. Though in Israel much of the cultus continued to be set according to a lunar calendar, this was no longer true of the sabbath, even in the biblical records. Separated from the lunar cycle, the sabbath had become a "secular" observance every seventh day. This account, relating the origin of the sabbath to the manna wonder, provides one more specific instance of the persistent tendency among Israel's historical interpreters to assimilate ancient cultic forms by providing them with a historical instead of a natural foundation.

22. The communication to Moses (vs. 5) had apparently not been shared with the people. In vs. 18 they were amazed that the amount gathered for each person came to just one omer. Here on Friday they are amazed that it comes to exactly two omers. The

---

all to lighten life if they do but have eyes to see and ears to hear. A preacher's wife, as he leaves the house, lifts the baby boy out of his high chair, and says, "You are growing so fast, soon you will be lifting me," but the preacher, seeking for some classical book illustration for his address on the younger generation, does not see, does not hear; so the congregation dwindles.

22-30. *Observance of the Sabbath.*—A study of the Hebrew text indicates that the manna story has been pieced together from several sources—the original narrative has been edited and added to. The word in vs. 15 translated "what" is not Hebrew, but the later Aramaic. The "quails" in Num. 11 arrive after the giving of the law on Sinai. Probably the priestly writ-

23 And he said unto them, This *is that* which the Lord hath said, To-morrow *is* the rest of the holy sabbath unto the Lord: bake *that* which ye will bake *to-day,* and seethe that ye will seethe; and that which remaineth over lay up for you to be kept until the morning.

24 And they laid it up till the morning, as Moses bade: and it did not stink, neither was there any worm therein.

25 And Moses said, Eat that to-day; for to-day *is* a sabbath unto the Lord: to-day ye shall not find it in the field.

26 Six days ye shall gather it; but on the seventh day, *which is* the sabbath, in it there shall be none.

27 ¶ And it came to pass, *that* there went out *some* of the people on the seventh day for to gather, and they found none.

28 And the Lord said unto Moses, How long refuse ye to keep my commandments and my laws?

and told Moses, 23 he said to them, "This is what the Lord has commanded: 'Tomorrow is a day of solemn rest, a holy sabbath to the Lord; bake what you will bake and boil what you will boil, and all that is left over lay by to be kept till the morning.'"

24 So they laid it by till the morning, as Moses bade them; and it did not become foul, and there were no worms in it. 25 Moses said, "Eat it today, for today is a sabbath to the Lord; today you will not find it in the field. 26 Six days you shall gather it; but on the seventh day, which is a sabbath, there will be none." 27 On the seventh day some of the people went out to gather, and they found none. 28 And the Lord said to Moses, "How long do you refuse to keep my commandments and my

---

leaders whom the writer cites as reporting the wonder to Moses probably reflect the organizational structure in Jerusalem after the Exile.

23. The explanation offered by Moses constitutes the sabbath decree. *Shabbāthôn,* an emphatic term for sabbath in the late era, is the term translated a day of solemn rest. The last part of the verse is clearly concerned with the issue of preparing food for the sabbath on the previous day. Later manuals such as the tractate on the sabbath in the Mishnah greatly elaborate this provision.

24-27. The preservation of the manna until the sabbath vindicates Moses' institution of it as a holy day. Those who were faithless were disappointed.

28. The narrator clearly has a didactic concern. The protecting care of God comes to those who keep the sabbath laws, as attested by the double supply of manna. But now, as then, some refuse to keep the commandments, i.e., they are without faith in the exodus revelation.

---

ers found in telling the original story that it created the dangerous impression that the Israelites gathered manna on the sabbath, and so inserted a modification of the tale by which the manna did not fall on that day. Still later the modified narrative gave the impression that it was an account of the origin of the sabbath. Auditors objected that the people could not have lived on manna alone, so the quails were inserted to provide enough nourishment for the multitude. The old story was changed to suit conditions as they existed after the giving of the law on Sinai, and to meet objections which had been met with in retelling. As is indicated in Gen. 1:14, the origin of the seven-day week was in the stars (see Gen. 29:27; Judg. 14:12), and was familiar to the people of Israel in early

times (see Exeg.). Its connection with moon and stars was forgotten in the growing religion of Yahweh. It became a day when man and beast could rest from their labors (23:12). All the burdensome sabbath regulations were developed later, but at first it was a holy day of rest (vss. 23, 29): so the people rested on the seventh day.

Thus an ancient superstitious custom was adapted by the religion of Yahweh to a religious and humanitarian use. The attitude of the missionaries of a new faith to the religious and superstitious customs of the people among whom they work has always been a difficult problem. One famous example is the work of one of the first Christian missionaries in China, Father Matteo Ricci, a Jesuit priest who entered

29 See, for that the LORD hath given you the sabbath, therefore he giveth you on the sixth day the bread of two days: abide ye every man in his place, let no man go out of his place on the seventh day.

30 So the people rested on the seventh day.

31 And the house of Israel called the name thereof Manna: and it *was* like coriander seed, white; and the taste of it *was* like wafers *made* with honey.

32 ¶ And Moses said, This *is* the thing which the LORD commandeth, Fill an omer of it to be kept for your generations; that they may see the bread wherewith I have fed you in the wilderness, when I brought you forth from the land of Egypt.

33 And Moses said unto Aaron, Take a pot, and put an omer full of manna therein, and lay it up before the LORD, to be kept for your generations.

laws? 29 See! The LORD has given you the sabbath, therefore on the sixth day he gives you bread for two days; remain every man of you in his place, let no man go out of his place on the seventh day." 30 So the people rested on the seventh day.

31 Now the house of Israel called its name manna; it was like coriander seed, white, and the taste of it was like wafers made with honey. 32 And Moses said, "This is what the LORD has commanded: 'Let an omer of it be kept throughout your generations, that they may see the bread with which I fed you in the wilderness, when I brought you out of the land of Egypt.'" 33 And Moses said to Aaron, "Take a jar, and put an omer of manna in it, and place it before the LORD, to be kept

---

29-31. As vs. 23 is the starting point for an elaboration of the rules for preparing for the sabbath, so vs. 29 is the basis for the many later laws relating to sabbath travel and activity.

(2) THE MEMORIAL MANNA (16:31-36)

32. The P writer affirms a tradition, no longer verifiable in his own day, that an omer of manna had been placed before the ark. His purpose was to remind Israel of God's presence and care in the desert.

33. The **jar**, described as of gold in the LXX, was to be set **before the LORD.** Moses asks Aaron to carry out the command.

---

the country in 1582. He held that a missionary must

conform to the opinions and customs of the people he is sent to, provided they be not manifestly inconsistent with the faith he is commissioned to preach. . . . He must make use of whatever has the appearance of truth and piety in the religion of the country where he preaches, and endeavour to reconcile it to his own doctrine. . . . Whoever in *China* neglects the usual reverence to his ancestors, forfeits the character of an honest man and good citizen; and whoever neglects that paid to Confucius, forfeits all pretensions to public honours and employments. [So] he permitted his converts to reverence their ancestors and Confucius.[2]

The result was a long controversy with Rome ending in papal bulls forbidding the practice, although Pope Alexander had been inclined to agree with the Jesuit. In 1704 the holy office decreed "that christians should by no means

assist at those sacrifices, which are offered in spring and autumn . . . to Confucius and their ancestors," and that the tablets of their ancestors should be removed from all Christian houses.[3] Yet the adaptation of ancient superstitious customs to modern religious and humanitarian uses is a part of all religious growth throughout the ages (Mark 2:27), and can be studied in actual operation in country districts of Mexico today.

31-36. *The Sacred Token of Remembrance.*—In the light of all that the manna had meant for Israel, Moses bids Aaron, **Take a pot, and put an omer full of manna therein, and lay it up before the LORD, to be kept for your generations** . . . so Aaron laid it up before the Testimony. The **Testimony** is ʿ*ēdhûth,* the ark, before which or in which were also laid the two tables on which the law was inscribed.

Every church and every home should have such a museum to preserve the remembrance of things past. A great philosopher, fumbling in his pocket for a pencil, brought out a pebble.

[2] Thomas Percy, ed., *Miscellaneous Pieces Relating to the Chinese* (London: R. & J. Dodsley, 1762), II, 15-16, 24, 28.

[3] *Ibid.,* II, 52.

34 As the LORD commanded Moses, so Aaron laid it up before the Testimony, to be kept.

35 And the children of Israel did eat manna forty years, until they came to a land inhabited: they did eat manna, until they came unto the borders of the land of Canaan.

36 Now an omer *is* the tenth *part* of an ephah.

17 And all the congregation of the children of Israel journeyed from the wilderness of Sin, after their journeys, according to the commandment of the LORD, and pitched in Rephidim: and *there was no water* for the people to drink.

throughout your generations." 34 As the LORD commanded Moses, so Aaron placed it before the Testimony, to be kept. 35 And the people of Israel ate the manna forty years, till they came to a habitable land; they ate the manna, till they came to the border of the land of Canaan. 36 (An omer is the tenth part of an ephah.)

17 All the congregation of the people of Israel moved on from the wilderness of Sin by stages, according to the commandment of the LORD, and camped at Reph'idim; but there was no water for the

---

34. It is said that Aaron placed the jar **before the Testimony,** i.e., before the ark. Num. 17:10 (=Hebrew 17:25) reports that Aaron's rod was also kept there. Heb. 9:4 reports that both the rod and the (golden) pot of manna, together with the tablets of the Lord (25:16), were *in* the ark rather than before it.

c) MASSAH-MERIBAH (17:1-7)

This is the second of three accounts of murmuring caused by thirst (cf. 15:22-27; Num. 20:1-13): Marah-Massah, Massah-Meribah, and Meribah-Kadesh. It is possible, though not demonstrable, that all three accounts rest on a single occurrence. In all three the main issue is faith versus disobedience. They seem to present transgression as an ever-deeper evil in Israel. In the first account (15:22-27) Yahweh provides Israel with a law or statute by which to test its faithfulness toward him. This account features the spirit of rebellion in the people. The third account (Num. 20:1-13 [P]) cites Moses' own lack of faith.

17:1. Day by day the Israelites travel at **the commandment of the LORD** (cf. Num. 10:33-36). The location of **Rephidim** is unknown. It should probably be sought in the

---

He looked at it and smiled, "My little boy picked that up and gave it to me on our last walk before I left home, and I have carried it around the world ever since." The baby's first shoes, the first report cards with "A" for effort, the broken vase, the rag doll—of such trifles are the riches of a home museum made; an old church has one of the original warming pans for the cold feet of the unheated congregation, the old bass viol, the hourglass that ran for forty-five minutes and was sometimes turned twice in the sermon. Real piety is connected with such trifles. Progress forgets that the discarded may be interesting in twenty years.

So long thy power hath blest me, sure it still
    Will lead me on.[4]

That is what the pot of manna in the ark meant.

17:1-6. *Water from the Rock.*—The scene at Rephidim has greatly impressed the imagina-

[4] John Henry Newman, "Lead, Kindly Light."

tion of the world. The Arabs show at Petra a Moses Spring, which they identify with that spirited out of the rock by the sacred rod (see Exeg. on vss. 1, 6). There is an ancient belief, still current enough to have articles upon it written in *The Hibbert Journal,* etc., that certain people have the skill by a magic staff or wand to find water in dry lands (see Num. 21:18). W. F. Barrett was satisfied that the skill does exist among certain individuals who are especially gifted, though otherwise generally simple and unsophisticated. Like the homing instinct in birds, he thinks, the dowser's power lies beneath the level of conscious perception.

To the average reader the scene has been interpreted to mean that there is no such thing in life as an impossible situation: one has only to attack his problem with faith in its possible solution and by God's help there is always a noble way out, satisfying to the soul. As the old automobile guides used to say so often, "End of road; turn right." There is a right turn at

2 Wherefore the people did chide with Moses, and said, Give us water that we may drink. And Moses said unto them, Why chide ye with me? wherefore do ye tempt the LORD?

3 And the people thirsted there for water; and the people murmured against Moses, and said, Wherefore *is* this *that* thou hast brought us up out of Egypt, to kill us and our children and our cattle with thirst?

4 And Moses cried unto the LORD, saying, What shall I do unto this people? they be almost ready to stone me.

people to drink. 2 Therefore the people found fault with Moses, and said, "Give us water to drink." And Moses said to them, "Why do you find fault with me? Why do you put the LORD to the proof?" 3 But the people thirsted there for water, and the people murmured against Moses, and said, "Why did you bring us up out of Egypt, to kill us and our children and our cattle with thirst?" 4 So Moses cried to the LORD, "What shall I do with this people? They are almost

general region of Kadesh (Num. 20:1), near which Mount Horeb must also be looked for. The Amalekites (vs. 8), who here attacked Israel, lived in this Negeb area and not at the lower end of the peninsula where the old Sinai tradition has caused explorers to look for this stopping place.

2. The faultfinding with Moses (ריב) has the nature of a legal argument. The people challenged Moses to justify his leadership by providing water; rather, they insist their thirst denies the validity of his position. The contention, says Moses, is tantamount to putting **the LORD to the proof** (cf. 16:7-8). The Hebrew verb *nāṣāh* means "to test," "to see" (or "to doubt") whether one will act in a certain way. It does not imply provoking one to act in a certain way, as the English verb **tempt** (KJV) now does.

3. This verse repeats in other words what has been said in vss. 1*b*β-2. Two sources seem to have been woven together and vss. 4-5 continue vs. 3.

4. Stoning was a recognized form of mob action (I Sam. 30:6). The impatient petulance and self-pity of Moses (cf. Num. 11:10-15; 20:10 [?]) recorded here is balanced by citations of his capacity for self-effacement and pity (32:32-33).

the end of every road if one has but faith and perseverance to find it. It seemed, and was actually said in print, in 1922 that Franklin D. Roosevelt's political aspirations had been brought to an untimely close in 1921 when he was stricken by infantile paralysis which left him a cripple. The examination paper of life may set a question which you know you cannot answer, but do not be so sure about that: keep looking at it, thinking about it, and lo, from somewhere within long forgotten memories and ideas will begin to stir. On the lawn outside the robins are having hard picking as they seek for worms. One fellow gazes despairingly down a dead hole. He thinks he will give it up; there is nothing there. But on second thought he returns to it and begins to peck at it, idly at first, then with growing excitement, and before this sentence is finished, he has extracted from it one of the juiciest and most satisfying worms he ever tasted in his life! The threshold of religion is at that point where the thirsty soul stands squarely in front of the hopeless barren rock, the seemingly impossible. One may use mystic psychological words and say that he did not despair but began to draw upon unexpected

inner resources, or one may openly say, as Exodus does, **The LORD said unto Moses.**

1-4. The Cry for God.—The poignancy of this passage, and especially of the words, **And Moses cried unto the LORD,** is illustrated in *The Green Pastures,* "You's with me, ain't you, Lawd?" [5]

4-7. Is the LORD Among Us or Not?—The people are thirsty in the desert. They come to Moses and demand that he justify his leadership by producing water; Moses appeals to God to help him in this emergency, and God shows him how to produce water miraculously out of the rock. It is not necessary to expound this episode on the basis of the supposition that God worked differently in those days from the way he operates now. Yet preaching becomes unreal and sentimental when one ignores the fact that many thousands of believing people in our days have died in the agonies of thirst and want, even while praying for succor to God just as earnestly as the Israelites and Moses ever did. From Moses' administrative point of view it showed hardness of heart and lack of faith to ask, **Is the LORD among us or not?** In our days

[5] Marc Connelly (New York: Farrar & Rinehart, 1929), Part II, scene 4, p. 144.

5 And the Lord said unto Moses, Go on before the people, and take with thee of the elders of Israel; and thy rod, wherewith thou smotest the river, take in thine hand, and go.

6 Behold, I will stand before thee there upon the rock in Horeb; and thou shalt smite the rock, and there shall come water out of it, that the people may drink. And Moses did so in the sight of the elders of Israel.

7 And he called the name of the place Massah, and Meribah, because of the chiding of the children of Israel, and because they tempted the Lord, saying, Is the Lord among us, or not?

8 ¶ Then came Amalek, and fought with Israel in Rephidim.

ready to stone me." 5 And the Lord said to Moses, "Pass on before the people, taking with you some of the elders of Israel; and take in your hand the rod with which you struck the Nile, and go. 6 Behold, I will stand before you there on the rock at Horeb; and you shall strike the rock, and water shall come out of it, that the people may drink." And Moses did so, in the sight of the elders of Israel. 7 And he called the name of the place Massah[x] and Mer'ibah,[y] because of the faultfinding of the children of Israel, and because they put the Lord to the proof by saying, "Is the Lord among us or not?"

8 Then came Am'alek and fought with

[x] That is *Proof*
[y] That is *Contention*

---

5. The writer assumes that the **rod** with which Moses struck the Nile (7:17, 20) is lying "before the Lord," and that Moses took it from there (Num. 17:10). It seems that some place, now missing, must have been mentioned after the concluding words **and go.** That would have provided the adverb **there** in vs. 6 with an antecedent.

6. The assurance, **I will stand before you,** is a strikingly effective anthropomorphism assuring Moses of Yahweh's presence and power **there.** The Mekilta (*ad loc.*) offers the following interpretation of this, "God said to him: Wherever you find the mark of man's feet, there am I before thee." The commentator seems to shy away from the metaphor of his text. The reference is, it seems, to a particular rock on Mount Horeb. It is so interpreted by Josephus (*Antiquities* III. 1. 7). However, Targ. Onkelos, on Num. 21:17, reports that the rock Moses struck thereafter followed Israel on its pilgrimage to provide it with water. In I Cor. 10:4, Paul reveals his knowledge of this legend and seems to take it seriously, "The supernatural Rock which followed them."

7. The place was named **Massah and Meribah** to signify the two ways Israel had shown its lack of faith. "The waters of Meribah" are identified with Kadesh (Num. 20:13 [sanctified]; 27:14; Ezek. 48:28). Massah and Meribah became synonymous with "hardness of heart" and faithlessness (Deut. 6:16; 9:22; 33:8; Ps. 95:8).

d) The Amalekites (17:8-16)

The story of the Amalekite attack typifies the military crises Israel encountered on its pilgrimage, comparable to the crises of hunger and thirst. However, the real issue

---

we admit our hardness of heart and lack of faith and we do ask this question. We read this episode and wonder why such miracles seldom if ever happen today. Then it may dawn upon us that these verses are not meant to be read as literal history, but rather as a pictorial illustration of deeper spiritual truth in a setting not merely of the present moment but of the past and future eternities. God does not promise to give people what they want, but he does promise to satisfy abundantly those who trust in him. This incident is an old folk tale expressing in a popular way a truth which can be tested in personal experience by every believer, but which cannot

receive its objective proof till the secrets of all hearts are known at last. Hot for certainty, we demand a proof of God in an incident, in an instant; but one cannot prove God, one can only know him, and that only gradually in a lifelong friendship, the perpetual happy surprises of the years ever adding new wonder to our knowledge of the ways of him we love.

8-16. *The Prevailing Hands of Moses.*—Joshua, traditionally a descendant of the great national hero Joseph, is chosen to be the general in charge of the first battle against Amalek, a tribe with which the Israelites had to do a good deal of fighting. Moses himself does not enter

9 And Moses said unto Joshua, Choose us out men, and go out, fight with Amalek: to-morrow I will stand on the top of the hill with the rod of God in mine hand.

10 So Joshua did as Moses had said to him, and fought with Amalek: and Moses, Aaron, and Hur went up to the top of the hill.

11 And it came to pass, when Moses held up his hand, that Israel prevailed: and when he let down his hand, Amalek prevailed.

Israel at Reph'idim. 9 And Moses said to Joshua, "Choose for us men, and go out, fight with Am'alek; tomorrow I will stand on the top of the hill with the rod of God in my hand." 10 So Joshua did as Moses told him, and fought with Am'alek; and Moses, Aaron, and Hur went up to the top of the hill. 11 Whenever Moses held up his hand, Israel prevailed; and whenever he lowered

---

here, for the writers, is not Israel's faith. Their actual concern is etiological. They want to account for and keep alive the ancient and bitter feud between Israel and Amalek.

8. The Amalekites were related to the Edomites (Gen. 36:12). Like Edom, they were an older people than Israel (Num. 24:20). They lived just to the north of Kadesh, probably claiming that oasis (Gen. 14:7; Num. 14:25). Israel's historians list them, together with Amorites, Hittites, Jebusites, and Canaanites as among the population of Palestine (Num. 13:29; 14:25, 43, 45). The suggestion of Ernst Sellin (*Geschichte des israelitisch-jüdischen Volkes* [Leipzig: Quelle & Meyer, 1924], I, 69-70) that the Amalekites fought Israel for the possession of Kadesh seems very plausible.

9. Joshua is here presented, without introduction, as the chief warrior. In 33:11 he is presented as Moses' personal servant, "a young man" (cf. 24:13; 32:17; Num. 11:28). It is probable, therefore, that our present account once stood toward the end of the Moses stories. Moses seems to play the role of thaumaturge; he is the conjurer who assures victory. Defeat by oath and imprecation was considered normal (Num. 22:6); Bentzen (*Intro. to O.T.*, I, 139) lists vs. 16 as a sample of the literary type known as the oath or "conjuring song" (cf. Josh. 10:12-13; I Sam. 14:24). Moses takes with him the **rod of God** he had carried to Egypt (4:20).

10. The Bible offers us no further information about **Hur.** Josephus (*Antiquities* III. 2. 4) speaks of him as the husband of Miriam.

11. The Samar. and the LXX texts state that Moses lifted up both hands. This seems more probable in view of the picture in the next verse.

---

the fight, but stands above the battle with hands outstretched, invoking the power of Yahweh. When his strength fails him, his arms are supported by Aaron, his brother, and Hur, traditionally the husband of his sister Miriam. As he so stands and later is seated on a rock on a hill above the conflict, he can be clearly seen against the sky by the fighting people. Moses with arms outstretched is perhaps the first example in the Bible of the symbolic use of the cross (though cf. Exeg.), a figure employed by nearly all peoples in their early expression of thought and feeling. It is found among the pre-Christian symbols in India, China, Egypt, Greece, among the Gauls, in Mexico, and among the pictographs of the Dakotas. Two origins may be suggested for the use of this symbol: the horizontal cross may derive from the crossroads, the place of doubt and decision, where in early folklore crowds of good and evil spirits as-

sembled to guide or betray the traveler on his way; the vertical cross as the meeting of the ideal and the every day, the intersection of the divine and the human. In Moses this upright form is indeed a marvelous picture of prayer, bringing divine power into human affairs, prophetic of John 12:32; 19:18.

The hands of Moses had already become a symbol to this people. Through them the power of God had manifested itself. Moses had stretched them out, and through the plagues the people had been freed from slavery; the sea had been divided; they had been delivered from dying by thirst and hunger. Now Moses' hands bring power for victory in battle. When Amalek pressed forward, Moses' faith failed. He doubted if they could win. His hands fell and Israel lost courage till his kinsmen came to help his failing faith. In all past emergencies God had delivered, or God and Moses had delivered, by miracle.

12 But Moses' hands *were* heavy; and they took a stone, and put *it* under him, and he sat thereon; and Aaron and Hur stayed up his hands, the one on the one side, and the other on the other side; and his hands were steady until the going down of the sun.

13 And Joshua discomfited Amalek and his people with the edge of the sword.

his hand, Am'alek prevailed. 12 But Moses' hands grew weary; so they took a stone and put it under him, and he sat upon it, and Aaron and Hur held up his hands, one on one side, and the other on the other side; so his hands were steady until the going down of the sun. 13 And Joshua mowed down Am'alek and his people with the edge of the sword.

---

12. Moses assumes a specific corporal posture to insure a desired result (cf. I Kings 18:42). This is not a sign of prayer in our sense of the term. The hand or arm is the sign of power (Gen. 31:29; Mic. 2:1); and the outstretched hands of Moses communicate the divine power. The motion is not just symbolic but intrinsically effective in the same sense as the words of an oath or the acted parables of the prophets were considered to be effective. Whether his arms were stretched upward vertically, or outward horizontally, is not clear. Beer (*Exodus*, p. 93) thinks that they were held outward horizontally, so that the silhouette of Moses made the sign of the cross. He asserts that the sign of Cain (Gen. 4:15) and the mark placed on the foreheads of those to be saved (Ezek. 9:4) were also the cross. However it is not Moses' total silhouette but his outstretched arms, communicating the power of Yahweh, that are featured.

13-14. Thanks to the aid of Yahweh, Joshua won the battle which, we may assume, enabled Israel to hold Kadesh. The "eternal war" is now ordained. God himself will **utterly blot out the remembrance of Amalek;** no one must remain alive to utter the name of the ancient ancestor. Deut. 25:18 repeats the command and explains the reason. The oracles of Balaam (Num. 24:20*b*) repeat the prediction. Because he mitigated the sharpness of the command in one small way, Saul lost the favor of Yahweh (I Sam. 15) through his disobedience. David remembered the injunction (I Sam. 27:8; 30:1). The last remnant of the Amalekites seems to have been annihilated in the days of Hezekiah about five centuries later (I Chr. 4:41-43). To write down the command increases its lasting validity.

Now came the greater miracle, the infusion of faith into the people themselves as they struggled in battle. As ancient sayings have it, "The greatest miracle of God is the faith of Israel."

The idea that certain people by their intercession can protect and inspire others in time of need is central in religious experience. They themselves would say that all they can do is to make themselves channels by which God's power is made available to these other people. This is one of the most valuable and (as is true of most valuable things) most dangerous of religious ideas. It is dangerous when certain people are set apart professionally to spend all their lives in seclusion praying for the world, for all prayer is the by-product of an active, practical life; and a life devoted entirely to prayer (while a sentimental symbol for others) is in itself not conducive to real prayer at all. As Meister Eckhart mystically says, "Mary was Martha before she was Mary." [6] It is dangerous when the prayers aim to make other people "God's pets," because they are being prayed for. During the

blitz in World War II an old woman in London had escaped, while all the lower part of her street had been demolished with much loss of life. The rector called next morning, and she said, "I never prayed so hard in my life as I did last night. Every bomb I heard coming I prayed hard and pushed it farther down the street. I can never thank God enough." The rector said, "Yes, but wasn't it rather hard on the folk who live at the other end of your street?" She said, "Oh, they should have prayed as hard as I did and pushed it right out into the sea." Now prayer may not change the trajectory of a bomb (at least with our present knowledge such an idea is incapable of proof or disproof, and is so alien to our conceptions that we are apt to scoff at the idea), but at least the fact that she had to pray kept her in her house, and the naïveté of her religious faith may have saved her life. Otherwise she thought just as Moses did on the hill, "It is quite fair to pray this way: to lift up one's hands for one's own."

14. *A Memorial in a Book.*—This note by an editor may have been the origin of the legend

6 Pfeiffer, *Meister Eckhart*, II, 97.

14 And the LORD said unto Moses, Write this *for* a memorial in a book, and rehearse *it* in the ears of Joshua: for I will utterly put out the remembrance of Amalek from under heaven.

15 And Moses built an altar, and called the name of it Jehovah-nissi:

16 For he said, Because the LORD hath sworn *that* the LORD *will have* war with Amalek from generation to generation.

18 When Jethro, the priest of Midian, Moses' father-in-law, heard of all that God had done for Moses, and for Israel his

---

14 And the LORD said to Moses, "Write this as a memorial in a book and recite it in the ears of Joshua, that I will utterly blot out the remembrance of Am'alek from under heaven." 15 And Moses built an altar and called the name of it, The LORD is my banner, 16 saying, "A hand upon the banner of the LORD![z] The LORD will have war with Am'alek from generation to generation."

18 Jethro, the priest of Mid'ian, Moses' father-in-law, heard of all that God

[z] Cn. Heb obscure

---

15. This reference to the **altar** Moses built may represent an attempt to explain the existence of a shrine at Kadesh, just as in the patriarchal stories Canaanite centers of worship, notably Hebron and Bethel, are said to have been founded by the fathers, Abraham and Jacob. The phrase *Yahweh-niṣṣî* can mean "standard," **banner,** or "sign." The last term seems intended here. The "sign" must be understood as intrinsically effective, i.e., "Yahweh is the one who does things for me." Josephus (*Antiquities* III. 2. 5) interpreted the phrase as "the Lord the Conqueror." The LXX reads it as "my refuge."

16. The writer draws the scene of the oath in which Moses first pledged perpetual war against Amalek. The Hebrew reads "throne" rather than **banner. From generation to generation** the faithful Israelite, with his hand on the altar, the throne of Yahweh, was to swear perpetual war on Amalek until finally Amalek should be no more.

2. JETHRO VISITS MOSES (18:1-27)

This account of Jethro's visit must be supplemented by Num. 10:29-36; 11:11-17, 24-30. The story of Jethro's visit is of unusual interest because it is the focal point of the "Kenite hypothesis" (see Intro., pp. 839-40).

---

that Moses was the author of the first five books of the Bible; the idea is developed in 24:4; Num. 33:2; Deut. 31:9. English dictionaries up to the end of the seventeenth century attributed these books to Moses and also the book of Job. The KJV calls the first five books "The First Book of Moses," "The Second Book of Moses," and so on. The practice of ascribing works to great authors who had not written them was common in antiquity, and was due to simplicity rather than to any desire to deceive. Perhaps it was the earliest appearance of the advertising spirit.

15-16. *The Altar of War.*—This would seem to be the sacred stone on which Moses sat during the battle. It was a royal throne for Yahweh, who had conquered. The words **The LORD hath sworn** are a guess by the translators at the meaning of Hebrew words which seem to be "a hand upon the throne of Yahweh." These words seem rather to refer to Moses' hand which was held up from the throne during the battle, that hand which, holding the rod, had worked such wonders for the people (see Expos. on vss. 8-16).

The **altar** is also to be a memorial of ven-

geance against Amalek. (This hatred runs all through the Hebrew story; see Deut. 25:17; I Sam. 15; 27:8; 30:1 ff.; I Chr. 4:42-43.) As such, the altar or stone is one of the early examples of the fostering of war by keeping ancient wrongs in remembrance and exploiting the dislike of people for other people with customs different from their own. The treaty stone in Limerick preserved by the Irish as a remembrance of the alleged perfidy of the English, the German "Hymn of Hate" in World War I, the square in Budapest in which burned four eternal lights dedicated to the recovery from its dishonest neighbors of its stolen territory, all these are examples of this same attempt to perpetuate an ancient hate. The Statue of Liberty in New York Harbor, a gift from France to the United States, and hundreds of schools and hospitals over the world, gifts of the great foundations and missionary societies of the United States, are better altars to God.

18:1-6. *Moses' Wife.*—The text of vs. 2 is obscure, but seems to mean that whereas in 4:20 Moses had taken his wife and sons to

people, *and* that the LORD had brought Israel out of Egypt;

2 Then Jethro, Moses' father-in-law, took Zipporah, Moses' wife, after he had sent her back,

3 And her two sons; of which the name of the one *was* Gershom; for he said, I have been an alien in a strange land:

4 And the name of the other *was* Eliezer; for the God of my father, *said he, was* mine help, and delivered me from the sword of Pharaoh:

5 And Jethro, Moses' father-in-law, came with his sons and his wife unto Moses into the wilderness, where he encamped at the mount of God:

6 And he said unto Moses, I thy father-in-law Jethro am come unto thee, and thy wife, and her two sons with her.

7 ¶ And Moses went out to meet his father-in-law, and did obeisance, and kissed him; and they asked each other of *their* welfare; and they came into the tent.

had done for Moses and for Israel his people, how the LORD had brought Israel out of Egypt. 2 Now Jethro, Moses' father-in-law, had taken Zippo'rah, Moses' wife, after he had sent her away, 3 and her two sons, of whom the name of the one was Gershom (for he said, "I have been a sojourner[a] in a foreign land"), 4 and the name of the other, Elie'zer[b] (for he said, "The God of my father was my help, and delivered me from the sword of Pharaoh"). 5 And Jethro, Moses' father-in-law, came with his sons and his wife to Moses in the wilderness where he was encamped at the mountain of God. 6 And when one told Moses, "Lo,[c] your father-in-law Jethro is coming to you with your wife and her two sons with her," 7 Moses went out to meet his father-in-law, and did obeisance and kissed him; and they asked each other of their welfare, and went

[a] Heb *ger*
[b] Heb *Eli*, my God, *ezer*, help
[c] Sam Gk Syr: Heb *I*

---

a) THE SACRIFICIAL MEAL (18:1-12)

18:1. What Jethro heard was **how the LORD had brought Israel out of Egypt.** But, characteristically, late Jewish tradition (cf. Mekilta, *ad loc.*) said that the occasion on which the report of the great deed of Yahweh came to Jethro was the giving of the law of Sinai. The same Taanitic record interprets the phrase **priest of Midian** as "priest of idolatry." We are actually never told whose priest Jethro is.

2-4. These verses seek to reconcile the following verse with 2:22; 4:20, 25 (cf. above). Later tradition reported that Moses had sent back his wife at Aaron's request. Eliezer means "God is help." The popular "etymology" is, as usual, a later development.

5. For Gressmann and others who consider this chapter part of a Kadesh cycle the last half of this verse is a late editorial addition attempting to harmonize the account with the Sinai tradition.

6-7. The RSV has improved the translation by following the Samar. text, the LXX, and the Syriac. It might well have followed the last two on the first word also and read,

---

Egypt, yet he later had sent them back to her father. This is the last time Zipporah is mentioned. It is hard to be the wife of a famous man. No one seems to take any notice of Zipporah or her sons after these three are mentioned in vs. 6. The best wives seem to like it this way, so that they can cherish (as a secret too sacred to be profaned by common knowledge) the truth of their real power. But there have been instances in modern times of women whose public service has been as great as that of their distinguished husbands. Most historians have been men, so that men have come to have an exaggerated opinion of their own importance in history; and human mores in the past have been dominated by a church whose officers were

wholly male and largely celibate, so that woman is just beginning to get her chance. She is learning not to accept man's view of woman as the whole truth, and to see that it is a mistake to take at their face value either his views of himself or of her. Nothing is known about Zipporah, but the Talmud says with creative remembrance that Moses turned first of all to the women when he needed help in making the people obey the law; for he said, "Adam would never have sinned, if God had only given Eve the directions instead of Adam," thus showing how much he had learned from Zipporah of the wisdom and tact of women.

7-12. *Jethro and Moses.*—This passage, with its climactic statement, **Jethro . . . offered a**

8 And Moses told his father-in law all that the LORD had done unto Pharaoh and to the Egyptians for Israel's sake, *and* all the travail that had come upon them by the way, and *how* the LORD delivered them.

9 And Jethro rejoiced for all the goodness which the LORD had done to Israel, whom he had delivered out of the hand of the Egyptians.

10 And Jethro said, Blessed *be* the LORD, who hath delivered you out of the hand of the Egyptians, and out of the hand of Pharaoh, who hath delivered the people from under the hand of the Egyptians.

into the tent. 8 Then Moses told his father-in-law all that the LORD had done to Pharaoh and to the Egyptians for Israel's sake, all the hardship that had come upon them in the way, and how the LORD had delivered them. 9 And Jethro rejoiced for all the good which the LORD had done to Israel, in that he had delivered them out of the hand of the Egyptians.

10 And Jethro said, "Blessed be the LORD, who has delivered you out of the hand of the Egyptians and out of the hand

---

"It was reported," i.e., an emissary from Jethro came to announce the coming of Jethro. Moses greeted his elder in appropriate and formal Oriental manner. The Hebrew word behind **welfare** is the word normally translated "peace."

8-9. After the reunion Moses invited (Samar.) Jethro into his tent and gave him an account of the great acts of Yahweh both in Egypt and in the desert. This recital of the acts of divine care in story, psalm, and ritual was always a standard practice in Israel. The Hebrew text says that Jethro **rejoiced,** but the LXX reports that he was "astonished," or overcome, by the news. It stresses the notion that if Jethro knew Yahweh at all before this, he now learned something decisively new about him.

10. That a non-Israelite might bless the God of Israel, whether he had known him before or not, was considered possible (Dan. 3:28; II Kings 5:15-17). Opponents of the Kenite hypothesis interpret this verse as marking a pagan's acknowledgment of the true God or of his conversion to him. Mekilta (*ad loc.*) says that this is the point at which Jethro freed himself from idolatry and acquired torah. The acceptance of the traditional interpretation of this verse and the rejection of a reconstruction such as Gressmann's (cf. Intro., pp. 839-40) have too often proceeded from the dogmatic assumption that to affirm the uniqueness and truth of Israel's faith we must rule out its genetic and phenomenological relation to its wider environment. Our study of the book of Exodus

---

burnt offering and sacrifices to God, has been explained in three different ways. (*a*) That this feast was celebrated by Jethro, the priest of Midian, in honor of Yahweh, who had done such wondrous things for Moses, the husband of Zipporah. That it was a feast in which, by eating together, the invited Hebrews were admitted, according to custom, to blood kinship with the Midianites. Moses was not mentioned as among those invited, perhaps because he, by marriage, was already blood kin to the Midianites (see Exeg. for another explanation). Although priest of the gods of Midian, Jethro already knew that Yahweh was greater than all gods. The feast in this case was a wonderful example of courtesy and religious tolerance. One is reminded of II Kings 5:18-19.

(*b*) That Jethro had become a convert to the religion of Yahweh and had been ordained a priest in his worship. Ancient legend adds

details to emphasize the joy of God over his conversion, that when he approached the altar manna began to fall around him as a blessing from heaven.

(*c*) That the omission of the name of Moses from the list of those bidden to the feast indicates that a sentence has been dropped from the text, as not being approved by later scribes. In this case, Jethro had always been a priest of Yahweh in Midian. He came to instruct Moses in two departments, (i) how a sacrifice to Yahweh should be offered, and (ii) how judicial affairs should be arranged. Later writers did not like the idea of their great leader being instructed in the worship of Yahweh by a Midianite, and dropped that statement. If this surmise is correct, it is evident that Sinai and its environs were in the diocese of Jethro. Yahweh may originally have been the god in this particular district, particularly of the sacred moun-

11 Now I know that the LORD *is* greater than all gods: for in the thing wherein they dealt proudly *he was* above them.

12 And Jethro, Moses' father-in-law, took a burnt offering and sacrifices for God: and Aaron came, and all the elders of Israel, to eat bread with Moses' father-in-law before God.

of Pharaoh. 11 Now I know that the LORD is greater than all gods, because he delivered the people from under the hand of the Egyptians,*d* when they dealt arrogantly with them." 12 And Jethro, Moses' father-in-law, offered*e* a burnt offering and sacrifices to God; and Aaron came with all the elders of Israel to eat bread with Moses' father-in-law before God.

d Transposing the last clause of v. 10 to v. 11
e Syr Tg Vg: Heb *took*

---

leads us to the conclusion that such an assumption is invalid in that it contradicts the nature of revelation presupposed by the bulk of the biblical testimony. It implies an account of revelation that is gnostic rather than biblical.

11. The meaning of Jethro's statement seems to be that this story of the insolence of Egypt against the Israelites and the deliverance of the latter had convinced him of the power of Israel's God.

12. The word **took,** in contrast to the expressions found in the Syriac and Targ., is not the technical term used for bringing a sacrifice. It is a neutral word. Paul Heinisch (*Das Buch Exodus* [Bonn: Peter Hanstein, 1934], p. 141) says that the word is employed purposely to indicate that the sacrifice was not valid from the point of view of the Mosaic law. Jethro, he adds, offered a sacrifice to his own god, not to Yahweh. But that is difficult to maintain in view of vss. 10-11. Heinisch adds that Moses and Aaron could come to the sacrifice without scruples since, from their point of view, Jethro's sacrifice to his god was in effect a sacrifice to Yahweh, because he offered it to the God who delivered Israel. This shows a capacity for subtle casuistry rather than for an appreciation of the spirit of the account itself.

It should be noted that **Aaron came with all the elders.** Moses is not mentioned. Beer (*Exodus*, p. 95) interprets this to imply that Moses was already privy to the cultic rite of which Jethro was the custodian and teacher, and that Moses had been initiated as a refugee. According to such a view this is the occasion of the initiation of the others.

The chief part of the sacrifice is a sacred meal consumed by the group **before God** (cf. 24:9-11). Both in Palestine and in the Negeb the "high places" at which such sacrifices were offered are still extant. A rectangular area on top of a natural rock was smoothed off. At one end a somewhat higher rock surface sometimes projected slightly

---

tain of Sinai. Moses first learned about Yahweh in the home of his father-in-law, and it was while there that Yahweh revealed himself to Moses in the burning bush. This last explanation seems to be the most probable (yet cf. Exeg. on vss. 1-27; 19:1). In those happy years after his marriage, when he was out all day with Jethro's herds, he would come home in the evening to his wife and babes, and to long talks about Yahweh, the God of the country round about, the God of whom Jethro was the priest. He found himself when he dared to stand up for his oppressed brothers; he found love when he met Zipporah; in the experience of home and children, in converse with a good man, in meditation alone among the flocks, he found

God. It was not a strange, far-off god of deducted argument, it was the God of the country where he lived and worked, the God of the home where he lived; he found God in the ways of his children, in the love of his wife, in the talk with her father, in his curiosity about the trees and the thunderstorms around Sinai. And now Jethro had come to instruct him in the ancient lore of religious ritual, and make him too a priest of Yahweh.

There are grounds for holding that Moses was the first to call the God of Israel by the name Yahweh (but cf. Exeg. on vss. 1-27); that he had learned from his father-in-law about this God of the country; that his name was revealed to Israel through Moses about the time when

13 ¶ And it came to pass on the morrow, that Moses sat to judge the people: and the people stood by Moses from the morning unto the evening.

13 On the morrow Moses sat to judge the people, and the people stood about

---

into the rectangle: it represented the seat of the deity before whom the brotherhood gathered. Those who shared in the feast reclined along the sides and at the lower end of the rectangle. An altar on which certain parts of victims were burned, and at which libations were poured out, stood to one side of the rectangular place (Volz, *Biblischen Altertümer*, p. 22 and plate opposite). A striking picture of such a meal is given in the account of the choice of Saul as king (cf. I Sam. 9:11-14).

b) APPOINTMENT OF JUDGES (18:13-26)

This section tells us that the civil organization of Israel's society in a later day was founded by Moses, under Jethro's instruction. The account is both etiological and historical in purpose. In Num. 11:11-17, 24-30, later followed by the Deuteronomist (Deut. 1:9-18), Moses himself is said to have found the burden of his work too heavy; and the foundation of the more differentiated administration is represented as having been ordained by God, without any reference to Jethro.

13. The function of Moses was comparable to that of the Bedouin tribal sheik today. Each morning such a sheik "sits" briefly as judge. As Israel gradually became an ever-greater aggregate of clan and tribal units such simple judicial administration by one man became impossible. Moses may here be considered as priest as well as tribal chief or judge. Originally there was no differentiation between the sacral and civil power (cf. Bentzen, *Intro. to O.T.*, I, 215-16). This incident is part of a continual process of differentiation in which sacral and secular authorities become more separable. But they do not stand completely apart. The civil judges receive their authority from Moses, the sacral head. Besides, the oracular decision, whether by sacred lot or prophetic inspiration, constitutes the "precedents" on the basis of which the "civil" magistrates work.

---

the people were moved by great devoutness after the crossing of the Red Sea. The first name we find derived from the name of Yahweh is Joshua, of the first generation after Moses. There are two sets of stories, one placing the new revelation at Kadesh (chs. 16–18), the other at Sinai (ch. 19). The later stories transfer the events from Kadesh to Sinai, move Jethro into the background, and make less of the influence of Midian. That it was possible to give God a new name was due to the great wave of gratitude which swept over the people at their escape from bondage, and to the fact that Moses apparently did not say much as to the origins of Yahweh, but emphasized what this God had just done and would do for Israel. So the God of Mount Sinai moved from Sinai, his ancient seat, accompanied Israel on their march, and became the God of Palestine; in the later thought of Israel he was dissevered from any particular land and was God of all. Israel and Yahweh became one in the burning flames of Sinai. He

was still the God of their fathers, but he had a new name, a new law, a new ritual.

13. Moses as Judge.—Slaves cannot be turned into saints overnight. These people were living the simple life. They had returned to nature. There were no complicated city conditions, no artificial luxuries to quarrel over, no banks or real estate deals, and yet **the people stood about Moses from morning till evening.** It would have taken a panel of trained psychiatrists and jurists, one can imagine, to deal with all the difficulties that had arisen in the day. When a crisis is over people always have more time to think of their pet troubles and dislikes and of their neighbors' shortcomings. "Too much noise in the next tent when we are trying to sleep"; "Why can't they keep their children in their own tent?" "Our black lamb has been missing for two days"; "They put their goat on the bit of pasture we had found." Probably the cases Moses had to solve would seem very modern to us, for human nature is nothing new.

14 And when Moses' father-in-law saw all that he did to the people, he said, What *is* this thing that thou doest to the people? Why sittest thou thyself alone, and all the people stand by thee from morning unto even?

15 And Moses said unto his father-in-law, Because the people come unto me to inquire of God:

16 When they have a matter, they come unto me; and I judge between one and another, and I do make *them* know the statutes of God, and his laws.

17 And Moses' father in-law said unto him, The thing that thou doest *is* not good.

18 Thou wilt surely wear away, both thou, and this people that *is* with thee: for this thing *is* too heavy for thee; thou art not able to perform it thyself alone.

19 Hearken now unto my voice, I will give thee counsel, and God shall be with thee: Be thou for the people to Godward, that thou mayest bring the causes unto God:

Moses from morning till evening. 14 When Moses' father-in-law saw all that he was doing for the people, he said, "What is this that you are doing for the people? Why do you sit alone, and all the people stand about you from morning till evening?" 15 And Moses said to his father-in-law, "Because the people come to me to inquire of God; 16 when they have a dispute, they come to me and I decide between a man and his neighbor, and I make them know the statutes of God and his decisions." 17 Moses' father-in-law said to him, "What you are doing is not good. 18 You and the people with you will wear yourselves out, for the thing is too heavy for you; you are not able to perform it alone. 19 Listen now to my voice; I will give you counsel, and God be with you! You shall represent the people before God, and bring their cases to God;

---

14. The cause of Jethro's amazement must be sought in his question, **Why do you sit alone?** He can hardly have been unacquainted with the meaning of the daily session.

15. To inquire of God is to seek an answer for an issue for which no precedent can suffice. The person exercising this technical function was long known as "seer" (cf. I Sam. 9:9). He might be a priest (I Sam. 22:15), and the breastplate of judgment (28:15-30) was the symbol of this priestly oracular function. Later the prophet was so exclusively the "seer" that the very term was displaced (cf. I Kings 22:8; II Kings 3:11; 8:8; 22:14). The outcome of an inquiry, whether by sacred lot or prophet, had the value of revelation. It was the word of God, not only in rhetorical fashion but also in effect.

16. Moses did not only deliver oracles; he also made routine applications of precedents to specific cases. The **statutes of God and his decisions** Moses makes known seem to refer to oracular decisions (cf. vss. 19-20).

17-18. Jethro objects. Both Moses and the people suffer unnecessary fatigue. In Num. 11:11-17 Moses himself chafes under his burden.

19-20. Jethro counsels Moses to confine his work to making inquiry of God and promulgating new decisions. **And God be with you** should perhaps be translated "that God may be with you."

14-20. *Jethro's Advice.*—The scene is set at evening, around the campfire at Moses' tent, with the family and guests sitting together discussing the events of the day. The old man Jethro politely but courageously gives his son-in-law a little advice. "You really do not arrange things very well, my son. You are dead tired, and the poor folk who have been standing in line all these hours are also dead tired."

He suggests that it is an impractical way of administering justice. No doubt it is a great compliment to Moses to have the people trust him so implicitly. They recognize that he is motivated by the fear of God, by devotion to the truth, and by total unselfishness. Still more extraordinary is his tireless activity. He is doing the work of many men. But the father-in-law is worried both for the health of Moses and for the dignity of his position. So the political organization of Israel is born, as is told in the

20 And thou shalt teach them ordinances and laws, and shalt show them the way wherein they must walk, and the work that they must do.

21 Moreover thou shalt provide out of all the people able men, such as fear God, men of truth, hating covetousness; and place *such* over them, *to be* rulers of thousands, *and* rulers of hundreds, rulers of fifties, and rulers of tens:

22 And let them judge the people at all seasons: and it shall be, *that* every great matter they shall bring unto thee, but every small matter they shall judge: so shall it be easier for thyself, and they shall bear *the burden* with thee.

20 and you shall teach them the statutes and the decisions, and make them know the way in which they must walk and what they must do. 21 Moreover choose able men from all the people, such as fear God, men who are trustworthy and who hate a bribe; and place such men over the people as rulers of thousands, of hundreds, of fifties, and of tens. 22 And let them judge the people at all times; every great matter they shall bring to you, but any small matter they shall decide themselves; so it will be easier for you, and they will bear the bur-

---

21. Jethro now makes his constructive proposal. The word **choose** (**provide** KJV) is a translation of the Hebrew *ḥāzāh,* from which the noun "seer" is derived. This may mean that Moses must use his peculiar gifts of sacred inquiry to select the judges. But very concrete and empirical criteria are also prescribed. They must be men who **fear God,** i.e., take him seriously, and they must have personal character and integrity. The standards of moral conduct later exalted in Israel (cf. Ps. 15) are here attributed to the Midianite priest. The division of the people into units of **thousands, of hundreds, of fifties, and of tens** represents an essential military organization which may, however, have had a very real socio-economic bearing (cf. I Sam. 22:7). It cannot be decided with certainty how early such a division of society prevailed in Israel.

22. **Every great matter** must probably be understood as a case requiring original instruction, as opposed to **any small matter** for which a precedent was at hand.

---

text. Perhaps it was the way Jethro had arranged things in Midian where he was priest. A later version of the story in Num. 11 does not allow Midian or its priest so much credit.

"It is bad for your health and it is bad for your standing among the people"; for Jethro recognized the same truth which Herodotus tells us was discovered by Deïoces, king of the Medes, who established a ceremonial on the principle that if people did not see him too much, "they would think him quite a different sort of being from themselves." [7] It is natural for people to think this way about their leaders. If one wants to be a pope or king, he should not be seen in the crowd around the bargain counters in basement stores. The judge of a supreme court can have few close friends, and should not appear much in public without his robes of office. Jethro's suggestion was founded on common sense. "Become the supreme court of last resort and let others do the routine work. It will save your health and preserve your influence." It was also the first faint step toward a democratic form of government, foreshadowed in 19:6.

[7] *The History* I. 99.

21-27. *Religion and Government.*—Hugh Latimer, on April 5, 1549, preaching before King Edward VI, quoted vs. 21 as a basis for his exhortation that the king appoint good public officers; and he went on:

Some say preachers should not meddle with such matters; but did not our Saviour Jesus Christ meddle with matters of judgment, when he spake of the wicked judge, to leave example to us to follow, to do the same? . . . Holy scripture qualifieth the officers, and sheweth what manner of men they should be, and of what qualities. . . . "Men of activity," that have stomachs [courage] to do their office; they must not be milksops, nor white-livered knights; they must be wise, hearty, hardy, men of a good stomach. Secondarily, he qualifieth them with the fear of God. . . . For if he fear God, he shall be no briber, no perverter of judgment, faithful. Thirdly, they must be chosen officers, . . . "in whom is truth;" if he say it, it shall be done. Fourthly, . . . "hating covetousness:" far from it; he will not come near it that hateth it. . . . Such as be meet to bear office, seek them out, hire them, give them competent and liberal fees, that they shall not need to take any bribes. [8]

[8] Fifth Sermon Preached Before King Edward VI.

23 If thou shalt do this thing, and God command thee *so,* then thou shalt be able to endure, and all this people shall also go to their place in peace.

24 So Moses hearkened to the voice of his father-in-law, and did all that he had said.

25 And Moses chose able men out of all Israel, and made them heads over the people, rulers of thousands, rulers of hundreds, rulers of fifties, and rulers of tens.

26 And they judged the people at all seasons: the hard causes they brought unto Moses, but every small matter they judged themselves.

27 ¶ And Moses let his father-in-law depart; and he went his way into his own land.

den with you. 23 If you do this, and God so commands you, then you will be able to endure, and all this people also will go to their place in peace."

24 So Moses gave heed to the voice of his father-in-law and did all that he had said. 25 Moses chose able men out of all Israel, and made them heads over the people, rulers of thousands, of hundreds, of fifties, and of tens. 26 And they judged the people at all times; hard cases they brought to Moses, but any small matter they decided themselves. 27 Then Moses let his father-in-law depart, and he went his way to his own country.

---

23. To emphasize his conviction that God was the immediate author of Israel's social and cultic institutions, a late editor inserted the provision **and God so commands you.** Thus the counsel of Jethro is qualified and Jethro recognizes Moses as the human instrument through whom God speaks and works.

24-26. Moses accepted the counsel of his father-in-law and put it into effect.

c) Departure of Jethro (18:27)

27. It is not intimated here that Moses tried to dissuade Jethro from leaving. That is the burden of the parable account (J) in Num. 10:29-32. We are told that Moses wanted Jethro to act as guide in the wilderness. Twice over (Num. 10:29, 32) Moses sought to persuade Jethro by promising him a share in the blessings God would give to Israel in Canaan. No response to Moses' second effort is recorded. Instead, the narrative moves at once to an account of Israel's renewal of the journey with the ark as guide. On the basis of this fact, Gressmann concluded that instead of accepting the request of Moses, Jethro had provided Israel with the ark.

This was plain speaking before the king, and preachers who would emulate him should remember that Latimer was burned at the stake six years afterward. But he loved Exodus. Hear him on 14:15 in another sermon:

Go to Moses, who had the guiding of God's people; see how he used prayer as an instrument to be delivered out of adversity, when he had great rough mountains on every side of him, and before him the Red Sea; Pharao's host behind him, peril of death round about him. What did he? despaired he? No. Whither went he? He repaired to God with his prayer, and said nothing: yet with a great ardency of spirit he pierced God's ear: "Now help, or never, good Lord; no help but in thy hand," quoth he. Though he never moved his lips, yet the scripture saith he cried out, and the Lord heard him, and said, . . . "Why criest thou out so loud?" The people heard him say nothing, and yet God said, "Why criest thou out?" Straightway he struck the water with his rod, and divided it, and

it stood up like two walls on either side, between the which God's people passed, and the persecutors were drowned.[9]

The separation between the sacred and the secular referred to in the Exeg. cannot be adequately defined, for the simple reason that in essence there is no such distinction. God must be lord of all. "Render to Cæsar the things that are Cæsar's, and to God the things that are God's" (Mark 12:17); this practical precept is necessary only because of Caesar's imperfect vision and man's inadequate conception of God's omnipresence. The ecclesiastical, however, is never pure or inclusive enough to contain all of religion and nothing but religion. So in practice it is necessary to make a clear division between the field of ecclesiastical authority and that of secular authority. God works in the church, God

[9] Third Sermon Preached Before King Edward VI, March 22, 1549.

19 In the third month, when the children of Israel were gone forth out of the land of Egypt, the same day came they *into* the wilderness of Sinai.

2 For they were departed from Rephidim, and were come *to* the desert of Sinai, and had pitched in the wilderness; and there Israel camped before the mount.

3 And Moses went up unto God, and the LORD called unto him out of the mountain, saying, Thus shalt thou say to the house of Jacob, and tell the children of Israel;

19 On the third new moon after the people of Israel had gone forth out of the land of Egypt, on that day they came into the wilderness of Sinai. 2 And when they set out from Reph'idim and came into the wilderness of Sinai, they encamped in the wilderness; and there Israel encamped before the mountain. 3 And Moses went up to God, and the LORD called him out of the mountain, saying, "Thus you shall say to the house of Jacob, and tell the people of

---

IV. SINAI: THE IMPLEMENTATION OF THE REVELATION (19:1–40:38)

In this third main section of Exodus we have an interpretation of the institutions of Israel as seen in the light of the revelation of God and his election of Israel as attested in the second section (7:14–18:27).

A. THE COVENANT (19:1–24:18)

For a discussion of the Exodus and the covenant of Sinai, cf. Intro., pp. 840-42.

1. THE THEOPHANY (19:1-25)
a) THE INVITATION (19:1-8)

19:1-2a. Vs. 2a should precede vs. 1. In later times the feast of Unleavened Bread was kept on the fifteenth day after the waving of the barley sheaf. Orthodox tradition held that this waving took place on the first day of the Unleavened Bread. The feast of Weeks (Pentecost) therefore fell on the sixth day of the third month. It commemorated the giving of the law on Sinai. P's chronological note may have all this in mind. The arrival at Sinai must thus be placed very early in the third month. The RSV, following the Amer. Trans., says that it was on the first day of the month. This is also the interpretation of Mekilta (*ad loc.*). Nevertheless, in some ways the expression **in the third month** (KJV) seems more natural. **New moon** is a liturgical term not normally accompanied by an ordinal.

2b-3. They **encamped before the mountain.** The identity of the mountain is taken for granted. Moses has brought his people to the scene at which he received his commis-

---

works in the state, but in both through sinful men, so that it is better at present to keep the rights of both within strictly defined limits—till the time comes when church and state are one, and that will be the coming of the kingdom of God. The church welcomes all signs of a tenderer conscience on the part of the state, and the state recognizes more and more the lifting power of the leaven introduced into society by thousands of priests and ministers who have been constantly reminding the farmer and shopkeeper, the millowner and workman of the charity and humility of Jesus.

19:1-6. The Human Mind and the Heavenly Inspiration.—The truest description of what happened to Moses at Sinai is in these simple words, **The LORD called unto him.** Behind the message which came from God there may have

been many years of brooding thought and selection on the part of Moses, many years of sifting among the laws and customs of men as known to him. How to say what had been placed in his mind, briefly, clearly, simply enough to gain the ears, minds, and hearts of the people was the problem with which he had wrestled in prayer during the long years of his preparation for leadership. Then came the great experience of inspiration out of which the divine message came. Many great leaders, writers, and artists have tried to express what the mysterious experience of inspiration is really like. It is always the climax to long years of labor or fiery experience deeply felt. In the end, musicians, poets, and statesmen have all come to the same mode of expressing and describing it which was used by Moses, **The LORD called unto him out of**

4 Ye have seen what I did unto the Egyptians, and *how* I bare you on eagles' wings, and brought you unto myself.	Israel: 4 You have seen what I did to the Egyptians, and how I bore you on eagles' wings and brought you to myself. 5 Now
5 Now therefore, if ye will obey my voice indeed, and keep my covenant, then ye shall be a peculiar treasure unto me above all people: for all the earth *is* mine:	therefore, if you will obey my voice and keep my covenant, you shall be my own possession among all peoples; for all the

sion. The "sign" of promise (3:12) has been fulfilled. It is also assumed that Yahweh dwells on Sinai. As Moses ascends the mountain, apparently before he has gone far, God calls out to him and offers to make a covenant with **the children of Israel.** Moses is entrusted with announcing the nature of the proposed covenant to the people.

4. The pledge for God's faithfulness and power in the covenant is his redemptive action already seen in the deliverance: **You have seen what I did.** The resource of the God of the Exodus is offered to Israel in terms of a permanent relationship. But this covenant will rest on historic fact.

5. The covenant was one between Yahweh and his servants. Obedience was the central role of Israel. This obedience is basically expressed in faith and loyalty. In the Deuteronomic school, which seems to influence the vocabulary of this verse, obedience is given more static and formal terms. To **keep my covenant** probably must be understood here as obeying the law. Israel is to be God's **own possession** (Deut. 7:7; 14:2; 26:18). The term, as applied to people, always refers to the elect community. This is also true

the mountain. Here is one attempt at elucidation made by a modern writer:

There is only the slightest touch of superstition in the conviction from which I cannot escape of being merely an incarnation, a mouthpiece, a medium of tremendous powers. Revelation is the only word which describes the simple fact that suddenly, with unspeakable certainty and clarity, something is seen and heard, stirring one's being to the very depths. One does not merely seek, one hears a voice. Something is given from behind the veil. Like a flash of lightning the thought becomes plain, standing out as clear as day. . . . Everything happens; it is not an act of one's own will, and yet a torrential sense of freedom, power and divinity courses through one's being. Facts become words, the working laws of life learn speech from thee. . . . This is my experience of inspiration.[1]

5. The Law of God.—Alexander Whyte, of Edinburgh, once said to his congregation, "You can read the Bible as a lawyer reads a will, or as the heir reads the will." There is great inspiration in both ways of reading the Bible. No antagonism need exist between the two readers, the exegete and the expositor. They help one another. As the text stands, all the religious experience of the first tellers of the tale, of the various editors and annotators of later times, and of the translators of the original text have gone into the narrative. One Oxford scholar used to say that "in a certain sense the Author-

ized Version is more inspired than the original." [2] There is edification in both ways of reading the account of the giving of the law. One can take it as it stands and find in it great riches, or one can study it to discover that the law as given in the story could not have been expressed in its present form by anyone in the time of Moses. It is a mistake to make too much of doubts and negations. Study the text deeply enough to find its positive message. Read the Bible both ways and find inspiration both in what it says and in how it came to say what it does.

As Francis Thompson sings in his "Hound of Heaven," the heart of religious experience is the fact that we are sought of God, not that we seek God. Here the initiative comes from the side of Yahweh; Moses is the intermediary. The religion of Israel was a covenant (*berîth*) which Yahweh offered to make with his people. This chapter is an account of how this definite engagement was entered into by both parties. In vs. 3 Moses receives the offer from Yahweh; in vs. 8 we have the acceptance by the people of the arrangement and treaty. The terms offered and accepted were that Israel should separate itself from all other peoples and devote itself to the worship of the true God. Yahweh

[1] *Nietzsche's Werke* (Leipzig: Alfred Kroner, 1922), XV, 90-91.

[2] Evelyn Abbott and Lewis Campbell, *The Life and Letters of Benjamin Jowett* (New York: E. P. Dutton & Co., 1897), I, 406. See also René Guénon, *Man and His Becoming* (London: Rider & Co., n.d.), p. 179: "In Arabic the word for *translation* means also *commentary*, the one being regarded as inseparable from the other."

6 And ye shall be unto me a kingdom of priests, and a holy nation. These *are* the words which thou shalt speak unto the children of Israel.

earth is mine, 6 and you shall be to me a kingdom of priests and a holy nation. These are the words which you shall speak to the children of Israel."

---

of the Greek equivalent in the N.T. (Tit. 2:14; I Pet. 2:9; Eph. 1:14). The freedom of God in his choice of Israel, the pure graciousness of the act, is stressed by **for all the earth is mine.**

6. The covenant is with the people, not with its leaders or priesthood. Just as in Israel the priests had access to the altar and the Levites rejoiced in the service of God and

---

had proved his power by rescuing the people from Egypt, and had borne them **on eagles' wings** safe to his Mount of Sinai. If they will keep the covenant, he will make them **a kingdom of priests, and a holy nation.**

Among the old stories of Israel there is one telling that when it became known that God was about to make the revelation of his law (*tôrāh*) to the people of Israel from a mountaintop, then all the mountains appeared before God to plead, each one, that it might be chosen for this great honor. "God of All, choose me," said Mount Hermon, "I am the highest of the mountains. It was my summit which, alone of all, towered above the waters of the flood, even as thy torah stands as a great rock above all the sins of the world." "Choose me," said Mount Carmel, "for I am lovely as a garden. Plant upon me the tree of thy torah, as thou didst plant the tree of life in the Garden of Eden." "Choose me, choose me," said Mount Lebanon, "for the voice of my cedars sings of thy greatness, as thy torah turns all the storms of the world into music, hymning thy praise." But God said to Mount Sinai, "From thy summit shall my torah go forth to my people, for thou art set alone in the desert, even as Israel is alone among the peoples, even as I, Yahweh, am alone in the desert of the universe."

The rabbis asked why God had waited till now to reveal his torah unto men. Why had he not given it in the first times to the first men? And God replied to the questioning, "I gave but one commandment unto the first man, 'Thou shalt not eat of the fruit of this tree,' yet Adam did eat of it. How then could they have been able to receive the six hundred and thirteen commandments of the torah?' "

Rabbi Hija bar Abba adds, "Look . . . how much greater is the Torah than the world: to give the world to the world, God needed but seven days: He needed full forty to give to it the Torah." [3]

6. The Priesthood of All Believers.—This verse was written either before the rise of the

professional priesthood in Israel, or by one who believed that sacred officialdom represents a stage in religious growth which should be outgrown. We must, he thought, anticipate a time when people "come of age" religiously and are able to accept their own responsibilities (Jer. 31:34). This is one of the most rejuvenating religious ideas of all time.

When in matters of law or physical health one gets into difficulties, he is wise to consult an expert, a man who has spent his life in the study of these fields of knowledge. The lawyer or physician knows what is the right thing to do. So official churches and official priesthoods argue that when you need religious truth, you should come to religious experts: they know all that can be known about God. But there are fallacies in this line of argument. In the case of law or medicine, the authority of the profession rests entirely on the results which accrue by the knowledge or skill it uses for men's benefit. The majority of clients attain justice or health; otherwise the experts would be discredited in the minds of the people.

But religion deals with matters for which no such check or proof is possible; no one can prove that officials are vested with powers over life after death, or forgiveness of sins; one may even suspect that these supposed powers are used by the professional class in maintaining their power over the people. No one church can produce definite proof that its brand of faith produces a finer type of human being than any other. The claim of any religious group to be unique religious experts rests entirely on their own say-so, their own reading of history (unaccepted by anyone else). This is why all religious dictatorship has to depend on some magical virtue it claims to possess by divine authority. That here is another fallacy is seen from the fact that while one man's religion can learn much from the religion of others, no two experiences are identical. This is God's plenty. The relation of each child to its parents is unique. Every man, as this writer implies, must become his own priest. He cannot shirk this responsibility, though at

[3] Edmond Fleg, *The Life of Moses*, tr. S. H. Guest (New York: E. P. Dutton & Co., 1928), p. 102.

7 ¶ And Moses came and called for the elders of the people, and laid before their faces all these words which the LORD commanded him.

8 And all the people answered together, and said, All that the LORD hath spoken we will do. And Moses returned the words of the people unto the LORD.

7 So Moses came and called the elders of the people, and set before them all these words which the LORD had commanded him. 8 And all the people answered together and said, "All that the LORD has spoken we will do." And Moses reported the words of

---

the support of the faithful, so Israel will fulfill the role of priest in the world. It will be **a holy nation,** i.e., set apart for a peculiar task. Israel was to be the church. This is also the interpretation of the text in the N.T. (I Pet. 2:5, 9).

7-8. The proposal Yahweh has made to Moses he reports to the elders. The people respond to God's offer of the covenant, and Moses brings their reply to him.

---

times all of us wish that it were possible, as in law and medicine, simply to put our case in the hands of experts, do what they say, and be relieved from the anguish of decision.

God is tied to no officials. The only badge of his presence is a burning, beating pulse of goodness, radiant and electric with ideas, love, indignation, and high resolve. As soon as any group solemnly claims to be sole conservators of his truth, he is gone from them, to dwell in scattered places with humble folk here and there, mothers of families, sons of toil; in the gracious atmosphere of a classroom or the lonely vigil of a seeker after truth.

6. *Consecration of a People.*—Every nation and race has its peculiar gifts. As Greece was the classical nation of art and philosophy, as Rome was the classical nation in law and organization, so Israel was the classical religious nation of history as the Western world has known it. Every nation has its own contribution to make to human civilization. But most nations misread themselves: for a hundred years and more the German people seemed to others to be most mistaken about themselves, but the same is true of us all. England glories in itself as the home of "fair play" and is met across the channel with the sobriquet "perfidious Albion"; the United States sings of itself as "the land of the free and the home of the brave," but is more connected in other people's minds with the "almighty dollar." It has been said, "Whenever you get a brand-new idea, look up and see which Greek philosopher expressed it best"; the genius of Rome still is present in our law courts; the religious ideas of the Jews have permeated the whole world; perhaps some race or nation may be able through the coming centuries to become a holy nation by its pure and unique contribution to civilization. The whole of human history is the story of how God offers this great destiny

to one nation after another, each in turn, "called according to his purpose" (Rom. 8:28). Holy words consecrating a nation to God were spoken by Lincoln at Gettysburg in November, 1863: "That this nation, under God, shall have a new birth of freedom, and that government of the people, by the people, for the people, shall not perish from the earth."

7-8. *The Worth of Effort.*—It is said that James Harvey Robinson was once asked if he could give in a few words the essence of the thousands of books of history he had read. He replied in three words, "Don't expect anything." The truth lies halfway between this pronouncement and that of an eminent biographer who replied to the same question, "Expect anything." The people of Israel were not able to carry out in the coming years the high resolve they here made, but they probably did better than they would have done if they had never reached for a moment this high peak of self-consecration. When Henry A. Wallace jokingly said to Mme. Litvinov that the object of World War II was to ensure that everybody in the world might have the privilege of drinking a quart of milk a day, and she replied, "Yes, even a pint," they knew that the aim was impossibly high, yet even to have stated it was a step forward.[4] It is worth while to get people to express their best selves once in a while in hymns and sacraments, even if one knows that he will not be able to deliver a full quart of fulfillment, or even a pint. It is easier to scoff at the Kellogg Pact or the United Nations Charter than it is to be sure that the nations are not a little more decent to each other, less sure of their own rights, than they would have been without these moments of inspiration. It is something to have become aware of the right way, even if we have not the full determination to follow it.

[4] Carl Sandburg, *Home Front Memo* (New York: Harcourt, Brace & Co., 1942), p. 172; see also p. 167.

9 And the Lord said unto Moses, Lo, I come unto thee in a thick cloud, that the people may hear when I speak with thee, and believe thee for ever. And Moses told the words of the people unto the Lord.

10 ¶ And the Lord said unto Moses, Go unto the people, and sanctify them to-day and to-morrow, and let them wash their clothes,

the people to the Lord. 9 And the Lord said to Moses, "Lo, I am coming to you in a thick cloud, that the people may hear when I speak with you, and may also believe you for ever."

Then Moses told the words of the people to the Lord. 10 And the Lord said to Moses, "Go to the people and consecrate them today and tomorrow, and let them wash

---

b) The Preparation (19:9-15)

9. The **cloud** was the symbol of divine presence and protection. It led Israel on pilgrimage (13:21), resting over the tabernacle on the journey from Sinai (40:34-38), and finally abiding in the temple (I Kings 8:10-11). Here it appears as the sign of God's presence on the mount, to authenticate the prophetic role of Moses, that the people **may also believe you for ever.** Without fully beholding his presence, the people are to hear God's voice. God discloses his will but does not shed his mystery. When Isaiah had his vision of God in the temple we are told that the house was filled with smoke (Isa. 6:4), a metaphor of similar import.

10-11. The distance between man and God is set forth by the three-day period of ceremonial purification decreed for people who are to approach his presence. The emphasis is upon an inherent and permanent difference of status between God and man. The forms of sanctification are very ancient and often show traces of an earlier setting in animism. Thus the washing of garments or of the body could imply the acquisition of

---

9. **When the Truth Is Manifest.**—The rabbis say that Abiram and Dathan had been whispering to the people that it was not Yahweh at all, but only Moses who spoke. So that even though God had spoken through Moses, it was necessary at this time for the people to hear the actual voice of God. John Galsworthy has a short story called "The Voice of ———," which tells how God's voice once was heard under such circumstances that those who heard it realized by its overwhelming truth that it was the very voice of God. Many devout people seek, as the children of Israel did, for some external proof that the voice is God's. It is the longing for such an external proof which divides the churches. But the proof that it is our Father's voice is not in the affidavit of any doctrine; it is in the voice itself. Fundamentalists and liberals have often denounced each other, but in those rare moments when the storms are high and the floods are out and they need real religion, they find themselves clinging to the same rock. There they cease arguing about whether it is God's voice or Moses' voice that directed them thither; they have listened and helped others struggling in the waters; God has spoken and they have both known his voice.

10. **The Approach of Reverence.**—Only those who have especially prepared themselves can approach the Godhead. All trace of ritual un-

cleanness must be removed (vss. 14-15; I Sam. 7:3; 21:5; Amos 4:12; Matt. 22:11-12). Rites and abstentions preparatory to the meeting-house lingered on in Scotland and New England, especially on days before the celebration of the communion service. This verse is the origin of "Sunday clothes." The Scots had a rite known as "fencing the tables" before the Sacrament to keep out any who were doctrinally or morally unworthy. Communion tokens, special metal coins, were given out by the elders on the previous week to those deemed worthy to partake of the Sacrament, and only those who had them were admitted at the door. Only one who has had the privilege as a child of being one of such a company on its way to church on Sunday morning can feel its real significance. We were "prepared" in raiment, in body, and in soul to meet our Creator; and as we looked around the church among our friends, we felt that all of us were at our best. The grime and worry of the week were gone, the sound of the grand old psalms was in our ears, we were ready for a great experience. The pulpit with its open Bible was lifted on high far above us; tables were spread in the aisles for the Holy Supper; an atmosphere of mutual forgiveness and respect filled the familiar place as all anticipated the approach of the great mysterious invisible presence. One could almost see the cloud in

11 And be ready against the third day: for the third day the Lord will come down in the sight of all the people upon mount Sinai.

12 And thou shalt set bounds unto the people round about, saying, Take heed to yourselves, *that ye* go *not* up into the mount, or touch the border of it: whosoever toucheth the mount shall be surely put to death:

their garments, **11** and be ready by the third day; for on the third day the Lord will come down upon Mount Sinai in the sight of all the people. **12** And you shall set bounds for the people round about, saying, 'Take heed that you do not go up into the mountain or touch the border of it; whoever touches the mountain shall be put to

---

the holiness of Yahweh or its virtue (II Kings 5–10). The insistence upon the use of running water in such instances (Lev. 14) probably goes back to an era when divine power was thought to reside in stream or fountain. Sometimes washing had the effect of removing the untouchability of those who had been in immediate contact with the holy (Lev. 16:23-24), though the removal of priestly garments alone might suffice for this (Ezek. 44:19). Here the rite of washing is used to neutralize the garment of those who will come into the presence of the holy (cf. Gen. 35:2).

12-13. Even though purified, the common people do not have the privilege of access which is allowed to the priests. As in the later temple, the more holy area is reserved for

---

which was fire and hear the thunderings of a mighty and tender voice. He spoke and we heard him clearly and the whole congregation, filling every pew, arose and answered in the words of "Old Hundredth," thunder answering thunder:

> All people that on earth do dwell,
> Sing to the Lord with cheerful voice;
> Him serve with mirth, his praise forth tell,
> Come ye before him and rejoice.

This was our Sinai; for we were children of the N.T. as well as of the Old, and we worshiped one who sat not always in the flames of Sinai, but also among his disciples on another mount amid the flowers which are the care and love of God. And our minister told us that David foresaw that teacher when he wrote Ps. 100.

11-13. When the Trumpets Sound.—There were in ancient Israel two kinds of trumpets, neither of which was properly a musical instrument. Both were used for signals or to augment a joyous uproar among the people. Here the reference is to a sustained note on the ram's horn, the shophar of the contemporary synagogue, probably the most ancient form of wind instrument in use today. The trumpet referred to in vs. 16 is probably the sacred instrument (here supernaturally sounding from the mount) such as is seen leaning against the golden table of showbread on the Arch of Titus. The shophar was usually a curved horn; the *ḥaṣôṣᵉrāh*, the priestly horn, was straight and made of metal. A ram's horn, when blown,

makes a good signal for the group to gather together, but vibrating metal has always made an impression of urgency, importance, majesty, on the human race. One has but to watch and listen when the impressive passages come in the performance of a modern symphony orchestra to see that the human race in all its sophisticated civilization is the same in this respect as were the nomad peoples of the Sinai wilderness.

The trumpet whose call summons the people to worship and the trumpet which announces in the central rite the supreme event of the advent of the divine presence—both these trumpets are needed in any church in any age. The first trumpet is that which gathers the people,

> To walk together to the kirk
> With a goodly company!
>
> To walk together to the kirk,
> And all together pray,
> While each to his great Father bends,
> Old men, and babes, and loving friends
> And youths and maidens gay! [5]

The second trumpet is sounded at the consummation of the rite of worship, the rapturous moment when the end for which they came together is achieved,

> Earth breaks up, time drops away,
> In flows heaven, with its new day.[6]

[5] Coleridge, *The Rime of the Ancient Mariner*, Part VII, sts. xx-xxi.
[6] Browning, "Christmas-Eve," Part X.

13 There shall not a hand touch it, but he shall surely be stoned, or shot through; whether *it be* beast or man, it shall not live: when the trumpet soundeth long, they shall come up to the mount.

14 ¶ And Moses went down from the mount unto the people, and sanctified the people; and they washed their clothes.

15 And he said unto the people, Be ready against the third day: come not at *your* wives.

death; 13 no hand shall touch him, but he shall be stoned or shot; whether beast or man, he shall not live.' When the trumpet sounds a long blast, they shall come up to the mountain." 14 So Moses went down from the mountain to the people, and consecrated the people; and they washed their garments. 15 And he said to the people, "Be ready by the third day; do not go near a woman."

the priests. Transgressors, **whether beast or man,** would forfeit their life to Yahweh. They were to be put to death. Since the transgressors were taboo, the provision that they must not be touched is precautionary, to insure the safety of the people. The ram's horn gave its name to the year of jubilee. We must assume here that the sounding of the *yôbhēl* was a part of the theophany; it was not blown by a man. Since the people would not come up the mount, those summoned here may be the priests. In that case the provision belongs properly after vs. 22.

14-15. Moses conducts the ceremonial preparation. The demand for marital abstinence during the three-day period, not included in the prescriptions for the preparation, seems to rest on an accepted regulation in early Israel (cf. I Sam. 21:4-6).

Three things draw people to church: (*a*) the hope of acquiring merit with God or man by attending church; (*b*) the anticipation of partaking in a common sacramental ritual in which one's best self yearns upward and is met and purified by the spirit of God which yearns downward to meet one's aspiration; and (*c*) the delight of thinking with some good speaker who has schooled himself to express the challenge, comfort, and inspiration of life in sermons filled with understanding sympathy and spiritual insight. All three blend in the average man's blood. The first is of the earth and moves the savage humor of both God and his prophets at times to declare, "I hate, I despise your feasts" (Amos 5:21); it has a slight validity and may lead to deeper understanding. But the other two reasons are real, and in view of them every minister should ask himself, "If I were a layman living here, why in the world should I bestir myself to go to this church? Does the trumpet sound in calling to my church, and when the congregation gathers, is there a supreme experience worth their pilgrimage?" Motion-picture artists spend millions of dollars and thousands of hours of reiterated labor to produce a great effect, but the work of the Lord is too often idly and slovenly done. A great church, which may be the smallest of village sanctuaries, is one into whose services have gone much labor and co-operative energy by preacher, choirs, janitors,

and people. When the moment has been prepared for, then the trumpet will sound with no uncertain tones, "and the Lord will come down upon Mount Sinai and call to Moses, and Moses will tell the people."

For the sound of the trumpet thrills preacher and people alike only as the consummation of long preparation and the hardest kind of work. Frederic W. H. Myers, in 1867, knew of these labors:

How have I knelt with arms of my aspiring
  Lifted all night in irresponsive air,
Dazed and amazed with overmuch desiring,
  Blank with the utter agony of prayer! [7]

And afterward when he had won his way to the full fruition of these vigils, in later editions of *St. Paul,* he added these lines:

Then with a rush the intolerable craving
  Shivers throughout me like a trumpet-call—
Oh to save these! to perish for their saving,
  Die for their life, be offered for them all! [8]

For "the secret of all art . . . lies in the faculty of self oblivion." [9]

14-15. See Expos. on vs. 10.

[7] *St. Paul* (London: Macmillan & Co., 1867), p. 13.
[8] *Ibid.* (1905), p. 34.
[9] E. G. R. Canudo, quoted in A. Coomaraswamy, *The Dance of Siva* (New York: The Sunwise Turn, Inc., 1918), p. 42.

16 ¶ And it came to pass on the third day in the morning, that there were thunders and lightnings, and a thick cloud upon the mount, and the voice of the trumpet exceeding loud; so that all the people that *was* in the camp trembled.

17 And Moses brought forth the people out of the camp to meet with God; and they stood at the nether part of the mount.

18 And mount Sinai was altogether on a smoke, because the LORD descended upon it in fire: and the smoke thereof ascended as the smoke of a furnace, and the whole mount quaked greatly.

19 And when the voice of the trumpet sounded long, and waxed louder and louder, Moses spake, and God answered him by a voice.

16 On the morning of the third day there were thunders and lightnings, and a thick cloud upon the mountain, and a very loud trumpet blast, so that all the people who were in the camp trembled. 17 Then Moses brought the people out of the camp to meet God; and they took their stand at the foot of the mountain. 18 And Mount Sinai was wrapped in smoke, because the LORD descended upon it in fire; and the smoke of it went up like the smoke of a kiln, and the whole mountain quaked greatly. 19 And as the sound of the trumpet grew louder and louder, Moses spoke, and God answered him

c) THE APPEARANCE (19:16-25)

16-17. The third day had begun on the evening before. Metaphors descriptive of violent storms accompanied by thunder and lightning are frequently used to describe the manifestation of God. They stress the mystery and awesomeness of his being (cf. Judg. 5:4-5; Isa. 2:12-22; Ps. 29). It seems impossible to decide definitely whether this description is based on an actual recollection of meteorologic conditions at Sinai or represents a literary portrayal in metaphors that were considered appropriate to a theophany. Inasmuch as these are widely used stock metaphors, and inasmuch as this account, at least in its written form, must be several centuries removed from the event, the latter seems much more probable. The real point is that the covenant rests on an authentic self-disclosure of Yahweh. And whether this is so here or not, there are places where descriptions of this type, purely metaphorical in character, are used to assert the authenticity of one's experience of deity (Isa. 6:1-5). In Israel **the trumpet** (shophar) was used to summon men to war or to proclaim great events (Judg 3:27; I Kings 1:34). This is a heavenly trumpet by which God himself announces his coming. It has persisted as an eschatological metaphor: e.g., "Gabriel's horn" (Matt. 24:31; I Cor. 15:52; I Thess. 4:16).

18-19. Despite vs. 3, Yahweh is pictured as descending to the mountain enveloped in fire; hence the smoke (cf. Isa. 6:4; Joel 2:30 [Hebrew 3:3]). This picture also corresponds to a persistent set of eschatological metaphors. Originally it may have been derived from

16-20. The Mystery of the Divine.—"Verily thou art a God that hidest thyself" (Isa. 45:15); so Sinai was covered by a cloud; so ordinary circumstances hid the divine glory from the people around Jesus (Mark 6:3). Some of our poets have generalized so far as to say that real power is always unseen, its effects are manifest, but the sap in the tree, the infant flower in the bud, the root in the soil, the lifeblood in the heart, the steam in the cylinder, the current in the wire —all must be hidden to do their creative work aright. **Thunders and lightnings, and a thick cloud upon the mount;** so the presence of God was felt by the people, but God himself was not seen. The followers of Philip (John 14:8)

throughout history have always sensed that this was the chief weak point about religion. But for the truly spiritual this fact is one of the great contributions of Israel to the religious thought of the world. "Up, make us gods" (32:1) is the cry of the vulgar always. If God is invisible, they must have an infallible idol to worship— the torah, the Bible itself, the divine official, the human race, old mother nature, the creed of a "true church," the golden calf, something that is more tangible than a mere still small voice after the tempests of life's struggle, or the sense of a presence "felt like sunshine by the blind." [1] But religion is the inner view of life, not its

[1] James Russell Lowell, "The Captive," st. v.

20 And the Lord came down upon mount Sinai, on the top of the mount: and the Lord called Moses *up* to the top of the mount; and Moses went up.

21 And the Lord said unto Moses, Go down, charge the people, lest they break through unto the Lord to gaze, and many of them perish.

22 And let the priests also, which come near to the Lord, sanctify themselves, lest the Lord break forth upon them.

23 And Moses said unto the Lord, The people cannot come up to mount Sinai: for thou chargedst us, saying, Set bounds about the mount, and sanctify it.

in thunder. 20 And the Lord came down upon Mount Sinai, to the top of the mountain; and the Lord called Moses to the top of the mountain, and Moses went up. 21 And the Lord said to Moses, "Go down and warn the people, lest they break through to the Lord to gaze and many of them perish. 22 And also let the priests who come near to the Lord consecrate themselves, lest the Lord break out upon them." 23 And Moses said to the Lord, "The people cannot come up to Mount Sinai; for thou thyself didst charge us, saying, 'Set bounds about the

---

seismic phenomena. But as in the case of the storm picture (vss. 16-17), one should hesitate to conclude, especially in view of the standard role such metaphors play, that Sinai must have been a volcanically active mountain. In the midst of this terrible mystery and power—"earthquake, wind, and fire"—**Moses spake, and God answered him by a voice.** There is meaning as well as power. In this account God's holiness is explained by holding together the awesomeness and the voice (cf. I Kings 19:11-13).

20-25. Moses is summoned to enter the cloud resting on the top of the mount. But he has hardly entered the divine presence when Yahweh tells him to return **and warn the people lest they break through to the Lord to gaze.** In view of vss. 12, 16 this seems anomalous. Vs. 23 appears to be a redactor's note seeking to harmonize the discrepancy, a harmonization in which Yahweh is revealed as very absent-minded! Moses is also to command the priests who will **come near** to share in the solemnities to **consecrate themselves** (cf. vs. 10). The arrangements at the mountain with respect to order of relative holiness are probably consciously patterned upon those which later prevailed in the temple. It seems possible to read vs. 24 as it stands only by assuming that it refers

---

outer appearance, and life on its inner side is always responsibilty. Man rises to his greatest heights in knowing God.

> What a pity, we cannot see Buddha face to face,
> Though he is everywhere at any time;
> Yet, as in a vision, he appears to us
>> In the calm morning hour, when there is no human bustling.[2]

21-25. The Awesomeness of God.—Men of every age form their own symbols of the invisible God. To these primitive people the big noise of thunder, sudden death by lightning, the fright induced by the quaking earth, and the fierce blare of the trumpet—these things seemed fitting symbols of the divine. To us noise, sense of insecurity, sudden death, seem rather beggarly symbols of God's presence; they are symbols of war rather than of God. Bigness, frightfulness, and terror still impress us, but less and less with a sense of the divine presence. We are coming to learn that it takes more courage,

brains, resourcefulness, and heroism to make peace than to make war, and that violence in behavior is always an expression of failure.

How far such conceptions as divine majesty, *numen tremendum*, born of dictatorship and war, can be replaced by expressions of the inner awe and reverence of the free spirit for real greatness, remains to be seen. There is more religion in Millet's "Angelus" than in any picture made of Sinai; it is not the subject of the picture that makes it religious so much as the spirit, reverence, skill, and insight with which it is painted. Churches should be ashamed to have poor daubs of sacred subjects hanging in their buildings. Better to have pictures of what are called secular subjects painted by honest workmen whose souls are touched with reverence for God's presence wherever it is found. One of the great tasks of the church today is to provide fitting pictures and symbols of the divine for the young, in architecture, music, sculpture, and painting.

The experience at Sinai was designed to instill a sense of reverence into the people's inter-

---

[2] Twelfth-century Japanese hymn. See Hastings, *Encyclopaedia of Religion and Ethics*, VII, 46.

24 And the Lord said unto him, Away, get thee down, and thou shalt come up, thou, and Aaron with thee: but let not the priests and the people break through to come up unto the Lord, lest he break forth upon them. 25 So Moses went down unto the people, and spake unto them. **20** And God spake all these words, saying,	mountain, and consecrate it.' " 24 And the Lord said to him, "Go down, and come up bringing Aaron with you; but do not let the priests and the people break through to come up to the Lord, lest he break out against them." 25 So Moses went down to the people and told them. **20** And God spoke all these words, saying,

to those priests who were not to **come near** (vs. 22) to share in the ceremony. Otherwise one must either be content with RSV's translation, **Go down and come up, bringing Aaron with you; but do not let the priests and the people . . .** or conclude with Beer (*Exodus*, p. 97) that vss. 21-25 are a badly garbled repetition.

2. The Decalogue (20:1-17)

In general all the laws in Exodus associated with Sinai, including the ordinances for the sanctuary beginning at ch. 25, are covered by **all these words** God spoke. Specifically, however, the reference is to the commandments that follow immediately. In Hebrew the Decalogue is known as "The Ten Words." In its primitive Hebrew form it consists of ten brief phrases, each only two words long. From earliest times (34:28; Deut. 4:13; 10:4) it was agreed that these were ten in number, though there was some disagreement as to how that total was arrived at. These ten words God spoke directly to the people (cf. vs. 21). Later, so that they might be preserved for instruction, Moses was summoned to the summit of the mountain to receive the tables on which they were inscribed (24:12; cf. 34:1, 27-28). God gave all other laws indirectly, through the mouth of Moses (vs. 22; 21:1; 24:3; 25:1). Those are probably the words Moses is said to have written down (24:3). For further details see Intro., pp. 842-43.

20:1. That **God spoke** or wrote laws is a metaphor for the biblical view that all true orders and laws are an expression of God's character and will. In the Bible, law is God in action.

course with God. Reverence is the indefinable attitude of body and spirit with which a noble soul responds to greatness in any form. The response of an audience to a great artist; the attitude of a patient to a great surgeon ("You delivered me from hell and have given me four happy years of life," said a sufferer to the man whose skill had been his deliverance); the silence of the formerly chattering crowd in that room in Dresden in which used to hang alone the Sistine Madonna; the anticipation of the response in the service of Holy Communion ("Minister: Lift up your hearts. People: We lift them up unto the Lord"); the affectionate murmur among the group when Jesus took a child and set him in the midst of them; the way a real gardener touches the new blossom, or a real teacher greets an original idea in a student, or the children and grandchildren surround grandma at Thanksgiving—all these are soaked with reverence, the sense that there are some things in life which are not common and unclean, but filled with wonder and glory. This

was the lesson of these ritual preparations and practices around this mount in the wilderness.

Toward the end of his life Plato published his final conviction that the divine element in the world is to be conceived as a persuasive agency and not as a coercive agency—one of the greatest intellectual discoveries ever made. Hitler, Napoleon, Alexander were great noisemakers and commanders; but what came of it?

20:1-17. The Ten Commandments.—Another version of the Ten Commandments is in Deut. 5:6-21. There are minor differences between the two accounts as well as between the translations, some of which evidently were founded on an earlier version than that in the text. A still different set of commandments is given in 34:10-29. The order of the commandments differs in different texts and versions (see Exeg.).

As we have them, the Ten Commandments are edited by the priests of later generations, yet even as originally formulated, they were not anything new, but were a deft and inspired selection edited from the great mass of moral

2 I *am* the Lḏord thy God, which have brought thee out of the land of Egypt, out of the house of bondage.

3 Thou shalt have no other gods before me.

2 "I am the Lḏord your God, who brought you out of the land of Egypt, out of the house of bondage.

3 "You shall have no other gods before[f] me.

f Or *besides*

---

2. The conviction that the law expresses God's very character is also driven home by this "formula of self-predication" (cf. Lev. 11:44-45; 19:2). Israel must be holy because God is. But by predicating the law upon God, who out of his goodness redeemed Israel from slavery (cf. 19:4-5; Hos. 13:4), the law becomes the instrument of a mutual relationship in which faith responds to love. This transforms the law into a form for expressing gratitude. The law, as the outcome of the covenant relationship, is thus itself a form of grace. This opening formula counts as the first in the Jewish ordering of "The Ten Words."

3. Yahweh is to be the only God Israel recognizes and worships. The theoretical question about the existence of other gods is not raised. It is assumed that there is only

---

and religious precepts which had gained currency among the people. They have been divided: first through fourth, religious duties; fifth through tenth, moral duties. Sometimes the fifth has been included in the religious section, as respect for parents was a matter of religion with ancient peoples (as today in China). The moral duties have been divided: the sixth through the eighth command directed against mean deeds, the ninth against mean words, the tenth against mean thoughts. The two positive commandments come together, observance of the sabbath and respect for parents, the latter being "the first commandment with promise" (Eph. 6:2); one's curiosity is aroused as to why these two only were positive when it would have been so easy to make them uniform with the others, but nobody knows the answer to that question. It has been surmised that the present form of the Ten Commandments came into being about the time of the Exile. It was impossible in exile for the people to continue to observe the ritual worship of the tabernacle, so they asked for a brief statement of the covenant which bound them to Yahweh. The Ten Commandments were the result. In spite of its brevity and simplicity, the code contains the essence of the spiritual life of Israel (see Exeg.). It is extraordinary under the circumstances that more signs of national prejudice and racial peculiarities have not remained in the code as it stands. It is so universal in its appeal that it has become a world document. Perhaps the only passage in the O.T. which excels this section (vss. 1-17) in brevity of form and breadth of spirit is Mic. 6:6-8; indeed, both might feel at home in the N.T.

An ancient rabbi teaches that all souls of all times were gathered around Sinai to hear the revelation of the law, because each generation will find new applications and new meanings for the general commandments. As stated they seem to define the duty of the citizen as an individual. But later ages wonder how far the principles laid down have not further and wider application to men's official and social duties also. The words of genius have a wider meaning than the thoughts which prompted them, and this code may forbid and command more than individual acts. The common people at least have thought so; among the placards carried in every antiwar parade there has always been one containing the Sixth Commandment; the plain language of the Seventh Commandment insists on reading itself between the lines of many a newspaper account of a new "romance," and the simple language of the Eighth Commandment has been used to describe very pretentious financial structures. The Ten Commandments are a supreme factor in the age-long process of kneading decency into the human race, an endeavor which has been going on for these many thousand years.

2. The Lord the Deliverer.—The Lord does not at this solemn moment name himself as "Creator of the universe," "Lord of the whole world," but as the liberator of Israel from the foreign yoke. It is the Spirit in history, the guiding genius of nations and individuals alike, who speaks. Yahweh chose Israel, not Israel Yahweh. God gives before he asks. He has given freedom; he now asks righteousness and worship.

3. The First Commandment.—Israel was surrounded by people who worshiped other gods. Israel must not follow this practice, but must worship Yahweh only. While originally a device for preventing the mixing of cults and the degradation of religious rites, there is profound truth in the doctrine that no man can worship more than one god. A god cannot remain a god

4 Thou shalt not make unto thee any graven image, or any likeness *of any thing* that *is* in heaven above, or that *is* in the earth beneath, or that *is* in the water under the earth:

5 Thou shalt not bow down thyself to them, nor serve them: for I the LORD thy God *am* a jealous God, visiting the iniquity of the fathers upon the children unto the third and fourth *generation* of them that hate me;

4 "You shall not make yourself a graven image, or any likeness of anything that is in heaven above, or that is in the earth beneath, or that is in the water under the earth; 5 you shall not bow down to them or serve them; for I the LORD your God am a jealous God, visiting the iniquity of the fathers upon the children to the third and the fourth generation of those who hate me,

---

one God. This has been called monolatry; it can also be described as a practical monotheism. Lutherans and Roman Catholics add vss. 4-6 to this one to make the First Commandment. Jews do the same to count the second.

4-6. These verses, which constitute the Second Commandment for most Protestants, are for the Lutherans and Roman Catholics the completion of the first. This commandment has played a very great role in the arguments denying the Mosaic origin of the Decalogue. Mowinckel (*Le décalogue* [Paris: Félix Alcan, 1927: "Études d'histoire et de philosophie religieuses"], pp. 61-62) asserted that, unlike the arguments that proceed from the Deuteronomic spirit and vocabulary of the Decalogue or from the impossibility of fitting it into the social situation of Israel under Moses, the argument that the Decalogue does not agree with the cultic forms and practices of the time of Moses and long after is decisive against its Mosaic origin. And in that argument, both for Mowinckel and others, the Second Commandment plays the major role. The substance of the argument is that as instituted by Moses, and until the seventh century, the Israelite cultus was not without representations of Yahweh that constituted images or ideals. It is maintained that not until Hosea do we meet a single prophet who was an iconoclast. The war against images began with the preaching of Hosea and is accepted as a general policy in the Deuteronomic reforms of the next century. Therefore, it is said, the prohibition of images in the Second Commandment automatically puts the Decalogue in the era of Deuteronomy.

The Hebrew word *péṣel*, which stands back of **graven image**, comes from the root meaning "to carve." Strictly and originally the word means a sculptured object. But it also became a general term for image, whether graven or molten (Isa. 30:22; 40:19; 44:10; Jer. 10:14). When used of a molten image it is always with the signification of idol (cf. LXX on this verse). Molten images are prohibited in vs. 23 and 34:17. Some-

---

worthy of worship if he has to step down occasionally from his throne to allow another god to reign for a few moments. The reason is that if the first god really were supreme, he would have included in his nature whatever was worthy of worship in the second god, and so call forth from the worshiper all that is noblest in him. There is no place for a second god.

The clearest example of what is meant by the First Commandment is that incident in Mark 5:9, where the spirit of the man possessed of devils could not give his name to the Lord, for, he said, "We are many." There must be some sort of unity in our lives, otherwise no one can depend on us. We cannot even depend on ourselves when we are in another mood, or, as the Bible puts it, when we are possessed by another devil. To worship one God is to have one

supreme loyalty in one's life which all one's instincts and passions and vagaries obey. So that, like Luther, one can stand before other principalities and powers of the outer and inner world and refuse to bow to them, saying humbly and definitely, "I can do no other," i.e., "I obey one greater than all of you." Religion must have first place in one's life, otherwise it is only pious talk.

With deep prophetic understanding A. B. Davidson, commenting in 1900 in his class on Jer. 1:10, said, "The consciousness of one God has created the consciousness of one world and one mankind."

4-6. *The Second Commandment.*—The First Commandment stresses the unity, the Second, the spirituality of God. "Let the hands or the head be at labor, thy heart ought to rest in God.

6 And showing mercy unto thousands of them that love me, and keep my commandments.

6 but showing steadfast love to thousands of those who love me and keep my commandments.

---

times this has been taken as proof that these passages are older than the Decalogue. Molten images which were of Canaanite origin were prohibited, it is said, but not graven ones, which were an indigenous development in Israel. Then, later in the Second Commandment, runs the argument, graven images were also outlawed. But in view of the fact that *pésel* can mean a molten as well as a graven image, such an argument does not finally decide the dating of the Second Commandment in relation to vss. 23 and 34:17.

We must, however, recognize that this commandment implies the prohibition of all idolatrous representations of deity. It insists on an aniconic cultus. Whether Moses instituted such a cultus is hotly debated. Those who deny that he did, insist that the ark (Num. 10:35-36; I Sam. 4:3-8), the ephod (Judg. 8:26-27; 17:4-5), teraphim (Judg. 18:14, 17-18, 20; I Sam. 15:23; 19:13, 16), and the brazen serpent (Num. 21:8-9; II Kings 18:4) constituted idols. Further, on the basis of such metaphors as "to see the face of Yahweh" (23:15, 17; 34:23-24; Deut. 16:16) and to "stroke the face of Yahweh" (23:11; I Kings 13:6; Jer. 26:19) it is insisted (cf. McNeile, *Exodus*, p. lx) that Yahweh was visibly represented at the shrine, whether on the ark or on a bull pedestal. Besides, not until Hosea are the molten images of Yahweh at Bethel, in the form of little golden bulls (I Kings 12:28), condemned.

Those who insist that Moses instituted the aniconic cultus in Israel reply to the argument of Mowinckel, McNeile, and others by saying that the objects proffered as idols were not such in their original signification. When they began to be treated as such, they were destroyed. The ark, they say, was Yahweh's empty throne (cf. Eichrodt, *Theologie des A.T.*, I, 44-51, who concludes his argument with the reminder that "no actual image of Yahweh anywhere in the Old Testament has been documented beyond dispute"). The debate has reached a stalemate. It is possible to save the rest of the Decalogue for the Mosaic period by considering this entire commandment a Deuteronomic addition. All of it after the first clause is Deuteronomic in any case.

The three divisions of the cosmos made by ancients are illustrated by **heaven, . . . earth, . . . the water under the earth.**

God is a spirit. Remember thou also art a spirit, created in his image." [8] One of the most valuable religious truths is symbolized in the fact that when one penetrates to the most secret heart of the tabernacle, to the ark of the testimony in the holy of holies, one finds that it is empty. No image or picture of Yahweh can be made. The universe is here thought of as divided into three parts: man is forbidden to portray God (*a*) as sun, moon, or stars; (*b*) as human or in the form of a beast; (*c*) as dragon or fish. Israel is almost unique among ancient nations in its religious dislike of images (yet see Exeg.). Art for these people conducted one to the portals of the sanctuary but could not penetrate the veil. It is impossible to represent the ineffable and intangible. The dislike of images may have been one reason for the lack of aesthetic feeling in a book like Exodus. Glover says that Paul passed through some of the most magnificent scenery in the world on his travels, but there is

not so much as a blade of grass in his writings. So also one looks in vain for any sense of the majesty of the desert, or of the beauty of sunrise, or of the oases, in Exodus. Perhaps there is nothing very robust in the way either of humor or aesthetics in the Bible. Its interests are in other directions, though faint indications of these qualities can be found. This commandment has been responsible for much iconoclasm in the history of the church. The souls of religious men have been scared in the presence of beauty. They have always been afraid that beauty might be mistaken for goodness, for these are twins, and so they thought it safer to kill beauty. Lately they have come to see that only the combined efforts of both twins can win young people for the life which is better than goodness and lovelier than beauty, because it is both.

The fourth generation: an early commentator adds, "There would be no fifth generation—they would all be insane." One reason for the validity of this commandment is the fact that

[8] Jacob Boehme, *The Supersensual Life*, tr. William Law (London: Allenson, n.d.), Dialogue II, p. 48.

7 Thou shalt not take the name of the LORD thy God in vain: for the LORD will not hold him guiltless that taketh his name in vain.

8 Remember the sabbath day, to keep it holy.

7 "You shall not take the name of the LORD your God in vain; for the LORD will not hold him guiltless who takes his name in vain.

8 "Remember the sabbath day, to keep it

7. The Third Commandment (second for Lutherans and Roman Catholics) deals with the use of Yahweh's name **in vain,** i.e., for that which lacks reality or truth. The name of God expresses his character and power. To call upon unreality, i.e., that which is not an expression of the divine character, by means of the divine name is to use the name **in vain.** Not only perjury but also the practice of magic, which constitutes the invocation of ultimate powers with whom God stands in conflict, and the invocation of the dead, were in all probability among the specific prohibitions implied by this commandment at its inception.

8-11. The Fourth (Third) Commandment concerns the sabbath. Next to the commandment prohibiting images (cf. vss. 4-6) this law has been used as illustration of the

God seems to show a different face to every man. Religious persecution and bigotry spring from the desire of one man to force other men to worship his god. God speaks to us all as individuals, not as a mob. He is our Father in the N.T., but a good father's relation with each one of his children is unique. One cannot make an image of God that will satisfy everybody. Until all mankind has a common eye, no one person can wholly see God.

7. The Third Commandment.—The misuse of the divine name was especially heinous among people who believed that the name was an essential part of the personality. The very naming of the name invoked the power of the whole person of whom the name was a part. The magic use of the divine name seems to have lingered on among people who were only beginning to know that true religion is more nearly related to moral action than to magic formulas. The magic use of the name was frowned upon as a part of a campaign to banish superstitious ideas and practices from the people (see Num. 23:23; I Sam. 28:9). There may be reference here also to swearing falsely by God, and to light and blasphemous use of the divine name (see Exeg.). We still are subject to both kinds of temptations, to belief in the miraculous power of sacred names (recall the comfort which the old woman told her minister she received "from that blessed word Mesopotamia"), and to the blasphemous use of holy names.

Every minister is tempted to cater to the primitive urge on the part of some in the congregation to hear over and over again certain magic formulas which seem to them to guarantee soundness of faith and comfortable doctrine. Whether the phrase is "the blood of Jesus" or "the brotherhood of man," it is merely magical

when it is used as a spell. Religion for many people consists in the good feeling aroused by the repetition of certain beloved formulas. This type of piety can be recognized by its extreme harshness in the denunciation of those who do not use them. It is not an easy type of religion for others to live with. Its sin is disobedience to the Third Commandment, which forbids the cheap and easy use of the divine name to cover up poverty of real thought and feeling.

Common cursing and swearing are due to the desire on the part of inarticulate people to impress others. The easiest way to shock another person into attention seems to be by the use of some particularly sacred and holy name. But the effect wears off almost immediately, and blasphemy simply becomes a boring habit, an expression of impotence and weakness. Special punishments are noted as coming on those who break this commandment. One may at least observe that the punishment in these cases is evident to all in the growing bigotry of the phrase-bound partisan, or the helpless apoplexy of the habitually profane.

John Bunyan tells us how he suddenly left off the habit of swearing, and adds, "Now, I could, without it, speak better and with more pleasantness than ever I could before." [4]

8-11. The Fourth Commandment.—The observance of rest days was fairly common among most primitive races. The four quarters of the moon mark an obvious division of time. The new moon and the full moon are apt to be looked upon as sacred signs. Thus a cycle of fourteen or fifteen days is established, of which

[4] W. Hale White, *John Bunyan* (New York: Charles Scribner's Sons, 1904), p. 12. For the impious use of pious formulas, see the perfect example in the letters of Deacon Snale in *The Autobiography of Mark Rutherford* (London: Hodder & Stoughton, 1913), chs. iv, vi.

9 Six days shalt thou labor, and do all thy work:

10 But the seventh day *is* the sabbath of the Lord thy God: *in it* thou shalt not do any work, thou, nor thy son, nor thy daughter, thy manservant, nor thy maidservant, nor thy cattle, nor thy stranger that *is* within thy gates:

11 For *in* six days the Lord made heaven and earth, the sea, and all that in them *is*, and rested the seventh day: wherefore the Lord blessed the sabbath day, and hallowed it.

holy. 9 Six days you shall labor, and do all your work; 10 but the seventh day is a sabbath to the Lord your God; in it you shall not do any work, you, or your son, or your daughter, your manservant, or your maidservant, or your cattle, or the sojourner who is within your gates; 11 for in six days the Lord made heaven and earth, the sea, and all that is in them, and rested the seventh day; therefore the Lord blessed the sabbath day and hallowed it.

---

non-Mosaic origin of the Decalogue. It is held that even in its briefest form this commandment could not come from the nomadic period. For nomads, it is said, there can be no regularly appointed days of rest; life is too unpredictable. Further, it has been held that not until the Exile does the sabbath become a sign of the covenant to the degree here assumed. Though it is impossible to give a final answer to these objections, two qualifications must be noted. Even as "nomads" Israelites were not wild raiders "to whom every day was alike," but a semisedentary people, as the tradition of residence at Kadesh amply illustrates. In the second place, while sabbath keeping became a fine art in the Exile and after, there is no real proof that it was not an ancient form in Israel. That it was is made more probable by the general prevalence of the sabbath in the ancient Near East.

---

the week of seven or eight days is the half. In the older parts of the Hebrew scriptures the new moon and the sabbath are almost invariably mentioned together.

Whether or not there is a long tradition behind the sacred day, the sabbath as defined in this commandment is distinctively a Jewish institution. In spite of later definitions and the adoption in Scotland and New England of the term "Christian Sabbath" for Sunday, the sacred day of the Jews has only an analogous connection with the Lord's Day of the Christians. The early leaders of the Christian church gave no sanction to the idea that Sunday was the heir of the sabbath, but in the lay mind there was always a sense of some connection between the two observances, and this feeling was legalized in A.D. 789 by Charlemagne's decree which forbade all ordinary labor on Sunday as a breach of the Fourth Commandment. The reformers of the sixteenth century definitely stated that the Fourth Commandment was abrogated by the N.T., yet human nature requires a day of rest from labor, so, they felt, we cannot do better than follow the tradition which sets apart the first day of the week for worship and rest. The result of this stand was that there was a decided slackening in Sunday observance, so that in the seventeenth and eighteenth centuries Protestantism turned back to the O.T. for authority in enforcing sabbath observance. The West-

minster Shorter Catechism, in answer to the question "How is the Sabbath to be sanctified?" reverts to the Fourth Commandment for the pattern of its answer. A vast literature has grown up around the Sunday-Sabbath question, but it is noticeable that more of the books are in English than in all other languages combined. The fact that Jesus was in his day accused of breaking the sabbath, and that he enunciated the principle that the sabbath was made for man and not man for the sabbath, should incline us to let Sunday, the Christian Lord's Day, rest on its own merits.

For the Jew the sabbath was a sign of the covenant between God and his chosen people (Ezek. 20:12, 20). The sabbath table hymn of Abraham Ibn Ezra (twelfth century) runs, "I keep the sabbath, God keeps me: a covenant eternally!" It was a day of rest in remembrance of the rest of God after the creation (Gen. 2:3; Exod. 31:17), less perhaps "that the Israelite should rest himself, than that he should give others rest." [5] It was a day of thanksgiving for the deliverance from Egypt (see also Lev. 19:34; Deut. 5:15). It was a day of sanctification (Gen. 1:31–2:3): the kiddush prescribed for use in the home on Friday evening runs in part, "For thou hast chosen us and sanctified us above all

[5] S. R. Driver in James Hastings, ed., *Dictionary of the Bible* (New York: Charles Scribner's Sons, 1902), IV, 321.

12 ¶ Honor thy father and thy mother: that thy days may be long upon the land which the LORD thy God giveth thee.

12 "Honor your father and your mother, that your days may be long in the land which the LORD your God gives you.

In Babylon the sabbath was a day of ill omen. In Israel to **keep holy** the sabbath is to separate it from other days. It affirms the rule of God in Israel's temporal affairs. The Deuteronomic version of the Decalogue differs most sharply from the Exodus form with respect to this commandment. It adds the ox and the ass (Deut. 5:14) to the list singled out to illustrate the general prohibition of activity. In vs. 11 the reason for the sabbath is that God rested at the end of the Creation (Gen. 2:2-3). This rest constituted the creation of the sabbath, which thus expresses God's own nature. In Deuteronomy the concern is not so much with the ultimate meaning of the sabbath as with its function in Israel (Deut. 5:15). It is to remind Israelites that they were once slaves and that God by his power delivered them and made them his own people. It is, in short, a weekly reminder of Passover, just as for Christians Sunday is a weekly reminder of Easter. The "humanitarian motive" in the function of the sabbath as taught in Deut. 5:15, often stressed, is at best a corollary.

12. The Fifth (Fourth) Commandment stands at the point of transition from social to civil law. The honoring of parents is a form of piety, though not a cultic observance. In Deut. 5:16 prosperity is added to the promise of length of days **in the land** offered here. Minor children were bound to strict obedience (21:15, 17; Lev. 20:9; Prov. 30:17). This commandment most especially refers to the treatment of helpless aged dependents. They are not to be sent abroad to be eaten of beasts or to die of exposure, as was the case in some societies. The possession of **the land** which **your God gives** ("is giving," "will give"—as in Deuteronomy the locus is Sinai) depends upon the maintenance of family standards.

---

nations, and in love and favor hast given us thy holy sabbath as an inheritance." It was a prophetic day, as is seen in the grace after the sabbath meal, "May the All-merciful let us inherit the day which shall be wholly a Sabbath and rest in the life everlasting." [6] This idea was reiterated in the later Christian Sunday-school hymn, "Where congregations ne'er disperse, and sabbaths have no end." [7] It was a day of joy. The Midrash to Ps. 92 reads, "Sanctify or honor the sabbath by choice meals, beautiful garments; delight your soul with pleasure and I will reward you [for this very pleasure]" (see Isa. 58:13-14). It was a day of worship, a day of special synagogue services, of the reading of the Bible and religious books. The keeping of the sabbath has always been, and with orthodox Jews still is, a mark of differentiation between them and other races among whom they live.

The list of those who are to rest on the sabbath is interesting: when mother protests that after washing, dressing, and feeding the children, getting her husband's Sunday clothes ready, preparing the Sunday dinner, and arriving at church herself nearly on time, she

[6] Simeon Singer, *Authorised Daily Prayer Book* (London: Eyre & Spottiswoode, 1916), p. 284; see Mishnah, Tamid 7:4.

[7] William Burkitt, "Jerusalem, my happy home."

objects to the minister giving out as an opening hymn "O day of rest and gladness," her attention should be called to the fact that the Fourth Commandment says nothing at all about mother resting on the sabbath. The Bible never asks for the impossible. It was to Christiana, the woman in *The Pilgrim's Progress,* that the vision was vouchsafed of the unregarded celestial crown above the toiler who was cleaning up the house.[8]

12. *The Fifth Commandment.*—Family solidarity has always been one of the characteristics of Israel. It was so much a part of the social texture of life that it would seem that no special commandment was necessary to protect parents (see 21:15, 17; Lev. 20:9; Deut. 27:16; Prov. 20:20; 30:17). To a child growing up in a Jewish home the Fifth Commandment would be as superfluous as "Thou must breathe" or "Thou must eat." Like the others in this code of laws, it is directed to the adult citizen who is burdened with the care of an aged parent, and is a warning against the heathen habit of abandoning the aged when they can no longer support themselves. The reward for such piety as is here commanded is a stable society in which health and long life can be enjoyed. Medical and surgical science have respected this

[8] Part II, ch. iii.

13 Thou shalt not kill.	13 "You shall not kill.
14 Thou shalt not commit adultery.	14 "You shall not commit adultery.

13. The Hebrew text of the Sixth (Fifth) Commandment is **You shall not kill.** This is the first of three civil provisions whose order is reversed in the LXX (on the basis of B) thus: theft, adultery, murder. Philo, Luke 18:20; Rom. 13:9 have still a different order: adultery, murder, theft, which corresponds both to the order of the LXX for the Deuteronomic form of the Decalogue and the Nash Papyrus (cf. Hos. 4:2; Jer. 7:9 for a still different order).

The commandment is concerned with the protection of human life within the community of Israel, against destruction by fellow Israelites. The verb is not limited to murder in the criminal sense and may be used of unpremeditated killing (Deut. 4:42). It forbids all killing not explicitly authorized. This means that in Israelite society it did not forbid the slaying of animals, capital punishment, or the killing of enemies in war. It had no direct bearing, either, on suicide.

14. The Seventh (Sixth) Commandment treats the family as a social unit. Its real concern is the sacredness of marriage; only by implication does it relate to the whole range of sexual morals. The verb on which the prohibition rests is used exclusively in the O.T. of marital infidelity or adultery, not of fornication.

commandment so efficiently that modern nations tend to be composed more and more of elderly people. Many proposed plans for the support of the aged are founded on an entirely literal reading of both this commandment and its promise, subtly shifting the responsibility to society and the state, a questionable proceeding needing more study.

The old Semitic proverb reads, "Let a man obey his mother and his father," the scribe mentioning the mother first. Augustine relates that when his mother importuned the good bishop for her son, he said to her at last, "Go thy way, and God bless thee, for it is not possible that the son of these tears should perish." [9]

Blood is thicker than water. The family tie was taken by Jesus as the best illustration of all deep spiritual kinship, and the incident in Matt. 12:50 means that all good people should be as dear to us as our parents. Both Judaism and Christianity are family religions.

13. The Sixth Commandment.—Since this commandment comes in the series determining the citizen's duty to his neighbor, it evidently is not in opposition to Gen. 9:3 or Deut. 20:1-4, nor perhaps relevant to I Sam. 31:4-5; II Sam. 17:23; and certainly is not meant to cancel out 21:12; etc.

A man's life is his most precious earthly possession; his right to enjoy it must be protected from idle irresponsibility which would deprive him of it for "thirty pieces of silver." Yet "I'll kill you if you don't" will always remain the final threat of a will that is balked, or as Undershaft put it in *Major Barbara,* "Nothing is ever done in this world until men are prepared to

[9] *Confessions* III. 12.

kill one another if it is not done." [1] Killing another man will probably never become completely taboo to the human race, but growing understanding begins to bring home to us the fact that retail or mass murder never accomplishes anything except to work off the irritation or fury of the moment. It has been said that the trouble with all punishments is that people like to give them. If one were to appraise the success of the Ten Commandments in attaining their object since their promulgation, perhaps this one has been the most successful of all. The respect for human life has definitely grown. It is harder to pass off murder under a respectable name than any other of the forbidden acts here noted.

14. The Seventh Commandment.—The underlying conviction is that there is a growing and eternal element in the love of a man and a woman. This relationship grows gradually in depth. The first full experience of love should be one in which both souls and bodies, the whole being, glow incandescent in mutual transfiguration. This commandment warns against yielding to the dictatorship of the body. Youth especially is apt to be impatient and greedy; it is apt to imagine that it can reiterate an experience, instead of capturing the full riches of that experience and maturing with it. Hence the chain marriages of Hollywood which never any promises fulfill. The carefree school of occasional infidelities is having a field day in the literature of the twentieth century. A good time seems to be had by all, if enough alcohol is provided to dull a deep-seated fas-

[1] Act III. See *The Complete Plays of Bernard Shaw* (London: Oldham's Press, 1934), p. 497.

15 Thou shalt not steal.	15 "You shall not steal.

15. To the sacredness of life and of the family, the Eighth (Seventh) Commandment adds the sacredness of property.

tidiousness of which human nature cannot quite rid itself even in the most advanced circles. An English magazine ran a competition in 1946 for the best new set of Ten Commandments. After reading the large number of entries, the editor had to confess that Moses still had the advantage, that he had the virtue of being concrete and brief and did not allow himself to deteriorate into mere advice. This Seventh Commandment seemed to give the competitors most trouble to revise. One question was: "Can an initial mistake in matrimony never be remedied? Must it ruin the lives of husband, wife, and children?" The true answer seems to be that in spite of the vulgarization of divorce by the spoiled children of the day, it has a place in our social life under uniform laws administered with sympathetic dignity. An exquisite Botticelli form sometimes contains a poisonous brew of egoism and greed and cruelty willing to be adored and taken care of for the rest of its life, and nothing more. Nature does not play quite fair with youth, and mistakes have to be corrected; but this commandment still stands guard over the ideal which is so often realized of true love between a man and a woman, deepening with the years, an eternal devotion, as William Blake says:

> Every little act,
> Word, work, & wish that has existed, all remaining still.
> . . . .
> For every thing exists; & not one sigh nor smile nor tear,
> One hair nor particle of dust, not one can pass away.[2]

While originally this commandment expressed the male point of view and may have meant, "My wife is my property, and is taboo to all other men," while it has been often used as a defensive device to protect the marital comfort of negligent and unfaithful husbands, yet its enunciation has been of the greatest importance in its concern for the inviolability of the home, and its general form has made it equally applicable both to men and women. It was a step in the process of humanizing nature; it is a milestone in the long and devious road that leads from the brute to the human, from Gen. 9:1 downhill to Eph. 5:12, but also up to Matt. 5:28, 32, and at last to Matt. 22:30: for the

[2] *Jerusalem,* ch. i.

body is a schoolroom in which the soul does grow, and the soul loves it so that they become one, and at the resurrection none can tell whether it is the resurrection of the body or the resurrection of the soul. Nothing is lost.

15. *The Eighth Commandment.*—This is the basic commandment on which the idea of private property rests. It is the protection which the diligent and prudent have against the idle and careless. The underlying conviction is, "I have toiled to collect these possessions, and you who have been idle must not rob me of the fruits of my industry." Over a century ago the *Plaindealer* comfortably asserted, "In a great majority of cases the possession of property is the proof of merit." [3] The human race has as a whole been sure of the validity of this principle. Yet all through human history, in each generation, there have been some who have made themselves unpopular with the ruling classes by gnawing and nibbling around the principle of the sanctity of private property. They have requested that some attention be given to the rules of the game under which this property was acquired. They have asked, "Are the rules fair?" or "Are the dice loaded which give some people such Saratoga trunks full of splendor and other equally worthy people only a beggarly bundle of sorry rags?" Horace Greeley in 1845 defined this controversy in historic words as "the everlasting class war of a portion of those who HAVE NOT against the mass of those who HAVE." [4]

Thinking men strive toward an application of this commandment which will ensure that the products of industry will be fairly divided, that the rules may ensure that each man shall have his fair share of the good things of this life. They do not limit the application of the commandment to forbidding the poor man to steal the silver candlesticks from the rich man; they pry into the question whether the superior "merit" of the few is real or imaginary, whether our economic system itself does not permit the few privileged ones continually to steal from the many life, liberty, and the pursuit of happiness. Theodore Roosevelt symbolized this effort in the slogan he invented for his Progressive Party, "Pass Prosperity Around!" One might

[3] May 13, 1837.
[4] "The Tariff Question," *American Whig Review,* II (1845), 114.

| 16 Thou shalt not bear false witness against thy neighbor. | 16 "You shall not bear false witness against your neighbor. |
| 17 Thou shalt not covet thy neighbor's house, thou shalt not covet thy neighbor's wife, nor his manservant, nor his maidservant, nor his ox, nor his ass, nor any thing that *is* thy neighbor's. | 17 "You shall not covet your neighbor's house; you shall not covet your neighbor's wife, or his manservant, or his maidservant, or his ox, or his ass, or anything that is your neighbor's." |

16. The Ninth (Eighth) Commandment sets forth the principle of the sacredness of the judicial system. The verb in the prohibition means "to answer"; i.e., at court, whether as plaintiff, defendant, or witness, a man must speak the truth in a charge involving his neighbor. The more general notions of talebearing and "character assassination" are perhaps not ruled out (23:1a), but the central concern is the integrity of the judicial system. One is reminded that in the Code of Hammurabi 1-4 the bearer of false witness was upon discovery sentenced to the punishment normal to the crime of which he had falsely accused another.

17. Lutherans and Roman Catholics treat this verse as two separate commandments. Both in the LXX for this verse and in the parallel Decalogue in Deut. 5 the wife is mentioned before the house. This is often explained as indicating a rise in the estimate

---

use the illustration of the poet and ask, Who is stealing when

> The golf links lie so near the mill
> That almost every day
> The laboring children can look out
> And see the men at play? [5]

But the possessive instinct has its limits. The stars still are in their ancient places simply because they are out of the reach of predatory human hands.

16. *The Ninth Commandment.*—The Ten Commandments have been criticized because they do not contain a prohibition against such an elementary sin as lying. But this Ninth Commandment is at least a start in the right direction. It is true that it refers specifically to evidence given in court about the conduct of a member of one's own race, but other passages in the O.T. testify to the people's understanding of the importance of truth, i.e., the agreement between language and facts (Deut. 13:14; 17:4; 22:20; Jer. 9:5; Ps. 15:2 ["in his heart," i.e., cordially, gladly]; Prov. 12:19; 14:25; 22:21). There is much to be said for starting the teaching of virtue by a simple concrete case rather than with a general principle. If a people start with this commandment, it may be possible to continue in the school of virtue till the principle of truthtelling is established in the more difficult instances that arise between buyer and seller (Prov. 20:14); but it is probably true that in the early books of the O.T. lying artistically was looked upon as something of an art

[5] From *Portraits and Protests* by Sarah N. Cleghorn. Copyright, 1917, by Henry Holt & Co., Inc. Reprinted by permission of the publishers.

which had its masterpieces. So Laban seemed to have felt about his exploit in Gen. 29:21-27; but Jacob could not very well complain if he remembered the incident related in Gen. 27:6-36, of which he and his mother were also proud.

Truthtelling has never been what might be called an endearing virtue. George Washington has gained nothing in popularity among youthful Americans by Parson Weems's story of the cherry tree: there are too many people who pride themselves on telling unpleasant truths; and there are some races who, though possessing little of this virtue, seem to have most of the other virtues and yet are delightful people! Perhaps Moses went as far as he could at the time in this commandment; the world seems still to consist of two types of people—those who believe in principles like truthtelling, and those who believe in people and lay more stress on manners and courtesy and kindness. There are still too few who unite both types in themselves and love truth and people equally well, or almost equally well. These are the men and women who know the meaning of the text "speaking the truth in love" (Eph. 4:15).

17. *The Tenth Commandment.*—The word translated house really means "household," and the rest of the commandment is an explication of the scope of that word (see Exeg.). The commandments are briefer in Hebrew than in the English translation, and in their original form were briefer still. The fact that there are no ways in English to issue sharp, short "forbiddings" may indicate certain racial characteristics in those who speak the language. The peremptory orders in the Hebrew which could be represented in English only as "No murder!"

18 ¶ And all the people saw the thunderings, and the lightnings, and the noise of the trumpet, and the mountain smoking: and when the people saw *it*, they removed, and stood afar off.	18 Now when all the people perceived the thunderings and the lightnings and the sound of the trumpet and the mountain smoking, the people were afraid and trem-

of women. Although such an interpretation is possible, what seems more probable is that "house" is here the inclusive term for all the family and possessions of a man, as is still true among the Arabs today. Some of the people and possessions included in the general term were later itemized to point up this prohibition of jealous desire. As in vs. 12, this final principle lies in the realm of sentiment, attitude, and thought. It is recognized that from this realm flow the deeds and words in the four preceding commandments.

3. The People's Fear of God (20:18-20)

This brief section continues the account of the theophany begun in ch. 19 and interrupted by the Decalogue. It is concerned with the effect of the appearance upon the people and interprets its real meaning to them.

18. The scene in 19:16-19 is summarized. The **people were afraid and trembled.** The last word is synonymous with "swaying" or "reeling." The people fell back at the

"No adultery!" "No stealing!" lose much of their force when made to read "Thou shalt not commit adultery," etc. The word translated **covet** seems to mean "indulge in thoughts which tend to lead to the actions named in the previous commandments." In the early days when the first Greek translation of the Hebrew text was made, the scholars used a word in Greek which clearly means "to set one's heart upon a thing," and Deuteronomy uses another Hebrew word which makes it doubly sure that the intention here is to prohibit grasping thoughts that lead to grasping deeds.

Some have seen a great advance in social sense illustrated in the form in which the commandments are given here and in Deuteronomy. This Tenth Commandment is a case in point. There the wife is not included as a part of the household, but is distinguished from other property both in position and by the use of a special verb (see Exeg. on Deut. 5:21). Augustine (followed by the Roman Catholics and Lutherans) unites the first two commandments into one and divides the tenth into two. This was a further recognition of the unique position of the wife. The commandment is one of the early insights into the fact that the inner life of man determines destiny. Here we step from the outer world of act and word, of crime and punishment, into the secret place where all good and all evil begin, the heart of man. The Ten Commandments were one of the early attempts to clean up that place; and that project of slum clearance has been going forward slowly ever since. Religion is in essence the keeping of good company in one's inner life, and in the

Tenth Commandment begins the search for an understanding of how to organize the powers and presences of that hidden country so as to produce good lives, peace, and brotherhood.

The inwardness of the last words of the Decalogue make them the very threshold of the N.T. There is no doubt that Jesus, in the Sermon on the Mount, had the Ten Commandments in mind. Many interesting diagrams like the following might be made:

	1. One God		Our Father (Matt. 6:9)	
Ye	2. No images		No forms needed at all (Matt. 6:7)	
have	3. No blasphemy		Hallowed be thy name (Matt. 6:9)	
heard	4. Man for the sabbath	But	The sabbath for man (Mark 2:27)	
that		I		
it was	5. Honor your parents	say	And also all good people (Matt. 12:50)	
said	6. No killing	unto	No anger (Matt. 5:22)	
by	7. No adultery	you	No lust (Matt. 5:28)	
them	8. No stealing		Give freely (Matt. 5:42)	
of old	9. No false swearing		No swearing (Matt. 5:34)	
time	10. No coveting		Covet righteousness (Matt. 5:6)	

18-20. *Religious Dread.*—So far the people had only heard terrible sounds, but no words such

19 And they said unto Moses, Speak thou with us, and we will hear: but let not God speak with us, lest we die.	bled; and they stood afar off, 19 and said to Moses, "You speak to us, and we will hear; but let not God speak to us, lest we die."
20 And Moses said unto the people, Fear not: for God is come to prove you, and that his fear may be before your faces, that ye sin not.	20 And Moses said to the people, "Do not fear; for God has come to prove you, and that the fear of him may be before your eyes, that you may not sin."
21 And the people stood afar off, and Moses drew near unto the thick darkness where God *was*.	21 And the people stood afar off, while Moses drew near to the thick cloud where

display of God's glory **and they stood afar off.** The idea of the holy, in terms of God's mystery and transcendence, pervades the scene. For this narrator awe and respect are taken as the normative mood in religion. God is holy.

19. It is here explained how Moses, at the people's request, became the mediator of the law to the people. They promise to **hear,** i.e., to obey his words. If God should speak in words, even more intimate and powerful aspects of his nature would be disclosed than are seen in the natural phenomena. In terms of speech—meaning, will, and reason— God is at once most like and most unlike man. His word is the sword of the Spirit.

20. Moses explains the terrible scene as a manifestation of God's goodness to Israel. It is another "sign" (15:25) of his power, to authenticate himself beyond doubt, so **that you may not sin.** Sin is understood as a lack of faith in God, a doubt about or denial of his reality. To have **the fear of him** is to live by faith in his power and reality. One is left with the impression that God did speak at this point and that the Decalogue must be understood as the record of his speech (Deut. 5:4).

4. THE LAWS OF THE COVENANT (20:21–23:33)

See Intro., pp. 843-44.

as those in vss. 1-17; they had bad consciences and were afraid of condemnation and punishment. Moses reassures them that the awfulness of the manifestation is intended to produce reverence, not panic: it is not designed to scare them but (in the common phrase) "to put the fear of God into them." Robert Burton thinks that morbid and dangerous conditions of mind are caused by "thundering ministers" who dwell too much in their sermons on the terrors of the divine being to sinful man.[6] Jonathan Edwards, however, seemed to approve of the use of fear as one way of keeping man from sin. It seems to us that both sin and its punishment are things to be afraid of, and that God, even to the worst sinner, is not an object of fear but rather of reverent awe and humble affection. Reinhold Niebuhr's two presuppositions of a true religion might be taken as a commentary on Exod. 20:19-21: "The first is a sense of reverence for a majesty, and of dependence upon an ultimate source of being. The second is a sense of moral obligation laid upon one from beyond oneself, and of moral unworthiness before a judge."[7]

But fear in itself is barren. Montaigne says, "It is feare I stand most in feare of."[8] It is at best only a danger signal for immature minds, a fence on the way, leading us to the real goal of human action. As expressed by Seneca, "The reward for a good deed is to have done it," and Cicero, "The fruit of a service done is in the service itself," and by Paul (as in the French translation), "Our glory is the testimony of our conscience" (II Cor. 1:12).

The "dread" which Kierkegaard felt so deeply is not mere panic: "The man who has learned the meaning of Dread has learned the highest of all things. . . . Dread is the possibility of freedom."[9] It is what Augustine meant by the restlessness of the man God has made for himself. It is the state of mind of the man who is faced with the choice between two eternities. Every instant we make that choice; and in making it we really exist, are really human.

20:21–23:33. *The Book of the Covenant.*—It is believed that this section is that referred to in 24:7 as "the book of the covenant." It is also described in 24:3 as "judgments" or "ordinances," and as "words," and in 24:4 as "the

---

[6] *Anatomy of Melancholy,* ed. Floyd Dell and Paul Jordan-Smith (New York: Tudor Publishing Co., 1948), p. 942.

[7] In a radio broadcast.

[8] *Essayes,* Bk I, ch. xviii.

[9] Quoted by T. S. Gregory, "Kierkegaard: the Prophet of Now," *The Listener,* XXXVI (1946), 718.

22 ¶ And the LORD said unto Moses, Thus thou shalt say unto the children of Israel, Ye have seen that I have talked with you from heaven.	God was. 22 And the LORD said to Moses, "Thus you shall say to the people of Israel: 'You have seen for yourselves that I have

a) TWO CULT LAWS (20:21-26)

(1) THE UNITY OF GOD (20:21-23)

21. After God had addressed the people in the words of the Decalogue Moses entered the cloud of mystery which concealed God from the people.

22. The commandments God is about to promulgate are predicated upon his own character (cf. vs. 2) which has just been authenticated by his address to the people. This verse may be an editor's recasting of the meaning of vs. 20. Its point is to motivate obedience to the laws that follow.

words of the LORD" which were written down by Moses. **Now these are the ordinances which you shall set before them** (for its details see the Exeg.). The history of the compilation of the book of the covenant would be very complicated, but a study of the document tells us much about the conditions of life in which it was codified and edited.

The main body of the book is concerned with civil justice: there are precepts of ritual law at the beginning and end. As is usual in the Pentateuch, all laws, whether ritual or secular, derive from the will of Yahweh as their source and justification. Ritual and moral precepts are in the form of direct commmands (20:24; 22:20); legal decisions are introduced by an "if" clause stating the conditions followed by the "law" on the question (see 21:2-11, where there are ten "if" clauses). The whole style is very similar to that of the ancient codes of law of other nations such as are found in Sumerian inscriptions and the remains of the laws and precepts of the Babylonians, Assyrians, and Hittites.

An interesting experiment can be made by any reader who will study the book of the covenant verse by verse and note down as he goes along the actual social conditions presupposed by each precept and ordinance. He will find that the people who recorded these decisions were not nomads or wandering tent dwellers of the desert, nor were they city folk tempted to the luxurious life which in the eighth century angered the prophets, Amos and Hosea in Israel, Isaiah and Micah in Judah. Their wealth was in cattle. The ass, the cow, and the sheep are mentioned, but not the camel or the horse, although in the nomad period camels were well known (Gen. 12:16; 24:10) and Solomon brought horses in great numbers out of Egypt (I Kings 10:28; II Chr. 9:28). In addition to the raising of cattle, the people had farms, orchards, olive yards, and vineyards. Money both of gold

and silver was in circulation. There were loans to people who needed this help, but there was no right to charge interest. People lived in villages and towns. Some were free and some were slaves. There were priests, judges, doctors, artisans, peasants, and shepherds, but there is no mention of soldiers or shopkeepers.

There is embodied in the book a great deal of sympathy for the weak and defenseless in the community—widows, orphans, the poor, and strangers. The laws about slavery are distinguished by their comparative mildness. The power of the father in his family is nearly absolute—he can sell his children into slavery. Any offense against one's parents is punished severely, even with death itself. A limit is set to the private feud, and one must be kind even to his enemy when he is in trouble.

While there are vestiges of primitive barbarism (as in the *lex talionis* [tit for tat] of 21:23-25, and the right of the master to flog male and female slaves to death provided they do not actually die under his hand), yet the book of the covenant is an attempt to improve existing conditions and advance in justice and morality. "It compares favourably with the English criminal law in the eighteenth century, and with the statutes of the slave states of America in the earlier half of the nineteenth century." [1]

At the beginning of the twentieth century there were found in Susa the pieces of a block of black diorite nearly eight feet high, containing 3,600 lines of cuneiform. The pieces were fitted together and the Code of Hammurabi (as it was discovered to be) is now in Paris. It was a monument of this great king, one of the most important personalities in the history of western Asia, the founder of the greatness of Babylonia. He has been identified with the Amraphel of Gen. 14:1. The inscription is about half the length of Exodus. At the top of one side there is carved the figure of Hammurabi receiving these

---

[1] Bennett, *Exodus*, p. 13.

23 Ye shall not make with me gods of silver, neither shall ye make unto you gods of gold.

talked with you from heaven. 23 You shall not make gods of silver to be with me, nor shall you make for yourselves gods of gold.

23. The problem in this verse is whether it prohibits gods other than Yahweh (vss. 2; 22:20; 23:13), whether it prohibits molten images (34:17), or whether it does both. The LXX interprets the verse to mean that it prohibits molten images (cf. Amer. Trans.). The RSV leaves the impression that the verse both inculcates monolatry and prohibits images. This seems nearer to the real meaning, though these two may form a single item, i.e., to make molten images would constitute transgressing the first provision. The difficult Hebrew idiom, **gods of silver to be with me,** has its Arabic counterpart in the Koranic prohibitions of polytheism (*shirk*); e.g., "Serve Allah and do not associate [share] anything with him" (4:40), or "Verily, God will not forgive that there be associated [shared] with him . . ." (4:51; cf. also 6:80, 152; 7:31 [Flügel ed.]). The unity of the Godhead must not be destroyed by associating other entities with Allah, i.e., offering them worship. Similarly, the Hebrew command לא תעשון אתי ("You must not make with me") means that no one and nothing must be associated with Yahweh. To make molten gods would mean doing just that; the last half of the verse stands in apposition to the first half.

laws from Shamash the sun-god, "the judge of heaven and earth." Both the Code of Hammurabi and the book of the covenant are expressions of the ideas of law which were common to all the Semitic nations of the time. The similarities between the two documents seem sometimes almost too marked to be accounted for simply by this common origin of popular conceptions in the two peoples. The book of the covenant may show the indirect influence of the code. Perhaps through the Canaanites the Hebrews were touched by the spirit of the Babylonian law. But the book of the covenant is by no means a slavish imitation. Conditions were entirely different. The code was formulated for a much more complicated society of city dwellers and suburbanites, where there were priests, judges, doctors, oculists, soldiers, storekeepers, tailors, seamen, innkeepers, peasants, etc., and king and court. The children of Israel seem to have taken what they could use from the code which they found among the earlier inhabitants of the land, and adopted the laws there found to a simpler way of life (yet see Intro., pp. 842-43). The covenant might be said to be the laws of the people as contrasted to the laws of the king found in the code.

The Code of Hammurabi was evidently not a mere collection of existing laws and customs from different times, but was a revision and improvement of existing laws by a man who wished to make ancient crude justice more humane and temper it with more charity. In the same way, all that we know about Moses would incline him in the same direction, toward the humanizing of ancient rough justice and the injection into savage ways of more kindliness

and mercy. His name was connected with the book of the covenant as one of the first to revise and spiritualize its contents. It probably assumed its present form *ca.* 900-800 B.C. when Lycurgus was similarly revising the laws of Sparta. The sources from which the book of the covenant grew into being are in the dim beginnings of all Semitic civilization in Babylonia and elsewhere, in the reforms instituted by many forward-looking individuals like Hammurabi, in the customs and laws of the Canaanites into whose land the Hebrews came, but perhaps most of all in the scenes implied in 18:13-26, when Moses and his colleagues "judged the people at all seasons," for these verses perhaps show how God spoke to Moses and made it literal truth to say in 24:3, "Moses . . . told the people all the words of the LORD and all the ordinances."

There is a good historical parallel in the Pilgrims' experiences, in the Mayflower Compact, and in the "Laws of the Colony of New Plymouth, 1623," the first entry in which is, "It was ordained 17 days of December Anᵒ 1623 by the court then held that all criminall facts, and also all matters of trespasses and debts betweene man and man should be tried by the verdict of twelve honest men to be impanelled by authority in forme of a jury upon their oath." [2] As in the book of the covenant, we have here an ancient human custom adopted and modified and passed on to people starting on a new way of life, to be further developed by them as experience dictates, and treasured by them as a

[2] *The Compact with the Charter and Laws of the Colony of New Plymouth* (Boston: Dutton & Wentworth, 1836), p. 28.

24 ¶ An altar of earth thou shalt make unto me, and shalt sacrifice thereon thy burnt offerings, and thy peace offerings, thy sheep, and thine oxen: in all places where I record my name I will come unto thee, and I will bless thee.

25 And if thou wilt make me an altar of stone, thou shalt not build it of hewn stone: for if thou lift up thy tool upon it, thou hast polluted it.

24 An altar of earth you shall make for me and sacrifice on it your burnt offerings and your peace offerings, your sheep and your oxen; in every place where I cause my name to be remembered I will come to you and bless you. 25 And if you make me an altar of stone, you shall not build it of hewn stones; for if you wield your tool upon it

---

(2) THE ALTAR (20:24-26)

24. The simplest and most traditional was the **altar of earth** under the open sky. No altar is here singled out for special honor. The presupposition is that people sacrifice as families or clans **in every place** in which they are located. The **place** is roughly the equivalent of the high places (cf. I Sam. 9:13). The head of the clan, or perhaps a priest, is the officiant. Two sacrifices are specified: the *'ôlāh* or "burnt offering" in which the victim is entirely burned on the altar in an act of homage to God; and the *shélem* or "peace offering" which is a festival meal that seals the ties of brotherhood within the group and between the group and God.

25. An altar of unchiseled stones is also permitted (cf. Josh. 8:30; I Kings 18:31). It seems that the demand of this law was never forgotten (Deut. 27:5-6; I Macc. 4:47) though the fact that later altars had horns (I Kings 1:50-51) and the description of elaborate altars in 27:1-8; Ezek. 43:13-17, show that Israel found ways of circumventing the ancient rudeness!

---

national heritage, as is seen in references to the jury system in the Declaration of Independence, and in the third article of the Constitution of the United States. Most of the verses of the book of the covenant have equally long histories before and after their insertion.

24-26. *The Impulse to Localize God.*—As is seen in Gen. 28:16, "Surely the LORD is in this place," the idea of the omnipresence of God was not yet a part of the religious faith of the time. Far more real to these people was the certainty that God was mysteriously present in certain special places. The altar was in ancient days the home of the Godhead, where God received his worshipers as his guests, as his children, and as petitioners for his favor. The wishing-well of later folklore continued the idea of a place where longing and petition had special validity and power. Here the Israelites are urged to erect many such altars. They can be made of earth or of unhewn stone. It was perhaps for such an altar that Naaman wanted his two mules' burden of earth (II Kings 5:17). It is generally believed that the prohibition against hewing the stones sprang from a feeling that the deity was driven out of the stone by the blows of a tool (see vs. 4; Gen. 28:22; 31:46; I Kings 18:31-32 and 6:7, where a compromise was made by having the hewing done in the quarry).

No steps were permitted on these open-air altars. The reasons of modesty given may also lie at the root of the priestly garb throughout the ages. A Princeton theological professor used to express the same idea in other words when he urged his students to wear a gown in the pulpit, and quoted the last clause in Ps. 147:10; a vestment is not an expression of the personality of the wearer, but of the fact that he speaks not as an individual but as a divine messenger. Only the two most lofty sacrifices are mentioned: the burnt offering dedicated entirely to the god, and the peace offering, of which the god has his generous part but the balance of which serves as a happy meal for the participants. The first is an expression of the worshiper's sense of God's majesty, the second of the brotherhood which exists between God and his people and among the people themselves. That there were already signs of denominational differences in ritual can be seen by the fact that Solomon's altars did not conform to these regulations, but were heretical, being made of gold and brass (I Kings 7:48; 8:64; see also Isa. 65:3; Exod. 27:1). The idea that God is especially near one in certain places corresponds with something very deep in human experience. We lose something when there is no "sacred place" in our home or our town or our country. Children and grandchildren revere the little trail in the woods leading

26 Neither shalt thou go up by steps unto mine altar, that thy nakedness be not discovered thereon.

21 Now these *are* the judgments which thou shalt set before them.

2 If thou buy a Hebrew servant, six years he shall serve: and in the seventh he shall go out free for nothing.

you profane it. 26 And you shall not go up by steps to my altar, that your nakedness be not exposed on it.'

21 "Now these are the ordinances which you shall set before them. 2 When you buy a Hebrew slave, he shall serve six years, and in the seventh he shall

---

26. In 28:42 the priestly dress is designed to overcome this objection to altar steps. The provision presupposed that the officiant was the head of a household wearing a short skirt. The altar in Ezekiel (43:17) was provided with steps, but the altar of Herod was approached by an incline, out of respect to the ancient ruling (McNeile, *Exodus,* p. 125).

b) THE SOCIAL CODE (21:1–23:19)
(1) TITLE (21:1)

21:1. This ostensibly continues the audience begun in 20:22. The ordinances intended to be covered by the heading run through 23:19, even though perhaps originally 21:2–22:17 was an independent unit. **Ordinances** in this context must be understood as normative precedents, case law.

(2) CIVIL AND CRIMINAL LAWS (21:2–22:17)
(a) THE ISRAELITE SLAVE (21:2-11)

2. **When you buy a Hebrew slave:** This law does not deal with foreigners, such as prisoners of war, who have been made slaves for life, or with their children, or the sale of either. The concern is with the male slave. Because of need he may have sold himself as a slave (Lev. 25:39); he may have been claimed in payment for a debt (II Kings 4:1); or he may have been sold by his parents because of their need for money (Neh. 5:2). The value of such a six-year slave was thirty shekels (vs. 32). The term of a slave (**he shall serve six years**) is twice the length of a slave's term in ancient Babylonia (Code of Hammurabi 117). In most other respects greater humaneness is shown the Israelite slave. It has been suggested that the phrase "double the hire of a hireling" (Deut. 15:18) reflects a knowledge of the three-year rule for slaves in Babylonia. Before a slave's term was up he could be redeemed by purchase. If he were seriously injured he would also get his freedom (vss. 26-27). Later, no matter how briefly he had served, the year of jubilee would, if taken seriously, have given a slave his freedom (Isaac Mendelsohn, *Slavery in the Ancient Near East* [New York: Oxford University Press, 1949], p. 85).

---

to the spot where "father used to go to see the sunset"; a lovely shrine in a church attracts worshipers from all denominations; one cannot visit the Adams Monument in Rock Creek Cemetery, Washington, rain or shine, summer or winter, without being likely to find two or three other people who have likewise come to stay there for fifteen quiet minutes out of this world.

21:1-11. *Slavery.*—The institution of slavery is of incalculable antiquity, as is seen by the regulations about its abuses both in the Code of Hammurabi and in the book of the covenant. Mankind has always had a bad conscience about it, and many of the earliest historical references

to it are attempts to mitigate its admitted evils. Both Greek and Roman civilizations were founded on the implied presence in the body politic of masses of slaves to do the menial work. Both Christianity and Islam for centuries accepted slavery as an inevitable condition of civilized society. Slavery was earnestly discussed by the framers of the Constitution of the United States, but in the end any reference to it was consciously omitted from that document, and Congress was prohibited from abolishing the slave trade for twenty years. The abolition of slavery in British dominions in 1833 was largely the work of humanitarians like Wilberforce, and the Thirteenth Amendment to the Consti-

3 If he came in by himself, he shall go out by himself: if he were married, then his wife shall go out with him.

4 If his master have given him a wife, and she have borne him sons or daughters; the wife and her children shall be her master's, and he shall go out by himself.

5 And if the servant shall plainly say, I love my master, my wife, and my children; I will not go out free:

6 Then his master shall bring him unto the judges; he shall also bring him to the door, or unto the doorpost; and his master shall bore his ear through with an awl; and he shall serve him for ever.

7 ¶ And if a man sell his daughter to be a maidservant, she shall not go out as the menservants do.

go out free, for nothing. 3 If he comes in single, he shall go out single; if he comes in married, then his wife shall go out with him. 4 If his master gives him a wife and she bears him sons or daughters, the wife and her children shall be her master's and he shall go out alone. 5 But if the slave plainly says, 'I love my master, my wife, and my children; I will not go out free,' 6 then his master shall bring him to God, and he shall bring him to the door or the doorpost; and his master shall bore his ear through with an awl; and he shall serve him for life.

7 "When a man sells his daughter as a slave, she shall not go out as the male slaves

3. At the end of his term or, however freed, upon regaining his freedom the slave's status was that of his situation before enslavement. If he had a family at the time of enslavement, his master no longer had a claim upon it. Deut. 15:13-14 adds that the freed slave must be fitted out with gifts of cattle, grain, and wine.

4. A master might give a female slave (but not of the class discussed in vss. 7-11) to a single slave as wife. But on the completion of the slave's six-year term, this wife and the children remained the possession of the master. **He shall go out alone.**

5-6. If, under such circumstances, a man prefers to maintain his family in slavery rather than to leave them and **to go out free** he may voluntarily take a vow of perpetual slavery. It seems that a master was obligated to honor such a request. He must **bring him to God,** i.e., to the altar and shrine of the family or clan. The mutual obligation, witnessed by deity, was marked by boring a hole through the slave's ear with an awl as a mark of his perpetual slavery. This is the only knowledge we have of the marking of Hebrew slaves. In ancient Babylonia slaves had the hair cut in a prescribed manner (Code of Hammurabi 226); and a slave who denied his master had his ear cut off (Code of Hammurabi 282). The boring took place at **the door or the doorpost.** We are reminded that this was the place which originally was the locus of the Passover sacrifice (12:22). The rite of the boring of the ear is domestic and social at the same time.

7. If an Israelite in financial straits **sells his daughter as a slave, she shall not go out as the male slaves do,** i.e., she shall not serve for a period of six years or any other

tution was passed in 1865; yet the League of Nations in 1926 was still engaged in the work of abolishing slavery.

The RSV gives a clear account of these early attempts to humanize and regulate slavery among the Hebrews. The more advanced regulations in Deut. 15:12-18 testify to even greater moral sensitiveness at the time of the close of the monarchy (see also Lev. 25:39-41, and Exeg. on Jer. 34:8-22 for a case which suggests that these regulations had become something of a dead letter in Israel). Man always shies at the difficulties of abolishing a settled evil institution like slavery or war, and tries for centuries rather to humanize it and mitigate its evils, all in vain,

till at last it dawns upon him that the essence of such institutions is inhumanity.

In these times there was no such thing as free labor in the modern sense. Menservants and maidservants were the property of their master. But it must be remembered that freeborn wives and children were also legally under the power of the master of the house. He could sell his children to another Israelite just as well as his slaves. Once admit that one man can "own" another and it becomes apparent that these laws tried to minimize the degradation in the relation of slave to master; the slaves were looked upon as members of the family. Slavery probably started in the human race as a result of

8 If she please not her master, who hath betrothed her to himself, then shall he let her be redeemed: to sell her unto a strange nation he shall have no power, seeing he hath dealt deceitfully with her.

9 And if he have betrothed her unto his son, he shall deal with her after the manner of daughters.

10 If he take him another *wife,* her food, her raiment, and her duty of marriage, shall he not diminish.

11 And if he do not these three unto her, then shall she go out free without money.

12 ¶ He that smiteth a man, so that he die, shall be surely put to death.

do. **8** If she does not please her master, who has designated her for himself,ᵍ then he shall let her be redeemed; he shall have no right to sell her to a foreign people, since he has dealt faithlessly with her. **9** If he designates her for his son, he shall deal with her as with a daughter. **10** If he takes another wife to himself, he shall not diminish her food, her clothing, or her marital rights. **11** And if he does not do these three things for her, she shall go out for nothing, without payment of money.

12 "Whoever strikes a man so that he

ᵍ Another reading is *so that he has not designated her*

---

specified time. She shall become a concubine and have the protection due a concubine. In Deut. 15:12, 17 this prohibition of holding female slaves on the same conditions as male slaves seems to be modified. The term here translated **slave** (אמה) means concubine in 23:12; Gen. 20:17; 21:12; Judg. 9:18; 19:19.

8. If a master decides not to take as a concubine a girl whom he purchased on the assumption that he would, **he has dealt faithlessly with her.** He must **let her be redeemed,** i.e., she may become the concubine of another Israelite, with the privileges implied in the original purchase; she may not be sold to a foreigner (*nokhrî*). In Babylonia a husband's concubine could be sold even after she had borne him children (Code of Hammurabi 119).

9. If the purchaser of a girl decides he does not want her as a concubine, or from the first **designates her for his son,** she must be married to the son of a free woman, i.e., she shall be the son's wife, not his concubine; her purchaser must deal with the girl **as with a daughter.**

10. In case a man has a slave concubine and then takes another woman, whether concubine or wife (the Hebrew text simply says "another"), he may not deny her the rights guaranteed in the original agreement. These rights are specified.

11. It is often felt that **these three things** are synonymous with the three rights of the concubine specified in vs. 10. But it seems more sound to treat this statement as a summary of the ways in which a householder may dispose of a girl he purchases: (*a*) He may take her as a concubine (this is assumed to have been done in vs. 10); (*b*) he may permit another Israelite to take her as wife or concubine, **let her be redeemed** (vs. 8); or (*c*) he may give her to his son as wife (vs. 9). **If he does not do these three things for her,** she shall be free, **without payment of money,** i.e., she need not be redeemed.

(b) Capital Offenses (21:12-17)

12. The murderer must die; this is the basic law in terms of which all variations and exceptions must be justified. Its principle is the *lex talionis* (vss. 23-25). This same

---

victory and defeat in war. The slaves of another race did not have as great privileges as the Hebrew slave (see Exeg.). For the position attained by slaves, see I Sam. 9:6 ff., where Saul is indebted to a slave for information and for a loan; I Sam. 25:11 ff., where Abigail follows the advice of a slave rather than that of the master; Gen. 24:1 ff., where Eliezer is almost Isaac's guardian; I Chr. 2:34 ff., where a slave could

marry the daughter of the house, and in Gen. 15:2 ff. become the heir. The fact that slaves were circumcised (Gen. 17:12) and partook in family worship (Deut. 12:18) made them brothers in the faith.

12-17. *Capital Punishment.*—These verses list crimes punishable by death. In Israel stoning was the usual method, though other forms of capital punishment are mentioned. The sentence

13 And if a man lie not in wait, but God deliver *him* into his hand; then I will appoint thee a place whither he shall flee.

14 But if a man come presumptuously upon his neighbor, to slay him with guile; thou shalt take him from mine altar, that he may die.

dies shall be put to death. 13 But if he did not lie in wait for him, but God let him fall into his hand, then I will appoint for you a place to which he may flee. 14 But if a man willfully attacks another to kill him treacherously, you shall take him from my altar, that he may die.

---

principle underlies the Code of Hammurabi, in which the first paragraph implies the death penalty for murder.

13. As in the Code of Hammurabi (206-7) and in the Hittite Laws (I. 1-5) a distinction is made in Israel between intentional and unintentional manslaughter. Unintentional killing is described by **but God let him fall into his hand.** No *Moîra* or *Fatum* beyond God is made responsible for accidents. However inexplicably, accidents play a part in the divine intention. The words **let him fall** imply no satisfaction on the part of the slayer; they describe a chance occurrence. **I will appoint for you a place** refers to the asylum for the unintentional killer. Perhaps originally every altar was such a place of safety, where the "avenger of blood" could not touch him. Later, when the cultus was centralized in Jerusalem and local altars lost their sacred character, secularized places of asylum were appointed (Deut. 4:41; 19:1-13; Num. 35:12). The need for a place of asylum shows that the ancient custom of the blood feud, in which the "avenger" wrought the retribution for murder, had not disappeared and that there was no sure "police protection" everywhere available for the murderer awaiting trial. The Code of Hammurabi does not have the provision for asylum; it was perhaps not needed in ancient Babylonian society.

14. It is assumed that every slayer, also the murderer, will seek the refuge of the altar. In every case the guilt or innocence of the individual will have to be established by legal procedure. The elders of the slayer's community constitute the court (Deut. 21:1-9; I Kings 21:8 ff.). When the person is found guilty of murder he is removed from the sacred area, taken **from my altar,** to be executed (cf. I Kings 2:28-34). The normal form of execution was stoning. The slayer not guilty of intentional killing in all probability paid a redemption fine for the person whose death he had caused (cf. vs. 30).

---

was carried out by "the avengers of blood," the kinsfolk of the victim. Murder or accidental homicide are the only two types of killing treated. The idea that a murderer must forfeit his own life is one of the oldest convictions of the human race. The elders of the town or village where the murderer lived must investigate the crime. The idea of criminal solidarity exemplified in 20:5 made it necessary for the town to clear itself of guilt by convicting and executing the offender. This conception is capable of modern applications to the criminal actions of "the kids of Dead End," the slum dwellers to whom the community has never given a chance of decent living. In the earliest times the execution of the murderer was a peace offering made to the restless unsatisfied soul of the dead man. This idea still underlies popular conceptions of capital punishment. "Something must be done to make it right." "We owe it to our dead friend to kill his murderer." However, the ill effects of capital punishment upon those who carry it out and upon the community at

large seem to many in modern times to outweigh the satisfaction felt by many people that the criminal has got his due, and thus the public is safeguarded from his further crimes. There are those who hold that capital punishment will fade out of human folkways progressively as communities become unwilling to do the deed and other ways of reforming the criminal are perfected.

13. *The Place of Refuge.*—The right of asylum, afterwards restricted to six specified cities (Deut. 4:41 ff.; 19:1 ff.), was a necessary precaution where the blood feud was apt to result in lynchings. By such means a chance was given for an orderly trial. Hammurabi lived in a society from which the blood feud had disappeared, and his code knows nothing of the right of asylum. There are today parts of the civilized world which are in a more barbaric condition than society in the times of Moses, where no asylum exists for the victims of the most degraded of blood feuds, that founded **on race** prejudice.

15 ¶ And he that smiteth his father, or his mother, shall be surely put to death.	15 "Whoever strikes his father or his mother shall be put to death.
16 ¶ And he that stealeth a man, and selleth him, or if he be found in his hand, he shall surely be put to death.	16 "Whoever steals a man, whether he sells him or is found in possession of him, shall be put to death.
17 ¶ And he that curseth his father, or his mother, shall surely be put to death.	17 "Whoever curses his father or his mother shall be put to death.
18 ¶ And if men strive together, and one smite another with a stone, or with *his* fist, and he die not, but keepeth *his* bed:	18 "When men quarrel and one strikes the other with a stone or with his fist and the man does not die but keeps his bed,

15, 17. The striking and cursing of parents are put on the same level; a crime in words is as serious as one in deed. This reflects the effectiveness associated with the oath. Death is the punishment in both instances. The death sentence, meted out in both cases, bespeaks the respect for parents inculcated in Israelite society. The central point of this law is that children must obey their parents, as the Deuteronomic expansion of it makes clear (Deut. 21:18-21). In ancient Babylonian society a crime of this type was punished symbolically by cutting off the hand that had struck the parent (Code of Hammurabi 195). It is possible that this symbolic pattern was also at some stages followed in Israel with those who cursed parents (Deut. 27:16). The father and mother are accorded the same status in claiming obedience of children.

16. Manstealing and kidnaping, as well as the sale into slavery of those abducted, were capital offenses. This was also true in the ancient Babylonian code which, however, concentrates on kidnaping (Code of Hammurabi 14). Deut. 24:7 specifies that this penalty applies to the abduction of Israelites.

(c) Noncapital Crimes (21:18-32)

18-19. The one who injures another in a quarrel must compensate the injured man for his loss of time and also have him **thoroughly healed,** i.e., pay his medical expenses. The question of whether the blow was delivered with the intention to kill is not raised.

16. *Kidnaping.*—The modern counterpart of this verse is kidnaping and holding for a ransom; the inhumanity and cruelty of the crime seem almost to merit the severity of the punishment here prescribed. It is still today one of the most highly punishable felonies, and always raises terrific public resentment, as in the cases of Charley Ross in 1874 and Charles A. Lindbergh's son in 1932 (see Gen. 37:26 ff.).

17. *The Penalty of Filial Disrespect.*—The severity of the punishment for him who **curses his father or his mother** illustrates the dignity of the status of parent (20:12). The word "to curse" in Hebrew means to make light, reduce the power of, and the word "to honor" means to give weight to, to augment the power of. Cursing, for the ancients, was possessed of real power. Modern life has substituted for it the power of belittlement, as can be seen if one studies the popular stories told about (say) the presidents of the United States in their lifetime. Hammurabi says the hand with which the son struck his parent must be cut off (for the same idea see Prov. 20:20 [RSV]; 30:17). The "General Laws and Liberties of New Plimouth

Colony, published in 1671," read: "If any Childe or Children above sixteen years old, and of competent Understanding, shall Curse or Smite their Natural Father or Mother; he or they shall be put to Death, unless it can be sufficiently testified that the Parents have been very Unchristianly negligent in the Education of such Children, or so provoked them by extreme and cruel Correction, that they have been forced thereunto, to preserve themselves from Death or Maiming." [3] Human progress is very slow, as is seen by the thousands of years it seems to have taken from the time of Moses to the time of the Pilgrim Fathers to exempt children under sixteen from this penalty and introduce the last "unlesses."

18-19. *Payment for the Loss of Time.*—The just and merciful arrangement of payment for doctor and loss of time (Hammurabi also includes doctor's fee) is the beginning of a long social development leading ultimately to insurance societies, workmen's compensation acts, and compulsory insurance regulations. Cain (Gen. 4:9) asked the question which started it all, and

[3] Ch. ii, sec. 13. See *Compact and Laws of New Plymouth,* p. 245.

19 If he rise again, and walk abroad upon his staff, then shall he that smote *him* be quit: only he shall pay *for* the loss of his time, and shall cause *him* to be thoroughly healed.

20 ¶ And if a man smite his servant, or his maid, with a rod, and he die under his hand; he shall be surely punished.

21 Notwithstanding, if he continue a day or two, he shall not be punished: for he *is* his money.

22 ¶ If men strive, and hurt a woman with child, so that her fruit depart *from her,* and yet no mischief follow: he shall be surely punished, according as the woman's husband will lay upon him; and he shall pay as the judges *determine.*

19 then if the man rises again and walks abroad with his staff, he that struck him shall be clear; only he shall pay for the loss of his time, and shall have him thoroughly healed.

20 "When a man strikes his slave, male or female, with a rod and the slave dies under his hand, he shall be punished. 21 But if the slave survives a day or two, he is not to be punished; for the slave is his money.

22 "When men strive together, and hurt a woman with child, so that there is a miscarriage, and yet no harm follows, the one who hurt her shall[h] be fined, according as the woman's husband shall lay upon him; and he shall pay as the judges determine.

[h] Heb *he shall*

In the ancient Babylonian code the victim had to take an oath that he did not strike with intent to kill and pay the physician's fee (Code of Hammurabi 206), a fee which was stipulated by state law and varied accordingly to the social class of the patient. Should the patient die a fine would also be imposed. The Hittite Laws (I. 10) assign medical costs to the assailant and in addition put levies upon him to compensate for time lost and for pain endured.

20-21, 26-27. The laws governing the corporal injuring of slaves show the effect of resting on two irreconcilable postulates, i.e., that the slave is a human being, and that he is another man's property. If a master strikes a slave so that the latter **dies under his hand,** he must be punished for destroying a human life, probably by paying a fine. If, however, the slave **survives a day or two** and then dies, there is no punishment. The loss of property by death is equal to the fine to fit the crime!

Destroying a slave's eye or breaking his teeth also constitutes an injury that draws a fine equal to the slave's value. Hence, the slave is set free. In Babylonia if a third party struck a slave, causing similar injuries, a fine was paid to the owner of the slave (Code of Hammurabi 199).

22. The men fighting might presumably **hurt a woman with child** while she was making an effort to separate them (Deut. 25:11). If the woman does not lose her life as a result of the miscarriage there shall be a fine to compensate for the loss of the unborn

society is not yet sure of the scope of the real answer.

20-21. *Ancient Severity and Gradual Humaneness.*—In respect of striking there was a great difference between the status of the freeman and the slave. But vss. 20-21 and 26-27 must be read with the understanding that they were mitigations of the more primitive customs which gave the master absolute power of life and death over his slaves. They probably went as far as public opinion at that time would stand; more merciful laws would not have been obeyed, as they would have been thought to undermine the master's power too radically. The rod was believed in those times to be necessary to enforce discipline and obedience (Prov. 10:13; 13:24). If the slave dies as he is being flogged the master

must be punished, but not by death, as no master could deliberately plan to destroy his own property; in fact, if the slave did not actually die in the flogging but survived for a day or so, then the loss of his slave was deemed sufficient punishment for the master. If bodily injury resulted, the loss of an eye or a tooth, then the principle of tit for tat (vss. 23-25) did not apply as he was only a slave; but instead, the slave should receive his freedom (vss. 26-27). These laws were more humane than even those of Hammurabi.

22-25. *Eye for Eye, Tooth for Tooth.*—This *lex talionis* is inserted as a quotation from still more ancient codifications of the laws of the people. It was a universal principle with all the nations bordering on the Mediterranean Sea,

23 And if *any* mischief follow, then thou shalt give life for life,

24 Eye for eye, tooth for tooth, hand for hand, foot for foot,

25 Burning for burning, wound for wound, stripe for stripe.

26 ¶ And if a man smite the eye of his servant, or the eye of his maid, that it perish; he shall let him go free for his eye's sake.

27 And if he smite out his manservant's tooth, or his maidservant's tooth; he shall let him go free for his tooth's sake.

28 ¶ If an ox gore a man or a woman, that they die: then the ox shall be surely stoned, and his flesh shall not be eaten; but the owner of the ox *shall be* quit.

29 But if the ox were wont to push with his horn in time past, and it hath been testified to his owner, and he hath not kept him in, but that he hath killed a man or a

23 If any harm follows, then you shall give life for life, 24 eye for eye, tooth for tooth, hand for hand, foot for foot, 25 burn for burn, wound for wound, stripe for stripe.

26 "When a man strikes the eye of his slave, male or female, and destroys it, he shall let the slave go free for the eye's sake. 27 If he knocks out the tooth of his slave, male or female, he shall let the slave go free for the tooth's sake.

28 "When an ox gores a man or a woman to death, the ox shall be stoned, and its flesh shall not be eaten; but the owner of the ox shall be clear. 29 But if the ox has been accustomed to gore in the past, and its owner has been warned but has not kept it in,

child. The amount of the fine is set by the husband. **As the judges determine** renders the Hebrew word בפללים, which some scholars, following Budde, conjecturally emend to בנפלים, "for the miscarriage." But it does not seem meaningless to read the text as it stands and think of the judges as passing on the fairness of the demand made by the husband (cf. vs. 30).

23-25. This classic statement of the *lex talionis,* repeated in Lev. 24:19-20 and Deut. 19:21, is presented as the continuation of the case of miscarriage through injury by means of the phrase **if any harm follows** (cf. vs. 22). Beer (*Exodus,* p. 111), however, thinks it should follow vss. 18-19 on the ground that, while the former makes provisions for atonement for temporary damages, this statement relates to permanent injuries that cannot be healed except by retaliation. That the wicked must suffer for his deeds is the assumption underlying the law. The principle is widely held in ancient society, notably in the Code of Hammurabi.

26-27. See Exeg. on vss. 20-21, 26-27, p. 999.

28. The owner of cattle is responsible for the injury they may inflict upon human beings. In the Code of Hammurabi (250-52) the ox is also used to illustrate this principle. The injury such an animal may cause constitutes a crime only if its owner is proved guilty of "criminal negligence." If the animal, having no record of meanness, gores a person to death, it must **be stoned, and its flesh must not be eaten.** The flesh of the animal has acquired the taboo of bloodguilt and must therefore not be touched; the pattern for the treatment of guilt in human beings is applied to the animal.

29. **But if the ox has been accustomed to gore,** the owner would be guilty of gross negligence and of murdering the person the ox has killed. He is subject to the death penalty.

and represents a step toward the humanizing of acts of revenge, limiting them to tit for tat, no more. It is curious that the principle that the bad must be punished for his badness is much older than the idea that the good must be rewarded for his goodness. This is perhaps due to an early conviction that badness is abnormal, that goodness is just normality and takes care

of itself (Lev. 24:19 ff.; Deut. 19:21; Matt. 5:38 ff.) .

26-27. See Expos. on vss. 20-21.

28-36. *Indirect Responsibility.*—The ox was looked upon as a murderer and its flesh was unclean (Gen. 9:5; see Arthur Train, "The Dog Andrew" in *Mr. Tutt's Case Book* [4]) . The

[4] New York: Charles Scribner's Sons, 1936, pp. 174-200.

woman; the ox shall be stoned, and his owner also shall be put to death.

30 If there be laid on him a sum of money, then he shall give for the ransom of his life whatsoever is laid upon him.

31 Whether he have gored a son, or have gored a daughter, according to this judgment shall it be done unto him.

32 If the ox shall push a manservant or a maidservant; he shall give unto their master thirty shekels of silver, and the ox shall be stoned.

33 ¶ And if a man shall open a pit, or if a man shall dig a pit, and not cover it, and an ox or an ass fall therein;

34 The owner of the pit shall make *it* good, *and* give money unto the owner of them; and the dead *beast* shall be his.

35 ¶ And if one man's ox hurt another's, that he die; then they shall sell the live ox, and divide the money of it; and the dead *ox* also they shall divide.

and it kills a man or a woman, the ox shall be stoned, and its owner also shall be put to death. 30 If a ransom is laid on him, then he shall give for the redemption of his life whatever is laid upon him. 31 If it gores a man's son or daughter, he shall be dealt with according to this same rule. 32 If the ox gores a slave, male or female, the owner shall give to their master thirty shekels of silver, and the ox shall be stoned.

33 "When a man leaves a pit open, or when a man digs a pit and does not cover it, and an ox or an ass falls into it, 34 the owner of the pit shall make it good; he shall give money to its owner, and the dead beast shall be his.

35 "When one man's ox hurts another's, so that it dies, then they shall sell the live ox and divide the price of it; and the dead

---

30. He may pay for his life by means of a ransom, the sum of which is set by the next of kin of the slain man under proper legal controls (cf. vs. 22) .

31. If the ox has killed minors the case must also be settled **according to this same rule,** the death penalty with an implicit recommendation for substitution by ransom payments.

32. The owner of a slave killed by an ox is to be compensated for his slave according to the market price for a slave. The same holds true in the Code of Hammurabi. The slave is treated as property; but the stoning of the ox (cf. vs. 28) reminds one that he is also a human being.

(d) LAWS SECURING PROPERTY RIGHTS (21:33–22:17 [Hebrew 16])

33-34. Pits might be either cisterns or wells; animals would be killed by the fall. The provision that **the owner of the pit shall make it good** probably refers to the earlier custom of providing a substitute animal. This was later changed to a money payment. For a time, no doubt, the owner had the option to decide the manner of restitution. The dead carcass was now the property of the man who had paid for his neglect. He could use the hide. Perhaps in ancient times the meat was eaten, but with the rise of laws forbidding the eating of blood this was afterward no longer possible. In Deut. 14:21 sojourners in Israel still seem to be outside the law respecting dead animals.

35-36. If an ox kills another ox, the two owners must equally bear the loss. Only if the owner of the ox that killed the other has been guilty of negligence is he alone responsible for all the damage.

---

owner, if he had been careless, was not included in the list of criminals punishable by death, as apparently the usual custom was to pay a ransom for his life (vs. 30) . The animals that kill men today are not oxen but tiny organisms, germs of disease. If the possessors of these are careless in spreading them around, they too should be put to death, or charged a very high ransom.

The tempo, the customs, the scale of life have changed, but the same essential dangers exist unchanged, to be met by the same justice and foresight and magnanimity.

In law and morals one of the early truths recognized was that it is a man's responsibility to take care that his acts and example do not dig pits (vs. 33) into which the innocent may fall

36 Or if it be known that the ox hath used to push in time past, and his owner hath not kept him in; he shall surely pay ox for ox; and the dead shall be his own.

22 If a man shall steal an ox, or a sheep, and kill it, or sell it; he shall restore five oxen for an ox, and four sheep for a sheep.

2 ¶ If a thief be found breaking up, and be smitten that he die, *there shall* no blood *be shed* for him.

3 If the sun be risen upon him, *there shall be* blood *shed* for him; *for* he should make full restitution: if he have nothing, then he shall be sold for his theft.

4 If the theft be certainly found in his hand alive, whether it be ox, or ass, or sheep; he shall restore double.

beast also they shall divide. **36** Or if it is known that the ox has been accustomed to gore in the past, and its owner has not kept it in, he shall pay ox for ox, and the dead beast shall be his.

22 *i* "If a man steals an ox or a sheep, and kills it or sells it, he shall pay five oxen for an ox, and four sheep for a sheep. *j*He shall make restitution; if he has nothing, then he shall be sold for his theft. **4** If the stolen beast is found alive in his possession, whether it is an ox or an ass or a sheep, he shall pay double.

2ᵏ "If a thief is found breaking in, and is struck so that he dies, there shall be no bloodguilt for him; **3a** but if the sun has risen upon him, there shall be bloodguilt for him.

i Ch 21. 37 in Heb
j Restoring verses 3b and 4 to their place immediately following verse 1
k Ch 22. 1 in Heb

22:1-4. These verses constitute a section on the thief. Vss. 1, 3*b*, 4 provide for restitution of and penalites for stolen animals. Vss. 2-3*a* discuss the right of an owner to slay the thief whom he discovers in the act of stealing his property.

1 (Hebrew 21:37). The penalties for stealing an ox or sheep are determined by the principle of multiple restitution, fivefold for the ox, fourfold for the sheep (cf. II Sam. 12:4, where, however, LXX reads "sevenfold"). The higher penalty for the ox may be due to the fact that it was more apt to be stolen, being used as a draft animal. The Code of Hammurabi (8) has a much higher restitution ratio, ranging all the way from ten to thirty.

3b. The thief who had not sold his stolen goods when he was apprehended received milder treatment (cf. vss. 7, 9). In the Code of Hammurabi (120, 124, 160) the double restitution principle is applied to cases of broken trust, but not in instances of outright theft.

2. The basic principle is that an owner is justified in killing a thief whom he finds in the act of **breaking in.** The Hebrew verb indicates that the thief broke in by means of digging through the walls of a town or house. It is possible to interpret this verse so as to assume that all **breaking in** occurred during the night, or as Beer does (*Exodus,* p. 113), that originally this provision allowed no exceptions, whether the theft was committed by day or night.

3a. Beer interprets this as a later qualification of the law in vs. 2, justifying the slaying of a thief caught in the act. Preferably this law should be interpreted to mean that a thief may be slain with impunity *only* when caught in the act of stealing. The assumption is that a thief does his business at night. **If the sun has risen upon him,** some time later, he may not be killed. But this interpretation, as well as Beer's, rests on a different rendering from that of the RSV. The difficult Hebrew phrase *dāmîm lô* is translated by the RSV as **bloodguilt for him** in both vs. 2 and vs. 3*a*. In vs. 2 this clearly

(for further regulations as to the disposal of the carcass see Lev. 17:15; Deut. 14:21).

In vss. 35-36 is another example of rough justice out of which have developed all the laws and regulations of modern life about road ac-

cidents with automobiles, mad dogs, and all the complicated contents of those learned volumes seen in every lawyer's bookshelf upon "the law of torts." They are founded on the belief that "a man is answerable for the 'natural and proba-

5 ¶ If a man shall cause a field or vine-yard to be eaten, and shall put in his beast, and shall feed in another man's field; of the best of his own field, and of the best of his own vineyard, shall he make restitution.

6 ¶ If fire break out, and catch in thorns, so that the stacks of corn, or the standing corn, or the field, be consumed *therewith;* he that kindled the fire shall surely make restitution.

7 ¶ If a man shall deliver unto his neigh-bor money or stuff to keep, and it be stolen out of the man's house; if the thief be found, let him pay double.

8 If the thief be not found, then the mas-ter of the house shall be brought unto the judges, *to see* whether he have put his hand unto his neighbor's goods.

5 "When a man causes a field or vineyard to be grazed over, or lets his beast loose and it feeds in another man's field, he shall make restitution from the best in his own field and in his own vineyard.

6 "When fire breaks out and catches in thorns so that the stacked grain or the standing grain or the field is consumed, he that kindled the fire shall make full restitu-tion.

7 "If a man delivers to his neighbor money or goods to keep, and it is stolen out of the man's house, then, if the thief is found, he shall pay double. 8 If the thief is not found, the owner of the house shall come near to God, to show whether or not he has put his hand to his neighbor's goods.

---

means that with respect to the slaying of the thief there is no guilt upon the slayer. The point of vs. 3a is that after **the sun has risen upon him** the thief's case is altered whether because he is no longer in the act of stealing or because he is doing it by daylight (cf. LXX).

5. The law presupposes the small owner-operated farm. In Babylonia the principle of making restitution for damage done to fields and crops was also in operation (Code of Hammurabi 55, 65), but the provisions reflect the tenant status of the individual farmer. There the custom of assessing fines of this sort on the basis of yield of adjacent land, or of **the best in his own field,** was apparently already giving way to the statistical standard based on the average yield per measure of land (Code of Hammurabi 56-58).

6. The case of damage by **fire** calls for the application of the same principle: **he that kindled the fire shall make full restitution.** In Babylonia, where irrigation was a high art, most of the examples are drawn from cases involving carelessness or neglect respecting the canals (Code of Hammurabi 53-56).

7-8. The simplicity and informality of Israelite society is revealed by the fact that the man who wants to put goods in storage gives them into the keeping of **his neighbor.**

---

ble' consequences of his acts; i.e., such conse-quences as a reasonable man in his place should have forseen as probable." [5]

22:5-15. *More Cases of Indirect Responsibility.* —It is hard to understand the Hebrew word in vs. 5—some guess it means **cause to be grazed over,** others, "cause to be burned over." The fact that the Code of Hammurabi (57) has a regula-tion about sheep feeding on another man's land inclines one to think that these verses refer first to the wandering herds and then to the wander-ing flames (vs. 6). Both the LXX and the Samar. texts make things a little plainer by inserting after the words **another man's field** this sen-tence: "He shall make compensation from his own field according to the produce thereof, and

[5] Frederick Pollock, "Tort," *Encyclopaedia Britannica,* XXII, 307.

if he has caused the whole field to be eaten. . . ." Then follow, as in our text, the words, **from the best in his own field.** The modern cattle who graze "off the lot" are the prospectors and in-vestors who long for the better grazing in other lands and then must be protected by the armed forces of the homeland.

The plight of the man who lights a pile of rubbish on his own land and sees it fanned by the wind till it spreads in flames toward his neighbor's property has given heart failure to farmers of all generations. War spreads just like the flames from one country to another, and the awful moment is just as poignant when one waits and fears to see the buildings of a neighbor burst into that frightful blaze.

8. *"So Help Me God."*—This coming before God is also the expression used in a like case by Hammurabi, but there was in the code a

9 For all manner of trespass, *whether it be* for ox, for ass, for sheep, for raiment, *or* for any manner of lost thing, which *another* challengeth to be his, the cause of both parties shall come before the judges; *and* whom the judges shall condemn, he shall pay double unto his neighbor.

10 If a man deliver unto his neighbor an ass, or an ox, or a sheep, or any beast, to keep; and it die, or be hurt, or driven away, no man seeing *it:*

11 *Then* shall an oath of the LORD be between them both, that he hath not put his hand unto his neighbor's goods; and the owner of it shall accept *thereof,* and he shall not make *it* good.

12 And if it be stolen from him, he shall make restitution unto the owner thereof.

13 If it be torn in pieces, *then* let him

9 "For every breach of trust, whether it is for ox, for ass, for sheep, for clothing, or for any kind of lost thing, of which one says, 'This is it,' the case of both parties shall come before God; he whom God shall condemn shall pay double to his neighbor.

10 "If a man delivers to his neighbor an ass or an ox or a sheep or any beast to keep, and it dies or is hurt or is driven away, without any one seeing it, 11 an oath by the LORD shall be between them both to see whether he has not put his hand to his neighbor's property; and the owner shall accept the oath, and he shall not make restitution. 12 But if it is stolen from him, he shall make restitution to its owner. 13 If it is torn by beasts, let him bring it as evi-

---

In Babylonia the wardens of goods in storage undertake their responsibility with the aid of an inventory-contract and witnesses (Code of Hammurabi 122). In Israel no such formality seems to have existed. A thief who is caught with goods stolen from storage must make double restitution (vs. 4). **If the thief is not found,** the **neighbor** to whom the goods were entrusted comes under suspicion. He must **come near to God** to convince the owner of the goods that he is innocent. Beer's suggestion (*Exodus,* p. 114) that the decision was by means of an oracle cannot be ruled out absolutely, but it seems that an oath was commonly taken in such cases (cf. vs. 11; I Kings 8:31-32). The possibility that the owner of the goods may be making false claims is not dealt with here, but the following verse is aware of it and provides for the right to challenge false claims.

9. A single principle covers cases of failure in trusteeship and false claims. The party who lies is to be treated as a thief, i.e., he **shall pay double** to his fellow (Code of Hammurabi 1-4). This holds also for articles found whose ownership is in doubt, and which are claimed by more than one party.

10-11. The case of animals entrusted to others rests on the same principle as holds for goods put in storage. But account is taken of the fact that animals can die or be hurt. Death or injury from natural causes involves no obligation for whoever has the animals in his care. It is possible that the Hebrew for **driven away** is a dittography for **is hurt.** If no one saw the manner of the death or injury of the animal concerned, the custodian of the animal must take an oath that **he has not put his hand to his neighbor's property.** Instead of **the oath by the LORD,** the LXX reads "oath of God." The RSV reads **the owner shall accept the oath.** The Hebrew phrase *welāqaḥ be'ālāw* has also been taken to mean that the owner will accept the dead or injured animal, signifiying thereby that he is satisfied and considers the case closed (McNeile, *Exodus,* p. 133; cf. Beer, *Exodus,* p. 114). This seems a much more significant interpretation of the phrase than that given in the RSV. To **accept the oath** is implicit in the manner of settling the issue and needs no elaboration.

12. The demand for restitution of animals lost by theft must be compared with the exemption from restitution of stored goods that have been stolen (vs. 8). The implication is that a shepherd or herdsman is constantly with the cattle and would, if responsible, make theft impossible.

13. If the herdsman can produce a part of the animal **torn by beasts,** it is proof that he was on the alert (I Sam. 17:35; see Amos 3:12), even though he may have been

bring it *for* witness, *and* he shall not make good that which was torn.

14 ¶ And if a man borrow *aught* of his neighbor, and it be hurt, or die, the owner thereof *being* not with it, he shall surely make *it* good.

15 But if the owner thereof *be* with it, he shall not make *it* good: if it *be* a hired *thing*, it came for his hire.

16 ¶ And if a man entice a maid that is not betrothed, and lie with her, he shall surely endow her to be his wife.

17 If her father utterly refuse to give her unto him, he shall pay money according to the dowry of virgins.

dence; he shall not make restitution for what has been torn.

14 "If a man borrows anything of his neighbor, and it is hurt or dies, the owner not being with it, he shall make full restitution. 15 If the owner was with it, he shall not make restitution; if it was hired, it came for its hire.[l]

16 "If a man seduces a virgin who is not betrothed, and lies with her, he shall give the marriage present for her, and make her his wife. 17 If her father utterly refuses to give her to him, he shall pay money equivalent to the marriage present for virgins.

[l] Or *it is reckoned in* (Heb *comes into*) *its hire*

unable to save it from the bear or the lion. Since he acted responsibly, no restitution need be made.

14-15. The Hebrew has only "If a man borrows of his fellow." One text of the LXX and the Syriac version insert "animal" (Amer. Trans.) and the Vulg. inserts "any of these," the substance of which is adopted in the RSV. However, the following phrase, **is hurt or dies,** speaks in favor of "animal." Restitution of a borrowed item implies abuse of it. Therefore, if the owner, who would oppose abuse of his own property, were present, no restitution could be demanded. The translation in the RSV of the last clause interprets it as making a distinction between a rented article and a borrowed article. In the case of the rented item restitution for damage or death in the absence of the owner cannot be sought, it is implied, since the rental is meant to absorb such losses, **it is reckoned in its hire.** It is possible, however, to translate the Hebrew in such a way as to continue the case of the borrowed item, viz., "If it was a hireling [who did the damage] it comes into his hire," i.e., the cost of restitution would be taken out of his wages.

16-17. Laws dealing with marriage and the family are missing in the Covenant Code proper. Many students feel that Deut. 22:13-26, made up of such laws, was originally a part of the code but later became misplaced. The provision regarding the seduction of the unbetrothed virgin appears here with the laws concerning the security of property. The central concern of the law is not marriage but the payment of **the marriage present.** This, according to the Deuteronomic form of the law, amounted to fifty shekels. It was assumed that she became the wife of her seducer, though in exceptional cases the father

written receipt to help keep things straight between depositor and conservator. There is some question whether God was invoked in the house or at a special sanctuary, also how the test of the veracity of the defendant was made. Perhaps it was a simple asseveration as in vs. 11, or some such ceremony as in Num. 5:11-31, or sacred lots (I Sam. 14:41). The lie detector of our day is the most recent of a long series of attempts made by the race to decide whether or not a person is telling the truth.

16. Concerning Seduction.—The principle underlying this regulation is that a daughter is the property of her father. The seducer has cheated the father of the money he could have received for her when she was married. Up to the twentieth century, English law on this ques-

tion was founded on the same idea that the value of the girl to her father is the basis for action. He has to prove, however, if she is over twenty-one, that she rendered actual service to him. Even such slight services as making tea for him or looking after the children are recognized as a basis for a suit. In the United States the woman usually can bring suit herself, but must prove deceit or breach of promise.

It has been generally thought that the honor of the family demands that the man shall marry the girl, thus leading to "shotgun weddings"; the fact that these so often turn out unhappily has brought many to doubt the wisdom of such forced marriages unless both parties are given time to decide of their own free will. The stigma of illegitimacy, if a child is involved, is of less

18 ¶ Thou shalt not suffer a witch to live.

19 ¶ Whosoever lieth with a beast shall surely be put to death.

20 ¶ He that sacrificeth unto *any* god, save unto the LORD only, he shall be utterly destroyed.

18 "You shall not permit a sorceress to live.

19 "Whoever lies with a beast shall be put to death.

20 "Whoever sacrifices to any god, save to the LORD only, shall be utterly destroyed.

---

might withhold her. In the Assyrian Code (A55) the case is treated in precisely the same way, except that the price is three times the normal marriage price.

(3) MORAL AND RELIGIOUS LAWS (22:18–23:9)

This second division of the social code is palpably permeated by the spirit of Israelite religion to an extent not discernible in the first half.

(a) CAPITAL OFFENSES (22:18-20)

18. The condemnation of the **sorceress** is in the apodictic form in which the Decalogue is written. For the most part sorcery is considered a preoccupation of women (I Sam. 28; Jer. 7:18; 44:15), but sorcerers are also mentioned (Deut. 18:10; Mal. 3:5). There were periodic efforts to stamp out all sorts of divination and witchcraft (I Sam. 28:3), but forms of it continued throughout the entire biblical period, and indeed into modern times. This verse was used to justify the punishment of witchcraft in the Middle Ages and in early New England. Sorcery constitutes a denial of the freedom and unity of God.

19. Bestiality is punishable by death, both for men and women (Lev. 20:15-16; Deut. 27:21). The Hittite laws have similar prohibitions (II. 187, 199, 200A), but it is not dealt with in the Babylonian code.

20. Only Yahweh may be worshiped in sacrifices. Transgressors are put under the sacred ban (*ḥērem*) and destroyed as in an *auto da fé* (cf. Deut. 13:13-18). The commandment reiterates and clarifies 20:3, 23. For a long time the same ban applied to captives and booty taken in war (cf. I Sam. 15:8 ff.).

---

import in modern life than the mismatched couple. In all such cases hasty action should be avoided and the best arrangement should be worked out for all three parties, father, mother, and child.

18. Witchcraft.—This and the following capital offense have been included throughout the ages in most codes of law.[6] Sorcery generally consists in superstitious rites connected with earlier forms of religion now discarded. But the religion of Yahweh demanded absolute loyalty, and to participate in other cults was regarded as religious high treason, punishable by death. The persecution of witches throughout the ages, for which this verse has to bear much of the responsibility (see Chancy's report cited in Willison), was due to many causes: the fact that the gods of an older religion generally become the devils of the new religion; etc. There is always evil and misfortune in life and it must be blamed on somebody. The easiest person on whom to blame it is the old woman who is ob-

served engaging in some ancient religious cult, gathering herbs, mumbling spells, and making brews. Just as the Nazis blamed the Jews for all their ills, and we must have a two-party system in order to have the other party to blame, so ancient people vented all their hate and fear on these old women, and sometimes on younger ones, who were often persuaded by their neighbors that they did possess strange powers. The attempt to scare and exploit fellow human beings by the assumption of supernatural powers is found not merely in some church circles today, but in all fields.[7] Note the superstitious faith many hold in the infallibility of the scientific method, "Scientific truth is exact, but it is incomplete and penultimate; [it] floats in a medium of mythology." [8]

20. The Danger of Distorted Emphasis.—This verse must bear some of the blame for the religious wars of history and for sectarian bigotry

[6] See Willison, *Saints and Strangers*, pp. 359-60; *Compact and Laws of New Plymouth*, p. 244.

[7] See Thurman Arnold, *The Folklore of Capitalism* (New Haven: Yale University Press, 1937), pp. 79-82.

[8] José Ortega Gasset, *Toward a Philosophy of History* (New York: W. W. Norton, 1941), p. 15.

21 ¶ Thou shalt neither vex a stranger, nor oppress him: for ye were strangers in the land of Egypt.

22 ¶ Ye shall not afflict any widow, or fatherless child.

23 If thou afflict them in any wise, and they cry at all unto me, I will surely hear their cry;

24 And my wrath shall wax hot, and I will kill you with the sword; and your wives shall be widows, and your children fatherless.

25 ¶ If thou lend money to *any of* my people *that is* poor by thee, thou shalt not

21 "You shall not wrong a stranger or oppress him, for you were strangers in the land of Egypt. 22 You shall not afflict any widow or orphan. 23 If you do afflict them, and they cry out to me, I will surely hear their cry; 24 and my wrath will burn, and I will kill you with the sword, and your wives shall become widows and your children fatherless.

25 "If you lend money to any of my peo-

(*b*) HUMANE AND PIOUS DUTIES (22:21-31)

21. The alien (*gêr*) whose protection is here guaranteed is a permanent resident in the community. He is to be differentiated from the foreigner (*nokhrî*), though he may in some cases be of foreign origin, and also from the **stranger** (*zār*), though his ways may in some cases be different. The term must be understood in the light of the originally normative organization of society by tribes and clans. Anyone not related by blood to a particular tribe or clan, but permanently associated with it and under its protection, was a *gêr*. The classification was tribal and social, not primarily religious. The Levite priest of Micah was a *gêr* (Judg. 17:7-13); and the Beerothites, who were surely Yahwists, of the tribe of Benjamin, were "residing" in Gittaim (II Sam. 4:3). The word points out a resident who is not indigenous to a place and who is ethnically unrelated to its people; the other distinctions it may occasionally have are derived from this. The verse is repeated with slight variations in 23:9.

22-24. God himself provides justice for the widows and orphans, as well as for the alien (Deut. 10:18-19). If Israelites should stand in the way of that justice by afflicting them, their own wives and children will be widowed and orphaned; the principle of the *lex talionis* is embodied in the law and the warning. Israel's protection of the weak was not a novel concern in the ancient world. In the conclusion of his famous code, Hammurabi boasts that with the help of his gods he has seen to it that under his rule the strong did not oppress the weak, and the widows and orphans were given justice (Hugo Gressmann, *Altorientalische Texte zum Alten Testament* [2nd ed; Berlin: Walter de Gruyter, 1926], p. 407). What is uniquely stressed here is the immediate and dynamic role the God of Israel plays in this concern for and accomplishment of justice. He is directly related to the historical process and has not, like an absentee, entrusted his work to an agent, such as Hammurabi, who can play an independent role.

25-27. The admonition—none of these "humane and pious duties" (vss. 21-31) are laws in a strict sense—not to demand interest from a poor fellow Israelite is to be closely

---

today. See Expos. on 20:3 for what is good in the command, but remember that in religious and international affairs the first step toward peace, and indeed toward truth, takes place when each group escapes from the notion that nothing but its own theory is correct.

21-24. *A Wider Mercy.*—The constantly reiterated commands to be merciful to strangers, widows, etc., testify to the miserable condition of the weak and helpless in Israel. The grounds given for charity are religious, as in many ancient codes—which suggests that it is histori-

cally true that more good has been done in the world by those who set out to love God than by those who set out to love man. If you set out to do other people good, it is difficult to avoid feeling that you are able to do them good because you are better than they are. As Kierkegaard is always insisting, it is through seeing God that everything human becomes really human.

25-27. *"Neither Shall You Exact Interest."*—The Bible consistently forbids the Jews to take interest from their own people (Deut. 23:20;

be to him as a usurer, neither shalt thou lay upon him usury.

26 If thou at all take thy neighbor's raiment to pledge, thou shalt deliver it unto him by that the sun goeth down:

27 For that *is* his covering only, it *is* his raiment for his skin: wherein shall he sleep? and it shall come to pass, when he crieth unto me, that I will hear; for I *am* gracious.

28 ¶ Thou shalt not revile the gods, nor curse the ruler of thy people.

29 ¶ Thou shalt not delay *to offer* the first of thy ripe fruits, and of thy liquors: the firstborn of thy sons shalt thou give unto me.

ple with you who is poor, you shall not be to him as a creditor, and you shall not exact interest from him. 26 If ever you take your neighbor's garment in pledge, you shall restore it to him before the sun goes down; 27 for that is his only covering, it is his mantle for his body; in what else shall he sleep? And if he cries to me, I will hear, for I am compassionate.

28 "You shall not revile God, nor curse a ruler of your people.

29 "You shall not delay to offer from the fullness of your harvest and from the outflow of your presses.

"The first-born of your sons you shall

---

associated, in its original form, with the provision about pledges in vss. 26-27. It is possible that the last clause, **you shall not exact interest from him,** is an explanatory gloss added to define **creditor** (cf. Deut. 23:19). The real point is that in his relations with a poor man, possibly his own employee, an Israelite must be generous. If he gives him an advance payment on his wage, he must not insist on payment by the end of the day at the risk of the man's doing without the **garment** he has given as pledge for the loan (vs. 26). The original admonition was not so much a prohibition of interest as a demand that one be ready to "risk an advance" without material security. Amos 2:6 condemns Israelites for having treated such advances in a strictly legal manner, even at the cost of making the poor destitute. As a barter economy developed into a money economy the problem of interest became increasingly acute (Deut. 23:19-20; Lev. 25:26); between Israelites interest on commercial loans was prohibited. (In Hebrew the word "interest" means "bite"!) To take a **neighbor's garment in pledge** for any time longer than the working hours of the day, when he does not wear it, is equivalent to making him pledge his life (cf. Deut. 24:6, 17). This prohibition ultimately makes enslavement for debt impossible.

28. **Revile** and **curse** represent two Hebrew words closely synonymous. Blasphemy was punished by death (Lev. 24:15-16). Beer (*Exodus,* p. 123) feels that the association of lese majesty with blasphemy presupposes the Davidic monarchy. The cursing of the ruler was a capital crime in the monarchic period (II Sam. 16:9; I Kings 2:8-9; 21:10).

29a. This provision, which must be interpreted as the offering of the first fruits, is stated in the briefest form in Hebrew, "You must not delay your produce and your juice." The produce refers to grains and the juice to grapes and, probably, olives. Later, at least, the amount was set at a tenth of the yield (Deut. 14:22; 26:1-12). The system

---

Lev. 25:36; Prov. 28:8). This has always been an awkward point with "influential" Christians, and has led to the word used here being translated **usury** in the KJV and the Vulg. Even the article on "Banks" in the *Encyclopaedia Britannica* states that interest was never forbidden to the Jews. Ruskin's example in refusing to take interest and spending only his capital is related in *Fors Clavigera.* But Deuteronomy expressly permits the charging of interest to strangers, and what the Bible means is that it is both awkward and embarrassing to have business relations with near relatives—better give to your

relatives than lend to them. But the whole history of the prejudice against exacting interest as told by an author like Sombart is interesting. The best tip in the financial market is that the only absolutely safe loan is one made to the Lord, and that we lend to him by giving to the poor (Prov. 19:17).[9]

29. *The Role of the First-Born.*—This passage sounds as if Yahweh demanded human sacrifice.

[9] We might all strive to be worthy of the epitaph on a tombstone in a colored servants' graveyard at Cooperstown, N. Y.: "Jennie York, Died Feb. 22, 1837, at 50 yrs. She had her faults but was kind to the poor."

30 Likewise shalt thou do with thine oxen, *and* with thy sheep: seven days it shall be with his dam; on the eighth day thou shalt give it me.	give to me. **30** You shall do likewise with your oxen and with your sheep: seven days it shall be with its dam; on the eighth day you shall give it to me.
31 ¶ And ye shall be holy men unto me: neither shall ye eat *any* flesh *that is* torn of beasts in the field; ye shall cast it to the dogs.	**31** "You shall be men consecrated to me; therefore you shall not eat any flesh that is torn by beasts in the field; you shall cast it to the dogs.
23 Thou shalt not raise a false report: put not thine hand with the wicked to be an unrighteous witness.	**23** "You shall not utter a false report. You shall not join hands with a wicked man, to be a malicious witness.

of the tithe in later Israel rested on this originally agricultural custom (cf. 23:19*a*; 34:26*a*). The LXX interprets the provision to mean "first fruits."

29b. As the offering of tithes is made to recognize God's title to the land, so the offering of the first-born of man and beast shows that they too are his. The manner in which **the first-born of your sons** shall be given to God is not discussed here (cf. 13:1-2, 11-16). The admonition is as terse as that respecting the first fruits; both presuppose that the way of offering is known. It is therefore hardly justifiable to use this provision in support of a view, sometimes advanced, that in early Israel the physical life of every first-born male child was devoted to God. The custom of slaying the first-born was at certain times probably very common (Ezek. 20:26; Mic. 6:7), but there is no good evidence that it was ever specifically demanded by the law of Yahweh. Ezekiel and Micah refer to the practice as an illustration of a lack of faith, implying that it is a recent aberration. The forms of redemption by which this law was fufilled, at least in later times, are set out under 12:1-2, 11-16.

30. The first-born male of **oxen** and **sheep** was to be offered **on the eighth day.** This offering was in the form of a sacrificial meal in which Yahweh shared. The provision that this must take place on the eighth day stands in the way, it is felt, of identifying Passover and the offering of the first-born as a single rite (cf. Beer, *Exodus,* p. 71). The first-born of all animals except the ox and the sheep could be redeemed (Num. 18:15-17). This makes the stipulation of the day on which these were to be sacrificed necessary, though this explanatory note may be of later origin.

31. It is a very ancient and very general custom among pastoral nomads to refuse to eat animals of their flock or herd that have been torn by wild beasts. The flesh is rendered taboo because of the evil power represented by the wild animal. This taboo was in all probability current in Israel from the earliest times. But here its meaning has been changed: **You shall be men consecrated to me.** Israelites must not eat the unclean or blood because of their relation to Yahweh. The practice is omitted in relation to the sanctity within which Israel lives rather than the taboo standing over against it. It seems impossible to say with certainty how long before the era of the Levitical Code (Lev. 7:24-27; 17:15 [H]) this reorientation took place.

(c) The Spirit of Justice (23:1-9)

This group of principles and admonitions—they are scarcely laws—are held together by the fact that their main purpose is to create the moral attitudes which shall permeate

Elsewhere substitution for the first-born is permitted (34:20). But the story of the proposed sacrifice of Isaac would not have been told except to discourage a custom which already existed. Either we have in these verses a vestigial part of a more ancient religion such as was preserved by the witches, or a custom of neighbor-ing tribes which Israel was apt to copy. The idea here is one of the origins of the special privileges of the eldest child throughout history (see Jer. 7:31; 19:5; Ezek. 20:25-26).

23:1-9. *Nonconductors of Evil.*—The substance of these verses (for detailed analysis see the Exeg.) might be expressed simply: Watch

2 ¶ Thou shalt not follow a multitude to *do* evil; neither shalt thou speak in a cause to decline after many to wrest *judgment:*

3 ¶ Neither shalt thou countenance a poor man in his cause.

4 ¶ If thou meet thine enemy's ox or his ass going astray, thou shalt surely bring it back to him again.

5 If thou see the ass of him that hateth thee lying under his burden, and wouldest forbear to help him, thou shalt surely help with him.

2 You shall not follow a multitude to do evil; nor shall you bear witness in a suit, turning aside after a multitude, so as to pervert justice; 3 nor shall you be partial to a poor man in his suit.

4 "If you meet your enemy's ox or his ass going astray, you shall bring it back to him. 5 If you see the ass of one who hates you lying under its burden, you shall refrain from leaving him with it, you shall help him to lift it up.*m*

m Gk: Heb obscure

---

all legal decisions. No penalties are specified for transgressions: the concern is not with specific cases but with an all-pervasive sense of justice. In the ancient Oriental world Israel alone was able, despite periodic delinquency such as that attacked by the prophets, to make this sense of justice and honor an ineradicable part of its ethos. Vss. 1-3, 6-9, are in the apodictic form of the Ten Words (20:1-17) ; vss. 4-5, in the specific form of case law, give two examples of moral character and social responsibility.

23:1. This verse is a repetition and illustration of the commandment against false witness (20:16). Connivance in matters of judicial testimony was subject to the severest penalties (Deut. 19:16-21).

2. A man must have the courage of his convictions. Instead of **to do evil** one can read "in evil things" (LXX). Instead of **in a suit** one can read "with a multitude." The will of the mob must not be confused with truth and justice, even at the risk of personal safety (cf. Ps. 15).

3. That a court would **be partial to a poor man** has seemed so unlikely to interpreters that they have often sought to emend the text of this verse in order to get the supposedly real meaning. Indeed, if, as seems probable, vs. 3 was originally followed by vs. 6 it becomes virtually impossible to make sense of vs. 3 as it stands. Lev. 19:15 is Beer's justification (*Exodus,* p. 118) for adding "nor to a great man" after **to a poor man.** Whether upward or downward, whether because of sentimentality or ambition, justice must not be forsaken. God is no respecter of persons (Deut. 10:17; Acts 10:34). The emendation suggested by Quell (Kittel, *Biblia Hebraica, ad loc.*) eliminates the poor man from this verse entirely (ודל to גדל). *"A* **great** *man* is probably the true reading" (McNeile, *Exodus,* p. 138). Since vs. 6, however, deals with the poor man, Beer's real concern is still served, and at the cost of a much more minor change.

4-5. Moral and social responsibility transcends personal enmities. Fulfilling it may heal the enmities. The primary concern is with responsibility (Deut. 22:1-4). It demands that a domestic animal found wandering about at large be returned to its owner by his "brother." In the second example the maintenance of the principle of responsibility is more difficult to achieve in view of the presence of the enemy with the donkey "stretched out" under his burden. Yet he must offer help. In both cases the enmity proceeds from the person to be aided; "one who is hostile to you" and **who hates you.** These examples belie the assertion of Matt. 5:43.

---

that you do not retail lies, nor talk maliciously and help an evil cause along. Do not be so anxious to agree with the majority, but decide honestly yourself. Be impartial both to the small and great, and see that you take particular pains to be fair to our poor. Keep far away from any shady dealings, have no part in destroying the

innocent or in helping to acquit the wicked— and have nothing to do with bribes.

Nothing could be more up to date today. It was and is an appeal to the conscience of the reader and is as pertinent to behavior in a law court as in a casual conversation. Be a nonconductor of evil. Be an individual, not merely a

6 Thou shalt not wrest the judgment of thy poor in his cause.

7 Keep thee far from a false matter; and the innocent and righteous slay thou not: for I will not justify the wicked.

8 ¶ And thou shalt take no gift: for the gift blindeth the wise, and perverteth the words of the righteous.

9 ¶ Also thou shalt not oppress a stranger: for ye know the heart of a stranger, seeing ye were strangers in the land of Egypt.

10 And six years thou shalt sow thy land, and shalt gather in the fruits thereof:

6 "You shall not pervert the justice due to your poor in his suit. 7 Keep far from a false charge, and do not slay the innocent and righteous, for I will not acquit the wicked. 8 And you shall take no bribe, for a bribe blinds the officials, and subverts the cause of those who are in the right.

9 "You shall not oppress a stranger; you know the heart of a stranger, for you were strangers in the land of Egypt.

10 "For six years you shall sow your

---

6. In the suit of **your poor** you must **not pervert the justice,** i.e., the decision or the basis on which it is given (*mishpāṭ*). The poor also belong to the community of Israel; they are **your poor.**

7. The **false charge** must be interpreted as a complaint without basis filed by a plaintiff against innocent persons. Such false charges must be treated for what they are. Every responsible person must keep far from them, lest he become an accomplice in the slaying of **the innocent and righteous** that might follow if such a false charge were established in court. The Hebrew text underlying **for I will not acquit the wicked** is in doubt. The LXX reads, "and you must not justify the wicked for a bribe," but this seems too much to anticipate vs. **8.**

8. The subtle psychological effect of becoming indebted to one partner in a suit through the acceptance of "favors" is well made by the metaphor about the blinding of **the officials** (Deut. 16:19).

9. This verse repeats the rule about the *gēr* in 22:21. It sums up the rule by adding that Israelites know the outlook of resident aliens.

(4) A CHURCH CALENDAR (23:10-19)

The second half of the social code (21:1–23:19), beginning at 22:18, probably ended originally at 23:3, for that verse has all the earmarks of the conclusion of an audience. However, the concluding provisions of what was probably the original code and those now found in vss. 13-19 belong together in our interpretation of Exodus since they are all concerned with the same subject, the manner and times of cultic observances incumbent upon all Israelites.

(a) THE SABBATHS (23:10-13)

10-11. The fallow year is not described as a sabbath here. Nor is it given a specifically religious meaning. Later its humanitarian function, stressed here, is not lost, but it is primarily a sabbath signifying Yahweh's possession of the land (Lev. 25:2-7). The custom

---

member of a mob (respectable or not). Be fair. Avoid the suburbs of the evil place.

10-13. Mercy for Man and Beast.—This whole chapter is filled with kindliness and thoughtfulness for others, love for one's enemies (vss. 4-5), showing that Matt. 5:42 was reflecting one school of ancient doctrine, and thought even for the beasts, showing that the famous final words of the book of Jonah were not unique and reminding one of the inclusion of the cattle in the

historic scene at Bethlehem.[1] Regulations which elsewhere are founded upon religious motives (see Lev. 25:4) are here based on humanitarian considerations only; even the sabbath (vs. 12) exists for the benefit of the ox and the ass (see Num. 22:28 ff.; Prov. 12:10; I Cor. 9:9). The poetry and pity that lie deep in the human heart conceived the idea of leaving the ground

[1] See Kipling's poem, "Eddi, the Priest of St. Wilfrid."

11 But the seventh *year* thou shalt let it rest and lie still; that the poor of thy people may eat: and what they leave the beasts of the field shall eat. In like manner thou shalt deal with thy vineyard, *and* with thy oliveyard.

12 Six days thou shalt do thy work, and on the seventh day thou shalt rest: that thine ox and thine ass may rest, and the son of thy handmaid, and the stranger, may be refreshed.

13 And in all *things* that I have said unto you be circumspect: and make no mention of the name of other gods, neither let it be heard out of thy mouth.

land and gather in its yield; 11 but the seventh year you shall let it rest and lie fallow, that the poor of your people may eat; and what they leave the wild beasts may eat. You shall do likewise with your vineyard, and with your olive orchard.

12 "Six days you shall do your work, but on the seventh day you shall rest; that your ox and your ass may have rest, and the son of your bondmaid, and the alien, may be refreshed. 13 Take heed to all that I have said to you; and make no mention of the names of other gods, nor let such be heard out of your mouth.

---

of letting land **lie fallow** is quite common among primitive people. The original function of the custom is probably religious, to appease the spiritual powers controlling the land or to give them opportunity to restore its fertility. That this was once true as well of the custom in Israel is rendered more likely by the fact that the laws about not cutting the corners (Lev. 23:22) or gathering the gleanings (Lev. 19:9-10), later also given a humanitarian explanation, are founded upon the conviction that the spirits ruling the soil must share in its products. It is not stated here that all land was to rest during the same year, but the analogy of vs. 12 implies it. In Lev. 25:2-7 this point is explicitly made. It is seriously doubtful that this was originally the case. We have little evidence to show that the fallow year was strictly observed by many until the era of the Maccabees; Lev. 26:34-35 seems to imply that it was not. So does Jer. 17:4, if it is a reference to the custom. In later times the law of the release of creditors and of slaves at the end of six years was combined with that of the fallow year, thus preserving it for an economy no longer purely agricultural (Deut. 15:2; Neh. 10:31).

12. With its humanitarian motivation, this form of the sabbath law corresponds most closely to Deut. 5:14-15. But in the complete absence of any Israelite religious interpretation it is like 34:21. This does not compel us to conclude that the sabbath had no religious meaning when this provision was written. The brevity of the provisions in the latter half of the code (cf. 22:29) leads one to assume that the code offers no innovations but serves as a reminder of what is well known.

13. This verse was once the conclusion to a series of admonitions, possibly from 21:1. The use of the name of another god is forbidden. The word **mention** rests on a Hebrew word meaning "cause to remember"; it has a cultic significance, i.e., in worship other gods may not be "remembered" by having their name mentioned. Nor is their name to pass one's lips in private. The law corresponds to 20:3 (cf. Exeg. on 22:20 and 34:14).

---

fallow on every seventh year; partly because it reminded the tenants that they were only borrowers from the real owner of the land who was Yahweh (Lev. 25:23); partly so that the poor and the beasts of the field should not be exterminated by the march of civilization, but like Ruth (2:15-16) should have a little left on which they could glean; partly, as it turned out, for the good of the land itself. So the modern science of agriculture was born!

It was a lovely idea, but the fact that Deuter-

onomy omits it suggests that it did not prove to be workable (Lev. 26:34-35), as it certainly would not be feasible in the case of vineyards and olive yards (which were added in vs. 11 by someone who was a scribe rather than a farmer). But the phrase in Leviticus "Then shall the land enjoy her sabbaths" is a fair picture of surcease from profit for momentary benefit to all, to the animals, to the poor, even to the character of the owner. And yet today the similar idea that industry should be operated **not**

14 ¶ Three times thou shalt keep a feast unto me in the year.

15 Thou shalt keep the feast of unleavened bread: (thou shalt eat unleavened bread seven days, as I commanded thee, in the time appointed of the month Abib; for in it thou camest out from Egypt: and none shall appear before me empty:)

16 And the feast of harvest, the firstfruits of thy labors, which thou hast sown in the field: and the feast of ingathering, *which is* in the end of the year, when thou hast gathered in thy labors out of the field.

17 Three times in the year all thy males shall appear before the Lord GOD.

18 Thou shalt not offer the blood of my sacrifice with leavened bread; neither shall the fat of my sacrifice remain until the morning.

19 The first of the firstfruits of thy land thou shalt bring into the house of the LORD thy God. Thou shalt not seethe a kid in his mother's milk.

14 "Three times in the year you shall keep a feast to me. 15 You shall keep the feast of unleavened bread; as I commanded you, you shall eat unleavened bread for seven days at the appointed time in the month of Abib, for in it you came out of Egypt. None shall appear before me empty-handed. 16 You shall keep the feast of harvest, of the first fruits of your labor, of what you sow in the field. You shall keep the feast of ingathering at the end of the year, when you gather in from the field the fruit of your labor. 17 Three times in the year shall all your males appear before the Lord GOD.

18 "You shall not offer the blood of my sacrifice with leavened bread, or let the fat of my feast remain until the morning.

19 "The first of the first fruits of your ground you shall bring into the house of the LORD your God.

"You shall not boil a kid in its mother's milk.

(b) THE GREAT FESTIVALS (23:14-19)

14. The three festivals of obligation are mentioned immediately after the sabbaths. **To keep a feast** and **appear before the Lord** are the same in this context (vs. 18; 34:25; cf. Deut. 16:16). These observances were originally held at many centers and only later centralized in Jerusalem, which is the place to be chosen of which Deuteronomy speaks. In I Sam. 1:3, 21 there is apparently an annual pilgrimage to Shiloh.

15. The first festival is designated in this E section as **unleavened bread.** In 34:24 [J] it is known as a Passover. This lends support to the view that it was known by the former title in the north and the latter in the south. The ancient festival has already been reoriented to celebrate Israel's deliverance. The admonition not to delay bringing the first fruits (22:29) is matched by the provision that **none shall appear before me empty-handed.** The terseness characteristic of so many laws from 22:18–23:19 is also exhibited in the summary of the festivals (cf. 12:15-28). The provisions serve as reminders rather than as instruction.

16. The feast of Weeks (34:22; Deut. 16:10, 16) is here called **the feast of harvest** (lit., "of the cutting") of crops sown in the field. The feast of Tabernacles is also known by its more primitive name: **the feast of ingathering** (cf. 34:22). In both instances the ancient titles bespeak the pre-Israelite history of the feasts.

18-19. These final rubrics are virtually identical with 34:24-25. The **fat of my feast** is that part of a sacrifice which was burned on the altar. It is doubtful that at the Passover anything except **the blood** was offered to Yahweh. In any case, the real concern is that the eating of the Passover must be completed before morning (34:25). This E section, however, knows the festival only as Unleavened Bread. In the Ugaritic texts (Birth of the Gods, 1. 14) we learn that at a sacrificial meal a kid was cooked in milk and a

---

solely for the benefit of the owners, but for the good of all, owners, workers, and the public, is slightly heretical if taken seriously. ("I am not running my business for the purpose of providing a quart of milk per diem for every

Hottentot," is still apt to be the reaction to any suggestion of public service rather than private profit.)

14-19. See Lev. 23; Deut. 16; for vs. 19, see Expos., pp. 850-51.

20 ¶ Behold, I send an Angel before thee, to keep thee in the way, and to bring thee into the place which I have prepared.

21 Beware of him, and obey his voice, provoke him not; for he will not pardon your transgressions: for my name *is* in him.

22 But if thou shalt indeed obey his voice, and do all that I speak; then I will be an enemy unto thine enemies, and an adversary unto thine adversaries.

23 For mine Angel shall go before thee, and bring thee in unto the Amorites, and the Hittites, and the Perizzites, and the Canaanites, the Hivites, and the Jebusites; and I will cut them off.

24 Thou shalt not bow down to their gods, nor serve them, nor do after their works: but thou shalt utterly overthrow them, and quite break down their images.

25 And ye shall serve the LORD your God, and he shall bless thy bread, and thy water; and I will take sickness away from the midst of thee.

20 "Behold, I send an angel before you, to guard you on the way and to bring you to the place which I have prepared. 21 Give heed to him and hearken to his voice, do not rebel against him, for he will not pardon your transgression; for my name is in him.

22 "But if you hearken attentively to his voice and do all that I say, then I will be an enemy to your enemies and an adversary to your adversaries.

23 "When my angel goes before you, and brings you in to the Amorites, and the Hittites, and the Per'izzites, and the Canaanites, the Hivites, and the Jeb'usites, and I blot them out, 24 you shall not bow down to their gods, nor serve them, nor do according to their works, but you shall utterly overthrow them and break their pillars in pieces. 25 You shall serve the LORD your God, and I[n] will bless your bread and your water; and I will take sickness away

[n] Gk Vg: Heb *he*

---

lamb in butter. The categorical rejection of such a practice in Israel, which develops as a primary principle in Jewish dietary laws, shows that while certain Canaanite practices were assimilated in order to serve the Israelite revelation, others were rejected outright. This is a striking illustration of the integrity maintained in the midst of a most comprehensive process of cultural assimilation.

c) A FAREWELL EXHORTATION (23:20-33)

This final section in the laws of the covenant (20:21–23:33) consists not of laws but of promises, warnings, and reminders. It is a farewell speech, spoken apparently as Israel set out from Sinai for Canaan. Though a conclusion to the laws of the covenant, it does not admonish the people to keep the code. Its burden is that Israel must obey the angel (vs. 22) who will lead it into its inheritance. And it warns against making covenants with the Canaanites or their gods, to whom the code makes no direct reference. Much of the discourse has a Deuteronomic cast.

20. The **angel** is God's presence in the midst of his people, to guide them in the wilderness (cf. 14:19). The cloud (13:21) and the ark (Num. 10:33) were also symbols of his presence. Canaan is the **place . . . prepared** (cf. 15:17).

21. The presence is personified so that God speaks of **him** in the third person. He has the full power and authority of God. The angel is God in one of his capacities or functions.

22. Israel's safety lies in obedience to the divine will. Israel's enemies were often the means of God's judgment. It was the prophets' role to explicate this.

23-25. The list of Canaanite peoples, the orders to uproot them, to avoid their gods, and to destroy the **pillars** are typically Deuteronomic (Deut. 7:1-5). Israelites had

---

20-33. *The Accompanying Angel.*—This passage forms the concluding paragraph of the book of the covenant, but originally was directed from Sinai to the children of Israel as they set out toward the Promised Land. Yahweh remains in Sinai but his word to Israel is, **I send an Angel**

before thee. The implication of the whole passage is that if Israel had obeyed the law of God and walked in his ways, its people would have been the happiest on earth. God had looked after everything for them. It is a sober truth for us all. God has anticipated and looked after

26 ¶ There shall nothing cast their young, nor be barren, in thy land: the number of thy days I will fulfil.

27 I will send my fear before thee, and will destroy all the people to whom thou shalt come; and I will make all thine enemies turn their backs unto thee.

28 And I will send hornets before thee, which shall drive out the Hivite, the Canaanite, and the Hittite, from before thee.

29 I will not drive them out from before thee in one year; lest the land become desolate, and the beast of the field multiply against thee.

30 By little and little I will drive them out from before thee, until thou be increased, and inherit the land.

31 And I will set thy bounds from the Red sea even unto the sea of the Philistines, and from the desert unto the river: for I will deliver the inhabitants of the land into your hand; and thou shalt drive them out before thee.

from the midst of you. 26 None shall cast her young or be barren in your land; I will fulfill the number of your days. 27 I will send my terror before you, and will throw into confusion all the people against whom you shall come, and I will make all your enemies turn their backs to you. 28 And I will send hornets before you, which shall drive out Hivite, Canaanite, and Hittite from before you. 29 I will not drive them out from before you in one year, lest the land become desolate and the wild beasts multiply against you. 30 Little by little I will drive them out from before you, until you are increased and possess the land. 31 And I will set your bounds from the Red Sea to the sea of the Philistines, and from the wilderness to the Eu-phra′tes; for I will deliver the inhabitants of the land into your hand, and you shall drive them out

probably taken over the pillar as a religious symbol from the Canaanites (II Kings 17:10; 18:4). Its abolition was a feature of the reforms of Hezekiah and Josiah and is prescribed in Deut. 12:3. The sickness that Yahweh would take away is also a Deuteronomic touch (Exod. 15:24b-26; Deut. 7:15; 28:27, 60).

26. In most of the O.T., and especially in the Deuteronomic writings, fruitfulness, prosperity, and long life were the hallmarks of the divine favor. The earth is "good" and its gifts desirable. There is little otherworldliness. The meaning of history is to be sought in historical fulfillment. Living is the reward of life.

27-29. The terror of the nations at the approach of God and his people (15:14-18) is here repeated. The Hebrew word for hornets (cf. Josh. 24:12; Deut. 7:20) is a collective noun. The writer draws a picture of some swarm of insects pursuing the fleeing natives of Canaan. His power in Canaan will be as great as it was in Egypt (cf. 8:20-32). A picture such as this could be drawn only when the harsh and difficult conditions of Israel's early centuries in Canaan had become a vague memory, romanticized because of a later prosperity.

30. Something of the actual ruggedness is still recalled in the qualification of this verse. The possession of the land had been a piecemeal process. It was not complete until the era of David. The reasons for this delay were seriously pondered (Judg. 2:21-23; 3:1-6).

31-33. These boundaries represent in idealized form the extent of Solomon's empire (I Kings 4:21). Actually, even in Solomon's time, Israel did not hold Philistia or any site on the Mediterranean, the sea of the Philistines.

everything for us. It depends entirely upon us whether we walk in the way of peace or stray into the byways of distress. I will be an enemy unto thine enemies, and an adversary unto thine adversaries. . . . God . . . shall bless thy bread, and thy water. . . . By little and little I will drive [thine enemies] out from before

thee, until thou . . . inherit the land. Well, what more could you ask? God will take care of you. But there are conditions—you must co-operate with God; "you must obey the voice of my Angel"; "you must not worship the gods of the enemy"; "you shall not let the gods of the heathen ensnare you, nor make any covenant

32 Thou shalt make no covenant with them, nor with their gods.

33 They shall not dwell in thy land, lest they make thee sin against me: for if thou serve their gods, it will surely be a snare unto thee.

24 And he said unto Moses, Come up unto the Lord, thou, and Aaron, Nadab, and Abihu, and seventy of the elders of Israel; and worship ye afar off.

2 And Moses alone shall come near the Lord: but they shall not come nigh; neither shall the people go up with him.

before you. 32 You shall make no covenant with them or with their gods. 33 They shall not dwell in your land, lest they make you sin against me; for if you serve their gods, it will surely be a snare to you."

24 And he said to Moses, "Come up to the Lord, you and Aaron, Nadab, and Abi'hu, and seventy of the elders of Israel, and worship afar off. 2 Moses alone shall come near to the Lord; but the others shall not come near, and the people shall not come up with him."

5. The Ratification of the Covenant (24:1-18)

The establishment of the covenant, which began with a theophany (ch. 19) and the conditions for which are laid down in the laws (chs. 20-23), is completed by the ceremonies of ratification here described. There are two ceremonies. The present text seeks to leave the impression that they were performed in succession. Before the first ceremony, while Moses is still on the mount, the directions for the second rite are given (vss. 1-2). Then follows the first rite in which Moses consecrates the people (vss. 3-8). The second ceremony, the sacred meal of Yahweh with the nobles of Israel (vss. 9-11), follows. Thereafter Moses and Joshua approach the Presence to receive the stone tablets of the law (vss. 12-14). The elders, with Aaron and Hur, remain behind to judge the people. The stage is set for ch. 32. It seems probable, however, that these two ceremonies represent two different ways of describing the ratification which have an origin independent of each other. Vss. 3-8 continue 23:32 and belong to the E source. Vss. 1-2, 9-11, 12-14 have traditionally been assigned to J (cf. McNeile, *Exodus,* pp. xxxi-xxxii; S. R. Driver, *The Book of Exodus* [Cambridge: Cambridge University Press; "The Cambridge Bible"], pp. 251-52). Otto Eissfeldt adheres to this by assigning them to his "L," i.e., to the lay strand he finds in J (*Einleitung in das Alte Testament* [Tübingen: J. C. B. Mohr, 1934], pp. 214-16).

24:1. And he said to Moses: After speaking to others Yahweh turns to Moses. We must perhaps return to the scene in 20:21. God has just addressed the people; now he speaks to Moses. Beer, who ascribes all of the core of ch. 24 to E¹ (i.e., to a strand in E that continues to use the name "Elohim" after 3:15), emends **to the Lord** to read, "to me" (*Exodus,* p. 126), since God himself is speaking. The inclusion of the two older sons of Aaron, **Nadab and Abihu,** has survived their repudiation in the later tradition (Lev. 10:1-3). The **elders** represent the people. In both ceremonies the covenant is sealed with the people as a whole.

2. Moses alone, or with Joshua (vs. 13), must approach the Presence (33:7-11). As in the temple, later, the gradations in holiness are carefully observed. The LXX reads "God" instead of "Lord" (cf. *ibid.*).

---

with them, but be wholly a sincere servant of God." The testimony of all saints in all ages answers, "Yes, this is literally true."

24:1-11. *In the Presence of the Infinite.*—Sapphire stone was lapis lazuli, a deep blue stone filled with starlike, goldlike particles of iron pyrites, a lovely symbol of the heavens, "this brave o'erhanging firmament, this majestical roof fretted with golden fire."[2] It was much

² Shakespeare, *Hamlet,* Act II, scene 2.

prized by the ancients, one of the seven stones placed on the breast of Babylonian kings. Most museums show Egyptian articles of luxury made from it, though with the original polish lost they look duller there than they did to the first proud owners.

Confronted with the words **they saw God,** the Greek translators of the Hebrew felt the contradiction with other passages concerning the fatal effects of looking upon God, and so they

<table>
<tr>
<td>

3 ¶ And Moses came and told the people all the words of the LORD, and all the judgments: and all the people answered with one voice, and said, All the words which the LORD hath said will we do.

4 And Moses wrote all the words of the LORD, and rose up early in the morning, and builded an altar under the hill, and twelve pillars, according to the twelve tribes of Israel.

5 And he sent young men of the children of Israel, which offered burnt offerings, and sacrificed peace offerings of oxen unto the LORD.

6 And Moses took half of the blood, and put *it* in basins; and half of the blood he sprinkled on the altar.

7 And he took the book of the covenant, and read in the audience of the people: and they said, All that the LORD hath said will we do, and be obedient.

8 And Moses took the blood, and sprinkled *it* on the people, and said, Behold the

</td>
<td>

3 Moses came and told the people all the words of the LORD and all the ordinances; and all the people answered with one voice, and said, "All the words which the LORD has spoken we will do." 4 And Moses wrote all the words of the LORD. And he rose early in the morning, and built an altar at the foot of the mountain, and twelve pillars, according to the twelve tribes of Israel. 5 And he sent young men of the people of Israel, who offered burnt offerings and sacrificed peace offerings of oxen to the LORD. 6 And Moses took half of the blood and put it in basins, and half of the blood he threw against the altar. 7 Then he took the book of the covenant, and read it in the hearing of the people; and they said, "All that the LORD has spoken we will do, and we will be obedient." 8 And Moses took the blood and threw it upon the people, and said, "Behold the blood of the covenant which the LORD has

</td>
</tr>
</table>

3. Here begins the account of the first ceremony. **The words of the LORD** must mean the contents of the laws. The phrase **all the ordinances** is probably a redactor's insertion since it is not included in the people's statement of acceptance.

4. Here and in vs. 7 Moses is said to have written the laws in a book and read them out to the people, though in vs. 3 the people had already accepted them following an oral report. Vss. 4 and 7 probably constitute a D addition (cf. Deut. 31:9, 24, 26) that forms a doublet to vs. 3. The **altar** Moses prepares is to be thought of as conforming to the type commanded in 20:24. The **twelve pillars** are here to be understood as symbolizing the people by clans rather than deity. Since **pillars** were also used to represent deity, and since this practice was outlawed in the era of Deuteronomy, the LXX renders this word as simply "stones."

5. The **burnt offerings** are to praise God; the **peace offerings** celebrate fellowship with him (cf. 20:24).

6-7. Moses serves as priest. The altar against which **he threw the blood** stands as a testimony to the act of consecration; it represents the active presence of God in the relationship. By the sprinkling of the same blood upon the people and upon the altar, God and people are united in a sacred fellowship. The sacred meal (vss. 9-11) was also a common way of establishing such fellowship. It was probably the oldest form, and the sprinkling of the blood symbolizes what was once no doubt an actual drinking of it. The people's acceptance repeats their words in vs. 3.

8. **The blood of the covenant** means the blood by means of which the covenant is established. In later tradition the book too was said to have been sprinkled by the blood

<table>
<tr>
<td>

translated, "They were seen in the place of God"; but the original text is explicit, and all of vs. 11*b* is a true suggestion of the sacrament of Holy Communion: The vision of God (the word for "see" is a poetical one in the Hebrew) is united to practical living. The poets saw God standing above the starry universe, and in so

</td>
<td>

doing were conscious of how small is man's body, yet how great is his mind that can embrace all this dazzling immensity, and soaring above it, picture to itself the Creator and Director of it all, nay, see him also, and talk with him as friend with friend. But the highest flight of poetic imagination was in the possi-

</td>
</tr>
</table>

blood of the covenant, which the LORD hath made with you concerning all these words.

9 ¶ Then went up Moses, and Aaron, Nadab, and Abihu, and seventy of the elders of Israel;

10 And they saw the God of Israel: and *there was* under his feet as it were a paved work of a sapphire stone, and as it were the body of heaven in *his* clearness.

11 And upon the nobles of the children of Israel he laid not his hand: also they saw God, and did eat and drink.

12 ¶ And the LORD said unto Moses, Come up to me into the mount, and be there: and I will give thee tables of stone, and a law, and commandments which I have written; that thou mayest teach them.

13 And Moses rose up, and his minister Joshua; and Moses went up into the mount of God.

14 And he said unto the elders, Tarry ye here for us, until we come again unto you: and, behold, Aaron and Hur *are* with you: if any man have any matters to do, let him come unto them.

made with you in accordance with all these words."

9 Then Moses and Aaron, Nadab, and Abi'hu, and seventy of the elders of Israel went up, 10 and they saw the God of Israel; and there was under his feet as it were a pavement of sapphire stone, like the very heaven for clearness. 11 And he did not lay his hand on the chief men of the people of Israel; they beheld God, and ate and drank.

12 The LORD said to Moses, "Come up to me on the mountain, and wait there; and I will give you the tables of stone, with the law and the commandment, which I have written for their instruction." 13 So Moses rose with his servant Joshua, and Moses went up into the mountain of God. 14 And he said to the elders, "Tarry here for us, until we come to you again; and, behold, Aaron and Hur are with you; whoever has a cause, let him go to them."

(Heb. 9:20). Blood becomes the metaphor for the covenant in the N.T. (Matt. 26:28; I Cor. 11:25). There the blood symbolizes especially the grace of God in man's redemption, a meaning borne by the Exodus in the O.T.

9-11. The sacred meal, provided for in vss. 1-2, now takes place. **They saw the God of Israel.** They did not behold a figure face to face (33:20). They looked up at the sky, **a pavement of sapphire stone,** on which the feet of God were supposed to rest. God was thought of as throned above the waters that were over the canopy of heaven (Ps. 29:10). The Presence is so real that it is as if "the heavens were opened" (Ezek. 1:1). The transfiguration scene in the N.T. is indebted to this account (cf. Matt. 17:5). In this sacred Presence the nobles were safe. Israel is holy by virtue of the covenant; it is not God, but it shares his life.

12-14. Moses is asked to **come up** to God, to enter what in the temple was known as the holy of holies. He was summoned to receive **the tables of stone** (cf. 31:18*b*) on

---

bility that man and his ways were directed and cared for by the same great power that laid the cornerstone of the earth, "when the morning stars sang together, and all the sons of God shouted for joy," that in him (to talk sacramentally) we may **eat and drink** and have our being.

12-18. *Alone with God.*—So Moses was, for **forty days and forty nights.** Forty was a symbolic number used generally for a period of time. Its use indicates many days or many years (see 16:35; Judg. 3:11; 5:31; 8:28; 13:1; I Sam. 4:18; I Kings 19:8; Amos 2:10; Matt. 4:2; Acts 1:3). The leader disappears for a considerable time, during which God speaks to him and he talks

with God. Leaders in our day lack such an opportunity. The president of the United States, the prime minister of Great Britain, are provided with presidential yachts or country homes by the nation; but business follows them by radio and special wire and messenger. Clergymen are supposed to have their mornings free for prayer and study, but they must fight friends, busybodies, and their own lazy selves, if their retreat is to be kept inviolate.

Moses went up the mount to meet and talk with God. Is there anything which corresponds with this in modern life? The sentimental pietist claims that he has had an identical experience, but the fruits in thought and life which he

15 And Moses went up into the mount, and a cloud covered the mount.

16 And the glory of the LORD abode upon mount Sinai, and the cloud covered it six days: and the seventh day he called unto Moses out of the midst of the cloud.

17 And the sight of the glory of the LORD *was* like devouring fire on the top of the mount in the eyes of the children of Israel.

18 And Moses went into the midst of the cloud, and gat him up into the mount: and Moses was in the mount forty days and forty nights.

15 Then Moses went up on the mountain, and the cloud covered the mountain. 16 The glory of the LORD settled on Mount Sinai, and the cloud covered it six days; and on the seventh day he called to Moses out of the midst of the cloud. 17 Now the appearance of the glory of the LORD was like a devouring fire on the top of the mountain in the sight of the people of Israel. 18 And Moses entered the cloud, and went up on the mountain. And Moses was on the mountain forty days and forty nights.

---

which the laws were written. These are also known as "the two tables of stone" (34:1, 4 [J]), "the tables of the covenant" (Deut. 9:9, 11, 15), and "the tables of testimony" (31:18a; 32:15; 34:29 [P]). That God had written the law meant that it expressed his character. The law in written form gave it permanence and made it serviceable as a cultural instrument; it was **written for their instruction.** The terms law and instruction rest on the same Hebrew root which means "to throw," "to shoot," or by derivation, "to point"; hence, from pointing, "to direct," "to instruct." Law is *tôrāh,* instruction. It is not primarily a precept in legal form; it is revelation in living cultural forms.

Joshua is Moses' **servant** or chaplain (33:11; Josh. 1:1). They leave the scene together. The LXX says that "they" **went up into the mountain.** The Hebrew text, perhaps for the sake of harmony with 32:15, offers no clue as to where Joshua went. Of all those left in charge only Aaron is held responsible when Moses returns (ch. 32).

15-18. This note, by a priestly editor, is really an introduction to the account of the deliverance of the cultic ordinances to Moses (chs. 25–31). For P these, and all laws, were given at Sinai. But they are not set in the framework of the covenant or considered as the conditions of it. For P the covenant with Abraham (Gen. 17) was the real covenant; further, laws were not part of the covenant, which constituted a sacramental relationship; they were only signs of it.

---

brings down from the mount too often do not justify his claim in the minds of his fellows. The scientist brings back from his vigil the new discovery and invention to be appraised by the world for what it is worth. The poet and composer and artist have proofs to offer of the authenticity of their "forty days." Moses brought down the tables of the law, tangible proof that something great had happened on the mount. Nor can it be otherwise with the religious man. He must justify his faith by thoughts and life which, tested by the standards of ordinary human beings, prove to be great. Mere pious words are not enough; mere assertions that God told him this are empty air. The proof is in the texture of what he is and thinks and does. The accents of the Holy Ghost are heard in truth that, like cold water to the thirsty soul, commends itself to the best in all men, in kindliness and courtesy of life.

Many an honest religious man has asked himself at times, "Have I ever heard God's voice or spoken to him and been sure of his answer?" Perhaps for most men the beginning of such an experience is in thanksgiving. After fulfilling some difficult assignment, one's whole being goes up to God in a simple acknowledgment, "Unless you had helped me, I could not have come through with it even as well as I have; a thousand thanks"; and at such a moment there is such a conscious relation as of father to beloved son, an interchange of affection, that the hand held out seems to be grasped and held for a moment. We are sure that someone greater than ourselves has been operating in and through us. Such was Moses' experience. "We have got this people so far upon their way; they are safely out of Egypt; we have the first beginnings of an organization started; we have escaped several pitfalls. I never could have done it by myself. To thee, Yahweh, all my gratitude and loyalty!" [3]

[3] See the last words of Moses in Connelly, *The Green Pastures,* Part II, scene 4.

25 And the Lord spake unto Moses, saying,

2 Speak unto the children of Israel, that they bring me an offering: of every man that giveth it willingly with his heart ye shall take my offering.

3 And this *is* the offering which ye shall take of them; gold, and silver, and brass,

4 And blue, and purple, and scarlet, and fine linen, and goats' *hair,*

25 The Lord said to Moses, 2 "Speak to the people of Israel, that they take for me an offering; from every man whose heart makes him willing you shall receive the offering for me. 3 And this is the offering which you shall receive from them: gold, silver, and bronze, 4 blue and purple and scarlet stuff and fine twined linen, goats'

B. THE P ORDINANCES FOR THE CULTUS (25:1–31:18)

See Intro., pp. 844-46.

1. THE OFFERING (25:1-9)

25:1. Moses had entered the cloud (24:18) to receive "the tables of stone" (24:12) inscribed with the law. But now the priestly writer summons him to make an oral communication to the people. Kurt Galling feels that the version PA did not contain the prescription for an offering, so that vss. 8-9 followed immediately upon vs. 1 (Beer, *Exodus,* p. 130).

2. Moses is to ask the people for **an offering** that will make construction of **the tabernacle** possible. The Hebrew word *terûmāh* means "heave offering" (Num. 18:8, 19; Neh. 12:44; 13:5). The phrase **whose heart makes him willing** shows that the **offering** here prescribed can also be equated with a freewill offering (cf. 35:29). Both offerings were expressions of personal loyalty and gratitude over and beyond the levies required of all. When Jehoash renovated the temple (II Kings 12:4-15) freewill offerings and the poll tax provided the means (cf. Exod. 30:13). In Ezekiel's plan for the restoration of the temple, the temple area itself is spoken of as a *terûmāh* (Ezek. 45:1; 48:8).

3. The items proper to the **offering** are listed. The metals were to be offered from stocks available (35:22, 24). There is no mention of iron, a metal which seems to have had a function only in tools of war and agriculture.

4. The woven supplies are made by the women (35:23, 25). Both available supplies and new manufacture can be included in the offering. The woolen fabrics are classified by the colors of the costly dyes used in their manufacture. The blue or violet and the purple were dyes obtained from two different species of shellfish found in the Mediterranean. The Hebrew "worm of scarlet" still indicates the origin of the third color. Women also spun the **fine twined linen** and the **goats' hair** (35:25-26).

Hard study, deep thought, a quiet mind receptive to the subtle suggestions that flow therefrom, an opening of the heart to a universal spirit, a purging of oneself from narrow meanness—these are the elements of prayer as Moses experienced it on the mount, when he felt a great spirit flow in upon his own and found his own ideas surrounded by and at last lost in the wider thoughts of God. God's revelation of himself is always progressive, growing. Moses' case as he came in contact with the religions of his day is like our own, "The keynote of idolatry is contentment with the prevalent gods." [4]

25:1-9. *The Sanctuary as Man's Response.*—Thus the first church was built: the dwelling or

[4] A. N. Whitehead, *Adventures of Ideas* (New York: The Macmillan Co., 1933), p. 12.

tabernacle, the tent of meeting, the holy place, the most holy place. It was God's house, a sublime reproduction of an ordinary dwelling house: with its laver in front of the entrance, as in every Eastern home, where hands and feet were washed for the visitor (Gen. 18:4; 43:24; John 13:5, foreshadowing Tit. 3:5); with its lampstand (Zech. 4:2); with a table for food; with its inner rooms not open to every visitor. It was a tent, a symbol of transitoriness, pointing onward to some more substantial dwelling for God in the Temple in Jerusalem, and at long last to the perfect tabernacle of Heb. 9:11; Rev. 21:3. It was a tent of witness containing the law of God. The writers of the description of the tabernacle were systematizers of tradition and they carried back into the twelfth century the

5 And rams' skins dyed red, and badgers' skins, and shittim wood,

6 Oil for the light, spices for anointing oil, and for sweet incense,

7 Onyx stones, and stones to be set in the ephod, and in the breastplate.

8 And let them make me a sanctuary; that I may dwell among them.

9 According to all that I show thee, *after* the pattern of the tabernacle, and the pattern of all the instruments thereof, even so shall ye make *it*.

hair, 5 tanned rams' skins, goatskins, acacia wood, 6 oil for the lamps, spices for the anointing oil and for the fragrant incense, 7 onyx stones, and stones for setting, for the ephod and for the breastpiece. 8 And let them make me a sanctuary, that I may dwell in their midst. 9 According to all that I show you concerning the pattern of the tabernacle, and of all its furniture, so you shall make it.

---

5. **Skins** and **wood** also constitute part of the offering. The **rams' skins** were "reddened," probably as a result of the tanning process. The other leather cited was also used to make sandals (Ezek. 16:10). This and the fact that the Hebrew word may be related to an Arabic word for "dolphin" has led some to conclude that it or some other marine mammal was the source of the second leather mentioned (cf. Amer. Trans. and ASV). **Acacia wood** had a reputation for durability (cf. LXX *ad loc.*) which modern study confirms. There is a desert species of acacia (*acacia seyal*), still extant, as well as an Egyptian species (*acacia nilotica*). It seems probable that the ark was made from the former (Deut. 10:3; cf. Isa. 41:19; cf. also G. E. Post, "Shittah Tree," in *A Dictionary of the Bible*, ed. James Hastings [New York: Charles Scribner's Sons, 1902], IV, 507).

6. This verse is omitted in the LXX. The **oil for the lamps** is olive oil (27:20-21). So is the oil mixed with spices for anointing (30:22-33). The spices for the **incense** are detailed in 30:34-38. The **oil** and **spices** were part of the offering brought by the leaders (35:27-28). Gifts of this type were often made to the temple by friendly foreigners of rank in the late Jewish era.

7. The translation of **onyx stones** for "stones of the *shōham*" (M.T.) rests mainly on the LXX. The true nature of the stones is uncertain. Other stones reportedly used in the breastplate (28:15-30) are not specified in any of the summaries (cf. 35:9, 27), though clearly referred to.

8-9. **Sanctuary** here means the whole sacred area, **the tabernacle** and the court surrounding it. It is the place set apart for God's abode. The dwelling is to be constructed according to **the pattern** God shows Moses on the mount (cf. vs. 40; 26:30; 27:8). There is revealed in the statement both a concern for preciseness about the appointment for the cultus and, as in the case of the law, the conviction that the cultic arrangements were ordained by God. The **pattern** is explicitly cited only for the ark, the lampstand, the table, the tent, and the altar. The temple was also thought to be the expression of a divine **pattern** (I Chr. 28:19). The notion of a heavenly model for temples, cult objects, and laws is universal in the ancient Near East.

---

ecclesiastical atmosphere of the fifth or fourth. The writers felt that the ideals of their own time must have been ideals for Israel ever since they began to worship Yahweh. The untrained nomads around Sinai, just escaped from brickmaking and slavery, could not have had the skill in carpentry work, weaving, embroidery, forging and casting of metals, toolmaking and the many other crafts necessary for such an elaborate structure. Not even with all the loot from the Egyptians could they have had enough of precious materials for such splendor, nor could

they have moved it about with them on their wanderings. As it stands, it is the enlarged vision which Moses saw upon the mount of what would be worthy for the home of Yahweh. As the Creator made the earth for man to dwell in, so man must make a dwelling for the Creator. The symbolic number seven runs all through the narrative. As the work of creation took seven days, as the building of Solomon's Temple took seven years (I Kings 6:38), so the work on the tabernacle took seven months (compare the following passages: 19:1 ff.; 24:18;

10 ¶ And they shall make an ark *of* shittim wood: two cubits and a half *shall be* the length thereof, and a cubit and a half the breadth thereof, and a cubit and a half the height thereof.

11 And thou shalt overlay it with pure gold, within and without shalt thou overlay

10 "They shall make an ark of acacia wood; two cubits and a half shall be its length, a cubit and a half its breadth, and a cubit and a half its height. 11 And you shall overlay it with pure gold, within and

---

2. THE ARK (25:10-22)

In the promulgation of the appointments for the cultus the ark comes first; in the account of the execution it is constructed after the tabernacle is ready. The mention of Bezalel by name in 37:1, however, suggests the possibility that the original order of the latter was changed (cf. 36:1). In the pre-Deuteronomic period the boxlike object (II Kings 12:9-10) was known as "the ark of Yahweh" (I Sam. 4:6) or "the ark of God" (I Sam. 3:3). In Deuteronomy it is called "the ark of the covenant of Yahweh" (Deut. 10:8; 31:9, 25-26). Here in P it is **the ark of the testimony** (vs. 22). The ark in early Israel was associated with the shrine at Shiloh (I Sam. 3–6) just as the tent of meeting was, perhaps, at Gibeon (II Chr. 1:3, 13). There is no good reason to doubt that this ark existed in Israel from the time of the nomadic era under Moses (cf. Num. 10:33-36). This is true whether it was taken over from the priest Jethro, from the shrine at Kadesh (cf. ch. 18), or whether it was built by Moses himself (Deut. 10:1-3). Modern research has shown that objects that serve as a palladium still exist among Arab tribes (Alois Musil, *The Manners and Customs of the Rwala Bedouins* [New York: American Geographical Society, 1928]; also, Julian Morgenstern, *The Ark, the Ephod, and the "Tent of Meeting"* [Cincinnati: Union of American Hebrew Congregations, 1945], pp. 5-55). The role of the ark in early Israel seems to have been very similar to these Arabic parallels: it led Israel on pilgrimage and in battle. The significance of the ark waned with the gradual fading of the nomadic spirit and role, and it may have ceased to exist even before the Exile (Jer. 3:16). In any event it did not survive the first temple. When P's account was written no ark existed any more. There may once have been an earlier description of the ark which was suppressed by P editors in favor of their own (33:1-6, 7-11; Deut. 10:1-5). We now know little about the appearance of the actual ark. It was perhaps a rather rude wooden box, open at the top, with few decorative parts.

10. Instead of reading **they shall make** it is better to read "thou shalt make" (so LXX and Samar.; cf. vss. 13, 17, 18, 23). The cubit was an Egyptian as well as an Israelite unit of length. A cubit is approximately eighteen inches. Thus the measurements of the ark were forty-five by twenty-seven by twenty-seven inches.

11. The **molding of gold round about** is often interpreted as a rim at the top into which perhaps the cover fitted (cf. ASV *ad loc.*). But it is also possible that the "wreath"

34:28; 40:17). The narrative in 39:1-31 is in seven paragraphs, punctuated by the formula "As Yahweh commanded Moses"; so also in 40:17-32. The editor has arranged the whole series of commands into seven sections (25:1 ff.), each beginning with the words "And Yahweh spake unto Moses saying." Some of the sections are in turn divided into seven parts, each beginning with the words "And thou shalt make." So later scribes tried to symbolize and systematize the pattern that was shown to Moses on the mount.

Whether or not the tabernacle was ever built in all its magnificence, it does seem clear that there was in the time of Moses an ark and a

tent with table, lampstand, and altar, dwelling in which there was a mysterious spiritual presence, who made his home with the people and received their offerings. It was built by the gifts of the people and with the skills that they possessed—a labor of love.

10-16. The Fashioning of the Ark.—The ark was the sacred and mysterious medium by which the guiding and protecting presence of Yahweh abode among his people. It was originally a box (see Exeg.). Ornaments and contents apparently were added later. The earliest descriptions do not mention them. Before it were placed relics and remembrances of God's mercies, the pot of manna, Aaron's rod that

it, and shalt make upon it a crown of gold round about.

12 And thou shalt cast four rings of gold for it, and put *them* in the four corners thereof; and two rings *shall be* in the one side of it, and two rings in the other side of it.

13 And thou shalt make staves *of* shittim wood, and overlay them with gold.

14 And thou shalt put the staves into the rings by the sides of the ark, that the ark may be borne with them.

15 The staves shall be in the rings of the ark: they shall not be taken from it.

16 And thou shalt put into the ark the testimony which I shall give thee.

17 And thou shalt make a mercy seat *of* pure gold: two cubits and a half *shall be* the length thereof, and a cubit and a half the breadth thereof.

without shall you overlay it, and you shall make upon it a molding of gold round about. 12 And you shall cast four rings of gold for it and put them on its four feet, two rings on the one side of it, and two rings on the other side of it. 13 You shall make poles of acacia wood, and overlay them with gold. 14 And you shall put the poles into the rings on the sides of the ark, to carry the ark by them. 15 The poles shall remain in the rings of the ark; they shall not be taken from it. 16 And you shall put into the ark the testimony which I shall give you. 17 Then you shall make a mercy seat⁰ of pure gold; two cubits and a half shall be its length, and a cubit and a half its breadth.

⁰ Or *cover*

---

or "crown" was a ropelike cable or band meant to go around the box at its middle, or lower down.

12. The word for **feet** (RSV) is not the one commonly used. It means a recurrent point or motion and may be translated **corners** (KJV; cf. I Kings 7:30). If the **rings** were attached to the corner post of the box they need not have been at the bottom.

13-15. The ark was mobile by virtue of the **poles.** When the original ark was brought to its final location in the holy of holies in the temple its poles were visible from the holy place (I Kings 8:8). As a symbol of the mobility of Yahweh, they were never to be removed from the rings.

16. Vss. 16, 21*b* give evidence of the composite character of this account. Deut. 10:2 also relates that the tables of the law were placed inside the ark; but in P the idea produces a change in its name. Instead of "the ark of the covenant," it becomes **the ark of the testimony** (vs. 22). Many scholars, among them Hugo Gressmann, have maintained that the original ark at first contained images of a deity or fetishes, and that these were later exchanged for, or rather interpreted as, the tablets of the laws. Others deny this, partly on the ground that there was no need for anything to be in the ark (Eichrodt, *Theologie des A.T.*, I, 44-45).

17. The *kappōreth* or **mercy seat** was a **cover** (RSV mg.) for the box. Its name, however, denotes the function it had in the cultus of P. It was the place where by blood the sins of Israel were "covered," i.e., atoned for (Lev. 16:2, 13-15). It was the most sacred object in the most holy place; it was the very throne of Yahweh.

---

blossomed. Later editors placed them inside the ark. Later tradition also places inside the ark the two tablets of the law. If, as is suggested by a study of the text, the original box was empty and unornamented, it is a nice example of early tendencies in the history of religion, tendencies to move from simplicity, silence, emptiness, and awe to ritual, splendor, and dogmatism, from the Quaker meeting to the High Mass at St. Peter's, from Ps. 23 to the Nicene Creed. Those who seek for fundamentals in religion must be careful not to move too many

of their revered relics from "before Yahweh" (16:33) and place them in the ark itself. A nineteenth-century traveler tells of finding in the hill country of British India a native who said he was a "Southern Baptist," which seems perilously near placing the American Civil War in the ark.

17-22. *The Mercy Seat and the Cherubim.*— The voice of God came from between the cherubs who stood upon the cover of the ark. The presence of God is just above the earth, not touching it. The sonorous Hebrew plural

18 And thou shalt make two cherubim *of* gold, *of* beaten work shalt thou make them, in the two ends of the mercy seat.

19 And make one cherub on the one end, and the other cherub on the other end: *even* of the mercy seat shall ye make the cherubim on the two ends thereof.

20 And the cherubim shall stretch forth *their* wings on high, covering the mercy seat with their wings, and their faces *shall look* one to another; toward the mercy seat shall the faces of the cherubim be.

21 And thou shalt put the mercy seat above upon the ark; and in the ark thou shalt put the testimony that I shall give thee.

22 And there I will meet with thee, and I will commune with thee from above the mercy seat, from between the two cherubim which *are* upon the ark of the testimony, of all *things* which I will give thee in commandment unto the children of Israel.

23 ¶ Thou shalt also make a table *of* shittim wood: two cubits *shall be* the length thereof, and a cubit the breadth thereof, and a cubit and a half the height thereof.

18 And you shall make two cherubim of gold; of hammered work shall you make them, on the two ends of the mercy seat. 19 Make one cherub on the one end, and one cherub on the other end; of one piece with the mercy seat shall you make the cherubim on its two ends. 20 The cherubim shall spread out their wings above, overshadowing the mercy seat with their wings, their faces one to another; toward the mercy seat shall the faces of the cherubim be. 21 And you shall put the mercy seat on the top of the ark; and in the ark you shall put the testimony that I shall give you. 22 There I will meet with you, and from above the mercy seat, from between the two cherubim that are upon the ark of the testimony, I will speak with you of all that I will give you in commandment for the people of Israel.

23 "And you shall make a table of acacia wood; two cubits shall be its length, a cubit its breadth, and a cubit and a half its height.

18-21a. Cherubim were guardians of sacred places of the tombs of the great (Gen. 3:24; Ezek. 28:14; for illustrations see Volz, *Biblischen Altertümer*, p. 12). They are also the servants of God (Ezek. 10:18; Ps. 18:10 [Hebrew 11]). As such they help to determine the representation of angels. They are usually given a human face and the body of an animal. Here in P the cherubim are attached to the **mercy seat** and their function, as in the temple, is to overshadow the divine Presence.

22. There will I meet with you: With these words P transfers a role that originally belonged to the tent of meeting (33:7-11) to the ark. For him the ark is no longer only a symbol of the constant presence of God with his people, in a rather gross form, as was true of the ancient ark. It is at the same time the symbol of God's nearness and of his transcendence. P's ark combines the functions of the ancient ark and the tent.

3. The Table (25:23-30)

23. Instead of **a table of acacia wood** the LXX prescribes "a table of pure gold." The table is for the **bread of the Presence** (vs. 30). The most ancient reference to this "holy bread" (I Sam. 21:6) does not mention a table. As in the case of the ark, the

---

cherubim has been of much value in hymnology. In the countries around, many such winged figures—griffins, bulls, etc.—were found in sacred shrines (see reference to Volz in Exeg.). They combined the ideas of strength and swiftness. According to the old rabbis, the name of the one was Righteousness and of the other Mercy; but some ancient interpreters have said that while usually their faces were half turned away from each other, yet when peace and righteous-

ness ruled among the people they turned toward each other, and bending forward kissed each other (Ps. 85:10).

23-40. *The Table and the Candlestick.*—The altar table seems to be mentioned in I Kings 6:20; Ezek. 41:22. Josephus says the legs were square at the top but that the feet were carved.[5] The "table bread for the presence" (I Sam. 21:5) was also found among the Babylonians,

[5] *Antiquities* III. 6. 6.

24 And thou shalt overlay it with pure gold, and make thereto a crown of gold round about.

25 And thou shalt make unto it a border of a handbreadth round about, and thou shalt make a golden crown to the border thereof round about.

26 And thou shalt make for it four rings of gold, and put the rings in the four corners that *are* on the four feet thereof.

27 Over against the border shall the rings be for places of the staves to bear the table.

28 And thou shalt make the staves *of* shittim wood, and overlay them with gold, that the table may be borne with them.

29 And thou shalt make the dishes thereof, and spoons thereof, and covers thereof, and bowls thereof, to cover withal: *of* pure gold shalt thou make them.

30 And thou shalt set upon the table showbread before me always.

24 You shall overlay it with pure gold, and make a molding of gold around it. 25 And you shall make around it a frame a handbreadth wide, and a molding of gold around the frame. 26 And you shall make for it four rings of gold, and fasten the rings to the four corners at its four legs. 27 Close to the frame the rings shall lie, as holders for the poles to carry the table. 28 You shall make the poles of acacia wood, and overlay them with gold, and the table shall be carried with these. 29 And you shall make its plates and dishes for incense, and its flagons and bowls with which to pour libations; of pure gold you shall make them. 30 And you shall set the bread of the Presence on the table before me always.

original must have been a simple wooden object. It was destroyed in the burning of the temple (II Kings 25:9). The story that Jeremiah preserved it in a cave (II Macc. 2:5) must be considered legendary. But, unlike the ark, the table was replaced in the second temple. However, we cannot be certain that the same table served it and the temple of Herod (cf. I Macc. 1:22; 4:49). In any case, later accounts stress the gold ornamentation rather than the wooden structure of the table (vss. 24, 26, 29 [PB]; vs. 23 [LXX]; Josephus *Antiquities* VIII. 3. 7). Only here is it explicitly stated that it was made of wood. The appearance of the table on the Titus Arch in Rome (Volz, *Biblischen Altertümer,* pp. 52-53) suggests that the sides of the table were open.

24-25. Sometimes the table was called "the pure table" (Lev. 24:6) because of the **pure gold** with which it was overlaid. The word for **molding** is the same as in vs. 11. Galling (Beer, *Exodus,* p. 133) thinks that it designates the same item as the word for frame, i.e., vs. 25a is PB's way of saying the same thing PA has said in vs 24b. Later an editor, failing to recognize the identity, added another molding on the frame (vs. 25b)! On the Titus Arch parts of the frame are visible. They are attached to the legs midway between the table top and the clawlike "feet." It seems possible to conclude that there was only one **molding**—on the frame, i.e., vs. 25b is an explanatory elaboration of vs. 24b.

26-27. The **rings** are apparently nearer the end of the legs in vs. 26 than in vs. 27; separate sources seem indicated.

29. The vessels are symbolized by a single bowl on the table in the Titus Arch (cf. Num. 4:7). This was for the offering of wine which accompanied the bread.

30. The **bread of the Presence** is also called "holy bread" (I Sam. 21:4, 6), and "continual bread" (I Chr. 9:32; Neh. 10:33; etc.). It is so designated in the N.T. (Matt. 12:4;

where it was likewise called bread of the Presence. It was a reminder that man's food is the gift of God and that it should be used in God's service. The term **showbread** is formed on the same analogy as Luther's *Schaubrot.* The idea that God himself would eat of the bread lingered on from primitive times (Jer. 7:18; Isa. 65:11). In one village church in England may

be seen a common loaf of bread prominently displayed every Sunday (paid for by an ancient legacy), to be given at the close of the service to the poorest person present—a good example of the complete humanizing of a faith born in superstition and perpetuated by ritual symbolism; a loaf first for the god to eat, then as a symbol of man's dependence and duty, and

31 ¶ And thou shalt make a candlestick *of* pure gold: *of* beaten work shall the candlestick be made: his shaft, and his branches, his bowls, his knops, and his flowers, shall be of the same.	31 "And you shall make a lampstand of pure gold. The base and the shaft of the lampstand shall be made of hammered work; its cups, its capitals, and its flowers shall be of one piece with it; 32 and there

31 ¶ And thou shalt make a candlestick *of* pure gold: *of* beaten work shall the candlestick be made: his shaft, and his branches, his bowls, his knops, and his flowers, shall be of the same.

32 And six branches shall come out of the sides of it; three branches of the candlestick out of the one side, and three branches of the candlestick out of the other side:

33 Three bowls made like unto almonds, *with* a knop and a flower in one branch; and three bowls made like almonds in the other branch, *with* a knop and a flower: so in the six branches that come out of the candlestick.

34 And in the candlestick *shall be* four bowls made like unto almonds, *with* their knops and their flowers.

35 And *there shall be* a knop under two branches of the same, and a knop under two branches of the same, and a knop under two branches of the same, according to the six branches that proceed out of the candlestick.

36 Their knops and their branches shall be of the same: all of it *shall be* one beaten work *of* pure gold.

31 "And you shall make a lampstand of pure gold. The base and the shaft of the lampstand shall be made of hammered work; its cups, its capitals, and its flowers shall be of one piece with it; 32 and there shall be six branches going out of its sides, three branches of the lampstand out of one side of it and three branches of the lampstand out of the other side of it; 33 three cups made like almonds, each with capital and flower, on one branch, and three cups made like almonds, each with capital and flower, on the other branch — so for the six branches going out of the lampstand; 34 and on the lampstand itself four cups made like almonds, with their capitals and flowers, 35 and a capital of one piece with it under each pair of the six branches going out from the lampstand. 36 Their capitals and their branches shall be of one piece with it, the whole of it one piece of hammered work of

Mark 2:26). The bread was an "offering" to Yahweh in which he was recognized as the source of the earth's fruitfulness and of Israel's sustenance. The table stood in the holy place, to the right of the entrance into the holy of holies.

4. THE LAMPSTAND (25:31-40)

P's description of the **lampstand** (*menôrāh*) corresponds to the object of the post-exilic period. We do not know whether the lamp (*nēr*) at Shiloh (I Sam. 3:3) was on a lampstand. In Solomon's temple there were ten lampstands (I Kings 7:48-50). Kurt Galling (*Biblisches Reallexikon* [Tübingen: J. C. B. Mohr, 1937; "Handbuch zum Alten Testament"], p. 349) is of the view that the seven-branched lampstand did not originate until the fifth century. The oil-burning lamps (vs. 37) are apparently of the terra-cotta variety. These lamps (*nēróth*) **shall be set up** on the lampstand. They are separable from it. Each lamp would consist of a single bowl for oil, but might support more than one wick. W. F. Albright reports that at Tell Beit Mirsim he found terra-cotta lamps that were pinched in seven places to hold seven wicks (*The Archaeology of Palestine and the Bible* [New York: Fleming H. Revell, 1932], pp. 161-62). Those found all dated from 900 B.C. or before. Vss. 31*b*, 33-36, 38-39 (PB) introduce extensive ornamentation.

The function of the lamps was to illuminate the holy place. Natural light could come in only by the eastern entrance. They also had an aesthetic function. But increasingly the lampstand served as a religious symbol. It was the sign of God's presence in the midst of his people (Zech. 4:1-14). For the lamps to go out was a sign of impending

finally in full understanding of the divine words, "Inasmuch as ye have done it unto one of the least, . . . ye have done it unto me" (Matt. 25:40). But this loaf soon again became a symbol in its turn as time marches on. a symbol of social justice.

33. Almond Blossoms.—The Hebrew word means "awaken." As the almond blossom is the first to appear in the spring, it has the same happy connotation as "May" in English poetry, "Mayflower" or "trailing arbutus" in the eastern United States (cf. Jer. 1:11-12).

37 And thou shalt make the seven lamps thereof: and they shall light the lamps thereof, that they may give light over against it.

38 And the tongs thereof, and the snuff-dishes thereof, *shall be of* pure gold.

39 *Of* a talent of pure gold shall he make it, with all these vessels.

40 And look that thou make *them* after their pattern, which was showed thee in the mount.

26 Moreover thou shalt make the tabernacle *with* ten curtains *of* fine twined linen, and blue, and purple, and scarlet: *with* cherubim of cunning work shalt thou make them.

pure gold. 37 And you shall make the seven lamps for it; and the lamps shall be set up so as to give light upon the space in front of it. 38 Its snuffers and their trays shall be of pure gold. 39 Of a talent of pure gold shall it be made, with all these utensils. 40 And see that you make them after the pattern for them, which is being shown you on the mountain.

26 "Moreover you shall make the tabernacle with ten curtains of fine twined linen and blue and purple and scarlet stuff; with cherubim skilfully worked shall you

disaster (II Esdras 10:22). It may be inferred from 27:21; 30:8 that the lamps were lit only at night. Later tradition affirmed that the lamps burned perpetually (cf. Josephus *Antiquities* III. 8. 3). The religious meaning of the ancient Menorah is perpetuated for Christians in the sanctuary lamp. In the tabernacle the lampstand stood opposite the bread of the Presence, to the left as one looked toward the most holy place.

38-39. In Isa. 6:6 the **snuffers** are tongs with which coals are picked up off the altar. These are perhaps tweezerlike instruments for adjusting the wicks. The **trays** are receptacles for holding them. A **talent** of gold weighed about 108 pounds.

40. The recurrence of the formula of vs. 9 shows that we are at the conclusion of a section. Ark, table, and lampstand constitute a unit.

5. The Tabernacle (26:1-37)

The tabernacle here presented never actually existed. It is a product of the priestly imagination, an ideal structure. Two historical objects helped to give shape to the imaginary structure which was to illustrate a new theological conviction. First, it drew on the tent of meeting of the ancient tradition. Galling (Beer, *Exodus*, pp. 134-35) shows persuasively that the oldest strand (PA in vss. 7-14) drew the tabernacle in the shape of a tent. The later development of the document (PB) added two items: (a) vss. 15-30, which provide a rectangular wooden structure to take the place of the original tent shape; (b) vss. 1-6, which provide the goat's hair tent cover of the tabernacle with a "lining" decorated after the patterns on the walls of Solomon's temple (cf. vs. 1; I Kings 6:29). Thus, on the basis of the history of the text as analyzed by von Rad and Galling, we must allow a chronological priority of influence to the tent in giving rise to this ideal structure.

As Gerhard von Rad has shown ("Zelt und Lade," *Neue kirchliche Zeitschrift*, XLII [1931], 476-98), P's theological concern was to work out a synthesis between tent and ark.

26:1-37. *Blue, Purple, and Scarlet.*—Symbolism and beauty in the sanctuary are one. Everything that can be done to inspire reverence should help the congregation in every church. Here emphasis is placed on color,[6] on skilled craftsmanship, on precious stones and metals, on lovely robes, on light, and trumpet tones.

[6] See Mary Webb's essay "The Beauty of Colour," *Poems and the Spring of Joy* (New York: E. P. Dutton & Co., 1929), pp. 202-11.

Dignity, form, seemliness rule throughout the making of the sanctuary and the performance of its services. It is probably not edifying for the modern man to study too curiously all the details of the following chapters, but it is most important to note how carefully and lovingly everything was planned. Nothing was left to chance. Every act was symbolic. The church ought to be, like the tabernacle, the most lovely, well-cared for, clean building in the community.

2 The length of one curtain *shall be* eight and twenty cubits, and the breadth of one curtain four cubits: and every one of the curtains shall have one measure.

3 The five curtains shall be coupled together one to another; and *other* five curtains *shall be* coupled one to another.

4 And thou shalt make loops of blue upon the edge of the one curtain from the selvedge in the coupling; and likewise shalt thou make in the uttermost edge of *another* curtain, in the coupling of the second.

5 Fifty loops shalt thou make in the one curtain, and fifty loops shalt thou make in the edge of the curtain that *is* in the coupling of the second; that the loops may take hold one of another.

6 And thou shalt make fifty taches of gold, and couple the curtains together with the taches: and it shall be one tabernacle.

make them. 2 The length of each curtain shall be twenty-eight cubits, and the breadth of each curtain four cubits; all the curtains shall have one measure. 3 Five curtains shall be coupled to one another; and the other five curtains shall be coupled to one another. 4 And you shall make loops of blue on the edge of the outmost curtain in the first set; and likewise you shall make loops on the edge of the outmost curtain in the second set. 5 Fifty loops you shall make on the one curtain, and fifty loops you shall make on the edge of the curtain that is in the second set; the loops shall be opposite one another. 6 And you shall make fifty clasps of gold, and couple the curtains one to the other with the clasps, that the tabernacle may be one whole.

He wanted to re-establish the idea of the transcendence of God in relation to his people symbolized by the ancient tent and its cloud. Creatively and theologically, "P stands in the Tent of Meeting tradition" (*ibid.*, p. 495). He was moving away from that which the ark at Shiloh or the holy of holies in Solomon's temple had stood for. This interpretation of the tabernacle does away with Wellhausen's view that the tabernacle represented an attempt to project the temple and its service back into the era of nomadism (cf. Intro., pp. 844-46).

a) The Tent (26:1-14)

26:1. You shall make the tabernacle with ten curtains: The number refers to the panels, each four cubits wide, which are to be brought together to form an "inner lining" for the **tent over the tabernacle** (vs. 7). The word **with** rests on no Hebrew form. It is used in an attempt to translate what is seen as an accusative of specification (cf. Amer. Trans., "out of").

The cherubim which provided the decorative motifs were apparently to be woven into the fabric. They were to be "the work of the skillful designers" in weaving (cf. Amer. Trans., "work of artists"). In contrast, the decorative work on the screen is spoken of as "the work of the embroiderer" (vs. 36).

2. This inner lining of the tentlike cover of the tabernacle is two cubits shorter than the goats' hair cover over it. Also there are only ten panels, while the latter has eleven. When placed over the frame, it would have lacked a cubit from reaching to the ground on either side (cf. illustration in Hastings, *Dictionary of the Bible*, IV, 661). It is not hinted how the ten extra cubits of width, which hung over at the rear of the frame when the completed whole was put over the thirty-cubit-long frame, were to be arranged. This lack of provisions for arranging the tent on the frame not only reminds us that the frame is probably a later intrusion but also that the whole is an imaginary structure.

3-6. How the five separate panels in each half were to be **coupled to one another** we are not told. The two halves were to be laid alongside of each other, the ends even. Then, where they met, along the side of each, fifty **loops of blue, opposite one another,** were to be provided. Golden clasps put through these loops were to hold the two halves

7 ¶ And thou shalt make curtains *of goats' hair* to be a covering upon the tabernacle: eleven curtains shalt thou make.

8 The length of one curtain *shall be* thirty cubits, and the breadth of one curtain four cubits: and the eleven curtains *shall be all* of one measure.

9 And thou shalt couple five curtains by themselves, and six curtains by themselves, and shalt double the sixth curtain in the forefront of the tabernacle.

10 And thou shalt make fifty loops on the edge of the one curtain *that is* outmost in the coupling, and fifty loops in the edge of the curtain which coupleth the second.

11 And thou shalt make fifty taches of brass, and put the taches into the loops, and couple the tent together, that it may be one.

12 And the remnant that remaineth of the curtains of the tent, the half curtain that remaineth, shall hang over the back side of the tabernacle.

13 And a cubit on the one side, and a cubit on the other side of that which remaineth in the length of the curtains of

7 "You shall also make curtains of goats' hair for a tent over the tabernacle; eleven curtains shall you make. 8 The length of each curtain shall be thirty cubits, and the breadth of each curtain four cubits; the eleven curtains shall have the same measure. 9 And you shall couple five curtains by themselves, and six curtains by themselves, and the sixth curtain you shall double over at the front of the tent. 10 And you shall make fifty loops on the edge of the curtain that is outmost in one set, and fifty loops on the edge of the curtain which is outmost in the second set.

11 "And you shall make fifty clasps of bronze, and put the clasps into the loops, and couple the tent together that it may be one whole. 12 And the part that remains of the curtains of the tent, the half curtain that remains, shall hang over the back of the tabernacle. 13 And the cubit on the one side, and the cubit on the other side, of

---

together. The central seam of the complete cover was directly over the veil which separated the holy from the most holy place.

7. As suggested above, vss. 7-14 may constitute the original core of the P account on the tabernacle. The **curtains of goats' hair** suggest standard Bedouin tent material. But it is stated that the curtains are **for a tent over the tabernacle.** The phrase is curious and suggests two pictures. Contrary to vss. 1, 15 the expression **over the tabernacle** suggests that the rectangular frame was, in essence, the tabernacle. Further *'ōhel* normally refers to a structure in its own right, not to a roof over another structure. It seems possible that originally the title "tent of meeting" stood here and that it was later changed to the present "double" form (cf. Beer, *Exodus,* p. 134).

8. There were to be **eleven curtains** or panels. Their length was to be **thirty cubits,** two cubits longer than the inner cover described in vss. 1-6. When hung over the frame specified in vss. 15-30 the ends would just reach the ground. However, it seems possible that this is an original account that envisioned the tabernacle as a tent with sloping sides, tent ropes and pins, and the poles to hold it up. Such a tent would have been forty cubits long (cf. *ibid.,* Fig. 1, p. 135). It would have been open at both ends. Galling has suggested that any description of it that may once have been a part of P would have been suppressed in favor of the frame of vss. 15-30 (*ibid.*). An echo of it may have survived in vs. 13.

9. The sixth panel of the foremost half was to **double over at the front of the tent** (cf. 28:16). In vs. 12, probably a gloss, a contradictory explanation is offered (cf. McNeile, *Exodus,* p. lxxvii). The manner of coupling the separate panels is not specified (cf. vs. 3).

10-11. The two halves are to be joined as in vss. 3-6. But the loops are probably of the **goats' hair** of which the curtains are made, and there are **fifty clasps of bronze.** These would be immediately over those in vs. 6 and, like them, over the veil.

13. This verse seems to presuppose the "lining" of vss. 1-6, which is twenty-eight cubits long. There is a surplus of two cubits in the length of the curtains.

the tent, it shall hang over the sides of the tabernacle, on this side and on that side, to cover it.

14 And thou shalt make a covering for the tent *of* rams' skins dyed red, and a covering above *of* badgers' skins.

15 ¶ And thou shalt make boards for the tabernacle *of* shittim wood standing up.

16 Ten cubits *shall be* the length of a board, and a cubit and a half *shall be* the breadth of one board.

17 Two tenons *shall there be* in one board, set in order one against another: thus shalt thou make for all the boards of the tabernacle.

what remains in the length of the curtains of the tent shall hang over the sides of the tabernacle, on this side and that side, to cover it. 14 And you shall make for the tent a covering of tanned rams' skins and goatskins.

15 "And you shall make upright frames for the tabernacle of acacia wood. 16 Ten cubits shall be the length of a frame, and a cubit and a half the breadth of each frame. 17 There shall be two tenons in each frame, for fitting together; so shall you do for all

---

14. **Tanned rams' skins and goatskins** (cf. 25:5) were to cover the black goats' hair tent. They may have been as a protection against the weather.

b) THE WOODEN STRUCTURE (26:15-30)

The wooden structure represents an attempt to make the tent-tabernacle conform to the Solomonic temple. The floor space measures thirty by ten cubits. Solomon's temple measured sixty by twenty. The most holy place is, as in the temple, a cube: ten by ten by ten, compared to thirty by twenty by twenty. But since the structure must be accommodated to the tent, the similarities end here. It consists of only two sides and a west end. Moreover, the walls are ten cubits high all around. The fact that the walls of the holy place in Solomon's temple were higher than in the most holy place is ignored. Finally, nothing is said about a roof or about any sort of central support such as is normally provided for a tent by tent poles (cf. vs. 8).

15-16. Galling's title for the wooden structure is *Brettergerüst* ("board frame"; Beer, *Exodus*, p. 136; note especially Fig. 3, p. 135). The Hebrew term *qerāshîm* was traditionally translated as **boards** (KJV, ASV). Galling continues to translate it so. Outside of this context it occurs only in Ezek. 27:6, where it is usually translated "deck," though the meaning is not clear. A. R. S. Kennedy (cf. "Tabernacle," Hastings, *Dictionary of the Bible*, IV, 659-61) reinterpreted the whole context of the word in the plan of the tabernacle and so arrived at the meaning **frames**. He proceeded on the dubious assumption that, in the writers of P, the tent cover and the wooden structure had been fully integrated. Specifically, Kennedy was convinced that the writers would have wanted the beautiful inner cover (vss. 1-6) with its colored cherubim visible along the walls as well as overhead. Therefore he decided that the wooden walls consisted of open frames through which the cover was visible. Also, Kennedy did not think that the writers would have portrayed a structure whose materials would have been so very difficult to transport in the desert. He perhaps overestimated the concerns of P with such practical matters. There is ample evidence of a lack of harmonization between tent and frame to warrant the possibility that the finely woven cherubim would have been invisible behind solid walls. The Kennedy hypothesis seeks to impute to the writers a concern for architectural niceties and interior decoration they do not seem to have had. Nevertheless, on simple linguistic grounds and for the sake of giving meaning to the text, his theory is still the best solution proposed (cf. Exeg. on vss. 17-19).

17-19. **Each frame** (or **board**) shall have two "hands" or **tenons** (cf. I Kings 7:32-33, "axletrees"; also vss. 35-36, "stays"). Kennedy identified the two uprights of

18 And thou shalt make the boards for the tabernacle, twenty boards on the south side southward.

19 And thou shalt make forty sockets of silver under the twenty boards; two sockets under one board for his two tenons, and two sockets under another board for his two tenons.

20 And for the second side of the tabernacle on the north side *there shall be* twenty boards,

21 And their forty sockets *of* silver; two sockets under one board, and two sockets under another board.

22 And for the sides of the tabernacle westward thou shalt make six boards.

the frames of the tabernacle. 18 You shall make the frames for the tabernacle: twenty frames for the south side; 19 and forty bases of silver you shall make under the twenty frames, two bases under one frame for its two tenons, and two bases under another frame for its two tenons; 20 and for the second side of the tabernacle, on the north side twenty frames, 21 and their forty bases of silver, two bases under one frame, and two bases under another frame; 22 and for the rear of the tabernacle westward you

---

his "frames" as the **tenons.** Since the tenons are to be joined, each to its opposite, he provided each frame with "cross rings" (Amer. Trans.). Traditionally the view has been that the two tenons were pins at the bottom of the boards, to be fitted into the socket of the silver bases (vss. 18-19). Galling, however, thinks of the **two tenons** as pins along the side of each board. The mates for these pins are thought of as mortising locks along the side edge of the board immediately opposite (cf. Beer, *Exodus*, Fig. 3, p. 135). The **fitting together** consists, then, of mortising the boards by inserting the pegs in their corresponding locks. Galling's interpretation is full of difficulties. Notably, in vs. 19 we are told that the two bases under each **frame** are for **its two tenons.** These must be the two tenons referred to in vs. 17. But if they are to be fitted into the base sockets, they must be at the bottom of the frame, not along its sides. Without warrant Galling interprets the tenons in vs. 19 as another pair than those in vs. 17, calling them "base pins" (*Standzapfen*). Nor, indeed, is there any real evidence for locks in the boards. The Hebrew text says that "they shall be joined, each to the one corresponding to it" (lit., "a woman to her sister"; cf. vs. 3). The antecedent of "they" is tenons, not boards as the KJV almost implies.

Galling saw this, but since he thought of the frames as boards he invented another pair of tenons for the base in vs. 19. It is not the boards that are to be fitted together or **set in order one against another;** nor are pins or tenons to be fitted into locks along the sides of the boards. Tenons are to be joined together. This, says Kennedy, is done by means of "cross rungs" (in late and modern Hebrew the word for rung is actually derived from the root involved in **fitting together**). The brilliance and proof of Kennedy's solution are here seen in the satisfactory interpretation it gives of vs. 17 and in the manner in which it reconciles vs. 17 with vs. 19.

18. The total length of the side walls would be thirty cubits. We do not know how deep the frames were. It is generally felt that if the frames were open outside measurements are indicated.

20-21. The bases or pedestals of silver are each to be provided with one socket.

22. The length of **six frames** would total nine cubits. It has often been suggested that this indicates that the depth of the frames was approximately nine inches. The **six frames** would then just fit between the north and south walls at the west end, giving an outside measurement of ten cubits (cf. McNeile, *Exodus*, p. lxxvi; also Kennedy, "Tabernacle," in Hastings, *op. cit.*, IV, 659-61). This interpretation automatically removes the two additional frames of vs. 23 from the wall proper.

23 And two boards shalt thou make for the corners of the tabernacle in the two sides.

24 And they shall be coupled together beneath, and they shall be coupled together above the head of it unto one ring: thus shall it be for them both; they shall be for the two corners.

25 And they shall be eight boards, and their sockets *of* silver, sixteen sockets; two sockets under one board, and two sockets under another board.

26 ¶ And thou shalt make bars *of* shittim wood; five for the boards of the one side of the tabernacle,

27 And five bars for the boards of the other side of the tabernacle, and five bars for the boards of the side of the tabernacle, for the two sides westward.

28 And the middle bar in the midst of the boards shall reach from end to end.

29 And thou shalt overlay the boards with gold, and make their rings *of* gold *for* places for the bars: and thou shalt overlay the bars with gold.

30 And thou shalt rear up the tabernacle according to the fashion thereof which was showed thee in the mount.

shall make six frames. 23 And you shall make two frames for corners of the tabernacle in the rear; 24 they shall be separate beneath, but joined at the top, at the first ring; thus shall it be with both of them; they shall form the two corners. 25 And there shall be eight frames, with their bases of silver, sixteen bases; two bases under one frame, and two bases under another frame.

26 "And you shall make bars of acacia wood, 27 five for the frames of the one side of the tabernacle, and five bars for the frames of the other side of the tabernacle, and five bars for the frames of the side of the tabernacle at the rear westward. 28 The middle bar, halfway up the frames, shall pass through from end to end. 29 You shall overlay the frames with gold, and shall make their rings of gold for holders for the bars; and you shall overlay the bars with gold. 30 And you shall erect the tabernacle according to the plan for it which has been shown you on the mountain.

23-24. In these verses the RSV owes much to the interpretation of the wooden structure provided by Kennedy. The **two** additional **frames** do not stand in the wall as properly a part of it, but are treated as **corners . . . in the rear.** The Hebrew term means "corner structure" (Ezek. 41:22). It does not seem impossible that it could signify buttress (Neh. 3:19-20). Once it is granted that the frames are buttresses it must be decided how they were placed. The RSV decides that they shall **be separate beneath, but joined at the top.** This emphasizes the sloping angle of the pieces. The word translated **separate** really means "twins"; here, "double." The word given as **joined** means "complete," "integrated." But in the Samar. and the LXX, instead of this word, there is a second occurrence of "double" (cf. ASV; Amer. Trans.). The sloping buttress shall be double or **separate** from the wall all the way up to the ring near the top of the wall (cf. vs. 28). **Thus shall it be with both of them,** i.e., with both corner pieces.

Galling (Beer, *Exodus,* p. 135) still holds to the view that the two additional frames were a part of the end wall itself, "corner pieces."

26-27. Wooden or iron **bars** were used especially to shut the gates of walled towns from within (cf. Deut. 3:5). Here they are to be run through loops or **rings of gold** (!) attached perhaps to the outside of the frames.

28. It seems that there were three bands of bars, but that only the middle band was to run the whole length of a wall, **from end to end.** On the side this would have meant a bar forty-five feet long!

30. This formula is an attempt to duplicate the one in 25:9, 40. It differs in that instead of speaking of the "pattern . . . on the mountain," it speaks of **the plan** (*mishpāṭ*). It does not really come at the conclusion of the instructions. Hence, it seems that the late writer who inserted that section into the P account (PB) must also have provided the formula.

31 ¶ And thou shalt make a veil *of* blue, and purple, and scarlet, and fine twined linen of cunning work: with cherubim shall it be made.

32 And thou shalt hang it upon four pillars of shittim *wood* overlaid with gold: their hooks *shall be of* gold, upon the four sockets of silver.

33 ¶ And thou shalt hang up the veil under the taches, that thou mayest bring in thither within the veil the ark of the testimony: and the veil shall divide unto you between the holy *place* and the most holy.

34 And thou shalt put the mercy seat upon the ark of the testimony in the most holy *place.*

35 And thou shalt set the table without the veil, and the candlestick over against the table on the side of the tabernacle toward the south: and thou shalt put the table on the north side.

36 And thou shalt make a hanging for the door of the tent, *of* blue, and purple, and scarlet, and fine twined linen, wrought with needlework.

37 And thou shalt make for the hanging five pillars *of* shittim *wood,* and overlay them with gold, *and* their hooks *shall be of* gold: and thou shalt cast five sockets of brass for them.

31 "And you shall make a veil of blue and purple and scarlet stuff and fine twined linen; in skilled work shall it be made, with cherubim; 32 and you shall hang it upon four pillars of acacia overlaid with gold, with hooks of gold, upon four bases of silver. 33 And you shall hang the veil from the clasps, and bring the ark of the testimony in thither within the veil; and the veil shall separate for you the holy place from the most holy. 34 You shall put the mercy seat upon the ark of the testimony in the most holy place. 35 And you shall set the table outside the veil, and the lampstand on the south side of the tabernacle opposite the table; and you shall put the table on the north side.

36 "And you shall make a screen for the door of the tent, of blue and purple and scarlet stuff and fine twined linen, embroidered with needlework. 37 And you shall make for the screen five pillars of acacia, and overlay them with gold; their hooks shall be of gold, and you shall cast five bases of bronze for them.

---

c) THE VEIL AND THE SCREEN (26:31-37)

31. The Hebrew word for **veil** used here occurs seventeen times in all and is always used of the screen separating the most holy from the holy place. It apparently had the same decorations as the inner lining of the tent and, like it, was the work of "the skillful designers" who were apparently weavers of colored figures (cf. vs. 1).

32. The veil was a hanging that was to be suspended from golden hooks at the top of four acacia wood **pillars.** These were overlaid with gold and set in **sockets** or **bases of silver** (cf. vs. 19). The **hooks** were to be **of gold.** The veil would presumably reach all the way up to the tent overhead.

33. The **clasps** with which the two halves of the inner and outer tent covers had been hooked together (vss. 6, 11) were immediately over the veil.

34-35. This veil, together with the **mercy seat,** is for the author a supreme symbol of God's transcendent freedom. But even the freedom of God can deteriorate into a static concept. Heb. 9:7-8; 10:19-22 depict the veil as the symbol of God's unapproachability.

36-37. The word for **screen,** here used of the hanging at the entrance to the holy place (cf. 35:15; 39:38; 40:8, 28), is also used for the fabric at the entrance to the court (27:16; 35:17; etc.); and with the word for veil it is used of the separation of the holy from the most holy (35:12; 39:34; 40:21). The screen that would constitute the door to the holy place was not as rich as the veil at the most holy place. The beautifully colored yarns were not to be woven into figures in the fabric but would be used by the

27 And thou shalt make an altar *of* shittim wood, five cubits long, and five cubits broad; the altar shall be four-square: and the height thereof *shall be* three cubits.

2 And thou shalt make the horns of it upon the four corners thereof: his horns shall be of the same: and thou shalt overlay it with brass.

3 And thou shalt make his pans to receive his ashes, and his shovels, and his basins, and his fleshhooks, and his firepans:

27 "You shall make the altar of acacia wood, five cubits long and five cubits broad; the altar shall be square, and its height shall be three cubits. 2 And you shall make horns for it on its four corners; its horns shall be of one piece with it, and you shall overlay it with bronze. 3 You shall make pots for it to receive its ashes, and

embroiderer. There were to be **five pillars** instead of four, gold covered and with golden hooks for the hanging. But the **sockets** were to be of bronze instead of silver, probably because of the distance from the holiest place.

6. THE BRASS ALTAR (27:1-8)

Beginning with the ark and moving outward, the instructions (chs. 25–31) treat each item of the cultic apparatus in order, whether of building or of furniture. The cover and walls of the tabernacle were described after the instructions concerning the furniture in the holy place. Now, before turning to the wall of the great court (vss. 9-19), we meet the great altar of burnt offering which is to occupy the central place in the court east of the tabernacle (40:29-30; I Kings 8:64; cf. illustration, Hastings, *Dictionary of the Bible,* IV, 657).

27:1. The term **the altar** implies that only one altar is contemplated. The altar of incense is not in mind at all. This altar is "the altar of burnt offering" (30:28; 31:9), also known as "the bronze altar" (38:30; 39:39) because it is finished entirely in bronze. In this respect it is patterned on Solomon's great altar (I Kings 8:64; II Kings 16:10-15; II Chr. 4:1). The bronze is to cover the acacia wood which will constitute the hollow frame of the structure (vs. 8). It is possible that it was contemplated that this hollow center would be filled with earth, thus conforming to the ancient law of the altar (20:24). Ezekiel's model altar was to be made of four stone squares, superimposed one on another, of which the topmost one measured twelve cubits, about ten cubits above the ground. Solomon's altar also is said to have stood ten cubits high with a flat surface measuring twenty by twenty cubits. This altar is much smaller: five by five by three cubits, which corresponds precisely to the size of the brass platform from which Solomon is said to have blessed the people at the consecration of the temple (II Chr. 6:12).

2. The **horns** of the altar were to be **of one piece with it** (cf. 25:19, 35) made of wood and brass. These horns were almost the heart of the altar. The blood of the sin offerings was applied to them (29:12). Those seeking asylum at the altar had to touch its horns (I Kings 1:50; 2:28). And the breaking of the horns constituted the destruction of the altar (Amos 3:14). Brass altars with horns were of Canaanite origin, adapted to the worship of Yahweh.

3. The **ashes,** as the Hebrew indicates, consisted of the encrustations of burned fat on the altar. These were to be removed from the altar whenever it was dismantled for

27:1-2. *The Horns of the Altar.*—The horns at the four corners of the altar were found also on Assyrian altars. When Israel adopted them, they became the most sacred part of the altar. In I Kings 1:50; 2:28 we find that those seeking refuge from revengeful enemies were safe if they caught hold of them. Every religion, every sermon, every creed must have points at which ordinary folk can take hold. All the sweet incense, the gold and blue and purple and scarlet, the bells and pomegranates, and vestments, are vanity if there is not some place for the fugitive and the sinner to hold on to in his day of distress.

all the vessels thereof thou shalt make *of* brass.

4 And thou shalt make for it a grate of network *of* brass; and upon the net shalt thou make four brazen rings in the four corners thereof.

5 And thou shalt put it under the compass of the altar beneath, that the net may be even to the midst of the altar.

6 And thou shalt make staves for the altar, staves *of* shittim wood, and overlay them with brass.

7 And the staves shall be put into the rings, and the staves shall be upon the two sides of the altar, to bear it.

8 Hollow with boards shalt thou make it: as it was showed thee in the mount, so shall they make *it*.

9 ¶ And thou shalt make the court of the tabernacle: for the south side southward *there shall be* hangings for the court *of* fine twined linen of a hundred cubits long for one side:

10 And the twenty pillars thereof and their twenty sockets *shall be of* brass; the hooks of the pillars and their fillets *shall be of* silver.

shovels and basins and forks and fire pans; all its utensils you shall make of bronze. **4** You shall also make for it a grating, a network of bronze; and upon the net you shall make four bronze rings at its four corners. **5** And you shall set it under the ledge of the altar so that the net shall extend half way down the altar. **6** And you shall make poles for the altar, poles of acacia wood, and overlay them with bronze; **7** and the poles shall be put through the rings, so that the poles shall be upon the two sides of the altar, when it is carried. **8** You shall make it hollow, with boards; as it has been shown you on the mountain, so shall it be made.

9 "You shall make the court of the tabernacle. On the south side the court shall have hangings of fine twined linen a hundred cubits long for one side; **10** their pillars shall be twenty and their bases twenty, of bronze, but the hooks of the pillars and

travel (Num. 4:13), and perhaps daily. The **ashes** could be kept temporarily to the east of the altar, probably in the **pots** or urns prescribed (cf. Lev. 1:16). For final disposal the priests had to carry them outside the camp, along with other waste of the sacrifices (Lev. 4:12; 6:10-11).

4-5. The **ledge of the altar** is suddenly introduced without further description. It was apparently **half way down the altar,** one and one-half cubits from its top. The width is not given. In Ezekiel's model altar, consisting of four tiers of stone, the ledge was formed by the difference in size between the third and fourth tiers (Ezek. 43:13-17). The ledge may have been intended as a substitute for the forbidden steps (20:26), though steps are also mentioned in Ezek. 43:17. In P's altar the ledge could have had only an aesthetic or symbolic function. The priests would not have needed to stand on a special elevation to serve at an altar only three cubits high.

The **network of bronze** was a sort of grille superimposed on the wooden shell. The carrying rings were to be attached to the altar at the corners, somewhere below the ledge.

6-7. The **poles** correspond to those for the ark and the table, except that they are gilded in **bronze** rather than in gold (25:13, 28).

7. The Tabernacle Court (27:9-19)

9. The **court of the tabernacle** is the sacred area surrounding it. Every temple and temple plan in Israel's history was provided with such a court. It is generally agreed that Solomon's temple, like these instructions for the tabernacle, contained only one court. Later temples had two or more.

10-12. The dimensions of the court are one hundred by fifty cubits, a rectangle consisting of two squares. The writer's love of symmetry is clearly apparent. But in his account of the **pillars** or posts on which the hangings will be put he becomes confusing. For each side there shall be twenty pillars, and for the **breadth of the court on the west**

11 And likewise for the north side in length *there shall be* hangings of a hundred *cubits* long, and his twenty pillars and their twenty sockets *of* brass; the hooks of the pillars and their fillets *of* silver.

12 ¶ And *for* the breadth of the court on the west side *shall be* hangings of fifty cubits: their pillars ten, and their sockets ten.

13 And the breadth of the court on the east side eastward *shall be* fifty cubits.

14 The hangings of one side *of the gate shall be* fifteen cubits: their pillars three, and their sockets three.

15 And on the other side *shall be* hangings fifteen *cubits:* their pillars three, and their sockets three.

16 ¶ And for the gate of the court *shall be* a hanging of twenty cubits, *of* blue, and purple, and scarlet, and fine twined linen, wrought with needlework: *and* their pillars *shall be* four, and their sockets four.

17 All the pillars round about the court *shall be* filleted with silver; their hooks *shall be of* silver, and their sockets *of* brass.

18 ¶ The length of the court *shall be* a hundred cubits, and the breadth fifty every where, and the height five cubits *of* fine twined linen, and their sockets *of* brass.

19 All the vessels of the tabernacle in all the service thereof, and all the pins thereof,

their fillets shall be of silver. 11 And likewise for its length on the north side there shall be hangings a hundred cubits long, their pillars twenty and their bases twenty, of bronze, but the hooks of the pillars and their fillets shall be of silver. 12 And for the breadth of the court on the west side there shall be hangings for fifty cubits, with ten pillars and ten bases. 13 The breadth of the court on the front to the east shall be fifty cubits. 14 The hangings for the one side of the gate shall be fifteen cubits, with three pillars and three bases. 15 On the other side the hangings shall be fifteen cubits, with three pillars and three bases. 16 For the gate of the court there shall be a screen twenty cubits long, of blue and purple and scarlet stuff and fine twined linen, embroidered with needlework; it shall have four pillars and with them four bases. 17 All the pillars around the court shall be filleted with silver; their hooks shall be of silver, and their bases of bronze. 18 The length of the court shall be a hundred cubits, the breadth fifty, and the height five cubits, with hangings of fine twined linen and bases of bronze. 19 All the utensils of the tabernacle

side ten pillars, each with a single bronze base. The numbers ten and twenty would have yielded completely symmetrical results, also for the more complicated east end (vss. 13-16), if they had applied to the units of hangings between posts rather than to the posts as such. As it is, it is impossible to reconcile the demands with the complete symmetry at which the writer obviously aims. Even Kennedy's clever interpretation fails because it results in putting the screen out of center in the east end (Hastings, *Dictionary of the Bible*, IV, 657; cf. McNeile, *Exodus*, pp. lxxviii-lxxix). It seems clear that we are here face to face with the sort of inadvertent slip typical of an amateur, which, however obvious, often escapes discovery until one is confronted by the impasse it implies. It reminds us that this plan, produced in the study, was never actually implemented.

13-16. In the east end of the court the central **twenty cubits** would constitute the entrance to the court. Whereas the **hangings** roundabout consist of **fine twined linen,** without ornamentation, the gate screen is to be embroidered with the **blue and purple and scarlet,** so constantly used in the plan. The **pillars and bases** are apparently meant to be the same as all the others.

17. This verse repeats what has already been said in vs. 10; vss. 9, 17-18 are perhaps the oldest (P^A) portion of this account. The pillars were all to be **filleted with silver.** This probably means that each pillar was to have a thin band of silver surrounding it.

18. The wall of the court was to be five cubits high. In Ezekiel's plan for the temple the outer wall was six cubits high (Ezek. 40:5).

19. The **utensils** are not specified here. The account of the brass laver (30:17-21) is added later. These are, however, the utensils for use at the altar (vs. 3). It seems

and all the pins of the court, *shall be of* brass.

20 ¶ And thou shalt command the children of Israel, that they bring thee pure oil olive beaten for the light, to cause the lamp to burn always.

21 In the tabernacle of the congregation without the veil, which *is* before the testimony, Aaron and his sons shall order it from evening to morning before the LORD: *it shall be* a statute for ever unto their generations on the behalf of the children of Israel.

28 And take thou unto thee Aaron thy brother, and his sons with him, from among the children of Israel, that he may minister unto me in the priest's office, *even* Aaron, Nadab and Abihu, Eleazar and Ithamar, Aaron's sons.

for every use, and all its pegs and all the pegs of the court, shall be of bronze.

20 "And you shall command the people of Israel that they bring to you pure beaten olive oil for the light, that a lamp may be set up to burn continually. **21** In the tent of meeting, outside the veil which is before the testimony, Aaron and his sons shall tend it from evening to morning before the LORD. It shall be a statute for ever to be observed throughout their generations by the people of Israel.

28 "Then bring near to you Aaron your brother, and his sons with him, from among the people of Israel, to serve me as priests — Aaron and Aaron's sons, Nadab and Abi'hu, Elea'zar and Ith'amar.

---

impossible to include any but utensils in the **court** in the provision that **all the utensils of the tabernacle** should be of bronze. Those inside the dwelling were all of gold. It also seems probable that only **pegs of the court** are actually intended (cf. 35:18; 39:40; Num. 3:37).

8. OIL FOR THE LAMP (27:20-21)

20-21. This regulation was probably inserted here by an editor to serve as an introduction to the section on the priest (chs. 28–29). The care of the lamp was a part of the priest's daily duty. It prescribes the bringing of oil for the lamp, **to be observed throughout their generations by the people of Israel.** The word **statute** also means "due" or "obligation." From year to year and age to age oil for the temple **lamp** (only one is mentioned, despite 25:31-40) must be provided by the faithful.

9. THE PRIESTHOOD AND ITS DRESS (28:1-43)

The setting is in the Mosaic era. Therefore Aaron and his sons are the priests. The latter are only incidentally introduced. The real preoccupation is with Aaron. We must see in him the symbol of the high priest of the postexilic era and in his sons the priests of that time. The description of the garments and functions corresponds to those of the priest in the postexilic period (Ecclus. 45:6-24; 50:1-24). The term "high priest" was not technically employed until after the Exile. There are various forms of it: "high priest" (II Chr. 34:9), "chief priest" (Ezra 7:5; II Chr. 19:11), "ruler of the house of God" (I Chr. 9:11). In the later Hasmonaean period the high priest was primarily a political figure. But here Aaron is singled out for attention because of his religious

---

20. *The Lamp to Burn Continually.*—A burning light is the finest symbol of a continuing spiritual presence. To the Hebrews light, the first begotten of God, was the finest, most immaterial substance known, for which no idolatrous corporeal form could be made.

28:1-43. *The Vestments of the Priests.*—There has always been great difference of opinion in every age of the world's history, both in religious and secular circles, as to whether priests as a profession have exercised on society an influence

more good or evil. The priest in every age owes his office partly to untenable ancestral beliefs and superstitions, partly to his present-day usefulness to society. Most of the evils of clericalism are due to the former element in his calling, especially the priest's assumption of special privileges and of supposed miraculous powers. When these are at a minimum, and his special training and skills and knowledge are on a par with those of other professions (such as medicine and law), then the priest performs a real service

2 And thou shalt make holy garments for Aaron thy brother, for glory and for beauty.

3 And thou shalt speak unto all *that are* wise-hearted, whom I have filled with the spirit of wisdom, that they may make Aaron's garments to consecrate him, that he may minister unto me in the priest's office.

4 And these *are* the garments which they shall make; a breastplate, and an ephod, and a robe, and a broidered coat, a mitre, and a girdle: and they shall make holy garments for Aaron thy brother, and his sons, that he may minister unto me in the priest's office.

5 And they shall take gold, and blue, and purple, and scarlet, and fine linen.

2 And you shall make holy garments for Aaron your brother, for glory and for beauty. 3 And you shall speak to all who have ability, whom I have endowed with an able mind, that they make Aaron's garments to consecrate him for my priesthood. 4 These are the garments which they shall make: a breastpiece, an ephod, a robe, a coat of checkerwork, a turban, and a girdle; they shall make holy garments for Aaron your brother and his sons to serve me as priests.

5 "They shall receive gold, blue and purple and scarlet stuff, and fine twined

function. Priestly religion is basically a religion of reconciliation, and in the person of the high priest this reconciliation is effected (cf. 33:12-23). Through Aaron the grace of Yahweh will be mediated to Israel. But Moses is to "put into his hand" this gift of God. Moses remains supreme over the priest.

a) INTRODUCTION (28:1-5)

28:1. Moses must **bring near** Aaron and his sons to make them priests. **To bring near** is a technical term denoting consecration. On the basis of the analogous Arabic word *kahin*, it is probable that etymologically the Hebrew word for priest (*kôhēn*) meant "seer." Originally a priest was especially one who counseled and gave oracles (I Sam. 9). The Urim and Thummim on Aaron's breastplate are a relic of this ancient function. The Zadokite priesthood, which was the one probably considered legitimate by P, claimed an Aaronic pedigree through Eleazar. This late and probably unauthentic claim illustrates that the Mosaic authority and unbroken heredity of the priesthood were held indispensable to its legitimacy.

2. The **holy garments** served a cultic purpose. They granted the priests access to the sacred precincts not open to laymen. They also served a social purpose—they were **for glory and for beauty.** They were the sign of the priest's dignity and of his social rank.

3. As Galling suggests (cf. Beer, *Exodus,* pp. 138-39), vss. 2-3 probably represent this unit in its oldest form (cf. 39:1). The **wise-hearted,** whom Moses is to command to make Aaron's garments, are not mentioned by name.

4-5. The usual offerings of colored yarn and **fine twined linen** are to be received by the skillful workers. In addition, gold thread is asked for. In the list of items the golden diadem to be placed on Aaron's turban is not included (cf. vss. 36-38). The short "breeches" (vs. 42) are also left out.

to society. This service consists in his knowledge and appreciation of the history and place of religion in human society throughout the past, in his skill as leader of men toward a more worthy religious life, in his personal character as the fullest expression of religious faith, in his power of expressing through ritual and imaginative presentation the tested truths of real religion. The real priest is characterized by a deep

and growing secret religious life, by the common virtues such as are admired by all men, and by a love for men and a real touch with God. He realizes more than most men that the house of truth has many mansions, that others may find God by other ways than his. By meditation and long practice he has attained skill in prayer, in the attainment of an infectiously healthy inner life, in influencing the lives of

6 ¶ And they shall make the ephod *of* gold, *of* blue, and *of* purple, *of* scarlet, and fine twined linen, with cunning work.

7 It shall have the two shoulderpieces thereof joined at the two edges thereof; and *so* it shall be joined together.

8 And the curious girdle of the ephod, which *is* upon it, shall be of the same, according to the work thereof; *even of* gold, *of* blue, and purple, and scarlet, and fine twined linen.

9 And thou shalt take two onyx stones, and grave on them the names of the children of Israel:

10 Six of their names on one stone, and *the other* six names of the rest on the other stone, according to their birth.

linen. 6 And they shall make the ephod of gold, of blue and purple and scarlet stuff, and of fine twined linen, skilfully worked. 7 It shall have two shoulder-pieces attached to its two edges, that it may be joined together. 8 And the skilfully woven band upon it, to gird it on, shall be of the same workmanship and materials, of gold, blue and purple and scarlet stuff, and fine twined linen. 9 And you shall take two onyx stones, and engrave on them the names of the sons of Israel, 10 six of their names on the one stone, and the names of the remaining six on the other stone, in the order of their

---

b) The Ephod (28:6-12)

6. The **ephod** is to be skillfully worked, i.e., the colored patterns shall be woven into the fabrics (cf. 26:1). The ephod was perhaps the oldest cultic garment in Israel. It was in use at Shiloh (I Sam. 2:18-19, 28). David wore an apronlike linen ephod when he brought up the ark (II Sam. 6:14, 15). The ephod was the indispensable piece of equipment for the delivery of an oracle (I Sam. 14:3 ff.; 23:6, 9 ff.). But this raises the question whether in such instances it was a garment worn by the priest or an image or object from which the oracle was obtained. In certain instances the term refers unmistakably to an image or similar object (Judg. 8:27; 17:5; 18:14; Hos. 3:4). The more doubtful cases in which the phrases "bringing the ephod" or "bearing the ephod" occur may indicate the same meaning (I Sam. 2:28; 23:9; 30:7). In P the word is no longer used of an image. The garment seems to have a symbolic function synonymous with the breastpiece.

7. With the aid of the Samar. one may perhaps read this verse as stating two separate facts about the ephod: it will have uniting **shoulderpieces** or straps, and the two edges of the main piece will be joined, thus making of it a single garment, pull-over style (cf. 39:4). This joining of the edges may have meant the joining of two pieces, front and back, under each of the arms.

8. The **skilfully woven band** seems to have been a girdle with which to fasten the ephod close about the waist (Lev. 8:7). It was permanently attached to the ephod and made of the same material.

9-10. The **two onyx stones** (cf. 25:7), on which the names of the **sons of Israel** are to be engraved, **in the order of their birth**, is paralleled by the twelve stones of the breastpiece in vss. 17-21. The latter is probably the more recent account. The function

---

others through sympathy and insight. He seeks nothing for himself; and for his church he asks only that it be judged by its fruits in producing good people, fairly criticized for its failings, and allowed to have its place as one among the many ways by which men find God. These are the real sacred garments of the priesthood; breastpieces, ephods, robes, turbans, and girdles are nothing if they are not the outward signs of these inner graces, and they are a very poor substitute for them.

Whitehead says: "Music, ceremonial clothing, ceremonial smells, and ceremonial rhythmic visual appearances, also have symbolic truth, or symbolic falsehood." [7] He means that they may suggest the emotion which votaries dumbly feel ought to be attached to the occasion; they provide an emotional clothing which changes the dim objective reality sought for into clear appearance, just as music organizes confused feeling into more distinct apprehension.

[7] *Adventures of Ideas*, p. 319.

11 With the work of an engraver in stone, *like* the engravings of a signet, shalt thou engrave the two stones with the names of the children of Israel: thou shalt make them to be set in ouches of gold.

12 And thou shalt put the two stones upon the shoulders of the ephod *for* stones of memorial unto the children of Israel: and Aaron shall bear their names before the Lord upon his two shoulders for a memorial.

13 ¶ And thou shalt make ouches *of* gold;

14 And two chains *of* pure gold at the ends; *of* wreathed work shalt thou make them, and fasten the wreathed chains to the ouches.

15 ¶ And thou shalt make the breastplate of judgment with cunning work; after the work of the ephod thou shalt make it; *of* gold, *of* blue, and *of* purple, and *of* scarlet, and *of* fine twined linen, shalt thou make it.

16 Foursquare it shall be *being* doubled; a span *shall be* the length thereof, and a span *shall be* the breadth thereof.

17 And thou shalt set in it settings of stones, *even* four rows of stones: *the first* row *shall be* a sardius, a topaz, and a carbuncle: *this shall be* the first row.

birth. 11 As a jeweler engraves signets, so shall you engrave the two stones with the names of the sons of Israel; you shall enclose them in settings of gold filigree. 12 And you shall set the two stones upon the shoulder-pieces of the ephod, as stones of remembrance for the sons of Israel; and Aaron shall bear their names before the Lord upon his two shoulders for remembrance. 13 And you shall make settings of gold filigree, 14 and two chains of pure gold, twisted like cords; and you shall attach the corded chains to the settings.

15 "And you shall make a breastpiece of judgment, in skilled work; like the work of the ephod you shall make it; of gold, blue and purple and scarlet stuff, and fine twined linen shall you make it. 16 It shall be square and double, a span its length and a span its breadth. 17 And you shall set in it four rows of stones. A row of sardius, topaz, and carbuncle shall be the first row;

of the stones in the two is the same: to emphasize that the priestly service represents the entire people (cf. vs. 29).

11-12. The **two stones,** set in rosette fillings of gold, are likened to **signets.** These were symbols of authority and commitment in all the ancient world (Gen. 41:42; Jer. 22:24; Hag. 2:23). Aaron's role as priest and his authority are provided by the covenant of grace Yahweh gives to Israel. He must **bear their names before the Lord.** Israel is the concern of his service.

c) The Breastpiece (28:13-30)

13-14. The **chains of pure gold** are not links but continuous and interwoven lines of gold cord, "cordage-work" (Amer. Trans., cf. I Kings 7:17).

15-16. The **breastpiece** is so designated because of its position when worn by the high priest. The Hebrew name of the object is *ḥōshen.* This could mean "beautiful object" but can also be linguistically interpreted as "pouch," and because of its function as the container of the Urim and Thummim this seems the more probable meaning. The same yarns used for the ephod are to be employed. The fabric is to be **in skilled work** (cf. vs. 6), i.e., there are to be patterns woven in color. The pouch was to be **square and double.** A span was one half a cubit. It consisted therefore of a piece of fabric a cubit long and folded over. It is usually assumed that the ends were sewed together. Possibly also one end of the resulting pouch was closed.

17-21. The function of the twelve precious stones which are to be set in four rows of three on the outer side of the pouch is identical with that of the two stones on the shoulders of the ephod (vss. 11-12): to bring the **twelve tribes** of Israel **to continual**

18 And the second row *shall be* an emerald, a sapphire, and a diamond.

19 And the third row a ligure, an agate, and an amethyst.

20 And the fourth row a beryl, and an onyx, and a jasper: they shall be set in gold in their inclosings.

21 And the stones shall be with the names of the children of Israel, twelve, according to their names, *like* the engravings of a signet; every one with his name shall they be according to the twelve tribes.

22 ¶ And thou shalt make upon the breastplate chains at the ends *of* wreathed work *of* pure gold.

23 And thou shalt make upon the breastplate two rings of gold, and shalt put the two rings on the two ends of the breastplate.

24 And thou shalt put the two wreathed *chains* of gold in the two rings *which are* on the ends of the breastplate.

25 And *the other* two ends of the two wreathed *chains* thou shalt fasten in the two ouches, and put *them* on the shoulderpieces of the ephod before it.

26 ¶ And thou shalt make two rings of gold, and thou shalt put them upon the two ends of the breastplate in the border thereof, which *is* in the side of the ephod inward.

27 And two *other* rings of gold thou shalt make, and shalt put them on the two sides of the ephod underneath, toward the forepart thereof, over against the *other* coupling thereof, above the curious girdle of the ephod.

18 and the second row an emerald, a sapphire, and a diamond; **19** and the third row a jacinth, an agate, and an amethyst; **20** and the fourth row a beryl, an onyx, and a jasper; they shall be set in gold filigree. **21** There shall be twelve stones with their names according to the names of the sons of Israel; they shall be like signets, each engraved with its name, for the twelve tribes. **22** And you shall make for the breastpiece twisted chains like cords, of pure gold; **23** and you shall make for the breastpiece two rings of gold, and put the two rings on the two edges of the breastpiece. **24** And you shall put the two cords of gold in the two rings at the edges of the breastpiece; **25** the two ends of the two cords you shall attach to the two settings of filigree, and so attach it in front to the shoulder-pieces of the ephod. **26** And you shall make two rings of gold, and put them at the two ends of the breastpiece, on its inside edge next to the ephod. **27** And you shall make two rings of gold, and attach them in front to the lower part of the two shoulder-pieces of the ephod, at its joining above the skilfully

---

remembrance before the Lord (vs. 29). Two other lists of precious stones, probably inspired by this one, and bearing many close resemblances to it in details are found in the Bible. In Ezek. 28:13 the king of Tyre is said to have had a shield of precious stones in which nine of the stones mentioned here are listed (in the LXX all twelve are given). Also, in Rev. 21:19-20 there is a list of twelve precious stones, decorations on the foundation stones of the Holy City, that closely resemble the stones decorating the breastpiece.

22-25. The **cords of gold,** already mentioned in vs. 14, are to hold up the oracle pouch. For each cord there is a ring of gold at the upper corners of the pouch. The other end of each cord is attached to the two **settings of filigree** on the forward part of the two shoulderpieces.

26-28. At the lower corners of the pouch there are also to be two rings. Since they are to be used to tie back the pouch so as to prevent it from swinging **loose from the ephod,** they are placed on the inside fold of the pouch, at the corners. Two other rings are to be put on the ephod (vs. 27). The location of these rings on the ephod has been very difficult. They are said to be on **the lower part of the two shoulderpieces.** It is literally more correct to say that they are "below the shoulderpieces" (cf. KJV) of the

28 And they shall bind the breastplate by the rings thereof unto the rings of the ephod with a lace of blue, that it may be above the curious girdle of the ephod, and that the breastplate be not loosed from the ephod.

29 And Aaron shall bear the names of the children of Israel in the breastplate of judgment upon his heart, when he goeth in unto the holy place, for a memorial before the LORD continually.

30 ¶ And thou shalt put in the breastplate of judgment the Urim and the Thummim; and they shall be upon Aaron's heart, when he goeth in before the LORD: and Aaron shall bear the judgment of the children of Israel upon his heart before the LORD continually.

woven band of the ephod. 28 And they shall bind the breastpiece by its rings to the rings of the ephod with a lace of blue, that it may lie upon the skilfully woven band of the ephod, and that the breastpiece shall not come loose from the ephod. 29 So Aaron shall bear the names of the sons of Israel in the breastpiece of judgment upon his heart, when he goes into the holy place, to bring them to continual remembrance before the LORD. 30 And in the breastpiece of judgment you shall put the Urim and the Thummim, and they shall be upon Aaron's heart, when he goes in before the LORD; thus Aaron shall bear the judgment of the people of Israel upon his heart before the LORD continually.

ephod, near its seam, i.e., where the edges of the ephod were joined (cf. vs. 7). It has been suggested that there was a "seam" under each of the arms. And thus these rings would be at the two sides of the ephod, just in front of the seams, and just above the "skilfully woven band" or girdle which went about the waist (cf. vs. 8). A lace of blue ran through the rings of the lower corners of the pouch, tied back from the pouch by means of these rings on the ephod under the arms just above the waist.

29-30. The priest has a double function. He must make intercession for the people before God, and he must declare God's will to the people. Originally the Urim and Thummim dealt solely with the latter. They were oracular media by which the priest obtained God's decision for the people (Num. 27:21; Deut. 33:8; I Sam. 28:6). The use of Urim and Thummim was apparently a prerogative of the priests. In this account the pouch is still called the breastpiece of judgment, but by means of the twelve beautiful stones it has become a symbol of the intercessory role of the priest. There is no evidence that the Urim and Thummim were actually used as oracular media in the postexilic era. Ezra 2:63 seems to show that they were not.

30. *The Urim and Thummim.*—John Newton in the eighteenth century said,

[They] were something in Aaron's breast-plate; but what, criticks and commentators are by no means agreed. . . . It is most probable that they were only names given to signify the clearness and certainty of the divine answers which were obtained by the high priest consulting God with his breast-plate on, in contradistinction to the obscure, enigmatical, uncertain, and imperfect answers of the heathen oracles.[8]

I Sam. 14:41-42; 28:6 seem to indicate that originally they had been two stones used for casting lots to discover the guilt or innocence of suspected parties. Every court of law has to have some similar device for suggesting to the public

that its decisions are not merely personal judgments. The difficulty about the use of Urim and Thummim, as is seen by the references to its application in the O.T., was that there are so many questions which cannot be answered by a mere yes or no, and that it was necessary to agree beforehand on the exact way in which the oracle was to be interpreted. The same difficulty exists today when the Constitution and precedent take the place of Urim and Thummim.

It was also early recognized that the use of such oracles placed too much power in the hands of the priests. At the beginning of the thirteenth century Gottfried von Strassburg comments on the use of similar tests with the words, "so the blessed Lord can be blown this way or that like the sleeve of a coat." [9]

[8] Samuel Johnson, *A Dictionary of the English Language* (London: W. Strahan, 1755-56), s.v. "Urim."

[9] *Tristan*, ed. Reinhold Bechstein (3rd ed.; Leipzig: F. A. Brockhaus, 1891), p. 187.

31 ¶ And thou shalt make the robe of the ephod all *of* blue.

32 And there shall be a hole in the top of it, in the midst thereof: it shall have a binding of woven work round about the hole of it, as it were the hole of an habergeon, that it be not rent.

33 ¶ And *beneath* upon the hem of it thou shalt make pomegranates *of* blue, and *of* purple, and *of* scarlet, round about the hem thereof; and bells of gold between them round about:

34 A golden bell and a pomegranate, a golden bell and a pomegranate, upon the hem of the robe round about.

35 And it shall be upon Aaron to minister: and his sound shall be heard when he goeth in unto the holy *place* before the LORD, and when he cometh out, that he die not.

31 "And you shall make the robe of the ephod all of blue. 32 It shall have in it an opening for the head, with a woven binding around the opening, like the opening in a garment,*ᵖ* that it may not be torn. 33 On its skirts you shall make pomegranates of blue and purple and scarlet stuff, around its skirts, with bells of gold between them, 34 a golden bell and a pomegranate, a golden bell and a pomegranate, round about on the skirts of the robe. 35 And it shall be upon Aaron when he ministers, and its sound shall be heard when he goes into the holy place before the LORD, and when he comes out, lest he die.

ᵖ The Hebrew word is of uncertain meaning

d) THE ROBE OF THE EPHOD (28:31-35)

31-35. The robe of the ephod is a separate garment, the *me'il,* over which the ephod and breastpiece are placed. Their wearing is the prerogative of the high priest alone. It is called **the robe of the ephod** to indicate its distinctly cultic character when worn by the priest. Originally it was the robe of the nobleman (I Sam. 18:4). But here this civil dress, fringed with pomegranates and bells, is set aside for sacred use. It was woven all of blue or rather of purple (cf. 25:4). In postexilic Israel, when Israel was a semi-autonomous religious community within a larger political state, the high priest also commonly carried the "princely" function of being the political representative of his people before the foreign ruler. The robe was symbolic of this role.

The **opening for the head**—"in the midst of it" (Hebrew)—speaks for the view commonly expressed (cf. Driver, *Exodus,* p. 307; Beer, *Exodus,* p. 142) that the *me'il* was a garment that had to be put on over the head. As such, in the Fourth Gospel it becomes the prototype for the seamless robe of Christ. A closely woven band bordered the edge of the head opening, **like the opening in a garment,** to prevent tearing. The pomegranates, in mixed colors, were ultimately perhaps derived from the nature mysticism of Canaanite Palestine. They were also used for decorative purposes in Solomon's temple (I Kings 7:20, 42). The sound of the robe would be heard when Aaron entered and left the temple. We are not told that the bells made the sound, though that must perhaps be assumed. Nor are we told whether God or the people would hear. In view of the phrase **lest he die** the implication is that either demons or God

34. *A Golden Bell and a Pomegranate.*—The best explanation of these is in vs. 40, **for glory and for beauty.** There may have been archaeological reasons for them, but they had been forgotten, and the people sewed them around the high priest's skirts for much the same reason that Browning used them as the title of several of his books of verse—because they liked the look and the sound of them. Bells and pome-

granates, a sweet sound and a sweet savor, still a good text upon which to speak of the beautiful place a church should be. The picture of the priest in all his robes, with the names of all the families of the congregation carved, each on a jewel on his breast, going into the holy place, the people following his progress by the sound of the bells, fragrant incense rising to heaven like the prayers of the faithful, makes

36 ¶ And thou shalt make a plate *of* pure gold, and grave upon it, *like* the engravings of a signet, HOLINESS TO THE LORD.

37 And thou shalt put it on a blue lace, that it may be upon the mitre; upon the forefront of the mitre it shall be.

38 And it shall be upon Aaron's forehead, that Aaron may bear the iniquity of the holy things, which the children of Israel shall hallow in all their holy gifts; and it shall be always upon his forehead, that they may be accepted before the LORD.

39 ¶ And thou shalt embroider the coat of fine linen, and thou shalt make the mitre *of* fine linen, and thou shalt make the girdle *of* needlework.

36 "And you shall make a plate of pure gold, and engrave on it, like the engraving of a signet, 'Holy to the LORD.' 37 And you shall fasten it on the turban by a lace of blue; it shall be on the front of the turban. 38 It shall be upon Aaron's forehead, and Aaron shall take upon himself any guilt incurred in the holy offering which the people of Israel hallow as their holy gifts; it shall always be upon his forehead, that they may be accepted before the LORD.

39 "And you shall weave the coat in checkerwork of fine linen, and you shall make a turban of fine linen, and you shall make a girdle embroidered with needlework.

would hear. The priestly robe was a protection against the demons who might want to slay one seeking an audience with God.

e) THE DIADEM, TURBAN, AND COAT (28:36-39)

Vss. 36-38 were apparently inserted after vs. 39, for the turban which is assumed in vs. 37 is first provided for in the instructions in vs. 39. In the parallel account (ch. 39), reporting the manufacture of the objects, the coats for Aaron and his sons, the turban for Aaron, the caps for the sons, and the girdle come first (39:27-29). The making of the plate and its attachment to the turban follow (39:30-31).

36. The **plate of pure gold** was equivalent to a diadem or crown. Its name is taken from the root meaning "to shine" (cf. Ps. 132:18). The diadem reminds us that in the postexilic community the high priest had the role of a "prince" (vss. 31-35). The phrase **Holy to the LORD** inscribed on the plate signifies that the priest, and through him all Israel, belongs to Yahweh or is set apart for his peculiar service.

37. The **turban** or **mitre** means lit., "that which is wrapped." It was probably a tall cone-shaped headdress. In Ezek. 21:26 (Hebrew vs. 31) the **turban** is a royal sign (cf. Zech. 3:5).

39. The **turban** was for Aaron alone. The **coat,** which was the long tunic worn underneath the purple robe, was part of the normal dress of every man. For the priest it is to be woven **in checkerwork of fine linen;** 39:27 seems to indicate that the coats for Aaron and his sons were identical (cf. vs. 40). In 39:29 only one girdle is reported as having been made **with needlework.** We do not learn how or whether the girdles for the sons were made, but we may assume that they were the same as Aaron's. The turban with its diadem, the ephod, the robe and the breastpiece are the distinctive objects of the high priest.

one wonder about the contrast with some modern methods of worshiping God, as Browning did in his *Christmas-Eve and Easter-Day.*[1] In Christian times the sound deemed most abhorrent to the ears of fiends and goblins has been the sweet and solemn sound of church bells.

36. *Holy to the Lord.*—These words refer neither to the turban nor to the priest as an

individual (19:6), but to the relation of Israel (in the person of their representative) to God. The people are a sacred object belonging to Yahweh. The meaning is the same as the motto on the seal in II Tim. 2:19, prophetic of Heb. 7:25. The responsibility for the service rests largely upon the priest (Num. 18:1). He must see to it that, in the words of the communion collect, "We may . . . worthily magnify thy holy Name."

[1] See also Frazer, *Folk-lore in O.T.,* III, 446-80.

40 ¶ And for Aaron's sons thou shalt make coats, and thou shalt make for them girdles, and bonnets shalt thou make for them, for glory and for beauty.

41 And thou shalt put them upon Aaron thy brother, and his sons with him; and shalt anoint them, and consecrate them, and sanctify them, that they may minister unto me in the priest's office.

42 And thou shalt make them linen breeches to cover their nakedness; from the loins even unto the thighs they shall reach:

43 And they shall be upon Aaron, and upon his sons, when they come in unto the tabernacle of the congregation, or when they come near unto the altar to minister in the holy *place;* that they bear not iniquity, and die: *it shall be* a statute for ever unto him and his seed after him.

29 And this *is* the thing that thou shalt do unto them to hallow them, to minister unto me in the priest's office: Take one young bullock, and two rams without blemish,

40 "And for Aaron's sons you shall make coats and girdles and caps; you shall make them for glory and beauty. 41 And you shall put them upon Aaron your brother, and upon his sons with him, and shall anoint them and ordain them and consecrate them, that they may serve me as priests. 42 And you shall make for them linen breeches to cover their naked flesh; from the loins to the thighs they shall reach; 43 and they shall be upon Aaron, and upon his sons, when they go into the tent of meeting, or when they come near the altar to minister in the holy place; lest they bring guilt upon themselves and die. This shall be a perpetual statute for him and for his descendants after him.

29 "Now this is what you shall do to them to consecrate them, that they may serve me as priests. Take one young

---

f) The Garments for Aaron's Sons (28:40-43)

40-41. The **caps** for Aaron's sons were apparently different from the turban of the high priest. A different Hebrew word is used for them (cf. Lev. 8:13). It implies a high or cuplike covering. The **girdles** were sashes with which the coats were bound about the waist; they seem to have been very long (cf. Josephus *Antiquities* III. 7. 2). Today in some parts of the Near East, notably among the Kurds, the social status of a man is indicated by the length of his sash.

42-43. The **linen breeches,** from **the loins to the thighs,** may have been loincloths (cf. LXX *ad loc.;* Josephus *Antiquities* III. 7. 1). The word is taken from a root meaning "to gather." The term **breeches** rests chiefly on the interpretation of it as a dual. The actual function of the loincloth dates back to the period when the ephod was the only garment prescribed for the priest (cf. 20:26; II Sam. 6:12-19). The tabernacle is designated as the **tent of meeting. The holy place** probably refers to the great court in which the altar of burnt offering stood, although strictly it refers to the interior of the tabernacle or temple. In later postexilic times only priests could approach the altar of burnt offering.

10. The Consecration of Priests (29:1-42a)

The instructions for the consecration of the priests were probably suggested by the report on their consecration by Moses in Lev. 8. Driver (*Exodus,* p. 315) has pointed out that the manner of the ceremonial, especially with respect to the manner of

---

29:1-28. *The Prerogatives of the Priests.*—Chs. 28–30 are best studied in connection with Lev. 8; Num. 8. Even at this early date the clergy received remuneration. A part of the sacrificed animal was reserved for their use after it had been offered to the Lord. This custom has led to many abuses and the enrichment of the priest-

hood both personally and corporately. Among others, the Quakers protested against the appointment of professional clergy, holding that the appointment of one man to preach to the exclusion of others was a limitation to the work of the Spirit. However, Robert Barclay in 1676 recognized that the care of a group might re-

2 And unleavened bread, and cakes unleavened tempered with oil, and wafers
unleavened anointed with oil: *of* wheaten
flour shalt thou make them.

3 And thou shalt put them into one
basket, and bring them in the basket, with
the bullock and the two rams.

4 And Aaron and his sons thou shalt
bring unto the door of the tabernacle of
the congregation, and shalt wash them with
water.

5 And thou shalt take the garments, and
put upon Aaron the coat, and the robe of
the ephod, and the ephod, and the breastplate, and gird him with the curious girdle
of the ephod:

bull and two rams without blemish, 2 and
unleavened bread, unleavened cakes mixed
with oil, and unleavened wafers spread with
oil. You shall make them of fine wheat flour.
3 And you shall put them in one basket
and bring them in the basket, and bring the
bull and the two rams. 4 You shall bring
Aaron and his sons to the door of the tent
of meeting, and wash them with water.
5 And you shall take the garments, and put
on Aaron the coat and the robe of the
ephod, and the ephod, and the breastpiece,
and gird him with the skilfully woven

---

the sacrifices, presupposes the regulations of Lev. 1–7, which tends to the conclusion that
the Levitical code was extant when this P account was written.

a) THE PRESENTATION (29:1-9)

29:1-3. The bread, cakes, and wafers, along with the bullock and the two rams are to
be "brought near," i.e., presented in ritual fashion. The **unleavened cakes** made of
"wheat germ" (Lev. 24:5) were a normal part of a peace offering (Lev. 7:12). They
were **mixed with oil.** In contrast, the very thin **unleavened wafers** were **anointed with oil.**
The name of the latter means, lit., "thin." A bread of this type, by the same name, is still
common in the Near East (*khubzun raqīqun*). The **bullock** will serve as sin offering
(vss. 10-14). One of the rams is a whole burnt offering (vss. 15-18). The other constitutes
the sacrifice of consecration.

4. Three steps are involved in the preparation of Aaron and his sons. Moses was to
cause them to "draw near" **to the door of the tent of meeting** where the presentation
took place. First he was to **wash them.** In contrast to the daily ablutions of hands and
feet (30:19-21), this was a washing of the entire body (cf. John 13:10; Heb. 10:22).

5-6. The second step in the preparation is the vesting of the priests. For this Aaron
is singled out for special attention (cf. Lev. 8:7-9).

---

quire a man's whole time, to the exclusion of
other remunerative work. He wrote:

Also they who have received this holy and unspotted gift, as they have freely received it, so are
they freely to give it, without hire or bargaining,
far less to use it as a Trade to get money by: Yet
if God hath called any one from their employment
or trades, by which they acquire their livelihood,
it may be lawful for such, according to the liberty
which they feel given them in the Lord, to receive
such temporals (to wit, what may be needful for
them for meat and clothing) as are given them
freely and cordially by those to whom they have
communicated spirituals.[2]

This seems to be a similar arrangement to that
commended in the text.

   [2] *An Apology for the True Christian Divinity* (Providence: Knowles & Vose, 1840), Prop. X, p. 271.

George Tyrrell wrote in one of his letters:

I will do what I can with the problem of the
absolute necessity and the absolute impossibility of
Churches. . . . As long as priests make their living
by the altar they will be suspected (even where
they are not guilty) of self-interested teaching. This
is a great source of the weakness of religion in all
ages and nations; not only as bringing priests (and
consequently their cause) into discredit, but as
separating Church life from civil-life to the great
detriment of both.[3]

He felt that the corporate self-interestedness of
all the churches was the great obstacle in the
way of Christianity. Albert Schweitzer in Lam-
baréné and the Friends in every stricken land
point us toward a better way.

   [3] M. D. Petre, *Autobiography and Life of George
Tyrrell* (New York: Longmans, Green & Co., 1912), II,
376.

6 And thou shalt put the mitre upon his head, and put the holy crown upon the mitre.

7 Then shalt thou take the anointing oil, and pour *it* upon his head, and anoint him.

8 And thou shalt bring his sons, and put coats upon them.

9 And thou shalt gird them with girdles, Aaron and his sons, and put the bonnets on them: and the priest's office shall be theirs for a perpetual statute: and thou shalt consecrate Aaron and his sons.

10 And thou shalt cause a bullock to be brought before the tabernacle of the congregation; and Aaron and his sons shall put their hands upon the head of the bullock.

11 And thou shalt kill the bullock before the LORD, *by* the door of the tabernacle of the congregation.

12 And thou shalt take of the blood of the bullock, and put *it* upon the horns of the altar with thy finger, and pour all the blood beside the bottom of the altar.

band of the ephod: **6** and you shall set the turban on his head, and put the holy crown upon the turban. **7** And you shall take the anointing oil, and pour it on his head and anoint him. **8** Then you shall bring his sons, and put coats on them, **9** and you shall gird them with girdles*q* and bind caps on them; and the priesthood shall be theirs by a perpetual statute. Thus you shall ordain Aaron and his sons.

10 "Then you shall bring the bull before the tent of meeting. Aaron and his sons shall lay their hands upon the head of the bull, **11** and you shall kill the bull before the LORD, at the door of the tent of meeting, **12** and shall take part of the blood of the bull and put it upon the horns of the altar with your finger, and the rest of*r* the blood you shall pour out at the base of the

q Gk: Heb *girdles, Aaron and his sons*
r Heb *all*

---

7. The third step consists in the anointing of Aaron with **oil** as a sign of his consecration to the priestly office. The oil, scented with precious perfumes (30:22-33), was poured out on the high priest's head (cf. Ps. 133:2). The anointing of priests is reported first in the P stratum. First only the high priest was anointed; so here (cf. Lev. 16:32; 21:10). Later the anointing of all priests became mandatory (28:41; 30:30; 40:15).

8-9. The vesting of the sons of Aaron is left to the last. While the high priest lives they serve as auxiliary priests (Ecclus. 50:12). Their chief distinction was that they were the heirs of Aaron; the priesthood was theirs **by a perpetual statute.** To **ordain Aaron and his sons** consisted in "filling their hands" with priestly authority. The supremacy of Moses consisted in God's choice of him for this task.

b) THE SIN OFFERING AND BURNT OFFERING (29:10-18)

10. Sin offerings were made on certain high occasions, both for individuals and for the entire community. First in this respect stands the great day of Atonement. But also on great festal occasions, such as Passover week (Ezek. 45:22, 23), sin offerings were appropriate. The bullock was the prescribed sin offering for the priest (Lev. 4:1-12). But this sacrifice, to induct **Aaron and his sons,** differs in that he does not offer in his own behalf, but brings his sacrifice to Moses.

11. The provision that the bullock be killed **at the door of the tent of meeting** is synonymous with "before the LORD" (Lev. 1:5; 3:7; 4:4, 15) and also, it seems, with the specific direction that the slaying shall take place to the north of the great altar (Lev. 1:11).

12. The officiating priest must dip his finger in the blood, not only to anoint **the horns of the altar** with it but to sprinkle the blood seven times before the veil that separates the holy place from the most holy (Lev. 4:5, 17). The blood is a "covering" for the sin for which the sacrifice is brought, whether this sin is specifiable or not (Lev. 4:26, 35). It is the sign of forgiveness.

13 And thou shalt take all the fat that covereth the inwards, and the caul *that is* above the liver, and the two kidneys, and the fat that *is* upon them, and burn *them* upon the altar.

14 But the flesh of the bullock, and his skin, and his dung, shalt thou burn with fire without the camp: it *is* a sin offering.

15 ¶ Thou shalt also take one ram; and Aaron and his sons shall put their hands upon the head of the ram.

16 And thou shalt slay the ram, and thou shalt take his blood, and sprinkle *it* round about upon the altar.

17 And thou shalt cut the ram in pieces, and wash the inwards of him, and his legs, and put *them* unto his pieces, and unto his head.

18 And thou shalt burn the whole ram upon the altar: it *is* a burnt offering unto the LORD: it *is* a sweet savor, an offering made by fire unto the LORD.

19 ¶ And thou shalt take the other ram; and Aaron and his sons shall put their hands upon the head of the ram.

altar. 13 And you shall take all the fat that covers the entrails, and the appendage of the liver, and the two kidneys with the fat that is on them, and burn them upon the altar. 14 But the flesh of the bull, and its skin, and its dung, you shall burn with fire outside the camp; it is a sin offering.

15 "Then you shall take one of the rams, and Aaron and his sons shall lay their hands upon the head of the ram, 16 and you shall slaughter the ram, and shall take its blood and throw it against the altar round about. 17 Then you shall cut the ram into pieces, and wash its entrails and its legs, and put them with its pieces and its head, 18 and burn the whole ram upon the altar; it is a burnt offering to the LORD; it is a pleasing odor, an offering by fire to the LORD.

19 "You shall take the other ram; and Aaron and his sons shall lay their hands

13-14. Of a sin offering nothing is eaten. Only certain pieces of **fat, . . . the appendage of the liver, and the two kidneys** were to be burned on the altar (Lev. 4:8-10). All the rest was to be burned outside the camp. When the sin offering was made in behalf of another than the priests, the priests could eat what was not burned on the altar (Lev. 5:13; 6:26).

15-18. Unlike the sin offering, the burnt offering for which **one of the rams** is used has only a casual relation to the ordination ceremony as such. It is a very traditional form of sacrifice, appropriate for every occasion. Its central religious theme is adoration. Because **Aaron and his sons** lay their hands upon it, the ram is presented as their offering of praise.

c) THE SACRIFICE OF INSTALLATION (29:19-36a)

The sacrifice of installation follows the general pattern of the peace offering. It consists of both animal and cereal portions. Also Aaron and his sons, who in this case occupy the role of ordinary worshipers, are to consume the major portion of the offering as a fellowship meal. The peace offering was chiefly the sacrifice of fellowship, as the whole burnt offering was the sacrifice of adoration.

19-21. Aaron and his sons play the role of ordinary worshipers. They **lay their hands upon the head of the ram** and so identify themselves with it. We are given the impression that Moses slew the ram (cf. vs. 11). He is to use some of the blood to apply to **the tips of the right ears of** [Aaron and] **his sons, . . . the thumbs of their right hands, and . . . the great toes of their right feet.** The same procedure is followed in the rite for the purification of lepers, both oil and blood being used (Lev. 14:14, 17). But in that rite the blood is obtained from a guilt offering and so has an expiatory significance. That seems ruled out in this case. A less formalized analogy to the ceremony prescribed here may be represented in 24:6, 8. The later symbolic significance of this application of

20 Then shalt thou kill the ram, and take of his blood, and put *it* upon the tip of the right ear of Aaron, and upon the tip of the right ear of his sons, and upon the thumb of their right hand, and upon the great toe of their right foot, and sprinkle the blood upon the altar round about.

21 And thou shalt take of the blood that *is* upon the altar, and of the anointing oil, and sprinkle *it* upon Aaron, and upon his garments, and upon his sons, and upon the garments of his sons with him: and he shall be hallowed, and his garments, and his sons, and his sons' garments with him.

22 Also thou shalt take of the ram the fat and the rump, and the fat that covereth the inwards, and the caul *above* the liver, and the two kidneys, and the fat that *is* upon them, and the right shoulder; for it *is* a ram of consecration:

23 And one loaf of bread, and one cake of oiled bread, and one wafer out of the basket of the unleavened bread that *is* before the Lord.

24 And thou shalt put all in the hands of Aaron, and in the hands of his sons; and shalt wave them *for* a wave offering before the Lord.

25 And thou shalt receive them of their hands, and burn *them* upon the altar for a burnt offering, for a sweet savor before the Lord: it *is* an offering made by fire unto the Lord.

upon the head of the ram, 20 and you shall kill the ram, and take part of its blood and put it upon the tip of the right ear of Aaron and upon the tips of the right ears of his sons, and upon the thumbs of their right hands, and upon the great toes of their right feet, and throw the rest of the blood against the altar round about. 21 Then you shall take part of the blood that is on the altar, and of the anointing oil, and sprinkle it upon Aaron and his garments, and upon his sons and his sons' garments with him; and he and his garments shall be holy, and his sons and his sons' garments with him.

22 "You shall also take the fat of the ram, and the fat tail, and the fat that covers the entrails, and the appendage of the liver, and the two kidneys with the fat that is on them, and the right thigh (for it is a ram of ordination), 23 and one loaf of bread, and one cake of bread with oil, and one wafer, out of the basket of unleavened bread that is before the Lord; 24 and you shall put all these in the hands of Aaron and in the hands of his sons, and wave them for a wave offering before the Lord. 25 Then you shall take them from their hands, and ·burn them on the altar in addition to the burnt offering, as a pleasing odor before the Lord; it is an offering by fire to the Lord.

---

blood (McNeile, *Exodus*, p. 190) may well have been that the priests were to heed God's word, do his work, and walk in his ways. But it is admitted by all that the rite has a very long history, and that in its primitive forms it represented a protection against demonic forces. Exegetes all recognize in vs. 21 a very late addition (Galling, McNeile) which seeks to extend the anointing (vs. 7) and the application of blood to the priests' garments.

22-23. The portions of the **fat** and the **kidneys** set aside to be burned on the altar correspond to the portions of the peace offering so assigned in Lev. 3:3-5. To these the **right thigh** is added. This was normally **of the priests' portion** (vs. 27; cf. Lev. 7:31-32), but this is a **ram of ordination**. Except for Moses, there are as yet no priests to claim the portion. One of each of the kinds of bread in the basket (vs. 3) is added to the portion of Yahweh.

24. The portions to be burned are first put into the hands of the priests. This "filling of the hands" is the very heart of the ordination rite. It symbolizes two things: (*a*) the priests are authorized to receive the sacrifices and prepare them for presentation to God, which is their chief function; (*b*) it is the prerogative of the priests to "live off the altar." The term **wave offering** is not applicable to the portion to be burned on the altar. Those portions that go to the priests are waved. Here it may signify the future prerogative of the priests in this respect.

26 And thou shalt take the breast of the ram of Aaron's consecration, and wave it *for* a wave offering before the LORD: and it shall be thy part.

27 And thou shalt sanctify the breast of the wave offering, and the shoulder of the heave offering, which is waved, and which is heaved up, of the ram of the consecration, *even* of *that* which *is* for Aaron, and of *that* which is for his sons:

28 And it shall be Aaron's and his sons' by a statute for ever from the children of Israel; for it *is* a heave offering: and it shall be a heave offering from the children of Israel of the sacrifice of their peace offerings, *even* their heave offering unto the LORD.

29 ¶ And the holy garments of Aaron shall be his sons' after him, to be anointed therein, and to be consecrated in them.

30 *And* that son that is priest in his stead shall put them on seven days, when he cometh into the tabernacle of the congregation to minister in the holy *place*.

31 ¶ And thou shalt take the ram of the consecration, and seethe his flesh in the holy place.

32 And Aaron and his sons shall eat the flesh of the ram, and the bread that *is* in the basket, *by* the door of the tabernacle of the congregation.

26 "And you shall take the breast of the ram of Aaron's ordination and wave it for a wave offering before the LORD; and it shall be your portion. 27 And you shall consecrate the breast of the wave offering, and the thigh of the priests' portion, which is waved, and which is offered from the ram of ordination, since it is for Aaron and for his sons. 28 It shall be for Aaron and his sons as a perpetual due from the people of Israel, for it is the priests' portion to be offered by the people of Israel from their peace offerings; it is their offering to the LORD.

29 "The holy garments of Aaron shall be for his sons after him, to be anointed in them and ordained in them. 30 The son who is priest in his place shall wear them seven days, when he comes into the tent of meeting to minister in the holy place.

31 "You shall take the ram of ordination, and boil its flesh in a holy place; 32 and Aaron and his sons shall eat the flesh of the ram and the bread that is in the basket, at

26. **The breast of the ram** was also a regular part of the priests' portion (Lev. 7:34; 10:14). This Moses is to take for himself, since he is the priest, and as officiating priest he is to **wave it for a wave offering**, i.e., move it out toward the altar and then draw it back, much as offering plates are handled in some churches.

27-28. These two verses are best understood as not directly related to this sacrifice. They are rather an explanatory note to the effect that the **breast of the wave offering and the thigh of the priests' portion** are for the personal use of Aaron and his sons. They are to take them from all peace offerings brought by the children of Israel.

29-30. These verses constitute another general note. The garments of Aaron become the hereditary possession of the priesthood. They are **to be anointed in them.** Only the high priest is anointed. Apparently it is assumed that the ceremony of installation (vs. 24) is repeated upon accession to the high priesthood. The seven-day period of the ceremony is to be inferred (cf. vs. 35).

31-32. In peace offering, after the portions for the altar and the priest had been contributed (vs. 27), the worshipers who brought the sacrifice were to consume the remainder in the sacred precincts while in a state of ritual purity (Lev. 7:15-21). The priest boiled the flesh for them (I Sam. 2:13). Here Moses seems to act as priest and the sacrifice is brought by **Aaron and his sons** (cf. Lev. 8:31). The boiling of the flesh is generally considered an older form of its preparation than roasting (cf. 12:8; Deut. 16:7). Beer (*Exodus*, p. 65), however, thinks roasting was a very primitive form and this P reference to boiling offers some support to his contention.

33 And they shall eat those things wherewith the atonement was made, to consecrate *and* to sanctify them: but a stranger shall not eat *thereof,* because they *are* holy.

34 And if aught of the flesh of the consecrations, or of the bread, remain unto the morning, then thou shalt burn the remainder with fire: it shall not be eaten, because it *is* holy.

35 And thus shalt thou do unto Aaron, and to his sons, according to all *things* which I have commanded thee: seven days shalt thou consecrate them.

36 And thou shalt offer every day a bullock *for* a sin offering for atonement: and thou shalt cleanse the altar, when thou hast made an atonement for it, and thou shalt anoint it, to sanctify it.

37 Seven days thou shalt make an atonement for the altar, and sanctify it; and it shall be an altar most holy: whatsoever toucheth the altar shall be holy.

38 ¶ Now this *is that* which thou shalt offer upon the altar; two lambs of the first year day by day continually.

39 The one lamb thou shalt offer in the morning; and the other lamb thou shalt offer at even:

the door of the tent of meeting. 33 They shall eat those things with which atonement was made, to ordain and consecrate them, but an outsider shall not eat of them, because they are holy. 34 And if any of the flesh for the ordination, or of the bread, remain until the morning, then you shall burn the remainder with fire; it shall not be eaten, because it is holy.

35 "Thus you shall do to Aaron and to his sons, according to all that I have commanded you; through seven days shall you ordain them, 36 and every day you shall offer a bull as a sin offering for atonement. Also you shall offer a sin offering for the altar, when you make atonement for it, and shall anoint it, to consecrate it. 37 Seven days you shall make atonement for the altar, and consecrate it, and the altar shall be most holy; whatever touches the altar shall become holy.

38 "Now this is what you shall offer upon the altar: two lambs a year old day by day continually. 39 One lamb you shall offer in the morning, and the other lamb you shall

---

33-34. The newly installed priests shall eat of the ram as the bread **with which atonement was made** at their induction. **Atonement,** "covering," is used here with respect to a peace offering. The idea of the removal of guilt is not included in the meaning of **atonement** as used here (cf. S. R. Driver, "Atonement," in Hastings, *Dictionary of the Bible,* IV, 128). The unhallowed person or **stranger** here means anyone not being consecrated to the priesthood. The term stranger as used in P often means the layman as over against the priest (Num. 3:10, 38). The Hebrew word (*zār*) should be distinguished from *gēr* (a person socially or tribally different) and *nokhrî* (a foreigner).

35-36a. The ceremony of installation lasted **seven days.** The ceremonial washing, dressing, and anointing were performed only on the first day. But the sacrifices were to be repeated **every day.** During this period the priests were to remain in the sacred enclosure (Lev. 8:33).

The **sin offering for atonement** here prescribed seems to be a late addition. Nothing is said about such an offering for the priests in the description of the installation ceremony, either here or in Lev. 8.

d) THE GREAT ALTAR (29:36b-42a)

36b-37. The prescription of **a sin offering for the altar** has nothing to do with the consecration of the priests as such. Its appearance here is anachronistic. These verses must represent a late editor's attempt to harmonize the tabernacle instructions respecting the altar with Ezek. 43:18-27.

38-42a. The prescription for the daily burnt offering given here corresponds exactly to Num. 28:3-8. In the pre-exilic period the **lamb** of the burnt offering was sacrificed in the morning, and the **cereal offering** was made at night (II Kings 16:15). This custom was so well established that to refer to the cereal offering (*minḥāh*) was synonymous

40 And with the one lamb a tenth deal of flour mingled with the fourth part of a hin of beaten oil; and the fourth part of a hin of wine *for* a drink offering.

41 And the other lamb thou shalt offer at even, and shalt do thereto according to the meat offering of the morning, and according to the drink offering thereof, for a sweet savor, an offering made by fire unto the LORD.

42 *This shall be* a continual burnt offering throughout your generations *at* the door of the tabernacle of the congregation before the LORD, where I will meet you, to speak there unto thee.

43 And there I will meet with the children of Israel, and *the tabernacle* shall be sanctified by my glory.

44 And I will sanctify the tabernacle of the congregation, and the altar: I will sanctify also both Aaron and his sons, to minister to me in the priest's office.

offer in the evening; 40 and with the first lamb a tenth measure of fine flour mingled with a fourth of a hin of beaten oil, and a fourth of a hin of wine for a libation. 41 And the other lamb you shall offer in the evening, and shall offer with it a cereal offering and its libation, as in the morning, for a pleasing odor, an offering by fire to the LORD. 42 It shall be a continual burnt offering throughout your generations at the door of the tent of meeting before the LORD, where I will meet with you, to speak there to you. 43 There I will meet with the people of Israel, and it shall be sanctified by my glory; 44 I will consecrate the tent of meeting and the altar; Aaron also and his sons I

---

with a reference to evening (I Kings 18:29, 36; cf. Dan. 9:21). In Ezekiel's plan for a restored service (Ezek. 46:18-25) both of the daily sacrifices were placed in the morning. They consisted of one lamb, one sixth of an ephah of meal, and one third of a hin of oil. The libation of wine is omitted. In this plan, as in Num. 28:3-8, the cereal offering has lost its independent status. Also, as compared with Ezek. 46:13-15, the cereal is reduced in proportion to the animal sacrifice. For there are to be two lambs, one in the morning and another in the evening. To accompany each one-tenth ephah of meal and one-quarter hin each of oil and of wine are required. An ephah is about a bushel, a hin about one and one-half gallons.

11. Conclusion (29:42b-46)

We are here at the conclusion of the main body (P^A and P^B) of the P instructions concerning the tabernacle. The mixed items that follow are all of very late origin (P^S). Galling (Beer, *Exodus*, p. 147) would except from this 31:12-17, which he thinks was originally, with 29:42b-46, part of a single conclusion.

42b-43. In the conclusion we sense again the attempt of P, frequently noted, to hold together the experience of God as grace and as demand or as transcendence and immanence. It is **at the door of the tent of meeting,** i.e., at the great altar (cf. vs. 4), that Yahweh will meet with Moses and **with the children of Israel.** In vs. 42b the phrase **meet with you** indicates a plural pronoun, second person. This might make it apply to the priests. However, the next phrase, **to speak there to you,** has a singular pronoun and must indicate Moses.

In vs. 43 the Hebrew of **it shall be sanctified** is problematic. The only possible antecedent of the subject is **the door of the tent** (vs. 42), not **the tabernacle** as such (KJV). The **door** in the context means the altar, however (cf. Exeg. on vs. 11). Consequently, the Vulg. rightly supplies that word. But the original Hebrew form is in doubt since the LXX, Syriac, and Targ. Onkelos agree in reading, "I shall be sanctified." We must either adopt that form or with Quell (Kittel, *Biblia Hebraica*, 3rd ed. *ad loc.*) drop the word altogether and read, "there will I meet with the children of Israel in my glory."

44. The consecration of **tent** and **altar** in this verse militates against supplying either **tabernacle** (KJV) or "altar" (Vulg.) in vs. 43.

45 ¶ And I will dwell among the children of Israel, and will be their God.

46 And they shall know that I *am* the LORD their God, that brought them forth out of the land of Egypt, that I may dwell among them: I *am* the LORD their God.

30 And thou shalt make an altar to burn incense upon: *of* shittim wood shalt thou make it.

2 A cubit *shall be* the length thereof, and a cubit the breadth thereof; foursquare shall it be: and two cubits *shall be* the height thereof: the horns thereof *shall be* of the same.

3 And thou shalt overlay it with pure gold, the top thereof, and the sides thereof round about, and the horns thereof; and thou shalt make unto it a crown of gold round about.

4 And two golden rings shalt thou make to it under the crown of it, by the two corners thereof, upon the two sides of it shalt thou make *it;* and they shall be for places for the staves to bear it withal.

5 And thou shalt make the staves *of* shittim wood, and overlay them with gold.

6 And thou shalt put it before the veil that *is* by the ark of the testimony, before

will consecrate, to serve me as priests. 45 And I will dwell among the people of Israel, and will be their God. 46 And they shall know that I am the LORD their God, who brought them forth out of the land of Egypt that I might dwell among them; I am the LORD their God.

30 "You shall make an altar to burn incense upon; of acacia wood shall you make it. 2 A cubit shall be its length, and a cubit its breadth; it shall be square, and two cubits shall be its height; its horns shall be of one piece with it. 3 And you shall overlay it with pure gold, its top and its sides round about and its horns; and you shall make for it a molding of gold round about. 4 And two golden rings shall you make for it; under its molding on two opposite sides of it shall you make them, and they shall be holders for poles with which to carry it. 5 You shall make the poles of acacia wood, and overlay them with gold. 6 And you shall put it before the veil that

---

45-46. In the tabernacle, which is hallowed by his majestic presence, rather than in the tables of the law, Yahweh **will dwell among the people of Israel.** God's purpose in the Exodus is affirmed to have been the establishment of this relationship of grace which the program of sacrificial worship implies.

12. LATE ADDITIONS (30:1-38)
a) THE ALTAR OF INCENSE (30:1-10)

Like many other cultic forms, the use of incense and of an altar of incense was taken over from Canaanite religion. Albright (*Archaeology of Palestine and the Bible,* pp. 161-62) directs us to the *ḥammánîm* he discovered at Tell Beit Mirsim in Iron Age deposits from ca. 1200-900. He tends to the view that the incense altar was a feature of pre-exilic worship in the temple, but that it incurred the wrath of the prophets and was for a time eclipsed. It still seems probable, however, that the incense altar, as opposed to incense as such, was among the forms that were assimilated very late to the worship of Yahweh. The burning of incense proceeded for a long time without an altar of incense (Lev. 16:12; Num. 16:6-7), and it seems probable that the censers reposed on the table when not in use. The other evidences for the existence of the altar of incense are all very late (vs. 27; 31:8; 35:15; 37:25; 39:38; 40:5, 26; Lev. 4:7; Num. 4:16; I Macc. 4:49; Luke 1:11; Heb. 9:4; Josephus *Jewish War* V. 5. 5). An altar of incense was probably introduced in the second temple, after the main account of the tabernacle cultus was complete. Hence we find it in this late supplementary section. In vss. 1-5 the pattern of the altar—**acacia wood** with an **overlay of pure gold, a molding of gold, golden rings** for the **poles of acacia wood**—corresponds very closely to the pattern of the ark and the table (25:1-30).

30:6. The golden altar, as it was known in contrast to the bronze altar of burnt offering in the courtyard (38:30; 39:39), was set **before the veil** of the most holy place between

the mercy seat that *is* over the testimony, where I will meet with thee.

7 And Aaron shall burn thereon sweet incense every morning: when he dresseth the lamps, he shall burn incense upon it.

8 And when Aaron lighteth the lamps at even, he shall burn incense upon it, a perpetual incense before the LORD throughout your generations.

9 Ye shall offer no strange incense thereon, nor burnt sacrifice, nor meat offering; neither shall ye pour drink offering thereon.

10 And Aaron shall make an atonement upon the horns of it once in a year with the blood of the sin offering of atonements; once in the year shall he make atonement upon it throughout your generations: it *is* most holy unto the LORD.

11 ¶ And the LORD spake unto Moses, saying,

12 When thou takest the sum of the children of Israel after their number, then shall they give every man a ransom for his soul

is by the ark of the testimony, before the mercy seat that is over the testimony, where I will meet with you. 7 And Aaron shall burn fragrant incense on it; every morning when he dresses the lamps he shall burn it, 8 and when Aaron sets up the lamps in the evening, he shall burn it, a perpetual incense before the LORD throughout your generations. 9 You shall offer no unholy incense thereon, nor burnt offering, nor cereal offering; and you shall pour no libation thereon. 10 Aaron shall make atonement upon its horns once a year; with the blood of the sin offering of atonement he shall make atonement for it once in the year throughout your generations; it is most holy to the LORD."

11 The LORD said to Moses, 12 "When you take the census of the people of Israel,

---

the table and the lampstand (40:23-26). Because it stands **before the mercy seat,** Heb. 9:4 mistakenly assumed that it stood inside the most holy place.

7-9. The burning of incense, together with the care of the lamps, became a daily duty, morning and evening, of the priests in active service. This service was arranged on a rotational basis in the later temple.

10. On the great day of Atonement, as described in Lev. 16, the priest carried a censer of coals taken from the great altar and incense into the most holy place. But there is no reference to the altar of incense. From this we must perhaps conclude that the account in Lev. 16 antedates the introduction of the altar of incense.

b) THE POLL TAX (30:11-16)

At the opening of the Christian Era all adult male Jews paid an annual temple tax of half a shekel (Matt. 17:24-27). This was "the shekel of the sanctuary" (Lev. 27:25) or the "Phoenician shekel," whose value was greater than the Babylonian shekel (A. R. S. Kennedy, "Money," in Hastings, *Dictionary of the Bible,* III, 422). It weighed 112 grams. As an annual levy this tax seems to have been introduced very late. In Neh. 10:32 (Hebrew vs. 33) the community is reported to have resolved to pay one third of a shekel annually. On the ground that the Hebrew or Phoenician shekel was divided only into

---

30:11-16. *Census Taking, Ancient and Modern.* —Widespread throughout the human race is the conviction that it is unlucky to take the census, to count people.[4] Even so late as 1753, fear was expressed by one member in the British House of Commons that the proposed census would be followed by "some great public misfortune or epidemical distemper," and in 1926 the authorities were afraid that there would be trouble with

[4] See Frazer, *Folk-lore in O.T.,* II, 555-63.

certain tribes in Kenya when the intention of taking a census became known. There is no doubt that certain people in all professions are "census-minded," e.g., superintendents of schools, denominational officials, etc. They delight in getting people to fill in forms, in publishing statistics, in reporting that so many thousand pieces of mail went out from their offices during the calendar year; their walls are adorned by framed graphs showing the variations in se-

unto the Lord, when thou numberest them; that there be no plague among them, when *thou* numberest them.

13 This they shall give, every one that passeth among them that are numbered, half a shekel after the shekel of the sanctuary: (a shekel *is* twenty gerahs:) a half shekel *shall be* the offering of the Lord.

14 Every one that passeth among them that are numbered, from twenty years old and above, shall give an offering unto the Lord.

15 The rich shall not give more, and the poor shall not give less, than half a shekel, when *they* give an offering unto the Lord, to make an atonement for your souls.

then each shall give a ransom for himself to the Lord when you number them, that there be no plague among them when you number them. **13** Each who is numbered in the census shall give this: half a shekel according to the shekel of the sanctuary (the shekel is twenty gerahs), half a shekel as an offering to the Lord. **14** Every one who is numbered in the census, from twenty years old and upward, shall give the Lord's offering. **15** The rich shall not give more, and the poor shall not give less, than the half shekel, when you give the Lord's offering

---

halves and quarters, this is interpreted as having been the lighter Babylonian shekel (one third of a shekel weighing 56-58 grams), i.e., the tax which was standard in Jesus' day, and the amount of which is indicated in this instruction, was double the tax that Nehemiah established. In this passage, probably based on Num. 1:1-3, the tax is designated as a ransom to protect men from the wrath of God when a census is taken (Num. 26:1-3). It is to be used **for the service of the tent of meeting** (vs. 16). This account is an attempt by a late P editor to establish the view that the temple tax was indeed "the commandment of Moses the servant of the Lord (II Chr. 24:6).

11-12. At the **census,** which is a military act, **each shall give a ransom** [i.e., provide a "covering"] **for himself.** The mustering of Israel's power, implicit in a census, was felt to provoke Yahweh's jealousy, for he was Israel's strength.

13. The term **shekel of the sanctuary** is here a technical term (Lev. 27:25) referring to the Phoenician coinage which was the standard for the temple tax. The parenthetical note that **the shekel is twenty gerahs** (Lev. 27:25; Num. 3:47; 18:16; Ezek. 45:12)

---

lected churches in the ratio of giving to home and foreign benevolences; they display maps with pins on them locating every home subscribing to the denominational paper; their chief delight is in issuing questionnaires asking for the exact number of hymnbooks in each church room during the year. Other people, regarded by these officials as superstitious, do not have much faith in continual counting. They instinctively fear the census in its many forms; they distrust organizations with large staffs of salaried officials, where the filing cabinet is the sacred shrine; they even feel that people should be stimulated to give freely rather than under the duress of the every member canvass; they talk about the log with Mark Hopkins at one end and the student at the other as the ideal college or church school; they suspect that most organizations exist chiefly for the benefit of the organization.

We shall always have these two types of people with us. The Lord's suggestion in these verses was that both sides should compromise. Let the counters count if they want to do it, but the

other side should see to it that there are some good results besides the mere resultant statistics. In fact, conduct an every member canvass to get everyone to give to the church, but without undue pressure or salesmanship. For there is still something unlucky about organization applied to human affairs. Even the poll tax suggested here has proved in our day an instrument of racial discrimination, and churches are apt to count their membership and attendance to prove themselves better than other churches; Rev. 7:9 is true not only of the redeemed, but of all spiritual things, "which no man could number."

By seeing the crowds of men about him, by getting engaged in all sorts of worldly affairs, by becoming wise about how things go in this world, such a man forgets himself, forgets what his name is, does not dare to believe in himself, finds it a too venturesome thing to be himself, far easier and safer to be like others, to become a "me too," a number, a cipher in the crowd.[5]

[5] Kierkegaard, quoted by T. S. Gregory, "Kierkegaard: the Prophet of Now," p. 717.

16 And thou shalt take the atonement money of the children of Israel, and shalt appoint it for the service of the tabernacle of the congregation; that it may be a memorial unto the children of Israel before the Lord, to make an atonement for your souls.

17 ¶ And the Lord spake unto Moses, saying,

18 Thou shalt also make a laver *of* brass, and his foot *also of* brass, to wash *withal:* and thou shalt put it between the tabernacle of the congregation and the altar, and thou shalt put water therein.

19 For Aaron and his sons shall wash their hands and their feet thereat:

20 When they go into the tabernacle of the congregation, they shall wash with water, that they die not; or when they come near to the altar to minister, to burn offering made by fire unto the Lord:

21 So they shall wash their hands and their feet, that they die not: and it shall be a statute for ever to them, *even* to him and to his seed throughout their generations.

to make atonement for yourselves. 16 And you shall take the atonement money from the people of Israel, and shall appoint it for the service of the tent of meeting; that it may bring the people of Israel to remembrance before the Lord, so as to make atonement for yourselves."

17 The Lord said to Moses, 18 "You shall also make a laver of bronze, with its base of bronze, for washing. And you shall put it between the tent of meeting and the altar, and you shall put water in it, 19 with which Aaron and his sons shall wash their hands and their feet. 20 When they go into the tent of meeting, or when they come near the altar to minister, to burn an offering by fire to the Lord, they shall wash with water, lest they die. 21 They shall wash their hands and their feet, lest they die: it shall be a statute for ever to them, even to him and to his descendants throughout their generations."

---

represents an attempt at interpreting the temple coinage in terms of the Babylonian weights, the gerah being a Babylonian unit (cf. *ibid.*).

16. The tax, like the gems on the high priest's shoulderpiece and breastpiece, would bring **the people of Israel to remembrance before the Lord**. The Levites and priests, whose lives were dedicated to the temple, were not subject to the tax. By means of it those in secular pursuit were **to make atonement**.

c) The Brass Laver (30:17-21)

In Solomon's temple stood a large circular tank, about forty-five feet in circumference, known as the "molten sea" (I Kings 7:23-26). It was all of brass and rested on twelve oxen. According to II Chr. 4:6, the "sea" was for the priestly ablutions. This late notice in P about the **laver of bronze** for the court of the tabernacle, reference to which had been omitted in the main body of the ordinances, bears no resemblance to the Solomonic precedents. In contrast to the other equipment few details are given. It had a **base of bronze** and was to stand **between the tent of meeting and the altar** (cf. I Kings 7:39). In 38:8 we are told that the women who served the tabernacle had provided their brass mirrors for its production. The writer's main concern seems to be to stress the importance

---

The methods of census decree that the workers in general must be liberated, even by means that make every worker a slave; that happiness can come by administration; that democracy works by numbers rather than by inner intellectual and moral responsibility. Think what might have been the condition of our world today if men had listened to Kierkegaard, rather than to the popular idealists, utilitarians, and optimists of his day!

17-21. *Values in Ritual.*— (Cf. 38:8.) The Exeg. points out how deeply the liturgical ablutions of Judaism have influenced Christianity. The Protestant Reformation was interested in supplanting most ritual observances by their spiritual counterparts. There was loss as well as gain in this attempt theoretically to spiritualize worship. The Protestant minister usually bows in silent prayer as he enters the sanctuary for a service; the people are sometimes urged **on the**

22 ¶ Moreover the LORD spake unto Moses, saying,

23 Take thou also unto thee principal spices, of pure myrrh five hundred *shekels*, and of sweet cinnamon half so much, *even* two hundred and fifty *shekels*, and of sweet calamus two hundred and fifty *shekels*,

24 And of cassia five hundred *shekels*, after the shekel of the sanctuary, and of oil olive a hin:

25 And thou shalt make it an oil of holy ointment, an ointment compound after the art of the apothecary: it shall be a holy anointing oil.

26 And thou shalt anoint the tabernacle of the congregation therewith, and the ark of the testimony,

22 Moreover, the LORD said to Moses, 23 "Take the finest spices: of liquid myrrh five hundred shekels, and of sweet-smelling cinnamon half as much, that is, two hundred and fifty, and of aromatic cane two hundred and fifty, 24 and of cassia five hundred, according to the shekel of the sanctuary, and of olive oil a hin; 25 and you shall make of these a sacred anointing oil blended as by the perfumer; a holy anointing oil it shall be. 26 And you shall anoint with it the tent of meeting and the ark of the testimony,

of the daily ritual ablutions for the priests. They must **wash with water, lest they die.** It is an everlasting obligation (*ḥōq*, cf. 28:43). The liturgical ablutions of Judaism have deeply influenced both Islam and Christianity.

d) THE HOLY OIL (30:22-33)

Oil, usually mixed with spices or aromatic fluids, was commonly used for adornment and for healing in Israel and in all the ancient Near East. It also served religious or liturgical purposes from earliest times. It symbolized the consecration of persons—notably kings, prophets, and priests—to specific vocations. The hallowed character of sacred objects or persons, lost by sin or impurity, was restored by anointing. Thus, after the sin offering, the altar was anointed (29:36); and the healed leper, restored to the fellowship of Israel, was anointed (Lev. 14:14-17). A great supply of oil was customarily in store, partly because the best oils, properly stored, were believed to improve with age. Alabaster jars or boxes (Matt. 26:7) were considered ideal for this purpose (A. Macalister, "Ointment," in Hastings, *Dictionary of the Bible*, III, 593).

22-25. **The finest spices** were valued like gold. They constituted a suitable royal gift (I Kings 10:2, 10, 15). Liquid myrrh is now known as "Balsam of Mecca" (Driver, *Exodus*, p. 335), as distinguished from more solid and less fragrant balsams. The **sweet-smelling cinammon** probably came from the Far East and the **aromatic cane** from India. **Cassia** is related to the **cinnamon** bark and also came from the Far East. The quantities are to be weighed **according to the shekel of the sanctuary**, which was heavier than the usual commercial weight (cf. Exeg. on vss. 11-16). With the oil, which amounted to about one and one-half gallons, the total weight of the quantities in the recipe would be about a hundred pounds.

26-29. All the utensils were to be anointed for consecration, **that they may be most holy.** With less specific detail the instruction is repeated in 40:9-11. The actual anointing of the tabernacle is not reported in Exodus (cf. Num. 7:1), possibly because the cloud of Yahweh's presence is stressed as the real hallowing of the shrine (40:34-38).

church calendar to say a prayer as they enter their pews. But more definite results might be obtained by some ritual observance like that by which the priest washes his hands in water before celebrating the service or some similar rite in which the people participate as they enter the church. It is perhaps true that for most people the symbolic vividness of some such act might really bring home to everyone the need of cleansing oneself, body and soul, before entering on the worship of God. The original idea was not that one had to be unnaturally clean for such service. No, people's normal life ought to be a holy life, and the ablution was "to impart

27 And the table and all his vessels, and the candlestick and his vessels, and the altar of incense,

28 And the altar of burnt offering with all his vessels, and the laver and his foot.

29 And thou shalt sanctify them, that they may be most holy: whatsoever toucheth them shall be holy.

30 And thou shalt anoint Aaron and his sons, and consecrate them, that *they* may minister unto me in the priest's office.

31 And thou shalt speak unto the children of Israel, saying, This shall be a holy anointing oil unto me throughout your generations.

32 Upon man's flesh shall it not be poured, neither shall ye make *any other* like it, after the composition of it: it *is* holy, *and* it shall be holy unto you.

33 Whosoever compoundeth *any* like it, or whosoever putteth *any* of it upon a stranger, shall even be cut off from his people.

34 ¶ And the Lord said unto Moses, Take unto thee sweet spices, stacte, and onycha, and galbanum; *these* sweet spices

27 and the table and all its utensils, and the lampstand and its utensils, and the altar of incense, 28 and the altar of burnt offering with all its utensils and the laver and its base; 29 you shall consecrate them, that they may be most holy; whatever touches them will become holy. 30 And you shall anoint Aaron and his sons, and consecrate them, that they may serve me as priests. 31 And you shall say to the people of Israel, 'This shall be my holy anointing oil throughout your generations. 32 It shall not be poured upon the bodies of ordinary men, and you shall make no other like it in composition; it is holy, and it shall be holy to you. 33 Whoever compounds any like it or whoever puts any of it on an outsider shall be cut off from his people.'"

34 And the Lord said to Moses, "Take sweet spices, stacte, and onycha, and gal-

---

30. The anointing of **Aaron and his sons** must be compared with 29:7. Whereas in that instruction the chief concern is for the establishment of the priesthood, this verse is concerned with its perpetuation (cf. 40:15). Generation after generation, the descendants of the high priest shall inherit his office and be established in it by sacred anointing.

31-33. The priests themselves make the oil (cf. 31:11). To stress the holiness of God and of his service, the people are commanded not to duplicate the recipe of the sacred oil for secular purposes.

e) The Incense Recipe (30:34-38)

As in the case of oil, the use of incense in the cultus was an adaptation for religious ends of its great and valued role in social usage. The capacity of a cultic form, thus derived, to persist long after the social forms that started it off have disappeared is notably illustrated by the continued use of oil and incense in the Christian churches. While originally the smoke of incense may have symbolized the deity's assimilation of the gifts burned on the altar, it early becomes a figure of the prayers of the faithful (Ps. 141:2; Rev. 5:8; 8:3-4).

34. The Hebrew word for **sweet spices** seems to come from a Semitic root that means "to smell." Since **an equal part** of each of the four aromatic items is to be used, there are

---

to one who has lost it the measure of sanctity that puts him on the level of ordinary social life." [6]

27-38. Fragrance in Religion.—Pleasant-smelling perfumes are agreeable to men, and it was assumed also to God. Heaven, in later

[6] W. Robertson Smith, *Lectures on the Religion of the Semites* (3rd ed.; London: A. & C. Black, 1927), p. 426.

Jewish writings, is a place of fragrance. The sense of smell is most potent in the remembrance of things past, in recalling to the mind scenes and situations of earlier days. The whiff of incense to the Roman Catholic at the Mass before the battle brings back to him the whole religious experience of his youth. Protestants have ignored or despised this fact. Too often the

with pure frankincense: of each shall there be a like *weight:*

35 And thou shalt make it a perfume, a confection after the art of the apothecary, tempered together, pure *and* holy:

36 And thou shalt beat *some* of it very small, and put of it before the testimony, in the tabernacle of the congregation, where I will meet with thee: it shall be unto you most holy.

37 And *as for* the perfume which thou shalt make, ye shall not make to yourselves according to the composition thereof: it shall be unto thee holy for the Lord.

38 Whosoever shall make like unto that, to smell thereto, shall even be cut off from his people.

31 And the Lord spake unto Moses, saying,

2 See, I have called by name Bezaleel the son of Uri, the son of Hur, of the tribe of Judah:

banum, sweet spices with pure frankincense (of each shall there be an equal part), 35 and make an incense blended as by the perfumer, seasoned with salt, pure and holy; 36 and you shall beat some of it very small, and put part of it before the testimony in the tent of meeting where I shall meet with you; it shall be for you most holy. 37 And the incense which you shall make according to its composition, you shall not make for yourselves; it shall be for you holy to the Lord. 38 Whoever makes any like it to use as perfume shall be cut off from his people."

31 The Lord said to Moses, 2 "See, I have called by name Bez'alel the son of Uri, son of Hur, of the tribe of Judah:

---

no specific amounts given. Like its Hebrew counterpart, the term **stacte,** used in the LXX, means "that which drips." In the Hellenistic world it designated a type of myrrh oil. The term **onycha** also rests on the LXX form and refers to the "mouth" or flap of a mollusk found in the Red Sea. The term **galbanum** is taken directly from the Hebrew and indicates a resin now found chiefly in Iran. **Frankincense** also accompanied the meal offering (Lev. 2:1-2, 15-16) and was placed with the bread of the Presence on the table (Lev. 24:7). It was a prized perfume (Song of S. 3:6) and was made from a gum resin, whitish in color as the Hebrew shows, found in Somaliland and South Arabia. Its cultic employment is criticized by Jeremiah (6:20).

35. The word for **incense** means "odor" or "smoke." **Salt** also figures in the meal offering (cf. Lev. 2:13). It may symbolize the ancient conviction that the covenant between God and Israel had been sealed in a fellowship meal (24:9-11). In such a meal, as among Arabs today, salt was peculiarly the sign that fellowship was established (II Chr. 13:5).

36-37. The compound must probably be understood to have been stored in a dry form and in relatively large pieces. For use a small portion was pulverized and placed in the censer or on the altar of incense.

13. Appointment of Bezalel and Oholiab (31:1-11)

In many respects this account, in which Yahweh instructs Moses to appoint Bezalel and Oholiab to make the tabernacle and its equipment, differs from its parallel in

---

stuffy atmosphere of buildings closed all week recall his childhood church to the Protestant boy. But the tabernacle and the temple for the Jew were intertwined with memories of fragrance. The priest was anointed with sweet-smelling oil, and there was the incense. Incense was first of all a costly offering pleasing to God; then it was a way of uniting sacred experiences with pleasant memories in man's subconscious

mind. It neutralized the smells of sacrifice and of crowds of men in hot climates. It was like-wise a lovely symbol of prayer rising in fragrance to heaven (cf. Ps. 141:2; Rev. 5:8; 8:3-4; John 12:3; st. ii of the hymn "Jesus shall reign where'er the sun").

31:1-11. *The Holiness of Beauty.*—The best commentary on the words of vs. 6, "I have endowed the minds of all craftsmen with skill,"

3 And I have filled him with the spirit of God, in wisdom, and in understanding, and in knowledge, and in all manner of workmanship,

4 To devise cunning works, to work in gold, and in silver, and in brass,

5 And in cutting of stones, to set *them,* and in carving of timber, to work in all manner of workmanship.

6 And I, behold, I have given with him Aholiab, the son of Ahisamach, of the tribe of Dan: and in the hearts of all that are wise-hearted I have put wisdom, that they may make all that I have commanded thee;

7 The tabernacle of the congregation, and the ark of the testimony, and the mercy seat that *is* thereupon, and all the furniture of the tabernacle,

8 And the table and his furniture, and the pure candlestick with all his furniture, and the altar of incense,

9 And the altar of burnt offering with all his furniture, and the laver and his foot,

10 And the clothes of service, and the holy garments for Aaron the priest, and the garments of his sons, to minister in the priest's office,

3 and I have filled him with the Spirit of God, with ability and intelligence, with knowledge and all craftsmanship, 4 to devise artistic designs, to work in gold, silver, and bronze, 5 in cutting stones for setting, and in carving wood, for work in every craft. 6 And behold, I have appointed with him Oho'liab, the son of Ahis'amach, of the tribe of Dan; and I have given to all able men ability, that they may make all that I have commanded you: 7 the tent of meeting, and the ark of the testimony, and the mercy seat that is thereon, and all the furnishings of the tent, 8 the table and its utensils, and the pure lampstand with all its utensils, and the altar of incense, 9 and the altar of burnt offering with all its utensils, and the laver and its base, 10 and the finely worked garments, the holy garments for Aaron the priest and the garments of his

35:30–36:7. It itemizes the objects to be made, including **the altar of incense** (vs. 8) and **the laver and its base** (vs. 9), reference to which is of very late origin in the instructions (cf. ch. 30). There is here no reference to the other workers co-operating with the leaders, nor about the offerings made for the work. It seems most probable that the section stems from the same late editor as ch. 30 (PS). He may have used 35:30–36:7 as a source for composing his addition.

31:1-2. Bezalel is designated as **of the tribe of Judah.** In I Chr. 2:18-20 his genealogy is traced to Caleb. The Caleb clan, originally a separate unit (Judg 1:11-15, 20; I Sam. 30:14), was absorbed by Judah.

3. The **Spirit of God** is virtually synonymous here with the divine wisdom or skill (vs. 6; cf. 36:2) which expresses itself in a mastery of arts and crafts.

6. Oholiab is mentioned only in this context. The reason for his association with the tribe of Dan is unknown.

10. The LXX reads "liturgical garments" instead of **finely worked garments.** The Samar. has "garments of the service." The Hebrew has **finely worked** also in 35:19; 39:1, 41. In all three cases it is followed by the phrase **for their service as priests.** Some MSS add the same phrase here. The translation of the Hebrew word (שׂרד) as **finely**

is in Ecclus. 38:24-34. Note especially the Revised Translation (1894) of the last verse:

But they will maintain the fabric of the world;
And in the handywork of their craft is their prayer.

See also "The Praise of Moses" (Ecclus. 45:1-5).

There is a lovely appreciation of craftsmen in Victoria Sackville-West's poem "The Land."

In one English church the end panel of each pew on the aisle was left of plain wood, to be carved by each pewholder according to his taste and ability. One of the high forms of worship

11 And the anointing oil, and sweet incense for the holy *place:* according to all that I have commanded thee shall they do.

12 ¶ And the LORD spake unto Moses, saying,

13 Speak thou also unto the children of Israel, saying, Verily my sabbaths ye shall keep: for it *is* a sign between me and you throughout your generations; that *ye* may know that I *am* the LORD that doth sanctify you.

14 Ye shall keep the sabbath therefore; for it *is* holy unto you. Every one that defileth it shall surely be put to death: for whosoever doeth *any* work therein, that soul shall be cut off from among his people.

15 Six days may work be done; but in the seventh *is* the sabbath of rest, holy to the LORD: whosoever doeth *any* work in the sabbath day, he shall surely be put to death.

16 Wherefore the children of Israel shall keep the sabbath, to observe the sabbath throughout their generations, *for* a perpetual covenant.

sons, for their service as priests, 11 and the anointing oil and the fragrant incense for the holy place. According to all that I have commanded you shall do."

12 And the LORD said to Moses, 13 "Say to the people of Israel, 'You shall keep my sabbaths, for this is a sign between me and you throughout your generations, that you may know that I, the LORD, sanctify you. 14 You shall keep the sabbath, because it is holy for you; every one who profanes it shall be put to death; whoever does any work on it, that soul shall be cut off from among his people. 15 Six days shall work be done, but the seventh day is a sabbath of solemn rest, holy to the LORD; whoever does any work on the sabbath day shall be put to death. 16 Wherefore the people of Israel shall keep the sabbath, observing the sabbath throughout their generations, as a per-

---

worked is achieved by treating it as synonymous with the Aramaic word (סרדא) meaning plaited or braided work. Galling doubts that the garments of Aaron's sons could have been included in such a description (Beer, *Exodus,* p. 151). He prefers to derive the Hebrew term from a Babylonian word (*serdu*) carrying the concept of agreement to perform. Thus he translates, "and the prescribed garments, even the sacred garments of Aaron."

14. THE SABBATH (31:12-17)

P's formulation of the sabbath law, both as to its source and function, appears here for the first time. It is absent from P's account of the Abrahamic covenant (Gen. 17), where circumcision is the chief sign. In Gen. 2:2-3 God consecrated the seventh day as a sign of his rule; here the seventh day becomes a sign and a commandment for Israel. For P it is rooted in the Creation and is a sign of the relationship of grace in which Israel stands to God, the sign of its election (cf. Ezek. 20:12). In 35:1-3 the law is reduced to a rule without any explanation and is primarily related to the tabernacle project.

12-13. All **sabbaths** are a part of the sabbath institution, which **is a sign** between the Lord and Israel.

16-17. The sabbath is a **perpetual covenant,** i.e., a sign of the relationship which

---

is art. God enjoys perhaps most of all a gift of something our hands have made. It was thus that painting and sculpture and woodcarving and music were born "to the glory of God." One who strives to bring perfection to the slightest thing he sets his hand to lives in the great tradition of art and religion.

A servant with this clause
Makes drudgery divine;

Who sweeps a room, as for Thy laws,
Makes that and th' action fine.[7]

The artist is not a special kind of man, but every man is a special kind of artist. The magnificent temple of God wherein he shines in all his glory is intellect, and his gift to those who worship therein is skill.

12-17. Cf. Expos. on 16:22-30.

[7] George Herbert, "The Elixir," st. v.

17 It *is* a sign between me and the children of Israel for ever: for *in* six days the LORD made heaven and earth, and on the seventh day he rested, and was refreshed.

18 ¶ And he gave unto Moses, when he had made an end of communing with him upon mount Sinai, two tables of testimony, tables of stone, written with the finger of God.

32 And when the people saw that Moses delayed to come down out of the mount, the people gathered themselves

petual covenant. 17 It is a sign for ever between me and the people of Israel that in six days the LORD made heaven and earth, and on the seventh day he rested, and was refreshed.' "

18 And he gave to Moses, when he had made an end of speaking with him upon Mount Sinai, the two tables of the testimony, tables of stone, written with the finger of God.

32 When the people saw that Moses delayed to come down from the moun-

---

Yahweh sets up (6:4) with Israel. This relationship is inherent in creation; it is a divine decree.

15. CONCLUSION (31:18)

The audience which began in 25:1 ends here. The gift of the **tables of stone, written with the finger of God,** reported here, probably comes from E and ties together 24:12-18 with ch. 32.

C. MOSES AND THE RESTORATION OF THE COVENANT (32:1–34:35)

As a literary structure these three chapters are a composite. Not only J and E, but also more than one editorial hand seem to have contributed to it. But despite this variety of sources and its piecemeal development, the section represents a dramatic whole. It

---

18. *A Message from Heaven.*—What proof was there that these tables were in God's handwriting? There are those who depend for this assurance on objective historic proof, just as handwriting experts are produced in courts of law today. But it is notorious that such experts often contradict one another in their testimony. They differ as to whether a letter was written by a particular person. How can we be sure that this particular statement was written by God?

There are some who profess to be able to pronounce authoritatively on this matter. Meister Eckhart dismisses all such with the statement that God has no individual style, "God's idiosyncrasy is being." [8] A French writer puts it this way: "O Lord, it is not because I have been told that you were the Son of God that I listen to your word; but your word is beautiful beyond any human word, and that is how I recognize that you are the Son of God." [9] We are saved by faith, not faith in inerrant documents, or in God's especially appointed experts on earth, but by faith in the truth, made clear by God's spirit in our own minds and hearts. Says Browning:

But here is the finger of God, a flash of the will that can,
Existent behind all laws, that made them and, lo, they are! [1]

This is a much more substantial rock on which to found one's faith. There is a democratic element in religion which depends on the general acceptance of truth by men of good will everywhere, as God breathed into man's nostrils the breath of life so that he partook of God's spirit and became a living soul (Gen. 2:7). All scripture is the purifier of that essential enlightened conscience and vision. Herbert Butterfield, professor of modern history in the University of Cambridge, says:

The conditions for a universal religion would not be satisfied by a religion which demanded that men should be experts in New Testament criticism—and capable of making up their minds where the highest experts differ—before they were in a state to make the essential choice between belief and unbelief. [2]

Edith Sichel says, "All the clergymen in the world cannot make one disbelieve in God," [3]

[8] Pfeiffer, *Meister Eckhart*, I, 206; see also Ananda K. Coomaraswamy, *The Transformation of Nature in Art* (Cambridge: Harvard University Press, 1934), p. 86.
[9] *The Journals of André Gide*, tr. Justin O'Brien (New York: Alfred A. Knopf, 1948), II, 170.

[1] "Abt Vogler," st. vii.
[2] *Christianity and History* (London: G. Bell & Sons, 1949), p. 126.
[3] *New and Old* (New York: E. P. Dutton & Co., 1918), p. 58.

together unto Aaron, and said unto him, Up, make us gods, which shall go before us; for *as for* this Moses, the man that brought

tain, the people gathered themselves together to Aaron, and said to him, "Up, make us gods, who shall go before us; as for this

---

deals with the relation of God's grace to his law in the covenant relationship in which Israel stands.

The covenant relationship was made possible by God's initial revelation in his act of deliverance. It is founded on grace. But the covenant demanded obedience of Israel. And the laws were the sign of this demand. What would happen to Israel's covenant relationship if Israel disobeyed? Is there forgiveness for apostates as well as redemption for slaves? Does God by grace restore those who have forfeited their covenant privilege? Can punishment and grace be correlatives? Given the fact of sin and disobedience, chs. 32–34 raise issues that are inescapable when chs. 1–15 and 19–24 are taken seriously. The covenant was broken when Israel denied Yahweh as King (32:1, 4, 8). The basic question is, Will Yahweh again lead a people who have once rejected his leadership (33:1-6)?

The answer seems to be that while Yahweh in a sense cannot lead the people again, he promises to be with Moses (33:12-16), who is the leader of the people. There is thus no explicit solution for the problem of the apostates and their forgiveness. The impasse is overcome by the exaltation of Moses. His faithfulness has an atoning value. Because of Moses, Israel will enjoy God's leadership even though the sin of apostasy is not canceled (32:34). In these chapters, as nowhere else, Moses is put in a class apart. He becomes a mediator who, because of what he is, effects a relationship between God and Israel which but for him could not have been restored. Moses is presented as a prophetic figure, perhaps modeled on the prophet Elijah. He is the angry iconoclast who pulverizes the idol and subjects his people to ordeal (32:20). His heroic zeal and anger make Aaron wither as a pathetic nonentity (32:21-24), and in the manner of Elijah he blesses the Levites for slaughtering all deviationists (32:25-29). But Moses is also the intercessor who loves his people more than himself. He is the priest whose prayers save Israel (32:11-14, 30-35). He is the unselfish servant without ambitions of his own, by whose devotion Israel is saved (33:12-16). Further, he is the divine companion, the intimate of Yahweh. Though he remains mortal and human, he has access to God as no other man has. In the restoration of the covenant Moses alone witnesses the theophany (34:3-10); in a sense it is restored with him, or in terms of his person. His own halo is the "sign" that seals the covenant (34:29-35). Thus in these chapters Moses becomes more than a prophet. He is the mediator of the covenant in the sense that what he is in faith and character makes the covenant possible. Israel can be restored to a relationship of grace only because of the perfect obedience of Moses.

1. The Golden Calf (32:1-35)

The calf was a molten image. Molten images were forbidden in Israel, both because it was wrong to represent God in any way and because they were associated with the

---

which is a sly way of saying that you must take nobody's word, you must know God yourself. It was in this way that the children of Israel knew that these words graven on the stones were in the handwriting of God. We can see them reading as Moses held the tablets up before them—the fruit of all their experience and aspiration, of all their tenderest and deepest relationships with their fellows and with God—then bowing their heads and saying, "These indeed are the words of God!"

32:1-35. The Molten Calf.—The history of this tale must be long and is certainly obscure,

but the underlying truth which has given it its longevity makes it impossible for any generation to forget it. The narrative as we have it dates from a later controversy about the validity of the use of images in the worship of Yahweh (see Exeg.). But the story itself is one of the classic tales of the human race. As Paul points out (I Cor. 10:7), and as is illustrated in Ps. 106·20 ff., it portrays three types of people: the mobsman, the politician, and the statesman: the man who so easily forgets the lovingkindness he has received and reverts to his evil ways; Aaron, the ecclesiastical politician, the apostle of the second

| us up out of the land of Egypt, we wot not what is become of him. | Moses, the man who brought us up out of the land of Egypt, we do not know what has |

cultus of the nature mysticism that was the prevalent religion of Canaan. The northern kingdom worshiped Yahweh under the form of two golden calves of this type. The adulteration of Israel's faith by Canaanite elements was certainly facilitated by this syncretistic adaptation. But it is not evident that any voice before Hosea spoke out against the practice. Not until the reformation of Josiah of Judah is it radically attacked. Even the puritan Elijah seems to have left the images at Bethel untouched. Therefore it has been generally felt that the story of the golden calf, as well as the prohibition of molten images, cannot date from a time earlier than the eighth century (cf. e.g., McNeile, *Exodus,* pp. 203-4). This story, it is thought, was set in the Mosaic era to throw the weight of tradition and of the great name of Moses to the support of the position of the reformers in the eighth and seventh centuries. Molten images, it is said, not only lacked attraction for the nomads Moses led, but were unknown to them. There can be no doubt that the story received its present form very much later than the Mosaic era and that it was developed and used for polemic purposes in the struggle of the Jerusalem priests against the Bethel shrine. But it would be difficult to demonstrate that Moses could not have been confronted with apostasy in this form. This is especially true if we take seriously the possibility that Israel borrowed heavily from such established shrine centers as Kadesh (cf. Beer, *Exodus,* pp. 155-56). Archaeological research has made it clear that even the most outlying oasis and settlement shared in the substance of the Canaanite fertility religion and its cultus. And further, however we may dispose of this particular illustration, the point it makes, that Moses taught that the covenant demanded faith in and loyalty to Yahweh alone, seems almost incontrovertible.

a) The People's Apostasy (32:1-6)

32:1. Aaron and the elders had been left in charge when Moses went up the mountain (24:14-18). They were to await his return. Aaron had no authority of his own; he was only a voice for Moses (4:15). The people do not ask for another god than Yahweh; they want Moses replaced as leader, for they **do not know what has become of him.** In his stead they want **gods, who shall go before us.** The charismatic leadership of the prophet is rejected in favor of what, it is hoped, will be a more stable representation of deity. The request has much in common with the people's request for a king (I Sam. 8:5). Unlike Samuel, Aaron does not consult Yahweh. He is ready to exchange charismatic leadership for more manageable forms (vss. 2-3). As in the case of the tabernacle (ch. 35), the materials for the cult are a gift of the people.

---

best, the feeble excuser of supine subservience to popular clamor; and Moses, the real leader of men with his white-hot indignation against sin and his tender intercession for sinners.

In *The Pilgrim's Progress* the pilgrims are welcomed by shepherds to the Delectable Mountains:

So they went forth with them, and walked a while, having a pleasant prospect on every side. . . . Then I saw in my dream that the shepherds had them to another place in a bottom, where was a door on the side of a hill. . . . The shepherds told them, "This is a byway to hell." [4]

So the Israelites discovered, after the delectable experience of their release from Egypt.

[4] Part I, ch. viii.

The *Autobiography of William Allen White* [5] gives one of the most vivid pictures of the Aaron politicians of his day in Kansas and the United States. In fact "The Worship of the Golden Calf" would be a fitting title for the history in many of his chapters.

It has been observed that God calls the Israelites **thy** people when angry with them (vs. 7). Moses seems to resent this and says in effect, "They are thy people too; thou didst bring them up out of Egypt. Yesterday they were slaves, and dost thou expect them to be heroes of the faith today?" They wanted a god whom they could see and had set up an image, perhaps meant to be one of Yahweh (vs. 5), like the images they had become accustomed to see in Egypt. But

[5] New York: The Macmillan Co., 1946.

2 And Aaron said unto them, Break off the golden earrings, which *are* in the ears of your wives, of your sons, and of your daughters, and bring *them* unto me.

3 And all the people brake off the golden earrings which *were* in their ears, and brought *them* unto Aaron.

4 And he received *them* at their hand, and fashioned it with a graving tool, after he had made it a molten calf: and they said, These *be* thy gods, O Israel, which brought thee up out of the land of Egypt.

5 And when Aaron saw *it,* he built an altar before it; and Aaron made proclamation, and said, To-morrow *is* a feast to the LORD.

6 And they rose up early on the morrow, and offered burnt offerings, and brought peace offerings; and the people sat down to eat and to drink, and rose up to play.

become of him." 2 And Aaron said to them, "Take off the rings of gold which are in the ears of your wives, your sons, and your daughters, and bring them to me." 3 So all the people took off the rings of gold which were in their ears, and brought them to Aaron. 4 And he received the gold at their hand, and fashioned it with a graving tool, and made a molten calf; and they said, "These are your gods, O Israel, who brought you up out of the land of Egypt!" 5 When Aaron saw this, he built an altar before it; and Aaron made proclamation and said, "Tomorrow shall be a feast to the LORD." 6 And they rose up early on the morrow, and offered burnt offerings and brought peace offerings; and the people sat down to eat and drink, and rose up to play.

4. The **graving tool** or stylus was probably used on the image after it had been cast. The word **calf** does not preclude the figure of a mature ox (Ps. 106:20). In all probability the figure was gold-plated. The people recognize in the image a representation of the **gods** who led them **out of the land of Egypt**. It may be that the use of the plural reflects a common concern with the polemics about the two bull images in Israel (I Kings 12:28).

5. Aaron proclaims a feast of dedication, **a feast to the LORD**. He builds an altar at which he officiates as priest. But it is an altar and a priesthood without the prophetic sanction of Moses. In later Israel the cultus claimed to be founded on the prophets.

6. The usual sacrifices of praise and of fellowship take place. Even in the Deuteronomic prescriptions worship is an occasion for feasting and "rejoicing" (Deut. 12:7, 18; 14:26; 16:11, 14). It is probable, however, that here some of the immoral practices that came with infiltrations from the Canaanite cultus are implied by the statement that the people **rose up to play** (cf. Num. 25:1-9; I Kings 14:24; Amos 2:7). Against these the Deuteronomic movement was directed.

Moses did not want to found a new dynasty, a new nation (vs. 10); he loved the people, and persuaded God to modify his wrath toward them. They were his children. They had been bad, but were they not little children? He was angry at what they had done, but sorry for them (Deut 9:12-14). For Aaron's excuse see Phillips Brooks's sermon "The Fire and the Calf." [6] It is a relief to see, as close study will reveal (see Exeg.), that vss. 25-29 were not a part of this story, but have been taken from the account of some other mass rebellion.

6. *Feasting and Dancing.*—This verse was the text of many a medieval sermon. Preachers were continually reminding their hearers that the first biblical account of dancing occurs in the story of the golden calf; and in the *Book of Homilies,* which was ordered to be read in the churches of England by the Convocation of 1542, "for stay of such errors as were then by ignorant preachers sparkled among the people," we find a comment on this message: "If the Israelites had not given themselves to belly-cheare, they had never so often fallen to idolatrie. Neyther would wee at this day be so addict to superstition were it not that wee so much esteemed the filling of our bellies." [7] Yet such leaders of the church as Thomas Aquinas could not rule out dancing and feasting altogether, for they found them mentioned without reprobation in other passages in scripture; many of them therefore allowed the dance and the feast on very exceptional occasions, such as a national victory, the homecoming of a friend, or even sometimes at weddings.

[6] *Sermons Preached in English Churches* (New York: E. P. Dutton & Co., 1883), pp. 43-64.

[7] *The Second Tome of Homilies,* Homily VI, "Against Gluttony and Drunkenness."

7 ¶ And the LORD said unto Moses, Go, get thee down; for thy people, which thou broughtest out of the land of Egypt, have corrupted *themselves:*

8 They have turned aside quickly out of the way which I commanded them: they have made them a molten calf, and have worshipped it, and have sacrificed thereunto, and said, These *be* thy gods, O Israel, which have brought thee up out of the land of Egypt.

9 And the LORD said unto Moses, I have seen this people, and, behold, it *is* a stiff-necked people:

10 Now therefore let me alone, that my wrath may wax hot against them, and that I may consume them: and I will make of thee a great nation.

11 And Moses besought the LORD his God, and said, LORD, why doth thy wrath wax hot against thy people, which thou hast brought forth out of the land of Egypt with great power, and with a mighty hand?

12 Wherefore should the Egyptians speak, and say, For mischief did he bring them out, to slay them in the mountains, and to consume them from the face of the earth? Turn from thy fierce wrath, and repent of this evil against thy people.

13 Remember Abraham, Isaac, and Israel, thy servants, to whom thou swarest by thine own self, and saidst unto them, I will multiply your seed as the stars of heaven, and all this land that I have spoken of will I give unto your seed, and they shall inherit *it* for ever.

14 And the LORD repented of the evil which he thought to do unto his people.

7 And the LORD said to Moses, "Go down; for your people, whom you brought up out of the land of Egypt, have corrupted themselves; 8 they have turned aside quickly out of the way which I commanded them; they have made for themselves a molten calf, and have worshiped it and sacrificed to it, and said, 'These are your gods, O Israel, who brought you up out of the land of Egypt!'" 9 And the LORD said to Moses, "I have seen this people, and behold, it is a stiff-necked people; 10 now therefore let me alone, that my wrath may burn hot against them and I may consume them; but of you I will make a great nation."

11 But Moses besought the LORD his God, and said, "O LORD, why does thy wrath burn hot against thy people, whom thou has brought forth out of the land of Egypt with great power and with a mighty hand? 12 Why should the Egyptians say, 'With evil intent did he bring them forth, to slay them in the mountains, and to consume them from the face of the earth'? Turn from thy fierce wrath, and repent of this evil against thy people. 13 Remember Abraham, Isaac, and Israel, thy servants, to whom thou didst swear by thine own self, and didst say to them, 'I will multiply your descendants as the stars of heaven, and all this land that I have promised I will give to your descendants, and they shall inherit it for ever.'" 14 And the LORD repented of the evil which he thought to do to his people.

---

b) MOSES' FIRST INTERCESSION (32:7-14)

7-10. The calf represents Yahweh to the people. But **they have made** [it] **for themselves.** It is their attempt to define the nature and way of Yahweh according to their own desires. This worship is a form of disobedience because it rests on an attempt to control deity. The wrath of God is stayed by the figure of Moses. Israel is here called his people (vs. 7). They are no longer God's people. The nobility of Moses as intercessor is stressed by the promise that if Moses would only let him destroy Israel, God would **make a great nation** of Moses himself.

11-14. Moses reminds God that he cannot deny his own people (cf. vs. 7). To destroy Israel would mean that God would undo what he has done (vs. 11). The meaning of what he has done would be obscured for the nations (vs. 12). It would mean going back on the oath to the fathers (Gen. 22:16), an oath backed by God's own character. The intercession assumes that God will be true to himself. Moses appeals to the rock of Israel's faith, the living God (Ps. 90).

15 ¶ And Moses turned, and went down from the mount, and the two tables of the testimony *were* in his hand: the tables *were* written on both their sides; on the one side and on the other *were* they written.

16 And the tables *were* the work of God, and the writing *was* the writing of God, graven upon the tables.

17 And when Joshua heard the noise of the people as they shouted, he said unto Moses, *There is* a noise of war in the camp.

18 And he said, *It is* not the voice of *them that* shout for mastery, neither *is it* the voice of *them that* cry for being overcome; *but* the noise of *them that* sing do I hear.

19 ¶ And it came to pass, as soon as he came nigh unto the camp, that he saw the calf, and the dancing: and Moses' anger waxed hot, and he cast the tables out of his hands, and brake them beneath the mount.

15 And Moses turned, and went down from the mountain with the two tables of the testimony in his hands, tables that were written on both sides; on the one side and on the other were they written. 16 And the tables were the work of God, and the writing was the writing of God, graven upon the tables. 17 When Joshua heard the noise of the people as they shouted, he said to Moses, "There is a noise of war in the camp." 18 But he said, "It is not the sound of shouting for victory, or the sound of the cry of defeat, but the sound of singing that I hear." 19 And as soon as he came near the camp and saw the calf and the dancing, Moses' anger burned hot, and he threw the tables out of his hands and broke

c) Moses the Prophet (32:15-24)

Vss. 7-14 are not presupposed in this section. Moses leaves the mountain because the tables are ready. He seems unaware that anything is amiss. Not until he sees the calf (vs. 19) is he angry. Then he assumes the role of a zealous and violent prophet, comparable to Elijah.

15-16. The **tables of the testimony** are the stones with the laws. These inscribed laws bear witness to God's will. The phrase is typical of P (cf. 25:16). The stones, **written on both sides,** had been inscribed by God himself. This is a graphic metaphor to impress the conviction that the law is an expression of God's character. Yahweh is not just the sanction for the laws in a theocracy: the laws constitute his own decisions. God cut out the stones as well. They were **the work of God** (cf. 24:12). The second set were hewn by Moses, and also apparently inscribed by him (34:1, 4, 27-28).

17-18. Joshua had been nearest to Moses (24:13); he now rejoins him but plays no further role in the events that follow. The Hebrew word (*'anôth*) translated **shouting** and **cry** is virtually repeated in the third clause (*'annôth*) where it is translated **singing.** The LXX felt that it must have the same root meaning in this third clause as in the previous two and consequently translated it so by adding the word "wine," i.e., "a voice set off by [for] wine." The picture is that of the orgiastic type of worship associated with fertility cults.

19-20. Moses breaks the tablets as a sign that the covenant relationship no longer exists between Israel and God. Israel is apostate. Moses is the prophet of judgment who

16. *The Language of Heaven.*—There has been much controversy by the literalists as to what language the tables were written in. It is most plausible to believe that they were written in the language of heaven, the characteristic of which is that, when read, everyone of every language hears them in his own tongue. For God has a language of his own, and he who hears it knows it is the voice of God. Among men there has been only one who has ever spoken it perfectly, and he spoke it and wrote it not in words and sentences but in a life and in a death. He wrote no book. All that he said has merely been reported to us by those who faintly understood, but his life is a language that all nations and peoples can understand.

19. *The Breaking of the Tablets.*—In the Talmud there is the suggestion that this was not entirely an act of temper. God is threatening to destroy the whole people for disobedience, ac-

20 And he took the calf which they had made, and burnt *it* in the fire, and ground *it* to powder, and strewed *it* upon the water, and made the children of Israel drink *of it*.

21 And Moses said unto Aaron, What did this people unto thee, that thou hast brought so great a sin upon them?

22 And Aaron said, Let not the anger of my lord wax hot: thou knowest the people, that they *are set* on mischief.

23 For they said unto me, Make us gods, which shall go before us: for *as for* this Moses, the man that brought us up out of the land of Egypt, we wot not what is become of him.

24 And I said unto them, Whosoever hath any gold, let them break *it* off. So they gave *it* me: then I cast it into the fire, and there came out this calf.

25 ¶ And when Moses saw that the people *were* naked, (for Aaron had made them naked unto *their* shame among their enemies,)

them at the foot of the mountain. 20 And he took the calf which they had made, and burnt it with fire, and ground it to powder, and scattered it upon the water, and made the people of Israel drink it.

21 And Moses said to Aaron, "What did this people do to you that you have brought a great sin upon them?" 22 And Aaron said, "Let not the anger of my lord burn hot; you know the people, that they are set on evil. 23 For they said to me, 'Make us gods, who shall go before us; as for this Moses, the man who brought us up out of the land of Egypt, we do not know what has become of him.' 24 And I said to them, 'Let any who have gold take it off'; so they gave it to me, and I threw it into the fire, and there came out this calf."

25 And when Moses saw that the people had broken loose (for Aaron had let them break loose, to their shame among their

---

announces a "full end," more final than any of his successors in the eighth and seventh centuries. He destroys the image in a manner reminiscent of Josiah's reforms (II Kings 23:4, 6, 12, 15). To make the people drink the water containing the dust of the accursed idol was probably a trial by ordeal (Num. 5:16-22). Those who were guilty would be indicated by the evil effects that would follow. The soul-shattering experience of the prophets who pronounced doom upon the people for whom they also made intercession is nowhere more graphically set forth than in this account.

21-24. Moses holds Aaron responsible. He has **brought a great sin upon them.** Aaron calls Moses **my lord** (cf. Num. 11:28; 12:11). In the Hebrew text as it now stands his excuse is very lame; the people are "in evil" or **set on evil.** Aaron had merely acted as the barometer of public opinion. His role is the antithesis of the prophet's role, which is here exalted in the person of Moses. Aaron disowns responsibility even for the form of the idol: **there came out this calf.**

d) The Levites (32:25-29)

This story of the punishment for the sin of apostasy also seeks to account for the origin of the Levitical priesthood. It was probably added to the account of the golden

---

cording to the Torah. Moses pleads for them apparently in vain. At the end of his patience, he at last says to God: "You cannot slay these people on the basis of a law which they have not known about. It is true that the punishment of death for idolatry or the making of images is prescribed on these tablets, but I am just coming down the mount with these laws. The people have not as yet heard them read. That there may be no proof that such a law existed, Behold, I take upon me thy wrath, and I break them to pieces! Now, if thou dost exterminate them, thou dost act as a tyrant, condemning them to

death for disobeying a law of which they were ignorant!" Rabbi Samuel bar Nahman illustrates it by the story of a man whose betrothed wife had been unfaithful to him, but he loved her and so tore up her marriage contract, for he said, "It will go easier with her if she faces the judges as a maiden than as a betrothed wife." [8] It was a prayer of defiance against an outmoded idea of God, and has many parallels in history. It is poignantly expounded in *The Green Pastures.* [1]

[8] Quoted by Fleg, *Moses,* pp. 111-14.
[1] Part II, scenes 6, 8.

26 Then Moses stood in the gate of the camp, and said, Who *is* on the Lord's side? *let him come* unto me. And all the sons of Levi gathered themselves together unto him.

27 And he said unto them, Thus saith the Lord God of Israel, Put every man his sword by his side, *and* go in and out from gate to gate throughout the camp, and slay every man his brother, and every man his companion, and every man his neighbor.

28 And the children of Levi did according to the word of Moses: and there fell of the people that day about three thousand men.

29 For Moses had said, Consecrate yourselves to-day to the Lord, even every man upon his son, and upon his brother; that he may bestow upon you a blessing this day.

30 ¶ And it came to pass on the morrow, that Moses said unto the people, Ye have sinned a great sin: and now I will go up unto the Lord; peradventure I shall make an atonement for your sin.

31 And Moses returned unto the Lord, and said, Oh, this people have sinned a great sin, and have made them gods of gold.

32 Yet now, if thou wilt forgive their sin — ; and if not, blot me, I pray thee, out of thy book which thou hast written.

enemies), **26** then Moses stood in the gate of the camp, and said, "Who is on the Lord's side? Come to me." And all the sons of Levi gathered themselves together to him. **27** And he said to them, "Thus says the Lord God of Israel, 'Put every man his sword on his side, and go to and fro from gate to gate throughout the camp, and slay every man his brother, and every man his companion, and every man his neighbor.'" **28** And the sons of Levi did according to the word of Moses; and there fell of the people that day about three thousand men. **29** And Moses said, "Today you have ordained yourselves[s] for the service of the Lord, each one at the cost of his son and of his brother, that he may bestow a blessing upon you this day."

30 On the morrow Moses said to the people, "You have sinned a great sin. And now I will go up to the Lord; perhaps I can make atonement for your sin." **31** So Moses returned to the Lord and said, "Alas, this people have sinned a great sin; they have made for themselves gods of gold. **32** But now, if thou wilt forgive their sin — and if not, blot me, I pray thee, out of thy book

[s] Gk Vg See Tg: Heb *ordain yourselves*

---

calf from another source. As an etiological story it has a parallel in the account of the establishment of the priesthood of Aaron by the zeal of Phinehas (Num. 25:7-13). The Levites elsewhere were held to owe their status by virtue of being the dedicated substitutes for the redeemed first-born (Num. 3:44-46; 8:5-19).

25-27. Moses challenges those loyal to Yahweh to kill the apostate brethren. He institutes a purge.

28-29. The Levites obey Moses and kill **about three thousand** Israelites. The term **ordained yourselves** is literally translated, "filled your [two] hands." It is used almost without exception of the consecration of priests (cf. Judg. 17:5, 12; I Kings 13:33). The Levites are not consecrated by other priests through the offering of sacrifices; they have consecrated themselves because for the name of Yahweh, in obedience to Moses, they have slain their sons and brothers (cf. Matt. 10:37).

e) Moses' Second Intercession (32:30-35)

30. The occasion **on the morrow** seems to follow Moses' descent from the mountain on the previous day. The punishment of the people by the Levitical massacre (vss. 25-29) cannot be presupposed. Moses **will go up to the Lord** as the great priest-intercessor to see if he **can make atonement.** The account exalts Moses.

31-32. The atonement Moses offers is his own faithfulness (cf., however, vss. 7-14, where he pleads God's character). If Israel cannot be forgiven, Moses himself wants to die: **blot me . . . out of thy book.** The **book** in the O.T. is the list of those who live on

33 And the LORD said unto Moses, Whosoever hath sinned against me, him will I blot out of my book.

34 Therefore now go, lead the people unto *the place* of which I have spoken unto thee: behold, mine Angel shall go before thee: nevertheless, in the day when I visit, I will visit their sin upon them.

35 And the LORD plagued the people, because they made the calf, which Aaron made.

33 And the LORD said unto Moses, Depart, *and* go up hence, thou and the people which thou hast brought up out of the land of Egypt, unto the land which I sware unto Abraham, to Isaac, and to Jacob, saying, Unto thy seed will I give it:

which thou hast written." 33 But the LORD said to Moses, "Whoever has sinned against me, him will I blot out of my book. 34 But now go, lead the people to the place of which I have spoken to you; behold, my angel shall go before you. Nevertheless, in the day when I visit, I will visit their sin upon them."

35 And the LORD sent a plague upon the people, because they made the calf which Aaron made.

33 The LORD said to Moses, "Depart, go up hence, you and the people whom you have brought up out of the land of Egypt, to the land of which I swore to Abraham, Isaac, and Jacob, saying, 'To

earth (Isa. 4:3; Mal. 3:16; Ps. 69:28). Sinners die young; the righteous live out the full span of life.

33-34. Moses' desire to die unless his people could be forgiven is both noble and tragic. The tragedy consists in his inability to provide what he most desires. He must live with the tragedy. He must continue to obey: go, lead the people. The day of visitation, however, will always be the prophetic day of judgment. There are no indulgences. The outcome of this tragedy is not provided simply by the discovery that in Yahweh justice and love are held together (as in Isa. 40–55); the deliverance from the tragedy depends upon the insight that the fulfillment of God's purpose transcends history. Prophetism must be followed by apocalypticism and the N.T.

35. This verse hardly follows from the preceding one. It may originally have followed vs. 20.

2. THE PROMISE OF GOD'S PRESENCE (33:1-23; 34:5b-9)

Though ch. 33 stands in its present position and seems to be a part of the general context, it is best to study it on the assumption that it was once a unit with a concern of its own. The incident of the golden calf is not a specific concern here, though it has a general relevance to the problem of God's presence with a sinful people. The scene is the imminent departure from Sinai (cf. Num. 10–11). Moses seeks assurance from God that he will indeed be present with him in his task of leadership after God has told him that he will not go up among them (vs. 3). The tent (vss. 7-11), a separable unit, must be understood as the means of God's presence. In a theophany Moses is given proof of God's promise (vss. 18-23).

a) DEPARTURE FROM SINAI (33:1-6)

33:1, 3. Chronologically this command to leave Sinai belongs at the conclusion of the promulgation of all the laws. Israel must leave for the land of which I swore. The

33:1-23. *Moses' Persistence with God.*—The argument between Yahweh and Moses may be likened to that with Abraham (Gen. 18:22-23). The more Moses gets from God, the more he is emboldened to ask, but he does not cease his wrestling with God till, unlike Abraham, he has obtained God's highest blessing. It is probably meant that the persistence of Moses in petition and argument was due to his initial misunder-

standing of God's first reply (vs. 17); as such it is a perfect picture of much of our praying, coming to a climax in vs. 14. We should all take to heart the fact that persistence in prayer is emphasized so much both in the O.T. and the N.T.; "Because of his importunity" (Luke 11:8). This passage in Exodus makes it clear that the persistence is necessary not for the purpose of persuading God, but in order that in

2 And I will send an Angel before thee; and I will drive out the Canaanite, the Amorite, and the Hittite, and the Perizzite, the Hivite, and the Jebusite:

3 Unto a land flowing with milk and honey: for I will not go up in the midst of thee; for thou *art* a stiffnecked people: lest I consume thee in the way.

4 ¶ And when the people heard these evil tidings, they mourned: and no man did put on him his ornaments.

5 For the Lord had said unto Moses, Say unto the children of Israel, Ye *are* a stiff-necked people: I will come up into the midst of thee in a moment, and consume thee: therefore now put off thy ornaments from thee, that I may know what to do unto thee.

6 And the children of Israel stripped themselves of their ornaments by the mount Horeb.

7 And Moses took the tabernacle, and pitched it without the camp, afar off from the camp, and called it the Tabernacle of

your descendants I will give it.' 2 And I will send an angel before you, and I will drive out the Canaanites, the Amorites, the Hittites, the Per'izzites, the Hivites, and the Jeb'usites. 3 Go up to a land flowing with milk and honey; but I will not go up among you, lest I consume you in the way, for you are a stiff-necked people."

4 When the people heard these evil tidings, they mourned; and no man put on his ornaments. 5 For the Lord had said to Moses, "Say to the people of Israel, 'You are a stiff-necked people; if for a single moment I should go up among you, I would consume you. So now put off your ornaments from you, that I may know what to do with you.' " 6 Therefore the people of Israel stripped themselves of their ornaments, from Mount Horeb onward.

7 Now Moses used to take the tent and

oath of God's promise still stands (32:13). God will not be immediately present with Israel as he has been at Sinai; he will not **go up among them.** His holiness prevents his unveiled presence. It would **consume** the people. This is doubly true: Israel is **a stiff-necked people,** rebellious as well as mortal.

2. This verse interrupts the continuity of vss. 1, 3. God says **I will send an angel** (LXX, "my angel") before he has been asked if or whom he will send. And in vs. 12 Moses says that God has not yet told whom he will send. The stock reference to the nations (cf. 3:8, 17; 34:11; etc.) also stamps it as an interpolation.

4-6. The Israelites **mourned** at the **evil tidings** that God would not personally accompany them. That this was for their own safety did not lessen the sorrow. Rather, it showed the tragedy of their situation. That **no man put on his ornaments** was not a sign of mourning but compliance with God's command by Moses (vs. 5). In 32:3-4 the people at the command of Aaron, not sanctioned by God or Moses his prophet, brought their trinkets for the manufacture of an illegitimate representation of deity. Here they are asked to bring the same sort of items for the construction of a legitimate instrument of the Presence (cf. 25:2-8; 35:20-29).

b) The Tent (33:7-11)

7. **The tent** is the '*ōhel mō'ēdh,* the tent of meeting, in contrast to the tabernacle (*mishkān*), from which the KJV fails to distinguish it. It is Moses' tent. He alone **used to take . . . and pitch it.** The LXX calls it "his tent." The Hebrew text says that he

the operation of prayer the petitioner's mind and imagination may be prepared for the answer already granted. As William Law says, "The Spirit of Prayer . . . is the Opener of all that is good within us, and the Receiver of all that is good without us." [2] The problem of prayer is

[2] *The Spirit of Prayer,* Part II, Dialogue 3, p. 116.

not to get God to answer our prayers, but to adjust ourselves to receive the answer. The Gulf Stream will flow through a straw if it is turned in the direction of that tremendous current.

7-10. *The Holy Place of Prayer.*—These verses are a fragment of some very old record which

11 And the LORD spake unto Moses face to face, as a man speaketh unto his friend. And he turned again into the camp; but his servant Joshua, the son of Nun, a young man, departed not out of the tabernacle.

12 ¶ And Moses said unto the LORD, See, thou sayest unto me, Bring up this people: and thou hast not let me know whom thou wilt send with me. Yet thou hast said, I know thee by name, and thou hast also found grace in my sight.

13 Now therefore, I pray thee, if I have found grace in thy sight, show me now thy way, that I may know thee, that I may find grace in thy sight: and consider that this nation *is* thy people.

11 Thus the LORD used to speak to Moses face to face, as a man speaks to his friend. When Moses turned again into the camp, his servant Joshua the son of Nun, a young man, did not depart from the tent.

12 Moses said to the LORD, "See, thou sayest to me, 'Bring up this people'; but thou hast not let me know whom thou wilt send with me. Yet thou hast said, 'I know you by name, and you have also found favor in my sight.' 13 Now therefore, I pray thee, if I have found favor in thy sight, show me now thy ways, that I may know thee and find favor in thy sight. Consider too that

---

11. Moses was the greatest of the prophets. God was in the habit (**used to**) of speaking to him **as a man speaks to his friend** (cf. Num. 12:7-8). The counterweight to these statements is provided by vss. 18-23. These do not contradict vs. 11 but underscore the cleft between Creator and creature which exists even in the case of a Moses, who is "faithful in all my house" (Num. 12:7; cf. Heb. 3:2, 5) "as a servant."

c) GOD REVEALS HIMSELF TO MOSES (33:12-23; 34:5*b*-9)

The renewal of the covenant relationship with Israel, symbolized by the new **tables of stone** (34:1) is made possible by the faith of Moses and is preceded by a theophany made to him alone. In this theophany God, by means of a revelation of his character (34:5*b*-9), pledges Moses his presence in the task of leadership. The account of the revelation has become separated from the account of the theophany by 34:1-5*a*, which serves to introduce the promulgation of the code beginning at 34:10. Aside from this intrusion, it is difficult to see a progressive order in the text as it now stands. Thus, vs. 12 presupposed vs. 17. But when vs. 17 is placed before vs. 12 it is difficult to find a situation to which it is God's response (McNeile, *Exodus*, p. 210, devised a solution as follows: Num. 11:11-12, 14-15; Exod. 33:17, 12-13, 18-23; 34:8-9; 33:14-16. But Num. 11:11-12, 14-15 do not seem to present a request to which vs. 17 could be a reply. The transposition of vss. 14-16 after 34:9 seems sound). It is impossible to account satisfactorily for vs. 12*b*.

12. The scene is still Sinai, despite vss. 7-11. The situation is that created by God who, in his wrath, commanded the people to go up to possess Palestine even though he would not go up among them. Moses asks God what this means, **Thou hast not let me know whom thou wilt send with me.** He is stunned. He simply cannot understand Yahweh's purpose. Surely God will not forsake Moses or his people.

13. Moses retains his faith but seeks knowledge: **Show me now thy ways.** The LXX reads, "Show me thyself" (cf. vss. 18, 20). **Consider too that this nation is thy people.**

---

at every morning service: the minister at his prayers suggesting to the congregation to do likewise.

11. *The Friend of God.*—Thomas Aquinas uses this passage as an example of the necessity to guard against gross literalism, saying, "When Scripture states that He spoke to him face to face, this is to be understood as expressing the opinion of the people, who thought that Moses

was speaking with God, mouth to mouth."[3] But it is a picture of a spiritual communion. The relationship between God and man in prayer is here one of close friendship; in Ps. 123:2 it is pictured as that of master and servant (cf. Neh. 1:5-6); in Jer. 3:19 the relationship is one of father to children. Sometimes several such

[3] *Summa Theologica*, Part II, Second Part, Q. XCVIII, art. 3. See also Pfeiffer, *Meister Eckhart*, I, 447.

14 And he said, My presence shall go *with thee,* and I will give thee rest.

15 And he said unto him, If thy presence go not *with me,* carry us not up hence.

16 For wherein shall it be known here that I and thy people have found grace in thy sight? *is it* not in that thou goest with us? So shall we be separated, I and thy people, from all the people that *are* upon the face of the earth.

17 And the Lord said unto Moses, I will do this thing also that thou hast-spoken: for thou hast found grace in my sight, and I know thee by name.

18 And he said, I beseech thee, show me thy glory.

this nation is thy people." 14 And he said, "My presence will go with you, and I will give you rest." 15 And he said to him, "If thy presence will not go with me, do not carry us up from here. 16 For how shall it be known that I have found favor in thy sight, I and thy people? Is it not in thy going with us, so that we are distinct, I and thy people, from all other people that are upon the face of the earth?"

17 And the Lord said to Moses, "This very thing that you have spoken I will do; for you have found favor in my sight, and I know you by name." 18 Moses said, "I

In the expected clarification he wants God to show what this means in the light of the disturbing command in vss. 1, 3. Moses' request for revelation is at the same time an intercession that God may assure them of his continued protection.

14-16. These verses should probably follow 34:9 (cf. *ibid.*). They accede to the request (34:9) that God **go in the midst. My presence will go with you.** Thus Moses' intercession has warded off God's threat in 33:1, 3. The Hebrew for **presence** is "face." It means that the fullness of God in his function as protector and leader will continue to be Israel's strength and safety. The judgment in which God "turns away his face" is removed. Only when Israel enjoys God's **presence** can it be a visible illustration of God's grace: only thus **shall it be known that I have found favor in thy sight, I and thy people.** Judgment is, after all, only the negative side of revelation!

17. The **very thing** God will do, Moses had asked for in vs. 13; God's declaration of his ways. **I know you by name** is a synonym for **thou hast found grace in my sight.** Moses' sincerity and faith move God to grant his request.

18. Moses is delighted. **Show me thy glory,** he says to God. The glory of God is the manifestation of God's character in its fullness. Moses wants God to disclose himself completely. Thus there is in Moses a poignant eagerness; he is entirely pure of heart, but he wants to know more than man can ever know (cf. vs. 21).

---

relationships are united, as in Mal. 1:6. All the prayers of Jesus begin with "Father" (except the cry of agony on the cross, "My God"). This was so characteristic of Jesus' way, and made such an impression on the Greek authors of the Gospels that they, recalling his very word, use the Aramaic *Abba.* In that word we feel that we are really listening to one who heard Jesus pray and remembered the sound of his voice.

15. *Nowhere Without God.*—"Moses was rather for dying where he stood, than to go one step without his God," so Christian comments in *The Pilgrim's Progress.*[4] Indeed, both parts of that tale have this text as their theme. God goes with anyone, even the weakest and most afraid, who will take him for guide. The children asked when they would be "at an end of this doleful place," the Valley of the Shadow of

Death, and Mr. Great-heart's answer was for them to "be of good courage and look well to their feet." The essentials of the story can be recalled: Christiana espied in front of them a thing of such a shape as she had never beheld before. Mr. Great-heart directed those who were afraid, to keep close to him. The fiend came on, "but when it was just come to him, it vanished to all their sights." In the ditch lay one Heedless, all rent and torn, a warning "not to set out lightly on pilgrimage, and to come without a guide." Mercy then, "looking behind her, saw, as she thought, something most like a lion, and it came a great padding pace after," and roared so loud that the valley echoed, and all their hearts, save the heart of their guide, did ache. But when Mr. Great-heart addressed himself to give him battle, it drew back and went no farther. And Christiana said, "Many have

[4] Part I, ch. ix.

19 And he said, I will make all my goodness pass before thee, and I will proclaim
the name of the Lord before thee; and will
be gracious to whom I will be gracious, and
will show mercy on whom I will show
mercy.

20 And he said, Thou canst not see my
face: for there shall no man see me, and
live.

21 And the Lord said, Behold, *there is*
a place by me, and thou shalt stand upon
a rock:

22 And it shall come to pass, while my
glory passeth by, that I will put thee in a
cleft of the rock, and will cover thee with
my hand while I pass by:

23 And I will take away mine hand, and
thou shalt see my back parts; but my face
shall not be seen.

pray thee, show me thy glory." 19 And he
said, "I will make all my goodness pass before you, and will proclaim before you my
name 'The Lord'; and I will be gracious
to whom I will be gracious, and will show
mercy on whom I will show mercy. 20 But,"
he said, "you cannot see my face; for man
shall not see me and live." 21 And the Lord
said, "Behold, there is a place by me where
you shall stand upon the rock; 22 and while
my glory passes by I will put you in a cleft
of the rock, and I will cover you with my
hand until I have passed by; 23 then I will
take away my hand, and you shall see my
back; but my face shall not be seen."

19. God accedes to Moses' request. He will let all his **goodness pass before** him. The
LXX reads "my glory." God's anger is past. Israel's sin is forgiven. God's revelation will
proclaim that he is as free in graciousness and mercy as in judgment. This new aspect of
the name as reconciliation God promises to disclose (cf. Rom. 9:15-16).

20. But though a new dimension of God, **my goodness** in forgiveness, will be revealed,
the **face** of God, his very being, cannot be disclosed in the glory that is manifest: **Thou
canst not see my face** (cf. 24:10).

21-23. Moses is to see the **glory** as it **passes by.** But God's **face shall not be seen.**
The poetic character of the bold anthropomorphism is evident from the statement that
there is a place beside God where Moses shall stand while God **passes by.** Moses will see
God's **glory** but not his **face;** he can know his will but not plumb his mystery.

34:5b. The revelation God promised Moses in 33:19 now actually begins. God **stood
with him there** (cf. 33:21) and **proclaimed the name** (cf. 33:19). This verse is in part the
conclusion of 34:1-4 and in part an editorial "bridge" from 33:23 to 34:6.

6-7. The Lord **passed before him:** Cf. 33:22; Moses stands in **a cleft of the rock**
as God commanded. The revelation, as anticipated (33:19), declares God's character.
The emphasis is upon his power to forgive. God is gracious, true, and merciful; full of
goodness and lovingkindness. But, supremely, he forgives **iniquity and transgression
and sin.** The Deuteronomic outlook pervades the passage (cf. 20:5; Num. 14:18;
Deut. 5:9).

spoke of it, but none can tell what the Valley
of the Shadow of Death should mean, until
they come to it themselves." But how God took
care of them all! Mr Ready-to-halt at the brink
of the last river cried, "Now I shall have no
more need of these crutches," and threw them
away; Much-afraid "went through the river
singing, but none could understand what she
said"; there was hope for all Bunyan's neighbors, even the meanest, who would take God for
guide, perhaps also in the end for the one of
whom he says least, "a young woman, her name
was Dull." [5] Bunyan's sympathetic understand-

ing of all kinds of people is filled with his assurance that this prayer is answered abundantly
for them all.

22. *The Cleft of the Rock.*—This is the scriptural basis for the famous hymn, "Rock of Ages,
cleft for me." In Exodus the **cleft** protects one
from the overwhelming glory of God, too daz-
zling for human eyes. It has been used in the
Fathers as a symbol of the Incarnation, in which
man saw as much of the divine being as was
intelligible by him and practical for him to live
by, God in man.

23. *The Revelation and the Mystery.*—A
salutary admonition to all dogmatic souls who

[5] Part II, chs. iii, vi-ix.

34 And the LORD said unto Moses, Hew thee two tables of stone like unto the first: and I will write upon *these* tables the words that were in the first tables, which thou brakest.

34 The LORD said to Moses, "Cut two tables of stone like the first; and I will write upon the tables the words that were on the first tables, which you broke.

8-9. Moses prostrates himself. He addresses God as "Adonai," not as Yahweh. This heightens the emphasis upon God's holiness and transcendence. Moses, knowing now that God forgives, asks for a reversal of God's expressed intention in 33:1, 3: **I pray thee, go in the midst of us.** The request is granted (cf. 33:14-16).

3. The Renewal of the Covenant (34:1-5a, 10-35)

The heart of this chapter is the so-called "ritual decalogue" (vss. 14-26). As it now stands it is integral to the main concerns of chs. 32–33: the religious significance of the person of Moses and the doctrine of forgiveness of sins. It presupposes 32:1, 4. The duplication of the tables of the law, following sin, ostensibly embodied in this chapter, is already cited in Deut. 10:1-5. Nevertheless, these laws have a history prior to their integration in chs. 32–34 as an illustration of God's restoration in forgiveness.

The laws are related to and must be compared with the cultic sections of the Covenant Code (20:21-26; 22:18–23:19), not with the Decalogue. Most of the provisions are parallel to those of 23:13-19 (cf. 34:14-26). Practically all of the others are virtually duplicated in various places of the larger code (34:17=20:23; 34:19-20=22:29-30; 34:21=23:12). The Covenant Code is included in the E document; the "ritual decalogue" in J. On all of this there is considerable agreement. The literary-historical question under dispute is whether the Covenant Code, in its cultic sections, has borrowed from 34:14-26, or whether 34:14-26 is what was left of J's version of the Covenant Code after E's version was incorporated in the JE history. The former view is held, among others, by R. H. Pfeiffer (*Introduction to the Old Testament* [New York: Harper & Bros., 1941], pp. 220-21). He considers the "ritual decalogue" an actual (Deuteronomic) edition of an ancient Canaanite code antedating 1200. The Covenant Code is also an edition of this code, he says, even earlier. But it is one in which the text of the original Canaanite code is badly disarranged. Hence 34:14-26 becomes the primary resource in the Bible for the recovery of Israel's early religious history, or even of its early social and political history (cf. H. H. Rowley, *The Re-discovery of the Old Testament* [Philadelphia: Westminster Press, 1946], pp. 120-21). However, some share the view of Eichrodt (*Theologie des A.T.,* I, 25) that 34:14-26 is only a "wreck" of J's version of Israel's laws, which was originally

---

would discourse upon the "Mind of God." The radio broadcasting of sermons has mercilessly exposed the weakness of much preaching. For the first time the microphone in the pulpit is a sign to the preacher that he may be speaking to many not of his fold. Try to conceal them as he may, his unspoken dogmatic assumptions annoy those whose prejudices are different from his. The blare of the Kremlin from all dictator camps, or of some ecclesiastical authoritarianism, seems for the time being to drown out the humble, varied testimony of liberal minds who accept the others as brethren, yet refuse to admit that their voices are the pure voice of God. Even Moses can see God's glory but not his face (see Exeg.). The souls of the saints came up to stand in the presence of the Eternal. They were a little distant with each other, but each one laid his gift before the throne. God

looked on each one and at his gift and smiled. At last came one magnificently dressed. As he approached the throne, he cleared all the other gifts away with his foot, and set his own in the center, saying, "This is the only one after thine own mind and law, O God." He smiled and was stepping back, but before he could reach his place again, the devil broke loose from hell and grabbed his gift and made off with it. And God rose from his throne, and, kneeling down, set all the other gifts in place again. When the givers saw this they shook hands, and some even kissed one another and wept. The giver of the rejected gift did likewise; and then, kneeling in astonished penitence, prayed, "Forgive me, for till now I had not seen thy face." And God laid his hand on him too, and said, "My son."

34:1-28. *The Growing Revelation.*—It is clear that there have been a number of editorial

the congregation. And it came to pass, *that* every one which sought the LORD went out unto the tabernacle of the congregation, which *was* without the camp.

8 And it came to pass, when Moses went out unto the tabernacle, *that* all the people rose up, and stood every man *at* his tent door, and looked after Moses, until he was gone into the tabernacle.

9 And it came to pass, as Moses entered into the tabernacle, the cloudy pillar descended, and stood *at* the door of the tabernacle, and *the* LORD talked with Moses.

10 And all the people saw the cloudy pillar stand *at* the tabernacle door: and all the people rose up and worshipped, every man *in* his tent door.

pitch it outside the camp, far off from the camp; and he called it the tent of meeting. And every one who sought the LORD would go out to the tent of meeting, which was outside the camp. 8 Whenever Moses went out to the tent, all the people rose up, and every man stood at his tent door, and looked after Moses, until he had gone into the tent. 9 When Moses entered the tent, the pillar of cloud would descend and stand at the door of the tent, and the LORD would speak with Moses. 10 And when all the people saw the pillar of cloud standing at the door of the tent, all the people would rise up and worship, every man at his tent door.

---

pitched the tent "for [to] him," i.e., for God. All accounts of the tent exalt Moses. Only for him was it a tent of revelation, the place at which God met him (cf. Num. 11:16-17, 24-30; 12:1-8; Deut. 31:14-15). As opposed to the ark, which stresses the nearness or presence of Yahweh (cf. Num. 10:35-36), the tent stresses God's separation from his people. It is a reminder that God is not among his people (vs. 3). The ark was preeminently the symbol of the priests. It is striking that the tent provides no role for the priest, not even Aaron. It seems to stand as the symbol of the most exalted form of prophecy (Num. 11:24–12:8). It is the tent of Moses, the prophet without fear.

But all who sought the LORD would go out to the tent of meeting, i.e., ordinary judgment, whether by oath or by lot, was given at the tent. It was for this purpose perhaps that Joshua was constantly in the tent (vs. 11). This constitutes an entirely different function, a function that does not presuppose the Presence, symbolized by the cloud, which Moses' entrance into the tent produced. It leads to the supposition that the ark may have stood inside the tent, though this must not obscure the point that the tent was an instrument in its own right, Moses' tent of revelation. The fact that the tent is called the "tent of the testimony" (Num. 9:15; 17:7-8 [Hebrew vss. 22-23]) lends support to the view that it also housed the ark. Eichrodt (*Theologie des A.T.*, I, 45-46) has made the point that the tabernacle tradition of P, which seeks to absorb the tradition of the tent, serves to establish an ineradicable connection between tent and ark despite the tension involved in the religious meanings they set forth.

8. Since every man . . . at his tent door could see Moses enter the tent, Beer (*Exodus*, p. 159), following Gressmann, discounts the statement that the tent was outside the camp. Only if the tent, like the tabernacle, were in the center of the camp, he says, could it be seen by all. But Num. 11:24-30 speaks strongly against this view. Since the tent was in all probability pitched on a high place above the camp, the objection Beer makes seems unnecessary.

9. The Hebrew says that "he spoke" with Moses, for the pillar of cloud is here a synonym for the Lord.

---

has drifted into this context. It refers to a time before the "tabernacle" was erected. At that time there was a smaller tent which Moses and Joshua could carry; it was pitched outside the camp; it was used only by Moses and was cared for in his absence by Joshua. It is a fitting picture of the personal devotional life of the min-

ister. There is a story of the white flag which flew at times over the tent of General Gordon in the desert and was the sign that he was not to be disturbed, that he was in prayer. The scene in which every man stood at the door of his tent and looked after Moses, saw the pillar of cloud descend, and worshiped, ought to be the scene

2 And be ready in the morning, and come up in the morning unto mount Sinai, and present thyself there to me in the top of the mount.

3 And no man shall come up with thee, neither let any man be seen throughout all the mount; neither let the flocks nor herds feed before that mount.

4 ¶ And he hewed two tables of stone like unto the first; and Moses rose up early in the morning, and went up unto mount Sinai, as the LORD had commanded him, and took in his hand the two tables of stone.

5 And the LORD descended in the cloud, and stood with him there, and proclaimed the name of the LORD.

6 And the LORD passed by before him, and proclaimed, The LORD, The LORD God, merciful and gracious, long-suffering, and abundant in goodness and truth,

7 Keeping mercy for thousands, forgiving iniquity and transgression and sin, and

2 Be ready in the morning, and come up in the morning to Mount Sinai, and present yourself there to me on the top of the mountain. 3 No man shall come up with you, and let no man be seen throughout all the mountain; let no flocks or herds feed before that mountain." 4 So Moses cut two tables of stone like the first; and he rose early in the morning and went up on Mount Sinai, as the LORD had commanded him, and took in his hand two tables of stone. 5 And the LORD descended in the cloud and stood with him there, and proclaimed the name of the LORD. 6 The LORD passed before him, and proclaimed, "The LORD, the LORD, a God merciful and gracious, slow to anger, and abounding in steadfast love and faithfulness, 7 keeping steadfast love for thousands, forgiving iniquity and trans-

---

a parallel to E's. This version, like that of E, may have been an edition of earlier materials, even pre-Mosaic materials. But on the view that E's edition was preserved, the main resource in the Bible for the recovery of Israel's early religious history is not the "ritual decalogue" of 34:14-26, but the Covenant Code.

a) PREPARATION (34:1-5a, 10-11)

34:1-2. Moses is to take **two tables of stone** up the mount (cf. 24:12). The addition of **like the first**, perhaps of Deuteronomic origin (Deut. 10:1-5), relates the account to chs. 32–33 and makes it function as a renewal of the covenant. The theophany is confined to Moses and has been provided in 33:12-23. Moses is to **present** himself to God. The Hebrew is the same as the word for "stand" in 33:21. Moses is to come up **in the morning**. In Deut. 10:3 he is first to make the ark. That may have been excised here because of 37:1.

3. The holiness of the mount separates it from all but Moses (cf. 19:12). The prohibition against grazing in sacred areas was common in ancient religion, and survives today at Sheikh Adi, the central shrine of the Yezidis in northern Iraq.

4-5a. Moses chiseled out two tablets and with these in his hands ascended the mount. The Lord came down in **the cloud and stood with him there.** Most commentators (Driver, *Exodus,* p. 366; Beer, *Exodus,* p. 160; cf. also, LXX *ad loc.*) designate Moses as the subject of the verb **stood.** That means also that Moses called upon **the name of the LORD.** The last part of vs. 5 then has no connection with 33:19 or vs. 6 immediately following.

5b-9. See Exeg. on 34:5b, 6-7, 8-9, pp. 1075-76.

---

changes, so that the second Decalogue as given here is not the same as the first. A table of contents would run as follows: only Yahweh is to be worshiped (vs. 14); no molten images are to be made (vs. 17); the feast of unleavened bread is to be observed (vs. 18); concerning firstlings of cattle (vss. 19-20); the sabbath (vs. 21); harvest and vintage feasts (vs. 22); all males to

appear before Yahweh thrice in the year (vs. 23); leavened bread not to be offered (vs. 25a); firstfruits to be offered (26a); a kid not to be boiled in its mother's milk (vs. 26b). See Expos., pp. 850-51. A study of the two forms of the Decalogue gives one some conception of the gradual ways of God's revelation of truth to man.

that will by no means clear *the guilty;* visiting the iniquity of the fathers upon the children, and upon the children's children, unto the third and to the fourth *generation.*

8 And Moses made haste, and bowed his head toward the earth, and worshipped.

9 And he said, If now I have found grace in thy sight, O Lord, let my Lord, I pray thee, go among us; for it *is* a stiffnecked people; and pardon our iniquity and our sin, and take us for thine inheritance.

10 ¶ And he said, Behold, I make a covenant: before all thy people I will do marvels, such as have not been done in all the earth, nor in any nation: and all the people among which thou *art* shall see the work of the LORD: for it *is* a terrible thing that I will do with thee.

11 Observe thou that which I command thee this day: behold, I drive out before thee the Amorite, and the Canaanite, and the Hittite, and the Perizzite, and the Hivite, and the Jebusite.

12 Take heed to thyself, lest thou make a covenant with the inhabitants of the land whither thou goest, lest it be for a snare in the midst of thee:

13 But ye shall destroy their altars, break their images, and cut down their groves:

14 For thou shalt worship no other god: for the LORD, whose name *is* Jealous, *is* a jealous God.

15 Lest thou make a covenant with the inhabitants of the land, and they go a whoring after their gods, and do sacrifice unto their gods, and *one* call thee, and thou eat of his sacrifice;

16 And thou take of their daughters unto thy sons, and their daughters go a whoring after their gods, and make thy sons go a whoring after their gods.

gression and sin, but who will by no means clear the guilty, visiting the iniquity of the fathers upon the children and the children's children, to the third and the fourth generation." 8 And Moses made haste to bow his head toward the earth, and worshiped. 9 And he said, "If now I have found favor in thy sight, O LORD, let the LORD, I pray thee, go in the midst of us, although it is a stiff-necked people; and pardon our iniquity and our sin, and take us for thy inheritance."

10 And he said, "Behold, I make a covenant. Before all your people I will do marvels, such as have not been wrought in all the earth or in any nation; and all the people among whom you are shall see the work of the LORD; for it is a terrible thing that I will do with you.

11 "Observe what I command you this day. Behold, I will drive out before you the Amorites, the Canaanites, the Hittites, the Per'izzites, the Hivites, and the Jeb'usites. 12 Take heed to yourself, lest you make a covenant with the inhabitants of the land whither you go, lest it become a snare in the midst of you. 13 You shall tear down their altars, and break their pillars, and cut down their Ashe'rim 14 (for you shall worship no other god, for the LORD, whose name is Jealous, is a jealous God), 15 lest you make a covenant with the inhabitants of the land, and when they play the harlot after their gods and sacrifice to their gods and one invites you, you eat of his sacrifice, 16 and you take of their daughters for your sons, and their daughters play the harlot after their gods and make your sons play the harlot after their gods.

---

10. The **covenant** is made as a promise. God **will do marvels.** The wonder of Israel's deliverance from Egypt is no longer the sanction for the law (cf. 20:2). Historical revelation is replaced by a species of sacramental mysticism. This verse is characteristic of P, as is also shown by the use of the word "created" (ברא) for the wonders God will do.

11. The preface closes with a Deuteronomic promise as the basis of exhortation (cf. 23:27-31; 33:2).

b) THE LAWS (34:12-28)

12-16. In Palestine Israel must make no treaties with native peoples (cf. 23:22). This Deuteronomic attempt to segregate Israel cultically and ethnically overlooks much of Israel's early social and religious history. The destruction of the altars, pillars, and sacred poles of the Canaanites was an accomplishment of the reign of Josiah in the seventh

17 Thou shalt make thee no molten gods.

18 ¶ The feast of unleavened bread shalt thou keep. Seven days thou shalt eat unleavened bread, as I commanded thee, in the time of the month Abib: for in the month Abib thou camest out from Egypt.

19 All that openeth the matrix *is* mine; and every firstling among thy cattle, *whether* ox or sheep, *that is male.*

20 But the firstling of an ass thou shalt redeem with a lamb: and if thou redeem *him* not, then shalt thou break his neck. All the firstborn of thy sons thou shalt redeem. And none shall appear before me empty.

21 ¶ Six days thou shalt work, but on the seventh day thou shalt rest: in earing time and in harvest thou shalt rest.

22 ¶ And thou shalt observe the feast of weeks, of the firstfruits of wheat harvest, and the feast of ingathering at the year's end.

23 ¶ Thrice in the year shall all your men children appear before the Lord GOD, the God of Israel.

24 For I will cast out the nations before thee, and enlarge thy borders: neither shall

17 "You shall make for yourself no molten gods.

18 "The feast of unleavened bread you shall keep. Seven days you shall eat unleavened bread, as I commanded you, at the time appointed in the month Abib; for in the month Abib you came out from Egypt. 19 All that opens the womb is mine, all your male cattle, the firstling of cow and sheep. 20 The firstlings of an ass you shall redeem with a lamb, or if you will not redeem it you shall break its neck. All the first-born of your sons you shall redeem. And none shall appear before me empty.

21 "Six days you shall work, but on the seventh day you shall rest; in plowing time and in harvest you shall rest. 22 And you shall observe the feast of weeks, the first fruits of wheat harvest, and the feast of ingathering at the year's end. 23 Three times in the year shall all your males appear before the LORD God, the God of Israel. 24 For I will cast out nations before you, and enlarge your borders; neither shall any man

century (cf. 23:24; Deut. 7:5; 12:3). Israel must **worship no other god** (cf. 23:23). This basic law (20:3) is here applied solely to the problem of Israel's dealings with the Canaanites. Yahweh's **name is Jealous.** His nature is such as to permit no rivals (20:5; Deut. 4:24). Therefore treaties must be avoided, for treaties would imply the coexistence of Canaanite and Israelite altars. Canaanites would **invite** (plural in LXX) Israelites to share in their sacrifices by offering them meat consecrated to their gods (cf. I Cor. 8:10). Intermarriage is a particularly fertile source of syncretism of this sort (Deut. 7:3-4).

17. The question of hewn representations is left open (cf. 20:23).

18. The provision for the feast of Unleavened Bread is identical with 23:15. In neither case is the Passover associated with it (cf. vs. 25). It seems plausible, as suggested by Beer (*Exodus,* p. 160), that the verse was inserted by the editor of JE.

19. The law of the first-born as stated here corresponds to 22:30. The first-born males of cow and sheep must be offered to God.

20a. The provision for the redemption of the ass and of the sons is identical with 13:13.

20b. Cf. 22:29. The offerings of the first fruits at the festivals and the offerings of first-born must be punctually observed.

21. The sabbath must be kept even when, because of the pressure of work **in plowing time and in harvest,** it might seem better not to do so (cf. 20:8-11; 23:12).

22-23. These verses are nearly identical with 23:16-17. Pentecost is here called **feast of weeks,** which is its specifically Israelite title. Tabernacles is still called by its older title, **feast of ingathering.** In ch. 22 the equivalent of vs. 18 immediately precedes the reference to these two festivals, thus accounting for the **three times in the year.**

24. This idyllic picture describes the blessing that will ensue if Israelites are faithful to the law. Their nation will be strong; and no man will molest their property when they make their three yearly pilgrimages.

any man desire thy land, when thou shalt go up to appear before the LORD thy God thrice in the year.

25 Thou shalt not offer the blood of my sacrifice with leaven; neither shall the sacrifice of the feast of the passover be left unto the morning.

26 The first of the firstfruits of thy land thou shalt bring unto the house of the LORD thy God. Thou shalt not seethe a kid in his mother's milk.

27 And the LORD said unto Moses, Write thou these words: for after the tenor of these words I have made a covenant with thee and with Israel.

28 And he was there with the LORD forty days and forty nights; he did neither eat bread, nor drink water. And he wrote upon the tables the words of the covenant, the ten commandments.

29 ¶ And it came to pass, when Moses came down from mount Sinai with the two tables of testimony in Moses' hand, when he came down from the mount, that Moses wist not that the skin of his face shone while he talked with him.

desire your land, when you go up to appear before the LORD your God three times in the year.

25 "You shall not offer the blood of my sacrifice with leaven; neither shall the sacrifice of the feast of the passover be left until the morning. 26 The first of the first fruits of your ground you shall bring to the house of the LORD your God. You shall not boil a kid in its mother's milk." 27 And the LORD said to Moses, "Write these words; in accordance with these words I have made a covenant with you and with Israel." 28 And he was there with the LORD forty days and forty nights; he neither ate bread nor drank water. And he wrote upon the tables the words of the covenant, the ten commandments.[t]

29 When Moses came down from Mount Sinai, with the two tables of the testimony in his hand as he came down from the mountain, Moses did not know that the skin of his face shone because he had been talk-

[t] Heb words

25-26. These three provisions are identical with 23:18-19, except that the Passover is mentioned here. Consequently, the fat which burned on the altar in other sacrifices is here changed to **the sacrifice**, i.e., to the lamb eaten at Passover.

27-28. As in 24:4, Moses writes the laws, though here in Yahweh's presence. They condition the covenant relationship which is here established with Moses and with Israel. Moses is given an exalted place in the relationship corresponding to the general spirit of chs. 32–34. As stated above (pp. 1076-77) the original words of the **covenant** can no longer be specified with any degree of certainty. Here the phrase probably refers to whatever poem of the Covenant Code was in the J document before it was combined with E. The **ten commandments** (Deut. 4:13; 10:4) is probably a later addition. Here it designates what is now left of the J version of the code (vss. 12-26), the so-called "ritual decalogue." It is possible, though scarcely mandatory, to order its provisions in ten parts. In Deut. 9:18; 10:10 it is held that Moses spent two vigils of **forty days and forty nights** on the mount (cf. 24:18). This tells us that when Deuteronomy was written, chs. 32–34 were already treated as an account of the breaking and renewal of the covenant.

c) THE TRANSFIGURATION OF MOSES (34:29-35)

29. The quasi divine status of Moses is here indicated by making the transfiguration of his face a sign and seal for the divine origin of the law. The phrase **two tables of the testimony** shows that this concluding section belongs to P (cf. also **Aaron and all the people** [vs. 31]). But in its exaltation of Moses it compares with chs. 32–34. When Moses talked with God, **the skin of his face shone**. The LXX says it was "glorified." The light of the Shekinah or divine Presence was communicated to him. This account is the antetype for the account of the transfiguration in the N.T. (Matt. 17:1-7). Moses **did not know** that the glory for which he had prayed (33:18) was actually effected in him personally.

30 And when Aaron and all the children of Israel saw Moses, behold, the skin of his face shone; and they were afraid to come nigh him.

31 And Moses called unto them; and Aaron and all the rulers of the congregation returned unto him: and Moses talked with them.

32 And afterward all the children of Israel came nigh: and he gave them in commandment all that the LORD had spoken with him in mount Sinai.

33 And *till* Moses had done speaking with them, he put a veil on his face.

34 But when Moses went in before the LORD to speak with him, he took the veil off, until he came out. And he came out, and spake unto the children of Israel *that* which he was commanded.

35 And the children of Israel saw the face of Moses, that the skin of Moses' face shone: and Moses put the veil upon his face again, until he went in to speak with him.

ing with God. 30 And when Aaron and all the people of Israel saw Moses, behold, the skin of his face shone, and they were afraid to come near him. 31 But Moses called to them; and Aaron and all the leaders of the congregation returned to him, and Moses talked with them. 32 And afterward all the people of Israel came near, and he gave them in commandment all that the LORD had spoken with him in Mount Sinai. 33 And when Moses had finished speaking with them, he put a veil on his face; 34 but whenever Moses went in before the LORD to speak with him, he took the veil off, until he came out; and when he came out, and told the people of Israel what he was commanded, 35 the people of Israel saw the face of Moses, that the skin of Moses' face shone; and Moses would put the veil upon his face again, until he went in to speak with him.

30-32. Moses impresses Aaron and all the others as possessing a measure of holiness beyond their range. **They were afraid to come near him.** God's holiness is treated as though it were a semifluid substance with which no one must be charged beyond his capacity. Moses stands at the border of heaven and earth. **But Moses called to them.** First to the leaders and then to the people he communicates God's will. The covenant is sealed in his person in contrast to 24:9-11.

33-35. These verses refer to a habitual practice of Moses, which, it is intimated, was adopted because of the single incident cited above. Except when appearing in the presence of God and when communicating his word to the people, he kept his face covered with a veil. The word occurs only here. Beer (*Exodus*, p. 164), following Gressmann, suggests that it is a mask such as is common among primitive priesthoods. Such masks are a protection against demons and also protect the common people from the excessive holiness of the priest. They are often worn by the priest to protect him in his approach to the god. Here it is noteworthy that Moses faces Yahweh with his face uncovered. In II Cor. 3:7-18 Paul accounts for the veiling of Moses' face on the assumption that the

---

33-35. *Moses Veils His Face.*—The verb translated **shone** occurs only twice in Hebrew literature: here and in Ps. 69:31, where it is used of a bullock displaying horns. The verb is derived from the noun "horn." The Vulg. translates it "horned," hence the representation by the old painters and Michelangelo of Moses with horns. In Job. 3:4 "horns" denote rays of light or lightning flashes. So the translation in English is probably what was meant. Vss. 34-35 are an editorial attempt to explain the veil, for which no meaning has been given. The implication is that the veil was used because the reflection of the divine glory was too sacred to be gazed at

by human eyes (see Exeg.). The episode has endless applications. Many a doctor and minister can testify that the phenomenon of the shining face was not only to be seen in Moses. Often they and others have been confronted with it shining on them from beds of pain, so that they too seemed to need the intervention of a veil to shield them from the piercing splendor of the divine soul shining through the frail body. It was noted at martyrdoms that the face of the agonizing sufferer sometimes seemed alight with a flame more triumphant than that consuming the faggots. In simpler ways the same experience

35 And Moses gathered all the congregation of the children of Israel together, and said unto them, These *are* the words which the Lord hath commanded, that *ye* should do them.

2 Six days shall work be done, but on the seventh day there shall be to you a holy day, a sabbath of rest to the Lord: whosoever doeth work therein shall be put to death.

3 Ye shall kindle no fire throughout your habitations upon the sabbath day.

4 ¶ And Moses spake unto all the congregation of the children of Israel, saying, This *is* the thing which the Lord commanded, saying,

5 Take ye from among you an offering unto the Lord: whosoever *is* of a willing heart, let him bring it, an offering of the Lord; gold, and silver, and brass,

6 And blue, and purple, and scarlet, and fine linen, and goats' *hair*,

7 And rams' skins dyed red, and badgers' skins, and shittim wood,

8 And oil for the light, and spices for anointing oil, and for the sweet incense,

9 And onyx stones, and stones to be set for the ephod, and for the breastplate.

10 And every wise-hearted among you shall come, and make all that the Lord hath commanded;

35 Moses assembled all the congregation of the people of Israel, and said to them, "These are the things which the Lord has commanded you to do. 2 Six days shall work be done, but on the seventh day you shall have a holy sabbath of solemn rest to the Lord; whoever does any work on it shall be put to death; 3 you shall kindle no fire in all your habitations on the sabbath day."

4 Moses said to all the congregation of the people of Israel, "This is the thing which the Lord has commanded. 5 Take from among you an offering to the Lord; whoever is of a generous heart, let him bring the Lord's offering: gold, silver, and bronze; 6 blue and purple and scarlet stuff and fine twined linen; goats' hair, 7 tanned rams' skins, and goatskins; acacia wood, 8 oil for the light, spices for the anointing oil and for the fragrant incense, 9 and onyx stones and stones for setting, for the ephod and for the breastpiece.

10 "And let every able man among you come and make all that the Lord has com-

---

"glory" faded quickly after Moses had left the presence of Yahweh; rather than remind people of the frailty of their means of access to God, Moses veils his face!

D. The Execution of the Cult Ordinances (35:1–40:38)

1. The Sabbath (35:1-3)

35:1-3. The sabbath law as here stated ignores the rich account of its source and meaning provided by P in 31:12-17. In its provision that on **six days shall work be done** it seems to concentrate on the work of the tabernacle, the announcement of which the brief statement of the law serves to introduce. Galling accentuates this particular reference by emending the Hebrew text in vs. 3 to read, "For all the work you have planned you shall kindle no fire . . . on the sabbath day," making the fires refer to those needed for the work in metals (Beer, *Exodus*, p. 164).

2. The Offering (35:4-29)

Moses carefully communicates God's instructions concerning the offering (cf. 25:1-9) **to all the congregation of the people of Israel** (vss. 4-9). In vs. 10 there is an invitation

---

is noted among kindly, humble folks. "Grandma," said one child, "must sleep in heaven, she is always so happy at breakfast," and the epitaph of a minister on the Hill in Andover states that even to meet him on the street made one feel that life was more worth while: "He wist not that his face shone."

35:1–39:43. These are almost exact repetitions of previous chapters with changes of person and tense.

11 The tabernacle, his tent, and his covering, his taches, and his boards, his bars, his pillars, and his sockets;

12 The ark, and the staves thereof, *with* the mercy seat, and the veil of the covering;

13 The table, and his staves, and all his vessels, and the showbread;

14 The candlestick also for the light, and his furniture, and his lamps, with the oil for the light;

15 And the incense altar, and his staves, and the anointing oil, and the sweet incense, and the hanging for the door at the entering in of the tabernacle;

16 The altar of burnt offering, with his brazen grate, his staves, and all his vessels, the laver and his foot;

17 The hangings of the court, his pillars, and their sockets, and the hanging for the door of the court;

18 The pins of the tabernacle, and the pins of the court, and their cords;

19 The clothes of service, to do service in the holy *place,* the holy garments for Aaron the priest, and the garments of his sons, to minister in the priest's office.

20 ¶ And all the congregation of the children of Israel departed from the presence of Moses.

21 And they came, every one whose heart stirred him up, and every one whom his spirit made willing, *and* they brought the Lord's offering to the work of the tabernacle of the congregation, and for all his service, and for the holy garments.

22 And they came, both men and women, as many as were willing-hearted, *and* brought bracelets, and earrings, and rings, and tablets, all jewels of gold: and every man that offered, *offered* an offering of gold unto the Lord.

23 And every man, with whom was found blue, and purple, and scarlet, and fine linen, and goats' *hair,* and red skins of rams, and badgers' skins, brought *them.*

24 Every one that did offer an offering of silver and brass brought the Lord's offering: and every man, with whom was found shittim wood for any work of the service, brought *it.*

manded: the tabernacle, 11 its tent and its covering, its hooks and its frames, its bars, its pillars, and its bases; 12 the ark with its poles, the mercy seat, and the veil of the screen; 13 the table with its poles and all its utensils, and the bread of the Presence; 14 the lampstand also for the light, with its utensils and its lamps, and the oil for the light; 15 and the altar of incense, with its poles, and the anointing oil and the fragrant incense, and the screen for the door, at the door of the tabernacle; 16 the altar of burnt offering, with its grating of bronze, its poles, and all its utensils, the laver and its base; 17 the hangings of the court, its pillars and its bases, and the screen for the gate of the court; 18 the pegs of the tabernacle and the pegs of the court, and their cords; 19 the finely wrought garments for ministering in the holy place, the holy garments for Aaron the priest, and the garments of his sons, for their service as priests."

20 Then all the congregation of the people of Israel departed from the presence of Moses. 21 And they came, every one whose heart stirred him, and every one whose spirit moved him, and brought the Lord's offering to be used for the tent of meeting, and for all its service, and for the holy garments. 22 So they came, both men and women; all who were of a willing heart brought brooches and earrings and signet rings and armlets, all sorts of gold objects, every man dedicating an offering of gold to the Lord. 23 And every man with whom was found blue or purple or scarlet stuff or fine linen or goats' hair or tanned rams' skins or goatskins, brought them. 24 Every one who could make an offering of silver or bronze brought it as the Lord's offering; and every man, with whom was found acacia wood of

to **every able man** to produce the goods asked for. In all probability this verse was originally followed immediately by vss. 20-29. Vss. 11-19 constitute a list of the objects to be made from the materials offered, including the **bread of the Presence** (vs. 13). This

25 And all the women that were wise-hearted did spin with their hands, and brought that which they had spun, *both* of blue, and of purple, *and* of scarlet, and of fine linen.

26 And all the women whose heart stirred them up in wisdom spun goats' *hair.*

27 And the rulers brought onyx stones, and stones to be set, for the ephod, and for the breastplate;

28 And spice, and oil for the light, and for the anointing oil, and for the sweet incense.

29 The children of Israel brought a willing offering unto the LORD, every man and woman, whose heart made them willing to bring for all manner of work, which the LORD had commanded to be made by the hand of Moses.

30 ¶ And Moses said unto the children of Israel, See, the LORD hath called by name Bezaleel the son of Uri, the son of Hur, of the tribe of Judah;

31 And he hath filled him with the spirit of God, in wisdom, in understanding, and in knowledge, and in all manner of workmanship;

32 And to devise curious works, to work in gold, and in silver, and in brass,

33 And in the cutting of stones, to set *them,* and in carving of wood, to make any manner of cunning work.

34 And he hath put in his heart that he may teach, *both* he, and Aholiab, the son of Ahisamach, of the tribe of Dan.

35 Them hath he filled with wisdom of heart, to work all manner of work, of the engraver, and of the cunning workman, and of the embroiderer, in blue, and in purple, in scarlet, and in fine linen, and of

any use in the work, brought it. 25 And all women who had ability spun with their hands, and brought what they had spun in blue and purple and scarlet stuff and fine twined linen; 26 all the women whose hearts were moved with ability spun the goats' hair. 27 And the leaders brought onyx stones and stones to be set, for the ephod and for the breastpiece, 28 and spices and oil for the light, and for the anointing oil, and for the fragrant incense. 29 All the men and women, the people of Israel, whose heart moved them to bring anything for the work which the LORD had commanded by Moses to be done, brought it as their freewill offering to the LORD.

30 And Moses said to the people of Israel, "See, the LORD has called by name Bez'alel the son of Uri, son of Hur, of the tribe of Judah; 31 and he has filled him with the Spirit of God, with ability, with intelligence, with knowledge, and with all craftsmanship, 32 to devise artistic designs, to work in gold and silver and bronze, 33 in cutting stones for setting, and in carving wood, for work in every skilled craft. 34 And he has inspired him to teach, both him and Oho'liab the son of Ahis'amach of the tribe of Dan. 35 He has filled them with ability to do every sort of work done by a craftsman or by a designer or by an embroiderer in blue

---

would hardly have been provided until after the dwelling was complete. Vs. 23 is out of place between vss. 22, 24, which tell of the contributions of precious metals. It belongs with vss. 25-26.

3. BEZALEL AND OHOLIAB (35:30–36:7)

This section was partly dealt with under 31:1-11 above. It is probably the original from which that passage was developed by a very late editor. Note that before actually calling Bezalel and Oholiab to their task (36:2), Moses communicates God's will in this matter to all Israel (vss. 30-35).

34. The two leaders were **inspired** by God **to teach** the men who were endowed by God with wisdom or skill. This is an instructive correlation of education with inspiration!

35. To be **filled . . . with ability** in this context is to be filled with the Spirit of God (31:3).

the weaver, *even* of them that do any work, and of those that devise cunning work.

36 Then wrought Bezaleel and Aholiab, and every wise-hearted man, in whom the LORD put wisdom and understanding to know how to work all manner of work for the service of the sanctuary, according to all that the LORD had commanded.

2 And Moses called Bezaleel and Aholiab, and every wise-hearted man, in whose heart the LORD had put wisdom, *even* every one whose heart stirred him up to come unto the work to do it:

3 And they received of Moses all the offering, which the children of Israel had brought for the work of the service of the sanctuary, to make it *withal*. And they brought yet unto him free offerings every morning.

4 And all the wise men, that wrought all the work of the sanctuary, came every man from his work which they made;

5 ¶ And they spake unto Moses, saying, The people bring much more than enough for the service of the work, which the LORD commanded to make.

6 And Moses gave commandment, and they caused it to be proclaimed throughout the camp, saying, Let neither man nor woman make any more work for the offering of the sanctuary. So the people were restrained from bringing.

7 For the stuff they had was sufficient for all the work to make it, and too much.

8 ¶ And every wise-hearted man among them that wrought the work of the tabernacle made ten curtains *of* fine twined linen, and blue, and purple, and scarlet: *with* cherubim of cunning work made he them.

and purple and scarlet stuff and fine twined linen, or by a weaver — by any sort of workman or skilled designer. 1 Bez'alel and Oho'liab and every able man in whom the LORD has put ability and intelligence to know how to do any work in the construction of the sanctuary shall work in accordance with all that the LORD has commanded."

2 And Moses called Bez'alel and Oho'liab and every able man in whose mind the LORD had put ability, every one whose heart stirred him up to come to do the work; 3 and they received from Moses all the freewill offerings which the people of Israel had brought for doing the work on the sanctuary. They still kept bringing him freewill offerings every morning, 4 so that all the able men who were doing every sort of task on the sanctuary came, each from the task that he was doing, 5 and said to Moses, "The people bring much more than enough for doing the work which the LORD has commanded us to do." 6 So Moses gave command, and word was proclaimed throughout the camp, "Let neither man nor woman do anything more for the offering for the sanctuary." So the people were restrained from bringing; 7 for the stuff they had was sufficient to do all the work, and more.

8 And all the able men among the workmen made the tabernacle with ten curtains; they were made of fine twined linen and blue and purple and scarlet stuff, with

---

36:2. Not only Bezalel and Oholiab, but **every able man in whose mind the LORD had put ability,** i.e., wisdom, was to share in the task.

3-7. The **freewill offering** (25:2) which the people brought to Moses proved to be more than sufficient, **much more than enough,** so Moses requests them to stop. The late account of the poll tax (30:11-16) is as completely ignored here as in ch. 25. This section belongs to the main body of the P narrative.

4. THE TABERNACLE (36:8-38)

See Exeg. on 26:1-37.

a) THE TENT (36:8-19)

See Exeg. on 26:1-14.

9 The length of one curtain *was* twenty and eight cubits, and the breadth of one curtain four cubits: the curtains *were* all of one size.

10 And he coupled the five curtains one unto another: and *the other* five curtains he coupled one unto another.

11 And he made loops of blue on the edge of one curtain from the selvedge in the coupling: likewise he made in the uttermost side of *another* curtain, in the coupling of the second.

12 Fifty loops made he in one curtain, and fifty loops made he in the edge of the curtain which *was* in the coupling of the second: the loops held one *curtain* to another.

13 And he made fifty taches of gold, and coupled the curtains one unto another with the taches: so it became one tabernacle.

14 ¶ And he made curtains *of* goats' *hair* for the tent over the tabernacle: eleven curtains he made them.

15 The length of one curtain *was* thirty cubits, and four cubits *was* the breadth of one curtain: the eleven curtains *were* of one size.

16 And he coupled five curtains by themselves, and six curtains by themselves.

17 And he made fifty loops upon the uttermost edge of the curtain in the coupling, and fifty loops made he upon the edge of the curtain which coupleth the second.

18 And he made fifty taches *of* brass to couple the tent together, that it might be one.

19 And he made a covering for the tent *of* rams' skins dyed red, and a covering *of* badgers' skins above *that.*

20 ¶ And he made boards for the tabernacle *of* shittim wood, standing up.

21 The length of a board *was* ten cubits, and the breadth of a board one cubit and a half.

22 One board had two tenons, equally distant one from another: thus did he make for all the boards of the tabernacle.

23 And he made boards for the tabernacle; twenty boards for the south side southward:

cherubim skilfully worked. 9 The length of each curtain was twenty-eight cubits, and the breadth of each curtain four cubits; all the curtains had the same measure.

10 And he coupled five curtains to one another, and the other five curtains he coupled to one another. 11 And he made loops of blue on the edge of the outmost curtain of the first set; likewise he made them on the edge of the outmost curtain of the second set; 12 he made fifty loops on the one curtain, and he made fifty loops on the edge of the curtain that was in the second set; the loops were opposite one another. 13 And he made fifty clasps of gold, and coupled the curtains one to the other with clasps; so the tabernacle was one whole.

14 He also made curtains of goats' hair for a tent over the tabernacle; he made eleven curtains. 15 The length of each curtain was thirty cubits, and the breadth of each curtain four cubits; the eleven curtains had the same measure. 16 He coupled five curtains by themselves, and six curtains by themselves. 17 And he made fifty loops on the edge of the outmost curtain of the one set, and fifty loops on the edge of the other connecting curtain. 18 And he made fifty clasps of bronze to couple the tent together that it might be one whole. 19 And he made for the tent a covering of tanned rams' skins and goatskins.

20 Then he made the upright frames for the tabernacle of acacia wood. 21 Ten cubits was the length of a frame, and a cubit and a half the breadth of each frame. 22 Each frame had two tenons, for fitting together; he did this for all the frames of the tabernacle. 23 The frames for the tabernacle he made thus: twenty frames for the south

b) The Wooden Structure (36:20-34)

See Exeg. on 26:15-30.

24 And forty sockets of silver he made under the twenty boards; two sockets under one board for his two tenons, and two sockets under another board for his two tenons.

25 And for the other side of the tabernacle, *which is* toward the north corner, he made twenty boards,

26 And their forty sockets of silver; two sockets under one board, and two sockets under another board.

27 And for the sides of the tabernacle westward he made six boards.

28 And two boards made he for the corners of the tabernacle in the two sides.

29 And they were coupled beneath, and coupled together at the head thereof, to one ring: thus he did to both of them in both the corners.

30 And there were eight boards; and their sockets *were* sixteen sockets of silver, under every board two sockets.

31 ¶ And he made bars of shittim wood; five for the boards of the one side of the tabernacle,

32 And five bars for the boards of the other side of the tabernacle, and five bars for the boards of the tabernacle for the sides westward.

33 And he made the middle bar to shoot through the boards from the one end to the other.

34 And he overlaid the boards with gold, and made their rings *of* gold *to be* places for the bars, and overlaid the bars with gold.

35 ¶ And he made a veil *of* blue, and purple, and scarlet, and fine twined linen: *with* cherubim made he it of cunning work.

36 And he made thereunto four pillars *of* shittim *wood,* and overlaid them with gold: their hooks *were of* gold; and he cast for them four sockets of silver.

37 ¶ And he made a hanging for the tabernacle door *of* blue, and purple, and scarlet, and fine twined linen, of needlework;

38 And the five pillars of it with their hooks: and he overlaid their chapiters and their fillets with gold: but their five sockets *were of* brass.

side; 24 and he made forty bases of silver under the twenty frames, two bases under one frame for its two tenons, and two bases under another frame for its two tenons. 25 And for the second side of the tabernacle, on the north side, he made twenty frames 26 and their forty bases of silver, two bases under one frame and two bases under another frame. 27 And for the rear of the tabernacle westward he made six frames. 28 And he made two frames for corners of the tabernacle in the rear. 29 And they were separate beneath, but joined at the top, at the first ring; he made two of them thus, for the two corners. 30 There were eight frames with their bases of silver: sixteen bases, under every frame two bases.

31 And he made bars of acacia wood, five for the frames of the one side of the tabernacle, 32 and five bars for the frames of the other side of the tabernacle, and five bars for the frames of the tabernacle at the rear westward. 33 And he made the middle bar to pass through from end to end halfway up the frames. 34 And he overlaid the frames with gold, and made their rings of gold for holders for the bars, and overlaid the bars with gold.

35 And he made the veil of blue and purple and scarlet stuff and fine twined linen; with cherubim skilfully worked he made it. 36 And for it he made four pillars of acacia, and overlaid them with gold; their hooks were of gold, and he cast for them four bases of silver. 37 He also made a screen for the door of the tent, of blue and purple and scarlet stuff and fine twined linen, embroidered with needlework; 38 and its five pillars with their hooks. He overlaid their capitals, and their fillets were of gold, but their five bases were of bronze.

c) THE VEIL AND THE SCREEN (36:35-38)

See Exeg. on 26:31-37.

37 And Bezaleel made the ark *of* shittim wood: two cubits and a half *was* the length of it, and a cubit and a half the breadth of it, and a cubit and a half the height of it:

2 And he overlaid it with pure gold within and without, and made a crown of gold to it round about.

3 And he cast for it four rings of gold, *to be set* by the four corners of it; even two rings upon the one side of it, and two rings upon the other side of it.

4 And he made staves *of* shittim wood, and overlaid them with gold.

5 And he put the staves into the rings by the sides of the ark, to bear the ark.

6 ¶ And he made the mercy seat *of* pure gold: two cubits and a half *was* the length thereof, and one cubit and a half the breadth thereof.

7 And he made two cherubim *of* gold, beaten out of one piece made he them, on the two ends of the mercy seat;

8 One cherub on the end on this side, and another cherub on the *other* end on that side: out of the mercy seat made he the cherubim on the two ends thereof.

9 And the cherubim spread out *their* wings on high, *and* covered with their wings over the mercy seat, with their faces one to another; *even* to the mercy seat-ward were the faces of the cherubim.

10 ¶ And he made the table *of* shittim wood: two cubits *was* the length thereof, and a cubit the breadth thereof, and a cubit and a half the height thereof:

11 And he overlaid it with pure gold, and made thereunto a crown of gold round about.

12 Also he made thereunto a border of a handbreadth round about; and made a crown of gold for the border thereof round about.

13 And he cast for it four rings of gold, and put the rings upon the four corners that *were* in the four feet thereof.

14 Over against the border were the rings, the places for the staves to bear the table.

37 Bez'alel made the ark of acacia wood; two cubits and a half was its length, a cubit and a half its breadth, and a cubit and a half its height. 2 And he overlaid it with pure gold within and without, and made a molding of gold around it. 3 And he cast for it four rings of gold for its four corners, two rings on its one side and two rings on its other side. 4 And he made poles of acacia wood, and overlaid them with gold, 5 and put the poles into the rings on the sides of the ark, to carry the ark. 6 And he made a mercy seat of pure gold; two cubits and a half was its length, and a cubit and a half its breadth. 7 And he made two cherubim of hammered gold; on the two ends of the mercy seat he made them, 8 one cherub on the one end, and one cherub on the other end; of one piece with the mercy seat he made the cherubim on its two ends. 9 The cherubim spread out their wings above, overshadowing the mercy seat with their wings, with their faces one to another; toward the mercy seat were the faces of the cherubim.

10 He also made the table of acacia wood; two cubits was its length, a cubit its breadth, and a cubit and a half its height; 11 and he overlaid it with pure gold, and made a molding of gold around it. 12 And he made around it a frame a handbreadth wide, and made a molding of gold around the frame. 13 He cast for it four rings of gold, and fastened the rings to the four corners at its four legs. 14 Close to the frame were the rings, as holders for the poles to carry the

5. THE ARK (37:1-9)

See Exeg. on 25:10-22.

6. THE TABLE (37:10-16)

See Exeg. on 25:23-30.

15 And he made the staves *of* shittim wood, and overlaid them with gold, to bear the table.

16 And he made the vessels which *were* upon the table, his dishes, and his spoons, and his bowls, and his covers to cover withal, *of* pure gold.

17 ¶ And he made the candlestick *of* pure gold: *of* beaten work made he the candlestick; his shaft, and his branch, his bowls, his knops, and his flowers, were of the same:

18 And six branches going out of the sides thereof; three branches of the candlestick out of the one side thereof, and three branches of the candlestick out of the other side thereof:

19 Three bowls made after the fashion of almonds in one branch, a knop and a flower; and three bowls made like almonds in another branch, a knop and a flower: so throughout the six branches going out of the candlestick.

20 And in the candlestick *were* four bowls made like almonds, his knops, and his flowers:

21 And a knop under two branches of the same, and a knop under two branches of the same, and a knop under two branches of the same, according to the six branches going out of it.

22 Their knops and their branches were of the same: all of it *was* one beaten work *of* pure gold.

23 And he made his seven lamps, and his snuffers, and his snuffdishes, *of* pure gold.

24 *Of* a talent of pure gold made he it, and all the vessels thereof.

25 ¶ And he made the incense altar *of* shittim wood: the length of it *was* a cubit, and the breadth of it a cubit; *it was* four-square; and two cubits *was* the height of it; the horns thereof were of the same.

26 And he overlaid it with pure gold, *both* the top of it, and the sides thereof round about, and the horns of it: also he made unto it a crown of gold round about.

table. 15 He made the poles of acacia wood to carry the table, and overlaid them with gold. 16 And he made the vessels of pure gold which were to be upon the table, its plates and dishes for incense, and its bowls and flagons with which to pour libations.

17 He also made the lampstand of pure gold. The base and the shaft of the lampstand were made of hammered work; its cups, its capitals, and its flowers were of one piece with it. 18 And there were six branches going out of its sides, three branches of the lampstand out of one side of it and three branches of the lampstand out of the other side of it; 19 three cups made like almonds, each with capital and flower, on one branch, and three cups made like almonds, each with capital and flower, on the other branch — so for the six branches going out of the lampstand. 20 And on the lampstand itself were four cups made like almonds, with their capitals and flowers, 21 and a capital of one piece with it under each pair of the six branches going out of it. 22 Their capitals and their branches were of one piece with it; the whole of it was one piece of hammered work of pure gold. 23 And he made its seven lamps and its snuffers and its trays of pure gold. 24 He made it and all its utensils of a talent of pure gold.

25 He made the altar of incense of acacia wood; its length was a cubit, and its breadth was a cubit; it was square, and two cubits was its height; its horns were of one piece with it. 26 He overlaid it with pure gold, its top, and its sides round about, and its horns; and he made a molding of gold round about

---

7. THE LAMPSTAND (37:17-24)

See Exeg. on 25:31-40.

8. THE ALTAR OF INCENSE (37:25-28)

See Exeg. on 30:1-10.

27 And he made two rings of gold for it under the crown thereof, by the two corners of it, upon the two sides thereof, to be places for the staves to bear it withal.

28 And he made the staves *of* shittim wood, and overlaid them with gold.

29 ¶ And he made the holy anointing oil, and the pure incense of sweet spices, according to the work of the apothecary.

38 And he made the altar of burnt offering *of* shittim wood: five cubits *was* the length thereof, and five cubits the breadth thereof; *it was* foursquare; and three cubits the height thereof.

2 And he made the horns thereof on the four corners of it; the horns thereof were of the same: and he overlaid it with brass.

3 And he made all the vessels of the altar, the pots, and the shovels, and the basins, *and* the fleshhooks, and the firepans: all the vessels thereof made he *of* brass.

4 And he made for the altar a brazen grate of network, under the compass thereof, beneath unto the midst of it.

5 And he cast four rings for the four ends of the grate of brass, *to be* places for the staves.

6 And he made the staves *of* shittim wood, and overlaid them with brass.

7 And he put the staves into the rings on the sides of the altar, to bear it withal; he made the altar hollow with boards.

8 ¶ And he made the laver *of* brass, and the foot of it *of* brass, of the looking-glasses of *the women* assembling, which assembled *at* the door of the tabernacle of the congregation.

9 ¶ And he made the court: on the south side southward the hangings of the court *were of* fine twined linen, a hundred cubits:

10 Their pillar *were* twenty, and their brazen sockets twenty; the hooks of the pillars and their fillets *were of* silver.

it, 27 and made two rings of gold on it under its molding, on two opposite sides of it, as holders for the poles with which to carry it. 28 And he made the poles of acacia wood, and overlaid them with gold.

29 He made the holy anointing oil also, and the pure fragrant incense, blended as by the perfumer.

38 He made the altar of burnt offering also of acacia wood; five cubits was its length, and five cubits its breadth; it was square, and three cubits was its height. 2 He made horns for it on its four corners; its horns were of one piece with it, and he overlaid it with bronze. 3 And he made all the utensils of the altar, the pots, the shovels, the basins, the forks, and the fire pans: all its utensils he made of bronze. 4 And he made for the altar a grating, a network of bronze, under its ledge, extending halfway down. 5 He cast four rings on the four corners of the bronze grating as holders for the poles; 6 he made the poles of acacia wood, and overlaid them with bronze. 7 And he put the poles through the rings on the sides of the altar, to carry it with them; he made it hollow, with boards.

8 And he made the laver of bronze and its base of bronze, from the mirrors of the ministering women who ministered at the door of the tent of meeting.

9 And he made the court; for the south side the hangings of the court were of fine twined linen, a hundred cubits; 10 their pillars were twenty and their bases twenty, of bronze, but the hooks of the pillars and

9. THE HALLOWED INCENSE AND OIL (37:29)

See Exeg. on 30:22-38.

10. THE BRASS ALTAR (38:1-7)

See Exeg. on 27:1-8.

11. THE BRASS LAVER (38:8)

See Exeg. on 30:17-21.

12. THE TABERNACLE COURT (38:9-20)

See Exeg. on 27:9-19.

11 And for the north side *the hangings were* a hundred cubits, their pillars *were* twenty, and their sockets of brass twenty; the hooks of the pillars and their fillets *of* silver.

12 And for the west side *were* hangings of fifty cubits, their pillars ten, and their sockets ten; the hooks of the pillars and their fillets *of* silver.

13 And for the east side eastward fifty cubits.

14 The hangings of the one side *of the gate were* fifteen cubits; their pillars three, and their sockets three.

15 And for the other side of the court gate, on this hand and that hand, *were* hangings of fifteen cubits; their pillars three, and their sockets three.

16 All the hangings of the court round about *were* of fine twined linen.

17 And the sockets for the pillars *were of* brass; the hooks of the pillars and their fillets *of* silver; and the overlaying of their chapiters *of* silver; and all the pillars of the court *were* filleted with silver.

18 And the hanging for the gate of the court *was* needlework, *of* blue, and purple, and scarlet, and fine twined linen: and twenty cubits *was* the length, and the height in the breadth *was* five cubits, answerable to the hangings of the court.

19 And their pillars *were* four, and their sockets *of* brass four; their hooks *of* silver, and the overlaying of their chapiters and their fillets *of* silver.

20 And all the pins of the tabernacle, and of the court round about, *were of* brass.

21 ¶ This is the sum of the tabernacle, *even* of the tabernacle of testimony, as it was counted, according to the commandment of Moses, *for* the service of the Levites, by the hand of Ithamar, son to Aaron the priest.

22 And Bezaleel the son of Uri, the son of Hur, of the tribe of Judah, made all that the LORD commanded Moses.

23 And with him *was* Aholiab, son of Ahisamach, of the tribe of Dan, an en-

their fillets were of silver. 11 And for the north side a hundred cubits, their pillars twenty, their bases twenty, of bronze, but the hooks of the pillars and their fillets of silver. 12 And for the west side were hangings of fifty cubits, their pillars ten, and their sockets ten; the hooks of the pillars and their fillets were of silver. 13 And for the front to the east, fifty cubits. 14 The hangings for one side of the gate were fifteen cubits, with three pillars and three bases. 15 And so for the other side; on this hand and that hand by the gate of the court were hangings of fifteen cubits, with three pillars and three bases. 16 All the hangings round about the court were of fine twined linen. 17 And the bases for the pillars were of bronze, but the hooks of the pillars and their fillets were of silver; the overlaying of their capitals was also of silver, and all the pillars of the court were filleted with silver. 18 And the screen for the gate of the court was embroidered with needlework in blue and purple and scarlet stuff and fine twined linen; it was twenty cubits long and five cubits high in its breadth, corresponding to the hangings of the court. 19 And their pillars were four; their four bases were of bronze, their hooks of silver, and the overlaying of their capitals and their fillets of silver. 20 And all the pegs for the tabernacle and for the court round about were of bronze.

21 This is the sum of the things for the tabernacle, the tabernacle of the testimony, as they were counted at the commandment of Moses, for the work of the Levites under the direction of Ith'amar the son of Aaron the priest. 22 Bez'alel the son of Uri, son of Hur, of the tribe of Judah, made all that the LORD commanded Moses; 23 and with him was Oho'liab the son of Ahis'a-

---

13. SUMMARY OF OFFERINGS (38:21-31)

In this summary of materials used in the manufacture of the tabernacle and its equipment the Levites, under Ithamar (vs. 20), are associated with Bezalel and Oholiab (cf. 31:1-11; 35:30–36:7). It appears therefore to be a very late addition to P (P^S). The census (Num. 1:13) is assumed to have taken place before the tabernacle was built (cf.

graver, and a cunning workman, and an embroiderer in blue, and in purple, and in scarlet, and fine linen.

24 All the gold that was occupied for the work in all the work of the holy *place,* even the gold of the offering, was twenty and nine talents, and seven hundred and thirty shekels, after the shekel of the sanctuary.

25 And the silver of them that were numbered of the congregation *was* a hundred talents, and a thousand seven hundred and threescore and fifteen shekels, after the shekel of the sanctuary:

26 A bekah for every man, *that is,* half a shekel, after the shekel of the sanctuary, for every one that went to be numbered, from twenty years old and upward, for six hundred thousand and three thousand and five hundred *men.*

27 And of the hundred talents of silver were cast the sockets of the sanctuary, and the sockets of the veil; a hundred sockets of the hundred talents, a talent for a socket.

28 And of the thousand seven hundred seventy and five *shekels* he made hooks for the pillars, and overlaid their chapiters, and filleted them.

29 And the brass of the offering *was* seventy talents, and two thousand and four hundred shekels.

30 And therewith he made the sockets to the door of the tabernacle of the congregation, and the brazen altar, and the brazen grate for it, and all the vessels of the altar,

31 And the sockets of the court round about, and the sockets of the court gate, and all the pins of the tabernacle, and all the pins of the court round about.

39 And of the blue, and purple, and scarlet, they made clothes of service, to do service in the holy *place,* and made the holy garments for Aaron; as the Lord commanded Moses.

mach, of the tribe of Dan, a craftsman and designer and embroiderer in blue and purple and scarlet stuff and fine twined linen.

24 All the gold that was used for the work, in all the construction of the sanctuary, the gold from the offering, was twenty-nine talents and seven hundred and thirty shekels, by the shekel of the sanctuary. 25 And the silver from those of the congregation who were numbered was a hundred talents and a thousand seven hundred and seventy-five shekels, by the shekel of the sanctuary: 26 a beka a head (that is, half a shekel, by the shekel of the sanctuary), for every one who was numbered in the census, from twenty years old and upward, for six hundred and three thousand, five hundred and fifty men. 27 The hundred talents of silver were for casting the bases of the sanctuary, and the bases of the veil; a hundred bases for the hundred talents, a talent for a base. 28 And of the thousand seven hundred and seventy-five shekels he made hooks for the pillars, and overlaid their capitals and made fillets for them. 29 And the bronze that was contributed was seventy talents, and two thousand and four hundred shekels; 30 with it he made the bases for the door of the tent of meeting, the bronze altar and the bronze grating for it and all the utensils of the altar, 31 the bases round about the court, and the bases of the gate of the court, all the pegs of the tabernacle, and all the pegs round about the court.

39 And of the blue and purple and scarlet stuff they made finely wrought garments, for ministering in the holy place; they made the holy garments for Aaron; as the Lord had commanded Moses.

30:11-16). The Hebrew for contribution (vs. 24) is here not *terûmāh,* as in 30:13, but *tenûphāh,* i.e., gift of dedication, to conform to the view presented that the poll tax was used in the building of the sanctuary.

14. The Priesthood and Its Dress (39:1-31)

See Exeg. on 28:1-43.

a) Introduction (39:1)

See Exeg. on 28:1-5.

2 And he made the ephod *of* gold, blue, and purple, and scarlet, and fine twined linen.

3 And they did beat the gold into thin plates, and cut *it into* wires to work *it* in the blue, and in the purple, and in the scarlet, and in the fine linen, *with* cunning work.

4 They made shoulderpieces for it, to couple *it* together: by the two edges was it coupled together.

5 And the curious girdle of his ephod, that *was* upon it, *was* of the same, according to the work thereof; *of* gold, blue, and purple, and scarlet, and fine twined linen; as the LORD commanded Moses.

6 ¶ And they wrought onyx stones inclosed in ouches of gold, graven, as signets are graven, with the names of the children of Israel.

7 And he put them on the shoulders of the ephod, *that they should be* stones for a memorial to the children of Israel; as the LORD commanded Moses.

8 ¶ And he made the breastplate *of* cunning work, like the work of the ephod; *of* gold, blue, and purple, and scarlet, and fine twined linen.

9 It was foursquare; they made the breastplate double: a span *was* the length thereof, and a span the breadth thereof, *being* doubled.

10 And they set in it four rows of stones: *the first* row *was* a sardius, a topaz, and a carbuncle: this *was* the first row.

11 And the second row, an emerald, a sapphire, and a diamond.

12 And the third row, a ligure, an agate, and an amethyst.

13 And the fourth row, a beryl, an onyx, and a jasper: *they were* inclosed in ouches of gold in their inclosings.

14 And the stones *were* according to the names of the children of Israel, twelve according to their names, *like* the engravings of a signet, every one with his name, according to the twelve tribes.

2 And he made the ephod of gold, blue and purple and scarlet stuff, and fine twined linen. **3** And gold leaf was hammered out and cut into threads to work into the blue and purple and the scarlet stuff, and into the fine twined linen, in skilled design. **4** They made for the ephod shoulder-pieces, joined to it at its two edges. **5** And the skilfully woven band upon it, to gird it on, was of the same materials and workmanship, of gold, blue and purple and scarlet stuff, and fine twined linen; as the LORD had commanded Moses.

6 The onyx stones were prepared, enclosed in settings of gold filigree and engraved like the engravings of a signet, according to the names of the sons of Israel. **7** And he set them on the shoulder-pieces of the ephod, to be stones of remembrance for the sons of Israel; as the LORD had commanded Moses.

8 He made the breastpiece, in skilled work, like the work of the ephod, of gold, blue and purple and scarlet stuff, and fine twined linen. **9** It was square; the breastpiece was made double, a span its length and a span its breadth when doubled. ·**10** And they set in it four rows of stones. A row of sardius, topaz, and carbuncle was the first row; **11** and the second row, an emerald, a sapphire, and a diamond; **12** and the third row, a jacinth, an agate, and an amethyst; **13** and the fourth row, a beryl, an onyx, and a jasper; they were enclosed in settings of gold filigree. **14** There were twelve stones with their names according to the names of the sons of Israel; they were like signets, each engraved with its name, for the

---

b) THE EPHOD (39:2-7)

See Exeg. on 28:6-12.

c) THE BREASTPIECE (39:8-21)

See Exeg. on 28:13-30.

15 And they made upon the breastplate chains at the ends, *of* wreathed work *of* pure gold.

16 And they made two ouches *of* gold, and two gold rings, and put the two rings in the two ends of the breastplate.

17 And they put the two wreathed chains of gold in the two rings on the ends of the breastplate.

18 And the two ends of the two wreathed chains they fastened in the two ouches, and put them on the shoulderpieces of the ephod, before it.

19 And they made two rings of gold, and put *them* on the two ends of the breastplate, upon the border of it, which *was* on the side of the ephod inward.

20 And they made two *other* golden rings, and put them on the two sides of the ephod underneath, toward the forepart of it, over against the *other* coupling thereof, above the curious girdle of the ephod.

21 And they did bind the breastplate by his rings unto the rings of the ephod with a lace of blue, that it might be above the curious girdle of the ephod, and that the breastplate might not be loosed from the ephod; as the LORD commanded Moses.

22 ¶ And he made the robe of the ephod *of* woven work, all *of* blue.

23 And *there was* a hole in the midst of the robe, as the hole of an habergeon, *with* a band round about the hole, that it should not rend.

24 And they made upon the hems of the robe pomegranates *of* blue, and purple, and scarlet, *and* twined *linen.*

25 And they made bells *of* pure gold, and put the bells between the pomegranates upon the hem of the robe, round about between the pomegranates;

26 A bell and a pomegranate, a bell and a pomegranate, round about the hem of the robe to minister *in;* as the LORD commanded Moses.

27 ¶ And they made coats *of* fine linen *of* woven work for Aaron, and for his sons,

twelve tribes. 15 And they made on the breastpiece twisted chains like cords, of pure gold; 16 and they made two settings of gold filigree and two gold rings, and put the two rings on the two edges of the breastpiece; 17 and they put the two cords of gold in the two rings at the edges of the breastpiece. 18 Two ends of the two cords they had attached to the two settings of filigree; thus they attached it in front to the shoulder-pieces of the ephod. 19 Then they made two rings of gold, and put them at the two ends of the breastpiece, on its inside edge next to the ephod. 20 And they made two rings of gold, and attached them in front to the lower part of the two shoulder-pieces of the ephod, at its joining above the skilfully woven band of the ephod. 21 And they bound the breastpiece by its rings to the rings of the ephod with a lace of blue, so that it should lie upon the skilfully woven band of the ephod, and that the breastpiece should not come loose from the ephod; as the LORD had commanded Moses.

22 He also made the robe of the ephod woven all of blue; 23 and the opening of the robe in it was like the opening in a garment, with a binding around its opening, that it might not be torn. 24 On the skirts of the robe they made pomegranates of blue and purple and scarlet stuff and fine twined linen. 25 They also made bells of pure gold, and put the bells between the pomegranates upon the skirts of the robe round about, between the pomegranates; 26 a bell and a pomegranate, a bell and a pomegranate round about upon the skirts of the robe for ministering; as the LORD had commanded Moses.

27 They also made the coats, woven of

---

d) THE ROBE OF THE EPHOD (39:22-26)

See Exeg. on 28:31-35.

e) THE DIADEM, TURBAN, COAT, AND GARMENTS FOR AARON'S SONS (39:27-31)

See Exeg. on 28:36-43.

28 And a mitre *of* fine linen, and goodly bonnets *of* fine linen, and linen breeches *of* fine twined linen,

29 And a girdle *of* fine twined linen, and blue, and purple, and scarlet, *of* needlework; as the LORD commanded Moses.

30 ¶ And they made the plate of the holy crown *of* pure gold, and wrote upon it a writing, *like to* the engravings of a signet, HOLINESS TO THE LORD.

31 And they tied unto it a lace of blue, to fasten *it* on high upon the mitre; as the LORD commanded Moses.

32 ¶ Thus was all the work of the tabernacle of the tent of the congregation finished: and the children of Israel did according to all that the LORD commanded Moses, so did they.

33 ¶ And they brought the tabernacle unto Moses, the tent, and all his furniture, his taches, his boards, his bars, and his pillars, and his sockets;

34 And the covering of rams' skins dyed red, and the covering of badgers' skins, and the veil of the covering;

35 The ark of the testimony, and the staves thereof, and the mercy seat;

36 The table, *and* all the vessels thereof, and the showbread;

37 The pure candlestick, *with* the lamps thereof, *even with* the lamps to be set in order, and all the vessels thereof, and the oil for light;

38 And the golden altar, and the anointing oil, and the sweet incense, and the hanging for the tabernacle door;

39 The brazen altar, and his grate of brass, his staves, and all his vessels, the laver and his foot;

40 The hangings of the court, his pillars, and his sockets, and the hanging for the court gate, his cords, and his pins, and all the vessels of the service of the tabernacle, for the tent of the congregation;

fine linen, for Aaron and his sons, 28 and the turban of fine linen, and the caps of fine linen, and the linen breeches of fine twined linen, 29 and the girdle of fine twined linen and of blue and purple and scarlet stuff, embroidered with needlework; as the LORD had commanded Moses.

30 And they made the plate of the holy crown of pure gold, and wrote upon it an inscription, like the engraving of a signet, "Holy to the LORD." 31 And they tied to it a lace of blue, to fasten it on the turban above; as the LORD had commanded Moses.

32 Thus all the work of the tabernacle of the tent of meeting was finished; and the people of Israel had done according to all that the LORD had commanded Moses; so had they done. 33 And they brought the tabernacle to Moses, the tent and all its utensils, its hooks, its frames, its bars, its pillars, and its bases; 34 the covering of tanned rams' skins and goatskins, and the veil of the screen; 35 the ark of the testimony with its poles and the mercy seat; 36 the table with all its utensils, and the bread of the Presence; 37 the lampstand of pure gold and its lamps with the lamps set and all its utensils, and the oil for the light; 38 the golden altar, the anointing oil and the fragrant incense, and the screen for the door of the tent; 39 the bronze altar, and its grating of bronze, its poles, and all its utensils; the laver and its base; 40 the hangings of the court, its pillars, and its bases, and the screen for the gate of the court, its cords, and its pegs; and all the utensils for the service of the tabernacle, for the tent of

---

15. THE PRESENTATION OF THE TABERNACLE (39:32-43)

Vss. 32-33a and 42-43 constitute the core of this section. The list of completed items brought to Moses, including as it does **the golden altar** and **the laver and its base**, must be viewed as a late addition. Two strands are also apparently combined in vss. 32-33a. The term **the tabernacle of the tent of meeting** (vs. 32), characteristic of PB, stands alongside **the tent** in vs. 33. The latter is more characteristic of PA (cf. 26:36; 29:43). The structure of vs. 33 in Hebrew suggests that **the tabernacle** is a later insertion. The theme of the passage is the importance of obedience.

41 The clothes of service to do service in the holy *place,* and the holy garments for Aaron the priest, and his sons' garments, to minister in the priest's office.

42 According to all that the Lord commanded Moses, so the children of Israel made all the work.

43 And Moses did look upon all the work, and, behold, they had done it as the Lord had commanded, even so had they done it: and Moses blessed them.

40 And the Lord spake unto Moses, saying,

2 On the first day of the first month shalt thou set up the tabernacle of the tent of the congregation.

3 And thou shalt put therein the ark of the testimony, and cover the ark with the veil.

4 And thou shalt bring in the table, and set in order the things that are to be set in order upon it; and thou shalt bring in the candlestick, and light the lamps thereof.

5 And thou shalt set the altar of gold for the incense before the ark of the testimony, and put the hanging of the door to the tabernacle.

6 And thou shalt set the altar of the burnt offering before the door of the tabernacle of the tent of the congregation.

7 And thou shalt set the laver between the tent of the congregation and the altar, and shalt put water therein.

8 And thou shalt set up the court round about, and hang up the hanging at the court gate.

9 And thou shalt take the anointing oil, and anoint the tabernacle, and all that *is* therein, and shalt hallow it, and all the vessels thereof: and it shall be holy.

10 And thou shalt anoint the altar of the burnt offering, and all his vessels, and sanctify the altar: and it shall be an altar most holy.

11 And thou shalt anoint the laver and his foot, and sanctify it.

meeting; 41 the finely worked garments for ministering in the holy place, the holy garments for Aaron the priest, and the garments of his sons to serve as priests. 42 According to all that the Lord had commanded Moses, so the people of Israel had done all the work. 43 And Moses saw all the work, and behold, they had done it; as the Lord had commanded, so had they done it. And Moses blessed them.

40 The Lord said to Moses, 2 "On the first day of the first month you shall erect the tabernacle of the tent of meeting. 3 And you shall put in it the ark of the testimony, and you shall screen the ark with the veil. 4 And you shall bring in the table, and set its arrangements in order; and you shall bring in the lampstand, and set up its lamps. 5 And you shall put the golden altar for incense before the ark of the testimony, and set up the screen for the door of the tabernacle. 6 You shall set the altar of burnt offering before the door of the tabernacle of the tent of meeting, 7 and place the laver between the tent of meeting and the altar, and put water in it. 8 And you shall set up the court round about, and hang up the screen for the gate of the court. 9 Then you shall take the anointing oil, and anoint the tabernacle and all that is in it, and consecrate it and all its furniture; and it shall become holy. 10 You shall also anoint the altar of burnt offering and all its utensils, and consecrate the altar; and the altar shall be most holy. 11 You shall also anoint the

16. The Assembly of the Tabernacle and Its Equipment (40:1-33)

The account of the assembly of the tabernacle and its service (vss. 16-33) is preceded by Yahweh's instructions to Moses concerning it. We are not told when or where the Lord spoke to Moses (vs. 1). Most of the instructions are actually drawn from 25:1–31:17. As in ch. 25, they begin with the ark; the manner of erecting the tabernacle itself (vss. 16-19) is not specified in this summary of the instructions. Reference to the mercy seat is also omitted (but cf. vs. 20).

12 And thou shalt bring Aaron and his sons unto the door of the tabernacle of the congregation, and wash them with water.

13 And thou shalt put upon Aaron the holy garments, and anoint him, and sanctify him; that he may minister unto me in the priest's office.

14 And thou shalt bring his sons, and clothe them with coats:

15 And thou shalt anoint them, as thou didst anoint their father, that they may minister unto me in the priest's office: for their anointing shall surely be an everlasting priesthood throughout their generations.

16 Thus did Moses: according to all that the LORD commanded him, so did he.

17 ¶ And it came to pass in the first month in the second year, on the first *day* of the month, *that* the tabernacle was reared up.

18 And Moses reared up the tabernacle, and fastened his sockets, and set up the boards thereof, and put in the bars thereof, and reared up his pillars.

19 And he spread abroad the tent over the tabernacle, and put the covering of the tent above upon it; as the LORD commanded Moses.

20 ¶ And he took and put the testimony into the ark, and set the staves on the ark, and put the mercy seat above upon the ark:

21 And he brought the ark into the tabernacle, and set up the veil of the covering, and covered the ark of the testimony; as the LORD commanded Moses.

22 ¶ And he put the table in the tent of the congregation, upon the side of the tabernacle northward, without the veil.

23 And he set the bread in order upon it before the LORD; as the LORD had commanded Moses.

24 ¶ And he put the candlestick in the tent of the congregation, over against the table, on the side of the tabernacle southward.

25 And he lighted the lamps before the LORD; as the LORD commanded Moses.

26 ¶ And he put the golden altar in the tent of the congregation before the veil:

27 And he burnt sweet incense thereon; as the LORD commanded Moses.

28 ¶ And he set up the hanging *at* the door of the tabernacle.

laver and its base, and consecrate it. **12** Then you shall bring Aaron and his sons to the door of the tent of meeting, and shall wash them with water, **13** and put upon Aaron the holy garments, and you shall anoint him and consecrate him, that he may serve me as priest. **14** You shall bring his sons also and put coats on them, **15** and anoint them, as you anointed their father, that they may serve me as priests: and their anointing shall admit them to a perpetual priesthood throughout their generations."

16 Thus did Moses; according to all that the LORD commanded him, so he did. **17** And in the first month in the second year, on the first day of the month, the tabernacle was erected. **18** Moses erected the tabernacle; he laid its bases, and set up its frames, and put in its poles, and raised up its pillars; **19** and he spread the tent over the tabernacle, and put the covering of the tent over it, as the LORD had commanded Moses. **20** And he took the testimony and put it into the ark, and put the poles on the ark, and set the mercy seat above on the ark; **21** and he brought the ark into the tabernacle, and set up the veil of the screen, and screened the ark of the testimony; as the LORD had commanded Moses. **22** And he put the table in the tent of meeting, on the north side of the tabernacle, outside the veil, **23** and set the bread in order on it before the LORD; as the LORD had commanded Moses. **24** And he put the lampstand in the tent of meeting, opposite the table on the south side of the tabernacle, **25** and set up the lamps before the LORD; as the LORD had commanded Moses. **26** And he put the golden altar in the tent of meeting before the veil, **27** and burnt fragrant incense upon it; as the LORD had commanded Moses. **28** And he put in place the

29 And he put the altar of burnt offering *by* the door of the tabernacle of the tent of the congregation, and offered upon it the burnt offering and the meat offering; as the LORD commanded Moses.

30 ¶ And he set the laver between the tent of the congregation and the altar, and put water there, to wash *withal*.

31 And Moses and Aaron and his sons washed their hands and their feet thereat:

32 When they went into the tent of the congregation, and when they came near unto the altar, they washed; as the LORD commanded Moses.

33 And he reared up the court round about the tabernacle and the altar, and set up the hanging of the court gate. So Moses finished the work.

34 ¶ Then a cloud covered the tent of the congregation, and the glory of the LORD filled the tabernacle.

35 And Moses was not able to enter into the tent of the congregation, because the cloud abode thereon, and the glory of the LORD filled the tabernacle.

36 And when the cloud was taken up from over the tabernacle, the children of Israel went onward in all their journeys:

37 But if the cloud were not taken up, then they journeyed not till the day that it was taken up.

38 For the cloud of the LORD *was* upon the tabernacle by day, and fire was on it by

screen for the door of the tabernacle. 29 And he set the altar of burnt offering at the door of the tabernacle of the tent of meeting, and offered upon it the burnt offering and the cereal offering; as the LORD had commanded Moses. 30 And he set the laver between the tent of meeting and the altar, and put water in it for washing, 31 with which Moses and Aaron and his sons washed their hands and their feet; 32 when they went into the tent of meeting, and when they approached the altar, they washed; as the LORD commanded Moses. 33 And he erected the court round the tabernacle and the altar, and set up the screen of the gate of the court. So Moses finished the work.

34 Then the cloud covered the tent of meeting, and the glory of the LORD filled the tabernacle. 35 And Moses was not able to enter the tent of meeting, because the cloud abode upon it, and the glory of the LORD filled the tabernacle. 36 Throughout all their journeys, whenever the cloud was taken up from over the tabernacle, the people of Israel would go onward; 37 but if the cloud was not taken up, then they did not go onward till the day that it was taken up. 38 For throughout all their journeys the cloud of the LORD was upon the tabernacle

---

17. CONCLUSION (40:34-38)

The heart of this conclusion, and its oldest portion, is found in vss. 34-35. These reiterate the main theme of P with respect to the tabernacle: it is the symbol of the relationship of grace in which Israel stands to a transcendent deity. The phrase **the glory of the LORD filled the tabernacle** occurs twice. The conclusion stresses the interior of the structure and uses the temple as its model. From that model, too, is derived the notion that Moses could not enter the tabernacle because of **the glory** (cf. I Kings 8:10-11), a note which contradicts the general outlook of P (25:22; 29:43-46; Lev. 9:23). This close

---

40:38. *The Tokens of the Presence.*—So the book of Exodus ends in glory with the descent of the presence of the Most High upon the house built by the skill and devotion of all the people. This is the fulfillment of the promise of 25:8, "Let them make me a sanctuary; that I may dwell among them." The people have done their part; now God does his part, and **the cloud . . . by day and the fire . . . by night** testify that he is indeed living among them.

The presence of God is for most men a dim

and faltering consciousness flickering in vague waves of feeling or in tenuous experiences admitting no objective proof. We say his hand is felt, his voice is heard. But the moment is fleeting, and there are long days of waiting for the chance that his quickening spirit may visit us again. Sustained by nothing but that faint hope, how little we have to carry us over those barren hours of doubt and worldliness and despair!

But in the sacraments, as in the tabernacle, we find the orderliness of a father's love who

night, in the sight of all the house of Israel, | by day, and fire was in it by night, in the
throughout all their journeys. | sight of all the house of Israel.

---

association of the tabernacle with the Solomonic temple is characteristic of P^B. On the
other hand, P^A thinks of the tabernacle as a tent and draws on the ancient tent of Moses
(33:7-11) as its model.

---

has given us regular outward signs of a continuous inner peace. Within, we may not be able except at rare moments to be sure that he is with us. But without, the table of the Holy Communion is always set. At noonday in the midst of men's business a cloud hovers above the place of God; in the darkest, loneliest night there is the glow of his presence. The door to the inner, unseen world opens to those who follow the visible signposts God places before their feet **throughout all their journeys.**

St. Augustine says, at first the scriptures will amuse and attract the child, and in the end, when he tries to understand them, they make fools of the wise, for none is so simple-minded but can find his level there nor none so wise but when he tries to fathom them will find they are beyond his depth.[6]

[6] Pfeiffer, *Meister Eckhart*, I, 257.